Keep on the Sunny Side.

At Days Inns our promise is as sure as the sun.

A sunny, warm welcome. A fresh Daybreak® Breakfast.*

More rewards more often with TripRewards,®

the world's largest hotel rewards program.** At Days Inns,

it's not just about the change we put in your pocket.

It's about the change we make in your journey.

**AAA Members: Save up to 10%†
at more than 65 AAA approved
Days Inn® hotels in Florida.**

DAYS INN
The Best Value Under The Sun™

For specific locations and reservations, call
**1-800-432-9755 or
daysinn.com**

A reflection of how you travel today.

How you take a vacation hasn't changed—your travel money choices have.

Today there are many ways to take your vacation money with you, and the prepaid AAA Visa TravelMoney® card is the most secure, convenient way to carry your funds. Simply preload your card with your travel funds before you leave, and you are ready to use your card for payment at any Visa® debit merchant or withdraw local currency at any Visa® Interlink/PLUS ATM around the world. Vacation with the Visa TravelMoney card—it is safer than cash.

The AAA Visa TravelMoney Card:

- Accepted at millions of Visa® debit merchants and hundreds of thousands of Visa® Interlink/PLUS ATMs worldwide
- More secure because it is not linked to your other cards or accounts
- Reloadable to help you track spending
- Includes Purchase Security, Zero Liability, and Emergency Assistance

AAA Visa TravelMoney card, safer than cash.

*Terms and conditions apply, see detailed terms and conditions provided with your card fulfillment kit. Information correct at time of printing, subject to change.

Visit Participating AAA offices
Click aaa.com/travelmoney
Call 866-339-3378

Other Travel Money products include:

Foreign Currency

Travelers Cheques

Florida

Are we meeting your travel needs?
Send written comments to:

AAA Member Comments
1000 AAA Drive, Box 61
Heathrow, FL 32746-5063

Published by AAA Publishing
1000 AAA Drive
Heathrow, FL 32746-5063
Copyright AAA 2005

Hospital information
© 2005 HealthForum, LLC

**Advertising Rate and Circulation
Information: (407) 444-8280**

**Printed in the USA by
Quebecor World, Buffalo, NY**

*Photo Credit: (Cover & Title Page)
Daytona International Speedway,
Daytona Beach
© International Speedway Corporation*

Printed on recyclable paper.
Please recycle whenever possible.

Mixed Sources
Product group from well-managed
forests and other controlled sources
www.fsc.org Cert no. SW-COC-1610
© 1996 Forest Stewardship Council

FSC

Stock #4609

◆ ◆

Florida

Featured Information

A STAY WORTH YOUR WHILE

Stay at participating Hilton hotels and enjoy our **Stay and Save**™ rates with your AAA/CAA membership. We offer members a special discounted AAA rate at over 240 AAA-approved locations in the U.S., Canada, and Mexico. Choose conveniently located luxury beach resorts or city-center accommodations.

Hilton HHonors® members can also earn hotel points *and* airline miles. Your stay isn't just about the bed or the linen, the food or the location. It's something more. Enjoy our upgraded amenities and high-speed internet access available in most guest rooms.

 Show Your Card & Save® at any participating property and enjoy special rates.

To make advance reservations, call our dedicated AAA number at **1-877-655-5694** or your local AAA travel office. Visit us at **hilton.com**.

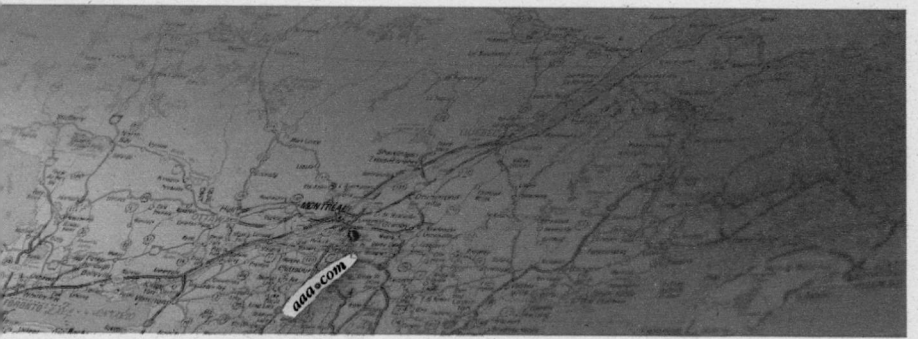

For hotel reservations and vacation planning, get right to the point on *aaa•com*. Reserve AAA Approved and Diamond rated hotels at the lowest online prices. Plus, enjoy these additional tools and benefits:

Online TourBook® – Find thousands of AAA Approved and Diamond rated hotels and restaurants, plus thousands of things to see and do.

Internet TripTik® – Get complete trip routings with hotel reservations, sightseeing stops, member discount locations, and more.

AAA Drive Trips* – Enjoy nearly 100 flexible, preplanned driving itineraries for popular destinations.

Vacation Getaways – Get exclusive benefits on flights, tours, cruises, and Disney vacation packages from AAA's Preferred Travel Partners.

AAA Map Gallery* – Print your own AAA maps for top destinations.

Hertz Rental – Save up to 20% on car rental.

Show Your Card & Save® – Search for exclusive member savings at 150,000 locations worldwide.

AAA Travel Money – Get no-fee travelers cheques, foreign currency, and prepaid cards.

Books – Save 5% on AAA travel, childrens, specialty, and automotive publications at aaa.com/barnesandnoble.

AAA Credit Card – Get up to 5% gas rebate.

AAA Approved Auto Repair – Find reliable service locations at home and away.

Plan your next trip on *aaa•com* — the only travel Web site backed by thousands of highly trained travel professionals at more than 1,000 AAA/CAA offices!

aaa•com
Plan to go.

*Products and services available through participating AAA and CAA clubs.

Getting away just got better.

LUXURY COLLECTION

WESTIN

The Atlantic, Ft. Lauderdale

The Diplomat Country Club & Spa

The Westin Diplomat Resort & Spa, Hollywood

The Westin Innisbrook Golf Resort, Palm Harbor

Walt Disney World Swan and Dolphin

The Westin Grand Bohemian, Orlando

Sheraton Studio City Hotel, Orlando

Sheraton World Resort, Orlando

Sheraton Sand Key Resort, Clearwater Beach

Sheraton Suites Tampa Airport

Sheraton Bal Harbour Beach Resort

Sheraton Suites Cypress Creek, Ft. Lauderdale

Sheraton Ft. Lauderdale Airport Hotel

Sheraton Suites Plantation, Ft. Lauderdale West

Sheraton Beach Resort, Key Largo

Sheraton Suites Key West

Whether you travel by plane, train, or automobile, simply show your AAA card and receive exclusive savings at Starwood Hotels & Resorts Worldwide.

To make reservations or to learn about
AAA special rates and member benefits call **866 782 7737**
starwood.com/aaa

MEMBER OF ⓢ STARWOOD PREFERRED GUEST®

©2005-2006 Starwood Hotels & Resorts Worldwide, Inc.
Not responsible for any typographical errors

Attractions, lodgings and restaurants are listed on the basis of merit alone after careful evaluation and approval by one of AAA/CAA's full-time, professionally trained Tourism Editors. Evaluations are unannounced to ensure that we see an establishment just as you would see it.

An establishment's decision to advertise in the TourBook guide has no bearing on its evaluation or rating. Advertising for services or products does not imply AAA endorsement.

All information in this guide was reviewed for accuracy before publication. However, since changes inevitably occur between annual editions, we suggest you work with your AAA travel professional or check on aaa.com to confirm prices and schedules.

How the TourBook Guide is Organized

The TourBook guide is organized into three distinct sections.

The **Points of Interest** section helps you plan daily activities and sightseeing excursions and provides details about the city or attraction you are visiting.

The **Lodgings and Restaurants** section helps you select AAA Approved accommodations and dining facilities meeting your specific needs and expectations.

The **Reference** section provides indexes for locating information within this guide and items to aid the trip planning process.

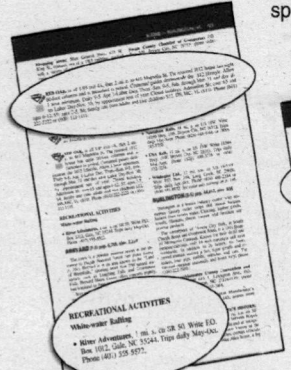
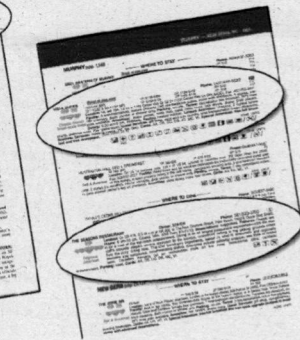
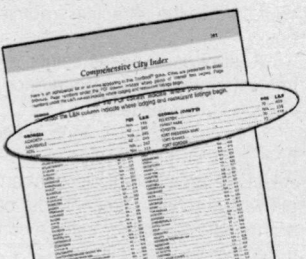

Locating the Attractions, Lodgings and Restaurants

Attractions, lodgings and restaurants are listed under the city in which they physically are located - or in some cases under the nearest recognized city. Most listings are alphabetically organized by state, province, region or island, then by city and establishment name.

A color is assigned to each state or province so that you can match the color bars at the top of the page to switch from the **Points of Interest** section to the **Lodgings and Restaurants** section.

Spotting maps help you physically locate points of interest, lodgings and restaurants in the major destinations.

The Comprehensive City Index located in the **Reference** section contains an A-to-Z list of cities.

Destination Cities and Destination Areas

Destination cities, established based on government models and local expertise, include metropolitan areas plus nearby vicinity cities. **Destination areas** are regions with broad tourist appeal; several cities will comprise the area.

If a city falls within a destination's vicinity, the city name will appear at its alphabetical location in the book, and a cross reference will give you the exact page on which listings for that city begin.

An orientation map appears at the beginning of each destination section to orient you to that destination.

Understanding the Points of Interest Listing

GEM Designation

A ⬙ indicates the attraction has been rated a AAA GEM, a "must see" point of interest that offers a *Great Experience for Members®*. These attractions have been judged to be of exceptional interest and quality by AAA Tourism Editors.

A GEM listing page with a brief description of individual GEM attractions follows the Orientation map near the beginning of each state or province Points of Interest section. Cross-references guide the reader to the attraction's listing page.

Discount Savings

The 〔SAVE〕 icon denotes those attractions offering AAA/CAA, AAA MasterCard, AAA VISA or international Show Your Card & Save discount cardholders a discount off the attraction's standard admission. Present your card at the attraction's admission desk.

A list of participating points of interest appears in the Reference section of this guide.

Shopping establishments preceded by a 〔SAVE〕 icon also provide to AAA/CAA members a discount and/or gift with purchase; present your card at the mall's customer service center to receive your benefit.

Exceptions

- Members should inquire in advance concerning the validity of the discount for special rates.
- The 〔SAVE〕 discount may not be used in conjunction with other discounts.
- Attractions that already provide a reduced senior or child rate may not honor the 〔SAVE〕 discount for those age groups.
- All offers are subject to change and may not apply during special events, particular days or seasons or for the entire validity period of the TourBook guide.

Shopping areas: Mast General Store, 630 W. King St., operates out of a 1913 building, stocked with a variety of goods incl... ware...

⬙ 〔SAVE〕 **RED OAK,** is off I-95 exit 4A, just n. to Dogwoo... restored 1812 house has eight 60-foot columns and... Allow 1 hour minimum. Daily 9-5, Apr. 1-Labor D... Labor Day-Nov. 30; by appointment rest of year. C... 6-12, $5; ages 2-5, $4; family rate (two adults and two chil... 5555 or (800) 555-5555.

⬙ 〔SAVE〕 **RED OAK,** is off I-95 exit 4A, just n. to Dogwood Dr., then 2 mi. e. to 610 Magnolia St. The restored 1812 house has eight 60-foot columns and is furnished in period. Costumed guides demonstrate the 1812 lifestyle. Allow 1 hour minimum. Daily 9-5, Apr. 1-Labor Day; Thurs.-Sun. 9-5, Feb.-Mar. 31 and day after Labor Day-Nov. 30; by appointment rest of year. Closed holidays. Admission $8; over 65 and ages 6-12, $5; ages 2-5, $4; family rate (two adults and two children) $12. DS, MC, VI. ($10). Phone (828) 555-5555 or (800) 555-5555.

RECREATIONAL ACTIVITIES

White-water Rafting

- **River Adventures,** 1 mi. s. on SR 50. Write P.O. Box 1012, Gale, NC 35244. Trips daily May-Oct. Phone (828) 555-5555.

BREVARD (F-3) pop. 6,789, elev. 2,229'

The town is a popular summer resort at the entrance to Pisgah National Forest *(see place listing p. 165).* Brevard is in an area known as the "Land of Waterfalls," sporting more than 250 named waterfalls such as Laughing Falls and Courthouse Falls. Brevard Music Center offers concerts nightly, last weekend in June to mid-August.

Brevard i...
por...

RECREATIONAL ACTIVITI...

White-water Rafting

- **River Adventures,** 1 mi. s. o... Box 1012, Gale, NC 35244... Phone (828) 555-5555.

NE — BURLINGTON, NC 125

Chamber of Commerce: P.O.
on City, NC 28713; phone (828)
267-0246.

hen 2 mi. e. to 610 Magnolia St. The
shed in period. Costumed guided tours.
rs.-Sun. 9-5, Feb.-Mar. 31 and day after
lidays. Admission $8, over 65 and ages
2. DS, MC, VI. ($10). Phone (828) 555-

vy. 19W. Write
y. 19W, Bryson City, NC 28713. Trips
y-Sept. Phone (828) 488-9366 or (800)

aft, 12 mi. s. on US 19W. Write 11040
JW, Bryson City, NC 28713. Trips daily
pt. Phone (828) 488-3316 or (800)
88.

ater Ltd., 12 mi. s.w. on US 19/74W.
P.O. Box 309, Long Creek, SC 29658.
daily Apr.-Oct. Phone (828) 488-2384 or
451-9972. See color ads starting on p. 146.

INGTON (B-5) pop. 44,917, elev. 656'

ngton is a textile industry center with nu-
factory outlet shops that attract bargain
from nearby states. Clothing, leather goods,
blankets, sheets, carpets and furniture are
r products.
centerpiece of 76-acre City Park, at South
n Street and Overbrook Road, is a 1910 Dent-
enagerie Carousel. Known for their detail and
ate carvings, only 14 such carousels still exist
wide. In addition to 26 horses, the hand-
d animals include a lion, tiger, giraffe and re-
r, four pigs, rabbits, ostriches and cats. The
sel operates seasonally and hours vary; phone
222-5030.

ington/Alamance County Convention and
eau: 610 S. Lexington Ave., P.O.
ington, NC 27216-0519; phone
637-3804.

ington Manufacturer's
r 145, houses more

TATE HISTORIC
5 mi. s.w. on SR
e between Royal-
tia and an inexpe-
ners known as the
50. Write P.O.   axes, corrupt officials
daily May-Oct.   John Allen house, a log

Directions

Unless otherwise specified, directions are given from the center of town, using the following highway designations:

I=interstate highway	**US**=federal highway
SR=state route	**CR**=county road
FM=farm to market	**FR**=forest road
Mex.=Mexican highway	**Hwy.**=Canadian or Caribbean highway

Prices and Dates of Operations

Admission prices are quoted without sales tax. Children under the lowest age specified are admitted free when accompanied by an adult. Days, months and age groups written with a hyphen are inclusive.

Prices pertaining to points of interest in the United States are quoted in U.S. dollars; points of interest in Canada are quoted in Canadian dollars; prices for points of interest in Mexico and the Caribbean are quoted as an approximate U.S. dollar equivalent.

Credit Cards Accepted

AX=American Express	**JC**=Japan Credit Bureau
CB=Carte Blanche	**MC**=MasterCard
DC=Diners Club	**VI**=VISA
DS=Discover	

Bulleted Listings

Casino gambling establishments are visited by AAA personnel to ensure safety; casinos within hotels are presented for member information regardless of whether the lodging is AAA Approved.

Recreational activities of a participatory nature (requiring physical exertion or special skills) are not inspected.

Wineries are inspected by AAA Tourism Editors to ensure they meet listing requirements and offer tours.

All are presented in an abbreviated bulleted format for informational purposes.

Understanding the Lodging Listing

Official Appointment

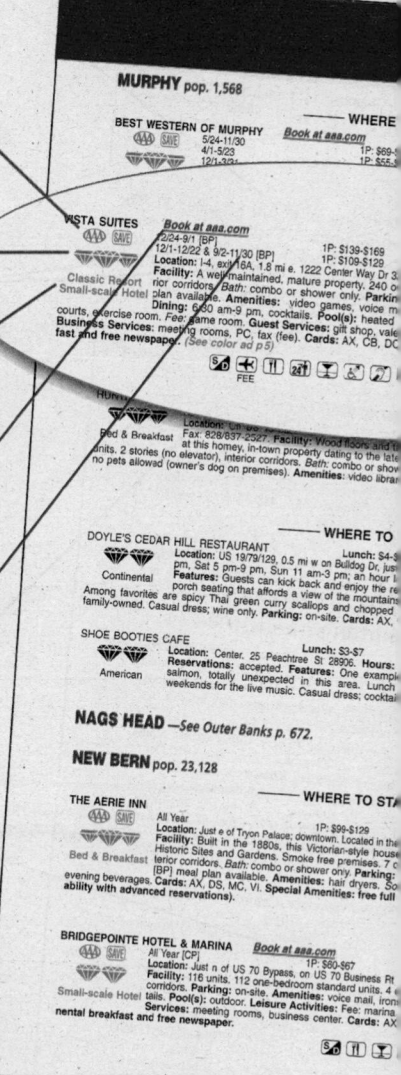

[AAA] or [CAA] indicates our Official Appointment (OA) lodgings. These properties guarantee members the lowest public rate available at the time of booking for the dates of stay or a minimum 10% discount off the standard room rates published in TourBook guides. We highlight these properties with red and a [SAVE] icon to help you quickly identify them.

Diamond Rating

The number of diamonds informs you of the overall complexity of a lodging's amenities and service. Red indicates an Official Appointment lodging. An [fyi] in place of diamonds indicates the property has not been rated but is included as an "information only" service. A detailed description of each rating level appears on page 20.

Classification

All diamond rated lodgings are classified using three key elements: style of operation, overall concept and service level. See pages 22-23 for details on our classifications.

Online Reservations

This notation indicates AAA/CAA members can conveniently check room availability, validate room rates and make reservations for this property in a secure online environment at aaa.com.

Rates

Shown from left to right: dates the rates are effective; any meal plan included in the rates (see below); standard room rates for 1 person (1P) or 2 persons (2P); extra person charge (XP); and any applicable family plan indicator (see below).

Rates are provided to AAA by each lodging and represent the regular (rack) rate ranges for a standard room. Rates are rounded to the nearest dollar and do not include taxes. U.S., Mexican and Caribbean rates are in U.S. dollars; rates for Canadian lodgings are in Canadian dollars.

Meal Plan Indicators

AP = American Plan of three meals daily
BP = Breakfast Plan of full hot breakfast
CP = Continental Plan of pastry, juice and another beverage
ECP = Expanded Continental Plan, which offers a wider variety of breakfast items
MAP = Modified American Plan of two meals daily

See individual listing "Terms" for additional meal plans not included in the room rate.

Family Plan Indicators

F = Children stay free
D = Discounts for children
F17 = Children 17 and under stay free
D17 = Discount for children 17 or under

The number displayed will reflect the property's age policy.

Credit Cards Accepted

AX=American Express
CB=Carte Blanche
DC=Diners Club
DS=Discover

JC=Japan Credit Bureau
MC=MasterCard
VI=VISA

Spotting Symbol

Black ovals with white numbers are used to locate, or "spot," lodgings on maps we provide for larger cities.

Service Availability

Unit types, amenities and room features preceded by the word "Some" indicate the item is available on a limited basis, potentially within only one unit.

Special Amenities

Some OA properties offer special amenities such as free continental breakfast; expanded continental breakfast or full breakfast; early check-in and late check-out; free room upgrade or preferred room; free local phone calls; or free daily newspaper. This does not imply that only these properties offer these amenities.

Icons

Lodging icons represent some of the member values, services and facilities offered.

Discounts

ASK May offer discount

S/D Offers minimum 10% senior discount to members over 59

Member Services

➤ Airport transportation

🐾 Pets allowed

🍴 Restaurant on premises

🍴→ Restaurant off premises (walking distance)

24🍴 24-hour room service

🍸 Cocktail lounge

👶 Child care

Accessibility Features

♿M Accessible features

🦻 Hearing-impaired equipment available

🚿 Roll-in showers

In-Room Amenities

✕ Designated non-smoking rooms

VCR VCR

🎬 Movies

DATA PORT Data port/modem line

🍱 Refrigerator

🍲 Microwave

☕ Coffee maker

A/C No air conditioning

TV No TV

CTV No cable TV

☎ No telephones

Leisure Activities

🎰 Full-service casino

🏊 Pool

💪 Health club on premises

💪 Health club off premises

🎯 Recreational activities

Safety Features (see page 24)
(Mexico and Caribbean only)

S Sprinklers

D Smoke detectors

SOME UNITS printed above the icons indicates the amenity is available on a limited basis, potentially in only one unit. **FEE** appearing below an icon indicates that an extra charge applies.

Understanding the Restaurant Listing

Official Appointment

⚠⚠⚠ or ⚠⚠ indicates our Official Appointment (OA) restaurants. The OA program permits properties to display and advertise the AAA or CAA emblem. We highlight these properties in red to help you quickly identify them. The AAA or CAA Approved sign helps traveling members find restaurants that want member business.

Diamond Rating

The number of diamonds informs you of the overall complexity of food, presentation, service and ambience. Red indicates an Official Appointment restaurant. A detailed description of each diamond level appears on page 21.

Cuisine Type

The cuisine type helps you select a dining facility that caters to your individual taste. AAA currently recognizes more than 90 different cuisine types.

Menus

This notation indicates AAA/CAA members can conveniently view the restaurant's menu in a secure online environment at aaa.com.

Credit Cards Accepted

AX=American Express

CB=Carte Blanche

DC=Diners Club

DS=Discover

JC=Japan Credit Bureau

MC=MasterCard

VI=VISA

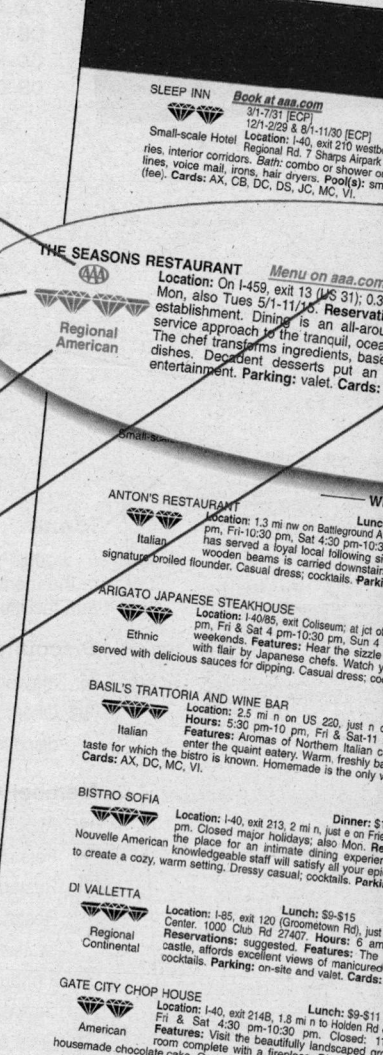

Prices

Rates shown represent the minimum and maximum entree cost per person. Exceptions may include one-of-a-kind or special market priced items. Rates are rounded to the nearest dollar and do not include taxes. U.S., Mexican and Caribbean rates are in U.S. dollars; rates for Canadian restaurants are in Canadian dollars.

Spotting Symbol

White ovals with black numbers serve as restaurant locators and are used to locate, or "spot," restaurants on maps we provide for larger cities.

Icons

Icons provide additional information about services and facilities.

🅰️	No air-conditioning
♿M	Accessible features
🍸	Cocktail lounge
🚬	Designated smoking section available

Classifications

If applicable, a restaurant may be defined as:

Classic - renowned and/or landmark restaurant in business longer than 25 years, known for unique style and ambience.

Historic - properties must meet one of the following criteria:
- Listed on the U.S. National Register of Historic Places
- Designated a U.S. National Historic Landmark
- Located in a U.S. National Register Historic District

Separate criteria designate historic properties in Canada, Mexico and the Caribbean.

(sample guide listings, partially visible)

GREENSBORO, NC 625

-$89 2P: $64-$104 Phone: (236)931-1272
-$79 2P: $54-$84 XP: $5 F18
Rd), just n; exit 210 eastbound, just e on Albert Pick Rd, then just n on XP: $5 F18
: 336/931-1496. **Facility:** 116 one-bedroom standard units. 7 sto-
on-site. **Terms:** cancellation fee imposed. **Amenities:** dual phone
uest Services: valet and coin laundry. **Business Services:** fax

SOME UNITS

Dinner: $16-$36 Phone: 336/555-5555 [5]
R 802. 1000 Ocean Blvd 35244. **Hours:** 6 pm-10 pm. Closed:
ested. **Features:** Guests are in for a treat at this top-notch
rable experience—from the wait staff's casually elegant
ng to the striking grounds views from the cozy dining area.
is seasonally and regionally available, into mouthwatering
n mark on the meal. Dressy casual attire; cocktails;
C, DS, MC, VI. **Classic**

DINE

Dinner: $8-$19 Phone: 336/273-1386
andover Ave. 1628 Battleground Ave 27408. **Hours:** 11 am-10
major holidays; also 12/24 & Sun. **Features:** This eatery
ustic Italian theme with black and white table cloths and a
- dining area. Famous for its lasagna, it also features a
ards: AX, MC, VI.

$18-$30
d Patterson St. 1200 S Holden Rd 27407. Phone: 336/299-1003
Closed: 11/25, 12/24, 12/25. **Hours:** 5 pm-10
eak, chicken, shrimp and sauteed vegetables prepared
ng cooked right at your table and enjoy huge portions
g: on-site. **Cards:** AX, MC, VI.

19-$30
ve; in Irving Park Plaza. 1720 Battleground Ave 27408. Phone: 336/333-9833
najor holidays; also Sun. **Reservations:** suggested.
m the wood-burning oven and reach diners as they
ped in olive oil is one small example of the delicious
sual dress; cocktails; entertainment. **Parking:** on-site.

just s. 616 Dolley Madison Rd 27410. Phone: 336/855-1313
suggested. **Features:** Elegant but not stuffy, this
French cuisine served by extremely helpful and
s. The Bistro was a house that has been converted
ards: AX, DC, MC, VI.

er: $19-$30
Grandover Pkwy; in Grandover Resort & Conference Phone: 336/294-1800
:30 pm, Sun 6-11 am, 11:30-2:30 & 6-10 pm.
g, which reflects the ambience of a European
the 18th hole of the east course. Casual dress;
DS, MC, VI.

ner: $19-$30
08 S Holden Rd 27407. **Hours:** 11:30 am-10 pm, Phone: 336/294-9977
12/25; also Sun. **Reservations:** suggested.
upscale bistro, which features a private dining
and end your meal with the creamy, mile-high
X, DC, DS, MC, VI.

ner: $4-$10
435B Dolley Madison Rd 27410. **Hours:** 11 am-8 Phone: 336/856-0070
an entrees, fresh fruits and vegetable juices;
dishes. Casual dress; beer only. **Parking:**

Lodging Rates Guaranteed

AAA/CAA members are guaranteed they will not be charged more than the maximum regular rate printed in the TourBook guide in each rate range for a standard room. Rates may vary within the range, depending on season and room type. Listed rates are based on last standard room availability. Obtain current AAA/CAA member rates and make reservations at aaa.com.

Discounts

Member discounts will apply to rates quoted within the rate range and are applicable at the time of booking. Special rates used in advertising, as well as special short-term promotional rates lower than the lowest listed rate in the range, are not subject to additional member discounts.

Exceptions

Rates for properties operating as concessionaires for the U.S. National Park Service are not guaranteed due to governing regulations. Rates in the Mexico TourBook are not guaranteed and may fluctuate based on the exchange rate of the peso.

Lodgings may temporarily increase room rates, not recognize discounts or modify pricing policies during special events. Examples of special events range from Mardi Gras and the Kentucky Derby (including pre-Derby events) to college football games, holidays, holiday periods and state fairs. Although some special events are listed in AAA/CAA TourBook guides and on aaa.com, it is always wise to check in advance with AAA travel professionals for specific dates.

Get the Room You Reserved

When making your reservation, identify yourself as a AAA or CAA member and request written confirmation to guarantee: type of room, rate, dates of stay, and cancellation and refund policies. At registration, show your membership card.

When you find your room is not as specified, and you have written confirmation of reservations for a certain type of accommodation, you should be given the option of choosing a different room or finding one elsewhere. Should you choose to go elsewhere and a refund is refused or resisted, submit the matter to AAA/CAA within 30 days, along with complete documentation, including your reasons for refusing the room and copies of your written confirmation and any receipts or canceled checks associated with this problem.

If you are charged more than the maximum rate listed in the TourBook guide for a standard

room, question the additional charge. If management refuses to adhere to the published rate, pay for the room and submit your receipt and membership number to AAA/CAA within 30 days. Include all pertinent information: dates of stay, rate paid, itemized paid receipts, number of persons in your party and the room number you occupied, and list any extra room equipment used. A refund of the amount paid in excess of the stated maximum will be made if our investigation indicates that unjustified charging occurred.

Deposit, Refund and Cancellation Policies

Most establishments give full deposit refunds if they have been notified at least 48 hours before the normal check-in time. Listing prose will note if more than 48 hours' notice is required for cancellation. Some properties may charge a cancellation or handling fee. When this applies, "cancellation fee imposed" will appear in the listing. If you cancel too late, you have little recourse if a refund is denied.

When an establishment requires full or partial payment in advance and your trip is cut short, a refund may not be given.

When canceling a reservation, phone the lodging immediately. Make a note of the date and time you called, the cancellation number if there is one, and the name of the person who handled the cancellation. If your AAA/CAA club made your reservation, allow them to make the cancellation for you as well, so you will have proof of cancellation.

Check-in and Check-out Times

Check-in and check-out times are shown in the lodging listings, under Terms, only if they are before 10 a.m. or after 3 p.m. respectively.

Members Save With Our Partners

These National Show Your Card & Save® partners provide the listed member benefits. Admission tickets that offer greater discounts may be available for purchase at the local AAA/CAA club. A maximum of six tickets is available at the discount price at the gate. Visit aaa.com to discover all of the great Show Your Card & Save® discounts in your area.

Attraction Partners

SeaWorld/Busch Gardens aaa.com/SeaWorld

- Save $5 at SeaWorld and Busch Gardens
- Save $3 at Sesame Place, Water Country USA and Adventure Island
- Save 10% on select aaa.com/BuschGardens up-close dining. Reservations are required; visit Guest Relations for details

Six Flags Theme Parks

- Save $4 on general admission at the gate
- Save $12 on general admission at the gate each Wednesday
- Save 10% on selected souvenirs and dining (check at main gate for details)

Universal Orlando aaa.com/Universal

- Save $4 on a 2-day/2-park pass or $5 on a 3-day/2-park pass at Universal Orlando's theme parks (savings apply to tickets purchased at the gate)
- Save 10% on select dining and souvenirs at both Universal Orlando theme parks and at select Universal CityWalk Orlando restaurants (excludes Emeril's)

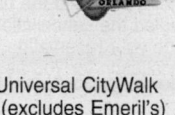

Universal Studios Hollywood

- Save $3 on a 1-day aaa.com/Universal Universal Studios Hollywood pass (savings applies to tickets purchased at the gate)

- Save 10% on select dining and souvenirs at Universal Studios Hollywood and Universal CityWalk

Gray Line aaa.com/GrayLine

- Save 10% on sightseeing tours of 1 day or less

Restaurant Partners

Landry's Seafood House, The Crab House, Chart House, Muer Seafood Restaurants, Joe's Crab Shack

- Save 10% on food and non-alcoholic beverages at all restaurants
- Save 10% on merchandise at Joe's Crab Shack
- Savings applicable to AAA/CAA members and up to six people

Hard Rock Cafe

- Save 10% on food, beverage and merchandise at all U.S. and select Canadian and international locations

- Savings applicable to AAA/CAA members and up to six people

AAA Dining Network aaa.com/dining

Save an average of 10% or more at over 2,500 restaurants across the United States and Canada simply by showing your AAA membership card

Lodging Partners

SAVINGS. SELECTION. SATISFACTION.—When contacting one of these lodging partners, you will be given AAA's best rates for your dates of stay. Your valid membership card must be presented at check-in. Select the chain you want and have your membership card available when making a reservation and checking in. Let the property know if you are dissatisfied with any part of your stay. If the matter cannot be resolved, you are entitled to recompense (see page 17).

Offer good at time of publication; chains and offers may change without notice. Lodging partners offering discounts to AAA/CAA members may vary in Mexico and the Caribbean.

Visit Over 1,100 AAA Offices **Click** aaa.com **Call** 866-AAA-SAVE

CHOICE HOTELS INTERNATIONAL ®

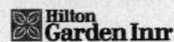   

Understanding the Diamond Ratings

AAA/CAA Tourism Editors have evaluated and rated each of the 55,000 lodging and restaurant establishments in the TourBook series to ensure quality travel information for our members. Listings are provided free of charge to AAA Approved establishments that have met AAA's 27 minimum requirements (for lodgings) concerning cleanliness, comfort and security - or - AAA's 12 minimum requirements (for restaurants) pertaining to cleanliness, food preparation and service.

Eligible applicants receive an unannounced evaluation by a AAA/CAA Tourism Editor that includes two distinct components:

- AAA Approval: The Tourism Editor first must determine whether the property meets the criteria required to be AAA Approved. Every establishment that meets these strict guidelines offers AAA members the assurance that, regardless of the diamond rating, it provides acceptable quality, cleanliness, service and value.
- AAA Diamond Rating: Once an establishment becomes AAA Approved, it is then assigned a rating of one to five diamonds, indicating the extensiveness of its facilities, amenities and services, from basic to moderate to luxury. These diamond ratings guide members in selecting establishments appropriately matched to their needs and expectations.

LODGINGS

1 Diamond

One diamond lodgings typically appeal to the budget-minded traveler. They provide essential, no-frills accommodations and basic comfort and hospitality.

2 Diamond

Two diamond lodgings appeal to family travelers seeking affordable yet more than the basic accommodations. Facilities, decor and amenities are modestly enhanced.

3 Diamond

Three diamond lodgings offer a distinguished style. Properties are multi-faceted, with marked upgrades in physical attributes, amenities and guest comforts.

4 Diamond

Four diamond lodgings are refined and stylish. Physical attributes are upscale. The fundamental hallmarks at this level include an extensive array of amenities combined with a high degree of hospitality, service and attention to detail.

5 Diamond

Five diamond lodgings provide the ultimate in luxury and sophistication. Physical attributes are extraordinary in every manner. Service is meticulous, exceeding guest expectations and maintaining impeccable standards of excellence. Extensive personalized services and amenities provide first-class comfort.

fyi The lodging listings with **fyi** in place of diamonds are included as an *information only* service for members. The icon indicates that a property has not been rated for one or more of the following reasons: too new to rate, under construction, under major renovation, not evaluated, may not meet all AAA requirements.

A property not meeting all AAA requirements is included for either its member value or because it may be the only accommodation available in the area. Listing prose will give insight as to why the **fyi** designation was assigned.

4 Diamond

Four diamond restaurants provide a distinctive fine-dining experience that is typically expensive. Surroundings are highly refined with upscale enhancements throughout. Highly creative chefs use imaginative presentations to augment fresh, top-quality ingredients. A proficient service staff meets or exceeds guest expectations. A wine steward may offer menu-specific knowledge to guide selection.

5 Diamond

Five diamond restaurants are luxurious and renowned for consistently providing a world-class experience. Highly acclaimed chefs offer artistic menu selections that are imaginative and unique, using only the finest ingredients available. A maitre d' leads an expert service staff in exceeding guest expectations, attending to every detail in an effortless and unobtrusive manner.

RESTAURANTS

1 Diamond

One diamond restaurants provide simple, familiar specialty food (such as burgers, chicken, pizza or tacos) at an economical price. Often self-service, basic surroundings complement a no-nonsense approach.

2 Diamond

Two diamond restaurants offer a familiar, family-oriented experience. Menu selection includes home-style foods and family favorites, often cooked to order, modestly enhanced and reasonably priced. Service is accommodating yet relaxed, a perfect complement to casual surroundings.

 The restaurants with **fyi** in place of diamonds are included as an *information only* service for members. These listings provide additional dining choices but have not yet been evaluated.

3 Diamond

Three diamond restaurants convey an entry into fine dining and are often positioned as adult-oriented experiences. The atypical menu may feature the latest cooking trends and/or traditional cuisine. Expanded beverage offerings complement the menu. The ambiance is well coordinated, comfortable and enhanced by a professional service staff.

Understanding the Lodging Classifications

To ensure that your lodging needs and preferences are met, we recommend that you consider an establishment's classification when making your travel choices. While the quality and comfort at properties with the same diamond rating should be consistent (regardless of the classification), there are differences in typical decor/theme elements, range of facilities and service levels.

Large-scale Hotel

A multistory establishment with interior room entrances. A variety of guest unit styles is offered. Public areas are spacious and

Hotel Royal Plaza, Lake Buena Vista, FL

include a variety of facilities such as a restaurant, fitness center, spa, business center, shops or meeting rooms.

Small-scale Hotel

A multistory establishment typically with interior room entrances. A variety of guest unit styles is offered. Public areas are limited

Baymont Inn, Dallas Ft. Worth-Airport N, TX

in size and/or the variety of facilities available.

Motel

A 1- to 3-story establishment typically with exterior room entrances facilitating convenient access to parking. The

Best Western Deltona Inn, Deltona, FL

standard guest units have one bedroom with a bathroom and are typically similar in decor and design throughout. Public areas are limited in size and/or the variety of facilities available.

Country Inn

Similar in definition to a bed and breakfast but usually larger in scale, with spacious public areas offering a

Greenville Inn, Greenville, ME

dining facility that serves at least breakfast and dinner.

Bed & Breakfast

Small-scale properties emphasizing a high degree of personal touches that provide guests an "at home" feeling. Guest units tend to be individually

1884 Paxton House Inn, Thomasville, GA

decorated. Rooms may not include some modern amenities such as televisions and telephones, and may have a shared bathroom. Usually owner-operated with a common room or parlor separate from the innkeeper's living quarters, where guests and operators can interact during evening and breakfast hours. Evening office closures are normal. A continental or full, hot breakfast is served and is included in the room rate.

Condominium

Vacation-oriented or extended-stay, apartment-style accommodations that are routinely available for rent through a management company. Units vary in design and decor and often contain one or more bedrooms, a living room,

Sands of Kahana, Kahana, Maui, HI

full kitchen and an eating area. Studio-type models combine the sleeping and living areas into one room. Typically, basic cleaning supplies, kitchen utensils and complete bed and bath linens are supplied. The guest registration area may be located off-site.

Cabin/Cottage

Vacation-oriented, small-scale, freestanding houses or cabins. Units vary in design and decor and often contain one

Desert Rose Inn, Bluff, UT

or more bedrooms, a living room, kitchen, dining area and bathroom. Studio-type models combine the sleeping and living areas into one room. Typically, basic cleaning supplies, kitchen utensils, and complete bed and bath linens are supplied. The guest registration area may be located off-site.

Ranch

Typically a working ranch with an obvious rustic, Western theme. In general, equestrian-related activities are featured, but ranches may

C Lazy U Ranch, Granby, CO

include other animals and activities as well. A variety of guest unit styles is offered in a family-oriented atmosphere.

Vacation Home

Vacation-oriented or extended-stay, large-scale, freestanding houses that are routinely available for rent through a management company. Houses

ResortQuest, Hilton Head Island, SC

vary in design and decor and often contain two or more bedrooms, a living room, full kitchen, dining room and multiple bathrooms. Typically, basic cleaning supplies, kitchen utensils, and complete bed and bath linens are supplied. The guest registration area may be located off-site.

Lodging Subclassifications

The following are subclassifications that may appear along with the classifications listed previously to provide a more specific description of the lodging.

Casino

Extensive gaming facilities are available such as blackjack, craps, keno and slot machines. Note: This subclassification will not appear beneath its diamond rating in the listing. It will be indicated by a ⊕ icon and will be included in the row of icons immediately below the lodging listing.

Classic

Renowned and landmark properties, older than 50 years, well-known for their unique style and ambience.

Historic

These properties are typically over 75 years of age and exhibit many features of a historic nature with respect to architecture, design, furnishings, public record or acclaim. Properties must meet one of the following criteria:

- Maintained the integrity of the historical aspect
- Listed on the U.S. National Register of Historic Places
- Designated a U.S. National Historic Landmark
- Located in a U.S. National Register Historic District

Separate criteria designate historic properties in Canada, Mexico and the Caribbean.

Resort

Recreation-oriented, geared to vacation travelers seeking a specific destination experience. Travel packages, meal plans, themed entertainment, and social and recreational programs are typically available. Recreational facilities are extensive and may include spa treatments, golf, tennis, skiing, fishing, water sports, etc. Larger resorts may offer a variety of guest accommodations.

Guest Safety

Room Security

In order to be approved for listing in AAA/CAA TourBook guides for the United States and Canada, accommodations must have dead-bolt locks on all guest room entry doors and connecting room doors.

If the area outside the guest room door is not visible from inside the room through a window or door panel, viewports must be installed on all guest room entry doors. Bed and breakfast properties and country inns are not required to have viewports. Ground floor and easily accessible sliding doors must be equipped with some type of secondary security locks.

Tourism Editors view a percentage of rooms at each property since it is not feasible to evaluate every room in every lodging establishment. Therefore, AAA cannot guarantee that there are working locks on all doors and windows in all guest rooms.

Fire Safety

Because of the highly specialized skills needed to conduct professional fire safety inspections, AAA/CAA Tourism Editors cannot assess fire safety.

Properties must meet all federal, state and local fire codes. Each guest unit in all U.S. and Canadian lodging properties must be equipped with an operational, single-station smoke detector. A AAA/CAA Tourism Editor has evaluated a sampling of the rooms to verify this equipment is in place.

Mexico and the Caribbean

Requirements for some features, such as door locks and smoke detectors/sprinkler systems, differ in Mexico and the Caribbean. If a property met AAA's security requirements at the time of the evaluation, the phrase "Meets AAA guest room security requirements" appears in the listing.

Service Animals

The Americans With Disabilities Act (ADA) prohibits U.S. businesses that serve the public from discriminating against persons with disabilities. Some businesses have mistakenly denied access to persons who use service animals. Businesses must permit entry to guests and their service animals, as well as allow service animals to accompany guests to all public areas of a property.

A property is permitted to ask whether the animal is a service animal or a pet, and whether the guest has a disability. The property may not, however, ask questions about the nature of the disability, the service provided by the animal or require proof of a disability or certification that the animal is a service animal. These regulations may not apply in Canada, Mexico or the Caribbean.

No fees or deposits, even those normally charged for pets, may be charged for service animals. Service animals fulfill a critical need for their owners—they are not pets.

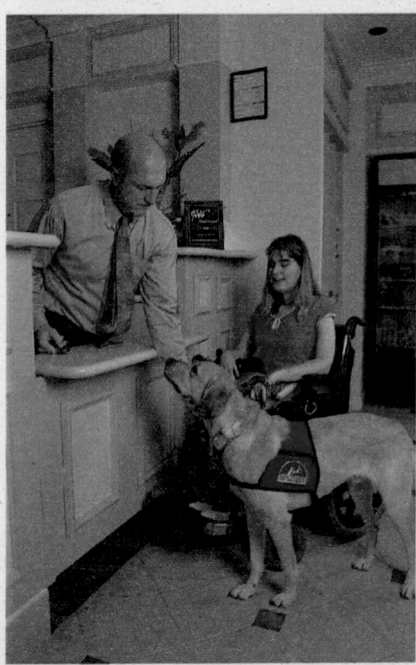

Savings for all Seasons

Hertz rents Fords and other fine cars. ® REG. U.S. PAT. OFF. © HERTZ SYSTEM INC., 1999/2006-99.

No matter the season, Hertz offers AAA members exclusive discounts and benefits.

Operating in 150 countries at over 7,400 locations, Hertz makes traveling more convenient and efficient wherever and whenever you go. Hertz offers AAA members discounts up to 20% on car rentals worldwide.

To receive your exclusive AAA member discounts and benefits, mention your AAA membership card at time of reservation and present it at time of rental. **In addition**, to receive a free one car class upgrade on daily, weekly or weekend rental in the United States and Canada, mention PC# 969194, and in Puerto Rico mention PC# 969183 at the time of reservation. Offer available through 12/15/06.

For reservations and program details, call your AAA Travel office or the Hertz/AAA Desk at **1-800-654-3080**.

FLORIDA ESSENTIALS

Plenty of sunshine and beaches make Florida the perfect place to play. And nobody makes playing more rewarding than the Florida Lottery. Every week a million people win at SCRATCH-OFF Games, FLORIDA LOTTO™, MEGA MONEY™, FANTASY 5®, PLAY 4™, and CASH 3™. And you could be one of them.

Vacation's a great time to play.

Florida

Sandy Beaches
Sun and fun are found in abundance along the expansive coast

Theme Park Adventures
Amusements range from water slides to roller coasters

Manatees & Alligators
Placid waters harbor Florida's native creatures

Relaxing in the Keys
Clear water and coral characterize this diving paradise

Journey into Space
Awesome launches light up the sky at Cape Canaveral

The Florida Keys
© William Harrigan
Lonely Planet Images

Stuart / Visit Florida

W hen you hear the word "Florida," there's a good chance that you conjure a vivid mental picture.

It probably includes swaying palms, sandy beaches and piercing rays of sunlight reflecting off the surface of the surrounding waters.

Perhaps you envision the emerald-green waters that caress the Gulf beaches at Pensacola. Or the sharks' teeth sprinkled across the sand in Venice. Or the colorful varieties of seashells blanketing the coast on the islands of Captiva and Sanibel. Or the rolling waves lapping at the sugary shore of Ponce Inlet.

Without a doubt, the state's seascapes are spectacular. But Florida boasts an

a whimsical paradise

appeal that stretches far beyond its handsome coast.

Images of lush inland landscapes are just as plentiful. Towering pine trees and stolid oaks rise from dense thickets of palmettos in the Apalachicola, Ocala and Osceola national forests. Prairies of saw grass interrupt mangrove stands and mazes of gnarled cypress roots that emerge from the murky swampland in the Everglades.

And Florida's most notable man-made enticements can't be overlooked: Glittery theme parks encourage young and old to make time for a day of play beneath a sun that almost always shines.

Florida is as close as you can get to seeing the world through the eyes of an artist with a mischievous sense of humor and a wildly creative genius.

The Sunshine State is a place of stunning extremes—a place where the sun shines brighter, the water runs bluer, the slash pines reach higher, the sands feel softer.

It's a place in which the Northerners live way down south around Miami and Fort Lauderdale and where Southern accents ring out from such northern enclaves as Pensacola and Tallahassee.

Strange creatures inhabit the water, the land and the air. Oafish manatees—thought to have given rise to the legend of the mermaid—ply the waters of coastal waterways and placid springs. Garish roseate spoonbills, whose showy pink plumes topped the chapeaus of many a society matron in the early 1900s, grace shorelines once dotted with flocks of flamingos.

Dog-sized Key deer skirt the brush on Big Pine Key. Libidinous lovebugs, known for their mating-while-flying rendezvous, make their impact as they smash two-by-two into the windshields of passing cars.

Exotic plants enliven the landscape with splashes of vivid color—the purple of the spiky pontederia, the fiery crimson of the hibiscus and poinciana, the violet-bluish cast of the Blewit mushroom, the orange, yellow and green of the citrus growing in the state's ubiquitous groves.

They Came with a Dream

This naturally varied canvas has reached out like a beckoning finger to visionaries far and wide.

Juan Ponce de León, who came in search of the legendary Fountain of Youth, blazed a trail for the conquistadores who followed in his footsteps. A pair of Henrys—Flagler and Plant—laid the framework, or rather the railroad tracks, that enabled the state to become a major vacation destination.

Building on that framework, an entrepreneur named Walt Disney turned a central Florida cow pasture into the home of the rodent with arguably the state's most recognized face—if not surely its most recognized pair of ears.

The stylistic touches left behind by architects of many eras give Florida a rich sense of texture. A Spanish flair prevails in historic St. Augustine, where buildings are distinguished by walled patios, stately arches and roofs of

---

Florida Historical Timeline

Juan Ponce de León, searching for the Fountain of Youth, sails around Florida and lands near the site that later becomes St. Augustine.

1513

Spanish explorer Pedro Menéndez de Aviles destroys a French Huguenot colony and establishes St. Augustine.

1565

Visit Florida

1819

Spain sells Florida to the United States.

1763

Under the First Treaty of Paris, England gains possession of the region; in 1783 the Second Treaty of Paris returns all of Florida to Spain.

Library of Congress

1817

Gen. Andrew Jackson comes to punish the Indians for attacking the settlers, thus instigating the First Seminole War.

burnt-orange clay tile. Ybor City's showier flourishes—wrought-iron balconies, sidewalk cafes and plazas—point to a profoundly Latin influence. Synthetic materials, pastel hues and rectilinear forms characterize the Art Deco hotels along Ocean Drive in Miami's trendy South Beach.

As diverse as the state's architecture are the people who call Florida home. Sharing a place under the sun is a seemingly haphazard mix of retirees, jet setters, refugees and adventurers, of young and old, of "conch" fishermen, business tycoons and developers, and of tourists who came to visit but decided to stay.

Endless Days of Sunshine

One of the state's very few constants is its weather. Florida's climate is sultry, whether you visit in February or August. Its thermostat has but two settings: warm and hot.

For the most part Mother Nature smiles kindly, although she is prone to excess when angered. Hurricanes, tornadoes, floods and fires are among the punishments mercilessly inflicted when she unleashes sporadic fits of fury.

But Floridians take it all in stride. It's considerably easier in a state that simply refuses to take itself too seriously.

As much as Florida is rolling oceans, saw grass prairies and mangrove and cypress swamps, it is bicycle-riding birds, leaping alligators, and sea lions and walruses masquerading as actors.

As much as you can make a living here growing sugar cane, catching fish or manufacturing semiconductors, you can pull on a tail to perform as a mermaid, choose a sunny sidewalk spot from which to draw caricatures of passersby or stroll through gardens bedecked as a prim Southern belle.

What other state's identity ties so closely to the unabashedly seedy treasures that lurk behind signs of brash neon? Plastic yard flamingos, seashell figurines with glued-on rolling eyes, the simple word "Florida" set amid the chaos of unrestrained tie-dye on a 50/50 cotton blend T-shirt—like no other state, Florida has its kitsch in sync.

It's a place that brings forth smiles and laughter and lets us see things in a different light. A whimsical light. A humorous light.

Florida achieves statehood.

1845

Walt Disney World opens, bringing with it an explosion of new tourist attractions and thousands of new jobs – along with millions of tourists – to central Florida.

© Charles E. Rotkin/Corbis

1971

George W. Bush is named the 43rd president after Florida's election controversy is resolved by the U.S. Supreme Court.

2001

1958
Shortly after the first U.S. satellite, Explorer I, is launched from Cape Canaveral, the National Aeronautics and Space Administration (NASA) is created.

1986
The space shuttle *Challenger* explodes seconds after liftoff, killing all seven aboard.

© Jack Novak/SuperStock

2004
In an unprecedented hurricane season, four storms ranging from Category 2 to Category 4 struck Florida within 6 weeks.

Recreation

Water, water everywhere, and most is great for play. Recreation is a way of life in the Sunshine State, and what better way to catch some rest 'n' relaxation than to get wet.

Not only is Florida nearly surrounded by ocean and gulf waters, but it also harbors thousands of lakes and hundreds of miles of rivers and canals. The prevalence of boat ramps and the impressive facilities of municipal marinas testify to the popularity of **boating**. Boaters should take caution to watch for endangered manatees in springs and coastal waterways.

To appreciate the beauty of the Everglades' narrow creeks and shallow bays, set out on a **canoeing** adventure. A tranquil weeklong escape awaits serious paddlers who tackle the 100-mile-long Wilderness Waterway. Although the Turner River and Mud Lake Loop trails are considerably shorter, the scenery is no less spectacular. Also worth navigating are the myriad rivers, lakes and ponds of the Apalachicola and Ocala national forests.

Looking for a lazy way to pass the day? Grab a tube and go **river floating** at Coldwater Creek in Blackwater River State Forest or at Ichetucknee Springs, west of High Springs.

In Motion in the Ocean

Surfing is a sure-fire way to beat the heat. The best waves crash on the Atlantic beaches, most notably from New Smyrna Beach south to Sebastian Inlet. Swells occasionally kick up south of Mayport Naval Base near Jacksonville and around Deerfield Beach and South Beach in south Florida.

Off the Miami coast, shipwrecks and other sunken items—such as a Boeing 727 jet lowered to the ocean floor in 1993—function as artificial reefs. Rich coral growth makes **scuba diving** ventures here particularly attractive. **Snorkeling,** especially popular at John Pennekamp Coral Reef State Park in Key Largo, allows for similar encounters with marine life at a more shallow depth.

The nearly 600 varieties of fish that live off the coast lure anglers to cast their lines into the brine. Many marinas provide **saltwater fishing** equipment, bait and guides for deep-sea or offshore charters. Record-size specimens also swim in the state's rivers and lakes, making **freshwater fishing** equally rewarding.

Don't neglect to pick up a license from the county tax collector. Saltwater licenses, required for all anglers ages 16 to 64, cost nonresidents $6.50 for 3 days, $16.50 for 7 days or $31.50 for 1 year; a resident license costs $13.50 for 1 year. Stamps that allow you to reel in snook and net crawfish cost an additional $2 each. Freshwater licenses cost nonresidents $16.50 for 7 days or $31.50 for 1 year; a 1-year resident license costs $13.50. Combination fresh- and saltwater licenses are available for $25.50. Subagents such as tackle shops, fish camps or hardware or sporting goods stores charge 50c extra for some licenses.

Taking to the Terrain

Set out on foot to explore the more than 1,300 miles of **hiking** trails that comprise the Florida Trail; write the Florida Trail Association, 5415 S.W. 13th St., Gainesville, FL 32608, or phone (352) 378-8823, or (877) 445-3352. Supplement your strides with spectacular ocean views by walking along the coastline at Canaveral National Seashore; the Klondike stretch is open only to hikers. Leashed pets are welcomed at Smyrna Dunes Park, at the northern tip of the New Smyrna Beach peninsula.

If you prefer your exertion on the easy to moderate end of the spectrum, catch a breeze while **bicycling** on the relatively flat Florida terrain. Although you won't experience many downhill thrills, you won't grunt through many uphill struggles either. The town of White Springs is near 15 trails, including the looping Gar Pond Trail and the Big Shoals Trail, which passes one of the state's scant white-water stretches on the Suwannee River.

Public and semiprivate courses all over the state make **golf** immensely popular. And there's a good chance you'll work up a sweat just watching a spectator sport. Major and minor league **baseball** and professional **football, basketball, hockey** and **soccer** teams play statewide, while **dog racing, horse racing, jai-alai** and **polo** draw their own crowds.

Recreational Activities

Throughout the TourBook, you may notice a Recreational Activities heading with bulleted listings of recreation-oriented establishments listed underneath. Similar operations also may be mentioned in Destination City recreation sections. Since normal AAA inspection criteria cannot be applied, these establishments are presented only for information. Age, height and weight restrictions may apply. Reservations often are recommended and sometimes are required. Addresses and/or phone numbers are provided so visitors can contact the attraction for additional information.

Fast Facts

POPULATION: 15,982,378.

AREA: 58,560 square miles; ranks 22nd.

CAPITAL: Tallahassee.

HIGHEST POINT: 345 ft., Walton County.

LOWEST POINT: Sea level, Atlantic Ocean.

TIME ZONE(S): Eastern/Central. DST.

MINIMUM AGE FOR GAMBLING: 18.

MINIMUM AGE FOR UNRESTRICTED DRIVER'S LICENSE: 18.

SEAT BELT/CHILD RESTRAINT LAWS: Seat belts required for driver and front-seat passengers 18 and over. Seat belt or child restraint required for ages 4-18. Child restraints required for under 4.

HELMETS FOR MOTORCYCLISTS: Required for under 21.

RADAR DETECTORS: Permitted, except in some municipalities.

FIREARMS LAWS: Vary by state and/or county. Contact the Florida Department of Agriculture, Division of Licensing, P.O. Box 6687, Tallahassee, FL 32314-6687; phone (850) 488-5381.

HOLIDAYS: Jan. 1; Martin Luther King Jr. Day, Jan. (3rd Mon.); Memorial Day, May (4th Mon.); July 4; Labor Day, Sept. (1st Mon.); Veterans Day, Nov. 11; Thanksgiving, Nov. (4th Thurs.); Christmas, Dec. 25.

TAXES: Florida's statewide sales tax is 6 percent, with counties allowed to levy up to an additional 1 percent. Counties also may levy on accommodations and meals a Tourist Development Tax or a Tourist Impact Tax of varying increments.

SPECIAL REGULATIONS: All motorists who drive trucks or pull trailers must stop at road guard agricultural inspection stations. Recreational vehicles and private passenger vehicles without trailers are not required to stop at these stations.

Permanently disabled persons with "handicapped" license plates from any state receive special parking privileges in Florida.

SPECIAL NOTE: Lovebugs are unlovely insects that swarm during daylight hours April through May and September through October, often clogging car radiators and smearing windshields. These insects are extremely sticky and contain an acid which, if allowed to remain on a car, can corrode the finish.

To lessen the problems posed by these insects, place a bug screen over your car's front grille, restrict travel to the early morning or late afternoon hours and drive at slower speeds.

INFORMATION CENTERS: State welcome centers can be found just south of the Florida/Georgia border on US 231 at Campbellton, south of the Florida/Georgia border off I-75 near Jennings, near the Florida/Alabama border off I-10 16 miles west of Pensacola, south of the Florida/Georgia border off I-95 near Yulee, and in the Capitol in Tallahassee.

FURTHER INFORMATION FOR VISITORS:

Visit Florida Inc.
P.O. Box 1100
Tallahassee, FL 32302
(888) 735-2872

NATIONAL FOREST INFORMATION:

National Forests in Florida
325 John Knox Rd., Suite F-100
Tallahassee, FL 32303-4160
(850) 523-8500
(877) 444-6777 (reservations)

FISHING AND HUNTING REGULATIONS:

Freshwater:
Florida Fish and Wildlife Conservation
   Commission, Freshwater
2590 Executive Center Cir.
Berkley Building, Suite 200
Tallahassee, FL 32301
(850) 488-4676

Saltwater:
Florida Fish and Wildlife Conservation
   Commission, Saltwater
Division of Marine Fisheries
2590 Executive Center Cir.
Berkley Building, Suite 101
Tallahassee, FL 32301
(850) 487-3122

RECREATION INFORMATION:

Florida Department of Environmental
   Protection
Division of Recreation and Parks
3900 Commonwealth Blvd.
Mail Station 535
Tallahassee, FL 32399-3000
(850) 245-2157

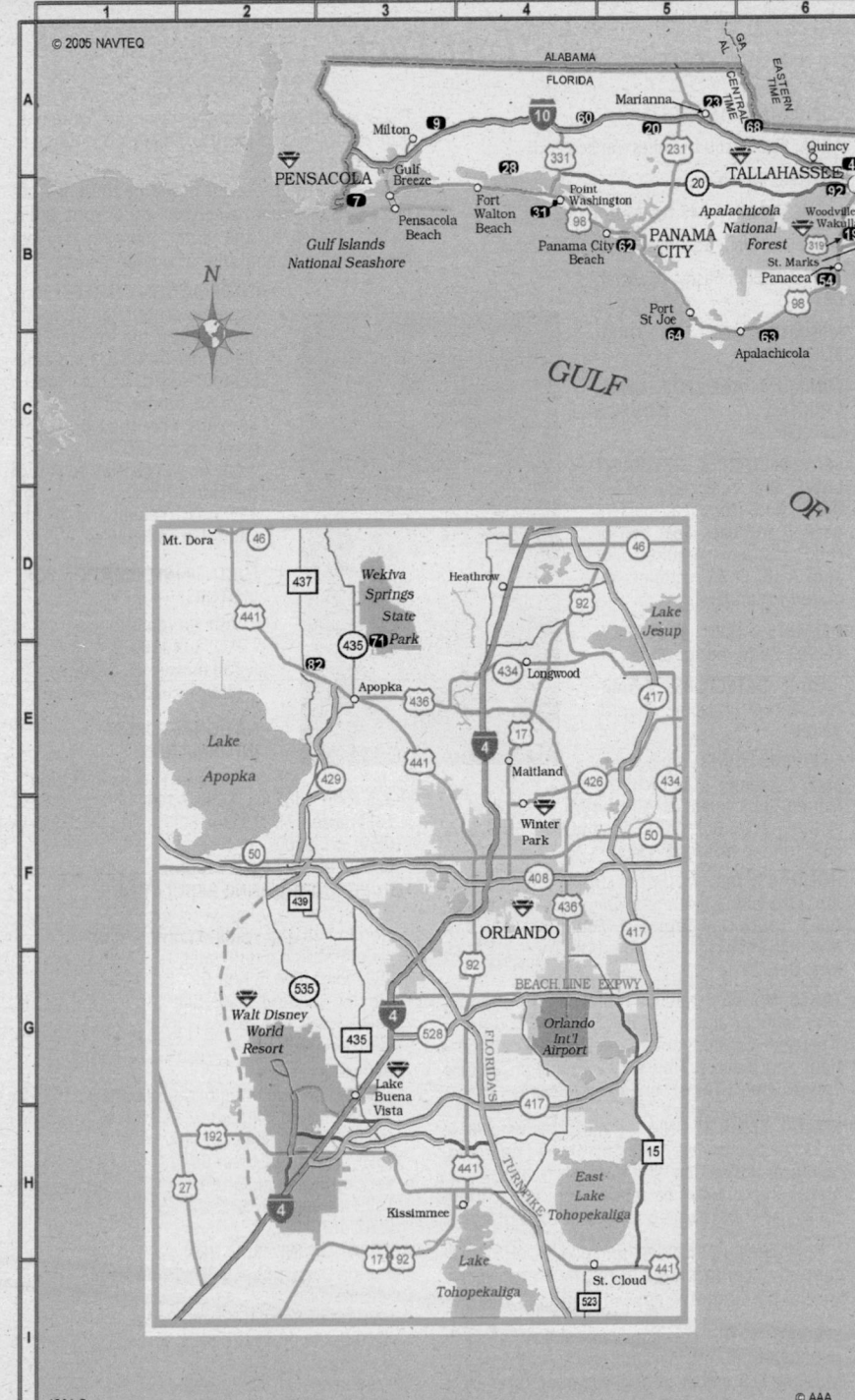

© 2005 NAVTEQ

4004-C

© AAA

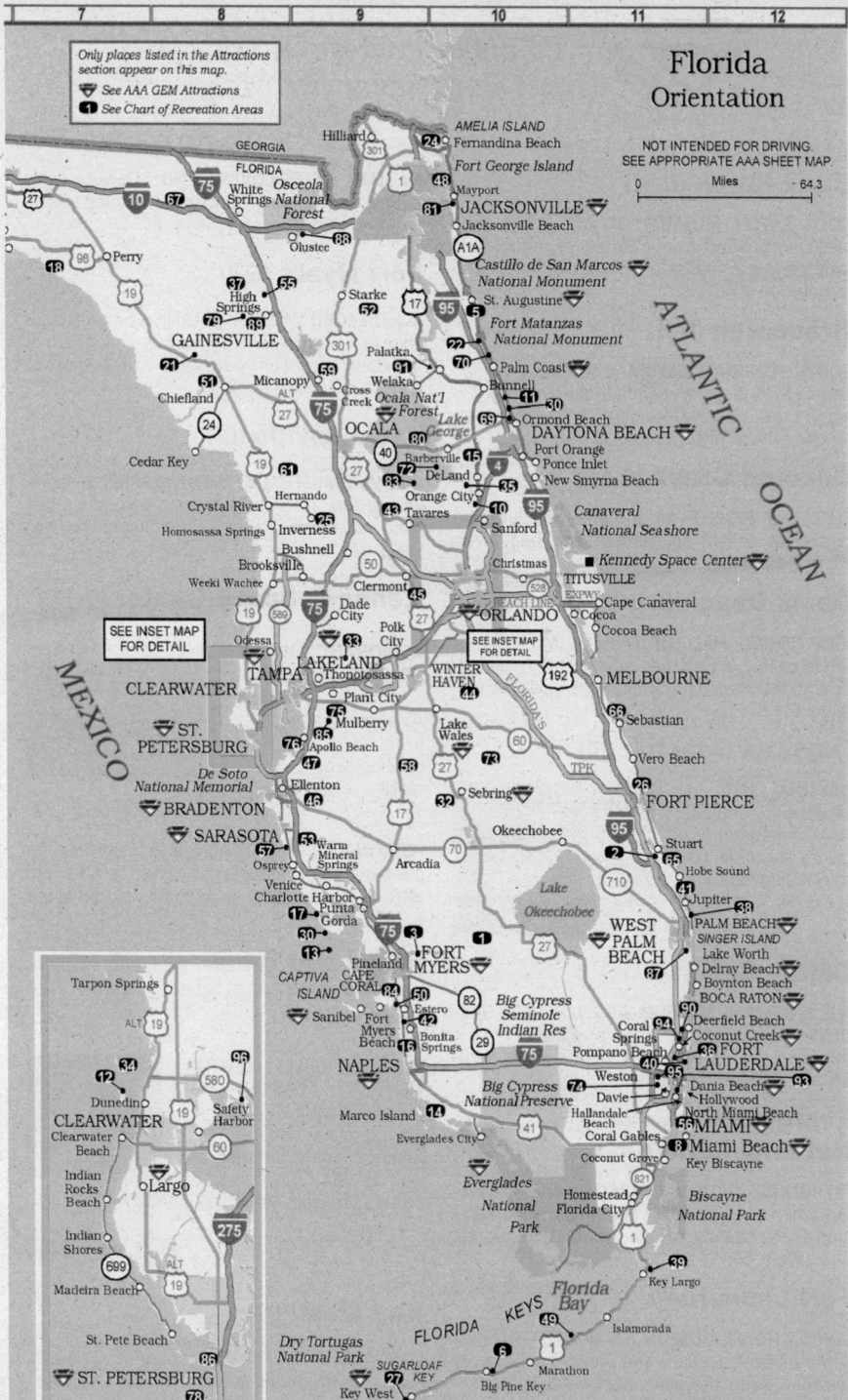

Florida
Orientation

NOT INTENDED FOR DRIVING.
SEE APPROPRIATE AAA SHEET MAP.

0   Miles   64.3

GEORGIA

FLORIDA

ATLANTIC

OCEAN

MEXICO

Hilliard

AMELIA ISLAND
Fernandina Beach
Fort George Island
Mayport
JACKSONVILLE
Jacksonville Beach

Castillo de San Marcos
National Monument
St. Augustine

Fort Matanzas
National Monument

Palm Coast
Bunnell
Ormond Beach
DAYTONA BEACH
Port Orange
Ponce Inlet
New Smyrna Beach

White Springs
Osceola National Forest
Olustee
Perry

High Springs
GAINESVILLE
Micanopy
Chiefland
Cross Creek
Starke
Palatka
Welaka
Ocala Nat'l Forest
Lake George
Cedar Key
OCALA
Barberville
DeLand
Orange City
Tavares
Sanford
Christmas

Canaveral National Seashore
Kennedy Space Center
TITUSVILLE
Cape Canaveral
Cocoa
Cocoa Beach

Crystal River
Hernando
Homosassa Springs
Inverness
Bushnell
Brooksville
Weeki Wachee
Clermont
Dade City
Polk City
Odessa
TAMPA
LAKELAND
Thonotosassa
CLEARWATER
ST. PETERSBURG
Plant City
Mulberry
Apollo Beach
De Soto National Memorial
Ellenton
BRADENTON
SARASOTA
Osprey
Warm Mineral Springs
Venice
Charlotte Harbor
Punta Gorda
Pineland
CAPTIVA ISLAND
CAPE CORAL
Sanibel
Fort Myers Beach
FORT MYERS
Estero
Bonita Springs
NAPLES
Marco Island

WINTER HAVEN
Lake Wales
Sebring
Okeechobee
Arcadia
Lake Okeechobee
Big Cypress Seminole Indian Res
Big Cypress National Preserve
Everglades City

ORLANDO
MELBOURNE
Sebastian
Vero Beach
FORT PIERCE
Stuart
Hobe Sound
Jupiter
WEST PALM BEACH
PALM BEACH
SINGER ISLAND
Lake Worth
Delray Beach
Boynton Beach
BOCA RATON
Deerfield Beach
Coconut Creek
Coral Springs
Pompano Beach
FORT LAUDERDALE
Weston
Davie
Dania Beach
Hollywood
North Miami Beach
Hallandale Beach
MIAMI
Coral Gables
Miami Beach
Coconut Grove
Key Biscayne
Homestead
Florida City
Biscayne National Park
Everglades National Park
Marathon
Big Pine Key
Key West
SUGARLOAF KEY
Dry Tortugas National Park
FLORIDA KEYS
Florida Bay
Key Largo
Islamorada

SEE INSET MAP FOR DETAIL

ATLANTIC OCEAN

Tarpon Springs
Dunedin
CLEARWATER
Clearwater Beach
Safety Harbor
Largo
Indian Rocks Beach
Indian Shores
Madeira Beach
St. Pete Beach
ST. PETERSBURG

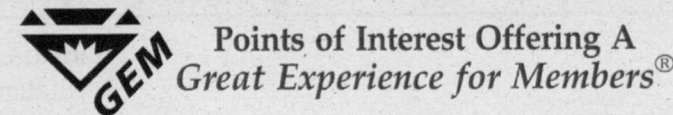

Points of Interest Offering A
Great Experience for Members®

Boca Raton (G-11)

BOCA RATON MUSEUM OF ART—More than 4,000 works of art from a variety of cultures and time periods comprise a diverse permanent collection. See p. 46.

Bradenton (F-8)

SOUTH FLORIDA MUSEUM—The renowned Tallant Collection of Paleo-Indian period artifacts is among the exhibits documenting Florida's natural and cultural history. See p. 47.

Coconut Creek (G-11)

BUTTERFLY WORLD—More than 4,000 fluttering butterflies delight shutterbugs and bug lovers alike. See p. 84.

Dania Beach (G-11)

IGFA FISHING HALL OF FAME & MUSEUM—A tackle gallery, a wetlands exhibit and simulated-fishing stations will lure you to this expansive museum. See p. 85.

Daytona Beach (C-10)

DAYTONA USA—Interactive displays, IMAX films and trivia games chronicle the city's racing heritage. See p. 54.

Delray Beach (G-11)

THE MORIKAMI MUSEUM AND JAPANESE GARDENS—Tranquility is the prevailing theme throughout a 200-acre park dedicated to traditional and modern Japanese culture. See p. 58.

Everglades National Park (H-10)

EVERGLADES NATIONAL PARK—Labyrinthine waters creep through salt prairies, hardwood hammocks and stands of mangroves and cypress trees. See p. 60.

Fort Lauderdale (G-11)

BONNET HOUSE MUSEUM & GARDENS—The residence of artists Frederic and Evelyn Bartlett is resplendent with the pair's works and decorative personal touches. See p. 77.

MUSEUM OF DISCOVERY AND SCIENCE—More than 200 stimulating exhibits draw young visitors into the realm of science. See p. 80.

Fort Myers (G-9)

EDISON-FORD WINTER ESTATES—Good friends Thomas Edison and Henry Ford wintered here as neighbors after Ford purchased a house next to Edison's in 1916. See p. 87.

Jacksonville (B-10)

CUMMER MUSEUM OF ART & GARDENS—Noteworthy features include Meissen porcelain tableware and a formal garden extending to the river. See p. 97.

Kennedy Space Center (D-11)

ASTRONAUT HALL OF FAME—The hall of fame honors America's space pioneers and traces the development of space exploration. See p. 107.

ASTRONAUTS MEMORIAL SPACE MIRROR—The black granite memorial pays tribute to American astronauts who died in the line of duty. See p. 107.

KENNEDY SPACE CENTER—The facility operates as America's center of space operations. See p. 106.

KENNEDY SPACE CENTER VISITOR COMPLEX—The complex features multimedia displays about the American space program as well as IMAX theaters and actual spacecraft. See p. 107.

Key West (I-9)

CONCH TOUR TRAINS—Narration centers on area history as the trains navigate old and new Key West. See p. 71.

Lake Buena Vista (G-3)

WALT DISNEY WORLD® RESORT—The sprawling complex includes the Magic Kingdom® Park, Epcot®, Disney-MGM Studios, Disney's Animal Kingdom®, family water parks and numerous entertainment, shopping and dining facilities. See p. 167.

Lakeland (E-9)

FLORIDA AIR MUSEUM AT SUN 'N FUN—If the aircraft displayed here seem a bit unusual, it is because many are either homebuilt or experimental models (or both). See p. 108.

Lake Wales (E-10)

HISTORIC BOK SANCTUARY—Landscaped gardens surround a marble and coquina stone tower that contains 60 bronze bells. See p. 109.

Largo (H-7)

PINEWOOD CULTURAL PARK—This 182-acre site features an art museum, botanical gardens and more than two dozen historic buildings representing the early days of Pinellas County. See p. 233.

Miami (H-11)

DEERING ESTATE AT CUTLER—The park's beautifully landscaped grounds comprise two historic homes, an American Indian burial ground and nature trails. See p. 120.

MIAMI-DADE CULTURAL CENTER—The center comprises a museum that outlines the history of south Florida; a museum that features the artwork of international contemporary artists; and a library. See p. 122.

MIAMI SEAQUARIUM—Watch performing marine mammals or have a personal encounter with dolphins on this 38-acre tropical island. See p. 123.

MIAMI METROZOO—Animal shows complement cageless environments inhabited by species of African, Asian and European animals. See p. 123.

PARROT JUNGLE ISLAND—Parrots and other exotic birds thrive in this subtropical flowery paradise. See p. 123.

VIZCAYA MUSEUM AND GARDENS—Opulent furnishings in the impressive 34-room villa represent the renaissance, baroque, rococo and neoclassical eras. See p. 124.

Miami Beach (H-11)

THE HOLOCAUST MEMORIAL—The 6 million Jews who died at the hands of the Nazis are remembered here. See p. 125.

Naples (G-9)

NAPLES MUSEUM OF ART—Entrance gates by metal artist Albert Paley and two gigantic Dale Chihuly glass chandeliers proclaim the caliber of this museum's art holdings. See p. 137.

Ocala (C-9)

THE APPLETON MUSEUM OF ART—The museum is a showcase for European, pre-Columbian, West African, Islamic and Asian art as well as antiquities. See p. 139.

Orlando (D-10)

DISCOVERY COVE ORLANDO—Swim with the sharks and hug dolphins at this resort-style park geared towards intimate, safe and un-  forgettable encounters between humans and animals. See p. 150.

DIXIE STAMPEDE DINNER & SHOW—Stampeding buffalo, spirited horses and a cast of singers, dancers and comedians entertain while guests enjoy a four-course feast. See p. 150.

SEAWORLD ORLANDO—The theme park lets visitors experience marine life up close through varied displays and shows, such as the one featuring the famed Shamu. See p. 155..

UNIVERSAL ORLANDO RESORT— The park features Universal Studios, where rides and  shows are based on popular films and TV shows; Universal's Islands of Adventure, with five lands representing legendary characters and super heroes; as well as an entertainment section with restaurants and clubs. See p. 156.

Palm Beach (F-11)

FLAGLER MUSEUM— This Gilded-Age mansion, furnished in original and period pieces, contains historical exhibits. See p. 187.

Palm Coast (C-10)

WASHINGTON OAKS GARDENS STATE PARK— Covering more than 400 acres of Florida coastal scenery, the gardens feature exotic plants from around the world. See p. 187.

Pensacola (B-2)

NATIONAL MUSEUM OF NAVAL AVIATION—Highlights of the museum collection are an NC-4 Flying Boat, a World War II SBD Dauntless and the Skylab Command Module. See p. 190.

St. Augustine (B-10)

CASTILLO DE SAN MARCOS NATIONAL MONUMENT—The Spanish fortress, which features massive diamond-shaped bastions at each corner, defended the city until the mid-18th century. See p. 193.

COLONIAL SPANISH QUARTER—Costumed guides depict the 1740s lifestyle in this quarter of restored and reconstructed buildings. See p. 195.

GOVERNMENT HOUSE MUSEUM—American Indian artifacts, treasure from Spanish shipwrecks and religious items are among the exhibits detailing area history. See p. 195.

HISTORIC OLD JAIL COMPLEX—The complex comprises a museum that depicts Florida's growth; the jail, which displays weaponry and outlines prison life; and narrated trolley tours. See p. 198.

LIGHTNER MUSEUM—Tiffany stained glass, Oriental art and art nouveau works are noteworthy in the Lightner collection. See p. 195.

OLDEST HOUSE—Also known as the González-Alvarez House, the structure is home to two museums: one tracing city history and one devoted to Florida's army. See p. 195.

ST. AUGUSTINE ALLIGATOR FARM—All 23 crocodilian species are represented at the farm, which also features tropical birds. See p. 198.

WORLD GOLF HALL OF FAME AT WORLD GOLF VILLAGE—The showcase for this sport honors golfing legends; an IMAX theater is part of the complex. See p. 199.

St. Petersburg (E-8)

THE FLORIDA HOLOCAUST MUSEUM—Tolerance and understanding are the lessons taught at this museum commemorating the millions who perished during this tragic period. See p. 218.

SALVADOR DALI MUSEUM—The Spanish artist's creative diversity is captured in works ranging from small impressionistic pieces to gigantic surrealistic montages. See p. 222.

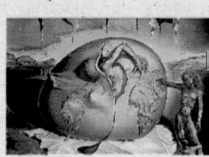

Sanibel (G-9)

THE BAILEY-MATTHEWS SHELL MUSEUM—Seashells from the nearby beaches of Sanibel and Captiva islands as well as locations around the world are displayed. See p. 200.

Sarasota (F-8)

THE JOHN AND MABLE RINGLING MUSEUM OF ART—An extensive collection of pieces by Peter Paul Rubens is the centerpiece of the Italian Renaissance museum. See p. 204.

Sebring (F-10)

HIGHLANDS HAMMOCK STATE PARK—Lush vegetation flourishes in the dense jungle and swampland in this easy-to-explore park. See p. 206.

Silver Springs (C-9)

FLORIDA'S SILVER SPRINGS—Glass-bottom boats cruise the clear artesian springs, offering views of underwater life as far as 40 feet below the water's surface. See p. 207.

Tallahassee (B-6)

ALFRED B. MACLAY GARDENS STATE PARK—Colorful azaleas, camellias and Oriental magnolias decorate the grounds of this Southern estate. See p. 208.

Tampa (E-8)

BUSCH GARDENS TAMPA BAY—A late 19th-century African motif punctuates the rides, entertainment, animal exhibits and shows in the park. See p. 223.

THE FLORIDA AQUARIUM—Florida's ecosystem and aquatic habitats are detailed in aquarium exhibits. See p. 223.

MOSI (MUSEUM OF SCIENCE & INDUSTRY)—In addition to a planetarium and an IMAX *Dome* theater, the museum presents displays  that explain aspects of science and technology. See p. 224.

Wakulla (B-6)

EDWARD BALL WAKULLA SPRINGS STATE PARK—The clear, deep springs are believed to have been discovered by Ponce de León, who claimed them to be the "fountain of youth." See p. 236.

West Palm Beach (F-11)

NORTON MUSEUM OF ART—The museum's holdings include a distinguished collection of 19th- and 20th-century European and American masterpieces. See p. 238.

Winter Park (F-4)

CHARLES HOSMER MORSE MUSEUM OF AMERICAN ART—Most noteworthy in the museum is an extensive collection of works by art nouveau master Louis Comfort Tiffany, whose stained glass gained him fame. See p. 184.

RECREATION AREAS

	MAP LOCATION	CAMPING	PICNICKING	HIKING TRAILS	BOATING	BOAT RAMP	BOAT RENTAL	FISHING	SWIMMING	PETS ON LEASH	BICYCLE TRAILS	SKIN/SCUBA	VISITOR CENTER	LODGE/CABINS	FOOD SERVICE
NATIONAL PARKS *(See place listings)*															
Biscayne (H-11) 173,000 acres. Scenic.		•	•	•	•	•		•	•	•			•	•	
Dry Tortugas (I-8) 64,657 acres. Scenic.		•	•		•	•		•	•				•	•	
Everglades (H-10) 1,506,539 acres. Scenic. Pets on leash in campgrounds only.		•	•	•	•	•	•	•		•	•		•	•	•
NATIONAL FORESTS *(See place listings)*															
Apalachicola 565,543 acres. Northwestern Florida.		•	•	•	•	•		•	•	•					
Ocala 383,573 acres. North-central Florida. Horse rental.		•	•	•	•	•	•	•	•	•	•	•	•	•	•
Osceola 198,484 acres. Northeastern Florida. Horse rentals and trails.		•	•	•	•	•		•	•	•					
NATIONAL SEASHORES *(See place listings)*															
Canaveral (D-10) 57,000 acres. East-central Florida. Canoe rental.		•	•	•	•	•	•	•	•				•		
Gulf Islands (B-3) 137,000 acres. Northwestern Florida.		•	•	•	•	•		•	•		•	•	•		
ARMY CORPS OF ENGINEERS															
Ortona Lock (G-10) 10 mi. e. of La Belle off SR 80 to campground unit; 12 mi. e off SR 78A to day use unit.	❶	•	•		•	•		•		•					
St. Lucie Lock (F-11) 140 acres comprising campground and day-use areas 8 mi. s.w. of Stuart off SR 76.	❷	•	•	•	•	•		•		•			•		
W.P. Franklin Lock (G-9) 12 mi. e. of Fort Myers off SR 78 to campground unit; 7 mi. e. off SR 80 to day use unit.	❸	•	•		•	•		•		•			•		
STATE															
Alfred B. Maclay Gardens (B-6) 1,179 acres 5 mi. n.e. of Tallahassee on US 319. Scenic. Horse trails. *(See Tallahassee p. 208)*	❹		•	•	•	•		•	•	•	•		•		
Anastasia (C-10) 1,643 acres at St. Augustine Beach off SR A1A.	❺	•	•	•	•			•	•	•	•				•
Bahia Honda (I-10) 490 acres on Bahia Honda Key on US 1 at mile marker 37. Snorkeling tours; kayak rentals.	❻	•	•	•	•	•	•	•	•	•		•		•	•
Big Lagoon (B-3) 730 acres 10 mi. s.w. of Pensacola on SR 292A.	❼	•	•	•	•	•		•	•	•					
Bill Baggs Cape Florida (H-11) 431 acres off US 1 on Key Biscayne. Historic. Lighthouse tour.	❽		•	•				•	•	•					•

RECREATION AREAS

Recreation Areas	MAP LOCATION	CAMPING	PICNICKING	HIKING TRAILS	BOATING	BOAT RAMP	BOAT RENTAL	FISHING	SWIMMING	PETS ON LEASH	BICYCLE TRAILS	SKIN/SCUBA	VISITOR CENTER	LODGE/CABINS	FOOD SERVICE
Blackwater River (A-3) 635 acres 15 mi. n.e. of Milton off US 90. Historic. Tubing; canoe rentals, guided walks.	9	•	•	•	•			•	•	•					
Blue Spring (D-10) 2,643 acres 2 mi. w. of Orange City off US 17/92 on W. French Ave. *(See Orange City p. 140)*	10	•	•	•	•			•	•	•			•	•	•
Bulow Plantation Ruins Historic (C-10) 152 acres 9 mi. s.e. of Bunnell off CR 2001 (Old Kings Rd.), between SR 100 and Old Dixie Hwy. Historic. Canoeing; interpretive center. *(See Bunnell p. 48)*	11		•	•	•	•		•		•					
Caladesi Island (G-7) 2,470 acres in the Gulf of Mexico w. of Dunedin. Bird-watching, boat camping. *(See Dunedin p. 232)*	12		•	•	•			•	•	•			•		•
Cayo Costa (G-9) 2,427 acres accessible by boat from Boca Grande or Fort Myers. Bird-watching.	13	•	•	•	•			•	•	•	•			•	
Collier-Seminole (H-9) 7,271 acres 17 mi. s. of Naples on US 41. Historic. Bird-watching. *(See Naples p. 136)*	14	•	•	•	•	•		•		•			•		
De Leon Springs (C-10) 600 acres 1 mi. w. of De Leon Springs off US 17. Historic. Canoe, kayak and paddleboat rentals. *(See De Leon Springs p. 58)*	15		•	•	•		•	•	•				•		•
Delnor-Wiggins Pass (G-9) 166 acres 11 mi. n.w. of Naples off SR 846. Shell gathering, turtle watching in nesting season; boardwalks, observation tower. *(See Naples p. 135)*	16		•		•	•		•	•	•			•		
Don Pedro Island (F-8) 230 acres accessible only by boat.	17		•	•	•			•	•	•					
Econfina River (B-7) 4,528 acres s. of Lamont at the end of CR 14. Horse trails.	18		•	•	•			•		•					
Edward Ball Wakulla Springs (B-6) 5,882 acres .5 mi. e. of Wakulla Springs at jct. SRs 61 and 267. Bird-watching; boat tours. *(See Wakulla p. 236)*	19		•	•					•	•				•	•
Falling Waters (A-5) 173 acres 3 mi. s. of Chipley off SR 77.	20	•	•	•					•	•					
Fanning Springs (C-8) 198 acres on US 19/98 on the e. bank of the Suwannee River in Fanning Springs.	21		•	•	•			•	•		•				
Faver-Dykes (C-10) 1,465 acres 15 mi. s. of St. Augustine off US 1.	22	•	•	•	•			•		•					
Florida Caverns (A-5) 1,280 acres 3 mi. n. of Marianna on SR 166. Bird-watching; horse trails. *(See Marianna p. 111)*	23	•	•	•	•	•		•	•	•	•		•		
Fort Clinch (A-10) 1,361 acres 2 mi. e. of Fernandina Beach on SR A1A at n. end of Amelia Island. Historic. Bird-watching. *(See Fernandina Beach p. 104)*	24	•	•	•				•	•	•	•		•		
Fort Cooper (D-8) 753 acres 2 mi. s. of Inverness off US 41. Historic.	25		•	•	•			•	•	•					
Fort Pierce Inlet (F-11) 1,137 acres 3 mi. e. of Fort Pierce on SR A1A. Bird-watching, surfing. *(See Fort Pierce p. 21)*	26	•	•	•				•	•	•	•	•			
Fort Zachary Taylor Historic (I-9) 53 acres at the s.w. end of Key West via Southard St. Historic. *(See Key West p. 72)*	27		•	•				•	•	•					•
Fred Gannon Rocky Bayou (B-4) 362 acres 5 mi. e. of Niceville on SR 20.	28	•	•	•	•	•		•	•	•					
Gamble Rogers Memorial State Recreation Area (C-10) 133 acres .5 mi. s. of Flagler Beach on SR A1A.	29	•	•	•	•	•		•	•	•					
Gasparilla Island (G-9) 127 acres 3 mi. s. of Placida on CR 775. Historic. Interpretive center, lighthouse.	30		•					•	•	•	•		•		
Grayton Beach (B-3) 2,127 acres adjacent to Grayton Beach on SR 30A.	31	•	•	•	•	•		•	•	•	•			•	
Highlands Hammock (F-10) 9,251 acres 3.5 mi. w. of US 27 on CR 634. Scenic. Bird-watching; horse trails, museum. *(See Sebring p. 206)*	32	•	•	•						•	•		•		•
Hillsborough River (E-8) 3,035 acres 6 mi. s. of Zephyrhills off US 301. Living-history program.	33	•	•	•	•				•	•					
Honeymoon Island (G-7) 2,810 acres 3 mi. n. of Dunedin on SR 586, w. of US 19A. Bird-watching.	34		•	•				•	•	•					•
Hontoon Island (D-10) 1,654 acres 6 mi. w. of DeLand off SR 44.	35	•	•	•				•		•			•	•	
Hugh Taylor Birch (G-11) 174 acres at Sunrise Blvd. and SR A1A in Fort Lauderdale.	36		•	•	•			•	•	•			•		

RECREATION AREAS

Recreation Area	MAP LOCATION	CAMPING	PICNICKING	HIKING TRAILS	BOATING	BOAT RAMP	BOAT RENTAL	FISHING	SWIMMING	PETS ON LEASH	BICYCLE TRAILS	SKIN/SCUBA	VISITOR CENTER	LODGE/CABINS	FOOD SERVICE
Ichetucknee Springs (B-8) 2,356 acres off US 27 .5 mi. e. of Hildreth. Scenic. Bird-watching, tubing. *(See High Springs p. 95)*	37		•	•	•				•	•			•		•
John D. MacArthur Beach (F-12) 437 acres on SR A1A, 2.8 mi. s. of jct. US 1 on Singer Island. Bird-watching. *(See Singer Island p. 207)*	38		•	•				•	•	•			•		•
John Pennekamp Coral Reef (I-11) 178 nautical miles on US 1 near Key Largo mile marker 102.5. *(See Key Largo p. 70)*	39	•	•	•	•	•	•	•	•	•		•	•		•
John U. Lloyd Beach (G-12) 310 acres 3 mi. s. of Fort Lauderdale on SR A1A.	40		•	•	•	•	•	•	•	•			•		•
Jonathan Dickinson (F-11) 11,500 acres 2 mi. s. of Hobe Sound on US 1. Historic. Scenic. Bird-watching; bicycle rental, horse trails. *(See Hobe Sound p. 95)*	41	•	•	•	•	•	•	•	•	•	•			•	•
Koreshan (G-9) 195 acres .5 mi. s. of Estero on US 41. Historic. Bird-watching; canoe rentals. *(See Estero p. 59)*	42	•	•	•	•	•		•	•				•		
Lake Griffin (D-9) 464 acres 1 mi. e. of Fruitland Park off US 27.	43	•	•	•	•	•		•		•					
Lake Kissimmee (E-10) 5,933 acres 8 mi. e. of Lake Wales via SR 60, 4 mi. n. on Boy Scout Rd., then 5 mi. n. on Camp Mack Rd. following signs. Bird-watching; horse trails, living-history program. *(See Lake Wales p. 110)*	44	•	•	•	•	•		•		•					
Lake Louisa (D-9) 4,407 acres 7 mi. s.e. of Clermont on Lake Nellie Rd. Horse trails.	45	•	•	•				•	•	•				•	
Lake Manatee (F-9) 548 acres 14 mi. e. of Bradenton on SR 64. Bird-watching.	46	•	•		•	•	•	•	•	•					
Little Manatee River (E-9) 2,417 acres 5 mi. s. of Sun City off US 301. Equestrian camping; horse trails.	47	•	•		•			•	•	•					
Little Talbot Island (B-10) 1,766 acres 17 mi. n.e. of Jacksonville on SR A1A. Pier.	48	•	•	•				•	•	•	•				
Long Key (I-10) 978 acres on Long Key at Layton on US 1.	49	•	•	•				•	•	•			•		
Lovers Key (G-9) 443 acres on CR 865, 2 mi. s. of Big Carlos Pass on Lovers Key.	50		•	•	•	•		•	•	•					•
Manatee Springs (C-8) 2,200 acres 6 mi. w. of Chiefland on SR 320. Bird-watching.	51	•	•	•	•			•	•	•					•
Mike Roess Gold Head Branch (C-9) 2,174 acres 6 mi. n.e. of Keystone Heights on SR 21. Bird-watching; bicycle, canoe and paddleboat rentals.	52	•	•	•	•		•	•	•	•			•		
Myakka River (F-9) 28,937 acres 17 mi. e. of Sarasota on SR 72. Bird-watching; airboat and tram tours, bicycle rentals, horse trails. *(See Sarasota p. 205)*	53	•	•	•	•	•	•	•		•	•		•	•	•
Ochlockonee River (B-6) 385 acres 4 mi. s. of Sopchoppy on US 319.	54	•	•	•	•	•		•	•	•					
O'Leno (B-8) 6,700 acres 6 mi. n. of High Springs off US 41. Historic. Bird-watching. *(See High Springs p. 95)*	55	•	•	•	•			•	•	•					
Oleta River (H-11) 1,032 acres at 3400 N.E. 163rd St. in North Miami Beach.	56		•	•	•			•	•	•				•	•
Oscar Scherer (F-8) 1,383 acres 2 mi. s. of Osprey on US 41. Bird-watching.	57	•	•	•	•			•	•	•			•		
Paynes Creek Historic (E-9) 400 acres .5 mi. e. of Bowling Green at 888 Lake Branch Rd. Historic. Bird-watching, canoeing; interpretive center.	58		•	•				•		•			•		
Paynes Prairie Preserve (C-9) 21,000 acres 1 mi. n. of Micanopy on US 441. Bird-watching, canoeing; horse trail. *(See Micanopy p. 135)*	59	•	•	•	•			•		•	•				
Ponce de Leon Springs (A-5) 382 acres .5 mi. s. of Ponce de Leon on US 90.	60		•	•					•	•					
Rainbow Springs (D-8) 1,083 acres 3 mi. n. of Dunnellon on US 41. Tubing; waterfalls.	61	•	•	•	•				•	•			•		
St. Andrews (B-5) 1,168 acres 3 mi. e. of Panama City Beach via SR 392. *(See Panama City Beach p. 187)*	62	•	•	•	•	•	•	•	•	•	•		•		•

RECREATION AREAS

	MAP LOCATION	CAMPING	PICNICKING	HIKING TRAILS	BOATING	BOAT RAMP	BOAT RENTAL	FISHING	SWIMMING	PETS ON LEASH	BICYCLE TRAILS	SKIN/SCUBA	VISITOR CENTER	LODGE/CABINS	FOOD SERVICE
St. George Island (C-6) 2,023 acres off US 98 via CRs G1A and 300 on St. George Island. Bird-watching.	63	•	•	•	•	•		•	•						
St. Joseph Peninsula (C-5) 2,600 acres 20 mi. s.w. of Port St. Joe. Bird-watching.	64	•	•	•	•	•	•	•	•	•			•		•
St. Lucie Inlet Preserve (F-11) 4,492 acres accessible by boat from Port Salerno on the Intracoastal Waterway. Bird-watching.	65		•	•				•	•	•					
Sebastian Inlet (E-11) 917 acres 15 mi. n. of Vero Beach on SR A1A. Bird-watching; museums. *(See Vero Beach p. 236)*	66	•	•	•	•	•	•	•	•	•		•	•		•
Suwannee River (B-8) 1,928 acres 13 mi. w. of Live Oak on US 90. Historic.	67	•	•	•	•	•		•	•						
Three Rivers (A-5) 667 acres 2 mi. n. of Sneads off US 90.	68	•	•	•	•	•		•	•						
Tomoka (C-10) 1,610 acres 3 mi. n. of Ormond Beach. Museum.	69	•	•	•	•	•	•	•		•			•		•
Washington Oaks Gardens (C-10) 425 acres at 6400 Oceanshore Blvd. Interpretive center. *(See Palm Coast p. 187)*	70		•	•				•		•			•	•	
Wekiwa Springs (E-3) 7,725 acres 4 mi. n.w. of I-4, off US 441 near Apopka. Bird-watching; horse trails.	71	•	•	•	•		•	•	•	•					•
OTHER															
Alexander Springs (D-9) 30 acres 13 mi. n.e. of Umatilla via SR 19 and CR 445. *(See Ocala National Forest p. 140)*	72	•	•	•	•		•	•	•	•		•	•		•
Avon Park Air Force Range (E-10) 84,000 acres on SR 64 in Avon Park.	73	•	•	•	•	•		•	•	•			•		
C.B. Smith (G-11) 320 acres at Flamingo Rd. and Hollywood Blvd. in Pembroke Pines. Tennis; miniature golf course, waterslide.	74		•	•	•	•	•	•	•	•			•		•
Edward Medard (E-9) 1,284 acres off Turkey Creed Rd. in Plant City. Beach, horse trails, observation tower. *(See Plant City p. 234)*	75	•	•	•	•	•		•	•	•					
E.G. Simmons (E-8) 469 acres on Tampa Bay, 1 mi. w. of US 41 in Ruskin.	76	•	•		•	•		•	•	•		•			
Everglades Holiday (G-11) 10 acres 20 mi. w. of Dania off Griffin Rd. Airboat rides.	77		•		•	•	•	•		•					•
Fort De Soto (E-8) 1,136 acres off I-275 exit 17 at Pinellas Bayway. Historic. *(See St. Petersburg p. 218)*	78	•	•	•	•	•		•	•	•	•				•
Ginnie Springs (C-8) 200 acres 7 mi. w. of High Springs off CR 340. Canoeing. *(See High Springs p. 95)*	79	•	•	•	•	•		•	•	•		•		•	•
Juniper Springs (C-9) 47 acres 28 mi. e. of Ocala on SR 40. Canoeing, kayaking; canoe rental, pool. *(See Ocala National Forest p. 140)*	80	•	•	•	•		•	•	•	•			•		•
Kathryn Abbey Hanna (B-9) 450 acres next to Mayport Naval Station off SR A1A in Jacksonville Beach. Canoeing, horseback riding; horse rentals.	81	•	•	•	•	•	•	•	•	•	•	•			
Kelly (E-3) 200 acres 6 mi. n. of Apopka on SR 435. Tubing. *(See Apopka p. 164)*	82	•	•	•				•	•	•					•
Lake Dorr (D-9) 10 acres 5 mi. n. of Umatilla on SR 19. *(See Ocala National Forest p. 140)*	83	•	•		•	•		•	•				•		
Lakes (G-9) 279 acres 6 mi. s.w. of I-75 exit 131, via Six Mile Cypress. Bicycle rental, jogging trails.	84		•	•				•	•	•	•				•
Lithia Springs (E-9) 200 acres 7.2 mi. s. of Brandon off Lithia Pinecrest Rd. Canoeing.	85	•	•	•				•	•	•					•
Maximo (I-8) 65 acres in St. Petersburg at 34th St. and Pinellas Point Dr. S. Observation tower, playground.	86		•		•	•		•		•					•
Okeeheelee (G-11) 1,000 acres in Palm Beach, 6 mi. w. of I-95 on Forest Hills Blvd. Ball fields, water-skiing course.	87		•	•	•	•	•	•		•	•	•			•
Olustee Beach (B-9) 15 acres .25 mi. n. of Olustee on CR 231.	88		•		•	•		•	•	•					
Poe Springs (C-8) 202 acres 3 mi. w. of High Springs on CR 340. *(See High Springs p. 95)*	89		•	•	•	•		•	•	•					•

RECREATION AREAS

	MAP LOCATION	CAMPING	PICNICKING	HIKING TRAILS	BOATING	BOAT RAMP	BOAT RENTAL	FISHING	SWIMMING	PETS ON LEASH	BICYCLE TRAILS	SKIN/SCUBA	VISITOR CENTER	LODGE/CABINS	FOOD SERVICE
Quiet Waters (G-11) 430 acres 2 mi. w. from I-95 via SR 810, then .25 mi. s. on SR 845 in Deerfield Beach. Cable water skiing; canoe, paddleboat and bicycle rentals. *(See Deerfield Beach p. 85)*	90	•	•		•	•	•	•	•	•	•	•			•
Rodman Reservoir (C-9) 10 mi. s.w. of Palatka off SR 19 access roads on the Ocklawaha River. Horse trails.	91	•	•	•	•	•		•	•						
Silver Lake (B-6) 25 acres 8 mi. w. of Tallahassee off SR 20.	92		•	•				•	•		•				
Topeekeegee Yugnee (G-11) 150 acres .5 mi. w. of I-95 on Sheridan St. (SR 822) in Hollywood. Canoe and paddleboat rentals, miniature golf course, waterslide.	93	•	•					•	•	•	•	•			•
Tradewinds (G-11) 90 acres at 3600 Sample Rd. in Coconut Creek. Botanical gardens, horse rental, museum, pony rides, hayrides.	94		•	•				•	•		•	•			•
Tree Tops (G-11) 256 acres at 3900 S.W. 100th Ave. in Davie. Canoe, horse and paddleboat rentals.	95	•	•					•	•		•	•	•		
Upper Tampa Bay (G-8) 596 acres w. of Tampa off SR 580. Canoeing. Boardwalk, nature center; playground.	96		•	•					•		•				

Florida Temperature Averages
Maximum / Minimum
From the records of the National Weather Service

	JAN	FEB	MAR	APR	MAY	JUNE	JULY	AUG	SEPT	OCT	NOV	DEC
Jacksonville	65/44	67/46	72/50	79/57	85/64	88/70	90/72	90/72	86/70	79/62	71/51	66/45
Key West	76/66	77/66	79/70	82/74	85/76	88/79	89/80	89/80	88/79	84/75	80/71	76/67
Miami	76/59	77/59	79/63	83/67	85/71	88/74	89/75	90/76	88/75	85/71	80/64	77/60
Orlando	70/50	72/51	76/56	81/61	87/66	89/71	90/73	90/73	88/72	82/66	76/57	71/51
Tallahassee	64/41	66/43	72/48	80/56	87/63	90/70	91/72	90/72	87/69	81/58	71/46	65/41
Tampa	71/50	72/52	76/56	82/62	87/67	90/72	90/74	90/74	89/73	84/65	77/56	72/51
West Palm Beach	75/56	76/56	79/60	83/65	86/69	88/72	90/74	90/74	88/75	84/70	79/62	76/57

Points of Interest

AMELIA ISLAND—*see Jacksonville p. 104.*

APALACHICOLA (C-6) pop. 2,334, elev. 17'

Apalachicola is a Hitchiti Indian word meaning "people on the other side." More than 80 percent of the state's oyster crop (10 percent of the nation's total) is cultivated in Apalachicola's more than 6,000 acres of oyster beds.

Apalachicola Bay Chamber of Commerce: 122 Commerce St., Apalachicola, FL 32320-1776; phone (850) 653-9419.

JOHN GORRIE MUSEUM STATE PARK, 46 Sixth St. at Ave. D, is 1 blk. e. of US 98 on Gorrie Square. The museum is named for Dr. John Gorrie, recipient of the first U.S. patent for mechanical refrigeration in 1851. A replica of Gorrie's ice-making machine and area history exhibits are featured. Allow 30 minutes minimum. Thurs.-Mon. 9-5; closed Jan. 1, Thanksgiving and Dec. 25. Admission $1, under 6 free. Phone (850) 653-9347.

APALACHICOLA NATIONAL FOREST

Elevations in the forest range from 10 ft. to 100 ft.

Stretching across four northwestern counties, the Apalachicola National Forest is the largest of Florida's three national forests. Its 550,000 acres of varied terrain include pine flatwoods, hardwood hammocks, swamp rivers, lakes and two wilderness areas: Bradwell Bay and Mud Swamp/New River. Secluded lakes and streams and canoe trails on the Sopchoppy and lower Ochlockonee rivers are popular with canoeists. Several lake areas have campgrounds and hiking trails. Hunting and fishing also are popular activities.

A portion of the 1,300-mile Florida National Scenic Trail passes through the forest, showcasing a wide variety of plants and wildlife native to the area. Hikers may catch glimpses of alligators and such rare and endangered species as the red-cockaded woodpecker, indigo snake and bald eagle.

Further information about the forest can be obtained at the district headquarters offices in Crawfordville, (850) 926-3561, and in Bristol, (850) 643-2282. *See Recreation Chart.*

APOLLO BEACH—*see Tampa Bay p. 231.*

APOPKA—*see Orlando p. 164.*

ARCADIA (F-9) pop. 6,604

(SAVE) **RIVERBOAT TOURS AT THE NAV-A-GATOR** is, off I-75 exit 170, then 3 mi. e. on Kings Hwy., following sign 1 mi. s. on Peace River St. to 9700 S.W. Riverview Cir. Offered are 2-hour narrated pontoon boat tours of the tranquil Peace River. A ghost town, parks and wildlife may be spotted. Food is available. Daily at 1. Fare $20.95; under 10, $10.95. Reservations are required. AX, DS, MC, VI. Phone (941) 627-3474.

BARBERVILLE (C-9) pop. 400, elev. 44'

THE PIONEER SETTLEMENT FOR THE CREATIVE ARTS is just w. of jct. US 17 on SR 40. Guided tours take visitors through buildings from the early 1900s. Many of the houses, stores and barns are Florida originals that were relocated to the site. During special events the settlement features music, crafts and art from the turn of the 20th century. Allow 2 hours minimum. Mon.-Fri. 9-4, Sat. 9-2; closed holidays. Admission $3; ages 5-12, $2. Phone (386) 749-2959.

BIG CYPRESS
NATIONAL PRESERVE (G-10)

Two major highways, Alligator Alley (I-75) and Tamiami Trail (US 41), cross the preserve and make it accessible from both coasts. Big Cypress National Preserve is part of Big Cypress Swamp, which encompasses more than 2,400 square miles of south Florida.

These areas are a major source of water for the fragile Everglades and the southwestern part of the state. Big Cypress National Preserve protects this valuable resource and provides sanctuary for varied wildlife, including alligators, herons, egrets, woodpeckers, bald eagles, deer and the endangered Florida panther. Hunting and fishing are permitted under special regulations; licenses are required.

Although referred to as a swamp, the preserve has marshlands, dry prairies, estuarine mangrove forests and islands of hardwoods. Its most distinctive feature is the broad belts of bald and dwarf pond cypress trees lining the sloughs and wet prairies.

Big Cypress Visitor Center, 20 miles east of Ochopee on US 41, presents a 13-minute film about the preserve as well as exhibits about natural resources and native animal and plant life. In winter ranger-led walks and canoe and bicycle tours are offered. Phone (239) 695-4111, ext. 0.

The visitor center is open daily 9-4:30; closed Dec. 25. Free. For further information contact the Chief of Interpretation, Big Cypress National Preserve, HCR 61, Box 110, Ochopee, FL 34141; phone (239) 695-1107 or (239) 695-1201.

BIG CYPRESS SEMINOLE INDIAN RESERVATION (G-10) pop. 500

AH-TAH-THI-KI MUSEUM, 16 mi. n. of I-75 exit 49 on CR 833, tells the story of Florida's Seminole Indians through a short film, exhibits about life in the Everglades in the 1800s, artifacts from the Smithsonian National Museum of the American Indian and a living-history village featuring arts and crafts demonstrations. Allow 1 hour, 30 minutes minimum. Tues.-Sun. 9-5; phone for holiday hours. Admission $6; over 61 and ages 4-12, $4. AX, CB, DC, DS, MC, VI. Phone (863) 902-1113. *See color ad p. 44.*

[SAVE] **BILLIE SWAMP SAFARI,** 19 mi. n. of I-75 exit 49, gives 20-minute airboat rides and 60-minute "swamp buggy" eco-tours of Billie Swamp Safari Park and Big Cypress. Views of such wildlife as panthers, alligators, snakes, razorback hogs and deer are common. Daylong and overnight safaris also are offered. Food is available. Tours depart daily 10-5; closed Dec. 25. Airboat ride $14. Swamp buggy tour $22; over 61, $20; ages 4-12, $12. Reservations 2 weeks in advance are required for overnight safaris; phone for daylong and overnight fares. AX, DS, MC, VI. Phone (863) 983-6101 or (800) 949-6101. *See color ad p. 44.*

BIG PINE KEY—see *The Florida Keys p. 68.*

BISCAYNE NATIONAL PARK (H-11)

Elevations in the land portion of the park are at sea level. Ninety-five percent of the park is water.

Reached via Florida's Turnpike (exit 2, Campbell Drive) and S.W. 328th St. (North Canal Drive), Biscayne National Park encompasses a huge part of southeast Florida. The park offers a look at an unspoiled part of Florida. Only 4,370 of its 173,000 acres are land; the rest are water, and there is as much to see below its surface as there is above it.

Biscayne National Park has four biological systems: the mainland mangrove forests, Biscayne Bay, the upper Florida Keys and the underwater reefs. Shallow Biscayne Bay, which is between the coast and the northernmost Florida Keys, has clear water and is home to sponges, crabs, dolphins and manatees, endangered mammals that favor the bay's warm waters.

The undeveloped upper Florida Keys are the result of many thousands of years of construction by the tiny animals collectively known as coral. The 20 miles of the park's reefs were formed by more than 100 species of coral and harbor more than 200 different kinds of fish, including brilliantly colored parrotfish, angelfish and wrasses. Moray eels also inhabit many of the underwater crevices.

To preserve the fragile reefs, visitors must anchor boats in the sandy bottoms, not on the coral. Do not touch the coral; doing so will kill it. Also, do not sit or stand on the coral, as it breaks easily and can cause painful cuts. Collecting coral, plants, animals, shipwreck artifacts or any other "souvenir" is prohibited.

The upper keys support other endangered species. Bald eagles, ospreys, pelicans, egrets and other large birds find refuge in the dense vegetation. Arsenicker and West Arsenicker keys are important nesting areas and therefore are closed to the public.

The islands feature many tropical plants that originated from seeds either blown here by West Indian winds or deposited by birds. On the mainland are forests of mangroves, easily recognized by their twisted roots, which trap and filter out sediment that would otherwise harm the water and its inhabitants. The mangrove roots provide excellent hiding places and food sources for young fish—another function vital to the region's food chain.

Biscayne National Park is an undeveloped wilderness. Camping is permitted only on Elliott Key and Boca Chita Key, which can be reached only by boat. Because the park is accessible primarily by boat, it is helpful to get a tour boat schedule from the headquarters on Convoy Point, reached via Florida's Turnpike (exit 2, Campbell Drive) and S.W. 328th St. (North Canal Drive). The facility is open daily 9-5.

Canoe rentals also are available. Reservations are required for all trips and rentals and must be confirmed before departure; phone (305) 230-1100.

For further park information contact Biscayne National Park, 9700 S.W. 328th St., Homestead, FL 33033-5634; phone (305) 230-7275. *See Recreation Chart and the AAA Southeastern CampBook.*

BISCAYNE NATIONAL UNDERWATER PARK BOAT TOURS, whose trips depart from Convoy Point Visitor Center at 9710 S.W. 328th St., offers 3-hour glass-bottom boat tours on a 53-foot vessel and snorkeling and scuba diving excursions on a 45-foot catamaran.

Glass-bottom boat trips depart daily at 10. Snorkeling trips depart daily at 1:30. Scuba diving trips depart Sat.-Sun. 8:30-1 (weather permitting). Glass-bottom boat fare $24.45; over 62, $19.45; under 12, $16.45. Snorkeling fare (includes equipment) $35. Scuba fare $54. Reservations are required. AX, MC, VI. Phone (305) 230-1100.

BOCA RATON (G-11) pop. 74,764, elev. 15'

Long a haven for the wealthy, Boca Raton has become a center for commerce, finance and technology while maintaining its "small-town" appeal. It is known for its visionary use of green space and parks.

The city's oldest unaltered wooden structure, built in 1912 with timber found on the beach, now houses the Children's Museum. The building on Crawford Boulevard features interactive exhibits highlighting history, science and the arts and humanities.

The Gulf Stream comes closest to the Florida shore at Boca Raton, making the climate ideal for sports and recreation.

Greater Boca Raton Chamber of Commerce: 1800 N. Dixie Hwy., Boca Raton, FL 33432; phone (561) 395-4433.

Shopping areas: Boca Center, at Military Trail and Town Center Road, offers boutiques, art galleries and restaurants. Mizner Park, on Federal Highway between Palmetto Park and Glades roads, is an outdoor mall with an amphitheater, upscale boutiques, eateries and a movie theater. Royal Palm Shopping Plaza, US 1 and Mizner Boulevard, features boutiques and specialty shops in a Mediterranean setting. Town Center Mall, half a mile west of I-95 on Glades Road, contains 187 stores including Bloomingdales, Macy's, Nordstrom, Saks Fifth Avenue and Sears.

BOCA RATON HISTORICAL SOCIETY, 71 N. Federal Hwy. at Palmetto Park Rd., is housed in the restored 1927 town hall, noted for its gilded dome. The Mediterranean Revival-style building, designed by Addison Mizner, has such architectural features as cypress millwork, a pecky cypress ceiling and fan-lit windows. Changing art and history exhibits are shown regularly. Allow 30 minutes minimum. Mon.-Fri. 10-4; closed holidays. Free. Phone (561) 395-6766.

BOCA RATON MUSEUM OF ART, just e. of US 1 (N. Federal Hwy.) between Glades Rd. and Palmetto Park Rd., in Mizner Park at 501 Plaza Real, houses changing exhibits of varied art media. The permanent collection contains 19th- and 20th-century European and American works, including pieces by Degas, Matisse and Picasso, and contemporary art by significant artists. Cultural art from Central American and West African civilizations includes stone carvings, pottery, textiles and utilitarian objects.

The history of photography can be traced through a collection of lantern slides, tintypes, ambrotypes, cibachromes and silver prints. Lithographs, silk screen prints and etchings are among the graphics displayed. An outdoor sculpture garden with contemporary works is among the museum's highlights.

Allow 1 hour minimum. Tues.-Fri. 10-5 (also Wed. 5-9), Sat.-Sun. noon-5; closed holidays. Admission $8; over 65, $6; students with ID $4; under 12 free. Admission during special exhibits $15; over 65, $12; students with ID $7. AX, MC, VI. Phone (561) 392-2500.

GUMBO LIMBO NATURE CENTER, 1 mi. n. of Palmetto Park Rd. on SR A1A, features sea turtles, sharks, stingrays and native tropical fish in four outdoor tanks. Also offered is a variety of habitats, including tropical hardwood hammock and mangrove wetlands that can be seen from a boardwalk and a 40-foot-high tower. Allow 30 minutes minimum. Mon.-Sat. 9-4, Sun. noon-4; closed holidays. Donations. Phone (561) 338-1473.

SAVE **LOXAHATCHEE EVERGLADES TOURS** is 10 mi. w. off I-95 exit 42B on Hillsboro Blvd., then 5 mi. w. on Loxahatchee Rd. On this guided airboat tour visitors learn about the environmental aspect and history of the Everglades. Wildlife sightings may include alligators and a variety of bird species. Food is available. Allow 1 hour minimum. Daily 9:30-4, May 15-Sept. 15; 10-4, rest of year (weather permitting). Closed Jan. 1, Thanksgiving and Dec. 25. Last tour departs at 4. Fare $30; ages 6-12, $15. AX, DS, VI. Phone (561) 482-6107 or (800) 683-5873.

SAVE **SPORTS IMMORTALS MUSEUM,** 1 mi. n. of Yamato Rd. to 6830 N. Federal Hwy. (US 1), features rotating displays from a collection of more than a million mementos. Among memorabilia are racing helmets, autographed baseballs, uniforms, World Series pins and varied equipment used by sporting greats. Mon.-Fri. 10-6, Sat. 10-5. Admission $7; under 12, $5. MC, VI. Phone (561) 997-2575.

BONITA SPRINGS (G-9)
pop. 32,797, elev. 12'

At the edge of Cypress Swamp, Bonita Springs offers good fishing in both the Gulf of Mexico and the Imperial River. Greyhound racing is the focus of attention at The Naples-Fort Myers Greyhound Track; phone (239) 992-2411.

Note: Policies vary concerning admittance of children to pari-mutuel betting facilities. Phone for information.

Bonita Springs Area Chamber of Commerce and Visitor Center: 25071 Chamber of Commerce Dr., Bonita Springs, FL 34135; phone (239) 992-2943 or (800) 226-2943.

EVERGLADES WONDER GARDENS, 27180 Old US 41, was opened in 1936 as a refuge for injured animals. The facility now is home to a large collection of native birds as well as panthers, alligators,

Florida crocodiles, flamingos, bears and otters. Otter shows and alligator feedings are offered. The grounds include botanical gardens and trees from around the world. A natural history museum also is on the premises. Guided tours are available. Allow 1 hour, 30 minutes minimum. Daily 9-5. Last tour begins 1 hour before closing. Admission $12; ages 3-12, $6. Phone (239) 992-2591.

BOYNTON BEACH (G-11)
pop. 60,389, elev. 30'

ARTHUR R. MARSHALL LOXAHATCHEE NATIONAL WILDLIFE REFUGE is on US 441/SR 7, 2 mi. s. of jct. SR 804 (Boynton Beach Blvd.) or 3 mi. n. of jct. SR 806 (Atlantic Ave.). The 143,874-acre refuge is home to endangered and threatened species such as the snail kite, the wood stork and the American alligator. Migrating waterfowl gather in the winter. Features include an observation tower, nature trails, a 12-mile bicycle trail, a 5.5-mile canoe trail, a visitor center with exhibits, and facilities for fishing, boating and bird-watching.

Refuge daily 6 a.m.-dusk. Visitor center Mon.-Fri. 9-4, Sat.-Sun. 9-4:30, mid-Oct. through Apr. 30; Wed.-Fri. 9-4, Sat.-Sun. 9-4:30, rest of year. Closed Thanksgiving and Dec. 25. Admission $5 per private vehicle or $1 per person arriving by bicycle or on foot. Phone (561) 734-8303.

SCHOOLHOUSE CHILDREN'S MUSEUM is at 129 E. Ocean Ave. Exhibits housed in a restored 1913 schoolhouse relate South Florida history. Interactive stations include a post office, a train depot and activities centered on farm life. An orientation film is offered. Allow 1 hour minimum. Tues.-Sat. 10-5. Admission $5; senior citizens $4; ages 2-17, $3. MC, VI. Phone (561) 742-6780.

BRADENTON (F-8) pop. 45,504, elev. 21'

See map page 204.

Nearby Gulf beaches attract visitors to Bradenton (BRAY-den-ton), on Florida's west coast. The Art League of Manatee County, 209 Ninth St. W., displays works of local artists. Classes, demonstrations and workshops are offered September through July; phone (941) 746-2862.

Pirate City, (941) 747-3031, at 1701 27th St. E., is the Pittsburgh Pirates' minor league and spring training facility. The major league team trains here in February, while the Pirates' minor-leaguers play here March through May. The Gulf Coast League plays here June through August, and the Instructional League plays September through October. Visitors can watch the Pirates prepare for the regular season as they battle other major league teams in March at McKechnie Field, Ninth Street and 17th Avenue W.; phone (941) 748-4610.

Bradenton also is the home of Pittsburgh's teams in the Gulf Coast Rookie League and the Florida Instructional League, providing baseball games from June to mid-October; phone (941) 747-3031.

From January through March the world-renowned Royal Lipizzan Stallions from Austria are trained at Colonel Herrmann's Ranch on Singletary Road in nearby Myakka City. Visitors are welcome at the training sessions; phone (941) 322-1501.

Bradenton Area Convention & Visitors Bureau—Bradenton: P.O. Box 1000, Bradenton, FL 34206; phone (941) 729-9177 or (800) 462-6283.

Shopping areas: De Soto Square Mall, US 41 and Cortez Road, features Dillard's, JCPenney and Sears among its 106 stores.

DE SOTO NATIONAL MEMORIAL—
see place listing p. 58.

FAMILY HERITAGE HOUSE MUSEUM, 5840 26th St. W. on the Manatee Community College campus, features exhibits tracing the African-American experience and has a large collection of reference material, including photographs, books, articles, artifacts and memorabilia. Topics of interest include the Underground Railroad, sports notables and Florida communities. Allow 1 hour minimum. Tues.-Thurs. 11-6, otherwise by appointment; closed holidays. Free. Phone (941) 752-5319.

HUNSADER FARMS is 10 mi. e. of I-75 exit 217 on SR 70, then 3 mi. n. to 5500 CR 675. Geared toward educating children about farming and farm life, the facility features a small zoo with chickens, cows, ducks, emus, goats, pheasants, pigs and turkeys. Picnicking is permitted. Allow 1 hour minimum. Mon.-Sat. 8-4, mid-Sept. to mid-June; closed major holidays. Free. Phone (941) 322-2168.

MANATEE VILLAGE HISTORICAL PARK is at 604 15th St. E. The park includes an 1860 courthouse, 1887 church, 1912 settler's house, 1903 general store and 1908 one-room schoolhouse. Other highlights include a replica of a typical Florida barn as well as a boat exhibit, restored smokehouse, turpentine still and working blacksmith shop. Visitors can tour the 1850 Old Manatee Burial Grounds by appointment. Picnicking is permitted. Allow 2 hours minimum. Mon.-Fri. 9-4:30, Sun. 1:30-4:30, Sept.-June; Mon.-Fri. 9-4:30, rest of year. Free. Phone (941) 749-7165.

SOUTH FLORIDA MUSEUM, 201 10th St. W., interprets regional history from prehistoric times to the present. Highlights include fossil evidence of Florida's earliest mammals and marine species and an extensive collection of prehistoric artifacts removed from archeological sites in the state.

Other exhibits cover local maritime traditions, early 20th-century medical practices and Spanish exploration in the New World. Spanish Plaza has full-scale replicas of 16th-century buildings.

Bishop Planetarium presents astronomy films and space science programs in a dome theater. The Parker Manatee Aquarium, part of Florida's manatee rehabilitation network, is home to Snooty, the oldest known manatee in captivity. Visitors can watch feedings on a Web cam and hear Snooty "speak" through a hydrophone.

Allow 1 hour, 30 minutes minimum. Museum/Aquarium open Mon.-Sat. 10-5, Sun. noon-5, Jan.-Apr. and in July; Tues.-Sat. 10-5, Sun. noon-5, rest of year. Planetarium shows Fri.-Sat. at 7, 8 and 9. Closed Jan. 1, Thanksgiving and Dec. 25. Museum/Aquarium admission $10; over 59, $8; ages 4-12, $6. Evening planetarium shows $7; over 59, $6; ages 4-12, $5. Combination tickets are available. MC, VI. Phone (941) 746-4131.

RECREATIONAL ACTIVITIES

Canoeing

- **Ray's Canoe Hideaway** is 2 mi. e. of I-75 exit 220 on SR 64. Other activities are offered. Mon.-Tues. and Thurs.-Sun. dawn-dusk. Phone (941) 747-3909.

BROOKSVILLE (D-8) pop. 7,264, elev. 126′

The rolling terrain surrounding Brooksville is rich in limestone, making its quarrying and distribution the city's major industry. The limestone also makes this a fertile agricultural and grazing area, as evidenced by the number of cattle ranches and horse farms. The founding of Brooksville predates the Civil War, and many of its residential streets are lined with turn-of-the-20th-century Victorian homes. Murals on downtown buildings depict historic events.

In the center of town, Hernando Park has an outdoor band shell, a playground and recreational facilities. The park also is the site of arts and crafts shows. Winding through nearby countryside are miles of hiking and biking trails, including those of nearby Withlacoochee State Forest.

Hernando County Welcome Center: 30305 Cortez Blvd., Brooksville, FL 34602; phone (800) 601-4580. *See color ad.*

Self-guiding tours: Brochures for a self-guiding walking or driving tour of the historic district are available from the welcome center.

MAY STRINGER HERITAGE MUSEUM is at 601 Museum Ct., 1 blk. n. of jct. SRs 50 and 41. Guides conduct tours of the four-story gabled building, which was built in the mid-19th century. Furnished rooms and a re-created schoolroom depict area history. Also featured is a collection of period medical equipment. Allow 1 hour minimum. Tues.-Sat. noon-3, Sept.-July. Admission $3; under 13, $1. Phone (352) 799-0129.

ROGERS' CHRISTMAS HOUSE VILLAGE is at 103 S. Saxon Ave. The village sits on a hilltop and consists of five turn-of-the-20th-century houses with gardens. The main house is decorated in a Christmas theme and displays gift items from around the world. Country Cottage, Magnolia House and Little House Under the Oak Tree also feature decorations and gifts. Storybook Land has animated displays. Daily 9:30-5; closed Thanksgiving and Dec. 25. Free. Phone (352) 796-2415 or (877) 312-5046.

BUNNELL (C-10) pop. 2,122, elev. 25′

BULOW PLANTATION RUINS HISTORIC STATE PARK, 9 mi. s.e. on CR 2001 (Old Kings Rd.) to 3501 S. Old Kings Rd., following signs, contains the remnants of Bulowville, a territorial period sugar mill and plantation destroyed by Seminoles in 1836. Interpretive center exhibits relate the story of the plantation and its destruction. The 152-acre site features the sugar mill ruins, a canoe trail and picnic and playground facilities.

Canoe rental is available. Fishing is permitted with a license. Allow 30 minutes minimum. Daily 9-5. Admission $3 per private vehicle, $1 for persons arriving by bicycle or on foot. Phone (386) 517-2084. *See Recreation Chart.*

BUSHNELL (D-8) pop. 2,050, elev. 75′

Rural Bushnell, where the Withlacoochee River flows through a cypress swamp as a small stream, features small lakes once fished by American Indians and Spanish explorers. Most are still popular with anglers today, as is Lake Panasoffkee, to the north. Withlacoochee State Forest, which covers 113,000 acres in three units, is west of town.

Florida National Veterans Cemetery, off I-75 exit 309 on SR 476B, is among the largest in the nation.

On SR 471 in nearby Webster shoppers enjoy Monday events at the Webster Flea Market, one of the largest flea markets in the country.

Sumter County Chamber of Commerce: 225 S. US 301, P.O. Box 100, Sumterville, FL 33585; phone (352) 793-3099.

DADE BATTLEFIELD HISTORIC STATE PARK, off I-75 exit 314, e. on CR 48, 1.5 mi. s. on US 301, then 1 mi. w. on CR 603, commemorates the massacre of Maj. Franeis L. Dade and his troops, who were ambushed by Seminole Indians the morning of Dec. 28, 1835. Highlights include reproductions of the log barricade used in the battle and monuments to the valor of Dade and his men. A visitor center has exhibits and artifacts, and an interpretive trail marks the military road and battlefield.

Picnicking is permitted. Allow 1 hour minimum. Grounds open daily 8-dusk. Visitor center open daily 9-5. Admission $2 per private vehicle (maximum eight people), $1 per person arriving by bicycle or on foot. Phone (352) 793-4781.

CANAVERAL NATIONAL SEASHORE (D-11)

Canaveral National Seashore lies north of the Kennedy Space Center *(see place listing p. 106)*. This 57,000-acre unit of the National Park Service encompasses 24 miles of unspoiled barrier beaches, shallow lagoons and dunes. Alligators, turtles, manatees and a variety of birds are among the abundant wildlife.

Swimming, boating, surf fishing and ranger-led activities can be enjoyed at Playalinda Beach at the southern tip of the seashore and at Apollo Beach at the area's northern end. The Merritt Island National Wildlife Refuge *(see Titusville p. 236)* adjoins the national seashore. An information center at 7611 S. Atlantic Ave. in New Smyrna Beach is open daily; phone (386) 428-3384.

The seashore is open daily 6 a.m.-8 p.m., late Apr.-late Oct.; 6-6, rest of year. Playalinda Beach is closed 3 days before a shuttle launch and reopens the following day. Admission $5 per vehicle. An annual pass is $28. For further information contact the Superintendent, Canaveral National Seashore, 308 Julia St., Titusville, FL 32796; phone (321) 267-1110. For a recorded daily beach report, phone (321) 867-0677. *See Recreation Chart.*

CAPE CANAVERAL (D-11)
pop. 8,829, elev. 9'

CASINOS
- **Sterling Casino,** departing from the Sterling Casino Lines terminal at Port Canaveral. Cruises daily at 11 a.m. and 7 p.m. Phone (321) 784-8558 or (800) 765-5711.

CAPE CORAL (G-9) pop. 102,286, elev. 5'

SAVE **SUN SPLASH FAMILY WATERPARK,** off I-75 exit 143, w. 12 mi. on SR 78, then s. 0.5

mi. to 400 Santa Barbara Blvd., offers 12 acres of recreational activities, including giant waterslides, activity and family pools, otter slides, an inner tube river, a children's play area and a game arcade.

Food is available. Allow 2 hours minimum. Sun.-Wed. and Fri. 10-6, Thurs. and Sat. 10-9, mid-May to mid-Aug.; Wed.-Sun. 11-5, early Mar. to mid-May; Sat.-Sun. and Labor Day 11-5, mid-Aug. to late Sept. Days may be added to the schedule during spring break. Phone to confirm schedule. Admission $11.95; under 48 inches tall $9.95; over 55, $5.95; under age 3, $2.95. MC, VI. Phone (239) 574-0557.

CAPTIVA (G-9) pop. 379, elev. 3'

Captiva is on Captiva Island, which is joined to Sanibel Island *(see Sanibel p. 200)* by a bridge. Some historians believe that the incident that gave Captiva its name mirrors that of Pocahontas. In 1528 Juan Ortiz was captured by the Calusa Indians and held on the island. Facing execution, Ortiz escaped to a friendly Indian tribe with help from the chief's daughter. In 1539 he was released to Hernando de Soto and became his interpreter. Visitors to Captiva can see the remains of the ceremonial shell mounds built by the Calusa.

The Calusa were skilled boatmen. From their tribal capital on Mound Key in Estero Bay they frequented neighboring barrier islands, including Useppa Island and Cabbage Key.

Useppa Island became an exclusive resort in the late 1890s. After the sport of tarpon fishing was introduced here, presidents, industrial tycoons and celebrities came to the Tarpon Inn, built by Chicago streetcar magnate John Roach, with hopes of reeling in the mighty "silver king." In 1960 the federal government briefly occupied Useppa Island while planning operations for the Bay of Pigs invasion.

Banyan trees, exotic flowers and lush vegetation line a walking path along the island's central ridge. The Useppa Museum traces local history through

DID YOU KNOW

Boca Raton
is
Spanish
for
"rat's mouth."

detailed exhibits about archeology, the Calusa Indians, Civil War activities, tarpon fishing and the Bay of Pigs connection; phone (239) 283-9600.

Cabbage Key features Indian shell mounds, walking paths and shelling beaches. Both Useppa Island and Cabbage Key are north of Captiva in Pine Island Sound and are accessible by private boat or seaplane, or on sightseeing cruises. *(see attraction listing).*

CAPTIVA CRUISES departs from McCarthy's Marina on Captiva Island. Among the cruises offered are 1- to 3-hour dolphin/wildlife and sunset cruises, 3-hour shelling trips, 4- to 5-hour cruises to Cabbage Key or Useppa Island, and 5- and 6-hour excursions to Boca Grande or Cayo Costa State Park.

Cruises are offered daily. Dolphin/wildlife and sunset cruises depart at 4 and dusk; shelling trips at 10 and 1; island cruises at 10. Closed Dec. 25. Fare $17.50-$35; ages 4-12, $10-$17.50. Reservations are required. Inquire about policies regarding refunds, inclement weather and minimum number of passengers. AX, DS, MC, VI. Phone (239) 472-5300.

CASTILLO DE SAN MARCOS NATIONAL MONUMENT—*see St. Augustine p. 193.*

CEDAR KEY (C-7) pop. 790, elev. 8′

Due to its location among a group of small barrier islands off the Gulf Coast of Florida, Cedar Key was a strategic point from which blockade runners exported cotton and lumber and imported food and supplies for the Confederacy during the Civil War. Following the war, lumbering and then fishing and shipbuilding formed the town's economic base.

An 1896 hurricane leveled the original town. Now primarily a resort area, the town relies on commercial fishing, crabbing, clam farming, oystering and tourism to sustain its economy. Cedar Key is home to many artists and its surrounding area is popular with bird-watchers.

Cedar Key Area Chamber of Commerce: P.O. Box 610, Cedar Key, FL 32625; phone (352) 543-5600.

Self-guiding tours: The Cedar Key Historical Society Museum *(see attraction listing)* offers brochures with tours of the historic district.

CEDAR KEY HISTORICAL SOCIETY MUSEUM, on SR 24 at Second St., depicts the town's history through photographs dating to the 1850s. Other displays include Seminole and Timucuan Indian artifacts and an exhibit about the fishing industry. Allow 30 minutes minimum. Sun.-Fri. 1-4, Sat. 11-5; closed Jan. 1, Thanksgiving and Dec. 25. Admission $1; ages 12-18, 50c. Phone (352) 543-5549.

CEDAR KEY STATE PARK MUSEUM is 1.75 mi. n. off SR 24 following signs to 12231 S.W. 166th Ct. Exhibits contain household articles from the past as well as a Confederate salt kettle and the St. Clair

Whitman Shell Collection, said to be one of the most complete collections ever assembled. Displays also relate the history of the area's railroad and fishing industries. Allow 30 minutes minimum. Thurs.-Mon. 9-5. Admission $1, under 6 free. Phone (352) 543-5350.

CHARLOTTE HARBOR (F-8)
pop. 3,647, elev. 4′

CHARLOTTE COUNTY HISTORICAL CENTER is at 22959 Bayshore Rd. This interactive museum houses changing exhibits exploring regional and natural history and permanent exhibits about Charlotte County. Allow 30 minutes minimum. Mon.-Fri. 10-5, Sat. 10-3; closed major holidays. Admission $2; under 13, $1. Phone (941) 629-7278.

CHIEFLAND (C-8) pop. 1,993, elev. 40′

LOWER SUWANNEE NATIONAL WILDLIFE REFUGE, 17 mi. s. on CR 347, is home to more than 90 species of birds that make their nests in the refuge's 52,935 acres. Hikers may spot such wildlife as bald eagles, white-tailed deer, wood ducks, swallow-tailed kites and alligators. River Trail offers visitors a view of the Suwanee River and the cypress trees and hardwood swamps that surround it. The refuge is open daily dawn-dusk; the refuge office is open Mon.-Fri. 7:30-4. Free. Phone (352) 493-0238.

CHRISTMAS—*see Orlando p. 164.*

CLEARWATER—*see Tampa Bay p. 231.*

CLEARWATER BEACH—*see Tampa Bay p. 231.*

CLERMONT—*see Orlando p. 165.*

COCOA (D-10) pop. 16,412, elev. 25′

Cocoa's first families arrived at this site along the Indian River in 1860, and the town was platted beginning in 1882. Although there are differing accounts of the name's origin, records do show that Cocoa was selected in the 1880s when the town's original name, Indian River City, was deemed by postal authorities to be too long for a postmark.

Throughout its early history, Cocoa experienced periodic growth spurts interrupted by such reversals as a catastrophic fire, a freeze that damaged the area's citrus crops and the Great Depression. The town's prospects improved considerably in the latter half of the 20th century thanks to its proximity to the Kennedy Space Center.

The Brevard Museum of History and Science, 2201 Michigan Ave., offers local history exhibits as well as a hands-on science discovery room for children; phone (321) 632-1830. The museum's grounds include a 22-acre nature preserve with trails.

Walking tours of the Cocoa Village historic district depart from the welcome center at 216 Florida Ave.; phone (321) 433-0362.

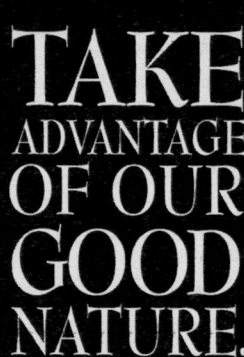

TAKE
ADVANTAGE
OF OUR
GOOD
NATURE.

Safety at Florida's Beaches

Florida's expansive coastline provides numerous opportunities for fun in the sun, but it also requires an extra degree of caution when taking a dip: A large number of Florida beaches are unguarded. Swimming at an unguarded beach presents a risk to swimmers not only through injury or drowning, but also through the dangers of rip currents, dangerous or poisonous marine animals and other hidden hazards.

However, many Florida beaches are guarded by trained, certified ocean lifeguards. To ensure your safety and that of

Digital Archives

your family, be sure to swim only when ocean lifeguards are present. A list of guarded beaches is available from the United States Lifesaving Association and the Florida Beach Patrol Chiefs Association, 340 S. Ocean Blvd., Delray Beach, FL 33483; phone (561) 243-7352.

Cocoa Beach Area Chamber of Commerce—Cocoa: 400 Fortenberry Rd., Merritt Island, FL 32952; phone (321) 459-2200.

SAVE **ASTRONAUT MEMORIAL PLANETARIUM & OBSERVATORY** is 2.5 mi. e. of I-95 exit 201 on SR 520, then 1.75 mi. n. on SR 501 to 1519 Clearlake Rd. Visitors can look through a 24-inch telescope to see objects in the solar system and deep space. The International Hall of Space Explorers honors men and women who have flown in space. The Science Quest Demonstration Hall features hands-on space science exhibits. Other options include planetarium shows, large-format films in the Iwerks Discovery Theatre and a laser show.

Fri.-Sat. 6:30-10:30 p.m. Other days and times vary; phone ahead. Film or planetarium show $6; over 55, $5; under 12, $4. Film and planetarium show $10; over 55, $8; under 12, $6. Laser show $6. Three shows $14. Rooftop observatory free. MC, VI. Phone (321) 433-7373.

COCOA BEACH (D-11) pop. 12,842, elev. 12′

Long a popular spot with locals, Cocoa Beach also is known for its location at the heart of the Space Coast. Cocoa Beach Pier extends 800 feet into the Atlantic, affording opportunities for fishing, surfing, dining and dancing.

Florida's Space Coast Office of Tourism—Cocoa Beach: 2725 Judge Fran Jamieson Way, Suite B-105, Viera, FL 32940; phone (877) 572-3224.

COCONUT CREEK—
see Fort Lauderdale p. 84.

COCONUT GROVE—
see Miami-Miami Beach p. 133.

CORAL GABLES—
see Miami-Miami Beach p. 133.

CORAL SPRINGS—*see Fort Lauderdale p. 84.*

CROSS CREEK (C-9) elev. 69′

MARJORIE KINNAN RAWLINGS HISTORIC STATE PARK, on CR 325, 4 mi. w. of jct. US 301 next to the county park, is the restored home of Marjorie Kinnan Rawlings, author of the Pulitzer Prize-winning novel "The Yearling." Cross Creek was the setting for several of Rawlings' books. Grounds open daily 9-5. Guided house tours are given Thurs.-Sun. at 10, 11, 1, 2, 3 and 4, Oct.-July; closed Jan. 1, Thanksgiving and Dec. 25. Grounds $2 per private vehicle. Tours $3; ages 6-12, $2. Phone (352) 466-3672. *See color ad p. 452.*

CRYSTAL RIVER (D-8) pop. 3,485, elev. 4′

Crystal River denotes both a town and the river that runs through it into Kings Bay. The waters accommodate anglers and scuba divers.

Citrus County Chamber of Commerce at Crystal River: 28 N.W. US 19, Crystal River, FL 34428-3900; phone (352) 795-3149.

CRYSTAL RIVER ARCHEOLOGICAL STATE PARK, 2 mi. n. on US 19, then 1 mi. w. on State Park St. to N. Museum Point, preserves the ceremonial mound complex built by American Indians who occupied the site from 200 B.C. to 1400 A.D. In addition to temple and burial mounds, there are middens, or refuse mounds, formed in part by the empty shells of the seafood that was an important part of the Indians' diet. Artifacts are displayed and an 8-minute videotape interprets the site's past.

Allow 1 hour, 30 minutes minimum. Grounds open daily 8-dusk. Visitor center open daily 9-5. Admission $2 per private vehicle (maximum eight people), $1 per person arriving by bicycle, motorcycle or on foot. Phone (352) 795-3817.

DADE CITY—*see Tampa Bay p. 232.*

DANIA BEACH—*see Fort Lauderdale p. 84.*

DAVIE—*see Fort Lauderdale p. 85.*

DAYTONA BEACH (C-10)
pop. 64,112, elev. 10′

Daytona Beach was more speedway than beach in the early days of the automobile. Between 1903 and 1935 some 15 speed records were set on the beach racecourse by Barney Oldfield, Sir Henry Segrave and Sir Malcolm Campbell. The racing tradition continues at Daytona International Speedway (*see attraction listing*).

During the day cars may be driven on several miles of the hard-packed sand. For safety, beach driving should be done during a low or outgoing tide and never in the water, however shallow. The speed limit on the beach is 10 miles per hour. Drivers should heed all signs, including those indicating conservation areas, where vehicles are prohibited. Overnight parking or camping on the beach is not permitted.

The beach is not open to motor vehicles between Seabreeze and International Speedway boulevards; south of Emelia Avenue in Daytona Beach Shores to Beach Street in Ponce Inlet; at Lighthouse Point Park in Ponce Inlet; or north of Granada Boulevard in Ormond Beach. A daily beach access toll of $5 per vehicle is charged February through November;

tollbooths are at each approach. For beach information phone (386) 239-7873.

A wide promenade along the ocean is the center of an amusement area anchored on the south by the Daytona Beach Pier, which features a sightseeing tower and sky ride. The bandshell at the north end of the promenade is the setting for concerts and events.

A scenic portion of SR A1A extends along the ocean from Ormond Beach north to Fernandina Beach, a distance of 110 miles.

Ocean lovers enjoy sailing, surfing and riding personal watercraft; the Halifax River is a favorite for scenic boat tours as well as boating, fishing, kayaking and sailboarding. Greyhounds race at Daytona Beach Kennel Club, next to the speedway; phone (386) 252-6484.

Note: Policies vary concerning admittance of children to pari-mutuel betting facilities. Phone for information.

Mary McLeod Bethune founded Bethune-Cookman College for the training of African-American women in 1904; it later became an accredited coed college. The campus, off International Speedway Boulevard, includes Bethune's home and gravesite (*see attraction listing*), early buildings and the Mary McLeod Bethune Performing Arts Center.

Daytona Beach Area Convention and Visitors Bureau: 126 E. Orange Ave., Daytona Beach, FL 32114; phone (386) 255-0415 or (800) 854-1234. *See color ad.*

Shopping areas: Ocean Walk Shoppes, 250 N. Atlantic Ave. at Ocean Walk Village, houses Maui Nix Surf Shop, a Harley-Davidson apparel store and other specialty shops in addition to food and entertainment venues in a three-story complex overlooking the historic bandshell. Daytona Flea Market, 1 mile west of Daytona International Speedway at the junction of I-95 and US 92, provides weekend browsing. Fresh produce, citrus and seafood are available at the Farmers Market, downtown on City Island. Volusia Mall, 1700 International Speedway Blvd. (US 92), features Dillard's, JCPenney, Macy's and Sears among its 120 stores.

ANGELL & PHELPS CHOCOLATE FACTORY TOUR, just s. of US 92 (International Speedway Blvd.) at 154 S. Beach St., offers tours of a working

AAA and Motorsports

AAA, a pioneer in the development and growth of auto racing during the first half of the 20th century, has returned to the racetrack. Today the association is the "Official Auto Club" and "Official Roadside Assistance Provider" of 11 tracks owned and operated by the International Speedway Corporation (ISC), which hosts the NASCAR NEXTEL Cup Series and Indy Racing League (IRL) events.

As part of an agreement with ISC, AAA's widely recognized logo appears on track safety and recovery vehicles as well as on track signs, in racing programs and at other promotional venues. ISC, a leading promoter of motorsports activities in the United States, conducts more than 100 events annually. ISC/AAA facilities include California Speedway in Fontana, Calif.; Darlington Raceway in Darlington, S.C.; Daytona International Speedway in Daytona Beach, Fla.; Homestead-Miami Speedway in Homestead, Fla.; Kansas Speedway in Kansas City, Kan.; Martinsville Speedway in Martinsville, Va.; Michigan International Speedway in Cambridge Junction, Mich.; Phoenix International Raceway in Phoenix, Ariz.; Richmond International Raceway in Richmond, Va.; Talladega Superspeedway in Talladega, Ala.; and Watkins Glen International in Watkins Glen, N.Y.

© International Speedway Corporation

factory where visitors can watch handmade chocolates being created. Allow 30 minutes minimum. Tours are given on the hour Mon.-Fri. 10-11 and 1-4. Free. Phone (386) 252-6531.

DAYTONA INTERNATIONAL SPEEDWAY is 1 mi. e. of I-95 exit 261 on US 92 (International Speedway Blvd.). NASCAR founder Bill France opened the tri-oval racetrack in 1959 with the inaugural Daytona 500 race. Every February the Daytona 500 thrills racing fans and is the culmination of Speedweeks, a series of sports- and stock-car races and test runs held throughout January. With 10 major race weekends each year, the speedway's busy calendar includes the Pepsi 400 in July, motorcycle events during Bike Week in March and Biketoberfest in October, vintage sports car racing in November and karting finals in December.

Daytona International Speedway features a 2.5-mile superspeedway and a 3.56-mile infield road course. When races are not scheduled, the 480-acre complex is used for vehicle testing and development and for automobile-related shows and events. Entrance for self-guiding tours is through DAYTONA USA *(see attraction listing)*. Guided tram tours of the speedway are given by DAYTONA USA daily 9:30-6 (weather and track schedule permitting). Self-guiding tours free. Phone (386) 253-7223 for race information and tickets, or TTY (386) 947-6700.

See color ad p. 55.

© International Speedway Corporation

AAA is the Official Auto Club of Daytona International Speedway.

DAYTONA USA is 1 mi. e. of I-95 exit 261A (southbound) or exit 261 (northbound) on the grounds of Daytona International Speedway. Visitors enter through a replica of the raceway's famed twin tunnels and are greeted by "The Heritage of Daytona," an exhibit that offers a chronological look at racing history.

Through interactive displays guests can broadcast a race, test their motor sports knowledge at a six-station trivia game and participate in a timed pit stop. The IMAX theater features NASCAR 3D: The IMAX Experience, a 45-minute, 3-D movie highlighting drivers and teams in action, and a 14-minute film that captures the excitement of the Daytona 500 race. Daytona Dream Laps is an exhilarating motion-simulator ride. A 30-minute speedway tram tour features stops at Pit Road, the Start/Finish Line, the 31-degree banking and Victory Lane.

Food is available. Allow 1 hour, 30 minutes minimum. Daily 9-7; closed Dec. 25. Extended hours

during race events. Speedway tours daily 9:30-6 (weather and track schedule permitting). Admission $21.50; over 60, $18.50; ages 6-12, $15.50. Speedway tour $7.50, under 6 free. MC, VI. Phone (386) 947-6800. *See color ad.*

SAVE **HALIFAX HISTORICAL SOCIETY AND MUSEUM** is 2 blks. s. of US 92 at 252 S. Beach St. Housed in the restored 1911 Merchants Bank building, the museum's displays of artifacts detail local history. Of special interest are prehistoric American Indian artifacts, a scale model of the 1938 boardwalk and a racing exhibit. Grandma's Attic is a large exhibit containing vintage toys, children's clothing and memorabilia dating to the early 1900s.

Allow 1 hour minimum. Tues.-Sat. 10-4; closed Thanksgiving weekend, Dec. 25 and Jan. 1. Admission $4; under 12, $1; free to children under 12 on Sat.; Thurs. afternoon adult admission by donation. Phone (386) 255-6976.

MARY MCLEOD BETHUNE HOME, 628 Dr. Mary McLeod Bethune Blvd. on the Bethune-Cookman College campus, was the residence of college founder Mary McLeod Bethune 1915-1955. A guided tour covers most of the rooms in the two-story structure, including the guest bedroom where Eleanor Roosevelt stayed. Bethune's gravesite is adjacent to the house. Allow 30 minutes minimum. Mon.-Fri. 9:30-4. Reservations are required. Free. Phone (386) 481-2122.

SAVE **MUSEUM OF ARTS AND SCIENCES** is .5 mi. s. of jct. US 92 and Nova Rd. (SR 5A). On a 90-acre plot, this Smithsonian Institution affiliate museum features permanent and changing exhibits. Included are African, American, Chinese, Cuban and French art; Coca-Cola memorabilia; race cars; and Florida history exhibits with a giant ground sloth. The museum also maintains a planetarium, environmental complex and sculpture garden.

Allow 1 hour minimum. Museum open Tues.-Fri. 9-4, Sat.-Sun. noon-5; closed major holidays. Planetarium shows Tues.-Fri. at 2, Sat.-Sun. at 1 and 3. Museum admission $8, students with ID $4, under 6 free. Planetarium admission an additional $3, children $2. Phone (386) 255-0285.

SOUTHEAST MUSEUM OF PHOTOGRAPHY is at 1200 W. International Speedway Blvd., Building 100, on the Daytona Beach Community College campus. The gallery of changing photography exhibits features both early and contemporary selections. Allow 30 minutes minimum. Mon. and Wed.-Fri. 10-4, Tues. 11-7, Sat.-Sun. 1-5; closed holidays. Donations. Phone (386) 506-4475.

A TINY CRUISE LINE departs from Halifax Harbor Marina dock E at 425 S. Beach St. Narrated cruises along the Halifax River are aboard a replica of an 1890s excursion boat. A 2-hour midday waterway trip offers chances to see dolphins and wildlife. One-hour cruises travel past riverfront estates or historic downtown. Sunset cruises also are available April through October.

Two-hour waterway cruise departs Mon.-Sat. at 11:30. One-hour riverfront estate cruise departs Mon.-Sat. at 2; historic downtown trip departs Mon.-Sat. at 3:30. Fare for 1-hour cruises $11.03; ages 4-12, $6.57. Fare for 2-hour cruise $16.43; ages 4-12, $9.62. Reservations are required for sunset cruises. Phone (386) 226-2343.

DEERFIELD BEACH—
see Fort Lauderdale p. 85.

DeLAND (D-9) pop. 24,904, elev. 27′

The stately oaks lining the streets of DeLand are the result of the arboreal interests and endeavors of Henry A. DeLand, who founded the city in 1876. Another local entrepreneur was Chinese emigrant Lue Gim Gong, who produced highly successful strains of oranges and grapefruit in the late 1800s.

During World War II Navy combat bomber pilots were trained in DeLand. DeLand Naval Air Station Museum and Historical Hangar, 910 Biscayne Blvd., contains aircraft, ammunition, practice bombs and military memorabilia; phone (386) 738-4149.

Stetson University, established in 1886 by DeLand and named for hat magnate John Stetson, contains Gillespie Museum of Minerals and Duncan Gallery of Art; phone (386) 822-7000. The university is on N. Woodland Boulevard. A booklet describing a campus walking tour is available at the public relations office.

Bill Dreggors Park on Stone Street is a popular picnic spot; phone (386) 740-5800. On the grounds

is the DeLand Memorial Hospital Museum, with a re-created 1920s surgery room and apothecary exhibits. Other highlights include military memorabilia, vintage electrical appliances and artifacts related to local African-American history; phone (386) 740-5800.

DeLand Area Chamber of Commerce: 336 N. Woodland Blvd., DeLand, FL 32720; phone (386) 734-4331.

AFRICAN AMERICAN MUSEUM OF THE ARTS, off US 17/92 at 325 S. Clara Ave., presents permanent displays of more than 150 artifacts, including masks and carvings. Changing exhibits feature works by established and emerging artists. A cultural park with an amphitheater honors the achievements of outstanding African-Americans. Allow 30 minutes minimum. Wed.-Sat. 10-4. Free. Phone (386) 736-4004.

CULTURAL ARTS CENTER, .5 mi. n. of jct. US 17/92 and SR 44 at 600 N. Woodland Blvd., offers changing exhibits in two galleries of the DeLand Museum of Art. Plays, concerts and children's programs are presented in the 240-seat Sands Theater Center. Allow 30 minutes minimum. Galleries open Tues.-Sat. 10-4, Sun. 1-4; closed holidays. Theater performance schedule varies; phone ahead. Museum admission $2. Theater admission varies with performance. Phone (386) 734-4371 for the museum, (386) 738-7156 for theater information or (386) 736-7456 for theater reservations.

HENRY A. DeLAND HOUSE MUSEUM, 137 W. Michigan Ave., was built in 1886 for attorney Arthur George Hamlin, DeLand's first attorney and developer of the Hamlin orange. It is filled with period furnishings and collectibles. An extensive collection of period photographs is on display. Guided tours are available. Allow 1 hour minimum. Tues.-Sat. noon-4; closed holidays. Donations. Phone (386) 740-6813.

MANATEE SEEKER SCENIC RIVER TOUR departs from Pier 44 Marina, 3 mi. w. on SR 44. Two-hour narrated cruises along the St. Johns River offer insights into the history of Florida and the river. Sightings of native wildlife in their natural environment might include manatees, alligators, otters, ospreys, bald eagles and egrets. Cruises depart daily at 10, 12:30 and 3; closed the last 2 weeks in May and Dec. 20-26. Departures require a minimum of four people. Fare $20; over 65 and ages 6-11, $16; under 6, $10. Reservations are recommended. Phone (800) 587-7131.

DE LEON SPRINGS (C-10)
pop. 2,358, elev. 60′

DE LEON SPRINGS STATE PARK is 1 mi. w. off US 17. The springs of this 600-acre park send 14 million gallons of water daily over a spillway into Spring Garden Creek. Swimming is permitted in the spring pool. Canoe, kayak and paddleboat rentals are available. Other features include nature trails, a

visitor information center with exhibits and an old sugar mill. Guests can cook pancakes at their table in a restaurant in the sugar mill. *See Recreation Chart.* Allow 1 hour minimum. Park open daily 8-dusk. Visitor center open Sat.-Sun. and holidays 10-12:30. Admission $5 per private vehicle (maximum of eight people), $1 per person arriving by bicycle or on foot. Phone (386) 985-4212.

DELRAY BEACH (G-11)
pop. 60,020, elev. 20′

A resort community, Delray Beach offers its residents simplicity and a relaxed pace.

Greater Delray Beach Chamber of Commerce: 64 S.E. Fifth Ave., Delray Beach, FL 33483; phone (561) 278-0424.

 THE MORIKAMI MUSEUM AND JAPANESE GARDENS are 3.5 mi. w. of I-95 exit 51 on Linton Blvd., then 1 mi. s. on Jog Rd. to 4000 Morikami Park Rd. The museum includes exhibitions dedicated to the living culture of Japan. An exhibit chronicles the history of the area's Yamato Colony, an early 20th-century Japanese farming settlement. The 200-acre park features whispering waterfalls, peaceful lakes, fish ponds, rock and bonsai gardens and pagodas.

Food is available. Allow 1 hour, 30 minutes minimum. Tues.-Sun. 10-5; closed holidays. Admission $9; over 65, $8; ages 6-18, $6. Phone (561) 495-0233.

OLD SCHOOL SQUARE CULTURAL ARTS CENTER AND NATIONAL HISTORIC SITE is 5 blks. w. of US 1 at 51 N. Swinton Ave., or 1 mi. e. of I-95 on Atlantic Ave. The center consists of restored, early 20th-century school buildings that house Cornell Museum of Art & History, Crest Theatre and Vintage Gymnasium. The theater presents professional plays, music, dance and Broadway cabaret productions from November to April. The museum features rotating regional, national and international exhibits.

Allow 30 minutes minimum. Mon.-Sat. 10:30-4:30, Sun. 1-4:30, Oct.-Apr.; Tues.-Sat. 10:30-4:30, rest of year. Closed holidays. Admission $6; over 59 and ages 14-21, $4. Phone (561) 243-7922.

DE SOTO NATIONAL MEMORIAL (E-8)

On the south shore of the Manatee River, 5 miles west of Bradenton on SR 64, then 2 miles north on 75th Street N.W., De Soto National Memorial commemorates the first major European exploration of what is now the southeastern United States.

The expedition began in 1539 when Hernando de Soto and about 600 Spanish soldiers landed somewhere in the Tampa Bay area. Marked by many Indian battles, the expedition covered 4,000 miles to the north and west. De Soto crossed the Mississippi River in 1541 and was buried in it when he died a year later. About half the group survived the 4-year ordeal.

The visitor center contains artifacts and exhibits explaining the expedition's effect on American Indians. A 21-minute film depicting the expedition is shown hourly. Talks by costumed rangers as well as crossbow and arquebus (matchlock musket) demonstrations are given hourly 10:30-3:30, mid-December to early April. There also is a nature trail. Allow 1 hour minimum. Daily 9-5; closed Jan. 1, Thanksgiving and Dec. 25. Free. Phone (941) 792-0458.

 **DISNEY WORLD, WALT—**
see Lake Buena Vista in Orlando p. 167.

DRY TORTUGAS NATIONAL PARK—
see The Florida Keys p. 68.

DUNEDIN—
see Tampa Bay p. 232.

ELLENTON (F-9) pop. 3,142, elev. 11′

Ellenton, a small community on the northern bank of the Manatee River, offers fine fishing opportunities, nearby white sandy beaches and a climate favorable to agricultural endeavors.

Bradenton Area Convention & Visitors Bureau—Ellenton: P.O. Box 1000, Bradenton, FL 34206; phone (941) 729-9177 or (800) 462-6283.

Shopping areas: [SAVE] Prime Outlets Ellenton, off I-75 exit 224, features more than 135 factory outlet stores, including Mikasa, Nike, Off 5th Saks Fifth Avenue and Samsonite.

GAMBLE PLANTATION HISTORIC STATE PARK AND JUDAH P. BENJAMIN CONFEDERATE MEMORIAL, on US 301, was a prosperous 3,500-acre sugar plantation from about 1845 to the late 1850s. The antebellum mansion is furnished in period. At the end of the Civil War, Judah P. Benjamin, secretary of state of the Confederacy, found refuge here before escaping to England. Picnicking is permitted. Allow 1 hour minimum. Grounds open daily 8 a.m.-dusk. Visitor Center open Thurs.-Mon. 8-11:45 and 12:45-4:30; closed Jan. 1, Thanksgiving and Dec. 25. Mansion tours are given Thurs.-Mon. at 9:30, 10:30, 1, 2, 3 and 4. Grounds and visitor center free. Mansion tour $5; ages 6-12, $3. Phone (941) 723-4536.

EPCOT—*see Lake Buena Vista in Orlando p. 171.*

ESTERO (G-9) pop. 9,503, elev. 11′

KORESHAN STATE HISTORIC SITE, US 41 at Corkscrew Rd. on the banks of the Estero River, was the site of the religious community established in 1894 when Cyrus Reed Teed and his followers, members of the Koreshan Unity, arrived from Chicago. Restored historical buildings and gardens occupy the site. Camping and canoe rentals are available; reservations are recommended. Campfire programs also are offered seasonally.

Insect repellent is recommended. Allow 1 hour minimum. Park open daily 8-dusk. Settlement open daily 8-5. Guided tours are given Sat.-Sun. at 10. Admission $3 (one person per private vehicle), $4 (maximum eight per private vehicle), $1 per person arriving by bicycle or on foot. AX, DS, MC, VI. Phone (239) 992-0311. *See Recreation Chart and the AAA Southeastern CampBook.*

EVERGLADES CITY (H-9) pop. 479, elev. 3′

Because of its location at the northwest corner of the Everglades, Everglades City is a popular point of departure for fishing trips into Everglades National Park. Some hotels will send a box lunch with the angler and prepare the day's catch for the evening meal.

Everglades Area Chamber of Commerce: P.O. Box 130, Everglades City, FL 34139; phone (239) 695-3941 or (800) 914-6355.

EDEN OF THE EVERGLADES, 2 mi. s. of jct. US 41 on SR 29, offers scenic pontoon boat tours on the waterways of the Ten Thousand Islands area. Airboat rides and safari-style land tours also are available. Insect repellent is recommended. Daily 9-5. Pontoon boat fare $19.50; ages 3-10, $10. MC, VI. Phone (239) 695-2800 or (800) 543-3367.

EVERGLADES EXCURSIONS—*see Naples p. 137.*

EVERGLADES NATIONAL PARK BOAT TOURS leave from the park's ranger station .5 mi. s. on CR 29. The Mangrove Wilderness tour cruises past Calusa Indian shell mounds to native mangrove forests, and the Ten Thousand Islands tour cruises through this island group bordering the Gulf of Mexico. Both tours offer bird and wildlife sightings. Cruises depart at intervals daily 8:30-5. Mangrove Wilderness tour $25; under 13, $12.50. Ten Thousand Islands tour $16; ages 6-12, $8. AX, DS, MC, VI. Phone (239) 695-2591.

MUSEUM OF THE EVERGLADES is at 105 W. Broadway. The museum is housed in a former laundry built in 1927 for workers constructing the Tamiami Trail across the Everglades. Exhibits recount the

DID YOU KNOW

There are 882 islands in the Florida Keys.

early history of this erstwhile company town and describe the region's first trading post. The life of Collier County developer and self-made millionaire Barron G. Collier also is highlighted. Allow 30 minutes minimum. Tues.-Sat. 10-4; closed holidays. Donations. Phone (239) 695-0008.

EVERGLADES NATIONAL PARK (H-10)

Elevations in the park range from sea level to 8 ft.

The park's main entrance is reached via SR 9336 from US 1 at Florida City. Everglades National Park, the largest remaining subtropical wilderness in the nation, is a diverse and intricately linked series of habitats sheltering a variety of plants and animals, many of them threatened or endangered. The park contains more than 1.5 million acres of natural habitat, half of them water, including Cape Sable, the southernmost point on the U.S. mainland. From Cape Sable the park extends 45 miles north along the Gulf of Mexico and 30 miles east, including Florida Bay.

The Everglades was originally a slow-moving freshwater river, 50 miles wide and a few inches deep, fed by Lake Okeechobee. Much of the region is a labyrinth of mangrove waterways and saw grass marsh dotted with hammocks and salt prairies. Except for the pinelands and the highest hammocks, any spot can become a swamp in the rainy season.

Increased development in southern Florida imperils the area. Canals alternately drain and flood the region to meet the water demands of nearby cities, but in doing so they reverse the natural wet and dry cycles of the Everglades. Although fire occurs naturally in this environment, drought and canal drainage have magnified its destructive impact.

The land areas are not more than 8 feet above mean sea level, and bay bottoms are not more than 16 feet below mean sea level. The Ten Thousand Islands area conceals a strange kind of beauty and tranquility within its tide-swept maze of islets, oyster bars and mud shallows.

Trees and flowers are much the same as those found in Cuba and the West Indies. At least six species of palms grow within the park. The stately royal palm is found in greatest numbers at the Royal Palm Visitor Center. In addition to the tropical and subtropical trees and shrubs, there are more species belonging to the temperate zone and multitudes of ferns, orchids and air plants. Beware of the saw

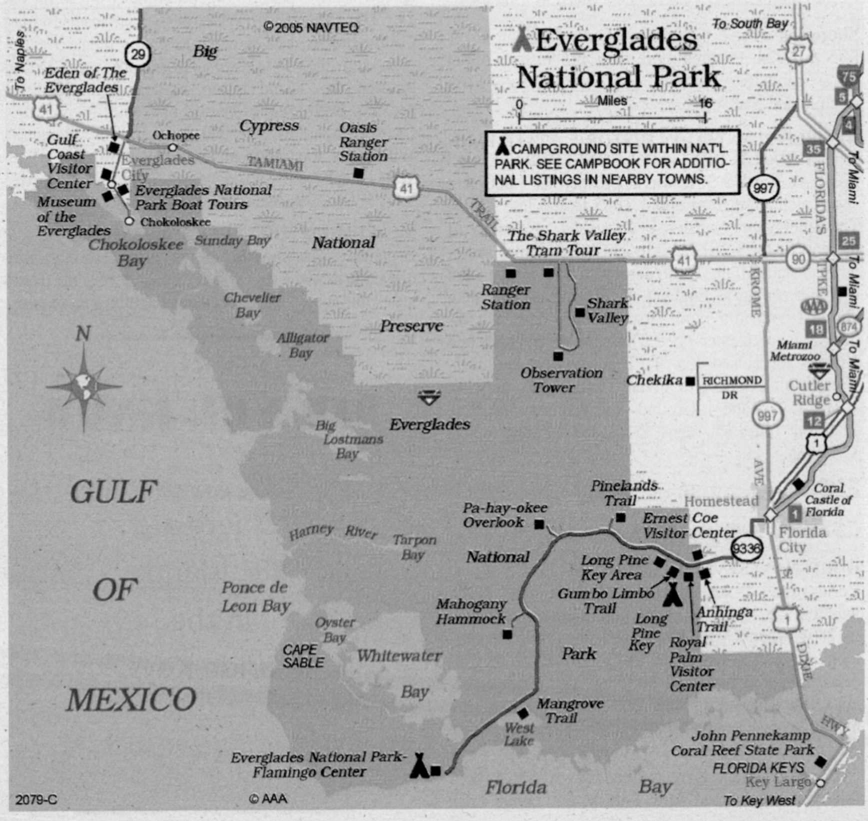

Find Hotels As Easy As 1-2-3-4-5!

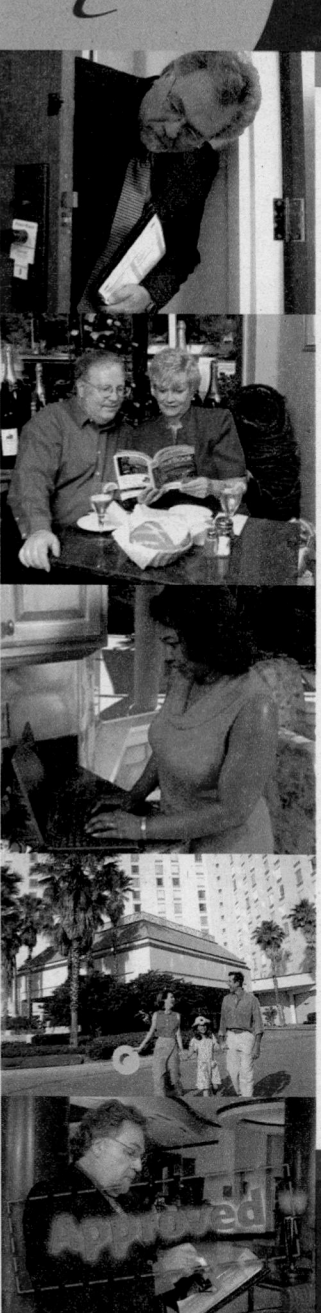

For reliable hotel stays matched to your needs, every time, use AAA's valuable two-part rating system:

- First, rest assured that *every* hotel designated **AAA Approved** upholds qualities important to members – cleanliness, service, and value.

- Focus your selection using the descriptive one-to-five **AAA Diamond Ratings** assigned exclusively to Approved properties to help you match your expectations.

Find AAA Approved and Diamond rated properties in the TourBook®, in print and on aaa.com. Look for the AAA logo on signage and billboards.

Read about **AAA Lodging Diamond Rating** requirements on page 20-21

grass; its sharp barbs can easily slash bare skin and thin clothing.

The park is home to more than 350 species of birds, 60 percent of which leave during summer. Among those that stay are two species found only in the southernmost tip of the Florida peninsula: the Cape Sable seaside sparrow and the great white heron. One species that does proliferate is the mosquito; strong insect repellent is a necessity from May to November and is recommended all year.

The Everglades is among the few remaining places where the manatee, or sea cow, and the rare American crocodile are assured a permanent sanctuary. Along with more than 600 species of fish, alligators, snakes and sea turtles are common. Bottlenose dolphins occasionally are seen. A fishing license is required for all fishing areas, and bag limits are strictly enforced for both freshwater and saltwater fishing.

General Information and Activities

Everglades National Park is open all year. From the headquarters and visitor center at the main entrance, this road continues to Flamingo. The scenic Tamiami Trail (US 41) skirts the park's northern border and leads to the Shark Valley and Everglades City entrances.

Few people really know the waterways of the Everglades. Most of the waters have been charted by the U.S. Coast and Geodetic Survey, and visitors traveling by boat should obtain these charts at area bait and tackle shops before starting their trips. Permits are required for overnight backcountry camping and must be applied for in person at ranger stations, no more than 24 hours in advance. As a safety precaution, park officials urge boaters to file trip plans before their departures.

Six marked canoe trails offer 4- to 22-mile round trips from the Flamingo area, and the 99-mile Wilderness Waterway winds between Flamingo and Everglades City. The Shark River is navigable for most small boats. Canoe rentals are available at outfitters in Flamingo and Everglades City; visitor centers distribute trail maps.

Along the main park road between park headquarters and Flamingo are five major boardwalk or blacktop nature trails (see Points of Interest). Flamingo has accommodations, eateries, sightseeing and charter fishing boats, a service station, marina, campground and visitor center which is open November through April. A visitor center and ranger station on the south side of Everglades City on SR 29 is open daily 7:30-5, Nov.-Apr.; 8-4:30, rest of year; phone (239) 695-3311. See Recreation Chart and the AAA Southeastern CampBook.

Sightseeing opportunities are abundant. Boat trips through a portion of the Ten Thousand Islands area leave from nearby cities (see Everglades City p. 59 and Naples p. 137). Other sightseeing trips are available from Flamingo, within the park. Self-guiding bicycle, kayak and canoe trips originate in Flamingo; phone (239) 695-3101.

Boat tours depart from Flamingo Marina. The 2-hour Backcountry cruises leave daily at 9, noon and 1:30, late Dec. to mid-Apr.; schedule varies rest of year. A 1.5-hour Florida Bay Cruise is offered daily at 2:30 and sunset, late Dec. to mid-Apr.; schedule varies rest of year. Boarding is 10 minutes before departure. Boat tours also leave from the visitor center in Everglades City.

Backcountry cruise $18; ages 6-12, $10. Florida Bay Cruise $12; ages 6-12, $7. Reservations are recommended for all boat tours. For further information about all boat tours phone the lodge at (239) 695-3101.

Airboat rides, available outside the park, are offered by private operators along the Tamiami Trail (US 41) west of Miami.

VISITOR CENTERS offer information that can enhance a visit to the park.

Ernest Coe Visitor Center, at the entrance at 40001 SR 9336, has exhibits about the park. Naturalists are on duty daily 8-5. Free. Phone (305) 242-7700.

Flamingo Visitor Center, 38 mi. s.w. of the main park entrance via SR 9336, has natural history exhibits and a marina opening onto Florida Bay. Rentals are available at the marina. Daily 8-5, Nov.-Apr.; staffing is intermittent rest of year. Free with park admission. Phone (239) 695-2945.

Gulf Coast Visitor Center, in Everglades City in the northwest corner of the park, contains natural-history exhibits. Daily 8:30-5. Free. Phone (239) 695-3311.

Royal Palm Visitor Center is 4 mi. inside the park. The center provides park information and, in winter, naturalist-led walks and illustrated talks. Daily 8-4:15. Free with park admission. Phone (305) 242-7700.

ADMISSION to the park is $10 per private vehicle or $5 per person arriving by bicycle, motorcycle or on foot.

PETS are permitted only in the park campgrounds and only if they are leashed, crated or otherwise physically restrained at all times. They are not allowed on developed trails, in the backcountry or in the visitor centers.

ADDRESS inquiries to the Superintendent, Everglades National Park, 40001 SR 9336, Homestead, FL 33034; phone (305) 242-7700.

Points of Interest

ANHINGA TRAIL starts at the Royal Palm Visitor Center and follows an elevated boardwalk. During the winter, alligators, snowy egrets, water turkeys and garfish can be seen.

CHEKIKA, 18 mi. n.w. of Homestead off SR 997, offers 640 acres of hardwood hammocks and wetlands with more than 100 species of birds. A boardwalk is available. **Note:** Access is limited due to flooding. The boardwalk is open.

GUMBO LIMBO TRAIL, starts at the Royal Palm Visitor Center and penetrates the interior of Paradise Key hammock, where many species of native plants can be seen.

LONG PINE KEY AREA, 7 mi. from the park entrance, contains camping and picnic facilities, and nature and hiking trails. *See the AAA Southeastern CampBook.*

MAHOGANY HAMMOCK, 19.5 mi. from the park entrance, is a region of mahogany trees and many other subtropical plants labeled for easy identification. An elevated boardwalk winds through the forest.

MANGROVE TRAIL, 30.5 mi. from the park entrance, extends through a mangrove forest at West Lake on an elevated boardwalk. The restored trail, which was badly damaged by a hurricane in 1960, passes through a landscape that shows the devastation such storms can cause.

PA-HAY-OKEE OVERLOOK is 12.5 mi. from the park entrance. The overlook consists of a 12-foot tower at Shark River Basin that affords views of the vast saw grass wilderness.

PINELANDS TRAIL, 6.5 mi. from the park entrance, extends into an area of southern pines, scrub palmetto and related plants.

SHARK VALLEY, off US 41, has several short self-guiding trails that explore the area. Bobcat Boardwalk passes through a saw grass slough, while Otter Cave Trail leads through limestone formations and a tropical hammock. Self-guiding bicycle trails and bicycle rentals are available. Visitor center open daily 9-5. Admission $8 per private vehicle, $4 per person arriving by bicycle, motorcycle or on foot (fee deductible from entrance fee to Everglades National Park). Phone (305) 221-8776.

The Shark Valley Tram Tour departs from Shark Valley off US 41. The 2-hour, 15-mile excursion explores the saw grass wilderness of Shark Valley and includes a 20-minute stop at the observation tower at the southern end of the valley. Tours operate daily 9-4, Dec.-Apr.; at 9:30, 11, 1 and 3, rest of year (weather permitting). Fare $13.25; over 62, $12.25; under 13, $8. Reservations are required 1 to 3 weeks in advance Nov.-Apr. AX, DS, MC, VI. Phone (305) 221-8455.

FERNANDINA BEACH—
see Jacksonville p. 104.

FLORIDA CITY—*see Miami-Miami Beach p. 134.*

FLORIDA'S SILVER SPRINGS—
see Silver Springs p. 207.

The Florida Keys

Bahia Honda State Park / © Peter Titmuss / Alamy

A watercolor sky glows lavender, cobalt, carmine, sienna—another sunset. The street performers pause. The audience applauds.

And then, on with the show. Back to shuffling for a better spot to watch the sword-swallower, kilted bagpiper, painted human "statue" and tip-pleading tightrope walker. Back to dodging oncoming onlookers, observing the people parade and eyeing vendors' wares. Back to the raucous ritual.

End the Beginning

You could only be in Key West, Florida's accessible slice of island spice. The final course in The Florida Keys' full menu of fun.

Imbued with a tropical flavor that extends to its ubiquitous dishes—conch chowder, conch fritters and, of course, Key lime pie—this tiny town at The End of the Road is a slightly sugary, slightly tart, somehow sublime little custard of sights, sounds, tastes and tempos. As impious as eating dessert first, it's perfectly placed to introduce this curving island chain's curious charisma.

Like its sister Keys that Henry Flagler's railroad linked, Key West's influences have been Bahamian, Cuban, military, visionary. Its industries have ranged from shipwreck salvaging to turtle hunting to cigar making to tourism. Its wealth has been vast (in the 1880s, before lighthouses helped treasure-laden ships avoid treacherous reefs) and lost (in the 1930s, after 42 miles of railroad succumbed to storm-tossed seas).

Its Old Town historic district—pedestrian-friendly and architecturally rich—is where wreckers' and shipbuilders' hybrid homes are now high-end bed-and-breakfasts admired for their tin roofs, gingerbread trim, signature shutters and wraparound verandas. Where former hangouts of hard-drinking heroes and hippies are now vacation-photo backdrops for families *and* frat boys. Where fierce, fighting roosters' docile descendents quaintly roam free, legally protected. That's Key West: tradition with a Key lime twist.

But of all its aspects, the self-nicknamed Conch Republic is arguably best known for having perpetuated a simple habit of nightly saluting the blazing horizon, albeit with an atmosphere increasingly more theme park than Thoreau.

In fact, if you strayed there straight from the airport or cruise ship, today's Mallory Square sundown scene could cause culture shock. Amid the pet-toting locals and souvenir T-shirt masses, first-timers tend to feel a bit like bit players on a crowded movie set. But for those who've been before, or who drove in through all those other quirky Keys, well, you've seen enough to know it's all for real. Surreal as it may be.

Driving the mostly two-lane Road That Went to Sea from Miami to Key West is like backtracking to the days predating endless exit ramps. Through the car windows—interspersed with mangroves, cattails and "passing lane 3 miles" signs—appear pirates posed in full regalia, monster lobsters, towering mermaid cutouts, lots of crusty cannons, a few giant anchors. Conspicuously placed as if to encourage a pull-off photo op, followed by a stop inside the air-conditioned comfort of whatever restaurant or shop sits close by, such oddities lend the landscape an innocent charm.

Then there are the signs: "Seafood" spelled in seashell mosaic; a neon turtle; even a rhinoceros-topped billboard. After many miles of this sort of scenery, one reaches the landlocked concrete buoy emblazoned "Southernmost Point" a little more prepared for Key West's mystique.

But don't think you have to head all the way to that oft-photographed red, yellow and black landmark to have *arrived*. Simply stop at almost any populated Key (taken from the Spanish *cayo*, or "small island") along the way and you'll usually be well fixed with great R & R opportunities. A good number of Florida Keys vacationers do just that, making family traditions out of annual stays at tuck-away campgrounds, easygoing efficiencies, "botels"—lodgings where marinas replace parking

lots—or sport-fishing hot spots flush with charter boats, guides and all-inclusive resorts.

Getting There *Is* Half the Fun

In the Upper Keys, where most of the kitsch is confined, Key Largo and the unparalleled John Pennekamp Coral Reef State Park beckon snorkelers and scuba divers. Here, experienced divers can find everything needed to explore the fantastically diverse and extremely fragile reef system several miles offshore. But amateurs aren't left out; many lodgings offer on-site diving instruction. The park's main beach even has a staged shipwreck that especially delights children, who can be heard shouting to shore their discovery of what surely is the long-lost cannon of an unfortunate Spanish galleon.

Anchoring the Upper Keys stretch is sport-fishing-focused Islamorada, boasting one of the region's largest concentrations of charter boats as well as the midwaylike atmosphere of lively Holiday Isle; complete with beach, pools, shops, boardwalk and marina, the resort is famous for appealing to a festive crowd.

Marathon, in the Middle Keys, combines residential side roads, numerous fishing tournaments and several resorts ideal for tropical retreats, and the sunset's just as pretty from here. The Museums of Crane Point Hammock offers an educational look at area animals, marine life and ecosystems. If time allows, a kayak jaunt through the Florida Bay "back-country" can provide a fascinating close-up glimpse of similar sights; rentals are readily available.

Once over the Seven Mile Bridge, be sure to visit Bahia Honda State Park. A sandy beach and walkable segment of old bridge—providing incredible views of the new bridge—make this a must-see spot

Theater of the Sea, Islamorada
© Focus Group / Alamy

to stretch your legs *and* shift your perspective into "island time."

Back in the car now and heading to the Lower Keys, you're in the homestretch. Be sure to slow for the endangered Key deer in Big Pine Key; it's the law. Then prepare for the sameness of mangroves, scrub, Australian pines and power lines, sights whose monotony instills an antsy appetite for what lies ahead.

The feeling heightens as you close in on Key West proper. You may know you're there by the sound of Navy fighter jets shredding air overhead; Naval Air Station Key West, on nearby Boca Chica Key, is one of the Navy's premier pilot-training facilities. Or by the "T" where U.S. 1 hits Roosevelt Boulevard (and New Town's jumble of condos and commerce commences). Or perhaps it won't fully register till you've reached Old Town itself and done the obligatory "Duval crawl"—head swiveling from T-shirt shop to tavern to tree-shaded courtyard eatery.

Destination The Florida Keys

*B*lame Henry Flagler. He laid the track that became the roadbed that put the Keys in easy reach.

*N*ow, millions visit. Some drop in, some drop out, some just drop anchor. And why not? With its warm breezes, top-notch water sports and weekend way of life, this enigmatic island chain is hard to resist.

Historic Tours of America

Conch Tour Trains, Key West.
Henry Flagler's preferred mode of transportation is a fitting way to explore the Island City. (See listing page 71)

Historic Tours of America

Little White House Museum, Key West.
Presidents Harry Truman, Dwight Eisenhower and John F. Kennedy slept here. (See listing page 72)

Big Pine Key

Sugarloaf Key

Key West

*P*laces included in this AAA Destination Area:

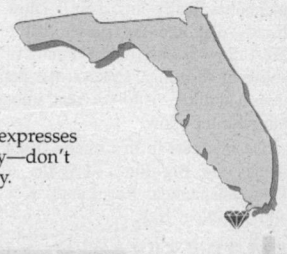

© James Urbach / SuperStock

Key West resident.
This grinning gator expresses
the Keys' philosophy—don't
take life too seriously.

Key
Largo

© Stephen Frink Collection / Alamy

Islamorada

Marathon

Florida Keys

*John Pennekamp Coral
Reef State Park,
Key Largo.*
In addition to its
natural wonders, this
scuba diver's delight
also is home to the
serene statue "Christ
of the Deep." (See
listing page 70)

Key West Lighthouse Museum.
Climb the stairs if you dare,
or just enjoy the historical
exhibits and life-size lens that
accompany this 1847 structure.
(See listing page 72)

© Wendell Metzen / Index Stock

However you reach it, once that mile-marker-zero mentality finally hits, you'll know The End of the Road—just like the sunset that closes every Key West day—is only the beginning of the bar-hopping, souvenir-shopping, conch-fritter-popping party more than a million visitors a year sojourn here to savor. On with the show.

Destinations in this region listed under their own names are Big Pine Key, Dry Tortugas National Park, Islamorada, Key Largo, Key West, Marathon and Sugarloaf Key.

BIG PINE KEY (I-10) pop. 5,032, elev. 5'

Big Pine Key, between Marathon and Key West, is home to the Key deer, a miniature species maturing to the size of a large dog. By the 1950s hunting had almost annihilated this subspecies of the Virginia whitetail. With only 800 of the animals remaining, the deer still is an endangered species.

Many deer have collided with vehicles and been injured or killed. Visitors are asked to observe the speed limit and not pull over to feed or photograph deer, as doing so encourages them to approach the road.

Great White Heron and Key West national wildlife refuges also preserve area bird life. The Key West refuge also provides a safe haven for sea turtle nests. Both are accessible only by boat.

The headquarters for both wildlife refuges—in Big Pine Shopping Plaza, a half-mile north of US 1 on Key Deer Boulevard at mile marker 30.5 at the traffic light—is open Mon.-Fri. 8-5.

Many reefs and their undersea inhabitants are protected in the Florida Keys National Marine Sanctuary, at nearby Looe Key. Characterized by coral reefs and clear water, the sanctuary is a delight to divers. Snorkel and scuba trips can be arranged from Looe Key Dive Center on Ramrod Key at mile marker 27.5; phone (305) 872-2215 or (800) 942-5397.

LOWER KEYS CHAMBER OF COMMERCE: P.O. Box 430511, Big Pine Key, FL 33043-0511; phone (305) 872-2411 or (800) 872-3722.

NATIONAL KEY DEER REFUGE, at mile marker 30.5 on US 1, is a designated refuge for the endangered diminutive deer. It encompasses approximately 8,700 acres. Blue Hole, 1.25 miles north of Key Deer and Watson boulevards, is a former quarry that attracts such wildlife as alligators and turtles. Two self-guiding nature trails begin off Key Deer Boulevard. Early morning and evening hours are the best times to view the deer. Daily dawn-dusk. Free. Phone (305) 872-0774.

DRY TORTUGAS NATIONAL PARK (I-8)

Elevations in the land portion of the park are at sea level. Most of the park is water.

The Tortugas are 68 nautical miles west of Key West. The seven Tortugas Keys, or Dry Tortugas Islands, and the surrounding waters in the Gulf of

© Denise Campbell Photography

Mexico constitute Dry Tortugas National Park. Discovered by Ponce de León in 1513 and named Las Tortugas for their great number of turtles, the islands are called Dry Tortugas because they lack fresh water.

For centuries the islands were inhabited by pirates who were protected from detection by passing vessels by the rocks and shallow waters. Lighthouses were built on Garden Key in 1825 and on Loggerhead Key in 1856. Discoveries of sunken Spanish treasure ships nearby bear witness to the shipwrecks that occurred along these shoals.

Strategically located between the United States and South America, the Tortugas attract many species of migratory birds. The most noted inhabitant is the sooty tern, which breeds on Bush Key between March and September. Another familiar inhabitant is the sea turtle, four endangered species of which nest in the park.

Fort Jefferson was begun on Garden Key in 1846, but after 30 years of construction it was still incomplete. Intended to protect vital shipping access to the Gulf, its 8-foot-thick walls and 450 guns were never tested. During the Civil War Federal troops occupied the fort, but by 1866 the introduction of rifled cannon and the fall of Fort Pulaski had made brick and masonry forts obsolete.

In 1861 Fort Jefferson became a prison for army deserters and in 1865 received the four "Lincoln Conspirators," condemned for their part in the assassination of President Abraham Lincoln. The fort was abandoned in 1874 following a hurricane and a second yellow fever outbreak. The Navy used it as the site for a wireless station in the early 1900s, then as a seaplane base in World War I. In 1935 President Franklin Roosevelt proclaimed the area a national monument.

Access to the park is by private boat or by commercial ferry or seaplane departing from Key West *(see place listing p. 70)*. Camping is permitted on the fort's grassy apron, and its shores lend themselves to swimming and snorkeling. No fresh water, food, fuel, supplies or public telephones are available.

Dry Tortugas National Park is open daily 24 hours. Fort open daily 9-5. Admission $5. A fee is charged for camping. A brief audiovisual presentation is available in the visitor center. For further information contact the Superintendent, Dry Tortugas National Park, 40001 SR 9336, Homestead, FL 33034; phone (305) 242-7700. *See Recreation Chart.*

ISLAMORADA (I-11) pop. 6,846, elev. 5′

Islamorada (I-lah-mor-AH-dah) is a fishing haven spread over the islands of Lower Matecumbe Key, Plantation Key, Upper Matecumbe Key and Windley Key. Its purplish appearance from a distance caused the Spanish to call it the "purple isle" *(isla morada)*. The wreck of the galleon *Herrera*, 2.5 miles off Whale Harbour Bridge, offers opportunities for underwater exploration and photography.

Indian Key Historic State Park, a half-mile southeast of Lower Matecumbe Key, is a 10-acre uninhabited island. This lavish paradise of notorious wrecker Capt. Jacob Housman was destroyed in 1840 when the captain's misuse of power prompted an Indian uprising. The ruins of houses and cisterns are now choked by vegetation planted by physician and botanist Dr. Henry Perrine, who conducted plant experiments at the settlement in 1838. The site is accessible only by private or chartered boat. For information phone (305) 664-9814 or (800) 322-5397.

Lignumvitae Key Botanical State Park can be reached only by private or chartered boat from the marinas at the western end of Islamorada. Because of its high elevation and the sensitive management of former owner William Matheson, the island retains a singular plant community and is a fine example of a West Indian hardwood hammock. Indigenous and introduced trees blossom at various times but are best viewed in spring or early summer.

Matheson House, built of coral in 1919 and furnished in 1930s styles, remains unchanged. A stone wall, possibly built by Spanish explorers as a navigation aid, extends the length of the island. Walking shoes and mosquito repellent are musts. For information phone (305) 664-2540.

Islamorada Chamber of Commerce: P.O. Box 915, Islamorada, FL 33036; phone (305) 664-4503 or (800) 322-5397.

Shopping areas: Bass Pro Shops World Wide Sportsman, 81576 Overseas Hwy., features an Everglades aquarium, several wildlife exhibits and sporting demonstrations.

THEATER OF THE SEA is at 84721 Overseas Hwy. The park features live performances by dolphins and sea lions, a guided tour of the marine life exhibits and a trip through a natural saltwater lagoon in a "bottomless" boat. Special events and programs also are offered at an additional cost and include a 4-hour adventure cruise and a swim with the dolphins. Food is available. Allow 2 hours, 30 minutes minimum. Daily 9:30-4. Open 10:30-4 on Dec. 25. Admission $23.95; ages 3-12, $15.95. Prices may vary; phone ahead. AX, MC, VI. Phone (305) 664-2431. *See color ad p. 69.*

KEY LARGO (I-11) pop. 11,886, elev. 6′

At 30 miles, Key Largo is the longest of the Florida Keys. Linked to the mainland by the first of 42 bridges along the Overseas Highway—the scenic 113-mile section of US 1 between the Florida mainland and Key West—Key Largo introduces the lifestyle of the keys with its marinas and diving and tackle shops.

Key Largo Chamber of Commerce: 105950 Overseas Hwy., Key Largo, FL 33037; phone (305) 451-1414 or (800) 822-1088.

JOHN PENNEKAMP CORAL REEF STATE PARK, on US 1 at mile marker 102.5, combines a land area with 178 nautical square miles of protected ocean waters. Features include a living coral reef, the underwater bronze statue "Christ of the Deep," two beaches, a boardwalk through a mangrove area and a visitor center with an aquarium. Snorkel, sail-and-snorkel, scuba and glass-bottom boat tours are available along with kayak and canoe rentals.

Park open daily 8-dusk (weather permitting). Visitor center open daily 8-5. A 2.5-hour glass-bottom boat tour departs daily at 9:15, 12:15 and 3. Scuba tours depart at 9:30 and 1:30. A 2.5-hour snorkel tour departs daily at 9, noon and 3. The 4-hour sail-and-snorkel tour departs daily at 9:30 and 1:30.

Admission $5 per private vehicle plus 50c per person; $1.50 per person arriving by bicycle or on foot. Glass-bottom boat tours $21; under 18, $14. Scuba tour $41. Snorkeling tour $27.95; under 12, $22.95. Sail-and-snorkel tour $33.95; under 18, $28.95. Reservations are recommended. Phone (305) 451-1202, or (305) 451-6300 for tour information and reservations. *See Recreation Chart and the AAA Southeastern CampBook.*

CASINOS

- **SunCruz Casino**, on US 1 at Holiday Inn Key Largo Resort and Marina at mile marker 100. Afternoon and evening departures available daily;

phone for schedule. After each day's first sailing, guests are shuttled out to the ship on a water taxi. Phone (305) 451-0000.

KEY WEST (I-9) pop. 25,478, elev. 22′

To its rocky shores, sandy beaches and weathered homes reminiscent of a coastal New England town, Key West adds another feature: its subtropical climate, which nourishes lush vegetation, especially palm trees, hibiscus and bougainvillea. Ship carpenters, using wooden pegs instead of nails, built many of the older houses, which are predominantly Bahamian in architecture.

The southernmost city in the continental United States, Key West once served as a base of operation against pirates; today it is the southern terminus of the scenic Overseas Highway (US 1). The prosperity of mid-19th century Key West was based on the thriving salvage business. At one time these enterprises provided the town with the highest per capita income in the nation.

Because of its proximity to Havana, about 90 miles south, the town was later a haven for Cuban political exiles. San Carlos Institute on Duval Street dates from the late 19th century, when it was used as a meeting place for the local Cuban community. City Cemetery on Margaret Street is the gravesite of the victims of the USS *Maine*, whose sinking precipitated the Spanish-American War.

Home at various times to Ernest Hemingway, Tennessee Williams and Robert Frost, Key West remains a popular retreat for artists and writers.

Although turtle hunting was once a major industry, federal laws protecting the endangered reptiles were enacted in the 1970s. The remains of a turtle-canning factory stand behind Turtle Kraals Bar and Restaurant on the harborfront at the north end of Margaret Street.

Donkey Milk House Museum, 613 Eaton St., derives its name from the alley in back where donkeys used to pull milk delivery carts. The restored 1860s home is open by appointment only; phone (305) 296-1866.

Of Key West's many natural attractions, its sunsets are among the most popular. Every night, weather permitting, more than two dozen street vendors and performers gather at Mallory Square Dock in Old Town off Duval Street. Jugglers, palm readers, contortionists, musicians and other entertainers vie for the attention and donations of the many spectators who begin gathering about an hour before sunset.

Nature also puts on a daily show in the shady confines of Nancy Forrester's Secret Garden, an environmental earthwork at 1 Free School Ln., off Simonton Street, where an extensive collection of rain forest plants creates a junglelike atmosphere complete with (caged) parrots; phone (305) 294-0015.

The Caribbean influence extends to the town's cuisine. Along Duval Street and its side streets, imaginative cafes and open-air restaurants serve foods ranging from gourmet specialties to ethnic snacks.

Various types of cruises, including those offering underwater viewing of the denizens of the deep, sailing, snorkeling and reef diving, depart from several private and city marinas. Of particular interest are bed and breakfasts cruises that incorporate snorkeling and gourmet meals. Deep-sea fishing trips leave from City Marina on Garrison Bight off Roosevelt Boulevard. Contact the chamber of commerce for more information.

Note: Parking regulations are strictly enforced throughout the city. Motor scooters should be parked in the areas designated for that purpose. There is no street parking available for recreational vehicles; follow signs to designated RV parking areas.

Key West Chamber of Commerce: Mallory Square, 402 Wall St., Key West, FL 33040; phone (305) 294-2587 or (800) 527-8539.

Self-guiding tours: Pelican Path—a route marked with pelican signs—leads visitors through historic Key West. A descriptive brochure outlining the tour and its sights can be picked up at the chamber of commerce.

[SAVE] **AUDUBON HOUSE AND TROPICAL GARDENS,** 205 Whitehead St., is where John James Audubon stayed while painting the wildlife of the Florida Keys in 1832. Chippendale furniture and Staffordshire pottery are among the 18th- and 19th-century furnishings in the restored home of noted harbor pilot and wrecker Capt. John Geiger. Original Audubon engravings are displayed. Tropical gardens feature exotic native plants. Allow 1 hour minimum. Daily 9:30-5. Admission $10; ages 6-12, $5. AX, MC, VI. Phone (305) 294-2116.

[GEM] **CONCH TOUR TRAINS** leave from Mallory Square. The 90-minute, 14-mile tour through old and new Key West features an informative narration about area history. Local points of interest along the tour include Old Town, Hemingway's house, Duval Street, Southernmost Point and the waterfront. Trains depart daily every half-hour 9-4:30. Fare $22.50; ages 4-12, $10.80. AX, DS, MC, VI. Phone (305) 294-5161.

[SAVE] **DISCOVERY UNDERSEA TOURS** departs from the historic Key West Seaport at 251 Margaret St. Offering narrated excursions aboard an 80-foot, glass-bottom vessel, this cruise company takes passengers out to nearby living coral reefs. Twenty windows set at an angle in the hull provide a panoramic view of the reef and its colorful denizens. Food is available. Allow 2 hours minimum. Cruises depart daily at 11:30, 2:30 and dusk, early Apr.-late Oct.; at 10:30, 1:30 and dusk, rest of year. Passengers should arrive 30 minutes before departure. Fare $35; ages 5-12, $16. Two children under age 5 admitted free with an adult on first cruise of the day. DS, MC, VI. Phone (305) 293-0099 or (800) 262-0099.

DRY TORTUGAS NATIONAL PARK FERRY departs from the Key West Seaport at 240 Margaret St. The ferry service offers a round-trip excursion to Fort Jefferson aboard a high-speed catamaran with air-conditioned cabins and open decks. Before returning to Key West, passengers spend 4.5 hours within the park during which they can swim, snorkel and take a 45-minute guided tour of the fort. Food is available. Allow a full day. Daily 8-5:30; closed Dec. 25. Fare (includes breakfast and lunch) $129; over 62, $119; ages 4-16, $89. AX, DS, MC, VI. Phone (305) 294-7009 or (800) 634-0939.

ERNEST HEMINGWAY HOME AND MUSEUM is at 907 Whitehead St. Hemingway bought the 1851 Spanish colonial-style mansion in 1931. Among works written here is "For Whom the Bell Tolls." The house, set in a lush tropical garden planted by the author, is home to more than 50 cats, descendants of Hemingway's felines. A penny embedded in the concrete at the head of the pool supposedly was tossed there when Hemingway discovered the pool's $20,000 price tag. Allow 30 minutes minimum. Daily 9-5. Admission $11; ages 6-12, $6. AX, MC, VI. Phone (305) 294-1136.

FLAGLER STATION OVER-SEA RAILWAY HISTOREUM is at 901 Caroline St. Henry Flagler completed the overseas railroad from Miami to Key West in 1912. Through photographs, memorabilia, audiotaped eyewitness accounts, old newsreels and a film of the historic arrival of the first train in Key West, visitors follow the story of the 7-year engineering feat from beginning to end. A restored Florida East Coast Railway car is on the grounds. Allow 1 hour minimum. Daily 9-5. Admission $5; under 12, $2.50. AX, DS, MC, VI. Phone (305) 295-3562 or (800) 868-7482.

FORT ZACHARY TAYLOR HISTORIC STATE PARK, at the s.w. end of the island via Southard St., was built 1845-66 as part of Florida's coastal defense system. The cannons within the walls constitute one of the largest collections of Civil War armaments. Swimming, fishing and picnicking on a tropical beach are among the recreational activities available.

Allow 3 hours minimum. Daily 8-dusk. Guided tours are given daily at noon and 2. Admission $6 per private vehicle plus 50c each passenger up to eight; $1.50 per person arriving by bicycle or on foot. Phone (305) 292-6713. *See Recreation Chart.*

KEY WEST AQUARIUM, at the foot of Whitehead St. on Mallory Sq., was one of the first open-air aquariums when it opened in 1934. Shark and turtle feedings take place daily, and a touch tank lets visitors interact with the marine life. Guided tours are available. Allow 1 hour minimum. Daily 10-6. Admission $10; ages 4-12, $5. Phone (305) 296-2051.

SAVE **KEY WEST BUTTERFLY & NATURE CONSERVATORY** is at 1316 Duval St. More than 50 butterfly species flourish amid tropical plants and trees in a climate-controlled atrium. A learning center provides an orientation film and tips for identifying butterflies by country of origin. Allow 1 hour minimum. Daily 9-5; closed Thanksgiving and Dec. 25. Last admission is at 4:30. Admission $10; ages 4-12, $7.50. AX, MC, VI. Phone (305) 296-2988 or (800) 839-4647.

SAVE **KEY WEST LIGHTHOUSE MUSEUM,** 938 Whitehead St., recounts Florida lighthouse history through exhibits featuring historical items, including a complete light assembly. The museum is in the former keeper's quarters. A spiral 88-step staircase leads to the top of the 1847 Key West Lighthouse. Allow 30 minutes minimum. Daily 9:30-4:30; closed Dec. 25. Admission $8; over 62, $7; students with ID $4; under 6 free. AX, MC, VI. Phone (305) 294-0012.

SAVE **KEY WEST MUSEUM OF ART & HISTORY AT THE CUSTOM HOUSE** is at 281 Front St. Built in 1891, the Romanesque Revival-style U.S. Custom House served as a customs processing station and later housed a post office, a district court and civil service offices until the 1930s. The museum's 10 galleries feature folk art, portraits of local notables and WPA artwork. History exhibits highlight the age of piracy, Ernest Hemingway's life and 25 years of Fantasy Fest costumes. Allow 1 hour minimum. Daily 9-5; closed Dec. 25. Admission $7; over 65, $6; students with ID $5. MC, VI. Phone (305) 295-6616.

KEY WEST SHIPWRECK HISTOREUM, 1 Whitehead St. in Old Mallory Square, is in a reproduction of the wreckers warehouse that originally stood on the site. Costumed actors interact with visitors and recreate the events of the wreck and salvage of the *Isaac Allerton,* which sank in 1856. Artifacts from the shipwreck are on display. A 65-foot observation tower provides a magnificent view of the Atlantic Ocean and the Gulf of Mexico. Allow 1 hour minimum. Daily 9:45-4:45. Admission $10; ages 4-12, $5. AX, DS, MC, VI. Phone (305) 292-8990.

THE LIBERTY FLEET OF TALL SHIPS departs from Hilton Resort and Marina, jct. Front and Greene sts. The schooner cruises around Key West and allows passengers the chance to steer and sail. Dinner cruises also are available. Cruises depart daily at 11, 2:30 and 5 (sunset cruise), Nov. 1-Apr. 1; daily at 11, 2:30 and 6:30 (sunset cruise), rest of year. Fare for 11 and 2:30 cruises $35; under 12, $25. Fare for sunset cruise $49; under 12, $35. Reservations are required. DS, MC, VI. Phone (305) 292-0332.

LITTLE WHITE HOUSE MUSEUM, 111 Front St. inside the Truman Annex, is the vacation retreat that Presidents Harry Truman, Dwight Eisenhower and John F. Kennedy used during their administrations. The house has been restored to its 1948 appearance. A 10-minute videotape introduces visitors to Truman, and a 40-minute guided tour gives insight into both his experiences in Key West and his presidency. Allow 1 hour minimum. Daily 9-4:30. Admission $11; ages 5-12, $5. AX, DS, JC, MC, VI. Phone (305) 294-9911.

MARTELLO TOWERS, on the south side of the island, are reached via SR A1A (S. Roosevelt Blvd.). The two brick fortifications were begun in 1858 by Union engineers to protect the defenses east of Fort Zachary Taylor.

[SAVE] **East Martello Museum and Gallery,** 3501 S. Roosevelt Blvd. at the airport entrance, exhibits Key West memorabilia relating to trade and the development of the island, including shipbuilding tools, treasure chests and boat models. The works of Mario Sanchez, a local artist and woodcarver, and metal sculpture by folk artist Stanley Papio are displayed. The citadel, accessible by stairs, provides a scenic overlook. Allow 30 minutes minimum. Daily 9:30-4:30; closed Dec. 25. Admission $6; over 65, $4; students with ID $3. AX, MC, VI. Phone (305) 296-3913.

Key West Garden Center is on a county beach on Atlantic Blvd. and White St. Tropical plants grow among the ruins of the west tower. Tues.-Sat. 9:30-3:15. Donations. Phone (305) 294-3210.

MEL FISHER MARITIME MUSEUM, Greene and Front sts., displays both precious and functional artifacts recovered from the wreckage of two Spanish galleons. While en route to Spain from Havana, the ships sank 40 miles off Key West in a hurricane Sept. 6, 1622. Highlights of the collection include a 77.76-carat emerald as well as gold and silver religious objects. Informative exhibits illustrate techniques of underwater archeology. Allow 1 hour minimum. Daily 9:30-5. Admission $11; students with ID $9; ages 6-12, $6. AX, MC, VI. Phone (305) 294-2633.

OLD TOWN TROLLEY tours leave from Mallory Square downtown or can be joined at any of the 10 stops as the trolley tours the island. The 1.5-hour tours of old Key West provide a narrated introduction to the history, legends and geography of the island. Points of interest along the tour include Key West Aquarium, Duval Street and Ernest Hemingway's house. Departures daily every 30 minutes 9:30-4:30. Fare $22; ages 4-12, $11. Tickets include one full loop around the island. AX, DS, MC, VI. Phone (305) 296-6688.

SEAPLANES OF KEY WEST departs from Key West International Airport, 3471 S. Roosevelt Blvd. Narrated, 40-minute, low-altitude flights to Fort Jefferson in Dry Tortugas National Park *(see place listing p. 68)* allow good views of marine life, shipwrecks and treasure salvaging operations. Visitors have ample time to explore the island. Beverages and snorkeling gear are provided. Allow 4 hours minimum. Full and half-day trips are available daily; closed Dec. 25. Fare for full-day trip $325; ages 7-12, $245; ages 2-6, $170. Half-day trip $189; ages 7-12, $139; ages 2-6, $109. Park entry fee $5. Reservations are required. AX, DC, MC, VI. Phone (305) 294-0709 or (800) 950-2359.

STARS & STRIPES—**KEY WEST,** departing from Land's End Marina at Caroline and Margaret sts., offers trips aboard a 54-foot catamaran. A full-day excursion includes sailing, snorkeling and beachcombing. A 2-hour sunset cruise offers a full view of Key West's legendary sunsets; complimentary refreshments are served.

Full-day trip departs daily at 9:30. Sunset cruise departs daily; times vary according to season. Boarding is 30 minutes before departure. Full-day fare (includes snorkel gear, instruction and food) $79.95; ages 7-17, $49.95. Sunset sail $35; ages 7-17, $17.50. Reservations are recommended. AX, MC, VI. Phone (305) 294-7877 or (800) 634-6369.

SUNNY DAYS *FAST CAT,* departing from 201 Elizabeth St., offers ferry service to Dry Tortugas National Park *(see place listing p. 68).* The trip includes a 2-hour ride (each way) on a high-speed catamaran and a 4.5-hour stay at the park. Knowledgeable guides provide a tour of the fort, and visitors have ample time to explore the island before the boat returns to Key West. Snorkeling gear is available. Food and beverages are included in the fare. Allow a full day. Departure is at 8; passengers should arrive 30 minutes early to check in. Fare $115; over 61, $110; ages 3-16, $80. Park entrance fee $5. AX, DS, MC, VI. Phone (305) 292-6100 or (800) 236-7937.

WRECKERS' MUSEUM/OLDEST HOUSE, 322 Duval St., is said to be the oldest house in south

Florida. The construction of the 1829 house includes horizontal wall boards, a ship's hatch in the roof and the "landlubber's tilt" in the office. Furnished with American antiques, the house contains maritime documents, ship models and displays about the history of 19th-century ship wrecking. The garden has a separate cookhouse and an exhibit pavilion. Allow 30 minutes minimum. Daily 10-4. Admission $5; ages 3-12, $1. Phone (305) 294-9502.

RECREATIONAL ACTIVITIES
Kayaking
- **Mosquito Coast Kayak Tours** departs from 310 Duval St. Write 32 King Fisher Ln., Key West, FL 33040. Tour departs daily at 9. Phone (305) 294-7178.

MARATHON (I-10) pop. 10,255

Marathon, named for the lament of an East Coast Railroad engineer when told to continue the line still farther, is the commercial and sport fishing center of the Middle Keys.

Marathon Chamber of Commerce: 12222 Overseas Hwy., Marathon, FL 33050; phone (305) 743-5417 or (800) 352-5397.

MUSEUMS AND NATURE CENTER OF CRANE POINT HAMMOCK, gulfside at mile marker 50, is a historic site. The natural history museum features models of marine life, animals and birds in naturalistic settings, while the children's museum features touch tanks. Also on the site are a model ship's deck, nature trails and an early Bahamian homestead. Allow 1 hour minimum. Mon.-Sat. 9-5, Sun. noon-5. Tours are available upon request. Admission $7.50; over 65, $6; students with ID $4; under 7 free. Phone (305) 743-9100.

SUGARLOAF KEY (I-9)

Sugarloaf Key gained its name from the sugarloaf pineapples once grown in the area. Just north of US 1 at the airport entrance is Bat Tower, an island landmark and a monument to a futile attempt to manipulate nature. Built in 1929 by fishing resort owner R.C. Perky, the tower was to become home to a colony of bats intended to feed on the resident mosquito population; once the bats were released they flew away, and the mosquitoes remained.

Visit Florida

This ends listings for The Florida Keys.
The following page resumes the alphabetical listings of cities in Florida.

Fort Lauderdale

© Walter Bibikow / Index Stock

City Population: 152,397   **Elevation:** 7 ft.

Editor's Picks:

Honeycombed by rivers, bays, inlets and canals, Fort Lauderdale is a city of islands, where the boat rivals the automobile as a mode of transportation. One-tenth of the city surface is water; 85 miles of navigable waters provide either home or temporary port for boats of all sizes. The Intracoastal Waterway, a canal system reminiscent of Venice, connects downtown office buildings, the galleries and boutiques on Las Olas Boulevard, and the museums, theaters and nightspots of Riverwalk.

Fort Lauderdale is primarily residential; with the exception of the waterfront and beach areas, it does not give the appearance of a resort community. The canals and waterways furnish a striking setting for many beautiful homes, the most lavish of which are east of US 1. However, residential does not necessarily mean sedate—Fort Lauderdale's clubs and discotheques offer a flourishing nightlife.

Although settled in 1838 by Maj. William Lauderdale, the resort did not begin to grow until after its incorporation in 1911. In Fort Lauderdale proper almost all hotels, motels and stores are just west of SR A1A. The beach to the east provides a pristine, 3-mile-long strip of sand that has proven to be one of Fort Lauderdale's foremost attractions. Fort Lauderdale Beach Boulevard, the stretch of A1A from Bahia Mar Marina to Sunrise Boulevard, is nationally noted for its integration of urban streetscape and beachfront scenery.

Miles of lagoons, waterways and beaches make Fort Lauderdale one of the most popular areas on the Gold Coast. Water taxis provide a convenient and relaxing way to navigate the inland waterways that wind through the city.

In addition to being a leading resort area, Fort Lauderdale also is an active commercial center. The marine industry and citrus groves play important roles. Port Everglades, 2 miles south, has one of the deepest harbors south of Norfolk, Va. The 10 modern terminals provide facilities for Caribbean-bound luxury liners as well as for the handling of millions of tons of cargo each year.

Getting There
By Car

SR A1A, US 1, Florida's Turnpike (toll), I-95 and US 441 are the major approaches to Fort Lauderdale from the north and I-75/I-595, known as Alligator Alley, is the major western approach. The roads are well-marked; the only trouble drivers might have is with US 1, variously posted as US 1 and Federal Highway. Downtown this route is known as N.E. or S.E. Sixth Avenue.

Getting Around
Street System

The street plan of Fort Lauderdale is a fairly simple grid. Broward Boulevard and Andrews Avenue divide the city into quadrants (N.E., S.W., etc.). Boulevards,

Getting There — *starting on p. 76*

Getting Around — *starting on p. 76*

What To See — *starting on p. 77*

What To Do — *starting on p. 81*

Where To Stay — *starting on p. 374*

Where To Dine — *starting on p. 389*

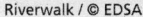

courts, drives and streets run east and west; avenues, terraces and ways run north and south.

The speed limit is 25 mph or as posted. Do not try to follow an unfamiliar route during rush hours (7 to 9 a.m. and 4:30 to 6 p.m.) or during lunch time.

Parking

Parking on downtown streets is metered; there are ample lots at rates of $1.25 per hour. Municipal parking in the beach areas costs $3-$6 per day. No parking is available along SR A1A. Parking along side streets costs 25c-$1.50 per hour.

Riverwalk / © EDSA

What To See

BONNET HOUSE MUSEUM & GARDENS, 900 N. Birch Rd., just s. of Sunrise Blvd., is a 35-acre beachfront estate that was the winter home of two artists, Frederic and Evelyn Bartlett. Designed by Bartlett during the 1920s, the plantation-style house features loggias accented with inlaid shellwork and balconies enclosed with lacy wrought iron made in New Orleans. The residence is surrounded by lagoons, gardens, fruit groves, a mangrove jungle and a desert garden planted from seeds collected on the couple's world travels.

Of note are pieces of artwork, decorative accents and hand-painted ceilings created by the Bartletts as well as collections of porcelains, religious figures, furnishings and objects found on the beach. A shell museum and an orchid greenhouse also are on the grounds.

Guided house and grounds tours are available. Allow 1 hour, 30 minutes minimum. Open Tues.-Sat. 10-4, Sun. noon-4, Dec.-Apr.; Wed.-Fri. 10-3, Sat. 10-4, Sun. noon-4, May-Aug. and Oct.-Nov. Last tour begins 90 minutes before closing. Schedule may vary; phone ahead. Admission $10; over 60, $9; ages 6-18, $8. Grounds only $6. AX, DS, MC, VI. Phone (954) 563-5393.

(SAVE) **INTERNATIONAL SWIMMING HALL OF FAME** is 1 blk. s. of Las Olas Blvd., just w. of SR A1A at 1 Hall of Fame Dr. The hall highlights the achievements of notable swimmers and contains aquatic artifacts dating to the 15th century. An art gallery features aquatic art from around the world. The Fort Lauderdale Aquatic Complex swimming pools adjoin the museum.

Allow 1 hour minimum. Museum and art gallery daily 9-5. Pool daily 9-4 (also Mon.-Fri. 6-7:30 p.m.); closed during swim meets. Museum and art gallery admission $3, over 55 and military and students with ID $1, under 12 free; family rate $5. Pool $4; senior citizens and military and students with ID $3. Parking $1 per hour. Phone (954) 462-6536, or (954) 828-4580 for the pool.

Destination Fort Lauderdale

*C*asual and laid-back. Sophisticated and energetic. Contradictory terms, but all appropriate for describing Fort Lauderdale.

*B*reezy resortwear is perfect for a day at the beach, a riverfront stroll or a museum visit. Or indulge in a little *haute couture*, fast-paced jai alai or Thoroughbred action. Set your own style and pace in Fort Lauderdale.

Greater Fort Lauderdale CVB

Fort Lauderdale waterways.
Sleek white boats serenely sandwiched between sky and water reflect the dreams of owners and visitors alike.

© L. Clarke / Corbis

Fort Lauderdale skyline.
High-rise lodgings mark the location of Fort Lauderdale's prime beachfront property.

International Game Fish Association

IGFA Fishing Hall of Fame & Museum, Dania Beach.
This soaring swordfish greets anglers making their way to celebrate the sport of game fishing. (See listing page 85)

See Vicinity map page 81

Greater Fort Lauderdale CVB

Flamingo Gardens, Davie.
This symbol of Florida kitsch is distinct among his feathered friends. (See listing page 85)

*P*laces included in this AAA Destination City:

The Informed Traveler

Sales Tax: The sales tax in Broward County is 6 percent. A tourist development tax of 5 percent is levied on rental accommodations.

WHOM TO CALL

Emergency: 911

Police (non-emergency): (954) 828-5700; sheriff (954) 765-4321.

Fire: (954) 828-6800

Time and Temperature: (954) 748-4444

Hospitals: Broward General Medical Center, (954) 355-4400; Memorial Regional Hospital, (954) 987-2000; Imperial Point Medical Center, (954) 776-8500.

WHERE TO LOOK

Newspapers

The *South Florida Sun Sentinel* and the *Miami Herald* are published daily and are available throughout the city. Many weekly publications supplement these papers.

Radio

Fort Lauderdale radio station WFTL (850 AM) is an all-news/weather station; WLRN (91.3 FM) is a member of National Public Radio.

Visitor Information

Greater Fort Lauderdale Chamber of Commerce: 512 N.E. Third Ave., Fort Lauderdale, FL 33301; phone (954) 462-6000.

The chamber distributes maps, brochures and a variety of other local information Mon.-Fri. 8-5.

Greater Fort Lauderdale Convention and Visitors Bureau: 100 Broward Blvd., Suite 200, Fort Lauderdale, FL 33316; phone (954) 765-4466 or (800) 356-1662, or the events hotline at (954) 357-5700. *See color ad p. 82.*

The bureau is open Mon.-Fri. 8:30-5.

The Fort Lauderdale Parks and Recreation events hotline is (954) 828-5363.

TRANSPORTATION

Air Travel

The Fort Lauderdale-Hollywood International Airport is between I-95 and US 1, just south of SR 84.

Rental Cars

Hertz, 3030 Holiday Dr. in Marriott Harbor Beach Hotel, (800) 654-3080, and at the airport, (954) 764-1199 or (800) 654-3080, offers discounts to AAA members. Many car rental agencies are listed in the telephone directory.

Rail Service

The Amtrak station is at 200 S.W. 21st Terr. For arrival information phone (954) 587-6692; for reservations and other information phone (800) 872-7245.

Buses

The bus terminal serving the city is Greyhound Lines Inc., 515 N.E. Third St.; phone (954) 764-6551, or (800) 231-2222 for schedule and rate information.

Taxis

Cabs are plentiful. Fares are metered and are $3.25 for the first mile and $2 for each additional mile (plus 30c per minute during stops). The largest company is Yellow Cab, (954) 565-5400; consult the telephone directory for others.

Public Transport

Broward County Transit, (954) 357-8400, provides transportation to all sections of Fort Lauderdale and its outlying areas. Buses also are available between the downtown area and the beach. City Cruiser Community Bus offers free shuttle service in the downtown and beach areas; for information phone (954) 761-3543.

MUSEUM OF ART FORT LAUDERDALE, 1 E. Las Olas Blvd., features a collection of 20th-century European and American art. Holdings include American Impressionist William Glackens' works, art from the Northern European Expressionist CoBrA movement and significant contemporary Latin American art.

Photography and videotaping are not permitted. Allow 2 hours minimum. Wed.-Mon. 11-7 (also Thurs. 7-9 p.m.); closed holidays. Admission $6; over 65, $5; ages 12-18, $3. Parking is available for a fee in nearby City Garage. Additional admission may be charged during special exhibits. Phone (954) 525-5500.

MUSEUM OF DISCOVERY AND SCIENCE, 401 S.W. Second St., is a hands-on science museum with more than 200 interactive exhibits. Florida Ecoscapes, focusing on the state's ecology, has sea turtles, sharks, alligators and a large captive Atlantic coral reef. Runways to Rockets features space science exhibits and a simulated flight to Mars.

Entertaining live science programs are offered daily in the Science Cafe. Discovery Center is designed for pre-school children. Other exhibits cover such topics as health, sound, gravity, technology and the Florida Everglades. The IMAX Theater presents 2-D and 3-D films on a five-story screen with a surround-sound system. National traveling exhibits are featured quarterly.

Food is available. Allow 2 hours minimum. Mon.-Sat. 10-5, Sun. noon-6. IMAX shows are presented daily; schedule varies with each film. Museum admission (includes exhibits and one IMAX show) $14; over 64, $13; ages 3-12, $12. Museum or theater admission only $9; over 64, $8; ages 3-12, $7. Metered parking is available. AX, MC, VI. Phone (954) 467-6637 for museum or (954) 463-4629 for theater.

OLD DILLARD CULTURAL ARTS MUSEUM, 1009 N.W. Fourth St. at jct. N.W. 11th Ave., is housed in the restored 1924 Dillard High School, which served as the area's first African-American school. Heritage exhibits include artifacts, photographs and interactive galleries. An exhibit about local jazz music centers on musician Julian "Cannonball" Adderly, the school's band director in the 1940s. Allow 1 hour minimum. Mon.-Fri. 11-4; closed holidays. Free. Phone (754) 322-8828.

OLD FORT LAUDERDALE VILLAGE & MUSEUM, 231 S.W. Second Ave., presents exhibitions of artifacts from prehistoric times to the present. The changing exhibits, archives and library offer information about local and regional history. Guided tours, which include the 1907 King-Cromartie House, a museum of pioneer lifestyles, are available. Allow 1 hour minimum. Tues.-Fri. 11-5, Sat.-Sun. noon-5; closed Jan. 1, Easter, Thanksgiving and Dec. 25. Tours are given Wed. and Sat.-Sun. 1-4. Admission $5; ages 6-16, $3. Admission (includes tours of museum and King-Cromartie House) $8; ages 6-16, $5. Phone (954) 463-4431.

Fort Lauderdale Beach / Visit Florida

RIVERWALK, downtown at S.W. Second Ave., is a meandering promenade through lush tropical landscaping along the New River. The walkway links attractions, arts and cultural institutions, restaurants and shops. Riverboat cruises are available and evening entertainment is offered year-round. Esplanade Park features an interactive scientific display that contains a human sundial and "whisper dishes"—satellite-like dishes that amplify whispered messages from 25 feet away. Daily 24 hours. Free. Phone (954) 468-1541.

SAWGRASS RECREATION PARK is 2 mi. n. of jct. I-75 and US 27N. Thirty-minute airboat tours of the Everglades feature an environmental and historical narration. Guides point out native flora and fauna; alligators sometimes can be seen. Tour guides explain tribal customs and history as visitors are led through a replica of a typical 18th-century Seminole Indian village. Snakes and alligators are displayed in separate exhibit areas. Fishing guides and boat rentals are available. Daily 9-5; closed Thanksgiving and Dec. 25. Admission $19.50; over 60, $17.55; ages 4-12, $10. AX, DS, MC, VI. Phone (954) 389-0202 or (800) 457-0788.

SAVE **STRANAHAN HOUSE** is at Las Olas Blvd. and S.E. Sixth Ave. Owned by one of Fort Lauderdale's founding families, this 1901 building has served as a trading post, restaurant and private home. Events are held throughout the year. Allow 30 minutes minimum. Wed.-Sat. 10-4, Sun. 1-4; closed major holidays. Guided tours are given on the hour. Last tour begins 1 hour before closing. Admission $6; under 12, $3. Phone (954) 524-4736.

What To Do

Sightseeing

Boat Tours

Discovery Cruise Line, departing Port Everglades, offers day-long cruises to Freeport, Grand Bahama Island, where, for additional fees, visitors can scuba or snorkel, fish or golf, or just shop and eat. Food, a sun deck and swimming pool, casino gambling and entertainment are featured aboard ship. Departures are daily at 7:45 a.m., with return arrival at 10 p.m. United States and Canadian citizens must carry proof of citizenship, such as a passport, an Alien Registration Receipt Card or an original birth certificate accompanied by a photo ID. For reservations phone (800) 937-4477 in Fla. or (800) 866-8687 out of Fla.

Sightseeing cruises along the Intracoastal Waterway and the New River are available aboard the Water Bus. The bus also offers transportation to restaurants, hotels, shops and attractions. For schedules and information phone (954) 467-6677.

JUNGLE QUEEN RIVERBOAT CRUISE, s. side of Bahia-Mar Yachting Center on SR A1A, offers a 3-hour sightseeing cruise along the New River past luxurious homes and downtown Fort Lauderdale. Dinner/entertainment cruises also are available.

Sightseeing cruises depart daily at 10 and 2; closed Dec. 25. Three-hour fare $13.50; ages 2-10, $9.25. Reservations are required. Phone (954) 462-5596. *See color ad p. 83.*

SAVE **RIVERFRONT CRUISES,** New River dock at Las Olas Riverfront Marketplace, 1 blk. w. of Andrews Ave., offers a 90-minute cruise along the New River and Intracoastal Waterway to the mansion-lined canals nicknamed "The Venice of America." Cruises depart every two hours Mon.-Fri. 12:30-6:30, Sat.-Sun. 10:30-6:30. Fare $14; ages 4-10, $8. AX, MC, VI. Phone (954) 463-3440.

Sports and Recreation

Fort Lauderdale has a public beach and excellent inland and ocean **fishing** waters. Many species of fish are caught in the "inside" waters. The Everglades and deep-sea fishing rank with the best in Florida. Fishing boats can be rented at Bahia-Mar and Pier 66. Area piers are good spots for fishing; bait, tackle and food are available.

Boating is another popular sport. There are numerous canals to be explored, and sailing around the

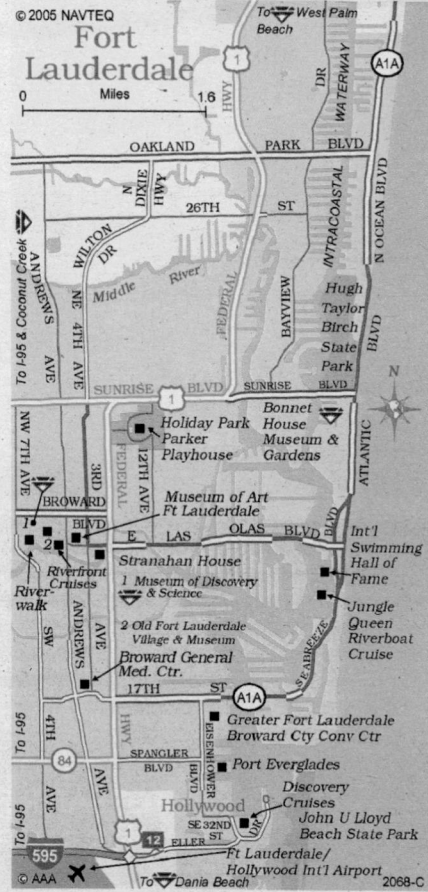

Let the sun go to your head.

There must be something in the South Florida air that makes you smile bigger. Laugh harder. And remember what it's like to be you. From strolling along palm tree fringed Blue Wave beaches, to boating along the Intracoastal Waterway, even diving through colorful coral reefs, a vacation in Greater Fort Lauderdale makes everything in life seem a little brighter. For our free Vacation Planning Guides, including Superior Small Lodgings, visit www.sunny.org or call (800) 22-SUNNY.

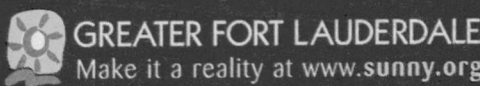

GREATER FORT LAUDERDALE
Make it a reality at www.**sunny**.org

barrier islands is a favorite pastime. Most marinas rent boats.

Scuba diving is rewarding along three lines of reefs, where clear water permits views of sea fans, branched coral and tropical fish. Many firms offer instruction and rental equipment; consult the telephone directory.

Water skiing is popular on the city's protected waterways and canals. Instruction is offered by the McGinnis School, 2421 S.W. 46th Ave., (954) 321-0221, and Ski-Rixen at Quiet Waters Park in Deerfield Beach, (954) 429-0215.

The Broward County Brian Piccolo Velodrome in nearby Cooper City consists of two tracks: one for competitive **bicycle racing** and one for recreational riding and **in-line skating**; phone (954) 437-2626.

The Broward County Parks system includes 17 regional parks, 15 neighborhood parks and more than 20 natural areas for outdoor recreation. In addition, community centers offer activities ranging from bridge for beginners to instruction in shellcraft. For more information, phone the Parks and Recreation Department at (954) 357-8100.

The Baltimore Orioles head south each year for **baseball** spring training in Fort Lauderdale; phone (954) 776-1921. **Hockey** comes to sunny South Florida in October when the Florida Panthers of the National Hockey League take to the ice at Office Depot Center in Sunrise; phone (954) 835-7000, or (954) 835-8326 for tickets.

Golf in the area is excellent. Most courses are semiprivate, with play governed by local regulations. Many hotels have agreements allowing guests to play on certain courses; check with your hotel manager.

Tennis is popular throughout the area; many hotels and motels have their own courts. Supplementing these are the public courts at Jimmy Everett Tennis Center, 701 N.E. 12th Ave., (954) 828-5379; and Joseph C. Carter Park, 1450 W. Sunrise Blvd., (954) 828-5411.

Shopping

Broward County shopping is diverse and plentiful. The Galleria at Fort Lauderdale, 2414 E. Sunrise Blvd., features anchor stores Macy's, Neiman Marcus and Saks Fifth Avenue as well as dining and entertainment venues. In nearby Plantation are Broward Mall, University Drive and Broward Boulevard, and Fashion Mall at Plantation, 321 N. University Dr.

Offerings in the western suburbs include Coral Square Mall, 9469 W. Atlantic Blvd. in Coral Springs, and Pembroke Lakes Mall, 11401 Pines Blvd. in Pembroke Pines.

The shops along Las Olas Boulevard between Federal Highway and the beach offer a unique experience. Specialty shops line US 1 at both the north and south entrances to the city.

More than 300 outlet stores, including many upscale and high-fashion retailers, comprise Sawgrass Mills, 12801 W. Sunrise Blvd. in Sunrise.

True bargain hunters may enjoy the Swap Shop, 3291 W. Sunrise Blvd. The 80-acre flea market features more than 2,000 vendors with wares ranging from brand-name electronics to antiques.

Theater and Concerts

Broward Center for the Performing Arts, 201 S.W. Fifth Ave. in the 22-block Riverwalk Arts and Entertainment District, is the setting for events including ballet, opera, Broadway shows, children's theater and concerts; phone (954) 522-5334 or (954) 462-0222.

Parker Playhouse, in Holiday Park at US 1 and N.E. Eighth Street, offers Broadway shows; phone (954) 763-2444.

War Memorial Auditorium, at 800 N.E. Eighth St. in Holiday Park, seats 2,100 people. Plays, concerts, sports events and exhibitions are presented throughout the year; phone (954) 828-5380.

Broward County supports an opera company, symphony orchestra and ballet, as well as other dance and musical programs. For performance information contact the Arts and Entertainment Hotline, (954) 357-5700, or (800) 249-2787 out of Fla.

Special Events

During January, March and September artists from across North America show their efforts at the Las

Olas Art Fair. Canada Fest and the Greek Festival are held during January. In mid-February the Seminole Tribal Fair takes place in nearby Hollywood.

April brings the Florida Derby, a thoroughbred racing event at Gulfstream Park in Hallandale Beach, and the Pompano Beach Seafood Festival. The 3-day consumer show and celebration Ocean Fest, held mid-month, draws more than 200 exhibitors to Fort Lauderdale for diving, treasure hunts, entertainment and seafood.

The 2-day Fort Lauderdale Air & Sea Show, featuring demonstrations of military and civilian aircraft along 4 miles of the city's beachfront, takes place in early May. The Pompano Fishing Rodeo and the Cajun/Zydeco Crawfish Festival also are in May.

Celebrate Independence Day with family activities, concerts and a fireworks display at the Fourth Along the Coast Family Celebration on Fort Lauderdale Beach.

Live music, children's activities and food spice up the Hollywood Beach Latin Festival, held in August on the Hollywood Beach Broadwalk.

During the Fort Lauderdale International Film Festival, held from mid-October to early November, celebrities flock to town to preview films from around the globe. The Fort Lauderdale International Boat Show takes place in late October and early November.

Also in November is the Hollywood Jazz Festival. Mid-November through January, Tradewinds Park dresses up for the Holiday Fantasy of Lights.

On a mid-December Saturday yachts at Port Everglades don holiday lights in preparation for a night's cruise up the Intracoastal Waterway—the spectacular and festive Winterfest Boat Parade. For further event information phone (954) 767-0686.

The Fort Lauderdale Vicinity

COCONUT CREEK (G-11)
pop. 43,566, elev. 17'

BUTTERFLY WORLD, in Tradewinds Park South at 3600 W. Sample Rd., includes a breeding laboratory, a butterfly museum and an insectarium with displays of unusual insects and butterflies from around the world. Two-story aviaries present gardens and a simulated tropical rain forest in which butterflies live restricted only by the buildings' screen construction.

In the Secret Garden, hummingbirds and rare bird species fly among a collection of passionflower and Dutchman's-pipe vines. Visitors can feed playful lorikeets in the Lorikeet Encounter. Also featured are a botanical garden and an English rose garden.

Allow 1 hour minimum. Mon.-Sat. 9-5, Sun. 1-5; closed Easter, Thanksgiving and Dec. 25. Last admission 1 hour before closing. Butterfly World admission $17.95; ages 4-12, $12.95. Tradewinds Park entrance fee on weekends and holidays $1 per person. AX, MC, VI. Phone (954) 977-4400.

CORAL SPRINGS (G-11) pop. 117,549

SAVE CORAL SPRINGS MUSEUM OF ART, off SR 868 exit 8, 1.5 mi. e. on Sample Rd., then .5 mi. s. to 2855 Coral Springs Dr., displays paintings, sculpture and mixed-media works by local and regional artists. Allow 1 hour minimum. Mon.-Sat. 10-5. Admission $4; over 65 and college students with ID, $3; under 18 free; free to all Wed. AX, MC, VI. Phone (954) 340-5000.

DANIA BEACH (G-11) pop. 20,061, elev. 11'

Dania Beach is a winter beach resort. Jai-alai is played year-round at Dania Jai-Alai Fronton on Dania Beach Boulevard, one-half mile east of US 1; for schedule phone (954) 927-2841.

Note: Policies vary concerning admittance of children to pari-mutuel betting facilities. Phone for information.

Greater Dania Beach Chamber of Commerce: 102 W. Dania Beach Blvd., P.O. Box 1017, Dania Beach, FL 33004; phone (954) 926-2323.

Shopping areas: Antique hunters will find remembrances of early Americana in the shops along Federal Highway. Bass Pro Shops Outdoor World, jct. I-95 and Griffin Rd. at 200 Gulf Stream Way, features an indoor waterfall and 33,000-gallon aquarium, wildlife exhibits and sporting demonstrations.

IGFA FISHING HALL OF FAME & MUSEUM is off I-95 exit 23, w. on Griffin Rd. (SR 818) to Anglers Ave., then s. to 300 Gulfstream Way. Included are a tackle gallery, a re-created saltwater marsh and wetland with alligators and turtles, a children's Discovery Room and an 18-minute film. Interactive fishing simulator stations demonstrate the effort required to reel in various species.

Touch-screen computers in the Legacy Gallery follow the histories of recreational fishing and the International Game Fish Association. The facility also houses the E.K. Harry Library of Fishes, a comprehensive collection of angling literature. Other galleries feature mounted world-record catches as well as trophies and fish stories. Three fishing boats are displayed in the marina.

Allow 2 hours minimum. Daily 10-6; closed Thanksgiving and Dec. 25. Admission $6; over 61 and ages 4-12, $5. AX, DS, MC, VI. Phone (954) 922-4212.

DAVIE (G-11) pop. 75,720, elev. 5'

BUEHLER PLANETARIUM & OBSERVATORY, on the A. Hughes Adams central campus of Broward Community College, 1 mi. s. of I-595 at 3501 S.W. Davie Rd., offers programs with time and space themes. Allow 1 hour minimum. Main features Fri. at 7 p.m., Sat. at 3 and 7 p.m., Sun. at 3. Family features Sat.-Sun. at 1:30. Star show Wed. at 7 p.m. Doors to the shows close on time. Afternoon show $4; evening show $5. Star show $2. For information phone (954) 201-6681.

FLAMINGO GARDENS, off I-595 exit 1B, then 3 mi. s. to 3750 S. Flamingo Rd., contains trees and plants indigenous to subtropical forests. A wildlife sanctuary is home to river otters, alligators and flamingos, while a free-flight aviary houses birds native to Florida. American bald eagles can be seen in the Birds of Prey Center. Visitors may take a 25-minute narrated tram tour through citrus groves and native oak hammocks.

Allow 2 hours, 30 minutes minimum. Daily 9:30-5:30, Oct.-May; Tues.-Sun. 9:30-5:30, rest of year. Tram tours depart on the hour 11-4. Admission $15; ages 4-11, $8. Tram tour $4; ages 4-11, $3. Phone (954) 473-2955.

YOUNG AT ART CHILDREN'S MUSEUM is off I-595 exit 2 (Hiatus Rd.), then just s. to 11584 SR 84W. Geared to children under 13, this hands-on museum includes a painting center, toddler play area, multicultural "village" and recycled-arts center where kids make sculptures from donated materials. The museum also hosts traveling exhibits. Mon.-Sat. 10-5, Sun. noon-5. Admission $5; over 60, $4.50; under 2 free. AX, MC, VI. Phone (954) 424-0085.

DEERFIELD BEACH (G-11)
pop. 64,583, elev. 16'

QUIET WATERS COUNTY PARK, is 2 mi. w. from I-95 via SR 810 (Hillsboro Blvd.), then .2 mi. s. on SR 845 (Powerline Rd.). Within its 430 acres this water-oriented park offers canoeing, paddleboating, freshwater fishing, swimming, camping, picnicking, bicycling and a mechanical water-ski tow. A children's water playground and a skate park also are available. A fishing license may be required for over 16 years of age.

Daily 8-7:30, last Sun. in Apr.-last Sat. in Oct.; 8-6, rest of year. Park admission Mon.-Fri. free; Sat.-Sun. and holidays $1 for vehicle driver and per passenger over age 5. Phone (954) 360-1315, or (954) 429-0215 for ski tow information. *See Recreation Chart.*

HALLANDALE BEACH (G-11)
pop. 31,000, elev. 10'

Primarily a retirement community, Hallandale Beach is the home of Gulfstream Park and the Hollywood Greyhound Track. The dog track presents races December through May; phone (954) 924-3200. Gulfstream Park, at US 1 and Hallandale Beach Boulevard, is open for horse racing from early January to late April; phone (954) 454-7000.

Note: Policies vary concerning admittance of children to pari-mutuel betting facilities. Phone for information.

DID YOU KNOW

The Gulf Between It, the first film to be shot in Technicolor, was filmed in Jacksonville in 1917.

HOLLYWOOD (G-11) pop. 139,357, elev. 7′

A resort and residential city between Fort Lauderdale and Miami, Hollywood is bordered with palmlined ocean beaches. The city's redeveloped downtown district sports an Art Deco touch. Entertainment is offered throughout the year at the Beach Theater bandshell, on the Hollywood Beach Broadwalk.

Hollywood Office of Tourism: 330 N. Federal Hwy., Hollywood, FL 33020; phone (954) 923-4000 or (800) 231-5562. *See color ad.*

Shopping areas: Oakwood Plaza, 2900 Oakwood Blvd., features a cluster of nationally-known book, clothing and household retail stores as well as restaurants and theaters. Downtown Hollywood offers boutique shopping and art galleries along with the Harrison Street Design District, known for its selection of antiques, collectibles, artwork, and home furnishings and accessories. Upscale clothing, jewelry and lifestyle accessory shops are the specialty at Seminole Paradise, 5804 Seminole Way next to the Seminole Hard Rock Hotel & Casino.

ANN KOLB NATURE CENTER is off I-95 exit 21, then 2.8 mi. e. to 751 Sheridan St. The center has nature trails, and an observation tower overlooking a mangrove estuary and a tour boat. An exhibit hall houses interactive displays and several aquariums.

Canoe and kayak rentals are available. Allow 1 hour minimum. Park open daily 8-7:30, Apr.-Oct.; 8-6, rest of year. Exhibit hall open daily 9-5. Admission $1. Phone (954) 926-2415 or (954) 926-2480.

SAVE **ART AND CULTURE CENTER OF HOLLYWOOD,** 1650 Harrison St., is a multidisciplinary art center that presents contemporary visual art exhibits, theater performances, lectures, cultural and educational programs and workshops. Allow 1 hour minimum. Galleries open Tues.-Sat. 10-5 (also Thurs. 5-8), Sun. 1-4; closed holidays. Gallery admission $5, students with ID $3, under 13 free. Performance ticket prices vary. Phone (954) 921-3274 for performance information.

CASINOS

- **Seminole Hard Rock Casino** is at 1 Seminole Way, Hollywood, FL 33314. Daily 24 hours. Phone (866) 502-7529.

POMPANO BEACH (G-11)
pop. 78,191, elev. 13′

Settled in 1880 and named for a local fish, Pompano Beach is known for its abundant sunshine and variety of recreational opportunities. Tourism became the city's focus in the 1920s after the Dixie Highway was completed. Warmed by the Gulf Stream, Pompano Beach is a popular resort. The city has approximately 20 parks, many of which offer tennis, softball, fishing and swimming.

Horse racing takes place at Pompano Park Racing, west of I-95 on Powerline Road (Race Track Road), October through August; phone (954) 972-2000.

Note: Policies vary concerning admittance of children to pari-mutuel betting facilities. Phone for information.

Greater Pompano Beach Chamber of Commerce: 2200 E. Atlantic Blvd., Pompano Beach, FL 33062; phone (954) 941-2940.

Shopping areas: Pompano Citi Center, 1 Pompano Sq. at the corner of Federal Highway and Copans Road, counts JCPenney, Macy's and Sears among its 100 stores. Festival Flea Market Mall, 2900 W. Sample Rd. in Pompano, offers a farmer's market and more than 800 vendors selling bargains Tuesday through Sunday.

WESTON (G-11) pop. 49,286, elev. 500′

EVERGLADES HOLIDAY PARK AIRBOAT TOURS depart from 21940 Griffin Rd., 5.7 mi. w. of I-75 exit 13B. One-hour excursions provide a well-rounded Everglades experience that includes historical narration, wildlife sightings, an alligator show and an exhilarating ride on a river of vegetation. Passengers sit in a covered compartment. Allow 1 hour minimum. Departures daily 9-5. Fare $18; ages 3-11, $9.50. MC, VI. Phone (954) 434-8111 or (800) 226-2244.

The previous listings were for the Fort Lauderdale Vicinity. This page resumes the alphabetical listings of cities in Florida.

FORT MATANZAS NATIONAL MONUMENT (C-10)

Off SR A1A 14 miles south of St. Augustine, Fort Matanzas National Monument includes the southern tip of Anastasia Island and the northern third of Rattlesnake Island. There is ferry service to the fort from which the monument took its name every hour on the half hour daily 9:30-4:30; to determine if the ferry is operating phone (904) 471-0116. The fort can be seen from the dock on Anastasia Island.

Built of coquina 1740-42 by the Spaniards, Fort Matanzas replaced temporary watch stations that had guarded the southern approach to St. Augustine since 1569. During the 16th century French Huguenots established bases in the area, threatening the Spaniards with territorial encroachment and what the latter considered to be religious heresy. The fort became United States property in 1821.

In 1565 Pedro Menéndez de Avilés set up his headquarters at what later became known as St. Augustine; following a hurricane that scattered the attacking French ships, he captured the enemy base about 35 miles north of St. Augustine. Upon returning to St. Augustine, Menéndez located the shipwrecked survivors of the French fleet some 14 miles south of town, where most of them surrendered and were killed. This engagement led the Spaniards to christen it the site of *matanzas,* or "slaughters."

A small visitor center on Anastasia Island contains exhibits pertaining to the fort's history. Swimming east of SR A1A at Matanzas Inlet is dangerous because of the currents. Grounds open daily 9-5:30. Visitor center open daily 9-4:30. Closed Dec. 25. Free. Phone (904) 471-0116.

FORT MYERS (G-9) pop. 48,208, elev. 9'

Majestic royal palms line the streets of Fort Myers, a city with more than 70 varieties of palms and a profusion of exotic flowers and tropical fruit. March through early April Fort Myers is the spring training home of the Boston Red Sox and the Minnesota Twins. The Red Sox play exhibition games at City of Palms Park, 2201 Edison Ave.; phone (239) 334-4700. The Twins play their games at Lee County Sports Complex off Daniels Road and Six Mile Cypress; phone (239) 768-4270 or (800) 338-9467.

Another sporting option is the Florida Everblades, who play their East Coast Hockey League home games at Everblades Arena, at I-75 exit 123 (Corkscrew Road); phone (239) 948-7825. The hockey season is mid-October through April.

The City Yacht Basin area is the town's boating center. Boating is popular on the Caloosahatchee River; a tropical cruise leaves from the yacht basin regularly.

Greater Fort Myers Chamber of Commerce: 2310 Edwards Dr., P.O. Box 9289, Fort Myers, FL 33902; phone (239) 332-3624 or (800) 366-3622.

Shopping areas: Edison Mall, 4125 Cleveland Ave. (US 41), features Dillard's, JCPenney, Macy's and Sears among its 155 stores. Bell Tower Shops, 13499 US 41 S.E., includes Saks Fifth Avenue and upscale boutiques. Royal Palm Square, 1400 Colonial Blvd., offers many boutiques and restaurants. Outlet shoppers will find more than 55 stores at [SAVE] Tanger Sanibel Factory Stores, between McGregor Boulevard and Summerlin Road. More than 100 shops, including Brooks Brothers, Polo Ralph Lauren and Tommy Hilfiger, can be found at Miromar Outlets, I-75 and Corkscrew Road (exit 123).

[SAVE] **CALUSA NATURE CENTER AND PLANETARIUM** is off I-75 exit 136, .5 mi. w. on Colonial Blvd. (SR 884), then n. to 3450 Ortiz Ave. The center is home to snakes, turtles, alligators, birds of prey, bobcats, bald eagles and crocodiles. It also features a walk-through butterfly aviary and 2.5 miles of nature trails. Planetarium shows are offered.

Allow 2 hours, 30 minutes minimum. Mon.-Sat. 9-5, Sun. 11-5; closed Easter, July 4, Thanksgiving and Dec. 25. Planetarium open daily; phone for show schedule. Admission $8; ages 3-12, $4. MC, VI. Phone (239) 275-3435.

ECHO is off I-75 exit 143, then 1 mi. e. on SR 78, then n. to 17391 Durrance Rd. ECHO, Educational Concerns for Hunger Organization, is a 50-acre farm demonstrating tropical food plants and techniques useful to farmers and urban gardeners in developing countries. The Global Village is divided into separate areas that represent urban gardens, a rain forest clearing, semi-arid land, hillside farming and tropical lowlands. The farm is open only by guided tour.

Allow 1 hour, 30 minutes minimum. Edible Landscape Nursery open Mon.-Sat. 9-noon; closed holidays. Guided farm tours are given Tues.-Sat. at 10 and 2, Jan.-Mar.; Tues. and Fri.-Sat. at 10, rest of year. Donations. Phone (239) 543-3246.

[GEM] **EDISON-FORD WINTER ESTATES,** 1 mi. s.w. on SR 867 at 2350 McGregor Blvd., includes historic buildings and the adjacent winter homes of early 20th-century industrialists Thomas Edison and Henry Ford. Docents stationed at various stops on the grounds provide information about the houses and gardens.

A highlight is a banyan tree said to be the largest in the continental United States; it was a gift from Harvey Firestone to Edison in 1925. A replica of the *Reliance,* Edison's battery-powered boat, offers cruises on the Caloosahatchee River.

Allow 4 hours minimum. Mon.-Sat. 9-5:30, Sun. noon-5:30; closed Thanksgiving and Dec. 25. River cruises depart every 30 minutes Mon.-Fri. 9-3 (weather permitting). Admission (includes both estates) $16; ages 6-12, $8.50. Edison museum and laboratory tour $9. River cruise $5.50. MC, VI. Phone (239) 334-7419. *See color ad p. 89.*

Henry Ford Winter Home was restored and furnished in the style of the 1920s using photographs and records of the house. Bought by Ford in 1916 because of its proximity to his good friend Edison, this winter residence of the world's first billionaire features grounds planted with citrus, bamboo and tropical foliage. A garage houses antique Ford cars. *See color ad p. 89.*

Thomas A. Edison's Winter Home is where the inventor spent his "working vacations" from 1886 until his death in 1931. Here he perfected such earlier inventions as the incandescent light bulb, the phonograph, the motion picture camera and the storage battery. He also cultivated a 14-acre botanical garden. The complex also includes a laboratory and a museum containing a large collection of Edison's inventions. *See color ad p. 89.*

[SAVE] **IMAGINARIUM HANDS-ON MUSEUM,** 2000 Cranford Ave., contains more than 60 interactive exhibits that allow visitors to explore the sciences, arts and humanities. Aquariums and touch tanks hold various types of marine life. An outdoor freshwater lagoon features fish, turtles, ducks, geese and swans. The museum also is home to alligators, snakes, iguanas, tortoises, birds and a kinkajou.

Allow 1 hour, 30 minutes minimum. Mon.-Sat. 10-5, Sun. noon-5; closed Thanksgiving and Dec. 25. Admission $8; over 55, $7; ages 3-12, $5. Under 13 must be with an adult. AX, DS, MC, VI. Phone (239) 337-3332.

J.C. CRUISES depart from the Fort Myers Yacht Basin at Lee St. and Edwards Dr. Offered are jungle cruises on the Caloosahatchee and Orange rivers past historic sites and lush wooded areas to a manatee sanctuary. Dolphins, alligators, exotic birds and other wildlife are often seen along the way. Lunch and dinner sightseeing excursions of varying lengths also are available aboard a triple-deck, 600-passenger paddle wheeler.

Allow 2 hours minimum. Jungle cruises depart Mon.-Sat. at 10 and 2, Sun. at 2. Lunch and dinner cruise schedule varies; phone ahead. Arrive 30 minutes before departure. Jungle cruise fare $14; ages 3-11, $6. Lunch and dinner cruise fares range $16-$78; ages 3-11, $8-$12.50. Reservations are required. MC, VI. Phone (239) 334-7474.

LEE COUNTY MANATEE PARK, off I-75 exit 141, then 1.5 mi. e. to 10901 SR 80, features observation platforms on a canal where manatees sometimes congregate during cooler winter months. Prime viewing season extends November through mid-March; phone ahead for recorded updates. A boardwalk and trail system wind through native plant habitats and a butterfly garden.

Pets are not permitted. Allow 1 hour minimum. Grounds daily 8-dusk, Apr.-Oct.; 8-5, rest of year.

Interpretive talks are given and kayak rentals are available Nov.-Mar. Admission free. Parking 75c per hour, maximum $3. Phone (239) 694-3537.

[SAVE] **MANATEE WORLD BOAT TOURS** is off I-75 exit 141, then e. to 5605 Palm Beach Blvd. (SR 80). Passengers may see manatees, alligators and a variety of native birds on guided ecotours of the Orange River, where hundreds of manatees congregate during winter months. A 45-minute educational videotape precedes the 1-hour boat trip. Allow 2 hours minimum. Trips depart daily at 10, noon, 2 and 4, Oct.-Apr.; otherwise varies. Closed Dec. 25. Fare $15; ages 3-12, $7. MC, VI. Phone (239) 693-1434 or (239) 694-4042.

MURPHY-BURROUGHS HOME, Fowler and First sts. (SR 80) at 2505 First St., overlooks the Caloosahatchee River and was built in 1901 as a winter residence for wealthy Montana cattle baron John T. Murphy. Of Georgian Revival architecture, the three-story house is furnished with original family pieces. **Note:** The house is closed for renovations; reopening is scheduled for late fall 2005. Allow 30 minutes minimum. Tours are given on request Wed.-Fri. 10-2, Nov.-Apr.; by appointment rest of year. Admission $4. Guided tour $6; ages 6-12, $3. Self-guiding tour $4. Free parking is available at the adjacent Ramada Inn. Phone (239) 332-5955.

SEMINOLE GULF RAILWAY departs from Colonial Station, 3.5 mi. w. of I-75 exit 136 on Colonial Blvd. The 1 hour, 45-minute RiverRail Explorer excursion travels north over the Caloosahatchee trestle to Bayshore and back. A narrator recounts the railroad's history and points out sights along the way. Three-hour murder mystery dinner trips also are available year-round and a holiday excursion is offered in December.

Sightseeing trips depart Wed. and Sat. at 10 and 12:15, Sun. at 12:15, late Nov.-day before Labor Day; closed holidays. Sightseeing fare $19.95; ages 3-12, $11.95; family rate (two adults and two children ages 3-12) $39.95. DS, MC, VI. Phone (239) 275-8487 or (800) 736-4853.

SIX MILE CYPRESS SLOUGH PRESERVE is 4 mi. w. off I-75 exit 131 on Daniels Pkwy., then 1.8 mi. n. on Ben Pratt-Six Mile Cypress Pkwy. While walking along a milelong boardwalk trail visitors can explore the wetland and observe such inhabitants as turtles, wading birds and alligators. Allow 1 hour minimum. Daily 8-8, Apr.-Sept.; 8-5, rest of year. Tours are given daily at 9:30 and 1:30, Jan.-Mar.; daily at 9:30 in Apr. and Nov.-Dec.; Wed. at 9:30, rest of year. Free. Parking 75c an hour (maximum of $3 a day). Phone (239) 432-2004.

[SAVE] **SOUTHWEST FLORIDA MUSEUM OF HISTORY** is 1.5 mi. e. of US 41 on Dr. Martin Luther King Blvd., then 1 blk. s. on Jackson to 2300 Peck St. In a restored railroad depot, artifacts depict the history of Fort Myers from the Paleo-Indian period to the present. Also displayed is *The Esperanza,* the longest and the last-built Pullman private

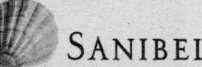

railroad car. Tues.-Sat. 10-5, Sun. noon-4; closed holidays. Admission $9.50; over 65, $8.50; ages 3-11, $4. Increased admission may be charged for special exhibits; phone ahead. MC, VI. Phone (239) 332-5955.

RECREATIONAL ACTIVITIES

Kayaking

- [SAVE] **GAEA Guides** picks up passengers in the area for tours departing from various locations. Write 340 Kingston Dr. W., Fort Myers, FL 33905. Daily 8-8. Reservations are required. Phone (239) 694-5513 or (866) 256-6388.

FORT MYERS BEACH (G-9)
pop. 6,561, elev. 8′

Fort Myers Beach traces its history from 1513, when Ponce de León passed this way. The town includes Estero Island, San Carlos Island and part of the mainland. Recreational activities include golf, tennis, jet skiing, parasailing and fishing. Full- and half-day charter fishing trips provide opportunities to haul in flounder, trout, mullet, pompano, bluefish, snook, grouper and tarpon. The catch from a pier or bridge is likely to be a sheepshead. A ferry service, Sea Key West Express, offers daily 3.5-hour high-speed trips to Key West aboard a catamaran (weather permitting); phone (239) 765-0808.

A barrier island on the Gulf of Mexico, Estero Island includes seven miles of white sand beaches.

Lynn Hall Memorial Park, south of Matanzas Pass Bridge, offers a public beach area with picnic facilities and hosts outdoor concerts throughout the year. Next to the park is the public fishing pier, frequented not only by anglers but also by dolphins, pelicans and, of course, sea gulls. On the north end of Estero Island, Bowditch Point Park is accessible by foot, bicycle or trolley. The 56-acre Matanzas Pass Wilderness Preserve is mid-island, and to the south is Lovers Key State Park *(see Recreation Chart).*

To facilitate beach traffic, trolley transportation is provided for a fee; phone (239) 275-8726.

Greater Fort Myers Beach Area Chamber of Commerce: 17200 San Carlos Blvd., Fort Myers Beach, FL 33931; phone (239) 454-7500 or (800) 782-9283.

FORT PIERCE (F-11) pop. 37,516, elev. 16′

Beef, citrus and vegetables from nearby ranching and farming areas find a market in Fort Pierce, which developed on the site of a U.S. Army post established in 1838 as a defense against the Seminoles. Native trees, flowers and colorful birds can be seen along Indian River Drive, which follows the river's west shore toward Jensen Beach.

Ball games are played at Tradition Field in nearby Port St. Lucie. In early February this stadium becomes the spring training site for the New York

Mets, and the St. Lucie Mets play minor league baseball here April through September; for further information phone (772) 871-2100.

The Indian River Community College McAlphin Fine Arts Center presents live performances throughout the year; phone (772) 462-4750.

East of Fort Pierce on SR A1A, Fort Pierce Inlet State Park includes Jack Island, a bird and wildlife refuge accessible by footbridge, as well as recreational facilities *(see Recreation Chart)*.

St. Lucie County Tourist Development Council: 2300 Virginia Ave., Fort Pierce, FL 34982; phone (772) 462-1535 or (800) 344-8443.

HEATHCOTE BOTANICAL GARDENS, between Virginia Ave. and Edwards Rd. at 210 Savannah Rd., features varied gardens that include Japanese bonsai, flowers and foliage of the subtropics and rain forest, palm trees and herbs. Events are held throughout the year. Allow 1 hour minimum. Tues.-Sat. 9-5, Sun. 1-5, Nov.-Apr.; Tues.-Sat. 9-5, rest of year. Closed major holidays. Admission $4; ages 6-12, $2. Phone (772) 464-4672.

MANATEE OBSERVATION AND EDUCATION CENTER, 480 N. Indian River Dr., offers indoor educational displays about manatees, and the fragile Treasure Coast ecosystem, as well as aquariums and displays of live animals. Outdoors, the covered observation walkway and the observation tower offer views of the Indian River and potential sightings of manatees in their natural habitat. A garden planted to attract butterflies also is on the grounds.

Allow 30 minutes minimum. Grounds open daily 24 hours. Indoor exhibits open Tues.-Sat. 10-5, Sun. noon-4, Oct.-June; Thurs.-Sat. 10-5, rest of year. Closed Jan. 1, Labor Day, Thanksgiving and Dec. 25. Admission $1, under 6 free. Phone (772) 466-1600, ext. 3333.

NAVY SEAL MUSEUM, 3 mi. n.e. of US 1 at 3300 N. SR A1A, depicts the history and development of the U.S. Navy's UDTs (Underwater Demolition Teams), SEALs (Sea, Air, Land Teams), Naval Combat Demolition Units, Scouts and Raiders through photographs and artifacts. The collection features weapons, equipment and underwater suits. Outdoor displays include boats, submersibles, small landing craft, a helicopter and Apollo training modules.

Allow 1 hour minimum. Mon.-Sat. 10-4, Sun. noon-4, Jan.-Apr.; Tues.-Sat. 10-4, Sun. noon-4, rest of year. Closed major holidays. Admission $5; ages 6-12, $2. AX, DS, MC, VI. Phone (772) 595-5845.

ST. LUCIE COUNTY HISTORICAL MUSEUM, 414 Seaway Dr. (S. SR A1A), is at the east end of South Beach Bridge. Spanish shipwreck treasures, artifacts from Old Fort Pierce and Seminole relics are displayed. The complex also includes a restored 1919 American LaFrance fire engine, a restored 1907 early Florida home, a memorial garden and changing exhibits. Allow 1 hour minimum. Tues.-Sat. 10-4, Sun. noon-4; closed holidays. Admission $4; over 65, $3.50; ages 6-17, $1.50. Phone (772) 462-1795.

Manatees

If you see a manatee while in Florida, both you and the manatee are lucky. You would be lucky to see one of Florida's most endangered animals, and the manatee will be lucky simply to exist. Despite protection efforts, the large gray mammals that inspired the legend of mermaids are threatened by human activity, and their future is uncertain.

Also called sea cows, manatees once ranged from North Carolina to Texas but now live almost exclusively in Florida. In winter they gather in the Crystal and Homosassa rivers, near Sanibel Island and Fort Myers,  throughout the tip of the peninsula and along the St. Johns River. Blue Spring State Park in Orange City is a manatee refuge,

Digital Archives

and the animals are protected by state and federal law.

Manatees can be 8 to 10 feet long and weigh almost 2,000 pounds. They have round bodies, two front appendages, a large round tail and a square, whiskery snout. Since each eats 50 to 100 pounds of vegetation a day, they act as underwater lawnmowers, helping keep waterways open.

Although they have no natural predators, pollution and development can destroy their habitats. Manatees must be near the surface to breathe, but they have poor eyesight and move too slowly to avoid motorboats, the greatest cause of injury and death. Motorboat propellers kill up to 50 manatees per year.

Females take 2 to 3 years to bear and raise a calf, and the population grows slowly. Manatees are bred in captivity at the Miami Seaquarium in the hope that those calves can be released into the wild to benefit future generations of manatees and humans.

FORT WALTON BEACH (B-4)
pop. 19,973, elev. 18′

Warm Gulf waters and a wide variety of recreational activities make Fort Walton Beach a popular area for family vacations. The sugar white sand beaches have attracted people since 500 B.C., when various Indian tribes conducted ceremonies in the area.

Emerald Coast Science Center, 139 Brooks St., offers interactive science exhibits for children; phone (850) 664-1261.

Just north is Eglin Air Force Base, where Gen. Jimmy Doolittle's "Raiders" trained and which is the headquarters of the USAF Air Armament Center and home of the McKinley Climatic Laboratory.

Emerald Coast Convention & Visitors Bureau: 1540 S.E. Miracle Strip Pkwy., Fort Walton Beach, FL 32548; phone (850) 651-7131 or (800) 322-3319. *See color ad p. 93.*

AIR FORCE ARMAMENT MUSEUM is 6 mi. n. of US 98 on SR 85, Near SR 189 and Eglin Air Force Base's west gate. The museum exhibits static aircraft including B-52 and B-17 bombers, an SR-71A Blackbird spy plane, an F-16 jet fighter, a Soviet MiG 21 and a MOAB (Massive Ordinance Air Blast). The armament collection features missiles, bombs and rockets. A film depicts the history and development of Eglin Air Force Base. Daily 9:30-4:30; closed federal holidays. Free. Phone (850) 882-4062.

GULFARIUM, 1 mi. e. on US 98, features the Living Sea, a glass-enclosed natural habitat for sharks, moray eels and sea turtles. Penguins, otters and alligators reside in separate exhibits. Live shows present the antics of dolphins and sea lions. Tues.-Sun. 9-8, June 1-early Aug.; 9-6, early Aug. to mid-May. Closed Thanksgiving and Dec. 24-25. Last admission is 2 hours before closing. Shows are given throughout the day. Admission $17.50; over 61, $15.50; ages 4-11, $10.50. Phone ahead to verify hours and rates. MC, VI. Phone (850) 244-5169.

INDIAN TEMPLE MOUND MUSEUM, 139 Miracle Strip Pkwy. S.E., depicts 10,000 years of Indian occupation of the northwest Florida coast as well as the history of European exploration and settlement in the area. The museum houses one of the largest collections of prehistoric ceramics in the Southeast. The temple mound, next to the museum, is topped by a replica temple. The mound was constructed around A.D. 1400.

Allow 30 minutes minimum. Mon.-Sat. 9-4:30, Sun. 12:30-4:30, June-Aug.; Mon.-Fri. 10-4, Sat. 9-4, rest of year. Admission $3; over 55 and military with ID $2; ages 4-17, $1. Phone (850) 833-9595.

GAINESVILLE (C-8) pop. 95,447, elev. 170′

Gainesville was founded in 1853 and named for Edmund P. Gaines, a U.S. Army officer who served in the War of 1812, a Seminole Indian battle and the

Mexican War. Both an agricultural and educational center, the community is home to the University of Florida and Santa Fe Community College. A map of the University of Florida campus is available at the AAA office at 1201 N.W. 13th St., or by contacting the university at (352) 392-2241.

Hippodrome State Theatre offers professional theater performances in a renovated 1911 federal building that once housed a post office, courtrooms and government offices. The theater also offers a cinema series and a gallery with the work of local artists. The Thomas Center, on Sixth Avenue, is a Mediterranean Revival-style villa built in 1907 that serves as a cultural center and features changing art exhibits, children's theater and formal gardens.

Opportunities to observe wildlife and geological formations are within a few miles of town. The 6,900-acre San Felasco Hammock Preserve State Park is 4 miles northwest on SR 232. Ranger-guided weekend activities, including walks, hikes, overnight trips and classes in wilderness orientation, are offered October through April. Reservations are required; phone (386) 462-7905.

The Gainesville to Hawthorne Rail Trail, a 17-mile trail designed for walking, bicycling and horseback riding, extends from Boulware Springs, on S.E. 15th Street in Paynes Prairie Preserve State Park *(see Micanopy p. 135 and Recreation Chart)*, through Lochloosa Wildlife Management Area to the town of Hawthorne.

Most Saturday mornings, and by appointment, guided tours are available to nearby Rosewood, site of the 1923 tragedy in which thirty African-American families were driven from their homes and their village destroyed; phone (800) 250-4645.

Alachua County Visitors and Convention Bureau: 30 E. University Ave., Gainesville, FL 32601; phone (866) 778-5002. *See color ad p. 452.*

Shopping areas: Among the 175 stores at Oaks Mall, 6419 Newberry Rd., are Belk Lindsey, Dillard's, JCPenney, Macy's and Sears.

DEVIL'S MILLHOPPER GEOLOGICAL STATE PARK is at 4732 Millhopper Rd. (SR 232), following signs. Measuring 120 feet deep and 500 feet across, this sinkhole formed as early as 10,000 years ago. The area is home to plants and animals normally found in the ravines of the Appalachian Mountains. A half-mile walking path circles the sinkhole while a 232-step wooden walkway descends it. An interpretive center houses natural history exhibits and an audiovisual presentation about sinkholes.

Picnicking is permitted. Allow 30 minutes minimum. Wed.-Sun. 9-5. Guided tours depart Saturday at 10. Admission $2 per private vehicle, $1 per person arriving by bicycle, bus or on foot. Phone (352) 955-2008 or (386) 462-7905.

FLORIDA MUSEUM OF NATURAL HISTORY is at Hull Rd. and S.W. 34th St. in the University of Florida Cultural Plaza. The Butterfly Rainforest features waterfalls, tropical foliage and thousands of

It DOESN'T take a

ROLLER COASTER

to make a child

✳ SCREAM ✳

with DELIGHT.

NORTHWEST FLORIDA'S

EMERALD COAST

OKALOOSA ISLAND • DESTIN • FORT WALTON BEACH

EMERALD COAST CONVENTION & VISITORS BUREAU, INC.

1-800-322-3319   WWW.DESTIN-FWB.COM

DESTIN   FORT WALTON BEACH   OKALOOSA ISLAND
CINCO BAYOU   MARY ESTHER

free-flying butterflies. Museum exhibits include a full-scale North Florida limestone cave replica and mammoth and mastodon skeletons standing more than 12 feet tall. More than 700 objects tell the story of South Florida's Indian peoples. The Hall of Fossils traces 65 million years of Earth's history. Allow 1 hour minimum. Mon.-Sat. 10-5, Sun. 1-5; closed Thanksgiving and Dec. 25. Butterfly Rainforest $7.50; ages 3-12, $4.50. Museum free. Phone (352) 846-2000. *See color ad p. 212.*

KANAPAHA BOTANICAL GARDENS is 1 mi. w. off I-75 exit 384 (SR 24) at 4700 S.W. 58th Dr. Paved walkways traverse 62 acres of specialty gardens lush with rare and unusual plants from around the world. In addition to butterfly, hummingbird, herb, bamboo and rock gardens, the grounds feature a vinery, palm hammock and hardwood forest. A water garden demonstrates the use of reclaimed water. Picnicking is permitted. Allow 1 hour minimum. Mon.-Wed. and Fri. 9-5, Sat.-Sun. 9-dusk. Admission $5; ages 6-13, $3. Phone (352) 372-4981. *See color ad p. 212.*

SAMUEL P. HARN MUSEUM OF ART, on the University of Florida campus at jct. S.W. 34th St. and Hull Rd., houses more than 6,000 works in a variety of mediums. The collection includes African and Asian art, modern art from Europe and the Americas, photography, and international contemporary works. Some collections are exhibited on a rotating basis. Allow 1 hour minimum. Tues.-Fri. 11-5, Sat. 10-5, Sun. 1-5; closed state holidays. Guided tours are given Sat.-Sun. at 2. Last admission 15 minutes before closing. Free. Phone (352) 392-9826. *See color ad p. 212.*

UNIVERSITY GALLERY is in the College of Fine Arts at the University of Florida at the intersection of S.W. 13th St. and S.W. 4th Ave. The gallery displays contemporary and experimental art, with an emphasis on the works of mid-career and established artists. Allow 1 hour minimum. Tues.-Fri. 10-5 (also Tues. 5-8), Sun. 1-5; closed holidays. Free. Phone (352) 392-0201.

DID YOU KNOW

Harriet Beecher Stowe, author of *Uncle Tom's Cabin,* had a winter home on the St. Johns River 1867-84.

GULF BREEZE (B-3) pop. 5,665, elev. 14′

Incorporating miles of bays and lagoons between Pensacola and Pensacola Beach, this peninsula is 1 mile from the Gulf of Mexico. Surrounded by water on three sides, it's a haven for water lovers and offers a variety of recreational activities including swimming, boating, sailing, fishing, diving and golfing.

Gulf Breeze Area Chamber of Commerce: 409 Gulf Breeze Pkwy., P.O. Box 337, Gulf Breeze, FL 32562; phone (850) 932-7888.

SAVE **THE ZOO,** 8 mi. e. on US 98 at 5701 Gulf Breeze Pkwy., is home to more than 900 animals in naturalistic habitats. Highlights include a Japanese garden, chimpanzee and gorilla islands, a children's zoo and wildlife demonstrations. Visitors ride the Safari Line train through a 30-acre wildlife preserve with free-roaming animals. Daily 9-6, Apr.-Sept. (weather permitting); 9-5, rest of year. Closed Thanksgiving and Dec. 24-25. Last admission 1 hour before closing. Admission $10.95; over 62, $9.95; ages 3-11, $7.95. Phone for train fares. AX, DS, MC, VI. Phone (850) 932-2229.

GULF ISLANDS
NATIONAL SEASHORE (B-3)

Stretching west 160 miles from Fort Walton Beach to Cat Island off Gulfport, Miss., Gulf Islands National Seashore covers more than 137,000 acres, 80 percent of which are submerged lands. Most of Florida's portion is accessible by car and includes Naval Live Oaks Reservation; part of Perdido Key; Fort Barrancas and the Advanced Redoubt on Pensacola Naval Air Station; the Okaloosa area near Fort Walton Beach; and portions of Santa Rosa Island including the Fort Pickens area.

Guided tours of Fort Barrancas and Fort Pickens are offered daily, and tours of the restored Advanced Redoubt *(see Pensacola p. 190)* are offered Saturdays. A visitor center at Naval Live Oaks Reservation features an orientation film and exhibits.

On the bay side of Santa Rosa Island is a recreation area with picnic facilities. Entrance fees are charged at Perdido Key, Fort Pickens and Santa Rosa areas.

Note: Access to some areas may be limited or prohibited due to ongoing repairs of damage caused by hurricanes in 2004. Phone ahead for details. For further information contact Gulf Islands National Seashore, 1801 Gulf Breeze Pkwy., Gulf Breeze, FL 32563; phone (850) 934-2600. *See Recreation Chart and the AAA Southeastern CampBook.*

HALLANDALE BEACH—
see Fort Lauderdale p. 85.

HEATHROW—*see Orlando p. 165.*

HERNANDO (D-8) pop. 8,253, elev. 50′

SAVE **TED WILLIAMS MUSEUM AND HITTERS HALL OF FAME** is 3.2 mi. w. of jct. US 41 on CR 486 in The Villages of Citrus Hills. Built in the shape of a baseball diamond, the museum houses photographs, artwork, memorabilia and other items from the life and career of Ted Williams, one of baseball's greatest hitters, and other notable players. The museum also features the Hitters Hall of Fame and continuous showings of the "20 Greatest Hitters," and the "Up Close Interview with Ted Williams."

Allow 1 hour, 30 minutes minimum. Tues.-Sun. 10-4; closed major holidays. Admission $6; under 13, $2. MC, VI. Phone (352) 527-6566.

HIGH SPRINGS (B-8) pop. 3,863, elev. 69′

High Springs, once a mining and railroad town, now offers antiquing and recreational opportunities in a small-town atmosphere. The downtown business section, representative of old Florida, features antique shops and several historic buildings.

O'Leno State Park *(see Recreation Chart and the AAA Southeastern CampBook)*, one of the first state parks developed in Florida, is 6 miles north and offers primitive camping, swimming, boating, fishing, nature trails, horseback riding trails, bicycle trails and a playground.

Other state and privately owned parks with natural springs surround High Springs. Blue Springs, west off CR 340, features a boardwalk and offers swimming. Ginnie Springs *(see the AAA Southeastern CampBook)* and Poe Springs, west off CR 340, and Ichetucknee Springs State Park, north off US 27, offer swimming, tubing, canoeing and underwater cave exploration *(see Recreation Chart)*.

High Springs Chamber of Commerce: P.O. Box 863, High Springs, FL 32655; (386) 454-3120.

RECREATIONAL ACTIVITIES
Canoeing
• **Santa Fe Canoe Outpost** is on US 441 at the Santa Fe River Bridge. Write P.O. Box 592, High Springs, FL 32655. Daily year-round. Reservations are recommended. Phone (386) 454-2050.

HILLIARD—*see Jacksonville p. 104.*

HOBE SOUND (F-11) pop. 11,376, elev. 24′

HOBE SOUND NATIONAL WILDLIFE REFUGE is at 13640 S.E. US 1. Occupying more than 1,000 acres of coastal sand dunes, mangrove swamps, sand pine and scrub oak forests, and sea turtle nesting areas, the refuge offers trails, a white sand beach and observation platforms. At the nature center visitors can observe live animals as well as shell and taxidermy displays. The beach is on Jupiter Island, accessible from North Beach Road.

Allow 1 hour minimum. Refuge daily 6 a.m.-dusk. Nature center Mon.-Fri. 9-3; closed Jan. 1, Memorial Day and Dec. 25. Beach parking $5 per private vehicle. Phone (772) 546-6141 for the refuge or (772) 546-2067 for the nature center.

JONATHAN DICKINSON STATE PARK, 2 mi. s. on US 1, comprises 11,500 acres, including the Loxahatchee River. Bald eagles, scrub jays and sandhill cranes are among the birds that thrive amid the park's abundant plant life. Guided tours depart to Trapper Nelson History Site on the river; it is accessible only by boat. Canoe rentals are available. A 2-hour river tour is available on the *Loxahatchee Queen.*

Park open daily 8-dusk. River tours depart daily at 9, 11, 1 and 3. Admission $4 per private vehicle (maximum eight people), $1 per person arriving by bicycle, bus or on foot. River tour fare $12; ages 6-12, $7. Phone (772) 546-2771, or (561) 746-1466 for river tour information. *See Recreation Chart.*

HOLLYWOOD—*see Fort Lauderdale p. 86.*

HOMESTEAD—*see Miami-Miami Beach p. 134.*

HOMOSASSA SPRINGS (D-8)
pop. 12,458, elev. 6′

HOMOSASSA SPRINGS WILDLIFE STATE PARK is on US 19 at 4150 S. Suncoast Blvd., 6 mi. n. of jct. US 19/98, following signs. Source of the Homosassa River, the freshwater spring emits millions of gallons each hour at a constant temperature of 72 F. Manatees and fresh- and saltwater fish can be seen through the windows of a floating observatory. The Wildlife Walk provides views native wildlife. Manatee programs and wildlife encounters are presented daily. Pontoon boats and trams shuttle visitors to and from the park.

Allow 3 hours minimum. Daily 9-5:30. Last admission and boat tour are 1 hour, 30 minutes before closing. Admission $9; ages 3-12, $5. AX, DS, MC, VI. Phone (352) 628-5343.

YULEE SUGAR MILL RUINS HISTORIC STATE PARK is 2.5 mi. w. of US 19/98 via CR 490. Now a ruin, the 1851 mill was built by Florida's first U.S. senator, David Levy Yulee, as part of a 5,100-acre sugar plantation. During the Civil War the mill supplied the Confederate Army with sugar products. Picnicking is permitted. Daily 8-dusk. Free. Phone (352) 795-3817.

INDIAN ROCKS BEACH—
see Tampa Bay p. 233.

INDIAN SHORES—*see Tampa Bay p. 233.*

INVERNESS (D-8) pop. 6,789, elev. 38′

WILD BILL'S AIRBOAT TOURS is on SR 44, 6.3 mi. e. of jct. US 41, 9 mi. w. of I-75. Narrated 45-minute airboat rides on the Withlacoochee River provide sightings of native wildlife, including wading birds, ospreys, eagles, deer and alligators. Allow 1 hour minimum. Daily 10-5; closed Jan. 1, Thanksgiving and Dec. 25. Fare $24; ages 3-12, $12. Reservations are required. AX, DS, MC, VI. Phone (352) 726-6060.

ISLAMORADA—*see The Florida Keys p. 69.*

Jacksonville

City Population: 735,617 **Elevation: 20 ft.**

Editor's Picks:

Cummer Museum of Art............ *(see p. 97)*
Kingsley Plantation................ *(see p. 102)*
Museum of Southern History ..... *(see p. 102)*

Visit Florida

Jacksonville is in the great double loop of the St. Johns River, the nation's longest north-flowing river. A busy seaport, it is one of Florida's major cultural, financial, industrial, transportation and commercial centers. The city also is a wholesale lumber market and coffee importation port and is home to a naval stores yard.

The city's history began in 1562, decades before the English settled Jamestown, when French Protestants known as Huguenots founded a colony on the banks of the St. Johns River. Named Fort Caroline, the ill-fated settlement was destroyed just 3 years later by Spanish troops from the garrison at nearby St. Augustine, and for the next 200 years Spain controlled Florida.

Spanish rule ended in 1763 when Spain traded Florida to Britain in return for Havana, which the British had conquered the year before. Ownership by Britain lasted only 20 years, but during that time The King's Road between Savannah, Georgia, and St. Augustine was completed. A settlement developed where the road crossed the St. Johns River, roughly where downtown Jacksonville is today.

As a result of the 1783 Treaty of Paris, which officially ended the American War of Independence, Britain returned Florida to Spain. But despite Spanish ownership, citizens of the new United States of America began settling in northern Florida, and during the War of 1812 both British and American forces made several incursions into the region.

To contend with the threat of American expansionism, Spain struck a deal with the United States in 1819 trading its interests in the Oregon Country and Florida in exchange for recognition of Spanish sovereignty over Texas.

After the United States took formal possession of Florida in 1821, settlers poured into the territory. The next year residents founded Jacksonville and named it after Gen. Andrew Jackson, the first military governor of the territory.

The town prospered as a port of entry until the Civil War, during which it was burned and abandoned several times. A major yellow fever outbreak killed hundreds of citizens in the late 1880s and forced many more to flee. In 1901 tragedy visited the city yet again when a fire destroyed nearly the entire downtown area.

The resurrected town became the leading metropolitan area in Florida for the next 40 years thanks to the railroad and the wealthy tourists who flocked to the city each winter. During these years several movie studios opened in the area, giving Jacksonville the nickname, "the World's Winter Film Capital." Naval bases built during World War II contributed to the city's further growth, and later, banking and insurance became important parts of the local economy.

City and county governments consolidated in 1968, which made Jacksonville the largest U.S. city in land area at the time; at 841 square miles, it is still the largest. In 1996 the metropolitan area's population passed the 1 million mark, and today Jacksonville remains a major port, financial center, site of military bases and a health center that continues to grow rapidly.

Getting There — *starting on p. 97*

Getting Around — *starting on p. 97*

What To See — *starting on p. 97*

What To Do — *starting on p. 102*

Where To Stay — *starting on p. 475*

Where To Dine — *starting on p. 486*

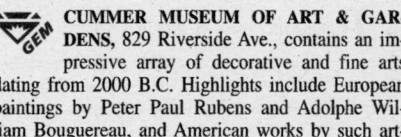

Getting There

By Car

Two important interstate highways, I-95 and I-10, intersect in the Jacksonville downtown area. I-95 traverses the United States from north to south beginning in Maine and ending in Miami. It is frequently congested as it approaches downtown.

I-10 connects Jacksonville on the East Coast with Los Angeles by way of New Orleans, Houston, San Antonio, Tucson and Phoenix.

I-295 arcs northeast and southwest of downtown, connecting with I-95 both south and north of downtown. I-295 also intersects with I-10 directly west of the city.

A more scenic approach is SR A1A, which follows the coastline through Jacksonville. Northeast of the city, SR A1A travels through historic Fernandina Beach.

US 1 is another important route. This highway runs the length of America's east coast, from Lubec, Maine, to Key West, Fla. US 17 approaches from the west and provides yet another route into Jacksonville.

Getting Around

Street System

Like most newer cities, the street system of downtown Jacksonville is a simple grid. Bay Street divides the city north-south, while Main Street is the east-west divider. The city does not adhere to a street naming convention, and thus a road's name (that is, whether it is called a street, avenue or boulevard) does not indicate its compass orientation.

The downtown speed limit is 30 mph. Traffic is most congested 7 to 9 a.m. and 4 to 6 p.m.

Jacksonville and the Beaches CVB

Parking

Both on-street parking and several parking garages are available downtown. A parking area under the Main Street bridge is convenient to Jacksonville Landing and other businesses. Parking meters require 25c per half hour.

What to See

ALEXANDER BREST MUSEUM, 6 mi. n. on the Jacksonville University campus at 2800 University Blvd. N., features a permanent collection of decorative arts and pre-Colombian objects, in addition to works by guest artists, faculty and students. Mon.-Fri. 9-4:30. Free. Phone (904) 256-73741.

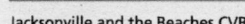 **CUMMER MUSEUM OF ART & GARDENS,** 829 Riverside Ave., contains an impressive array of decorative and fine arts dating from 2000 B.C. Highlights include European paintings by Peter Paul Rubens and Adolphe William Bouguereau, and American works by such artists as Thomas Moran and Winslow Homer. Of

Destination Jacksonville

© Steve Vidler / SuperStock

Jacksonville skyline.
A skyline enhanced by contemporary skyscrapers and riverfront marketplaces defines northeast Florida's hub city.

*F*or many visitors heading south Jacksonville is, geographically at least, Florida's unofficial welcome center—and the city is a fine example of what the Sunshine State is all about.

*T*ake beaches for example. Jacksonville and its environs have miles of sand to wiggle your toes in. Add to that an assortment of museums to suit individual tastes, professional sports and abundant recreational activities.

© Gibson Stock Photography

Cummer Museum of Art & Gardens, Jacksonville. Gardens grace the grounds of this museum, while fine and decorative arts adorn its galleries. (See listing page 97)

© Lee Snider / Corbis

Museum of Science and History, Jacksonville. Highlights include life-size models of Florida's marine mammals and interactive physical science exhibits. (See listing page 102)

Fort Clinch State Park, Fernandina Beach. A pre-Civil War fortification is the centerpiece of this park. (See listing page 104)

See Vicinity map page 101

*P*laces included in this AAA Destination City:

Amelia Island	104	Jacksonville Beach	104
Fernandina Beach	104	Mayport	105
Hilliard	104		

Amelia Island Tourist Development Council

The Informed Traveler

Sales Tax: The sales tax is 7 percent in Clay and Nassau counties, 7 percent in Duval County and 6 percent in St. Johns County. A 6 percent bed tax is levied in Duval and St. Johns counties; the tourist development tax in Clay County is 2 percent.

WHOM TO CALL

Emergency: 911

Police (non-emergency): (904) 630-0500

Fire: (904) 630-0529

Weather: (904) 741-4311

Hospitals: Baptist Medical Center, (904) 202-2000; St. Vincent's Medical Center, (904) 308-7300; Shands Jacksonville Medical Center, (904) 244-0411.

WHERE TO LOOK

Newspapers

Jacksonville's daily paper, *The Florida Times-Union,* is distributed in the morning.

Radio

Radio station WOKV (690 AM) is a news-talk station; WJCT (89.9 FM) is a member of National Public Radio.

Visitor Information

Jacksonville and the Beaches Convention and Visitors Bureau: 550 S. Water St., Suite 1000, Jacksonville, FL 32202; phone (904) 798-9111 or (800) 733-2668.

TRANSPORTATION

Air Travel

More than a dozen major and regional carriers serve Jacksonville International Airport, which is about 13 miles north of downtown near the northern junction of I-95 and I-295.

Several taxi and limousine companies serve the airport, although the baggage claim area is served exclusively by Gator City Taxi, (904) 355-8294. Taxi fares to downtown average $27.

Rental Cars

Hertz, at the airport, offers discounts to AAA members; phone (904) 741-2151 or (800) 654-3080. For listings of other agencies check the telephone directory.

Rail Service

The Amtrak station is at 3570 Clifford Ln., 5 miles northwest of downtown. For arrival information phone (904) 766-5110; for reservations and information phone (800) 872-7245.

Buses

The main Greyhound Lines Inc. bus terminal is at 10 N. Pearl St.; phone (904) 356-9976. A sub-station is at 5732 Normandy Blvd.; phone (904) 786-4323. For rate and schedule information phone (800) 231-2222.

Taxis

Major cab companies are Checker Cab Co., (904) 764-2472, Citicab, (904) 425-2222, and Gator City Taxi, (904) 355-8294. Base fare is $1.25 with a rate of $1.50 per mile.

Public Transport

Jacksonville Transportation Authority operates city buses. Stops include the transfer center at Florida Community College Jacksonville and the SouthBank area. Fare for buses on the beaches is $1.35; town routes are 75c. Downtown trolley buses are free. For information phone (904) 630-3100. The Skyway Express, an automated monorail system, provides transportation between the Prime Osborn Convention Center, Hemming Plaza and Jacksonville Landing on the North Bank and Dupont Station across the river for 35c; phone (904) 630-3181.

Boats

River taxi service between points along the St. Johns River is available from S.S. Marine Taxi, (904) 733-7782.

particular interest is early 18th-century Meissen porcelain tableware said to be one of the world's most significant collections.

Changing exhibits complement the permanent collection. A formal garden modeled after the gardens of Villa Gamberaia in Florence, Italy, extends from the museum to the St. Johns River. Art Connections, in the Art Education Center, features an interactive teaching gallery.

Allow 2 hours minimum. Tues.-Sat. 10-5 (also Tues. and Thurs. 5-9), Sun. noon-5; closed major holidays. Admission $6; senior citizens and military with ID $4; students with ID $3; under 6, $1; free to college students with ID Tues.-Fri. 1:30-4:30; free to all Tues. 4-9. Phone (904) 356-6857.

FORT CAROLINE NATIONAL MEMORIAL, 13 mi. e. near jct. Monument and Fort Caroline rds., is within the Timucuan Ecological and Historic Preserve and marks the site near which French colonials established a settlement in 1564. A year later Spaniards massacred many of them at Matanzas Inlet. The memorial contains a model of the fort, interpretive trails and Ribault Monument, an obelisk commemorating the first landing at St. Johns in 1562. The visitor center has displays. Allow 1 hour minimum. Daily 9-5; closed Jan. 1, Thanksgiving and Dec. 25. Donations. Phone (904) 641-7155.

JACKSONVILLE HISTORICAL CENTER, on S. Riverwalk just e. of Main St. Bridge, features displays depicting Jacksonville's history. Mon.-Fri. 11-5, Sat. 10:30-4:30; closed Jan. 1, Thanksgiving and Dec. 25. Free. Phone (904) 398-4301.

JACKSONVILLE MARITIME MUSEUM, on the s. bank of the Riverwalk at 1015 Museum Cir., Unit 2, maintains exhibits depicting the origin, development and current impact of the maritime trade upon Florida. The importance of the St. Johns River and the port of Jacksonville are emphasized. Among displays are scale-model ships, paintings and photographs. Mon.-Fri. 10:30-3, Sat.-Sun. 1-5. Free. Phone (904) 398-9011.

JACKSONVILLE MUSEUM OF MODERN ART is downtown at 333 N. Laura St. The museum presents a collection of contemporary art dating from after World War II through the 20th century. Food is available. Allow 30 minutes minimum. Tues. and Fri. 11-5, Wed.-Thurs. 11-9, Sat. 11-4, Sun. noon-4. Admission $6; over 65, military and students with ID and under 13, $4; free to all Wed. 5-9; free to families with children Sun. AX, MC, VI. Phone (904) 366-6911.

SAVE **JACKSONVILLE ZOO AND GARDENS,** I-95 exit 358A, off Heckscher Dr. at 370 Zoo Pkwy., features more than 2,000 animals from around the world on 89 acres. In addition to Great Apes of the World, Plains of East Africa and Range of the Jaguar, the park has Giraffe Overlook, an exhibit that allows visitors to feed giraffes. Savannah Blooms is a botanical garden. A train ride is available.

Jacksonville Maritime Museum / © Gibson Stock Photography

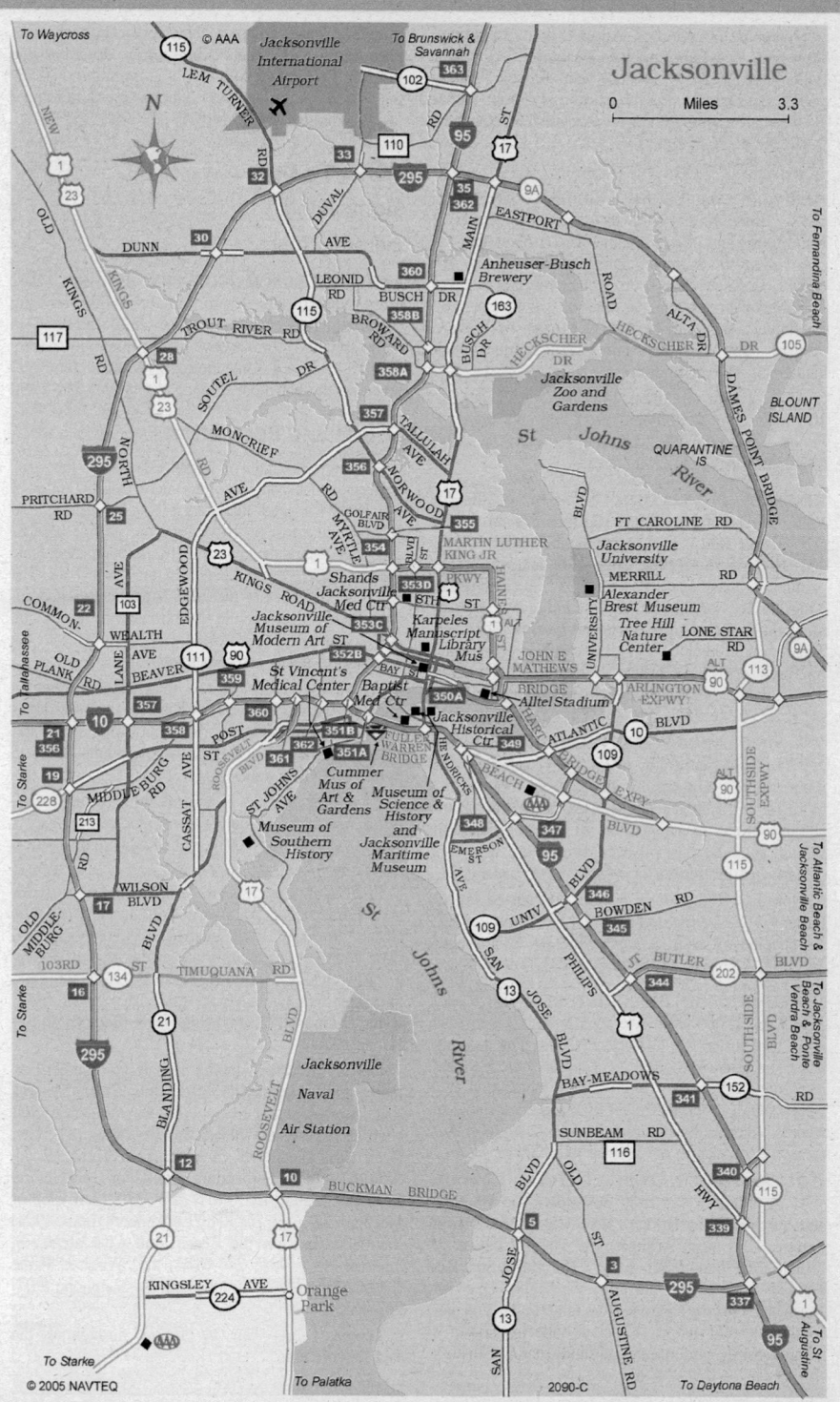

Jacksonville

Picnicking is permitted. Allow 2 hours minimum. Mon.-Fri. 9-5, Sat.-Sun. 9-6, early Mar.-day after Labor Day; daily 9-5, rest of year. Closed Thanksgiving and Dec. 25. Last admission is 1 hour before closing. Admission $9.50; senior citizens $8; ages 3-12, $6.50. Train ride $4; ages 3-12, $2. AX, DS, MC, VI. Phone (904) 757-4462.

KARPELES MANUSCRIPT LIBRARY MUSEUM, 101 W. First St. at Laura, has changing exhibits of historic and significant documents. Displays that rotate within the Karpeles museum system may include letters by Napoleon Bonaparte and George Washington or the musical notations of Ludwig van Beethoven, Wolfgang Amadeus Mozart or Richard Wagner. Sprinkles' Museum is an educational, hands-on area for children.

Allow 1 hour minimum. Museum open Tues.-Sat. 10-3. Museum admission free. Children's area $4. Phone (904) 356-2992 for the museum or (904) 632-2386 for the children's area.

KINGSLEY PLANTATION, .5 mi. n. of the St. Johns River Ferry on SR A1A, then 2.5 mi. w. on Fort George Rd., is part of the Timucuan Ecological and Historic Preserve. This 19th-century cotton plantation was operated 1813-39 by Zephaniah Kingsley. It is one of the last remaining examples of the plantation system of territorial Florida. The main lodge and the remains of 23 slave cabins are visible. Interpretive displays reflect 19th-century plantation life. Daily 9-5; closed Jan. 1, Thanksgiving and Dec. 25. Free. Phone (904) 251-3537.

SAVE **MUSEUM OF SCIENCE AND HISTORY** is at 1025 Museum Cir. In this playground for the mind, where "do touch" is the rule, visitors can explore far off galaxies in the Alexander Brest Planetarium, view the collection of live northeastern Florida animals, or stroll back through 12,000 years of northeast Florida history.

Mon.-Fri. 10-5, Sat. 10-6, Sun. 1-6; closed Jan. 1, Easter, Thanksgiving and Dec. 24-25. Admission $7; senior citizens and military with ID $5.50; ages 3-12, $5. AX, MC, VI. Phone (904) 396-6674.

MUSEUM OF SOUTHERN HISTORY is off I-10 exit 358, 3 mi. s. on Cassat Ave., 1.5 mi. e. on San Juan Ave., then just n. to 4304 Herschel St. The museum houses an extensive collection of artifacts, clothing and memorabilia from the Civil War era, in addition to a 5,000-volume research library and genealogical records. Allow 1 hour minimum. Tues.-Sat. 10-4. Admission $3, under 16 free. Phone (904) 388-3574.

SAVE **TREE HILL NATURE CENTER** is across the St. Johns River from downtown via US 90A and the Matthews Bridge. Take US 90A/Arlington Expwy. 4 mi. e. to Arlington Rd., then .5 mi. n. to Lillian Rd., then .5 mi. e. to 7152 Lone Star Rd. The 70-acre nature preserve is a showcase for Northeast Florida's native flora and fauna and encompasses four nature trails, a butterfly house, a hummingbird garden and a small natural history

museum. Turtle Town is home to the protected gopher tortoise; another exhibit area describes the Florida black bear. Allow 1 hour minimum. Mon.-Sat. 8-4:30. Admission $2; senior citizens and under 18, $1. Phone (904) 724-4646.

What To Do

Sightseeing

Industrial Tours

ANHEUSER-BUSCH BREWERY, 111 Busch Dr., offers guided tours. Visitors may view the brewing and bottling processes and then sample products in the hospitality room. Allow 1 hour minimum. Mon.-Sat. 10-4; closed some holidays. Guided tours are given on the half hour. Free. Phone (904) 751-8116.

Sports and Recreation

The intricate chain of barrier islands off the coast adjacent to Jacksonville offers more than 50 miles of white sandy beaches that are great for **swimming.** Just 20 miles northeast of the city are the pristine beaches and wild natural beauty of Little Talbot Island State Park and Fort George Island Cultural State Park. The beach communities of the area—Atlantic Beach, Neptune Beach, Jacksonville Beach and, to the south, Ponte Vedra Beach—combine surf and sand with the amenities of hotels and restaurants.

With Jacksonville's access to water, **boating** is a popular pastime in the area. The city operates docks at the following locations: Huguenot Memorial Park, Kathryn Abbey Hanna Park, Metropolitan Park and SouthBank Riverwalk.

Kayaking services offer trips through the coastal salt marshes and on quiet waterways; contact Kayak Amelia, (904) 251-0016, or Kayak Adventures, (904) 249-6200.

Fishing can be enjoyed along the St. Johns River and Intracoastal Waterway and in the Atlantic Ocean. Speckled trout, striped bass, bluefish, redfish, flounder and whiting are a few of the fish frequently caught at Little Talbot Island State Park. Saltwater fishing and more than 60 acres of freshwater fishing lakes are available at Kathryn Abbey Hanna Park.

Golf and Florida's balmy climate go together perfectly, and Jacksonville offers more than 50 area golf courses. Courses include Baymeadows Golf Club at 7981 W. Baymeadows Cir., (904) 731-5701; Deerfield Lakes Golf Club off Lem Turner Road, (904) 879-7279; Fernandina Municipal Golf Club at 2800 Bill Melton Rd., (904) 277-7370; Golf Club of Jacksonville at 10440 Tournament Ln., (904) 779-0800; Jacksonville Beach Golf Club at 605 S. Penman Rd., (904) 247-6184; and Windsor Parke Golf Club at 13823 Sutton Park Dr. N., phone (904) 223-4653.

Tennis courts can be found throughout the Jacksonville area.

Timucuan Ecological & Historic Preserve, 12713 Fort Caroline Rd., offers numerous **hiking** and **biking** trails through several distinct ecological communities; phone (904) 641-7155. Three self-guiding nature trails are at the University of North Florida Nature Preserve. Bird-watching is a popular pastime along the hiking trails of both Big and Little Talbot islands.

Local fans of professional **football** were given a gift in 1993 when the city was awarded a National Football League franchise. The Jacksonville Jaguars play at Alltel Stadium, One Alltel Stadium Place; phone (904) 633-2000.

The Jacksonville Suns, a farm team of the Los Angeles Dodgers, play AA Southern League **baseball** at the Baseball Grounds of Jacksonville, 301 Randolph Blvd., in the sports complex; phone (904) 630-3690.

Greyhound racing takes place at Orange Park Kennel Club from early September to late May and at Jacksonville Kennel Club from early June through late August. For more information about either track, phone (904) 646-0001.

Note: Policies vary concerning admittance of children to pari-mutuel betting facilities. Phone for information.

Shopping

In addition to major shopping malls, a multitude of small shopping centers and an array of antique stores and flea markets, the city boasts Jacksonville Landing, on Independent Drive along the St. Johns River. This downtown marketplace features shops, riverfront cafes and restaurants. A water taxi takes patrons across the river to the SouthBank Riverwalk.

St. Johns Town Center, 4775 Town Center Pkwy., has more than 1 million square feet of shopping and dining space in an open-air configuration anchored by Dillard's.

Avenues Shopping Mall, 10300 Southside Blvd., has 110 stores including Belk, Dillard's, JCPenney, Parisian and Sears. Orange Park Mall, 1910 Wells Rd., counts Belk, Dillard's, JCPenney and Sears among its 134 stores. Regency Square, 9501 Arlington Expwy., has 170 stores including Belk, Dillard's, JCPenney and Sears.

Theater and Concerts

The Jacksonville Symphony Orchestra presents performances throughout the year including a guest artist series, an outdoor concert series and smaller group concerts. Times-Union Center for the Performing Arts, 300 Water St., is a state-of-the-art performance venue overlooking the St. Johns River downtown. Its three halls include Robert E. Jacoby Hall, home of the Jacksonville Symphony Orchestra; Moran Theater, which can accommodate large-scale concerts and Broadway touring shows; and Terry Theater, which is used for smaller performances. For more information phone (904) 354-5479.

The Florida Community College at Jacksonville Artist Series brings Broadway productions along with national and international ballet, opera and contemporary dance companies; phone (904) 632-3373.

Located downtown, the lavish Florida Theater was built in 1927 and serves as a performing arts center; phone (904) 355-5661 for information or (904) 355-2787 for tickets.

Special Events

Jacksonville is host to exciting events throughout the year. College football fans celebrate the new year with the Gator Bowl, which is played Jan. 1 and is one of the city's top sporting events.

In March the Gate River Run attracts 10,000 runners for a 15-kilometer race along the city's roads and bridges. Also taking place in March is The Players Championship golf tournament, the Professional Golf Association's premier spring event.

Early April brings the Springing the Blues Music Festival, three days of blues music held at SeaWalk Pavilion, and the Jacksonville Jazz Festival, which features concerts at various indoor and outdoor venues. In late April, the World of Nations Celebration focuses on Jacksonville's cultural mix; the event is held in Metropolitan Park.

In mid-May, visitors to the Jacksonville Film Festival have numerous opportunities to screen feature, documentary and short films.

The Greater Jacksonville Kingfish Tournament features prizes, a fish fry, seafood festival and entertainment in July.

The Greater Jacksonville Agricultural Fair in October offers livestock, a petting zoo, horticultural exhibits, arts and crafts, carnival rides and country entertainment.

Ring in the new year during the Gator Bowl New Year's Eve Street Festival on the riverfront in downtown Jacksonville.

DID YOU KNOW

The oldest place name in North America is Florida.

The Jacksonville Vicinity

AMELIA ISLAND (A-10)

Miles of Appalachian quartz beaches and towering sand dunes distinguish Amelia Island, a picturesque island off the northeast tip of Florida's Atlantic coast. Formerly a haven for smugglers of slaves, liquor and foreign goods, in the mid-19th-century the island became the site of Florida's first cross-state railroad and, consequently, the state's first resort. The many Victorian buildings in Fernandina Beach, the island's only city *(see place listing p. 104)*, remain a testament to the island's "Golden Age."

Ironically, another railroad—Henry Flagler's Florida East Coast Railway—soon lured tourists farther south, locking the island in its Victorian atmosphere. Once thought a disaster, this development is now heralded as a blessing, as visitors seek relief from the modern world in Amelia Island's old-fashioned charm and pace.

A popular resort area, the island offers many recreational opportunities including golf, swimming and horseback riding. At the southern end of the island is American Beach, one of the country's last predominately African-American beaches. The town of American Beach was founded in the 1930s, an era during which many beaches were closed to African-Americans.

Amelia Island/Fernandina Beach/Yulee Chamber of Commerce—Amelia Island: 961687 Gateway Blvd., Suite 101-G, Amelia Island, FL 32034; phone (904) 261-3248 or (800) 226-3542.

RECREATIONAL ACTIVITIES
Horseback Riding
• **Kelly Seahorse Ranch** is at 7500 First Coast Hwy., Amelia Island, FL 32034. Rides daily at 10, noon, 2 and 4. Reservations are recommended. Phone (904) 491-5166.

FERNANDINA BEACH (A-10)
pop. 10,549, elev. 10′

Fernandina Beach is the northern terminus for a portion of scenic highway extending 105 miles south via SR A1A to Daytona Beach. Once called a "festering fleshpot" by President James Monroe because of the pirates and smugglers who anchored here, the town later became Florida's first resort.

This centuries-old town on Amelia Island features a variety of architectural styles. The Victorian district is scattered across 50 blocks, including residential and commercial buildings and a popular shopping area. On Centre Street at Second Avenue is the Palace Saloon, built in 1878 and reputedly the oldest in the state. A hand-carved, 40-foot mahogany bar and hand-painted murals decorate the interior.

The first week in May the town celebrates the local shrimping industry and its early days under the flags of eight nations with the Isle of Eight Flags Shrimp Festival.

Amelia Island/Fernandina Beach/Yulee Chamber of Commerce—Fernandina Beach: 961687 Gateway Blvd., Suite 101-G, Amelia Island, FL 32034; phone (904) 261-3248 or (800) 226-3542.

Self-guiding tours: A brochure outlining a tour of the historic district is available from the chamber of commerce.

AMELIA ISLAND MUSEUM OF HISTORY, 233 S. Third St., is in Nassau County's former jailhouse. The museum depicts the history of Amelia Island through photographs and artifacts. One-hour guided tours of the first floor exhibit hall depict the island's past and tell of the eight nations whose flags have flown over its harbor. Allow 1 hour minimum. Museum open Mon.-Sat. 10-4; closed holidays. Guided tours are given Mon.-Sat. at 11 and 2. Admission $5, students with ID $3. Phone (904) 261-7378.

FORT CLINCH STATE PARK, 2 mi. e. on SR A1A at the n. end of Amelia Island, comprises 1,361 acres. The brick and masonry fort was begun in 1847 but never completed. Occupied by Federal forces in 1862, it was instrumental in introducing Northerners to Florida's warm climate, which resulted in a tourist boom after the Civil War. Rangers dressed in Union uniforms carry out the daily chores of garrison soldiers of the Civil War era. Campsites are available; reservations are required.

Park open daily 8-dusk. Fort open daily 9-5; candlelight tours are available by reservation Fri.-Sat., early May-Labor Day. Park admission $5 per private vehicle (maximum eight people), $1 per person arriving by bicycle or on foot. Fort admission $2, under 6 free. Candlelight tours $3. Phone (904) 277-7274. *See Recreation Chart and the AAA Southeastern CampBook.*

HILLIARD (A-9) pop. 2,702, elev. 69′

RECREATIONAL ACTIVITIES
Horseback Riding
• **Country Day Stable** is at 2940 Jane Ln., Hilliard, FL 32046. Daily 10-5; closed Thanksgiving and Dec. 25. Reservations are required. Phone (904) 879-9383.

JACKSONVILLE BEACH (B-10)
pop. 20,990, elev. 14′

The Jacksonville and Atlantic Railway Company built a railway from Jacksonville to the beach in 1886 while simultaneously acquiring large tracts of oceanfront property for development. Within a few years Pablo Beach, as it was know then, was on its way to becoming a resort. Further growth ensued around the turn of the 20th century when Henry

Flagler folded the failing local railroad company into his Florida East Coast Railway System. Pablo Beach was renamed Jacksonville Beach in 1925.

SAVE **ADVENTURE LANDING,** 1 mi. w. of SR A1A at 1944 Beach Blvd., features Shipwreck Island Water Park, with three extreme waterslides, a wave pool and a pirate play village with 12 slides. Among other amusements are go-karts, laser tag and miniature golf. Amusements open daily at 10; closing times vary. Water park open daily 10-7, late Apr.-late Sept.; otherwise varies. Closed Dec. 25. Admission $23.99, under 42 inches tall $19.99, under 3 free when accompanied by an adult. After 4 p.m. $14.99. AX, DS, MC, VI. Phone (904) 246-4386.

PABLO HISTORICAL PARK, 380 Pablo Ave., houses the Beaches Area Historical Society, which interprets local history. A guided tour of the complex includes a railroad foreman's house built in 1900, a train depot relocated from Mayport and a 1911 steam locomotive. The house contains photographs of early beach life and antique furniture; the depot features railroad memorabilia. Allow 30 minutes minimum. Mon.-Sat. 10-3; closed holidays. Admission $2; senior citizens $1.50; ages 7-17, $1. Phone (904) 241-5657.

MAYPORT (B-10) elev. 10'

CASINOS

• **Harbor Light Casino,** 4738 Ocean St. Tues., Thurs. and Fri. 7 p.m.-midnight, Wed. and Sat. 11 a.m.-4 p.m. and 7 p.m.-midnight; Sun. 1-6. Phone (904) 241-7200 or (800) 752-1778.

SouthBank Riverwalk / Jacksonville & the Beaches Convention and Visitors Bureau

This ends listings for the Jacksonville Vicinity.
The following page resumes the alphabetical listings of cities in Florida.

JACKSONVILLE BEACH—
see Jacksonville p. 104.

JENSEN BEACH (F-11) pop. 11,100, elev. 8′

While Jensen Beach offers innumerable recreational possibilities, it also harbors sea turtles in a protected nesting zone. During June and July, approximately 6,000 sea turtles can be observed making their annual journey from ocean to shore and back. The turtles should not be disturbed.

Jensen Beach Chamber of Commerce: 1900 Ricou Terr., Jensen Beach, FL 34957; phone (772) 334-3444.

FPL'S ENERGY ENCOUNTER, on Hutchinson Island at 6501 S. Ocean Dr. at the St. Lucie nuclear power plant (Gate B), offers more than 30 interactive displays and exhibits pertaining to energy, electricity and nuclear power. Highlights include an energy treasure hunt and computer games. The College of Turtle Knowledge focuses on turtles that nest nearby. Allow 1 hour minimum. Sun.-Fri. 10-4; closed holidays. Free. Phone (772) 468-4111 or (877) 375-4386.

JUPITER (F-11) pop. 39,328, elev. 28′

Once the transportation hub of southeastern Florida, Jupiter was the starting point for the Celestial Railroad, which ran through Mars, Venus, Neptune and Juno to Lake Worth. The town since has become a center for recreation and light industry while retaining its quaint atmosphere.

The Florida Marlins, 2003 World Series champions, and the St. Louis Cardinals both take up residence in Jupiter during spring training. Exhibition baseball games are played in March at Roger Dean Stadium, 4751 Main St.; phone (561) 775-1818.

Jupiter-Tequesta-Juno Beach Chamber of Commerce: 800 N. US 1, Jupiter, FL 33477-4440; phone (561) 746-7111.

BURT REYNOLDS AND FRIENDS MUSEUM is at 100 US 1N at Indiantown Rd. (SR 706). Memorabilia and personal collections highlight Burt Reynolds' 40-year acting career. Exhibits feature movie props, Western artifacts, sports trophies and autographed photographs. Allow 1 hour minimum. Wed.-Sun. 10-4; closed major holidays. Admission $3. AX, DS, MC, VI. Phone (561) 743-9955.

JUPITER INLET LIGHTHOUSE is 1 mi. n. on US 1, .1 mi. e. on Beach Rd., then .2 mi. s. on Captain Armours Way. Completed in 1860, the lighthouse still guides ships approaching the Florida coast with a beam that is visible from 18 miles at sea. On 45-minute guided tours, visitors can climb 105 feet for a view of the Atlantic Ocean. Allow 1 hour minimum. Sat.-Wed. 10-4. Last admission 45 minutes before closing. Sunset tours are available. Admission (includes climbing tour) $6. Sunset tour $15. Under 48 inches tall not permitted on tour. Proper shoes are required. Phone (561) 747-8380.

LOXAHATCHEE RIVER HISTORICAL MUSEUM is off I-95 exit 87, 4 mi. e. on Indiantown Rd, then n. to 805 US 1N in Burt Reynolds Park. Regional history is depicted through photographs and artifacts. Exhibits focus on the natural environment, pioneer history, shipwrecks and Seminole Indian history. Tours of the nearby 1898 DuBois Pioneer Home are available.

Allow 1 hour minimum. Museum open Tues.-Fri. 10-5, Sat.-Sun. noon-5, Sept.-June; Tues-Fri. 10-5, rest of year. Closed major holidays. Tours of the DuBois house are offered Tues.-Wed. 1-4. Museum admission $5; over 55, $4; ages 6-18, $3. House tour $2. AX, MC, VI. Phone (561) 747-6639.

KENNEDY SPACE CENTER (D-11)

Forty-seven miles east of Orlando via the Beachline Line Expressway (toll) or SR 50, the John F. Kennedy Space Center (KSC) is accessible from the mainland off US 1, 6 miles across the SR 405 causeway over the Indian River, or from the beaches across the SR 520 or 528 causeways to Merritt Island, then north on SR 3 and Space Commerce Way. The center is located within the 140,000-acre Merritt Island National Wildlife Refuge *(see Titusville p. 236)* and extends some 34 miles along the coast.

Kennedy Space Center is the launch and landing site for the space shuttle, NASA's reusable space transportation system that first flew into Earth orbit when *Columbia* launched in 1981. It is home to two launch pads, one of the world's longest runways and the nation's third-largest building, the Vehicle Assembly Building. KSC also is the only place in the world where man has launched from Earth and traveled to the moon.

Cape Canaveral Air Station, east of the space center, was the site of the historic Mercury and Gemini flights, including America's first suborbital space flight taken by Navy Cmdr. Alan B. Shepard Jr. on May 5, 1961, and the country's first manned orbital flight by Marine Lt. Col. John H. Glenn Jr. on Feb. 20, 1962. Cape Canaveral is now the site for unmanned rocket launches.

The most current launch information can be obtained from the visitor center, which generally offers the best views; phone (321) 449-4444. Launches also can be viewed from US 1 along the Indian River in Titusville. Good vantage points include SR A1A in Cocoa Beach, Jetty Park in Port Canaveral and the coastline south of the Cape Canaveral Air Force Station border. With the purchase of a Launch Transportation Ticket, visitors parking at the KSC Visitor Complex can board shuttle buses to a launch viewing site on the NASA causeway. The shuttle operates only on scheduled launch dates. For additional information phone (321) 449-4444, or TTY (321) 454-4198. *See color ad p. 157.*

KENNEDY SPACE CENTER VISITOR COMPLEX is 11 mi. e. of I-95 on SR 405.

Built in 1967 to allow the families of NASA astronauts and employees to view space center operations, the modern facility explores the past, present and future of the U.S. space program. The complex features multimedia displays and hands-on exhibits, IMAX films, spacecraft and artifacts, encounters with astronauts and behind-the-scenes tours.

Admission to the complex includes a bus tour of NASA restricted areas, offering a view of the shuttle launch pads from the four-story LC 39 Observation Gantry. At the Apollo/Saturn V Center, visitors can walk beneath the 363-foot Saturn V rocket and watch footage of Neil Armstrong's history-making walk on the moon. The Firing Room Theater simulates an earth-shaking Apollo 8 rocket launch.

Food and free pet kennels are available. Allow 5 hours minimum to see the visitor complex and take the KSC bus tour. To avoid crowds arrive early. Complex open daily at 9, closing times vary; closed Dec. 25 and certain launch days. Bus tours depart continuously 9:45-2:15. Maximum Access admission (includes all shows, exhibits, IMAX films, KSC bus tour and Astronaut Hall of Fame) $37; ages 3-11, $27. Standard admission $30; ages 3-11, $20. Phone ahead to verify prices. AX, DC, DS, MC, VI. Phone (321) 449-4444. *See color ad p. 157.*

Astronaut Hall of Fame is s. of jct. SR 405 and US 1 at 6225 Vectorspace Blvd.

Dedicated to honoring America's space pioneers, the hall of fame traces the development of space exploration through video footage, personal memorabilia and historic spacecraft. Simulators let visitors experience the pull of gravity, negotiate a shuttle landing and ride a Mars rover.

Allow 3 hours minimum. Daily 10-6:30; closed Dec. 25 and certain launch days. Admission $13.95; ages 3-11, $9.95. Combination ticket with Kennedy Space Center Visitor Complex (includes all shows and exhibits, Astronauts Memorial Space Mirror, IMAX films and bus tour) $37; ages 3-11, $27. Phone ahead to verify prices. AX, DC, DS, MC, VI. Phone (321) 449-4444.

Astronauts Memorial Space Mirror is accessible through the entrance to the Kennedy Space Center Visitor Complex. Dedicated to American astronauts who died in the line of duty, this 60-ton black granite monument is carved with the names of 24 men and women, including the *Columbia* crew. The mirrored surface reflects each name against the sky. Allow 30 minutes minimum. Daily 9-dusk; closed Dec. 25 and certain launch days. Admission included in Kennedy Space Center Visitor Complex admission. Phone (321) 452-2887.

KEY BISCAYNE—
see Miami-Miami Beach p. 134.

KEY LARGO—*see The Florida Keys p. 70.*

KEY WEST—*see The Florida Keys p. 70.*

KISSIMMEE—*see Orlando p. 165.*

LAKE BUENA VISTA—*see Orlando p. 167.*

LAKELAND (E-9) pop. 78,452, elev. 227'

Lakeland encompasses 13 lakes that provide many opportunities for fishing, boating and water skiing. The area also offers pleasant surroundings for such sports as golf and tennis. Long known for its citrus growing and phosphate mining industries, Lakeland also boasts an infusion of high-tech and service industries into the commercial mix.

The world's largest group of buildings designed by Frank Lloyd Wright is on the Florida Southern College campus at Ingraham Avenue and McDonald Street. The 1938 Annie Pfeiffer Chapel was the first structure here; others were patterned after its "Child of the Sun" theme. A visitor center has exhibits about Wright's work. Maps for a self-guiding tour are available at the center or outside the administration building; phone (863) 680-4597.

During March the city is the spring-training camp for baseball's Detroit Tigers, and from April through August it is the home of the Lakeland Tigers. Exhibition games are played at Joker Marchant Stadium; phone (863) 688-7911. Ice hockey games, concerts, ballet performances and trade shows are among the entertainment presented at The Lakeland Center, 700 W. Lemon St.

Every spring Lakeland is the site of the 7-day Sun 'n Fun EAA Fly-In, which attracts visitors from around the world. In addition to 500 commercial exhibitors, there are workshops, forums and daily air shows, and the exhibits and aircraft of the Florida Air Museum at Sun 'n Fun *(see attraction listing).* Dates for the 2005 Fly-In are Apr. 12-18. For Fly-In information phone (863) 644-2431.

DID YOU KNOW

Except for their cream-colored bellies, alligators are black, not green.

Lakeland Chamber of Commerce: 35 Lake Morton Dr., Lakeland, FL 33801; phone (863) 688-8551.

Self-guiding tours: Information about tours of the downtown historic district is available from the chamber of commerce.

Shopping areas: Lakeland Square, on US 98 at I-4, contains Belk Lindsey, Dillard's, JCPenney, Macy's and Sears. Antique lovers can find more than 60 shops and dealers in the city's antiques district, located 2 blocks north of Main Street along Kentucky Avenue and Pine Street.

(SAVE) **EXPLORATIONS V CHILDREN'S MUSEUM,** 109 N. Kentucky Ave., offers changing hands-on exhibits, materials and activities allowing children ages 2-12 to explore the realms of nature, science, the continents, business and fantasy. The interactive programs are designed to promote learning and cultural growth. Allow 1 hour minimum. Mon.-Sat. 9-5:30; closed holidays. Admission for ages 2-15, $4; over 15, $2. Phone (863) 687-3869.

FLORIDA AIR MUSEUM AT SUN 'N FUN is at 4175 Medulla Rd. at the Lakeland Linder Airport. The museum houses more (SAVE) than 60 collectible aircraft including many unusual experimental and homebuilt models. Amphibious aircraft, biplanes, gyrocopters, sailplanes, sports planes, ultralights, simulators and vintage military planes, along with a collection of aircraft engines, are among the various items on display. Visitors can see aeronautical memorabilia from tycoon Howard Hughes' collection. A library contains several thousand aviation-related books and magazines.

Guided tours are available. Allow 1 hour minimum. Mon.-Fri. 9-5, Sat. 10-4, Sun. noon-4; closed holidays. Admission $8; over 54, $6; ages 8-12, $4. AX, MC, VI. Phone (863) 644-0741.

POLK MUSEUM OF ART, 800 E. Palmetto St. just off Lake Morton Dr., has changing exhibits of contemporary and historical art. The museum's permanent collection includes pre-Columbian artifacts; Asian ceramics, ivory and fabrics; European ceramics; decorative arts from South Africa, Georgian silver; and American art of the 19th and 20th centuries. Allow 1 hour minimum. Tues.-Sat. 10-5, Sun. 1-5; closed holidays. Admission $5, senior citizens $3, students with ID and under 6 free. Hours and prices may vary during special exhibitions. Phone (863) 688-7743.

LAKE PLACID (F-10) pop. 1,668, elev. 136'

Lake Stearns was renamed Lake Placid in the late 1920s by Melvil Dewey, creator of the Dewey Decimal Classification, a system for cataloging library books. A resident of Lake Placid, N.Y., Dewey wintered in Florida and was instrumental in the town's development as a resort.

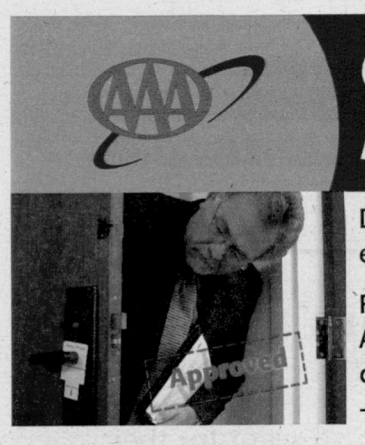

Lake Placid is surrounded by 27 lakes that provide innumerable opportunities for fishing and boating. Lake Wales Ridge National Wildlife Refuge is approximately 7 miles south off US 27.

Greater Lake Placid Chamber of Commerce: 18 N. Oak St., Lake Placid, FL 33852; phone (863) 465-4331.

THE MURALS OF LAKE PLACID are downtown. More than 35 colorful renderings of significant people, places and events in Florida history adorn town buildings and other structures, including fences and trash cans. Maps for self-guiding tours are available at shops and from the Chamber of Commerce. Allow 1 hour minimum. Daily 9-4. Free. Phone (863) 531-0211 or (863) 465-4331.

LAKE WALES (E-10) pop. 10,194, elev. 252′

On North Wales Drive at North Avenue in Lake Wales a bizarre phenomenon occurs: Through optical illusion, cars appear to roll uphill. To experience this mystery, park your car at the bottom of the incline known as Spook Hill and release the brake.

It is said that the Spook Hill mystery stems from a Seminole legend in which Chief Cufcowellax and his tribe settled on Lake Wales. Soon a huge bull alligator moved into the lake and regularly attacked the Indians. Aided by the Great Spirit, the chief stalked the beast and engaged him in a month-long battle, after which the chief rose from the water in victory.

During the battle a small lake, now North Lake Wales, appeared next to the big one. The chief was later buried on the shores of the new lake. Some attribute the Spook Hill enigma to the alligator seeking revenge, while others speculate that Cufcowellax has returned to defend his homeland from encroachment.

Housed in a 1927 mission-style structure that served as a Catholic church for 60 years, the Lake Wales Arts Center at 1099 SR 60 E. provides gallery and performance space for actors and artists; phone (863) 676-8426. Florida's Natural Grove House Visitor Center on US 27 offers information about the citrus industry and local attractions, as well as a free glass of juice; phone (863) 679-4110 or (800) 237-7805.

Lake Wales Area Chamber of Commerce: 340 W. Central Ave., P.O. Box 191, Lake Wales, FL 33859-0191; phone (863) 676-3445.

Shopping areas: Eagle Ridge Mall, 5 miles north on US 27, has Dillard's, JCPenney and Sears as its anchor stores. Art galleries, antique shops and specialty stores can be found in the downtown Lake Wales Historic District.

THE DEPOT—LAKE WALES MUSEUM AND CULTURAL CENTER, 325 S. Scenic Hwy. (US 27A), is the former 1928 Atlantic Coast Line train depot. Displays include photographs and memorabilia pertaining to local history and the railroad, cattle, citrus and turpentine industries. Also featured are a 1926 restored caboose and a 1944 engine. Allow 30 minutes minimum. Mon.-Fri. 9-5, Sat. 10-4; closed some holidays. Free. Phone (863) 678-4209.

HISTORIC BOK SANCTUARY, 3 mi. n. off CR 17A (Burns Ave.), consists of 250 acres with gardens, a 205-foot marble and coquina bell tower and Pinewood Estate, a Mediterranean Revival-style mansion. One of Florida's oldest attractions, the tower and gardens were dedicated to the American people in 1929 by President Calvin Coolidge on behalf of founder Edward Bok, a Dutch immigrant.

Other features include daily recitals from the 60-bell carillon, a nature observatory and Pine Ridge Nature Preserve Trail. The Education and Visitor Center presents art exhibits, an orientation videotape about the life and legacy of Edward Bok, and exhibits about the carillon and endangered plants and animals found on the property.

Picnicking is permitted. Food is available. Sanctuary daily 8-6. Last admission 1 hour before closing. Visitor center daily 9-5. Mansion tours are available daily. Admission $8; ages 5-12, $3. Phone (863) 676-1408. *See color ad p. 109.*

LAKE KISSIMMEE STATE PARK is 8 mi. e. via SR 60, 5 mi. n. on Boy Scout Rd., then 5 mi. e. on Camp Mack Rd. following signs. Wildlife abounds in this part of Florida's Osceola Plain between lakes Kissimmee, Rosalie and Tiger, an area that forms the headwaters of the Everglades. During the ice ages this plain lay beneath the sea; the ancient shoreline and beach dunes still are recognizable in the form of a rise and dips on Camp Mack Road. The park has an observation tower and hiking trails.

Daily 7-dusk. Admission $4 per private vehicle (two to eight people), $3 per private vehicle (single occupant), $1 per person arriving by bicycle or on foot. Phone (863) 696-1112. *See Recreation Chart and the AAA Southeastern CampBook.*

Kissimmee Cow Camp, 14248 Camp Mack Rd., is a living-history interpretation of the area's cattle

country days in 1876. Sat.-Sun. and major holidays 9:30-4:30. Admission included in park entrance fee.

LAKE WORTH (G-11) pop. 35,133, elev. 19′

Development of Lake Worth began in the 1900s when lakeshore lots were offered as giveaways to those who bought nearby tracts of fruit and truck land. The area became so popular that land to the west intended for development was virtually abandoned until the late 1930s, while the lake settlement expanded and was named for Gen. William Jenkins Worth of Seminole Indian Wars fame.

A variety of recreational programs is offered throughout the city for visitors and residents alike, including golf, concerts in the park, shuffleboard, tennis and boating. Local theater groups perform at the Lake Worth Playhouse; phone (561) 586-6410. Concerts are held at Watson B. Duncan III Theater on the Palm Beach Community College campus; phone (561) 868-3309.

Lake Worth offers fine fishing. Freshwater varieties are caught in Lake Osborne and from bridges spanning Lake Worth; saltwater species are snagged from one of Florida's longest municipally owned Atlantic Ocean piers as well as from charter craft for deep-sea and reef fishing. A trackless trolley provides service to the beach, shopping areas, parks and downtown businesses.

A 65-foot mural depicting the construction of King Solomon's Temple occupies one wall inside the Scottish Rite Masonic Center at 2000 North D St. A guide describes the mural and its Biblical subject along with the history of the masons; phone (561) 582-6794 for tour information.

Lake Worth Chamber of Commerce: 807A Lucerne Ave., Lake Worth, FL 33460; phone (561) 582-4401.

LARGO—*see Tampa Bay p. 233.*

LONGWOOD—*see Orlando p. 182.*

LOXAHATCHEE (F-11) pop. 19,103, elev. 22′

SAVE **LION COUNTRY SAFARI,** 15.5 mi. w. of I-95 exit 68 on US 98/441 and SR 80 (Southern Blvd.), is a 500-acre drive-through wildlife preserve in which giraffes, wildebeests, rhinoceroses, African elephants, lions, zebras, chimpanzees, Aldabra tortoises, Asiatic water buffalo and many other animals roam freely. Visitors must stay in their cars with doors and windows closed. Convertibles are not permitted; rental vehicles are available.

Picnicking is permitted. Food and free kennels are available. Allow 3 hours minimum. Daily 9:30-5:30. Last vehicle admitted 1 hour before closing. Admission $19.95; over 65, $17.95; ages 3-9, $15.95. Rental vans $8 per 1.5 hours. Parking $3. AX, DS, MC, VI. Phone (561) 793-1084. *See color ad p. 237.*

MADEIRA BEACH—*see Tampa Bay p. 233.*

MAITLAND—*see Orlando p. 182.*

MARATHON—*see The Florida Keys p. 75.*

MARCO ISLAND (H-9) pop. 14,879

At the northern tip of the Ten Thousand Islands, Marco Island is reached from US 41 via either SR 92 or 951; both bridges are free. This shell-gatherer's paradise on Florida's southern Gulf Coast was transformed from a fishermen's retreat into a lively resort community. Golf, tennis and swimming are among the recreational activities.

Marco Island Area Chamber of Commerce: 1102 N. Collier Blvd., Marco Island, FL 34145; phone (239) 394-7549 or (800) 788-6272.

Shopping areas: Marco Town Center Mall, downtown at North Collier Boulevard and Bald Eagle Drive, features chic, one-of-a-kind boutiques. Chico's is among the apparel shops at Marco Walk, on South Collier Boulevard. [SAVE] Prime Outlets Naples, 5 miles north on SR 951, offers 40 outlet shops representing manufacturers such as Bass Shoes, Geoffrey Beene, Liz Claiborne and Mikasa.

MARCO ISLAND TROLLEY TOURS, boarded at most accommodations on Marco Island and Goodland Island, provides a 90-minute narrated tour of the island's historic sites, including seashell mounds built by Calusa Indians. Departures Mon.-Sat. 10-3:30 with extended hours during summer months. Last boarding at 3:15. Fare (includes an all-day boarding pass) $20; ages 1-12, $9. Phone (239) 394-1600.

[SAVE] **VANTASTIC TOURS** picks up passengers from area hotels. Narrated safari-style tours of the Everglades include a 1-hour airboat ride, a nature drive through Big Cypress Preserve, a tour of Everglades City and a visit to a Seminole Indian trading post and wildlife habitat. Visitors may see alligators, bald eagles, manatees, ospreys, otters, hawks and other native wildlife. Allow 5 hours minimum. Tours depart daily at 8 and 1, Oct.-Apr.; at 8, rest of year. Fare $72; ages 3-10, $42. AX, DS, MC, VI. Phone (239) 394-7699 or (866) 826-8687.

MARIANNA (A-5) pop. 6,230, elev. 89′

FLORIDA CAVERNS STATE PARK, 3 mi. n. on SR 166, has extensive limestone caverns with calcite formations, a museum, natural rock gardens and a horse trail (no horse rental). The Chipola River Canoe Trail, part of the Florida Canoe Trail System, begins here. Guided cavern tours explore a lighted passageway.

The park is open daily 8-dusk. Cavern tours are conducted daily 9-4. Park admission $4 per private vehicle (maximum eight people), $1 per person arriving by bicycle or on foot. Cavern admission $6; ages 3-12, $3. Canoe rental $10 per half-day, $15 per full day. Phone (850) 482-9598 for recorded information. *See Recreation Chart and the AAA Southeastern CampBook.*

MAYPORT—*see Jacksonville p. 105.*

MELBOURNE (E-11) pop. 71,382, elev. 21′

The town was named after the postmaster's Australian hometown in 1879. Economic growth came in the late 1890s with the arrival of the Florida East Coast Railway. The introduction of another innovative form of travel—space flight—led to the development of high-tech and electronics industries, an additional benefit of the city's proximity to the Kennedy Space Center *(see place listing p. 106).*

Florida's Space Coast Office of Tourism—Melbourne: 2725 Judge Fran Jamieson Way, Suite B-105, Viera, FL 32940; phone (877) 572-3224. *See color ad p. 155.*

Shopping areas: Melbourne Square Mall, on US 192, 2 miles east of I-95, contains Belk Lindsey, Dillard's, JCPenney and Macy's. The downtown Historic District has specialty and antique shops.

BREVARD MUSEUM OF ART AND SCIENCE, 2 blks. e. of US 1 at 1463 Highland Ave., presents changing exhibits of works by artists of regional, national and international acclaim. Lectures, workshops and classes are given on a regular basis. The Ruth Cote Clemente Children's Science Center offers more than 35 interactive exhibits. Allow 1 hour minimum. Tues.-Sat. 10-5, Sun. 1-5; closed major holidays. Admission $5; over 62, $3; students with ID $2; free to all Thurs. AX, MC, VI. Phone (321) 242-0737.

[SAVE] **BREVARD ZOO,** .5 mi. e. of I-95 exit 191 to 8225 N. Wickham Rd., features more than 500 animals representing some 150 species in regional habitats that include North and South America, Australia and Africa. Visitors can feed giraffes and lorikeets. Kayak tours allow visitors to get a unique perspective of selected habitats. Train rides are available.

Allow 2 hours minimum. Daily 9:30-5; closed Thanksgiving and Dec. 25. Last admission is 45 minutes before closing. Kayak tours daily 10:30-3:30. Admission $9; over 60, $8; ages 2-12, $6. Kayak tours $5; under 13 must be with an adult, and under 5 are not permitted. Train $3. AX, DS, MC, VI. Phone (321) 254-9453.

LIBERTY BELL MEMORIAL MUSEUM, 1601 Oak St., has as its centerpiece a replica of the Liberty Bell cast by the foundry in England that made the original bell. Other exhibits include military uniforms and weapons, war memorabilia, a plaza of flags and reproductions of significant historical documents relating to freedom. Monuments dedicated to military branches and major wars are displayed in an adjacent military park. Allow 30 minutes minimum. Mon.-Fri. 10-4; closed Martin Luther King Jr. Day, July 4, Labor Day, Thanksgiving and Dec. 24-Jan. 3. Donations. Phone (321) 727-1776.

Miami-Miami Beach

Population:
Miami 362,470 Miami Beach 87,933
Elevation:
Miami 20 ft. Miami Beach 4 ft.

Editor's Picks:

The Holocaust Memorial ....(see p. 125)

Miami Metrozoo....................(see p. 123)

Vizcaya Museum and Gardens....(see p. 124)

Ocean Drive / Greater Miami CVB

Cultivated from a tropical wilderness, Miami celebrated its centennial in 1996. Even Julia Tuttle and Henry Flagler, the visionaries who saw the potential of this seemingly inhospitable portion of south Florida, would be amazed to see the transformation the area has undergone. The former wilderness is now a thriving, colorful city, young and vibrant despite its 100 years. Mediterranean architecture and a contemporary skyline blend with Art Deco styling, just as the smell of orange blossoms now coexists with the scent of *arroz con pollo.*

Then there are the colors: flamingo pink, lime green, Caribbean blue. The landscape is punctuated with marzipan hues, predominant in the tropical deco of hip Miami Beach. And it is surely the image of a fuzzy orange Miami sun, green palms and azure waters that draw some 11 million vacationers annually to this new Casablanca.

Miami and Miami Beach, interchangeable in the minds of most tourists, in reality are vastly different. Miami is a larger and more diverse metropolis that caters to tourism but also supports light industry. Miami Beach, almost exclusively tourist-oriented, consists mostly of condos and hotels. In fact, squeezed into an area of only 7.5 square miles, sandwiched between the Atlantic Ocean and Biscayne Bay, is a dazzling array of hotels that can accommodate three times the city's usual population.

One of the first to recognize Miami's potential was Julia Tuttle. The Chicagoan arrived in 1891, enchanted by the sunshine and mild ocean breezes. South Florida then was frontier territory and Miami amounted to little more than the ruins of a U.S. army outpost and a few plantations. But the coastal location and commercial promise of the Miami River led to Tuttle's bold prediction—that the area would become one of the world's busiest seaports and a vital link for trade with the Americas and the Caribbean.

Tuttle unsuccessfully tried to persuade millionaire industrialist Henry Morrison Flagler to extend his rail line south from West Palm Beach. Then, in a fateful twist, an 1895 freeze destroyed most of Florida's northern citrus crop. Tuttle sent a bouquet of orange blossoms to Flagler, proof of a frost-free Miami. It was enough to change Flagler's mind: The Florida East Coast Railway arrived in April 1896, and the city of Miami was incorporated 3 months later.

Among the first of the tourists and Northern transplants was New Jersey businessman John Collins, who had bought, sight unseen, a coconut plantation on one of Miami's barrier islands. Collins sought to link the isles with the mainland by building a bridge, but ran out of money before finishing the project.

Exclusive Fisher Island is named for the businessman who came to Collins' aid. Carl Fisher, inventor

𝒢etting 𝒯here — *starting on p. 118*

𝒢etting 𝒜round — *starting on p. 118*

𝒲hat 𝒯o 𝒮ee — *starting on p. 120*

𝒲hat 𝒯o 𝒟o — *starting on p. 125*

𝒲here 𝒯o 𝒮tay — *starting on p. 571*

𝒲here 𝒯o 𝒟ine — *starting on p. 586*

of the automobile headlight and owner of the Indianapolis Speedway, traded completion of the bridge for part of Collins' island property—and Miami Beach was born. Dredging Biscayne Bay to build up the narrow, sandy stretch, Collins sculpted paradise, constructing golf courses, hotels, tennis courts and polo fields, beginning the halcyon days of winter retreats and sun-splashed resorts.

The first real estate boom was barely in full swing when it rocked out of control. Property sold for mere pennies, hawked on street corners by binder boys who would bind the sale with a slip of paper. Speculation was such that entire communities were designed and auctioned without so much as a brick laid, though there might be an imposing archway leading nowhere.

The whimsical, pastel-painted Art Deco hotels on South Beach today are gentle reminders of a re-awakening city after the dismal Depression era. Created in the streamlined moderne style, lodgings sported the mixture of austere and cheerful favored by designers of the day. Charmed by the look and Miami's affordability, vacationers, retirees and Northern transplants flocked to the area in the 1930s and '40s.

Miami's modern expansion saw a changing social climate and a growth of business opportunities. A second building boom was on, as servicemen who trained in Miami Beach during World War II returned with their families after the war. And the advent and increasing popularity of commercial aviation brought the city its first flush of international sun worshippers.

There were other firsts, such as the bittersweet press reviews of the 1950s when the city made national headlines during the U.S. Senate committee

© Miami Seaquarium

hearings on organized crime. Miami had attracted mafiosi, including the infamous Al Capone. The '50s were, nonetheless, heydays, as Arthur Godfrey and Jackie Gleason televised nationally from Miami studios and high fashion held sway in such stores as Saks Fifth Avenue, Bonwit Teller and Cartier. Few could conceive the turning point of 1959 and its profound implications.

When Fidel Castro overthrew Fulgencio Batista Zaldivar on Jan. 1, 1959, the first Cubans exiled to Miami were the deposed dictator's political and military henchmen. Wealthy Havana citizens and a brain drain of professionals—doctors, journalists, lawyers, conservative politicians—followed, suspicious of Castro's socialist drift. When widespread disillusion with the regime set in, an exodus began, and Miami's Cuban population swelled to 300,000 before the freedom flights ended in 1973.

By sheer numbers, Cuban expatriates transformed Miami; their entrepreneurial skills and desire for a new life formed the basis for a multinational society.

Although the changing face of the city brought with it ethnic tensions, industry flourished. The next decade saw Miami's harbor become the world's largest cruise ship port.

Events in Cuba once again changed the face of the city. When Castro opened the port of Mariel, 140,000 Cuban refugees arrived in 1980. Liberty City and other overcrowded areas erupted in violence, and longtime residents, disheartened by the crime and commotion, headed north out of Miami-Dade County.

But Miami surmounted its crisis in a timely and spectacular fashion. The criminal-justice system worked to blot up hard-core criminals, and a $3 billion building boom downtown resulted in the glass skyscrapers and fanciful architecture along Biscayne Bay's boulevards.

Other Spanish-speaking groups also have made Miami their home, and Spanish is heard everywhere. Whether street signs and billboards are in English or Spanish first (nearly all display both) depends on how close they are to "Little Havana," the Latin district centering on S.W. Eighth Street, or *Calle Ocho.*

When producers discovered the city's unpredictable shapes and dazzling colors, Miami became the locale of a new television series. "Miami Vice" premiered in 1984, transforming the city into a cool, hip, hot metropolis. Property values rose, tourism boomed and investors rushed in. When "Miami Vice" ended in 1989, the city's international reputation had been set, and city leaders looked forward to capitalizing on the resulting mystique. They did not, of course, anticipate the devastating results of Hurricane Andrew, which demolished billions of dollars worth of real estate in 1992. But Miami survived.

As the cultural complexion of Miami continues to evolve, Hispanics, Central and South Americans and those of Caribbean heritage are joined by Asians and Europeans, transforming the city's social and economic fabric. Nowhere is this more apparent than in South Beach, where the Art Deco gems of yesterday are now the ultra-hip backdrop for America's Riviera.

Though much of the action centers on the Art Deco District's refurbished landmarks, sidewalk cafes, nightclubs and beaches, the mainland is thriving as well. Little Havana and Little Haiti are reminders of Miami's cultural heritage, while downtown the highest concentration of international banks in the Southeast adds muscle to Miami's transcontinental economy.

Central to Miami-Dade County's worldwide air, sea and ground transportation networks is the Port of Miami, handling more than 5 million tons of containerized cargo annually. Miami International Airport ranks first among U.S. airports for international cargo, moving more than 1 million tons each year.

As America's new Ellis Island, Miami may very well be the most foreign of U.S. cities. The entrepreneurial spirit, however, that fostered its evolution

Coconut Grove / Visit Florida

The Informed Traveler

Sales Tax: Miami-Dade County sales tax is 7 percent. An additional hotel room tax is 4 percent in Bal Harbour and Surfside and 6 percent in Miami Beach and the rest of Miami-Dade County.

WHOM TO CALL

Emergency: 911

Police (non-emergency): (305) 595-6263 (Miami-Dade County) or (305) 579-6111 (Miami)

Fire: (305) 595-6263 (Miami-Dade County) or (305) 579-6231 (Miami)

Time and Temperature: (305) 324-8811

Weather: (305) 229-4522

Hospitals: Baptist Hospital of Miami, (305) 596-1960; South Miami, (786) 662-4000.

WHERE TO LOOK

Newspapers

Miami's two main papers are the *Miami Herald* (morning) and *Diario Las Americas* (Spanish, afternoon). Miami Beach has the *Miami Beach Sun Post* (weekly).

Radio

Miami radio station WINZ (940 AM) is an all-news/weather station; WLRN (91.3 FM) is a member of National Public Radio.

Visitor Information

Greater Miami Convention and Visitors Bureau: 701 Brickell Ave., Suite 2700, Miami, FL 33131; phone (305) 539-3000 or (800) 933-8448.

The bureau distributes information and a vacation planner Mon.-Fri. 8:30-5.

WHAT TO PACK

Miami's average annual temperature is a balmy 76 degrees. December through March is delightful, with daytime highs in the mid-70s, comfortable lows around 60 and little rain. Miami is hot and humid the rest of the year. June through September can be sweltering, with daytime temperatures averaging around 90. Ocean breezes temper the heat along the coast.

The sun's ultraviolet rays are insidiously strong, especially when reflected off the water. Wear sunscreen—an SPF rating of at least 15 is recommended—and a hat.

Thunderstorms are common from May through October; carry an umbrella to be prepared for sudden showers. Severe storms and hurricanes are unlikely but do occur; Hurricane Andrew in 1992 is the most recent example. The hurricane season lasts from June through November. *For additional information see temperature chart p. 43.*

Lightweight resort wear is appropriate almost everywhere although there are ample opportunities to dress up. A light sweater is handy in some air-conditioned interiors.

Destination Miami-Miami Beach

L inked by causeways and an easygoing lifestyle, Miami and Miami Beach are an energizing mix of natural beauty and contemporary entertainment.

S napshots of swaying palm trees and gently breaking waves share space in vacation albums with souvenir programs from professional sporting events. And reminiscences of exotic bougainvillea and hibiscus linger with memories of performing dolphins and rare wildlife.

Beach and palm trees, Miami Beach.
Miami Beach is known worldwide for its sunny days and sandy beaches.

See Vicinity map page 121

Fairchild Tropical Botanic Garden, Coral Gables.
Flamingoes enhance the beauty of this tropical oasis known for its many rare plant collections.
(See listing page 133)

Greater Miami CVB

The Holocaust Memorial, Miami Beach.
The memorial includes gardens, sculpture, photographs and vignettes dedicated to the memory of the experience.
(See listing page 125)

Homestead •

Florida City •

P laces included in this AAA Destination City:

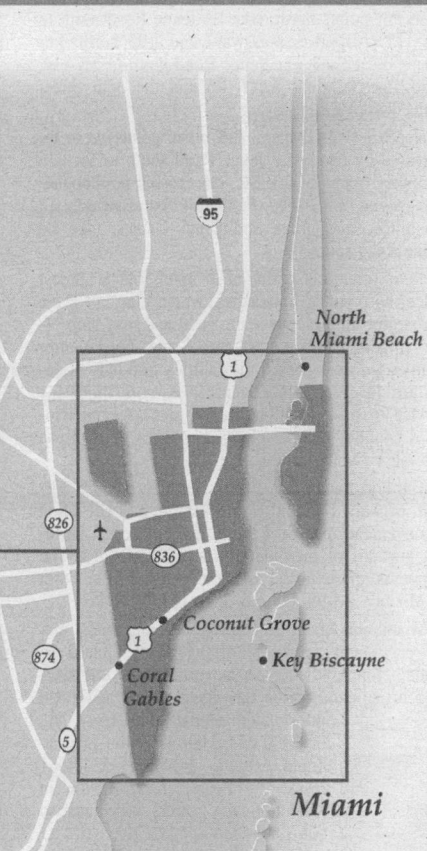

North
Miami Beach

Coconut Grove

Key Biscayne

Coral
Gables

Miami

*Vizcaya Museum and
Gardens, Miami.*
Allow plenty of time to explore
the 10 acres of formal gardens
and the 34 rooms of this Italian
Renaissance-style villa built in
1916. (See listing page 124)

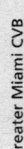

Miami Seaquarium, Miami.
Flipper and friends frolic during daily
performances at this Miami landmark.
(Hint: Don't sit too close if you don't
want to get wet.) (See listing page 123)

from swampy wetland to diverse, international metropolis is distinctly American. The intriguing contrasts of hedonism and hardship are unmistakably Miami.

Getting There

By Car

Moving from the coast inland, the major north-south routes are SR A1A, US 1, I-95, US 441 and Florida's Turnpike. The coastal route—SR A1A—is by far the most scenic but is slow. It is the only approach to Miami Beach from the north. US 1 travels through cities and commercial areas. I-95 is a congested four- to six-lane freeway. Two- to four-lane US 441 traverses developed and industrial land with heavy traffic.

From farther north, through the central part of the state, comes Florida's Turnpike (toll), which swings in a wide arc to the west around Miami; it also is linked directly with the I-95 connection into downtown. SR 826 (Palmetto Expressway) provides another western bypass closer to the city limits. SR 836 (Dolphin Expressway) runs east and west, connecting to the turnpike, I-95 and SR 826.

From the west come I-75, US 27 and US 41 (Tamiami Trail), all of which become congested as they approach the city limits.

Seven causeways span Biscayne Bay to link Miami and Miami Beach: MacArthur (US 41 and SR A1A), Venetian (toll), Julia Tuttle (I-195), 79th Street, Broad (96th Street), 163rd Street and William Lehman (SR 856).

Metrorail / © Royalty Free / Corbis

Air Travel

Miami International Airport, northwest at Le Jeune Road and N.W. 36th Street, is centrally located 7 miles from downtown. It ranks 12th in the United States for total passenger traffic, serving approximately 30 million travelers annually. A $5.4 billion airport expansion is expected to be completed in 2010.

Exit the airport on Central Boulevard east to Le Jeune Road (S.W. 42nd Avenue). To go directly downtown, take Le Jeune Road south to SR 836 East. For points north, take Le Jeune Road north to SR 112 (Airport Expressway) and I-95 north. For Miami Beach, take Le Jeune Road north to SR 112, following the signs for I-195 and the 36th Street (Julia Tuttle) Causeway.

Kendall, West Miami and other points west are accessed by taking Le Jeune Road south to SR 836 (Dolphin Expressway). SR 836 crosses northbound/southbound SR 826 (Palmetto Expressway). To reach Coconut Grove and Coral Gables, take Le Jeune Road south.

Taxis offer transportation to hotels but at almost twice the price of limousines, which may not leave the airport until all seats are filled and may stop often to discharge passengers. Some hotels offer shuttles for their guests; the shuttles stop only at departure level airport entrances. Airport limousine service to most locations in Miami-Dade and Broward counties may be charged at a flat rate; return trip rates usually are less.

The Fort Lauderdale-Hollywood International Airport, between I-95 and US 1, just south of SR 84, is a convenient option for those traveling to the northern portions of the Miami-Miami Beach area. The airport is approximately 45-minutes to 1-hour north of Miami via I-95, US 1 or Florida's Turnpike.

Miami and Miami Beach are served by many major car rental agencies. Arrangements should be made before you leave on your trip; your local AAA club office can provide this assistance or additional information. Hertz, (800) 654-3080, or (305) 871-0300 at Miami International Airport, and (305) 534-4661 inside the Fontainebleau Hilton in Miami Beach, offers discounts to AAA members.

Rail Service

The Amtrak Station is at 8303 N.W. 37th Ave. For arrival information phone (305) 835-1221; for reservations and other information phone (800) 872-7245.

Buses

Greyhound Lines Inc. stations are at 4111 N.W. 27th St., (305) 871-1810, in Miami; at 16560 N.E. Sixth Ave., (305) 945-0801, in North Miami. For fares phone (800) 231-2222.

Getting Around

Street System

Negotiating the streets of Miami can be mastered easily despite its sprawling layout. Two helpful points of reference are the city's cluster of skyscrapers, downtown at the geographical center, and Biscayne Bay, always to the east.

Miami is divided into four quadrants: Northeast, Northwest, Southeast and Southwest. Should you be looking for a particular address within the city, the section designation (N.E., N.W., S.E., S.W.) is an important factor.

Flagler Street divides the city north-south, while Miami Avenue is the east-west divider. Avenues, courts and places run north and south; streets and terraces run east and west. Except for the communities of Hialeah and Coral Gables, which have their own numbering systems, all street numbers start at Flagler Street and at Miami Avenue.

Unless otherwise posted, the speed limit is 30 mph in business and residential areas and 55 mph on highways. It is 65 or 70 mph on Florida's Turnpike and other designated highways. Miami has a typical big city rush hour (7 to 9 a.m. and 4:30 to 6 p.m.). Expressway traffic is particularly slow. Right turns on red are permitted after a complete stop, unless otherwise posted. Left turns on red are permitted from a one-way street onto another one-way street after a complete stop. U-turns are permitted except where otherwise posted.

The primary point of reference in Miami Beach is Collins Avenue (SR A1A), the city's major north-south through street. Along or near this thoroughfare is the famed string of hotels and motels, with the residential area lying west to Bay Road.

In both cities the speed limit is 25 mph or as posted. Motorists should not try to follow an unfamiliar route during rush hours. The lunch hour also is busy.

Directional signs sporting an orange sunburst on a blue background begin at the airport and guide motorists to some of the more popular destinations within the Miami area as well as pointing out the quickest routes to such resort areas as Orlando and Key West.

Parking

Both Miami and Miami Beach have downtown, on-street metered parking, parking lots and garages. Downtown metered street parking is available in Miami at the rate of $1 per hour.

Miami has six municipal parking garages: at 40 N.W. Third, 190 N.W. Third, 90 S.W. First, 100 S.E. Second, 90 N.W. First and 100 S.E. Second streets. Rates at the first two are $1.50 for 1 hour to a daily maximum of $9.55; at the third and fourth the rates are $2 and $3 respectively per half-hour with daily maximums of $14.50 (on S.W. First) and $21 (at S.E. Second); and the latter two run $2.25 per half-hour ($14.75 daily maximum) and $3 per half-hour ($18.50 daily maximum), respectively. Some specialty districts, such as Bayside Marketplace, have

their own lots and fee schedules. Lot rates vary according to location, but they generally start at about 50c to $1 for the first hour and about 50c for each additional half-hour. Bayside Marketplace charges $2 per hour for parking after 9 a.m.

On-street parking in Miami Beach often is difficult to find. Visiting drivers should look carefully for signs when parking on Miami Beach streets due to the number of areas where parking is restricted.

Ocean Drive, Miami Beach / © R. Kord / Robertstock

Metered parking is available throughout Miami Beach at the rate of 25¢ per 15 minutes to half-hour. There are five municipal parking garages: at 42nd Street between Sheridan and Royal Palm avenues; 17th Street between Penna and Meridian avenues; Collins Avenue at 13th Street; at the intersection of Michigan Avenue and Lincoln Road; and Drexel Avenue at 12th Street.

There are also numerous public parking lots in the Miami Beach area. Rates vary by lot and location. Lots with daily rates generally charge $1 an hour. Some lots are served by electronic meters that charge the standard metered rate; these lots offer a daily rate only during events.

Taxis & Limousines

Cabs are plentiful and operate on the meter system. Fares are $1.50 base fee plus $2 per mile and 30c for each minute of waiting. The largest companies are Yellow Cab Co., (305) 444-4444, and Metro Taxi, (305) 888-8888. Consult the telephone directory for others.

Private limousine service is $50 to $75 an hour, with a 2-hour minimum; most companies add a 20 percent driver gratuity.

Public Transportation

The Miami-Dade County Transit Agency links greater Miami with buses, Metrorail and Metromover. Metrorail is an elevated rail system serving downtown Miami; it also runs north and west to Hialeah and south to Kendall. Metromover is a 4.4-mile elevated rail system that loops around downtown.

Buses operate countywide. The fare is $1.25, plus 25c for a transfer to another bus or to Metrorail; transfers to Metromover are free. Express bus fare is $1.50. Exact change is required. Reduced-fare Golden Passports are available for senior citizens.

Metrorail fare is $1.25; exact change is required. Bus transfers are 25¢; transfers to Metromover are free. Regular Metromover fare is free; there is a $1 fee to transfer from Metromover to a bus or Metrorail. Both trains operate daily 24 hours. Metromover trains arrive every 10 seconds; Metrorail trains arrive approximately every 10 minutes weekdays (every 6 minutes during high-volume hours, 2:30-6:30) and every 20 minutes Saturday and Sunday. For schedules and route information about both systems phone (305) 770-3131.

What To See

MIAMI

DEERING ESTATE AT CUTLER is off S.W. 168th St. at 16701 S.W. 72nd Ave.
The 450-acre bayfront estate, once part of the town of Cutler, was purchased by Charles Deering in 1913. On the grounds is the circa 1900 Richmond Cottage, which served as Cutler's inn and is said to be the first hotel between Coconut Grove and Key West. In 1922 Deering built the adjacent, Mediterranean Revival-style Stone House.

The property consists of landscaped grounds, a keyhole-shaped boat basin, a palm grove, a boardwalk through a mangrove forest and a nature trail featuring exotic plants and a hardwood hammock. The Tequesta Burial Mound is an American Indian site dating from 1500. Guided tours of the mangroves, houses and natural areas are offered as well as butterfly tours and canoe tours to Chicken Key, just offshore.

Picnicking is permitted. Allow 2 hours minimum. Park open daily 10-5. Ticket office open daily 10-4. Both closed Thanksgiving and Dec. 25. House tours depart at 10:30 and 2. Natural area tours depart at 11:30 and 3. Admission $7; ages 4-17, $5. AX, MC, VI. Phone (305) 235-1668.

GOLD COAST RAILROAD MUSEUM is at 12450 S.W. 152nd St. (Coral Reef Dr.), at the entrance to Miami Metrozoo; take Florida's Tpke. (SR 821) exit 16. Featured exhibits include 15 passenger cars, 14 locomotives, 14 freight cars, two cranes, four cabooses, and the *Ferdinand Magellan*, the Pullman car built for President Franklin Roosevelt. Rides on a small-scale train are offered on weekends for a fee. The museum is on the site of a former World War II blimp airship base; an exhibit details base history.

Picnicking is permitted. Allow 1 hour minimum. Mon.-Fri. 10-4, Sat.-Sun. 11-4. Admission $5; ages 3-11, $3. AX, MC, VI. Phone (305) 253-0063.

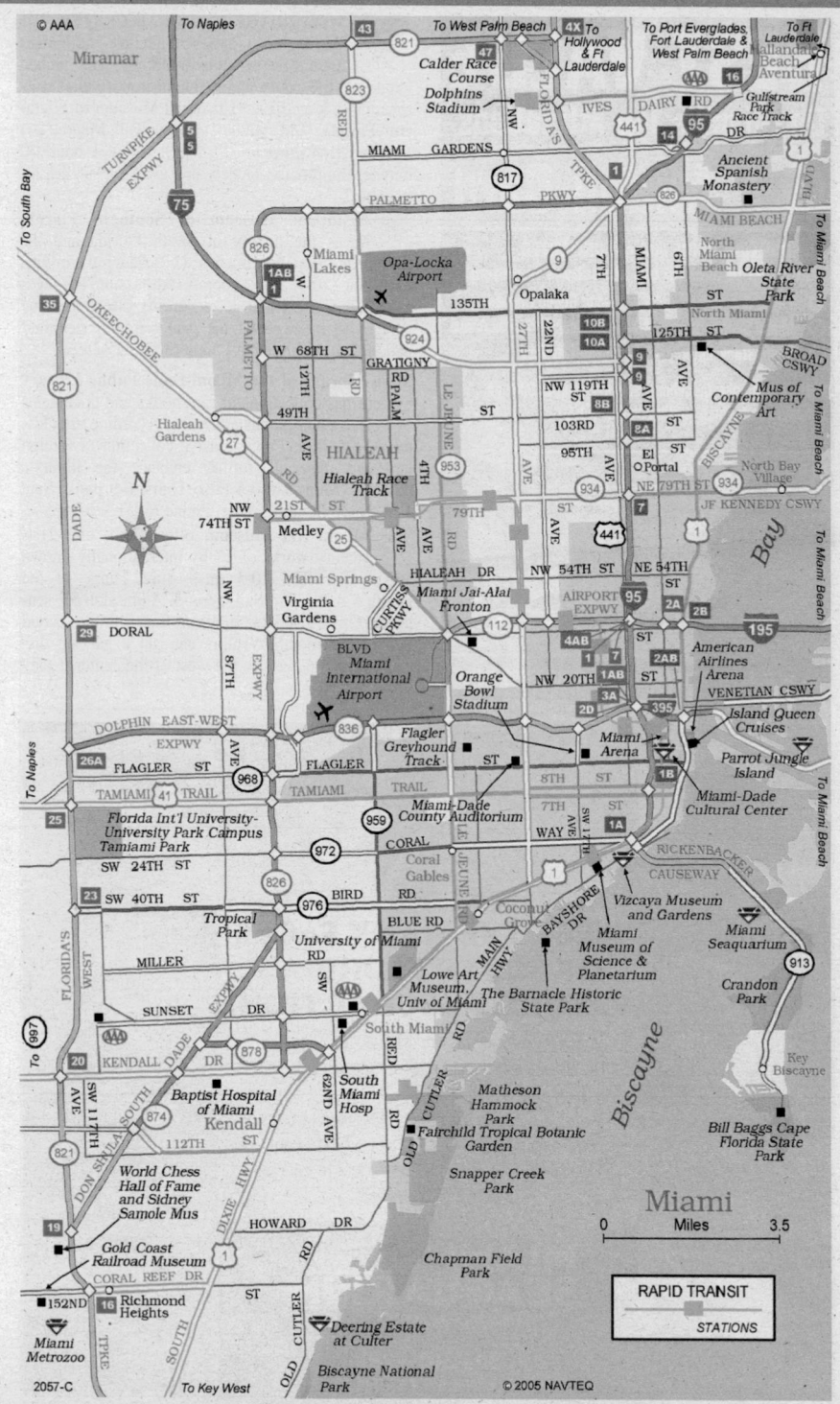

MIAMI-DADE CULTURAL CENTER, 101 W. Flagler St. at S.W. First Ave., comprises three Spanish-style buildings with arched windows, tile roofs and wrought-iron fixtures surrounding a large plaza: Historical Museum of Southern Florida, the public library and Miami Art Museum *(see attraction listings).* Allow 1 hour, 30 minutes minimum. Tickets are available at the attractions.

[SAVE] **Historical Museum of Southern Florida** traces the history of South Florida and the Caribbean through permanent and changing exhibits. Mon.-Sat. 10-9, Sun. noon-5. Admission $5; ages 6-12, $2. Visitors can get a parking discount at the garages to the west of the center if they get their parking stubs validated. Phone (305) 375-1492.

Main Library of the Miami-Dade Public Library System has collections of rare books and documents as well as photographs and prints recording area history. Artwork and an extensive collection of foreign language materials further enhance the library's holdings. Mon.-Sat. 9-6 (also Thurs. 6-9 p.m.), Sun. 1-5; closed holidays. Free. Phone (305) 375-2665.

[SAVE] **Miami Art Museum** offers 20th- and 21st-century works of art by internationally known artists. Tues.-Fri. 10-5 (also third Thurs. of the month 5-8:30), Sat.-Sun. noon-5. Admission $5, senior citizens $2.50, free to all on Sun. and the second Sat. of the month. Visitors can get a parking discount at the garages to the west of the center if they

get their parking stubs validated. Phone (305) 375-3000.

MIAMI METROZOO is at 12400 S.W. 152nd St. (Coral Reef Dr.), .2 mi. w. of jct. SR 821 (Florida's Tpke.). Metrozoo is a cageless zoo where animals roam in settings similar to their natural habitats. The spacious exhibits cover the continents of Africa, Asia and Europe with such inhabitants as chimpanzees, orangutans, elephants, bongo antelopes, Malayan sun bears and Cuban crocodiles.

Winding paths lead visitors through animal exhibits in the Asian Loop, which includes an aviary with 80 Asian bird species. Also featured are rare white Bengal tigers, a gorilla family and an African plains exhibit, where giraffes, zebras and ostriches coexist as they do in the wild.

Animal shows are presented three times daily. An air-conditioned monorail traverses the zoo's 290 acres. Viewing caves are offered. The Children's Zoo has an ecology theater.

Food is available. Allow 3 hours minimum. Daily 9:30-5:30. Last admission is 1 hour, 30 minutes before closing. Admission $11.50; ages 3-12, $6.75. AX, MC, VI. Phone (305) 251-0400.

MIAMI MUSEUM OF SCIENCE & PLANETARIUM is s.e. of jct. I-95 and US 1 at 3280 S. Miami Ave. and can be reached via the pedestrian overpass from the Vizcaya Metrorail station. The museum presents national traveling exhibitions spanning topics from archeology to zoology. Newton's Notions, a series of interactive science and math experiments, is among the permanent exhibits. The outdoor Wildlife Center is a rehabilitation facility for injured birds of prey. Multimedia and star shows are presented daily in the planetarium.

Allow 1 hour, 30 minutes minimum. Daily 10-6; closed Thanksgiving and Dec. 25. Planetarium shows daily on the hour 10-6. Observatory open Fri. 8-10 p.m. (weather permitting); free star show Fri. at 7:30 p.m. (except first Fri. of the month). Last admission is 1 hour before closing. Admission $10; over 61 and students with ID $8; ages 3-12, $6; half-off admission Mon.-Fri. after 4:30. AX, MC, VI. Phone (305) 646-4200, or (305) 646-4420 for planetarium show information.

MIAMI SEAQUARIUM, 4400 Rickenbacker Cswy., offers shows, presentations and marine mammal exhibits. Divers hand feed reef fish and moray eels in a 250,000-gallon saltwater aquarium. Popular shows feature TV dolphin "star" Flipper, the funny exploits of Salty the Sea Lion and his friends, and the graceful beauty of the Pacific white-sided dolphins that perform with Lolita the killer whale. Other highlights include sharks and endangered manatees and sea turtles.

The 2-hour Water and Dolphin Exploration lets participants interact one-on-one with dolphins in the water. The full experience includes a tour of the facility, a presentation by a trainer and a 30-minute session of feeding, touching, training and riding dolphins. Wet suits are provided.

Parrott Jungle Island / Greater Miami CVB

Food is available. Allow 4 hours, 30 minutes minimum. Daily 9:30-6. Water and Dolphin Exploration sessions daily at 8:30, noon and 3:30. Last admission is 1 hour, 30 minutes before closing. Admission $25.95; over 55, $23.95; ages 3-9, $20.95. Water and Dolphin Exploration $149, with additional fees for observers; reservations are required. Parking $5. AX, MC, VI. Phone (305) 361-5705. *See color ad p. 122.*

MONKEY JUNGLE is 22 mi. s.w. on US 1, then 3 mi. w., or Florida Tpke. exit 11 and then 4 mi. w., at 14805 S.W. 216th St. Visitors take a jungle safari to the wilds of South America, Asia and Africa. Habitats include the Camaroon Forest, Mandrills and Parrots of the World and the Amazonian Rain Forest. Various shows are presented daily.

Allow 2 hours, 30 minutes minimum. Daily 9:30-5. Last admission 1 hour before closing. Admission $17.95; over 645, $14.95; ages 3-9, $11.95. AX, DC, DS, MC, VI. Phone (305) 235-1611.

PARROT JUNGLE ISLAND is at 1111 Parrot Jungle Tr. on Watson Island, off the MacArthur Cswy. The sanctuary is home to 500 species of plants and some 3,000 exotic and rare animals, including a variety of parrots, twin orangutans and one of the largest crocodiles in the world. Visitors can interact with trainers and animals that stroll through the park.

Among the shows offered are Winged Wonders, featuring free-flying and singing birds; Reptile Giants, with monitor lizards, pythons and an albino alligator; and Wild Encounters, showcasing chimpanzees, baboons, honey bears and other creatures.

The grounds feature lush tropical gardens, a lake, an Everglades habitat, a rare plant nursery and an 800-seat amphitheater for concerts and touring animal shows.

Allow 4 hours minimum. Daily 10-6. Admission $24.95; ages 3-10, $19.95. AX, MC, VI. Phone (305) 400-7000. *See color ad p. 120.*

VIZCAYA MUSEUM AND GARDENS is at 3251 S. Miami Ave. Formerly the winter residence of agricultural industrialist James Deering, the 50-acre, European-inspired estate features 34 rooms lavishly furnished with European decorative arts representing the Renaissance, baroque, rococo and neoclassic eras. The once open-air home has been enclosed unobtrusively with glass to protect the valuable furnishings from the weather.

Hedges and walls divide the estate into many small gardens. Extensive gardens with pools and fountains contain sculptures from France and Italy. At the foot of the steps leading to Biscayne Bay, an unusual sculptured barge creates an area of calm water.

Note: Visitors are required to ascend and descend stairs. Photography is not permitted in the house. Allow 2 hours minimum. House open daily 9:30-5. Gardens open daily 9:30-5:30. Closed Dec. 25. Last admission at 4:30. Admission $12; over 61, $9; ages 6-12, $5. AX, MC, VI. Phone (305) 250-9133. *See color ad.*

SAVE **WINGS OVER MIAMI** is at 14710 S.W. 128th St. at the Kendall-Tamiami Airport. A large hangar houses a number of antique, restored aircraft, some from World Wars I and II, the Korean War and Vietnam. Two videos offer historical information, and display cases contain model planes and other aviation-related items. Allow 30 minutes minimum. Thurs.-Sun. 10-5:30; closed holidays. Admission $9.95; over 59 and under 12, $5.95. AX, MC, VI. Phone (305) 233-5197.

WORLD CHESS HALL OF FAME AND SIDNEY SAMOLE MUSEUM is off Florida's Tpke. exit 16, s. on 117th Ave., .5 mi. w. on S.W. 152nd St., .5 mi. n. on S.W. 122nd Ave., just e. on S.W. 144th St., then .5 mi. n. to 13755 S.W. 119th Ave. Displays relating to the game include various chess clocks, literature, full chess sets and Staunton chess pieces. A timeline explores the history of the game from prehistory to 1845. The Hall of Fame honors inductees, U.S. and world chess champions and Sid Samole, who created the first computer chess set. Allow 30 minutes minimum. Thurs.-Sat. 10:30-5, Sun. 1-5. Admission $5; under 12, $3. Phone (786) 242-4255.

MIAMI BEACH

BASS MUSEUM OF ART, 2121 Park Ave. in Miami Beach, features a permanent collection of European paintings, sculpture and textiles as well as temporary exhibitions of art from around the

world in five galleries of the 1930 Art Deco building. Lectures, a film series and live performances also are offered. Allow 1 hour minimum. Tues.-Sat. 10-5 (also second Thurs. of the month 5-9); closed holidays. Admission $6, senior citizens and students with ID $4, under 6 free. AX, MC, VI. Phone (305) 673-7530.

CARL FISHER MONUMENT is in Fisher Park at Alton Rd. and Lake Vista Dr. in Miami Beach. The monument, which consists of a bust of Fisher mounted on a large keystone, commemorates the man who helped to establish Miami Beach and who deeded many public beaches and parks to the city.

THE HOLOCAUST MEMORIAL, 1933-45 Meridian Ave., is dedicated to the memory of the 6 million Jewish men, women and children who suffered and died at the hands of the Nazis during their rule of Germany. The focus of the memorial is a 42-foot-high bronze arm rising from the ground; sculptured people climb it, looking for an escape.

Other features include a memorial wall with black granite panels etched with names of victims; a series of vignettes displaying victims helping victims; a photographic mural of holocaust history; a meditation garden; and the Dome of Contemplation with an eternal flame. Allow 30 minutes minimum. Daily 9-9. Free. Phone (305) 538-1663.

(SAVE) **JEWISH MUSEUM OF FLORIDA**, 2 blks. s. of Fifth St. at 301 Washington Ave., is housed in a restored Art Deco building formerly used as a synagogue. The core exhibit depicts Jewish life since 1763. Temporary exhibits change three times annually. Films, a timeline wall of Jewish history and a research center are available. Allow 1 hour minimum. Tues.-Sun. 10-5; closed Jewish holidays. Admission $6; over 65, $5; under 6 free; family rate $12; free to all Sat. Phone (305) 672-5044.

THE WOLFSONIAN-FLORIDA INTERNATIONAL UNIVERSITY is at 1001 Washington Ave. in Miami Beach's Art Deco District. Housed in a renovated 1920s Mediterranean-style warehouse, the museum features furniture, paintings, ceramics, architectural models, posters, books and memorabilia that depict the history, art, architecture and design of the late 19th and early 20th centuries.

Allow 1 hour minimum. Mon.-Tues. and Sat-Sun. noon-6, Thurs.-Fri. noon-9; closed major holidays. Admission $5, senior citizens and students with ID $3.50, under 6 free. Phone (305) 531-1001.

What To Do

Sightseeing

Boat Tours

(SAVE) **ISLAND QUEEN CRUISES** depart from Bayside Marketplace at 401 Biscayne Blvd. Passengers embark on a 1.5-hour sightseeing cruise through the harbor and port and around Star Island, where million-dollar homes owned by celebrities are identified. Narration is provided in English and

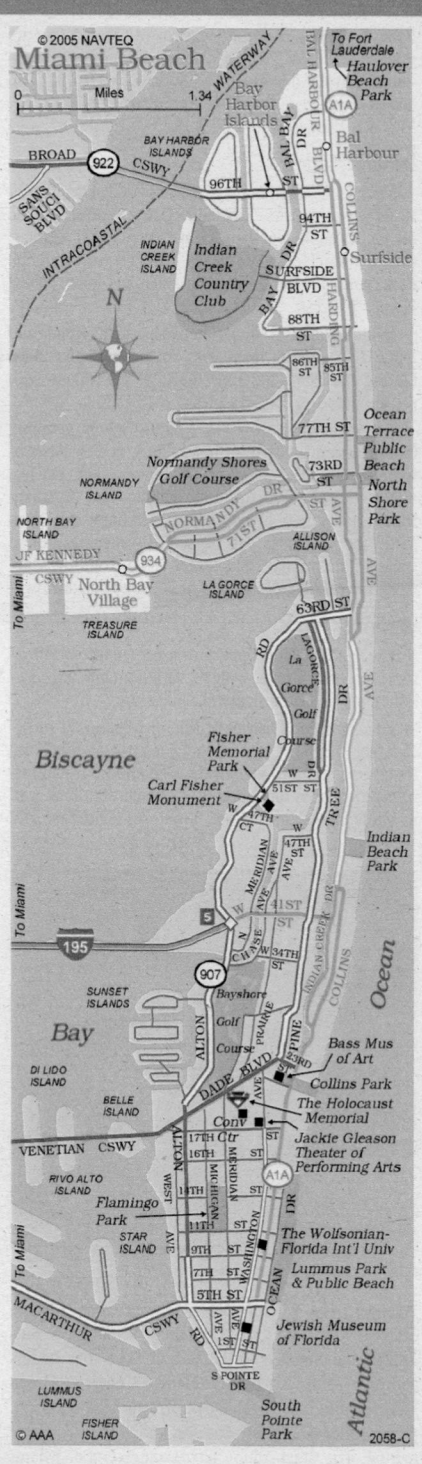

Spanish. Views of the downtown Miami skyline are especially scenic. Allow 1 hour, 30 minutes minimum. Cruises depart on the hour Mon.-Thurs. 11-6 and at 7:30, Fri.-Sun. 11-7. Fare $16; ages 4-12, $7. MC, VI. Phone (305) 379-5119.

Driving Tours

Main and Ingraham highways and Old Cutler Road, south from Coconut Grove, offer scenic drives through Coconut Grove and Coral Gables. Old Cutler Highway passes Matheson Hammock Park and Fairchild Tropical Garden (see Coral Gables p. 133).

South Miami Avenue, between 15th Road and Dixie Highway, is lined with royal poinciana trees. During late May and June the trees are ablaze with red flowers.

An interesting drive in Miami Beach is along Collins Avenue, with its hotels and motels. Also of interest are the magnificent homes and estates, which run the architectural gamut from Spanish-Mediterranean to bold modern. Although not open to the public, these can be seen by driving around some of the private islands accessible from the MacArthur, Venetian, North Bay and Broad causeways.

Walking Tours

There are several opportunities for exploration on foot. Coconut Grove, with its varied architecture and bohemian air, is particularly appealing.

The Art Deco District in Miami Beach is a showcase for the movement's characteristic architectural touches: porthole windows, geometric patterns, rounded corners and glass-block construction as well as walls bathed in fuchsia, turquoise, chartreuse and

Miami Beach / © Uripos / eStock Photo

lavender. The Miami Design Preservation League offers a 90-minute tour of the area Wednesdays, Saturdays and Sundays at 10:30 a.m. The tour begins and ends at the Art Deco Welcome Center at Ocean Front Auditorium, 1001 Ocean Dr. in Miami Beach; phone (305) 672-2014. The fee is $20, $15 for over age 64. The organization also arranges other Miami

Beach area tours and provides audiotapes for self-guided tours.

Little Havana, S.W. 12th Avenue to S.W. 27th Avenue, has open-air markets, music, shops, restaurants and a plaza, all of which reflect the Cuban culture.

Spectator Sports

In addition to year-round sunshine and white, sandy beaches, Miami is blessed with an abundance of professional sport offerings, including four major-league teams. No matter what your preference might be, you'll find a venue and a crowd of like-minded fans ready to cheer on their favorites.

Auto Racing

The 5,000-seat stadium at **Hialeah Speedway,** 3300 Okeechobee Rd., holds weekly stock-car races in five divisions; phone (305) 821-6644.

Homestead-Miami Speedway (see Homestead p. 134) has a 1.5-mile oval track that is negotiated by some of the sport's top names.

Baseball

Fans of the National League **Florida Marlins** passionately support their team during home games at **Dolphin Stadium,** 2267 Dan Marino Blvd., east of 27th Avenue in North Miami; phone (305) 626-7400. The Marlins brought the World Series title home to Miami in 1997 and 2003. The national pastime also is played locally in the college ranks when the **University of Miami Hurricanes** take the field on the UM campus at **Mark Light Stadium.**

Basketball

The **Miami Heat,** Atlantic division champions, have been a hot ticket in town since their 1988 debut. During their October to April season, the Heat play at the **American Airlines Arena,** downtown on Biscayne Boulevard adjacent to Bayside Marketplace; phone (786) 777-4328 for information.

Football

Backed by legions of "dolfans," the **Miami Dolphins** suit up for battle at the 75,000-seat Dolphin Stadium; phone (954) 452-7000 for the Dolphins or (305) 623-6100 for the stadium. The **Orange Bowl** stadium at 1501 N.W. Third St. is home turf for the University of Miami Hurricanes; phone (305) 643-7100. Despite five national championship titles, the 'Canes seldom fill up the stadium, so tickets are not difficult to come by.

Greyhound Racing

The dogs average a swift 40 mph at **Flagler Greyhound Track,** 401 N.W. 38th Ct., from June through November; phone (305) 649-3000.

Horse Racing

Thoroughbreds run to the roar of the crowd December through May at **Gulfstream Park,** 901 S. Federal Hwy. in nearby Hallandale *(see Hallandale Beach p. 85),* about a half-hour drive north from downtown Miami. The scenic track, encircling an artificial lake, is host to numerous major races; phone (305) 931-7223.

The usual March-to-May season is extended at **Calder Race Course,** just south of County Line Road (SR 852) at 21001 N.W. 27th Ave., where the horses run from late April to early January on a 1-mile course in a glass-enclosed, air-conditioned sports facility. Phone (305) 625-1311 for specific starting and wrap-up dates.

Jai-Alai

In this high-speed, indoor version of lacrosse, players climb the walls to catch and hurl balls *(pelotas)* with woven baskets *(cestas).* Spectators place bets on the evening's players behind a protective wall of glass. See the action for yourself at America's oldest jai-alai arena *(fronton),* the **Miami Jai-Alai Fronton,** 3500 N.W. 37th Ave.; phone (305) 633-6400.

Note: Policies on admitting children to pari-mutuel betting facilities vary. Phone in advance for specific information.

Recreation

A wealth of clear blue skies and a climate conducive to outdoor activity any time of the year make Miami a "hot" spot for those in search of fun in the sun. This tropical playground, with an average annual temperature of 76 F, comes equipped with aquamarine waters and more than enough land-based activities to suit all tastes.

Bicycling

Few places offer such diverse cycling environments as Miami. Pedal the hard-packed sands of **Miami Beach** while enjoying the sun and sights, or take the bicycle path that winds beneath a canopy of trees in **Coconut Grove,** where you can hop off and cruise through the neighborhood's colorful downtown area. Slightly more removed is the tropical escape of **Key Biscayne.** Here, on an island just 7 miles long and 2 miles wide, are 12 miles of bicycling trails. Bicycle rentals are available at all of the above locations; helmets are required for those under 17.

Experienced bicyclists desiring more extensive routes can contact the Miami-Dade Bicycle Pedestrian Program, which distributes maps about bicycling and bicycling safety and outlines some of Miami's more than 180 miles of bicycle trails; phone (305) 375-1647. A color-coded map of Miami-Dade County's suitable roads also is available.

Fishing

An abundance of water naturally brings plenty of fishing opportunities, and the popularity of bridge

fishing, seen all over Miami, is just a prelude to the opportunities available in a city where fishing is serious business. **South Pointe Park** in south Miami Beach offers excellent surf casting. Although bridge fishing generally is not allowed, it is permitted on the old **Rickenbacker Causeway,** which was left standing for that purpose when the new bridge was constructed for automobile traffic. Several piers in Miami Beach, as well as the **Tamiami Canal,** also are favorites of anglers.

Numerous marinas offer deep-sea fishing excursions, where avid anglers haul in prizes that range from snapper and bonito to big game catches like sailfish, tarpon and bluefish.

Kelley Fishing Fleet, 10800 Collins Ave. at Haulover Marina, provides party boats for half-day or full-day excursions out of Miami Beach; phone (305) 945-3801. Private charter boats abound at Haulover, with many offering 2-, 3- and 4-day fishing trips to the Bahamas; make the rounds and choose the one that suits your needs.

Licenses, required for freshwater fishing, are available at bait and tackle shops, sporting goods and discount department stores, as well as the county tax collector's office in the Miami-Dade County Courthouse, 140 W. Flagler St., Miami, FL 33130. Licenses also are available by mail; phone (888) 347-4356 (a credit card is required).

Golf

More than 30 golf courses provide a wide choice of greens for hackers and seasoned golfers alike. Crandon Park Golf Course, 6700 Crandon Blvd. in Key Biscayne, (305) 361-9129, is recognized by

CocoWalk, Coconut Grove / © Angelo Cavalli / SuperStock

most Florida golfers as the No. 1-ranked public course in the state; it also is among the top public links in the country. All courses listed below offer at least 18 holes and are open to the public.

Sites in the Miami area include Bayshore, 2401 Biarritz Dr. in Miami Beach, (305) 868-6502; Biltmore, 1210 Anastasia in Coral Gables, (305) 460-5364; Don Shula's Hotel and Golf Club, 6842

Main St. in Miami Lakes, (305) 821-1150; Doral Park Golf and Country Club, 5001 N.W. 104th Ave., (305) 591-8800; Golf Club of Miami, 6801 Miami Gardens Dr., (305) 829-8449; International Links Miami-Melreese, 1802 N.W. 37th Ave., (305) 633-4583; Killian Green, 9980 S.W. 104th St., (305) 271-0917; Miami Springs Golf Course, 650 Curtiss Pkwy. in Miami Springs, (305) 805-5180; and Miccosukee Golf & Country Club, 6401 Kendall Lakes Dr., (305) 382-3930.

The two city-owned Miami Beach courses welcome guests, and many hotels and motels have arrangements with private and semiprivate courses that allow guests to play.

Tennis

Miami's balmy climate allows for year-round tennis dates, and nearly 500 public courts cater to the racket. A majority of the hotels and motels in Miami and Miami Beach have private tennis facilities for their guests. Nearly all charge an hourly fee for use by nonresidents.

Best bets include the **Tennis Center at Crandon Park,** 7300 Crandon Blvd. in Key Biscayne, with hard courts; phone (305) 365-2300. Miami Beach's **Flamingo Tennis Center,** at Jefferson and 11th streets, offers 19 well-maintained clay courts; phone (305) 673-7761. For additional information about public courts phone the Miami-Dade County Parks Department at (305) 755-7800.

Water Sports

Whether you like zipping across its surface or exploring the world below it, everything you need to enjoy the water can be found in Miami, and all of it can be rented—from kayaks, windsurfers and boogie boards to catamarans, sailboats, personal watercraft and scuba equipment.

Many scuba and sail shops offer day-trip packages that include rental equipment and lessons for windsurfing, scuba diving and snorkeling. Sunken hulls; reefs and underwater gardens provide excellent opportunities for photography or exploration. North of Snapper Creek and south of Matheson Hammock Park is one of the better snorkeling sites. Another favorite location is near **Fowley Rocks Light** just south of Key Biscayne.

Boating is popular in Miami. Boats of all sizes and descriptions are for hire, whether for pleasure cruising, fishing or water skiing. **Dinner Key** and waterfront Coconut Grove are pristine and popular sites for launching sailboats. Other locations for sailboat rentals are available around the bay and on the **Miami River.** Boating events, whose locations and schedules are printed in area newspapers, take place throughout the year.

Powerboat rentals are available from **Club Nautico** at several locations: Monty's Stone Crab/Seafood House and Row Bar in Coconut Grove, (305) 858-6258; Crandon Park Marina in Key Biscayne, (305) 361-9217; and Miami Beach Marina, in Miami Beach, (305) 673-2502. Renters must be at least 21 years of age.

Water skiing and windsurfing instruction and equipment are available throughout the area. Many shops are clustered around the 79th Street Causeway (North Bay). Skiing is good all along the bay. Personal watercraft also can be rented. Surfing, while not the best in the country, attracts many enthusiasts. Two of the best spots are **South Beach** and **Haulover Beach.**

Some of the most popular white sand beaches in the Miami area are at **Bill Baggs Cape Florida State Park** and **Crandon Park.** Miami Beach's oceanfront restoration program added 150 to 200 feet to the width of the city's 10.5-mile stretch of beach, southward from 87th Terrace to the south end of Miami Beach.

Shopping

Greater Miami can easily accommodate those with a shop-'til-you-drop mentality. Although big city congestion can mean rare parking spaces and a frenzied atmosphere, such inconveniences are quickly forgotten by those who browse the shops' enticements. And, because of Miami's tourist orientation, the area is a treasure trove of souvenirs, from colorful T-shirts to opulent *objets d'art.*

Antiques

Miami's tastes in antiques are far from mainstream. Shops are hidden around the region, to be uncovered like sunken treasure. In Coral Gables, fine European furniture, clocks, bronzes and art glass are found at **Alhambra Antiques Center,** 2850 Salzedo St.; **Olde Tyme Shoppe,** 1423 Ponce de Leon Blvd., offers vintage pocket watches, chiming watches, clocks and other unique collector pieces. And, of course, where else would you expect to find a wealth of Art Deco wares but in the heart of the trendy Art Deco District?

Malls

More than 160 specialty shops fill the spacious **Dadeland Mall,** 7535 N. Kendall Dr. in Kendall. Anchored by Florida's largest Macy's department store, Dadeland features JCPenney, Saks Fifth Avenue and The Limited/Express. Also in Kendall, the open-air **The Falls,** 8888 S.W. 136th St., has Bloomingdale's and more than 100 ritzy shops in a lush, tropical setting.

Just west of the airport, **Miami International Mall,** 1455 N.W. 107th Ave., has JCPenney, Macy's and Sears in addition to 140 smaller stores. Off the

Palmetto Expressway at the N.W. 103rd Street exit in Hialeah is **Westland Mall.** JCPenney, Macy's and Sears join 100 smaller shops.

At 19501 Biscayne Blvd. in Aventura, a short hop off the William Lehman Causeway (SR 856), **Aventura Mall** is anchored by Bloomingdale's, JCPenney, Macy's and Sears. Specialty boutiques are among the mall's 250 shops and restaurants. **Southland Mall,** US 1S and Caribbean Boulevard, has JCPenney, Macy's and Sears among its 125 stores.

Jackie Gleason Theater of the Performing Arts / © Andre Jenny / Alamy

Outlets

Dolphin Mall, 5 miles west of Miami International Airport off the Dolphin Expressway at 11401 N.W. 13th St., offers discount stores with a wide variety of merchandise, including clothing, shoes, china, leather, toys and home accessories.

Specialty Districts

In addition to a multitude of malls, Miami also features upscale and themed shopping districts. The boutique district along **Collins Avenue** in South Beach features Armani Exchange, Banana Republic and Nicole Miller. Continental cafes and the boutiques of Bulgari, Cartier, Gucci, Louis Vuitton, Tiffany & Co. and Ungaro, to name a few, give credence to the internationally renowned status of **Bal Harbour Shops,** 9700 Collins Ave. in Bal Harbour; the shops also claim Florida's largest Neiman Marcus store. In this area it is not just business as usual; gracious transactions and outstanding service are customary in Bal Harbour's elegant setting.

Fun, funky and favored for drinks by an after-work crowd, the **Bayside Marketplace,** 401 Biscayne Blvd., is a downtown shopping, dining and entertainment mecca on Biscayne Bay. Designed after the historic Faneuil Hall Marketplace in Boston, the waterfront arcade combines more than 100 specialty boutiques, street performers, restaurants and outdoor eateries, and nightly open-air concerts to create a festive atmosphere. The **Pier 5 Market,** part of the complex, highlights the works of local artisans, entrepreneurs and inventors.

Rustic outdoor push carts, avant-garde clothing stores and lavishly decorated plazas are the hallmarks of **Coconut Grove,** Miami's tropical, pedestrian-friendly shopping and dining village. A smorgasbord of funky import shops, European salons and vintage clothing boutiques, the Grove is centered on Main Highway and Grand Avenue. At its heart is **CocoWalk,** 3015 Grand Ave., a colorful, casual open-air shopping center that includes cafes and trendy nightspots.

Some of the region's finest boutiques, gourmet restaurants and art galleries line the famed **Miracle Mile** in Coral Gables. The neighborhood's central boulevard and an integral part of George Merrick's original city plan, Miracle Mile is actually a half mile, between 37th and 42nd avenues, of small, picturesque 1970s storefronts along a wide, tree-lined boulevard. The significance here is historical as well as commercial. **The Village of Merrick Park,** at Ponce de Leon Boulevard and San Lorenzo Avenue in Coral Gables, is anchored by Neiman Marcus and Nordstrom and includes such high-end retailers as Ann Taylor, Gucci and Tiffany & Co.

A unique assortment of art galleries, antique shops and offbeat boutiques provides blocks of inspired browsing along South Miami Beach's

Lincoln Road. This 7-block pedestrian mall near the north end of the Art Deco District is the center of the city's happening art scene. It is surrounded by the district's two main commercial arteries, Collins and Washington avenues.

Performing Arts

The 1981 development of the National Foundation for the Arts was the springboard for cultural evolution in south Florida. Patrons of the arts enjoy an expanding array of performing arts venues. Included are the handsomely refurbished **Colony Theater** on Lincoln Road in south Miami Beach, (305) 674-1026; the 1,710-seat, Moorish-styled **Gusman Center for the Performing Arts,** 174 E. Flagler Street in downtown Miami, (305) 374-2444; and the Art Deco **Jackie Gleason Theater of the Performing Arts** (known as "TOPA") on Washington Avenue in south Miami Beach, (305) 673-7300.

Dance

Among the professional dance troupes in the Miami area is the **Miami City Ballet,** Florida's first fully professional resident ballet company. Artistic director Edward Villella premiered in the New York City Ballet under George Balanchine; works by Balanchine are included in the company's repertoire. Performances take place October through March at the Jackie Gleason Theater of the Performing Arts and at other venues throughout south Florida; phone (305) 929-7010 for ticket information.

The professional dance company **Ballet Flamenco La Rosa** moves to a flamenco and Latin-style beat; for ticket and schedule information phone (305) 672-0552.

Music

Although Miami does not have a resident symphony orchestra, the void is filled by the **New World Symphony.** Conductor Michael Tilson Thomas created the only advanced-training orchestra in the world as an interim step for young musicians who have completed their academic instruction. For subscriptions, season or single tickets phone (305) 673-3331, or phone the main office at (305) 673-3330.

Lovers of classical music appreciate the high-caliber offerings of the **Concert Association of Florida.** The long-running series features such luminaries as Itzhak Perlman and Andre Watts; phone (305) 808-7446.

Performing primarily at Gusman Center for the Performing Arts downtown, the **Florida Philharmonic** maintains its main office at 3401 N.W. 9th Ave. in Fort Lauderdale. South Florida's premier

symphony orchestra presents a full season of concerts, including children's programs; phone (954) 561-2997 for schedule and ticket information.

Opera

The celebrated **Florida Grand Opera,** 2901 W. Flagler St., which has provided South Florida with operatic performances since the early 1940s, offers five productions annually in the **Miami-Dade County Auditorium,** at Flagler Street and 29th Avenue; phone (305) 854-7890. Included among those honored during the opera's International Series are

© Jeff Greenberg / Alamy

Placido Domingo and Luciano Pavarotti. Promising singers make their mark in lead roles during the lower-priced National Series.

Theater

Housed in a lovely Spanish rococo-style palace, **Coconut Grove Playhouse,** 3500 Main Hwy. in Coconut Grove, has been one of Miami's most respected theaters since its inception in 1956, offering star casts in hit shows. Check the local newspapers for rates and schedules or phone (305) 442-4000. Broadway-bound plays and musical reviews are staged in its 1,100-seat main section; the playhouse also presents productions in the intimate **Encore Room.**

Area Stage Company presents off-Broadway plays throughout the year. **Actor's Playhouse** offers year-round productions for adults and children and is host to the National Children's Theater Festival.

Special Events

On New Year's Day Miami honors the orange with the **Orange Bowl Festival.** The festival is capped that night by the **Orange Bowl** football game. Runners join in the celebration during the **Orange Bowl 5K/10K.** The **Junior Orange Bowl International Youth Festival,** held in December, is a children's counterpart to the Orange Bowl festivities and features arts and crafts shows and competitions in football, tennis, soccer, golf and bowling.

Art Deco Weekend, a 3-day festival in mid-January where South Beach's fanciful architecture takes center stage, celebrates the Miami Beach historic district with a street fair, a 1930s-style ball, a film series, lectures, entertainment and a parade. The **Royal Caribbean Classic** golf tournament beckons devotees of that sport late January to early February.

The February calendar is filled with such events as the **Miami/Coconut Grove Art Festival,** one of the state's largest, offering works in almost every medium; the **Miami International Boat Show** at Miami Beach Convention Center; and the **Mid-Winter Sailing Regatta.** Miami-bound foreign and independent film fans will enjoy the **Miami International Film Festival,** which takes place during 10 days in February at Gusman Center for the Performing Arts. This increasingly important affair attracts more than 45,000 cinema aficionados. In late

South Beach / Visit Florida

February or early March, galleries of fans attend the **Celebrity Golf Championship.**

In the jubilant tradition of Rio de Janeiro, 9 days of merrymaking begin with the pageantry of **Carnival Miami,** said to be the nation's largest Hispanic celebration and Miami's largest event. This week-long Cuban celebration in early March has parades, concerts, fireworks and entertainment. Festivities culminate in the famous **Calle Ocho,** where more than 1 million people, mostly of Latin American descent, fill a 23-block area along S.W. Eighth Street in the heart of the Cuban district to enjoy music, food and each other's company.

Villa Vizcaya fills with period costumes, food and craft vendors, music and performances at the **Italian**

Renaissance Festival in mid-March. In June the **Royal Poinciana Festival** coincides with the blooming of the trees in Bayfront Park. Also in June, the **Miami-Bahamas Goombay Festival** celebrates the city's ties to Caribbean culture with street dances and other entertainment; this event takes place in Coconut Grove.

Handmade arts and crafts, alligator wrestling, food and American Indian music are all part of the festivities that take place in late July at the Miccosukee Indian Village during the **Everglades Music and Craft Festival.** Amid more than 150 exhibits of arts, crafts and novelties, south Florida jazz musicians perform on three stages in mid-September at **Taste of Art and Jazz** in Miami Lakes.

Cultural heritage comes to the forefront at three fall events. At the beginning of October is the **West Indian American Day Carnival,** a celebration of the Caribbean, featuring concerts, arts and crafts, food, costumed galas and street festivals. **Caribbean Carnival,** also in October, is a celebration of the Caribbean people and cultures, featuring concerts, arts and crafts, food, costumed galas and street festivals, all taking place at Hialeah Park race track in Hialeah.

In November the **NASCAR NEXTEL Cup Championship** and the **NASCAR Busch and Craftsman Truck series** are run at the Homestead-Miami Speedway *(see Homestead p. 134).* The **Harvest Festival,** a popular craft extravaganza the weekend before Thanksgiving, includes historical re-enactments, music, a quilt sale and antique cars.

The **Marion Edwards Jr. Memorial Race** for late-model stock cars is held in December at the Hialeah Speedway. In a zany spoof of the beloved King Orange Jamboree Parade, the **King Mango Strut** in late December features such wacky entries as the Precision Briefcase Drill Team and the Marching Freds. To round out the year the **Big Orange New Year's Eve Celebration and Parade** snakes along Biscayne Bay to kick off a weekend of New Year's celebrations.

The Latin Chamber of Commerce (CAMACOL) sponsors Hispanic festivals throughout the year. For information contact the chamber at 1417 W. Flagler St., Miami, FL 33135; phone (305) 642-3870.

The Miami-Miami Beach Vicinity

BISCAYNE NATIONAL PARK—*see place listing p. 45.*

COCONUT GROVE (H-11) elev. 10′

THE BARNACLE HISTORIC STATE PARK is at 3485 Main Hwy. Commodore Ralph Munroe, an area pioneer and noted designer of shallow-draft sailing yachts, built the cottage in 1891 and later enlarged it by raising the seven rooms to accommodate another floor underneath. Most furnishings belonged to Munroe, and many of his photographs are displayed. A boat house also is on the property. The cottage may be viewed only by guided tour.

Allow 1 hour minimum. Grounds open Fri.-Mon. 9-4. Free guided tours of the cottage are given at 10, 11:30, 1 and 2:30; closed Jan. 1, Thanksgiving and Dec. 25. Park admission $1, under 6 free. Phone (305) 442-6866.

CORAL GABLES (H-11)
pop. 42,249, elev. 11′

A planned community, Coral Gables is noted for its landscaped plazas and parkways, gateways of coral rock and royal poinciana trees. Spanish, Mediterranean and contemporary architecture blend in the downtown area. Many estates are in the older section of the city; modern mansions line the bayfront. Coral Gables Merrick House, 907 Coral Way, was the home of founder George Merrick, who named the city after his family home.

The Spanish architecture, lagoons and grottoes of the Venetian Pool, a public swimming pool at 2701 De Soto Blvd., reflect the lavish Coral Gables lifestyle of the 1920s. Also of interest are the Dutch-South African, Chinese and French villages.

Coral Gables is home to the University of Miami.

Coral Gables Chamber of Commerce: 360 Greco Ave., Suite 100, Coral Gables, FL 33146; phone (305) 446-1657.

FAIRCHILD TROPICAL BOTANIC GARDEN is next to Matheson Hammock Park at 10901 Old Cutler Rd. Narrated tram tours take visitors through this 83-acre botanical garden, which features rare tropical plants, palms, flowering trees and vines, exotic orchids and striking vistas. The garden features a tropical rain forest with plants from around the world. Food is available. Gardens open daily 9:30-4:30; closed Dec. 25. Tram tours depart hourly Mon.-Fri. 10-3, Sat.-Sun. 10-4. Admission (includes tram tour) $15; over 64, $12; ages 3-12, $5. AX, DS, MC, VI. Phone (305) 667-1651.

LOWE ART MUSEUM, UNIVERSITY OF MIAMI is w. of jct. US 1 and Stanford Dr. at 1301 Stanford Dr. Opened in 1952, the museum houses more than 12,000 objects representing western and non-western art from classical to contemporary. Spanning 5,000 years, the collection includes Greco-Roman antiquities, Italian renaissance and baroque art, pre-Columbian and southwest American Indian pieces and artworks from the Americas, Europe, Asia and Africa.

Allow 1 hour minimum. Tues.-Wed. and Fri.-Sat. 10-5, Thurs. noon-7, Sun. noon-5; closed major holidays. Admission $5, over 65 and students with ID $3, under 12 free. AX, DS, MC, VI. Phone (305) 284-3535.

MATHESON HAMMOCK PARK, 9610 Old Cutler Rd., is a man-made atoll pool separated from Biscayne Bay by a walkway. Trails wind among native shrubs and virgin forest. A boat ramp and bathhouse are available. Picnicking is permitted. Daily 6 a.m.-dusk. Parking $4 for automobiles, $10 for recreational vehicles, buses or vehicles with trailers. Phone (305) 665-5475.

FLORIDA CITY (H-10) pop. 7,843, elev. 6′

Florida City is surrounded by agricultural fields often referred to as the nation's "winter vegetable basket." Snap and pole beans, zucchini and squash are winter crops, while okra, limes, avocados and mangoes grow during the summer. Florida City State Farmer's Market, 300 N. Krome Ave. west of the junction of US 1 and Florida's Turnpike, is a wholesale and retail outlet. The retail outlet is open November through June, the wholesale outlet year-round; phone (305) 246-6334.

Greater Homestead-Florida City Chamber of Commerce: 43 N. Krome Ave., Homestead, FL 33030; phone (305) 247-2332.

Shopping areas: SAVE Prime Outlets Florida City, junction SR 821 (Florida's Turnpike) and US 1 at 250 E. Palm Dr., offers 60 outlet shops including Bass, Mikasa and Nike.

EVERGLADES ALLIGATOR FARM is off Florida's Turnpike exit 0, 1.5 mi. w. on Palm Dr. (S.W. 344th St.), then 4 mi. s. on S.W. 192nd Ave. The farm features more than 2,000 alligators as well as snakes, crocodiles and caimans. Alligator shows and snake demonstrations are given hourly. Narrated airboat rides also are offered. Allow 2 hours minimum. Daily 9-6; closed Dec. 25. Admission $17; over 65, $16; ages 4-11, $10. AX, DS, MC, VI. Phone (305) 247-2628.

HOMESTEAD (H-10) pop. 31,909, elev. 9′

The center of south Florida's fruit and nursery production, Homestead serves as a gateway to Everglades National Park *(see place listing p. 60)*, Biscayne National Park *(see place listing p. 45)* and The Florida Keys *(see place listing p. 64)*. The city's historic district offers shops and restaurants in a landscaped setting.

Tropical Everglades Visitor Center: 160 US 1, Florida City, FL 33034; phone (305) 245-9180 or (800) 388-9669.

CORAL CASTLE OF FLORIDA, 2 mi. n. on US 1, was constructed of massive blocks of hand-hewn coral rock. Using primitive tools, Latvian immigrant Ed Leedskalnin worked alone 1923-51 to build the structure and its furnishings. Audiotapes for self-guiding tours are available. Allow 1 hour minimum. Daily 7 a.m.-8 p.m. Admission $9.75; over 62, $6.50; ages 7-12, $5. AX, DS, MC, VI. Phone (305) 248-6345.

HOMESTEAD-MIAMI SPEEDWAY is off Florida's Turnpike exit 6, then s. 3 mi. on Speedway Blvd. (137th St.). NASCAR races top the list of motor sports that attract top-name drivers and thousands of fans to this 434-acre facility. The premier event is the Ford Championship Weekend, held in November, which features three season-finale races: the NEXTEL Cup competition, run at night under the lights, and the Busch and Craftsman Truck series.

Motorcycle and sports-car races are held on the 2.2-mile, 14-turn infield road course. The facility seats 65,000 and sports an Art Deco look with bright colors indicative of Miami architecture. Visitors may view and photograph the track from the Turn One Tower. Entry is through the gift shop Mon.-Fri. 10-3. Free. Phone (305) 230-7223 or (866) 409-7223 for event and ticket information.

© International Speedway Corporation

AAA is the Official Auto Club of Homestead-Miami Speedway.

KEY BISCAYNE (H-11) pop. 10,507, elev. 5′

CRANDON PARK, 4000 Crandon Blvd., is reached via the Rickenbacker Causeway over Biscayne Bay; toll $1. This scenic park has historic gardens, landscaped picnic areas and a 2.5-mile public beach. Kayak rentals and guided historical tours are available. Allow 1 hour minimum. Daily 8-dusk. Admission $4 per private vehicle, $10 per bus or recreational vehicle. Phone (305) 361-5421.

NORTH MIAMI BEACH (H-11)
pop. 40,786, elev. 10′

ANCIENT SPANISH MONASTERY (Episcopal) is at 16711 W. Dixie Hwy. Built in 12th-century Spain, the structure was dismantled and shipped to the United States in 1925. The monastery was rebuilt in 1952 and now houses ancient artworks and furniture. Allow 2 hours minimum. Mon.-Sat. 9-5, Sun. 2-5; closed Easter, Thanksgiving and Dec. 25. May close for private parties on weekends, so phone ahead. Admission $5; over 65 and students with ID $2.50; under 12, $2. Phone (305) 945-1461.

SAVE **MUSEUM OF CONTEMPORARY ART,** off I-95 exit 10A, then 1.5 mi. e. to 770 N.E. 125th St., offers changing exhibits in various media from sculpture to photography. Allow 1 hour minimum. Tues.-Sat. 11-5; Sun. noon-5; closed major holidays. Admission $5, over 65 and students with ID $3, under 12 free. AX, MC, VI. Phone (305) 893-6211.

The previous listings were for the Miami-Miami Beach Vicinity. This page resumes the alphabetical listings of cities in Florida.

MICANOPY (C-8) pop. 653, elev. 100′

The former site of a Timucuan Indian village, Micanopy (MIK-uh-no-pee) is the state's oldest inland town not on a waterway. Many antique, art and curio shops help to create an atmosphere of a small Florida village during the 19th century.

MICANOPY HISTORICAL SOCIETY MUSEUM, off I-75 exit 374, e. on SR 234, then n. to jct. Cholokka Blvd. and Early St., features historical artifacts housed in an 1890s warehouse. Guided tours are available. Allow 30 minutes minimum. Daily 1-4. Donations. Phone (352) 466-3200.

PAYNES PRAIRIE PRESERVE STATE PARK, 1 mi. n. on US 441, encompasses 21,000 acres of freshwater marsh, hammocks, pine flatwoods, swamps and ponds. More than 30 miles of trails are available. Visitor center exhibits interpret the natural and cultural history of this important ecological area. A 50-foot observation tower stands near the center of the preserve and a recreation area is at Lake Wauberg.

Allow 1 hour minimum. Park open daily 8-dusk. Visitor center open daily 9-4. Ranger-led activities are available November through April by reservation. Admission $4 per private vehicle (maximum eight people), $1 per person arriving by bicycle or on foot. Phone (352) 466-3397 or (352) 466-4100. *See Recreation Chart and the AAA Southeastern CampBook.*

MILTON (A-3) pop. 7,200, elev. 15′

A heavy growth of briars along the Blackwater River elicited Milton's early name, Scratch Ankle. The Blackwater, one of the state's most pristine rivers, has retained its importance to modern Milton as a carrier of recreational canoeists rather than commerce; canoes and tubes can be rented in the area. Blackwater River State Park *(see Recreation Chart)* and Blackwater River State Forest are northeast. Historic old homes date back to the Civil War days. Whiting Field Naval Air Station is north on SR 87.

Santa Rosa County Chamber of Commerce and Tourist Information Center: 5247 Stewart St., Milton, FL 32570; phone (850) 623-2339.

RECREATIONAL ACTIVITIES
Canoeing

- **Adventures Unlimited** is 12 mi. n. on SR 87, then 4 mi. e. following signs. Write 8974 Tomahawk Landing, Milton, FL 32570. Other activities are offered. Daily 8-6, Mar.-Sept.; 8-4, rest of year. Closed Thanksgiving and Dec. 25. Phone (850) 623-6197 or (800) 239-6864.

MOUNT DORA—*see Orlando p. 182.*

MULBERRY (E-9) pop. 3,230, elev. 140′

Long known as the center of phosphate production in central Florida, Mulberry was founded in 1901. The city today covers about 6 square miles.

MULBERRY PHOSPHATE MUSEUM, 1 blk. s. of jct. SRs 37 and 60 at 101 S.E. First St., features a collection of fossilized remains of prehistoric animals, area memorabilia and exhibits related to the phosphate industry. A phosphate train also is displayed. Allow 1 hour minimum. Tues.-Sat. 10-4:30. Donations. Phone (863) 425-2823.

NAPLES (G-9) pop. 20,976, elev. 9′

With trendy boutiques, art galleries, cozy restaurants and other upscale accouterments, Naples quickly is becoming one of the most sophisticated cities on Florida's west coast. This image is a far cry from the days in 1885 when development began and the area was accessible only by water. The Naples Pier is a relic of that period.

Naples' greatest treasures are not found in the shops and malls—the city has long been famous for its 10 miles of public beaches. Shell gathering and other beachfront activities are available at Delnor-Wiggins Pass State Park *(see Recreation Chart),* 11 miles northwest via SR 846.

Rookery Bay, 5 miles south, is an area of mangrove islands that shelter rare birds and marine life. Maintained as a national estuarine research reserve, it features an environmental learning center that is reached from Collier Boulevard in East Naples.

Golfing is popular in the Naples area. Swamp buggy races, first held in 1949, take place in January, March and October at the Florida Sports Park off Collier Boulevard; phone (800) 897-2701.

DID YOU KNOW

Of the 50 states, only Alaska has more islands than Florida.

Philharmonic Center for the Arts, at 5833 Pelican Bay Blvd., presents varied entertainment; phone (239) 597-1900 or (800) 597-1900.

Naples Visitors Information Center: 2390 Tamiami Tr. N., Naples, FL 34103; phone (239) 262-6141.

Shopping areas: Among the 140 stores at Coastland Center, 1900 N. Tamiami Tr., are Dillard's, JCPenney, Macy's and Sears. Tin City, at the corner of US 41 (Tamiami Trail) and SR 851 (Goodlette-Frank Road), is restored to capture the flavor of pioneer-era Naples. The Village on Venetian Bay, 4200 Gulf Shore Blvd. N., offers boutiques, restaurants and galleries in a Mediterranean setting.

Waterside Shops, US 41 and Seagate Drive, has a wide selection of shops including Banana Republic, Saks Fifth Avenue and Talbots. The Third Street South Shopping Area in the historic district of Old Naples, just 2 blocks from the Naples Pier, has more than 100 shops, galleries, restaurants and cafes.

[SAVE] **CARIBBEAN GARDENS: THE ZOO IN NAPLES** is 1.75 mi. n. via US 41 to jct. Fleischmann Blvd., then .5 mi. e. to 1590 Goodlette-Frank Rd. Founded in 1919, the 52-acre zoo features a self-guiding trail that winds through a botanical garden populated by animals. Visitors can observe natural animal behavior complemented by wildlife footage and graphics during two feature shows, Planet Predator and Serpents: Fangs & Fiction. A 20-minute boat cruise offers views of primates roaming freely on island habitats. Scheduled activities include Alligator Bay Feeding and Meet the Keeper.

Picnicking is permitted. Allow 4 hours minimum. Daily 9:30-5:30; closed Easter, Thanksgiving and Dec. 25. Last admission 1 hour before closing. Admission (including boat cruise) $15.95; ages 4-15, $9.95. DS, MC, VI. Phone (239) 262-5409.

COLLIER COUNTY MUSEUM is at jct. US 41E and Airport-Pulling Rd., in the County Government Center. Exhibits trace the history of Collier County from the Calusa Indian period to the present. A steam logging locomotive also is featured. Allow 30 minutes minimum. Mon.-Fri. 9-5, Sat. 9-4; closed holidays. Free. Phone (239) 774-8476.

COLLIER-SEMINOLE STATE PARK BOAT TOURS is 17 mi. s. on US 41 at 20200 E. Tamiami Tr. One-hour tours aboard a pontoon boat take passengers along the Black Water River, which runs through Collier-Seminole State Park. Narration is provided about the early settlements and pioneers of the area as well as the animals and plants that populate the Everglades.

Departures daily at 9:30, 11, 12:30, 2 and 3:30; closed Dec. 25. Departures require a minimum of four adults. Fare $10; ages 6-12, $7.50. MC, VI. Phone (239) 642-8898. *See Recreation Chart and the AAA Southeastern CampBook.*

THE CONSERVANCY NATURE CENTER, off Goodlette-Frank Rd. at 1450 Merrihue Dr., features a wildlife rehabilitation center, nature trails, and canoe and kayak rentals. A Museum of Natural History features snakes, a loggerhead sea turtle and hands-on displays. Changing exhibits also are offered. Among the highlights is a 45-minute narrated boat tour of a mangrove forest and a lagoon.

Allow 1 hour minimum. Mon.-Sat. 9-4:30, Sun. noon-4, Nov.-Apr.; Mon.-Sat. 9-4:30, rest of year. Closed major holidays. Center $7.50; ages 3-12, $2. Phone (239) 262-0304.

CORKSCREW SWAMP SANCTUARY, off I-75 exit 111, then 16 mi. e. on Immokalee Rd to 375 Sanctuary Rd., is an 11,000-acre wilderness area and wildlife sanctuary of the National Audubon Society, with nearly 200 bird species in temporary or permanent residence. The sanctuary contains the largest known stand of virgin bald cypress, some more than 500 years old. Alligators can be seen regularly from the 2.25-mile boardwalk.

Allow 1 hour minimum. Daily 7 a.m.-7:30 p.m., Apr. 11-Sept. 30, 7-5:30, rest of year. Admission $10; college students with ID $6; ages 6-18, $4. MC, VI. Phone (239) 348-9151. *See color ad*

DOUBLE SUNSHINE SIGHTSEEING CRUISES departs from Tin City on US 41. During 90-minute

narrated sightseeing cruises of Naples Bay, passengers can enjoy views of waterfront mansions, mangrove-lined islands, dolphins, manatees and such birds as bald eagles and pelicans. Also available are half-day deep-sea fishing trips aboard the *Lady Brett,* and half-day bay fishing trips aboard the *Capt. Paul.*

Sightseeing cruises depart daily at 10, noon, 2, 4 and 1 hour before dusk. Deep-sea trips depart daily at 7:45 and 1. Bay fishing trips depart at 9 and 1. Sightseeing fare $28.30; under 12, $14.15. Deep-sea fare $60; under 12, $55. Bay fishing fare $55; under 12, $50. Reservations are recommended. Phone (239) 263-4949.

SAVE **EVERGLADES EXCURSIONS,** departing from the Old Naples General Store downtown, offers full- and half-day excursions throughout the Everglades. Highlights include a narrated jungle cruise through Everglades National Park, a visit to Everglades City, an airboat ride through the Ten Thousand Islands and a tour of Fakahatchee Strand Preserve State Park and Big Cypress National Preserve.

Allow 4 hours minimum. Trips depart daily at 8 and noon; closed Dec. 25. Half-day fare $65; ages 4-12, $49. Full-day fare (including lunch) $99; ages 4-12, $69. Reservations are required. AX, DS, MC, VI. Phone (239) 262-1914 or (800) 592-0848. *See color ad.*

NAPLES DEPOT MUSEUM, 1051 Fifth Ave. S. at 10th St., is in a renovated 1927 train station. A collection of railroad memorabilia, including an operating Lionel train, is displayed inside the depot; a baggage car stands outside, where a children's train ride is offered. Thurs.-Sat. noon-4. Hours may vary; phone for schedule. Donations. Phone (239) 262-1776.

GEM **NAPLES MUSEUM OF ART** is off I-75 exit 107, 5 mi. w. on Pine Ridge Rd., then .4 mi. n. on US 41 to 5833 Pelican Bay Blvd., in the Philharmonic Center for the Arts complex. The museum's permanent collection includes American paintings and drawings, modern Mexican art, sculpture, miniature rooms and furniture by renowned miniaturists and two large chandeliers by glass artist Dale Chihuly.

Allow 2 hours minimum. Tues.-Sat. 10-4, Sun. noon-4, mid-Sept. to late July; closed major holidays. Guided tours are given at 11 and 2, Oct.-May. Admission $8, students with ID $4, under 5 free. AX, MC, VI. Phone (239) 597-1900 or (800) 597-1900.

NAPLES TROLLEY TOURS boards at Naples Trolley Depot and Old Naples General Store, downtown on Sixth Ave. S., and at many stops along the route. The area's historic sites, shopping areas and residential sections are highlighted in a narrated 1.75-hour tour that includes Naples Pier, Fifth Avenue S., Pelican Bay, Venetian Village and Tin City. Daily 8:30-5:30.

Fare (includes an all-day reboarding pass) $19; ages 3-12, $9. AX, DS, MC, VI. Phone (239) 262-7300 or (800) 592-0848. *See color ad p. 137.*

[SAVE] **SEE MANATEES GUARANTEED** is 22 mi. s. on US 41, in the Port of the Islands complex. Guided 90-minute trips aboard a six-passenger boat offer close-up glimpses of submerged and surfacing manatees as well as sightings of alligators and birds. Allow 1 hour, 30 minutes minimum. Trips depart daily 8:30-4. Reservations are required. Fare $35; under 7, $15. Fare may vary; phone ahead. MC, VI. Phone (239) 642-8818 or (800) 379-7440.

THE TEDDY BEAR MUSEUM OF NAPLES, 1.75 mi. w. of I-75 exit 107 at 2511 Pine Ridge Rd., displays more than 5,000 teddy bears, ranging in size from less than 1 inch to larger than life. The collection includes bears made of fabric, marble and bronze as well as antique and limited-edition bears. Teddy bear art and memorabilia also are featured, and teddy bear-making classes are available seasonally. Allow 30 minutes minimum. Tues.-Sat. 10-5; closed major holidays. Admission $8; over 60, $6; ages 4-12, $3. AX, DS, MC, VI. Phone (239) 598-2711 or (866) 365-2327.

NEW SMYRNA BEACH (D-10)
pop. 20,048, elev. 10'

On this beach north of Cape Canaveral, automobiles may be driven along the stretch of firm white sand from the inlet south to 27th Avenue. Drivers should heed signs noting unsafe areas. Overnight parking or camping are not permitted on the beach. February through mid-November, a daily driving toll of $5 per car is charged; season passes are available for both residents ($20) and nonresidents ($40). Toll booths are at each approach.

The foundations of the Turnbull Ruins/Old Fort, built of coquina, are on N. Riverside Drive between Washington and Julia streets. These ruins, made of walls 3 feet thick, represent a local mystery—it has never been established if the foundation is the unfinished remains of a pre-colonial fort or the incomplete beginnings of a mansion for the Turnbull family. The remains of a large plantation's sugar mill can be seen at Sugar Mill Ruins, 1050 Old Mission Rd. Built in the early 1800s, the mill was destroyed during the Second Seminole War.

The Atlantic Center for the Arts, 1414 Art Center Ave., provides studio space and facilities for resident artists and offers exhibitions and events throughout the year; phone (386) 427-6975 or (800) 393-6975.

New Smyrna Beach Visitors Bureau: 2238 SR 44, New Smyrna Beach, FL 32168; phone (386) 428-1600 or (800) 541-9621.

THE *MANATEE* SCENIC CRUISES departs from Sea Harvest Marina on Riverside Dr. between the North and South causeways. Narrated cruises aboard

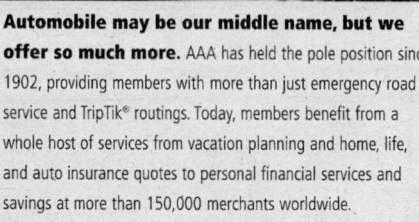

the *Manatee* navigate the protected wetland and scenic mangrove shores along the Intracoastal Waterway. Sights include Ponce de Leon Lighthouse, waterfront homes and native wildlife, such as dolphins. Lunch cruises also are available. Narrated cruises depart daily; times vary. Boarding is 15 minutes before departure. Fare $19; under 12, $14. Reservations are required. Phone (386) 428-0201 or (800) 881-2628.

NORTH MIAMI BEACH—
see Miami-Miami Beach p. 134.

NORTH PORT (F-9) pop. 22,797, elev. 11′

SAVE THE SPRINGS is off I-75 exit 191, s. on US 41, .8 mi. e. on Ortiz Blvd., then just s. to 12200 San Servando Ave. This warm mineral spring has an average temperature of 87 degrees Fahrenheit year-round and produces 9 million gallons of fresh mineral water a day. Picnicking is permitted. Food and lockers are available. Allow 2 hours minimum. Daily 9-5; closed Dec. 25. Admission $14; senior citizens and military with ID $12; students with ID $9; ages 3-12, $5. AX, DS, MC, VI. Phone (941) 426-1692.

OCALA (C-9) pop. 45,943, elev. 104′

Ocala (oh-KAL-a) has moss-draped oaks and stately old Southern homes along many of its streets. The surrounding area is considered the heartland of Florida's Thoroughbred industry. It is possible to visit some of the horse farms. Particularly scenic segments of two highways approach Ocala: US 301 from Waldo and US 27 from Williston.

Ocala-Marion County Chamber of Commerce: 110 E. Silver Springs Blvd., Ocala, FL 34470; phone (352) 629-8051.

Shopping areas: Paddock Mall, a half-mile east of I-75 on SR 200, features Belk Lindsey, JCPenney, Macy's and Sears.

GEM SAVE **THE APPLETON MUSEUM OF ART,** 4333 N.E. Silver Springs Blvd., houses European paintings, sculpture and decorative arts; contemporary art; pre-Columbian artworks; West African, Islamic and Asian artworks; as well as antiquities. The Edith-Marie Appleton wing features a library, a workshop and additional galleries. Lectures and films also are offered. Allow 1 hour minimum. Tues.-Sun. 10-6; closed Jan. 1, Thanksgiving and Dec. 25. Admission $6; over 55 and college students with ID $4; ages 10-18, $3. AX, MC, VI. Phone (352) 291-4455.

E-ONE FACTORY TOURS is .5 mi. e. of I-75 exit 352 (SR 40), .5 mi. s. on S.W. 33rd Ave., then 1 mi. s.w. on S.W. Seventh St. to 1601 S.W. 37th Ave. Guided tours of three factories where fire trucks are manufactured are offered. Tours cover 2 miles of walking and can be noisy and hot during the summer. Safety goggles are provided and shoes with closed toes must be worn.

Note: Children under 6 are not allowed on the factory tour, but they may go on an abbreviated tour of the Vehicle Delivery Center, which includes sitting in the cab of a fire truck, subject to availability. Allow 1 hour, 30 minutes minimum. Tours offered Mon.-Fri. at 9, 11 and 1 (weather permitting); closed holidays and Dec. 26-31. Admission $6; over 55, $4; fire service members with ID and ages 6-12 free. Phone (352) 861-3524.

GEM **FLORIDA'S SILVER SPRINGS—**
see Silver Springs p. 207

GARLITS' AUTO MUSEUM is 8 mi. s. on I-75 to exit 341, .25 mi. e. on CR 484, then .25 mi. s. on

CR 475A. In addition to displaying 100 antique automobiles in a separate building, the museum traces the evolution of the sport of drag racing through the 50-year collection of "Big Daddy" Don Garlits' cars and artifacts. Allow 1 hour minimum. Daily 9-5; closed Dec. 25. Admission $12; over 59 and ages 13-18, $10; ages 5-12, $3. Under 16 must be with an adult. MC, VI. Phone (352) 245-8661 or (877) 271-3278.

OCALA NATIONAL FOREST

Elevations in the forest range from 10 ft. to 125 ft.

In central Florida, the 383,573-acre forest contains numerous plant species of vegetation and clear lakes, springs and streams. The forest is said to have the world's largest stand of sand pine. Other predominant trees types include longleaf and slash pine, cypress and hardwood. In addition to several shorter trails, a well-traveled section of the Florida National Scenic Trail winds through the forest and is popular with hikers. Hunting is allowed by permit from the Florida Fish and Wildlife Conservation Commission *(see Fast Facts).*

Developed recreation sites include Alexander Springs, Juniper Springs, Lake Dorr, Fore Lake, Mill Dam, Clearwater Lake, Salt Springs and Silver Glen Springs. Juniper Prairie Wilderness is home to Pat's Island, where parts of the movie "The Yearling" were filmed. Juniper Springs was constructed in 1935 by the Civilian Conservation Corps. *See Recreation Chart.*

Brochures and information on forest recreational opportunities are available at Ocklawaha Visitor Center on SR 40 at SR 315, between Silver Springs and the Ocklawaha River; phone (352) 236-0288. The center is open daily 9-5.

ODESSA—*see Tampa Bay p. 233.*

OKEECHOBEE (F-10) pop. 5,376, elev. 29'

At the crossroads of SR 70, US 98 and US 441, Okeechobee serves as a center for such outdoor activities as boating, fishing, camping and air boat rides. The town also is a commercial center for cattle, which is evident in the several festivals and rodeos that take place throughout the year.

Okeechobee Chamber of Commerce: 55 S. Parrott Ave., Okeechobee, FL 34972; phone (863) 763-6464.

LAKE OKEECHOBEE, covering approximately 750 square miles, is the second largest freshwater lake in the continental United States. Its greatest depth is 10 feet, but the water is so shallow in most places that birds can be seen wading a mile from shore. A lighted pier at Lock 7 (US 441 and SR 78) provides day and night fishing. A hiking and biking trail winds 110 miles along a levee that surrounds the entire lake. Recreational facilities are available.

OLUSTEE (B-8) elev. 140'

OLUSTEE BATTLEFIELD HISTORIC STATE PARK, about 2.5 mi. e. on US 90, marks the site of the largest Civil War battle on Florida soil. Union forces were defeated decisively at the site on Feb. 20, 1864; the battle is re-enacted every February. Highlights include a museum featuring Civil War artifacts. Site open daily 8-5. Museum open daily 9-5. Site and museum free. Phone (386) 758-0400.

ONA (F-9) elev. 90'

SOLOMON'S CASTLE is 8 mi. s. of SR 64 on CR 663, 5 mi. w. on CR 665, then .7 mi. n. to 4533 Solomon Rd. Built entirely by hand and covered with discarded newspaper printing plates, this shiny castle-like structure features a tower, dungeon, moat and more than 80 interpretive stained glass windows created by the owner/artist. Sculptures made from recycled objects are displayed in galleries throughout the residence. Food is available. Allow 1 hour, 30 minutes minimum. Tues.-Sun. 11-4, Oct.-June. Last tour begins 30 minutes before closing. Admission $10; under 13, $4. Phone (863) 494-6077.

ORANGE CITY (D-9) pop. 6,604, elev. 43'

Orange City's early residents were the Timucuan Indians, who lived along the St. Johns River and ate the snails that inhabited the river's sandbars. The mound formed by the accumulation of centuries of snail shells later served as a foundation for the area's first permanent home, the 1872 Thursby House. Today the residence is preserved in Blue Spring State Park, a winter habitat of the endangered manatee.

Chambers of Commerce of West Volusia: 520 N. Volusia Ave., Orange City, FL 32763; phone (386) 775-2793.

BLUE SPRING STATE PARK, 2 mi. w. off US 17/92 on W. French Ave., contains a spring run that maintains a temperature of 73 degrees Fahrenheit. Manatees come here mid-November through March to escape the cooler waters of the St. Johns River. Viewing platforms, ranger interpretation programs and a video presentation introduce visitors to these gentle creatures. Visitors may not swim with or feed the manatees. Canoe rentals are available.

Allow 2 hours minimum. Park daily 8-dusk. Video presentation shown Mon.-Fri. at 1:30, 2:30 and 3:30, Sat.-Sun. at 11, 1:30, 2:30 and 3:30, mid-Nov. to mid-Mar. Admission $5 per private vehicle (maximum eight people), $1 per person arriving by bicycle or on foot. Phone (386) 775-3663. *See Recreation Chart and the AAA Southeastern CampBook.*

St. Johns River Cruises, in Blue Spring State Park at 2100 W. French Ave., offers narrated cruises and nature tours along the St. Johns River. Allow 2 hours minimum. Cruises depart daily at 10 and 1 (also at 3:30, Jan.-Apr.). Fare $16; over 60, $14; ages 3-12, $10. Park admission $5. Reservations are required. AX, DS, MC, VI. Phone (407) 330-1612 or (386) 917-0724.

Drive America With AAA

See America

*from s e a   t o   s h i n i n g   s e a and **everything in between.***

Let AAA help you plan your next drive vacation. Whether you're taking a weekend trip or visiting one of North America's major travel destinations, *AAA Drive Trips* provide all the information you need.

Each *AAA Drive Trip* includes a route map, estimated driving time, mileage, and details on where to stay and what to see and do along the way.

So, on your next drive vacation, trust a AAA for all your vacation needs, including TourBooks®, TripTiks®, the lowest online hotel rates, member discounts and much more.

Visit us online at <u>aaa.com</u> or stop by your local AAA office.

aaa.com

Orlando

City Population: 185,951 **Elevation:** 111 ft.

Editor's Picks:

SeaWorld Orlando...................*(see p. 155)*

Universal Orlando Resort..........*(see p. 156)*

Walt Disney World® Resort.......*(see p. 167)*

Lake Eola Park / © Paul Thompson / imagestate

Walt Disney World. It is the dream destination of every young child, the first stop on a Super Bowl champion's victory tour. It conjures up images of azure swimming pools, life-size cartoon characters and a fantasy castle where dreams come true. And it has made the young city of Orlando the world's most popular vacation spot.

Central Florida's Disney story began in the mid-1960s, when entertainment visionary "Uncle Walt" Disney paid a series of hush-hush visits to the swamplands of southwest Orange County. Secretive property deals soon followed, piquing locals' interest and sparking questions about the mysterious doings south of town. The answer—and instant fame—came in 1971 when the Magic Kingdom became the area's first theme park.

Bolstered by Walt Disney World's phenomenal success, Orlando began a rapid growth spurt. Hotels and restaurants sprang up around the park practically overnight, swiftly followed by a legion of souvenir shops and tourist strips. A diverse mix of people flocked to the area, lured by Disney's magic spell and the promise of easy living in the nation's new vacation capital.

But while Disney is the centerpiece of Orlando's appeal, the City Beautiful offers more than just theme parks. Summer rainstorms and a warm climate promote lush vegetation. Pines, palms and oaks draped with Spanish moss line the streets, and landscaped gardens display many varieties of flowers.

In the midst of the state's lake country, central Florida offers more than 2,000 lakes and dozens of parks in which to hike, lounge, bike or engage in water sports. Even in the throes of rapid growth, the downtown streets, many of them brick, seem clean and friendly, the skies are smog-free and subtropical vegetation graces almost every view.

Of course, success breeds risks along with rewards. New residents arrive by the thousands each year, and as a result, Orlando natives make up less than half the population and the best-known citizens are the mascots of the local theme parks.

Surprisingly, Orlando is no stranger to the boom-town hustle and bustle, having experienced several boom-and-bust cycles in its short but tumultuous past. The city began as a small settlement founded by brothers Aaron and Isaac Jernigan, who in 1843 established a cattle ranch and trading post on what is now Lake Holden.

More than one story explains the origin of the town's name, but the most reliable claims it honors a member of a company of U.S. soldiers and volunteers, Orlando Reeves. One night in 1835 Reeves was at his post as sentry along Sandy Beach—the shores of today's Lake Eola—when he noticed a "log" in the lake. Realizing it was an Indian creeping toward the camp, Reeves gave the alarm to warn his company.

The frontier outpost grew quickly, and by the 1860s cattle ranches and cotton plantations were a common sight. By virtue of its remote location, Orlando was far removed from the ravages of the Civil War. It was very much a Confederate city, however, and so became a haven for displaced Southerners.

Getting There — starting on p. 144

Getting Around — starting on p. 149

What To See — starting on p. 150

What To Do — starting on p. 158

Where To Stay — starting on p. 687

Where To Dine — starting on p. 689

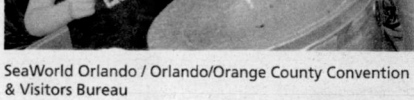

They came seeking a fresh start among the thriving cattle herds and the thick groves of a new industry: citrus production.

The first success story belonged to William Harrison Holden, who in 1875 planted a commercial orange grove on the shore of the lake that would later take his name. Countless would-be citrus kings followed his lead, and soon lemons, oranges and grapefruit constituted the area's leading business.

The pioneer period came to a close in 1880 with the completion of the South Florida Railroad, which offered a link to the North. The advent of rail travel was a defining moment for the city: Along with increased commercial opportunities came multitudes of sun-seeking tourists escaping harsh Northern winters.

By 1890 the cowtown had become a real town, with all the trappings of 19th-century success. Stores and businesses prospered along the main thoroughfare, Orange Avenue, and Orlando's first population boom was well under way. Even a minor freeze in 1886—a harbinger of larger disasters to come—had little effect on the growth of the citrus and real estate industries.

Those heady days ended soon enough. Another, more devastating freeze gripped central Florida during the winter of 1894-95, destroying crops and ruining growers' fortunes overnight. A gradual recovery eventually offset the losses, and citrus production continued to be an economic staple through the 1950s. But increasing urbanization and colder winters steadily pushed the industry south into warmer, more rural areas, and Orange County's once-abundant groves now are a distant memory.

In the waning years of the 1920s, growth had escalated to unsupportable levels and the local economy destabilized. A serious fruit fly infestation in

SeaWorld Orlando / Orlando/Orange County Convention & Visitors Bureau

1929 derailed the citrus business, leading to an eerily prophetic crash. As the boom ground to a halt, the Great Depression struck a heavy blow, leaving the city and its residents in dire financial straits.

World War II brought defense manufacturing and related businesses, helping to erase the effects of the Depression. But it was the postwar period that ushered in the region's most dynamic growth. Defense build-ups and the space race—the major fronts of the Cold War—soon became central Florida's primary industries. The Glenn L. Martin Co. (now Lockheed Martin Corp.) opened its first Orlando plant in 1957, bringing in hundreds of workers from the North and creating thousands of jobs for locals. The Kennedy Space Center soon followed, and the resulting economic activity spawned numerous supporting businesses, attracting a tremendous influx of new residents.

These developments were spurred in large part by the area's most rewarding transaction: Walt Disney's purchase of the land where he would build the Walt

Disney World Resort. When plans for developing the site were formally announced late in 1965, they fueled yet another land rush. Real estate prices skyrocketed as speculators bought their own piece of the action. In an unprecedented move, the state legislature granted the company the autonomy to rule itself. Disney promptly set up its own government within an area called the Reedy Creek Improvement District, complete with taxing privileges and municipal services.

The Magic Kingdom's price tag topped $400 million at its Oct. 1, 1971, opening. Though Disney himself was not alive to see it, the park quickly exceeded all expectations and remains one of the world's most popular destinations. In fact, Walt Disney World's allure helped make Orlando something of a theme park mecca. In the decades since the first guests walked through the turnstiles, such attractions as SeaWorld Orlando, Epcot, Disney-MGM Studios and Universal Orlando Resort have opened their gates to the visitors thronging Mickey Mouse's hometown. Gone are the quiet days of orange groves and rural simplicity.

Today Orlando is a far cry from the small Southern town it was in the 1840s. The perennial boomtown is well on its way to becoming a major international city. The Orlando International Airport has undergone a series of renovations and expansions that have made it an important transportation center. The Orlando Arena (renamed T.D. Waterhouse Centre in 2000) opened in 1989, mainly to serve as home court for the city's popular NBA team, the Orlando Magic. The area also has attracted new businesses, even as others like Lockheed Martin began to downsize.

With the coming of two major players in the entertainment market, Universal Studios and Disney-MGM Studios, Orlando has emerged as an up-and-coming center for the motion picture industry. Technology also remains a key component in Orlando's business picture. Although defense has taken a big hit, the high-tech fields of software, telecommunications, lasers and electro-optics are filling the gap.

Recent developments indicate that the city's growth shows no signs of ending any time soon. With the closure of the Naval Training Center, Orlandoans optimistically embraced conversion of the site to a residential development touting upscale living within minutes of downtown. The University of Central Florida (UCF), founded in 1968, continues to grow and now has one of the region's finest technology programs. Disney's planned residential community, Celebration, is patterned after the progressive village that Walt himself envisioned as the solution to modern urban problems.

Getting There

By Car

Orlando is laced with busy thoroughfares. Primary among these is I-4, a trans-Florida route that combines direct travel through the city with strategic controlled access. From the Daytona Beach area it

Visit Florida

The Informed Traveler

Sales Tax: In Osceola County the sales tax is 7 percent; in Orange County it is 6.5 percent; and in Lake and Seminole counties it is 7 percent. Orange and Osceola counties levy a 5 percent resort tax, while in Lake and Seminole counties the tax is 3 percent.

WHOM TO CALL

Emergency: 911

Police (non-emergency): (407) 246-2414; Sheriff (407) 737-2400

Fire: (407) 422-7121

Time and Temperature: (407) 646-3131

Hospitals: Florida Hospital, (407) 303-6611; Orlando Regional Medical Center, (407) 841-5111.

WHERE TO LOOK

Newspapers

The Orlando Sentinel is distributed in the morning. Friday's *Calendar* section summarizes the coming week's events.

Radio

Radio station WWNZ (740 AM) is an all-news/talk station; WDBO (580 AM) is an all-talk/weather station; WMFE (90.7) is a member of National Public Radio.

Visitor Information

Orlando/Orange County Convention & Visitors Bureau Official Visitor Center: 8723 International Dr., Orlando, FL 32819; phone (407) 363-5872 or (800) 551-0181.

The bureau distributes a variety of information daily 8-7.

Greater Orlando Chamber of Commerce: 75 S. Ivanhoe Blvd., Orlando, FL 32804; phone (407) 425-1234 Mon.-Fri. 8:30-5.

A free monthly magazine titled *See Orlando* is distributed at hotels and motels throughout the city.

WHAT TO PACK

Orlando is as renowned for its warm weather as for its theme parks. The winter months especially are a relief from colder climates, with lows generally in the 50s and highs in the 70s. Sudden cold snaps lend a certain unpredictability to central Florida winters, but these usually are short-lived.

Summer months tend to be hot and muggy, with temperatures routinely in the 90s. The intense humidity is alleviated many afternoons by brief thunderstorms. These sudden storms are the worst facet of Orlando's weather. (Note: Seek shelter indoors to wait out storms, as lightning strikes and pounding rain pose serious hazards, especially to the uninitiated driver. If you can't pull over safely, turn on your headlights and proceed with extreme caution.)

It is always a good idea to wear sunblock if you will be outdoors for any length of time, as the strong Florida sun can burn unprotected skin even on cool or overcast days. *For additional information see temperature chart p. 43.*

Comfort is the driving fashion force in Florida, and Orlando is a typically casual city. Shorts and sandals are acceptable in all but the most exclusive restaurants. Winters are fairly mild, but cold snaps necessitate sweaters, jackets or light coats from December through February.

A word to the wise: Warm temperatures outside often make for cold temperatures inside, as air conditioners are turned full blast against the summer heat.

Destination Orlando

*I*t all started with a mouse—the emergence of Orlando as everyone's favorite vacation destination, that is.

*O*nce a quiet town surrounded by citrus groves, Orlando was almost overnight transformed into a tourist mecca. Other attractions followed Mickey, and Orlando soon grew into a vibrant metropolitan area with world-class cultural offerings.

Richard Petty Driving Experience, Lake Buena Vista.
A variety of programs puts guests in the driver's seat. (See listing page 167)

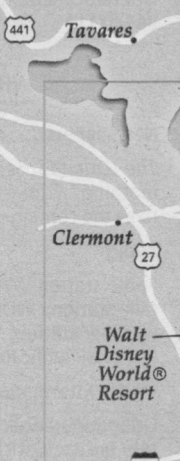

The Magic Kingdom® Park, Lake Buena Vista.
The only unsmiling face you'll see in this enchanted land will likely belong to Grumpy. (See listing page 173)

*P*laces included in this AAA Destination City:

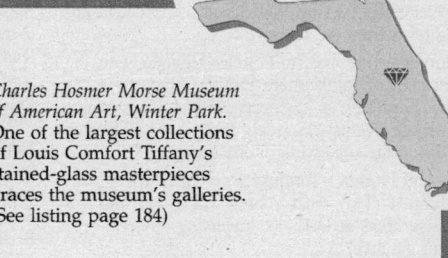

Charles Hosmer Morse Museum of American Art, Winter Park. One of the largest collections of Louis Comfort Tiffany's stained-glass masterpieces graces the museum's galleries. (See listing page 184)

Orange County Regional History Center, Orlando. From gators to space shuttles, the natural and cultural history of Central Florida is symbolized in this dome. (See listing page 154)

See Vicinity map page 151

Wet 'n Wild, Orlando. You can go wild on rides like Disco H_2O, or take it slow on the Lazy River float trip. (See listing page 158)

forks off I-95 and enters Orlando on the northeast side; from the Gulf Coast it comes from Tampa and St. Petersburg, passing Walt Disney World and entering town from the southwest.

Florida's Turnpike (toll) links Orlando with the resort areas of southeastern Florida. About 35 miles to the northwest it connects with I-75, a major north-south freeway. Florida's Turnpike interchanges with I-4 at the southwestern city limits.

I-4 and Florida's Turnpike form an X across central Florida. Two older routes, US 17/92 and US 441, also cross at Orlando, traversing different portions of the area.

SR 528, more commonly known as the Beachline Line Expressway (toll), passes south of the city. It channels traffic between Orlando and the Cape Canaveral area and connects with routes leading downtown.

SR 50 (Colonial Drive) is an east-west route that passes through downtown and connects smaller communities near the Gulf with Atlantic coast areas. To avoid traffic an alternative is SR 408, the East-West Expressway (toll), which links with SR 50 both east and west of downtown. The expressway also connects with the Central Florida Greeneway (SR 417) just south of SR 50. An expansion to the eastern terminus brings the toll road to US 17/92 in Sanford; other eastern and western expansions are planned and sections of the expressway may be undergoing construction.

SR 436 (Semoran Boulevard) swings in a wide northwesterly arc from the airport and Beachline Expressway southeast of town to US 441 northwest at Apopka and offers an alternative—although often busy—route to I-4.

Air Travel

The Orlando area is served by two airports: Orlando International Airport (OIA), at SR 436 and the Beachline Expressway, and Orlando Sanford Airport in Sanford, which serves commercial and private aircraft. OIA, about 15 miles from both downtown and the tourist district, is a primary destination for many major domestic and international airlines. Serving more than 26 million passengers in 2003, it is one of the world's fastest growing major airports. Its four satellite terminals are linked to the main terminal by automated people movers, making it easy to navigate. (**Note:** Orlando's tourist volume often leads to traffic congestion during peak vacation seasons. Allow plenty of transit time—coming and going—between the airport and your destination.)

To reach downtown Orlando, follow Airport Boulevard north as it merges into SR 436. Though heavily traveled, SR 436 offers direct access to central, east and north Orlando via SRs 50 or 408 (toll). To reach the International Drive area, take Airport Boulevard to SR 528 (toll), then head west to SR 482, which intersects International just east of I-4. Take Airport Boulevard south to SR 417 (toll) to go to the Disney resort via SR 536 or to reach Kissimmee via US 17/92/441.

Cab fares from the Orlando airport to downtown or International Drive average $36; limousines are approximately $90 plus a 20-percent tip to downtown and $115 to International Drive; shuttle vans are $15 one way, or $25 round trip; and public transportation is $1. Cab fare to the Disney resort averages $48. Many hotels and motels have courtesy car service.

Orlando is served by several major rental car agencies. Arrangements should be made before you depart, especially during peak seasons. Your local AAA club can provide this service or additional information. Hertz, (407) 859-8400 or (800) 654-3080, offers discounts to AAA members.

Rail Service

Amtrak provides train service to four stations in the metro area. Passenger-only trains stop at the stations at 1400 Sligh Blvd. in downtown Orlando and 150 W. Morse Blvd. in downtown Winter Park; Kissimmee's passenger station is at 111 Dakin St. The AutoTrain, which runs south from Lorton, VA, stops at the Sanford station at 800 Persimmon Ave. Phone (800) 872-7245 for both rail services.

Buses

A Greyhound Lines Inc. terminal, (407) 292-3422 for customer service, (407) 292-3424 for tickets, (800) 231-2222, or (800) 531-5332 for Spanish-speaking persons, is off West SR 50 (Colonial Drive) at 555 N. John Young Pkwy.

Getting Around

Street System

Because much of Orlando's growth occurred during the 1960s and '70s, the city is remarkably car-friendly. Roads are generally in good shape, although construction caused by near-constant expansion is a fact of life around the tourist district and downtown. Points of interest are usually on or near the main thoroughfares, most of which are accessible via I-4. For a small city, Orlando has surprisingly lengthy rush-hour periods, 6:30-9 a.m. and 4-6:30 p.m. Try to avoid traveling on I-4, US 17/92, SR 50 and SR 436 during these times.

Downtown Orlando is basically a grid, with several one-way streets. All street numbering begins at the intersection of Central Boulevard and Orange Avenue, the main strip through downtown. Orange is a one-way road south through the downtown core; its northbound counterpart is Rosalind Avenue. East-west roads accessing important downtown sites include Amelia Street (T.D. Waterhouse Centre), Livingston Street (Bob Carr Performing Arts Center, Expo Center), Robinson Street (Lake Eola), Central (Orlando Public Library, Lake Eola), Church Street (Downtown Farmer's Market) and South Street (City Hall).

International Drive, the heart of the tourist area, is south Orlando's busiest road. A profusion of hotels, shopping centers, outlet stores, restaurants, strolling vacationers and cruising teenagers usually combine to create crowded conditions and frequent delays.

Unless otherwise posted, the speed limit on most streets is 30 mph. Rush-hour traffic, 6:30 to 9 a.m. and 4 to 6:30 p.m., should be avoided. Unless otherwise posted, right turns are permitted on red after a complete stop.

Parking

Metered street parking downtown is available at 75¢ per hour, but spaces are generally hard to find at peak periods, which are on weekdays and weekend evenings. Downtown parking also is available in an open-air lot underneath I-4 on Garland Avenue between Central Boulevard and Pine Street.

Municipal garages can be found throughout downtown, including at Amelia Street, between Revere Street and Hughey Avenue; Church Street, between Division and Hughey avenues; Pine Street, between Garland and Orange avenues; Central Boulevard, between Garland and Orange avenues; and Central Boulevard, between Rosalind and Magnolia avenues. Rates range $1-$1.50 per half-hour or $12 per day.

Winter Park has free parking along Park Avenue, but spaces can be hard to come by during peak hours. Public lots are located just west of Park Avenue off New England Avenue, Morse Boulevard and Canton Avenue.

Most attractions and shopping centers have ample parking, but parking fees for the major theme parks

I-Ride Trolley / Orlando/Orange County CVB

can run as high as $8 per day. Check with your hotel to see if it offers free shuttle service to the theme parks.

Taxis and Limousines

Local taxis are metered and charge $3.50-$3.75 for the first mile, $2 for each additional mile. Major cab companies are Ace Metro, (407) 855-0564; Checker, (407) 699-9999; City, (407) 422-5151; and Yellow, (407) 422-4455.

Limousine service is available throughout most of the city; the ride from the airport to downtown Orlando or International Drive is about $90 plus a 20-percent tip, and $115 to International Drive.

Public Transportation

Brightly painted buses are a colorful sight in the metro area, thanks to LYNX, the transit authority for Orange, Osceola and Seminole counties, which operates more than 200 buses on 50-plus routes.

Bus stops, called Links, are marked by fuchsia paw-print signs listing all the routes that are immediately accessible from that stop. The system serves most of the city, including downtown, the tourist district and major shopping centers. Main routes are 4, between south Orlando and Kissimmee; 10, through Kissimmee; 38, downtown to the International Drive area; 41, between SR 436 and the airport; 42, between International Drive and the airport; and 50, between downtown to the Walt Disney World Resort.

I-Ride Trolleys cater exclusively to tourist traffic along International Drive 8 a.m.-10:30 p.m.; the wait is 15 minutes. Trolley fare is 75¢; over 65, 25¢; under 12 free with adult. LYNX also offers Lymmo, a free bus service that uses a bus-only lane to transport passengers throughout the downtown area, including stops at city hall and T.D. Waterhouse Centre. Lymmo runs Mon.-Thurs. 6 a.m.-10 p.m., Fri. 6 a.m.-midnight, Sat. 10-midnight, Sun. 10-10.

LYNX fare is $1.50; transfers are free. Exact change is required. Buses run Mon.-Fri. 4:15 a.m.-3:05 a.m., Sat. 4:45-a.m.-1:05 a.m., Sun. 4:45 a.m.-10:35 p.m.; holiday schedules may vary. For additional information about routes and schedules phone (407) 841-8240.

What To See

DISCOVERY COVE ORLANDO is at 6000 Discovery Cove Way next to SeaWorld Orlando. The all-inclusive park allows visitors, at their own pace, to encounter a variety of animals up-close and in a lush island resort setting.

Three beautiful lagoons are home to playful dolphins with which guests, under the supervision of trainers, can swim and have their pictures taken. An artificial reef beckons snorkelers with its realistic coral and colorful tropical fish. Nearby, swimmers, protected by clear underwater partitions, come face-to-face with sharks and barracudas. A tropical river allows guests to float through a free-flight aviary where they can hand-feed exotic birds. Stingrays, sloths and anteaters are among the other touchable creatures at the park.

Allow a full day. Daily 9-5:30, Mar.-Oct.; schedule varies rest of year. Admission, including dolphin swim, $239-$269 (depending on the season); without dolphin swim, $139-$169 (depending on the season); under age 3 free. Prices may vary; phone ahead. Admission to Discovery Cove Orlando also includes 7 consecutive days admission to SeaWorld Orlando or Busch Gardens Tampa Bay, lunch and all swim gear. Guests may upgrade to a 14-day combination pass for unlimited admission to SeaWorld Orlando and Busch Gardens Tampa Bay for $30. Children under 6 are not permitted to interact with the dolphins. Reservations are required. AX, DS, MC, VI. Phone (877) 877-9455. *See color ad p. 152.*

DIXIE STAMPEDE DINNER & SHOW is off I-4 exit 68, .2 mi. e. on SR 535, then 1 mi. n. to 8251 Vineland Ave. The main show celebrates America through lively vignettes depicting life in the North and the South, during which the audience participates in a friendly regional rivalry. Entertainment includes a buffalo stampede; horseback competitions, trick riding feats and graceful equestrian drills; musical performances; comedy routines; and chicken, pig and ostrich races. The show concludes with a patriotic musical finale written by Dolly Parton. A four-course feast is served during the show.

Live entertainment in the Carriage Room precedes the main show. Before entering the building, guests can stroll along a covered walkway and view the horses in open stables. Allow 3 hours minimum. Performances daily; schedule varies. Carriage Room show begins 1 hour before main show. Admission $46.99; ages 3-11, $19.99. Under 3 on adult's lap free. AX, DS, MC, VI. Phone (407) 238-4455 or (866) 443-4943.

EPCOT—*see Lake Buena Vista p. 172.*

GATORLAND is 6 mi. s. of the Beachline Expwy. (SR 528) on US 17/92/441 at 14501 S. Orange Blossom Tr. Opened as a roadside attraction in 1949, the 110-acre park and wildlife preserve is home to thousands of alligators, crocodiles, snakes and other reptiles. Highlights include a children's petting zoo, a train ride, an aviary and a breeding marsh with observation tower. Daily shows include Gator Wrestlin', Gator Jumparoo, Jungle Crocs of the World and Up-Close Encounters.

Food is available. Allow 3 hours minimum. Daily 9-5. Closing times may vary; phone ahead. Admission $19.95; ages 3-12, $9.95. AX, DS, MC, VI. Phone (407) 855-5496 or (800) 393-5297.

HARRY P. LEU GARDENS is at 1920 N. Forest Ave.; I-4 exit 85 to Princeton Ave., s. on Mills Ave., then .5 mi. e. via Virginia Dr. The 50-acre botanical garden feature camellias, roses, a home demonstration garden, vegetable and herb plots, a butterfly garden and a tropical stream garden with a large banana tree collection. The Leu House Museum, dating from the 1880s, can be viewed by guided tour. Allow 1 hour, 30 minutes minimum. Gardens open daily 9-5; closed Dec. 25. House tours are given

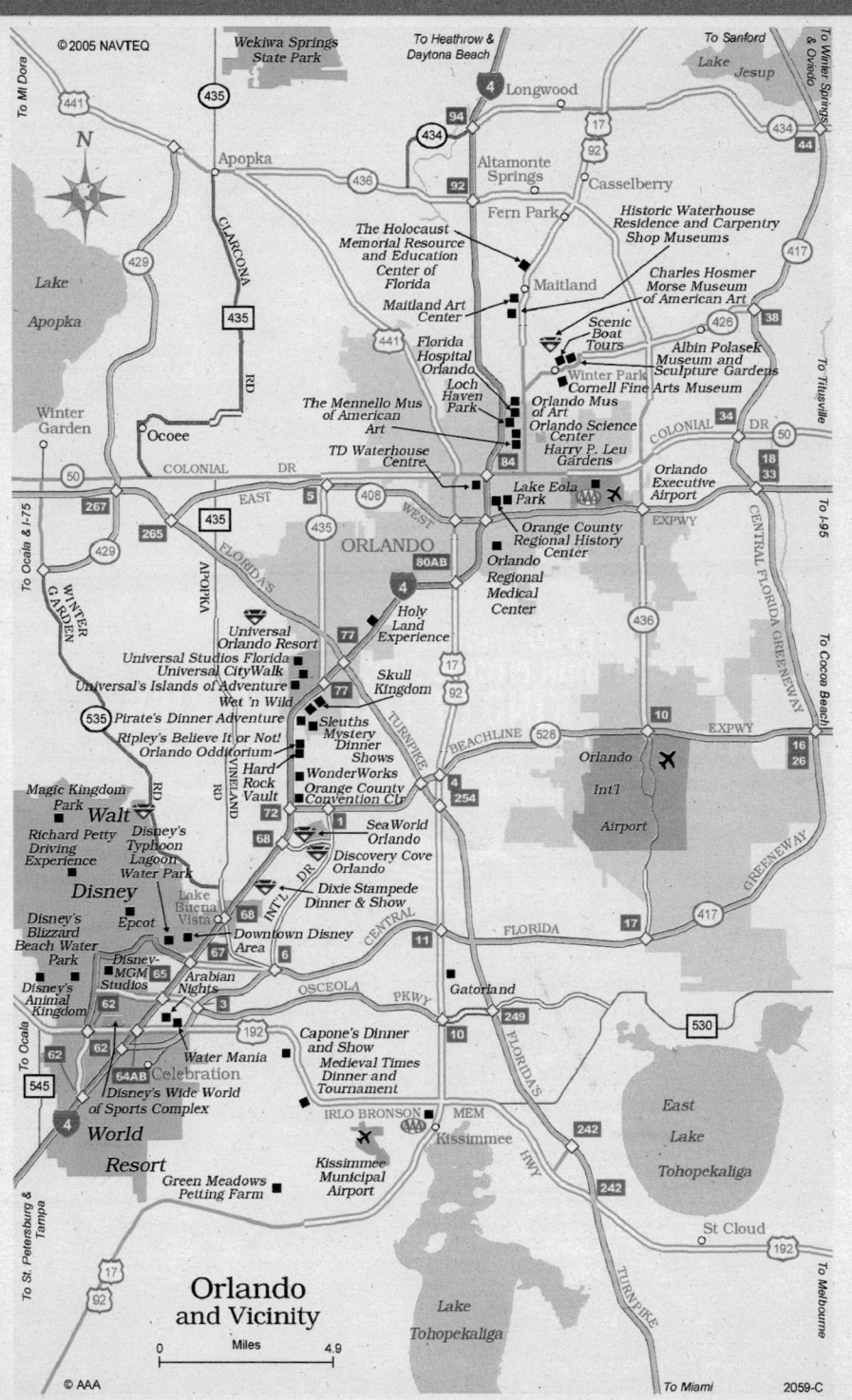

© 2005 NAVTEQ

To Mt Dora
To Heathrow &
Daytona Beach
To Sanford
To Winter Springs
& Oviedo

Wekiwa Springs
State Park

Longwood

Lake
Jesup

Apopka

Altamonte
Springs

Casselberry

Fern Park

Lake
Apopka

The Holocaust
Memorial Resource
and Education
Center of
Florida

Historic Waterhouse
Residence and Carpentry
Shop Museums

Maitland

Charles Hosmer
Morse Museum
of American Art

Maitland Art
Center

Scenic
Boat
Tours

Winter
Garden

Florida
Hospital
Orlando

Ocoee

The Mennello Mus
of American
Art

Loch
Haven
Park

Albin Polasek
Museum and
Sculpture Gardens

Winter Park

Cornell Fine Arts Museum

Orlando Mus
of Art

Orlando Science
Center

TD Waterhouse
Centre

Harry P. Leu
Gardens

COLONIAL

DR

ORLANDO

Orlando
Executive
Airport

Lake Eola
Park

Orange County
Regional History
Center

Orlando
Regional
Medical
Center

EXPWY

Holy
Land
Experience

Universal
Orlando Resort

Skull
Kingdom

Universal Studios Florida
Universal CityWalk
Universal's Islands of Adventure
Wet 'n Wild

Sleuths
Mystery
Dinner
Shows

Pirate's Dinner Adventure
Ripley's Believe It or Not!
Orlando Odditorium

WonderWorks

Orange County
Convention Ctr

Hard
Rock
Vault

Orlando
Int'l
Airport

Magic Kingdom
Park

SeaWorld
Orlando

Walt

Richard Petty
Driving
Experience

Disney's
Typhoon
Lagoon
Water Park

Discovery Cove
Orlando

Disney

Lake
Buena
Vista

Dixie Stampede
Dinner & Show

Epcot

Disney's
Blizzard
Beach Water
Park

Downtown Disney
Area

Disney-
MGM
Studios

Arabian
Nights

Disney's
Animal
Kingdom

Gatorland

Water Mania

Capone's Dinner
and Show

World

Celebration

Medieval Times
Dinner and
Tournament

East
Lake
Tohopekaliga

Disney's Wide World
of Sports Complex

IRLO BRONSON

MEM

Resort

Kissimmee

Kissimmee
Municipal
Airport

St Cloud

Green Meadows
Petting Farm

Orlando
and Vicinity

0   Miles   4.9

Lake
Tohopekaliga

To Miami

2059-C

© AAA

THEY COMMUNICATE THROUGH
A SERIES OF HIGH PITCHED SQUEAKS.
KIND OF LIKE YOUR KIDS.

COME TO DISCOVERY COVE IN ORLANDO, where you can swim with dolphins, snorkel with thousands of tropical fish or simply relax on our pristine beaches. For the daylong adventure that will stay with you and your family for a lifetime, visit DiscoveryCove.com, call I-877-4-DISCOVERY or purchase your Discovery Cove admission package at participating AAA offices.

DISCOVERY COVE
ORLANDO
The memory that never fades.

daily 10-3:30. Reservations are required for guided garden tours. Admission $5; ages 5-17, $1. Phone (407) 246-2620.

HOLY LAND EXPERIENCE, off I-4 exit 78 (Conroy Rd.), then just w. to 4655 Vineland Rd., is a recreation of Jerusalem at the time of Christ. Exhibits and live musical performances are offered. Allow 4 hours minimum. Mon.-Fri. 10-5, Sat. 9-6, Sun. noon-6. Hours vary; phone ahead. Admission $29.99; ages 6-12, $19.99. AX, DS, MC, VI. Phone (407) 367-2065 or (866) 872-4659. *See color ad p. 153.*

LAKE EOLA PARK, 3 blks. from the center of town on E. Central Blvd., has stately trees and flowering plants and shrubs. In the center of Lake Eola is the colorfully lighted Clinton Allen Fountain. The park also has swan paddleboats and a playground. Food is available. Playground open daily 8 a.m.-11 p.m. Paddleboats daily noon-dusk. Park and playground free. Paddleboats $12 per half-hour (three people per boat). Phone (407) 246-2827 for the park or (407) 232-0111 for paddleboat information.

LOCH HAVEN PARK, bounded by Mills (US 17/92) and Orange aves. and bisected by Princeton St., contains three museums and a theater. The Orlando Repertory Theatre stages productions. Phone (407) 896-7365.

SAVE **The Mennello Museum of American Art** is at 900 E. Princeton St. next to the Orlando Science Center's parking garage. The museum houses a permanent collection of the works of Earl Cunningham, a prominent 20th-century American

folk artist. Traveling exhibits also are featured. Allow 30 minutes minimum. Tues.-Sat. 10:30-4:30, Sun. noon-4:30; closed holidays. Admission $4; over 60, $3; students with ID $1; under 12 free. Phone (407) 246-4278.

Orlando Museum of Art, 2416 N. Mills Ave., maintains permanent collections of American and African art, including art of the ancient Americas. Also featured are changing exhibits, a discovery center and hands-on family activities. Allow 1 hour minimum. Tues.-Fri. 10-4, Sat.-Sun. noon-4; closed holidays. Admission $8; over 55 and college students with ID $7; ages 6-18, $5. Phone (407) 896-4231.

SAVE **Orlando Science Center,** 777 E. Princeton St., features hundreds of hands-on exhibits. Visitors can journey through the human body, encounter Florida wildlife, unearth dinosaur mysteries and gaze at stars in the observatory. Large-format films and planetarium shows can be viewed in the eight-story CineDome.

Allow 2 hours minimum. Mon.-Thurs. 9-5, Fri.-Sat. 9-9, Sun. noon-5, Memorial Day to mid-Aug.; Tues.-Thurs. and Mon. school holidays 9-5, Fri-Sat. 9-9, Sun. noon-5, rest of year. Closed Easter, Thanksgiving and Dec. 25. Admission $14.95; over 54 and students with ID $13.95; ages 3-11, $9.95. Reduced admission Fri.-Sat. after 6 p.m. Parking $3.50. Phone (407) 514-2000 or (888) 672-4386.

SAVE **ORANGE COUNTY REGIONAL HISTORY CENTER,** 65 E. Central Blvd., offers permanent and special exhibits tracing the area's history from 12,000 years ago to the present. In the orientation theater, visitors view a 15-minute audiovisual presentation from rocking chairs on a "Florida back porch." Other features include a Florida Cracker-style pioneer cabin, a tin-can tourist camp, a re-created Seminole Indian village and interactive displays about Florida industries.

Allow 1 hour, 30 minutes minimum. Mon.-Sat. 11-5, Sun. noon-5; closed holidays. Admission $7; over 59 and students with ID $6.50; ages 3-12, $3.50. MC, VI. Phone (407) 836-8500 or (800) 965-2030. *See color ad p. 164.*

PIRATE'S DINNER ADVENTURE is .25 mi. s. of International Dr. at 6400 Carrier Dr. Guests at this interactive dinner show enjoy a feast while musical comedy, swashbuckling stunts and live-action performances take place aboard a pirate galleon. After the show, guests may attend the Buccaneer Bash dance party and visit the Pirate's Maritime Museum. Evening shows daily; phone for performance times and matinee information. Admission $49.95; ages 3-11, $29.95. Reservations are recommended. AX, CB, DS, MC, VI. Phone (407) 248-0590 or (800) 866-2469.

SAVE **RIPLEY'S BELIEVE IT OR NOT! ORLANDO ODDITORIUM** is .5 mi. s.e. of I-4 exit 74A (Sand Lake Rd.) at 8201 International Dr. Odd and unusual exhibits and video presentations from around the world are featured in 16 themed galleries that include interactive illusions, human and animal oddities, weird

Gatorland / © David Sanger / Alamy Images

art and dinosaurs and fossils. Allow 1 hour minimum. Daily 9 a.m.-1 a.m. Last admission 1 hour before closing. Admission $16.95; ages 4-12, $11.95. AX, DS, MC, VI. Phone (407) 345-0501 or (800) 998-4418, ext. 3.

SEAWORLD ORLANDO is at 7007 Sea World Dr., at jct. I-4 and SR 528 (Beachline Expwy.). This marine life adventure park has sea-themed shows and up-close animal encounters, attractions and rides, including Kraken, a floorless roller coaster, and Journey to Atlantis, a water coaster thrill ride. A simulated helicopter ride takes visitors to Wild Arctic, where whales, walruses and polar bears coexist.

Waterfront at SeaWorld is a 5-acre neighborhood with entertainment, dining and shopping. Shows include Blue Horizons, showcasing animals, performers and exotic birds in a Broadway-style production; Odyssea, a .5-hour spectacular with acrobatic feats and special effects; Pets Ahoy; Clyde and Seamore Take Pirate Island; and The Shamu Adventure.

Key West at SeaWorld has live entertainment and sea turtles, and visitors can feed dolphins and stingrays. Manatees: The Last Generation? explores the endangered creatures' world, and California sea lions and seals reside at Pacific Point Preserve.

Shamu's Happy Harbor; Penguin Encounter; Dolphin Nursery; Tropical Reef; Shark Encounter; and The Anheuser-Busch Hospitality Center are other features. The 5.5- to 6-hour Adventure Express offers reserved seating at certain shows; back-door access to rides; animal feedings; and a tour guide.

Several other guided tours are offered. Kennels, strollers, lockers and wheelchair rentals are available. Allow a full day. Park generally opens daily at 9; closing times vary. Last admission 1 hour before closing.

Admission $61.75; ages 3-9, $49.95. There is an additional fee for Adventure Express tours. Parking $8 for automobiles, $9 for recreational vehicles or campers, $10 for preferred parking. AAA members save on Luau dining. Reservations are required; visit Guest Relations for details. AX, DS, MC, VI. Phone (888) 800-5447.

SKULL KINGDOM, off I-4 exit 75A at 5933 American Way, is a haunted castle complete with special effects and robotics as well as night creatures and fiends. Sudden encounters and gruesome scenes await visitors as they make their way through two floors of mazes and caverns. Daily noon-11, July-Aug. and major holidays; Mon.-Fri. 6 p.m.-11 p.m., Sat.-Sun. noon-11, rest of year. Admission $14.95. Not recommended for under 8. AX, CB, DS, JC, MC, VI. Phone (407) 354-1564.

SLEUTHS MYSTERY DINNER SHOWS is 8267 International Dr. Guests become detectives to help solve a crime in these comedy-mystery dinner shows. Allow 3 hours minimum. Shows daily

at 7:30; phone for additional seatings. Show times vary; phone ahead. Tickets $44.95; ages 3-11, $24.95. Reservations are required. AX, DC, DS, MC, VI. Phone (407) 363-1985 or (800) 393-1985.

SAVE **TITANIC—THE EXHIBITION,** 8445 International Dr. in The Mercado, features re-created ship interiors, more than 200 artifacts, movie memorabilia and interactive tours. Allow 1 hour minimum. Daily 10-8. Admission $17.95; ages 6-12, $12.95. AX, MC, VI. Phone (407) 248-1166.

GEM **UNIVERSAL ORLANDO RESORT** is off I-4 exit 75A (eastbound) or 74B (westbound). The resort brings movies to life through rides and shows at Universal Studios, visits the universe of myths, legends and superheroes at Universal's Islands of Adventure, and offers Universal CityWalk for shopping, dining and nighttime entertainment.

The theme parks, entertainment complex and on-site hotels are within walking distance of each other. All shopping, dining and entertainment facilities also are available to day guests. Because of the popularity of the parks, large crowds and long lines can be expected, especially during holiday periods.

Strollers, wheelchairs and electric carts can be rented. Kennels are available. The theme parks open daily at 9; closing hours vary by season. Universal CityWalk open daily 11 a.m.-2 a.m. CityWalk hours may vary; phone ahead.

A 1-day ticket to either Universal Studios or Universal's Islands of Adventure is $63; ages 3-9, $52. Two- and 3-day tickets provide unlimited admission to both parks on the same day. Multi-day tickets also include access to all clubs at Universal CityWalk. Two-day ticket $107.95; ages 3-9, $97.95. Three-day ticket $122.95; ages 3-9, $112.95. Most multi-day tickets do not expire until all days are used. Parking $9; valet parking $16. Discounted tickets are available at participating AAA offices. See page 18 for more information. AX, DS, MC, VI. Phone (407) 363-8000.

Universal CityWalk, off I-4 exit 75A (eastbound) or 74B (westbound), is an entertainment complex featuring dining in themed restaurants, nightclubs, specialty shopping and a 20-screen movie theater. Live performances at restaurants and clubs are evening highlights. Daily 11 a.m.-2 a.m. Hours may vary; phone ahead. Admission to CityWalk complex free. Evening cover charges vary by club. A pass covering evening admission to all clubs is $9.95, or $13 with movie admission included. Parking free at the Universal Orlando lot after 6 p.m. (excluding valet parking). Members save 10 percent on dining and souvenirs at select restaurants. AX, DS, MC, VI. Phone (407) 363-8000.

SAVE **UNIVERSAL'S ISLANDS OF ADVENTURE,** off I-4 exit 74B (westbound) or 75A (eastbound), has five themed islands with thrill rides and attractions.

Marvel Super Hero Island includes the 3-D thrill ride The Amazing Adventures of Spider-Man, the Incredible Hulk Coaster and the gravity-defying Doctor Doom's Fearfall. Toon Lagoon's attractions are based on cartoons and comic strips, such as Dudley Do-Right's Ripsaw Falls log flume ride and Popeye & Bluto's Bilge-Rat Barges white-water raft ride.

Jurassic Park re-creates a land inhabited by prehistoric creatures. Jurassic Park River Adventure, a raft ride through dinosaur habitats, features a T-Rex on the loose. Unearth mysteries from the past at Jurassic Park Discovery Center. Camp Jurassic is an interactive play area, and Pteranodon Flyers offers kids a prehistoric birds-eye view.

The Lost Continent features the inverted double roller coasters Dueling Dragons and the Eighth Voyage of Sindbad stunt show. Theodor "Dr. Seuss" Geisel's characters come to life at Seuss Landing. The Cat In The Hat takes visitors on a ride through the childhood classic, and a menagerie of characters serves as steeds on the Caro-Seuss-el. Other areas include the If I Ran The Zoo play area and the One Fish, Two Fish, Red Fish, Blue Fish ride.

Allow a full day. Park opens daily at 9; closing hours vary according to season. One-day admission $63; ages 3-9, $52. Parking $9; valet parking $16. Discounted tickets available at participating AAA offices. Members save 10 percent on in-park dining and souvenirs (excludes food or merchandise carts, tobacco, candy, film, collectibles, clearance

and sundry items). AX, DS, MC, VI. Phone (407) 363-8000.

UNIVERSAL STUDIOS, off I-4 exit 75A (eastbound) or 74B (westbound), takes visitors into the worlds of movies and television. The theme park, also a working television and motion picture production studio, has a back lot, sound stages and realistic street sets.

Fear Factor Live, based on the reality TV show, allows audience participation. Riders are plunged into darkness in Revenge of the Mummy the Ride, and Ogrevision lets guests see, hear and feel the action in Shrek 4-D. The interactive ride Men in Black Alien Attack allows visitors to save the galaxy by zapping creatures as the ride moves through city streets.

Terminator 2: 3-D is a futuristic mix of live action and 3-D film. Visitors hurtle through time and space in Back to the Future the Ride and come face-to-face with a tornado in Twister. . .Ride It Out.

Jimmy Neutron's Nicktoon Blast takes visitors on a wild chase through favorite cartoons, including "SpongeBob SquarePants" and "Rugrats." Woody Woodpecker's KidZone features the Curious George Goes to Town play area, Woody Woodpecker's Nuthouse Coaster and E.T. Adventure.

Allow a full day. Park opens daily at 9; closing hours vary according to season. One-day admission $63; ages 3-9, $52. Parking $9; valet parking $16. Discounted tickets available at participating AAA offices. Members save 10 percent on in-park dining and souvenirs (excludes food or merchandise carts, tobacco, candy, film, collectibles, clearance and sundry items). AX, DS, MC, VI. Phone (407) 363-8000.

Suess Landing, Universal's Islands of Adventure
Orlando/Orange County CVB

WALT DISNEY WORLD® RESORT—
see Lake Buena Vista p. 167.

WET 'N WILD is off I-4 exit 75A at 6200 International Dr. This water recreation park features a variety of water rides and activity pools. Highlights include Disco H20, a raft adventure accompanied by 1970s music; The Blast, a twisting tubing course that propels riders along at intervals with gusts of water; and Lazy River, a float journey to bubbling springs.

Picnicking is permitted. Food, locker rooms and showers are available. Bathing suits are required—no shorts, cutoffs or items with metal fasteners, rivets, zippers or buckles are permitted. Allow 6 hours minimum. Open daily at 9, early June-late July and late Mar.-early Apr.; at 9:30, late May-early June and early Aug.-early Sept.; at 10, rest of year. Closing times vary; phone ahead.

Admission $33.95; ages 3-9, $27.95; over 55, $16.98. Parking $6; recreational vehicles $7. Lockers $7. AX, DS, MC, VI. Phone (407) 351-1800 or (800) 992-9453.

WONDERWORKS is .8 mi. n. of SR 528 at 9067 International Dr. An upside-down building contains this interactive attraction, which features more than 100 hands-on exhibits and a laser tag arena. Virtual reality technology and simulations enable visitors to experience an earthquake and hurricane force winds, design and ride their own roller-coaster, walk away from their shadow, swim with sharks and lay on a bed of nails.

Food is available. Allow 1 hour minimum. Daily 9 a.m.-midnight. Admission $17.95; over 55 and ages 4-12, $12.95. Laser tag is additional. Fee for parking. AX, DS, MC, VI. Phone (407) 351-8800.

What To Do

Sightseeing

Bus, Carriage, Limousine or Train Tours

Guided tours are a good way to make the best use of time in Orlando. Gator Tours, (407) 522-5911 or (800) 537-0917, offers day and overnight narrated tours, with pickup at your lodging.

Spectator Sports

From downtown Orlando to Walt Disney World Resort, fans have several venues to choose from when it comes to the city's various professional sports offerings. Orlando's premier sports arena, **T.D. Waterhouse Centre,** 600 W. Amelia St., hosts arena football, basketball and hockey games.

Baseball

Disney's Wide World of Sports® Complex, Osceola Parkway and Victory Way, is the spring training home of the **Atlanta Braves.** For game schedules and ticket information phone (407) 939-1500.

Osceola County Stadium, 1000 Bill Beck Blvd. in Kissimmee, is the site of the **Houston Astros** spring training camp.

Basketball

Orlando basketball enthusiasts root for their home team, the NBA's **Orlando Magic.** Fans can attend games at T.D. Waterhouse Centre. The city's two colleges also have basketball teams. For schedule and ticket information phone the Orlando Magic, (407) 916-2400; Rollins College, (407) 646-2663, in Winter Park; and the University of Central Florida Arena, (407) 823-6006, in Orlando.

Football

The **Florida Citrus Bowl** hosts college football games, including the annual Capital One Bowl, the Mazda Tangerine Bowl and home games for the Division I **UCF Knights.** The city has an arena football team, the **Orlando Predators,** who were league champions in 1998 and 2000; games are played in the T.D. Waterhouse Centre downtown.

Greyhound Racing

Dog racing is a year-round diversion. **Sanford-Orlando Kennel Club,** (407) 831-1600, at 301 Dog Track Rd. in Longwood, holds matinee and evening races.

Note: Policies concerning admittance of children to pari-mutuel betting facilities vary. Phone for information.

Hockey

The **Florida Seals,** members of the Atlantic Coast Hockey League, play in the Kissimmee's Silver Spurs Arena. For schedule and ticket information phone (321) 939-2465.

Jai-Alai

Played in only a few states, jai-alai is one of Orlando's most unusual offerings. The game is similar to handball, except the athletes field the ball not with their bare hands, but with a curved basket worn on one arm. Pari-mutuel betting adds to the excitement of this fast-paced sport at **Orlando-Seminole Jai-Alai Fronton,** (407) 339-6221, in Fern Park on US 17/92. The live jai-alai season in Orlando is January through March, although the facility is open year-round for televised jai-alai and racing events.

Note: Policies concerning admittance of children to pari-mutuel betting facilities vary. Phone for information.

Recreation

Lengthy summers and mild winters create ideal recreation conditions in central Florida year-round, and locals make the most of it. The area's many waterways host a wide variety of activities, and drier pastimes abound as well. Phone the Orange County Parks & Recreation Department 24-Hour Parks Info-Line, (407) 836-6280, for more information.

Bicycling

Although bicycling is growing in popularity in Orlando, there are few dedicated bike paths in the city, and traffic is always a concern. Exercise caution and obey all traffic laws when bicycling on the street. If possible, ride in a park—both **Turkey Lake** and **Lake Underhill** parks offer trails—or other specially designated area. Locals enjoy the **Cady Way Trail,** running 3.5 miles from the Fashion Square Mall on SR 50 to Cady Way in Winter Park, as well as the quiet, tree-lined streets of **Rollins College, College Park** and **downtown Orlando.**

Wet 'n Wild / Orlando/Orange County CVB

The **Walt Disney World Resort** offers a variety of trails as well as bicycle rentals.

Fishing

With hundreds of lakes and several rivers to choose from, anglers will have no problem finding a place to cast their lines—bass, bream and catfish are among the available catches. Some favorite spots are **Gaston Edwards Park** on Lake Ivanhoe near downtown; **Lake Fairview,** north of College Park; Lake Underhill Park, east of town off Conway Road; **Lake Cane/Marsha Park** and **Turkey Lake Park,** both just off Conroy-Windermere Rd.; **Wekiwa Springs State Park,** on SR 435 in northwest Orange County; and **Lake Tohopekaliga** in Kissimmee, south of US 192. The Walt Disney World complex also affords angling opportunities for tourists and residents alike. A freshwater license is required for those age 16 or older; phone Fisheries Management, (407) 846-5300, for additional details.

Deep-sea fishing is a popular pastime, and charters are available in many beachfront towns. Anglers age 16 and over must purchase saltwater licenses, which are available at many bait and tackle shops, most Wal-Marts and Kmarts and at all tax assessors' offices. For further information phone the Florida Fish and Wildlife Conservation Commission, (850) 488-6058.

Golf

Golf is a way of life for many Orlando residents; an abundance of courses—more than 150—graces the metropolitan area, from the city-bound links of small municipal properties to the spectacular settings of the luxury resorts. All of the following courses offer at least 18 holes and are open to the public year round: Casselberry Golf Club, (407) 699-9310, 300 S. Triplet Lake Dr.; Celebration Golf Club, (407) 566-4653, 701 Golf Park Dr.; Dubsdread, (407) 246-2551, 549 W. Par St.; Eastwood Golf Club, (407) 281-4653, 13950 Golfway Blvd.; Hunter's Creek, (407) 240-4653, 14401 Sports Club Way; Mayfair Country Club, (407) 322-2531, in Sanford; MetroWest Country Club, (407) 299-1099, 2100 S. Hiawassee Rd.; Stoneybrook Orlando, (407) 384-6888, 2900 Northampton Ave.; Walt Disney World Golf Complex, (407) 939-4653, in Lake Buena Vista; and Wedgefield Golf and Country Club, (407) 568-2116, 20550 Maxim Pkwy.

Hot Air Ballooning

[SAVE] **Blue Water Balloons,** (407) 894-5040, **Bob's Balloon Charters,** (407) 466-6380, and **Orange Blossom Balloons,** (407) 239-7677, offer aerial views of the Orlando area via hot air balloons. Some scenic trips include breakfast and champagne.

Jogging and Walking

Orlando also boasts two scenic, paved recreation trails built on old railway beds. Both provide opportunities for walking and jogging. The 22.5-mile **West Orange Trail** runs between the Lake/Orange county line through abandoned orange groves to Apopka. For information contact the Orange County Parks and Recreation Department at (407) 654-1108. Closer to downtown Orlando, the 3.5-mile Cady Way Trail connects Winter Park to Fashion Square

Orlando/Orange County CVB

Mall. For information contact the Transportation Planning Bureau (407) 246-2775.

One can walk or jog just about anywhere in central Florida, but the following spots are exceptionally nice. Downtown Orlando features **Lake Eola,** noted for Centennial Fountain, as well as **Langford Park** on Central Boulevard. Just outside downtown

are College Park's charming streets and the serene oasis of Lake Ivanhoe's **Gaston Edwards Park. Winter Park** is a good place for a stroll, particularly along popular **Park Avenue** or on the **Rollins College** campus. Other appealing sites include **Mead Gardens** and **Kraft Azalea Gardens and Park** in Winter Park. Due to the relentless Florida sun, early morning and late afternoon are the best times for either activity.

Tennis

Tennis courts are nearly as numerous as lakes in metropolitan Orlando, with more than 800 throughout the area. Many hotels offer court privileges to their guests. The courts at county parks are always open to the general public; for further details phone the City of Orlando Recreation Bureau, (407) 246-2288, or the Orange County Parks and Recreation Department, (407) 836-6200. Some resorts offer public access, including **Cypress Creek Country Club** at 5353 S. Vineland Rd., (407) 351-2187; the **Grand Cypress Racquet Club,** 55 Grand Cypress Blvd., (407) 239-1944; and Kissimmee's **Poinciana Golf & Racquet Resort,** 500 E. Cypress Pkwy., (407) 933-5300.

Water Sports

The abundance of lakes in central Florida—more than 2,000 by some counts—provides endless opportunities for water sports of all kinds, including boating, canoeing, swimming, water skiing and windsurfing. Some of the most popular sites include Lake Underhill; Lake Ivanhoe; and the **Butler Chain of Lakes** and **Winter Park Chain of Lakes.** For information about the Butler Chain of Lakes contact the Orange County Parks and Recreation Department at (407) 246-2238; for information about the Winter Park Chain of Lakes, phone (407) 599-3334; or phone the City of Orlando Aquatics Department at (407) 246-2288.

Just north of Orlando near Apopka is Wekiwa Springs State Park *(see Recreation Chart and the AAA Southeastern CampBook),* where swimming in the crystal clear spring water is popular. The Wekiva River is considered one of the state's best canoeing rivers; canoe rental information is available at the marina, (407) 884-2008.

Boating is a favorite recreation; residents have their choice of several inland waterways to explore. The Butler and Winter Park Chain of Lakes are groupings of connected lakes. The Rollins College campus and beautiful homes line the shores of the lakes in Winter Park's chain, and boat tours are available *(see place listing p. 184).* Another active waterway, the **St. Johns River,** connects nearby Sanford with

Jacksonville and boat tours are available *(see De-Land p. 56)*. Houseboats can be rented on a daily basis in DeLand, allowing visitors to navigate the river in style.

Shopping

With an influx of tourists from all over the world, Orlando's shopping areas must satisfy a variety of tastes and styles. From high fashion and international selections to famous labels at bargain-hunter prices, Orlando has them. Weather-related items such as lightweight sportswear and swimsuits are stocked all year, and area citrus products are sold at many roadside stands.

Antiques

The best antiquing downtown is in the **North Orange Avenue Antiques District,** running south from the 2900 block to the 1600 block. This funky strip is lined with stores selling everything from 1930s radios to 19th-century furniture to housewares from the 1950s and '60s. Particularly charming is a little cluster of buildings known as **Ivanhoe Row,** along the 1200 block across from Lake Ivanhoe. The College Park section of **Edgewater Drive** and **Fairbanks Avenue** east of I-4 also have a number of antiques dealers. Pricier items can be found at the shops along **Park Avenue** in Winter Park.

Malls

In south Orlando, the massive **Florida Mall,** 8001 S. Orange Blossom Tr., boasts more than 200 shops and a bustling food court anchored by such major retailers as Dillard's, JCPenney, Nordstrom, Saks Fifth Avenue and Sears. Chanel, Gucci, Macy's and Neiman Marcus are among the upscale tenants of **The Mall at Millenia,** off I-4 at 4200 Conroy Rd., which includes more than 150 shops, services and restaurants. Northeast of downtown is **Orlando Fashion Square Mall,** 3201 E. Colonial Dr., featuring Dillard's, JCPenney, Macy's, Sears, a second-floor food court and 165 smaller stores, including such mall standards as The Limited and the Gap. **Altamonte Mall,** 451 E. Altamonte Dr., offers four anchors—Dillard's, JCPenney, Macy's and Sears—along with a food court and two floors containing 175 boutiques from the Banana Republic to the Body Shop.

Sanford's **Seminole Towne Center,** 200 Towne Center Cir., is the northernmost of the area malls. It has about 120 shops, a food court and five department stores: Dillard's, JCPenney, McRae's, Macy's and Sears. East of Orlando is the **Oviedo Marketplace** with Dillard's, Macy's and Sears. West of downtown, **West Oaks Mall** at Clarke Road and SR 50 in Ocoee is anchored by Dillard's, JCPenney, McRae's and Sears.

Outlets

International Drive is a mecca for bargain hunters. In addition to the abundance of souvenir shops, there are outlet stores scattered along the length of the road throughout the tourist area. Goods run the

Boggy Creek Airboat Rides
© Mike and Carol Gibson of Versatile Photography

gamut from shoes to cookware, representing such manufacturers as Corning-Revere, Dansk, Mikasa and Royal Doulton.

Festival Bay, a shopping and entertainment complex at 5250 International Dr., sports an elegant tropical design. Festively decorated tiled walkways connect theaters, eateries and such retails stores as Bass Pro Shops Outdoor World and Ron Jon Surf Shop.

At 8200 Vineland Ave., which connects International Drive and SR 535 (or take I-4 exit 68), is **Orlando Premium Outlets,** which offers mid- to high-end designer labels and name brands in a Mediterranean village atmosphere. The mall's amenities include a food court, parcel lockers and a currency exchange. Stores include Banana Republic, Bottega Veneta, Coach, DKNY, Louis Feraud, Nautica, Nike Factory, Oilily, Polo Ralph Lauren, Tommy Hilfiger and Timberland.

The largest conglomeration of outlet stores is off International Drive. [SAVE] **Prime Outlets Orlando,** 5401 W. Oakridge Rd., features apparel, electronics, jewelry, shoes, housewares and other items from more than 170 vendors; the Annex also offers a food court and a carrousel. Expect to find the likes of Calvin Klein, Easy Spirit, Etienne Aigner, London Fog and Oneida, among many others. Just south at 5211 International Dr. is a second [SAVE] **Prime Outlets Orlando,** a large plaza ringed with discount shops for Ann Taylor, Coach, Cole Haan, Fossil, Lenox, Saks Fifth Avenue and more. The **Kissimmee Manufacturer's Outlet,** 4673 W. Irlo Bronson Memorial Pkwy., features several dozen stores, including Bass and Nike.

Specialty Districts

Large malls aren't the only game in town—there are many interesting boutiques to be found in the area's themed shopping areas and independent districts. The **Winter Park Farmer's Market** fills Saturday mornings with fresh produce, herbs, baked goods and hot coffee in a refurbished train depot at 200 W. New England Ave. One block east is Winter Park's heart and soul, **Park Avenue.** The European-flavored promenade is lined with an eclectic assortment of boutiques, galleries and eateries ranging from the upscale to the funky, making the avenue a favorite for shopping, browsing or just meandering. Especially interesting are the shops in the courtyards and the **Hidden Garden.** Tired shoppers can take a break across the street in **Central Park** or at one of the many charming cafes along the way.

The Mercado, 8445 International Dr., features specialty shops with beachwear, collectibles, casual clothing and imported goods as well as live entertainment in the courtyard every night.

Downtown Disney Marketplace is the place to go for international purchases. Here boutiques filled with items from around the world line the shores of Buena Vista Lagoon, and artisans demonstrate their skills for passersby. Also in the Downtown Disney area on Buena Vista Drive is **Planet Hollywood,**

Mount Dora / Visit Florida

where the fascination with all that is Hollywood is captured in souvenirs ranging from designer T-shirts to key chains to leather jackets. Farther south, near the intersection of I-4 and US 192, is **Disney's Town of Celebration,** a planned community with all the amenities of a small town including a downtown area complete with nearly two dozen shops and restaurants.

Yet another shopping destination on International Drive is **Pointe* Orlando,** at 9101 International Dr. near the Orange County Convention Center. This six-building complex features more than 80 shops, restaurants and attractions, including IMAX and conventional theaters and WonderWorks *(see attraction listing p. 158),* an entertainment center in what appears to be a three-story, upside-down building.

Flea World, on US 17/92 in Sanford, features merchants, eateries, amusement rides and live entertainment. A half-hour northwest of Orlando, historic Mount Dora is known for its abundance of antiques shops. Hundreds of dealers gather each weekend at **Renninger's Antique Market** on SR 441. Antiques lovers also can search for finds in downtown Sanford.

Kissimmee's **Old Town,** 5770 W. Irlo Bronson Memorial Pkwy., evokes a turn-of-the-20th-century atmosphere with brick walkways, a Ferris wheel, a roller coaster and a wooden train exhibit. More than 70 shops offer an extensive selection of wares ranging from music boxes to magic tricks.

Performing Arts

The strength of Orlando's appeal lies mainly with its family-oriented attractions and entertainment. While this is good news for the folks at Disney and Universal, it has detracted some focus from the city's cultural scene. Arts enthusiasts need not despair, though—local arts groups have begun to expand their presence. Theater offers the most varied slate, with dance and music filling in the gaps. As the film industry gains a foothold in the area, it is likely that the fine arts will enjoy even greater success, attracting new artists to practice their crafts in the City Beautiful.

Dance

The **Orlando Ballet** is the city's professional dance company. The season, which lasts from September to May, features concerts and programs ranging from classical to modern. The troupe also stages the Nutcracker ballet every Christmas, accompanied by a live orchestra of local musicians. Performances generally are held at the **Bob Carr Performing Arts Centre;** for information phone (407) 426-1733.

Rollins College brings in some of the dance world's brightest stars, including the Alvin Ailey Repertory and Pilobolus, to the **Annie Russell Theatre** to supplement the **Rollins Dance** student program; phone (407) 646-2145.

Film

Alternative cinema finds a home at the **Enzian Theater,** 1300 S. Orlando Ave., offering filmgoers a varied menu of critically acclaimed American independent and foreign films. The theater itself is unusual—it is set in an old house, with audience seating at tables rather than in an auditorium. For information phone (407) 629-1088.

Music

Despite lacking a full-time professional orchestra, Orlando does have a variety of groups dedicated to making beautiful music. The **Orlando Philharmonic** gives three concert series during the year. Performances are held at the Bob Carr Performing Arts Centre; the **Orlando Museum of Art,** 2416 N. Mills Ave., in Loch Haven Park; and the **John and Rita Lowndes Shakespeare Center,** in Loch Haven Park behind the Orlando Museum of Art; for additional information phone (407) 896-6700. The **Festival of Orchestras,** (407) 539-0245, imports full-size symphonies, featuring such esteemed groups as the Cleveland Orchestra; guests also play at the Bob Carr.

A favorite local event is the Bach Festival, a celebration of masterworks by Bach and other major composers. Held in late February or early March, the program is performed by the **Bach Festival Choir and Orchestra,** which also offers the Festival Concert Series from October through April. The group performs at the **Knowles Memorial Chapel** at Rollins College; phone (407) 646-2182.

Opera

Opera in central Florida is presented by the **Orlando Opera Company,** staging three major works from November through March, as well as special programs during the season. Performances are at the Bob Carr Performing Arts Centre with the venue for the company's operettas being the **Dr. Phillips Center for the Performing Arts** at 1111 N. Orange Ave. For season and ticket information phone (407) 426-1717 or (407) 426-1700 for the box office.

Theater

One of the area's most popular theaters is the **UCF Civic Theatre,** 1001 Princeton St., (407) 896-7365. Another local favorite is the **SunTrust Broadway in Orlando** series, sponsoring touring Broadway shows at the Bob Carr Performing Arts Centre. Tickets for the biggest hits often require several weeks' notice; phone (800) 448-6322. **Theatre Downtown,** (407) 841-0083, offers avant-garde and mainstream works just north of the city center at 2113 N. Orange Ave. The **Orlando Theatre Project,** (407) 328-2040, puts on a similar mix at **Seminole Community College's Fine Arts Theatre,** 100 Weldon Blvd. in Sanford.

The play's the thing at the **Orlando-UCF Shakespeare Festival,** (407) 447-1700, dedicated to staging the bard's timeless plays in innovative ways.

The festival, held each April at the **Walt Disney Amphitheater at Lake Eola Park,** produces additional works throughout the year, from classically-inspired independent pieces to the **PlayLab Series,** a selection of experimental plays, presented at the John and Rita Lowndes Shakespeare Center at Loch Haven Park, 812 E. Rollins St.

The University of Central Florida features a full season of performances through **Theatre UCF,**

Bob Carr Performing Arts Centre / Orlando/Orange County CVB

(407) 823-1500. Rollins College also mounts a full season, with four productions at the Annie Russell Theatre running the gamut of theatrical genres; phone (407) 646-2145.

Special Events

On New Year's Day two top college football teams test their skills during the **Capital One Bowl** Football Classic. A parade and other related activities precede the big game.

In late January the **Zora Neale Hurston Festival of Arts and Humanities** celebrates the life of the noted interpreter of Southern rural African-American culture. This culture is celebrated further throughout February at varied events during the **Black History Month Festival.**

Orlando's moderate temperatures are ideal for art festivals. Most popular are the **Mount Dora Arts Festival** in early February; the **Downtown Orlando Arts Festival** in early March; the **Winter Park Sidewalk Art Festival** on the third weekend in March; and the **Maitland Arts & Fine Crafts Festival** in mid-April. A pair of **Fiesta in the Park** celebrations take place in April and November on the shores of Lake Eola.

For 10 days in mid-May, entertainers from around the world converge on downtown Orlando, treating theatergoers to a variety of unusual and cutting edge performances as part of the **International Fringe**

Festival. Later in May more than 200,000 ears of corn are eaten during the **Zellwood Sweet Corn Festival,** also a showcase for big-name country musicians.

Two PGA golf tournaments are on Orlando's calendar of events. In March the **Bay Hill Invitational** is held at Arnold Palmer's Bay Hill Club & Lodge, while the **Funai Classic at Walt DisneyWorld** is held at the Palm and Magnolia courses at Walt Disney Wórld in October.

In early November the **Walt Disney World Festival of the Masters** is held at Downtown Disney Marketplace. During this 3-day event, major American artists display their works. The city of Winter Park rings in the holiday season with **Christmas in the Park,** which combines a concert by the Bach Festival Choir and stunning outdoor displays of lighted Tiffany windows on loan from the nearby Charles Hosmer Morse Museum of American Art.

The Orlando Vicinity

APOPKA (E-2) pop. 26,642

ROCK SPRINGS AND KELLY PARK are 6 mi. n. on SR 435. Rock Springs, a half-mile east of the park entrance on Kelly Park Road, discharges 26,000 gallons of clear, 68-degree Fahrenheit water per minute into a spring that is popular for tubing and swimming. Shelters, bathhouses, tube rentals (outside park), hiking trails and camping facilities are available. Picnicking is permitted. Daily 9-7, Apr.-Oct.; 8-6, rest of year. Admission $1, under 6 free. Phone (407) 889-4179. *See Recreation Chart.*

CHRISTMAS (D-10) pop. 1,162, elev. 44'

Every yuletide the town of Christmas receives thousands of pieces of mail, which are stamped with the Christmas postmark and sent on their way. Four miles south on Taylor Creek Road is the headquarters of the Tosohatchee State Preserve. The preserve's 28,000 acres of woodlands and wetlands along the St. Johns River offer hiking and bicycling trails, fishing and nature study.

FORT CHRISTMAS HISTORICAL PARK is 2 mi. n. of SR 50 on CR 420 (Fort Christmas Rd.). The

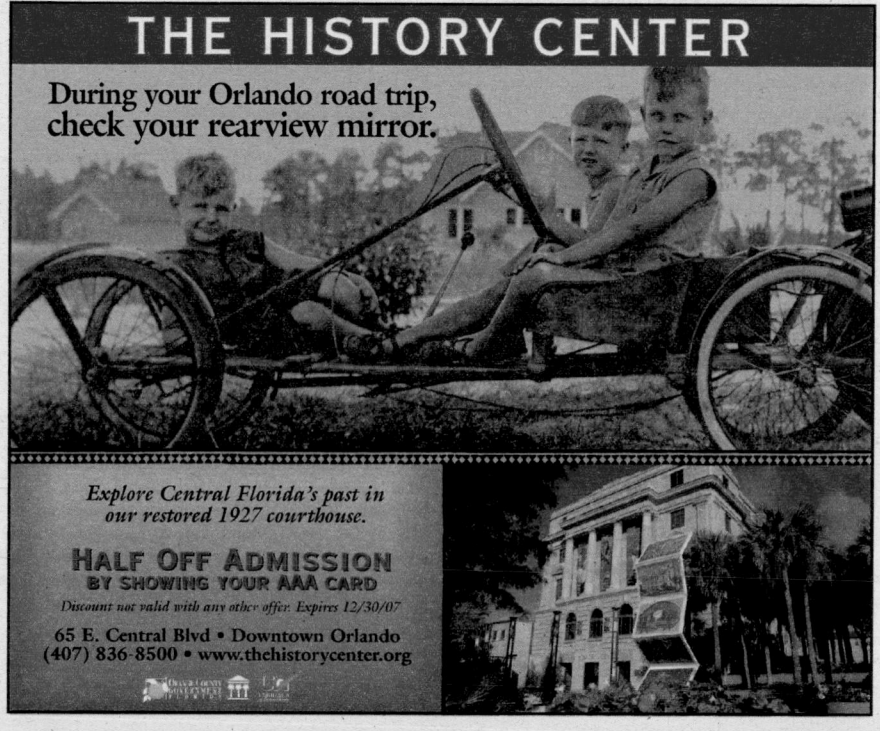

park contains a replica of a fort begun Dec. 25, 1837, during the Second Seminole Indian War. Two blockhouses contain exhibits about the Seminole Indian Wars and area pioneers. Guided tours of seven restored pioneer houses are available for viewing. Recreation facilities also are available. Picnicking is permitted. Allow 1 hour minimum. Tues.-Sat. 10-5, Sun. 1-5; closed holidays. Free. Phone (407) 568-4149.

[SAVE] **JUNGLE ADVENTURES**, 26205 E. SR 50, lets visitors view alligators in their natural habitat. A swamp cruise on board a pontoon boat; a wildlife show including endangered Florida panthers; and alligator feeding demonstrations are featured. An American Indian village re-creates the lifestyle of native Florida Indians. Guided tours are available. Allow 2 hours, 30 minutes minimum. Daily 9:30-5:30. Admission $17.50; over 60, $14; ages 3-11, $8.50. AX, DS, MC, VI. Phone (877) 424-2867.

MIDWAY AIRBOAT RIDES is at 28501 E. Colonial Dr. (SR 50). Airboat rides on the St. John's River provide views of wildlife and swamp vegetation. Sightings might include alligators, otters and a variety of native bird species. Allow 1 hour minimum. Mon.-Sat. 9-5, Sun. 10-5. Last tour departs at 4:15. Fare $15, ages 3-11, $7. MC, VI. Phone (407) 568-6790.

CLERMONT (D-9) pop. 9,333, elev. 190′

Clermont founder A.F. Wrotnoski named this town of wide, shady streets and rolling hills after his French birthplace. Lake Louisa State Park *(see Recreation Chart)*, 7 miles southeast of Clermont on Lake Nellie Road, is one of 13 in a chain of lakes connected by the Palatkahah River.

South Lake Chamber of Commerce: 691 W. Montrose St., P.O. Box 120417, Clermont, FL 34712-0417; phone (352) 394-4191.

CITRUS TOWER CENTRE is 1 mi. n. of the SR 50 jct. at 141 US 27N. Reached by elevator, the 226-foot-tall tower's observation deck provides a panorama of the surrounding lakes and rolling hills. Food is available. Allow 30 minutes minimum. Mon.-Thurs. 9-6, Fri.-Sat. 9-9; closed Thanksgiving and Dec. 25. Admission $3.50; ages 3-15, $1. AX, DS, MC, VI. Phone (352) 394-4061.

NATIONAL PRESIDENTS HALL OF FAME, just n. of SR 50 at 123 US 27N, features changing exhibits of memorabilia related to U.S. presidents and their first ladies. Among displays are campaign and inaugural artifacts, first ladies' evening gowns, replicas of china place settings and miniature re-creations of White House rooms. Videotape presentations include a tour of the White House and presidential biographies. Allow 2 hours minimum. Daily 9-5. Admission $11.95; ages 6-11, $6.95. DS, MC, VI. Phone (352) 394-2836.

WINERIES

• **Lakeridge Winery and Vineyards**, 2.5 mi. s. off Florida's Tpke. exit 285 to 19239 US 27N. Mon.-Sat. 10-5, Sun. 11-5; closed Jan. 1, Easter, Thanksgiving and Dec. 25. Phone (352) 394-8627 or (800) 768-9463.

HEATHROW (D-4) pop. 4,068, elev. 50′

Heathrow is the site of the AAA National Office. North of Orlando at I-4 and Lake Mary Boulevard, the Heathrow community includes recreational, commercial and residential areas.

KISSIMMEE (H-3) pop. 47,814, elev. 62′

Kissimmee (Kiss-SEM-mee), or "Heaven's Place" in the Calusa Indian language, is near the southern terminus of a scenic portion of Florida's Turnpike, which extends 65 miles southeast from Wildwood. It is more widely known to visitors to the central Florida region as being a near neighbor of Walt Disney World® Resort. Many downtown businesses occupy structures dating from the late 1800s; landscaping and renovations preserve the town's old-time aura.

Area industries include plastics, engineering, electronics and agriculture. The Florida Cattlemen's Association has its headquarters in town. Kissimmee also attracts the sports-minded to Osceola County Stadium, in Osceola Heritage Park, where the Houston Astros conduct spring training during March; phone (321) 697-3200 for Astros ticket information.

Silver Spurs Arena, US 192 and Bill Beck Blvd. in Osceola Heritage Park, hosts the popular Silver Spurs Rodeo, concerts and major sports events. Picnic tables and boat ramps are available at Lake Front Park, .25 mile southeast of US 17/92. Also in the park is the Monument of States, a stone pyramid consisting of stones from various states and 22 countries.

A taste of the exotic can be found at A World of Orchids, 2501 Old Lake Wilson Rd., where plants are showcased in an enclosed tropical rain forest setting; phone (407) 396-1887.

Kissimmee Convention & Visitors Bureau: 1925 E. Irlo Bronson Memorial Hwy., Kissimmee, FL 34744-4413; phone (407) 847-5000 or (800) 333-5477. *See color ad p. 772.*

Shopping areas: Old Town, just east of I-4 on US 192, features 75 specialty shops as well as restaurants and amusement rides in a re-created turn-of-the-20th-century setting. Hundreds of classic cars cruise the streets of Old Town every Friday and Saturday night.

ARABIAN NIGHTS, off I-4 exit 64A at 6225 W. Irlo Bronson Memorial Hwy., is a 1-hour, 45-minute dinner show featuring equestrian acts in an indoor arena. The performances include a Wild West act and a Broadway-style production with special effects and magic. A three-course dinner is served during the show. Allow 2 hours, 30 minutes minimum.

Performances nightly; occasional noon matinee. Admission $47; ages 3-11, $29. Reservations are recommended. AX, CB, DC, DS, MC, VI. Phone (407) 239-9223 or (800) 553-6116.

[SAVE] **BOGGY CREEK AIRBOAT RIDES** is 19 mi. s. on Poinciana Blvd. in Southport Park, following signs. The company offers trips in 18-passenger airboats from Lake Tohopekaliga through the wetlands and Everglades headwaters. Passengers are likely to see eagles, turtles, alligators and other Florida wildlife during the voyage. Allow 30 minutes minimum. Daily 9-5:30. Fare $18.95; ages 3-12, $14.95. AX, MC, VI. Phone (407) 344-9550. *See color ad.*

[SAVE] **CAPONE'S DINNER AND SHOW,** 4740 W. Irlo Bronson Memorial Hwy. (US 192), .7 mi. e. of jct. SR 535, presents a musical dinner show based on the 1930s escapades of gangster Al Capone. Allow 2 hours, 30 minutes minimum. Performances nightly at 8. Matinees are offered; phone for schedule. Admission $43.99; ages 4-12, $25.99. Reservations are suggested. AX, DS, MC, VI. Phone (407) 397-23 *See color ad p. 692.*

[SAVE] **GREEN MEADOWS PETTING FARM,** 3 mi. e. of I-4 exit 64A on US 192, then 5 mi. s. on Poinciana Blvd., offers guided tours of a 50-acre farm with more than 300 farm animals. The hands-on philosophy encourages learning as visitors milk a cow, ride a pony or hold a chicken. Petting pens with various farm animals are a highlight of the tour. Tractor-drawn hayrides and a train ride are included.

Picnicking is permitted. Allow 2 hours minimum. Daily 9:30-4; closed Thanksgiving and Dec. 25. Admission $19, under 2 free. DS, MC, VI. Phone (407) 846-0770.

LAKE KISSIMMEE STATE PARK— *see Lake Wales p. 110.*

MEDIEVAL TIMES DINNER AND TOURNAMENT, 6 mi. e. of I-4 exit 64A at 4510 W. Irlo Bronson Memorial Hwy. (US 192), is in a replica of an 11th-century European castle. A medieval feast is served by staff members costumed in period attire. Spectators feast a few feet from tournament action in the Great Ceremonial Arena, where knights on Andalusian stallions compete in jousting matches and medieval games of skill.

Allow 2 hours minimum. Performances nightly; show times vary. Admission $49.95; ages 3-11, $33.95. Reservations are required. AX, DS, MC, VI. Phone (407) 396-1518 or (888) 935-6878.

Medieval Life, 6 mi. e. of I-4 exit 64A at 4510 W. Irlo Bronson Memorial Hwy. (US 192), is a permanent re-creation of a medieval village. This 10-cottage hamlet showcases medieval artifacts and costumed artisans working their trades. Allow 1 hour minimum. Open daily 2 hours before dinner show time. Admission $3.50.

[SAVE] **WATER MANIA,** .5 mi. e. of I-4 at 6073 W. Irlo Bronson Memorial Hwy. (US 192), is a 36-acre park containing raft rides, waterslides, flumes, a wave pool, a surfing simulator, an inner tube river ride, children's play areas and an arcade. Raft rentals, life vests, showers, changing rooms and lockers are available. Picnicking is permitted. Food is available. Allow 4 hours minimum. Daily 10-5, mid-Mar. through Labor Day; Thurs.-Sun. 11-5, day after Labor Day-Oct. 31 Admission $29.95; ages 3-9, $26.95. Locker rentals $9.28-$11.42 with a $5 deposit. Parking $6. MC, VI. Phone (407) 396-2626 or (800) 527-3092.

LAKE BUENA VISTA (G-3)
pop. 16, elev. 100'

RICHARD PETTY DRIVING EXPERIENCE, off US 192 exit World Dr., following signs to Magic Kingdom, puts race fans in the seat of a stock car on a 1-mile, tri-oval track. A ride-along program allows guests 16 and older to ride with a professional instructor at speeds up to 140 mph. A variety of programs for drivers 18 and older includes behind-the-wheel experiences; reservations and a valid driver's license are required.

Daily 8-4; closed Jan. 1, Easter, Oct. 20-23, Thanksgiving and Dec. 25. Ride-along program $99; riders 16-18 must be accompanied by parent or legal guardian. Driving programs start at $379. AX, DS, MC, VI. Phone (407) 939-0130 or (800) 237-3889.

WALT DISNEY WORLD® RESORT is accessible from US 192, Osceola Pkwy. and several exits off I-4 s. of Orlando, depending on the park destination. Covering 30,500 acres, the complex includes four theme parks: the Magic Kingdom® Park, Epcot®, Disney-MGM Studios and Disney's Animal Kingdom®; two themed water parks; 22 resorts; Disney's Fort Wilderness Resort and Campground; five championship golf courses; two luxurious spas; Disney's Wide World of Sports® Complex; and the Downtown Disney® area, a shopping, dining and entertainment district.

Walt Disney's Florida legacy is a land of vision, imagination and innovation. The news that the creator of California's popular Disneyland® was going to build a theme park just south of the small town of Orlando was announced in 1965. Drawn to the area by its climate, highway access and inexpensive land, Disney and his "Imagineers" began transforming acres of swamps and orange groves into a magical vacationland that opened in 1971.

The Magic Kingdom Park, where childhood dreams and fantasies are brought to life, was an instant success. Other theme parks were soon on the drawing board, and Epcot, a celebration of technology and world cultures, joined the Magic Kingdom Park in 1982. Disney-MGM Studios, a natural addition considering Disney's background in animation and television and film production, followed in 1989. Disney's Animal Kingdom brought both wild and imaginary creatures to the public in 1998.

The resort is in a near-constant state of expansion and modernization. This process may include enhancements to existing attractions as well as new development.

The golf, recreational, shopping, dining and entertainment facilities of the resort also are open to day visitors. Monorail, boat and motor coach transportation are available throughout the resort.

Navigating the Walt Disney World property is greatly simplified by clear, concise road signs. Tram service is provided from parking areas to the main entrance of Disney's Animal Kingdom, Epcot, Disney-MGM Studios and to the Transportation and Ticket Center near the Magic Kingdom Park. From the Transportation and Ticket Center, ferryboats and a monorail transport visitors to the Magic Kingdom Park.

Disney's FASTPASS® is an easy-to-use computerized system that helps guests avoid waiting in long lines at many attractions. This free service is available for the most popular rides at each of the four theme parks. By choosing the FASTPASS option, guests are assigned a time when they can return and experience the attraction with little or no wait.

To obtain a FASTPASS, a guest inserts his theme park ticket into the FASTPASS machine located near the entrance to the chosen attraction. A timed ticket is delivered, printed with a 1-hour window of time during which the guest may return and enter the attraction at a special FASTPASS entrance. Park maps list participating FASTPASS attractions.

To honor Walt Disney's legacy of theme park magic that began with Disneyland park 50 years ago, Walt Disney World Resort kicked off the Happiest Celebration on Earth on May 5, 2005.

Theme parks open generally at 9; closing times vary. Multi-day ticket options provide admission to all four theme parks and other entertainment areas. One-day, One-park admission $63; ages 3-9, $52. AX, DC, DS, JC, MC, VI. Phone (407) 824-4321. *See color ads starting on p.175.*

Disney-MGM Studios, 2 mi. n. of US 192 off World Dr., is a theme park and working production studio featuring attractions, Broadway-style shows and live entertainment, all centered around popular films, television, music and animation. The centerpiece of the park is the 122-foot Sorcerer's Hat, designed to resemble the pointed hat worn by Mickey Mouse in Disney's animated film "Fantasia."

Hollywood and Sunset boulevards re-create the glamorous golden age of Hollywood. The Twilight Zone Tower of Terror$_{TM}$, which begins with a journey through the haunted hallways of the vintage Hollywood Tower Hotel, culminates in multiple 13-story drops in a runaway service elevator. Rock 'n' Roller Coaster Starring Aerosmith is an indoor thrill ride featuring a soundtrack by the renowned rock 'n' roll band. The coaster ride, complete with rock concert lighting, takes visitors on a high-speed, looping trip through the Hollywood Hills.

Disney characters riding in retrofitted classic cars lead a motorcade during the Disney Stars and Motor Cars Parade.

At Who Wants to be a Millionaire-Play It!, guests can participate in a re-creation of the hit TV game show. The game's high-tech set is complete with its signature dramatic lighting. The "fastest finger" determines who will sit in the hot seat, though all audience members can play along using their own keypads.

Fantasmic! is a nighttime water spectacular that takes you inside the dreams of Sorcerer Mickey. The show is a battle of good versus evil in which Sorcerer Mickey's magic creates dancing waters, dazzling lasers, shooting comets, animated fountains, swirling stars, balls of fire and

other wonders. Mickey himself conducts the musical score as the presentation lights up the night sky.

Death-defying stunts are the cornerstone of the Indiana Jones™ Epic Stunt Spectacular, inspired by the film "Raiders of the Lost Ark." The new Lights, Motors, Action!™ Extreme Stunt Show combines tire-squealing cars and high-flying motorcycles with special effects and pyrotechnics to demonstrate how stunts are filmed for Hollywood movies.

A Broadway-style rendition of "Beauty and the Beast" is performed at the Theater of the Stars, where highlights from the animated film about Belle and the Beast's love story are brought to life on stage. Voyage of the Little Mermaid brings the story of Ariel and her colorful undersea world to the stage.

Visitors will feel as if they are bursting into outer space aboard Star Tours, a ride based on the movie "Star Wars." Disney-MGM Studios Backlot Tour shows how filmmakers create special-effect movie and television disasters. Riders are taken on a shuttle tour of movie sets, the highlight of which is an explosive journey through Catastrophe Canyon, where fires erupt and a flash flood threatens to tip the shuttle over.

Guests can travel into classic moments from the movies on The Great Movie Ride as well as see Kermit, Miss Piggy and friends in a 3-D misadventure in Jim Henson's Muppet*Vision 3-D.

Meet Bear in the Big Blue House™, Stanley and JoJo and Goliath as they sing and laugh with visitors and other Disney Channel characters in Playhouse Disney-Live on Stage!

Park opens daily generally at 9; closing times vary. Admission $63; ages 3-9, $52. AX, DC, DS, JC, MC, VI.

Phone (407) 824-4321. *See color ads starting on p. 175.*

Disney's Animal Kingdom, n. of US 192 on World Dr. then following signs along Osceola Pkwy., features real and imaginary animals as well as attractions and live shows. Entering through The Oasis, a lush area of streams, gardens and waterfalls, visitors can go back in time to encounter dinosaurs, take an African safari amid free-roaming animals, be transported to southeast Asia and come face-to-face with Disney characters in entertaining settings.

At the center of the park in Discovery Island™ is the majestic Tree of Life, which reaches 14 stories high and represents the diversity of animal life through intricate carvings of more than 300 animal life forms. Shown in a theater deep inside the Tree of Life, It's Tough to be a Bug!® is a comical, 3-D, special effects adventure offering a bug's-eye view of the world from the perspective of Flik, the hero of the Disney/Pixar movie "A Bug's Life."

DinoLand U.S.A.®, devoted to the Age of Dinosaurs, is entered by walking under a 50-foot-tall brachiosaurus. The thrill ride DINOSAUR blasts

back 65 million years to rescue a dinosaur from the edge of extinction as a deadly asteroid speeds towards Earth. Also in this land are Chester & Hester's Dino-Rama!, a roadside carnival featuring dinosaur-themed games and rides; Primeval Whirl, a time machine-themed coaster that spins riders back through the ages to encounter crazy prehistoric creatures; and TriceraTop Spin, which enables kids to ride flying dinosaurs, though cautions them to watch out for flying comets.

The Boneyard is an open-air playground and dig site in which children can maneuver their way through a maze of dinosaur skeletons and help unearth the bones of a giant mammoth.

Africa features a journey into one of the last wild sanctuaries of our planet. Beginning in the modern-day town of Harambe, the Kilimanjaro Safaris® expedition takes you on a chase for poachers through a 120-acre African savanna where hippos, zebras, gazelles, giraffes and elephants roam freely.

After exiting their vehicle, visitors can traverse the Pangani Forest Exploration Trail and observe a troop of gorillas interacting in this naturalistic habitat.

Another option is the Wildlife Express Train; riders are transported to Rafiki's Planet Watch, an interactive experience where conservation efforts are explained and small animals can be seen and touched.

The land of Asia features a soaking, white-water rafting adventure at Kali River Rapids. Coming in 2006 is a new adventure—Expedition Everest™, a high-speed train ride through the Himalayas. Beware, though; your route to Mount Everest crosses the forbidden realm of the legendary yeti, or, as he's also known, the abominable snowman.

Costumed actors and storytellers, Disney characters, puppets, stage floats and live animals entertain in Disney's Animal Kingdom. Elaborate puppets, giant animal stilt walkers and drummers join Mickey, Minnie, Donald and Goofy during Mickey's Jammin' Jungle Parade. Festival of the Lion King at Camp Minnie-Mickey turns song, dance and characters from the popular movie into a Broadway-style extravaganza.

Park generally opens daily at 9; closing time varies. Admission $63; ages 3-9, $52. AX, DC, DS, JC, MC, VI. Phone (407) 824-4321. *See color ads starting on p. 175.*

 **Disney's Blizzard Beach Water Park**, 2 mi. n. of US 192 off World Dr., features a mix of Florida sun and a theme of alpine snow. "Snow"-capped Mt. Gushmore is where you'll find side-by-side racing waterslides and Summit Plummet, where those who dare can plunge down a 90-foot drop at 55 mph.

Tamer offerings include a family raft ride down Teamboat Springs, "icy" bobsled runs, an inner tube run, a chair lift ride, flumes, a wave pool and a children's area. Food is available. Hours vary. Admission $35; ages 3-9, $29. AX, DC, DS, JC, MC, VI. Phone (407) 560-9283. *See color ads starting on p. 175.*

Disney's Typhoon Lagoon Water Park, US 192 w. to World Dr., then e. on Buena Vista Dr., re-creates a tropical village that has just experienced a great storm.

A new adventure awaits thrill-seekers on Crush 'n' Gusher, a white-knuckle coaster-style water ride featuring gravity-defying uphill climbs, hairpin turns and sudden drops. Also featured are a children's water playground and one of the world's largest wave pools. Food is available. Hours vary. Admission $35; ages 3-9, $29. AX, DC, DS, JC, MC, VI. Phone (407) 560-9283. *See color ads starting on p. 175.*

Disney's Wide World of Sports Complex, w. on US 192 to World Dr., then e. on Osceola Pkwy., is a state-of-the-art sports venue where amateur and professional athletes hone their skills and compete in their particular sport. The complex is the spring-training home of the Atlanta Braves and the summer training camp for the Tampa Bay Buccaneers.

Admission $10.28; ages 3-9, $7.71. Admission may increase for special events. Some events may require a separate admission charge. Parking is free. AX, DC, DS, JC, MC, VI. Phone (407) 363-6600. *See color ads starting on p. 175.*

Downtown Disney Area, w. on US 192 to World Dr. then e. on Buena Vista Dr., is a 120-acre waterfront shopping, themed dining and entertainment complex. The area is a showplace of celebrity restaurants, night clubs, a 24-screen movie theater and specialty shops.

In addition, Downtown Disney Marketplace has restaurants and retail options, including Rainforest Café; the interactive toy playground Once Upon A Toy; and World of Disney, featuring an expansive selection of character merchandise.

Downtown Disney West Side also is home to DisneyQuest®, a five-story indoor interactive theme park where visitors can design and take a simulated ride on their own roller coaster or battle virtual villains. Other options include the extravagant theatrical production of the Cirque du Soleil® show La Nouba™, which is performed only at the Walt Disney World Resort.

For adult nighttime fun Downtown Disney Pleasure Island is an evening entertainment complex featuring themed clubs, including an improv comedy club; a '70s- and '80s-themed dance club; Mannequins Dance Palace, with a rotating dance floor; the BET SoundStage™ Club, featuring rhythm & blues, soul and hip-hop; and high-energy dance clubs.

The island is open to all daily at 7 p.m. A $20.95 entrance fee provides admission to Pleasure Island clubs. An annual pass is $55.95. There may be additional charges for special events. Age restrictions may apply for certain facilities. DisneyQuest $35; ages 3-9, $29. Cirque du Soleil $61-$95; ages 3-9, $49-$76. AX, DC, DS, JC, MC, VI. Phone (407) 934-7781, or (407) 939-7600 for Cirque du Soleil reservations. *See color ads starting on p. 175.*

Epcot is 3 mi. s. of the Magic Kingdom Park off World Dr. The park encompasses Future World and World Showcase— two major areas designed to combine Disney fun and imagination with the wonders of the real world.

Attractions in Future World include the park's symbol, Spaceship Earth, where human communication is explored in a time travel adventure from Earth's earliest days to the present, and Innoventions, which lets guests discover the world's latest technology in a constantly changing, hands-on showcase.

The Land, which examines our environment and food resources, features a boat ride through greenhouses of the future. New in 2005, Soarin' takes guests on a simulated hang gliding adventure over California. Riders fly over such memorable landmarks as the Golden Gate Bridge, Yosemite National Park, redwood forests and Napa Valley, while gentle breezes provide scents of orange blossoms and pine trees.

"Honey I Shrunk the Audience," in the Imagination pavilion, has 3-D effects that virtually jump off the screen. Journey into Imagination stars a purple dragon named Figment who shows how our five senses influence our imagination.

Wonders of Life and The Living Seas explore advances in science and technology in a fun and interactive way. Body Wars takes visitors on a virtual reality ride through the human body, while a saltwater aquarium is home to a coral reef inhabited by sharks, rays and dolphins. Nemo & Friends showcases the live fish that are depicted as animated characters in the film "Finding Nemo," including Mr. Ray, Dory and Nemo himself. Guests also can engage in live, animated conversation with Crush, the turtle.

Test Track, based on a General Motors automotive proving grounds, takes guests on a thrilling high-speed ride filled with turns, climbs and evasive maneuvers. Mission: SPACE launches guests on a realistic space adventure to Mars, from the exhilarating lift-off to a soaring journey into deep space.

World Showcase presents the best of Mexico, China, Norway, Germany, Italy, Japan, France, Morocco, the United Kingdom, Canada and America, all of which can be reached by foot or boat across the World Showcase Lagoon from Future World. Guests can experience the cultures, traditions, holidays, architecture, food and entertainment of all 11 countries.

Visitors to Mexico can enjoy a boat ride on El Rio del Tiempo, while in Norway the Maelstrom boat ride transports guests back to the days of the Vikings. Other pavilions spotlight artists performing traditional music, dance and theatrical works. All pavilions are staffed by nationals of that country and bilingual Disney cast members.

IllumiNations: Reflections of Earth is a nighttime spectacular that features fireworks, original music, lasers and magic.

For daily entertainment schedules visit Guest Relations. Reservations for lunch or dinner at any full-service restaurant should be made at Guest Relations or by phoning (407) 939-3463. Epcot is connected to the Magic Kingdom Park by an 8-mile monorail circuit.

Future World opens daily generally at 9. World Showcase opens daily generally at 11. Closing times vary. Admission $63; ages 3-9, $52. AX, DC, DS, JC, MC, VI. Phone (407) 824-4321. *See color ads starting on p. 175.*

Magic Kingdom

Magic Kingdom Park, US 192 exit World Dr. following signs, is divided into seven themed "lands," all featuring attractions, entertainment, restaurants and shops. The park is entered through Main Street, U.S.A., a representation of a typical late 19th-century boulevard complete with cafes, shops and horse-drawn streetcars.

The park's centerpiece is Cinderella Castle, which serves as the backdrop for the new Cinderellabration musical spectacular, where guests witness the magical moment when Cinderella is crowned a princess. The castle also is the gateway to Fantasyland, where adventures are based on Disney films. Hundreds of dolls in international costumes perform at the newly refurbished "it's a small world." Join in the adventures of other favorite Disney characters at the Mad Tea Party, Dumbo the Flying Elephant, Snow White's Scary Adventure and Peter Pan's Flight rides.

The cast of Mickey's PhilharMagic, a 3-D film spectacular designed with families in mind, includes Mickey, Donald, Ariel, Peter Pan, Tinkerbell, Aladdin and Simba as Disney music, 3-D computer-generated animation and special effects come together on a 150-foot-wide screen in the PhilharMagic Concert Hall.

At Mickey's Toontown Fair children can see Mickey Mouse and visit his house, Minnie's cottage and Donald's boat. The Barnstormer, a children's roller coaster, is featured at Goofy's Wiseacre Farm.

The futuristic Tomorrowland features Space Mountain, a high-speed race through the darkness of space; Astro Orbiter, a rocket to the stars; and Tomorrowland Indy Speedway. Buzz Lightyear's Space Ranger Spin, an interactive space fantasy, arms guests with infrared lasers to zap Emperor Zurg's forces in this ride based on the Disney/Pixar movie "Toy Story." In Stitch's Great Escape the audience is caught in the middle of the mayhem as Stitch busts loose in a galaxy of gross-out fun.

Liberty Square depicts early America with boat trips on the *Liberty Belle*. The Hall of Presidents offers a patriotic salute to the 42 individuals who have served this nation and features animatronic figures of each president engaged in animated conversation. Visitors can expect to encounter a lively collection of 999 ghosts and ghouls in the Haunted Mansion.

Adventureland offers a swashbuckling voyage with the Pirates of the Caribbean as well as an opportunity to ride a four-passenger carpet while trying to avoid water-spewing camels on The Magic Carpets of Aladdin. Jungle Cruise journeys through four continents and encounters "wild" animals from tropical jungles.

Big Thunder Mountain Railroad, a runaway mine train, is the focus of Frontierland, which also is the site of Splash Mountain, a log flume ride with a five-story drop. Take a ride on a log raft to reach and explore Tom Sawyer Island, then join a zany group of singing bears at the foot stompin' Country Bear Jamboree. Frontierland also is one of the starting points for a ride on the Walt Disney World Railroad.

Wishes, a fireworks spectacular narrated by Jiminy Cricket, explodes over and around Cinderella Castle most nights. The 12-minute display brings together classic Disney songs, character voices and pyrotechnic effects.

Park opens daily generally at 9; closing times vary. Admission $63; ages 3-9, $52. AX, DC, DS, JC, MC, VI. Phone (407) 824-4321. *See color ads starting on p. 175.*

General Information

Disney's Magic Kingdom Park, Epcot, Disney-MGM Studios and Disney's Animal Kingdom open daily generally at 9. Closing times vary between each park, depending on the season.

Large crowds and long lines are to be expected, especially during holiday periods. Individual park maps are available at Guest Relations Information Centers near the entrance of each park.

Parking and Pets

The entrance road leads to parking (fee $9 per day). Free tram service connects the parking area with the Ticket and Transportation Center, Epcot, Disney-MGM Studios and Disney's Animal Kingdom. Transportation also is available to all guest areas. Kennels—at Magic Kingdom Park (Ticket and Transportation Center), Epcot, Disney-MGM Studios, Disney's Animal Kingdom and Disney's Fort Wilderness Resort and Campground—charge a nominal fee to care for and feed pets.

Admissions

"Magic Your Way," Walt Disney World Resort's ticket pricing structure effective Jan. 1, 2006, allows visitors to customize their stay at Disney's theme parks, attractions and entertainment areas based on their interests and the length of their visit. To compute their ticket price, guests first determine the base ticket price, which varies depending on the number of days they plan on spending at the resort. They then choose from a list of options, all available as add-on prices, that enable them to tailor their stay to their own needs.

Base Ticket, the starter pass, provides admission to one theme park for each day purchased. Guests can visit Magic Kingdom Park or Epcot or Disney-MGM Studios or Disney's Animal Kingdom. One-day admission $63; ages 3-9, $52. Two-day ticket $125; ages 3-9, $103. Three-day $181; ages 3-9, $149. Four-day $195; ages 3-9, $160. Five-day $199; ages 3-9, $162. Six-day $202; ages 3-9, $164. Seven-day $204; ages 3-9, $165.

Park Hopper® Option allows guests to visit more than one theme park on the same day, any combination of parks in a day. The add-on price is $40, whether the ticket is 1 day or 7 days.

Water Park Fun & More offers visitors the chance to experience other Disney attractions and entertainment areas. A specified number of visits (between two and five) can be made, based on the length of the ticket purchased. Choices are DisneyQuest, Disney's Blizzard Beach Water Park, Disney's Typhoon Lagoon Water Park, Disney's Wide World of Sports Complex and Pleasure Island. The add-on price is $50, whether the ticket is 1 day or 7 days.

No Expiration Option, when added on to the ticket, means unused admission days never expire and can be used at some future date. This option is available on multi-day tickets. Two- and 3-day add-on price $10; 4 days $20; 5 days $40; 6 days $50; 7 days $65.

Visitors can take advantage of advance purchase savings on tickets of 5 or more days with Park Hopper and/or Magic Plus Pack options selected when the tickets are purchased in advance of arrival at Walt Disney World Resort.

Select tickets are available at participating AAA Travel offices.

Tickets are valid during regular hours and include unlimited use of the Walt Disney World transportation system. All tickets expire 14 days from first use, unless the No Expiration option has been selected. No refunds for unused tickets are issued for any reason. Tickets are non-transferable. Some activities or events may be separately priced. Prices quoted above do not include tax. Prices and entitlements may change without notice. AX, DC, DS, JC, MC, VI. For ticket information phone (407) 824-4321 or TTY (407) 827-5141.

Walt Disney World

the happiest
celebration
on earth

A quick and easy guide to the biggest celebration in Disney history, commemorating 50 years of magic at Disney destinations around the world! In the next few pages, check out new attractions and entertainment at all four *Walt Disney World* Theme Parks from Disney destinations worldwide.

MAGIC KINGDOM®

Welcome to a place where storybook fantasy becomes everyday reality. Where elephants fly, teacups dance, and every day ends happily ever after in seven lands of fun.

As part of the Happiest Celebration On Earth, the new Cinderellabration musical is here, inspired by the *Tokyo Disneyland*® show. It's a lavish look beyond the storybook ending to the golden moment when our reigning princess received her crown.

For an encounter of the gross-out kind, there's Stitch's Great Escape!™ attraction, where the mischievous little blue alien wreaks hilarious havoc all around you! Then, join Donald Duck on a 3-D musical misadventure in Mickey's PhilharMagic.

Challenge the famous *Magic Kingdom* mountain range with a Space Mountain® rocket ride; a raucous, runaway Big Thunder Mountain Railroad adventure; and a five-story Splash Mountain® free-fall into Brer Rabbit's laughin' place.

For the grand finale— fireworks, music and color give a joyous, moving "performance" in the Wishes™ nighttime spectacular.

celebrate
more
enchantment
MAGIC KINGDOM

Get more time in the Theme Parks! Enjoy the *Extra Magic Hours* Benefit as a *Disney Resort* hotel Guest. Find out how in the *Disney Resort* section of this TourBook, on the GOLD Disney pages.

celebrate
more
excite-
ment

EPCOT®

EPCOT®

Epcot® offers the best of both worlds: a world where high-tech meets big fun, and a World Showcase of international culture and cuisine. The newest wonder is the exhilarating **Soarin'**™ attraction—direct from *Disneyland*® Resort—a sensational experience that sails you into the sky on a hang gliding adventure over natural wonders from the Golden Gate Bridge to Yosemite National Park.

Feel the power of liftoff on **Mission: SPACE**®, the most intense thrill ride in any Disney Park, on a journey to Mars. Shift into the fast lane for **Test Track** and face the rigors of a real automobile proving ground.

At **The Living Seas**, check out the delightful **Turtle Talk With Crush** and see the real-life "Nemo" clown fish and his friends from the Walt Disney Pictures presentation of a Pixar Animation Studios film, *Finding Nemo.* Nearby, go for big laughs as you shrink down to the size of a flea in **Honey, I Shrunk the Audience.** For the finale, the eleven World Showcase nations are the backdrop for **IllumiNations: Reflections of Earth**, a symphony of lasers and fireworks.

DISNEY-MGM STUDIOS

Get cast into an exciting day of showbiz, high-speed attractions and sensational shows! The newest thrills come from *Disneyland®* Resort Paris, as **Lights, Motors, Action!**™ Extreme Stunt Show brings you white-knuckle action with flying motorcycles and airborne sports cars for the ultimate behind-the-scenes look at super stunt driving. Scream through 13 floors on a random elevator ride through the fifth dimension on **The Twilight Zone Tower of Terror.**™ Take a wild, twisting road trip on **Rock 'n' Roller Coaster®** Starring Aerosmith. Then, let the kids sing along with their TV pals from *Bear in the Big Blue House,*™ *JoJo's Circus* and *Stanley* in **Playhouse Disney–Live on Stage!** Get a behind-the-scenes glimpse at how animated classics are made at the newly enhanced **The Magic of Disney Animation.** Blast into hyperspace on **Star Tours,** the ultimate *Star Wars*™ thrill ride. And cheer on one very brave mouse as he conquers Disney villains in the nighttime spectacular, **Fantasmic!**

celebrate
more
action

DISNEY-MGM
STUDIOS

DISNEY'S ANIMAL KINGDOM®

Explore an amazing kingdom where every day comes alive with creatures from our world—and our imagination. The newest adventure is **Expedition Everest–Legend of the Forbidden Mountain,**™ a high-speed train trek forward and backward through the treacherous Himalayan unknown where the dreaded Yeti lurks! (Opening Spring 2006.) Set off for a **Kilimanjaro Safaris**® expedition, exploring through 110 acres of African savannah to encounter freely roaming wildlife. Dodge flaming meteors and ferocious beasts as you scream your way through the thrill-packed **DINOSAUR** ride. Sing along with Timon, Pumbaa, Simba and company at the musical extravaganza, **Festival of the Lion King**. View the world through bug-colored glasses in **It's Tough to be a Bug!**®, a 3-D show inspired by the Walt Disney Pictures presentation of a Pixar Animation Studios film, *A Bug's Life*. Hang on for a watery **Kali River Rapids**® ride. And every day, your Disney character pals are waiting for you to laugh along with **Mickey's Jammin' Jungle** Parade.

celebrate **more thrills**

DISNEY'S ANIMAL KINGDOM

WATER PARKS

Disney's two Water Parks are magically themed and equally brimming with exhilaration and relaxation for all ages.

Disney's Typhoon Lagoon Water Park is a paradise of shady palms and sandy shores, where you can kick back under the sun, float along the creek, or bodysurf in one of the world's largest wave pools. For all-new thrills, check out **Crush 'n' Gusher**, a white-knuckle water coaster with powerful water jets that launch you up and beyond gravity's scope! You can even ride over a thriving reef with real sharks.

Disney's Blizzard Beach Water Park immerses you in the fantasy of a "snowstorm" in Florida. But instead of freezing, you can chill out for a lazy day on the ice floes. Or freak out on the coolest slides and hottest flume rides, even racing up to 55 mph down **Summit Plummet**, one of the tallest and fastest water slides in the nation!

Did you know?
Disney Resort Guests receive special benefits! See the GOLD Disney pages in this TourBook to find out more.

splash into **Disney's** water parks

Discover Downtown Disney, day or night!

The *Downtown Disney®* area is a waterfront metropolis at the heart of *Walt Disney World®* Resort, featuring some of the most unique shopping anywhere. For kids of all ages, you'll find that perfect Disney treasure at **World of Disney®** store—the largest Disney character merchandise shop on earth—as well as innovative toys and classic favorites at **Once Upon a Toy**, sports fan fun at **Team Mickey Athletic Club**, dreams to build at **LEGO Imagination Center®**, and holiday magic at **Disney's Days of Christmas**. The delights never seem to end, from music, movies and collectibles to fashion, food and fine Disney art. For grown-ups, every night is a party at *Downtown Disney* Pleasure Island* with its eight outrageous clubs. And gather the whole gang at *Downtown Disney* West Side for the astounding Cirque du Soleil® show, *La Nouba*™

*Certain age restrictions may apply for access to certain facilities.

AAA Members have the edge

Call or visit your local AAA Travel office now and save on select *Disney Resort* accommodations with the AAA Disney *Magic Moments®* Savings plan or other special *AAA Vacations®* packages. They include a *Disney Resort* stay, Disney's *Magic Your Way* Tickets and these EXCLUSIVE *AAA Vacations®* benefits:

- *AAA Vacations® Diamond Card* for special savings on meals, merchandise and recreation at participating Disney locations.

- *AAA Diamond Parking* – Preferred Parking in special AAA spaces at all four *Walt Disney World* Theme Parks (subject to availability, voucher required, some block-out dates apply).

  Ask about the new exclusive **Disney Character Storytelling Experience** available on select *AAA Vacations®* packages. Restrictions apply.

All AAA benefits subject to change without notice.

Buy your Disney tickets before you leave home

With Disney's **Magic Your Way** Tickets*, you can enjoy attractions and shows at all four *Walt Disney World* Theme Parks for 1-10 days. The more you play, the less you pay per day! Add on the **Park Hopper®** Option and visit multiple Parks on the same day. Or add the **Water Park Fun & More** Option** to enjoy Disney Water Parks, *Downtown Disney* Pleasure Island, *DisneyQuest®* Indoor Interactive Theme Park and more. Buy select tickets through AAA Travel before you leave home and enjoy Preferred Parking in AAA Diamond Spaces at all four Disney Theme Parks (subject to availability, voucher required, some block-out dates apply).
To find out how to purchase Disney tickets, visit aaa.com or contact your local AAA office.

NOTE: Select *AAA Vacations®* packages already include Disney tickets.
Theme Parks, rides, attractions, entertainment, operating hours, and other programs may be changed or discontinued. Sometimes, only one Water Park is open and, on occasion, both may be closed due to inclement weather.

*Theme Park tickets must be used within 14 days of first use unless the *No Expiration* Option is purchased. Except for activities/events separately priced. **The number of options varies with the number of days on your ticket. Visiting more than one Theme Park on the same day requires the *Park Hopper®* option.

LONGWOOD (D-4) pop. 13,745, elev. 75′

BIG TREE PARK is n. on US 17/92, then 1.5 mi. w. on Gen. J.C. Hutcheson Pkwy. A boardwalk in the 11-acre park leads to The Senator, a 3,500-year-old giant cypress tree that is one of the largest in the United States. The tree is 138 feet high, with a diameter of 17.5 feet and a circumference of 47 feet. Picnicking is permitted. Daily 8 a.m.-dusk. Free. Phone (407) 788-0405.

MAITLAND (E-4) pop. 12,019, elev. 91′

Maitland's 19th-century growth followed a pattern familiar to many central Florida towns. A pioneer fort in the Second Seminole War, the settlement prospered during the citrus producing era and later swelled as the railroad brought an influx of climate-conscious tourists and entrepreneurs.

The Maitland Historical Museum, 221 W. Packwood, highlights area history and houses the Telephone Museum, which traces the growth of the family-owned Winter Park Telephone Co. 1910-76 through photographs, telephone equipment and related memorabilia. The company got its start when a Maitland grocer installed telephones in customers' houses to take orders. For additional information phone (407) 644-2451.

Audubon of Florida, 1101 Audubon Way, is a rehabilitation center for injured birds of prey and a permanent home for those that cannot be released; phone (407) 644-0190.

Maitland Area Chamber of Commerce: 110 N. Maitland Ave., Maitland, FL 32751; phone (407) 644-0741.

HISTORIC WATERHOUSE RESIDENCE AND CARPENTRY SHOP MUSEUMS are .9 mi. n. of SR 423 on US 17/92, then e. to 820 Lake Lily Dr. The 1884 Waterhouse residence is a house museum that highlights the experiences of one of Maitland's pioneer families. Antique tools and woodworking techniques are exhibited at the Carpentry Shop Museum. Allow 30 minutes minimum. Thurs.-Sun. noon-4; closed major holidays. Admission $2, family rate $5. Phone (407) 644-2451.

THE HOLOCAUST MEMORIAL RESOURCE AND EDUCATION CENTER OF FLORIDA is 1.25 mi. e. of I-4 exit 90A at 851 N. Maitland Ave. (SR 414). The center illustrates key events of the Holocaust through chronological displays, photographs and audiovisual presentations. A memorial wall built of Jerusalem stone remembers the 6 million Jews who died at the hands of the Nazis. Allow 1 hour minimum. Mon.-Thurs. 9-4, Fri. 9-1, Sun. 1-4; closed major national and Jewish holidays. Free. Phone (407) 628-0555.

MAITLAND ART CENTER is 1.5 mi. e. of I-4 exit 90A on SR 414 (Maitland Blvd.), .7 mi. s. on CR 427 (Maitland Ave.), then .2 mi. w. to 231 W. Packwood Ave. One of the few surviving examples of "fantasy" architecture in the southeast United States, this 23-building complex is ornamented with murals, bas-reliefs and carvings in Aztec and Mayan styles. Walkways wind through courtyards and gardens at the center, which was founded as an artist's colony in the 1930s. Changing exhibits showcase local, regional and national artists and craftspersons.

Guided tours are available. Allow 1 hour minimum. Mon.-Fri. 9-4:30, Sat.-Sun. noon-4:30; closed major holidays. Donations. Phone (407) 539-2181.

MOUNT DORA (D-2) pop. 9,418, elev. 175′

Established in 1880, Mount Dora—about 25 miles northwest of Orlando—is a mecca for antiques collectors and dealers alike. Equally known as a festival city, Mount Dora is home to top-rated arts and crafts festivals.

Sightseers can take train, carriage, trolley or boat trips, rent a bicycle or canoe, or simply stroll along the shore of picturesque Lake Dora. Gilbert Park, with a playground, croquet field and boating facilities, is a popular spot for picnics. The 1,700-foot-long Palm Island Boardwalk is said to be Florida's longest lakeside boardwalk.

Mount Dora Chamber of Commerce: 341 Alexander St., P.O. Box 196, Mount Dora, FL 32756; phone (352) 383-2165.

Shopping areas: Boutiques, gift shops and antiques galleries line Mount Dora's downtown streets, and as many as 1,500 antiques dealers gather for the fairs and extravaganzas held at Renninger's Antique Center. There, collectors and window shoppers can find anything from furniture and jewelry to Art Deco items and World's Fair collectibles.

ST. CLOUD (I-4) pop. 20,074, elev. 63′

FOREVER FLORIDA AND THE CRESCENT J RANCH is 7.5 mi. s. of jct. US 192 on US 441, then e. to 4755 N. Kenansville Rd. Tours in an elevated swamp buggy introduce guests to several ecosystems and wildlife species within a 4,700-acre working cattle ranch and nature preserve. A pony riding ring and a petting zoo are available for children. Horseback riding trips also are offered. Food is available. Allow 2 hours minimum. Ranch and preserve open daily 9-5. Swamp buggy tours depart at 10 and 1. Tour fare $19.95, children $14.95. Reservations are recommended for tours. MC, VI. Phone (407) 957-9794 or (866) 854-3837.

REPTILE WORLD SERPENTARIUM, 4.5 mi. e. on US 192, 1 mi. e. of jct. CR 532, houses more than 50 species of snakes from around the world in glass display cases. Also featured are turtle, alligator and lizard exhibits. Venom programs are given daily at noon and 3. Allow 1 hour, 30 minutes minimum. Tues.-Sun. 9-5:30, Oct.-Aug.; closed Jan. 1, Thanksgiving weekend and Dec. 25. Admission $5.75; ages 6-17, $4.75; ages 3-5, $3.75. Phone (407) 892-6905.

Step into Paradise!

*A*nd step into a world of fun and relaxation with world-class beaches, dining, activities and so much more!

For more information or reservations, call or visit your local AAA Travel Office or log on to www.aaa.com.

Pleasant Holidays

SANFORD (D-10) pop. 38,291, elev. 20′

On Lake Monroe at the head of navigation on the St. Johns River, Sanford was established as a trading post in 1837. Gen. Henry R. Sanford bought 12,000 acres, including the townsite, in 1871 and established citrus groves.

The historic district, centered on First Street, contains structures dating back to 1883 and includes a former office building and hotel erected in 1887 for railroad entrepreneur Henry B. Plant. A refurbished 1922 silent movie and vaudeville house on S. Magnolia Avenue serves as home to the elen Stairs Theatre for the Performing Arts, a venue for the theatre's repertory company, the Central Florida Lyric Opera, the Orlando City Ballet and other area performance troupes.

RiverWalk, a 1.2-mile pedestrian way skirting the lake north of the historic district, provides waterfront picnicking and recreation space.

Amtrak's Auto Train transports passengers and their cars to and from Lorton, Va. To reach the station, take SR 46 (I-4 exit 101C) east to 400 Persimmon Ave.

Sanford/Seminole County Chamber of Commerce: 400 E. First St., Sanford, FL 32771; phone (407) 322-2212.

Shopping areas: First Street, in the downtown historic district, features a variety of shops with antiques and collectibles.

Self-guiding tours: Brochures for walking tours of the historic district are available from the chamber of commerce.

CENTRAL FLORIDA ZOO is n.w. on US 17/92, .7 mi. s. of I-4 exit 104. The park contains mammals, birds, reptiles and a children's zoo as well as a miniature train and a carousel. Picnicking is permitted. Allow 2 hours minimum. Daily 9-5; closed Thanksgiving and Dec. 25. Admission $8.95; over 60, $6.95; ages 3-12, $4.95. MC, VI. Phone (407) 323-4450.

MUSEUM OF SEMINOLE COUNTY HISTORY is 1 mi. s. on US 17/92, then w. to 300 Bush Blvd. Two buildings feature displays about the area's early citrus, celery, turpentine and fishing industries. Other exhibits highlight transportation, law enforcement and period artifacts. Allow 30 minutes minimum. Mon.-Fri. 9-5, Sat. 9-4; closed holidays. Free. Phone (407) 665-2489.

SAVE **RIVERSHIP** *ROMANCE* is off I-4 exit 101C, 4.5 mi. e. on SR 46, then n. on Palmetto Ave. to Monroe Harbour Marina. Luncheon sightseeing cruises are offered along the St. Johns River aboard a 100-foot, 1940s-style Great Lakes steamer. Dinner/dance cruises also are available. Three-hour luncheon cruise departs Wed. and Sat.-Sun. at 11; 4-hour luncheon cruise departs Mon.-Tues. and Thurs.-Fri. at 11. Three-hour lunch fares start at $36.75; 4-hour

lunch fares begin at $47.25. Reservations are required. AX, DS, MC, VI. Phone (407) 321-5091 or (800) 423-7401.

THE SANFORD MUSEUM, 520 E. First St., houses exhibits depicting the city's history. Two rooms dedicated to city founder Henry Shelton Sanford include his art collection, books and papers. Tues.-Fri. 11-4, Sat. 1-4; closed holidays. Free. Phone (407) 302-1000.

TAVARES (D-9) pop. 9,700, elev. 66′

CAPTAIN DAVE'S DORA CANAL CRUISES departs from the dock at the intersection of US 441 and Lake Shore Blvd. Captain Dave's offers narrated cruises of Lake Eustis, Lake Dora and the Dora Canal during which passengers can see a variety of local wildlife. Allow 1 hour, 30 minutes minimum. Cruises depart at 10:30, 1 and 3, mid-Oct. through Apr. 30. Fare $10. Reservations are required. Phone (352) 343-3889.

WINTER PARK (F-4) pop. 24,090, elev. 96′

Moss-draped oaks line the residential streets of Winter Park, a community of beautiful homes and picturesque lakes. The campus of Rollins College features brick streets and Mediterranean-style buildings on the shores of Lake Virginia. The small, private college is at the foot of Park Avenue, a popular shopping district with a varied selection of upscale boutiques, galleries and restaurants.

Winter Park Chamber of Commerce: 150 N. New York Ave., Winter Park, FL 32787; phone (407) 644-8281.

SAVE **ALBIN POLASEK MUSEUM AND SCULPTURE GARDENS** is 1.3 mi. e. of US 17/92 at 633 Osceola Ave. (SR 426). Three galleries and the gardens display the sculptures and paintings of the Czech-American artist. Noteworthy is a wooden nativity Polasek created at age 15. Guided tours are available. Tues.-Sat. 10-4, Sun. 1-4, Sept.-June; closed holidays. Admission $5, seniors $4, students with ID $3, under 12 free. Phone (407) 647-6294.

GEM **CHARLES HOSMER MORSE MUSEUM OF AMERICAN ART,** 445 N. Park Ave., contains works by Louis Comfort Tiffany, a celebrated and influential designer of the late 19th and early 20th century. Many of the stained-glass windows on exhibit were installed at Laurelton Hall, Tiffany's mansion on Long Island. A highlight is the chapel Tiffany designed for the 1893 Exposition at the Chicago World's Fair.

The museum houses art and historical documents including works by Tiffany's contemporaries, a collection of American art pottery and American paintings from the late 19th century to the early 20th century. Guided tours are available. Allow 1 hour minimum. Tues.-Sat. 9:30-4 (also Fri. 4-8, Sept.-May), Sun. 1-4; closed major holidays. Admission $3; students over 12, $1; free to all Fri. 4-8 in season, Easter, July 4 and Dec. 24. Phone (407) 645-5311.

CORNELL FINE ARTS MUSEUM, 2.25 mi. e. of I-4 exit 87 at the end of Holt Ave. on the Rollins College campus, displays permanent and changing exhibits of American and European paintings, decorative arts and sculpture. Representative artists include William Merritt Chase, Childe Hassam and Louis Comfort Tiffany. **Note:** The museum is closed for renovations; reopening is scheduled for fall 2005. Allow 1 hour minimum. Tues.-Fri. 10-5, Sat.-Sun. 1-5; closed holidays. Free. Phone (407) 646-2526.

SCENIC BOAT TOURS, leaving from the foot of Morse Blvd., provide narrated 1-hour cruises past many of Winter Park's opulent lakeside estates and landmarks. Allow 1 hour, 30 minutes minimum. Departures daily on the hour 10-4; closed Dec. 25. Fare $9; under 12, $4. Phone (407) 644-4056.

Men in Black Alien Attack, Universal Studios / Orlando/Orange County CVB

This ends listings for the Orlando Vicinity.
The following page resumes the alphabetical listings of cities in Florida.

ORMOND BEACH (C-10)
pop. 36,301, elev. 6'

Charles and Frank Duryea, Barney Oldfield, R.E. Olds, Alexander Winton and others raced cars on the sands of Ormond Beach in the early and mid-1900s, giving the city its reputation as the birthplace of speed.

Ormond Beach Chamber of Commerce: 165 W. Granada Blvd., Ormond Beach, FL 32174; phone (386) 677-3454.

THE CASEMENTS, 25 Riverside Dr., was the winter home of John D. Rockefeller from 1914 until his death in 1937. The house is now a cultural and civic center, with a collection of Hungarian folk art, Boy Scout memorabilia and an exhibit of Rockefeller furnishings and personal items. Allow 30 minutes minimum. Mon.-Fri. 9-5, Sat. 9-noon; closed holidays. Tours are given Mon.-Fri. 10-2:30, second Sat. of the month 10-11:30. Donations. Phone (386) 676-3216.

ORMOND MEMORIAL ART MUSEUM AND GARDENS, 1 mi. e. of US 1 at 78 E. Granada Blvd., contains a 4.5-acre botanical memorial garden with a waterfall, nature trails and turtle ponds as well as changing exhibits of contemporary Florida art and fine crafts. Allow 30 minutes minimum. Gardens open daily dawn-dusk. Gallery open Mon.-Fri. 10-4, Sat.-Sun. noon-4; closed major holidays. Admission $2; senior citizens and students free. Phone (386) 676-3347.

OSCEOLA NATIONAL FOREST
Elevations in the forest range from 120 ft. to 180 ft.

Near the Georgia border, Osceola National Forest encompasses 201,364 acres consisting of flat country dotted with ponds and swamps. Fishing is available in numerous creeks and rivers. Hunting is permitted, but a special license is required in the Osceola Wildlife Management Area; for information phone the Florida Fish and Wildlife Conservation Commission at (850) 488-4676. Ocean Pond *(see the AAA Southeastern CampBook)* and Olustee Beach are major recreation areas within the forest. Phone (386) 752-2577. *See Recreation Chart.*

OSPREY (F-8) pop. 4,143, elev. 10'

HISTORIC SPANISH POINT, 337 N. Tamiami Trail (US 41), is a 30-acre historic site on Little Sarasota Bay. Florida pioneer life is interpreted through a homestead house, a chapel, a citrus packing house and boat-building exhibits. Spanish Point was the site of the winter estate of Bertha Palmer, widow of a Chicago businessman; the grounds contain formal gardens she created in the early 1900s and a butterfly garden. Visitors can view an archeology display inside a prehistoric shell mound.

Guided tours are available. Picnicking is permitted. Allow 1 hour, 30 minutes minimum. Mon.-Sat.

9-5, Sun. noon-5; closed Jan. 1, Easter, Thanksgiving and Dec. 25. Admission $7; over 55, $5 on Mon.; ages 6-12, $3. DS, MC, VI. Phone (941) 966-5214.

PALATKA (C-9) pop. 10,033, elev. 28'

Judge Isaac Bronson, one of Palatka's foremost residents, was a member of the 25th U.S. Congress and was responsible for proposing the act by which Florida became a state. His restored home, Bronson-Mulholland House, 100 Mulholland Park, was built in 1854 and is open to the public.

Rodman Reservoir, 10 miles southwest off SR 19, is a popular recreation destination, particularly for bass fishing. Several boat ramps are available in the area. *See Recreation Chart.*

Putnam County Chamber of Commerce: 1100 Reid St., P.O. Box 550, Palatka, FL 32178; phone (386) 328-1503.

RAVINE GARDENS STATE PARK, on Twigg St., is 1.25 mi. s. off SR 20. Formed by water erosion from the St. Johns River, the steep ravines provide a rich environment for wild plants. Two swinging bridges cross the ravines, and nature trails wind through the 59-acre gardens, which have been landscaped extensively with azaleas and camellias. A children's playground and a fitness trail are available. Picnicking is permitted. Daily 8-dusk. The road is closed to motorized vehicles at 4 p.m. Admission $4 per private vehicle (maximum of eight people), $1 per person arriving by bicycle or on foot. Phone (386) 329-3721.

PALM BEACH (F-11) pop. 10,468, elev. 32'

In 1878 the Spanish ship *Providentia,* bound from the West Indies to Spain, went aground at Palm Beach, spilling its cargo of coconuts along the sandy, barrier island. When Henry Flagler visited the area in the early 1890s, he found a small community of settlers amid a growth of coconut palms. Recognizing the potential of South Florida, he chose Palm Beach for the site of his next luxury hotel and laid out a fashionable resort that has retained the quiet charm and tropical beauty of his original vision.

A scenic portion of SR A1A meanders along the ocean as it extends from Palm Beach south to Fort Lauderdale, a drive of 47 miles.

Also see West Palm Beach p. 237.

Palm Beach Chamber of Commerce: 45 Cocoanut Row, Palm Beach, FL 33480; phone (561) 655-3282.

Shopping areas: Shops such as Cartier, Gucci and Tiffany line tree-shaded Worth Avenue.

BETHESDA-BY-THE-SEA, S. County Rd. and Barton Ave., is an Episcopal church of modified 15th-century Gothic design. Adjacent are the attractive, formally landscaped Cluett Memorial Gardens. Church and gardens open daily 8-5. Free. Phone (561) 655-4554.

FLAGLER MUSEUM is at Cocoanut Row and Whitehall Way. Original and period furnishings and Flagler family memorabilia grace Whitehall, the opulent 1902 Gilded Age mansion railroad magnate Henry Flagler built for his bride. The 55-room house was hailed as "grander and more magnificent than any other private dwelling in the world."

The house was restored as a museum in 1959. Among the highlights are the grand entrance hall, a Louis XIV music room and a Louis XV ballroom. The museum also features changing exhibits and special programs. Visitors can see Flagler's private railroad car in a pavilion on the south lawn.

Guided and audiotape tours are available. Allow 1 hour, 30 minutes minimum. Tues.-Sat. 10-5, Sun. noon-5; closed Jan. 1, Thanksgiving and Dec. 25. Admission $12; ages 6-12, $3. AX, MC, VI. Phone (561) 655-2833. *See color ad p. 238.*

SOCIETY OF THE FOUR ARTS, Four Arts Plaza just off Royal Palm Way, comprises a library, art gallery, auditorium, and sculpture and botanical gardens. Lectures by authors and noted speakers are presented weekly, early December through mid-April. **Note:** The gardens are closed for renovations; phone ahead for reopening date. Allow 30 minutes minimum. Gallery open Mon.-Fri. 10-5, Sat. 9-1, Nov.-Apr. Library open Mon.-Fri. 10-5 (also Sat. 9-1, Nov.-Apr.). Free. A fee may be charged during special events. Phone (561) 655-7226 or (561) 655-2766 for the library.

PALM COAST (C-10) pop. 32,732, elev. 10′

WASHINGTON OAKS GARDENS STATE PARK, 6400 N. Oceanshore Blvd., originally was part of Bella Vista Plantation owned by Gen. Joseph Hernandez, a militia general who commanded troops during the Second Seminole War. Extending from the Atlantic Ocean to the Matanzas River, the preserve covers more than 400 acres of Florida coastal scenery. Included are scenic tidal marshes, a scrub community, a beach and a hammock. Coquina rock outcroppings worn into unusual shapes by the sea give the beach area an unearthly appearance. Many species of shorebirds and marine and forest animals make their home in the area.

Formal gardens contain exotic plants from around the world; a history of the area is presented at the Young House. Guided walks are provided on weekends and by request. Picnicking is permitted. Allow 3 hours minimum. Daily 8-dusk. Admission $4 per private vehicle. Phone (386) 446-6780. *See Recreation Chart.*

PANACEA (B-6) elev. 5′

GULF SPECIMEN MARINE LABORATORY, just s. of US 98, following signs to 222 Clark Dr., features a 25,000-gallon marine aquarium and touch tanks housing sea horses, crabs, rays, sponges, starfish and small sharks. Allow 1 hour minimum. Mon.-Fri. 9-5,

Sat. 10-4, Sun. noon-4. Admission $5; ages 3-11, $3. Phone (850) 984-5297.

PANAMA CITY (B-4) pop. 36,417, elev. 33′

Panama City, county seat of Bay County, is a leading port on St. Andrew Bay off the Gulf of Mexico and is the eastern terminus for a scenic portion of US 98 extending 98 miles to Gulf Breeze, just south of Pensacola. Spanish expeditions visited this site 1516-40, but it was not until 1765 that an English settlement was made at St. Andrew, now part of Panama City.

The area also is home to Tyndall Air Force Base and Naval Support Activity-Panama City. The city is known for its sugar-white beaches. A marina at the foot of Harrison Avenue includes berths for about 400 boats. Fishing boats can be chartered on St. Andrew Bay.

Bay County Chamber of Commerce: 235 W. Fifth St., P.O. Box 1850, Panama City, FL 32402-1850; phone (850) 785-5206.

JUNIOR MUSEUM OF BAY COUNTY, 1731 Jenks Ave., offers child-oriented hands-on exhibits including Body Works, Hands-On Science, Nature Corner, Imagine Me and Discovery Depot. Highlights include the Pioneer Homestead, a re-created farm from the late 1800s, and a boardwalk nature trail through a swamp and forest area. Allow 30 minutes minimum. Mon.-Fri. 9-4:30, Sat. 10-4; closed major holidays. Donations. Phone (850) 769-6128.

PANAMA CITY BEACH (B-4)
pop. 7,671, elev. 7′

Powdery white sand beaches and emerald waters of the Gulf of Mexico give Panama City Beach its status as a popular shore resort. The Yucatan Current, part of the Gulf Stream, runs close to the shores of Panama City Beach, bringing with it nutrient-rich Caribbean water and blue marlin, sailfish, big bull dolphin (fish), wahoo and tuna. One fishing pier extends 1,600 feet into the Gulf.

More than 27 miles of beach give access to numerous recreational pursuits, on- or offshore. Activities include pleasure boating, sailing, jet skiing, wind surfing and parasailing. Dozens of shipwrecks and almost 50 artificial reefs provide plenty of scuba diving options.

St. Andrews State Park *(see Recreation Chart and the AAA Southeastern CampBook)* flanks the pass separating Panama City Beach from Shell Island, the barrier isle guarding the mouth of St. Andrew Bay. The mainland portion of the park, reached via Thomas Drive, contains a restored turpentine still. The Shell Island segment, an excellent spot for swimming, snorkeling and shell gathering, is accessible only by boat. Shuttles depart from the end of Thomas Drive in the recreation area daily every 30 minutes 9-5.

With nearly 320 days of sunny skies and temperate climate, Panama City Beach is known for its "golfability" factor. Five championship golf courses are in close proximity to the beaches.

Shipwreck Island Waterpark, 12000 Front Beach Rd., is a popular family attraction.

Ebro Greyhound Park, on SR 79 at SR 20, offers live greyhound racing February through October; phone (850) 234-3943.

Note: Policies vary concerning admittance of children to pari-mutuel betting facilities. Phone for information.

Panama City Beach Convention and Visitors Bureau: P.O. Box 9473, Panama City Beach, FL 32417; phone (850) 233-6503 or (800) 722-3224. *See color ad.*

CAPT. ANDERSON CRUISES, at Capt. Anderson's Marina, 5550 N. Lagoon Dr. at jct. Thomas Dr., offers 3-hour sightseeing cruises to Shell Island and a 75-minute sunset Dolphin Watch cruise aboard a glass-bottom boat. Dinner/dance, gospel music and deep-sea fishing cruises also are available. Shell Island cruises depart daily at 9 and 1, Dolphin Watch daily at 5:15, Mar.-Oct. Shell Island cruise $16; ages 6-11, $10; ages 2-5, $7. Dolphin Watch $8; ages 2-11, $5. MC, VI. Phone (850) 234-5940 or (800) 874-2415.

THE MUSEUM OF MAN IN THE SEA, .25 mi. w. of jct. SR 79 at 17314 Panama City Beach Pkwy. (US 98), illustrates the history of undersea exploration using dioramas and written records. Highlights include rare and antique diving equipment and related displays. Changing exhibits are featured. Allow 1 hour minimum. Daily 9-5; closed Jan. 1, Thanksgiving and Dec. 25. Admission $5; over 65, $4.50; ages 6-16, $2.50. AX, DS, MC, VI. Phone (850) 235-4101.

THE OCEAN OPRY MUSIC SHOW, 2 mi. w. of Hathaway Bridge to 8400 Front Beach Rd., presents a comedy and country music stage show in a 1,000-seat theater. Nashville stars appear throughout the year. Food is available. Allow 2 hours minimum. Performances Mon.-Sat. at 8 p.m., June-Aug. (also Sun. performances Memorial Day, July 4 and Labor Day weekends); Tues. and Fri.-Sat. at 7:30 p.m., rest of year. Admission $19.95; ages 5-11, $9.95. Prices vary for special shows. DS, MC, VI. Phone (850) 234-5464 for reservations and schedule.

PENSACOLA (B-2) pop. 56,255, elev. 39′

Although an attempt was made in 1559 by Don Tristan de Luna, permanent settlement at Pensacola was not established until 1698. The town has flown the flags of Spain, France, England, the Confederate States and the United States, and its government has changed hands 13 times.

In 1814 the British used the harbor as a base in their war with the United States, but withdrew when the city was attacked by Gen. Andrew Jackson. Here Jackson completed the transaction by which Spain sold Florida to the United States in 1821. In the city's historic downtown at Plaza Ferdinand VII is the site where the Spanish flag was lowered for the last time. Pensacola was the territorial capital until 1822, and Andrew Jackson was a resident while governor of Florida.

The Seville Square historic district, bounded on the north by Government Street and on the east by Alcaniz Street, is an area of restored 19th-century buildings that now houses shops, restaurants, museums and art galleries.

Pensacola's Naval Air Station is a center for electronic warfare and cartographic training as well as headquarters for the Blue Angels precision flying team.

Gulf Islands National Seashore *(see place listing p. 94 and Recreation Chart)* offers miles and miles

of unspoiled sugar-white beaches and emerald waters. Recreational activities include boating, swimming and sun-bathing. Other outdoor activities can be enjoyed on the area's numerous waterways, including the Blackwater and Perdido rivers and Coldwater and Sweetwater-Juniper creeks *(see Milton p. 135)*.

The Wildlife Sanctuary of Northwest Florida, 105 N. S St., cares for injured and orphaned wildlife, including foxes, deer, eagles, egrets, herons, owls, pelicans and hawks; for information phone (850) 433-9453.

West of the city on Dog Track Road, Pensacola Greyhound Track presents dog races Wednesday through Saturday evenings and Saturday and Sunday afternoons. Phone (850) 455-8595.

Note: Policies vary concerning admittance of children to pari-mutuel betting facilities. Phone for information.

Pensacola Bay Area Convention and Visitors Center: 1401 E. Gregory St., Pensacola, FL 32501; phone (850) 434-1234 or (800) 874-1234.

Self-guiding tours: The convention and visitors center, at the foot of the 3-mile bay bridge, offers free information about tours of the city.

Shopping areas: Cordova Mall, 5100 N. Ninth Ave., contains more than 150 stores including Dillard's and Parisian. University Mall, 7171 N. Davis Hwy., features JCPenney, McRae's and Sears among its 85 stores. Old buildings have been transformed into specialty shops at Palafox Place.

HISTORIC PENSACOLA VILLAGE, bounded north by Government St., south by Main St., east by Seville Square and west by Plaza Ferdinand, is a complex of 10 museum buildings reflecting 450 years of Pensacola's history. Allow 1 hour minimum. Mon.-Sat. 10-4; closed holidays. Village admission $6; over 65 and military with ID $5; ages 4-16, $2.50. Phone (850) 595-5985.

Dorr House, 311 S. Adams St., is an example of Greek Revival architecture. Built in 1871 by Clara Barkley Dorr, the widow of a lumber baron, the two-story house is furnished with late Victorian pieces.

Julee Cottage, 210 E. Zaragoza St., was built in 1805 and once belonged to Julee Panton, a free woman of color.

Lavalle House, 205 E. Church St., was built by Carlos Lavalle and Marianna Bonifay in 1805 during Florida's second Spanish period. A rare example of French Creole Colonial architecture, the house is furnished to reflect the 1820s Pensacola frontier.

Museum of Commerce, 201 E. Zaragoza St., features a full-scale replica of an 1890s Pensacola street inside a 19th-century warehouse. Printing presses, a hardware store, a toy shop and a horse-drawn buggy collection are among the exhibits.

Museum of Industry, 200 E. Zaragoza St., displays photographs, tools and equipment related to the 19th-century industrial boom in west Florida. Exhibits focus on Pensacola's fishing, brickmaking, railroad and lumber industries.

T.T. Wentworth Jr. Florida State Museum, 330 S. Jefferson St., was built in the Renaissance Revival style in 1907 as Pensacola's city hall. The elaborate building now houses changing exhibits about the region's history, architecture and archeology.

NATIONAL MUSEUM OF NAVAL AVIATION, on the Naval Air Station, Pensacola, traces the development of American naval aviation from its beginnings to the present. Highlighted among more than 170 historic naval aircraft are the NC-4 Flying Boat, which in 1919 became the first plane to cross the Atlantic; the only surviving SBD Dauntless from the Battle of Midway; and the Skylab Command Module.

Four A-4 Skyhawks are suspended from the ceiling in formation in the Blue Angels Atrium. Bus tours of the flight line feature additional aircraft. Walk-through displays portray a World War II carrier hangar bay, a South Pacific Sea Island forward Marine base and the wartime home front. Other exhibits range from pre-World War I memorabilia to items used by Navy prisoners of war during the Vietnam War. An IMAX theater presents films every hour.

Food is available. Allow 1 hour, 30 minutes minimum. Daily 9-5; closed Jan. 1, Thanksgiving and Dec. 25. Museum free. IMAX film $7; senior citizens, military with ID and ages 4-12, $6.50. Phone (850) 453-6289 or (800) 327-5002. *See color ad p. 189.*

NAVAL AIR STATION, PENSACOLA, s. end of Navy Blvd., provides maps and visitor information at the front gate, Building 777. For historical maps and base information contact the public affairs office. The air station is open daily; hours vary. Free. Phone (850) 452-2311.

Fort Barrancas is one of several U.S. forts built by the U.S. Corps of Engineers in the 19th century along northwestern Florida's coastline. A dry moat surrounds the inner walls and makes access to the fort possible only by way of a drawbridge. Allow 45 minutes minimum. Daily 9:30-4:45, Mar.-Oct.; 8:30-3:45, rest of year. Hours may vary; phone ahead. Closed Dec. 25. Tours are given at 2. Free. Phone (850) 455-5167.

PENSACOLA HISTORICAL MUSEUM, in the Arbona Building at 115 E. Zaragoza St., relates the military and maritime history of the town from its early days to the present. Exhibits of local historical items include flags, photographs, military buttons and American Indian artifacts. A resource center on E. Church Street maintains genealogical information, maps, government records and manuscripts.

Allow 30 minutes minimum. Museum Mon.-Sat. 10-4:30. Resource center Tues.-Fri. 10-4, Sat. by appointment. Closed holidays. Museum $2. Resource

center research fee $5. Phone (850) 433-1559 for museum, or (850) 434-5455 for resource center.

PLAZA FERDINAND VII, S. Palafox St. between E. Government and Zaragoza sts., was part of Pensacola's original Spanish settlement. A statue of Andrew Jackson commemorates the transfer of Florida to the United States.

VETERANS MEMORIAL PARK, at the corner of Bayfront Pkwy. and Ninth Ave., contains a replica of the Vietnam Veterans Memorial in Washington, D.C., and memorials to veterans of World War I, World War II, the Korean War and the Vietnam War. Daily 24 hours. Free. Phone (850) 456-0040.

PENSACOLA BEACH (B-3) elev. 7'

Snow white sand and aquamarine water make Pensacola Beach one of Florida's most beautiful beaches. Bordered by two preserved seashores, the area offers more than 20 miles of beach front covered in sugarlike sand composed of 99 percent pure quartz.

Wide paths parallel beach roads to offer skaters, cyclists, walkers and joggers a place for recreation. Other popular pursuits include fishing, golf and a wide array of water sports.

Pensacola Beach Chamber of Commerce Visitor Information Center: 735 Pensacola Beach Blvd., Pensacola Beach, FL 32561; phone (850) 932-1500 or (800) 635-4803.

PERRY (B-7) pop. 6,847, elev. 30'

FOREST CAPITAL MUSEUM STATE PARK, 1 mi. s. on US 19 at 204 Forest Park Dr., depicts the development of the forest industry. Exhibits illustrate modern forestry, turpentine production, regional wildlife and the cutting of virgin forests, cypress swamps and hardwood hammocks. The adjacent North Florida Cracker Homestead, built in the 1860s, interprets the lifestyle of early settlers. A playground is available. Picnicking is permitted. Allow 30 minutes minimum. Thurs.-Mon. 9-noon and 1-5; closed Jan. 1, Thanksgiving and Dec. 25. Admission $1, under 6 free. Phone (850) 584-3227.

PINELAND (G-9) pop. 444, elev. 20'

SAVE *TROPIC STAR* OF PINE ISLAND is 3.5 mi. n. of jct. SR 78 and CR 767 to 13921 Waterfront Dr. at Pineland Marina on Pine Island. Offered are full-day narrated nature cruises through the protected waters of Pine Island Sound to Cabbage Key and a rustic state park on Cayo Costa; a tram carries visitors to the beach on the Gulf of Mexico. Visitors can view porpoises, manatees and birds as well as explore islands accessible only by boat. Picnicking is permitted on Cayo Costa. Allow a full day. Cruises depart daily at 9:30 and return at 4. Fare $29; ages 2-7, $17. State park fee including tram $1. Reservations are required. Phone (239) 283-0015.

PLANT CITY—*see Tampa Bay p. 233.*

POINT WASHINGTON (B-4) elev. 16′

EDEN GARDENS STATE PARK AND WESLEY HOUSE is 1 mi. n. of US 98 on CR 395. Magnolias, colorful camellias and azaleas, a historic rose garden and live oaks draped in Spanish moss surround an 1898 Greek Revival mansion filled with Colonial, Empire and Victorian furnishings. The house was built on the site of a lumber mill owned by William Wesley. Two Civil War encampments are held during the year. Forty-five minute guided tours of the mansion are offered.

Grounds open daily 8-dusk. Mansion tours Thurs.-Mon. on the hour 10-3. Admission to grounds $3 per private vehicle (up to six persons plus $1 each additional person). Mansion tour $3; under 12, $1. Phone (850) 231-4214.

POLK CITY (E-9) pop. 1,516, elev. 173′

Incorporated in 1925, Polk City is near the Lake Wales Ridge, the highest ground on the Florida peninsula. Hundreds of thousands of years ago, when most of Florida was underwater, the ridge was part of an island chain that was isolated from the rest of North America. As a result of this isolation, the area today includes sandhill and scrub habitats that are home to a host of rare, threatened and endangered species.

The Water Ski Museum and Hall of Fame at 1251 Holy Cow Rd. contains vintage water ski paraphernalia from the early days of the sport including two pine boards that are said to be the very first water skis ever used; phone (863) 324-2472.

Central Florida Visitors & Convention Bureau: 600 N. Broadway, Suite 300, Bartow, FL 33830; phone (863) 534-2500.

FANTASY OF FLIGHT, I-4 exit 44, then .5 mi. n. on SR 559, features vintage aircraft portraying various eras of aviation, including the Short Sunderland—purportedly the world's last airworthy civilian four-engine flying boat. A walk-through diorama of a World War II bombing mission aboard a B-17 Flying Fortress is complete with films and audiotapes. Fightertown lets visitors experience an aerial dogfight. Guided aircraft shop tours are available.

Food is available. Allow 1 hour, 30 minutes minimum. Daily 9-5; closed Thanksgiving and Dec. 25. Admission $24.95; over 59, $22.95; ages 5-12, $13.95. AX, MC, VI. Phone (863) 984-3500.

POMPANO BEACH—
see Fort Lauderdale p. 86.

PONCE INLET (C-10) pop. 2,513, elev. 10′

THE *MANATEE* SCENIC CRUISES—
see New Smyrna Beach p. 138.

MARINE SCIENCE CENTER is just w. of SR A1A (S. Atlantic Ave.) at 100 Lighthouse Dr. Dioramas, nature trails, an observation tower and a 5,000-gallon aquarium provide marine life discovery experiences. Visitors can observe sea turtle and bird

rehabilitation centers. Allow 1 hour minimum. Mon.-Sat. 10-4, Sun. noon-4; closed Dec. 25. Last admission is 30 minutes before closing. Admission $3; ages 5-12, $1. AX, DS, MC, VI. Phone (386) 304-5545.

PONCE DE LEON INLET LIGHT STATION, just w. of SR A1A (S. Atlantic Ave.) at 4931 S. Peninsula Dr., features a 175-foot-high lighthouse that has been in service since 1887. Visitors may climb to the top of the lighthouse for a panorama of the Daytona Beach area. Also on the grounds are three keepers' cottages, a Fresnel lens museum, a nature trail and historic boats.

Picnicking is permitted in an adjacent park. Allow 1 hour minimum. Daily 10-9, Memorial Day-Labor Day; 10-5, rest of year. Closed Dec. 25. Last admission is 1 hour before closing. Admission $5; under 11, $1.50. Phone (386) 761-1821.

PORT ORANGE (C-10) pop. 45,823, elev. 20′

SUGAR MILL BOTANICAL GARDENS, 1 mi. w. of US 1 off Herbert St. on Old Sugar Mill Rd., encompasses 12 acres of landscaped grounds surrounding the restored ruins of an 1836 English sugar mill burned by Seminole Indians. A life-size statue of a prehistoric ground sloth and four dinosaur statues are along the garden trails. Guided tours are available. Daily 8-6. Tours are given Wed. 9-3. Donations. Phone (386) 767-1735.

PORT ST. JOE (C-5) pop. 3,644, elev. 5′

CONSTITUTION CONVENTION MUSEUM STATE PARK, 1.5 mi. s. on US 98, preserves the site of Florida's first constitutional convention. Exhibits pertain to this event and other local history. Animated talking mannequins provide 2 minutes of closing remarks at the end of the tour. Allow 30 minutes minimum. Thurs.-Mon. 9-noon and 1-5 Eastern Time; closed Jan. 1, Thanksgiving and Dec. 25. Admission $1, under 6 free. Phone (850) 229-8029.

PUNTA GORDA (F-9) pop. 14,344, elev. 61′

Punta Gorda, the county seat, is Charlotte County's only incorporated community. The old city dock, on the banks of the Peace River, has been transformed into Fisherman's Village, a marina and shopping complex. Across the street, the Visual Arts Center houses several galleries and features revolving exhibits. The area offers cruises, boat rentals and fishing charters.

Octagon Wildlife Sanctuary, on Horseshoe Road off SR 31, provides refuge for injured or unwanted wild and exotic animals; phone (239) 543-1130. Another organization that assists orphaned or injured animals is the Peace River Wildlife Center in Ponce de Leon Park, which attempts to rehabilitate and release native wildlife to their natural habitats; phone (941) 637-3830.

Charlotte County Chamber of Commerce: 326 W. Marion, Suite 112, Punta Gorda, FL 33950; phone (941) 639-2222. *See color ad p. 51.*

BABCOCK WILDERNESS ADVENTURES is off I-75S exit 164 (southbound), 1 mi. n. on US 17, 15 mi. e. on SR 74, then 6 mi. s. on SR 31; or off I-75N exit 143 (northbound), 3 mi. e. on SR 78, then 9 mi. n. on SR 31, to 8000 SR 31. Visitors get a close look at rare Florida panthers, alligators, snakes, birds, cattle and other native fauna and flora during the 1.5-hour swamp buggy tours through a working cattle ranch and the surrounding cypress swamp and other ecosystems. A museum with exhibits also is available.

Allow 2 hours minimum. Swamp buggy tours daily 9-3, Oct.-May; schedule varies rest of year. Fare $17.95; under 12, $10.95. Reservations are required. AX, DS, MC, VI. Phone (800) 500-5583 for reservations.

KING FISHER CRUISE LINES, 1200 W. Retta Esplanade in Fishermen's Village, offers day cruises to the offshore islands of Cabbage Key or to Cayo Costa State Park. Half-day river and harbor cruises, deep-sea fishing trips, afternoon and evening cruises and seasonal trips, including a Christmas Canal Cruise, also are available. Cabbage Key cruises depart Tues., Thurs. and Sat. at 9. Cayo Costa cruises depart Tues., Thurs. and Sun. at 9. Schedules may vary; phone ahead. Full-day cruises $21.95; ages 3-12, $11. Reservations are recommended. AX, MC, VI. Phone (941) 639-0969.

MILITARY HERITAGE & AVIATION MUSEUM is at 1200 W. Retta Esplanade in Fisherman's Village. Exhibits feature artifacts, uniforms, equipment and memorabilia chronicling American military history. Allow 1 hour minimum. Mon.-Sat. 10-6, Sun. noon-5; closed Jan. 1 and Dec. 25. Free. Phone (941) 575-9002.

QUINCY (A-6) pop. 6,982, elev. 187'

Established in 1828, the agricultural town of Quincy owed its early prosperity to the tobacco industry. The Quincy State Bank eventually persuaded its patrons to invest in the fledgling Coca-Cola Co., resulting in economic fortune for both the town and its citizens.

Soldiers from the battles of Natural Bridge and Olustee were treated in Quincy, a medical center during the Civil War. The town also served as a supply commissary for the Confederate Army. In 1868 a fire destroyed more than half the town, leading to an ordinance requiring that all new buildings be constructed of brick.

The 36-block historic district features landscaping, period lighting and Victorian-style buildings. Most structures were built in the late 1880s, although several houses date back to the 1840s.

Gadsden County Chamber of Commerce: 208 N. Adams St., P.O. Box 389, Quincy, FL 32353; phone (850) 627-9231.

Self-guiding tours: A brochure outlining a tour of the historic district is available from the chamber of commerce.

SAFETY HARBOR—*see Tampa Bay p. 234.*

ST. AUGUSTINE (B-10) pop. 11,592, elev. 7'

See map page 194.

As the oldest, continuously occupied European settlement in the United States, St. Augustine has played varied and prominent historic roles. Juan Ponce de León, in search of the legendary Fountain of Youth, landed in this area Apr. 3, 1513, and took possession of the region for Spain. In 1565 King Phillip II sent Pedro Menéndez de Avilés to colonize the new territory. Menéndez de Avilés arrived in Florida on the Feast Day of St. Augustine and named the landing site after the saint.

Its coastal location made the town both strategic and vulnerable. Pirates sacked St. Augustine in both the 16th and 17th centuries. Military importance soon came to the forefront as England extended its holdings southward down the coast. Spain responded by starting to build Castillo de San Marcos in 1672.

By the time St. Augustine was ceded to England in 1763, it had served as the seat of government for 30 missions as well as for all Spanish possessions in the regions of Florida and coastal Georgia. British loyalists from adjacent states sought refuge during the Revolutionary War.

In 1783 Florida was traded back to Spain. Encouraged by Spanish land grants, many Americans moved onto property vacated by the English. Florida became a U.S. possession in 1821, and during the Second Seminole War in the 1830s, St. Augustine resumed a military role.

The quiet coastal town came to life in the 1880s when Henry Flagler began to develop the area as a winter resort and playground. With a railway link provided from New York, plush hotels were built and leisure activities such as golf and yachting awaited the city's guests.

Still preserving strong evidence of its Spanish origin, the Old City is being restored to a likeness of its colonial days; much of the historic area north of the Plaza de la Constitución is complete. Typical Spanish houses, with walled patios enclosing Old World gardens, line the many narrow streets.

Tolomato Cemetery, also known as the Old Spanish Cemetery, is at Cordova Street between Orange and Saragossa streets. Formerly the site of the Christian Indian village of Tolomato, the cemetery served as a Catholic burial ground 1784-1892 and is the burial site of Augustin Verot, the first bishop of St. Augustine. The cemetery is only open by request; information is available at the rectory entrance of the Cathedral of St. Augustine on Treasury Street.

South of the city, St. Augustine Beach provides a return to the present. Miles of wide, hard-packed sand beaches afford beach driving, swimming and surfing opportunities. Boating also is popular.

Tours of area attractions by horse-drawn carriage depart from the bayfront area next to Castillo de San Marcos. The city's historic sites can be seen in a different light during nightly ghost tours. Costumed guides tell eerie stories about the city and its historic buildings as part of walking tours conducted by Ghost Tours of St. Augustine; phone (904) 461-4604. The Trolley of the Doomed provides transportation to haunted sites such as the Old Drug Store, the Spanish Military Hospital Museum and The Old Jail on tours offered by Ghosts & Gravestones; phone (904) 826-3663.

The Huguenot cemetery, between the City Gate and the Visitor Information Center, is open to the public anytime the gate is unlocked.

Note: Parking regulations are enforced strictly throughout the city. Yellow curbs are no-parking zones. Several parking lots are available. *See St. Augustine Walking Tour map.*

St. Augustine, Ponte Vedra and The Beaches Visitors and Convention Bureau: 88 Riberia St., Suite 400, St. Augustine, FL 32084; phone (904) 829-1711 or (800) 653-2489. *See color ad.*

Shopping areas: St. Augustine Outlet Center and Belz Factory Outlet World are both off I-95 exit 318 on SR 16.

The Old City

CASTILLO DE SAN MARCOS NATIONAL MONUMENT, a Spanish fortress, is at Castillo Dr. and Avenida Menéndez. The oldest masonry fort in the United States, it was built 1672-95 of coquina, a soft local shellrock, as part of the defenses along the route of the treasure fleets. For many years the fort was the northernmost point of Spain's New World holdings.

The symmetrical fort has massive diamond-shaped bastions at each of its four corners, and 60 to 77 cannons once occupied the gun deck. Its walls, 12 feet thick at the base, 8 feet thick at the top and 33 feet high, are skirted by a moat on three sides. Part of the "Cubo Line," a palisaded city wall, has been rebuilt. A stairway leads to the gun deck overlooking the Old City Gate, quaint old streets and Matanzas Bay. Exhibits trace fort history.

Metal detectors are not permitted. Allow 1 hour minimum. Daily 8:45-4:45; closed Dec. 25. Cannons are fired Saturday and Sunday from Memorial Day through Labor Day. Admission $5; ages 6-16, $2. Phone (904) 829-6506.

CATHEDRAL-BASILICA OF ST. AUGUSTINE, on Cathedral Pl. facing the plaza, is the seat of the oldest Catholic parish in the nation. Built in the 1790s, it was reconstructed after a fire in 1887. The original structure forms the nave. Brochures for self-guiding tours are available at the entrance. Daily 7-5. Donations. Phone (904) 824-2806.

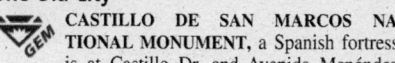

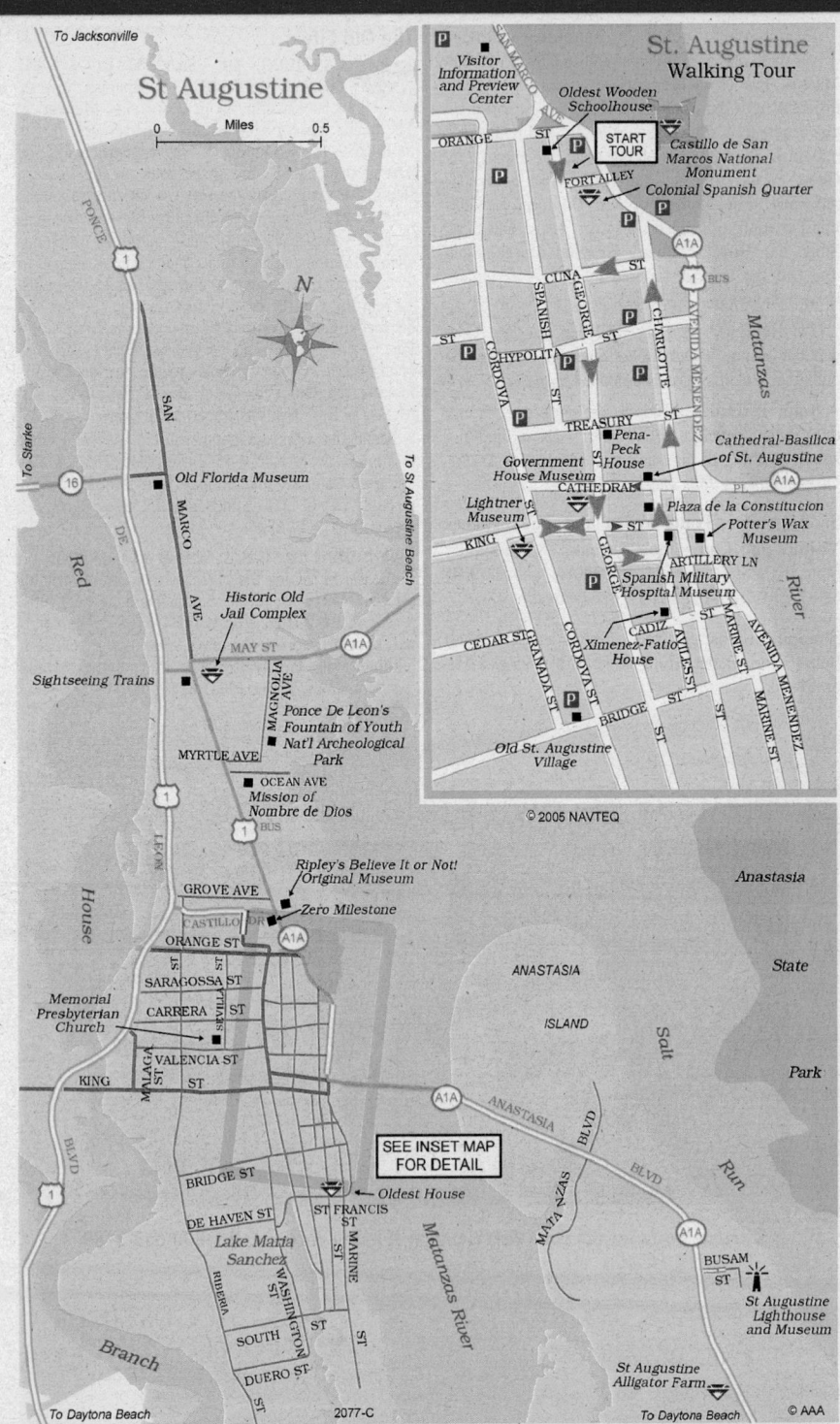

To Jacksonville

St Augustine

Miles
0   0.5

To Starke

To St Augustine Beach

Ponce

1

16

Red

DE

SAN

MARCO

AVE

Old Florida Museum

House

Historic Old
Jail Complex

MAY ST

A1A

Sightseeing Trains

MAGNOLIA AVE

Ponce De Leon's
Fountain of Youth
Nat'l Archeological
Park

MYRTLE AVE

OCEAN AVE
Mission of
Nombre de Dios

1   BUS

Ripley's Believe It or Not!
Original Museum

GROVE AVE

Zero Milestone

CASTILLO DR

ORANGE ST

A1A

LEON

1

SARAGOSSA ST

Memorial
Presbyterian
Church

CARRERA   ST

SEVILLA ST

VALENCIA ST

MALAGA ST

KING   ST

BLVD

Anastasia

State

ANASTASIA

ISLAND

Salt

Park

A1A

ANASTASIA

MATANZAS BLVD

BLVD

Run

A1A

SEE INSET MAP
FOR DETAIL

BRIDGE ST

DE HAVEN ST

Lake Maria
Sanchez

ST FRANCIS ST

MARINE ST

WASHINGTON ST

RIBERA

Oldest House

Matanzas River

BUSAM
ST

St Augustine
Lighthouse
and Museum

SOUTH   ST

Branch

DUERO ST

To Daytona Beach

2077-C

St Augustine
Alligator Farm

To Daytona Beach

© AAA

St. Augustine Walking Tour

P

Visitor
Information
and Preview
Center

Oldest Wooden
Schoolhouse

ORANGE   ST

P

START
TOUR

Castillo de San
Marcos National
Monument

FORT ALLEY

Colonial Spanish Quarter

P

A1A

1
BUS

CUNA   GEORGE   ST

SPANISH   ST

P

ST

CHYPOLITA   ST

P

CORDOVA   ST

CHARLOTTE   ST

AVENIDA MENENDEZ

Matanzas

TREASURY   ST

P

Pena-
Peck
House

Government
House Museum

CATHEDRAL

Cathedral-Basilica
of St. Augustine

PL

A1A

Lightner
Museum

Plaza de la Constitucion

KING   ST

Potter's Wax
Museum

GEORGE   ST

ARTILLERY LN

P

Spanish Military
Hospital Museum

CEDAR ST

GRANADA ST

CORDOVA ST

CADIZ   ST

Ximenez-Fatio
House

MARINE ST

AVILES ST

AVENIDA MENENDEZ

MARINE ST

River

P

BRIDGE   ST

Old St. Augustine
Village

© 2005 NAVTEQ

COLONIAL SPANISH QUARTER, 53 St. George St., is a living-history museum that consists of restored and reconstructed buildings depicting daily life in 1740 St. Augustine. Demonstrations of blacksmithing, carpentry, leatherworking, coopering and candle making are given by costumed interpreters. Military quarters reflect how soldiers and their families lived in a presidio town.

De Mesa/Sánchez Site began as a two-room coquina (shell-rock) house in the mid-18th century. Additions and modifications continued until the end of the 19th century. Much information about the area has been gleaned from the excavation. Guided tours are given on a regular basis. Other structures include Casa de Gallegos, a tabby (oyster shell and lime) house typical of the 1750s; Casa de Gómez, a wooden house; and the Spanish colonial-style De Hita/González Houses.

Allow 1 hour minimum. Daily 9-5:30; closed major holidays. Last admission is at 4:45. Admission $6.50; over 62 and military with ID $5.50; ages 6-18, $4. Phone (904) 823-4569.

FLAGLER COLLEGE TOURS, 74 King St., explores several rooms of the former Ponce de León Hotel, built in 1888 by Henry Flagler. Highlights include the rotunda, which features an ornate dome ceiling, carved columns, Tiffany glass windows and decorative mosaic tile floors. The 800-seat grand dining hall has massive Tiffany windows and is furnished with the original tables and carved oak chairs. Eight Tiffany crystal chandeliers, artwork and Flagler family portraits adorn the grand parlor.

Allow 1 hour minimum. Tours are given daily on the hour 10-3, mid-May to mid- Aug.; daily at 10 and 2, rest of year. Closed Dec. 25. Visitors should arrive 20 minutes early to purchase tickets and view a videotape. Tours are subject to cancellation during school events; phone ahead to verify schedule. Fee $6; under 12, $2. Tickets also are available at Flagler's Legacy, 59 St. George St. Phone (904) 819-6400.

GOVERNMENT HOUSE MUSEUM, 48 King St., illustrates area history through a chronological series of exhibits and presentations. Displays feature an archeological exhibit, American Indian artifacts, treasure from Spanish shipwrecks and military and religious items. Allow 1 hour minimum. Daily 9-4:30; closed major holidays. Last admission is at 3:45. Admission $2.50; senior citizens $2; ages 6-12, $1. Phone (904) 825-5033.

LIGHTNER MUSEUM, at King and Cordova sts., is housed in the former Alcazar Hotel, built by Henry Flagler in 1888. In 1948 Otto C. Lightner, the Chicago publisher and editor of *Hobbies* magazine, converted the empty hotel into a museum to contain his vast collection of art, antiques and other items.

Three floors display furnishings, costumes, Victorian art glass and natural history specimens. One room is devoted to a collection of Tiffany stained glass. Other highlights include Oriental art, art nouveau works and a Victorian village.

Nineteenth-century mechanical musical instruments are demonstrated daily at 11 and 2. The hotel's steam baths still exist on the second floor. The site of the former indoor swimming pool, one of the largest of its day, is now an antiques mall. Food is available. Allow 2 hours minimum. Daily 9-5; closed Dec. 25. Last admission 1 hour before closing. Admission $8; ages 12-18, $2. Phone (904) 824-2874.

OLD ST. AUGUSTINE VILLAGE, entrance on Cordova St. at Bridge St., occupies an entire city block. Nine buildings, all in their original locations, were built from 1790 to 1910. Archeological records reveal the block was the site of a 16th-century hospital and cemetery, an 18th-century Spanish Colonial defense line and an early bridge. Interpreters, various programs, art and textile galleries, and exhibits provide a vivid depiction of early Florida. Allow 1 hour minimum. Mon.-Sat. 10-4:30, Sun. 11-4:30; closed Thanksgiving and Dec. 24-25. Admission $7; over 61, $6; students with ID $5. Phone (904) 823-9722.

OLDEST HOUSE, 14 St. Francis St. at the s. end of the seawall, is said to be Florida's oldest documented Spanish Colonial dwelling. Built on a site occupied since the early 1600s, the present structure, with coquina walls and hand-hewn cedar beams, dates from the early 1700s.

A number of alterations brought the house into its current shape and size, reflecting both Spanish and British architectural styles. The house is furnished to represent its different periods. An ornamental garden typifies plants grown by the Spanish, British and American occupants. The complex includes two museums tracing 400 years of city history and the state's military history.

Allow 1 hour minimum. Daily 9-5; closed Easter, Thanksgiving and Dec. 25. Tours are given daily every half hour. Last admission is 30 minutes before closing. Admission $7; over 55, $6; ages 6-18, $4; family rate (two adults and five children) $15. MC, VI. Phone (904) 824-2872.

OLDEST WOODEN SCHOOLHOUSE, 14 St. George St., was built 1750-60 of cypress and cedar and is among the nation's oldest. Automated mannequins representing the professor and his students dressed in period clothing relate the school's history and explain the barter system, subjects studied and the use of the dunce cap. Schoolbooks, slates, old maps and other artifacts are displayed. The kitchen, separated from the main building to reduce the risk of fire, is open to the public. Allow 30 minutes minimum. Daily 9-5; closed Dec. 25. Admission $3; over 65 and military with ID $2.50; ages 6-12, $2. Phone (904) 824-0192.

PEÑA-PECK HOUSE, 143 St. George St., was built in the 1740s of native coquina stone. Originally the home of Royal Treasurer Juan Estaban de Peña, Dr. Seth Peck bought the property in

1834. Displays include early Spanish artifacts and Peck family furnishings from the 18th century. Allow 30 minutes minimum. Mon.-Fri. 12:30-4:30, Sat. 10:30-4:30; closed holidays. Admission $4.50; over 55, $3.50; ages 12-18, $2.50. AX, DS, MC, VI. Phone (904) 829-5064.

PLAZA DE LA CONSTITUCIÓN, bounded by Cathedral, King, Charlotte and St. George sts., was the central square around which the business section of the Old City was built and where the slave market was held. One end overlooks Matanzas Bay and opens into the approach to the Bridge of Lions. Spaniards erected the monument in the center of the plaza in 1813. The public marketplace at the east end is a reconstruction of one built in 1824.

POTTER'S WAX MUSEUM, 17 King St., faces the plaza. More than 170 life-size figures depict historically significant persons and events. In summer visitors may watch the craftspersons at work. Allow 30 minutes minimum. Daily 9-9, June 15-Labor Day; 9-5, rest of year. Closed Dec. 25. Admission $9.95; over 55, $8.95; ages 6-12, $6.75. AX, DS, MC, VI. Phone (904) 829-9056.

SIGHTSEEING TRAINS, 170 San Marco Ave., provides stop-offs at major points of interest, shops and restaurants over a 7-mile tour. Tours depart every 15-20 minutes daily 8:30-5. Fare (good for 3 consecutive days) $18; ages 6-12, $5. Package tours are available. Phone (904) 829-6545 or (800) 226-6545.

SPANISH MILITARY HOSPITAL MUSEUM is at 3 Aviles St. Costumed guides re-enact the daily life of patients and staff in a reconstruction of a military hospital of the second Spanish colonial period. Five exhibit areas illustrate medical practices of the time and include an apothecary with period artifacts. Allow 30 minutes minimum. Mon.-Sat. 10-5, Sun. noon-4; closed Dec. 25. Admission $3.50; under 18, $2. Phone (904) 827-0807.

XIMENEZ-FATIO HOUSE, 20 Aviles St., is a well-preserved merchant's house and store dating to the Second Spanish Period 1783-1819. The house has been restored to the Territorial Period 1821-61, when it was operated as an inn. Guided tours are available. Allow 30 minutes minimum. Mon.-Sat. 11-4, Sun. 1-4. Tours are conducted every half-hour. Last tour begins 30 minutes before closing. Admission $5; ages 6-17, $4; over 64, $3. Phone (904) 829-3575.

▲▲▲ Walking Tour: The Old City

See map page 194.

The tour will take 1-2 hours, depending on your pace as well as the number of listed sites you visit and plaques you stop to read along the way. Those attractions appearing in bold type have detailed listings in The Old City section. Even if you decide not to visit a listed site, reading the listing when you reach that point should make the tour more interesting.

The best place to park is at the Visitor Information Center, 10 Castillo Dr., in front of the Castillo

de San Marcos. Keep in mind that no automobiles are permitted on St. George Street in the restoration area.

St. Augustine, compact and full of history, is a great place for a stroll. Influenced by the Timucuan Indians and placed under Spanish and English rule before becoming a U.S. territory, the city retains the flavors of its multicultured past. In the early 18th century, the walled city was entered through the City Gates, and this remains a logical place to begin a walk through Old St. Augustine. The Spanish built the wall surrounding the city in 1739 for defense; this gateway connected the wall, which was constructed of palm logs, dirt, cacti and coquina (soft limestone containing shell and coral fragments, quarried locally on Anastasia Island). The pillars, also made of coquina, were added in 1808. Closed at dusk, the gates protected the north end of the city. A replica of the log wall runs from the gates to the **Castillo de San Marcos,** which you can see by looking east toward the water.

The Huguenot Cemetery, just north of the City Gates, serves as a final resting place for many non-Catholics, not solely French immigrants. An outbreak of yellow fever coupled with the fact that the Catholic cemetery inside the city walls would not accept Protestants brought about its founding in 1821.

Begin by heading south on narrow St. George Street, where second-story balconies add interest to simple buildings and whitewashed walls hide courtyards. More than 50 houses and craft shops have been restored or reconstructed on this pedestrians-only lane, where it seems there are always groups of school children on field trips.

The first spot the kids flock to is the **Oldest Wooden Schoolhouse,** on the right at 14 St. George St. The cedar building also served as a guardhouse during the Seminole Wars due to its proximity to the City Gates. If you can beat the crowd, check out its tabby floors (a mixture of crushed oyster shells and lime) and wooden peg construction.

The major part of the restoration area begins as you cross Fort Alley. Note the National Greek Orthodox Shrine, 41 St. George St., dedicated to the Greek colony of New Smyrna, where Greek immigrants were kept as servants. Its St. Photios Chapel is decorated with icons and frescoes depicting Greek Orthodox theology. Gold leaf highlights much of the chapel's artwork, and sounds of Byzantine music fill the halls.

Colonial workers at the reconstructed **Colonial Spanish Quarter** (the entrance is via the Triay House at 29 St. George St.) go about their work as if it's just another day in the mid-18th century. Clad in period dress, gardeners tend to their vegetables; woodworkers repair furniture under a thatched hut; and blacksmiths fashion nails. Note the citrus tree planted by the Spanish to aid in the prevention of scurvy. You might find Señora Gallegos cooking dinner on a fogon (Mediterranean stove) in the two-room **Casa de Gallegos.** Casa de Ribera is decorated with antique furnishings, and **Casa de Gómez** is a Spanish soldier's dwelling with a small store. Other noteworthy structures in the village are the **De Hita/González Houses** and the coquina **De Mesa/ Sánchez Site,** where costumed interpreters perform various household chores.

On the west side of the block at the corner of Cuna Street is the Sánchez de Ortigosa House. Nearby are the reconstructed wooden buildings comprising the Peso de Burgo/Pellicer House, occupied by a Minorcan family 1763-83.

Proceed along St. George, enjoying the warm tones of ancient coquina stonework and the glimpses of courtyards between many of the buildings. At 105 St. George is the Sánchez House, a restored coquina and masonry building (now home to a crystal shop); house tours are offered.

As you cross Hypolita Street, look out for the sightseeing tram that shuffles by, accompanied by clanging bells.

Glance down Treasury Street, one of the narrowest streets in the Old City. On the left, the **Peña-Peck House** occupies the corner of Treasury and St. George; built in the 1690s for the Spanish treasurer, it was later occupied by a British doctor whose wife often used the house for high-society get-togethers. The art and furnishings reflect an extravagant lifestyle.

The tower on your left is part of the large **Cathedral-Basilica of St. Augustine,** which faces the Plaza de la Constitución. Founded in 1565, the parish holds what are said to be the country's oldest parish records, dating from 1594. The present cathedral was built in 1797 in the Spanish Mission style; following a fire in 1887 it was restored and its adjacent Spanish Renaissance-style bell tower was added. Inside the church, oil paintings are replicas of those found in the Vatican's Pauline Chapel. Victorian stained glass and sculpted marble also adorn the interior. (You might choose to visit the church later, as the route circles back this way.)

Cross Cathedral Street and continue south along St. George. To your left is the **Plaza de la Constitución,** which extends east toward the bay. Established in 1598 by an edict from King Phillip II, it was the hub of the original settlement. In the center is a monument dedicated to the Spanish Constitution of 1812.

The building to your right on the corner of St. George and King streets is the **Government House Museum.** Dating to the 1700s, the site served as the headquarters for Spanish, English and territory governors 1595-1821. It is now home to the St. Augustine Preservation Board and contains interesting artifacts and Spanish treasure.

Turn right at King Street. At Cordova Street, the Casa Monica Hotel will be on your left. This Spanish/Moorish-style structure, one of three hotels owned by railroad magnate Henry Flagler, has a long history. Born as a grand hotel in 1887, it later served as the county courthouse for nearly 30 years before reopening in its present state.

Now look to the right. You can't miss the former Ponce de León Hotel—a huge Moorish-style palace with tall spires, turrets and a red-tiled roof. Built in 1888 by Henry Flagler as part of his grand plan to turn the city into an exclusive winter retreat, the hotel was the country's first major building to be crafted using poured concrete. The interior is posh: It features Tiffany stained glass, imported marble and carved oak. A beautiful courtyard, open to the public, leads to the foyer. Since 1968 the building has served as the main hall of Flagler College; it is what is arguably the fanciest student dining room. Guided tours are available.

Across the street from Flagler College is the third of Henry Flagler's hotels—the Spanish Renaissance Revival-style Alcazar Hotel, which also opened in 1888. Its design was based on the royal palace in Seville, Spain. Palm trees, fountains and a statue of Pedro Menéndez front the large building, which shelters City Hall and the **Lightner Museum.** Flagler would be proud—the museum's collection of decorative arts is quite affluent.

If you like, continue 1 block west on King Street to the **Museum of Weapons and Early American History.** Next door is the funky Zorayda Castle, a smaller re-creation of the 13th-century Spanish Alhambra in Granada.

Retrace your steps along King to St. George. At the corner of St. George and King is Trinity Episcopal Church, established in 1830 and said to be the oldest Protestant church in Florida. Turn right onto St. George and make a left on narrow Artillery Lane to enter the city's oldest section.

At Aviles Street, turn right. At the corner of Cadiz Street is the two-story **Ximenez-Fatio House** (it's the one surrounded by the white picket fence). This late 18th-century coquina house has been restored and is furnished to reflect an 1850s boarding house.

Traipse back on Aviles, where galleries and boutiques reside. On the right, at 3 Aviles, is the **Spanish Military Hospital Museum** (once called the Hospital of our Lady Guadalupe), which has displays depicting day-to-day operations of the 18th century.

Head back to the Plaza de la Constitución by continuing north on Aviles. The market building to your right is a replica of the original. Turn right on Cathedral Street and walk for one block to Charlotte Street. From here you can see the statue (on the east end of the plaza) of Juan Ponce de León, who landed in 1513—he points east toward Matanzas Bay and the Bridge of Lions, a Mediterranean-style bridge built in 1927. Tile-roofed towers, arches and lion statues grace the structure, which is on the National Register of Historic Places.

Turn left on Charlotte and proceed north. A three-block walk past boutiques, antiques shops and bed and breakfast inns leads to Cuna Street. Look northeast from the corner of Charlotte and Cuna for a good view of the fort and bay. Turn left on Cuna, where more stores in restored buildings entice shoppers. At St. George, turn right. The City Gates, where you began your tour, is about a block north.

Other Points of Interest

HISTORIC OLD JAIL COMPLEX, 167 San Marco Ave., encompasses the Florida Heritage Museum, The Old Jail and Old Town Trolley Tours of St. Augustine. Daily 9:30-5; closed Easter, Thanksgiving and Dec. 25. Combination rates are available. Phone (904) 829-3800.

Florida Heritage Museum depicts Florida's growth from early Indian cultures through the Flagler era. Personal items and pictures of Henry Flagler are displayed along with a model railroad tracing the route he established between Jacksonville and Key West. Additional exhibits focus on the Florida Cracker, Fort Mose, Confederate items, 16th-century Spanish weapons, a life-size sunken ship and its treasures, and a replica of an Indian village. Allow 1 hour minimum. Mon.-Sat. 10-9, Sun. 10-6. Admission $5; ages 6-12, $4.

The Old Jail contains a large collection of weapons and displays that illustrate prison life in early St. Augustine. Costumed guides portray the sheriff and his deputies. Visitors may tour the family's living quarters, which are in the same building as the prisoners' cells. Newspaper articles and photographs depict the history of the jail. Allow 30 minutes minimum. Guided tours depart every 15 minutes daily 9:30-5; closed Easter, Thanksgiving and Dec. 25. Admission $6; ages 6-12, $4.

Old Town Trolley Tours of St. Augustine offers a narrated 1-hour tour of the city with stops at 20 sites. Passengers may reboard the open-air trolleys at their own pace. Tours depart every 15-20 minutes daily 8:30-4:30; closed Easter and Dec. 25. Fare (includes admission to Florida Heritage Museum) $18; ages 6-12, $5. MC, VI. Phone (904) 829-3800.

MEMORIAL PRESBYTERIAN CHURCH is at Valencia and Sevilla sts. Henry Flagler built the Venetian Renaissance structure in 1890 as a memorial to his daughter. Construction was completed in less than a year, although the stained-glass windows took an additional 11 years to complete. Guides provide a brief overview of the church's history. Allow 30 minutes minimum. Mon.-Sat. 9-4, Sun. 12:30-4. Donations. Phone (904) 829-6451.

MISSION OF NOMBRE DE DIOS is 5 blks. n. of the city gate on San Marco Ave. Pedro Menéndez de Avilés landed here Sept. 8, 1565, and established the first permanent community. A 208-foot stainless-steel cross marks the site of the founding of St. Augustine. The Shrine of Our Lady of La Leche and a small museum are on the grounds. Allow 1 hour minimum. Daily 8-5; closed major holidays. Donations. Phone (904) 824-2809.

NORTH AMERICAN TOP-GUN, at the St. Augustine Airport on US 1, offers flights and air-to-air combat training in World War II fighter-type aircraft. Passengers can choose sightseeing, aerobatic or fighter pilot flights, from a 15-minute ride to a 5-hour air-combat mission. A videotape of the flight is offered. Daily 9-5. Fare $195-$1,690. Reservations are required. AX, DS, MC, VI. Phone (904) 823-3505 or (800) 257-1636.

OLD FLORIDA MUSEUM is at jct. SR 16 and San Marco Ave. Hands-on exhibits of weapons, tools, games and domestic relics allow visitors to experience everyday activities in various periods of Florida history. Allow 30 minutes minimum. Daily 10-5. Admission $6; senior citizens and under 18, $5; family rate (two adults and two children) $15. MC, VI. Phone (904) 824-8874 or (800) 813-3208.

PONCE DE LEÓN'S FOUNTAIN OF YOUTH NATIONAL ARCHEOLOGICAL PARK, e. of SR A1A (San Marco Ave.) on Williams St. to 11 Magnolia Ave., is on the site claimed to be Ponce de León's landing place Apr. 3, 1513. The park contains the Timucuan Indian spring Ponce de León hoped was the Fountain of Youth. A cross of coquina stones excavated in 1909 is thought to be the claiming landmark. Remains of Christian Indian burials and archeological exhibits are on the grounds. A planetarium offers a display about star navigation.

Allow 1 hour minimum. Daily 9-5; closed Dec. 25. Admission $6; over 60, $5; ages 6-12, $3. Phone (904) 829-3168 or (800) 356-8222.

RIPLEY'S BELIEVE IT OR NOT! ORIGINAL MUSEUM is at 19 San Marco Ave. The museum of oddities and curiosities opened here in 1950. Castle Warden, a Moorish Revival mansion built in 1887 for a Philadelphia industrialist and later operated as a hotel by Marjorie Kinnan Rawlings, now houses more than 800 exhibits, from shrunken heads and torture devices to life-size wax figures and unusual works of art.

Allow 1 hour minimum. Daily 9-8, Memorial Day-Labor Day; Sun.-Thurs. 9-7, Fri.-Sat. 9-8, rest of year. Admission $12.95; over 54, $8.95; ages 5-12, $7.95. AX, DS, MC, VI. Phone (904) 824-1606.

ST. AUGUSTINE ALLIGATOR FARM, 1.75 mi. s.e. on SR A1A, on Anastasia Island, features a complete collection of the 23 crocodilian species, including rare white alligators. An elevated walkway winds through a rookery and over an alligator swamp. Florida wildlife shows are presented hourly. Allow 2 hours minimum. Daily 9-6, June-Aug.; 9-5, rest of year. Admission $17.95; ages 5-11, $9.95. AX, DS, MC, VI. Phone (904) 824-3337.

ST. AUGUSTINE LIGHTHOUSE AND MUSEUM is 1 mi. s.e. on SR A1A, then n. on Red Cox Dr. on Anastasia Island. St. Augustine's maritime past is reflected in this working lighthouse and restored keeper's house. Visitors may climb the 219 stairs to the top of the tower for a panoramic view of the city and its beaches. Highlights include exhibits illustrating the lives of lightkeepers and U.S. Coast Guard personnel who were stationed in St. Augustine during World War II. Shipwreck artifacts also are featured.

Daily 9-6; closed Easter, Thanksgiving and Dec. 24-25. Lighthouse tower opens 15 minutes after the museum. Lighthouse and museum $7.50; over 55, $5.95; ages 5-11, $5. Museum only $5; over 55, $4; ages 5-11, $3. Under 44 inches tall are not admitted to the lighthouse tower. Phone (904) 829-0745.

SAVE **ST. AUGUSTINE SCENIC CRUISE** departs from the Municipal Marina, 111 Avenida Menendez. Narrated sightseeing tours of Matanzas Bay offer views of historic landmarks. Allow 1 hour, 30 minutes minimum. Daily at 11, 1, 2:45, 4:30, 6:45 and 8:30, May 22-Labor Day; at 11, 1, 2:45, 4:30 and 6:15, Apr. 1-May 21 and day after Labor Day-Oct. 15; at 11, 1, 2:45 and 4:30, rest of year. Closed Dec. 25. Fare $15; over 59, $9; ages 13-18, $8; ages 5-12, $6. Phone (904) 824-1806 or (800) 542-8316.

WHETSTONE CHOCOLATE FACTORY, 2 Coke Rd., offers self-guiding tours of candy making operations with information about the origins of chocolate and the history of the Whetstone company. **Note:** Tours are not available. The factory is scheduled to move to 100 S. Ponce de Leon Blvd. in late 2005. Tours will resume at the new location; phone ahead for information. Allow 1 hour minimum. Mon.-Sat. 10-5; closed Jan. 1, Thanksgiving and Dec. 25. Free. Phone (904) 825-1700, ext. 25.

GEM **WORLD GOLF HALL OF FAME AT WORLD GOLF VILLAGE,** .5 mi. w. of I-95 exit 323, is a showcase for the game of **SAVE** golf. The World Golf Hall of Fame pays tribute to the history of the game and honors its members through exhibits of memorabilia and artifacts, videotape presentations and interactive golfing activities. The 300-seat IMAX theater shows films on an 80-foot-wide, 6-story-high screen. Film topics vary.

The village consists of the World Golf Hall of Fame, an IMAX theater, an 18-hole natural grass putting course, two golf courses, a golf academy, resort hotels, restaurants and retail shops.

Guided tours are available. World Golf Hall of Fame open Mon.-Sat. 10-6, Sun. noon-6; closed Thanksgiving and Dec. 25. IMAX schedule varies; phone ahead. Inclusive admission to World Golf Hall of Fame, one IMAX film and putting course $15; over 55 and students and military with ID $13; ages 4-12, $10. IMAX theater $7.50; over 55 and students and military with ID $6.50; ages 4-12, $5. AX, DS, MC, VI. Phone (904) 940-4123.

ZERO MILESTONE is at Castillo Dr. and San Marco Ave. The coquina ball marks the eastern terminus of both the Old Spanish Trail, which linked the missions between St. Augustine and Pensacola, and the first transcontinental highway within the United States. Daily 24 hours. Free.

WINERIES

- **San Sebastian Winery**, 157 King St. Mon.-Sat. 10-6, Sun. 11-6; closed Jan. 1, Easter, Thanksgiving and Dec. 25. Phone (904) 826-1594 or (888) 352-9463.

ST. CLOUD—*see Orlando p. 182.*

ST. MARKS (B-6) pop. 272, elev. 7'

In 1836 a railroad was built to connect Tallahassee with St. Marks. Now dismantled, the Tallahassee-St. Marks Historic Railroad State Trail offers a 16-mile paved trail for bicyclists, hikers, horseback riders and skaters. For additional information phone (850) 922-6007.

ST. MARKS NATIONAL WILDLIFE REFUGE, off US 98 s. of Newport, covers approximately 68,500 acres along the Gulf of Mexico. The refuge borders Apalachee Bay and extends from the Aucilla River west to the Ochlockonee River. Forty-nine miles of the Florida Trail pass through the refuge. Varied wildlife can be observed all year. The refuge is home to St. Marks Lighthouse, built in 1831, and several other historic sites.

Refuge visitor center open Mon.-Fri. 8-4, Sat.-Sun. 10-5. The refuge is open daily dawn-dusk; closed federal holidays. Admission $4 per private vehicle, $1 per person arriving by bicycle. Phone (850) 925-6121.

SAN MARCOS DE APALACHE HISTORIC STATE PARK, off SR 363, 1 mi. s.w. on Old Fort Rd., displays Indian, Spanish and Civil War artifacts. The interpretive center is on the site of a fort built by the Spanish in 1679 at the confluence of the Wakulla and St. Marks rivers and later occupied by English, Confederate and Federal troops. Outside are a military cemetery and the remains of the fort and earthworks. Allow 30 minutes minimum. Thurs.-Mon. 9-5; closed Jan. 1, Thanksgiving and Dec. 25. Grounds free. Museum $1, under 6 free. Phone (850) 925-6216 or (850) 922-6007.

ST. PETE BEACH—*see Tampa Bay p. 234.*

ST. PETERSBURG—*see Tampa Bay p. 210.*

SANFORD—*see Orlando p. 184.*

SANIBEL (G-9) pop. 6,064, elev. 6'

Sanibel is on a resort island of the same name; access to the island is by a toll causeway ($6 access, free egress) from Punta Rassa. This barrier island is known for its lighthouse, lush vegetation, extensive beaches, abundant bird life and, perhaps most of all, seashells. Each tide brings thousands of shells onto the fine sand beaches.

When Ponce de León discovered the southwest coast of Florida in 1513, he named it *Costa de Caracoles,* or "Coast of Seashells." The apparently smooth harbor at the southern end of this chain of islands later was designated on a Spanish map as *Puerto S. Nibel,* south level port. *S.* also is the Spanish abbreviation for *San,* or saint; through an error, subsequent maps designated this harbor as *Puerto de San Nibel.*

The traditional, and less prosaic, explanation of Sanibel's name is that pirate José Gaspar was so charmed by this lovely island that he named it after Santa Isabella, a beautiful queen of Spain.

The many paved paths make bicycling a favorite mode of transportation. Moped and bicycle rentals are available. Public beach parking is limited on Sanibel Island and regulations are enforced strictly. For information about designated parking areas contact the Sanibel Visitors Center.

A bridge connects Sanibel Island with Captiva Island *(see Captiva p. 49).*

Sanibel Visitors Center: 1159 Causeway Rd., Sanibel, FL 33957; phone (239) 472-1080.

THE BAILEY-MATTHEWS SHELL MUSEUM, 3075 Sanibel-Captiva Rd., features 30 exhibits of seashells from around the world. Displays are devoted to shells in art and history, shell habitat, rare specimens, fossil shells and common Sanibel-Captiva shells. A children's learning lab features hands-on play areas, games, displays and a tank with indigenous mollusks. A 30-minute videotape presentation is given on the hour, and a children's videotape also is shown. Allow 1 hour minimum. Daily 10-4; closed major holidays.

Admission $6; ages 5-16, $3. Phone (239) 395-2233 or (888) 679-6450.

J.N. "DING" DARLING NATIONAL WILDLIFE REFUGE, 1 Wildlife Dr., is named for the editorial cartoonist and pioneer conservationist. The refuge encompasses more than 6,500 acres of wetlands and island uplands. Amenities include canoe trails, a birdwatching tower, a self-guiding wildlife drive, an interpretive trail and a boat ramp. A list of more than 200 bird species that can be viewed is available from the headquarters at the refuge entrance.

Wildlife drive open Sat.-Thurs. 7:30 a.m.-30 minutes before dusk. Visitor center open daily 9-4. Bailey Tract and walking trails open dawn-dusk. Admission $5 per private vehicle, $1 for pedestrians and bicyclists. Phone (239) 472-1100.

Sanibel-Captiva Conservation Foundation, 3333 Sanibel-Captiva Rd., has guided nature trail tours, a butterfly house, an exhibit with a touch tank, and a nature center with displays about the ecology of area wetlands. Mon.-Fri. 8:30-4, Oct.-Apr.; Mon.-Fri. 8:30-3, rest of year. Admission $3, under 17 free. AX, DS, MC, VI. Phone (239) 472-2329.

Take the Tram Wildlife Drive departs from the visitor center within J.N. "Ding" Darling National Wildlife Refuge. Island history, folklore, archeology and wildlife are highlighted during 90-minute, narrated tram tours. The tram follows the refuge driving tour path and makes various stops to allow ample viewing of mangroves and wildlife. Allow 2 hours minimum. Tours depart Sat.-Thurs. 10-4. Fare $10; under 13, $7. Reservations are required. MC, VI. Phone (239) 472-1351 or (239) 472-8900.

Tarpon Bay Explorers Nature and Sea Life Cruise departs from the foot of Tarpon Bay Rd. within J.N. "Ding" Darling National Wildlife Refuge. Ninety-minute programs include a 1-hour boat tour of Tarpon Bay with opportunities for viewing pelicans, herons, dolphins and manatees as well as a 30-minute interactive presentation by marine biologists at touch tanks filled with sea horses, sea stars, puffer fish and other marine life. Breakfast and sunset cruises also are available. Allow 2 hours minimum. Cruises depart Sat.-Thurs. 9-6. Ninety-minute program $20; under 13, $12. Breakfast and sunset cruises $25; under 13, $15. MC, VI. Phone (239) 472-8900.

SANIBEL HISTORICAL VILLAGE AND MUSEUM, 950 Dunlop Rd., exhibits local artifacts and memorabilia in a 1913 Florida Cracker house. Early photographs and documents trace the history of Sanibel from its pioneer days, while archeological finds document the prehistory of the island. Several restored late 19th-century cottages and early 20th-century buildings are on the site. A 1926 Model T pickup truck is displayed. Wed.-Sat. 10-4, Nov.-Apr.; Wed.-Sat. 10-1, May 1 to mid-Aug. Admission $5. Phone (239) 472-4648.

SANIBEL LIGHTHOUSE is 1.5 mi. e. of the causeway on Periwinkle Way. Built in 1884, this Sanibel landmark was electrified in 1962 and is operated today by the U.S. Coast Guard. The lighthouse and cottages are closed to visitors, however the parklike grounds and nearby beach are popular places to view sunsets. The lighthouse is reached via a boardwalk through dense foliage inhabited by wildlife. Local lore credits an 1890s lightkeeper with planting the first periwinkles on Sanibel Island. Allow 1 hour minimum. Daily dawn-dusk. Free. Parking $2 per hour. Phone (239) 472-4135.

SARASOTA (F-8) pop. 52,715, elev. 18′

See map page 204.

Although the origin of its name is not clear, the city has been a fixture on Sarasota Bay since the 1700s. The population was augmented by Scottish settlers in the 1880s, and the area became popular as a resort in the early part of the 20th century.

The circus is an integral part of Sarasota's past. In 1927 John Ringling selected the town for his Ringling Brothers and Barnum & Bailey Circus and made it his home. He exerted a major influence on the growth and development of the city because people from all over the world came to Sarasota to star in his show.

Sarasota, including the offshore islands of Casey Key, Lido Key, Longboat Key, St. Armand Key and Siesta Key, is a beach resort and art community. Hotels and residential and commercial areas ring Sarasota Bay, and the islands offer 35 miles of beaches that border the blue waters of the Gulf.

In the mainland section of the city is an array of performing arts groups, including the Asolo Theatre Company, The Players, Sarasota Opera, the Florida West Coast Symphony, Sarasota Ballet of Florida, the Florida String Quartet, Florida Symphonic Band and several vocal and chamber ensembles as well as an active theater district.

Performing arts facilities include The F.S.U. Center for the Performing Arts *(see attraction listing)*; Van Wezel Performing Arts Hall, 777 N. Tamiami Tr.; the Sarasota Opera House, 61 N. Pineapple Ave.; and the Florida West Coast Symphony Center, 709 N. Tamiami Tr. The Golden Apple Dinner Theatre, 25 N. Pineapple Ave., and the Florida Studio Theatre, 1241 N. Palm Ave., present entertainment from drama to musicals.

Since Sarasota is the city where golf was introduced to Florida from Scotland and where the first course was laid out in 1886, it is understandable that the sport remains popular; more than 30 courses are within minutes of downtown.

During March, Ed Smith Sports Complex at 12th Street and Tuttle Avenue is the spring training home for baseball's Cincinnati Reds; phone (941) 954-4101, ext. 5200. Beginning Dec. 1 and throughout spring training, ticket information for Reds games is available at (941) 954-4464. The Sarasota Red Sox, class A affiliate of the Boston Red Sox, take to the field April through early September; phone (941) 365-4460.

Sarasota Ski-A-Rees presents a free water ski show each Sunday from late January through the end of April at Ken Thompson Park on City Island near the aquarium; phone (941) 388-1666.

Greyhound racing takes place from late December to mid-April at Sarasota Kennel Club on Old Bradenton Road; phone (941) 355-7744.

Note: Policies vary concerning admittance of children to pari-mutuel betting facilities. Phone for information.

Visitor Information Center: 655 N. Tamiami Tr., Sarasota, FL 34236; phone (941) 957-1877 or (800) 522-9799. *See color ad p. 203.*

Shopping areas: Westfield Shoppingtown Sarasota, 8201 S. Tamiami Tr., includes Dillard's, JCPenney, Macy's and Sears among its 90 stores. St. Armands Circle and the vicinity contain more than 150 shops. Dillard's, Macy's and Saks Fifth Avenue are at Westfield Shoppingtown South Gate, 3501 S. Tamiami Tr.

CROWLEY MUSEUM & NATURE CENTER is off I-75 exit 210, 11. mi. e. on Fruitville Rd., then 2.5 mi. s. on Myakka Rd. This 190-acre nature preserve includes trails through five habitats, a boardwalk through swamps and marshes, an observation tower overlooking the Myakka River and a pioneer history area with a museum, homesteader's cabin, sugar cane mill, Cracker house and blacksmith shop. Allow 3 hours minimum. Tues.-Sun. 10-4, Jan.-Apr.; Thurs.-Sun. 10-4, rest of year. Admission $5; ages 5-12, $3. Phone (941) 322-1000.

ENTERPRISE SAILING CHARTERS depart from Marina Jack Slip E19 near jct. John Ringling Blvd. and US 41. The tour company offers excursions in the waters of Sarasota Bay and the Gulf of Mexico aboard a three-sail sailboat that can accommodate up to 12 passengers. A sunset cruise is available. Food is included. Allow 2 hours minimum. Daily 8-8. Fare $35-$60. Reservations are required. AX, DS, MC, VI. Phone (941) 951-1833 or (888) 232-7768.

THE F.S.U. CENTER FOR THE PERFORMING ARTS, 5555 N. Tamiami Tr., is an arts complex whose mainstage theater has ornate interior replicating a 1903 Scottish opera house. The complex houses the Florida State University Asolo Conservatory for Actor Training and the professional Asolo Theatre Company. Professional performances in rotating repertory are given in the 500-seat Mertz Theatre November-May, while student performances are staged in the 161-seat Cook Theatre. Tours generally are given Mon., Wed. and Fri.-Sat. at 10 and 11, Nov.-May. Hours may vary; phone ahead. Phone (941) 351-8000 or (800) 361-8388.

G.WIZ—THE HANDS-ON SCIENCE MUSEUM, 1001 Boulevard of the Arts, encourages learning through more than 85 interactive exhibits. In addition to exploring science, visitors can play a tune on the laser harp, create an animated video or test their physical performance at a sprinting station. A Kids' Lab area is aimed at preschoolers.

Picnicking is permitted. Allow 1 hour minimum. Tues.-Sat. 10-5, Sun 1-5; closed Jan. 1, Easter, Thanksgiving and Dec. 25. Admission $7; over 55, $6; ages 2-18, $5. All children must be with an adult. Phone (941) 309-4949.

HISTORIC SPANISH POINT—see Osprey p. 186.

THE JOHN AND MABLE RINGLING MUSEUM OF ART is 4 mi. n., just w. of US 41 at 5401 Bay Shore Blvd. The fortune John Ringling derived from his circus and vast real estate investments was well spent on his art museum and 1920s estate. The 66-acre complex, decorated with statues and dotted with banyan trees and Cuban

laurels, offers rose gardens, sitting areas and a view of Sarasota Bay.

The museum was built in Italian Renaissance style, with an inner courtyard studded with reproductions of many world-famous sculptures, including a bronze cast of Michelangelo's "David." The art collection includes significant holdings of American, European and non-Western art, with masterpieces from the 17th-century baroque period. Noteworthy is the Peter Paul Rubens collection.

Food is available. Allow 3 hours minimum. Daily 10-5:30; closed Jan. 1, Thanksgiving and Dec. 25. Admission (also includes Cà d'Zan and The Circus Museum) $15; over 64, $12; under 13 free with an

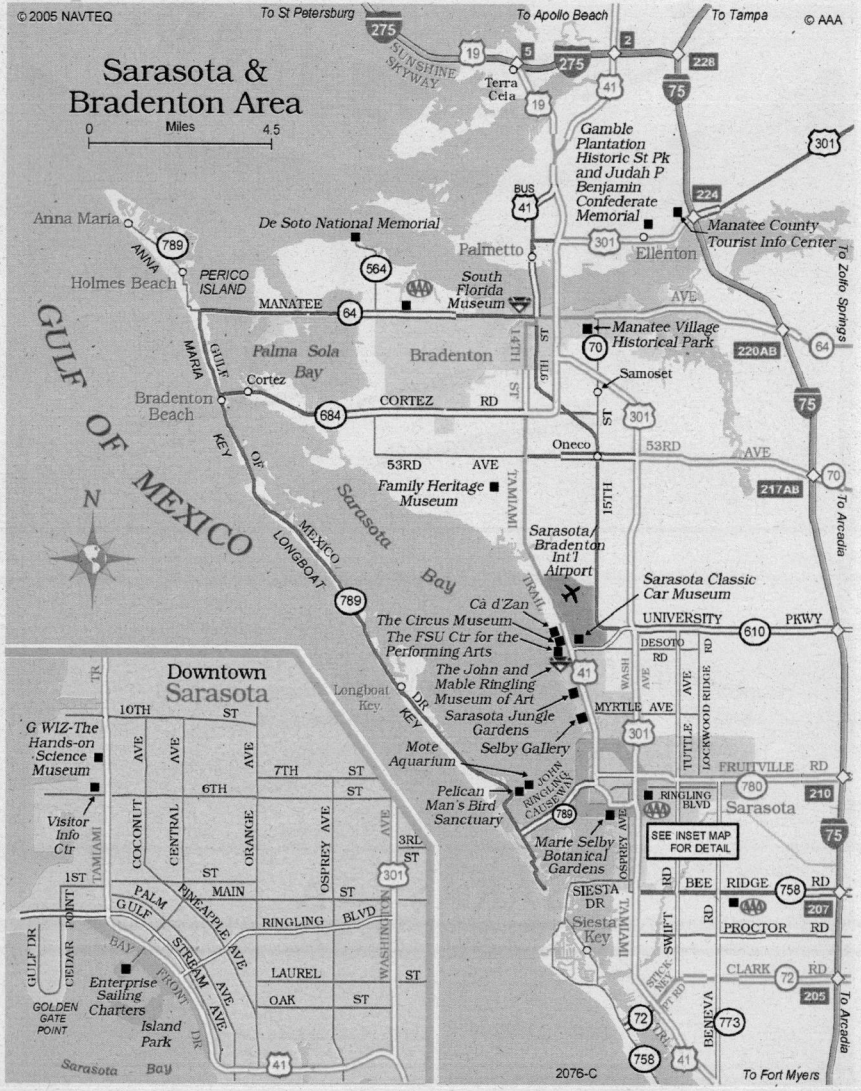

adult; Museum of Art free to all Mon.; Cà d'Zan and The Circus Museum combination admission Mon. $10. Advance tickets are recommended. AX, MC, VI. Phone (941) 351-1660, or (941) 358-3180 for advance ticket information.

Cà d'Zan (Ringling's Winter Residence) was completed in 1926 at a cost of $1.5 million. The 32-room, terra-cotta mansion resembles a Venetian palace. Marble, tapestries and elaborately carved and gilded furniture dominate the interior. Tour sizes are limited; an admission time is provided with art museum ticketing. Admission price included with John and Mable Ringling Museum of Art. Phone (941) 359-5700.

The Circus Museum consists of displays of gilded parade wagons, calliopes, costumes, posters, photographs and a variety of circus memorabilia. Daily 10-5:30; closed Jan. 1, Thanksgiving and Dec. 25. Admission price included with John and Mable Ringling Museum of Art. Phone (941) 359-5700.

SAVE **MARIE SELBY BOTANICAL GARDENS,** US 41S at 811 S. Palm Ave., occupies 9 acres of lush gardens. The gardens specialize in epiphytes, or air plants. Among plants featured are orchids, Amazonian bromeliads, carnivorous pitcher plants, cypress trees, water lilies, succulent plants, and giant bamboo and banyan trees. An elevated boardwalk winds through a mangrove swamp. Other features include a butterfly garden and a museum of botanical art.

Food is available. Allow 1 hour, 30 minutes minimum. Daily 10-5; closed Dec. 25. Admission $12; ages 6-11, $6. Phone (941) 366-5731, ext. 221.

SAVE **MOTE AQUARIUM** is on City Island Sarasota between Longboat Key and St. Armands Key at 1600 Ken Thompson Pkwy. On view are dolphins, manatees, sharks, sea turtles, eels and many of Southwest Florida's plants, fish and invertebrates. Visitors can touch stingrays, horseshoe crabs and other marine life in a 30-foot tank and view research areas at Mote Marine Laboratory. Boat tours of local waters are available aboard the *Sarasota Bay Explorer.*

Food is available. Allow 1 hour minimum. Daily 10-5. Admission $15; ages 4-12, $10. Additional fee for boat tours. AX, DS, MC, VI. Phone (941) 388-4441 or (800) 691-6683 for the aquarium, or (941) 388-4200 for the boat.

MYAKKA WILDLIFE TOURS, 9 mi. e. of I-75 exit 205 via SR 72, offers narrated tram tours through the wildlife habitats in Myakka River State Park (*see Recreation Chart and the AAA Southeastern CampBook*). Narrated airboat cruises on Upper Myakka Lake interpret the ecology of the lake and offer views of the animals.

Binoculars are recommended. Allow 1 hour minimum. Tram tours daily at 1 and 2:30, Dec. 16-May 31. Airboat cruises daily at 10, 11:30 and 1 (also at 2:30, Dec. 16-May 31). Fare for each tour $8; ages 6-12, $4. Apply for boarding pass upon arrival. Phone (941) 365-0100.

PELICAN MAN'S BIRD SANCTUARY is s. of Longboat Key at s. end of New Pass Bridge at 1708 Ken Thompson Pkwy., off SR 789. Dedicated to the rehabilitation of sick and injured birds, the sanctuary also serves as an education center. A boardwalk winds through the lush tropical setting, which contains habitats for a variety of permanently disabled birds including pelicans, herons, storks and sandhill cranes. Guided tours are available. Allow 30 minutes minimum. Daily 10-5. Admission $6; ages 12-17, $4; ages 4-11, $2. Phone (941) 388-4444.

SARASOTA CLASSIC CAR MUSEUM is 3.5 mi. n. at jct. US 41 and University Pkwy., 1 blk. s. of Sarasota/Bradenton Airport. More than 100 vintage, classic, muscle and exotic cars spanning 100 years of automobile history are featured. Included are John Lennon's Mercedes Roadster, Paul McCartney's Mini Cooper, a dragster owned by Don Garlits and several cars belonging to John and Mable Ringling. Guided tours are available. Allow 1 hour, 30 minutes minimum. Daily 9-6; closed Dec. 25. Admission $8.50; over 64, $7.65; ages 13-17, $5.75; ages 6-12, $4. AX, MC, VI. Phone (941) 355-6228.

SARASOTA JUNGLE GARDENS is .25 mi. w. of US 41 via Myrtle St., at 3701 Bayshore Rd. Trails wind through a 10-acre tropical jungle with palms, seasonal flowering shrubs and unusual plants that houses alligators, monkeys, macaws and wallabies. A lagoon features flamingos and swans. The Gardens of Christ display hand-carved dioramas depicting the life of Jesus. Children's highlights include a playground, a bird posing area and pony rides. Five wildlife shows are presented twice daily.

Food is available. Allow 2 hours minimum. Daily 9-5; closed Dec. 25. Pony rides are available Sat.-Sun. Admission $11; over 62, $10; ages 3-12, $7. AX, DS, MC, VI. Phone (941) 355-5305.

SELBY GALLERY, on the campus of Ringling School of Art and Design on Dr. Martin Luther King Jr. Way, just e. of 2700 N. Tamiami Tr., showcases exhibits by national and international artists and designers. Lectures and films are presented throughout the year. Allow 30 minutes minimum. Mon.-Sat. 10-4 (also Tues. 4-7); closed holidays and between exhibits. Free. Phone (941) 359-7563.

SEBASTIAN (E-11) pop. 16,181, elev. 19'

In July 1715 several ships were lost in Sebastian Inlet during a hurricane. The 1,500 men, women and children who survived formed a camp to recover for the Spanish Crown the gold and silver that had been lost to the sea. Their efforts were aided by Ais Indians in the area.

Several early attempts at cutting through the barrier island off Sebastian to connect the Atlantic Ocean and Indian River Lagoon failed due to weather, shifting dunes or lack of maintenance. A permanent inlet was dredged in 1948.

Sebastian River Area Chamber of Commerce: 700 Main St., Sebastian, FL 32958; phone (772) 589-5969.

SEBRING (F-10) pop. 9,667, elev. 160'

Sebring (SEE-bring) was founded in 1911 by George E. Sebring, an ardent prohibitionist from Ohio; some early deeds contained bans against the use or sale of alcohol on the premises. The Atlantic Coast Railroad reached the town in 1912 and the land boom began. By 1920 there were nine resorts and the area was a popular winter resort for the affluent, and in 1926, the residents numbered 7,000. Following the land bust of 1924-26, the population dwindled to approximately 3,000. The establishment of the B-17 training facility Hendricks Field in World War II began the town's rebirth.

Today Sebring boasts some of the state's largest groves of citrus, lime and avocado trees. Sebring International Raceway plays host to automobile races, including March's grueling 12 Hours of Sebring Endurance Race, part of the American Le Mans Series; phone (800) 626-7223. Medal of Honor Park, on US 27 at the Agricultural Center, is an outside memorial dedicated to veterans.

Sebring Chamber of Commerce: 309 Circle Park Dr., Sebring, FL 33870; phone (863) 385-8448.

THE CHILDREN'S MUSEUM OF THE HIGHLANDS, 219 N. Ridgewood Dr., has a child-size supermarket complete with shopping carts, a scanner and a cash register. Other hands-on exhibits include a waterworks and a television station. Children can make music, paint their faces and make huge bubbles using materials provided by the museum. Allow 1 hour, 30 minutes minimum. Tues.-Sat. 10-5 (also Thurs. 5-8); closed Jan. 1, Thanksgiving and Dec. 24-25. Admission $3. Children must be with an adult. Phone (863) 385-5437.

HIGHLANDS HAMMOCK STATE PARK, 3.5 mi. w. of US 27 on CR 634, is a 9,251-acre wilderness of lush vegetation, dense jungle and swamps, all accessible by an excellent system of paved drives and well-marked trails. Trees range in age from more than 400 years to nearly 1,000 years. Highland Hammocks was Florida's first state park, and was developed by the CCC in the 1930s. The Florida State Civilian Conservation Corps Museum features displays about park history.

Ranger-narrated tram tours are available; inquire at the ranger station. Park rangers conduct nature programs on Thursday evenings, November-April. Slide presentations about a variety of topics are offered on Saturday evenings.

Food is available during winter months. Park open daily 8-dusk (also open Fri.-Sat. dusk-9 p.m. for camper check-in, Oct.-May). Museum open daily 8-4. Nature walk Mon. at 10, Nov.-Apr. Admission $4 per private vehicle (maximum of eight people), $1 per person arriving by bicycle or on foot. Phone (863) 386-6094. *See Recreation Chart and the AAA Southeastern CampBook.*

SILVER SPRINGS (C-9) pop. 9,770, elev. 47'

FLORIDA'S SILVER SPRINGS, on SR 40, is reputedly the world's largest formation of clear artesian springs. One major spring, 65 feet long and 12 feet high, and more than a dozen minor springs form the headwaters of the crystalline Silver River, part of the inland waterway that links the springs to the St. Johns River and Jacksonville. The springs release more than 550 million gallons every 24 hours.

A narrated cruise in a glass-bottom boat offers a clear view of underwater life as far as 40 feet below the surface. The Fort King River Cruise travels past exhibits representative of 10,000 years of springs history, and visitors can view native wildlife along the way. Wilderness Trail Ride is a four-wheel adventure through a 35-acre area where llamas, emus and deer roam free.

Picnicking is permitted only in the picnic area outside the park. Free pet kennels are available. Allow 5 hours minimum. Daily 10-5. Last admission is 1 hour before closing. All-inclusive admission $32.99; over 55, $29.99; ages 3-10, $23.99. Combination ticket with Wild Waters $35.99; over 55, $32.99; under 48 inches tall $26.99; under age 2 free. Parking $6. AX, DS, MC, VI. Phone (352) 236-2121. *See color ad p. 139.*

Wild Waters is adjacent to Silver Springs. The water park features a 450,000-wave pool, eight waterslide flumes including the Twin Twister; and Cool Kids Cove, a children's play area and volleyball facilities. Picnicking is permitted. Daily 10-6, June-July, days and hours vary Mar.-May and Aug.-Sept. Admission $23.99; under 48 inches tall $20.99; under age 2 free. Parking $6. Phone (352) 236-2121.

SINGER ISLAND (F-11)

Known for its wide beaches and proximity to the Gulf Stream a mile away, Singer Island was owned in the 1920s by Paris Singer, son of the sewing machine magnate. He planned to develop the island as Palm Beach had been, but it became the property of one of Singer's ex-wives, who did not appreciate its potential. The island now supports a resort community.

JOHN D. MacARTHUR BEACH STATE PARK is on SR A1A, 1.75 mi. s. of jct. US 1, SR A1A and SR 786 or 3 mi. n. of jct. US 1, SR A1A and SR 708. Sandwiched between the Atlantic Ocean and Lake Worth, the park features nature trails and a footbridge over a cove to sand dunes. Free tram service from the parking lot to the beach front is available daily 10-4. Snorkeling (must have a dive flag—rentals are available), swimming, fishing and picnic sites also are available. The nature center has exhibits and presents a movie about the area's ecosystem.

Allow 1 hour, 30 minutes minimum. Park open daily 8-dusk. Nature center open 9-5. Admission $4 per private vehicle (maximum eight people), $1 per person arriving by bicycle or on foot. Phone (561) 624-6950. *See Recreation Chart.*

STARKE (B-9) pop. 5,593, elev. 150'

CAMP BLANDING MUSEUM AND MEMORIAL PARK is 11 mi. e. of jct. US 301 on SR 16, at the main gate of Camp Blanding. The museum, housed in a refurbished World War II barracks, contains photographs, artifacts and exhibits honoring the camp, which was a major training center during World War II. Outdoor exhibits include weapons and vehicles as well as monuments and memorials to those who served in World War II and other 20th-century conflicts. Guided tours are available. Allow 1 hour minimum. Daily noon-4; closed holidays. Donations. Phone (904) 682-3196.

STUART (F-11) pop. 14,633, elev. 12'

Stuart is known by boating enthusiasts as the eastern terminus of the Okeechobee Waterway, which crosses the state to the Gulf of Mexico. Fishing is excellent in nearby Indian River as well as in the Gulf Stream about 10 miles offshore, where larger species, especially sailfish, are caught.

Florida Oceanographic Coastal Center, 890 N.E. Ocean Blvd. on Hutchinson Island, has aquariums, touch tanks, nature trails and educational exhibits about marine life; phone (772) 225-0505.

Stuart/Martin County Chamber of Commerce: 1650 S. Kanner Hwy., Stuart, FL 34994; phone (772) 287-1088.

Self-guiding tours: The chamber of commerce provides a walking tour map of downtown.

ELLIOTT MUSEUM is on Hutchinson Island, 4.5 mi. n.e. of US 1 on SR A1A. The museum houses the many inventions and patents of Sterling Elliott and his son. The Americana Wing contains turn-of-the-20th-century barber and apothecary shops and an ice cream parlor. Collectible dolls and toys are displayed. Other galleries house decorative arts, antique bicycles, baseball memorabilia and vintage cars, including a 1926 Bugatti Grand Prix race car.

Allow 1 hour minimum. Mon.-Sat. 10-4, Sun. 1-4; closed Jan. 1, Easter, July 4, Thanksgiving and Dec. 25. Admission $6; ages 6-13, $2. Phone (772) 225-1961.

GILBERT'S BAR HOUSE OF REFUGE MUSEUM, on Hutchinson Island, is 4 mi. n.e. via SR A1A, then 1.25 mi. e. through the Marriott Resort. The restored 1875 lifesaving station houses a museum of nautical and marine history. A restored boathouse contains a maritime exhibit. **Note:** The museum is closed for restoration until spring 2006; phone ahead to verify hours. Allow 30 minutes minimum. Mon.-Sat. 10-4, Sun. 1-4; closed July 4 and Dec. 25. Admission $4; ages 6-12, $2. Phone (772) 225-1875.

SUGARLOAF KEY—
see The Florida Keys p. 75.

TALLAHASSEE (B-6) pop. 150,624, elev. 216'

In 1823 two explorers set out to find a permanent seat of government for the newly formed territory of Florida. The site they chose—midway between St. Augustine and Pensacola—was called "tallahassee" (tal-a-HASS-ee) by the Creek and Seminole Indians, a name meaning "old town." The rendezvous point became the state capital.

A convention in 1861 declared Florida an independent nation and a member of the Confederate States of America. In 1865 during the Civil War, Confederate Floridian soldiers repelled Union forces at the Battle of Natural Bridge *(see attraction listing p. 239)* to protect Tallahassee, making it the only uncaptured Confederate capital east of the Mississippi River.

Tallahassee's first state house was a log cabin; two more impressive structures were constructed in later years. The Old Capitol, built in 1845, is now an elegant centerpiece to the Florida State Capitol complex, which was completed in 1977. *(See attraction listings.)*

The oldest building in the city is the Columns, begun in 1830 by wealthy banker William "Money" Williams. It served as the focal point of financial, political and social development in the state's early

history and was saved from demolition by being moved to 100 N. Duval St. in 1973.

The Governor's Mansion at Brevard and Adams streets is open for tours during legislative sessions and the Christmas season. Highlights include hollowware from the battleship USS *Florida* and French impressionist paintings. Another historic landmark is Union Bank at Apalachee Parkway and Calhoun Street. The oldest surviving bank building in the state, the restored 1841 structure houses an extension office of the Southeast Regional Black Archives Research Center and Museum *(see attraction listing).*

In a region of rolling hills, live oak forests and rivers, Tallahassee has beautiful gardens and large lakes. The city also is noted for its many canopy roads; Miccosukee, Centerville, Meridian and Old St. Augustine are just a few. The 419-acre campus of Florida A&M University stands on the highest of Tallahassee's seven hills, and Florida State University is on a 463-acre campus slightly west of downtown. The Flying High Circus offers collegiate performances under Florida State University's big top in April.

Tallahassee Little Theatre presents comedic and dramatic productions from September to July. Both evening and matinee performances are offered; phone (850) 224-8474.

Tallahassee Area Visitor Information Center: 106 E. Jefferson St., Tallahassee, FL 32301; phone (850) 413-9200 or (800) 628-8662. *See color ad.*

Shopping areas: Among the 150 stores at Governors Square Mall, 1500 Apalachee Pkwy., are Dillard's, JCPenney, Macy's and Sears. Tallahassee Mall, 2415 N. Monroe St., features Dillard's and Parisian among its 100 stores. Antique stores and art galleries line Main Street in downtown Havana, a small town 13 miles north of Tallahassee.

▲ **ALFRED B. MACLAY GARDENS STATE PARK,** at 3540 Thomasville Rd. 1 mi. n. of I-10 exit 203 on US 319, consists of more than 1,100 acres, including 28 acres of ornamental gardens that are the focal point of the park. New York businessman Alfred B. Maclay and his wife Louise began the gardens in 1923. Colorful azaleas, camellias and Oriental magnolias as well as many native plants bloom January through April. The Maclay House has restored living and dining rooms and serves as a center for information about the Maclays, camellias and the gardens.

Nearly 8 miles of hiking, biking and horse trails run through the park, which also features a picturesque picnic/recreation area with covered shelters, a swimming area, a boat launch and a playground.

Allow 1 hour minimum. Park open daily 8-dusk. Gardens open daily 9-5. House open daily 9-5, Jan.-Apr. Park admission $4 per private vehicle (maximum eight persons, $1 extra for every person over the maximum), $1 per person arriving by bicycle or on foot. Garden admission Jan.-Apr. (includes park and house) $4; ages 2-12, $2. Garden admission rest of year free. MC, VI. Phone (850) 487-4556. *See Recreation Chart.*

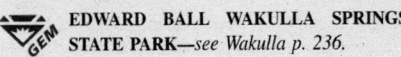 **EDWARD BALL WAKULLA SPRINGS STATE PARK**—*see Wakulla p. 236.*

FLORIDA STATE CAPITOL, 401 S. Monroe St., is a 22-story tower with house and senate chambers on either side, both with public viewing galleries. There is an observation deck on the top floor and a Florida information center just inside the west plaza entrance. Florida's legislature is in session from March through April.

Allow 1 hour minimum. Building open Mon.-Fri. 8-5; closed holidays. Free. Phone (850) 488-6167 for guided tour information.

GOODWOOD MUSEUM AND GARDENS is at 1600 Miccosukee Rd. The restored antebellum house is appointed with marble fireplaces, mahogany staircases and a fresco depicting Aesop's Fables. Originally a composite of Greek Revival, Federal and Italianate architectural styles, the house was modified with the addition of columns in the early 1900s. The estate was home to several prominent Floridians, including Sen. William C. Hodges. Allow 1 hour minimum. Grounds open Mon.-Fri. 10-5, Sat. 10-2. Guided tours are given Mon.-Fri. 10-4, Sat. 10-2. Admission $5. Phone (850) 877-4202.

THE KNOTT HOUSE MUSEUM, 301 E. Park Ave., was built in 1843 as a private home. Restored to its 1930s appearance, this stately house has been restored and is fully furnished with the Victorian pieces acquired by the Knott family when they bought the house in 1928. Colorful stories of William Knott, career politician, and his wife Luella, a poet, musician and community activist, are recounted. Narrated tours are given on the hour Wed.-Fri. 1-3, Sat. 10-3; closed Thanksgiving and Dec. 25. Free. Phone (850) 922-2459.

LAKE JACKSON MOUNDS ARCHAEOLOGICAL STATE PARK is 2 mi. n. of I-10 at the s. tip of Lake Jackson. The mounds are remains of a ceremonial center that existed A.D. 1200-1500. Six earth temple mounds are within the site. Daily 8-dusk. Admission $3 per private vehicle, $1 per person arriving by bicycle or on foot. Phone (850) 922-6007.

THE MARY BROGAN MUSEUM OF ART AND SCIENCE, 350 S. Duval St., houses art exhibits and interactive science experiences. The museum is an affiliate of the Smithsonian Institution. Mon.-Sat. 10-5, Sun. 1-5; closed major holidays. Admission $6, over 61 and military and students with ID $3.50. AX, DS, MC, VI. Phone (850) 513-0700.

MISSION SAN LUIS is off US 90 at 2021 Mission Rd. Marked trails connect re-created dwellings and other structures on this hilly, oak-shaded site, home to a Spanish-Indian village 1656-1704. Tues.-Sun.

10-4; closed Thanksgiving and Dec. 25. Donations. Phone (850) 487-3711.

MUSEUM OF FLORIDA HISTORY, in the R.A. Gray Building at 500 S. Bronough St., has exhibits depicting Florida's colorful past. Visitors can view a mastodon skeleton and a giant armadillo mannequin from the Pleistocene era, gold and silver from Spanish shipwrecks, flags flown during the Civil War, a partial replica of a Florida steamboat and various artifacts from the changing gallery. Touring exhibits and educational programs also are featured.

Allow 30 minutes minimum. Mon.-Fri. 9-4:30, Sat. 10-4:30, Sun. and holidays noon-4:30; closed Thanksgiving and Dec. 25. Donations. Phone (850) 245-6400.

THE OLD CAPITOL, jct. Monroe St. and Apalachee Pkwy., has been restored to its 1902 appearance. Self-guiding tours of the building cover the house and senate chambers, the governor's suite, the supreme court and the rotunda. The Florida Center for Political History and Governance explores the political process and individuals who have played important roles in Florida's colorful history. Allow 30 minutes minimum. Mon.-Fri. 9-4:30, Sat. 10-4:30, Sun. and holidays noon-4:30; closed Thanksgiving and Dec. 25. Donations. Phone (850) 487-1902.

SOUTHEASTERN REGIONAL BLACK ARCHIVES RESEARCH CENTER AND MUSEUM is on the Florida A&M University campus, off Monroe St. between Gaines St. and Orange Ave. Housed in the 1907 Carnegie Library, the museum contains artifacts, photographs, manuscripts, art works, oral history tapes and rare maps that document the history and culture of Africans and African Americans. A visitor parking permit is available at the campus police department on Wahnish Way. Allow 1 hour minimum. Mon.-Fri. 9-4; closed holidays. Free. Phone (850) 599-3020.

[SAVE] **TALLAHASSEE AUTOMOBILE MUSEUM** is at 3550 Mahan Dr. Among the vehicles in this collection are a 1948 Tucker Torpedo, two Batmobiles used in Batman movies and the hearse that carried Abraham Lincoln's body. Automotive collectibles and related memorabilia also are displayed. Allow 1 hour minimum. Mon.-Sat. 10-5, Sun. noon-5. Admission $7.50; ages 11-15, $5; under 11, $4. AX, DS, MC, VI. Phone (850) 942-0137.

TALLAHASSEE MUSEUM OF HISTORY AND NATURAL SCIENCE, 6.5 mi. s.w. at Lake Bradford, depicts north Florida's natural and human history. A nature trail winds through 52 acres of woodlands and cypress swamps, which are home to more than 100 indigenous animals. Also on the grounds are a restored 1880s farm complex, the antebellum home of the great-grandniece of George Washington, a one-room schoolhouse, a church and a caboose.

Food is available. Allow 2 hours minimum. Mon.-Sat. 9-5, Sun. 12:30-5. Admission $8; over 65 and college students with ID $7.50; ages 4-15, $5. AX, MC, VI. Phone (850) 575-8684.

Tampa Bay including St. Petersburg, Tampa and Clearwater

Tampa / © Scott Berner / Camerique Inc. / Robertstock

Population:
St. Petersburg 248,232   Tampa 303,447
Elevation:
St. Petersburg 45 ft.   Tampa 27 ft.

Editor's Picks:

Busch Gardens Tampa Bay ....*(see p. 223)*

The Florida Aquarium ....*(see p. 223)*

Salvador Dali Museum.............*(see p. 222)*

With the world's tourism mecca—Orlando—just 70 miles up the road, it's easy to overlook the cities by the bay as major travel destinations. But Tampa, St. Petersburg, Clearwater and their adjoining communities have a great deal to offer the visitor. And yes, there's a theme park here, too: Busch Gardens Tampa Bay preceded Walt Disney's dream by 12 years.

But there are also some things Mickey and friends don't have. Stretching for almost 35 miles from Crystal Beach south to Fort De Soto Park are the Gulf Coast's broad, graceful, white-sand beaches—some of the prettiest in the country. With varied cultural offerings, water recreation opportunities and savory Spanish- and Cuban-influenced cuisine, Tampa Bay merits a closer look.

Spanish explorer Hernando de Soto apparently agreed when he led a band of men ashore on the southern Pinellas coast in 1539. But de Soto wasn't the first foreign visitor. Fellow countryman Panfilo de Narváez had stopped off 11 years earlier, and some historians believe that Juan Ponce de Léon may have come ashore as early as 1513.

Yet the Timucuan and Tocobaga tribes inhabited the area centuries before the first Spaniards arrived. The Pinellas Peninsula takes its name from the Spanish phrase meaning "point of pines," and the city of Clearwater borrowed from the Tocobagan word *pocotopaug,* "clear water." But the name "Tampa" is a cartographic typo. Local American Indians called their village *Tanpa,* meaning "sticks of fire" (an allusion to the lightning so common in central Florida), but the area's first maps read "Tampa."

During the 18th century the bay belonged to pirates who left a decided influence on the area. One of them, the legendary Jose Gaspar, may have pillaged and kidnapped his way to annual celebrity—Tampa's first Gasparilla Pirate Festival was held in 1904, and the weeklong extravaganza continues each February. The area's NFL team, the Tampa Bay Buccaneers, also takes its name from this era.

In 1824 the U.S. Army arrived to establish Fort Brooke. Tampa was chartered within a decade and became the center of the Florida territory's cattle industry due to nearby pastureland and convenient water transportation. The Civil War interrupted growth;the defenseless settlement was shelled by

Getting There — starting on p. 216

Getting Around — starting on p. 217

What To See — starting on p. 218

What To Do — starting on p. 225

Where To Stay — starting on p. 961

Where To Dine — starting on p. 965

St. Petersburg/Clearwater Area CVB

Union troops and ravaged by a yellow fever epidemic in the early 1870s. Prosperity returned when railroad tycoon Henry B. Plant brought his South Florida Railroad to town in 1884. Plant also built several deep-water piers, setting the stage for the city's development as a port.

Meanwhile, Dr. Odet Philippe arrived on the Pinellas Peninsula in the mid-1830s. Philippe brought with him Bahamian citrus stock and planted the area's first groves at what is now Safety Harbor. Nearby Clearwater took shape after the 1841 establishment of Fort Harrison; the town was incorporated in 1891, 3 years after Russian immigrant Peter A. Demens brought his Orange Belt Railroad through en route to St. Petersburg. Following the 1894-95 freeze (which damaged local citrus groves), Plant took over the railroad and in 1896 built the Gulf Coast's first luxury hotel, the Belleview. Shortly thereafter wealthy winter residents built estates overlooking Clearwater Harbor.

St. Petersburg saw its first influx of homesteaders around 1856. Union blockaders forced inhabitants across the bay during the Civil War, yet farmers and fishermen trickled back to the peninsula following the war, and citrus groves were planted. About the time Plant was making tracks to Tampa, Demens' Orange Belt Railroad arrived. He named the city for his Russian birthplace, and St. Petersburg was incorporated in 1892. Although somewhat isolated, it became a popular winter resort.

Tampa, however, maintained a developmental edge. By 1890 the Ybor City cigar industry was booming. In the early 1900s, sponge beds were found in gulf waters near Tarpon Springs; Greek immigrants arrived by the hundreds to cultivate them. Railroads stimulated the tourist trade, and the area attracted wealthy Northern vacationers. The exclusive Tampa Bay Hotel, now part of the University of Tampa, was built by Plant in an effort to outdo railroad rival Henry Flagler, who was developing a string of luxury properties southward down Florida's east coast. The hotel's 1891 opening was attended by royalty, financial bigwigs and luminaries.

With the outbreak of the Spanish-American War in 1898 came another group of visitors—the U.S. military. Theodore Roosevelt and his Rough Riders set up camp in Tampa and staged their Cuban invasion from the port on Old Tampa Bay.

Tampa's population grew to nearly 16,000 by 1900—after Jacksonville, it was the state's largest city. The cigar industry peaked shortly before World War I, but cigar makers continued to produce high-quality, handmade Havanas. Most of the '20s roared by in a series of successive land booms. During this period O.H. Platt developed Tampa's first subdivision—the stately Victorian homes comprising Hyde Park, west of the Hillsborough River. David P.

Davis, meanwhile, reclaimed the land south of downtown known as the Davis Islands. These man-made islands were a showcase of winding streets, substantial homes and ornamental landscaping.

By 1934 two bridges—the Gandy and the Courtney Campbell—linked Tampa with St. Petersburg and Clearwater respectively, establishing the Pinellas Peninsula as a major travel destination in its own right. (A third, the Howard Frankland Bridge, opened in 1960.) Tampa's MacDill Air Force Base received its first troops in 1940, and the port became an important shipbuilding center during World War II.

Cigars were once the city's mainstay, and brick and frame buildings housing such companies as the Hav-a-Tampa Cigar Factory and the Cuesta-Rey Cigar Factory provided employment for Spanish, Italian and Cuban immigrants who labored at long tables hand-rolling tobacco leaves. Cigars are still produced, but the area business community has diversified. Tourism has the biggest economic impact—visitors spend some $2.8 billion here every year—but varied industries include electronic equipment and biomedical manufacturing, citrus canning, shrimping, paint production, brewing, phosphate mining, transportation and finance and government sectors.

Tampa is the foremost port of Florida's west coast and one of the nation's busiest. The port's strategic location contributes to some 108,000 jobs and $13 billion each year to the local economy.

Tampa Bay also is known to some as "Technology Bay." More than 30 percent of Florida's high-tech employees work at such firms as AT&T Paradyne, General Electric, Honeywell Avionics, Verizon and Unisys. Nearly half of Florida's medical technology companies reside in the bay area, and the Home Shopping Network's headquarters is in St. Petersburg. Of the seven Fortune 1000 companies headquartered in the Tampa Bay region, three are ranked in the Fortune 500.

Architecturally, Tampa admirably records the different periods of its growth. Older stucco homes with flat roofs, patios and wrought-iron balconies show a marked Spanish influence. Scattered throughout the central city are old frame dwellings and compact single-story bungalows surrounded by moss-draped oaks, towering palms and blooming hibiscus.

Tampa's vertical profile was fairly thin before the building boom of the 1980s and early 1990s. The addition of Tampa Convention Center, Tampa Bay Performing Arts Center and several office skyscrapers heightened the city's once modest business district to a stature worthy of more established corporate centers. Adding an exotic—albeit low-lying—touch to the lofty skyscrapers are the bulbous silver-domed minarets and intricate Moorish accents of the University of Tampa.

The 1990s brought further development. A $110 million expansion enhanced the Tampa International Airport, and next door to the Florida Aquarium on

The Florida Aquarium / © Lee Snider / Corbis

The Informed Traveler

Sales Tax: Sales tax is 7 percent in Hillsborough County, 7 percent in Pinellas County and 6 percent in Pasco County. An accommodations tax is 5 percent in Hillsborough County and 4 percent in Pinellas County.

WHOM TO CALL

Emergency: 911

Police (non-emergency): *St. Petersburg:* (727) 893-7780; Sheriff (727) 582-6200. *Tampa:* (813) 231-6130; Sheriff (813) 247-8200.

Fire: *St. Petersburg:* (727) 893-7694; *Tampa:* (813) 274-7005.

Hospitals: *St. Petersburg:* Bayfront Medical Center, (727) 823-1234; Edward White Hospital, (727) 323-1111. *Tampa:* Tampa General, (813) 844-7000.

WHERE TO LOOK

Newspapers

The area is served by two daily newspapers, the *St. Petersburg Times* and *The Tampa Tribune*. Several publications with smaller circulations serve local areas; one such paper is the trilingual *La Gaceta*.

Radio

WUSF (89.7 FM) is a member of National Public Radio.

Visitor Information

St. Petersburg Chamber of Commerce: 100 Second Ave. N., St. Petersburg, FL 33701; phone (727) 821-4715 Mon.-Fri. 8-5.

The St. Petersburg Chamber of Commerce information center at The Pier is open Mon.-Sat. 10-8, Sun. 11-6; phone (727) 821-6164.

St. Petersburg/Clearwater Area Convention & Visitors Bureau: 13805 58th St. N., Suite 2-200, Clearwater, FL 33700; phone (727) 464-7200.

Tampa Bay Convention & Visitors Bureau: 400 N. Tampa St., Suite 2800, Tampa, FL 33602; phone (813) 223-2752 or (800) 448-2672.

Tampa Bay Visitor Information Center: 615 Channelside Dr., Suite 108-A, Tampa, FL 33602; phone (813) 223-2752 or (800) 448-2672.

The Tampa Bay Visitor Information Center is open Mon.-Sat. 9:30-5:30, Sun. 11-5.

WHAT TO PACK

Winter temperatures in the Tampa Bay area rarely fall below freezing. Skies are mostly sunny, and humidity is moderate. However, from May into October highs hover around 90 degrees. The "heat index" reading—a combination of heat and the relative humidity—may make it feel more like 100. Afternoon thunderstorms offer relief but can be capable of producing high winds, lightning, driving rain, local flooding, occasional hail and, possibly, tornadoes. *For additional information see temperature chart p. 43.*

Even though **Tampa** is more businesslike than **St. Petersburg** and **Clearwater** when it comes to attire, dress tends to be informal. Few restaurants require a jacket and tie, and most nightspots are decidedly casual. When sightseeing, dress for comfort.

Destination Tampa Bay including St. Petersburg, Tampa and Clearwater

Florida Botanical Gardens, Largo.
Native plants, fountains and ponds grace this lovely 150-acre setting. (See listing page 233)

St. Petersburg / Clearwater Area CVB

*T*he Tampa Bay area has all the ingredients for one heck of a vacation.

*T*here are theme and water parks for the active crowd; world-class museums for the culturally inclined; recreational pursuits for athletic types; and shopping and spectator sports for everyone in between.

© Gibson Stock Photography

Baseball spring training, St. Petersburg.
Fans gather in March to watch major league teams practice and play exhibition games. (See mention page 225)

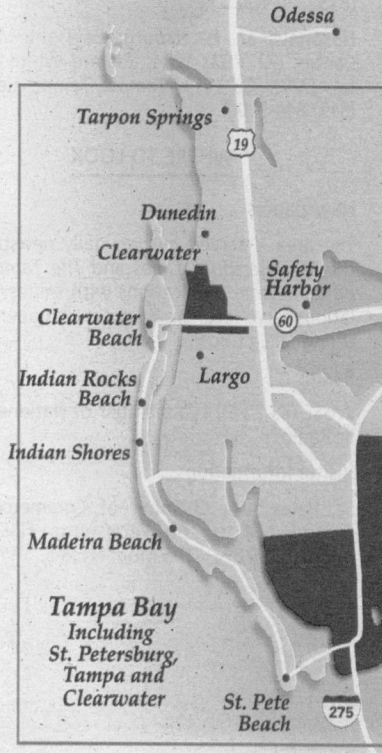

Odessa

Tarpon Springs
19
US 19

Dunedin

Clearwater
Safety Harbor
60

Clearwater Beach

Indian Rocks Beach
Largo

Indian Shores

Madeira Beach

Tampa Bay
Including
St. Petersburg,
Tampa and
Clearwater

St. Pete Beach
275

*P*laces included in this AAA Destination Area:

Captain Memo's Pirate Cruise,
Clearwater Beach.
Explore the Gulf of Mexico
buccaneer style aboard the
Pirates Ransom. (See listing
page 232)

St. Petersburg / Clearwater Area CVB

© Richard Cummins / SuperStock

Chaise lounges on beach.
Sparkling sand and warm Gulf waters
lure vacationers and inspire soft
dreams of early retirement.

See Vicinity map page 220

St. Petersburg / Clearwater Area CVB

St. Petersburg Museum of History,
St. Petersburg.
Early flight and other topics specific to
the Pinellas Peninsula are covered here.
(See listing page 222)

Channelside Drive is Channelside, a dining, shopping and entertainment complex centered on the new cruise ship terminals. A Riverwalk connects Curtis Hixon Park and Washington Street and the Tampa Convention Center.

St. Petersburg, too, embraced development in the last decade of the 20th century with the addition of BayWalk, a multimillion dollar entertainment complex. Cultural offerings increased to nearly 30 art galleries and museums while momentum picked up on the sports scene with the addition of Major League Baseball's Tampa Bay Devil Rays.

The Tampa Bay area's blend of big-time industry and leisure pursuits proves to be a combination that works.

Getting There

By Car

When approaching *St. Petersburg* from the north, take I-75 and US 19. I-75, the fast freeway route, merges with other routes in Tampa and becomes I-275 as it heads for St. Petersburg over the Howard Frankland Bridge. Divided US 19 and two-lane US 19A diverge at Tarpon Springs to offer a choice of slower approaches from the northern Gulf Coast.

Coming from the south on I-75, US 19 and I-275, enter *St. Petersburg* over the mouth of Tampa Bay via the Sunshine Skyway Bridge (toll). Approaching from the east, I-4 provides direct access to the I-275/Howard Frankland Bridge into St. Petersburg.

The major direct route to *Tampa* from the north is I-75, which traverses Florida's north-central lake district: The 62-mile stretch south of Wildwood is

Ybor City / © David R. Frazier Photolibrary, Inc. / Alamy

especially scenic. It is roughly paralleled by US 301 on the east and US 41 on the west. North of downtown I-75 changes to I-275, which merges with I-4 in mid-city. I-75 bypasses the city proper to the east, rejoining I-275 north of Bradenton.

Driving into *Tampa* from the south, US 41 parallels I-75, the main corridor from the southern Gulf

Coast. From Daytona Beach in the east, I-4 angles across central Florida through Orlando, while older US 92 runs parallel from Lakeland. SR 60, a four-lane, divided highway, leads from Lake Wales. Running from the Gulf Coast west of Tampa, SR 60 connects to *Clearwater,* and I-275 travels to St. Petersburg.

Air Travel

Commercial flights entering *Tampa* land at Tampa International Airport. Several commercial airlines and private planes use St. Petersburg-Clearwater International Airport. Private and corporate planes have access to Albert Whitted Municipal Airport in *St. Petersburg* and Peter O. Knight Airport in Tampa.

Tampa International Airport is on the city's west side along Old Tampa Bay. To reach downtown *Tampa,* take I-275 north—though you'll actually be traveling east—and take the Ashley Street exit. Past this exit I-275 turns sharply northward, bisecting the city. Continue along I-275 to reach such destinations as the University of South Florida and Busch Gardens Tampa Bay. Exit to I-4 east if you're heading for Ybor City, Plant City or Lakeland. Or take a cab: United and Yellow cabs provide service from the airport. Both have a minimum $10 fare; average fare to downtown (about 6 miles) is about $17.

To reach downtown *St. Petersburg,* take I-275 south. Cross the bay on the 7-mile Howard Frankland Bridge and proceed another 10 miles or so due south. From I-275, take I-375 into the northern half of downtown or I-175 into the southern half. Transportation from Tampa International to St. Petersburg is easily acquired. Supershuttle provides transfers from Tampa International to St. Petersburg and cities in Hernando, Pasco and Sarasota counties; phone (727) 572-1111. Bay Shuttle, (866) 259-9929, provides service within Hillsborough County.

St. Petersburg-Clearwater International Airport is about 10 miles across the bay from Tampa on SR 686 (Roosevelt Boulevard), near the west side of the Howard Frankland Bridge. Airport traffic exits northwest toward Clearwater or south, providing access to St. Petersburg and Tampa. To reach *Clearwater,* take SR 686 about 3 miles west to US 19, US 19 another 3 miles north to SR 60 (Gulf-to-Bay Boulevard), then SR 60 a mile or so west into town. Downtown St. Petersburg is about 10 miles due south of the airport via I-275. To get to the interstate, exit south from the airport on SR 686 to SR 688 (Ulmerton Road). Go a mile or so east to another segment of SR 686 and take it a mile south to I-275.

Hertz, which offers discounts to AAA members, is at Tampa International Airport, (813) 874-3232;

St. Petersburg-Clearwater International Airport, (727) 531-3774; and at St. Pete Beach, (727) 360-1631; or phone (800) 654-3080. Check the telephone directory for other agencies.

Rail Service

Tampa's Amtrak station is at 601 N. Nebraska Ave. in downtown Tampa, behind historic Union Station. Daily service is offered; phone (813) 221-7600 or (800) 872-7245. Buses from *St. Petersburg* to the Amtrak station leave from the junction of Park Boulevard and US 19N; phone (727) 522-9475 or (800) 872-7245.

Bus service to Union Station also is available via HARTline routes 2, 9 and 12; phone (813) 254-4278. In addition, the Pinellas Suncoast Transit Authority (PSRA) maintains two bus routes to the terminal: The 100X runs from Gateway Mall, Ninth Street N. and 77th Avenue, and the 200X runs from near US 19 and Gulf to Bay Boulevard. For PSTA schedules phone (727) 530-9911.

Buses

Greyhound Lines Inc. is at 180 Ninth St. N. in *St. Petersburg* and 610 Polk St. in *Tampa;* phone (800) 231-2222 or (813) 229-2174, respectively.

Getting Around

Street System

St. Petersburg's street system is essentially a compass-oriented grid. All avenues, terraces and places run east-west; streets and ways run north-south. Central Avenue (CR 150) is the north-south divider; parallel to Tampa Bay is First Street. Numbering of north-south streets begins at the bay and progresses westward 81 blocks to Boca Ciega Bay on the Gulf.

From I-275, I-375 accesses the northern half of downtown *St. Petersburg* and I-175 the southern half. US 92 (Fourth Street) and SR 689 (Ninth Street) provide downtown access from I-275 as well.

Downtown *Tampa* is bracketed by water and has only a few major access routes. From I-275, take the Ashley Street exit. Also from the north, Nebraska Avenue SR 45 and one-way US 41 Bus. Rte. lead into downtown. Cass Street approaches from the west. From the east, use SR 60 (John F. Kennedy Boulevard).

Tampa also is laid out in a basic grid, with a few geographic variations. US 41 Bus. Rte. (Florida Avenue) divides east from west; John F. Kennedy Boulevard/Frank Adamo Drive (SR 60) separates north from south. Many streets in the downtown area are one way.

Five major east-west thoroughfares support cross-town traffic: SR 582 (Fowler Avenue), SR 580

(Busch Boulevard), US 92/US 41 (Hillsborough Avenue), SR 574 (Martin Luther King Jr. Boulevard), and the Crosstown Expressway (toll). Three others parallel I-275: on the west, SR 597/SR 580/US 92 (Dale Mabry Highway); through the central city, US 41/SR 45 (Nebraska Avenue); and on the east, SR 583 (56th Street).

Besides I-275, US 19 and US 19 Alt. are the main north-south routes on the Pinellas Peninsula.

Fort De Soto, Mullet Key, St. Petersburg / © Tony Arruza / Corbis

Congested SR 699 (Gulf Boulevard), lined with shops, restaurants and motels, connects the beach communities from Clearwater Beach south to St. Pete Beach. Running east-west are SR 60 (Gulf-to-Bay Boulevard/Courtney Campbell Causeway) to Clearwater, SR 688 (Ulmerton Road) to the beaches, and SR 694/CR 694 (Gandy Boulevard/Park Boulevard) through the communities of Pinellas Park and Seminole to the beaches.

Generally, downtown speed limits for *Clearwater, St. Petersburg* and *Tampa* are 30 mph or as posted. Unless otherwise posted, a right turn is allowed on a red light after a complete stop. It is best to avoid taking an unfamiliar route during rush hours (about 7 to 9 a.m. and 4:30 to 6 p.m.).

Parking

Clearwater, St. Petersburg and *Tampa* all have limited on-street parking in the downtown business sections and along major thoroughfares. Rates for municipal parking garages start at $1.25 per hour and range from $5.40 to $7 for 6-24 hours. Metered lot parking and use of the Fort Brooke parking garage in Tampa cost $1.25 per hour (if using the garage for 6-24 hours, the rate is $7). For downtown parking information phone (813) 221-3686.

Metered parking at the beaches is available on the street and in lots at 25c-$1 per hour; beach parking is not allowed. For additional parking information phone (813) 274-8179.

Taxis and Limousines

Major companies include *Tampa*-based United Cab Co., (813) 253-2424, and Tampa Taxi, (813) 888-5008; and Yellow Cab Co., (813) 253-0121 in Tampa and (727) 821-7777 in *St. Petersburg*.

Taxis are metered. Most cabs in *Clearwater* and *St. Petersburg* charge $1.50 to enter and $1.60 per mile; most *Tampa* cabs are $2 to enter and $2 per mile. A taxi ride between Tampa International Airport and downtown Tampa, the Ybor City area and the cruise terminals costs a flat rate of $20 in either direction. Limousine service averages $65 per hour in the Tampa Bay area.

Public Transportation

Pinellas Suncoast Transit Authority serves *St. Petersburg* and Pinellas County; for bus fares and schedules phone (727) 530-9911. HARTline serves *Tampa* and its immediate suburbs, including shopping malls and area attractions. The In-Town Connector provides free transportation around downtown Tampa. Service also includes the TECO Line Streetcar System, which makes 11 stops along a 2.3-mile track between downtown Tampa and Ybor City. For HARTline bus and streetcar fares and schedules, phone (813) 254-4278.

St. Petersburg, Clearwater and the beach communities have three trolley systems for visitors. Suncoast Beach Trolley, operated by PSTA, travels Gulf Boulevard north to Clearwater's Sand Key and south to St. Pete Beach; phone (727) 530-9911. The Looper circles downtown St. Petersburg, and the Jolley Trolley route covers Clearwater and Clearwater Beach.

Sunken Gardens, St. Petersburg
© Gibson Stock Photography

What To See

ST. PETERSBURG

See map page 220.

BOYD HILL NATURE PARK, 1101 Country Club Way S., is reached by taking I-275 exit 17, 1.75 mi. e. on 54th Ave. S. to Martin Luther King Jr. St., n. to Country Club Way, then w. 2 blks. This 245-acre preserve on the west side of Lake Maggiore has nature and bicycle trials, a birds of prey aviary and an environmental education center with interpretive displays. Guided walks and special programs are available; phone for schedule.

Picnicking is permitted. Allow 1 hour, 30 minutes minimum. Park open Tues.-Thurs. 9-8, Fri.-Sat. 9-6, Sun. 11-6; closed Jan. 1, Thanksgiving and Dec. 25. A 60- to 90-minute guided tram tour is offered daily at 1. Park free. Nature trail $2; ages 3-16, $1. Tram fare $1. Phone (727) 893-7326.

Lake Maggiore Park, Dr. Martin Luther King Jr. St. between 37th and 40th aves. S., covers 721 acres around Lake Maggiore. Fishing facilities and bicycle trails are available. Picnicking is permitted. Daily dawn-dusk. Free.

THE FLORIDA HOLOCAUST MUSEUM, downtown at 55 Fifth St. S. at jct. First Ave. S., is one of the largest Holocaust museums in the Southeast. Eleven eternal flames, symbolizing the 11 million victims of the Nazis, are part of the three-story building's facade. The 12 sections of the permanent exhibit trace the Holocaust's beginnings in medieval eastern Europe to its implications in modern times.

A boxcar from Nazi-occupied Poland rests on a section of railroad tracks from the Treblinka camp. Changing exhibits feature art, photography and artifacts related to the Holocaust and human rights. An audiotape tour is included with admission.

Allow 2 hours minimum. Mon.-Fri. 10-5, Sat.-Sun. noon-5; closed Jan. 1, Rosh Hashana, Yom Kippur, Thanksgiving and Dec. 25. Last admission is 1 hour before closing. Admission $8; over 60 and students with ID $7; under 18, $3. AX, CB, DS, MC, VI. Phone (727) 820-0100 or (800) 960-7448. *See color ad p. 219.*

FLORIDA INTERNATIONAL MUSEUM is at 100 Second St. N. With emphasis on the arts and popular themes, this Smithsonian affiliate presents major traveling exhibitions from national and international museums, including The Smithsonian, and rotating exhibits from a permanent collection of artifacts.

Note: The museum is scheduled to move to 244 Second Ave. N. in fall 2005. Tues.-Sat. 10-5, Sun noon-5. Last admission 1 hour before closing. Admission $10; senior citizens and military with ID $8; ages 7-18, $6. Hours may vary during special exhibitions; phone ahead. MC, VI. Phone (727) 341-7900.

FORT De SOTO PARK is off I-275 exit 17 at Pinellas Bayway; two toll causeways are crossed en route. The 1,136-acre park occupies five keys: Madeleine, St. Jean, St. Christopher, Bonne Fortune and Mullet. Plants and wildlife are protected; pets must be leashed except at Paw Playground. Daily dawn-dusk. Nature tours begin at various locations Sat.-Sun. at 10. Free. Toll 85c. Phone (727) 582-2267. *See Recreation Chart and the AAA Southeastern CampBook.*

Fort De Soto, on the southern end of Mullet Key, was begun during the Spanish-American War but was incomplete at war's end. Its guns never were fired in battle. There are walkways around the fort area. A pamphlet outlining a self-guiding tour along the Historical Trail is available. A 90-minute guided walking tour of the fort is offered Sat. at 10.

SAVE **GREAT EXPLORATIONS** is off I-275 exit 24, 1 mi. e. on 22nd Ave. N., then .5 mi. s. to 1925 Fourth St. N. This children's museum offers hands-on exhibits exploring such topics as computer animation, robotics, sailing, music and sound. Visitors can climb a wall using foot and toe holds, launch tennis balls to the top of the museum, and design and race a vehicle. Allow 1 hour minimum. Mon.-Sat. 10-4:30, Sun. noon-4:30; closed Jan. 1, Thanksgiving and Dec. 25. Admission $9; over 55 and ages 3-11, $8. A combination ticket with Sunken Gardens is available. MC, VI. Phone (727) 821-8992.

MUSEUM OF FINE ARTS is at 255 Beach Dr. N.E. on the waterfront. French Impressionist paintings and 20th-century photography are among the highlights of the collection, which includes works by Cézanne, Gauguin, Monet, Rodin and O'Keeffe. Also displayed are ancient Greek and Roman, pre-Columbian, Asian, African and American Indian works and decorative arts, including Steuben glass. Special exhibitions also are presented.

Guided tours are available. Open Tues.-Sat. 10-5, Sun. 1-5; closed Jan. 1, Martin Luther King Jr. Day, July 4, Thanksgiving and Dec. 25. Admission $8; over 65, $7; students with ID $2; under 6 free. Prices may vary during special exhibits. AX, MC, VI. Phone (727) 896-2667. *See color ad.*

THE PIER, extending 2,400 feet into Tampa Bay at the foot of Second Ave. N.E., downtown, is one of the most recognized landmarks on Florida's west coast. The complex is an inverted five-story pyramidal that offers fishing, an aquarium, dolphin sightseeing cruises *(see What To Do, Sightseeing p. 225)*, sailboat charters, pelican feeding, entertainment, shops, restaurants and a Concierge Center. A free trolley runs between the parking lot and the pier.

Allow 2 hours minimum. Mon.-Thurs. 10-9, Fri.-Sat. 10-10, Sun. 11-7. Concierge Center open Mon.-Sat. 10-8, Sun. 11-6. Parking $3; $5 for special events. Phone (727) 821-6443.

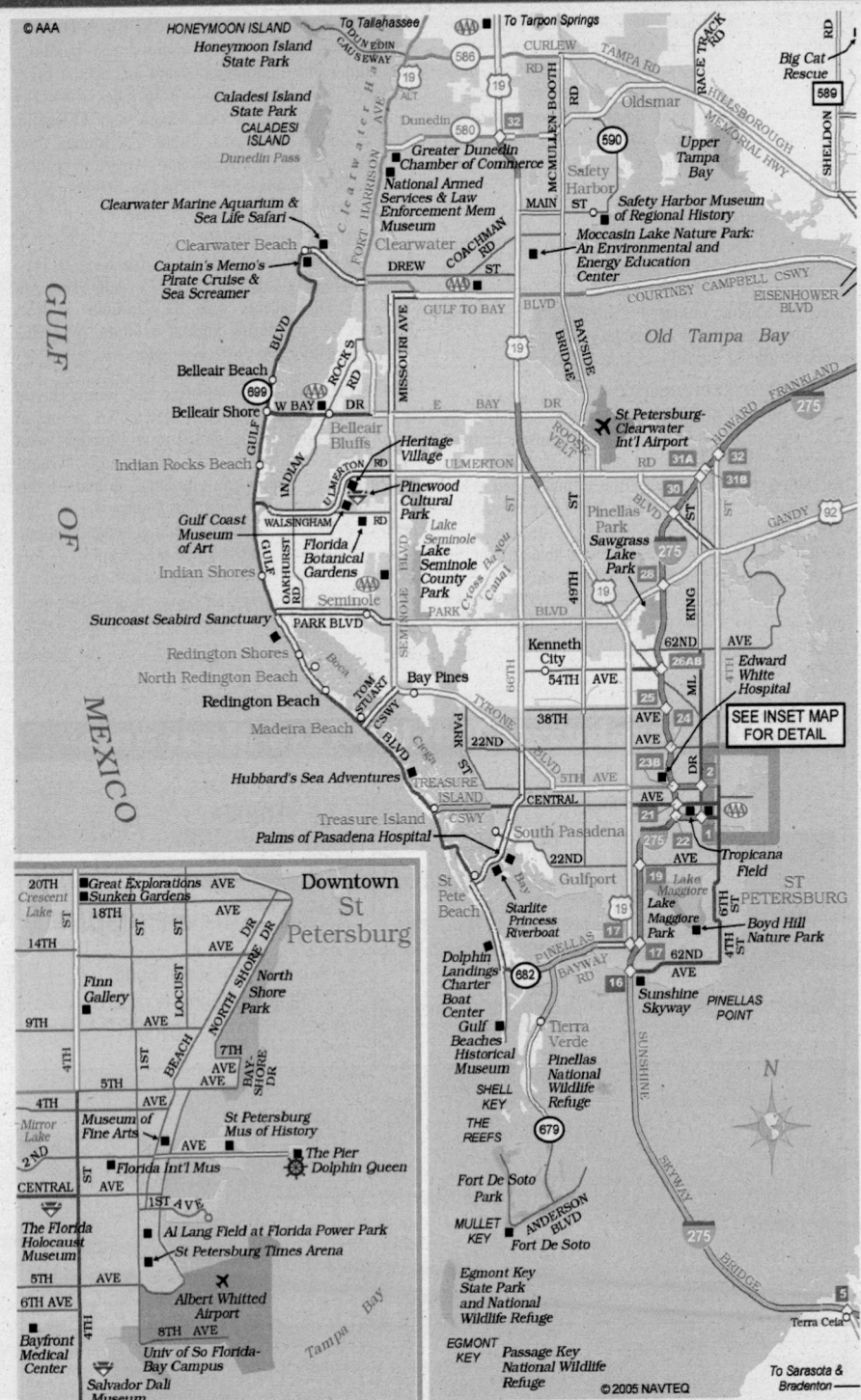

© AAA

HONEYMOON ISLAND
Honeymoon Island State Park

To Tallahassee
To Tarpon Springs

Caladesi Island State Park
CALADESI ISLAND
Dunedin Pass

CURLEW
TAMPA RD

Big Cat Rescue

Oldsmar

Greater Dunedin Chamber of Commerce
National Armed Services & Law Enforcement Mem Museum

Upper Tampa Bay

Clearwater Marine Aquarium & Sea Life Safari
Clearwater Beach
Captain's Memo's Pirate Cruise & Sea Screamer

Safety Harbor
Safety Harbor Museum of Regional History
Moccasin Lake Nature Park: An Environmental and Energy Education Center

Clearwater
DREW   ST

GULF TO BAY   BLVD

COURTNEY CAMPBELL CSWY
EISENHOWER BLVD

Old   Tampa   Bay

Belleair Beach
Belleair Shore
Indian Rocks Beach

W BAY   DR
Belleair Bluffs

St Petersburg-Clearwater Int'l Airport

Heritage Village
Pinewood Cultural Park
Gulf Coast Museum of Art

Pinellas Park
Sawgrass Lake Park

Indian Shores
Florida Botanical Gardens

Lake Seminole
Lake Seminole County Park

Suncoast Seabird Sanctuary
PARK BLVD

Redington Shores
North Redington Beach
Redington Beach
Madeira Beach

Bay Pines

Kenneth City
54TH   AVE
38TH   AVE

Edward White Hospital

SEE INSET MAP FOR DETAIL

Hubbard's Sea Adventures

22ND   AVE

GULF

OF

MEXICO

Treasure Island
Palms of Pasadena Hospital

CENTRAL   AVE

South Pasadena
22ND
Gulfport

Tropicana Field

ST PETERSBURG

Boyd Hill Nature Park

Lake Maggiore
Lake Maggiore Park

Downtown
St Petersburg

20TH   AVE
Crescent Lake
18TH

Great Explorations
Sunken Gardens

14TH

Finn Gallery

North Shore Park

9TH   AVE

St Pete Beach

Starlite Princess Riverboat

Sunshine Skyway
PINELLAS POINT

Dolphin Landings Charter Boat Center
Gulf Beaches Historical Museum

Tierra Verde
Pinellas National Wildlife Refuge

4TH   AVE
Mirror Lake

Museum of Fine Arts
St Petersburg Mus of History

2ND   AVE

St Petersburg

Florida Int'l Mus

The Pier
Dolphin Queen

CENTRAL   AVE
1ST AVE

The Florida Holocaust Museum

Al Lang Field at Florida Power Park
St Petersburg Times Arena

SHELL KEY
THE REEFS

5TH   AVE

6TH AVE

Albert Whitted Airport
8TH   AVE

Fort De Soto Park
MULLET KEY

ANDERSON BLVD
Fort De Soto

Bayfront Medical Center

Univ of So Florida-Bay Campus
Salvador Dali Museum

Tampa Bay

Egmont Key State Park and National Wildlife Refuge
EGMONT KEY

Passage Key National Wildlife Refuge

© 2005 NAVTEQ

To Sarasota & Bradenton

Terra Ceia

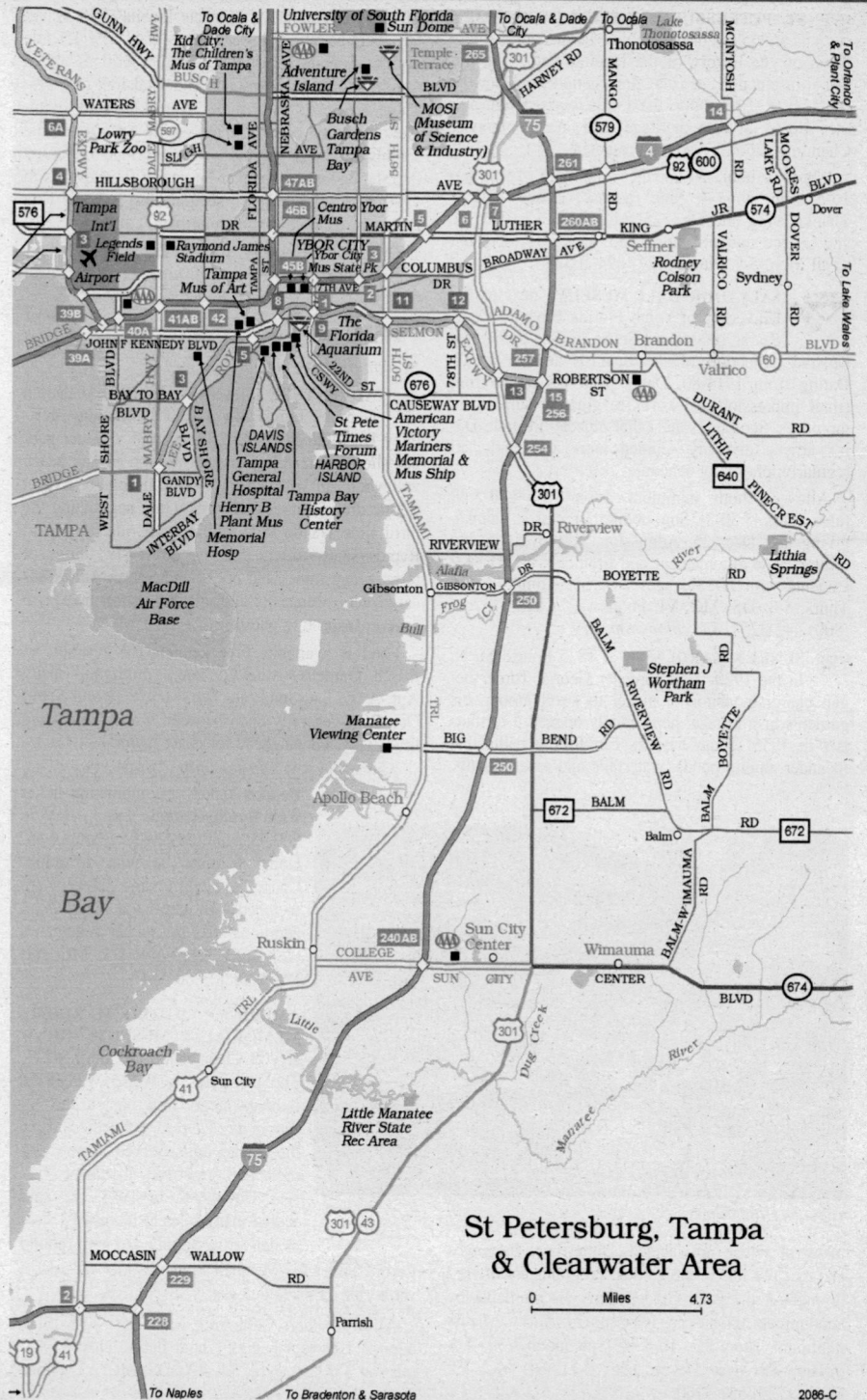

St Petersburg, Tampa
& Clearwater Area

0   Miles   4.73

2086-C

SAVE **ST. PETERSBURG MUSEUM OF HISTORY** is at 335 Second Ave. N.E. Permanent exhibits focus on the history of the Pinellas Peninsula, the 1914 origination of the first commercial airline flight in St. Petersburg, the 1920s tourist boom and the area's diverse heritage and neighborhoods. Changing exhibits also are presented.

Allow 1 hour, 30 minutes minimum. Tues.-Sat. 10-5, Sun. noon-4, Mon. noon-7; closed Jan. 1, Thanksgiving and Dec. 25. Admission $7; over 61 and college students with ID $5; ages 7-17, $3. Free to all Mon. 5-7. Phone (727) 894-1052.

GEM **SALVADOR DALI MUSEUM,** next to the University of South Florida Bayboro Campus at 1000 Third St. S., houses a comprehensive collection of the Spanish artist's works. Dating from 1914-80, Dali's paintings range from small impressionistic works to gigantic surrealistic montages. Sculptures and other objects illustrate Dali's artistic diversity. Guided tours are conducted regularly; phone for schedule.

Allow 1 hour minimum. Mon.-Sat. 9:30-5:30 (also Thurs. 5:30-8), Sun. noon-5:30; closed Thanksgiving and Dec. 25. Admission $14; over 65 and military, law enforcement and firemen with ID $12; students with ID $9; ages 5-9, $3. Admission $5 Thurs. 5-8. DS, MC, VI. Phone (727) 823-3767 or (800) 442-3254. *See color ad p. 219.*

SAVE **SUNKEN GARDENS** is at 1825 Fourth St. N. In the 1920s avid gardener George Turner began charging visitors a nickel to stroll among his garden's lush foliage; he officially opened it to tourists in 1935. Today visitors can follow paths that meander among ponds, waterfalls and exotic plants,

Ybor City / Visit Florida

many of which are labeled. Butterflies, flamingos and macaws live in the garden. Programs are offered throughout the year. Guided tours are available by appointment. Picnicking is permitted. Allow 2 hours minimum. Mon.-Sat. 10-4:30, Sun. noon-4:30. Admission $8; over 54, $6; ages 2-11, $4. MC, VI. Phone (727) 551-3100.

SUNSHINE SKYWAY connects Pinellas and Manatee counties across lower Tampa Bay. The 15-mile bridge is made up of three smaller bridges and a 4-mile concrete skyway and is a vital link of I-275. There are areas for fishing, picnicking and swimming off the roadway. The central section of the southbound span of the original bridge collapsed into the bay when a tanker hit one of the supports in 1980. The original north section now is home to a three-quarter-mile-long fishing pier.

Open daily 24 hours. Toll $1. Fishing pier $3 per vehicle. There is a separate fishing fee of $2; over 65, $1.50; ages 6-12, $1. Phone (727) 865-0668.

TAMPA

See map page 220.

SAVE **ADVENTURE ISLAND** is .25 mi. n. of Busch Gardens Tampa Bay at 10001 Malcolm McKinley Dr. (40th St.). The 25-acre tropical water park has slides, water play areas, a wave pool and beach volleyball, all with a Key West atmosphere. Expect twists, drops, curves and turns while negotiating the thrill slide Wahoo Run, a tunnel raft ride. Key West Rapids sends rafters cruising down six stories of turns, water mines and pools, and Splash Attack has cargo nets, waterfalls and a 1,000-gallon bucket to soak unsuspecting guests.

Food is available. Free kennels are available at Busch Gardens. Allow 5 hours minimum. Daily Apr.-Aug.; Sat.-Sun., late Feb.-March 31 and Sept.-Oct. Park generally open between 9 and 10; closing times vary. Phone ahead for exact hours.

Admission $33.95; ages 3-9, $31.95. The 2-day Bounce Ticket, a combination ticket with Busch Gardens Tampa Bay, is $69.95; children $59.95. Parking $5. Under 8 must be with an adult. Changing facilities and showers are included with admission. There is an additional fee for locker rental and the games area. AX, DS, MC, VI. Phone (888) 800-5447.

AMERICAN VICTORY MARINERS MEMORIAL & MUSEUM SHIP is at 705 Channelside Dr. Berth #271. The memorial, a World War II-era military cargo ship named the SS *American Victory,* is dedicated to those who built, served aboard and protected American merchant vessels. Completed in 1945, the ship served many roles in its history, such as delivering supplies to help rebuild Europe under the Marshall Plan. Visitors can tour a variety of rooms and decks.

Allow 2 hours minimum. Mon.-Sat. 10-5, Sun. noon-5. Last tour begins 1 hour before closing. Admission $8; ages 3-12, $4. AX, DS, MC, VI. Phone (813) 228-8766.

SAVE **BIG CAT RESCUE** is at 12802 Easy St. Specializing in rare and endangered cats, this 40-acre wildlife sanctuary and rehabilitation center offers guided walking tours of its grounds and facilities. More than 20 cat species live in the sanctuary including Bengal tigers, bobcats, caracals, leopards, lions, lynxes, ocelots and servals. Specialty tours also are available. Allow 3 hours minimum. Tours depart Mon.-Fri. at 9 and 3, Sat. at 9:30, 11:30 and 1:30. Fee $20. Under 10 are not permitted. MC, VI. Phone (813) 920-4130.

 GEM SAVE **BUSCH GARDENS TAMPA BAY** is at 3000 E. Busch Blvd. (SR 580), 2 mi. e. of jct. I-275 exit 50 or 2 mi. w. of I-75 exit 265. The 335-acre African-themed park features more than 2,000 animals as well as thrill rides, live entertainment, shopping and dining.

Roller coasters include SheiKra, a dive coaster that sends riders 200 feet up, then 90 degrees down at 70 mph.; Gwazi, a double wooden coaster; Montu, an inverted steel coaster; the loops and spirals of Kumba; and hairpin turns on Cheetah Chase. Edge of Africa, with a world-class zoo as its showcase, offers a safari experience with naturalistic animal habitats, remote encampments and African villages.

The Serengeti Safari Tour takes riders through herds of free-roaming giraffes, zebras, antelopes and ostriches. Lory Landing's aviary is populated with tropical birds, including lorikeets, hornbills and touracos. Myombe Reserve: The Great Ape Domain allows visitors to see lowland gorillas and chimpanzees in a naturalistic setting. Rhino Rally combines an off-road safari through white rhino, cape buffalo and elephant habitats with a raging white-water river ride.

The show, KaTonga: Musical Tales from the Jungle, tells animal fables through music, dance and costumes. In the 4-D movie, R.L. Stine's Haunted Lighthouse, mischievous children lead visitors on an adventure to uncover the lighthouse's haunted legend.

Food, free kennels, and stroller, wheelchair and locker rentals are available. Allow a full day. Park open generally daily at 9; closing hours vary. Phone ahead for exact hours.

Admission $57.95; ages 3-9, $47.95. There is an additional fee for the Serengeti Safari Tour. The 2-day Bounce Ticket, a combination ticket with Adventure Island, is $69.95; children $59.95. Parking $7 for automobiles, $11 for recreational vehicles and campers. AX, DS, MC, VI. Phone (888) 800-5447.

CENTRO YBOR MUSEUM is at 1600 E. Eighth Ave., Suite B-104. Located within Tampa's historic cigar-manufacturing district, the museum features cigar trade exhibits and a 7-minute videotape tracing the area's transformation from quiet swampland to bustling city. The building also houses the Ybor City Visitor Information Center. Allow 1 hour minimum. Mon.-Sat. 10-6, Sun. noon-5. Free. Phone (813) 241-8838.

GEM SAVE **THE FLORIDA AQUARIUM,** 701 Channelside Dr. on the downtown waterfront, is a 200,000-square-foot aquarium that features more than 10,000 aquatic plants from

Bayshore Boulevard / © Tony Arruza / Corbis

Florida and around the world. Exhibits highlight wetlands, bays, beaches and coral reefs and feature ocean predators and rare Australian leafy sea dragons.

A children's playground has interactive aquatic discovery zones. Also available are behind-the-scenes tours, close-up animal encounters, dive shows, touch tanks and opportunities to swim in a 500,000-gallon coral reef tank. Wild Dolphin Eco-tours of the bay take passengers aboard a catamaran in search of manatees and bottle nose dolphins.

Food is available. Allow 2 hours minimum. Aquarium open daily 9:30-5; closed Thanksgiving and Dec. 25. Eco-tours depart daily; phone for schedule. Aquarium admission $17.95; over 60, $14.95; ages 3-12, $11.95. Eco-tour fare $18.95; over 60, $17.95; ages 3-12, $13. Combination tickets are available. Parking $5. AX, DS, MC, VI. Phone (813) 273-4000.

SAVE **KID CITY: THE CHILDREN'S MUSEUM OF TAMPA** is next to Lowry Park Zoo at 7550 North Blvd. In this interactive museum, children can explore a child-friendly city and shop for groceries, dress like a firefighter, deliver mail or ride bikes and scooters on city streets. A play space for toddlers also is available. Picnicking is permitted. Allow 1 hour minimum. Mon.-Thurs. 9-2, Fri. 9-5, Sat. 10-5, Sun. noon-5. Admission $5, under 1 free. Phone (813) 935-8441.

LOWRY PARK ZOO, I-275 exit 48 w. to 1101 W. Sligh Ave., is 46 acres of lush natural habitats comprising six main exhibit areas: The Florida Manatee and Aquatic Center, Native Florida Wildlife Center, Asian Domain; Primate World, Wallaroo Station Children's Zoo and Safari Africa. Visitors can feed the birds in Lorikeet Landing and touch and feed stingrays at Stingray Bay. Manatee Encounter offers a behind-the-scenes look into a manatee hospital.

Food is available. Daily 9:30-5. Last admission 15 minutes before closing. Admission $14.95; over 60, $13.95; ages 3-11, $10.50. AX, DS, MC, VI. Phone (813) 935-8552.

MOSI (MUSEUM OF SCIENCE & INDUSTRY), 4801 E. Fowler Ave., is 3 mi. e. on SR 582 from I-275 exit 51 or 3 mi. w. of I-75 exit 265. One of the largest science centers in the country, MOSI contains more than 280,000 square feet of hands-on exhibits and demonstrations pertaining to science and technology, health and the human body, and flight and space.

The Gulf Coast Hurricane simulates 84-mph winds. Visitors can follow the life cycle of a butterfly in the BioWorks Butterfly Garden or explore nature trails in the Back Woods, a 40-acre wilderness. Kids in Charge uses interactive exhibits to show connections between science and everyday life.

The Saunders Planetarium offers presentations daily; phone for schedule. Telescope viewing sessions also are available. The IMAX *Dome* Theatre features large-format films on a 10,500-square-foot domed screen.

Allow 4 hours minimum. Opens Mon.-Fri. 9-5, Sat.-Sun. 9-7. Closing times may vary, phone ahead. Admission, including the IMAX *Dome* Theater,

Tampa Bay / Tampa Bay Convention & Visitors Bureau

$15.95; over 59, $13.95; ages 2-12, $11.95. AX, DS, MC, VI. Phone (813) 987-6300, (813) 987-6100 or (800) 995-6674.

TAMPA BAY HISTORY CENTER, I-275 exit 44, then 1.5 mi. e. following signs to 225 S. Franklin St., interprets regional history covering such topics as Florida's first people, wars, railroads and

shipping, and the cigar, citrus and cattle industries. Allow 1 hour minimum. Tues.-Sat. 10-5; closed holidays. Free. Phone (813) 228-0097.

(SAVE) **TAMPA MUSEUM OF ART**, 600 N. Ashley Dr., displays permanent and major traveling art exhibitions. Permanent collections include Greek and Roman antiquities as well as contemporary art. Tues.-Sat. 10-5 (also third Thurs. of the month 5-9), Sun. 11-5; closed major holidays. Admission $7; over 61, $6; students with ID and ages 6-18, $3; all ages by donation third Thurs. of the month 5-9 and Sat. 10-noon. AX, MC, VI. Phone (813) 274-8130.

UNIVERSITY OF SOUTH FLORIDA, 4202 Fowler Ave. in n.e. Tampa, was founded in 1956 and occupies 1,695 acres. The campus features a contemporary art museum and botanical gardens. Guided campus tours can be arranged. Phone (877) 873-2855.

UNIVERSITY OF TAMPA, 401 W. Kennedy Blvd., was established in 1931. Today it offers more than 80 fields of study. Encompassing 100 acres, the campus centers on the former Tampa Bay Hotel, a Victorian-style building with Moorish revival architecture featuring minarets, domes and cupolas. The hotel was built in 1891 by transportation magnate Henry B. Plant, who was instrumental in the reconstruction of the South.

Allow 30 minutes minimum. University tours are given Tues. and Thurs. at 1:30, Sept.-May; closed Jan. 1, Thanksgiving and Dec. 18-25. Free. Phone (813) 253-6220.

(SAVE) **Henry B. Plant Museum** is housed in the south wing of Plant Hall. Once the Tampa Bay Hotel, the museum displays the Moorish Revival-style building's original collection of decorative arts and furnishings. Exhibits re-create the first-class accommodations and activities of 1891. A video presentation highlights Tampa's Victorian-era lifestyle and tourism, and a live stage performance features character vignettes of the hotel's staff and guests.

Museum open Tues.-Sat. 10-4, Sun. noon-4. Stage show Sun. at 2, Sept.-Nov. and Jan.-May. Admission $5; under 13, $2. Stage show free with admission. A fee is charged for the Victorian Christmas Stroll in Dec. Phone (813) 254-1891.

YBOR CITY MUSEUM STATE PARK, 3 blks. s. of I-4 exit 1 at 1818 E. Ninth Ave., is in a former bakery with huge brick ovens still intact. Displays depict Ybor City's founding by Vicente Martinez-Ybor as well as the cigar industry, which brought many nationalities to Tampa. An 1895 cigar worker's cottage, furnished in period, is open by guided tour. Allow 30 minutes minimum. Daily 9-5. Admission $3, under 6 free. Phone (813) 247-6323.

CASINOS

• **Seminole Hard Rock Casino** is at 5223 N. Orient Rd., Tampa, FL 33610. Daily 24 hours. Phone (866) 502-7529.

What To Do In Tampa Bay

Sightseeing

Boat Tours

Sightseeing tours as well as lunch, dinner, evening, ecology, jazz and pirate-themed cruises depart from marinas in Clearwater Beach, Madeira Beach, St. Pete Beach and St. Petersburg.

DOLPHIN QUEEN departs from The Pier, at the foot of Second Ave. in St. Petersburg. Narrated, 90-minute sightseeing cruises on Tampa Bay include sightings of dolphins, manatees and native birds as well as views of the historic waterfront and the U.S. Coast Guard Base. Photo opportunities are plentiful. Allow 1 hour minimum. Cruises daily at 11:30, 1, 3 and 5. Fare $16; over 54 and military with ID $14; ages 3-12, $9.50. MC, VI. Phone (727) 647-1538.

[SAVE] *STARLITE PRINCESS* RIVERBOAT boards at the Corey Causeway at 3400 Pasadena Ave. S. in St. Petersburg. The paddlewheel excursion boat offers a variety of sightseeing cruises on scenic inland waterways. Dinner dance cruises also are offered.

Two-hour luncheon/sightseeing cruise departs Tues. and Fri.-Sat. at noon. A 3-hour luncheon/sightseeing cruise departs Wed. at noon. Dixieland Jazz cruise departs Sun. at 1. Boarding begins 30 minutes before departure. Closed major holidays.

Two-hour luncheon/sightseeing cruise (meal optional) $11.25; ages 3-12, $8.20. Three-hour sightseeing and Dixieland Jazz cruises (meal optional) $13.80; ages 3-12, $10. Reservations are required. AX, MC, VI. Phone (727) 462-2628 or (800) 444-4814.

Driving Tours

With its scenic views of Hillsborough Bay, Bayshore Boulevard in *Tampa* is not only a popular walking and exercise area but also a preferred driving route. Among the beautiful residential neighborhoods to explore is Davis Islands, built on three man-made islands in the 1920s, and historic Hyde Park.

Walking Tours

The 4.5-mile sidewalk along Bayshore Boulevard in *Tampa*, which skirts the west side of Hillsborough Bay, is an excellent recreation area. The sidewalk is reputedly the world's longest continuous walkway.

St. Petersburg/Clearwater Area CVB

The Ybor City Chamber of Commerce and Ybor City Museum offer a guided walking tour of historic Ybor City; the fee is $5. The 2-hour tour departs from the museum Saturdays at 10:30. For further information contact the museum at 1818 E. Ninth Ave., Tampa, FL 33605; phone (813) 247-0323.

Spectator Sports

Tampa Bay area fans have the option to root for a home run; slap high-fives after a touchdown; count down the time during a power play; watch dogs chase a stuffed rabbit; or applaud as a favorite horse makes a photo finish. Whatever your pleasure, the following options will have you cheering.

Baseball

Professional baseball is played at several locations. The **Tampa Bay Devil Rays** play major league baseball April through September at **Tropicana Field**, 1 Tropicana Dr. in *St. Petersburg;* phone (727) 825-3137 for general information, or (727) 898-7297 for tickets. The Devil Rays remain in St. Petersburg during the off-season; spring training games take place at Al Lang Field at **Progress Energy Park**, 180 Second Ave. S.E.; phone (727) 825-3137 for ticket information. Both the Devil Rays major and minor league teams train at 7901 30th Ave. N.

The **New York Yankees** major and minor league teams call *Tampa* home in the spring. They play at **Legends Field**, N. Dale Mabry Highway and Martin Luther King Jr. Boulevard. The facility's 10,000-seat stadium is a replica of New York's Yankee Stadium. Play is March to September; for information phone (813) 875-7753.

Two other major league teams hold spring training on the Pinellas Peninsula: the Philadelphia Phillies and the Toronto Blue Jays, both of which have minor league affiliates that play ball locally. In summer the Phillies' **Clearwater Threshers** train at *Clearwater's* **Bright House Networks Field,** 601 N. Old Coachman Rd., and the **Dunedin Blue Jays** work out at **Knology Park,** 373 Douglas Ave. in Dunedin. Both teams play a full minor league schedule; phone (727) 442-8496 for the Threshers or (727) 733-9302 for the Blue Jays.

Football

The NFL's **Tampa Bay Buccaneers** play at **Raymond James Stadium** between N. Dale Mabry Highway and N. Himes Avenue; for ticket information phone (813) 879-2827. The stadium also is the setting for the Outback Bowl game, played on New Year's Day. The **Tampa Bay Storm** play arena football from February to May at the **St. Pete Times Forum,** downtown *Tampa* at Channelside Drive and Morgan Street; phone (813) 276-7300.

Greyhound Racing

The *St. Petersburg* Kennel Club's **Derby Lane** track at 10490 Gandy Blvd. features greyhound racing most evenings and weekends from early January to late June; phone (727) 812-3339. **Tampa Greyhound Track,** 8300 N. Nebraska Ave. at Waters Street in the Sulphur Springs section of *Tampa,* does the same July through December; phone (813) 932-4313.

Note: Policies vary concerning admittance of children to pari-mutuel betting facilities. Phone for information.

Channelside / Tampa Bay Convention & Visitors Bureau

Hockey

The NHL's **Tampa Bay Lightning,** winners of the 2004 Stanley Cup, hit the ice at the St. Pete Times Forum October through April. For information and tickets phone (813) 301-6600.

Horse Racing

Horse racing devotees can go to the only Thoroughbred track on Florida's west coast, **Tampa Bay Downs,** 11225 Race Track Rd. in Tampa. The track holds races mid-December to early May. For more information phone (813) 855-4401.

Note: Policies vary concerning admittance of children to pari-mutuel betting facilities. Phone for information.

Recreation

The American Medical Association was on to the bay area's bounty of recreational riches back in 1885, when it named St. Petersburg as an ideal location for a "world health city." Near year-round warmth, broad beaches, a varied system of waterways and some 400 public parks and playgrounds make the region a true haven for outdoor enthusiasts.

Bicycling

Tampa's busy roadways generally are not conducive to safe bicycling; however, scenic, 4.5-mile **Bayshore Boulevard** is a delightful exception. It offers a breezy ride along the western shore of Hillsborough Bay with pretty water views as a backdrop. **Suncoast Parkway Trail** parallels the toll-road of the same name between the Veterans Expressway and State Road 50, and is generally separated from it by a buffer zone of plants and trees.

The **Friendship Trail Bridge,** once the Old Gandy Bridge connecting *Tampa* and *St. Petersburg,* now serves as an over-the-water recreation trail for bicyclists, in-line skaters and joggers.

Fishing

The central Gulf Coast offers some of the best saltwater fishing in the state. More than 300 species roam these warm waters. Tarpon appear in late spring and early summer, and kingfish run in spring and fall. Sea trout, bluefish, mackerel and grouper are commonly caught, and the waters of Hillsborough County yield bass, bream and perch.

Boats can be chartered for inshore and offshore saltwater and freshwater fishing; make arrangements at **Clearwater Municipal Marina, St. Pete Beach** or **Isla del Sol.** Boats equipped for 30-100 passengers venture into deep Gulf waters; they can be rented for half-day or all-day trips, which cost $20-$40 per person, depending on the amenities offered. For details about what may be caught where and when, pick up a *Guide to Florida Fishing* at local tackle shops.

Lake Thonotosassa, northeast of *Tampa* via SR 582, attracts freshwater fishing enthusiasts. The docks off **Davis Islands** and Bayshore Boulevard in

Tampa offer ample casting sites. **The Skyway Fishing Pier,** next to the Sunshine Skyway Bridge, extends 3,350 feet into lower Tampa Bay; its northern end has concession stands, showers, picnic tables and parking lots.

Freshwater and saltwater fishing licenses are sold at some tackle shops, sporting goods and discount department stores and at the county tax collector's office. Phone (813) 307-6549 for information.

Golf

With some 50 courses to choose from and weather that allows for year-round play, the bay area is a true golfer's paradise. Some of the public and semiprivate courses in the *St. Petersburg* area are Bardmoor Golf and Tennis Club, 8001 Cumberland Rd. in Largo, (727) 392-1234; Baypointe, 9399 Commodore Dr., (727) 595-2095; Mainlands, 9445 Mainlands Blvd., (727) 577-4847; Mangrove Bay, 875 62nd Ave. N.E., (727) 893-7800; Tides, 11832 66th Ave. N. in Seminole, (727) 393-8483; and Twin Brooks, 3800 22nd Ave. S., (727) 893-7445. East Bay Golf Club of Largo, 702 Country Club Dr., offers night golf until 11:30 p.m.; phone (727) 581-3333.

Tampa area courses include Bloomingdale, 4113 Great Golfers Pl., (813) 653-6823; Heritage Harbor, 19502 Heritage Harbor Pkwy., (813) 949-4886; Northdale, 4417 Northdale Blvd., (813) 962-0428; Rocky Point, 4151 Dana Shores Dr., (813) 673-4316; Rogers Park, 7910 30th St., (813) 673-4396; TPC, 5300 W. Lutz Lake Fern Rd., (866) 752-9872; USF, 4202 E. Fowler Ave., (813) 632-6893; and Westchase, 11602 Westchase, (813) 854-2331.

Hot Air Ballooning

Hot air balloon flights offer views of the Tampa Bay area accompanied by a champagne brunch. For fares, flight schedules and departure locations phone **Big Red Balloon Sightseeing Adventures,** (813) 969-1518, or **Crystal Magic Balloon Co.,** (727) 536-3005.

Jogging and Walking

Sunny weather encourages both visitors and locals to enjoy the outdoors. The **Pinellas Trail,** a former railroad corridor stretching 37 miles from Tarpon Springs to *St. Petersburg,* provides opportunities for walking, jogging, bicycling and in-line skating. Many entry and exit points exist along the trail. For information contact the Pinellas County Park Department, 631 Chestnut St. in Clearwater; phone (727) 464-3347.

Some 8 miles of nature trails wind through scenic hardwood hammocks at **Hillsborough River State Park,** about 12 miles northeast of *Tampa* via US 301; phone (813) 987-6771.

Tennis

The **St. Petersburg Tennis Center,** 650 18th Ave. S., features 15 clay tennis courts; phone (727) 823-2225. For additional information phone the St. Petersburg Recreation Department at (727) 893-7441.

In *Tampa* the city-operated facility at **Hillsborough Community College,** west of Raymond James Stadium, has both hard and soft courts; phone (813)

Raymond James Stadium / Tampa Bay Convention & Visitors Bureau

348-1173. There are eight clay courts at **Marjorie Park,** on Davis Islands just south of downtown Tampa; phone (813) 259-1664. There are six clay and two hard courts at the **Treasure Island Golf, Tennis and Recreation Center,** 10315 Paradise Blvd.; phone (727) 360-6062. Tampa Parks and Recreation Department, (813) 274-8615, can provide a complete list of playing courts.

Water Sports

The Pinellas Peninsula's many beaches, with their attendant pleasures—swimming, skin diving and water skiing—line the slender offshore islands.

While there are two public beaches on the *Tampa* side of the bay—**Ben T. Davis Beach,** along Courtney Campbell Causeway (SR 60) near the airport, and **Picnic Island Park** near Port Tampa—it's the gulf beaches that draw water lovers. Some of the popular island towns are **Indian Rocks Beach, Madeira Beach,** St. Pete Beach, **Treasure Island** and **North Redington Beach.**

Water sports of all kinds, including parasailing, are the focal point at **John's Pass Village and Boardwalk,** 140 128th Ave. in Madeira Beach, (727) 391-7373. The **Tackle Shack** in Pinellas Park offers instruction and rentals for kayaking, sailboating and scuba diving; phone (727) 546-5080 or (800) 537-6099.

The Pinellas County park system provides several areas throughout the county where picnicking, boating and swimming can be enjoyed. **Fort De Soto Park,** south of St. Pete Beach, is one of the most developed *(see Recreation Chart and the AAA Southeastern CampBook).*

Hillsborough County parks also offer aquatic variety. Swimmers can dip into 72-degree spring water year-round at **Lithia Springs Park,** off Lithia Pinecrest Road *(see Recreation Chart).* The springs feed the Alafia River, the county's most popular canoeing destination; launches are available in Lithia Springs Park and in **Alderman's Ford Park,** off CR 39 near Lithia.

Picnic Island Park, near the original encampment of Theodore Roosevelt's Rough Riders during the Spanish-American War, beckons boaters, swimmers, picnickers and anglers. The park is south of the Gandy Bridge (US 92) near MacDill Air Force Base and accessible via Commerce Street in *Tampa.*

Other Diversions

One of the world's largest shuffleboard clubs is at **Mirror Lake Recreation Park** in downtown *St. Petersburg.* A daily guest membership is available. The **St. Petersburg Shuffleboard Club,** next to Mirror Lake Recreation Park, provides lawn bowling lanes; phone (727) 822-2083. If you'd rather exercise gray matter than muscles, try the **St. Petersburg Chess Club** any day of the week at 540 Fourth Ave. N. in Mirror Lake Recreation Park; phone (727) 822-1171. For trapshooting enthusiasts, the **Deer Creek Sporting Clays** in Land O' Lakes offers 5-stand sporting clays and courses through palmetto and pine woods; phone (813) 996-1970.

Shopping

Tampa Bay's retail front offers a great deal of activity, whether it be expansive malls, factory outlet centers or specialty shopping districts.

Antiques

In *St. Petersburg* the **Gas Plant Antique Arcade,** 1246 Central Ave., offers wares from more than 100 dealers. Unusual shops contain a variety of finds from jewelry to antiques along **Beach Drive.**

An antiques district of sorts centers on the shops along **Euclid Avenue** and **El Prado Boulevard** near south *Tampa's* Palma Ceia neighborhood. And **Antique & Decorative Arts,** 917 N. Franklin St., carries European furniture, glassware, rugs, silver jewelry, porcelain and works of art.

Malls

Want to shop until you drop? *St. Petersburg's* selection of malls can get you started. The four anchors at **Tyrone Square Mall,** Tyrone Boulevard and 22nd Avenue N., are Dillard's, JCPenney, Macy's and Sears. The mall also contains more than 170 other stores and restaurants. **Crosswinds Shopping Center** is at 66th Street and 20th Avenue N., Downtown St. Petersburg is home to **Baywalk,** 153 Second. Ave. N., a shopping complex that includes Ann Taylor.

The largest mall on the Pinellas Peninsula is *Clearwater's* **Countryside Mall,** US 19N and SR 580, which features Dillard's, JCPenney, Macy's and

Sears in addition to restaurants and more than 170 boutiques and specialty outlets. Countryside also contains the state's only in-mall ice-skating rink.

If you're heading for the beach and need to pick up a few things, **Seminole Mall,** at the corner of 113th Street and Park Boulevard in Seminole, has a Bealls Outlet and some 70 other stores.

There's more shopping across the bay in *Tampa.* **Westfield Shoppingtown Citrus Park** is off Veterans Expressway and Gunn Highway in west Tampa. **Westfield Shoppingtown Brandon** is at the intersection of I-75 and SR 60 on Tampa's east side. The major anchor stores are Dillard's, JCPenney, Macy's and Sears, complemented by 120 specialty shops and boutiques.

University Mall, west of the University of South Florida at 2200 E. Fowler Ave., is the region's largest at 1.3 million square feet. The major stores operating here are Dillard's, JCPenney, Macy's and Sears, along with more than 130 specialty shops and restaurants.

Next to Tampa International Airport, **International Plaza** is an upscale, two-story mall with a large restaurant courtyard and approximately 200 stores. It is anchored by Dillard's, Neiman Marcus and Nordstrom, and includes Christian Dior, Godiva and Tiffany & Co. Last but not least, **West Shore Plaza,** off I-275 exit 40A, opened in 1967 and was the first of *Tampa's* enclosed malls. JCPenney, Macy's, Saks Fifth Avenue and Sears anchor the mall, which has more than 130 other stores and an international food court.

Outlets

The area's factory outlets are a good bet for good buys. In *Clearwater,* **Crossroads Mall,** Roosevelt Boulevard and US 19, has Bass Shoes, 9 West, TJ Maxx, Van Heusen and about 60 other stores.

Specialty Districts

The Pinellas side of the bay offers intriguing shopping, much of it with an appropriately waterside theme. At Gulf Boulevard and 128th Avenue in Madeira Beach is **John's Pass Village & Boardwalk,** where a fishing village atmosphere permeates more than 100 stores, boutiques and restaurants. The shopping experience is enhanced by a scenic 1,000-foot boardwalk. The **Wagon Wheel Flea Market,** 7801 Park Blvd. in Pinellas Park, has more than 2,000 vendors and is open Sat.-Sun. 7:30-4.

A bit farther down the peninsula, at 5501 Gulf Blvd. in St. Pete Beach, is **Silas Bayside Market,** a small complex of shops and restaurants in a tropical setting. **The Pier,** at the end of Second Avenue N.E. in downtown *St. Petersburg,* has shops, restaurants and a food court, all under one inverted pyramid roof facing Tampa Bay.

The atmosphere is as enticing as the offerings at the bay area's assorted specialty emporiums. Just off Bayshore Boulevard at Swann and Dakota avenues in Hyde Park—a stone's throw from downtown *Tampa*—is **Old Hyde Park Village,** which contains a delightful collection of more than 50 shops, restaurants and cafes. The area offers an Old World charm complemented by a cosmopolitan tempo. Shoppers can settle at a shady outdoor table after perusing the upscale merchandise at the likes of Brooks Brothers, Restoration Hardware, The Sharper Image and Williams-Sonoma.

More eclectic offerings are available in Ybor City, *Tampa's* Latin Quarter just northeast of downtown. Shopping and dining establishments are focused around **Centro Ybor,** between 15th and 17th streets and 7th and 9th avenues. Here and in the surrounding area shoppers may delight in boutiques and specialty stores. A short drive from Ybor City and adjacent to the Florida Aquarium is **Channelside,** an entertainment and dining complex featuring several boutiques and gift shops.

Performing Arts

Tampa Bay's spectrum of arts encompasses blockbuster Broadway musicals, symphony and chamber music concerts, children's shows and holiday spectaculars. Its keystone is the 300,000-square-foot **Tampa Bay Performing Arts Center** (TBPAC), the largest performing arts facility south of Washington, D.C.'s Kennedy Center. On the east bank of the Hillsborough River in downtown *Tampa,* the TBPAC plays host to a great variety of cultural events at its venues: the 2,557-seat **Carol Morsani Hall;** 1,000-seat **Ferguson Hall;** 300-seat **Jaeb Theater;** and 150-seat **Shimberg Playhouse.**

Phone (813) 229-7827 for schedule and ticket information regarding each of these venues.

Be sure to grab a free copy of the *Weekly Planet,* which is available throughout the city. The publication is filled with local news features; sections on restaurants, theater, film and music; and listings of upcoming events.

Film

Downtown's 1,500-seat **Tampa Theatre,** a restored 1926 movie palace at 711 Franklin St. Mall, is a great spot to catch foreign films, cult movies, Hollywood classics and occasional concerts. Tours of the historic building also are offered; phone (813) 274-8981. **Beach Theatre,** 315 Corey Ave. in St. Pete Beach, shows foreign and offbeat, low-budget films; phone (727) 360-6697.

Music

A full season of symphonic presentations is brought to the Tampa Bay area by the **Florida Orchestra Inc.** and by local dance companies. Performances take place at TBPAC; *Clearwater's* acoustically acclaimed **Ruth Eckerd Hall** in the Richard B. Baumgardner Center for the Performing Arts; and the **Mahaffey Theater** in *St. Petersburg.* Phone (813) 286-2403 or (800) 662-7286 for ticket and schedule information.

Works for voice are presented by the **Master Chorale of Tampa Bay,** (813) 258-9468; **Tampa Oratorio Singers,** (813) 247-3866; and **Tampa Bay**

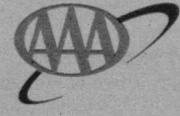

Arts Inc., (727) 865-9004. Performance locations vary.

Free band concerts are held January through March at **Williams Park** in downtown *St. Petersburg.* **Straub Park,** next to the Museum of Fine Arts overlooking the inner harbor, and bayside **Vinoy Park,** near Straub Park, are settings for many events in St. Petersburg.

Theater

Broadway and off-Broadway plays are a big hit in the bay area. Try the **American Stage Theater,** 211 Third St. S. in *St. Petersburg,* for classical and contemporary plays in an intimate setting; phone (727) 823-7529. The **St. Petersburg Little Theater,** 4025 31st St. S., stages six major productions September through June; phone (727) 866-1973.

The Carrollwood Players, 4333 Gunn Hwy. in *Tampa,* is a little-theater group presenting a variety of productions; phone (813) 265-4000. Comedies, musical revues and stage readings are offered at **Gorilla Theatre,** 4419 N. Hubert Ave.; phone (813) 879-2914. TBPAC's Shimberg Playhouse features local performing companies and improvisational groups, and the cozy Jaeb Theater presents plays and cabaret shows.

The **Tampa Bay Broadway Series** brings the best of Broadway to TBPAC's Carol Morsani Hall; phone (813) 229-7827.

Special Events

St. Petersburg recognizes its ethnic groups during the **International Folk Fair** in March; offerings include ethnic foods and folk dances.

Fiesta Day, Ybor City / © Ace Stock Limited / Alamy

St. Petersburg's biggest celebration is the **Festival of States,** which is held in early April and pays tribute to the city's winter visitors; waterfront fireworks, an arts festival, music festival, the election of royalty, a ball and a parade fill the agenda.

St. Petersburg also is host to **St. Anthony's Tampa Bay Triathlon,** which takes place in April; **Shakespeare in the Park,** which offers several weeks of professional productions of Shakespeare's works redone in a lighter, humorous mode mid-April to mid-May; and **Tarpon Round-Up,** a popular fishing event held during May and June. To round out the year, the holiday **Lighted Boat Parade** takes place downtown at the waterfront in early December.

Tampa's calendar of events begins with **The Outback Bowl** at **Raymond James Stadium** on Dale Mabry Highway. This New Year's Day event matches college football's Southeastern Conference and Big 10 Conference champions. Mid-month brings the **Black Heritage Festival,** a celebration of the area's ethnic diversity.

But of all the goings-on, the **Gasparilla Pirate Fest** is the biggest, maddest and most colorful of *Tampa's* events. Florida's answer to Mardi Gras, Gasparilla is held the first Saturday in February with the capturing of Tampa by pirates, followed by several parades throughout the city. The festivities continue throughout the month with **Fiesta Day,** a celebration of ethnic diversity in Ybor City, and the 5- and 15-kilometer **Gasparilla Distance Classic** the first weekend in March. The **Gasparilla Festival of the Arts** wraps up the celebration with artists and craftspersons from around the world.

Not to be outdone by "the invasion" and all its associated activities, the **Florida State Fair** in February is the showcase for the state's finest agriculture, handicrafts, arts and industry. A midway, entertainment, shows and exhibits add to the festivities. The **Outback Steakhouse Pro-Am,** held at Tournament Players Club of Tampa Bay, tees off in mid-February. The **Best of Tampa Bay,** sponsored by the Tampa Bay Performing Arts Center in April, features culinary creations from the area's top restaurants.

Guavaween, *Tampa's* Latin-style Halloween celebration, includes a street party, satirical parade, contests and entertainment. The event, held in Ybor City in October, takes its name from a succulent tropical fruit and echoes a Tampa nickname: "The Big Guava."

Celebrate another delicious fruit at the **Florida Strawberry Festival** in Plant City, where visitors can indulge in strawberry shortcakes and enjoy musical performances. Festivities coincide with the fruit's harvest in early March.

Aficionados of performing arts won't want to miss the **Clearwater Jazz Holiday.** The 4-day festival, held the third weekend in October at downtown *Clearwater's* Coachman Park, features performers of national and international acclaim.

The Tampa Bay Vicinity

APOLLO BEACH (E-9) pop. 7,444

MANATEE VIEWING CENTER is 2.5 mi. w. of I-75 exit 246 (Big Bend Rd.) at jct. Big Bend (CR 672) and Dickman rds. The center is across the warm-water discharge canal from the Tampa Electric Big Bend power plant and features an observation platform for manatee watching and a movie about manatees. Other displays cover Florida yard landscaping, power plant generation and by-product recycling. A nature trail provides closer glimpses of native plants and wildlife.

Allow 1 hour, 30 minutes minimum. Daily 10-5, Nov.-Apr.; closed Easter, Thanksgiving and Dec. 25. Free. Phone (813) 228-4289 to verify operating dates.

CLEARWATER (H-7) pop. 108,787, elev. 29'

A resort city and popular retirement community on the Pinellas Peninsula, Clearwater overlooks the Gulf of Mexico.

The Philadelphia Phillies hold spring training and play exhibition games from early March to early April at Bright House Networks Field; their Class A affiliates, the Clearwater Threshers, train and play April through August; phone (727) 467-4457.

Broadway shows, orchestral and jazz performances, ballet, opera and children's theater are staged throughout the year at Ruth Eckerd Hall in Richard B. Baumgardner Center, 1111 McMullen Booth Rd.; phone (727) 791-7400.

Clearwater Regional Chamber of Commerce: 1130 Cleveland St., P.O. Box 2457, Clearwater, FL 33755; phone (727) 461-0011.

Shopping areas: Westfield Shoppingtown, 27001 US 19 N., features Dillard's, JCPenney, Macy's and Sears as well as an ice skating rink.

(SAVE) **CLEARWATER MARINE AQUARIUM,** 249 Windward Passage, is a working aquarium dedicated to public education, marine research and the rescue, rehabilitation and release of injured or sick whales, dolphins, otters and sea turtles. Marine exhibits, underwater viewing tanks, daily eco-cruises and animal care presentations are offered. Allow 1 hour, 30 minutes minimum. Mon.-Fri. 9-5, Sat. 9-4, Sun. 11-4; closed major holidays. Admission $9; ages 3-12, $6.50. MC, VI. Phone (727) 441-1790.

MOCCASIN LAKE NATURE PARK: AN ENVIRONMENTAL AND ENERGY EDUCATION CENTER, 2750 Park Trail Ln., is a 51-acre nature preserve. The interpretive center features wildlife, plant and energy exhibits. Nature trails wind through upland hardwoods and wetlands to a 5-acre lake. Picnicking is permitted. Allow 1 hour minimum. Tues.-Fri. 9-5, Sat.-Sun. 10-6; closed Jan. 1, Thanksgiving, day after Thanksgiving and Dec. 25. Admission $3; ages 3-12, $2. Guided tours are available for a fee with advance notification. Phone (727) 462-6024.

SEA LIFE SAFARI departs from Clearwater Marine Aquarium at 249 Windward Passage or from slip 58 at Clearwater Marina, 25 Causeway Blvd. A 2-hour sightseeing cruise on Clearwater Bay and the Intracoastal Waterway is narrated by a marine biologist and may provide a rare opportunity to touch sea creatures gathered in a licensed trawl net. Dolphins are often spotted. The boat passes a bird sanctuary and stops at an island for shelling. Sunset cruises are available.

Allow 3 hours minimum. Trips leave the aquarium daily at 11, 1:30 and 4. Fare $17.75; ages 3-12, $11.45. A combination ticket with Clearwater Marine Aquarium is available. AX, MC, VI. Phone (727) 462-2628 or (800) 444-4814.

CLEARWATER BEACH (H-7) elev. 5'

Clearwater Beach is connected with the mainland by the Clearwater Memorial Causeway, a landscaped, 2-mile drive. The broad, white-sand beach attracts both residents and visitors.

Outdoor entertainment is plentiful. The Clearwater Marina harbors a large sport-fishing fleet of

deep-sea charter boats and a variety of sightseeing cruise boats. The Dolphin Encounter offers an opportunity to view dolphins and feed seabirds; for schedule and fare information, phone (727) 442-7433.

Magicians, jugglers, musicians, and craftspeople gather on Pier 60 daily at dusk for Sunsets at Pier 60, a celebration patterned after Key West's legendary homage to the setting sun.

CAPTAIN MEMO'S PIRATE CRUISE, just off SR 60 at Clearwater Marina, offers 2-hour cruises in the Gulf of Mexico aboard a reproduction of a pirate ship. Cruise departs daily at 10, 2, 4:30 and 7 p.m. Boarding is 30 minutes before departure. Schedule may vary; phone ahead. Fare $32 ($35 for 4:30 and 7 p.m. cruises); over 65 and ages 13-17, $25; ages 3-12, $20. Reservations are recommended. AX, DS, MC, VI. Phone (727) 446-2587. *See color ad p. 231.*

[SAVE] *SEA SCREAMER* departs from slip 10 at Clearwater Marina. Narrated, 1-hour speedboat rides begin with a slow cruise out of Clearwater Harbor. The boat accelerates as it enters the Gulf of Mexico, providing an exhilarating trip accompanied by dolphins. Allow 1 hour, 30 minutes minimum. Departures daily at noon, 2, 4 and 6, June 1-Sept. 15; at noon, 2 and 4, rest of year. Tickets are sold 30 minutes before departure. Fare $15; ages 5-12, $10. AX, CB, DC, DS, MC, VI. Phone (727) 447-7200.

[SAVE] *SHOW QUEEN* CRUISES departs from Clearwater Marina at 25 Causeway Blvd. The captain gives a historical narration during sightseeing/ lunch and dinner cruises along Clearwater Harbor and the Intracoastal Waterway. The open top deck provides opportunities for viewing seabirds and marine life. Afternoon cruises depart Mon.-Sat. at 12:30, Sun. at 1:30. Sightseeing cruise $9.95; ages 4-10, $6.95. Sightseeing cruise with lunch $18.95; ages 4-10, $9.95. Reservations are recommended. AX, DS, MC, VI. Phone (727) 461-3111.

[SAVE] *STARLITE MAJESTY* is just off SR 60 at Clearwater Marina. The tri-deck yacht offers 2- and 3-hour sightseeing tours of Clearwater Harbor. Dinner/dance cruises also are available. Two-hour sightseeing tours depart Tues.-Wed. and Fri.-Sat. at noon. Three-hour cruise departs Thurs. at noon. Boarding is 30 minutes before departure. Two-hour sightseeing cruise $11.25; ages 3-12, $8.20 (meals extra). Three-hour cruise $14.95; ages 3-12, $11 (meals extra). Reservations are required for luncheon and dinner/dance cruises. AX, MC, VI. Phone (727) 462-2628 or (800) 444-4814.

DADE CITY (D-9) pop. 6,188, elev. 89'

Originally settled as Fort Dade in the 1840s, the settlement's name was changed to Dade City in 1884. Historic Church Avenue, the restored Old Courthouse, antiques shops, and a lively calendar of events add to the community's quaint atmosphere.

Greater Dade City Chamber of Commerce: 14112 8th St., Dade City, FL 33525; phone (352) 567-3769.

[SAVE] **PIONEER FLORIDA MUSEUM AND VILLAGE** is 1.5 mi. n. via US 301, then e. on Pioneer Museum Rd. Highlights include a one-room pioneer schoolhouse, the 1860s John Overstreet House, Enterprise Methodist Church, an 1896 depot with a 1913 Porter steam engine, sawmill buildings, a general store, and a moonshine still. The museum also displays early farm machinery, vintage carriages, American Indian artifacts, Roseville pottery, textiles, and antique toys and dolls. Allow 2 hours minimum. Tues.-Sat. 10-5; Sun. 1-5; closed holidays. Admission $5; over 54, $4; ages 6-18, $2. Phone (352) 567-0262.

DUNEDIN (G-7) pop. 35,691, elev. 13'

Dunedin, a name closely resembling the Gaelic word from which Edinburgh is derived, traces its Scottish heritage to the town's early days as a seaport and trading center. Its villagelike image has been preserved in a rejuvenated downtown with boutiques and antiques shops, while subtropical surroundings and almost four miles of waterfront account for its tranquil atmosphere.

Home of the spring training camp of the Toronto Blue Jays baseball club, Knology Park on Douglas Avenue features exhibition games from early March to early April and the Class A Florida State League Dunedin Blue Jays throughout the summer; phone (727) 733-9302.

Just off the coast, two barrier islands are available to water and nature enthusiasts. The Gulf beaches of Honeymoon Island State Park, accessible via Dunedin Causeway, are popular for swimming and sunbathing. Caladesi Island State Park *(see Recreation Chart)* is reached by passenger ferry departing from the recreation area at regular intervals; phone (727) 734-5263. Both parks are refuges for endangered birds, including egrets, herons, ospreys and storks. Between the mainland and the islands outdoor enthusiasts can windsurf, sail catamarans and ride personal watercraft on the protected waters of St. Joseph Sound.

Bicycling, walking, jogging and inline skating can be enjoyed on a portion of the Pinellas Trail that winds through the downtown area.

Transportation memorabilia and historical documents, photographs and artifacts are found at Dunedin Historical Society and Museum, 341 Main St., in the former railroad depot; phone (727) 736-1176.

Greater Dunedin Chamber of Commerce: 301 Main St., Dunedin, FL 34698; phone (727) 733-3197.

NATIONAL ARMED SERVICES & LAW ENFORCEMENT MEMORIAL MUSEUM is at 500 Douglas Ave. Exhibits feature military and law enforcement weapons, uniforms, photographs, artifacts and memorabilia dating from the Revolutionary War to the present. A full-size replica of an electric chair anchors an exhibit about capital punishment in Florida. Allow 1 hour minimum. Tues.-Fri. 10-2, Sat. 10-4; closed Jan. 1, Thanksgiving and Dec. 25. Admission $5; over 60, $4.50; students with ID $3; under 7 free. MC, VI. Phone (727) 734-0700.

INDIAN ROCKS BEACH (H-7)
pop. 5,072, elev. 10′

Indian Rocks Beach is a resort community near the midpoint of Sand Key, a long, narrow island in the Gulf off the Pinellas County coast. It is accessible by SR 688 north of St. Petersburg.

Tampa Bay Beaches Chamber of Commerce—Indian Rocks Beach: 105 Fifth Ave., Indian Rocks Beach, FL 33785; phone (727) 595-4575 or (800) 944-1847.

INDIAN SHORES (H-7) pop. 1,705, elev. 5′

SUNCOAST SEABIRD SANCTUARY, on the Gulf Coast at 18328 Gulf Blvd., houses and treats injured pelicans, herons, egrets, owls, hawks and other birds. Rehabilitated birds are released into the wild; those with permanent impairments remain at the sanctuary or are sent to other wildlife parks around the world. Educational programs are presented the first Sunday of each month at 2. Daily 9-dusk. Guided tours and lectures are offered Wed. and Sun. at 2. Donations. Phone (727) 391-6211.

LARGO (H-7) pop. 69,371, elev. 50′

Largo is bordered on three sides by water—the Gulf of Mexico circles around the west and south sides, and Tampa Bay is on the eastern border. In 1905 when it became a city, it had 291 residents and covered 1 square mile.

Largo/Mid-Pinellas Chamber of Commerce: 151 3rd St. N.W., Largo, FL 33779-0326; phone (727) 584-2321.

Shopping areas: Largo Mall, on the corner of Ulmerton Road (SR 688) and Seminole Boulevard, has more than 75 stores and restaurants.

PINEWOOD CULTURAL PARK is just off Ulmerton Rd. at 125th St. N. This 182-acre site is home to three attractions and the Pinellas County Extension office of the University of Florida. Daily 7-7. Free. Phone (727) 582-2200.

Florida Botanical Gardens is at 12175 125th St. N. Among the many themed areas at this 150-acre garden are those dedicated to herbs, palms, roses and topiaries. Native Florida plants and exotic specimens suited to the local climate are represented in both natural and formal settings. Visitors can wander along paths that wind around ponds bordered by colorful flowers and splashing fountains. Allow 2 hours minimum. Daily 7-7. Welcome Center Mon.-Sat. 8-5, Sun. noon-4. Closed Thanksgiving and Dec. 25. Free. Phone (727) 582-2100.

Gulf Coast Museum of Art is at 12211 Walsingham Rd. Permanent and changing displays of contemporary art include works by Florida artists from 1960 onward and fine contemporary craft media objects from the southeastern United States. Allow 1 hour, 30 minutes minimum. Tues.-Sat., Sun. noon-4. Admission $5; over 61, $4; students with ID $3; under 10 free; free to all Sat. 10-noon. Phone (727) 518-6833.

Heritage Village is at 11909 125th St. N. More than two dozen structures relocated to this 21-acre site depict life during the early days of Pinellas County. A museum in the center of the complex displays maps and photographs of early Pinellas County. Guided tours are available. Open Tues.-Sat. 10-4, Sun. 1-4; closed major holidays. Donations. Phone (727) 582-2123.

MADEIRA BEACH (I-7) pop. 4,511, elev. 6′

Joined to the mainland near St. Petersburg by a free causeway, Madeira Beach offers good swimming and parasailing as well as rentals of personal watercraft. Boats can be chartered from several marinas for fishing in the Gulf of Mexico.

Tampa Bay Beaches Chamber of Commerce—Madeira Beach: 500 105th Ave., Madeira Beach, FL 33708; phone (727) 391-7373 or (800) 944-1847.

Shopping areas: John's Pass Village and Boardwalk, 12901 Gulf Blvd. E., is a shopping area with a nautical theme; it contains more than 100 gift and specialty shops, restaurants and art galleries.

HUBBARD'S SEA ADVENTURES, departing from 150 John's Pass Boardwalk, offers a narrated 1.5-hour dolphin-watch nature cruise aboard a catamaran. Passengers can view dolphins and a variety of bird life along the way. Deep-sea fishing trips also are available. Allow 2 hours minimum. Sightseeing cruise departs daily at 1, 3 and 5 (also at 7, Apr.-Sept.); closed Dec. 25. Fare $11.95; ages 3-11, $6. Reservations are suggested. MC, VI. Phone (727) 398-6577.

ODESSA (E-8) pop. 3,173, elev. 58′

SAVE **J.B. STARKEY'S FLATWOODS ADVENTURES** is at 12959 SR 54. Visitors board an open-sided buggy for narrated 2-hour tours of a vast, working cattle ranch; visitors are likely to see a variety of wildlife. An elevated boardwalk through a cypress swamp leads to an observation deck overlooking an alligator hole. Tour guides interpret Cracker cowboy skills and the Florida cattle rancher's way of life. Horseback trail rides also are available.

Allow 3 hours minimum. Buggy tours Mon.-Sat. 9-5. Fare $16.75; senior citizens $15.75; ages 3-12, $9. Reservations are required. MC, VI. Phone (813) 926-1133 or (877) 734-9453.

PLANT CITY (E-9) pop. 29,915, elev. 37′

Plant City was named after Henry Bradley Plant, a wealthy railroad magnate, but the town is best known for its plant crop, the strawberry. The majority of all the winter strawberries in the United States is grown on farms surrounding Plant City. The annual Florida Strawberry Festival draws some 800,000 visitors in early March.

The town is home to the International Softball Federation, the world governing body for softball competition. The Tampa Bay Polo Club plays at Polo Players Plantation on Cowart Road Sunday afternoons at 2, December through May; phone (813) 764-8064.

A 700-acre reservoir created from a reclaimed phosphate mining area is the center of recreational activities in Edward Medard Park, off Turkey Creek Rd.; phone (813) 757-3802. *See Recreation Chart.*

The Pioneer/Heritage Museum, in the 1914 Plant City High School Community Center at 605 N. Collins St., has several exhibit rooms with period themes such as clothing, furnishings, medical equipment, farm implements and railroading; phone (813) 757-9226.

Plant City Visitor Information Center: 31702 N. Park Rd., Plant City, FL 33563; phone (813) 754-7045.

DINOSAUR WORLD, off I-4 exit 17, just n. on Branch Forbes Rd., then just w. to 5145 Harvey Tew Rd., features more than 150 life-size fiberglass models of dinosaurs in a variety of settings, including a forest, a boneyard, simulated caves and a fossil dig. Picnicking and pets are permitted. Allow 1 hour minimum. Daily 9-6. Admission $9.75; senior citizens $8.95; ages 3-12, $7.75. AX, DS, MC, VI. Phone (813) 717-9865.

SAFETY HARBOR (H-8)
pop. 17,203, elev. 14′

Local Indians dipped into the area's five mineral springs long before the 1539 arrival of Hernando de Soto, who named the springs *Espiritu Santo*, meaning water of the Holy Spirit. Said to possess healing powers, the water first lured health-minded visitors to the area in the mid-1800s; by the early 1900s it was being bottled and shipped around the world. Today, Safety Harbor's calling card is its spa culture.

Safety Harbor Chamber of Commerce: 200 Main St., Safety Harbor, FL 34695; phone (727) 726-2890.

[SAVE] **SAFETY HARBOR MUSEUM OF REGIONAL HISTORY** is at 329 Bayshore Blvd. S. Exhibits tracing regional habitation from prehistoric times to the Spanish exploration period include pottery, tools, beads and fossils. The importance of the mineral springs in area development is explained through photographs and memorabilia. Allow 1 hour minimum. Tues.-Fri. 10-4, Sat.-Sun. 1-4; closed holidays. Admission $3; over 62 and ages 12-18, $2. MC, VI. Phone (727) 726-1668.

ST. PETE BEACH (I-7) pop. 9,929, elev. 5′

A resort community on Long Key, St. Pete Beach is connected to the mainland by the St. Pete Beach Causeway and the Pinellas Bayway (toll). The town has good swimming beaches, several fishing piers and charter boat operations.

Tampa Bay Beaches Chamber of Commerce— St. Pete Beach: 6990 Gulf Blvd., St. Pete Beach, FL 33706; phone (727) 360-6957 or (800) 944-1847.

Shopping areas: Silas Bayside Shopping Center, 5505 Gulf Blvd., features specialty shops in a tropical setting. Dolphin Village Shopping Center, 4615 Gulf Blvd., has 30 specialty shops. The historic Corey Avenue area offers varied shops, and the 8th Avenue Shopping District at Pass-a-Grill Beach offers galleries, shops and restaurants.

DOLPHIN LANDINGS CHARTER BOAT CENTER is at 4737 Gulf Blvd. (SR 699), .5 mi. s. of jct. SRs 693 and 699, in Dolphin Village Shopping Center. The 2-hour dolphin watch cruise on a 51-foot sailboat affords opportunities for spotting the playful creatures. Other cruises are available, including sunset, snorkeling, fishing and shelling excursions. Allow 2 hours minimum. Dolphin watch departures daily at 9:30, noon and 2:15. Departures require a minimum of four adults. Reservations are required. Dolphin watch fare $30; under 12, $20. AX, MC, VI. Phone (727) 367-4488.

GULF BEACHES HISTORICAL MUSEUM, 115 10th Ave., is housed in the first church built on the Gulf Coast barrier islands. Exhibits portray the history of the area. Allow 1 hour minimum. Thurs.-Sat. 10-4, Sun. 1-4, otherwise by appointment; closed major holidays. Free. Phone (727) 552-1610.

TARPON SPRINGS (G-7)
pop. 21,003, elev. 18′

Tarpon Springs became an important center for sponge fishing when Greek divers came to the area in the early 1900s. Although the industry has diminished, the Greek influence still is evident in the remaining sponge boats and in the dock area, where sponge shops and Greek restaurants and bakeries are plentiful. Sponge-diving exhibitions, scenic cruises and deep-sea fishing charters are available from the dock area.

A replica of St. Sophia's in Constantinople, the 1943 Greek Orthodox Cathedral of St. Nicholas, at the corner of Pinellas Avenue (US 19A) and Orange Street, is the center of colorful pageantry during Greek festivals.

The ancient craft of brass rubbing, transferring designs from brass engravings to paper, can be attempted daily 10-7 at the Medieval Brass Rubbing Centre on Dodecanese Boulevard; phone (727) 934-6760.

Tarpon Springs Chamber of Commerce: 11 E. Orange St., Tarpon Springs, FL 34689; phone (727) 937-6109.

GEORGE INNESS JR. PICTURES, in the Unitarian Universalist Church at Grand Blvd. and Read St., contains 12 paintings by George Inness Jr., son of the American 19th-century landscape artist. The paintings depict his extraordinary treatment of light and use of the green tones that were named after him. Guided tours are available. Allow 30 minutes minimum. Tues.-Sun. 2-5, Nov.-Apr.; closed holidays. Last tour begins 30 minutes before closing. Donations. Phone (727) 937-4682.

SAVE **KONGER TARPON SPRINGS AQUARIUM** is at 850 Dodecanese Blvd. A simulated coral reef, complete with native plants and tropical fish, illustrates life under the sea in a 120,000-gallon tank. Visitors may watch a shark-feeding show, and a tidal pool offers a close look at such sea creatures as starfish and hermit crabs. Allow 30 minutes minimum. Mon.-Sat. 10-5, Sun. noon-5. Admission $5.25; over 55, $4.50; ages 3-11, $3.25. Phone (727) 938-5378.

SAVE **ST. NICHOLAS BOAT LINE**, .4 mi. w. of jct. Alt. US 19 at 693 Dodecanese Blvd., offers 35-minute, narrated, round-trip cruises through the historic sponge docks of Tarpon Springs. A diver in traditional diving gear provides a demonstration of sponge harvesting. The boat has been used in the filming of several movies and television shows. Allow 1 hour minimum. Departures daily approximately every 45 minutes 10-4:30; closed Greek Orthodox Easter and Dec. 25. Fare $8; ages 6-13, $4. Phone (727) 942-6425.

THONOTOSASSA (E-9) pop. 6,091, elev. 49′

Fort Foster, on the Hillsborough River in nearby Hillsborough River State Park *(see Recreation Chart)*, was used as a battle post and supply depot during the Second Seminole War. Abandoned in 1838 because of disease and the miserable, damp conditions, the fort and the bridge it guarded have been reconstructed on the original site. A tram transports visitors to the fort for a fee. Seasonal guided tours are available; phone (813) 987-6771.

RECREATIONAL ACTIVITIES
Canoeing
• **Canoe Escape** is off I-75 exit 265, then .5 mi. e. Write 9335 E. Fowler Ave., Thonotosassa, FL 33592. Mon.-Fri. 9-5, Sat.-Sun. 8-6; closed Thanksgiving and Dec. 24-25. Last 2-hour trip departs at 2. Phone (813) 986-2067.

Sunshine Skyway Bridge, St. Petersburg / © Robert Harding World Imagery / Alamy

This ends listings for the Tampa Bay Vicinity.
The following page resumes the alphabetical listings of cities in Florida.

TAVARES—see Orlando p. 184.

THONOTOSASSA—see Tampa Bay p. 235.

TITUSVILLE (D-10) pop. 40,670, elev. 18′

Named for founder Col. Henry T. Titus in 1874, Titusville once was a citrus shipping point and commercial fishing port. The establishment of Kennedy Space Center (see place listing p. 106) brought the Space Age—and increased tourism—to this small mainland city.

Florida's Space Coast Office of Tourism—Titusville: 2725 Judge Fran Jamieson Way, Suite B-105, Viera, FL 32940; phone (877) 572-3224.

SAVE **AMERICAN POLICE HALL OF FAME & MUSEUM,** 6350 Horizon Dr., displays more than 10,000 items relating to law enforcement. Exhibits include a mock crime scene, execution equipment, specialty cars and replicas of jail cells. A memorial lists the names of U.S. police officers killed in the line of duty since 1960. A shooting range is available. Allow 1 hour minimum. Daily 10-6; closed Dec. 25. Admission $12; over 65, military with ID and ages 4-12, $8; active and retired law enforcement officers and family survivors free. MC, VI. Phone (321) 264-0911.

MERRITT ISLAND NATIONAL WILDLIFE REFUGE, 5 mi. e. on SR 402 across the Titusville Cswy., is a habitat for wintering migratory waterfowl. A visitor center offers educational displays, wildlife exhibits and a 20-minute video about the refuge. Behind the center, a boardwalk takes visitors over a pond and through an oak hammock to a freshwater marsh. Special interpretive programs are offered November through March.

Daily dawn-dusk. Visitor center Mon.-Fri. 8:30-4:30, Sat. 9-5 (also Sun. 9-5, Nov.-Mar.). Free. Phone (321) 861-0667.

SAVE **VALIANT AIR COMMAND WARBIRD AIR MUSEUM,** 6600 Tico Rd. at the Space Coast Regional Airport, following signs, features aviation memorabilia dating from World War I to the present. Exhibits include model planes, uniforms and up to 30 restored aircraft in restoration and exhibition hangars. Allow 2 hours minimum. Daily 10-6; closed Jan. 1, Thanksgiving and Dec. 25. Admission $9; over 60 and military with ID $8; ages 4-12, $5. MC, VI. Phone (321) 268-1941.

VENICE (F-8) pop. 17,764, elev. 13′

As its name implies, Venice has a distinct Mediterranean ambience with Northern Italian influences. The city's location on the Gulf makes it a popular destination for boating, fishing and golfing. Visitors can comb the beaches for fossilized shark teeth, which range in size from one-eighth-inch to 3 inches.

Venice Area Chamber of Commerce: 597 Tamiami Trail S., Venice, FL 34285-2424; phone (941) 488-2236.

VERO BEACH (E-11) pop. 20,362, elev. 17′

Vero Beach plays host to the Los Angeles Dodgers baseball team during spring training. Exhibition games are played at Holman Stadium from March to early April; phone (772) 569-4900. The Vero Beach Dodgers offer games during their regular season from mid-April to early September.

McKee Botanical Garden, 350 US 1, features orchids, palm trees and dense tropical vegetation on the remaining 18 acres of an 80-acre jungle garden created in the 1930s by William Lyman Phillips for northern industrialist Arthur McKee. It was one of Florida's first public gardens; phone (772) 794-0601.

Sebastian Inlet State Park (see Recreation Chart), 15 miles north on SR A1A, preserves more than 900 acres of barrier island for recreation and wildlife protection. In addition to 3 miles of beach for swimming, surfing and snorkeling, the park has nature trails and a Volksport walking trail. Interpretive programs and two museums also are available.

Indian River County Chamber of Commerce: 1216 21st St., Vero Beach, FL 32960; phone (772) 567-3491.

McLARTY TREASURE MUSEUM, 13 mi. n. on SR A1A, is at the s. end of Sebastian Inlet State Park. The museum's historical displays include artifacts and a diorama of the 1715 Spanish Plate Fleet and the shipwreck salvors' camp, including salvage materials. An audiovisual presentation highlights the modern-day treasure salvaging operations off the coast. Allow 1 hour minimum. Daily 10-4:30. Last show begins 1 hour, 15 minutes before closing. Admission $1, under 6 free. Phone (772) 589-2147.

WAKULLA (B-6)

GEM **EDWARD BALL WAKULLA SPRINGS STATE PARK,** jct. SRs 61 and 267, was known to early Indians for its plentiful wildlife The main spring, with a water temperature of 70 F, is considered one of the state's deepest, having been explored to a depth of 300 feet. The maximum flow was recorded in 1973 at 1.2 billion gallons a day; in 1931 the minimum flow was measured at 16.2 million gallons. The average is 576 million gallons of crystal-clear water daily.

A popular "birding mecca," the park offers hiking, bicycle and nature trails and swimming opportunities. Narrated river cruises provide glimpses of animals in their native habitats, while glass-bottom boat tours provide views of marine life.

Allow 2 hours minimum. Park daily 8-dusk. River cruises depart daily every half hour 9:30-5, during DST; 9:15-4:30, rest of year (weather permitting). Glass-bottom boat cruises depart daily 11-3 (only when the water has clear visibility). Admission $4 per private vehicle (maximum eight people), $1 extra for every person over the maximum. Glass-bottom boat or river cruise $6; under 13, $4. Phone (850) 224-5950. See Recreation Chart.

WEEKI WACHEE (D-8) pop. 12, elev. 34'

WEEKI WACHEE SPRINGS WATERPARK, on US 19 at jct. SR 50, is built around a spring that flows at a rate of 170 million gallons a day and maintains a temperature of 72 F. The Wilderness River Cruise explores the flora and fauna of a typical Florida ecosystem. "Mermaids" perform in an underwater theater. A natural spring on the Weeki Wachee River feeds Buccaneer Bay, which features a white sand beach, six flume rides, a river tube ride and a children's play area.

Picnicking is permitted only at Buccaneer Bay. Food, lockers and kennels are available. Allow 6 hours minimum. Park opens daily at 10; closing times vary. Buccaneer Bay is open seasonally; phone ahead. Last admission 1 hour before closing. Admission $21.95; ages 3-10, $14.95. AX, MC, VI. Phone (352) 596-2062.

WELAKA (C-9) pop. 586, elev. 28'

WELAKA NATIONAL FISH HATCHERY AQUARIUM, on CR 309, displays reptiles and 22 tanks containing specimens of about 50 species of native freshwater fish. Allow 30 minutes minimum. Daily 8-3. Free. Phone (386) 467-2374.

WEST PALM BEACH (F-11)
pop. 82,103, elev. 21'

Founded in 1894 by railroad tycoon Henry Flagler, West Palm Beach has grown into a center for commerce and business. Fifty miles north of Miami, the city is a popular destination for beach recreation, sport fishing, shopping and cultural activities.

Kravis Center for the Performing Arts includes a 2,200-seat concert hall, a black box theater, a restaurant and an outdoor amphitheater. Performances range from classical to country and feature well-known entertainers; for information phone (561) 833-8300 or (800) 572-8471. CityPlace in downtown West Palm Beach offers a mix of upscale shopping, gourmet dining and entertainment, including dancing fountains choreographed to light and music. Clematis Street is known for its trendy shops, restaurants, theaters and nightlife.

Approximately 15 miles west of town in Wellington, the Palm Beach Polo Grounds is the site of polo matches and horse shows from December through April; phone (561) 798-7000. The Palm Beach Kennel Club, Belvedere Road and Congress Avenue, holds greyhound races year round; phone (561) 683-2222.

Note: Policies vary concerning admittance of children to pari-mutuel betting facilities. Phone for information.

Chamber of Commerce of the Palm Beaches: 401 N. Flagler Dr., West Palm Beach, FL 33401; phone (561) 833-3711.

Shopping areas: Palm Beach Mall, 1 block east of I-95 exit 71, features Dillard's, JCPenney, Macy's

and Sears among its 100 stores. The Mall at Wellington Green, 15 miles west at US 441 and Forest Hill Boulevard, features more than 120 stores, including Dillard's, JCPenney, Macy's and Nordstrom.

LION COUNTRY SAFARI—
see Loxahatchee p. 110

MOUNTS BOTANICAL GARDEN, off I-95 exit 68, 2.5 mi. w. on Southern Blvd., then .4 mi. n. to 531 N. Military Tr., features more than 2,000 tropical and subtropical plants from six continents; a paved loop walkway and a network of secondary paths; and a pond with fish, turtles and other wildlife. The 14-acre garden is in bloom all year long. Allow 1 hour minimum. Mon.-Sat. 8:30-4:30, Sun. and holidays 1-5; closed Jan. 1, Thanksgiving and Dec. 24-25. Guided tours are given Sat. at 11 and Sun. at 2. Free. Admission is charged during special events. Phone (561) 233-1749.

THE MUSEUM AT RAGTOPS MOTORCARS, 2119 S. Dixie Hwy., displays classic and special-interest automobiles in a 1925 Art Deco showroom. Other exhibits include a vintage soda bar, a replica of a drive-in theater, automotive memorabilia and antiques. Allow 1 hour minimum. Mon.-Sat. 10-5; closed Easter, Thanksgiving and Dec. 25. Admission $5; over 65, $4; under 13, $3. AX, MC, VI. Phone (561) 655-2836 or (877) 724-8677.

NORTON MUSEUM OF ART is .5 mi. s. of Okeechobee Blvd. on US 1, at 1451 S. Olive Ave. The museum is recognized for its collection of European, American and contemporary art; Chinese art and photography, including ancient bronzes, jades and ceramics. Highlights include 19th- and 20th-century paintings and sculpture by such European artists as Paul Gauguin, Henri Matisse, Claude Monet and Pablo Picasso; and American artists including Edward Hopper, Georgia O'Keeffe and Jackson Pollock.

Allow 1 hour minimum. Tues.-Sat. 10-5, Sun. 1-5 (also Mon. 10-5, Nov.-Apr.); closed major holidays. Guided tours are given daily at 2. Admission $8; ages 13-21, $3. An additional fee may be charged for special exhibits. AX, DS, MC, VI. Phone (561) 832-5196.

PALM BEACH ZOO is e. of I-95 at 1301 Summit Blvd. in Dreher Park. The 23-acre zoo is home to more than 1,000 animals from Florida, South and Central America, Asia and Australia. Exhibits include a Florida panther, a Bengal tiger, giant tortoises, exotic birds, kangaroos, emus and reptiles. The Tropics of the Americas exhibit features Mayan pyramids and ruins. Children's attractions include an interactive fountain and a carousel.

Food is available. Allow 2 hours minimum. Daily 9-5; closed Thanksgiving and Dec. 25. Last admission 45 minutes before closing. Admission $10.95; over 60, $7.95; ages 3-12, $6.95. AX, MC, VI. Phone (561) 533-0887.

SAVE **SOUTH FLORIDA SCIENCE MUSEUM,** 4801 Dreher Tr. N. in Dreher Park, has a variety of permanent and changing exhibits and interactive displays. The Egypt gallery features an authentic mummy and Roman Period artifacts. Tanks at the McGinty Aquarium display Atlantic and Pacific species of ocean life, including live corals. The Buzz Aldrin Planetarium offers star and laser light shows, and the Gibson Observatory features one of the largest telescopes in the state.

Allow 1 hour minimum. Museum open Mon.-Fri. 10-5, Sat. 10-6, Sun. noon-6; closed Thanksgiving and Dec. 25. Planetarium shows daily at 1 and 2. Laser light shows Fri.-Sun. at 3 (also Fri. at 9 and 10 p.m.). Museum $7; ages 3-12, $5. Fees may change for special exhibits. Planetarium shows $2. Laser light shows $4. Galaxy Golf $2. Phone (561) 832-1988.

WESTON—*see Fort Lauderdale p. 86.*

WHITE SPRINGS (B-8) pop. 819, elev. 125′

Once a health resort, White Springs is built around sulphur springs. Seminole and Timucuan Indians considered the springs sacred and believed their warriors were impervious to attack while recuperating.

STEPHEN FOSTER FOLK CULTURE CENTER STATE PARK, 3 mi. e. of I-75 on US 41, covers 850 wooded acres beside the Suwannee River, which the composer immortalized in his song "Old Folks At Home." In the visitor center are animated dioramas depicting Foster's songs. Dioramas and exhibits are in the 200-foot carillon tower. The Crafts Square features Florida Cracker-style buildings with craft studios. Hiking and bicycling trails are available.

Picnicking and camping are permitted. Allow 4 hours minimum. Park open daily 8-dusk. Buildings open daily 9-5. Admission $4 per private vehicle (maximum eight people) or motorcycle, $1 per person arriving by bicycle, bus or on foot. Some events have varying admission charges. Phone (386) 397-2733.

WINTER HAVEN (E-9)
pop. 26,487, elev. 170′

Winter Haven is surrounded by more than 40 freshwater lakes, many of which are joined by canals to form a navigable chain of lakes ideal for family recreation and water sports such as boating, fishing and skiing.

Cleveland Indians spring training baseball thrills locals and visitors in March at Chain of Lakes Park, 500 Cletus Allen Dr. at SR 540; phone (863) 293-3900.

Greater Winter Haven Area Chamber of Commerce: 401 Ave. B N.W., P.O. Box 1420, Winter Haven, FL 33882; phone (863) 293-2138 or (800) 871-7027. *See color ad p. 240.*

SAVE **CYPRESS GARDENS ADVENTURE PARK,** 5 mi. s.e. on SR 540, is an updated version of Cypress Gardens, founded in 1936 and long known for its botanical gardens, Southern belles and water skiing shows. This family amusement park also features more than 35 rides, a water park, a butterfly conservatory and a craftsmen's village. A concert series and daily shows are offered.

Food is available. Wheelchair, stroller and locker rentals are available. Park opens daily at 10; closing times vary. Phone ahead for exact hours. Admission $34.95; over 54 and ages 3-9, $29.95. Admission includes a second day free within six days. Parking $7 for automobiles, $9 for recreational vehicles. AX, MC, VI. Phone (863) 324-2111. *See color ad p. 240.*

WINTER PARK—*see Orlando p. 184.*

WOODVILLE (B-6) pop. 3,006, elev. 39′

NATURAL BRIDGE BATTLEFIELD HISTORIC STATE PARK is a 6-acre site 6 mi. e. off SR 363. The Battle of Natural Bridge was fought Mar. 6, 1865, to prevent Union troops from capturing the Capitol at Tallahassee. Picnicking and fishing are permitted. Daily 8-dusk. Free. Phone (850) 922-6007.

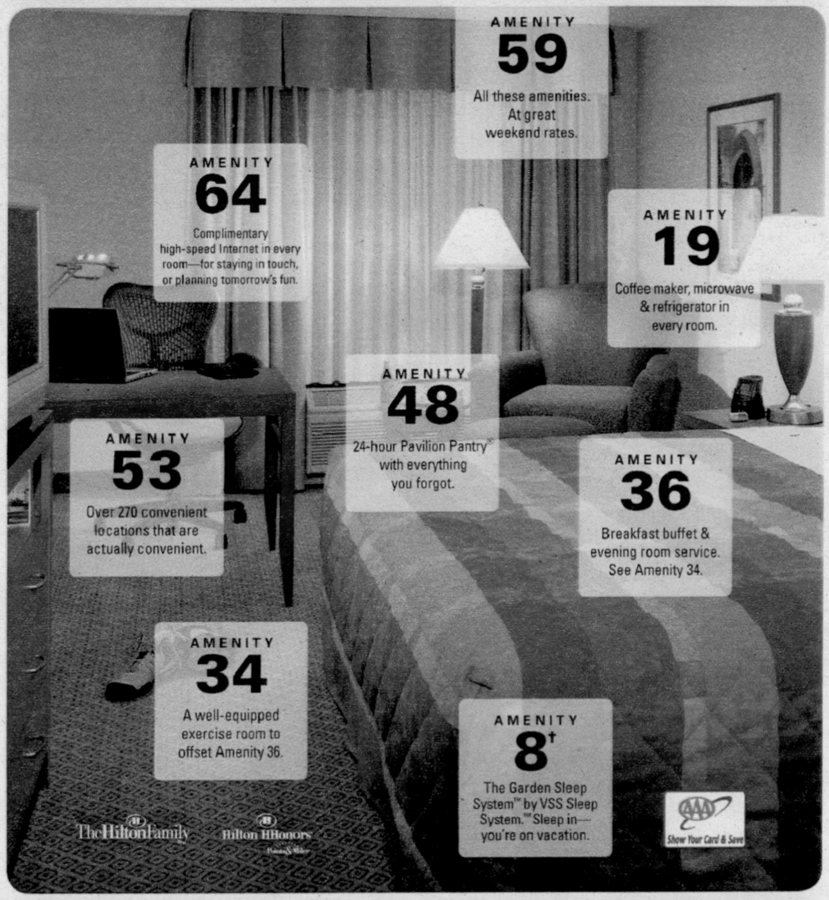

Florida

The Florida Keys
© William Harrigan
Lonely Planet Images

Florida Orientation Map to Destinations

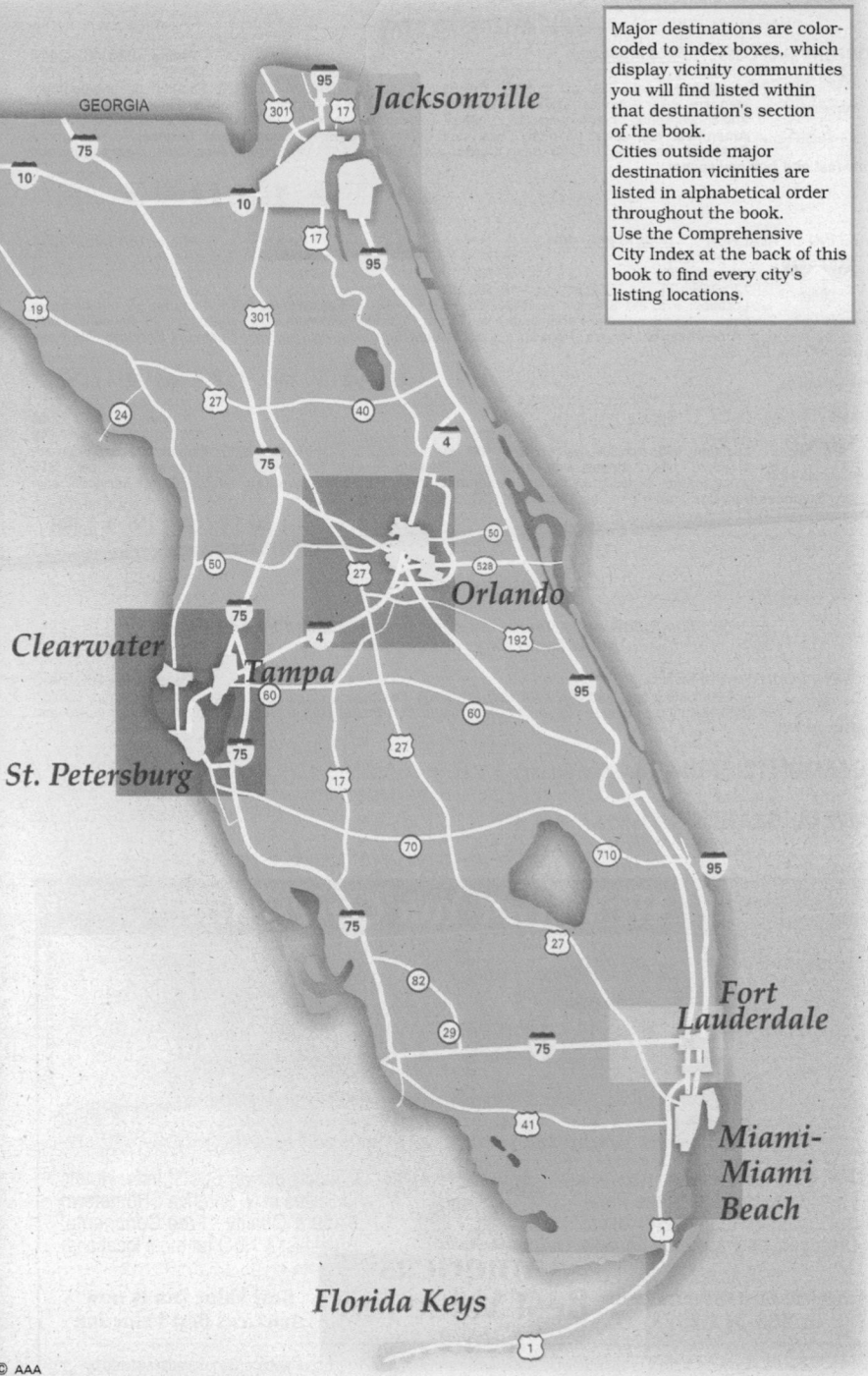

GEORGIA

Jacksonville

Major destinations are color-coded to index boxes, which display vicinity communities you will find listed within that destination's section of the book.
Cities outside major destination vicinities are listed in alphabetical order throughout the book.
Use the Comprehensive City Index at the back of this book to find every city's listing locations.

Orlando

Clearwater

Tampa

St. Petersburg

Fort Lauderdale

Miami-Miami Beach

Florida Keys

© AAA

ALACHUA pop. 6,098

——— WHERE TO STAY ———

COMFORT INN/FL-339   *Book at aaa.com*   Phone: (386)462-2414

AAA SAVE   All Year   1P: $70   2P: $85   XP: $5   D12
WWW WWW   **Location:** I-75, exit 399, just e. 15920 NW Hwy 441 32615. Fax: 386/462-2220. **Facility:** 62 one-bedroom
Small-scale Hotel   standard units. 2 stories, exterior corridors. **Parking:** on-site. **Terms:** 2-4 night minimum stay - seasonal
and/or weekends, 7 day cancellation notice, package plans, pets ($10 extra charge, in smoking units). **Amenities:** high-speed Internet, irons, hair dryers. **Pool(s):** outdoor. **Guest Services:** coin laundry. **Business Services:** PC, fax (fee). **Cards:** AX, DC, DS, MC, VI. **Special Amenities:** free continental
breakfast and free newspaper.

SOME UNITS

🖥️ 📞 🍽️ 🏊 📷 DATA⁣PORT 🛗 📺 📱 / ✕ /
FEE

DAYS INN OF ALACHUA   *Book at aaa.com*   Phone: (386)462-3251

WWW WWW   3/1-3/31 [CP]   1P: $100-$140   2P: $110-$160   XP: $10   F
          4/1-11/30 [CP]   1P: $80-$100   2P: $90-$120   XP: $10   F
Motel   12/1-2/28 [CP]   1P: $80-$100   2P: $85-$105   XP: $10   F
Location: I-75, exit 399, just w. 16100 NW Hwy 441 32615. Fax: 386/462-3251. **Facility:** 55 one-bedroom
standard units. 2 stories, exterior corridors. **Parking:** on-site. **Terms:** 1-3 night minimum stay - weekends, 15 day cancellation
notice-fee imposed. **Amenities:** hair dryers. **Pool(s):** outdoor. **Guest Services:** coin laundry. **Business Services:** fax (fee).
Cards: AX, DC, DS, MC, VI.

SOME UNITS

ASK 🖥️ 🍽️ 🏊 📷 🛗 📺 📱 / ✕ /

QUALITY INN ALACHUA   *Book at aaa.com*   Phone: 386/462-2244

WWW WWW   All Year   1P: $90   2P: $90   XP: $10   F18
Small-scale Hotel   **Location:** I-75, exit 399, just e. 15960 NW Hwy 441 32615. Fax: 386/462-2012. **Facility:** 92 one-bedroom
standard units. 2 stories, exterior corridors. **Parking:** on-site. **Terms:** [CP] meal plan available, pets ($10
extra charge, in designated units). **Amenities:** irons, hair dryers. **Pool(s):** outdoor. **Guest Services:** coin
laundry. **Business Services:** meeting rooms. **Cards:** AX, DC, DS, JC, MC, VI.

SOME UNITS

ASK 🖥️ 🐕 🍽️ 🏊 📷 📱 / ✕ 🛗 📺 /
FEE

——— WHERE TO DINE ———

——— **The following restaurant has not been evaluated by AAA** ———
but is listed for your information only.

BROWN'S COUNTRY BUFFET   Phone: 386/462-3000

fyi   Not evaluated. **Location:** 14423 NW Hwy 441 32606. **Features:** The eatery ofers homestyle Southern comfort
food featuring barbecue ribs, whole catfish and homemade salads along with plenty of vegetables and
desserts as well.

ALTAMONTE SPRINGS —See Orlando p. 743.

AMELIA ISLAND —See Jacksonville p. 492.

ANNA MARIA pop. 1,814 (See map and index starting on p. 904)

——— WHERE TO DINE ———

BISTRO AT ISLAND'S END

Dinner: $8-$27
Phone: 941/779-2444 (54)

▽▽▽ (diamonds)

Continental

Location: On north end, jct Gulf Dr and Pine Ave; 3 mi n of jct SR 64. 10101 Gulf Dr 34216. **Hours:** 5:30 pm-9:30 pm, Fri & Sat-10:30 pm. **Reservations:** suggested. **Features:** Enjoy steak, seafood and pasta in a cozy, bistro-style setting. Excellent presentation, quality ingredients and good flavor are all elements of this superb menu. Whet your appetite with Gulf Coast gumbo, then sample the first-rate grilled salmon. Dressy casual; cocktails; entertainment. **Parking:** on-site. **Cards:** AX, CB, DC, DS, MC, VI.

SANDBAR

Lunch: $6-$13   **Dinner:** $11-$21   **Phone:** 941/778-0444 (55)

▽▽ (diamonds)

Seafood

Location: 2.8 mi n of SR 64 on Gulf Dr, then just w. 100 Spring Ave 34216. **Hours:** 11:30 am-10 pm. **Closed:** 12/25. **Features:** "Old Florida" is the theme of this popular, casual restaurant overlooking the Gulf of Mexico. Vintage photos set a nostalgic mood and each table is afforded a wonderful view of the gulf. Enjoy live entertainment nightly on the outdoor dining deck. Casual dress; cocktails. **Parking:** on-site. **Cards:** AX, CB, DC, DS, MC, VI.

APALACHICOLA pop. 2,334

——— WHERE TO STAY ———

BEST WESTERN APALACH INN

Phone: (850)653-2116

(AAA) (SAVE)

▽▽▽

Small-scale Hotel

All Year   1P: $90-$140   2P: $100-$160   XP: $10   F12
Location: 1.5 mi w. 249 Hwy 98 W 32320. Fax: 850/653-9136. **Facility:** 42 one-bedroom standard units, some with whirlpools. 2 stories, exterior corridors. **Parking:** on-site. **Terms:** cancellation fee imposed. **Amenities:** high-speed Internet, irons, hair dryers. **Pool(s):** outdoor. **Business Services:** fax (fee). **Cards:** AX, CB, DC, DS, MC, VI. **Special Amenities:** free continental breakfast and free local telephone calls.

SOME UNITS

COOMBS HOUSE INN

Phone: (850)653-9199

(AAA) (SAVE)

▽▽▽

Bed & Breakfast

All Year [BP]   1P: $89-$169   2P: $89-$169   XP: $15   F5
Location: Corner of US 98 and 6th St; center. 80 6th St 32320. Fax: 850/653-2785. **Facility:** The inn consists of two Victorian homes built in 1905 and 1911. Each of the distinctively decorated guest rooms features antique furniture and accents, some with Jacuzzi tub and fireplace. Designated smoking area. 19 units. 18 one-bedroom standard units, some with whirlpools. 1 one-bedroom suite ($149-$225) with efficiency. 2-3 stories (no elevator), interior corridors. *Bath:* combo or shower only. **Parking:** on-site and street. **Terms:** 5 day cancellation notice-fee imposed, package plans, pets ($15 extra charge). **Amenities:** hair dryers. **Leisure Activities:** bicycles. *Fee:* massage. **Guest Services:** complimentary evening beverages: Fri & Sat, airport transportation-Apalachicola Airport. **Business Services:** meeting rooms, fax. **Cards:** AX, DS, MC, VI. **Special Amenities:** free full breakfast and free local telephone calls.

SOME UNITS

FEE

GIBSON INN

Phone: (850)653-2191

(AAA) (SAVE)

▽▽▽

Historic
Country Inn

All Year   1P: $85-$185   XP: $10   F8
Location: On US 98 at west end of bridge. Market St & Ave C 32320 (PO Box 221, 32329). Fax: 850/653-3521. **Facility:** Victorian accents and antiques from around the world furnish the individually decorated guest rooms of this restored 1907 inn. Designated smoking area. 30 units. 29 one-bedroom standard units. 1 one-bedroom suite ($140-$185). 3 stories (no elevator), interior corridors. *Bath:* combo or shower only. **Parking:** street. **Terms:** 2-3 night minimum stay - seasonal and/or weekends, 14 day cancellation notice-fee imposed, package plans, pets ($25 extra charge). **Business Services:** meeting rooms, fax (fee). **Cards:** AX, MC, VI.

FEE

APOLLO BEACH —See Tampa Bay p. 1000.

APOPKA —See Orlando p. 747.

ARCADIA pop. 6,604

——— WHERE TO STAY ———

BEST WESTERN ARCADIA INN   *Book at aaa.com*

Phone: (863)494-4884

(AAA) (SAVE)

▽▽

Motel

All Year [ECP]   1P: $69-$149   2P: $69-$149   XP: $5   F18
Location: 0.6 mi s of SR 70 on US 17. 504 S Brevard Ave 34266. Fax: 863/494-2006. **Facility:** 37 units. 36 one-bedroom standard units, some with whirlpools. 1 one-bedroom suite with kitchen. 1 story, exterior corridors. *Bath:* combo or shower only. **Parking:** on-site. **Terms:** cancellation fee imposed, package plans, small pets only ($15 extra charge, with prior approval). **Amenities:** high-speed Internet, safes, irons, hair dryers. **Pool(s):** heated outdoor. **Leisure Activities:** covered picnic area, grills. **Guest Services:** gift shop, valet and coin laundry. **Business Services:** fax (fee). **Cards:** AX, CB, DC, DS, JC, MC, VI. **Special Amenities:** free expanded continental breakfast and free local telephone calls.

SOME UNITS

FEE

HOLIDAY INN EXPRESS HOTEL & SUITES   *Book at aaa.com*   **Phone:** (863)494-5900

2/1-4/30	1P: $119-$159	2P: $119-$159	XP: $10	F18
12/1-1/31	1P: $99-$139	2P: $99-$139	XP: $10	F18
5/1-11/30	1P: $89-$139	2P: $89-$139	XP: $10	F18

Small-scale Hotel
Location: On SR 70, 1.9 mi e at jct SR 31. 2709 SE Hwy 70 34266. **Fax:** 863/231-0219. **Facility:** 63 one-bedroom standard units, some with whirlpools. 4 stories, interior corridors. *Bath:* combo or shower only. **Parking:** on-site. **Terms:** 3 day cancellation notice. **Amenities:** high-speed Internet, dual phone lines, voice mail, irons, hair dryers. **Pool(s):** outdoor. **Leisure Activities:** exercise room. **Guest Services:** valet and coin laundry. **Business Services:** meeting rooms, business center. **Cards:** AX, DS, MC, VI. **Special Amenities:** free continental breakfast and free local telephone calls.

SOME UNITS

—— WHERE TO DINE ——

ARCADIA TEA ROOM & WINE CELLAR BISTRO   **Lunch:** $4-$10   **Dinner:** $8-$18   **Phone:** 863/494-2424

American
Location: Just n of jct SR 70; downtown. 117 W Oak St 34265. **Hours:** 8 am-2 & 4:30-7 pm, Sat-9 pm; Sunday brunch 10 am-2 pm. **Closed:** 1/1, 12/25. **Reservations:** accepted. **Features:** Step into history in these quaint dining rooms decorated with lavish antiques. Fresh, home-cooked entrees are offered at reasonable prices, like the hearty classic liver and onions with real mashed potatoes and savory gravy. Dressy casual; beer & wine only. **Parking:** on-site and street. **Cards:** DS, MC, VI.

NAV-A-GATOR GRILL   **Lunch:** $4-$23   **Dinner:** $11-$25   **Phone:** 941/627-3474

Seafood
Location: I-75, exit 170, 3.1 mi ne on CR 769, then 1.5 mi s on Peace River St. 9700 SW Riverview Cir 34269. **Hours:** 11 am-8 pm, Fri-Sun to 9 pm. **Closed:** 4/16, 11/23, 12/25. **Reservations:** not accepted. **Features:** On the Peace River in the DeSoto Marings, the active and loud restaurant is a local favorite. Its menu offers grouper, captain's platter, shrimp, alligator, seafood baskets and sandwiches. Enjoy deck dining, where you can watch fishermen bringing in their latest catch and marvel at the scenery. Or take a stroll through the small on-site museum. Casual dress; cocktails; entertainment. **Parking:** on-site. **Cards:** AX, DC, DS, MC, VI.

WHEELER'S CAFE   **Lunch:** $3-$6   **Phone:** 863/993-1555

American
Location: Just n of jct SR 70; downtown. 130 Monroe 34266. **Hours:** Open 12/1-7/31 & 8/21-11/30; 6 am-3 pm. **Features:** Casual surroundings evoke the feel of an old roadside cafe. On this site in various inceptions since 1929, this place prepares good home-cooked items, such as meatloaf, fried catfish, ham steak with pineapple and roast beef with gravy. Also served are sandwiches, salads, soups and a full selection of breakfast foods for early risers. Casual dress. **Parking:** on-site.

ASTOR —See Orlando p. 748.

ATLANTIC BEACH —See Jacksonville p. 494.

AVENTURA —See Miami-Miami Beach p. 593.

AVON PARK pop. 8,542

—— WHERE TO STAY ——

ECONO LODGE   *Book at aaa.com*   **Phone:** (863)453-2000

2/1-3/18	1P: $70-$90	2P: $70-$90
12/1-1/31	1P: $60-$80	2P: $60-$80
3/19-11/30	1P: $60-$70	2P: $60-$70

Motel
Location: On US 27; 2.5 mi s of jct SR 17 and 64. 2511 US Hwy 27 S 33825. **Fax:** 863/453-0820. **Facility:** 57 one-bedroom standard units. 2 stories, exterior corridors. **Parking:** on-site. **Terms:** cancellation fee imposed, pets ($10 extra charge). **Pool(s):** outdoor. **Guest Services:** coin laundry. **Business Services:** fax (fee). **Cards:** AX, DS, MC, VI. **Special Amenities:** free continental breakfast and free local telephone calls.

SOME UNITS

FEE

BALDWIN —See Jacksonville p. 496.

BAL HARBOUR —See Miami-Miami Beach p. 594.

BARTOW pop. 15,340

—— WHERE TO STAY ——

THE STANFORD INN   **Phone:** 863/533-2393

All Year   1P: $95-$140   2P: $95-$140   XP: $10

Bed & Breakfast
Location: Main St, s on S Broadway to E Stanford St; downtown. 555 E Stanford St 33830. **Fax:** 863/519-0238. **Facility:** Set amongst towering trees and featuring many Victorian accents, this 1900s Georgian revival structure has an inviting porch that beckons for company. Designated smoking area. 6 units. 4 one-bedroom standard units, some with whirlpools. 2 cottages. 2 stories, interior/exterior corridors. *Bath:* combo or shower only. **Parking:** on-site. **Terms:** 3 day cancellation notice, [BP] meal plan available, package plans. **Amenities:** irons. *Some:* hair dryers. **Pool(s):** outdoor. **Leisure Activities:** whirlpool. **Business Services:** fax (fee). **Cards:** AX, DS, MC, VI.

SOME UNITS

BAY HARBOR ISLANDS —See Miami-Miami Beach p. 594.

BELLEAIR BLUFFS —See Tampa Bay p. 1001.

BELLE GLADE pop. 14,906

──── **WHERE TO STAY** ────

TRAVELERS MOTOR LODGE
AAA SAVE
◆◆ ◆◆
Motel

All Year 1P: $72-$78 2P: $75-$79 XP: $10 F12
Phone: 561/996-6761
Location: 1 mi sw on SR 80. 1300 S Main St 33430. Fax: 561/996-6763. **Facility:** 26 one-bedroom standard units. 1 story, exterior corridors. **Parking:** on-site. **Terms:** office hours 7 am-11 pm, cancellation fee imposed. **Cards:** AX, DS, MC, VI. **Special Amenities: free local telephone calls and free newspaper.**

SOME UNITS
📷 / 🛢 /

BOCA RATON pop. 74,764

──── **WHERE TO STAY** ────

BEST WESTERN UNIVERSITY INN *Book at aaa.com*
AAA SAVE
◆◆◆
Motel

12/21-4/30 [CP] 1P: $107-$139 2P: $107-$139
12/1-12/20 & 5/1-11/30 [CP] 1P: $67-$79 2P: $67-$79
Phone: (561)395-5225
Location: US 1, 1 mi n of jct SR 808 (Glades Rd). 2700 N Federal Hwy 33431. Fax: 561/338-9180. **Facility:** 90 one-bedroom standard units. 2 stories (no elevator), interior/exterior corridors. *Bath:* combo or shower only. **Parking:** on-site. **Terms:** cancellation fee imposed. **Amenities:** high-speed Internet, voice mail, safes (fee), irons, hair dryers. **Dining:** 11 am-11 pm, cocktails. **Pool(s):** heated outdoor. **Leisure Activities:** whirlpool, exercise room. **Guest Services:** coin laundry, airport transportation-Ft. Lauderdale-Hollywood Int'l & West Palm Beach airports. **Cards:** AX, CB, DC, DS, MC, VI. **Special Amenities: free continental breakfast and free local telephone calls.**
(See color ad below)

SOME UNITS
🅂🅳 ✈ 🍴 📺 🎾 🏊 🐕 📷 🗄 🛗 🛏 💻 / ⊠ /

BOCA RATON BRIDGE HOTEL *Book at aaa.com*
◆◆◆◆
Large-scale Hotel

12/16-4/30 1P: $259 2P: $259 XP: $10 F
12/1-12/15 & 11/17-11/30 1P: $199 2P: $199 XP: $10 F
5/1-11/16 1P: $149 2P: $149 XP: $10 F
Phone: (561)368-9500
Location: Just w of SR A1A, 1 mi s of jct SR 798 (Palmetto Park Rd). Across from the ocean. 999 E Camino Real 33432. Fax: 561/362-0492. **Facility:** 121 units. 96 one-bedroom standard units. 25 one-bedroom suites ($179-$399). 11 stories, interior corridors. *Bath:* combo or shower only. **Parking:** on-site and valet. **Terms:** 3 day cancellation notice-fee imposed, [AP] meal plan available. **Amenities:** dual phone lines, voice mail, irons, hair dryers. *Fee:* video games, high-speed Internet. *Some:* CD players. **Dining:** Carmen's at the Top of the Bridge, see separate listing. **Pool(s):** heated outdoor. **Leisure Activities:** rental boats, exercise room. *Fee:* bicycles. **Guest Services:** gift shop, valet laundry. **Business Services:** meeting rooms, fax (fee). **Cards:** AX, DC, DS, MC, VI.

SOME UNITS
(A$K) 🅂🅳 🍴 📺 🎾 🏊 🐕 ⊠ 📷 🗄 💻 / ⊠ / VCR .FEE 🛏 FEE /

BOCA RATON MARRIOTT *Book at aaa.com*
◆◆◆
Large-scale Hotel

1/1-11/30 1P: $189-$349 2P: $189-$349
12/1-12/31 1P: $149-$189 2P: $149-$189
Phone: (561)392-4600
Location: I-95, exit 44 (Palmetto Park Rd), 0.8 mi n on Military Tr. 5150 Town Center Cir 33486. Fax: 561/368-9223. **Facility:** 256 units. 255 one-bedroom standard units. 1 one-bedroom suite. 11 stories, interior corridors. *Bath:* combo or shower only. **Parking:** on-site and valet. **Terms:** package plans. **Amenities:** dual phone lines, voice mail, honor bars, irons, hair dryers. *Fee:* video games, high-speed Internet. **Pool(s):** heated outdoor. **Leisure Activities:** whirlpool, exercise room. **Guest Services:** gift shop, valet laundry. **Business Services:** conference facilities, business center. **Cards:** AX, MC, VI.

SOME UNITS
(A$K) 🅂🅳 🍴 📺 🚶 🎾 🏊 📷 🗄 💻 / ⊠ / VCR FEE 🛏 FEE /

BOCA RATON RESORT & CLUB

Book at aaa.com Phone: (561)447-3000

AAA [SAVE]

12/1-4/30	1P: $310-$775	2P: $310-$775	XP: $30	F16
5/1-6/30	1P: $215-$600	2P: $215-$600	XP: $30	F16
9/1-11/30	1P: $185-$600	2P: $185-$600	XP: $30	F16
7/1-8/31	1P: $160-$495	2P: $160-$495	XP: $30	F16

Resort
Large-scale Hotel

Location: I-95, exit 44 (Palmetto Park Rd), 1.9 mi e to Federal Hwy, s to Camino Real, then 0.5 mi e. 501 E Camino Real 33432 (PO Box 5025, 33431). Fax: 561/447-3183. **Facility:** Historic Florida resort built in 1926 on Intracoastal Waterway. Rooms in original Cloister Inn, high-rise tower villas or beach club. Meticulous grounds. 1043 units. 851 one-bedroom standard units. 180 one- and 12 two-bedroom suites ($360-$9500), some with kitchens. 3-27 stories, interior corridors. *Bath:* combo or shower only. **Parking:** valet. **Terms:** cancellation fee imposed, [BP] & [MAP] meal plans available, package plans, $18 service charge. **Amenities:** dual phone lines, voice mail, fax, safes, honor bars, irons, hair dryers. *Fee:* video games, high-speed Internet. *Some:* DVD players, CD players. **Dining:** 12 restaurants, 6 am-11 pm; guests only; 18% service charge, cocktails, entertainment. **Pool(s):** 6 heated outdoor. **Leisure Activities:** whirlpool, lifeguard on duty, limited beach access, rental sailboats, recreation programs, croquet, rental bicycles, jogging, spa, volleyball. *Fee:* marina, waterskiing, scuba diving, snorkeling, charter fishing, aqua cycles, golf-36 holes, 30 tennis courts (9 lighted), golf & tennis instruction, game room. **Guest Services:** gift shop, valet laundry, area transportation-shopping & beach club. **Business Services:** conference facilities, business center. **Cards:** AX, CB, DC, DS, MC, VI. **Special Amenities: free local telephone calls and free newspaper.**

SOME UNITS

COURTYARD BY MARRIOTT

Book at aaa.com Phone: (561)241-7070

AAA [SAVE]

12/1-3/31	1P: $119-$219	2P: $119-$219
4/1-5/27 & 10/1-11/30	1P: $159-$179	2P: $159-$179
5/28-9/30	1P: $109-$129	2P: $109-$129

Small-scale Hotel

Location: I-95, exit 45 (SR 808/Glades Rd). 2000 NW Executive Center Ct 33431. Fax: 561/241-7080. **Facility:** 152 units. 140 one-bedroom standard units. 12 one-bedroom suites ($159-$259). 4 stories, interior corridors. *Bath:* combo or shower only. **Parking:** on-site. **Terms:** [BP] meal plan available, package plans. **Amenities:** high-speed Internet, dual phone lines, voice mail, irons, hair dryers. **Dining:** 6:30-10:30 am, Sat & Sun 7-11 am. **Pool(s):** heated outdoor. **Leisure Activities:** whirlpool, exercise room. **Business Services:** meeting rooms, business center. **Cards:** AX, CB, DC, DS, JC, MC, VI. **Special Amenities: free newspaper.**

SOME UNITS

DISCOVERY INN & SUITES

Phone: (561)395-7172

AAA [SAVE]

1/21-4/22	1P: $109-$139	2P: $119-$159	XP: $10	F18
12/21-1/20	1P: $89-$109	2P: $99-$129	XP: $10	F18
12/1-12/20	1P: $79-$89	2P: $89-$99	XP: $10	F18
4/23-11/30	1P: $69-$89	2P: $79-$99	XP: $10	F18

Motel

Location: US 1, 1 mi n of jct SR 808 (Glades Rd). 2899 N Federal Hwy 33431. Fax: 561/750-7351. **Facility:** 48 one-bedroom standard units. 2 stories (no elevator), exterior corridors. **Parking:** on-site. **Terms:** [ECP] meal plan available. **Amenities:** irons, hair dryers. **Pool(s):** outdoor. **Guest Services:** valet laundry. **Business Services:** meeting rooms, fax (fee). **Cards:** AX, DC, DS, MC, VI. **Special Amenities: free expanded continental breakfast and free local telephone calls.**

SOME UNITS

DOUBLETREE GUEST SUITES-BOCA RATON

Book at aaa.com Phone: (561)997-9500

AAA [SAVE]

1/17-4/16	1P: $89-$229	2P: $89-$229	XP: $10	F18
12/1-1/16 & 10/1-11/30	1P: $79-$209	2P: $79-$209	XP: $10	F18
4/17-9/30	1P: $69-$209	2P: $69-$209	XP: $10	F18

Small-scale Hotel

Location: I-95, exit 48B (Yamato Rd), just w; in Arvida Corporate Park. 701 NW 53rd St 33487. Fax: 561/994-3565. **Facility:** 180 one-bedroom suites. 4 stories, exterior corridors. *Bath:* combo or shower only. **Parking:** on-site. **Terms:** small pets only ($50 fee, $10 extra charge). **Amenities:** video games (fee), high-speed Internet, dual phone lines, voice mail, irons, hair dryers. **Dining:** 6 am-10 pm, Sat & Sun from 6:30 am, cocktails. **Pool(s):** heated outdoor. **Leisure Activities:** whirlpool, putting green. **Guest Services:** sundries, valet and coin laundry, area transportation-within 5 mi. **Business Services:** meeting rooms, fax (fee). **Cards:** AX, DC, DS, MC, VI. **Special Amenities: free full breakfast and free newspaper.**

SOME UNITS

EMBASSY SUITES-BOCA RATON

Book at aaa.com Phone: (561)994-8200

12/18-4/22 [AP]	1P: $109-$259	2P: $109-$259	XP: $10	F
4/23-11/30 [AP]	1P: $89-$209	2P: $89-$209	XP: $10	F
12/1-12/17 [AP]	1P: $79-$199	2P: $79-$199	XP: $10	F

Small-scale Hotel

Location: I-95, exit 48B (Yamato Rd), just w. Located in Arvida Corporate Park. 661 NW 53rd St 33487. Fax: 561/995-9821. **Facility:** 263 units. 261 one- and 2 two-bedroom suites. 7 stories, interior corridors. *Bath:* combo or shower only. **Parking:** on-site and valet. **Terms:** cancellation fee imposed. **Amenities:** high-speed Internet (fee), voice mail, safes, irons, hair dryers. **Pool(s):** heated outdoor. **Leisure Activities:** saunas, whirlpool, exercise room. *Fee:* massage. **Guest Services:** gift shop, valet and coin laundry, area transportation. **Business Services:** meeting rooms, business center. **Cards:** AX, CB, DC, DS, JC, MC, VI.

SOME UNITS

FAIRFIELD INN & SUITES BY MARRIOTT

Book at aaa.com Phone: (561)417-8585

AAA [SAVE]

12/1-4/15	1P: $99-$199	2P: $99-$199
4/16-11/30	1P: $59-$109	2P: $59-$109

Small-scale Hotel

Location: I-95, exit 45 (SR 808/Glades Rd), just e, then 1.1 mi n. 3400 Airport Rd 33431. Fax: 561/417-5355. **Facility:** 119 one-bedroom standard units. 4 stories, interior corridors. *Bath:* combo or shower only. **Parking:** on-site. **Terms:** 3 day cancellation notice. **Amenities:** high-speed Internet, dual phone lines, voice mail, irons, hair dryers. **Pool(s):** small heated outdoor. **Leisure Activities:** whirlpool, limited exercise equipment. **Guest Services:** valet laundry. **Business Services:** meeting rooms, fax (fee). **Cards:** AX, DC, DS, MC, VI.

SOME UNITS

HAMPTON INN-BOCA RATON   *Book at aaa.com*   Phone: 561/988-0200

▼▼▽▽
Small-scale Hotel

Property failed to provide current rates

Location: I-95, exit 48A northbound; exit 48B southbound. 1455 Yamato Rd 33431. **Fax:** 561/988-0203. **Facility:** 94 one-bedroom standard units. 4 stories, interior corridors. *Bath:* combo or shower only. **Parking:** on-site. **Amenities:** high-speed Internet, dual phone lines, voice mail, irons, hair dryers. **Pool(s):** heated outdoor. **Guest Services:** valet laundry. **Business Services:** fax (fee).

SOME UNITS

🕎 ⬥M ⬥ ⟲ ➤ ✈ 📷 DATA PORT 🗄 💻 / ✕ VCR 📷 / FEE

HILTON GARDEN INN BOCA RATON   *Book at aaa.com*   Phone: (561)988-6110

AAA SAVE
▽▽▽▽
Small-scale Hotel

12/16-4/30	1P: $139-$209	2P: $139-$209	XP: $10 F18
12/1-12/15	1P: $109-$189	2P: $109-$189	XP: $10 F18
5/1-11/30	1P: $99-$189	2P: $99-$189	XP: $10 F18

Location: I-95, exit 50, just w. 8201 Congress Ave 33487. **Fax:** 561/988-9256. **Facility:** 149 one-bedroom standard units. 4 stories, interior corridors. *Bath:* combo or shower only. **Parking:** on-site. **Terms:** cancellation fee imposed. **Amenities:** video games (fee), high-speed Internet, dual phone lines, voice mail, irons, hair dryers. **Dining:** 6:30-10 am, 11-2 & 5-10 pm, cocktails. **Pool(s):** heated outdoor. **Leisure Activities:** limited exercise equipment. **Guest Services:** sundries, valet and coin laundry, area transportation-within 2 mi. **Business Services:** meeting rooms, business center. **Cards:** AX, CB, DC, DS, JC, MC, VI. **Special Amenities:** free newspaper. *(See color ad below)*

SOME UNITS

S⬥ 🕎 🍸 ⬥M ⬥ ⟲ ➤ ✈ DATA PORT 🗄 📷 💻 / ✕ /

HILTON SUITES BOCA RATON   *Book at aaa.com*   Phone: (561)483-3600

AAA SAVE
▽▽▽▽
Small-scale Hotel

1/1-4/30	1P: $199-$269	2P: $219-$289	XP: $10 F18
10/1-11/30	1P: $179-$209	2P: $199-$229	XP: $10 F18
12/1-12/31	1P: $159-$199	2P: $179-$199	XP: $10 F18
5/1-9/30	1P: $149-$179	2P: $169-$199	XP: $10 F18

Location: Florida Tpke, exit 75 (SR 808/Glades Rd); in Arvida Parkway Center. 7920 Glades Rd 33434. **Fax:** 561/479-2280. **Facility:** 200 units. 199 one- and 1 two-bedroom suites. 7 stories, interior corridors. *Bath:* combo or shower only. **Parking:** on-site. **Terms:** cancellation fee imposed, small pets only ($100 fee). **Amenities:** dual phone lines, voice mail, honor bars, irons, hair dryers. *Fee:* video games, high-speed Internet. **Pool(s):** heated outdoor. **Leisure Activities:** whirlpool, exercise room. **Guest Services:** valet and coin laundry, area transportation-within 5 mi. **Business Services:** meeting rooms, fax (fee). **Cards:** AX, CB, DC, DS, JC, MC, VI. **Special Amenities:** free full breakfast and free newspaper. *(See color ad below)*

SOME UNITS

S⬥ 🛏 FEE 🕎 ⬥ ⟲ ➤ VCR ✈ DATA PORT 📷 💻 / ✕ 🗄 / FEE

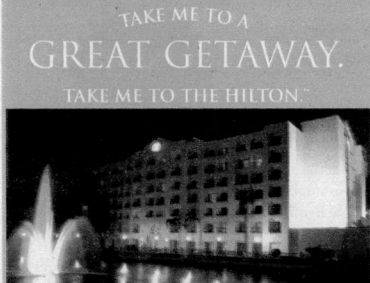

HOLIDAY INN EXPRESS   *Book at aaa.com*   Phone: (561)482-7070

(AAA) SAVE
▼▼▼

Small-scale Hotel

2/1-3/31	1P: $139-$159	2P: $139-$159
12/1-1/31 & 4/1-4/20	1P: $129-$139	2P: $129-$139
4/21-11/30	1P: $79-$99	2P: $79-$99

Location: SR 808 (Glades Rd), w of Florida Tpke, exit 75; in Lakeside Centre Shops. 8144 Glades Rd 33434. **Fax:** 561/482-6076. **Facility:** 97 one-bedroom standard units. 4 stories, interior corridors. *Bath:* combo or shower only. **Parking:** on-site. **Terms:** check-in 4 pm. **Amenities:** high-speed Internet, voice mail, irons, hair dryers. **Pool(s):** heated outdoor. **Leisure Activities:** exercise room. **Guest Services:** sundries, valet laundry. **Business Services:** meeting rooms, fax (fee). **Cards:** AX, CB, DC, DS, JC, MC, VI. **Special Amenities: free continental breakfast and free local telephone calls.** *(See color ad below)*

SOME UNITS
[S][D] [†↑] [⚷] [➘] [🐾] [DATA PORT] [▣] / [✕] [🛏] / FEE

HOLIDAY INN HOTEL & SUITES BOCA RATON
TOWN CENTER   *Book at aaa.com*   Phone: (561)368-5200

▼▼▼

Small-scale Hotel

12/1-4/15	1P: $129-$209	2P: $129-$209
4/16-11/30	1P: $69-$189	2P: $69-$189

Location: I-95, exit 45 (SR 808/Glades Rd), just w. 1950 Glades Rd 33431. Fax: 561/395-4783. **Facility:** 184 units. 146 one-bedroom standard units. 38 one-bedroom suites. 5 stories, interior/exterior corridors. *Bath:* combo or shower only. **Parking:** on-site. **Terms:** package plans. **Amenities:** high-speed Internet, dual phone lines, voice mail, irons, hair dryers. **Dining:** Mario's of Boca, see separate listing. **Pool(s):** heated outdoor, wading. **Leisure Activities:** whirlpool, exercise room. **Guest Services:** valet and coin laundry. **Business Services:** meeting rooms, fax (fee). **Cards:** AX, CB, DC, DS, JC, MC, VI. *(See color ad below)*

SOME UNITS
[ASK] [S][D] [†↑] [🍸] [⚷M] [🖉] [➘] [🐾] [DATA PORT] [▣] / [✕] [🛏] / FEE FEE

HOMESTEAD STUDIO SUITES HOTEL-BOCA
RATON/COMMERCE   *Book at aaa.com*   Phone: (561)994-2599

▼▼▼

Motel

1/2-4/15	1P: $85-$109	2P: $90-$114	XP: $5	F17
12/1-1/1 & 4/16-11/30	1P: $59-$74	2P: $64-$79	XP: $5	F17

Location: I-95, exit 50, just s on Congress Ave to NW 6th Ave. Located in a commercial office park complex. 501 NW 77th St 33487. Fax: 561/994-2792. **Facility:** 115 units. 91 one-bedroom standard units with efficiencies. 22 one- and 2 two-bedroom suites with efficiencies. 2 stories, exterior corridors. *Bath:* combo or shower only. **Parking:** on-site. **Terms:** office hours 6:30 am-11 pm, pets ($75 fee). **Amenities:** high-speed Internet (fee), voice mail, irons, hair dryers. *Some:* dual phone lines. **Guest Services:** coin laundry. **Business Services:** fax (fee). **Cards:** AX, DC, DS, MC, VI.

SOME UNITS
[ASK] [S][D] [🐾] [⚷] [🐾] [DATA PORT] [🛏] [📷] [▣] / [✕] / FEE

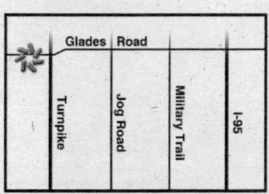

THE INN AT OCEAN BREEZE
Book at aaa.com
Phone: (561)994-0400

| | 12/1-4/14 | 1P: $89-$99 | 2P: $89-$99 | XP: $10 | F |
| | 4/15-11/30 | 1P: $49-$59 | 2P: $49-$59 | XP: $10 | F |

Resort
Small-scale Hotel

Location: I-95, exit 48A (Yamato Rd), 0.5 mi e, then 0.5 mi n; in Boca Teeca Country Club. 5800 NW 2nd Ave 33487. Fax: 561/998-8279. **Facility:** Most rooms with balcony or patio. 46 one-bedroom standard units. 3 stories, interior corridors. **Parking:** on-site. **Terms:** check-in 4 pm, 3 day cancellation notice-fee imposed. **Pool(s):** heated outdoor. **Leisure Activities:** sauna, whirlpool, 6 tennis courts, exercise room. *Fee:* golf-27 holes. **Guest Services:** coin laundry. **Business Services:** meeting rooms, fax (fee). **Cards:** AX, DS, MC, VI.

SOME UNITS
(ASK) (SD) (⊞) (🍴) (➜) (⊠) (🖥) (💻) / (⊠) /
FEE

LA BOCA CASA
Book at aaa.com
Phone: (561)392-0885

AAA SAVE
Motel

All Year | 1P: $119-$164 | 2P: $119-$164

Location: On SR A1A, just n of jct Palmetto Park Rd. Across from the beach. 365 N Ocean Blvd 33432. Fax: 561/367-8127. **Facility:** 19 one-bedroom suites with kitchens. 2 stories (no elevator), exterior corridors. **Parking:** on-site. **Terms:** office hours 8:30 am-4:30 pm, 3 night minimum stay - seasonal and/or weekends, 3 day cancellation notice-fee imposed, weekly rates available. **Amenities:** voice mail, irons, hair dryers. **Pool(s):** heated outdoor. **Leisure Activities:** whirlpool, beach access. **Guest Services:** complimentary laundry. **Business Services:** fax (fee). **Cards:** AX, MC, VI.

(➜) (VCR) (DATA PORT) (🖥) (💻)

RENAISSANCE BOCA RATON HOTEL
Book at aaa.com
Phone: (561)368-5252

	12/1-5/26	1P: $129-$309	2P: $129-$309
	10/1-11/30	1P: $109-$249	2P: $109-$249
	5/27-9/30	1P: $109-$189	2P: $109-$189

Large-scale Hotel

Location: I-95, exit 45 (SR 808/Glades Rd), just w to NW 19th St. 2000 NW 19th St 33431. Fax: 561/750-5437. **Facility:** 189 units. 184 one-bedroom standard units. 5 one-bedroom suites. 5 stories, interior corridors. **Parking:** on-site and valet. **Terms:** cancellation fee imposed. **Amenities:** high-speed Internet, dual phone lines, voice mail, safes, honor bars, irons, hair dryers. *Some:* DVD players, fax. **Pool(s):** heated outdoor. **Leisure Activities:** whirlpool, limited exercise equipment. **Guest Services:** valet laundry, area transportation. **Business Services:** meeting rooms, business center. **Cards:** AX, DC, DS, JC, MC, VI.

SOME UNITS
(ASK) (SD) (⊞) (🍴) (Y) (➜) (🎥) (DATA PORT) (💻) / (⊠) /

RESIDENCE INN-BY MARRIOTT-BOCA RATON
Book at aaa.com
Phone: (561)994-3222

AAA SAVE

	12/26-5/27 [BP]	1P: $199-$229
	10/1-11/30 [BP]	1P: $139-$169
	12/1-12/25 [BP]	1P: $129-$159
	5/28-9/30 [BP]	1P: $99-$129

Small-scale Hotel

Location: I-95, exit 50, just w of Congress Ave. 525 NW 77th St 33487. Fax: 561/994-3339. **Facility:** 120 units. 81 one-bedroom standard units with kitchens. 9 one- and 30 two-bedroom suites with kitchens. 2 stories (no elevator), exterior corridors. *Bath:* combo or shower only. **Parking:** on-site. **Terms:** cancellation fee imposed, package plans, pets ($75 fee). **Amenities:** high-speed Internet, voice mail, irons, hair dryers. **Pool(s):** heated outdoor. **Leisure Activities:** whirlpools, barbecue grills, sports court, basketball, volleyball. **Guest Services:** complimentary evening beverages: Mon-Thurs, valet and coin laundry, area transportation-within 5 mi. **Business Services:** meeting rooms. **Cards:** AX, DC, DS, MC, VI. **Special Amenities:** free expanded continental breakfast and free newspaper.

SOME UNITS
(SD) (🐾) (🎿) (🔌) (➜) (♿) (⊠) (🎥) (DATA PORT) (🖥) (💻) (💻) / (⊠) /
FEE

SPRINGHILL SUITES BY MARRIOTT
Book at aaa.com
Phone: (561)994-2107

| | 12/1-4/22 | 1P: $169-$189 | 2P: $169-$189 |
| | 4/23-11/30 | 1P: $89-$109 | 2P: $89-$109 |

Small-scale Hotel

Location: I-95, exit 48B (Yamato Rd), just w; in Arvida Corporate Park. 5130 NW 8th Ave 33487. Fax: 561/994-0226. **Facility:** 146 one-bedroom standard units. 5 stories, interior corridors. *Bath:* combo or shower only. **Parking:** on-site. **Terms:** 3 day cancellation notice-fee imposed. **Amenities:** high-speed Internet, dual phone lines, voice mail, irons, hair dryers. **Pool(s):** heated outdoor. **Leisure Activities:** whirlpool, exercise room. **Guest Services:** sundries, valet and coin laundry. **Business Services:** meeting rooms, business center. **Cards:** AX, CB, DC, DS, JC, MC, VI.
(See color ad below)

SOME UNITS
(ASK) (SD) (⊞) (♿M) (🎿) (🔌) (➜) (🎥) (DATA PORT) (🖥) (💻) (💻) / (⊠) /

TOWNEPLACE SUITES BY MARRIOTT — *Book at aaa.com* Phone: (561)994-7232

| 12/1-4/22 | 1P: $179-$239 |
| 4/23-11/30 | 1P: $99-$159 |

Small-scale Hotel **Location:** I-95, exit 48B (Yamato Rd), just w; in Arvida Corporate Park. 5110 NW 8th Ave 33487. Fax: 561/994-2134. **Facility:** 91 units. 66 one-bedroom standard units with efficiencies. 6 one- and 19 two-bedroom suites with kitchens. 4 stories, interior corridors. *Bath:* combo or shower only. **Parking:** on-site. **Terms:** 3 day cancellation notice-fee imposed, small pets only ($75 fee). **Amenities:** video games (fee), high-speed Internet, dual phone lines, voice mail, irons, hair dryers. **Pool(s):** heated outdoor. **Leisure Activities:** limited exercise equipment. **Guest Services:** valet and coin laundry. **Business Services:** business center. **Cards:** AX, CB, DC, DS, JC, MC, VI. *(See color ad p 253)* SOME UNITS

ASK 🅂🄳 🐾 🎮 🛗 🖥 🎵 ➡ 🍽 DATA PORT 🔒 🖥 📺 / ✕ /
FEE

——— WHERE TO DINE ———

ARTURO'S RISTORANTE Lunch: $15-$25 Dinner: $20-$35 Phone: 561/997-7373

Italian **Location:** On US 1, 1 mi n of jct Yamato Rd. 6750 N Federal Hwy 33487. **Hours:** 11:30 am-3 & 5:30-10 pm, Sat & Sun from 5:30 pm. Closed: 11/23, 12/25; also Super Bowl Sun. **Reservations:** suggested. **Features:** This gem has family working in every facet of the restaurant. You will find all the traditional Italian favorites as well as the house favorites. There are two dining rooms: one is rather on the formal side, while the other has more of a garden feel to it. The restaurant offers an award-winning wine list as well. Dressy casual; cocktails; entertainment. **Parking:** on-site and valet. **Cards:** AX, CB, DC, DS, MC, VI. 🍸

BACIO Lunch: $10-$17 Dinner: $12-$28 Phone: 561/391-3993

Italian **Location:** I-95, exit 45 (Glades Rd W); in the Simon Town Center Mall near Nordstrom's. 6000 Glades Rd, Suite 1230 33431. **Hours:** 11:30 am-9 pm, Fri & Sat-11 pm. Closed: 4/16, 11/23. **Reservations:** suggested. **Features:** Guests dine on the attractive patio or in the indoors dining room, which nurtures a warm atmosphere. The expansive menu lists prepared-to-order foods. Cocktails. **Parking:** on-site and valet. **Cards:** AX, DC, MC, VI. 🛗 🍸

BIG CITY TAVERN Lunch: $10-$13 Dinner: $11-$30 Phone: 561/362-6754

American **Location:** I-95, exit 44 (Palmetto Park Rd), 0.3 mi w, then 1 mi w on Military Tr; in Boca Center. 5250 Town Center Cir 33486. **Hours:** 11:30 am-2 & 5-11 pm. **Features:** The atmosphere alternates between quiet and bustling. Outside, it's just Florida, but inside resembles a classical tavern. Food is distinctive in its presentation, and the flavors will knock you out. The menu lists fresh seafood, chops, steaks, huge salads and a large beverage selection. Dressy casual; cocktails. **Parking:** on-site and valet. **Cards:** AX, MC, VI. 🛗 🍸 🔪

BISTRO ZENITH Lunch: $8-$14 Dinner: $12-$30 Phone: 561/997-2570

American **Location:** Jct Yamato and Jog/Powerline rds; in Regency Court Shopping Center. 3011 Yamato Rd 33434. **Hours:** 11:30 am-2:30 & 5:30-9 pm, Fri-10 pm, Sat 5:30 pm-10 pm. Closed: 5/29, 7/4. **Reservations:** suggested. **Features:** The overview menu includes fresh seafood, pasta and American comfort foods. Those seated in the dining room get glimpses of the fast-paced kitchen. At night, the lighting is soft with some Art Deco neon accenting the decor. Dressy casual; cocktails. **Parking:** on-site. **Cards:** AX, MC, VI. 🍸

BOCA RATON ALE HOUSE Lunch: $7-$12 Dinner: $8-$18 Phone: 561/487-2889

American **Location:** Florida Tpke, exit 8, 1.7 mi w; just w of Lyons Rd; in Boca Lyons Plaza. 9244 W Glades Rd 33434. **Hours:** 11 am-2 am, Thurs-Sat to 3 am. **Features:** Patrons munch on huge onion rings or piles of cheese fries and revel in the lively sport bar atmosphere, with more than 50 TVs to help. A menu of fun favorites includes burgers, pasta and some seafood items. Wash it all down with more than 85 beers on tap and bottled versions. Casual dress; cocktails. **Parking:** on-site. **Cards:** AX, CB, DC, DS, JC, MC, VI. 🛗 🍸

BONG Lunch: $7-$15 Dinner: $12-$30 Phone: 561/368-3338

Asian **Location:** Just e of US 1 (Federal Hwy); in Bank of America building. 150 E Palmetto Park Rd 33432. **Hours:** 11:30 am-3 & 5-10 pm, Fri-midnight, Sat 5 pm-midnight, Sun 5 pm-10 pm. Closed: Mon. **Reservations:** suggested. **Features:** Sushi and Kobe beef are among starters at this great setting for Asian cuisine. The chef adds his own touches to distinctive Thai and Chinese presentations. The dining rooms are uncommon. Dressy casual; cocktails. **Parking:** valet. **Cards:** AX, DC, MC, VI. 🛗 🍸

BREWZZI Lunch: $9-$25 Dinner: $9-$25 Phone: 561/392-2739

American **Location:** I-95, exit 45 (SR 808/Glades Rd), just w; in Glades Plaza. 2222 Glades Rd 33431. **Hours:** 11:30 am-10:30 pm, Fri & Sat-11:30 pm. **Features:** Hand-crafted beer and fresh seafood go hand in hand here. The brewmaster has won awards for his brews and ales, which also pair with other menu choices, including sandwiches, large salads, chicken selections, pasta, big chops and meatloaf. Brick-oven pizza also makes an appearance on the menu. Casual dress; cocktails. **Parking:** on-site. **Cards:** AX, MC, VI. 🛗 🍸

CARMEN'S AT THE TOP OF THE BRIDGE — *Menu on aaa.com* Dinner: $18-$36 Phone: 561/368-9500

Continental **Location:** Just w of SR A1A, 1 mi s of jct SR 798 (Palmetto Park Rd); in Boca Raton Bridge Hotel. 999 E Camino Real 33432. **Hours:** 5:30 pm-10 pm, Fri & Sat-11 pm, Sun 11 am-3 pm. Closed: Mon & Tues. **Reservations:** suggested. **Features:** Enjoy your meal overlooking the Intracoastal Waterway or the Atlantic Ocean; the diverse menu offers fresh seafood as well as meat and pasta selections. Dressy casual; cocktails; entertainment. **Parking:** on-site and valet. **Cards:** AX, CB, DC, DS, JC, MC, VI. 🛗 🍸

CHESAPEAKE BAY CRAB CAKE FACTORY Lunch: $7-$18 Dinner: $7-$18 Phone: 561/912-1114

American **Location:** 1.1 mi w of Yamato Rd; in Polo Club Shoppes. 5030 Champion Blvd 33496. **Hours:** 10:30 am-8 pm, Sat-6 pm. Closed major holidays; also Sun. **Features:** Not only can you get the house specialty of lump crab cake; they offer a variety of salads, sandwiches, quiches and signature side dishes. This little eatery offers inside or sidewalk seating. Casual dress. **Parking:** on-site. **Cards:** AX, MC, VI.

CUCINA D'ANGELO
Lunch: $7-$15 **Dinner:** $14-$35 **Phone:** 561/750-2344
Location: I-95, exit 44 (Palmetto Park Rd), 0.3 mi w, 1 mi n on Military Trail; in Boca Center. 5050 Town Center Dr 33431. **Hours:** 11 am-2:30 & 5:30-10:30 pm, Fri-11 pm, Sat 5:30 pm-11 pm, Sun 5:30 pm-10:30 pm.
Italian
Reservations: suggested. **Features:** The menu transports diners to Italy. Let the waiter suggest something or explore the menu. The atmosphere is soothing both inside and outside under the stars. Dressy casual; cocktails. **Parking:** on-site and valet. **Cards:** MC, VI.

FRAN'S CHICKEN HAVEN
Lunch: $4-$9 **Dinner:** $4-$9 **Phone:** 561/395-0781
Location: I-95, exit 45 (SR 808), 2.2 mi e, then 0.5 mi n on US 1 (Federal Hwy); in 20th St Plaza. 1925 N Federal Hwy 33432. **Hours:** 11 am-8 pm. Closed major holidays; also Sun. **Features:** Casual is the atmosphere, and chicken is the feature. Food doesn't sit long because it's good. The menu also lists some seafood and Southern-style veggies. Casual dress. **Parking:** on-site. **Cards:** AX, MC, VI.
American

GARY WOO ASIAN BISTRO
Lunch: $6-$8 **Dinner:** $9-$22 **Phone:** 561/368-8803
Location: 1.5 mi n of SR 808 (Glades Rd). 3400 N Federal Hwy 33431. **Hours:** 11:30 am-2:30 & 4-10 pm, Sat & Sun from 3 pm. **Features:** The large menu covers all of the regions of China. Patrons can specify the desired spiciness of their favorite meal. The staff is friendly in the casual dining room. Casual dress; cocktails. **Parking:** on-site. **Cards:** MC, VI.
Chinese

GOLD COAST GRILL
Lunch: $8-$12 **Dinner:** $12-$24 **Phone:** 561/955-8884
Location: I-95, exit 45 (Glades Rd/SR 808), just w to Butts Rd, then s to Glades Plaza. 2200 W Glades Rd 33431. **Hours:** 11 am-2:30 & 4-10:30 pm, Fri & Sat-11:30 pm, Sun 4 pm-10 pm. Closed: 11/23, 12/25. **Features:** A calming dining room inside and a relaxing courtyard outside, the restaurant has a menu that centers on fresh seafood, but steaks and pasta dishes are also available; don't forget the lobsters. Dressy casual; cocktails. **Parking:** on-site. **Cards:** AX, CB, DC, DS, JC, MC, VI.
Seafood

GRINDER'S HOT GRILL
Lunch: $5-$13 **Dinner:** $5-$13 **Phone:** 561/620-0099
Location: I-95, exit 45 (SR 808/Glades Rd), 1.9 mi e; corner of Glades Rd and Dixie Hwy. 1198 N Dixie Hwy 33432. **Hours:** 11 am-9 pm, Fri & Sat-10 pm. Closed: 9/4, 11/23. **Features:** Comfort food is the big feature. Among selections are meatloaf, ribs, pot roast and both hot and cold grinders (submarine sandwiches). Pizza can be ordered by the slice or pie. The atmosphere is comfortable. Casual dress; beer & wine only. **Parking:** on-site. **Cards:** MC, VI.
Italian

ICHIBAN JAPANESE RESTAURANT AT BOCA RATON
Lunch: $9-$15 **Dinner:** $12-$30 **Phone:** 561/451-2429
Location: I-95, exit 45 (SR 808/Glades Rd), 3.7 mi w; Florida Tpke, exit 75, 0.8 mi w; in The Sommerset Shoppes. 8841 Glades Rd 33434. **Hours:** 11:30 am-10:15 pm, Fri & Sat-10:45 pm. Closed: 11/23, 12/25. **Reservations:** accepted. **Features:** The restaurant offers three seating areas: a delightful patio for lighter fare and drinks, a casually decorated dining room for menu items, or a communal table where diners can have their meals cooked in front of them. The regular menu features sushi, sashimi, a generous selection of custom hand rolls and a good selection of fresh seafood and Kobe beef. Casual dress; cocktails. **Parking:** on-site. **Cards:** MC, VI.
Japanese

KATHY'S GAZEBO CAFE
Lunch: $9-$18 **Dinner:** $24-$35 **Phone:** 561/395-6032
Location: US 1, 0.5 mi s of Yamato Rd. 4199 N Federal Hwy 33431. **Hours:** Open 12/1-7/31 & 9/1-11/30; 11:30 am-3 & 5:30-10 pm, Sat from 5:30 pm. Closed major holidays. **Reservations:** suggested. **Features:** This popular, European-style restaurant features fine dining with generous portions of freshly prepared entrees. Subdued lighting, fresh flowers and comfortable booths enhance the intimate, cozy setting. Patio dining is also offered. Semi-formal attire; cocktails. **Parking:** on-site. **Cards:** AX, MC, VI.
Continental

KYOJIN JAPANESE SEAFOOD BUFFET
Lunch: $9-$11 **Dinner:** $16-$20 **Phone:** 561/218-1708
Location: From Glades Rd, just s; in The Shops of Boca Grove. 21073 Powerline Rd 33433. **Hours:** 11:30 am-2:30 & 5-9:30 pm, Fri-10 pm, Sat noon-3 & 5-10 pm, Sun noon-3 & 5-9:30 pm. **Features:** Try what you haven't before at this sushi buffet. If sushi and sashimi aren't your taste, then try the hibachi grill items cooked right in front of you. They also offer traditional Chinese and Japanese items on the all-you-can-eat buffet. Casual dress; beer & wine only. **Parking:** on-site. **Cards:** AX, MC, VI.
Japanese

LA TRE
Lunch: $6-$10 **Dinner:** $12-$18 **Phone:** 561/392-4568
Location: I-95, exit 44 (Palmetto Park Rd), 2.2 mi e, then just e of US 1 (N Federal Hwy). 249 E Palmetto Park Rd 33432. **Hours:** noon-2:30 & 5-10 pm, Mon-Wed to 2:30 pm. **Reservations:** accepted. **Features:** The bright, cozy restaurant is just off the busy streets. The chef adds his own twist to Vietnamese preparations of fresh seafood, chicken, pork and beef. He has not forgotten the roots of the cuisine, and many vegetarian selections are offered. Casual dress; beer & wine only. **Parking:** on-site and street. **Cards:** AX, CB, DC, MC, VI.
Vietnamese

LA VIEILLE MAISON
Dinner: $18-$46 **Phone:** 561/391-6701
Location: Just w of SR A1A. 770 E Palmetto Park Rd 33432. **Hours:** 6 pm-9:30 pm; to 10 pm in season. **Reservations:** required. **Features:** This restored Mizner-style mansion with a lovely courtyard is set among lush tropical gardens. Several intimate dining rooms, each tastefully appointed, provide the backdrop for nouvelle and classic French cuisine. An extensive wine list is available. Semi-formal attire; cocktails. **Parking:** valet. **Cards:** AX, DC, DS, MC, VI. **Historic**
French

LEGAL SEA FOODS
Lunch: $8-$13 **Dinner:** $14-$35 **Phone:** 561/447-2112
Location: I-95, exit 45, 1 mi n; in the Town Center Mall. 6000 W Glades Rd 33431. **Hours:** 11:30 am-10 pm, Fri & Sat-11 pm, Sun noon-9 pm. Closed: 11/23, 12/25. **Reservations:** accepted. **Features:** New England-style seafood has arrived; experience the clam chowder and the New England clam bake as well as other favorites. Casual dress; cocktails. **Parking:** on-site. **Cards:** AX, CB, DC, DS, JC, MC, VI.
Seafood

LINDA B. OF BOCA RATON
▼▼▼▼
Continental
Dinner: $18-$39 **Phone:** 561/367-0200
Location: Just e of US 1/Federal Hwy. 41 E Palmetto Park Rd 33432. **Hours:** 5:30 pm-10 pm.
Reservations: suggested. **Features:** Come relax and enjoy a great meal in this cozy and comfortable dining room where the menu is all about steaks, seafood, and Linda's favorites. Dressy casual; cocktails. **Parking:** valet and street. **Cards:** MC, VI.

LINDBURGER'S
▼
American
Lunch: $5-$12 **Dinner:** $5-$12 **Phone:** 561/620-3882
Location: I-95, exit 45 (SR 808/Glades Rd), 2.1 mi e, then just n on US 1 (Federal Hwy). 1654 N Federal Hwy 33432. **Hours:** 11 am-9 pm, Fri & Sat-9:30 pm, Sun-8 pm. Closed: 11/23, 12/25. **Features:** The eatery may not have sold 50 million burgers, but it does prepare more than 50 burger combinations, in addition to large salads, hot dogs and hot and cold sandwiches. This is a fun place to eat and relax. Patio seating is an option. Casual dress; beer & wine only. **Parking:** on-site. **Cards:** AX, MC, VI.

MARIO'S OF BOCA
▼▼▼ ▼▼▼
Italian
Lunch: $8-$15 **Dinner:** $8-$25 **Phone:** 561/392-5595
Location: I-95, exit 45 (SR 808/Glades Rd), just w; in Holiday Inn Hotel & Suites Boca Raton Town Center. 1901 N Military Tr 33431. **Hours:** 7:30 am-10:30 & 11-10 pm, Fri & Sat-11 pm, Sun 7 am-9:30 pm. **Features:** The restaurant offers two seating options: in the spacious and comfortable dining room or at the counter where the chefs toss pasta and saute veal and scallops. The large menu lists many Italian favorites. Casual dress; cocktails. **Parking:** on-site and valet. **Cards:** AX, CB, DC, DS, JC, MC, VI.

MARK'S AT THE PARK
▼▼▼ ▼▼▼
Mediterranean
Lunch: $8-$15 **Dinner:** $15-$35 **Phone:** 561/395-0770
Location: I-95, exit 45 (SR 808/Glades Rd), 2.2 mi e, 0.4 mi s on US 1 (N Federal Hwy), then e to Mizner Park; opposite fountains. 344 Plaza Real 33432. **Hours:** 11:30 am-3 & 5-11 pm, Fri & Sat-midnight, Sun-10:30 pm. **Reservations:** suggested. **Features:** "New Mediterranean" cuisine reflects the delicate balance of flavors of the different countries of the region. Fresh, local ingredients contribute to the outstanding taste of preparations of fish, poultry, fresh pasta and meat. The atmosphere is modern contemporary, with muted colors accented with mild tones. Soft, indirect lighting lends sophistication. Among seating options are the chef's counter, which offers a view of the kitchen, and an outdoor patio. Dressy casual; cocktails. **Parking:** valet. **Cards:** AX, DC, DS, MC, VI.

MISSISSIPPI SWEETS BBQ CO.
▼
Barbecue
Cards: MC, VI.
Lunch: $5-$7 **Dinner:** $9-$15 **Phone:** 561/394-6779
Location: 1 mi n of jct SR 808 (Glades Rd); in 2399 Plaza. 2399 N Federal Hwy 33431. **Hours:** 11 am-9:30 pm, Fri-10 pm, Sat 4 pm-10 pm. Closed: 4/16, 11/23, 12/25; also Sun. **Reservations:** not accepted. **Features:** The menu is not as long as the river, but the food is serious barbecue. They offer pulled pork, ribs and chicken. If you want something different, try the sweet potato fries. Casual dress; beer & wine only. **Parking:** on-site.

MON AMI AN AMERICAN BRASSERIE
▼▼▼ ▼▼▼
American

MC, VI.
Lunch: $8-$12 **Dinner:** $8-$22 **Phone:** 561/394-2428
Location: I-95, exit 45 (SR 808/Glades Rd), just e. 1400 Glades Rd 33431. **Hours:** 11:30 am-10 pm, Fri & Sat-10:30 pm, Sun-9:30 pm; hours vary in summer. **Features:** The atmosphere is like a restaurant in Paris but the food is All-American, including meat loaf, pork loin and some pasta entrees. A sidewalk cafe area is available and is open later than the dining room. Casual dress; cocktails. **Parking:** on-site. **Cards:** AX, DS,

NEW YORK PRIME, A STEAKHOUSE
▼▼▼▼
Steak House
Cards: AX, DC, DS, MC, VI.
Dinner: $26-$45 **Phone:** 561/998-3881
Location: I-95, exit 45 (SR 808/Glades Rd). 2350 NW Executive Center Dr 33431. **Hours:** 5 pm-10 pm. **Reservations:** required. **Features:** Steak, the prime entree, is not to be overlooked on a menu that also includes other meat selections and seafood. The steaks are large, and the lobsters are larger. The dining room is upbeat and bustling. An extensive wine list is offered. Dressy casual; cocktails. **Parking:** valet.

THE ORIGINAL STEAKHOUSE & SPORTS THEATRE
▼▼▼ ▼▼▼
Steak House
Cards: AX, MC, VI.
Lunch: $9-$23 **Dinner:** $9-$23 **Phone:** 561/488-1131
Location: Florida Tpke, exit 75 (SR 808/Glade Rd); in Corporate Centre. 7875 Glades Rd 33434. **Hours:** 4 pm-11 pm, Fri-midnight, Sat noon-midnight, Sun noon-10 pm. Closed major holidays. **Features:** The theme here: Lots of food, lots of TVs and lots of sports. The menu lists a nice selection of steaks, seafood, chicken and ribs. Guests have lots of fun in the relaxed atmosphere. Casual dress; cocktails. **Parking:** on-site.

P.F. CHANG'S CHINA BISTRO
▼▼▼ ▼▼▼
Chinese
CB, DC, DS, JC, MC, VI.
Lunch: $6-$12 **Dinner:** $10-$20 **Phone:** 561/393-3722
Location: I-95, exit 45 (SR 808/Glades Rd), just e; in University Commons. 1400 Glades Rd 33431. **Hours:** 11 am-11 pm, Fri & Sat-midnight, Sun-10 pm. Closed: 11/23, 12/25. **Features:** The bistro-style eatery's menu emphasizes traditional and innovative Asian and modern Chinese cuisine. The softly lit room is accented with statues and a mural of the China countryside. Casual dress; cocktails. **Parking:** on-site. **Cards:** AX,

THE RASCAL HOUSE
▼▼▼
Deli/Subs
Sandwiches
Lunch: $8-$26 **Dinner:** $8-$26 **Phone:** 561/982-8899
Location: I-95, exit 45 (SR 808/Glade Rd), just w. 2006 Executive Center Dr 33431. **Hours:** 8 am-10 pm, Fri & Sat-11 pm. **Features:** The restaurant has been around for generations in Miami. The huge menu comprises traditional Jewish delicatessen items. Diners can sit and nibble on pickles while they decide on a tall sandwich or give in to the temptation of fresh bakery items. Casual dress; cocktails. **Parking:** on-site. **Cards:** AX, MC, VI.

SMOKEY BONES BBQ
▼▼▼ ▼▼▼
Barbecue
Lunch: $7-$21 **Dinner:** $7-$21 **Phone:** 561/852-7870
Location: 1 mi s of Glades Rd; in The Target Shopping Place. 21733 SR 7 33428. **Hours:** 11 am-10 pm, Fri & Sat-11 pm. Closed: 11/23, 12/25. **Features:** The sports-oriented atmosphere appeals to families. Table speakers enable diners to hear the action they see on the TVs around the room. On the menu are ribs and a variety of other barbecue meats. Casual dress; cocktails. **Parking:** on-site. **Cards:** AX, MC, VI.

STIR CRAZY
♦♦♦ ♦♦♦
Asian

Lunch: $8-$14   **Dinner:** $9-$16   **Phone:** 561/338-7500
Location: I-95, exit 45 (SR 808/Glades Rd), 1 mi w on Glades Rd; in Towne Center Mall, northside. 6000 Glades Rd, #1015 33431. **Hours:** 11:30 am-10 pm, Fri & Sat-11:30 pm. **Features:** A fun place to eat for the whole family, the restaurant has patrons pick their noodles and meat then build their bowl of vegetables and sauce. Then everything is cooked in front of them. An alternative is a dish from the menu of traditional Asian fare. Casual dress; cocktails. **Parking:** on-site and valet. **Cards:** AX, CB, DC, DS, JC, MC, VI. &M

UNCLE TAI'S
AAA
♦♦♦ ♦♦♦
Chinese

Lunch: $8-$15   **Dinner:** $11-$26   **Phone:** 561/368-8806
Location: I-95, exit 44 (Palmetto Park Rd), 0.3 mi w, then 1 mi n on Military Tr; in Boca Center. 5250 Town Center Cir 33486. **Hours:** 11:30 am-2:30 & 5-10 pm, Fri & Sat-10:30 pm, Sun from 5 pm. **Reservations:** suggested. **Features:** The menu takes diners to the high mountain areas in the Central Province of Hunan. The menu is large, and the flavors are to be experienced. Classic touches decorate the dining room. The wait staff will help guests determine an appropriate spice level. Casual dress; cocktails. **Parking:** on-site and valet. **Cards:** AX, MC, VI.   Y

WILT CHAMBERLIN'S
♦♦♦ ♦♦♦
American

Lunch: $6-$12   **Dinner:** $6-$18   **Phone:** 561/488-8881
Location: I-95, exit 45 (SR 808/Glades Rd), 3.7 mi w; or Florida Tpke, 0.8 mi w; in Sommerset Shoppes. 8903 Glades Rd 33434. **Hours:** 11:30 am-11:30 pm, Fri & Sat-12:30 am. **Features:** The restaurant's menu features a wide variety of comfort foods such as meat loaf, burgers, some pasta and seafood items. There is entertainment for both children and adults: for the child, there are video games galore; for the adult, a basketball court to see if you can dunk like Wilt. Casual dress; cocktails. **Parking:** on-site. **Cards:** AX, DC, DS, MC, VI.

ZYNG ASIAN GRILL
♦♦♦
Asian

Lunch: $8-$12   **Dinner:** $8-$18   **Phone:** 561/394-9994
Location: From SR 808/Glades Rd, just s; in Boca Village Square. 21210 St. Andrews Blvd 33431. **Hours:** 11 am-10 pm. **Features:** A casual way to enjoy fresh Asian dishes; the menu has many options to suit your taste and flavors. Casual dress; beer & wine only. **Parking:** on-site. **Cards:** AX, DC, DS, MC, VI.

———— *The following restaurants have not been evaluated by AAA but are listed for your information only.* ————

FLANIGAN'S SEAFOOD BAR & GRILL
fyi

Phone: 561/395-4699
Not evaluated. **Location:** 45 S Federal Hwy 33432. **Features:** The family-friendly restaurant is known for its baby back ribs, burgers and seafood.

WATER COLORS
fyi

Phone: 561/368-9500
Not evaluated. **Location:** In Radisson Bridge Resort of Boca. 999 E Camino Real 33432. **Features:** Patrons are treated to views of the boats and other activity along the Intracoastal Waterway. The menu lists fresh local seafood and steak, as well as sandwiches for those who prefer something lighter.

BOKEELIA pop. 1,997

———— WHERE TO STAY ————

BOKEELIA TARPON INN
♦♦♦ ♦♦♦
Historic Bed & Breakfast

Phone: (239)283-8961

12/1-4/15	1P: $225-$275	2P: $245-$295	XP: $25 F3
4/16-7/31	1P: $175-$225	2P: $195-$255	XP: $25 F3
8/1-11/30	1P: $139-$175	2P: $159-$195	XP: $25 F3

Location: On Pine Island; on CR 767; center. 8241 Main St 33922. Fax: 239/283-8215. **Facility:** Built in 1914 in a relaxing, quiet area, the property offers elegantly decorated guest rooms; enjoy harbor views from the screened second floor lanai. 6 one-bedroom standard units. 2 stories, interior/exterior corridors. *Bath:* combo or shower only. **Parking:** on-site. **Terms:** office hours 9 am-5 pm, age restrictions may apply, 10 day cancellation notice-fee imposed. **Amenities:** hair dryers. *Some:* irons. **Leisure Activities:** beach access, boat dock, bicycles. *Fee:* charter fishing. **Guest Services:** gift shop, complimentary evening beverages, complimentary laundry. **Business Services:** business center. **Cards:** AX, CB, DC, DS, JC, MC, VI.   ASK YI+ ✕ ⚠ DATA PORT

BONITA SPRINGS pop. 32,797 (See map and index starting on p. 428)

———— WHERE TO STAY ————

AMERICINN HOTEL & SUITES
♦♦♦ ♦♦♦
Small-scale Hotel

Book at aaa.com   **Phone:** (239)495-9255

12/1-4/11	1P: $149-$200	2P: $149-$200
4/12-11/30	1P: $79-$170	2P: $79-$170

Location: I-75, exit 116, 0.7 mi s of Bonita Beach Rd on US 41. 28600 Trails Edge Blvd 34134. Fax: 239/495-6448. **Facility:** 87 units. 78 one-bedroom standard units. 9 one-bedroom suites. 4 stories, interior corridors. *Bath:* combo or shower only. **Parking:** on-site. **Terms:** [ECP] meal plan available, small pets only ($10 fee, in designated units). **Amenities:** irons, hair dryers. **Pool(s):** heated outdoor. **Leisure Activities:** exercise room. **Guest Services:** valet and coin laundry. **Business Services:** meeting rooms, fax (fee). **Cards:** AX, DC, DS, MC, VI. *(See color ad p 969)*

SOME UNITS
ASK SD 📞 YI+ &M 🐾 🛁 ≈ DATA PORT 🖥 /✕/
FEE

(See map and index starting on p. 428)

BAYMONT INN-BONITA SPRINGS   *Book at aaa.com*
Phone: (239)949-9400

	1/17-4/16	1P: $100-$130	2P: $100-$130
	12/22-1/16	1P: $90-$100	2P: $90-$100
Small-scale Hotel	12/1-12/21 & 4/17-11/30	1P: $60-$90	2P: $60-$90

Location: I-75, exit 116, just w. 27991 Oakland Dr 34135. Fax: 239/948-4480. **Facility:** 60 one-bedroom standard units. 3 stories, interior corridors. *Bath:* combo or shower only. **Parking:** on-site. **Terms:** [ECP] meal plan available. **Amenities:** video games (fee), voice mail, irons, hair dryers. **Pool(s):** outdoor. **Leisure Activities:** whirlpool, exercise room. **Guest Services:** coin laundry. **Business Services:** fax (fee). **Cards:** AX, CB, DC, DS, JC, MC, VI.

SOME UNITS

BONITA RESORT & CLUB   *Book at aaa.com*
Phone: 239/992-5198

	1/22-4/22 Wkly	1P: $915	2P: $915
	12/1-1/21 & 4/23-9/9 Wkly	1P: $665	2P: $665
Condominium	9/10-11/30 Wkly	1P: $600	2P: $600

Location: I-75, exit 116, 7.9 mi w on Bonita Beach Rd/CR 865; US 41 (S Tamiami Tr), 4.4 mi w. 26101 Hickory Blvd 34134. Fax: 239/992-2649. **Facility:** 26 units. 24 one- and 2 two-bedroom suites with kitchens. 4 stories, interior corridors. **Parking:** on-site. **Terms:** office hours 8:30 am-4:30 pm, 3 night minimum stay, 30 day cancellation notice-fee imposed. **Amenities:** irons. **Pool(s):** heated outdoor. **Leisure Activities:** whirlpool, beach access, boating, boat dock, fishing, recreation programs, rooftop sun deck, barbecue grills, bicycles, horseshoes. **Guest Services:** complimentary laundry. **Cards:** MC, VI.

COMFORT INN HOTEL   *Book at aaa.com*
Phone: (239)992-5001

| | All Year | 1P: $49-$159 | 2P: $49-$159 | XP: $10 | F |

Location: I-75, exit 116, 2.5 mi w on CR 865. 9800 Bonita Beach Rd 34135. Fax: 239/992-9283. **Facility:** 69 one-bedroom standard units. 3 stories, interior corridors. **Parking:** on-site. **Terms:** cancellation fee imposed, small pets only ($25 fee). **Amenities:** voice mail, safes, irons, hair dryers. **Pool(s):** heated outdoor. **Leisure Activities:** whirlpool. **Guest Services:** coin laundry. **Business Services:** meeting rooms, fax (fee). **Cards:** AX, CB, DC, DS, JC, MC, VI. **Special Amenities:** free continental breakfast and free local telephone calls.

SOME UNITS
FEE

HAMPTON INN   *Book at aaa.com*
Phone: (239)947-9393

| | All Year [BP] | 1P: $69-$169 | 2P: $69-$169 |

Location: I-75, exit 116, 3.3 mi w on CR 865; jct US 41 (Tamiami Tr) and Bonita Beach Rd. 27900 Crown Lake Blvd 34135. Fax: 239/947-3966. **Facility:** 91 one-bedroom standard units. 3 stories, interior corridors. *Bath:* combo or shower only. **Parking:** on-site. **Terms:** package plans. **Amenities:** high-speed Internet, voice mail, irons, hair dryers. **Pool(s):** heated outdoor. **Guest Services:** valet laundry. **Business Services:** meeting rooms, fax (fee). **Cards:** AX, DC, DS, MC, VI.

SOME UNITS

HOLIDAY INN EXPRESS   *Book at aaa.com*
Phone: (239)948-0699

| | 1/20-4/30 | 1P: $129-$149 |
| | 12/1-1/19 & 5/1-11/30 | 1P: $119-$139 |

Location: I-75, exit 116, 0.4 mi to CR 865, 3.2 mi w, then n. 27891 Crown Lake Blvd 34135. Fax: 239/948-0676. **Facility:** 108 one-bedroom standard units. 4 stories, interior corridors. *Bath:* combo or shower only. **Parking:** on-site. **Terms:** [ECP] meal plan available. **Amenities:** dual phone lines, voice mail, safes, irons, hair dryers. **Pool(s):** small outdoor. **Guest Services:** valet and coin laundry. **Business Services:** fax (fee).

SOME UNITS

HYATT REGENCY COCONUT POINT RESORT & SPA   *Book at aaa.com*
Phone: (239)444-1234   89

| | 12/1-4/30 | 1P: $265-$420 | 2P: $265-$420 | XP: $25 | F18 |
| | 5/1-11/30 | 1P: $179-$300 | 2P: $179-$300 | XP: $25 | F18 |

Location: I-75, exit 123 (CR 850/Corkscrew Rd), 1.9 mi w to US 41 (Tamiami Tr), 2.3 mi s, then 1.5 mi w. 5001 Coconut Rd 34134. Fax: 239/390-4344. **Facility:** Water views and balconies enhance most accommodations at this resort decorated with a tropical touch. 454 units. 426 one-bedroom standard units. 28 one-bedroom suites. 18 stories, interior corridors. *Bath:* combo or shower only. **Parking:** on-site (fee) and valet. **Terms:** check-in 4 pm, 3 day cancellation notice-fee imposed, $10 service charge. **Amenities:** DVD players, CD players, dual phone lines, voice mail, safes, irons, hair dryers. *Fee:* video games, high-speed Internet. **Dining:** 5 restaurants, 6:30 am-10 pm, cocktails, also, Tanglewood, see separate listing, entertainment. **Pool(s):** outdoor, 2 heated outdoor. **Leisure Activities:** whirlpools, waterslide, recreation programs, rental bicycles, playground, spa. *Fee:* charter fishing, kayaks, golf-18 holes, golf and tennis instruction, 2 lighted tennis courts. **Guest Services:** gift shop, valet laundry, area transportation-beach & golf course. **Business Services:** conference facilities, business center. **Cards:** AX, CB, DC, DS, JC, MC, VI.
(See color ad p 631)

SOME UNITS

STAYBRIDGE SUITES BY HOLIDAY INN   *Book at aaa.com*
Phone: 239/949-5913

| | All Year [ECP] | 1P: $149-$249 | 2P: $149-$249 |

Location: I-75, exit 116, 3.5 mi w on CR 865, 1.4 mi n on US 41 (Tamiami Tr), then e on Highland Woods Blvd. 8900 Brighton Ln 34135. Fax: 239/949-5914. **Facility:** 106 units. 53 one-bedroom standard units with kitchens. 35 one- and 18 two-bedroom suites with kitchens. 4 stories, interior corridors. *Bath:* combo or shower only. **Parking:** on-site. **Terms:** cancellation fee imposed, weekly rates available, package plans, small pets only ($100 fee). **Amenities:** high-speed Internet, dual phone lines, voice mail, irons, hair dryers. **Pool(s):** heated outdoor. **Leisure Activities:** exercise room. **Guest Services:** sundries, complimentary evening beverages: Tues-Thurs, valet and coin laundry. **Business Services:** meeting rooms, business center. **Cards:** AX, CB, DC, DS, MC, VI.

SOME UNITS
FEE

(See map and index starting on p. 428)

TRIANON BONITA BAY *Book at aaa.com* Phone: (239)948-4400

▼▼▼

12/1-12/31 [ECP]	1P: $103-$250	2P: $103-$250	XP: $10	F18
1/1-4/10 [ECP]	1P: $160-$225	2P: $160-$225	XP: $10	F18
4/11-11/30 [ECP]	1P: $98-$130	2P: $98-$130	XP: $10	F18

Small-scale Hotel **Location:** I-75, exit 123, just w of US 41 (Tamiami Tr); 6 mi s of Corkscrew Rd. Adjacent to The Promenade Shops. 3401 Bay Commons Dr 34134. Fax: 239/948-4401. **Facility:** 100 one-bedroom standard units. 4 stories, interior corridors. *Bath:* combo or shower only. **Parking:** on-site. **Terms:** cancellation fee imposed. **Amenities:** voice mail, safes, irons, hair dryers. *Some:* CD players. **Pool(s):** heated outdoor. **Leisure Activities:** exercise room. **Guest Services:** valet laundry. **Business Services:** meeting rooms, fax (fee). **Cards:** AX, DC, DS, MC, VI.

SOME UNITS

ASK 🅢🄳 ▮†▮ ▤ ⟨M⟩ 🖏 ⇨ 🎥 DATA PORT ▦ / ✕ VCR ▬ /
FEE

─────── **WHERE TO DINE** ───────

MEL'S DINER BONITA Lunch: $5-$9 Dinner: $5-$15 Phone: 239/949-3080

▼▼ **Location:** 0.7 mi s of Bonita Beach Rd. 28601 Trails Edge 34134. **Hours:** 6:30 am-9:30 pm, Fri & Sat-10 pm, Sun-
9 pm. **Features:** American comfort foods—from sandwiches to burgers to ribs—are served in a pleasant
American setting. Casual dress. **Parking:** on-site. **Cards:** AX, DS, MC, VI.

NOODLES ITALIAN CAFE Lunch: $6-$10 Dinner: $10-$21 Phone: 239/498-0050

▼▼▼ **Location:** From Bonita Beach Rd, 0.7 mi s on US 41 (Tamiami Tr) to Trails Edge Blvd. 28340 Trails Edge Blvd #9
34134. **Hours:** 11 am-10 pm, Sat & Sun from 4 pm. Closed: 11/23. **Features:** The family-friendly restaurant's
Italian walls are painted with pasta characters. Italian favorites are served in large portions. Casual dress;
cocktails. **Parking:** on-site. **Cards:** AX, DS, MC, VI.

⟨M⟩ ▤

ROY'S Dinner: $22-$29 Phone: 239/498-7697

▼▼▼ **Location:** I-75, exit 116, 3.3 mi w on CR 565 (Bonita Beach Rd), 1 mi n on US 41 (Tamiami Tr) to W Terry St/Bonita Bay
Blvd, then w, just n; in The Promenade Shops. 26831 S Bay Dr, Suite 100 34134. **Hours:** 5 pm-9:30 pm, Fri & Sat-
Pacific Rim 10 pm. Closed: 7/4, 11/23, 12/25. **Reservations:** suggested. **Features:** An open-air kitchen, from which
many interesting aromas arise, greets diners as they enter the dining room. The menu's many entrees—
including many seafood dishes not seen on this coast—reflect a Hawaiian fusion style. A large wine list complements the food.
Dressy casual; cocktails. **Parking:** on-site. **Cards:** AX, CB, DC, DS, JC, MC, VI.

⟨M⟩ ▤

SKILLETS OF BONITA *Menu on aaa.com* Lunch: $5-$9 Phone: 239/992-9333

ⒶⒶⒶ **Location:** I-75, exit 116, 2.9 mi w; US 41 (Tamiami Tr), just e; in The Sunshine Plaza. 9174 Bonita Beach Rd, #100
34135. **Hours:** 7 am-2:30 pm. Closed: 11/23, 12/25. **Features:** Breakfast and lunch are served all the time.
▼ Offerings range from omelets and other egg specialties to pancakes, blintzes and waffles to a large
American selection of sandwiches. Casual dress. **Parking:** on-site. **Cards:** MC, VI.

TANGLEWOOD Lunch: $11-$17 Dinner: $18-$30 Phone: 239/444-1234 72

▼▼ ▼▼ **Location:** I-75, exit 123 (CR 850/Corkscrew Rd), 1.9 mi w to US 41 (Tamiami Tr), 2.3 mi s, then 1.5 mi w; in Hyatt
Regency Coconut Point Resort & Spa. 5001 Coconut Rd 34134. **Hours:** 6:30-11 am, 11:30-3 & 5:30-10 pm, Wed
Continental & Thurs-3 pm. **Reservations:** suggested. **Features:** The room's decor is soft, with earthy tones and
accents of a tropical plantation home. Continental cuisine is prepared with a Florida twist: fresh local
ingredients. The chef changes the menu seasonally to take advantage of the freshest available products. Dressy casual;
cocktails. **Parking:** on-site and valet. **Cards:** AX, CB, DC, DS, JC, MC, VI.

▤

BOWLING GREEN pop. 2,892

─────── **WHERE TO STAY** ───────

BEST WESTERN HERITAGE INN & SUITES *Book at aaa.com* Phone: (863)773-2378

ⒶⒶⒶ SAVE All Year [CP] 1P: $69-$150 2P: $69-$150

▼▼▼ **Location:** US 17, 3 mi n; 0.3 mi n of SR 62. 2727 Hwy 17 N 33834 (401 S 6th Ave, WAUCHULA, 33873).
Facility: Designated smoking area. 48 units. 46 one-bedroom standard units, some with whirlpools. 2 one-
Small-scale Hotel bedroom suites with kitchens (no utensils). 3 stories, interior corridors. *Bath:* some combo or shower only.
Parking: on-site. **Terms:** cancellation fee imposed. **Amenities:** high-speed Internet, voice mail, irons, hair
dryers. **Pool(s):** heated outdoor. **Leisure Activities:** whirlpool, exercise room. **Guest Services:** coin
laundry. **Business Services:** meeting rooms, fax (fee). **Cards:** AX, CB, DC, DS, MC, VI. **Special Amenities:** free continental
breakfast.

🅢🄳 ⇨ ✕ 🖏 DATA PORT ▬ 📷 ▦

BOYNTON BEACH pop. 60,389 (See map and index starting on p. 843)

──── WHERE TO STAY ────

ATLANTIC LODGE
Phone: 561/732-4446 **73**

🔷 (AAA) (SAVE)

12/15-4/14	1P: $70-$77	2P: $80-$90	XP: $10	D12
12/1-12/14 & 4/15-11/30	1P: $46-$50	2P: $50-$55	XP: $10	D12

Motel
Location: US 1, 0.8 mi s of jct Woolbright Rd. Located in a quiet area. 2607 S Federal Hwy 33435. Fax: 561/731-0325. **Facility:** 20 one-bedroom standard units, some with efficiencies. 1 story, exterior corridors. *Bath:* combo or shower only. **Parking:** on-site. **Terms:** office hours 9 am-8 pm, 14 day cancellation notice-fee imposed, weekly rates available. **Pool(s):** heated outdoor. **Guest Services:** coin laundry. **Cards:** AX, DC, DS, MC, VI.

SOME UNITS

⟦S⟧⟦D⟧ ⟦⟧ ⟦⟧ ⟦⟧ / ⟦⟧ ⟦⟧ /

HAMPTON INN & SUITES BOYNTON BEACH *Book at aaa.com*
Phone: 561/369-0018 **70**
Property failed to provide current rates

▽▽▽▽

Small-scale Hotel
Location: I-95, exit 59 (Gateway Blvd), 1.2 mi w. 1475 W Gateway Blvd 33426. Fax: 561/738-5235. **Facility:** 161 units. 146 one-bedroom standard units. 15 one-bedroom suites. 4 stories, interior corridors. *Bath:* combo or shower only. **Parking:** on-site. **Amenities:** video games (fee), high-speed Internet, dual phone lines, voice mail, irons, hair dryers. **Pool(s):** heated outdoor. **Leisure Activities:** exercise room. **Guest Services:** sundries, complimentary evening beverages: Mon-Thurs, valet and coin laundry. **Business Services:** meeting rooms, business center.

SOME UNITS

⟦⟧ ⟦M⟧ ⟦⟧ ⟦⟧ ⟦⟧ ⟦⟧ ⟦DATA PORT⟧ ⟦⟧ / ⟦X⟧ ⟦VCR⟧ ⟦⟧ ⟦⟧ /

HOLIDAY INN-BOYNTON BEACH *Book at aaa.com*
Phone: (561)737-4600 **71**

▽▽▽

12/20-4/18	1P: $139-$149	2P: $139-$149
12/1-12/19 & 4/19-11/30	1P: $99-$109	2P: $99-$109

Small-scale Hotel
Location: I-95, exit 59 (Gateway Blvd), 1.2 mi w to SR 807 (Congress Ave); 0.3 mi s of jct SR 806 (Gateway Blvd); adjacent to Catalina Shopping Center. 1601 N Congress Ave 33426. Fax: 561/734-6523. **Facility:** 170 units. 152 one-bedroom standard units. 4 one- and 14 two-bedroom suites with kitchens. 4 stories, interior/exterior corridors. *Bath:* combo or shower only. **Parking:** on-site. **Terms:** pets ($40 fee). **Amenities:** high-speed Internet, voice mail, irons, hair dryers. **Pool(s):** heated outdoor. **Leisure Activities:** whirlpool, exercise room. *Fee:* game room. **Guest Services:** valet and coin laundry. **Business Services:** meeting rooms, business center. **Cards:** AX, CB, DC, DS, JC, MC, VI. *(See color ad below)*

SOME UNITS

(ASK) ⟦S⟧⟦D⟧ ⟦⟧ ⟦⟧ ⟦⟧ ⟦⟧ ⟦⟧ ⟦X⟧ ⟦⟧ ⟦DATA PORT⟧ ⟦⟧ / ⟦X⟧ ⟦⟧ ⟦⟧ /
FEE

(See map and index starting on p. 843)

HOLIDAY INN EXPRESS I-95 *Book at aaa.com* **Phone:** (561)734-9100 72

12/1-4/14 [ECP]	1P: $149-$249	2P: $149-$249	XP: $10 F18
11/22-11/30 [ECP]	1P: $94-$154	2P: $94-$154	XP: $10 F18
4/15-5/29 [ECP]	1P: $94-$134	2P: $94-$134	XP: $10 F18
5/30-11/21 [ECP]	1P: $84-$124	2P: $84-$124	XP: $10 F18

Small-scale Hotel **Location:** I-95, exit 57, jct SR 804 (Boynton Beach Blvd). 480 W Boynton Beach Blvd 33435. Fax: 561/738-7193. **Facility:** 102 one-bedroom standard units. 4 stories, interior corridors. *Bath:* combo or shower only. **Parking:** on-site. **Terms:** cancellation fee imposed. **Amenities:** video games (fee), high-speed Internet, voice mail, irons, hair dryers. *Some:* dual phone lines. **Pool(s):** heated outdoor. **Guest Services:** complimentary evening beverages: Mon-Sat, coin laundry. **Business Services:** meeting rooms, fax (fee). **Cards:** AX, DC, DS, MC, VI. **Special Amenities:** free expanded continental breakfast and free local telephone calls. *(See color ad below)*

SOME UNITS / FEE FEE

(See map and index starting on p. 843)

──────── WHERE TO DINE ────────

MAMA JENNIE'S ITALIAN RESTAURANT
Ⓐ
▼▼ ◆◆
South Italian

Dinner: $8-$15   Phone: 561/737-2407   64
Location: I-95, exit 57, just w on SR 804. 706 W Boynton Beach Blvd 33426. **Hours:** 4 pm-9 pm, Fri & Sat-10 pm. **Reservations:** accepted. **Features:** Generous portions at reasonable prices make the restaurant a good choice if you're seeking an excellent value. Well-prepared homemade dishes—such as baked stuffed lobster, seafood pomodoro and traditional pasta—are served in a casual, family atmosphere. Casual dress; cocktails. **Parking:** on-site. **Cards:** AX, DS, MC, VI.

MICHAEL'S SONOMA GRILLE
Ⓐ
▼▼▼ ▼
Continental

Dinner: $15-$23   Phone: 561/752-2252   66
Location: I-95, exit 56, 2.8 mi w; 1.7 mi w of Congress Ave (SR 807); in Village Square Shopping Plaza. 3441 Woolbright Rd 33436. **Hours:** 4 pm-10 pm. **Closed:** 12/25. **Reservations:** suggested. **Features:** Contemporary decor and very good food — a great combination that is coupled with friendly service. The dishes are creative, utilizing local seafood and fresh produce from local markets. Dressy casual; beer & wine only. **Parking:** on-site. **Cards:** AX, DC, DS, MC, VI.

TWO GEORGES WATERFRONT GRILLE
▼▼▼
Seafood

Lunch: $7-$11   Dinner: $14-$30   Phone: 561/736-2717   65
Location: From S Federal Hwy, e on E Ocean Ave, then n. 728 Casa Loma Blvd 33435. **Hours:** 11 am-10 pm, Fri & Sat-11 pm, Sun 9-11 am. **Closed:** 11/23, 12/25. **Features:** The open-air restaurant features fresh seafood, of course, and friendly service. Early-bird specials are among options. Casual dress; cocktails. **Parking:** valet. **Cards:** AX, DS, MC, VI.

BRADENTON pop. 45,504   (See map and index starting on p. 904)

──────── WHERE TO STAY ────────

COMFORT INN-BRADENTON   Book at aaa.com   Phone: (941)747-7500   39
Ⓐ SAVE
▼▼ ▼
Motel

1/15-4/20 [ECP]	1P: $100-$120	2P: $120-$140	XP: $10	F12
12/16-1/14 [ECP]	1P: $90-$100	2P: $100-$110	XP: $10	F12
12/1-12/15 [ECP]	1P: $80-$90	2P: $90-$100	XP: $10	F12
4/21-11/30 [ECP]	1P: $60-$70	2P: $70-$80	XP: $10	F12

Location: I-75, exit 220 southbound; exit 220B northbound, 0.3 mi w on SR 64. 580 E 66th St Ct 34208. **Fax:** 941/748-8002. **Facility:** 70 units. 64 one-bedroom standard units. 6 one-bedroom suites ($129-$179), some with kitchens and/or whirlpools. 2 stories, exterior corridors. *Bath:* combo or shower only. **Parking:** on-site. **Terms:** 7 day cancellation notice. **Amenities:** irons, hair dryers. **Pool(s):** outdoor. **Leisure Activities:** whirlpool, gazebo. **Guest Services:** valet and coin laundry. **Business Services:** meeting rooms. **Cards:** AX, DC, DS, MC, VI. **Special Amenities:** free expanded continental breakfast and free local telephone calls.

SOME UNITS

DAYS INN BRADENTON   Book at aaa.com   Phone: (941)746-1141   42
▼▼▼ ▼▼▼
Motel

1/27-4/22	1P: $89-$139	2P: $99-$149	XP: $10	F16
12/1-1/26 & 4/23-11/30	1P: $59-$89	2P: $69-$99	XP: $10	F16

Location: On US 41, just e of jct US 301. 3506 1st St W 34208. **Fax:** 941/745-2382. **Facility:** 130 one-bedroom standard units. 2 stories, exterior corridors. *Bath:* combo or shower only. **Parking:** on-site. **Terms:** cancellation fee imposed, pets ($50 deposit, $7 extra charge). **Amenities:** safes (fee), hair dryers. *Some:* irons. **Pool(s):** outdoor. **Leisure Activities:** shuffleboard. **Guest Services:** valet laundry. **Business Services:** meeting rooms, fax (fee). **Cards:** AX, CB, DC, DS, MC, VI.

SOME UNITS

DAYS INN I-75   Book at aaa.com   Phone: (941)746-2505   37
▼▼ ▼▼
Motel

1/1-3/31	1P: $110	2P: $110	
12/1-12/31 & 4/1-11/30	1P: $48	2P: $48	XP: $10 F

Location: I-75, exit 220 southbound; exit 220B northbound, 0.3 mi w on SR 64. 644 67th St Cir E 34208. **Fax:** 941/745-1839. **Facility:** 60 units. 59 one-bedroom standard units. 1 one-bedroom suite with kitchen. 2 stories, exterior corridors. **Parking:** on-site. **Terms:** [CP] meal plan available. **Amenities:** voice mail, hair dryers. *Some:* irons. **Pool(s):** outdoor. **Guest Services:** coin laundry. **Business Services:** PC, fax (fee). **Cards:** AX, CB, DC, DS, MC, VI.

SOME UNITS

ECONO LODGE AIRPORT   Book at aaa.com   Phone: 941/758-7199   45
▼▼ ▼
Motel

Property failed to provide current rates
Location: On US 41, 2 mi s of jct SR 70. 6727 14th St W 34207. **Fax:** 941/751-4947. **Facility:** 78 one-bedroom standard units. 2 stories, exterior corridors. **Parking:** on-site. **Terms:** check-in 4 pm, small pets only ($10 extra charge). **Amenities:** dual phone lines, voice mail. *Some:* high-speed Internet, irons, hair dryers. **Pool(s):** heated outdoor. **Guest Services:** coin laundry. **Business Services:** fax (fee).

SOME UNITS

HOLIDAY INN EXPRESS   Book at aaa.com   Phone: (941)748-6610   38
Ⓐ SAVE
▼▼ ▼
Small-scale Hotel

12/21-4/30 [CP]	1P: $109-$199	2P: $109-$199
12/1-12/20 & 5/1-11/30 [CP]	1P: $89-$199	2P: $89-$199

Location: I-75, exit 220 southbound; exit 220B northbound, 0.3 mi w on SR 64. 648 67th Cir E 34208. **Fax:** 941/748-0922. **Facility:** 60 units. 57 one-bedroom standard units. 3 one-bedroom suites with whirlpools. 3 stories, interior corridors. *Bath:* combo or shower only. **Parking:** on-site. **Terms:** 1-3 night minimum stay. **Amenities:** high-speed Internet, dual phone lines, voice mail, irons, hair dryers. **Pool(s):** heated outdoor. **Guest Services:** valet and coin laundry. **Business Services:** fax. **Cards:** AX, CB, DC, DS, JC, MC, VI. **Special Amenities:** free continental breakfast and free local telephone calls.

SOME UNITS

(See map and index starting on p. 904)

HOLIDAY INN-RIVERFRONT Book at aaa.com

Phone: (941)747-3727 **36**

AAA SAVE

| | 1/1-5/31 | 1P: $129-$199 | 2P: $129-$199 | XP: $25 | F17 |
| | 12/1-12/31 & 6/1-11/30 | 1P: $89-$199 | 1P: $89-$199 | XP: $25 | F17 |

Small-scale Hotel

Location: W of US 41 and 301; south side of Hernando Desoto Bridge via 3rd St W. 100 Riverfront Dr W 34205. Fax: 941/746-4289. **Facility:** 153 units. 96 one-bedroom standard units. 57 one-bedroom suites. 5 stories, interior corridors. **Parking:** on-site. **Amenities:** high-speed Internet, dual phone lines, voice mail, irons, hair dryers. **Dining:** 2 restaurants, 7 am-1:30 & 5-10 pm, cocktails. **Pool(s):** heated outdoor. **Leisure Activities:** whirlpool, fishing, lending library, exercise room. **Guest Services:** valet laundry. **Business Services:** conference facilities, business center. **Cards:** AX, CB, DC, DS, JC, MC, VI. **Special Amenities:** free newspaper and free room upgrade (subject to availability with advance reservations). *(See color ad below)*

SOME UNITS

HOWARD JOHNSON EXPRESS INN Book at aaa.com

Phone: (941)756-8399 **44**

AAA SAVE

	2/1-4/15	1P: $74-$119	2P: $79-$124	XP: $10	F16
	12/22-1/31	1P: $60-$104	2P: $65-$109	XP: $10	F16
	12/1-12/21	1P: $55-$94	2P: $60-$104	XP: $10	F16
	4/16-11/30	1P: $55-$84	2P: $69-$89	XP: $10	F16

Motel

Location: On US 41, 1.5 mi s of jct SR 70. 6511 14th St W 34207. Fax: 941/755-1387. **Facility:** 48 one-bedroom standard units, some with efficiencies. 2 stories, exterior corridors. **Parking:** on-site. **Terms:** cancellation fee imposed, [ECP] meal plan available, pets ($10 extra charge). **Amenities:** voice mail, irons, hair dryers. *Some:* high-speed Internet. **Pool(s):** heated outdoor. **Guest Services:** coin laundry. **Business Services:** fax. **Cards:** AX, DS, MC, VI. **Special Amenities:** free expanded continental breakfast and free newspaper.

SOME UNITS

FEE

MOTEL 6 #678 Book at aaa.com

Phone: 941/747-6005 **40**

	1/27-3/26	1P: $54-$65	2P: $60-$70	XP: $3	F17
	3/27-11/30	1P: $39-$55	2P: $45-$61	XP: $3	F17
	1/1-1/26	1P: $42-$52	2P: $48-$58	XP: $3	F17
	12/1-12/31	1P: $39-$49	2P: $45-$55	XP: $3	F17

Motel

Location: I-75, exit 220 southbound; exit 220B northbound, just w on SR 64. 660 67th St Cir E 34208. Fax: 941/745-1388. **Facility:** 121 one-bedroom standard units. 2-3 stories, exterior corridors. **Parking:** on-site. **Terms:** small pets only. **Pool(s):** heated outdoor. **Guest Services:** coin laundry. **Business Services:** fax (fee). **Cards:** AX, CB, DC, DS, MC, VI.

SOME UNITS

QUALITY INN & SUITES Book at aaa.com

Phone: 941/747-6465 **41**

Property failed to provide current rates

Motel

Location: On US 41, 1 mi s of jct SR 64. 2303 1st St E 34208. Fax: 941/747-1070. **Facility:** 186 units. 160 one-bedroom standard units. 26 one-bedroom suites. 2 stories, exterior corridors. **Parking:** on-site. **Amenities:** irons, hair dryers. **Pool(s):** heated outdoor. **Leisure Activities:** 2 tennis courts, playground, shuffleboard. **Guest Services:** coin laundry. **Business Services:** meeting rooms, business center.

SOME UNITS

SHOREWALK VACATION VILLAS RESORT Book at aaa.com

Phone: (941)794-9800 **43**

	2/1-4/24	1P: $133-$135	2P: $133-$135
	12/16-1/31	1P: $110-$112	2P: $110-$112
	4/25-11/30	1P: $96-$98	2P: $96-$98
	12/1-12/15	1P: $92-$94	2P: $92-$94

Condominium

Location: Just s of jct SR 684 (Cortez Rd) on 47th St W. 4601 46th Street Ct W 34210. Fax: 941/795-2163. **Facility:** 188 two-bedroom suites with kitchens. 2 stories, exterior corridors. **Parking:** on-site. **Terms:** office hours 8:30 am-8 pm, check-in 5 pm, 14 day cancellation notice. **Amenities:** irons. *Some:* hair dryers. **Pool(s):** 2 heated outdoor. **Leisure Activities:** whirlpools, fishing, 2 lighted tennis courts, recreation programs, playground, basketball, shuffleboard. *Fee:* game room. **Guest Services:** complimentary laundry. **Business Services:** fax (fee). **Cards:** AX, DS, MC, VI.

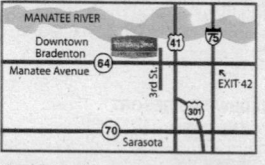

(See map and index starting on p. 904)

——— WHERE TO DINE ———

ANNA MARIA OYSTER BAR **Lunch:** $5-$25   **Dinner:** $5-$25   **Phone:** 941/792-0077   **65**
Seafood
Location: On SR 684 (Cortez Rd), just w of jct 66th St W; in Cortez Village. **Hours:** 11 am-9 pm, Fri & Sat-10 pm. Closed: 11/23, 12/25. **Reservations:** accepted. **Features:** In the neat establishment, the dining room is loaded with eye-pleasing nautical goodies that are offered for sale. The menu offers seafood and more seafood, with all types of broiled, fried or blackened items to try. Casual dress; cocktails. **Parking:** on-site.
Cards: AX, DS, MC, VI.

ANNA MARIA OYSTER BAR **Lunch:** $5-$25   **Dinner:** $5-$25   **Phone:** 941/758-7880   **68**
Seafood
Location: On US 41, jct 69th Ave. 6906 14th St W 34207. **Hours:** 11:30 am-9 pm, Fri & Sat-10 pm. Closed: 11/23, 12/25. **Features:** Island-style dining is offered in a fun, contemporary setting with lots of nautical touches. The menu has a multitude of choices, ranging from seafood to poultry to meat dishes. Fried shrimp is an outstanding selection. Casual dress; cocktails. **Parking:** on-site. **Cards:** AX, DS, MC, VI.

BART'S FAMILY DINER **Lunch:** $5-$13   **Dinner:** $5-$13   **Phone:** 941/748-7143   **62**
American
Location: On SR 64; jct 24th St E. 2230 Manatee Ave E 34208. **Hours:** 6:30 am-7 pm, Sun-2 pm. **Features:** True to its name, the diner-style establishment employs a helpful wait staff and serves good home cooking. Casual dress; beer & wine only. **Parking:** on-site. **Cards:** MC, VI.

D'ARITINO'S PASTA & PIZZA **Lunch:** $6-$12   **Dinner:** $6-$12   **Phone:** 941/727-4900   **67**
Italian
Location: I-75, exit 217, just w on SR 70. 7230 52nd Pl E 34203. **Hours:** 11 am-9 pm, Fri & Sat-10 pm. Closed: 11/23, 12/25. **Reservations:** not accepted. **Features:** A local favorite for more than 20 years, the popular spot prepares great Italian/Mediterranean specialties: designer pizzas, soups, salads, seafood dishes and such traditional dishes as veal, eggplant and chicken parmigiana, lasagna, manicotti, moussaka and ravioli. Casual dress; beer & wine only. **Parking:** on-site. **Cards:** AX, DS, MC, VI.

MILLER'S DUTCH KITCH'N **Lunch:** $5-$14   **Dinner:** $5-$14   **Phone:** 941/746-8253   **64**
American
Location: On US Business Rt 41 at 35th Ave W; downtown. 3401 14th St W 34205. **Hours:** 11 am-8 pm. Closed: 12/25; also Sun. **Features:** Amish cooking and courteous service are the attractions, with simple meals to remind you of home-like pan-fried chicken with potatoes and gravy; or come in for a cup of coffee and a slice of one of 20 made-from-scratch pies, like the rich coconut cream. Casual dress. **Parking:** on-site.
Cards: MC, VI.

R.J. GATORS HOMETOWN GRILL & BAR **Lunch:** $7-$16   **Dinner:** $7-$16   **Phone:** 941/795-6633   **66**
American
Location: On SR 684, jct 60th St Ct W. 6100 Cortez Rd W 34210. **Hours:** 11 am-midnight, Fri & Sat-1 am. Closed: 11/23, 12/25. **Features:** Many colorful elements and an alligator motif about the walls lend to the rustic appeal of the fun spot. The menu is just as fun, including such dishes as grinders, wraps, steaks, ribs, sandwiches, combination dishes and seafood items. Casual dress; cocktails; entertainment. **Parking:** on-site. **Cards:** AX, DC, DS, MC, VI.

SONNY'S REAL PIT BAR-B-Q **Lunch:** $7-$13   **Dinner:** $7-$13   **Phone:** 941/746-6166   **63**
Barbecue
Location: I-75, exit 220 southbound; exit 220B northbound, 0.3 mi w on SR 64. 631 67th St Cir E 34208. **Hours:** 11 am-9:30 pm. **Features:** Around since 1968, the restaurant prepares outstanding barbecue, including dinner plates, combination platters and mouthwatering baby back ribs. It's hard to go wrong with any of the choices. The extensive salad bar lines up all types of fresh fruits, vegetables, soups and fixings. Casual dress. **Parking:** on-site. **Cards:** MC, VI.

BRADENTON BEACH pop. 1,482   (See map and index starting on p. 904)

——— WHERE TO STAY ———

TORTUGA INN BEACH RESORT **Phone:** (941)778-6611   **49**
Motel

2/1-5/1	1P: $155-$270
5/2-11/30	1P: $119-$263
12/1-12/15	1P: $115-$255
12/16-1/31	1P: $135-$240

Location: On SR 789, 0.3 mi n of jct SR 684. 1325 Gulf Dr N 34217. Fax: 941/778-6748. **Facility:** Designated smoking area. 37 units. 20 one-bedroom standard units, some with efficiencies and/or whirlpools. 17 two-bedroom suites with kitchens, some with whirlpools. 2 stories, exterior corridors. **Bath:** combo or shower only. **Parking:** on-site. **Terms:** office hours 8 am-6 pm, check-in 4 pm, 14 day cancellation notice-fee imposed, pets ($25 extra charge, in designated units). **Amenities:** video library, irons, hair dryers. **Pool(s):** heated outdoor. **Leisure Activities:** beach access, boat dock, fishing, boat slips, gas grills, beach chairs, umbrellas, beach towels. **Guest Services:** coin laundry. **Business Services:** meeting rooms, fax. **Cards:** AX, MC, VI. **Special Amenities:** free local telephone calls.

FEE

TRADEWINDS RESORT **Phone:** 941/779-0010   **48**
Cottage

12/17-4/21	1P: $205-$325	2P: $205-$325
4/22-11/30	1P: $150-$245	2P: $150-$245
12/1-12/16	1P: $145-$240	2P: $145-$240

Location: On SR 789, 0.5 mi n of jct SR 684. On Sarasota Bay. 1603 Gulf Dr N 34217. Fax: 941/778-6114. **Facility:** A Key West-style ambience imbues this hotel on the Intracoastal Waterway. Designated smoking area. 34 cottages. 1-2 stories, exterior corridors. **Bath:** combo or shower only. **Parking:** on-site. **Terms:** office hours 10 am-6 pm, 14 day cancellation notice-fee imposed, weekly rates available, pets ($25 extra charge, in designated units). **Amenities:** video library, irons, hair dryers. **Pool(s):** small heated outdoor. **Leisure Activities:** beach access, fishing, fishing pier, fishing equipment, picnic tables, barbecue area with grills. **Guest Services:** coin laundry. **Business Services:** fax. **Cards:** AX, MC, VI.

FEE

(See map and index starting on p. 904)

——— WHERE TO DINE ———

BEACH HOUSE RESTAURANT

Lunch: $5-$13   **Dinner:** $7-$20   **Phone:** 941/779-2222   [71]

Seafood

DS, MC, VI.

Location: On SR 789 at SR 684. 200 Gulf Dr N 34216. **Hours:** 11:30 am-10 pm. **Closed:** 12/25. **Features:** Directly on the Gulf of Mexico, the casual restaurant lets guests enjoy great sunset views while dining on tasty seafood. Among selections are snapper, shrimp, scallops, mahi mahi and catfish dishes, as well as chicken and steak choices for landlubbers. Casual dress; cocktails. **Parking:** on-site. **Cards:** AX,

BRIDGE TENDER INN

Lunch: $5-$12   **Dinner:** $5-$30   **Phone:** 941/778-4849   [72]

American

Location: Just e of jct SR 789. 135 Bridge St 34217. **Hours:** noon-1 am. **Features:** In the historic Bridge Street District, the casual, rustic setting invites patrons to enjoy views of the waterway and, if they're lucky, a dolphin or two. Menu choices include New York strip, pasta preparations and Dijon-glazed salmon. Casual dress; cocktails. **Parking:** street. **Cards:** AX, DS, MC, VI.

BRANDON —See Tampa Bay p. 1001.

BROOKSVILLE pop. 7,264

——— WHERE TO STAY ———

BEST WESTERN BROOKSVILLE I-75   *Book at aaa.com*

Motel

12/1-4/15 [ECP]	1P: $79-$99	2P: $79-$99	XP: $10 F18
4/16-11/30 [ECP]	1P: $69-$89	2P: $69-$89	XP: $5 F18

Phone: (352)796-9481

Location: I-75, exit 301, just w on US 98/SR 50. 30307 Cortez Blvd 34602. Fax: 352/799-7595. **Facility:** 121 one-bedroom standard units. 2 stories, exterior corridors. *Bath:* combo or shower only. **Parking:** on-site. **Terms:** package plans, pets ($25 extra charge). **Amenities:** irons, hair dryers. **Pool(s):** outdoor, wading. **Leisure Activities:** exercise room. **Guest Services:** valet and coin laundry. **Business Services:** meeting rooms, business center. **Cards:** AX, DC, DS, MC, VI. *(See color ad below)*

DAYS INN HERITAGE INN   *Book at aaa.com*

Motel

12/1-4/14	1P: $74-$109	2P: $74-$109	XP: $5
4/15-11/30	1P: $64-$89	2P: $64-$89	XP: $5

Phone: (352)796-9486

Location: I-75, exit 301, just e on US 98/SR 50. 6320 Windmere Rd 34602. Fax: 352/754-8721. **Facility:** 117 one-bedroom standard units. 2 stories, exterior corridors. **Parking:** on-site. **Terms:** [ECP] meal plan available, pets ($15 fee). **Amenities:** irons, hair dryers. **Pool(s):** outdoor. **Leisure Activities:** barbecue grills, picnic area. *Fee:* game room. **Guest Services:** coin laundry. **Business Services:** meeting rooms, fax (fee). **Special Amenities:** free continental breakfast and free local telephone calls. **Cards:** AX, CB, DC, DS, MC, VI.

HAMPTON INN   *Book at aaa.com*

Motel

12/1-5/1 [ECP]	1P: $120-$165	2P: $120-$165	XP: $10 F18
5/2-11/30 [ECP]	1P: $105-$145	2P: $105-$145	XP: $10 F18

Phone: (352)796-1000

Location: I-75, exit 301, just w on US 98/SR 50. 30301 Cortez Blvd 34602. Fax: 352/796-9170. **Facility:** 75 units. 73 one- and 2 two-bedroom standard units. 2 stories, interior/exterior corridors. *Bath:* combo or shower only. **Parking:** on-site. **Amenities:** high-speed Internet, voice mail, irons, hair dryers. **Guest Services:** complimentary evening beverages: Mon-Thurs, valet laundry. **Business Services:** meeting rooms, business center. **Cards:** AX, DC, DS, MC, VI. *(See color ad below)*

—— WHERE TO DINE ——

PAPA JOE'S ITALIAN RESTAURANT Lunch: $7-$18 Dinner: $10-$18 **Phone:** 352/799-3904
♦♦ ♦♦
Italian
Location: I-75, exit 301, 4 mi w on US 98/SR 50, then just s. 6244 Spring Lake Hwy 34601. **Hours:** 11 am-9 pm, Fri & Sat-10:30 pm, Sun noon-8 pm. Closed major holidays; also 4/14 & 4/15. **Features:** This well-established local favorite offers a wide variety of homemade items. Try the seafood pasta loaded with lobster, crab, shrimp, oysters and scallops in a creamy sauce. A deli, capricci and gift shop appeal to after-dinner browsers. Casual dress; cocktails. **Parking:** on-site. **Cards:** AX, DS, MC, VI.

BUSHNELL pop. 2,050

—— WHERE TO STAY ——

BEST WESTERN GUEST HOUSE INN *Book at aaa.com* **Phone:** (352)793-5010
12/1-4/30 [ECP]	1P: $59-$99	2P: $59-$99	XP: $3	F12
5/1-11/30 [ECP]	1P: $49-$89	2P: $49-$89	XP: $3	F12

(AAA) (SAVE)
♦♦ ♦♦
Motel
Location: I-75, exit 314, just e. 2224 W Hwy 48 33513 (PO Box 847). **Fax:** 352/793-1310. **Facility:** 48 one-bedroom standard units. 2 stories, exterior corridors. **Parking:** on-site. **Terms:** weekly rates available, small pets only ($12.50 extra charge). **Amenities:** high-speed Internet, irons, hair dryers. **Pool(s):** outdoor. **Business Services:** fax (fee). **Cards:** AX, CB, DC, DS, MC, VI. **Special Amenities:** free expanded continental breakfast and early check-in/late check-out.

SOME UNITS

FEE   FEE

CYPRESS HOUSE RANCH BED & BREAKFAST **Phone:** 352/568-0909
♦♦♦♦
Bed & Breakfast
12/1-5/1	1P: $70-$100	2P: $80-$120	XP: $10	F18
5/2-11/30	1P: $65-$90	2P: $60-$100	XP: $5	F18

Location: I-75, exit 309, 2 mi n on CR 476B. Located in a rural area. 5175 CR 631 C 33513. **Fax:** 352/568-7971. **Facility:** Set on 10 acres, this log home built of cypress features rustic, country decor with modern amenities. Designated smoking area. 5 units. 3 one-bedroom standard units. 1 one- and 1 two-bedroom suites ($90-$110). 2 stories, interior/exterior corridors. *Bath:* shower only. **Parking:** on-site. **Terms:** 3 day cancellation notice-fee imposed, no pets allowed (owner's pets on premises). **Amenities:** video library, irons. **Pool(s):** outdoor. **Leisure Activities:** canoeing, bicycles, hiking trails, horseshoes. *Fee:* horseback riding. **Business Services:** meeting rooms, fax. **Cards:** AX, DS, MC, VI.

SOME UNITS
ASK ⬛ ⊗ ⊗ CTV VCR Z /🗄 🖼 /

MICROTEL INN & SUITES *Book at aaa.com* **Phone:** (352)568-2111
1/15-3/31	1P: $59-$99	2P: $59-$99	XP: $5	F18
12/1-1/14 & 4/1-11/30	1P: $49-$74	2P: $49-$74	XP: $5	F18

(AAA) (SAVE)
♦♦ ♦♦
Motel
Location: I-75, exit 314, just w. 2612 Hwy 48 33513 (PO Box 385). **Fax:** 352/568-2113. **Facility:** 69 units. 45 one-bedroom standard units. 24 one-bedroom suites ($59-$109), some with whirlpools. 3 stories, interior corridors. *Bath:* combo or shower only. **Parking:** on-site. **Amenities:** high-speed Internet, irons. *Some:* hair dryers. **Pool(s):** outdoor. **Business Services:** meeting rooms, fax. **Cards:** AX, CB, DC, DS, MC, VI. **Special Amenities:** free continental breakfast and free local telephone calls.

SOME UNITS
⬛ 🍴 ⬛ ⬛ 🚶 🐕 DATA PORT /⊗ 🗄 🖼 🖥 /

—— WHERE TO DINE ——

SONNY'S REAL PIT BAR-B-Q Lunch: $5-$18 Dinner: $5-$18 **Phone:** 352/569-0200
♦♦ ♦♦
Barbecue
Location: I-75, exit 314, just w. 2684 W CR 48 33513. **Hours:** 11 am-9:30 pm. Closed: 12/25. **Features:** Around since 1968, the restaurant prepares outstanding barbecue, including dinner plates, combination platters and mouthwatering baby back ribs. It's hard to go wrong with any of the choices. The extensive salad bar lines up all types of fresh fruits, vegetables, soups and fixings. Casual dress. **Parking:** on-site. **Cards:** MC, VI.

⬛

CALLAWAY pop. 14,233

—— WHERE TO DINE ——

LARRY'S REAL PIT BAR-B-Q Lunch: $5-$10 Dinner: $5-$10 **Phone:** 850/522-9600
♦♦ ♦♦
American
Location: 1.8 mi e of jct US 98 and Transmitter Rd. 532 N Tyndall Pkwy 32404. **Hours:** 10:30 am-9 pm, Sun-9:30 pm. Closed: 12/25. **Features:** Slow-cooked barbecue is the focus of the menu. Pulled pork is tasty, and dishes can be wrapped to go for diners in a hurry. Casual dress; beer only. **Parking:** on-site. **Cards:** AX, DS, MC, VI.

CAPE CANAVERAL pop. 8,829

——— WHERE TO STAY ———

CAPE WINDS RESORT
Phone: 321/783-6226

(AAA) SAVE

◆◆◆◆◆

Condominium

All Year   1P: $160-$190   2P: $160-$190   XP: $12   F14
Location: Jct SR 520, 1.8 mi n on SR A1A, 0.3 mi e via Taylor Ave. 7400 Ridgewood Ave 32920. Fax: 321/799-2676. **Facility:** The hotel's apartment-style guest units have two bathrooms. 44 units. 17 one- and 27 two-bedroom suites ($160-$190) with kitchens. 5 stories, exterior corridors. **Parking:** on-site. **Terms:** office hours 8:30 am-5:30 pm, 5 night minimum stay, 14 day cancellation notice, weekly rates available. **Amenities:** high-speed Internet, voice mail, irons, hair dryers. *Some:* DVD players. **Pool(s):** heated outdoor. **Leisure Activities:** sauna, whirlpool, 2 lighted tennis courts, basketball. **Guest Services:** coin laundry. **Cards:** AX, CB, DC, DS, JC, MC, VI.

SOME UNITS

🏊 ⊗ VCR DATA/PORT 🖨 📺 💻 / ⊗ /

COUNTRY INN & SUITES, CAPE CANAVERAL
Phone: 321/784-8500

(fyi)

Small-scale Hotel

2/3-11/30   1P: $139-$199
12/1-2/2   1P: $119-$159
Too new to rate. **Location:** SR 528 E, exit 26 to Astronaut Blvd. 9009 Astronaut Blvd 32920. **Amenities:** 156 units, pets, coffeemakers, microwaves, refrigerators, pool. **Terms:** 10 day cancellation notice. **Cards:** AX, DC, DS, MC, VI.

RADISSON RESORT AT THE PORT   *Book at aaa.com*
Phone: (321)784-0000

◆◆◆

Small-scale Hotel

Bath: combo or shower only.

1/31-4/22   1P: $129-$199   2P: $129-$199
12/1-1/30 & 4/23-11/30   1P: $119-$179   2P: $119-$179
Location: SR A1A. 8701 Astronaut Blvd 32920. Fax: 321/784-3737. **Facility:** 284 units. 212 one-bedroom standard units. 72 one-bedroom suites ($149-$219) with whirlpools. 2-3 stories, interior/exterior corridors. **Parking:** on-site. **Terms:** cancellation fee imposed, [BP] meal plan available, package plans. **Amenities:** voice mail, irons, hair dryers. *Some:* dual phone lines. **Pool(s):** heated outdoor, wading. **Leisure Activities:** whirlpool, lighted tennis court, exercise room. **Fee:** game room. **Guest Services:** gift shop, valet and coin laundry, area transportation. **Business Services:** conference facilities, business center. **Cards:** AX, CB, DC, DS, JC, MC, VI. *(See color ad p 280)*

SOME UNITS

(ASK) (SD) 🍴 🍸 (&M) 🛗 📶 🏊 ⊗ 🎥 DATA/PORT 💻 / ⊗ 🖨 📺 🍽

RON JON CAPE CARIBE RESORT
Phone: (321)799-4900

(AAA) SAVE

◆◆◆◆

Resort Condominium

All Year   1P: $120-$525   2P: $120-$525
Location: SR 528 (Bee Line Expwy) to "Cruise Terminal B" exit, 1.2 mi e on George King Blvd. 1000 Shorewood Dr 32920. Fax: 321/784-3949. **Facility:** Convenient to the port of Cape Canaveral, this resort has ample facilities on site; beach access is a few feet away. Smoke free premises. 206 units. 55 one-bedroom standard units with whirlpools. 53 one- and 98 two-bedroom suites with kitchens, some with whirlpools. 1-5 stories, exterior corridors. *Bath:* combo or shower only. **Parking:** on-site. **Terms:** check-in 4 pm, 2-3 night minimum stay - seasonal and/or weekends, 3 day cancellation notice-fee imposed. **Amenities:** voice mail, irons, hair dryers. **Dining:** 11 am-9 pm, cocktails. **Pool(s):** heated outdoor, 2 wading. **Leisure Activities:** whirlpool, waterslide, miniature golf, 2 lighted tennis courts, recreation programs in summer, children's play center, lazy river, movie theatre, picnic area, water park, board games, jogging, exercise room, basketball, shuffleboard. **Fee:** massage, game room. **Guest Services:** gift shop, coin laundry. **Business Services:** business center. **Cards:** AX, DC, DS, MC, VI. *(See color ad below)*

🛗 🍴 (&) 🏊 ⊗ ⊗ 🎥 DATA/PORT 🖨 📺 💻

ROYAL MANSIONS CONDOMINIUM RESORT   *Book at aaa.com*
Phone: (321)784-8484

(AAA) SAVE

◆◆◆

Condominium

All Year Wkly   1P: $999-$1559   2P: $999-$1559
Location: Jct SR 520, 2.8 mi n on SR A1A, then 1 mi e via Central Blvd. 8600 Ridgewood Ave 32920. Fax: 321/799-2907. **Facility:** On the ocean, the condo is designed and furnished in a French-Caribbean style. Smoke free premises. 107 units. 71 one- and 36 two-bedroom suites ($999-$1559) with kitchens. 3 stories (no elevator), exterior corridors. **Parking:** on-site. **Terms:** office hours 8:30 am-6 pm, 7 night minimum stay, 7 day cancellation notice, [CP] meal plan available. **Amenities:** DVD players, voice mail, safes (fee), irons, hair dryers. **Pool(s):** heated outdoor. **Leisure Activities:** whirlpool, basketball. **Guest Services:** complimentary evening beverages, valet and coin laundry. **Business Services:** fax (fee). **Cards:** AX, DC, DS, MC, VI.

SOME UNITS

(SD) (&) 🏊 ⊗ 🎥 🖨 📺 💻 / DATA/PORT /

—————— WHERE TO DINE ——————

KELSEY'S PIZZERIA

Italian

Lunch: $4-$15   **Dinner:** $4-$15   **Phone:** 321/783-9191

Location: On SR A1A. 8699 Astronaut Blvd 32920. **Hours:** 11 am-9:30 pm, Sun from 4 pm. Closed: 4/16, 11/23, 12/25. **Features:** The menu mixes Italian and Greek items, including such choices as meat lovers' pizza and chicken souvlaki. For those in a hurry, express lunch is offered from 11 am to 2 pm. Casual dress; beer & wine only. **Parking:** on-site. **Cards:** AX, MC, VI.

ZACHARY'S FAMILY RESTAURANT

Greek

Lunch: $4-$20   **Dinner:** $8-$20   **Phone:** 321/784-9007

Location: On SR A1A. 8799 Astronaut Blvd 32920. **Hours:** 6 am-10 pm, Sat from 7 am, Sun 7 am-3 pm. Closed: 11/23, 12/25. **Reservations:** accepted. **Features:** A combination of Greek and American cuisine inspired the eclectic menu of traditional favorites. Succulent leg of lamb and breaded veal parmigiana are among menu items. Casual dress; beer & wine only. **Parking:** on-site. **Cards:** AX, DC, DS, MC, VI.

CAPE CORAL pop. 102,286 (See map and index starting on p. 428)

—————— WHERE TO STAY ——————

CASA LOMA MOTEL ON THE WATERFRONT

Motel

Phone: 239/549-6000   **33**

1/15-4/5	1P: $125-$175	2P: $135-$185	XP: $10
12/1-1/14	1P: $100-$150	2P: $110-$160	XP: $10
4/6-5/31	1P: $90-$150	2P: $90-$150	XP: $10
6/1-11/30	1P: $70-$85	2P: $70-$85	XP: $10

Location: 1.5 mi n of jct Cape Coral Pkwy. 3608 Del Prado Blvd 33904. **Fax:** 239/549-4877. **Facility:** Designated smoking area. 49 one-bedroom standard units with efficiencies. 2 stories (no elevator), interior/exterior corridors. *Bath:* combo or shower only. **Parking:** on-site. **Terms:** 15 day cancellation notice-fee imposed, weekly rates available, package plans. **Amenities:** irons, hair dryers. **Pool(s):** heated outdoor. **Leisure Activities:** boat dock, fishing, sun deck, exercise room. **Guest Services:** coin laundry. **Business Services:** fax (fee). **Cards:** AX, DS, MC, VI.

SOME UNITS

DOCKSIDE INN

Motel

Phone: (239)542-0061   **34**

12/16-4/15	1P: $115-$145	2P: $125-$155	XP: $10	D12
4/16-11/30	1P: $85-$115	2P: $95-$125	XP: $10	D12
12/1-12/15	1P: $75-$95	2P: $85-$105	XP: $10	D12

Location: 1.2 mi n of jct Cape Coral Pkwy. 3817 Del Prado Blvd 33904. **Fax:** 239/542-3678. **Facility:** 15 one-bedroom suites with kitchens. 2 stories (no elevator), exterior corridors. **Parking:** on-site. **Terms:** office hours 9 am-8 pm, 7 day cancellation notice, pets ($20 fee). **Amenities:** voice mail, irons, hair dryers. **Pool(s):** heated outdoor. **Leisure Activities:** boat dock, fishing, boat slips, gas grills, picnic area. **Guest Services:** coin laundry. **Cards:** AX, DS, MC, VI. **Special Amenities:** free local telephone calls.

SOME UNITS

FEE   FEE

HAMPTON INN & SUITES

fyi

Small-scale Hotel

Phone: 239/540-1050

Under construction, scheduled to open January 2006. **Location:** 619 SE 47th Terrace 33904-8520. **Fax:** 239/598-5300. **Planned Amenities:** coffeemakers, microwaves, pool.

MALAGA RESORT MOTEL

Motel

Phone: 239/542-3464   **35**

12/1-4/15 Wkly		2P: $455-$700	XP: $10
4/16-11/30 Wkly		2P: $260-$400	XP: $10

Location: I-75, exit 136, just e of jct Del Prado Blvd. 1721 SE 46th Ln 33904. **Fax:** 239/542-5294. **Facility:** 22 units. 21 one- and 1 two-bedroom standard units, some with efficiencies or kitchens. 2 stories (no elevator), exterior corridors. **Parking:** on-site. **Terms:** office hours 7 am-10 pm, 30 day cancellation notice, in season-fee imposed, daily rates available. **Amenities:** *Some:* irons, hair dryers. **Pool(s):** heated outdoor. **Leisure Activities:** fishing, badminton, gas grills, picnic area, shuffleboard, volleyball. *Fee:* boat dock. **Guest Services:** coin laundry. **Cards:** DS, MC, VI. **Special Amenities:** free local telephone calls and preferred room (subject to availability with advance reservations).

QUALITY HOTEL

Small-scale Hotel

Book at aaa.com

Phone: (239)542-2121   **36**

1/1-4/21	1P: $95-$125	2P: $105-$135	XP: $10	F18
12/1-12/31	1P: $90-$110	2P: $100-$130	XP: $10	F18
4/22-11/30	1P: $75-$115	2P: $80-$125	XP: $10	F18

Location: Jct Del Prado Blvd. 1538 Cape Coral Pkwy 33904. **Fax:** 239/542-6319. **Facility:** 142 one-bedroom standard units. 5 stories, interior corridors. *Bath:* combo or shower only. **Parking:** on-site. **Terms:** check-in 4 pm, pets ($8 extra charge, 1st floor units). **Amenities:** high-speed Internet, voice mail, irons, hair dryers. **Pool(s):** heated outdoor. **Leisure Activities:** exercise room. **Guest Services:** valet and coin laundry. **Business Services:** meeting rooms, fax (fee). **Cards:** AX, CB, DC, DS, JC, MC, VI.

SOME UNITS

FEE   FEE

—————— WHERE TO DINE ——————

ARIANI NORTHERN ITALIAN GRILL

Northern Italian

Dinner: $15-$25   **Phone:** 239/772-8000   **16**

Location: I-75, exit 143, just e of Del Prado Blvd; in Del Prado Mall. 1529 SE 15th Terrace 33990. **Hours:** 5 pm-10 pm. Closed: 4/16, 12/25; also Mother's Day. **Reservations:** suggested. **Features:** Specializing in northern Italian cuisine, the restaurant has a casually elegant dining room attended by thoughtful, well-attired servers. Many fresh pasta dishes are available, as are grilled and roasted meats and fresh seafood. Among favorite choices are lambuco, veal scallopini, salmon, tuna, pork medallions Florentine and chicken breast prepared in varied ways: alla Riveria, Marsala mushroom, pizzaiola, Milanese or alla parmigiana. Casual dress; cocktails. **Parking:** on-site. **Cards:** AX, MC, VI.

(See map and index starting on p. 428)

BRIGANDS STEAK & SEAFOOD GRILL **Lunch:** $5-$9 **Dinner:** $13-$24 **Phone:** 239/540-4665 [18]

Steak & Seafood

Location: In Cay West Pavilion. 1708 Cape Coral Pkwy W 33914. **Hours:** 11 am-10 pm, Sun noon-9 pm. Closed: 1/1, 12/25. **Features:** This clean dining room with a nautical decor is tucked away in a small shopping mall. The menu features grilled, fried, broiled or blackened seafood, and other specialties like prime rib and chicken. Love spicy food? Try the Jamaican jerk chicken. Casual dress; cocktails. **Parking:** on-site.
Cards: AX, MC, VI.

BUBBA'S ROADHOUSE & SALOON **Lunch:** $6-$10 **Dinner:** $9-$30 **Phone:** 239/282-5520

American

Location: 0.6 mi w of jct Chiquita Blvd. 2121 SW Pine Island Rd 33991. **Hours:** 11:30 am-10 pm, Fri & Sat-11 pm. Closed: 11/23, 12/25. **Reservations:** accepted. **Features:** As the name says, the restaurant nurtures a rustic roadhouse mood. Patrons can try some good finger foods, as well as soups, salads and sandwich platters. Casual dress; cocktails. **Parking:** on-site. **Cards:** AX, DS, MC, VI.

IGUANA MIA **Lunch:** $7-$12 **Dinner:** $12-$15 **Phone:** 239/945-7755 [17]

Mexican

Location: Cape Coral Pkwy, just e of jct SE 10th Pl (Leonard St). 1027 E Cape Coral Pkwy 33904. **Hours:** 11 am-10 pm. Closed: 7/4, 11/23, 12/25. **Features:** Hop into this lively, yet simple, cantina, where you'll find a good variety of standard favorites such as sour cream chicken, fajitas and beef burritos with black beans. Frozen margaritas and fried ice cream cool the jalapeno-heated palate. Casual dress; cocktails. **Parking:** on-site.
Cards: AX, DS, MC, VI.

MORETTI'S SEAFOOD RESTAURANT **Lunch:** $8-$10 **Dinner:** $11-$23 **Phone:** 239/283-5825

Seafood

Location: On SR 78, 1.5 mi w of Tamiami Trail. 4200 Pine Island Rd NW 33993. **Hours:** 11 am-9 pm. Closed major holidays. **Features:** A terrific spot for casual dining and good food. The seafood is wonderful and fresh, the staff is accommodating and knowledgeable and the ambiance casual and nautical. Casual dress; cocktails. **Parking:** on-site. **Cards:** AX, MC, VI.

RUM RUNNERS **Lunch:** $6-$12 **Dinner:** $7-$20 **Phone:** 239/542-0200 [19]

American

Location: 3 mi s from Cape Coral Pkwy W. 5848 Cape Harbour Dr 33914. **Hours:** 11:30 am-3 & 5-9 pm. **Reservations:** accepted. **Features:** The upbeat atmosphere invites you to dine at your leisure; seafood specialties are abundant and the lounge is lively. Dressy casual; cocktails. **Parking:** on-site. **Cards:** AX, DS, MC, VI.

CAPE HAZE

——— WHERE TO STAY ———

COLONY DON PEDRO **Phone:** 941/697-2192

Condominium

Property failed to provide current rates

Location: On Don Pedro Island, access by car ferry from Island Transit Ferry terminal, just w of CR 775. Located in a remote area. 40 S Gulf Blvd 34224 (7025 Placida Rd #A, ENGLEWOOD). Fax: 941/697-8441. **Facility:** Located on an island, the hotel is reachable by ferry. 34 units. 27 two-bedroom suites with kitchens. 7 vacation homes. 2 stories (no elevator), exterior corridors. **Parking:** on-site. **Terms:** office hours 8:30 am-5 pm. **Amenities:** video library, irons. Some: DVD players, CD players. **Pool(s):** 2 heated outdoor. **Leisure Activities:** boat dock, fishing, 2 lighted tennis courts, rental bicycles. **Guest Services:** complimentary laundry. **Business Services:** fax.

PALM ISLAND RESORT **Phone:** (941)697-4800

Resort
Condominium

All Year 2P: $145-$695 XP: $20 F6

Location: Jct CR 771/775/776, 5 mi s to Panama Blvd, just w to Ferry Landing (Gulf Blvd), then 1.1 mi w. 7092 Placida Rd 33946. Fax: 941/697-0696. **Facility:** The resort's spacious, one- to three-bedroom condominium villas on Palm Island can be reached by car ferry from 7 am to 10 pm. 92 units. 30 one-, 44 two- and 15 three-bedroom suites with kitchens. 3 vacation homes. 2-3 stories (no elevator), exterior corridors. **Parking:** on-site. **Terms:** office hours 8 am-6 pm, 2 night minimum stay, 14 day cancellation notice-fee imposed, weekly rates available. **Amenities:** video library (fee), irons, hair dryers. **Dining:** 8:30 am-9 pm, Fri & Sat-9:30 pm, cocktails, entertainment. **Pool(s):** 5 heated outdoor. **Leisure Activities:** whirlpools, rental boats, fishing, 11 tennis courts, recreation programs, rental bicycles, playground, exercise room. Fee: canoes, marina, charter fishing, kayaks, water aerobics, golf carts, tennis instruction, nature tours, fitness training, massage. **Guest Services:** gift shop, complimentary laundry. **Business Services:** meeting rooms, fax (fee). **Cards:** AX, DS, MC, VI. **Special Amenities:** free local telephone calls.

——— WHERE TO DINE ———

JAM'S OF CAPE HAZE **Dinner:** $13-$26 **Phone:** 941/697-2080

Italian

Location: 0.6 mi n on CR 775; in Cape Haze Plaza. 8501 Placida Rd 33946. **Hours:** Open 12/1-7/1 & 8/1-11/30; 4 pm-9:30 pm. Closed: 11/23, 12/25. **Reservations:** suggested. **Features:** The restaurant offers a good selection of Italian and American dishes, as well as sandwiches and pizza. Dressy casual; cocktails. **Parking:** on-site. **Cards:** AX, DS, MC, VI.

CAPTIVA pop. 379 (See map and index starting on p. 428)

——— WHERE TO STAY ———

SOUTH SEAS RESORT & YACHT HARBOR   *Book at aaa.com*   **Phone:** (239)472-1400   **39**

AAA SAVE
▽▽▽▽▽
Resort
Condominium

2/10-4/22	1P: $389-$1299
1/1-2/9	1P: $309-$1299
4/23-5/28	1P: $269-$1299
5/29-11/30	1P: $249-$1299

Location: At north tip of Captiva Island. 5400 South Seas Plantation Rd 33924 (PO Box 194). Fax: 239/472-6518. **Facility:** On a secluded site adjoining the gulf and bay, this extensive property offers a variety of room types. 587 units. 105 one-bedroom standard units. 146 one-, 245 two- and 70 three-bedroom suites. 21 vacation homes. 1-3 stories, exterior corridors. *Bath:* combo or shower only. **Parking:** on-site. **Terms:** open 1/1-11/30, check-in 4 pm, 14 day cancellation notice-fee imposed, package plans, $8 service charge. **Amenities:** voice mail, safes, irons, hair dryers. **Dining:** 4 restaurants, 7:30 am-10 pm; 18% service charge, cocktails, also, Chadwick's Restaurant, see separate listing, nightclub, entertainment. **Pool(s):** 18 heated outdoor. **Leisure Activities:** saunas, whirlpools, rental boats, fishing, recreation programs, aerobic & aqua exercise instruction, jogging, playground, shuffleboard. *Fee:* canoes, sailboats, marina, aqua bikes, fishing guides, parasailing, personal watercraft, sailing school & instruction, shelling charters, golf-9 holes, 18 tennis courts (5 lighted), sun cats, fishing equipment, sightseeing cruises, bicycles, massage, game room. **Guest Services:** gift shop, valet and coin laundry, area transportation-within resort, beauty salon. **Business Services:** conference facilities, business center. **Cards:** AX, CB, DC, DS, MC, VI. **Special Amenities:** free local telephone calls and free newspaper. *(See color ad below)*

SOME UNITS

[icons]

WHO SAYS THE BEST THINGS COME IN SMALL PACKAGES?

South Seas Resort & Yacht Harbour

Captiva Island, Florida

www.south-seas-resort.com

GET READY TO BE CAPTIVATED

(See map and index starting on p. 428)

——— WHERE TO DINE ———

THE BUBBLE ROOM RESTAURANT   Lunch: $8-$10   Dinner: $19-$29   Phone: 239/472-5558   26
American
Location: Jct Andy Rosse Ln. 15001 Captiva Dr 33924. **Hours:** 11:30 am-3 & 4:30-9 pm, Fri & Sat-9:30 pm. Closed: 12/25. **Reservations:** not accepted. **Features:** The decor is a whimsical mix of Christmas, nostalgia, '30s and '40s memorabilia and Hollywood. Friendly servers efficiently manage their tables. The menu features steak, fresh fish and thick cut prime rib. Portions are generous and the desserts are not to be ignored. Casual dress; cocktails. **Parking:** on-site. **Cards:** AX, DC, DS, MC, VI.

CHADWICK'S RESTAURANT   Lunch: $7-$14   Dinner: $19-$27   Phone: 239/472-7575   22
Seafood
Location: At north tip of Captiva Island; in South Seas Resort & Yacht Harbor. 5400 South Seas Plantation Rd 33924. **Hours:** 11 am-2 & 5:30-9:30 pm; Sunday brunch 10 am-2 pm. **Reservations:** suggested, 2/1-4/30. **Features:** Located at the entrance to the South Seas Resort, it features an extensive themed dinner buffet and a lovely brunch on Sundays. A limited standard menu is also available. Please note the 18% service charge added to each bill. Casual dress; cocktails; entertainment. **Parking:** on-site. **Cards:** AX, CB, DC, DS, MC, VI.

THE GREEN FLASH   Lunch: $5-$15   Dinner: $14-$28   Phone: 239/472-3337   29
American
Location: Jct Murmond Ln. 15183 Captiva Dr 33924. **Hours:** 11:30 am-3:30 & 5:30-9:30 pm. Closed: 12/25. **Reservations:** required, for dinner. **Features:** Directly on the water, this restaurant treats diners to sightings of Pine Island Sound's wildlife and offers such preparations as fettuccine Alfredo, steamed shrimp and the popular surf and turf dish. Dressy casual; cocktails. **Parking:** on-site. **Cards:** AX, DS, MC, VI.

KEYLIME BISTRO   Lunch: $6-$12   Dinner: $22-$34   Phone: 239/395-4000   28
American
Location: Jct Captiva Rd. 11509 Andy Rosse Ln 33924. **Hours:** 8 am-10 pm. **Features:** Known for its seafood, sushi, pasta and prime rib, the cozy restaurant in historic Captiva Village serves breakfast, lunch and dinner. Casual dress; cocktails. **Parking:** on-site. **Cards:** AX, DC, DS, MC, VI.

MAMA ROSA'S PIZZERIA   Lunch: $7-$19   Dinner: $7-$19   Phone: 239/472-7672   23
Pizza
Location: At north tip of Captiva Island; in Chadwick's Square. 402 Captiva Rd 33924. **Hours:** 11 am-7 pm. **Features:** The pizzeria is popular for its Italian fare, which includes anything from vegetable pizza to antipasto to hot and cold submarine sandwiches. Casual dress. **Parking:** on-site. **Cards:** MC, VI.

THE MUCKY DUCK   Lunch: $4-$16   Dinner: $17-$37   Phone: 239/472-3434   25
Seafood
Location: Just w of jct Captiva Rd. 11546 Andy Rosse Ln 33924. **Hours:** 11:30 am-3 & 5-9:30 pm, Sun-3 pm. Closed: 4/16, 11/23, 12/25. **Reservations:** not accepted. **Features:** Established in 1976, the restaurant is popular on the island for watching gorgeous sunsets or listening to local musicians while waiting to dine on fabulous food. Patrons should get here early to minimize their wait for a table. Although seafood is always a favorite choice, many diners opt for a beef or poultry dish. Casual dress; cocktails; entertainment. **Parking:** on-site. **Cards:** AX, DS, MC, VI.

OLD CAPTIVA HOUSE   Lunch: $18-$34   Dinner: $18-$34   Phone: 239/472-5161   30
American
Location: 2 mi n of jct Blind Pass. 15951 Captiva Rd 33924. **Hours:** 7:30 am-11 & 5:30-10 pm. **Features:** Guests can step into a bit of history via the surroundings of the popular restaurant, known for its Continental cuisine. Dressy casual; cocktails. **Parking:** on-site. **Cards:** MC, VI.

R C OTTER'S ISLAND EATS   Lunch: $6-$15   Dinner: $8-$25   Phone: 239/395-1142   27
American
Location: Jct Captiva Rd. 11506 Andy Ross Ln 33924. **Hours:** 8 am-9 pm. **Features:** In historic Captiva Village, the popular spot welcomes patrons for breakfast, lunch and dinner. Fresh seafood and steaks share menu space with chops and creative pasta dishes. Casual dress. **Parking:** on-site. **Cards:** AX, DC, DS, MC, VI.

REDFISH BLUFISH   Lunch: $8-$13   Dinner: $9-$13   Phone: 239/472-1956   24
Continental
Location: Just w of Andy Rosse Ln; jct Wightman Ln; in Captiva Village Square. 14970 Captiva Dr 33924. **Hours:** 11 am-3 & 6-9:30 pm, Sun-3 pm. Closed: Mon. **Features:** In the heart of historic Captiva, the dining spot serves preparations of French cuisine ranging from steaks to seafood to pasta dishes. Casual dress; cocktails. **Parking:** on-site. **Cards:** DS, MC, VI.

CARRABELLE pop. 1,303

——— WHERE TO STAY ———

THE MOORINGS AT CARRABELLE   Phone: 850/697-2800
Small-scale Hotel
3/1-9/30	2P: $125-$175	XP: $15	F12
12/1-2/28 & 10/1-11/30	2P: $100-$150	XP: $15	F12

Location: On US 98, just e of bridge. 1000 US 98 32322 (PO Box M). Fax: 850/697-3950. **Facility:** 22 units. 21 one- and 1 two-bedroom standard units. 2 stories, exterior corridors. **Parking:** on-site. **Terms:** weekly rates available, pets ($50 deposit, $10 extra charge). **Amenities:** high-speed Internet. **Pool(s):** outdoor. **Leisure Activities:** marina, fishing. **Fee:** scuba diving, charter fishing. **Guest Services:** coin laundry. **Business Services:** meeting rooms, fax (fee). **Cards:** AX, DS, MC, VI.

SOME UNITS

CASSELBERRY —See Orlando p. 748.

CEDAR KEY pop. 790

——— WHERE TO STAY ———

DOCKSIDE MOTEL
Phone: 352/543-5432

(AAA) (SAVE)
All Year   1P: $67-$87   2P: $67-$87   XP: $5   F
Location: SR 24, just w on Front St to Dock St, then just w. Located adjacent to public marina and fishing pier. 491 Dock St 32625 (PO Box 55). **Facility:** 10 one-bedroom standard units. 2 stories, interior corridors. **Parking:** street. **Business Services:** fax.

Motel

ISLAND PLACE OF CEDAR KEY
Phone: 352/543-5307

2/1-7/31	1P: $115-$185	2P: $115-$185	XP: $6	F5
8/1-11/30	1P: $100-$175	2P: $100-$175	XP: $6	F5
12/1-1/31	1P: $95-$165	2P: $95-$165	XP: $6	F5

Condominium
Location: On SR 24. 550 First St 32625 (PO Box 687). Fax: 352/543-9141. **Facility:** Enjoy all the comforts of home in these nicely appointed gulf-front condominiums with full-size living room, kitchen and balcony. 30 units. 27 one- and 3 two-bedroom standard units with kitchens. 3 stories (no elevator), exterior corridors. **Parking:** on-site. **Terms:** 2 night minimum stay - weekends, 3 day cancellation notice-fee imposed, weekly rates available, package plans. **Amenities:** voice mail. **Pool(s):** outdoor. **Leisure Activities:** whirlpool. **Guest Services:** complimentary laundry. **Business Services:** business center. **Cards:** AX, DS, MC, VI.

SOME UNITS

NATURE'S LANDING CONDOMINIUMS
Phone: 352/543-9161

All Year   1P: $120-$170   2P: $120-$170
Location: 0.5 mi e of downtown. 7041 Depot & 3rd St 32625 (PO Box 697). Fax: 352/543-6119. **Facility:** These 1- and 2- bedroom condominiums are situated on historical old railroad property overlooking the back bayou
Condominium
area of Cedar Key. Designated smoking area. 26 units. 14 one- and 12 two-bedroom standard units with kitchens. 3 stories, exterior corridors. **Parking:** on-site. **Terms:** office hours 9:30 am-6 pm, 2 night minimum stay - weekends, 3 day cancellation notice-fee imposed, package plans. **Amenities:** DVD players. **Pool(s):** heated outdoor. **Leisure Activities:** whirlpool. **Guest Services:** complimentary laundry. **Cards:** AX, MC, VI.

PARK PLACE MOTEL & CONDOMINIUMS
Phone: 352/543-5737

(AAA) (SAVE)
2/1-5/31	1P: $70-$100	2P: $70-$100	XP: $5	F13
12/1-1/31 & 6/1-11/30	1P: $65-$85	2P: $65-$85	XP: $5	F13

Location: At A St. 211 2nd St 32625 (PO Box 613). Fax: 352/543-8011. **Facility:** 30 units. 22 one-bedroom standard units with efficiencies. 8 one-bedroom suites with efficiencies. 3 stories (no elevator), exterior corridors. **Parking:** on-site. **Terms:** 2 night minimum stay - seasonal and/or weekends, small pets only ($7 extra charge). **Amenities:** voice mail. **Leisure Activities:** gazebo with grill. **Business Services:** fax.
Motel
Cards: AX, DS, MC, VI. **Special Amenities:** free local telephone calls.

SOME UNITS

FEE   FEE

SEAHORSE LANDING CONDOMINIUMS
Phone: 352/543-5860

(AAA) (SAVE)
All Year   1P: $150-$165   2P: $150-$165
Location: Just w on 6th St. 4050 G St 32625. Fax: 352/543-5861. **Facility:** These attractive gulf-front condominiums with Florida style decor offer full-length balconies for lounging. 13 two-bedroom standard units with kitchens. 2 stories, exterior corridors. **Parking:** on-site. **Terms:** check-in 4 pm, 2 night minimum
Condominium
stay, weekly rates available, pets ($15-$20 extra charge, in designated units). **Amenities:** irons. **Pool(s):** outdoor. **Leisure Activities:** whirlpool, boat dock, fishing, barbecue grill. **Guest Services:** complimentary laundry. **Business Services:** meeting rooms, fax. **Cards:** AX, DS, MC, VI. **Special Amenities:** free local telephone calls and free newspaper.

FEE

——— WHERE TO DINE ———

ISLAND HOTEL & RESTAURANT
Lunch: $7-$12   **Dinner:** $18-$26   Phone: 352/543-5111
Location: Center. 373 2nd St 32625. **Hours:** 6 pm-9 pm, Sat & Sun also 11:30 am-2 pm. Closed: Mon. **Features:** On the National Register of Historic Places, the hotel features a quaint, full-service lounge with beers from around the world and a "special occasion" dining room. Fresh seafood, including seasonal
American
Florida rock lobster, Cedar Key oysters and stone crab. Shrimp and grouper are specialties. Lamb, pork, chicken, Angus beef and a few vegetarian dishes round out the menu. Casual dress; cocktails. **Parking:** on-site. **Cards:** MC, VI.

THE ISLAND ROOM AT CEDAR COVE
Lunch: $8-$9   **Dinner:** $11-$28   Phone: 352/543-6520

(AAA)
Location: At Cedar Cove Beach and Yacht Club. 192 2nd St 32625. **Hours:** 5 pm-10 pm, Sat from 2 pm, Sun 11 am-9 pm. Closed: 12/25. **Reservations:** suggested. **Features:** Adjacent to the public beach and overlooking the bay to the south, the dining room is on the ground floor of Cedar Cove condominiums. The
Seafood
menu leans toward fish, but preparations are multiregional. Pasta can be ordered Alfredo, primavera, or marinara, and grouper is particularly good cooked Cajun-style. Crab cakes, oysters, shrimp, lamb, chicken, Angus beef and surf 'n' turf are all featured. Desserts include a Key lime tart, New Orleans bread pudding and creme brulee. Casual dress; cocktails. **Parking:** on-site. **Cards:** AX, DS, MC, VI.

CELEBRATION —See Orlando p. 749.

CHARLOTTE HARBOR pop. 3,647

——— WHERE TO STAY ———

BANANA BAY WATERFRONT MOTEL   **Phone:** (941)743-4441

◈   1/1-3/31 Wkly   1P: $550-$850   XP: $8
        12/1-12/31 & 11/1-11/30 Wkly   1P: $450-$675   XP: $8
Motel   4/1-10/31 Wkly   1P: $450-$660   XP: $8

Location: Jct US 41. 23285 Bayshore Rd 33980. Fax: 941/743-4172. **Facility:** 16 one-bedroom standard units, some with efficiencies. 1-2 stories, exterior corridors. *Bath:* shower only. **Parking:** on-site. **Terms:** office hours 9 am-9 pm, small pets only ($4 extra charge). **Amenities:** high-speed Internet. *Some:* irons, hair dryers. **Leisure Activities:** boat dock, fishing, shuffleboard. *Fee:* paddleboats. **Guest Services:** coin laundry. **Business Services:** fax (fee). **Cards:** AX, DS, MC, VI.

SOME UNITS

CHIEFLAND pop. 1,993

——— WHERE TO STAY ———

BEST WESTERN SUWANNEE VALLEY INN   *Book at aaa.com*   **Phone:** (352)493-0663

Ⓐ Ⓢ𝖠𝖵𝖤   All Year [CP]   1P: $60-$75   2P: $70-$85   XP: $10   F16

Location: On US 19/98, just n of jct US 129. 1125 N Young Blvd 32626. Fax: 352/493-0663. **Facility:** 60 one-bedroom standard units. 2 stories, exterior corridors. **Parking:** on-site. **Terms:** small pets only ($10 extra charge). **Amenities:** irons, hair dryers. **Pool(s):** outdoor. **Guest Services:** coin laundry. **Business**
Small-scale Hotel **Services:** meeting rooms, fax (fee). **Cards:** AX, DC, DS, MC, VI. **Special Amenities:** free continental breakfast and free local telephone calls.

SOME UNITS

HOLIDAY INN EXPRESS   *Book at aaa.com*   **Phone:** 352/493-9400

◈◈◈   Property failed to provide current rates
Small-scale Hotel   **Location:** US 19/98, 1.5 mi n of jct US 129. 809 NW 21st Ave 32626 (PO Box 789, 32644-0789). Fax: 352/493-4050. **Facility:** 66 one-bedroom standard units. 2 stories, exterior corridors. *Bath:* combo or shower only. **Parking:** on-site. **Terms:** pets ($10 extra charge). **Amenities:** irons, hair dryers. **Pool(s):** outdoor. **Leisure Activities:** whirlpool. **Guest Services:** coin laundry. **Business Services:** meeting rooms, fax (fee).

SOME UNITS

——— WHERE TO DINE ———

BAR-B-Q BILL'S   **Lunch:** $4-$10   **Dinner:** $4-$15   **Phone:** 352/493-4444

◈   **Location:** On US 19 at NW 19th Ave. 1901 N Young Blvd 32626. **Hours:** 7 am-10 & 11-9 pm, Fri & Sat-10 pm. Closed: 11/23, 12/25. **Reservations:** not accepted. **Features:** Under oak trees in the middle of a
American   commercial area, the eatery serves succulent barbecue beef, chicken, pork and turkey. A salad bar with several hot items is also an option. Barbecue meats can be ordered by the pound or as a sandwich or plate. Also on the menu are fried fish, fried or grilled chicken, soup, chili and even hot dogs and knockwurst. Service is casual and folksy, and it seems everybody knows everybody. Casual dress; beer only. **Parking:** on-site. **Cards:** DS, MC, VI.

CHIPLEY pop. 3,592

——— WHERE TO STAY ———

SUPER 8 MOTEL   *Book at aaa.com*   **Phone:** 850/638-8530

◈◈◈   All Year   1P: $59-$74   2P: $59-$74   XP: $5   F12

Motel   **Location:** I-10, exit 120, just n. 1150 Motel Dr 32428. Fax: 850/638-9895. **Facility:** 40 one-bedroom standard units. 1 story, exterior corridors. **Parking:** on-site. **Terms:** package plans, small pets only ($5 extra charge). **Business Services:** fax (fee). **Cards:** AX, DC, DS, MC, VI.

SOME UNITS

——— WHERE TO DINE ———

CANCUN'S MEXICAN GRILL   **Lunch:** $4-$8   **Dinner:** $5-$10   **Phone:** 850/415-1655

◈   **Location:** I-10, exit 120, just n. 1511 Main St 32428. **Hours:** 11 am-9 pm, Fri & Sat-10 pm. Closed: 1/1, 11/23, 12/25. **Features:** Tacos, enchiladas, chimichangas and burritos are some of the traditional choices. Platters
Mexican   and combination plates are popular. Casual dress; beer & wine only. **Parking:** on-site. **Cards:** AX, MC, VI.

CLEARWATER —*See Tampa Bay p. 1007.*

CLEARWATER BEACH —*See Tampa Bay p. 1015.*

CLERMONT —*See Orlando p. 749.*

CLEWISTON pop. 6,460

------ WHERE TO STAY ------

BEST WESTERN OF CLEWISTON   *Book at aaa.com*   Phone: (863)983-3400

(AAA) (SAVE)

12/1-3/31	1P: $119-$179	2P: $129-$189	XP: $10	F12
4/1-5/31	1P: $119-$169	2P: $129-$169	XP: $10	F12
6/1-11/30	1P: $69-$109	2P: $79-$119	XP: $10	F12

Motel

Location: On US 27/SR 80. Located in a quiet area. 1020 W Sugarland Hwy 33440. Fax: 863/983-3441. **Facility:** 51 units. 50 one-bedroom standard units, some with efficiencies. 1 one-bedroom suite ($79-$189). 2 stories, exterior corridors. *Bath:* combo or shower only. **Parking:** on-site. **Terms:** cancellation fee imposed. **Amenities:** voice mail, safes (fee), irons, hair dryers. **Pool(s):** heated outdoor. **Guest Services:** coin laundry. **Business Services:** meeting rooms, fax (fee). **Cards:** AX, CB, DC, DS, MC, VI. **Special Amenities:** free continental breakfast and free newspaper.

SOME UNITS

COCOA pop. 16,412

------ WHERE TO STAY ------

BEST WESTERN COCOA INN   *Book at aaa.com*   Phone: (321)632-1065

All Year	1P: $65-$139	2P: $65-$139

Small-scale Hotel

Location: I-95, exit 201 (SR 520), 0.3 mi e. 4225 W King St 32926. Fax: 321/631-3302. **Facility:** 120 one-bedroom standard units. 2 stories (no elevator), exterior corridors. *Bath:* combo or shower only. **Parking:** on-site. **Terms:** package plans, pets ($6 extra charge). **Amenities:** voice mail, safes, irons, hair dryers. *Some:* DVD players (fee). **Pool(s):** heated outdoor. **Leisure Activities:** *Fee:* game room. **Guest Services:** valet and coin laundry. **Business Services:** meeting rooms, fax (fee). **Cards:** AX, DC, DS, MC, VI.

SOME UNITS

CAMPBELL MOTEL   Phone: 321/636-6111

(AAA) (SAVE)

All Year	1P: $45-$65	2P: $65-$75	XP: $10	F12

Motel

Location: 1.5 mi s of jct SR 528. 1084 N Cocoa Blvd 32922. Fax: 321/636-6111. **Facility:** 18 one-bedroom standard units. 1 story, exterior corridors. *Bath:* combo or shower only. **Parking:** on-site. **Terms:** 7 day cancellation notice. **Cards:** DS, MC, VI. **Special Amenities:** free local telephone calls and early check-in/late check-out.

SOME UNITS

ECONO LODGE-SPACE CENTER   *Book at aaa.com*   Phone: (321)632-4561

(AAA) (SAVE)

All Year	1P: $55-$175	2P: $55-$175	XP: $5	F17

Small-scale Hotel

Location: US 1, just n of jct SR 528. 3220 N Cocoa Blvd 32926. Fax: 321/631-3756. **Facility:** 144 one-bedroom standard units. 3 stories, exterior corridors. **Parking:** on-site. **Terms:** weekly rates available, [BP] meal plan available, package plans, small pets only ($10 fee). **Dining:** 6:30-10 am, Sat & Sun-11 am. **Pool(s):** outdoor. **Leisure Activities:** shuffleboard. **Guest Services:** coin laundry. **Business Services:** meeting rooms, fax (fee). **Cards:** AX, CB, DC, DS, MC, VI. **Special Amenities:** free full breakfast and free local telephone calls.

SOME UNITS

HOLIDAY INN EXPRESS HOTEL & SUITES   *Book at aaa.com*   Phone: 321/635-9975

(AAA) (SAVE)

12/1-3/31 & 9/1-11/30	1P: $109-$199
4/1-8/31	1P: $99-$169

Small-scale Hotel

Location: I-95, exit 201 (SR 520), just w. 301 Tucker Ln 32926. Fax: 321/639-3698. **Facility:** 75 one-bedroom standard units. 3 stories, interior corridors. *Bath:* combo or shower only. **Parking:** on-site. **Terms:** cancellation fee imposed, [CP] meal plan available, small pets only ($30 extra charge). **Amenities:** high-speed Internet, dual phone lines, voice mail, irons, hair dryers. **Pool(s):** outdoor. **Leisure Activities:** sauna, whirlpool, exercise room. **Guest Services:** valet and coin laundry. **Business Services:** meeting rooms, business center. **Cards:** AX, DC, DS, MC, VI. **Special Amenities:** free expanded continental breakfast and free newspaper.

SOME UNITS

RAMADA INN COCOA BEACH AREA/KSC   *Book at aaa.com*   Phone: (321)631-1210

(AAA) (SAVE)

12/1-6/30 [CP]	1P: $109	2P: $109-$119	XP: $10	F12
7/1-11/30 [CP]	1P: $69	2P: $79	XP: $10	F12

Small-scale Hotel

Location: I-95, exit 202 (SR 524), just w. 900 Friday Rd 32926. Fax: 321/636-8661. **Facility:** 99 one-bedroom standard units. 2 stories, exterior corridors. **Parking:** on-site. **Terms:** cancellation fee imposed, weekly rates available, package plans, small pets only ($50 fee, $5 extra charge). **Amenities:** voice mail, safes (fee), irons, hair dryers. **Dining:** 7 am-10 & 4:30-9 pm, cocktails. **Pool(s):** heated outdoor. **Leisure Activities:** boat dock, fishing, jogging, shuffleboard. **Guest Services:** coin laundry. **Business Services:** meeting rooms. **Cards:** AX, CB, DC, DS, MC, VI. **Special Amenities:** free continental breakfast and early check-in/late check-out.

SOME UNITS

SUPER 8 MOTEL COCOA BEACH AREA/KSC   *Book at aaa.com*   Phone: (321)631-1212

(AAA) (SAVE)

12/1-6/30 [CP]	1P: $99-$109	2P: $99-$109	XP: $10	F12
7/1-11/30 [CP]	1P: $69-$79	2P: $69-$79	XP: $10	F12

Motel

Location: I-95, exit 202 (SR 524), 0.5 mi sw. 900A Friday Rd 32926. Fax: 321/636-8661. **Facility:** 53 one-bedroom standard units. 2 stories (no elevator), exterior corridors. **Parking:** on-site. **Terms:** cancellation fee imposed, weekly rates available, small pets only ($50 fee, $5 extra charge). **Amenities:** voice mail, safes (fee). **Pool(s):** heated outdoor. **Leisure Activities:** fishing, jogging, shuffleboard. **Guest Services:** coin laundry. **Cards:** AX, CB, DC, DS, MC, VI. **Special Amenities:** free continental breakfast and early check-in/late check-out.

SOME UNITS

――――― **WHERE TO DINE** ―――――

BLACK TULIP

Continental

| Lunch: $7-$10 | Dinner: $15-$23 | Phone: 321/631-1133 |

Location: On SR 520, 0.3 mi e of jct US 1. 207 Brevard Ave 32922. **Hours:** 11:30 am-2 & 5:30-9 pm. Closed major holidays; also Sun 6/1-11/30. **Reservations:** suggested. **Features:** This charming and comfortable cafe features classic dishes with innovative touches. For a flavorful lunch, try the traditional chunky gazpacho with the quiche of the day, and finish with the delicious flan from a Brazilian recipe. At night, subdued lighting sets a romantic mood. Daylight is prime time to enjoy dining on the outdoor patio. Casual dress; cocktails; entertainment. **Parking:** on-site. **Cards:** AX, DC, DS, MC, VI.

CAFE MARGAUX

French

| Lunch: $5-$13 | Dinner: $16-$28 | Phone: 321/639-8343 |

Location: Off SR 520, just e of US 1; in Historic Cocoa Village. 220 Brevard Ave 32922. **Hours:** 11 am-3 & 5-9:30 pm. Closed: Sun & 7/1-7/21. **Reservations:** suggested. **Features:** Bright during the day and romantic at night, the cozy dining areas and outside courtyard terrace are reminiscent of New Orleans. An extensive wine list includes selections to complement a nice variety of seafood, lamb, beef, pasta and mixed grill dishes. Dressy casual; cocktails. **Parking:** street. **Cards:** AX, CB, DC, DS, MC, VI.

COCOA BEACH pop. 12,842

――――― **WHERE TO STAY** ―――――

BEST WESTERN OCEANFRONT RESORT   *Book at aaa.com*

Small-scale Hotel

All Year   1P: $79-$219   2P: $89-$229   XP: $10   Phone: (321)783-7621 F17

Location: SR A1A, 0.8 mi n of jct SR 520. 5600 N Atlantic Ave 32931. Fax: 321/799-4576. **Facility:** 180 one-bedroom standard units, some with efficiencies or kitchens. 2-7 stories, interior/exterior corridors. *Bath:* combo or shower only. **Parking:** on-site. **Amenities:** video games (fee), voice mail, irons, hair dryers. *Some:* high-speed Internet. **Pool(s):** heated outdoor. **Leisure Activities:** sun deck, barbecue grills, playground, exercise room, shuffleboard. **Guest Services:** complimentary evening beverages: Tues, coin laundry. **Business Services:** meeting rooms, PC. **Cards:** AX, CB, DC, DS, MC, VI. **Special Amenities:** free local telephone calls and free newspaper. *(See color ad below)*

     SOME UNITS

COCOA BEACH OCEANSIDE INN

Book at aaa.com

Phone: (321)784-3126

12/25-9/1 [ECP]	1P: $99-$179	2P: $99-$179	XP: $10	F21
12/1-12/24 & 9/2-11/30 [ECP]	1P: $79-$179	2P: $79-$179	XP: $10	F21

Location: Just e of SR A1A; 0.8 mi n of jct SR 520. 1 Hendry Ave 32931. Fax: 321/799-0883. **Facility:** 76 units. 74 one-bedroom standard units. 2 one-bedroom suites ($250-$350), some with whirlpools. 5-6 stories, exterior corridors. **Parking:** on-site. **Terms:** 2-3 night minimum stay - seasonal and/or weekends, cancellation fee imposed, package plans. **Amenities:** safes, hair dryers. **Pool(s):** heated outdoor. **Leisure Activities:** rooftop observation deck for shuttle launches. **Cards:** AX, DC, DS, MC, VI. **Special Amenities:** free expanded continental breakfast. *(See color ad below)*

Small-scale Hotel

SOME UNITS

COMFORT INN & SUITE RESORT *Book at aaa.com*

Phone: (321)783-2221

2/1-8/12	1P: $99-$229	2P: $99-$229	XP: $10 F18
8/13-11/30	1P: $89-$229	2P: $89-$229	XP: $10 F18
12/1-1/31	1P: $89-$209	2P: $89-$209	XP: $10 F18

Location: SR A1A, 0.3 mi s of jct SR 520. 3901 N Atlantic Ave 32931. Fax: 321/783-0461. **Facility:** 170 units. 80 one-bedroom standard units, some with efficiencies. 90 one-bedroom suites, some with whirlpools. 1-6 stories, exterior corridors. *Bath:* combo or shower only. **Parking:** on-site. **Terms:** 2-7 night minimum stay - seasonal, 3 day cancellation notice-fee imposed, [AP] meal plan available, package plans. **Amenities:** high-speed Internet, voice mail, safes, irons, hair dryers. *Some:* dual phone lines. **Pool(s):** heated outdoor. **Leisure Activities:** whirlpool, poolside grills, pool tables, table tennis, playground, exercise room, shuffleboard, volleyball. *Fee:* game room. **Guest Services:** valet and coin laundry. **Business Services:** meeting rooms. **Cards:** AX, CB, DC, DS, JC, MC, VI. **Special Amenities:** free local telephone calls and free newspaper. *(See color ad p 276)*

SOME UNITS

COURTYARD BY MARRIOTT COCOA BEACH *Book at aaa.com*

Phone: (321)784-4800

All Year   1P: $119-$199   2P: $119-$199

Location: 0.5 mi s of jct SR 520. 3435 N Atlantic Ave 32931. Fax: 321/784-4812. **Facility:** 131 units. 119 one-bedroom standard units, some with whirlpools. 12 one-bedroom suites ($179-$219). 7 stories, interior corridors. *Bath:* combo or shower only. **Parking:** on-site. **Terms:** check-in 4 pm, [BP] meal plan available. **Dining:** 6:30 am-10:30 & noon-9 pm, Sat & Sun-11 am. **Pool(s):** heated outdoor. **Leisure Activities:** whirlpool, exercise room. *Fee:* beach equipment. **Guest Services:** sundries, valet and coin laundry. **Business Services:** meeting rooms, PC. **Cards:** AX, CB, DC, DS, JC, MC, VI. **Special Amenities:** free newspaper and early check-in/late check-out. *(See color ad below)*

SOME UNITS

DAYS INN COCOA BEACH   *Book at aaa.com*   Phone: (321)784-2550
AAA SAVE   All Year   1P: $69-$169   2P: $79-$179   XP: $10   F17
Location: SR A1A, 0.8 mi n of jct SR 520. 5500 N Atlantic Ave 32931. Fax: 321/868-7124. **Facility:** 103 one-bedroom standard units, some with efficiencies. 2 stories, exterior corridors. **Parking:** on-site. **Amenities:** video games (fee), voice mail, irons, hair dryers. *Some:* safes. **Pool(s):** heated outdoor. **Leisure**
Small-scale Hotel **Activities:** sun deck, barbecue grills, picnic area, exercise room. **Guest Services:** coin laundry. **Cards:** AX, CB, DC, DS, MC, VI. **Special Amenities:** free local telephone calls and free newspaper.
(See color ad below)

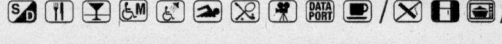

DISCOVERY BEACH RESORT & TENNIS CLUB   *Book at aaa.com*   Phone: (321)868-7777
AAA SAVE   2/12-11/30   1P: $180   2P: $215
     12/1-2/11   1P: $135   2P: $165
Location: Just e of SR A1A; 0.8 mi s of jct SR 520. 300 Barlow Ave 32931. Fax: 321/868-0086. **Facility:** This upscale condominium features washer/dryers and two or more bathrooms in each guest unit. 66 units. 6
Condominium one-, 56 two- and 4 three-bedroom suites with kitchens. 8 stories, exterior corridors. *Bath:* combo or shower only. **Parking:** on-site. **Terms:** check-in 4 pm, 3 day cancellation notice, weekly rates available. **Amenities:** video library, voice mail, irons. *Some:* DVD players. **Dining:** 5 pm-midnight; closed Mon, cocktails. **Pool(s):** heated outdoor. **Leisure Activities:** sauna, whirlpool, 2 lighted tennis courts, recreation programs, exercise room, basketball, horseshoes, volleyball. *Fee:* game room. **Guest Services:** complimentary laundry. **Cards:** MC, VI.

DOUBLETREE HOTEL COCOA BEACH
OCEANFRONT   *Book at aaa.com*   Phone: (321)783-9222
   All Year   1P: $109-$189   2P: $124-$204   XP: $15   F18
Location: SR A1A, 1 mi s of jct SR 520. 2080 N Atlantic Ave 32931. Fax: 321/799-3234. **Facility:** 148 units. 136
Small-scale Hotel one-bedroom standard units. 12 one-bedroom suites ($149-$229). 6 stories, interior corridors. **Parking:** on-site. **Terms:** check-in 4 pm, cancellation fee imposed. **Amenities:** video games (fee), dual phone lines, voice mail, irons, hair dryers. **Pool(s):** heated outdoor, wading. **Leisure Activities:** exercise room. **Guest Services:** gift shop, valet and coin laundry. **Business Services:** conference facilities, business center. **Cards:** AX, CB, DC, DS, JC, MC, VI.

FOUR POINTS BY SHERATON COCOA BEACH   Phone: 321/783-8717
fyi   12/1-5/1 [CP]   1P: $119-$259   2P: $119-$259
     5/2-11/30 [CP]   1P: $109-$259   2P: $109-$259
Small-scale Hotel Too new to rate. **Location:** I-95, exit 205 (SR 528 E) to SR A1A; 4 mi s of Port Canaveral. 4001 N Atlantic Ave 32931. Fax: 321/783-8719. **Amenities:** 75 units, pets, restaurant, coffeemakers, pool. **Terms:** cancellation fee imposed. **Cards:** AX, DC, DS, MC, VI.

HAMPTON INN COCOA BEACH   *Book at aaa.com*   Phone: (321)799-4099
AAA SAVE   All Year [ECP]   1P: $109-$189   2P: $109-$189
Location: 0.5 mi s of jct SR 520. 3425 N Atlantic Ave 32931. Fax: 321/799-4991. **Facility:** 150 one-bedroom standard units. 8 stories, interior/exterior corridors. *Bath:* combo or shower only. **Parking:** on-site. **Terms:** check-in 4 pm. **Amenities:** video games (fee), high-speed Internet, dual phone lines, voice mail,
Small-scale Hotel irons, hair dryers. **Pool(s):** heated outdoor. **Leisure Activities:** walkway to beach, exercise room. **Guest Services:** sundries, valet and coin laundry. **Business Services:** meeting rooms, PC. **Cards:** AX, CB, DC, DS, JC, MC, VI. **Special Amenities:** free expanded continental breakfast and free local telephone calls.
(See color ad p 279)

HILTON COCOA BEACH OCEANFRONT   *Book at aaa.com*   Phone: (321)799-0003
AAA SAVE   1/1-11/30   1P: $130-$260   2P: $145-$275   XP: $15   F18
     12/1-12/31   1P: $120-$250   2P: $135-$265   XP: $15   F18
Location: SR A1A, 1.5 mi s of jct SR 520. 1550 N Atlantic Ave 32931. Fax: 321/799-0344. **Facility:** 296 units. 290
Small-scale Hotel one-bedroom standard units. 6 one-bedroom suites. 7 stories, interior corridors. *Bath:* combo or shower only. **Parking:** on-site. **Terms:** check-in 4 pm, package plans. **Amenities:** dual phone lines, voice mail, irons, hair dryers. *Fee:* video games, high-speed Internet. **Dining:** 2 restaurants, 6:30 am-10 pm, cocktails. **Pool(s):** heated outdoor. **Leisure Activities:** exercise room, volleyball. *Fee:* boogie boards, surfboards, massage. **Guest Services:** gift shop, valet and coin laundry. **Business Services:** conference facilities. **Cards:** AX, CB, DC, DS, JC, MC, VI. **Special Amenities:** free newspaper. *(See color ad p 279)*

HOLIDAY INN COCOA BEACH OCEANFRONT RESORT
Book at aaa.com

(AAA) (SAVE)
◆◆◆◆◆

Small-scale Hotel

2/12-4/29	1P: $150-$350
4/30-9/3	1P: $120-$350
12/1-2/11 & 9/4-11/30	1P: $120-$300

Phone: (321)783-2271

Location: SR A1A, 1.8 mi s of jct SR 520. 1300 N Atlantic Ave 32931. **Fax:** 321/799-8569. **Facility:** 501 units. 459 one-bedroom standard units. 42 one-bedroom suites, some with kitchens. 2-3 stories (no elevator), exterior corridors. *Bath:* combo or shower only. **Parking:** on-site. **Terms:** check-in 4 pm, 2-4 night minimum stay - weekends, cancellation fee imposed, package plans, small pets only ($25 deposit, $10 extra charge). **Amenities:** video games (fee), voice mail, irons, hair dryers. **Dining:** 2 restaurants, 6:30 am-10 pm, cocktails. **Pool(s):** heated outdoor, wading. **Leisure Activities:** whirlpool, boogie boards, surfboards, cabanas, umbrellas, beach chairs, 2 lighted tennis courts, playground, exercise room, shuffleboard, volleyball. *Fee:* game room. **Guest Services:** gift shop, valet and coin laundry. **Business Services:** conference facilities. **Cards:** AX, CB, DC, DS, JC, MC, VI. **Special Amenities:** free newspaper.

SOME UNITS

HOLIDAY INN EXPRESS HOTEL & SUITES *Book at aaa.com*　　　　　Phone: 321/868-2525
All Year　　　1P: $119-$159　　2P: $119-$159　　XP: $10　　　F18
Location: SR A1A, 0.7 mi n of jct SR 520. 5575 N Atlantic Ave 32931. Fax: 321/868-6302. **Facility:** 60 units. 47
Small-scale Hotel one-bedroom standard units, some with whirlpools. 11 one- and 2 two-bedroom suites ($189-$299), some
with whirlpools. 4 stories, interior corridors. *Bath:* combo or shower only. **Parking:** on-site. **Amenities:** high-
speed Internet, dual phone lines, voice mail, irons, hair dryers. **Pool(s):** outdoor. **Leisure Activities:** whirlpool, limited exercise
equipment. **Guest Services:** valet and coin laundry. **Business Services:** meeting rooms, PC. **Cards:** AX, CB, DC, DS, JC,
MC, VI.

SOME UNITS

(ASK) [symbols]

THE INN AT COCOA BEACH　　　　　　　　　　　　　　　　　Phone: (321)799-3460
2/1-5/31 [ECP]　　1P: $135-$325　　2P: $135-$325　　XP: $20
12/1-1/31 & 6/1-11/30 [ECP]　1P: $125-$295　　2P: $125-$295　　XP: $20
Small-scale Hotel **Location:** Just s of SR 520; just e of SR A1A. 4300 Ocean Beach Blvd 32931. Fax: 321/784-8632. **Facility:** Smoke
free premises. 50 one-bedroom standard units, some with whirlpools. 2-4 stories, interior/exterior corridors.
Parking: on-site. **Terms:** age restrictions may apply, 7 day cancellation notice. **Amenities:** video library, safes. **Pool(s):**
outdoor. **Leisure Activities:** bicycles, shuffleboard. *Fee:* massage. **Guest Services:** gift shop, complimentary evening
beverages, valet laundry. **Business Services:** meeting rooms. *Fee:* administrative services, fax. **Cards:** AX, DS, MC, VI.

SOME UNITS

[symbols]

LA QUINTA INN COCOA BEACH *Book at aaa.com*　　　　　　Phone: (321)783-2252
(AAA) (SAVE)　All Year [ECP]　1P: $59-$279　　2P: $59-$279　　XP: $15　　F18
Location: On SR A1A, 1.7 mi s. 1275 N Atlantic Ave 32931. Fax: 321/323-5045. **Facility:** 127 one-bedroom
standard units. 2 stories, exterior corridors. *Bath:* combo or shower only. **Parking:** on-site. **Terms:** package
plans. **Amenities:** high-speed Internet, dual phone lines, voice mail, irons, hair dryers. **Dining:** 7 am-2 am,
Small-scale Hotel cocktails. **Pool(s):** heated outdoor. **Leisure Activities:** barbecue grills, picnic tables, pool tables,
shuffleboard. **Guest Services:** valet and coin laundry. **Business Services:** meeting rooms, fax (fee).
Cards: AX, CB, DC, DS, JC, MC, VI. **Special Amenities:** free expanded continental breakfast and free newspaper.
(See color ad below)

SOME UNITS

[symbols]

LUNA SEA MOTEL *Book at aaa.com*　　　　　　　　　　　　Phone: (321)783-0500
(AAA) (SAVE)　All Year [ECP]　1P: $49-$199　　2P: $49-$199　　XP: $6　　F12
Location: 0.7 mi s of SR 520 on SR A1A. 3185 N Atlantic Ave 32931. Fax: 321/784-6515. **Facility:** 44 one-
bedroom standard units, some with efficiencies. 2 stories, exterior corridors. **Parking:** on-site.
Amenities: hair dryers. **Pool(s):** heated outdoor. **Leisure Activities:** picnic area. **Guest Services:** coin
Motel laundry. **Cards:** AX, DC, DS, MC, VI. **Special Amenities:** free expanded continental breakfast.

SOME UNITS

[symbols]

OCEAN SUITE HOTEL *Book at aaa.com*
Phone: (321)784-4343

Small-scale Hotel
All Year 1P: $99-$259 2P: $99-$259 XP: $10 F8
Location: Just n of SR 520; just e of SR A1A. 5500 Ocean Beach Blvd 32931. Fax: 321/783-6514. **Facility:** 50 one-bedroom suites. 5 stories, exterior corridors. **Parking:** on-site. **Terms:** 2-4 night minimum stay - seasonal, 7 day cancellation notice. **Amenities:** high-speed Internet, voice mail, irons, hair dryers. **Pool(s):** outdoor. **Guest Services:** valet and coin laundry. **Business Services:** meeting rooms. **Cards:** AX, DC, DS, MC, VI.

SOME UNITS

QUALITY SUITES COCOA BEACH *Book at aaa.com*
Phone: (321)783-6868

Small-scale Hotel
2/11-4/20 [CP] 1P: $129-$299 2P: $129-$299
4/21-11/30 [CP] 1P: $99-$259 2P: $99-$259
12/1-2/10 [CP] 1P: $109-$219 2P: $109-$219
Location: SR A1A, 0.3 mi s of jct SR 520. 3655 N Atlantic Ave 32931. Fax: 321/783-6784. **Facility:** 48 one-bedroom suites. 5 stories, interior corridors. *Bath:* combo or shower only. **Parking:** on-site. **Terms:** package plans. **Amenities:** high-speed Internet, dual phone lines, voice mail, irons, hair dryers. **Leisure Activities:** whirlpool. **Guest Services:** valet and coin laundry. **Business Services:** meeting rooms. **Cards:** AX, CB, DC, DS, JC, MC, VI.

SOME UNITS

THE RESORT ON COCOA BEACH *Book at aaa.com*
Phone: (321)783-4000

Condominium
All Year 1P: $130-$310 2P: $130-$310
Location: SR A1A, 2 mi s of jct SR 520. 1600 N Atlantic Ave 32931. Fax: 321/799-0272. **Facility:** This beachside resort offers numerous activites for visitors of all ages; lively colors decorate each suite and most have balconies with beach views. 124 two-bedroom suites with kitchens and whirlpools. 8 stories, exterior corridors. **Parking:** on-site. **Terms:** check-in 4 pm, 3 day cancellation notice, weekly rates available. **Amenities:** video library (fee), voice mail, irons, hair dryers. **Dining:** 11 am-10 pm, Sat & Sun from 4 pm, cocktails. **Pool(s):** heated outdoor. **Leisure Activities:** sauna, whirlpool, water sprite for kids, 2 lighted tennis courts, recreation programs, exercise room, basketball, volleyball. *Fee:* beach furniture, kids play area, movie theater, game room. **Guest Services:** gift shop, complimentary laundry. **Cards:** AX, DC, DS, MC, VI.

SURF STUDIO BEACH RESORT
Phone: 321/783-7100

Motel
1/16-11/30 1P: $100-$195 2P: $100-$195 XP: $15 F10
12/1-1/15 1P: $85-$155 2P: $85-$155 XP: $15 F10
Location: SR A1A northbound, 5 mi s of jct SR 520 at Francis St; 1.3 mi n of Partrick AFB. 1801 S Atlantic Ave 32931. Fax: 321/783-2695. **Facility:** 11 units. 4 one-bedroom standard units, some with efficiencies. 7 one-bedroom suites with kitchens. 1 story, exterior corridors. *Bath:* combo or shower only. **Parking:** on-site. **Terms:** 7 day cancellation notice-fee imposed, weekly rates available, pets ($20 extra charge). **Amenities:** voice mail. **Pool(s):** heated outdoor. **Guest Services:** coin laundry. **Cards:** AX, DS, MC, VI.

FEE

WAKULLA SUITES *Book at aaa.com*
Phone: (321)783-2230

Small-scale Hotel
All Year 1P: $109-$199 2P: $109-$199 XP: $10 F18
Location: SR A1A, 0.5 mi s of jct SR 520. 3550 N Atlantic Ave 32931. Fax: 321/783-3938. **Facility:** 116 two-bedroom suites with kitchens. 2 stories, exterior corridors. **Parking:** on-site. **Terms:** check-in 4 pm, 7 day cancellation notice-fee imposed, weekly rates available, package plans. **Amenities:** voice mail. *Some:* high-speed Internet. **Pool(s):** heated outdoor, wading. **Leisure Activities:** oceanside deck, barbecue grills, shuffleboard. *Fee:* game room. **Guest Services:** valet and coin laundry. **Cards:** AX, CB, DC, DS, MC, VI.
Special Amenities: preferred room (subject to availability with advance reservations).

WHERE TO DINE

ANACAPRI PIZZERIA
Lunch: $5-$14 Dinner: $5-$14 Phone: 321/868-2266

Italian
Location: SR A1A northbound, 2.3 mi s of jct SR 520. 605 N Atlantic Ave 32931. **Hours:** 11 am-10 pm. Closed: Sun. **Features:** Pizza pies, hot and cold submarine sandwiches and baked dishes are staples at the popular pizza shop. Casual dress. **Parking:** on-site. **Cards:** AX, MC, VI.

BERNARD'S SURF
Dinner: $17-$30 Phone: 321/783-2401

Steak & Seafood
Location: SR A1A northbound, 2.3 mi s of jct SR 520 at Minutemen Cswy. 2 S Atlantic Ave 32931. **Hours:** 4 pm-10 pm, Fri & Sat-11 pm. Closed: 12/25. **Reservations:** suggested. **Features:** This family-owned restaurant has been a Cocoa Beach favorite since 1948. Excellent steak and market-fresh seafood is served in a relaxed, fine-dining atmosphere. A lengthy wine list and a very nice variety of appetizers make happy hour a celebration. Casual dress; cocktails. **Parking:** on-site. **Cards:** AX, DC, DS, MC, VI.

HEIDELBERG RESTAURANT
Lunch: $6-$14 Dinner: $16-$23 Phone: 321/783-6806

German
Location: SR A1A, 3 mi s of jct SR 520. 7 N Orlando Ave 32931. **Hours:** 10 am-10 pm, Sun from 5 pm. Closed: 7/4, 11/23, 12/25; also Mon. **Reservations:** suggested, weekends. **Features:** Such specialties as goulash, stroganoff and luscious Viennese pastries make up the decidedly German and Austrian menu in the romantic restaurant. European decor enhances the cozy, classical feel. A pianist performs on Friday and Saturday evenings. Casual dress; cocktails; entertainment. **Parking:** street. **Cards:** AX, MC, VI.

THE MANGO TREE RESTAURANT
Dinner: $15-$39 Phone: 321/799-0513

Continental
Location: SR A1A northbound, 2.5 mi s of jct SR 520. 118 N Atlantic Ave 32931. **Hours:** 6 pm-10 pm. Closed: 1/1, 12/25; also Mon. **Reservations:** suggested. **Features:** Several cozy areas—from an elegantly formal dining room to the tropically decorated garden terrace complete with graceful swans, all lend to the intimate plantation-home ambience of the restaurant. Attractive presentation is a trademark of every dish. Semi-formal attire; cocktails; entertainment. **Parking:** on-site. **Cards:** AX, MC, VI.

PUNJAB INDIAN CUISINE   Lunch: $5-$15   Dinner: $9-$15   Phone: 321/799-4696

Indian

Location: On SR 520, just w of jct SR A1A; in White Rose Shopping Center. 285 W Cocoa Beach Cswy 32931. **Hours:** 11:30 am-2 & 5-9:30 pm. Closed major holidays. **Reservations:** accepted. **Features:** A Northern influence is evident in the excellent menu variety, which includes breads, lassi and kulfi. Favorites include shrimp curry, tandoori chicken and lamb, as well as seafood and vegetarian dishes. Textured walls and subdued lighting set the mood. Casual dress; beer & wine only. **Parking:** on-site. **Cards:** AX, DS, MC, VI.

ROBERTO'S LITTLE HAVANA RESTAURANT   Lunch: $7-$11   Dinner: $7-$11   Phone: 321/784-1868

Cuban

Location: SR A1A southbound, 2.7 mi s of jct SR 520. 26 N Orlando Ave 33931. **Hours:** 6 am-3 & 5-9 pm, Fri & Sat-10 pm, Mon-3 pm. Closed major holidays. **Reservations:** accepted. **Features:** The unpretentious downtown eatery serves up a delicious variety of Cuban dishes, such as yucca, plantain, French-bread Cuban sandwiches and beans with rice, as well as beef, chicken and pork entrees. Locals often drop by for breakfast. Casual dress; beer & wine only. **Parking:** on-site. **Cards:** AX, DS, MC, VI.

YEN YEN CHINESE RESTAURANT   Lunch: $5-$12   Dinner: $8-$16   Phone: 321/783-9512

Chinese

Location: On SR A1A. 2 N Atlantic Ave 32931. **Hours:** 11:30 am-10 pm, Fri-11 pm, Sat noon-11 pm, Sun noon-10 pm. Closed: one week in summer (call ahead 7/5-7/31). **Reservations:** suggested. **Features:** Delicate sauces and exotic seasonings flavor such entrees as Shelly's chicken and the signature snow white prawn. Comfortable and quiet, the atmosphere borrows from the discrete cultures of Europe and Asia to create a distinct and elegant feel. Casual dress; cocktails. **Parking:** on-site. **Cards:** AX, DC, DS, MC, VI.

———— *The following restaurant has not been evaluated by AAA* ————
but is listed for your information only.

OLD FISH HOUSE RESTAURANT   Phone: 321/799-9190

[fyi]   Not evaluated. **Location:** Jct SR 520 and A1A; in White Rose Shopping Center. 249 W Cocoa Beach Cswy 32931. **Features:** The popular seafood restaurant serves fresh catches of the day and seafood native to Florida waters.

COCONUT CREEK —See Fort Lauderdale p. 396.

COCONUT GROVE —See Miami-Miami Beach p. 595.

CORAL GABLES —See Miami-Miami Beach p. 599.

CORAL SPRINGS —See Fort Lauderdale p. 396.

CORTEZ pop. 4,491

———— WHERE TO STAY ————

———— *The following lodging was either not evaluated or did not* ————
meet AAA rating requirements but is listed for your information only.

CHARLIE'S COTTAGES   Phone: 941/794-5980

[fyi]   Not evaluated. **Location:** Just s of jct SR 684 (Cortez Rd), enter via 125th St W. 4512 124th St Ct W 34215 (PO Box 671). Facilities, services, and decor characterize a basic property.

CRESCENT BEACH pop. 985   (See map and index starting on p. 874)

———— WHERE TO STAY ————

BEACHER'S LODGE   Phone: (904)471-8849   [62]

2/1-9/3	1P: $109-$225	2P: $109-$225	
12/1-1/31 & 9/4-11/30	1P: $79-$155	2P: $79-$155	

Small-scale Hotel

Location: Just s of jct SR 206. 6970 A1A S 32080. Fax: 904/471-3002. **Facility:** 94 units. 9 one-bedroom standard units with efficiencies. 85 one-bedroom suites, some with efficiencies or kitchens. 4 stories, exterior corridors. *Bath:* some combo or shower only. **Parking:** on-site. **Terms:** weekly rates available, package plans, small pets only ($50 fee, in designated units). **Amenities:** DVD players, voice mail, irons, hair dryers. **Pool(s):** heated outdoor. **Guest Services:** coin laundry. **Business Services:** meeting rooms. **Cards:** AX, DS, MC, VI. **Special Amenities:** free local telephone calls.

SOME UNITS

FEE

CHANNEL MARKER 71 BARRIER ISLAND INN AND RESTAURANT   Phone: 904/461-4288

12/27-11/30	1P: $84-$149	2P: $118-$298	XP: $75	F10
12/1-12/23	1P: $84-$149	2P: $118-$248	XP: $75	F10

Small-scale Hotel

Location: 1.4 mi s of SR 206. 7601 A1A S 32080. Fax: 904/461-4881. **Facility:** Smoke free premises. 10 one-bedroom standard units, some with whirlpools. 2 stories, interior corridors. *Bath:* combo or shower only. **Parking:** on-site. **Terms:** open 12/1-12/23 & 12/27-11/30, 2 night minimum stay - weekends, 14 day cancellation notice-fee imposed, package plans, small pets only. **Amenities:** video library, hair dryers. **Dining:** 9 am-2:30 & 5-10 pm, Sat & Sun 9 am-10 pm; closed Mon & Tues. **Leisure Activities:** whirlpool, fishing, jet spa swimming pool, kayaks. *Fee:* massage. **Guest Services:** gift shop. **Cards:** AX, DC, DS, MC, VI.

CRESCENT CITY pop. 1,776

———— WHERE TO STAY ————

LAKE VIEW MOTEL
Phone: 386/698-1090
All Year   1P: $48-$80   2P: $55-$85   XP: $5   D5
Motel
Location: 1 mi n on US 17. 1004 N Summit St 32112. Fax: 386/698-4616. **Facility:** 19 one-bedroom standard units, some with efficiencies (no utensils). 1 story, exterior corridors. *Bath:* combo or shower only. **Parking:** on-site. **Terms:** cancellation fee imposed, small pets only ($5 extra charge). **Amenities:** voice mail. **Pool(s):** outdoor. **Cards:** AX, DS, MC, VI.

SOME UNITS
(ASK) (🛏) (📶) (🏊) / (✕) (📠) (📶) (🍽) (💻) /
FEE

———— WHERE TO DINE ————

The following restaurant has not been evaluated by AAA but is listed for your information only.

3 BANANAS
Phone: 386/698-2861
[fyi]
Not evaluated. **Location:** 0.3 mi e of US 17. 11 S Lake St 32112. **Features:** Guests can dine amid island decor inside or relax on the patio. Moderately priced seafood makes up the core of the menu.

CRESTVIEW pop. 14,766

———— WHERE TO STAY ————

COMFORT INN   *Book at aaa.com*
Phone: (850)423-1200
3/1-9/1 [ECP]   1P: $90-$149   2P: $99-$149   XP: $10   F10
9/2-11/30 [ECP]   1P: $89-$149   2P: $89-$149   XP: $10   F10
Small-scale Hotel   12/1-2/28 [ECP]   1P: $80-$149   2P: $89-$149   XP: $10   F10
Location: I-10, exit 56, just s. 4040 S Ferdon Blvd 32536. Fax: 850/423-1210. **Facility:** 50 one-bedroom standard units, some with whirlpools. 2 stories, exterior corridors. **Parking:** on-site. **Terms:** 1-2 night minimum stay - seasonal. **Amenities:** irons, hair dryers. **Pool(s):** outdoor. **Guest Services:** valet laundry. **Business Services:** PC. **Cards:** AX, CB, DC, DS, JC, MC, VI.

SOME UNITS
(ASK) (S/D) (📶) (🏊) (✳) (📠) (💻) (🍽) (💻) / (✕) /

ECONO LODGE   *Book at aaa.com*
Phone: 850/682-6255
Property failed to provide current rates
Motel
Location: I-10, exit 56, 0.3 mi n. 3101 S Ferdon Blvd 32536 (PO Box 1466). Fax: 850/682-0638. **Facility:** 84 one-bedroom standard units. 2 stories, exterior corridors. **Parking:** on-site.

SOME UNITS
(📶) / (✕) (📶) (🍽) (💻) /

HAMPTON INN   *Book at aaa.com*
Phone: 850/689-2378
Property failed to provide current rates
Small-scale Hotel
Location: I-10, exit 56. 3709 S Ferdon Blvd 32536. Fax: 850/689-4465. **Facility:** 70 one-bedroom standard units. 3 stories, exterior corridors. *Bath:* combo or shower only. **Parking:** on-site. **Amenities:** high-speed Internet, voice mail, irons, hair dryers. *Some:* safes. **Pool(s):** outdoor. **Leisure Activities:** whirlpool. **Guest Services:** coin laundry. **Business Services:** meeting rooms.

SOME UNITS
(📶) (🏊) (🛁) (✳) (📠) (💻) / (✕) (📶) (🍽) /
FEE

HOLIDAY INN   *Book at aaa.com*
Phone: (850)682-6111
(AAA) (SAVE)   All Year.   1P: $90
(▽▽) (▽▽)   **Location:** I-10, exit 56, 0.5 mi s. 4050 S Ferdon Blvd 32536 (PO Box 1358). Fax: 850/689-1189. **Facility:** 118 one-bedroom standard units. 2 stories, exterior corridors. *Bath:* combo or shower only. **Parking:** on-site.
Small-scale Hotel   **Terms:** [BP] meal plan available, small pets only ($25 fee). **Amenities:** voice mail, irons, hair dryers. *Some:* dual phone lines. **Dining:** 6-9 am, 11-2 & 5-9 pm, Sat 11 am-1 & 5-9 pm, cocktails. **Pool(s):** outdoor. **Leisure Activities:** exercise room. **Guest Services:** valet and coin laundry. **Business Services:** meeting rooms. **Cards:** AX, CB, DC, DS, MC, VI. **Special Amenities:** free newspaper and free room upgrade (subject to availability with advance reservations).

SOME UNITS
(S/D) (🛏) (🍴) (🍷) (👤) (🏊) (✳) (📠) (💻) / (✕) (📶) /
FEE

JAMESON INN   *Book at aaa.com*
Phone: (850)683-1778
All Year [ECP]   1P: $54-$104   **Location:** I-10, exit 56, just s. 151 Cracker Barrel Dr 32536. Fax: 850/683-1779. **Facility:** 55 units. 53 one-bedroom standard units. 2 one-bedroom suites. 3 stories, interior corridors. *Bath:* combo or shower only.
Small-scale Hotel   **Parking:** on-site. **Terms:** cancellation fee imposed. **Amenities:** voice mail, irons, hair dryers. **Pool(s):** outdoor. **Leisure Activities:** exercise room. **Guest Services:** valet laundry. **Business Services:** meeting rooms. **Cards:** AX, CB, DC, DS, MC, VI.

SOME UNITS
(ASK) (🛏) (📶) (🏊) (✳) (📠) / (✕) (📶) (🍽) (💻) /

SUPER 8 MOTEL
Phone: (850)682-9649
(AAA) (SAVE)   All Year   1P: $44-$64   2P: $49-$69   XP: $5   F12
(▽▽) (▽▽)   **Location:** I-10, exit 56, 0.3 mi s. 3925 S Ferdon Blvd 32539. Fax: 850/682-9649. **Facility:** 63 one-bedroom standard units. 2 stories, exterior corridors. **Parking:** on-site. **Terms:** pets ($5 fee). **Amenities:** *Some:* hair dryers. **Guest Services:** coin laundry. **Cards:** AX, DC, DS, MC, VI. **Special Amenities:** free continental breakfast and free local telephone calls.

SOME UNITS
(S/D) (🛏) (📶) (🍽) (💻) / (✕) /
FEE

CROSS CITY pop. 1,775

------ WHERE TO STAY ------

CARRIAGE INN

Motel

Phone: (352)498-0001

All Year	1P: $36-$42	2P: $42-$52	XP: $10 D12

Location: 0.5 mi s on US 19, 27A and 98. 16872 SE Hwy 19 32628 (PO Box 1360). Fax: 352/498-5054. **Facility:** 25 one-bedroom standard units. 2 stories, exterior corridors. *Bath:* combo or shower only. **Parking:** on-site. **Pool(s):** outdoor. **Leisure Activities:** basketball. **Guest Services:** airport transportation-Cross City Airport. **Business Services:** fax. **Cards:** AX, DC, DS, MC, VI. **Special Amenities:** free local telephone calls and preferred room (subject to availability with advance reservations).

SOME UNITS

CRYSTAL RIVER pop. 3,485

------ WHERE TO STAY ------

BEST WESTERN CRYSTAL RIVER RESORT   *Book at aaa.com*
Resort
Small-scale Hotel

Phone: (352)795-3171

11/10-11/30	1P: $102-$135	2P: $107-$140	XP: $5 F18
12/1-4/30	1P: $94-$127	2P: $99-$132	XP: $5 F18
5/1-11/9	1P: $87-$119	2P: $92-$125	XP: $5 F18

Location: On US 19/98, 0.8 mi n of jct SR 44. 614 NW Hwy 19 34428. Fax: 352/795-3179. **Facility:** On King's Bay. 114 one-bedroom standard units, some with whirlpools. 2 stories, exterior corridors. *Bath:* combo or shower only. **Parking:** on-site. **Terms:** check-in 4 pm, small pets only ($3 extra charge). **Amenities:** safes, irons, hair dryers. *Some:* high-speed Internet. **Pool(s):** heated outdoor. **Leisure Activities:** whirlpool, rental boats, boat dock, fishing. *Fee:* scuba diving, snorkeling, diving instruction. **Guest Services:** gift shop, coin laundry. **Business Services:** meeting rooms, fax (fee). **Cards:** AX, CB, DC, DS, MC, VI. **Special Amenities:** free local telephone calls and free newspaper.

SOME UNITS

FEE   FEE

DAYS INN   *Book at aaa.com*
Small-scale Hotel

Phone: (352)795-2111

12/1-4/30	1P: $65-$130	2P: $65-$130	XP: $5 F17
5/1-11/30	1P: $60-$120	2P: $60-$125	XP: $5 F17

Location: US 19, 2.2 mi n of jct SR 44. 2380 NW US 19 34428. Fax: 352/795-4126. **Facility:** 104 one-bedroom standard units, some with whirlpools. 2 stories, exterior corridors. *Bath:* combo or shower only. **Parking:** on-site. **Terms:** pets ($10 extra charge). **Amenities:** hair dryers. **Dining:** 24 hours. **Guest Services:** coin laundry. **Business Services:** meeting rooms. **Cards:** AX, DC, DS, MC, VI. **Special Amenities:** free local telephone calls and free newspaper.

SOME UNITS

FEE

PLANTATION INN & GOLF RESORT   *Book at aaa.com*
Resort
Small-scale Hotel

Phone: (352)795-4211

1/1-4/30	1P: $119-$391	2P: $119-$391	XP: $15 F17
10/1-11/30	1P: $112-$328	2P: $112-$328	XP: $15 F17
12/1-12/31	1P: $109-$318	2P: $109-$318	XP: $15 F17
5/1-9/30	1P: $96-$295	2P: $96-$295	XP: $15 F17

Location: On SR 44, 0.5 mi w of jct US 19/98. 9301 W Fort Island Tr 34429. Fax: 352/795-1156. **Facility:** On King's Bay. 144 units. 142 one-bedroom standard units. 2 one-bedroom suites. 2 stories, interior/exterior corridors. *Bath:* combo or shower only. **Parking:** on-site. **Terms:** cancellation fee imposed, package plans. **Amenities:** voice mail, irons, hair dryers. *Some:* video games (fee). **Dining:** 6-11 am, 11:30-2 & 5:30-10 pm; Sunday brunch, cocktails. **Pool(s):** heated outdoor. **Leisure Activities:** whirlpool, rental boats, rental canoes, marina, fishing, driving range, croquet, horseshoes, shuffleboard, volleyball. *Fee:* scuba diving, snorkeling, pontoon, golf-27 holes, 2 lighted tennis courts, tennis instruction. **Guest Services:** valet and coin laundry. **Business Services:** conference facilities, fax (fee). **Cards:** AX, DC, DS, MC, VI.

SOME UNITS

FEE

------ WHERE TO DINE ------

CHARLIE'S FISH HOUSE
Seafood

Lunch: $4-$15   **Dinner:** $4-$15   **Phone:** 352/795-2468

Location: US 19, just n of jct SR 44. 224 US 19 NW 34228. **Hours:** 11 am-9 pm. Closed: 4/16, 11/23, 12/25; also for dinner 12/24. **Features:** This eatery is a seafood tradition in this part of Florida, and not just because they are close to the Gulf; the food is what keeps them coming back. Casual dress; beer & wine only. **Parking:** on-site. **Cards:** AX, DS, MC, VI.

CUTLER RIDGE —*See Miami-Miami Beach p. 602.*

DADE CITY —*See Tampa Bay p. 1022.*

DANIA BEACH —*See Fort Lauderdale p. 398.*

DAVENPORT —*See Orlando p. 750.*

DAVIE —*See Fort Lauderdale p. 400.*

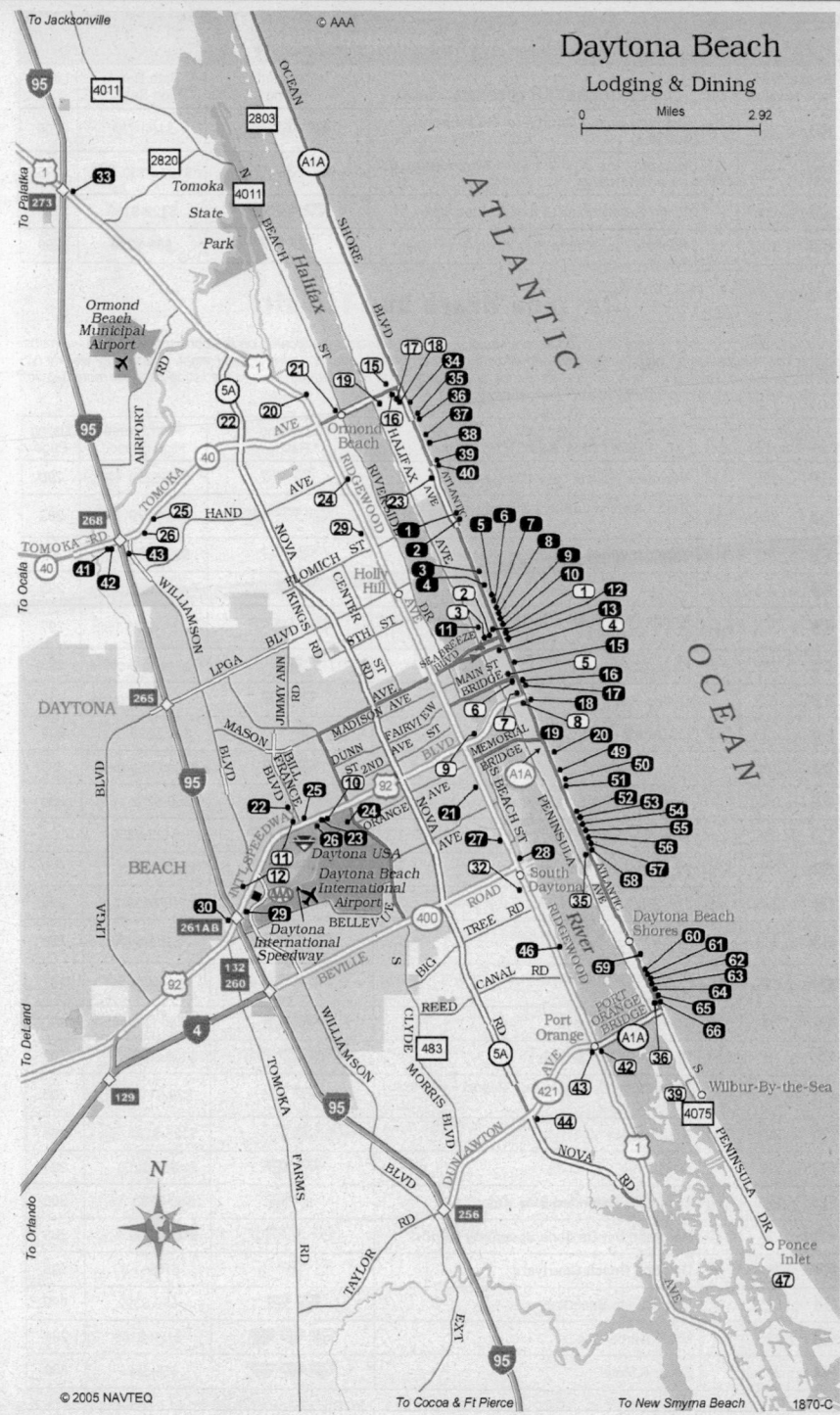

Daytona Beach
Lodging & Dining

Miles
0   2.92

✈ Airport Accommodations

Spotter/Map Page Number	OA	DAYTONA BEACH INTERNATIONAL	Diamond Rating	Rate Range High Season	Listing Page
24 / p. 285	AAA	Daytona Beach Courtyard, 0.5 mi from terminal	▽▽▽	$169 SAVE	295
23 / p. 285	AAA	Hampton Inn Daytona Speedway-Airport, 0.6 mi n of terminal	▽▽▽	$104-$350 SAVE	295
26 / p. 285		Hilton Garden Inn, 0.6 mi nw of terminal	▽▽▽	$129-$189	296
25 / p. 285		Ramada Inn Speedway, 1 mi nw of terminal	▽▽	$89-$399	299

Daytona Beach and Vicinity

This index helps you "spot" where approved accommodations and restaurants are located on the corresponding detailed maps. Lodging rate ranges are for comparison only and show the property's high season; rates are per night, unless only weekly (W) rates are available. Restaurant rate range is for dinner, unless only lunch (L) is served. Turn to the listing page for more detailed rate information and consult display ads for special promotions.

Spotter/Map Page Number	OA	DAYTONA BEACH - Lodgings	Diamond Rating	Rate Range High Season	Listing Page
1 / p. 285	AAA	Bermuda House - see color ad p 291	▽▽	$59-$350 SAVE	290
2 / p. 285	AAA	Best Western LaPlaya Resort - see color ad p 291	▽▽▽	$79-$479 SAVE	292
3 / p. 285	AAA	Tropical Winds Oceanfront Resort	▽▽	$59-$329 SAVE	301
4 / p. 285		Days Inn on the Beach	▽	Failed to provide	295
5 / p. 285	AAA	Holiday Inn Hotel & Suites Oceanfront - see color ad p 297	▽▽▽	$129-$279 SAVE	297
6 / p. 285		Capri Motel	▽	Failed to provide	293
7 / p. 285		Ocean Villa Motel	▽▽	Failed to provide	298
8 / p. 285	AAA	La Quinta Inn & Suites - see color ad p 298	▽▽	$89-$299 SAVE	298
9 / p. 285		Del-Aire Motel	▽▽	Failed to provide	295
10 / p. 285	AAA	Comfort Inn & Suites - see color ad p 293	▽▽▽	$89-$259 SAVE	294
11 / p. 285		The Villa Bed & Breakfast	▽▽▽	$125-$250	301
12 / p. 285	AAA	Plaza Ocean Club - see color ad p 291	▽▽▽	$129-$429 SAVE	299
13 / p. 285	AAA	The Plaza Resort & Spa - see color ad p 291	▽▽▽	$149-$459 SAVE	299
15 / p. 285		Hilton Daytona Beach Ocean Front Resort - see color ad p 296	▽▽▽	$189-$509	296
16 / p. 285	AAA	Best Western Mayan Inn Beachfront - see color ad p 291	▽▽	$69-$479 SAVE	292
17 / p. 285		Super 8-Oceanfront	▽▽	Failed to provide	300
18 / p. 285	AAA	Boardwalk Inn & Suites	▽▽	$129-$149 SAVE	292
19 / p. 285	AAA	Travelodge Ocean Jewels Resort - see color ad p 300	▽▽	$79-$119 SAVE	300
20 / p. 285	AAA	Nautilus Inn	▽▽	$125-$170 SAVE	298
21 / p. 285		Days Inn	▽▽	$60-$260	294
22 / p. 285	AAA	Suburban Extended Stay Hotel	▽▽	$50-$280 SAVE	300
23 / p. 285	AAA	Hampton Inn Daytona Speedway-Airport	▽▽▽	$104-$350 SAVE	295
24 / p. 285	AAA	Daytona Beach Courtyard	▽▽▽	$169 SAVE	295
25 / p. 285		Ramada Inn Speedway	▽▽	$89-$399	299
26 / p. 285		Hilton Garden Inn	▽▽▽	$129-$189	296
27 / p. 285		Super 8 Motel	▽▽▽	$59-$289	300

Spotter/Map Page Number	OA	DAYTONA BEACH - Lodgings (continued)	Diamond Rating	Rate Range High Season	Listing Page
28 / p. 285		Scottish Inns	◆	$36-$245	299
29 / p. 285	AAA	La Quinta Inn Daytona Beach	◆◆	$75-$95 SAVE	298
30 / p. 285	AAA	Days Inn Speedway	◆	$69-$249 SAVE	295
		DAYTONA BEACH - Restaurants			
1 / p. 285		Byron's Grill	◆◆	$7-$20	301
2 / p. 285		The Oyster Pub	◆	$7-$25	302
3 / p. 285		Sapporo Japanese Steak House	◆◆	$8-$16	302
4 / p. 285		Starlite Diner	◆	$4-$11	302
5 / p. 285		Hog Heaven Bar-B-Q	◆◆	$8-$12	301
6 / p. 285		Cruisin' Cafe Bar & Grill	◆	$5-$17	301
7 / p. 285		Shells Great Casual Seafood	◆◆	$8-$14	302
8 / p. 285		Neelam Indian Cuisine	◆	$10-$16	301
9 / p. 285		Martinis on Bay	◆◆◆	$13-$20	301
10 / p. 285	AAA	Cancun Lagoon Bar & Grill	◆◆	$8-$17	301
11 / p. 285		Mr. Goodcents	◆	$4-$6	301
12 / p. 285		Buca di Beppo	◆◆	$11-$30	301
		ORMOND BEACH - Lodgings			
33 / p. 285	AAA	Comfort Inn Interstate	◆◆	$250 SAVE	839
34 / p. 285	AAA	The Cove On Ormond Beach A Club Navigo Resort - see color ad p 771	◆◆◆	$79-$299 SAVE	839
35 / p. 285	AAA	Best Western Mainsail Inn and Suites - see color ad p 292	◆◆	$90-$420 SAVE	839
36 / p. 285		Econo Lodge on the Beach	◆◆	$95-$225	840
37 / p. 285		Symphony Beach Club	◆◆	$59-$95	840
38 / p. 285	AAA	Comfort Inn On The Beach	◆◆	$95-$225 SAVE	839
39 / p. 285	AAA	Driftwood Beach Motel - see color ad p 295	◆◆	$45-$175 SAVE	839
40 / p. 285	AAA	Coral Beach Motel	◆◆	$65-$350 SAVE	839
41 / p. 285		Hampton Inn Ormond Beach	◆◆◆	$84-$255	840
42 / p. 285		Jameson Inn	◆◆◆	$54-$104	840
43 / p. 285		Sleep Inn	◆◆	$75-$200	840
		ORMOND BEACH - Restaurants			
15 / p. 285		Peach Valley Cafe	◆◆	$5-$7(L)	841
16 / p. 285	AAA	La Crepe En Haut	◆◆◆	$26-$50	841
17 / p. 285	AAA	Julian's	◆◆	$12-$20	841
18 / p. 285		Stonewood Grill & Tavern	◆◆◆	$14-$28	841
19 / p. 285	AAA	Billy's Tap Room & Grill	◆◆	$9-$22	840
20 / p. 285		Barry's Patio Bar & Grill	◆	$5-$12	840
21 / p. 285		English Rose Tea Room	◆◆	$8-$10(L)	841
22 / p. 285		Ormond Steakhouse	◆◆	$10-$25	841
23 / p. 285		Charlie Horse Restaurant	◆◆	$6-$19	840
24 / p. 285		Mario's	◆◆	$10-$19	841
25 / p. 285		Dustin's Bar-B-Q	◆	$8-$13	840

Spotter/Map Page Number	OA	ORMOND BEACH - Restaurants (continued)	Diamond Rating	Rate Range High Season	Listing Page
26 / p. 285		Royal Dynasty Restaurant & Lounge	◇	$8-$17	841
		SOUTH DAYTONA - Lodgings			
46 / p. 285	AAA	Sunset Inn	◇	$39-$155 SAVE	925
		SOUTH DAYTONA - Restaurant			
32 / p. 285		Maria Bonita	◇◇	$8-$14	925
		DAYTONA BEACH SHORES - Lodgings			
49 / p. 285	AAA	Oceanside Inn - see color ad p 307	◇◇	$49-$199 SAVE	306
50 / p. 285	AAA	Bahama House - see color ad p 303	◇◇◇	$186-$224 SAVE	302
51 / p. 285		Treasure Island Resort - see color ad p 291	fyi	Failed to provide	309
52 / p. 285	AAA	Perry's Ocean-Edge Resort - see color ad p 308	◇◇◇	$75-$174 SAVE	308
53 / p. 285	AAA	Best Western-Aku Tiki Inn - see color ad p 293	◇◇	$169-$229 SAVE	305
54 / p. 285	AAA	Tropical Manor Motel - see color ad p 309	◇◇	$80-$150 SAVE	309
55 / p. 285	AAA	Hawaiian Inn - see color ad p 306	◇◇	$79-$149 SAVE	306
56 / p. 285	AAA	Sun Viking Lodge - see color ad p 294	◇◇◇	$99-$329 SAVE	308
57 / p. 285	AAA	Shoreline All Suites Inn - see color ad p 294	◇◇	$79-$169 SAVE	308
58 / p. 285	AAA	Acapulco Hotel & Resort - see color ad p 291	fyi	$119-$199 SAVE	302
59 / p. 285	AAA	Hampton Inn Oceanfront - see color ad p 693	◇◇	$89-$299 SAVE	305
60 / p. 285	AAA	Holiday Inn Daytona Beach Shores	◇◇	$89-$139 SAVE	306
61 / p. 285	AAA	Dream Inn	◇◇	$79-$299 SAVE	305
62 / p. 285	AAA	Beach House Oceanfront Motel	◇◇	$59-$89 SAVE	303
63 / p. 285	AAA	Atlantic Ocean Palm Inn - see color ad p 303	◇◇	$69-$189 SAVE	302
64 / p. 285	AAA	Palm Plaza Oceanfront Resort - see color ad p 304	◇◇	$119-$169 SAVE	306
65 / p. 285	AAA	Beachside Motel - see color ad p 304	◇◇	$119-$159 SAVE	304
66 / p. 285		Days Inn Oceanfront South Tropical Seas	◇◇	$59-$329	305
		DAYTONA BEACH SHORES - Restaurants			
35 / p. 285	AAA	China-American Garden	◇◇	$7-$14	310
36 / p. 285		Ocean Diner	◇	$6-$8(L)	310
		HOLLY HILL - Restaurant			
29 / p. 285		Steaks and Eggs	◇	$4-$9	461
		WILBUR-BY-THE-SEA - Restaurant			
39 / p. 285	AAA	Boondocks	◇	$5-$15	1070
		PORT ORANGE - Restaurants			
42 / p. 285		Aunt Catfish's On The River	◇◇	$9-$29	869
43 / p. 285		Sorrento's Deli	◇	$5-$15	870
44 / p. 285		Port Orange Steakhouse	◇◇	$8-$22	869
		PONCE INLET - Restaurant			
47 / p. 285	AAA	Inlet Harbor Marina & Restaurant	◇◇	$9-$23	869

DAYTONA BEACH pop. 64,112   (See map and index starting on p. 285)

———— WHERE TO STAY ————

BELLA COSTA CONDO HOTEL   **Phone:** 386/255-0921
[fyi]   Under construction, scheduled to open February 2006. **Location:** On SR A1A, 1.3 mi s of jct US 92. 1615 S
Small-scale Hotel   Atlantic Ave 32118. Fax: 386/255-3849. **Planned Amenities:** 195 units, restaurant, coffeemakers,
                    microwaves, refrigerators, pool. **Terms:** 3-5 night minimum stay - seasonal, 7 day cancellation notice,
                    (See color ad below)

BERMUDA HOUSE   *Book at aaa.com*   **Phone:** (386)672-1440   ❶
AAA SAVE   All Year   1P: $59-$350   2P: $59-$350   XP: $10   F13
◆◆ ◆◆   **Location:** On SR A1A, 4 mi n of jct US 92. 2560 N Atlantic Ave 32118. Fax: 386/677-8811. **Facility:** 142 one-
                bedroom standard units, some with efficiencies or kitchens. 4-8 stories, interior/exterior corridors. *Bath:*
Small-scale Hotel combo or shower only. **Parking:** on-site. **Terms:** 2-7 night minimum stay - seasonal, 7 day cancellation
                notice, pets ($25 deposit, $10 extra charge). **Amenities:** safes (fee). **Pool(s):** outdoor, wading. **Leisure
Activities:** whirlpool. **Guest Services:** coin laundry. **Cards:** AX, CB, DC, DS, MC, VI. **Special Amenities:**
free room upgrade **(subject to availability with advance reservations).** *(See color ad p 291)*   SOME UNITS

(See map and index starting on p. 285)

BEST WESTERN LAPLAYA RESORT   *Book at aaa.com*   **Phone:** (386)672-0990   ❷

12/1-4/9	1P: $79-$479	
6/9-9/4	1P: $99-$359	
9/5-11/30	1P: $79-$269	
4/10-6/8	1P: $69-$189	

Small-scale Hotel **Location:** On SR A1A, 3.3 mi n of jct US 92. 2500 N Atlantic Ave 32118. Fax: 386/677-0982. **Facility:** 238 units. 204 one-bedroom standard units, some with efficiencies. 34 one-bedroom suites ($139-$479) with efficiencies. 10 stories, exterior corridors. *Bath:* combo or shower only. **Parking:** on-site. **Terms:** check-in 4 pm, 7 day cancellation notice, package plans, pets ($25 fee). **Amenities:** voice mail, safes (fee), irons, hair dryers. **Dining:** 7-10 am; to 1:30 pm in season. **Pool(s):** heated outdoor, heated indoor, wading. **Leisure Activities:** whirlpools, recreation programs in season, gazebo, exercise room, shuffleboard. *Fee:* game room. **Guest Services:** valet and coin laundry. **Business Services:** meeting rooms. **Cards:** AX, DC, DS, MC, VI. **Special Amenities:** free local telephone calls. *(See color ad p 291)*

SOME UNITS

BEST WESTERN MAYAN INN BEACHFRONT   *Book at aaa.com*   **Phone:** (386)252-2378   ⓰

12/1-4/9	1P: $69-$479	2P: $69-$479
6/9-9/4	1P: $89-$359	2P: $89-$359
9/5-11/30	1P: $69-$269	2P: $69-$269
4/10-6/8	1P: $69-$189	2P: $69-$189

Small-scale Hotel **Location:** Jct US 92 and SR A1A, just n, just e, then just n. 103 S Ocean Ave 32118. Fax: 386/252-8670. **Facility:** 110 one-bedroom standard units, some with efficiencies and/or whirlpools. 8 stories, interior/exterior corridors. *Bath:* combo or shower only. **Parking:** on-site. **Terms:** 7 day cancellation notice, package plans. **Amenities:** voice mail, safes (fee), irons, hair dryers. *Some:* high-speed Internet. **Pool(s):** outdoor. **Leisure Activities:** *Fee:* game room. **Guest Services:** coin laundry. **Cards:** AX, CB, DC, DS, MC, VI. **Special Amenities:** free continental breakfast and free local telephone calls. *(See color ad p 291)*

SOME UNITS

BOARDWALK INN & SUITES   *Book at aaa.com*   **Phone:** (386)253-8300   ⓲

3/3-8/13 [CP]	1P: $129-$149	2P: $129-$149	XP: $8 F18
12/1-3/2 [CP]	1P: $99-$129	2P: $99-$129	XP: $8 F18
8/14-11/30 [CP]	1P: $99-$119	2P: $99-$119	XP: $8 F18

Small-scale Hotel **Location:** Jct SR A1A and US 92. 301 S Atlantic Ave 32118. Fax: 386/255-8277. **Facility:** 101 units. 73 one-bedroom standard units. 28 one-bedroom suites ($129-$169) with kitchens, some with whirlpools. 5 stories, exterior corridors. *Bath:* combo or shower only. **Parking:** on-site. **Terms:** 3 day cancellation notice, package plans. **Amenities:** voice mail, safes, hair dryers. **Dining:** 11 am-midnight. **Pool(s):** heated outdoor. **Leisure Activities:** sauna, whirlpool, limited exercise equipment. *Fee:* game room. **Guest Services:** coin laundry. **Business Services:** meeting rooms, fax. **Cards:** AX, DS, MC, VI. **Special Amenities:** free continental breakfast and free local telephone calls.

(See map and index starting on p. 285)

CAPRI MOTEL

Motel

Property failed to provide current rates

Phone: 386/252-2555   **6**

Location: Oceanfront. On SR A1A, 1.5 mi n of jct US 92. 832 N Atlantic Ave 32118. **Fax:** 386/255-7378. **Facility:** 24 one-bedroom standard units, some with efficiencies or kitchens. 1-2 stories, exterior corridors. **Parking:** on-site. **Amenities:** safes (fee). **Pool(s):** 2 outdoor, wading. **Leisure Activities:** waterslide, shuffleboard. *Fee:* game room. **Guest Services:** coin laundry.

SOME UNITS

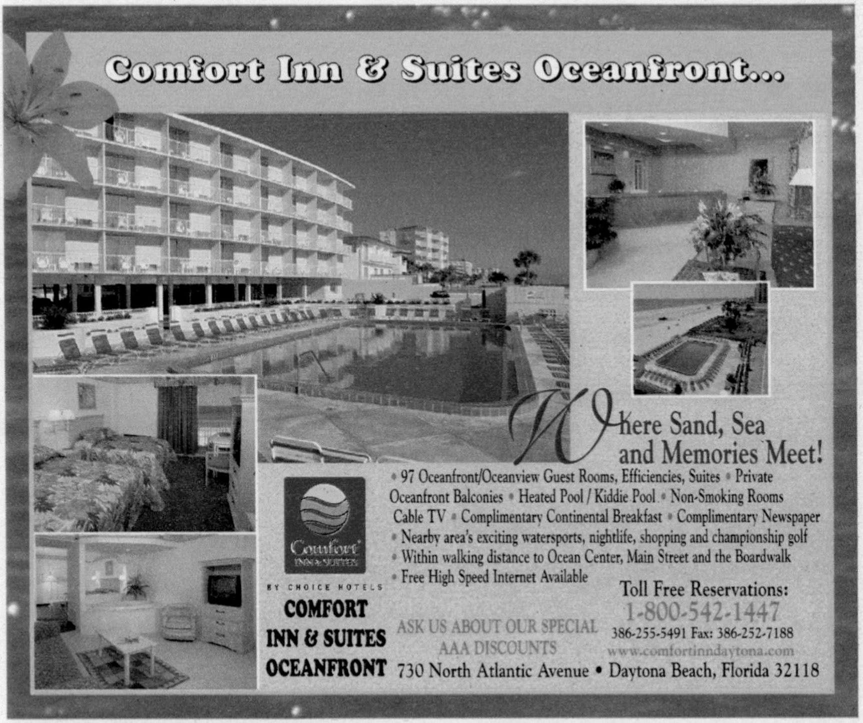

(See map and index starting on p. 285)

COMFORT INN & SUITES   *Book at aaa.com*   Phone: (386)255-5491   **10**

AAA SAVE

Motel

All Year   1P: $89-$259

Location: On SR A1A, 1.1 mi n of jct US 92. 730 N Atlantic Ave 32118. Fax: 386/252-7188. **Facility:** 97 units. 85 one-bedroom standard units, some with efficiencies. 12 one-bedroom suites, some with efficiencies and/or whirlpools. 5 stories, interior/exterior corridors. **Bath:** combo or shower only. **Parking:** on-site. **Terms:** 5 day cancellation notice-fee imposed, [ECP] meal plan available. **Amenities:** dual phone lines, voice mail, safes, irons, hair dryers. **Pool(s):** heated outdoor, wading. **Guest Services:** valet and coin laundry. **Cards:** AX, CB, DC, DS, MC, VI. **Special Amenities:** free continental breakfast and free newspaper. *(See color ad p 293)*

SOME UNITS

DAYS INN   *Book at aaa.com*   Phone: 386/255-4500   **21**

Small-scale Hotel

All Year   1P: $60-$250   2P: $70-$260   XP: $10   F13

Location: I-95, exit 260A, 2.5 mi e on SR 400, then 0.5 mi n on US 1. 544 S Ridgewood Ave 32114. Fax: 386/323-9558. **Facility:** 42 one-bedroom standard units. 2 stories, exterior corridors. **Bath:** combo or shower only. **Parking:** on-site. **Amenities:** voice mail, hair dryers. *Some:* irons. **Pool(s):** outdoor. **Guest Services:** coin laundry. **Cards:** AX, DC, DS, MC, VI.

SOME UNITS

(See map and index starting on p. 285)

DAYS INN ON THE BEACH   Phone: 386/255-2745 **4**

Property failed to provide current rates
Location: On SR A1A; 1.9 mi n of jct US 92. 1220 N Atlantic Ave 32118. **Fax:** 386/238-1646. **Facility:** 75 one-bedroom standard units, some with kitchens (utensils extra charge). 4 stories, exterior corridors. **Parking:** on-site. **Amenities:** hair dryers. **Pool(s):** outdoor. **Leisure Activities:** whirlpool. **Guest Services:** coin laundry.

Small-scale Hotel

SOME UNITS

DAYS INN SPEEDWAY   *Book at aaa.com*   Phone: (386)255-0541 **30**

2/1-7/15	1P: $69-$249	2P: $69-$249	XP: $10	F
7/16-11/30	1P: $59-$189	2P: $59-$189	XP: $10	F
12/1-1/31	1P: $59-$89	2P: $59-$89	XP: $10	F

Motel

Location: I-95, exit 261B southbound; exit 261 northbound, just w on US 92. 2900 W International Speedway Blvd 32124. **Fax:** 386/253-1468. **Facility:** 170 one-bedroom standard units. 2 stories (no elevator), exterior corridors. *Bath:* combo or shower only. **Parking:** on-site. **Terms:** 1-5 night minimum stay, 30 day cancellation notice-fee imposed, package plans, pets ($10 extra charge). **Amenities:** hair dryers. **Dining:** 6 am-10 pm, Fri & Sat-11 pm. **Pool(s):** outdoor. **Guest Services:** coin laundry. **Cards:** AX, CB, DC, DS, JC, MC, VI. **Special Amenities:** free local telephone calls and free newspaper.

SOME UNITS

FEE   FEE

DAYTONA BEACH COURTYARD   *Book at aaa.com*   Phone: (386)255-3388 **24**

1/1-4/30	1P: $169	2P: $169	
12/1-12/31 & 5/1-11/30	1P: $139	2P: $139	

Small-scale Hotel

Location: I-95, exit 261, 2.6 mi e, then just e. 1605 Richard Petty Blvd 32114. **Fax:** 386/255-3391. **Facility:** 122 units. 118 one-bedroom standard units, some with whirlpools. 4 one-bedroom suites. 3 stories, interior corridors. *Bath:* combo or shower only. **Parking:** on-site. **Terms:** [BP] & [CP] meal plans available, package plans. **Amenities:** high-speed Internet, dual phone lines, voice mail, irons, hair dryers. **Dining:** 6-10 am, Sat & Sun 7-11 am. **Pool(s):** heated outdoor. **Leisure Activities:** whirlpool, exercise room. **Guest Services:** valet and coin laundry. **Business Services:** meeting rooms, business center. **Cards:** AX, DC, DS, MC, VI. **Special Amenities:** free newspaper and early check-in/late check-out.

SOME UNITS

DEL-AIRE MOTEL   Phone: 386/252-2563 **9**

Property failed to provide current rates
Location: Oceanfront. On SR A1A, 1.3 mi n of jct US 92. 744 N Atlantic Ave 32118. **Fax:** 386/252-4866. **Facility:** 20 units. 19 one-bedroom standard units, some with efficiencies or kitchens. 1 one-bedroom suite with kitchen. 2 stories, exterior corridors. **Parking:** on-site. **Terms:** office hours 8:30 am-10 pm. **Amenities:** *Some:* safes (fee). **Pool(s):** heated outdoor. **Leisure Activities:** playground, shuffleboard.

Motel

SOME UNITS

HAMPTON INN DAYTONA SPEEDWAY-AIRPORT   *Book at aaa.com*   Phone: (386)257-4030 **23**

All Year [ECP]   1P: $104-$350   2P: $114-$350

Location: I-95, exit 261, 2.1 mi e on US 92; adjacent to Daytona International Speedway. 1715 W International Speedway Blvd 32114. **Fax:** 386/257-5721. **Facility:** 122 one-bedroom standard units. 4 stories, interior corridors. **Parking:** on-site. **Terms:** 13% service charge. **Amenities:** high-speed Internet, voice mail, irons, hair dryers. **Pool(s):** outdoor. **Leisure Activities:** whirlpool, limited exercise equipment. **Guest Services:** valet laundry, area transportation-within 2 mi. **Business Services:** conference facilities, PC. **Cards:** AX, CB, DC, DS, JC, MC, VI. **Special Amenities:** free expanded continental breakfast and free local telephone calls.

Small-scale Hotel

SOME UNITS

FEE

(See map and index starting on p. 285)

HILTON DAYTONA BEACH OCEAN FRONT RESORT . *Book at aaa.com* Phone: (386)254-8200 **15**

2/1-4/15	1P: $189-$509	2P: $189-$509	XP: $25	F17
4/16-9/5	1P: $189-$459	2P: $189-$459	XP: $25	F17
9/6-11/30	1P: $179-$259	2P: $179-$259	XP: $25	F17
12/1-1/31	1P: $109-$199	2P: $109-$199	XP: $25	F17

Large-scale Hotel

Location: On SR A1A, 0.5 mi n of US 92. Located opposite the convention center. 100 N Atlantic Ave 32118. Fax: 386/253-0275. **Facility:** 742 units. 741 one-bedroom standard units. 1 one-bedroom suite with whirlpool. 11-16 stories, interior corridors. *Bath:* combo or shower only. **Parking:** valet. **Terms:** check-in 4 pm, 5-7 night minimum stay - seasonal, 3 day cancellation notice, package plans. **Amenities:** video games (fee), high-speed Internet, voice mail, irons, hair dryers. *Some:* dual phone lines. **Pool(s):** heated indoor/outdoor, 2 wading, lap. **Leisure Activities:** whirlpools, playground, exercise room, volleyball. *Fee:* massage. **Guest Services:** gift shop, valet and coin laundry. **Business Services:** conference facilities, business center. **Cards:** AX, CB, DC, DS, MC, VI. *(See color ad below)*

SOME UNITS

FEE

HILTON GARDEN INN *Book at aaa.com* Phone: (386)944-4000 **26**

All Year 1P: $129-$189 2P: $129-$189

Small-scale Hotel

Location: I-95, exit 261A, 2 mi e, then just s; next to Daytona International Speedway. 189 Midway Ave 32114. Fax: 386/944-4001. **Facility:** 115 units. 101 one-bedroom standard units, some with whirlpools. 14 one-bedroom suites, some with whirlpools. 5 stories, interior corridors. *Bath:* combo or shower only. **Parking:** on-site. **Terms:** check-in 4 pm, [AP] meal plan available, package plans. **Amenities:** video games (fee), high-speed Internet, dual phone lines, voice mail, irons, hair dryers. **Pool(s):** outdoor. **Leisure Activities:** whirlpool, exercise room. **Guest Services:** sundries, coin laundry, area transportation. **Business Services:** meeting rooms, business center. **Cards:** AX, CB, DC, DS, MC, VI.

SOME UNITS

(See map and index starting on p. 285)

HOLIDAY INN HOTEL & SUITES OCEANFRONT   *Book at aaa.com*   Phone: (386)255-5494   **5**

(AAA) (SAVE)
12/1-4/15 & 6/29-8/15	1P: $129-$279	2P: $129-$279	XP: $10	F17
4/16-6/28 & 8/16-11/30	1P: $114-$199	2P: $114-$199	XP: $10	F17

Location: On SR A1A, 1.3 mi n of US 92. 930 N Atlantic Ave 32118. Fax: 386/255-5495. **Facility:** 123 units. 103 one-bedroom standard units, some with whirlpools. 20 one-bedroom suites ($149-$299). 6 stories, interior/exterior corridors. *Bath:* combo or shower only. **Parking:** on-site. **Terms:** 7 day cancellation notice-fee imposed. **Amenities:** dual phone lines, voice mail, safes, irons, hair dryers. **Dining:** 7 am-10 & 5-9 pm.

Small-scale Hotel

Pool(s): heated outdoor. **Leisure Activities:** exercise room. *Fee:* game room. **Guest Services:** gift shop, valet and coin laundry. **Business Services:** meeting rooms. **Cards:** AX, DC, DS, MC, VI. *(See color ad below)*   SOME UNITS

(See map and index starting on p. 285)

LA QUINTA INN & SUITES *Book at aaa.com*    **Phone: (386)944-0060** 8

AAA SAVE

2/1-4/30 [ECP]	1P: $89-$299	2P: $89-$299	XP: $10 F17
5/1-9/3 [ECP]	1P: $79-$149	2P: $79-$149	XP: $10 F17
9/4-11/30 [ECP]	1P: $69-$129	2P: $69-$129	XP: $10 F17
12/1-1/31 [ECP]	1P: $69-$119	2P: $69-$119	XP: $10 F17

Small-scale Hotel **Location:** On SR A1A, 1.4 mi n of US 92. 816 N Atlantic Ave 32118. Fax: 386/944-0070. **Facility:** 77 units. 65 one-and 8 two-bedroom standard units, some with whirlpools. 4 one-bedroom suites ($109-$189). 2-3 stories, exterior corridors. *Bath:* combo or shower only. **Parking:** on-site. **Terms:** 1-5 night minimum stay - seasonal, 3 day cancellation notice, package plans, small pets only ($50 deposit). **Amenities:** high-speed Internet, dual phone lines, voice mail, safes, irons, hair dryers. **Pool(s):** outdoor. **Leisure Activities:** whirlpool, limited beach access, exercise room. **Guest Services:** coin laundry. **Business Services:** meeting rooms. **Cards:** AX, MC, VI. **Special Amenities:** free expanded continental breakfast and free local telephone calls. *(See color ad below)*

SOME UNITS

🅂🄳 🐕 ⓕ 🛆 🚠 📹 📠 DATA PORT 🖥 🖥 🖥 /✕/ FEE

LA QUINTA INN DAYTONA BEACH *Book at aaa.com*   **Phone: (386)255-7412** 29

AAA SAVE

All Year   1P: $75-$95   XP: $7   F18

Motel **Location:** I-95, exit 261 northbound; exit 261B southbound, just e. Located in a commercial area. 2725 International Speedway Blvd 32114. Fax: 386/255-5350. **Facility:** 143 units. 142 one-bedroom standard units. 1 one-bedroom suite. 2 stories (no elevator), interior corridors. *Bath:* combo or shower only. **Terms:** [ECP] meal plan available, small pets only. **Amenities:** video games (fee), voice mail, irons, hair dryers. **Pool(s):** heated outdoor. **Leisure Activities:** whirlpool. **Guest Services:** coin laundry. **Business Services:** meeting rooms, fax. **Cards:** AX, CB, DC, DS, MC, VI. **Special Amenities:** free expanded continental breakfast and free local telephone calls.

SOME UNITS

🐕 🍴 🅵M ⓕ 🎮 🚠 📹 DATA PORT 🖥 /✕🖥/

NAUTILUS INN   **Phone: (386)254-8600** 20

AAA SAVE

6/2-8/5	1P: $125-$170	2P: $125-$170	XP: $10 F17
2/3-6/1	1P: $114-$160	2P: $114-$160	XP: $10 F17
8/6-11/30	1P: $105-$135	2P: $105-$135	XP: $10 F17
12/1-2/2	1P: $94-$125	2P: $94-$125	XP: $10 F17

Small-scale Hotel **Location:** On SR A1A, 1.5 mi s of jct US 92. 1515 S Atlantic Ave 32118. Fax: 386/254-8427. **Facility:** Smoke free premises. 99 one-bedroom standard units, some with efficiencies. 10 stories, interior corridors. **Parking:** on-site. **Terms:** 10 day cancellation notice. **Amenities:** safes. **Pool(s):** heated outdoor. **Leisure Activities:** whirlpool, recreation programs, shuffleboard. **Guest Services:** complimentary evening beverages, coin laundry. **Business Services:** meeting rooms. **Cards:** AX, DS, MC, VI. **Special Amenities:** free continental breakfast.

🍴 🚠 ✕ ✕ 🖥 🖥

OCEAN VILLA MOTEL *Book at aaa.com*   **Phone: 386-252-4644** 7

Motel

Property failed to provide current rates

Location: On SR A1A, 1.5 mi n of jct US 92. Located on the beach. 828 N Atlantic Ave 32118. Fax: 386/255-7378. **Facility:** 37 units. 32 one-bedroom standard units, some with efficiencies or kitchens. 5 one-bedroom suites with kitchens. 2 stories, exterior corridors. *Bath:* combo or shower only. **Parking:** on-site. **Amenities:** safes (fee). **Pool(s):** 2 outdoor, wading. **Leisure Activities:** waterslide, shuffleboard. **Fee:** game room. **Guest Services:** coin laundry.

SOME UNITS

🍴 🚠 ✕ DATA PORT 🖥 /🖥 🖥/

(See map and index starting on p. 285)

PLAZA OCEAN CLUB   Book at aaa.com   Phone: (386)239-9800 12

	2/1-4/16	1P: $129-$429	2P: $129-$429	XP: $10	F
	4/17-8/20	1P: $139-$339	2P: $139-$339	XP: $10	F
	8/21-11/30	1P: $119-$309	2P: $119-$309	XP: $10	F
	12/1-1/31	1P: $89-$199	2P: $89-$199	XP: $10	F

Small-scale Hotel **Location:** Oceanfront. On SR A1A, 1 mi n of jct SR 90. 640 N Atlantic Ave 32118. Fax: 386/253-0735. **Facility:** 206 one-bedroom standard units. 11 stories, interior corridors. *Bath:* combo or shower only. **Parking:** valet. **Terms:** check-in 4 pm, package plans, small pets only ($15 fee). **Amenities:** video games (fee), voice mail, safes, irons, hair dryers. **Dining:** 6:30 am-10 pm; lunch and dinner times vary in season, cocktails. **Pool(s):** heated outdoor, wading. **Leisure Activities:** exercise room. **Guest Services:** valet and coin laundry. **Business Services:** meeting rooms. **Cards:** AX, CB, DC, DS, JC, MC, VI. **Special Amenities:** free room upgrade (subject to availability with advance reservations). *(See color ad p 291)*

THE PLAZA RESORT & SPA   Book at aaa.com   Phone: (386)255-4471 13

	2/1-4/16	1P: $149-$459	2P: $149-$459	XP: $10	F
	4/17-8/20	1P: $159-$359	2P: $159-$359	XP: $10	F
	8/21-11/30	1P: $139-$329	2P: $139-$329	XP: $10	F
	12/1-1/31	1P: $99-$219	2P: $99-$219	XP: $10	F

Large-scale Hotel **Location:** On SR A1A, 1 mi n of US 92. 600 N Atlantic Ave 32118. Fax: 386/238-7984. **Facility:** 320 units. 315 one-bedroom standard units, some with whirlpools. 5 one-bedroom suites. 14 stories, interior corridors. *Bath:* combo or shower only. **Parking:** on-site (fee). **Terms:** check-in 4 pm, package plans. **Amenities:** voice mail, safes (fee), irons, hair dryers. **Dining:** 2 restaurants, 7 am-10 pm, cocktails, nightclub. **Pool(s):** heated outdoor. **Leisure Activities:** whirlpool, putting green, recreation programs in season, exercise room, spa, sports court. **Guest Services:** gift shop, valet and coin laundry. **Business Services:** conference facilities, administrative services (fee). **Cards:** AX, CB, DC, DS, JC, MC, VI. **Special Amenities:** free room upgrade (subject to availability with advance reservations). *(See color ad p 291)*

RAMADA INN SPEEDWAY   Book at aaa.com   Phone: (386)255-2422 25

All Year   1P: $89-$399   2P: $89-$399

Small-scale Hotel **Location:** I-95, exit 261A southbound; exit 261 northbound, 2 mi e on US 92. Located across from Daytona International Speedway. 1798 W International Speedway Blvd 32114. Fax: 386/253-1749. **Facility:** 127 one-bedroom standard units. 2 stories (no elevator), exterior corridors. *Bath:* combo or shower only. **Parking:** on-site. **Terms:** 1-7 night minimum stay - seasonal, 7 day cancellation notice, [AP] meal plan available, pets ($25 fee). **Amenities:** voice mail, safes, irons, hair dryers. **Pool(s):** outdoor. **Guest Services:** valet laundry, area transportation. **Business Services:** meeting rooms. **Cards:** AX, DC, DS, MC, VI.

SCOTTISH INNS   Book at aaa.com   Phone: (386)258-5742 28

	9/1-11/30	1P: $36-$149	2P: $49-$245	XP: $8	D11
Motel	4/26-8/31	1P: $39-$165	2P: $49-$220	XP: $8	D11
	12/1-4/25	1P: $39-$149	2P: $49-$199	XP: $8	D11

Location: I-95, exit 260A, 2.5 mi e on SR 400, then just n on US 1. 1515 S Ridgewood Ave 32114. Fax: 386/253-7635. **Facility:** 20 one-bedroom standard units. 1 story, exterior corridors. **Parking:** on-site. **Terms:** 30 day cancellation notice-fee imposed, small pets only ($8 extra charge). **Amenities:** high-speed Internet (fee). **Pool(s):** outdoor. **Cards:** AX, DS, MC, VI.

(See map and index starting on p. 285)

SUBURBAN EXTENDED STAY HOTEL   *Book at aaa.com*   Phone: (386)274-4200   **22**
AAA (SAVE)   All Year   1P: $50-$280   2P: $50-$280   XP: $20   F12
Location: I-95, exit 261, 2 mi e, then just n. 220 Bill France Blvd 32114. Fax: 386/274-3383. **Facility:** 135 one-bedroom standard units with efficiencies. 3 stories, exterior corridors. *Bath:* combo or shower only. **Parking:** on-site. **Terms:** 30 day cancellation notice-fee imposed. **Amenities:** voice mail. **Pool(s):** heated outdoor.
Motel   **Guest Services:** coin laundry. **Cards:** AX, DS, MC, VI.

SOME UNITS

SUPER 8 MOTEL   *Book at aaa.com*   Phone: (386)255-5540   **27**
All Year [CP]   1P: $59-$269   2P: $69-$289   XP: $10   F6
Location: I-95, exit 260A, 2.5 mi e on SR 400, then 0.5 mi n on US 1 (Ridgewood Ave). 1242 S Ridgewood Ave 32114.
Small-scale Hotel   Fax: 386/255-9942. **Facility:** 45 one-bedroom standard units, some with whirlpools. 2 stories, interior corridors. *Bath:* combo or shower only. **Parking:** on-site. **Terms:** cancellation fee imposed. **Amenities:** high-speed Internet, voice mail, irons, hair dryers. **Pool(s):** outdoor. **Guest Services:** coin laundry. **Cards:** AX, DS, MC, VI.

SOME UNITS

SUPER 8-OCEANFRONT   *Book at aaa.com*   Phone: 386/253-0666   **17**
Property failed to provide current rates
Location: Jct US 92 and SR A1A N, just e, then n. 133 S Ocean Ave 32118. Fax: 386/239-0858. **Facility:** 76 units.
Motel   74 one-bedroom standard units, some with efficiencies. 2 one-bedroom suites with whirlpools. 2 stories (no elevator), exterior corridors. *Bath:* combo or shower only. **Parking:** on-site. **Amenities:** safes (fee). **Pool(s):**
outdoor. **Guest Services:** coin laundry.

SOME UNITS

TRAVELODGE OCEAN JEWELS RESORT   *Book at aaa.com*   Phone: (386)252-2581   **19**
AAA (SAVE)   3/3-6/8   1P: $79-$119   2P: $79-$119   XP: $10   F18
6/9-8/12   1P: $69-$109   2P: $69-$109   XP: $10   F18
12/1-3/2 & 8/13-11/30   1P: $59-$99   2P: $59-$99   XP: $10   F18
Location: On SR A1A, 0.6 mi s of jct US 92. Located ocean side. 935 S Atlantic Ave 32118. Fax: 386/257-3608.
Condominium   **Facility:** 118 units. 117 one-bedroom standard units with efficiencies. 1 two-bedroom suite ($79-$149) with kitchen. 2-6 stories, exterior corridors. **Parking:** on-site. **Terms:** cancellation fee imposed, package plans.
Amenities: voice mail. **Dining:** 2 pm-2 am. **Pool(s):** outdoor, heated outdoor, wading. **Leisure Activities:** barbecue grills, picnic tables, exercise room. **Fee:** game room. **Guest Services:** coin laundry. **Business Services:** meeting rooms. **Cards:** AX, CB, DC, DS, MC, VI. **Special Amenities:** free newspaper and early check-in/late check-out. *(See color ad below)*

SOME UNITS

(See map and index starting on p. 285)

TROPICAL WINDS OCEANFRONT RESORT   *Book at aaa.com*   Phone: (386)258-1016   **3**

AAA SAVE   All Year   1P: $59-$329   2P: $59-$329   XP: $10   F18

Small-scale Hotel

Location: On SR A1A; 2 mi n of jct US 92. 1398 N Atlantic Ave 32118. **Fax:** 386/255-6462. **Facility:** 94 units. 85 one- and 7 two-bedroom standard units, some with efficiencies. 2 one-bedroom suites with kitchens. 8 stories, interior corridors. **Parking:** on-site. **Terms:** 2 night minimum stay - seasonal and/or weekends, package plans. **Amenities:** hair dryers. **Dining:** 7 am-2 pm. **Pool(s):** outdoor, heated indoor. **Leisure Activities:** shuffleboard. *Fee:* game room. **Guest Services:** valet and coin laundry. **Cards:** AX, CB, DC, MC, VI.

SOME UNITS
🅂🄳 🍽 🏊 DATA PORT 🔒 🖨 / ⊠ 💻 /

THE VILLA BED & BREAKFAST   Phone: (386)248-2020   **11**

All Year   1P: $125-$250   2P: $125-$250

Bed & Breakfast

Location: On SR A1A, 1 mi n from jct US 92, just w on Seabreeze Blvd, then just n. 801 N Peninsula Dr 32118. **Fax:** 386/248-2020. **Facility:** Flower gardens and a tiled patio accent this 1920s Spanish Revival mansion on two acres of manicured grounds fronted by a gated entry. Smoke free premises. 4 one-bedroom standard units. 2 stories, interior corridors. **Parking:** on-site. **Terms:** age restrictions may apply, 7 day cancellation notice-fee imposed, [ECP] meal plan available, no pets allowed (owner's pets on premises). **Amenities:** video library, hair dryers. *Some:* CD players. **Pool(s):** outdoor. **Leisure Activities:** whirlpool, bicycles. **Business Services:** PC. **Cards:** AX, MC, VI.

SOME UNITS
🏊 ⊠ VCR 🎥 ☎ / 🔒 /

──────── **WHERE TO DINE** ────────

BUCA DI BEPPO   Lunch: $11-$30   Dinner: $11-$30   Phone: 386/253-6523   **12**

Italian

Location: I-95, exit 261 northbound; exit 261A southbound, 1 mi e. 2514 W International Speedway Blvd 32114. **Hours:** 4 pm-10 pm, Fri-11 pm, Sat 3 pm-11 pm, Sun noon-9 pm. **Closed:** 11/23, 12/25. **Features:** There isn't an inch of wall space not covered by photographs or memorabilia in some form. Food is served family-style in a fun atmosphere. The cuisine has been described as "immigrant Southern Italian.". Casual dress. **Parking:** on-site. **Cards:** AX, DC, DS, MC, VI.

BYRON'S GRILL   Lunch: $7-$20   Dinner: $7-$20   Phone: 386/257-6606   **1**

Greek

Location: SR A1A, 1 mi n of jct SR 90. 701 N Atlantic Ave 32118. **Hours:** 11 am-10 pm. **Closed:** 12/25. **Features:** A varied menu of steaks, chops, seafood, pizza, pasta and salads is presented. Take-out service is available. Casual dress; beer & wine only. **Parking:** on-site. **Cards:** MC, VI.

CANCUN LAGOON BAR & GRILL   Lunch: $6-$17   Dinner: $8-$17   Phone: 386/255-6500   **10**

AAA

Mexican

Location: I-95, exit 261, 2 mi e. 1735 W International Speedway Blvd 32114. **Hours:** 11 am-1 am, Fri & Sat-2 am, Sun & Mon-11 pm. **Closed:** 12/25. **Features:** The menu comprises well-prepared traditional Mexican selections. The use of quality ingredients is evident in the good flavors of the food. The inviting, upbeat dining room, use of upscale accents and friendly, attentive staff set the mood for enjoyable dining that is relaxed and informal. Casual dress; cocktails. **Parking:** on-site. **Cards:** AX, DC, DS, MC, VI.

&M

CRUISIN' CAFE BAR & GRILL   Lunch: $5-$17   Dinner: $5-$17   Phone: 386/253-5522   **6**

American

Location: Just n of jct US 92 and SR A1A. 2 S Atlantic Ave 32118. **Hours:** 11 am-3 am. **Reservations:** accepted. **Features:** Eat your burger in a race car while you watch replays of auto races. After the meal you can purchase authentic racing memorabilia. Casual dress; cocktails; entertainment. **Parking:** on-site and street. **Cards:** AX, DS, MC, VI.

�

HOG HEAVEN BAR-B-Q   Lunch: $8-$12   Dinner: $8-$12   Phone: 386/257-1212   **5**

Barbecue

Location: On SR A1A, 0.5 mi n of US 92. 37 N Atlantic Ave 32118. **Hours:** 11 am-11 pm. **Features:** Slow cooked barbecue abounds; the pulled pork sandwich is very tasty with sweet slaw and fries as the traditional accompaniment. Casual dress; beer & wine only. **Parking:** on-site. **Cards:** AX, MC, VI.

MARTINIS ON BAY   Lunch: $8-$14   Dinner: $13-$20   Phone: 386/258-1212   **9**

American

Location: 2 blks n of US 92 at Beach St; downtown. 101 Bay St 32114. **Hours:** 11 am-4:30 & 5-10 pm, Fri-11 pm, Sat 5 pm-11 pm. **Closed:** 12/25; also Sun. **Reservations:** accepted. **Features:** Retro surroundings make for a contemporary setting for casual dining. The skilled kitchen's flavorful creations, which change daily based on the market availability of fresh ingredients, appeal to both taste and visual sensations. The congenial wait staff is knowledgeable and attentive. Casual dress; cocktails. **Parking:** street. **Cards:** AX, MC, VI.

MR. GOODCENTS   Lunch: $4-$6   Dinner: $4-$6   Phone: 386/238-2368   **11**

American

Location: I-95, exit 261 northbound; exit 261A southbound, 1.5 mi e. 1808 W International Speedway Blvd 32114. **Hours:** 11 am-9 pm, Sun-6 pm. **Closed:** 1/1, 11/23, 12/25. **Features:** Offering quick-serve sandwiches and sides made to order, the eatery has limited seating, so get it and go. Casual dress. **Parking:** on-site. **Cards:** AX, DS, MC, VI.

NEELAM INDIAN CUISINE   Lunch: $7-$16   Dinner: $10-$16   Phone: 386/238-1022   **8**

Indian

Location: Jct US 92 and SR A1A, just s. 318 S Atlantic Ave 32118. **Hours:** 11:30 am-2 & 5-10:30 pm. **Features:** The casual restaurant's well-prepared dishes include such favorites as shrimp curry and tandoori chicken. Options include not only choices from the menu but also from the varied buffet. Casual dress; beer & wine only. **Parking:** on-site. **Cards:** AX, DS, MC, VI.

(See map and index starting on p. 285)

THE OYSTER PUB　　　**Lunch:** $5-$7　　　**Dinner:** $7-$25　　　**Phone:** 386/255-6348　②
　　　Location: Jct US 92 and SR A1A, 1 mi n, just w. 555 Seabreeze Blvd 32118. **Hours:** 11:30 am-3 am.
　　　Reservations: not accepted. **Features:** The restaurant has a fun pub atmosphere. The game room in the
American　back has pool tables and video games for guests' enjoyment. Choices range from burgers to seafood, but
　　　the oysters come most highly recommended. Casual dress; cocktails. **Parking:** on-site. **Cards:** AX, DS,
MC, VI.

SAPPORO JAPANESE STEAK HOUSE　　　**Lunch:** $4-$9　　　**Dinner:** $8-$16　　　**Phone:** 386/257-4477　③
　　　Location: Jct US 92 and SR A1A, 1 mi n, just w. 501 Seabreeze Blvd 32118. **Hours:** 11:30 am-10 pm, Fri-11 pm,
　　　Sat 5 pm-11 pm, Sun 5 pm-10 pm. Closed: 11/23. **Reservations:** accepted. **Features:** The Japanese
Japanese　steakhouse has two dining areas: one with eight tables where chefs grill the food in front of diners and the
　　　other regular dining room, which also includes a sushi bar. Good food is value-priced. Casual dress;
cocktails. **Parking:** on-site. **Cards:** AX, DC, DS, MC, VI.

SHELLS GREAT CASUAL SEAFOOD　　　**Lunch:** $5-$8　　　**Dinner:** $8-$14　　　**Phone:** 386/258-0007　⑦
　　　Location: On SR A1A, just n of US 92. 200 S Atlantic Ave 32118. **Hours:** 11:30 am-10 pm, Fri & Sat-11 pm.
　　　Closed: 11/23, 12/25. **Features:** Shellfish and pasta, a few chicken and one steak item served in a very
Seafood　casual, informal setting with bare table tops by servers in jeans and brightly colored tropical shirts. Casual
　　　dress; cocktails. **Parking:** on-site. **Cards:** AX, DS, MC, VI.

STARLITE DINER　　　**Lunch:** $4-$8　　　**Dinner:** $4-$11　　　**Phone:** 386/255-9555　④
　　　Location: On SR A1A, 0.8 mi n of US 92. 401 N Atlantic Ave 32118. **Hours:** 7 am-11 pm, Fri & Sat-midnight, Sun-
　　　9 pm. Closed: 12/25. **Features:** This '60s-era jukebox joint is the place to go for comfort food and lots of it.
American　Mom's meatloaf, juicy burgers, homemade cakes and pies and decadent fountain creations might not do
　　　much for your waistline, but they'll work wonders for your state of mind. Casual dress. **Parking:** on-site.
Cards: AX, DC, DS, MC, VI.

DAYTONA BEACH SHORES pop. 4,299　(See map and index starting on p. 285)

────── WHERE TO STAY ──────

ACAPULCO HOTEL & RESORT　　　　　　　　　　　**Phone:** (386)761-2210　58
　AAA SAVE　All Year　　　1P: $119-$199　　　2P: $119-$199　　　XP: $10　　　F16
　fyi　Under major renovation, scheduled to be completed October 2005. **Last rated:** ▽▽▽ **Location:** On SR
　　　A1A, 2.8 mi s of jct US 92. 2505 S Atlantic Ave 32118. Fax: 386/761-2216. **Facility:** 133 one-bedroom standard
　　　units, some with efficiencies. 8 stories, interior corridors. **Bath:** combo or shower only. **Parking:** on-site.
Small-scale Hotel　**Terms:** 5 night minimum stay - seasonal, 7 day cancellation notice-fee imposed. **Amenities:** voice mail,
safes (fee), hair dryers. **Dining:** 7-11 am. **Pool(s):** heated outdoor, wading. **Leisure Activities:** whirlpools, recreation programs,
shuffleboard. **Guest Services:** gift shop, coin laundry. **Business Services:** fax. **Cards:** AX, CB, DC, DS, MC, VI.
Special Amenities: free room upgrade (subject to availability with advance reservations). (See color ad p 291)

SOME UNITS

ATLANTIC OCEAN PALM INN　　　　　　　　　　　**Phone:** (386)761-8450　63
　AAA SAVE　2/1-8/31　　　1P: $69-$189　　　2P: $69-$189　　　XP: $10　　　F12
　　　12/1-1/31 & 9/1-11/30　1P: $59-$149　　　2P: $59-$149　　　XP: $10　　　F12
▽▽ ▽▽　**Location:** On SR A1A, 5 mi s of jct US 92. 3247 S Atlantic Ave 32118. Fax: 386/304-3079. **Facility:** 50 one-
　　　bedroom standard units, some with efficiencies and/or whirlpools. 3 stories, exterior corridors. **Parking:** on-
Motel　site. **Terms:** office hours 8 am-10 pm, 1-7 night minimum stay - seasonal and/or weekends, 30 day
　　　cancellation notice-fee imposed, weekly rates available, small pets only ($15 fee, in designated units).
Amenities: hair dryers. **Pool(s):** heated outdoor. **Leisure Activities:** sun deck, shuffleboard. **Guest Services:** coin laundry.
Cards: AX, DS, MC, VI. (See color ad p 303)

SOME UNITS

FEE

BAHAMA HOUSE　　**Book at aaa.com**　　　　　　　　**Phone:** (386)248-2001　50
　AAA SAVE　6/2-8/12 [ECP]　　1P: $186-$224　　2P: $186-$224　　XP: $10　　F17
　　　2/3-6/1 [ECP]　　　1P: $134-$202　　2P: $134-$202　　XP: $10　　F17
▽▽ ▽▽　12/1-2/2 & 8/13-11/30 [ECP]　1P: $134-$162　　2P: $134-$162　　XP: $10　　F17
Small-scale Hotel　**Location:** On SR A1A, 1.5 mi s of jct US 92. 2001 S Atlantic Ave 32118. Fax: 386/248-0991. **Facility:** 95 units. 91
　　　one-bedroom standard units, some with efficiencies and/or whirlpools. 4 one-bedroom suites with
　　　efficiencies, some with whirlpools. 10 stories, interior corridors. **Bath:** combo or shower only. **Parking:** on-
site. **Terms:** 2 night minimum stay - seasonal, 7 day cancellation notice, package plans. **Amenities:** high-speed Internet, voice
mail, safes (fee), irons, hair dryers. **Pool(s):** heated outdoor. **Leisure Activities:** whirlpool, recreation programs. **Guest
Services:** complimentary evening beverages, coin laundry. **Cards:** AX, CB, DC, DS, MC, VI. **Special Amenities: free
expanded continental breakfast and free newspaper.** (See color ad p 303)

SOME UNITS

(See map and index starting on p. 285)

BEACH HOUSE OCEANFRONT MOTEL

Phone: (386)788-7107   **62**

◆◆◆ SAVE All Year   1P: $59-$89   2P: $59-$89   XP: $10   F12
▽▽ ▽▽   **Location:** On SR A1A, 0.5 mi n of Port Orange Bridge. 3221 S Atlantic Ave 32118. Fax: 386/760-3672. **Facility:** 10
Motel   units. 9 one-bedroom standard units, some with efficiencies. 1 three-bedroom suite with kitchen. 1 story,
exterior corridors. *Bath:* combo or shower only. **Parking:** on-site. **Terms:** 30 day cancellation notice-fee
imposed, weekly rates available. **Amenities:** irons, hair dryers. *Some:* DVD players. **Pool(s):** heated
outdoor. **Leisure Activities:** whirlpool. **Guest Services:** coin laundry. **Cards:** AX, DS, MC, VI.
Special Amenities: free local telephone calls.

SOME UNITS

⬛ 🛢 📶 🅿 🏊 🛏 🖥 💻 / ✕ VCR /

(See map and index starting on p. 285)

BEACHSIDE MOTEL   *Book at aaa.com*   Phone: (386)788-5569   ⑥⑤

AAA SAVE   2/3-9/3 [ECP]   1P: $119-$159   2P: $119-$159
            12/1-2/2 [ECP]   1P: $79-$109   2P: $79-$109
◆◆◆◆   9/4-11/30 [ECP]   1P: $79-$104   2P: $79-$104

            Location: On SR A1A, 5.3 mi s of US 92, 0.3 mi n of Port Orange Bridge. 3309 S Atlantic Ave 32118.
Small-scale Hotel Fax: 386/271-0000. **Facility:** Smoke free premises. 31 one-bedroom standard units with efficiencies. 5
            stories, interior corridors. **Parking:** on-site. **Terms:** 10 day cancellation notice, package plans.
Amenities: irons, hair dryers. **Pool(s):** heated outdoor, wading. **Leisure Activities:** whirlpool. *Fee:* game room. **Guest Services:** valet and coin laundry. **Business Services:** meeting rooms. **Cards:** AX, CB, DC, DS, MC, VI. **Special Amenities:** free expanded continental breakfast and early check-in/late check-out. *(See color ad below)*

(See map and index starting on p. 285)

BEST WESTERN-AKU TIKI INN   *Book at aaa.com*

Phone: (386)252-9631   **53**

2/3-4/22	1P: $169-$229	2P: $169-$229	XP: $10 F17
4/23-8/19	1P: $139-$199	2P: $139-$199	XP: $10 F17
12/1-2/2 & 8/20-11/30	1P: $109-$169	2P: $109-$169	XP: $10 F17

Location: On SR A1A, 2.2 mi s of jct US 92. 2225 S Atlantic Ave 32118. Fax: 386/252-1198. **Facility:** 132 one-bedroom standard units, some with efficiencies. 5 stories, interior corridors. **Parking:** on-site. **Terms:** 7 day cancellation notice, package plans. **Amenities:** high-speed Internet, voice mail, safes, irons, hair dryers. **Dining:** 7 am-9 pm, cocktails. **Pool(s):** heated outdoor, wading. **Leisure Activities:** shuffleboard. **Guest Services:** complimentary evening beverages, coin laundry. **Business Services:** meeting rooms. **Cards:** AX, CB, DC, DS, JC, MC, VI. **Special Amenities:** free local telephone calls and free newspaper. *(See color ad p 293)*

SOME UNITS

DAYS INN OCEANFRONT SOUTH TROPICAL SEAS   *Book at aaa.com*

Phone: (386)767-8737   **66**

All Year	1P: $59-$329	2P: $59-$329	XP: $10 F18

Location: On SR A1A, just n of Port Orange Bridge; 5.8 mi s of US 92. 3357 S Atlantic Ave 32118. Fax: 386/756-9612. **Facility:** 75 one-bedroom standard units, some with efficiencies. 7 stories, interior corridors. **Terms:** 2 night minimum stay - seasonal and/or weekends, package plans. **Amenities:** hair dryers. **Pool(s):** heated outdoor. **Leisure Activities:** whirlpool, shuffleboard. *Fee:* game room. **Guest Services:** coin laundry. **Cards:** AX, CB, DC, DS, MC, VI.

SOME UNITS

DREAM INN   *Book at aaa.com*

Phone: (386)767-2821   **61**

12/25-11/30	1P: $79-$299	2P: $79-$299	XP: $10 D12

Location: On SR A1A, 0.5 mi n of Port Orange Bridge. 3217 S Atlantic Ave 32118. Fax: 386/767-7778. **Facility:** 26 one-bedroom standard units, some with efficiencies and/or whirlpools. 2 stories, exterior corridors. *Bath:* combo or shower only. **Terms:** open 12/25-11/30, 60 day cancellation notice-fee imposed. **Amenities:** voice mail, safes, hair dryers. **Pool(s):** heated outdoor. **Leisure Activities:** *Fee:* boogie boards, beach chairs. **Guest Services:** coin laundry. **Cards:** AX, DS, MC, VI. **Special Amenities:** free newspaper and preferred room (subject to availability with advance reservations).

SOME UNITS

HAMPTON INN OCEANFRONT   *Book at aaa.com*

Phone: (386)767-8533   **59**

All Year [BP]	1P: $89-$299	2P: $99-$299	XP: $10 F18

Location: On SR A1A, 4.5 mi s of jct US 92. 3135 S Atlantic Ave 32118. Fax: 386/788-1609. **Facility:** 114 one-bedroom standard units. 8 stories, interior/exterior corridors. *Bath:* combo or shower only. **Terms:** check-in 4 pm, cancellation fee imposed, package plans. **Amenities:** voice mail, irons, hair dryers. **Pool(s):** heated outdoor. **Leisure Activities:** whirlpool, volleyball. **Guest Services:** valet and coin laundry. **Cards:** AX, DC, DS, MC, VI. **Special Amenities:** free full breakfast and free local telephone calls. *(See color ad p 693)*

SOME UNITS

(See map and index starting on p. 285)

HAWAIIAN INN   *Book at aaa.com*   Phone: (386)255-5411   **55**

AAA (SAVE)   2/1-5/25   1P: $79-$149   2P: $79-$149
            8/22-11/30   1P: $69-$129   2P: $69-$129
▼▼▼ ▼▼   12/1-1/31   1P: $59-$119   2P: $59-$119
            5/26-8/21   1P: $59-$109   2P: $59-$109
Condominium   **Location:** On SR A1A, 2.3 mi s of jct US 92. 2301 S Atlantic Ave 32118. Fax: 386/253-1209. **Facility:** Smoke free premises. 208 units. 167 one-bedroom standard units with efficiencies. 38 one- and 3 two-bedroom suites with kitchens. 5 stories, interior/exterior corridors. *Bath:* combo or shower only. **Parking:** on-site. **Terms:** check-in 4 pm, 3 day cancellation notice-fee imposed, package plans. **Amenities:** safes (fee). *Some:* hair dryers. **Dining:** 2 restaurants, 7 am-6 pm; dinner show 5:30 pm, cocktails. **Pool(s):** outdoor, heated indoor, wading. **Leisure Activities:** miniature golf, shuffleboard. *Fee:* game room. **Guest Services:** gift shop, coin laundry. **Business Services:** meeting rooms, fax (fee). **Cards:** AX, DS, MC, VI.
(See color ad below)

🆂ᴰ 🍴 🍸 🏊 ⚔ ✕ 📷 🔌 📺 ▦ 💻

HOLIDAY INN DAYTONA BEACH SHORES   *Book at aaa.com*   Phone: (386)761-2050   **60**

AAA (SAVE)   All Year   1P: $89-$139   2P: $89-$139   XP: $10   F18
▼▼▼ ▼▼   **Location:** On SR A1A, 5 mi s of jct US 92. 3209 S Atlantic Ave 32118. Fax: 386/761-3922. **Facility:** 193 units. 190 one-bedroom standard units. 3 one-bedroom suites. 8 stories, interior corridors. **Parking:** on-site.
Small-scale Hotel   **Terms:** cancellation fee imposed, package plans. **Amenities:** safes (fee), irons, hair dryers. **Dining:** 7 am-11 & 5-8 pm seasonally, cocktails. **Pool(s):** heated outdoor, wading. **Leisure Activities:** exercise room. *Fee:* game room. **Guest Services:** gift shop, valet and coin laundry. **Business Services:** meeting rooms.
Cards: AX, CB, DC, DS, JC, MC, VI. **Special Amenities:** free newspaper.

SOME UNITS
🆂ᴰ 🍴 🍸 🏊 ⚔ 📷 🔌 📺 /✕ 🔌 ▦ /

OCEANSIDE INN   *Book at aaa.com*   Phone: (386)255-4492   **49**

AAA (SAVE)   2/1-4/30   1P: $79-$349   2P: $79-$349
            5/1-8/31   1P: $59-$269   2P: $59-$269
▼▼▼ ▼▼   9/1-11/30   1P: $49-$199   2P: $49-$199
            12/1-1/31   1P: $49-$109   2P: $49-$109
Small-scale Hotel   **Location:** 0.5 mi s of jct US 92. 1909 S Atlantic Ave 32118. Fax: 386/258-0354. **Facility:** 191 units. 185 one-bedroom standard units. 6 one-bedroom suites with kitchens. 9 stories, interior corridors. *Bath:* combo or shower only. **Parking:** on-site. **Terms:** check-in 4 pm, 3 day cancellation notice-fee imposed, [CP] meal plan available, package plans. **Amenities:** voice mail, safes (fee), irons, hair dryers. **Dining:** 7:30 am-10 & 11:30-2 am. **Pool(s):** heated outdoor, wading. **Leisure Activities:** garden deck, exercise room. **Guest Services:** coin laundry. **Business Services:** meeting rooms, fax (fee). **Cards:** AX, DS, MC, VI. **Special Amenities:** free continental breakfast. *(See color ad p 307)*

SOME UNITS
🆂ᴰ 🍴 🍸 🅜 🏊 📷 🔌 📺 /✕ 🔌 ▦ /

PALM PLAZA OCEANFRONT RESORT   *Book at aaa.com*   Phone: (386)767-1711   **64**

AAA (SAVE)   2/3-9/3 [ECP]   1P: $119-$169   2P: $119-$169
            12/1-2/2 [ECP]   1P: $79-$114   2P: $79-$114
▼▼▼ ▼▼▼   9/4-11/30 [ECP]   1P: $79-$104   2P: $79-$104
Small-scale Hotel   **Location:** On SR A1A, 5.3 mi s of US 92; 0.3 mi n of Port Orange Bridge. 3301 S Atlantic Ave 32118-6308. Fax: 386/756-8394. **Facility:** 98 units. 88 one-bedroom standard units with efficiencies. 10 one-bedroom suites ($109-$299) with efficiencies. 12 stories, exterior corridors. *Bath:* combo or shower only. **Parking:** on-site. **Terms:** 10 day cancellation notice, package plans. **Amenities:** safes (fee), irons, hair dryers. **Pool(s):** heated outdoor, wading. **Leisure Activities:** whirlpool. *Fee:* game room. **Guest Services:** valet and coin laundry. **Business Services:** meeting rooms. **Cards:** AX, CB, DC, DS, MC, VI. **Special Amenities:** free expanded continental breakfast and early check-in/late check-out. *(See color ad p 304)*

SOME UNITS
🆂ᴰ 🍴 🏊 🎥 🔌 🔌 ▦ 📺 /✕ /

Easy, hassle-free vehicle battery testing or replacement

A battery jump gets you on your way fast … but, to where? Another breakdown? A garage waiting room so you can sit while your battery is being tested or a new one installed? AAA Battery Service provides members on-the-scene battery testing and replacement at competitive prices.

Call **1-800-AAA-HELP** to find out how it works!*

Emergency Services

*This service is not available in all areas. Contact your AAA representative for details.

(See map and index starting on p. 285)

PERRY'S OCEAN-EDGE RESORT   *Book at aaa.com*   Phone: (386)255-0581   52
| | | |
12/1-8/5   1P: $75-$174   2P: $75-$174
8/6-11/30   1P: $75-$140   2P: $75-$140
Location: On SR A1A, 2 mi s of jct US 92. 2209 S Atlantic Ave 32118. Fax: 386/258-7315. **Facility:** 200 one-bedroom standard units, some with efficiencies or kitchens. 2-6 stories, interior/exterior corridors. **Parking:** on-site.
Small-scale Hotel   **Terms:** check-in 4 pm, 3 day cancellation notice-fee imposed, [CP] meal plan available. **Amenities:** voice mail. *Fee:* video library, safes. *Some:* high-speed Internet, irons, hair dryers. **Dining:** 7 am-2 pm. **Pool(s):** 2 outdoor, heated indoor, wading. **Leisure Activities:** whirlpool, putting green, recreation programs, bocci, lawn games, tetherball, playground, exercise room, basketball, horseshoes, shuffleboard, volleyball. *Fee:* game room. **Guest Services:** gift shop, coin laundry. **Business Services:** meeting rooms, PC, fax (fee). **Cards:** AX, DC, DS, MC, VI. **Special Amenities:** free continental breakfast. Affiliated with Best Value Inn Brand Membership. *(See color ad below)*

SOME UNITS
🅢🅓 🍴 🏊 ⊠ DATA PORT / VCR 🔲 🖳 /
FEE

SHORELINE ALL SUITES INN   *Book at aaa.com*   Phone: (386)252-1692   57
| | | |
1/31-9/10 [CP]   2P: $79-$169   XP: $20   F18
12/1-1/30 & 9/11-11/30 [CP]   2P: $69-$149   XP: $20   F18
Location: On SR A1A, 2.8 mi s of jct US 92. 2435 S Atlantic Ave 32118. Fax: 386/239-7068. **Facility:** 17 units. 13 one- and 4 two-bedroom suites ($69-$169) with kitchens. 1-2 stories (no elevator), exterior corridors. *Bath:* **Small-scale Hotel**   combo or shower only. **Parking:** on-site. **Terms:** 30 day cancellation notice, package plans. **Amenities:** video library, DVD players, CD players, hair dryers. **Pool(s):** heated outdoor. **Leisure Activities:** sun deck, barbecue grills, shuffleboard, volleyball. **Guest Services:** coin laundry. **Cards:** AX, DS, MC, VI. **Special Amenities:** free continental breakfast and free local telephone calls.

🅢🅓 🍴 🏊 ⊠ ⊠ 🏃 🔲 🖳 🖳

SUN VIKING LODGE   Phone: (386)252-6252   56
| | | |
2/1-8/19   1P: $99-$329   2P: $99-$329   XP: $15   F17
8/20-11/30   1P: $85-$199   2P: $85-$199   XP: $10   F17
12/1-1/31   1P: $79-$159   2P: $79-$159   XP: $10   F17
Location: On SR A1A, 2.5 mi s of jct US 92. 2411 S Atlantic Ave 32118. Fax: 386/252-5463. **Facility:** 91 units. 69 **Small-scale Hotel**   one-bedroom standard units, some with efficiencies. 22 one-bedroom suites ($129-$399) with kitchens. 2-8 stories, interior/exterior corridors. **Parking:** on-site. **Terms:** check-in 5 pm, 2-5 night minimum stay – seasonal and/or weekends, 7 day cancellation notice. **Amenities:** *Fee:* video library, safes. **Dining:** 7:30 am-2:30 pm. **Pool(s):** heated outdoor, heated indoor, wading. **Leisure Activities:** sauna, whirlpool, waterslide, recreation programs, playground, exercise room, basketball, shuffleboard, volleyball. *Fee:* game room. **Guest Services:** coin laundry. **Business Services:** meeting rooms, PC. **Cards:** AX, CB, DC, DS, MC, VI. **Special Amenities:** free newspaper. *(See color ad p 294)*

SOME UNITS
🅢🅓 🍴 🏊 ⊠ 🔲 🖳 / ⊠ VCR /
FEE

(See map and index starting on p. 285)

TREASURE ISLAND RESORT

Phone: 386/255-8371 **51**

[fyi]

Property failed to provide current rates

Large-scale Hotel
Under major renovation, scheduled to be completed January 2006. **Last rated:** ♛♛♛ **Location:** On SR A1A, 1.8 mi s of jct US 92. 2025 S Atlantic Ave 32118. Fax: 386/255-4984. **Facility:** 227 units. 223 one-bedroom standard units, some with efficiencies. 4 one-bedroom suites with kitchens. 11 stories, interior/exterior corridors. *Bath:* combo or shower only. **Parking:** on-site. **Terms:** check-in 4 pm. **Amenities:** voice mail, safes (fee), irons, hair dryers. **Pool(s):** outdoor, heated outdoor, wading. **Leisure Activities:** whirlpools, recreation programs. *Fee:* game room. **Guest Services:** gift shop, valet and coin laundry. **Business Services:** meeting rooms, fax. *(See color ad p 291)*

SOME UNITS

TROPICAL MANOR MOTEL

Phone: 386/252-4920 **54**

⊕⊕⊕ [SAVE]

2/1-9/4   2P: $80-$150   XP: $7
12/1-1/31 & 9/5-11/30   2P: $65-$130   XP: $7

♛♛ ♛♛

Motel

Location: On SR A1A, 2.2 mi s of jct US 92. 2237 S Atlantic Ave 32118. Fax: 386/258-9415. **Facility:** 36 units. 16 one-bedroom standard units, some with efficiencies. 20 one-bedroom suites with kitchens. 1-2 stories, exterior corridors. *Bath:* combo or shower only. **Parking:** on-site. **Terms:** office hours 8 am-1 am, 2 night minimum stay - seasonal and/or weekends, 14 day cancellation notice, weekly rates available. **Pool(s):** heated outdoor, wading. **Leisure Activities:** pavilion with grill, shuffleboard. **Guest Services:** coin laundry. **Cards:** AX, DS, MC, VI. *(See color ad below)*

(See map and index starting on p. 285)

─────── *The following lodging was either not evaluated or did not* ───────
meet AAA rating requirements but is listed for your information only.

THE SHORES RESORT & SPA
[fyi] Not evaluated. **Location:** On SR A1A, 3.2 mi s of jct US 92. 2637 S Atlantic Ave 32118. Facilities, services, and decor characterize a mid-range property.
Phone: 386/767-7350

─────── **WHERE TO DINE** ───────

CHINA-AMERICAN GARDEN **Dinner:** $7-$14 Phone: 386/788-6269 **③⑤**
⚠️ **Location:** On SR A1A, 2.8 mi s of jct US 92; in Pappas Plaza Shopping Center. 2516 S Atlantic Ave 32118.
Hours: Open 12/26-11/30; 4 pm-11 pm. **Reservations:** accepted. **Features:** The hot and sour soup rates
💎💎 high on the list of favorites. This is casual family dining specializing in Cantonese cuisine with some
Chinese   Szechuan and Mandarin dishes. Thai cuisine is also served. Casual dress; cocktails. **Parking:** on-site.
Cards: AX, MC, VI.
🍴

OCEAN DINER **Lunch:** $6-$8 Phone: 386/322-6867 **③⑥**
💎 **Location:** On SR A1A, just n of Port Orange Bridge, then 5.8 mi s of US 92. 3344 S Atlantic Ave 32118. **Hours:** 6 am-
2 pm. **Features:** Serving breakfast all day, the restaurant offers traditional omelettes, french toast and
American   waffles as well as sandwich platters, burgers and specialty cakes. Casual dress. **Parking:** on-site.

DEBARY pop. 15,559

─────── **WHERE TO STAY** ───────

HAMPTON INN DEBARY/DELTONA *Book at aaa.com* Phone: (386)668-5758
💎💎💎 All Year [ECP] 1P: $79-$109 2P: $89-$119
Location: I-4, exit 108, just nw. 308 Sunrise Blvd 32713. Fax: 386/668-1284. **Facility:** 76 one-bedroom standard
Small-scale Hotel   units, some with whirlpools. 3 stories, interior corridors. *Bath:* combo or shower only. **Parking:** on-site.
Terms: 30 day cancellation notice, package plans. **Amenities:** voice mail, irons, hair dryers. **Pool(s):**
outdoor. **Leisure Activities:** whirlpool, exercise room. **Guest Services:** coin laundry. **Business Services:** fax (fee). **Cards:** AX,
DC, DS, MC, VI.
SOME UNITS
(ASK) 🆂🅳 🍴 ⚙️ &M ♿ ⊘ 🏊 📷 🎛️ ☕ /✕/

─────── **WHERE TO DINE** ───────

SWAMP HOUSE GRILL **Lunch:** $5-$7 **Dinner:** $7-$17 Phone: 386/668-8891
💎💎 **Location:** 2.7 mi w of US 17-92. 488 W Highbanks Rd 32713. **Hours:** 11 am-9 pm, Fri-10 pm, Sat 8 am-10 pm,
Sun 8 am-9 pm. Closed: 1/1, 12/25; also Mon. **Features:** Nestled in a casual tropical setting by a marina,
American   the crowd flocks here by boat and by foot. The catfish is the most popular entree, but don't miss out on the
other fresh seafood. Casual dress; cocktails. **Parking:** on-site. **Cards:** AX, DS, MC, VI.

DEERFIELD BEACH —*See Fort Lauderdale p. 401.*

DE FUNIAK SPRINGS pop. 5,089

─────── **WHERE TO STAY** ───────

BEST WESTERN CROSSROADS INN *Book at aaa.com* Phone: 850/892-5111
💎💎💎 All Year 1P: $69-$99 2P: $69-$99 XP: $5 F17
Location: I-10, exit 85, just s. Located in a rural quiet area. 2343 Freeport Rd 32435 (PO Box 852).
Small-scale Hotel   Fax: 850/892-2439. **Facility:** 100 one-bedroom standard units. 2 stories, interior/exterior corridors. **Parking:**
on-site. **Amenities:** high-speed Internet, irons, hair dryers. **Pool(s):** outdoor. **Business Services:** meeting
rooms, fax (fee). **Cards:** AX, DC, DS, MC, VI.
SOME UNITS
(ASK) 🆂🅳 🛏️ 🍴 🍸 🏊 📷 🎛️ ☕ /✕ 📶 🖥️/

DAYS INN *Book at aaa.com* Phone: 850/892-6115
💎💎 Property failed to provide current rates
Location: I-10, exit 85, just n. 472 Hugh Adams Rd 32433. Fax: 850/892-0707. **Facility:** 58 one-bedroom
Small-scale Hotel   standard units. 1 story, exterior corridors. **Parking:** on-site. **Terms:** pets ($10 extra charge). **Amenities:** hair
dryers. **Pool(s):** outdoor. **Business Services:** fax.
SOME UNITS
🛏️ 🍴 🏊 📷 📶 🖥️ /✕/
FEE

HOTEL DE FUNIAK Phone: 850/892-4383
💎💎💎 Property failed to provide current rates
Location: On US 90; center. 400 E Nelson 32433. Fax: 850/892-5346. **Facility:** Smoke free premises. 11 units.
Small-scale Hotel   9 one-bedroom standard units. 2 one-bedroom suites. 2 stories, interior/exterior corridors. *Bath:* combo or
shower only. **Parking:** street. **Amenities:** high-speed Internet. **Business Services:** meeting rooms, fax.
🍴 ♿ ✕

DELAND pop. 24,904

—— WHERE TO STAY ——

COMFORT INN & SUITES *Book at aaa.com*
Phone: (386)736-3100

2/1-4/30 [CP]	1P: $95-$235	2P: $95-$235
12/1-1/31 [CP]	1P: $85-$165	2P: $85-$165
5/1-9/30 [CP]	1P: $75-$150	2P: $75-$150
10/1-11/30 [CP]	1P: $75-$125	2P: $75-$125

AAA SAVE 🔷🔷🔷

Small-scale Hotel **Location:** 0.5 mi ne on US 92 at jct US 17. 400 E International Speedway Blvd 32724. Fax: 386/740-0570. **Facility:** 68 one-bedroom standard units, some with whirlpools. 3 stories, interior corridors. *Bath:* combo or shower only. **Parking:** on-site. **Amenities:** voice mail, irons, hair dryers. **Pool(s):** outdoor. **Leisure Activities:** whirlpool. **Guest Services:** coin laundry. **Business Services:** meeting rooms. **Cards:** AX, DC, DS, MC, VI. **Special Amenities:** free continental breakfast and free local telephone calls.

SOME UNITS

DELAND ARTISAN INN
Phone: 386/736-3484

🔷🔷🔷

Historic Country Inn

All Year	1P: $95-$185	2P: $95-$185

Location: Downtown. 215 S Woodland Blvd 32720. Fax: 386/822-9065. **Facility:** Built in 1924, this hotel has been completely renovated; the Spanish facade and the stucco walls add to its historic charm. Smoke free premises. 8 one-bedroom suites ($95-$185), some with whirlpools. 3 stories, interior corridors. **Parking:** on-site. **Terms:** check-in 4 pm, age restrictions may apply, 3 day cancellation notice. **Amenities:** voice mail, hair dryers. **Dining:** restaurant, see separate listing. **Business Services:** meeting rooms, fax (fee). **Cards:** AX, DC, DS, MC, VI.

HOLIDAY INN *Book at aaa.com*
Phone: (386)738-5200

2/2-3/31	1P: $199-$229
6/27-11/30	1P: $79-$209
4/1-6/26	1P: $69-$99
12/1-2/1	1P: $59-$79

AAA SAVE 🔷🔷🔷

Small-scale Hotel **Location:** 0.3 mi ne on US 92 from jct US 17. 350 E International Speedway Blvd 32724. Fax: 386/734-7552. **Facility:** 148 units. 137 one-bedroom standard units. 11 one-bedroom suites. 6 stories, interior corridors. *Bath:* combo or shower only. **Parking:** on-site. **Terms:** 2-3 night minimum stay - seasonal, cancellation fee imposed, pets ($25 fee). **Amenities:** voice mail, irons, hair dryers. **Dining:** 6:30 am-2 & 5:30-9 pm, cocktails. **Pool(s):** heated outdoor. **Leisure Activities:** whirlpool, exercise room. **Guest Services:** valet and coin laundry. **Business Services:** conference facilities, PC. **Cards:** AX, DC, DS, MC, VI. **Special Amenities:** free newspaper.

SOME UNITS

FEE

HONTOON LANDING RESORT & MARINA
Phone: (386)734-2474

All Year	1P: $90-$225	2P: $90-$225 XP: $10

AAA SAVE 🔷🔷🔷

Motel **Location:** US 17-92, 2.1 mi w on SR 44, 1.9 mi sw on CR 4110 (Old New York), then 3.4 mi s on CR 4125 (Hontoon Rd). 2317 River Ridge Rd 32720. Fax: 386/738-9743. **Facility:** 18 units. 15 one-bedroom standard units, some with kitchens. 2 one- and 1 two-bedroom suites ($135-$225) with kitchens, some with whirlpools. 1-2 stories (no elevator), exterior corridors. *Bath:* combo or shower only. **Parking:** on-site. **Terms:** 30 day cancellation notice-fee imposed. **Amenities:** voice mail. *Some:* irons. **Pool(s):** outdoor. **Leisure Activities:** rental boats, fishing, gas grills. *Fee:* marina, fishing boats, houseboats, pontoon boats. **Guest Services:** gift shop. **Cards:** DS, MC, VI.

SOME UNITS

UNIVERSITY INN
Phone: (386)734-5711

4/1-11/30	1P: $79-$179	2P: $79-$179
2/1-3/31	1P: $89-$175	2P: $89-$175
1/1-1/31	1P: $79-$89	2P: $79-$89
12/1-12/31	1P: $69-$79	2P: $69-$79

AAA SAVE 🔷🔷🔷

Motel **Location:** US 17, 0.9 mi n of jct SR 44. Located next to Stetson University. 644 N Woodland Blvd 32720. Fax: 386/734-5716. **Facility:** 59 units. 58 one-bedroom standard units. 1 one-bedroom suite with kitchen. 2 stories (no elevator), exterior corridors. *Bath:* combo or shower only. **Parking:** on-site. **Terms:** 2-3 night minimum stay - seasonal, cancellation fee imposed, [CP] meal plan available, pets ($20 extra charge). **Pool(s):** outdoor. **Leisure Activities:** limited exercise equipment. **Business Services:** meeting rooms. **Cards:** AX, DS, MC, VI. **Special Amenities:** free continental breakfast and free local telephone calls.

SOME UNITS

FEE

—— WHERE TO DINE ——

CEDAR RIVER SEAFOOD
Lunch: $5-$17   **Dinner:** $5-$17   **Phone:** 386/738-1968

🔷🔷

Seafood

Location: 0.3 mi ne on US 92 from jct US 17. 310 E International Speedway Blvd 32724. **Hours:** 11 am-9 pm, Fri & Sat-10 pm. Closed: 11/23, 12/25. **Features:** Fishing nets, driftwood and boat oars are part of the decor, but they're not the reason people come to the kid-friendly seafood restaurant. The big draw is the menu, which lists such fresh catches of the day as mahi mahi, as well as crabs, shrimp and scallops. The staff is friendly. Casual dress; beer & wine only. **Parking:** on-site. **Cards:** MC, VI.

DELAND ARTISAN INN
Lunch: $5-$12   **Dinner:** $12-$21   **Phone:** 386/736-3484

🔷🔷

Continental

Location: Downtown; in Deland Artisan Inn. 215 S Woodland Blvd 32720. **Hours:** 11 am-9 pm, Fri-10 pm, Sat 4 pm-10 pm. Closed major holidays; also Sun. **Features:** This downtown eatery is housed in a historic old hotel now known as the Deland Artisan Inn. Casual atmosphere and creative menu offerings make this a great place for lunch or dinner. Casual dress; cocktails. **Parking:** on-site. **Cards:** AX, DC, DS, MC, VI.

EL RANCHO MEXICANO

Lunch: $6-$10   **Dinner:** $6-$10   **Phone:** 386/822-9171

Mexican

Location: Just n of jct US 17-92 and CR 472. 2420 S Woodland Blvd 32724. **Hours:** 11 am-9 pm, Fri & Sat-10 pm. Closed: 1/1, 11/23, 12/25. **Features:** In a shopping center, the restaurant presents a menu of traditional Mexican favorites, as well as flavorful house specialties. The informal dining room is suited for a casual dining experience. Casual dress; beer & wine only. **Parking:** on-site. **Cards:** AX, DS, MC, VI.

EL RANCHO MEXICANO

Lunch: $6-$10   **Dinner:** $6-$10   **Phone:** 386/738-9047

Mexican

Location: Jct US 92 and 17; in shopping center. 1564 N Woodland Blvd 32724. **Hours:** 11 am-9 pm, Fri & Sat-10 pm. Closed: 1/1, 11/23, 12/25. **Features:** In a shopping center, the restaurant presents a menu of traditional Mexican favorites, as well as flavorful house specialties. The informal dining room is suited for a casual dining experience. Casual dress; beer & wine only. **Parking:** on-site. **Cards:** AX, DS, MC, VI.

GRAM'S KITCHEN

Lunch: $1-$8   **Phone:** 386/736-9340

American
Cards: MC, VI.

Location: On SR 44, 1.6 mi e of US 17-92. 844 E New York Ave 32724. **Hours:** 6 am-4 pm, Sun-3 pm. Closed: 11/23, 12/25. **Reservations:** not accepted. **Features:** Breakfast is served all day. Patron can get eggs cooked their way, French toast or omelets. Lunch options include homemade chili, egg salad, tuna melts and open-faced sandwiches. Save room for one of the homemade desserts. Casual dress. **Parking:** on-site.

HAMPTON'S DRIVE-IN

Lunch: $4-$12   **Dinner:** $4-$12   **Phone:** 386/734-3860

American

Location: Just ne on US 92 from jct US 17. 250 International Speedway Blvd 32724. **Hours:** 6 am-8 pm, Sun 7 am-8 pm. Closed: 11/23, 12/25. **Features:** Drivers need not leave the comfort of their car, as curbside service is the norm. While this place is known for its tender and juicy chicken dinners, other favorites are sandwiches and surf and turf dinners. Casual dress. **Parking:** on-site.

HAVANA CUBA RESTAURANT

Lunch: $7-$9   **Dinner:** $7-$9   **Phone:** 386/736-7726

Cuban

Location: Downtown. 210 N Woodland Blvd 32720. **Hours:** 11 am-8 pm, Thurs & Fri-9 pm. Closed major holidays; also Sat & Sun. **Features:** In historic downtown, the restaurant serves traditional Cuban cuisine and homemade sangria. Begin the meal with shredded flank steak, fried pork or chicken and mojo criollo, and end with delicious flan. Also on the menu are empanadas, fried plantains, tostones and Cuban sandwiches. Casual dress; beer & wine only. **Parking:** street. **Cards:** MC, VI.

HUNTER'S RESTAURANT

Lunch: $3-$7   **Phone:** 386/736-7954

American

Location: Downtown. 202 N Woodland Blvd 32720. **Hours:** 6 am-2 pm, Sat-noon. Closed major holidays; also Sun & Martin Luther King Jr Day. **Reservations:** accepted. **Features:** The restaurant has been serving the area with the same down-home cooking that made it known 54 years ago. Breakfast choices include omelets and fried eggs with a side of grits, hash browns and a pancake. Among lunch options are PB&J and triple-decker club sandwiches, as well as patty melts, egg salad, roast beef sandwich, chef salad, homemade chili and soup. Casual dress. **Parking:** street. **Cards:** MC, VI.

LE JARDIN CAFE

Lunch: $4-$8   **Dinner:** $7-$23   **Phone:** 386/740-0303

French

Location: Jct of Woodland Blvd and Indiana Ave; downtown. 103 W Indiana Ave 32720. **Hours:** 11 am-2 & 5-10 pm, Sat from 5 pm. Closed major holidays; also Sun. **Features:** On a quiet side street, the cafe presents a menu of French and Vietnamese cuisine. Selections might include escargot and lobster Martinique or fried wontons and pan-fried grouper Mekong style. Also on the menu are duck pate, scampi, shrimp Basquaise and Vietnamese curry chicken, pork or beef. Casual dress. **Parking:** street. **Cards:** AX, DS, MC, VI.

MICHAEL'S COOK'S CAFE

Lunch: $3-$8   **Dinner:** $3-$8   **Phone:** 386/738-5030

Deli/Subs
Sandwiches

Location: Downtown. 101 N Woodlands Blvd 32720. **Hours:** 8 am-5 pm, Sat 11 am-4 pm. Closed major holidays; also Sun. **Features:** The busy downtown eatery serves burgers, pitas, Reubens, hot and cold sandwiches and vegetarian selections. This place also tempts guests with delicious pies and cakes for dessert. Casual dress. **Parking:** on-site.

THE ORIGINAL HOLIDAY HOUSE

Lunch: $9   **Dinner:** $10   **Phone:** 386/734-6319

American

Location: US 17, 0.8 mi n of jct SR 44. 704 N Woodland Blvd 32720. **Hours:** 11:30 am-8:30 pm, Sun from 11 am. Closed: Mon. **Features:** Informal dining in a homey setting features signature items like carved lamb, turkey, roast beef and ham. An excellent selection of homemade desserts like the triple-layer chocolate cake and peach cobbler round out this comfort-food buffet. Casual dress. **Parking:** on-site. **Cards:** DS, MC, VI.

THEY CALL IT MACARONI

Lunch: $5-$14   **Dinner:** $5-$14   **Phone:** 386/740-0169

Italian

Location: Downtown. 124 N Woodland Blvd 32720. **Hours:** 11 am-2 & 5-9 pm, Sat 11 am-9 pm, Sun 11 am-7 pm. Closed major holidays. **Features:** Located in historic downtown, this quaint Italian restaurant has homemade pasta, sauces and bread all prepared fresh daily by the owner. Casual dress; cocktails. **Parking:** street. **Cards:** AX, DS, MC, VI.

DE LEON SPRINGS pop. 2,358

——— WHERE TO DINE ———

KARLING'S INN

Dinner: $14-$24   **Phone:** 386/985-5535

American

Location: On US 17, 5 mi n of jct US 92. 4640 N US 17 32130. **Hours:** 5 pm-9 pm; Sunday brunch 11 am-3 pm. Closed: Mon. **Reservations:** suggested. **Features:** The simple Tudor-style building, in an out-of-the-way location, is well worth visiting for its attentive service, European country setting and pleasingly presented Continental dishes. The house specialty is duck in a dark bing cherry sauce. Casual dress; beer & wine only. **Parking:** on-site. **Cards:** DS, MC, VI.

DELRAY BEACH pop. 60,020

———— WHERE TO STAY ————

BUDGET INN

AAA **SAVE**

Motel

Phone: 561/276-8961

12/1-4/15	1P: $79-$89	2P: $89-$99	XP: $10 F16
4/16-11/30	1P: $49-$59	2P: $59-$69	XP: $10 F16

Location: US 1, 1.8 mi n of jct SR 806 (Atlantic Ave). Located in a quiet area. 2500 N Federal Hwy 33483. Fax: 561/276-1455. **Facility:** 17 one-bedroom standard units. 1 story, exterior corridors. *Bath:* shower only. **Parking:** on-site. **Terms:** office hours 7 am-11 pm, 3 day cancellation notice. **Pool(s):** outdoor. **Cards:** AX, DS, MC, VI. **Special Amenities:** free local telephone calls and early check-in/late check-out.

SOME UNITS

THE COLONY HOTEL & CABANA CLUB   *Book at aaa.com*

AAA **SAVE**

Historic Small-scale Hotel

Phone: (561)276-4123

2/1-3/31 [ECP]	2P: $220-$310
12/1-1/31 [ECP]	2P: $180-$250
4/1-4/30 [ECP]	2P: $185-$245
5/1-11/30 [ECP]	2P: $125-$185

Location: On SR 806 (Atlantic Ave) at US 1 northbound; center. 525 E Atlantic Ave 33483. Fax: 561/276-0123. **Facility:** This intimate 1926 hotel is on a historic main street near many shops and eateries; beach facilities are close by. Smoke free premises. 70 units. 49 one- and 21 two-bedroom standard units. 3 stories, interior corridors. *Bath:* combo or shower only. **Parking:** on-site. **Terms:** 3 day cancellation notice, package plans, pets ($25 extra charge). **Amenities:** high-speed Internet, voice mail, safes, irons, hair dryers. **Pool(s):** saltwater. **Leisure Activities:** limited exercise equipment. **Guest Services:** gift shop, valet and coin laundry. **Business Services:** meeting rooms, fax (fee). **Cards:** AX, DS, MC, VI. **Special Amenities:** free expanded continental breakfast and free newspaper.

SOME UNITS

FEE

MARRIOTT DELRAY BEACH   *Book at aaa.com*

AAA **SAVE**

Small-scale Hotel

Phone: (561)274-3200

2/1-4/30	1P: $309-$359
12/1-1/31	1P: $259-$309
10/1-11/30	1P: $189-$249
5/1-9/30	1P: $169-$229

Location: I-95, exit 52, 1.8 mi e, then just s; jct SR A1A and Atlantic Ave. Located across from the beach. 10 N Ocean Blvd 33483. Fax: 561/274-3202. **Facility:** 268 units. 264 one-bedroom standard units. 4 one-bedroom suites ($209-$359). 6 stories, interior corridors. *Bath:* combo or shower only. **Parking:** on-site and valet. **Terms:** check-in 4 pm, package plans. **Amenities:** high-speed Internet, dual phone lines, voice mail, safes, honor bars, irons, hair dryers. **Dining:** 3 restaurants, 6:30 am-11 pm, cocktails, entertainment. **Pool(s):** heated outdoor. **Leisure Activities:** whirlpool, beach access, exercise room. **Fee:** massage. **Guest Services:** gift shop, valet laundry. **Business Services:** meeting rooms, business center. **Cards:** AX, DC, DS, JC, MC, VI. **Special Amenities:** free newspaper and early check-in/late check-out.

SOME UNITS

FEE

PARLIAMENT INN   Phone: (561)276-6245

Motel

All Year   2P: $64-$290   XP: $15   D11
Location: I-95, exit 52A (SR 806 E/Atlantic Ave), 1.9 mi e to SR A1A, then w. 1236 George Bush Blvd 33483. Fax: 561/279-4528. **Facility:** 8 units. 2 one-bedroom standard units, some with efficiencies or kitchens. 5 one- and 1 two-bedroom suites ($77-$290) with kitchens. 1 story, exterior corridors. *Bath:* combo or shower only. **Parking:** on-site. **Terms:** office hours 9 am-6 pm, 3 night minimum stay, age restrictions may apply, cancellation fee imposed. **Amenities:** irons. **Pool(s):** heated outdoor. **Leisure Activities:** barbecue gas grill. **Guest Services:** coin laundry. **Special Amenities:** free local telephone calls and preferred room (subject to availability with advance reservations).

RESIDENCE INN DELRAY BEACH   *Book at aaa.com*   Phone: (561)276-7441

All Year   1P: $199-$659
Location: I-95, exit 52, 1.7 mi e. 1111 E Atlantic Ave 33483. Fax: 561/276-7445. **Facility:** 95 units. 54 one-bedroom standard units with efficiencies. 39 one- and 2 two-bedroom suites with kitchens. 11 stories, interior corridors. *Bath:* combo or shower only. **Parking:** on-site. **Terms:** check-in 4 pm, cancellation fee imposed, small pets only ($150 deposit). **Amenities:** video games (fee), high-speed Internet, dual phone lines, voice mail, irons, hair dryers. **Pool(s):** heated outdoor. **Leisure Activities:** whirlpool, exercise room. **Guest Services:** sundries, complimentary evening beverages: Mon-Thurs, valet and coin laundry. **Business Services:** meeting rooms, fax (fee). **Cards:** AX, DC, DS, MC, VI. *(See color ad p 313)*

Small-scale Hotel

SOME UNITS

SEAGATE HOTEL & BEACH CLUB   *Book at aaa.com*   Phone: (561)276-2421

Small-scale Hotel

12/21-4/30 [CP]   1P: $140-$756   2P: $140-$756
12/1-12/20 [CP]   1P: $140-$506   2P: $140-$506
5/1-11/30 [CP]   1P: $104-$338   2P: $104-$338
Location: SR A1A, 0.5 mi s of jct SR 806 (Atlantic Ave). 400 S Ocean Blvd 33483. Fax: 561/243-4714. **Facility:** 70 units. 11 one-bedroom standard units with efficiencies. 51 one-, 7 two- and 1 three-bedroom suites with kitchens. 3 stories, exterior corridors. *Bath:* combo or shower only. **Parking:** on-site. **Terms:** check-in 4 pm, 30 day cancellation notice, 12/15-4/30-fee imposed, weekly rates available. **Amenities:** video games (fee), voice mail, safes, irons, hair dryers. **Dining:** 11:30 am-2:30 & 6-9:30 pm, guests only, cocktails. **Pool(s):** 2 heated outdoor. **Leisure Activities:** beach access, rental paddleboats, guided kayak tours. *Fee:* sailboats, windsurfing, water sports. **Guest Services:** coin laundry. **Business Services:** meeting rooms. **Cards:** AX, DS, MC, VI. **Special Amenities:** free continental breakfast and free newspaper.

SOME UNITS

WRIGHT BY THE SEA

Phone: (561)278-3355

2/1-4/23	1P: $219-$399	2P: $219-$399	XP: $20
12/21-1/31	1P: $189-$359	2P: $189-$359	XP: $20
12/1-12/20	1P: $149-$289	2P: $149-$289	XP: $20
4/24-11/30	1P: $109-$249	2P: $109-$249	XP: $20

Motel

Location: Oceanfront. SR A1A, just s of jct Linton Blvd. 1901 S Ocean Blvd 33483. Fax: 561/278-2871. **Facility:** Designated smoking area. 28 units. 4 one-bedroom standard units with kitchens. 22 one- and 2 two-bedroom suites with kitchens. 2 stories (no elevator), exterior corridors. *Bath:* combo or shower only. **Parking:** on-site. **Terms:** office hours 8 am-8 pm, 30 day cancellation notice, weekly rates available. **Amenities:** voice mail, irons, hair dryers. **Pool(s):** heated outdoor. **Leisure Activities:** barbecue grills, table tennis, basketball, shuffleboard. **Guest Services:** coin laundry. **Cards:** AX, DC, DS, MC, VI. **Special Amenities:** free newspaper.

----- **WHERE TO DINE** -----

32 EAST

Dinner: $18-$28   **Phone:** 561-276-7868

American

Location: I-95, exit 52A, 1 mi e; just e of Swinton Ave. 32 E Atlantic Ave 33444. **Hours:** 5:30 pm-10 pm, Fri & Sat-11 pm. Closed: 12/25; also 1/2 & Super Bowl Sun. **Reservations:** required. **Features:** Fresh local and regional seafood and produce go into preparations of contemporary American cuisine, complemented by a fantastic wine list. The upbeat atmosphere and comfortable dining room make this restaurant a fun place to eat. Dressy casual; cocktails. **Parking:** valet. **Cards:** AX, DS, MC, VI.

THE BLUE ANCHOR

Lunch: $8-$22   **Dinner:** $8-$22   **Phone:** 561/272-7272

British

Location: Jct of E Atlantic Ave and Palm Square; just w of bridge. 804 E Atlantic Ave 33483. **Hours:** 11:30 am-2 am, Sun from noon. Closed: 11/23. **Features:** The pub serves many traditional foods such as shepherd's pie, bangers n' mash, fish n' chips, mixed grill and home-baked pies, including steak and English Stilton pie. The outside of the pub was shipped from England where it welcomed Londoners for almost 150 years at the Old Blue Anchor pub at London's historic Chancery Lane. Casual dress; cocktails. **Parking:** on-site. **Cards:** AX, DS, MC, VI.

JIMMY'S STONE CRABS & GRILL

Dinner: $17-$54   **Phone:** 561/278-0036

Steak & Seafood

Location: I-95, exit Atlantic Ave, 1.5 mi e; 1 blk w of US 1. 411 E Atlantic Ave 33483. **Hours:** 5 pm-9 pm, Fri & Sat-10 pm. **Reservations:** suggested. **Features:** The newly removated spacious restaurant offers fresh Florida stone crab, of course (when in season), fresh seafood that includes Florida lobster tail, prime steaks and gourmet salads; outside seating is available. Casual dress; cocktails. **Parking:** valet and street. **Cards:** AX, DC, MC, VI.

LINDBURGERS

Lunch: $5-$15   **Dinner:** $5-$15   **Phone:** 561/495-1722

American

Location: I-95, exit 52 (SR 806/Atlantic Ave), 2 mi w; Florida Tpke, exit 81, 3 mi e; on northwest corner of Military Tr and Atlantic Ave; in the Market Place of Delray. 14535B S Military Tr 33484. **Hours:** 11:30 am-9 pm, Sun from 3 pm. Closed: 1/1, 4/16, 12/25. **Reservations:** not accepted. **Features:** The relaxed restaurant may not have sold 50 million burgers, but it lines up more than 50 combinations of burgers. Also on the menu are hot dogs and hot and cold sandwiches. Casual dress; beer & wine only. **Parking:** on-site. **Cards:** AX, DS, MC, VI.

MANCINI'S

Dinner: $14-$32   **Phone:** 561/272-7300

Italian

Location: I-95, exit 52; at Railway and Atlantic Ave. 290 E Atlantic Ave 33444. **Hours:** 5 pm-10 pm, Fri & Sat-11 pm. Closed: 11/23. **Reservations:** suggested, required in season. **Features:** The contemporary, trendy restaurant presents fresh seafood, steaks and innovative pastas in the Tuscan style. Cocktails. **Parking:** valet and street. **Cards:** AX, MC, VI.

PINEAPPLE GRILLE

Lunch: $6-$9   **Dinner:** $12-$25   **Phone:** 561/265-1368

Caribbean

Location: US 1, 0.3 mi e on George Bush Blvd; SR A1A, 0.4 mi w on George Bush Blvd; in Palm Trail Plaza. 800 Palm Tr 33483. **Hours:** 11 am-2 & 5-10 pm, Fri & Sat-11 pm, Sun 9:30 am-10 pm. Closed: 4/16, 12/25. **Reservations:** suggested. **Features:** Look no further to taste the cuisine of the islands. The Trinidadian chef reveals his secrets in seafood and meat entrees. Also on the menu are brick-oven pizzas and burgers for the kids. The dining room's atmosphere evokes a beachfront feel. Dressy casual; cocktails; entertainment. **Parking:** on-site. **Cards:** AX, MC, VI.

DELTONA pop. 69,543

----- **WHERE TO STAY** -----

BEST WESTERN DELTONA INN

Book at aaa.com   **Phone:** (386)860-3000

2/1-4/30	1P: $89-$239	2P: $89-$239	XP: $10	F18
12/1-1/31	1P: $79-$239	2P: $79-$239	XP: $10	F18
10/1-11/30	1P: $79-$199	2P: $79-$199	XP: $10	F18
5/1-9/30	1P: $79-$109	2P: $79-$109	XP: $10	F18

Small-scale Hotel **Location:** I-4, exit 108, just ne. 481 Deltona Blvd 32725. Fax: 386/860-2687. **Facility:** 130 units. 128 one-bedroom standard units. 2 one-bedroom suites ($109-$299), some with whirlpools. 2 stories, interior corridors. **Parking:** on-site. **Terms:** small pets only ($10 fee). **Amenities:** voice mail, irons, hair dryers. *Some:* high-speed Internet. **Dining:** 6:30-11 am, 11:30-1:45 & 4:30-9 pm, Fri & Sat-10 pm, cocktails. **Pool(s):** outdoor. **Guest Services:** coin laundry. **Business Services:** meeting rooms. **Cards:** AX, DC, DS, MC, VI. **Special Amenities:** free local telephone calls and free newspaper.

SOME UNITS

DESTIN pop. 11,119

—— WHERE TO STAY ——

BAY CLUB OF SANDESTIN
Phone: (850)837-8866

(AAA) (SAVE)
♢♢ ♢♢
Condominium

3/1-10/31	1P: $150-$235	2P: $150-$235
11/1-11/30	1P: $100-$150	2P: $100-$150
12/1-2/28	1P: $90-$150	2P: $90-$150

Location: Next to Conference Centre Bayside. 120 N Sandestin Blvd 32550. Fax: 850/654-9188. **Facility:** 44 one-bedroom standard units, some with whirlpools. 6 stories, interior corridors. *Bath:* combo or shower only. **Parking:** on-site. **Terms:** age restrictions may apply, 3 day cancellation notice. **Amenities:** voice mail, irons, hair dryers. **Pool(s):** 4 outdoor, 3 wading. **Leisure Activities:** saunas, whirlpools, rental boats, fishing, recreation programs, jogging. *Fee:* sailboats, marina, waterskiing, charter fishing, personal watercraft, golf-72 holes, 18 tennis courts (4 lighted), bicycles, massage. **Guest Services:** complimentary laundry. **Business Services:** meeting rooms, PC, fax (fee). **Cards:** AX, DS, MC, VI.

🆘 🍴 🍸 🏊 👪 ⊠ 📼 ⚓ 🖧 📞 ▣ ▣
FEE

BEST WESTERN SUMMERPLACE INN *Book at aaa.com*
Phone: (850)650-8003

(AAA) (SAVE)
♢♢♢♢

Small-scale Hotel

6/1-8/14	1P: $119-$169	2P: $119-$169	XP: $10	F17
4/1-5/31	1P: $89-$139	2P: $89-$139	XP: $10	F17
12/1-3/31	1P: $69-$119	2P: $69-$119	XP: $10	F17
8/15-11/30	1P: $59-$109	2P: $59-$109	XP: $10	F17

Location: US 98, 2.2 mi e. 14047 Emerald Coast Pkwy 32541. Fax: 850/650-8004. **Facility:** 72 units. 70 one-bedroom standard units. 2 one-bedroom suites. 4 stories, interior corridors. *Bath:* combo or shower only. **Parking:** on-site. **Terms:** check-in 4 pm, 3 day cancellation notice-fee imposed. **Amenities:** high-speed Internet, voice mail, irons, hair dryers. **Pool(s):** small outdoor, heated indoor. **Leisure Activities:** whirlpool, limited exercise equipment. **Guest Services:** valet and coin laundry. **Business Services:** meeting rooms. **Cards:** AX, DS, MC, VI. **Special Amenities: free continental breakfast and free local telephone calls.**

SOME UNITS

🆘 🍴 👨‍🦽 🏊 ⚓ 🖧 📞 ▣ / ⊠ ▣ /

COMFORT INN *Book at aaa.com*
Phone: (850)654-8611

♢♢ ♢♢♢

Small-scale Hotel

All Year	1P: $79-$300	2P: $79-$300	XP: $10	F18

Location: Jct US 98 and SR 293, 1 mi w. 19001 Emerald Coast Pkwy 32541. Fax: 850/654-8815. **Facility:** 100 units. 87 one-bedroom standard units. 13 one-bedroom suites, some with whirlpools. 4 stories, interior corridors. *Bath:* combo or shower only. **Parking:** on-site. **Terms:** check-in 4 pm. **Amenities:** voice mail, irons, hair dryers. **Pool(s):** outdoor, heated indoor. **Leisure Activities:** exercise room. **Guest Services:** gift shop, valet and coin laundry. **Business Services:** meeting rooms. **Cards:** AX, CB, DC, DS, MC, VI.

SOME UNITS

(ASK) 🆘 🍴 👨‍🦽 🏊 ⚓ 🖧 📞 ▣ ▣ / ⊠ /

COUNTRY INN & SUITES BY CARLSON *Book at aaa.com*
Phone: (850)650-9191

♢♢ ♢♢♢

Small-scale Hotel

5/23-9/6	1P: $127-$229	2P: $127-$229	XP: $10	F17
3/4-5/22	1P: $115-$229	2P: $115-$229	XP: $10	F17
9/7-11/30	1P: $89-$229	2P: $89-$229	XP: $10	F17
12/1-3/3	1P: $79-$229	2P: $79-$229	XP: $10	F17

Location: Off US 98; behind the TGIF Restaurant. 4415 Commons Dr E 32541. Fax: 850/654-1802. **Facility:** 83 units. 37 one-bedroom standard units. 46 one-bedroom suites. 3 stories, interior corridors. *Bath:* combo or shower only. **Parking:** on-site. **Amenities:** high-speed Internet, voice mail, irons, hair dryers. **Pool(s):** heated outdoor. **Leisure Activities:** whirlpool, exercise room. **Guest Services:** valet and coin laundry. **Business Services:** meeting rooms, fax. **Cards:** AX, DC, DS, MC, VI.

SOME UNITS

(ASK) 🆘 🍴 👨‍🦽 📷 🏊 📼 ⚓ 🖧 ▣ / ⊠ 📞 ▣ /

EMBASSY SUITES HOTEL *Book at aaa.com*
Phone: (850)337-7000

♢♢ ♢♢♢

Large-scale Hotel

5/26-8/15 [BP]	1P: $159-$289	2P: $159-$289	XP: $15	F16
3/1-5/25 & 8/16-11/30 [BP]	1P: $129-$189	2P: $129-$189	XP: $15	F16
12/1-2/28 [BP]	1P: $89-$129	2P: $89-$129	XP: $15	F16

Location: 8 mi e of the bridge, just w. 570 Scenic Gulf Dr 32550. Fax: 850/337-7080. **Facility:** 155 one-bedroom standard units, some with whirlpools. 4 stories, interior corridors. *Bath:* combo or shower only. **Parking:** on-site. **Amenities:** video games, high-speed Internet, dual phone lines, voice mail, safes, irons, hair dryers. **Pool(s):** heated outdoor. **Leisure Activities:** whirlpool, exercise room. **Guest Services:** gift shop, complimentary evening beverages, valet and coin laundry, area transportation. **Business Services:** conference facilities, fax (fee). **Cards:** AX, CB, DC, DS, MC, VI.

SOME UNITS

(ASK) 🍴 🍸 🏊 ⚓ 🖧 📞 ▣ ▣ / ⊠ /

HAMPTON INN *Book at aaa.com*
Phone: (850)654-2677

♢♢♢♢

Small-scale Hotel

5/21-8/31	1P: $169-$269	2P: $169-$269	
3/1-5/20	1P: $119-$199	2P: $119-$199	
9/1-11/30	1P: $89-$199	2P: $89-$199	
12/1-2/28	1P: $79-$159	2P: $79-$159	

Location: US 98, 1 mi e. 1625 Hwy 98 E 32541. Fax: 850/654-0745. **Facility:** 104 units. 89 one-bedroom standard units. 15 one-bedroom suites, some with efficiencies. 2 stories, exterior corridors. *Bath:* combo or shower only. **Parking:** on-site. **Terms:** check-in 4 pm, 2-3 night minimum stay - seasonal and/or weekends. **Amenities:** high-speed Internet, voice mail, irons, hair dryers. **Pool(s):** heated outdoor. **Leisure Activities:** whirlpool, basketball. **Guest Services:** valet and coin laundry. **Business Services:** meeting rooms. **Cards:** AX, CB, DC, DS, JC, MC, VI.

SOME UNITS

(ASK) 🍴 👨‍🦽 🏊 ⚓ 🖧 📞 ▣ ▣ / ⊠ /

HILTON SANDESTIN BEACH GOLF RESORT & SPA   *Book at aaa.com*   Phone: (850)267-9500

| | All Year | 1P: $99-$499 | 2P: $109-$499 | XP: $10 | F18 |

Location: 10 mi e at Sandestin Blvd. 4000 S Sandestin Blvd 32550. Fax: 850/267-3076. **Facility:** A full-service
Resort   beachfront hotel with gulf views from all angles, the property offers family units with bunk beds and a range
Large-scale Hotel   of leisure activities. 598 units. 574 one-bedroom standard units. 24 one-bedroom suites, some with
whirlpools. 15 stories, interior corridors. *Bath:* some combo or shower only. **Parking:** on-site (fee) and valet.
Terms: check-in 4 pm, 7 day cancellation notice-fee imposed, package plans. **Amenities:** dual phone lines,
voice mail, safes, honor bars, irons, hair dryers. *Some:* CD players, high-speed Internet. **Dining:** 2
restaurants, 7 am-11 pm, cocktails, also, Seagar's Prime Steaks and Seafood, see separate listing. **Pool(s):** 2 heated outdoor,
heated indoor, wading. **Leisure Activities:** saunas, whirlpools, recreation programs in season, spa, volleyball. *Fee:* marina,
scuba diving, snorkeling, charter fishing, kayak, golf-72 holes, 15 tennis courts (4 lighted), bicycles, game room. **Guest
Services:** gift shop, valet and coin laundry, area transportation (fee)-around Sandestin Resort & outlet mall. **Business
Services:** conference facilities, business center. **Cards:** AX, CB, DC, DS, JC, MC, VI. **Special Amenities:** free newspaper.

SOME UNITS

HOLIDAY INN EXPRESS HOTEL & SUITES   *Book at aaa.com*   Phone: (850)654-9383

	5/26-8/15	1P: $149-$199	2P: $149-$199	XP: $10	F18
	3/1-5/25	1P: $79-$169	2P: $79-$169	XP: $10	F18
Small-scale Hotel	8/16-11/30	1P: $79-$159	2P: $79-$159	XP: $10	F18
	12/1-2/28	1P: $79-$139	2P: $79-$139	XP: $10	F18

Location: Jct Hutchinson St and US 98. 108 Hutchinson St 32541. Fax: 850/654-9348. **Facility:** 74 one-bedroom standard units. 3
stories, interior corridors. *Bath:* combo or shower only. **Parking:** on-site. **Amenities:** high-speed Internet, dual phone lines,
voice mail, irons, hair dryers. **Pool(s):** outdoor. **Guest Services:** valet laundry. **Business Services:** meeting rooms, PC, fax.
Cards: AX, DC, DS, MC, VI.

SOME UNITS

HOLIDAY INN OF DESTIN   *Book at aaa.com*   Phone: (850)837-6181

	3/11-8/12	1P: $179-$235	2P: $170-$235	
	8/13-10/14	1P: $125-$195	2P: $125-$195	
Small-scale Hotel	12/1-3/10 & 10/15-11/30	1P: $85-$125	2P: $85-$125	

Location: On US 98, 2.2 mi e of bridge. 1020 Hwy 98 E 32541 (PO Box 577). Fax: 850/837-1523. **Facility:** 233
one-bedroom standard units. 9 stories, interior corridors. *Bath:* combo or shower only. **Parking:** on-site. **Terms:** 3 day
cancellation notice-fee imposed. **Amenities:** voice mail, safes, irons, hair dryers. *Some:* DVD players, video games. **Pool(s):**
outdoor, heated indoor, wading. **Leisure Activities:** sauna, whirlpool, recreation programs in summer, exercise room. *Fee:*
game room. **Guest Services:** gift shop, valet and coin laundry. **Business Services:** meeting rooms. **Cards:** AX, DC, DS,
MC, VI.

SOME UNITS

SANDESTIN BAYSIDE INN

Phone: (850)267-8000

Small-scale Hotel

All Year   1P: $95-$746   2P: $95-$746

Location: 10 mi e on US 98. 9300 Emerald Coast Pkwy W 32550. Fax: 850/267-8221. **Facility:** Smoke free premises. 175 units. 159 one-bedroom standard units. 16 one-bedroom suites. 8 stories, interior corridors. **Parking:** on-site. **Terms:** check-in 4 pm, 14 day cancellation notice, [AP], [BP] & [MAP] meal plans available, package plans. **Amenities:** DVD players, voice mail, irons, hair dryers. **Pool(s):** 9 outdoor, 4 heated outdoor, 3 wading. **Leisure Activities:** saunas, whirlpools, rental boats, fishing, recreation programs, bicycles, jogging, playground, spa, basketball. *Fee:* sailboats, marina, charter fishing, golf-72 holes, 20 tennis courts (2 lighted). **Guest Services:** valet laundry. **Business Services:** meeting rooms. **Cards:** AX, CB, DC, DS, JC, MC, VI.

SANDESTIN GOLF AND BEACH RESORT

Phone: (850)267-8000

Condominium

All Year   1P: $90-$882

Location: 10 mi e on US 98. 9300 Emerald Coast Pkwy W 32550. Fax: 850/267-8221. **Facility:** Well appointed condominiums set in an inviting village with access to all the amenities the resort has to offer. 391 units. 297 one- and 63 two-bedroom standard units, some with efficiencies or kitchens. 31 three-bedroom suites with kitchens. 5-11 stories, interior corridors. **Parking:** on-site. **Terms:** check-in 4 pm, 14 day cancellation notice-fee imposed, weekly rates available, [MAP] meal plan available, package plans. **Amenities:** high-speed Internet, dual phone lines, voice mail, irons, hair dryers. **Pool(s):** 9 outdoor, 4 heated outdoor, 3 wading. **Leisure Activities:** saunas, whirlpools, rental boats, fishing, recreation programs, bicycles, jogging, playground, spa, basketball. *Fee:* sailboats, marina, charter fishing, golf-72 holes, 20 tennis courts (2 lighted). **Guest Services:** gift shop, valet and coin laundry, area transportation. **Business Services:** conference facilities. **Cards:** AX, CB, DC, DS, MC, VI.

SOME UNITS

SANDESTIN GOLF AND BEACH RESORT

Book at aaa.com   **Phone:** (850)267-8000

Resort
Large-scale Hotel

All Year   1P: $95-$190   2P: $95-$190

Location: On US 98, 10 mi e. 9300 Emerald Coast Pkwy W 32550. Fax: 850/267-8221. **Facility:** Surrounded by extensive resort facilities, the property offers high-rise beach condos, waterfront housekeeping villas and designer-decorated homes. 592 units. 90 one-, 271 two- and 181 three-bedroom suites ($131-$240), some with whirlpools. 50 vacation homes. 11 stories, interior/exterior corridors. **Parking:** on-site. **Terms:** check-in 4 pm, age restrictions may apply, 14 day cancellation notice, [AP], [BP] & [MAP] meal plans available, package plans. **Amenities:** dual phone lines, voice mail, irons. **Dining:** 3 restaurants, 6:30 am-9:30 pm, cocktails. **Pool(s):** 9 outdoor, 4 heated outdoor, 3 wading. **Leisure Activities:** saunas, whirlpools, rental boats, fishing, recreation programs, bicycles, jogging, playground, spa, basketball. *Fee:* sailboats, marina, charter fishing, kayaks, parasailing, personal watercraft, golf-72 holes, 20 tennis courts (2 lighted). **Guest Services:** gift shop, valet and coin laundry, area transportation. **Business Services:** conference facilities, fax (fee). **Cards:** AX, CB, DC, DS, JC, MC, VI. *(See color ad p 317)*

SOME UNITS

TOPS'L BEACH & RACQUET RESORT

Phone: 850/337-1682

Resort
Condominium

Property failed to provide current rates

Location: On US 98, 10.2 mi e. 9011 Hwy 98 W 32550. Fax: 850/267-9168. **Facility:** This resort may be centered around tennis, but its comfortable accommodations are designed with leisure in mind. 310 units. 31 one- and 232 two-bedroom standard units. 37 three-bedroom suites. 10 vacation homes. 1-15 stories, interior/exterior corridors. **Parking:** on-site. **Amenities:** DVD players, voice mail, safes, irons. **Pool(s):** outdoor, 4 heated outdoor, heated indoor/outdoor. **Leisure Activities:** saunas, whirlpools, steamroom, sailboats, putting green, 14 tennis courts (12 lighted), racquetball court, recreation programs, hiking trails, exercise room, basketball, shuffleboard, volleyball, game room. *Fee:* massage. **Guest Services:** gift shop, complimentary laundry, area transportation. **Business Services:** meeting rooms, fax (fee).

WINGATE INN

Book at aaa.com   **Phone:** (850)654-4678

Small-scale Hotel

5/1-8/15	1P: $169-$209	2P: $169-$209	XP: $10	F18
12/1-4/30	1P: $79-$139	2P: $79-$139	XP: $10	F18
8/16-11/30	1P: $99	2P: $99	XP: $10	F18

Location: 2.5 mi w of Midbay Bridge. Adjacent to Big Kahuna's Water Park. 117 Palms St 32541. Fax: 850/654-4263. **Facility:** 94 one-bedroom standard units. 3 stories, interior corridors. **Bath:** combo or shower only. **Parking:** on-site. **Terms:** 3 day cancellation notice-fee imposed. **Amenities:** high-speed Internet, dual phone lines, voice mail, irons, hair dryers. **Pool(s):** outdoor. **Leisure Activities:** whirlpool, exercise room. **Guest Services:** valet laundry. **Business Services:** meeting rooms, business center. **Cards:** AX, CB, DC, DS, JC, MC, VI.

SOME UNITS

——— WHERE TO DINE ———

ANOTHER BROKEN EGG CAFE

Lunch: $4-$13   **Phone:** 850/622-2050

American

Location: On US 98, 10 mi e; in Sandestin Golf and Beach Resort. 9100 Baytowne Wharf Blvd 32550. **Hours:** 7 am-3 pm; to 2 pm in winter. Closed: 12/25. **Reservations:** not accepted. **Features:** Enjoy a breakfast experience you will not soon forget; huge cinnamon buns, Popeye's omelette and fruit and nut pancakes or french toast are some of the menu specialties. Casual dress; cocktails. **Parking:** on-site. **Cards:** AX, DS, MC, VI.

BEACH WALK - CRYSTAL BEACH

Lunch: $12-$26   **Dinner:** $18-$35   **Phone:** 850/650-7100

Seafood

Location: 0.5 mi s on Crystal Beach Dr. 2996 Scenic Hwy 98 32541. **Hours:** 11:30 am-2:30 & 5-10 pm, Sun 11 am-3 & 5-10 pm; Sunday brunch. Closed: 1/1. **Reservations:** suggested. **Features:** The dramatic entrance down a lovely staircase to the host stand sets the mood for the dining experience. Meals here aren't soon forgotten. Dressy casual; cocktails. **Parking:** on-site and valet. **Cards:** AX, DC, DS, MC, VI.

BONEFISH GRILL

Seafood

Dinner: $14-$21   **Phone:** 850/650-3161

Location: Jct US 98 and SR 293; in shopping plaza. 4447 Commons Dr, #105 32541. **Hours:** 4 pm-10:30 pm, Fri & Sat-11:30 pm, Sun-10 pm. **Closed:** 11/23, 12/25. **Reservations:** accepted. **Features:** Fresh fish is the specialty of the house and the menu and nightly specials offer a variety from which to choose. The food is well prepared and cooked to perfection; service is casual in nature and staff are skilled and attentive. Casual dress; cocktails. **Parking:** on-site. **Cards:** AX, DS, MC, VI.

CAFE GRAZIE

Italian

Dinner: $10-$19   **Phone:** 850/837-7240

Location: 1.6 mi w of jct US 331. 1771 Old Hwy 98 32541. **Hours:** 4 pm-10 pm; to 9 pm 11/1-2/28. **Closed:** 11/23, 12/25; also Super Boul Sun. **Features:** Country Italian is the dining room's decor theme, combining colors and various media to create a comfortable, casual experience. The ingredients are fresh and the food prepared to order — much is made in-house. Service is casual yet very attentive and all elements of the restaurant combine for an enjoyable meal. Dressy casual; cocktails. **Parking:** on-site. **Cards:** AX, DC, DS, MC, VI.

CHAN'S MARKET CAFE

Specialty

Lunch: $5-$13   **Dinner:** $6-$19   **Phone:** 850/837-1334

Location: 10 mi e; at the Market at Sandestin. 9375 Emerald Coast Pkwy 32550. **Hours:** 11 am-10 pm; hours may vary. **Closed:** 11/23, 12/25. **Features:** It's hard to believe this charming setting is just off the main highway. It offers both inside and outside dining with a good selection of deli items and signature sandwiches. The gourmet deli and bakery that are part of this establishment entice you to try not only the local seafood but also the selection of meats and freshly baked breads. At breakfast, linger over freshly brewed coffee, pancakes, biscuits, eggs and sausage while overlooking the duck pond. Casual dress; cocktails. **Parking:** on-site. **Cards:** AX, DS, MC, VI.

THE CRAB TRAP

Seafood

Lunch: $6-$19   **Dinner:** $8-$20   **Phone:** 850/654-2722

Location: On US 98; at James Lee Park. 3500 Old Hwy 98 32541. **Hours:** 11 am-10 pm. **Closed:** 12/25. **Features:** Some tables and booths at this beachside restaurant afford good views. Among the inexpensive offerings are seafood specialties and sandwiches. Casual dress; cocktails. **Parking:** on-site. **Cards:** AX, DS, MC, VI.

CUVEE BEACH

International

Dinner: $16-$30   **Phone:** 850/650-8900

Location: 1 mi e of bridge. 36120 Emerald Coast Pkwy 32541. **Hours:** 5:30 pm-10 pm. **Closed:** 11/23, 12/25; also Sun. **Reservations:** accepted. **Features:** The restaurant serves wine country cuisine, and designs meals to enhance the wine experience. Dressy casual; cocktails. **Parking:** on-site. **Cards:** AX, DS, MC, VI.

DESTIN DINER

American

Lunch: $4-$6   **Dinner:** $5-$8   **Phone:** 850/654-5843

Location: On US 98, 0.8 mi e. 1083 Hwy 98 E 32541. **Hours:** 6 am-10 pm; hours may vary in winter. **Closed:** 12/25. **Features:** The nostalgic, charming diner offers simple home cooking with '50s-era hospitality. Casual dress. **Parking:** on-site. **Cards:** AX, DS, MC, VI.

GRAFFITI

Mediterranean

Dinner: $8-$23   **Phone:** 850/654-2764

Location: On US 98, 2.9 mi w of bridge. 707 E Hwy 98 32541. **Hours:** 5 pm-9 pm, Fri & Sat-10 pm. Closed major holidays. **Features:** The walls and ceiling are adorned with an eclectic collection of artwork that keeps guests occupied between courses. This place is one of the locals' best-kept secrets. Casual dress; cocktails; entertainment. **Parking:** on-site. **Cards:** MC, VI.

THE LIGHTHOUSE RESTAURANT

Seafood

DC, DS, MC, VI.

Dinner: $8-$27   **Phone:** 850/654-2828

Location: On US 98, 2 mi e; in Shoreline Village Plaza. 878 Hwy 98 E, Shoreline Mall 32541. **Hours:** 4:30 pm-9 pm. **Closed:** 4/16, 9/4, 12/24, 12/25. **Reservations:** not accepted. **Features:** Bring your whole family and enjoy the relaxed atmosphere. An extensive menu offers a wide selection with an emphasis on seafood. An authentic Key lime pie offers a taste of the tropics. Casual dress; cocktails. **Parking:** on-site. **Cards:** AX,

MARLIN GRILL

Steak & Seafood

Dinner: $18-$50   **Phone:** 850/351-1990

Location: On US 98, 10 mi e; in The Village of Baytowne Wharf. 9100 Baytowne Wharf Blvd 32550. **Hours:** 5 pm-10 pm. **Reservations:** suggested. **Features:** In the heart of Baytowne Wharf, the fine dining establishment presents chef's creations that look too good to eat, but patrons don't seem to have a problem cleaning their plates. Dressy casual; cocktails. **Parking:** on-site. **Cards:** AX, DS, MC, VI.

MCALISTER'S DELI

American

Lunch: $5-$10   **Dinner:** $5-$10   **Phone:** 850/650-6646

Location: On US 98, 8 mi e. 10859 Hwy 98 W, Suite 105 32541. **Hours:** 10:30 am-9 pm. Closed major holidays. **Features:** Your favorite deli selections with sides like potato salad or fruit cup and dessert are served in a casual, comfortable setting. Casual dress. **Parking:** on-site. **Cards:** AX, DS, MC, VI.

MCGUIRE'S IRISH PUB

Steak House

Lunch: $8-$12   **Dinner:** $12-$22   **Phone:** 850/650-0000

Location: On US 98, at east end of Destin Pass Bridge. 33 Hwy 98 E 32541. **Hours:** 11 am-2 am. **Closed:** 11/23, 12/25. **Features:** A pleasant experience, this restaurant features steaks, seafood and tasty, oversized burgers. Sing along to nostalgic music or watch the action on the gulf and bay from an open upper deck. Homemade bread and butter pudding makes a delicious treat. Casual dress; cocktails; entertainment. **Parking:** on-site. **Cards:** AX, DC, DS, MC, VI.

O SOLE MIO TRATTORIA ITALIANO

Italian

Dinner: $12-$22   **Phone:** 850/650-5950

Location: 2.5 mi e of bridge. 12273 Emerald Coast Pkwy 32541. **Hours:** 5 pm-10 pm. **Closed:** 11/23, 12/25; also Sun. **Reservations:** accepted. **Features:** Dimmed lighting creates a soft mood and pleasant atmosphere. The delectable creations are worth the wait. Casual dress; cocktails. **Parking:** on-site. **Cards:** AX, DS, MC, VI.

RUTHERFORDS 465 RESTAURANT   Lunch: $9-$18   Dinner: $20-$40   Phone: 850/337-8888
▼▼▼▼   **Location:** 0.7 mi e of Mid-Bay Bridge. 4460 Legendary Dr, Suite 400 32541. **Hours:** 11 am-7 pm.
American   **Features:** Nestled in the far corner of a country club, the fine-dining establishment traverses American, Pan Asian and French fusion cuisine. Selections such as the jasmine lobster appetizer, Chilean sea bass entree and berries Rutherford dessert wake up the nostrils and tickle the palate. The award-winning wine list is likely to impress even elite wine connoisseurs. Dressy casual; cocktails. **Parking:** on-site. **Cards:** AX, DS, MC, VI.

SAKURA ORIENTAL CUISINE AND SUSHI BAR   Lunch: $5-$16   Dinner: $10-$16   Phone: 850/654-5818
▼▼   **Location:** Downtown; in Destin K-Mart Shopping Center. 763 Hwy 98 E 32541. **Hours:** 11 am-2:30 & 5-9:30 pm,
Chinese   Fri-10 pm, Sat 5 pm-10 pm. Closed major holidays; also Sun. **Features:** A limited menu enables the casual and intimate restaurant to focus on a small assortment of tasty dishes, including sushi. Especially good are the piquant sweet and sour soup and a shrimp and beef dish served in a spicy brown sauce. Casual dress; beer & wine only. **Parking:** on-site. **Cards:** AX, CB, DC, MC, VI.

SEAGAR'S PRIME STEAKS AND SEAFOOD   *Menu on aaa.com*   Dinner: $30-$45   Phone: 850/267-9500
ⒶⒶⒶ   **Location:** 10 mi e at Sandestin Blvd; in Hilton Sandestin Beach Golf Resort & Spa. 4000 Sandestin Blvd S 32550.
▼▼▼▼   **Hours:** 6 pm-10 pm, Fri & Sat-11 pm. Closed: 11/23, 12/25. **Reservations:** suggested. **Features:** A sophisticated setting features lavish appointments and an upscale dress code. An open kitchen offers prime
Steak & Seafood   steaks and seafood with an innovative use of fresh ingredients. A separate lounge with a cigar steward is perfect for after-dinner relaxation. Dressy casual; cocktails; entertainment. **Parking:** valet. **Cards:** AX, CB, DC, DS, MC, VI.

─── *The following restaurant has not been evaluated by AAA* ───
but is listed for your information only.

PANCAKE CREPERIE & BAKERY   Phone: 850/654-9999
[fyi]   Not evaluated. **Location:** 11225 Hwy 98 W 32541. **Features:** This creperie serves pancakes of every variety with a multitude of toppings from which to choose. The sandwiches are made on freshly baked bread and croissants; pastries and baguettes are also available.

DUNEDIN —*See Tampa Bay p. 1022.*

EAST PALATKA pop. 1,707

─── WHERE TO STAY ───

BEST WESTERN INN OF PALATKA   *Book at aaa.com*   Phone: (386)325-7800
▼▼   2/13-6/1 [ECP]   1P: $110-$150   2P: $110-$150   XP: $5   F12
      12/1-2/12 & 6/2-11/30 [ECP]   1P: $90-$150   2P: $90-$150   XP: $5   F12
Small-scale Hotel   **Location:** On US 17, just s of St John's River Bridge. 119 Hwy 17 S 32131. Fax: 386/328-4008. **Facility:** 56 one-bedroom standard units. 2 stories (no elevator), exterior corridors. *Bath:* combo or shower only. **Parking:** on-site. **Terms:** cancellation fee imposed. **Amenities:** irons, hair dryers. *Some:* high-speed Internet. **Pool(s):** outdoor. **Leisure Activities:** whirlpool. **Guest Services:** valet and coin laundry. **Business Services:** meeting rooms. **Cards:** AX, CB, DC, DS, JC, MC, VI.

SOME UNITS

ELKTON   (See map and index starting on p. 874)

─── WHERE TO STAY ───

COMFORT INN ST. AUGUSTINE   *Book at aaa.com*   Phone: (904)829-3435   [65]
ⒶⒶⒶ [SAVE]   1/31-4/30 & 10/1-11/30 [CP]   1P: $79-$109   2P: $79-$109
      5/1-9/30 [CP]   1P: $69-$109   2P: $69-$109
▼▼ ▼▼   12/1-1/30 [CP]   1P: $69-$99   2P: $69-$99
Small-scale Hotel   **Location:** I-95, exit 311, just w. 2625 SR 207 32033. Fax: 904/824-1558. **Facility:** 62 one-bedroom standard units. 2 stories (no elevator), exterior corridors. **Parking:** on-site. **Terms:** pets ($10 extra charge). **Amenities:** irons, hair dryers. **Pool(s):** outdoor. **Guest Services:** coin laundry. **Cards:** AX, CB, DC, DS, MC, VI. **Special Amenities:** free continental breakfast and free local telephone calls.

SOME UNITS

ELLENTON pop. 3,142   (See map and index starting on p. 904)

─── WHERE TO STAY ───

GUESTHOUSE INTERNATIONAL INN   *Book at aaa.com*   Phone: (941)729-0600   [29]
▼▼   1/25-4/15 [ECP]   1P: $90-$110   2P: $90-$110   XP: $10   F18
      12/1-1/24 [ECP]   1P: $80-$89   2P: $80-$89   XP: $10   F18
Motel   4/16-11/30 [ECP]   1P: $60-$80   2P: $60-$80   XP: $10   F18
      Location: I-75, exit 224, 0.3 mi s on US 301, just w on 51st Ave E, then just n. 4915 17th St E 34222.
Fax: 941/722-5908. **Facility:** 63 one-bedroom standard units. 2 stories, exterior corridors. *Bath:* combo or shower only. **Parking:** on-site. **Terms:** pets ($10 extra charge). **Amenities:** voice mail, safes, irons, hair dryers. **Pool(s):** heated outdoor. **Leisure Activities:** whirlpool. **Guest Services:** coin laundry. **Business Services:** fax (fee). **Cards:** AX, CB, DC, DS, JC, MC, VI.

SOME UNITS

(See map and index starting on p. 904)

HAMPTON INN   *Book at aaa.com*   Phone: (941)721-4000   **27**

12/1-5/1 & 11/2-11/30	1P: $129-$159	2P: $129-$159
5/2-11/1	1P: $99-$109	2P: $99-$109

Small-scale Hotel   **Location:** I-75, exit 224, just n on US 301, then just w on 60th Ave E. 5810 20th Ct E 34222. Fax: 941/721-4100. **Facility:** 116 one-bedroom standard units, some with whirlpools. 5 stories, interior corridors. *Bath:* combo or shower only. **Parking:** on-site. **Amenities:** video games (fee), high-speed Internet, voice mail, irons, hair dryers. *Some:* dual phone lines. **Pool(s):** heated outdoor. **Guest Services:** valet and coin laundry. **Business Services:** meeting rooms, business center. **Cards:** AX, CB, DC, DS, JC, MC, VI.

SOME UNITS

(ASK) (SD) (🍽) (ⓜ) (♿) (⊘) (≋) (†🏊) (📷) (DATA PORT) (💻) / (✕) (🔒) (🖥) /

SLEEP INN & SUITES RIVERFRONT   *Book at aaa.com*   Phone: (941)721-4933   **28**

1/1-4/15 [CP]	1P: $99-$199	2P: $99-$199	XP: $10	F
12/1-12/31 & 4/16-11/30 [CP]	1P: $69-$149	2P: $69-$149	XP: $10	F

Motel   **Location:** I-75, exit 224, just n on US 301, just e on 19th St E, then 0.3 mi sw. 5605 18th St E 34222. Fax: 941/721-4934. **Facility:** 67 units. 59 one-bedroom standard units, some with whirlpools. 8 one-bedroom suites. 4 stories, interior corridors. *Bath:* combo or shower only. **Parking:** on-site. **Terms:** cancellation fee imposed, weekly rates available, pets ($5 extra charge). **Amenities:** high-speed Internet, dual phone lines, voice mail, irons, hair dryers. **Pool(s):** heated outdoor. **Leisure Activities:** exercise room. **Guest Services:** coin laundry. **Business Services:** meeting rooms, business center. **Cards:** AX, CB, DC, DS, JC, MC, VI.

SOME UNITS

(🐾) (🍽) (ⓜ) (♿) (≋) (📷) (DATA PORT) (💻) / (✕) (🔒) (🖥) /
FEE

──── WHERE TO DINE ────

BEEF'O'BRADY'S   Lunch: $6-$9   Dinner: $6-$9   Phone: 941/722-6500   **40**

American   **Location:** I-75, exit 224, 0.5 mi ne on US 301, 0.6 mi nw on 60th Ave E, then 0.4 mi w; in J.P. Igloo Ice & Inline Skating Complex. 5309 29th St E 34222. **Hours:** 11 am-11 pm, Sun noon-10 pm. **Features:** Established in 1985, the popular sports-themed restaurant is known for its great burgers, sandwiches, baskets, soups, salads and the favorite, buffalo wings. Patrons can savor a meal while watching a sports program on any one of the strategically placed TVs. Casual dress; cocktails. **Parking:** on-site. **Cards:** MC, VI.

(ⓜ) (🍸)

BIG L RESTAURANT   Lunch: $2-$7   Phone: 941/722-7866   **46**

American   **Location:** I-75, exit 224, 0.9 mi s on US 301; at jct 42nd Ave Dr E. 4219 US 301 34222. **Hours:** 6 am-2 pm, Sun 6:30-11:30 am. **Features:** Decorated in '50s memorabilia, the family-owned-and-operated diner-style restaurant has been a local favorite for years for its friendly staff and good food. Diners can treat themselves to a hearty breakfast; any number of submarines, sandwiches or platters for lunch; or a yummy ice cream sundae when a craving strikes. Casual dress. **Parking:** on-site.

HICKORY HOLLOW   Lunch: $5-$15   Dinner: $7-$17   Phone: 941/722-3932   **45**

American   **Location:** I-75, exit 224, 0.6 mi s. 4705 US Hwy 301 N 34222. **Hours:** 11 am-close. Closed major holidays; also Sun, Mon & 7/1-7/15. **Reservations:** not accepted. **Features:** The casual restaurant focuses on home-style country cooking—from its many sandwiches to its many dinner platters. Casual dress; beer & wine only. **Parking:** on-site.

LEE'S CRAB TRAP II   Lunch: $5-$12   Dinner: $9-$30   Phone: 941/729-7777   **44**

Seafood   **Location:** I-75, exit 224, 0.4 mi s on US 301, just w on 51st Ave, then s. 4815 Memphis Rd 34222. **Hours:** 11:30 am-9 pm, Fri & Sat-10 pm. Closed: 11/23, 12/25. **Features:** The bustling and rustic shanty overlooking a small pond and bird refuge is noted for quality seafood as well as such exotic temptations as kangaroo, buffalo, alligator, ostrich and barbecued wild pig. Wood carvings, mounted wildlife and pictures add effect to the rustic spot. Casual dress; cocktails. **Parking:** on-site. **Cards:** DS, MC, VI.

(🍸)

PEACH'S   Lunch: $4-$8   Phone: 941/721-7838   **41**

American   **Location:** I-75, exit 224, just n on US 301, then just w. 2215 60th Ave E 34222. **Hours:** 6 am-2:30 pm. Closed: 11/23, 12/25. **Features:** Peaches are central to the neat little eatery's cozy country theme. Open for breakfast and lunch, this place offers anything from the popular omelets to salads, burgers and pocket sandwiches. A slice of homemade peach cobbler with a scoop of ice cream is a must try. Casual dress. **Parking:** on-site. **Cards:** MC, VI.

(ⓜ)

ROARING 20'S PIZZA AND PIPES   Lunch: $5-$16   Dinner: $5-$16   Phone: 941/723-1733   **42**

Pizza   **Location:** I-75, exit 224, 1 mi e. 6750 N US 301 34222. **Hours:** 4:30 pm-9 pm, Fri-10 pm, Sat noon-2:30 & 4:30-10 pm, Sun noon-2:30 & 4:30-9 pm. Closed major holidays. **Features:** The establishment is an attraction and restaurant rolled into one. Representative of casual fare are pizzas, sandwiches, and pasta and salad bar offerings. Trained organists put on a fabulous show on the breathtaking 4/42 Mighty Wurlitzer Theatre pipe organ. Guests can while away the hours listening to old-time tunes and tapping their toes. Casual dress; beer & wine only. **Parking:** on-site. **Cards:** MC, VI.

(ⓜ)

RUBY TUESDAY   Lunch: $8-$18   Dinner: $8-$18   Phone: 941/721-6341   **43**

American   **Location:** I-75, exit 224, just n on US 301, then just w on 60th Ave E. 5802 20th St E 34222. **Hours:** 11 am-11 pm, Fri & Sat-midnight, Sun-10 pm. Closed: 12/25. **Features:** After a harried day of trolling the nearby outlet mall, shoppers can stop in for a pick-me-up. The eatery offers an extensive salad bar, burgers, sandwiches, ribs, combination platters, fajitas and steaks. Casual dress; cocktails. **Parking:** on-site. **Cards:** AX, DS,
MC, VI.

(ⓜ) (🍸)

ENGLEWOOD pop. 16,196

------ **WHERE TO STAY** ------

PALM MANOR CONDOMINIUMS   Phone: (941)474-3700

12/5-4/30	1P: $115	2P: $115
12/1-12/4 & 5/1-11/30	1P: $80	2P: $80

Condominium **Location:** On SR 775, just se of jct SR 776; opposite Merchants Crossing Plaza. Located in a commercial area. 1531 Placida Rd 34223. Fax: 941/475-5366. **Facility:** 30 two-bedroom standard units with kitchens. 2 stories (no elevator), exterior corridors. **Parking:** on-site. **Terms:** office hours 8:30 am-4 pm, 3 night minimum stay, 30 day cancellation notice-fee imposed, weekly rates available. **Amenities:** irons. *Some:* hair dryers. **Pool(s):** heated outdoor. **Leisure Activities:** tennis court, horseshoes, shuffleboard. **Guest Services:** complimentary laundry. **Cards:** DS, MC, VI.

SOME UNITS
🏊 ❌ 📠 🛏 🧳 💻 / ❌ 📹 /
FEE.

SEAFARER BEACH RESORT   Phone: 941/474-4388

2/1-4/30	1P: $170-$255	2P: $170-$255	XP: $15
12/1-1/2	1P: $155-$230	2P: $155-$230	XP: $15
1/3-1/31	1P: $140-$205	2P: $140-$205	XP: $15
5/1-11/30	1P: $120-$180	2P: $120-$180	XP: $15

Motel **Location:** Oceanfront. On Manasota Key; 1.7 mi w on Manasota Beach Rd from jct SR 776 (Englewood Rd), just s. 8520 Manasota Key Rd 34223. Fax: 941/474-4388. **Facility:** Designated smoking area. 9 units. 4 one-bedroom standard units with efficiencies. 5 one-bedroom suites with kitchens. 1 story, exterior corridors. *Bath:* combo or shower only. **Parking:** on-site. **Terms:** office hours 9 am-5 pm, 30 day cancellation notice-fee imposed, weekly rates available. **Pool(s):** heated outdoor. **Leisure Activities:** fishing, barbecue grills, gazebo. **Guest Services:** coin laundry. **Business Services:** fax. **Cards:** AX, DS, MC, VI. **Special Amenities: free local telephone calls and free newspaper.**

🏊 ❌ 🎿 📠 🛏 🧳 💻

SEA OATS BEACH CLUB   Phone: 941/474-3611

Property failed to provide current rates

Condominium **Location:** Oceanfront. On Manasota Key; from jct SR 776, 1.4 mi w on Beach Rd, then just s. 1720 Gulf Blvd 34223. Fax: 941/474-3611. **Facility:** 25 units. 11 one- and 14 two-bedroom suites with kitchens. 2 stories, exterior corridors. **Parking:** on-site. **Terms:** office hours 9 am-5 pm. **Amenities:** video library, irons, hair dryers. **Pool(s):** heated outdoor. **Leisure Activities:** whirlpool, bicycles, shuffleboard. **Guest Services:** coin laundry. **Business Services:** fax.

🍴 🏊 ❌ 📹 🛏 🧳 💻

------ **WHERE TO DINE** ------

PRIME TIME STEAK & SPIRITS   Dinner: $5-$31   Phone: 941/697-7799

American **Location:** On CR 775, 4.2 mi w of jct SR 776; in Rotonda Plaza. 5855 Placida Rd, Suite 100 34224. **Hours:** 4 pm-10:30 pm, Fri & Sat-11:30 pm, Sun 11 am-10:30 pm. Closed: 11/23, 12/25. **Reservations:** not accepted. **Features:** A Southwestern aura punctuates this restaurant, where the menu dabbles in seafood, Mexican dishes, pasta, steak and poultry, all prepared from scratch. Watch romantic sunsets over Lemon Bay, or slip into the sports-themed bar for a livelier experience. Casual dress; cocktails. **Parking:** on-site. **Cards:** AX, DC, DS, MC, VI.

🍽

EUSTIS —*See Orlando p. 753.*

EVERGLADES CITY pop. 479

------ **WHERE TO DINE** ------

THE OYSTER HOUSE RESTAURANT   *Menu on aaa.com*   Lunch: $5-$20   Dinner: $5-$20   Phone: 239/695-2073

Seafood **Location:** 3 mi s on SR 29 (Chokoloskee Cswy). 901 Copeland Ave 34139. **Hours:** Open 12/1-6/1 & 9/1-11/30; 11 am-10 pm. Closed: 11/23, 12/25. **Reservations:** suggested, 1/1-4/30. **Features:** Serving seasonal offerings of fresh local seafood, alligator, frog legs and stone crab claws, this rustic restaurant feels like old Florida, with stuffed wildlife and maritime decor. The bright and airy dining room looks out over the Gulf of Mexico. Casual dress; cocktails; entertainment. **Parking:** on-site. **Cards:** AX, CB, DC, DS, JC, MC, VI.

🍽

FERN PARK —See Orlando p. 753.

FLAGLER BEACH pop. 4,954

——— WHERE TO STAY ———

BEACH FRONT MOTEL
Phone: (386)439-0089

▼▼ ▼▼
Motel

	1P: $64-$69	2P: $64-$69	XP: $5	F18
2/11-9/3	1P: $54-$59	2P: $54-$59	XP: $5	F18
12/1-2/10 & 9/4-11/30				

Location: On SR A1A, 1 mi s of SR 100. 1544 S A1A 32136. Fax: 386/439-0083. **Facility:** 20 one-bedroom standard units, some with efficiencies. 2 stories, exterior corridors. **Parking:** on-site. **Terms:** 3 day cancellation notice, weekly rates available, pets (dogs only, $15 fee). **Cards:** DS, MC, VI.

SOME UNITS
(ASK) (S⊘) 🍴 🖥 / ✕ 🖨 🖵 /
FEE

FLAGLER BEACH MOTEL & RENTALS
Phone: 386/439-7717

▼
Motel

Property failed to provide current rates
Location: On SR A1A, 1.5 mi s of SR 100. 1820 S Oceanshore Blvd 32136. Fax: 386/439-7717. **Facility:** Smoke free premises. 23 units. 20 one-bedroom standard units with efficiencies. 3 one-bedroom suites with efficiencies. 1 story, exterior corridors. *Bath:* combo or shower only. **Parking:** on-site. **Pool(s):** outdoor.

🍴 🏊 ✕ 🕿 🖥 🖨 🖵

TOPAZ MOTEL
Phone: (386)439-3301

(AAA) (SAVE)
▼▼ ▼▼
Small-scale Hotel

| All Year | 1P: $65-$180 | 2P: $65-$180 | XP: $10 | F12 |

Location: On SR A1A, 0.5 mi s of SR 100. 1224 S Oceanshore Blvd 32136. Fax: 386/439-3942. **Facility:** 58 one-bedroom standard units, some with efficiencies and/or whirlpools. 2 stories, interior/exterior corridors. *Bath:* combo or shower only. **Parking:** on-site. **Terms:** weekly rates available, pets (dogs only, $11 fee). **Amenities:** video library, voice mail. *Some:* hair dryers. **Dining:** 11 am-3 & 5:30-10 pm, Sat from 5:30 pm, Sun from 3 pm, wine/beer only. **Pool(s):** outdoor. **Guest Services:** coin laundry. **Business Services:** meeting rooms. **Cards:** AX, DS, MC, VI. **Special Amenities:** preferred room (subject to availability with advance reservations).

SOME UNITS
🖥 🍴 🐾 🏊 / ✕ (VCR) 🖥 🖨 🖵 /
FEE

THE WHITE ORCHID OCEANFRONT INN & SPA
Phone: 386/439-4944

(AAA) (SAVE)
▼▼ ▼▼

2/15-10/31	1P: $149-$269	2P: $149-$269	XP: $45
11/1-11/30	1P: $129-$249	2P: $129-$249	XP: $45
12/1-2/14	1P: $119-$219	2P: $119-$219	XP: $45

Location: On SR A1A, 0.5 mi s of SR 100. 1104 S Oceanshore Blvd 32136. Fax: 386/439-4946. **Facility:** Featuring a main house and a carriage house decorated in Art Deco style, this property is across the street from the ocean. Smoke free premises. 10 one-bedroom standard units, some with whirlpools. 2 stories, interior/exterior corridors. *Bath:* combo or shower only. **Parking:** on-site. **Terms:** 2 night minimum stay - weekends, age restrictions may apply, 10 day cancellation notice-fee imposed, [BP] meal plan available, package plans. **Amenities:** voice mail, irons, hair dryers. **Pool(s):** heated outdoor, small heated outdoor. **Leisure Activities:** beach accessories, bicycles, spa. **Guest Services:** gift shop. **Business Services:** fax. **Cards:** AX, DS, MC, VI. **Special Amenities:** free full breakfast and free local telephone calls.

🖥 🏊 ✕ ✕ 📹 🖥

Bed & Breakfast

——— WHERE TO DINE ———

CHRISTINA'S OCEANVIEW RESTAURANT
Lunch: $10-$15   Dinner: $16-$30   Phone: 386/439-2232

▼▼ ▼▼
American
Cards: AX, DS, MC, VI.

Location: 2.5 mi s of SR 100. 2444 S Oceanshore Blvd 32136. **Hours:** 11 am-9 pm, Fri & Sat-10 pm. Closed: 12/25; also Tues. **Features:** Patrons can sit on the patio while eating sandwiches, wings or fish and chips. Prime rib, lobster tail and snow crab legs are among dishes preferred in the inside dining room. Save room for fried ice cream and chocolate sauce served in a tortilla shell. Casual dress; cocktails. **Parking:** on-site.

🍽

FISHERMAN'S NET
Lunch: $5-$15   Dinner: $6-$18   Phone: 386/439-1818

▼▼ ▼▼
Seafood

Location: Just s of SR 100. 500 S Oceanshore Blvd 32136. **Hours:** 11 am-9 pm, Fri & Sat-10 pm. Closed: Mon. **Features:** Across from the pier so the seafood is fresh, the restaurant invites you to choose your pleasure and have it blackened, fried or baked. Casual dress; cocktails. **Parking:** on-site. **Cards:** MC, VI.

FLORAL CITY pop. 4,989

——— WHERE TO STAY ———

MOONRISE RESORT
Phone: 352/726-2553

▼▼ ▼▼
Cottage

| All Year | 1P: $70-$100 | 2P: $70-$110 | XP: $5 |

Location: Just e on CR 48, then 1.5 mi n on Old Floral City Rd. 8801 E Moonrise Ln, Lot 18 34436. Fax: 352/726-2553. **Facility:** 10 cottages. 1 story, exterior corridors. *Bath:* combo or shower only. **Parking:** on-site. **Terms:** 2 night minimum stay - weekends, 21 day cancellation notice, weekly rates available, pets ($20 fee). **Leisure Activities:** boat dock, fishing, shuffleboard. *Fee:* boats, canoes, paddleboats. **Guest Services:** coin laundry. **Business Services:** fax.

🖥 ✕ 🕿 🖥 🖨 🖵
FEE

FLORIDA CITY —See Miami-Miami Beach p. 603.

Destination
The Florida Keys

T hey've been called a string of pearls, draped across a sweep of turquoise water.

T hat's only half the truth. Fact is, these Keys are many things to many people. From sport-fishers' gold mine to scuba divers' sunken treasure, they offer a pirate's chest full of activities for all.

Visit Florida

Seven Mile Bridge connecting the Keys.
With a seascape this stunning, who needs a big-city skyline? (See mention page 65)

National Oceanic & Atmospheric Admin/William Folsom

Shark art, Islamorada.
Better to face this denizen on a sunny seaside deck than in the deep blue sea.

Little Torch Key

Key West

See Vicinity map page 334

P laces included in this AAA Destination Area:

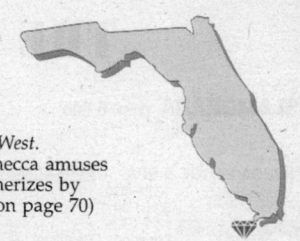

Duval Street, Key West.
This main-drag mecca amuses
by day and mesmerizes by
night. (See mention page 70)

(9336)

(1)

*Key
Largo*

Islamorada

(1)
Long Key

*Key Colony
Beach*

Marathon

Florida Keys

© Gibson Stock Photography

Land's End Marina, Key West.
From Key Largo to Key
West, this chain of islands
is sport-fishing central.

Historic Tours of America

Southernmost Point, Key West.
A colorful landlocked buoy marks the
end of the road. (See mention page 64)

THE FLORIDA KEYS

ISLAMORADA pop. 6,846

——— WHERE TO STAY ———

CHEECA LODGE & SPA　*Book at aaa.com*　　　　　　　　　　Phone: (305)664-4651

(AAA) (SAVE)　12/25-4/30　　　　1P: $269-$1400　　2P: $269-$1400　　XP: $30　　F17
　　　　　　　5/1-11/30　　　　1P: $159-$1049　　2P: $159-$1049　　XP: $30　　F17
♦♦♦♦ ♦♦♦♦　12/1-12/24　　　　1P: $169-$929　　　2P: $169-$929　　XP: $30　　F17

Resort　　　　**Location:** Oceanfront. US 1 at MM 82. Located in a quiet area. 81801 Overseas Hwy 33036 (PO Box 527).
Large-scale Hotel　**Fax:** 305/664-2893. **Facility:** Notable for its ocean pier, this luxurious beach resort also offers a saltwater swimming lagoon, lush landscaping and comfortable rooms. Designated smoking area. 203 units. 140 one-bedroom standard units. 63 one-bedroom suites with kitchens. 2-4 stories, interior/exterior corridors. *Bath:* combo or shower only. **Parking:** on-site and valet. **Terms:** check-in 4 pm, 14 day cancellation notice-fee imposed, [ECP] & [MAP] meal plans available, package plans, $39 service charge. **Amenities:** video library, DVD players, CD players, dual phone lines, voice mail, safes, honor bars, irons, hair dryers. *Some:* high-speed Internet (fee). **Dining:** 2 restaurants, 7 am-10 pm, cocktails, also, Atlantic's Edge, see separate listing. **Pool(s):** 2 heated outdoor. **Leisure Activities:** saunas, whirlpools, steamrooms, limited beach access, rental paddleboats, boat dock, snorkeling, fishing, saltwater lagoon, 525 ft fishing pier, golf-9 holes, 6 lighted tennis courts, recreation programs, yoga instruction, bicycles, jogging, playground, spa, volleyball. *Fee:* boats, sailboats, windsurfing, scuba diving, charter fishing, dive trips, sunset cruises, parasailing, eco tours. **Guest Services:** gift shop, valet laundry, airport transportation (fee)-Miami International Airport, area transportation. **Business Services:** meeting rooms, business center. **Cards:** AX, DC, DS, MC, VI. **Special Amenities:** free local telephone calls and free newspaper.
(See color ad below)

SOME UNITS

（⑤⑥）（✈）（🅱️）（🍴）（♿）（💪）（🏊）（✕）（✕）（DATA PORT）（📧）（🖥️）／（VCR）（🖼️）／
　　　　　　　　FEE

DAYS INN-ISLAMORADA　*Book at aaa.com*　　　　　　　　　Phone: 305/664-3681

♦♦ ♦♦　　　　　　　　Property failed to provide current rates

Motel　　　**Location:** US 1 at MM 82.7. 82749 Overseas Hwy 33036. Fax: 305/664-9020. **Facility:** 36 units. 16 one-bedroom standard units, some with efficiencies. 19 one- and 1 two-bedroom suites with kitchens. 1-5 stories, exterior corridors. **Parking:** on-site. **Amenities:** voice mail, hair dryers. **Pool(s):** outdoor. **Leisure Activities:** *Fee:* bicycles. **Business Services:** fax (fee).

SOME UNITS

（🍴）（🏊）（DATA PORT）／（✕）（📧）（🖥️）／

HAMPTON INN & SUITES　*Book at aaa.com*　　　　　　　　Phone: 305/664-0073

♦♦♦ ♦♦　　　　　　　　Property failed to provide current rates

Small-scale Hotel　**Location:** Oceanfront. US 1 at MM 80. 80001 Overseas Hwy 33036. Fax: 305/664-0807. **Facility:** 79 units. 20 one-bedroom standard units. 37 one- and 22 two-bedroom suites with efficiencies. 5 stories, interior corridors. *Bath:* combo or shower only. **Parking:** on-site. **Amenities:** video games (fee), high-speed Internet, voice mail, safes, irons, hair dryers. **Pool(s):** heated outdoor. **Leisure Activities:** whirlpool, limited beach access, rental paddleboats, fishing, playground, exercise room, shuffleboard. *Fee:* boats, canoes, boat dock, scuba diving, snorkeling, charter fishing, bicycles, massage. **Guest Services:** gift shop, coin laundry. **Business Services:** fax (fee).

SOME UNITS

（🍴）（🅱️）（♿M）（✉）（💪）（🏊）（✕）（VCR）（🎮）（DATA PORT）（🖥️）／（✕）（📧）（🖼️）／

THE ISLANDER RESORT **Book at aaa.com** Phone: (305)664-2031

▽▽▽ 12/25-4/30 1P: $209-$425 2P: $209-$425 XP: $10 F12
5/1-11/30 1P: $139-$375 2P: $139-$375 XP: $10 F12
Motel 12/1-12/24 1P: $119-$199 2P: $119-$199 XP: $10 F12
Location: Oceanfront. US 1 at MM 82.1. 82100 Overseas Hwy 33036 (PO Box 766). Fax: 305/664-5503. **Facility:** 114 units. 101 one-bedroom standard units with kitchens. 12 one- and 1 two-bedroom suites with kitchens, some with whirlpools. 1 story, exterior corridors. *Bath:* combo or shower only. **Parking:** on-site. **Terms:** cancellation fee imposed, [CP] meal plan available, package plans. **Amenities:** high-speed Internet, safes, irons, hair dryers. **Pool(s):** 2 heated outdoor. **Leisure Activities:** whirlpool, fishing, exercise room, basketball, horseshoes, shuffleboard, volleyball. **Guest Services:** coin laundry. **Business Services:** meeting rooms. **Cards:** AX, DC, DS, MC, VI. *(See color ad below)*

(ASK) (⊓) (☿) (🛥) (✕) (CTV) (DATA PORT) (⊟) (🖭) (▭)

PELICAN COVE RESORT & MARINA Phone: (305)664-4435

(AAA) (SAVE) 12/23-4/16 [CP] 1P: $195-$765 2P: $195-$765 XP: $20 F12
4/17-11/30 [CP] 1P: $155-$615 2P: $155-$615 XP: $20 F12
▽▽▽▽ 12/1-12/22 [CP] 1P: $135-$515 2P: $135-$515 XP: $20 F12
Small-scale Hotel **Location:** Oceanfront. US 1 at MM 84.5. Located behind the Theater of the Sea. 84457 Old Overseas Hwy 33036 (PO Box 633). Fax: 305/664-5134. **Facility:** 63 units. 54 one-bedroom standard units, some with efficiencies. 9 one-bedroom suites ($265-$365) with kitchens and whirlpools. 3 stories, exterior corridors. **Parking:** on-site. **Terms:** check-in 4 pm, 2 night minimum stay - weekends, 5 day cancellation notice-fee imposed. **Amenities:** voice mail, irons, hair dryers. **Pool(s):** heated outdoor. **Leisure Activities:** whirlpool, fishing, tennis court. *Fee:* boats, boat dock, snorkeling, charter fishing, snorkel trips, waverunners, kayaks. **Guest Services:** valet laundry. **Business Services:** meeting rooms, fax (fee). **Cards:** AX, CB, DC, DS, MC, VI. **Special Amenities:** free continental breakfast and free newspaper. *(See color ad below)*

SOME UNITS
(S⊡) (⊓+) (☿) (🛆) (🛥) (✕) (⊟) (▭) / (VCR) (🖭) /

SANDS OF ISLAMORADA Phone: (305)664-2791

(AAA) (SAVE) 12/22-9/4 1P: $140-$285 XP: $15
9/5-11/30 1P: $105-$235 XP: $15
▽▽▽ 12/1-12/21 1P: $99-$225 XP: $15
Motel **Location:** Oceanfront. US 1 at MM 80. 80051 Overseas Hwy 33036. Fax: 305/664-2886. **Facility:** 9 units. 8 one-bedroom standard units, some with efficiencies. 1 one-bedroom suite with efficiency. 1-2 stories, exterior corridors. *Bath:* combo or shower only. **Parking:** on-site. **Terms:** office hours 8 am-9 pm, 3 day cancellation notice-fee imposed, pets ($15 fee). **Amenities:** video library, voice mail, hair dryers. **Pool(s):** outdoor. **Leisure Activities:** whirlpool, barbecue grill. *Fee:* boat dock. **Business Services:** fax (fee). **Cards:** MC, VI.

SOME UNITS
(🛏) (⊓+) (🖫) (🛥) (✕) (DATA PORT) (⊟) (🖭) (▭) / (VCR) /
FEE

——— **WHERE TO DINE** ———

ATLANTIC'S EDGE **Dinner:** $16-$42 **Phone:** 305/664-4651
▼▼▼ ▼▼▼ **Location:** US 1 at MM 82; in Cheeca Lodge & Spa. 81801 Overseas Hwy 33036. **Hours:** 6 pm-10 pm.
Regional American **Reservations:** suggested. **Features:** "Barefoot elegance" is the motto at the comfortable yet elegant restaurant, where local seafood specialties dominate the menu. Atlantic Ocean views capture diners' attention while a pianist provides background music. This place satisfies those out celebrating a special occasion or those taking in an occasional treat. The menu is varied, and servers are friendly. Dressy casual; cocktails. **Parking:** on-site. **Cards:** AX, CB, DC, DS, MC, VI.

ISLAMORADA FISH COMPANY **Lunch:** $8-$13 **Dinner:** $8-$24 **Phone:** 305/664-9271
▼▼▼ **Location:** US 1 at MM 81.5. 81532 Overseas Hwy 33036. **Hours:** 11 am-10 pm. Closed: 11/23, 12/25.
Seafood **Features:** On the waterfront, the restaurant offers the freshest seafood. The dining room has no walls, which makes for outstanding views of the gulf, mangroves and sunset from every table. Casual dress; cocktails. **Parking:** on-site. **Cards:** AX, DS, MC, VI.

ISLAMORADA RESTAURANT AND BAKERY **Lunch:** $4-$8 **Phone:** 305/664-8363
▼▼▼ **Location:** US 1 at MM 81.6 (gulfside). 81620 Overseas Hwy 33036. **Hours:** 6 am-2 pm. Closed: 12/25.
American **Features:** Locals line up for hours to partake of the famous breakfasts at this diner-style restaurant and bakery. Casual dress; beer & wine only. **Parking:** on-site. **Cards:** AX, MC, VI.

MARKER 88 RESTAURANT **Lunch:** $7-$15 **Dinner:** $17-$30 **Phone:** 305/852-9315
◈◈◈ **Location:** On US 1 at MM 88. US 1, MM 88 33036. **Hours:** 11 am-10 pm. Closed: 11/23, 12/25.
▼▼▼ **Reservations:** suggested. **Features:** An elaborate menu offers local seafood specials. The dining room overlooks Florida Bay. Both the soup and salad are very good. Try the yellowtail rangoon for a tropical twist.
Seafood The service is pleasant and very professional. Casual dress; cocktails. **Parking:** on-site. **Cards:** AX, DC, DS, MC, VI.

SQUID ROW RESTAURANT **Lunch:** $4-$7 **Dinner:** $10-$25 **Phone:** 305/664-9865
◈◈◈ **Location:** US 1 at MM 81.9. 81901 Overseas Hwy 33036. **Hours:** 11:30 am-9:30 pm, Fri & Sat-10 pm. Closed:
▼▼▼ 11/23, 12/25. **Reservations:** suggested, for dinner. **Features:** A wide range of fresh seafood, steak, chicken and pasta is prepared to order. Bouillabaisse is a house specialty, and dessert, bread and dressing are
Steak & Seafood made on the premises. A tasty grilled fish sandwich with french fries provides a satisfying lunch for those on the go. Casual dress; cocktails. **Parking:** on-site. **Cards:** AX, CB, DC, DS, MC, VI.

UNCLE'S RESTAURANT **Dinner:** $12-$30 **Phone:** 305/664-4402
▼▼▼ ▼▼▼ **Location:** US 1 at MM 80.9. 80900 Overseas Hwy 33036. **Hours:** 5 pm-10 pm, Fri & Sat-10:30 pm. Closed:
Steak & Seafood 12/25; also Sun. **Reservations:** required. **Features:** Steaks and wild game are available, but the restaurant specializes in fresh, local seafood prepared in many different styles. The atmosphere is subtle, with pictures of local catches on the wall. Casual dress; cocktails. **Parking:** on-site. **Cards:** AX, DS, MC, VI.

WHALE HARBOR RESTAURANT & MARINA **Lunch:** $6-$20 **Dinner:** $10-$30 **Phone:** 305/664-4959
▼▼▼ **Location:** Jct Whale Harbor Channel. 83413 Overseas Hwy 33036. **Hours:** 11:30 am-10 pm. **Reservations:** not
Seafood accepted. **Features:** Directly on Whale Harbor Channel, the restaurant lets guests watch harbor and waterway activities while savoring all sorts of seafood. Choices range from the cracked conch platter to the catch of the day. Diners with hearty appetites might try the combination platter, which has loads of oysters, clams, shrimp, mussels, crayfish, smoked fish and crab legs. Casual dress; cocktails. **Parking:** on-site. **Cards:** AX, DC, DS, MC, VI.

KEY COLONY BEACH pop. 788

——— **WHERE TO STAY** ———

CONTINENTAL INN **Phone:** 305/289-0101
◈◈◈ SAVE
▼▼▼

12/1-1/2	2P: $150	XP: $10	F5
1/3-4/1	2P: $130	XP: $10	F5
4/2-8/31	2P: $125	XP: $10	F5
9/1-11/30	2P: $109	XP: $10	F5

Condominium **Location:** Oceanfront. 1.2 mi sw from jct US 1 and Sadowski Cswy (MM 53.8). 1121 W Ocean Dr 33051 (PO Box 510209). Fax: 305/743-8150. **Facility:** 42 units. 40 one-bedroom standard units with kitchens. 2 two-bedroom suites with kitchens. 2 stories (no elevator), exterior corridors. *Bath:* combo or shower only. **Parking:** on-site. **Terms:** office hours 9 am-5 pm, cancellation fee imposed. **Amenities:** *Some:* DVD players, irons, hair dryers. **Pool(s):** heated outdoor. **Leisure Activities:** limited beach access, barbecue area, recreational room, tiki huts, shuffleboard. **Guest Services:** coin laundry. **Business Services:** fax (fee). **Cards:** MC, VI. **Special Amenities:** free local telephone calls.

SOME UNITS

KEY LARGO pop. 11,886

——— **WHERE TO STAY** ———

BAY BREEZE MOTEL **Phone:** 305/852-5248
▼▼▼ ▼▼▼ Property failed to provide current rates
Motel **Location:** 7.5 mi s from center of town, at MM 92.5. Located in a quiet area. 160 Sterling Rd 33070. Fax: 305/852-5758. **Facility:** 19 units. 12 one-bedroom standard units, some with efficiencies. 1 two-bedroom suite. 6 cottages. 2 stories (no elevator), exterior corridors. *Bath:* combo or shower only. **Parking:** on-site. **Terms:** office hours 9 am-6 pm. **Pool(s):** heated outdoor. **Leisure Activities:** boating, boat dock. **Business Services:** fax (fee).

SOME UNITS
FEE

BAYSIDE RESORT   *Book at aaa.com*   Phone: (305)451-4450

Motel

1/29-4/22   2P: $129-$199
12/1-1/28 & 4/23-11/30   2P: $89-$199
Location: US 1 at MM 99.5. 99490 Overseas Hwy 33037 (PO Box 1050). Fax: 305/451-9650. **Facility:** 56 units. 54 one-bedroom standard units. 2 one-bedroom suites ($189-$299) with efficiencies. 2-3 stories, exterior corridors. **Parking:** on-site. **Terms:** 3 night minimum stay - seasonal, 3 day cancellation notice. **Amenities:** high-speed Internet, hair dryers. *Some:* safes, irons. **Dining:** noon-3 & 5-11 pm, Sat & Sun from 5 pm, wine/beer only. **Pool(s):** small heated outdoor. **Leisure Activities:** limited beach access, fishing, barbecue grills, volleyball. **Guest Services:** sundries. **Business Services:** fax (fee). **Cards:** AX, DC, DS, MC, VI. **Special Amenities:** free continental breakfast and free local telephone calls. *(See color ad below)*

SOME UNITS

FEE

BEST WESTERN SUITES AT KEY LARGO   *Book at aaa.com*   Phone: (305)451-5081

Condominium

12/1-3/31 [ECP]   1P: $119-$139   2P: $119-$139   XP: $10   F18
4/1-11/30 [ECP]   1P: $99-$139   2P: $99-$139   XP: $10   F18
Location: 0.3 mi e of US 1 at MM 100. Located on a waterway. 201 Ocean Dr 33037. Fax: 305/451-4173. **Facility:** 40 one-bedroom suites with kitchens. 2 stories, exterior corridors. **Parking:** on-site. **Terms:** package plans. **Amenities:** high-speed Internet, safes (fee), irons, hair dryers. **Pool(s):** outdoor. **Leisure Activities:** fishing. *Fee:* scuba diving, snorkeling, charter fishing. **Guest Services:** coin laundry. **Business Services:** fax (fee). **Cards:** AX, CB, DC, DS, JC, MC, VI. **Special Amenities:** free expanded continental breakfast and free local telephone calls.

SOME UNITS

HOLIDAY INN RESORT *Book at aaa.com* Phone: (305)451-2121
▼▼▼▼ All Year 1P: $199-$289
Location: US 1 at MM 100. 99701 Overseas Hwy 33037. Fax: 305/451-5592. Facility: 132 one-bedroom
Small-scale Hotel standard units. 2 stories, interior/exterior corridors. Bath: combo or shower only. Parking: on-site.
Terms: cancellation fee imposed. Amenities: voice mail, irons, hair dryers. Pool(s): 2 heated outdoor.
Leisure Activities: whirlpool, fishing, playground, exercise room. Fee: boats, marina, scuba diving, snorkeling, charter fishing,
bicycles. Guest Services: gift shop, coin laundry. Business Services: meeting rooms, fax (fee). Cards: AX, DS, MC, VI.
(See color ad below)
SOME UNITS

(A$K) (S/▫) (†¶) (Y) (⌾) (⊅) (⇌) (⊠) (✖) (DATA PORT) (⊟) (▱) / (⊠) /

HOWARD JOHNSON RESORT KEY LARGO *Book at aaa.com* Phone: (305)451-1400
(AAA) (SAVE) 1/13-4/23 1P: $119-$199 2P: $119-$199
10/19-11/30 1P: $109-$199 2P: $109-$199
▼▼ ▼▼ 12/1-1/12 & 4/24-10/18 1P: $99-$189 2P: $99-$189
Location: Oceanfront. US 1 at MM 102 (Bayside). Located on the bayfront. 102400 Overseas Hwy 33037 (PO Box
Small-scale Hotel 1024). Fax: 305/451-3953. Facility: 100 one-bedroom standard units. 2 stories (no elevator), interior
corridors. Bath: combo or shower only. Parking: on-site. Terms: cancellation fee imposed, [BP] meal plan
available, small pets only ($10 extra charge). Amenities: safes. Dining: 7-11 am. Pool(s): heated outdoor. Leisure
Activities: fishing. Fee: canoes, scuba diving, snorkeling. Guest Services: coin laundry. Business Services: meeting rooms.
Cards: AX, DC, DS, MC, VI. Special Amenities: free local telephone calls and free newspaper.
SOME UNITS

(S/▫) (🛏) (†¶) (Y) (⌾M) (⌾) (⊅) (⇌) (⊠) (✖) (DATA PORT) (▱) / (⊠) (⊟) (▱) /
FEE

MARINA DEL MAR RESORT & MARINA *Book at aaa.com* Phone: 305/451-4107
▼▼▼▼ Property failed to provide current rates
Location: US 1 at MM 100. Located adjacent to Holiday Inn. 527 Caribbean Dr 33037. Fax: 305/451-1891.
Small-scale Hotel Facility: 76 units. 64 one-bedroom standard units, some with efficiencies. 8 one-, 3 two- and 1 three-
bedroom suites with kitchens. 2-4 stories, exterior corridors. Parking: on-site. Terms: office hours 7 am-11
pm, small pets only ($50 deposit). Amenities: irons, hair dryers. Some: DVD players (fee). Dining: Coconuts Restaurant &
Lounge, see separate listing. Pool(s): heated outdoor. Leisure Activities: whirlpool, 2 lighted tennis courts, jogging, exercise
room. Fee: marina, scuba diving, snorkeling, fishing, charter fishing, bicycles, massage. Guest Services: gift shop, coin
laundry. Business Services: meeting rooms, fax (fee). *(See color ad below)*
SOME UNITS

(🛏) (†¶) (Y) (⊅) (⇌) (⊠) (✖) (⊟) (▱) / (⊠) (VCR) (▱) /
FEE FEE

MARRIOTT KEY LARGO BAY BEACH RESORT *Book at aaa.com*

Phone: (305)453-0000

▼▼▼▼ 12/1-4/30   1P: $289-$699   2P: $289-$699   XP: $20   F16
      5/1-11/30   1P: $199-$629   2P: $199-$629   XP: $20   F16

Resort   **Location:** Oceanfront. US 1 at MM 103.8. 103800 Overseas Hwy 33037. **Fax:** 305/453-0093. **Facility:** The resort
Large-scale Hotel   features tropical-themed guest rooms and suites on extensive grounds which overlook the bay. 153 units. 133 one-bedroom standard units, some with efficiencies. 20 two-bedroom suites ($629-$1500) with kitchens. 4 stories, exterior corridors. *Bath:* combo or shower only. **Parking:** on-site. **Terms:** 4 day cancellation notice-fee imposed. **Amenities:** high-speed Internet, voice mail, safes, honor bars, irons, hair dryers. **Pool(s):** heated outdoor. **Leisure Activities:** whirlpool, limited beach access, rental boats, rental canoes, rental paddleboats, boat dock, fishing, tennis court, recreation programs, jogging, exercise room, spa, basketball, shuffleboard, volleyball. *Fee:* scuba diving, snorkeling, charter fishing, bicycles. **Guest Services:** gift shop, valet and coin laundry. **Business Services:** conference facilities, fax (fee). **Cards:** AX, DC, DS, JC, MC, VI. *(See color ad below)*

SOME UNITS

(ASK) (S/D) (TIＰ) (Y) (⊘) (⇆) (✕) (🐾) (DATA PORT) (🛏) / (✕) (VCR) (🔒) (🖥) /

RAMADA LIMITED RESORT AND MARINA *Book at aaa.com*

Phone: (305)451-3939

▼▼▼▼ All Year [BP]   1P: $89-$229   2P: $89-$229   XP: $9   F18

     Location: US 1 at MM 100. 99751 Overseas Hwy 33037. **Fax:** 305/453-0222. **Facility:** 92 units. 89 one-bedroom
Small-scale Hotel   standard units. 3 one-bedroom suites with whirlpools. 5 stories, interior corridors. **Parking:** on-site. **Terms:** cancellation fee imposed. **Amenities:** voice mail, irons, hair dryers. **Pool(s):** heated outdoor. **Leisure Activities:** whirlpool, rental boats. *Fee:* marina, scuba diving, snorkeling, fishing, charter fishing. **Guest Services:** coin laundry. **Business Services:** meeting rooms, fax (fee). **Cards:** AX, DS, MC, VI. *(See color ad below)*

SOME UNITS

(ASK) (S/D) (TIＰ) (⇆) (❖) (✕) (🐾) (DATA PORT) (🔒) (🖥) / (✕) /

ROCK REEF RESORT

Phone: 305/852-2401

(AAA) (SAVE)   12/18-4/29   2P: $119-$200   XP: $15   D10
▼▼ ▼▼   4/30-9/9   2P: $115-$180   XP: $15   D10
     12/1-12/17 & 9/10-11/30   2P: $108-$150   XP: $15   D10

Motel   **Location:** US 1 at MM 98. 97850 Overseas Hwy 33037 (PO Box 73). **Fax:** 305/852-5355. **Facility:** 21 units. 12 one- and 3 two-bedroom standard units, some with efficiencies. 3 one- and 1 two-bedroom suites ($170-$275) with kitchens. 2 cabins ($170-$235). 1-2 stories (no elevator), exterior corridors. *Bath:* combo or shower only. **Parking:** on-site. **Terms:** office hours 9 am-8 pm, 2 night minimum stay - weekends, 21 day cancellation notice-fee imposed, weekly rates available. **Leisure Activities:** paddleboats, boat dock, fishing, fishing pier, barbecue area, tetherball, tropical gardens, shuffleboard. **Guest Services:** coin laundry. **Business Services:** fax (fee). **Cards:** AX, DS, MC, VI. **Special Amenities:** free local telephone calls and free room upgrade (subject to availability with advance reservations).

SOME UNITS

(S/D) (TIＰ) (✕) (✕) (🔒) / (🖥) (🖥) /

SHERATON BEACH RESORT, KEY LARGO   *Book at aaa.com*   **Phone:** (305)852-5553

AAA SAVE | 12/18-4/29 | 1P: $139-$409 | 2P: $139-$409 | XP: $15 | F17
| 12/1-12/17 & 4/30-11/30 | 1P: $109-$369 | 2P: $109-$369 | XP: $15 | F17

Location: US 1 at MM 97. 97000 S Overseas Hwy 33037. Fax: 305/852-8669. **Facility:** The hotel, nestled within a hammock of hardwood trees along the gulf, offers some water-view rooms. 200 one-bedroom standard

Resort
Large-scale Hotel

units, some with whirlpools. 4 stories, exterior corridors. *Bath:* combo or shower only. **Parking:** on-site. **Terms:** cancellation fee imposed, $7 service charge, small pets only ($50 fee). **Amenities:** voice mail, safes, honor bars, irons, hair dryers. *Fee:* video games, high-speed Internet. **Dining:** 4 restaurants, 6:30 am-11 pm, cocktails. **Pool(s):** 2 heated outdoor. **Leisure Activities:** sauna, whirlpool, limited beach access, rental paddleboats, rental sailboats, boat dock, fishing, kayaks, parasailing, personal watercraft, 2 lighted tennis courts, jogging, exercise room. *Fee:* windsurfing, charter fishing, massage, game room. **Guest Services:** gift shop, valet laundry. **Business Services:** conference facilities. **Cards:** AX, CB, DC, DS, MC, VI. **Special Amenities:** free local telephone calls and free newspaper.
(See color ad below)

SOME UNITS

FEE

TARPON FLATS INN & MARINA   **Phone:** (305)453-1313

AAA SAVE | 12/1-4/30 [ECP] | 1P: $175-$225 | 2P: $175-$225 | XP: $10 | F11
| 5/1-11/30 [ECP] | 1P: $140-$175 | 2P: $140-$175 | XP: $10 | F11

Location: US 1 at MM 103.5, 0.3 mi e on Transylvania, then s on Oceanview to Shoreland Dr. Located on the bayfront. 29 Shoreland Dr 33037. Fax: 305/453-1305. **Facility:** The inn has a tranquil setting, overlooking Largo

Bed & Breakfast

Sound amid the aromas of fragrant tropical flowers; rooms are decorated with a Caribbean flair. Designated smoking area. 6 one-bedroom standard units, some with kitchens. 3 stories (no elevator), interior/exterior corridors. *Bath:* combo or shower only. **Parking:** on-site. **Terms:** office hours 9 am-5 pm, 2 night minimum stay - weekends, 7 day cancellation notice-fee imposed, weekly rates available, package plans, no pets allowed (owner's pet on premises). **Amenities:** CD players, voice mail, hair dryers. **Leisure Activities:** whirlpool, barbecue grills. *Fee:* sailboats, boat dock, scuba diving, snorkeling, fishing, charter fishing, kayaks. **Guest Services:** complimentary laundry. **Cards:** AX, CB, DC, DS, MC, VI. **Special Amenities:** free expanded continental breakfast and free local telephone calls.

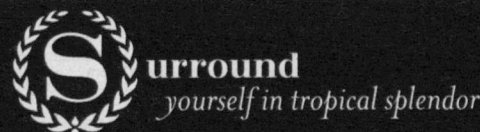

———— WHERE TO DINE ————

BALLYHOO'S HISTORIC SEAFOOD GRILLE   **Lunch:** $7-$22   **Dinner:** $7-$22   **Phone:** 305/852-0822
Location: US 1 at MM 97.8 (in the median). MM 97.8 33037. **Hours:** 11 am-10 pm. Closed: 11/23, 12/25.
Reservations: accepted. **Features:** This 1930s conch house is where the locals dine. Main draws are the
Seafood   relaxed ambience and the abundance of tasty seafood. Locally caught yellowtail snapper prepared in a
variety of ways is a highlight on a menu that also includes shrimp, scallops and stone crab in season.
Delicious homemade Key lime pie makes for a perfect ending. Beer & wine only. **Parking:** on-site. **Cards:** AX, MC, VI.

BAYSIDE GRILL   **Lunch:** $6-$10   **Dinner:** $8-$23   **Phone:** 305/451-3380
Location: US 1 at MM 99.5. 99530 Overseas Hwy 33037. **Hours:** 11:30 am-10 pm. Closed: 11/23, 12/25.
Features: Offering Caribbean-style dishes with local seafood and steaks, this popular spot also features a
lovely sunset view of Florida Bay. A very good wine list and a wide selection of imported beers will help you
American   choose just the right beverage for your meal. Casual dress; cocktails. **Parking:** on-site. **Cards:** AX, MC, VI.

CAFE LARGO   **Dinner:** $9-$25   **Phone:** 305/451-4885
Location: US 1 at MM 99.5. 99530 Overseas Hwy 33037. **Hours:** 4:30 pm-11 pm. Closed: 11/23, 12/25.
Features: Fresh local seafood, certified steak, pasta dishes and other Italian specialties are well
complemented by a very good wine list and extensive selections of imported beer. Soup is homemade and
Italian   changes daily at this spot, perfect for a quick meal. Casual dress; cocktails. **Parking:** on-site. **Cards:** AX, MC, VI.

COCONUTS RESTAURANT & LOUNGE   **Lunch:** $6-$8   **Dinner:** $10-$17   **Phone:** 305/453-9794
Location: US 1 at MM 100; in Marina Del Mar Resort & Marina. 528 Caribbean Dr 33037-1050. **Hours:** 11 am-10
pm. **Features:** No need to dress up for this casual restaurant with a wooden deck overlooking the marina.
Steak & Seafood   Watch the yachts dock for lunch and enjoy a delicious meal with consistent service. The stuffed shrimp with
crab meat is accompanied by summer squash and zucchini. Casual dress; cocktails; entertainment.
Parking: on-site. **Cards:** AX, DC, MC, VI.

THE FISH HOUSE RESTAURANT &
SEAFOOD MARKET   *Menu on aaa.com*   **Lunch:** $9-$15   **Dinner:** $14-$30   **Phone:** 305/451-4665
Location: US 1 at MM 102.4. 102401 Overseas Hwy 33037. **Hours:** Open 12/1-9/8 & 10/3-11/30; 11:30 am-10
pm. Closed: 11/23; also for lunch 12/25. **Features:** Small but always bustling, the restaurant boasts ample
portions of seafood, such as pan-sauteed fish, as well as shrimp and lobster specials that change daily. The
wait staff is energetic, and the meringue-topped Key lime pie is a tempting treat. Casual dress; cocktails.
Seafood   **Parking:** on-site. **Cards:** AX, DC, DS, MC, VI.

GANIM'S - KEY LARGO   **Lunch:** $4-$10   **Phone:** 305/451-2895
Location: US 1 at MM 99.6. 99696 Overseas Hwy 33037. **Hours:** 6 am-2 pm. **Features:** Whether it's breakfast
or lunch, diners find generous portions of diner-style comfort food at this roadside restaurant. Casual dress;
American   beer & wine only. **Parking:** on-site. **Cards:** AX, DS, MC, VI.

GANIM'S RESTAURANT-PENNEKAMP   **Lunch:** $6-$9   **Dinner:** $9-$12   **Phone:** 305/451-3337
Location: US 1 at MM 102.2. 102250 Overseas Hwy 33037. **Hours:** 6 am-9 pm, Sun-2 pm. Closed: 12/25.
Features: Whether it's breakfast, lunch or dinner, diners find generous portions of diner-style comfort food
American   at this roadside restaurant. Casual dress; beer & wine only. **Parking:** on-site. **Cards:** AX, DS, MC, VI.

SNOOKS BAYSIDE   **Lunch:** $6-$9   **Dinner:** $15-$30   **Phone:** 305/453-3799
Location: US 1 at MM 99.9; between Marina del Mar Bayside and Largo Honda. 99470 Overseas Hwy 33037.
Hours: 11:30 am-10 pm, Sun 10 am-9:30 pm. **Reservations:** accepted. **Features:** Choose either the
terrace or an attractive dining room overlooking Florida Bay. Featuring seafood, steak, veal and chicken, the
cuisine is fresh and served by a capable staff. Select tastefully arranged dessert choices brought to you on
American   a silver tray. An extensive wine list is available. Casual dress; cocktails; entertainment. **Parking:** on-site.
Cards: AX, DC, DS, MC, VI.

———— *The following restaurant has not been evaluated by AAA* ————
but is listed for your information only.

RIB DADDY   **Phone:** 305/451-0900
[fyi]   Not evaluated. **Location:** US 1 at MM 102.5. 102570 Overseas Hwy 33037. **Features:** This family-oriented spot is
decked out in a rustic Western motif. Efficient servers bring you traditional barbecue favorites like
charbroiled steak, chicken, seafood, ribs and homemade baked beans; try the onion rings for a treat.

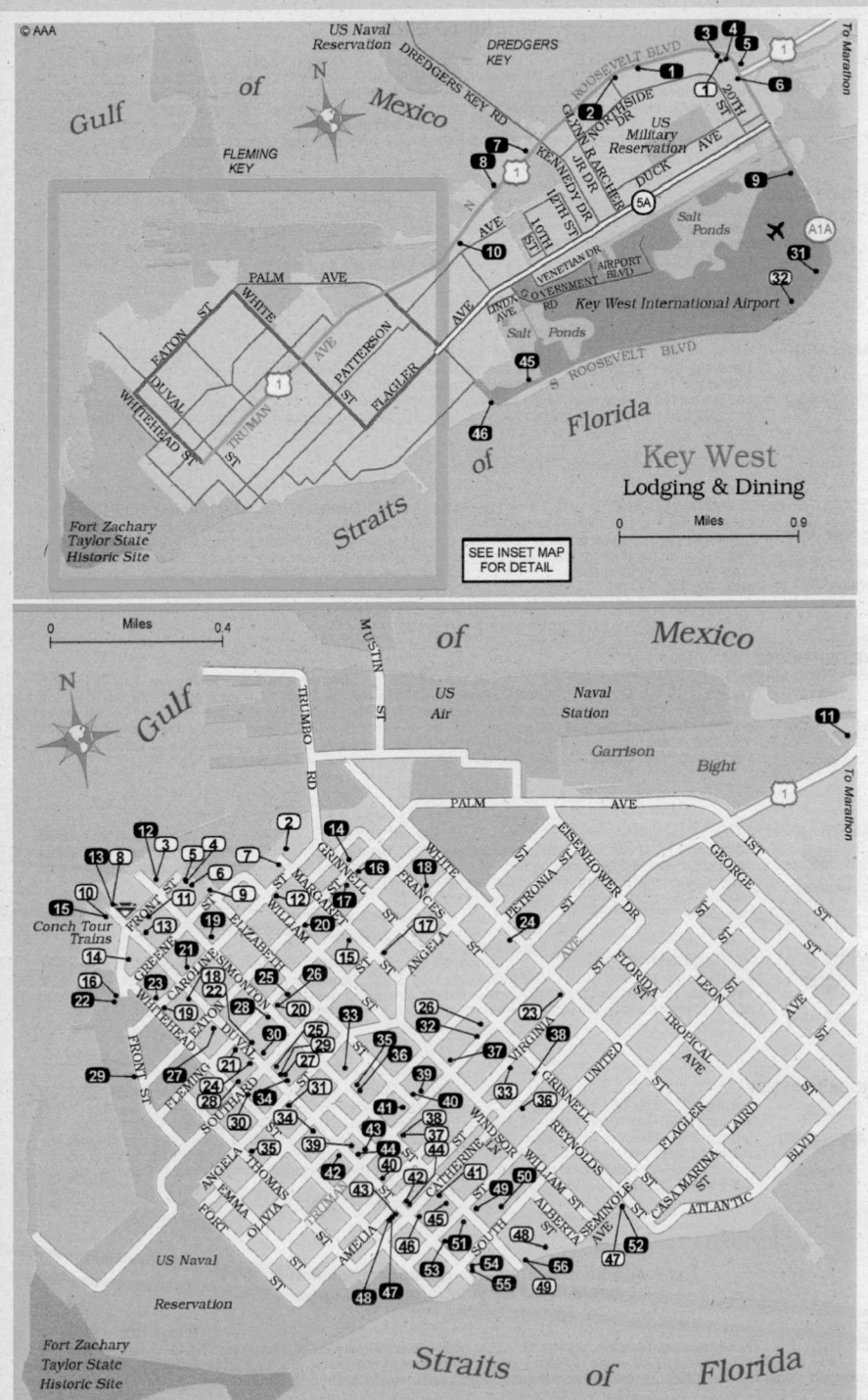

© AAA

Gulf of Mexico

US Naval Reservation

DREDGERS KEY

DREDGERS KEY RD

ROOSEVELT BLVD

To Marathon

FLEMING KEY

US Military Reservation

Salt Ponds

Key West International Airport

Salt Ponds

S ROOSEVELT BLVD

Florida

of

Straits

Fort Zachary Taylor State Historic Site

PALM AVE

WHITE ST

EATON ST

DUVAL ST

WHITEHEAD ST

TRUMAN

PATTERSON AVE

FLAGLER ST

Key West
Lodging & Dining

0   Miles   0.9

SEE INSET MAP FOR DETAIL

0   Miles   0.4

Gulf of Mexico

US Air

Naval Station

Garrison Bight

PALM AVE

To Marathon

Conch Tour Trains

Fort Zachary Taylor State Historic Site

US Naval

Reservation

Straits of Florida

1877-C

© 2005 NAVTEQ

Key West

This index helps you "spot" where approved accommodations and restaurants are located on the corresponding detailed maps. Lodging rate ranges are for comparison only and show the property's high season; rates are per night, unless only weekly (W) rates are available. Restaurant rate range is for dinner, unless only lunch (L) is served. Turn to the listing page for more detailed rate information and consult display ads for special promotions.

Spotter/Map Page Number	OA	KEY WEST - Lodgings	Diamond Rating	Rate Range High Season	Listing Page
① / p. 334	⟨AAA⟩	Travelodge Key West Hotel - see color ad p 352	◇◇	$79-$599 SAVE	353
② / p. 334		Inn at Key West	◇◇◇	$129-$289	347
③ / p. 334	⟨AAA⟩	Radisson Hotel Key West - see color ad p 351	◇◇◇	$119-$399 SAVE	351
④ / p. 334	⟨AAA⟩	Comfort Inn - see color ad p 343	◇◇◇	$129-$299 SAVE	342
⑥ / p. 334		Days Inn-Key West	◇◇◇	$109-$450	344
⑦ / p. 334		Courtyard by Marriott-Key West Waterfront	◇◇◇	$209-$319	343
⑧ / p. 334		Hampton Inn - see color ad p 346	◇◇◇	$104-$289	346
⑨ / p. 334		DoubleTree Grand Key Resort - see color ad p 344	◇◇◇	$189-$819	344
⑩ / p. 334		Fairfield Inn by Marriott Key West	◇◇	$259-$299	345
⑪ / p. 334		Banana Bay Resort-Key West	◇◇◇	$155-$300	338
⑫ / p. 334	⟨AAA⟩	Hyatt Key West Resort & Marina - see color ad p 347	◇◇◇	$273-$500 SAVE	347
⑬ / p. 334	⟨AAA⟩	Pier House Resort & Caribbean Spa - see color ad p 351	◇◇◇	$290-$2000 SAVE	351
⑭ / p. 334	⟨AAA⟩	Budget Key West - see color ad p 348	◇	$119-$299 SAVE	342
⑮ / p. 334	⟨AAA⟩	Ocean Key Resort, A Noble House Resort	◇◇◇◇	$339-$1149 SAVE	350
⑯ / p. 334	⟨AAA⟩	Knowles House B & B	◇◇◇	$159-$219 SAVE	348
⑰ / p. 334	⟨AAA⟩	Westwinds Inn	◇◇	$150-$210 SAVE	353
⑱ / p. 334	⟨AAA⟩	Frances Street Bottle Inn	◇◇	$89-$209 SAVE	345
⑲ / p. 334	⟨AAA⟩	Cypress House Bed & Breakfast	◇◇◇	$150-$400 SAVE	344
⑳ / p. 334		Island City House Hotel	◇◇◇	$125-$375	347
㉑ / p. 334	⟨AAA⟩	Curry Mansion Inn	◇◇◇	$240-$325 SAVE	344
㉒ / p. 334		Hilton Key West Resort & Marina	◇◇◇◇	$329-$579	346
㉓ / p. 334	⟨AAA⟩	The Banyan Resort - see color ad p 338	◇◇◇	$225-$400 SAVE	338
㉔ / p. 334	⟨AAA⟩	The Palms Hotel	◇◇	$185-$205 SAVE	350
㉕ / p. 334		Ambrosia Too At Fleming St	◇◇◇	$125-$445	338
㉖ / p. 334		The Marquesa Hotel	◇◇◇◇	$285-$430	350
㉗ / p. 334		Crowne Plaza La Concha Hotel Resorts	◇◇◇	$199-$406	343
㉘ / p. 334	⟨AAA⟩	Heron House	◇◇◇◇	$199-$369 SAVE	346
㉙ / p. 334		The Weatherstation Inn	◇◇◇	$215-$335	353
㉚ / p. 334	⟨AAA⟩	Pegasus International Hotel	◇◇	$159-$250 SAVE	350
㉛ / p. 334	⟨AAA⟩	Best Western Key Ambassador Resort Inn - see color ad p 340	◇◇◇	$109-$349 SAVE	340
㉜ / p. 334	⟨AAA⟩	Lightbourn Inn	◇◇◇	$178-$328 SAVE	349
㉝ / p. 334	⟨AAA⟩	Courtney's Place Historic Cottages & Inn	◇◇	$139-$259 SAVE	343
㉞ / p. 334	⟨AAA⟩	Duval Inn	◇◇◇	$110-$199 SAVE	345

Spotter/Map Page Number	OA	KEY WEST - Lodgings (continued)	Diamond Rating	Rate Range High Season	Listing Page
35 / p. 334	AAA	The Merlin Inn - see color ad p 348	◆◆	$145-$349 SAVE	350
36 / p. 334	AAA	The Paradise Inn - see color ad p 341	◆◆◆	$329-$759 SAVE	350
37 / p. 334	AAA	La Pensione	◆◆◆	$168-$178 SAVE	349
38 / p. 334		The Grand	◆◆	$148-$248	345
39 / p. 334	AAA	Key Lime Inn - see color ad p 348	◆◆◆	$159-$349 SAVE	348
40 / p. 334	AAA	Chelsea House - see color ad p 342	◆◆◆	$155-$275 SAVE	342
41 / p. 334	AAA	The Conch House Heritage Inn - see color ad p 291	◆◆◆	$148-$228 SAVE	343
42 / p. 334	AAA	Andrews Inn	◆◆◆	$179-$199 SAVE	338
43 / p. 334		Center Court Historic Inn & Cottages	◆◆◆	$158-$708	342
44 / p. 334	AAA	Duval House - see color ad p 345	◆◆◆	$155-$390 SAVE	345
45 / p. 334	AAA	Sheraton Suites-Key West - see color ad p 352, p 8	◆◆◆	$209-$425 SAVE	352
46 / p. 334	AAA	1800 Atlantic Condominiums	◆◆◆	$370-$550 SAVE	338
47 / p. 334		The Cuban Club Suites	◆◆◆	$129-$599	343
48 / p. 334		La Casa de Luces	◆◆◆	$129-$599	348
49 / p. 334	AAA	Best Western Hibiscus Motel - see color ad p 341	◆◆	$169-$319 SAVE	340
50 / p. 334	AAA	Ocean Breeze Inn	◆◆	$139-$239 SAVE	350
51 / p. 334	AAA	Blue Marlin Motel - see color ad p 341	◆◆	$179-$319 SAVE	340
52 / p. 334	AAA	Wyndham Casa Marina Resort	◆◆◆	$379 SAVE	353
53 / p. 334		Southernmost Hotel in the USA - see color ad p 349	◆◆◆	$195-$285	352
54 / p. 334		Southernmost on the Beach - see color ad p 349	◆◆◆	$259-$359	352
55 / p. 334		La Mer Hotel & Dewey House - see color ad p 349	◆◆◆◆	$285-$435	349
56 / p. 334	AAA	Wyndham Reach Resort	◆◆◆	$379 SAVE	353
		KEY WEST - Restaurants			
1 / p. 334		El Meson de Pepe on the Boulevard	◆◆	$12-$22	355
2 / p. 334		Half Shell Raw Bar	◆	$6-$24	355
3 / p. 334		Nicola Seafood	◆◆◆	$22-$29	357
4 / p. 334		A & B Lobster House	◆◆◆	$22-$39	353
5 / p. 334		Alonzo's Oyster Bar	◆◆	$14-$24	354
6 / p. 334		The Commodore Waterfront Restaurant	◆◆◆	$18-$30	354
7 / p. 334		Turtle Kraals Restaurant & Bar	◆	$8-$20	358
8 / p. 334	AAA	One Duval	◆◆◆	$25-$36	357
9 / p. 334		Conch Republic Seafood Company	◆◆	$8-$18	355
10 / p. 334	AAA	Hot Tin Roof	◆◆◆◆	$18-$35	355
11 / p. 334		Two Friends Patio Restaurant	◆◆	$17-$24	358
12 / p. 334		Pepe's Cafe	◆◆	$10-$20	357
13 / p. 334		Bagatelle Restaurant	◆◆	$15-$25	354
14 / p. 334		Roof Top Cafe	◆◆◆	$13-$32	357
15 / p. 334	AAA	Michaels	◆◆◆	$17-$30	357

Spotter/Map Page Number	OA	KEY WEST - Restaurants (continued)	Diamond Rating	Rate Range High Season	Listing Page
⑯ / p. 334		Latitudes Beach Cafe	▽▽▽	$18-$35	356
⑰ / p. 334	◬◬◬	**Mangia Mangia**	▽▽	$9-$15	356
⑱ / p. 334		Grand Cafe Key West	▽▽▽	$16-$34	355
⑲ / p. 334		Kelly's Caribbean Bar, Grill & Brewery	▽▽	$12-$27	355
⑳ / p. 334		Cafe Marquesa	▽▽▽▽	$28-$39	354
㉑ / p. 334		Jimmy Buffett's Margaritaville Cafe	▽▽	$14-$18	355
㉒ / p. 334		Key West Seafood & Beer Garden	▽▽	$15-$22	356
㉓ / p. 334		Sandy's Cafe	▽	$5-$9	357
㉔ / p. 334		La Trattoria	▽▽▽	$15-$29	356
㉕ / p. 334		The Upper Crust	▽	$10-$20	358
㉖ / p. 334		Kyushu	▽▽	$12-$20	356
㉗ / p. 334		Lobo's Mixed Grill	▽	$6-$10	356
㉘ / p. 334		Martin's	▽▽▽	$18-$35	356
㉙ / p. 334		Antonia's Restaurant	▽▽▽	$12-$32	354
㉚ / p. 334		Meteor Smokehouse Restaurant	▽	$8-$24	357
㉛ / p. 334		Mangoes Restaurant and Catering	▽▽▽	$4-$26	356
㉜ / p. 334		Martha's Steak & Seafood	▽▽▽	$16-$28	356
㉝ / p. 334		Ambrosia Japanese Restaurant	▽▽	$16-$30	354
㉞ / p. 334		Croissants de France	▽▽	$6-$14(L)	355
㉟ / p. 334		Blue Heaven	▽▽	$19-$39	354
㊱ / p. 334		El Siboney	▽	$6-$14	355
㊲ / p. 334		Duffy's Steak & Lobster House	▽▽	$13-$20	355
㊳ / p. 334		Pisces Seafood Restaurant	▽▽▽▽	$23-$44	357
㊴ / p. 334		Nine One Five Restaurant	▽▽▽	$17-$26	357
㊵ / p. 334		Origami Sushi Bar & Japanese Restaurant	▽▽	$8-$23	357
㊶ / p. 334		Camille's	▽▽	$11-$22	354
㊷ / p. 334	◬◬◬	**Square One Restaurant**	▽▽▽	$16-$32	358
㊸ / p. 334	◬◬◬	**Alice's Key West**	▽▽▽	$16-$32	354
㊹ / p. 334		La Te Da Ocean Grill	▽▽▽	$14-$30	356
㊺ / p. 334		Abbondanza Italian Restaurant	▽▽	$9-$17	354
㊻ / p. 334		Banana Cafe	▽▽	$8-$24	354
㊼ / p. 334		Flagler's Restaurant & Lounge	▽▽▽	$17-$38	355
㊽ / p. 334		Louie's Backyard	▽▽▽	$24-$39	356
㊾ / p. 334		Shula's on the Beach	▽▽▽	$25-$40	357

KEY WEST pop. 25,478   (See map and index starting on p. 334)

───── WHERE TO STAY ─────

1800 ATLANTIC CONDOMINIUMS   *Book at aaa.com*   Phone: (305)294-8877   46
(AAA) (SAVE)   12/20-4/21   2P: $370-$550
▼▼▼▼   12/1-12/19 & 4/22-11/30   2P: $245-$450
Location: Jct US 1 and SR A1A, 3.1 mi on SR A1A. Located in a small shopping center. 1800 Atlantic Blvd 33040 (1722 N
Condominium   Roosevelt Blvd). Fax: 305/294-7356. **Facility:** Rooms are individually decorated and all have private balconies,
some with ocean views and some with courtyard views. 55 units. 3 one-, 50 two- and 2 three-bedroom suites
with kitchens and whirlpools. 4 stories, interior/exterior corridors. **Parking:** on-site. **Terms:** office hours 9 am-6
pm, check-in 4 pm, 3 night minimum stay, 14 day cancellation notice-fee imposed, weekly rates available, $35 service charge.
Amenities: voice mail, irons. *Some:* CD players. **Pool(s):** heated outdoor. **Leisure Activities:** whirlpool, limited beach access,
3 lighted tennis courts, racquetball court, barbecue grills. **Guest Services:** complimentary laundry. **Business Services:** meeting
rooms. **Cards:** AX, DS, MC, VI. **Special Amenities: free local telephone calls.**
SOME UNITS
[⊤⊦] [⇌] [⊠] [VCR] [▯] [▱] / [⊠] /

AMBROSIA TOO AT FLEMING ST   Phone: (305)296-9838   25
▼▼▼▼   All Year [ECP]   1P: $125-$445   2P: $125-$445   XP: $25   F7
Location: Just n of Simonton St; in Old Town. 622 Fleming St 33040. Fax: 305/296-2425. **Facility:** Spacious
Bed & Breakfast   rooms and a tropical setting characterize this property which is close to the center of town. Designated
smoking area. 12 units. 6 one-bedroom standard units. 5 one- and 1 two-bedroom suites, some with
kitchens. 2-4 stories, exterior corridors. *Bath:* combo or shower only. **Parking:** on-site. **Terms:** office hours 8 am-6 pm, 3 night
minimum stay - weekends, 30 day cancellation notice-fee imposed, pets ($25 fee). **Amenities:** voice mail, irons, hair dryers.
Pool(s): small heated outdoor, lap. **Cards:** AX, DS, MC, VI.
SOME UNITS
[🐾] [⊤⊦] [⇌] [⊠] [⚑] [DATA PORT] [▯] [▱] / [▱] /
FEE

ANDREWS INN   Phone: (305)294-7730   42
(AAA) (SAVE)   12/21-4/30   1P: $179-$199   2P: $179-$199   XP: $15
▼▼▼▼   12/1-12/20 & 5/1-11/30   1P: $115-$159   2P: $115-$159   XP: $15
Location: Just s of Duval St; between US 1 and Olivia St; in Old Town. Located in a quiet area. 0 Whalton Ln 33040.
Fax: 305/294-0021. **Facility:** Rooms surround a tranquil pool set amid tall shade trees and tropical foliage.
Bed & Breakfast   Designated smoking area. 6 one-bedroom standard units. 1-2 stories (no elevator), exterior corridors.
Parking: street. **Terms:** office hours 9 am-6 pm, 3-7 night minimum stay, age restrictions may apply, 14 day
cancellation notice-fee imposed, no pets allowed (owner's pets on premises). **Pool(s):** small heated outdoor. **Leisure
Activities:** *Fee:* bicycles. **Cards:** AX, DS, MC, VI. **Special Amenities: free expanded continental breakfast and free local
telephone calls.**
[⊤⊦] [⇌] [⊠]

BANANA BAY RESORT-KEY WEST   *Book at aaa.com*   Phone: (305)296-6925   11
▼▼▼▼   1/1-11/30   1P: $155-$300   2P: $155-$300   XP: $30
12/1-12/31   1P: $155-$250   2P: $155-$250   XP: $25
Motel   **Location:** On US 1, 1 mi s of entrance to island. 2319 N Roosevelt Blvd 33040. Fax: 305/296-2004. **Facility:** 48
units. 34 one-bedroom standard units, some with efficiencies. 14 one-bedroom suites ($175-$300), some
with efficiencies or kitchens. 2 stories (no elevator), exterior corridors. **Parking:** on-site. **Terms:** office hours 7 am-10 pm, age
restrictions may apply, 7 day cancellation notice-fee imposed, [CP] meal plan available, package plans. **Amenities:** voice mail,
irons, hair dryers. **Pool(s):** outdoor. **Leisure Activities:** whirlpool, snorkeling, fishing, exercise room. *Fee:* boat dock, charter
fishing. **Guest Services:** gift shop, coin laundry. **Business Services:** meeting rooms, fax (fee). **Cards:** AX, DC, DS, MC, VI.
SOME UNITS
[ASK] [⊤⊦] [⇌] [⊠] [⚑] [DATA PORT] [▯] [▱] / [⊠] [▱] /

THE BANYAN RESORT   Phone: (305)296-7786   23
(AAA) (SAVE)   12/1-5/1   2P: $225-$400   XP: $20   F12
▼▼▼▼   5/2-11/30   2P: $165-$300   XP: $20   F12
Location: Just s of Duval St; in Old Town. 323 Whitehead St 33040. Fax: 305/294-1107. **Facility:** 38 units. 5 one-
bedroom standard units with kitchens. 28 one- and 5 two-bedroom suites with kitchens. 2-3 stories (no
Small-scale Hotel   elevator), interior/exterior corridors. *Bath:* combo or shower only. **Parking:** on-site (fee). **Terms:** office hours
9 am-10 pm, check-in 4 pm, 3 night minimum stay - weekends, age restrictions may apply, 14 day
cancellation notice. **Amenities:** voice mail, safes, irons, hair dryers. *Some:* DVD players (fee). **Pool(s):** outdoor, heated outdoor.
Leisure Activities: whirlpool, barbecue areas, rental bicycles. **Guest Services:** valet and coin laundry. **Business Services:** fax
(fee). **Cards:** AX, CB, DC, DS, JC, MC, VI. *(See color ad below)*
SOME UNITS
[S⊡] [⊤⊦] [⇌] [⊠] [▯] [▱] [▱] / [VCR] /
FEE

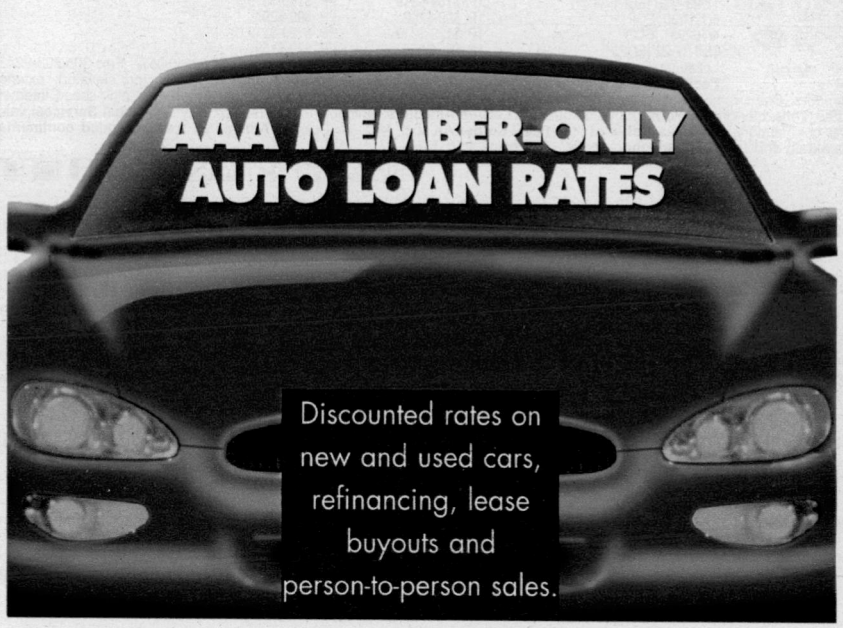

BEST WESTERN HIBISCUS MOTEL   *Book at aaa.com*   Phone: (305)294-3763   49

(AAA) (SAVE)   12/23-4/15 [ECP]   1P: $169-$319   2P: $169-$319
◆◆◆◆   6/1-11/30 [ECP]   1P: $99-$299   2P: $99-$299
          4/16-5/31 [ECP]   1P: $129-$219   2P: $129-$219
Motel   12/1-12/22 [ECP]   1P: $99-$159   2P: $99-$159
          Location: Corner of United and Simonton sts; in Old Town. 1313 Simonton St 33040-0552. Fax: 305/293-9243.
Facility: Designated smoking area. 61 one-bedroom standard units. 2 stories (no elevator), exterior
corridors. *Bath:* combo or shower only. **Parking:** on-site. **Terms:** 3 day cancellation notice. **Amenities:** high-speed Internet,
safes, irons, hair dryers. **Pool(s):** heated outdoor. **Leisure Activities:** whirlpool, scooters. *Fee:* bicycles. **Guest Services:** valet
and coin laundry. **Business Services:** fax (fee). **Cards:** AX, DS, MC, VI. **Special Amenities:** free expanded continental
breakfast and free local telephone calls. *(See color ad p 341)*

⊞ ⟨⟩ ⊘ ⟲ ⊠ ⊠ ⟨⟩ [DATA PORT] ⊟ ⟨⟩ ⟨⟩

BEST WESTERN KEY AMBASSADOR RESORT INN   *Book at aaa.com*   Phone: (305)296-3500   31

(AAA) (SAVE)   12/1-2/16 & 5/29-11/30 [ECP]   1P: $109-$349   2P: $109-$349   XP: $15   F12
◆◆◆◆   2/17-4/16 [ECP]   1P: $189-$299   2P: $189-$299   XP: $15   F12
          4/17-5/28 [ECP]   1P: $129-$269   2P: $129-$269   XP: $10   F12
Motel   **Location:** On SR A1A, 1 mi s of jct US 1. 3755 S Roosevelt Blvd 33040. Fax: 305/296-9961. **Facility:** 100 one-
          bedroom standard units. 2 stories (no elevator), exterior corridors. *Bath:* combo or shower only. **Parking:**
          on-site. **Terms:** 3 day cancellation notice. **Amenities:** high-speed Internet, voice mail, irons, hair dryers.
Pool(s): heated outdoor. **Leisure Activities:** barbecue/picnic area, outdoor fitness center, shuffleboard. **Guest Services:** coin
laundry. **Business Services:** fax (fee). **Cards:** AX, CB, DC, DS, MC, VI. **Special Amenities:** free expanded continental
breakfast and free local telephone calls. *(See color ad below)*

[S/D] ⊞ ⊘ ⟲ ⟨⟩ [DATA PORT] ⊟ ⟨⟩

BLUE MARLIN MOTEL   Phone: (305)294-2585   51

(AAA) (SAVE)   12/23-4/15 [CP]   1P: $179-$319   2P: $179-$319
◆◆◆◆   4/16-5/31 [CP]   1P: $109-$299   2P: $109-$299
          6/1-11/30 [CP]   1P: $79-$229   2P: $79-$229
Motel   12/1-12/22 [CP]   1P: $89-$179   2P: $89-$179
          Location: Just s of US 1; in Old Town. 1320 Simonton St 33040. Fax: 305/296-1209. **Facility:** 53 one-bedroom
          standard units. 2 stories (no elevator), exterior corridors. **Terms:** 3 day cancellation notice.
Amenities: irons, hair dryers. **Pool(s):** heated outdoor. **Guest Services:** valet and coin laundry. **Business Services:** fax (fee).
Cards: AX, DS, MC, VI. **Special Amenities:** free continental breakfast. *(See color ad p 341)*   SOME UNITS

⊞ ⟲ ⟨⟩ [DATA PORT] ⊟ ⟨⟩ /⊠/

(See map and index starting on p. 334)

BUDGET KEY WEST *Book at aaa.com* Phone: (305)294-3333 **14**

Motel

12/23-4/15	1P: $119-$299	2P: $119-$299
4/16-11/30	1P: $99-$229	2P: $99-$229
12/1-12/22	1P: $89-$149	2P: $89-$149

Location: Just n of Grinnell St; in Old Town. 1031 Eaton St 33040. Fax: 305/293-8892. **Facility:** 17 one-bedroom standard units. 2 stories (no elevator), exterior corridors. *Bath:* shower only. **Parking:** street. **Terms:** office hours 8 am-10 pm, 2 night minimum stay - weekends, 7 day cancellation notice. **Business Services:** fax (fee). **Cards:** AX, DS, MC, VI. **Special Amenities: free local telephone calls and preferred room (subject to availability with advance reservations).** *(See color ad p 348)*

CENTER COURT HISTORIC INN & COTTAGES Phone: (305)296-9292 **43**

Bed & Breakfast

12/15-4/30	1P: $158-$708	2P: $158-$708	XP: $15
5/1-5/31	1P: $128-$503	2P: $128-$503	XP: $15
12/1-12/14 & 6/1-11/30	1P: $98-$398	2P: $98-$398	XP: $15

Location: 0.5 mi n of jct US 1; between Duval and Simonton sts; in Old Town. 915 Center St 33040. Fax: 305/294-4104. **Facility:** Just off Truman Street, this property is in a quiet area yet close to shops and eateries; rooms feature Caribbean-style decor. Designated smoking area. 32 units. 7 one-bedroom standard units, some with efficiencies, kitchens and/or whirlpools. 25 one-bedroom suites ($128-$318) with kitchens, some with whirlpools. 1-2 stories (no elevator), interior/exterior corridors. *Bath:* combo or shower only. **Parking:** street. **Terms:** office hours 9 am-6 pm, 3-7 night minimum stay - seasonal and/or weekends, 30 day cancellation notice-fee imposed, pets ($10 extra charge, in designated units). **Amenities:** video games, CD players, voice mail, safes, irons, hair dryers. *Some:* DVD players. **Pool(s):** 3 heated outdoor. **Leisure Activities:** whirlpools, limited exercise equipment. *Fee:* bicycles. **Guest Services:** valet laundry. **Cards:** AX, DS, MC, VI.

CHELSEA HOUSE *Book at aaa.com* Phone: (305)296-2211 **40**

Historic Bed
& Breakfast

12/23-4/1	1P: $155-$275	2P: $155-$275	XP: $10
4/2-5/28	1P: $104-$159	2P: $104-$159	XP: $10
12/1-12/22 & 5/29-11/30	1P: $89-$150	2P: $89-$150	XP: $10

Location: Corner of Elizabeth St and Truman Ave. 707 Truman Ave 33040. Fax: 305/296-4822. **Facility:** Close to shopping, restaurants and the historic district, this property includes two 1870 Victorian homes surrounded by lush tropical foliage. Smoke free premises. 21 one-bedroom standard units, some with kitchens. 2 stories (no elevator), interior/exterior corridors. *Bath:* combo or shower only. **Parking:** on-site. **Terms:** office hours 8 am-8 pm, 2 night minimum stay - weekends, age restrictions may apply, 10 day cancellation notice-fee imposed, small pets only ($15 extra charge). **Amenities:** safes, hair dryers. **Pool(s):** heated outdoor. **Business Services:** fax (fee). **Cards:** AX, DC, DS, MC, VI. **Special Amenities: free expanded continental breakfast.** *(See color ad below)*

COMFORT INN *Book at aaa.com* Phone: (305)294-3773 **4**
F

Motel

2/1-4/16	1P: $129-$299	2P: $129-$299	XP: $25
12/1-1/31 & 4/17-11/30	1P: $99-$299	2P: $99-$299	XP: $25

Location: On US 1; in New Town. 3824 N Roosevelt Blvd 33040-6552. Fax: 305/294-5739. **Facility:** 100 one-bedroom standard units. 2 stories (no elevator), exterior corridors. *Bath:* combo or shower only. **Parking:** on-site. **Terms:** cancellation fee imposed, [CP] meal plan available. **Amenities:** voice mail, safes (fee), irons, hair dryers. **Pool(s):** outdoor. **Guest Services:** coin laundry. **Business Services:** fax (fee). **Cards:** AX, DC, DS, MC, VI. *(See color ad p 343)*

(See map and index starting on p. 334)

THE CONCH HOUSE HERITAGE INN

(AAA) (SAVE)
△▽△▽△▽

12/21-4/30 [ECP]   2P: $148-$228   XP: $15
5/1-5/31 [ECP]   2P: $118-$178   XP: $15
12/1-12/20 & 6/1-11/30 [ECP]   2P: $98-$158   XP: $15

Phone: (305)293-0020 **41**

Classic Historic Bed & Breakfast

Location: On US 1, just n of Duval St; in Old Town. 625 Truman Ave 33040. Fax: 305/293-8447. **Facility:** A wraparound porch adds character to this centrally located Conch house featuring spacious rooms and some antique furnishings. Smoke free premises. 8 one-bedroom standard units. 2 stories (no elevator), interior/exterior corridors. *Bath:* combo or shower only. **Parking:** on-site. **Terms:** office hours 9 am-8 pm, 2 night minimum stay - seasonal and/or weekends, age restrictions may apply, 14 day cancellation notice-fee imposed. **Pool(s):** outdoor. **Business Services:** fax (fee). **Cards:** AX, DS, MC, VI. **Special Amenities: free local telephone calls and free newspaper.** *(See color ad p 291)*

COURTNEY'S PLACE HISTORIC COTTAGES & INN

(AAA) (SAVE)
△▽△▽△▽

12/21-5/1 [ECP]   2P: $139-$259   XP: $20   F12
12/1-12/20 & 5/2-11/30 [ECP]   2P: $79-$169   XP: $20   F12

Phone: (305)294-3480 **33**

Historic Cottage

Location: Just e of jct Petronia and Simonton sts; in Old Town. 720 Whitmarsh Ln 33040-6552. Fax: 305/294-7019. **Facility:** In the historic district, this property features pine-paneled walls in many guest rooms. 16 cottages. 2 stories (no elevator), exterior corridors. *Bath:* combo or shower only. **Parking:** on-site. **Terms:** office hours 9 am-6 pm, 3 night minimum stay - seasonal and/or weekends, 21 day cancellation notice-fee imposed, package plans, pets (owner's pets on premises). **Amenities:** DVD players, irons. **Pool(s):** small heated outdoor. **Leisure Activities:** barbecue grills. *Fee:* bicycles. **Guest Services:** valet laundry. **Cards:** AX, DS, MC, VI.

COURTYARD BY MARRIOTT-KEY WEST

WATERFRONT   *Book at aaa.com*
△▽△▽△▽

12/26-4/23   1P: $209-$309   2P: $219-$319   XP: $10   F12
4/24-9/16   1P: $159-$229   2P: $169-$239   XP: $10   F12
9/17-11/30   1P: $109-$199   2P: $119-$209   XP: $10   F12
12/1-12/25   1P: $119-$159   2P: $129-$169   XP: $10   F12

Phone: (305)296-6595 **7**

Small-scale Hotel

Location: On US 1, 1 mi w of jct SR A1A; in New Town. 3041 N Roosevelt Blvd 33040. Fax: 305/296-8351. **Facility:** 67 units. 43 one-bedroom standard units. 22 one- and 2 two-bedroom suites ($199-$899), some with efficiencies and/or whirlpools. 3 stories, interior/exterior corridors. *Bath:* combo or shower only. **Parking:** on-site. **Terms:** cancellation fee imposed, [AP], [BP] & [CP] meal plans available. **Amenities:** high-speed Internet, dual phone lines, voice mail, irons, hair dryers. **Pool(s):** heated outdoor. **Leisure Activities:** whirlpool, exercise room. **Guest Services:** valet and coin laundry, area transportation (fee). **Business Services:** meeting rooms, business center. **Cards:** AX, CB, DC, DS, JC, MC, VI.

SOME UNITS

CROWNE PLAZA LA CONCHA HOTEL RESORTS

Book at aaa.com
△▽△▽△▽

12/1-4/30   1P: $199-$371   2P: $234-$406   XP: $35   F18
5/1-11/30   1P: $149-$371   2P: $184-$406   XP: $35   F18

Phone: (305)296-2991 **27**

Large-scale Hotel

Location: Corner of Duval and Fleming sts; in Old Town. 430 Duval St 33040. Fax: 305/294-3283. **Facility:** 160 units. 158 one-bedroom standard units. 2 one-bedroom suites ($399-$1100). 2-7 stories, interior corridors. **Parking:** on-site. **Terms:** check-in 4 pm, 2 night minimum stay, 3 day cancellation notice. **Amenities:** video games (fee), dual phone lines, voice mail, irons, hair dryers. **Leisure Activities:** rental bicycles, exercise room. **Guest Services:** gift shop, valet laundry. **Business Services:** meeting rooms, fax (fee). **Cards:** AX, DS, MC, VI.

SOME UNITS

THE CUBAN CLUB SUITES

△▽△▽△▽

All Year [CP]   2P: $129-$599   XP: $15

Phone: 305/294-5269 **47**

Motel

Location: Corner of Duval and Amelia sts; in Old Town. 1108 Duval St 33040 (419 Amelia St). Fax: 305/292-7665. **Facility:** 8 units. 4 one- and 4 two-bedroom suites with kitchens. 2 stories (no elevator), interior corridors. **Parking:** on-site. **Terms:** office hours 8 am-9 pm, off-site registration, age restrictions may apply, 14 day cancellation notice-fee imposed, small pets only ($10 extra charge). **Amenities:** irons. **Pool(s):** 2 small outdoor. **Leisure Activities:** whirlpool. **Guest Services:** complimentary laundry. **Business Services:** fax (fee). **Cards:** AX, MC, VI.

FEE

(See map and index starting on p. 334)

CURRY MANSION INN
Phone: (305)294-5349 **21**

🔵 SAVE

▽▽▽▽

Historic Bed
& Breakfast

1/16-4/15	1P: $240-$325	2P: $240-$325	XP: $50	F
12/1-1/15 & 4/16-11/30	1P: $175-$245	2P: $175-$245	XP: $50	F

Location: Just n of jct Duval St; in Old Town. 511 Caroline St 33040-6604. Fax: 305/294-4093. **Facility:** Tall trees surround this historic mansion built in the late 1800s; room decor ranges from period antiques to wicker and tropical colors. Designated smoking area. 28 units. 24 one-bedroom standard units, some with whirlpools. 4 one-bedroom suites. 2 stories (no elevator), interior/exterior corridors. *Bath:* combo or shower only. **Parking:** on-site. **Terms:** office hours 8:30 am-8 pm, 14 day cancellation notice-fee imposed, small pets only. **Amenities:** irons, hair dryers. **Pool(s):** heated outdoor. **Leisure Activities:** whirlpools, billiard room, beach privileges. *Fee:* massage. **Guest Services:** complimentary evening beverages, complimentary and valet laundry. **Business Services:** meeting rooms, business center. **Cards:** AX, DC, DS, MC, VI. **Special Amenities:** free full breakfast and free local telephone calls.

SOME UNITS

🛏 🍴 🏊 ✕ ✕ 🎥 📶 📞 / VCR /

CYPRESS HOUSE BED & BREAKFAST
Phone: (305)294-6969 **19**

🔵 SAVE

▽▽▽▽

Historic Bed
& Breakfast

12/1-4/30 [ECP]	1P: $150-$400	2P: $150-$400	XP: $25
5/1-11/30 [ECP]	1P: $125-$325	2P: $125-$325	XP: $25

Location: Jct Simonton St; in Old Town. 601 Caroline St 33040. Fax: 305/296-1174. **Facility:** A Bahamian-style house dating from 1888, this B&B offers spacious rooms decorated with some period antiques. Designated smoking area. 22 units. 20 one-bedroom standard units. 1 one- and 1 two-bedroom suites with efficiencies. 3 stories (no elevator), interior/exterior corridors. *Bath:* some shared or private, combo or shower only. **Parking:** street. **Terms:** office hours 9 am-8 pm, 3-5 night minimum stay - seasonal, age restrictions may apply, 30 day cancellation notice-fee imposed, no pets allowed (owner's pets on premises). **Amenities:** high-speed Internet, voice mail, hair dryers. *Some:* irons. **Pool(s):** small heated outdoor. **Leisure Activities:** *Fee:* bicycles. **Guest Services:** complimentary evening beverages, valet laundry. **Business Services:** fax (fee). **Cards:** AX, DS, MC, VI. **Special Amenities:** free expanded continental breakfast and free newspaper.

SOME UNITS

🆂 🍴 🏊 ✕ 🎥 📶 📞 / 📺 /

DAYS INN-KEY WEST
Book at aaa.com Phone: (305)294-3742 **6**

▽▽▽

Motel

All Year 1P: $109-$450 2P: $109-$450

Location: Just e of jct US 1 and SR A1A. 3852 N Roosevelt Blvd 33040. Fax: 305/296-7260. **Facility:** 133 units. 115 one-bedroom standard units. 18 one-bedroom suites ($139-$470). 2 stories, exterior corridors. *Bath:* combo or shower only. **Parking:** on-site. **Terms:** check-in 4 pm, 3 day cancellation notice. **Amenities:** dual phone lines, voice mail, safes, hair dryers. **Pool(s):** heated outdoor. **Guest Services:** coin laundry. **Business Services:** fax (fee). **Cards:** AX, CB, DC, DS, JC, MC, VI.

SOME UNITS

ASK 🆂 🍴 🏊 🎥 📶 / ✕ 📞 📺 💻 /

DOUBLETREE GRAND KEY RESORT
Book at aaa.com Phone: (305)293-1818 **9**

▽▽▽

Large-scale Hotel

12/22-4/22	1P: $189-$819	2P: $189-$819	XP: $10	F18
4/23-5/28	1P: $145-$619	2P: $145-$619	XP: $10	F18
5/29-11/30	1P: $109-$529	2P: $109-$529	XP: $10	F18
12/1-12/21	1P: $105-$529	2P: $105-$529	XP: $10	F18

Location: From US 1, 0.5 mi s on SR A1A. Located in a quiet area. 3990 S Roosevelt Blvd 33040. Fax: 305/296-6962. **Facility:** 216 units. 208 one-bedroom standard units, some with whirlpools. 6 one- and 2 two-bedroom suites, some with whirlpools. 4 stories, interior corridors. *Bath:* combo or shower only. **Parking:** on-site (fee). **Terms:** check-in 4 pm, 3 day cancellation notice, package plans. **Amenities:** video games (fee), high-speed Internet, dual phone lines, voice mail, safes, honor bars, irons, hair dryers. *Some:* CD players. **Pool(s):** heated outdoor. **Leisure Activities:** whirlpool, rental sailboats, exercise room. *Fee:* scuba diving, snorkeling, fishing, massage. **Guest Services:** gift shop, valet and coin laundry, area transportation. **Business Services:** meeting rooms, business center. **Cards:** AX, CB, DC, DS, JC, MC, VI. *(See color ad below)*

SOME UNITS

ASK ✈ 🍴 🍸 🏋 💪 🏊 ✕ 🎥 📶 💻 / ✕ 📞 📺 /

(See map and index starting on p. 334)

DUVAL HOUSE   Book at aaa.com   Phone: (305)294-1666   44

(AAA) [SAVE]

[diamond][diamond][diamond]

Historic Bed
& Breakfast

12/25-4/30	1P: $155-$390	2P: $155-$390	XP: $20
12/1-12/24 & 5/1-11/30	1P: $125-$265	2P: $125-$265	XP: $20

Location: Just n of jct Truman Ave and Duval St; in Old Town. 815 Duval St 33040. Fax: 305/292-1701. **Facility:** This property includes seven Conch houses surrounded by a lush tropical courtyard and pool; rooms vary in size. Designated smoking area. 28 units. 26 one- and 1 two-bedroom standard units, some with efficiencies. 1 one-bedroom suite with kitchen. 2 stories (no elevator), exterior corridors. *Bath:* combo or shower only. **Parking:** on-site (fee). **Terms:** office hours 9 am-9 pm, 2 night minimum stay - seasonal and/or weekends, age restrictions may apply, 7 day cancellation notice-fee imposed. **Amenities:** voice mail, hair dryers. **Pool(s):** outdoor. **Business Services:** fax (fee). **Cards:** AX, CB, DC, DS, JC, MC, VI. **Special Amenities:** free expanded continental breakfast. *(See color ad below)*

SOME UNITS

[S] [TV] [paddle] [X] [cross] / [coffee] [B] [microwave] /

DUVAL INN   Phone: (305)295-9531   34

(AAA) [SAVE]

[diamond][diamond][diamond]

Historic Bed
& Breakfast

12/24-4/30 [CP]	1P: $110-$199	2P: $110-$199	XP: $15	D18
12/1-12/23 [CP]	1P: $79-$199	2P: $79-$199	XP: $15	D18
5/1-11/30 [CP]	1P: $79-$169	2P: $79-$169	XP: $15	D18

Location: Truman Ave, 0.3 mi w on Simonton St, just s. 511 Angela St 33040. Fax: 305/295-9525. **Facility:** These two Conch houses just off Duval Street offer cozy, nicely furnished rooms; shopping and many restaurants are nearby. Designated smoking area. 7 one-bedroom standard units. 2 stories (no elevator), interior corridors. *Bath:* combo or shower only. **Parking:** on-site (fee). **Terms:** office hours 8:30 am-8 pm, 14 day cancellation notice-fee imposed. **Amenities:** voice mail, hair dryers. *Some:* irons. **Pool(s):** small heated indoor. **Leisure Activities:** rental bicycles. **Business Services:** fax (fee). **Cards:** AX, DS, MC, VI.

[S] [TV] [paddle] [X] [B]

FAIRFIELD INN BY MARRIOTT KEY WEST   Book at aaa.com   Phone: (305)296-5700   10

[diamond][diamond]

Motel

12/1-6/1 [CP]	1P: $259-$299	2P: $259-$299
6/2-11/30 [CP]	1P: $149-$299	2P: $149-$299

Location: On US 1, 1 mi s of entrance to island. 2400 N Roosevelt Blvd 33040. Fax: 305/292-9840. **Facility:** 106 units. 80 one-bedroom standard units. 26 one-bedroom suites. 2 stories, exterior corridors. *Bath:* combo or shower only. **Parking:** on-site. **Terms:** cancellation fee imposed. **Amenities:** video games (fee), high-speed Internet, irons, hair dryers. **Pool(s):** heated outdoor. **Leisure Activities:** *Fee:* bicycles. **Guest Services:** valet laundry. **Business Services:** fax. **Cards:** AX, DC, DS, MC, VI.

SOME UNITS

[ASK] [TV] [symbol] [P] [paddle] [cross] [DATA PORT] [plate] / [X] [B] [microwave] /

FRANCES STREET BOTTLE INN   Phone: (305)294-8530   18

(AAA) [SAVE]

[diamond][diamond][diamond]

Historic Bed
& Breakfast

All Year [ECP]	1P: $89-$209	2P: $89-$209
		XP: $25 F12

Location: US 1/Roosevelt Blvd, w on White St, then just s on Southard St; corner of Frances and Southard sts; in Old Town. Located in a residential area. 535 Frances St 33040. Fax: 305/294-1628. **Facility:** Palm trees shade a courtyard and hot tub and Caribbean colors decorate the guest rooms at this property not far from shopping. Designated smoking area. 8 one-bedroom standard units. 2 stories (no elevator), interior corridors. *Bath:* combo or shower only. **Parking:** street. **Terms:** office hours 8 am-8 pm, 2-3 night minimum stay - seasonal and/or weekends, 14 day cancellation notice-fee imposed, small pets only ($25 fee). **Amenities:** *Some:* CD players. **Leisure Activities:** hot tub. **Cards:** AX, MC, VI. **Special Amenities:** free expanded continental breakfast and free local telephone calls.

SOME UNITS

[bed] [TV] [X] [Z] / [VCR] [B] /
FEE

THE GRAND   Phone: (305)294-0590   38

[diamond][diamond]

Historic Bed
& Breakfast

12/16-4/30	1P: $148-$248	2P: $148-$248
5/1-11/30	1P: $88-$248	2P: $88-$248
12/1-12/15	1P: $88-$118	2P: $88-$118

Location: From Truman Ave, just e; between Virginia and Catherine sts. 1116 Grinnell St 33040. Fax: 305/294-0477. **Facility:** The rooms are comfortable with a tropical color scheme; the courtyard or "gathering place" has the same color scheme along with tropical plants. Designated smoking area. 7 units. 3 one- and 4 two-bedroom standard units, some with efficiencies. 2 stories (no elevator), exterior corridors. *Bath:* combo or shower only. **Parking:** on-site. **Terms:** office hours 9 am-5 pm, 2-3 night minimum stay - seasonal and/or weekends, age restrictions may apply, cancellation fee imposed. **Leisure Activities:** whirlpool. **Cards:** AX, DS, MC, VI.

SOME UNITS

[TV] [X] [B] / [coffee] [microwave] /

(See map and index starting on p. 334)

HAMPTON INN

▼▼▼ Motel

Book at aaa.com   **Phone: (305)294-2917**   **8**

5/29-11/30	1P: $104-$289	2P: $104-$289
2/17-4/16	1P: $179-$229	2P: $179-$229
12/1-2/16	1P: $104-$189	2P: $104-$189
4/17-5/28	1P: $134-$184	2P: $134-$184

Location: On US 1, 1.5 mi w of jct SR A1A. Located on the gulf side. 2801 N Roosevelt Blvd 33040. Fax: 305/296-0221. **Facility:** 159 one-bedroom standard units, some with whirlpools. 2 stories, exterior corridors. **Bath:** combo or shower only. **Parking:** on-site. **Terms:** cancellation fee imposed, [ECP] meal plan available. **Amenities:** high-speed Internet, voice mail, safes, irons, hair dryers. **Pool(s):** heated outdoor. **Leisure Activities:** whirlpool. *Fee:* bicycles. **Guest Services:** gift shop, coin laundry. **Business Services:** meeting rooms, fax. **Cards:** AX, CB, DC, DS, MC, VI. *(See color ad below)*

HERON HOUSE

🔺🔺🔺 Bed & Breakfast

Book at aaa.com   **Phone: (305)294-9227**   **28**

12/1-4/30 [ECP]	1P: $199-$369	2P: $199-$369	XP: $35
5/1-5/31 & 10/19-11/30 [ECP]	1P: $159-$329	2P: $159-$329	XP: $35
6/1-10/18 [ECP]	1P: $129-$249	2P: $129-$249	XP: $35

Location: From Truman Ave, w on Simonton St; near corner of Fleming St; in Old Town. 512 Simonton St 33040. Fax: 305/294-5692. **Facility:** Island-style touches enhance the contemporary decor of guest rooms at this property made up of four Conch houses dating from 1856. Designated smoking area. 23 one-bedroom standard units, some with whirlpools. 2 stories, exterior corridors. **Bath:** combo or shower only. **Parking:** on-site (fee) and street. **Terms:** office hours 8 am-8 pm, 2 night minimum stay, age restrictions may apply, 30 day cancellation notice, 14 day 5/1-11/30-fee imposed. **Amenities:** CD players, voice mail, safes, irons, hair dryers. **Pool(s):** heated outdoor. **Leisure Activities:** sun deck. **Guest Services:** complimentary evening beverages. **Business Services:** fax. **Cards:** AX, DC, DS, MC, VI. **Special Amenities:** free expanded continental breakfast and free newspaper.

HILTON KEY WEST RESORT & MARINA

🔺🔺🔺 Resort Large-scale Hotel

Book at aaa.com   **Phone: (305)294-4000**   **22**

1/1-4/29	1P: $329-$579	2P: $329-$579	XP: $20	F18
4/30-11/30	1P: $199-$579	2P: $199-$579	XP: $20	F18
12/1-12/31	1P: $199-$559	2P: $199-$559	XP: $20	F18

Location: Adjacent to Mallory Square; in Old Town. 245 Front St 33040. Fax: 305/294-4086. **Facility:** This Key West/Caribbean-style property features large guest rooms, many with balconies; a walking bridge connects to the Mallory Square Dock. 215 units. 146 one-bedroom standard units. 14 one- and 18 two-bedroom suites ($499-$1299), some with whirlpools. 37 cottages ($825-$2025). 3-4 stories, interior/exterior corridors. **Bath:** combo or shower only. **Parking:** on-site (fee) and valet. **Terms:** check-in 4 pm, 14 day cancellation notice, [AP] meal plan available. **Amenities:** video games (fee), high-speed Internet, voice mail, safes, honor bars, irons, hair dryers. *Some:* DVD players, CD players, dual phone lines. **Dining:** Latitudes Beach Cafe, see separate listing. **Pool(s):** 2 heated outdoor. **Leisure Activities:** whirlpools, recreation programs, exercise room. *Fee:* boats, marina, scuba diving, snorkeling, charter fishing, massage. **Guest Services:** gift shop, valet laundry. **Business Services:** conference facilities, business center. **Cards:** AX, CB, DC, DS, JC, MC, VI.

(See map and index starting on p. 334)

HYATT KEY WEST RESORT & MARINA   *Book at aaa.com*   Phone: (305)809-1234   🔟

12/1-4/22	1P: $273-$500	2P: $273-$500
4/23-8/31	1P: $217-$500	2P: $217-$500
9/1-11/30	1P: $175-$500	2P: $175-$500

Large-scale Hotel   **Location:** Simonton and Front sts; just n of Mallory Square; in Old Town. 601 Front St 33040. Fax: 305/809-4050. **Facility:** 120 one-bedroom standard units, some with whirlpools. 5 stories, exterior corridors. **Bath:** combo or shower only. **Parking:** on-site (fee) and valet. **Terms:** check-in 4 pm, 3 day cancellation notice-fee imposed, $10 service charge. **Amenities:** high-speed Internet (fee), dual phone lines, voice mail, safes, honor bars, irons, hair dryers. *Some:* DVD players, CD players. **Dining:** 11 am-9 pm, also, Nicola Seafood, see separate listing. **Pool(s):** heated outdoor. **Leisure Activities:** whirlpool, exercise room. *Fee:* boats, scuba diving, snorkeling, charter fishing, charter sailing, parasailing, personal watercraft, scuba & sunset cruises, snorkeling & scuba instruction, bicycles, massage. **Guest Services:** gift shop, valet laundry. **Business Services:** meeting rooms, fax (fee). **Cards:** AX, CB, DC, DS, JC, MC, VI.
(See color ad below)

SOME UNITS

🍴 ♿ 🛎 🛟 ✕ 📡 💻 / ✕ VCR /

INN AT KEY WEST   Phone: (305)294-5541   ②

12/1-4/30	1P: $129-$289	2P: $129-$289	XP: $10 F
5/1-11/30	1P: $129-$159	2P: $129-$159	XP: $10 F

Small-scale Hotel   **Location:** On US 1; in New Town. 3420 N Roosevelt Blvd 33040. Fax: 305/294-7932. **Facility:** 105 one-bedroom standard units, some with efficiencies. 2 stories (no elevator), interior/exterior corridors. **Bath:** combo or shower only. **Parking:** on-site. **Terms:** 3 day cancellation notice. **Amenities:** high-speed Internet, dual phone lines, voice mail, irons, hair dryers. **Pool(s):** heated outdoor. **Leisure Activities:** whirlpool, exercise room. **Guest Services:** valet and coin laundry. **Business Services:** meeting rooms, fax (fee). **Cards:** AX, DC, DS, MC, VI.

SOME UNITS

ASK S♿ 🍴 Y ♿ 🛟 🛎 📡 💻 / ✕ 🖥 🖨 /
FEE FEE

ISLAND CITY HOUSE HOTEL   *Book at aaa.com*   Phone: (305)294-5702   ⑳

All Year	1P: $125-$375	2P: $125-$375	XP: $20 F12

Historic Bed & Breakfast   **Location:** Jct Eaton St; in Old Town. 411 William St 33040. Fax: 305/294-1289. **Facility:** The property includes a tropical courtyard, two Victorian homes dating from 1880 and a replica of a cigar factory. Designated smoking area. 24 units. 20 one- and 4 two-bedroom suites, some with efficiencies or kitchens. 2-3 stories (no elevator), interior/exterior corridors. **Parking:** street. **Terms:** office hours 8 am-8 pm, 2-3 night minimum stay - seasonal and/or weekends, 14 day cancellation notice-fee imposed. **Amenities:** video library (fee), voice mail, irons, hair dryers. *Some:* high-speed Internet. **Pool(s):** heated outdoor. **Leisure Activities:** *Fee:* bicycles. **Business Services:** fax (fee). **Cards:** AX, DC, MC, VI.

SOME UNITS

🍴 🛎 ✕ 🖥 💻 / VCR 📡 🖨 /
FEE

(See map and index starting on p. 334)

KEY LIME INN   *Book at aaa.com*   Phone: (305)294-5229   **39**

AAA SAVE

◆◆◆

Historic Bed & Breakfast

12/23-4/15 [CP]	1P: $159-$349	2P: $159-$349
4/16-11/30 [CP]	1P: $109-$249	2P: $109-$249
12/1-12/22 [CP]	1P: $109-$169	2P: $109-$169

Location: On US 1, just n of Duval St. 725 Truman Ave 33040. **Fax:** 305/294-9623. **Facility:** This Bahamian-style inn offers cottage-like rooms, some poolside with private outdoor sitting areas overlooking quiet, tree-shaded grounds. Designated smoking area. 37 one-bedroom standard units. 1-2 stories (no elevator), exterior corridors. *Bath:* shower only. **Parking:** on-site. **Terms:** office hours 7 am-midnight, 2 night minimum stay - weekends, 7 day cancellation notice. **Amenities:** safes, hair dryers. *Some:* irons. **Pool(s):** outdoor. **Cards:** AX, DS, MC, VI. **Special Amenities: free continental breakfast and preferred room (subject to availability with advance reservations).** *(See color ad below)*

SOME UNITS

   / /

KNOWLES HOUSE B & B   Phone: 305/296-8132   **16**

AAA SAVE

◆◆◆

Historic Bed & Breakfast

12/23-5/1 [ECP]	1P: $159-$219	2P: $159-$219	XP: $20
12/1-12/22 & 5/2-11/30 [ECP]	1P: $119-$149	2P: $119-$149	XP: $20

Location: Just s of Grinnell St. 1004 Eaton St 33040. **Fax:** 305/296-2093. **Facility:** Just blocks from the hub of town and from waterfront shops and eateries, the property offers a cozy courtyard with many flowering plants and shade. Designated smoking area. 8 one-bedroom standard units, some with whirlpools. 2 stories (no elevator), exterior corridors. *Bath:* combo or shower only. **Parking:** on-site and street. **Terms:** office hours 8 am-8 pm, 2-3 night minimum stay, age restrictions may apply, 21 day cancellation notice-fee imposed, package plans. **Amenities:** hair dryers. **Pool(s):** small heated outdoor. **Leisure Activities:** whirlpool. *Fee:* bicycles. **Guest Services:** complimentary evening beverages. **Business Services:** fax (fee). **Cards:** DS, MC, VI. **Special Amenities: free expanded continental breakfast and free local telephone calls.**

LA CASA DE LUCES   Phone: 305/294-5269   **48**

◆◆◆

Historic Bed & Breakfast

All Year [CP]	2P: $129-$599	XP: $15

Location: Truman Ave, e on Duval St, then just s. 419 Amelia St 33040. **Fax:** 305/292-7665. **Facility:** Some small rooms. Attractive room decor. 8 units. 1 one-bedroom standard unit with efficiency. 7 one-bedroom suites with kitchens, some with whirlpools. 2 stories (no elevator), exterior corridors. *Bath:* combo or shower only. **Parking:** on-site. **Terms:** office hours 8 am-9 pm, age restrictions may apply, 14 day cancellation notice-fee imposed. **Cards:** AX, MC, VI.

ASK SD

(See map and index starting on p. 334)

LA MER HOTEL & DEWEY HOUSE   *Book at aaa.com*   **Phone:** (305)296-6577 **55**

▼▼▼ ▼▼▼ ▼▼▼	12/25-4/29	1P: $285-$435	2P: $285-$435	XP: $25
	4/30-5/29	1P: $230-$395	2P: $230-$395	XP: $15
Classic Historic	5/30-11/30	1P: $185-$375	2P: $185-$375	XP: $15
Bed & Breakfast	12/1-12/24	1P: $179-$365	2P: $179-$365	XP: $15

Location: Oceanfront. South St below Simonton St; in Old Town. 504-506 South St 33040. Fax: 305/294-2108. **Facility:** This property's two buildings face the beach and allow views of the sunrise; shops and restaurants are nearby. 19 one-bedroom standard units, some with efficiencies and/or whirlpools. 2 stories (no elevator), interior/exterior corridors. **Parking:** on-site. **Terms:** 2 night minimum stay - weekends, age restrictions may apply, 10 day cancellation notice, [ECP] meal plan available. **Amenities:** high-speed Internet, voice mail, safes, irons, hair dryers. **Leisure Activities:** whirlpool. **Guest Services:** valet laundry. **Business Services:** fax (fee). **Cards:** AX, DS, MC, VI. *(See color ad below)*

SOME UNITS

⟦ 🛎️ ⟧ ⟦ ✕ ⟧ ⟦ DATA PORT ⟧ ⟦ 🛄 ⟧ ⟦ 🖥️ ⟧ / ⟦ 💼 ⟧ /

LA PENSIONE   **Phone:** 305/292-9923 **37**

(AAA) [SAVE]

▼▼▼▼▼▼	12/21-11/30	2P: $168-$178	XP: $25
	12/1-12/20	2P: $118-$128	XP: $25
Historic Bed			
& Breakfast			

Location: On US 1, just n of Duval St; in Old Town. 809 Truman Ave 33040. Fax: 305/296-6509. **Facility:** Dating from 1891, this house has classical architecture and spacious, tastefully appointed rooms; a small pool area offers additional lounging space. Designated smoking area. 9 one-bedroom standard units. 2 stories (no elevator), interior/exterior corridors. *Bath:* combo or shower only. **Parking:** on-site. **Terms:** office hours 7 am-7 pm, age restrictions may apply, cancellation fee imposed. **Pool(s):** small outdoor. **Business Services:** fax (fee). **Cards:** AX, DC, DS, MC, VI. **Special Amenities: free continental breakfast and free local telephone calls.**

⟦ S🅿️ ⟧ ⟦ 🛎️ ⟧ ⟦ 🏊 ⟧ ⟦ ✕ ⟧ ⟦ 📺 ⟧

LIGHTBOURN INN   **Phone:** (305)296-5152 **32**

(AAA) [SAVE]

▼▼▼▼▼▼	1/2-4/15 [ECP]	1P: $178-$328	2P: $178-$328	XP: $25
	12/1-1/1 & 4/16-5/31 [ECP]	1P: $128-$328	2P: $128-$328	XP: $25
Historic Bed	6/1-11/30 [ECP]	1P: $98-$328	2P: $98-$328	XP: $25
& Breakfast			

Location: US 1, just n of Duval St. 907 Truman Ave 33040. Fax: 305/294-9490. **Facility:** This 1903 Queen Anne-style inn is furnished with antiques as well as artifacts from the owners' extensive travels. Designated smoking area. 10 one-bedroom standard units. 2 stories (no elevator), interior/exterior corridors. *Bath:* shower only. **Parking:** on-site. **Terms:** office hours 8 am-6 pm, 2 night minimum stay - seasonal and/or weekends, age restrictions may apply, 14 day cancellation notice-fee imposed. **Amenities:** voice mail. **Pool(s):** heated outdoor. **Business Services:** fax (fee). **Cards:** AX, DS, MC, VI. **Special Amenities: free expanded continental breakfast and free local telephone calls.**

⟦ 🛎️ ⟧ ⟦ 🏊 ⟧ ⟦ ✕ ⟧

(See map and index starting on p. 334)

THE MARQUESA HOTEL   *Book at aaa.com*   Phone: (305)292-1919   26

12/1-4/10 & 10/24-11/30	1P: $285-$430	2P: $285-$430	XP: $25
4/11-5/30	1P: $235-$370	2P: $235-$370	XP: $25
5/31-10/23	1P: $175-$300	2P: $175-$300	XP: $25

Classic Historic Small-scale Hotel **Location:** Jct Simonton and Fleming sts; in Old Town. 600 Fleming St 33040. Fax: 305/294-2121. **Facility:** Several varieties of orchids grow in the garden of this service-oriented hotel occupying a restored 1884 house. Designated smoking area. 27 one-bedroom standard units. 1-3 stories (no elevator), interior/exterior corridors. **Parking:** on-site. **Terms:** age restrictions may apply, 10 day cancellation notice, [CP] meal plan available. **Amenities:** CD players, safes, irons, hair dryers. **Dining:** Cafe Marquesa, see separate listing. **Pool(s):** outdoor, heated outdoor. **Leisure Activities:** *Fee:* bicycles. **Guest Services:** valet laundry. **Business Services:** fax (fee). **Cards:** AX, DC, MC, VI.

THE MERLIN INN   *Book at aaa.com*   Phone: (305)296-3336   35

12/23-4/15 [CP]	1P: $145-$349	2P: $145-$349	XP: $20	F12
4/16-11/30 [CP]	1P: $99-$349	2P: $99-$349	XP: $20	F12
12/1-12/22 [CP]	1P: $99-$199	2P: $99-$199	XP: $20	F12

Historic Bed & Breakfast **Location:** Just n of US 1 (Truman Ave); corner of Simonton and Petrona sts; in Old Town. 811 Simonton St 33040. Fax: 305/296-3524. **Facility:** Varied room types are comfortable and decorated with an accent on natural woods; a tropical courtyard and pool area are well-suited for relaxing. Designated smoking area. 20 units. 15 one-bedroom standard units. 5 one-bedroom suites, some with efficiencies. 2 stories (no elevator), exterior corridors. *Bath:* combo or shower only. **Parking:** street. **Terms:** office hours 8 am-8 pm, 2 night minimum stay - weekends, 7 day cancellation notice. **Amenities:** safes, hair dryers. **Pool(s):** outdoor. **Cards:** AX, DS, MC, VI. **Special Amenities:** free continental breakfast and preferred room (subject to availability with advance reservations). *(See color ad p 348)*

OCEAN BREEZE INN   Phone: 305/296-2829   50

12/1-4/30	1P: $139-$239	2P: $139-$239	XP: $15
5/1-11/30	1P: $99-$169	2P: $99-$169	XP: $10

Motel **Location:** Just n of Duval St. 625 South St 33040. Fax: 305/296-2092. **Facility:** 15 one-bedroom standard units, some with efficiencies. 1 story, exterior corridors. *Bath:* shower only. **Parking:** on-site. **Terms:** office hours 8 am-6 pm, 3-5 night minimum stay - seasonal and/or weekends, age restrictions may apply, 14 day cancellation notice-fee imposed. **Amenities:** hair dryers. *Some:* DVD players, irons. **Pool(s):** small heated outdoor. **Business Services:** fax (fee). **Cards:** AX, DS, MC, VI.

OCEAN KEY RESORT, A NOBLE HOUSE RESORT   *Book at aaa.com*   Phone: (305)296-7701   15

12/23-5/31	1P: $339-$1149	XP: $35	F
6/1-11/30	1P: $239-$1149	XP: $35	F
12/1-12/22	1P: $239-$1049	XP: $35	F

Large-scale Hotel **Location:** At Mallory Square; in Old Town. Zero Duval St 33040. Fax: 305/292-7685. **Facility:** Many of the property's large, Caribbean-themed rooms overlook the water or Mallory Square. 100 units. 55 one-bedroom standard units, some with whirlpools. 33 one- and 12 two-bedroom suites, some with kitchens and/or whirlpools. 2-5 stories, exterior corridors. *Bath:* combo or shower only. **Parking:** valet. **Terms:** check-in 4 pm, 5 day cancellation notice-fee imposed. **Amenities:** CD players, high-speed Internet (fee), voice mail, irons, hair dryers. **Dining:** 7 am-10 pm, also, Hot Tin Roof, see separate listing, entertainment. **Pool(s):** heated outdoor. **Leisure Activities:** fishing, personal watercraft. *Fee:* charter fishing. **Guest Services:** gift shop, valet laundry. **Business Services:** meeting rooms, fax (fee). **Cards:** AX, CB, DC, DS, MC, VI.

THE PALMS HOTEL   Phone: (305)294-3146   24

12/21-4/30	1P: $160	2P: $185-$205	XP: $10	F13
5/1-11/30	1P: $110	2P: $120-$205	XP: $10	F13
12/1-12/20	1P: $110	2P: $120-$130	XP: $10	F13

Historic Bed & Breakfast **Location:** Just w of Truman Ave. 820 White St 33040. Fax: 305/294-8463. **Facility:** The hotel offers a variety of lodgings in the 1889 main house or in outbuildings around a courtyard. 30 units. 27 one-bedroom standard units. 3 one-bedroom suites, some with efficiencies or kitchens. 2 stories (no elevator), exterior corridors. *Bath:* some shared or private, combo or shower only. **Parking:** street. **Terms:** office hours 8 am-10 pm, 2 night minimum stay - weekends, 7 day cancellation notice-fee imposed, [ECP] meal plan available, small pets only. **Pool(s):** heated outdoor. **Leisure Activities:** sun deck, pool table, exercise room. *Fee:* bicycles. **Cards:** AX, DS, MC, VI.

THE PARADISE INN   Phone: (305)293-8007   36

12/23-4/15 [ECP]	1P: $329-$759	2P: $329-$759
12/1-12/22 & 4/16-5/31 [ECP]	1P: $199-$599	2P: $199-$599
6/1-11/30 [ECP]	1P: $179-$599	2P: $179-$599

Bed & Breakfast **Location:** US 1, just n; in Old Town. 819 Simonton St 33040. Fax: 305/293-0807. **Facility:** These elegantly contemporary rooms, suites and cottages are set on lush grounds. Designated smoking area. 18 units. 8 one-bedroom standard units. 7 one-bedroom suites. 3 cottages with whirlpools. 1-2 stories (no elevator), exterior corridors. **Parking:** on-site. **Terms:** 3 day cancellation notice. **Amenities:** CD players, voice mail, safes, irons, hair dryers. **Pool(s):** small heated outdoor. **Leisure Activities:** whirlpool. **Guest Services:** valet laundry. **Business Services:** fax (fee). **Cards:** AX, DS, MC, VI. *(See color ad p 341)*

PEGASUS INTERNATIONAL HOTEL   *Book at aaa.com*   Phone: 305/294-9323   30

All Year	1P: $159-$250	XP: $20	F4

Small-scale Hotel **Location:** Corner of Duval and Southard sts; in Old Town. 501 Southard St 33040. Fax: 305/294-4741. **Facility:** 25 one-bedroom standard units. 3 stories, interior/exterior corridors. *Bath:* shower only. **Parking:** on-site. **Terms:** 7 day cancellation notice-fee imposed. **Amenities:** high-speed Internet, hair dryers. **Pool(s):** heated outdoor. **Leisure Activities:** whirlpool, sun deck. **Guest Services:** valet laundry. **Cards:** AX, CB, DC, DS, JC, MC, VI.

(See map and index starting on p. 334)

PIER HOUSE RESORT & CARIBBEAN SPA   *Book at aaa.com*   Phone: (305)296-4600   🔟🔟

🔺🔺🔺 SAVE

12/24-4/15	1P: $290-$2000	2P: $290-$2000	XP: $35	F7
4/16-5/14	1P: $245-$1585	2P: $245-$1585	XP: $35	F7
12/1-12/23 & 5/15-11/30	1P: $200-$1400	2P: $200-$1400	XP: $35	F7

Large-scale Hotel   **Location:** Oceanfront. At the foot of Duval St; in Old Town. One Duval St 33040. Fax: 305/296-7569. **Facility:** Designated smoking area. 142 units. 126 one-bedroom standard units. 13 one- and 3 two-bedroom suites. 1-5 stories, interior/exterior corridors. *Bath:* combo or shower only. **Parking:** on-site. **Terms:** check-in 4 pm, 2-4 night minimum stay - seasonal, 7 day cancellation notice-fee imposed, [AP] meal plan available, package plans, small pets only ($100 fee). **Amenities:** voice mail, honor bars, irons, hair dryers. *Fee:* video games, high-speed Internet. *Some:* CD players. **Dining:** 3 restaurants, 7:30 am-midnight, cocktails, also, One Duval, see separate listing, entertainment. **Pool(s):** heated outdoor. **Leisure Activities:** whirlpools, limited beach access, rental bicycles, spa. *Fee:* motor scooters. **Guest Services:** valet laundry, beauty salon. **Business Services:** meeting rooms, fax (fee). **Cards:** AX, CB, DC, DS, MC, VI. **Special Amenities:** free newspaper. *(See color ad below)*

SOME UNITS

🔲🔲🔲🔲🔲🔲🔲🔲🔲🔲🔲🔲🔲🔲🔲🔲 /🔲/
FEE FEE   FEE

RADISSON HOTEL KEY WEST   *Book at aaa.com*   Phone: (305)294-5511   ③

🔺🔺🔺 SAVE

12/1-4/2	1P: $119-$399	2P: $119-$399	XP: $20	F17
4/3-11/30	1P: $109-$399	2P: $109-$399	XP: $20	F17

Small-scale Hotel   **Location:** On US 1; in New Town. 3820 N Roosevelt Blvd 33040-6552. Fax: 305/296-1939. **Facility:** 145 units. 141 one-bedroom standard units. 4 one-bedroom suites. 6 stories, exterior corridors. *Bath:* combo or shower only. **Parking:** on-site. **Terms:** 1-3 night minimum stay - seasonal, cancellation fee imposed. **Amenities:** voice mail, safes (fee), irons, hair dryers. **Dining:** 2 restaurants, 24 hours. **Pool(s):** heated outdoor. **Leisure Activities:** sun deck, exercise room. **Guest Services:** valet and coin laundry. **Business Services:** meeting rooms, fax (fee). **Cards:** AX, CB, DC, DS, JC, MC, VI. **Special Amenities:** free room upgrade and preferred room (each subject to availability with advance reservations). *(See color ad below)*

SOME UNITS

🔲🔲🔲🔲🔲🔲🔲🔲🔲🔲🔲🔲 /🔲/

(See map and index starting on p. 334)

SHERATON SUITES-KEY WEST   *Book at aaa.com*   Phone: (305)292-9800   **45**

AAA SAVE	12/1-4/9	1P: $209-$425	2P: $209-$425	XP: $15	F17
	8/21-11/30	1P: $149-$425	2P: $149-$425	XP: $15	F17
	4/10-5/30	1P: $190-$389	2P: $190-$389	XP: $15	F17
	5/31-8/20	1P: $159-$349	2P: $159-$349	XP: $15	F17

Large-scale Hotel **Location:** Jct US 1 and SR A1A, 3 mi s. Located across from the beach. 2001 S Roosevelt Blvd 33040. Fax: 305/294-6009. **Facility:** 180 one-bedroom suites, some with whirlpools. 4 stories, interior/exterior corridors. *Bath:* combo or shower only. **Parking:** on-site. **Terms:** 3 day cancellation notice-fee imposed, pets ($50 fee). **Amenities:** video games (fee), dual phone lines, voice mail, safes, irons, hair dryers. **Dining:** 7 am-10 pm, cocktails. **Pool(s):** heated outdoor. **Leisure Activities:** whirlpool, beach access, exercise room. *Fee:* bicycles. **Guest Services:** gift shop, valet and coin laundry, area transportation-downtown. **Business Services:** meeting rooms, fax (fee). **Cards:** AX, CB, DC, DS, MC, VI. *(See color ad below & p 8)*

SOME UNITS

SOUTHERNMOST HOTEL IN THE USA   *Book at aaa.com*   Phone: (305)296-6577   **53**

	12/25-4/29	1P: $195-$285	2P: $195-$285	XP: $15	F18
	4/30-5/29	1P: $124-$245	2P: $124-$245	XP: $10	F18
Motel	5/30-11/30	1P: $105-$220	2P: $105-$220	XP: $10	F18
	12/1-12/24	1P: $99-$199	2P: $99-$199	XP: $10	F18

Location: Jct Duval and United sts; in Old Town. 1319 Duval St 33040. Fax: 305/294-3380. **Facility:** 127 one-bedroom standard units, some with efficiencies. 2-3 stories, exterior corridors. **Parking:** on-site. **Terms:** 2 night minimum stay - weekends, 5 day cancellation notice. **Amenities:** voice mail, safes, irons, hair dryers. **Pool(s):** 2 heated outdoor. **Leisure Activities:** whirlpool, rental bicycles. **Guest Services:** gift shop, coin laundry. **Business Services:** meeting rooms, fax (fee). **Cards:** AX, DS, MC, VI. *(See color ad p 349)*

SOME UNITS

SOUTHERNMOST ON THE BEACH   *Book at aaa.com*   Phone: (305)296-6577   **54**

	12/25-4/29	1P: $259-$359	2P: $259-$359	XP: $15	F18
	4/30-5/29	1P: $184-$304	2P: $184-$304	XP: $15	F18
Motel	5/30-11/30	1P: $164-$279	2P: $164-$279	XP: $10	F18
	12/1-12/24	1P: $154-$250	2P: $154-$250	XP: $10	F18

Location: Oceanfront. South St below Simonton St; in Old Town. 508 South St 33040. Fax: 305/294-2108. **Facility:** 48 one-bedroom standard units, some with efficiencies. 2 stories (no elevator), exterior corridors. *Bath:* combo or shower only. **Parking:** on-site. **Terms:** 2 night minimum stay - weekends, 10 day cancellation notice. **Amenities:** high-speed Internet, voice mail, safes, irons, hair dryers. **Pool(s):** outdoor. **Leisure Activities:** *Fee:* scuba diving, bicycles. **Guest Services:** gift shop, coin laundry. **Business Services:** fax (fee). **Cards:** AX, DS, MC, VI. *(See color ad p 349)*

SOME UNITS

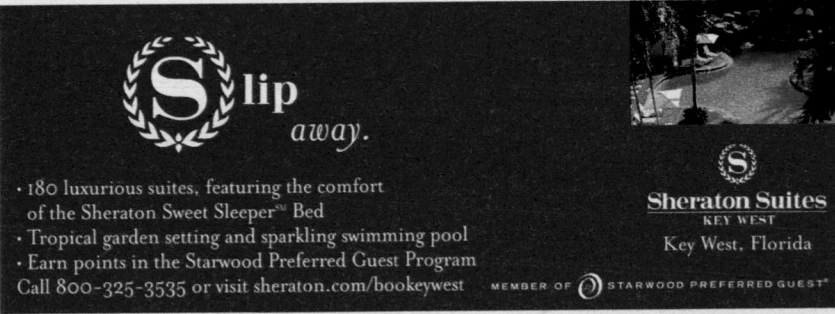

(See map and index starting on p. 334)

TRAVELODGE KEY WEST HOTEL   *Book at aaa.com*   Phone: (305)296-7593   ❶

(AAA) (SAVE)   All Year   1P: $79-$599

Small-scale Hotel   **Location:** On US 1; in New Town. 3444 N Roosevelt Blvd 33040. Fax: 305/294-5246. **Facility:** 64 units. 32 one-bedroom standard units. 24 one-, 3 two- and 5 three-bedroom suites with kitchens (utensil deposit required). 2-4 stories, exterior corridors. *Bath:* combo or shower only. **Parking:** on-site. **Terms:** cancellation fee imposed. **Amenities:** voice mail, irons, hair dryers. **Pool(s):** heated outdoor. **Leisure Activities:** whirlpool. **Business Services:** fax. **Cards:** AX, CB, DC, DS, JC, MC, VI. **Special Amenities:** free continental breakfast and free newspaper. *(See color ad p 352)*

SOME UNITS
🅂 🍽️ 🏊 ⚗️ DATA PORT 🖥️ / ✕ VCR 🔌 🖥️ /

THE WEATHERSTATION INN   Phone: (305)294-7277   ❷⑨

▽▽▽▽   12/20-4/30 [CP]   1P: $215-$335   2P: $215-$335   XP: $20
12/1-12/19 & 5/1-11/30 [CP]   1P: $170-$235   2P: $170-$235   XP: $20

Classic Historic Bed & Breakfast   **Location:** US 1 to Whitehead St, turn right, then left on Southard St; in Truman Annex Complex. 57 Front St 33040. Fax: 305/294-0544. **Facility:** A stately white building, the inn sits on picket-fence-enclosed grounds containing a variety of tropical trees and flowering plants. Smoke free premises. 8 one-bedroom standard units. 2 stories (no elevator), interior corridors. *Bath:* shower only. **Parking:** on-site. **Terms:** office hours 8 am-6 pm, 2 night minimum stay - weekends, age restrictions may apply, 15 day cancellation notice-fee imposed. **Amenities:** video library, voice mail, hair dryers. **Pool(s):** small heated outdoor. **Guest Services:** valet laundry. **Cards:** AX, DC, DS, JC, MC, VI.

(ASK) 🍽️ ♿ 🏊 ✕ VCR DATA PORT

WESTWINDS INN   *Book at aaa.com*   Phone: 305/296-4440   ❶⑦

(AAA) (SAVE)   12/1-4/22   1P: $150-$210   2P: $150-$210   XP: $25
▽▽ ▽▽   4/23-5/29   1P: $110-$170   2P: $110-$170   XP: $25
5/30-11/30   1P: $75-$135   2P: $75-$135   XP: $25

Bed & Breakfast   **Location:** Just n of Duval St; near Historic Seaport District; in Old Town. 914 Eaton St 33040. Fax: 305/293-0931. **Facility:** 22 units. 18 one-bedroom standard units. 4 two-bedroom suites, some with efficiencies or kitchens. 1-2 stories (no elevator), interior/exterior corridors. *Bath:* combo or shower only. **Parking:** street. **Terms:** office hours 8 am-8 pm, 2 night minimum stay - seasonal, age restrictions may apply, 14 day cancellation notice-fee imposed, no pets allowed (owner's pets on premises). **Amenities:** high-speed Internet, voice mail, hair dryers. **Pool(s):** outdoor, heated outdoor. **Guest Services:** gift shop, coin laundry. **Business Services:** meeting rooms. **Cards:** DS, MC, VI. **Special Amenities:** free expanded continental breakfast and free local telephone calls.

SOME UNITS
🍽️ 🏊 / 🅆 🔌 🖥️ 🖥️ /

WYNDHAM CASA MARINA RESORT   *Book at aaa.com*   Phone: (305)296-3535   ❺②

(AAA) (SAVE)   2/16-4/15   1P: $379   2P: $379   XP: $20   F17
▽▽▽▽   12/1-2/15   1P: $359   2P: $359   XP: $20   F17
4/16-10/28   1P: $319   2P: $319   XP: $20   F17
10/29-11/30   1P: $309   2P: $309   XP: $20   F17

Historic Large-scale Hotel   **Location:** Oceanfront. 4 mi s on Flagler (CR 5A) from jct SR A1A. 1500 Reynolds St 33040-6552. Fax: 305/296-4633. **Facility:** This historic hotel was built in 1921 by Henry Flagler; rooms and suites are available with ocean views and with balconies or patios. 311 units. 242 one-bedroom standard units. 64 one- and 5 two-bedroom suites ($384-$454). 3-4 stories, interior/exterior corridors. *Bath:* combo or shower only. **Parking:** on-site. **Terms:** check-in 4 pm, 7 day cancellation notice, $14 service charge. **Amenities:** dual phone lines, voice mail, safes, honor bars, irons, hair dryers. *Fee:* video games, high-speed Internet. *Some:* CD players. **Dining:** 2 restaurants, 7 am-10 pm, also, Flagler's Restaurant & Lounge, see separate listing, entertainment. **Pool(s):** 2 heated outdoor. **Leisure Activities:** sauna, whirlpool, limited beach access, fishing, pier, 3 lighted tennis courts, recreation programs, rental bicycles, exercise room, horseshoes, volleyball. *Fee:* windsurfing, scuba diving, snorkeling, charter fishing, catamaran, parasailing, personal watercraft, catamaran, scuba instruction, mopeds, massage. **Guest Services:** gift shop, valet laundry. **Business Services:** conference facilities, business center. **Cards:** AX, CB, DC, DS, JC, MC, VI.

SOME UNITS
🔀 🍽️ ♿ 📶 🏊 ✕ ⚗️ DATA PORT 🖥️ / ✕ VCR 🔌 /
FEE

WYNDHAM REACH RESORT   *Book at aaa.com*   Phone: (305)296-5000   ❺⑥

(AAA) (SAVE)   2/16-4/15   1P: $379   2P: $379   XP: $20   F17
▽▽▽▽   12/1-2/15   1P: $359   2P: $359   XP: $20   F17
4/16-10/28   1P: $319   2P: $319   XP: $20   F17
10/29-11/30   1P: $309   2P: $309   XP: $20   F17

Large-scale Hotel   **Location:** Oceanfront. Just s of jct Truman Ave and Simonton St. 1435 Simonton St 33040. Fax: 305/296-2830. **Facility:** 150 units. 71 one-bedroom standard units. 79 one-bedroom suites ($384-$454). 2-5 stories, exterior corridors. *Bath:* combo or shower only. **Parking:** on-site and valet. **Terms:** check-in 4 pm, 7 day cancellation notice, $14 service charge. **Amenities:** dual phone lines, voice mail, safes, honor bars, irons, hair dryers. *Fee:* video games, high-speed Internet. *Some:* CD players. **Dining:** 7 am-7 pm, cocktails, also, Shula's on the Beach, see separate listing. **Pool(s):** heated outdoor. **Leisure Activities:** sauna, whirlpool, rental paddleboats, rental sailboats, snorkeling, fishing, scuba instruction, recreation programs, exercise room, massage, horseshoes, volleyball. *Fee:* windsurfing, scuba diving, charter fishing, kayaks, personal watercraft. **Guest Services:** gift shop, valet laundry. **Business Services:** meeting rooms, business center. **Cards:** AX, CB, DC, DS, JC, MC, VI.

SOME UNITS
🔀 🍽️ 🍷 📶 🏊 ✕ ⚗️ DATA PORT 🖥️ / ✕ /

———— WHERE TO DINE ————

A & B LOBSTER HOUSE   Dinner: $22-$39   Phone: 305/294-5880   ④

▽▽▽   **Location:** Duval St, just n. 700 Front St 33040. **Hours:** 6 pm-11 pm. Closed: 12/24. **Reservations:** accepted.
Steak & Seafood   **Features:** Located just off the harbor docks, this restaurant is elevated in order to present a wonderful view. Fresh seafood at its best is available in a tablecloth atmosphere. Dressy casual; cocktails. **Parking:** on-site. **Cards:** AX, DS, MC, VI.

(See map and index starting on p. 334)

ABBONDANZA ITALIAN RESTAURANT
Dinner: $9-$17   **Phone:** 305/292-1199   45
Italian
Location: Corner of Louise and Simonton sts. 1208 Simonton St 33040. **Hours:** 5 pm-10 pm. **Features:** The restaurant's name means "lots of food"—and appropriately so. Well-prepared entrees are made with local seafood, pasta and flavorful sauces. The ambience and decor are fresh and inviting. Casual dress; cocktails. **Parking:** street. **Cards:** MC, VI.

ALICE'S KEY WEST
Lunch: $9-$16   **Dinner:** $16-$32   **Phone:** 305/292-5733   43
Caribbean
Location: Just e of Truman Ave; corner of Duval and Amelia sts. 1114 Duval St 33040. **Hours:** 8:30 am-2 & 6-11 pm, Sun from 10 am. **Reservations:** suggested. **Features:** Take a trip to the islands where fresh seafood, spices and tropical fruits come together. If seafood is not your taste, the restaurant offers a variety of meat selections including meatloaf and a Cuban-style ostrich dish. Casual dress; cocktails. **Parking:** street. **Cards:** AX, DS, MC, VI.

ALONZO'S OYSTER BAR
Lunch: $8-$13   **Dinner:** $14-$24   **Phone:** 305/294-5880   5
Seafood
Location: Duval St, just n; at end of Front St. 700 Front St 33040. **Hours:** 11 am-11 pm. **Features:** This restaurant is located on the water, and offers the freshest of seafood. The dining room offers great views of the harbor and the boats. The decor resembles the casualness of a dockside eatery. Casual dress; cocktails. **Parking:** on-site. **Cards:** AX, DS, MC, VI.

AMBROSIA JAPANESE RESTAURANT
Lunch: $7-$16   **Dinner:** $16-$30   **Phone:** 305/293-0304   33
Japanese
Location: From Truman Ave, just e; corner of Parker and Virginia sts. 1100 Packer St 33040. **Hours:** 11:30 am-2 & 6-10 pm, Sat from 6 pm. Closed: 11/23, 12/25; also Sun. **Reservations:** suggested. **Features:** The small corner house serves foods with big flavors. Patrons often are amazed at the selection of sushi, sashimi and more than sushi rolls. Tempura- and teriyaki-style foods also are available. Casual dress; beer & wine only. **Parking:** street. **Cards:** AX, MC, VI.

ANTONIA'S RESTAURANT
Dinner: $12-$32   **Phone:** 305/294-6565   29
Regional Italian
Location: In Old Town. 615 Duval St 33040. **Hours:** 6 pm-11 pm; from 6:30 pm in summer. Closed: 11/23. **Reservations:** suggested. **Features:** Regional Italian food features homemade pasta, fresh seafood, veal, beef and lamb. Innovative presentations, warm surroundings and an extensive wine list make this a place for special occasions. A complimentary cookie plate will satisfy your sweet tooth. Dressy casual; cocktails. **Parking:** street. **Cards:** AX, MC, VI.

BAGATELLE RESTAURANT
Lunch: $7-$13   **Dinner:** $15-$25   **Phone:** 305/296-6609   13
Regional American
Location: Downtown. 115 Duval St 33040. **Hours:** 11 am-10:30 pm, Fri & Sat-10:30 pm. Closed: 9/4. **Reservations:** suggested. **Features:** An inviting wraparound porch makes this 1884 sea captain's revival home a great location for leisurely dining. Seafood specialties are featured with other traditional entrees. Casual dress; cocktails. **Parking:** street. **Cards:** AX, DS, MC, VI.

BANANA CAFE
Lunch: $6-$10   **Dinner:** $8-$24   **Phone:** 305/294-7227   46
French
Location: Just s of jct US 1; in Old Town. 1211 Duval St 33040. **Hours:** Open 12/1-8/31 & 10/1-11/30; 8 am-4 pm. Closed: Tues. **Features:** A charming, casual restaurant, it offers a variety of dishes you may enjoy on the covered patio or in the outdoor dining area. The shredded tuna sandwich with spinach leaves, capers and a hard-boiled egg is a fresh twist on the traditional lunch entree. Casual dress; beer & wine only. **Parking:** street. **Cards:** AX, DC, DS, MC, VI.

BLUE HEAVEN
Lunch: $7-$15   **Dinner:** $19-$39   **Phone:** 305/296-8666   35
American
Location: Just s of Duval St; corner of Petronia and Thomas sts. 729 Thomas St 33040. **Hours:** Open 12/1-9/8 & 10/16-11/30; 8 am-3 & 6-10:30 pm. Closed: 11/23, 12/25. **Features:** The Caribbean-influenced menu features seafood and a popular Sunday brunch with lobster Benedict and shrimp in grits. Roosters run around the converted barn house; a rooster graveyard is the resting place of prize cockfighters from the early 1900s. Casual dress; cocktails. **Parking:** street. **Cards:** DS, MC, VI.

CAFE MARQUESA
Dinner: $28-$39   **Phone:** 305/292-1244   20
Northern American
Location: Jct Simonton and Fleming sts; in Old Town; in The Marquesa Hotel. 600 Fleming St 33040. **Hours:** 6 pm-11 pm; from 7 pm 6/1-11/1. **Reservations:** suggested. **Features:** Featuring "Contemporary American cuisine" (a cross-cultural blend of food from the Americas, Asia and the Caribbean), the changing menu includes meat and fresh seafood presented with artistic skill and preparation. Attentive service adds to the cozy atmosphere. Dressy casual; cocktails. **Parking:** street. **Cards:** AX, DC, MC, VI.

CAMILLE'S
Lunch: $6-$13   **Dinner:** $11-$22   **Phone:** 305/296-4811   41
American
Location: Just s of US 1; in Old Town. 1202 Simonton St 33040. **Hours:** 8 am-3 & 6-10 pm. **Features:** Resembling a roadside diner, this funky, Key West-style eatery projects a casual atmosphere with modest tables and counter seating. Breakfast is the most popular meal, with an assortment of sandwiches, seafood and beef entrees served later in the day. Casual dress; cocktails. **Parking:** on-site. **Cards:** AX, DS, MC, VI.

CHICO'S CANTINA
Lunch: $2-$18   **Dinner:** $7-$18   **Phone:** 305/296-4714
Mexican
Location: On US 1, 0.6 mi n of jct US 1 and SR A1A. 5230 US 1, Stock Island 33040. **Hours:** 11:30 am-9:30 pm. Closed major holidays; also 9/1-9/16. **Reservations:** not accepted. **Features:** The menu rounds up the traditional Tex-Mex items, but the chef's specials, which change daily or as the market allows, are the choices worth watching for. The casual spot offers inside and patio seating. Casual dress; beer & wine only. **Parking:** on-site. **Cards:** AX, DS, MC, VI.

THE COMMODORE WATERFRONT RESTAURANT
Dinner: $18-$30   **Phone:** 305/294-9191   6
Steak House
Location: From Duval St, just n; in A & B Marina area. 700 Front St 33040. **Hours:** 5:30 pm-10 pm. **Reservations:** suggested. **Features:** Set your appetite for fresh seafood and large steaks at this restaurant, which offers views of the harbor from almost every table. The rewarding wine selection is a must-see. Dressy casual; cocktails. **Parking:** street. **Cards:** AX, MC, VI.

(See map and index starting on p. 334)

CONCH REPUBLIC SEAFOOD COMPANY   Lunch: $8-$18   Dinner: $8-$18   Phone: 305/294-4403   (9)
Seafood
Location: Corner of Greene and Elizabeth sts; in Historic Seaport District. 631 Greene St 33040. **Hours:** 11 am-2 am. **Features:** In the harbor, the restaurant has many tables that offer a view of the boats. Fresh seafood is the key here. Casual dress; cocktails. **Parking:** on-site (fee) and street. **Cards:** AX, CB, DC, DS, MC, VI.

CROISSANTS DE FRANCE   Lunch: $6-$14   Phone: 305/294-2624   (34)
French
Location: In Old Town. 816 Duval St 33040. **Hours:** 7:30 am-2 pm, Sat & Sun-3 pm. **Reservations:** not accepted. **Features:** Gazpacho, brioche, quiche and assorted croissants are among the popular, light offerings of the tropical, outdoor cafe. Fountains and plants add to the European character. An adjacent bakery stays open in the evenings for take-out customers. Casual dress; beer & wine only. **Parking:** street.
Cards: AX, CB, DC, DS, JC, MC, VI.

DUFFY'S STEAK & LOBSTER HOUSE   Lunch: $7-$12   Dinner: $13-$20   Phone: 305/294-4900   (37)
Steak House
Location: Corner of Simonton St and Truman Ave. 1007 Simonton St 33040. **Hours:** 11:30 am-11 pm. **Reservations:** not accepted. **Features:** For steak and lobster, this casual restaurant is the place to go. Fresh local seafood is the specialty, but landlubbers' favorites are also available. Casual dress; cocktails. **Parking:** street. **Cards:** MC, VI.

EL MESON DE PEPE ON THE BOULEVARD   Lunch: $7-$16   Dinner: $12-$22   Phone: 305/295-9448   (1)
Cuban
Location: On US 1 (Roosevelt Blvd), just s of SR A1A. 3800 N Roosevelt Blvd 33040. **Hours:** 11 am-10 pm, Fri & Sat-11 pm. **Features:** The restaurant is a great place to just relax. In addition to Cuban favorites and some house specialties, the menu lists some American dishes. Meat and seafood entrees are prepared in many traditional ways. Casual dress; cocktails. **Parking:** on-site. **Cards:** MC, VI.

EL SIBONEY   Lunch: $6-$14   Dinner: $6-$14   Phone: 305/296-4184   (36)
Cuban
Location: Just s of US 1; corner of Margaret and Catherine sts. 900 Catherine St 33040. **Hours:** 11 am-9:30 pm. Closed major holidays; also Sun. **Features:** Casual and family-oriented, the energetic restaurant is decorated with original Cuban paintings. The roast pork, shrimp paella, grilled chicken breast and signature Siboney steak are menu favorites. Large windows make for excellent people-watching. Casual dress; beer & wine only. **Parking:** on-site.

FLAGLER'S RESTAURANT & LOUNGE   Lunch: $8-$12   Dinner: $17-$38   Phone: 305/296-3535   (47)
Steak & Seafood
Location: 4 mi s on Flagler (CR 5A) from jct SR A1A; in Wyndham Casa Marina Resort. 1500 Reynolds St 33040. **Hours:** 7 am-11:30 & 6-10:30 pm, Sun 11 am-2 & 6-10 pm. **Reservations:** suggested. **Features:** A pleasant, comfortable setting overlooks a pool and the beach. This place is known for its aged steak and fresh seafood. The cooked-to-order steak is smothered in a delicious onion butter, and the Cuban creme brulee perfectly ends a great meal. Dressy casual; cocktails; entertainment. **Parking:** on-site. **Cards:** AX, CB, DC, DS, JC, MC, VI.

GRAND CAFE KEY WEST   Lunch: $7-$16   Dinner: $16-$34   Phone: 305/292-4740   (18)
American
Location: On Duval St, just e of Caroline St. 314 Duval St 33040. **Hours:** 11 am-11:30 pm. **Features:** Eat outside and enjoy the garden-like setting and the peoplewatching, or sit inside with local art decorating the dining room. The food is wonderful; a changing menu has a worldly flair, with pastas, fresh local seafood and gourmet brick oven pizzas. Casual dress; cocktails. **Parking:** street. **Cards:** AX, DS, MC, VI.

HALF SHELL RAW BAR   Lunch: $6-$24   Dinner: $6-$24   Phone: 305/294-7496   (2)
Seafood
Location: At the very west end of Margaret St; in Historic Seaport District. 231 Margaret St 33040. **Hours:** 11 am-11 pm. Closed: 11/23, 12/25. **Features:** Right on the water, this place is as casual as casual gets. At the heart of the menu is fresh seafood. Casual dress; cocktails. **Parking:** on-site (fee) and street. **Cards:** AX, DS, MC, VI.

HOT TIN ROOF   Menu on aaa.com   Lunch: $7-$13   Dinner: $18-$35   Phone: 305/295-7056   (10)
Regional American
Location: At Mallory Square; in Old Town; in Ocean Key Resort, A Noble House Resort. Zero Duval St 33040. **Hours:** 7:30 am-11:30 & 6-10 pm. **Reservations:** suggested. **Features:** The restaurant presents "Conch Fusion" island cuisine, a blend of Latin American and American flavors. The menu lists fresh local and regional seafood and meats. Guests may choose to sit inside amid palm fronds and painted tiles, or outside watching the sunset—either location provides a memorable experience. Dressy casual; cocktails. **Parking:** street. **Cards:** AX, CB, DC, DS, JC, MC, VI.

JIMMY BUFFETT'S MARGARITAVILLE CAFE   Lunch: $5-$10   Dinner: $14-$18   Phone: 305/292-1435   (21)
American
Location: On Duval St; between Southard St and Fleming. 500 Duval St 33040. **Hours:** 10 am-midnight. **Reservations:** not accepted. **Features:** The original cafe in the chain, this restaurant—the capital of Margaritaville—is where it all got started. Patrons can get a big burger, fresh seafood or a pasta dish. It goes without saying that margaritas, in many types and sizes, are a favorite in Margaritaville. Casual dress; cocktails; entertainment. **Parking:** street. **Cards:** AX, MC, VI.

KELLY'S CARIBBEAN BAR, GRILL & BREWERY   Lunch: $6-$11   Dinner: $12-$27   Phone: 305/293-8484   (19)
Continental
Location: Jct Caroline St; in Old Town. 301 Whitehead St 33040. **Hours:** 11 am-close. **Reservations:** not accepted. **Features:** A short walk from popular Duval Street, the restaurant enables patrons to dine under the stars in the tropical patio area. Among enjoyable creations are Caribbean apple chicken, camarones Curacao and the chop: tasty pork chops marinated in citrus, teriyaki and garlic. Microbrewed beers are made on site. Casual dress; cocktails. **Parking:** street. **Cards:** AX, DC, DS, MC, VI.

(See map and index starting on p. 334)

KEY WEST SEAFOOD & BEER GARDEN **Dinner:** $15-$22 **Phone:** 305/296-2038 ㉒
Seafood
Location: In Old Town. 517 Duval St 33040. **Hours:** 5 pm-10 pm. **Reservations:** suggested. **Features:** Fresh is the key word at this casually styled restaurant: the fish are caught from local captains and brought straight to the kitchen. The atmosphere is calming with a canopy of trees and small fountains; sometimes the stars peek through for a visit. Casual dress; cocktails. **Parking:** street. **Cards:** MC, VI.

KYUSHU **Lunch:** $7-$12 **Dinner:** $12-$20 **Phone:** 305/294-2995 ㉖
Japanese
Location: On US 1; in Old Town. 921 Truman Ave 33040. **Hours:** 11:30 am-2 & 5:30-10:30 pm, Fri-11 pm, Sat 5:30 pm-11 pm. Closed: Mon. **Reservations:** suggested. **Features:** Attentive and friendly service at the sushi bar and in the tatami rooms makes for a pleasant visit. The sushi is fresh and presented with a touch of class. Order the fried pork loin cooked with an egg splash and served on a bed of rice with sauteed onions. Casual dress; cocktails. **Parking:** on-site. **Cards:** AX, CB, DC, DS, MC, VI.

LA TE DA OCEAN GRILL **Lunch:** $9-$17 **Dinner:** $14-$30 **Phone:** 305/296-6706 ㊹
American
Location: Corner of Duval and Catherine sts; in historic La Te Da Guest House. 1125 Duval St 33040. **Hours:** 8 am-midnight. **Reservations:** accepted. **Features:** New World fusion cuisine captures the flavors of the Caribbean, Asia and the American Southwest with great use of fresh local seafood, meat and tropical fruits. Dine outdoors under the stars or inside with the signed Picasso lithographs. Casual dress; cocktails. **Parking:** street. **Cards:** AX, CB, DC, DS, JC, MC, VI.

LATITUDES BEACH CAFE **Lunch:** $9-$18 **Dinner:** $18-$35 **Phone:** 305/292-5394 ⑯
Seafood
Location: Adjacent to Mallory Square; in Old Town; in Hilton Key West Resort & Marina. 245 Front St 33040. **Hours:** 7 am-10 pm; you must pick up your boat tickets at the hotel concierge's desk; boat leaves on quarter to the hour. **Reservations:** required. **Features:** On an island 500 yards from downtown, the breezy restaurant focuses on seafood but also offers other selections. Because there are no walls, this eatery closes during inclement weather. The fresh air and views are invigorating. Dressy casual; cocktails. **Parking:** on-site (fee). **Cards:** AX, CB, DC, DS, JC, MC, VI.

LA TRATTORIA **Dinner:** $15-$29 **Phone:** 305/296-1075 ㉔
Italian
Location: In Old Town. 524 Duval St 33040. **Hours:** 5:30 pm-10:30 pm, Fri & Sat-1 am. **Reservations:** accepted. **Features:** This cozy place offers many house speciality Italian dishes as well as traditional favorites. Casual dress; cocktails. **Parking:** street. **Cards:** AX, DS, MC, VI.

LOBO'S MIXED GRILL **Lunch:** $6-$10 **Dinner:** $6-$10 **Phone:** 305/296-5303 ㉗
American
Location: Just off Duval St. 5 Key Lime Square 33040. **Hours:** 11 am-6 pm, Sun noon-5 pm. **Reservations:** not accepted. **Features:** Diners can unwind in the gardenlike setting with a great sandwich or wrap. Fresh is the key word when it comes to ingredients. Casual dress. **Parking:** street.

LOUIE'S BACKYARD **Lunch:** $11-$16 **Dinner:** $24-$39 **Phone:** 305/294-1061 ㊽
Regional American
Location: Just s of Truman Ave via Simonton St to South St, just e to Vernon, then s. 700 Waddell Ave 33040. **Hours:** 11:30 am-2:30 & 6-10 pm. Closed: 9/5-9/17 & for dinner 9/18-9/30. **Reservations:** suggested. **Features:** The charming 1908 Victorian house features hardwood floors and a facade with many windows. Outdoor decks on both floors offer great views of the ocean. Beautifully prepared fish and steaks and an excellent wine list make the restaurant notable. Dressy casual; cocktails. **Parking:** street. **Cards:** AX, DC, MC, VI.

MANGIA MANGIA **Dinner:** $9-$15 **Phone:** 305/294-2469 ⑰

Italian
Location: Just n of US 1; corner of Margaret and Southard sts. 900 Southard St 33040. **Hours:** 5:30 pm-10 pm. Closed major holidays; also Super Bowl Sun. **Features:** Rigatoni with jumbo shrimp, fresh pasta and homemade tiramisu encourage you to "eat eat" at the casual, small restaurant. Palms, plants and herbs envelop the outdoor garden. Caribbean decor is the theme inside. Casual dress; beer & wine only. **Parking:** street. **Cards:** AX, MC, VI.

MANGOES RESTAURANT AND CATERING **Lunch:** $4-$15 **Dinner:** $4-$26 **Phone:** 305/292-4606 ㉛
Ethnic
Location: At Angela St; in Old Town. 700 Duval St 33040. **Hours:** 11:30 am-3 & 5:30-11 pm, Sun from noon. **Reservations:** accepted. **Features:** In the heart of Key West, the restaurant lets diners eat or nurse a libation under the stars in the courtyard or linger over dinner in a romantic dining room with soft diverse lighting and original artwork. Preparations of meat and fresh local seafood creatively fuse American and Caribbean styles. Casual dress; cocktails. **Parking:** street. **Cards:** AX, DC, DS, MC, VI.

MARTHA'S STEAK & SEAFOOD **Dinner:** $16-$28 **Phone:** 305/294-3466 ㉜
Steak & Seafood
Location: On SR A1A, 2 mi s of jct US 1; in New Town. 3591 S Roosevelt Blvd 33040. **Hours:** 5:30 pm-10 pm, Fri & Sat-10:30 pm. **Reservations:** suggested. **Features:** The popular establishment has been a local fixture since 1979. Dishes ranging from steak au poivre to stuffed pork chops to the filet mignon and lobster tail platter can be had at the lovely spot. Casual dress; cocktails; entertainment. **Parking:** on-site. **Cards:** AX, CB, DC, DS, MC, VI.

MARTIN'S **Dinner:** $18-$35 **Phone:** 305/296-1183 ㉘
Continental
Location: Between Duval and Whitehead sts; between Southard St and Fleming; in Old Town. 416 Applerouth Ln 33040. **Hours:** Open 12/1-5/30 & 9/6-11/30; 6 pm-11 pm. **Reservations:** suggested. **Features:** It may be hard to find, but when you do it will be a treasure. Inside is a cozy, cottagelike room, while outside is a romantic courtyard with white pin lights and reflections of the stars. Casual dress; cocktails. **Parking:** street. **Cards:** AX, MC, VI.

(See map and index starting on p. 334)

METEOR SMOKEHOUSE RESTAURANT
Lunch: $8-$12   **Dinner:** $8-$24   **Phone:** 305/294-5602   ㉚

Barbecue

Location: 1 blk s of Duval St; at Whitehead and Southard sts. 404 Southard St 33040. **Hours:** 11 am-10 pm, Fri & Sat-11 pm, Sun noon-11 pm. **Features:** Ribs are the real thing at the smokehouse. Barbecue meats are prepared with a Memphis dry rub application and special sauce. The atmosphere inside is eclectic, while outside has a local feel. Casual dress; cocktails. **Parking:** on-site and street. **Cards:** AX, CB, DC, DS, JC, MC, VI.

MICHAELS
Dinner: $17-$30   **Phone:** 305/295-1300   ⑮

Steak & Seafood

Location: Just n of US 1; corner of Margaret and Southard sts. 532 Margaret St 33040. **Hours:** 5:30 pm-11 pm. Closed: 9/21-10/4. **Reservations:** suggested. **Features:** The restaurant exudes a garden atmosphere with help from large umbrellas and a focal-point fountain. The cozy dining room incorporates a mural by Maurizio Mancioli. Prime beef and local seafood feature heavily on the menu. Casual dress; cocktails. **Parking:** street. **Cards:** AX, MC, VI.

NICOLA SEAFOOD
Lunch: $8-$14   **Dinner:** $22-$29   **Phone:** 305/296-9900   ③

East Seafood

Location: Simonton and Front sts; just n of Mallory Square; in Old Town; in Hyatt Key West Resort & Marina. 601 Front St 33040. **Hours:** 7 am-3 & 6-10 pm. **Reservations:** suggested. **Features:** Have a drink and enjoy an excellent sunset view on the gulf with indoor or terrace dining. Seafood is the house specialty with local fresh fish, lobster and crab cakes. Cocktails. **Parking:** on-site. **Cards:** AX, CB, DC, DS, JC, MC, VI.

NINE ONE FIVE RESTAURANT
Dinner: $17-$26   **Phone:** 305/296-0669   ㊴

Continental

Location: Just w of jct US 1; in Old Town. 915 Duval St 33040. **Hours:** 6 pm-midnight. **Features:** Right on popular Duval Street, the relaxing spot is a favorite for its tapas. However, guests also can order from the main menu, which lists such courses as seared sea scallops, black grouper, roasted organic breast of chicken and salads, including the delicious watercress and Belgian endive with Gorgonzola cheese. Casual dress; wine only. **Parking:** on-site (fee) and street. **Cards:** MC, VI.

ONE DUVAL
Dinner: $25-$36   **Phone:** 305/296-4600   ⑧

Regional American

Location: At the foot of Duval St; in Old Town; in Pier House Resort & Caribbean Spa. One Duval St 33040. **Hours:** 5:30 pm-10:30 pm. **Reservations:** suggested. **Features:** A stylish waterfront dining room also features a patio for viewing the activity in Mallory Square. Market-fresh seafood and a conch chowder that will give you a taste of the Keys are offered with other excellent choices like spinach salad and veal. Dressy casual; cocktails; entertainment. **Parking:** on-site. **Cards:** AX, CB, DC, DS, MC, VI.

ORIGAMI SUSHI BAR & JAPANESE RESTAURANT
Dinner: $8-$23   **Phone:** 305/294-0092   ㊵

Japanese

Location: Just e of Truman Ave. 1075 Duval St, C-3 33040. **Hours:** 6 pm-9:30 pm. **Features:** Locals come here for fresh sushi, sashimi and tempura dishes. The artistic presentations can be enjoyed inside or under the stars. Casual dress; beer & wine only. **Parking:** on-site. **Cards:** AX, DS, MC, VI.

PEPE'S CAFE
Lunch: $6-$10   **Dinner:** $10-$20   **Phone:** 305/294-7192   ⑫

American

Location: Just e of Duval St. 806 Caroline St 33040. **Hours:** 6:30 am-4 & 5:30-10 pm. **Features:** The oldest restaurant in Key West, it features pleasant service and picnic-style seating on a patio shaded by blooming bougainvillea. Feast on homemade meals like meatloaf with mashed potatoes and an authentic, onion-and-sausage-filled black bean soup. Casual dress; cocktails. **Parking:** street. **Cards:** DS, MC, VI.

PISCES SEAFOOD RESTAURANT
Dinner: $23-$44   **Phone:** 305/294-7100   ㊳

Regional American

Location: Corner of Truman Ave and Simonton St. 1007 Simonton St 33040-6552. **Hours:** 6 pm-11 pm. **Reservations:** suggested. **Features:** Dine on the cafe-terrasse or in the intimate indoor dining room. Local seafood entrees are creatively prepared and presented with a tropical French flair, like the snail appetizer served in a puff pastry with goat cheese and bits of red bell pepper. Dressy casual; cocktails. **Parking:** street. **Cards:** AX, MC, VI.

ROOF TOP CAFE
Lunch: $6-$15   **Dinner:** $13-$32   **Phone:** 305/294-2042   ⑭

Seafood

Location: Jct Fitzpatrick; in Old Town. 308 Front St 33040. **Hours:** Open 12/1-9/1 & 10/1-11/30; 10:30 am-10:30 pm. **Features:** Just as the name suggests, the restaurant affords patrons a lofty vantage point. The rooftop setting, which is near Duval Street, is decidedly elegant. Representative of the food are such fabulous choices as Jamaican jerk chicken, roast duck and grilled salmon nicoise. Casual dress; cocktails. **Parking:** on-site (fee) and street. **Cards:** AX, DS, MC, VI.

SANDY'S CAFE
Lunch: $5-$9   **Dinner:** $5-$9   **Phone:** 305/295-0159   ㉓

Cuban

Location: Just e of US 1; in Window of M & M Laundry Building. 1026 White St 33040. **Hours:** 5 am-8 pm. Closed: 11/23, 12/25. **Features:** The little walk-up restaurant is known for Cuban sandwiches and other island favorites. Casual dress. **Parking:** street.

SHULA'S ON THE BEACH
Dinner: $25-$40   **Phone:** 305/296-6144   ㊾

Steak House

Location: Just s of jct Truman Ave and Simonton St; in Wyndham Reach Resort. 1435 Simonton St 33040. **Hours:** 5:30 pm-11 pm. **Reservations:** suggested. **Features:** Certified Angus steaks, as well as lobster and other seafood selections, are served in large portions at this place, which affords ocean views. Dressy casual; cocktails. **Parking:** on-site. **Cards:** AX, CB, DC, DS, MC, VI.

(See map and index starting on p. 334)

SQUARE ONE RESTAURANT   *Menu on aaa.com*   **Lunch:** $5-$18   **Dinner:** $16-$32   **Phone:** 305/296-4300   42
Location: At Duval Square. 1075 Duval St 33040. **Hours:** 9 am-3 & 6-10 pm. **Reservations:** suggested.
Features: Expect creative steak and seafood entrees—such as grilled filet mignon, New Zealand rack of lamb and sauteed sea scallops—in this intimate restaurant. The tropical courtyard is illuminated at night. For dessert, try Key lime pie or creme brulee. Dressy casual; cocktails; entertainment. **Parking:** on-site.
American   **Cards:** AX, DS, MC, VI.

TURTLE KRAALS RESTAURANT & BAR   **Lunch:** $8-$20   **Dinner:** $8-$20   **Phone:** 305/294-2640   7
Location: Jct Caroline and Margaret sts; in Land End Village; in Old Town. 1 Lands End Village 33040. **Hours:** 7 am-10 pm. **Features:** Just a short walk from Duval Street, the historic spot was the previous site of a turtle cannery. On the menu are great local seafood and other tasty dishes, including mojo roast pork and the house specialty mango crab cakes with Key lime-mustard sauce. Diners can watch a sunset or the dockside activity of boats coming and going. Lucky folks might catch a turtle race. Casual dress; cocktails. **Parking:** on-site. **Cards:** AX, DS, MC, VI.

TWO FRIENDS PATIO RESTAURANT   **Lunch:** $8-$18   **Dinner:** $17-$24   **Phone:** 305/296-3124   11
Location: Just n of jct Duval St; in Old Town. 512 Front St 33040. **Hours:** 8 am-11 pm. Closed: last week of Sept. **Reservations:** not accepted. **Features:** A local landmark since 1967, the casual restaurant prepares great seafood dishes. Patrons often visit after milling about Duval Street for yummy fried grouper or the great Caribbean crab cakes dish. Service is friendly and welcoming. Casual dress; cocktails; entertainment. **Parking:** on-site. **Cards:** AX, DC, MC, VI.

THE UPPER CRUST   **Lunch:** $10-$20   **Dinner:** $10-$20   **Phone:** 305/293-8890   25
Location: Just s of Southard St; in Old Town. 611 Duval St 33040. **Hours:** noon-11 pm. **Features:** Freshly made Neapolitan-style pizza can be grabbed by the slice or the pie. Among fresh ingredient choices are four varieties of cheese. Those who prefer a calzone or salad can find those here, as well. The atmosphere is casual and friendly. Casual dress; beer only. **Parking:** street. **Cards:** MC, VI.
Italian

———— *The following restaurants have not been evaluated by AAA* ————
but are listed for your information only.

DUVAL BEACH CLUB   **Phone:** 305/295-6550
fyi   Not evaluated. **Location:** At east end of Duval St. 1405 Duval St 33040. **Features:** At the beachfront restaurant, patrons can have breakfast while watching the sun rise or listen to the waves at sunset. Tropical beverages match with a variety of comfort foods. Beach chairs can be rented during the day.

(See map and index starting on p. 334)

SEVEN FISH   Phone: 305/296-2777

[fyi]   Not evaluated. **Location:** 632 Olive St 33040. **Features:** A very little restaurant that offers big food featuring fresh seafoods and meats prepared in their own style. Reservations are a must to get a table.

LITTLE TORCH KEY

-------- WHERE TO STAY --------

LITTLE PALM ISLAND RESORT & SPA   *Book at aaa.com*   Phone: 305/872-2524

Property failed to provide current rates

Location: Oceanfront. Shore Station on US 1 at MM 28.5; jct Pirate Rd; 10 minute launch ride to island leaving hourly. Located on a remote island. 28500 Overseas Hwy 33042. Fax: 305/872-4843. **Facility:** 5.5 acres of lush foliage welcomes you to an island hideaway. Enjoy a thatched bungalow-style suite decorated with opulent furnishings. Designated smoking area. 30 one-bedroom standard units with whirlpools. 1 story, exterior corridors. **Parking:** on-site. **Terms:** office hours 9 am-8 pm, age restrictions may apply. **Amenities:** safes, honor bars, irons, hair dryers. *Some:* DVD players. **Dining:** The Dining Room at Little Palm Island, see separate listing. **Pool(s):** heated outdoor. **Leisure Activities:** rental boats, canoeing, paddleboats, sailboats, windsurfing, snorkeling, fishing, jogging, exercise room. **Fee:** marina, scuba diving, charter fishing, massage. **Guest Services:** gift shop, valet laundry, area transportation (fee).

Resort / Small-scale Hotel

-------- WHERE TO DINE --------

THE DINING ROOM AT LITTLE PALM ISLAND   **Lunch:** $18-$36   **Dinner:** $43-$46   Phone: 305/872-2551

Nouvelle Continental

Location: Shore Station on US 1 at MM 28.5; jct Pirate Rd; 10 minute launch ride to island leaving hourly; in Little Palm Island Resort & Spa. 28500 Overseas Hwy 33042. **Hours:** 8 am-10:30, noon-2:30 & 6:30-9:30 pm. **Reservations:** required. **Features:** Florida and French regional dishes are featured with a nouvelle presentation. Outdoor tables and a lengthy wine list are available. You must be at least 16 years old. Dressy casual; cocktails. **Parking:** on-site. **Cards:** AX, CB, DC, DS, MC, VI.

LONG KEY

-------- WHERE TO STAY --------

LIME TREE BAY RESORT   *Book at aaa.com*   Phone: (305)664-4740

(AAA) [SAVE]   All Year   1P: $79-$295   2P: $79-$295   XP: $15   F8

Location: US 1 at MM 68.5. 68500 Overseas Hwy 33001 (PO Box 839). Fax: 305/664-0750. **Facility:** 36 units. 28 one- and 2 two-bedroom standard units, some with efficiencies or kitchens. 6 one-bedroom suites, some with efficiencies or kitchens. 1-2 stories (no elevator), exterior corridors. *Bath:* combo or shower only. **Parking:** on-site. **Terms:** office hours 8 am-10 pm, 15 day cancellation notice. **Amenities:** voice mail. **Pool(s):** outdoor. **Leisure Activities:** whirlpool, fishing, tennis court. **Fee:** sailboats. **Cards:** AX, DC, DS, MC, VI. **Special Amenities:** free local telephone calls.

Motel

SOME UNITS

MARATHON pop. 10,255

-------- WHERE TO STAY --------

BANANA BAY RESORT-MARATHON KEY   *Book at aaa.com*   Phone: (305)743-3500

12/26-4/30 [CP]	1P: $125-$225	2P: $125-$225	XP: $15	F5
12/1-12/25 [CP]	1P: $85-$225	2P: $85-$225	XP: $15	F5
5/1-11/30 [CP]	1P: $85-$185	2P: $85-$185	XP: $15	F5

Small-scale Hotel   **Location:** Oceanfront. US 1 at MM 49.5; gulfside. 4590 Overseas Hwy 33050. Fax: 305/743-2670. **Facility:** 61 one-bedroom standard units. 2 stories (no elevator), interior corridors. **Parking:** on-site. **Terms:** office hours 7 am-10 pm, 2-3 night minimum stay - weekends, 7 day cancellation notice, package plans. **Amenities:** voice mail, irons, hair dryers. **Pool(s):** heated outdoor. **Leisure Activities:** whirlpool, limited beach access, rental sailboats, fishing, 2 tennis courts, exercise room, horseshoes. **Fee:** boats, boat dock, scuba diving, snorkeling, charter fishing. **Guest Services:** gift shop, coin laundry. **Business Services:** meeting rooms, fax (fee). **Cards:** AX, CB, DC, DS, JC, MC, VI.

SOME UNITS

COCO PLUM BEACH & TENNIS CLUB   Phone: (305)743-0240

12/18-4/22 Wkly	2P: $1338-$2528
4/23-8/19 Wkly	2P: $918-$1960
8/20-11/30 Wkly	2P: $918-$1680
12/1-12/17 Wkly	2P: $857-$1365

Vacation Home

Location: Off US 1 at MM 54.5, then 1.5 mi. 109 Coco Plum Dr 33050. Fax: 305/743-9351. **Facility:** All of the units are spacious and offer views of the tropical courtyard; a beach is close by. 20 vacation homes, some with pools. 2 stories (no elevator), exterior corridors. **Parking:** on-site. **Terms:** office hours 9 am-5 pm, 3 night minimum stay, 30 day cancellation notice-fee imposed, daily rates available. **Amenities:** voice mail, hair dryers. **Leisure Activities:** whirlpool, tennis court. **Guest Services:** complimentary laundry. **Business Services:** fax (fee). **Cards:** AX, MC, VI.

CORAL LAGOON RESORT & MARINA

Phone: 305/289-0121

AAA SAVE

12/1-4/20		2P: $135-$160	XP: $10	F3
4/21-9/6	1P: $110-$135	2P: $110-$135	XP: $10	F3
9/7-11/30	1P: $85-$110	2P: $85-$110	XP: $10	F3

Cottage

Location: US 1 at MM 53.5; oceanside. 12399 Overseas Hwy 33050. Fax: 305/289-0195. **Facility:** Designated smoking area. 18 cottages. 1 story, exterior corridors. *Bath:* combo or shower only. **Parking:** on-site. **Terms:** office hours 8 am-6 pm, 3 night minimum stay - seasonal and/or weekends, 30 day cancellation notice-fee imposed. **Amenities:** video library (fee), safes, hair dryers. **Leisure Activities:** boat dock, fishing, beach & pool privileges. *Fee:* charter fishing, diving tours. **Guest Services:** coin laundry. **Business Services:** fax (fee). **Cards:** AX, CB, DC, DS, JC, MC, VI. **Special Amenities:** free local telephone calls and early check-in/late check-out.

FLAMINGO INN

Phone: 305/289-1478

AAA SAVE

12/16-4/18	1P: $89-$119	2P: $89-$119	XP: $10	F7
4/19-9/5	1P: $79-$109	2P: $79-$109	XP: $10	F7
12/1-12/15	1P: $50-$103	2P: $50-$103	XP: $5	F7
9/6-11/30	1P: $59-$89	2P: $59-$89	XP: $5	F7

Motel

Location: On Grassy Key; US 1 at MM 59.5. 59299 Overseas Hwy 33050. Fax: 305/743-4399. **Facility:** 11 units. 7 one-bedroom standard units. 3 one- and 1 two-bedroom units. 1 story, exterior corridors. *Bath:* combo or shower only. **Parking:** on-site. **Terms:** office hours 8 am-10 pm, 7 day cancellation notice-fee imposed. **Pool(s):** outdoor. **Leisure Activities:** barbecue facilities. **Business Services:** fax (fee). **Cards:** MC, VI.

SOME UNITS

HAWK'S CAY RESORT   *Book at aaa.com*

Phone: (305)743-7000

AAA SAVE

12/25-4/22	1P: $300-$1350	2P: $300-$1350	XP: $25	F12
4/23-11/30	1P: $250-$1250	2P: $250-$1250	XP: $25	F12
12/1-12/24	1P: $220-$1200	2P: $200-$1200	XP: $25	F12

Resort
Large-scale Hotel

Location: Oceanfront. On Duck Key; 0.5 mi s of US 1. Located in a remote area. MM 61 33050 (61 Hawk's Cay Blvd, DUCK KEY). Fax: 305/743-0641. **Facility:** Though this property offers conference facilities and a corporate team-building program, its atmosphere is casual and family oriented. 472 units. 177 one-bedroom standard units. 290 two- and 5 three-bedroom suites with kitchens. 2-5 stories, interior/exterior corridors. **Parking:** on-site. **Terms:** check-in 4 pm, 2-4 night minimum stay - seasonal and/or weekends, 7 day cancellation notice-fee imposed, $20 service charge. **Amenities:** video library, voice mail, irons, hair dryers. *Some:* high-speed Internet (fee). **Dining:** 5 restaurants, 7 am-11 pm, cocktails. **Pool(s):** 4 heated outdoor, wading. **Leisure Activities:** sauna, whirlpools, steamroom, fishing, salt water lagoon, putting green, recreation programs, eco tours, kayak trips, sunset cruise, dolphin encounter program, playground, exercise room, spa, sports court, basketball, volleyball. *Fee:* boats, waterskiing, scuba diving, snorkeling, charter fishing, diving trip & scuba instruction, parasailing, sailing instruction, 8 tennis courts (2 lighted), bicycles, game room. **Guest Services:** gift shop, airport transportation-Marathon Airport. **Business Services:** conference facilities, business center. **Cards:** AX, DS, MC, VI. *(See color ad below)*

SOME UNITS

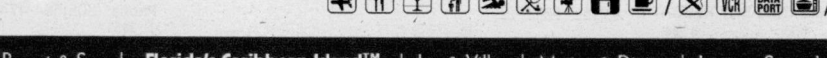

HOLIDAY INN & MARINA, FLORIDA KEYS   *Book at aaa.com*   Phone: 305/289-0222

▽▽▽▽   All Year   1P: $79-$259   2P: $79-$259   XP: $10   F18

Small-scale Hotel   **Location:** US 1 at MM 54. 13201 Overseas Hwy 33050. Fax: 305/743-5460. **Facility:** 134 one-bedroom standard units. 2 stories, exterior corridors. *Bath:* combo or shower only. **Parking:** on-site. **Terms:** check-in 4 pm, 3 day cancellation notice-fee imposed. **Amenities:** high-speed Internet, dual phone lines, voice mail, safes, irons, hair dryers. **Pool(s):** heated outdoor, wading. **Leisure Activities:** fishing, exercise room. *Fee:* boats, scuba diving, snorkeling, charter fishing. **Guest Services:** gift shop, coin laundry. **Business Services:** meeting rooms, fax (fee). **Cards:** AX, DC, DS, MC, VI.

SOME UNITS

🍽 🍸 🉑 ⇆ 🗙 🐾 DATA PORT 🗄 🖵 / 🗙 /

RAMADA MARATHON OCEANVIEW FLORIDA KEYS   Phone: 305/743-8550

▽▽▽ ▽▽▽   Property failed to provide current rates

Small-scale Hotel   **Location:** US 1 at MM 54. 13351 Overseas Hwy 33050. Fax: 305/743-8832. **Facility:** 80 one-bedroom standard units. 2 stories (no elevator), interior corridors. *Bath:* combo or shower only. **Parking:** on-site. **Terms:** small pets only ($20 extra charge). **Amenities:** voice mail, irons, hair dryers. **Pool(s):** heated outdoor. **Leisure Activities:** *Fee:* boats. **Guest Services:** valet and coin laundry.

SOME UNITS

🐕 🛏➔ ⇆ 🐾 DATA PORT 🗄 🖵 / 🗙 /
FEE

ROYAL HAWAIIAN MOTEL/BOTEL   Phone: (305)743-7500

🔺🔺🔺 [SAVE]   12/1-4/15   1P: $89-$150   2P: $89-$150   XP: $10

4/16-9/5   1P: $89-$135   2P: $89-$135   XP: $10

▽▽▽   9/6-11/30   1P: $69-$99   2P: $69-$99   XP: $10

Motel   **Location:** US 1 at MM 53; gulfside. 12020 Overseas Hwy 33050. Fax: 305/743-0577. **Facility:** 8 one-bedroom standard units, some with efficiencies. 1 story, exterior corridors. *Bath:* shower only. **Parking:** on-site. **Terms:** office hours 8 am-10 pm, 7 day cancellation notice-fee imposed. **Pool(s):** small outdoor. **Leisure Activities:** boat dock, fishing, barbecue grills, picnic area. **Cards:** DS, MC, VI. **Special Amenities:** free local telephone calls and preferred room (subject to availability with advance reservations).

🛏➔ ⇆ 🗙 🐾 DATA PORT 🗄 🖵

TRANQUILITY BAY BEACH HOUSE RESORT   Phone: 305/289-0888

[fyi]   12/23-4/30   1P: $499-$869   2P: $499-$869

5/1-7/31   1P: $399-$629   2P: $399-$629

Vacation Home   8/1-11/30   1P: $299-$499   2P: $299-$499

12/1-12/22   1P: $199-$499   2P: $199-$499

Too new to rate, opening scheduled for August 2005. **Location:** US 1 to Overseas Hwy at MM 48.5. 2600 Overseas Hwy 33050. Fax: 305/289-0667. **Amenities:** 87 units, restaurant, coffeemakers, microwaves, refrigerators, pool. **Terms:** 14 day cancellation notice. $10 service charge. **Cards:** AX, CB, DC, DS, MC, VI. *(See color ad below)*

Tranquility Bay
BEACH HOUSE RESORT
MARATHON, FLORIDA KEYS

NEWEST LUXURY BEACH HOUSE RESORT IN THE HEART OF THE FLORIDA KEYS ON 2.5 ACRES OF PRISTINE SANDY BEACH.

1-866-MID KEYS
WWW.TRANQUILITYBAY.COM

─────── WHERE TO DINE ───────

ANNETTE'S LOBSTER & STEAKHOUSE   **Lunch:** $6-$13   **Dinner:** $13-$48   **Phone:** 305/743-5516
◆◆ ◆◆   **Location:** US 1 at MM 49.5. 3660 Overseas Hwy 33050. **Hours:** 11 am-3 & 5-9 pm. **Reservations:** suggested.
Features: Diners who are looking to taste and experience the seafood of coastal Florida will find it at this
Steak & Seafood   bustling roadside restaurant. Casual dress; cocktails. **Parking:** on-site. **Cards:** AX, DS, MC, VI.

BARRACUDA GRILL   **Dinner:** $18-$27   **Phone:** 305/743-3314
◆◆ ◆◆   **Location:** US 1 at MM 49.5. 4290 Overseas Hwy 33050. **Hours:** 5:55 pm-10 pm; from 6:55 pm 3/24-11/27.
Closed: Sun. **Features:** The atmosphere is casual, but the food is serious. Fresh is another keyword here,
American   and the fish comes in daily. The owner/chef presents his foods as art. Soothing decor prevails indoors and
on the patio. Casual dress; beer & wine only. **Parking:** on-site. **Cards:** AX, MC, VI.
◣

THE QUAY OF MARATHON   **Lunch:** $7-$14   **Dinner:** $10-$36   **Phone:** 305/289-1810
◆◆ ◆◆   **Location:** US 1 at MM 54. 12650 Overseas Hwy 33050. **Hours:** 11 am-10 pm, Fri & Sat-11 pm.
Reservations: suggested, in season. **Features:** Relaxing gulf views enhance the mellow experience for
Steak & Seafood   diners who unwind in the cozy dining room as well as those who opt for the breezy patio. The woodwork
and decor suggest a nautical theme. Prime rib, dolphin, alligator, swordfish and homemade cheesecake are
among tasty offerings. Casual dress; cocktails. **Parking:** on-site. **Cards:** AX, CB, DC, DS, MC, VI.
Ⴘ

Visit Florida

This ends listings for The Florida Keys.
The following page resumes the alphabetical listings of cities in Florida.

Destination Fort Lauderdale
pop. 152,397

Canals, lagoons, rivers, the Atlantic Ocean and the Intracoastal Waterway—Fort Lauderdale is literally shaped by various bodies of H_2O.

Cruise ships depart its port for Caribbean destinations, divers snorkel in crystal blue waters, waterfront cafes prepare feasts of locally caught seafood, sailboats and yachts mingle in marinas and a floating taxi takes you from here to there.

The beach at Hollywood.
Palm trees line Fort Lauderdale's beachfront promenade.

Las Olas Boulevard, Fort Lauderdale. Eateries, nightclubs and shops entice visitors to this popular district. (See mention page 83)

A Fort Lauderdale marina. Several marinas provide docking sites for seacraft and seabirds.

Deerfield Beach

Hillsboro • Beach

Coral Springs
Coconut Creek
Margate •
• Lighthouse Point
Pompano Beach

Tamarac
95
Lauderdale-by-the-Sea

870

Lauderhill
• Lauderdale Lakes

869

Sunrise •
Plantation •

75

Weston •

595

Davie •
• Dania Beach

Hollywood •

75

Pembroke Pines
Hallandale Beach

Miramar

Fort Lauderdale

See Vicinity map page 365

Golf courses in Fort Lauderdale. Scores of courses beckon pros and duffers alike to chase birdies.

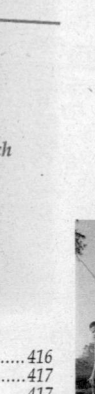

P*laces included in this AAA Destination City:*

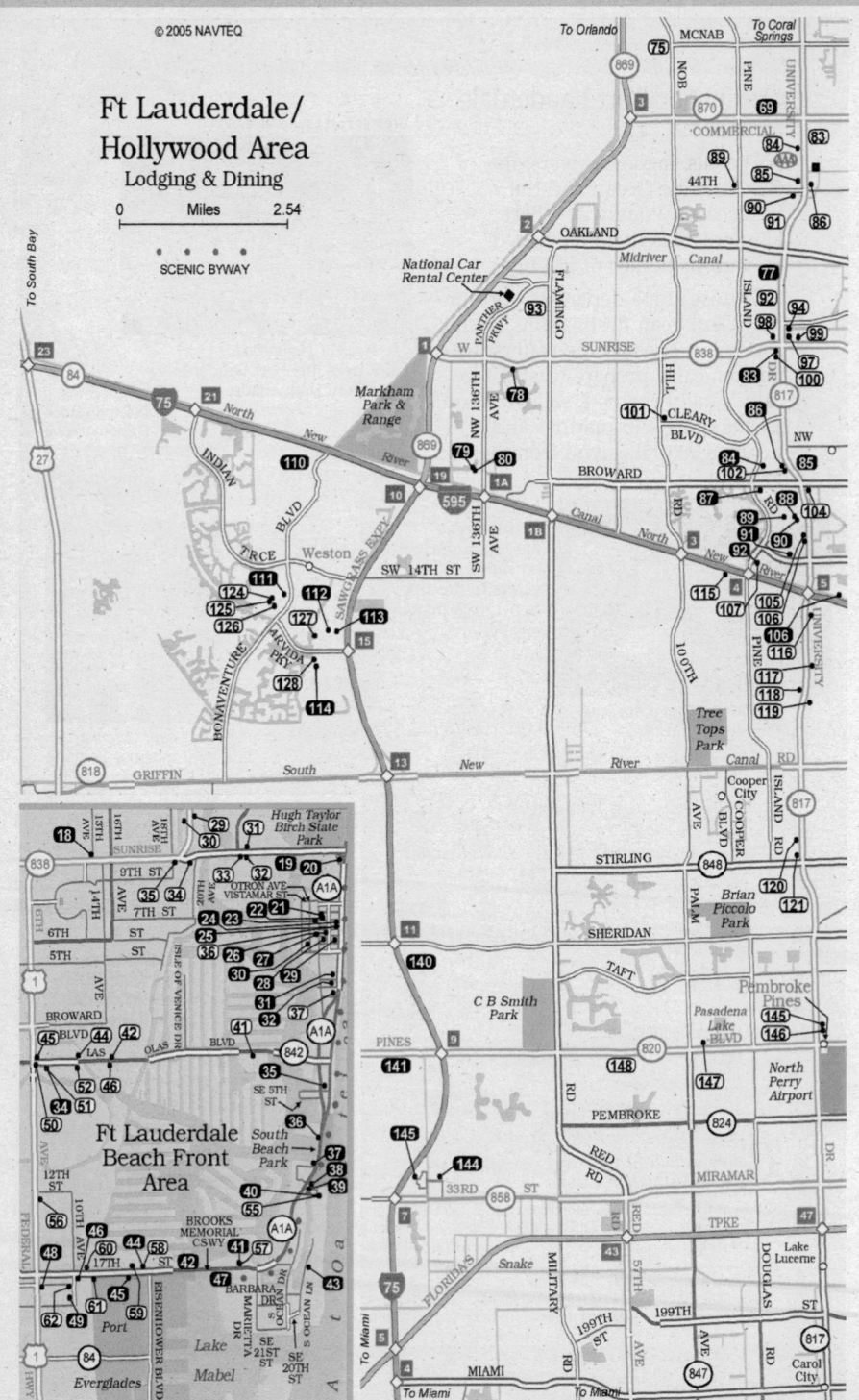

© 2005 NAVTEQ

Ft Lauderdale/
Hollywood Area
Lodging & Dining

0   Miles   2.54

SCENIC BYWAY

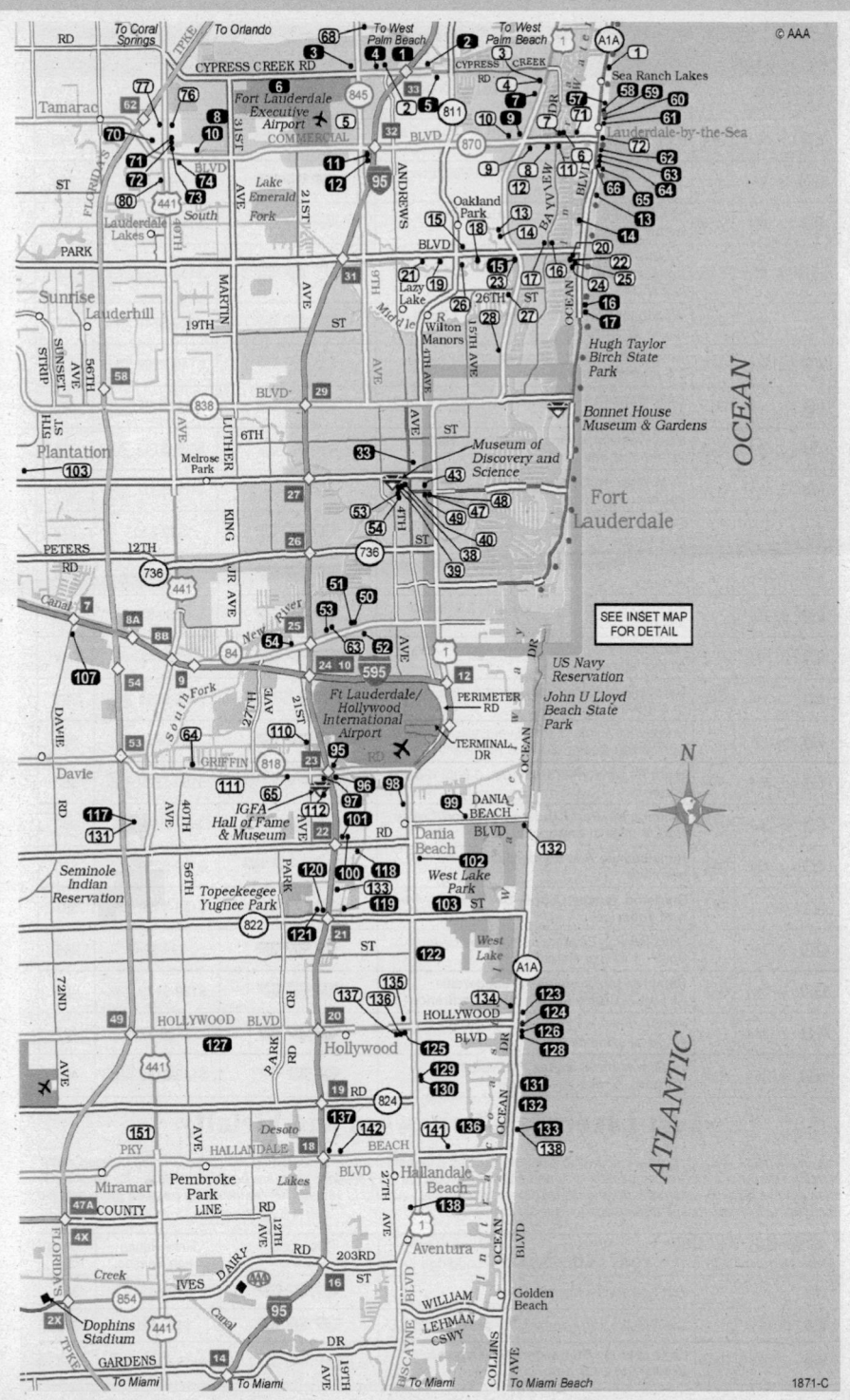

© AAA

1871-C

✈ Airport Accommodations

Spotter/Map Page Number	OA	FORT LAUDERDALE-HOLLYWOOD INT'L	Diamond Rating	Rate Range High Season	Listing Page
97 / p. 364	AAA	Courtyard by Marriott Airport & Cruise Port, 2.5 mi s of entrance	▽▽▽	$159-$219 SAVE	398
100 / p. 364		Hilton Garden Inn Ft. Lauderdale/Hollywood Airport, 3 mi s of entrance	▽▽▽	$169-$209	399
96 / p. 364	AAA	Sheraton Fort Lauderdale Airport Hotel, 2 mi sw of entrance	▽▽▽	$150-$309 SAVE	399
101 / p. 364	AAA	SpringHill Suites by Marriott Fort Lauderdale Airport & Cruise Port, 3 mi s of entrance	▽▽▽	$139-$159 SAVE	399
95 / p. 364	AAA	Wyndham Fort Lauderdale Airport Hotel, 2 mi sw of entrance	▽▽▽	$189-$249 SAVE	400
49 / p. 364	AAA	AmeriSuites (Fort Lauderdale/17th Street), 2.6 mi n of entrance	▽▽▽	$149-$169 SAVE	374
51 / p. 364	AAA	Best Western Fort Lauderdale Inn, 3.5 mi n of entrance	▽▽	$89-$159 SAVE	375
47 / p. 364	AAA	Best Western Marina Inn & Yacht Harbor, 3.2 mi n of entrance	▽▽▽	$139-$149 SAVE	375
39 / p. 364	AAA	Best Western-Oceanside Inn, 4 mi n of entrance	▽▽▽	$169-$209 SAVE	376
48 / p. 364		Comfort Suites Airport & Cruise Port, 1.8 mi n of entrance	▼▼▼	$99-$209	378
46 / p. 364		Embassy Suites-Fort Lauderdale, 2.3 mi n of entrance	▼▼▼	$229-$299	379
42 / p. 364		Fort Lauderdale Marina Marriott, 2.9 mi n of entrance	▼▼▼	$159-$389	380
50 / p. 364		Hampton Inn Fort Lauderdale Airport North, 3.5 mi n of entrance	▼▼▼	$143	381
40 / p. 364	AAA	Harbor Beach Marriott Resort & Spa, 4 mi n of entrance	▽▽▽▽	$399-$599 SAVE	381
45 / p. 364		Holiday Inn Express Port Everglades Cruise & Convention Center, 2.5 mi n of entrance	▼▼▼	$139-$159	382
41 / p. 364	AAA	Hyatt Regency Pier Sixty Six, 3.2 mi n of entrance	▽▽▽▽	$165-$279 SAVE	382
54 / p. 364	AAA	Ramada Inn-Fort Lauderdale Airport/Cruise Port, 2 mi n of entrance	▽▽	$95-$124 SAVE	385
44 / p. 364	AAA	Renaissance Fort Lauderdale, 2.6 mi n of entrance	▽▽▽▽	$199-$259 SAVE	386
38 / p. 364	AAA	Sheraton Yankee Clipper Beach Hotel, 4 mi n of entrance	▽▽▽	$189-$329 SAVE	387
120 / p. 364		Days Inn Fort Lauderdale/Hollywood Airport South, 4 mi s of entrance	▼▼▼	$99-$249	405
118 / p. 364	AAA	Hampton Inn & Suites-Ft. Lauderdale Airport & Cruise Port, 3 mi s of entrance	▽▽▽	$129-$179 SAVE	407
121 / p. 364		Holiday Inn Fort Lauderdale/Hollywood Airport, 4 mi s of entrance	▼▼▼	$129-$299	407
119 / p. 364	AAA	La Quinta Inn & Suites Ft. Lauderdale (Airport), 4 mi s of entrance	▽▽▽	$149-$169 SAVE	408

Fort Lauderdale/Hollywood and Vicinity

This index helps you "spot" where approved accommodations and restaurants are located on the corresponding detailed maps. Lodging rate ranges are for comparison only and show the property's high season; rates are per night, unless only weekly (W) rates are available. Restaurant rate range is for dinner, unless only lunch (L) is served. Turn to the listing page for more detailed rate information and consult display ads for special promotions.

Spotter/Map Page Number	OA	FORT LAUDERDALE - Lodgings	Diamond Rating	Rate Range High Season	Listing Page
1 / p. 364		Fort Lauderdale Marriott North	▼▼▼	$129-$349	380
2 / p. 364		The Westin, Fort Lauderdale - see color ad p 8	▼▼▼	$169-$209	389
3 / p. 364	AAA	La Quinta Inn Ft. Lauderdale (Cypress Creek/I-95) - see color ad p 384	▽▽▽	$115-$130 SAVE	384

Spotter/Map Page Number	OA	FORT LAUDERDALE - Lodgings (continued)	Diamond Rating	Rate Range High Season	Listing Page
4 / p. 364		Sheraton Suites Cypress Creek	▽▽▽	$169	387
5 / p. 364		Hampton Inn	▽▽▽	$99-$149	380
6 / p. 364		Courtyard by Marriott Fort Lauderdale North Cypress Creek	▽▽▽	$69-$179	378
7 / p. 364		Fairfield Inn by Marriott-Ft Lauderdale North	▽▽▽	$129-$159	379
8 / p. 364		TownePlace Suites by Marriott - see color ad p 388	▽▽▽	$149-$199	388
9 / p. 364		Courtyard by Marriott, Fort Lauderdale East	▽▽▽	$139-$189	378
10 / p. 364	ⒶⒶⒶ	**Comfort Inn**	▽▽	$79-$209 SAVE	377
11 / p. 364		El Palacio Sports Hotel & Conference Center	▽▽▽	$89-$129	379
12 / p. 364		Red Roof Inn	▽▽	$65-$85	385
13 / p. 364		Ramada Plaza Beach Resort	▽▽▽	$189-$239	385
14 / p. 364	ⒶⒶⒶ	**Fort Lauderdale Beach Palace Hotel & Suites**	▽▽	$89-$129 SAVE	380
15 / p. 364	ⒶⒶⒶ	**Best Western Oakland Park Inn**	▽▽▽	$99-$159 SAVE	376
16 / p. 364	ⒶⒶⒶ	**Ireland's Inn Beach Resort -** see color ad p 383	▽▽▽	$149-$262 SAVE	383
17 / p. 364	ⒶⒶⒶ	**Best Western Pelican Beach Resort -** see color ad p 377	▽▽▽	$239-$559 SAVE	376
18 / p. 364	ⒶⒶⒶ	**By-Eddy Apartment Motel**	▽	$70-$80 SAVE	377
19 / p. 364		The Doubletree Guest Suites/Fort Lauderdale Galleria	▽▽▽	$189-$369	379
20 / p. 364	ⒶⒶⒶ	**Holiday Inn Ft. Lauderdale Beach -** see color ad p 382	▽▽▽	$159-$249 SAVE	382
21 / p. 364	ⒶⒶⒶ	**Tropi Rock Resort**	▽▽▽	$96-$178 SAVE	389
22 / p. 364		Sans Souci Hotel	▽▽	$89-$200	387
23 / p. 364		Birch Patio Motel	▽▽	$75-$140	376
24 / p. 364	ⒶⒶⒶ	**Sea Club Resort**	▽▽	$90-$350 SAVE	387
25 / p. 364		The Atlantic	▽▽▽▽	$609	374
26 / p. 364	ⒶⒶⒶ	**Royal Saxon Apartments**	▽▽	$65-$175 SAVE	386
27 / p. 364		Sea Chateau Resort Motel	▽	$65-$100	387
28 / p. 364		Angela's Beach Resort	▽▽	$89-$230	374
29 / p. 364	ⒶⒶⒶ	**Ft. Lauderdale Waterfront Inns Beach Resort**	▽▽	$130-$299 SAVE	380
30 / p. 364		Flying Cloud Motel	▽▽	$95-$135	379
31 / p. 364	ⒶⒶⒶ	**Sheraton Yankee Trader Beach Hotel -** see color ad p 8	▽▽▽	$189-$329 SAVE	387
32 / p. 364		Ocean Holiday Motel	▽▽	$85-$200	385
33 / p. 364		Hampton Inn Fort Lauderdale Downtown City Center	▽▽▽	$179-$219	381
34 / p. 364	ⒶⒶⒶ	**Riverside Hotel -** see color ad p 386	▽▽▽	$199-$295 SAVE	386
35 / p. 364		Fort Lauderdale Oceanfront Hotel	▽▽▽	$119-$299	380
36 / p. 364	ⒶⒶⒶ	**Bahia Mar Beach Resort & Yachting Center**	▽▽▽	$179-$229 SAVE	375
37 / p. 364	ⒶⒶⒶ	**Days Inn Bahia Cabana Beach Resort & Marina**	▽▽	$159 SAVE	379
38 / p. 364	ⒶⒶⒶ	**Sheraton Yankee Clipper Beach Hotel -** see color ad p 8	▽▽▽	$189-$329 SAVE	387
39 / p. 364	ⒶⒶⒶ	**Best Western-Oceanside Inn -** see color ad p 376	▽▽▽	$169-$209 SAVE	376

Spotter/Map Page Number	OA	FORT LAUDERDALE - Lodgings (continued)	Diamond Rating	Rate Range High Season	Listing Page
40 / p. 364	AAA	**Harbor Beach Marriott Resort & Spa** - see color ad p 381	◆◆◆◆	$399-$599 SAVE	381
41 / p. 364	AAA	**Hyatt Regency Pier Sixty Six** - see color ad p 382	◆◆◆◆	$165-$279 SAVE	382
42 / p. 364		Fort Lauderdale Marina Marriott	◆◆◆	$159-$389	380
43 / p. 364	AAA	**Lago Mar Resort & Club**	◆◆◆◆	$285-$580 SAVE	383
44 / p. 364	AAA	**Renaissance Fort Lauderdale** - see color ad p 386	◆◆◆◆	$199-$259 SAVE	386
45 / p. 364		Holiday Inn Express Port Everglades Cruise & Convention Center	◆◆◆	$139-$159	382
46 / p. 364		Embassy Suites-Fort Lauderdale	◆◆◆	$229-$299	379
47 / p. 364	AAA	**Best Western Marina Inn & Yacht Harbor** - see color ad p 375	◆◆◆	$139-$149 SAVE	375
48 / p. 364		Comfort Suites Airport & Cruise Port - see color ad p 378	◆◆◆	$99-$209	378
49 / p. 364	AAA	**AmeriSuites (Fort Lauderdale/17th Street)**	◆◆◆	$149-$169 SAVE	374
50 / p. 364		Hampton Inn Fort Lauderdale Airport North	◆◆◆	$143	381
51 / p. 364	AAA	**Best Western Fort Lauderdale Inn**	◆◆◆	$89-$159 SAVE	375
52 / p. 364	AAA	**Holiday Inn Express Hotel & Suites**	◆◆◆	$129-$159 SAVE	381
53 / p. 364		Motel 6 - Ft. Lauderdale #55	◆	$59-$75	384
54 / p. 364	AAA	**Ramada Inn-Fort Lauderdale Airport/Cruise Port** - see color ad p 385	◆◆◆	$95-$124 SAVE	385
		FORT LAUDERDALE - Restaurants			
1 / p. 364		Sea Watch Restaurant	◆◆	$15-$31	394
2 / p. 364		Moonlite Diner	◆	$9-$17	393
3 / p. 364		Buca di Beppo	◆◆	$14-$25	390
4 / p. 364		Sagami Japanese Restaurant	◆◆	$8-$25	394
5 / p. 364		Sonny's Real Pit Bar-B-Q	◆	$8-$15	394
6 / p. 364		Andre's Steakhouse	◆◆	$16-$35	389
7 / p. 364		Umberto's of Long Island Pizza & Restaurant	◆◆	$6-$20	395
8 / p. 364	AAA	**Eduardo de San Angel**	◆◆◆	$19-$32	391
9 / p. 364		Chuck's Steak House	◆◆	$12-$28	391
10 / p. 364		Big Louie's Italian Restaurant	◆	$4-$14	389
11 / p. 364		The Ambry	◆◆	$14-$31	389
12 / p. 364		Ferdo's Grill	◆◆	$8-$18	391
13 / p. 364		Mai-Kai Restaurant	◆◆	$18-$32	393
14 / p. 364		Kyojin Japanese Seafood Buffet	◆◆	$16-$18	392
15 / p. 364		By Word of Mouth	◆◆◆	$20-$30	390
16 / p. 364		Las Vegas	◆◆	$9-$12	392
17 / p. 364	AAA	**Rainbow Palace**	◆◆◆◆	$19-$51	393
18 / p. 364		Food Lovers American Cafe	◆◆	$13-$25	391
19 / p. 364	AAA	**Primavera Restaurant**	◆◆◆	$16-$30	393
20 / p. 364		J's Waterfront Grille	◆◆◆	$15-$34	392
21 / p. 364		Jack's Bar-B-Q Smokehouse	◆	$6-$18	392
22 / p. 364		Shooters Waterfront Cafe USA	◆◆	$7-$23	394
23 / p. 364		Gauchos Steak House	◆◆	$24	391

Spotter/Map Page Number	OA	FORT LAUDERDALE - Restaurants (continued)	Diamond Rating	Rate Range High Season	Listing Page
24 / p. 364		Charley's Crab	◆◆◆	$12-$34	390
25 / p. 364		Black Orchid Cafe	◆◆◆	$15-$40	390
26 / p. 364		Gibby's Steaks & Seafood	◆◆	$17-$30	391
27 / p. 364		Ruth's Chris Steak House	◆◆◆	$23-$38	394
28 / p. 364		Try My Thai Cafe Too	◆◆	$9-$17	395
29 / p. 364		Fuddruckers, World's Greatest Burgers	◆	$6-$12	391
30 / p. 364		Casa D' Angelo	◆◆◆	$12-$36	390
31 / p. 364		Jade Palace Chinese Cuisine Restaurant	◆◆	$8-$19	392
32 / p. 364		Seasons 52	◆◆◆	$8-$22	394
33 / p. 364		Red Star Tavern	◆◆	$9-$25	393
34 / p. 364		Big Louie's Italian Restaurant	◆	$5-$13	389
35 / p. 364		Canyon Southwest Cafe	◆◆◆	$19-$39	390
36 / p. 364		Trina Restaurant & Lounge	◆◆◆◆	$19-$38	395
37 / p. 364		Casablanca Cafe	◆◆	$11-$19	390
38 / p. 364		TarponBend Food & Tackle	◆◆	$6-$19	394
39 / p. 364		Himmarshee Bar & Grille	◆◆◆	$13-$27	392
40 / p. 364		Creolina's Cuisine	◆◆	$12-$21	391
41 / p. 364		Chima Steakhouse	◆◆◆	$44	391
42 / p. 364		Louie Louie Italian Bistro	◆◆	$10-$25	393
43 / p. 364		Brasserie Las Olas	◆◆	$12-$28	390
44 / p. 364		Mancini's Restaurant	◆◆◆	$15-$36	393
45 / p. 364		Johnny V Restaurant/Lounge	◆◆◆	$22-$38	392
46 / p. 364		Floridian Restaurant	◆	$8-$16	391
47 / p. 364		Timpano Italian Chophouse	◆◆◆	$9-$30	394
48 / p. 364		Jackson's Steakhouse	◆◆◆	$16-$36	392
49 / p. 364		Samba Room	◆◆◆	$18-$28	394
50 / p. 364		Cheesecake Factory	◆◆◆	$8-$25	390
51 / p. 364	AAA	**The Grill Room on Las Olas - see color ad p 386**	◆◆◆◆	$20-$40	392
52 / p. 364		Mark's Las Olas	◆◆◆◆	$17-$36	393
53 / p. 364		The River House	◆◆◆	$12-$28	393
54 / p. 364	AAA	**Shirttail Charlie's Restaurant**	◆◆	$10-$22	394
55 / p. 364		3030 Ocean	◆◆◆	$25-$40	389
56 / p. 364		Tom Jenkins Bar-B-Q	◆	$5-$18	395
57 / p. 364		Grille 66 and Bar	◆◆◆	$15-$49	392
58 / p. 364		Bistro 17 - see color ad p 386	◆◆◆	$17-$30	389
59 / p. 364		Bimini Boatyard Bar & Grill	◆◆	$12-$30	389
60 / p. 364		Chuck's Steak House	◆◆	$12-$28	391
61 / p. 364		Carlos & Pepe's 17th Street Cantina	◆	$8-$18	390
62 / p. 364		Cafe Del Rio	◆◆	$9-$19	390
63 / p. 364		Lil' Red's Cookin	◆	$5-$14	393
64 / p. 364		Royal India	◆◆	$9-$16	394

Spotter/Map Page Number	OA	FORT LAUDERDALE - Restaurants (continued)	Diamond Rating	Rate Range High Season	Listing Page
65 / p. 364		Tropical Acres Restaurant	▽▽	$11-$17	395
		LAUDERDALE-BY-THE-SEA - Lodgings			
57 / p. 364	AAA	Clarion Lauderdale Beach Resort - see color ad p 413	▽▽▽	$169-$249 SAVE	412
58 / p. 364	AAA	Tropic Seas Resort - see color ad p 388	▽▽	$200-$300	414
59 / p. 364		Great Escape Motel	▽▽	$80-$150	412
60 / p. 364	AAA	A Little Inn By The Sea - see color ad p 384	▽▽▽	$139-$189 SAVE	412
61 / p. 364		Blue Seas Courtyard	▽▽	$120-$136	412
62 / p. 364	AAA	Courtyard Villa On The Ocean - see color ad p 378	▽▽▽	$179-$272 SAVE	412
63 / p. 364	AAA	Sea Spray Inn	▽▽▽	$80-$185 SAVE	414
64 / p. 364	AAA	Buena Vista Hotel & Conference Center - see color ad p 378	▽▽▽	$149-$239 SAVE	412
65 / p. 364	AAA	Holiday Inn-Lauderdale-By-The-Sea North Beach	▽▽▽	$159-$179 SAVE	412
66 / p. 364		Sea Lord Hotel & Suites	▽▽▽	$145-$275	413
		LAUDERDALE-BY-THE-SEA - Restaurants			
71 / p. 364		Blue Moon Fish Co.	▽▽▽▽	$25-$36	414
72 / p. 364		Aruba Beach Cafe	▽▽	$5-$22	414
		TAMARAC - Lodgings			
69 / p. 364	AAA	Comfort Suites Sawgrass	▽▽▽	$109-$299 SAVE	424
70 / p. 364	AAA	Hampton Inn, Commercial Blvd	▽▽▽	$129-$179 SAVE	425
71 / p. 364		Ramada Plaza Hotel	▽▽	Failed to provide	425
72 / p. 364	AAA	Wellesley Inn (Ft. Lauderdale/Tamarac)	▽▽	$59-$79 SAVE	425
73 / p. 364		Homestead Studio Suites Hotel-Ft Lauderdale/Tamarac	▽▽	$59-$84	425
74 / p. 364	AAA	Baymont Inn & Suites Ft. Lauderdale	▽▽	$89-$109 SAVE	424
		TAMARAC - Restaurants			
75 / p. 364		Char-Hut of Nob Hill	▽	$3-$10	425
76 / p. 364		G G's of New York Italian Restaurant	▽	$9-$22	425
77 / p. 364		Hong Kong City BBQ	▽▽	$7-$25	425
		SUNRISE - Lodgings			
77 / p. 364	AAA	Hilton Fort Lauderdale Sunrise	▽▽▽	$139-$169 SAVE	423
78 / p. 364		Crowne Plaza Fort Lauderdale Hotel at Sawgrass Mills	▽▽▽	$184-$314	423
79 / p. 364	AAA	Baymont Inn & Suites Sunrise at Sawgrass - see color ad p 560	▽▽▽	$109-$129 SAVE	423
80 / p. 364	AAA	Wellesley Inn & Suites (Sunrise)	▽▽	$109-$159 SAVE	423
		SUNRISE - Restaurants			
89 / p. 364		Emerald Coast	▽▽	$19	424
90 / p. 364		Rio Vista Isle Cafe	▽▽	$11-$25	424
91 / p. 364		La Stella South	▽▽	$13-$26	424
92 / p. 364		Char-Hut of Sunrise	▽	$3-$10	424
93 / p. 364		Legal Sea Foods	▽▽	$14-$30	424
94 / p. 364	AAA	Mario the Baker Italian Restaurant & Pizza	▽▽	$6-$13	424

Spotter/Map Page Number	OA	PLANTATION - Lodgings	Diamond Rating	Rate Range High Season	Listing Page
83 / p. 364		Holiday Inn Plantation/Sawgrass	◆◆◆	$99-$149	418
84 / p. 364	AAA	**Staybridge Suites Ft Lauderdale-Plantation**	◆◆◆	$154-$219 SAVE	419
85 / p. 364		Residence Inn by Marriott-Ft. Lauderdale/Plantation	◆◆◆	Failed to provide	418
86 / p. 364	AAA	**Sheraton Suites-Plantation** - see color ad p 8	◆◆◆	$299-$700 SAVE	419
87 / p. 364		AmeriSuites Plantation	◆◆◆	$119-$149	417
88 / p. 364		Hampton Inn Plantation	◆◆◆	$139-$159	418
89 / p. 364	AAA	**Wellesley Inn (Plantation)**	◆◆	$109-$169 SAVE	419
90 / p. 364	AAA	**Courtyard by Marriott**	◆◆	$209 SAVE	418
91 / p. 364	AAA	**La Quinta Inn & Suites Ft. Lauderdale (Plantation)** - see color ad p 384	◆◆◆	$129-$149 SAVE	418
92 / p. 364		Renaissance Ft. Lauderdale/Plantation Hotel	◆◆◆◆	$199-$499	418
		PLANTATION - Restaurants			
97 / p. 364		Al-Salan Middle East Restaurant	◆◆	$8-$15	419
98 / p. 364		Jalapenos Mexican Kitchen	◆◆	$9-$14	420
99 / p. 364		Caspian Persian Grill	◆◆	$11-$17	419
100 / p. 364		Fuddruckers, World's Greatest Hamburgers	◆	$5-$13	419
101 / p. 364		The Original Steakhouse & Sports Theatre	◆◆	$9-$23	420
102 / p. 364		Bonefish Grill	◆◆◆	$14-$25	419
103 / p. 364		Takeyama	◆◆	$11-$30	420
104 / p. 364		Grapevine Gourmet Cuisine	◆◆	$7-$12(L)	420
105 / p. 364		Smokey Bones	◆◆	$7-$21	420
106 / p. 364		Grumpy Dick's Seafood Grill & Bar	◆◆	$8-$23	420
107 / p. 364		Bin 595	◆◆◆	$15-$34	419
		DANIA BEACH - Lodgings			
95 / p. 364	AAA	**Wyndham Fort Lauderdale Airport Hotel**	◆◆◆	$189-$249 SAVE	400
96 / p. 364	AAA	**Sheraton Fort Lauderdale Airport Hotel -** see color ad p 8	◆◆◆	$150-$309 SAVE	399
97 / p. 364	AAA	**Courtyard by Marriott Airport & Cruise Port**	◆◆◆	$159-$219 SAVE	398
98 / p. 364	AAA	**Luckey's Motel**	◆◆	$69-$169 SAVE	399
99 / p. 364		Motel 6 - Dania Beach #376	◆	$51-$70	399
100 / p. 364		Hilton Garden Inn Ft. Lauderdale/Hollywood Airport	◆◆◆	$169-$209	399
101 / p. 364	AAA	**SpringHill Suites by Marriott Fort Lauderdale Airport & Cruise Port**	◆◆◆	$139-$159 SAVE	399
102 / p. 364		Super 8 Motel	◆◆	$109-$190	399
103 / p. 364	AAA	**Sleep Inn & Suites**	◆◆◆	$109-$249 SAVE	399
		DANIA BEACH - Restaurants			
110 / p. 364	AAA	**Rustic Inn Crabhouse**	◆◆	$12-$30	400
111 / p. 364		Le Petit Cafe	◆◆	$8-$20	400
112 / p. 364		Islamorada Fish Company	◆◆	$5-$21	400
		DAVIE - Lodgings			
106 / p. 364		Homestead Studio Suites Hotel-Plantation/Davie	◆◆	$69-$104	400

Spotter/Map Page Number	OA	DAVIE - Lodgings (continued)	Diamond Rating	Rate Range High Season	Listing Page
107 / p. 364	⚫	Comfort Suites Fort Lauderdale Airport West	◈◈◈	$129-$179 [SAVE]	400
		DAVIE - Restaurants			
115 / p. 364		Char-Hut 84	◈	$3-$10	401
116 / p. 364		Davie Ale House	◈	$7-$13	401
117 / p. 364		Sonny's Real Pit Bar-B-Q	◈	$8-$15	401
118 / p. 364		Buca di Beppo	◈◈	$14-$25	401
119 / p. 364		Geronimo's Casual Gourmet Grill & Bar	◈◈	$9-$18	401
120 / p. 364		Bob Gilbert's Kansas City Seafood & Steakhouse Restaurant	◈◈	$12-$32	401
121 / p. 364		Shorty's Bar-B-Q	◈	$5-$14	401
		WESTON - Lodgings			
110 / p. 364	⚫	Wyndham Resort & Golden Door Spa at Weston	◈◈◈	$119-$250 [SAVE]	426
111 / p. 364		TownePlace Suites by Marriott Weston	◈◈◈	$69-$209	426
112 / p. 364	⚫	AmeriSuites (Ft. Lauderdale/Weston)	◈◈◈	$135-$199 [SAVE]	426
113 / p. 364	⚫	Courtyard by Marriott Weston	◈◈◈	$89-$239 [SAVE]	426
114 / p. 364		Residence Inn by Marriott Weston	◈◈◈	$179-$249	426
		WESTON - Restaurants			
124 / p. 364		Japan Inn	◈◈	$11-$25	427
125 / p. 364	⚫	East City Grill	◈◈◈	$20-$35	426
126 / p. 364		Tarpon Bend Food & Tackle	◈◈	$5-$17	427
127 / p. 364		IL Toscano	◈◈◈	$11-$30	427
128 / p. 364		Flanigan's Seafood Bar & Restaurant	◈◈	$6-$18	427
		HOLLYWOOD - Lodgings			
117 / p. 364	⚫	Seminole Hard Rock Hotel & Casino Hollywood	◈◈◈◈	$229-$349 [SAVE]	409
118 / p. 364	⚫	Hampton Inn & Suites-Ft. Lauderdale Airport & Cruise Port - see color ad p 406	◈◈◈	$129-$179 [SAVE]	407
119 / p. 364	⚫	La Quinta Inn & Suites Ft. Lauderdale (Airport) - see color ad p 384	◈◈◈	$149-$169 [SAVE]	408
120 / p. 364		Days Inn Fort Lauderdale/Hollywood Airport South	◈◈◈	$99-$249	405
121 / p. 364		Holiday Inn Fort Lauderdale/Hollywood Airport	◈◈◈	$129-$299	407
122 / p. 364		Econo Lodge	◈◈	$79-$139	406
123 / p. 364	⚫	Villa Sinclair Beach Suites & Spa - see color ad p 410	◈◈◈	$190-$350 [SAVE]	410
124 / p. 364	⚫	Ramada Inn Hollywood Beach Resort - see color ad p 408	◈◈◈	$189-$209 [SAVE]	408
125 / p. 364		Ramada Plaza Hotel	◈◈◈	$99-$199	409
126 / p. 364	⚫	Sandy Shores Motel & Family Lodging	◈	$75-$95 [SAVE]	409
127 / p. 364	⚫	Econo Lodge Inn & Suites Hollywood Blvd - see color ad p 406	◈◈◈	$59-$199 [SAVE]	406
128 / p. 364		Hollywood By The Sea Bed & Breakfast	◈◈◈	Failed to provide	408
129 / p. 364	⚫	Shell Motel - see color ad p 410	◈◈	$45-$95 [SAVE]	410
130 / p. 364	⚫	Richards Motel - see color ad p 409	◈	$36-$79 [SAVE]	409
131 / p. 364	⚫	Greenbríar Beach Club	◈◈	$129-$329	406
132 / p. 364	⚫	Holiday Inn Hollywood Beach	◈◈◈	$149-$289 [SAVE]	407

Spotter/Map Page Number	OA	HOLLYWOOD - Lodgings (continued)	Diamond Rating	Rate Range High Season	Listing Page
133 / p. 364	AAA	**The Westin Diplomat Resort & Spa -** see color ad p 8	◆◆◆◆	$450-$540 SAVE	410
		HOLLYWOOD - Restaurants			
131 / p. 364		The Council Oak	◆◆◆	$25-$45	411
132 / p. 364		Martha's on the Intracoastal	◆◆◆	$15-$30	411
133 / p. 364		Hollywood Ale House & Raw Bar	◆	$6-$11	411
134 / p. 364		Giorgio's Grill	◆◆◆	$12-$30	411
135 / p. 364		Universe Cafe	◆◆	$7-$18	411
136 / p. 364		Try My Thai Cafe	◆◆	$9-$19	411
137 / p. 364		Sushi Blues Cafe	◆◆	$9-$28	411
138 / p. 364	AAA	**Hollywood Prime**	◆◆◆◆	$24-$42	411
		HALLANDALE BEACH - Lodgings			
136 / p. 364	AAA	**The Diplomat Country Club & Spa**	◆◆◆◆	$450-$540 SAVE	405
137 / p. 364	AAA	**Best Western Hallandale**	◆◆◆	$79-$199 SAVE	404
138 / p. 364	AAA	**Hampton Inn - Hallandale/Aventura -** see color ad p 404	◆◆◆	$119-$169 SAVE	405
		HALLANDALE BEACH - Restaurants			
141 / p. 364		Hometown Buffet	◆	$10	405
142 / p. 364		The Dog House	◆	$4-$7(L)	405
		PEMBROKE PINES - Lodgings			
140 / p. 364		Hampton Inn Pembroke Pines	◆◆◆	Failed to provide	417
141 / p. 364	AAA	**Grand Palms Hotel-Spa & Golf Resort**	◆◆◆	$135-$170 SAVE	417
		PEMBROKE PINES - Restaurants			
145 / p. 364		Scruby's B.B.Q.	◆	$6-$19	417
146 / p. 364		Jalapanos Mexican Kitchen	◆◆	$9-$15	417
147 / p. 364		The Roasted Pepper Italian Seafood & Grill	◆◆	$10-$20	417
148 / p. 364		Dragon Gate Chinese Restaurant	◆◆	$8-$19	417
		MIRAMAR - Lodgings			
144 / p. 364		Hilton Garden Inn Ft. Lauderdale SW/Miramar - see color ad p 416	◆◆◆	$149-$199	416
145 / p. 364		Wingate Inn	◆◆◆	$129-$159	416
		MIRAMAR - Restaurant			
151 / p. 364		Sonny's Real Pit Bar-B-Q	◆	$8-$15	416
		POMPANO BEACH - Restaurant			
68 / p. 364		Madras Cafe	◆◆	$10-$20	422
		LAUDERDALE LAKES - Restaurant			
80 / p. 364		Pho Nam Do	◆◆	$5-$9	414
		LAUDERHILL - Restaurants			
83 / p. 364		Makino Japanese Seafood Buffet	◆◆	$16-$18	415
84 / p. 364		Gabose Restaurant	◆◆	$8-$23	414
85 / p. 364		Le Creperie	◆◆◆	$15-$28	414
86 / p. 364		Joe's Crab Shack	◆◆	$9-$21	414

FORT LAUDERDALE pop. 152,397 (See map and index starting on p. 364)

--- WHERE TO STAY ---

AMERISUITES (FORT LAUDERDALE/17TH STREET) *Book at aaa.com* **Phone:** 954/763-7670 **49**

(AAA) [SAVE]
⬥⬥⬥

Small-scale Hotel

1/1-4/30 [ECP]	1P: $149-$169	2P: $149-$169	XP: $10	F18
12/1-12/31 & 5/1-11/30 [ECP]	1P: $119-$129	2P: $119-$129	XP: $10	F18

Location: SR A1A/17th St Cswy, just s. 1851 SE Tenth Ave 33316. Fax: 954/763-6269. **Facility:** 128 one-bedroom standard units. 6 stories, interior corridors. *Bath:* combo or shower only. **Parking:** on-site. **Terms:** pets ($10 fee). **Amenities:** high-speed Internet (fee), voice mail, irons, hair dryers. *Some:* dual phone lines. **Pool(s):** heated outdoor. **Leisure Activities:** exercise room. **Guest Services:** valet and coin laundry, airport transportation-Fort Lauderdale-Hollywood International Airport, area transportation-Port Everglades. **Business Services:** meeting rooms, fax (fee). **Cards:** AX, DC, DS, JC, MC, VI. **Special Amenities:** free full breakfast.

SOME UNITS

✈ 📶 🍴 ⚅M 🗝 ⊘ 🛥 VCR 🐾 DATA PORT 🛢 🖥 ⬛ / ✕ /
FEE

ANGELA'S BEACH RESORT **Phone:** (954)563-7926 **28**

⬥⬥ ⬥⬥

Motel

12/1-5/8	1P: $89-$230	2P: $89-$230	XP: $20	D12
10/2-11/30	1P: $60-$130	2P: $69-$160	XP: $20	D12
5/9-10/1	1P: $52-$130	2P: $52-$140	XP: $20	D12

Location: On SR A1A, 6 blks s of SR 838 (Sunrise Blvd); west corner of Breakers Ave and Windamar St. 3016 Windamar St 33304. **Facility:** Designated smoking area. 19 units. 12 one-bedroom standard units, some with efficiencies. 6 one- and 1 two-bedroom suites ($52-$160) with kitchens. 3 stories (no elevator), exterior corridors. **Parking:** on-site. **Terms:** office hours 10 am-6 pm, 21 day cancellation notice-fee imposed. **Amenities:** *Some:* safes (fee). **Pool(s):** heated outdoor. **Leisure Activities:** sauna. **Guest Services:** coin laundry. **Cards:** AX, MC, VI.

[ASK] 🛥 ✕ 🛢 🖥 ⬛

THE ATLANTIC *Book at aaa.com* **Phone:** (954)567-8020 **25**

⬥⬥⬥⬥ ⬥⬥⬥⬥

Small-scale Hotel

12/1-4/16	1P: $609	2P: $609	XP: $20	F17
4/17-6/1 & 9/28-11/30	1P: $559	2P: $559	XP: $20	F17
6/2-9/27	1P: $459	2P: $459	XP: $20	F17

Location: From Sunrise Blvd (SR 838), 0.5 mi s. Across from the ocean/beach. 601 N Ft. Lauderdale Beach Blvd 33304. Fax: 954/567-8040. **Facility:** This property is located across from the ocean and many of the rooms offer that view; spacious rooms feature a modern decor package. Designated smoking area. 124 units. 60 one-bedroom standard units with efficiencies. 57 one-, 6 two- and 1 three-bedroom suites ($649-$799) with kitchens, some with whirlpools. 16 stories, interior corridors. **Parking:** valet. **Terms:** 3 day cancellation notice-fee imposed, package plans, $18 service charge. **Amenities:** CD players, dual phone lines, voice mail, safes, honor bars, irons, hair dryers. *Fee:* video games, high-speed Internet. *Some:* DVD players, fax. **Dining:** Trina Restaurant & Lounge, see separate listing. **Pool(s):** heated outdoor. **Leisure Activities:** saunas, whirlpools, steamrooms, spa. **Guest Services:** gift shop, valet and coin laundry. **Business Services:** meeting rooms, business center. **Cards:** AX, DC, DS, JC, MC, VI.

[ASK] 🛢S 🅿 ✈ 🍴 24 🍸 🛥 ♿ ✕ ✕ 🐾 DATA PORT 🛢 🖥 ⬛
FEE

(See map and index starting on p. 364)

BAHIA MAR BEACH RESORT & YACHTING CENTER   *Book at aaa.com*   Phone: (954)764-2233   **36**

(AAA) (SAVE)	12/1-4/30	1P: $179-$229	2P: $179-$229	XP: $10 F18
	5/1-9/30	1P: $109-$199	2P: $109-$199	XP: $10 F18
▼▼▼▼	10/1-11/30	1P: $139-$179	2P: $139-$179	XP: $10 F18

Location: SR A1A, 0.5 mi s of Las Olas Blvd. Located across from the beach. 801 Seabreeze Blvd 33316. Large-scale Hotel Fax: 954/523-5424. **Facility:** 296 units. 294 one-bedroom standard units. 2 one-bedroom suites. 16 stories, interior corridors. *Bath:* combo or shower only. **Parking:** on-site (fee) and valet. **Terms:** check-in 4 pm, 3 day cancellation notice-fee imposed, package plans. **Amenities:** dual phone lines, voice mail, safes, honor bars, irons, hair dryers. *Fee:* video games, high-speed Internet. **Dining:** 4 restaurants, 6:30 am-10:30 pm, cocktails. **Pool(s):** heated outdoor. **Leisure Activities:** 4 lighted tennis courts, exercise room. *Fee:* marina, scuba diving, snorkeling, fishing, charter fishing, golf privileges, massage. **Guest Services:** gift shop, valet and coin laundry, water taxi stop. *Fee:* PADI dive instruction. **Business Services:** meeting rooms, business center. **Cards:** AX, DC, DS, MC, VI.

SOME UNITS / FEE

BEST WESTERN FORT LAUDERDALE INN   *Book at aaa.com*   Phone: (954)462-7005   **51**

(AAA) (SAVE)	12/15-4/30 [ECP]	1P: $89-$159	2P: $89-$159	XP: $10 F17
	12/1-12/14 & 5/1-11/30 [ECP]	1P: $79-$109	2P: $79-$109	XP: $10 F17
▼▼▼▼				

Location: I-95, exit 25 (SR 84), 0.7 mi e. 1221 SR 84 33315. Fax: 954/462-5949. **Facility:** 50 one-bedroom Small-scale Hotel standard units. 2 stories, interior corridors. *Bath:* combo or shower only. **Parking:** on-site. **Amenities:** high-speed Internet, dual phone lines, voice mail, irons, hair dryers. **Pool(s):** heated outdoor. **Guest Services:** airport transportation-Fort Lauderdale-Hollywood International Airport, area transportation-Port Everglades & Convention Center. **Business Services:** meeting rooms, fax (fee). **Cards:** AX, CB, DC, DS, JC, MC, VI. **Special Amenities:** free expanded continental breakfast and free local telephone calls.

SOME UNITS /

BEST WESTERN MARINA INN & YACHT HARBOR   *Book at aaa.com*   Phone: (954)525-3484   **47**

(AAA) (SAVE)	1/1-5/8	1P: $139-$149	2P: $139-$149	XP: $10 F18
	12/1-12/31	1P: $119-$129	2P: $119-$129	XP: $10 F18
▼▼▼▼	10/16-11/30	1P: $99-$109	2P: $99-$109	XP: $10 F18
	5/9-10/15	1P: $79-$89	2P: $79-$89	XP: $10 F18

Small-scale Hotel **Location:** SR A1A, 1.2 mi e of US 1 (Federal Hwy). Located across from Port Everglades and convention center. 2150 SE 17th St Cswy 33316. Fax: 954/764-2915. **Facility:** 166 one-bedroom standard units. 4 stories, exterior corridors. *Bath:* combo or shower only. **Parking:** on-site. **Terms:** check-in 4 pm. **Amenities:** voice mail, safes, irons, hair dryers. *Some:* high-speed Internet. **Dining:** 7 am-10 pm, cocktails, entertainment. **Pool(s):** heated outdoor. **Leisure Activities:** whirlpool. *Fee:* marina. **Guest Services:** coin laundry, airport transportation-Fort Lauderdale/Hollywood International Airport, area transportation-Port Everglades & convention center. **Business Services:** fax (fee). **Cards:** AX, DS, MC, VI. **Special Amenities:** free continental breakfast. *(See color ad below)*

SOME UNITS / FEE

(See map and index starting on p. 364)

BEST WESTERN OAKLAND PARK INN *Book at aaa.com*   Phone: (954)565-4601 **15**

(AAA) [SAVE]

▼▼▼▼

Motel

1/1-4/15 [ECP]	1P: $99-$159	2P: $99-$159	XP: $10 F12
12/1-12/31 & 4/16-11/30 [ECP]	1P: $79-$119	2P: $79-$119	XP: $10 F12

Location: US 1 (Federal Hwy), just s of jct SR 816 (Oakland Park Blvd). 3001 N Federal Hwy 33306. **Fax:** 954/565-0384. **Facility:** 105 one-bedroom standard units, some with whirlpools. 3 stories, exterior corridors. **Parking:** on-site. **Terms:** cancellation fee imposed. **Amenities:** safes, irons, hair dryers. *Some:* CD players, high-speed Internet. **Dining:** 11 am-11 pm, cocktails. **Pool(s):** heated outdoor. **Guest Services:** coin laundry. **Business Services:** meeting rooms, fax (fee). **Cards:** AX, DC, DS, MC, VI. **Special Amenities:** free expanded continental breakfast and preferred room (subject to availability with advance reservations).

SOME UNITS

$\boxed{S_D^\bullet}$ ⑪ ⛱ 🏊 ⟨DATA PORT⟩ 🔒 🖥 🖵 / ☒ /

BEST WESTERN-OCEANSIDE INN *Book at aaa.com*   Phone: (954)525-8115 **39**

(AAA) [SAVE]

▼▼▼▼

Small-scale Hotel

12/25-4/30 [BP]	1P: $169-$209	2P: $169-$209	XP: $10 F12
10/1-11/30 [BP]	1P: $109-$209	2P: $109-$209	XP: $10 F12
12/1-12/24 [BP]	1P: $109-$149	2P: $109-$149	XP: $10 F12
5/1-9/30 [BP]	1P: $99-$139	2P: $99-$139	XP: $10 F12

Location: SR A1A, just s of Bahia Mar Marina. 1180 Seabreeze Blvd 33316. **Fax:** 954/527-0957. **Facility:** Designated smoking area. 101 units. 100 one-bedroom standard units. 1 one-bedroom suite. 5 stories, interior corridors. *Bath:* combo or shower only. **Parking:** on-site (fee). **Terms:** 3 day cancellation notice-fee imposed. **Amenities:** high-speed Internet, voice mail, safes (fee), irons, hair dryers. **Dining:** 7 am-10:30 pm, cocktails. **Pool(s):** heated outdoor. **Leisure Activities:** beach access, sun deck. **Guest Services:** valet and coin laundry, area transportation-Port Everglades. **Business Services:** meeting rooms, fax (fee). **Cards:** AX, CB, DC, DS, MC, VI. **Special Amenities:** free full breakfast and free local telephone calls. *(See color ad below)*

$\boxed{S_D^\bullet}$ ✈ ⑪ ⛱ 🏊 ☒ 📷 ⟨DATA PORT⟩ 🔒 🖥 🖵

BEST WESTERN PELICAN BEACH RESORT *Book at aaa.com*   Phone: (954)568-9431 **17**

(AAA) [SAVE]

▼▼▼▼

Large-scale Hotel

12/23-5/7	1P: $239-$559	2P: $239-$559	XP: $10 F12
12/1-12/22 & 5/8-11/30	1P: $130-$399	2P: $130-$399	XP: $10 F12

Location: Oceanfront. On SR A1A, 0.8 mi s of SR 816 (Oakland Park Blvd). 2000 N Atlantic Blvd 33305. **Fax:** 954/565-2622. **Facility:** 180 units. 66 one-bedroom standard units, some with efficiencies. 114 one-bedroom suites. 11 stories, exterior corridors. *Bath:* combo or shower only. **Parking:** valet. **Terms:** 2 night minimum stay - weekends, 14 day cancellation notice-fee imposed. **Amenities:** video games (fee), high-speed Internet, voice mail, safes, irons, hair dryers. *Some:* dual phone lines. **Dining:** 7 am-midnight, cocktails. **Pool(s):** 2 heated outdoor. **Leisure Activities:** lifeguard on duty, limited beach access, fishing, recreation programs, exercise room. *Fee:* paddleboats, sailboats, windsurfing, scuba diving, snorkeling, bicycles, massage, game room. **Guest Services:** gift shop. **Business Services:** meeting rooms, business center. **Cards:** AX, DC, DS, MC, VI. **Special Amenities:** free local telephone calls and free newspaper. *(See color ad p 377)*

SOME UNITS

$\boxed{S_D^\bullet}$ ⑪ ⛱ 🏊 ☒ 📷 ⟨DATA PORT⟩ 🔒 🖥 🖵 / ☒ / VCR /

BIRCH PATIO MOTEL   Phone: (954)563-9540 **23**

◆◆ ◆◆

Motel

12/1-4/15		2P: $75-$140	XP: $10 F12
4/16-11/30		2P: $50-$90	XP: $10 F12

Location: 0.4 mi s on SR A1A from jct SR 838 (Sunrise Blvd), w on Aurumar St. 617 N Birch Rd 33304. **Fax:** 954/563-4037. **Facility:** Designated smoking area. 20 units. 5 one-bedroom standard units. 15 one-bedroom suites, some with efficiencies or kitchens. 1-2 stories (no elevator), exterior corridors. *Bath:* combo or shower only. **Parking:** on-site. **Terms:** office hours 8:30 am-9:30 pm, 5-7 night minimum stay, 28 day cancellation notice-fee imposed, pets ($50 deposit, $10 extra charge). **Pool(s):** heated outdoor. **Leisure Activities:** shuffleboard. **Guest Services:** coin laundry. **Cards:** AX, DS, MC, VI.

SOME UNITS

[ASK] 🛏 🏊 ☒ 🔒 🖵 / 🖥 /
FEE

(See map and index starting on p. 364)

BY-EDDY APARTMENT MOTEL — Phone: 954/764-7555 **18**

(AAA) (SAVE)

12/1-4/17	1P: $70-$80	2P: $70-$80	XP: $8	F12
4/18-5/8	1P: $60-$70	2P: $60-$70	XP: $8	F12
5/9-11/30	1P: $50-$60	2P: $50-$60	XP: $8	F12

Motel **Location:** 0.6 mi w of US 1 (Federal Hwy) and SR 838 (Sunrise Blvd). 1021 NE 13th Ave 33304. Fax: 954/764-7577. **Facility:** 16 one-bedroom standard units, some with kitchens, 2 stories (no elevator), exterior corridors. **Parking:** on-site. **Terms:** 30 day cancellation notice-fee imposed, weekly rates available. **Pool(s):** heated outdoor. **Leisure Activities:** barbecue grills, picnic tables. **Guest Services:** coin laundry. **Cards:** MC, VI. **Special Amenities:** preferred room (subject to availability with advance reservations).

SOME UNITS

COMFORT INN — *Book at aaa.com* — Phone: (954)315-2900 **10**

(AAA) (SAVE)

12/22-4/15	1P: $79-$209	2P: $79-$209	XP: $10	F17
12/1-12/21 & 4/16-11/30	1P: $59-$169	2P: $59-$169	XP: $10	F17

Small-scale Hotel **Location:** SR 870 (Commercial Blvd), 0.9 mi e of Florida Tpke, exit 62; 0.3 mi e of jct SR 7 and US 441. 3551 W Commercial Blvd 33309. Fax: 954/733-1557. **Facility:** 70 one-bedroom standard units, some with whirlpools. 3 stories, interior corridors. *Bath:* combo or shower only. **Parking:** on-site. **Terms:** [ECP] meal plan available. **Amenities:** high-speed Internet, dual phone lines, voice mail, safes (fee), irons, hair dryers. **Pool(s):** small heated outdoor. **Leisure Activities:** whirlpool, exercise room. **Guest Services:** valet and coin laundry. **Business Services:** meeting rooms, business center. **Cards:** AX, CB, DC, DS, JC, MC, VI. **Special Amenities:** free expanded continental breakfast and free local telephone calls.

SOME UNITS

(See map and index starting on p. 364)

COMFORT SUITES AIRPORT & CRUISE PORT   *Book at aaa.com*   Phone: (954)767-8700   **48**

12/22-5/5 [ECP]	1P: $99-$209	2P: $99-$209	XP: $10	F18
12/1-12/21 [ECP]	1P: $79-$159	2P: $79-$159	XP: $10	F18
5/6-11/30 [ECP]	1P: $69-$159	2P: $69-$159	XP: $10	F18

Small-scale Hotel   **Location:** US 1 (Federal Hwy), 0.5 mi s of jct SR A1A. 1800 S Federal Hwy 33316. Fax: 954/767-8629. **Facility:** 111 units. 100 one-bedroom standard units. 11 one-bedroom suites. 7 stories, interior corridors. *Bath:* combo or shower only. **Parking:** on-site. **Terms:** cancellation fee imposed. **Amenities:** high-speed Internet, voice mail, irons, hair dryers. **Pool(s):** heated outdoor. **Guest Services:** valet laundry, area transportation. **Business Services:** meeting rooms, fax (fee). **Cards:** DC, DS, MC, VI. *(See color ad below)*

SOME UNITS
[ASK] [S/D] [+] [T+] [&] [√] [~] [★] [DATA PORT] [■] [▭] / [✕] [▤] /

COURTYARD BY MARRIOTT, FORT LAUDERDALE EAST   *Book at aaa.com*   Phone: (954)771-8100   **9**

1/1-5/6	1P: $139-$189	2P: $139-$189
7/2-11/30	1P: $79-$149	2P: $79-$149
5/7-7/1	1P: $99-$139	2P: $99-$139
12/1-12/31	1P: $75-$135	2P: $75-$135

Small-scale Hotel

Location: US 1 (Federal Hwy), jct SR 870 and Commercial Blvd. 5001 N Federal Hwy 33308. Fax: 954/776-7980. **Facility:** 104 units. 100 one-bedroom standard units. 4 one-bedroom suites. 5 stories, interior corridors. *Bath:* combo or shower only. **Parking:** on-site. **Terms:** [BP] meal plan available, package plans. **Amenities:** high-speed Internet, dual phone lines, voice mail, safes, irons, hair dryers. **Pool(s):** heated outdoor. **Leisure Activities:** whirlpool, exercise room. **Guest Services:** valet and coin laundry. **Business Services:** meeting rooms, fax (fee). **Cards:** AX, CB, DC, DS, JC, MC, VI.

SOME UNITS
[ASK] [S/D] [T+] [Y] [&] [√] [~] [★] [DATA PORT] [■] [▭] / [✕] [▤] /

COURTYARD BY MARRIOTT FORT LAUDERDALE NORTH CYPRESS CREEK   *Book at aaa.com*   Phone: (954)772-7770   **6**

All Year   1P: $69-$179

Small-scale Hotel

Location: I-95, exit 33B, 2.3 mi w; at Fort Lauderdale Executive Airport. 2440 W Cypress Creek Rd 33309. Fax: 954/772-4780. **Facility:** 136 units. 131 one-bedroom standard units. 5 one-bedroom suites. 4 stories, interior corridors. *Bath:* combo or shower only. **Parking:** on-site. **Terms:** cancellation fee imposed, package plans. **Amenities:** high-speed Internet (fee), dual phone lines, voice mail, irons, hair dryers. **Pool(s):** heated outdoor. **Leisure Activities:** whirlpool, exercise room. **Guest Services:** valet and coin laundry. **Business Services:** meeting rooms, fax (fee). **Cards:** AX, DC, DS, MC, VI.

SOME UNITS
[ASK] [S/D] [T+] [Y] [&] [√] [~] [★] [DATA PORT] [▭] / [✕] [■] [▤] /

(See map and index starting on p. 364)

DAYS INN BAHIA CABANA BEACH RESORT &
MARINA *Book at aaa.com* Phone: (954)524-1555 ㊲

	12/16-4/17	1P: $159	2P: $159	XP: $10	F12
	4/18-11/30	1P: $85	2P: $85	XP: $5	F12
	12/1-12/15	1P: $75	2P: $75	XP: $5	F12

Motel
Location: On SR A1A; 0.7 mi s of jct Las Olas Blvd. 3001 Harbor Dr (A1A) 33316. Fax: 954/764-5951. **Facility:** 70 units. 62 one-bedroom standard units, some with efficiencies. 7 one- and 1 two-bedroom suites ($130-$225), some with kitchens. 2-6 stories (no elevator), exterior corridors. *Bath:* combo or shower only. **Parking:** on-site and valet. **Terms:** cancellation fee imposed. **Amenities:** voice mail, safes, hair dryers. **Dining:** 7 am-11 pm, cocktails, entertainment. **Pool(s):** heated outdoor. **Leisure Activities:** whirlpool, beach access. *Fee:* boat dock. **Guest Services:** gift shop. **Business Services:** fax (fee). **Cards:** AX, DC, DS, MC, VI. **Special Amenities:** free newspaper.

THE DOUBLETREE GUEST SUITES/FORT
LAUDERDALE GALLERIA *Book at aaa.com* Phone: (954)565-3800 ⑲

	12/26-4/30	1P: $189-$369	2P: $189-$369	XP: $20	F18
	10/1-11/30	1P: $189-$269	2P: $189-$269	XP: $20	F18
	5/1-9/30	1P: $149-$259	2P: $149-$259	XP: $20	F18

Small-scale Hotel | 12/1-12/25 | 1P: $129-$199 | 2P: $129-$199 | XP: $20 | F18 |
Location: Intracoastal Bridge on SR 838 (Sunrise Blvd); 3 blks w of jct SR A1A. 2670 E Sunrise Blvd 33304. Fax: 954/561-0387. **Facility:** 229 units. 207 one- and 22 two-bedroom suites with kitchens. 14 stories, interior corridors. **Parking:** on-site (fee) and valet. **Terms:** 3 day cancellation notice-fee imposed, [BP], [CP] & [ECP] meal plans available, package plans. **Amenities:** high-speed Internet (fee), dual phone lines, voice mail, irons, hair dryers. **Pool(s):** heated outdoor. **Leisure Activities:** saunas, whirlpool, exercise room. *Fee:* boat dock. **Guest Services:** valet and coin laundry. **Business Services:** meeting rooms, business center. **Cards:** AX, CB, DC, DS, JC, MC, VI.

EL PALACIO SPORTS HOTEL & CONFERENCE
CENTER Phone: (954)776-4880 ⑪

| | 12/1-4/15 | 1P: $89-$129 | 2P: $89-$129 | XP: $10 | F17 |
| | 4/16-11/30 | 1P: $65-$95 | 2P: $69-$95 | XP: $10 | F17 |

Small-scale Hotel **Location:** I-95, exit 32, jct Commercial Blvd and Powerline Rd. 4900 Powerline Rd 33309. Fax: 954/315-9188. **Facility:** 190 one-bedroom standard units. 5 stories, exterior corridors. *Bath:* combo or shower only. **Parking:** on-site. **Terms:** cancellation fee imposed, [AP], [BP] & [CP] meal plans available, $5 service charge. **Amenities:** high-speed Internet, voice mail, safes, irons, hair dryers. *Some:* dual phone lines. **Pool(s):** heated outdoor. **Leisure Activities:** exercise room. **Guest Services:** valet and coin laundry. **Business Services:** meeting rooms, fax (fee). **Cards:** AX, DC, DS, MC, VI.

EMBASSY SUITES-FORT LAUDERDALE *Book at aaa.com* Phone: (954)527-2700 ㊻

	12/1-5/26	1P: $229-$299	XP: $10	F18
	10/1-11/30	1P: $179-$299	XP: $10	F18
	5/27-9/30	1P: $139-$199	XP: $10	F18

Large-scale Hotel **Location:** On SR A1A, just e of jct US 1 (Federal Hwy). 1100 SE 17th St Cswy 33316. Fax: 954/760-7202. **Facility:** 358 one-bedroom suites ($309-$369). 12 stories, interior corridors. *Bath:* combo or shower only. **Parking:** on-site (fee) and valet. **Terms:** 1-2 night minimum stay - seasonal and/or weekends, cancellation fee imposed, small pets only ($25 fee). **Amenities:** dual phone lines, voice mail, irons, hair dryers. *Fee:* video games, high-speed Internet. **Pool(s):** heated outdoor. **Leisure Activities:** sauna, whirlpool, steamroom, exercise room. **Guest Services:** gift shop, complimentary evening beverages, valet and coin laundry. **Business Services:** conference facilities, business center. **Cards:** AX, CB, DC, DS, JC, MC, VI.

FAIRFIELD INN BY MARRIOTT-FT LAUDERDALE
NORTH *Book at aaa.com* Phone: (954)491-2500 ⑦

	12/15-4/15	1P: $129-$159	2P: $129-$159	
	12/1-12/14	1P: $89-$109	2P: $89-$109	
	4/16-11/30	1P: $69-$99	2P: $69-$99	

Small-scale Hotel **Location:** 0.5 mi n on US 1 (Federal Hwy) from SR 870 (Commercial Blvd). 5727 N Federal Hwy 33308. Fax: 954/491-7945. **Facility:** 162 one-bedroom standard units. 2 stories (no elevator), exterior corridors. *Bath:* combo or shower only. **Parking:** on-site. **Terms:** 3 day cancellation notice, [CP] meal plan available. **Amenities:** voice mail, irons, hair dryers. *Some:* high-speed Internet. **Pool(s):** heated outdoor. **Leisure Activities:** whirlpool, exercise room. *Fee:* game room. **Guest Services:** valet and coin laundry. **Business Services:** meeting rooms, fax (fee). **Cards:** AX, CB, DC, DS, JC, MC, VI.

FLYING CLOUD MOTEL Phone: (954)563-7062 ㉚

	12/1-3/15	1P: $95-$135	2P: $95-$135	XP: $10	D18
	3/16-5/31 & 10/1-11/30	1P: $69-$99	2P: $69-$99	XP: $10	D18
	6/1-9/30	1P: $49-$79	2P: $49-$79	XP: $10	D18

Motel **Location:** Just w of SR A1A; between Terramar and Rio Mar sts, 0.5 mi s of SR 838 (Sunrise Blvd). 533 Orton Ave 33304. Fax: 954/563-0463. **Facility:** 26 units. 19 one-bedroom standard units, some with efficiencies. 7 one-bedroom suites with kitchens. 2 stories (no elevator), exterior corridors. *Bath:* combo or shower only. **Parking:** on-site. **Terms:** office hours 9 am-6 pm, 14 day cancellation notice, small pets only ($50 fee). **Amenities:** safes, voice mail. **Pool(s):** heated outdoor. **Guest Services:** coin laundry. **Business Services:** fax (fee). **Cards:** AX, DS, MC, VI.

(See map and index starting on p. 364)

FORT LAUDERDALE BEACH PALACE HOTEL & SUITES *Book at aaa.com*

Phone: 954/563-3400 **14**

(AAA) [SAVE]

| | 12/25-4/16 | 1P: $89-$129 | 2P: $89-$129 | XP: $10 | F |
| | 12/1-12/24 & 4/17-11/30 | 1P: $49-$79 | 2P: $49-$79 | XP: $10 | F |

Motel

Location: SR A1A, 1.1 mi s of Commercial Blvd (SR 870). 3711 N Ocean Blvd 33308. Fax: 954/563-6633. **Facility:** 66 one-bedroom standard units. 4 stories, exterior corridors. **Parking:** on-site. **Terms:** [CP] meal plan available. **Amenities:** safes (fee). **Dining:** 11:30 am-1 am, cocktails. **Pool(s):** heated outdoor. **Guest Services:** coin laundry. **Business Services:** fax (fee). **Cards:** AX, DS, MC, VI.

SOME UNITS

FORT LAUDERDALE MARINA MARRIOTT *Book at aaa.com*

Phone: (954)463-4000 **42**

	1/1-5/28	1P: $159-$389
	10/1-11/30	1P: $159-$279
	12/1-12/31	1P: $119-$259
Large-scale Hotel	5/29-9/30	1P: $129-$229

Location: Located across from Port Everglades and convention center. 1881 SE 17th St 33316. Fax: 954/527-6705. **Facility:** 580 units. 570 one-bedroom standard units. 10 one-bedroom suites. 3-14 stories, interior corridors. *Bath:* combo or shower only. **Parking:** on-site (fee) and valet. **Terms:** check-in 4 pm, 3 day cancellation notice, package plans. **Amenities:** dual phone lines, voice mail, safes, irons, hair dryers. *Fee:* video games, high-speed Internet. *Some:* DVD players, CD players. **Pool(s):** heated outdoor. **Leisure Activities:** saunas, whirlpool, exercise room. *Fee:* marina, charter fishing, massage. **Guest Services:** gift shop, valet and coin laundry, area transportation. **Business Services:** conference facilities, business center. **Cards:** AX, DC, DS, MC, VI.

SOME UNITS

FORT LAUDERDALE MARRIOTT NORTH *Book at aaa.com*

Phone: (954)771-0440 **1**

	12/1-5/26	1P: $129-$349
	9/30-11/30	1P: $109-$209
Large-scale Hotel	5/27-9/29	1P: $89-$189

Location: I-95, exit 33B, just nw; 0.5 mi n of jct Cypress Creek Rd. 6650 N Andrews Ave 33309. Fax: 954/772-9834. **Facility:** 315 units. 311 one-bedroom standard units. 4 one-bedroom suites. 16 stories, interior corridors. *Bath:* combo or shower only. **Parking:** on-site and valet. **Terms:** cancellation fee imposed, package plans. **Amenities:** dual phone lines, voice mail, safes, irons, hair dryers. *Fee:* video games, high-speed Internet. *Some:* honor bars. **Pool(s):** heated outdoor. **Leisure Activities:** sauna, whirlpool, exercise room. **Guest Services:** gift shop, valet and coin laundry, area transportation. **Business Services:** conference facilities, business center. **Cards:** AX, CB, DC, DS, MC, VI.

SOME UNITS

FORT LAUDERDALE OCEANFRONT HOTEL *Book at aaa.com*

Phone: (954)524-8733 **35**

	12/1-4/30	1P: $119-$299	2P: $119-$299	XP: $20	F18
	5/1-5/31	1P: $99-$179	2P: $99-$179	XP: $20	F18
Large-scale Hotel	6/1-11/30	1P: $79-$139	2P: $79-$139	XP: $20	F18

Location: SR A1A, just s of Las Olas Blvd. 440 Seabreeze Blvd 33316. Fax: 954/467-7489. **Facility:** 230 units. 224 one-bedroom standard units, some with whirlpools. 6 one-bedroom suites with whirlpools. 12 stories, interior corridors. *Bath:* combo or shower only. **Parking:** valet. **Amenities:** voice mail, irons, hair dryers. *Fee:* video games, high-speed Internet. **Pool(s):** heated outdoor. **Leisure Activities:** whirlpool, exercise room. **Guest Services:** valet laundry. **Business Services:** meeting rooms, business center. **Cards:** AX, CB, DC, DS, JC, MC, VI.

SOME UNITS
FEE

FT. LAUDERDALE WATERFRONT INNS BEACH RESORT *Book at aaa.com*

Phone: 954/564-4341 **29**

(AAA) [SAVE]

	12/24-5/12	1P: $130-$299	2P: $130-$299	XP: $10	F12
	12/1-12/23 & 10/26-11/30	1P: $109-$199	2P: $109-$199	XP: $10	F12
	5/13-10/25	1P: $89-$169	2P: $89-$169	XP: $10	F12

Motel

Location: 0.5 mi s of SR 838 (Sunrise Blvd), on SR A1A; corner of Atlantic Blvd and Viramar St. 521 Fort Lauderdale Beach Blvd 33304. Fax: 954/565-9564. **Facility:** Designated smoking area. 59 units. 47 one-bedroom standard units, some with efficiencies. 11 one- and 1 two-bedroom units with kitchens. 3 stories (no elevator), exterior corridors. *Bath:* combo or shower only. **Parking:** on-site. **Terms:** 2-3 night minimum stay - weekends, 3 day cancellation notice, package plans. **Amenities:** voice mail, irons, hair dryers. *Some:* safes. **Pool(s):** 2 heated outdoor. **Leisure Activities:** beach access, barbecue grills, exercise room, shuffleboard. *Fee:* bicycles. **Guest Services:** coin laundry. **Business Services:** fax (fee). **Cards:** AX, CB, DC, DS, JC, MC, VI. **Special Amenities:** free continental breakfast and free newspaper.

SOME UNITS

HAMPTON INN *Book at aaa.com*

Phone: (954)776-7677 **5**

| | 12/1-4/30 | 1P: $99-$149 |
| Small-scale Hotel | 5/1-11/30 | 1P: $89-$109 |

Location: I-95, exit 33 southbound, 0.5 mi e; exit 33A northbound, then e. 720 E Cypress Creek Rd 33334. Fax: 954/776-0805. **Facility:** 122 one-bedroom standard units. 4 stories, interior corridors. *Bath:* combo or shower only. **Parking:** on-site. **Amenities:** high-speed Internet, voice mail, irons, hair dryers. **Pool(s):** outdoor. **Leisure Activities:** whirlpool, exercise room. **Guest Services:** valet laundry. **Business Services:** meeting rooms, fax (fee). **Cards:** AX, CB, DC, DS, JC, MC, VI.

SOME UNITS
FEE FEE

(See map and index starting on p. 364)

HAMPTON INN FORT LAUDERDALE AIRPORT
NORTH   *Book at aaa.com*   Phone: 954/524-9900   50

1/1-4/30	1P: $143	2P: $143
12/1-12/31	1P: $107	2P: $107
5/1-11/30	1P: $99	2P: $99

Small-scale Hotel   **Location:** I-95, exit 25 (SR 84), 0.7 mi e to SW 12th Ave, then just n. Located in a quiet area. 2301 SW 12th Ave 33315. Fax: 954/524-5155. **Facility:** 108 one-bedroom standard units. 5 stories, interior corridors. *Bath:* combo or shower only. **Parking:** on-site. **Terms:** package plans, small pets only. **Amenities:** high-speed Internet, dual phone lines, voice mail, irons, hair dryers. **Pool(s):** outdoor. **Leisure Activities:** limited exercise equipment. **Guest Services:** sundries, valet laundry, area transportation. **Business Services:** meeting rooms, fax (fee). **Cards:** AX, CB, DC, DS, MC, VI.

SOME UNITS

HAMPTON INN FORT LAUDERDALE DOWNTOWN
CITY CENTER   *Book at aaa.com*   Phone: (954)924-2700   33

10/1-11/30 [ECP]	1P: $179-$209	2P: $189-$219	XP: $10 F12
12/1-4/30 [ECP]	1P: $169-$199	2P: $179-$209	XP: $10 F12
5/1-9/30 [ECP]	1P: $129-$149	2P: $139-$159	XP: $10 F12

Small-scale Hotel   **Location:** SR 842 (Broward Blvd), just n; entrance on NE 3rd St. 250 N Andrews Ave 33301. Fax: 954/924-2717. **Facility:** 156 one-bedroom standard units. 11 stories, interior corridors. *Bath:* combo or shower only. **Parking:** on-site. **Terms:** cancellation fee imposed. **Amenities:** video games (fee), high-speed Internet, dual phone lines, voice mail, safes, irons, hair dryers. **Pool(s):** heated outdoor. **Leisure Activities:** whirlpool, exercise room. **Guest Services:** sundries, valet and coin laundry. **Business Services:** meeting rooms, business center. **Cards:** AX, DC, DS, MC, VI.

SOME UNITS

HARBOR BEACH MARRIOTT RESORT & SPA   *Book at aaa.com*   Phone: 954/525-4000   40

12/24-6/8	1P: $399-$599	2P: $399-$599
9/5-11/30	1P: $289-$399	2P: $289-$399
12/1-12/23	1P: $269-$369	2P: $269-$369
6/9-9/4	1P: $199-$329	2P: $199-$329

Resort   **Location:** E of SR A1A; s of Bahia Mar Marina. 3030 Holiday Dr 33316. Fax: 954/766-6152. **Facility:** A private Large-scale Hotel   beach, a full luxury spa, a large tropical pool and spacious rooms add appeal to this property. 637 units. 602 one-bedroom standard units. 35 one-bedroom suites ($700-$3000), some with whirlpools. 15 stories, interior corridors. *Bath:* combo or shower only. **Parking:** on-site (fee) and valet. **Terms:** check-in 4 pm, 7 day cancellation notice, 3 day in summer-fee imposed, package plans. **Amenities:** CD players, dual phone lines, voice mail, safes, honor bars, irons, hair dryers. **Fee:** video games, high-speed Internet. *Some:* DVD players, fax. **Dining:** 3 restaurants, 6 am-midnight, cocktails, also, 3030 Ocean, see separate listing, entertainment. **Pool(s):** 2 heated outdoor. **Leisure Activities:** saunas, whirlpools, steamrooms, fishing, private beach, charter sailing, recreation programs, spa, basketball, volleyball, game room. *Fee:* windsurfing, waterskiing, scuba diving, snorkeling, parasailing, personal watercraft, segway tours, sunfish, golf privileges, 4 tennis courts, tennis instruction, bicycles. **Guest Services:** gift shop, valet and coin laundry. **Business Services:** conference facilities, business center. **Cards:** AX, CB, DC, DS, MC, VI. **Special Amenities:** free newspaper. *(See color ad below)*

SOME UNITS

HOLIDAY INN EXPRESS HOTEL & SUITES   Phone: (954)828-9905   52

12/16-4/15 [ECP]	1P: $129-$149	2P: $139-$159	XP: $10 F16
12/1-12/15 & 4/16-11/30 [ECP]	1P: $119-$139	2P: $129-$149	XP: $10 F16

Small-scale Hotel   **Location:** I-95, exit 25 (SR 84 E), 0.8 mi e. 1150 SR 84 33315. Fax: 954/828-9904. **Facility:** 100 one-bedroom standard units. 5 stories, interior corridors. *Bath:* combo or shower only. **Parking:** on-site. **Amenities:** high-speed Internet, dual phone lines, voice mail, irons, hair dryers. **Pool(s):** heated outdoor. **Leisure Activities:** limited exercise equipment. **Guest Services:** sundries, valet and coin laundry, airport transportation-Ft Lauderdale/Hollywood International Airport, area transportation-Port Everglades. **Business Services:** meeting rooms, business center. **Cards:** AX, CB, DC, DS, JC, MC, VI. **Special Amenities:** free expanded continental breakfast and free newspaper.

SOME UNITS

(See map and index starting on p. 364)

HOLIDAY INN EXPRESS PORT EVERGLADES
CRUISE & CONVENTION CENTER *Book at aaa.com* **Phone: (954)728-2577** **45**

	2/1-4/15 [ECP]	1P: $139-$159	2P: $139-$159
	12/24-1/31 [ECP]	1P: $109-$129	2P: $109-$129
Small-scale Hotel	4/16-11/30 [ECP]	1P: $99-$119	2P: $99-$119
	12/1-12/23 [ECP]	1P: $89-$109	2P: $89-$109

Location: SR A1A, 1 mi e of US 1 (Federal Hwy). 1500 SE 17th St Cswy 33316. Fax: 954/728-2591. **Facility:** 78 one-bedroom standard units. 5 stories, interior corridors. *Bath:* combo or shower only. **Parking:** on-site. **Amenities:** high-speed Internet, voice mail, irons, hair dryers. **Guest Services:** valet laundry, area transportation. **Business Services:** meeting rooms, fax (fee). **Cards:** AX, DC, DS, JC, MC, VI.

SOME UNITS
(ASK) SD ⊕ ⊕ &M ⊗ ⊘ ⊛ DATA PORT ⊟ / ⊠ ⊟ /
FEE

HOLIDAY INN FT. LAUDERDALE BEACH *Book at aaa.com* **Phone: (954)563-5961** **20**

| | 12/1-4/30 & 10/1-11/30 | 1P: $159-$249 | 2P: $159-$249 |
| | 5/1-9/30 | 1P: $99-$159 | 2P: $99-$159 |

Location: SR A1A, jct SR 838 (E Sunrise Blvd). 999 Ft Lauderdale Beach Blvd 33304. Fax: 954/564-5261. **Facility:** 240 units. 236 one-bedroom standard units. 4 one-bedroom suites. 12 stories, interior corridors. **Large-scale Hotel** *Bath:* combo or shower only. **Parking:** on-site (fee). **Terms:** [AP], [BP] & [CP] meal plans available, package plans. **Amenities:** video games (fee), high-speed Internet, voice mail, safes, irons, hair dryers. **Dining:** 7 am-10 pm, cocktails. **Pool(s):** heated outdoor. **Leisure Activities:** exercise room. **Guest Services:** valet laundry. **Business Services:** meeting rooms. **Cards:** AX, CB, DC, DS, MC, VI. **Special Amenities:** free newspaper and free room upgrade **(subject to availability with advance reservations).** *(See color ad below)*

SOME UNITS
SD ⊕ ⊤ ⊗ ⊘ ⊛ ⊛ DATA PORT ⊟ ⊟ / ⊠ /

HYATT REGENCY PIER SIXTY SIX *Book at aaa.com* **Phone: (954)525-6666** **41**

| | 12/1-5/31 & 10/1-11/30 | 1P: $165-$279 | 2P: $165-$279 | XP: $30 | F18 |
| | 6/1-9/30 | 1P: $110-$205 | 2P: $110-$205 | XP: $30 | F18 |

Location: SR A1A, 1.3 mi e of jct US 1 (Federal Hwy). 2301 SE 17th St Cswy 33316. Fax: 954/728-3541. **Facility:** On the Intracoastal Waterway, the hotel features tropical foliage, a large deck and a pool with a waterfall. 388 units. 380 one-bedroom standard units. 8 one-bedroom suites, some with whirlpools. 1-17 **Large-scale Hotel** stories, interior/exterior corridors. *Bath:* combo or shower only. **Parking:** on-site (fee) and valet. **Terms:** check-in 4 pm, 3 day cancellation notice-fee imposed, $10 service charge. **Amenities:** high-speed Internet (fee), dual phone lines, voice mail, safes, honor bars, irons, hair dryers. *Some:* DVD players, CD players, fax. **Dining:** 4 restaurants, 6:30 am-11 pm, cocktails, also, Grille 66 and Bar, see separate listing, nightclub, entertainment. **Pool(s):** 2 heated outdoor. **Leisure Activities:** whirlpool, steamroom, rental boats, fishing, golf privileges, spa. *Fee:* sauna, marina, scuba diving, snorkeling, charter fishing, scuba instruction, 2 lighted tennis courts. **Guest Services:** gift shop, valet laundry, beauty salon. **Business Services:** conference facilities, business center. **Cards:** AX, CB, DC, DS, JC, MC, VI. *(See color ad below)*

SOME UNITS
⊤ ⊤ ⊛ &M ⊗ ⊘ ⊛ ⊕ ⊠ ⊛ DATA PORT ⊟ / ⊠ VCR ⊟ /
FEE FEE

(See map and index starting on p. 364).

IRELAND'S INN BEACH RESORT   *Book at aaa.com*   Phone: (954)565-6661   🔟⑥

(AAA) (SAVE)

▼▼♦▼▼

12/1-4/20	1P: $149-$262	2P: $149-$262	XP: $10	F16
10/30-11/30	1P: $169-$250	2P: $169-$250	XP: $10	F16
4/21-10/29	1P: $129-$179	2P: $129-$179	XP: $10	F16

Small-scale Hotel

Location: Oceanfront. 0.8 mi s of SR 816 (Oakland Park Blvd); just e of SR A1A. 2220 N Atlantic Blvd 33305. Fax: 954/565-8893. **Facility:** 95 units. 85 one-bedroom standard units, some with efficiencies. 10 one-bedroom suites ($209-$315), some with efficiencies and/or whirlpools. 3-7 stories, exterior corridors. *Bath:* combo or shower only. **Parking:** on-site and valet. **Terms:** 3 day cancellation notice-fee imposed. **Amenities:** video games (fee), voice mail, safes, irons, hair dryers. *Some:* high-speed Internet. **Dining:** 7:30 am-10 pm, entertainment. **Pool(s):** 3 heated outdoor. **Leisure Activities:** limited beach access. **Guest Services:** gift shop, valet laundry. **Business Services:** meeting rooms, fax (fee). **Cards:** AX, DS, MC, VI. *(See color ad below)*

SOME UNITS

LAGO MAR RESORT & CLUB   *Book at aaa.com*   Phone: (954)523-6511   4③

(AAA) (SAVE)

▼▼♦▼▼

12/20-4/30	1P: $285-$580	2P: $285-$580	XP: $10	F
10/25-11/30	1P: $195-$305	2P: $195-$305	XP: $10	F
12/1-12/19	1P: $185-$295	2P: $185-$295	XP: $10	F
5/1-10/24	1P: $160-$260	2P: $160-$260	XP: $10	F

Resort
Large-scale Hotel

Location: Oceanfront. Just e of SR A1A; 0.5 mi ne of 17th St Cswy Bridge to Mayan Dr, to Ocean Dr, s to Grace, e to S Ocean Ln, then just n. 1700 S Ocean Ln 33316. Fax: 954/524-6627. **Facility:** A mosaic floor mural adds interest to the lobby of this hotel, which faces the beach on one side and a lake on the other. 204 units. 40 one-bedroom standard units. 146 one- and 18 two-bedroom suites, some with kitchens. 3-5 stories, interior/exterior corridors. *Bath:* combo or shower only. **Parking:** on-site and valet. **Terms:** check-in 4 pm, 7 day cancellation notice, 3 day off season-fee imposed, [AP], [BP], [CP] & [ECP] meal plans available, package plans. **Amenities:** video games (fee), CD players, high-speed Internet, dual phone lines, voice mail, safes, irons, hair dryers. **Dining:** 4 restaurants, 7:30 am-10 pm, cocktails, entertainment. **Pool(s):** 2 heated outdoor. **Leisure Activities:** miniature golf, tennis instruction, recreation programs, playground, exercise room, spa, shuffleboard, volleyball. *Fee:* 4 tennis courts, game room. **Guest Services:** gift shop, valet and coin laundry. **Business Services:** conference facilities, business center. **Cards:** AX, DC, MC, VI.

SOME UNITS

(See map and index starting on p. 364)

LA QUINTA INN FT. LAUDERDALE (CYPRESS
CREEK/I-95)   *Book at aaa.com*   Phone: (954)491-7666   ▣3
   (AAA) (SAVE)   2/1-4/30   1P: $115-$130   XP: $7   F18
   ▽▽▽▽   5/1-11/30   1P: $75-$95   XP: $7   F18
             12/1-1/31   1P: $69-$89   XP: $7   F18
Small-scale Hotel **Location:** I-95, exit 33 southbound, 0.8 mi; exit 33B northbound, at Powerline Rd. 999 W Cypress Creek Rd 33309.
Fax: 954/491-7669. **Facility:** 145 one-bedroom standard units. 4 stories, interior corridors. *Bath:* combo or shower only. **Parking:** on-site. **Terms:** [ECP] meal plan available, small pets only. **Amenities:** video games (fee), dual phone lines, voice mail, irons, hair dryers. **Pool(s):** outdoor. **Leisure Activities:** whirlpool, exercise room. **Guest Services:** valet and coin laundry. **Business Services:** meeting rooms, fax (fee). **Cards:** AX, CB, DC, DS, MC, VI.
Special Amenities: free expanded continental breakfast and free local telephone calls. *(See color ad below)*

SOME UNITS
🐾 🛗 ⊘ 🛏 🎥 [DATA PORT] 📺 / ⊠ 🛄 📷 /
                                                   FEE   FEE

MOTEL 6 - FT. LAUDERDALE #55   *Book at aaa.com*   Phone: 954/760-7999   ▣53
   ▽   1/2-11/30   1P: $59-$69   2P: $65-$75   XP: $3   F17
        12/1-1/1   1P: $49-$59   2P: $55-$65   XP: $3   F17
Small-scale Hotel **Location:** I-95, exit 25 (SR 84 E), just e, then U-turn at light. 1801 SR 84 33315. Fax: 954/832-0653. **Facility:** 106 one-bedroom standard units. 2 stories (no elevator), interior corridors. *Bath:* shower only. **Parking:** on-site.
Pool(s): heated outdoor. **Guest Services:** coin laundry. **Cards:** AX, CB, DC, DS, MC, VI.

SOME UNITS
🅢ᴅ 🐾 🛗 ⊘ 🛏 🎥 [DATA PORT] / ⊠ /

(See map and index starting on p. 364)

OCEAN HOLIDAY MOTEL   Phone: 954/761-9933   **32**

	12/1-4/15	1P: $85-$200	2P: $85-$200	XP: $10 F3
	4/16-11/30	1P: $55-$175	2P: $55-$175	XP: $10 F3

Motel   **Location:** SR A1A; between Seville and Alhambra sts, from SR 838 (Sunrise Blvd) 0.9 mi s; from Las Olas Blvd 0.4 mi n. 205 N Atlantic Blvd (A1A) 33304. Fax: 954/761-9933. **Facility:** 18 one-bedroom standard units. 3 stories. *Bath:* combo or shower only. **Parking:** on-site. **Terms:** office hours 10 am-8 pm, 14 day cancellation notice-fee imposed, weekly rates available. **Leisure Activities:** beach access. **Business Services:** fax (fee). **Cards:** AX, DC, DS, MC, VI.

SOME UNITS

[🛜] [🛏] / [✕] [🖨] /

RAMADA INN-FORT LAUDERDALE
  AIRPORT/CRUISE PORT   *Book at aaa.com*   Phone: (954)584-4000   **54**

	12/23-4/30 [BP]	1P: $95-$124	2P: $95-$124	XP: $10 F17
	10/1-11/30 [BP]	1P: $75-$95	2P: $75-$95	XP: $10 F17
	12/1-12/22 [BP]	1P: $73-$95	2P: $73-$95	XP: $10 F17
	5/1-9/30 [BP]	1P: $69-$85	2P: $69-$85	XP: $10 F17

Motel   **Location:** I-95, exit 25 (SR 84), just w. 2275 SR 84/Marina Mile Rd 33312. Fax: 954/797-6038. **Facility:** 144 one-bedroom standard units. 2 stories (no elevator), exterior corridors. *Bath:* combo or shower only. **Parking:** on-site. **Terms:** small pets only ($25 fee). **Amenities:** voice mail, safes (fee), irons, hair dryers. **Dining:** 3 restaurants, 6 am-11 pm, cocktails, nightclub. **Pool(s):** outdoor. **Guest Services:** valet and coin laundry, airport transportation-Fort Lauderdale-Hollywood International Airport, area transportation-cruise port & Port Everglades. **Business Services:** meeting rooms, business center. **Cards:** AX, CB, DC, DS, MC, VI. **Special Amenities:** free full breakfast. *(See color ad below)*

SOME UNITS

[🅂] [✚] [🐾] [🍴] [🍸] [♿] [🎣] [🏊] [🎥] [DATA PORT] [🖥] / [✕] [🛏] [🖨] /
     FEE

RAMADA PLAZA BEACH RESORT   *Book at aaa.com*   Phone: 954/565-6611   **13**

	12/23-4/30	1P: $189-$239	2P: $189-$239	XP: $10 F17
	5/1-11/30	1P: $109-$189	2P: $109-$189	XP: $10 F17
	12/1-12/22	1P: $109-$159	2P: $109-$159	XP: $10 F17

Large-scale Hotel   **Location:** Oceanfront. Just e of SR A1A; 0.5 mi n of jct SR 816 (Oakland Park Blvd). 4060 Galt Ocean Dr 33308-6597. Fax: 954/564-7730. **Facility:** 225 units. 210 one-bedroom standard units. 15 one-bedroom suites ($199-$399) with efficiencies and whirlpools. 9 stories, interior corridors. *Bath:* combo or shower only. **Parking:** valet. **Terms:** check-in 4 pm, cancellation fee imposed. **Amenities:** voice mail, safes (fee), irons, hair dryers. **Pool(s):** heated outdoor. **Leisure Activities:** whirlpool, limited beach access, rental sailboats, exercise room. *Fee:* snorkeling, game room. **Guest Services:** gift shop, valet and coin laundry. **Business Services:** meeting rooms, fax (fee). **Cards:** AX, DC, DS, MC, VI.

SOME UNITS

[ASK] [🅂] [🍴] [🍸] [♿] [🎣] [🏊] [✕] [DATA PORT] [🛏] [🖨] [🖥] / [✕] /

RED ROOF INN   *Book at aaa.com*   Phone: (954)776-6333   **12**

	1/1-3/26	1P: $65-$80	2P: $70-$85	XP: $5 F18
	3/27-9/24	1P: $60-$75	2P: $65-$80	XP: $5 F18
	12/1-12/31 & 9/25-11/30	1P: $50-$70	2P: $55-$75	XP: $5 F18

Small-scale Hotel   **Location:** I-95, exit 32, just w of jct Commercial Blvd, then n. 4800 Powerline Rd 33309. Fax: 954/776-3648. **Facility:** 104 one-bedroom standard units. 4 stories, interior corridors. *Bath:* combo or shower only. **Parking:** on-site. **Terms:** small pets only. **Amenities:** video games (fee), voice mail. **Pool(s):** heated outdoor. **Business Services:** fax (fee). **Cards:** AX, CB, DC, DS, MC, VI.

SOME UNITS

[🐾] [✚] [♿] [🎣] [🏊] [🎥] [DATA PORT] / [✕] /

(See map and index starting on p. 364)

RENAISSANCE FORT LAUDERDALE *Book at aaa.com* Phone: (954)626-1700

(AAA) [SAVE]
	1/1-3/31	1P: $199-$259	2P: $199-$259	XP: $10	F18
	10/1-11/30	1P: $169-$229	2P: $169-$229	XP: $10	F18
	12/1-12/31	1P: $149-$209	2P: $149-$209	XP: $10	F18
	4/1-9/30	1P: $109-$159	2P: $109-$159	XP: $10	F18

Large-scale Hotel **Location:** SR A1A, just e of US 1 (Federal Hwy). 1617 SE 17th St Cswy 33316. Fax: 954/626-1717. **Facility:** Near the beach, airport and seaport, this hotel boasts a stylishly decorated lobby and finely appointed rooms. 233 units. 229 one-bedroom standard units, some with whirlpools. 4 one-bedroom suites. 12 stories, interior corridors. *Bath:* combo or shower only. **Parking:** valet. **Terms:** package plans. **Amenities:** dual phone lines, voice mail, safes, honor bars, irons, hair dryers. *Fee:* video games, high-speed Internet. **Dining:** 6 am-11 pm, cocktails, also, Bistro 17, see separate listing. **Pool(s):** heated outdoor. **Leisure Activities:** whirlpool, exercise room. **Guest Services:** valet laundry. **Business Services:** meeting rooms, business center. **Cards:** AX, CB, DC, DS, JC, MC, VI. *(See color ad below)*

SOME UNITS

RIVERSIDE HOTEL *Book at aaa.com* Phone: (954)467-0671

(AAA) [SAVE]
	12/1-4/16	1P: $199-$295	2P: $199-$295	XP: $15	F18
	10/1-11/30	1P: $165-$249	2P: $165-$249	XP: $15	F18
	4/17-5/31	1P: $169-$245	2P: $169-$245	XP: $15	F18
	6/1-9/30	1P: $125-$205	2P: $125-$205	XP: $15	F18

Classic Historic **Location:** 2 mi w of SR A1A, jct US 1 underpass; main entrance on SE 4th St. Located in a fashionable historic district.
Small-scale Hotel 620 E Las Olas Blvd 33301. Fax: 954/462-2148. **Facility:** On the New River, and replete with Old World charm, the property includes a recently added tower complex where modern touches enhance the ambience. 217 units. 207 one-bedroom standard units. 10 one-bedroom suites, some with whirlpools. 12 stories, interior corridors. *Bath:* combo or shower only. **Parking:** on-site and valet. **Terms:** cancellation fee imposed. **Amenities:** dual phone lines, voice mail, honor bars, irons, hair dryers. *Fee:* video games, high-speed Internet. **Dining:** 2 restaurants, 7 am-11:30 pm, cocktails, also, The Grill Room on Las Olas, see separate listing. **Pool(s):** heated outdoor. **Leisure Activities:** *Fee:* boat dock. **Guest Services:** gift shop, valet laundry. **Business Services:** meeting rooms. **Cards:** AX, DC, DS, MC, VI. **Special Amenities:** free newspaper and free room upgrade (subject to availability with advance reservations). *(See color ad below)*

SOME UNITS

ROYAL SAXON APARTMENTS Phone: 954/566-7424

(AAA) [SAVE]
| | All Year | 1P: $65-$175 | 2P: $65-$175 | XP: $20 | F12 |

Motel **Location:** Just w of SR A1A, 0.5 mi s of SR 838 (Sunrise Blvd); corner of Breakers Ave and Terramar St. 551 Breakers Ave 33304. Fax: 954/566-8305. **Facility:** 15 units. 2 one-bedroom standard units with efficiencies. 13 one-bedroom suites with kitchens. 2 stories, exterior corridors. **Parking:** on-site. **Terms:** office hours 8 am-10 pm, 14 day cancellation notice, weekly rates available, small pets only ($100 deposit). **Pool(s):** heated outdoor. **Leisure Activities:** barbecue grills. **Guest Services:** coin laundry. **Cards:** DC, MC, VI. **Special Amenities:** free local telephone calls and free newspaper.

FEE

(See map and index starting on p. 364)

ST. REGIS RESORT - FORT LAUDERDALE

[fyi]

Large-scale Hotel

4/1-5/31	1P: $529-$709	2P: $529-$709	XP: $40	F16
10/1-11/30	1P: $479-$609	2P: $479-$609	XP: $40	F16
6/1-9/30	1P: $359-$509	2P: $359-$509	XP: $40	F16

Phone: 954/465-2300

Too new to rate. Location: On SR A1A, 1 mi s of SR 838 (Sunrise Blvd). Across from the beach. 1 N Ft Lauderdale Beach Blvd 33304. **Fax:** 954/465-2340. **Amenities:** 192 units, restaurant, coffeemakers, microwaves, refrigerators, pool, exercise facilities. **Terms:** open 4/1-11/30, check-in 4 pm, 21 day cancellation notice-fee imposed. **Cards:** AX, CB, DC, DS, MC, VI.

SANS SOUCI HOTEL   *Book at aaa.com*   **Phone: (954)564-4311**   **22**

Motel

12/1-5/10	1P: $89-$200	2P: $89-$200	XP: $10	F12
5/11-11/30	1P: $59-$200	2P: $59-$200	XP: $10	F12

Location: 0.4 mi s on SR A1A from Sunrise Blvd (SR 838), w on Aurumar St, on corner. 618 N Birch Rd 33304. **Fax:** 954/564-4472. **Facility:** 20 units. 12 one-bedroom standard units, some with efficiencies. 8 one-bedroom suites with kitchens. 3 stories (no elevator), exterior corridors. **Parking:** on-site. **Terms:** office hours 7:30 am-9:30 pm, 2-7 night minimum stay, 21 day cancellation notice-fee imposed. **Amenities:** voice mail, safes (fee). **Pool(s):** heated outdoor. **Guest Services:** coin laundry. **Business Services:** fax (fee). **Cards:** AX, DS, MC, VI.

(ASK) (TI+) (🏊) (DATA PORT) (🛗) (📶)

SEA CHATEAU RESORT MOTEL   **Phone: (954)566-8331**   **27**

Motel

All Year	1P: $65-$100 XP: $10 F12

Location: 2 blks w of SR A1A; 0.5 mi s of SR 838 (Sunrise Blvd). 555 N Birch Rd & Terramar St 33304. **Fax:** 954/564-2411. **Facility:** 19 one-bedroom standard units, some with efficiencies. 2 stories (no elevator), exterior corridors. **Parking:** on-site. **Terms:** office hours 8 am-7 pm, 10 day cancellation notice-fee imposed, weekly rates available, small pets only. **Pool(s):** outdoor.

SOME UNITS

(ASK) (SD) (🐾) (🏊) (CTV) (🛗) (📶)

SEA CLUB RESORT   **Phone: (954)564-3211**   **24**

(AAA) (SAVE)

Small-scale Hotel

12/16-4/15	1P: $90-$250	2P: $90-$350	XP: $10	F12
12/1-12/15 & 4/16-11/30	1P: $59-$79	2P: $69-$89	XP: $10	F12

Location: On SR A1A, 0.4 mi s of SR 838 (Sunrise Blvd). Located across from the beach. 619 N Fort Lauderdale Beach Blvd 33304. 99 units. 98 one-bedroom standard units. 1 one-bedroom suite ($150-$450). 3-6 stories, interior/exterior corridors. *Bath:* combo or shower only. **Parking:** on-site. **Terms:** cancellation fee imposed, [AP], [BP] & [CP] meal plans available, package plans. **Amenities:** voice mail, safes (fee), irons, hair dryers. **Dining:** 7 am-2 am, cocktails. **Pool(s):** outdoor. **Guest Services:** gift shop, valet and coin laundry. **Business Services:** meeting rooms, fax (fee). **Cards:** AX, CB, DC, DS, JC, MC, VI.

SOME UNITS

(SD) (TI) (Y) (🏊) (🎥) (DATA PORT) (🛗) (💻) / (✕) (📶) /

SHERATON SUITES CYPRESS CREEK   *Book at aaa.com*   **Phone: (954)772-5400**   **4**

Large-scale Hotel

12/1-4/30	1P: $169	2P: $169	XP: $10	F17
10/1-11/30	1P: $129	2P: $129	XP: $10	F17
5/1-9/30	1P: $99	2P: $99	XP: $10	F17

Location: I-95, exit 33B northbound, then w; exit 33 southbound, then w (Cypress Creek Rd). 555 NW 62nd St 33309. **Fax:** 954/772-5490. **Facility:** 253 one-bedroom suites. 8 stories, interior corridors. *Bath:* combo or shower only. **Parking:** on-site and valet. **Terms:** cancellation fee imposed, small pets only. **Amenities:** dual phone lines, voice mail, irons, hair dryers. *Fee:* video games, high-speed Internet. *Some:* fax. **Pool(s):** heated outdoor. **Leisure Activities:** whirlpool, exercise room. **Guest Services:** gift shop, valet and coin laundry, area transportation. **Business Services:** meeting rooms, business center. **Cards:** AX, DC, DS, MC, VI.

SOME UNITS

(ASK) (SD) (🐾) (TI) (Y) (🏊) (🎥) (DATA PORT) (🛗) (💻) / (✕) (VCR) /
FEE

SHERATON YANKEE CLIPPER BEACH HOTEL   *Book at aaa.com*   **Phone: (954)524-5551**   **38**

(AAA) (SAVE)

Large-scale Hotel

12/1-4/15	1P: $189-$329	2P: $189-$329	XP: $15	F17
10/6-11/30	1P: $169-$309	2P: $169-$309	XP: $15	F17
4/16-6/3	1P: $159-$299	2P: $159-$299	XP: $15	F17
6/4-10/5	1P: $119-$229	2P: $119-$229	XP: $15	F17

Location: Oceanfront. SR A1A, just s of Bahia Mar Marina. 1140 Seabreeze Blvd (A1A) 33316. **Fax:** 954/523-5376. **Facility:** 500 units. 492 one-bedroom standard units. 8 one-bedroom suites ($329-$689) with whirlpools. 5-11 stories, interior/exterior corridors. *Bath:* combo or shower only. **Parking:** on-site (fee) and valet. **Terms:** cancellation fee imposed. **Amenities:** dual phone lines, voice mail, safes, irons, hair dryers. *Fee:* video games, high-speed Internet. **Dining:** 2 restaurants, 6:30 am-11 pm, cocktails, entertainment. **Pool(s):** 2 heated outdoor. **Leisure Activities:** parasailing, personal watercraft, putting green, recreation programs, exercise room, sports court, basketball, shuffleboard, volleyball. **Guest Services:** gift shop, valet and coin laundry. **Business Services:** meeting rooms, business center. **Cards:** AX, CB, DC, DS, MC, VI. *(See color ad p 8)*

SOME UNITS

(SD) (TI) (Y) (&M) (♿) (🎥) (🏊) (✕) (🐾) (DATA PORT) (💻) / (✕) (🛗) /
FEE

SHERATON YANKEE TRADER BEACH HOTEL   *Book at aaa.com*   **Phone: (954)467-1111**   **31**

(AAA) (SAVE)

Large-scale Hotel

12/1-4/15	1P: $189-$329	2P: $189-$329	XP: $15	F17
10/6-11/30	1P: $169-$309	2P: $169-$309	XP: $15	F17
4/16-6/3	1P: $159-$299	2P: $159-$299	XP: $15	F17
6/4-10/5	1P: $119-$229	2P: $119-$229	XP: $15	F17

Location: On SR A1A, 0.8 mi s of SR 838 (Sunrise Blvd). Located across from the beach. 321 N Fort Lauderdale Beach Blvd, A1A 33304. **Fax:** 954/462-2342. **Facility:** 457 units. 442 one-bedroom standard units. 15 one-bedroom suites ($329-$689). 14-15 stories, interior corridors. *Bath:* combo or shower only. **Parking:** on-site (fee) and valet. **Terms:** cancellation fee imposed, package plans. **Amenities:** dual phone lines, voice mail, safes, irons, hair dryers. *Fee:* video games, high-speed Internet. **Dining:** 2 restaurants, 6:30 am-11 pm, cocktails, entertainment. **Pool(s):** 2 heated outdoor. **Leisure Activities:** beach access, 2 tennis courts, exercise room, sports court, game room. **Guest Services:** gift shop, valet and coin laundry. **Business Services:** conference facilities, business center. **Cards:** AX, CB, DC, DS, MC, VI. *(See color ad p 8)*

SOME UNITS

(SD) (TI) (Y) (🏠) (&M) (🎥) (🏊) (✕) (🐾) (DATA PORT) (💻) / (✕) (🛗) /
FEE

(See map and index starting on p. 364)

TOWNEPLACE SUITES BY MARRIOTT   *Book at aaa.com*   Phone: (954)484-2214   ❽

▼▼▼   12/1-4/22   1P: $149-$199
4/23-11/30   1P: $99-$159

Small-scale Hotel   **Location:** I-95, exit 33, 2.7 mi w, then 0.5 mi s on NW 31st St. 3100 Prospect Rd 33309. Fax: 954/484-4533.
Facility: 95 units. 69 one-bedroom standard units with efficiencies. 4 one- and 22 two-bedroom suites with kitchens. 2-3 stories, interior corridors. *Bath:* combo or shower only. **Parking:** on-site. **Terms:** 3 day cancellation notice-fee imposed, small pets only ($70 fee). **Amenities:** video games (fee), high-speed Internet, dual phone lines, voice mail, irons, hair dryers. **Pool(s):** small heated outdoor. **Leisure Activities:** limited exercise equipment. **Guest Services:** valet and coin laundry. **Business Services:** business center. **Cards:** AX, CB, DC, DS, JC, MC, VI. *(See color ad below)*

SOME UNITS

(A$K) (S D) 🐕 [ ] 🚭 ⌐ 🏊 🎦 (DATA PORT) 🛢 🖥 💻 / (X) /
FEE

(See map and index starting on p. 364)

TROPI ROCK RESORT   *Book at aaa.com*   Phone: (954)564-0523   [21]

[AAA] [SAVE]

12/15-5/15	1P: $96-$178	2P: $96-$178	XP: $10	F12
5/16-11/30	1P: $74-$118	2P: $74-$118	XP: $5	F12
12/1-12/14	1P: $72-$115	2P: $72-$115	XP: $5	F12

Motel

Location: 0.3 mi s of jct SR 838 (Sunrise Blvd) on SR A1A, then just right. 2900 Belmar St 33304. **Fax:** 954/564-1313. **Facility:** Designated smoking area. 31 units. 30 one-bedroom standard units, some with efficiencies or kitchens. 1 one-bedroom suite with kitchen. 3 stories, exterior corridors. **Parking:** on-site. **Terms:** office hours 7:30 am-11:30 pm, 3 night minimum stay - seasonal, 14 day cancellation notice, weekly rates available. **Amenities:** voice mail, hair dryers. *Some:* CD players. **Pool(s):** heated outdoor. **Leisure Activities:** rooftop sun deck, 2 tennis courts, barbecue grills, exercise room, shuffleboard. **Guest Services:** coin laundry. **Business Services:** fax (fee). **Cards:** AX, DC, DS, MC, VI. **Special Amenities:** free local telephone calls and early check-in/late check-out.

SOME UNITS

[icons] / [VCR] [icon] /

THE WESTIN, FORT LAUDERDALE   *Book at aaa.com*   Phone: (954)772-1331   [2]

12/1-4/28	1P: $169-$209	2P: $169-$209	XP: $20
10/2-11/30	1P: $159-$199	2P: $159-$199	XP: $20
4/29-5/27	1P: $129-$149	2P: $129-$149	XP: $20
5/28-10/1	1P: $109-$149	2P: $109-$149	XP: $20

Large-scale Hotel

Location: I-95, exit 33 southbound, then e; exit 33A northbound; in Radice Corporate Park. 400 Corporate Dr 33334-3642. **Fax:** 954/491-9087. **Facility:** 293 units. 291 one-bedroom standard units. 2 one-bedroom suites. 14 stories, interior corridors. **Bath:** combo or shower only. **Parking:** on-site and valet. **Terms:** cancellation fee imposed, weekly rates available, small pets only ($50 deposit). **Amenities:** dual phone lines, voice mail, safes, honor bars, irons, hair dryers. **Fee:** video games, high-speed Internet. *Some:* CD players. **Pool(s):** heated outdoor. **Leisure Activities:** saunas, whirlpool, jogging, exercise room. **Guest Services:** gift shop, valet laundry, area transportation. **Business Services:** conference facilities, business center. **Cards:** AX, DC, DS, MC, VI. *(See color ad p 8)*

SOME UNITS

[ASK] [icons] FEE FEE   [icons] / [icons] /

WHERE TO DINE

3030 OCEAN   **Dinner:** $25-$40   Phone: 954/525-4000   [55]

Continental

Location: E of SR A1A; s of Bahia Mar Marina; in Harbor Beach Marriott Resort & Spa. 3030 Holiday Dr 33316. **Hours:** 6 pm-10:30 pm. **Reservations:** suggested. **Features:** Besides an upbeat, sophisticated ambience, the restaurant's claim to fame is an innovative menu that changes monthly. Fresh local and regional seafood is always at the top of the menu, and highlights include lobster, prawns and various fish selections. Other temptations include grilled Kansas City strip steak and rack of lamb. The chef delights diners with creative and detailed presentations. Dressy casual; cocktails. **Parking:** on-site (fee) and valet. **Cards:** AX, CB, DC, DS, JC, MC, VI.

THE AMBRY   **Lunch:** $9-$14   **Dinner:** $14-$31   Phone: 954/771-7342   [11]

Regional German

Location: Just e of US 1 (Federal Hwy). 3016 E Commercial Blvd 33308. **Hours:** 11:30 am-2 & 5-10 pm, Sat from 5 pm. Closed: 9/15-10/1. **Reservations:** suggested. **Features:** Such classics as sauerbraten and Wiener schnitzel make up the tasty Teutonic fare at the intimate restaurant, which also caters to the more timid with steak and seafood selections. Dark, windowless dining areas and cordial servers set a cozy mood. Dressy casual; cocktails. **Parking:** on-site. **Cards:** AX, DC, MC, VI.

ANDRE'S STEAKHOUSE   **Dinner:** $16-$35   Phone: 954/489-7411   [6]

Steak House

Location: Just e of US 1 (Federal Hwy). 3031 E Commercial Blvd 33308. **Hours:** 5 pm-10 pm. Closed: Mon 5/1-11/30. **Reservations:** suggested. **Features:** The restaurant is known for its aged steaks and big side dishes, but if seafood is on the agenda, that also can be taken care of. Casual dress; cocktails. **Parking:** on-site. **Cards:** AX, CB, DC, DS, JC, MC, VI.

[M] [icon]

BIG LOUIE'S ITALIAN RESTAURANT   **Lunch:** $4-$14   **Dinner:** $4-$14   Phone: 954/771-2288   [10]

Italian

Location: Commercial Blvd at NE 20th Ave; just w of jct US 1 (Federal Hwy). 2103 E Commercial Blvd 33308. **Hours:** 11 am-midnight, Fri & Sat-1 am, Sun noon-midnight. Closed: 11/23. **Features:** You can find no-frills dining at this small, family-oriented restaurant which offers oversized pizzas, made-to-order pizzas and an extensive list of homemade pastas. One visit and you'll know why Big Louie's is a local favorite. Casual dress; beer & wine only. **Parking:** on-site. **Cards:** AX, DC, DS, MC, VI.

BIG LOUIE'S ITALIAN RESTAURANT   **Lunch:** $4-$13   **Dinner:** $5-$13   Phone: 954/467-1166   [34]

Pizza

Location: Jct US 1 (Federal Hwy); in Gateway Shopping Center. 1990 E Sunrise Blvd 33304. **Hours:** 11 am-1 am, Sun from noon. Closed: 11/23. **Features:** Servers have to hustle in this bustling atmosphere, but they keep on smiling as they deliver oversized sandwiches and copious portions of homemade pasta. You won't find any sissy pizza in this joint; if it isn't huge, it isn't worth it. Casual dress; beer & wine only. **Parking:** on-site. **Cards:** AX, DC, DS, MC, VI.

[M]

BIMINI BOATYARD BAR & GRILL   **Lunch:** $8-$18   **Dinner:** $12-$30   Phone: 954/525-7400   [59]

American

Location: SR A1A, 0.8 mi e of jct US 1 (Federal Hwy). 1555 SE 17th St 33316. **Hours:** 11:30 am-4 & 5-10 pm, Sun 11 am-3 & 5-10 pm; Sunday brunch. Closed: 11/23, 12/25. **Reservations:** accepted. **Features:** A relaxing, casual atmosphere makes dining in this waterfront eatery a great get-away-from-it-all experience. The menu includes gourmet pizzas, sandwiches and salads, as well as pasta, seafood, meat and poultry dishes. The Sunday brunch is a special treat. Casual dress; cocktails. **Parking:** on-site and valet. **Cards:** AX, CB, DC, DS, MC, VI.

[M] [icon]

BISTRO 17   **Lunch:** $9-$14   **Dinner:** $17-$30   Phone: 954/626-1701   [58]

Regional American

Location: SR A1A, just e of US 1 (Federal Hwy); in Renaissance Fort Lauderdale. 1617 17th St Cswy 33316. **Hours:** 6-10 am, 11-2:30 & 5:30-11 pm. **Reservations:** suggested. **Features:** The cozy restaurant offers a balanced menu of meat and fresh seafood dishes that blend exciting flavors. Cuisines of many regions combine to make up the regional Floridian taste. An extensive list of wines by the bottle or glass complements the menu. Dressy casual; cocktails. **Parking:** valet. **Cards:** AX, CB, DC, DS, JC, MC, VI. *(See color ad p 386)*

[M] [icon]

(See map and index starting on p. 364)

BLACK ORCHID CAFE
▼▽▼▽▼
Continental
Dinner: $15-$40   **Phone:** 954/561-9398   ㉕
Location: Jct N Ocean Blvd/SR A1A and 30th St, just s of Oakland Park Blvd. 2985 N Ocean Blvd 33308. **Hours:** 5 pm-10 pm, Fri & Sat-11 pm. **Reservations:** suggested. **Features:** This eatery is cozy and features French, American and Continental fare with some exotic wild game entrees. Dressy casual; cocktails. **Parking:** on-site. **Cards:** AX, DS, MC, VI.   🔥M Ⓨ

BRASSERIE LAS OLAS
▼▽▼▽▼
American
Lunch: $8-$15   **Dinner:** $12-$28   **Phone:** 954/779-7374   ㊸
Location: Just w of US 1 (Federal Hwy); just e of Andrews Ave. 333 E Las Olas Blvd 33301. **Hours:** 11:30 am-10 pm, Fri & Sat-11 pm. Closed: 11/23, 12/25. **Features:** Patrons can relax in the wide-open dining room or outside on the square with the fountain, lights and tall buildings of downtown. Food selections include comforting home favorites, fresh seafood dishes, chops and steaks. Dressy casual; cocktails. **Parking:** on-site and valet. **Cards:** AX, DS, MC, VI.   🔥M ◥

BUCA DI BEPPO
▼▽ ▼▽
South Italian
Dinner: $14-$25   **Phone:** 954/229-0922   ③
Location: Commercial Blvd (SR 870), 0.8 mi n; in Imperial Square Shopping Center. 5975 N Federal Hwy 33308. **Hours:** 5 pm-10 pm, Fri & Sat-11 pm, Sun noon-9 pm. Closed: 11/23, 12/25. **Reservations:** suggested. **Features:** A fun place to eat, the restaurant offers family-style—which translates to "huge"—portions. The various dining rooms display an eclectic collection of more than 2,500 pictures of Italy, figurines related to the country and famous, as well as not-so-famous, natives. Casual dress; cocktails. **Parking:** on-site. **Cards:** AX, CB, DC, DS, JC, MC, VI.   🔥M Ⓨ

BY WORD OF MOUTH
▼▽▼▽▼
American
Lunch: $8-$15   **Dinner:** $20-$30   **Phone:** 954/564-3663   ⑮
Location: I-95, exit 31A northbound; exit 31 southbound, 2.5 mi to Old Dixie Hwy, 0.4 mi n to NE 34th Ct, e to NE 12th Ave, then just s. 3200 NE 12th Ave 33334. **Hours:** 11 am-3 & 5-10 pm, Tues-3 pm. Closed: 11/23, 12/25; also Sun & Mon. **Reservations:** suggested. **Features:** The deli case displays a show-and-tell of the day's dishes, described in detail by the wait staff. The flavorful main courses represent a variety of several cuisines; desserts are as fancy as the setting is simple. Service is efficient and hospitable. Dressy casual; beer & wine only. **Parking:** on-site. **Cards:** AX, DC, DS, MC, VI.

CAFE DEL RIO
▼▽ ▼▽
Tex-Mex
Lunch: $7-$10   **Dinner:** $9-$19   **Phone:** 954/463-5490   ㊷
Location: SR A1A/12th St Cswy, just s. 1821 SE 10th Ave 33316. **Hours:** 11:30 am-10 pm, Fri & Sat-11 pm. Closed: 11/23, 12/25. **Reservations:** accepted. **Features:** The menu blends traditional Tex-Mex entrees with house specialties. Dining room walls sport murals depicting a festive Mexican countryside. Casual dress; cocktails. **Parking:** on-site. **Cards:** AX, DC, DS, MC, VI.   🔥M Ⓨ

CANYON SOUTHWEST CAFE
▼▽▼▽▼
Southwest American
Dinner: $19-$39   **Phone:** 954/765-1950   ㉟
Location: Just w of jct US 1 (Federal Hwy) and 19th Ave. 1818 E Sunrise Blvd 33304. **Hours:** 5:30 pm-11 pm, Fri & Sat-11 pm. Closed: 7/4, 11/23, 12/25. **Features:** Fabulous green chilies are used in many dishes on this eclectic menu. You'll also find an unusual group of Southwestern dishes with some Asian touches. The decor is very warm and Southwestern, and the service will fulfill your every need. Dressy casual; cocktails. **Parking:** street. **Cards:** AX, DC, DS, MC, VI.   Ⓨ

CARLOS & PEPE'S 17TH STREET CANTINA
▼▽▼
Tex-Mex
Lunch: $8-$12   **Dinner:** $8-$18   **Phone:** 954/467-7192   ㊱
Location: Just e of US 1 (Federal Hwy) on SR A1A/17th St Cswy. 1302 SE 17th St 33316. **Hours:** 5 pm-10 pm, Fri & Sat 11:30 am-11 pm, Sun 11:30 am-10 pm. Closed: 11/23, 12/25. **Features:** The atmosphere is casual and child-friendly. Fresh chips and salsa are served alongside Mexican favorites. Casual dress; cocktails. **Parking:** on-site. **Cards:** MC, VI.   Ⓨ

CASABLANCA CAFE
▼▽▼▽
International
Lunch: $8-$14   **Dinner:** $11-$19   **Phone:** 954/764-3500   ㊲
Location: Jct Alhambra St and Atlantic Blvd. 3049 Alhambra St 33305. **Hours:** 11:30 am-11 pm, Fri & Sat-11:30 pm. **Features:** An extraordinary menu combines influences from the cuisines of Morocco, Mexico, Japan, Italy, Spain, Cuba, the Caribbean and even Louisiana Cajun country. Fresh, authentic ingredients and a chic Moroccan setting make this a truly exotic experience. Casual dress; cocktails; entertainment. **Parking:** on-site (fee). **Cards:** AX, CB, DC, DS, MC, VI.   🔥M ◥

CASA D' ANGELO
▼▽▼▽▼
Northern Italian
Dinner: $12-$36   **Phone:** 954/564-1234   ㉚
Location: Just n of SR 838 (Sunrise Blvd); in the Sunrise Square. 1201 N Federal Hwy (US 1) 33304. **Hours:** 5:30 pm-10 pm, Fri & Sat-11 pm. Closed major holidays. **Reservations:** required. **Features:** The atmosphere, the enticing food and an award-winning wine list are a combination that will result in a culinary trip to Northern Italy. The chef offers his and your favorites of pastas, meat and fresh seafoods for your journey. Dressy casual; cocktails. **Parking:** on-site. **Cards:** AX, CB, DC, DS, JC, MC, VI.   🔥M Ⓨ

CHARLEY'S CRAB
▼▽▼▽▼
Seafood
Lunch: $6-$17   **Dinner:** $12-$34   **Phone:** 954/561-4800   ㉔
Location: Off SR A1A, just s of jct Oakland Park Blvd via NE 30th St. 3000 NE 32nd Ave 33308. **Hours:** 11:30 am-10 pm, Fri & Sat-11 pm, Sun from 11 am. **Reservations:** suggested. **Features:** A knowledgeable wait staff can reel off the characteristics of the tantalizing array of dishes on the restaurant's menu. On the Intracoastal Waterway, the eatery features cozy, indoor dining as well as a comfortable, breezy terrace. Dressy casual; cocktails. **Parking:** valet. **Cards:** AX, DC, DS, MC, VI.   Ⓨ ◥

CHEESECAKE FACTORY
▼▽▼▽▼
American
Lunch: $8-$25   **Dinner:** $8-$25   **Phone:** 954/463-1999   ㊿
Location: 2 mi w of SR A1A, jct US 1 (Federal Hwy) underpass and Las Olas Blvd. 600 E Las Olas Blvd 33301. **Hours:** 11:30 am-11:30 pm, Fri & Sat-12:30 am, Sun 10 am-11 pm. Closed: 11/23, 12/25. **Features:** Diners can eat outside on the walk or inside the bustling dining room. The large menu lists more than 200 items. "Large" also describes the size of the portions. Forty cheesecake varieties are offered, and adding toppings further increases the options. Casual dress; cocktails. **Parking:** on-site (fee). **Cards:** AX, CB, DC, DS, MC, VI.   🔥M Ⓨ

(See map and index starting on p. 364)

CHIMA STEAKHOUSE   Lunch: $22   Dinner: $44   Phone: 954/712-0580   ④①
Location: US 1 (Federal Hwy), 1.4 mi e; SR A1A (Fort Lauderdale Beach Blvd/Seabreeze Blvd), 0.5 mi w. 2400 E Las Olas Blvd 33301. **Hours:** noon-2 & 5-10:30 pm, Sat & Sun 1 pm-3:30 & 5-10:30 pm.
Brazilian   **Reservations:** suggested. **Features:** The Gauchos will bring you steaks all night long on long skewers, but before you are tempted with that you have to try the salad buffet with all of its temptations. The wines are matched to the menu with an international selection. Dressy casual; cocktails. **Parking:** valet. **Cards:** MC, VI.

CHUCK'S STEAK HOUSE   Lunch: $7-$15   Dinner: $12-$28   Phone: 954/772-2850   ⑨
Location: Just e of US 1 (Federal Hwy). 2428 E Commercial Blvd 33308. **Hours:** 11:30 am-11 pm, Sat & Sun from 4 pm. **Reservations:** accepted. **Features:** Finally, there's a place where the family can go for hand-cut
Steak House   steaks and moderate prices. Those who don't want steak might try the fresh catch or one of the chops. The contemporary atmosphere is relaxing. Don't overlook the salad bar. Casual dress; cocktails. **Parking:** on-site. **Cards:** AX, DC, DS, MC, VI.

CHUCK'S STEAK HOUSE   Lunch: $7-$15   Dinner: $12-$28   Phone: 954/764-3333   ⑥⓪
Location: Just e of US 1 (Federal Hwy). 1207 SE 17th St Cswy 33316. **Hours:** 11:30 am-11 pm, Sat & Sun from 4 pm. **Reservations:** accepted. **Features:** Finally, there's a place where the family can go for hand-cut
Steak House   and moderate prices. Those who don't want steak might try the fresh catch or one of the chops. The contemporary atmosphere is relaxing. Don't overlook the salad bar. Casual dress; cocktails. **Parking:** on-site. **Cards:** AX, MC, VI.

CREOLINA'S CUISINE   Lunch: $7-$12   Dinner: $12-$21   Phone: 954/524-2003   ④⓪
Location: From W Broward Blvd, s on Nugent/SW 3rd aves, then just e. 209 SW 2nd St 33301. **Hours:** 11 am-2:30 & 5-10 pm, Fri & Sat-11 pm, Sun & Mon-9 pm. Closed major holidays. **Reservations:** suggested.
Cajun   **Features:** The chef enhances the jambalaya, etoufee and gumbo with his style of Cajun cooking. He also adds a Southern twist in some of his creations. The dining room is cozy, but sidewalk seating is also available. Dressy casual; beer & wine only. **Parking:** street. **Cards:** DS, MC, VI.

EDUARDO DE SAN ANGEL   *Menu on aaa.com*   Dinner: $19-$32   Phone: 954/772-4731   ⑧
Location: Just e of US 1 (N Federal Hwy). 2822 E Commercial Blvd 33308. **Hours:** 5:30-10 pm. Closed major holidays; also Sun. **Reservations:** suggested. **Features:** Not your typical Mexican cuisine, the fare on this restaurant's menu includes masterfully presented gourmet specialties. The surroundings are sophisticated.
Mexican   Dressy casual; beer & wine only. **Parking:** street. **Cards:** AX, CB, DC, DS, MC, VI.

FERDO'S GRILL   Lunch: $6-$12   Dinner: $8-$18   Phone: 954/492-5552   ①②
Location: From Oakland Park Blvd (SR 816), 0.8 mi n on US 1 (Federal Hwy). 4300 N Federal Hwy 33308. **Hours:** 11:30 am-10 pm, Fri-11 pm, Sat 5 pm-11 pm. Closed major holidays; also Sun.
Mediterranean   **Reservations:** accepted. **Features:** The menu blends Middle Eastern and Mediterranean cuisine. Meat, poultry and some vegetarian entrees are infused with the flavors of the Mediterranean. Lending to the relaxed atmosphere are art pieces of the area and of the owners. Casual dress; beer & wine only. **Parking:** on-site. **Cards:** AX, DS, MC, VI.

FLORIDIAN RESTAURANT   Lunch: $7-$13   Dinner: $8-$16   Phone: 954/463-4041   ④⑥
Location: Just w of SR A1A. 1410 Las Olas Blvd 33301. **Hours:** 24 hours. **Features:** In the same location since 1937, the eatery has been a beacon to locals and tourists alike for quick service and wholesome food.
American   Burgers, wings and fried seafood are the most popular items. Casual dress; beer & wine only. **Parking:** street.

FOOD LOVERS AMERICAN CAFE   Dinner: $13-$25   Phone: 954/566-9606   ①⑧
Location: Just e of Dixie Hwy on SR 816 (Oakland Park Blvd). 1576 E Oakland Park Blvd 33334. **Hours:** 5:30 pm-9:30 pm, Fri & Sat-10:30 pm. Closed: Mon. **Reservations:** suggested, weekends. **Features:** Excellent fare
Continental   with a French flair is the norm in this polished, yet homey, atmosphere. Although the menu comprises primarily seafood, meat and poultry dishes, it also boasts a multi-cultural flavor with such entrees as Hungarian goulash over linguine. Dressy casual; beer & wine only. **Parking:** on-site. **Cards:** DS, MC, VI.

FUDDRUCKERS, WORLD'S GREATEST BURGERS   Lunch: $6-$12   Dinner: $6-$12   Phone: 954/565-0077   ②⑨
Location: Just n of Sunrise (SR 838). 1200 Federal Hwy/US 1 33304. **Hours:** 11 am-9 pm, Fri & Sat-10 pm. Closed: 11/23, 12/25. **Features:** Size matters at this fun spot, as is evidenced in the difference between an
American   average burger and a really big one. A video game area occupies both big and little kids. Diners can customize their burgers at a bar with fixings. Casual dress; cocktails. **Parking:** on-site. **Cards:** AX, DS, MC, VI.

GAUCHOS STEAK HOUSE   Lunch: $15   Dinner: $24   Phone: 954/630-1330   ②③
Location: US 1, just s of jct SR 816 (Oakland Park Blvd). 3001 N Federal Hwy 33306. **Hours:** noon-3 & 5-10 pm. **Reservations:** accepted. **Features:** A 100-item buffet accompanies all-you-can-eat gaucho-style steaks,
Argentine   lamb and ribs in the casual and soothing setting. Casual dress; cocktails. **Parking:** on-site. **Cards:** MC, VI.

GIBBY'S STEAKS & SEAFOOD   Dinner: $17-$30   Phone: 954/565-2929   ②⑥
Location: I-95, exit 31A northbound; exit 31 southbound, 1.5 mi e, just s of Oakland Park Blvd (SR 816). 2900 NE 12 Terr 33334. **Hours:** 5 pm-10 pm. **Reservations:** accepted. **Features:** A mouth-watering menu features such
Steak & Seafood   entrees as prime-aged steak, rack of lamb, stone crab and live Maine lobster as well as homemade pastries and straight-from-the-oven cracked wheat bread. The country-club-style dining rooms offer relaxed comfort. Casual dress; cocktails. **Parking:** on-site. **Cards:** AX, DS, MC, VI.

(See map and index starting on p. 364)

GRILLE 66 AND BAR **Dinner:** $15-$49 **Phone:** 954/728-3500 [57]
▼▼▼▼
Regional Steak House
Location: SR A1A, 1.3 mi e of jct US 1 (Federal Hwy); in Hyatt Regency Pier Sixty Six. 2301 SE 17th St Cswy 33316. **Hours:** 5:30 pm-11 pm, Sun-10 pm. **Reservations:** not accepted. **Features:** While savoring aged steaks and fresh seafood, guests can watch the boats and yachts in the marina from their tables. Dressy casual; cocktails; entertainment. **Parking:** valet. **Cards:** AX, DC, DS, MC, VI.

THE GRILL ROOM ON LAS OLAS **Dinner:** $20-$40 **Phone:** 954/467-2555 [51]
ⒶⒶⒶ
▼▼▼▼
Continental
Location: 2 mi w of SR A1A, jct US 1 underpass; main entrance on SE 4th St; in Riverside Hotel. 620 E Las Olas Blvd 33301. **Hours:** 6 pm-11 pm. Closed: Sun & Mon. **Reservations:** suggested. **Features:** Excellent preparations feature aged meat and fresh fish and are served in a contemporary dining room. Cordial servers ably explain exquisitely presented dishes. Diners can consult an extensive wine list to find the right bottle to complement their meal. Dressy casual; cocktails; entertainment. **Parking:** valet. **Cards:** AX, CB, DC, MC, VI. *(See color ad p 386)*

HIMMARSHEE BAR & GRILLE **Lunch:** $7-$12 **Dinner:** $13-$27 **Phone:** 954/764-5154 [39]
▼▼▼
American
Location: W Broward Blvd, s on Nugent Ave/SW 3rd Ave, then just e. 210 SW 2nd St 33301. **Hours:** 11:30 am-2 & 5:30-10 pm, Fri & Sat-11 pm, Sun 4:30 pm-9 pm. Closed: 12/25; also 5/24. **Reservations:** suggested. **Features:** The chef calls his creations "eclectic American cuisine" because they borrow from Mediterranean, Asian, Italian and European influences. Only the freshest seafood, meat and poultry are used in the innovative preparations. Be sure to save room for the sinful desserts. The dining room has great color with changing local art, and tables also are available on the sidewalk. Entertainment is offered weekends at the great bar on the second floor. Dressy casual; cocktails. **Parking:** valet and street. **Cards:** AX, MC, VI.

JACK'S BAR-B-Q SMOKEHOUSE **Lunch:** $6-$10 **Dinner:** $6-$18 **Phone:** 954/567-9595 [21]
▲▲▲
Barbecue
Location: I-95, exit 31A, 1.2 mi e. 500 E Oakland Park Blvd 33334. **Hours:** 11 am-10 pm, Fri & Sat-11 pm, Sun-8:30 pm. Closed major holidays. **Features:** Barbecue—in the form of pulled pork, beef, ham and unforgettable ribs—is king here. As for the sides, try the collards. Casual dress; beer & wine only. **Parking:** on-site. **Cards:** MC, VI.

JACKSON'S STEAKHOUSE **Dinner:** $16-$36 **Phone:** 954/522-4450 [48]
▼▼▼
Steak House
Location: Just w of US 1 (S Federal Hwy). 450 E Las Olas Blvd 33301. **Hours:** 5 pm-10 pm, Fri & Sat-11 pm. Closed: 12/25. **Reservations:** suggested. **Features:** In the trendy heart of the city, the restaurant gives the impression of a private club to diners who step inside. Such touches as wood-paneled walls, a beamed ceiling, lots of artwork and adequate brightness characterize the dining room. Menu selections of fine meat and fresh seafood are well-paired with choices from the extensive wine list. Dressy casual; cocktails; entertainment. **Parking:** valet. **Cards:** AX, CB, DC, DS, MC, VI.

JADE PALACE CHINESE CUISINE RESTAURANT **Lunch:** $7-$9 **Dinner:** $8-$19 **Phone:** 954/561-1601 [31]
▲▲▲ ▲▲▲
Chinese
Location: Just e of US 1 (Federal Hwy); across from Galleria Mall. 2465 E Sunrise Blvd 33304. **Hours:** 11:30 am-11 pm, Sun noon-10:30 pm. Closed: 11/23. **Reservations:** accepted. **Features:** The relaxed restaurant presents a menu with more than 100 Cantonese and Szechuan items, as well as some house specialties. Guests have come to expect good meals. Casual dress; cocktails. **Parking:** on-site. **Cards:** AX, MC, VI.

JOHNNY V RESTAURANT/LOUNGE **Lunch:** $12-$20 **Dinner:** $22-$38 **Phone:** 954/761-7920 [45]
▼▼▼
Regional American
Location: Just e of S Federal Hwy/US 1. 625 E Las Olas Blvd 33301. **Hours:** 11:30 am-2:30 & 5:30-11 pm, Fri & Sat-midnight. **Reservations:** suggested. **Features:** The menu will take you the islands and part of it has a southwest twist to bring you back to the mainland. The decor is eclectic with modern looks but a slight retro feel, and can be real cozy in the back section. They offer a wide assortment of cheeses, and yes, the chef has included Cheese Whiz for your enjoyment. A vast wine list will accommodate your every whim and want. Dressy casual; cocktails. **Parking:** on-site (fee). **Cards:** AX, MC, VI.

J'S WATERFRONT GRILLE **Dinner:** $15-$34 **Phone:** 954/566-2427 [20]
▼▼▼▼
Steak & Seafood
Location: Off SR A1A, just s of Oakland Park Blvd. 3003 NE 32nd Ave 33308. **Hours:** 5 pm-10 pm, Fri & Sat-11 pm. **Reservations:** accepted. **Features:** The waterfront restaurant's menu lists the freshest of seafood, as well as thick steaks and chops. The open-air dining room is trendy, and outside guests can watch boats pass. Leave room for one of the big desserts. Dressy casual; cocktails. **Parking:** on-site (fee) and valet. **Cards:** AX, DS, MC, VI.

KYOJIN JAPANESE SEAFOOD BUFFET **Lunch:** $9-$11 **Dinner:** $16-$18 **Phone:** 954/568-2208 [14]
▼▼ ▼▼
Japanese
Location: On US 1 (Federal Hwy), just n of Oakland Park Blvd. 3485 N Federal Hwy 33306. **Hours:** 11:30 am-2:30 & 5-9:30 pm, Fri-10 pm, Sat noon-3 & 5-10 pm, Sun noon-3 & 5-9:30 pm. **Features:** Try what you haven't before at this sushi buffet. If sushi and sashimi aren't your taste, then try the hibachi grill items cooked right in front of you. They also offer traditional Chinese and Japanese items on the all-you-can-eat buffet. Casual dress; beer & wine only. **Parking:** on-site. **Cards:** MC, VI.

LAS VEGAS **Lunch:** $6-$8 **Dinner:** $9-$12 **Phone:** 954/564-1370 [16]
▲▲▲ ▲▲▲
Cuban
Location: I-95, exit 31A northbound; exit 31, 2 mi e; just w of SR A1A and Intracoastal Waterway Bridge. 2807 E Oakland Park Blvd 33306. **Hours:** 11:30 am-10 pm. Closed: 12/25. **Reservations:** accepted. **Features:** Authentic Cuban food, music and decor contribute to the restaurant's atmosphere. Popular standbys grilled chicken and roast pork co-exist with more sophisticated dishes, such as Argentine-style grilled flank steak, to create a tasty and diverse menu. Casual dress; beer & wine only. **Parking:** street. **Cards:** MC, VI.

(See map and index starting on p. 364)

LIL' RED'S COOKIN'   Lunch: $5-$14   Dinner: $5-$14   Phone: 955/463-7883   ⑥③
Location: I-95, exit 25, just e on SR 84 to SW 15th Ave, make U-turn, then just w. 1705 SR 84 33315. **Hours:** 6:30 am-10 pm, Fri & Sat-11 pm. **Closed:** 11/23, 12/25. **Features:** Those who fancy barbecue will have found a home at the casual spot. Although barbecue platters stand out, other choices from the large menu include such comfort foods as sandwiches and meat platters. Casual dress; beer & wine only. **Parking:** on-site.

Barbecue

LOUIE LOUIE ITALIAN BISTRO   Lunch: $8-$18   Dinner: $10-$25   Phone: 954/524-5200   ④②
Location: E of US 1 (Federal Hwy); corner of SE 15th Ave. 1313 E Las Olas Blvd 33301. **Hours:** 11:30 am-11 pm, Fri-midnight, Sat 8 am-midnight, Sun 8 am-11 pm. **Closed:** 11/23. **Reservations:** accepted. **Features:** Just on the edge of busy Las Olas Boulevard, the Italian bistro offers good food in a comfortable setting. Brick-oven pizza shouldn't be overlooked on the large menu. Casual dress; cocktails. **Parking:** on-site and valet.
Cards: AX, DS, MC, VI.

Italian

MAI-KAI RESTAURANT   Dinner: $18-$32   Phone: 954/563-3272   ①③
Location: US 1 (Federal Hwy), 0.3 mi n of jct SR 816 (Oakland Park Blvd). 3599 N Federal Hwy 33308. **Hours:** 5 pm-10:30 pm, Fri & Sat-11:30 pm. **Reservations:** required. **Features:** A bright, exotic atmosphere spices up the restaurant, noted for its lobster Bora Bora, filet mignon and Mandarin pressed duck. Pay a cover charge to enjoy the Polynesian revue, or instead opt to sit in a secluded, romantic dining room or on the patio. Dressy casual; cocktails; entertainment. **Parking:** on-site (fee) and valet. **Cards:** AX, DC, DS, MC, VI.

Chinese

MANCINI'S RESTAURANT   Lunch: $16-$17   Dinner: $15-$36   Phone: 954/764-5510   ④④
Location: Between SE 10th St and SR A1A. 1017 E Las Olas Blvd 33301. **Hours:** noon-3 & 6-11 pm. **Reservations:** required. **Features:** The Tuscan trattoria offers a choice of indoor seating near the exhibition kitchen or al fresco seating streetside. On the menu are innovative pasta dishes, as well as Italian-inspired steak, seafood and chicken preparations. Seafood-packed risotto with a light saffron sauce and fresh roma tomatoes is heavenly, as is the savory center-cut veal topped with wild mushrooms in Borolo sauce. Guests can enjoy live music most nights while imbibing one of the designer martinis. Dressy casual; cocktails. **Parking:** valet. **Cards:** MC, VI.

Italian

MARK'S LAS OLAS   Dinner: $17-$36   Phone: 954/463-1000   ⑤②
Location: E of US 1, on south side of street. 1032 E Las Olas Blvd 33301. **Hours:** 6 pm-10 pm, Fri & Sat-11 pm; dinner hours vary in winter. **Closed:** 11/23, 12/25. **Reservations:** suggested. **Features:** Located in the heart of the shopping and dining district, New Florida fusion cuisine is showcased by a South Florida celebrity chef. Open kitchen design sets off the dining room's Art Deco accents. There is an extensive wine list and bustling ambience at this popular spot. Dressy casual; cocktails. **Parking:** valet and street. **Cards:** AX, DC, MC, VI.

American

MOONLITE DINER   Lunch: $6-$9   Dinner: $9-$17   Phone: 954/938-1116   ②
Location: I-95, exit 33, just w on Cypress Creek Rd (SR 811), jct Cypress Creek Rd and Andrews Ave. 6201 N Andrews Ave 33309. **Hours:** 24 hours. **Reservations:** accepted. **Features:** On the outside, this place resembles a diner car, but inside it looks like a diner from New Jersey. Walls display old food-product pictures, and the counter has short stools. The menu is all over the place with its breakfast, lunch and dinner items. Burgers and malts are a big hit. Casual dress; beer & wine only. **Parking:** on-site. **Cards:** AX, DS, MC, VI.

American

PRIMAVERA RESTAURANT   Lunch: $7-$15   Dinner: $16-$30   Phone: 954/564-6363   ①⑨
Location: I-95, exit 31A northbound; exit 31 southbound, 1.5 mi e. 830 E Oakland Park Blvd 33334. **Hours:** noon-3 & 5:30-10 pm. **Closed:** 12/25. **Reservations:** suggested. **Features:** In addition to homemade pasta and dessert, there is a wide variety of seafood and meat that makes for difficult decisions. The owner visits each table keeping diners happy. Dressy casual; cocktails; entertainment. **Parking:** on-site. **Cards:** AX, DC, DS, MC, VI.

Northern Italian

RAINBOW PALACE   Lunch: $8-$14   Dinner: $19-$51   Phone: 954/565-5652   ①⑦
Location: 0.5 mi e of US 1 (Federal Hwy). 2787 E Oakland Park Blvd 33306. **Hours:** noon-3 & 5-10 pm, Fri-11 pm, Sat 5 pm-11 pm, Sun 5 pm-10 pm. **Closed:** 7/4, 11/23. **Reservations:** suggested. **Features:** Gourmet selections in a plush setting include nine vegetarian offerings. Start with an exquisite mushroom appetizer with portobellos, shiitakes and buttons in a light scallion sauce. An extensive wine list is available. Gentlemen's jackets are suggested. Dressy casual; cocktails. **Parking:** on-site. **Cards:** AX, CB, DC, DS, MC, VI.

Chinese

RED STAR TAVERN   Lunch: $7-$15   Dinner: $9-$25   Phone: 954/565-8858   ③③
Location: Just e of US 1 (Federal Hwy); in Galleria Mall. 2418 Sunrise Blvd 33304. **Hours:** 11 am-midnight. **Features:** In a great place, the eatery affords tired shoppers a spot to rest and recharge their batteries. The large menu lists not only burgers, sandwiches and large salads but also chops, a fresh fish entree and some pasta dishes. The atmosphere is that of a modern tavern, with many food and beverage choices. Dressy casual; cocktails. **Parking:** on-site and valet. **Cards:** AX, CB, DC, DS, JC, MC, VI.

American

THE RIVER HOUSE   Dinner: $12-$28   Phone: 954/525-7661   ⑤③
Location: From W Broward Blvd, 0.3 mi s on Nugent Ave/SW 3rd Ave. 301 SW 3rd Ave 33301. **Hours:** 5:30 pm-11 pm, Sun 11:30 am-3 & 5:30-10 pm. **Closed:** 5/29, 12/25. **Reservations:** suggested. **Features:** Built in 1903, the riverfront restaurant lures diners to sit under the canopy of trees and stars to eat and watch the passing boats. Seating also is offered indoors and on the porch. On the menu are New American preparations of fresh seafood, meat and poultry. Dressy casual; cocktails. **Parking:** valet. **Cards:** AX, MC, VI. **Historic**

American

(See map and index starting on p. 364)

ROYAL INDIA **Lunch:** $7-$8   **Dinner:** $9-$16   **Phone:** 954/964-0071   64
Indian
Location: I-95, exit 23 (Griffin Rd), 2 mi w. 3801 Griffin Rd 33312. **Hours:** 11:30 am-3 & 5-10:30 pm.
Reservations: suggested, on weekends. **Features:** The user-friendly menu adeptly describes the savory
dishes on this varied menu. If the tangy and heady roasting doesn't add enough flavor to your entree, you
can sample from a sizable assortment of chutneys and other relishes to achieve the taste you favor. Dressy
casual; beer & wine only. **Parking:** on-site. **Cards:** AX, DC, DS, MC, VI.

RUTH'S CHRIS STEAK HOUSE   **Dinner:** $23-$38   **Phone:** 954/565-2338   27
Steak House
Location: 0.7 mi s from Oakland Park Blvd (SR 816). 2525 N Federal Hwy 33305. **Hours:** 5 pm-11 pm, Fri & Sat-11
pm. **Reservations:** accepted. **Features:** Patrons sit and relax in the comforting and soothing dining room.
The many steaks are cooked in the steakhouse's special way. Fresh seafood and chops are among other
offerings. Dressy casual; cocktails. **Parking:** valet. **Cards:** AX, DC, MC, VI.

SAGAMI JAPANESE RESTAURANT   **Lunch:** $7-$15   **Dinner:** $8-$25   **Phone:** 954/771-4447   4
Japanese
Location: SR 870 (Commerical Blvd), 0.8 mi n; in Imperial Square Shopping Center. 5975 N Federal Hwy 33308.
Hours: noon-10:45 pm, Sat from 5 pm, Sun 5 pm-11:45 pm. Closed: 11/23, 12/25. **Features:** A comfortable
setting for fresh sushi and sashimi, the restaurant also serves tempura, stir-fry and teriyaki-style entrees.
Casual dress; beer & wine only. **Parking:** on-site. **Cards:** AX, MC, VI.

SAMBA ROOM   **Lunch:** $10-$18   **Dinner:** $18-$28   **Phone:** 954/468-2000   49
Cuban
Location: Just w of US 1 (Federal Hwy). 350 E Las Olas Blvd 33301. **Hours:** 11 am-11 pm.
Reservations: suggested. **Features:** Located in the heart of Fort Lauderdale's trendy Las Olas Blvd. It
features affordable Latin fusion entrees, meats and seafoods. Dressy casual; cocktails. **Parking:** valet.
Cards: AX, MC, VI.

SEASONS 52   **Lunch:** $8-$22   **Dinner:** $8-$22   **Phone:** 954/537-1052   32
American
Location: Just e of US 1 (Federal Hwy); in Galleria Mall. 2428 E Sunrise Blvd 33304. **Hours:** 11:30 am-10 pm, Fri &
Sat-11 pm. **Reservations:** suggested. **Features:** Exhibiting a four seasons concept, the menu changes with
the seasons and sometimes sooner; "fresh" is the key ingredient and the selection available is extreme.
There are small plates and regular portions of foods, but the calories are under control. The dining room is
very contemporary and offers an open-air feeling. Dressy casual; cocktails. **Parking:** on-site and valet. **Cards:** AX, CB, DC, DS,
JC, MC, VI.

SEA WATCH RESTAURANT   **Lunch:** $6-$18   **Dinner:** $15-$31   **Phone:** 954/781-2200   1
Steak & Seafood
Location: SR A1A, 1 mi n of jct SR 870 (Commercial Blvd). 6002 N Ocean Blvd 33308. **Hours:** 11:30 am-3:30 & 5-
10 pm. Closed: 12/25. **Features:** Several dining rooms in this nautically decorated restaurant give diners
beautiful views of the beach and ocean. Widely varied entrees are served by a friendly, attentive wait staff.
Dressy casual; cocktails. **Parking:** on-site and valet. **Cards:** AX, CB, DS, MC, VI.

SHIRTTAIL CHARLIE'S RESTAURANT   **Lunch:** $5-$10   **Dinner:** $10-$22   **Phone:** 954/463-3474   54
Seafood
Location: On south bank of the New River; just sw of Andrews Ave, via SW 5th St; downtown. 400 SW 3rd Ave 33315.
Hours: 11:30 am-10 pm. Closed: 11/23, 12/25. **Reservations:** accepted. **Features:** Overlooking the scenic
New River, the restaurant lets you unwind while enjoying fried alligator and stuffed yellowtail snapper. Indoor
and outdoor dining both lend the same tropical experience. After eating, take advantage of a complimentary
boat ride. Casual dress; cocktails. **Parking:** on-site. **Cards:** AX, DS, MC, VI.

SHOOTERS WATERFRONT CAFE USA   **Lunch:** $7-$12   **Dinner:** $7-$23   **Phone:** 954/566-2855   22
Seafood
Location: Off SR A1A, just s of Oakland Park Blvd via NE 32nd Ave. 3033 NE 32nd Ave 33308. **Hours:** 11:30 am-10
pm, Fri & Sat-11 pm. **Features:** The food is great and the view even better. Guests can watch the boats go
by while noshing on sandwiches, fresh seafood, pasta or landlubber standbys. Indoor and outdoor seating is
available. Casual dress; cocktails. **Parking:** on-site (fee) and valet. **Cards:** AX, MC, VI.

SONNY'S REAL PIT BAR-B-Q   **Lunch:** $4-$9   **Dinner:** $8-$15   **Phone:** 954/776-4994   5
Barbecue
Location: I-95, exit 32 (Commercial Blvd), just e, then just n. 5401 Powerline Rd 33309. **Hours:** 10:30 am-9:30 pm,
Fri & Sat-10 pm. Closed: 11/23, 12/25. **Features:** Barbecue chicken, ribs and pulled pork are done right:
slowly cooked over a hardwood fire then coated in sauce. Also tempting are smoked turkey, fried catfish and
charbroiled chicken. A casual family atmosphere surrounds patrons. Casual dress; beer only. **Parking:** on-
site. **Cards:** AX, MC, VI.

TARPONBEND FOOD & TACKLE   **Lunch:** $6-$10   **Dinner:** $6-$19   **Phone:** 954/523-3233   38
Seafood
Location: From W Broward Blvd, s on Nugent Ave/SW 3rd Ave, then just e. 200 SW 2nd St 33301. **Hours:** 11:30 am-
11 pm, Fri & Sat-midnight. Closed: 5/29, 11/23, 12/25. **Features:** On the corner of the street, the fun,
friendly restaurant has sidewalk tables and a dining room bedecked in fishing memorabilia, including tackle
and scores of pictures. The menu features fish, burgers, chicken and pasta. Entertainment is offered
Thursday through Sunday. Casual dress; cocktails. **Parking:** valet and street. **Cards:** AX, DS, MC, VI.

TIMPANO ITALIAN CHOPHOUSE   **Lunch:** $6-$17   **Dinner:** $9-$30   **Phone:** 954/462-9119   47
Italian
Location: Just w of US 1 (Federal Hwy), just e of Andrew Ave; corner of 5th Ave and E Las Olas Blvd. 450 E Las Olas
Blvd 33301. **Hours:** 11 am-10 pm, Fri-11 pm, Sat 4 pm-11 pm, Sun 5 pm-10 pm. Closed: 11/23, 12/25.
Reservations: suggested. **Features:** Soft lighting and dark wood accents characterize the dining room.
Menu offerings include large steaks, chops and fresh pasta, as well as great combinations. A few fresh
seafood choices, all prepared with an Italian flair, also are thrown into the mix. Casual dress; cocktails; entertainment. **Parking:**
on-site (fee) and valet. **Cards:** AX, CB, DC, DS, MC, VI.

(See map and index starting on p. 364)

TOM JENKINS BAR-B-Q   **Lunch:** $4-$9   **Dinner:** $5-$18   **Phone:** 954/522-5046   **56**

Barbecue   **Location:** Just s of Davie Blvd (SR 736). 1236 S Federal Hwy 33316. **Hours:** 11 am-8:30 pm, Fri & Sat-10 pm. Closed: Sun & Mon. **Features:** Ribs, pulled and sliced pork, chicken, sliced beef and Mississippi catfish are all good at this casual eatery. Great aromas lure patrons through the door. Only cash is accepted. Casual dress. **Parking:** on-site.

TRINA RESTAURANT & LOUNGE   **Lunch:** $10-$18   **Dinner:** $19-$38   **Phone:** 954/567-8070   **36**

Mediterranean   **Location:** From Sunrise Blvd (SR 838), 0.5 mi s; in The Atlantic. 601 N Ft. Lauderdale Beach Blvd 33304. **Hours:** 11 am-10 pm, Fri & Sat-11 pm. **Features:** Views of the Atlantic Ocean can be enjoyed from the dining room, which has an upbeat feel with tall ceilings and colored walls, or the patio. Fresh land and sea ingredients factor into creative preparations of Mediterranean fare. Dressy casual; entertainment. **Parking:** valet. **Cards:** AX, CB, DC, DS, JC, MC, VI.

TROPICAL ACRES RESTAURANT   **Dinner:** $11-$17   **Phone:** 954/989-2500   **65**

Steak & Seafood   **Location:** I-95, exit 23 (Griffin Rd), 0.3 mi w. 2500 Griffin Rd 33312. **Hours:** 4:30 pm-10 pm, Sun 3 pm-9 pm. Closed: 12/24, 12/25. **Reservations:** accepted. **Features:** Family-owned since 1949, the popular restaurant serves cuts of meat on sizzling skillets plucked straight out of the fireplace grill. The menu also lists 40 other tempting entrees. Cozy banquet facilities make the place a top choice for private parties. Dressy casual; cocktails. **Parking:** on-site and street. **Cards:** AX, CB, DC, MC, VI. **Classic**

TRY MY THAI CAFE TOO   **Lunch:** $6-$9   **Dinner:** $9-$17   **Phone:** 954/630-0030   **28**

Thai   **Location:** 0.6 mi n of Sunrise Blvd (SR 83B); in Plaza Del Mar. 1507 N Federal Hwy 33304. **Hours:** 10:30 am-2:30 & 5-10:30 pm, Sat from 5 pm, Sun 5 pm-10 pm. Closed: 11/23, 12/25; also Mon. **Reservations:** accepted. **Features:** Menu descriptions pump up the appeal of meat and fresh fish dishes prepared with curry flavors. Patrons can decide on the spice level. The atmosphere is bright and bistro-like. Casual dress; beer & wine only. **Parking:** on-site. **Cards:** AX, DC, DS, MC, VI.

UMBERTO'S OF LONG ISLAND PIZZA & RESTAURANT   **Lunch:** $6-$20   **Dinner:** $6-$20   **Phone:** 954/776-0258   **7**

Italian   **Location:** Just e of US 1 (Federal Hwy). 3051 E Commercial Blvd 33308. **Hours:** 11 am-10 pm, Fri & Sat-11 pm. **Features:** The food is Italian and the atmosphere casual. On the menu are brick-oven pizzas, pasta dishes and traditional veal, chicken and seafood specialties. Casual dress; beer & wine only. **Parking:** on-site. **Cards:** MC, VI.

The following restaurants have not been evaluated by AAA but are listed for your information only.

DAN MARINO'S TOWN TAVERN   **Phone:** 954/522-1313

(fyi)   Not evaluated. **Location:** 300 SW 1st Ave 33301. **Features:** Football memorabilia decorates the casual restaurant, which offers pasta, burgers, sandwiches, seafood and ribs.

FLANIGAN'S SEAFOOD BAR & GRILL   **Phone:** 954/493-5329

(fyi)   Not evaluated. **Location:** 1479 E Commercial Blvd 33334. **Features:** The family-friendly restaurant is known for its baby back ribs, burgers and seafood.

FLANIGAN'S SEAFOOD BAR & GRILL   **Phone:** 954/267-4877

(fyi)   Not evaluated. **Location:** 1721 N Andrews Ave 33311. **Features:** The family-friendly restaurant is known for its baby back ribs, burgers and seafood.

The Fort Lauderdale Vicinity

COCONUT CREEK pop. 43,566

—— WHERE TO DINE ——

COCONUT CREEK ALE HOUSE   **Lunch:** $7-$19   **Dinner:** $7-$19   **Phone:** 954/354-0414

American

Location: Florida Tpke, exit 16, just s; in Winston Park Plaza. 5331 Lyons Rd 33073. **Hours:** 11:30 am-2 am, Fri & Sat from 11 am. Closed: 11/23, 12/25. **Features:** For watching sporting events and eating comfort foods, such as burgers and meatloaf, this place is hard to beat. Guests have a choice of more than 40 TVs and more than 55 beers. Casual dress; cocktails. **Parking:** on-site. **Cards:** AX, CB, DC, DS, JC, MC, VI.

CORAL SPRINGS pop. 117,549

—— WHERE TO STAY ——

CORAL SPRINGS MARRIOTT HOTEL GOLF CLUB & CONVENTION CENTER   *Book at aaa.com*   **Phone:** 954/753-5598

	1P:	2P:
12/1-4/15	1P: $159-$189	2P: $159-$189
10/1-11/30	1P: $119-$159	2P: $119-$159
4/16-9/30	1P: $99-$139	2P: $99-$139

Resort
Large-scale Hotel

Location: Sawgrass Expwy/SR 869, exit 10 (Coral Ridge Dr), 0.3 mi n, then 0.3 mi w. 11775 Heron Bay Blvd 33076. **Fax:** 954/753-2888. **Facility:** The hotel has an atrium lobby and offers some rooms with golf course views. 224 units. 217 one-bedroom standard units. 7 one-bedroom suites, some with whirlpools. 7 stories, interior corridors. *Bath:* combo or shower only. **Parking:** on-site. **Terms:** 1-3 night minimum stay, cancellation fee imposed, package plans, small pets only ($50 fee). **Amenities:** dual phone lines, voice mail, irons, hair dryers. *Fee:* video games, high-speed Internet. **Dining:** 6:30 am-10 pm, cocktails. **Pool(s):** heated outdoor. **Leisure Activities:** sauna, whirlpool, exercise room. *Fee:* golf-18 holes, golf instruction. **Guest Services:** gift shop, valet and coin laundry, area transportation-within 5 mi. **Business Services:** meeting rooms, business center. **Cards:** AX, CB, DC, DS, JC, MC, VI. **Special Amenities:** free newspaper. *(See color ad below)*

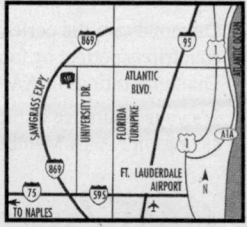

COURTYARD BY MARRIOTT CORAL SPRINGS   *Book at aaa.com*   Phone: (954)227-1300
▼▼▼▼ All Year   1P: $89-$149
Small-scale Hotel   **Location:** Atlantic Blvd, just s on University Dr, then w on NW 6th Ct. Located behind McDonalds. 620 N University Dr 33071. Fax: 954/227-1500. **Facility:** 110 units. 106 one-bedroom standard units. 4 one-bedroom suites ($139-$199). 4 stories, interior corridors. *Bath:* combo or shower only. **Parking:** on-site. **Terms:** 3 day cancellation notice-fee imposed. **Amenities:** high-speed Internet, dual phone lines, voice mail, irons, hair dryers. **Pool(s):** heated outdoor. **Leisure Activities:** whirlpool, exercise room. **Guest Services:** valet and coin laundry. **Business Services:** meeting rooms, business center. **Cards:** AX, DC, DS, JC, MC, VI. *(See color ad p 396)*   SOME UNITS

ASK SD ⛐ ⬚ ⌨ ⛵ ⚐ DATA PORT ▣ / ✕ ▤ ▣ /

LA QUINTA INN FT. LAUDERDALE (CORAL SPRINGS)   *Book at aaa.com*   Phone: (954)753-9000
AAA SAVE   1/18-4/30   1P: $120-$135   XP: $7   F18
▼▼▼▼   12/1-1/17 & 5/1-11/30   1P: $89-$99   XP: $7   F18
Small-scale Hotel   **Location:** SR 817, just n or jct SR 834 (Sample Rd). 3701 University Dr 33065. Fax: 954/755-4012. **Facility:** 121 units. 118 one-bedroom standard units. 3 one-bedroom suites. 5 stories, interior corridors. *Bath:* combo or shower only. **Parking:** on-site. **Terms:** [ECP] meal plan available, small pets only. **Amenities:** voice mail, irons, hair dryers. *Fee:* video games, high-speed Internet. **Pool(s):** heated outdoor. **Guest Services:** valet and coin laundry. **Business Services:** meeting rooms, fax (fee). **Cards:** AX, CB, DC, DS, MC, VI. **Special Amenities:** free expanded continental breakfast and free local telephone calls. *(See color ad p 384)*   SOME UNITS

🐾 ⛐ ⬚ ⌨ ⛵ ⚐ DATA PORT ▣ / ✕ ▤ ▣ /
FEE FEE

STUDIO 6 #6027   *Book at aaa.com*   Phone: 954/796-0011
▼▼▼▼   1/6-3/30   1P: $65-$75   2P: $69-$79   XP: $4   F17
Motel   12/1-1/5   1P: $64-$74   2P: $68-$78   XP: $4   F17
    3/31-11/30   1P: $54-$64   2P: $58-$68   XP: $4   F17
Location: SR 869 (Sawgrass Expwy), exit 12 (University Dr), just s. 5645 University Dr 33067. Fax: 954/796-7530. **Facility:** 124 one-bedroom standard units with efficiencies. 2 stories, exterior corridors. *Bath:* combo or shower only. **Parking:** on-site. **Terms:** office hours 7 am-8 pm, weekly rates available, small pets only ($10-$50 fee). **Amenities:** voice mail, irons, hair dryers. **Guest Services:** coin laundry. **Business Services:** fax (fee). **Cards:** AX, CB, DC, DS, MC, VI.   SOME UNITS

SD 🐾 ⛐ ⬚ ⌨ ⛵ ⚐ DATA PORT ▤ ▣ ▣ / ✕ /
FEE

WELLESLEY INN (CORAL SPRINGS)   *Book at aaa.com*   Phone: (954)344-2200
AAA SAVE   12/1-4/15   1P: $119   2P: $119   XP: $10   F18
▼▼▼   4/16-11/30   1P: $99   2P: $99   XP: $10   F18
Small-scale Hotel   **Location:** SR 817, just s of jct Sample Rd (SR 834). 3100 N University Dr 33065. Fax: 954/344-7885. **Facility:** 103 units. 101 one-bedroom standard units. 2 one-bedroom suites. 4 stories, interior corridors. *Bath:* combo or shower only. **Parking:** on-site. **Terms:** small pets only ($10 fee). **Amenities:** voice mail, irons, hair dryers. *Fee:* video games, high-speed Internet. *Some:* dual phone lines. **Pool(s):** heated outdoor. **Guest Services:** valet laundry. **Business Services:** fax (fee). **Cards:** AX, CB, DC, DS, MC, VI.   SOME UNITS

SD 🐾 ⛐ ⬚ ⌨ ⛵ ⚐ DATA PORT ▤ ▣ ▣ / ✕ /
FEE

──────── **WHERE TO DINE** ────────

ANITA'S GRILL MEXICANO   Dinner: $18-$25   Phone: 954/255-1778
AAA   **Location:** On SR 834 (Sample Rd), 0.8 mi w of University Blvd, 2 mi e of Sawgrass Expwy. 10288 W Sample Rd 33065. **Hours:** 5:30 pm-10:30 pm. Closed: 7/4, 11/23, 12/25; also Sun; Mon 6/1-10/31. **Reservations:** accepted. **Features:** Gourmet food with the freshest ingredients from the land and sea is accented with the spices of Mexico. A dimly lit room accented with pictures of the Mexican countryside softens the impact of the spices. Dressy casual; beer & wine only. **Parking:** on-site. **Cards:** AX, CB, DC, DS, JC, MC, VI.
Mexican   ⛐

BIG BEAR BREWING COMPANY   Lunch: $7-$12   Dinner: $10-$24   Phone: 954/341-5545
▼▼▼   **Location:** From Atlantic Blvd (SR 814), 0.9 mi n. 1800 N University Dr 33065. **Hours:** 11:30 am-10:30 pm, Fri & Sat-11:30 pm, Sun 11 am-10 pm. Closed: 11/23, 12/25. **Reservations:** accepted, weekdays.
American   **Features:** Dark, wood-paneled walls and large pictures contribute to the warm setting. Beers are made on the premises, as evidenced in the brew tanks at the entrance. Entrees—including chops, steaks, ribs and seafood—are served in plentiful portions. Casual dress; cocktails. **Parking:** on-site. **Cards:** AX, DC, DS, MC, VI.   ⛐ ⍾

BIG TOMATO MARKET GRILL   Lunch: $7-$17   Dinner: $7-$17   Phone: 954/753-4244
▼▼▼   **Location:** Corner of Atlantic Blvd and University Dr; in Coral Square Mall. 9457 W Atlantic Blvd 33065. **Hours:** 11 am-close. Closed: 11/23, 12/25. **Features:** Near the food court in the mall, the restaurant delivers comfort from shopping and lots of food, including pizza, pasta dishes and veal and chicken selections. Portions are large enough that patrons need a shopping bag to take home what isn't finished. Casual dress; cocktails.
Italian   **Parking:** on-site. **Cards:** AX, DC, DS, MC, VI.   ⛐ ⍾

BONEFISH GRILL   Dinner: $15-$27   Phone: 954/509-0405
▼▼▼   **Location:** 0.6 mi n of Atlantic Blvd. 1455 N University Dr 33071. **Hours:** 4 pm-10:30 pm, Fri & Sat-11:30 pm, Sun-10 pm. **Reservations:** accepted. **Features:** A cozy, soft setting for relaxing, the restaurant presents a menu centering on fresh seafood grilled over wood. Also in the mix are steaks and chops, as well as pasta dishes with seafood. Casual dress; cocktails. **Parking:** on-site. **Cards:** AX, CB, DC, DS, JC, MC, VI.   ⍾
Seafood

DAN MARINO'S TOWN TAVERN   Lunch: $8-$12   Dinner: $8-$27   Phone: 954/341-4658
▼▼▼   **Location:** From Atlantic Blvd, just n. 901 N University Dr 33071. **Hours:** 11:30 am-10 pm, Fri & Sat-11 pm. Closed: 11/23, 12/25. **Features:** The restaurant has the feel of an American bistro. The menu lists a local fresh seafood item daily, along with Dan's ribs and other comfort foods. Casual dress; cocktails. **Parking:**
American   on-site. **Cards:** AX, MC, VI.   ⛐ ⍾ ◣

EL MARIACHI MEXICAN & SPANISH RESTAURANT   Lunch: $6-$10   Dinner: $10-$17   Phone: 954/753-3788

Mexican

Location: Just n of Atlantic Blvd, jct Ramblewood Dr; in Ramblewood Plaza. 1203 N University Dr 33071. **Hours:** 11:30 am-10 pm, Fri & Sat-11:30 pm, Sun noon-10 pm. Closed: 7/4, 11/23, 12/25. **Reservations:** accepted, Fri & Sat. **Features:** The diverse menu lists Mexican and Spanish favorites as well as a few Tex-Mex options. The comfortable dining room displays art from each country. Service is attentive and well-paced. Casual dress; cocktails. **Parking:** on-site. **Cards:** AX, CB, DC, DS, JC, MC, VI.

GOLD COAST GRILL   Lunch: $6-$9   Dinner: $9-$19   Phone: 954/255-3474

Steak & Seafood

Location: On SR 817 (University Dr), 0.4 mi s from Sample Rd (SR 834); in The Walk on University. 2752 N University Dr 33065. **Hours:** 11 am-2:30 & 4-10:30 pm, Fri & Sat-11:30 pm, Sun 4 pm-10 pm. Closed: 11/23, 12/25. **Features:** Soothing is the word in the lounge and in the comfortable dining room. Outdoor seats afford views of the lit fountain. Menu selections center on good fresh seafood and steaks. Lighter choices also are available. Dressy casual; cocktails. **Parking:** on-site. **Cards:** AX, CB, DC, DS, JC, MC, VI.

MAMBO JAMBO A LATIN AMERICAN CAFE   Lunch: $8-$16   Dinner: $8-$23   Phone: 954/575-0533

Latino

Location: From Atlantic Blvd, 1.3 mi n on University Dr, jct NW 19th St and University Dr. 1933 University Dr 33071. **Hours:** 11:30 am-3:30 & 4:30-10 pm, Fri & Sat 4:30 pm-midnight, Sun 4:30 pm-10 pm. Closed major holidays. **Features:** Those who can't decide between South American or Cuban food are in for a treat. Favorites from each region include a variety of seviches, as well as beef, lamb, pork, poultry and fresh seafood dishes. The decor is warm and upbeat. Patrons can sample tequilas and wines with dinner inside or on the patio. Casual dress; cocktails. **Parking:** on-site. **Cards:** AX, MC, VI.

MILLER'S CORAL SPRINGS ALE HOUSE   Lunch: $5-$11   Dinner: $6-$11   Phone: 954/825-0574

American

Location: Atlantic Blvd (SR 817), 1.3 mi n on University Dr; jct NW 19th St and University Dr. 1915 N University Dr 33071. **Hours:** 11 am-2 am, Thurs-Sat to 3 am. Closed: 11/23. **Features:** For watching sporting events and eating comfort foods, this place is hard to beat. Guests have a choice of more than 40 TVs and more than 90 beers. Casual dress; cocktails. **Parking:** on-site. **Cards:** AX, MC, VI.

NINJA JAPANESE RESTAURANT   Lunch: $5-$22   Dinner: $9-$25   Phone: 954/796-9810

Japanese

Location: Corner of University Dr and Royal Palm Blvd; on the northwest corner; in a small shopping plaza. 2554 University Dr 33065. **Hours:** 11:30 am-10:30 pm, Fri & Sat-11 pm, Sun 4 pm-9:30 pm. Closed: 11/23, 12/25. **Reservations:** accepted. **Features:** A serious array of sushi and sashimi, including 32 varieties of rolls, is served in a casual atmosphere. Also on the menu are chicken and beef dishes, as well as tempura choices. Casual dress; beer & wine only. **Parking:** on-site. **Cards:** AX, DC, MC, VI.

THE ORIGINAL STEAKHOUSE & SPORTS THEATRE   Lunch: $9-$23   Dinner: $9-$23   Phone: 954/757-5575

Steak House

Location: Corner of University and Ramblewood drs; just n of Atlantic Blvd; in a shopping plaza across from Coral Springs Mall. 1000 University Dr 33071. **Hours:** 4 pm-11 pm, Fri-midnight, Sat noon-midnight, Sun noon-10 pm. Closed major holidays. **Features:** The theme here: Lots of food, lots of TVs and lots of sports. The menu lists a nice selection of steaks, seafood, chicken and ribs. Guests have lots of fun in the relaxed atmosphere. Casual dress; cocktails. **Parking:** on-site. **Cards:** AX, CB, DC, DS, JC, MC, VI.

RUNYON'S   Lunch: $8-$20   Dinner: $20-$34   Phone: 954/752-2333

American

Location: On SR 834 (Sample Rd), 0.5 mi w of jct SR 817 (University Dr). 9810 W Sample Rd 33065. **Hours:** 11 am-2:30 & 4-10:30 pm, Fri-11 pm, Sat & Sun 4 pm-11 pm. Closed: Super Bowl Sun. **Reservations:** suggested. **Features:** Dining rooms are decorated with recognizable black-and-white photographs and autographed pictures of celebrities who have been seen here. On the menu are well-prepared steaks, chops and seafood. Dressy casual; cocktails; entertainment. **Parking:** on-site. **Cards:** AX, DC, DS, MC, VI.

The following restaurant has not been evaluated by AAA but is listed for your information only.

CORAL SPRINGS SUPER BUFFET   Phone: 954/796-6777

(fyi)

Not evaluated. **Location:** Just s of Royal Palm Blvd; in Coral Palm Plaza. 2101 N University Dr 33071. **Features:** Among offerings are a large selection of Chinese favorites, some American fare and raw bar choices.

DANIA BEACH pop. 20,061   (See map and index starting on p. 364)

WHERE TO STAY

COURTYARD BY MARRIOTT AIRPORT & CRUISE PORT   *Book at aaa.com*   Phone: (954)342-8333   97

	1P	2P
1/1-4/30	1P: $159-$219	2P: $159-$219
12/1-12/31	1P: $119-$189	2P: $119-$189
10/1-11/30	1P: $99-$169	2P: $99-$169
5/1-9/30	1P: $79-$149	2P: $79-$149

Small-scale Hotel **Location:** I-95, exit 23, w on Griffen Rd (SR 818) to Anglers Ave, then s. 400 Gulf Stream Way 33004. Fax: 954/342-8555. **Facility:** 174 units. 171 one-bedroom standard units. 3 one-bedroom suites ($179-$289). 6 stories, interior corridors. *Bath:* combo or shower only. **Parking:** on-site. **Amenities:** high-speed Internet, dual phone lines, voice mail, irons, hair dryers. **Dining:** 6:30-11 am, Sat & Sun from 7 am, cocktails. **Pool(s):** heated outdoor. **Leisure Activities:** whirlpool, exercise room. **Guest Services:** airport transportation-Fort Lauderdale-Hollywood International Airport, area transportation-Port Everglades only. **Business Services:** meeting rooms, business center. **Cards:** AX, CB, DC, DS, JC, MC, VI. **Special Amenities:** free newspaper.

SOME UNITS

La Quinta: Spanish for "AAA members rest easy."

Wherever the road takes you, there are more than 375 La Quinta locations nationwide ready to greet you. And, as a AAA member, you can save up to 30% when you stay with us.*

So whether you stretch your legs in our spacious rooms or recharge with a free continental breakfast, La Quinta has got you covered. Plus, if you join the Returns program, you can earn points to redeem for valuable rewards.

To make a reservation, contact your AAA travel professional, call La Quinta at **1-800-221-4731** or visit **LQ.com**. (See back for map of locations.)

La Quinta ©2005

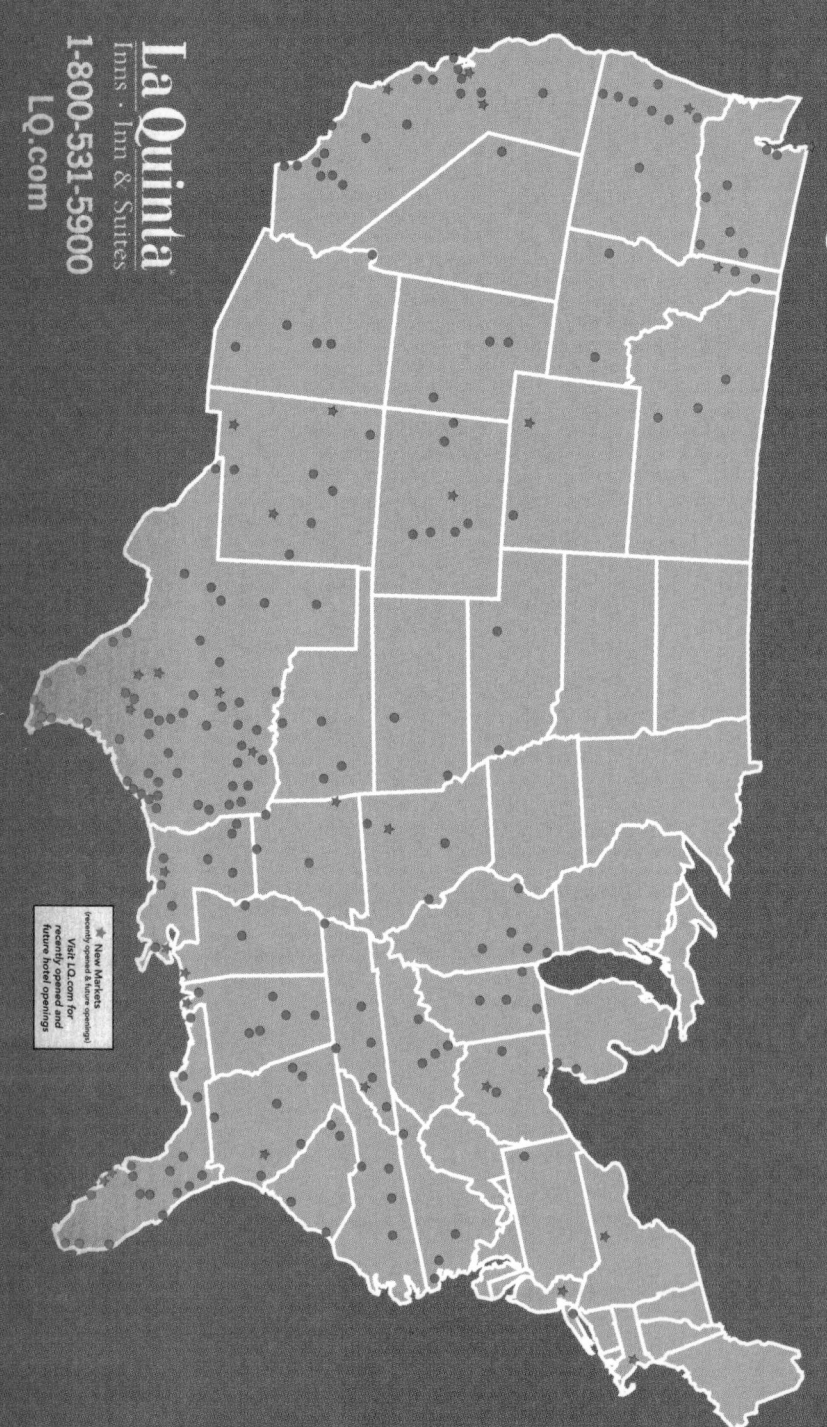

(See map and index starting on p. 364)

HILTON GARDEN INN FT. LAUDERDALE/HOLLYWOOD AIRPORT — Book at aaa.com
Phone: (954)924-9204 **100**

	1P: $169-$209	2P: $169-$209	XP: $10	F18
1/1-4/30				
12/1-12/31 & 10/1-11/30	1P: $129-$149	2P: $129-$149	XP: $10	F18
5/1-9/30	1P: $99-$119	2P: $99-$119	XP: $10	F18

Small-scale Hotel **Location:** I-95, exit 22 (Stirling Rd), just e. 180 SW 18th Ave 33004. Fax: 954/924-9042. **Facility:** 156 one-bedroom standard units. 6 stories, interior corridors. *Bath:* combo or shower only. **Parking:** on-site. **Terms:** cancellation fee imposed, package plans. **Amenities:** video games (fee), high-speed Internet, dual phone lines, voice mail, safes, irons, hair dryers. **Pool(s):** heated outdoor. **Leisure Activities:** whirlpool, exercise room. **Guest Services:** sundries, valet and coin laundry, area transportation. **Business Services:** meeting rooms, business center. **Cards:** AX, CB, DC, DS, JC, MC, VI.

SOME UNITS

LUCKEY'S MOTEL
Phone: (954)925-5500 **98**

| 12/15-4/15 | 1P: $69-$169 | 2P: $69-$169 | XP: $10 | F12 |
| 12/1-12/14 & 4/16-11/30 | 1P: $59-$79 | 2P: $59-$79 | XP: $10 | F12 |

Location: US 1, 0.5 mi n of jct Sterling Rd; 0.5 mi s of jct Griffin Rd; center. 205 N Federal Hwy 33004. Fax: 954/424-9825. **Facility:** 15 one-bedroom standard units, some with efficiencies. 1 story, exterior corridors. *Bath:* shower only. **Parking:** on-site. **Amenities:** irons, hair dryers. **Guest Services:** coin laundry. **Cards:** AX, DS, MC, VI.

SOME UNITS

MOTEL 6 - DANIA BEACH #376 — Book at aaa.com
Phone: 954/921-5505 **99**

12/23-3/26	1P: $51-$64	2P: $57-$70	XP: $3	F17
3/27-5/25	1P: $45-$55	2P: $51-$61	XP: $3	F17
12/1-12/22 & 5/26-11/30	1P: $39-$49	2P: $45-$55	XP: $3	F17

Motel **Location:** I-95, exit 22, 1.1 mi e on Stirling Rd, just n on US 1 (Federal Hwy), then 0.8 mi e. 825 E Dania Beach Blvd 33004. Fax: 954/920-0591. **Facility:** 163 one-bedroom standard units. 2 stories (no elevator), exterior corridors. *Bath:* combo or shower only. **Parking:** on-site. **Terms:** small pets only (limit 1). **Pool(s):** heated outdoor. **Guest Services:** coin laundry. **Business Services:** fax (fee). **Cards:** AX, CB, DC, DS, MC, VI.

SOME UNITS

SHERATON FORT LAUDERDALE AIRPORT HOTEL — Book at aaa.com
Phone: (954)920-3500 **96**

1/1-3/31	1P: $150-$309	2P: $150-$309	XP: $10	F17
12/1-12/31 & 4/1-6/30	1P: $120-$209	2P: $120-$209	XP: $10	F17
7/1-11/30	1P: $110-$199	2P: $110-$199	XP: $10	F17

Location: I-95, exit 23. Adjoins Design Center of the Americas. 1825 Griffin Rd 33004. Fax: 954/920-3571. Large-scale Hotel **Facility:** 250 units. 246 one-bedroom standard units. 4 one-bedroom suites. 12 stories, interior corridors. *Bath:* combo or shower only. **Parking:** on-site (fee) and valet. **Terms:** cancellation fee imposed, pets ($50 fee). **Amenities:** dual phone lines, voice mail, irons, hair dryers. *Some: Fee:* high-speed Internet. **Dining:** 6 am-11 pm, cocktails. **Pool(s):** heated outdoor. **Leisure Activities:** whirlpool, 2 lighted tennis courts, exercise room. **Guest Services:** gift shop, valet laundry, airport transportation-Fort Lauderdale-Hollywood International Airport. **Business Services:** meeting rooms, business center. **Cards:** AX, CB, DC, DS, JC, MC, VI. **Special Amenities:** free newspaper. *(See color ad p 8)*

SOME UNITS
FEE   FEE

SLEEP INN & SUITES — Book at aaa.com
Phone: (954)874-1800 **103**

2/1-4/15 [ECP]	1P: $109-$249	2P: $109-$249	XP: $10	F17
12/1-1/31 [ECP]	1P: $99-$229	2P: $99-$229	XP: $10	F17
10/1-11/30 [ECP]	1P: $89-$199	2P: $89-$199	XP: $10	F17
4/16-9/30 [ECP]	1P: $79-$189	2P: $79-$189	XP: $10	F17

Small-scale Hotel **Location:** I-95, exit 21, 1.7 mi e, then just n. 1500 SE 5th Ave 33004. Fax: 954/874-1818. **Facility:** 69 one-bedroom standard units. 3 stories, interior corridors. *Bath:* combo or shower only. **Parking:** on-site. **Terms:** cancellation fee imposed. **Amenities:** high-speed Internet, dual phone lines, voice mail, irons, hair dryers. **Pool(s):** small heated outdoor. **Leisure Activities:** whirlpool, limited exercise equipment. **Guest Services:** valet and coin laundry, airport transportation-Fort Lauderdale-Hollywood International Airport, area transportation-Port Everglades. **Business Services:** business center. **Cards:** AX, CB, DC, DS, JC, MC, VI.

SOME UNITS

SPRINGHILL SUITES BY MARRIOTT FORT LAUDERDALE AIRPORT & CRUISE PORT — Book at aaa.com
Phone: 954/920-9696 **101**

2/26-4/15	1P: $139-$159			
12/1-2/25 & 9/30-11/30	1P: $119-$139			
4/16-9/29	1P: $99-$119			

Location: I-95, exit 22, just e on Stirling, then n. 151 SW 18th Ct 33004. Fax: 954/929-3577. **Facility:** 168 one-bedroom standard units. 7 stories, interior corridors. *Bath:* combo or shower only. **Parking:** on-site. Small-scale Hotel **Terms:** cancellation fee imposed. **Amenities:** high-speed Internet, dual phone lines, voice mail, irons, hair dryers. **Pool(s):** heated outdoor. **Leisure Activities:** whirlpool, exercise room. **Guest Services:** sundries, valet and coin laundry, airport transportation-Fort Lauderdale-Hollywood International Airport, area transportation. **Business Services:** meeting rooms, business center. **Cards:** AX, DC, DS, MC, VI.

SOME UNITS

SUPER 8 MOTEL
Phone: (954)921-6500 **102**

| 12/1-4/15 [CP] | 1P: $109-$190 | 2P: $109-$190 | XP: $10 | F |
| 4/16-11/30 [CP] | 1P: $69-$119 | 2P: $69-$119 | XP: $10 | F |

Motel **Location:** I-95, exit 22 (Stirling Rd), 1.1 mi e, then just s. 333 S Federal Hwy 33004. Fax: 954/921-0430. **Facility:** 36 one-bedroom standard units. 2 stories, exterior corridors. **Parking:** on-site. **Amenities:** irons, hair dryers. **Guest Services:** area transportation. **Cards:** AX, DS, MC, VI.

SOME UNITS

(See map and index starting on p. 364)

WYNDHAM FORT LAUDERDALE AIRPORT HOTEL   *Book at aaa.com*   Phone: (954)920-3300   95

12/1-4/16	1P: $189-$249	2P: $189-$249	XP: $10 F12
10/1-11/30	1P: $149-$209	2P: $149-$209	XP: $10 F12
4/17-5/31	1P: $149-$189	2P: $149-$189	XP: $10 F12
6/1-9/30	1P: $129-$169	2P: $129-$169	XP: $10 F12

Large-scale Hotel **Location:** I-95, exit 23. 1870 Griffin Rd 33004. Fax: 954/920-3348. **Facility:** 388 units. 383 one-bedroom standard units. 5 one-bedroom suites. 8 stories, interior/exterior corridors. *Bath:* combo or shower only. **Parking:** on-site (fee) and valet. **Amenities:** dual phone lines, voice mail, irons, hair dryers. *Fee:* video games, high-speed Internet. **Dining:** 6 am-11 pm, cocktails. **Pool(s):** heated outdoor. **Leisure Activities:** whirlpool, 2 lighted tennis courts, exercise room. *Fee:* massage. **Guest Services:** gift shop, valet and coin laundry, airport transportation-Fort Lauderdale-Hollywood International Airport. **Business Services:** meeting rooms, business center. **Cards:** AX, DC, DS, MC, VI.

———— WHERE TO DINE ————

ISLAMORADA FISH COMPANY   Lunch: $5-$21   Dinner: $5-$21   Phone: 954/927-7737   112
Seafood   **Location:** I-95, exit 23, w on Griffin Rd (SR 818) to Anglers Ave, then s; in Bass Pro Shop Outdoor World. 220 Gulfstream Way 33004. **Hours:** 11 am-10 pm. Closed: 12/25. **Features:** An aquatic tank sits in the middle of the dining room, where you can dine on selections of local seafood. The casual atmosphere spills over to the outdoor porch, which overlooks the man-made lake. Families are welcomed. Casual dress; cocktails. **Parking:** on-site. **Cards:** AX, DS, VI.

LE PETIT CAFE   Lunch: $8-$20   Dinner: $8-$20   Phone: 954/967-9912   111
French   **Location:** I-95, exit 23, 1.4 mi w. 3308 Griffin Rd 33004. **Hours:** 11:30 am-2:30 & 4:30-9:30 pm, Sat & Sun from 4:30 pm. Closed: 11/23; also Mon. **Features:** Familiar classics dominate the menu in this spiffy creperie. Hearts-of-palm salad, frog legs, beef bourguignonne and, of course, many crepe choices are served in a quietly charming atmosphere featuring the music of Edith Paif. Don't leave without dessert. Dressy casual; beer & wine only. **Parking:** on-site. **Cards:** MC, VI.

RUSTIC INN CRABHOUSE   *Menu on aaa.com*   Lunch: $5-$12   Dinner: $12-$30   Phone: 954/584-1637   110
Seafood   **Location:** I-95, exit 23, just w on Griffin Rd (SR 818), then n, across the bridge. 4331 Ravenswood Rd 33312. **Hours:** 11:30 am-10:45 pm, Sun 2 pm-9:45 pm. Closed: 11/23. **Features:** The classic crab house is known for its garlic crabs. Also on the menu are other fresh seafood items, ribs and pasta dishes. Patrons can sit dockside or inside with pictures of the famous who have cracked crabs here. Casual dress; cocktails. **Parking:** on-site. **Cards:** AX, CB, DC, DS, JC, MC, VI.

———— *The following restaurant has not been evaluated by AAA but is listed for your information only.* ————

HOT DIGGITY DOGS   Phone: 954/981-7827
fyi   Not evaluated. **Location:** I-95, exit 23, 0.7 mi w. 2641 Griffin Rd 33004. **Features:** Hot dogs are king, with the Chicago and New York styles topping the list. Rounding out the menu are Polish sausages, Italian sausages and grilled chicken sandwiches.

DAVIE pop. 75,720   (See map and index starting on p. 364)

———— WHERE TO STAY ————

COMFORT SUITES FORT LAUDERDALE AIRPORT
WEST   *Book at aaa.com*   Phone: (954)585-7071   107

12/16-4/15 [ECP]	1P: $129-$169	2P: $139-$179
4/16-11/30 [ECP]	1P: $109-$139	2P: $119-$149
12/1-12/15 [ECP]	1P: $109-$129	2P: $119-$139

Small-scale Hotel   **Location:** I-595, exit 7, just s. 2540 Davie Rd 33317. Fax: 954/585-8201. **Facility:** 77 units. 74 one-bedroom standard units. 3 one-bedroom suites. 5 stories, interior corridors. *Bath:* combo or shower only. **Parking:** on-site. **Amenities:** video games (fee), high-speed Internet, dual phone lines, voice mail, irons, hair dryers. **Leisure Activities:** whirlpool, exercise room. **Guest Services:** valet and coin laundry, airport transportation-Fort Lauderdale-Hollywood International Airport, area transportation-Port Everglades, within 5 mi. **Business Services:** meeting rooms, business center. **Cards:** AX, CB, DC, DS, JC, MC, VI. **Special Amenities:** free expanded continental breakfast and free local telephone calls.

HOMESTEAD STUDIO SUITES
HOTEL-PLANTATION/DAVIE   *Book at aaa.com*   Phone: (954)476-1211   106

1/2-4/15	1P: $69-$99	2P: $74-$104 XP: $5 F17
12/1-1/1 & 4/16-11/30	1P: $59-$84	2P: $64-$89 XP: $5 F17

Motel   **Location:** I-595, exit University Dr/SR 817, 0.3 mi. 7550 SR 84 E 33317. Fax: 954/476-0026. **Facility:** 126 one-bedroom standard units with efficiencies. 2 stories, exterior corridors. *Bath:* combo or shower only. **Parking:** on-site. **Terms:** office hours 6:30 am-10 pm, small pets only ($75 fee). **Amenities:** high-speed Internet (fee), voice mail, irons. **Guest Services:** coin laundry. **Cards:** AX, DC, DS, MC, VI.

(See map and index starting on p. 364)

──────── WHERE TO DINE ────────

BOB GILBERT'S KANSAS CITY SEAFOOD & STEAKHOUSE RESTAURANT Dinner: $12-$32 Phone: 954/680-0322 (120)
▼▼ ▲▲▲▲
Location: I-595, exit 5, 2.8 mi s on University Dr (SR 819), just s of Griffin Rd; in the Davie Square Shopping Plaza. 5645 S University Dr 33328. **Hours:** 5 pm-11 pm. **Reservations:** accepted. **Features:** This restaurant is an example of what is fast becoming a rarity in America: a mid-range priced steakhouse; the decor is warm as well. Casual dress; cocktails. **Parking:** on-site. **Cards:** AX, DC, DS, MC, VI.
Steak & Seafood

BUCA DI BEPPO Dinner: $14-$25 Phone: 954/577-3287 (118)
▼▼ ▲▲▲▲
Location: I-595, exit 5, 1.5 mi s; in Rolling Hills Plaza. 3355 S University Dr 33328. **Hours:** 5 pm-10 pm, Fri & Sat-11 pm, Sun noon-9 pm. **Reservations:** suggested. **Features:** A fun place to eat, the restaurant offers family-style—which translates to "huge"—portions. The various dining rooms display an eclectic collection of more than 2,500 pictures of Italy, figurines related to the country and famous, as well as not-so-famous, natives. Casual dress; cocktails. **Parking:** on-site. **Cards:** AX, CB, DC, DS, JC, MC, VI.
South Italian

CHAR-HUT 84 Lunch: $3-$10 Dinner: $3-$10 Phone: 954/474-9312 (115)
▼ ▲▲▲
Location: I-595, exit 4, just w; in Pine Island Ridge Plaza. 9000 W SR 84 33324. **Hours:** 11 am-9:30 pm, Fri & Sat-10 pm, Sun-9 pm. Closed: 11/23, 12/25. **Features:** The locally owned spot has great burgers and a quarter-pound hot dog, as well as chicken and fish dishes. It's casual and good. Casual dress. **Parking:** on-site. **Cards:** AX, DS, MC, VI.
American

DAVIE ALE HOUSE Lunch: $7-$13 Dinner: $7-$13 Phone: 954/236-0062 (116)
▼ ◆◆◆
Location: I-95, exit 5, just s. 2080 University Dr 33324. **Hours:** 11 am-2 am. Closed: 11/23. **Features:** Munch on huge onion rings or cheese fries and revel in the lively sports bar atmosphere. A menu of fun favorites includes burgers, steak, chicken, pasta and a nice raw bar. Wash it all down with one of an extensive list of draft and bottled beers. Casual dress; cocktails. **Parking:** on-site. **Cards:** AX, DC, DS, MC, VI.
American

GERONIMO'S CASUAL GOURMET GRILL & BAR Lunch: $8-$11 Dinner: $9-$18 Phone: 954/474-9992 (119)
▼▼ ◆◆◆◆
Location: On University Dr (SR 817), 1.5 mi s of jct SR 84; in University Park Plaza. 3528 S University Dr 33328. **Hours:** 5 pm-4 am, Fri & Sat from 7 pm, Thurs & Fri 11:30 am-5 pm, Mon 9 pm-4 am. Closed major holidays. **Features:** A creative menu featuring California and international dishes with fresh ingredients brings repeat business to this eatery. The atmosphere is simple and casual. Sample the black bean soup or order the grilled swordfish topped with sun-dried tomato salsa. Casual dress; cocktails; entertainment. **Parking:** on-site. **Cards:** AX, MC, VI.
American

SHORTY'S BAR-B-Q Lunch: $5-$14 Dinner: $5-$14 Phone: 954/680-9900 (121)
▼ ▲▲▲
Location: Just n of Sheridan St. 5989 S University Dr 33328. **Hours:** 11 am-10 pm, Fri & Sat-11 pm. **Features:** Hungry folks in the mood for barbecue ribs, brisket, chicken or pulled pork will find it at the fun and upbeat spot. The walls and ceilings offer plenty to look at while the food is being prepared. The menu offers enough diversity to appeal to all ages. Casual dress; beer & wine only. **Parking:** on-site. **Cards:** AX, MC, VI.
Barbecue

SONNY'S REAL PIT BAR-B-Q Lunch: $4-$9 Dinner: $8-$15 Phone: 954/476-7611 (117)
▼ ▲▲▲
Location: I-595, exit 5 (University Dr), 0.7 mi s; in Arrowhead Plaza Shops. 2699 S University Dr 33328. **Hours:** 11 am-9:30 pm, Fri & Sat-10:30 pm. **Features:** Serving barbecue done right, slowly cooked over a hardwood fire, this is the place for chicken, ribs, and pulled pork; they also offer smoked turkey, fried catfish, and charbroiled chicken, all surrounded by a family atmosphere. Casual dress; beer only. **Parking:** on-site. **Cards:** AX, MC, VI.
Barbecue

DEERFIELD BEACH pop. 64,583

──────── WHERE TO STAY ────────

BEST WESTERN DEERFIELD BEACH HOTEL & SUITES *Book at aaa.com* Phone: (954)570-8888
AAA SAVE

1/20-3/31	1P: $125-$195	2P: $125-$195	XP: $10	F17
11/1-11/30	1P: $95-$165	2P: $95-$165	XP: $10	F17
12/1-1/19	1P: $89-$149	2P: $89-$149	XP: $10	F17
4/1-10/31	1P: $85-$125	2P: $85-$125	XP: $10	F17

▼▼▼
Small-scale Hotel **Location:** I-95, exit 41, SW 10th St to SW 12th Ave, then s. 1050 E Newport Center Dr 33442. Fax: 954/570-5346. **Facility:** 107 one-bedroom suites. 5 stories, exterior corridors. *Bath:* combo or shower only. **Parking:** on-site. **Terms:** cancellation fee imposed, [BP] meal plan available. **Amenities:** voice mail, irons, hair dryers. *Fee:* video games, safes. *Some:* high-speed Internet. **Dining:** 4 pm-9 pm, Sat also 6:30-10 am, Sun 6:30-10 am, cocktails. **Pool(s):** heated outdoor. **Leisure Activities:** whirlpool, jogging, limited exercise equipment. **Guest Services:** sundries, valet and coin laundry. **Business Services:** meeting rooms, fax (fee). **Cards:** AX, CB, DC, DS, JC, MC, VI. **Special Amenities:** early check-in/late check-out. *(See color ad p 374)*

SOME UNITS

CARRIAGE HOUSE RESORT MOTEL *Book at aaa.com* Phone: 954/427-7670
▼▼ ▲▲▲▲

	1P: $124-$227	2P: $124-$227	XP: $12	F13
2/1-3/14	1P: $124-$227	2P: $124-$227	XP: $12	F13
12/1-1/31 & 3/15-4/16	1P: $98-$155	2P: $98-$155	XP: $12	F13
4/17-11/30	1P: $66-$120	2P: $66-$120	XP: $12	F13

Motel **Location:** SR A1A, just s of jct SR 810 (Hillsboro Blvd). 250 S Ocean Blvd 33441. Fax: 954/428-4790. **Facility:** 30 units. 19 one-bedroom standard units, some with efficiencies. 10 one- and 1 two-bedroom suites with kitchens. 2 stories (no elevator), exterior corridors. *Bath:* combo or shower only. **Parking:** on-site. **Terms:** office hours 7 am-8 pm, 3 night minimum stay - seasonal and/or weekends, 45 day cancellation notice. **Amenities:** voice mail, safes (fee). **Pool(s):** heated outdoor. **Guest Services:** coin laundry. **Cards:** DS, MC, VI.

SOME UNITS

COMFORT INN-OCEANSIDE   *Book at aaa.com*   Phone: (954)428-0650

(AAA) (SAVE)

12/23-4/22	1P: $109-$199	2P: $109-$199	XP: $10	F16
4/23-11/30	1P: $89-$149	2P: $89-$149	XP: $10	F16
12/1-12/22	1P: $89-$129	2P: $89-$129	XP: $10	F16

Motel   **Location:** SR A1A, jct SR 810 (Hillsboro Blvd). 50 SE 20th Ave 33441. Fax: 954/427-2666. **Facility:** 69 one-bedroom standard units. 6 stories, interior corridors. *Bath:* combo or shower only. **Parking:** on-site. **Amenities:** voice mail, irons, hair dryers. *Fee:* video games, safes. **Pool(s):** outdoor, wading. **Guest Services:** valet and coin laundry. **Business Services:** meeting rooms, fax (fee). **Cards:** AX, CB, DC, DS, JC, MC, VI. **Special Amenities: free continental breakfast and free newspaper.**

SOME UNITS

FEE FEE

COMFORT SUITES   *Book at aaa.com*   Phone: (954)570-8887

(AAA) (SAVE)

12/1-3/31 [CP]	1P: $109-$169	2P: $109-$169	XP: $10	F17
4/1-11/30 [CP]	1P: $79-$149	2P: $79-$149	XP: $10	F17

Small-scale Hotel   **Location:** I-95, exit 41, jct SW 10th St to SW 12th Ave, then s; in Newport Center Complex. 1040 E Newport Center Dr 33442. Fax: 954/428-7638. **Facility:** 101 one-bedroom standard units. 4 stories, exterior corridors. *Bath:* combo or shower only. **Parking:** on-site. **Terms:** cancellation fee imposed, pets ($25 fee, $10 extra charge). **Amenities:** voice mail, irons, hair dryers. *Fee:* video games, safes. **Pool(s):** heated outdoor. **Leisure Activities:** whirlpool, jogging. **Guest Services:** valet and coin laundry. **Business Services:** meeting rooms, fax (fee). **Cards:** AX, CB, DC, DS, JC, MC, VI. **Special Amenities: free room upgrade (subject to availability with advance reservations).** *(See color ad p 374)*

SOME UNITS

FEE

EMBASSY SUITES-DEERFIELD BEACH RESORT   *Book at aaa.com*   Phone: (954)426-0478

All Year	1P: $119-$450	2P: $119-$450	XP: $30	F16

Large-scale Hotel   **Location:** SR A1A, 0.5 mi s of jct SR 810 (Hillsboro Blvd). 950 Ocean Dr (SR A1A) 33441. Fax: 954/360-0539. **Facility:** 244 one-bedroom units. 7 stories, interior corridors. *Bath:* combo or shower only. **Parking:** on-site (fee) and valet. **Terms:** 1-7 night minimum stay - seasonal and/or weekends, cancellation fee imposed, [BP] meal plan available, pets (small dogs only, $30 extra charge). **Amenities:** video library (fee), dual phone lines, voice mail, safes, irons, hair dryers. *Some:* high-speed Internet (fee). **Pool(s):** heated outdoor. **Leisure Activities:** whirlpool, beach access, snorkeling, recreation programs, exercise room. **Guest Services:** gift shop, complimentary evening beverages, valet and coin laundry. **Business Services:** meeting rooms, fax (fee). **Cards:** AX, CB, DC, DS, JC, MC, VI.

SOME UNITS

(ASK) FEE

HAMPTON INN DEERFIELD BEACH   *Book at aaa.com*   Phone: (954)481-1221

12/19-4/30	1P: $139-$279	2P: $139-$279	
12/1-12/18 & 5/1-11/30	1P: $89-$179	2P: $89-$179	

Small-scale Hotel   **Location:** I-95, exit 42A, just e; in Hillsboro Center. 660 W Hillsboro Blvd 33441. Fax: 954/481-3432. **Facility:** 106 units. 98 one-bedroom standard units. 8 one-bedroom suites ($299-$399). 4 stories, interior corridors. *Bath:* combo or shower only. **Parking:** on-site. **Amenities:** video games (fee), high-speed Internet, dual phone lines, voice mail, irons, hair dryers. **Pool(s):** heated outdoor. **Leisure Activities:** exercise room. **Guest Services:** sundries, valet and coin laundry. **Business Services:** meeting rooms, business center. **Cards:** AX, CB, DC, DS, JC, MC, VI.

SOME UNITS

HILTON DEERFIELD BEACH/BOCA RATON   *Book at aaa.com*   Phone: (954)427-7700

(AAA) (SAVE)

1/1-4/7	1P: $109-$250	XP: $10	F18
4/8-5/19	1P: $79-$199	XP: $10	F18
5/20-11/30	1P: $69-$199	XP: $10	F18
12/1-12/31	1P: $75-$190	XP: $10	F18

Large-scale Hotel   **Location:** I-95, exit 42A southbound, just e on Hillsboro Blvd; exit 37A northbound. 100 Fairway Dr 33441. Fax: 954/427-2308. **Facility:** 221 units. 216 one-bedroom standard units. 5 one-bedroom suites ($275-$450). 8 stories, interior corridors. *Bath:* combo or shower only. **Parking:** on-site. **Terms:** cancellation fee imposed, package plans. **Amenities:** high-speed Internet (fee), dual phone lines, voice mail, safes, irons, hair dryers. **Dining:** 6:30 am-11 pm, cocktails. **Pool(s):** heated outdoor. **Leisure Activities:** whirlpool, exercise room. **Guest Services:** gift shop, valet laundry, area transportation-within 5 mi. **Business Services:** meeting rooms, business center. **Cards:** AX, CB, DC, DS, JC, MC, VI.

SOME UNITS

FEE

HOLIDAY PARK HOTELS & SUITES   Phone: (954)427-2200

12/24-2/4 [CP]	1P: $110	2P: $110
12/1-12/23 & 2/25-11/30 [CP]	1P: $59	2P: $59

Motel   **Location:** I-95, exit 42B, just w on SR 810 (Hillsboro Blvd), then just s on 12th Ave SW. 1250 W Hillsboro Blvd 33442. Fax: 954/481-2094. **Facility:** 157 units. 151 one-bedroom standard units. 6 one-bedroom suites with kitchens. 2 stories (no elevator), exterior corridors. *Bath:* combo or shower only. **Parking:** on-site. **Terms:** open 12/1-2/4 & 2/25-11/30, $1 service charge, small pets only ($10 extra charge). **Amenities:** voice mail, safes (fee), irons, hair dryers. **Pool(s):** heated outdoor. **Leisure Activities:** exercise room. **Guest Services:** coin laundry. **Business Services:** meeting rooms, fax (fee). **Cards:** AX, CB, DC, DS, MC, VI.

SOME UNITS

(ASK) FEE   FEE FEE

HOWARD JOHNSON PLAZA RESORT HOTEL   *Book at aaa.com*   Phone: (954)428-2850

12/17-4/22	1P: $189-$229	2P: $199-$239	XP: $10	F18
4/23-11/30	1P: $129-$169	2P: $139-$179	XP: $10	F18
12/1-12/16	1P: $125-$165	2P: $135-$175	XP: $10	F18

Small-scale Hotel   **Location:** SR A1A, just n of jct SR 810 (Hillsboro Blvd). 2096 NE 2nd St 33441. Fax: 954/480-9639. **Facility:** 177 one-bedroom standard units. 8 stories, interior corridors. *Bath:* combo or shower only. **Parking:** on-site. **Terms:** 3 night minimum stay - seasonal, 3 day cancellation notice-fee imposed, package plans. **Amenities:** safes (fee), irons, hair dryers. **Pool(s):** heated outdoor. **Leisure Activities:** exercise room. *Fee:* game room. **Guest Services:** valet laundry. **Business Services:** meeting rooms, fax (fee). **Cards:** AX, CB, DC, DS, MC, VI.

SOME UNITS

FEE

LA QUINTA INN FT. LAUDERDALE (DEERFIELD BEACH)   *Book at aaa.com*

Phone: (954)421-1004

	12/1-4/30	1P: $89-$129	XP: $7	F18
	5/1-11/30	1P: $72-$82	XP: $7	F18

Location: I-95, exit 42A, 0.3 mi e on SR 810. 351 W Hillsboro Blvd 33441-1801. Fax: 954/427-8069. **Facility:** 128 one-bedroom standard units. 3 stories, exterior corridors. *Bath:* combo or shower only. **Parking:** on-site.
Motel   **Terms:** [ECP] meal plan available, small pets only. **Amenities:** video games (fee), voice mail, irons, hair dryers. **Pool(s):** heated outdoor. **Guest Services:** coin laundry. **Business Services:** meeting rooms, fax (fee). **Cards:** AX, CB, DC, DS, MC, VI. **Special Amenities:** free expanded continental breakfast and free local telephone calls. *(See color ad p 384)*

SOME UNITS
🛏 🍴➕ 🅼 🚳 🏊 🎥 DATA PORT ☕ / ✖ 📼 📺 /

PANTHER MOTEL & APARTMENTS

Phone: 954/427-0700

	1/15-3/31 Wkly	1P: $495-$595	2P: $495-$595	XP: $10
	12/1-1/14 Wkly	1P: $420-$477	2P: $420-$477	XP: $10
Motel	4/1-4/30 Wkly	1P: $325-$350	2P: $325-$350	XP: $10
	5/1-11/30 Wkly	1P: $270-$320	2P: $270-$320	XP: $10

Location: SR A1A, 0.5 mi s of jct SR 810 (Hillsboro Blvd). 715 S A1A 33441. Fax: 954/481-2389. **Facility:** 20 units. 16 one-bedroom standard units with efficiencies. 4 one-bedroom suites with kitchens. 2 stories (no elevator), exterior corridors. **Parking:** on-site. **Terms:** office hours 8 am-10 pm, age restrictions may apply, 30 day cancellation notice, daily rates available. **Amenities:** safes. **Pool(s):** heated outdoor. **Leisure Activities:** shuffleboard. **Guest Services:** coin laundry. **Cards:** MC, VI.

🏊 📼 📺 📺

RETTGER RESORTS BEACH CLUB

Phone: 954/427-7900

	12/1-4/15	1P: $109-$149	2P: $109-$149	XP: $10	F3
	4/16-11/30	1P: $59-$89	2P: $59-$89	XP: $10	F3

Motel   **Location:** Just n on SR A1A from SR 810 (Hillsboro Blvd) to 20th Tr. Across from ocean. 100 NE 20th Terrace 33441. Fax: 954/427-7978. **Facility:** Smoke free premises. 18 units. 16 one-bedroom standard units. 2 one-bedroom suites ($119-$249) with kitchens and whirlpools. 2 stories (no elevator), exterior corridors. **Parking:** on-site. **Terms:** office hours 8 am-10 pm, 7 day cancellation notice. **Amenities:** dual phone lines, voice mail. **Pool(s):** heated outdoor. **Leisure Activities:** beach access. **Cards:** AX, CB, DC, DS, JC, MC, VI.

SOME UNITS
(ASK) 🍴➕ 🏊 ✖ 🎥 DATA PORT 📼 / 📺 📺 /

TRAVELERS INN

Phone: (954)421-5000

	2/1-3/31	1P: $89-$149	2P: $99-$169	XP: $10	F17
	12/21-1/31	1P: $69-$129	2P: $79-$149	XP: $10	F17
	12/1-12/20 & 4/1-11/30	1P: $55-$99	2P: $59-$109	XP: $10	F17

Motel   **Location:** On US 1, 1.3 mi s of jct SR 810 (Hillsboro Blvd). 1401 S Federal Hwy 33441. Fax: 954/426-2811. **Facility:** 107 units. 106 one-bedroom standard units, some with efficiencies. 1 one-bedroom suite ($99-$349). 2 stories, interior/exterior corridors. **Parking:** on-site. **Terms:** [AP] & [CP] meal plans available, pets ($10 extra charge, in limited units). **Amenities:** voice mail, irons, hair dryers. **Dining:** 7 am-10 pm, cocktails. **Pool(s):** heated outdoor. **Guest Services:** coin laundry, beauty salon. **Business Services:** meeting rooms, fax (fee). **Cards:** AX, CB, DC, DS, JC, MC, VI. **Special Amenities:** free newspaper and preferred room (subject to availability with advance reservations).

SOME UNITS
[S/D] 🐾 🍴 🍽 🏊 🎥 DATA PORT / ✖ (VCR) 📺 📺 📺 /
FEE   FEE

TROPIC ISLE BEACH RESORT

Phone: 954/427-1000

Property failed to provide current rates

Motel   **Location:** SR A1A, 0.3 mi s of jct SR 810 (Hillsboro Blvd). 370 S A1A 33441. Fax: 954/429-9754. **Facility:** 15 units. 13 one-bedroom standard units with efficiencies. 2 one-bedroom suites with kitchens. 2 stories, exterior corridors. *Bath:* combo or shower only. **Parking:** on-site. **Terms:** office hours 9 am-5 pm. **Amenities:** voice mail, safes. *Some:* irons. **Pool(s):** heated outdoor. **Guest Services:** coin laundry.

🏊 📺 📺 📺

WELLESLEY INN (DEERFIELD BEACH)   *Book at aaa.com*

Phone: (954)428-0661

	12/16-4/30	1P: $89-$159	2P: $89-$159	XP: $10	F16
	12/1-12/15 & 5/1-11/30	1P: $65-$109	2P: $65-$109	XP: $10	F16

Small-scale Hotel   **Location:** I-95, exit 42B, just w on SR 810 (Hillsboro Blvd), then just s. 100 12th Ave SW 33442. Fax: 954/427-6701. **Facility:** 79 units. 76 one-bedroom standard units. 3 one-bedroom suites. 4 stories, interior corridors. *Bath:* combo or shower only. **Parking:** on-site. **Terms:** package plans, small pets only ($10 fee). **Amenities:** video games (fee), voice mail, irons, hair dryers. **Pool(s):** heated outdoor. **Leisure Activities:** exercise room. **Guest Services:** coin laundry, area transportation. **Business Services:** meeting rooms, fax (fee). **Cards:** AX, CB, DC, DS, MC, VI.

SOME UNITS
(ASK) [S/D] 🛏 🍴➕ 🅼 🚳 🎥 🏊 🎥 DATA PORT 📺 📺 📺 / ✖ /
FEE

─────── **WHERE TO DINE** ───────

BROOKS RESTAURANT

Dinner: $20-$45   **Phone:** 954/427-9302

Location: US 1, 0.5 mi s of jct SR 810 (Hillsboro Blvd). 500 S Federal Hwy 33441. **Hours:** 6 pm-10 pm. Closed: 12/25; also Mon & Tues 5/8-11/25. **Reservations:** suggested. **Features:** Although patrons normally come here dressed up, they can feel comfortable amid the subdued, attractive decor. Generous portions of well-prepared entrees are presented in an inviting manner. Semi-formal attire; cocktails. **Parking:** on-site and
Continental   valet. **Cards:** AX, CB, DC, MC, VI.

🍽

CAFE CLAUDE

Lunch: $10-$15   **Dinner:** $17-$25   **Phone:** 954/421-7337

Location: 0.5 mi e of jct US 1; in Cove Plaza. 1544 SE 3rd Ct 33441. **Hours:** Open 12/1-7/14 & 9/16-11/30; 5:15 pm-10 pm, also Fri 11:30 am-2 pm. **Reservations:** suggested. **Features:** Claude Pottier, the French owner and chef, prepares authentic French cuisine in a nice, casual atmosphere. Each entree has visual appeal with decoratively carved vegetables accented with sauce. The homemade desserts top off the superb
French   presentation. Semi-formal attire; cocktails. **Parking:** on-site. **Cards:** AX, CB, DC, MC, VI.

🍽

THE COVE RESTAURANT & LOUNGE   Lunch: $8-$15   Dinner: $10-$33   Phone: 954/421-9272

Seafood
Location: Just off Hillsboro Blvd; 0.5 mi e of US 1; on Intracoastal Waterway; in Cove Plaza. 1754 SE Third Ct 33441. **Hours:** 11 am-10 pm, Fri & Sat-midnight. Closed: 11/23, 12/25. **Features:** On the Intracoastal Waterway, the restaurant affords views of the water from most tables. Many patrons come for fresh seafood, others come for the relaxed atmosphere combined with the boats that pass, and still others stop in for friendly service. Casual dress; cocktails. **Parking:** on-site and valet. **Cards:** AX, DC, MC, VI.

PAL'S CHARLEY'S CRAB   Lunch: $6-$14   Dinner: $12-$29   Phone: 954/427-4000

Seafood
Location: On Intracoastal Waterway, just off Hillsboro Blvd (SR 810), 0.5 mi e of jct US 1; in Cove Plaza. 1755 SE 3rd Ct 33441. **Hours:** 11:30 am-10 pm. **Reservations:** suggested. **Features:** A well-established restaurant, it overlooks the scenic Intracoastal Waterway. A wide variety of delicious seafood dishes are served along with featured pasta specials. Start with the spicy black bean soup and order a fresh catch from Florida waters. Dressy casual; cocktails; entertainment. **Parking:** on-site and valet. **Cards:** AX, DC, DS, MC, VI.

WHALE'S RIB   Lunch: $7-$16   Dinner: $14-$22   Phone: 954/429-3954

Seafood
Location: From Hillsboro Blvd (SR 810), just n on SR A1A. 2031 NE 2nd St 33441. **Hours:** 11 am-11 pm, Fri-Sun to midnight. Closed: 11/23, 12/25; also for dinner 12/24. **Reservations:** not accepted. **Features:** The restaurant is close to the ocean so the fish is fresh. Casual is the attire and so is the atmosphere at the longtime local favorite. Casual dress; cocktails. **Parking:** on-site and street. **Cards:** AX, DC, MC, VI.

YUCATAN MEXICAN BAR & GRILL   Lunch: $7-$12   Dinner: $8-$18   Phone: 954/481-9933

Mexican
Location: 0.5 mi n of Hillsboro Blvd (SR 810); jct S Federal Hwy and SE 5th St. 525 S Federal Hwy 33441. **Hours:** 11:30 am-9 pm, Fri & Sat-10 pm. **Features:** The casual little cantina presents a large menu with all the favorite Mexican dishes. A large drink menu satisfies most thirsts. Casual dress; cocktails. **Parking:** on-site. **Cards:** MC, VI.

The following restaurant has not been evaluated by AAA but is listed for your information only.

FLANIGAN'S SEAFOOD BAR & GRILL   Phone: 954/427-9304

(fyi)
Not evaluated. **Location:** 2041 NE 2nd St 33441. **Features:** The family-friendly restaurant is known for its baby back ribs, burgers and seafood.

HALLANDALE BEACH   (See maps and indexes starting on p. 364, 534)

--- WHERE TO STAY ---

BEST WESTERN HALLANDALE   *Book at aaa.com*   Phone: (954)456-8333   **137**

(AAA) (SAVE)	12/23-4/15 [ECP]	1P: $79-$199	2P: $89-$199	XP: $10	D17
	12/1-12/22 & 4/16-11/30 [ECP]	1P: $69-$149	2P: $69-$149	XP: $6	D17

Small-scale Hotel
Location: I-95, exit 18 (SR 855/Hallandale Beach Blvd), just e. 101 Ansin Blvd 33009. Fax: 954/455-0324. **Facility:** 100 one-bedroom standard units. 5 stories, interior corridors. *Bath:* combo or shower only. **Parking:** on-site. **Terms:** 2-4 night minimum stay - seasonal. **Amenities:** high-speed Internet, voice mail, irons, hair dryers. **Pool(s):** outdoor. **Leisure Activities:** exercise room. **Guest Services:** valet and coin laundry. **Business Services:** meeting rooms, fax (fee). **Cards:** AX, CB, DC, DS, MC, VI. **Special Amenities:** free local telephone calls and free newspaper.

SOME UNITS

(See maps and indexes starting on p. 364, 534)

THE DIPLOMAT COUNTRY CLUB & SPA   *Book at aaa.com*   Phone: (954)883-4000   136

(AAA) (SAVE)	12/1-4/17	1P: $450-$540	XP: $25
	10/31-11/30	1P: $335-$425	XP: $25
▼▼▼▼ ▼▼▼▼	4/18-10/30	1P: $315-$405	XP: $25

Resort
Small-scale Hotel

Location: I-95, exit 18 (SR 858/Hallandale Beach Blvd), 2.3 mi e, then 0.4 mi n; SR A1A, 0.5 mi w, then 0.4 mi n. Located on the golf course. 501 Diplomat Pkwy 33009. Fax: 954/883-4009. **Facility:** Located just off the waterway and surrounded by a golf course on beautiful grounds. The rooms are large and beautifully decorated and furnished. 60 units. 54 one-bedroom standard units. 6 one-bedroom suites. 4 stories, interior corridors. *Bath:* combo or shower only. **Parking:** valet. **Terms:** 3 day cancellation notice-fee imposed, package plans, $16 service charge. **Amenities:** CD players, dual phone lines, voice mail, fax, safes, honor bars, irons, hair dryers. *Fee:* video games, high-speed Internet. *Some:* DVD players. **Dining:** 6:30 am-10 pm, cocktails. **Pool(s):** 2 heated outdoor. **Leisure Activities:** saunas, whirlpools, steamrooms, beach access, fishing, spa. *Fee:* boat dock, charter fishing, golf-18 holes, golf & tennis instruction, 10 tennis courts (6 lighted). **Guest Services:** gift shop, valet laundry. **Business Services:** meeting rooms, business center. **Cards:** AX, CB, DC, DS, JC, MC, VI. **Special Amenities:** free newspaper.

SOME UNITS

[icons] / [icons]

HAMPTON INN - HALLANDALE/AVENTURA   *Book at aaa.com*   Phone: (954)874-1111   138

(AAA) (SAVE)	12/1-4/23 & 10/2-11/30 [ECP]	1P: $119-$169	2P: $119-$169
	4/24-6/4 [ECP]	1P: $109-$159	2P: $109-$159
▼▼▼▼	6/5-10/1 [ECP]	1P: $89-$139	2P: $89-$139

Small-scale Hotel

Location: I-95, exit 18 (SR 858/ Hallandale Beach Blvd), 1.4 mi, then 0.8 mi s on US 1 (Federal Hwy). Located across from Gulfstream Park. 1000 S Federal Hwy. 33009. Fax: 954/874-1112. **Facility:** 151 one-bedroom standard units. 8 stories, interior corridors. *Bath:* combo or shower only. **Parking:** on-site. **Terms:** package plans. **Amenities:** video games (fee), high-speed Internet, dual phone lines, voice mail, irons, hair dryers. **Pool(s):** heated outdoor. **Leisure Activities:** exercise room. **Guest Services:** valet laundry. **Business Services:** meeting rooms, fax (fee). **Cards:** AX, CB, DC, DS, JC, MC, VI. **Special Amenities:** free expanded continental breakfast and free newspaper.
(See color ad p 404)

SOME UNITS

[icons] / [icons]
   FEE   FEE

--------- **WHERE TO DINE** ---------

THE DOG HOUSE   **Lunch:** $4-$7   Phone: 954/458-3787   142

▼▼

American

Location: I-95, exit 18 (SR 858/Hallandale Beach Blvd), just e. 1040 W Hallandale Beach Blvd 33009. **Hours:** 11 am-6 pm. **Features:** First-timers shouldn't let the name fool them. Certainly hot dogs are at the heart of the menu, but burgers also can be had. Guests can watch a video about hot dogs while waiting for their food. Not surprisingly, the atmosphere is casual. Casual dress. **Parking:** on-site. **Cards:** AX, DC, DS, MC, VI.

HOMETOWN BUFFET   **Lunch:** $7   **Dinner:** $10   Phone: 954/456-5155   141

▼▼

American

MC, VI.

Location: I-95, exit 18 (SR 858/Hallandale Beach Blvd), 2.5 mi e. 1403 E Hallandale Beach Blvd 33009. **Hours:** 11 am-9 pm, Fri-10 pm, Sat 8 am-10 pm, Sun 8 am-9 pm. **Features:** The all-you-can-eat buffet lines up good comfort foods such as those guests might find at home. Varied tables display salad ingredients, meats and vegetables, as well as tempting desserts. The setting is casual. Casual dress. **Parking:** on-site. **Cards:** DS,

[icon]

--------- *The following restaurant has not been evaluated by AAA but is listed for your information only.* ---------

FLANIGAN'S SEAFOOD BAR & GRILL   Phone: 954/458-2566

(fyi)

Not evaluated. **Location:** 4 N Federal Hwy 33009. **Features:** The family-friendly restaurant is known for its baby back ribs, burgers and seafood.

HILLSBORO BEACH pop. 2,163

--------- **WHERE TO STAY** ---------

ROYAL FLAMINGO VILLAS   Phone: (954)427-0660

▼▼▼▼▼	12/1-4/30	1P: $154-$215	2P: $193-$270	XP: $15	F12
	5/1-11/30	1P: $93-$154	2P: $110-$171	XP: $15	F12

Cottage

Location: SR A1A, 0.8 mi s of jct SR 810 (Hillsboro Blvd). 1225 Hillsboro Mile 33062. Fax: 954/427-6110. **Facility:** The property's manicured grounds extend from the ocean to the Intracoastal Waterway; many of its spacious cottages have water views. 40 cottages. 1 story, exterior corridors. **Parking:** on-site. **Terms:** office hours 9 am-5 pm, check-in 4 pm, 5 night minimum stay, 45 day cancellation notice. **Amenities:** voice mail, irons. **Pool(s):** heated outdoor. **Leisure Activities:** shuffleboard. **Guest Services:** coin laundry. **Cards:** DS, MC, VI.

(ASK) [icons]

HOLLYWOOD pop. 139,357 (See map and index starting on p. 364)

--------- **WHERE TO STAY** ---------

DAYS INN FORT LAUDERDALE/HOLLYWOOD
AIRPORT SOUTH   *Book at aaa.com*   Phone: (954)923-7300   120

	12/1-4/15 [CP]	1P: $99-$249	2P: $99-$249
▼▼▼▼	4/16-11/30 [CP]	1P: $79-$159	2P: $79-$159

Small-scale Hotel

Location: I-95, exit 21, just nw on SR 822 (Sheridan St). 2601 N 29th Ave 33020. Fax: 954/921-6706. **Facility:** 114 one-bedroom standard units. 7 stories, interior corridors. **Parking:** on-site. **Terms:** small pets only ($10 extra charge). **Amenities:** voice mail, irons, hair dryers. **Pool(s):** outdoor. **Leisure Activities:** exercise room. **Guest Services:** valet and coin laundry, area transportation (fee). **Business Services:** meeting rooms, business center. **Cards:** AX, CB, DC, DS, JC, MC, VI.

SOME UNITS

(ASK) [icons] / [icons]
   FEE   FEE

(See map and index starting on p. 364)

ECONO LODGE   *Book at aaa.com*   Phone: (954)920-3001   122
♦♦♦♦ ♦♦♦♦   2/1-4/9 [CP]   1P: $79-$139   2P: $79-$139   XP: $10   F17
             12/1-1/31 [CP]   1P: $69-$109   2P: $69-$109   XP: $10   F17
Motel   4/10-11/30 [CP]   1P: $59-$99   2P: $59-$99   XP: $10   F17
             Location: 1 mi n on US 1 from SR 820 (Hollywood Blvd), then e. 1725 Taft St 33020. Fax: 954/923-7294.
Facility: 34 one-bedroom standard units. 2 stories (no elevator), exterior corridors. *Bath:* combo or shower only. **Parking:** on-site. **Terms:** cancellation fee imposed. **Amenities:** hair dryers. **Pool(s):** heated outdoor. **Cards:** AX, CB, DC, DS, JC, MC, VI.

SOME UNITS

(ASK) (SD) (▥+) (➔) (ฃ) (DATA PORT) / (✕) (▯) (▭) (▭) /

ECONO LODGE INN & SUITES HOLLYWOOD BLVD   *Book at aaa.com*   Phone: (954)981-1800   127
(AAA) (SAVE)   All Year [ECP]   1P: $59-$199   2P: $59-$199   XP: $10   F16
             Location: I-95, exit 20, 1.6 mi w; Florida Tpke, exit 49, 1.3 mi e. 4900 Hollywood Blvd 33021. Fax: 954/961-6628.
♦♦♦♦ ♦♦♦♦   **Facility:** 40 units. 32 one-bedroom standard units. 8 one-bedroom suites with whirlpools. 2 stories, exterior
Motel   corridors. *Bath:* combo or shower only. **Parking:** on-site. **Terms:** package plans, small pets only ($15 extra
             charge). **Amenities:** high-speed Internet, dual phone lines, voice mail, irons, hair dryers. *Some:* DVD
             players, CD players, safes (fee). **Pool(s):** heated outdoor. **Guest Services:** sundries, valet and coin
laundry. **Business Services:** meeting rooms. **Cards:** AX, CB, DC, DS, JC, MC, VI. **Special Amenities:** free local telephone
calls and early check-in/late check-out. *(See color ad below)*

SOME UNITS

(SD) (🐾) (▥+) (👤) (⊘) (➔) (ฃ) (DATA PORT) (▯) (▭) (▭) / (✕) (VCR) /
FEE

GREENBRIAR BEACH CLUB   Phone: (954)922-2606   131
(AAA) (SAVE)   12/1-5/1 [ECP]   2P: $129-$329   XP: $15   F12
             5/2-11/30 [ECP]   2P: $94-$229   XP: $15   F12
♦♦♦♦ ♦♦♦♦   **Location:** Oceanfront. Hollywood Blvd, 0.8 mi s on SR A1A/Ocean Blvd to Iris Terrace, turn left to S Surf Rd, then just
Motel   n. 1900 S Surf Rd 33019. Fax: 954/923-0897. **Facility:** 47 units. 37 one-bedroom standard units with kitchens.
             10 one-bedroom suites with kitchens. 2-3 stories (no elevator), exterior corridors. **Parking:** on-site.
             Terms: office hours 9 am-7 pm, 30 day cancellation notice, 7 day off season, weekly rates available.
Amenities: high-speed Internet (fee), voice mail, safes, hair dryers. **Pool(s):** heated outdoor. **Leisure Activities:** barbecue
grills, rental bicycles, shuffleboard, volleyball. **Guest Services:** coin laundry. **Business Services:** meeting rooms, fax (fee).
Cards: AX, DC, DS, MC, VI. **Special Amenities:** free expanded continental breakfast.

SOME UNITS

(▥+) (➔) (✕) (ฃ) (DATA PORT) (▯) (▭) (▭) / (✕) (VCR) /

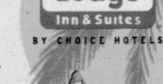

(See map and index starting on p. 364)

HAMPTON INN & SUITES-FT. LAUDERDALE
AIRPORT & CRUISE PORT   *Book at aaa.com*
Phone: (954)922-0011   **118**

12/1-4/30 [ECP]	1P: $129-$179	2P: $129-$179	XP: $10 F18
10/1-11/30 [ECP]	1P: $129-$169	2P: $129-$169	XP: $10 F18
5/1-9/30 [ECP]	1P: $89-$109	2P: $89-$109	XP: $10 F18

Small-scale Hotel   **Location:** I-95, exit 22, just e; 2 mi s of airport. 2500 Stirling Rd 33020. Fax: 954/929-7118. **Facility:** 104 units. 53 one-bedroom standard units. 51 one-bedroom suites ($109-$229) with efficiencies. 5 stories, interior corridors. *Bath:* combo or shower only. **Parking:** on-site. **Terms:** 11% service charge. **Amenities:** video games (fee), high-speed Internet, dual phone lines, voice mail, irons, hair dryers. **Pool(s):** small heated outdoor. **Guest Services:** sundries, complimentary evening beverages: Mon-Thurs, valet and coin laundry, airport transportation-Fort Lauderdale-Hollywood International Airport, area transportation-Amtrak Station, Hard Rock Casino & Port Everglades. **Business Services:** meeting rooms, business center. **Cards:** AX, CB, DC, DS, JC, MC, VI. *(See color ad p 406)*

SOME UNITS

HOLIDAY INN FORT LAUDERDALE/HOLLYWOOD
AIRPORT   *Book at aaa.com*
Phone: (954)925-9100   **121**

12/25-4/30	1P: $129-$299	2P: $129-$299
12/1-12/24 & 5/1-11/30	1P: $99-$169	2P: $99-$169

Small-scale Hotel   **Location:** I-95, exit 21, just w on SR 822 (Sheridan St). 2905 Sheridan St 33020. Fax: 954/925-5512. **Facility:** 150 units. 146 one-bedroom standard units. 4 one-bedroom suites ($129-$399). 6 stories, interior corridors. *Bath:* combo or shower only. **Parking:** on-site. **Terms:** [CP] meal plan available, 11% service charge. **Amenities:** high-speed Internet, dual phone lines, voice mail, irons, hair dryers. **Pool(s):** heated outdoor. **Leisure Activities:** whirlpool, exercise room. **Guest Services:** valet and coin laundry, area transportation (fee). **Business Services:** meeting rooms, business center. **Cards:** AX, CB, DC, DS, MC, VI.

SOME UNITS

HOLIDAY INN HOLLYWOOD BEACH   *Book at aaa.com*
Phone: (954)923-8700   **132**

12/23-4/16	1P: $149-$289	2P: $149-$289 XP: $10 F19
12/1-12/22 & 4/17-11/30	1P: $99-$209	2P: $99-$209 XP: $10 F19

Small-scale Hotel   **Location:** Oceanfront. SR A1A, 0.5 mi n of jct SR 858 (Hallandale Beach Blvd). 2711 S Ocean Dr 33019. Fax: 954/923-7059. **Facility:** 201 one-bedroom standard units. 5 stories, interior corridors. *Bath:* combo or shower only. **Parking:** valet. **Terms:** check-in 4 pm, 3 day cancellation notice-fee imposed, package plans. **Amenities:** high-speed Internet, voice mail, safes, irons, hair dryers. **Dining:** 2 restaurants, 7 am-10 pm, cocktails. **Pool(s):** heated outdoor. **Leisure Activities:** limited beach access, recreation programs, exercise room, shuffleboard. **Guest Services:** gift shop, valet and coin laundry. **Business Services:** meeting rooms, fax (fee). **Cards:** AX, CB, DC, DS, MC, VI. **Special Amenities:** free local telephone calls and free newspaper.

SOME UNITS
FEE

(See map and index starting on p. 364)

HOLLYWOOD BEACH MARRIOTT   Phone: 954/924-2202

[fyi]   12/1-4/30   1P: $349   2P: $349
               5/1-5/31 & 10/1-11/30 1P: $269   2P: $269
Large-scale Hotel 6/1-9/30   1P: $219   2P: $219
Too new to rate. **Location:** Oceanfront. From SR 820 (Hollywood Blvd), 1 mi n on SR A1A (N Ocean Dr). 2501 N Ocean Dr 33019. Fax: 954/925-1411. **Amenities:** 229 units, restaurant, coffeemakers, pool. **Cards:** AX, CB, DC, DS, JC, MC, VI. *(See color ad p 407)*

HOLLYWOOD BY THE SEA BED & BREAKFAST   Phone: 954/927-5301   [128]

Property failed to provide current rates

▼▼▼▼   **Location:** From SR 820 (Hollywood Blvd), just s on SR A1A, then just e. Located near the beach. 301 Jackson St
Classic Bed   33019. Fax: 954/367-1703. **Facility:** A home with an Eclectic Vintage Florida decor. The rooms take on their
& Breakfast   own personality with the colors and furnishings. The beach, real close. Designated smoking area. 7 one-
bedroom standard units, some with whirlpools. 2 stories (no elevator). *Bath:* combo or shower only.
Parking: street. **Amenities:** voice mail, safes, hair dryers. *Some:* DVD players. **Pool(s):** small heated outdoor. **Leisure Activities:** beach access.

LA QUINTA INN & SUITES FT. LAUDERDALE
(AIRPORT)   *Book at aaa.com*   Phone: (954)922-2295   [119]
ⒶⒶⒶ [SAVE]   1/1-4/30   1P: $149-$169   XP: $7   F18
               5/1-11/30   1P: $109-$125   XP: $7   F18
▼▼▼▼   12/1-12/31   1P: $99-$119   XP: $7   F18
Small-scale Hotel **Location:** I-95, exit 21, just e to Oakwood, then just left. 2620 N 26th Ave 33020. Fax: 954/922-2995. **Facility:** 131
units. 125 one-bedroom standard units. 6 one-bedroom suites ($135-$205). 6 stories, interior corridors.
Bath: combo or shower only. **Parking:** on-site. **Terms:** [ECP] meal plan available, small pets only.
Amenities: voice mail, irons, hair dryers. *Fee:* video games, high-speed Internet. *Some:* dual phone lines. **Pool(s):** heated
outdoor. **Leisure Activities:** whirlpool, fishing, exercise room. **Guest Services:** valet and coin laundry, airport transportation-
Fort Lauderdale-Hollywood International Airport, area transportation-Port Everglades. **Business Services:** meeting rooms, fax
(fee). **Cards:** AX, CB, DC, DS, MC, VI. **Special Amenities: free expanded continental breakfast and free local telephone
calls.** *(See color ad p 384)*   SOME UNITS

RAMADA INN HOLLYWOOD BEACH RESORT   *Book at aaa.com*   Phone: (954)921-0990   [124]
ⒶⒶⒶ [SAVE]   12/22-4/22 [CP]   1P: $189-$209   2P: $189-$209   XP: $15   F18
               4/23-11/30 [CP]   1P: $139-$149   2P: $139-$149   XP: $15   F18
▼▼▼▼   12/1-12/21 [CP]   1P: $99-$129   2P: $99-$129   XP: $15   F18
Large-scale Hotel **Location:** Oceanfront. Jct SR 820 (Hollywood Blvd) and SR A1A (N Ocean Dr). 101 N Ocean Dr 33019.
Fax: 954/920-9480. **Facility:** 220 units. 190 one-bedroom standard units with efficiencies. 30 one-bedroom
suites ($169-$269) with kitchens, some with whirlpools. 8 stories, interior corridors. *Bath:* combo or shower
only. **Parking:** on-site (fee) and valet. **Terms:** check-in 4 pm, cancellation fee imposed. **Amenities:** high-speed Internet, safes,
irons, hair dryers. **Dining:** 5 restaurants, 7 am-11 pm, cocktails. **Pool(s):** heated outdoor, wading. **Leisure Activities:** whirlpool,
lifeguard on duty, limited beach access, exercise room. *Fee:* bicycles, massage, game room. **Guest Services:** gift shop, valet
and coin laundry, beauty salon. *Fee:* airport transportation-Fort Lauderdale-Hollywood International Airport, area transportation-
Port Everglades. **Business Services:** meeting rooms, fax (fee). **Cards:** AX, DS, MC, VI. **Special Amenities: free continental
breakfast and free newspaper.** *(See color ad below)*   SOME UNITS

(See map and index starting on p. 364)

RAMADA PLAZA HOTEL   *Book at aaa.com*   Phone: (954)927-3341   125
     12/1-4/30   1P: $99-$199   2P: $99-$199
     5/1-11/30   1P: $69-$159   2P: $69-$159
Small-scale Hotel **Location:** I-95, exit 20 (SR 820/Hollywood Blvd), 1.2 mi e to S 20th St, turn right, then left. 1925 Harrison St 33020.
Fax: 954/925-1695. **Facility:** 95 units. 84 one-bedroom standard units. 11 one-bedroom suites ($99-$199).
6 stories, exterior corridors. **Parking:** on-site (fee). **Terms:** package plans. **Amenities:** voice mail, safes, irons, hair dryers.
Pool(s): outdoor. **Leisure Activities:** exercise room. **Guest Services:** valet and coin laundry. *Fee:* beauty salon. **Business
Services:** meeting rooms, fax (fee). **Cards:** AX, CB, DC, DS, MC, VI.

SOME UNITS

(A$K) (S$_D$) (+) (⫴) (Y) (⇌) (⟐) (DATA PORT) (🖥) / (✕) (🖪) (🖨) /
     FEE   FEE   FEE

RICHARDS MOTEL   Phone: 954/921-6418   130
     12/1-4/30   1P: $36-$79   2P: $39-$79   XP: $15
     5/1-11/30   1P: $36-$56   2P: $39-$56   XP: $15
     Location: US 1, 0.7 mi s of Hollywood Cir; 0.3 mi n of jct Pembroke Rd. 1219 S Federal Hwy 33020.
Motel   **Fax:** 954/925-1797. **Facility:** 33 units. 25 one-bedroom standard units, some with efficiencies. 7 one- and 1
     two-bedroom suites ($89-$149), some with efficiencies or kitchens. 1-2 stories (no elevator), exterior
     corridors. *Bath:* combo or shower only. **Parking:** on-site. **Terms:** office hours 8 am-midnight, cancellation
fee imposed, weekly rates available. **Pool(s):** heated outdoor. **Leisure Activities:** barbecue grills, shuffleboard. **Guest
Services:** coin laundry. **Business Services:** fax (fee). **Cards:** AX, CB, DC, DS, MC, VI. *(See color ad below)*

SOME UNITS

(S$_D$) (⫴) (⇌) (⟐) (🖪) / (🖨) (🖥) /

SANDY SHORES MOTEL & FAMILY LODGING   Phone: 954/923-3750   126
     12/17-4/30   1P: $75-$95   2P: $75-$95   XP: $10
     5/1-11/30   1P: $60-$70   2P: $60-$70   XP: $10
     12/1-12/16   1P: $55-$65   2P: $55-$65   XP: $10
     Location: From SR 820 (Hollywood Blvd), just s on SR A1A (S Ocean Dr), then e. Located near the beach. 342 Van
Motel   Buren St 33019. **Fax:** 954/923-3076. **Facility:** Designated smoking area. 16 one-bedroom standard units,
     some with efficiencies or kitchens. 1 story, exterior corridors. *Bath:* combo or shower only. **Parking:** on-site.
Terms: office hours 8 am-8 pm, 7 day cancellation notice-fee imposed, small pets only ($100 deposit, $5 extra charge).
Amenities: high-speed Internet. *Some:* irons. **Leisure Activities:** gas barbecue grill. **Guest Services:** coin laundry. **Business
Services:** fax (fee). **Cards:** MC, VI.

                                                    (🗒) (⫴) (✕) (⟐) (DATA PORT) (🖪) (🖨)
                                                    FEE

SEMINOLE HARD ROCK HOTEL & CASINO
HOLLYWOOD   *Book at aaa.com*   Phone: (954)327-7625   117
     12/1-4/30   1P: $229-$349   2P: $229-$349   XP: $30   F12
     5/1-9/30 & 10/1-11/30   1P: $189-$349   2P: $189-$349   XP: $30   F12
     Location: I-95, exit 22, 2.9 mi w, then just n on SR 7/US 441; Florida Tpke, exit 53, 0.5 mi e, then 0.8 mi s. 1 Seminole
Large-scale Hotel Way 33314. **Fax:** 954/327-7655. **Facility:** Rock n' roll is the theme: the public areas have memorabilia from
     your favorite groups. Try the slots and poker tables or the shops out on the mall. 481 units. 418 one-
     bedroom standard units. 63 one-bedroom suites ($650-$4500). 12 stories, interior corridors. *Bath:* combo or
shower only. **Parking:** on-site and valet. **Terms:** check-in 4 pm, 7 day cancellation notice-fee imposed, package plans, 11%
service charge, small pets only ($200 deposit, in limited units). **Amenities:** video games (fee), CD players, high-speed Internet,
dual phone lines, voice mail, safes, honor bars, irons, hair dryers. **Dining:** 5 restaurants, 24 hours, cocktails, also, The Council
Oak, see separate listing, nightclub, entertainment. **Pool(s):** heated outdoor, wading. **Leisure Activities:** whirlpools, waterslide,
lifeguard on duty, man-made beach area at the pool, spa, volleyball, game room. **Guest Services:** gift shop, valet laundry.
Business Services: conference facilities, business center. **Cards:** AX, CB, DC, DS, MC, VI.

SOME UNITS

(🎲) (+) (🐾) (⫴) (24⁺) (Y) (⟟M) (⌔) (🎵) (⇌) (🎮) (✕) (⟐) (DATA PORT) (🖥) / (✕) (🖪) (🖨) /
     FEE   FEE

(See map and index starting on p. 364)

SHELL MOTEL   Phone: (954)923-8085 129

(AAA) (SAVE)

◆◆◆◆◆◆
Motel

12/1-4/30	1P: $45-$90	2P: $49-$95	XP: $10 F10
5/1-11/30	1P: $39-$75	2P: $45-$80	XP: $10 F10

Location: US 1, 0.7 mi s of Hollywood Cir; 0.3 mi n of jct Pembroke Rd. 1201 S Federal Hwy 33020. Fax: 954/925-8750. **Facility:** 35 units. 26 one-bedroom standard units, some with efficiencies. 9 one-bedroom suites with kitchens. 1 story, exterior corridors. *Bath:* combo or shower only. **Parking:** on-site. **Terms:** office hours 9 am-midnight, 30 day cancellation notice-fee imposed, weekly rates available. **Pool(s):** heated outdoor. **Leisure Activities:** barbecue grills, shuffleboard. **Guest Services:** coin laundry. **Business Services:** fax (fee). **Cards:** AX, DS, MC, VI. *(See color ad below)*

SOME UNITS

VILLA SINCLAIR BEACH SUITES & SPA   Phone: (954)662-1955 123

(AAA) (SAVE)

◆◆◆/◆◆◆
Small-scale Hotel

All Year	2P: $190-$350	XP: $50 F

Location: From Hollywood Blvd (SR 820), just n on Ocean Dr (SR A1A), e on Arizona St, then e. Located 1/2 block from the beach. 317 Polk St 33019 (10760 Paris St, 33026). Fax: 954/450-0000. **Facility:** Designated smoking area. 6 units. 2 one-bedroom standard units with efficiencies. 3 one- and 1 two-bedroom suites ($250-$350) with kitchens. 2 stories (no elevator), interior corridors. **Parking:** on-site and street. **Terms:** office hours noon-6 pm, check-in 4 pm, 60 day cancellation notice-fee imposed, weekly rates available, package plans. **Amenities:** DVD players, CD players, voice mail, fax, safes, honor bars, irons, hair dryers. **Leisure Activities:** sauna, whirlpool, barbecue grill. *Fee:* massage. **Guest Services:** sundries. **Cards:** DC, MC, VI. **Special Amenities:** early check-in/late check-out and preferred room (subject to availability with advance reservations). *(See color ad below)*

THE WESTIN DIPLOMAT RESORT & SPA   *Book at aaa.com*   Phone: (954)602-6000 133

(AAA) (SAVE)

◆◆◆◆/◆◆◆◆
Large-scale Hotel

12/1-4/17	1P: $450-$540	XP: $25
10/1-11/30	1P: $335-$425	XP: $25
4/18-9/30	1P: $315-$405	XP: $25

Location: Oceanfront. Just n on SR A1A (S Ocean Dr) from SR 858 (Hallendale Beach Blvd). 3555 S Ocean Dr 33019. Fax: 954/602-7000. **Facility:** This beachfront resort impresses guests with its large lobby, two-level pool and spacious, luxuriously appointed rooms. 998 units. 902 one-bedroom standard units. 94 one- and 2 two-bedroom suites, some with whirlpools. 36 stories, interior corridors. *Bath:* combo or shower only. **Parking:** on-site (fee) and valet. **Terms:** 3 day cancellation notice-fee imposed, package plans, $16 service charge. **Amenities:** dual phone lines, voice mail, safes, honor bars, irons, hair dryers. *Fee:* video games, high-speed Internet. *Some:* DVD players, CD players, fax. **Dining:** 6 restaurants, 6:30 am-11 pm, also, Hollywood Prime, see separate listing, entertainment. **Pool(s):** 2 heated outdoor. **Leisure Activities:** whirlpools, fishing, golf & tennis instruction, golf school, recreation programs, exercise room, spa. *Fee:* boat dock, charter fishing, golf-18 holes, 10 tennis courts (6 lighted). **Guest Services:** gift shop, valet laundry, area transportation-The Country Club. **Business Services:** conference facilities, business center. **Cards:** AX, CB, DC, DS, JC, MC, VI. **Special Amenities:** free local telephone calls. *(See color ad p 8)*

SOME UNITS

(See map and index starting on p. 364)

─────── **WHERE TO DINE** ───────

THE COUNCIL OAK   Dinner: $25-$45   Phone: 954/327-7625   [131]
▽▼▽▼▽
Steak House
Location: I-95, exit 22, 2.9 mi w, then just n on SR 7/US 441; Florida Tpke, exit 53, 0.5 mi e, then 0.8 mi s; in Seminole Hard Rock Hotel & Casino Hollywood. 1 Seminole Way 33314. **Hours:** 5 pm-midnight. **Reservations:** suggested. **Features:** Enjoy great steak and seafood offerings. The large room offers a contemporary decor and comfortable surroundings; the wine selection is very large and complements the menu. Dressy casual; cocktails. **Parking:** on-site and valet. **Cards:** AX, CB, DC, DS, JC, MC, VI.

GIORGIO'S GRILL   Dinner: $12-$30   Phone: 954/929-7030   [134]
▽▼▽▼
Italian
Location: SR A1A (S Ocean Dr), just n of SR 820 (Hollywood Blvd). 606 N Ocean Dr 33019. **Hours:** 4 pm-midnight. **Reservations:** accepted. **Features:** On the Intracoastal Waterway, the restaurant invites diners to relax indoors or on the outdoor patio. Seafood is the specialty on a menu that also includes Mediterranean entrees of pasta, pizza, beef and chicken. Dressy casual; cocktails. **Parking:** on-site (fee) and valet. **Cards:** AX, DS, MC, VI.

HOLLYWOOD ALE HOUSE & RAW BAR   Lunch: $5-$11   Dinner: $6-$11   Phone: 954/925-7275   [133]
▼▽▼
American
Location: I-95, exit 21 (Sheridan St/SR 882), just e to Oakwood, then left; in Oakwood Plaza are. 3215 Oakwood Blvd 33020. **Hours:** 11 am-2 am, Thurs-Sat to 3 am. **Features:** Sports-lovers munch on huge onion rings or piles of cheese fries while reveling in the lively sports-bar atmosphere, which incorporates more than 50 TVs. Fun favorites include burgers, pasta and some seafood items. All can be washed down with one of the more than 85 draft beer and bottled beer choices. Casual dress; cocktails. **Parking:** on-site. **Cards:** AX, MC, VI.

HOLLYWOOD PRIME   Dinner: $24-$42   Phone: 954/602-6000   [138]
ⒶⒶⒶ
▽▼▽▼▽
Steak House
Location: Just n on SR A1A (S Ocean Dr) from SR 858 (Hallendale Beach Blvd); in The Westin Diplomat Resort & Spa. 3555 S Ocean Dr 33019. **Hours:** 5:30 pm-11 pm. Closed: Sun & Mon. **Reservations:** suggested. **Features:** Contributing to the traditional steakhouse decor are white linens and leather chairs. Many wine choices are suited to the succulent dry-aged steaks and fresh seafood. Dressy casual; cocktails. **Parking:** on-site (fee) and valet. **Cards:** AX, CB, DC, DS, JC, MC, VI.

MARTHA'S ON THE INTRACOASTAL   Lunch: $7-$14   Dinner: $15-$30   Phone: 954/923-5444   [132]
▽▼▽▼
American
Location: Between Dania Beach Blvd Bridge and Sheridan St, just s. 6024 N Ocean Dr 33019. **Hours:** 11:30 am-4 & 4:30-10 pm, Fri & Sat-11 pm. **Reservations:** suggested. **Features:** An island feel tinges the cuisine and decor of this waterfront eatery. The views are outstanding. Seafood dazzlers dominate the first plates, and the main plates are equally enticing and innovative. Fresh seafood is always available. Dressy casual; cocktails; entertainment. **Parking:** valet. **Cards:** AX, DC, DS, MC, VI.

SUSHI BLUES CAFE   Lunch: $8-$22   Dinner: $9-$28   Phone: 954/929-9560   [137]
▽▼▽▼
Japanese
Location: From Hollywood Blvd, just s on Dixie Hwy, just e. 2009 Harrison St 33020. **Hours:** 11 am-11:30 pm, Fri & Sat-1:30 am. Closed: 11/23, 12/25. **Reservations:** accepted. **Features:** The sushi rocks, the meat items rock and the decor is casual; jazzy music is available weeknights. Dressy casual; cocktails. **Parking:** street. **Cards:** AX, MC, VI.

TRY MY THAI CAFE   Lunch: $6-$9   Dinner: $9-$19   Phone: 954/926-5585   [136]
▼▽▼ ▼▽▼
Thai
Location: From Hollywood Blvd, just s on Dixie Hwy, then just e. 2003 Harrison St 33020. **Hours:** 11 am-2:30 & 5-10:30 pm, Sat & Sun from 5 pm. Closed: 11/23, 12/25. **Reservations:** accepted. **Features:** Some resources call the decor funky, while others find it modern and bistrolike. The food is traditional, but the names of entrees are comical. Caring servers know the menu. This is a fun, casual place to eat. Casual dress; beer & wine only. **Parking:** street. **Cards:** AX, DC, DS, MC, VI.

UNIVERSE CAFE   Lunch: $7-$18   Dinner: $7-$18   Phone: 954/920-3774   [135]
▼▽▼ ▼▽▼
American
Location: On Hollywwod Blvd (SR 820); between N 20th and N 18th aves. 1925 Hollywood Blvd 33020. **Hours:** 11:30 am-10 pm, Fri & Sat-11 pm. **Features:** This restaurant's menu is all over the globe (thus the name); you can choose from fresh seafood to boutique pizzas with a meat item to select from. Eat inside in a soft colored room or outside and watch the people wander by. Casual dress; cocktails. **Parking:** street. **Cards:** AX, MC, VI.

──────── *The following restaurant has not been evaluated by AAA* ────────
but is listed for your information only.

FLANIGAN'S SEAFOOD BAR & GRILL   Phone: 954/964-3793
[fyi]
Not evaluated. **Location:** 2505 N University Dr 33024. **Features:** The family-friendly restaurant is known for its baby back ribs, burgers and seafood.

LAUDERDALE-BY-THE-SEA pop. 2,563 (See map and index starting on p. 364)

──────── WHERE TO STAY ────────

A LITTLE INN BY THE SEA   Phone: (954)772-2450   [60]

(AAA) (SAVE)   12/16-4/30 [ECP]   1P: $139-$189   2P: $139-$189   XP: $15   F12
               5/1-11/30 [ECP]   1P: $99-$149   2P: $99-$149   XP: $10   F12
▼▼▼▼▼   12/1-12/15 [ECP]   1P: $89-$139   2P: $89-$139   XP: $10   F12
   Motel   **Location:** Oceanfront. Just e of SR A1A; 0.4 mi n of SR 870 (Commercial Blvd). 4546 El Mar Dr 33308.
            Fax: 954/938-9354. **Facility:** 29 one-bedroom standard units, some with efficiencies or kitchens. 2-3 stories
            (no elevator), interior/exterior corridors. **Parking:** on-site. **Terms:** office hours 8 am-9:30 pm, 30 day
cancellation notice-fee imposed. **Amenities:** high-speed Internet, voice mail, safes (fee). **Pool(s):** heated outdoor. **Leisure
Activities:** limited beach access, rooftop sun deck, barbecue grill, bicycles. **Business Services:** fax (fee). **Cards:** AX, DC,
MC, VI. **Special Amenities:** free expanded continental breakfast and free newspaper. *(See color ad p 384)*

                                                                                            SOME UNITS
                                           [icons] FEE

BLUE SEAS COURTYARD   Phone: 954/772-3336   [61]

▼▼▼ ▼▼▼   12/1-4/15   1P: $120-$136   2P: $120-$136   XP: $15
               4/16-5/1   1P: $92-$110   2P: $92-$110   XP: $15
               10/1-11/30   1P: $91-$106   2P: $91-$106   XP: $15
   Motel   5/2-9/30   1P: $88-$103   2P: $88-$103   XP: $15
Location: 0.5 mi n of SR 870 (Commercial Blvd). Located across from the ocean. 4525 El Mar Dr 33308. **Fax:** 954/772-6337.
Facility: Designated smoking area. 12 one-bedroom standard units, some with efficiencies. 2 stories (no elevator), exterior
corridors. *Bath:* combo or shower only. **Parking:** on-site. **Terms:** office hours 7 am-4 pm, age restrictions may apply, 30 day
cancellation notice-fee imposed. **Pool(s):** heated outdoor. **Cards:** MC, VI.

                                           [icons]

BUENA VISTA HOTEL & CONFERENCE CENTER   Phone: 954/489-9870   [64]

(AAA) (SAVE)   12/1-4/30   1P: $149-$239   2P: $149-$239   XP: $15
               5/1-11/30   1P: $89-$149   2P: $89-$149   XP: $15
▼▼▼▼▼   **Location:** Just s of SR 870 (Commercial Blvd). Located in a quiet area across from the ocean. 4225 El Mar Dr 33308.
            Fax: 954/489-1044. **Facility:** Designated smoking area. 13 units. 10 one-bedroom standard units. 1 one-
Small-scale Hotel and 2 two-bedroom suites with efficiencies. 3 stories, interior/exterior corridors. *Bath:* combo or shower only.
               Parking: on-site. **Terms:** office hours 8:30 am-5 pm, 30 day cancellation notice. **Amenities:** video library,
dual phone lines, voice mail, irons, hair dryers. **Leisure Activities:** hot tub, limited exercise equipment. *Fee:* massage. **Guest
Services:** coin laundry. **Business Services:** meeting rooms, business center. **Cards:** AX, MC, VI. **Special Amenities:** free
continental breakfast and free newspaper. *(See color ad p 378)*

                                                                                            SOME UNITS
                                           [icons]

CLARION LAUDERDALE BEACH RESORT   *Book at aaa.com*   Phone: (954)776-5660   [57]

(AAA) (SAVE)   12/22-4/16   1P: $169-$249   2P: $169-$249   XP: $10   F17
               12/1-12/21 & 4/17-11/30   1P: $89-$139   2P: $89-$139   XP: $10   F17
▼▼▼▼▼   **Location:** SR A1A, 0.5 mi n of SR 870 (Commercial Blvd). 4660 N Ocean Dr 33308. **Fax:** 954/776-4689.
            Facility: 178 units. 161 one-bedroom standard units. 17 one-bedroom suites ($139-$249) with kitchens. 1-5
Small-scale Hotel stories, interior/exterior corridors. *Bath:* combo or shower only. **Parking:** on-site. **Terms:** cancellation fee
imposed, $3 service charge. **Amenities:** high-speed Internet, dual phone lines, voice mail, safes, irons, hair
dryers. **Dining:** 2 restaurants, 7 am-11:30 pm, cocktails. **Pool(s):** 2 heated outdoor. **Leisure Activities:** exercise room,
shuffleboard, volleyball. **Guest Services:** valet and coin laundry. **Business Services:** fax (fee). **Cards:** AX, CB, DC, DS,
MC, VI. *(See color ad p 413)*

                                                                                            SOME UNITS
                                           [icons]

COURTYARD VILLA ON THE OCEAN   Phone: 954/776-1164   [62]

(AAA) (SAVE)   12/1-4/30   1P: $179-$272   2P: $179-$272   XP: $15
               5/1-11/30   1P: $115-$167   2P: $115-$167   XP: $15
▼▼▼▼▼   **Location:** Oceanfront. SR 870 (Commerical Blvd), just s. 4312 El Mar Dr 33308. **Fax:** 954/491-0768.
            Facility: Designated smoking area. 8 one-bedroom standard units. 2 stories (no elevator), exterior corridors.
   Motel   *Bath:* shower only. **Parking:** on-site. **Terms:** office hours 8:30 am-5 pm, age restrictions may apply, 30 day
            cancellation notice. **Amenities:** video library, voice mail, irons, hair dryers. **Leisure Activities:** scuba diving,
snorkeling, beach towels, sun deck, pool spa, tennis court, barbecue grills, bicycles. **Cards:** AX, MC, VI. **Special Amenities:**
free continental breakfast and free newspaper. *(See color ad p 378)*

                                           [icons]

GREAT ESCAPE MOTEL   Phone: 954/772-1002   [59]

▼▼ ▼▼   12/1-4/30   1P: $80-$150   2P: $80-$150   XP: $10   F
               4/21-11/30   1P: $55-$125   2P: $55-$125   XP: $10   F
   Motel   **Location:** On SR A1A, just n of SR 870 (Commercial Blvd). 4620 N Ocean Dr 33308. **Fax:** 954/772-6488.
            Facility: Designated smoking area. 11 units. 9 one-bedroom standard units, some with efficiencies. 2 one-
bedroom suites ($125-$150) with kitchens. 2 stories (no elevator), exterior corridors. **Parking:** on-site. **Terms:** office hours 9
am-9 pm, 30 day cancellation notice-fee imposed, weekly rates available. **Amenities:** *Some:* irons. **Pool(s):** heated outdoor.
Guest Services: coin laundry. **Business Services:** fax (fee). **Cards:** AX, DS, MC, VI.

                                           [icons]

HOLIDAY INN-LAUDERDALE-BY-THE-SEA NORTH
BEACH   *Book at aaa.com*   Phone: (954)776-1212   [65]

(AAA) (SAVE)   12/1-4/20   1P: $159-$179   2P: $159-$179
               4/21-11/30   1P: $139-$169   2P: $139-$169
▼▼▼▼▼   **Location:** SR A1A, just s of jct SR 870 (Commercial Blvd). 4116 N Ocean Dr 33308. **Fax:** 954/776-1411.
            Facility: 186 one-bedroom standard units. 5 stories, exterior corridors. *Bath:* combo or shower only.
Small-scale Hotel **Parking:** on-site. **Terms:** 3 day cancellation notice-fee imposed. **Amenities:** high-speed Internet, voice
               mail, irons, hair dryers. **Dining:** 6:30 am-10 pm, cocktails. **Pool(s):** heated outdoor. **Leisure
Activities:** beach access, limited exercise equipment. *Fee:* scuba diving, snorkeling. **Guest Services:** gift shop, valet and coin
laundry. **Business Services:** meeting rooms, fax (fee). **Cards:** AX, DC, DS, MC, VI.

                                                                                            SOME UNITS
                                           [icons]

(See map and index starting on p. 364)

SEA LORD HOTEL & SUITES   *Book at aaa.com*   Phone: (954)776-1505   66

	12/16-4/30	1P: $145-$275	2P: $145-$275	XP: $8	F12
	11/1-11/30	1P: $125-$225	2P: $125-$225	XP: $8	F12
Small-scale Hotel	12/1-12/15	1P: $115-$201	2P: $115-$201	XP: $8	F12
	5/1-10/31	1P: $105-$201	2P: $105-$201	XP: $8	F12

Location: Oceanfront. Just s of Commercial Blvd (SR 870). 4140 El Mar Dr 33308. Fax: 954/776-1981. **Facility:** 48 units. 39 one-bedroom standard units, some with efficiencies. 9 one-bedroom suites with kitchens. 5 stories, exterior corridors. **Parking:** on-site. **Terms:** office hours 8 am-10 pm, 14 night minimum stay - seasonal, 30 day cancellation notice-fee imposed, $1 service charge. **Amenities:** voice mail, safes (fee), irons, hair dryers. **Pool(s):** heated outdoor. **Guest Services:** coin laundry. **Business Services:** fax (fee). **Cards:** AX, DS, MC, VI.

SOME UNITS
ASK SD ⏸ ⤢ ⚅ DATA PORT 🛏 🍽 💻 / ⊠ /

(See map and index starting on p. 364)

SEA SPRAY INN

Phone: (954)776-1311   **63**

AAA SAVE

	2P: $80-$185	XP: $8	F12
12/1-4/15			
4/16-11/30	2P: $75-$145	XP: $8	F12

Motel

Location: SR 870 (Commercial Blvd), just s. 4245 El Mar Dr 33308. **Fax:** 954/772-3178. **Facility:** 6 units. 2 one-bedroom standard units with efficiencies. 4 one-bedroom suites with kitchens. 3 stories (no elevator), exterior corridors. *Bath:* combo or shower only. **Parking:** on-site. **Terms:** office hours 9 am-5 pm, 2 night minimum stay - weekends, 21 day cancellation notice. **Amenities:** voice mail, irons, hair dryers. *Some:* DVD players, safes. **Leisure Activities:** beach access. **Cards:** MC, VI. **Special Amenities: free local telephone calls and preferred room (subject to availability with advance reservations).**

TROPIC SEAS RESORT

Phone: (954)772-2555   **58**

AAA SAVE

	1P: $200-$300	2P: $200-$300	XP: $20	F12
2/1-4/30 [CP]				
12/1-1/31 [CP]	1P: $180-$280	2P: $180-$280	XP: $20	F12
10/1-11/30 [CP]	1P: $120-$180	2P: $120-$180	XP: $20	F12
5/1-9/30 [CP]	1P: $110-$170	2P: $110-$170	XP: $20	F12

Motel

Location: Oceanfront. Just e of SR A1A; 0.5 mi n of jct SR 870 (Commercial Blvd). 4616 El Mar Dr 33308. Fax: 954/771-5711. **Facility:** 16 units. 9 one-bedroom standard units, some with efficiencies. 7 one-bedroom suites with kitchens. 2 stories (no elevator), exterior corridors. **Parking:** on-site. **Terms:** office hours 8 am-8 pm, 15 day cancellation notice. **Amenities:** voice mail. *Some:* DVD players, CD players. **Pool(s):** heated outdoor. **Leisure Activities:** barbecue grills. **Guest Services:** coin laundry. **Cards:** AX, DS, MC, VI. **Special Amenities: free continental breakfast and free newspaper.** *(See color ad p 388)*

SOME UNITS

--- **WHERE TO DINE** ---

ARUBA BEACH CAFE

Lunch: $5-$18   **Dinner:** $5-$22   **Phone:** 954/776-0001   **72**

Caribbean

Location: Just e of SR A1A. One Commercial Blvd 33308. **Hours:** 11 am-close. **Reservations:** not accepted. **Features:** A casual, fun place to eat, the restaurant affords a panoramic view of the beach and offers fresh seafood items and meat entrees, some of which reflect an island twist. Casual dress; cocktails; entertainment. **Parking:** valet. **Cards:** AX, CB, DC, DS, MC, VI.

BLUE MOON FISH CO.

Lunch: $10-$15   **Dinner:** $25-$36   **Phone:** 954/267-9888   **71**

Regional Seafood

Location: From SR A1A (Ocean Dr), just w on SR 870 (Commercial Blvd), then n. 4405 W Tradewinds Ave 33308. **Hours:** 11:30 am-10 pm, Fri & Sat-11 pm. **Reservations:** suggested. **Features:** The waterfront restaurant's menu lines up the freshest of the sea, as well as chops, steaks and some foods with a New Orleans twist. Great desserts are artful in presentation. The interior shows art deco flair, while outside guests can sit and watch the boat activity. Dressy casual; cocktails. **Parking:** valet. **Cards:** MC, VI.

LAUDERDALE LAKES pop. 31,705   (See map and index starting on p. 364)

--- **WHERE TO DINE** ---

PHO NAM DO

Lunch: $5-$8   **Dinner:** $5-$9   **Phone:** 954/485-6079   **80**

Vietnamese

Location: Just s of SR 870 (Commercial Blvd); in Lake Town Center. 4461 N SR 7 33319. **Hours:** 11:30 am-9 pm, Sun 11 am-8 pm. Closed: Wed. **Features:** In a small shopping center, the restaurant musters big flavors in its wide variety of fresh Vietnamese foods. Casual dress. **Parking:** on-site. **Cards:** AX, DS, MC, VI.

LAUDERHILL pop. 57,585   (See map and index starting on p. 364)

--- **WHERE TO DINE** ---

GABOSE RESTAURANT

Lunch: $8-$15   **Dinner:** $8-$23   **Phone:** 954/572-4800   **84**

Asian

Location: Jct Inverrary Blvd and SR 817 (University Dr); just s of SR 870 (Commercial Blvd); in Los Madres Plaza. 4991 N University Dr 33351. **Hours:** 11:30 am-10:30 pm, Fri & Sat-11 pm, Sun 1 pm-10:30 pm. Closed: 11/23, 12/25. **Features:** Guests can ponder a large menu in the cozy dining room. Traditional Korean barbecue preparation is applied to fish, beef and pork items, while other offerings include hot pot casseroles, soups and noodle dishes. Sushi cravings also can be sated here. Casual dress; beer & wine only. **Parking:** on-site. **Cards:** MC, VI.

JOE'S CRAB SHACK

Lunch: $5-$10   **Dinner:** $9-$21   **Phone:** 954/749-2722   **86**

Seafood

Location: SR 817 (University Dr), 1 mi s of Commercial Blvd at NW 44th St. 4402 N University Dr 33351. **Hours:** 11 am-10 pm, Fri & Sat-11 pm. **Features:** In a warehouse-style building, this popular, casual restaurant is decorated in a nautical theme. Fresh seafood, including several varieties of crab, is the menu staple. Hungry patrons should head for the all-you-can-eat shellfish and salad bar. Casual dress; cocktails. **Parking:** on-site. **Cards:** AX, CB, DC, DS, MC, VI.

LE CREPERIE

Dinner: $15-$28   **Phone:** 954/741-9035   **85**

French

Location: From SR 870 (Commercial Blvd), just n; in Sunset Plaza. 4589 N University Dr 33351. **Hours:** 5:30 pm-10 pm, Sun 5 pm-9 pm. Closed: Mon. **Features:** The restaurant's name suggests its specialty, and more than two dozen crepe varieties are among offerings. In addition to French crepes, some large enough to be meals or shared, the menu lists some regular entrees. This place is known for its dessert crepes. The atmosphere is comfortable, and service is friendly and informative. Casual dress; beer & wine only. **Parking:** on-site. **Cards:** AX, DS, MC, VI.

(See map and index starting on p. 364)

MAKINO JAPANESE SEAFOOD BUFFET   **Lunch:** $9-$11   **Dinner:** $16-$18   **Phone:** 954/748-3788   (83)
Japanese
Location: Just s of SR 870 (Commercial Blvd). 5200 N University Blvd 33351. **Hours:** 11:30 am-2 & 5-9 pm, Fri-10 pm, Sat noon-3 & 5-10 pm, Sun noon-3 & 5-9 pm. **Features:** Try what you haven't before at this sushi buffet. If sushi and sashimi aren't your taste, then try the hibachi grill items cooked right in front of you. They also offer traditional Chinese and Japanese items on the all-you-can-eat buffet. Casual dress; beer & wine only. **Parking:** on-site. **Cards:** MC, VI.

LIGHTHOUSE POINT pop. 10,767

------- **WHERE TO DINE** -------

CAP'S PLACE-ISLAND RESTAURANT & BAR   **Dinner:** $13-$25   **Phone:** 954/941-0418
Seafood
Location: Just n on US 1 (Federal Hwy) from jct Copans Rd, 1.1 mi e and n via NE 24th St, follow signs to Cap's Dock for short boat ride to the island. 2765 NE 28th Ct, #2 33064. **Hours:** 5:30 pm-10 pm, Fri & Sat-11 pm. Closed: 11/23, 12/24, 12/25; also Super Bowl Sun. **Reservations:** suggested. **Features:** Operating out of a building that once was a gambling casino, the restaurant sits on an island in the Intracoastal Waterway and has been a source of rich history since 1929. Grouper chowder, hearts of palm salad and fresh broiled fish are menu favorites. Casual dress; cocktails. **Parking:** on-site. **Cards:** AX, MC, VI. **Historic**

CIELITO LINDO DOS   **Lunch:** $6-$10   **Dinner:** $8-$17   **Phone:** 954/941-8226
Mexican
Location: From SR 834 (Sample Rd), 0.7 mi n. 4480 N Federal Hwy 33064. **Hours:** noon-10 pm, Wed-10:30 pm, Fri & Sat-11 pm. Closed: 11/23, 12/25. **Reservations:** accepted. **Features:** Mexican and Spanish items decorate the dining room. Foods come from various regions of Mexico and pick up some influences from Spanish and Cuban cuisine. Casual dress; cocktails. **Parking:** on-site. **Cards:** AX, DC, DS, MC, VI.

FIFTH AVENUE GRILL   **Lunch:** $6-$15   **Dinner:** $14-$30   **Phone:** 954/782-4433
Steak House
Location: On US 1 (Federal Hwy), 1.1 mi n of Sample Rd (SR 834). 4650 N Federal Hwy 33064. **Hours:** 11:30 am-4 & 5-10 pm, Fri & Sat-11 pm. Closed: Super Bowl Sun. **Reservations:** accepted. **Features:** An award-winning wine list complements flame-broiled steak and chops, as well as fresh seafood preparations. The dining room is cozy and inviting. Dressy casual; cocktails. **Parking:** on-site and valet. **Cards:** AX, DC, MC, VI.

LE BISTRO   **Dinner:** $15-$28   **Phone:** 954/946-9240
French
Location: From SR 834 (Sample Rd), just n; in Main St Plaza. 4626 N Federal Hwy 33064. **Hours:** 5 pm-10 pm. Closed: 1/1, 12/25; also Mon. **Reservations:** suggested. **Features:** Classic cuisine is served in generous portions at this small, quaint eatery. Great attention is given to every detail from preparation to presentation, from service to atmosphere. Beer & wine only. **Parking:** on-site. **Cards:** MC, VI.

MANGIA BENE RISTORANTE   **Dinner:** $12-$28   **Phone:** 954/943-7055
Italian
Location: 0.8 mi n of Copans Rd; in The 3110 Plaza. 3150 N Federal Hwy/US 1 33064. **Hours:** 6 pm-10 pm. **Reservations:** accepted. **Features:** The soothing and comfortable dining room welcomes guests to sit and enjoy larger-than-normal-size dishes. Most Italian favorites are on the menu, as are desserts worth saving room for. Granny's pound cake won't disappoint. Casual dress; cocktails. **Parking:** on-site. **Cards:** AX, CB, DC, DS, JC, MC, VI.

MARGATE pop. 53,909

------- **WHERE TO DINE** -------

JASMINE THAI & SUSHI BAR   *Menu on aaa.com*   **Lunch:** $8-$13   **Dinner:** $10-$20   **Phone:** 954/979-5530
Thai
Location: Atlantic Blvd (SR 814), 0.7 mi n on SR 7 and US 441, then just e; in Cocogate Plaza. 5103 Coconut Creek Pkwy 33063. **Hours:** 11 am-3 & 4:30-10 pm, Sat & Sun from 4:30 pm. Closed major holidays; also Super Bowl Sun. **Reservations:** accepted. **Features:** Fresh, carefully prepared cuisine such as snapper with chili garlic sauce, roast duckling, panang curry and tornado chicken is served by a friendly wait staff. A quaint bridge and large pictures in the small, comfortable setting convey an Oriental feel. Casual dress; beer & wine only. **Parking:** on-site. **Cards:** AX, CB, DC, DS, MC, VI.

LA BAMBA MEXICAN & SPANISH RESTAURANT   **Lunch:** $6-$13   **Dinner:** $6-$13   **Phone:** 954/978-6377
Mexican
Location: Just s of US 441; in The Peppertree Plaza. 5452 W Sample Rd 33073. **Hours:** 11:30 am-10 pm, Fri & Sat-11 pm. Closed: 7/4, 11/23, 12/25. **Features:** In a small shopping center, the restaurant is decorated with art objects from many regions of Mexico and Spain. The menu lists both Mexican favorites and Spanish dishes. Casual dress; cocktails. **Parking:** on-site. **Cards:** AX, CB, DC, DS, MC, VI.

L J DINER   **Lunch:** $5-$11   **Dinner:** $5-$15   **Phone:** 954/956-7111
American
Location: From Sawgrass Expwy, 1.6 mi s on SR 441, just e of SR 441; in Peppertree Plaza. 5660 W Sample Rd 33063. **Hours:** 24 hours. **Features:** The exterior is that of a dining car, while the inside is eclectic with pictures of the past, posters and other nostalgic items. The menu blends comfort foods and some Greek items. Casual dress; cocktails. **Parking:** on-site. **Cards:** AX, MC, VI.

MIRAMAR pop. 72,739   (See map and index starting on p. 364)

──────── **WHERE TO STAY** ────────

COURTYARD BY MARRIOTT FORT LAUDERDALE
SW/MIRAMAR   **Phone: 954/450-1801**
(fyi)   Under construction, scheduled to open September 2006. **Location:** I-75, exit 7A (Miramar Pkwy), just e to SW
145th Ave, then n. 14500 SW 29th St (Hotel Rd) 33027. Fax: 954/450-9130. **Planned Amenities:** coffeemakers,
Small-scale Hotel   pool.

HILTON GARDEN INN FT. LAUDERDALE
SW/MIRAMAR   *Book at aaa.com*   **Phone: (954)438-7700**   **144**
▼▼▼▼   1/1-4/30   1P: $149-$199   2P: $149-$199
12/1-12/31 & 5/1-11/30   1P: $129-$169   2P: $129-$169
Small-scale Hotel   **Location:** I-75, exit 7A, e to SW 145th Ave, then n. 14501 Hotel Rd 33027. Fax: 954/392-8606. **Facility:** 149 one-
bedroom standard units. 5 stories, interior corridors. *Bath:* combo or shower only. **Parking:** on-site.
Terms: [BP], [CP] & [MAP] meal plans available. **Amenities:** video games (fee), high-speed Internet, dual phone lines, voice
mail, irons, hair dryers. **Pool(s):** heated outdoor. **Leisure Activities:** limited exercise equipment. **Guest Services:** sundries,
valet and coin laundry. **Business Services:** meeting rooms, business center. **Cards:** AX, CB, DC, DS, MC, VI.
(See color ad below)
SOME UNITS
🍽️ 🍸 📶 🛗 ⊘ 🚲 🎥 🔌 🅿️ 🛏️ 🖥️ / 🚫 /

RESIDENCE INN BY MARRIOTT FORT
LAUDERDALE SW/MIRAMAR   **Phone: 954/450-2717**
(fyi)   Under construction, scheduled to open September 2006. **Location:** I-75, exit 7A (Miramar Pkwy), just e to 145th
Ave, then n. 14700 SW 29th St (Hotel Rd) 33027. Fax: 954/450-9395. **Planned Amenities:** pets, coffeemakers,
Small-scale Hotel   microwaves, refrigerators, pool.

WINGATE INN   *Book at aaa.com*   **Phone: (954)441-0122**   **145**
▼▼▼   12/1-4/30 [ECP]   1P: $129-$149   2P: $139-$159   XP: $10   F12
10/1-11/30 [ECP]   1P: $119-$129   2P: $129-$139   XP: $10   F12
5/1-9/30 [ECP]   1P: $109-$119   2P: $119-$129   XP: $10   F12
Small-scale Hotel   **Location:** I-75, exit 7A, just e to SW 148th Ave to Huntington Corporate Park. 2800 SW 149th Ave 33027.
Fax: 954/441-0328. **Facility:** 100 one-bedroom standard units. 4 stories, interior corridors. *Bath:* combo or shower only.
Parking: on-site. **Terms:** cancellation fee imposed. **Amenities:** video games (fee), high-speed Internet, dual phone lines, voice
mail, safes, irons, hair dryers. **Pool(s):** outdoor. **Leisure Activities:** whirlpool, exercise room. **Guest Services:** valet and coin
laundry. **Business Services:** meeting rooms, business center. **Cards:** AX, DC, DS, MC, VI.
SOME UNITS
(ASK) 🛗 🍽️ 🛗 ⊘ 🚲 🎥 🔌 🅿️ 🛏️ 🖥️ / 🚫 /

──────── **WHERE TO DINE** ────────

SONNY'S REAL PIT BAR-B-Q   **Lunch:** $4-$9   **Dinner:** $8-$15   **Phone:** 954/987-2336   **151**
▼▼▼   **Location:** I-95, exit 19 (Pembroke Rd), 2.5 mi w, then just s on SR 441/SR Rd 7 (S Powerline Rd). 2100 S SR Rd
7/Powerline Rd 33023. **Hours:** 11 am-9:30 pm, Fri & Sat-10:30 pm. Closed: 11/23, 12/25. **Features:** Barbecue
Barbecue   chicken, ribs and pulled pork are done right: slowly cooked over a hardwood fire then coated in sauce. Also
tempting are smoked turkey, fried catfish and charbroiled chicken. A casual family atmosphere surrounds
patrons. Casual dress. **Parking:** on-site. **Cards:** AX, MC, VI.

PEMBROKE PINES pop. 137,427 (See map and index starting on p. 364)

—— WHERE TO STAY ——

GRAND PALMS HOTEL-SPA & GOLF RESORT **Book at aaa.com** Phone: (954)431-8800 **141**

(AAA) (SAVE)

12/21-4/15 [CP]	1P: $135-$170	2P: $135-$170	XP: $10 F16
12/1-12/20 & 4/16-11/30 [CP]	1P: $119-$144	2P: $119-$144	XP: $10 F16

Location: I-75, exit 9B (Pines Blvd), 0.4 mi w on SR 820. 110 Grand Palms Dr 33027. Fax: 954/435-5988.
Resort
Small-scale Hotel **Facility:** The resort's lush landscaping and numerous recreational offerings give it the ambience of a retreat. 137 units. 101 one-bedroom standard units. 36 one-bedroom suites ($144-$170). 2 stories (no elevator), exterior corridors. *Bath:* combo or shower only. **Parking:** on-site and valet. **Terms:** cancellation fee imposed. **Amenities:** voice mail, irons, hair dryers. *Some:* dual phone lines. **Dining:** 7 am-9 pm, cocktails. **Pool(s):** outdoor. **Leisure Activities:** exercise room, spa. *Fee:* golf-27 holes, golf instruction, 6 tennis courts (2 lighted). **Guest Services:** valet and coin laundry. **Business Services:** meeting rooms. **Cards:** AX, DC, DS, MC, VI.
Special Amenities: free continental breakfast and free local telephone calls.

SOME UNITS

🅵 🍴 🛏 🕃 ♿ 🏊 ⊠ 🎥 DATA PORT 💻 / ⊠ 🖥 🖥 /
FEE

HAMPTON INN PEMBROKE PINES **Book at aaa.com**

Property failed to provide current rates Phone: 954/441-4242 **140**

Location: I-75, exit 11A, 0.4 mi e on Sheridan St (SR 822) to NW 146th Ave, then 0.4 mi s. 1900 NW 150th Ave 33028.
Small-scale Hotel Fax: 954/441-1118. **Facility:** 107 one-bedroom standard units, some with whirlpools. 5 stories, interior corridors. *Bath:* combo or shower only. **Parking:** on-site. **Amenities:** video games (fee), high-speed Internet, voice mail, safes, irons, hair dryers. **Pool(s):** outdoor. **Leisure Activities:** whirlpool, exercise room. **Guest Services:** valet and coin laundry. **Business Services:** meeting rooms, business center.

SOME UNITS

🍴 ♿ 🕃 🔈 🏊 🎥 DATA PORT 🖥 🖥 💻 / ⊠ /

—— WHERE TO DINE ——

DRAGON GATE CHINESE RESTAURANT Lunch: $5-$9 Dinner: $8-$19 Phone: 954/438-9982 **148**

Location: I-75, exit 9A, 2.5 mi e; corner of Hiatus Rd and Pines Blvd; in Michael's Plaza. 11232 Pines Blvd 33026.
Chinese **Hours:** 11:30 am-10 pm, Fri & Sat-11 pm, Sun noon-10 pm. Closed: 11/23. **Features:** The large menu offers many Chinese, as well as American, favorites from the land and sea. Heat and spice levels can be
JC, MC, VI. altered to the diner's preference. Casual dress; beer & wine only. **Parking:** on-site. **Cards:** AX, CB, DC, DS,
♿

JALAPANOS MEXICAN KITCHEN Lunch: $6-$8 Dinner: $9-$15 Phone: 954/965-8088 **146**

Location: Florida Tpke, exit 49, 2.1 mi w on Hollywood Blvd/Pine Blvd, then just n; in University Plaza. 207 N University
Mexican Dr 33024. **Hours:** 11:30 am-10 pm, Fri & Sat-11 pm. **Features:** Traditional Mexican favorites share same
DC, DS, JC, MC, VI. space with some regional favorites. Guests can eat inside, where there is plenty of color, or outside on the patio. A wide selection of tequilas is available. Casual dress; cocktails. **Parking:** on-site. **Cards:** AX, CB,
🍸

THE ROASTED PEPPER ITALIAN SEAFOOD &
  GRILL Lunch: $5-$12 Dinner: $10-$20 Phone: 954/450-8800 **147**

Location: I-75, exit 9A, 4.4 mi e; in The Roasted Pepper Pine Plaza Center. 9893 Pines Blvd 33024. **Hours:** 4 pm-11
Italian pm, Fri also 11 am-3 pm, Sat 2 pm-11 pm, Sun 2 pm-10 pm. Closed major holidays; also Mon.
Features: This busy family restaurant serves traditional favorites like brick-oven pizza. When the singer
takes a break, the servers dance and sing to keep the beat going. A neat, entertaining place to go for
generous portions of authentic Italian food. Casual dress; cocktails; entertainment. **Parking:** on-site. **Cards:** AX, DS, MC, VI.
🍸

SCRUBY'S B.B.Q. Lunch: $5-$8 Dinner: $6-$19 Phone: 954/987-1933 **145**

Location: Florida Tpke, exit 49, 2.1 mi w on Hollywood Blvd/Pines Blvd, then just n. 251 N University Blvd 33024.
Barbecue **Hours:** 11 am-9:30 pm, Fri & Sat-10 pm. **Features:** The restaurant is casual and lively, and the barbecue is
plentiful. Ribs, chicken, pulled pork and big burgers are among choices. The staff's friendliness earns a
special mention. Casual dress; beer & wine only. **Parking:** on-site. **Cards:** AX, MC, VI.
♿

—— *The following restaurant has not been evaluated by AAA* ——
but is listed for your information only.

BAHAMA BREEZE
  [fyi] Not evaluated. **Location:** 11000 Pines Blvd 33025. **Features:** The atmosphere is tropical and the foods Phone: 954/450-6450
featured are that of the islands with meats, pastas and fresh seafoods.

PLANTATION pop. 66,700 (See map and index starting on p. 364)

—— WHERE TO STAY ——

AMERISUITES PLANTATION **Book at aaa.com** Phone: (954)370-2220 **87**

12/26-4/30 [BP]	1P: $119-$149	2P: $119-$149	XP: $10 F18
12/1-12/25 & 5/1-11/30 [BP]	1P: $99-$109	2P: $99-$109	XP: $10 F18

Location: I-595, exit 4 (Pine Island Rd), 1.3 mi n. Located behind the Westside Corporate Center. 8530 W Broward Blvd
Small-scale Hotel 33324. Fax: 954/370-2272. **Facility:** 128 one-bedroom standard units. 6 stories, interior corridors. *Bath:*
combo or shower only. **Parking:** on-site. **Terms:** cancellation fee imposed. **Amenities:** video games (fee), high-speed Internet,
voice mail, irons, hair dryers. *Some:* dual phone lines. **Pool(s):** heated outdoor. **Leisure Activities:** exercise room. **Guest
Services:** valet and coin laundry, area transportation. **Business Services:** meeting rooms, business center. **Cards:** AX, DC,
DS, MC, VI.

SOME UNITS

(ASK) (S/D) ♿ 🍴 ♿ 🕃 🔈 🏊 VCR 🎥 DATA PORT 🖥 🖥 💻 / ⊠ /

(See map and index starting on p. 364)

COURTYARD BY MARRIOTT   *Book at aaa.com*   Phone: (954)475-1100   **90**

12/26-5/27	1P: $209	2P: $209	
12/1-12/25	1P: $179-$199	2P: $179-$199	
9/25-11/30	1P: $189	2P: $189	
5/28-9/24	1P: $129	2P: $129	

Small-scale Hotel   **Location:** Just w of SR 817 (University Dr); 0.5 mi sw of SR 842 (Broward Blvd). Located next to Broward Mall. 7780 SW 6th St 33324. Fax: 954/424-8402. **Facility:** 149 units. 138 one-bedroom standard units. 11 one-bedroom suites ($159-$239). 3 stories, interior corridors. *Bath:* combo or shower only. **Parking:** on-site. **Amenities:** high-speed Internet, voice mail, irons, hair dryers. **Dining:** 6:30-10 am, Sat & Sun 7-11 am. **Pool(s):** heated outdoor. **Leisure Activities:** whirlpool, exercise room. **Guest Services:** valet and coin laundry. **Business Services:** meeting rooms, fax (fee). **Cards:** AX, CB, DC, DS, JC, MC, VI. **Special Amenities:** free newspaper.

SOME UNITS

HAMPTON INN PLANTATION   *Book at aaa.com*   Phone: (954)382-4500   **88**

12/26-4/15	1P: $139-$159
4/16-11/30	1P: $129-$149
12/1-12/25	1P: $119-$139

Small-scale Hotel   **Location:** Just w of SR 817 (University Dr); 0.5 mi sw of SR 842 (Broward Blvd). Located next to the Broward Mall. 7801 SW 6th St 33324. Fax: 954/382-4510. **Facility:** 128 one-bedroom standard units. 5 stories, interior corridors. *Bath:* combo or shower only. **Parking:** on-site. **Terms:** [CP] meal plan available, 11% service charge. **Amenities:** high-speed Internet, dual phone lines, voice mail, irons, hair dryers. **Pool(s):** heated outdoor. **Leisure Activities:** whirlpool, exercise room. **Guest Services:** valet and coin laundry, area transportation. **Business Services:** meeting rooms, fax. **Cards:** AX, CB, DC, DS, JC, MC, VI.

SOME UNITS

HOLIDAY INN PLANTATION/SAWGRASS   *Book at aaa.com*   Phone: (954)472-5600   **83**

1/1-4/15	1P: $99-$149	2P: $99-$149	XP: $10	F18
12/1-12/31 & 4/16-11/30	1P: $79-$129	2P: $79-$129	XP: $10	F18

Small-scale Hotel   **Location:** SR 817, just s of jct SR 838 (Sunrise Blvd). 1701 N University Dr 33322. Fax: 954/370-3201. **Facility:** 335 units. 319 one-bedroom standard units. 16 one-bedroom suites. 2-5 stories, interior/exterior corridors. *Bath:* combo or shower only. **Parking:** on-site. **Terms:** cancellation fee imposed, [CP] meal plan available, package plans, small pets only ($25 fee). **Amenities:** video games (fee), dual phone lines, voice mail, irons, hair dryers. **Pool(s):** heated outdoor. **Leisure Activities:** exercise room. **Guest Services:** valet and coin laundry, area transportation. **Business Services:** meeting rooms, business center. **Cards:** AX, DC, DS, MC, VI.

SOME UNITS

FEE

LA QUINTA INN & SUITES FT. LAUDERDALE   Phone: (954)476-6047   **91**
   (PLANTATION)   *Book at aaa.com*

2/1-4/30	1P: $129-$149	XP: $7	F18
5/1-11/30	1P: $99-$109	XP: $7	F18
12/1-1/31	1P: $95-$105	XP: $7	F18

Small-scale Hotel   **Location:** I-595, exit 5 (SR 817 N/University Dr), just n, then just w; in Crossroad Office Park. 8101 Peters Rd 33324. Fax: 954/476-6547. **Facility:** 131 units. 127 one-bedroom standard units. 4 one-bedroom suites ($130-$185). 4 stories, interior corridors. *Bath:* combo or shower only. **Parking:** on-site. **Terms:** [ECP] meal plan available, small pets only. **Amenities:** video games (fee), high-speed Internet, voice mail, irons, hair dryers. **Pool(s):** heated outdoor. **Leisure Activities:** whirlpool, exercise room. **Guest Services:** valet and coin laundry. **Business Services:** meeting rooms, fax (fee). **Cards:** AX, CB, DC, DS, MC, VI. **Special Amenities:** free expanded continental breakfast and free local telephone calls. *(See color ad p 384)*

SOME UNITS

RENAISSANCE FT. LAUDERDALE/PLANTATION   Phone: (954)472-2252   **92**
   HOTEL   *Book at aaa.com*

12/1-6/1	1P: $199-$499	2P: $219-$499
9/13-11/30	1P: $189-$399	2P: $209-$419
6/2-9/12	1P: $169-$299	2P: $189-$319

Large-scale Hotel   **Location:** I-595, exit 4 (Pine Island Rd), n to N New River Canal Rd. 1230 Pine Island Rd 33324. Fax: 954/308-4600. **Facility:** Conviently located to shopping and office parks, the property's rooms are decorated in dark wood tones reminiscent of the British West Indies style. 250 units. 241 one-bedroom standard units. 9 one-bedroom suites. 9 stories, interior corridors. *Bath:* combo or shower only. **Parking:** on-site and valet. **Terms:** cancellation fee imposed, package plans. **Amenities:** CD players, dual phone lines, voice mail, irons, hair dryers. *Fee:* video games, high-speed Internet. *Some:* safes. **Dining:** Bin 595, see separate listing. **Pool(s):** heated outdoor. **Leisure Activities:** exercise room. *Fee:* massage. **Guest Services:** sundries, valet and coin laundry, area transportation. **Business Services:** meeting rooms. **Cards:** AX, CB, DC, DS, JC, MC, VI.

SOME UNITS

RESIDENCE INN BY MARRIOTT-FT.   Phone: 954/723-0300   **85**
   LAUDERDALE/PLANTATION   *Book at aaa.com*

Property failed to provide current rates

Location: I-595, exit 5 (SR 817/University Dr), 0.7 mi n; just n of jct SR 842 (Broward Blvd). 130 N University Dr 33324. Fax: 954/474-7385. **Facility:** 138 units. 34 one-bedroom standard units with kitchens. 74 one- and 30 two-bedroom suites with kitchens. 1-4 stories, interior corridors. *Bath:* combo or shower only. **Parking:** on-site. **Terms:** small pets only ($75 fee). **Amenities:** video games (fee), high-speed Internet, dual phone lines, voice mail, irons, hair dryers. **Pool(s):** heated outdoor. **Leisure Activities:** whirlpool, exercise room, sports court. **Guest Services:** sundries, complimentary evening beverages: Mon-Thurs, valet and coin laundry. **Business Services:** meeting rooms, fax (fee).

SOME UNITS

FEE

(See map and index starting on p. 364)

SHERATON SUITES-PLANTATION   *Book at aaa.com*   Phone: (954)424-3300   [86]

(AAA) [SAVE]

12/1-4/14	1P: $299-$700	2P: $299-$700	XP: $20 F18
4/15-11/30	1P: $279-$700	2P: $279-$700	XP: $20 F18

Location: I-595, exit 5 (SR 817/University Dr), 0.7 mi n; 0.3 mi n of jct Broward Blvd (SR 842); at Fashion Mall. 311 N University Dr 33324. Fax: 954/452-8887. **Facility:** 263 units. 262 one- and 1 two-bedroom suites, some with **Large-scale Hotel** whirlpools. 9 stories, interior corridors. *Bath:* combo or shower only. **Parking:** on-site and valet. **Terms:** small pets only ($25 extra charge). **Amenities:** video games (fee), dual phone lines, voice mail, honor bars, irons, hair dryers. *Some:* high-speed Internet (fee), fax. **Dining:** 6:30 am-2:30 & 5:30-10:30 pm, Sat & Sun from 7 am, cocktails. **Pool(s):** heated outdoor. **Leisure Activities:** sauna, whirlpool, exercise room. **Guest Services:** valet laundry, airport transportation-Fort Lauderdale-Hollywood International Airport. **Business Services:** meeting rooms, business center. **Cards:** AX, DC, DS, MC, VI. **Special Amenities:** free newspaper. *(See color ad p 8)*

SOME UNITS

STAYBRIDGE SUITES FT
LAUDERDALE-PLANTATION   *Book at aaa.com*   Phone: (954)577-9696   [84]

(AAA) [SAVE]

12/26-4/30	1P: $154-$219	2P: $154-$219
5/1-11/30	1P: $134-$189	2P: $134-$199
12/1-12/25	1P: $124-$189	2P: $124-$199

Location: I-595, exit 4, 1.7 mi n. 410 N Pine Island Rd 33324. Fax: 954/577-9648. **Facility:** 141 units. 61 one-**Small-scale Hotel** bedroom standard units with efficiencies. 49 one- and 31 two-bedroom suites with kitchens. 4 stories, interior corridors. *Bath:* combo or shower only. **Parking:** on-site. **Terms:** cancellation fee imposed, [ECP] meal plan available, package plans, small pets only ($30 fee, $100 deposit). **Amenities:** DVD players, high-speed Internet, dual phone lines, voice mail, irons, hair dryers. **Pool(s):** heated outdoor. **Leisure Activities:** gas barbecue grill, exercise room, sports court. **Guest Services:** sundries, complimentary evening beverages: Tues-Thurs, valet and coin laundry. **Business Services:** meeting rooms, business center. **Cards:** AX, DC, DS, MC, VI. **Special Amenities:** free expanded continental breakfast and free local telephone calls.

SOME UNITS

WELLESLEY INN (PLANTATION)   *Book at aaa.com*   Phone: (954)473-8257   [89]

(AAA) [SAVE]

12/26-4/15	1P: $109-$159	2P: $119-$169	XP: $10 F17
12/1-12/25 & 4/16-11/30	1P: $79-$109	2P: $89-$119	XP: $10 F17

Location: 0.3 mi w of SR 817 (University Dr); 0.5 mi sw of jct SR 842 (Broward Blvd). Located next to the Broward Mall. 7901 SW 6th St 33324. Fax: 954/473-9804. **Facility:** 105 units. 92 one-bedroom standard units. 13 one-**Small-scale Hotel** bedroom suites. 4 stories, interior corridors. *Bath:* combo or shower only. **Parking:** on-site. **Terms:** small pets only ($10 extra charge). **Amenities:** voice mail, irons, hair dryers. *Fee:* video games, high-speed Internet. *Some:* dual phone lines. **Pool(s):** heated outdoor. **Guest Services:** valet laundry. **Business Services:** fax (fee). **Cards:** AX, CB, DC, DS, JC, MC, VI.

SOME UNITS

━━━━━ **WHERE TO DINE** ━━━━━

AL-SALAN MIDDLE EAST RESTAURANT   **Lunch:** $3-$4   **Dinner:** $8-$15   **Phone:** 954/916-5193   [97]

South Mediterranean

Location: On University Dr (SR 817); corner of Sunrise Blvd (SR 838); in back section of Mercede Executive Plaza. 1816 N University Dr 33322. **Hours:** 8:30 am-10 pm, Fri-Sun to 11 pm. **Features:** Recipes at this family-owned Middle Eastern restaurant have been handed down from and cooked by generations. Try kebabs, baba ghanoush, Cornish hens or any of a variety of salads. Be sure to leave room for the pasty. A small store section carries some of the spices. Casual dress; beer only. **Parking:** on-site. **Cards:** AX, DC, MC, VI.

BIN 595   **Lunch:** $7-$17   **Dinner:** $15-$34   **Phone:** 954/308-4595   [107]

Regional American

Location: I-595, exit 4 (Pine Island Dr), n to N New River Canal Rd; in Renaissance Ft. Lauderdale/Plantation Hotel. 1230 S Pine Island Rd 33324. **Hours:** 6:30 am-11 pm. **Reservations:** suggested. **Features:** The comfortable, upbeat room has hanging Deco lighting and a hand-painted ceiling. Distinctive interpretations of American fusion cuisine blend flavors from the islands with tropical fruit sauces, herbs, fresh seafood and quality meats. Complementing the menu is a good selection of wines. Dressy casual; cocktails. **Parking:** on-site. **Cards:** AX, CB, DC, DS, JC, MC, VI.

BONEFISH GRILL   **Dinner:** $14-$25   **Phone:** 954/723-9660   [102]

Seafood

Location: Corner of Broward Blvd and University Dr; in The Fashion Mall. 321 N University Dr 33324. **Hours:** 4 pm-10:30 pm, Fri & Sat-11:30 pm, Sun-10 pm. **Closed:** 11/23, 12/25. **Reservations:** accepted. **Features:** Patrons can unwind in the soft, cozy setting and peruse a menu of fresh seafood dishes grilled over wood. Also in the mix are steaks and chops, as well as pasta dishes with seafood. Dressy casual; cocktails. **Parking:** on-site. **Cards:** AX, DC, MC, VI.

CASPIAN PERSIAN GRILL   **Lunch:** $8   **Dinner:** $11-$17   **Phone:** 954/236-9955   [99]

Persian

Location: Just w of University Blvd (SR 817). 7821 W Sunrise Blvd 33322. **Hours:** 11:30 am-2:30 & 5:30-9 pm, Fri-10 pm, Sat noon-10 pm, Sun noon-9 pm. **Closed:** 7/4, 11/23. **Reservations:** accepted. **Features:** Each food item reflects a tradition dating back thousands of years. Among choices are soups, kebabs and stews from the region of what was once Persia. The casual restaurant's friendly staff guides patrons. Casual dress. **Parking:** on-site. **Cards:** AX, DC, DS, MC, VI.

FUDDRUCKERS, WORLD'S GREATEST
HAMBURGERS   **Lunch:** $5-$13   **Dinner:** $5-$13   **Phone:** 954/476-8111   [100]

American

Location: Corner of Sunrise Blvd (SR 838) and University Blvd (SR 817). 1801 N University Blvd 33351. **Hours:** 11 am-9 pm, Fri & Sat-10 pm. **Closed:** 11/23, 12/25. **Features:** Size matters at this fun spot, as is evidenced in the difference between an average burger and a really big one. A video game area occupies both big and little kids. Diners can customize their burgers at a bar with fixings. Casual dress; cocktails. **Parking:** on-site. **Cards:** AX, DS, MC, VI.

(See map and index starting on p. 364)

GRAPEVINE GOURMET CUISINE Lunch: $7-$12 Phone: 954/475-1357 (104)

▼▼ ▼▼

Deli/Subs
Sandwiches

Location: I-595, exit 5, 1.4 mi n on University (SR 817), just s of Broward Blvd (SR 842); in the Plantation Community Plaza. 256 S University Dr 33324. **Hours:** 8:30 am-6 pm, Fri-5:30 pm, Sat 9:30 am-5:30 pm. Closed major holidays; also Sun, Rosh Hashanah, Yom Kippur. **Reservations:** accepted. **Features:** Whether seated inside the store-like area or outside, guests can savor gourmet sandwiches, salads, desserts and meal selections. Patrons select from a chalkboard or deli case, and staffers bring the choices to the table. Casual dress; wine only. **Parking:** on-site. **Cards:** AX, DC, MC, VI.

GRUMPY DICK'S SEAFOOD GRILL & BAR Lunch: $8-$12 Dinner: $8-$23 Phone: 954/452-1952 (106)

▼▼ ▼▼

Seafood

Location: I-595, exit 5, just n of I-595 on University Dr (SR 817); in The Fountains Promenade Plaza. 801 S University Dr 33324. **Hours:** 11:30 am-10 pm, Fri & Sat-11 pm. **Features:** Only the name is grumpy, as the staff is pleasant and the menu food-friendly. In addition to the ocean's freshest, diners can sample burgers, ribs and chicken. Casual dress; cocktails. **Parking:** on-site. **Cards:** AX, CB, DC, DS, JC, MC, VI. (access) (M) (Y)

JALAPENOS MEXICAN KITCHEN Lunch: $6-$8 Dinner: $9-$14 Phone: 954/473-5351 (98)

▼▼ ▼▼

Mexican

Location: From University Blvd (SR 817), just w; in Jacaranda Plaza. 8229 Sunrise Blvd 33322. **Hours:** 11:30 am-10 pm, Fri & Sat-11 pm. **Closed:** 11/23, 12/25. **Reservations:** accepted. **Features:** In addition to traditional entrees, the menu lists some choices from Central Mexico. The atmosphere is festive—from the colorful tables and chairs to the art on the wall. Beverages include a large assortment of tequilas. Casual dress; cocktails. **Parking:** on-site. **Cards:** AX, CB, DC, DS, JC, MC, VI. (access M) (Y)

THE ORIGINAL STEAKHOUSE & SPORTS THEATRE Lunch: $9-$23 Dinner: $9-$23 Phone: 954/382-1018 (101)

▼▼ ▼▼

Steak House

Location: Jct Nob Hill Rd and Cleary Blvd; southeast corner of Plantation Promenade Plaza. 10199 Cleary Blvd 33324. **Hours:** 4 pm-11 pm, Fri-midnight, Sat noon-midnight, Sun noon-10 pm. **Closed:** 11/23, 12/24, 12/25. **Features:** Guests find lots of food, lots of TVs and lots of sports. That is the theme here. On the menu is a nice selection of steaks, seafood, chicken and ribs. Fun is encouraged in the relaxed atmosphere. Casual dress; cocktails. **Parking:** on-site. **Cards:** MC, VI. (access M) (Y)

SMOKEY BONES Lunch: $7-$21 Dinner: $7-$21 Phone: 954/474-3833 (105)

▼▼ ▼▼

Barbecue

Location: I-595, exit 5, just n of I-595 on University Dr (SR 817); in The Fountains Complex. 809 S University Dr 33324. **Hours:** 11 am-10 pm, Fri & Sat-11 pm. **Closed:** 11/23, 12/25. **Features:** Families are welcomed in the sports-oriented environment. Speakers at each table allow guests to listen to the activity on the many TVs around the dining area. The menu lists ribs and a variety of barbecue meats. Casual dress; cocktails. **Parking:** on-site. **Cards:** AX, CB, DC, DS, JC, MC, VI. (access M) (Y)

TAKEYAMA Lunch: $8-$12 Dinner: $11-$30 Phone: 954/792-0350 (103)

▼▼ ▼▼

Japanese

Location: Just n of Broward Blvd (SR 842) at NW 69th Ave and Cypress Rd; in Cypress Square Center. 6920 Cypress Rd 33317. **Hours:** 11:30 am-2 & 5:30-9:30 pm, Fri & Sat-10 pm. Closed major holidays; also Mon. **Reservations:** suggested, weekends. **Features:** This sushi bar presents a variety of dishes that could be considered edible works of art. The Takeyama inside-out roll has a unique stone crab filling. Vegetarian sushi is offered with sukiyaki, teriyaki and tempura dishes. Try the unusual pizza sushi. Dressy casual; beer & wine only. **Parking:** on-site. **Cards:** AX, DC, MC, VI.

POMPANO BEACH pop. 78,191 (See map and index starting on p. 364)

———— WHERE TO STAY ————

THE BAREFOOT PLACE *Book at aaa.com* Phone: 954/941-8856

(AAA) (SAVE)

▼▼

Motel

	1P: $65-$95	2P: $65-$95	XP: $8	F10
2/1-3/31				
12/1-1/31	1P: $56-$85	2P: $56-$85	XP: $8	F10
4/1-4/30	1P: $49-$77	2P: $49-$77	XP: $8	F10
5/1-11/30	1P: $41-$66	2P: $41-$66	XP: $8	F10

Location: SR 814 (Atlantic Blvd), 1.1 mi n on SR A1A, then w. 3221 NE 8th Ct 33062. Fax: 954/943-0521. **Facility:** 9 units. 8 one-bedroom standard units, some with efficiencies. 1 one-bedroom suite with kitchen. 2 stories (no elevator), exterior corridors. **Bath:** combo or shower only. **Parking:** on-site. **Terms:** office hours 8:30 am-9 pm, 3 day cancellation notice-fee imposed. **Pool(s):** heated outdoor. **Cards:** AX, MC, VI. **Special Amenities:** free newspaper and free room upgrade (subject to availability with advance reservations). (S/D) (symbols)

BEACHCOMBER RESORT & VILLAS *Book at aaa.com* Phone: (954)941-7830

(AAA) (SAVE)

▼▼▼▼

Small-scale Hotel

2/1-5/1	1P: $169-$369	2P: $169-$369	XP: $10	F10
12/1-12/31	1P: $129-$329	2P: $129-$329	XP: $10	F10
1/1-1/31	1P: $116-$250	2P: $116-$250	XP: $10	F10

Location: Oceanfront. SR A1A, 0.5 mi s of jct SR 814 (Atlantic Blvd). 1200 S Ocean Blvd 33062. Fax: 954/942-7680. **Facility:** 143 units. 139 one-bedroom standard units, some with efficiencies (no utensils). 4 two-bedroom suites ($329-$450) with kitchens (no utensils). 1-8 stories, interior/exterior corridors. **Bath:** combo or shower only. **Parking:** on-site. **Terms:** open 12/1-5/1, 7 day cancellation notice-fee imposed. **Amenities:** video games (fee), high-speed Internet, voice mail, safes, irons, hair dryers. **Dining:** 7 am-3 & 5-9 pm, cocktails. **Pool(s):** outdoor, heated outdoor. **Leisure Activities:** putting green, shuffleboard, volleyball. **Guest Services:** gift shop, coin laundry. **Business Services:** meeting rooms, fax (fee). **Cards:** AX, CB, DC, DS, MC, VI. **Special Amenities:** free local telephone calls and free newspaper.

SOME UNITS
(symbols)

(See map and index starting on p. 364)

CROTON ARMS RESORT APARTMENTS
Phone: (954)941-1766

1/26-3/31	1P: $80-$125	2P: $80-$125	XP: $20 F5
12/19-1/25	1P: $70-$105	2P: $70-$105	XP: $10 F5
12/1-12/18 & 4/1-11/30	1P: $50-$75	2P: $50-$75	XP: $10 F5

Motel

Location: Just w of SR A1A; 1.3 mi n of jct SR 814 (Atlantic Blvd). Located in a quiet area. 3237 NE 11th St 33062. Fax: 954/941-1775. **Facility:** 20 units. 3 one-bedroom standard units with efficiencies. 17 one-bedroom suites with kitchens. 1-2 stories (no elevator), exterior corridors. **Bath:** combo or shower only. **Parking:** on-site. **Terms:** office hours 8 am-10:30 pm, 3 night minimum stay, 60 day cancellation notice-fee imposed. **Pool(s):** heated outdoor. **Leisure Activities:** whirlpool, shuffleboard. **Guest Services:** coin laundry.

DOLPHIN APARTMENT MOTEL
(AAA) [SAVE]
Phone: (954)941-7373

2/1-3/31	1P: $75-$107	2P: $75-$107	XP: $8 F10
12/1-1/31	1P: $65-$98	2P: $65-$98	XP: $8 F10
4/1-4/30	1P: $50-$80	2P: $50-$80	XP: $8 F10
5/1-11/30	1P: $45-$70	2P: $45-$70	XP: $8 F10

Motel

Location: 0.8 mi n on SR A1A from jct SR 814 (Atlantic Blvd), just w. 3215 NE 7th St 33062. Fax: 954/941-7388. **Facility:** 20 units. 17 one-bedroom standard units, some with efficiencies or kitchens. 3 one-bedroom suites with kitchens. 2 stories (no elevator), exterior corridors. **Parking:** on-site. **Terms:** office hours 9 am-10 pm. **Amenities:** voice mail. *Some:* CD players, irons, hair dryers. **Pool(s):** heated outdoor. **Leisure Activities:** barbecue grill, bicycles, shuffleboard. **Guest Services:** coin laundry. **Cards:** MC, VI.

EXTENDED STAY DELUXE   *Book at aaa.com*
Phone: 954/783-1050

Property failed to provide current rates

Small-scale Hotel

Location: I-95, exit 33B (Cypress Creek Rd) to Andrews Ave, just s, then left on McNab St. 1401 SW 15th St 33069. Fax: 954/783-1610. **Facility:** 129 units. 109 one-bedroom standard units with kitchens. 20 one-bedroom suites with kitchens. 3 stories, interior corridors. **Bath:** combo or shower only. **Parking:** on-site. **Terms:** small pets only ($10 fee). **Amenities:** dual phone lines, voice mail, irons, hair dryers. *Fee:* video games, high-speed Internet, safes. **Pool(s):** heated outdoor. **Leisure Activities:** limited exercise equipment. **Guest Services:** valet and coin laundry. **Business Services:** fax (fee).

SOME UNITS

FEE

FAIRFIELD ROYAL VISTA
Phone: 954/233-7500

Property failed to provide current rates

Condominium

Location: SR 814 (Atlantic Blvd), 0.6 mi s on SR A1A. 1110 S Ocean Blvd 33062. Fax: 954/233-7513. **Facility:** On the ocean, the property offers some rooms with water views; all rooms have balconies and feature colorful decor packages. 91 units. 31 one- and 60 two-bedroom suites with kitchens. 6-9 stories, interior corridors. **Parking:** on-site. **Terms:** check-in 4 pm. **Amenities:** video library (fee), CD players, voice mail, safes, honor bars, irons, hair dryers. **Pool(s):** 2 heated outdoor, wading. **Leisure Activities:** fishing, playground, exercise room, horseshoes, volleyball. *Fee:* sailboats, game room. **Guest Services:** complimentary laundry. **Business Services:** fax (fee).

THE FAIRWAYS OF PALM-AIRE RESORT
(AAA) [SAVE]
Phone: (954)972-3300

All Year	1P: $89-$349	2P: $99-$359

Resort Condominium

Location: I-95, exit 36, 1 mi w on SR 814 (Atlantic Blvd), then 0.4 mi s on Powerline Rd. 2601 Palm Aire Dr N 33069. Fax: 954/968-2711. **Facility:** The resort offers supervised spa facilities, transportation while on the grounds, and large, nicely decorated rooms, some overlooking a golf course. 398 units. 15 one-bedroom standard units with efficiencies. 70 one-, 308 two-, and 5 three-bedroom suites, some with whirlpools. 2-10 stories, interior corridors. **Bath:** combo or shower only. **Parking:** on-site. **Terms:** check-in 4 pm, 2-7 night minimum stay - seasonal and/or weekends, 30 day cancellation notice. **Amenities:** video library (fee), CD players, voice mail, irons, hair dryers. *Some:* DVD players, safes. **Pool(s):** 4 heated outdoor, wading. **Leisure Activities:** sauna, whirlpools, waterslide, miniature golf, recreation programs, playground, spa, volleyball. *Fee:* golf-90 holes, 2 lighted tennis courts, game room. **Guest Services:** complimentary laundry. **Business Services:** meeting rooms, fax (fee). **Cards:** AX, DS, MC, VI.

SOME UNITS

MOTEL 6 - POMPANO BEACH #371   *Book at aaa.com*
Phone: 954/977-8011

1/14-3/26	1P: $49-$59	2P: $55-$65	XP: $3 F17
12/1-1/13 & 3/27-11/30	1P: $44-$54	2P: $50-$60	XP: $3 F17

Motel

Location: Florida Tpke, exit 67 (Coconut Creek Pkwy/Martin Luther King Blvd), just s. 1201 NW 31st Ave 33069. Fax: 954/972-0814. **Facility:** 127 one-bedroom standard units. 2 stories (no elevator). **Bath:** shower only. **Parking:** on-site. **Terms:** small pets only. **Pool(s):** heated outdoor. **Guest Services:** coin laundry. **Business Services:** fax (fee). **Cards:** AX, CB, DC, DS, MC, VI.

SOME UNITS

FEE FEE

RONNY DEE MOTEL
(AAA) [SAVE]
Phone: 954/943-3020

2/1-11/30	2P: $82-$106	XP: $7
12/20-1/31	2P: $69-$90	XP: $7
12/1-12/19	2P: $55-$72	XP: $5

Motel

Location: SR A1A, just s of jct SR 814 (Atlantic Blvd). Located across from beach. 717 S Ocean Blvd 33062. Fax: 954/783-5112. **Facility:** Designated smoking area. 32 units. 31 one-bedroom standard units, some with efficiencies or kitchens. 1 two-bedroom suite with kitchen. 1-2 stories (no elevator), exterior corridors. **Bath:** combo or shower only. **Parking:** on-site. **Terms:** office hours 8 am-8 pm, 21 day cancellation notice, weekly rates available. **Amenities:** voice mail. **Pool(s):** heated outdoor. **Leisure Activities:** barbecue grills, shuffleboard. **Guest Services:** coin laundry. **Cards:** DS, MC, VI.

SOME UNITS

(See map and index starting on p. 364)

SPA ATLANTIS *Book at aaa.com*   **Phone:** (954)590-1000

▼▼▼ ▼▼▼
12/1-4/30	1P: $169-$450	2P: $169-$450
10/1-11/30	1P: $129-$400	2P: $129-$400
5/1-9/30	1P: $109-$350	2P: $109-$350

Large-scale Hotel **Location:** Oceanfront. On SR A1A, 1.4 mi n of SR 814 (Atlantic Blvd). 1350 N Ocean Blvd 33062. Fax: 954/590-1001. **Facility:** Smoke free premises. 89 units. 79 one-bedroom standard units. 10 one-bedroom suites. 10 stories, interior corridors. **Bath:** combo or shower only. **Parking:** on-site and valet. **Terms:** weekly rates available, [AP] meal plan available, package plans, 18% service charge. **Amenities:** video library, voice mail, safes, irons, hair dryers. **Pool(s):** 2 heated outdoor. **Leisure Activities:** whirlpool, spa. **Guest Services:** gift shop, valet and coin laundry, area transportation. **Business Services:** meeting rooms, fax (fee). **Cards:** AX, DS, MC, VI.

ASK ✈ ⑪ &M 🖥 🅿 ⇨ ⇪ ✕ VCR 🐾 DATA PORT 🛏 🖥

SUPER 8 MOTEL *Book at aaa.com*   **Phone:** 954/943-3500

AAA SAVE
2/1-4/30 [CP]	1P: $69-$169	2P: $69-$169	XP: $5	F16
12/1-1/31 [CP]	1P: $49-$119	2P: $49-$119	XP: $5	F16
5/1-11/30 [CP]	1P: $49-$99	2P: $49-$99	XP: $5	F16

▼▼ ▼▼
Small-scale Hotel **Location:** Just e of US 1 and NE 10th St; 0.8 mi n from SR 814 (Atlantic Blvd). 2300 NE 10th St 33062. Fax: 954/943-3500. **Facility:** 60 one-bedroom standard units. 2 stories, interior corridors. **Parking:** on-site. **Terms:** 3 day cancellation notice-fee imposed. **Pool(s):** small outdoor. **Business Services:** fax (fee). **Cards:** AX, CB, DC, DS, MC, VI. **Special Amenities:** free continental breakfast and free newspaper.

SOME UNITS
S🅳 ⑪➕ ⇨ 🐾 DATA PORT 🛏 / ✕ 🖥 /

SURF SIDE MOTEL *Book at aaa.com*   **Phone:** (954)942-5507

AAA SAVE
12/1-3/31	1P: $110-$150	2P: $125-$150	XP: $10	F12
4/1-5/1	1P: $79-$99	2P: $89-$109	XP: $10	F12
5/2-11/30	1P: $59-$79	2P: $69-$89	XP: $10	F12

▼▼▼ ▼
Motel **Location:** I-95, exit 36A, SR 814 (Atlantic Blvd E) to SR A1A, then just s. 710 S Ocean Blvd 33062. Fax: 954/785-9713. **Facility:** 35 units. 31 one-bedroom standard units, some with kitchens. 4 one-bedroom suites with kitchens. 2 stories, exterior corridors. *Bath:* combo or shower only. **Parking:** on-site. **Terms:** office hours 8 am-10 pm, 21 day cancellation notice. **Amenities:** voice mail. **Pool(s):** heated outdoor. **Leisure Activities:** beach access, barbecue grills, shuffleboard. **Guest Services:** coin laundry. **Business Services:** fax (fee). **Cards:** AX, DC, DS, MC, VI.

SOME UNITS
⇨ 🐾 DATA PORT 🛏 🖥 / ✕ 🖥 /

─────── **WHERE TO DINE** ───────

CALYPSO RAW BAR & RESTAURANT   **Lunch:** $8-$15   **Dinner:** $8-$23   **Phone:** 954/942-1633
▼▼▼ ▼▼▼
Caribbean **Location:** I-95, exit 34, 0.9 mi e on SR 814 (Atlantic Blvd), then 0.5 mi s; in Garden Isles Shopping Center. 460 S Cypress Rd 33060. **Hours:** Open 12/1-9/1 & 10/1-11/30; 11 am-10 pm, Fri & Sat-10:30 pm, Sun noon-9:30 pm. Closed: 11/23, 12/25; also Mon. **Features:** A taste of the islands comes to the mainland. The menu lists fresh seafood and other Caribbean favorites. Start with scorched conch and maybe end up with a cutter (island word for sandwich). Hungrier patrons might go for a jerk item or curry dish. Steaks and chops can be spiced to the diner's liking. Casual dress; beer & wine only. **Parking:** on-site. **Cards:** AX, DC, DS, MC, VI.

&M

CHEZ PORKY'S   **Lunch:** $5-$16   **Dinner:** $7-$19   **Phone:** 954/946-5590
▼▼ ▼
American **Location:** I-95, exit 36A, 0.9 mi e on Atlantic Blvd (SR 814), 0.6 mi s on Old Dixie Hwy, then 0.3 mi e; in Robert Thomas Plaza. 105 SW Sixth St 33060. **Hours:** 11:30 am-9:30 pm, Sat 4:30 pm-10:30 pm, Sun 4:30 pm-9 pm. Closed major holidays. **Features:** Hard to find friendlier folks than at this Louisiana kitchen and barbecue. Baby back ribs, chicken and Cajun seafood dishes are served with your choice of two delicious side dishes. This restaurant is worth any wait, so sit back and relax for a spell. Casual dress; beer & wine only. **Parking:** on-site. **Cards:** AX, MC, VI.

DARREL & OLIVER'S CAFE MAXX   **Dinner:** $16-$38   **Phone:** 954/782-0606
AAA
▼▼▼ ▼▼▼
Regional American **Location:** SR 814 (Atlantic Blvd), 0.3 mi e of jct US 1. 2601 E Atlantic Blvd at NE 26th St 33062. **Hours:** 5:30 pm-11 pm, Sun-10 pm. Closed: 7/4; also Super Bowl Sun. **Reservations:** suggested. **Features:** A cafe ambience contributes to the casually elegant experience diners have come to expect here. Innovatively prepared and presented dishes, which incorporate the freshest of ingredients, are well-complemented by an award-winning wine list. Dressy casual; beer & wine only. **Parking:** valet. **Cards:** AX, DC, DS, MC, VI.

FRANK'S RISTORANTE   **Dinner:** $10-$24   **Phone:** 954/785-4140
▼▼ ▼
Italian **Location:** Just e of SR A1A. 3428 E Atlantic Blvd 33062. **Hours:** 5 pm-11 pm. **Reservations:** accepted. **Features:** This place has the neighborhood pizzeria written all over it. Walk in and just get a slice or order by the pie. Traditional pasta dishes, chicken and veal specials are also available, and there is always a fresh seafood special. Casual dress; cocktails. **Parking:** street. **Cards:** AX, MC, VI.

FRANK'S RISTORANTE & PIZZA   **Lunch:** $5-$25   **Dinner:** $5-$25   **Phone:** 954/785-1480
▼
Italian **Location:** Just e of SR A1A. 3428 E Atlantic Blvd 33062. **Hours:** 11 am-11 pm. **Features:** This place has "neighborhood pizzeria" written all over it. Guests walk in and grab just a slice or a whole pie. Seats are available on the sidewalk or inside. Also on the menu are traditional pasta dishes, chicken and veal entrees and always a fresh seafood special. Casual dress; cocktails. **Parking:** street. **Cards:** AX, MC, VI.

MADRAS CAFE   **Lunch:** $8   **Dinner:** $10-$20   **Phone:** 954/977-5434   (68)
▼▼ ▼
Indian **Location:** SR 814 (Atlantic Blvd), 1.4 mi s; in 1400 Gateway Plaza. 1434 S Powerline Rd 33069. **Hours:** 11:30 am-2:30 & 5-10 pm, Fri & Sat 11:30 am-3 & 5-10:30 pm, Sun 11:30 am-3 & 6-10 pm. **Reservations:** suggested. **Features:** Those who haven't traveled to India might make this a first stop. The expansive menu lists all of the favorites, ranging from rice specialties and tandoori chicken to lamb dishes and seven types of naan. Guests can dial in their preferred heat level for the varied curry dishes. Dressy casual; cocktails. **Parking:** on-site. **Cards:** AX, CB, DC, DS, MC, VI.

🍸

(See map and index starting on p. 364)

PEKING DUCK HOUSE CHINESE RESTAURANT   **Lunch:** $4-$7   **Dinner:** $7-$19   **Phone:** 954/946-0436
Chinese
Location: I-95, exit 36A, 2.1 mi e on SR 814 (Atlantic Blvd); at corner of NE 13th Ave and Atlantic Blvd 33060. **Hours:** noon-10 pm, Fri & Sat-11 pm. **Features:** Peking duck is a specialty at the aptly named restaurant, which features a wide range of traditional Cantonese favorites. Casual dress; beer & wine only. **Parking:** on-site. **Cards:** AX, MC, VI.

RONNIE B'S   **Lunch:** $5-$13   **Dinner:** $5-$18   **Phone:** 954/781-9494
American
Location: I-95, exit 38A, 2 mi e on Copans Rd, then just s at US 1 and NE 16th St. 1600 N Federal Hwy 33062. **Hours:** 7 am-10 pm, Fri & Sat-11 pm; from 8 am, Sat 7 am-11 pm, Sun 7 am-10 pm 5/1-10/31. **Features:** You won't find the Fonz here, but the 50s diner does have malts and milkshakes along with big burgers, sandwiches and banana splits. Casual dress; beer only. **Parking:** on-site. **Cards:** AX, DC, MC, VI.

SUNFISH GRILL   **Dinner:** $22-$36   **Phone:** 954/788-2434
American
Location: Just e of US 1, just over the Intracoastal Bridge on the north side; in small shopping complex. 2771 E Atlantic Blvd 33062. **Hours:** 5:30 pm-9:30 pm, Fri & Sat-10 pm. Closed major holidays; also Sun & Mon 5/1-12/31. **Reservations:** required. **Features:** Chef Anthony Sindaco calls his artistic creations "contemporary American seafood," but he also prepares some meat dishes. Aromas from the open kitchen are enticing, and desserts are worth the splurge. The lengthy wine list includes hard-to-find selections as well as the traditionals. The decor is eclectic. Dressy casual; beer & wine only. **Parking:** on-site. **Cards:** AX, MC, VI.

VESUVIO'S RESTAURANT   **Dinner:** $12-$28   **Phone:** 954/941-1594
Italian
Location: 0.3 mi e of jct US 1. 2715 E Atlantic Blvd 33062. **Hours:** Open 12/1-6/30 & 8/1-11/30; 5:30 pm-11 pm. Closed: Mon. **Reservations:** suggested. **Features:** You'll have to wait for the made-to-order entrees, but every second will be worth it. The many offerings of veal, chicken, beef, vegetables and seafood are just delicious. Cozy and crowded at the same time, the restaurant boasts a friendly wait staff. Cocktails. **Parking:** on-site. **Cards:** AX, CB, DC, DS, MC, VI.

SUNRISE pop. 85,779   (See map and index starting on p. 364)

———— WHERE TO STAY ————

BAYMONT INN & SUITES SUNRISE AT SAWGRASS   *Book at aaa.com*   **Phone:** (954)846-1200   **79**

Small-scale Hotel

12/1-4/30	1P: $109-$129		XP: $7	F18
5/1-11/30	1P: $95-$105		XP: $7	F18

Location: SW 136th Ave, 0.3 mi n of jct I-595, exit 1A and SR 84; 0.5 mi e of jct I-75 and Sawgrass Expwy. 13651 NW 2nd St 33325. Fax: 954/845-0100. **Facility:** 101 units. 98 one-bedroom standard units. 3 one-bedroom suites. 4 stories, interior corridors. **Bath:** combo or shower only. **Parking:** on-site. **Terms:** [ECP] meal plan available, small pets only. **Amenities:** video games (fee), voice mail, irons, hair dryers. **Pool(s):** heated outdoor. **Leisure Activities:** exercise room. **Guest Services:** valet and coin laundry. **Business Services:** meeting rooms, fax (fee). **Cards:** AX, CB, DC, DS, MC, VI. **Special Amenities:** free expanded continental breakfast and free local telephone calls. *(See color ad p 560)*

SOME UNITS

CROWNE PLAZA FORT LAUDERDALE HOTEL AT SAWGRASS MILLS   *Book at aaa.com*   **Phone:** (954)851-1020   **78**
Large-scale Hotel

1/1-4/15	1P: $184-$299	2P: $199-$314	XP: $15	F18
4/16-11/30	1P: $159-$214	2P: $174-$229	XP: $15	F18
12/1-12/31	1P: $154-$199	2P: $169-$214	XP: $15	F18

Location: I-75 to Sawgrass Expwy N (SR 869), exit Sunrise Blvd E, then 1 mi. Located across from Sawgrass Mills Mall. 13400 W Sunrise Blvd 33323. Fax: 954/851-0500. **Facility:** 250 units. 236 one-bedroom standard units. 14 one-bedroom suites, some with whirlpools. 10 stories, interior corridors. **Bath:** combo or shower only. **Parking:** on-site. **Terms:** cancellation fee imposed, package plans. **Amenities:** CD players, dual phone lines, voice mail, safes, irons, hair dryers. **Fee:** video games, high-speed Internet. **Some:** DVD players. **Pool(s):** heated outdoor. **Leisure Activities:** whirlpool, exercise room. **Guest Services:** gift shop, valet and coin laundry, area transportation. **Business Services:** meeting rooms, business center. **Cards:** AX, CB, DC, DS, MC, VI.

SOME UNITS

HILTON FORT LAUDERDALE SUNRISE   *Book at aaa.com*   **Phone:** (954)748-7000   **77**
Small-scale Hotel

1/1-5/31	1P: $139-$169	XP: $25	F12
12/1-12/31	1P: $99-$139	XP: $25	F12
6/1-11/30	1P: $99-$139		

Location: University Dr (SR 817), just s of jct Oakland Park Blvd. 3003 N University Dr 33322. Fax: 954/572-0799. **Facility:** 297 units. 200 one-bedroom standard units. 97 one-bedroom suites. 6 stories, interior corridors. **Bath:** combo or shower only. **Parking:** on-site and valet. **Terms:** cancellation fee imposed, package plans. **Amenities:** high-speed Internet (fee), dual phone lines, voice mail, honor bars, irons, hair dryers. **Dining:** 7 am-10 pm, cocktails. **Pool(s):** heated outdoor. **Leisure Activities:** whirlpool, exercise room, spa. **Guest Services:** gift shop, valet laundry, area transportation-local shopping malls. **Business Services:** meeting rooms, business center. **Cards:** AX, CB, DC, DS, MC, VI. **Special Amenities:** free newspaper and early check-in/late check-out.

SOME UNITS

WELLESLEY INN & SUITES (SUNRISE)   *Book at aaa.com*   **Phone:** (954)845-9929   **80**
Small-scale Hotel

12/26-4/15 [CP]	1P: $109-$159	2P: $109-$159	XP: $10	F
12/1-12/25 & 4/16-11/30 [CP]	1P: $79-$119	2P: $79-$119	XP: $10	F

Location: SW 136th Ave, 0.3 mi n of jct I-595, exit 1A and SR 84; 0.5 mi e of jct I-75 and Sawgrass Expwy. 13600 NW 2nd St 33325. Fax: 954/845-9996. **Facility:** 103 one-bedroom standard units. 4 stories, interior corridors. **Bath:** combo or shower only. **Parking:** on-site. **Terms:** small pets only ($10 extra charge). **Amenities:** voice mail, irons, hair dryers. **Fee:** video games, high-speed Internet. **Pool(s):** heated outdoor. **Guest Services:** valet and coin laundry. **Business Services:** meeting rooms, fax (fee). **Cards:** AX, DC, DS, MC, VI.

SOME UNITS

(See map and index starting on p. 364)

———— WHERE TO DINE ————

CHAR-HUT OF SUNRISE
American

Lunch: $3-$10   **Dinner:** $3-$10   **Phone:** 954/749-0671   92
Location: From Oakland Park Blvd, 0.7 mi s at jct NW 25th Court and University Dr. 2601 N University Dr 33322. **Hours:** 11 am-9:30 pm, Fri & Sat-10 pm, Sun-9 pm. Closed: 11/23, 12/25. **Features:** The locally owned spot has great burgers and a quarter-pound hot dog, as well as chicken and fish dishes. It's casual and good. Casual dress. **Parking:** on-site. **Cards:** AX, DS, MC, VI.

EMERALD COAST
Chinese

Lunch: $8   **Dinner:** $19   **Phone:** 954/572-3822   89
Location: Sawgrass Expwy (SR 869), 1.8 mi e on Commercial Blvd (SR 870), then 0.9 mi s; in Gold's Plaza. 4519 N Pine Island Rd 33351. **Hours:** 11:30 am-2:30 & 4-9 pm, Fri-10 pm, Sat 4 pm-10 pm, Sun noon-2:30 & 4-9:30 pm. **Reservations:** accepted. **Features:** The Chinese buffet lays out more than 100 tasty food items on several different island stations. Most favorites are represented, as are such choices as crab legs, carved prime rib and sushi rolls. Save room for dessert, as you'll have plenty of selections from which to choose. Casual dress; cocktails. **Parking:** on-site. **Cards:** AX, DC, MC, VI.

LA STELLA SOUTH
Italian

Dinner: $13-$26   **Phone:** 954/748-4788   91
Location: At Springtree and University Dr; in Country Club Plaza. 3801 N University Dr 33351. **Hours:** 5 pm-10 pm. Closed: 11/23, 12/25; also Mon & Tues in summer. **Reservations:** suggested. **Features:** This old-fashioned restaurant presents dishes of veal, chicken, seafood and fish, including the distinctive fish marechiara. Photographs of such celebrities as Jackie Gleason and Natalie Cole decorate the walls of the pleasant, dimly lit dining room. Beer & wine only. **Parking:** on-site. **Cards:** AX, DC, DS, MC, VI.

LEGAL SEA FOODS
Seafood

Lunch: $5-$13   **Dinner:** $14-$30   **Phone:** 954/846-9011   93
Location: Sawgrass Expwy (SR 869), exit 1 (Sunrise Blvd and SR 838), 1 mi e to Sawgrass Mills Mall. 2602 Sawgrass Mills Cir 33323. **Hours:** 11:30 am-10 pm, Fri & Sat-11 pm, Sun noon-9 pm. Closed: 11/23, 12/25. **Reservations:** accepted. **Features:** Step into the unusual and sophisticated dining room at The Oasis at Sawgrass for a taste of fresh seafood with an emphasis on New England. The wine list includes a good selection of complementary vintages. Dressy casual; cocktails. **Parking:** on-site. **Cards:** AX, DC, DS, MC, VI.

MARIO THE BAKER ITALIAN RESTAURANT & PIZZA
Italian

Lunch: $5-$8   **Dinner:** $6-$13   **Phone:** 954/742-3333   94
Location: Just n of Sunrise Blvd (SR 838). 2220 N University Dr 33322. **Hours:** 11 am-10 pm, Fri & Sat-11 pm, Sun noon-10 pm. Closed major holidays. **Features:** Families frequent the restaurant for its varied pizzas, as well as pasta, veal, chicken, subs and a few seafood choices. Casual dress; beer & wine only. **Parking:** on-site. **Cards:** AX, MC, VI.

RIO VISTA ISLE CAFE
American

Dinner: $11-$25   **Phone:** 954/749-8118   90
Location: Just w of University Blvd; in Lincoln Park West Shopping Plaza. 7836 NW 44th St 33351. **Hours:** 5 pm-10 pm, Sat & Sun from 4:30 pm. Closed: Mon, also Tues in summer. **Reservations:** suggested. **Features:** Tucked away in a small shopping plaza, the upscale, intimate restaurant offers a seasonally changing menu and don't-miss specials. Another must: one of the excellent desserts. Beer & wine only. **Parking:** on-site. **Cards:** DS, MC, VI.

———— *The following restaurant has not been evaluated by AAA but is listed for your information only.* ————

RAINFOREST CAFE
fyi

Phone: 954/851-1015
Not evaluated. **Location:** Sawgrass Expwy (SR 869), exit 1 to Sawgrass Mills Mall. 12801 Sunrise Blvd 33323. **Features:** The dining room has robotic animals from the rain forest as well as a simulated tropical storm and many large aquariums. The menu lists kid-friendly choices as well as those catering to adults.

TAMARAC pop. 55,588   (See map and index starting on p. 364)

———— WHERE TO STAY ————

BAYMONT INN & SUITES FT. LAUDERDALE   *Book at aaa.com*   **Phone:** (954)485-7900   74
Small-scale Hotel

12/1-4/30	1P: $89-$109	XP: $7	F18
5/1-11/30	1P: $69-$89	XP: $7	F18

Location: On SR 870 (Commercial Blvd), 0.8 mi e of Florida Tpke, exit 62; just e of jct SR 7 and US 441. 3800 W Commercial Blvd 33309. Fax: 954/733-5469. **Facility:** 98 units. 96 one-bedroom standard units. 2 one-bedroom suites. 3 stories, interior corridors. *Bath:* combo or shower only. **Parking:** on-site. **Terms:** [ECP] meal plan available, small pets only ($25 deposit). **Amenities:** video games (fee), voice mail, irons, hair dryers. **Pool(s):** small outdoor. **Guest Services:** coin laundry. **Business Services:** meeting rooms, fax (fee). **Cards:** AX, CB, DC, DS, MC, VI. **Special Amenities:** free expanded continental breakfast and free local telephone calls.

SOME UNITS

COMFORT SUITES SAWGRASS   *Book at aaa.com*   **Phone:** (954)343-1322   69
Small-scale Hotel

1/16-4/15 [ECP]	1P: $109-$299	2P: $109-$299	XP: $10	F17
12/1-1/15 [ECP]	1P: $89-$199	2P: $89-$199	XP: $10	F17
4/16-11/30 [ECP]	1P: $79-$169	2P: $79-$169	XP: $10	F17

Location: Sawgrass Expwy, exit 3, 2.1 mi e. 8301 W Commercial Blvd 33351. Fax: 954/343-1360. **Facility:** 80 units. 76 one-bedroom standard units. 4 one-bedroom suites with whirlpools. 4 stories, interior corridors. *Bath:* combo or shower only. **Parking:** on-site. **Terms:** cancellation fee imposed. **Amenities:** high-speed Internet, dual phone lines, voice mail, safes (fee), irons, hair dryers. **Pool(s):** small heated outdoor. **Leisure Activities:** whirlpool, limited exercise equipment. **Guest Services:** valet and coin laundry. **Business Services:** meeting rooms, business center. **Cards:** AX, CB, DC, DS, JC, MC, VI.

SOME UNITS

(See map and index starting on p. 364)

HAMPTON INN, COMMERCIAL BLVD *Book at aaa.com* Phone: (954)735-7575 **70**

2/1-3/31	1P: $129-$179	2P: $129-$179
12/1-1/31	1P: $99-$139	2P: $99-$139
4/1-4/30	1P: $89-$129	2P: $89-$129
5/1-11/30	1P: $79-$109	2P: $79-$109

Small-scale Hotel Location: On SR 870 (Commercial Blvd); Florida Tpke, exit 62, just e to NW 47th Terrace; just w of jct US 441 and SR 7. 4499 W Commercial Blvd 33319. Fax: 954/735-7330. **Facility:** 81 one-bedroom standard units. 3 stories, interior corridors. *Bath:* combo or shower only. **Parking:** on-site. **Terms:** check-in 4 pm, 5 day cancellation notice, [ECP] meal plan available. **Amenities:** high-speed Internet, dual phone lines, voice mail, irons, hair dryers. **Pool(s):** small heated outdoor. **Leisure Activities:** whirlpool, limited exercise equipment. **Business Services:** meeting rooms, fax (fee). **Cards:** AX, CB, DC, DS, MC, VI. **Special Amenities:** free expanded continental breakfast and free local telephone calls.

SOME UNITS

HOMESTEAD STUDIO SUITES HOTEL-FT
LAUDERDALE/TAMARAC *Book at aaa.com* Phone: (954)733-6644 **73**

1/2-4/15	1P: $59-$79	2P: $64-$84	XP: $5 F17
12/1-1/1 & 4/16-11/30	1P: $39-$59	2P: $44-$64	XP: $5 F17

Motel **Location:** SR 870 (Commercial Blvd), 0.7 mi e of Florida Tpke, exit 62; just e of jct US 441 and SR 7. 3873 W Commercial Blvd 33309. Fax: 954/733-9301. **Facility:** 146 one-bedroom standard units with kitchens. 2 stories (no elevator), exterior corridors. *Bath:* combo or shower only. **Parking:** on-site. **Terms:** office hours 6:30 am-10 pm, pets ($75 fee). **Amenities:** voice mail, irons. **Guest Services:** coin laundry. **Cards:** AX, DC, DS, MC, VI.

SOME UNITS

RAMADA PLAZA HOTEL *Book at aaa.com* Phone: 954/739-4000 **71**

Property failed to provide current rates
Location: 0.5 mi e of Florida Tpke, exit 62, just n on SR 7 and US 441. 5100 N SR 7 33319. Fax: 954/733-5037. **Small-scale Hotel** **Facility:** 269 units. 264 one-bedroom standard units. 5 one-bedroom suites. 5 stories, interior corridors. *Bath:* combo or shower only. **Parking:** on-site. **Amenities:** video games (fee), voice mail, safes, irons, hair dryers. **Pool(s):** heated outdoor. **Leisure Activities:** whirlpool, 2 tennis courts, exercise room. **Guest Services:** gift shop, beauty salon. **Business Services:** meeting rooms, business center.

SOME UNITS

WELLESLEY INN (FT. LAUDERDALE/TAMARAC) Phone: (954)484-6909 **72**

All Year	1P: $59-$69	2P: $62-$79	XP: $10 F

Location: SR 7 and US 441, just n of jct SR 870 (Commercial Blvd); 0.5 mi e of Florida Tpke, exit 62, then n. 5070 N SR 7 33319. Fax: 954/731-2374. **Facility:** 100 units. 94 one-bedroom standard units. 6 one-bedroom suites ($99-$120). 4 stories, interior corridors. *Bath:* combo or shower only. **Parking:** on-site. **Terms:** 1-15 night **Small-scale Hotel** minimum stay - seasonal and/or weekends, weekly rates available, $2 service charge. **Amenities:** voice mail, irons, hair dryers. *Some:* safes. **Pool(s):** heated outdoor. **Guest Services:** coin laundry. **Business Services:** fax (fee). **Cards:** AX, DS, MC, VI. **Special Amenities:** free continental breakfast and free local telephone calls.

SOME UNITS

WHERE TO DINE

CHAR-HUT OF NOB HILL Lunch: $3-$10 Dinner: $3-$10 Phone: 954/720-5566 **75**

American **Location:** From University Dr, 1.4 mi w on W McNab Rd at corner of Nob Hill Rd. 10000 W McNab Rd 33321. **Hours:** 11 am-9:30 pm, Fri & Sat-10 pm, Sun-9 pm. Closed: 11/23, 12/25. **Features:** The locally owned spot has great burgers and a quarter-pound hot dog, as well as chicken and fish dishes. It's casual and good. Casual dress. **Parking:** on-site. **Cards:** AX, DS, MC, VI.

G G'S OF NEW YORK ITALIAN RESTAURANT Lunch: $6-$8 Dinner: $9-$22 Phone: 954/484-0400 **76**

Italian **Location:** 0.5 mi n of SR 870 (Commercial Blvd); in San Casa Plaza. 5440 N State Rd 7 33319. **Hours:** 11 am-10 pm. Closed: 4/16, 11/23, 12/25. **Reservations:** accepted. **Features:** Families that visit the neighborhood-style restaurant enjoy pasta dishes, hand-tossed pizza and other traditional and house favorites. Casual dress; beer & wine only. **Parking:** on-site. **Cards:** AX, DS, MC, VI.

HONG KONG CITY BBQ Lunch: $6-$8 Dinner: $7-$25 Phone: 954/777-3832 **77**

Cantonese **Location:** Florida Tpke, exit 62, e on SR 870 (Commercial Blvd), then just n; in Commercial Plaza. 5301 N SR 7 (SR 441) 33319. **Hours:** 11 am-11 pm, Sun from 10:30 am. **Features:** The restaurant brings New York Chinatown cuisine to Florida. On the menu are many favorites, including dim sum, from all over China. The atmosphere is casual, but the flavors are serious. Casual dress; beer & wine only. **Parking:** on-site. **Cards:** AX, CB, DC, DS, JC, MC, VI.

The following restaurant has not been evaluated by AAA but is listed for your information only.

FLANIGAN'S SEAFOOD BAR & GRILL Phone: 954/733-0514

fyi Not evaluated. **Location:** 5450 N SR 7 33319. **Features:** The family-friendly restaurant is known for its baby back ribs, burgers and seafood.

WESTON pop. 49,286 (See map and index starting on p. 364)

——— WHERE TO STAY ———

AMERISUITES (FT. LAUDERDALE/WESTON) **Book at aaa.com** Phone: (954)659-1555 **112**

(AAA) (SAVE)	1/1-3/31 [ECP]	1P: $135-$199	2P: $135-$199	XP: $10 F18
▽▽▽▽	4/1-9/30 [ECP]	1P: $109-$169	2P: $109-$169	XP: $10 F18
	10/1-11/30 [ECP]	1P: $129-$159	2P: $129-$159	XP: $10 F18
	12/1-12/31 [ECP]	1P: $119-$135	2P: $119-$135	XP: $10 F18

Small-scale Hotel **Location:** I-75, exit 15, 0.5 mi w on Arvida Pkwy to Weston Rd, n to N Commerce Pkwy, then just e. 2201 N Commerce Pkwy 33326. Fax: 954/659-1191. **Facility:** 128 one-bedroom standard units. 6 stories, interior corridors. *Bath:* combo or shower only. **Parking:** on-site. **Terms:** cancellation fee imposed, weekly rates available, small pets only ($10 fee). **Amenities:** dual phone lines, voice mail, irons, hair dryers. *Fee:* video games, high-speed Internet. **Pool(s):** small heated outdoor. **Leisure Activities:** limited exercise equipment. **Guest Services:** valet and coin laundry. **Business Services:** meeting rooms, fax (fee). **Cards:** AX, CB, DC, DS, JC, MC, VI. **Special Amenities:** free full breakfast.

SOME UNITS
🐾 🍴 ⓂＭ ᓚᘏ 📷 🐟 🐕 DATA PORT 🖥 🖨 ▣ / ✕ VCR /
FEE

COURTYARD BY MARRIOTT WESTON **Book at aaa.com** Phone: (954)343-2225 **113**

(AAA) (SAVE) All Year 1P: $89-$239 2P: $89-$239
▽▽▽▽ **Location:** I-75, exit 15 to Weston Rd, n to Commerce Pkwy, then just e. 2000 N Commerce Pkwy 33326. Fax: 954/343-2277. **Facility:** 174 units. 171 one-bedroom standard units. 3 one-bedroom suites. 6 stories, interior corridors. *Bath:* combo or shower only. **Parking:** on-site. **Terms:** cancellation fee imposed, package Small-scale Hotel plans. **Amenities:** video games (fee), high-speed Internet, dual phone lines, voice mail, irons, hair dryers. **Dining:** 6:30-10:30 am, Sat & Sun 7-11:30 am, cocktails. **Pool(s):** heated outdoor. **Leisure Activities:** whirlpool, exercise room. **Guest Services:** sundries, valet and coin laundry. **Business Services:** meeting rooms, business center. **Cards:** AX, CB, DC, DS, JC, MC, VI. **Special Amenities:** free newspaper.

SOME UNITS
ⓈＤ 🍴 📺 🐟 🐕 DATA PORT 🖥 / ✕ ▣ 🖨 ▣ /

RESIDENCE INN BY MARRIOTT WESTON **Book at aaa.com** Phone: (954)659-8585 **114**

▽▽▽ 12/18-4/17 1P: $179-$249 2P: $179-$249
| | 4/18-11/30 | 1P: $129-$219 | 2P: $129-$219 |
Small-scale Hotel 12/1-12/17 1P: $119-$209 2P: $119-$209
Location: I-75, exit 15 to Weston Rd, just s. 2605 Weston Rd 33331. Fax: 954/659-3130. **Facility:** 100 units. 50 one-bedroom standard units with kitchens. 34 one- and 16 two-bedroom suites with kitchens. 3 stories, interior corridors. *Bath:* combo or shower only. **Parking:** on-site. **Terms:** weekly rates available, small pets only ($75 deposit). **Amenities:** high-speed Internet, dual phone lines, voice mail, irons, hair dryers. **Pool(s):** small heated outdoor. **Leisure Activities:** whirlpool, limited exercise equipment, sports court. **Guest Services:** valet and coin laundry. **Business Services:** meeting rooms, fax (fee). **Cards:** AX, CB, DC, DS, JC, MC, VI.

SOME UNITS
(ASK) ⓈＤ 🐾 🍴 ⓂＭ ᓚᘏ 📷 🐟 ✕ 🐕 DATA PORT 🖥 🖨 ▣ / ✕ /
FEE

TOWNEPLACE SUITES BY MARRIOTT WESTON **Book at aaa.com** Phone: (954)659-2234 **111**

▽▽▽ All Year 1P: $69-$209
Location: I-75, exit 15, 1 mi e on Arvida Pkwy to Bonaventure Blvd, n to Three Village Rd, then w. Located across from Small-scale Hotel Weston Town Center. 1545 Three Village Rd 33326. Fax: 954/659-2282. **Facility:** 95 units. 69 one-bedroom standard units with kitchens. 4 one- and 22 two-bedroom suites with kitchens. 2-3 stories, interior corridors. *Bath:* combo or shower only. **Parking:** on-site. **Terms:** [CP] meal plan available, small pets only ($75 fee). **Amenities:** high-speed Internet, dual phone lines, voice mail, irons, hair dryers. **Pool(s):** small heated outdoor. **Leisure Activities:** limited exercise equipment. **Guest Services:** valet and coin laundry. **Business Services:** fax (fee). **Cards:** AX, CB, DC, DS, JC, MC, VI.

SOME UNITS
(ASK) ⓈＤ 🐾 🍴 ⓂＭ 🐟 🐕 DATA PORT 🖥 🖨 ▣ / ✕ /
FEE

WYNDHAM RESORT & GOLDEN DOOR SPA AT WESTON **Book at aaa.com** Phone: (954)389-3300 **110**

(AAA) (SAVE) All Year 1P: $119-$250 2P: $119-$250 XP: $20 F12
▽▽▽▽ **Location:** I-75, exit 21 (Indian Trace) southbound, 1.6 mi e on SR 84 to E Mall Dr, then just s; exit northbound, U-turn to Resort SR 84, 1.6 mi to E Mall Dr, then just s. 250 Racquet Club Rd 33326. Fax: 954/384-1416. **Facility:** The resort offers Large-scale Hotel full-service, European-style spa facilities; a waterfall pool area is surrounded by tropical trees and plants. 496 units. 389 one-bedroom standard units. 87 one- and 20 two-bedroom suites ($250-$395), some with whirlpools. 4 stories, exterior corridors. *Bath:* combo or shower only. **Parking:** on-site and valet. **Terms:** check-in 4 pm, $10 service charge. **Amenities:** video library (fee), DVD players, voice mail, irons, hair dryers. *Some:* CD players. **Dining:** 6:30 am-11 pm, cocktails. **Pool(s):** 3 heated outdoor. **Leisure Activities:** whirlpools, recreation programs, jogging, playground, spa. *Fee:* golf-36 holes, golf & tennis instruction, 15 lighted tennis courts, racquetball courts. **Guest Services:** gift shop, valet laundry, area transportation-within 5 mi. **Business Services:** conference facilities, business center. **Cards:** AX, DC, DS, JC, MC, VI. **Special Amenities:** free local telephone calls and free newspaper.

SOME UNITS
✈ 🍴 📺 🏋 ᓚᘏ 🐟 ➕ ✕ 🐕 DATA PORT ▣ / ✕ VCR 🖥 /
FEE FEE

——— WHERE TO DINE ———

EAST CITY GRILL Lunch: $8-$14 Dinner: $20-$35 Phone: 954/659-3339 **125**

(AAA) **Location:** I-75, exit 15, 1 mi e on Arvida Pkwy to Bonaventure Blvd, then just n to The Bell Tower Shops. 1800 Bell Tower Ln 33326. **Hours:** 11:30 am-3:30 & 5:30-10:30 pm, Fri-11 pm, Sat 5:30 pm-11 pm, Sun 5:30 pm-10 ▽▽▽ pm. Closed: Super Bowl Sun. **Reservations:** suggested. **Features:** The chef draws upon an eclectic array Continental of international cuisines to create fresh seafood and meat dishes. An extensive wine list complements the menu. Seating is offered in the cozy dining room and on the patio, which overlooks a small lake. Dressy casual; cocktails. **Parking:** on-site. **Cards:** AX, DC, DS, MC, VI.

ⓂＭ 📺

(See map and index starting on p. 364)

FLANIGAN'S SEAFOOD BAR & RESTAURANT   Lunch: $6-$18   Dinner: $6-$18   Phone: 954/385-8080

American

Location: I-75, exit 15, 0.5 mi w on Arvida Pkwy, then just n. 2460 Weston Rd 33326. **Hours:** 11 am-12:30 am, Fri & Sat-1:30 am. **Features:** In a small shopping center, the room has settings with many pictures of fishing trips and sport items. The back patio area has a water view. The menu lists a wide variety of fresh seafood items, in addition to the well-known ribs. Casual dress; cocktails. **Parking:** on-site. **Cards:** AX, CB, DC, DS, JC, MC, VI.

IL TOSCANO   Lunch: $8-$15   Dinner: $11-$30   Phone: 954/385-5883

Northern
Italian

Location: I-75, exit 15, 0.5 mi w on Arvida Pkwy to Weston Rd, then just n; in Waterway Shoppes of Weston. 2282 Weston Rd 33326. **Hours:** 11:30 am-11 pm, Fri & Sat-midnight. Closed: 11/23, 12/25. **Reservations:** accepted. **Features:** Guests can request seating in the upbeat, cozily lit dining room or on the back patio. Northern Italian recipes combine local seafood, fresh pasta and top-quality meats. Dressy casual; cocktails. **Parking:** on-site. **Cards:** AX, CB, DC, DS, JC, MC, VI.

JAPAN INN   Lunch: $7-$16   Dinner: $11-$25   Phone: 954/659-7847   124

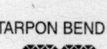
Asian

Location: I-75, exit 15, 1 mi e on Arvida Pkwy to Bonaventure Blvd, then just n to The Bell Tower Shopps. 1798 Market St 33326. **Hours:** 11:30 am-3 & 4:30-11 pm, Fri & Sat-midnight, Sun-10:30 pm. **Reservations:** accepted. **Features:** Patrons can take their appetite to eastern Asia. Sit in the dining room and peruse the bountiful menu, which is diverse in foods from Thailand and north to Japan, or sit at the cooking tables and watch food cooked at the communal tables. Casual dress; cocktails. **Parking:** on-site. **Cards:** MC, VI.

TARPON BEND FOOD & TACKLE   Lunch: $5-$10   Dinner: $5-$17   Phone: 954/888-9118   126

Seafood

Location: I-75, exit 15, 1 mi e on Arvida Pkwy to Bonaventure Blvd, then just n; in Weston Towne Center. 1630 Bell Tower Ln 33326. **Hours:** 11:30 am-11 pm, Sat from noon, Sun noon-10 pm. Closed: 11/23, 12/25. **Features:** The casual, fun eatery serves up fresh seafood items—in both sandwiches and dinner-size entrees—from local waters. Sports fans who need to see the game can do so on one of the many TVs around the room. Casual dress; cocktails. **Parking:** on-site. **Cards:** AX, DS, MC, VI.

Flamingo Gardens, Davie / Greater Fort Lauderdale Convention & Visitors Bureau

This ends listings for the Fort Lauderdale Vicinity.
The following page resumes the alphabetical listings of cities in Florida.

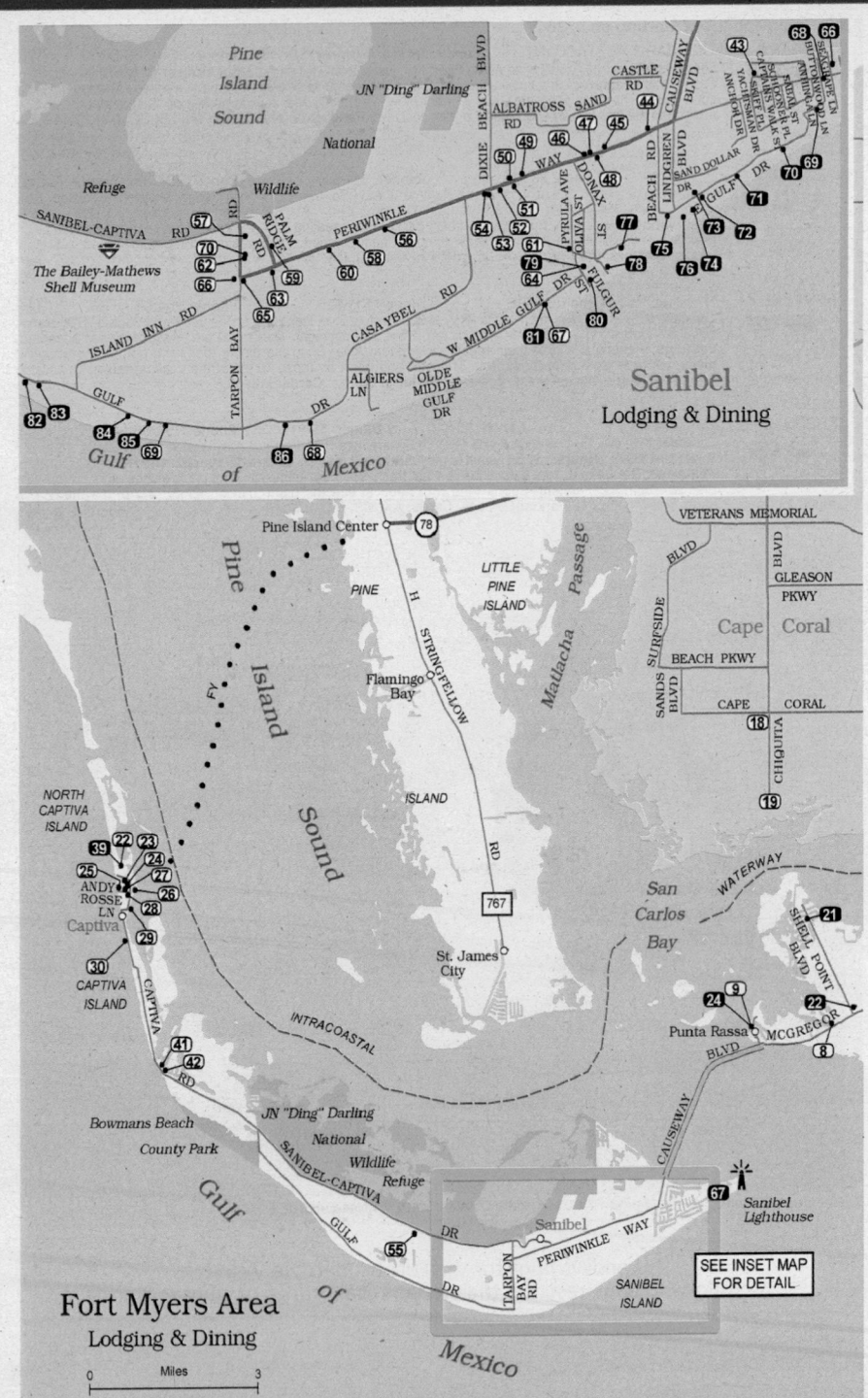

Sanibel
Lodging & Dining

Fort Myers Area
Lodging & Dining

1752-A

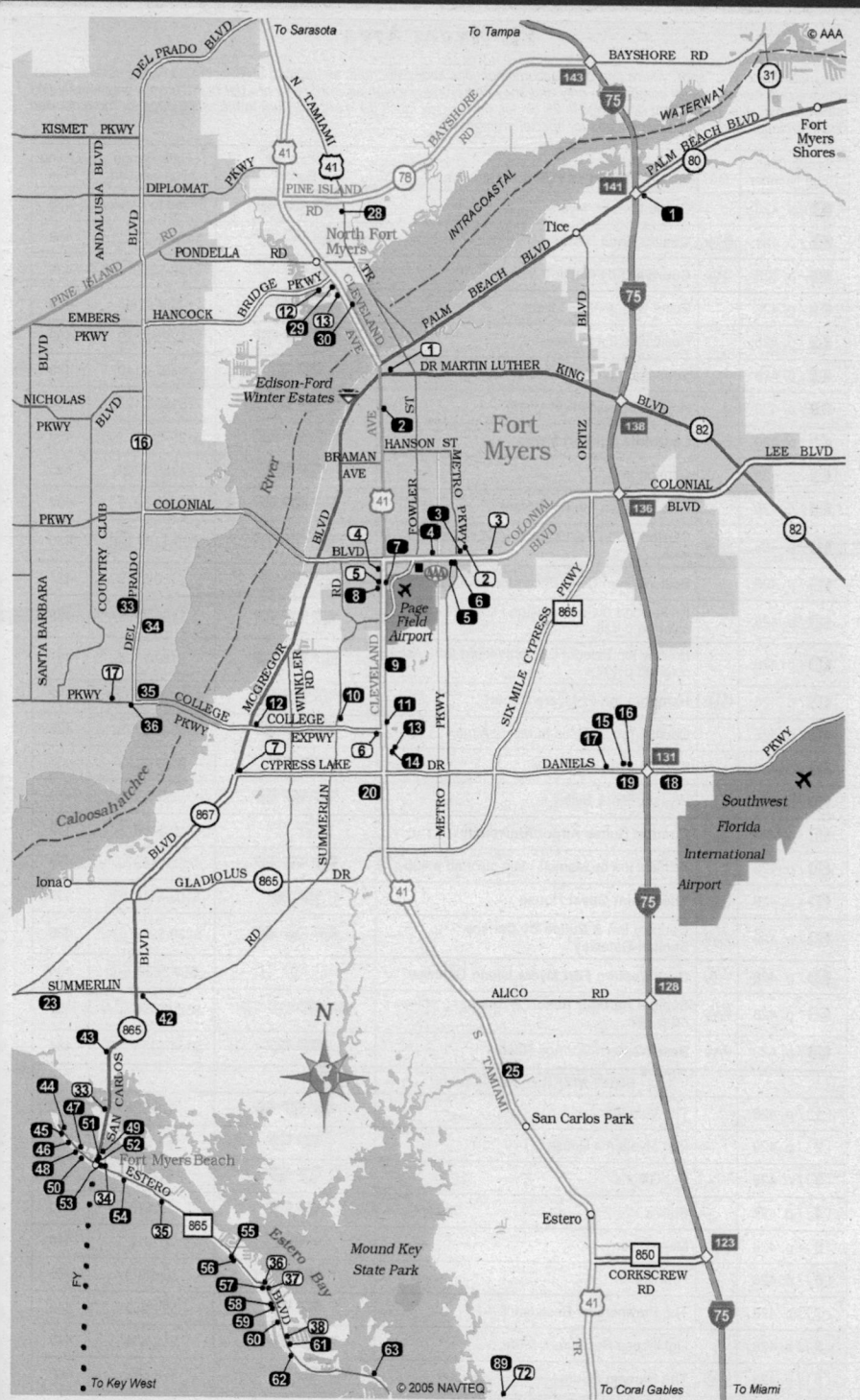

Ft. Myers Area

This index helps you "spot" where approved accommodations and restaurants are located on the corresponding detailed maps. Lodging rate ranges are for comparison only and show the property's high season; rates are per night, unless only weekly (W) rates are available. Restaurant rate range is for dinner, unless only lunch (L) is served. Turn to the listing page for more detailed rate information and consult display ads for special promotions.

Spotter/Map Page Number	OA	FORT MYERS - Lodgings	Diamond Rating	Rate Range High Season	Listing Page
1 / p. 428		Comfort Inn-Ft. Myers	◆◆◆	Failed to provide	435
2 / p. 428	AAA	Quality Hotel Historic District	◆◆◆	$119-$179 SAVE	438
3 / p. 428	AAA	Courtyard by Marriott	◆◆◆	$159-$269 SAVE	436
4 / p. 428		Super 8 Motel-Fort Myers	◆◆	$69-$189	439
5 / p. 428		Residence Inn by Marriott	◆◆◆	$229-$329	439
6 / p. 428		Suburban Extended Stay Hotel	◆◆	$107-$140	439
7 / p. 428		Howard Johnson-Fort Myers	◆◆	$120-$125	438
8 / p. 428	AAA	La Quinta Inn Fort Myers	◆◆	$129-$149 SAVE	438
9 / p. 428		Comfort Inn	◆◆	$159-$209	435
10 / p. 428		Hilton Garden Inn Fort Myers	◆◆◆	$199-$279	437
11 / p. 428	AAA	Clarion Hotel Fort Myers - see color ad p 435	◆◆◆	$99-$189 SAVE	435
12 / p. 428		Best Western Coral Bridge Inn & Suites	◆◆◆	$129-$159	434
13 / p. 428		Homewood Suites by Hilton-Ft. Myers - see color ad p 438	◆◆◆	$159-$289	438
14 / p. 428		Holiday Inn Select Ft. Myers Airport Area - see color ad p 437	◆◆◆	$189-$309	437
15 / p. 428	AAA	Hampton Inn-Ft Myers Airport	◆◆◆	$199-$249 SAVE	437
16 / p. 428		Country Inn & Suites Ft Myers-Airport	◆◆◆	$140-$175	436
17 / p. 428		Best Western Airport Inn	◆◆	$169-$189	434
18 / p. 428		Wynstar Inn & Suites	◆◆◆	$59-$259	439
19 / p. 428	AAA	Comfort Suites Airport/University	◆◆	$119-$169 SAVE	435
20 / p. 428		Fairfield Inn by Marriott - see color ad p 436	◆◆◆	$179-$279	436
21 / p. 428	AAA	Shell Point Guest House	◆◆	$103-$118 SAVE	439
22 / p. 428	AAA	Country Inn & Suites By Carlson Sanibel-Gateway	◆◆◆	$239-$289 SAVE	436
23 / p. 428	AAA	Best Western Fort Myers Island Gateway	◆◆◆	$69-$229 SAVE	434
24 / p. 428	AAA	Sanibel Harbour Resort & Spa - see color ad p 897	◆◆◆◆	$329-$499 SAVE	439
25 / p. 428	AAA	Best Western Springs Resort	◆◆	$134-$144 SAVE	434
		FORT MYERS - Restaurants			
1 / p. 428		The Veranda	◆◆◆	$20-$28	440
2 / p. 428		Fort Myers Ale House	◆◆	$6-$13	440
3 / p. 428		R J Gator's	◆◆	$7-$18	440
4 / p. 428		Shell's	◆◆	$8-$18	440
5 / p. 428		Mel's Diner	◆	$7-$11	440
6 / p. 428		First Watch	◆◆	$6-$8(L)	440
7 / p. 428		The Prawnbroker Restaurant	◆◆	$14-$30	440
8 / p. 428		Lighthouse Restaurant & Bar	◆◆	$10-$24	440
9 / p. 428	AAA	The Banyan Room	◆◆◆	$28-$42	440

Spotter/Map Page Number	OA	**NORTH FORT MYERS - Lodgings**	Diamond Rating	Rate Range High Season	Listing Page
28 / p. 428		Cactus Motel	◈	$69-$120	643
29 / p. 428	AAA	**Econo Lodge**	◈◈	$95-$145 SAVE	643
30 / p. 428		Howard Johnson Express Inn	◈◈	$159-$209	644
		NORTH FORT MYERS - Restaurants			
12 / p. 428		Hurricane Harry's	◈	$8-$17	644
13 / p. 428		Land & Sea Family Restaurant	◈	$5-$20	644
		CAPE CORAL - Lodgings			
33 / p. 428	AAA	**Casa Loma Motel on the Waterfront**	◈◈	$125-$185 SAVE	268
34 / p. 428	AAA	**Dockside Inn**	◈	$115-$155 SAVE	268
35 / p. 428	AAA	**Malaga Resort Motel**	◈	$455-$700(W) SAVE	268
36 / p. 428		Quality Hotel	◈◈◈	$95-$135	268
		CAPE CORAL - Restaurants			
16 / p. 428		Ariani Northern Italian Grill	◈◈◈	$15-$25	268
17 / p. 428		Iguana Mia	◈◈	$12-$15	269
18 / p. 428		Brigands Steak & Seafood Grill	◈◈	$13-$24	269
19 / p. 428		Rum Runners	◈◈◈	$7-$20	269
		CAPTIVA - Lodgings			
39 / p. 428	AAA	**South Seas Resort & Yacht Harbor** - see color ad p 270	◈◈◈	$389-$1299 SAVE	270
		CAPTIVA - Restaurants			
22 / p. 428	AAA	**Chadwick's Restaurant**	◈◈	$19-$27	271
23 / p. 428		Mama Rosa's Pizzeria	◈	$7-$19	271
24 / p. 428		Redfish Blufish	◈◈	$9-$13	271
25 / p. 428		The Mucky Duck	◈◈	$17-$37	271
26 / p. 428		The Bubble Room Restaurant	◈◈	$19-$29	271
27 / p. 428		R C Otter's Island Eats	◈◈	$8-$25	271
28 / p. 428	AAA	**Keylime Bistro**	◈◈	$22-$34	271
29 / p. 428		The Green Flash	◈◈	$14-$28	271
30 / p. 428		Old Captiva House	◈◈◈	$18-$34	271
		FORT MYERS BEACH - Lodgings			
42 / p. 428		Hampton Inn & Suites	◈◈◈	$279-$310	442
43 / p. 428		Mariner's Lodge and Marina	◈◈	$99-$149	443
44 / p. 428	AAA	**Pink Shell Beach Resort and Spa** - see color ad p 444	◈◈◈	$349-$619 SAVE	444
45 / p. 428	AAA	**Beach Club I**	◈◈	$100-$233 SAVE	441
47 / p. 428		Island House Motel	◈◈	$49-$139	443
48 / p. 428	AAA	**Best Western Beach Resort**	◈◈	$249-$269 SAVE	441
49 / p. 428	AAA	**Matanzas Inn**	◈	$99-$175 SAVE	443
50 / p. 428		Bay To Beach Resort	◈◈◈	$2400-$3900(W)	441
51 / p. 428		Sun Deck Resort	◈	$129-$235	448
52 / p. 428	AAA	**Lighthouse Resort Inn & Suites** - see color ad p 445	◈◈	$115-$295 SAVE	443
53 / p. 428		Silver Sands Villas	◈◈	$79-$219	446

Spotter/Map Page Number	OA	FORT MYERS BEACH - Lodgings (continued)	Diamond Rating	Rate Range High Season	Listing Page
54 / p. 428	AAA	DiamondHead Beach Resort - see color ad p 447	◆◆◆	$350-$400 SAVE	441
55 / p. 428		Cornerstone Beach Resort	◆◆◆	Failed to provide	441
56 / p. 428	AAA	Sandpiper Gulf Resort - see color ad p 446	◆◆◆	$100-$245 SAVE	446
57 / p. 428		Outrigger Beach Resort - see color ad p 445	◆◆	$160-$245	444
58 / p. 428	AAA	GullWing Beach Resort - see color ad p 447	◆◆◆	$410-$550 SAVE	442
59 / p. 428	AAA	Pointe Estero Resort Hotel - see color ad p 447	◆◆◆	$360-$540 SAVE	444
60 / p. 428	AAA	Holiday Inn	◆◆◆	$259-$425 SAVE	443
61 / p. 428	AAA	Santa Maria Harbour Resort - see color ad p 447	◆◆◆	$280-$420 SAVE	446
62 / p. 428	AAA	Caribbean Beach Club	◆◆	$840-$1050(W) SAVE	441
63 / p. 428	AAA	Lovers Key Beach Club & Resort - see color ad p 445	◆◆◆	$230-$300 SAVE	443
		FORT MYERS BEACH - Restaurants			
33 / p. 428		The Fish Monger	◆◆	$12-$18	448
34 / p. 428		The Beached Whale	◆◆	$7-$20	448
35 / p. 428		Anthony's On The Gulf	◆◆	$11-$21	448
36 / p. 428		Munch Box Family Restaurant	◆	$6-$15	448
37 / p. 428		Charley's Boat House Grill	◆◆	$16-$26	448
38 / p. 428		Loggerhead's	◆◆	$9-$18	448
		SANIBEL - Lodgings			
67 / p. 428		Shell Island Beach Club	◆◆◆	$2450-$2625(W)	900
68 / p. 428	AAA	Brennen's Tarpon Tale Inn	◆◆◆	$139-$209 SAVE	895
69 / p. 428	AAA	Colony Resort	◆◆	$175-$210 SAVE	895
70 / p. 428	AAA	Seaside Inn - see color ad p 899	◆◆◆	$319-$419 SAVE	900
71 / p. 428		Sandalfoot Condominium - see color ad p 896	◆◆◆	$1545-$2395(W)	896
72 / p. 428		Sanibel Arms West Condominium	◆◆◆	$725-$2150(W)	897
73 / p. 428	AAA	Sanibel Moorings - see color ad p 898	◆◆◆	$227-$392 SAVE	898
74 / p. 428	AAA	Sanibel's Song of the Sea, a European-style seaside inn - see color ad p 899	◆◆◆	$299-$449 SAVE	898
75 / p. 428		Tortuga Beach Club	◆◆	$2800(W)	900
76 / p. 428	AAA	The Sanibel Inn - see color ad p 899	◆◆◆	$213-$427 SAVE	898
77 / p. 428		Sanibel Beach Club	◆◆◆	$2325(W)	897
78 / p. 428		Pelicans Roost - see color ad p 896	◆◆◆	$2500(W)	896
79 / p. 428	AAA	Holiday Inn Sanibel Island	◆◆◆	$299-$399 SAVE	895
80 / p. 428	AAA	Sanibel Siesta Condominium	◆◆◆	$1456-$2470(W) SAVE	898
81 / p. 428	AAA	Sundial Beach Resort - see color ad p 899, p 200	◆◆◆	$359-$679 SAVE	900
82 / p. 428	AAA	West Wind Inn	◆◆◆	$267-$334 SAVE	900
83 / p. 428	AAA	Best Western Sanibel Island Beach Resort - see color ad p 899	◆◆	$320-$352 SAVE	895
84 / p. 428		Hurricane House	◆◆◆	$2485(W)	896
85 / p. 428	AAA	Shalimar Cottage & Motel	◆◆	$265-$345 SAVE	900
86 / p. 428		Sanibel Cottages	◆◆◆	$2800(W)	897

Spotter/Map Page Number	OA	SANIBEL - Restaurants	Diamond Rating	Rate Range High Season	Listing Page
41 / p. 428		Mad Hatter	◇◇◇	$27-$30	902
42 / p. 428		Lazy Flamingo	◇	$8-$16	902
43 / p. 428		Gramma Dot's	◇◇	$17-$24	901
44 / p. 428		Lazy Flamingo Seafood Grill	◇	$9-$19	902
45 / p. 428		Matzaluna The Italian Kitchen!	◇◇	$9-$20	902
46 / p. 428		The Mermaid Kitchen & Cake Factory	◇◇	$9-$23	902
47 / p. 428		Dolce Vita Restaurant & Lounge	◇◇◇	$17-$27	901
48 / p. 428		The Jacaranda	◇◇	$17-$35	901
49 / p. 428		The Sanibel Steakhouse	◇◇◇	$16-$28	903
50 / p. 428		Schnapper's Hots	◇	$4-$8	903
51 / p. 428		McT's Shrimp House & Tavern	◇◇	$14-$26	902
52 / p. 428		Traders Store & Cafe	◇◇	$14-$26	903
53 / p. 428		Sanibel Island Pizza & Pasta	◇	$9-$14	902
54 / p. 428		LaVigna Italian Restaurant & Grille	◇◇	$9-$29	901
55 / p. 428		Doc Ford's Rum Bar & Grille	◇◇	$8-$29	901
56 / p. 428		The Sanibel Cafe	◇◇	$5-$16	902
57 / p. 428	AAA	**Twilight Cafe**	◇◇◇	$20-$30	903
58 / p. 428		Gully's of Sanibel Family Restaurant	◇◇	$8-$16	901
59 / p. 428		Hungry Heron	◇◇	$7-$21	901
60 / p. 428		The Island Cow	◇◇	$6-$25	901
61 / p. 428		Beachview Steakhouse & Seafood Restaurant	◇◇	$18-$31	901
62 / p. 428		The Timbers Restaurant & Fish Market	◇◇	$13-$34	903
63 / p. 428		Cheeburger Cheeburger	◇	$5-$12	901
64 / p. 428		Morgan's Forest	◇◇	$16-$28	902
65 / p. 428		The Seafood Factory	◇◇	$15-$25	903
66 / p. 428		Amy's Over Easy Cafe	◇◇	$7-$12(L)	901
67 / p. 428		Windows on the Water	◇◇	$17-$25	903
68 / p. 428		Thistle Lodge Beachfront Restaurant	◇◇◇	$15-$25	903
69 / p. 428		Riviera Restaurant	◇◇◇	$17-$30	902
		BONITA SPRINGS - Lodgings			
89 / p. 428	AAA	**Hyatt Regency Coconut Point Resort & Spa** - see color ad p 631	◇◇◇◇	$265-$420 SAVE	258
		BONITA SPRINGS - Restaurant			
72 / p. 428		Tanglewood	◇◇◇◇	$18-$30	259

FORT MYERS pop. 48,208   (See map and index starting on p. 428)—*See also FORT MYERS BEACH & NORTH FORT MYERS.*

─────── **WHERE TO STAY** ───────

BEST WESTERN AIRPORT INN   *Book at aaa.com*   Phone: (239)561-7000   **17**

◆◆ ◆◆

2/1-4/15 [CP] 1P: $169-$189	2P: $169-$189
12/21-1/31 [CP] 1P: $119-$139	2P: $119-$139
12/1-12/20 & 4/16-11/30 [CP] 1P: $90-$119	2P: $90-$119

Small-scale Hotel   **Location:** I-75, exit 131, 0.6 mi w. 8955 Daniels Pkwy 33912. Fax: 239/561-5963. **Facility:** 106 units. 91 one-bedroom standard units. 15 one-bedroom suites, some with kitchens and/or whirlpools. 4 stories, interior corridors. *Bath:* combo or shower only. **Parking:** on-site. **Terms:** pets ($10 extra charge). **Amenities:** high-speed Internet, voice mail, safes (fee), irons, hair dryers. **Pool(s):** outdoor. **Leisure Activities:** whirlpool, exercise room. **Guest Services:** valet and coin laundry. **Business Services:** meeting rooms, fax (fee). **Cards:** AX, CB, DC, DS, JC, MC, VI.

SOME UNITS

BEST WESTERN CORAL BRIDGE INN & SUITES   *Book at aaa.com*   Phone: (239)454-6363   **12**

▽▽▽

3/1-4/15 1P: $129-$159	2P: $129-$159
12/1-2/28 & 4/16-11/30 1P: $60-$90	2P: $60-$90

Small-scale Hotel   **Location:** 1.3 mi w of US 41 at McGregor Blvd; in Southpointe Commons. 9200 College Pkwy 33919. Fax: 239/454-4329. **Facility:** 100 units. 30 one-bedroom standard units. 70 one-bedroom suites with efficiencies. 5 stories, interior corridors. *Bath:* combo or shower only. **Parking:** on-site. **Terms:** package plans, pets ($10 extra charge). **Amenities:** video library (fee), high-speed Internet, dual phone lines, voice mail, safes, irons, hair dryers. **Pool(s):** heated outdoor. **Leisure Activities:** whirlpool, exercise room. **Guest Services:** valet and coin laundry. **Business Services:** meeting rooms, business center. **Cards:** AX, CB, DC, DS, MC, VI.

SOME UNITS

BEST WESTERN FORT MYERS ISLAND GATEWAY   *Book at aaa.com*   Phone: (239)466-1200   **23**

(AAA) (SAVE)

All Year 1P: $69-$229	XP: $5 F18

▽▽▽▽

Small-scale Hotel   **Location:** Jct John Morris Rd. 20091 Summerlin Rd SW 33908. Fax: 239/466-3797. **Facility:** 158 one-bedroom standard units, some with whirlpools. 3 stories. *Bath:* combo or shower only. **Parking:** on-site. **Terms:** cancellation fee imposed, pets ($25 extra charge). **Amenities:** video games (fee), voice mail, irons, hair dryers. *Some:* high-speed Internet. **Dining:** 7 am-10 pm, cocktails. **Pool(s):** heated outdoor. **Leisure Activities:** whirlpool, table tennis. **Guest Services:** valet and coin laundry. **Business Services:** meeting rooms, fax (fee). **Cards:** AX, CB, DC, DS, JC, MC, VI. **Special Amenities:** free local telephone calls and free newspaper.

SOME UNITS

BEST WESTERN SPRINGS RESORT   *Book at aaa.com*   Phone: (239)267-7900   **25**

(AAA) (SAVE)

2/1-4/1 1P: $134-$144	2P: $134-$144
12/1-1/31 & 4/2-4/29 1P: $99-$109	2P: $99-$109
4/30-11/30 1P: $79-$95	2P: $79-$95

▽▽▽▽

Motel   **Location:** On US 41 at Constitution Blvd. 18051 S Tamiami Tr 33908. Fax: 239/267-9763. **Facility:** 49 one-bedroom standard units. 2 stories (no elevator), exterior corridors. **Parking:** on-site. **Terms:** check-in 4 pm, pets ($15 extra charge). **Amenities:** high-speed Internet, safes (fee), irons, hair dryers. **Dining:** 6 am-9 pm, cocktails. **Pool(s):** outdoor. **Leisure Activities:** boat dock, fishing, 2 warm natural mineral springs soaking pools. **Guest Services:** complimentary evening beverages, valet and coin laundry. **Business Services:** meeting rooms, fax (fee). **Cards:** AX, CB, DC, DS, MC, VI. **Special Amenities:** free local telephone calls and free newspaper.

SOME UNITS

(See map and index starting on p. 428)

CLARION HOTEL FORT MYERS
Phone: (239)936-4300 **11**

AAA SAVE

Large-scale Hotel

| | 1/16-4/30 | 1P: $99-$189 | 2P: $99-$189 | XP: $10 | F18 |
| | 12/1-1/15 & 5/1-11/30 | 1P: $69-$109 | 2P: $69-$109 | XP: $10 | F18 |

Location: On US 41, 0.8 mi n of jct Daniels Pkwy. Located in a commercial area. 12635 S Cleveland Ave 33907. Fax: 239/936-2058. **Facility:** 192 units. 181 one-bedroom standard units. 11 one-bedroom suites. 2-5 stories (no elevator), interior/exterior corridors. **Parking:** on-site. **Terms:** check-in 4 pm. **Amenities:** high-speed Internet, dual phone lines, voice mail, irons, hair dryers. **Dining:** 6:30 am-10 pm, cocktails. **Pool(s):** heated outdoor. **Leisure Activities:** exercise room. **Guest Services:** valet and coin laundry, airport transportation-Southwest Regional Airport. **Business Services:** conference facilities, fax (fee). **Cards:** AX, CB, DC, DS, JC, MC, VI. **Special Amenities:** free local telephone calls and free room upgrade (subject to availability with advance reservations).
(See color ad below)

SOME UNITS
[icons] / X 🔒 🖥 /

COMFORT INN *Book at aaa.com*
Phone: (239)936-3993 **9**

Motel

	2/2-4/30	1P: $159-$199	2P: $169-$209	XP: $10	F12
	12/1-2/1	1P: $109-$159	2P: $119-$169	XP: $10	F12
	5/1-11/30	1P: $79-$109	2P: $89-$119	XP: $10	F12

Location: On US 41, 1.5 mi n of jct Daniels Pkwy. 11501 S Cleveland Ave 33907. Fax: 239/936-7234. **Facility:** 80 one-bedroom standard units. 2 stories (no elevator), exterior corridors. *Bath:* combo or shower only. **Parking:** on-site. **Terms:** [ECP] meal plan available. **Amenities:** high-speed Internet, voice mail, safes (fee), irons, hair dryers. **Pool(s):** outdoor. **Business Services:** meeting rooms, fax (fee). **Cards:** AX, CB, DC, DS, JC, MC, VI.

SOME UNITS
[ASK] [icons] / X /

COMFORT INN-FT. MYERS *Book at aaa.com*
Phone: 239/694-9200 **1**

Small-scale Hotel

Property failed to provide current rates

Location: I-75, exit 141, just e on SR 80, then just s on Orange River Blvd. 4171 Boatways Rd 33905. Fax: 239/690-0180. **Facility:** 61 one-bedroom standard units. 3 stories, interior corridors. *Bath:* combo or shower only. **Parking:** on-site. **Terms:** pets ($10 extra charge). **Amenities:** *Some:* irons, hair dryers. **Pool(s):** heated outdoor. **Leisure Activities:** whirlpool. **Guest Services:** valet and coin laundry. **Business Services:** meeting rooms, fax (fee).

SOME UNITS
[icons] FEE / X 🔒 🖥 🖥 /

COMFORT SUITES AIRPORT/UNIVERSITY *Book at aaa.com*
Phone: (239)768-0005 **19**

AAA SAVE

Motel

	1/17-4/30	1P: $119-$149	2P: $129-$169	XP: $10	F18
	1/1-1/16	1P: $99-$129	2P: $109-$149	XP: $10	F18
	12/1-12/31 & 5/1-11/30	1P: $89-$109	2P: $109-$129	XP: $10	F18

Location: I-75, exit 131, just w. 13651 Indian Paint Ln 33912. Fax: 239/768-5458. **Facility:** 65 units. 64 one-bedroom standard units, some with whirlpools. 1 one-bedroom suite. 2 stories, interior corridors. **Parking:** on-site. **Terms:** pets ($10 extra charge). **Amenities:** video library, voice mail, safes (fee), irons, hair dryers. **Pool(s):** heated outdoor. **Leisure Activities:** whirlpool, billiards, exercise room. **Guest Services:** complimentary evening beverages, valet and coin laundry. **Business Services:** meeting rooms, fax. **Cards:** AX, DC, DS, MC, VI. **Special Amenities:** free expanded continental breakfast and free local telephone calls.

SOME UNITS
[icons] FEE / X /

(See map and index starting on p. 428)

COUNTRY INN & SUITES BY CARLSON
SANIBEL-GATEWAY *Book at aaa.com*   Phone: (239)454-9292   22

AAA SAVE	2/1-4/22 [CP]	1P: $239-$289	2P: $239-$289
▽▽▽▽	12/1-1/31 [CP]	1P: $150-$190	2P: $150-$190
	4/23-11/30 [CP]	1P: $109-$159	2P: $109-$159

Small-scale Hotel **Location:** Jct McGregor Blvd; in Shell Point. 13901 Shell Point Plaza 33908. Fax: 239/454-9159. **Facility:** 112 units. 74 one-bedroom standard units. 38 one-bedroom suites ($124-$269), some with kitchens. 4 stories, interior corridors. *Bath:* combo or shower only. **Parking:** on-site. **Terms:** cancellation fee imposed, pets ($10 extra charge). **Amenities:** high-speed Internet, dual phone lines, voice mail, irons, hair dryers. **Pool(s):** heated outdoor. **Leisure Activities:** exercise room. *Fee:* golf club privileges. **Guest Services:** sundries, valet and coin laundry. **Business Services:** meeting rooms, fax (fee). **Cards:** AX, CB, DC, DS, JC, MC, VI. **Special Amenities: free continental breakfast and free local telephone calls.**

SOME UNITS
[icons]
FEE

COUNTRY INN & SUITES FT MYERS-AIRPORT   *Book at aaa.com*   Phone: (239)454-0040   16

▽▽▽▽	12/1-4/22	1P: $140-$170	2P: $145-$175	XP: $5	F18
	4/23-11/30	1P: $89-$128	2P: $99-$135	XP: $5	F18

Small-scale Hotel **Location:** I-75, exit 131, just w on Daniels Pkwy, then just n on Danport Blvd. 9401 Market Place Rd 33912. Fax: 239/454-6006. **Facility:** Designated smoking area. 85 units. 65 one-bedroom standard units. 20 one-bedroom suites. 4 stories, interior corridors. *Bath:* combo or shower only. **Parking:** on-site. **Terms:** cancellation fee imposed, [CP] & [ECP] meal plans available. **Amenities:** video games (fee), dual phone lines, voice mail, irons, hair dryers. **Pool(s):** heated outdoor. **Leisure Activities:** whirlpool, exercise room. **Guest Services:** coin laundry. **Business Services:** meeting rooms, business center. **Cards:** AX, DC, DS, MC.

SOME UNITS
[icons]

COURTYARD BY MARRIOTT   *Book at aaa.com*   Phone: (239)275-8600   3

AAA SAVE	3/1-4/23	1P: $159-$269
▽▽▽▽	2/1-2/28	1P: $109-$229
	12/1-1/31 & 4/24-11/30	1P: $99-$149

Small-scale Hotel **Location:** I-75, exit 136, 3.4 mi w on SR 884 (Colonial Blvd). 4455 Metro Pkwy 33916. Fax: 239/275-7087. **Facility:** 149 units. 137 one-bedroom standard units. 12 one-bedroom suites. 3 stories, interior corridors. *Bath:* combo or shower only. **Parking:** on-site. **Terms:** cancellation fee imposed, [AP], [BP] & [CP] meal plans available. **Amenities:** high-speed Internet, voice mail, irons, hair dryers. **Dining:** 6:30-10:30 am, Sat & Sun 7 am-noon. **Pool(s):** heated outdoor. **Leisure Activities:** whirlpool, exercise room. **Guest Services:** valet and coin laundry. **Business Services:** meeting rooms, PC, fax. **Cards:** AX, DC, DS, JC, MC, VI. **Special Amenities: free newspaper.**

SOME UNITS
[icons]

FAIRFIELD INN BY MARRIOTT   *Book at aaa.com*   Phone: (239)437-5600   20

▽▽▽	1/23-4/16	1P: $179-$279	2P: $179-$279
	12/1-1/22	1P: $89-$199	2P: $89-$199
	4/17-11/30	1P: $89-$119	2P: $89-$119

Small-scale Hotel **Location:** On US 41, just s of jct Daniels Pkwy; in Cypress Lake Center. 7090 Cypress Terrace 33907. Fax: 239/437-5616. **Facility:** 104 one-bedroom standard units, some with whirlpools. 3 stories, interior corridors. *Bath:* combo or shower only. **Parking:** on-site. **Amenities:** high-speed Internet, voice mail, irons, hair dryers. **Pool(s):** heated outdoor. **Leisure Activities:** whirlpool. **Guest Services:** valet laundry. **Business Services:** fax. **Cards:** AX, DC, DS, JC, MC, VI. *(See color ad below)*

SOME UNITS
[icons]
FEE   FEE FEE

(See map and index starting on p. 428)

HAMPTON INN-FT MYERS AIRPORT *Book at aaa.com* Phone: 239/768-2525 **15**

1/16-4/16 [ECP]	1P: $199-$219	2P: $229-$249	XP: $10	F18
4/17-11/30 [ECP]	1P: $139-$159	2P: $149-$169	XP: $10	F18
12/26-1/15 [ECP]	1P: $129-$149	2P: $139-$159	XP: $10	F18
12/1-12/25 [ECP]	1P: $109-$129	2P: $119-$139	XP: $10	F18

Small-scale Hotel **Location:** I-75, exit 131, just w on Daniels Pkwy, then just n on Danport Blvd. 9241 Marketplace Rd 33912. Fax: 239/768-6049. **Facility:** 87 one-bedroom standard units. 3 stories, interior corridors. **Bath:** combo or shower only. **Parking:** on-site. **Terms:** cancellation fee imposed. **Amenities:** video games (fee), high-speed Internet, voice mail, irons, hair dryers. **Pool(s):** outdoor. **Leisure Activities:** exercise room. **Guest Services:** valet laundry. **Business Services:** meeting rooms, fax (fee). **Cards:** AX, CB, DC, DS, MC, VI. **Special Amenities:** free expanded continental breakfast and free local telephone calls.

SOME UNITS

HILTON GARDEN INN FORT MYERS *Book at aaa.com* Phone: (239)790-3500 **10**

2/1-4/30	1P: $199-$279	2P: $199-$279	XP: $10	F18
12/1-1/31	1P: $89-$169	2P: $89-$169	XP: $10	F18
5/1-11/30	1P: $79-$159	2P: $79-$159	XP: $10	F18

Small-scale Hotel **Location:** 1 mi w of US 41 on College Pkwy at Summerlin; in University Commons. 12600 University Dr 33907. Fax: 239/790-3501. **Facility:** 126 units. 109 one-bedroom standard units. 17 one-bedroom suites. 5 stories, interior corridors. **Bath:** combo or shower only. **Parking:** on-site. **Terms:** cancellation fee imposed, package plans. **Amenities:** video games (fee), high-speed Internet, dual phone lines, voice mail, irons, hair dryers. **Pool(s):** heated outdoor. **Leisure Activities:** whirlpool, exercise room. **Guest Services:** sundries, valet and coin laundry. **Business Services:** meeting rooms, business center. **Cards:** AX, CB, DC, DS, JC, MC, VI.

SOME UNITS

HOLIDAY INN SELECT FT. MYERS AIRPORT AREA *Book at aaa.com* Phone: (239)482-2900 **14**

1/30-4/30	1P: $189-$299	2P: $199-$309	XP: $10	
5/1-6/1	1P: $159-$189	2P: $169-$199	XP: $10	
12/1-1/29	1P: $139-$189	2P: $139-$199	XP: $10	
6/2-11/30	1P: $139-$189	2P: $149-$189	XP: $10	

Location: Jct Daniels Pkwy; in Bell Tower Shops. 13051 Bell Tower Dr 33907. Fax: 239/482-4668. **Facility:** 227 units. 223 one-bedroom standard units. 4 one-bedroom suites. 5 stories, interior corridors. **Bath:** combo or shower only. **Parking:** on-site. **Terms:** 3 day cancellation notice, [AP] meal plan available, small pets only ($50 fee). **Amenities:** high-speed Internet, dual phone lines, voice mail, irons, hair dryers. **Pool(s):** heated outdoor. **Leisure Activities:** jogging, exercise room. **Guest Services:** valet and coin laundry, area transportation. **Business Services:** conference facilities, business center. **Cards:** AX, DC, DS, MC, VI. *(See color ad below)*

SOME UNITS

(See map and index starting on p. 428)

HOMEWOOD SUITES BY HILTON-FT. MYERS   *Book at aaa.com*   Phone: (239)275-6000   **13**

1/1-4/16 [BP]	1P: $159-$289	2P: $159-$289	XP: $10	F21
4/17-6/4 [BP]	1P: $139-$219	2P: $139-$219	XP: $10	F21
12/1-12/31 [BP]	1P: $139-$189	2P: $139-$189	XP: $10	F21
6/5-11/30 [BP]	1P: $99-$179	2P: $99-$179	XP: $10	F21

Small-scale Hotel

Location: Just e of jct US 41; in Bell Tower Shops. 5255 Big Pine Way 33907. Fax: 239/275-6601. **Facility:** 130 one-bedroom suites with kitchens. 3 stories, interior corridors. *Bath:* combo or shower only. **Parking:** on-site. **Terms:** 1-14 night minimum stay - seasonal, 3 day cancellation notice, seasonal, package plans, pets ($75 fee). **Amenities:** video library (fee), high-speed Internet, dual phone lines, voice mail, irons, hair dryers. **Pool(s):** heated outdoor. **Leisure Activities:** whirlpool, exercise room. **Guest Services:** gift shop, complimentary evening beverages: Mon-Thurs, valet and coin laundry, area transportation. **Business Services:** meeting rooms, business center. **Cards:** AX, CB, DC, DS, JC, MC, VI. *(See color ad below)*

SOME UNITS

HOWARD JOHNSON-FORT MYERS   *Book at aaa.com*   Phone: (239)936-3229   **7**

1/9-4/20	1P: $120	2P: $125	XP: $5	F
12/17-1/8	1P: $104	2P: $109	XP: $5	F
12/1-12/16 & 4/21-11/30	1P: $79	2P: $89	XP: $5	F

Motel

Location: On US 41, just s of jct N Airport Rd. 4811 S Cleveland Ave 33907. Fax: 239/939-0424. **Facility:** 116 units. 111 one-bedroom standard units. 5 one-bedroom suites ($100-$175). 2 stories (no elevator), exterior corridors. *Bath:* combo or shower only. **Parking:** on-site. **Terms:** pets ($25 extra charge). **Amenities:** high-speed Internet, voice mail, safes (fee), irons, hair dryers. **Pool(s):** outdoor. **Leisure Activities:** exercise room. **Guest Services:** coin laundry. **Business Services:** meeting rooms, fax (fee). **Cards:** AX, CB, DC, DS, JC, MC, VI.

SOME UNITS

LA QUINTA INN FORT MYERS   *Book at aaa.com*   Phone: (239)275-3300   **8**

1/20-4/30	1P: $129-$149	XP: $7	F18
5/1-11/30	1P: $85-$95	XP: $7	F18
12/1-1/19	1P: $79-$89	XP: $7	F18

Motel

Location: On US 41, just s of jct N Airport Rd. 4850 S Cleveland Ave 33907-1320. Fax: 239/275-6661. **Facility:** 129 units. 128 one-bedroom standard units. 1 one-bedroom suite. 2 stories (no elevator), exterior corridors. *Bath:* combo or shower only. **Parking:** on-site. **Terms:** [ECP] meal plan available, small pets only. **Amenities:** video games (fee), voice mail, irons, hair dryers. *Some:* dual phone lines, fax. **Pool(s):** heated outdoor. **Guest Services:** valet and coin laundry. **Business Services:** meeting rooms, fax. **Cards:** AX, CB, DC, DS, MC, VI. **Special Amenities:** free expanded continental breakfast and free local telephone calls.

SOME UNITS

QUALITY HOTEL HISTORIC DISTRICT   *Book at aaa.com*   Phone: (239)332-3232   **2**

2/15-4/16	1P: $119-$179
1/1-2/14	1P: $79-$129
12/1-12/31 & 4/17-11/30	1P: $69-$125

Small-scale Hotel

Location: On US 41, just n. 2431 Cleveland Ave 33901. Fax: 239/332-0590. **Facility:** 123 one-bedroom standard units. 4 stories, interior corridors. *Bath:* combo or shower only. **Parking:** on-site. **Terms:** cancellation fee imposed, small pets only ($15 extra charge). **Amenities:** high-speed Internet, irons, hair dryers. *Some:* safes. **Dining:** 7 am-2 & 5-10 pm, cocktails. **Pool(s):** outdoor. **Leisure Activities:** exercise room. **Guest Services:** valet and coin laundry. **Business Services:** meeting rooms, business center. **Cards:** AX, DC, DS, MC, VI.

SOME UNITS

(See map and index starting on p. 428)

RESIDENCE INN BY MARRIOTT — *Book at aaa.com* — Phone: (239)936-0110 **5**

	12/19-4/16 [ECP]	1P: $229-$329
	10/1-11/30 [ECP]	1P: $144-$174
Small-scale Hotel	4/17-9/30 [ECP]	1P: $134-$164
	12/1-12/18 [ECP]	1P: $134-$154

Location: I-75, exit 136, 3.5 mi w on SR 884 (Colonial Blvd). 2960 Colonial Blvd 33912. Fax: 239/936-4144. **Facility:** 78 units. 66 one- and 12 two-bedroom suites with kitchens. 3 stories, interior corridors. *Bath:* combo or shower only. **Parking:** on-site. **Terms:** pets ($75 extra charge). **Amenities:** high-speed Internet, voice mail, irons, hair dryers. *Some:* DVD players. **Pool(s):** heated outdoor. **Leisure Activities:** whirlpool, exercise room, sports court. **Guest Services:** complimentary evening beverages: Mon-Thurs, valet and coin laundry. **Business Services:** meeting rooms, PC, fax (fee). **Cards:** AX, DC, DS, MC, VI.

SOME UNITS

[ASK] [S/D] 🐕 [🍴] [&M] [🐾] [📷] [🏊] [✖] [📺] [DATA PORT] [🛏] [📺] [📺] / [✖] [VCR] /
FEE

SANIBEL HARBOUR RESORT & SPA — *Book at aaa.com* — Phone: (239)466-4000 **24**

[AAA] [SAVE]	12/24-5/15	1P: $329-$499	2P: $329-$499	XP: $20	F17
	10/16-11/30	1P: $219-$399	2P: $219-$399	XP: $20	F17
	12/1-12/23	1P: $219-$359	2P: $219-$359	XP: $20	F17
	5/16-10/15	1P: $179-$309	2P: $179-$309	XP: $20	F17

Resort
Large-scale Hotel

Location: At Sanibel Island Cswy entrance overlooking San Carlos Bay, enter at Punta Rassa Rd. 17260 Harbour Pointe Dr 33908. Fax: 239/466-6050. **Facility:** Water-view balconies grace all of the upscale hotel rooms and condo units at this resort on 80 unspoiled acres overlooking the Intracoastal Waterway. 398 units. 280 one-bedroom standard units. 65 one- and 53 two-bedroom suites ($429-$1600), some with kitchens. 3-12 stories, interior/exterior corridors. *Bath:* combo or shower only. **Parking:** on-site. **Terms:** 7 day cancellation notice-fee imposed, package plans, $15 service charge. **Amenities:** video games (fee), voice mail, irons, hair dryers. *Some:* CD players, high-speed Internet, dual phone lines, safes, honor bars. **Dining:** 4 restaurants, 6 am-1 am, cocktails, also, The Banyan Room, see separate listing, entertainment. **Pool(s):** 5 heated outdoor, heated indoor. **Leisure Activities:** whirlpools, rental boats, fishing, 7 lighted tennis courts, recreation programs, kids club, jogging, spa, basketball. *Fee:* sailboats, marina, charter fishing, kayaks, fishing pier, golf privileges, tennis instruction, dinner cruises on 100-ft yacht. **Guest Services:** gift shop, valet laundry, area transportation-Sanibel Island, beauty salon. **Business Services:** conference facilities, business center. **Cards:** AX, DC, DS, MC, VI.

(See color ad p 897)

SOME UNITS

[S/D] [🍴] [24hr] [🍸] [🎾] [&M] [🐾] [📷] [🏊] [💆] [✖] [📺] [DATA PORT] [📺] / [✖] [VCR] [🛏] [📺] /
FEE FEE

SHELL POINT GUEST HOUSE — Phone: (239)466-1111 **21**

[AAA] [SAVE]	12/1-4/30	1P: $103	2P: $118	XP: $6	F18
	5/1-11/30	1P: $55	2P: $55	XP: $6	F18

Motel

Location: 2 mi nw of jct McGregor Blvd; in gated community Shell Point Village. 15040 Shell Point Blvd 33908. Fax: 239/454-2266. **Facility:** 38 one-bedroom standard units. 2 stories, exterior corridors. **Parking:** on-site. **Terms:** office hours 7 am-9 pm. **Amenities:** *Some:* irons. **Dining:** 2 restaurants, 7 am-6:30 pm, Sun-6 pm. **Pool(s):** heated outdoor. **Leisure Activities:** putting green, 2 lighted tennis courts, exercise room, shuffleboard. *Fee:* golf-18 holes. **Guest Services:** gift shop, coin laundry. **Business Services:** meeting rooms, fax (fee). **Cards:** MC, VI.

SOME UNITS

[S/D] [🍴] [🏊] [✖] / [✖] /

SUBURBAN EXTENDED STAY HOTEL — *Book at aaa.com* — Phone: (239)938-0100 **6**

	1/16-4/14	1P: $107-$135	2P: $112-$140	XP: $5	F18
	4/15-11/30	1P: $60-$70	2P: $65-$75	XP: $5	F18
Small-scale Hotel	12/1-1/15	1P: $49-$70	2P: $54-$75	XP: $5	F18

Location: I-75, exit 136, 3.5 mi w on SR 884 (Colonial Blvd). 10150 Metro Pkwy 33912. Fax: 239/938-0370. **Facility:** 101 units. 92 one-bedroom standard units with efficiencies. 9 one-bedroom suites ($75-$135) with kitchens. 4 stories, interior corridors. *Bath:* combo or shower only. **Parking:** on-site. **Terms:** cancellation fee imposed, weekly rates available, pets ($25 fee). **Amenities:** high-speed Internet, voice mail, irons. **Pool(s):** heated outdoor. **Guest Services:** coin laundry. **Business Services:** meeting rooms, fax (fee). **Cards:** AX, DC, DS, MC, VI.

SOME UNITS

[ASK] [S/D] 🐕 [🍴] [&M] [🐾] [📷] [🏊] [📺] [DATA PORT] [🛏] [📺] [📺] / [✖] /
FEE

SUPER 8 MOTEL-FORT MYERS — *Book at aaa.com* — Phone: (239)275-3500 **4**

	All Year [ECP]	1P: $69-$189	2P: $69-$189	XP: $6	F12

Small-scale Hotel

Location: I-75, exit 136, 4 mi w on SR 884 (Colonial Blvd). 2717 Colonial Blvd 33907. Fax: 239/275-5426. **Facility:** 117 one-bedroom standard units. 4 stories, exterior corridors. *Bath:* combo or shower only. **Parking:** on-site. **Amenities:** voice mail, irons, hair dryers. **Pool(s):** outdoor. **Guest Services:** valet laundry. **Business Services:** fax (fee). **Cards:** AX, DC, DS, MC, VI.

SOME UNITS

[ASK] [S/D] [🍴] [&M] [🐾] [📷] [🏊] [📺] [DATA PORT] [🛏] [📺] [📺] / [✖] /

WYNSTAR INN & SUITES — *Book at aaa.com* — Phone: (239)791-5000 **18**

	4/16-11/30	1P: $59-$259	2P: $59-$259	XP: $10	F16
	1/16-4/15	1P: $89-$249	2P: $89-$249	XP: $10	F16
Small-scale Hotel	12/1-1/15	1P: $59-$249	2P: $59-$249	XP: $10	F16

Location: I-75, exit 131, just e. 10150 Daniels Pkwy 33913. Fax: 239/791-5001. **Facility:** Designated smoking area. 77 units. 72 one-bedroom standard units. 5 one-bedroom suites with kitchens. 3 stories, interior corridors. *Bath:* combo or shower only. **Parking:** on-site. **Terms:** cancellation fee imposed, pets ($100 deposit, $25 extra charge, in designated units). **Amenities:** high-speed Internet, voice mail, irons, hair dryers. *Some:* dual phone lines. **Pool(s):** heated outdoor. **Leisure Activities:** exercise room. **Guest Services:** valet and coin laundry. **Business Services:** meeting rooms, fax. **Cards:** AX, DC, DS, MC, VI.

SOME UNITS

[ASK] [S/D] [✈] 🐕 [🍴] [&M] [🐾] [📷] [🏊] [✖] [📺] [DATA PORT] [🛏] [📺] [📺] / [VCR] /
FEE FEE

(See map and index starting on p. 428)

———— WHERE TO DINE ————

THE BANYAN ROOM   Dinner: $28-$42   Phone: 239/466-4000   9
(AAA)
Location: At Sanibel Island Cswy entrance overlooking San Carlos Bay, enter at Punta Rassa Rd; in Sanibel Harbour Resort & Spa. 17260 Harbour Pointe Dr 33908. **Hours:** 5 pm-9:30 pm. Closed: Sun, Mon & 7/1-10/31.
Reservations: suggested. **Features:** The upscale restaurant employs delightful staff members who are eager to ensure a memorable dining experience. The chef prepares each dish with individual creativity and delicious flavor. Guests may find fresh ahi tuna, braised mallard duck or filet mignon on the varied menu. The pastry chef creates incredible desserts, most notably a sinful chocolate souffle. Dressy casual; cocktails. **Parking:** on-site and valet. **Cards:** AX, DS, MC, VI.

Mediterranean

FIRST WATCH   Lunch: $6-$8   Phone: 239/274-5551   6
Location: Jct US 41; in College Parkway. 7091 College Pkwy 33907. **Hours:** 7 am-2:30 pm. **Features:** Open for breakfast and lunch, the comfy restaurant prepares great omelets and such healthy dishes as orchard oatmeal, fruit bowls and veggie roll-ups. Also on the menu are many sandwiches and salads. Casual dress. **Parking:** on-site. **Cards:** AX, DS, MC, VI.

American

FORT MYERS ALE HOUSE   Lunch: $6-$13   Dinner: $6-$13   Phone: 239/931-4160   2
Location: I-75, exit 136, 3.5 mi w; adjacent to Courtyard by Marriott. 4400 Kernel Cir 33916. **Hours:** 11 am-2 am. Closed: 11/23, 12/25. **Features:** Ample portions of familiar foods make this casual restaurant popular with tourists and locals. Casual dress; cocktails. **Parking:** on-site. **Cards:** AX, DC, MC, VI.

American

LIGHTHOUSE RESTAURANT & BAR   Lunch: $10-$24   Dinner: $10-$24   Phone: 239/489-0770   8
Location: Just n of jct McGregor Blvd; at Port Sanibel Marina. 14301 Port Lomfort Rd 33908. **Hours:** 11 am-10 pm. **Features:** Diners can enjoy fresh seafood, aged prime beef or a rich pasta dish while enjoying a breathtaking sunset view from the restaurant's waterfront locale. From January through May, the Sunday brunch is a popular attraction. Casual dress; cocktails. **Parking:** on-site. **Cards:** AX, CB, DC, DS, JC, MC, VI.

American

MEL'S DINER   Lunch: $6-$11   Dinner: $7-$11   Phone: 239/275-7850   5
Location: On US 41, just s of jct N Airport Rd. 4820 Cleveland Ave 33907. **Hours:** 6:30 am-10 pm. Closed: 12/25. **Features:** Guests can listen to rock 'n' roll while taking a walk down memory lane. The dining room is decorated with scads of '50s memorabilia. In addition to hamburgers and milkshakes, the menu lists a good array of standard diner fare. Casual dress. **Parking:** on-site. **Cards:** AX, DS, MC, VI.

American

THE PRAWNBROKER RESTAURANT   Dinner: $14-$30   Phone: 239/489-2226   7
Location: Jct Cypress Lake Dr; 2.6 mi w of US 41. 13451-16 McGregor Blvd 33919. **Hours:** 4 pm-9:30 pm, Fri & Sat-10 pm. Closed: 11/23. **Reservations:** suggested. **Features:** The intimate restaurant is a prime spot for moderately upscale dining. Although there are numerous steak and pasta selections, seafood is the specialty, and such dishes as crunchy grouper won't disappoint. The two dining rooms overlook lush tropical gardens. Casual dress; cocktails. **Parking:** on-site. **Cards:** AX, MC, VI.

Seafood

RIB CITY GRILL   Lunch: $6-$20   Dinner: $6-$20   Phone: 239/693-2223
Location: I-75, exit 141, 3 mi e on SR 80. 13908 SR 80 33905. **Hours:** 11 am-9 pm, Fri & Sat-10 pm, Sun 11:30 am-9 pm. Closed: 11/23, 12/25. **Features:** The staff is a pleasure at the fun restaurant. Rustic decor and great food, especially the mouthwatering ribs, make for a great dining experience for lunch or dinner. Casual dress; cocktails. **Parking:** on-site. **Cards:** AX, MC, VI.

American

R J GATOR'S   Lunch: $7-$18   Dinner: $7-$18   Phone: 239/278-3336   3
Location: I-75, exit 136, 3 mi w on SR 884 (Colonial Blvd). 4451 Veronica Shoemaker Blvd 33916. **Hours:** 11 am-midnight, Fri-1 am. Closed: 11/23, 12/25. **Reservations:** accepted. **Features:** This is a fun spot to enjoy anything from grilled steaks, ribs or seafood platters to sandwiches, burgers or one of their various wraps. The gator nibs are a great way to start your meal and the fried shrimp is excellent. Casual dress; cocktails. **Parking:** on-site. **Cards:** AX, DS, MC, VI.

American

SHELL'S   Lunch: $8-$10   Dinner: $8-$18   Phone: 239/278-9011   4
Location: On US 41, just s of SR 884. 4606 S Cleveland Ave 33907. **Hours:** 11:30 am-10 pm. Closed major holidays. **Features:** This popular Florida chain is focused on fried, broiled and grilled seafood but a few landlubber items are offered. A great location for families, the pleasant staff is accommodating, and dishes are nicely prepared. Casual dress; cocktails. **Parking:** on-site. **Cards:** AX, DS, MC, VI.

Seafood

THE VERANDA   Lunch: $6-$10   Dinner: $20-$28   Phone: 239/332-2065   1
Location: Corner of Second at Broadway; across from City Hall; center. 2122 Second St 33901. **Hours:** 11 am-2:30 & 5:30-10 pm. Closed: 1/1, 12/25; also Sun. **Reservations:** suggested. **Features:** A restored house built circa 1900 boasts a brick courtyard and koi pond. Choose from an interesting selection of local seafood, beef, lamb, veal, pasta and chicken. Finish your meal with an outstanding Key lime pie. Casual dress; cocktails; entertainment. **Parking:** on-site and street. **Cards:** AX, MC, VI.

American

FORT MYERS BEACH pop. 6,561   (See map and index starting on p. 428)—See also FORT MYERS.

—— WHERE TO STAY ——

BAY TO BEACH RESORT
Phone: (239)463-5846   🔟50

▼◈▼◈▼
Condominium

	1P	2P
12/1-4/7 Wkly	1P: $2400-$3900	2P: $2400-$3900
10/29-11/26 Wkly	1P: $1500-$2900	2P: $1500-$2900
4/8-10/28 Wkly	1P: $1125-$2900	2P: $1125-$2900
11/27-11/30 Wkly	1P: $1125-$2525	2P: $1125-$2525

Location: Oceanfront. 0.3 mi n of Matanzas Pass Bridge. 740 Estero Blvd 33931. Fax: 239/463-4364. **Facility:** Relax and enjoy the gulf sunsets from the balcony of your suite; the nifty pool area features a dolphin waterfall. Designated smoking area. 14 units. 2 one- and 12 two-bedroom suites with kitchens. 4 stories, exterior corridors. **Parking:** on-site. **Terms:** office hours 9 am-5 pm, 3-7 night minimum stay - seasonal, 30 day cancellation notice-fee imposed, package plans. **Amenities:** high-speed Internet (fee), irons, hair dryers. *Some:* DVD players. **Pool(s):** heated outdoor. **Leisure Activities:** fishing, rental bicycles. **Guest Services:** sundries, complimentary laundry. **Business Services:** fax (fee). **Cards:** AX, DS, MC, VI.

SOME UNITS
🍴 ⊠ ✕ 🛄 📷 🖥 / VCR / FEE

BEACH CLUB I
Phone: 239/463-2882   🔟45

AAA SAVE
▼◈▼◈▼
Condominium

	1P	2P
All Year	1P: $100-$195	2P: $128-$233

Location: Oceanfront. 0.6 mi n of jct Matanzas Pass Bridge. 326 Estero Blvd 33931. Fax: 239/463-4244. **Facility:** Designated smoking area. 15 units. 5 one- and 10 two-bedroom suites with kitchens. 6 stories, exterior corridors. **Parking:** on-site. **Terms:** office hours 8 am-4 pm, 3 night minimum stay, age restrictions may apply, 30 day cancellation notice-fee imposed, weekly rates available. **Amenities:** voice mail, safes, irons, hair dryers. *Some:* DVD players (fee). **Pool(s):** heated outdoor. **Leisure Activities:** gazebo and barbecue grill area, shuffleboard, volleyball. *Fee:* massage. **Guest Services:** coin laundry. **Business Services:** fax. **Cards:** AX, MC, VI.

SOME UNITS
🍴 ⊠ ✕ 📷 📠 🛄 📷 🖥 / VCR / FEE

BEST WESTERN BEACH RESORT   *Book at aaa.com*
Phone: (239)463-6000   🔟48

AAA SAVE
▼◈▼◈▼
Small-scale Hotel

2/1-4/23	1P: $249-$269	2P: $249-$269	XP: $10	F17
12/24-1/31	1P: $179-$259	2P: $179-$259	XP: $10	F17
4/24-11/30	1P: $119-$189	2P: $119-$189	XP: $10	F17
12/1-12/23	1P: $109-$139	2P: $109-$139	XP: $10	F17

Location: Oceanfront. 0.4 mi n of Matanzas Pass Bridge. 684 Estero Blvd 33931. Fax: 239/463-3013. **Facility:** 75 units. 69 one-bedroom standard units with efficiencies. 2 one- and 4 two-bedroom suites ($179-$409) with kitchens. 5 stories, exterior corridors. *Bath:* combo or shower only. **Parking:** on-site. **Terms:** 7 day cancellation notice-fee imposed, weekly rates available, [CP] meal plan available, small pets only ($10 extra charge, in smoking units). **Amenities:** safes, irons, hair dryers. **Pool(s):** heated outdoor. **Leisure Activities:** rental sailboats, playground, shuffleboard, volleyball. *Fee:* parasailing, personal watercraft. **Guest Services:** coin laundry. **Business Services:** fax (fee). **Cards:** AX, DC, DS, MC, VI. **Special Amenities: free continental breakfast and free local telephone calls.**

SOME UNITS
$ 🐾 🍴 📷 🌊 ⊠ ✕ 📷 📠 🛄 📷 🖥 / ✕ / FEE

CARIBBEAN BEACH CLUB   *Book at aaa.com*
Phone: (239)463-6111   🔟62

AAA SAVE
▼◈▼◈▼
Condominium

	1P	2P
12/1-4/22 Wkly	1P: $840-$1050	2P: $840-$1050
9/4-11/30 Wkly	1P: $615-$740	2P: $615-$740
4/23-9/3 Wkly	1P: $555-$680	2P: $555-$680

Location: Oceanfront. 5 mi s of jct SR 865 (Matanzas Pass Bridge). 7600 Estero Blvd 33931. Fax: 239/463-9579. **Facility:** 44 units. 3 one-bedroom standard units with efficiencies. 40 one- and 1 two-bedroom suites with kitchens. 2-3 stories (no elevator), exterior corridors. *Bath:* combo or shower only. **Parking:** on-site. **Terms:** office hours 9 am-5 pm, 3-7 night minimum stay - seasonal, age restrictions may apply, 30 day cancellation notice-fee imposed, $45 service charge. **Amenities:** voice mail, irons, hair dryers. **Pool(s):** heated outdoor. **Leisure Activities:** whirlpool, boating, boat dock, fishing, bicycles, horseshoes, shuffleboard, volleyball. **Guest Services:** complimentary laundry. **Business Services:** meeting rooms, fax (fee). **Cards:** AX, MC, VI.

SOME UNITS
$ 🍴 🌊 ⊠ ✕ 📷 📠 🛄 📷 🖥 / VCR / FEE

CORNERSTONE BEACH RESORT
Phone: 239/463-2401   🔟55

▼◈▼◈▼
Condominium

Property failed to provide current rates

Location: Oceanfront. 2.9 mi s of Matanzas Pass Bridge (SR 865). 5480 Estero Blvd 33931. Fax: 239/463-2404. **Facility:** Very nicely decorated guest units all feature fully equipped kitchens, washers and dryers, and large rooms. All have great views of the Gulf. Designated smoking area. 12 units. 8 one- and 4 two-bedroom suites with kitchens. 5 stories, exterior corridors. **Parking:** on-site. **Terms:** office hours 9 am-5 pm. **Amenities:** high-speed Internet (fee), irons, hair dryers. *Some:* DVD players (fee). **Pool(s):** heated outdoor. **Leisure Activities:** putting green, rental bicycles. **Guest Services:** complimentary laundry. **Business Services:** fax (fee).

🍴 🦽M 🌊 ✕ 📠 🛄 📷 🖥

DIAMONDHEAD BEACH RESORT   *Book at aaa.com*
Phone: (239)765-7654   🔟54

AAA SAVE
▼◈▼◈▼
Large-scale Hotel

2/10-4/22	1P: $350-$400	2P: $350-$400	XP: $10	F
12/1-1/1	1P: $190-$385	2P: $190-$385	XP: $10	F
1/2-2/9	1P: $240-$280	2P: $240-$280	XP: $10	F
4/23-11/30	1P: $200-$240	2P: $200-$240	XP: $10	F

Location: Oceanfront. 0.8 mi s of Matanzas Pass Bridge (SR 865). 2000 Estero Blvd 33931. Fax: 239/765-1694. **Facility:** 124 one-bedroom suites. 12 stories, interior/exterior corridors. *Bath:* combo or shower only. **Parking:** on-site. **Terms:** 3 day cancellation notice, package plans. **Amenities:** video games (fee), high-speed Internet, voice mail, irons, hair dryers. *Some:* dual phone lines. **Dining:** 7:30 am-10 pm; Sunday brunch, cocktails. **Pool(s):** heated outdoor. **Leisure Activities:** whirlpools, exercise room, volleyball. *Fee:* parasailing, cabanas, personal watercraft, massage. **Guest Services:** sundries, coin laundry. **Business Services:** conference facilities, fax (fee). **Cards:** AX, DS, MC, VI. **Special Amenities: free newspaper and free room upgrade (subject to availability with advance reservations).**
(See color ad p 447)

SOME UNITS
$ 🍴 🍸 🦽M 🌊 🌊 ⊠ ✕ 📷 📠 🛄 📷 🖥 / ✕ /

(See map and index starting on p. 428)

GULLWING BEACH RESORT *Book at aaa.com*   **Phone:** (239)765-4300 🔢58

AAA SAVE
▽▽▽▽
Condominium

2/10-4/22	1P: $410-$550	2P: $410-$550
12/1-1/1	1P: $215-$530	2P: $215-$530
1/2-2/9	1P: $285-$460	2P: $285-$460
4/23-11/30	1P: $225-$360	2P: $225-$360

Location: Oceanfront. 4.5 mi se of Matanzas Pass Bridge (SR 865). 6620 Estero Blvd 33931. Fax: 239/765-4646. **Facility:** Play in the crystal white sand or catch the action from your room overlooking the beach and pool areas. Designated smoking area. 62 units. 10 one-, 12 two- and 40 three-bedroom suites with kitchens and whirlpools. 12 stories, interior corridors. *Bath:* combo or shower only. **Parking:** on-site. **Terms:** office hours 8 am-10 pm, 14 day cancellation notice, package plans. **Amenities:** video library (fee), DVD players, dual phone lines, voice mail, irons, hair dryers. *Some:* video games (fee). **Pool(s):** heated outdoor. **Leisure Activities:** whirlpool, tennis court, recreation programs, barbecue grills at gazebo area, exercise room, volleyball. *Fee:* cabanas, massage. **Guest Services:** gift shop, complimentary laundry. **Business Services:** meeting rooms, business center. **Cards:** AX, DS, MC, VI. **Special Amenities:** free newspaper.
(See color ad p 447)

SOME UNITS

🆂🅳 📶 ♿M ♿ 🎧 🏊 ✂ ✉ 📷 DATA PORT ⬛ 📺 💻 / VCR / FEE

HAMPTON INN & SUITES *Book at aaa.com*   **Phone:** 239/437-8888 🔢42

▽▽▽
Motel

2/1-3/31 [ECP]	1P: $279	2P: $310
12/1-1/31 [ECP]	1P: $159	2P: $279
4/1-11/30 [ECP]	1P: $109	2P: $129

Location: Just e of jct San Carlos Blvd (SR 865). 11281 Summerlin Square Rd 33931. Fax: 239/437-8889. **Facility:** 120 units. 78 one-bedroom standard units. 42 one-bedroom suites with kitchens. 4 stories, interior corridors. *Bath:* combo or shower only. **Parking:** on-site. **Terms:** cancellation fee imposed. **Amenities:** video games (fee), dual phone lines, voice mail, irons, hair dryers. **Pool(s):** heated outdoor. **Leisure Activities:** exercise room. **Guest Services:** sundries. **Business Services:** meeting rooms, PC, fax (fee). **Cards:** AX, DS, MC, VI.

SOME UNITS

ASK 📶 ♿M ♿ 🎧 🏊 📷 DATA PORT 💻 / ✉ ⬛ 📺 /

(See map and index starting on p. 428)

HOLIDAY INN — *Book at aaa.com* — Phone: (239)463-5711 — 60

AAA SAVE
Motel

12/25-11/30	1P: $259-$425	2P: $259-$425	
12/1-12/24	1P: $159-$325	2P: $159-$325	

Location: Oceanfront. 4.3 mi se of Matanzas Pass Bridge (SR 865). 6890 Estero Blvd 33931. Fax: 239/463-7038. **Facility:** 103 units. 101 one-bedroom standard units. 2 one-bedroom suites ($325-$425) with kitchens. 2 stories, exterior corridors. *Bath:* combo or shower only. **Parking:** on-site. **Terms:** cancellation fee imposed, [AP], [BP] & [CP] meal plans available. **Amenities:** voice mail, safes (fee), irons, hair dryers. **Dining:** 7 am-9 pm, cocktails, entertainment. **Pool(s):** heated outdoor. **Leisure Activities:** putting green, foosball, picnic areas, pool table, table tennis, exercise room, shuffleboard, volleyball. *Fee:* cabanas, parasailing, personal watercrafts, game room. **Guest Services:** valet and coin laundry, area transportation (fee)-trolley stop. **Business Services:** meeting rooms, fax (fee). **Cards:** AX, CB, DC, DS, JC, MC, VI. **Special Amenities:** free newspaper and early check-in/late check-out.

SOME UNITS

ISLAND HOUSE MOTEL — Phone: 239/463-9282 — 47

Motel

All Year	1P: $49-$139	2P: $49-$139	XP: $15 D18

Location: 0.4 mi n of Matanzas Pass Bridge (SR 865). 701 Estero Blvd 33931. Fax: 239/463-2080. **Facility:** Designated smoking area. 5 one-bedroom suites with kitchens. 1 story, exterior corridors. **Parking:** on-site. **Terms:** office hours 9 am-6 pm. **Amenities:** DVD players, irons, hair dryers. **Pool(s):** heated outdoor. **Leisure Activities:** beach access, boat dock, fishing, bicycles. **Guest Services:** coin laundry. **Business Services:** fax (fee). **Cards:** MC, VI.

LIGHTHOUSE RESORT INN & SUITES — *Book at aaa.com* — Phone: (239)463-9392 — 52

AAA SAVE
Small-scale Hotel

1/3-4/15	1P: $115-$295	2P: $115-$295	XP: $15 F
12/16-1/2	1P: $110-$295	2P: $110-$295	XP: $15 F
12/1-12/15 & 4/16-11/30	1P: $79-$150	2P: $79-$150	XP: $15 F

Location: Jct Matanzas Pass Bridge (SR 865). 1051 5th St 33931. Fax: 239/765-5297. **Facility:** Designated smoking area. 79 units. 35 one-bedroom standard units, some with efficiencies. 34 one- and 10 two-bedroom suites with kitchens. 2-4 stories, exterior corridors. *Bath:* combo or shower only. **Parking:** on-site. **Terms:** office hours 7 am-11 pm, 3 day cancellation notice-fee imposed, small pets only ($25 fee). **Amenities:** video library (fee), voice mail, hair dryers. *Some:* irons. **Dining:** noon-10 pm, cocktails, entertainment. **Pool(s):** 2 heated outdoor. **Leisure Activities:** tennis privileges, barbecue grills & picnic areas, limited exercise equipment. *Fee:* boat slips. **Guest Services:** gift shop, coin laundry. **Business Services:** PC (fee). **Cards:** AX, DC, DS, MC, VI. *(See color ad p 445)*

FEE   SOME UNITS   FEE

LOVERS KEY BEACH CLUB & RESORT — *Book at aaa.com* — Phone: (239)765-1040 — 63

AAA SAVE
Condominium

2/1-4/30 [ECP]	1P: $230-$300	2P: $230-$300	XP: $10 F16
12/20-1/31 [ECP]	1P: $175-$230	2P: $175-$230	XP: $10 F16
5/1-11/30 [ECP]	1P: $155-$210	2P: $155-$210	XP: $10 F16
12/1-12/19 [ECP]	1P: $140-$195	2P: $140-$195	XP: $10 F16

Location: 6 mi s of Matanzas Pass Bridge (SR 865). 8771 Estero Blvd 33931. Fax: 239/765-1055. **Facility:** Enjoy frolicking in the lagoon-like pool with a cascading waterfall or take a stroll on the beach while watching the dolphins in the surf. 85 one-bedroom suites with kitchens, some with whirlpools. 13 stories, interior corridors. *Bath:* combo or shower only. **Parking:** on-site. **Terms:** 3 night minimum stay - seasonal, 3 day cancellation notice. **Amenities:** voice mail, safes, irons, hair dryers. *Fee:* video games, high-speed Internet. **Dining:** 7:30 am-9 pm. **Pool(s):** heated outdoor. **Leisure Activities:** whirlpool, exercise room. **Guest Services:** coin laundry. **Business Services:** meeting rooms, fax (fee). **Cards:** AX, DS, MC, VI. **Special Amenities:** free expanded continental breakfast and free local telephone calls. *(See color ad p 445)*

SOME UNITS

MARINER'S LODGE AND MARINA — *Book at aaa.com* — Phone: (239)466-9700 — 43

Motel

12/1-4/20	1P: $99-$149	2P: $99-$149	XP: $10 F16
4/21-11/30	1P: $65-$80	2P: $65-$80	XP: $5 F16

Location: 1.5 mi e of Matanzas Pass Bridge (SR 865). 17990 San Carlos Blvd 33931. Fax: 239/466-6116. **Facility:** 34 units. 32 one-bedroom standard units. 2 one-bedroom suites with kitchens. 1-2 stories (no elevator), exterior corridors. *Bath:* combo or shower only. **Parking:** on-site. **Terms:** 3 day cancellation notice, weekly rates available. **Pool(s):** heated outdoor. **Leisure Activities:** whirlpool, fishing, shuffleboard. *Fee:* boat dock. **Guest Services:** coin laundry. **Cards:** AX, DC, DS, MC, VI.

SOME UNITS

MATANZAS INN — Phone: (239)463-9258 — 49

AAA SAVE
Motel

12/1-4/30		2P: $99-$175	XP: $10 F13
5/11-11/30		2P: $59-$145	XP: $10 F13

Location: Just e of the Matanza Pass Bridge (SR 865); just n. 414 Crescent St 33931. Fax: 239/765-9258. **Facility:** Designated smoking area. 26 units. 13 one-bedroom standard units. 12 one- and 1 two-bedroom suites with kitchens. 1-2 stories (no elevator), exterior corridors. **Parking:** on-site. **Terms:** office hours 8 am-10 pm, check-in 4 pm, 30 day cancellation notice, weekly rates available. **Pool(s):** heated outdoor. **Leisure Activities:** whirlpool, fishing, barbecue grills. *Fee:* boat dock, charter fishing. **Guest Services:** coin laundry. **Business Services:** fax. **Cards:** AX, DC, MC, VI.

SOME UNITS   FEE

(See map and index starting on p. 428)

OUTRIGGER BEACH RESORT *Book at aaa.com* Phone: (239)463-3131 57

2/5-4/22	1P: $160-$245	2P: $160-$245	XP: $10	F11
4/23-11/30	1P: $105-$160	2P: $105-$206	XP: $10	F11
12/25-2/4	1P: $125-$195	2P: $125-$195	XP: $10	F11
12/1-12/24	1P: $95-$160	2P: $95-$160	XP: $10	F11

Small-scale Hotel

Location: Oceanfront. 4 mi s of Matanzas Pass Bridge (SR 865). 6200 Estero Blvd 33931-1281. Fax: 239/463-6577. **Facility:** Designated smoking area. 144 units. 143 one-bedroom standard units, some with efficiencies. 1 one-bedroom suite with kitchen. 1-4 stories, exterior corridors. *Bath:* combo or shower only. **Parking:** on-site. **Terms:** check-in 4 pm, 3 day cancellation notice. **Amenities:** voice mail, safes, hair dryers. *Some:* irons. **Pool(s):** heated outdoor. **Leisure Activities:** recreation programs, rental bicycles. **Guest Services:** gift shop, coin laundry. **Business Services:** meeting rooms. *Fee:* PC, fax. **Cards:** AX, MC, VI. *(See color ad p 445)*

SOME UNITS

PINK SHELL BEACH RESORT AND SPA *Book at aaa.com* Phone: (239)463-6181 44

2/17-4/22	1P: $349-$619	2P: $349-$619	XP: $20	F17
1/3-2/16	1P: $199-$619	2P: $199-$619	XP: $20	F17
4/23-11/30	1P: $159-$619	2P: $159-$619	XP: $20	F17
12/1-1/2	1P: $149-$619	2P: $149-$619	XP: $20	F17

Resort
Condominium

Location: Oceanfront. 0.7 mi n of jct Matanzas Pass Bridge (SR 865). 275 Estero Blvd 33931. Fax: 239/463-1229. **Facility:** Located on 12 acres, the expansive resort offers beach to bayfront views. The meandering pool delights guests of all ages. Designated smoking area. 235 units. 60 one-bedroom standard units with efficiencies. 94 one-, 80 two- and 1 three-bedroom suites with kitchens. 1-9 stories, exterior corridors. *Bath:* combo or shower only. **Parking:** on-site. **Terms:** check-in 4 pm, 14 day cancellation notice-fee imposed, package plans. **Amenities:** high-speed Internet, voice mail, safes, irons, hair dryers. **Dining:** 2 restaurants, 7:30 am-9 pm, cocktails. **Pool(s):** 4 heated outdoor. **Leisure Activities:** rental boats, rental paddleboats, rental sailboats, fishing, 2 tennis courts, recreation programs, butterfly garden, recreation center, rental bicycles, playground, spa, volleyball. *Fee:* boat dock, charter fishing, excursion boats, parasailing, personal watercraft. **Guest Services:** gift shop, valet and coin laundry, area transportation-trolley stop. **Business Services:** meeting rooms, business center. **Cards:** AX, CB, DC, DS, MC, VI. *(See color ad below)*

SOME UNITS

POINTE ESTERO RESORT HOTEL *Book at aaa.com* Phone: (239)765-1155 59

2/10-4/22	1P: $360-$540
12/1-1/1	1P: $195-$520
1/2-2/9	1P: $245-$450
4/23-11/30	1P: $205-$340

Condominium

Location: Oceanfront. 4.5 mi se of Matanzas Pass Bridge (SR 865). 6640 Estero Blvd 33931. Fax: 239/765-0657. **Facility:** A majestic highrise overlooking the gulf affords views beyond the horizon. Spacious suites offer all the amenities of a home away from home. Designated smoking area. 60 two-bedroom suites with kitchens and whirlpools. 16 stories, interior corridors. **Parking:** on-site. **Terms:** office hours 8 am-10 pm, 2-7 night minimum stay - seasonal, 14 day cancellation notice. **Amenities:** video library (fee), DVD players, voice mail, irons, hair dryers. **Pool(s):** heated outdoor. **Leisure Activities:** whirlpool, tennis court, recreation programs, barbecue grills, exercise room. **Guest Services:** gift shop, complimentary laundry. **Business Services:** PC. **Cards:** AX, DS, MC, VI. *(See color ad p 447)*

SANDPIPER GULF RESORT *Book at aaa.com*   **Phone:** (239)463-5721   56

[AAA] [SAVE]   All Year   1P: $100-$245   2P: $100-$245   XP: $10   F12

Small-scale Hotel   **Location:** Oceanfront. 3.1 mi s of Matanzas Pass Bridge. 5550 Estero Blvd 33931. Fax: 239/765-0039. **Facility:** Designated smoking area. 63 units. 58 one-bedroom standard units with efficiencies. 5 one-bedroom suites with kitchens. 2-5 stories, interior/exterior corridors. **Parking:** on-site. **Terms:** office hours 7 am-6 pm, 2-3 night minimum stay - seasonal, 14 day cancellation notice-fee imposed, weekly rates available. **Amenities:** CD players, voice mail, hair dryers. *Some:* irons. **Pool(s):** 2 heated outdoor. **Leisure Activities:** whirlpool, barbecue grills, shuffleboard. *Fee:* personal watercraft, parasailing. **Guest Services:** coin laundry. **Business Services:** fax (fee). **Cards:** DS, MC, VI. *(See color ad below)*

SANTA MARIA HARBOUR RESORT *Book at aaa.com*   **Phone:** (239)765-6700   61

[AAA] [SAVE]   2/10-4/22   1P: $280-$420   2P: $280-$420

    12/1-1/1   1P: $150-$400   2P: $150-$400

    1/2-2/9   1P: $160-$270   2P: $160-$270

Condominium   4/23-11/30   1P: $155-$260   2P: $155-$260

Location: 5 mi s of Matanzas Pass Bridge (SR 865). 7317 Estero Blvd 33931. Fax: 239/765-6909. **Facility:** Set back from road among water canals. Designated smoking area. 50 units. 4 one-, 44 two- and 2 three-bedroom suites with kitchens. 4 stories, exterior corridors. **Parking:** on-site. **Terms:** office hours 8 am-8 pm, age restrictions may apply, 14 day cancellation notice. **Amenities:** video library (fee), DVD players, voice mail, irons, hair dryers. **Pool(s):** heated outdoor. **Leisure Activities:** sauna, whirlpools, fishing, recreation programs, barbecue grills, gazebo. *Fee:* boat dock. **Guest Services:** sundries, complimentary laundry. **Business Services:** PC, fax (fee). **Cards:** AX, DS, MC, VI.

(See color ad p 447)

SILVER SANDS VILLAS   **Phone:** (239)463-6554   53

    4/1-11/30   1P: $79-$219   2P: $79-$219   XP: $15   F3

    12/1-3/31   1P: $79-$199   2P: $79-$199   XP: $15   F3

Motel   **Location:** Just s of Matanzas Pass Bridge (SR 865). 1207 Estero Blvd 33931. Fax: 239/463-2260. **Facility:** Designated smoking area. 17 units. 4 one-bedroom standard units, some with efficiencies (no utensils). 13 one- and 4 two-bedroom suites ($79-$219) with kitchens. 2 stories, exterior corridors. *Bath:* combo or shower only. **Parking:** on-site. **Terms:** office hours 7 am-8 pm, age restrictions may apply, 21 day cancellation notice, small pets only ($50 fee). **Amenities:** video library. *Some:* irons, hair dryers. **Pool(s):** heated outdoor. **Guest Services:** coin laundry. **Business Services:** PC, fax. **Cards:** AX, MC, VI.

SOME UNITS

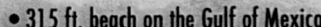

Home. Conveniently found in five tropical locations.

DiamondHead

GullWing

Pointe Estero

Santa Maria

FEATURING:

· Spacious suites

· Fully appointed kitchens

· Private balconies

· Watersports & activities

· Shopping nearby

· Heated pools & spas

· Great local dining

Save 10~25%

(off published rates)

Prepare to free your mind as you sink your toes into the softest, white sand and listen to the tide break. The truly unrivaled settings showcase all that Southwest Florida has to offer. Our unsurpassed amenities, attentive staff, private suites and many ways to relax will fulfill every one of your getaway plans.

SUNSTREAM
Hotels & Resorts

An exclusive collection of condo resorts offering the comforts and freedom of home.

FORT MYERS BEACH, FLORIDA • WWW.SUNSTREAM.COM/AAA

888-702-0782

(See map and index starting on p. 428)

SUN DECK RESORT   *Book at aaa.com*   Phone: (239)463-1842   **51**

	2/11-4/1	1P: $129-$235	2P: $129-$235	XP: $10	F12
	12/21-2/10	1P: $75-$190	2P: $75-$190	XP: $10	F12
Motel	12/1-12/20 & 4/2-11/30	1P: $49-$135	2P: $49-$135	XP: $10	F12

Location: Just s of Matanzas Pass Bridge (SR 865). 1051 Third St 33931. Fax: 239/463-9823. **Facility:** Designated smoking area. 7 units. 5 one-bedroom standard units, some with efficiencies or kitchens. 2 two-bedroom suites with kitchens. 3 stories (no elevator), exterior corridors. *Bath:* combo or shower only. **Parking:** on-site. **Terms:** office hours 7 am-9 pm, 30 day cancellation notice-fee imposed, small pets only ($20 fee). **Guest Services:** complimentary laundry. **Cards:** MC, VI.

——— WHERE TO DINE ———

ANTHONY'S ON THE GULF   Lunch: $9-$21   Dinner: $11-$21   Phone: 239/463-2600   **35**

Italian

Location: On SR 865, 2 mi s of Matanzas Pass Bridge. 3040 Estero Blvd 33931. **Hours:** 11:30 am-10 pm, Fri & Sat-11 pm. **Features:** Picturesque beach views and a tropical decor await diners at this casual gulf-shore restaurant. The menu dips into both American and Italian cuisine to assemble enticing dishes, such as baked stuffed mushrooms, buffalo shrimp and manicotti with sausage. Also available is standard fare—pizza, burgers and sandwiches. Casual dress; cocktails. **Parking:** on-site. **Cards:** AX, DS, MC, VI.

THE BEACHED WHALE   Lunch: $7-$20   Dinner: $7-$20   Phone: 239/463-5505   **34**

Seafood

Location: 0.5 mi s of Matanzas Pass Bridge. 1249 Estero Blvd 33931. **Hours:** 11:30 am-2 am. **Features:** Set just across from the beach and within walking distance of many shops and beach sights is this popular little restaurant. Guests enjoy the rustic charm and fresh seafood offerings. Casual dress; cocktails. **Parking:** on-site. **Cards:** AX, DS, MC, VI.

CHARLEY'S BOAT HOUSE GRILL   Dinner: $16-$26   Phone: 239/765-4800   **37**

Steak & Seafood

Location: 4.1 mi s of Matanzas Pass Bridge (SR 865). 6241 Estero Blvd 33931. **Hours:** 5 pm-10 pm. **Features:** Enjoy a great flame broiled steak or any one of their many seafood choices: red snapper, swordfish, grouper, salmon, lobster tail and shrimp just to name a few. Finish with a yummy slice of Key lime pie or the popular "Death by Chocolate" and you have treated yourself to a fine, filling meal. Casual dress; cocktails. **Parking:** on-site. **Cards:** MC, VI.

THE FISH MONGER   Dinner: $12-$18   Phone: 239/765-5544   **33**

Seafood

Location: Just n of Matanzas Pass Bridge. 19030 San Carlos Blvd 33931. **Hours:** 4 pm-10 pm. Closed major holidays. **Reservations:** accepted. **Features:** The casual, family-friendly seafood restaurant specializes in fresh fish brought in by a local fleet. The menu includes grouper, snapper, mahi mahi, tuna, tilefish, cobia, amberjack, salmon, swordfish and Pompano catfish, as well as New York steak, ribs and chicken. Diners can have their fresh catch cooked on the premises. Casual dress; cocktails. **Parking:** on-site. **Cards:** MC, VI.

LOGGERHEAD'S   Lunch: $6-$11   Dinner: $9-$18   Phone: 239/463-4644   **38**

American

Location: 4.5 mi se of Matanzas Pass Bridge; in Villa Santini Plaza. 7205 Estero Blvd 33931. **Hours:** 11 am-midnight. Closed: 1/1, 11/23, 12/25. **Features:** Popular with the local crowd, this casual restaurant specializes in seafood but also offers a wide range of comfort foods, including burgers, sandwiches, soups and salads. Casual dress; cocktails. **Parking:** on-site. **Cards:** AX, DS, MC, VI.

MUNCH BOX FAMILY RESTAURANT   Lunch: $4-$12   Dinner: $6-$15   Phone: 239/463-1889   **36**

American

Location: On SR 865, 3.8 mi s of Matanzas Pass Bridge. 6101 Estero Blvd 33931. **Hours:** 8 am-2 & 4:30-8:30 pm, Sun-noon. Closed: Mon. **Features:** Families on a budget will favor the meat-and-potatoes fare and child-friendly atmosphere of this comfortable mom-and-pop restaurant. It serves such home-style staples as omelets, hash browns, sandwiches, meatloaf and pot roast. Casual dress; beer & wine only. **Parking:** on-site.

FORT PIERCE pop. 37,516

——— WHERE TO STAY ———

COMFORT SUITES   *Book at aaa.com*   Phone: (772)409-1420

	1/16-4/15 [ECP]	1P: $109-$169	2P: $109-$169	XP: $10	F18
	12/1-1/15 [ECP]	1P: $89-$139	2P: $89-$139	XP: $10	F18
Small-scale Hotel	4/16-11/30 [ECP]	1P: $79-$129	2P: $79-$129	XP: $10	F18

Location: I-95, exit 129, just w, then s. 6505 Metal Dr 34945. Fax: 772/409-1430. **Facility:** 68 units. 65 one-bedroom standard units. 3 one-bedroom suites, some with whirlpools. 4 stories, interior corridors. *Bath:* combo or shower only. **Parking:** on-site. **Amenities:** high-speed Internet, voice mail, safes (fee), irons, hair dryers. **Pool(s):** heated outdoor. **Leisure Activities:** whirlpool, limited exercise equipment. **Guest Services:** complimentary evening beverages: Mon-Thurs, coin laundry. **Business Services:** meeting rooms, PC. **Cards:** AX, CB, DC, DS, JC, MC, VI.

SOME UNITS

DAYS INN HUTCHINSON ISLAND   *Book at aaa.com*   Phone: 772/461-8737

Property failed to provide current rates

Motel

Location: SR A1A southbound, Hutchinson Island, 2.5 mi e of jct US 1. 1920 Seaway Dr 34949. Fax: 772/460-2218. **Facility:** 36 one-bedroom standard units, some with kitchens. 1 story, interior/exterior corridors. **Parking:** on-site. **Terms:** pets ($10 fee). **Amenities:** dual phone lines, voice mail, safes (fee), irons, hair dryers. **Pool(s):** heated outdoor. **Leisure Activities:** fishing. **Guest Services:** coin laundry. **Business Services:** fax (fee).

SOME UNITS

DOCKSIDE HARBORLIGHT RESORT
Phone: (772)468-3555

(AAA) [SAVE]

Small-scale Hotel

All Year [CP]   1P: $79-$250   2P: $79-$250   XP: $10   F16
Location: SR A1A southbound, 2 mi e of jct US 1. 1160 Seaway Dr 34949. Fax: 772/489-9848. **Facility:** 20 one-bedroom standard units, some with kitchens. 2 stories, exterior corridors. **Parking:** on-site. **Terms:** 1-3 night minimum stay - seasonal and/or weekends, 3 day cancellation notice. **Amenities:** voice mail. **Pool(s):** heated outdoor. **Leisure Activities:** whirlpool, rental boats, fishing, fishing pier. *Fee:* boat dock. **Guest Services:** coin laundry. **Business Services:** meeting rooms, fax (fee). **Cards:** AX, CB, DC, DS, MC, VI.
Special Amenities: free continental breakfast and preferred room (subject to availability with advance reservations).

SOME UNITS

[icons]

HOLIDAY INN EXPRESS   *Book at aaa.com*
Phone: (772)464-5000

2/1-4/30	1P: $101-$165	2P: $101-$165	XP: $8	F18
12/1-1/31	1P: $79-$125	2P: $79-$125	XP: $8	F18
10/1-11/30	1P: $80-$110	2P: $80-$110	XP: $8	F18
5/1-9/30	1P: $79-$109	2P: $79-$109	XP: $8	F18

Small-scale Hotel

Location: I-95, exit 129, 0.7 mi w on SR 70; Florida Tpke, exit 152. 7151 Okeechobee Rd 34945. Fax: 772/461-9573. **Facility:** 100 one-bedroom standard units. 2 stories, exterior corridors. *Bath:* combo or shower only. **Parking:** on-site. **Terms:** cancellation fee imposed, small pets only ($25 deposit). **Amenities:** voice mail, irons, hair dryers. *Some:* dual phone lines. **Pool(s):** outdoor, wading. **Guest Services:** valet and coin laundry. **Business Services:** meeting rooms, fax (fee). **Cards:** AX, CB, DC, DS, MC, VI.

SOME UNITS

[icons] FEE

MOTEL 6-FORT PIERCE #1207   *Book at aaa.com*
Phone: 772/461-9937

2/11-5/29	1P: $53-$63	2P: $59-$69	XP: $3	F17
1/1-2/10 & 5/30-11/30	1P: $49-$59	2P: $55-$65	XP: $3	F17
12/1-12/31	1P: $41-$51	2P: $47-$57	XP: $3	F17

Motel

Location: I-95, exit 129, just w, then n. 2500 Peters Rd 34945. Fax: 772/460-9472. **Facility:** 120 one-bedroom standard units. 2 stories, exterior corridors. *Bath:* combo or shower only. **Parking:** on-site. **Pool(s):** outdoor. **Guest Services:** coin laundry. **Cards:** AX, CB, DC, DS, MC, VI.

SOME UNITS

[icons]

QUALITY INN
Phone: (772)460-9855

(AAA) [SAVE]

Small-scale Hotel

12/1-4/16	1P: $79-$159	2P: $79-$159	XP: $5	F12
4/17-11/30	1P: $59-$139	2P: $59-$139	XP: $5	F12

Location: I-95, exit 129, 0.4 mi w on SR 70; 0.3 mi e of Florida Tpke, exit 152. 2831 Reynolds Dr 34945. Fax: 772/465-7117. **Facility:** 72 one-bedroom standard units. 2 stories, exterior corridors. *Bath:* combo or shower only. **Parking:** on-site. **Terms:** weekly rates available. **Amenities:** high-speed Internet, dual phone lines, voice mail, irons, hair dryers. **Guest Services:** valet laundry. **Business Services:** fax. **Cards:** AX, DC, DS, MC, VI. **Special Amenities:** free continental breakfast and free local telephone calls.

SOME UNITS

[icons] FEE

SLEEP INN   *Book at aaa.com*
Phone: (772)595-6080

Small-scale Hotel

12/1-5/1 [CP]	1P: $150-$170	2P: $150-$170	XP: $10	F18
5/2-11/30 [CP]	1P: $90-$110	2P: $90-$110		

Location: I-95, exit 129, just w. 2715 Crossroads Pkwy 34945. Fax: 772/595-6070. **Facility:** 67 one-bedroom standard units. 4 stories, interior corridors. *Bath:* combo or shower only. **Parking:** on-site. **Terms:** [CP] meal plan available. **Amenities:** high-speed Internet, irons, hair dryers. **Leisure Activities:** exercise room. **Guest Services:** coin laundry. **Cards:** AX, CB, DC, DS, MC, VI.

SOME UNITS

[icons]

VILLA NINA ISLAND INN BED & BREAKFAST
Phone: 772/467-8969

Bed & Breakfast

All Year [CP]   1P: $125-$215   2P: $125-$215
Location: SR A1A (North Hutchinson Island), 4 mi ne of jct US 1. Located across the street from beach. 3851 N A1A 34949. **Facility:** Lovely home. All rooms with private entrance. Smoke free premises. 5 units. 3 one-bedroom standard units. 2 one-bedroom suites. 1 story, exterior corridors. *Bath:* combo or shower only. **Parking:** on-site. **Terms:** check-in 4 pm, age restrictions may apply, 21 day cancellation notice-fee imposed, weekly rates available. **Amenities:** high-speed Internet, voice mail, irons, hair dryers. **Pool(s):** outdoor. **Guest Services:** coin laundry. **Business Services:** fax (fee). **Cards:** DS, MC, VI.

[icons]

--- **WHERE TO DINE** ---

MANGROVE MATTIES
Phone: 772/466-1044

Seafood

Lunch: $7-$15   **Dinner:** $12-$19
Location: SR A1A southbound; 2.3 mi e of jct US 1. 1640 Seaway Dr 34949. **Hours:** 11:30 am-10 pm, Sun from 10:30 am. Closed: 12/25. **Reservations:** suggested. **Features:** Feast on fresh seafood on an open air terrace only 20 feet from the inlet. To continuously offer a good variety, the menu changes daily and features such dishes as crab and shrimp Alfredo and coco shrimp. Be sure to save room for homemade Key lime pie. Casual dress; cocktails. **Parking:** on-site. **Cards:** AX, DC, DS, MC, VI.

[icon]

R. J. GATORS
Phone: 772/461-0068

American

Lunch: $5-$14   **Dinner:** $5-$14
Location: I-95, exit 129, 1.4 mi e. 5000 Okeechobee Rd 34947. **Hours:** 11 am-11 pm. Closed major holidays. **Features:** Multiple televisions and video games are a few ways to keep entertained while you feast on wings, ribs, seafood specials or a specialty sandwich. Casual dress; cocktails. **Parking:** on-site. **Cards:** AX, DS, MC, VI.

FORT WALTON BEACH pop. 19,973

———— WHERE TO STAY ————

BEST WESTERN FORT WALTON BEACHFRONT
HOTEL *Book at aaa.com*   Phone: (850)243-9444

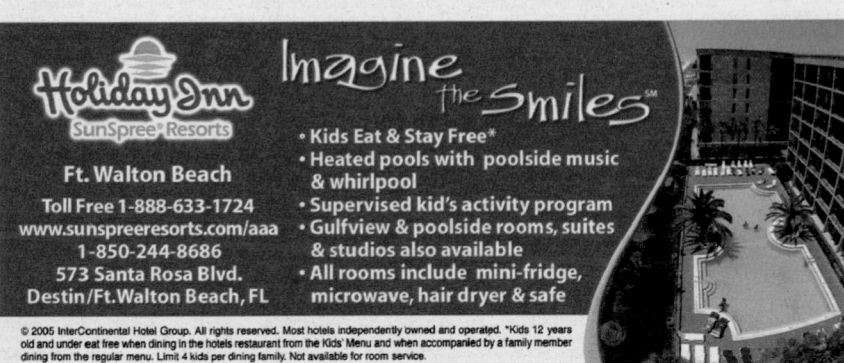

(AAA) (SAVE)   3/18-9/3 [ECP]   1P: $169-$199   2P: $169-$199   XP: $10   F12
◆◆◆◆   2/14-3/17 & 9/4-11/30 [ECP]   1P: $119-$149   2P: $119-$149   XP: $10   F12
          12/1-2/13 [ECP]   1P: $99-$129   2P: $99-$129   XP: $10   F12
Small-scale Hotel **Location:** US 98, just sw on Okaloosa Island. 380 Santa Rosa Blvd 32548. Fax: 850/243-5445. **Facility:** 100 one-bedroom standard units, some with whirlpools. 6 stories, exterior corridors. *Bath:* combo or shower only. **Parking:** on-site. **Terms:** 2-3 night minimum stay - seasonal, package plans. **Amenities:** voice mail, irons, hair dryers. *Some:* high-speed Internet. **Dining:** entertainment. **Pool(s):** heated outdoor. **Leisure Activities:** recreation programs in summer, volleyball. *Fee:* kayak, beach chairs & umbrellas. **Guest Services:** valet and coin laundry. **Business Services:** meeting rooms. **Cards:** AX, CB, DC, DS, JC, MC, VI. **Special Amenities: free expanded continental breakfast and free local telephone calls.**

SOME UNITS

CAYO GRANDE SUITES HOTEL *Book at aaa.com*   Phone: (850)862-7540

(AAA) (SAVE)   5/1-8/31   1P: $115-$215   2P: $115-$215
◆◆◆◆   3/1-4/30   1P: $100-$170   2P: $100-$170
          9/1-11/30   1P: $85-$170   2P: $85-$170
          12/1-2/28   1P: $69-$115   2P: $69-$115
Small-scale Hotel **Location:** US 98, n on SR 393 to SR 189, 1.6 nw on SR 189 to Racetrack Rd, then 0.9 mi e. 214 Racetrack Rd NW 32547. Fax: 850/862-7467. **Facility:** 103 units. 5 one-bedroom standard units. 74 one- and 24 two-bedroom suites, some with kitchens and/or whirlpools. 6 stories, interior/exterior corridors. **Terms:** 3 day cancellation notice, weekly rates available, package plans. **Amenities:** voice mail, irons, hair dryers. *Some:* DVD players, video games, honor bars. **Dining:** 6:30 am-2 pm, Sat & Sun-10:30 am. **Pool(s):** 3 outdoor. **Leisure Activities:** saunas, putting green, tennis court, exercise room. **Guest Services:** valet and coin laundry. **Business Services:** meeting rooms, business center. **Cards:** AX, DC, DS, MC, VI. **Special Amenities: free full breakfast and free newspaper.**

SOME UNITS
FEE

FOUR POINTS HOTEL SHERATON *Book at aaa.com*   Phone: (850)243-8116

◆◆◆◆   5/1-9/3   1P: $175-$295   2P: $175-$295   XP: $10   F18
          3/3-4/30   1P: $145-$220   2P: $145-$220   XP: $10   F18
          9/4-11/30   1P: $100-$180   2P: $100-$180   XP: $10   F18
Large-scale Hotel 12/1-3/2   1P: $100-$145   2P: $100-$145   XP: $10   F18
Location: US 98, 0.7 mi e. 1325 Miracle Strip Pkwy 32548. Fax: 850/244-3064. **Facility:** 216 one-bedroom standard units, some with whirlpools. 2-7 stories, interior/exterior corridors. *Bath:* combo or shower only. **Parking:** on-site. **Amenities:** video games (fee), high-speed Internet, dual phone lines, voice mail, irons, hair dryers. **Pool(s):** 2 heated outdoor. **Leisure Activities:** whirlpools, exercise room, volleyball. **Guest Services:** gift shop, valet and coin laundry. **Business Services:** meeting rooms, business center. **Cards:** AX, CB, DC, DS, MC, VI.

SOME UNITS

HAMPTON INN FORT WALTON BEACH *Book at aaa.com*   Phone: 850/301-0906

◆◆◆◆   All Year [CP]   1P: $79-$229   2P: $79-$229
Small-scale Hotel **Location:** Just w of US 98. 1112 Santa Rosa Blvd 32548. Fax: 850/244-2531. **Facility:** 100 one-bedroom standard units. 2 stories, interior corridors. *Bath:* combo or shower only. **Parking:** on-site. **Terms:** check-in 4 pm, cancellation fee imposed. **Amenities:** video games (fee), voice mail, irons, hair dryers. **Pool(s):** outdoor. **Leisure Activities:** exercise room. **Business Services:** PC. **Cards:** AX, DC, DS, MC, VI.

SOME UNITS

HOLIDAY INN SUNSPREE RESORT   *Book at aaa.com*   **Phone: (850)244-8686**

AAA SAVE

5/21-8/10	1P: $179-$199	2P: $189-$359	XP: $10	F18
3/2-5/20	1P: $149-$169	2P: $149-$199	XP: $10	F18
8/11-11/30	1P: $109-$149	2P: $119-$149	XP: $10	F18
12/1-3/1	1P: $109-$119	2P: $119-$129	XP: $10	F18

Resort
Large-scale Hotel

Location: 1 mi sw of US 98. 573 Santa Rosa Blvd 32548. **Fax:** 850/244-5926. **Facility:** The fun never stops around the pool. Many rooms are open to patios at poolside. 195 units. 151 one-bedroom standard units. 44 one-bedroom suites with kitchens. 3-7 stories, interior/exterior corridors. *Bath:* combo or shower only. **Parking:** on-site. **Terms:** 3 day cancellation notice-fee imposed, package plans. **Amenities:** dual phone lines, voice mail, safes, irons, hair dryers. *Some:* video games. **Dining:** 7 am-2 & 4:30-10 pm, cocktails. **Pool(s):** 2 heated outdoor. **Leisure Activities:** whirlpool, recreation programs, exercise room. *Fee:* game room. **Guest Services:** valet and coin laundry. **Business Services:** meeting rooms. **Cards:** AX, CB, DC, DS, JC, MC, VI. *(See color ad p 450)*

SOME UNITS

(icons) FEE / VCR /

QUALITY INN BAYSIDE   *Book at aaa.com*   **Phone: (850)275-0300**

AAA SAVE

5/19-9/4	1P: $109-$149	2P: $109-$149	
3/13-5/18	1P: $99-$149	2P: $99-$149	
12/1-3/12 & 9/5-11/30	1P: $79-$109	2P: $79-$109	

Small-scale Hotel

Location: 1.5 mi w of Eglin Pkwy on US 98. 322 Miracle Strip Pkwy 32548. **Fax:** 850/275-0315. **Facility:** 100 one-bedroom standard units. 2 stories, interior corridors. *Bath:* combo or shower only. **Parking:** on-site. **Terms:** [CP] & [ECP] meal plans available. **Amenities:** high-speed Internet, voice mail, safes, irons, hair dryers. **Pool(s):** outdoor. **Leisure Activities:** boat dock, exercise room. **Guest Services:** coin laundry. **Business Services:** meeting rooms, PC. **Cards:** AX, DC, DS, MC, VI.

SOME UNITS

(icons) / X /

RAMADA PLAZA BEACH RESORT   *Book at aaa.com*   **Phone: (850)243-9161**

All Year	1P: $158-$175	2P: $158-$175	XP: $20 F18

Large-scale Hotel

Location: US 98, 1 mi e. 1500 Miracle Strip Pkwy SE 32548. **Fax:** 850/243-2391. **Facility:** 335 units. 317 one-bedroom standard units. 18 one-bedroom suites ($240-$300). 6 stories, interior/exterior corridors. **Parking:** on-site. **Terms:** 3 day cancellation notice-fee imposed. **Amenities:** high-speed Internet, voice mail, safes, irons, hair dryers. **Pool(s):** outdoor, heated outdoor, wading. **Leisure Activities:** whirlpool, exercise room. **Guest Services:** gift shop, valet and coin laundry. **Business Services:** conference facilities. **Cards:** AX, CB, DC, DS, MC, VI.

SOME UNITS

(icons) ASK / X /

—— WHERE TO DINE ——

BELLISSIMO   **Lunch: $6-$15**   **Dinner: $6-$15**   **Phone: 850/243-5555**

Italian

Location: 1.6 mi n of US 98. 178 Elgin Pkwy NE 32547. **Hours:** 11 am-3 & 5-9 pm, Fri-10 pm, Sat 5 pm-9 pm. **Features:** The casual and cozy pizza place offers homestyle Italian specialties like baked ziti and lasagna. Casual dress; beer & wine only. **Parking:** street. **Cards:** AX, DS, MC, VI.

LOS RANCHEROS MEXICAN RESTAURANT   **Lunch: $4-$7**   **Dinner: $7-$11**   **Phone: 850/862-2007**

Mexican

Location: 0.5 mi n of US 98. 300 Elgin Pkwy. **Hours:** 11 am-10 pm, Sun noon-9 pm. **Features:** Inexpensive Mexican restaurant; fajitas a specialty. Casual dress; cocktails. **Parking:** on-site. **Cards:** AX, MC, VI.

MULHOLLOWS BISTRO 215   **Lunch: $8-$15**   **Dinner: $15-$20**   **Phone: 850/796-3663**

American

Location: Just w of Elgin Pkwy. 215 Miracle Strip Pkwy 32548. **Hours:** 11 am-9 pm, Fri & Sat-10 pm. **Closed:** Sun. **Reservations:** suggested. **Features:** The eclectic bistro features good service and food made to order. Dressy casual; cocktails. **Parking:** on-site. **Cards:** AX, MC, VI.

OLD BAY STEAMER   **Dinner: $6-$23**   **Phone: 850/664-2795**

Seafood

Location: US 98, just s. 104 Santa Rosa Blvd 32548. **Hours:** 4 pm-9 pm, Fri & Sat-10 pm. **Closed:** 1/1, 4/16, 12/25; also Super Bowl Sun. **Features:** What more can guests ask for than a warm, welcoming atmosphere and fresh, tasty food? A new location hasn't changed this restaurant's good reputation. Casual dress; cocktails. **Parking:** on-site. **Cards:** AX, CB, DC, DS, JC, MC, VI.

PANDORA'S STEAK HOUSE   **Dinner: $13-$22**   **Phone: 850/244-8669**

Steak House

Location: US 98, just s. 1120B Santa Rosa Blvd 32548. **Hours:** 5 pm-10 pm, Fri & Sat-10:30 pm. **Closed:** 11/23, 12/24, 12/25; also Mon 9/1-5/25. **Reservations:** accepted. **Features:** On Okaloosa Island, the restaurant specializes in moderately priced preparations of seafood and steak. Casual dress; cocktails; entertainment. **Parking:** on-site. **Cards:** AX, DC, DS, MC, VI.

PRANZO ITALIAN RISTORANTE   **Dinner: $8-$22**   **Phone: 850/244-9955**

Italian

Location: US 98, just n. 1225 Santa Rosa Blvd 32548. **Hours:** 5 pm-10 pm. **Closed:** 1/1, 11/23, 12/25; also Sun. **Reservations:** accepted. **Features:** The restaurant nurtures a traditional Italian atmosphere, with cozy booths and subdued lighting. Couple this with authentic cuisine, and diners are transported to Italy and its family-oriented culture. Portions are ample and desserts delicious. Casual dress; cocktails. **Parking:** on-site. **Cards:** AX, DS, MC, VI.

FRUITLAND PARK —See Orlando p. 753.

GAINESVILLE pop. 95,447

——— **WHERE TO STAY** ———

BEST WESTERN GATEWAY GRAND   *Book at aaa.com*   Phone: (352)331-3336

(AAA) [SAVE]   All Year   1P: $89-$129   2P: $89-$129
◈◈◈◈   **Location:** I-75, exit 390, just n of SR 222, then just w. 4200 NW 97th Blvd 32606. **Fax:** 352/331-3337. **Facility:** 152
units. 151 one-bedroom standard units, some with whirlpools. 1 two-bedroom suite ($159-$250). 3 stories,
interior corridors. *Bath:* combo or shower only. **Parking:** on-site. **Terms:** check-in 4 pm, [CP] & [ECP] meal
Small-scale Hotel   plans available, small pets only ($15 extra charge). **Amenities:** video games, high-speed Internet, voice
mail, irons, hair dryers. **Dining:** 11 am-10 pm, cocktails. **Pool(s):** outdoor. **Leisure Activities:** whirlpool,
exercise room. *Fee:* golf-18 holes, massage. **Guest Services:** valet and coin laundry, beauty salon. **Business Services:**
conference facilities, fax. **Cards:** AX, CB, DC, DS, MC, VI. **Special Amenities: free expanded continental breakfast and free
local telephone calls.** *(See color ad below)*

SOME UNITS
[S㊉] [✈] [🛏] [¶] [♈] [🚹M] [📠] [🏊] [✕] [🐾] [DATA PORT] [💻] / [✕] [🛋] [🖨] /
            FEE

CABOT LODGE   *Book at aaa.com*   Phone: 352/375-2400
◈◈   Property failed to provide current rates
Location: I-75, exit 384, just e on SR 24. 3726 SW 40th Blvd 32608. **Fax:** 352/335-2321. **Facility:** 208 one-
Small-scale Hotel   bedroom standard units. 3 stories, interior corridors. **Parking:** on-site. **Amenities:** high-speed Internet, voice
mail, irons, hair dryers. **Pool(s):** outdoor. **Leisure Activities:** exercise room. **Guest Services:**
complimentary evening beverages, valet laundry. **Business Services:** meeting rooms, business center.

SOME UNITS
[¶✦] [📠] [🏊] [🐾] [DATA PORT] / [✕] [🛋] [💻] /

COMFORT INN
Book at aaa.com

Phone: (352)373-6500

All Year 1P: $58-$140 2P: $58-$140 XP: $5 F18

Location: I-75, exit 382, 2 mi ne on SR 331, then 1 mi n on US 441. 2435 SW 13th St 32608. Fax: 352/224-3311. **Facility:** 60 one-bedroom standard units, some with kitchens and/or whirlpools. 2 stories, exterior corridors. *Bath:* combo or shower only. **Parking:** on-site. **Terms:** 1-4 night minimum stay. **Amenities:** high-speed Internet, irons, hair dryers. **Pool(s):** outdoor. **Leisure Activities:** whirlpool. **Guest Services:** coin laundry. **Business Services:** fax (fee). **Cards:** AX, CB, DC, DS, JC, MC, VI. **Special Amenities:** free continental breakfast and early check-in/late check-out.

Small-scale Hotel

SOME UNITS

COMFORT INN WEST
Book at aaa.com

Phone: (352)264-1771

All Year 1P: $79-$169 2P: $79-$169 XP: $5 F18

Location: I-75, exit 384, just e, then just n. 3440 SW 40th Blvd 32608. Fax: 352/264-9996. **Facility:** 83 units. 78 one-bedroom standard units, some with whirlpools. 5 one-bedroom suites ($99-$219), some with whirlpools. 4 stories, interior corridors. *Bath:* combo or shower only. **Parking:** on-site. **Terms:** [CP] meal plan available, pets ($10 extra charge). **Amenities:** high-speed Internet, voice mail, safes (fee), irons, hair dryers. **Pool(s):** small outdoor. **Leisure Activities:** exercise room. **Guest Services:** valet and coin laundry. **Business Services:** meeting rooms, fax (fee). **Cards:** AX, DC, DS, JC, MC, VI. **Special Amenities:** free continental breakfast and free local telephone calls.

Small-scale Hotel

SOME UNITS

FEE

COURTYARD BY MARRIOTT
Book at aaa.com

Phone: (352)335-9100

1/1-11/30 1P: $109-$129 2P: $109-$129 XP: $10 F
12/1-12/31 1P: $99-$119 2P: $99-$119 XP: $10 F

Small-scale Hotel **Location:** I-75, exit 384, just e on SR 24. 3700 SW 42nd St 32608. Fax: 352/335-1502. **Facility:** 81 units. 78 one-bedroom standard units. 3 one-bedroom suites ($149-$159). 3 stories, interior corridors. *Bath:* combo or shower only. **Parking:** on-site. **Terms:** cancellation fee imposed, [BP] & [CP] meal plans available, package plans. **Amenities:** high-speed Internet, voice mail, irons, hair dryers. **Pool(s):** heated outdoor. **Leisure Activities:** whirlpool, exercise room. **Guest Services:** valet and coin laundry. **Business Services:** meeting rooms, business center. **Cards:** AX, DC, DS, JC, MC, VI.

SOME UNITS

ECONO LODGE UNIVERSITY
Book at aaa.com

Phone: (352)373-7816

2/1-4/30 & 8/1-11/30 1P: $43-$109 2P: $47-$119 XP: $5 F15
5/1-7/31 1P: $39-$55 2P: $44-$65 XP: $5 F15
12/1-1/31 1P: $39-$55 2P: $43-$60 XP: $5 F15

Motel **Location:** I-75, exit 382, 2 mi e on SR 331, then 0.5 mi n on US 441. 2649 SW 13th St 32608. Fax: 352/372-9099. **Facility:** 53 one-bedroom standard units. 2 stories, exterior corridors. **Parking:** on-site. **Terms:** 3 day cancellation notice, pets ($10 extra charge). **Pool(s):** outdoor. **Cards:** AX, DC, DS, MC, VI. **Special Amenities:** free local telephone calls and free newspaper.

SOME UNITS

FEE

EXTENDED STAYAMERICA
Book at aaa.com

Phone: (352)375-0073

All Year 1P: $56-$71 2P: $61-$86 XP: $5 F12

Location: I-75, exit 384, just e. 3600 SW 42nd St 32608. Fax: 352/375-0960. **Facility:** 120 one-bedroom standard units with efficiencies. 3 stories, exterior corridors. *Bath:* combo or shower only. **Parking:** on-site. *Small-scale Hotel* **Terms:** weekly rates available, pets ($25 extra charge). **Amenities:** voice mail. **Guest Services:** coin laundry. **Business Services:** fax (fee). **Cards:** AX, CB, DC, DS, MC, VI.

SOME UNITS

FEE

HAMPTON INN
Book at aaa.com

Phone: (352)371-4171

All Year [ECP] 1P: $97-$165 2P: $97-$165

Location: I-75, exit 384, just e, then s. 4225 SW 40th Blvd 32608. Fax: 352/371-4234. **Facility:** 105 units. 96 one-bedroom standard units. 9 one-bedroom suites with whirlpools. 4 stories, interior/exterior corridors. *Bath:* combo or shower only. **Parking:** on-site. **Amenities:** high-speed Internet, voice mail, irons, hair dryers. *Small-scale Hotel* **Pool(s):** heated outdoor. **Leisure Activities:** exercise room. **Guest Services:** valet laundry. **Business Services:** meeting rooms, fax (fee). **Cards:** AX, CB, DC, DS, JC, MC, VI.

SOME UNITS

HILTON UNIVERSITY OF FLORIDA CONFERENCE
CENTER GAINESVILLE
Book at aaa.com

Phone: (352)371-3600

All Year 1P: $99-$179 2P: $99-$179 XP: $15 F17

Location: I-75, exit 384, 0.9 mi e on SR 24, then 0.7 mi n on SR 121; in University of Florida. 1714 SW 34th St 32607. Fax: 352/371-0306. **Facility:** 246 units. 245 one-bedroom standard units. 1 one-bedroom suite. 7 stories, interior corridors. *Bath:* combo or shower only. **Parking:** on-site. **Terms:** check-in 4 pm, package plans. *Large-scale Hotel* **Amenities:** video games, high-speed Internet, dual phone lines, voice mail, irons, hair dryers. **Pool(s):** outdoor. **Leisure Activities:** whirlpool, exercise room. **Guest Services:** valet laundry. **Business Services:** meeting rooms, business center. **Cards:** AX, CB, DC, DS, JC, MC, VI.

SOME UNITS

FEE FEE

HOLIDAY INN EXPRESS
Phone: (352)376-0004

All Year 1P: $82-$154 2P: $87-$189 XP: $5 F18

Location: I-75, exit 384, just w; behind Cracker Barrel Restaurant. 3905 SW 43rd St 32608. Fax: 352/376-1979. **Facility:** 115 units. 111 one-bedroom standard units, some with whirlpools. 4 one-bedroom suites with whirlpools, some with kitchens. 4 stories, interior corridors. *Bath:* combo or shower only. **Parking:** on-site. *Small-scale Hotel* **Terms:** [ECP] meal plan available, small pets only ($5-$10 extra charge, in designated units). **Amenities:** video games, dual phone lines, voice mail, irons, hair dryers. **Pool(s):** heated outdoor. **Leisure Activities:** exercise room. **Guest Services:** valet and coin laundry. **Business Services:** meeting rooms, fax. **Cards:** AX, DC, DS, MC, VI. **Special Amenities:** free expanded continental breakfast.

SOME UNITS

FEE

HOLIDAY INN UNIVERSITY CENTER *Book at aaa.com*   **Phone:** (352)376-1661

 All Year   1P: $107-$167   2P: $107-$167

Location: Jct US 441/SR 24; downtown; adjacent to University of Florida. 1250 W University Ave 32601. **Fax:** 352/336-8717. **Facility:** 166 one-bedroom standard units. 6 stories, interior corridors. *Bath:* combo or shower only. **Parking:** on-site. **Terms:** [AP] meal plan available, 3% service charge. **Amenities:** video games, Small-scale Hotel high-speed Internet, voice mail, irons, hair dryers. **Dining:** 24 hours. **Pool(s):** outdoor. **Leisure Activities:** exercise room. **Guest Services:** valet laundry, area transportation-hospital. **Business Services:** meeting rooms, fax. **Cards:** AX, CB, DC, DS, JC, MC, VI. **Special Amenities:** free newspaper and early check-in/late check-out.

SOME UNITS

HOLIDAY INN-WEST   *Book at aaa.com*   **Phone:** 352/332-7500

 12/1-4/30   1P: $89-$129   2P: $89-$129   XP: $10

5/1-11/30   1P: $79-$119   2P: $79-$119   XP: $10

Location: I-75, exit 387, just w. 7417 Newberry Rd 32605. **Fax:** 352/332-0487. **Facility:** 152 units. 150 one-bedroom standard units. 2 one-bedroom suites. 2 stories, exterior corridors. **Parking:** on-site. **Amenities:** video games, Small-scale Hotel high-speed Internet, voice mail, irons, hair dryers. **Dining:** 6 am-2 & 5-10 pm, cocktails. **Pool(s):** outdoor, heated outdoor, wading. **Leisure Activities:** exercise room. **Guest Services:** valet and coin laundry, area transportation-hospital. **Business Services:** conference facilities, fax (fee). **Cards:** AX, CB, DC, DS, JC, MC, VI. **Special Amenities:** free newspaper. *(See color ad below)*

SOME UNITS

LA QUINTA INN GAINESVILLE *Book at aaa.com*   Phone: (352)332-6466

3/1-8/31	1P: $79-$99	2P: $86-$106	XP: $7 F18
12/1-2/28 & 9/1-11/30	1P: $73-$93	2P: $80-$100	XP: $7 F18

Small-scale Hotel   **Location:** I-75, exit 387, just e, then just n. Located behind the Red Lobster Restaurant. 920 NW 69th Terrace 32605. **Fax:** 352/332-7074. **Facility:** 133 one-bedroom standard units. 3-4 stories, exterior corridors. **Parking:** on-site. **Terms:** [ECP] meal plan available, small pets only. **Amenities:** video games, voice mail, irons, hair dryers. **Pool(s):** heated outdoor. **Business Services:** meeting rooms, fax. **Cards:** AX, CB, DC, DS, MC, VI.

SOME UNITS

MOTEL 6 #414   *Book at aaa.com*   Phone: 352/373-1604

2/7-4/28	1P: $37-$47	2P: $43-$53	XP: $3 F17
12/1-2/6 & 4/29-11/30	1P: $35-$45	2P: $41-$51	XP: $3 F17

Small-scale Hotel   **Location:** I-75, exit 384, just e. 4000 SW 40th Blvd 32608. **Fax:** 352/335-8314. **Facility:** 121 one-bedroom standard units. 2 stories, exterior corridors. *Bath:* combo or shower only. **Parking:** on-site. **Terms:** small pets only. **Pool(s):** outdoor. **Guest Services:** coin laundry. **Cards:** AX, CB, DC, DS, MC, VI.

SOME UNITS

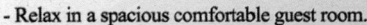 

PARAMOUNT PLAZA HOTEL & SUITES   *Book at aaa.com*

Phone: (352)377-4000

▼▼▼▼ All Year   1P: $89-$229   XP: $10   F

Small-scale Hotel   **Location:** I-75, exit 382, 2 mi ne on SR 331, then 0.8 mi n on US 441. 2900 SW 13th St 32608. Fax: 352/377-7766. **Facility:** 197 units. 191 one-bedroom standard units. 6 one-bedroom suites. 4 stories, interior corridors. *Bath:* combo or shower only. **Parking:** on-site. **Terms:** 3 day cancellation notice, weekly rates available, $3 service charge. **Amenities:** video games, dual phone lines, voice mail, safes, irons, hair dryers. *Some:* fax. **Pool(s):** heated outdoor. **Leisure Activities:** exercise room. **Guest Services:** valet and coin laundry, area transportation. **Business Services:** conference facilities. *Fee:* PC, fax. **Cards:** AX, MC, VI. *(See color ad p 455)*

SOME UNITS

(ASK) (S D) (+) (〒) (&) (〰) (⊇) (♨) (DATA PORT) (⊑) / (✕) (⬛) (⊡) /
FEE

QUALITY INN   *Book at aaa.com*

Phone: (352)378-2405

▼▼▼ All Year [CP]   1P: $54-$131   2P: $54-$131   XP: $5   F17

Small-scale Hotel   **Location:** I-75, exit 382, just w. 3455 SW Williston Rd 32608. Fax: 352/381-8742. **Facility:** 88 one-bedroom standard units. 2 stories, interior/exterior corridors. *Bath:* combo or shower only. **Parking:** on-site. **Terms:** cancellation fee imposed, pets ($50 deposit). **Amenities:** voice mail, irons, hair dryers. **Pool(s):** outdoor. **Leisure Activities:** exercise room. **Business Services:** meeting rooms, fax (fee). **Cards:** AX, CB, DC, DS, JC, MC, VI.

SOME UNITS

(ASK) (S D) (🛏) (〒+) (⊇) (♨) (DATA PORT) (⊑) / (✕) (⬛) (⊡) /
FEE

RAMADA LIMITED   *Book at aaa.com*

Phone: (352)332-8001

(AAA) (SAVE)   12/1-4/30   1P: $79-$109   2P: $79-$109   XP: $10   F18
▼▼▼   5/1-11/30   1P: $69-$99   2P: $69-$99   XP: $10   F18

Small-scale Hotel   **Location:** I-75, exit 387, just w. 7413 W Newberry Rd 32605. **Facility:** 119 units. 118 one-bedroom standard units. 1 one-bedroom suite. 2 stories, exterior corridors. *Bath:* combo or shower only. **Parking:** on-site. **Terms:** small pets only ($10 extra charge). **Amenities:** video games, high-speed Internet (fee), voice mail, irons, hair dryers. **Dining:** 6 am-2 & 5-10 pm, cocktails. **Pool(s):** outdoor, heated outdoor, wading. **Leisure Activities:** exercise room. **Guest Services:** valet and coin laundry, area transportation-hospital. **Business Services:** meeting rooms, fax (fee). **Cards:** AX, CB, DC, DS, JC, MC, VI. **Special Amenities:** free room upgrade and preferred room (each subject to availability with advance reservations).** *(See color ad p 454)*

SOME UNITS

(S D) (+) (🛏) (〒) (Y) (⊇) (♨) (DATA PORT) (⊑) / (✕) (⬛) (⊡) /
FEE

RED ROOF INN-GAINESVILLE   *Book at aaa.com*

Phone: (352)336-3311

▼▼▼ ▼▼▼   1/22-4/8   1P: $49-$59   2P: $56-$65   XP: $6   F18
  1/1-1/21 & 4/9-11/30   1P: $43-$59   2P: $49-$65   XP: $6   F18
Small-scale Hotel   12/1-12/31   1P: $44-$55   2P: $50-$61   XP: $6   F18

Location: I-75, exit 384, just e. 3500 SW 42nd St 32608. Fax: 352/336-7855. **Facility:** 129 units. 125 one-bedroom standard units. 4 one-bedroom suites. 4 stories, interior corridors. *Bath:* combo or shower only. **Parking:** on-site. **Amenities:** video games, voice mail. **Pool(s):** heated outdoor. **Guest Services:** coin laundry. **Business Services:** fax. **Cards:** AX, CB, DC, DS, MC, VI.

SOME UNITS

(🛏) (〒+) (&M) (&) (⊘) (⊇) (♨) (DATA PORT) / (✕) (⬛) (⊡) /

SWEETWATER BRANCH INN BED & BREAKFAST

Phone: 352/373-6760

(AAA) (SAVE)   All Year   1P: $85-$200   2P: $85-$200   XP: $25   D8
▼▼▼▼   **Location:** 1.3 mi e of the University on SR 26; 7.3 mi e of I-75, exit 387. Located in a light-business residential area. 625 E University Ave 32601. Fax: 352/371-3771. **Facility:** On landscaped grounds close to the center of town, this B&B is actually two 1895 houses, each with guest rooms decorated in period. Designated smoking Bed & Breakfast   area. 13 units. 9 one-bedroom standard units, some with whirlpools. 3 one-bedroom suites. 1 cottage ($75). 2-3 stories (no elevator), interior corridors. **Parking:** on-site. **Terms:** 7 day cancellation notice-fee imposed, weekly rates available. **Amenities:** high-speed Internet, voice mail, irons, hair dryers. *Some:* CD players. **Guest Services:** complimentary evening beverages. **Business Services:** meeting rooms, fax. **Cards:** AX, MC, VI. **Special Amenities:** free full breakfast and free local telephone calls.

SOME UNITS

(S D) (+) (✕) (DATA PORT) / (VCR) (⬛) (⊡) (⊑) /
FEE

─────── **WHERE TO DINE** ───────

43RD ST DELI AND BREAKFAST HOUSE

Lunch: $4-$9   **Phone:** 352/373-5656

▼▼ ▼▼   **Location:** I-75, exit 382, just w. 3483 SW Williston Rd 32603. **Hours:** 7 am-3 pm, Sun 8 am-2 pm. **Features:** You'll find good portions of fresh food made to order with plenty of side items to choose from American   inside this newly renovated building with country style decor. Casual dress. **Parking:** on-site. **Cards:** AX, DS, MC, VI.

AMELIA'S

Lunch: $9-$15   **Dinner:** $9-$19   **Phone:** 352/373-1919

▼▼ ▼▼   **Location:** Just s on SR 329, just e; in Sun Centre Mall; entrance through courtyard. 235 S Main St 32601. **Hours:** 5 pm-9:30 pm, Thurs also 11:30 am-2:30 pm, Fri 11:30 am-2:30 & 5-10:30 pm, Sat 5 pm-10:30 pm, Sun 5 pm-Italian   8:30 pm. Closed major holidays. **Reservations:** suggested, weekends. **Features:** In the historic district behind the Hippodrome Theatre is this restaurant with two cozy dining rooms. A large, covered patio runs the width of the restaurant and is accessed from the courtyard around the theater. Olive oil complements the warm loaf of Italian bread and crisp, green salad. Chicken, veal and fish, prepared in a variety of Italian and other European ways, are available. Servers are friendly. Casual dress; cocktails. **Parking:** street. **Cards:** AX, DC, MC, VI.

BALLYHOO GRILL
American

Lunch: $7-$12   **Dinner:** $7-$20   **Phone:** 352/373-0059
Location: Just e of jct NW 43rd St. 3700 W University Ave 32607. **Hours:** 11 am-10 pm, Fri & Sat-11 pm. Closed: 1/1, 11/23, 12/25. **Features:** The eatery offers fresh seafood served in a lively, nautical-themed atmosphere. Casual dress; cocktails. **Parking:** on-site. **Cards:** AX, DC, DS, MC, VI.

BENTO CAFE
Japanese

Lunch: $6-$9   **Dinner:** $6-$9   **Phone:** 352/377-8686
Location: I-75, exit 387, 2.4 mi e on SR 26; in Plaza Royale. 3832 W Newberry Rd 32607. **Hours:** 11 am-10:30 pm, Fri & Sat-11 pm. Closed major holidays. **Features:** Lighted tables are the highlight of the contemporary decor at this restaurant, where your favorite Pan-Asian cuisine is served up at the counter in a very casual setting. Casual dress. **Parking:** on-site. **Cards:** AX, DS, MC, VI.

BONEFISH GRILL
Seafood
DS, JC, MC, VI.

Dinner: $13-$21   **Phone:** 352/377-8383
Location: I-75, exit 384, just e. 3237 SW 35th Blvd 32608. **Hours:** 4 pm-10:30 pm, Fri & Sat-11:30 pm, Sun 3 pm-10 pm. **Features:** Fresh fish is the specialty of the house and the menu and nightly specials offer a variety from which to choose. The food is well-prepared and cooked to perfection. Service is casual in nature and staff are skilled and attentive. Dressy casual; cocktails. **Parking:** on-site. **Cards:** AX, CB, DC,

BONO'S REAL PIT BAR-B-Q
Barbecue

Lunch: $5-$9   **Dinner:** $5-$16   **Phone:** 352/331-3112
Location: I-75, exit 387, just e. 6760 Newberry Rd 32605. **Hours:** 11 am-10 pm. Closed: 1/1, 12/25. **Features:** Large portions of your favorite slow-cooked barbecue and side items are served in a very casual setting, or they can also be purchased to take home. Casual dress; beer only. **Parking:** on-site. **Cards:** AX, MC, VI.

CHICKEN KITCHEN
American

Lunch: $5-$9   **Dinner:** $5-$9   **Phone:** 352/377-5776
Location: Just s of jct Archer Rd. 3333 SW 34th St 32608. **Hours:** 11 am-10 pm, Sun-9 pm. Closed major holidays. **Features:** The eatery offers quick-serve chicken with several recipe combinations to choose from. Casual dress. **Parking:** on-site. **Cards:** AX, DC, MC, VI.

CHUTNEES
Indian

Lunch: $10-$22   **Dinner:** $13-$30   **Phone:** 352/333-1133
Location: I-75, exit 390, just w on 39th Ave. 3833 NW 97th Blvd 32606. **Hours:** 11:30 am-3 & 5-10 pm. Closed: 1/1, 12/25. **Reservations:** accepted. **Features:** Dressy casual; beer & wine only. **Parking:** on-site. **Cards:** AX, MC, VI.

CRISPERS
American

Lunch: $6-$9   **Dinner:** $6-$9   **Phone:** 352/335-6150
Location: Jct Archer Rd, just s. 3102 SW 34th St 32608. **Hours:** 10:30 am-10 pm, Sun from 11 am. **Features:** The quick-serve eatery offers great salads, soups and sandwiches; the single portions are a good size and they have larger portions for families or parties. Casual dress. **Parking:** on-site. **Cards:** AX, DS, MC, VI.

DINNER
Italian

Dinner: $10-$22   **Phone:** 352/378-7850
Location: Just s of University Ave; downtown. 11 SE 1st Ave 32601. **Hours:** 6 pm-10 pm, Fri & Sat-11 pm. Closed: Sun & Mon. **Reservations:** accepted. **Features:** The downtown locale of this upscale eatery adds to the ambience. Seating is limited, but the Mediterranean-inspired cuisine will make up for the wait. Dressy casual; cocktails. **Parking:** street. **Cards:** AX, DS, MC, VI.

EMILIANO'S CAFE
Italian
Parking: street. **Cards:** AX, DS, MC, VI.

Lunch: $7-$10   **Dinner:** $11-$22   **Phone:** 352/375-7381
Location: Downtown. 7 SE 1st Ave 32601. **Hours:** 11:30 am-4 & 5:30-10 pm, Fri & Sat-11 pm, Sun 5:30 pm-9 pm. Closed: 11/23, 12/25; also Mon. **Reservations:** accepted. **Features:** Patrons can gaze at passersby from the cozy patio while awaiting eclectic Spanish selections prepared with a Caribbean influence. Among offerings are puerco calypso, pollo Caribeno and homemade carrot cake. Casual dress; beer & wine only.

IVEY'S GRILL
American

Lunch: $5-$10   **Dinner:** $7-$15   **Phone:** 352/371-4839
Location: Jct 34th St. 3303 W University Ave 32608. **Hours:** 8:30 am-3 & 5-9 pm, Fri & Sat-10 pm, Sun-3 pm. Closed major holidays; also Mon. **Features:** Unique menu selections and daily creations will tempt you to step outside of your box. Many locals and college students frequent this quaint eatery. Casual dress; beer & wine only. **Parking:** on-site. **Cards:** AX, MC, VI.

LAS MARGARITAS MEXICAN RESTAURANT & CANTINA
Mexican

Lunch: $4-$7   **Dinner:** $7-$14   **Phone:** 352/374-6699
Location: From Newberry Rd, 2.5 mi n on NW 43rd St, just w. 4401 NW 25th Pl 32606. **Hours:** 11 am-10 pm, Sun noon-9 pm. Closed: 11/23, 12/25. **Reservations:** accepted, except Fri. **Features:** The extensive menu includes tacos, burritos, combination platters, vegetarian selections and children's choices. Casual dress; cocktails. **Parking:** on-site. **Cards:** AX, DS, MC, VI.

THE MELTING POT
Fondue

Dinner: $15-$30   **Phone:** 352/372-5623
Location: Downtown. 418 E University 32601. **Hours:** 5:30 pm-10 pm, Fri & Sat-11 pm. Closed major holidays. **Reservations:** suggested. **Features:** Enjoy fondue prepared right at your table at this restaurant, which is good for group fun or a romantic night out for couples. Dressy casual; cocktails. **Parking:** on-site. **Cards:** AX, CB, DC, DS, JC, MC, VI.

MI APA LATIN CAFE
Latino

Lunch: $4-$7   **Dinner:** $4-$7   **Phone:** 352/376-7020
Location: Just s of Newberry Rd/University Ave. 114 SW 34th St 32607. **Hours:** 7 am-9 pm, Sun from 11 am. Closed major holidays. **Features:** The local favorite offers Cuban cuisine at its best and is often bustling with locals and college students alike. Menu specialties include roast pork sandwich, Cuban burger and grilled chicken steak. Casual dress. **Parking:** on-site. **Cards:** AX, CB, DC, DS, JC, MC, VI.

MILDRED'S BIG CITY FOOD   *Menu on aaa.com*   **Lunch:** $6-$8   **Dinner:** $13-$29   **Phone:** 352/371-1711
American
Location: I-75, exit 387, 3 mi e on SR 26; at west end of Westgate Regency Shopping Center. 3445 W University Ave 32607. **Hours:** 11 am-9 pm, Fri & Sat-10 pm. Closed: 11/23, 12/25; also Sun. **Reservations:** suggested, for dinner. **Features:** By day, this place is a coffee shop serving estate coffees with unusual sandwiches, hummus, roast tomato and more standard fare. By night, it's a trendy bistro with sophisticated fare. Alligator fritters and roast butternut and scallop bisque lead to a baby green salad with blue cheese and spiced walnuts. Entrees include pecan-crusted chicken with brandied sweet potatoes, as well as varied beef, lamb and seafood choices. To ensure freshness, the menu changes almost daily. Casual dress; cocktails. **Parking:** on-site. **Cards:** AX, DS, MC, VI.

MR HAN'S RESTAURANT   **Lunch:** $5-$12   **Dinner:** $10-$26   **Phone:** 352/331-6400
Chinese
Location: I-75, exit 387, just e, then just n on NW 69th Terrace. 6944 NW 10th Pl 32605. **Hours:** 11:30 am-9 pm. **Features:** This is one of Gainesville's long-standing restaurants and is a local favorite. Traditional Chinese cuisine is served in a sophisticated atmosphere. Casual dress; cocktails. **Parking:** on-site. **Cards:** AX, MC, VI.

MORAGHOT THAI RESTAURANT   **Lunch:** $6-$15   **Dinner:** $6-$22   **Phone:** 352/336-9097
Thai
Location: I-75, exit 390, 2.5 mi e. 4780 NW 39th Ave 32606. **Hours:** 11:30 am-2:30 & 5-10 pm, Fri & Sat-11 pm. **Features:** Traditional Thai recipes make up a well rounded menu. The selections are well prepared and presented in a casual setting that includes televisions mounted to the walls. Sushi bar and vegetarian entrees also available. Casual dress; cocktails. **Parking:** on-site. **Cards:** AX, MC, VI.

POMODORO CAFE   **Lunch:** $8-$11   **Dinner:** $7-$14   **Phone:** 352/380-9886
Italian
Location: I-75, exit 390, just e. 9200 NW 39th Ave, Suite 100 32606. **Hours:** 11 am-10 pm. Closed: 12/25; also 11/25. **Reservations:** accepted. **Features:** Colorful murals adorn the walls and help create a lively, festive feeling. The menu is steeped in Italian tradition, with offerings of bruschetta, cappellini Francesco and tiramisu. Casual dress; beer & wine only. **Parking:** on-site. **Cards:** AX, DS, MC, VI.

RAFFERTY'S RESTAURANT AND BAR   **Lunch:** $6-$12   **Dinner:** $6-$12   **Phone:** 352/374-0675
American
Location: Jct 34th St. 3410 SW Archer Rd 32606. **Hours:** 11 am-10 pm, Fri & Sat-11 pm. Closed major holidays. **Features:** This is a family-style restaurant. Casual dress; cocktails. **Parking:** on-site. **Cards:** AX, DC, DS, MC, VI.

RIGATELLI'S ITALIAN GRILL   **Lunch:** $4-$8   **Dinner:** $8-$17   **Phone:** 352/331-7226
Italian
Location: I-75, exit 387, just e; in The Oaks Mall. 6233 W Newberry Rd 32606. **Hours:** 11 am-10 pm. Closed: 11/23, 12/25. **Reservations:** accepted. **Features:** The Italian restaurant serves baked pasta dishes as well as double cut pork chops, scampi and everyone's favorite: pizza. Casual dress; cocktails. **Parking:** on-site. **Cards:** AX, CB, DC, DS, JC, MC, VI.

SONNY'S REAL PIT BBQ   **Lunch:** $6-$9   **Dinner:** $6-$15   **Phone:** 352/378-7881
Barbecue
Location: I-75, exit 382, just e. 2700 N Waldo Rd 32609. **Hours:** 11:30 am-9:30 pm. **Features:** The country themed restaurant offers slow-cooked barbecue, daily all-you-can-eat specials and a salad bar. Casual dress; beer only. **Parking:** on-site. **Cards:** AX, DS, MC, VI.

SONNY'S REAL PIT BBQ   **Lunch:** $6-$9   **Dinner:** $6-$15   **Phone:** 352/375-6667
Barbecue
Location: I-75, exit 384, 0.4 mi e. 3635 SW Archer Rd 32606. **Hours:** 11 am-9:30 pm. **Features:** The country themed restaurant offers slow-cooked barbecue, daily all-you-can-eat specials and a salad bar. Casual dress. **Parking:** on-site. **Cards:** AX, DS, MC, VI.

THE SOVEREIGN RESTAURANT   **Dinner:** $18-$27   **Phone:** 352/378-6307
Continental
Location: Just e of SR 329. 12 SE 2nd Ave 32601. **Hours:** 5:30 pm-10 pm. Closed major holidays; also Sun. **Reservations:** suggested. **Features:** Just east of Main Street in a converted turn-of-the-20th-century carriage house, this restaurant almost has become a Gainesville institution. The menu borrows from Europe in style of preparation. Specialties are aged beef and veal on a menu that also includes lamb, chicken, fish and seafood dishes, as well as a few vegetarian choices and even some game. Service has some formal touches but is friendly and not at all stuffy. The owner/chef has been in this location since 1976. Dressy casual; cocktails. **Parking:** valet. **Cards:** AX, CB, DC, DS, MC, VI.

STEVE'S CAFE AMERICAIN   **Dinner:** $15-$26   **Phone:** 352/377-9337
American
Location: Just w of Main St (SR 329) on SR 26. 12 W University Ave 32601. **Hours:** 5 pm-10 pm. Closed major holidays. **Reservations:** accepted. **Features:** In a storefront at the center of downtown, the restaurant is convenient to theater and other nightlife, just a short distance from the University of Florida campus. The kitchen—in the center of the dining room—hides nothing. As the name implies, the food is American with preparation styles borrowed from the classic French. The menu changes seasonally. Desserts, including ice creams, are made on site and are worth saving room for. Prix fixe menus are also available. Casual dress; cocktails. **Parking:** street. **Cards:** AX, DC, DS, MC, VI.

STONEWOOD TAVERN & GRILL   **Dinner:** $10-$28   **Phone:** 352/379-5982
Steak & Seafood
Location: Just e of jct NW 43rd St. 3812 Newberry Rd 32607. **Hours:** 5 pm-10 pm, Fri & Sat 4 pm-11 pm, Sun noon-9 pm. Closed: 11/23, 12/25. **Reservations:** accepted. **Features:** Well-prepared dishes range from filet mignon to rack of lamb to grilled scallops. The dining room is comfortably appointed, with the decor reflecting a beautiful use of stone, wood and earth tones. Servers are knowledgeable and attentive. Dressy casual; cocktails. **Parking:** on-site. **Cards:** AX, CB, DC, DS, JC, MC, VI.

——— The following restaurants have not been evaluated by AAA ———
but are listed for your information only.

GATORS DOCKSIDE   Phone: 352/338-4445
[fyi]   Not evaluated. **Location:** 3842 Newberry Rd 32603. **Features:** Known for wings, ribs and seafood, this sports
          bar chain offers casual food in a fun setting.

WING ZONE   Phone: 352/377-2473
[fyi]   Not evaluated. **Location:** 923 University Ave 32601. **Features:** The eatery offers a casual, sports bar style
          atmosphere with many choices of wing sauces.

GREEN COVE SPRINGS —See Jacksonville p. 496.

GULF BREEZE pop. 5,665

——— WHERE TO DINE ———

BILLY-BOB'S BEACH BARBECUE   **Lunch:** $7-$16   **Dinner:** $7-$16   **Phone:** 850/934-2999
◆◆   **Location:** On US 98, 1.5 mi e of Pensacola Bay Bridge. 911 Gulf Breeze Pkwy 32561. **Hours:** 11 am-9 pm. Closed:
Barbecue   11/23, 12/25. **Features:** With the wood tables, chairs and benches, this eatery is like picnicking indoors. The
            owner smokes his own meats to perfection; guests can add sauce or simply enjoy the flavor of the meat.
            Tempting homemade desserts are offered, such as the Pig Puddin' (pecan pie combined with a whipped
cream mixture). Casual dress; beer only. **Parking:** on-site. **Cards:** AX, DS, MC, VI.   [&M]

CREAMERY CAFE   **Lunch:** $7-$9   **Dinner:** $12-$15   **Phone:** 850/932-1525
◆◆ ◆◆   **Location:** US 98; at Gulf Breeze Shopping Center. 348 Gulf Breeze Pkwy 32561. **Hours:** 8 am-9 pm. Closed:
Regional German   11/23, 12/25. **Reservations:** accepted. **Features:** Stop on the way to or from the coast at this family-run
            cafe. As the name so aptly describes, creamy delicious ice cream is a must at this delightful eatery. This is
and entrees. A complimentary glass of wine is served with a dinner entree. Casual dress; beer & wine only. **Parking:** on-site.
Cards: AX, DS, MC, VI.

GULFPORT —See Tampa Bay p. 1023.

HAINES CITY pop. 13,174

——— WHERE TO STAY ———

BEST WESTERN LAKE HAMILTON   *Book at aaa.com*   **Phone:** (863)421-6929
(AAA) [SAVE]   2/10-4/30 [CP]   1P: $81-$87   2P: $81-$87   XP: $7   F13
               12/1-12/31 [CP]   1P: $74-$79   2P: $74-$79   XP: $7   F13
◆◆◆◆   1/1-2/9 & 5/1-11/30 [CP]   1P: $59-$79   2P: $59-$79   XP: $7   F13
Motel   **Location:** On US 27, just s of jct SR 544; 2 mi s of jct US 17-92. 605 B Moore Rd 33844. **Fax:** 863/422-0409.
               Facility: 50 units. 45 one-bedroom standard units. 5 one-bedroom suites ($84-$94). 1 story, exterior
               corridors. **Parking:** on-site. **Terms:** pets ($5 deposit). **Amenities:** irons, hair dryers. *Some:* high-speed
Internet. **Pool(s):** heated outdoor. **Leisure Activities:** lighted tennis court, shuffleboard. **Guest Services:** coin laundry.
Business Services: meeting rooms, fax (fee). **Cards:** AX, CB, DC, DS, JC, MC, VI. **Special Amenities: free continental
breakfast and free local telephone calls.**
                                                                      SOME UNITS
         [S/D] [🛏] [&M] [🍴] [📷] [DATA PORT] [☕] / [⊠] [🛡] [🖥] /
                   FEE   FEE FEE

HOWARD JOHNSON INN   *Book at aaa.com*   **Phone:** 863/422-8621
(AAA) [SAVE]   2/1-5/1   1P: $69-$99   2P: $69-$99   XP: $5   F17
               5/2-11/30   1P: $55-$99   2P: $59-$99   XP: $5   F17
◆◆ ◆◆   12/1-1/31   1P: $55-$89   2P: $59-$89   XP: $5   F17
Motel   **Location:** On US 27, 1.8 mi s of jct US 17-92. 33224 Hwy 27 S 33844. **Fax:** 863/421-4745. **Facility:** 120 one-
               bedroom standard units. 2 stories, exterior corridors. **Parking:** on-site. **Terms:** 1-4 night minimum stay -
               seasonal, cancellation fee imposed, pets ($10 fee). **Dining:** 7 am-9 pm. **Pool(s):** outdoor. **Guest Services:**
coin laundry. **Business Services:** meeting rooms, fax (fee). **Cards:** AX, CB, DC, DS, JC, MC, VI. **Special Amenities: free
newspaper.**
                                                                      SOME UNITS
         [🛏] [🍴] [📶] [🍴] [📷] [DATA PORT] [☕] / [⊠] [🛡] [🖥] /
                   FEE

——— WHERE TO DINE ———

FISH TALES   **Lunch:** $6-$8   **Dinner:** $9-$18   **Phone:** 863/421-3474
◆◆ ◆◆   **Location:** On US 27, 1 mi n of US 17. 35510 US Hwy 27 33844. **Hours:** 11 am-9 pm. Closed: 11/23, 12/25.
Seafood   **Reservations:** accepted. **Features:** The fun family restaurant serves Southern-style seafood, steak and
            grits. House specials include jumbo butterfly shrimp, coconut-fried shrimp and fresh catfish. Desserts, which
            are homemade daily, are displayed in the restaurant entry area. Don't pass up the deep-fried Twinkies.
Casual dress; cocktails. **Parking:** on-site. **Cards:** AX, DS, MC, VI.   [Y]

HALLANDALE BEACH —See Fort Lauderdale p. 404.

HAVANA pop. 1,713

──────── **WHERE TO DINE** ────────

NICHOLSON FARMHOUSE   **Dinner:** $10-$26   **Phone:** 850/539-5931

Steak House
Location: On SR 12, 3.5 mi w of US 27. 200 Coca Cola Ave (SR 12) 32333. **Hours:** 4 pm-10 pm. Closed major holidays; also Sun & Mon. **Reservations:** suggested. **Features:** This complex of five historic houses on 40 rustic acres is an unusual location in which to enjoy monstrous portions of quality beef, well-aged and cooked to order. Down-to-earth servers are attentive and friendly. Save room for strawberry shortcake. Casual dress. **Parking:** on-site. **Cards:** AX, DS, MC, VI. **Historic**

HEATHROW —See Orlando p. 754.

HERNANDO pop. 8,253

──────── **WHERE TO STAY** ────────

BEST WESTERN CITRUS HILLS LODGE   *Book at aaa.com*   **Phone:** (352)527-0015
1/1-4/30	1P: $93-$103	2P: $93-$103	XP: $7	F
12/1-12/31 & 11/1-11/30	1P: $88-$98	2P: $88-$98	XP: $7	F
5/1-10/31	1P: $78-$88	2P: $78-$88	XP: $7	F

Small-scale Hotel **Location:** CR 486 at Citrus Hills Blvd, 3.3 mi w of US 41. 350 E Norvell Bryant Hwy 34442. **Fax:** 352/527-2360. **Facility:** 50 one-bedroom standard units, some with whirlpools. 2 stories, exterior corridors. **Parking:** on-site. **Terms:** weekly rates available, [CP] meal plan available, small pets only ($10 extra charge). **Amenities:** voice mail, irons, hair dryers. **Pool(s):** heated outdoor. **Leisure Activities:** *Fee:* massage. **Guest Services:** coin laundry, beauty salon. **Business Services:** meeting rooms, fax (fee). **Cards:** AX, CB, DC, DS, MC, VI.

SOME UNITS

HIALEAH —See Miami-Miami Beach p. 604.

HIALEAH GARDENS —See Miami-Miami Beach p. 605.

HIGHLAND BEACH pop. 3,775

──────── **WHERE TO STAY** ────────

HOLIDAY INN-HIGHLAND BEACH   *Book at aaa.com*   **Phone:** (561)278-6241
12/19-5/1	1P: $249-$299	2P: $249-$299	
5/2-11/30	1P: $139-$179	2P: $139-$179	
12/1-12/18	1P: $129-$169	2P: $129-$169	

Location: Oceanfront. SR A1A, 1 mi s of Linton Blvd. 2809 S Ocean Blvd 33487. **Fax:** 561/278-7133. **Facility:** 115
Small-scale Hotel units. 112 one-bedroom standard units. 3 one-bedroom suites. 6 stories, interior/exterior corridors. *Bath:* combo or shower only. **Parking:** on-site. **Terms:** check-in 4 pm, cancellation fee imposed. **Amenities:** high-speed Internet, dual phone lines, voice mail, safes, irons, hair dryers. **Dining:** 7 am-10 pm, cocktails. **Pool(s):** heated outdoor, wading. **Leisure Activities:** whirlpool, exercise room. *Fee:* beach cabanas. **Guest Services:** gift shop, valet and coin laundry. **Business Services:** meeting rooms, fax (fee). **Cards:** AX, DC, DS, MC, VI. **Special Amenities:** free local telephone calls and free newspaper. *(See color ad below)*

SOME UNITS

HIGH SPRINGS pop. 3,863

──────── **WHERE TO STAY** ────────

GRADY HOUSE BED AND BREAKFAST   **Phone:** (386)454-2206
All Year [BP]   1P: $95-$205   2P: $95-$205   XP: $15
Historic Bed
& Breakfast
Location: 0.5 mi n on US 27. 420 NW 1st Ave 32643 (PO Box 205, 32655). **Fax:** 386/454-3486. **Facility:** Built in 1917, this B&B is decorated with an extensive collection of reproduction and original artwork. Designated smoking area. 5 units. 1 one-bedroom standard unit. 4 one-bedroom suites. 2 stories, interior corridors. *Bath:* combo or shower only. **Parking:** on-site. **Terms:** age restrictions may apply, 7 day cancellation notice-fee imposed. **Cards:** AX, DS, MC, VI.

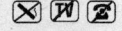

THE RUSTIC INN BED & BREAKFAST
Motel
Phone: (386)454-1223
All Year [ECP]   1P: $69-$89   2P: $79-$119   XP: $15
Location: 2.1 mi s on US 27/41. 15529 NW SR 45 32643. **Fax:** 386/454-1225. **Facility:** Designated smoking area. 6 one-bedroom standard units. 1 story, exterior corridors. **Parking:** on-site. **Terms:** 7 day cancellation notice-fee imposed, package plans. **Amenities:** video library. **Pool(s):** outdoor. **Cards:** MC, VI.

HILLSBORO BEACH —See Fort Lauderdale p. 405.

HOLLY HILL pop. 12,119 (See map and index starting on p. 285)

——— **WHERE TO DINE** ———

STEAKS AND EGGS
American
Lunch: $4-$9   **Dinner:** $4-$9   **Phone:** 386/671-7878   **29**
Location: 1.8 mi s of SR 40. 1702 Ridgewood Ave 32117. **Hours:** 6 am-7 pm, Sat-2 pm, Sun 7 am-2 pm. Closed: 4/16, 11/23, 12/25. **Reservations:** not accepted. **Features:** Enjoy simple comfort food anytime of the day, from pancakes and eggs for dinner to steak for breakfast. Casual dress. **Parking:** on-site.

HOLLYWOOD —See Fort Lauderdale p. 405.

HOLMES BEACH pop. 4,966 (See map and index starting on p. 904)

——— **WHERE TO STAY** ———

HALEY'S MOTEL
Motel
Phone: (941)778-5405   **32**
2/1-4/30   1P: $109-$259   2P: $109-$259   XP: $10   F4
5/1-11/30   1P: $89-$219   2P: $89-$219   XP: $10   F4
12/1-1/31   1P: $79-$189   2P: $79-$189   XP: $10   F4
Location: On CR 789, 1.2 mi n of jct SR 64, jct Palm Dr; on Anna Maria Island. 8102 Gulf Dr N 34217. **Fax:** 941/779-0079. **Facility:** Designated smoking area. 13 units. 10 one-bedroom standard units, some with efficiencies or kitchens. 2 one- and 1 two-bedroom suites with kitchens. 1-2 stories, exterior corridors. *Bath:* combo or shower only. **Parking:** on-site. **Terms:** office hours 9:30 am-10 pm, 3-7 night minimum stay - seasonal and/or weekends, 30 day cancellation notice-fee imposed, pets ($30 fee). **Amenities:** *Some:* DVD players, CD players, irons, hair dryers. **Pool(s):** heated outdoor. **Leisure Activities:** beach umbrellas, chairs & towels, gas barbecue, hammock, bicycles. **Guest Services:** complimentary laundry. **Business Services:** PC, fax. **Cards:** AX, DS, MC, VI.
SOME UNITS
FEE

HARRINGTON HOUSE BEACHFRONT BED & BREAKFAST
Historic Bed & Breakfast
Phone: (941)778-5444   **33**
12/17-11/30 [BP]   1P: $189-$329   2P: $189-$329   XP: $25
12/1-12/16 [BP]   1P: $139-$289   2P: $139-$289   XP: $25
Location: Oceanfront. On CR 789, 1.2 mi n of jct SR 64. Located on Anna Maria Island. 5626 Gulf Dr 34217. **Fax:** 941/778-0527. **Facility:** Made from indigenous coquina, this 1925 B&B fronting on the gulf features individually decorated rooms, some with fireplaces. Designated smoking area. 19 units. 15 one-bedroom standard units, some with whirlpools. 1 one- and 2 two-bedroom suites. 1 cottage. 1-3 stories (no elevator), interior/exterior corridors. *Bath:* combo or shower only. **Parking:** on-site. **Terms:** 2 night minimum stay - weekends, age restrictions may apply, 14 day cancellation notice. **Amenities:** video library, CD players, high-speed Internet, voice mail, irons, hair dryers. **Pool(s):** heated outdoor. **Leisure Activities:** sea kayaks, gazebo, lending library, bicycles. *Fee:* massage. **Guest Services:** gift shop. **Business Services:** PC, fax. **Cards:** AX, MC, VI. **Special Amenities:** free full breakfast and free local telephone calls.
SOME UNITS

——— **WHERE TO DINE** ———

BEACH BISTRO
American
Dinner: $36-$61   **Phone:** 941/778-6444   **58**
Location: On CR 789, 1.5 mi n of jct SR 64. 6600 Gulf Dr 34217. **Hours:** 5:30 pm-10 pm. Closed: 11/23, 12/25. **Reservations:** suggested. **Features:** The award-winning, beachfront restaurant is noted for its creative appetizers, main dishes and desserts. Casual dress; cocktails. **Parking:** on-site. **Cards:** AX, CB, DC, DS, MC, VI.

OOH LA LA!
French
Lunch: $5-$15   **Dinner:** $18-$36   **Phone:** 941/778-5320   **59**
Location: Just off Gulf Dr; in Island Shopping Center. 5406 Marina Dr 34217. **Hours:** 11 am-3 pm, Sun 8 am-3 & 5:30-9:30 pm. Closed: 12/25. **Reservations:** suggested. **Features:** Located in an older strip mall, this small but quaint bistro-type setting with its French flair for decor offers a friendly, welcoming staff ready to serve such items as veal, salmon, lamb, duck, venison, omelets and croissants, all freshly prepared by the owner/chef. Try the potato-crusted grouper with its rich variety of spices and a wonderful gravy blend. Wine is available with top California selections. Dressy casual; beer & wine only. **Parking:** on-site. **Cards:** AX, DC, DS, MC, VI.

HOMESTEAD —See Miami-Miami Beach p. 605.

HOMOSASSA pop. 2,294

——— **WHERE TO STAY** ———

THE LAST RESORT
Cottage
Phone: 352/628-7117
All Year   1P: $120-$150   2P: $120-$150   XP: $20   F6
Location: 2.5 mi w of US 19/98. 10738 W Halls River Rd 34448. **Facility:** 6 cottages. 1 story, exterior corridors. **Parking:** on-site. **Terms:** 2 night minimum stay - weekends, 7 day cancellation notice-fee imposed, weekly rates available. **Leisure Activities:** boat dock, fishing. **Guest Services:** coin laundry. **Business Services:** fax. **Cards:** MC, VI.

———— WHERE TO DINE ————

SUB STATION

Deli/Subs
Sandwiches

Lunch: $4-$11   **Dinner:** $4-$11   **Phone:** 352/628-7827
Location: Just s of jct CR 490 and US 19. 4075 S Suncoast Blvd 34448. **Hours:** 11 am-9 pm, Sun-8 pm.
Features: Not your average sandwich shop; the menu also offers country favorites like fried chicken and
meatloaf. Casual dress. **Parking:** on-site.

HOMOSASSA SPRINGS pop. 12,458

———— WHERE TO STAY ————

PARK INN   *Book at aaa.com*   **Phone:** (352)628-4311

1/15-4/20	1P: $79-$89	2P: $79-$89	XP: $10 F18
12/1-1/14 & 4/21-11/30	1P: $69-$79	2P: $69-$79	XP: $10 F18

Small-scale Hotel   **Location:** Just s of jct CR 490 and US 19. 4076 S Suncoast Blvd 34448. **Fax:** 352/628-0650. **Facility:** 103 one-bedroom standard units. 2 stories, exterior corridors. **Parking:** on-site. **Terms:** weekly rates available, pets
($15 extra charge). **Amenities:** voice mail, irons, hair dryers. **Pool(s):** heated outdoor. **Leisure Activities:** playground, spa,
game room. **Fee:** exercise room. **Guest Services:** coin laundry, area transportation. **Business Services:** meeting rooms, fax
(fee). **Cards:** AX, DC, DS, MC, VI.

SOME UNITS

(ASK) (SD) [icons] FEE / [icons] /

HOWEY-IN-THE-HILLS —See Orlando p. 754.

HUDSON —See Tampa Bay p. 1023.

INDIALANTIC pop. 2,944—See also MELBOURNE.

———— WHERE TO STAY ————

CROWNE PLAZA MELBOURNE OCEANFRONT   **Phone:** (321)777-4100

(AAA) (SAVE)

1/15-11/30	1P: $159-$229	2P: $159-$229	
12/1-1/14	1P: $139-$209	2P: $139-$209	

(fyi)   Under major renovation, scheduled to be completed July 2005. **Last rated:** ▼▼▼ **Location:** On SR A1A, 2.3
mi n of jct US 192. 2605 N SR A1A 32903. **Fax:** 321/773-6132. **Facility:** 295 units. 283 one-bedroom standard
Small-scale Hotel   units. 12 one-bedroom suites. 5-8 stories, interior/exterior corridors. **Parking:** on-site. **Terms:** check-in 4
pm, cancellation fee imposed, [AP] meal plan available. **Amenities:** voice mail, irons, hair dryers. **Dining:** 6:30 am-2 & 5-10 pm,
cocktails. **Pool(s):** heated outdoor. **Leisure Activities:** whirlpool, 2 tennis courts, exercise room, volleyball. **Guest Services:**
gift shop, valet and coin laundry. **Business Services:** conference facilities, fax (fee). **Cards:** AX, CB, DC, DS, JC, MC, VI.
Special Amenities: free local telephone calls and free newspaper.

SOME UNITS

(SD) [icons] /

GUESTHOUSE INTERNATIONAL INN   *Book at aaa.com*   **Phone:** (321)779-9994

(AAA) (SAVE)

12/1-4/30	1P: $89-$159	2P: $99-$169	XP: $10 F10
5/1-11/30	1P: $69-$159	2P: $79-$149	XP: $10 F10

Motel   **Location:** 0.4 mi s of SR 518 (Eau Gallie Cswy). 2900 N A1A Hwy 32903. **Fax:** 321/779-3933. **Facility:** 26 one-bedroom standard units, some with efficiencies. 2 stories, exterior corridors. **Parking:** on-site. **Terms:** 7 day
cancellation notice. **Amenities:** irons, hair dryers. **Dining:** 7 am-11 pm. **Pool(s):** small outdoor. **Leisure
Activities:** whirlpool. **Guest Services:** coin laundry. **Business Services:** fax (fee). **Cards:** AX, DC, DS,
MC, VI. **Special Amenities:** free local telephone calls and early check-in/late check-out.

SOME UNITS

[icons] /

HILTON MELBOURNE BEACH OCEANFRONT   **Phone:** (321)777-5000

(fyi)

All Year	1P: $159-$229	2P: $169-$239	XP: $10 F18

Under major renovation, scheduled to be completed December 2005. **Last rated:** ▼▼▼ **Location:** On N SR
Small-scale Hotel   A1A, 3 mi n of jct US 192. 3003 N SR A1A 32903. **Fax:** 321/777-3713. **Facility:** 118 one-bedroom standard units.
11 stories, interior corridors. **Parking:** on-site. **Terms:** cancellation fee imposed, pets ($50 fee).
Amenities: high-speed Internet (fee), dual phone lines, voice mail, irons, hair dryers. **Pool(s):** heated outdoor. **Leisure
Activities:** whirlpool, exercise room, horseshoes, volleyball. **Guest Services:** gift shop, valet laundry. **Business Services:**
conference facilities, fax (fee). **Cards:** AX, DC, DS, MC, VI.

SOME UNITS

[icons] FEE / [icons] /

MELBOURNE SUITES BEACH HOTEL   **Phone:** (321)723-4222

(fyi)

2/1-4/30	1P: $119-$299	2P: $119-$299	XP: $10 F18
5/1-11/30	1P: $99-$189	2P: $99-$189	XP: $10 F18
12/1-1/31	1P: $99-$169	2P: $99-$169	XP: $10 F18

Small-scale Hotel   Under major renovation, scheduled to be completed December 2005. **Last rated:** ▼▼▼ **Location:** On SR
A1A, 1.5 mi n of jct US 192. 1665 N SR A1A 32903. **Fax:** 321/768-2438. **Facility:** 208 one-bedroom suites. 9 stories, exterior
corridors. **Parking:** on-site. **Terms:** small pets only ($25 deposit, $10 extra charge). **Amenities:** voice mail, safes, irons, hair
dryers. **Fee:** video games, high-speed Internet. **Pool(s):** heated outdoor. **Leisure Activities:** whirlpool. **Fee:** game room. **Guest
Services:** gift shop, valet and coin laundry. **Business Services:** meeting rooms, fax. **Cards:** AX, DS, MC, VI.

SOME UNITS

(ASK) (SD) [icons] FEE / [icons] /

OCEANFRONT COTTAGES   **Phone:** 321/725-8474

▼▼▼

12/11-9/11 Wkly	1P: $990-$1190	2P: $990-$1190	XP: $50 F
12/1-12/10 & 9/12-11/30 Wkly	1P: $790-$990	2P: $790-$990	XP: $50 F

Cottage   **Location:** Just s of east end of US 192. 612 Wavecrest Ave 32903. **Facility:** The property has a poolside
courtyard and some rooms with fireplaces. Designated smoking area. 6 cottages. 2 stories, exterior
corridors. *Bath:* shower only. **Parking:** on-site. **Terms:** age restrictions may apply, 60 day cancellation notice-fee imposed, small
pets only ($50 fee). **Amenities:** DVD players, irons, hair dryers. **Pool(s):** small outdoor. **Guest Services:** complimentary
laundry. **Cards:** MC, VI.

[icons] FEE

RADISSON SUITE HOTEL OCEANFRONT *Book at aaa.com* Phone: (321)773-9260

▽▼▽▼▽▼

1/1-11/30	1P: $209-$269	2P: $209-$269	XP: $10 F18
12/1-12/31	1P: $189-$269	2P: $189-$269	XP: $10 F18

Small-scale Hotel **Location:** 3.2 mi n of jct US 192. 3101 N Hwy A1A 32903. Fax: 321/777-3190. **Facility:** 168 units. 30 one-bedroom standard units with whirlpools. 138 one-bedroom suites ($209-$269). 16 stories, exterior corridors. **Parking:** on-site. **Terms:** check-in 4 pm, package plans. **Amenities:** video games (fee), voice mail, safes, irons, hair dryers. **Pool(s):** heated outdoor. **Leisure Activities:** whirlpools. **Guest Services:** valet and coin laundry. **Business Services:** conference facilities. **Cards:** AX, DC, DS, MC, VI.

SOME UNITS

(ASK) 🍴 🍸 🌀 ⛵ 📹 [DATA PORT] 🖥 🖨 🖥 /✖/

TUCKAWAY SHORES RESORT Phone: (321)723-3355

AAA [SAVE]

▽▼ ▽▼

Motel

1/31-8/31	1P: $110-$125	2P: $110-$125	XP: $10
12/1-1/30	1P: $95-$109	2P: $95-$109	XP: $10
9/1-11/30	1P: $85-$99	2P: $85-$99	XP: $10

Location: SR A1A, 0.8 mi s of jct US 192. 1441 S Miramar Ave (A1A) 32903. Fax: 321/727-1441. **Facility:** Smoke free premises. 31 one-bedroom suites with efficiencies. 3 stories (no elevator), exterior corridors. **Parking:** on-site. **Terms:** weekly rates available. **Amenities:** voice mail. **Pool(s):** outdoor. **Guest Services:** coin laundry. **Business Services:** meeting rooms, fax. **Cards:** AX, DS, MC, VI.

[S🚭] ⛵ ✖ 🖥 🖨 🖥

WINDEMERE INN BY THE SEA BED AND BREAKFAST Phone: 321/728-9334

AAA [SAVE]

▽▼▽▼

Bed & Breakfast

All Year [BP]	1P: $120-$250	2P: $120-$250	XP: $25

Location: Jct US 192, 0.3 mi s on SR A1A. 815 S Miramar Ave (A1A) 32903. Fax: 321/728-2741. **Facility:** While contemporary on the exterior, the interior of this property is a Victorian setting; ocean views from the beachside property are wonderful. Smoke free premises. 9 units. 7 one-bedroom standard units, some with whirlpools. 2 one-bedroom suites ($280-$400), some with whirlpools. 1-3 stories (no elevator), interior/exterior corridors. **Bath:** combo or shower only. **Parking:** on-site. **Terms:** 2 night minimum stay - weekends, 14 day cancellation notice, 5% service charge, no pets allowed (owner's pet on premises). **Amenities:** irons, hair dryers. **Leisure Activities:** beach deck, massage. **Business Services:** fax (fee). **Cards:** DS, MC, VI. **Special Amenities:** free full breakfast and free local telephone calls.

SOME UNITS

✖ 📞 /📺/

——— WHERE TO DINE ———

BIZZARRO'S FAMOUS NEW YORK Lunch: $4-$9 Dinner: $4-$9 Phone: 321/724-4799

▽▼

Italian

Location: Jct US 192/SR A1A, just n on SR A1A. 4 Wavecrest Ave 32903. **Hours:** 11 am-9 pm, Fri & Sat-11 pm, Sun noon-9 pm. **Closed:** 11/23, 12/25. **Features:** Families enjoy dining at the Italian eatery, which specializes in pizza, stuffed pizza and hot submarine sandwiches. Pizza is available by the slice. Salads also make a menu appearance. Casual dress; beer & wine only. **Parking:** on-site.

🚫

BLUEBERRY MUFFIN RESTAURANT Lunch: $5-$10 Phone: 321/725-7117

▽▼

American

Location: Jct US 192/SR A1A, 0.8 mi n on SR A1A. 1130 N Hwy A1A 32903. **Hours:** 6:30 am-3 pm. **Closed:** 12/25. **Reservations:** not accepted. **Features:** Known for serving hearty breakfasts, the beachside restaurant also prepares lunch items. Casual dress. **Parking:** on-site. **Cards:** AX, DC, DS, MC, VI.

CITY TROPICS BISTRO Lunch: $7-$18 Dinner: $9-$18 Phone: 321/723-1300

▽▼ ▽▼

American

Location: On US 192, just w of SR A1A. 249 Fifth Ave 32903. **Hours:** 11 am-midnight, Fri & Sat-2 am. **Closed:** 12/25. **Features:** Just a mile from the beach, the Caribbean bistro prepares sushi, brick-oven pizza and fresh seafood with an island twist. More than 1,000 varieties of wine can be had in the adjacent wine shop. Casual dress; cocktails. **Parking:** on-site. **Cards:** AX, DS, MC, VI.

PAPPAGALLO'S Lunch: $3-$14 Dinner: $3-$14 Phone: 321/773-7272

▽▼

Italian

Location: 0.4 mi s of SR 518 (Eau Gallie Cswy). 2910 N A1A 32903. **Hours:** 11 am-9:30 pm, Fri & Sat-11 pm, Sun noon-9:30 pm. **Closed** major holidays. **Features:** Just across from the beach, the pizzeria serves favorite pasta dishes, pizzas and salads to patrons coming in from a long day at the beach. Casual dress; beer & wine only. **Parking:** on-site. **Cards:** AX, DC, DS.

SKEWERS Lunch: $4-$11 Dinner: $8-$19 Phone: 321/727-8944

AAA

▽▼ ▽▼

Lebanese

Location: On US 192, just w of SR A1A; center. 144 Fifth Ave 32903. **Hours:** 11 am-4 & 5-9:30 pm. **Closed:** 1/1, 11/23, 12/25; also Sun. **Features:** The restaurant's authentic Middle Eastern atmosphere is enhanced by nightly belly-dancing performances via satellite from Lebanon. The menu blends delicious classic Middle East and Lebanese cuisine with some Continental items. Knafeh is an outstanding choice for dessert. Casual dress; beer & wine only. **Parking:** on-site. **Cards:** AX, DC, DS, MC, VI.

VALORA'S RESTAURANT Lunch: $7-$10 Dinner: $14-$22 Phone: 321/953-1919

▽▼▽▼

American

Location: 1.5 mi n of US 192. 1500 N Hwy A1A 32903. **Hours:** 9 am-9 pm, Sat from 8 am, Sun 8 am-2 pm, Mon 9 am-2 pm. **Closed** major holidays. **Reservations:** suggested, weekends. **Features:** Although the atmosphere and decor suggest bistro, the food is more of the fine-dining variety. Flavor combinations that result from the blending of fresh ingredients tantalize the taste buds. The bakery turns out rich, luscious desserts. Jazz performances enhance the atmosphere on Friday and Saturday nights. Casual dress; wine only. **Parking:** on-site. **Cards:** AX, DC, DS, MC, VI.

[♿M]

VILLA PALMA RISTORANTE Dinner: $11-$22 Phone: 321/951-0051

▽▼▽▼

Italian

Location: 0.3 mi n of US 192; in Indialantic Shopping Plaza. 874 N Hwy A1A 32903. **Hours:** 5 pm-9 pm, Fri & Sat-10:30 pm. **Closed:** 11/23, 12/25. **Reservations:** suggested. **Features:** The owner/chef makes pasta from scratch. For a treat, try shrimp parmigiana. Entrees include preparations of beef, chicken, veal and seafood. Casual dress; beer & wine only. **Parking:** on-site. **Cards:** AX, DC, DS, MC, VI.

INDIAN HARBOUR BEACH pop. 8,152

─────── WHERE TO STAY ───────

WELLESLEY INN-MELBOURNE/INDIAN HARBOUR BEACH *Book at aaa.com*

Phone: (321)773-0325

(AAA) (SAVE)
WW WW

Small-scale Hotel

12/1-3/31 & 7/1-11/30	1P: $99-$139
4/1-5/31	1P: $89-$109
6/1-6/30	1P: $79-$109

Location: I-95, exit 183, 8 mi e, then 1 mi n on SR 513. 1894 S Patrick Dr 32937. Fax: 321/773-0320. **Facility:** 76 one-bedroom standard units. 2 stories (no elevator), interior/exterior corridors. *Bath:* combo or shower only. **Parking:** on-site. **Terms:** cancellation fee imposed, [CP] meal plan available, small pets only ($25 extra charge). **Amenities:** voice mail, safes (fee), irons, hair dryers. **Pool(s):** outdoor. **Leisure Activities:** fishing. *Fee:* game room. **Guest Services:** coin laundry. **Cards:** AX, DS, MC, VI.

SOME UNITS
(S/D) 🛏️ 📺 🍴 ≈ 🎥 [DATA PORT] 💻 / ✕ 🛗 🖥️ /
FEE

─────── WHERE TO DINE ───────

MELO'S ITALIAN RISTORANTE
WWW WW
Italian

Dinner: $8-$23

Phone: 321/773-3555

Location: Jct SR A1A, 0.3 mi w. 1000 Eau Gallie Blvd 32937. **Hours:** 4:30 pm-10 pm. Closed major holidays; also Mon. **Features:** Representative of chef Carmelo's scrumptious homemade dishes are veal Marsala, shrimp fra diavolo and gnocchi gorgonzola. Tony Bennett once was a guest of the eatery, which is just minutes from the beach, and sang a capella for the guests. Casual dress; cocktails. **Parking:** on-site. **Cards:** DS, MC, VI.

INDIAN ROCKS BEACH —*See Tampa Bay p. 1023.*

INDIAN SHORES —*See Tampa Bay p. 1024.*

INVERNESS pop. 6,789

─────── WHERE TO STAY ───────

CENTRAL MOTEL
WWW WW
Motel

Phone: (352)726-4515

| 12/1-4/30 | 1P: $50-$67 | 2P: $59-$69 |
| 5/1-11/30 | 1P: $50-$67 | 2P: $57-$67 |

Location: On US 41, 1 mi s. 721 US 41S 34450. Fax: 352/726-0915. **Facility:** 38 one-bedroom standard units. 2 stories, exterior corridors. *Bath:* combo or shower only. **Parking:** on-site. **Pool(s):** outdoor. **Leisure Activities:** *Fee:* bicycles. **Business Services:** fax (fee). **Cards:** AX, DC, DS, MC, VI.

SOME UNITS
(ASK) (S/D) 🍴 ≈ 🐾 🎥 [DATA PORT] 🛗 💻 / ✕ /

VAN DER VALK INVERNESS
WW WW
Vacation Home

Phone: (352)637-1140

| All Year | 2P: $125-$275 |

Location: 2.7 mi n on US 41. 4555 E Windmill Dr 34453. Fax: 352/637-2552. **Facility:** These 3- and 4- bedroom executive-style pool homes features a garage and is professionally decorated and located in a residential community. 85 vacation homes with pools. 1 story. **Parking:** on-site. **Terms:** check-in 4 pm, 4 night minimum stay, 28 day cancellation notice, $65 service charge, pets ($100 fee). **Amenities:** irons, hair dryers. **Guest Services:** complimentary laundry, area transportation (fee). **Business Services:** meeting rooms. **Cards:** AX, DC, DS, MC, VI.

SOME UNITS
(ASK) (S/D) 🛏️ 🐾 🛗 🖥️ 💻 / ✕ /
FEE

─────── WHERE TO DINE ───────

CINNAMON STICKS
WWW WW
American

Lunch: $4-$12 **Dinner:** $6-$16 **Phone:** 352/726-7333

Location: Just w of jct US 41. 2120 W Hwy 44 34453. **Hours:** 7 am-9 pm. Closed: 12/25. **Reservations:** accepted. **Features:** This casual dining room has a country theme and offers American traditions like pot roast in puff pastry and Dutch apple pie. Casual dress. **Parking:** on-site. **Cards:** DS, MC, VI.

COACH'S PUB & EATERY
WW
American

Lunch: $5-$8 **Dinner:** $7-$12 **Phone:** 352/344-3333

Location: Downtown; adjacent to courthouse. 114 W Main St 34450. **Hours:** 11 am-midnight, Fri-2 am, Sun-10 pm. Closed: 4/16, 12/25. **Features:** Racing car hoods and college and professional sports banners highlight an entire wall in this sports bar-themed restaurant. Try the pub fare featuring sandwiches, salads and chili. Extensive selection of 40 drafts and 70 bottled beers are available. Casual dress; cocktails. **Parking:** on-site and street. **Cards:** AX, MC, VI.

🍸

COCKADOODLES CAFE
WW
American

Lunch: $3-$7 **Phone:** 352/637-0335

Location: Center. 206 W Tompkins St 34450. **Hours:** 6:30 am-2 pm. Closed: 4/16, 11/23, 12/25; also 6/28-7/4. **Reservations:** suggested. **Features:** Wake up to great breakfast food cooked to order in this downtown cafe, including serves traditional favorites like eggs any way you like them, pancakes and french toast. Casual dress. **Parking:** on-site and street.

HEIDI'S ITALIAN RESTAURANT
WW
Italian

Lunch: $3-$6 **Dinner:** $3-$6 **Phone:** 352/637-1355

Location: Jct SR 44 W. 901 Hwy 41 N 34450. **Hours:** 11 am-9 pm, Sat from 4 pm. **Features:** This quaint Italian restaurant is located at the junction of the town's two main streets. Casual dress; beer & wine only. **Parking:** on-site. **Cards:** MC, VI.

SONNY'S REAL PIT BBQ
WWW WW
Barbecue

Lunch: $6-$9 **Dinner:** $6-$15 **Phone:** 352/341-2686

Location: Center. 750 W Main St 34450. **Hours:** 11 am-9 pm, Fri & Sat-10 pm. **Features:** The country themed restaurant offers slow-cooked barbecue, daily all-you-can-eat specials and a salad bar. Casual dress. **Parking:** on-site. **Cards:** AX, DS, MC, VI.

STUMPKNOCKERS ON THE SQUARE
WW WW
Steak & Seafood

Lunch: $5-$8 **Dinner:** $10-$17 **Phone:** 352/726-2212

Location: Center. 110 W Main St 34450. **Hours:** 11 am-9 pm, Fri & Sat-10 pm. Closed: 11/23; also Mon. **Reservations:** accepted. **Features:** The casual, quaint restaurant serves meals prepared to order. House specialties include fried catfish, stuffed flounder, gator steaks, frog legs, sea scallops and mahi mahi. Casual dress; cocktails. **Parking:** on-site. **Cards:** MC, VI.

ISLAMORADA —*See The Florida Keys p. 326.*

Destination Jacksonville
pop. 735,617

T he principal city of Florida's First Coast, Jacksonville is no longer known just as a banking and insurance center.

I ts nearby beaches are meccas for sun worshipers. The PGA thought so much of the area it established its tour headquarters here. And architecture buffs revel in the Victorian atmosphere of Amelia Island.

Jacksonville and the Beaches CVB

Jacksonville Landing.
This downtown marketplace features shops, riverfront eateries and a water taxi to the Riverwalk. (See mention page 103)

ALLTEL Stadium, Jacksonville.
During football season, legions of fans root for the Jacksonville Jaguars at this stadium. (See mention page 103)

Visit Florida

Jacksonville and the Beaches CVB

See Vicinity map page 467

Jacksonville's skyline.
Pleasure craft bob in this marina on the St. Johns River, which runs through downtown Jacksonville, Florida's River City by the Sea.

Jacksonville

Baldwin

Yulee · Amelia Island

Atlantic Beach
Neptune Beach
Jacksonville Beach
Ponte Vedra Beach

Orange Park

Green Cove Springs

Dining in Fernandino Beach on Amelia Island.
The historic district offers unique dining places.

P laces included in this AAA Destination City:

Visit Florida

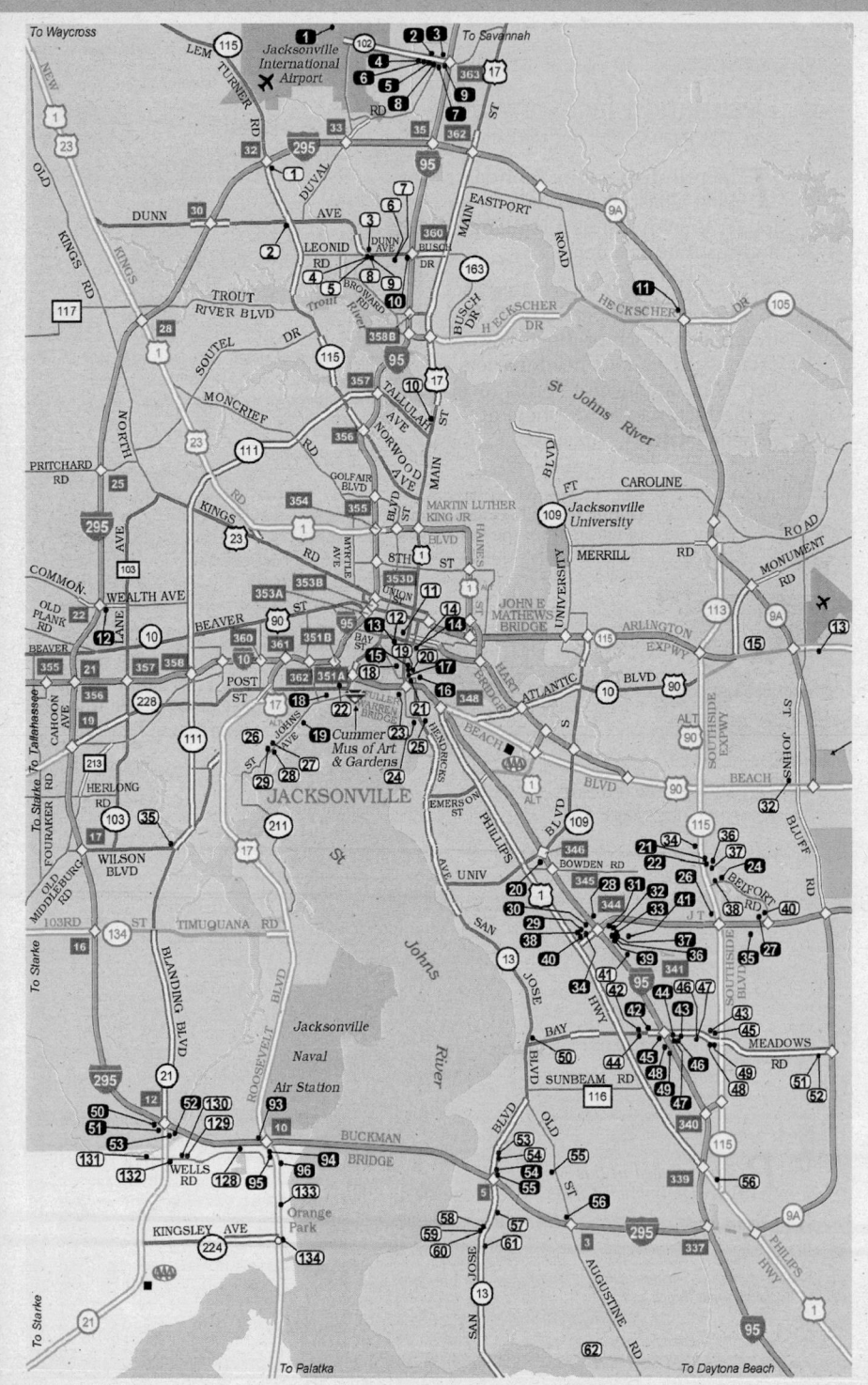

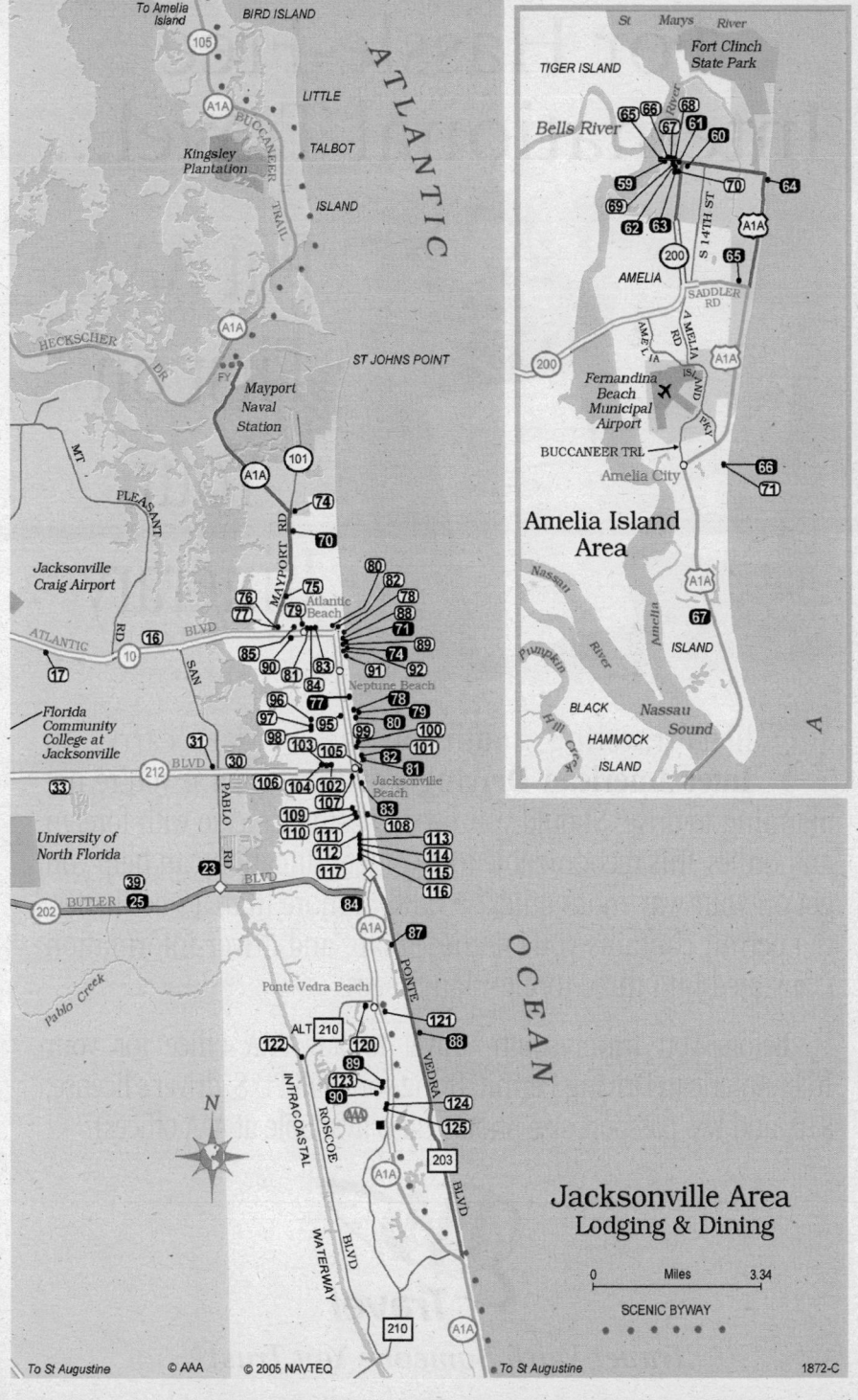

Jacksonville Area
Lodging & Dining

Amelia Island Area

For Hassle-Free International Travel...

Put AAA First on Your Itinerary

When traveling south of the border, carry an **Inter-American Driving Permit...** even if you're not planning to drive. Should you need to communicate with foreign authorities, this recognizable form of identification can help you get on your way more quickly. Valid in more than 15 countries, the permit contains your name, photo, and driver information translated into three foreign languages.

Before you travel south, travel to any AAA office for your Inter-American Driving Permit. Bring your valid U.S. driver's license, $10, and two passport-size photos (also available at AAA offices).

Travel

Travel With Someone You Trust®

✈ Airport Accommodations

Spotter/Map Page Number	OA	JACKSONVILLE INTERNATIONAL	Diamond Rating	Rate Range High Season	Listing Page
➊ / p. 466	AAA	Clarion Hotel Airport Conference Center, at terminal	◈◈◈	$104-$129 SAVE	476
➐ / p. 466		Courtyard by Marriott Jacksonville Airport I-95, 2.5 mi e of terminal	◈◈◈	$89-$175	476
➋ / p. 466	AAA	Days Inn Airport, 2.1 mi e of terminal	◈◈	$97-$107 SAVE	477
➍ / p. 466		Fairfield Inn Airport, 2.1 mi e of terminal	◈◈◈	$69-$139	477
➑ / p. 466	AAA	Hampton Inn Jacksonville Airport, 2.3 mi e of terminal	◈◈◈	$69-$119 SAVE	478
➏ / p. 466		Hilton Garden Inn Jacksonville Airport, 2.2 mi e of terminal	◈◈◈	$69-$199	479
➒ / p. 466		Holiday Inn Airport, 2.2 mi e of terminal	◈◈◈	$103-$139	479
➌ / p. 466		Red Roof Inn-Airport, 1.5 mi e of terminal	◈	$48-$61	484

Jacksonville Area

This index helps you "spot" where approved accommodations and restaurants are located on the corresponding detailed maps. Lodging rate ranges are for comparison only and show the property's high season; rates are per night, unless only weekly (W) rates are available. Restaurant rate range is for dinner, unless only lunch (L) is served. Turn to the listing page for more detailed rate information and consult display ads for special promotions.

Spotter/Map Page Number	OA	JACKSONVILLE - Lodgings	Diamond Rating	Rate Range High Season	Listing Page
➊ / p. 466	AAA	Clarion Hotel Airport Conference Center	◈◈◈	$104-$129 SAVE	476
➋ / p. 466	AAA	Days Inn Airport	◈◈	$97-$107 SAVE	477
➌ / p. 466		Red Roof Inn-Airport	◈	$48-$61	484
➍ / p. 466		Fairfield Inn Airport	◈◈◈	$69-$139	477
➎ / p. 466		Wingate Inn-Airport	◈◈◈	$89-$109	485
➏ / p. 466		Hilton Garden Inn Jacksonville Airport	◈◈◈	$69-$199	479
➐ / p. 466		Courtyard by Marriott Jacksonville Airport I-95	◈◈◈	$89-$175	476
➑ / p. 466	AAA	Hampton Inn Jacksonville Airport	◈◈◈	$69-$119 SAVE	478
➒ / p. 466		Holiday Inn Airport	◈◈◈	$103-$139	479
➓ / p. 466	AAA	La Quinta Inn Jacksonville (Airport/North) - see color ad p 482	◈◈◈	$79-$106 SAVE	482
⓫ / p. 466		Holiday Inn Express & Suites Jacksonville	◈◈◈	$82-$139	479
⓬ / p. 466	AAA	Holiday Inn-Commonwealth	◈◈◈	$69-$299 SAVE	479
⓭ / p. 466	AAA	Omni Jacksonville Hotel	◈◈◈◈	$119-$399 SAVE	483
⓮ / p. 466	AAA	Hyatt Regency Jacksonville Riverfront - see color ad p 481	◈◈◈	$105-$205 SAVE	481
⓯ / p. 466	AAA	Hilton Jacksonville Riverfront	◈◈◈	$99-$259 SAVE	479
⓰ / p. 466		Radisson Riverwalk Hotel	◈◈◈	Failed to provide	483
⓱ / p. 466		Hampton Inn Central	◈◈◈	$89-$149	478
⓲ / p. 466	AAA	Plantation Manor Inn	◈◈◈◈	$150-$250 SAVE	483
⓳ / p. 466		House On Cherry Street	◈◈◈	$85-$165	481
⓴ / p. 466	AAA	Days Inn South - see color ad p 477	◈◈	$52-$69 SAVE	477
㉑ / p. 466		SpringHill Suites by Marriott Jacksonville Deerwood Park	◈◈◈	Failed to provide	485
㉒ / p. 466		Hampton Inn & Suites	◈◈◈	$69-$289	478
㉓ / p. 466	AAA	Courtyard by Marriott	◈◈◈	$84-$168 SAVE	476

Spotter/Map Page Number	OA	JACKSONVILLE - Lodgings (continued)	Diamond Rating	Rate Range High Season	Listing Page
24 / p. 466		Hilton Garden Inn Deerwood Park	▽▽▽	$69-$199	478
25 / p. 466		Wingate Inn-Windsor Parke	▽▽▽	$79-$199	485
26 / p. 466		Extended Stay Deluxe	▽▽▽	Failed to provide	477
27 / p. 466		Homestead Studio Suites Hotel-Jacksonville/Southside	▽▽	$55-$105	480
28 / p. 466	◉	**Econo Lodge Inn and Suites**	▽▽	$111-$299 SAVE	477
29 / p. 466	◉	**Wingate Inn/Southside** - see color ad p 485	▽▽▽	$89-$169 SAVE	485
30 / p. 466		Jacksonville Courtyard at J T Butler Blvd	▽▽▽	Failed to provide	481
31 / p. 466	◉	**Best Western Hotel JTB/Southpoint** - see color ad p 475	▽▽▽	$70-$189 SAVE	475
32 / p. 466	◉	**Holiday Inn Express Hotel and Suites** - see color ad p 480	▽▽▽	$69-$159 SAVE	480
33 / p. 466		Jacksonville Marriott Hotel	▽▽▽	Failed to provide	481
34 / p. 466		La Quinta Inn & Suites Jacksonville (Butler Blvd) - see color ad p 482	▽▽▽	$93-$115	482
35 / p. 466		Residence Inn by Marriott	▽▽▽	$99-$179	484
36 / p. 466		Hampton Inn Jacksonville I-95 South	▽▽▽	Failed to provide	478
37 / p. 466		Homestead Studio Suites Hotel-Jacksonville/Southeast	▽▽▽	$65-$115	480
38 / p. 466	◉	**Masters Inn Butler Blvd/Southpoint**	▽▽	$44-$59 SAVE	483
39 / p. 466		Radisson Hotel Jacksonville Butler Boulevard	▽▽▽	$71-$139	483
40 / p. 466		Jameson Inn	▽▽▽	$54-$104	481
41 / p. 466		Candlewood Suites	▽▽▽	$79-$89	476
42 / p. 466		Homewood Suites by Hilton	▽▽▽	$99-$199	480
43 / p. 466		Embassy Suites Hotel	▽▽▽	$109-$174	477
44 / p. 466		Holiday Inn Baymeadows	▽▽▽	$79-$99	479
45 / p. 466		La Quinta Inn Jacksonville (Baymeadows) - see color ad p 482	▽▽▽	$79-$105	482
46 / p. 466		AmeriSuites (Jacksonville/Baymeadows)	▽▽	$69-$79	475
47 / p. 466		Homestead Studio Suites Hotel-Jacksonville/Baymeadows	▽▽▽	$55-$115	480
48 / p. 466		Quality Inn & Suites	▽▽▽	$72	483
49 / p. 466	◉	**Residence Inn by Marriott**	▽▽▽	$119-$299 SAVE	484
50 / p. 466	◉	**Hampton Inn-Orange Park**	▽▽▽	$89-$129 SAVE	478
51 / p. 466		Motel 6 Jacksonville SW (Orange Park) #415	▽	$39-$55	483
52 / p. 466	◉	**Country Inn & Suites**	▽▽▽	$91-$199 SAVE	476
53 / p. 466	◉	**La Quinta Inn Jacksonville (Orange Park)** - see color ad p 482	▽▽▽	$74-$96 SAVE	482
54 / p. 466	◉	**Baymont Inn & Suites Jacksonville** - see color ad p 475	▽▽	$89-$109 SAVE	475
55 / p. 466	◉	**Ramada Inn Conference Center** - see color ad p 484	▽▽	$89-$99 SAVE	484
56 / p. 466		Holiday Inn Express Hotel & Suites	▽▽▽	$90-$180	479
		JACKSONVILLE - Restaurants			
1 / p. 466		Cross Creek Steakhouse & Ribs	▽▽	$5-$19	487
2 / p. 466		Marco Polo Chinese Restaurant & Mongolian Barbecue	▽	$7-$14	489
3 / p. 466		St. John's Seafood and Steaks	▽	$7-$15	490

Spotter/Map Page Number	OA	JACKSONVILLE - Restaurants (continued)	Diamond Rating	Rate Range High Season	Listing Page
④ / p. 466		Sol Cuba Cafe	◈	$8-$14	490
⑤ / p. 466		La Rancherita	◈	$5-$12	488
⑥ / p. 466		Chan's Chinese Restaurant	◈◈	$7-$20	486
⑦ / p. 466		Bono's Pit Bar-B-Q	◈	$6-$15	486
⑧ / p. 466		JT's Smokehouse Bar-B-Q	◈	$7-$11	488
⑨ / p. 466		Be'Nays Restaurant	◈	$4-$9	486
⑩ / p. 466		Joseph's Pizza & Italian Restaurant	◈◈	$4-$18	488
⑪ / p. 466		Zodiac Grill	◈	$5-$8(L)	491
⑫ / p. 466		Juliette's	◈◈◈	$17-$32	488
⑬ / p. 466		Sushi & Wok	◈	$3-$11	490
⑭ / p. 466		Bravo Ristorante!	◈◈◈	$20-$30	486
⑮ / p. 466		Mt. Fuji Japanese Steak House & Sushi Bar	◈◈	$11-$30	489
⑯ / p. 466		Coal's Brick Oven Pizzeria	◈	$7-$15	487
⑰ / p. 466		Johnny Carino's	◈◈	$7-$13	488
⑱ / p. 466		River City Brewing Company	◈◈	$14-$30	490
⑲ / p. 466		Ruth's Chris Steak House	◈◈◈	$24-$38	490
⑳ / p. 466		Morton's The Steakhouse	◈◈◈	$43-$57	489
㉑ / p. 466		The Wine Cellar	◈◈◈	$20-$31	491
㉒ / p. 466		Mossfire Grill	◈◈	$10-$20	489
㉓ / p. 466		The Corner Brasserie	◈◈	$19-$24	487
㉔ / p. 466		Pom's Thai Bistro	◈◈◈	$27-$34	489
㉕ / p. 466	ⓐⓐⓐ	**Matthew's**	◈◈◈◈	$20-$32	489
㉖ / p. 466		Crush	◈◈◈	$19-$35	487
㉗ / p. 466		Sterlings of Avondale	◈◈◈	$19-$39	490
㉘ / p. 466		Biscotti's Espresso Cafe	◈◈	$10-$30	486
㉙ / p. 466		The Brick Restaurant	◈◈	$15-$28	486
㉚ / p. 466		Marker 32	◈◈◈	$16-$33	489
㉛ / p. 466		El Ranchito Restaurant	◈◈	$6-$12	487
㉜ / p. 466		Madrid	◈◈	$5-$12	488
㉝ / p. 466		Ginza Japanese Cuisine	◈◈	$9-$24	488
㉞ / p. 466		Copeland's of New Orleans	◈◈	$12-$28	487
㉟ / p. 466		China Super Buffet	◈	$9-$12	486
㊱ / p. 466		Mellow Mushroom	◈◈	$7-$25	489
㊲ / p. 466		Gallery Bistro	◈◈◈	$11-$25	488
㊳ / p. 466		Seven Bridges Grille & Brewery	◈◈	$9-$20	490
㊴ / p. 466		Basha Mediterranean Cuisine	◈◈	$5-$12	486
㊵ / p. 466		Bono's Pit Bar-B-Q	◈	$6-$15	486
㊶ / p. 466		Dave & Busters	◈◈	$7-$20	487
㊷ / p. 466	ⓐⓐⓐ	**Pagoda Chinese Restaurant**	◈◈	$8-$19	489
㊸ / p. 466		Celeno's Pizza	◈	$5-$10	486

Spotter/Map Page Number	OA	JACKSONVILLE - Restaurants (continued)	Diamond Rating	Rate Range High Season	Listing Page
44 / p. 466		Renna's Pizza	◆	$2-$8	489
45 / p. 466		Deerwood Deli & Diner	◆◆	$7-$9(L)	487
46 / p. 466		Foo House	◆◆	$7-$23	487
47 / p. 466		Souper Salad	◆	$6-$8	490
48 / p. 466		Panera Bread	◆	$3-$8	489
49 / p. 466		Joseph's Italian Restaurant	◆◆	$7-$15	488
50 / p. 466		Vito's Italian Restaurant	◆◆	$6-$18	491
51 / p. 466		Sweet Indulgence Cafe & Desserts	◆	$3-$7	490
52 / p. 466		Enricos Ristorante	◆◆◆	$10-$19	487
53 / p. 466		Rosalia's Italian Cafe	◆	$9-$20	490
54 / p. 466		Genghis Khan Mongolian Bar-B-Que	◆	$7-$12	488
55 / p. 466		Harmonius Monks	◆◆	$6-$19	488
56 / p. 466		Buca di Beppo	◆◆	$8-$19	486
57 / p. 466		The American Cafe	◆◆	$7-$15	486
58 / p. 466		Truffles Coffee House & Bakery	◆◆	$5-$9	491
59 / p. 466		The Tree Steak House	◆◆	$14-$30	490
60 / p. 466		Mandarin Dragon	◆◆	$6-$12	488
61 / p. 466		Santioni's Cucina Italiana	◆◆	$10-$22	490
62 / p. 466		Clark's Fish Camp	◆	$5-$14	487
AMELIA ISLAND - Lodgings					
59 / p. 466		Hampton Inn & Suites-Amelia Island	◆◆◆	$109-$182	493
60 / p. 466		Hoyt House	◆◆◆	$119-$219	493
61 / p. 466		Bailey House	◆◆◆	$149-$209	493
62 / p. 466		The Addison On Amelia Island	◆◆◆	Failed to provide	492
63 / p. 466		The Fairbanks House	◆◆◆	$180-$395	493
64 / p. 466	AAA	**Elizabeth Pointe Lodge**	◆◆◆	$175-$375 SAVE	493
65 / p. 466		Hampton Inn Amelia Island	◆◆◆	$89-$179	493
66 / p. 466	AAA	**The Ritz-Carlton, Amelia Island**	◆◆◆◆◆	$249-$449 SAVE	493
67 / p. 466	AAA	**Amelia Island Plantation -** see color ad p 492	◆◆◆◆	$191-$769 SAVE	492
AMELIA ISLAND - Restaurants					
65 / p. 466		Brett's Waterway Cafe	◆◆	$16-$27	494
66 / p. 466		Pompeo's Italian Restaurant	◆◆	$12-$23	494
67 / p. 466	AAA	**Centre Street Cafe**	◆◆	$20-$28	494
68 / p. 466		Lulu's Bra & Grill	◆◆	$7-$13	494
69 / p. 466		Senorita's Coffee and Wine	◆◆	$5-$8	494
70 / p. 466		Beech Street Grill	◆◆◆	$18-$30	494
71 / p. 466	AAA	**The Grill**	◆◆◆◆◆	$35-$65	494
ATLANTIC BEACH - Lodgings					
70 / p. 466	AAA	**Best Western Mayport Inn & Suites**	◆◆◆	$78-$220 SAVE	494
71 / p. 466		Sea Turtle Inn	◆◆◆	$105-$225	495

Spotter/Map Page Number	OA	**ATLANTIC BEACH** - Restaurants	Diamond Rating	Rate Range High Season	Listing Page
(74) / p. 466		Mayport Gardens Chinese Restaurant	▽	$5-$8	495
(75) / p. 466		Negril's Paradise	▽	$3-$10	495
(76) / p. 466		Ragtime Tavern & Seafood Grill	▽▽▽	$10-$20	495
(77) / p. 466		Sun Dog Diner	▽▽	$7-$17	495
(78) / p. 466		Plantains	▽▽	$17-$29	495
(79) / p. 466		Seafood Kitchen	▽	$5-$14	495
(80) / p. 466		Sticky Fingers Restaurant & Bar	▽▽	$6-$15	495
(81) / p. 466		Wasabi	▽▽	$10-$22	496
(82) / p. 466		Al's Pizza	▽▽	$6-$15	495
(83) / p. 466		Tijuana Flats Burrito Co.	▽	$7-$10	495
(84) / p. 466		The Tree Steak House	▽▽▽	$14-$30	496
(85) / p. 466		Ristorante Sequino's	▽▽▽	$11-$20	495
		NEPTUNE BEACH - Lodgings			
(87) / p. 466		Sea Horse Oceanfront Inn	▽▽	$99-$189	500
		NEPTUNE BEACH - Restaurants			
(88) / p. 466		Sunny Caribbee	▽▽	$14-$19	500
(89) / p. 466		Mezza Luna Vagabondo Ristorante	▽▽	$15-$25	500
(90) / p. 466		Bone's Pit Bar-B-Q	▽	$6-$14	500
(91) / p. 466		Beach Buns	▽	$2-$5(L)	500
(92) / p. 466		The Loop	▽	$6-$18	500
		JACKSONVILLE BEACH - Lodgings			
(77) / p. 466		Pelican Path B & B by the Sea	▽▽▽	$125-$175	497
(78) / p. 466	⚑	**Fairfield Inn & Suites**	▽▽▽	$109-$189 [SAVE]	497
(79) / p. 466		Holiday Inn SunSpree Resort	▽▽▽	$99-$259	497
(80) / p. 466	⚑	**Comfort Inn Oceanfront** - see color ad p 497	▽▽	$129-$189 [SAVE]	496
(81) / p. 466	⚑	**Best Western Oceanfront**	▽▽▽	$109-$349 [SAVE]	496
(82) / p. 466	⚑	**Quality Suites Oceanfront**	▽▽▽	$179-$299 [SAVE]	498
(83) / p. 466		The Fig Tree Inn	▽▽	$110-$185	497
(84) / p. 466	⚑	**Hampton Inn Ponte Vedra at Jacksonville Beach** - see color ad p 504	▽▽▽	$189 [SAVE]	497
		JACKSONVILLE BEACH - Restaurants			
(95) / p. 466		Matsu Japanese Steak House & Sushi Bar	▽▽	$11-$28	499
(96) / p. 466		Dwight's Bistro	▽▽▽	$10-$25	499
(97) / p. 466		D'Fontana Pizzeria and Ristorante	▽	$5-$12	498
(98) / p. 466		Gene's Seafood Restaurant	▽▽	$9-$15	499
(99) / p. 466		Harry's Seafood Bar & Grill	▽▽	$12-$20	499
(100) / p. 466		Dolphin Depot	▽▽	$19-$35	498
(101) / p. 466		Ichiban Japanese Steak House	▽▽	$8-$15	499
(102) / p. 466		Chan's Chinese	▽	$5-$7	498
(103) / p. 466		Danny's at the Beach	▽▽	$7-$12	498
(104) / p. 466	⚑	**Giovanni's Restaurant**	▽▽▽	$17-$38	499

Spotter/Map Page Number	OA	JACKSONVILLE BEACH - Restaurants (continued)	Diamond Rating	Rate Range High Season	Listing Page
105 / p. 466		Poncho-N-Charlie's Tex-Mex Cantina	◆◆	$10-$15	499
106 / p. 466		Lighthouse Grille	◆◆	$7-$23	499
107 / p. 466		Beachside Seafood	◆	$5-$9	498
108 / p. 466		Beach Hut Cafe	◆	$3-$7(L)	498
109 / p. 466		Thai Room	◆◆	$10-$32	500
110 / p. 466		Bono's Pit Bar-B-Q	◆	$6-$15	498
111 / p. 466		Castillo de Mexico	◆◆	$7-$15	498
112 / p. 466		Ellen's Kitchen	◆	$4-$6(L)	499
113 / p. 466		Mario's at the Beach	◆	$8-$18	499
114 / p. 466		Cruiser's Grill	◆	$5-$7	498
115 / p. 466		Jason's Deli	◆	$4-$9	499
116 / p. 466		Bonefish Grill	◆◆◆	$14-$19	498
117 / p. 466		Roy's	◆◆◆	$19-$34	500
		PONTE VEDRA BEACH - Lodgings			
87 / p. 466	AAA	**Ponte Vedra Inn and Club** - see color ad p 505	◆◆◆◆◆	$280-$640 SAVE	504
88 / p. 466	AAA	**The Lodge & Club at Ponte Vedra Beach**	◆◆◆◆	$360-$640 SAVE	504
89 / p. 466	AAA	**Hilton Garden Inn**	◆◆◆	$79-$209 SAVE	502
90 / p. 466	AAA	**The Sawgrass Marriott Resort & Beach Club** - see color ad p 505	◆◆◆	$240-$284 SAVE	504
		PONTE VEDRA BEACH - Restaurants			
120 / p. 466		Players Cafe	◆	$2-$6(L)	506
121 / p. 466		J J's Cuisine & Wine	◆◆	$14-$30	506
122 / p. 466		Lulu's Waterfront Grille	◆	$12-$20	506
123 / p. 466		Paddy Mac's Tavern	◆◆	$7-$18	506
124 / p. 466		Restaurant Medure	◆◆◆	$18-$29	506
125 / p. 466		Santioni's of Sawgrass	◆◆	$10-$17	506
		ORANGE PARK - Lodgings			
93 / p. 466	AAA	**Best Western Southside Hotel & Suites** - see color ad p 501	◆◆◆	$72-$92 SAVE	501
94 / p. 466		Holiday Inn Orange Park	◆◆◆	$79-$99	502
95 / p. 466		Fairfield Inn by Marriott	◆◆◆	$76-$89	501
96 / p. 466		Comfort Inn	◆◆	$65-$95	501
		ORANGE PARK - Restaurants			
128 / p. 466		Monique's Cafe & Imports	◆	$5-$10	502
129 / p. 466		Kyodai Sushi Rock	◆◆	$21-$34	502
130 / p. 466		Venezia's Italian Restaurant	◆◆	$7-$15	502
131 / p. 466		The Hilltop	◆◆	$12-$20	502
132 / p. 466		Johnny Carino's Country Italian	◆◆	$9-$13	502
133 / p. 466		Ramirez Restaurant	◆◆	$7-$15	502
134 / p. 466		Sarnelli's Ristorante	◆◆	$11-$25	502

JACKSONVILLE pop. 735,617   (See map and index starting on p. 466)

———— **WHERE TO STAY** ————

AMERISUITES (JACKSONVILLE/BAYMEADOWS)   *Book at aaa.com*   Phone: (904)737-4477   **46**
All Year [BP]   1P: $69   2P: $79   XP: $10   F
Location: I-95, exit 341, just e. 8277 Western Way Cir 32256. Fax: 904/739-1649. **Facility:** 112 one-bedroom
Small-scale Hotel   standard units, some with whirlpools. 6 stories, interior corridors. *Bath:* combo or shower only. **Parking:** on-
site. **Terms:** cancellation fee imposed, package plans, small pets only. **Amenities:** high-speed Internet
(fee), voice mail, irons, hair dryers. *Some:* dual phone lines. **Pool(s):** heated outdoor. **Leisure Activities:** exercise room. **Guest
Services:** complimentary evening beverages: Mon-Thurs, valet and coin laundry. **Business Services:** meeting rooms, fax (fee).
Cards: AX, CB, DC, DS, MC, VI.
SOME UNITS

BAYMONT INN & SUITES JACKSONVILLE   *Book at aaa.com*   Phone: (904)268-9999   **54**
12/1-4/30   1P: $89-$109   XP: $7   F18
5/1-11/30   1P: $67-$74   XP: $7   F18
Location: I-295, exit 5A northbound; exit 5 southbound at SR 13. 3199 Hartley Rd 32257. Fax: 904/268-9611.
Facility: 99 units. 96 one-bedroom standard units. 3 one-bedroom suites, some with kitchens. 3 stories,
Small-scale Hotel interior corridors. **Parking:** on-site. **Terms:** [ECP] meal plan available, small pets only. **Amenities:** video
games, voice mail, irons, hair dryers. **Pool(s):** outdoor. **Leisure Activities:** exercise room. **Guest Services:**
valet and coin laundry. **Business Services:** fax. **Cards:** AX, CB, DC, DS, MC, VI. **Special Amenities:** free expanded
continental breakfast and free local telephone calls. *(See color ad below)*
SOME UNITS

BEST WESTERN HOTEL JTB/SOUTHPOINT   *Book at aaa.com*   Phone: (904)281-0900   **31**
All Year   1P: $70-$189   2P: $80-$189   XP: $10   F17
Location: I-95, exit 344 (SR 202), just ne, then just s. 4660 Salisbury Rd 32256. Fax: 904/281-0417. **Facility:** 184
one-bedroom standard units. 6 stories, interior corridors. **Parking:** on-site. **Terms:** 14 day cancellation
notice-fee imposed, [ECP] meal plan available, small pets only ($15 extra charge). **Amenities:** video games
Large-scale Hotel (fee), voice mail, irons, hair dryers. *Some:* high-speed Internet, dual phone lines. **Pool(s):** outdoor. **Leisure
Activities:** sauna, exercise room. **Guest Services:** valet and coin laundry. **Business Services:** meeting
rooms, business center. **Cards:** AX, CB, DC, DS, JC, MC, VI. **Special Amenities:** early check-in/late check-out.
(See color ad below)
SOME UNITS

(See map and index starting on p. 466)

CANDLEWOOD SUITES   *Book at aaa.com*
Phone: (904)296-7785 **41**

▼▼▼▼▼
Small-scale Hotel

All Year   1P: $79-$89

Location: I-95, exit 344 (SR 202), ne to Belfort Rd, then just s. 4990 Belfort Rd 32256. Fax: 904/296-9281. **Facility:** 111 units. 87 one-bedroom standard units with efficiencies. 24 one-bedroom suites with efficiencies. 3 stories, interior corridors. *Bath:* combo or shower only. **Parking:** on-site. **Terms:** cancellation fee imposed, pets ($75-$150 fee). **Amenities:** video library, CD players, dual phone lines, voice mail, irons, hair dryers. **Leisure Activities:** exercise room. **Guest Services:** valet and coin laundry. **Business Services:** fax (fee). **Cards:** AX, CB, DC, DS, MC, VI.

SOME UNITS

ASK Ⓢⓓ 🛏 🍽️ 🏋M ♿ 🚳 VCR 📽 DATA/PORT 🛗 🖼️ 🖥️ / 🗙 /
FEE

CLARION HOTEL AIRPORT CONFERENCE CENTER   *Book at aaa.com*
Phone: (904)741-1997 **1**

(AAA) SAVE
▼▼▼▼▼
Large-scale Hotel

All Year   1P: $104-$129   2P: $104-$129   XP: $10   F18

Location: I-95, exit 363B, 2.6 mi w; at the airport. 2101 Dixie Clipper Rd 32218. Fax: 904/741-5520. **Facility:** 200 units. 196 one-bedroom standard units. 4 one-bedroom suites ($149-$309) with whirlpools. 2-6 stories, interior corridors. *Bath:* combo or shower only. **Parking:** on-site. **Terms:** [AP] meal plan available. **Amenities:** video games (fee), high-speed Internet, dual phone lines, voice mail, irons, hair dryers. **Dining:** 2 restaurants, 5:30 am-11 pm, cocktails. **Pool(s):** outdoor. **Leisure Activities:** whirlpool, exercise room. **Guest Services:** gift shop, valet and coin laundry, airport transportation-Jacksonville International Airport. **Business Services:** conference facilities, business center. **Cards:** AX, CB, DC, DS, JC, MC, VI. **Special Amenities: free continental breakfast and free local telephone calls.**

SOME UNITS

Ⓢⓓ ✈ 🍽️ 📺 🏊 📽 DATA/PORT 🖥️ / 🗙 VCR 🛗 🖼️ /
FEE

COUNTRY INN & SUITES   *Book at aaa.com*
Phone: (904)772-7771 **52**

(AAA) SAVE
▼▼▼▼▼
Small-scale Hotel

All Year   1P: $91-$199   2P: $91-$199

Location: I-295, exit 12, just s. 5945 Youngerman Cir E 32244. Fax: 904/772-7071. **Facility:** 61 units. 50 one-bedroom standard units. 11 one-bedroom suites ($109-$299), some with whirlpools. 3 stories, interior corridors. *Bath:* combo or shower only. **Parking:** on-site. **Terms:** [AP] & [ECP] meal plans available. **Amenities:** high-speed Internet, dual phone lines, voice mail, irons, hair dryers. **Pool(s):** outdoor. **Leisure Activities:** exercise room. **Guest Services:** coin laundry. **Business Services:** meeting rooms. *Fee:* PC, fax. **Cards:** AX, CB, DC, DS, JC, MC, VI. **Special Amenities: free expanded continental breakfast and early check-in/late check-out.**

SOME UNITS

Ⓢⓓ 🍽️ 🏋M ♿ 🏊 📽 DATA/PORT 🛗 🖼️ 🖥️ / 🗙 VCR /

COURTYARD BY MARRIOTT   *Book at aaa.com*
Phone: (904)223-1700 **23**

(AAA) SAVE
▼▼▼▼▼
Small-scale Hotel

All Year   1P: $84-$168   2P: $84-$168

Location: Just n of J Turner Butler Blvd. Located across from Mayo Clinic. 4600 San Pablo Rd 32224. Fax: 904/223-1026. **Facility:** 146 units. 134 one-bedroom standard units. 12 one-bedroom suites ($159-$169). 3 stories, interior corridors. *Bath:* combo or shower only. **Parking:** on-site. **Terms:** cancellation fee imposed, package plans. **Amenities:** high-speed Internet, voice mail, irons, hair dryers. **Dining:** 6:30 am-1:30 & 5-8 pm, Fri & Sat-11 am, Sun 7 am-11 & 5-8 pm, cocktails. **Pool(s):** outdoor. **Leisure Activities:** whirlpool, exercise room. **Guest Services:** valet and coin laundry, area transportation-Mayo Clinic. **Business Services:** meeting rooms, business center. **Cards:** AX, DC, DS, MC, VI. **Special Amenities: free newspaper.**

SOME UNITS

Ⓢⓓ 🍽️ ♿ 🚳 🏊 📽 DATA/PORT 🖥️ / 🗙 🛗 /

COURTYARD BY MARRIOTT JACKSONVILLE AIRPORT I-95   *Book at aaa.com*
Phone: 904/741-1122 **7**

▼▼▼▼▼
Small-scale Hotel

All Year   1P: $89-$175   2P: $89-$175

Location: I-95, exit 363B, just w on Airport Rd, then just s. 14668 Duval Rd 32218 (PO Box 18369, 32229). Fax: 904/741-0929. **Facility:** 81 units. 78 one-bedroom standard units. 3 one-bedroom suites, some with whirlpools. 3 stories, interior corridors. *Bath:* combo or shower only. **Parking:** on-site. **Amenities:** high-speed Internet, dual phone lines, voice mail, irons, hair dryers. **Pool(s):** outdoor. **Leisure Activities:** whirlpool, exercise room. **Guest Services:** valet and coin laundry. **Business Services:** meeting rooms, PC, fax. **Cards:** AX, DC, DS, MC, VI.

SOME UNITS

ASK Ⓢⓓ ✈ 🍽️ 🏋M ♿ 🚳 🏊 📽 DATA/PORT 🖥️ / 🗙 🛗 🖼️ /

(See map and index starting on p. 466)

DAYS INN AIRPORT   *Book at aaa.com*   Phone: (904)741-4000 **2**

AAA SAVE ▼▼ ▼▼
Motel

All Year   1P: $97   2P: $107   XP: $10   F10
Location: I-95, exit 363, just w. 1181 Airport Rd 32218. Fax: 904/741-0609. **Facility:** 62 one-bedroom standard units. 2 stories (no elevator), exterior corridors. **Parking:** on-site. **Terms:** 3 day cancellation notice-fee imposed, weekly rates available. **Amenities:** voice mail, hair dryers. **Pool(s):** outdoor. **Guest Services:** coin laundry. **Cards:** AX, CB, DC, DS, MC, VI. **Special Amenities:** free continental breakfast and free newspaper.

SOME UNITS

DAYS INN SOUTH   *Book at aaa.com*   Phone: (904)733-3890 **20**

AAA SAVE ▼▼ ▼▼
Small-scale Hotel

All Year [ECP]   1P: $52-$69   2P: $52-$69   XP: $10   F12
Location: I-95, exit 346B southbound; exit 345 northbound. 5649 Cagle Rd 32216. Fax: 904/636-9841. **Facility:** 120 one-bedroom standard units. 2 stories, exterior corridors. *Bath:* combo or shower only. **Parking:** on-site. **Terms:** package plans. **Amenities:** hair dryers. **Pool(s):** outdoor. **Leisure Activities:** exercise room. **Business Services:** meeting rooms, fax. **Cards:** AX, CB, DC, DS, MC, VI. **Special Amenities:** free expanded continental breakfast and free newspaper. *(See color ad below)*

SOME UNITS

ECONO LODGE INN AND SUITES   *Book at aaa.com*   Phone: (904)281-0198 **28**

AAA SAVE ▼▼ ▼▼
Motel

10/26-11/3   1P: $111-$299   2P: $111-$299   XP: $10   F18
12/1-10/25 & 11/4-11/30   1P: $59-$299   2P: $59-$299   XP: $10   F18
Location: I-95, exit 344, just nw to Salisbury Rd, then just n. Located in an office park. 4300 Salisbury Rd N 32216. Fax: 904/296-3580. **Facility:** 99 one-bedroom standard units. 3 stories, exterior corridors. **Parking:** on-site. **Terms:** package plans. **Amenities:** *Some:* irons, hair dryers. **Pool(s):** small outdoor. **Guest Services:** coin laundry. **Business Services:** fax (fee). **Cards:** AX, DS, MC, VI. **Special Amenities:** free continental breakfast and free local telephone calls.

SOME UNITS

EMBASSY SUITES HOTEL   *Book at aaa.com*   Phone: 904/731-3555 **43**

▼▼▼ ▼▼▼

Small-scale Hotel

1/1-11/30 [BP]   1P: $109-$174   2P: $109-$174   XP: $10   F18
12/1-12/31 [BP]   1P: $99-$169   2P: $99-$169   XP: $10   F18
Location: I-95, exit 341, 0.5 mi e. 9300 Baymeadows Rd 32256. Fax: 904/731-4972. **Facility:** 277 one-bedroom suites. 7 stories, interior corridors. *Bath:* combo or shower only. **Parking:** on-site. **Terms:** 1-3 night minimum stay - seasonal, cancellation fee imposed. **Amenities:** video games (fee), voice mail, irons, hair dryers. *Some:* dual phone lines. **Pool(s):** heated indoor. **Leisure Activities:** sauna, whirlpool, exercise room. **Guest Services:** gift shop, complimentary evening beverages, valet and coin laundry, area transportation. **Business Services:** conference facilities, fax (fee). **Cards:** AX, CB, DC, DS, JC, MC, VI.

SOME UNITS

EXTENDED STAY DELUXE   *Book at aaa.com*   Phone: 904/620-9008 **26**

▼▼▼ ▼▼▼

Small-scale Hotel

Property failed to provide current rates
Location: I-95, exit 344, 2.5 mi e on J Turner Butler Blvd to Southside Blvd, then just n on west side of road. 8801 Perimeter Park Blvd 32216. Fax: 904/620-9068. **Facility:** 126 units. 123 one-bedroom standard units. 3 one-bedroom suites. 3 stories, interior corridors. *Bath:* combo or shower only. **Parking:** on-site. **Amenities:** video games, high-speed Internet, dual phone lines, voice mail, safes (fee), irons, hair dryers. **Pool(s):** outdoor. **Leisure Activities:** exercise room. **Guest Services:** valet and coin laundry. **Business Services:** fax (fee).

SOME UNITS

FAIRFIELD INN AIRPORT   *Book at aaa.com*   Phone: 904/741-3500 **4**

▼▼▼ ▼▼▼

Small-scale Hotel

All Year [ECP]   1P: $69-$139   2P: $69-$139
Location: I-95, exit 363B, 0.3 mi w. 1300 Airport Rd 32218. Fax: 904/741-3600. **Facility:** 107 one-bedroom standard units, some with whirlpools. 3 stories, interior corridors. *Bath:* combo or shower only. **Parking:** on-site. **Amenities:** voice mail, irons, hair dryers. **Pool(s):** heated outdoor. **Leisure Activities:** whirlpool, exercise room. **Guest Services:** valet laundry. **Business Services:** meeting rooms, fax. **Cards:** AX, CB, DC, DS, JC, MC, VI.

SOME UNITS

(See map and index starting on p. 466)

HAMPTON INN *Book at aaa.com* Phone: (904)783-8277

WWWW
Small-scale Hotel

All Year [BP] 1P: $89-$139 2P: $89-$139
Location: I-10, exit 351, just se. 548 Chaffee Point Blvd 32221. Fax: 904/693-2480. **Facility:** 82 one-bedroom standard units. 3 stories, interior corridors. *Bath:* combo or shower only. **Parking:** on-site. **Amenities:** video games (fee), high-speed Internet, voice mail, irons, hair dryers. **Pool(s):** outdoor. **Leisure Activities:** exercise room. **Guest Services:** coin laundry. **Business Services:** meeting rooms, business center. **Cards:** AX, DC, DS, MC, VI.

SOME UNITS

(ASK) (SD) (T+) (&M) (⊙) (⊘) (⊇) (★) (DATA PORT) (□) / (X) (▤) (⊟) /

HAMPTON INN & SUITES *Book at aaa.com* Phone: (904)997-9100 [22]

WWWW
Small-scale Hotel

All Year [ECP] 1P: $69-$269 2P: $75-$289 XP: $6 F18
Location: I-95, exit 344, 2.5 mi e on J Turner Butler Blvd, then 0.9 mi n on SR 115. 4415 Southside Blvd 32216. Fax: 904/997-9102. **Facility:** 128 units. 123 one-bedroom standard units, some with whirlpools. 5 one-bedroom suites ($109-$189) with whirlpools. 6 stories, interior corridors. *Bath:* combo or shower only. **Parking:** on-site. **Amenities:** dual phone lines, voice mail, irons, hair dryers. *Some:* DVD players. **Pool(s):** outdoor. **Leisure Activities:** exercise room. **Guest Services:** sundries, valet and coin laundry, area transportation. **Business Services:** meeting rooms, business center. **Cards:** AX, DC, DS, MC, VI.

SOME UNITS

(ASK) (SD) (T+) (&⊙) (⊇) (★) (DATA PORT) (日) (▤) (□) / (X) /

HAMPTON INN CENTRAL *Book at aaa.com* Phone: (904)396-7770 [17]

WWWW
Small-scale Hotel

All Year 1P: $89-$149 2P: $89-$149
Location: South side of Main St Bridge. 1331 Prudential Dr 32207. Fax: 904/396-8044. **Facility:** 118 one-bedroom standard units, some with whirlpools. 5 stories, interior corridors. *Bath:* combo or shower only. **Parking:** on-site. **Amenities:** video games, high-speed Internet, dual phone lines, voice mail, irons, hair dryers. **Pool(s):** outdoor. **Guest Services:** sundries, valet laundry. **Business Services:** meeting rooms, fax. **Cards:** AX, DC, DS, MC, VI.

SOME UNITS

(ASK) (SD) (T+) (&M) (⊙) (⊇) (⊕) (★) (DATA PORT) (□) / (X) (日) (⊟) /

HAMPTON INN JACKSONVILLE AIRPORT *Book at aaa.com* Phone: (904)741-4980 [8]

(AAA) (SAVE)
WWWW
Small-scale Hotel

All Year 1P: $69-$119 2P: $69-$119
Location: I-95, exit 363B, just w, then just s on Duval Rd. Located in a gated property. 1170 Airport Entrance Rd 32218. Fax: 904/741-4186. **Facility:** 113 one-bedroom standard units. 2 stories (no elevator), exterior corridors. *Bath:* combo or shower only. **Parking:** on-site. **Terms:** [ECP] meal plan available, pets (in limited units). **Amenities:** video games (fee), voice mail, irons, hair dryers. **Pool(s):** outdoor. **Leisure Activities:** exercise room. **Guest Services:** coin laundry. **Business Services:** fax. **Cards:** AX, CB, DC, DS, MC, VI. **Special Amenities:** free expanded continental breakfast and free local telephone calls.

SOME UNITS

(SD) (⊀) (🐾) (T+) (&M) (⊙) (⊘) (⊇) (★) (DATA PORT) (□) / (X) (日) (⊟) /

HAMPTON INN JACKSONVILLE I-95 SOUTH *Book at aaa.com* Phone: 904/281-0443 [36]

WWWW
Small-scale Hotel

Property failed to provide current rates
Location: I-95, exit 344 (SR 202), just ne, then just s. 4690 Salisbury Rd 32256. Fax: 904/281-0144. **Facility:** 128 one-bedroom standard units. 4 stories, interior corridors. *Bath:* combo or shower only. **Parking:** on-site. **Amenities:** video games (fee), high-speed Internet, dual phone lines, voice mail, irons, hair dryers. **Pool(s):** small outdoor. **Leisure Activities:** limited exercise equipment. **Guest Services:** valet laundry. **Business Services:** meeting rooms, business center.

SOME UNITS

(T+) (⊙) (⊘) (⊇) (★) (DATA PORT) (日) (▤) (□) / (X) /

HAMPTON INN-ORANGE PARK *Book at aaa.com* Phone: (904)777-5313 [50]

(AAA) (SAVE)
WWWW
Small-scale Hotel

12/31-11/30 1P: $89-$129 2P: $89-$129
12/1-12/30 1P: $89-$109 2P: $89-$109
Location: I-295, exit 12, just w of SR 21. 6135 Youngerman Cir 32244. Fax: 904/778-1545. **Facility:** 121 one-bedroom standard units. 2 stories, exterior corridors. *Bath:* combo or shower only. **Parking:** on-site. **Terms:** [ECP] meal plan available. **Amenities:** video games, high-speed Internet, voice mail, irons, hair dryers. **Pool(s):** heated outdoor. **Leisure Activities:** limited exercise equipment. **Guest Services:** valet and coin laundry. **Business Services:** meeting rooms, fax. **Cards:** AX, CB, DC, DS, MC, VI. **Special Amenities:** free full breakfast and free local telephone calls.

SOME UNITS

(SD) (T+) (&M) (⊘) (⊇) (★) (DATA PORT) (□) / (X) (日) /

HILTON GARDEN INN DEERWOOD PARK *Book at aaa.com* Phone: (904)997-6600 [24]

WWWW
Small-scale Hotel

All Year 1P: $69-$199 2P: $69-$199
Location: I-95, exit 344, 2.5 mi e on J Turner Butler Blvd to SR 115, 0.8 mi n to Gate Pkwy, then just e. 9745 Gate Pkwy Dr N 32246. Fax: 904/997-6601. **Facility:** 119 units. 118 one-bedroom standard units. 1 one-bedroom suite. 5 stories, interior corridors. *Bath:* combo or shower only. **Parking:** on-site. **Terms:** cancellation fee imposed, [BP] & [CP] meal plans available, package plans. **Amenities:** video games (fee), high-speed Internet, dual phone lines, voice mail, irons, hair dryers. **Pool(s):** outdoor. **Leisure Activities:** whirlpool, exercise room. **Guest Services:** sundries, valet and coin laundry, area transportation. **Business Services:** meeting rooms, business center. **Cards:** AX, CB, DC, DS, JC, MC, VI.

SOME UNITS

(T|) (Y) (&M) (⊙) (⊘) (⊇) (★) (DATA PORT) (日) (▤) (□) / (X) /

(See map and index starting on p. 466)

HILTON GARDEN INN JACKSONVILLE AIRPORT   *Book at aaa.com*   Phone: (904)421-2700   **6**
▼▼▼▼ All Year   1P: $69-$199   2P: $69-$199
Location: I-95, exit 363B, 0.5 mi w. 13503 Ranch Rd 32218. Fax: 904/421-2701. **Facility:** 111 units. 102 one-bedroom standard units, some with whirlpools. 9 one-bedroom suites, some with whirlpools. 5 stories, interior corridors. *Bath:* combo or shower only. **Parking:** on-site. **Terms:** check-in 4 pm, [BP] meal plan available, package plans. **Amenities:** video games (fee), high-speed Internet, dual phone lines, voice mail, irons, hair dryers. **Pool(s):** outdoor. **Leisure Activities:** whirlpool, exercise room. **Guest Services:** sundries, valet and coin laundry. **Business Services:** meeting rooms, business center. **Cards:** AX, CB, DC, DS, JC, MC, VI.
Small-scale Hotel
SOME UNITS

HILTON JACKSONVILLE RIVERFRONT   *Book at aaa.com*   Phone: 904/398-8800   **15**
(AAA) (SAVE) All Year   1P: $99-$259   2P: $99-$259   XP: $10   F17
▼▼▼▼ **Location:** On south bank of river; just e of Main St Bridge; center. 1201 Riverplace Blvd 32207. Fax: 904/398-9170. **Facility:** Smoke free premises. 292 one-bedroom standard units. 8 stories, interior corridors. *Bath:* combo or shower only. **Parking:** on-site (fee) and valet. **Terms:** check-in 4 pm, cancellation fee imposed, [BP] meal plan available. **Amenities:** video games (fee), voice mail, irons, hair dryers. *Some:* high-speed Internet, dual phone lines. **Dining:** 2 restaurants, 6 am-11 pm, cocktails. **Pool(s):** heated outdoor. **Leisure Activities:** whirlpool, exercise room. *Fee:* charter fishing. **Guest Services:** gift shop, valet laundry. **Business Services:** conference facilities, business center. **Cards:** AX, DC, DS, MC, VI.
Large-scale Hotel
SOME UNITS

HOLIDAY INN AIRPORT   *Book at aaa.com*   Phone: (904)741-4404   **9**
▼▼▼▼ All Year   1P: $103-$139   2P: $103-$139
Location: I-95, exit 363, just w. 14670 Duval Rd 32218 (PO Drawer 18409, 32229-0409). Fax: 904/741-4907. **Facility:** 489 one-bedroom standard units. 2-6 stories, interior/exterior corridors. *Bath:* combo or shower only. **Parking:** on-site. **Terms:** package plans, pets (in selected units). **Amenities:** dual phone lines, voice mail, safes, irons, hair dryers. **Pool(s):** outdoor, heated indoor/outdoor, wading. **Leisure Activities:** 2 lighted tennis courts, exercise room, basketball. **Guest Services:** gift shop, valet and coin laundry. **Business Services:** conference facilities, business center. **Cards:** AX, CB, DC, DS, JC, MC, VI.
Small-scale Hotel
SOME UNITS

HOLIDAY INN BAYMEADOWS   *Book at aaa.com*   Phone: (904)737-1700   **44**
▼▼▼▼ All Year   1P: $79-$99   2P: $79-$99
Location: I-95, exit 341, 0.3 mi e. 9150 Baymeadows Rd 32256. Fax: 904/737-0207. **Facility:** 240 units. 232 one-bedroom standard units. 8 one-bedroom suites ($129). 2-4 stories, interior/exterior corridors. *Bath:* combo or shower only. **Parking:** on-site. **Terms:** small pets only. **Amenities:** voice mail, irons, hair dryers. **Pool(s):** outdoor. **Leisure Activities:** exercise room. **Guest Services:** valet and coin laundry. **Business Services:** meeting rooms, business center. **Cards:** AX, CB, DC, DS, JC, MC, VI.
Small-scale Hotel
SOME UNITS

HOLIDAY INN-COMMONWEALTH   *Book at aaa.com*   Phone: (904)781-6000   **12**
(AAA) (SAVE) All Year   1P: $69-$299   2P: $69-$299   XP: $5   F17
▼▼▼ **Location:** I-295, exit 22, just e. 6802 Commonwealth Ave 32254. Fax: 904/781-2784. **Facility:** 177 one-bedroom standard units. 2 stories (no elevator), interior/exterior corridors. *Bath:* combo or shower only. **Parking:** on-site. **Amenities:** video games (fee), voice mail, irons, hair dryers. **Dining:** 6 am-2 & 5-10 pm, cocktails. **Pool(s):** heated indoor. **Leisure Activities:** saunas, whirlpool, foosball, tennis table, exercise room. **Guest Services:** valet and coin laundry. **Business Services:** meeting rooms, fax. **Cards:** AX, CB, DC, DS, JC, MC, VI.
Small-scale Hotel
SOME UNITS

HOLIDAY INN EXPRESS & SUITES JACKSONVILLE   *Book at aaa.com*   Phone: (904)696-3333   **11**
▼▼▼ All Year   1P: $82-$139   2P: $82-$139   XP: $10   F18
Location: I-95, exit 362A southbound, 4.9 mi s on SR 9A to Heckscher Dr, then just w; exit 358A northbound, 5.8 mi ne on Heckscher Dr. 10148 New Berlin Rd 32226. Fax: 904/696-5700. **Facility:** 73 one-bedroom standard units. 3 stories, interior corridors. *Bath:* combo or shower only. **Parking:** on-site. **Terms:** cancellation fee imposed, [ECP] meal plan available, pets ($50 deposit). **Amenities:** high-speed Internet, voice mail, irons, hair dryers. **Pool(s):** heated outdoor. **Leisure Activities:** whirlpool, exercise room. *Fee:* game room. **Guest Services:** coin laundry. **Business Services:** meeting rooms, PC. **Cards:** AX, CB, DC, DS, JC, MC, VI.
Small-scale Hotel
SOME UNITS
FEE

HOLIDAY INN EXPRESS HOTEL & SUITES   Phone: 904/899-9000   **56**
▼▼▼ All Year   1P: $90-$150   2P: $100-$180   XP: $10   F12
Location: I-295, exit 3, just n. 11262 St. Augustine Rd 32257. Fax: 904/899-9001. **Facility:** Smoke free premises. 80 one-bedroom standard units. 3 stories, interior corridors. *Bath:* combo or shower only. **Parking:** on-site. **Terms:** [ECP] meal plan available. **Amenities:** video games (fee), dual phone lines, voice mail, irons, hair dryers. **Pool(s):** heated outdoor. **Leisure Activities:** exercise room. **Guest Services:** valet and coin laundry. **Business Services:** meeting rooms. **Cards:** AX, DC, DS, JC, MC, VI.
Small-scale Hotel
SOME UNITS

(See map and index starting on p. 466)

HOLIDAY INN EXPRESS HOTEL AND SUITES   *Book at aaa.com*   **Phone:** (904)332-9500   32

(AAA) (SAVE)   All Year   1P: $69-$139   2P: $79-$159   XP: $10   F15

▼▼▼▼   **Location:** I-95, exit 344 (SR 202), just ne, then s. 4675 Salisbury Rd 32256. **Fax:** 904/332-9222. **Facility:** 88 one-bedroom standard units. 4 stories, interior corridors. *Bath:* combo or shower only. **Parking:** on-site.

Small-scale Hotel   **Terms:** [ECP] meal plan available. **Amenities:** high-speed Internet, dual phone lines, voice mail, irons, hair dryers. **Pool(s):** small outdoor. **Leisure Activities:** exercise room. **Guest Services:** complimentary evening beverages: Wed, valet and coin laundry. **Business Services:** meeting rooms, business center. **Cards:** AX, CB, DC, DS, MC, VI. **Special Amenities:** free expanded continental breakfast. *(See color ad below)*

SOME UNITS
[S◎] [📶] [🛠] [🚗] [🛁] [📶] [🍴] / [✕] [📦] [🖥] /

HOMESTEAD STUDIO SUITES
HOTEL-JACKSONVILLE/BAYMEADOWS   *Book at aaa.com*   **Phone:** (904)739-1881   47

▼▼▼▼   All Year   1P: $55-$110   2P: $60-$115   XP: $5   F17

Small-scale Hotel   **Location:** I-95, exit 341, just e to Western Way, then just s. 8300 Western Way 32256. **Fax:** 904/739-0557. **Facility:** 125 units. 115 one-bedroom standard units. 10 one-bedroom suites. 3 stories, interior corridors. *Bath:* combo or shower only. **Parking:** on-site. **Terms:** pets ($75 fee). **Amenities:** high-speed Internet (fee), voice mail, irons. **Guest Services:** valet and coin laundry. **Business Services:** fax. **Cards:** AX, DC, DS, MC, VI.

SOME UNITS
[ASK] [S◎] [🛏] [📶] [🛁] [🚗] [✚] [📺] [📶] [📦] [🖥] [🖥] / [✕] [VCR] /
    FEE

HOMESTEAD STUDIO SUITES
HOTEL-JACKSONVILLE/SOUTHEAST   *Book at aaa.com*   **Phone:** (904)296-0661   37

▼▼▼▼   All Year   1P: $65-$110   2P: $70-$115   XP: $5   F17

Small-scale Hotel   **Location:** I-95, exit 344, e on J Turner Butler Blvd, then just s. 4693 Jacksonville-Salisbury Rd S 32256. **Fax:** 904/296-3965. **Facility:** 100 units. 78 one-bedroom standard units with efficiencies. 22 one-bedroom suites with efficiencies. 3 stories, interior corridors. *Bath:* combo or shower only. **Parking:** on-site. **Terms:** pets ($25 extra charge). **Amenities:** video games, high-speed Internet (fee), dual phone lines, voice mail, irons, hair dryers. **Pool(s):** outdoor. **Leisure Activities:** exercise room. **Guest Services:** complimentary evening beverages: Mon & Wed, valet and coin laundry. **Business Services:** fax. **Cards:** AX, DC, DS, MC, VI.

SOME UNITS
[ASK] [S◎] [🛏] [🛠M] [🛁] [🚗] [🏊] [📺] [📶] [📦] [🖥] [🖥] / [✕] [VCR] /
    FEE

HOMESTEAD STUDIO SUITES
HOTEL-JACKSONVILLE/SOUTHSIDE   *Book at aaa.com*   **Phone:** (904)642-9911   27

▼▼ ▼▼   All Year   1P: $55-$100   2P: $60-$105   XP: $5   F17

Motel   **Location:** I-95, exit 344, 3.5 mi e on J Turner Butler Blvd to Gate Pkwy, just n, then just w. Located in a quiet, partly residential area. 10020 Skinner Lake Rd 32246. **Fax:** 904/642-5673. **Facility:** 132 units. 127 one-bedroom standard units with efficiencies. 5 one-bedroom suites with efficiencies. 2 stories, exterior corridors. *Bath:* combo or shower only. **Parking:** on-site. **Terms:** pets ($75 fee). **Amenities:** high-speed Internet (fee), voice mail, irons. *Some:* dual phone lines. **Guest Services:** valet and coin laundry. **Business Services:** fax. **Cards:** AX, DC, DS, MC, VI.

SOME UNITS
[ASK] [S◎] [🛏] [📶] [🛠M] [🛁] [✚] [📺] [📶] [📦] [🖥] [🖥] / [✕] /
    FEE

HOMEWOOD SUITES BY HILTON   *Book at aaa.com*   **Phone:** (904)733-9299   42

▼▼▼▼   All Year [BP]   1P: $99-$199

Small-scale Hotel   **Location:** I-95, exit 341, 0.3 mi w. 8737 Baymeadows Rd 32256. **Fax:** 904/448-5889. **Facility:** 116 units. 108 one- and 8 two-bedroom standard units, some with kitchens. 2-3 stories, interior/exterior corridors. **Parking:** on-site. **Terms:** pets ($75 fee). **Amenities:** video games, high-speed Internet, voice mail, irons, hair dryers. **Pool(s):** outdoor. **Leisure Activities:** whirlpool, exercise room, sports court. **Guest Services:** complimentary evening beverages: Mon-Thurs, valet and coin laundry. **Business Services:** meeting rooms, business center. **Cards:** AX, DC, DS, MC, VI.

SOME UNITS
[ASK] [S◎] [🛏] [🚗] [✕] [📺] [📶] [📦] [🖥] [🖥] / [✕] /
    FEE

(See map and index starting on p. 466)

HOUSE ON CHERRY STREET

Phone: 904/384-1999 **19**

All Year [ECP]   1P: $85-$165   2P: $85-$165   XP: $10
Location: Just s of Riverside Ave; in Riverside Historic District. 1844 Cherry St 32205. Fax: 904/387-4007.
Bed & Breakfast   **Facility:** This 1909 house with a large lawn on the St. Johns River is furnished with American antiques from the Queen Anne period as well as many oriental rugs. Smoke free premises. 4 one-bedroom standard units. 2 stories, interior corridors. *Bath:* combo or shower only. **Parking:** on-site. **Terms:** age restrictions may apply, 4 day cancellation notice, weekly rates available, [BP] meal plan available. **Leisure Activities:** boat dock. **Guest Services:** complimentary evening beverages. **Business Services:** PC, fax. **Cards:** AX, DS, MC, VI.

SOME UNITS
(A$K) [X] [☎] / [VCR] [▯] /

HYATT REGENCY JACKSONVILLE RIVERFRONT   *Book at aaa.com*

Phone: (904)588-1234 **14**

(AAA) (SAVE)   All Year   1P: $105-$205   2P: $105-$205   XP: $25   F18
Location: Downtown; just e of The Landing. 225 Coast Line Dr E 32202. Fax: 904/634-4554. **Facility:** 966 units.
Large-scale Hotel   950 one-bedroom standard units. 16 one-bedroom suites. 4-19 stories, interior corridors. *Bath:* combo or shower only. **Parking:** on-site (fee) and valet. **Terms:** 3 day cancellation notice-fee imposed. **Amenities:** video games, high-speed Internet, dual phone lines, voice mail, irons, hair dryers. *Some: Fee:* DVD players. **Dining:** 4 restaurants, 6 am-10:30 pm, cocktails, entertainment. **Pool(s):** heated outdoor. **Leisure Activities:** sauna, whirlpool, exercise room. **Guest Services:** gift shop, complimentary evening beverages: Tues, valet and coin laundry, area transportation (fee)-within 3 mi. **Business Services:** conference facilities, business center. **Cards:** AX, CB, DC, DS, JC, MC, VI. *(See color ad below)*

SOME UNITS
[✈] [▯|] [Y] [➳] [X] [▯] [DATA PORT] [▯] / [X] [VCR] [▯] /
FEE   FEE FEE

JACKSONVILLE COURTYARD AT J T BUTLER BLVD   *Book at aaa.com*

Phone: 904/296-2828 **30**

Property failed to provide current rates
Location: I-95, exit 344 (SR 202), just sw, then just nw. 4670 Lenoir Ave S 32216. Fax: 904/296-9508. **Facility:** 137
Small-scale Hotel   units. 132 one-bedroom standard units. 5 one-bedroom suites. 5 stories, interior corridors. *Bath:* combo or shower only. **Parking:** on-site. **Amenities:** high-speed Internet, dual phone lines, voice mail, irons, hair dryers. **Pool(s):** small heated outdoor. **Leisure Activities:** whirlpool, exercise room. **Guest Services:** valet and coin laundry. **Business Services:** meeting rooms, fax (fee).

SOME UNITS
[▯|] [Y] [&M] [▯] [∅] [➳] [▯] [DATA PORT] [▯] / [X] [▯] [▣] /

JACKSONVILLE MARRIOTT HOTEL   *Book at aaa.com*

Phone: 904/296-2222 **33**

Property failed to provide current rates
Location: I-95, exit 344, southeast corner off J Turner Butler Blvd. 4670 Salisbury Rd 32256. Fax: 904/296-7561.
Large-scale Hotel   **Facility:** 256 units. 251 one-bedroom standard units. 5 one-bedroom suites, some with whirlpools. 9 stories, interior corridors. **Parking:** on-site. **Amenities:** high-speed Internet (fee), dual phone lines, voice mail, irons, hair dryers. **Pool(s):** outdoor, heated indoor. **Leisure Activities:** sauna, whirlpool, exercise room. *Fee:* massage. **Guest Services:** gift shop, valet laundry. **Business Services:** conference facilities, business center.

SOME UNITS
[▯|] [Y] [📟] [➳] [X] [▯] [DATA PORT] [▯] / [X] [▯] /

JAMESON INN   *Book at aaa.com*

Phone: (904)296-0968 **40**

All Year [ECP]   1P: $54-$104
Location: I-95, exit 344, just w. 7030 Bonneval Rd 32216. Fax: 904/296-0715. **Facility:** 79 units. 77 one-bedroom
Small-scale Hotel   standard units. 2 one-bedroom suites. 3 stories, interior corridors. *Bath:* combo or shower only. **Parking:** on-site. **Terms:** cancellation fee imposed. **Amenities:** voice mail, irons, hair dryers. **Pool(s):** outdoor. **Leisure Activities:** exercise room. **Guest Services:** valet laundry. **Business Services:** meeting rooms, fax (fee). **Cards:** AX, CB, DC, DS, MC, VI.

SOME UNITS
(A$K) [🛏] [▯|] [➳] [▯] [DATA PORT] / [X] [▯] [▣] [▯] /

(See map and index starting on p. 466)

LA QUINTA INN & SUITES JACKSONVILLE (BUTLER BLVD) *Book at aaa.com*
Phone: (904)296-0703 **34**

All Year   1P: $93-$109   2P: $99-$115   XP: $6   F18
Small-scale Hotel
Location: I-95, exit 344 (SR 202), just sw, then just nw. 4686 Lenoir Ave S 32216. Fax: 904/296-0709. **Facility:** 131 units. 125 one-bedroom standard units. 6 one-bedroom suites ($123-$139). 6 stories, interior corridors. *Bath:* combo or shower only. **Parking:** on-site. **Terms:** [ECP] meal plan available. **Amenities:** video games (fee), high-speed Internet, voice mail, irons, hair dryers. *Some:* dual phone lines. **Pool(s):** heated outdoor. **Leisure Activities:** whirlpool, exercise room. **Guest Services:** valet and coin laundry. **Business Services:** meeting rooms, fax (fee). **Cards:** AX, CB, DC, DS, MC, VI. *(See color ad below)*

SOME UNITS

LA QUINTA INN JACKSONVILLE (AIRPORT/NORTH) *Book at aaa.com*
Phone: (904)751-6960 **10**

2/1-3/31   1P: $79-$99   2P: $86-$106   XP: $7   F18
4/1-11/30   1P: $75-$92   2P: $82-$99   XP: $7   F18
12/1-1/31   1P: $73-$89   2P: $80-$96   XP: $7   F18
Small-scale Hotel
Location: I-95, exit 360, southwest corner. 812 Dunn Ave 32218. Fax: 904/751-9769. **Facility:** 128 units. 126 one-bedroom standard units. 2 one-bedroom suites. 3 stories, exterior corridors. **Parking:** on-site. **Terms:** [ECP] meal plan available, small pets only. **Amenities:** video games, voice mail, irons, hair dryers. **Pool(s):** heated outdoor. **Guest Services:** coin laundry. **Business Services:** fax (fee). **Cards:** AX, CB, DC, DS, MC, VI. **Special Amenities:** free expanded continental breakfast and free local telephone calls. *(See color ad below)*

SOME UNITS
FEE

LA QUINTA INN JACKSONVILLE (BAYMEADOWS) *Book at aaa.com*
Phone: (904)731-9940 **45**

5/1-9/30   1P: $79-$95   2P: $89-$105   XP: $10   F18
12/1-4/30 & 10/1-11/30   1P: $76-$86   2P: $86-$96   XP: $10   F18
Motel
Location: I-95, exit 341, southwest corner. 8255 Dix Ellis Tr 32256. Fax: 904/731-3854. **Facility:** 106 units. 104 one-bedroom standard units. 2 one-bedroom suites. 2 stories, exterior corridors. **Parking:** on-site. **Terms:** [CP] meal plan available, small pets only. **Amenities:** video games, high-speed Internet, voice mail, irons, hair dryers. *Some:* dual phone lines. **Pool(s):** heated outdoor. **Guest Services:** valet and coin laundry. **Business Services:** fax (fee). **Cards:** AX, CB, DC, DS, MC, VI. *(See color ad below)*

SOME UNITS

LA QUINTA INN JACKSONVILLE (ORANGE PARK) *Book at aaa.com*
Phone: (904)778-9539 **53**

All Year   1P: $74-$89   2P: $81-$96   XP: $7   F18
Location: I-295, exit 12, just s on SR 21. 8555 Blanding Blvd 32244-5797. Fax: 904/779-5214. **Facility:** 122 units. 121 one-bedroom standard units. 1 one-bedroom suite. 2 stories, exterior corridors. **Parking:** on-site.
Small-scale Hotel
Terms: [ECP] meal plan available, small pets only. **Amenities:** video games, voice mail, irons, hair dryers. **Pool(s):** outdoor. **Guest Services:** coin laundry. **Business Services:** meeting rooms, fax. **Cards:** AX, CB, DC, DS, MC, VI. **Special Amenities:** free expanded continental breakfast and free local telephone calls. *(See color ad below)*

SOME UNITS
FEE FEE

(See map and index starting on p. 466)

MASTERS INN BUTLER BLVD/SOUTHPOINT *Book at aaa.com* Phone: (904)281-2244 **38**
AAA SAVE All Year [ECP] 1P: $44-$49 2P: $49-$59 XP: $5 F18
Location: I-95, exit 344 (SR 202), just sw, then just nw. 4940 Mustang Rd 32216. Fax: 904/281-2243. **Facility:** 100
one-bedroom standard units. 3 stories, interior corridors. *Bath:* combo or shower only. **Parking:** on-site.
Terms: weekly rates available, package plans, small pets only ($10-$15 extra charge). **Business Services:**
Small-scale Hotel meeting rooms, fax (fee). **Cards:** AX, CB, DC, DS, JC, MC, VI. **Special Amenities:** free expanded
continental breakfast and free local telephone calls.
SOME UNITS

MOTEL 6 JACKSONVILLE SW (ORANGE PARK) #415 *Book at aaa.com* Phone: 904/777-6100 **51**
12/1-4/3 & 5/31-11/30 1P: $39-$49 2P: $45-$55 XP: $3 F17
4/4-5/30 1P: $37-$47 2P: $43-$53 XP: $3 F17
Motel Location: I-295, exit 12, just sw. 6107 Youngerman Cir 32244. Fax: 904/779-2223. **Facility:** 126 one-bedroom
standard units. 2 stories, exterior corridors. *Bath:* shower only. **Parking:** on-site. **Pool(s):** outdoor. **Guest**
Services: coin laundry. **Cards:** AX, CB, DC, DS, MC, VI.
SOME UNITS

OMNI JACKSONVILLE HOTEL *Book at aaa.com* Phone: (904)355-6664 **13**
AAA SAVE 9/5-11/30 1P: $119-$399 2P: $119-$399 XP: $10 F17
12/1-5/26 1P: $109-$399 2P: $109-$399 XP: $10 F17
5/27-9/4 1P: $105-$399 2P: $105-$399 XP: $10 F17
Location: Corner of Pearl and Water sts; on northside of St. Johns River; downtown; adjacent to The Landing. 245
Large-scale Hotel Water St 32202. Fax: 904/791-4810. **Facility:** This service-oriented hotel offers spacious rooms convenient to
the auditorium and stadium. 348 units. 344 one-bedroom standard units. 4 one-bedroom suites ($299-
$1299). 15 stories, interior corridors. **Parking:** on-site. **Terms:** cancellation fee imposed, package plans, small pets only ($50
deposit). **Amenities:** video games (fee), dual phone lines, voice mail, honor bars, irons, hair dryers. **Dining:** Juliette's, see
separate listing. **Pool(s):** heated outdoor. **Leisure Activities:** golf and tennis privileges, exercise room. **Guest Services:** gift
shop, valet laundry, area transportation-within 2 mi. **Business Services:** conference facilities, business center. **Cards:** AX, CB,
DC, DS, MC, VI.
SOME UNITS

PLANTATION MANOR INN Phone: 904/384-4630 **18**
AAA SAVE All Year [BP] 1P: $150-$200 2P: $175-$250 XP: $25
Location: Corner of Copeland and Oak sts; in the Riverside Historic District. 1630 Copeland St 32204.
Fax: 904/387-0960. **Facility:** Doric columns add a gracious touch to the wraparound porch of this 1905
Greek Revival plantation home; fireplaces are available in some units. Smoke free premises. 9 one-
Historic Bed bedroom standard units. 3 stories (no elevator), interior corridors. *Bath:* combo or shower only. **Parking:** on-
& Breakfast site. **Terms:** 7 day cancellation notice-fee imposed. **Amenities:** high-speed Internet, voice mail, irons, hair
dryers. **Pool(s):** heated outdoor. **Leisure Activities:** whirlpool. **Business Services:** PC, fax. **Cards:** AX,
DC, MC, VI. **Special Amenities:** free full breakfast and free local telephone calls.
SOME UNITS

QUALITY INN & SUITES *Book at aaa.com* Phone: (904)739-1155 **48**
AAA SAVE All Year 1P: $72 2P: $72 XP: $5 D
Location: I-95, exit 341, sw off Baymeadows Rd. 8333 Dix Ellis Tr 32256. Fax: 904/731-0752. **Facility:** 127 units.
109 one-bedroom standard units. 18 one-bedroom suites. 3 stories, exterior corridors. *Bath:* combo or
Small-scale Hotel shower only. **Parking:** on-site. **Terms:** cancellation fee imposed, [CP] meal plan available, small pets only
($50 fee). **Amenities:** voice mail, safes (fee), irons, hair dryers. **Pool(s):** outdoor. **Leisure Activities:** whirlpool, exercise room.
Guest Services: complimentary evening beverages: Mon-Thurs, valet and coin laundry. **Business Services:** meeting rooms.
Cards: AX, DC, DS, MC, VI.
SOME UNITS

RADISSON HOTEL JACKSONVILLE BUTLER
BOULEVARD *Book at aaa.com* Phone: (904)281-9700 **39**
All Year 1P: $71-$139 2P: $71-$139 XP: $10 F17
Location: I-95, exit 344, just e on Butler Blvd, then just s. 4700 Salisbury Rd 32256. Fax: 904/281-1957.
Small-scale Hotel **Facility:** 167 units. 164 one-bedroom standard units. 3 one-bedroom suites ($150-$199). 6 stories, interior
corridors. *Bath:* combo or shower only. **Parking:** on-site. **Terms:** cancellation fee imposed, package plans,
small pets only. **Amenities:** high-speed Internet, dual phone lines, voice mail, safes, irons, hair dryers. **Pool(s):** outdoor.
Leisure Activities: whirlpool, exercise room. **Guest Services:** sundries, valet and coin laundry. **Business Services:** meeting
rooms, business center. **Cards:** AX, DC, DS, MC, VI.
SOME UNITS

RADISSON RIVERWALK HOTEL *Book at aaa.com* Phone: 904/396-5100 **16**
Property failed to provide current rates
Location: South side of the St. Johns River; 0.3 mi e of Main Street Bridge; downtown. 1515 Prudential Dr 32207.
Fax: 904/396-8007. **Facility:** 322 units. 309 one-bedroom standard units. 13 one-bedroom suites, some
Large-scale Hotel with whirlpools. 5 stories, interior corridors. **Parking:** on-site. **Amenities:** voice mail, irons, hair dryers. Fee:
video games, high-speed Internet. **Pool(s):** outdoor. **Leisure Activities:** 2 lighted tennis courts, exercise room. **Guest**
Services: gift shop, valet and coin laundry. **Business Services:** conference facilities, business center.
SOME UNITS

(See map and index starting on p. 466)

RAMADA INN CONFERENCE CENTER   *Book at aaa.com*   **Phone:** (904)268-8080   **55**

(AAA) (SAVE)   All Year   1P: $89-$99   2P: $89-$99   XP: $5   F18

◆◆◆   **Location:** I-295, exit 5A northbound; exit 5 southbound, just n on SR 13. 3130 Hartley Rd 32257. Fax: 904/262-8718. **Facility:** 152 units. 150 one-bedroom standard units. 2 one-bedroom suites, some with kitchens. 2 stories, exterior corridors. **Parking:** on-site. **Terms:** small pets only ($50 fee, $100 deposit). **Amenities:** voice mail,

Small-scale Hotel   irons, hair dryers. **Dining:** 6:30-9:30 am, 11-2 & 5-9 pm, Fri & Sat-10 pm; Sunday brunch-2 pm, cocktails, nightclub. **Pool(s):** outdoor, wading. **Leisure Activities:** *Fee:* game room. **Guest Services:** valet and coin laundry. **Business Services:** meeting rooms. **Cards:** AX, CB, DC, DS, JC, MC, VI. **Special Amenities:** free full breakfast and free local telephone calls. *(See color ad below)*

SOME UNITS

FEE

RED ROOF INN-AIRPORT   *Book at aaa.com*   **Phone:** (904)741-4488   **3**

◆◆◆   1/1-11/30   1P: $48-$56   2P: $53-$61   XP: $5   F18

        12/1-12/31   1P: $45-$53   2P: $50-$58   XP: $5   F18

Motel   **Location:** I-95, exit 363, just w. 14701 Airport Entrance Rd 32218. Fax: 904/741-4493. **Facility:** 108 one-bedroom standard units. 2 stories, exterior corridors. **Parking:** on-site. **Terms:** small pets only. **Amenities:** video games (fee), voice mail. **Pool(s):** heated outdoor. **Cards:** AX, CB, DC, DS, MC, VI.

SOME UNITS

RESIDENCE INN BY MARRIOTT   *Book at aaa.com*   **Phone:** (904)996-8900   **35**

◆◆◆   All Year [BP]   1P: $99-$179   2P: $99-$179

        Location: I-95, exit 344, 3.5 mi e on J Turner Butler Blvd to Gate Blvd, just s, then just w. 10551 Deerwood Park Blvd

Small-scale Hotel   32256. Fax: 904/996-8904. **Facility:** 120 units. 60 one-bedroom standard units with efficiencies. 36 one- and 24 two-bedroom suites, some with efficiencies or kitchens. 3 stories, interior corridors. *Bath:* combo or shower only. **Parking:** on-site. **Terms:** pets ($150 fee). **Amenities:** video games, high-speed Internet, dual phone lines, voice mail, irons, hair dryers. **Pool(s):** outdoor. **Leisure Activities:** whirlpool, exercise room, sports court. **Guest Services:** complimentary evening beverages: Mon-Thurs, valet and coin laundry. **Business Services:** meeting rooms, fax (fee). **Cards:** AX, CB, DC, DS, JC, MC, VI.

SOME UNITS

RESIDENCE INN BY MARRIOTT   *Book at aaa.com*   **Phone:** (904)733-8088   **49**

(AAA) (SAVE)   All Year [BP]   1P: $119-$299

◆◆◆   **Location:** I-95, exit 341 (SR 152), just w to Freedom Commerce Pkwy, then just s to Dix Ellis Tr. 8365 Dix Ellis Tr 32256. Fax: 904/731-8354. **Facility:** 112 one-bedroom standard units with kitchens. 2 stories, exterior

Small-scale Hotel   corridors. *Bath:* combo or shower only. **Parking:** on-site. **Terms:** pets ($75 fee). **Amenities:** high-speed Internet, voice mail, irons, hair dryers. **Pool(s):** small heated outdoor. **Leisure Activities:** whirlpools, exercise room, sports court. **Guest Services:** complimentary evening beverages: Mon-Thurs, valet and coin laundry. **Business Services:** meeting rooms, fax (fee). **Cards:** AX, CB, DC, DS, MC, VI. **Special Amenities:** free full breakfast and free newspaper.

SOME UNITS

FEE

(See map and index starting on p. 466)

SPRINGHILL SUITES BY MARRIOTT JACKSONVILLE DEERWOOD PARK   *Book at aaa.com*   Phone: 904/997-6650   **21**

▼▼▼ Small-scale Hotel

Property failed to provide current rates

Location: I-95, exit 344, 2.5 mi e, then 1 mi n on SR 115. 4385 Southside Blvd 32216. Fax: 904/997-6610. **Facility:** 102 one-bedroom standard units. 5 stories, interior corridors. *Bath:* combo or shower only. **Parking:** on-site. **Amenities:** video games, high-speed Internet, dual phone lines, voice mail, irons, hair dryers. **Pool(s):** outdoor. **Leisure Activities:** whirlpool, exercise room. **Guest Services:** valet and coin laundry, area transportation. **Business Services:** meeting rooms, fax.

SOME UNITS

[icons]

WINGATE INN-AIRPORT   *Book at aaa.com*   Phone: (904)421-5000   **5**

▼▼▼ Small-scale Hotel

All Year   1P: $89-$109   2P: $89-$109   XP: $5   F17

Location: I-95, exit 363B, just w. 1200 Airport Rd 32218. Fax: 904/421-5001. **Facility:** 81 one-bedroom standard units, some with whirlpools. 4 stories, interior corridors. *Bath:* combo or shower only. **Parking:** on-site. **Terms:** check-in 4 pm, package plans. **Amenities:** video games (fee), high-speed Internet, dual phone lines, voice mail, safes, irons, hair dryers. **Pool(s):** heated indoor/outdoor. **Leisure Activities:** whirlpool, exercise room. **Guest Services:** valet and coin laundry, area transportation. **Business Services:** meeting rooms, business center. **Cards:** AX, CB, DC, DS, JC, MC, VI.

SOME UNITS

[icons]

WINGATE INN/SOUTHSIDE   *Book at aaa.com*   Phone: 904/281-2600   **29**

AAA SAVE   ▼▼▼ Small-scale Hotel

All Year   1P: $89-$169   2P: $89-$169

Location: I-95, exit 344, just w, then just n. 4681 Lenoir Ave S 32216. Fax: 904/281-1166. **Facility:** 102 one-bedroom standard units, some with whirlpools. 4 stories, interior corridors. *Bath:* combo or shower only. **Parking:** on-site. **Terms:** [BP] meal plan available. **Amenities:** video games, high-speed Internet, dual phone lines, voice mail, safes, irons, hair dryers. **Pool(s):** outdoor. **Leisure Activities:** whirlpool, exercise room. **Guest Services:** valet and coin laundry. **Business Services:** meeting rooms, business center. **Cards:** AX, DC, DS, MC, VI. **Special Amenities:** free full breakfast and free local telephone calls. *(See color ad below)*

SOME UNITS

[icons] FEE

WINGATE INN-WINDSOR PARKE   *Book at aaa.com*   Phone: (904)421-7000   **25**

▼▼▼ Small-scale Hotel

All Year   1P: $79-$199   2P: $79-$199   XP: $5   F

Location: I-95, exit 344, 7.5 mi e on SR 202, then just n on Hodges Blvd. 4791 Windsor Commons Court 32224. Fax: 904/421-7001. **Facility:** 104 one-bedroom standard units, some with whirlpools. 5 stories, interior corridors. *Bath:* combo or shower only. **Parking:** on-site. **Amenities:** video games (fee), high-speed Internet, dual phone lines, voice mail, safes, irons, hair dryers. **Pool(s):** heated indoor/outdoor. **Leisure Activities:** whirlpool, exercise room. **Guest Services:** complimentary evening beverages: Wed, coin laundry, area transportation. **Business Services:** meeting rooms, business center. **Cards:** AX, CB, DC, DS, MC, VI.

SOME UNITS

[icons]

When You Really Need to Speak Their Language... Let the IDP Speak for You

When traveling overseas, carry an **International Driving Permit...** even if you're not planning to drive. Should you need to communicate with foreign authorities, this recognizable form of identification can help you get on your way more quickly. Valid in over 150 countries, the permit contains information translated into ten languages.

Before you travel the world, travel to any AAA office for your International Driving Permit. Bring your valid U.S. driver's license, $10, and two passport-size photos (also available at AAA offices).

Travel With Someone You Trust®

(See map and index starting on p. 466)

———— WHERE TO DINE ————

THE AMERICAN CAFE
Lunch: $7-$15   **Dinner:** $7-$15   **Phone:** 904/886-8322   ⑤⑦
American
Location: I-295, exit 5, just s. 11113 San Jose Blvd 32223. **Hours:** 11 am-10 pm, Fri & Sat-11 pm. Closed: 11/23, 12/25. **Features:** Casual American dishes along the lines of burgers, gourmet pizza, oven-baked pies, ribs and pasta specialties make up the menu. Casual dress; cocktails. **Parking:** on-site. **Cards:** AX, CB, DC, DS, JC, MC, VI.

BASHA MEDITERRANEAN CUISINE
Lunch: $5-$12   **Dinner:** $5-$12   **Phone:** 904/821-4747   ㊈
Mediterranean
Location: I-95, exit 344, 7.5 mi e on SR 202, then just n; in Windsor Commons Shopping Center. 4765 Hodges Blvd 32224. **Hours:** 11 am-10 pm. Closed: Sun. **Features:** Food is made to order at the Lebanese restaurant. Tabbouleh and fattoush salads, kafta and tawook kebabs and Fatayer and lahem be ajin hot pies are a few of the tempting selections. Lebanese desserts pair well with Turkish coffee. Casual dress; beer & wine only.
Parking: on-site. **Cards:** AX, MC, VI.

BE'NAYS RESTAURANT
Lunch: $4-$9   **Dinner:** $4-$9   **Phone:** 904/714-0276   ⑨
Southern
Location: I-95, exit Dunn Ave, 0.7 mi w. 1440-22 Dunn Ave 32218. **Hours:** 11 am-8 pm, Sun-6 pm. Closed: Mon. **Features:** The storefront location is not ideal and the decor is not memorable, but the heaping servings of Caribbean favorites are well worth the trip. Casual dress. **Parking:** on-site. **Cards:** MC, VI.

BISCOTTI'S ESPRESSO CAFE
Lunch: $8-$20   **Dinner:** $10-$30   **Phone:** 904/387-2060   ㉘
American
Location: I-10, exit 360, 2 mi s on McDuff Ave, then 1 mi w. 3556 St. Johns Ave 32204. **Hours:** 10:30 am-10 pm, Fri-midnight, Sat 8 am-midnight, Sun 8 am-9 pm. Closed major holidays. **Features:** Indoor and outdoor seating is available in the relaxed neighborhood gathering spot, which overlooks the Avondale shopping district. On the eclectic menu are pizzas, salads and hearty sandwiches, which are nicely accompanied by freshly ground coffee, espresso and cappuccino. Desserts are decadent. Casual dress; beer & wine only. **Parking:** street.
Cards: AX, DC, DS, MC, VI.

BONO'S PIT BAR-B-Q
Lunch: $6-$15   **Dinner:** $6-$15   **Phone:** 904/998-1997   ㊴
Barbecue
Location: I-95, exit 344, 3.5 mi e on J Turner Butler Blvd to Gate Pkwy, just n, then just w. 10020 Skinner Lake Dr 32246. **Hours:** 11 am-9 pm. Closed major holidays. **Features:** Slow-cooked for over 12 hours, the meat is what sets this small chain apart from the others; the juicy and favorable ribs, pulled pork, chicken, beef and turkey are just some of the offerings available here. Try the different fried corn on the cob or slow-cooked baked beans for great tasting sides. Casual dress; beer only. **Parking:** on-site. **Cards:** AX, DS, MC, VI.

BONO'S PIT BAR-B-Q
Lunch: $6-$15   **Dinner:** $6-$15   **Phone:** 904/696-6968   ⑦
Barbecue
Location: I-295, exit 360, just w. 1036-2 Dunn Ave 32218. **Hours:** 11 am-9 pm, Fri & Sat-10 pm, Sun noon-9 pm. Closed major holidays. **Features:** Slow-cooked for over 12 hours, the meat is what sets this small chain apart from the others; the juicy and favorable ribs, pulled pork, chicken, beef and turkey are just some of the offerings available here. Try the different fried corn on the cob or slow-cooked baked beans for great tasting sides. Casual dress; beer only. **Parking:** on-site. **Cards:** AX, DS, MC, VI.

BRAVO RISTORANTE!
Lunch: $10-$15   **Dinner:** $20-$30   **Phone:** 904/633-9095   ⑭
Italian
Location: Downtown. 225 E Coastline Dr 32202. **Hours:** 11:30 am-1:30 & 5-10 pm, Fri & Sat-11 pm. Closed: Sun. **Reservations:** accepted. **Features:** Entertainment abounds at the performance-focused restaurant. Guests can be mesmerized by the culinary staff in the exhibition kitchen or the show-tune-singing servers atop the grand piano. Dressy casual; cocktails. **Parking:** valet. **Cards:** AX, CB, DC, DS, JC, MC, VI.

THE BRICK RESTAURANT
Lunch: $12-$20   **Dinner:** $15-$28   **Phone:** 904/387-0606   ㉙
International
Location: Just sw of S Edgewood Ave; s of downtown; in historic Avondale. 3585 St. John Ave 32205. **Hours:** 11 am-10 pm, Fri 10 am-midnight, Sat 10:30 am-midnight, Sun 10 am-10 pm. **Features:** A historic building with a large bar area featuring live music on some nights showcases a broad menu of both familiar and more trendy and creative preparations. The efficient service is performed by a pleasantly agreeable staff making it an ideal spot for early evening family or casual dining. Casual dress; cocktails; entertainment. **Parking:** street. **Cards:** AX, CB, DC, DS, JC, MC, VI.
Ⓛ Ⓜ

BUCA DI BEPPO
Dinner: $8-$19   **Phone:** 904/363-9090   ㊺
Italian
Location: I-95, exit 339, 0.3 mi e; in Avenues Mall parking lot. 10334 Southside Blvd 32256. **Hours:** 5 pm-10 pm, Sat & Sun from noon. **Features:** Experience Italian food the way it was meant to be: with the whole family. The menu is set up with family sized portions; if you are lacking in conversation, just look at the interesting items hanging on the walls. Casual dress; beer & wine only. **Parking:** on-site. **Cards:** AX, DS, MC, VI.

CELENO'S PIZZA
Lunch: $5-$10   **Dinner:** $5-$10   **Phone:** 904/646-9200   ㊸
Italian
Location: I-95, exit 341, 0.8 mi e; in Baymeadows Common Shopping Center. 9550 Baymeadows Rd, #7 32256. **Hours:** 11 am-10 pm, Fri & Sat-11 pm. Closed major holidays. **Features:** Pizza is the specialty on a menu that also includes hot and cold submarine sandwiches, salads and traditional Italian favorites. Casual dress. **Parking:** on-site. **Cards:** MC, VI.

CHAN'S CHINESE RESTAURANT
Lunch: $5-$12   **Dinner:** $7-$20   **Phone:** 904/751-1716   ⑥
Chinese
Location: I-95, exit Dunn Ave, 0.5 mi w. 1036 Dunn Ave, Suite 24 32218. **Hours:** 11 am-9:30 pm, Fri-10:30 pm, Sat-10 pm, Sun noon-9 pm. **Features:** The restaurant is a popular lunch spot for good reason: selections don't taste batch prepared and the service is pleasant. Casual dress. **Parking:** on-site. **Cards:** MC, VI.

CHINA SUPER BUFFET
Lunch: $4-$9   **Dinner:** $9-$12   **Phone:** 904/696-8588   ㉟
Chinese
Location: I-95, exit 360, 0.4 mi w; in Highland Square shopping center. 1038-003 Dunn Ave 32218. **Hours:** 11 am-10:30 pm, Fri & Sat-11 pm. **Features:** Guests are sure to find some of their favorite Chinese dishes on the extensive buffet. Choices include beef with broccoli and sweet and sour chicken, as well as a nice selection of desserts. Casual dress. **Parking:** on-site. **Cards:** MC, VI.

(See map and index starting on p. 466)

CLARK'S FISH CAMP
Seafood

Lunch: $5-$14 Dinner: $5-$14 Phone: 904/268-3474 (62)
Location: I-295, exit 3, 0.8 mi s, then 1.7 mi w. 12903 Hood Landing Rd 32217. **Hours:** 4:30 pm-9:30 pm, Fri-10 pm, Sat 11:30 am-10 pm, Sun 11:30 am-9 pm. **Closed:** 1/1, 11/23, 12/24, 12/25; also Super Bowl Sun. **Features:** Guests can appreciate old Florida charm at its best. The menu lists a slew of Southern favorites, starting with New England or Minorcan clam chowder or fried gator tail. Fried, charbroiled or the house special stuffed fish with hush puppies and cole slaw make up the core of the menu. Mounted animals surround the relaxing indoor dining rooms, while the patio overlooks the waterway. Most meals come with choices of vegetables and salad. Casual dress; cocktails. **Parking:** on-site. **Cards:** DS, MC, VI.

COAL'S BRICK OVEN PIZZERIA
Pizza

Lunch: $7-$15 Dinner: $7-$15 Phone: 904/220-0096 (16)
Location: Jct SR 9A/10, 4 mi e. 13245-1 Atlantic Blvd 32225. **Hours:** 11 am-9 pm, Fri & Sat-10 pm, Sun noon-9 pm. **Closed** major holidays. **Features:** Wood-fired ovens add tasty flavor to a wide selection of specialty pizzas. Also offered is an excellent selection of sandwiches, salads, well-prepared pasta dishes and oven-baked dinners. Casual dress; beer & wine only. **Parking:** on-site. **Cards:** AX, DS, MC, VI. (占M)

COPELAND'S OF NEW ORLEANS
Cajun

Lunch: $7-$15 Dinner: $12-$28 Phone: 904/998-4414 (34)
Location: I-95, exit 344, 0.3 mi e, then 1.4 mi n. 4310 Southside Blvd 32216. **Hours:** 11 am-11 pm, Sun-10 pm. **Closed:** 12/25. **Reservations:** accepted. **Features:** A taste of N'awlins awaits just inside the doors. The vast menu of Cajun specialties comprises temptations for everyone. Casual dress; cocktails. **Parking:** on-site. **Cards:** AX, CB, DC, DS, JC, MC, VI. (占M)

THE CORNER BRASSERIE
Regional American

Lunch: $7-$11 Dinner: $19-$24 Phone: 904/396-1414 (23)
Location: Between Childrens Way and Phillips St; in San Marco neighborhood. 1430 San Marco Blvd 32207. **Hours:** 11 am-3 & 5-10 pm, Sat from 5 pm, Mon-3 pm. **Closed:** 1/1, 11/23, 12/26; also Sun. **Reservations:** suggested. **Features:** The cozy and intimate dining room is comfortably casual. The talented chef creates delectable meals and creative dishes. Some favorites include Caribbean snapper, fried green tomatoes with goat cheese, Angus beef filet and prosciutto-wrapped Muscovy duck. For a refreshing treat, try the chilled anise-scented avocado soup with jumbo lump crab meat. Dressy casual; beer & wine only. **Parking:** on-site. **Cards:** AX, DS, MC, VI.

CROSS CREEK STEAKHOUSE & RIBS
American

Lunch: $5-$19 Dinner: $5-$19 Phone: 904/765-7420 (1)
Location: I-295, exit 32, just s. 12123 Lem Turner Rd 32218. **Hours:** 11 am-10 pm, Fri & Sat-11 pm. **Closed:** 11/23, 12/25. **Features:** Great tasting thick cut steaks and wonderful fall-off-the-bone ribs are just a few of the main entrees this popular restaurant is known for. They also feature great salads and numerous sandwiches for lunch and dinner. Casual dress; cocktails. **Parking:** on-site. **Cards:** AX, DS, MC, VI. (占M)(Y)

CRUSH
French

Dinner: $19-$35 Phone: 904/381-0909 (26)
Location: Just e of Roosevelt Blvd; s of downtown; in historic Avondale. 3630 Park St 32205. **Hours:** 5 pm-10 pm, Fri & Sat-2 am. **Closed:** 11/23, 12/25; also Sun & Mon. **Features:** Flawless service in cozy, refined surroundings epitomizes the dining experience at this relatively new restaurant. The gourmet cuisine is deftly prepared. Great for sharing are the petit or grand voyage which includes a dizzying array of seafood. Dressy casual; beer & wine only. **Parking:** on-site. **Cards:** AX, DS, MC, VI. (Y)

DAVE & BUSTERS
American

Lunch: $5-$8 Dinner: $7-$20 Phone: 904/296-1525 (41)
Location: I-95, exit 101, just s. 7025 Salisbury Rd 32256. **Hours:** 11:30 am-midnight, Thurs-Sat to 1 am. **Features:** Game aficionados can take time out from the bustling arcade, pocket billiards or shuffleboard to dine in the relaxed setting off in the corner. Casual dress; cocktails. **Parking:** on-site. **Cards:** AX, CB, DC, DS, MC, VI. (Y)

DEERWOOD DELI & DINER
American

Lunch: $7-$9 Phone: 904/641-4877 (45)
Location: I-95, exit 344, 3.5 mi e on J Turner Butler Blvd to Gate Blvd, just s, then w. 9934 Old Baymeadows Rd 32256. **Hours:** 7 am-4:30 pm. **Closed** major holidays; also Sun. **Reservations:** not accepted. **Features:** The classic diner decor takes you back in time as you enjoy excellent homemade sandwiches and shakes. Casual dress. **Parking:** on-site. **Cards:** AX, MC, VI.

EL RANCHITO RESTAURANT
Colombian

Lunch: $6-$12 Dinner: $6-$12 Phone: 904/992-4607 (31)
Location: On US 90, just w of jct San Pablo; in San Pablo Station. 1433-22 Beach Blvd 32250. **Hours:** 11 am-9 pm. **Closed:** Mon. **Features:** The restaurant is popular for its varied menu, which incorporates Colombian, Cuban and Mexican items. Sweet plantains, yuca, chicken with yellow rice, Cuban sandwiches, quesadillas, tacos and fajitas are among eclectic choices. Casual dress; beer & wine only. **Parking:** on-site. **Cards:** MC, VI.

ENRICOS RISTORANTE
Italian

Lunch: $6-$10 Dinner: $10-$19 Phone: 904/538-9882 (52)
Location: Jct Baymeadows Rd and SR 9A; in Reedy Branch Shopping Center. 10920-3 Baymeadows Rd 32256. **Hours:** 11 am-2 & 5-10 pm. **Features:** A relaxing atmosphere is not all that patrons find at the ristorante, where the pasta is homemade and fresh ingredients enhance the flavor of every dish. Gnocchi with bolognese sauce, shrimp scampi and chicken marshal are a few treats to tide guests over until dessert. The tiramisu should not be missed. Casual dress; cocktails. **Parking:** on-site. **Cards:** AX, DS, MC, VI. (占M)

FOO HOUSE
Chinese

Lunch: $5-$7 Dinner: $7-$23 Phone: 904/730-2468 (46)
Location: I-95, exit 341 (SR 152), 0.6 mi e; in Food Lion Shopping Center. 9550-32 Baymeadows Rd (SR 152) 32256. **Hours:** 11 am-2:30 & 4:30-9:30 pm, Sat & Sun from noon. **Closed:** 11/23, 12/25. **Features:** Beautiful Oriental decor, friendly service and a wide selection of made-to-order dishes set the restaurant apart. Lunch specials offer extra value. Casual dress; beer & wine only. **Parking:** on-site. **Cards:** AX, DS, MC, VI. (占M)

(See map and index starting on p. 466)

GALLERY BISTRO   Lunch: $5-$8   Dinner: $11-$25   Phone: 904/997-8320   (37)
Location: I-95, exit 344, 2.5 mi e on J Turner Butler Blvd, 0.9 mi n on SR 115, then just e. 9753 Deer Lake Ct 32246. **Hours:** 11 am-10 pm, Fri-11 pm, Sat 5 pm-11 pm, Sun 5 pm-10 pm. Closed: 11/23, 12/24, 12/25. **Reservations:** accepted. **Features:** Relax in a dining room of comfortable modern decor, accented by contemporary art, woods, metal and bold colors. Well-prepared menu selections have an upscale flare, and include comfort foods, Asian accents and fusion. Dressy casual; cocktails. **Parking:** on-site. **Cards:** AX, DS, MC, VI.
American

GENGHIS KHAN MONGOLIAN BAR-B-QUE   Dinner: $7-$12   Phone: 904/268-1668   (54)
Location: I-295, exit 5, just n. 10601 San Jose Blvd 32217. **Hours:** 5 pm-9:30 pm, Fri & Sat-11 pm. Closed: 11/23, 12/25. **Features:** Guests navigate a buffet-style setup while choosing meats and vegetables for the chef to prepare. Casual dress; beer & wine only. **Parking:** on-site. **Cards:** AX, MC, VI.
Mongolian

GINZA JAPANESE CUISINE   Lunch: $7-$10   Dinner: $9-$24   Phone: 904/928-1375   (33)
Location: US 90/SR 212/Beach Blvd, just s; in Kernan Plaza. 3503 Kernan Blvd S 32224. **Hours:** 11 am-8:30 pm, Fri & Sat-10:30 pm. **Features:** The small restaurant's big menu lists more than 30 traditional and custom rolls among its selection of sushi and sashimi. Also offered are special bowl meals and teriyaki- and tempura-style foods. Casual dress; beer & wine only. **Parking:** on-site. **Cards:** AX, MC, VI.
Japanese

HARMONIUS MONKS   Dinner: $6-$19   Phone: 904/880-3040   (55)
Location: I-295, exit 3, 1.2 mi n. 10550 Old Saint Augustine Rd 32223. **Hours:** 5 pm-2 am. Closed: Sun. **Reservations:** accepted. **Features:** While you satisfy your appetite, the singing wait staff will entertain you; don't be afraid to join in. Casual dress; cocktails. **Parking:** on-site. **Cards:** AX, DC, DS, MC, VI.
American

JOHNNY CARINO'S   Lunch: $6-$8   Dinner: $7-$13   Phone: 904/646-4822   (17)
Location: On SR 10, just w of Kernan Rd. 11892 Atlantic Ave 32225. **Hours:** 11 am-10 pm, Fri & Sat-11 pm. Closed: 11/23, 12/25. **Features:** The restaurant calls itself "country Italian." Menu selections include many traditional favorites, as well as some inventive and hot and spicy items. The atmosphere is casual, and the dining room is decorated in a Mediterranean theme. Casual dress; cocktails. **Parking:** on-site. **Cards:** AX, DC, DS, MC, VI.
Italian

JOSEPH'S ITALIAN RESTAURANT   Lunch: $6-$10   Dinner: $7-$15   Phone: 904/642-3444   (49)
Location: I-95, exit 344, 1.5 mi e; in Baymeadows Village Shopping Center. 9802 Baymeadows Rd 32216. **Hours:** 11 am-10 pm, Sun-9:30 pm. Closed major holidays; also Mon. **Features:** All entrees made to order using old Italian family recipies. Choose from traditional pizza's with gourmet toppings, fresh salads, homemade pasta dishes or delicious hot or cold sandwiches. Casual dress; beer & wine only. **Parking:** on-site. **Cards:** AX, DC, DS, MC, VI.
Italian

JOSEPH'S PIZZA & ITALIAN RESTAURANT   Lunch: $4-$18   Dinner: $4-$18   Phone: 904/765-0335   (10)
Location: I-95, exit 355, just e to Brentwood Ave, 0.5 mi n to W 44th St, 0.7 mi to N Main St, then 0.8 mi n. 7316 N Main St 32208. **Hours:** 11 am-10 pm, Fri & Sat-10:30 pm, Sun 11 am-9:30 pm. **Features:** All entrees at this restaurant are made to order using old Italian family recipies. Choose from traditional pizzas with gourmet toppings, fresh salads, homemade pasta dishes or delicious hot or cold sandwiches. Casual dress; beer & wine only. **Parking:** on-site. **Cards:** AX, DS, MC, VI.
Italian

JT'S SMOKEHOUSE BAR-B-Q   Lunch: $6-$10   Dinner: $7-$11   Phone: 904/751-2750   (8)
Location: I-95, exit 360, 0.8 mi n; in Dunn Avenue Plaza. 1440 Dunn Ave 32218. **Hours:** 11 am-9 pm, Thurs-Sat to 10 pm. Closed: 12/24, 12/25. **Features:** Guests find hearty barbecue favorites—ribs, turkey, chicken and other tasty fare—on the menu in the rustic eatery. A country lunch buffet featuring meats, vegetables, salad and desserts is offered six days a week. Casual dress; beer only. **Parking:** on-site. **Cards:** AX, MC, VI.
Barbecue

JULIETTE'S   Lunch: $4-$13   Dinner: $17-$32   Phone: 904/355-7118   (12)
Location: Corner of Pearl and Water sts; on northside of St. Johns River; downtown; adjacent to The Landing; in Omni Jacksonville Hotel. 245 Water St 32202. **Hours:** 6:30 am-2 & 5-10:30 pm, Fri & Sat-11 pm. **Reservations:** suggested. **Features:** The upscale bistro offers dining in an open-ceiling, high-rise atrium. The seasonally changing menu combines the flavors of America and Italy in its pasta, seafood, steak and chicken dishes. The wine list shows breadth, and the servers are knowledgeable. Dressy casual; cocktails. **Parking:** on-site. **Cards:** AX, CB, DC, DS, JC, MC, VI.
American

LA RANCHERITA   Lunch: $5-$10   Dinner: $5-$12   Phone: 904/751-5928   (5)

Location: I-95, exit 360, 0.8 mi w; in Dunn Plaza Shopping Center. 1440 Dunn Ave, 27A 32218. **Hours:** 11 am-9 pm, Sun-3 pm. Closed: 11/23, 12/25. **Features:** This place may be small, but the food and attentive service are plentiful. Enjoy authentic Mexican delights such as fajitas and chimichangas. A lunch buffet is served daily; come early as all the locals flock here. Casual dress. **Parking:** on-site. **Cards:** AX, MC, VI.
Mexican

MADRID   Lunch: $5-$10   Dinner: $5-$12   Phone: 904/642-3741   (32)
Location: Just e of SR 9A. 11233 Beach Blvd 32246. **Hours:** 10:30 am-9 pm. **Features:** Ample portions of your choice are served up quickly and bright, colorful decor sets the mood for a good meal. Casual dress. **Parking:** on-site. **Cards:** MC, VI.
Spanish

MANDARIN DRAGON   Lunch: $4-$6   Dinner: $6-$12   Phone: 904/260-4681   (60)
Location: I-295, exit 5, 1 mi s; in The Gates of Olde Mandarin Shopping Center. 11362-8 San Jose Blvd 32223. **Hours:** 11 am-9:30 pm, Fri & Sat-10 pm. Closed: 7/4, 11/23, 12/25. **Reservations:** suggested, weekends. **Features:** An Oriental motif featuring dragon decorations and exotic flowers weaves through the bi-level dining room of the restaurant. In addition to well-presented traditional dishes, you can choose from an interesting selection of Chinese beer and wine. Casual dress; beer & wine only. **Parking:** on-site. **Cards:** AX, DC, DS, MC, VI.
Chinese

(See map and index starting on p. 466)

MARCO POLO CHINESE RESTAURANT & MONGOLIAN BARBECUE
Lunch: $7-$14   **Dinner:** $7-$14   **Phone:** 904/768-8700   ②

Chinese

Location: I-295, exit 30, 1.5 mi e on SR 104; jct Lem Turner Rd. 3000-14 Dunn Ave 32218. **Hours:** 11 am-9:30 pm, Fri & Sat-10:30 pm. **Features:** An Oriental buffet makes this a popular spot. Guests also can hand pick bowls of fresh ingredients that will be cooked at the Mongolian grill as they wait. If neither of those options sounds appealing, a standard menu lists more than 100 items, including moo goo gai pan, sweet and sour pork, garlic shrimp and egg foo yong. Casual dress. **Parking:** on-site. **Cards:** MC, VI.

MARKER 32
Dinner: $16-$33   **Phone:** 904/223-1534   ㉚

Continental

Location: 0.5 mi w of Intracoastal Waterway Bridge. 14549 Beach Blvd 32225. **Hours:** 5:30 pm-10 pm, Fri & Sat-11:30 pm. Closed major holidays. **Reservations:** suggested. **Features:** Delicious, innovative dishes of polenta, grilled mahi mahi and the sinful chocolate comet attract an upscale crowd to this casual restaurant. Polished servers are knowledgeable about the menu, and the waterfront views are outstanding. Dressy casual; cocktails. **Parking:** on-site. **Cards:** AX, DC, MC, VI.

MATTHEW'S
AAA

Dinner: $20-$32   **Phone:** 904/396-9922   ㉕

Continental

Location: Just s of Atlantic Blvd; s of downtown; in historic San Marco. 2107 Hendricks Ave 32207. **Hours:** 5:30 pm-10 pm. Closed major holidays; also Sun. **Reservations:** required. **Features:** Recognized as one of Jacksonville's premiere dining rooms, the restaurant provides a showcase in which renowned chef Matthew Medure tantalizes guests with innovative cuisine and award-winning wines. Superbly refined service reaches each intimate booth and linen-clothed table, as well as the chef's barside tasting table near the kitchen. The diverse menu blends Southern, Mediterranean and Asian influences. Reservations typically fill up well in advance. Semi-formal attire; beer & wine only. **Parking:** on-site. **Cards:** AX, DC, DS, MC, VI.

MELLOW MUSHROOM
Lunch: $7-$18   **Dinner:** $7-$25   **Phone:** 904/997-1955   ㊱

Pizza

Location: I-95, exit 344 E, e on J Turner Butler Blvd, 2.4 mi to SR 115, then 1 mi n. 9734 Deer Lake Ct 32246. **Hours:** 11 am-10 pm, Fri & Sat-midnight, Sun noon-10 pm. Closed: 12/25. **Reservations:** accepted. **Features:** Large hoagies, honey-basted pretzels and 16-inch pizzas are a few favorites. Pizza by the slice is available. Casual dress; cocktails. **Parking:** on-site. **Cards:** AX, CB, DC, DS, JC, MC, VI.

MORTON'S THE STEAKHOUSE
Dinner: $43-$57   **Phone:** 904/399-3933   ⑳

Steak House

Location: Just n of corner of Prudential Dr and Riverplace Blvd; downtown. 1510 Riverplace Blvd 32207. **Hours:** 5:30 pm-11 pm, Sun 5 pm-10 pm. Closed major holidays. **Reservations:** suggested. **Features:** This is the king of kings steakhouse for the ardent carnivore. Polished service is executed in a relaxed and refined atmosphere. Besides the humongous Porterhouse steak, there is prime rib, filet mignon, New York strip and rib-eye along with accompaniments of creamed spinach and garlic mash potatoes. Dressy casual; cocktails. **Parking:** valet. **Cards:** AX, CB, DC, MC, VI.

MOSSFIRE GRILL
Lunch: $7-$9   **Dinner:** $10-$20   **Phone:** 904/355-4434   ㉒

Southwestern

Location: Just s of Park St. 1537 Margaret St 32204. **Hours:** 11 am-10 pm. Closed major holidays; also Sun. **Features:** The chef serves Southwestern foods with flair, from chile-fried plantains to BBQ shrimp tostada. In seasonal weather, the shady patio offers Southern charm in which to enjoy pecan chicken and key lime pie. Casual dress; cocktails. **Parking:** street. **Cards:** AX, CB, DC, MC, VI.

MT. FUJI JAPANESE STEAK HOUSE & SUSHI BAR
Lunch: $5-$30   **Dinner:** $11-$30   **Phone:** 904/724-8883   ⑮

Japanese

Location: 0.3 mi w of SR 9A. 10055 Atlantic Blvd 32225. **Hours:** 11:30 am-2:30 & 5-10 pm. **Features:** Watching the personal chefs prepare meals is a show in itself. Many Japanese combination platters are among choices, as is a great selection of sushi and sashimi. Casual dress; cocktails. **Parking:** on-site. **Cards:** AX, DS, MC, VI.

PAGODA CHINESE RESTAURANT
AAA

Lunch: $5-$7   **Dinner:** $8-$19   **Phone:** 904/731-0880   ㊷

Chinese

Location: I-95, exit 341, 0.5 mi w on SR 152. 8617 Baymeadows Rd 32256. **Hours:** 11 am-10 pm, Fri-11 pm, Sat noon-11 pm; also Sun. **Features:** 7/4, 11/23, 12/25; also Sun. **Features:** A family operation since the mid-1980s, the informal restaurant serves such traditional cuisine as sweet-and-sour chicken, curry chicken, fried rice and seafood with vegetables—all spiced to the diner's preference. Modern Chinese artifacts decorate the building's interior—a pagoda-like room with a beamed ceiling and 360-degree skylights. Casual dress; cocktails. **Parking:** on-site. **Cards:** AX, CB, DC, DS, MC, VI.

PANERA BREAD
Lunch: $3-$8   **Dinner:** $3-$8   **Phone:** 904/645-5747   ㊽

American

Location: I-95, exit 344, 1.5 mi e; in Baymeadows Village Shopping Center. 9810 Baymeadows Rd 32256. **Hours:** 6:30 am-9 pm, Sun 7 am-8 pm. **Features:** The restaurant is a great place for healthy sandwiches and homemade soups served in large bread bowls. Numerous varieties of freshly baked bread and bagels make this a popular stop for breakfast. Casual dress. **Parking:** on-site. **Cards:** AX, DS, MC, VI.

POM'S THAI BISTRO
Lunch: $13-$24   **Dinner:** $27-$34   **Phone:** 904/338-0269   ㉔

Thai

Location: Between Naldo Ave and Sorrento Rd; in San Marco neighborhood. 1974 San Marco Blvd 32207. **Hours:** 11:30 am-2 & 5-10 pm, Fri & Sat-10:30 pm. Closed major holidays; also Sun. **Reservations:** suggested. **Features:** This is a trendy restaurant above a lively bar in a pedestrian-friendly neighborhood. The savory seasoned dishes are both mouth-watering and exquisitely presented. Dressy casual; cocktails. **Parking:** street. **Cards:** AX, CB, DC, DS, JC, MC, VI.

RENNA'S PIZZA
Lunch: $2-$8   **Dinner:** $2-$8   **Phone:** 904/730-9313   ㊹

Pizza

Location: I-95, exit 341 (SR 152), 0.4 mi w; in Baymeadows Festival Shopping Center. 8642 Baymeadows Rd (SR 152) 32226. **Hours:** 10:30 am-9 pm, Fri & Sat-10 pm, Sun noon-9 pm. Closed major holidays. **Features:** With three successful area restaurants of the same name and a history that goes back decades, the New York-style pizzeria consistently has been rated in the top of its class. Pasta and soups also are available. Casual dress; beer & wine only. **Parking:** on-site. **Cards:** AX, DS, MC, VI.

(See map and index starting on p. 466)

RIVER CITY BREWING COMPANY **Lunch:** $6-$15 **Dinner:** $14-$30 **Phone:** 904/398-2299 [18]
Location: On south bank of St. Johns River; just w of Main Street Bridge. 835 Museum Cir 32207. **Hours:** 11 am-3 & 5-10 pm, Fri & Sat-11 pm, Sun 10:30 am-2:30 pm. **Closed:** 12/25; also for lunch 1/1. **Reservations:** accepted. **Features:** The restaurant carries out a mood of casual elegance with white linen tablecloths and servers working in teams. The nautically themed, tiered dining room offers scenic views of the city skyline, the St. Johns River and the marina. Eclectic menu choices include preparations of chicken, chops and pasta with an emphasis on local seafood. Inviting desserts are displayed on a tray. A spacious riverside deck and a brew pub are dining alternatives and a perfect setting for happy hour. Casual dress; cocktails. **Parking:** on-site. **Cards:** AX, CB, DC, DS, MC, VI.

American

ROSALIA'S ITALIAN CAFE **Lunch:** $5-$10 **Dinner:** $9-$20 **Phone:** 904/880-3989 [53]
Location: I-295, exit 5, just n. 10503-3 San Jose Blvd 32257. **Hours:** 11 am-10 pm, Sat from 4:30 pm. Closed major holidays; also Sun. **Reservations:** accepted. **Features:** Seat yourself in this storefront cafe with real Italian flair. Offers a variey of specialties, such as baked ziti. Casual dress; beer & wine only. **Parking:** on-site. **Cards:** AX, DC, DS, MC, VI.

Italian

RUTH'S CHRIS STEAK HOUSE **Dinner:** $24-$38 **Phone:** 904/396-6200 [19]
Location: Downtown on the St. John's River; in Hilton Jacksonville & Towers. 1201 Riverplace Blvd 32207. **Hours:** 5 pm-10:30 pm, Fri & Sat-11 pm, Sun-9:30 pm. **Closed:** 11/23, 12/25. **Reservations:** suggested. **Features:** Dressy casual; cocktails. **Parking:** on-site and valet. **Cards:** AX, CB, DC, DS, JC, MC, VI.

Steak House

ST. JOHN'S SEAFOOD AND STEAKS **Lunch:** $6-$7 **Dinner:** $7-$15 **Phone:** 904/696-1023 [3]
Location: I-95, exit 125, 0.7 mi w. 1403-21 Dunn Ave 32218. **Hours:** 11 am-10 pm, Fri & Sat-10:30 pm, Sun-9 pm. Closed major holidays. **Features:** Nautical-themed decor sets the tone in the dining room, where patrons gather for hearty steak and seafood dishes. Generous portions are a good value. Casual dress; beer & wine only. **Parking:** on-site. **Cards:** AX, DC, DS, MC, VI.

Steak & Seafood

SANTIONI'S CUCINA ITALIANA **Dinner:** $10-$22 **Phone:** 904/262-5190 [61]
Location: I-295, exit 5, 1.5 mi s. 11531 San Jose Blvd 32223. **Hours:** 5 pm-10 pm, Fri & Sat-11 pm. Closed major holidays. **Features:** Homemade pastas, sauces and breads are prepared daily in the old-style Italian eatery. Lobster pescatora, gnocchi and chicken parmigiana are some of the nightly offerings. Dressy casual; beer & wine only. **Parking:** on-site. **Cards:** AX, DS, MC, VI.

Italian

SEVEN BRIDGES GRILLE & BREWERY **Lunch:** $9-$12 **Dinner:** $9-$20 **Phone:** 904/997-1999 [38]
Location: I-95, exit 344, 2.5 mi e on J Turner Butler Blvd, 0.8 mi n on SR 115, then just e. 9735 Gate Pkwy N 32246. **Hours:** 11 am-midnight, Fri & Sat-2 am. **Reservations:** accepted. **Features:** Open warehouse feel with beer vats on the second level visible from most areas of the restaurant. Unique and tasty menu selections like hazelnut encrusted chicken. Large scale desserts are homemade and worth saving room for. Casual dress; cocktails. **Parking:** on-site. **Cards:** AX, DS, JC, MC, VI.

American

SOL CUBA CAFE **Lunch:** $6-$12 **Dinner:** $8-$14 **Phone:** 904/696-6660 [4]
Location: I-95, exit 360, just w. 1440-34 Dunn Ave 32218. **Hours:** 10:30 am-9 pm, Fri-11 pm, Sat noon-11 pm. Closed major holidays; also Sun. **Reservations:** accepted. **Features:** This unassuming eatery is where healthy portions of home-style Cuban cuisine is simply presented. It's also quite a popular spot for take-away but suitable for dining in as well. Casual dress; beer & wine only. **Parking:** on-site. **Cards:** MC, VI.

Cuban

SOUPER SALAD **Lunch:** $6-$8 **Dinner:** $6-$8 **Phone:** 904/732-7075 [47]
Location: I-95, exit 341 (SR 152), 0.6 mi e; in Food Lion Shopping Center. 9550-17 Baymeadows Rd (SR 152) 32256. **Hours:** 10:15 am-9 pm, Sun 10:30 am-8:30 pm. **Closed:** 11/23, 12/25. **Features:** Excellent value options, the meals satisfy not only the enormously hungry but also weight watchers. The self-service cafeteria line has soups, salads, potatoes, pasta, taco fixings, pizza, dessert and sundae bars and breads. All items are prepared daily. Casual dress. **Parking:** on-site. **Cards:** AX, DC, DS, MC, VI.

American

STERLINGS OF AVONDALE **Lunch:** $8-$12 **Dinner:** $19-$39 **Phone:** 904/387-0700 [27]
Location: Just w of S Edgewood Ave; s of downtown; in historic Avondale. 3551 St. Johns Ave 32205. **Hours:** 11 am-3 & 5:30-10 pm, Fri & Sat-11 pm, Sun 11 am-2 & 5-9 pm. **Reservations:** accepted. **Features:** Guests can sit back in an upscale atmosphere and dine on preparations of veal, rack of lamb, seafood and steak. The wine selection is extensive. Dressy casual; cocktails. **Parking:** street. **Cards:** AX, DS, MC, VI.

American

SUSHI & WOK **Lunch:** $3-$8 **Dinner:** $3-$11 **Phone:** 904/642-5522 [13]
Location: 1.3 mi e of jct SR 9A; in Justin Plaza. 10916 Atlantic Blvd, #23 32225. **Hours:** 11 am-10:30 pm, Fri & Sat-11:30 pm, Sun noon-10 pm. **Features:** The eatery serves batch prepared Chinese food for those in a hurry. Casual dress. **Parking:** on-site. **Cards:** AX, MC, VI.

Japanese

SWEET INDULGENCE CAFE & DESSERTS **Lunch:** $3-$7 **Dinner:** $3-$7 **Phone:** 904/538-0787 [51]
Location: Jct Baymeadows Rd and SR 9A; in Reedy Branch Shopping Center. 10920 Baymeadows Rd, Suite 33 32256. **Hours:** 7 am-10 pm, Sun from 8 am. **Features:** A display case of freshly made breads, desserts and pastries entices patrons as they order at the counter. Made-to-order sandwiches, specialty coffees, ice cream and tempting desserts will satisfy anyone. Casual dress. **Parking:** on-site. **Cards:** AX, DS, MC, VI.

American

THE TREE STEAK HOUSE **Dinner:** $14-$30 **Phone:** 904/262-0006 [59]
Location: I-295, exit 5, 1 mi s; in The Gates of Olde Mandarin Shopping Center. 11362-1 San Jose Blvd 32223. **Hours:** 5 pm-10 pm, Fri & Sat-10:30 pm, Sun-9 pm. Closed major holidays. **Reservations:** accepted. **Features:** Brick and low lighting contribute to the rustic atmosphere of the busy restaurant. The open-flame grill faces the dining room, and steaks are cut to order at the table. An extensive wine list and a varied salad bar complement the entrees. Casual dress; cocktails. **Parking:** on-site. **Cards:** AX, CB, DC, DS, MC, VI.

Steak House

(See map and index starting on p. 466)

TRUFFLES COFFEE HOUSE & BAKERY **Lunch:** $5-$9 **Dinner:** $5-$9 **Phone:** 904/260-5192 ⑤⑧
Bakery/Desserts
Location: I-295, exit 5, 1 mi s; in The Gates of Olde Mandarin Shopping Center. 11362-11 San Jose Blvd 32223. **Hours:** 7 am-9 pm, Fri & Sat-11 pm, Sun 8 am-7 pm. **Features:** Those with a sweet tooth should beware because the bakery is a trove of temptations. Homemade breakfast pastries, muffins, cookies, bars, cheesecakes, tortes, pies and cakes are offered in many varieties. Casual dress; beer & wine only. **Parking:** on-site. **Cards:** AX, DS, MC, VI.

VITO'S ITALIAN RESTAURANT **Lunch:** $6-$18 **Dinner:** $6-$18 **Phone:** 904/737-9236 ⑤⓪
Italian
Location: Jct San Jose Blvd. 3825 Baymeadows Rd 32217. **Hours:** 11 am-10 pm, Fri-11 pm, Sat 4 pm-11 pm, Sun 4:30 pm-10 pm. Closed: Mon. **Features:** Baked lasagna, manicotti and tortellini are among pasta dishes on the menu, but don't forget about chicken, seafood and grilled entrees. Pizza, calzones and submarine sandwiches round out the offerings. Casual dress; cocktails. **Parking:** on-site. **Cards:** AX, CB, DC, DS, JC, MC, VI.

THE WINE CELLAR **Lunch:** $10-$17 **Dinner:** $20-$31 **Phone:** 904/398-8989 ②①
International
Location: I-95, exit 350A, just ne. 1314 Prudential Dr 32207. **Hours:** 11 am-2 & 5:30-10 pm, Sat from 5:30 pm. Closed major holidays; also Sun & 7/2-7/8. **Reservations:** suggested. **Features:** The warm and inviting atmosphere is enhanced by elegant dark wood walls and large windows. Well-rounded menu with some unique selections such as banana chip-encrusted sea bass. There is an extensive wine list. Dressy casual; cocktails. **Parking:** on-site. **Cards:** AX, CB, DC, DS, MC, VI.

ZODIAC GRILL **Lunch:** $5-$8 **Phone:** 904/354-8283 ⑪
Mediterranean
Location: Corner of N Hogan and W Adams sts; downtown. 130 W Adams St 32202. **Hours:** 7 am-4 pm. Closed major holidays; also Sat & Sun. **Features:** Casual dress; beer & wine only. **Parking:** on-site (fee). **Cards:** AX, CB, DC, DS, JC, MC, VI.

The following restaurants have not been evaluated by AAA but are listed for your information only.

ATLANTA BREAD COMPANY BAKERY CAFE **Phone:** 904/928-3141
fyi
Not evaluated. **Location:** I-95, exit 344, 2.5 mi e, then 1 mi n on SR 115. 9700-5 Deer Lake Ct 32216. **Features:** Specialty sandwiches on a multitude of breads and numerous soups that rotate on a daily schedule. Salads, pastries and gourmet coffee drinks are ordered at the counters of this bright storefront cafe.

THAI PALACE RESTAURANT **Phone:** 904/880-5363
fyi
Not evaluated. **Location:** 9965 San Jose Blvd 32257. **Features:** Open for lunch and dinner, this family owned and operated restaurant offers a variety of curry dishes; the shrimp himapan is a favorite.

The Jacksonville Vicinity

AMELIA ISLAND   (See map and index starting on p. 466)

─────── WHERE TO STAY ───────

THE ADDISON ON AMELIA ISLAND   **Phone:** 904/277-1604   **62**

▼▼▼▼   Property failed to provide current rates

Location: In Fernandina Beach; just s of Centre St, corner of Ash and S 7th sts; in historic district. 614 Ash St 32034.
Bed & Breakfast   Fax: 904/277-8124. **Facility:** Guests are served cookies and lemonade every afternoon at this property offering lodgings in a garden house, a cottage or an 1876 Victorian house. Smoke free premises. 14 one-bedroom standard units, some with whirlpools. 2 stories, interior/exterior corridors. *Bath:* combo or shower only. **Parking:** street. **Terms:** age restrictions may apply. **Amenities:** video library, hair dryers. *Some:* CD players, irons. **Leisure Activities:** *Fee:* bicycles.

SOME UNITS

[symbols] / VCR /

AMELIA ISLAND PLANTATION   *Book at aaa.com*   **Phone:** (904)261-6161   **67**

AAA SAVE   All Year   1P: $191-$754   2P: $206-$769   XP: $15   F15
Location: In Fernandina Beach; SR A1A, 6.5 mi s of the bridge. 6800 First Coast Hwy 32034 (PO Box 3000,
▼▼▼▼   FERNANDINA BEACH). Fax: 904/277-5945. **Facility:** Secluded, wooded grounds envelope this waterfront
Resort   property offering accommodations ranging from hotel rooms to three-bedroom villas with private pools.
Large-scale Hotel   Smoke free premises. 635 units. 343 one-bedroom standard units. 110 one-, 110 two- and 72 three-bedroom suites. 1-8 stories, interior/exterior corridors. *Bath:* combo or shower only. **Parking:** on-site.
Terms: check-in 4 pm, 1-7 night minimum stay, 14 day cancellation notice-fee imposed, weekly rates available, package plans, $25 service charge, pets ($100 deposit, $50 extra charge, in designated units). **Amenities:** *Some:* video games (fee), high-speed Internet, dual phone lines, honor bars. **Dining:** 9 restaurants, 7 am-10 pm; 20% service charge, cocktails, entertainment. **Pool(s):** 21 outdoor, 2 heated outdoor, heated indoor, wading. **Leisure Activities:** saunas, whirlpools, steamrooms, rental canoes, boat dock, fishing, recreation programs, hiking trails, jogging, playground, spa, sports court. *Fee:* charter fishing, kayaks, golf-54 holes, 23 tennis courts (3 lighted), bicycles, horseback riding. **Guest Services:** gift shop, valet laundry, area transportation-Amelia Island Plantation. **Business Services:** conference facilities, business center. **Cards:** AX, DC, DS, MC, VI. *(See color ad below)*

SOME UNITS

[symbols] FEE FEE   / [symbols] /

(See map and index starting on p. 466)

BAILEY HOUSE

Historic Bed & Breakfast

All Year [BP]   1P: $149-$209   2P: $149-$209   XP: $25
Phone: (904)261-5390   61

Location: In Fernandina Beach; just s of Centre St; in historic district. 28 S 7th St 32034. Fax: 904/321-0103. **Facility:** Stained glass, heart-pine floors, oriental rugs, ornate mantelpieces, claw-foot bathtubs and Queen Anne furnishings distinguish this Victorian home. Smoke free premises. 10 one-bedroom standard units, some with kitchens and/or whirlpools. 2 stories, interior corridors. *Bath:* combo or shower only. **Parking:** on-site. **Terms:** age restrictions may apply, 5 day cancellation notice-fee imposed, no pets allowed (owner's dog on premises). **Amenities:** irons, hair dryers. **Leisure Activities:** bicycles. **Business Services:** fax. **Cards:** AX, DS, MC, VI.

SOME UNITS
(ASK) [icons] / (VCR) [icons] /

ELIZABETH POINTE LODGE

(AAA) (SAVE)

Bed & Breakfast

All Year [BP]   1P: $175-$350   2P: $205-$375   XP: $25
Phone: (904)277-4851   64
F6

Location: In Fernandina Beach; SR A1A, just s on the ocean. 98 S Fletcher Ave 32034. Fax: 904/277-6500. **Facility:** This New England-style house featuring a wraparound piazza and a lobby fireplace has nautical-themed guest rooms reminiscent of Nantucket. Smoke free premises. 25 units. 24 one-bedroom standard units, some with whirlpools. 1 two-bedroom suite. 4 stories, interior/exterior corridors. **Parking:** on-site. **Terms:** 7 day cancellation notice, package plans. **Amenities:** voice mail, irons, hair dryers. *Some:* DVD players, CD players. **Leisure Activities:** beach accessories. *Fee:* bicycles. **Guest Services:** valet laundry. **Business Services:** meeting rooms. **Cards:** AX, DS, MC, VI. **Special Amenities:** free full breakfast and free local telephone calls.

SOME UNITS
[icons] / (VCR) [icons] /

THE FAIRBANKS HOUSE

Historic Bed & Breakfast

All Year [BP]   1P: $180-$395   2P: $180-$395   XP: $50
Phone: (904)277-0500   63

Location: In Fernandina Beach; just s of Centre St; in historic district. 227 S 7th St 32034. Fax: 904/277-3103. **Facility:** This service-oriented property includes an 1885 Italianate-style villa and cottages; guest units are furnished with antiques and oriental rugs. Smoke free premises. 12 units. 8 one-bedroom standard units, some with whirlpools. 1 two-bedroom suite ($270-$395) with whirlpool. 3 cottages ($270-$395), some with whirlpools. 3 stories (no elevator), interior/exterior corridors. *Bath:* combo or shower only. **Parking:** on-site. **Terms:** 2-3 night minimum stay - seasonal and/or weekends, age restrictions may apply, 14 day cancellation notice-fee imposed, package plans. **Amenities:** irons, hair dryers. **Pool(s):** outdoor. **Leisure Activities:** bicycles. **Guest Services:** complimentary evening beverages. **Business Services:** meeting rooms. **Cards:** AX, DS, MC, VI.

SOME UNITS
[icons] / (VCR) [icons] /

HAMPTON INN AMELIA ISLAND

Small-scale Hotel

Book at aaa.com

All Year   1P: $89-$169   2P: $99-$179   XP: $10
Phone: (904)321-1111   65
F18

Location: In Fernandina Beach; just w of jct SR A1A and Sadler Rd. 2549 Sadler Rd 32034. Fax: 904/321-0115. **Facility:** 82 units. 77 one-bedroom standard units. 5 one-bedroom suites, some with whirlpools. 3 stories, interior corridors. *Bath:* combo or shower only. **Parking:** on-site. **Terms:** check-in 4 pm, cancellation fee imposed, package plans. **Amenities:** video games (fee), high-speed Internet, dual phone lines, voice mail, irons, hair dryers. **Pool(s):** small outdoor. **Guest Services:** valet laundry. **Cards:** AX, DS, MC, VI.

SOME UNITS
(ASK) [icons] / [icons] /

HAMPTON INN & SUITES-AMELIA ISLAND

Small-scale Hotel

Book at aaa.com

2/11-6/30 [ECP]   1P: $109-$182   XP: $10
12/1-2/10 & 7/1-11/30 [ECP]   1P: $99-$139   XP: $10
Phone: 904/491-4911   59
F18
F18

Location: In Fernandina Beach; I-95, exit 373 (SR A1A), 16 mi, then left on Ash St. 19 S 2nd St 32034. Fax: 904/491-4910. **Facility:** 122 units. 61 one-bedroom standard units, some with whirlpools. 61 one-bedroom suites ($119-$182), some with efficiencies and/or whirlpools. 4 stories, interior corridors. *Bath:* combo or shower only. **Parking:** on-site. **Terms:** 30 day cancellation notice, package plans. **Amenities:** high-speed Internet, dual phone lines, voice mail, irons, hair dryers. **Pool(s):** outdoor. **Leisure Activities:** exercise room. **Guest Services:** sundries, valet and coin laundry. **Business Services:** meeting rooms, business center. **Cards:** AX, DC, DS, JC, MC, VI.

SOME UNITS
(ASK) [icons] / [icons] / (VCR) [icons] /

HOYT HOUSE

Historic Bed & Breakfast

All Year [BP]   1P: $119-$219   2P: $119-$219   XP: $35
Phone: (904)277-4300   60

Location: In Fernandina Beach; on Atlantic Ave/SR 200 at Centre and S 8th sts; in the historic district. 804 Atlantic Ave 32034. Fax: 904/277-9626. **Facility:** Gourmet breakfasts are served in the dining room at this 1905 Queen Anne home decorated with antiques and reproductions. Designated smoking area. 10 one-bedroom standard units, some with whirlpools. 2 stories (no elevator), interior corridors. *Bath:* combo or shower only. **Parking:** on-site. **Terms:** 2 night minimum stay - weekends, age restrictions may apply, 7 day cancellation notice-fee imposed, weekly rates available, package plans, small pets only ($35 fee, owner's dog on premises). **Amenities:** irons, hair dryers. **Guest Services:** complimentary evening beverages. **Business Services:** meeting rooms. **Cards:** AX, DS, MC, VI.

SOME UNITS
(ASK) [icons] / (VCR) /
FEE

THE RITZ-CARLTON, AMELIA ISLAND

(AAA) (SAVE)

Resort Large-scale Hotel

Book at aaa.com

2/17-8/6   1P: $249-$449   2P: $249-$449
12/1-2/16 & 8/7-11/30   1P: $199-$389   2P: $199-$389
Phone: (904)277-1100   66

Location: In Fernandina Beach; on SR A1A. 4750 Amelia Island Pkwy 32034. Fax: 904/277-1145. **Facility:** All guest rooms have private balconies with views of the ocean at this beach-front hotel featuring extensive collections of art and antiques. 449 units. 404 one-bedroom standard units. 45 one-bedroom suites, some with whirlpools. 8 stories, interior corridors. **Parking:** valet. **Terms:** 7 day cancellation notice-fee imposed, package plans. **Amenities:** CD players, dual phone lines, voice mail, safes, honor bars, irons, hair dryers. *Fee:* video games, high-speed Internet. **Dining:** 2 restaurants, 6:30 am-10 pm, cocktails, also, The Grill, see separate listing, entertainment. **Pool(s):** heated outdoor, small heated outdoor, heated indoor. **Leisure Activities:** saunas, whirlpools, steamrooms, recreation programs, jogging, playground, spa, volleyball. *Fee:* charter fishing, golf-18 holes, 9 tennis courts (6 lighted), bicycles, game room. **Guest Services:** gift shop, valet laundry, area transportation (fee). **Business Services:** conference facilities, business center. **Cards:** AX, CB, DC, DS, JC, MC, VI.

SOME UNITS
[icons] / [icons] /
FEE

(See map and index starting on p. 466)

———— WHERE TO DINE ————

BEECH STREET GRILL   Dinner: $18-$30   Phone: 904/277-3662   (70)
🔻🔻 ◇ 🔻🔻   **Location:** In Fernandina Beach; corner of 8th and Beech sts. 801 Beech St 32034. **Hours:** 6 pm-10 pm. Closed:
American   1/1, 11/23, 12/25; also Super Bowl Sun. **Reservations:** suggested. **Features:** In an 1889 Victorian house
that exudes a contemporary feel inside, the restaurant is known for its progressive, imaginative treatments
of such fresh seafood specialties as macadamia nut-crusted grouper topped with curried citrus cream and
mango chili salsa. Also offered are such savory dishes as roasted venison loin with black currant sauce and apple chipotle-
glazed pork with roasted garlic. Dressy casual; cocktails. **Parking:** on-site. **Cards:** AX, DC, DS, MC, VI.   🅛M

BRETT'S WATERWAY CAFE   Lunch: $8-$15   Dinner: $16-$27   Phone: 904/261-2660   (65)
🔻🔻🔻 🔻🔻🔻   **Location:** In Fernandina Beach; at end of Centre St; on Amelia River (Intracoastal Waterway). 1 S Front St 32034.
American   **Hours:** 11:30 am-2:30 & 5:30-9:30 pm, Sun from 5:30 pm; to 8:30 pm in winter. Closed major holidays.
Features: Popular for its Southern hospitality, the restaurant is noted for its excellent seafood and beef
selections, a small but impressive wine list and homemade desserts. The dining rooms face the Fernandina
Harbor and a marina on the Amelia River. Casual dress; cocktails. **Parking:** on-site. **Cards:** AX, MC, VI.   🍸

CENTRE STREET CAFE   *Menu on aaa.com*   Dinner: $20-$28   Phone: 904/277-6600   (67)
(AAA)   **Location:** In Fernandina Beach; in downtown historic district. 316-D Centre St 32097. **Hours:** 6 pm-9 pm. Closed:
🔻🔻🔻 🔻🔻   12/25; also Sun & Mon. **Reservations:** accepted. **Features:** Creative dishes prepared by Danish
International   chef/owner are full of robust taste with a mixture of flavors. The Danish meatballs are a fun entree to enjoy.
The house salad is enhanced with asparagus and delightful homemade dressings. For dessert try the
coconut creme brulee. Only the freshest and finest ingredients are used. A superb wine list is enlighting and
features lesser known high-quality vineyards. Dressy casual; beer & wine only. **Parking:** street.
Cards: MC, VI.   🍸

THE GRILL   Dinner: $35-$65   Phone: 904/277-1100   (71)
(AAA)   **Location:** In Fernandina Beach; on SR A1A; in The Ritz-Carlton, Amelia Island. 4750 Amelia Island Pkwy 32034.
🔻🔻🔻 ◇ 🔻🔻🔻   **Hours:** 6:30 pm-9:30 pm; Sunday brunch 11 am-2:30 pm. Closed: Sun & Mon. **Reservations:** suggested.
Regional   **Features:** Overlooking the Atlantic Ocean, the airy, clublike dining room is a formal setting, but the service
American   is friendly and unpretentious. Creative international influences abound in preparations of Florida seafood,
grilled meat and wild game. Semi-formal attire; cocktails; entertainment. **Parking:** valet. **Cards:** AX, CB, DC,
DS, JC, MC, VI.   🍸

LULU'S BRA & GRILL   Lunch: $5-$8   Dinner: $7-$13   Phone: 904/261-7123   (68)
🔻🔻🔻 🔻🔻🔻   **Location:** Downtown. 11 B S 7th St 32034. **Hours:** 11 am-8 pm, Fri & Sat-9 pm. Closed: Sun. **Features:** Yes,
Mexican   "Bra" is correct — just a way to catch your attention. The grill has an eclectic array of salads, soups and
sandwiches on bread or pita. Casual dress. **Parking:** on-site. **Cards:** MC, VI.   🚭

POMPEO'S ITALIAN RESTAURANT   Lunch: $6-$9   Dinner: $12-$23   Phone: 904/261-7490   (66)
🔻🔻🔻 🔻🔻🔻   **Location:** Corner of Center and S 3rd sts. 302 Center St 32034. **Hours:** 11 am-4 & 5-10 pm. **Features:** The
Italian   flavors of Italy are brought to patrons via the secret sauces used by the owner. Guests can sit out on the
patio or inside and enjoy their and the chef's favorite foods. Casual dress; cocktails. **Parking:** street.
Cards: AX, CB, DC, DS, JC, MC, VI.

SENORITA'S COFFEE AND WINE   Lunch: $5-$8   Dinner: $5-$8   Phone: 912/576-9883   (69)
🔻🔻🔻 🔻🔻🔻   **Location:** Downtown. 31 S 5th St 32034. **Hours:** 10:30 am-8 pm. **Features:** The quaint cafe has a vast
American   selection of gourmet coffee and wine; the menu offers sandwiches and lite fare. Casual dress; beer & wine
only. **Parking:** street. **Cards:** MC, VI.

———— *The following restaurant has not been evaluated by AAA* ————
but is listed for your information only.

MARTI ROOM   Phone: 904/261-3300
(fyi)   Not evaluated. **Location:** In Fernandina Beach; just s of Centre St; in Florida House Inn. 22 S 3rd St 32034.
Features: Traditional Southern cooking is served boardinghouse-style all-you-care-to-eat. International beer
selections from over 100 countries are available.   🍸

ATLANTIC BEACH pop. 13,368   (See map and index starting on p. 466)

———— WHERE TO STAY ————

BEST WESTERN MAYPORT INN & SUITES   *Book at aaa.com*   Phone: (904)435-3500   (70)
(AAA) (SAVE)   All Year [ECP]   1P: $78-$180   2P: $99-$220
🔻🔻🔻 🔻🔻   **Location:** 2 mi n on SR A1A; 1.4 mi s of naval base. 2389 Mayport Rd 32233. **Fax:** 904/435-2080. **Facility:** 60 one-
Small-scale Hotel   bedroom standard units, some with whirlpools. 2 stories, interior corridors. *Bath:* combo or shower only.
Parking: on-site. **Terms:** cancellation fee imposed, package plans. **Amenities:** high-speed Internet, dual
phone lines, voice mail, safes, irons, hair dryers. **Pool(s):** outdoor. **Leisure Activities:** whirlpool, barbecue
deck with charcoal grill, exercise room, horseshoes. **Guest Services:** valet and coin laundry. **Cards:** AX,
CB, DC, DS, JC, MC, VI. **Special Amenities:** free expanded continental breakfast and free local telephone calls.
SOME UNITS

🆂🅳 [icons]   /✕/

(See map and index starting on p. 466)

SEA TURTLE INN   *Book at aaa.com*   Phone: (904)249-7402   **71**
F17
All Year   1P: $105-$225   2P: $105-$225   XP: $10
Location: End of Atlantic Blvd. 1 Ocean Blvd 32233. Fax: 904/247-1517. **Facility:** 193 units. 191 one-bedroom
Small-scale Hotel   standard units. 2 one-bedroom suites. 8 stories, interior corridors. *Bath:* combo or shower only. **Parking:** on-
site. **Terms:** check-in 4 pm, cancellation fee imposed, [BP] & [CP] meal plans available. **Amenities:** video
library (fee), high-speed Internet, dual phone lines, voice mail, irons, hair dryers. **Dining:** Plantains, see separate listing.
Pool(s): outdoor. **Leisure Activities:** volleyball. **Guest Services:** gift shop, valet and coin laundry. **Business Services:**
conference facilities, fax (fee). **Cards:** AX, DC, DS, MC, VI.

SOME UNITS

(ASK) (S&) (✕) FEE (T↑) (Y) (☇) (🛥) (➕) (VCR) (📷) (DATA PORT) (🛢) (💻) / (✕) /

──────── **WHERE TO DINE** ────────

AL'S PIZZA   Lunch: $4-$15   Dinner: $6-$15   Phone: 904/249-0002   **82**
Location: Jct US 1. 303 Atlantic Blvd 32233. **Hours:** 11 am-11 pm, Fri & Sat-midnight, Sun-10 pm.
Italian   **Features:** Location, location, location: this converted auto garage with three roll up doors still intact was
carefully transformed into a happening pizza place. Casual dress; beer only. **Parking:** on-site. **Cards:** AX,
CB, DS, MC, VI.

MAYPORT GARDENS CHINESE RESTAURANT   Lunch: $5-$8   Dinner: $5-$8   Phone: 904/246-2102   **74**
Location: 3 mi n of jct Atlantic Blvd on SR A1A; 1 mi s of naval base. 701-24 Mayport Crossing Blvd 32233. **Hours:** 11
Chinese   am-9:30 pm. Closed major holidays; also Sun. **Features:** The chef/owner uses the freshest ingredients to
make all your favorite traditional Chinese dishes. Although the simply decorated dining room is welcoming
enough, the restaurant is more popular for its takeout menu. Casual dress. **Parking:** on-site.
(✕)

NEGRIL'S PARADISE   Lunch: $3-$10   Dinner: $3-$10   Phone: 904/247-9590   **75**
Location: 2 mi n of Atlantic Blvd; in Mayport Square Plaza. 1447-5 Mayport Rd 32233. **Hours:** 10 am-9 pm, Sun-
Caribbean   7:30 pm. Closed: 11/23, 12/25; also Sat. **Features:** Welcome, mon! The restaurant dishes up Caribbean
food with flair. The Jamaican owner/chef prepares such island entrees as stew beef and curry chicken.
Casual dress. **Parking:** on-site. **Cards:** MC, VI.

PLANTAINS   Lunch: $8-$15   Dinner: $17-$29   Phone: 904/249-7402   **78**
Location: End of Atlantic Blvd; in Sea Turtle Inn. 1 Ocean Blvd 32233. **Hours:** 6:30 am-10:30 pm. **Features:** Daily
American   fresh seafood is at the heart of the beachside restaurant's menu. Outdoor seating affords partial views of
the ocean. Casual dress; cocktails. **Parking:** on-site. **Cards:** AX, DS, MC, VI.

RAGTIME TAVERN & SEAFOOD GRILL   Lunch: $7-$9   Dinner: $10-$20   Phone: 904/241-7877   **76**
Location: Just e of SR A1A; corner of Atlantic and Ocean blvds. 207 Atlantic Blvd 32233. **Hours:** 11 am-midnight, Fri
Seafood   & Sat-1:30 am. Closed: 11/23, 12/25; also for dinner 12/24. **Features:** This bustling microbrewery offers
New Orleans-style grilled Cajun specialties. Three bars feature a live band on some nights. Spicy food and
a lively atmosphere, along with fresh Florida vegetables like okra and corn, make this restaurant a winner.
Casual dress; cocktails. **Parking:** street. **Cards:** AX, DC, DS, MC, VI.
(Y) (✕)

RISTORANTE SEQUINO'S   Lunch: $6-$11   Dinner: $11-$20   Phone: 904/249-0101   **85**
Location: 1 mi e of Intracoastal Waterway Bridge; in Atlantic Village Shopping Center. 1021 Atlantic Blvd 32233.
Italian   **Hours:** 11 am-3 pm, Thurs & Fri also 6 pm-10 pm, Sat & Sun 6 pm-10 pm. Closed: 12/25. **Features:** The
restaurant offers a broad selection of seafood, steak and chicken entrees, emphasizing presentation and
MC, VI.   moving away from traditional dishes. Casual dress; cocktails. **Parking:** on-site. **Cards:** AX, CB, DS,
(✕)

SEAFOOD KITCHEN   Lunch: $4-$13   Dinner: $5-$14   Phone: 904/241-8470   **79**
Location: Jct SR A1A/10. 0.6 mi e. 31 Royal Palm Dr 32233. **Hours:** 11 am-10 pm. Closed: 11/23, 12/25.
Features: Simple, basic and fresh seafood is prepared at the popular restaurant. Creamy coleslaw, French
Regional Seafood fries and hushpuppies accompany each dish. Casual dress; beer & wine only. **Parking:** on-site. **Cards:** AX,
DC, DS, MC, VI.

STICKY FINGERS RESTAURANT & BAR   Lunch: $6-$15   Dinner: $6-$15   Phone: 904/241-7427   **80**
Location: Jct SR A1A; in Shoppes of North Shore. 363-1 Atlantic Blvd 32233. **Hours:** 11 am-10 pm, Fri & Sat-11
American   pm. Closed: 11/23, 12/25. **Features:** Delicious ribs are the focus at this restaurant, but there's much more!
Enjoy barbecue beef, chicken or pork with a selection of sauces, and be sure to leave room for a
homemade dessert. The outdoor covered seating is breezy and comfortable. Entertainment is offered on
weekends. Casual dress; cocktails. **Parking:** on-site. **Cards:** AX, DC, DS, MC, VI.
(Y) (✕)

SUN DOG DINER   Lunch: $7-$17   Dinner: $7-$17   Phone: 904/241-8221   **77**
Location: Just e of 3rd St (SR A1A). 207 Atlantic Blvd 32233. **Hours:** 11 am-2 am, Sun from 10 am; Sunday
brunch. Closed: 12/25. **Features:** An established favorite frequented by locals, this diner has it all.
American   Hamburgers and hot dogs share the menu with more sophisticated fare, including sesame seared tuna and
blackened NY strip. Half of the restaurant is a lively night spot with live music nightly. Cigar connoisseurs
can slip off to the Cobalt Room, which has comfy chairs and a TV. This is also a great place to slide up to the counter for a
thick, rich milkshake. Casual dress; cocktails; entertainment. **Parking:** street. **Cards:** AX, DC, DS, MC, VI.

TIJUANA FLATS BURRITO CO.   Lunch: $7-$10   Dinner: $7-$10   Phone: 904/242-0234   **83**
Location: Just w of jct 3rd Ave and Atlantic Blvd. 725-1 Atlantic Blvd 32211. **Hours:** 11 am-10 pm, Fri & Sat-10:30
Mexican   pm, Sun noon-9 pm. Closed major holidays. **Features:** This quick service chain eatery provides hearty
Mexican fare like burritos, tacos, quesadillas and enchiladas. For the hot sauce aficionado, there are more
than a dozen unique flavors to choose from. Casual dress; beer only. **Parking:** on-site. **Cards:** MC, VI.

(See map and index starting on p. 466)

THE TREE STEAK HOUSE   Dinner: $14-$30   Phone: 904/241-5600   [84]
▼▼▼▼   **Location:** Jct SR A1A/10, 0.6 mi e. 725-6 Atlantic Blvd 32233. **Hours:** 5 pm-9 pm. Closed major holidays.
Reservations: accepted. **Features:** More than 30 years of excellence hasn't spoiled the heralded tradition
Steak & Seafood   of tableside selection of Select prime rib, which is brought whole to the table, sliced and prepared as the
guests desires. Other entree selections include filet of beef, rack of lamb, pork tenderloin and fresh seafood
and are prepared with equal care. Casual dress; cocktails. **Parking:** on-site. **Cards:** AX, DC, MC, VI.   [&M] [Y]

WASABI   Lunch: $7-$9   Dinner: $10-$22   Phone: 904/246-8588   [81]
▼▼▼   **Location:** From intersection SR A1A and Atlantic Blvd, 1 mi w; in North Beach Plaza Atlantic Theater. 725-12 Atlantic
Blvd 32233. **Hours:** 11 am-2:30 & 5-9:30 pm, Fri-10:30 pm, Sat 11:30 am-3 & 5-10:30 pm, Sun 11:30 am-3 &
Japanese   5-9:30 pm. Closed major holidays. **Reservations:** accepted. **Features:** A huge assortment of Japanese
favorites including an extensive assortment of sushi, sashimi, various seafood items and noodle dishes are
all featured here. The decorations and friendly staff add to the enjoyment of this popular restaurant. Casual dress; cocktails.
Parking: on-site. **Cards:** AX, DC, DS, MC, VI.   [&M]

BALDWIN pop. 1,634

——— **WHERE TO STAY** ———

BEST WESTERN BALDWIN INN   Phone: (904)266-9759
(AAA) [SAVE]   All Year [CP]   1P: $60-$150   2P: $65-$155   XP: $5   F12
Location: I-10, exit 343, just s. 1088 US 301 S 32234. Fax: 904/266-9759. **Facility:** 42 one-bedroom standard
▼▼ ▼▼   units. 1 story, exterior corridors. **Parking:** on-site. **Terms:** cancellation fee imposed, pets ($8 extra charge).
Amenities: irons, hair dryers. *Some:* high-speed Internet. **Pool(s):** outdoor. **Cards:** AX, CB, DC, DS, JC,
Motel   MC, VI. **Special Amenities:** free continental breakfast.   SOME UNITS

[S&] [🛏] [¶] [🛌] [✈] [DATA PORT] [🖥] / [✕] /
            FEE

GREEN COVE SPRINGS pop. 5,378

——— **WHERE TO STAY** ———

RIVER PARK INN, THE 1887 HOUSE   Phone: 904/284-2994
▼▼ ▼▼   All Year [BP]   2P: $85-$195   XP: $10
Location: Corner of Spring St; in historic business district. 103 S Magnolia Ave 32043. **Facility:** Smoke free
premises. 5 one-bedroom standard units, some with whirlpools. 2 stories, interior corridors. *Bath:* combo or
Bed & Breakfast   shower only. **Parking:** on-site. **Terms:** check-in 4 pm, 14 day cancellation notice-fee imposed.
Amenities: voice mail, irons, hair dryers. *Some:* CD players. **Leisure Activities:** whirlpool. **Guest Services:** complimentary
laundry, area transportation (fee). **Cards:** AX, DS, MC, VI.   [✈] [¶] [✕] [VCR]
                                                                                        FEE

——— **WHERE TO DINE** ———

RONNIE'S WINGS, OYSTERS & MORE   Lunch: $5-$15   Dinner: $5-$15   Phone: 904/284-4728
▼▼▼   **Location:** Corner of Magnolia; across from park. 232 Walnut St 32043. **Hours:** 11 am-11 pm. **Features:** You'll be
amazed at the many selections on the menu. Choose lighter fare from a wide selection of such appetizers
American   as calamari, or chow down on one of the house specialties of shrimp, fish or chicken. Friendly servers are
eager to please. Casual dress; cocktails. **Parking:** on-site. **Cards:** AX, DS, MC, VI.

JACKSONVILLE BEACH pop. 20,990   (See map and index starting on p. 466)

——— **WHERE TO STAY** ———

BEST WESTERN OCEANFRONT   *Book at aaa.com*   Phone: (904)249-4949   [81]
(AAA) [SAVE]   All Year   1P: $109-$279   2P: $109-$349   XP: $10   F16
Location: Oceanfront. 0.4 mi n of Beach Blvd (US 90). 305 1st St N 32250. Fax: 904/249-6040. **Facility:** 51 one-
▼▼ ▼▼   bedroom standard units, some with whirlpools. 3 stories, interior corridors. *Bath:* combo or shower only.
Parking: on-site. **Terms:** 2-4 night minimum stay - seasonal and/or weekends, cancellation fee imposed.
Small-scale Hotel   **Amenities:** high-speed Internet (fee), voice mail, safes, irons, hair dryers. **Pool(s):** heated outdoor. **Guest
Services:** valet and coin laundry. **Business Services:** PC. **Cards:** AX, CB, DC, DS, MC, VI.
Special Amenities: free expanded continental breakfast and free local telephone calls.   SOME UNITS

[S&] [¶] [✈] [🛌] [✈] [DATA PORT] [📶] [🖥] [🖥] / [✕] [VCR]
                                                                                              FEE

COMFORT INN OCEANFRONT   *Book at aaa.com*   Phone: (904)241-2311   [80]
(AAA) [SAVE]   3/1-9/6 [ECP]   1P: $129-$189
12/1-2/28 [ECP]   1P: $119-$159
▼▼ ▼▼   9/7-11/30 [ECP]   1P: $109-$149
Location: Just e of SR A1A; at 14th Ave N. 1515 First St N 32250. Fax: 904/249-3830. **Facility:** 177 one-bedroom
Small-scale Hotel   standard units. 7 stories, interior corridors. *Bath:* combo or shower only. **Parking:** on-site. **Terms:** check-in 4
pm, cancellation fee imposed. **Amenities:** video games, voice mail, safes (fee), irons, hair dryers. **Dining:** 9
am-8 pm. **Pool(s):** heated outdoor. **Leisure Activities:** whirlpool, exercise room. **Guest Services:** gift shop, valet and coin
laundry. **Business Services:** meeting rooms, PC (fee). **Cards:** AX, DC, DS, MC, VI. **Special Amenities:** free expanded
continental breakfast and free local telephone calls. *(See color ad p 497)*   SOME UNITS

[¶] [Y] [🛁] [✈] [✈] [DATA PORT] [🖥] / [✕] [📶] [🖥] /

(See map and index starting on p. 466)

FAIRFIELD INN & SUITES   *Book at aaa.com*   Phone: (904)435-0100   **78**

AAA SAVE   2/1-9/30   1P: $109-$189
▼▼▼▼   12/1-1/31 & 10/1-11/30   1P: $89-$159
Location: Just e of SR A1A; at 16th Ave N. 1616 N 1st St 32250. Fax: 904/435-0106. **Facility:** 76 one-bedroom
standard units, some with whirlpools. 3 stories, interior corridors. **Parking:** on-site. **Terms:** 2 night minimum
Small-scale Hotel stay - seasonal and/or weekends, [CP] meal plan available. **Amenities:** high-speed Internet, voice mail,
irons, hair dryers. *Some:* CD players. **Pool(s):** heated outdoor. **Leisure Activities:** whirlpool, exercise room.
Guest Services: coin laundry. **Business Services:** meeting rooms, business center. **Cards:** AX, CB, DC, DS, MC, VI.

SOME UNITS

THE FIG TREE INN   Phone: 904-246-8855   **83**

▼▼▼   3/1-11/30   1P: $110-$170   2P: $145-$185   XP: $20   D12
     12/1-2/28   1P: $100-$160   2P: $135-$175   XP: $20   D12
Bed & Breakfast **Location:** Just e of SR A1A. 185 4th Ave S 32250. **Facility:** Smoke free premises. 6 one-bedroom standard
units, some with whirlpools. 2 stories (no elevator), interior corridors. *Bath:* combo or shower only. **Parking:**
on-site. **Terms:** check-in 4 pm, age restrictions may apply. 3 day cancellation notice-fee imposed, package plans.
Amenities: video library, DVD players, irons, hair dryers. **Leisure Activities:** bicycles. **Guest Services:** coin laundry.
Cards: AX, DS, MC, VI.

SOME UNITS

HAMPTON INN PONTE VEDRA AT JACKSONVILLE
BEACH   *Book at aaa.com*   Phone: (904)280-9101   **84**

AAA SAVE   All Year   1P: $189   2P: $189
▼▼▼▼   **Location:** Just s of J Turner Butler Blvd; e of Intercoastal Bridge. 1220 Marsh Landing Pkwy 32250.
Fax: 904/280-5903. **Facility:** 118 one-bedroom standard units, some with whirlpools. 5 stories, interior
corridors. *Bath:* combo or shower only. **Parking:** on-site. **Terms:** cancellation fee imposed, package plans.
Small-scale Hotel **Amenities:** dual phone lines, voice mail, irons, hair dryers. **Pool(s):** outdoor. **Guest Services:** sundries,
valet laundry. **Business Services:** meeting rooms, PC, fax (fee). **Cards:** AX, DC, DS, MC, VI.
Special Amenities: free expanded continental breakfast and free local telephone calls. *(See color ad p 504)*

SOME UNITS
FEE

HOLIDAY INN SUNSPREE RESORT   *Book at aaa.com*   Phone: (904)249-9071   **79**

▼▼▼   2/1-10/1   1P: $99-$259
     12/1-1/31 & 10/2-11/30   1P: $89-$159
Small-scale Hotel **Location:** Just e of SR A1A; at 16th Ave N. 1617 N 1st St 32250. Fax: 904/241-4321. **Facility:** 143 units. 137 one-
bedroom standard units. 6 one-bedroom suites. 4-7 stories, interior/exterior corridors. **Parking:** on-site.
Terms: check-in 4 pm, 2 night minimum stay - seasonal and/or weekends, cancellation fee imposed, [BP] meal plan available,
package plans. **Amenities:** video games (fee), voice mail, irons, hair dryers. **Pool(s):** outdoor. **Leisure Activities:** recreation
programs, exercise room. *Fee:* bicycles. **Guest Services:** gift shop, valet and coin laundry, area transportation. **Business
Services:** meeting rooms, PC. **Cards:** AX, CB, DC, DS, MC, VI.

SOME UNITS

PELICAN PATH B & B BY THE SEA   Phone: (904)249-1177   **77**

▼▼▼   All Year [BP]   1P: $125-$175   2P: $125-$175   XP: $40
     Location: Oceanfront at 1st St. 11 N 19th Ave 32250. **Facility:** Pan dowdy is a breakfast specialty at this B&B by
Bed & Breakfast the ocean; two spacious guest rooms overlook the water. Smoke free premises. 4 one-bedroom standard
units, some with whirlpools. 2 stories, interior corridors. **Parking:** on-site. **Terms:** age restrictions may apply,
7 day cancellation notice-fee imposed, package plans. **Amenities:** video library, hair dryers. **Leisure Activities:** bicycles.
Cards: AX, DS, MC, VI.

(See map and index starting on p. 466)

QUALITY SUITES OCEANFRONT   *Book at aaa.com*   Phone: (904)435-3535   82

AAA SAVE	3/3-9/3	1P: $179-$299	2P: $179-$299	XP: $10	F16
	12/1-3/2 & 9/4-11/30	1P: $159-$259	2P: $159-$259	XP: $10	F16

Location: Oceanfront. Just n of Beach Blvd (US 90). 11 1st St N 32250. Fax: 904/435-3536. **Facility:** Smoke free premises. 72 one-bedroom suites, some with whirlpools. 6 stories, interior corridors. *Bath:* combo or shower only. **Parking:** on-site. **Terms:** 1-2 night minimum stay - seasonal, package plans, pets ($25 extra charge, with prior approval). **Amenities:** high-speed Internet (fee), voice mail, safes, irons, hair dryers. **Pool(s):** heated outdoor. **Leisure Activities:** whirlpool, exercise room. **Guest Services:** sundries, complimentary evening beverages, valet and coin laundry. **Business Services:** meeting rooms, business center. **Cards:** AX, CB, DC, DS, JC, MC, VI.
Special Amenities: free full breakfast and free local telephone calls.

Small-scale Hotel

SOME UNITS

WHERE TO DINE

BEACH HUT CAFE   Lunch: $3-$7   Phone: 904/249-3516   108
Location: Just s of Beach Blvd. 1281 S 3rd St 32250. **Hours:** 6 am-2:30 pm. **Features:** The classic beach-style cafe offers fast, friendly service and hearty meal selections; grab a picnic table and dig in. Casual dress. **Parking:** on-site. **Cards:** MC, VI.

American

BEACHSIDE SEAFOOD   Lunch: $5-$9   Dinner: $5-$9   Phone: 904/241-2702   107
Location: 2.4 mi n at Butler Blvd. 120 S Third Ave 32250. **Hours:** 11 am-9 pm, Mon-5 pm. Closed major holidays. **Features:** Casual dress; beer & wine only. **Parking:** on-site. **Cards:** MC, VI.

Seafood

BONEFISH GRILL   Dinner: $14-$19   Phone: 904/247-4234   116
Location: On SR A1A, 1.5 mi s of Beach Blvd. 2400 S 3rd St 32250. **Hours:** 4 pm-10:30 pm, Fri & Sat-11:30 pm, Sun-10 pm. Closed: 11/23, 12/25. **Reservations:** accepted. **Features:** Fish is the house specialty, and the menu and nightly specials offer a variety of choices. Well-prepared food is cooked to perfection. Service is casual in nature, and the staff is skilled and attentive. Dressy casual; cocktails. **Parking:** on-site. **Cards:** AX, DC, DS, MC, VI.

Seafood

BONO'S PIT BAR-B-Q   Lunch: $6-$15   Dinner: $6-$15   Phone: 904/249-8704   110
Location: 1.5 mi n of Butler Blvd. 1266 Third St 32250. **Hours:** 11 am-9:30 pm, Sun 12:30 pm-4 pm. Closed major holidays. **Features:** Slow-cooked for over 12 hours, the meat is what sets this small chain apart from the others; the juicy and favorable ribs, pulled pork, chicken, beef and turkey are just some of the offerings available here. Try the different fried corn on the cob or slow-cooked baked beans for great tasting sides. Casual dress; beer only. **Parking:** on-site. **Cards:** AX, DS, MC, VI.

Barbecue

CASTILLO DE MEXICO   Lunch: $5-$11   Dinner: $7-$15   Phone: 904/339-0007   111
Location: 0.3 mi n of Beach Blvd. 1222 S 3rd St 32250. **Hours:** 11 am-10 pm, Fri-11:30 pm, Sat 11:30 am-11:30 pm, Sun noon-9:30 pm. **Features:** The restaurant serves traditional selections in a colorful environment; the walls are adorned with painted tiles and framed scenes of Mexico and there's a stage for live entertainment. Casual dress; cocktails. **Parking:** on-site. **Cards:** AX, DC, DS, MC, VI.

Mexican

CHAN'S CHINESE   Lunch: $5-$7   Dinner: $5-$7   Phone: 904/247-0123   102
Location: 0.5 mi w of SR A1A (3rd St) on Beach Blvd. 35 N 11th St 32250. **Hours:** 11:30 am-9:30 pm, Fri & Sat-10:30 pm. Closed major holidays. **Features:** Primarily a takeout operation, the eatery does have a few booths and tables. Guests order at the counter, then take a table to wait for their food. Although this is a basic operation with standard Oriental fare, the entrees are well-prepared and flavorful. **Parking:** on-site. **Cards:** MC, VI.

Chinese

CRUISER'S GRILL   Lunch: $5-$7   Dinner: $5-$7   Phone: 904/270-0356   114
Location: 1 mi n at Butler Blvd. 319 23rd Ave S 32250. **Hours:** 11 am-10 pm, Fri & Sat-11 pm, Sun noon-10 pm. Closed: 4/16, 11/23, 12/25. **Features:** American favorites of wings, burgers, steaks and salads are all on the menu here. Large portions and a friendly, relaxed atmosphere are also "part of the menu". Casual dress; beer & wine only. **Parking:** on-site. **Cards:** AX, DS, MC, VI.

American

DANNY'S AT THE BEACH   Lunch: $6-$7   Dinner: $7-$12   Phone: 904/242-8894   103
Location: 0.6 mi w of jct SR A1A (3rd St). 1183 Beach Blvd 32250. **Hours:** 7 am-9 pm, Sun & Mon-3 pm. **Features:** A Southern accent punctuates many of the comfort foods, and some selections may have a bit of a twist. The relaxed restaurant employs a helpful staff. Casual dress; cocktails. **Parking:** on-site. **Cards:** AX, DS, MC, VI.

American

D'FONTANA PIZZERIA AND RISTORANTE   Lunch: $5-$12   Dinner: $5-$12   Phone: 904/247-0470   97
Location: 1.3 mi n of Beach Blvd. 1269 Penman Rd 32250. **Hours:** 11 am-10 pm. Closed: Sun. **Features:** Well known by locals for their white pizza, this no-frills ristorante gets a little crowded, so carry-out is available. Casual dress. **Parking:** on-site. **Cards:** MC, VI.

Italian

DOLPHIN DEPOT   Dinner: $19-$35   Phone: 904/270-1424   100
Location: Corner of 6th Ave N and 1st St. 704 N 1st St 32221. **Hours:** 5 pm-10 pm, Fri & Sat-11 pm, Sun-9 pm. Closed major holidays. **Reservations:** suggested. **Features:** Preparations of eclectic Carolina coastal cuisine include lobster and a variety of fish dishes. Dressy casual; beer & wine only. **Parking:** on-site. **Cards:** AX, DC, DS, MC, VI.

Russian

(See map and index starting on p. 466)

DWIGHT'S BISTRO
Dinner: $10-$25   **Phone:** 904/241-4496   96

American

Location: 1.5 mi n of US 90. 1527 Penman Rd 32250. **Hours:** 5 pm-10 pm. **Reservations:** suggested. **Features:** A strong local reputation keeps this eclectic bistro in high demand. The decor will easily provide topics of conversation and the food will keep you coming back. Dressy casual; cocktails. **Parking:** on-site. **Cards:** MC, VI.

ELLEN'S KITCHEN
Lunch: $4-$6   **Phone:** 904/246-1572   112

American

Location: Pablo Plaza Shopping Center, north end. 1824 S 3rd St 32250. **Hours:** 7 am-2 pm. **Closed:** 11/23, 12/25. **Features:** The locals line up at this cheery diner for breakfast every day of the week. Make your own omelet with homemade biscuits. Eat breakfast and other fine Southern cooking all day long. The crab cake Benedict is a unique offering. Servers are informed and pleasant. Casual dress. **Parking:** on-site. **Cards:** AX, MC, VI.

GENE'S SEAFOOD RESTAURANT
Lunch: $6-$15   **Dinner:** $9-$15   **Phone:** 904/241-9333   98

Seafood

Location: 1 mi n of Beach Blvd. 1249 Penman Rd 32250. **Hours:** 11 am-9 pm, Fri & Sat-10 pm. **Closed:** 11/23, 12/25. **Features:** Specializing in seafood, the casual restaurant offers such choices as gator tail, crawfish and frog. Items can be fried, broiled, blackened or barbecued. Casual dress; cocktails. **Parking:** on-site. **Cards:** AX, DS, MC, VI.

GIOVANNI'S RESTAURANT   *Menu on aaa.com*
Dinner: $17-$38   **Phone:** 904/249-7787   104

Italian

Location: From intersection of SR A1A and US 90, 1.2 mi w. 1161 Beach Blvd 32250. **Hours:** 5:30 pm-10:30 pm, Fri & Sat-11 pm, Mon 6 pm-10 pm. Closed major holidays; also Sun. **Reservations:** accepted. **Features:** This upscale Italian restaurant has a modern feel with old taste charms. The entrees include numerous pasta dishes such as cannelloni florentina and spaghetti alla massigliese, as well as pan seared red snapper and scallops. Filet mignon, veal, duck and rack of lamb are also smong the wonderful dishes that await you here. Casual dress; cocktails. **Parking:** on-site and valet. **Cards:** AX, MC, VI.

HARRY'S SEAFOOD BAR & GRILL
Lunch: $8-$12   **Dinner:** $12-$20   **Phone:** 904/247-8855   99

American

Location: On 3rd St N/SR A1A; corner of N 10th Ave; in Sea Walk Plaza. 1018 3rd St N 32250. **Hours:** 11 am-10 pm, Fri & Sat-11 pm. **Features:** The casual atmosphere and menu both reflect a little New Orleans flair. Among cuisine selections are blackened entrees, crawfish done many ways, fried catfish and fresh fish prepared with several homemade sauces and garnishes. Casual dress; cocktails. **Parking:** on-site. **Cards:** AX, MC, VI.

ICHIBAN JAPANESE STEAK HOUSE
Dinner: $8-$15   **Phone:** 904/247-8228   101

Japanese

Location: Jct US 90 (Beach Blvd) and SR A1A, 0.4 mi n. 675 N 3rd St 32250. **Hours:** 5 pm-9:45 pm, Fri & Sat-10:45 pm. **Closed:** 11/23. **Reservations:** accepted. **Features:** Sushi, teriyaki, tempura and steak delicacies are all here. Combine the casual atmosphere with attentive service and hearty portions, and you end up with an Oriental feast for the senses. Choose sushi made-to-order as you watch or steak, seafood and beef combinations offered by a smiling chef at spotless steak table grills. Japanese cookery with an American accent is found in entrees such as hibachi shrimp, scallops, chicken, steak and lobster. Casual dress; cocktails. **Parking:** on-site. **Cards:** AX, DS, MC, VI.

JASON'S DELI
Lunch: $4-$9   **Dinner:** $4-$9   **Phone:** 904/246-7585   115

American

Location: Just n of JTB, then w; in Pablo Plaza Shopping Center. 2230 Third St S 32250. **Hours:** 10 am-9 pm, Fri & Sat-10 pm. **Features:** Soups, salads, wraps, muffulettas, submarine sandwiches and super spuds make up the bulk of the menu. Healthy selections are specially marked, and vegetarian dishes are available. Casual dress. **Parking:** on-site. **Cards:** AX, DS, MC, VI.

LIGHTHOUSE GRILLE
Lunch: $7-$23   **Dinner:** $7-$23   **Phone:** 904/242-8899   106

American

Location: Jct SR A1A, 1.5 mi w on US 90, just s. 2600 Beach Blvd 32250. **Hours:** 11 am-10 pm, Fri & Sat-11 pm. **Closed:** 11/23, 12/25. **Reservations:** accepted. **Features:** The menu at the casually upscale eatery lists steak, prime rib, chicken, ribs, seafood, burgers and salads. Views from the dining room and outdoor deck overlook the Intracoastal Waterway. Casual dress; cocktails. **Parking:** on-site. **Cards:** AX, DC, MC, VI.

MARIO'S AT THE BEACH
Lunch: $8-$18   **Dinner:** $8-$18   **Phone:** 904/246-0005   113

Italian

Location: On 3rd St S/SR A1A; in Office Depot Plaza. 1830 S 3rd St 32250. **Hours:** 11 am-10 pm, Fri & Sat-11 pm. **Closed:** 11/23, 12/25. **Features:** Patrons can relax over Neapolitan or Sicilian pizza, baked pasta dishes or traditional veal, chicken and seafood dishes. Patio seating is a sunny-day option. Casual dress; beer & wine only. **Parking:** on-site. **Cards:** MC, VI.

MATSU JAPANESE STEAK HOUSE & SUSHI BAR
Dinner: $11-$28   **Phone:** 904/249-4290   95

Japanese

Location: On 3rd St N/SR A1A; corner of 15th Ave N; in the North Beach Village Plaza. 1515 N 3rd St 32250. **Hours:** 5 pm-10 pm, Fri & Sat-10:30 pm, Sun 11:30 am-10 pm. **Closed:** 12/25. **Reservations:** accepted. **Features:** Guests can sit at one of the five cooking tables or at the sushi bar and watch their food made in front of them. A fun time will be had at either. Casual dress; cocktails. **Parking:** on-site. **Cards:** AX, MC, VI.

PONCHO-N-CHARLIE'S TEX-MEX CANTINA
Lunch: $10-$15   **Dinner:** $10-$15   **Phone:** 904/247-3055   105

Tex-Mex

Location: Between 2nd St and 3rd St S; center. 208 Beach Blvd 32250. **Hours:** 4 pm-10 pm, Fri-11 pm, Sat 11 am-11 pm, Sun 11 am-10 pm. **Closed:** 12/25; also Mon. **Features:** One of the newest Tex-Mex restaurants in the neighborhood, this place has something to suit every palate. There are tasty fish tacos, tamales, chili rellenos and enchiladas that are prepared in four different ways. For the hearty appetite, try the fajitas or create your own combination platter. There's also a gringo menu. Be sure and say "hola, amigo" to Poncho and Charlie. Casual dress; cocktails. **Parking:** on-site and valet. **Cards:** AX, DS, MC, VI.

(See map and index starting on p. 466)

ROY'S
Hawaiian

Dinner: $19-$34   **Phone:** 904/241-7697   117

Location: Corner of S 3rd St and Osceola; in South Third Shopping Plaza. 2400-101 S 3rd St 32250. **Hours:** 5 pm-10 pm, Fri & Sat-11 pm, Sun-9 pm. Closed: 11/23, 12/25. **Reservations:** suggested. **Features:** Patrons are transported to the shores of Hawaii and greeted with a warm aloha. The restaurant features the recipes of celebrity chef Roy Yamaguchi. Hawaiian fusion cuisine is prepared from fresh fish flown in from around the world. Great for sharing is Roy's Canoe, a sampler of appetizers. Entree temptations include roasted macadamia nut mahi mahi in lobster cognac sauce and hibachi-style grilled salmon in citrus ponzu sauce. The desserts are irresistible. Dressy casual; cocktails. **Parking:** on-site and valet. **Cards:** AX, DC, DS, JC, MC, VI.

THAI ROOM
Thai

Lunch: $7-$9   **Dinner:** $10-$32   **Phone:** 904/249-8444   109

Location: 13th Ave S on SR A1A. 1286 S 3rd St 32250. **Hours:** 11 am-2 & 5-9:30 pm, Fri-10:30 pm, Sat 5 pm-10:30 pm, Sun 5 pm-9:30 pm. Closed major holidays. **Reservations:** accepted. **Features:** This is what it's like to dine in Thailand. An attractive fountain and greenery-surrounded waterfall grace the center of the dining room, while a thatch-like mansard roof over the bar area fosters an outdoors feeling. Begin with a light spring roll or one of several homemade soups, then enjoy duck curry or other favorites such as prig pow, kra proa or a host of rice and noodle selections. Dishes are spiced to diners' preference. Casual dress; beer & wine only. **Parking:** on-site. **Cards:** AX, DC, DS, MC, VI.

NEPTUNE BEACH pop. 7,270   (See map and index starting on p. 466)

—— WHERE TO STAY ——

SEA HORSE OCEANFRONT INN
Small-scale Hotel

Phone: 904/246-2175   74

All Year   1P: $99-$189   2P: $99-$189   XP: $15

Location: Jct Atlantic Blvd and 1st St. 120 Atlantic Blvd 32266. **Fax:** 904/246-4256. **Facility:** 38 units. 37 one-bedroom standard units. 1 one-bedroom suite ($139-$189). 3 stories, exterior corridors. *Bath:* combo or shower only. **Parking:** on-site. **Amenities:** high-speed Internet. **Pool(s):** outdoor. **Leisure Activities:** shuffleboard. **Business Services:** fax (fee). **Cards:** AX, DC, DS, MC, VI.

SOME UNITS

—— WHERE TO DINE ——

BEACH BUNS
American

Lunch: $2-$5   **Phone:** 904/249-7557   91

Location: Jct Atlantic Blvd and 1st St, just s. 120 Lemon St 32266. **Hours:** 11:30 am-3 pm. Closed: Mon except on holidays. **Features:** Tasty hot dogs, cold drinks and delicious frozen desserts are here right on the beach for your enjoyment. Casual dress. **Parking:** on-site.

BONE'S PIT BAR-B-Q
Barbecue

Lunch: $6-$14   **Dinner:** $6-$14   **Phone:** 904/270-2666   90

Location: On SR A1A/10, just w of jct Penman Rd; in Penman Plaza. 1307 Atlantic Blvd 32266. **Hours:** 11 am-9:30 pm, Fri & Sat-10 pm. **Features:** A favorite since 1949, the eatery presents a menu of smoked beef, pork, turkey and chicken items. Also available are sandwiches and rib baskets, low-calorie choices and family-feast platters. Diners smother the various meats with one of the many original sauces. Casual dress; beer only. **Parking:** on-site. **Cards:** MC, VI.

THE LOOP
American

Lunch: $6-$18   **Dinner:** $6-$18   **Phone:** 904/241-8476   92

Location: Just s of Atlantic Blvd. 211 3rd St 32266. **Hours:** 11 am-10 pm, Fri-11 pm. Closed: 12/25. **Features:** Award-winning burgers, freshly made pizza, cool refreshing salads and thick malts are just a few of the great offerings at this casual and well known eatery; they have a light menu along with some wonderful rich desserts. Beer only. **Parking:** on-site. **Cards:** AX, DS, MC, VI.

MEZZA LUNA VAGABONDO RISTORANTE
Italian

Dinner: $15-$25   **Phone:** 904/246-5100   89

Location: Corner of Atlantic Blvd and 1st St; adjacent to courthouse. 110 1st St 32266. **Hours:** 5 pm-10:30 pm, Fri & Sat-11:30 pm, Sun 4 pm-10 pm. Closed: Mon. **Reservations:** suggested. **Features:** Enjoy special seafood and veal entrees and pizza made in a wood-burning oven. A trained and knowledgeable staff makes this restaurant seem like home. A scrumptious dessert menu includes a thin, caramelized layer of creme brulee in a thick raspberry sauce. Casual dress; cocktails. **Parking:** street. **Cards:** AX, MC, VI.

SUNNY CARIBBEE
Caribbean

Lunch: $7-$19   **Dinner:** $14-$19   **Phone:** 904/270-8940   88

Location: Jct Atlantic Ave. 100 N 1st St 32266. **Hours:** 11 am-2 am. Closed: 12/25. **Features:** With jerk spicing, herb rubs and tropical sauces, the restaurant's specialties show a decidedly Caribbean flair. The dining room is informal and the service style casual. The upper level offers outdoor seating. Casual dress; cocktails. **Parking:** street. **Cards:** AX, DS, MC, VI.

ORANGE PARK pop. 9,081 (See map and index starting on p. 466)

──────── WHERE TO STAY ────────

BEST WESTERN SOUTHSIDE HOTEL & SUITES *Book at aaa.com* Phone: 904/264-4466 93
(AAA) (SAVE)
1/2-11/30 1P: $72-$92 2P: $72-$92 XP: $10 F18
12/1-1/1 1P: $69-$89 2P: $69-$89 XP: $10 F18
Small-scale Hotel **Location:** I-295, exit 10 (US 17), just nw. 4580 Collins Rd 32073. Fax: 904/264-2193. **Facility:** 103 units. 71 one-bedroom standard units, some with whirlpools. 32 one-bedroom suites ($89-$110). 5 stories, interior corridors. **Parking:** on-site. **Terms:** [BP] meal plan available. **Amenities:** high-speed Internet, voice mail, irons, hair dryers. **Pool(s):** small heated outdoor. **Leisure Activities:** limited exercise equipment. **Guest Services:** valet and coin laundry, area transportation-within 10 mi. **Business Services:** meeting rooms, business center. **Cards:** AX, DC, DS, MC, VI. **Special Amenities:** free full breakfast and free newspaper. *(See color ad below)*

SOME UNITS
🅂🅳 🏊 ⊗ DATA/PORT 🖥 📷 📺 /⊠/

COMFORT INN *Book at aaa.com* Phone: (904)644-4444 96
Small-scale Hotel **Location:** I-295, exit 10 (US 17), just s. Located adjacent to a kennel club. 341 Park Ave 32073. Fax: 904/215-9585. All Year 1P: $65-$95 2P: $65-$95 2 stories (no elevator), exterior corridors. **Terms:** package plans, pets ($30 fee). **Amenities:** voice mail, irons, hair dryers. **Pool(s):** outdoor. **Leisure Activities:** tennis court. **Guest Services:** valet and coin laundry. **Business Services:** meeting rooms, business center. **Cards:** AX, CB, DC, DS, JC, MC, VI.

SOME UNITS
(ASK) 🅂🅳 🐕 🏊 ⊞ ⊗ DATA/PORT 🖥 📷 📺 /⊠/
FEE FEE

FAIRFIELD INN BY MARRIOTT *Book at aaa.com* Phone: 904/278-7442 95
All Year 1P: $76-$89 2P: $79-$89
Small-scale Hotel **Location:** I-295, exit 10 (US 17), 0.3 mi s to Wells Rd, then w. 450 Eldridge Ave 32073. Fax: 904/278-5022. **Facility:** 83 one-bedroom standard units. 3 stories, interior corridors. *Bath:* combo or shower only. **Parking:** on-site. **Terms:** cancellation fee imposed, [CP] meal plan available. **Amenities:** high-speed Internet, voice mail, irons, hair dryers. **Pool(s):** outdoor. **Leisure Activities:** whirlpool, exercise room. **Guest Services:** valet laundry. **Cards:** AX, CB, DC, DS, JC, MC, VI.

SOME UNITS
(ASK) 👓Ⓜ 🚹 🌙 🏊 ⊗ DATA/PORT /⊠ 🖥 📷 /

(See map and index starting on p. 466)

HOLIDAY INN ORANGE PARK   Phone: **(904)264-9513**   **94**
All Year   1P: $79-$99   2P: $79-$99

Small-scale Hotel
Location: I-295, exit 10 (US 17), just s. 150 Park Ave 32073. Fax: 904/278-1575. **Facility:** 299 units. 294 one-and 1 two-bedroom standard units. 4 one-bedroom suites, some with whirlpools. 2 stories, exterior corridors. *Bath:* combo or shower only. **Parking:** on-site. **Amenities:** video games (fee), voice mail, irons, hair dryers. **Pool(s):** outdoor, wading. **Leisure Activities:** exercise room. **Guest Services:** valet and coin laundry. **Business Services:** meeting rooms. **Cards:** AX, CB, DC, DS, JC, MC, VI.

SOME UNITS

——— WHERE TO DINE ———

THE HILLTOP   Dinner: $12-$20   Phone: 904/272-5959   **131**

American
Location: I-295, exit 12, s on Blanding Blvd, then 0.3 mi w. 2030 Wells Rd 32073. **Hours:** 5:30 pm-9:30 pm, Fri & Sat-10 pm. Closed: 12/25; also Sun & Mon. **Reservations:** accepted. **Features:** A prominent Orange Park landmark, this restaurant offers gracious Southern hospitality in the charming environment of the Old South. Enjoy dinner in the stately formal dining room. Extensive wine list. Dressy casual; cocktails. **Parking:** on-site. **Cards:** AX, DC, DS, MC, VI.

JOHNNY CARINO'S COUNTRY ITALIAN   Lunch: $7-$9   Dinner: $9-$13   Phone: 904/278-7880   **132**

Italian
DS, MC, VI.
Location: I-295, exit 12, 0.5 mi s, then just e. 1940 Wells Rd 32244. **Hours:** 11 am-10 pm, Fri & Sat-11 pm. Closed: 11/23, 12/25. **Features:** The restaurant calls itself "country Italian." Menu selections include many traditional favorites as well as some inventive and hot-and-spicy items; the atmosphere is casual and the dining room is decorated in a Mediterranean theme. Casual dress; cocktails. **Parking:** on-site. **Cards:** AX,

KYODAI SUSHI ROCK   Lunch: $14-$18   Dinner: $21-$34   Phone: 904/215-8228   **129**

Japanese
Location: 0.5 mi e of Blanding Blvd. 1861 Wells Rd 32073. **Hours:** 11:30 am-2 & 4:30-10 pm. **Features:** Located across from the Orange Park mall this upbeat restaurant offers an array of sushi and sashimi as well as full Japanese meals and performance tepenyaki cooking. Casual dress; cocktails. **Parking:** on-site. **Cards:** AX, MC, VI.

MONIQUE'S CAFE & IMPORTS   Lunch: $3-$8   Dinner: $5-$10   Phone: 904/215-0199   **128**

South American
Location: I-295, exit 12, 0.3 mi s to Wells Rd, then e. 1540 Wells Rd 32073. **Hours:** 7 am-9 pm, Sat from 8 am, Sun 9 am-6 pm. Closed major holidays. **Features:** The restaurant offers excellent Southern favorites cooked in an open kitchen as well as homemade desserts. Select a bottle of imported wine to enjoy at home. Casual dress; wine only. **Parking:** on-site. **Cards:** AX, MC, VI.

RAMIREZ RESTAURANT   Lunch: $5-$10   Dinner: $7-$15   Phone: 904/278-9040   **133**

Mexican
Location: I-295, exit 10, 1.2 mi s. 1237 Park Ave 32073. **Hours:** 11 am-10 pm, Fri & Sat-2 am. **Features:** This family-owned and -operated icon provides a great home-cooked meal; all the traditional favorites are available. Casual dress; cocktails. **Parking:** on-site. **Cards:** AX, MC, VI.

SARNELLI'S RISTORANTE   Dinner: $11-$25   Phone: 904/269-1331   **134**

Italian
Location: Corner of Kingsley and US 17. 2023 Park Ave 32073. **Hours:** 5 pm-10 pm. Closed: 11/23, 12/25; also Sun. **Reservations:** accepted. **Features:** The casual restaurant offers a menu focused on traditional Italian preparations. Casual dress; beer & wine only. **Parking:** on-site. **Cards:** AX, DS, MC, VI.

VENEZIA'S ITALIAN RESTAURANT   Lunch: $5-$9   Dinner: $7-$15   Phone: 904/278-1989   **130**

Italian
Cards: AX, CB, DC, DS, MC, VI.
Location: I-295, exit 12, 0.5 mi s on Blanding Blvd, then 0.3 mi e. 1871 Wells Rd 32073. **Hours:** 11 am-2 & 5-10 pm, Sun-9 pm. Closed: 4/16, 11/23, 12/25. **Reservations:** accepted. **Features:** A trellis-type archway, statues and pillars help to create a romantic ambience reminiscent of Old Italy. Traditional menu offerings include bruschetta, assorted pasta dishes and veal preparations. Casual dress; beer & wine only. **Parking:** on-site.

PONTE VEDRA BEACH   (See maps and indexes starting on p. 466, 874)

——— WHERE TO STAY ———

HILTON GARDEN INN   *Book at aaa.com*   Phone: **(904)280-1661**   **89**
12/1-5/31   1P: $79-$209   2P: $79-$209   XP: $10   F17
6/1-11/30   1P: $79-$199   2P: $79-$199   XP: $10   F17

Small-scale Hotel
Location: 5 mi s of jct J Turner Butler Blvd on SR A1A, just e; in Sawgrass Village Shopping Center. 45 PGA Tour Blvd 32082. Fax: 904/280-1544. **Facility:** 127 units. 76 one-bedroom standard units, some with whirlpools. 51 one-bedroom suites. 6 stories, interior corridors. *Bath:* combo or shower only. **Parking:** on-site. **Terms:** package plans. **Amenities:** video games (fee), high-speed Internet, dual phone lines, voice mail, irons, hair dryers. **Dining:** 6-9:30 am, Sat, Sun & holidays 7 am-noon, also, Paddy Mac's Tavern, see separate listing. **Pool(s):** heated outdoor. **Leisure Activities:** whirlpool, exercise room. *Fee:* golf privileges. **Guest Services:** sundries, valet and coin laundry, area transportation-Mayo Clinic. **Business Services:** meeting rooms, business center. **Cards:** AX, CB, DC, DS, MC, VI. **Special Amenities:** free local telephone calls and free newspaper.

SOME UNITS

At 60 mph, if you reach down to change the radio station you can travel the length of a football field.

Stay Focused
Keep your mind on the road.

THE LODGE & CLUB AT PONTE VEDRA BEACH   *Book at aaa.com*   Phone: (904)273-9500   88

3/1-5/31	1P: $360-$640	2P: $360-$640
2/1-2/28 & 6/1-11/30	1P: $270-$440	2P: $270-$440
12/1-1/31	1P: $230-$400	2P: $230-$440

Resort
Small-scale Hotel

Location: I-95, exit 344 (J. Turner Butler Blvd) to SR A1A, 0.5 mi n to 36th Ave, then 2 mi s. 607 Ponte Vedra Blvd 32082. Fax: 904/273-0210. **Facility:** On the ocean, this service-oriented, Mediterranean-style resort offers organized activities and waterfront guest rooms with balconies and fireplaces. 66 units. 64 one-bedroom standard units, some with whirlpools. 2 one-bedroom suites with whirlpools. 2 stories, exterior corridors. *Bath:* combo or shower only. **Parking:** on-site and valet. **Terms:** check-in 4 pm, 3 day cancellation notice-fee imposed, package plans, $15 service charge. **Amenities:** high-speed Internet, dual phone lines, voice mail, safes, honor bars, irons, hair dryers. *Some:* DVD players. **Dining:** 7-10:30 am, 11:30-2:30 & 5:30-10 pm, guests only; 18% service charge, cocktails, entertainment. **Pool(s):** 3 heated outdoor, wading. **Leisure Activities:** saunas, whirlpools, steamrooms, recreation programs, spa. *Fee:* paddleboats, sailboats, charter fishing, beach kayaks, golf-90 holes, 15 tennis courts (7 lighted), bicycles. **Guest Services:** gift shop, valet laundry, area transportation-Ponte Vedra. **Business Services:** meeting rooms, PC, fax (fee). **Cards:** AX, CB, DC, DS, MC, VI. **Special Amenities:** free local telephone calls and free newspaper. Affiliated with A Preferred Hotel.

SOME UNITS
FEE [icons] FEE

PONTE VEDRA INN AND CLUB   *Book at aaa.com*   Phone: (904)285-1111   87

3/1-5/31	1P: $280-$640	2P: $280-$640
6/1-11/30	1P: $210-$540	2P: $210-$540
2/1-2/28	1P: $200-$540	2P: $200-$540
12/1-1/31	1P: $180-$490	2P: $180-$490

Resort
Large-scale Hotel

Location: I-95, exit 344 (J Turner Butler Blvd) to SR A1A, 0.5 mi n to 36th Ave S, then s via CR 203 and Ponte Vedra Blvd. 200 Ponte Vedra Blvd 32082-9305. Fax: 904/285-2111. **Facility:** This service-oriented beach-club resort was founded in 1927; guest rooms are waterfront with balconies or patios. 249 units. 226 one-bedroom standard units, some with whirlpools. 23 one-bedroom suites ($340-$640), some with whirlpools. 2 stories, exterior corridors. **Parking:** on-site. **Terms:** 3 day cancellation notice, package plans, $16 service charge. **Amenities:** CD players, dual phone lines, voice mail, safes, honor bars, irons, hair dryers. *Some:* DVD players, high-speed Internet. **Dining:** 3 restaurants, 7 am-10 pm; guests only, cocktails, entertainment. **Pool(s):** 3 heated outdoor, wading, lap. **Leisure Activities:** saunas, whirlpools, steamrooms, rental paddleboats, fishing, beach equipment, kayaks, surf & boogie boards, driving range, recreation programs, jogging, playground, spa. *Fee:* boats, sailboats, windsurfing, charter fishing, golf-36 holes, 15 tennis courts (7 lighted), aerobics, spinning, pilates & yoga instruction, bicycles. **Guest Services:** gift shop, valet and coin laundry, area transportation-within 8 mi. **Business Services:** conference facilities, business center. **Cards:** AX, CB, DC, DS, MC, VI. **Special Amenities:** free local telephone calls and free newspaper. *(See color ad p 505)*

SOME UNITS
FEE [icons] FEE

THE SAWGRASS MARRIOTT RESORT & BEACH CLUB   *Book at aaa.com*   Phone: (904)285-7777   90

12/1-6/15	1P: $240-$284
9/11-11/30	1P: $175-$250
6/16-9/10	1P: $175-$208

Large-scale Hotel

Location: 2.5 mi s of J Turner Butler Blvd. 1000 PGA Tour Blvd 32082. Fax: 904/280-7003. **Facility:** 508 units. 403 one-bedroom standard units. 105 one-bedroom suites, some with kitchens. 7 stories, interior corridors. *Bath:* combo or shower only. **Parking:** on-site (fee) and valet. **Terms:** check-in 4 pm, cancellation fee imposed, pets ($75 deposit, in designated units). **Amenities:** video games (fee), high-speed Internet, voice mail, honor bars, irons, hair dryers. **Dining:** 5 restaurants, 6 am-midnight, cocktails. **Pool(s):** outdoor, 2 heated outdoor, 2 wading. **Leisure Activities:** whirlpools, miniature golf, bicycles, playground, exercise room, spa. *Fee:* golf-99 holes, tennis privileges. **Guest Services:** gift shop, valet and coin laundry, area transportation-within resort. **Business Services:** conference facilities, business center. **Cards:** AX, CB, DC, DS, JC, MC, VI. **Special Amenities:** free newspaper. *(See color ad p 505)*

SOME UNITS
FEE FEE [icons]

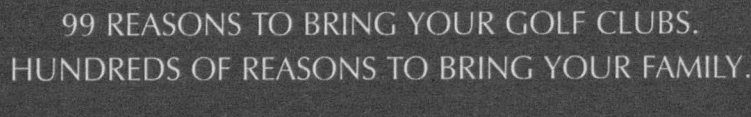
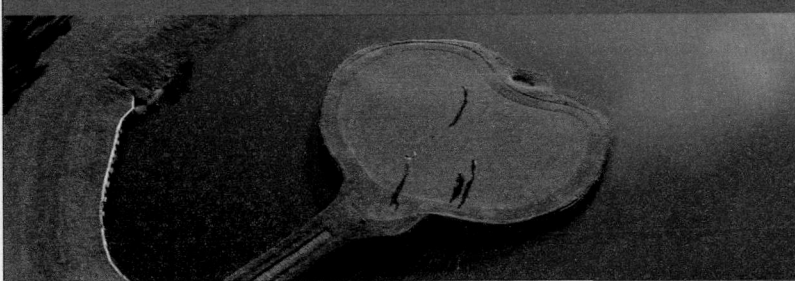

(See maps and indexes starting on p. 466, 874)

——— WHERE TO DINE ———

BARBARA JEAN'S

Regional Seafood

Lunch: $8-$20 **Dinner:** $8-$20 **Phone:** 904/280-7522 38

Location: Jct SR A1A and CR 210A (Solano Rd), 4.6 mi w and s. 15 S Roscoe Blvd 32082. **Hours:** 11 am-9 pm, Fri & Sat-10 pm. Closed: 12/25. **Features:** Nestled in the wooded scrub alongside the Intracoastal Waterway, is a casual eatery serving up great crab cakes, warm breads and other Southern comfort foods. Casual dress; cocktails. **Parking:** on-site. **Cards:** AX, DS, MC, VI.

J J'S CUISINE & WINE

French

Lunch: $6-$22 **Dinner:** $14-$30 **Phone:** 904/273-7980 121

Location: 2 mi s of jct J Turner Butler Blvd; in Shoppes at Ponte Vedra. 330 A1A N, Suite 209 32082. **Hours:** 10 am-9 pm, Fri & Sat-10 pm. Closed major holidays; also Sun & Mon. **Reservations:** accepted. **Features:** When you enter the relaxed restaurant, you enter the streets of Paris. Browse gourmet groceries and baked goods, then dine in the cafe. Choose from quiche, soup and sandwiches for lunch, or enjoy a heartier dinner of roast loin, salmon or seared tuna. Casual dress; beer & wine only. **Parking:** on-site. **Cards:** AX, DC, DS, MC, VI.

LULU'S WATERFRONT GRILLE

Seafood

Lunch: $7-$11 **Dinner:** $12-$20 **Phone:** 904/285-0139 122

Location: 1 mi s. 301 N Roscoe Blvd 32082. **Hours:** 11 am-10 pm. Closed: 11/23, 12/25. **Features:** Dining on the screened porch of this restaurant, which resembles a clapboard house, is darn close to what old Florida is all about. Feast on shrimp jambalaya, caper-coated catch of the day and the native dessert, Key lime pie. Casual dress; cocktails. **Parking:** on-site. **Cards:** AX, MC, VI.

PADDY MAC'S TAVERN

American

Lunch: $7-$13 **Dinner:** $7-$18 **Phone:** 904/285-3133 123

Location: 5 mi s of jct J Turner Butler Blvd on SR A1A, just e; in Sawgrass Village Shopping Center; in Hilton Garden Inn. 43 PGA Tour Blvd 32082. **Hours:** 11 am-11 pm. Closed: 11/23, 12/25. **Reservations:** accepted. **Features:** The popular neighborhood eatery affords a relaxed and friendly atmosphere. Enjoy a large selection of finger foods or such delicacies as salmon, one of the chef's specialties. Take time to look over framed pictures taken at local golfing events. Locally owned and operated. Casual dress; cocktails. **Parking:** on-site. **Cards:** AX, DC, DS, MC, VI.

PLAYERS CAFE

American

Lunch: $2-$6 **Phone:** 904/273-5595 120

Location: Corner of Solana Rd and SR A1A. 262 Solana Rd 32082. **Hours:** 6:30 am-2:30 pm. Closed: 11/23, 12/25. **Features:** Casual, friendly atmosphere in a coffee-shop setting. Walls are painted with amusing charicatures of people playing sports. Casual dress. **Parking:** on-site. **Cards:** AX, MC, VI.

RESTAURANT MEDURE

Continental

Dinner: $18-$29 **Phone:** 904/543-3797 124

Location: 5.3 mi s of J Turner Butler Blvd. 818 N SR A1A 32082. **Hours:** 5:30 pm-10 pm. Closed major holidays. **Reservations:** required. **Features:** This restaurant features Continental cuisine with a Mediterranean flair prepared in an exhibition-style kitchen. Select from various seafood and game in light stocks and broths. Natural wood colors and leather provide a comfortable yet upscale atmosphere. Live jazz five days a week. Dressy casual; cocktails. **Parking:** on-site. **Cards:** AX, CB, DC, DS, JC, MC, VI.

SANTIONI'S OF SAWGRASS

Italian

Dinner: $10-$17 **Phone:** 904/273-7272 125

Location: 1 mi n of jct SR A1A and CR 210; in Tournament Plaza Shopping Center. 832-1 A1A N 32082. **Hours:** 5 pm-10 pm. Closed: 4/16, 11/23, 12/25. **Reservations:** accepted. **Features:** The chef/owner has prepared classic Italian fare for more than 28 years. Featured entrees on a menu of all made-to-order dishes include shrimp fra diavolo, linguine with clam sauce and gnocchi. The wine list delivers a wide selection of California selections. Pizza is available as a carryout choice. Casual dress; beer & wine only. **Parking:** on-site. **Cards:** AX, DS, MC, VI.

YULEE pop. 8,392

——— WHERE TO STAY ———

COMFORT INN

Small-scale Hotel

Book at aaa.com

Phone: (904)225-2600

All Year 1P: $85-$99 2P: $85-$99 XP: $10 D16

Location: I-95, exit 373, just e on SR 200/A1A. 76043 Sidney Pl 32097. Fax: 904/225-1966. **Facility:** 59 one-bedroom standard units, some with whirlpools. 2 stories, interior corridors. *Bath:* combo or shower only. **Parking:** on-site. **Amenities:** irons, hair dryers. **Pool(s):** small outdoor. **Guest Services:** coin laundry. **Cards:** AX, DC, DS, MC, VI.

SOME UNITS

The previous listings were for the Jacksonville Vicinity.
This page resumes the alphabetical listings of cities in Florida.

JACKSONVILLE BEACH —*See Jacksonville p. 496.*

JENSEN BEACH pop. 11,100

———— WHERE TO STAY ————

RIVER PALM COTTAGES
Phone: 772/334-0401

12/1-4/30	1P: $99-$169	2P: $169-$199	XP: $10	F16
5/1-11/30	1P: $79-$99	2P: $149-$169	XP: $10	F16

Cottage
Location: On SR 707 (NE Indian River Dr); 1.4 mi s of jct SR 732. 2325 NE Indian River Dr 34957. **Fax:** 772/334-0527. **Facility:** 23 units. 4 one-bedroom standard units. 19 cottages ($289-$398). 1-2 stories, exterior corridors. *Bath:* combo or shower only. **Parking:** on-site. **Terms:** 14 day cancellation notice-fee imposed, weekly rates available, small pets only ($10 extra charge). **Amenities:** voice mail, irons, hair dryers. **Pool(s):** heated outdoor. **Leisure Activities:** boat dock, volleyball. **Guest Services:** coin laundry. **Cards:** AX, MC, VI.

SOME UNITS

VISTANA'S BEACH CLUB   *Book at aaa.com*
Phone: (772)229-9200

All Year   2P: $295
Location: SR A1A, Hutchinson Island, 2 mi n of jct SR 732. 10740 S Ocean Dr 34957. **Fax:** 772/229-3902.
Condominium   **Facility:** The spacious condos feature beach decor; one of the two buildings has oceanfront balconies with tranquil views. 76 two-bedroom suites with kitchens, some with whirlpools. 9 stories, exterior corridors. **Parking:** on-site. **Terms:** check-in 4 pm, 3 day cancellation notice-fee imposed. **Amenities:** video library, irons. *Some:* hair dryers. **Pool(s):** heated outdoor, wading. **Leisure Activities:** whirlpool, rental boats, fishing, 2 lighted tennis courts, recreation programs, playground, volleyball. **Fee:** charter fishing, bicycles, massage, game room. **Guest Services:** complimentary laundry. **Business Services:** fax (fee). **Cards:** AX, DC, DS, MC, VI.

JUNO BEACH pop. 3,262   (See map and index starting on p. 843)

———— WHERE TO STAY ————

HAMPTON INN JUNO BEACH   *Book at aaa.com*
Phone: (561)626-9090   [23]

12/1-4/30 [BP]	1P: $159-$299	2P: $179-$299	
5/1-11/30 [BP]	1P: $99-$199	2P: $109-$199	

Small-scale Hotel
Location: US 1, just s of jct Donald Ross Rd. 13801 US Hwy 1 33408. **Fax:** 561/624-9936. **Facility:** 89 units. 88 one-bedroom standard units, some with whirlpools. 1 one-bedroom suite ($199-$299). 2 stories, interior corridors. *Bath:* combo or shower only. **Parking:** on-site. **Terms:** cancellation fee imposed. **Amenities:** voice mail, irons, hair dryers. **Pool(s):** small heated outdoor. **Leisure Activities:** whirlpool. **Guest Services:** valet and coin laundry. **Business Services:** meeting rooms, PC. **Cards:** AX, CB, DC, DS, MC, VI.

SOME UNITS

HOLIDAY INN EXPRESS-NORTH PALM BEACH   *Book at aaa.com*
Phone: (561)622-4366   [22]

All Year [ECP]   1P: $99-$169   2P: $99-$169
Small-scale Hotel
Location: Jct Donald Ross Rd. 13950 US Hwy 1 33408. **Fax:** 561/625-5245. **Facility:** 108 units. 96 one-bedroom standard units. 12 one-bedroom suites. 3 stories, interior/exterior corridors. *Bath:* combo or shower only. **Parking:** on-site. **Terms:** pets ($25 fee). **Amenities:** voice mail, irons, hair dryers. **Pool(s):** outdoor. **Leisure Activities:** exercise room. **Guest Services:** valet and coin laundry. **Business Services:** meeting rooms, business center. **Cards:** AX, DC, DS, JC, MC, VI.

SOME UNITS

———— WHERE TO DINE ————

CLASSICO'S ITALIAN RESTAURANT   **Dinner:** $10-$23   Phone: 561/622-9772   [13]
Location: US 1, just n of jct Donald Ross Rd; in Loggerhead Plaza. 14133 US Hwy 1 33408. **Hours:** 4:30 pm-10 pm, Sun 5 pm-9 pm. **Closed:** 11/23, 12/25. **Features:** Candlelight dinners feature creative dishes of veal,
Italian   chicken, pasta and seafood, all cooked to order with only fresh ingredients. The eatery is noted for its displays of movie memorabilia from the '20s through the '50s and its sinful homemade desserts. Casual dress; cocktails. **Parking:** on-site. **Cards:** AX, MC, VI.

JUPITER pop. 39,328

———— WHERE TO STAY ————

BEST WESTERN INTRACOASTAL INN   *Book at aaa.com*
Phone: (561)575-2936

2/1-4/15	1P: $129-$179	2P: $139-$199	XP: $10	F17
12/1-1/31 & 4/16-11/30	1P: $89-$129	2P: $99-$149	XP: $10	F17

Small-scale Hotel
Location: 0.5 mi s of jct SR 706 (Indiantown Rd). 810 S US Hwy 1 33477. **Fax:** 561/575-9346. **Facility:** 53 one-bedroom standard units, some with whirlpools. 2 stories (no elevator), interior corridors. *Bath:* combo or shower only. **Parking:** on-site. **Amenities:** irons, hair dryers. **Pool(s):** outdoor. **Guest Services:** coin laundry. **Cards:** AX, CB, DC, DS, MC, VI. **Special Amenities:** free continental breakfast and free local telephone calls.

SOME UNITS

COMFORT INN & SUITES   *Book at aaa.com*   Phone: (561)745-7997

12/1-4/15 & 11/1-11/30 [ECP]	1P: $149-$270	2P: $149-$270	XP: $10 F18
4/16-10/31 [ECP]	1P: $110-$200	2P: $110-$200	XP: $10 F18

Small-scale Hotel **Location:** I-95, exit 87 (SR 706/Indiantown Rd), 0.8 mi e. 6752 W Indiantown Rd 33458. Fax: 561/768-022. **Facility:** 69 one-bedroom standard units, some with whirlpools. 4 stories, interior corridors. *Bath:* combo or shower only. **Parking:** on-site. **Amenities:** high-speed Internet, voice mail, safes (fee), irons, hair dryers. **Pool(s):** heated outdoor. **Leisure Activities:** exercise room. **Guest Services:** coin laundry. **Business Services:** meeting rooms, business center. **Cards:** AX, CB, DC, DS, MC, VI.

ASK SD 🍽 🛋 🏊 📷 DATA PORT 🖥 🖨 🖥 / ⊠ /

FAIRFIELD INN & SUITES BY MARRIOTT   *Book at aaa.com*   Phone: (561)748-5252

1/1-5/1 [ECP]	1P: $129-$179	2P: $129-$179	XP: $10 F
5/2-11/30 [ECP]	1P: $109-$139	2P: $109-$139	XP: $10 F
12/1-12/31 [ECP]	1P: $109-$129	2P: $109-$129	XP: $10 F

Small-scale Hotel **Location:** I-95, exit 87A, 0.8 mi e on SR 706 (Indiantown Rd). 6748 W Indiantown Rd 33458. Fax: 561/748-5251. **Facility:** 110 one-bedroom standard units, some with efficiencies. 4 stories, interior corridors. *Bath:* combo or shower only. **Parking:** on-site. **Terms:** 3 day cancellation notice-fee imposed, 11% service charge. **Amenities:** dual phone lines, voice mail, irons, hair dryers. *Some:* CD players, high-speed Internet. **Pool(s):** heated outdoor. **Leisure Activities:** whirlpool, exercise room. **Guest Services:** valet laundry. **Cards:** AX, DC, DS, JC, MC, VI.

ASK SD 🍽 🛋 🏊 📷 DATA PORT 🖥 / ⊠ 🖨 🖥 /

JUPITER BEACH RESORT   *Book at aaa.com*   Phone: (561)746-2511

12/1-4/30	1P: $409-$719	2P: $409-$719	XP: $25 F18
5/1-5/31 & 10/1-11/30	1P: $259-$419	2P: $259-$419	XP: $25 F18
6/1-9/30	1P: $229-$349	2P: $229-$349	XP: $25 F18

Large-scale Hotel **Location:** SR A1A, 1 mi se of jct US 1; jct SR 706 (Indiantown Rd). 5 N A1A 33477-5190. Fax: 561/744-1741. **Facility:** 159 units. 125 one-bedroom standard units. 34 one-bedroom suites ($1000-$1800). 9 stories, interior corridors. *Bath:* combo or shower only. **Parking:** on-site and valet. **Terms:** check-in 4 pm, 3 day cancellation notice-fee imposed. **Amenities:** high-speed Internet, dual phone lines, voice mail, safes, honor bars, irons, hair dryers. **Dining:** 7 am-11 pm, cocktails, entertainment. **Pool(s):** heated outdoor. **Leisure Activities:** lighted tennis court, exercise room, volleyball. **Fee:** scuba diving, snorkeling. **Guest Services:** gift shop, valet laundry. **Business Services:** meeting rooms, business center. **Cards:** AX, CB, DC, DS, MC, VI. **Special Amenities:** free newspaper and free room upgrade **(subject to availability with advance reservations).** *(See color ad below)*

SD 🍽 🍸 🛋 🏊 ⊠ 📷 DATA PORT 🖥 / ⊠ VCR FEE 🖨 🖥 /

WELLESLEY INN (JUPITER)   *Book at aaa.com*   Phone: (561)575-7201

12/16-5/15	1P: $149	2P: $149
5/16-11/30	1P: $89	2P: $89
12/1-12/15	1P: $79	2P: $79

Small-scale Hotel   **Location:** SR 706 (Indiantown Rd); 0.3 mi w of jct US 1; in Fisherman's Wharf Plaza. 34 Fishermans Wharf 33477. **Fax:** 561/575-1169. **Facility:** 102 one-bedroom standard units. 3 stories, interior corridors. *Bath:* combo or shower only. **Parking:** on-site. **Terms:** weekly rates available, package plans, small pets only ($10 fee). **Amenities:** video games (fee), dual phone lines, voice mail, irons, hair dryers. *Some:* safes. **Pool(s):** small heated outdoor. **Leisure Activities:** exercise room. **Guest Services:** valet and coin laundry. **Business Services:** PC. **Cards:** AX, CB, DC, DS, JC, MC, VI. **Special Amenities:** free expanded continental breakfast and free local telephone calls.

SOME UNITS

KENANSVILLE

──── **WHERE TO STAY** ────

LAKE MARIAN PARADISE CABINS & MARINA   Phone: 407/436-1464

Motel   All Year   1P: $70-$95   2P: $70-$95   XP: $10   F5
Location: Florida Tpke, exit 242, 4.6 mi s on US 192, then 31.7 mi on CR 523. 901 Arnold Rd 34739. **Facility:** 6 one-bedroom standard units with kitchens. 1 story, exterior corridors. *Bath:* shower only. **Parking:** on-site. **Terms:** office hours 6 am-6 pm, 7 day cancellation notice-fee imposed, weekly rates available. **Leisure Activities:** marina, fishing, hiking trails, shuffleboard. *Fee:* putting green. **Guest Services:** gift shop, coin laundry. **Cards:** MC, VI.

──── **WHERE TO DINE** ────

LAKE MARIAN RESTAURANT   **Lunch:** $4-$14   **Dinner:** $4-$14   Phone: 407/436-1051
Location: Florida Tpke, exit 242, 4.6 mi s on US 192, then 31.7 mi w on CR 523. 30 S Canoe Creek Rd 34739. **Hours:** 7 am-8 pm. **Features:** Enjoy country cooking in this quaint eatery located just off Lake Marian; the menu offers catfish as well as burgers and roast beef. **Parking:** on-site. **Cards:** MC, VI.

American

KENDALL —*See Miami-Miami Beach p. 606.*

KEY BISCAYNE —*See Miami-Miami Beach p. 607.*

KEY COLONY BEACH —*See The Florida Keys p. 328.*

KEY LARGO —*See The Florida Keys p. 328.*

KEY WEST —*See The Florida Keys p. 338.*

KISSIMMEE —*See Orlando p. 754.*

LADY LAKE —*See Orlando p. 790.*

LAKE BUENA VISTA —*See Orlando p. 791.*

LAKE CITY pop. 9,980

──── **WHERE TO STAY** ────

BEST WESTERN INN   *Book at aaa.com*   Phone: (386)752-3801

All Year   1P: $55-$105   2P: $60-$110   XP: $5   F17
Location: I-75, exit 427, just w. 3598 W US Hwy 90 32055. **Fax:** 386/755-4846. **Facility:** 82 units. 80 one-bedroom standard units. 2 one-bedroom suites. 2 stories, exterior corridors. **Parking:** on-site. **Terms:** small pets only ($10 extra charge, in designated units). **Amenities:** high-speed Internet, irons, hair dryers. Small-scale Hotel   **Pool(s):** outdoor. **Leisure Activities:** sauna, whirlpool, playground, exercise room. *Fee:* game room. **Guest Services:** coin laundry. **Business Services:** meeting rooms, business center. **Cards:** AX, CB, DC, DS, JC, MC, VI. **Special Amenities:** free expanded continental breakfast and free local telephone calls.

SOME UNITS

COUNTRY INN & SUITES   *Book at aaa.com*   Phone: (386)754-5944

All Year   1P: $95-$130
Location: I-75, exit 427, just w. 350 SW Florida Gateway Dr 32024. **Fax:** 386/754-1557. **Facility:** 60 units. 46 one-bedroom standard units, some with whirlpools. 14 one-bedroom suites ($110-$130). 3 stories, interior Small-scale Hotel   corridors. *Bath:* combo or shower only. **Parking:** on-site. **Terms:** 1-2 night minimum stay, 3 day cancellation notice, [ECP] meal plan available. **Amenities:** high-speed Internet, dual phone lines, voice mail, safes, irons, hair dryers. **Pool(s):** heated indoor. **Leisure Activities:** whirlpool, exercise room. **Guest Services:** valet and coin laundry. **Business Services:** meeting rooms, fax. **Cards:** AX, DC, DS, MC, VI.

SOME UNITS

DAYS INN

Book at aaa.com

AAA SAVE

Small-scale Hotel

All Year [ECP]   1P: $60-$110   2P: $69-$110   XP: $5   F12
Location: I-75, exit 427, 0.3 mi e. 3144 W US Hwy 90 32055. Fax: 386/752-9350. **Facility:** 120 one-bedroom standard units. 2 stories, exterior corridors. **Parking:** on-site. **Amenities:** hair dryers. **Pool(s):** outdoor. **Business Services:** fax. **Cards:** AX, CB, DC, DS, MC, VI. **Special Amenities:** free expanded continental breakfast and free newspaper.

Phone: (386)752-9350

SOME UNITS

DAYS INN I-10

Book at aaa.com

AAA SAVE

Small-scale Hotel

All Year   1P: $75-$200   2P: $75-$200   XP: $5   F14
Location: I-10, exit 303, just s. 3430 US Hwy 441 32055. Fax: 386/758-7612. **Facility:** 62 one-bedroom standard units. 2 stories, exterior corridors. **Parking:** on-site. **Terms:** [CP] meal plan available, small pets only ($5-$10 extra charge). **Amenities:** hair dryers. **Pool(s):** outdoor. **Guest Services:** coin laundry. **Business Services:** PC, fax. **Cards:** AX, DC, DS, MC, VI. **Special Amenities:** free continental breakfast and free local telephone calls.

Phone: (386)758-4224

SOME UNITS

FEE

DRIFTWOOD INN

AAA SAVE

Motel

All Year   1P: $36-$60   2P: $38-$60   XP: $5   D10
Location: I-75, exit 427, 0.7 mi e. 2764 W US Hwy 90 32055. Fax: 386/961-8798. **Facility:** 20 one-bedroom standard units. 1 story, exterior corridors. **Parking:** on-site. **Terms:** small pets only ($5-$10 extra charge). **Cards:** AX, DS, MC, VI. **Special Amenities:** free continental breakfast and free local telephone calls.

Phone: 386/755-3545

SOME UNITS

FEE

ECONO LODGE SOUTH

Book at aaa.com

AAA SAVE

Motel

All Year [CP]   1P: $50-$60   2P: $60-$70   XP: $5   F18
Location: I-75, exit 414, at US 441. Located adjacent to truck parking. 14113 S US Hwy 441 32024. Fax: 386/755-8864. **Facility:** 59 one-bedroom standard units. 1 story, exterior corridors. **Parking:** on-site. **Terms:** 7 day cancellation notice, small pets only. **Pool(s):** outdoor. **Cards:** AX, DC, DS, MC, VI. **Special Amenities:** free continental breakfast and free local telephone calls.

Phone: 386/755-9311

SOME UNITS

HAMPTON INN

Small-scale Hotel

All Year   1P: $88-$130   2P: $88-$130
Location: I-75, exit 427, just w, then 0.4 mi s. 414 SW Florida Gateway Dr 32024. Fax: 386/758-3196. **Facility:** 60 one-bedroom standard units, some with whirlpools. 2 stories, exterior corridors. *Bath:* combo or shower only. **Parking:** on-site. **Terms:** 2 night minimum stay, 3 day cancellation notice, [ECP] meal plan available. **Amenities:** high-speed Internet, voice mail, safes, irons, hair dryers. **Pool(s):** outdoor. **Leisure Activities:** whirlpool. **Guest Services:** valet laundry. **Business Services:** fax. **Cards:** AX, DC, DS, MC, VI.

Phone: (386)752-3419

SOME UNITS

FEE

HOLIDAY INN HOTEL & SUITES

AAA SAVE

Small-scale Hotel

6/1-7/31   1P: $119-$129   2P: $119-$129   XP: $35   F12
12/1-5/31 & 8/1-11/30   1P: $99-$109   2P: $99-$109   XP: $35   F12
Location: I-75, exit 427, just e. 213 SW Commerce Dr 32025. Fax: 386/758-2211. **Facility:** 127 one-bedroom standard units, some with whirlpools. 6 stories, interior corridors. *Bath:* combo or shower only. **Parking:** on-site. **Terms:** 14 day cancellation notice-fee imposed, package plans. **Amenities:** video games, CD players, high-speed Internet, dual phone lines, voice mail, irons, hair dryers. **Dining:** 6 am-11 pm. **Pool(s):** heated indoor. **Leisure Activities:** sauna, whirlpool, exercise room, game room. **Guest Services:** valet and coin laundry. **Business Services:** conference facilities, business center. **Cards:** AX, CB, DC, DS, JC, MC, VI. **Special Amenities:** free local telephone calls and free newspaper. *(See color ad p 455)*

Phone: (386)754-1411

SOME UNITS

JAMESON INN

Book at aaa.com

Small-scale Hotel

All Year [ECP]   1P: $54-$104
Location: I-75, exit 427, just e, then just s. 285 SW Commerce Blvd 32025. Fax: 386/758-8166. **Facility:** 55 units. 53 one-bedroom standard units. 2 one-bedroom suites. 3 stories, interior corridors. *Bath:* combo or shower only. **Parking:** on-site. **Terms:** cancellation fee imposed, small pets only. **Amenities:** voice mail, irons, hair dryers. **Pool(s):** outdoor. **Leisure Activities:** exercise room. **Guest Services:** valet laundry. **Business Services:** meeting rooms, fax (fee). **Cards:** AX, CB, DC, DS, MC, VI.

Phone: (386)758-8440

SOME UNITS

RODEWAY INN

Book at aaa.com

AAA SAVE

Motel

All Year   1P: $45-$75   2P: $45-$75   XP: $5   F12
Location: I-75, exit 427, just e. 205 SW Commerce Dr 32025. Fax: 386/752-4100. **Facility:** 44 one-bedroom standard units. 1 story, exterior corridors. **Parking:** on-site. **Terms:** weekly rates available, pets ($5 extra charge). **Guest Services:** coin laundry. **Business Services:** fax (fee). **Cards:** AX, DS, MC, VI. **Special Amenities:** free continental breakfast and preferred room (subject to availability with advance reservations).

Phone: 386/755-5203

SOME UNITS

FEE

SCOTTISH INNS *Book at aaa.com*

AAA SAVE

Motel

Phone: (386)755-0230

All Year   1P: $46   2P: $46   XP: $5   D11
Location: I-75, exit 427, 0.6 mi e. 2916 W US Hwy 90 32055. **Fax:** 386/755-5277. **Facility:** 34 one-bedroom standard units. 1 story, exterior corridors. **Parking:** on-site. **Terms:** cancellation fee imposed, package plans, pets ($5-$10 extra charge). **Cards:** AX, DS, MC, VI. **Special Amenities: free continental breakfast and free local telephone calls.**

SOME UNITS

FEE

SUPER 8 MOTEL

AAA SAVE

Motel

Phone: (386)752-6450

All Year   1P: $69-$120   2P: $74-$120   XP: $7   F13
Location: I-75, exit 423, 0.3 mi w on SR 47. Located in a quiet rural area. 3954 SW SR 47 32024. **Fax:** 386/752-6450. **Facility:** 87 one-bedroom standard units. 2 stories, exterior corridors. **Parking:** on-site. **Terms:** weekly rates available. **Dining:** 6:30 am-9 pm, Fri & Sat 6 am-10 pm, Sun & Mon 6 am-3 pm. **Pool(s):** outdoor. **Business Services:** fax. **Cards:** AX, CB, DC, DS, JC, MC, VI. **Special Amenities: free continental breakfast and free local telephone calls.**

SOME UNITS

———— WHERE TO DINE ————

CHASTEEN'S DOWNTOWN

American

Lunch: $4-$7   Phone: 386/752-7504
Location: Downtown. 204 N Marion Ave 32055. **Hours:** 7:30 am-4 pm. Closed: 11/23, 12/25. **Features:** The Chasteen family has been in the restaurant business for over 21 years and it shows. The menu boasts signature sandwiches like chicken cordon bleu panini, carnival burger and buffalo bits sandwich. Casual dress. **Parking:** street. **Cards:** MC, VI.

DESOTO DRUG STORE

American

Lunch: $4-$8   Phone: 386/752-9958
Location: Just n of US 90; downtown. 405 N Marion St 32055. **Hours:** 8 am-4:30 pm; to 4 pm off season. Closed major holidays; also Sat & Sun. **Features:** In the heart of the downtown antique shopping district, the authentic soda fountain entices you to come in, take a seat at the counter and sip on a frothy shake. Better yet, enjoy a scrumptious lunch of a chef specialty, such as Bordeaux chicken or steak Diane. It's worth a special trip for breakfast, when choices include pecan Belgian waffles, omelets and French toast. Casual dress. **Parking:** street. **Cards:** MC, VI.

EL POTRO

Mexican

Lunch: $5-$7   **Dinner:** $6-$10   Phone: 386/758-3100
Location: I-75, exit 427, 1 mi e; opposite Gleason Mall. 4290 Hwy 90 32055. **Hours:** 11 am-10 pm. Closed major holidays. **Features:** Authentic Mexican cuisine is served in semi-private booths around an open fireplace. Recipes reflect a true south-of-the-border taste. Attention to detail and professionalism go a long way here. Casual dress; cocktails. **Parking:** on-site. **Cards:** DS, MC, VI.

KEN'S BBQ

American

Lunch: $4-$8   **Dinner:** $4-$8   Phone: 386/752-5919
Location: 4 mi e of jct I-75. US Hwy 90 W 32056. **Hours:** 11 am-9 pm. Closed: Sun. **Features:** Locally-owned and operated for many years, this restaurant is a popular Lake City institution. One visit and ya'll have to come back! Friendly efficient service is a characteristic enjoyed at all locations. The barbecue sauces go well with the pork, ribs, chicken or beef. Most plates or dinners include a choice of baked beans and a side of cole slaw. Enjoy fresh Texas-style garlic bread with your dinner. Casual dress. **Parking:** on-site. **Cards:** AX, DS, MC, VI.

LAKE CITY DELI & CATERING

Deli/Subs Sandwiches

Lunch: $6-$8   Phone: 386/755-9393
Location: 4.5 mi e of jct I-75. 1115 US 90 W 32055. **Hours:** 10 am-3 pm. Closed: 1/1, 11/23, 12/25; also Sat & Sun. **Reservations:** not accepted. **Features:** The eatery offers enticing salads to please any taste, like the California Cobb and the peachy keen: peaches, tuna, egg salad and cottage cheese. Sandwiches (of course), wraps, and hot meals are also available. Dressy casual. **Parking:** on-site. **Cards:** AX, DS, MC, VI.

SONNY'S REAL PIT BBQ

Barbecue

Lunch: $6-$9   **Dinner:** $6-$15   Phone: 386/752-1117
Location: I-75, exit 427, 1.8 mi e. 3177 W Hwy 90 32055. **Hours:** 11:30 am-9:30 pm, Fri & Sat-10 pm. **Features:** Fresh smoked and barbecued meats are the main focus of the country-style eatery. Diners help themselves at the salad bar and shouldn't forget to ask about dessert. Casual dress; beer only. **Parking:** on-site. **Cards:** AX, DS, MC, VI.

WILDFLOWER CAFE

American

Lunch: $3-$6   Phone: 386/754-1150
Location: Downtown. 326 N Marion Ave 32055. **Hours:** 7:30 am-2:30 pm. Closed major holidays; also Sun. **Features:** Have a hearty homestyle breakfast in this downtown cafe. Traditional favorites like scrambled eggs, french toast and pancakes. Casual dress. **Parking:** street.

LAKE HELEN pop. 2,743

———— WHERE TO STAY ————

THE ANN STEVENS HOUSE

AAA SAVE

Bed & Breakfast

Phone: (386)228-0310

All Year [BP]   1P: $110-$150   2P: $120-$160   XP: $30
Location: I-4, exit 116, 1 mi e on Main St, 0.5 mi s on CR 4139, turn left on Ohio St, right on Pleasant Rd, then right. 201 E Kicklighter Rd 32744. **Fax:** 386/228-2337. **Facility:** Dating from the 1890s, this two-story carriage house features a pub on the lower level and has six modern guest units; a walking path leads to a lake. Smoke free premises. 8 one-bedroom standard units, some with whirlpools. 2 stories, interior/exterior corridors. *Bath:* combo or shower only. **Parking:** on-site. **Terms:** age restrictions may apply, 7 day cancellation notice-fee imposed, package plans. **Amenities:** video library, hair dryers. **Leisure Activities:** whirlpool, croquet, electronic darts, lending library, walking trails, bicycles. **Guest Services:** gift shop. **Cards:** AX, CB, DC, DS, JC, MC, VI. **Special Amenities: free full breakfast and free local telephone calls.**

LAKELAND pop. 78,452

———— WHERE TO STAY ————

AMERISUITES LAKELAND CENTER
Book at aaa.com
Phone: (863)413-1122

(AAA) (SAVE)

Small-scale Hotel

All Year   1P: $79-$159   2P: $79-$159
Location: I-4, exit 32, 3.2 mi s on US 98, then just w. Located at the Lakeland Center. 525 W Orange St 33815. Fax: 863/413-1133. **Facility:** 128 one-bedroom standard units. 6 stories, interior corridors. *Bath:* combo or shower only. **Parking:** on-site. **Terms:** pets ($10 fee). **Amenities:** voice mail, irons, hair dryers. *Fee:* video games, high-speed Internet. *Some:* dual phone lines. **Pool(s):** heated outdoor. **Leisure Activities:** exercise room. **Guest Services:** valet and coin laundry. **Business Services:** meeting rooms, fax (fee). **Cards:** AX, CB, DC, DS, JC, MC, VI. **Special Amenities: free full breakfast.**

SOME UNITS

SD 🐾 🛏 &M 🚪 🕰 ➷ VCR 🐾 DATA PORT 🛏 🖥 🖥 / ✕ /
    FEE

BAYMONT INN & SUITES LAKELAND
Book at aaa.com
Phone: (863)815-0606

(AAA) (SAVE)

Small-scale Hotel

1/1-4/30	1P: $109-$129	XP: $7	F18
5/1-11/30	1P: $89-$99	XP: $7	F18
12/1-12/31	1P: $85-$95	XP: $7	F18

Location: I-4, exit 33; jct SR 33, just nw. 4315 Lakeland Park Dr 33809. Fax: 863/815-9711. **Facility:** 104 units. 102 one-bedroom standard units. 2 one-bedroom suites, some with kitchens. 4 stories, interior corridors. *Bath:* combo or shower only. **Parking:** on-site. **Terms:** [ECP] meal plan available, pets ($20 deposit). **Amenities:** video games, voice mail, irons, hair dryers. **Pool(s):** outdoor. **Guest Services:** coin laundry. **Business Services:** meeting rooms, fax (fee). **Cards:** AX, CB, DC, DS, MC, VI. **Special Amenities: free expanded continental breakfast and free local telephone calls.**

SOME UNITS

🛏 🍴 &M 🚪 🕰 ➷ 🐾 DATA PORT 🖥 / ✕ 🛏 🖥 /
    FEE

BEST WESTERN DIPLOMAT INN
Book at aaa.com
Phone: 863/688-7972

Property failed to provide current rates

Small-scale Hotel

Location: I-4, exit 32, just s. 3311 US 98 N 33805. Fax: 863/688-8377. **Facility:** 120 one-bedroom standard units. 2 stories, exterior corridors. **Parking:** on-site. **Amenities:** irons, hair dryers. *Some:* high-speed Internet. **Pool(s):** outdoor, wading. **Guest Services:** valet and coin laundry. **Business Services:** meeting rooms, fax (fee).

SOME UNITS

🍴 🍸 🕰 ➷ 🐾 🐾 DATA PORT 🖥 / ✕ 🛏 🖥 /
                                       FEE

COMFORT INN & SUITES
Book at aaa.com
Phone: (863)859-0100

(AAA) (SAVE)

Small-scale Hotel

All Year   1P: $99-$149   2P: $99-$149   XP: $10   F21
Location: I-4, exit 32, just nw; at Lakeland Square Mall. 3520 Hwy US 98 N 33809. Fax: 863/859-0106. **Facility:** 106 one-bedroom standard units. 6 stories, interior corridors. *Bath:* combo or shower only. **Parking:** on-site. **Terms:** cancellation fee imposed, small pets only ($25 fee). **Amenities:** high-speed Internet, voice mail, irons, hair dryers. *Some:* DVD players. **Pool(s):** heated outdoor. **Guest Services:** coin laundry. **Business Services:** meeting rooms, fax (fee). **Cards:** AX, DC, DS, MC, VI. **Special Amenities: free continental breakfast and free local telephone calls.**

SOME UNITS

SD 🐾 🍴 &M 🚪 🕰 ➷ 🐾 🐾 DATA PORT 🖥 / ✕ 🛏 🖥 /
    FEE   FEE

COURTYARD BY MARRIOTT
Book at aaa.com
Phone: (863)802-9000

Small-scale Hotel

All Year   1P: $99-$115   2P: $99-$115
Location: I-4, exit 27 (Polk Pkwy), se on SR 570 (toll) to exit 5, then just n. 3725 Harden Blvd 33803. Fax: 863/802-5300. **Facility:** 78 units. 75 one-bedroom standard units. 3 one-bedroom suites ($145-$160). 3 stories, interior corridors. *Bath:* combo or shower only. **Parking:** on-site. **Terms:** [BP] meal plan available. **Amenities:** high-speed Internet, dual phone lines, voice mail, irons, hair dryers. **Pool(s):** heated outdoor. **Leisure Activities:** whirlpool, exercise room. **Guest Services:** valet and coin laundry. **Business Services:** meeting rooms, business center. **Cards:** AX, DC, DS, JC, MC, VI.

SOME UNITS

(ASK) SD 🍴 🍸 &M 🚪 🕰 ➷ 🐾 DATA PORT 🖥 / ✕ 🛏 🖥 /

HAMPTON INN
Book at aaa.com
Phone: (863)816-2525

(AAA) (SAVE)

Small-scale Hotel

1/1-4/30 [ECP]	1P: $85-$139	2P: $95-$149
12/1-12/31 & 5/1-11/30 [ECP]	1P: $75-$105	2P: $85-$105

Location: I-4, exit 33, just nw. 4420 N Socrum Loop Rd 33809. Fax: 863/816-2727. **Facility:** 70 one-bedroom standard units. 3 stories, interior corridors. *Bath:* combo or shower only. **Parking:** on-site. **Terms:** 15 day cancellation notice. **Amenities:** high-speed Internet, dual phone lines, voice mail, irons, hair dryers. **Pool(s):** heated outdoor. **Leisure Activities:** exercise room. **Guest Services:** coin laundry. **Business Services:** meeting rooms, fax (fee). **Cards:** AX, CB, DC, DS, JC, MC, VI. **Special Amenities: free expanded continental breakfast and free newspaper.**

SOME UNITS

SD 🍴 &M 🚪 🕰 ➷ 🐾 DATA PORT 🛏 🖥 🖥 / ✕ /

HOLIDAY INN LAKELAND HOTEL & CONFERENCE CENTER
Book at aaa.com
Phone: (863)688-8080

Small-scale Hotel

1/1-4/30	1P: $81-$99
5/1-11/30	1P: $72-$90
12/1-12/31	1P: $71-$90

Location: I-4, exit 32, just e. 3260 US Hwy 98 N 33805. Fax: 863/688-6820. **Facility:** 157 units. 156 one-bedroom standard units. 1 one-bedroom suite. 4 stories, interior corridors. *Bath:* combo or shower only. **Parking:** on-site. **Terms:** package plans, 12% service charge, pets ($25 fee). **Amenities:** video games (fee), high-speed Internet, dual phone lines, voice mail, irons, hair dryers. **Pool(s):** outdoor. **Leisure Activities:** exercise room. **Guest Services:** valet and coin laundry. **Business Services:** meeting rooms, fax (fee). **Cards:** AX, DS, JC, MC, VI.

SOME UNITS

(ASK) SD 🛏 🍴 🕰 🚪 🐾 🐾 DATA PORT 🖥 / ✕ 🛏 🖥 /
             FEE   FEE FEE

HOLIDAY INN LAKELAND SOUTH   *Book at aaa.com*   **Phone:** (863)646-5731

12/1-4/1	1P: $99	2P: $99
4/11-11/30	1P: $89	2P: $89

Small-scale Hotel   **Location:** 3 mi s on SR 37. 3405 S Florida Ave 33803. Fax: 863/646-5215. **Facility:** 171 one-bedroom standard units. 2 stories, exterior corridors. **Parking:** on-site. **Terms:** open 12/1-4/1 & 4/11-11/30. **Amenities:** high-speed Internet, voice mail, irons, hair dryers. **Pool(s):** outdoor. **Leisure Activities:** whirlpool, exercise room. **Guest Services:** complimentary evening beverages: Mon-Fri, valet laundry. **Business Services:** meeting rooms, fax. **Cards:** AX, DC, DS, MC, VI.

SOME UNITS

[ASK] [S/D] [📶] [🍴] [🍸] [🔊M] [📷] [🚲] [🎥] [DATA PORT] [💻] / [✕] [📁] [🖨] /   FEE   FEE

IMPERIAL SWAN HOTEL & SUITES   *Book at aaa.com*   **Phone:** (863)647-3000

AAA SAVE

All Year	1P: $99-$239	2P: $99-$239

Small-scale Hotel   **Location:** SR 37, 3.5 mi s of US 98 business route. 4141 S Florida Ave 33813. Fax: 863/644-0467. **Facility:** 168 units. 138 one-bedroom standard units, some with whirlpools. 30 one-bedroom suites ($129-$239) with whirlpools. 7 stories, interior corridors. *Bath:* combo or shower only. **Parking:** on-site. **Terms:** 30 day cancellation notice-fee imposed, package plans, pets ($10 fee). **Amenities:** video games (fee), dual phone lines, voice mail, irons, hair dryers. *Some:* high-speed Internet. **Dining:** 6:30-9:30 & 5:30-9 pm, cocktails. **Pool(s):** outdoor. **Leisure Activities:** exercise room. **Guest Services:** valet and coin laundry. **Business Services:** conference facilities, business center. **Cards:** AX, DS, MC, VI. **Special Amenities:** free local telephone calls and free newspaper.

SOME UNITS

[ASK] [🍴] [🍸] [🔊M] [📱] [📷] [🚲] [🎥] [DATA PORT] [💻] / [✕] [📁] [🖨] /   FEE

JAMESON INN   *Book at aaa.com*   **Phone:** (863)858-9070

All Year [ECP]	1P: $54-$104

Small-scale Hotel   **Location:** I-4, exit 33, just nw. 4375 Lakeland Park Dr 33809. Fax: 863/858-2491. **Facility:** 67 units. 65 one-bedroom standard units. 2 one-bedroom suites. 3 stories, interior corridors. *Bath:* combo or shower only. **Parking:** on-site. **Terms:** cancellation fee imposed, pets ($10 extra charge). **Amenities:** voice mail, irons, hair dryers. **Pool(s):** outdoor. **Leisure Activities:** exercise room. **Guest Services:** valet laundry. **Business Services:** meeting rooms, fax (fee). **Cards:** AX, CB, DC, DS, MC, VI.

SOME UNITS

[ASK] [🛏] [🍴] [🔊M] [♿] [📷] [🚲] [🎥] [DATA PORT] [💻] / [✕] [📁] [🖨] /   FEE

LAKELAND RESIDENCE INN BY MARRIOTT   *Book at aaa.com*   **Phone:** 863/680-2323

All Year	1P: $129-$200

Small-scale Hotel   **Location:** I-4, exit 27 (Polk Pkwy), se on SR 570 (toll) to exit 5, then just n. 3701 Harden Blvd 33803. Fax: 863/680-1717. **Facility:** 78 units. 33 one-bedroom standard units with kitchens, 33 one- and 12 two-bedroom suites with kitchens. 3 stories, interior corridors. *Bath:* combo or shower only. **Parking:** on-site. **Terms:** cancellation fee imposed, weekly rates available, [BP] meal plan available, pets ($125 fee). **Amenities:** high-speed Internet, dual phone lines, voice mail, irons, hair dryers. **Pool(s):** outdoor. **Leisure Activities:** whirlpool, exercise room, sports court. **Guest Services:** valet and coin laundry. **Business Services:** meeting rooms, fax (fee). **Cards:** AX, DC, DS, MC, VI.

SOME UNITS

[ASK] [🛏] [📱] [📷] [🚲] [✕] [🎥] [DATA PORT] [📁] [🖨] [🖨] / [✕] /   FEE

LA QUINTA INN & SUITES LAKELAND · *Book at aaa.com*

Phone: (863)859-2866

1/11-4/30	1P: $109-$129	XP: $7 · F18
12/1-1/10	1P: $79-$99	XP: $7 · F18
5/1-11/30	1P: $85-$95	XP: $7 · F18

(AAA) (SAVE) ◆◆◆

Small-scale Hotel

Location: I-4, exit 32, just n on US 98. 1024 Crevasse St 33809. Fax: 863/859-2956. **Facility:** 119 units. 113 one-bedroom standard units. 6 one-bedroom suites ($115-$169). 6 stories, interior corridors. *Bath:* combo or shower only. **Parking:** on-site. **Terms:** [ECP] meal plan available, small pets only. **Amenities:** video games, high-speed Internet, voice mail, irons, hair dryers. *Some:* dual phone lines. **Pool(s):** heated outdoor. **Leisure Activities:** whirlpool, exercise room. **Guest Services:** valet and coin laundry. **Business Services:** meeting rooms, fax (fee). **Cards:** AX, CB, DC, DS, MC, VI. **Special Amenities:** free expanded continental breakfast and free local telephone calls.

SOME UNITS

(icons)

ROYALTY INN

Phone: (863)858-4481

12/1-4/30 [ECP]	1P: $69-$109	2P: $79-$150	XP: $15 · F12
5/1-11/30 [ECP]	1P: $59-$79	2P: $69-$89	XP: $10 · F12

(AAA) (SAVE) ◆◆◆

Small-scale Hotel

Location: I-4, exit 32, just ne. 3425 Hwy 98 N 33809. Fax: 863/853-2514. **Facility:** 64 one-bedroom standard units. 2 stories, interior corridors. **Parking:** on-site. **Terms:** weekly rates available. **Amenities:** high-speed Internet, voice mail, safes (fee). *Some:* hair dryers. **Pool(s):** outdoor. **Leisure Activities:** exercise room. **Guest Services:** valet and coin laundry. **Business Services:** meeting rooms, fax (fee). **Cards:** AX, DS, VI. **Special Amenities:** free expanded continental breakfast and free newspaper. *(See color ad p 513).*

SOME UNITS

(icons)

SCOTTISH INNS · *Book at aaa.com*

Phone: 863/687-2530

2/1-4/10 [CP]	1P: $54-$62	2P: $64-$89	XP: $5 · F12
1/1-1/31 [CP]	1P: $54-$57	2P: $61-$68	XP: $5 · F12
4/11-11/30 [CP]	1P: $54-$56	2P: $60-$67	XP: $5 · F12
12/1-12/31 [CP]	1P: $53-$56	2P: $60-$67	XP: $5 · F12

(AAA) (SAVE) ◆

Motel

Location: I-4, exit 32 westbound, 2.4 mi s on US 98, then 0.5 mi s on US 37; exit 28 (Memorial Blvd) eastbound, 4 mi e, then 0.5 mi s on US 37. 244 N Florida Ave 33801. Fax: 863/688-1961. **Facility:** 46 one-bedroom standard units. 2 stories, exterior corridors. *Bath:* combo or shower only. **Parking:** on-site. **Terms:** 3 day cancellation notice. **Pool(s):** outdoor. **Guest Services:** coin laundry. **Business Services:** fax (fee). **Cards:** AX, CB, DC, DS, MC, VI. **Special Amenities:** free continental breakfast.

SOME UNITS

(icons)

SUBURBAN EXTENDED STAY HOTEL · *Book at aaa.com*

Phone: (863)816-1700

All Year	1P: $49-$105 · 2P: $49-$105	XP: $10 · F16

(AAA) (SAVE) ◆◆

Motel

Location: I-4, exit 32, 1 mi w. 4335 Williamson Blvd 33810. Fax: 863/816-9685. **Facility:** 138 one-bedroom standard units with kitchens. 3 stories, exterior corridors. *Bath:* combo or shower only. **Parking:** on-site. **Terms:** 10 day cancellation notice, weekly rates available. **Amenities:** voice mail. **Guest Services:** coin laundry. **Business Services:** fax (fee). **Cards:** AX, DC, DS, MC, VI.

(icons)

——— WHERE TO DINE ———

JIMBO'S PIT BAR B-Q

Lunch: $2-$9 · Dinner: $2-$9 · Phone: 863/683-3777

◆

Barbecue

Location: 1.5 mi e of jct US 98 and 92. 1215 E Memorial Blvd 33801. **Hours:** 10:30 am-9 pm, Fri & Sat-10 pm. Closed major holidays; also Sun. **Features:** For 20 years, the restaurant has served delicious barbecue. Guests can wash down ribs, chicken, pork or beef with a shake. A slice of apple pie makes the meal complete. Casual dress. **Parking:** on-site. **Cards:** MC, VI.

PAN YE'S CHINESE RESTAURANT

Lunch: $4-$12 · Dinner: $4-$12 · Phone: 863/686-2052

◆

Chinese

Location: I-4, exit 32, 2.8 mi s to jct US 92, then 0.4 mi e. 743 E Memorial Blvd 33801. **Hours:** 11 am-9 pm. Closed: 7/4, 11/23, 12/25; also Mon. **Features:** Reliable, Americanized Chinese fare is served by a friendly family. The house specials include pork, poultry, beef and seafood combinations. Egg rolls, fried rice and many other tasty entrees can be sampled at the buffet from 11 am-2:30 pm. Casual dress; beer & wine only. **Parking:** on-site. **Cards:** AX, DS, MC, VI.

RED BARN STEAK HOUSE

Lunch: $6-$25 · Dinner: $6-$25 · Phone: 863/686-2754

◆◆

Steak House

Location: I-4, exit 27, just s on Harden Blvd to Parkway Frontage Rd, 0.5 mi w to north frontage road, 1 mi w to SR 570, then 3.3 mi w. 6150 New Tampa Hwy (US 92) 33815. **Hours:** 11 am-10 pm. Closed: 11/23, 12/25. **Reservations:** suggested. **Features:** A Florida tradition for over fifty years, the restaurant offers fine Florida beef in a unique and rustic country setting. Guests choose the cut and slice preferred at the table and it is cooked to the guest's satisfaction. Save room for the Jack Daniels dessert! The lines are often long but the wait is worth the time. Casual dress; cocktails. **Parking:** on-site. **Cards:** AX, CB, DC, DS, JC, MC, VI.

LAKE MARY —See Orlando p. 821.

LAKE PARK pop. 8,721 (See map and index starting on p. 843)

——— WHERE TO DINE ———

CAFE DU PARK

Dinner: $16-$34 · Phone: 561/845-0529 · [32]

◆◆◆

French

Location: US 1, 1.3 mi n of jct SR A1A (Blue Heron Blvd). 612 N Federal Hwy 33403. **Hours:** Open 12/1-7/31 & 10/1-11/30; 5:30 pm-10 pm. Closed: Sun & Mon. **Reservations:** suggested. **Features:** Several cozy dining rooms in a former private home offer an intimate experience. The owner-chef prepares the cuisine with a Continental touch, and the servers are attentive and friendly. Try the snails wrapped in phyllo pastry with a white wine sauce. Semi-formal attire; beer & wine only. **Parking:** on-site. **Cards:** AX, DC, MC, VI.

LAKE WALES pop. 10,194

------ WHERE TO STAY ------

CHALET SUZANNE COUNTRY INN & RESTAURANT
Phone: (863)676-6011

(AAA) (SAVE)

◈◈◈

Historic Country Inn

All Year [BP]   1P: $169-$229   2P: $169-$229   XP: $12

Location: CR 17A, 1.5 mi e of jct US 27. 3800 Chalet Suzanne Dr 33859. Fax: 863/676-1814. **Facility:** Approached via wrought iron gates and a winding, palm-lined drive, the inn is nestled on 100 acres with a private lake, formal gardens and a gazebo. 28 one-bedroom standard units, some with whirlpools. 1-2 stories, exterior corridors. *Bath:* combo or shower only. **Parking:** on-site. **Terms:** 3 day cancellation notice-fee imposed, [MAP] meal plan available, package plans. **Amenities:** *Some:* irons, hair dryers. **Dining:** restaurant, see separate listing. **Pool(s):** outdoor. **Leisure Activities:** air strip, horseshoes, volleyball. *Fee:* massage. **Guest Services:** gift shop, valet laundry. **Business Services:** meeting rooms, fax (fee). **Cards:** AX, CB, DC, DS, MC, VI. **Special Amenities: free full breakfast and free local telephone calls.**

🍽️ 🛋️ ⚙️ ➰ ⊠

GREEN GABLES INN
Phone: 863/676-2511

(AAA) (SAVE)

◈◈◈

Motel

2/4-4/13 [CP]	1P: $87-$97	2P: $87-$97	XP: $3
12/1-12/31 [CP]	1P: $67-$77	2P: $67-$77	XP: $3
1/1-2/3 [CP]	1P: $61-$71	2P: $61-$71	XP: $3
4/14-11/30 [CP]	1P: $56-$66	2P: $56-$66	XP: $3

Location: 2 mi n of jct US 60. 21380 Hwy 27 33859. Fax: 863/676-3140. **Facility:** 56 one-bedroom standard units. 1 story, exterior corridors. **Parking:** on-site. **Terms:** office hours 6 am-12:30 pm. **Amenities:** video library (fee), hair dryers. **Pool(s):** heated outdoor. **Leisure Activities:** fishing, sun deck, 2 lighted tennis courts, picnic area with grill, exercise room, basketball, shuffleboard. **Guest Services:** coin laundry. **Business Services:** meeting rooms, fax (fee). **Cards:** AX, DS, MC, VI. **Special Amenities: free continental breakfast and free newspaper.** *(See color ad below)*

SOME UNITS

🅂🄳 🍽️ ➰ ⊠ 🎥 [DATA PORT] ▣ / ⊠ VCR 🔌 📟 /
                FEE   FEE   FEE

------ WHERE TO DINE ------

CHALET SUZANNE RESTAURANT
Menu on aaa.com   **Lunch:** $15-$42   **Dinner:** $35-$96   **Phone:** 863/676-6011

(AAA)

◈◈◈

American

Location: CR 17A, 1.5 mi e of jct US 27; in Chalet Suzanne Country Inn & Restaurant. 3800 Chalet Suzanne Dr 33859. **Hours:** 8 am-11 & noon-8 pm, Fri & Sat-9 pm. **Reservations:** suggested. **Features:** Quaint ambience is the overwhelming appeal of this multi-level, lakefront restaurant. Decorated with antiques and memorabilia, each dining room has its own individual charm. Six-course inclusive dinners feature cuisine with a Continental flair. Dressy casual; cocktails. **Parking:** on-site. **Cards:** AX, CB, DC, DS, MC, VI. **Country Inn**

🍸

LAKE WORTH pop. 35,133   (See map and index starting on p. 843)

------ WHERE TO STAY ------

HOLIDAY INN WEST PALM BEACH-TURNPIKE
Book at aaa.com   **Phone:** (561)968-5000   60

◈◈◈

Small-scale Hotel

12/1-4/15	1P: $135-$155	2P: $135-$155	XP: $6	F19
4/16-11/30	1P: $110-$115	2P: $110-$115	XP: $6	F19

Location: SR 802, just e of Florida Tpke, exit 93. 7859 Lake Worth Rd 33467. Fax: 561/968-2451. **Facility:** 114 one-bedroom standard units. 2 stories (no elevator), interior/exterior corridors. *Bath:* combo or shower only. **Parking:** on-site. **Amenities:** dual phone lines, voice mail, irons, hair dryers. **Pool(s):** heated outdoor. **Leisure Activities:** tennis court, exercise room. **Guest Services:** valet and coin laundry. **Business Services:** meeting rooms, fax (fee). **Cards:** AX, CB, DC, DS, JC, MC, VI.

SOME UNITS

(ASK) 🅂🄳 🍽️ 🛋️ ⚙️ ➰ 🎥 [DATA PORT] ▣ / ⊠ 🔌 /
                                             FEE

LAGO MOTOR INN
Phone: 561/585-5246   63

(AAA) (SAVE)

◈◈

Motel

All Year   1P: $85-$95   2P: $95-$115   XP: $10   D10

Location: I-95, exit 63, 0.7 mi e, then just s on US 1; US 1, just s of jct 6th Ave S. 714 S Dixie Hwy 33460. **Facility:** 17 one-bedroom standard units, some with efficiencies. 2 stories (no elevator), exterior corridors. **Parking:** on-site. **Terms:** 14 day cancellation notice-fee imposed, pets ($10 extra charge). **Pool(s):** outdoor. **Guest Services:** coin laundry. **Business Services:** fax (fee). **Cards:** AX, MC, VI.

SOME UNITS

🐾 ➰ 🔌 / ⊠ /
FEE

(See map and index starting on p. 843)

THE MANGO INN BED AND BREAKFAST　　　　　　　　　　**Phone: (561)533-6900**　　62

| | 12/1-4/30 [BP] | 1P: $140-$300 | 2P: $140-$300 | XP: $35 |
| | 5/1-11/30 [BP] | 1P: $125-$200 | 2P: $125-$200 | XP: $40 |

Bed & Breakfast　**Location:** I-95, exit 64, 0.9 mi e on N 10th Ave, then s. Located in a quiet residential area. 128 N Lakeside Dr 33460. Fax: 561/493-3748. **Facility:** Nestled in a conveniently located residential area, have breakfast on the patio overlooking the courtyard; rooms are warm, colorful and cozy. Smoke free premises. 10 units. 7 one-bedroom standard units. 2 one-bedroom suites, some with kitchens (no utensils). 1 cottage. 2 stories (no elevator), interior/exterior corridors. *Bath:* combo or shower only. **Parking:** on-site and street. **Terms:** office hours 6:30 am-6 pm, age restrictions may apply, 14 day cancellation notice, package plans. **Amenities:** video library, CD players, voice mail, irons, hair dryers. **Pool(s):** small heated outdoor. **Guest Services:** complimentary evening beverages. **Cards:** AX, DS, MC, VI.

SOME UNITS

ASK ⊇ ✕ DATA PORT / 🅿 VCR 🔳 🔲 🖵 /

NEW SUN GATE MOTEL　　　　　　　　　　　　　　　　**Phone: (561)588-8110**　　64

	12/1-4/15	1P: $69-$89	2P: $79-$89	XP: $5	F14
	10/1-11/30	1P: $59-$69	2P: $69-$79	XP: $5	F14
	4/16-9/30	1P: $49-$59	2P: $59-$69	XP: $5	F14

Motel　**Location:** I-95, exit 63, 1 mi e on 6th Ave S, then just s. 901 S Federal Hwy 33460. Fax: 561/588-8041. **Facility:** 33 one-bedroom standard units. 2 stories (no elevator), exterior corridors. *Bath:* shower only. **Parking:** on-site. **Terms:** office hours 9 am-10 pm, 14 day cancellation notice, 7 day off season, [AP] & [BP] meal plans available, $2 service charge. **Amenities:** *Some:* irons, hair dryers. **Dining:** 8 am-8 pm, Mon-2 pm; closed 6/1-9/30. **Pool(s):** outdoor. **Leisure Activities:** barbecue grills. *Fee:* sauna. **Guest Services:** coin laundry. **Cards:** DS, MC, VI.

SOME UNITS

S🔳 🍴 ⊇ 🅿 🔳 🖵 / ✕ 🔲 /

SABAL PALM HOUSE B & B INN　　　　　　　　　　　**Phone: 561/582-1090**　　61

| | 12/1-4/30 & 11/18-11/30 [BP] | 1P: $155-$250 | 2P: $155-$250 |
| | 5/1-11/17 [BP] | 1P: $125-$200 | 2P: $125-$200 |

Bed & Breakfast　**Location:** Just n of SR 802; west side of Intracoastal Bridge. 109 N Golfview Rd 33460. Fax: 561/582-0933. **Facility:** Guest rooms named after famous artists and decorated with their work add an unusual touch to this B&B located along the Intracoastal Waterway. Smoke free premises. 7 units. 6 one-bedroom standard units, some with whirlpools. 1 one-bedroom suite ($190-$250) with whirlpool. 2 stories (no elevator), interior/exterior corridors. *Bath:* combo or shower only. **Parking:** street. **Terms:** office hours 7 am-11 pm, age restrictions may apply, 14 day cancellation notice-fee imposed, no pets allowed (owner's dog on premises). **Amenities:** video library, CD players, safes, irons, hair dryers. *Some:* DVD players. **Leisure Activities:** pool privileges. **Business Services:** PC. **Cards:** DS, MC, VI. **Special Amenities:** free full breakfast and free local telephone calls.

🍴➕ ✕

━━━━━━ **WHERE TO DINE** ━━━━━━

BOHEMIAN GARDEN RESTAURANT　　**Dinner:** $10-$21　　　　**Phone:** 561/968-4111　　53

Steak & Seafood　**Location:** SR 802, 1 mi w of jct Military Tr. 5450 Lake Worth Rd 33463. **Hours:** 4:30 pm-10 pm, Sun 4 pm-9 pm, Mon 4:30 pm-9 pm. **Closed:** 5/29, 9/4. **Reservations:** suggested. **Features:** Old World charm can be found in this 53-year-old restaurant with paneled walls and oil paintings of Bohemia. An extensive menu offers chicken, beef and local seafood. The warm spinach salad will help nourish you as well as satisfy your taste buds. Casual dress; cocktails. **Parking:** on-site. **Cards:** AX, CB, DC, DS, MC, VI.　　Ⓨ

BROGUE'S IRISH PUB　　**Lunch:** $6-$16　　**Dinner:** $6-$16　　**Phone:** 561/585-1885　　58

Irish　**Location:** Center; between North K and North M sts. 621 Lake Ave 33460. **Hours:** 11:30 am-10 pm, Fri & Sat-11 pm. **Closed:** 12/25. **Reservations:** accepted. **Features:** Serving more than just Irish cuisine, the friendly and lively pub has something to suit most palates. Meals are served either in the rich, dark wood dining room with Irish and sports memorabilia or on the al fresco sidewalk seating area. Menu items range from shepherd's pie and gourmet burgers to fish n' chips as well as bangers and mash. Live music is featured most nights. Casual dress; cocktails; entertainment. **Parking:** street. **Cards:** AX, DS, MC, VI.　　Ⓨ

DAVE'S LAST RESORT & RAW BAR　　**Lunch:** $7-$20　　**Dinner:** $7-$20　　**Phone:** 561/588-5208　　55

American　**Location:** Jct K St. 632 Lake Ave 33468. **Hours:** 11 am-1 am, Fri & Sat-2 am, Sun noon-midnight. **Features:** Casual service and a fun nautical raw bar contribute to the restaurant's relaxed vibe. In addition to salads, wraps, burgers and sandwiches, the menu lists fajitas, burritos and nachos. Those with heartier appetites might try a 16-ounce porterhouse or baby back rib dinner. Casual dress; cocktails. **Parking:** street. **Cards:** MC, VI.　　Ⓨ

L'ANJOU　　　　　　　　　**Dinner:** $18-$36　　　　　　**Phone:** 561/582-7666　　56

French　**Location:** Downtown; corner of Lake Ave and J St. 717 Lake Ave 33460. **Hours:** 4:30 pm-10 pm; to 9 pm 6/1-9/30. **Closed:** 12/25; also Mon & 6/1-9/30. **Reservations:** accepted. **Features:** Classic refinement and French cuisine are hallmarks of the family-owned-and-operated restaurant. Great care and attentiveness helps ensure an enjoyable dining experience. On the well-rounded menu are such items as rabbit and veal, as well as fish entrees, including pompano. Try frog legs or foie gras as an appetizer. The wine list is broad enough to match easily with all courses. Casual dress; cocktails. **Parking:** on-site. **Cards:** AX, MC, VI.　　Ⓨ

RUSTICO ITALIANO　　　　　　**Dinner:** $15　　　　　　**Phone:** 561/547-2782　　54

Italian　**Location:** Between J and K sts; corner of Lucerne Ave and K St; downtown. 701 Lucerne Ave 33460. **Hours:** 5 pm-10 pm. **Closed:** 1/1, 12/25. **Reservations:** suggested. **Features:** In the heart of quaint downtown is the restaurant with a refined rustic interior. As Dean Martin croons in the background, prepare yourself for some flavorful and well prepared Italian dishes that range from veal to seafood. Save room for the in-house prepared desserts. Dressy casual; beer & wine only. **Parking:** street. **Cards:** AX, MC, VI.

(See map and index starting on p. 843)

SAITO BANGKOK **Lunch:** $9-$15 **Dinner:** $14-$22 **Phone:** 561/588-1785 (57)

Asian

Location: Center; between Lake Worth Rd and 1st Ave S. 15 North J St 33460. **Hours:** 11:30 am-2:30 & 5-10 pm. **Reservations:** accepted. **Features:** Those who can't decide between Japanese or Thai food might stop at this place, which offers both. Servers at the neighborhood eatery are young and quick. House specialties include sweet and sour duck or fish and Thai noodle dishes, such as pad thai. Ever-popular Thai soups—such as tom yum made with lemon grass, lime juice and hot pepper—burst with flavor. Included in the full array of Japanese dishes are teriyaki, tempura, stir-fry, sushi and sashimi choices. Casual dress; cocktails. **Parking:** street. **Cards:** AX, DS, MC, VI.

——— *The following restaurants have not been evaluated by AAA* ———
but are listed for your information only.

FLANIGAN'S SEAFOOD BAR & GRILL **Phone:** 561/964-4666

(fyi) Not evaluated. **Location:** 2401 10th Ave N 33461. **Features:** The family-friendly restaurant is known for its baby back ribs, burgers and seafood.

JOHN G'S **Phone:** 561/585-9860

(fyi) Not evaluated. **Location:** 10 S Ocean Blvd 33460. **Features:** Open for breakfast and lunch. Casual dining with ocean view. Inexpensive.

LANTANA pop. 9,437 (See map and index starting on p. 843)

——— **WHERE TO STAY** ———

BEST WESTERN INN OF AMERICA *Book at aaa.com* **Phone:** (561)588-0456 (78)

12/1-4/15 & 11/16-11/30 [ECP]	1P: $99-$169	2P: $99-$169	XP: $10	F16
4/16-11/15 [ECP]	1P: $69-$120	2P: $69-$120	XP: $10	F16

Small-scale Hotel

Location: I-95, exit 60, just e, then just s. 7051 Seacrest Blvd 33462. Fax: 561/585-0607. **Facility:** 92 one-bedroom standard units. 4 stories, interior corridors. *Bath:* combo or shower only. **Parking:** on-site. **Amenities:** voice mail, safes (fee), irons, hair dryers. *Some:* high-speed Internet. **Pool(s):** heated outdoor. **Guest Services:** coin laundry. **Cards:** AX, CB, DC, DS, MC, VI.

SOME UNITS

COMFORT INN & SUITES LANTANA/BOYNTON
BEACH *Book at aaa.com* **Phone:** (561)582-7878 (77)

12/1-4/30	1P: $79-$149	2P: $79-$149
10/1-11/30	1P: $75-$129	2P: $75-$129
5/1-9/30	1P: $59-$99	2P: $59-$99

Small-scale Hotel

Location: I-95, exit 60, 0.3 mi e. 1221 Hypoluxo Rd 33462. Fax: 561/582-8878. **Facility:** 60 units. 58 one-bedroom standard units, some with whirlpools. 2 one-bedroom suites ($79-$229) with whirlpools. 3 stories, interior corridors. *Bath:* combo or shower only. **Parking:** on-site. **Amenities:** voice mail, safes, irons, hair dryers. **Pool(s):** small heated outdoor. **Leisure Activities:** exercise room. **Guest Services:** coin laundry. **Business Services:** meeting rooms. **Cards:** AX, CB, DC, DS, JC, MC, VI. *(See color ad p 260)*

SOME UNITS

MOTEL 6 LANTANA #688 *Book at aaa.com* **Phone:** 561/585-5833 (76)

1/1-3/26	1P: $56-$66	2P: $62-$72	XP: $3	F17
3/27-5/29	1P: $49-$59	2P: $55-$65	XP: $3	F17
12/1-12/31 & 5/30-11/30	1P: $39-$49	2P: $45-$55	XP: $3	F17

Motel

Location: I-95, exit 61 (SR 812), just e, then s. 1310 W Lantana Rd 33462. Fax: 561/547-9701. **Facility:** 154 one-bedroom standard units. 2 stories, exterior corridors. **Parking:** on-site. **Terms:** small pets only. **Pool(s):** heated outdoor. **Guest Services:** coin laundry. **Cards:** AX, CB, DC, DS, MC, VI.

SOME UNITS

——— **WHERE TO DINE** ———

ANCHOR INN RESTAURANT **Dinner:** $16-$26 **Phone:** 561/965-4794 (70)

Steak House

Location: I-95, exit 60, 0.5 mi w. 2810 Hypoluxo Rd 33462. **Hours:** 4:30 pm-10 pm, Fri & Sat-11 pm. **Reservations:** accepted. **Features:** Long established in the area, the comfortable, casual lakefront restaurant offers a menu featuring such seafood dishes as shrimp scampi and broiled salmon. Other offerings include steak, chicken and chops. Casual dress; cocktails. **Parking:** on-site. **Cards:** AX, MC, VI.

RIGGINS CRABHOUSE **Lunch:** $7-$15 **Dinner:** $12-$25 **Phone:** 561/586-3000 (69)

Seafood

Location: I-95, exit 61 (SR 812), just e on Lantana Rd, then just n; in Lantana Shopping Center, northwest corner. 607 Ridge Rd 33462. **Hours:** noon-9:30 pm, Fri-10:30 pm, Sat 2 pm-10:30 pm, Sun 2 pm-9:30 pm. Closed major holidays. **Features:** Guests can crack the shells of Maryland-style crabs all they want. Among other offerings are fresh local seafood and some land foods. Casual dress; cocktails. **Parking:** on-site. **Cards:** AX, DC, DS, MC, VI.

LARGO —*See Tampa Bay p. 1025.*

LAUDERDALE-BY-THE-SEA —*See Fort Lauderdale p. 412.*

LAUDERDALE LAKES —*See Fort Lauderdale p. 414.*

LAUDERHILL —*See Fort Lauderdale p. 414.*

LEESBURG —*See Orlando p. 826.*

LEHIGH ACRES pop. 33,430

——— **WHERE TO STAY** ———

ADMIRAL LEHIGH GOLF RESORT
Phone: (239)369-2121

(AAA) (SAVE)

1/16-3/31	1P: $118	2P: $118	XP: $12	F14
6/1-11/30	1P: $68-$80	2P: $68-$80	XP: $12	F14
12/1-1/15 & 4/1-5/31	1P: $80	2P: $80	XP: $12	F14

Location: 2.5 mi n on CR 884. 225 E Joel Blvd 33972. Fax: 239/368-1660. **Facility:** 131 one-bedroom standard units. 2 stories, exterior corridors. *Bath:* combo or shower only. **Parking:** on-site. **Terms:** [BP] meal plan available, package plans. **Amenities:** voice mail, irons, hair dryers. **Dining:** 4 restaurants, 6:30 am-9 pm, cocktails, entertainment. **Pool(s):** heated outdoor. **Leisure Activities:** saunas, steamrooms, jogging, aerobics, sports court, basketball, shuffleboard. *Fee:* golf-18 holes, golf instruction, demonstration & privileges, massage. **Guest Services:** coin laundry, beauty salon. *Fee:* tanning facility. **Business Services:** conference facilities, business center. **Cards:** AX, DC, DS, MC, VI. **Special Amenities:** free room upgrade (subject to availability with advance reservations). *(See color ad p 434)*

Small-scale Hotel

SOME UNITS

🛋 📺 ⚙ 🏊 📶 ✕ 🎥 [DATA PORT] 🛏 / ✕ 🛗 🗄
FEE FEE

LEHIGH RESORT CLUB
Phone: 239/368-2022

(AAA) (SAVE)

All Year   1P: $54-$840   2P: $54-$840

Condominium

Location: 2.5 mi n on CR 884. 231 Joel Blvd 33972. Fax: 239/368-5088. **Facility:** 20 one-bedroom suites, some with efficiencies or kitchens. 2 stories, exterior corridors. **Parking:** on-site. **Terms:** office hours 8 am-5 pm, 3 night minimum stay, 3 day cancellation notice-fee imposed, weekly rates available. **Amenities:** video library (fee), voice mail, irons, hair dryers. **Pool(s):** heated outdoor, wading. **Leisure Activities:** whirlpool, miniature golf, golf cage, 2 lighted tennis courts, racquetball courts, recreation programs, gazebo picnic area, library, table tennis, playground, exercise room, basketball, horseshoes, shuffleboard, volleyball. *Fee:* fishing & Everglades trips, golf privileges, game room. **Guest Services:** gift shop, complimentary laundry. **Business Services:** business center. **Cards:** MC, VI.

🍽 🏊 ✕ [VCR] [DATA PORT] 🛗 🗄 🗄

——— **WHERE TO DINE** ———

INSIDE RESTAURANT AND TOUCAN BAR   *Menu on aaa.com*
Dinner: $10-$22   Phone: 239/369-2500

(AAA)

German

Location: 2.8 mi n of jct Joel Blvd. 2305 Lakeview Dr 33972. **Hours:** 4 pm-9:30 pm. Closed: Mon. **Reservations:** suggested. **Features:** Set on Lake Camille, the German-themed and decorated restaurant presents a menu with such specialties as bratwurst, sauerbraten, Wiener schnitzel, venison goulash and veal stew. An international favorite is grilled duck breast served in gooseberry sauce with gnocchi and red cabbage. Casual dress; cocktails. **Parking:** on-site. **Cards:** AX, CB, DC, DS, MC.

🖰

LIGHTHOUSE POINT —*See Fort Lauderdale p. 415.*

LITHIA —*See Tampa Bay p. 1026.*

LITTLE TORCH KEY —*See The Florida Keys p. 359.*

LIVE OAK pop. 6,300

——— **WHERE TO STAY** ———

ECONO LODGE   *Book at aaa.com*
Phone: (386)362-7459

(AAA) (SAVE)

All Year   1P: $55-$65   2P: $60-$69   XP: $5   F16

Location: I-10, exit 283, just s. 6811 N US 129 & I-10 32060 (PO Box 820, 32064). Fax: 386/364-6598. **Facility:** 53 one-bedroom standard units, some with whirlpools. 2 stories, exterior corridors. **Parking:** on-site. **Terms:** pets ($10 extra charge). **Amenities:** hair dryers. **Pool(s):** outdoor. **Leisure Activities:** whirlpool, picnic table. **Guest Services:** coin laundry. **Business Services:** meeting rooms, fax (fee). **Cards:** AX, CB, DC, DS, JC, MC, VI. **Special Amenities:** free continental breakfast and free local telephone calls.

Small-scale Hotel

SOME UNITS

📶 🐕 🍽 🏊 📶 🛗 / ✕ 🛗 🗄
FEE

HOLIDAY INN EXPRESS   *Book at aaa.com*
Phone: 386/362-2600

(AAA) (SAVE)

All Year   1P: $80-$169   2P: $80-$169   XP: $15

Location: I-10, exit 283, just s. 6694 US 129 N 32060. Fax: 386/362-4300. **Facility:** 69 one-bedroom standard units. 3 stories, interior corridors. *Bath:* combo or shower only. **Parking:** on-site. **Terms:** cancellation fee imposed. **Amenities:** high-speed Internet, dual phone lines, voice mail, irons, hair dryers. **Pool(s):** outdoor. **Leisure Activities:** whirlpool, exercise room. **Guest Services:** valet and coin laundry. **Business Services:** meeting rooms, fax. **Cards:** AX, DC, DS, MC, VI. **Special Amenities:** free continental breakfast and free local telephone calls.

Small-scale Hotel

SOME UNITS

📶 🏊 📶 [DATA PORT] 🛗 / ✕ 🛗 🗄 /

SUWANNEE RIVER BEST WESTERN INN   *Book at aaa.com*   Phone: (386)362-6000

[AAA] [SAVE]   All Year [CP]   1P: $50-$145   2P: $50-$175   XP: $10   F12
▼▼▼▼   **Location:** I-10, exit 283, 0.3 mi s. 6819 US 129 N 32060. Fax: 386/364-1308. **Facility:** 64 one-bedroom units. 2 stories, exterior corridors. **Parking:** on-site. **Terms:** 2-3 night minimum stay - weekends, 7 day cancellation notice-fee imposed, small pets only ($10 extra charge). **Amenities:** voice mail, irons, hair
Small-scale Hotel   dryers. **Pool(s):** outdoor. **Guest Services:** coin laundry. **Business Services:** fax (fee). **Cards:** AX, CB, DC, DS, MC, VI. **Special Amenities:** free continental breakfast and free local telephone calls.

SOME UNITS

[S⊘] [🛏] [🍴+] [⇌] [📷] [DATA PORT] [▣] / [✕] [📶] [🍳] /
[FEE]

──────── **WHERE TO DINE** ────────

──────── *The following restaurant has not been evaluated by AAA* ────────
but is listed for your information only.

DIXIE GRILL   Phone: 386/364-2810
▼▼   **Location:** 0.3 mi e of jct US 90 and 129; center. 101 Dowling Ave 32060. **Features:** Home cookin' doesn't get any better than this. An icon for decades, the Dixie Grill dishes out favorites including country fried steak,
German   chicken & dumplings and bread pudding. Come and get it!   [A/C]

LONGBOAT KEY pop. 7,603   (See map and index starting on p. 904)

──────── **WHERE TO STAY** ────────

THE COLONY BEACH & TENNIS RESORT   *Book at aaa.com*   Phone: (941)383-6464   [56]
▼▼▼▼   4/23-11/30   1P: $195-$1175
12/1-1/7 & 2/16-4/22   1P: $395-$695
Resort   1/8-2/15   1P: $280-$470
Condominium   **Location:** Oceanfront. On SR 789, 2 mi n of New Pass Bridge. 1620 Gulf of Mexico Dr 34228. Fax: 941/383-7549.
Facility: Located directly on the Gulf of Mexico, the property offers modern decor and amenities in suites within high rise, cottage or beach home type settings. Designated smoking area. 234 units. 125 one- and 109 two-bedroom suites ($195-$950) with kitchens, some with whirlpools. 3-6 stories, interior/exterior corridors. *Bath:* combo or shower only.
Parking: on-site. **Terms:** check-in 4 pm, 30 day cancellation notice-fee imposed, [AP] meal plan available, package plans.
Amenities: video library, high-speed Internet (fee), voice mail, safes, irons, hair dryers. *Some:* DVD players (fee). **Dining:** The Colony Dining Room, see separate listing. **Pool(s):** heated outdoor. **Leisure Activities:** saunas, whirlpools, steamrooms, fishing, 21 tennis courts (2 lighted), recreation programs, rental bicycles, playground, spa, basketball, volleyball. *Fee:* snorkeling, charter fishing. **Guest Services:** gift shop, valet and coin laundry, area transportation (fee). **Business Services:** conference facilities, business center. **Cards:** AX, DC, DS, MC, VI.

SOME UNITS

[ASK] [✈] [🍴] [🍸] [📶] [🐾] [⇌] [🚴] [✕] [✕] [DATA PORT] [🍳] [▣] [▣] / [VCR] /
[FEE]   [FEE]

DIPLOMAT RESORT   Phone: (941)383-3791   [55]
▼▼   2/1-4/23 Wkly   2P: $1077-$1784   XP: $12   F10
4/24-8/15 Wkly   2P: $769-$1500   XP: $12   F10
Condominium   8/16-11/30 Wkly   2P: $725-$1400   XP: $12   F10
12/1-1/31 Wkly   2P: $725-$1280   XP: $12   F10
Location: Oceanfront. On SR 789, 3.7 mi n of New Pass Bridge. 3155 Gulf of Mexico Dr 34228. Fax: 941/383-0983. **Facility:** 50 units. 20 one-bedroom standard units with efficiencies. 28 one- and 2 two-bedroom suites with kitchens. 2 stories, exterior corridors.
Parking: on-site. **Terms:** office hours 9 am-6 pm, 7 night minimum stay, 21 day cancellation notice-fee imposed.
Amenities: voice mail. *Some:* DVD players, CD players, irons, hair dryers. **Pool(s):** heated outdoor. **Leisure Activities:** fishing.
Guest Services: coin laundry. **Business Services:** fax (fee). **Cards:** DC, MC, VI.

SOME UNITS

[🍴+] [⇌] [DATA PORT] [🍳] [▣] / [✕] [VCR] /

HARBOUR VILLA CLUB   Phone: 941/383-9544   [52]
[AAA] [SAVE]   1/1-4/30 Wkly   1P: $1895   2P: $1895
12/1-12/31 & 11/1-11/30 Wkly   1P: $1335   2P: $1335
▼▼▼▼   5/1-10/31 Wkly   1P: $975   2P: $975
Condominium   **Location:** Just e of jct SR 789. 615 Dream Island Rd 34228. Fax: 941/383-8028. **Facility:** Overlooks the Intracoastal Waterway. Designated smoking area. 15 two-bedroom suites with kitchens and whirlpools. 3 stories, exterior corridors. **Parking:** on-site. **Terms:** check-in 4 pm, 7 night minimum stay, 21 day cancellation notice-fee imposed. **Amenities:** voice mail, irons. *Some:* DVD players, CD players. **Pool(s):** heated outdoor. **Leisure Activities:** whirlpool, fishing, 4 tennis courts (2 lighted), barbecue grills. *Fee:* marina. **Guest Services:** complimentary laundry. **Business Services:** fax. **Cards:** AX, MC, VI.

[⇌] [✕] [✕] [VCR] [DATA PORT] [🍳] [▣] [▣]

HILTON LONGBOAT KEY BEACHFRONT RESORT   *Book at aaa.com*   Phone: (941)383-2451   [54]
▼▼▼▼   2/1-5/31   1P: $295-$345   XP: $25   F
12/1-12/31   1P: $275-$325   XP: $25   F
Small-scale Hotel   1/1-1/31 & 6/1-11/30   1P: $195-$265   XP: $25   F
Location: Oceanfront. On SR 789, 6.2 mi n of New Pass Bridge. 4711 Gulf of Mexico Dr 34228. Fax: 941/383-7979.
Facility: 102 units. 80 one-bedroom standard units, some with efficiencies. 22 one-bedroom suites, some with kitchens. 5 stories, interior/exterior corridors. *Bath:* combo or shower only. **Parking:** on-site. **Terms:** check-in 4:30 pm, 3 day cancellation notice-fee imposed, package plans, small pets only ($50 fee). **Amenities:** high-speed Internet, voice mail, safes, honor bars, irons, hair dryers. **Pool(s):** heated outdoor. **Leisure Activities:** whirlpool, rental boats, rental sailboats, recreation programs in summer, exercise room, volleyball. *Fee:* bicycles. **Guest Services:** gift shop, valet laundry, area transportation. **Business Services:** conference facilities, fax. **Cards:** AX, CB, DC, DS, MC, VI.

SOME UNITS

[ASK] [S⊘] [🍴] [🍸] [📶] [🐾] [⇌] [✕] [📷] [DATA PORT] [▣] / [✕] [🍳] [▣] /
[FEE]   [FEE]

(See map and index starting on p. 904)

LONGBOAT KEY CLUB & RESORT   *Book at aaa.com*   Phone: (941)383-8821   **57**

(AAA) [SAVE]	2/1-4/22	1P: $350-$1160	2P: $350-$1160	XP: $20 F18
	12/1-1/31	1P: $270-$1160	2P: $270-$1160	XP: $20 F18
◆◆◆◆ ◆◆◆◆	4/23-11/30	1P: $235-$625	2P: $235-$625	XP: $20 F18

Resort
Condominium

Location: Oceanfront. On SR 789, just n of New Pass Bridge. 301 Gulf of Mexico Dr 34228. Fax: 941/383-0359. **Facility:** All units at this gulfside resort have a private balcony and most have a washer and dryer; a harborside complex is north of the main property. Designated smoking area. 204 units. 136 one-bedroom standard units, some with efficiencies. 23 one- and 45 two-bedroom suites. 4-10 stories, exterior corridors. *Bath:* combo or shower only. **Parking:** on-site. **Terms:** 14 day cancellation notice-fee imposed, package plans, $25 service charge. **Amenities:** video library, video games (fee), CD players, high-speed Internet, dual phone lines, voice mail, safes, honor bars, irons, hair dryers. *Some:* DVD players (fee), fax. **Dining:** 5 restaurants, 6:30 am-midnight, cocktails, entertainment. **Pool(s):** heated outdoor. **Leisure Activities:** whirlpool, recreation programs, kids club, aerobics, yoga, pilates, library, bicycles, jogging, playground, spa, basketball, volleyball. *Fee:* snorkeling, cabanas, catamarans, kayaks, golf-45 holes, golf instruction, 36 tennis courts (6 lighted), adult tennis clinic. **Guest Services:** gift shop, valet laundry, area transportation-within 5 mi. **Business Services:** conference facilities, business center. **Cards:** AX, CB, DC, MC, VI. **Special Amenities:** free local telephone calls and free newspaper.

[icons] FEE

RIVIERA BEACH RESORT   Phone: 941/383-2552   **53**

(AAA)	1/28-4/28 Wkly	1P: $913-$1258	2P: $913-$1258	XP: $10
	4/29-8/18 Wkly	1P: $850-$1100	2P: $850-$1100	XP: $10
◆◆◆	8/19-11/30 Wkly	1P: $800-$1050	2P: $800-$1050	XP: $10
Motel	12/1-1/27 Wkly	1P: $798-$1028	2P: $798-$1028	XP: $10

Location: Oceanfront. On SR 789, 5 mi s of jct SR 684 (Cortez Rd). 5451 Gulf of Mexico Dr 34228. Fax: 941/383-2245. **Facility:** Designated smoking area. 9 units. 7 one- and 2 two-bedroom standard units with kitchens. 1 story, exterior corridors. **Parking:** on-site. **Terms:** office hours 8:30 am-6:30 pm, 7 night minimum stay - seasonal, 30 day cancellation notice-fee imposed, small pets only ($100 deposit, $10 extra charge). **Amenities:** voice mail. *Some:* irons, hair dryers. **Pool(s):** heated outdoor. **Leisure Activities:** whirlpool, grills, shuffleboard. **Guest Services:** coin laundry. **Business Services:** fax. **Cards:** AX, DS, MC, VI. **Special Amenities:** free local telephone calls.

[icons] FEE

——— WHERE TO DINE ———

CAFE ON THE BAY   Lunch: $8-$14   Dinner: $18-$30   Phone: 941/383-0440   **79**

◆◆

American

Location: Gulf of Mexico Dr; just e on Bay Isles Pkwy, then just s; in The Moorings. 2630 Harbourside Dr 34228. **Hours:** 11 am-3 & 5-9 pm, Fri & Sat-10 pm; Sunday brunch 9 am-2 pm. Closed: for lunch weekdays in summer. **Reservations:** suggested. **Features:** Guests come by car or boat to the waterside eatery, where they can savor attractive, hearty dishes made from fresh ingredients. Casual dress; cocktails. **Parking:** on-site. **Cards:** AX, CB, DC, DS, MC, VI.

THE COLONY DINING ROOM   Lunch: $7-$19   Dinner: $20-$38   Phone: 941/383-5558   **80**

◆◆◆◆

American

Location: On SR 789, 2 mi n of New Pass Bridge; in The Colony Beach & Tennis Resort. 1620 Gulf of Mexico Dr 34228. **Hours:** 11:30 am-close. **Reservations:** suggested. **Features:** Adjacent to the sparkling gulf, the restaurant boasts an original, lavish menu of contemporary Continental dishes and an extensive wine list. Fresh seafood is always popular. Live entertainment contributes to the dining experience. Dressy casual; cocktails; entertainment. **Parking:** on-site and valet. **Cards:** AX, DS, MC, VI.

EUPHEMIA HAYE RESTAURANT   Dinner: $21-$44   Phone: 941/383-3633   **77**

◆◆◆

Continental

Location: On SR 789, 7.8 mi n of New Pass Bridge. 5540 Gulf of Mexico Dr 34228. **Hours:** Open 12/1-9/5 & 9/20-11/30; 5 pm-close. Closed: 12/25. **Reservations:** suggested. **Features:** The eclectic and creative menu features such delicacies as roast duckling served over stuffing with a seasonal fruit sauce. The clean, comfortable dining room, tasty food and thoughtful service should make diners want to mark their maps for the next trip to town. Dressy casual; cocktails; entertainment. **Parking:** on-site. **Cards:** CB, DC, DS, MC, VI.

HARRY'S CONTINENTAL KITCHENS   Lunch: $11-$24   Dinner: $20-$32   Phone: 941/383-0777   **76**

◆◆◆

Continental

Location: Just e of SR 789; 3.7 mi s of jct SR 684 (Cortez Rd). 525 St. Judes Dr 34228. **Hours:** 11:30 am-2 & 5-9 pm, Fri & Sat-9:30 pm, Sun 10 am-2 & 5-9 pm. Closed: 12/25; also Mon 5/1-10/31. **Reservations:** suggested. **Features:** Pleasant, professional service and an innovative menu with fresh herbs, homemade soups and delectable desserts make this quaint, tropical eatery perfect for a gourmet seafood meal. Casual dress; cocktails. **Parking:** on-site. **Cards:** AX, DS, MC, VI.

MAR VISTA DOCKSIDE RESTAURANT & PUB   Lunch: $7-$15   Dinner: $15-$20   Phone: 941/383-2391   **75**

◆◆

Seafood

Location: 2 mi s of jct SR 684 (Cortez Rd) on SR 789 (Gulf of Mexico Dr), 0.3 mi ne. 760 Broadway St 34228. **Hours:** 11:30 am-10 pm. Closed: 12/25. **Reservations:** not accepted. **Features:** On Sarasota Bay, the restaurant welcomes diners who arrive both by car and boat. Seafarers can tie up to one of 12 boat slips. The menu lists many seafood entrees, as well as sandwiches and salads. Casual dress; cocktails. **Parking:** on-site. **Cards:** AX, CB, DC, DS, MC, VI.

MAUREEN PALM GRILLE   Dinner: $11-$29   Phone: 941/383-7774   **78**

◆◆◆

Continental

Location: On SR 789, 7 mi n of New Pass Bridge; in Centre Shops. 5350 Gulf of Mexico Dr 34228. **Hours:** 5:30 pm-10 pm. Closed: Mon. **Features:** A trendy decor incorporates melon-colored walls with interesting artwork, and sets the right mood for adult fine dining. Creatively prepared and displayed entrees including seafood, lamb, and steak feature carpaccio and a fabulous bouillabaisse. Dressy casual; cocktails. **Parking:** on-site. **Cards:** AX, DC, DS, MC, VI.

LONG KEY —*See The Florida Keys p. 359.*

LONGWOOD —*See Orlando p. 827.*

LOXAHATCHEE   (See map and index starting on p. 843)

———— WHERE TO STAY ————

SOUTHERN PALM BED & BREAKFAST   **Phone:** (561)790-1413   **57**

▼▼▼▼   1/1-4/30   1P: $139-$239   2P: $139-$239   XP: $15
        12/1-12/31 & 5/1-11/30   1P: $99-$125   2P: $99-$125   XP: $15
Bed & Breakfast   **Location:** SR 7, 4.4 mi w on Southern Blvd, SR 90/S US 441 to D Rd, 0.3 mi n to Collection Canal Rd, 0.5 mi w to C Rd, then 0.3 mi n. 15130 Southern Palm Way 33470. Fax: 561/791-3035. **Facility:** A small pond can be seen from all rooms and balconies of this B&B in a quiet, country setting; furnishings include a variety of antiques. Smoke free premises. 6 units. 5 one-bedroom standard units. 1 one-bedroom suite. 2 stories (no elevator), interior/exterior corridors. **Parking:** on-site. **Terms:** 3 night minimum stay - seasonal, age restrictions may apply, 14 day cancellation notice-fee imposed. **Amenities:** hair dryers. **Guest Services:** coin laundry. **Cards:** AX, DS, MC, VI.

(ASK) (SₒD) ☒ ▯

MACCLENNY   pop. 4,459

———— WHERE TO STAY ————

ECONO LODGE   *Book at aaa.com*   **Phone:** (904)259-3000

(AAA) (SAVE)   3/1-5/31 & 9/1-11/30 [CP]   1P: $46-$85   2P: $51-$85   XP: $5   F18
                12/1-2/28 & 6/1-8/31 [CP]   1P: $44-$85   2P: $49-$85   XP: $5   F18
▼▼▼▼   **Location:** I-10, exit 335, just s of jct SR 121. 151 Woodlawn Rd 32063 (PO Box 425). Fax: 904/259-4418.
Motel   **Facility:** 53 one-bedroom standard units, some with whirlpools. 2 stories, exterior corridors. **Parking:** on-site. **Terms:** small pets only ($10 fee). **Amenities:** *Some:* hair dryers. **Pool(s):** outdoor. **Leisure Activities:** whirlpool. **Guest Services:** coin laundry. **Business Services:** meeting rooms. **Cards:** AX, CB, DC, DS, MC, VI. **Special Amenities: free continental breakfast and free local telephone calls.**

SOME UNITS
(SₒD) (¶¶+) (🐾) (🎦) (DATA PORT) / ☒ ▯ 🖾 🖵 /
                        FEE

MADEIRA BEACH —*See Tampa Bay p. 1027.*

MADISON   pop. 3,061

———— WHERE TO STAY ————

HOLIDAY INN EXPRESS-I-10 MADISON   *Book at aaa.com*   **Phone:** 850/973-2020

▼▼▼▼   All Year   1P: $82-$160   2P: $87-$180   XP: $5   F
        Location: I-10, exit 258, just n. 167 SE Bandit St 32340. Fax: 850/973-3366. **Facility:** 60 one-bedroom standard
Small-scale Hotel   units, some with whirlpools. 3 stories, interior corridors. *Bath:* combo or shower only. **Parking:** on-site. **Amenities:** high-speed Internet, voice mail, irons, hair dryers. *Some:* DVD players, CD players. **Pool(s):** outdoor. **Guest Services:** valet and coin laundry. **Business Services:** meeting rooms, business center. **Cards:** AX, CB, DC, DS, MC, VI.

SOME UNITS
(ASK) (¶¶+) (🌄M) (🎦) (🐾) (¶¶+) (🎦) (DATA PORT) ▯ 🖾 🖵 / ☒ (VCR)

MAITLAND —*See Orlando p. 828.*

MANALAPAN   pop. 321   (See map and index starting on p. 843)

———— WHERE TO STAY ————

THE RITZ-CARLTON, PALM BEACH   **Phone:** (561)533-6000   **67**

(AAA) (SAVE)   4/28-5/31 & 10/28-11/30   1P: $375-$4000   2P: $375-$4000
(fyi)   12/1-4/27   1P: $325-$4000   2P: $325-$4000
                6/1-10/27   1P: $265-$4000   2P: $265-$4000
Large-scale Hotel   Under major renovation, scheduled to be completed December 2005. **Last rated:** ▼▼▼▼▼ **Location:** On SR A1A; 9 mi s of Palm Beach. 100 S Ocean Blvd 33462. Fax: 561/588-4202. **Facility:** 270 units. 215 one-bedroom standard units. 55 one-bedroom suites, some with whirlpools. 5-6 stories (no elevator), interior corridors. **Parking:** valet. **Terms:** 14 day cancellation notice, 7 day 6/2-10/26-fee imposed, package plans, pets ($35 extra charge, with prior approval). **Amenities:** CD players, dual phone lines, voice mail, safes, honor bars, irons, hair dryers. *Fee:* video games, high-speed Internet. *Some:* DVD players, fax. **Dining:** 2 restaurants, 6:30 am-11 pm; to midnight in season, cocktails, also, The Grill, see separate listing, entertainment. **Pool(s):** heated outdoor. **Leisure Activities:** saunas, whirlpool, steamrooms, rental sailboats, snorkeling, recreation programs, bicycles, exercise room, spa, basketball, volleyball. *Fee:* scuba diving, charter fishing, parasailing, personal watercraft, scuba instruction, golf privileges, 6 tennis courts, tennis instruction. **Guest Services:** gift shop, valet laundry, area transportation (fee)-within 9 mi, beauty salon. **Business Services:** conference facilities, business center. **Cards:** AX, CB, DC, DS, JC, MC, VI.

SOME UNITS
(🍸) (¶¶) (24¶) (Y) (🎣) (∅) (🐾) (☒) (🎦) (DATA PORT) / ☒ (VCR) ▯ 🖾 🖵 /
FEE   FEE FEE

———— WHERE TO DINE ————

THE GRILL   **Dinner:** $22-$42   **Phone:** 561/533-6000   **61**
▼▼▼▼ ▼▼▼▼   **Location:** On SR A1A; 9 mi s of Palm Beach; in The Ritz-Carlton, Palm Beach. 100 S Ocean Blvd 33462. **Hours:** 6 pm-10 pm. **Closed:** Sun & Mon; days may vary in summer. **Reservations:** suggested. **Features:** The
Steak & Seafood   elegant clublike setting incorporates warm wood tones and original oil paintings. Fresh seafood and aged beef factor into basic grill items, as well as some more adventurous offerings. Service is professional. Semi-formal attire; cocktails; entertainment. **Parking:** valet. **Cards:** AX, CB, DC, DS, JC, MC, VI.

(Y)

MARATHON —*See The Florida Keys p. 359.*

MARCO ISLAND pop. 14,879 (See map and index starting on p. 620)

——— WHERE TO STAY ———

HILTON MARCO ISLAND BEACH RESORT *Book at aaa.com*

Phone: (239)394-5000 **45**

(AAA) [SAVE]

1/1-4/30	1P: $209-$399	2P: $209-$399	XP: $25	F18
12/1-12/31	1P: $149-$399	2P: $149-$399	XP: $25	F18
5/1-11/30	1P: $149-$259	2P: $149-$259	XP: $25	F18

Resort
Large-scale Hotel

Location: Oceanfront. I-75, exit 101, 9.8 mi s via SR 951; 1 mi s of SR 92 (San Marco Dr). 560 S Collier Blvd (SR 951) 34145. Fax: 239/394-5251. **Facility:** The resort offers large rooms with balconies, elegant public areas and such recreational opportunities as jet skiing. 297 units. 271 one-bedroom standard units. 26 one-bedroom suites, some with whirlpools. 11 stories, interior corridors. *Bath:* combo or shower only. **Parking:** on-site and valet. **Terms:** check-in 4 pm, 7 day cancellation notice-fee imposed, [BP] meal plan available. **Amenities:** dual phone lines, voice mail, safes, irons, hair dryers. *Fee:* video games, high-speed Internet. **Dining:** 2 restaurants, 7 am-11 pm, cocktails, also, Sandcastles, see separate listing, entertainment. **Pool(s):** heated outdoor. **Leisure Activities:** sauna, whirlpool, recreation programs. *Fee:* sailboats, windsurfing, waterskiing, charter fishing, parasailing, personal watercraft, sea kayaks, 3 lighted tennis courts, massage, game room. **Guest Services:** gift shop, complimentary evening beverages: Mon, valet laundry. **Business Services:** conference facilities, business center. **Cards:** AX, CB, DC, DS, MC, VI.

SOME UNITS

[icons] FEE

MARCO BEACH OCEAN RESORT *Book at aaa.com*

Phone: (239)393-1400 **43**

(AAA) [SAVE]

12/23-4/23	1P: $429-$1200	2P: $429-$1200	XP: $25	F13
4/24-5/28	1P: $329-$800	2P: $329-$800	XP: $25	F13
5/29-11/30	1P: $219-$550	2P: $219-$550	XP: $25	F13
12/1-12/22	1P: $219-$500	2P: $219-$500	XP: $25	F13

Large-scale Hotel **Location:** I-75, exit 101, 9.8 mi s via SR 951; 0.7 mi s of SR 92 (San Marco Dr). 480 S Collier Blvd 34145. Fax: 239/393-1401. **Facility:** Spacious suites have deluxe decor, overlook the gulf and feature either a balcony or patio. 100 units. 85 one- and 15 two-bedroom suites with kitchens. 12 stories, interior corridors. *Bath:* combo or shower only. **Parking:** on-site (fee) and valet. **Terms:** 7 day cancellation notice-fee imposed. **Amenities:** CD players, dual phone lines, voice mail, safes, irons, hair dryers. *Fee:* video games, high-speed Internet. *Some:* DVD players. **Dining:** 2 restaurants, 7 am-10 pm, cocktails, also, Sale e Pepe, see separate listing. **Pool(s):** heated outdoor. **Leisure Activities:** saunas, whirlpool, steamrooms, fishing, spa. *Fee:* charter fishing, golf privileges. **Guest Services:** valet laundry, shoeshine. **Business Services:** conference facilities, business center. **Cards:** AX, DC, DS, JC, MC, VI. **Special Amenities:** free local telephone calls and free newspaper.

SOME UNITS

[icons]

MARCO ISLAND MARRIOTT RESORT, GOLF CLUB & SPA *Book at aaa.com*

Phone: 239/394-2511 **42**

12/1-4/22 & 10/1-11/30	1P: $295-$660	2P: $295-$660	
4/23-5/28	1P: $295-$610	2P: $295-$610	
5/29-9/30	1P: $250-$600	2P: $250-$600	

Resort
Large-scale Hotel

Location: I-75, exit 101, 16.2 mi s on SR 951 to SR 92 (San Marco Blvd), then 0.5 mi s. 400 S Collier Blvd (SR 951) 34145. Fax: 239/642-2672. **Facility:** Boutiques and large rooms with balconies are features at this beachfront facility overlooking the gulf. 727 units. 665 one-bedroom standard units. 32 one- and 30 two-bedroom suites ($652-$3000), some with whirlpools. 11 stories, interior corridors. *Bath:* combo or shower only. **Parking:** on-site and valet. **Terms:** check-in 4 pm, 14 day cancellation notice-fee imposed, package plans. **Amenities:** voice mail, safes, honor bars, irons, hair dryers. *Fee:* video games, high-speed Internet. *Some:* DVD players. **Dining:** Kurrents, see separate listing. **Pool(s):** 3 heated outdoor, wading. **Leisure Activities:** whirlpools, waterslide, rental sailboats, recreation programs, rental bicycles, playground, exercise room, spa. *Fee:* charter fishing, 4 lighted tennis courts. **Guest Services:** gift shop, valet and coin laundry, area transportation (fee). **Business Services:** conference facilities, business center. **Cards:** AX, CB, DC, DS, JC, MC, VI.

SOME UNITS

[icons]

(See map and index starting on p. 620)

OLDE MARCO ISLAND INN & SUITES
Book at aaa.com   **Phone:** 239/394-3131   41

▼▼◇▼   12/1-4/25 & 11/1-11/30   1P: $199-$229   2P: $199-$229
            4/26-10/31   1P: $129-$149   2P: $129-$149

Small-scale Hotel **Location:** I-75, exit 101, 14.7 mi s on SR 951 to Bald Eagle Dr, 1.3 mi w to Palm St, then just s. 100 Palm St 34145. Fax: 239/394-4485. **Facility:** 53 units. 51 two- and 2 three-bedroom suites, some with kitchens. 4 stories, exterior corridors. **Parking:** on-site. **Terms:** office hours 8 am-10 pm, 3 day cancellation notice-fee imposed, $9 service charge. **Amenities:** high-speed Internet, dual phone lines, voice mail, irons, hair dryers. **Pool(s):** heated outdoor. **Leisure Activities:** exercise room. **Guest Services:** gift shop. **Business Services:** meeting rooms, fax (fee). **Cards:** AX, DC, DS, MC, VI.

[ASK] [🍴] [▽] [♨] [🏊] [✕] [VCR] [♦] [DATA PORT] [🔌] [🖥] [🖵]

RADISSON SUITE BEACH RESORT ON MARCO
ISLAND   **Book at aaa.com**   **Phone:** (239)394-4100   46

▼▼◇▼   1/1-4/30   1P: $269-$299   2P: $269-$299   XP: $10   F17
            5/1-11/30   1P: $169-$189   2P: $169-$189   XP: $10   F17
            12/1-12/31   1P: $145-$185   2P: $145-$185   XP: $10   F17

Large-scale Hotel **Location:** I-75, exit 101, 16.2 mi s on SR 951 to SR 92 (San Marco Blvd), then 1 mi s. 600 S Collier Blvd (SR 951) 34145. Fax: 239/394-0419. **Facility:** 268 units. 59 one-bedroom standard units. 163 one- and 46 two-bedroom suites ($165-$499) with kitchens, some with whirlpools. 14 stories, exterior corridors. *Bath:* combo or shower only. **Parking:** on-site. **Terms:** check-in 4 pm, 2 night minimum stay - weekends, 14 day cancellation notice-fee imposed, $9 service charge. **Amenities:** high-speed Internet, voice mail, safes, irons, hair dryers. *Some:* DVD players (fee). **Pool(s):** heated outdoor. **Leisure Activities:** whirlpool, lighted tennis court, recreation programs, exercise room, basketball, volleyball. *Fee:* sailboats, windsurfing, waterskiing, bicycles. **Guest Services:** gift shop, coin laundry. **Business Services:** conference facilities, fax (fee). **Cards:** AX, CB, DC, DS, JC, MC, VI. *(See color ad p 522)*

SOME UNITS

[ASK] [S🛏] [🍴] [▽] [♨] [🌙] [🏊] [✕] [♦] [DATA PORT] [🔌] [🖥] [🖵] / [✕] [VCR] / FEE

THE SURF CLUB OF MARCO
                          Phone: (239)642-5800   44

▼▼◇▼   All Year Wkly   1P: $1400-$1625   2P: $1400-$1625

Condominium **Location:** I-75, exit 101, 16.2 mi s on SR 951 to SR 92 (San Marco Blvd), then 0.9 mi s. 540 S Collier Blvd (SR 951) 34145. Fax: 239/642-7245. **Facility:** The property's two-bedroom apartments include queen-size sleeper sofas and private balconies; many of the units have either gulf or island views. 44 two-bedroom suites with kitchens. 8 stories, exterior corridors. **Parking:** on-site. **Terms:** 2 night minimum stay - seasonal, 14 day cancellation notice-fee imposed. **Amenities:** video library (fee), safes, irons. **Pool(s):** heated outdoor. **Leisure Activities:** whirlpool, 3 tennis courts. **Guest Services:** gift shop, coin laundry. **Business Services:** meeting rooms, fax (fee). **Cards:** AX, CB, DC, DS, MC, VI.

[ASK] [🍴] [🌙] [VCR] [♦] [DATA PORT] [🔌] [🖥] [🖵]

━━━━━━ **WHERE TO DINE** ━━━━━━

ARTURO'S RISTORANTE ITALIANO
          Dinner: $13-$35   **Phone:** 239/642-0550   47

▼▼◇▼   **Location:** Just n of SR 951. 844 Bald Eagle Dr 34145. **Hours:** 5 pm-close. Closed: 4/16, 12/25; also 2 weeks in early Sept. **Reservations:** suggested. **Features:** Casual, comfortable dining is what to expect at this bustling restaurant. Such well-prepared traditional dishes as bruscetta and the signature mozzarella and prosciutto-stuffed pork chop boast a flavorful taste and colorful presentation. Dressy casual; cocktails.

Italian

Parking: on-site. **Cards:** MC, VI.

KONRAD'S SEAFOOD & GRILLE ROOM
          Dinner: $13-$38   **Phone:** 239/642-3332   53

▼▼◇ ▼▼◇   **Location:** 1 mi s of SR 92 (San Marco Blvd); in Mission Plaza. 599 S Collier Blvd 34145. **Hours:** 5 pm-10 pm. Closed: 12/24, 12/25; also Super Bowl Sun. **Reservations:** suggested. **Features:** A slightly upscale ambience hangs in the air at this neoclassically decorated restaurant. The flavorful oak-grilled salmon is popular, as is the marinated flank steak with stuffed shrimp, plum tomatoes and cilantro. Jazz musicians perform seasonally. Dressy casual; cocktails. **Parking:** on-site and valet. **Cards:** AX, DC, DS, MC, VI.

Steak & Seafood

[▽]

KURRENTS
          Dinner: $22-$38   **Phone:** 239/642-2695   50

▼▼◇▼   **Location:** I-75, exit 101, 16.2 mi s on SR 951 to SR 92 (San Marco Blvd), then 0.5 mi s; in Marco Island Marriott Resort, Golf Club & Spa. 400 S Collier Blvd 34145. **Hours:** 5:30 pm-10 pm. **Reservations:** suggested. **Features:** The beauty of this place is the decor: a soft version of art deco. Representative of the serious food are large steaks and fresh seafood, as well as a few pasta dishes. Presentation and service are plusses here, and it's child-friendly. Dressy casual; cocktails. **Parking:** on-site and valet. **Cards:** AX, CB, DC, DS, MC, VI.

Continental

[♿M] [▽]

MAREK'S COLLIER HOUSE RESTAURANT
          Dinner: $23-$27   **Phone:** 239/642-9948   46

◆◆◆   **Location:** 1.2 mi n of SR 951. 1121 Bald Eagle Dr 34145. **Hours:** Open 12/1-8/1 & 10/1-11/30; 5:30 pm-close. Closed: Sun off season. **Reservations:** suggested. **Features:** In restored historic home of Capt. Bill Collier, this intimate restaurant has three dining areas: a main room, cozy library and quaint veranda. The chef prepares imaginative gourmet fare, such as Maine lobster, thermidor, lamb and duckling. Dressy casual; beer & wine only. **Parking:** on-site. **Cards:** DS, MC, VI. **Historic**

Continental

SALE E PEPE
    Lunch: $12-$22   **Dinner:** $22-$34   **Phone:** 239/393-1600   51

▼▼◇▼   **Location:** I-75, exit 101, 9.8 mi s via SR 951; 0.7 mi s of SR 92 (San Marco Dr); in Marco Beach Ocean Resort. 480 S Collier Blvd 34145. **Hours:** 7-10:30 am, 11-2 & 6-9 pm, Fri & Sat-10 pm. **Features:** The restaurant offers views of the Gulf, elegant decor and a casual side, too. The all-Italian menu is translated into English. The chef prepares fresh seafood, tender meats and freshly made pasta combined with his sauces and some traditional sauces. Artful food presentations are memorable. Semi-formal attire; cocktails. **Parking:** valet.

Northern Italian

Cards: AX, CB, DC, DS, JC, MC, VI.

[♿M]

(See map and index starting on p. 620)

SANDCASTLES
~~~~
American

**Dinner:** $18-$26      **Phone:** 239/394-5000   52

**Location:** I-75, exit 101, 9.8 mi s via SR 951; 1 mi s of SR 92 (San Marco Dr); in Hilton Marco Island Beach Resort. 560 S Collier Blvd 34145. **Hours:** 6 pm-10 pm. **Reservations:** suggested. **Features:** This intimate and classy restaurant is known for fine dining with many upscale specialties, including entrees of beef, veal, lamb and seafood. A good selection of decadent desserts; creme brulee, strawberry shortcake or Milky Way pie tame the sweet tooth. Dressy casual; cocktails; entertainment. **Parking:** valet and street. **Cards:** AX, DC, DS, JC, MC, VI.

**SNOOK INN**
~~
Seafood

**Lunch:** $8-$12      **Dinner:** $8-$25      **Phone:** 239/394-3313   45

**Location:** SR 951, 2.5 mi n. 1215 Bald Eagle Dr 34145. **Hours:** 11 am-10 pm. Closed: 11/23, 12/25; also for dinner 12/24. **Reservations:** not accepted. **Features:** Enjoy a drink at the bar while you take in a view of the Marco River. A casual nautical theme includes a large aquarium and tabletops inset with sand, shells and faux pieces of eight. The menu offers an abundance of fresh seafood, steak, sandwiches and appetizers. Casual dress; cocktails; entertainment. **Parking:** on-site. **Cards:** AX, DC, DS, MC, VI.

**SUSHI, BLUES & STEAKS**
~~~~
Japanese

Dinner: $6-$44   **Phone:** 239/642-4900   48

Location: Jct SR 951 and Bald Eagle Dr, 0.5 mi s on Bald Eagle Dr, then just e on Marco Lake Dr; corner of First Ave; in The Lakeside Inn. 155 First Ave 34145. **Hours:** 4:30 pm-10 pm. Closed: Sun. **Reservations:** suggested. **Features:** Memorable sushi and contemporary American fare are prepared at the newer eatery. Guests may request seating on a screened patio overlooking the lake or inside; both offer views of the natural wildlife. Knowledgeable servers welcome questions about dish preparations and willingly make suggestions. Casual dress; cocktails. **Parking:** on-site. **Cards:** AX, DC, DS, MC, VI.

VERDI'S - AN AMERICAN BISTRO
~~~~
American

**Dinner:** $17-$28      **Phone:** 239/394-5533   49

**Location:** Jct SR 951 and Bald Eagle Dr, 1 mi s; in Sand Dollar Plaza. 241 N Collier Blvd 34145. **Hours:** Open 12/1-7/31 & 10/1-11/30; 5:30 pm-9:30 pm; from 6 pm 5/1-7/31. Closed: 4/16, 12/25; also Mon 6/1-7/31 & Sun. **Reservations:** suggested. **Features:** Created with imagination and detail, the chef's fresh seafood, meat and pasta entrees are complemented by choices off the wine list. The dining room decor evokes a cozy feel. Dressy casual; beer & wine only. **Parking:** on-site. **Cards:** DC, DS, MC, VI.

# MARGATE —See Fort Lauderdale p. 415.

# MARIANNA pop. 6,230

## ———— WHERE TO STAY ————

**BEST WESTERN MARIANNA INN**   *Book at aaa.com*
AAA SAVE
~~~~
Small-scale Hotel

Phone: (850)526-5666

| All Year | 1P: $49-$59 | 2P: $59-$79 | XP: $10 | F |

Location: Jct I-10, exit 142, 0.3 mi s. 2086 Hwy 71 S 32448. **Facility:** 80 one-bedroom standard units. 2 stories, exterior corridors. **Parking:** on-site. **Terms:** 2-3 night minimum stay - weekends, small pets only ($10 extra charge). **Amenities:** high-speed Internet, voice mail, irons, hair dryers. **Pool(s):** outdoor. **Guest Services:** coin laundry. **Business Services:** fax. **Cards:** AX, CB, DC, DS, JC, MC, VI. **Special Amenities:** free continental breakfast and free local telephone calls.

SOME UNITS

COUNTRY INN & SUITES BY CARLSON   *Book at aaa.com*
~~~~
Small-scale Hotel

**Phone:** 850/526-0096

| All Year [CP] | 1P: $79-$109 | 2P: $85-$115 | XP: $6 | F17 |

**Location:** I-10, exit 142, just n. 2196 Post Oak Ln 32448. **Fax:** 850/482-0044. **Facility:** 70 units. 58 one-bedroom standard units, some with whirlpools. 10 one- and 2 two-bedroom suites ($109-$139). 3 stories, interior corridors. **Bath:** combo or shower only. **Parking:** on-site. **Terms:** cancellation fee imposed. **Amenities:** high-speed Internet, voice mail, irons, hair dryers. **Some:** dual phone lines. **Pool(s):** outdoor. **Leisure Activities:** whirlpool, exercise room. **Guest Services:** coin laundry. **Business Services:** meeting rooms. **Cards:** AX, CB, DC, DS, MC, VI.

SOME UNITS

**HAMPTON INN**   *Book at aaa.com*
~~~~
Small-scale Hotel

Phone: 850/526-1006

Property failed to provide current rates

Location: I-10, exit 142, just nw. 2185 Hwy 71 S 32448. **Fax:** 850/526-1824. **Facility:** 70 one-bedroom standard units. 2 stories, exterior corridors. **Bath:** combo or shower only. **Parking:** on-site. **Amenities:** high-speed Internet, voice mail, irons, hair dryers. **Pool(s):** outdoor. **Guest Services:** coin laundry. **Business Services:** fax (fee).

SOME UNITS

HINSON HOUSE BED & BREAKFAST
~~~~
Bed & Breakfast

**Phone:** (850)526-1500

| All Year [BP] | 1P: $64-$105 |

**Location:** Just w of downtown center. 4338 Lafayette St 32446. **Fax:** 850/482-4449. **Facility:** It's Christmas all year at this service-oriented property where the holiday decorations never come down; guests may access a stocked refrigerator. Designated smoking area. 5 one-bedroom standard units. 2 stories, interior/exterior corridors. **Parking:** on-site. **Terms:** check-in 4 pm, weekly rates available, package plans. **Cards:** AX, DC, DS, MC, VI.

**HOLIDAY INN EXPRESS**
~~~~
Small-scale Hotel

Phone: 850/526-2900

Property failed to provide current rates

Location: I-10, exit 21, just n. 2222 Hwy 71 N 32448. **Fax:** 850/526-7551. **Facility:** 61 one-bedroom standard units, some with whirlpools. 2 stories, exterior corridors. **Bath:** combo or shower only. **Parking:** on-site. **Amenities:** voice mail, irons, hair dryers. **Pool(s):** outdoor. **Guest Services:** coin laundry.

SOME UNITS

MICROTEL INN & SUITES

Phone: 850/526-5005

Small-scale Hotel

All Year [CP] 1P: $49-$54 2P: $61-$69 XP: $5 F

Location: I-10, exit 142, just n. 4959 White Tail Dr 32448. Fax: 850/526-5003. **Facility:** 64 one-bedroom standard units, some with whirlpools. 3 stories, interior corridors. *Bath:* combo or shower only. **Parking:** on-site. **Terms:** 1-2 night minimum stay - seasonal and/or weekends, 4 day cancellation notice. **Pool(s):** outdoor. **Guest Services:** coin laundry. **Business Services:** fax. **Cards:** AX, CB, DC, DS, JC, MC, VI.

SOME UNITS

ASK ⑤🚲 🍴 ⑤M 🛅 🛋 🐾 ⚡ 🖥 💻 / ✕ 🛑 🖥 /

QUALITY INN   *Book at aaa.com*

Phone: (850)526-5600

Small-scale Hotel

3/1-8/31 [ECP] 1P: $79-$99 2P: $79-$99 XP: $7 F17
9/1-11/30 [ECP] 1P: $69-$99 2P: $69-$99 XP: $7 F17
12/1-2/28 [ECP] 1P: $69-$89 2P: $69-$89 XP: $7 F17

Location: I-10, exit 142, just n. 2175 Hwy 71 S 32448. Fax: 850/482-7899. **Facility:** 80 one-bedroom standard units. 2 stories, exterior corridors. **Parking:** on-site. **Terms:** 2-3 night minimum stay - seasonal and/or weekends, cancellation fee imposed, package plans, pets ($12-$25 extra charge). **Amenities:** high-speed Internet, irons, hair dryers. **Pool(s):** outdoor. **Guest Services:** coin laundry. **Business Services:** fax (fee). **Cards:** AX, CB, DC, DS, JC, MC, VI.

SOME UNITS

ASK ⑤🚲 🐾 🍴 🛋 ⚡ 🖥 💻 / ✕ 🛑 🖥 /
FEE

SUPER 8 MOTEL   *Book at aaa.com*

Phone: 850/482-4770

Small-scale Hotel

Property failed to provide current rates

Location: I-10, exit 142, just n. 2226 Hwy 71 N 32448. Fax: 850/482-1133. **Facility:** 47 one-bedroom standard units, some with whirlpools. 2 stories, exterior corridors. *Bath:* combo or shower only. **Parking:** on-site. **Pool(s):** outdoor.

SOME UNITS

🍴 🛋 ⚡ 🖥 🛑 🖥 / ✕ /

--------- **WHERE TO DINE** ---------

MADISON WAREHOUSE

Lunch: $5-$8 Dinner: $6-$18 Phone: 850/526-4000

Steak House

Location: Downtown. 2881 Madison St 32425. **Hours:** 11 am-2 & 5-9 pm, Sat from 5 pm. Closed major holidays; also Sun. **Reservations:** accepted. **Features:** In a rustic warehouse building, the steakhouse offers comfort food at a good price. Casual dress; beer & wine only. **Parking:** street. **Cards:** AX, DS, MC, VI.

PESCE'S SEAFOOD & ITALIAN RESTAURANT

Lunch: $5-$9 Dinner: $8-$16 Phone: 850/482-8005

Italian

Cards: MC, VI.

Location: I-10, exit 136, 0.8 mi n, then just w. 2914 Optimist Dr 32446. **Hours:** 11 am-2 & 4:30-9 pm, Sat from 4:30 pm. Closed 1/1, 12/25; also Sun. **Reservations:** accepted. **Features:** Seafood and Italian specialties include sauteed tilapia over a bed of fresh spinach with balsamic dressing and chopped tomatoes, pistachio nut salmon, mandarin orange chicken and shrimp and veal francese. Casual dress. **Parking:** on-site.

RED CANYON GRILL

Dinner: $8-$15 Phone: 850/482-4256

Southwestern

Location: 2.5 mi n of jct US 90 on SR 166; across from Florida Caverns. 3297 Caverns Rd 32448. **Hours:** 5 pm-9 pm, Fri & Sat-9:30 pm. Closed major holidays; also Sun & Mon. **Reservations:** accepted. **Features:** The restaurant carries off its Southwestern theme with a large antler chandelier and assorted artifacts hanging on the walls. Such dishes as fajitas, mesquite-grilled shrimp, pasta with grilled vegetables, and corn soup are well-presented and flavorful. Casual dress; beer & wine only. **Parking:** on-site. **Cards:** AX, MC, VI.

🍸

SAN MARCOS MEXICAN RESTAURANT

Lunch: $4-$8 Dinner: $6-$10 Phone: 850/482-6654

Mexican

Location: 0.4 mi w of jct SR 71. 4727 Hwy 90 32446. **Hours:** 11 am-9 pm, Fri & Sat-10 pm. **Features:** The sound of fajitas sizzling on a platter makes heads turn and mouths water. Other favorites include burritos, enchiladas and bistec dinners. Casual dress; beer only. **Parking:** on-site. **Cards:** MC, VI.

TASTES OF THE OLD SOUTH

Lunch: $4-$7 Dinner: $5-$10 Phone: 850/482-7992

American

Location: Just w of jct US 90. 2809 Hwy 71 32446. **Hours:** 11 am-8 pm, Fri-9 pm, Sat 4 pm-9 pm, Mon 11 am-2 pm. Closed: 1/1, 11/23, 12/25; also Sun. **Features:** The small town eatery offers good food in a friendly environment, including fried chicken like Grandma used to make and other Old South favorites. Casual dress. **Parking:** on-site. **Cards:** AX, DS, MC, VI.

TONY'S RESTAURANT

Lunch: $3-$15 Dinner: $3-$16 Phone: 850/482-2232

Italian

Parking: on-site. **Cards:** AX, CB, DC, MC, VI.

Location: I-10, exit 136, just w on US 90. 4133 Lafayette St 32448. **Hours:** 11 am-8:30 pm. Closed major holidays; also Sat & Sun. **Features:** Expect long lines at this popular family-owned and family-friendly eatery. The atmosphere, red booths and soft rock music piped through speakers, is as comfortable and familiar as the basic, tasty fare of such dishes as chicken parmesan and spaghetti. Casual dress; beer only.

MELBOURNE pop. 71,382—*See also INDIALANTIC, MELBOURNE BEACH & WEST MELBOURNE.*

✈ Airport Accommodations

Spotter/Map Page Number	OA	MELBOURNE INTERNATIONAL	Diamond Rating	Rate Range High Season	Listing Page
N/A		Hilton Melbourne Rialto Place, 0.5 mi se of airport	◆◆◆	$119-$269	526

——— **WHERE TO STAY** ———

COURTYARD BY MARRIOTT *Book at aaa.com*
Phone: (321)724-6400

AAA SAVE
◆◆◆
Small-scale Hotel

12/1-4/27	1P: $94-$169	
4/28-6/29 & 9/5-11/30	1P: $109-$134	
6/30-9/4	1P: $104-$124	

Location: I-95, exit 180, 3 mi e on US 192. 2101 W New Haven Ave 32904. Fax: 321/984-4006. **Facility:** 146 units. 134 one-bedroom standard units. 12 one-bedroom suites ($109-$184). 3 stories, interior corridors. *Bath:* combo or shower only. **Parking:** on-site. **Terms:** cancellation fee imposed. **Amenities:** high-speed Internet, dual phone lines, voice mail, irons, hair dryers. **Dining:** 6-10 am, Sat & Sun 7-11 am. **Pool(s):** heated outdoor. **Leisure Activities:** whirlpool, exercise room. **Guest Services:** valet and coin laundry. **Business Services:** meeting rooms. **Cards:** AX, DC, DS, JC, MC, VI. **Special Amenities: free newspaper and preferred room (subject to availability with advance reservations).**

SOME UNITS

[icons]

CRANE CREEK INN WATERFRONT BED & BREAKFAST
Phone: (321)768-6416

◆◆◆
Bed & Breakfast

All Year [ECP]	1P: $100-$199	2P: $100-$199	XP: $25

Location: Jct US 192, just s on Babcock, then 0.9 mi e. 907 E Melbourne Ave 32901. **Facility:** Guests may arrive by car or boat at this Key West-style guest house on a creek navigable to the Intracoastal Waterway. Smoke free premises. 5 one-bedroom standard units, some with efficiencies and/or whirlpools. 2 stories (no elevator), interior/exterior corridors. *Bath:* combo or shower only. **Parking:** on-site. **Terms:** 2-3 night minimum stay - weekends, age restrictions may apply, 14 day cancellation notice-fee imposed, pets (dogs only, $10 extra charge). **Amenities:** irons, hair dryers. **Pool(s):** outdoor. **Leisure Activities:** whirlpool, canoeing, paddleboats, boat dock, fishing. **Cards:** AX, CB, DC, JC, MC, VI.

SOME UNITS

[icons] FEE

HILTON MELBOURNE RIALTO PLACE *Book at aaa.com*
Phone: (321)768-0200

◆◆◆
Small-scale Hotel

All Year	1P: $119-$259	2P: $129-$269	XP: $10 F18

Location: 1 mi w of US 1, 0.8 mi n of US 192 via Airport Blvd. 200 Rialto Pl 32901. Fax: 321/956-7247. **Facility:** 237 units. 235 one-bedroom standard units, some with whirlpools. 2 one-bedroom suites. 8 stories, interior corridors. *Bath:* combo or shower only. **Parking:** on-site. **Terms:** [AP], [BP] & [CP] meal plans available, package plans, pets ($50 deposit). **Amenities:** dual phone lines, voice mail, irons, hair dryers. *Fee:* video games, high-speed Internet. **Pool(s):** heated outdoor. **Leisure Activities:** whirlpool, lighted tennis court, exercise room, basketball. *Fee:* massage. **Guest Services:** gift shop, valet and coin laundry, area transportation. **Business Services:** conference facilities, business center. **Cards:** AX, DS, MC, VI.

SOME UNITS

[icons] FEE   FEE   FEE

IMPERIAL'S HOTEL & CONFERENCE CENTER *Book at aaa.com*
Phone: (321)255-0077

AAA SAVE
◆◆◆
Small-scale Hotel

2/3-4/29 [ECP]	1P: $89-$179	2P: $89-$179	XP: $10 F18
12/1-2/2 & 4/30-11/30 [ECP]	1P: $79-$149	2P: $79-$149	XP: $10 F18

Location: I-95, exit 191 (CR 509). 8298 N Wickham Rd 32940. Fax: 321/259-9633. **Facility:** 126 units. 125 one-bedroom standard units. 1 one-bedroom suite ($99-$199). 5 stories, interior corridors. **Parking:** on-site. **Amenities:** video games (fee), voice mail, irons, hair dryers. *Some:* high-speed Internet, dual phone lines, fax. **Dining:** 11:30 am-10 pm, Sat from 5 pm; closed Sun, cocktails. **Pool(s):** outdoor. **Leisure Activities:** exercise room, volleyball. **Guest Services:** valet and coin laundry. **Business Services:** conference facilities, fax (fee). **Cards:** AX, CB, DC, DS, MC, VI. **Special Amenities: free expanded continental breakfast and free newspaper.**

SOME UNITS

[icons]

LA QUINTA INN & SUITES MELBOURNE
Phone: (321)242-9400

AAA SAVE
◆◆◆
Small-scale Hotel

1/17-4/30	1P: $129-$159	XP: $7 F18
5/1-11/30	1P: $115-$125	XP: $7 F18
12/1-1/16	1P: $105-$195	XP: $7 F18

Location: I-95, exit 191 (CR 509), just w. 7200 George T Edwards Dr 32940. Fax: 321/242-9440. **Facility:** 102 units. 99 one-bedroom standard units. 3 one-bedroom suites. 4 stories, interior corridors. *Bath:* combo or shower only. **Parking:** on-site. **Terms:** [ECP] meal plan available. **Amenities:** video games (fee), voice mail, irons, hair dryers. *Some:* dual phone lines. **Pool(s):** heated outdoor. **Guest Services:** valet and coin laundry. **Business Services:** meeting rooms, fax (fee). **Cards:** AX, CB, DC, DS, MC, VI. **Special Amenities: free expanded continental breakfast and free local telephone calls.**

SOME UNITS

[icons]

SUPER 8 *Book at aaa.com*
Phone: (321)723-4430

AAA SAVE
◆◆
Motel

12/15-4/15 [CP]	1P: $69-$89	2P: $69-$89	XP: $6 F12
12/1-12/14 & 4/16-11/30 [CP]	1P: $59	2P: $69	XP: $6 F12

Location: I-95, exit 180, 7 mi e to US 1 on US 192, then 0.5 mi n. 1515 S Harbor City Blvd 32901. Fax: 321/723-4312. **Facility:** 56 one-bedroom standard units. 2 stories, interior corridors. *Bath:* combo or shower only. **Parking:** on-site. **Terms:** weekly rates available, small pets only ($10 deposit). **Amenities:** irons, hair dryers. **Guest Services:** coin laundry. **Cards:** AX, DC, DS, MC, VI. **Special Amenities: free continental breakfast and early check-in/late check-out.**

SOME UNITS

[icons] FEE

WISTERIA INN BED & BREAKFAST

▼▼▼ All Year   1P: $95-$145   2P: $95-$145   XP: $15   **Phone: (321)727-0717**

Bed & Breakfast **Location:** I-95, exit 180, 4.5 mi e US 192, then just n. 1924 Catterton Dr 32901. **Fax:** 321/733-1854. **Facility:** This B&B, built in 1924 as a private residence in the Spanish Colonial Revival style, features nine-foot ceilings and heart of pine floors. Smoke free premises. 4 one-bedroom standard units. 2 stories (no elevator), interior corridors. *Bath:* combo or shower only. **Parking:** on-site. **Terms:** office hours 7 am-10 pm, 14 day cancellation notice, weekly rates available, pets ($10 extra charge). **Amenities:** irons, hair dryers. **Leisure Activities:** bicycles. **Cards:** AX, DS, MC, VI.

SOME UNITS

✈ 🐾 🍴 🏨 ✕ 🐕 / 🗄 🗄 🖭 /
       FEE

——— WHERE TO DINE ———

CHARLIE & JAKES BREWERY GRILLE

▼▼ ▼▼   **Lunch: $5-$16**   **Dinner: $5-$16**   **Phone:** 321/752-7675

American **Location:** I-95, exit 191 (CR 509), 3.5 mi e. 6300 N Wickham Rd, #137 32940. **Hours:** 11 am-10 pm, Fri & Sat-11 pm, Sun noon-9 pm. Closed major holidays. **Features:** Fresh seafood, steaks, barbecue and hand-crafted beer are served in the friendly eatery. Casual dress; cocktails. **Parking:** on-site. **Cards:** AX, DS, MC, VI.

CONCHY JOE'S SEAFOOD RESTAURANT

▼▼ ▼▼   **Lunch: $5-$15**   **Dinner: $10-$27**   **Phone:** 321/253-3131

Seafood **Location:** 0.3 mi e of US 1 via Eau Gallie Blvd, north side of causeway. 1477 Pineapple Ave 32935. **Hours:** 11:30 am-2:30 & 4-10 pm. Closed: 11/23, 12/25; also for dinner 12/24. **Features:** Deep-fried alligator, conch salad and grouper Marsala are specialties in the nautically themed restaurant, on the site of the 1925 Oleander's Hotel. Photographs and memorabilia are displayed throughout the casual, riverfront establishment. Casual dress; cocktails; entertainment. **Parking:** on-site. **Cards:** AX, DS, MC, VI.

🍸

MEG O' MALLEY'S

▼▼ ▼▼   **Lunch: $5-$9**   **Dinner: $7-$23**   **Phone:** 321/952-5510

Irish **Location:** Jct US 1 and 192, just w on US 192; downtown. 812 E New Haven Ave 32901. **Hours:** 10:30 am-midnight. Closed: 1/1, 12/24, 12/25. **Reservations:** accepted. **Features:** Erin go eat! Probably the only Irish pub known as well for its food as its parties, this is a great place to meet, eat and enjoy. Great service, lovely beginnings and sweet endings are the traditions here. Traditional pub fare is available but the chef's full menu is an absolute treat. Soups, appetizers and entrees are all a delight. Casual dress; cocktails. **Parking:** on-site. **Cards:** AX, DS, MC, VI.

MELBOURNE BEACH pop. 3,335—*See also MELBOURNE.*

——— WHERE TO DINE ———

CAFE COCONUT COVE

▼▼ ▼▼   **Dinner: $13-$27**   **Phone:** 321/727-3133

German **Location:** On SR A1A, 6.8 mi s of jct US 192. 4210 SR A1A S 32951. **Hours:** Open 12/1-8/31 & 10/1-11/30; 5 pm-9 pm. Closed: 12/25; also Sun & Mon. **Features:** Diners can enjoy beautiful sunsets from a cozy dining room that overlooks the Indian River. Hearty German cuisine is prepared by the chef/owner, who extends a warm welcome to his guests. Favorites include spatzle, bratwurst and schnitzel. Casual dress; beer & wine only. **Parking:** on-site. **Cards:** DS, MC, VI.

DJON'S CHOP HOUSE

▼▼ ▼▼   **Dinner: $15-$28**   **Phone:** 321/722-2737

French **Location:** 2.5 mi s of jct US 192 and SR A1A, 0.5 mi w. 522 Ocean Ave 32951. **Hours:** 5 pm-10 pm, Fri & Sat-11 pm. Closed: 12/25; also Sun off season. **Reservations:** suggested. **Features:** This inn was started under the 1842 Homestead Act and used by steamboat crews. The unusual tile stove came from Europe. On the menu are a good variety of dishes, including escargots, salad, crab cakes, chicken, veal, filet, rack of lamb and desserts flambeed tableside. Wine is stored in a temperature-controlled cellar. Casual dress; cocktails; entertainment. **Parking:** street. **Cards:** AX, CB, DC, DS, MC, VI.

🍸

MERRITT ISLAND pop. 36,090

——— WHERE TO STAY ———

CLARION HOTEL-KENNEDY SPACE CENTER AREA   *Book at aaa.com*

🆔 SAVE   2/2-4/30   1P: $99-$179   2P: $99-$179   XP: $10   F18   **Phone: (321)452-7711**
         12/1-2/1 & 5/1-11/30   1P: $89-$159   2P: $89-$159   XP: $10   F18
▼▼▼ ▼
Small-scale Hotel **Location:** I-95, exit 201, 6 mi e. 260 E Merritt Island Cswy (SR 520) 32952. **Fax:** 321/452-9462. **Facility:** 128 one-bedroom standard units. 2 stories, exterior corridors. **Parking:** on-site. **Terms:** [ECP] meal plan available, package plans. **Amenities:** dual phone lines, voice mail, safes, irons, hair dryers. **Dining:** 4 pm-midnight, cocktails, nightclub. **Pool(s):** outdoor. **Leisure Activities:** pool deck and tropical courtyard, tennis court, exercise room, horseshoes, volleyball. **Guest Services:** valet and coin laundry. **Business Services:** meeting rooms, business center. **Cards:** AX, CB, DC, DS, JC, MC, VI. *(See color ad p 277)*

SOME UNITS

🆂 🍴 🍸 🐾 🏊 ✕ 🐕 DATA PORT 🖭 / ✕ 🗄 🗄 /

——— WHERE TO DINE ———

R.J. GATORS FLORIDA SEA GRILL & BAR

▼▼ ▼▼   **Lunch: $5-$17**   **Dinner: $8-$20**   **Phone:** 321/459-3313

American **Location:** I-95, exit 201, 5.8 mi e; located by Merritt Island Mall. 650 E Merritt Island Cswy 32952. **Hours:** 11 am-midnight. Closed: 11/23, 12/25. **Reservations:** accepted. **Features:** The fun, gator-themed family restaurant aims to please everyone. Although known for wings, this place also serves steaks, fresh seafood, burgers, wraps, chicken and salads. Trivia games are a hit in the large bar area. Casual dress; cocktails. **Parking:** on-site. **Cards:** AX, CB, DC, DS, JC, MC, VI.

Destination Miami-Miami Beach
pop. 362,470

Pioneering Julia Tuttle convinced millionaire Henry Flagler to extend his railroad farther south, and the rest has been history.

Now a cosmopolitan metropolis and a leader in the world of global commerce, Miami and the Beaches also are internationally known as a vacation paradise where cultures, both pop and ethnic, blend under a bright, tropical sun.

© Gibson Stock Photography

Art Deco District, Miami Beach. The bold outlines, geometric shapes, rounded corners and pastel colors of these Art Deco buildings are as striking today as they were in their 1920s and '30s heyday. (See mention page 126)

See Vicinity maps pages 530 and 535

Greater Miami CVB

© Gibson Stock Photography

Boating, Greater Miami. With a bay, a river and an ocean, light boating excursions are a popular pastime.

Shopping in Greater Miami. Malls and specialty districts accommodate shoppers of everything from beach gear to fine clothing.

Homestead

Florida City

Places included in this AAA Destination City:

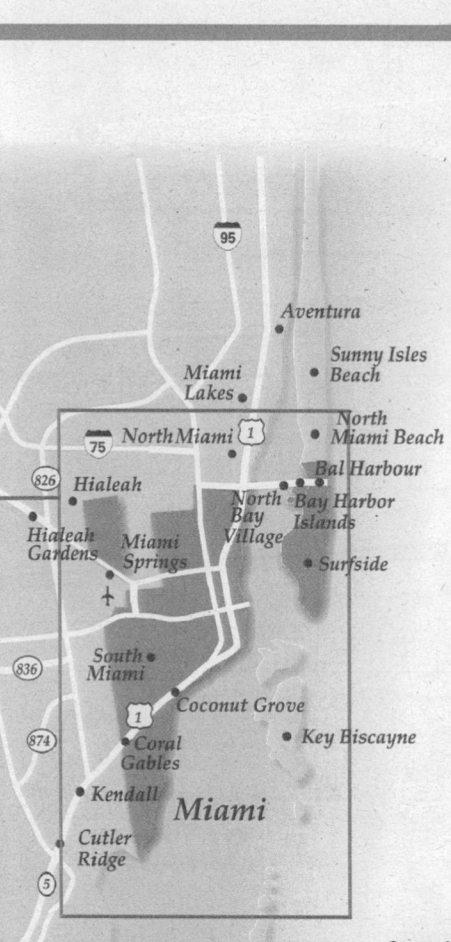

© HIRB / Index Stock

Alfresco dining, Greater Miami.
Sunshine and warm, gentle
breezes entice diners to shun
walls and roofs.

Greater Miami CVB

*Calle Ocho Festival,
Miami.*
A weeklong heritage
celebration heats up
the Cuban district in
March. (See mention
page 132)

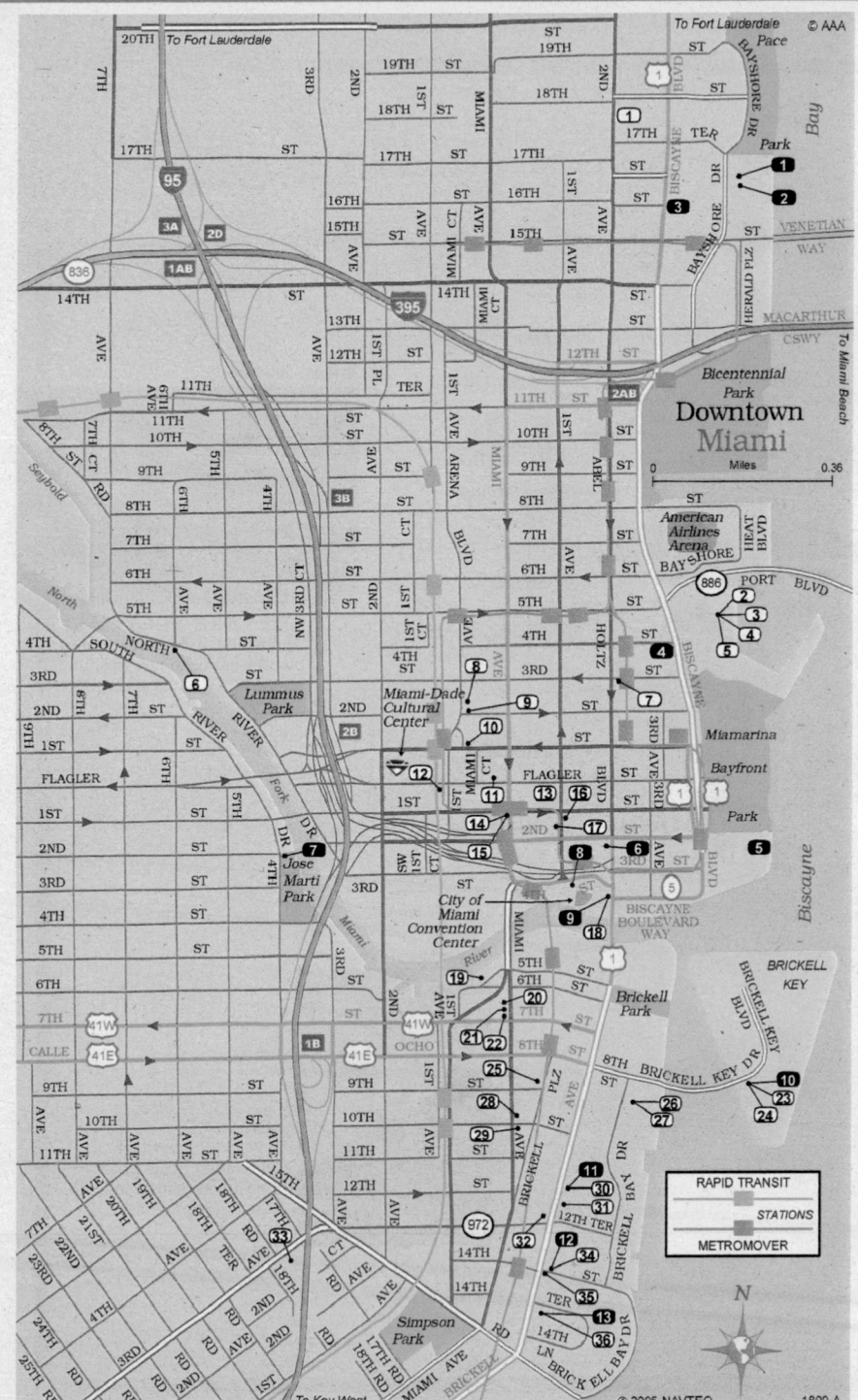

Downtown Miami

This index helps you "spot" where approved accommodations and restaurants are located on the corresponding detailed maps. Lodging rate ranges are for comparison only and show the property's high season; rates are per night, unless only weekly (W) rates are available. Restaurant rate range is for dinner, unless only lunch (L) is served. Turn to the listing page for more detailed rate information and consult display ads for special promotions.

Spotter/Map Page Number	OA	DOWNTOWN MIAMI - Lodgings	Diamond Rating	Rate Range High Season	Listing Page
1 / p. 530		Doubletree Grand-Biscayne Bay	◇◇◇	$129-$349	553
2 / p. 530		Miami Marriott Biscayne Bay Hotel	◇◇◇	$259-$500	555
3 / p. 530		Radisson Hotel Miami	◇◇◇	$149-$269	555
4 / p. 530	AAA	Holiday Inn Port of Miami-Downtown - see color ad p 554	◇◇◇	$123-$147 SAVE	554
5 / p. 530		InterContinental Miami	◇◇◇◇	$169-$309	555
6 / p. 530		Courtyard by Marriott Miami Downtown	◇◇◇	$115-$169	552
7 / p. 530		Miami River Inn	◇◇	$109-$199	555
8 / p. 530		Clarion Hotel & Suites - see color ad p 553	◇◇◇	$117-$144	552
9 / p. 530	AAA	Hyatt Regency Miami - see color ad p 554	◇◇◇	$135-$235 SAVE	554
10 / p. 530	AAA	Mandarin Oriental, Miami	◇◇◇◇◇	$625-$860 SAVE	555
11 / p. 530	AAA	JW Marriott Hotel-Miami	◇◇◇◇	$215-$245 SAVE	555
12 / p. 530		Conrad Miami	◇◇◇◇	$129-$429	552
13 / p. 530	AAA	Four Seasons Hotel Miami	◇◇◇◇	$375-$1950 SAVE	554
		DOWNTOWN MIAMI - Restaurants			
1 / p. 530		S & S Restaurant	◇	$6-$9	558
2 / p. 530		Mambo Cafe	◇◇	$6-$20	558
3 / p. 530		Lombardi's Restaurante Italiano	◇◇◇	$6-$23	557
4 / p. 530		Bubba Gump Shrimp Co	◇◇	$11-$19	556
5 / p. 530		Los Ranchos of Bayside	◇◇	$14-$27	558
6 / p. 530		Joe's Seafood Restaurant	◇◇	$12-$20	557
7 / p. 530		Off the Grill	◇	$4-$9(L)	558
8 / p. 530		Lil Anthony's Pizzeria	◇	$2-$15(L)	557
9 / p. 530		Golden Carrot	◇◇	$4-$13(L)	557
10 / p. 530		Diana's Cafe	◇	$4-$10(L)	557
11 / p. 530		Granny Feelgoods	◇◇	$9-$14(L)	557
12 / p. 530		Caciques Corner	◇	$6-$14(L)	556
13 / p. 530		La Loggia Ristorante	◇◇◇	$12-$18	557
14 / p. 530		Rigattis Cafe	◇	$5-$10	558
15 / p. 530		Hanami Sushi	◇	$4-$10	557
16 / p. 530		Camila's	◇	$8	556
17 / p. 530		Giovana Caffe	◇	$5-$12(L)	557
18 / p. 530		Riverwalk Cafe	◇◇◇	$8-$20	558
19 / p. 530		Big Fish	◇◇	$12-$25	556
20 / p. 530		Tobacco Road	◇	$7-$10	559
21 / p. 530		Indochine	◇◇	$13-$20	557
22 / p. 530		The River Oyster Bar	◇◇◇	$15-$36	558

Spotter/Map Page Number	OA	DOWNTOWN MIAMI - Restaurants (continued)	Diamond Rating	Rate Range High Season	Listing Page
㉓ / p. 530	AAA	**Azul**	▽▽▽▽▽	$26-$37	556
㉔ / p. 530	AAA	**Cafe Sambal at Mandarin Oriental, Miami**	▽▽▽▽	$10-$32	556
㉕ / p. 530		Chicken Kitchen	▽	$4-$15	556
㉖ / p. 530		Sushi Siam Restaurant	▽▽	$8-$24	559
㉗ / p. 530		Porcao	▽▽▽	$15-$40	558
㉘ / p. 530		Perricone's Marketplace & Cafe	▽▽	$14-$27	558
㉙ / p. 530		Provence Grill	▽▽	$10-$21	558
㉚ / p. 530		Isabela's	▽▽▽	$17-$25	557
㉛ / p. 530		Gordon Biersch Brewery Restaurant	▽▽▽	$10-$25	557
㉜ / p. 530		Morton's of Chicago The Steakhouse	▽▽▽	$22-$39	558
㉝ / p. 530		Tutto Pasta Ristorante	▽▽	$15-$24	559
㉞ / p. 530		Atrio	▽▽▽	$15-$30	556
㉟ / p. 530		Deli Lane Cafe	▽▽	$5-$13	556
㊱ / p. 530		ACQUA	▽▽▽▽	$13-$30	556

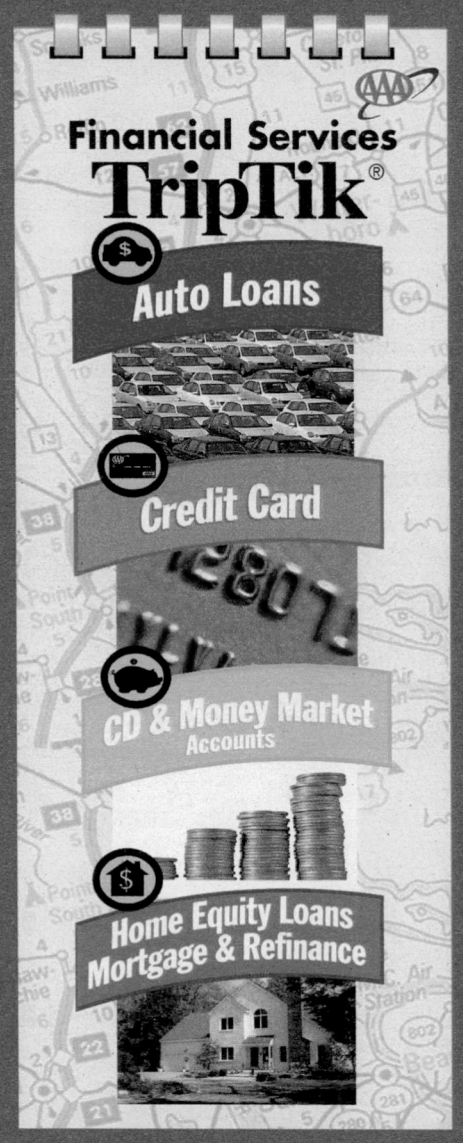

Smart Financial Decisions Start with AAA

With so many financial products on the market today, it's hard to know which way to go. AAA can help.

From vehicle financing and home mortgages, to credit cards and money market accounts, let AAA help map your way to a promising financial future.

Visit aaa.com for complete details and to apply.

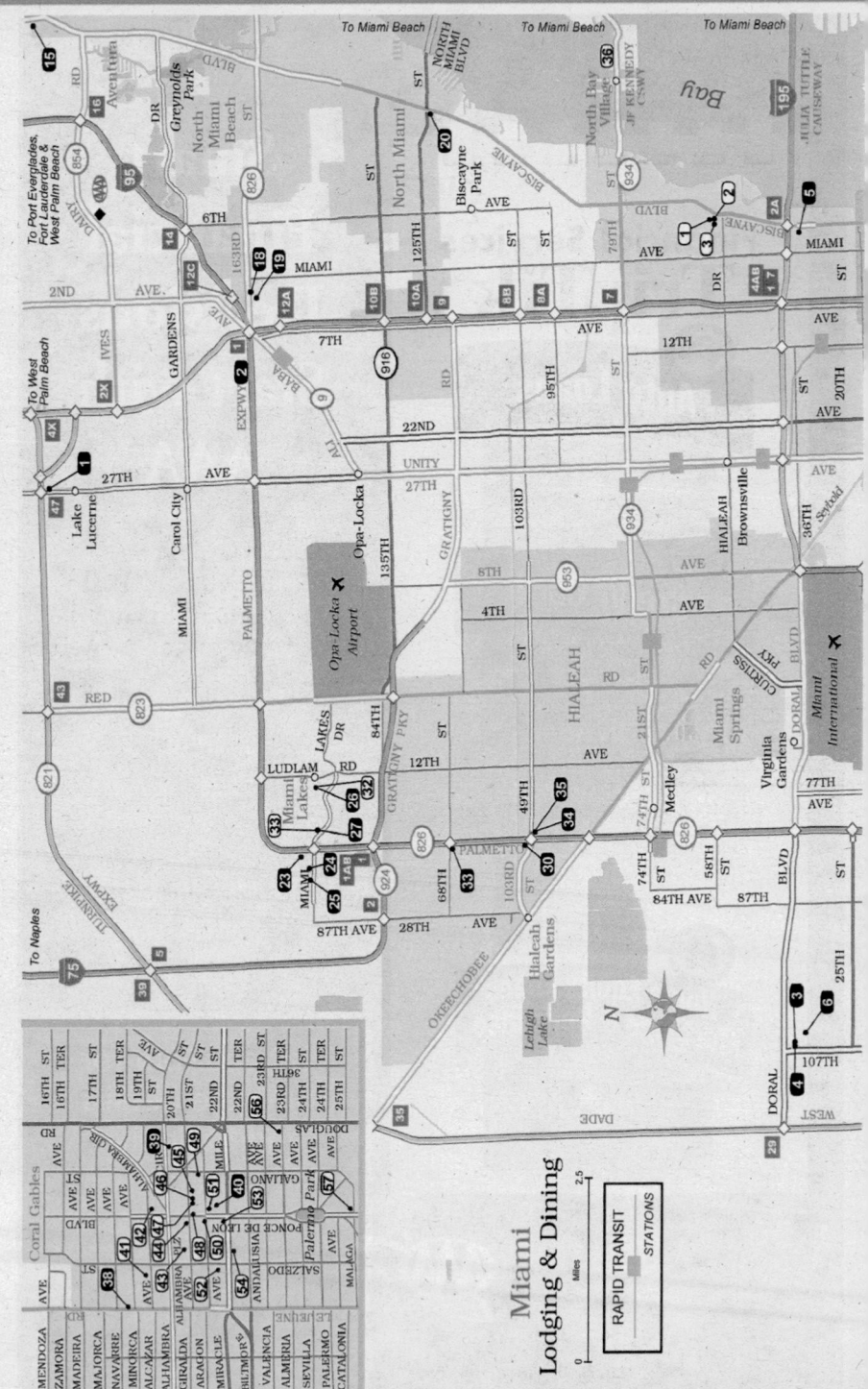

Miami
Lodging & Dining

RAPID TRANSIT
STATIONS

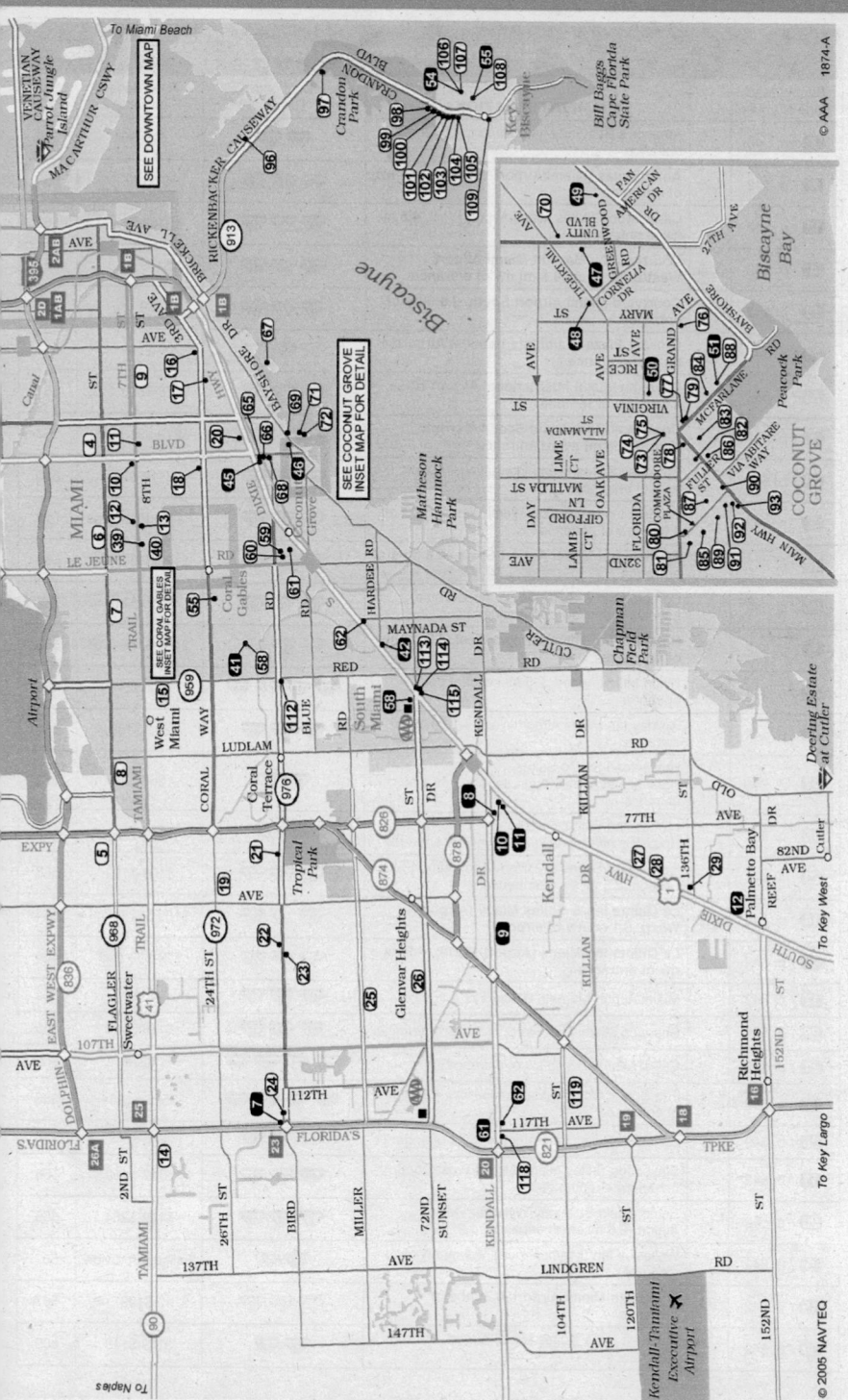

✈ Airport Accommodations

Spotter/Map Page Number	OA	MIAMI INTERNATIONAL	Diamond Rating	Rate Range High Season	Listing Page
7 / p. 542		America's Best Inn-Miami Airport, 4.5 mi nw of entrance	◆◆	$79-$99	559
8 / p. 542	AAA	AmeriSuites (Miami/Airport West), 4.9 mi nw of entrance	◆◆◆	$99-$139 SAVE	559
13 / p. 542		Candlewood Suites Miami Airport West, 4.5 mi nw of entrance	◆◆◆	$109-$129	560
4 / p. 542	AAA	Courtyard by Marriott-Miami Airport West/Doral Area, 4.8 mi nw of entrance	◆◆◆	$189 SAVE	561
18 / p. 542	AAA	Courtyard Miami Airport South, 0.8 mi s of entrance	◆◆◆	$169 SAVE	561
24 / p. 542	AAA	Crowne Plaza Miami International Airport, 1 mi s of entrance	◆◆◆	$209-$259 SAVE	561
25 / p. 542	AAA	Days Inn Miami International Airport Hotel, 4.3 mi sw of terminal	◆◆◆	$125-$500 SAVE	561
1 / p. 542	AAA	Doral Golf Resort and Spa, A Marriott Resort, 4.8 mi nw of entrance	◆◆◆◆	$219-$319 SAVE	562
33 / p. 542		Embassy Suites Miami International Airport, 0.8 mi n of entrance	◆◆◆	$119-$229	610
3 / p. 542		Fairfield Inn by Marriott-Miami West/Doral Area, 4.8 mi nw of entrance	◆◆◆	Failed to provide	562
16 / p. 542	AAA	Fairfield Inn Miami Airport South, 0.8 mi s of entrance	◆◆◆	$129-$159 SAVE	562
26 / p. 542		Hampton Inn & Suites-Miami Airport/Blue Lagoon, 2.5 mi sw of entrance	◆◆◆	$119-$219	562
9 / p. 542	AAA	Hampton Inn-Miami Airport West, 4.8 mi nw of entrance	◆◆◆	$129-$179 SAVE	563
22 / p. 542		Hilton Miami Airport, 2.5 mi sw of airport entrance	◆◆◆◆	$89-$249	563
12 / p. 542		Holiday Inn-Miami Airport West, 5.1 mi nw of entrance	◆◆◆	$92-$109	563
27 / p. 542		Homestead Studio Suites Hotel-Miami/Airport/Blue Lagoon, 2 mi s of entrance	◆◆	$64-$94	563
10 / p. 542		Homestead Studio Suites Hotel-Miami/Airport/Doral, 5.1 mi nw entrance	◆◆	$69-$99	563
23 / p. 542		Homewood Suites by Hilton-Miami Airport/Blue Lagoon, 2.5 mi sw of entrance	◆◆◆	$169-$199	563
14 / p. 542	AAA	La Quinta Inn & Suites Miami (Airport West), 5.1 mi nw of airport	◆◆◆	$109-$129 SAVE	564
5 / p. 542	AAA	La Quinta Inn Miami (Airport North), 4.5 mi nw of entrance	◆◆◆	$79-$99 SAVE	564
17 / p. 542		Miami Airport Marriott, 0.8 mi s of entrance	◆◆◆	$134	564
29 / p. 542		Sheraton Miami Mart Hotel, 4 mi sw of terminal	◆◆◆	$149-$229	565
21 / p. 542		Sofitel Miami, 2.5 mi sw of entrance	◆◆◆◆	$279	566
2 / p. 542		The Spa at Doral, A Marriott Resort, 4.8 mi nw of entrance	◆◆◆◆	$529-$1254	566
28 / p. 542		SpringHill Suites by Marriott, 2 mi s of entrance	◆◆◆	$99-$149	566
11 / p. 542		Staybridge Suites Miami-Airport West-Doral, 5.1 mi sw of entrance	◆◆◆	$112-$159	566
20 / p. 542		Summerfield Suites by Wyndham-Miami Airport, 2.5 mi sw of entrance	◆◆◆	$129-$284	566
6 / p. 542		Wellesley Inn (Miami Airport), 4.9 mi nw of entrance	◆◆	Failed to provide	567
15 / p. 542	AAA	Wyndham Miami Airport, 0.3 mi e of entrance	◆◆◆	$149-$199 SAVE	567
39 / p. 542		Baymont Inn & Suites Miami-Airport, 0.8 mi n of entrance	◆◆	$119-$149	609

Spotter/Map Page Number	OA	MIAMI INTERNATIONAL (continued)	Diamond Rating	Rate Range High Season	Listing Page
37 / p. 542	AAA	Comfort Inn & Suites-Miami International Airport, 2 mi nw of entrance	◈◈◈	$129-$259 SAVE	610
35 / p. 542		Days Inn Miami Airport North, 2 mi nw of entrance	◈◈	$65-$139	610
38 / p. 542		Embassy Suites Miami International Airport, 0.8 mi n of entrance	◈◈◈	$119-$229	610
36 / p. 542	AAA	Holiday Inn Express Miami International Airport, 2 mi nw of entrance	◈◈◈	$179-$199 SAVE	611
32 / p. 542	AAA	Holiday Inn-Miami International Airport, 0.5 mi n of entrance	◈◈◈	$139-$199 SAVE	611
34 / p. 542		Homestead Studio Suites Hotel-Miami/Airport/Miami Springs, 2 mi nw of entrance	◈◈◈	$79-$109	611
33 / p. 542	AAA	Sleep Inn-Miami Airport, 2 mi nw of entrance	◈◈	$109-$169 SAVE	611

Miami

This index helps you "spot" where approved accommodations and restaurants are located on the corresponding detailed maps. Lodging rate ranges are for comparison only and show the property's high season; rates are per night, unless only weekly (W) rates are available. Restaurant rate range is for dinner, unless only lunch (L) is served. Turn to the listing page for more detailed rate information and consult display ads for special promotions.

Spotter/Map Page Number	OA	MIAMI - Lodgings	Diamond Rating	Rate Range High Season	Listing Page
1 / p. 534		El Palacio Sports Hotel & Conference Center	◈◈◈	Failed to provide	562
2 / p. 534	AAA	El Palacio Resort Hotel & Suites	◈◈◈	$70-$140 SAVE	562
3 / p. 534	AAA	Best Western Miami Airport West Inn & Suites	◈◈◈	$119-$149 SAVE	560
4 / p. 534		Baymont Inn & Suites Miami Airport West - see color ad p 560	◈◈◈	$85-$105	560
5 / p. 534		Super 8 Motel	◈◈	Failed to provide	566
6 / p. 534		TownePlace Suites by Marriott	◈◈◈	$79-$179	567
7 / p. 534	AAA	Comfort Suites Miami/Kendall	◈◈◈	$109-$189 SAVE	560
8 / p. 534		Ramada Limited South Miami Dadeland	◈◈◈	$109-$155	565
9 / p. 534		Radisson Kendall Hotel & Suites Miami	◈◈◈	$179-$469	565
10 / p. 534		Courtyard by Marriott, Miami Dadeland	◈◈◈	$189-$239	561
11 / p. 534	AAA	Miami Marriott Dadeland	◈◈◈◈	$219-$249 SAVE	564
12 / p. 534	AAA	Quality Inn-South at The Falls - see color ad p 565	◈◈◈	$99-$119 SAVE	565
		MIAMI - Restaurants			
1 / p. 534		Sushi Siam Morningside	◈◈	$4-$26	570
2 / p. 534		Andiamo! Brick Oven Pizza	◈	$8-$19	567
3 / p. 534		Soyka	◈◈◈	$9-$23	570
4 / p. 534		Islas Canarias Restaurant	◈	$5-$19	568
5 / p. 534		La Casita	◈◈	$12-$18	569
6 / p. 534		"Fico" Key West Seafood	◈	$9-$21	568
7 / p. 534		Las Culebrinas	◈◈	$9-$25	569
8 / p. 534		Palomilla Grill	◈◈	$6-$20	569
9 / p. 534		Casa Panza	◈◈	$7-$18	568
10 / p. 534		Ayestaran Restaurant	◈	$3-$19	567
11 / p. 534		Casa Juancho Restaurant	◈◈	$16-$38	568

Spotter/Map Page Number	OA	MIAMI - Restaurants (continued)	Diamond Rating	Rate Range High Season	Listing Page
⑫ / p. 534		Versailles	◆	$9-$22	570
⑬ / p. 534		La Carreta Restaurant	◆◆	$6-$20	569
⑭ / p. 534		Cami's Seafood & Pasta	◆	$5-$17	567
⑮ / p. 534		Old San Juan	◆◆	$12-$30	569
⑯ / p. 534		Zuperpollo Restaurante Internacional	◆◆	$6-$26	570
⑰ / p. 534		Old Lisbon Restaurant & Bar	◆◆	$13-$20	569
⑱ / p. 534		El Farolito	◆◆◆	$9-$23	568
⑲ / p. 534		Lila's Restaurant	◆◆	$6-$13	569
⑳ / p. 534		The Original Daily Bread Marketplace	◆	$5-$9	569
㉑ / p. 534		Tropical Chinese Restaurant	◆◆◆	$10-$45	570
㉒ / p. 534		Graziano's Parilla Argentina	◆◆◆	$12-$35	568
㉓ / p. 534		Sergio's	◆	$7-$10	570
㉔ / p. 534		Shorty's Bar-B-Q	◆	$5-$14	570
㉕ / p. 534	AAA	**The Fish House**	◆◆	$10-$20	568
㉖ / p. 534		Scully's Tavern	◆◆	$8-$15	569
㉗ / p. 534		Tani Thai Restaurant	◆◆	$8-$23	570
㉘ / p. 534		Anacapri	◆◆	$11-$22	567
㉙ / p. 534		Fleming: A Taste of Denmark	◆◆◆	$12-$26	568
		HALLANDALE BEACH - Lodgings			
⓯ / p. 534	AAA	**Hampton Inn - Hallandale/Aventura - see color ad p 404**	◆◆◆	$119-$169 SAVE	405
		NORTH MIAMI - Lodgings			
⓲ / p. 534	AAA	**Holiday Inn North Miami Golden Glades**	◆◆◆	$129-$159 SAVE	613
⓳ / p. 534		Golden Glades Inn & Conference Center	◆◆◆	$89-$119	613
⓴ / p. 534		Best Western Windsor Inn	◆◆◆	$90-$189	613
		MIAMI LAKES - Lodgings			
㉓ / p. 534	AAA	**Courtyard by Marriott-Miami Lakes**	◆◆◆	$139-$209 SAVE	608
㉔ / p. 534	AAA	**Wellesley Inn (Miami Lakes)**	◆◆	$139-$169 SAVE	609
㉕ / p. 534		TownePlace Suites by Marriott	◆◆◆	$124-$144	609
㉖ / p. 534		Don Shula's Hotel	◆◆◆	$179-$209	609
㉗ / p. 534		Don Shula's Golf Club	◆◆◆	$159-$165	608
		MIAMI LAKES - Restaurants			
㉜ / p. 534		Shula's Steak 2	◆◆	$6-$30	609
㉝ / p. 534		Shula's Steakhouse	◆◆◆	$18-$50	609
		HIALEAH GARDENS - Lodgings			
㉚ / p. 534	AAA	**Howard Johnson Plaza Hotel & Conference Center-Miami Airport**	◆◆◆	$109-$199 SAVE	605
		HIALEAH - Lodgings			
㉝ / p. 534	AAA	**Holiday Inn Express Hotel & Suites**	◆◆◆	$69-$129 SAVE	605
㉞ / p. 534	AAA	**Ramada Inn-Miami Airport North**	◆◆	$99-$119 SAVE	605
㉟ / p. 534	AAA	**Days Inn Miami Lakes/Westland Mall**	◆◆	$84-$94 SAVE	604

Spotter/Map Page Number	OA	**CORAL GABLES** - Lodgings	Diamond Rating	Rate Range High Season	Listing Page
38 / p. 534		Holiday Inn Coral Gables Business District - see color ad p 599	◈◈◈	$139-$149	599
39 / p. 534	AAA	**Hyatt Regency Coral Gables**	◈◈◈◈	$159-$325 SAVE	600
40 / p. 534		Omni Colonnade Hotel	◈◈◈◈	$199-$359	600
41 / p. 534		The Biltmore Hotel Coral Gables	◈◈◈◈	$306-$369	599
42 / p. 534		Holiday Inn University of Miami	◈◈◈	$109-$189	599
		CORAL GABLES - Restaurants			
39 / p. 534		Caffe Italia	◈◈	$7-$14	600
40 / p. 534		Mylos Restaurant & Bar	◈◈	$10-$25	601
41 / p. 534		Francesco Restaurant	◈◈	$15-$26	600
42 / p. 534		Restaurant St. Michel	◈◈	$15-$33	602
43 / p. 534		Tambo Restaurant & Lounge	◈◈◈	$25-$34	602
44 / p. 534		La Provence French Bakery Gourmet Deli & Cafe	◈	$4-$9	601
45 / p. 534		Miss Saigon Bistro	◈◈	$15-$29	601
46 / p. 534		Puchetta Restaurant	◈◈◈	$11-$25	602
47 / p. 534		Archie's Gourmet Pizza	◈◈	$8-$12	600
48 / p. 534		Spris	◈◈	$7-$15	602
49 / p. 534		Gables Diner	◈◈	$9-$22	601
50 / p. 534		Sushi Maki	◈◈	$8-$18	602
51 / p. 534		Tula	◈◈◈	$13-$27	602
52 / p. 534		Caffe Abbracci	◈◈◈◈	$14-$28	600
53 / p. 534		Houston's	◈◈	$9-$34	601
54 / p. 534		Ortanique on the Mile	◈◈◈	$15-$32	601
55 / p. 534		Carmen the Restaurant	◈◈◈	$22-$43	600
56 / p. 534		NORMAN'S	◈◈◈	$26-$39	601
57 / p. 534		Christy's	◈◈◈	$18-$35	600
58 / p. 534		Palme d'Or	◈◈◈	$20-$40	601
59 / p. 534		Chispa	◈◈◈	$17-$34	600
61 / p. 534		The Palm Restaurant	◈◈◈	$18-$66	601
62 / p. 534		Moon	◈◈	$8-$30	601
		COCONUT GROVE - Lodgings			
45 / p. 534		Hampton Inn-Coconut Grove/Coral Gables	◈◈◈	Failed to provide	595
46 / p. 534		The Doubletree Hotel at Coconut Grove	◈◈◈	Failed to provide	595
47 / p. 534	AAA	**The Ritz-Carlton Coconut Grove, Miami**	◈◈◈◈◈	$299-$459 SAVE	595
48 / p. 534		Residence Inn by Marriott	◈◈◈	$172-$229	595
49 / p. 534	AAA	**Wyndham Grand Bay-Coconut Grove**	◈◈◈◈	$229-$239 SAVE	596
50 / p. 534	AAA	**Mayfair Hotel & Spa** - see color ad p 595	◈◈◈◈	$209-$389 SAVE	595
51 / p. 534		Sonesta Hotel & Suites Coconut Grove	◈◈◈	$159-$1039	596
		COCONUT GROVE - Restaurants			
65 / p. 534		Berries at the Grove	◈◈	$7-$22	596
66 / p. 534		Las Culebrinas in the Grove Restaurant	◈◈	$8-$28	597

Spotter/Map Page Number	OA	COCONUT GROVE - Restaurants (continued)	Diamond Rating	Rate Range High Season	Listing Page
67 / p. 534		Baleen	◆◆◆	$19-$40	596
68 / p. 534		Flanigan's	◆◆	$7-$23	597
69 / p. 534		Monty's Raw Bar	◆◆	$10-$19	598
70 / p. 534		Bizcaya	◆◆◆◆	$18-$35	596
71 / p. 534		Chart House	◆◆◆	$19-$40	596
72 / p. 534		Scotty's Landing	◆	$7-$24	598
73 / p. 534		Cafe' Tu Tu Tango	◆◆	$5-$9	596
74 / p. 534		Cafe Med	◆◆	$7-$23	596
75 / p. 534		The Cheesecake Factory	◆◆	$7-$26	597
76 / p. 534		Mezzanotte In The Grove	◆◆	$15-$26	597
77 / p. 534		Johnny Rockets	◆	$4-$12	597
78 / p. 534		Sandbar Grill	◆	$8-$13	598
79 / p. 534		New York Roma Pizza & Pasta	◆	$2-$7	598
80 / p. 534		Anokha Fine Indian Cuisine	◆◆	$11-$31	596
81 / p. 534		Red Lantern Chinese Restaurant	◆◆	$10-$28	598
82 / p. 534		Le Bouchon du Grove	◆◆	$18-$26	597
83 / p. 534		Cozzolis Pizza Cafe	◆	$3-$22	597
84 / p. 534		Oasis Internet Cafe	◆	$4-$10	598
85 / p. 534		Don Quixote	◆◆◆	$13-$20	597
86 / p. 534		Le Moulin du Grove	◆◆◆	$9-$16	597
87 / p. 534		Mr. Moe's	◆◆	$7-$22	598
88 / p. 534		Tara Steak & Lobster House	◆◆	$21-$51	598
89 / p. 534		Feelings Cafe	◆◆	$7-$15	597
90 / p. 534		Mambo Cafe	◆◆	$10-$18	597
91 / p. 534		Green Street Cafe	◆◆◆	$10-$18	597
92 / p. 534		Senor Frog's	◆◆	$12-$18	598
93 / p. 534		Tuscany Cafe	◆◆	$10-$20	598
		KEY BISCAYNE - Lodgings			
54 / p. 534		Sonesta Beach Resort Key Biscayne - see color ad p 541	◆◆◆◆	$239-$459	607
55 / p. 534		The Ritz-Carlton, Key Biscayne	◆◆◆◆◆	$429-$1599	607
		KEY BISCAYNE - Restaurants			
96 / p. 534	AAA	**Rusty Pelican**	◆◆◆	$16-$30	608
97 / p. 534		Sundays on the Bay	◆◆	$10-$20	608
98 / p. 534		La Carreta	◆	$14-$25	607
99 / p. 534		The Oasis	◆	$3-$10	608
100 / p. 534		Ad Gustum	◆	$6-$12	607
101 / p. 534		Le Croisic	◆◆◆	$15-$25	607
102 / p. 534		La Piazetta	◆◆	$12-$20	607
103 / p. 534		Linda B Steak House	◆◆◆	$17-$30	608
104 / p. 534		Chief's Seafood Market & Sushi Bar	◆	$15-$28	607

Spotter/Map Page Number	OA	**KEY BISCAYNE** - Restaurants (continued)	Diamond Rating	Rate Range High Season	Listing Page
⑩⑤ / p. 534		Tango Grill	◇◇	$12-$23	608
⑩⑥ / p. 534		Purple Dolphin	◇◇◇◇	$21-$28	608
⑩⑦ / p. 534		Two Dragons Restaurant	◇◇◇	$14-$25	608
⑩⑧ / p. 534		Cioppino	◇◇◇◇	$27-$43	607
⑩⑨ / p. 534		Sushi Siam	◇◇	$22-$35	608
		SOUTH MIAMI - Lodgings			
⑤⑧ / p. 534	◬	**Best Western South Miami** - see color ad p 614	◇◇◇	$130-$149 SAVE	614
		SOUTH MIAMI - Restaurants			
⑪② / p. 534		Picnic's at Allen's Drugs	◇	$7-$8	614
⑪③ / p. 534	◬	**Trattoria Sole**	◇◇◇	$11-$23	614
⑪④ / p. 534		Blu - La Pizzeria del Sole	◇◇◇	$8-$14	614
⑪⑤ / p. 534		Khoury's	◇◇	$11-$23	614
		KENDALL - Lodgings			
⑥① / p. 534	◬	**Wellesley Inn (Miami/Kendall)**	◇◇	$116-$146 SAVE	606
⑥② / p. 534	◬	**AmeriSuites (Miami/Kendall)**	◇◇◇	$129-$189 SAVE	606
		KENDALL - Restaurants			
⑪⑧ / p. 534		La Carreta	◇◇	$6-$22	606
⑪⑨ / p. 534		Gil Capa's Bistro	◇◇	$8-$16	606
		NORTH BAY VILLAGE - Restaurant			
㊱ / p. 534		The Crab House Seafood Restaurant	◇◇	$12-$39	613

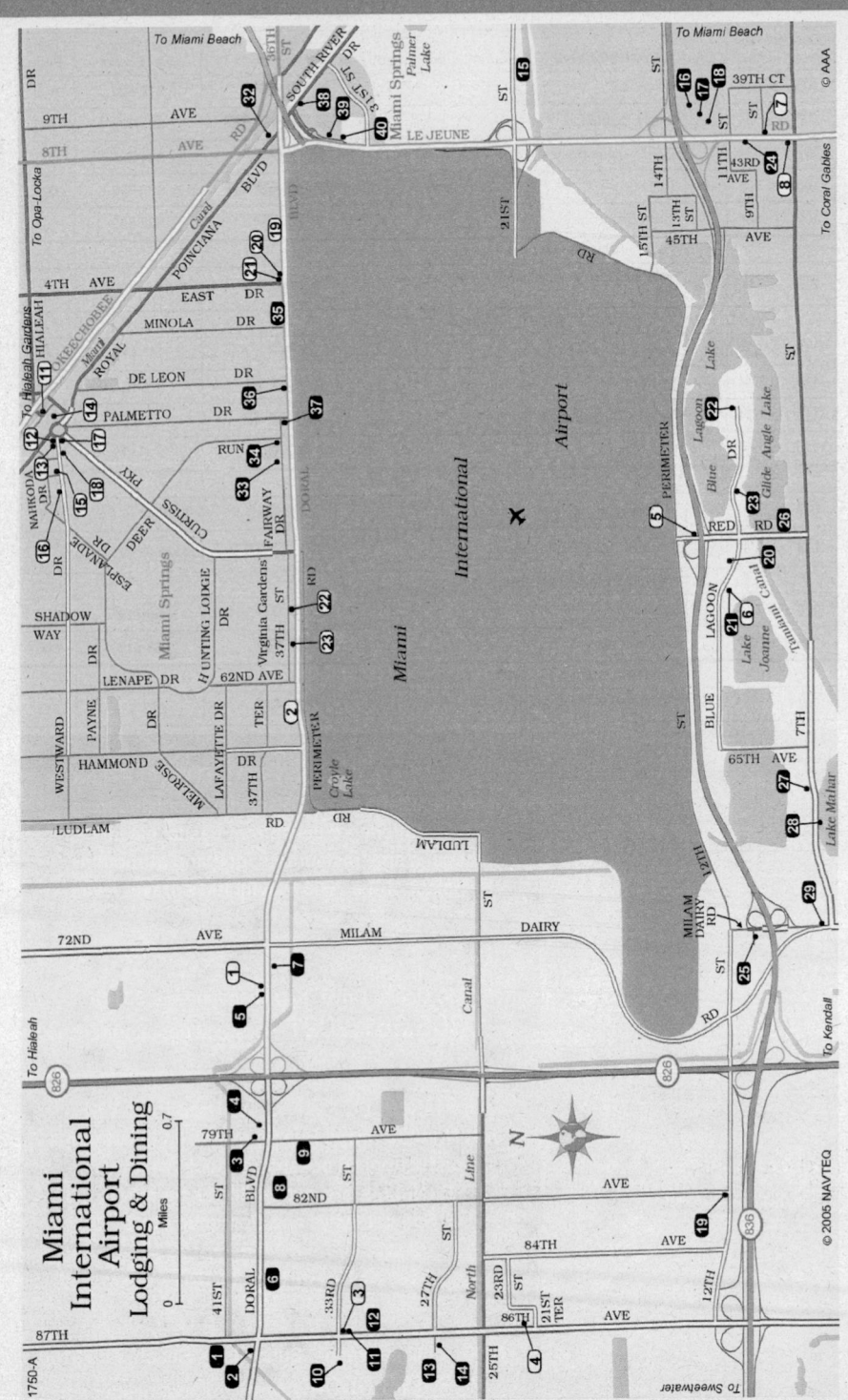

Miami
International
Airport
Lodging & Dining

Miami International Airport

This index helps you "spot" where approved accommodations and restaurants are located on the corresponding detailed maps. Lodging rate ranges are for comparison only and show the property's high season; rates are per night, unless only weekly (W) rates are available. Restaurant rate range is for dinner, unless only lunch (L) is served. Turn to the listing page for more detailed rate information and consult display ads for special promotions.

Spotter/Map Page Number	OA	MIAMI - Lodgings	Diamond Rating	Rate Range High Season	Listing Page
1 / p. 542	AAA	Doral Golf Resort and Spa, A Marriott Resort	◈◈◈◈	$219-$319 SAVE	562
2 / p. 542		The Spa at Doral, A Marriott Resort	◈◈◈◈	$529-$1254	566
3 / p. 542		Fairfield Inn by Marriott-Miami West/Doral Area	◈◈◈	Failed to provide	562
4 / p. 542	AAA	Courtyard by Marriott-Miami Airport West/Doral Area	◈◈◈	$189 SAVE	561
5 / p. 542	AAA	La Quinta Inn Miami (Airport North)	◈◈◈	$79-$99 SAVE	564
6 / p. 542		Wellesley Inn (Miami Airport)	◈◈	Failed to provide	567
7 / p. 542		America's Best Inn-Miami Airport	◈◈	$79-$99	559
8 / p. 542	AAA	AmeriSuites (Miami/Airport West)	◈◈	$99-$139 SAVE	559
9 / p. 542	AAA	Hampton Inn-Miami Airport West	◈◈	$129-$179 SAVE	563
10 / p. 542		Homestead Studio Suites Hotel-Miami/Airport/Doral	◈◈	$69-$99	563
11 / p. 542		Staybridge Suites Miami-Airport West-Doral	◈◈◈	$112-$159	566
12 / p. 542		Holiday Inn-Miami Airport West	◈◈	$92-$109	563
13 / p. 542		Candlewood Suites Miami Airport West	◈◈◈	$109-$129	560
14 / p. 542	AAA	La Quinta Inn & Suites Miami (Airport West)	◈◈◈	$109-$129 SAVE	564
15 / p. 542	AAA	Wyndham Miami Airport	◈◈◈	$149-$199 SAVE	567
16 / p. 542	AAA	Fairfield Inn Miami Airport South	◈◈◈	$129-$159 SAVE	562
17 / p. 542		Miami Airport Marriott	◈◈◈	$134	564
18 / p. 542	AAA	Courtyard Miami Airport South	◈◈◈	$169 SAVE	561
19 / p. 542		Residence Inn by Marriott	◈◈◈	$99-$189	565
20 / p. 542		Summerfield Suites by Wyndham-Miami Airport	◈◈◈	$129-$284	566
21 / p. 542		Sofitel Miami	◈◈◈◈	$279	566
22 / p. 542		Hilton Miami Airport	◈◈◈◈	$89-$249	563
23 / p. 542		Homewood Suites by Hilton-Miami Airport/Blue Lagoon	◈◈◈	$169-$199	563
24 / p. 542	AAA	Crowne Plaza Miami International Airport	◈◈◈	$209-$259 SAVE	561
25 / p. 542	AAA	Days Inn Miami International Airport Hotel	◈◈◈	$125-$500 SAVE	561
26 / p. 542		Hampton Inn & Suites-Miami Airport/Blue Lagoon	◈◈◈	$119-$219	562
27 / p. 542		Homestead Studio Suites Hotel-Miami/Airport/Blue Lagoon	◈◈	$64-$94	563
28 / p. 542		SpringHill Suites by Marriott	◈◈◈	$99-$149	566
29 / p. 542		Sheraton Miami Mart Hotel	◈◈◈	$149-$229	565
		MIAMI - Restaurants			
1 / p. 542		El Tropico	◈	$8-$14	568
2 / p. 542		Apo's Cafe	◈◈	$7-$14	567
3 / p. 542		Doral Ale House	◈	$8-$15	568
4 / p. 542		Shorty's Bar-B-Q	◈◈	$5-$14	570
5 / p. 542		94th Aero Squadron	◈◈	$13-$45	567

Spotter/Map Page Number	OA	**MIAMI** - Restaurants (continued)	Diamond Rating	Rate Range High Season	Listing Page
6 / p. 542		La Riviera Restaurant	◆◆◆	$9-$30	569
7 / p. 542		Latin Cafe 2000	◆◆	$7-$16	569
8 / p. 542		Hereford Grill	◆◆◆	$15-$44	568
		MIAMI SPRINGS - Lodgings			
32 / p. 542	AAA	Holiday Inn-Miami International Airport - see color ad p 610	◆◆◆	$139-$199 [SAVE]	611
33 / p. 542	AAA	Sleep Inn-Miami Airport - see color ad p 552	◆◆	$109-$169 [SAVE]	611
34 / p. 542		Homestead Studio Suites Hotel-Miami/Airport/Miami Springs	◆◆◆	$79-$109	611
35 / p. 542		Days Inn Miami Airport North	◆◆	$65-$139	610
36 / p. 542	AAA	Holiday Inn Express Miami International Airport - see color ad p 553	◆◆◆	$179-$199 [SAVE]	611
37 / p. 542	AAA	Comfort Inn & Suites-Miami International Airport - see color ad p 552	◆◆◆	$129-$259 [SAVE]	610
38 / p. 542		Embassy Suites Miami International Airport	◆◆◆	$119-$229	610
39 / p. 542		Baymont Inn & Suites Miami-Airport - see color ad p 560	◆◆	$119-$149	609
40 / p. 542		Red Roof Inn Miami Airport	◆◆◆	$80-$100	611
		MIAMI SPRINGS - Restaurants			
11 / p. 542		Holleman's	◆◆	$12-$26	612
12 / p. 542		Bangkok Sushi	◆◆	$8-$17	611
13 / p. 542		Garden Restaurant	◆◆	$7-$15	612
14 / p. 542		Thai Rama Sushi	◆◆	$8-$15	612
15 / p. 542		Westward Cafe	◆	$3-$8(L)	612
16 / p. 542		Treats Cafe	◆◆	$8-$12	612
17 / p. 542		Harvest Moon Bistro	◆	$4-$7(L)	612
18 / p. 542		Cozy Corner	◆	$6-$9	612
19 / p. 542		Thai Palace	◆◆	$9-$17	612
20 / p. 542		Peru Place	◆◆	$6-$12	612
21 / p. 542		Patio Tipico	◆	$3-$25	612
22 / p. 542		Basilico	◆◆	$10-$15	611
23 / p. 542		Cisco's Cafe	◆◆	$8-$16	612

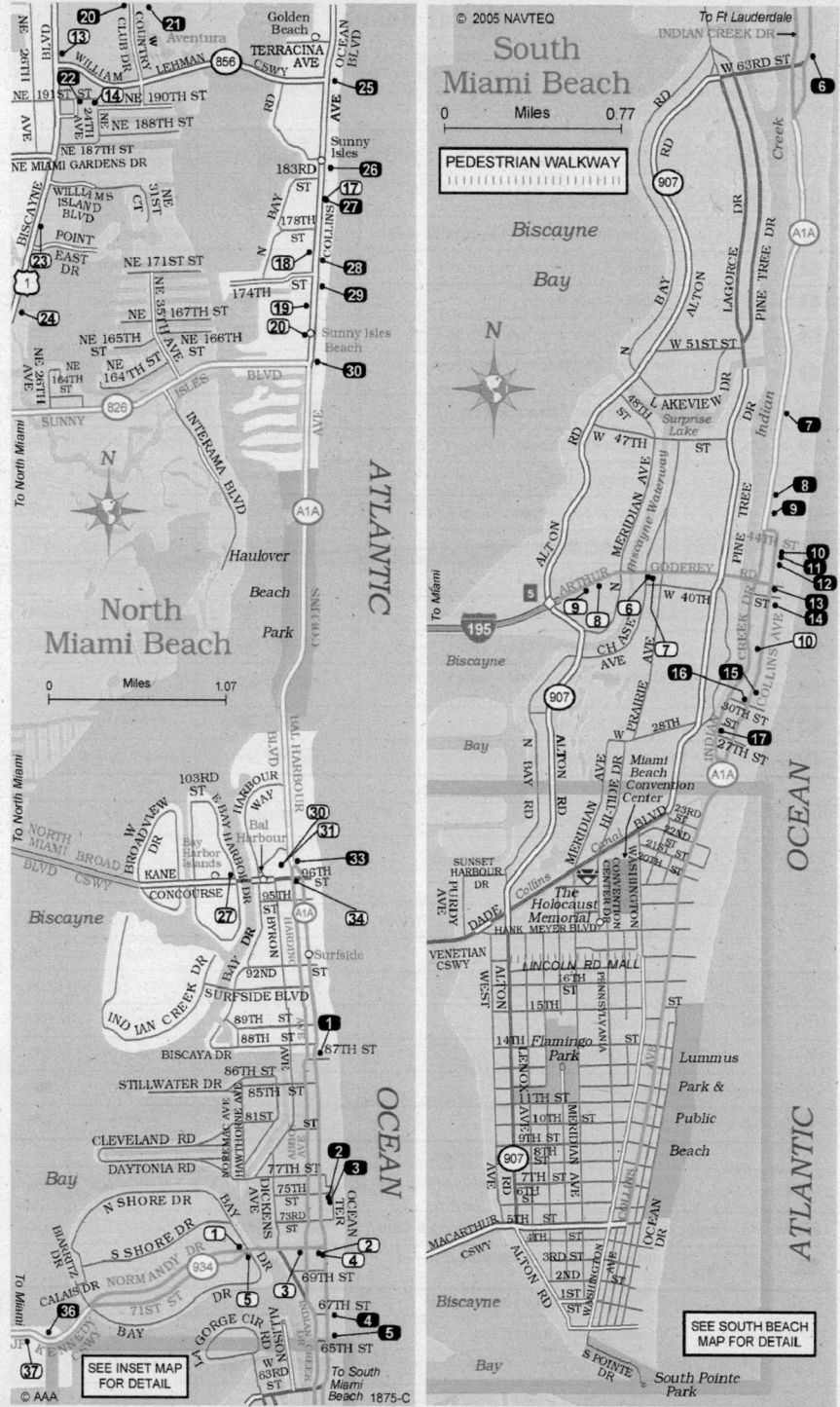

Miami Beach

This index helps you "spot" where approved accommodations and restaurants are located on the corresponding detailed maps. Lodging rate ranges are for comparison only and show the property's high season; rates are per night, unless only weekly (W) rates are available. Restaurant rate range is for dinner, unless only lunch (L) is served. Turn to the listing page for more detailed rate information and consult display ads for special promotions.

Spotter/Map Page Number	OA	MIAMI BEACH - Lodgings	Diamond Rating	Rate Range High Season	Listing Page
1 / p. 545	AAA	Howard Johnson Plaza Dezerland Beach & Spa - see color ad p 577	◈◈◈	$119-$169 SAVE	577
2 / p. 545	AAA	Days Inn North Beach - see color ad p 574	◈◈	$109-$259 SAVE	574
3 / p. 545		Ocean Surf Hotel - see color ad p 581	◈◈	$100-$200	581
4 / p. 545		Deauville Beach Resort	◈◈◈	Failed to provide	575
5 / p. 545		Mimosa Hotel & Spa - see color ad p 580	◈◈◈	Failed to provide	579
6 / p. 545	AAA	The New Casablanca On the Ocean - see color ad p 580	◈◈◈	$159-$199 SAVE	580
7 / p. 545	AAA	Wyndham Miami Beach Resort	◈◈◈	$259 SAVE	585
8 / p. 545	AAA	Eden Roc, A Renaissance Resort & Spa	◈◈◈	$159-$424 SAVE	575
9 / p. 545	AAA	Fontainebleau Resort	◈◈◈	$199-$1200 SAVE	575
10 / p. 545	AAA	Four Points by Sheraton Miami Beach	◈◈◈	$219-$319 SAVE	576
11 / p. 545	AAA	Best Western Beach Resort	◈◈◈	$159-$239 SAVE	571
12 / p. 545	AAA	Days Inn Oceanside	◈◈	$149-$229 SAVE	574
13 / p. 545	AAA	Fairfield Inn & Suites, Miami Beach	◈◈◈	$169-$249 SAVE	575
14 / p. 545		Courtyard by Marriott-Miami Beach Oceanfront	◈◈◈	$119-$299	573
15 / p. 545	AAA	RIU Florida Beach Hotel - see color ad p 582	◈◈◈	$185-$235 SAVE	582
16 / p. 545		Villa Capri All Suites Hotel	◈◈◈	$195-$415	584
17 / p. 545		The Indian Creek Hotel	◈◈◈	Failed to provide	577
		MIAMI BEACH - Restaurants			
1 / p. 545		Las Vacas Gordas	◈◈	$10-$17	588
2 / p. 545		Gil's Cafe	◈◈	$9-$25	587
3 / p. 545		Cafe Prima Pasta	◈◈◈	$14-$31	586
4 / p. 545		Sapori Di Roma Ristorante Italiano & Pizzeria	◈◈	$9-$20	591
5 / p. 545		Lemon Twist	◈◈◈	$9-$18	588
6 / p. 545		Cafe Avante Ristorante Italiano	◈◈◈	$14-$31	586
7 / p. 545		Crystal Cafe	◈◈◈◈	$13-$28	587
8 / p. 545		Yeung's Chinese	◈◈	$8-$40	592
9 / p. 545		Oasis Cafe	◈◈	$6-$10	589
10 / p. 545		La Spiaggia Ristorante	◈◈	$7-$18	588
		AVENTURA - Lodgings			
20 / p. 545		Residence Inn by Marriott-Aventura Mall - see color ad p 593	◈◈◈	$119-$409	594
21 / p. 545	AAA	The Fairmont Turnberry Isle Resort & Club	◈◈◈◈	$350-$4200 SAVE	593
22 / p. 545	AAA	Courtyard by Marriott Aventura Mall - see color ad p 593	◈◈◈	$152-$169 SAVE	593
		AVENTURA - Restaurants			
13 / p. 545		The Bamboo Club Asian Bistro	◈◈	$9-$19	594
14 / p. 545		Chef Allen's	◈◈◈◈	$26-$38	594

Spotter/Map Page Number	OA	SUNNY ISLES BEACH - Lodgings	Diamond Rating	Rate Range High Season	Listing Page
25 / p. 545		Marco Polo Beach Resort, A Ramada Plaza	◆◆◆	$129-$299	616
26 / p. 545	AAA	**Best Western Thunderbird Beach Resort**	◆◆	$109-$129 [SAVE]	615
27 / p. 545	AAA	**Trump International Sonesta Beach Resort**	◆◆◆◆	$325-$850 [SAVE]	616
28 / p. 545	AAA	**Travelodge Monaco Oceanfront Resort**	◆	$109-$129 [SAVE]	616
29 / p. 545		DoubleTree Ocean Point Resort & Spa-Miami Beach North	◆◆◆	$189-$479	615
30 / p. 545	AAA	**Newport Beachside Hotel & Resort**	◆◆◆	$139-$325 [SAVE]	616
		SUNNY ISLES BEACH - Restaurants			
17 / p. 545	AAA	**Neomi's Grill**	◆◆◆	$8-$30	616
18 / p. 545		Timo	◆◆◆	$12-$26	617
19 / p. 545		Jerry's Famous Deli	◆	$6-$36	616
20 / p. 545		Emerald Coast	◆◆	$14-$18	616
		BAL HARBOUR - Lodgings			
33 / p. 545	AAA	**Sheraton Bal Harbour Beach Resort - see color ad p 8**	◆◆◆	$399-$499 [SAVE]	594
		BAL HARBOUR - Restaurants			
30 / p. 545		Carpaccio	◆◆	$14-$21	594
31 / p. 545	AAA	**Bal Harbour Bistro**	◆◆	$9-$25	594
		NORTH BAY VILLAGE - Lodgings			
36 / p. 545	AAA	**Best Western on the Bay Inn & Marina - see color ad p 572**	◆◆	$74-$114 [SAVE]	613
		NORTH BAY VILLAGE - Restaurant			
37 / p. 545		Oggi Caffe Ristorante Italiano	◆◆◆	$14-$36	613
		NORTH MIAMI BEACH - Restaurants			
23 / p. 545		Fuddruckers World's Greatest Hamburger	◆	$5-$13	613
24 / p. 545		Tuna's Waterfront Grille	◆◆	$15-$28	614
		BAY HARBOR ISLANDS - Restaurant			
27 / p. 545	AAA	**Caffe DaVinci**	◆◆◆	$13-$30	594
		SURFSIDE - Restaurant			
34 / p. 545		Sushi Republic	◆◆	$5-$21	617

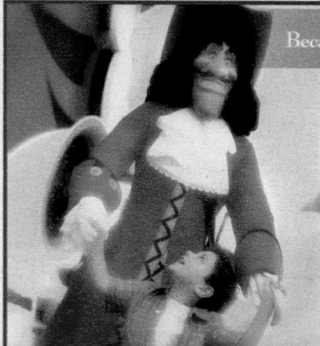

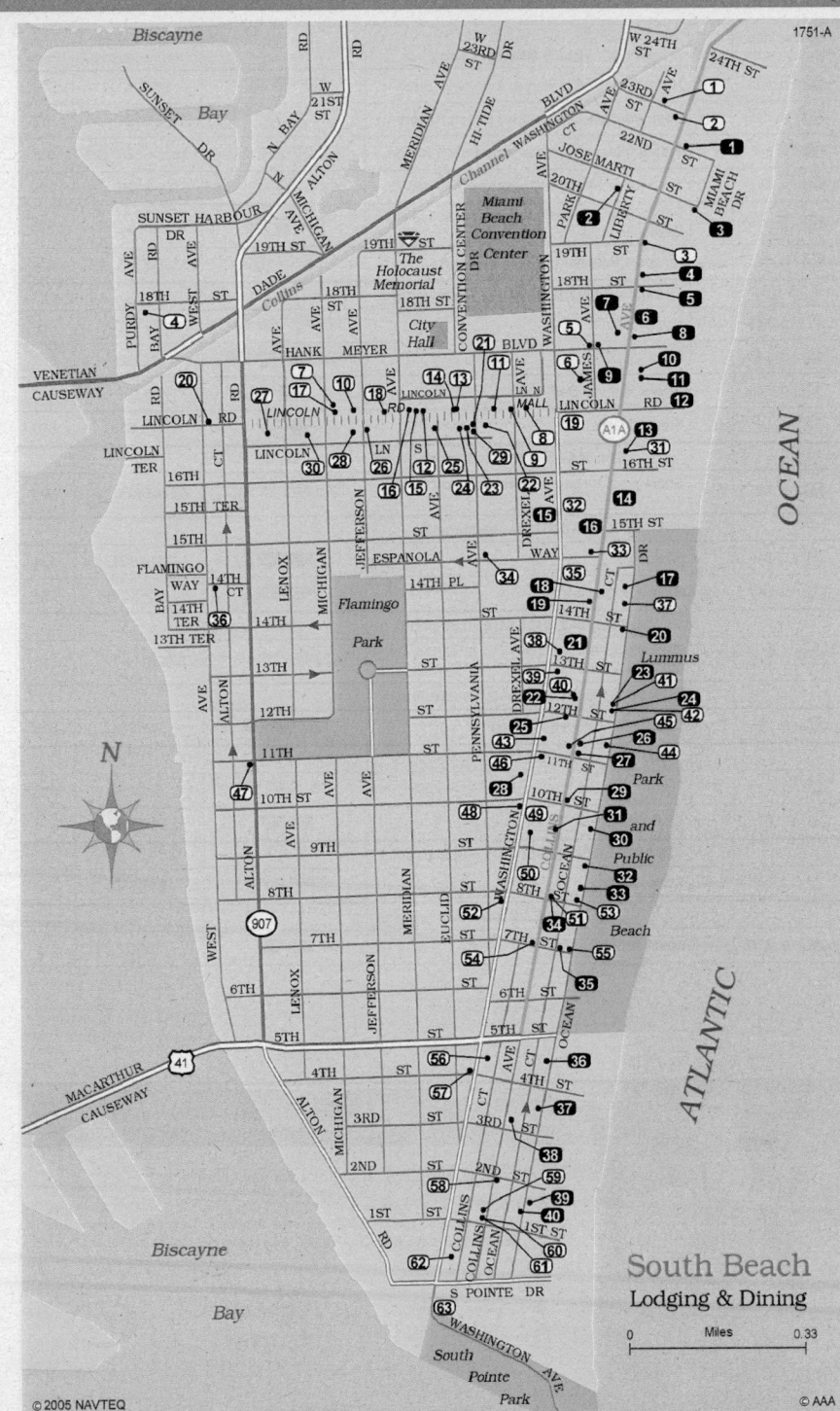

1751-A

© 2005 NAVTEQ

© AAA

South Beach
Lodging & Dining

0   Miles   0.33

South Beach

This index helps you "spot" where approved accommodations and restaurants are located on the corresponding detailed maps. Lodging rate ranges are for comparison only and show the property's high season; rates are per night, unless only weekly (W) rates are available. Restaurant rate range is for dinner, unless only lunch (L) is served. Turn to the listing page for more detailed rate information and consult display ads for special promotions.

Spotter/Map Page Number	OA	MIAMI BEACH - Lodgings	Diamond Rating	Rate Range High Season	Listing Page
1 / p. 548	AAA	Holiday Inn South Beach Resort - see color ad p 576	◈◈◈	$179-$299 SAVE	576
3 / p. 548	AAA	Days Inn South Beach	◈◈	$159-$239	574
4 / p. 548	AAA	Riande Continental South Beach Hotel	◈◈	$140-$199 SAVE	581
5 / p. 548	AAA	Shelborne Beach Resort-South Beach - see color ad p 583	◈◈◈	$185-$2500 SAVE	583
6 / p. 548	AAA	South Seas Hotel	◈◈◈	$239-$625 SAVE	583
7 / p. 548		Las Brisas South Beach Hotel - Dorset Hotel	◈◈◈	Failed to provide	578
8 / p. 548		DoubleTree Surfcomber Hotel	◈◈◈	$169-$329	575
9 / p. 548		Cadet Hotel	◈◈◈	$99-$225	572
10 / p. 548	AAA	The National Hotel	◈◈◈	$279-$3579 SAVE	579
11 / p. 548		Sagamore Hotel	◈◈◈◈	Failed to provide	583
12 / p. 548		The Ritz-Carlton, South Beach	◈◈◈◈	$599-$5500	582
13 / p. 548	AAA	Loews Miami Beach Hotel - see color ad p 578	◈◈◈◈	$339-$4000 SAVE	578
14 / p. 548		Crowne Plaza Royal Palm on South Beach	◈◈◈	Failed to provide	573
15 / p. 548	AAA	Courtyard By Marriott, Miami South Beach	◈◈◈	$219-$349 SAVE	573
16 / p. 548	AAA	Rodeway Inn South Beach	◈◈	$89-$129 SAVE	582
17 / p. 548	AAA	Crescent Resort and Spa on South Beach - see color ad p 771	◈◈◈	$99-$459 SAVE	573
18 / p. 548		The President Hotel	◈◈	$190-$300	581
19 / p. 548		Nassau Suite Hotel	◈◈◈	$230-$310	579
20 / p. 548		Winter Haven Hotel	◈◈◈	$169-$399	584
21 / p. 548		Beachcomber Hotel	◈◈	$140-$170	571
22 / p. 548		Comfort Inn & Suites South Beach	◈◈◈	$179	573
23 / p. 548		Hotel Ocean	◈◈◈	$210-$675	577
24 / p. 548		The Tides Hotel	◈◈◈◈	$550-$650	584
25 / p. 548		The Marlin	◈◈◈	$225-$895	579
26 / p. 548		The Kent Hotel	◈◈◈	$145-$175	578
27 / p. 548		Tudor Hotel & Suites	◈◈◈	Failed to provide	584
28 / p. 548	AAA	Best Western South Beach	◈◈◈	$145-$185 SAVE	572
29 / p. 548		Essex House Hotel & Suites	◈◈◈	$99-$399	575
30 / p. 548		Edison Hotel South Beach	◈◈	Failed to provide	575
31 / p. 548		The Blue Moon	◈◈◈◈	$99-$399	572
32 / p. 548		The Waldorf Towers Hotel	◈◈◈	$139-$219	584
33 / p. 548	AAA	Casa Grande Suite Hotel	◈◈◈	$315-$1500 SAVE	573
34 / p. 548	AAA	The Hotel	◈◈◈◈	$275-$450 SAVE	576
35 / p. 548	AAA	Avalon Hotel	◈◈◈	$209-$299 SAVE	571
36 / p. 548		Ocean Five Hotel - see color ad p 576	◈◈◈	$195-$345	581

Spotter/Map Page Number	OA	MIAMI BEACH - Lodgings (continued)	Diamond Rating	Rate Range High Season	Listing Page
37 / p. 548		The Wave Hotel	◆◆◆	$149-$249	584
38 / p. 548		Atlantica Hotel & Suites	◆◆	$79-$139	571
39 / p. 548	AAA	**Marriott South Beach**	◆◆◆	$359-$389 [SAVE]	579
40 / p. 548		Century Hotel	◆◆◆	$115-$215	573
		MIAMI BEACH - Restaurants			
1 / p. 548		Mama Vieja Restaurant & Night Club	◆	$7-$20	589
2 / p. 548		Talula	◆◆◆◆	$8-$28	591
3 / p. 548		Nobu Miami Beach	◆◆◆	$16-$38	589
4 / p. 548		Joe Allen	◆◆	$10-$25	588
5 / p. 548		Casa Tua	◆◆◆◆	$46-$57	587
6 / p. 548		One-Ninety Restaurant	◆◆	$18-$33	590
7 / p. 548		Icebox Cafe	◆◆	$28-$35	588
8 / p. 548		Little Mushroom Bar & Cafe	◆	$8-$24	589
9 / p. 548		Yuca Restaurant	◆◆◆	$7-$40	592
10 / p. 548		Pacific Time	◆◆◆	$17-$32	590
11 / p. 548		Rosinella	◆◆	$6-$26	590
12 / p. 548		World Resource Cafe	◆◆	$15-$45	592
13 / p. 548		Carnevale	◆◆◆	$9-$26	586
14 / p. 548		Aura	◆◆	$15-$25	586
15 / p. 548		Tiramesu	◆◆	$10-$32	592
16 / p. 548		Spris	◆◆	$7-$15	591
17 / p. 548		Lincoln Road Cafe	◆	$6-$10	589
18 / p. 548	AAA	**da Leo Trattoria**	◆◆	$17-$29	587
19 / p. 548		Rumi Restaurant & Lounge	◆◆◆	$25-$35	590
20 / p. 548		Kim's Chinese Restaurant	◆◆	$5-$16	588
21 / p. 548		Sushi Samba Dromo	◆◆◆	$10-$39	591
22 / p. 548		Dulcianna Cafe	◆	$6-$10	587
23 / p. 548		La Lupa Di Roma	◆◆	$12-$30	588
24 / p. 548		Ristoranti Il Sole	◆◆◆	$12-$26	590
25 / p. 548		Nexxt Cafe	◆◆	$8-$24	589
26 / p. 548		Van Dyke Cafe	◆◆	$12-$25	592
27 / p. 548		Doraku	◆◆	$7-$28	587
28 / p. 548		Touch Restaurant	◆◆◆	$14-$32	592
29 / p. 548		El Rancho Grande Mexican Restaurant	◆◆	$6-$18	587
30 / p. 548		Balans	◆◆◆	$10-$17	586
31 / p. 548		Emeril's Miami Beach	◆◆◆◆	$21-$33	587
32 / p. 548		Parrillada Argentina	◆◆	$10-$13	590
33 / p. 548		Jerry's Famous Deli South Beach	◆◆	$8-$25	588
34 / p. 548		Tantra	◆◆◆◆	$30-$90	591
35 / p. 548		Osteria del Teatro	◆◆◆	$16-$42	590

Spotter/Map Page Number	OA	**MIAMI BEACH** - Restaurants (continued)	Diamond Rating	Rate Range High Season	Listing Page
36 / p. 548		Barton G. The Restaurant	▽▽▽▽	$14-$34	586
37 / p. 548		The Front Porch	▽▽	$12-$18	587
38 / p. 548		Escopazzo Restaurant	▽▽▽	$10-$25	587
39 / p. 548		Playwright Irish Pub & Restaurant	▽▽	$18-$22	590
40 / p. 548		Spiga Ristorante Italiano	▽▽▽	$14-$25	591
41 / p. 548		Les 2 Fontaines	▽▽	$9-$31	588
42 / p. 548		Twelve Twenty	▽▽	$20-$35	592
43 / p. 548		Sushi Saigon	▽▽	$12-$20	591
44 / p. 548		Vix	▽▽▽▽	$26-$43	592
45 / p. 548		Mark's South Beach	▽▽▽▽	$26-$42	589
46 / p. 548		11th Street Diner	▽	$10-$15	586
47 / p. 548		Novecento	▽▽▽	$12-$25	589
48 / p. 548		Metro	▽▽	$27-$34	589
49 / p. 548		Ruen Thai and Sushi Bar	▽▽	$10-$28	590
50 / p. 548		B.E.D	▽▽	$30-$40	586
51 / p. 548	AAA	**Wish**	▽▽▽▽	$20-$33	592
52 / p. 548		Paesano's Ristorante	▽▽	$12-$25	590
53 / p. 548	AAA	**News Cafe**	▽▽	$12-$25	589
54 / p. 548		Puerto Sagua	▽	$6-$20	590
55 / p. 548	AAA	**A Fish Called Avalon**	▽▽▽	$18-$35	586
56 / p. 548		Tuscan Steak	▽▽	$27-$68	592
57 / p. 548		China Grill	▽▽▽	$21-$37	587
58 / p. 548		Big Pink	▽▽	$4-$20	586
59 / p. 548		La Factoria	▽▽	$9-$27	588
60 / p. 548		Shoji Sushi	▽▽▽	$9-$25	591
61 / p. 548		Nemo Restaurant	▽▽▽	$18-$28	589
62 / p. 548	AAA	**Joe's Stone Crab Restaurant**	▽▽▽	$5-$60	588
63 / p. 548		Smith & Wollensky Steak & Chop House	▽▽▽	$23-$39	591

DOWNTOWN MIAMI　(See map and index starting on p. 530)

------ **WHERE TO STAY** ------

CLARION HOTEL & SUITES　*Book at aaa.com*　　　　　　　　**Phone:** (305)374-5100　**8**
　　▼▼〰〰▼▼　12/1-4/30　　　1P: $117-$144　　　2P: $117-$144　　　XP: $10　　F14
　　　　　　　5/1-11/30　　　1P: $81-$117　　　2P: $81-$117　　　XP: $10　　F14
Small-scale Hotel　**Location:** Corner of Miami Ave. 100 SE 4th St 33131. Fax: 305/381-9826. **Facility:** 149 units. 117 one-bedroom standard units. 32 one-bedroom suites. 16 stories, interior corridors. *Bath:* combo or shower only. **Parking:** valet. **Amenities:** video games (fee), voice mail, irons, hair dryers. **Pool(s):** outdoor. **Leisure Activities:** exercise room. **Guest Services:** valet laundry. **Business Services:** meeting rooms, fax (fee). **Cards:** AX, CB, DC, DS, MC, VI.
(See color ad p 553)

SOME UNITS
(ASK) (S⊘) (¶¶) (Y) (⅋) (⌀) (⇌) (⚐) (DATA PORT) (▣) / (⊠) /

CONRAD MIAMI　*Book at aaa.com*　　　　　　　　　**Phone:** 305/503-6500　**12**
　▼▼▼▼ ▼▼▼▼　All Year　　　1P: $129-$429　　　2P: $129-$429　　　XP: $25　　F18
　　　　　　Location: On US 1 (Brickell Ave) and 13th St; in Expinito Santo Plaza. Located in the financial district. 1395 Brickell Ave
Large-scale Hotel　33131. Fax: 305/503-6599. **Facility:** Located in the banking district, the rooms are furnished in a modern and comfortable, contemporary style and offer great downtown views. 250 units. 203 one-bedroom standard units, some with efficiencies. 32 one- and 15 two-bedroom suites ($229-$529), some with kitchens. 16-22 stories, interior corridors. **Parking:** on-site (fee) and valet. **Terms:** check-in 4 pm, cancellation fee imposed. **Amenities:** DVD players, video games (fee), high-speed Internet, dual phone lines, voice mail, safes, honor bars, irons, hair dryers. **Dining:** Atrio, see separate listing. **Pool(s):** heated outdoor. **Leisure Activities:** whirlpool, exercise room, spa. **Guest Services:** gift shop, valet laundry, area transportation (fee). **Business Services:** conference facilities, business center. **Cards:** AX, CB, DC, DS, MC, VI.

SOME UNITS
(✈) (¶¶) (24¶) (Y) (⅋) (⌀) (⇌) (⊠) (⚐) (DATA PORT) (▣) / (⊠) (▤) (▥) /
FEE

COURTYARD BY MARRIOTT MIAMI DOWNTOWN　*Book at aaa.com*　**Phone:** (305)374-3000　**6**
　▼▼〰▼▼　12/1-4/30　　　1P: $115-$169　　　2P: $115-$169　　　XP: $10　　F
　　　　　9/15-11/20　　　1P: $109-$149　　　2P: $109-$149　　　XP: $10　　F
Small-scale Hotel　11/21-11/30　　1P: $99-$139　　　2P: $99-$139　　　XP: $10　　F
　　　　　5/1-9/14　　　1P: $99-$115　　　2P: $99-$115　　　XP: $10　　F
Location: Just s of Flagler St on US 1 and 41; 0.8 mi e of I-95, exit 2A. Adjoins the convention center. 200 SE 2nd Ave 33131. Fax: 305/358-4061. **Facility:** 231 units. 204 one-bedroom standard units. 27 one-bedroom suites ($179-$209). 13 stories, interior corridors. *Bath:* combo or shower only. **Parking:** on-site (fee). **Amenities:** video games (fee), high-speed Internet, dual phone lines, voice mail, safes, irons, hair dryers. **Pool(s):** heated outdoor. **Leisure Activities:** exercise room. **Guest Services:** sundries, valet and coin laundry. **Business Services:** meeting rooms, fax (fee). **Cards:** AX, DS, MC, VI.

SOME UNITS
(ASK) (S⊘) (¶¶) (Y) (⅋) (⌀) (⇌) (⚐) (DATA PORT) (▣) / (⊠) (▤) (▥) /

(See map and index starting on p. 530)

DOUBLETREE GRAND-BISCAYNE BAY	*Book at aaa.com*		Phone: (305)372-0313	①
12/1-4/16	1P: $129-$349	2P: $129-$349	XP: $10	F18
10/1-11/30	1P: $149-$289	2P: $149-$289	XP: $10	F18
4/17-9/30	1P: $119-$229	2P: $119-$229	XP: $10	F18

Small-scale Hotel **Location:** Just e of US 1 (Biscayne Blvd) at 15th St. Located on the Bay. 1717 N Bayshore Dr 33132. Fax: 305/372-9455. **Facility:** 220 units. 152 one-bedroom standard units. 40 one- and 28 two-bedroom suites ($169-$389) with kitchens. 6-42 stories, interior corridors. *Bath:* combo or shower only. **Parking:** valet. **Terms:** cancellation fee imposed. **Amenities:** voice mail, irons, hair dryers. *Some:* dual phone lines, safes, honor bars. *Fee:* video games, high-speed Internet. **Pool(s):** heated outdoor. **Leisure Activities:** sauna, whirlpool. **Guest Services:** gift shop, valet and coin laundry. **Business Services:** meeting rooms, fax (fee). **Cards:** AX, CB, DC, DS, MC, VI.

SOME UNITS

(See map and index starting on p. 530)

FOUR SEASONS HOTEL MIAMI   *Book at aaa.com*   Phone: (305)358-3535   **13**

12/1-5/31 & 10/1-11/30	1P: $375-$1950	2P: $375-$1950	XP: $25	F18
6/1-9/30	1P: $275-$1250	2P: $275-$1250	XP: $25	F18

Location: On US 1 (Brickell Ave) and 14th St. 1435 Brickell Ave 33131. Fax: 305/358-7758. **Facility:** Marble floors and large sculptures give common areas an Italian-villa ambience; in guest rooms, cushioned window seats overlook the bay or skyline. 305 units. 210 one-bedroom standard units, some with efficiencies. 67 one- and 28 two-bedroom suites ($675-$1950), some with kitchens. 20-36 stories, interior corridors. **Parking:** on-site (fee) and valet. **Terms:** [BP] meal plan available, package plans, small pets only. **Amenities:** DVD players, dual phone lines, voice mail, safes, honor bars, irons, hair dryers. *Fee:* video games, high-speed Internet. *Some:* fax. **Dining:** 6:30 am-11 pm, cocktails, also, ACQUA, see separate listing. **Pool(s):** heated outdoor, wading. **Leisure Activities:** whirlpool, spa. **Guest Services:** gift shop, valet laundry, area transportation (fee). **Business Services:** conference facilities, business center. **Cards:** AX, DC, DS, JC, MC, VI.

SOME UNITS

HOLIDAY INN PORT OF MIAMI-DOWNTOWN   *Book at aaa.com*   Phone: (305)371-4400   **4**

12/28-4/16	1P: $123-$147	2P: $123-$147	XP: $10	F17
4/17-11/30	1P: $103-$124	2P: $103-$124	XP: $10	F17
12/1-12/27	1P: $99-$109	2P: $99-$109	XP: $10	F17

Location: On US 1; facing Port of Miami. Located across from the Bayside Marketplace. 340 Biscayne Blvd 33132. Fax: 305/372-2862. **Facility:** 200 units. 192 one-bedroom standard units. 8 one-bedroom suites. 10 stories, interior corridors. *Bath:* combo or shower only. **Parking:** on-site (fee). **Terms:** cancellation fee imposed, 13% service charge. **Amenities:** video games (fee), dual phone lines, voice mail, safes, irons, hair dryers. *Some:* CD players. **Dining:** 6:30 am-10:30 pm, cocktails. **Pool(s):** outdoor. **Leisure Activities:** exercise room. **Guest Services:** sundries, valet and coin laundry. **Business Services:** meeting rooms, PC. **Cards:** AX, CB, DC, DS, JC, MC, VI. **Special Amenities:** free local telephone calls and free newspaper. *(See color ad below)*

SOME UNITS

HYATT REGENCY MIAMI   *Book at aaa.com*   Phone: (305)358-1234   **9**

12/1-5/31 & 10/1-11/30	1P: $135-$235	2P: $135-$235	XP: $25	F18
6/1-9/30	1P: $79-$179	2P: $79-$179	XP: $25	F18

Location: Corner of SE 4th St and SE 2nd Ave. Located next to the convention center. 400 SE 2nd Ave 33131-2107. Fax: 305/358-0529. **Facility:** All accommodations in this contemporary hotel have balconies offering views of the city as well as the Miami River and Biscayne Bay. 587 units. 575 one-bedroom standard units. 12 one-bedroom suites. 24 stories, interior corridors. *Bath:* combo or shower only. **Parking:** valet. **Terms:** cancellation fee imposed. **Amenities:** dual phone lines, voice mail, safes, irons, hair dryers. *Some:* CD players, high-speed Internet (fee). **Dining:** 2 restaurants, 7 am-10 pm, cocktails, also, Riverwalk Cafe, see separate listing. **Pool(s):** heated outdoor. **Leisure Activities:** exercise room. *Fee:* massage. **Guest Services:** gift shop, valet laundry. **Business Services:** conference facilities, business center. **Cards:** AX, CB, DC, DS, JC, MC, VI. *(See color ad below)*

SOME UNITS

(See map and index starting on p. 530)

INTERCONTINENTAL MIAMI *Book at aaa.com*   Phone: (305)577-1000   **5**
All Year   1P: $169-$309   XP: $30   F18
Location: At Biscayne Blvd and Chopin Plaza. Located on the bay. 100 Chopin Plaza 33131. Fax: 305/577-0384.
Large-scale Hotel   **Facility:** Deco furniture and warm colors comprise rooms with city views at the hotel complex, which overlooks Biscayne Bay and features a large, colorful lobby. 641 units. 606 one-bedroom standard units. 34 one- and 1 two-bedroom suites ($299-$799), some with whirlpools. 34 stories, interior corridors. *Bath:* combo or shower only. **Parking:** valet. **Terms:** check-in 4 pm. **Amenities:** CD players, dual phone lines, voice mail, safes, honor bars, irons, hair dryers. *Fee:* video games, high-speed Internet. *Some:* DVD players (fee). **Pool(s):** heated outdoor. **Leisure Activities:** jogging. *Fee:* massage. **Guest Services:** gift shop, valet laundry. **Business Services:** conference facilities, business center. **Cards:** AX, DC, DS, MC, VI.

SOME UNITS

JW MARRIOTT HOTEL-MIAMI *Book at aaa.com*   Phone: (305)374-1224   **11**
12/1-4/7   1P: $215-$245   2P: $215-$245
4/8-5/19 & 9/25-11/30   1P: $195-$225   2P: $195-$225
5/20-9/24   1P: $145-$175   2P: $145-$175
Location: On US 1, corner of SE 10th St. 1109 Brickell Ave 33131. Fax: 305/329-3675. **Facility:** Located in the Brickell Avenue business district, the hotel has rooms with views of the city or the bay front and elegant, warm decor. 300 units. 278 one-bedroom standard units. 22 one-bedroom suites. 7-22 stories, interior corridors. *Bath:* combo or shower only. **Parking:** valet. **Amenities:** CD players, dual phone lines, voice mail, safes, honor bars, irons, hair dryers. *Fee:* video games, high-speed Internet. *Some:* DVD players, fax. **Dining:** 6:30 am-11:30 pm, cocktails, also, Isabela's, see separate listing. **Pool(s):** heated outdoor. **Leisure Activities:** whirlpool, spa. **Guest Services:** gift shop, valet laundry. **Business Services:** conference facilities, business center. **Cards:** AX, CB, DC, DS, MC, VI. **Special Amenities:** free newspaper.

SOME UNITS

MANDARIN ORIENTAL, MIAMI *Book at aaa.com*   Phone: (305)913-8288   **10**
1/1-5/31   1P: $625-$860   2P: $625-$860   XP: $25   F
12/1-12/31   1P: $625-$800   2P: $625-$800   XP: $25   F
10/1-11/30   1P: $520-$735   2P: $520-$735   XP: $25   F
6/1-9/30   1P: $415-$620   2P: $415-$620   XP: $25   F
Large-scale Hotel   **Location:** US 1 (Brickell Ave), just e on SE 8th St (Brickell Key Dr). 500 Brickell Key Dr 33131. Fax: 305/913-8300. **Facility:** Many of the spacious, lavishly decorated rooms at this stunning hotel feature balconies offering great views of Biscayne Bay and the skyline. 327 units. 296 one-bedroom standard units. 31 one-bedroom suites ($1250-$5000), some with kitchens and/or whirlpools. 20 stories, interior corridors. *Bath:* combo or shower only. **Parking:** valet. **Terms:** cancellation fee imposed, [AP] & [CP] meal plans available, package plans, small pets only ($200 deposit). **Amenities:** high-speed Internet (fee), dual phone lines, voice mail, safes, honor bars, irons, hair dryers. *Some:* DVD players, CD players. **Dining:** 6 am-11 pm, cocktails, also, Azul, Cafe Sambal at Mandarin Oriental, Miami, see separate listings, entertainment. **Pool(s):** heated outdoor. **Leisure Activities:** saunas, whirlpool, steamrooms, jogging, spa. **Guest Services:** gift shop, valet laundry. **Business Services:** conference facilities, business center. **Cards:** AX, CB, DC, DS, JC, MC, VI.

SOME UNITS

MIAMI MARRIOTT BISCAYNE BAY HOTEL *Book at aaa.com*   Phone: (305)374-3900   **2**
12/1-4/30   1P: $259-$500
5/1-6/17 & 10/1-11/30   1P: $199-$400
6/18-9/30   1P: $159-$299
Large-scale Hotel   **Location:** Just e of US 1 (Biscayne Blvd) at 15th St. 1633 N Bayshore Rd 33132. Fax: 305/375-0597. **Facility:** 601 units. 597 one-bedroom standard units. 4 one-bedroom suites. 31 stories, interior corridors. *Bath:* combo or shower only. **Parking:** on-site (fee) and valet. **Terms:** check-in 4 pm, [AP] meal plan available, package plans. **Amenities:** high-speed Internet (fee), dual phone lines, voice mail, safes, irons, hair dryers. **Pool(s):** heated outdoor. **Leisure Activities:** whirlpool, rental boats, exercise room. *Fee:* charter fishing. **Guest Services:** gift shop, valet and coin laundry. **Business Services:** conference facilities, business center. **Cards:** AX, CB, DC, DS, JC, MC, VI.

SOME UNITS

MIAMI RIVER INN   Phone: (305)325-0045   **7**
12/16-3/15   1P: $109-$199   2P: $109-$199   XP: $15   F12
12/1-12/15 & 3/16-6/30   1P: $89-$129   2P: $89-$129   XP: $15   F12
7/1-11/30   1P: $69-$119   2P: $69-$119   XP: $15   F12
Bed & Breakfast   **Location:** I-95, exit 1B (SW 7th St), just w to SW 5th Ave, just n to SW 2nd St, then e. 118 SW South River Dr 33130. Fax: 305/325-9227. **Facility:** Smoke free premises. 40 one-bedroom standard units. 2-3 stories (no elevator), interior/exterior corridors. *Bath:* shared or private, combo, shower or tub only. **Parking:** on-site. **Terms:** office hours 8 am-11 pm, 3 day cancellation notice-fee imposed, [CP] meal plan available, package plans, small pets only ($25 extra charge, with prior approval). **Pool(s):** outdoor. **Leisure Activities:** whirlpool. **Guest Services:** coin laundry. **Business Services:** meeting rooms. **Cards:** AX, CB, DC, DS, MC, VI.

FEE

RADISSON HOTEL MIAMI *Book at aaa.com*   Phone: (305)374-0000   **3**
12/1-5/28   1P: $149-$269   2P: $149-$269
10/1-11/30   1P: $149-$229   2P: $149-$229
5/29-9/30   1P: $119-$189   2P: $119-$189
Large-scale Hotel   **Location:** US 1, 1 mi n of Flagler St. 1601 Biscayne Blvd 33132. Fax: 305/714-3811. **Facility:** 528 units. 503 one-bedroom standard units. 25 one-bedroom suites. 11-32 stories, interior corridors. *Bath:* combo or shower only. **Parking:** on-site (fee) and valet. **Terms:** cancellation fee imposed, package plans. **Amenities:** dual phone lines, voice mail, irons, hair dryers. *Fee:* video games, high-speed Internet. **Pool(s):** heated outdoor. **Leisure Activities:** sauna, exercise room. **Guest Services:** gift shop, valet laundry. **Business Services:** conference facilities, business center. **Cards:** AX, CB, DC, DS, MC, VI.

SOME UNITS

(See map and index starting on p. 530)

──────── WHERE TO DINE ────────

ACQUA
Italian
Lunch: $12-$22   **Dinner:** $13-$30   **Phone:** 305/381-3190   [36]
Location: On US 1 (Brickell Ave) and 14th St; in Four Seasons Hotel Miami. 1435 Brickell Ave 33131. **Hours:** 6:30 am-11 pm. **Reservations:** suggested. **Features:** The chef creatively incorporates regional favorites, such as Florida lobster and snapper, into traditional Italian cuisine. Guests can gaze out over Biscayne Bay while dining in the elegantly casual setting. The restaurant carries out the high standard of service characteristic of its location in the Four Seasons Hotel. Dressy casual; cocktails. **Parking:** on-site (fee) and valet. **Cards:** AX, CB, DC, DS, JC, MC, VI.

ATRIO
American
Lunch: $8-$14   **Dinner:** $15-$30   **Phone:** 305/503-6500   [34]
Location: On US 1 (Brickell Ave) and 13th St; in Expinito Santo Plaza; in Conrad Miami. 1395 Brickell Ave 33131. **Hours:** 6:30 am-10:30 pm. **Reservations:** suggested. **Features:** Diners can relax in the brightly colored dining room and take in views of downtown. Dishes, which incorporate fresh ingredients from the water and the land, reflect a blend of Spanish and American cooking styles. Dressy casual; cocktails. **Parking:** valet.
Cards: AX, CB, DC, DS, JC, MC, VI.

AZUL
New World
Lunch: $11-$28   **Dinner:** $26-$37   **Phone:** 305/913-8288   [23]
Location: US 1 (Brickell Ave), just e on SE 8th St (Brickell Key Dr); in Mandarin Oriental, Miami. 500 Brickell Key Dr 33131. **Hours:** noon-3 & 7-11 pm, Sat from 7 pm. Closed: Sun. **Reservations:** required. **Features:** The upscale dining room affords beautiful views of the Miami skyline and the waters of Biscayne Bay. The informal dining room is decidedly first-class but is unencumbered by trappings of opulence. Many dishes reflect Mediterranean origins but incorporate imaginative Asian influences typical of the Mandarin Oriental chain. Particularly refreshing are a number of meat and seafood dishes featuring multiple preparation styles. Dressy casual; cocktails. **Parking:** valet. **Cards:** AX, DC, DS, MC, VI.

BIG FISH
Seafood
Lunch: $9-$15   **Dinner:** $12-$25   **Phone:** 305/373-1770   [19]
Location: Jct US 1 (Brickell Ave), 0.5 mi w on SE 5th St; on the river. 55 SW Miami Ave Rd 33130. **Hours:** noon-3 & 6-midnight, Sat & Sun noon-11:30 pm. Closed: 11/23, 12/25. **Reservations:** accepted. **Features:** A nondescript building fronts this fabulous covered outdoor dining spot, perched along the river with the downtown skyline as a backdrop. Well-prepared seafood, such as honey-glazed salmon, shares menu space with steaks and Italian dishes with homemade pasta. Casual dress; cocktails. **Parking:** street. **Cards:** AX, MC, VI.

BUBBA GUMP SHRIMP CO
Seafood
Lunch: $11-$19   **Dinner:** $11-$19   **Phone:** 305/379-8866   [4]
Location: Just s of SR 836; in Bayside Market Place. 401 Biscayne Blvd 33132. **Hours:** 11:30 am-11 pm, Fri & Sat-midnight. Closed: 11/23, 12/25. **Features:** Just like the movie, shrimp with...(many choices) and prepared many ways too. You will find burgers and pastas also. Casual dress; cocktails. **Parking:** on-site (fee). **Cards:** AX, CB, DC, DS, JC, MC, VI.

CACIQUES CORNER
Cuban
Lunch: $6-$14   **Phone:** 305/371-8317   [12]
Location: Corner of NW 1st Ave and W Flagler Ave; just w of N Miami Ave; near County Courthouse. 100 W Flagler Ave 33130. **Hours:** 5 am-7 pm. **Features:** The hole-in-the-wall kind of place is popular with downtown workers and nearby museumgoers. The eatery's many sandwich choices include Cubans, medianoches, clubs and grouper. Among main menu offerings are steak milanese, churrasco, porterhouse, T-bone, whole red snapper and king fish. To top off the meal, try any of such desserts as Key lime pie, bread pudding and tres leches. Combinations make up a good section of the full breakfast menu. Take-out is a favorite option. Casual dress; beer & wine only. **Parking:** on-site (fee). **Cards:** AX, DC, DS, MC, VI.

CAFE SAMBAL AT MANDARIN ORIENTAL, MIAMI
Asian
Lunch: $9-$33   **Dinner:** $10-$32   **Phone:** 305/913-8251   [24]
Location: US 1 (Brickell Ave), just e on SE 8th St (Brickell Key Dr); in Mandarin Oriental, Miami. 500 Brickell Key Dr 33131. **Hours:** 6:30 am-11 pm. **Reservations:** suggested. **Features:** Lending to the dining room's "Zen" feel is a central waterfall that promotes an air of relaxed tranquility. The service staff is well trained. Among the many Asian-influenced items are Bangkok-style curry lobster, teriyaki-seared salmon, Hainan chicken rice and the crisp seafood wonton. Desserts please both the eyes and palate. The trained chef prepares creatively presented dishes a la minute. Dressy casual; cocktails. **Parking:** on-site (fee) and valet. **Cards:** AX, DC, MC, VI.

CAMILA'S
Brazilian
Lunch: $8   **Dinner:** $8   **Phone:** 305/375-0992   [16]
Location: SE 1st Ave, jct International Place. 129 SE 1st Ave 33131. **Hours:** 11 am-10 pm. **Features:** The all-you-can-eat buffet is the restaurant's only option. Patrons can choose from a variety of meats, salads, vegetables and desserts. Selections change daily. Casual dress; beer & wine only. **Parking:** on-site (fee). **Cards:** AX, MC, VI.

CHICKEN KITCHEN
American
Lunch: $4-$15   **Dinner:** $4-$15   **Phone:** 305/358-8646   [25]
Location: Between SW 11th and SW 13th; in Brickell Plaza. 842 SE 1st Ave 33138. **Hours:** 11 am-9 pm, Sat-8 pm. Closed major holidays. **Features:** Always fresh and never frozen is the key to the great tasting marinated and grilled chicken that awaits you at this local favorite. Casual dress. **Parking:** street. **Cards:** MC, VI.

DELI LANE CAFE
American
Lunch: $5-$13   **Dinner:** $5-$13   **Phone:** 305/377-8811   [35]
Location: Just n of Rickenbacker Causeway. 1401 Brickell Ave 33131. **Hours:** 7 am-9 pm, Sat & Sun 8 am-3 pm. Closed: 11/23, 12/25. **Features:** A great start would be stuffed artichokes or a brie and fruit platter, followed by a specialty sandwich of pressed duck or portabella club, toped off with gourmet cheesecake or "chocolate something". Fresh catch of the day, pizzas, calzones and quesadillas are also available. Casual dress; beer & wine only. **Parking:** street. **Cards:** AX, DC, MC, VI.

(See map and index starting on p. 530)

DIANA'S CAFE
Cuban

Lunch: $4-$10   Phone: 305/577-0838   [10]

Location: Between 1st and NE 2nd aves. 99 NW 1st St 33128. **Hours:** 6:30 am-5 pm. Closed major holidays; also Sat & Sun. **Features:** Sweet plantains with a cup of fresh black bean soup and your choice of Cuban-style sandwiches await you at this popular downtown cafe. Casual dress. **Parking:** street. **Cards:** DC, MC, VI.

GIOVANA CAFFE
Italian

Lunch: $5-$12   Phone: 305/374-1024   [17]

Location: Between SE 1st and SE 2nd sts. 154 SE 1st Ave 33131. **Hours:** 11 am-4 pm. Closed major holidays; also Sat & Sun. **Features:** Specialty sandwiches, freshly made salads, homemade pastas and desserts are available here at this friendly restaurant. Casual dress; beer & wine only. **Parking:** street. **Cards:** MC, VI.

GOLDEN CARROT
Natural/Organic

Lunch: $4-$13   Phone: 305/350-9988   [9]

Location: Intersection of NW 1st Ave and NW 2nd St. 201 NW 1st Ave 33128. **Hours:** 7 am-4 pm. Closed major holidays; also Sat & Sun. **Features:** "100% natural" jumps out from the menu; pita veggie sandwiches, focaccia sandwiches, organic 7-grain bread sandwiches and wraps are only the first page offerings. Grilled fish, pasta entrees and skinless and boneless chicken are also available from the extensive menu. Casual dress. **Parking:** street. **Cards:** AX, DS, MC, VI.

GORDON BIERSCH BREWERY RESTAURANT
American

Lunch: $8-$16   Dinner: $10-$25   Phone: 786/425-1130   [31]

Location: On US 1, jct 12th St SE. 1201 Brickell Ave 33131. **Hours:** 11:30 am-midnight. **Features:** The trendy, inviting spot bustles during lunch and dinner. Menu offerings range from stir-fried fare, pasta dishes, sandwiches and create-your-own pizzas to Hawaiian rib-eye, lemon-ginger-crusted salmon, chicken Marsala and the fabulous sesame-seared ahi tuna. Among lagers brewed on site are Marzen, Dunkles and Blonde Rock. The service staff is courteous. Casual dress; cocktails. **Parking:** on-site (fee) and valet. **Cards:** MC, VI.

GRANNY FEELGOODS
Natural/Organic

Lunch: $9-$14   Phone: 305/377-9600   [11]

Location: Corner of N Miami Ave and W Flagler St; center of downtown shopping district; in City National Bank Building. 25 W Flagler St 33130. **Hours:** 7 am-4 pm. Closed: 1/1, 12/25; also 12/31. **Features:** In the heart of Miami shopping district, the healthy-option eatery presents a menu of soups, salads, sandwiches and omelets, as well as a terrific selection of vitamin- and mineral-laden smoothies. Favorites also include baked ziti, eggplant parmigiana, chicken Marsala, spinach lasagna and vegetarian and tofu dishes. Service is quick and bright. Casual dress. **Parking:** on-site (fee). **Cards:** AX, CB, DC, DS, JC, MC, VI.

HANAMI SUSHI
Sushi

Lunch: $4-$10   Dinner: $4-$10   Phone: 305/373-7745   [15]

Location: Between S Miami and SW 1st aves. 100 S Miami Ave, Suite 3 33130. **Hours:** 10:30 am-7 pm. Closed: 1/1, 12/25; also 12/31, Sat & Sun. **Features:** Fancy sushi rolls of spicy tuna, smoked salmon or fresh salmon are just a few of the tasty delights that are offered at this convenient takeout restaurant. Various noodle and rice bowls, samurai and ninja combos and fresh soups are just a small sample of the menu items available. Casual dress. **Parking:** street. **Cards:** AX, DS, MC, VI.

INDOCHINE
Asian

Lunch: $8-$12   Dinner: $13-$20   Phone: 305/379-1525   [21]

Location: US 1 (Brickell Ave), w on SE 7th St, then just n. 638 S Miami Ave 33131. **Hours:** 11 am-3 & 6-11 pm, Sat from 6 pm. Closed: 11/23, 12/25; also Sun. **Reservations:** accepted. **Features:** The innovative eatery marries a sushi bar and an Italian ristorante. Entrees include warm panini sandwiches, sublime crepes with ricotta and pink sauce and skewered shrimp with garlic. Note that there is a fee for parking at lunch. Casual dress; beer & wine only. **Parking:** street. **Cards:** MC, VI.

ISABELA'S
Pacific Rim

Lunch: $8-$15   Dinner: $17-$25   Phone: 305/374-1224   [30]

Location: On US 1, corner of SE 10th St; in JW Marriott Hotel-Miami. 1109 Brickell Ave 33131. **Hours:** 6:30 am-2:30 & 6-11 pm. Closed: Sat & Sun. **Reservations:** suggested. **Features:** The dining room's colors reflect the tones of the sun with a touch of the sky. The fresh seafood of the oceans and the meats of the land are influenced by the Pacific Rim flavors. The wine list complements the food very well. Dressy casual; cocktails. **Parking:** valet. **Cards:** AX, CB, DC, DS, JC, MC, VI.

JOE'S SEAFOOD RESTAURANT
Seafood

Lunch: $7-$14   Dinner: $12-$20   Phone: 305/381-9329   [6]

Location: 0.8 mi w of I-95 on Miami River; corner of NW 4th St and North River Dr. 400 NW North River Dr 33128. **Hours:** 11 am-10 pm, Fri & Sat-11 pm. Closed: for dinner 12/24. **Reservations:** accepted. **Features:** The casual, bustling restaurant serves fish caught from its own fleet as well as appetizing preparations of stone crab, shrimp, scallops and lobster. An open-air terrace offers sunny, yet breezy, dining and the occasional glimpse of a celebrity yacht. Casual dress; cocktails. **Parking:** on-site. **Cards:** AX, CB, DC, MC, VI.

LA LOGGIA RISTORANTE
Italian

Lunch: $9-$16   Dinner: $12-$18   Phone: 305/373-4800   [13]

Location: Jct of W Flagler St and SE 1st Ave. 68 W Flagler St 33130. **Hours:** 11:30 am-9 pm, Fri-10 pm. Closed major holidays; also Sat & Sun. **Reservations:** suggested. **Features:** In the hustle and bustle of downtown, the restaurant boasts comfortable Old World decor and an interesting menu. Representative of choices are linguine with seafood, pumpkin ravioli and arugula, corn, avocado and hearts of palm salad with grilled shrimp and ginger dressing. Casual dress; cocktails. **Parking:** street. **Cards:** AX, MC, VI.

LIL ANTHONY'S PIZZERIA
Pizza

Lunch: $2-$15   Phone: 305/373-4100   [8]

Location: Between NW 2nd and 3rd sts. 221 NW 1st Ave 33128. **Hours:** 10 am-3 pm. Closed major holidays; also Sat & Sun. **Features:** The downtown location keeps this tiny pizzeria busy at lunchtime. In addition to panini and a few pasta entrees, crisp thin-crust pizza is available by the slice or the pie. Casual dress. **Parking:** street. **Cards:** MC, VI.

LOMBARDI'S RESTAURANTE ITALIANO
Italian

Lunch: $6-$23   Dinner: $6-$23   Phone: 305/381-9580   [3]

Location: Just s of SR 836; in Bayside Market Place. 401 Biscayne Blvd 33132. **Hours:** 11:30 am-11 pm, Fri & Sat-midnight. **Features:** After a long day of shopping at Bayside Market Place, diners can stop into the delightful restaurant for fresh seafood and pasta dishes. Outdoor seats offer wonderful views of the bay. Casual dress; cocktails. **Parking:** on-site (fee). **Cards:** AX, MC, VI.

(See map and index starting on p. 530)

LOS RANCHOS OF BAYSIDE   Lunch: $14-$27   Dinner: $14-$27   Phone: 305/375-0666   (5)
International
Location: Just s of jct SR 836; in Bayside Market Place. 401 Biscayne Blvd N-100 33132. **Hours:** 11:30 am-10:30 pm, Fri & Sat noon-11 pm. **Features:** Dining experiences are intimate at the cozy restaurant, which is known for its excellent beef dishes. Professional service delivered with a personal flair makes guests feel special. The Nicaraguan-themed menu lists such choices as tasty grilled red snapper, shrimp scampi, churrasco, grilled chicken breast and fajitas. Sweet fried plantains are a must-try. Dressy casual; cocktails. **Parking:** on-site (fee). **Cards:** MC, VI.

MAMBO CAFE   Lunch: $5-$11   Dinner: $6-$20   Phone: 305/374-7417   (2)
Cuban
Location: Just s of SR 836; in Bayside Market Place. 401 Biscayne Blvd 33131. **Hours:** 10 am-11 pm, Fri & Sat-midnight. **Features:** The open-air Cuban cafe enables patrons to enjoy a glance at the bay or people-watch. Tasty selections won't empty the wallet. Casual dress; cocktails. **Parking:** on-site (fee). **Cards:** AX, DC, MC, VI.

MORTON'S OF CHICAGO THE STEAKHOUSE   Lunch: $22-$39   Dinner: $22-$39   Phone: 305/400-9990   (32)
Steak House
Location: On US 1 (Brickell Ave), at corner of SE 12th St. 1200 Brickell Ave 33131. **Hours:** 11:30 am-2:30 & 5:30-11 pm, Sat from 5:30 pm, Sun 5:30 pm-10 pm. **Closed:** 12/25. **Reservations:** accepted. **Features:** In the heart of the banking district, the restaurant features soothing decor and an attentive wait staff. Steaks garner high interest, as do such fresh seafood items as lobster. Dressy casual; cocktails. **Parking:** valet. **Cards:** AX, CB, DC, DS, JC, MC, VI.

OFF THE GRILL   Lunch: $4-$9   Phone: 305/358-5852   (7)
American
Location: Just e of NE 2nd Ave; at College/Bayside Metro Station. 212 NE 3rd St 33132. **Hours:** 10 am-5 pm. Closed major holidays. **Features:** At the Caribbean bistro, diners will find a lengthy chalkboard menu describing a variety of flavorful dishes, ranging from wraps and salads to fajitas and pasta entrees. Guests order at the counter and have a seat upstairs or on the brick patio. Casual dress. **Parking:** street. **Cards:** MC, VI.

PERRICONE'S MARKETPLACE & CAFE   Lunch: $9-$25   Dinner: $14-$27   Phone: 305/374-9449   (28)
Italian
Location: SE 10th St at jct Miami Ave. 15 SE 10th St 33131. **Hours:** 11:30 am-10 pm, Fri-11 pm, Sat 8 am-11 pm, Sun 8 am-10 pm. **Closed:** 1/1, 11/23, 12/25. **Reservations:** suggested. **Features:** The cafe is the perfect place for a power lunch, with its fast, friendly, attentive service and extensive menu offerings. Diners can opt for porch, patio or indoor seating. Casual dress; cocktails; entertainment. **Parking:** on-site (fee) and valet. **Cards:** AX, DC, MC, VI.

PORCAO   Lunch: $15-$40   Dinner: $15-$40   Phone: 305/373-2777   (27)
Brazilian
Location: Jct of Brickell Bay Dr and SE 8th St. 801 Brickell Bay Dr 33131. **Hours:** noon-midnight, Sat & Sun from 1 pm. **Closed:** 12/25. **Reservations:** accepted. **Features:** From a waterfront location, guests can experience elegant Brazilian-style dining. The salad bar lines up an ample selection of exotic salads. Skewers of lamb, bacon-wrapped filet, marinated chicken and salmon are continuously served piping hot and sliced tableside onto patrons' plates. Dressy casual; cocktails. **Parking:** on-site (fee) and valet. **Cards:** AX, DC, MC, VI.

PROVENCE GRILL   Lunch: $9-$16   Dinner: $10-$21   Phone: 305/373-1940   (29)
French
Location: Jct 10th St SW. 1001 S Miami Ave 33130. **Hours:** 11 am-3 & 5:30-11 pm, Sat & Sun from 5:30 pm. **Features:** French-Mediterranean cuisine is at the heart of the menu at the trendy little bistro, which is a favorite of the business crowd at lunch. Among enticing items are pan-seared scallops, penne pasta with fresh sauteed salmon and sauteed veal scaloppine. A delightful ending is crepes suzette. Casual dress; cocktails. **Parking:** on-site (fee). **Cards:** AX, DS, MC, VI.

RIGATTIS CAFE   Lunch: $5-$10   Dinner: $5-$10   Phone: 305/377-1672   (14)
Italian
Location: Just s off E Flagler St. 100 S Miami Ave 33132. **Hours:** 8 am-9 pm. Closed major holidays; also Sat & Sun. **Features:** Fresh salads, soups, sandwiches and pasta meals are the specialty in this small and intimate streetside cafe. Casual dress. **Parking:** street. **Cards:** MC, VI.

THE RIVER OYSTER BAR   Lunch: $5-$21   Dinner: $15-$36   Phone: 305/530-1915   (22)
Seafood
Location: Just s of Tobacco Rd, downtown. 650 S Miami Ave 33131. **Hours:** 11:30 am-10:30 pm, Fri-11:30 pm, Sat 6 pm-11:30 pm. **Closed:** Sun. **Reservations:** suggested. **Features:** Oysters from far and wide abound at the fashionable restaurant. Diners can select from West Coast oysters, which come from Puget Sound or northern California; East Coast ones from Rhode Island; or Canadian ones found in Vancouver, British Columbia. Among other choices are cowboy steak, New Zealand lamb rack, yellowtail snapper and Australian barramundi. Dressy casual; cocktails. **Parking:** street. **Cards:** AX, DC, DS, MC, VI.

RIVERWALK CAFE   Lunch: $6-$20   Dinner: $8-$20   Phone: 305/358-1234   (18)
American
Location: Corner of SE 4th St and SE 2nd Ave; in Hyatt Regency Miami. 400 SE 2nd Ave 33131. **Hours:** 6:30 am-10 pm, Fri & Sat-11 pm. **Reservations:** accepted. **Features:** The casually elegant restaurant allows guests a variety of cuisine choices. The menu boasts an array of meats and seafood, as well as homemade desserts. Dressy casual; cocktails. **Parking:** on-site (fee). **Cards:** AX, CB, DC, DS, JC, MC, VI.

S & S RESTAURANT   Lunch: $6-$9   Dinner: $6-$9   Phone: 305/373-4291   (1)
American
Location: From US 1 (Biscayne Blvd), just w on NE 17th St, at corner. 1757 NE 2nd Ave 33132. **Hours:** 6 am-6 pm, Sat & Sun-2 pm. **Features:** The classic luncheonette has a slight retro decor, but it's the food that's king here. A menu of primarily comfort foods changes daily. Casual dress. **Parking:** street.

(See map and index starting on p. 530)

SUSHI SIAM RESTAURANT · **Lunch:** $8-$15   **Dinner:** $8-$24   **Phone:** 305/579-9944   [26]
Sushi   **Location:** Just s of Brickell Key Dr. 801 Brickell Bay Dr 33131. **Hours:** 11 am-3 & 5-10:30 pm, Sat from 5 pm. Closed major holidays; also Sun. **Features:** An extensive menu of Japanese soups, appetizers, noodles and sashimi as well as a fresh sushi bar are but a few of the available menu offerings. Casual dress; cocktails. **Parking:** on-site (fee) and street. **Cards:** AX, CB, DC, DS, JC, MC, VI.

TOBACCO ROAD **Lunch:** $7-$10   **Dinner:** $7-$10   **Phone:** 305/374-1198   [20]
American   **Location:** Just n of jct 7th St SW. 626 S Miami Ave 33130. **Hours:** 11:30 am-5 am. **Features:** The restaurant's decor is basic, as is the service, but it clearly works for this place, which has been around for more than 90 years. The establishment is reputed to be the oldest restaurant, bar and cabaret in Miami. Live music lends to the atmosphere daily: blues on six nights a week and jazz on Wednesdays. Casual dress; cocktails; entertainment. **Parking:** on-site (fee). **Cards:** MC, VI.

TUTTO PASTA RISTORANTE **Lunch:** $15-$24   **Dinner:** $15-$24   · **Phone:** 305/857-0709   [33]
Italian   **Location:** Just s of 15th St. 1751 SW 3rd Ave 33129. **Hours:** 11:30 am-10:30 pm, Fri & Sat-11 pm. Closed major holidays; also Sun. **Reservations:** accepted. **Features:** Offering good red sauce and cream sauce fare at reasonable prices, the eatery is both an Italian restaurant and a deli. Casual dress; cocktails. **Parking:** street. **Cards:** AX, CB, DC, DS, JC, MC, VI.

---

*The following restaurants have not been evaluated by AAA
but are listed for your information only.*

BONGOS CUBAN CAFE **Phone:** 786/777-2100
[fyi]   Not evaluated. **Location:** On US 1, jct 8th St NE; in American Airlines Arena. 601 Biscayne Blvd 33131. **Features:** At American Airlines Arena, the happening spot serves excellent Cuban cuisine. Hours vary depending on arena events, so call ahead for times.

CAPITAL GRILLE **Phone:** 305/374-4500
[fyi]   Not evaluated. **Location:** On US 1. 444 Brickell Ave 33131. **Features:** Popular steakhouse; rich and scrumptious desserts. Expensive.

MIAMI pop. 362,470   (See maps and indexes starting on p. 534, 542)

--- **WHERE TO STAY** ---

AMERICA'S BEST INN-MIAMI AIRPORT   *Book at aaa.com*   **Phone:** (305)592-5440   [7]
Motel
1/1-3/31	1P: $79-$89	2P: $89-$99
12/1-12/31 & 4/1-11/30	1P: $59-$69	2P: $69-$79

Location: Just e of jct SR 826 (Palmetto Expwy). 7330 NW 36th St 33166. Fax: 305/477-8155. **Facility:** 116 one-bedroom standard units. 2 stories (no elevator), interior corridors. *Bath:* combo or shower only. **Parking:** on-site. **Terms:** [ECP] meal plan available, small pets only. **Pool(s):** outdoor. **Guest Services:** valet and coin laundry. **Business Services:** meeting rooms, fax (fee). **Cards:** AX, CB, DC, DS, MC, VI.

SOME UNITS
(ASK) 〔S〕〔🛏〕〔🍴〕〔➳〕〔🐾〕〔▣〕/〔✕〕〔DATA PORT〕/

AMERISUITES (MIAMI/AIRPORT WEST)   *Book at aaa.com*   **Phone:** (305)718-8292   [8]
Small-scale Hotel
12/1-4/30	1P: $99-$139	2P: $99-$139
10/1-11/30	1P: $94-$134	2P: $94-$134
5/1-9/30	1P: $89-$129	2P: $89-$129

Location: 0.4 mi w on NW 36th St from jct SR 826 (Palmetto Expwy). 3655 NW 82nd Ave 33166. Fax: 305/718-8295. **Facility:** 126 one-bedroom standard units. 6 stories, interior corridors. *Bath:* combo or shower only. **Parking:** on-site. **Terms:** small pets only. **Amenities:** video games (fee), high-speed Internet, voice mail, irons, hair dryers. *Some:* dual phone lines. **Pool(s):** heated outdoor. **Leisure Activities:** exercise room. **Guest Services:** valet and coin laundry, airport transportation-Miami International Airport. **Business Services:** meeting rooms. **Cards:** AX, CB, DC, DS, JC, MC, VI. **Special Amenities:** free full breakfast.

SOME UNITS
〔S〕〔➔〕〔🛏〕〔🍴〕〔✆M〕〔▣〕〔📷〕〔➳〕〔VCR〕〔🐾〕〔DATA PORT〕〔▤〕〔▣〕〔💻〕/〔✕〕/

(See maps and indexes starting on p. 534, 542)

BAYMONT INN & SUITES MIAMI AIRPORT WEST   *Book at aaa.com*   Phone: (305)640-9896   **4**
F18
| | 12/1-4/15 & 10/16-11/30 | 1P: $85-$105 | 2P: $85-$105 | XP: $10 | |
| | 4/16-10/15 | 1P: $69-$99 | 2P: $69-$99 | XP: $10 | F18 |

Small-scale Hotel **Location:** Florida Tpke, exit 29, 1.2 mi e to 107th Ave, then right. 3805 NW 107th Ave 33178. Fax: 305/640-0608. **Facility:** 92 units. 84 one-bedroom standard units. 8 one-bedroom suites. 4 stories, interior corridors. *Bath:* combo or shower only. **Parking:** on-site. **Terms:** [ECP] meal plan available. **Amenities:** video games (fee), voice mail, irons, hair dryers. *Some:* high-speed Internet, dual phone lines, safes. **Pool(s):** outdoor. **Guest Services:** valet and coin laundry. **Business Services:** meeting rooms, fax (fee). **Cards:** AX, CB, DC, DS, MC, VI. *(See color ad below)*

SOME UNITS
(ASK) (SD) (TI+) 🍴 🐦 🎥 (DATA PORT) 🖥 / ✕ 🛏 🖨 /

BEST WESTERN MIAMI AIRPORT WEST INN &
SUITES   *Book at aaa.com*   Phone: 305/463-7195   **3**
(AAA) (SAVE)
	12/1-4/20	1P: $119-$149	2P: $119-$149	XP: $10	F17
	9/29-11/30	1P: $89-$129	2P: $89-$129	XP: $10	F17
	4/21-9/28	1P: $81-$119	2P: $81-$119	XP: $10	F17

Small-scale Hotel **Location:** Florida Tpke, exit 29, 1.2 mi e to 107th Ave, then s. 3875 NW 107th Ave 33178. Fax: 305/463-7154. **Facility:** 103 one-bedroom standard units, some with efficiencies. 4 stories, interior corridors. *Bath:* combo or shower only. **Parking:** on-site. **Terms:** 15 day cancellation notice, weekly rates available. **Amenities:** video games (fee), high-speed Internet, voice mail, irons, hair dryers. *Some:* dual phone lines. **Pool(s):** outdoor. **Leisure Activities:** putting green, exercise room. **Guest Services:** valet and coin laundry, airport transportation-Miami International Airport. **Business Services:** meeting rooms, business center. **Cards:** AX, CB, DC, DS, MC, VI. **Special Amenities:** free full breakfast and free local telephone calls.

SOME UNITS
✈ (TI+) (M) 🐦 🎥 (DATA PORT) 🛏 🖨 🖥 / ✕ /

CANDLEWOOD SUITES MIAMI AIRPORT WEST   *Book at aaa.com*   Phone: (305)591-9099   **13**
	1/1-4/30	1P: $109-$129	2P: $109-$129	
	5/1-11/30	1P: $89-$99	2P: $89-$99	
	12/1-12/31	1P: $79-$89	2P: $79-$89	

Small-scale Hotel **Location:** SR 826 (Palmetto Expwy), 0.8 mi w on nw 36th St, 0.4 mi s. 8855 NW 27th St 33172. Fax: 305/591-4117. **Facility:** 128 units. 104 one-bedroom standard units with efficiencies. 24 one-bedroom suites ($139-$169) with kitchens. 3 stories, interior corridors. *Bath:* combo or shower only. **Parking:** on-site. **Terms:** cancellation fee imposed, small pets only ($75 fee). **Amenities:** video library, CD players, dual phone lines, voice mail, irons, hair dryers. **Pool(s):** small heated outdoor. **Leisure Activities:** whirlpool, exercise room. **Guest Services:** valet and coin laundry. **Cards:** AX, DC, DS, MC, VI.

SOME UNITS
(ASK) (SD) 🛏 (TI+) (M) 🐦 (VCR) 🎥 (DATA PORT) 🛏 🖨 🖥 / ✕ /
FEE

COMFORT SUITES MIAMI/KENDALL   *Book at aaa.com*   Phone: (305)220-3901   **7**
(AAA) (SAVE)
| | 12/1-4/16 & 10/1-11/30 [ECP] | 1P: $109-$179 | 2P: $119-$189 | XP: $10 | F17 |
| | 4/17-9/30 [ECP] | 1P: $89-$149 | 2P: $99-$159 | XP: $10 | F17 |

Small-scale Hotel **Location:** Florida Tpke, exit 23 to SW 40th St, e to SW 117th Ave, then n to entrance. 3901 SW 117th Ave 33175. Fax: 305/221-1348. **Facility:** 132 units. 128 one-bedroom standard units. 4 one-bedroom suites ($149-$209) with whirlpools. 5 stories, interior corridors. *Bath:* combo or shower only. **Parking:** on-site. **Amenities:** high-speed Internet, dual phone lines, voice mail, irons, hair dryers. **Pool(s):** heated outdoor. **Leisure Activities:** whirlpool, exercise room. **Guest Services:** valet and coin laundry. **Business Services:** meeting rooms, business center. **Cards:** AX, CB, DC, DS, JC, MC, VI. **Special Amenities:** free expanded continental breakfast and free local telephone calls.

SOME UNITS
(SD) (TI+) (M) 🐦 🎥 (DATA PORT) 🛏 🖨 🖥 / ✕ /

(See maps and indexes starting on p. 534, 542)

COURTYARD BY MARRIOTT-MIAMI AIRPORT
WEST/DORAL AREA   *Book at aaa.com*   Phone: (305)477-8118   **4**

12/1-4/30	1P: $189	2P: $189
5/1-11/30	1P: $179	2P: $179

Location: Just w of jct SR 826 (Palmetto Expwy) and NW 36th St. 3929 NW 79th Ave 33166. Fax: 305/599-9363. **Facility:** 145 units. 133 one-bedroom standard units. 12 one-bedroom suites. 4 stories, interior corridors. Small-scale Hotel *Bath:* combo or shower only. **Parking:** on-site. **Terms:** cancellation fee imposed, package plans. **Amenities:** high-speed Internet, dual phone lines, voice mail, safes, irons, hair dryers. **Dining:** 6-10 am, Sat & Sun 7-11 am. **Pool(s):** heated outdoor. **Leisure Activities:** whirlpool, exercise room. **Guest Services:** valet and coin laundry, airport transportation-Miami International Airport, area transportation-within 3 mi. **Business Services:** meeting rooms. **Cards:** AX, CB, DC, DS, JC, MC, VI. **Special Amenities:** free newspaper.

SOME UNITS

COURTYARD BY MARRIOTT, MIAMI DADELAND   *Book at aaa.com*   Phone: (305)670-1220   **10**

12/1-4/29	1P: $189-$239	2P: $189-$239
9/25-11/30	1P: $169-$189	2P: $169-$189
4/30-6/10	1P: $169-$179	2P: $169-$179
6/11-9/24	1P: $149-$169	2P: $149-$169

Small-scale Hotel
Location: SR 826 (Palmetto Expwy), exit Kendall Dr E, then 2 blks s. 9075 S Dadeland Blvd 33156. Fax: 305/670-1730. **Facility:** 128 units. 122 one-bedroom standard units, some with whirlpools. 6 one-bedroom suites, some with whirlpools. 4 stories, interior corridors. *Bath:* combo or shower only. **Parking:** on-site (fee). **Terms:** package plans. **Amenities:** high-speed Internet, dual phone lines, voice mail, irons, hair dryers. **Pool(s):** heated outdoor. **Leisure Activities:** whirlpool, exercise room. **Guest Services:** sundries, valet and coin laundry. **Business Services:** meeting rooms. *Fee:* PC, fax. **Cards:** AX, CB, DC, DS, JC, MC, VI.

SOME UNITS
FEE FEE

COURTYARD MIAMI AIRPORT SOUTH   *Book at aaa.com*   Phone: (305)642-8200   **18**

12/1-3/30	1P: $169
10/1-11/30	1P: $159
3/31-5/28	1P: $149
5/29-9/30	1P: $129

Small-scale Hotel **Location:** Se of jct SR 836 (Dolphin Expwy). 1201 NW Le Jeune Rd 33126. Fax: 305/644-1168. **Facility:** 125 units. 124 one-bedroom standard units. 1 one-bedroom suite. 5 stories, interior corridors. *Bath:* combo or shower only. **Parking:** on-site (fee). **Terms:** check-in 4 pm, [BP] meal plan available, package plans. **Amenities:** video games (fee), high-speed Internet, voice mail, irons, hair dryers. **Dining:** 2 restaurants, 6:30 am-1 am. **Pool(s):** heated outdoor. **Leisure Activities:** whirlpools, jogging, exercise room, basketball, volleyball. *Fee:* 8 tennis courts (6 lighted), game room. **Guest Services:** valet and coin laundry, airport transportation-Miami International Airport, area transportation-Dolphin Mall. **Cards:** AX, CB, DC, DS, JC, MC, VI. **Special Amenities:** free newspaper and early check-in/late check-out.

SOME UNITS

CROWNE PLAZA MIAMI INTERNATIONAL AIRPORT   *Book at aaa.com*   Phone: 305/446-9000   **24**

10/1-11/30	1P: $209-$259	2P: $209-$259	XP: $15	F12
12/1-4/15	1P: $199-$259	2P: $199-$259	XP: $15	F12
4/16-6/1	1P: $179-$239	2P: $179-$239	XP: $15	F12
6/2-9/30	1P: $129-$199	2P: $129-$199	XP: $15	F12

Large-scale Hotel **Location:** 1 mi s of terminal entrance, just s of jct SR 836 (Dolphin Expwy). 950 NW Le Jeune Rd 33126. Fax: 305/441-0725. **Facility:** 304 one-bedroom standard units. 6 stories, interior corridors. *Bath:* combo or shower only. **Parking:** on-site. **Terms:** cancellation fee imposed, package plans. **Amenities:** CD players, voice mail, irons, hair dryers. *Some:* high-speed Internet. **Dining:** 6:30 am-midnight, cocktails. **Pool(s):** outdoor. **Leisure Activities:** saunas, whirlpool, exercise room. **Guest Services:** gift shop, valet and coin laundry, airport transportation-Miami International Airport. **Business Services:** meeting rooms, business center. **Cards:** AX, DC, DS, JC, MC, VI.

SOME UNITS
FEE

DAYS INN MIAMI INTERNATIONAL AIRPORT
HOTEL   *Book at aaa.com*   Phone: (305)261-4230   **25**

12/1-3/31 & 11/1-11/30	1P: $125-$500	2P: $125-$500	XP: $10	F12
4/1-10/31	1P: $54-$119	2P: $54-$119	XP: $10	F12

Small-scale Hotel **Location:** Just n of Milam Dairy Rd and NW 11th St off SR 836. 7250 NW 11th St 33126. Fax: 305/264-9685. **Facility:** 103 one-bedroom standard units. 4 stories, interior corridors. **Parking:** on-site. **Terms:** $2 service charge. **Amenities:** high-speed Internet, voice mail, safes (fee), irons, hair dryers. **Dining:** 7:30 am-10:30 & 11-10 pm, Fri & Sat-2 am, Sun 7 am-11:30 & 6-10 midnight, cocktails. **Pool(s):** outdoor. **Leisure Activities:** exercise room. **Guest Services:** coin laundry, airport transportation-Miami International Airport, area transportation-Port of Miami. **Business Services:** meeting rooms, business center. **Cards:** AX, CB, DC, DS, JC, MC, VI. **Special Amenities:** free newspaper and free room upgrade (subject to availability with advance reservations).

SOME UNITS

(See maps and indexes starting on p. 534, 542)

DORAL GOLF RESORT AND SPA, A MARRIOTT
RESORT *Book at aaa.com* Phone: (305)592-2000 **1**

(AAA) (SAVE)

12/1-3/31	1P: $219-$319	2P: $219-$319
4/1-5/15 & 10/1-11/30	1P: $219	2P: $219
5/16-9/30	1P: $164	2P: $164

Resort
Large-scale Hotel

Location: 1 mi w of jct SR 826 (Palmetto Expwy) at jct NW 36th St and NW 87th Ave. 4400 NW 87th Ave 33178. **Fax:** 305/594-4682. **Facility:** Rooms at the resort, some with balconies and others that overlook a golf course, vary in size, but all have quality decor; a European spa is nearby. 646 units. 581 one-bedroom standard units. 50 one- and 15 two-bedroom suites ($363-$1254), some with whirlpools. 3-4 stories, interior corridors. *Bath:* combo or shower only. **Parking:** on-site and valet. **Terms:** check-in 4 pm, 3 day cancellation notice-fee imposed, package plans, $18 service charge. **Amenities:** video games (fee), CD players, high-speed Internet, dual phone lines, voice mail, safes, honor bars, irons, hair dryers. **Dining:** 4 restaurants, 6:30 am-midnight, cocktails, entertainment. **Pool(s):** 2 heated outdoor, wading. **Leisure Activities:** whirlpool, waterslide, fishing, stocked lakes, recreation programs, jogging, playground, spa, sports court, basketball, volleyball. *Fee:* charter fishing, golf-90 holes, golf & tennis instruction, 12 tennis courts (6 lighted). **Guest Services:** valet laundry, airport transportation (fee)-Miami International Airport. **Business Services:** conference facilities, business center. **Cards:** AX, CB, DC, DS, JC, MC, VI. **Special Amenities:** free newspaper and early check-in/late check-out.

SOME UNITS

EL PALACIO RESORT HOTEL & SUITES *Book at aaa.com* Phone: 305/624-8401 **2**

(AAA) (SAVE)

All Year 1P: $70-$140 2P: $90-$140

Small-scale Hotel

Location: I-95, exit 12, w on SR 826 (Palmetto Expwy), then n. 16805 NW 12th Ave 33169. **Fax:** 305/625-0022. **Facility:** 104 units. 99 one-bedroom standard units, some with whirlpools. 5 one-bedroom suites with whirlpools. 4 stories, interior corridors. **Parking:** on-site. **Terms:** 3 day cancellation notice-fee imposed, $5 service charge. **Amenities:** voice mail, safes (fee), hair dryers. *Some:* irons. **Dining:** 8 am-10 pm, cocktails. **Pool(s):** outdoor. **Leisure Activities:** exercise room. **Guest Services:** airport transportation-Miami International Airport, area transportation-within 5 mi. **Business Services:** meeting rooms, fax (fee). **Special Amenities:** free newspaper and early check-in/late check-out.

SOME UNITS

EL PALACIO SPORTS HOTEL & CONFERENCE
CENTER *Book at aaa.com* Phone: 305/621-5801 **1**

Property failed to provide current rates

Large-scale Hotel

Location: SR 852 at jct SR 817 and Florida Tpke, exit 47; from south exit 4X. Located next to the racetrack and Pro Player Stadium. 21485 NW 27th Ave 33056. **Fax:** 305/624-8202. **Facility:** 214 one-bedroom standard units. 9 stories, interior corridors. *Bath:* combo or shower only. **Parking:** on-site. **Amenities:** video games (fee), voice mail, irons, hair dryers. **Pool(s):** heated outdoor. **Leisure Activities:** exercise room. *Fee:* game room. **Guest Services:** gift shop, valet and coin laundry. **Business Services:** meeting rooms, fax (fee).

SOME UNITS

FAIRFIELD INN BY MARRIOTT-MIAMI WEST/DORAL
AREA *Book at aaa.com* Phone: 305/599-5200 **3**

Property failed to provide current rates

Small-scale Hotel

Location: Just w of jct SR 826 (Palmetto Expwy) and NW 36th St. 3959 NW 79th Ave 33166. **Fax:** 305/436-2935. **Facility:** 129 one-bedroom standard units. 3 stories, interior/exterior corridors. **Parking:** on-site. **Amenities:** high-speed Internet, voice mail, irons, hair dryers. **Pool(s):** heated outdoor. **Guest Services:** valet laundry.

SOME UNITS

FAIRFIELD INN MIAMI AIRPORT SOUTH *Book at aaa.com* Phone: (305)643-0055 **16**

(AAA) (SAVE)

12/1-4/14	1P: $129-$159
10/1-11/30	1P: $89-$139
4/15-9/30	1P: $79-$129

Motel

Location: Se of jct SR 836 (Palmetto Expwy) and NW Le Jeune Rd. 1201 NW Le Jeune Rd 33126. **Fax:** 305/649-3997. **Facility:** 281 one-bedroom standard units. 3 stories, exterior corridors. *Bath:* combo or shower only. **Parking:** on-site. **Terms:** cancellation fee imposed, [ECP] meal plan available, package plans, 13% service charge. **Amenities:** voice mail, irons, hair dryers. **Dining:** 6:30 am-1 am. **Pool(s):** heated outdoor. **Leisure Activities:** whirlpools, jogging, exercise room, basketball, volleyball. *Fee:* 8 tennis courts (6 lighted), game room. **Guest Services:** valet and coin laundry, airport transportation-Miami International Airport, area transportation-Dolphin Mall. **Cards:** AX, CB, DC, DS, JC, MC, VI. **Special Amenities:** free expanded continental breakfast and free local telephone calls.

SOME UNITS

HAMPTON INN & SUITES-MIAMI AIRPORT/BLUE
LAGOON *Book at aaa.com* Phone: (305)262-5400 **26**

| 1/1-4/15 [BP] | 1P: $119-$209 | 2P: $129-$219 |
| 12/1-12/31 & 4/16-11/30 [BP] | 1P: $79-$169 | 2P: $89-$179 |

Small-scale Hotel

Location: SR 836 (Dolphin Expwy), exit Red Rd/57th Ave S, just s of NW 7th St. 777 NW 57th Ave 33126. **Fax:** 305/262-5488. **Facility:** 147 units. 110 one-bedroom standard units. 37 one-bedroom suites with kitchens. 11 stories, interior corridors. *Bath:* combo or shower only. **Parking:** on-site. **Terms:** 7 day cancellation notice. **Amenities:** video games (fee), high-speed Internet, dual phone lines, voice mail, safes, irons, hair dryers. **Pool(s):** outdoor. **Leisure Activities:** whirlpool, exercise room. **Guest Services:** valet and coin laundry, area transportation. **Business Services:** meeting rooms, business center. **Cards:** AX, CB, DC, DS, JC, MC, VI.

SOME UNITS

(See maps and indexes starting on p. 534, 542)

HAMPTON INN-MIAMI AIRPORT WEST   *Book at aaa.com*   Phone: (305)513-0777   **9**

(AAA) (SAVE)

1/1-4/30 [BP]	1P: $129-$179	2P: $129-$169	XP: $5	F16
5/1-11/30 [BP]	1P: $89-$109	2P: $89-$109	XP: $5	F16
12/1-12/31 [BP]	1P: $79-$102	2P: $79-$102	XP: $5	F16

Small-scale Hotel   **Location:** SR 826 (Palmetto Expwy), exit NW 36th St, just s of jct NW 58th St, just s; in Boykin Center. 3620 NW 79th Ave 33166. Fax: 305/513-9019. **Facility:** 127 one-bedroom standard units. 6 stories, interior corridors. *Bath:* combo or shower only. **Parking:** on-site. **Terms:** pets ($25 extra charge). **Amenities:** video games (fee), high-speed Internet, voice mail, irons, hair dryers. **Pool(s):** heated outdoor. **Leisure Activities:** exercise room. **Guest Services:** valet and coin laundry, airport transportation-Miami International Airport, area transportation-within 3 mi. **Business Services:** meeting rooms, business center. **Cards:** AX, DC, DS, MC, VI. **Special Amenities: free full breakfast and free local telephone calls.**

SOME UNITS

HILTON MIAMI AIRPORT   *Book at aaa.com*   Phone: (305)262-1000   **22**

All Year	1P: $89-$249	2P: $89-$249	XP: $10	F18

Large-scale Hotel   **Location:** Se of jct SR 836 (Dolphin Expwy), exit Red Rd, 0.7 mi e. 5101 Blue Lagoon Dr 33126. Fax: 305/267-0038. **Facility:** On a peninsula near a lagoon, the hotel offers units with views of water or runway; decor is contemporary, with warm, comfortable color schemes. 500 units. 430 one-bedroom standard units. 70 one-bedroom suites. 14 stories, interior corridors. *Bath:* combo or shower only. **Parking:** on-site (fee) and valet. **Terms:** cancellation fee imposed, [AP], [BP], [CP], [ECP] & [MAP] meal plans available. **Amenities:** dual phone lines, voice mail, honor bars, irons, hair dryers. *Fee:* video games, high-speed Internet. *Some:* DVD players, fax. **Pool(s):** heated outdoor. **Leisure Activities:** saunas, whirlpool, 2 lighted tennis courts, jogging, exercise room, basketball. **Guest Services:** gift shop, valet laundry, area transportation. **Business Services:** conference facilities, business center. **Cards:** AX, CB, DC, DS, MC, VI.

SOME UNITS

HOLIDAY INN-MIAMI AIRPORT WEST   *Book at aaa.com*   Phone: (305)500-9000   **12**

1/1-5/31	1P: $92-$109	2P: $92-$109	XP: $10	F12
6/1-11/30	1P: $85-$99	2P: $85-$99	XP: $10	F12
12/1-12/31	1P: $80-$95	2P: $80-$95	XP: $10	F12

Small-scale Hotel   **Location:** 0.4 mi s of jct NW 36th St. 3255 NW 87th Ave 33172. Fax: 305/500-9500. **Facility:** 120 units. 115 one-bedroom standard units. 5 one-bedroom suites. 6 stories, interior corridors. *Bath:* combo or shower only. **Parking:** on-site. **Terms:** cancellation fee imposed, [AP], [BP] & [CP] meal plans available, package plans. **Amenities:** video games (fee), high-speed Internet, dual phone lines, voice mail, safes, honor bars, irons, hair dryers. **Pool(s):** heated outdoor. **Leisure Activities:** exercise room, basketball. **Guest Services:** valet and coin laundry. **Business Services:** meeting rooms, business center. **Cards:** AX, DC, DS, MC, VI.

SOME UNITS

HOMESTEAD STUDIO SUITES
HOTEL-MIAMI/AIRPORT/BLUE LAGOON   *Book at aaa.com*   Phone: (305)260-0085   **27**

1/2-4/15	1P: $64-$89	2P: $69-$94	XP: $5	F17
12/1-1/1 & 4/16-11/30	1P: $49-$69	2P: $54-$74	XP: $5	F17

Motel   **Location:** SR 836 (Dolphin Expwy), exit Milam Dairy Rd S, 0.3 mi e; in Blue Lagoon Office Park. 6605 NW 7th St 33126. Fax: 305/260-0042. **Facility:** 149 one-bedroom standard units with efficiencies. 2 stories, exterior corridors. *Bath:* combo or shower only. **Parking:** on-site. **Terms:** office hours 6:30 am-10:30 pm, small pets only ($75 fee). **Amenities:** high-speed Internet (fee), voice mail, irons. **Guest Services:** sundries, valet and coin laundry. **Cards:** AX, DC, DS, MC, VI.

SOME UNITS

HOMESTEAD STUDIO SUITES
HOTEL-MIAMI/AIRPORT/DORAL   *Book at aaa.com*   Phone: (305)436-1811   **10**

1/2-4/15	1P: $69-$94	2P: $74-$99	XP: $5	F17
12/1-1/1 & 4/16-11/30	1P: $49-$69	2P: $54-$74	XP: $5	F17

Motel   **Location:** SR 826 (Palmetto Expwy), 0.8 mi w on NW 36th St, just s. Located in the Westpoint Office Park. 8720 NW 33rd St 33172. Fax: 305/436-1864. **Facility:** 150 one-bedroom standard units with efficiencies. 2 stories, exterior corridors. *Bath:* combo or shower only. **Parking:** on-site. **Terms:** office hours 7 am-11 pm, pets ($75 fee). **Amenities:** high-speed Internet (fee), voice mail, irons. **Pool(s):** small heated outdoor. **Guest Services:** coin laundry. **Cards:** AX, DC, DS, MC, VI.

SOME UNITS

HOMEWOOD SUITES BY HILTON-MIAMI
AIRPORT/BLUE LAGOON   *Book at aaa.com*   Phone: (305)261-3335   **23**

12/1-5/15	1P: $169-$199	2P: $169-$199	
10/1-11/30	1P: $129-$199	2P: $129-$199	
5/16-9/30	1P: $119-$179	2P: $119-$179	

Small-scale Hotel   **Location:** Se of jct SR 836 (Dolphin Expwy), exit Red Rd. 5500 Blue Lagoon Dr 33126. Fax: 305/261-1223. **Facility:** 159 units. 134 one- and 25 two-bedroom suites with efficiencies. 7 stories, interior corridors. *Bath:* combo or shower only. **Parking:** on-site. **Terms:** [BP] meal plan available, small pets only ($20-$100 fee, $20 extra charge). **Amenities:** high-speed Internet, dual phone lines, voice mail, safes (fee), irons, hair dryers. **Pool(s):** heated outdoor. **Leisure Activities:** whirlpool, fishing, exercise room, sports court. **Guest Services:** complimentary evening beverages: Mon-Thurs, valet and coin laundry, area transportation. **Business Services:** meeting rooms, business center. **Cards:** AX, CB, DC, DS, JC, MC, VI.

SOME UNITS

(See maps and indexes starting on p. 534, 542)

LA QUINTA INN & SUITES MIAMI (AIRPORT WEST)   *Book at aaa.com*   **Phone:** (305)436-0830   [14]

AAA SAVE	2/1-4/30	1P: $109-$129	XP: $7	F18
	5/1-11/30	1P: $92-$112	XP: $7	F18
◆◆◆	12/1-1/31	1P: $89-$109	XP: $7	F18

Small-scale Hotel **Location:** SR 836 (Dolphin Expwy), just n on 87th NW Ave. 8730 NW 27th St 33172. Fax: 305/436-0840. **Facility:** 143 units. 137 one-bedroom standard units. 6 one-bedroom suites. 6 stories, interior corridors. *Bath:* combo or shower only. **Parking:** on-site. **Terms:** [ECP] meal plan available, small pets only. **Amenities:** video games (fee), high-speed Internet, voice mail, irons, hair dryers. *Some:* dual phone lines. **Pool(s):** heated outdoor. **Leisure Activities:** whirlpool, exercise room. **Guest Services:** airport transportation-Miami International Airport. **Business Services:** meeting rooms, fax (fee). **Cards:** AX, CB, DC, DS, MC, VI. **Special Amenities:** free expanded continental breakfast and free local telephone calls.

SOME UNITS

[icons]

LA QUINTA INN MIAMI (AIRPORT NORTH)   *Book at aaa.com*   **Phone:** (305)599-9902   [5]

AAA SAVE	12/1-4/30	1P: $79-$99	XP: $7	F18
	5/1-11/30	1P: $75-$85	XP: $7	F18

Motel **Location:** Just e of jct SR 826 (Palmetto Expwy). 7401 NW 36th St 33166. Fax: 305/594-0552. **Facility:** 165 units. 162 one-bedroom standard units. 3 one-bedroom suites. 3 stories, exterior corridors. *Bath:* combo or shower only. **Parking:** on-site. **Terms:** [ECP] meal plan available, small pets only. **Amenities:** video games (fee), voice mail, irons, hair dryers. **Pool(s):** outdoor. **Guest Services:** valet and coin laundry, airport transportation-Miami International Airport. **Business Services:** fax (fee). **Cards:** AX, CB, DC, DS, MC, VI. **Special Amenities:** free expanded continental breakfast and free local telephone calls.

SOME UNITS

[icons]

MIAMI AIRPORT MARRIOTT   *Book at aaa.com*   **Phone:** (305)649-5000   [17]

◆◆◆	All Year	1P: $134

Large-scale Hotel **Location:** Se of jct SR 836 (Dolphin Expwy) and NW Le Jeune Rd. 1201 NW Le Jeune Rd 33126. Fax: 305/642-3369. **Facility:** 366 units. 361 one-bedroom standard units. 5 one-bedroom suites. 10 stories, interior corridors. *Bath:* combo or shower only. **Parking:** on-site (fee). **Terms:** check-in 4 pm, cancellation fee imposed, package plans. **Amenities:** dual phone lines, voice mail, irons, hair dryers. *Fee:* video games, high-speed Internet. *Some: Fee:* DVD players. **Pool(s):** heated outdoor. **Leisure Activities:** whirlpools, jogging, exercise room, basketball, volleyball. *Fee:* 8 tennis courts (6 lighted), game room. **Guest Services:** gift shop, valet and coin laundry, area transportation. **Business Services:** conference facilities, business center. **Cards:** AX, CB, DC, DS, JC, MC, VI.

SOME UNITS

[icons] FEE FEE

MIAMI MARRIOTT DADELAND   *Book at aaa.com*   **Phone:** (305)670-1035   [11]

AAA SAVE	12/1-4/29	1P: $219-$249	2P: $219-$249
	10/1-11/30	1P: $199-$249	2P: $199-$249
◆◆◆ ◆◆◆	4/30-5/27	1P: $199-$239	2P: $199-$239
	5/28-9/30	1P: $169-$209	2P: $169-$209

Large-scale Hotel **Location:** SR 826 (Palmetto Expwy), exit Kendall Dr E, then 2 blks. 9090 S Dadeland Blvd 33156. Fax: 305/670-5083. **Facility:** The hotel, near shopping and the University of Miami, offers spacious rooms with contemporary decor as well as a lobby with marble floor. 302 units. 300 one-bedroom standard units. 2 one-bedroom suites. 24 stories, interior corridors. *Bath:* combo or shower only. **Parking:** on-site (fee) and valet. **Terms:** check-in 4 pm, package plans. **Amenities:** dual phone lines, voice mail, safes, honor bars, irons, hair dryers. *Fee:* video games, high-speed Internet. *Some:* CD players. **Dining:** 2 restaurants, 6:30 am-2:30 & 4:30-11 pm, cocktails. **Pool(s):** heated outdoor. **Leisure Activities:** whirlpool, exercise room. **Guest Services:** gift shop, valet and coin laundry, airport transportation-Miami International Airport, area transportation-within 3 mi. **Business Services:** conference facilities, business center. **Cards:** AX, CB, DC, DS, JC, MC, VI. **Special Amenities:** free newspaper.

SOME UNITS

[icons]

(See maps and indexes starting on p. 534, 542)

QUALITY INN-SOUTH AT THE FALLS   *Book at aaa.com*   Phone: (305)251-2000   **12**

AAA SAVE	2/10-4/30	1P: $99-$119	2P: $99-$119	XP: $10	F18
	12/23-2/9	1P: $94-$111	2P: $94-$111	XP: $10	F18
	12/1-12/22	1P: $84-$100	2P: $84-$100	XP: $10	F18
Motel	5/1-11/30	1P: $79-$96	2P: $79-$96	XP: $10	F18

Location: US 1 at SW 145th St. 14501 S Dixie Hwy (US 1) 33176. Fax: 305/235-2225. **Facility:** 100 one-bedroom standard units. 2 stories (no elevator), exterior corridors. **Parking:** on-site. **Terms:** weekly rates available, small pets only ($10 extra charge). **Amenities:** dual phone lines, voice mail, irons, hair dryers. **Dining:** 6:30 am-10 pm, Fri & Sat-11 pm, cocktails. **Pool(s):** heated outdoor. **Leisure Activities:** *Fee:* game room. **Guest Services:** coin laundry. **Business Services:** meeting rooms, fax (fee). **Cards:** AX, CB, DC, DS, MC, VI. **Special Amenities:** free newspaper and free room upgrade (subject to availability with advance reservations). *(See color ad below)*

SOME UNITS

🅂🄳 🍴 🍸 🛋 🐾 📷 DATA PORT 💻 / ✕ 🛗 🖥 / FEE

RADISSON KENDALL HOTEL & SUITES MIAMI   *Book at aaa.com*   Phone: (305)279-7700   **9**

	1/16-4/30 & 10/2-11/30	1P: $179-$469	2P: $179-$469	XP: $10	F18
	5/1-10/1	1P: $149-$369	2P: $149-$369	XP: $10	F18
Small-scale Hotel	12/1-1/15	1P: $139-$369	2P: $139-$369	XP: $10	F18

Location: Florida Tpke, exit 20, 3 mi e; SR 874 (Don Shula), 0.6 mi e; US 1, 1.8 mi w. Located next to Baptist Hospital of Miami. 9100 N Kendall Dr 33176. Fax: 305/779-9179. **Facility:** 156 units. 108 one-bedroom standard units. 32 one- and 16 two-bedroom suites ($229-$479) with kitchens. 4 stories, interior corridors. *Bath:* combo or shower only. **Parking:** on-site. **Terms:** package plans. **Amenities:** dual phone lines, voice mail, safes, honor bars, irons, hair dryers. *Fee:* video games, high-speed Internet. **Pool(s):** outdoor. **Leisure Activities:** whirlpool, 2 lighted tennis courts, exercise room. **Guest Services:** valet laundry, area transportation. **Business Services:** meeting rooms, fax (fee). **Cards:** AX, CB, DC, DS, MC, VI.

SOME UNITS

ASK 🅂🄳 🍴 🍸 🛋 ✕ 📷 DATA PORT 💻 / ✕ 🛗 / FEE

RAMADA LIMITED SOUTH MIAMI DADELAND   *Book at aaa.com*   Phone: (305)595-6000   **8**

	12/1-4/30 [ECP]	1P: $109-$145	2P: $119-$155	XP: $10	F21
Small-scale Hotel	5/1-11/30 [ECP]	1P: $139-$369		XP: $10	F21

Location: SR 826 (Palmetto Expwy), exit Kendall Dr, just w. 7600 N Kendall Dr 33156. Fax: 305/279-6988. **Facility:** 122 one-bedroom standard units. 6 stories, interior corridors. **Parking:** on-site. **Amenities:** high-speed Internet, dual phone lines, voice mail, irons, hair dryers. **Pool(s):** outdoor. **Business Services:** meeting rooms, fax (fee). **Cards:** AX, CB, DC, DS, JC, MC, VI.

SOME UNITS

ASK 🅂🄳 🍴 🛋 🐾 ✕ 📷 DATA PORT 💻 / ✕ 🛗 /

RESIDENCE INN BY MARRIOTT   *Book at aaa.com*   Phone: (305)591-2211   **19**

	All Year	1P: $99-$189
Small-scale Hotel	

Location: SR 836 (Dolphin Expwy), exit 87th Ave NW, just n to NW 82nd Ave, then e. 1212 NW 82nd Ave 33126. Fax: 305/591-0902. **Facility:** 112 units. 64 one-bedroom standard units with kitchens. 48 one-bedroom suites with kitchens. 3 stories, exterior corridors. **Parking:** on-site. **Terms:** pets ($75 fee). **Amenities:** high-speed Internet, voice mail, irons, hair dryers. **Pool(s):** small outdoor. **Leisure Activities:** whirlpool, limited exercise equipment, sports court, basketball. **Business Services:** meeting rooms, fax (fee). **Cards:** AX, CB, DC, DS, JC, MC, VI.

SOME UNITS

ASK 🅂🄳 🐾 🍴 🛋 🐾 ✕ 📷 DATA PORT 🛗 🖥 💻 / ✕ / FEE

SHERATON MIAMI MART HOTEL   Phone: (305)261-3800   **29**

	1/1-3/31	1P: $149-$199	2P: $149-$229	XP: $20	F17
Large-scale Hotel	12/1-12/31 & 4/1-11/30	1P: $109-$199	2P: $109-$199	XP: $20	F17

Location: At Milam Dairy Rd off SR 836 (Dolphin Expwy). Located adjacent to the Merchandise Mart Complex. 711 NW 72nd Ave 33126. Fax: 305/261-7665. **Facility:** 334 units. 331 one-bedroom standard units, some with whirlpools. 3 one-bedroom suites ($239-$599). 12 stories, interior corridors. *Bath:* combo or shower only. **Parking:** on-site (fee). **Terms:** cancellation fee imposed. **Amenities:** high-speed Internet (fee), dual phone lines, voice mail, honor bars, irons, hair dryers. *Some:* CD players. **Pool(s):** heated outdoor. **Leisure Activities:** whirlpool, racquetball court, exercise room. **Guest Services:** gift shop, valet laundry. **Business Services:** conference facilities, business center. **Cards:** AX, DC, DS, MC, VI.

SOME UNITS

ASK 🅂🄳 ✚ 🍴 🍸 🛋 🐾 ✕ 📷 DATA PORT 💻 / ✕ 🛗 /

(See maps and indexes starting on p. 534, 542)

SOFITEL MIAMI   *Book at aaa.com*   Phone: (305)264-4888   **21**
All Year   1P: $279   2P: $279   XP: $20   F18
Location: Just sw of jct SR 836 (Dolphin Expwy), exit Red Rd. 5800 Blue Lagoon Dr 33126. Fax: 305/262-9049.
Large-scale Hotel   **Facility:** Striking modern architecture and Art Deco-style rooms distinguish this property, which overlooks a lagoon and is close to the airport. 281 units. 254 one-bedroom standard units. 27 one-bedroom suites. 15 stories, interior corridors. *Bath:* combo or shower only. **Parking:** on-site (fee) and valet. **Terms:** cancellation fee imposed, package plans, small pets only. **Amenities:** dual phone lines, voice mail, irons, hair dryers. *Fee:* video games, high-speed Internet. *Some:* CD players. **Dining:** La Riviera Restaurant, see separate listing. **Pool(s):** outdoor. **Leisure Activities:** 2 lighted tennis courts. *Fee:* massage. **Guest Services:** gift shop, valet laundry, area transportation. **Business Services:** conference facilities, business center. **Cards:** AX, DC, DS, MC, VI.

SOME UNITS
(ASK) [S/D] [✈] [🐾] [🍴] [24↑] [Y] [🏊] [👥] [✱] [DATA PORT] / [✕] [🔒] /
FEE

THE SPA AT DORAL, A MARRIOTT RESORT   Phone: (305)593-6030   **2**
4/9-5/15 & 10/1-11/30   1P: $529-$1254   2P: $529-$1254
5/16-9/30   1P: $352-$946   2P: $352-$946
Resort   12/1-4/8   1P: $352-$430   2P: $352-$430
Small-scale Hotel   **Location:** 1.3 mi w of jct SR 826 (Palmetto Expwy); on NW 36th St. Located on the grounds of the Doral Golf Resort. 8755 NW 36th St 33178. Fax: 305/591-9268. **Facility:** This property offers world-class spa services and features spacious and luxurious rooms decorated in soft colors. Designated smoking area. 48 one-bedroom standard units with whirlpools. 3 stories, interior corridors. **Parking:** on-site and valet. **Terms:** age restrictions may apply, 3 day cancellation notice-fee imposed, package plans. **Amenities:** video games (fee), CD players, high-speed Internet, dual phone lines, voice mail, safes, honor bars, irons, hair dryers. *Some:* fax. **Pool(s):** outdoor, heated indoor, lap. **Leisure Activities:** saunas, whirlpool, steamrooms, waterslide, fishing, jogging, spa. *Fee:* charter fishing, golf-90 holes, 12 tennis courts (6 lighted). **Guest Services:** gift shop, valet laundry. **Business Services:** meeting rooms, business center. **Cards:** AX, CB, DC, DS, JC, MC, VI.

(ASK) [S/D] [✈] [🍴] [🏊] [✱] [✕] [✕] [DATA PORT] [🔒] [💻]
FEE

SPRINGHILL SUITES BY MARRIOTT   Phone: (305)265-0144   **28**
1/1-4/16   1P: $99-$149   2P: $99-$149
10/2-11/30   1P: $99-$139   2P: $99-$139
Small-scale Hotel   4/17-10/1   1P: $89-$129   2P: $89-$129
12/1-12/31   1P: $89-$109   2P: $89-$109
Location: SR 836 (Dolphin Expwy), exit NW 72nd Ave S. 6700 NW 7th St 33126. Fax: 305/265-6213. **Facility:** 151 one-bedroom standard units. 7 stories, interior corridors. *Bath:* combo or shower only. **Parking:** on-site. **Terms:** small pets only ($10 fee). **Amenities:** high-speed Internet (fee), voice mail, irons, hair dryers. *Some:* dual phone lines. **Pool(s):** heated outdoor. **Leisure Activities:** exercise room. **Guest Services:** valet and coin laundry, area transportation. **Business Services:** meeting rooms, business center. **Cards:** AX, DC, DS, JC, MC, VI.

SOME UNITS
(ASK) [✈] [🐾] [📷] [🏊] [✱] [DATA PORT] [🔒] [🖼] [💻] / [✕] /
FEE

STAYBRIDGE SUITES MIAMI-AIRPORT
WEST-DORAL   *Book at aaa.com*   Phone: (305)500-9100   **11**
4/17-11/30 [BP]   1P: $112-$158   2P: $112-$159   XP: $10   F16
12/1-4/16 [BP]   1P: $102-$138   2P: $102-$138   XP: $10   F16
Small-scale Hotel   **Location:** 0.4 mi s of jct NW 36th St. 3265 NW 87th Ave 33172. Fax: 305/500-9200. **Facility:** 96 units. 56 one-bedroom standard units with efficiencies. 40 one-bedroom suites with kitchens. 8 stories, interior corridors. *Bath:* combo or shower only. **Parking:** on-site. **Terms:** 3 day cancellation notice-fee imposed, package plans, pets ($125 fee). **Amenities:** video library (fee), high-speed Internet, dual phone lines, voice mail, irons, hair dryers. **Pool(s):** outdoor. **Leisure Activities:** exercise room, basketball. **Guest Services:** valet and coin laundry, area transportation. **Business Services:** meeting rooms, business center. **Cards:** AX, CB, DC, DS, JC, MC, VI.

SOME UNITS
(ASK) [S/D] [✈] [🐾] [📷] [🏊] [VCR] [✱] [DATA PORT] [🔒] [🖼] [💻] / [✕] /
FEE

SUMMERFIELD SUITES BY WYNDHAM-MIAMI
AIRPORT   *Book at aaa.com*   Phone: (305)269-1922   **20**
1/1-4/30 & 10/1-11/30 [BP]   1P: $129-$264   2P: $129-$284   XP: $20   F17
12/1-12/31 & 5/1-9/30 [BP]   1P: $109-$224   2P: $109-$244   XP: $20   F17
Small-scale Hotel   **Location:** Se of jct SR 836 (Dolphin Expwy), exit Red Rd, just w. 5710 Blue Lagoon Dr 33126. Fax: 305/269-1925. **Facility:** 156 units. 99 one- and 57 two-bedroom suites ($109-$284) with kitchens. 3 stories, interior corridors. *Bath:* combo or shower only. **Parking:** on-site. **Terms:** pets ($200 fee). **Amenities:** dual phone lines, safes, irons, hair dryers. *Fee:* video library, high-speed Internet. **Pool(s):** heated outdoor. **Leisure Activities:** whirlpool, limited exercise equipment. **Guest Services:** sundries, complimentary evening beverages: Mon-Thurs, valet and coin laundry, area transportation. **Business Services:** meeting rooms, fax (fee). **Cards:** AX, CB, DC, DS, JC, MC, VI.

SOME UNITS
(ASK) [✈] [🐾] [🍴] [M] [📷] [🏊] [VCR] [✱] [DATA PORT] [🔒] [🖼] [💻] / [✕] /
FEE

SUPER 8 MOTEL   *Book at aaa.com*   Phone: 305/573-7700   **5**

Property failed to provide current rates
Motel   **Location:** I-195, exit 2A, just s on US 1 (Biscayne Blvd). 3400 Biscayne Blvd 33137. Fax: 305/573-7706.
Facility: 49 one-bedroom standard units. 2 stories (no elevator), exterior corridors. **Parking:** on-site.
Pool(s): outdoor. **Guest Services:** coin laundry. **Business Services:** fax (fee).

SOME UNITS
[🍴] [🏊] [✱] [DATA PORT] / [✕] [🔒] /

(See maps and indexes starting on p. 534, 542)

TOWNEPLACE SUITES BY MARRIOTT   *Book at aaa.com*   Phone: (305)718-4144   6

	1/1-4/30 [CP]	1P: $79-$179	2P: $79-$179
	5/1-11/30 [CP]	1P: $49-$129	2P: $49-$129
	12/1-12/31 [CP]	1P: $49-$119	2P: $49-$119

Small-scale Hotel   **Location:** Florida Tpke, exit 29, 1.2 mi e to 107th Ave, then just s. Located in an office park. 10505 NW 36th St 33178. Fax: 305/718-4480. **Facility:** 95 units. 59 one-bedroom standard units with efficiencies. 6 one- and 30 two-bedroom suites, some with kitchens. 4 stories, interior corridors. *Bath:* combo or shower only. **Parking:** on-site. **Terms:** 14 day cancellation notice, pets ($75 fee). **Amenities:** high-speed Internet, dual phone lines, voice mail, irons, hair dryers. **Pool(s):** small outdoor. **Leisure Activities:** limited exercise equipment. **Guest Services:** valet and coin laundry. **Business Services:** fax (fee). **Cards:** AX, CB, DC, DS, MC, VI.

SOME UNITS

WELLESLEY INN (MIAMI AIRPORT)   Phone: 305/592-4799   6

Property failed to provide current rates

Small-scale Hotel   **Location:** 0.8 mi w of jct SR 826 (Palmetto Expwy). 8436 NW 36th St 33166. Fax: 305/471-8461. **Facility:** 104 units. 91 one-bedroom standard units. 13 one-bedroom suites. 4 stories, interior corridors. **Parking:** on-site. **Terms:** pets ($25 fee). **Amenities:** video games (fee), high-speed Internet, voice mail, irons, hair dryers. **Pool(s):** heated outdoor. **Guest Services:** valet and coin laundry. **Business Services:** meeting rooms.

SOME UNITS

WYNDHAM MIAMI AIRPORT   *Book at aaa.com*   Phone: (305)871-3800   15

	10/1-11/30	1P: $149-$189	2P: $149-$199	XP: $10	F17
	1/1-4/30	1P: $119-$189	2P: $119-$199	XP: $10	F17
	12/1-12/31	1P: $139-$189	2P: $139-$189	XP: $10	F17
	5/1-9/30	1P: $99-$139	2P: $99-$149	XP: $10	F17

Large-scale Hotel   **Location:** Le Jeune Rd, 0.3 mi e on NW 25th St, then s on NW 39th Ave to end of street. 3900 NW 21st St 33142. Fax: 305/871-0447. **Facility:** 408 units. 402 one-bedroom standard units. 6 one-bedroom suites ($199-$299). 10 stories, interior corridors. *Bath:* combo or shower only. **Parking:** on-site (fee) and valet. **Amenities:** dual phone lines, voice mail, irons, hair dryers. *Fee:* video games, high-speed Internet. *Some:* CD players, fax. **Dining:** 6 am-2:30 & 5:30-10 pm, cocktails. **Pool(s):** heated outdoor. **Leisure Activities:** saunas, whirlpool, 3 lighted tennis courts, exercise room. *Fee:* golf-18 holes, golf instruction. **Guest Services:** gift shop, valet laundry, airport transportation-Miami International Airport. **Business Services:** meeting rooms, business center. **Cards:** AX, CB, DC, DS, JC, MC, VI.

SOME UNITS

------ **WHERE TO DINE** ------

94TH AERO SQUADRON   Lunch: $7-$17   Dinner: $13-$45   Phone: 305/261-4220   5

American   **Location:** E from SR 836, exit Red Rd; U-turn at light from SR 836 W, exit Red Rd. 1395 NW 57th Ave 33126. **Hours:** 11 am-10 pm, Fri & Sat-11 pm, Sun 10 am-10 pm; also Sunday brunch. **Reservations:** suggested. **Features:** Fans of flying appreciate this replica of a World War II French farmhouse for its runway views and for the headsets that let users get an earful of talk from the tower. The prime rib of beef, filet mignon and upside-down apple walnut cake are favorites. Casual dress; cocktails; entertainment. **Parking:** on-site. **Cards:** AX, DS, MC, VI.

ANACAPRI   Lunch: $8-$11   Dinner: $11-$22   Phone: 305/232-8001   28

Italian   **Location:** Just n of SW 128th and US 1 (S Dixie Hwy); in Southpark Centre. 12669 S Dixie Hwy 33156. **Hours:** 11:30 am-2:30 & 5-10:30 pm, Fri & Sat-11:30 pm, Sun 5 pm-9 pm. Closed major holidays; also Tues. **Reservations:** suggested, after 6:30 pm. **Features:** The friendly neighborhood restaurant brings all the favorite Italian dishes—from A to Z—to Miami. A cozy atmosphere tops it all off the right way. This place's market, with some menu favorites, is just a few steps away. Semi-formal attire; beer & wine only. **Parking:** on-site. **Cards:** AX, CB, DC, DS, JC, MC, VI.

ANDIAMO! BRICK OVEN PIZZA   Lunch: $8-$19   Dinner: $8-$19   Phone: 305/762-5751   2

Pizza   **Location:** I-195, exit 2A, 1 mi n. 5600 Biscayne Blvd 33137. **Hours:** 11 am-11 pm, Fri & Sat-midnight. Closed: 11/23, 12/25. **Reservations:** not accepted. **Features:** New York and classic Italian-style pizzas are cooked in a brick oven. Patrons can choose from many combinations or create their own pie. Most of the eating area is outside. Casual dress; beer & wine only. **Parking:** on-site and street. **Cards:** AX, MC, VI.

APO'S CAFE   Lunch: $7-$14   Dinner: $7-$14   Phone: 305/870-0207   2

Latino   **Location:** Just e of NW 62nd Ave; n of airport. 6301 NW 36th St 33166. **Hours:** 7 am-10 pm, Fri & Sat 11 am-11 pm. **Reservations:** accepted. **Features:** Offering authentic Puerto Rican fare, the restaurant also features attentive service in a spacious Hispanic Colonial dining room. Casual dress; cocktails. **Parking:** on-site. **Cards:** AX, CB, DC, DS, JC, MC, VI.

AYESTARAN RESTAURANT   Lunch: $3-$19   Dinner: $3-$19   Phone: 305/649-4982   10

Caribbean   **Location:** Jct US 1 and SW 27th Ave, just n. **Hours:** 7 am-1 am. **Features:** The friendly neighborhood restaurant serves Cuban and Spanish food. Representative of weekly specials are Cuban sandwiches, meatballs and white rice and arroz con pollo. Casual dress. **Parking:** on-site. **Cards:** AX, CB, DC, DS, MC, VI.

CAMI'S SEAFOOD & PASTA   Lunch: $4-$10   Dinner: $5-$17   Phone: 305/223-2911   14

Seafood   **Location:** Florida Tpke, exit 25, just w; corner of SW 122nd Ave and SW 8th St. 12170 SW 8th St 33175. **Hours:** 11 am-10 pm, Fri & Sat-11:30 pm. Closed: 11/23. **Features:** Here you will find fresh seafood served fast. Menu highlights include a shrimp pasta in cream sauce and stone crabs when in season. If you have a taste for garlic, choose penne pasta with spinach and shrimp. For dessert, try the local favorite, Key lime pie. Casual dress; beer & wine only. **Parking:** on-site. **Cards:** AX, DC, DS, MC, VI.

(See maps and indexes starting on p. 534, 542)

CASA JUANCHO RESTAURANT　　Lunch: $10-$38　　Dinner: $16-$38　　Phone: 305/642-2452　⑪
Spanish
Location: Just e of jct SW 8th St and SW 25th Ave. 2436 SW 8th St 33135. **Hours:** noon-midnight, Fri & Sat-1 am. Closed: for dinner 12/24. **Reservations:** suggested. **Features:** Freshly prepared dishes of authentic Spanish cuisine are served in a tranquil garden setting with lush plants and the rush of a waterfall. Choose from a display case of live lobsters and iced red snapper, or try the shrimp sauteed in olive oil and garlic. Dressy casual; cocktails; entertainment. **Parking:** valet. **Cards:** AX, CB, DC, DS, MC, VI.

CASA PANZA　　Lunch: $7-$18　　Dinner: $7-$18　　Phone: 305/643-5343　⑨
Spanish
Location: Between 16th and 17th aves; in the heart of Little Havana. 1620 SW 8th St 33135. **Hours:** 11 am-11 pm. Closed: 12/25. **Reservations:** accepted. **Features:** The eatery is just like dining in Madrid; dancing and singing keep this place lively. Casual dress; beer & wine only. **Parking:** on-site. **Cards:** AX, CB, DC, DS, MC, VI.

DORAL ALE HOUSE　　Lunch: $7-$9　　Dinner: $8-$15　　Phone: 305/629-9442　③
American
Location: 0.4 mi s of jct NW 36th St. 3271 NW 87th Ave 33172. **Hours:** 11 am-2 am, Fri & Sat-3 am. Closed: 11/23, 12/25. **Features:** Sports-lovers munch on huge onion rings or piles of cheese fries while reveling in the lively sports-bar atmosphere, which incorporates more than 50 TVs. Fun favorites include burgers, pasta and some seafood items. All can be washed down with one of the more than 85 draft beers and bottled choices. Casual dress; cocktails. **Parking:** on-site. **Cards:** AX, DC, DS, MC, VI.

EL FAROLITO　　Lunch: $6-$15　　Dinner: $9-$23　　Phone: 305/446-4122　⑱
Peruvian
Location: 0.3 mi e of Le Jeune Rd. 2885 Coral Way 33145. **Hours:** noon-10 pm. **Reservations:** accepted. **Features:** Seafood and barbecue are done Peruvian style. Among creations served at the fine-dining establishment are seco de carne (beef stew in cilantro sauce), pulpo al olivo (octopus in black olive sauce), and bistec a la plancha (flank-grilled steak). Dressy casual; cocktails. **Parking:** street. **Cards:** MC, VI.

EL TROPICO　　Lunch: $4-$12　　Dinner: $8-$14　　Phone: 305/477-6705　①
Cuban
Location: Just e of SR 826 (Palmetto Expwy). 7387 NW 36th St 33166. **Hours:** 7 am-9 pm. **Features:** The cafeteria-style eatery offers good food at reasonable prices. The only frills are the variety of selections and the taste. Casual dress. **Parking:** on-site. **Cards:** AX, DS, MC, VI.

"FICO" KEY WEST SEAFOOD　　Lunch: $5-$8　　Dinner: $9-$21　　Phone: 305/446-4040　⑥
Seafood
Location: Corner of 37th Ave and W Flagler; in The Shops at Flagler and Douglas. 3757 W Flagler St 33134. **Hours:** 11 am-11 pm, Fri & Sat-24 hours. Closed: 12/25. **Features:** Established in 1989, the restaurant builds its menu on fresh fish and seafood from Key West. A fish market is adjacent. Lining the extensive menu are five daily soups, such as lobster bisque and black bean; hot and cold appetizers, including shrimp seviche, mussels, cod fish fritters and seafood empanadas; and varied fish and chicken entrees. Desserts range from flan to tres leches cake to rice pudding. Casual dress; beer & wine only. **Parking:** on-site. **Cards:** MC, VI.

THE FISH HOUSE　　Lunch: $6-$9　　Dinner: $10-$20　　Phone: 305/595-8453　㉕
Seafood
Location: 2.3 mi w of 56th St, exit SR 826 (Palmetto Expwy); in Miller Road Plaza. 10000 SW 56th St 33165. **Hours:** 11:30 am-10 pm, Sat-11 pm. Closed: 11/23, 12/25. **Features:** This family-oriented restaurant features an adjacent seafood market. Wonderfully fresh and flavorful snapper, mahi mahi and salmon are the best entrees. Try a fried blue crab sandwich with coleslaw and with, perhaps, the savory fish soup on the side. Casual dress; beer & wine only. **Parking:** on-site. **Cards:** AX, DC, DS, MC, VI.

FLEMING: A TASTE OF DENMARK　　Dinner: $12-$26　　Phone: 305/232-6444　㉙
Danish
Location: Jct US 1, just e. 8511 SW 136th St 33156. **Hours:** 5:30 pm-10:30 pm. Closed: Mon. **Reservations:** suggested. **Features:** Salmon, duck and pan-seared sea bass over couscous are among the extensive menu offerings of this intimate, family-owned restaurant. Artifacts, copper pots and displays of antiques add authenticity to the Scandinavian aura. Dressy casual; cocktails. **Parking:** on-site. **Cards:** AX, DC, DS, MC, VI.

GRAZIANO'S PARILLA ARGENTINA　　Lunch: $12-$35　　Dinner: $12-$35　　Phone: 305/225-0008　㉒
Argentine
Location: Between SR 826 (Palmetto Expwy) and Florida Tpke. 9227 Bird Rd 33165. **Hours:** noon-3:30 & 5-10:30 pm, Fri & Sat-11:30 pm, Sun noon-10 pm. **Reservations:** suggested. **Features:** Grilled meat is why people visit the restaurant again and again. The family atmosphere makes everyone feel welcomed. An extensive wine list satisfies any palate. Dressy casual; cocktails. **Parking:** valet. **Cards:** MC, VI.

HEREFORD GRILL　　Lunch: $14-$24　　Dinner: $15-$44　　Phone: 305/441-6505　⑧
Regional Steak House
Location: 1.2 mi s of Miami International Airport entrance; corner of NW 42nd Ave (Le Jeune Rd) and NW 7th St. 782 NW 42nd Ave (Le Jeune Rd) 33133. **Hours:** 11:30 am-11 pm, Fri-midnight, Sat 6 pm-midnight, Sun 2 pm-10 pm. **Reservations:** suggested. **Features:** The sophisticated Old World style decor and the formally attired waiters set the mood for this upscale dining experience. Offering Certified Angus Beef, beef is by far the most popular item on the menu but there is an array of other choices as well. To whet the appetite try one of the many soups offered such as French onion, lobster bisque or cream of asparagus. For those with a sweet tooth there is a dessert cart presented tableside that is laden with heavenly temptations. Dressy casual; cocktails. **Parking:** valet. **Cards:** AX, CB, DC, DS, JC, MC, VI.

ISLAS CANARIAS RESTAURANT　　Lunch: $5-$16　　Dinner: $5-$19　　Phone: 305/649-0440　④
Cuban
Location: Just n of Flagler St. 285 NW 27th Ave 33125. **Hours:** 7 am-11 pm, Sun from 8 am. **Features:** A casual deli and diner located in Miami's "Little Havana" features authentic Cuban dishes. Decorated with an abundance of locally painted pictures of Cuba, the dining room is the perfect backdrop for well-prepared food and efficient service. Casual dress; beer & wine only. **Parking:** on-site. **Cards:** AX, MC, VI.

(See maps and indexes starting on p. 534, 542)

LA CARRETA RESTAURANT   Lunch: $6-$20   Dinner: $6-$20   Phone: 305/444-7501   13
Cuban
Location: In Little Havana; at SW 8th St (Calle Ocho) and 36th Ct. 3632 SW 8th St 33135. **Hours:** 24 hours. **Features:** The popular spot is the original "Carreta," a bustling local chain that serves a variety of typical Cuban foods. Charbroiled meats, beef, seafood, chicken and pork dishes share menu space with delicious sandwiches prepared in the Cuban style. Those who can't decide might opt for a sampler platter. Casual dress. **Parking:** on-site. **Cards:** DC, DS, MC, VI.

LA CASITA   Lunch: $6-$10   Dinner: $12-$18   Phone: 305/267-4444   5
Cuban
Location: Just w of Mall of the Americas; corner of NW 79th Ave and NW 2nd St. 7931 NW 2nd St 33126. **Hours:** 7 am-10 pm, Fri & Sat-11 pm. **Reservations:** accepted. **Features:** Tables at this quintessential place for Cuban comfort food are closely spaced, and service is snappy. The extensive menu lists more than 50 meals. Lechon—Cuban-style roasted pork—is a favorite, as are such seafood dishes as fried red snapper, grouper Creole, king fish and lobster. For a quick bite, try a sandwich or salad. Daily lunch specials are popular. For dessert, try one of the many flavored flans or tres leches cake. Casual dress; beer & wine only. **Parking:** on-site. **Cards:** AX, DC, DS, MC, VI.

LA RIVIERA RESTAURANT   Lunch: $9-$25   Dinner: $9-$30   Phone: 305/264-4888   6
Nouvelle French
Location: Just sw of jct SR 836 (Dolphin Expwy), exit Red Rd; in Sofitel Miami. 5800 Blue Lagoon Dr 33126. **Hours:** 6 am-11 pm. **Reservations:** suggested. **Features:** The room is decorated in soft whites with complementing soft pastels. A romantic feel characterizes the patio, which has pin lights and white colors. Foods are prepared with a French flair and presented in an artistic manner. Dressy casual; cocktails. **Parking:** on-site (fee) and valet. **Cards:** AX, CB, DC, DS, JC, MC, VI.

LAS CULEBRINAS   Lunch: $7-$18   Dinner: $9-$25   Phone: 305/445-2337   7
Spanish
Location: 0.6 mi w of Le Jeune Rd (42nd Ave), just s. 4700 W Flagler St 33133. **Hours:** 11:30 am-11 pm, Fri & Sat-midnight. **Closed:** 11/23, 12/25. **Features:** The cozy room has a comfortable feel. The menu lists preparations of local seafood and other dishes with Spanish and Cuban flavors. Casual dress; beer & wine only. **Parking:** on-site. **Cards:** AX, DS, MC, VI.

LATIN CAFE 2000   Lunch: $6-$16   Dinner: $7-$16   Phone: 305/642-3395   7
Cuban
Location: On Le Jeune Rd, just n of NW 7th St. 875 Le Jeune Rd 33126. **Hours:** 7 am-midnight, Fri & Sat-1 am. **Reservations:** accepted. **Features:** The menu puts forth a variety of dishes filled with Latin flavors. The Cuban sandwich is a signature item. In addition to inside seating, the restaurant has a small outdoor dining area with tropical foliage. The atmosphere is casual, relaxed and informal. Casual dress; beer & wine only. **Parking:** on-site. **Cards:** AX, CB, DC, DS, MC, VI.

LILA'S RESTAURANT   Lunch: $6-$13   Dinner: $6-$13   Phone: 305/553-6061   19
Cuban
Location: Jct SR 972 (SW 24th St) and SR 913 (SW 87th Ave); in Westchester Mall Shopping Center. 8518 SW 24th Ct 33155. **Hours:** 11 am-11 pm. **Closed:** 11/23. **Reservations:** not accepted. **Features:** The menu lists traditional Cuban preparations of beef, chicken, pork and seafood, and the portions are huge. The highlight is Lila's steak, a marinated steak covered with a mountain of french fries or plantains. Casual dress; cocktails. **Parking:** on-site. **Cards:** AX, DC, DS, MC, VI.

OLD LISBON RESTAURANT & BAR   Lunch: $8-$20   Dinner: $13-$20   Phone: 305/854-0039   17
Portuguese
Location: Jct SW 17th Ave and 24th St. 1698 SW 22 St 33145. **Hours:** noon-11 pm, Fri & Sat-11:30 pm, Sun-10 pm. **Reservations:** suggested. **Features:** Take a joyous journey to Portugal without a passport! This quaint neighborhood eatery serves appetizers like fresh octopus salad; entrees like codfish served five ways, Alentejana-style clams and grilled sardines; and, of course, decadent desserts. Semi-formal attire; cocktails. **Parking:** on-site and valet. **Cards:** AX, DS, MC, VI.

OLD SAN JUAN   Lunch: $5-$10   Dinner: $12-$30   Phone: 305/263-9911   15
Regional Caribbean
Location: Jct US 41 (SW 8th St) and SR 959 (SW 57th Ave), just s. 1200 SW 57th Ave 33144. **Hours:** 11 am-3 & 5-9 pm, Fri & Sat 5 pm-10 pm, Sun noon-10 pm. **Closed:** major holidays. **Reservations:** accepted. **Features:** A heavy Puerto Rican influence punctuates offerings of Caribbean cuisine. Sunday patrons can choose from the buffet or the full a la carte menu. Service is friendly, and each freshly prepared dish is delicious. Casual dress; beer & wine only. **Parking:** on-site. **Cards:** DS, MC, VI.

THE ORIGINAL DAILY BREAD MARKETPLACE   Lunch: $5-$9   Dinner: $5-$9   Phone: 305/856-0363   20
Middle Eastern
Location: From US 1 (Brickell Ave), w on SW 27th Ave, then just n. 2400 SW 27th St 33133. **Hours:** 9 am-8 pm, Sun 11 am-5 pm. **Closed:** major holidays; also Sat. **Features:** There are two outlets: one a small store with hard-to-find Greek and Middle Eastern foods and, on the other side, an eatery with dishes from the Middle East and Greece. Casual dress. **Parking:** on-site. **Cards:** AX, DC, MC, VI.

PALOMILLA GRILL   Lunch: $4-$6   Dinner: $6-$20   Phone: 305/261-3424   8
Argentine
Location: Just e of SR 826 (Palmetto Expwy). 6890 W Flagler St 33144. **Hours:** 11 am-10 pm. **Reservations:** accepted. **Features:** The atmosphere is cozy and warm, ideal for a special occasion. Grilled meat is the specialty, and all entrees are served with fried plantains or cassava. Casual dress; cocktails. **Parking:** on-site. **Cards:** AX, DS, MC, VI.

SCULLY'S TAVERN   Lunch: $3-$8   Dinner: $8-$15   Phone: 305/271-7404   26
American
Location: Just w of SW 97th Ave at SW 72nd St. 9809 Sunset Dr 33173. **Hours:** 11 am-1 am, Fri-3 am, Sat noon-3 am, Sun noon-1 am. **Closed:** 11/23, 12/25. **Features:** This lively sports bar serves reasonably priced pub dishes, including the house favorite: prime rib. Casual dress; cocktails. **Parking:** on-site. **Cards:** AX, CB, DC, DS, JC, MC, VI.

(See maps and indexes starting on p. 534, 542)

SERGIO'S
Cuban
MC, VI.
Lunch: $5-$7   **Dinner:** $7-$10   **Phone:** 305/552-9626   (23)
Location: SR 826 (Palmetto Expwy), 1.7 mi w. 9330 SW 40th St 33165. **Hours:** 6 am-midnight, Thurs-Sat 24 hours. Closed: 12/25. **Features:** The restaurant has both outside and inside seating. A Latin slant to the decor helps set the stage for the casual, informal atmosphere. On the menu are varied Cuban and Latin selections, including the signature Cuban sandwich. Casual dress. **Parking:** on-site. **Cards:** AX, DC,

SHORTY'S BAR-B-Q
Barbecue
Cards: AX, MC, VI.
Lunch: $5-$14   **Dinner:** $5-$14   **Phone:** 305/227-7732   (24)
Location: Florida Tpke, exit 23 to SW 40th St, then e. 11575 SW 40th St 33165. **Hours:** 11 am-10 pm, Fri & Sat-11 pm. **Features:** Hungry folks in the mood for barbecue ribs, brisket, chicken or pulled pork will find it at the fun and upbeat spot. The walls and ceilings offer plenty to look at while the food is being prepared. The menu offers enough diversity to appeal to all ages. Casual dress; beer & wine only. **Parking:** on-site.

SHORTY'S BAR-B-Q
Barbecue
MC, VI.
Lunch: $5-$14   **Dinner:** $5-$14   **Phone:** 305/471-5554   (4)
Location: SR 836, exit NW 87th Ave, then 0.7 mi n. 2255 NW 87th Ave 33172. **Hours:** 11 am-10 pm, Fri & Sat-11 am. **Features:** Hungry folks in the mood for barbecue ribs, brisket, chicken or pulled pork will find it at the fun and upbeat spot. The walls and ceilings offer plenty to look at while the food is being prepared. The menu offers enough diversity to appeal to all ages. Casual dress; cocktails. **Parking:** on-site. **Cards:** AX,

SOYKA
American
Lunch: $10-$15   **Dinner:** $9-$23   **Phone:** 305/759-3117   (3)
Location: 1 mi n of I-95, just w of US 1 (Biscayne Blvd), just n of NE 54th St. 5556 NE 4th Ct 33137. **Hours:** 11 am-11 pm, Fri & Sat-midnight. Closed: 7/4, 11/23, 12/25. **Reservations:** accepted. **Features:** Contributing to the restaurant's warehouse effect are dark woods, decorative ceiling fans and other touches that give a distinctive look. Friendly staff accommodate the customer's pace while giving attentive service. The kitchen puts out a variety of well-prepared dishes that offer eye appeal as well as taste. In addition to salads, sandwiches and burgers, the menu lists wood-fired oven pizzas as well as pasta, meat, chicken and seafood main courses. Limited outside seating is available. Casual dress; cocktails. **Parking:** on-site. **Cards:** AX, DC, DS, MC, VI.

SUSHI SIAM MORNINGSIDE
Japanese
Lunch: $4-$26   **Dinner:** $4-$26   **Phone:** 305/751-7818   (1)
Location: I-195, exit 2A, just n on US 1 (Biscayne Blvd). 5582 NE 4th Ct 33137. **Hours:** 11:30 am-10 pm, Fri & Sat-10:30 pm. Closed major holidays. **Features:** The trendy dining room is bathed in soothing colors. Topping the menu is sushi, served fresh and in innovative presentations. Casual dress; beer & wine only. **Parking:** street. **Cards:** MC, VI.

TANI THAI RESTAURANT
Thai
Casual dress; beer only. **Parking:** on-site. **Cards:** AX, MC, VI.
Lunch: $7-$12   **Dinner:** $8-$23   **Phone:** 305/253-3583   (27)
Location: US 1 (S Dixie Hwy). 12269 S Dixie Hwy 33156. **Hours:** 11:30 am-3 & 5-10 pm, Fri-11 pm, Sat noon-3 & 5-11 pm, Sun 5 pm-10 pm. Closed: 11/23. **Reservations:** suggested. **Features:** Peculiarly named dishes, such as Gang Dang and Cocky Bob, belie the sophisticated dishes for which the restaurant is known. Check out the pad ha pow with pork, a savory brown sauce with basil and pepper-flavored juicy white meat pork.

TROPICAL CHINESE RESTAURANT
Chinese
Lunch: $7-$15   **Dinner:** $10-$45   **Phone:** 305/262-7576   (21)
Location: SR 826 (Palmetto Expwy), just w. 7991 Bird Rd 33155. **Hours:** 11:30 am-10:30 pm, Fri-11:30 pm, Sat 11 am-11:30 pm, Sun 10:30 am-10 pm. **Reservations:** accepted. **Features:** In a small shopping plaza, this restaurant surprises diners with its menu. Authentic Hong Kong-style cooking is characterized by innovative preparation. Casual dress; cocktails. **Parking:** on-site. **Cards:** AX, DC, MC, VI.

VERSAILLES
Cuban
Lunch: $7-$12   **Dinner:** $9-$22   **Phone:** 305/445-7614   (12)
Location: Just e of Douglas Rd. 3555 SW 8th St 33135. **Hours:** 8 am-2 am, Fri & Sat-4:30 am, Sun 9 am-2 am. Closed: 11/23, 12/25. **Features:** This is the place to be seen in the Cuban community. Patrons can sample traditional favorites from a large menu. A Cuban bakery is just next door. Casual dress; beer & wine only. **Parking:** on-site. **Cards:** AX, DC, DS, MC, VI.

ZUPERPOLLO RESTAURANTE INTERNACIONAL
Argentine
Lunch: $4-$10   **Dinner:** $6-$26   **Phone:** 305/477-6556   (16)
Location: Just w of SW 12th Ave. 1247 Coral Way (SW 22nd St) 33145. **Hours:** 11 am-midnight. Closed major holidays. **Features:** Meat and seafood items cooked in the Argentinean style share menu space with pasta and other meat entrees. Lending personalized charm to the dining room are many pictures and prints of Argentina. Patio seating is an option. Casual dress; cocktails. **Parking:** street. **Cards:** MC, VI.

─────── *The following restaurant has not been evaluated by AAA* ───────
but is listed for your information only.

P. F. CHANG'S
[fyi]
Phone: 305/234-2338
Not evaluated. **Location:** US 1 (Dixie Hwy); in Falls Shopping Center. 8888 SW 136th St 33176. **Features:** This Oriental bistro features cuisine from five Chinese regions in a fun and upbeat atmosphere.

MIAMI BEACH   pop. 87,933   (See maps and indexes starting on p. 545, 548)

——— **WHERE TO STAY** ———

ATLANTICA HOTEL & SUITES   *Book at aaa.com*   Phone: (305)532-7077   38

12/1-5/31 & 10/1-11/30 [CP]	1P: $79-$129	2P: $89-$139
6/1-9/30 [CP]	1P: $69-$89	2P: $79-$99

Small-scale Hotel   **Location:** Just s of 5th Ave. 321 Collins Ave 33139. Fax: 305/532-8767. **Facility:** Designated smoking area. 26 units. 23 one-bedroom standard units. 3 one-bedroom suites ($99-$179). 2 stories (no elevator), interior corridors. *Bath:* combo or shower only. **Parking:** on-site (fee) and street. **Terms:** 2 night minimum stay - weekends, 7 day cancellation notice-fee imposed. **Amenities:** voice mail, safes, irons, hair dryers. **Business Services:** fax (fee). **Cards:** AX, DS, MC, VI.

SOME UNITS

ASK ▯+ ⊠ DATA PORT 🖥 / VCR 📷 🖵 / FEE

AVALON HOTEL   *Book at aaa.com*   Phone: (305)538-0133   35

AAA SAVE
Classic
Small-scale Hotel

12/1-4/16 [CP]	1P: $209-$299	2P: $209-$299	XP: $25	F12
4/17-6/4 [CP]	1P: $179-$269	2P: $179-$269	XP: $25	F12
10/2-11/30 [CP]	1P: $169-$269	2P: $169-$269	XP: $25	F12
6/5-10/1 [CP]	1P: $139-$229	2P: $139-$229	XP: $25	F12

Location: E of SR A1A (Collins Ave); jct 7th St and Ocean Dr. Located in the heart of the Art Deco District, across from beach. 700 Ocean Dr 33139. Fax: 305/534-0258. **Facility:** Located in the Art Deco district, the property offers modern comforts and bright decor; a patio seating area welcomes ocean breezes. 105 one-bedroom standard units. 3 stories, interior corridors. **Parking:** valet. **Terms:** 3 day cancellation notice-fee imposed. **Amenities:** high-speed Internet, voice mail, safes, irons, hair dryers. **Dining:** A Fish Called Avalon, see separate listing. **Leisure Activities:** beach access, pool privileges. **Guest Services:** valet laundry. **Business Services:** meeting rooms. **Cards:** AX, DC, DS, MC, VI.

SOME UNITS

▯+ ⊻ VCR 📷 / ⊠ 🖥 /

BEACHCOMBER HOTEL   *Book at aaa.com*   Phone: (305)531-3755   21

12/1-3/31 [CP]	1P: $140-$170	2P: $140-$170	XP: $20	F12
4/1-4/30 & 11/1-11/30 [CP]	1P: $130-$150	2P: $130-$150	XP: $20	F12
5/1-10/31 [CP]	1P: $110-$130	2P: $110-$130	XP: $20	F12

Small-scale Hotel   **Location:** On Collins Ave (SR A1A), just s of 14th St. 1340 Collins Ave 33139. Fax: 305/673-8609. **Facility:** 29 one-bedroom standard units. 2 stories (no elevator), interior corridors. **Parking:** on-site (fee). **Amenities:** voice mail, safes (fee), honor bars. **Guest Services:** valet laundry. **Business Services:** fax (fee). **Cards:** AX, DC, DS, MC, VI.

SOME UNITS

ASK S▯ ▯+ ▯++ 📷 / ⊠ /

BEST WESTERN BEACH RESORT   *Book at aaa.com*   Phone: (305)532-3311   11

AAA SAVE
Small-scale Hotel

12/23-4/30	1P: $159-$239	2P: $159-$239	XP: $10	F18
12/1-12/22 & 7/1-11/30	1P: $109-$199	2P: $109-$199	XP: $10	F18
5/1-6/30	1P: $99-$179	2P: $99-$179	XP: $10	F18

Location: Oceanfront. On SR A1A, just n of 43rd St. 4333 Collins Ave 33140. Fax: 305/531-5296. **Facility:** 253 units. 249 one-bedroom standard units. 4 one-bedroom suites. 11 stories, interior corridors. *Bath:* combo or shower only. **Parking:** valet. **Terms:** cancellation fee imposed, [AP], [BP], [CP], [ECP] & [MAP] meal plans available. **Amenities:** irons, hair dryers. *Fee:* video games, safes. *Some:* high-speed Internet. **Dining:** 7-11 am, noon-2:30 & 5-10 pm, cocktails. **Pool(s):** outdoor. **Leisure Activities:** limited beach access, limited exercise equipment. *Fee:* water sports. **Guest Services:** valet laundry. **Business Services:** meeting rooms, fax (fee). **Cards:** AX, CB, DC, DS, JC, MC, VI. **Special Amenities:** free local telephone calls and early check-in/late check-out.

SOME UNITS

S▯ ▯+ ⊻ 🛜 ⊘ 🏊 📷 DATA PORT 🖵 / ⊠ 🖥 🖴 / FEE

(See maps and indexes starting on p. 545, 548)

BEST WESTERN SOUTH BEACH   *Book at aaa.com*

 — AAA [SAVE] ▽▽▽

Phone: (305)674-1930   **28**

12/23-4/30 [CP]	1P: $145-$185	2P: $145-$185	XP: $10 F12
12/1-12/22 & 7/1-11/30 [CP]	1P: $85-$135	2P: $85-$135	XP: $10 F12
5/1-6/30 [CP]	1P: $65-$115	2P: $65-$115	XP: $10 F12

Location: Jct I-395 and 5th St, 0.6 mi n, just s of 11th St. 1050 Washington Ave 33139. Fax: 305/534-6591. **Facility:** Centrally located in the Art Deco area with shops and eateries close by, the property features cozy rooms with that "Deco" touch. 135 one-bedroom standard units. 2-3 stories, interior/exterior corridors. *Bath:* combo or shower only. **Parking:** street. **Amenities:** dual phone lines, voice mail, safes (fee), irons, hair dryers. **Pool(s):** heated outdoor. **Leisure Activities:** exercise room. **Guest Services:** valet laundry. **Business Services:** business center. **Cards:** AX, DC, DS, MC, VI. **Special Amenities: free continental breakfast and free local telephone calls.**

Classic Small-scale Hotel

SOME UNITS
[ad] [🛏] [📷] [DATA PORT] [💻] / [✕] [🛗]

THE BLUE MOON   *Book at aaa.com*

▽▽▽ ▽▽▽

Phone: (305)673-2262   **31**

4/1-11/30	1P: $99-$399	2P: $99-$399	XP: $20 F12
12/1-3/31	1P: $89-$399	2P: $89-$399	XP: $20 F12

Classic Small-scale Hotel

Location: On SR A1A (Collins Ave); between 9th and 10th sts; in Art Deco District. 944 Collins Ave 33139. Fax: 305/534-5399. **Facility:** Guest rooms are decorated in vivid colors; a small pool and deck are at the back of the property. 75 units. 72 one-bedroom standard units. 3 one-bedroom suites. 2-3 stories, interior corridors. *Bath:* combo or shower only. **Parking:** on-site (fee) and valet. **Terms:** 3 day cancellation notice-fee imposed, [MAP] meal plan available. **Amenities:** CD players, dual phone lines, voice mail, safes, honor bars, irons, hair dryers. *Some:* DVD players. **Pool(s):** small heated outdoor. **Leisure Activities:** whirlpool. **Guest Services:** valet laundry. **Business Services:** meeting rooms, fax (fee). **Cards:** AX, CB, DC, DS, MC, VI.

SOME UNITS
[ASK] [S/D] [🍴] [Y] [🛏] [👪] [📷] [DATA PORT] [💻] / [✕] [VCR]

CADET HOTEL   *Book at aaa.com*

▽▽▽

Phone: (305)672-6688   **9**

All Year	1P: $99-$225	XP: $50 F10

Classic Small-scale Hotel

Location: Just w of SR A1A (Collins Ave) on 17th St; corner of James Ave and 17th St. 1701 James Ave 33139. Fax: 305/532-1676. **Facility:** This Art Deco hotel features Egyptian cotton linens and is located between the beach, the convention center and the mall; what more could you ask for? Designated smoking area. 38 units. 37 one-bedroom standard units. 1 one-bedroom suite. 2 stories (no elevator), interior corridors. *Bath:* combo or shower only. **Parking:** valet. **Terms:** 3 day cancellation notice-fee imposed, [AP] & [CP] meal plans available, small pets only ($35 fee). **Amenities:** high-speed Internet, dual phone lines, voice mail, safes, honor bars, irons. *Some:* hair dryers. **Guest Services:** valet laundry. **Business Services:** meeting rooms, fax (fee). **Cards:** AX, DC, DS, MC, VI.

[ASK] [🛏] [🍴] [✕] [👪] [✕] [📷] [DATA PORT]
FEE

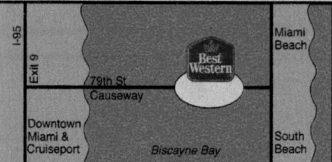

(See maps and indexes starting on p. 545, 548)

CASA GRANDE SUITE HOTEL *Book at aaa.com*   **Phone:** 305/672-7003 **33**

12/1-5/31	1P: $315-$1500	2P: $315-$1500	XP: $15	F10
6/1-11/30	1P: $215-$950	2P: $215-$950	XP: $15	F10

AAA [SAVE]
Small-scale Hotel
Location: E of SR A1A (Collins Ave) and 8th St. Located in heart of the Art Deco District, across from beach. 834 Ocean Dr 33139. Fax: 305/673-3669. **Facility:** 34 units. 9 one-bedroom standard units with kitchens. 22 one-, 2 two- and 1 three-bedroom suites ($215-$1500) with kitchens. 2-5 stories, interior corridors. *Bath:* combo or shower only. **Parking:** valet. **Terms:** 2-4 night minimum stay - seasonal, 3 day cancellation notice-fee imposed, package plans, small pets only ($100 fee). **Amenities:** CD players, dual phone lines, voice mail, safes, honor bars, irons, hair dryers. *Fee:* video library, high-speed Internet. **Guest Services:** valet laundry. **Business Services:** meeting rooms. **Cards:** AX, DC, DS, MC, VI. **Special Amenities:** free newspaper and free room upgrade (subject to availability with advance reservations).

SOME UNITS

CENTURY HOTEL *Book at aaa.com*   **Phone:** (305)674-8855 **40**

12/1-4/30	1P: $115-$215	2P: $115-$215
9/1-11/30	1P: $115-$165	2P: $115-$165
5/1-8/31	1P: $80-$115	2P: $80-$115

Small-scale Hotel
Location: Just e of SR A1A (Collins Ave), just s of 2nd St. Located across from the beach. 140 Ocean Dr 33139. Fax: 305/538-5733. **Facility:** 26 one-bedroom standard units. 2 stories (no elevator), interior corridors. *Bath:* shower only. **Parking:** on-site (fee) and valet. **Terms:** 2-3 night minimum stay - weekends, 7 day cancellation notice, small pets only ($250 deposit, $30 extra charge). **Amenities:** CD players, dual phone lines, voice mail, safes, honor bars, irons, hair dryers. **Leisure Activities:** beach access. **Cards:** AX, DS, MC, VI.

COMFORT INN & SUITES SOUTH BEACH *Book at aaa.com*   **Phone:** (305)531-3406 **22**

All Year	1P: $179	2P: $179

Small-scale Hotel
Location: On SR A1A; jct Collins Ave and 12th St; in heart of the Art Deco District. 1238 Collins Ave 33139. Fax: 305/538-0850. **Facility:** 28 units. 20 one-bedroom standard units. 8 one-bedroom suites ($189-$289). 3 stories, interior corridors. *Bath:* combo or shower only. **Parking:** valet. **Terms:** cancellation fee imposed, 13% service charge. **Amenities:** high-speed Internet, voice mail, honor bars, irons, hair dryers. **Leisure Activities:** limited exercise equipment. **Guest Services:** valet laundry. **Business Services:** meeting rooms. **Cards:** AX, DC, DS, MC, VI.

SOME UNITS

COURTYARD BY MARRIOTT-MIAMI BEACH OCEANFRONT *Book at aaa.com*   **Phone:** (305)538-3373 **14**

All Year	1P: $119-$299	2P: $119-$299	XP: $10	F

Large-scale Hotel
Location: Oceanfront. On SR A1A (Collins Ave), at Collins Ave and 40th St. 3925 Collins Ave 33140. Fax: 305/538-7077. **Facility:** 263 units. 251 one-bedroom standard units. 12 one-bedroom suites ($249-$899). 14 stories, interior corridors. *Bath:* combo or shower only. **Parking:** valet. **Terms:** check-in 4 pm, 2 night minimum stay - weekends, cancellation fee imposed, package plans, 13% service charge. **Amenities:** video games (fee), high-speed Internet, dual phone lines, voice mail, safes, honor bars, irons, hair dryers. **Pool(s):** heated outdoor. **Leisure Activities:** whirlpool, limited beach access, playground, exercise room. **Guest Services:** sundries, valet and coin laundry. **Business Services:** meeting rooms, business center. **Cards:** AX, DC, DS, MC, VI.

SOME UNITS

COURTYARD BY MARRIOTT, MIAMI SOUTH BEACH *Book at aaa.com*   **Phone:** (305)604-8887 **15**

12/22-4/30	1P: $219-$349	2P: $219-$349
5/1-9/23	1P: $119-$299	2P: $119-$299
9/24-11/30	1P: $139-$249	2P: $139-$249
12/1-12/21	1P: $179-$199	2P: $179-$199

AAA [SAVE]
Classic
Small-scale Hotel
Location: I-395 and 5th St, 1 mi n; just s of 16th St. 1530 Washington Ave 33139. Fax: 305/604-8868. **Facility:** This hotel, complemented by a rooftop pool, is located a block from the beach and is close to shops and eateries. 90 units. 86 one-bedroom standard units, some with whirlpools. 4 one-bedroom suites. 5 stories, interior corridors. *Bath:* combo or shower only. **Parking:** valet. **Terms:** [BP] meal plan available, package plans. **Amenities:** video games (fee), high-speed Internet, dual phone lines, voice mail, irons, hair dryers. **Dining:** 6:30-10 am, Sat & Sun 7-11 am. **Pool(s):** outdoor. **Leisure Activities:** exercise room. **Guest Services:** sundries, valet and coin laundry. **Business Services:** meeting rooms, fax (fee). **Cards:** AX, DC, DS, MC, VI. **Special Amenities:** free newspaper.

SOME UNITS

CRESCENT RESORT AND SPA ON SOUTH BEACH *Book at aaa.com*   **Phone:** (305)531-5197 **17**

All Year	1P: $99-$459	2P: $99-$459	XP: $15

AAA [SAVE]
Classic
Small-scale Hotel
Location: Just e of SR A1A (Collins Ave) and 14th St. Across the street from the beach. 1420 Ocean Dr 33139. Fax: 305/531-9734. **Facility:** On the famous Ocean Drive, this property offers some rooms with beach views; all rooms are spacious and nicely furnished with a slight nautical flair. Designated smoking area. 27 units. 24 one- and 3 two-bedroom suites ($99-$459) with kitchens, some with whirlpools. 4 stories, interior corridors. *Bath:* combo or shower only. **Parking:** valet. **Terms:** check-in 4 pm, 3 day cancellation notice-fee imposed, package plans. **Amenities:** CD players, dual phone lines, voice mail, safes, irons, hair dryers. *Fee:* video games, high-speed Internet. **Leisure Activities:** beach access, spa. **Guest Services:** valet laundry. **Cards:** AX, DC, DS, MC, VI. **Special Amenities:** preferred room (subject to availability with advance reservations). *(See color ad p 771)*

CROWNE PLAZA ROYAL PALM ON SOUTH BEACH *Book at aaa.com*   **Phone:** 305/604-5700 **14**

Property failed to provide current rates

Large-scale Hotel
Location: On SR A1A (Collins Ave), just s of 16th Ave. 1545 Collins Ave 33139. Fax: 305/604-2059. **Facility:** 417 units. 267 one-bedroom standard units. 145 one- and 5 two-bedroom suites. 17 stories, interior/exterior corridors. *Bath:* combo or shower only. **Parking:** valet. **Terms:** check-in 4 pm, small pets only ($100 deposit, $50 fee). **Amenities:** CD players, dual phone lines, voice mail, safes, honor bars, irons, hair dryers. *Fee:* video games, high-speed Internet. **Pool(s):** heated outdoor, small heated outdoor. **Leisure Activities:** snorkeling, exercise room. *Fee:* massage. **Guest Services:** gift shop, valet laundry. **Business Services:** meeting rooms, business center.

SOME UNITS

(See maps and indexes starting on p. 545, 548)

DAYS INN NORTH BEACH *Book at aaa.com*   Phone: (305)866-1631   **2**

AAA SAVE

12/16-4/15	1P: $109-$259	2P: $109-$259	XP: $10	F17
12/1-12/15 & 4/16-11/30	1P: $89-$199	2P: $89-$199	XP: $10	F17

Location: SR A1A (Collins Ave) and 75th St, just e on 75th St, then a right turn. Located across from the beach. 7450 Ocean Terrace 33141. Fax: 305/868-4617. **Facility:** 92 one-bedroom standard units. 7 stories, interior Small-scale Hotel corridors. *Bath:* combo or shower only. **Parking:** on-site (fee). **Amenities:** voice mail, safes (fee), hair dryers. **Dining:** 7 am-11 & 5-11 pm. **Pool(s):** outdoor. **Leisure Activities:** beach access. *Fee:* game room. **Guest Services:** coin laundry. **Business Services:** fax (fee). **Cards:** AX, CB, DC, DS, JC, MC, VI. **Special Amenities:** free newspaper and preferred room (subject to availability with advance reservations). *(See color ad below)*

SOME UNITS

⬛ 🍴 🍸 🏊 📷 🖥 📠 / ✖ /

DAYS INN OCEANSIDE *Book at aaa.com*   Phone: (305)673-1513   **12**

AAA SAVE

12/23-4/30	1P: $149-$229	2P: $149-$229	XP: $10	F18
12/1-12/22 & 7/1-11/30	1P: $99-$189	2P: $89-$189	XP: $10	F18
5/1-6/30	1P: $89-$169	2P: $89-$169	XP: $10	F18

Location: Oceanfront. On SR A1A; corner of 43rd St. 4299 Collins Ave 33140. Fax: 305/538-0727. **Facility:** 143 Small-scale Hotel one-bedroom standard units. 8 stories, interior corridors. *Bath:* combo or shower only. **Parking:** valet. **Terms:** cancellation fee imposed, [AP], [BP], [CP] & [MAP] meal plans available. **Amenities:** voice mail, safes (fee), irons, hair dryers. **Dining:** 2 restaurants, 7 am-11 pm, cocktails. **Pool(s):** outdoor. **Leisure Activities:** limited beach access. **Guest Services:** sundries, valet and coin laundry. **Business Services:** meeting rooms, PC (fee). **Cards:** AX, CB, DC, DS, JC, MC, VI. **Special Amenities:** free newspaper.

SOME UNITS

⬛ 🍴 🍸 🏊 📷 📠 / ✖ 🖥 📠 / 💻 /
FEE   FEE

DAYS INN SOUTH BEACH *Book at aaa.com*   Phone: (305)538-6631   **3**

AAA SAVE

12/23-4/30	1P: $159-$239	2P: $159-$239	XP: $10	F18
12/1-12/22 & 7/1-11/30	1P: $109-$199	2P: $109-$199	XP: $10	F18
5/1-6/30	1P: $99-$179	2P: $99-$179	XP: $10	F18

Location: Oceanfront. SR A1A (Collins Ave) at 21st St. 100 21st St 33139. Fax: 305/674-0954. **Facility:** 172 one-Small-scale Hotel bedroom standard units. 7 stories, interior/exterior corridors. *Bath:* combo or shower only. **Parking:** on-site (fee) and valet. **Terms:** cancellation fee imposed, [AP], [BP], [CP], [ECP] & [MAP] meal plans available. **Amenities:** safes (fee), hair dryers. **Dining:** 7-11 am, Sat & Sun-noon. **Pool(s):** outdoor. **Leisure Activities:** limited beach access. **Guest Services:** valet and coin laundry. **Cards:** AX, CB, DC, DS, JC, MC, VI.

SOME UNITS

⬛ 🍴 ♿ 📷 🏊 📷 📠 / ✖ 📠 💻 /
FEE

(See maps and indexes starting on p. 545, 548)

DEAUVILLE BEACH RESORT *Book at aaa.com* **Phone:** 305/865-8511 **4**

▼▼▼▼ Property failed to provide current rates
Location: Oceanfront. SR A1A at 67th St. 6701 Collins Ave 33141. Fax: 305/865-8154. **Facility:** 484 units. 471
Large-scale Hotel one-bedroom standard units. 13 one-bedroom suites, some with whirlpools. 17 stories, interior corridors.
Bath: combo or shower only. **Parking:** valet. **Amenities:** video games (fee), voice mail, safes, irons, hair
dryers. **Pool(s):** heated outdoor. **Leisure Activities:** whirlpool, limited beach access, exercise room, spa. **Guest Services:** gift
shop, valet and coin laundry. **Business Services:** conference facilities, business center.

SOME UNITS

DOUBLETREE SURFCOMBER HOTEL *Book at aaa.com* **Phone:** (305)532-7715 **8**

▼▼▼▼
	12/1-4/30	1P: $169-$329	2P: $169-$329	XP: $10	F17
	10/1-11/30	1P: $189-$289	2P: $189-$289	XP: $10	F17
	5/1-9/30	1P: $149-$289	2P: $149-$289	XP: $10.	F17

Classic **Location:** On SR A1A (Collins Ave) and 17th Ave. 1717 Collins Ave 33139. Fax: 305/532-7280. **Facility:** Styled in
Small-scale Hotel keeping with the Art Deco area where it's located, the hotel offers some ocean-view rooms and a pool; the
beach is a short walk away. 185 units. 181 one-bedroom standard units. 4 one-bedroom suites ($459-$559). 3 stories, interior
corridors. *Bath:* combo or shower only. **Parking:** valet. **Terms:** 2-3 night minimum stay - seasonal and/or weekends,
cancellation fee imposed, package plans, $7 service charge. **Amenities:** video games (fee), dual phone lines, voice mail, irons,
hair dryers. *Some:* CD players. **Pool(s):** heated outdoor. **Guest Services:** valet laundry. **Business Services:** meeting rooms.
Cards: AX, CB, DC, DS, JC, MC, VI.

SOME UNITS

FEE

EDEN ROC, A RENAISSANCE RESORT & SPA *Book at aaa.com* **Phone:** (305)531-0000 **8**

(AAA) (SAVE) All Year 1P: $159-$424 2P: $159-$424
▼▼▼▼ **Location:** Oceanfront. SR A1A (Collins Ave), just n of 41st St. 4525 Collins Ave 33140. Fax: 305/674-5555.
Facility: 349 units. 347 one-bedroom standard units, some with kitchens and/or whirlpools. 2 one-bedroom
Large-scale Hotel suites ($189-$424), some with kitchens and/or whirlpools. 13 stories, interior corridors. *Bath:* combo or
shower only. **Parking:** valet. **Terms:** 3 day cancellation notice-fee imposed, package plans, small pets only
($75 extra charge). **Amenities:** dual phone lines, voice mail, safes, honor bars, irons, hair dryers. *Fee:*
video games, high-speed Internet. **Dining:** 2 restaurants, 6:30 am-1 am, cocktails. **Pool(s):** 2 heated outdoor. **Leisure
Activities:** saunas, whirlpools, steamrooms, limited beach access, rental boats, water sports, racquetball court, squash court,
rock climbing wall, jogging, spa, volleyball. **Guest Services:** gift shop, valet laundry, beauty salon. **Business Services:** meeting
rooms, business center. **Cards:** AX, CB, DC, MC, VI.

SOME UNITS

FEE

EDISON HOTEL SOUTH BEACH **Phone:** 305/531-2744 **30**

▼▼▼ Property failed to provide current rates
Location: Corner of 10th St and Ocean Dr. 960 Ocean Dr 33139. Fax: 305/672-4153. **Facility:** 60 one-bedroom
Small-scale Hotel standard units. 6 stories, interior corridors. *Bath:* combo or shower only. **Parking:** valet. **Amenities:** irons,
hair dryers. **Pool(s):** outdoor. **Leisure Activities:** beach access. **Guest Services:** valet laundry. **Business
Services:** fax (fee).

SOME UNITS

/VCR/

ESSEX HOUSE HOTEL & SUITES *Book at aaa.com* **Phone:** (305)534-2700 **29**

▼▼▼▼ All Year 1P: $99-$399 2P: $99-$399 XP: $20 F12
Location: On SR A1A (Collins Ave) and 10th St. 1001 Collins Ave 33139. Fax: 305/532-3827. **Facility:** Art deco
Classic style historic motel. Boutique style room. 79 one-bedroom standard units, some with whirlpools. 3 stories,
Small-scale Hotel interior/exterior corridors. **Parking:** on-site (fee) and valet. **Terms:** 3 day cancellation notice-fee imposed,
package plans. **Amenities:** dual phone lines, voice mail, irons, hair dryers. *Some:* honor bars. **Pool(s):**
small heated outdoor. **Leisure Activities:** *Fee:* massage. **Guest Services:** valet laundry. **Business Services:** fax (fee).
Cards: AX, DC, DS, MC, VI.

SOME UNITS

(ASK) /VCR/

FAIRFIELD INN & SUITES, MIAMI BEACH *Book at aaa.com* **Phone:** (305)673-3337 **13**

(AAA) (SAVE)
	12/23-4/30 [ECP]	1P: $169-$249	2P: $169-$249	XP: $10	F18
	7/1-11/30 [ECP]	1P: $119-$219	2P: $119-$219	XP: $10	F18
	12/1-12/22 [ECP]	1P: $119-$209	2P: $119-$209	XP: $10	F18
	5/1-6/30 [ECP]	1P: $109-$209	2P: $109-$209	XP: $10	F18

Small-scale Hotel **Location:** Oceanfront. Jct SR A1A (Collins Ave) and 40th St. 4101 Collins Ave 33140. Fax: 305/673-3660.
Bath: combo or shower only. **Parking:** valet. **Terms:** cancellation fee imposed, [AP], [BP] & [CP] meal plans available.
Amenities: video games (fee), high-speed Internet, voice mail, safes, irons, hair dryers. **Pool(s):** heated outdoor. **Leisure
Activities:** beach access, limited exercise equipment. *Fee:* beach services. **Guest Services:** valet and coin laundry. **Business
Services:** meeting rooms, business center. **Cards:** AX, CB, DC, DS, JC, MC, VI. **Special Amenities:** free expanded
continental breakfast and free local telephone calls.

SOME UNITS

FONTAINEBLEAU RESORT *Book at aaa.com* **Phone:** (305)538-2000 **9**

(AAA) (SAVE) All Year 1P: $199-$1200 2P: $199-$1200 XP: $30 F18
▼▼▼▼ **Location:** On SR A1A. 4441 Collins Ave 33140. Fax: 305/674-4607. **Facility:** 876 units. 816 one-bedroom
standard units. 40 one- and 20 two-bedroom suites ($199-$1200), some with whirlpools. 4-17 stories,
Large-scale Hotel interior corridors. *Bath:* combo or shower only. **Parking:** valet. **Terms:** package plans, small pets only.
Amenities: dual phone lines, voice mail, honor bars, irons, hair dryers. *Fee:* video games, safes. **Dining:** 3
restaurants, 6:30 am-midnight, cocktails, nightclub, entertainment. **Pool(s):** heated outdoor, wading.
Leisure Activities: whirlpools, steamrooms, waterslide, rental boats, rental paddleboats, recreation programs, playground,
exercise room, spa. *Fee:* sailboats, windsurfing, charter fishing, jet ski, parasailing. **Guest Services:** gift shop, valet laundry.
Business Services: conference facilities, business center. **Cards:** AX, CB, DC, DS, MC, VI. **Special Amenities:** free
newspaper.

SOME UNITS

FEE

(See maps and indexes starting on p. 545, 548)

FOUR POINTS BY SHERATON MIAMI BEACH

(AAA) (SAVE)

Book at aaa.com   Phone: (305)531-7494   **10**

12/23-4/30	1P: $219-$319	2P: $219-$319	XP: $10	F18
12/1-12/22 & 7/1-11/30	1P: $169-$249	2P: $169-$249	XP: $10	F18
5/1-6/30	1P: $159-$239	2P: $159-$239	XP: $10	F18

Large-scale Hotel

Location: Oceanfront. On SR A1A, just n of 43rd St. 4343 Collins Ave 33140. Fax: 305/532-2490. **Facility:** 216 units. 197 one-bedroom standard units. 19 one-bedroom suites with whirlpools. 10 stories, interior corridors. *Bath:* combo or shower only. **Parking:** valet. **Terms:** cancellation fee imposed, [AP], [BP], [CP], [ECP] & [MAP] meal plans available. **Amenities:** video games (fee), high-speed Internet, dual phone lines, voice mail, safes, irons, hair dryers. **Dining:** 6:30 am-11 pm, cocktails. **Pool(s):** heated outdoor. **Leisure Activities:** whirlpool, lifeguard on duty, limited beach access, exercise room, volleyball. *Fee:* paddleboats, sailboats, water sports. **Guest Services:** gift shop, valet laundry. **Business Services:** meeting rooms, business center. **Cards:** AX, CB, DC, DS, JC, MC, VI. **Special Amenities:** free newspaper.

SOME UNITS

(icons) / (icons) FEE FEE FEE

HOLIDAY INN SOUTH BEACH RESORT

(AAA) (SAVE)

Book at aaa.com   Phone: (305)779-3200   **1**

| 12/23-4/16 | 1P: $179-$299 | 2P: $179-$299 | XP: $15 | F18 |
| 12/1-12/22 & 4/17-11/30 | 1P: $139-$229 | 2P: $139-$229 | XP: $15 | F18 |

Large-scale Hotel

Location: Oceanfront. SR A1A, at 22nd St. 2201 Collins Ave 33139. Fax: 305/532-1403. **Facility:** 355 units. 353 one-bedroom standard units. 2 one-bedroom suites. 2-12 stories, interior/exterior corridors. *Bath:* combo or shower only. **Parking:** on-site. **Terms:** check-in 4 pm, cancellation fee imposed, [AP] & [BP] meal plans available, package plans. **Amenities:** dual phone lines, voice mail, safes, irons, hair dryers. **Dining:** 2 restaurants, 7 am-11 pm, cocktails. **Pool(s):** heated outdoor. **Leisure Activities:** whirlpool, 2 lighted tennis courts, exercise room, volleyball. *Fee:* catamarans, parasailing, personal watercraft, game room. **Guest Services:** gift shop, valet and coin laundry. **Business Services:** fax (fee). **Cards:** AX, DC, DS, MC, VI. **Special Amenities:** free local telephone calls and free newspaper. *(See color ad below)*

SOME UNITS

(icons) / (icons) FEE

THE HOTEL

(AAA) (SAVE)

Book at aaa.com   Phone: (305)531-2222   **34**

12/1-5/31	1P: $275-$450	2P: $275-$450
10/1-11/30	1P: $255-$385	2P: $255-$385
6/1-9/30	1P: $225-$355	2P: $225-$355

Classic
Small-scale Hotel

Location: On SR A1A (Collins Ave) and 8th St. 801 Collins Ave 33139. Fax: 305/531-3222. **Facility:** Fashion designer Todd Oldham is credited with selecting the finishes and furnishings in the lobby and guest rooms of this Art Deco-area property. 53 units. 49 one-bedroom standard units. 4 one-bedroom suites with whirlpools. 4 stories, interior corridors. *Bath:* combo or shower only. **Parking:** on-site (fee) and valet. **Terms:** 2-3 night minimum stay - weekends, 7 day cancellation notice-fee imposed. **Amenities:** video library (fee), CD players, high-speed Internet, dual phone lines, voice mail, safes, honor bars, hair dryers. *Some:* irons. **Dining:** Wish, see separate listing. **Pool(s):** heated outdoor. **Leisure Activities:** beach services, exercise room. *Fee:* massage. **Guest Services:** gift shop, valet laundry. **Business Services:** meeting rooms. *Fee:* administrative services, fax. **Cards:** AX, DC, DS, MC, VI. **Special Amenities:** free newspaper.

(icons)

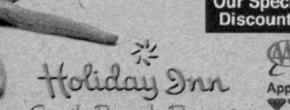

(See maps and indexes starting on p. 545, 548)

HOTEL OCEAN   Book at aaa.com   Phone: (305)672-2579   [23]
▼▼▼▼   12/1-5/31 [CP]   1P: $210-$675   2P: $210-$675   XP: $49   F3
               6/1-11/30 [CP]   1P: $190-$555   2P: $190-$555   XP: $49   F3
Small-scale Hotel Location: E of jct SR A1A (Collins Ave) and 12th St. Located in the heart of the Art Deco District, across from beach.
1230 Ocean Dr 33139. Fax: 305/672-7665. Facility: 27 units. 13 one-bedroom standard units. 14 one-
bedroom suites, some with whirlpools. 5 stories, interior corridors. Bath: combo or shower only. Terms: 2-3 night
minimum stay - seasonal and/or weekends, 3 day cancellation notice, package plans, small pets only ($15 extra charge).
Amenities: CD players, dual phone lines, voice mail, safes, irons, hair dryers. Some: DVD players. Dining: Les 2 Fontaines,
see separate listing. Leisure Activities: beach access. Guest Services: valet laundry. Business Services: meeting rooms, fax
(fee). Cards: AX, DC, DS, MC, VI.

SOME UNITS

HOWARD JOHNSON PLAZA DEZERLAND BEACH &
SPA   Book at aaa.com   Phone: (305)865-6661   [1]
(AAA) [SAVE]   12/23-4/30   1P: $119-$169   2P: $119-$169   XP: $10   F17
               5/1-11/30   1P: $69-$119   2P: $69-$119   XP: $10   F17
▼▼▼▼   12/1-12/22   1P: $65-$109   2P: $65-$109   XP: $10   F17
Large-scale Hotel Location: Oceanfront. SR 922 (Broad Cswy/96th St), just s on Harding Ave, then e on 87th St. 8701 Collins Ave 33154.
Fax: 305/866-2630. Facility: 225 units. 223 one-bedroom standard units, some with efficiencies. 2 one-
bedroom suites with kitchens. 10 stories, interior corridors. Bath: combo or shower only. Parking: on-site
(fee). Terms: check-in 4 pm, cancellation fee imposed, [BP] & [CP] meal plans available, package plans, $6 service charge.
Amenities: voice mail, safes (fee), irons, hair dryers. Dining: 7 am-11 pm, cocktails. Pool(s): outdoor. Leisure
Activities: sauna, whirlpool, steamroom, limited beach access, spa, volleyball. Fee: miniature golf, beach water sports
activities. Guest Services: area transportation-within 5 mi. Business Services: meeting rooms, fax (fee). Cards: AX, CB, DC,
DS, JC, MC, VI. (See color ad below)

SOME UNITS

THE INDIAN CREEK HOTEL   Book at aaa.com   Phone: 305/531-2727   [17]
▼▼▼▼   Property failed to provide current rates
               Location: SR A1A southbound, at 28th St, just w of Collins Ave. 2727 Indian Creek Dr 33140. Fax: 305/531-5651.
Small-scale Hotel Facility: 61 one-bedroom standard units. 3 stories, interior corridors. Parking: street. Amenities: voice mail,
irons, hair dryers. Some: CD players. Pool(s): outdoor. Guest Services: valet laundry. Business Services:
meeting rooms.

SOME UNITS

(See maps and indexes starting on p. 545, 548)

THE KENT HOTEL *Book at aaa.com* Phone: (305)604-5068 **26**

▼▼▼▼

12/1-4/30 [ECP]	1P: $145-$170	2P: $145-$175	XP: $25	F12
5/1-11/30 [ECP]	1P: $140-$145	2P: $140-$145	XP: $25	F12

Classic
Small-scale Hotel

Location: On SR A1A, at Collins Ave and 11th St. Located one block from the beach. 1131 Collins Ave 33139. Fax: 305/604-5180. **Facility:** Built during the Art Deco Era, the Kent offers a lovely/tropical courtyard off the lobby; rooms have brightly colored furniture. 54 units. 53 one-bedroom standard units. 1 one-bedroom suite with whirlpool. 3 stories, interior corridors. *Bath:* combo or shower only. **Parking:** valet. **Terms:** check-in 4 pm, 3 day cancellation notice-fee imposed, pets (dogs only, $25 extra charge). **Amenities:** CD players, voice mail, safes, irons, hair dryers. *Some:* DVD players. **Guest Services:** valet laundry. **Business Services:** meeting rooms, PC, fax (fee). **Cards:** AX, DC, DS, MC, VI.

SOME UNITS

(A$K) (S✎) (🛏) (🍴) (⛎) (🏊) (VCR) (📶) (DATA PORT) (📠) / (✕) /
FEE

LAS BRISAS SOUTH BEACH HOTEL - DORSET
HOTEL *Book at aaa.com* Phone: 305/938-6000 **7**

▼▼▼

Property failed to provide current rates

Location: On SR A1A; jct Collins Ave and 17th St; in heart of the Art Deco District. 1720 Collins Ave 33139.
Small-scale Hotel Fax: 305/938-6001. **Facility:** 52 units. 51 one-bedroom standard units. 1 one-bedroom suite. 3 stories, interior corridors. *Bath:* combo or shower only. **Parking:** valet. **Amenities:** DVD players, CD players, dual phone lines, voice mail, safes, irons, hair dryers. **Pool(s):** small heated outdoor. **Guest Services:** valet laundry.

SOME UNITS

(🍴) (🛥) (🏊) (📶) (DATA PORT) / (✕) /

LOEWS MIAMI BEACH HOTEL *Book at aaa.com* Phone: (305)604-1601 **13**

(AAA) (SAVE)

▼▼▼ ▼▼▼

12/22-4/30	1P: $339-$4000	2P: $339-$4000	XP: $30	F18
12/1-12/21	1P: $249-$4000	2P: $249-$4000	XP: $30	F18
5/1-5/31	1P: $289-$3500	2P: $289-$3500	XP: $30	F18
6/1-11/30	1P: $219-$3500	2P: $219-$3500	XP: $30	F18

Large-scale Hotel **Location:** On SR A1A, at Collins and 16th aves. 1601 Collins Ave 33139. Fax: 305/604-3999. **Facility:** This waterfront hotel in the Art Deco area features two buildings on grounds enhanced by tropical trees and fountains; the lobby has shops and eateries. 790 units. 724 one-bedroom standard units. 57 one- and 9 two-bedroom suites ($400-$4000). 12-18 stories, interior corridors. *Bath:* combo or shower only. **Parking:** valet. **Terms:** check-in 4 pm, 3 day cancellation notice-fee imposed, small pets only. **Amenities:** CD players, dual phone lines, voice mail, safes, honor bars, irons, hair dryers. *Fee:* video games, high-speed Internet. *Some: Fee:* DVD players. **Dining:** 5 restaurants, 7 am-11 pm, cocktails, also, Emeril's Miami Beach, see separate listing, entertainment. **Pool(s):** heated outdoor, wading. **Leisure Activities:** saunas, whirlpools, recreation programs, spa. *Fee:* water sports on the beach. **Guest Services:** gift shop, valet laundry. **Business Services:** conference facilities, business center. **Cards:** AX, DC, DS, MC, VI. **Special Amenities:** free newspaper. *(See color ad below)*

SOME UNITS

(🛏) (🍴) (24🕐) (🍸) (⛎M) (⛎) (🏊) (🛥) (📶) (✕) (📶) (📷) (DATA PORT) (💻) / (✕) (VCR) (📠) /
FEE FEE

(See maps and indexes starting on p. 545, 548)

THE MARLIN — *Book at aaa.com* Phone: (305)604-3595   **25**

12/1-6/1	1P: $225-$895	2P: $225-$895	XP: $25 F
6/2-11/30	1P: $135-$595	2P: $135-$595	XP: $25 F

Small-scale Hotel   **Location:** On SR A1A, at Collins Ave and 12th St. 1200 Collins Ave 33139. Fax: 305/673-9609. **Facility:** 12 units. 9 one-bedroom standard units with kitchens. 3 one-bedroom suites with kitchens, some with whirlpools. 3 stories, interior corridors. **Parking:** valet. **Terms:** 14 day cancellation notice-fee imposed, package plans, $5 service charge, pets (small dogs only, $100 fee). **Amenities:** video library (fee), DVD players, CD players, dual phone lines, voice mail, safes, honor bars, irons, hair dryers. **Leisure Activities:** *Fee:* massage. **Guest Services:** valet laundry. **Business Services:** fax (fee). **Cards:** AX, DC, DS, MC, VI.

MARRIOTT SOUTH BEACH   *Book at aaa.com* Phone: 305/536-7700   **39**

12/1-4/30	1P: $359-$389	2P: $359-$389	
5/1-9/25	1P: $289-$319	2P: $289-$319	
9/25-11/30	1P: $259-$289	2P: $259-$289	
6/1-9/24	1P: $199-$239	2P: $199-$239	

Large-scale Hotel   **Location:** Oceanfront. Just e of SR A1A (Collins Ave); just s of 2nd St. 161 Ocean Dr 33139. Fax: 305/536-9900. **Facility:** 236 units. 229 one-bedroom standard units. 7 one-bedroom suites. 10 stories, interior corridors. *Bath:* combo or shower only. **Terms:** 3 day cancellation notice-fee imposed, package plans, small pets only ($100 deposit). **Amenities:** dual phone lines, voice mail, safes, irons, hair dryers. *Fee:* video games, high-speed Internet. *Some:* CD players. **Dining:** 7 am-10 pm, cocktails. **Pool(s):** heated outdoor. **Leisure Activities:** whirlpool, limited beach access, fishing, exercise room. *Fee:* massage. **Guest Services:** gift shop, valet laundry. **Business Services:** meeting rooms, business center. **Cards:** AX, CB, DC, DS, JC, MC, VI.   SOME UNITS

MIMOSA HOTEL & SPA   *Book at aaa.com* Phone: 305/867-5000   **5**

Property failed to provide current rates

Location: Oceanfront. On SR A1A (Collins Ave) at 65th St. 6525 Collins Ave 33141. Fax: 305/864-4422. **Facility:** 60 Small-scale Hotel   units. 58 one-bedroom standard units with whirlpools, some with efficiencies. 2 one-bedroom suites with efficiencies and whirlpools. 3 stories, interior corridors. *Bath:* combo or shower only. **Parking:** valet. **Amenities:** DVD players, high-speed Internet, voice mail, safes, irons, hair dryers. **Pool(s):** heated outdoor. **Leisure Activities:** limited beach access, exercise room, spa. **Guest Services:** valet laundry. **Business Services:** meeting rooms, business center. *(See color ad p 580)*   SOME UNITS

NASSAU SUITE HOTEL   *Book at aaa.com* Phone: (305)532-0043   **19**

12/1-3/31 [CP]	1P: $230-$310	2P: $230-$310	XP: $20 F12
4/1-4/30 & 11/1-11/30 [CP]	1P: $210-$280	2P: $210-$280	XP: $20 F12
5/1-10/31 [CP]	1P: $160-$250	2P: $160-$250	XP: $20 F12

Small-scale Hotel   **Location:** On Collins Ave (SR A1A), just n of 13th St. 1414 Collins Ave 33139. Fax: 305/534-3133. **Facility:** 22 units. 15 one-bedroom standard units with kitchens. 7 one-bedroom suites with kitchens. 3 stories, interior corridors. **Parking:** on-site (fee). **Amenities:** DVD players, high-speed Internet, voice mail, safes (fee), irons, hair dryers. *Some:* CD players. **Guest Services:** valet laundry. **Business Services:** meeting rooms, business center. **Cards:** AX, DC, DS, MC, VI.   SOME UNITS

THE NATIONAL HOTEL   *Book at aaa.com* Phone: (305)532-2311   **10**

12/29-5/29	1P: $279-$3579	2P: $279-$3579	
9/29-11/30	1P: $249-$3569	2P: $249-$3569	
12/1-12/28	1P: $249-$3469	2P: $249-$3469	
5/30-9/28	1P: $179-$2789	2P: $179-$2789	

Classic   **Location:** Oceanfront. On SR A1A (Collins Ave) and 16th St. 1677 Collins Ave 33139. Fax: 305/534-1426. **Facility:** The Small-scale Hotel   lobby is reminiscent of the late '30s, and rooms in the tower also reflect the Deco era; a courtyard features a pool, and the beach is nearby. 151 units. 148 one-bedroom standard units. 3 one-bedroom suites ($309-$3579), some with whirlpools. 13 stories, interior corridors. *Bath:* combo or shower only. **Parking:** valet. **Terms:** check-in 4 pm, 3 day cancellation notice, package plans, $11 service charge. **Amenities:** DVD players, video games (fee), CD players, high-speed Internet, dual phone lines, voice mail, safes, honor bars, irons, hair dryers. **Dining:** 2 restaurants, 6 am-11 pm, cocktails, entertainment. **Pool(s):** heated outdoor, lap. **Leisure Activities:** limited beach access, exercise room. *Fee:* massage. **Guest Services:** sundries, valet laundry. **Business Services:** meeting rooms, business center. **Cards:** AX, DC, DS, JC, MC, VI.   SOME UNITS

(See maps and indexes starting on p. 545, 548)

THE NEW CASABLANCA ON THE OCEAN   *Book at aaa.com*   Phone: (305)868-0010   **6**

(AAA) (SAVE)
12/22-4/16 [CP]   1P: $159-$199   2P: $159-$199   XP: $5   D12
12/1-12/21 & 4/17-11/30 [CP]   1P: $139-$169   2P: $139-$169   XP: $5   D12

Location: Oceanfront. SR A1A (Collins Ave), just n of 63rd St. 6345 Collins Ave 33141. Fax: 305/865-7111.

Large-scale Hotel **Facility:** 150 units. 146 one-bedroom standard units with kitchens. 1 one- and 3 two-bedroom suites ($279-$349) with kitchens. 10 stories, interior corridors. **Parking:** valet. **Amenities:** voice mail, safes, irons, hair dryers. **Dining:** 7 am-10 pm, cocktails. **Pool(s):** heated outdoor. **Leisure Activities:** limited beach access, exercise room. **Guest Services:** gift shop, valet and coin laundry. **Business Services:** meeting rooms, fax (fee). **Cards:** AX, CB, DC, DS, JC, MC, VI. **Special Amenities:** free continental breakfast and free newspaper. *(See color ad below)*

SOME UNITS

(See maps and indexes starting on p. 545, 548)

OCEAN FIVE HOTEL   *Book at aaa.com*   Phone: (305)532-7093   36
♦♦♦♦   12/20-5/31 [CP]   1P: $195-S345   2P: $195-$345   XP: $15   F12
         12/1-12/19 & 6/1-11/30 [CP]   1P: $135-$245   2P: $135-$245   XP: $15   F12
Small-scale Hotel   **Location:** Just e of SR A1A (Collins Ave); between 4th and 5th sts. 436 Ocean Dr 33139. Fax: 305/534-7353. **Facility:** 56 units. 52 one-bedroom standard units. 4 one-bedroom suites, some with kitchens. 2-3 stories, interior corridors. *Bath:* shower only. **Parking:** valet. **Terms:** 3 day cancellation notice-fee imposed. **Amenities:** CD players, high-speed Internet, voice mail, safes, honor bars, irons, hair dryers. *Some:* dual phone lines. **Leisure Activities:** beach access, jogging. **Guest Services:** valet laundry. **Business Services:** fax (fee). **Cards:** AX, DC, DS, MC, VI.
(See color ad p 576)

                                             SOME UNITS
(ASK) (S/D) ✈ [†|] ⊤ (雫) DATA ⌷ /✕/
                    FEE   PORT

OCEAN SURF HOTEL   *Book at aaa.com*   Phone: (305)866-1648   3
♦♦♦   1/1-4/10 [CP]   2P: $100-$200
       12/1-12/31 & 4/11-11/30 [CP]   2P: $80-$200
Small-scale Hotel   **Location:** Collins Ave and 75th St, just e on 75th St, then a right turn. Located across from the beach. 7436 Ocean Terrace 33141. Fax: 305/866-1649. **Facility:** 49 one-bedroom standard units. 4 stories, interior corridors. *Bath:* combo or shower only. **Parking:** on-site (fee). **Terms:** cancellation fee imposed, weekly rates available, package plans. **Amenities:** safes (fee), hair dryers. **Leisure Activities:** beach access. **Guest Services:** valet laundry. **Cards:** AX, DC, DS, MC, VI. *(See color ad below)*

                                             SOME UNITS
(ASK) (S/D) [†|↑] (&M) (⌖) (雫) 🖥 /✕/

THE PRESIDENT HOTEL   *Book at aaa.com*   Phone: (305)538-2882   18
♦♦♦   4/15-11/30   1P: $190-$275   2P: $200-$300   XP: $15   F15
       12/1-4/14   1P: $140-$190   2P: $160-$209   XP: $15   F15
Classic   **Location:** On SR A1A/Collins Ave, just s of Espanola Way. 1423 Collins Ave 33139. Fax: 305/604-0350. **Facility:** A
Small-scale Hotel   block from the beach, this hotel in the Art Deco district has antique Spanish furniture. 64 one-bedroom standard units. 4 stories, interior corridors. *Bath:* combo or shower only. **Parking:** street. **Terms:** 3 day cancellation notice. **Amenities:** dual phone lines, voice mail, safes. *Some:* hair dryers. **Pool(s):** outdoor. **Guest Services:** valet laundry. **Business Services:** meeting rooms, fax (fee). **Cards:** AX, MC, VI.

                                             SOME UNITS
(ASK) (S/D) [†|] ⊤ (⌖) (≈) (雫) DATA 🖥 /✕/
                                         PORT

RIANDE CONTINENTAL SOUTH BEACH HOTEL   *Book at aaa.com*   Phone: (305)531-3503   4
(AAA) (SAVE)   12/27-3/31 [ECP]   1P: $140-S199   2P: $140-$199   XP: $10   F
♦♦♦ ♦♦   12/1-12/26 & 4/1-11/30 [ECP]   1P: $120-S199   2P: $120-$199   XP: $10   F
Large-scale Hotel   **Location:** On SR A1A (Collins Ave), just n of 18th St. 1825 Collins Ave 33139. Fax: 305/531-5602. **Facility:** 249 one-bedroom standard units. 8 stories, interior corridors. **Parking:** valet. **Terms:** 3 day cancellation notice-fee imposed. **Amenities:** high-speed Internet, voice mail, irons, hair dryers. *Some:* safes, honor bars. **Dining:** 7 am-4 & 5-10 pm, cocktails. **Pool(s):** outdoor. **Leisure Activities:** *Fee:* massage. **Guest Services:** gift shop, valet laundry. **Business Services:** meeting rooms, fax (fee). **Cards:** AX, DC, DS, MC, VI.

                                             SOME UNITS
(S/D) [†|] ⊤ (≈) DATA /✕ 🖥 /
                        PORT

(See maps and indexes starting on p. 545, 548)

THE RITZ-CARLTON, SOUTH BEACH   *Book at aaa.com*   **Phone:** (786)276-4000   🔟2️⃣
All Year   1P: $599-$5500   2P: $599-$5500
Location: Oceanfront. Jct SR A1A (Collins Ave) and Lincoln Rd. 1 Lincoln Rd 33139. **Fax:** 786/276-4001.
Large-scale Hotel   **Facility:** Located on the beach and in the heart of the Art Deco district. 376 units. 333 one-bedroom standard units. 43 one-bedroom suites, some with whirlpools. 3-11 stories, interior corridors. *Bath:* combo or shower only. **Parking:** valet. **Terms:** check-in 4 pm, 3 day cancellation notice-fee imposed, weekly rates available, small pets only ($250 fee). **Amenities:** CD players, dual phone lines, voice mail, safes, honor bars, irons, hair dryers. *Fee:* video library, video games, high-speed Internet. *Some:* DVD players. **Pool(s):** heated outdoor. **Leisure Activities:** whirlpool, limited beach access, spa. *Fee:* fishing, charter fishing. **Guest Services:** gift shop, valet laundry, area transportation. **Business Services:** conference facilities, business center. **Cards:** AX, CB, DC, DS, JC, MC, VI.

SOME UNITS
🛏️ 🍴 24️⃣ 🍷 📶 💪 ♿ 🌀 🏊 🛶 ✖️ 🎥 📠 / ✖️ 📦 /
FEE

RIU FLORIDA BEACH HOTEL   *Book at aaa.com*   **Phone:** (305)673-5333   1️⃣5️⃣
12/1-4/30   1P: $185-$235   2P: $185-$235   XP: $20   F12
5/1-11/30   1P: $155-$205   2P: $155-$205   XP: $20   F12
Location: On SR A1A at 31st St. Located in a quiet oceanfront area. 3101 Collins Ave 33140. **Fax:** 305/673-9335.
Large-scale Hotel   **Facility:** 284 one-bedroom standard units. 9 stories, interior corridors. *Bath:* combo or shower only. **Parking:** valet. **Terms:** check-in 4 pm, 3 day cancellation notice, [BP] meal plan available. **Amenities:** safes (fee), honor bars, irons, hair dryers. *Some:* DVD players. **Dining:** 2 restaurants, 7 am-10 pm, cocktails, entertainment. **Pool(s):** heated outdoor, wading. **Leisure Activities:** lifeguard on duty, limited beach access. **Guest Services:** gift shop, valet laundry. **Business Services:** meeting rooms, fax (fee). **Cards:** AX, DC, DS, MC, VI. *(See color ad below)*

SOME UNITS
  / ✖️ /

RODEWAY INN SOUTH BEACH   *Book at aaa.com*   **Phone:** (305)673-1199   1️⃣6️⃣
All Year   1P: $89-$129   2P: $89-$129   XP: $15   F12
Location: On SR A1A (Collins Ave), just s of 15th St. Across from the beach. 1506 Collins Ave 33139. **Fax:** 305/532-7418. **Facility:** 29 units. 27 one-bedroom standard units. 2 one-bedroom suites. 2-4 stories, exterior corridors. *Bath:* combo or shower only. **Parking:** on-site (fee). **Terms:** small pets only ($100 deposit, in limited units). **Amenities:** voice mail, safes. *Some:* DVD players, CD players, irons, hair dryers. **Dining:** 24 hours, wine/beer only. **Business Services:** business center. **Cards:** AX, DS, MC, VI.
Motel
Special Amenities: free full breakfast and free local telephone calls.

SOME UNITS
    / ✖️ 📦 /
FEE

(See maps and indexes starting on p. 545, 548)

SAGAMORE HOTEL   *Book at aaa.com*   Phone: 305/535-8088   ⓫

▼▼▼ ▼▼▼   Property failed to provide current rates

Small-scale Hotel   **Location:** Oceanfront. On Collins Ave (SR A1A); between 16th and 15th sts. 1671 Collins Ave 33139. Fax: 305/535-8185. **Facility:** Located on the beach in the heart of the deco area, the hotel features museum-like public areas and spacious and modern rooms. 93 units. 4 one-bedroom standard units with efficiencies and whirlpools. 89 one-bedroom suites with efficiencies and whirlpools. 5 stories, interior corridors. *Bath:* combo or shower only. **Parking:** valet. **Amenities:** video library, DVD players, CD players, high-speed Internet, dual phone lines, voice mail, safes, honor bars, irons, hair dryers. **Pool(s):** heated outdoor. **Leisure Activities:** lifeguard on duty, limited beach access, spa. **Guest Services:** valet laundry. **Business Services:** meeting rooms.

SOME UNITS

[icons: ✈ FEE | ❮❯ | 24 | ❨ | ➦ | ⊶ | VCR | ▣ | DATA PORT | � | ◳ | ▣ | / ⊠ /]

SHELBORNE BEACH RESORT-SOUTH BEACH   *Book at aaa.com*   Phone: (305)531-1271   ❺

AAA SAVE | 12/1-5/31 & 9/1-11/30 | 1P: $185-$2500 | 2P: $185-$2500 | XP: $10 | F12
         | 6/1-8/31 | 1P: $145-$2500 | 2P: $145-$2500 | XP: $10 | F12

▼▼ ▼▼   **Location:** Oceanfront. SR A1A at 18th St. 1801 Collins Ave 33139. Fax: 305/531-2206. **Facility:** 200 units. 191 one-bedroom standard units. 1 one- and 8 two-bedroom suites ($475-$2850) with kitchens, some with whirlpools. 2-16 stories, interior corridors. *Bath:* combo or shower only. **Parking:** valet. **Terms:** 3 day cancellation notice-fee imposed, $3 service charge. **Amenities:** voice mail, safes (fee), irons, hair dryers. *Some:* CD players. **Dining:** 7 am-11 pm, Fri & Sat-midnight, cocktails, nightclub. **Pool(s):** heated outdoor. **Leisure Activities:** sauna, whirlpools, exercise room, volleyball. **Guest Services:** valet laundry. **Business Services:** conference facilities, fax (fee). **Cards:** AX, CB, DC, DS, MC, VI. **Special Amenities: free room upgrade (subject to availability with advance reservations).** *(See color ad below)*

Large-scale Hotel

SOME UNITS

[icons: S/D | ❮❯ | ❨ | ➦ | ⊠ | ▣ | DATA PORT | / ⊠ | VCR FEE | ▣ | ◳ | ▣ /]

SOUTH SEAS HOTEL   *Book at aaa.com*   Phone: (305)538-1411   ❻

AAA SAVE | 12/1-4/16 [ECP] | 1P: $239-$625 | 2P: $239-$625 | XP: $25 | F12
         | 4/17-6/4 [ECP] | 1P: $219-$525 | 2P: $219-$525 | XP: $25 | F12
▼▼ ▼▼ | 10/2-11/30 [ECP]| 1P: $189-$525 | 2P: $189-$525 | XP: $25 | F12
         | 6/5-10/1 [ECP] | 1P: $149-$425 | 2P: $149-$425 | XP: $25 | F12

Small-scale Hotel   **Location:** Oceanfront. On SR A1A; at Collins Ave and 17th St. 1751 Collins Ave 33139. Fax: 305/532-9477. **Facility:** 111 one-bedroom standard units. 7 stories, interior corridors. *Bath:* combo or shower only. **Parking:** valet. **Terms:** 3 day cancellation notice-fee imposed. **Amenities:** high-speed Internet, voice mail, safes, irons, hair dryers. *Some:* DVD players, CD players, safes. **Dining:** 7 am-midnight, cocktails. **Pool(s):** heated outdoor. **Leisure Activities:** limited exercise equipment. *Fee:* massage. **Guest Services:** valet laundry. **Business Services:** meeting rooms, business center. **Cards:** AX, DC, DS, MC, VI. **Special Amenities: free expanded continental breakfast and free local telephone calls.**

SOME UNITS

[icons: ✈ FEE | ❮❯ | ♿M | ✎ | ➦ | ▣ | DATA PORT | / ⊠ | VCR | ▣ | ◳ | ▣ /]

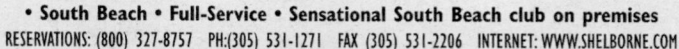

(See maps and indexes starting on p. 545, 548)

THE TIDES HOTEL   *Book at aaa.com*   Phone: (305)604-5070   24

▼▼▼ ▼▼▼	12/1-4/30	1P: $550-$650	2P: $550-$650	XP: $25	F12
	5/1-11/30	1P: $420-$520	2P: $420-$520	XP: $25	F12

Small-scale Hotel   **Location:** E of jct SR A1A (Collins Ave) and 12th St. 1220 Ocean Dr 33139. Fax: 305/604-5180. **Facility:** A restored Art Deco-style hotel, The Tides features a large lobby reminiscent of the 1930s; all guest rooms face the ocean. 45 units. 42 one-bedroom standard units. 3 one-bedroom suites ($1500-$3000) with whirlpools. 10 stories, interior corridors. **Parking:** valet. **Terms:** check-in 4 pm, 2-3 night minimum stay - weekends, 3 day cancellation notice-fee imposed, [AP] & [BP] meal plans available, package plans, pets (small dogs only, $100 extra charge). **Amenities:** video library (fee), DVD players, CD players, high-speed Internet, dual phone lines, voice mail, safes, honor bars, irons, hair dryers. *Some:* fax. **Dining:** Twelve Twenty, see separate listing. **Pool(s):** heated outdoor. **Leisure Activities:** beach access, exercise room. **Guest Services:** valet laundry. **Business Services:** meeting rooms. Fee: PC, fax. **Cards:** AX, DC, DS, MC, VI.

SOME UNITS
🐕 ⏹ 24⏹ 🍸 🚪M 🖊 📷 🐬 VCR 📶 DATA PORT / ✕ ☎ /
FEE

TUDOR HOTEL & SUITES   *Book at aaa.com*   Phone: 305/534-2934   27
▼▼▼   Property failed to provide current rates

Classic
Small-scale Hotel   **Location:** On SR A1A (Collins Ave) at 11th St. 1111 Collins Ave 33139. Fax: 305/531-1874. **Facility:** Centered in the Art Deco district, this hotel is a block from the beach. 107 units. 98 one-bedroom standard units. 8 one- and 1 two-bedroom suites with efficiencies (no utensils). 4 stories, interior corridors. **Parking:** valet. **Terms:** check-in 4 pm. **Amenities:** voice mail, safes, irons, hair dryers. **Guest Services:** valet and coin laundry. **Business Services:** meeting rooms, fax (fee).

SOME UNITS
⏹ 🍸 📷 DATA PORT 🖥 / ✕ ☎ 🖥 /

VILLA CAPRI ALL SUITES HOTEL   *Book at aaa.com*   Phone: (305)531-7742   16

▼▼▼	12/23-4/30	2P: $195-$415	XP: $20	F16
	12/1-12/22	2P: $175-$325	XP: $20	F16

Small-scale Hotel   5/1-11/30   2P: $170-$295   XP: $20   F16
Location: On SR A1A; at 30th St. Located in a quiet area, across from beach. 3010 Collins Ave 33140. Fax: 305/532-3030. **Facility:** 71 units. 30 one-bedroom suites. 41 one-bedroom suites with efficiencies. 4 stories, interior corridors. **Parking:** valet. **Terms:** check-in 4 pm, 3 day cancellation notice, [AP] meal plan available, small pets only ($35 fee). **Amenities:** CD players, voice mail, honor bars, irons, hair dryers. *Some:* DVD players. **Pool(s):** outdoor. **Leisure Activities:** sauna, beach access, exercise room. **Business Services:** business center. **Cards:** AX, DC, DS, MC, VI.

SOME UNITS
A$K S🐾 🐕 🍸 🍸 🐬 📷 DATA PORT ☎ 🖥 🖥 / ✕ VCR /
FEE

THE WALDORF TOWERS HOTEL   *Book at aaa.com*   Phone: (305)531-7684   32

▼▼▼	12/1-12/31	1P: $139-$219	2P: $139-$219	XP: $20	F3
	1/1-5/31	1P: $139-$189	2P: $139-$189	XP: $20	F3
	6/1-11/30	1P: $109-$129	2P: $109-$129	XP: $20	F3

Classic
Small-scale Hotel   **Location:** Corner of 8th St and Ocean Dr; just e of Collins Ave (SR A1A). Across from the beach. 860 Ocean Dr 33139. Fax: 305/672-6836. **Facility:** Located across the street from the beach, shopping and clubs nearby, the hotel's room sizes reflect the Art Deco era but are modernly furnished. 41 units. 38 one-bedroom standard units. 3 one-bedroom suites ($239-$599). 3 stories, interior corridors. *Bath:* shower only. **Parking:** valet. **Terms:** cancellation fee imposed, 13% service charge, small pets only ($20 fee). **Amenities:** DVD players, CD players, voice mail, safes, irons, hair dryers. *Some:* dual phone lines. **Guest Services:** gift shop, valet laundry. **Business Services:** meeting rooms. **Cards:** AX, DC, DS, MC, VI.

SOME UNITS
A$K S🐾 ➕ 🐕 🍸 🍸 💪 VCR 📷 DATA PORT ☎ / ✕ /
FEE FEE

THE WAVE HOTEL   *Book at aaa.com*   Phone: (305)673-0401   37

▼▼▼	4/21-9/30	1P: $149-$169	2P: $219-$249	XP: $25	F12
	12/1-4/20	1P: $199-$219	2P: $209-$249	XP: $25	F12

Small-scale Hotel   10/1-11/30   1P: $159-$179   2P: $179-$199   XP: $25   F12
Location: Just e of SR A1A (Collins Ave), at 4th St and Ocean Dr. 350 Ocean Dr 33139. Fax: 305/531-9385. **Facility:** 66 units. 64 one-bedroom standard units. 2 one-bedroom suites ($399-$449). 4 stories, interior corridors. **Parking:** on-site and valet. **Terms:** 3 day cancellation notice-fee imposed, [CP] meal plan available, package plans. **Amenities:** CD players, high-speed Internet, voice mail, safes, honor bars, irons, hair dryers. **Leisure Activities:** beach access, limited exercise equipment. **Guest Services:** valet laundry. **Business Services:** meeting rooms, fax (fee). **Cards:** AX, CB, DC, DS, JC, MC, VI.

SOME UNITS
A$K S🐾 🍸 🍸 DATA PORT / ✕ /

WINTER HAVEN HOTEL   *Book at aaa.com*   Phone: (305)531-5571   20

▼▼▼	12/27-3/31	1P: $169-$399	2P: $169-$399
	4/1-5/31	1P: $129-$399	2P: $129-$399
	6/1-11/30	1P: $99-$399	2P: $99-$399

Classic
Small-scale Hotel   12/1-12/26   1P: $99-$129   2P: $99-$129
Location: Corner of Ocean Dr and 14th St. Located across from the beach. 1400 Ocean Dr 33139. Fax: 305/538-6387. **Facility:** Located across the street from the beach, the hotel features an enormous lobby and rooms that vary in size, but all have rich mahogany wood furniture. 66 one-bedroom standard units. 6 stories, interior corridors. *Bath:* shower only. **Parking:** valet. **Terms:** 3 day cancellation notice-fee imposed, package plans. **Amenities:** dual phone lines, voice mail, safes, irons, hair dryers. **Guest Services:** valet laundry. **Business Services:** meeting rooms. **Cards:** AX, DC, DS, MC, VI.

SOME UNITS
A$K S🐾 🍸 DATA PORT / ✕ /

(See maps and indexes starting on p. 545, 548)

WYNDHAM MIAMI BEACH RESORT   *Book at aaa.com*   Phone: (305)532-3600   7

AAA SAVE	12/23-5/31	1P: $259	2P: $259	XP: $20	F17
▽▽▽▽	10/1-11/30	1P: $199	2P: $199	XP: $20	F17
	12/1-12/22 & 6/1-9/30	1P: $179	2P: $179	XP: $20	F17

Location: On SR A1A; 0.5 mi n of jct Arthur Godfrey Rd. 4833 Collins Ave 33140. Fax: 305/534-7409. **Facility:** 424
Large-scale Hotel units. 404 one-bedroom standard units. 20 one-bedroom suites ($294-$434), some with whirlpools. 18 stories, interior corridors. *Bath:* combo or shower only. **Parking:** valet. **Terms:** check-in 4 pm, 3 day cancellation notice, $10 service charge. **Amenities:** dual phone lines, voice mail, honor bars, irons, hair dryers. *Fee:* video games, high-speed Internet. **Dining:** 3 restaurants, 6:30 am-1:30 am; pool terrace dining; 17% service charge, cocktails. **Pool(s):** heated outdoor. **Leisure Activities:** saunas, steamrooms, jogging, exercise room. *Fee:* paddleboats, boat dock, waterskiing, scuba diving, snorkeling, charter fishing, jet skis, scuba instruction, massage. **Guest Services:** gift shop, valet laundry. **Business Services:** conference facilities, business center. **Cards:** AX, CB, DC, DS, JC, MC, VI.

SOME UNITS

[icons] 🍽 🍷 📶 📷 🚤 ✂ 📹 DATA PORT 💻 / ✕ VCR 📱 / FEE

The following lodging was either not evaluated or did not meet AAA rating requirements but is listed for your information only.

HOTEL VICTOR   Phone: 305/428-1234
fyi   Not evaluated. **Location:** E of jct SR A1A (Collins Ave) and 11th St. 1144 Ocean Dr 33139. Facilities, services, and decor characterize an upscale property.

(See maps and indexes starting on p. 545, 548)

—————— WHERE TO DINE ——————

11TH STREET DINER
American
Lunch: $8-$14   **Dinner:** $10-$15   **Phone:** 305/534-6373   46
Location: Between 10th and 11th sts. 1065 Washington Ave 33139. **Hours:** 24 hours. **Reservations:** not accepted. **Features:** This original art deco diner was built in 1948 and moved to Miami Beach from Pennsylvania in 1992 and restored to its original form. The classic diner serves up a large variety of salads and sandwiches, as well as traditional entrees and daily specials, all while rock & roll music plays in the background. Casual dress; cocktails. **Parking:** street. **Cards:** AX, DC, MC, VI.

A FISH CALLED AVALON
Seafood
Dinner: $18-$35   **Phone:** 305/532-1727   55
Location: E of SR A1A (Collins Ave); jct 7th and Ocean Dr; in Avalon Hotel. 700 Ocean Dr 33139. **Hours:** 6 pm-11 pm. Closed major holidays. **Reservations:** suggested. **Features:** On busy and popular Ocean Drive, the restaurant gives diners a choice of seating on the patio, where live jazz entertains, or in the casually elegant dining room. Guests can expect superior professional service and incredible food. Desserts such as the apple berry tart are so spectacular that diners may want to start there and work backward through the diverse menu. Dressy casual; cocktails. **Parking:** valet and street. **Cards:** AX, DS, MC, VI.

AURA
Continental
Lunch: $7-$15   **Dinner:** $15-$25   **Phone:** 305/695-1100   14
Location: Between Pennsylvania and Euclid aves; in Lincoln Road Mall. 613 Lincoln Rd 33139. **Hours:** 11 am-midnight. **Reservations:** accepted. **Features:** The widely varied menu in the tiny dining room covers seafood, such as Chilean sea bass and salmon, as well as steak, chicken and pasta dishes. Casual dress; cocktails. **Parking:** street. **Cards:** AX, DS, MC, VI.

BALANS
International
Lunch: $10-$17   **Dinner:** $10-$17   **Phone:** 305/534-9191   30
Location: Between Michigan and Lenox aves. 1022 Lincoln Rd 33139. **Hours:** 8 am-1 am. **Features:** The decor is eclectic at the inviting restaurant, which presents a menu that lists such offerings as sweet potato souffle, Chilean sea bass, grilled salmon and specialty salads. Among wonderful desserts are warm chocolate cake, lemon tart and crepes con dulce de leche. Dressy casual; cocktails. **Parking:** street. **Cards:** AX, MC, VI.

BARTON G. THE RESTAURANT
American
Dinner: $14-$34   **Phone:** 305/672-8881   36
Location: Jct 15th St. 1427 West Ave 33139. **Hours:** 6 pm-10 pm, Fri & Sat-1 am. **Reservations:** suggested. **Features:** Imagination, unique food presentations and fresh offerings from the seas and local markets await you. The menu will allow you hints to the presentation of the dishess and the taste you will be presented with. Dressy casual; cocktails. **Parking:** valet and street. **Cards:** AX, DC, MC, VI.

B.E.D
New World
Dinner: $30-$40   **Phone:** 305/532-9070   50
Location: Between 9th and 10th sts. 929 Washington Ave 33139. **Hours:** 8 pm-5 am. Closed: Sun. **Reservations:** required. **Features:** Enter this unbelievably cool and chic restaurant and relax while dining in a large, comfortable bed. The amiable waitstaff guides the guests through the menu and bed protocol. To maintain the ambiance (and to make sure the guests are not rushed) there are only two seatings per night. The talented chef combines French cooking techniques with global ingredients using artistic presentations. Foie gras, roasted quail, escargot, veal chops and ahi tuna are just a few of the items that grace the menu. Dressy casual; cocktails. **Parking:** on-site (fee) and valet. **Cards:** DC, DS, MC, VI.

BIG PINK
American
Lunch: $4-$20   **Dinner:** $4-$20   **Phone:** 305/531-0888   58
Location: Jct 2nd St. 157 Collins Ave 33139. **Hours:** 8 am-midnight, Thurs-2 am, Fri-Sun to 5:30 am. **Features:** The extremely popular and bustling South Beach eatery is just a block from the popular beach and the many art deco buildings and boutiques on Ocean Avenue. The restaurant is reminiscent of a subway tunnel and has a trendy yet industrial look about it. The extensive menu lists anything from breakfast to practically any type of sandwich, burger, gourmet pizza or wrap. Full entrees appeal to those with heartier appetites. Homemade desserts are a must try. Casual dress; cocktails. **Parking:** street. **Cards:** AX, DC, MC, VI.

CAFE AVANTE RISTORANTE ITALIANO
Italian
Lunch: $10-$14   **Dinner:** $14-$31   **Phone:** 305/538-4400   6
Location: On Arthur Godfrey Rd at Chase Ave. 732 41st St 33140. **Hours:** 11:30 am-3 & 5-10 pm, Fri & Sat-11 pm. **Features:** Guests can enjoy Northern Italian cuisine amid classic surroundings at this popular fine-dining spot. Mouthwatering dishes, such as Atlantic salmon in mustard-white wine sauce or gulf shrimp sauteed in spicy marinara sauce, are a treat. Desserts are a delight. Dressy casual; beer & wine only. **Parking:** street. **Cards:** AX, DS, MC, VI.

CAFE PRIMA PASTA
Italian
Lunch: $12-$22   **Dinner:** $14-$31   **Phone:** 305/867-0106   3
Location: Between Byron and Abbott sts. 414 71st St 33141. **Hours:** noon-midnight, Fri & Sat-1 am, Sun 5 pm-midnight. **Reservations:** suggested. **Features:** Even with a much-needed expansion, the bustling restaurant still often requires a wait for a table. Homemade pasta, succulent osso buco and a bottomless bread basket with homemade olive-oil dipping sauce are among temptations. The extensive menu—including the appetizer platter with in-house-marinated vegetables and Italian mozzarella—keeps this jewel one of the most popular places in Miami Beach. Dressy casual; cocktails. **Parking:** on-site and valet. **Cards:** AX, MC, VI.

CARNEVALE
Italian
Lunch: $9-$26   **Dinner:** $9-$26   **Phone:** 305/672-3333   13
Location: Between Euclid and Meridian aves; in Lincoln Road Mall area. 607 Lincoln Rd 33139. **Hours:** 11 am-midnight, Fri & Sat-1 am. **Reservations:** accepted. **Features:** From carpaccio de salmone to filet mignon salad to veal marsala and fresh dough pizzas, there is something for everyone at this restaurant. Fresh seafood, chicken, numerous pasta dishes and tasty sandwiches are some of the other items available. A large assortment of deserts are the finishing touch to this festive atmosphere restaurant. Casual dress; cocktails. **Parking:** street. **Cards:** AX, DC, MC, VI.

(See maps and indexes starting on p. 545, 548)

CASA TUA   Dinner: $46-$57   Phone: 305/673-1010   ⑤
International   **Location:** Just w of Collins Ave; between 17th and 18th sts. 1700 James St 33139. **Hours:** 6:30 pm-11:30 pm. Closed major holidays; also Sun. **Reservations:** required. **Features:** Inside a mansion on a hidden corner of South Beach is this refined oasis of gastronomic pleasure and superb comfort coupled with impeccable service. Choose to dine at one of the dining room tables or the 18-seat communal table in front of the exhibition kitchen. The upscale, country Italian cuisine menu is tweaked nightly. Start with the wine marinated beef carpaccio or spinach salad. Main dishes range from lamb chops to duck breast and baby clams. Save room for the double tower chocolate cake. Dressy casual; cocktails. **Parking:** valet. **Cards:** AX, MC, VI.

CHINA GRILL   Lunch: $21-$37   Dinner: $21-$37   Phone: 305/534-2211   ㊄
Asian   **Location:** Corner of 5th St and Washington Ave. 404 Washington Ave 33139. **Hours:** noon-midnight, Fri & Sat 6 pm-1 am, Sun 6 pm-midnight. **Reservations:** suggested. **Features:** Bustling and never boring, this club-like spot is the "see-and-be-seen" place for sake, vodka and ample portions of dramatically prepared delights such as porterhouse lobster. Just eyeing the sinful desserts is likely to stretch your waistband. Dressy casual; cocktails. **Parking:** valet. **Cards:** AX, DC, MC, VI.

CRYSTAL CAFE   Dinner: $13-$28   Phone: 305/673-8266   ⑦
Continental   **Location:** Just e of Chase Ave. 726 Arthur Godfrey Rd 33140. **Hours:** 5 pm-10 pm, Fri & Sat-11 pm. Closed: Mon. **Reservations:** suggested. **Features:** Cozy romantic dining room with soft, indirect lighting and good use of mirrors. One of the specialties is the osso bucco that is done with a French flair. A large menu offers a variety of meat, seafood and pasta entrees. A nice wine list complements this menu. Several half bottles are also available. Dressy casual; beer & wine only. **Parking:** on-site. **Cards:** AX, DS, MC, VI.

DA LEO TRATTORIA   Lunch: $7-$25   Dinner: $17-$29   Phone: 305/674-0350   ⑱

Italian   **Location:** Between Jefferson and Michigan aves; in Lincoln Road Mall area. 819 Lincoln Rd 33139. **Hours:** 5:30 pm-11:30 pm, Sat-midnight, Sun 11:30 am-3:30 & 5:30-11:30 pm; Sunday brunch. **Reservations:** accepted. **Features:** This place is Italy in Miami Beach. Diners can eat outside under the stars or inside what feels like a small Italian neighborhood place. The food speaks Italy with some Tuscan flavors. Among choices are some steak items, fresh seafood and not-to-be-forgotten pasta dishes. Dressy casual. **Parking:** street. **Cards:** AX, DC, DS, MC, VI.

DORAKU   Lunch: $7-$21   Dinner: $7-$28   Phone: 305/695-8383   ㉗
Japanese   **Location:** Corner of Alton Rd; in Lincoln Road Mall. 1104 Lincoln Rd 33139. **Hours:** noon-3:30 & 5-midnight, Fri-1 am, Sat 3 pm-1 am, Sun 3 pm-11:30 pm. Closed: 11/23, 12/25. **Reservations:** suggested. **Features:** The soft glow of paper lanterns lends to a peaceful setting. Guests also can unwind by sampling the large array of sake selections. On the menu is an extensive variety of sushi, sashimi, rolls and tempura-style foods. Casual dress; cocktails. **Parking:** on-site (fee) and street. **Cards:** AX, DC, DS, MC, VI.

DULCIANNA CAFE   Lunch: $6-$10   Dinner: $6-$10   Phone: 305/532-1101   ㉒
Bakery/Desserts   **Location:** Just w of Washington Ave; in Lincoln Road Mall. 532 Lincoln Rd 33139. **Hours:** 8:30 am-11 pm, Fri & Sat-midnight. Closed: 11/23, 12/25. **Features:** The busy Lincoln Road restaurant lets diners stop in for a quick bite—maybe a sandwich and a wonderful gelato—before running off on their way. Casual dress. **Parking:** on-site (fee) and street. **Cards:** MC, VI.

EL RANCHO GRANDE MEXICAN RESTAURANT   Lunch: $5-$8   Dinner: $6-$18   Phone: 305/673-0480   ㉙
Mexican   **Location:** Just s of Lincoln Rd. 1626 Pennsylvania Ave 33139. **Hours:** 11:30 am-10 pm. Closed: 1/1, 11/23. **Features:** The colorful cantina's menu centers on traditional fare, such as enchiladas and black bean soup. Casual dress; cocktails. **Parking:** street. **Cards:** AX, DS, MC, VI.

EMERIL'S MIAMI BEACH   Lunch: $12-$25   Dinner: $21-$33   Phone: 305/695-4550   ㉛
Regional American   **Location:** On SR A1A, at Collins and 16th aves; in Loews Miami Beach Hotel. 1601 Collins Ave 33139. **Hours:** 11:30 am- 2 & 5:30-10 pm, Fri & Sat-11 pm. **Reservations:** suggested. **Features:** Celebrity chef Emeril Lagasse brings his style of cooking to Miami and incorporates it in fresh area seafood. The setting is soft with a variety of colors and fabrics. Dressy casual; cocktails. **Parking:** on-site (fee) and valet. **Cards:** AX, CB, DC, DS, JC, MC, VI.

ESCOPAZZO RESTAURANT   Dinner: $10-$25   Phone: 305/674-9450   ㉛
Italian   **Location:** Just n of jct 13th St. 1311 Washington Ave 33139. **Hours:** 6 pm-midnight, Sat-1 am, Sun-11 pm. **Reservations:** suggested. **Features:** Guests are transported to Little Italy as they cross the cozy restaurant's threshold. Italian recipes are prepared on the premises, and the staff is attentive and accommodating. Semi-formal attire; cocktails. **Parking:** valet. **Cards:** AX, DS, MC, VI.

THE FRONT PORCH   Lunch: $8-$12   Dinner: $12-$18   Phone: 305/531-8300   ㊲
International   **Location:** Corner of Ocean Dr and 14th St; inside the Penguin Hotel. 1418 Ocean Dr 33139. **Hours:** 8 am-10 pm, Fri-Sun to 10:30 pm. Closed: for dinner 12/24, 12/25 & Thanksgiving. **Features:** In the heart of South Beach is this great people-watching eatery. Choose from porch, interior or sidewalk seating with views of the ocean and beach. The international menu offers sandwiches, soups, salads and full-size entrees with Italian, Cuban and Italian influences. They are well known for hearty breakfast plates as well. Casual dress; cocktails. **Parking:** on-site (fee). **Cards:** AX, CB, DC, DS, MC, VI.

GIL'S CAFE   Lunch: $6-$10   Dinner: $9-$25   Phone: 305/867-0779   ②
Brazilian   **Location:** Jct SR A1A (Collins Ave) and 71st St, just w. 216 71st St 33141. **Hours:** 11:30 am-midnight, Fri & Sat-2 am, Sun 5 pm-midnight. Closed: 11/23. **Reservations:** suggested. **Features:** The Brazilian restaurant has live music, sidewalk seating and a wonderful menu featuring ginger-carrot soup, shrimp and salmon cooked in coconut milk and banana bread pudding. Casual dress; cocktails; entertainment. **Parking:** street. **Cards:** DS, MC, VI.

(See maps and indexes starting on p. 545, 548)

ICEBOX CAFE **Lunch:** $15-$20 **Dinner:** $28-$35 **Phone:** 305/538-8448 ⑦

◆◆ Continental

Location: Between Lincoln Rd and 17th St; just n of Lincoln Road Mall. 1657 Michigan Ave 33139. **Hours:** 11 am-4 & 6-11 pm. Closed: 11/23; also 12/24 & 12/31. **Features:** The open kitchen creates unique dishes using the freshest ingredients. The dining area is casual with friendly service. This eatery is best known for the fabulous array of desserts offered, and the weekend brunch is also very popular. Casual dress; beer & wine only. **Parking:** no self-parking. **Cards:** AX, DC, DS, MC, VI.

JERRY'S FAMOUS DELI SOUTH BEACH **Lunch:** $8-$15 **Dinner:** $8-$25 **Phone:** 305/532-8030 ㉝

◆◆ American

Location: On US 1 (Collins Ave) at corner of Espanola Way. 1450 Collins Ave 33139. **Hours:** 24 hours. **Reservations:** not accepted. **Features:** The restaurant features deli characteristics, such as big desserts and tall sandwiches, but the menu has just about anything you want. The dining room is decorated in the Art Deco style. Casual dress; cocktails. **Parking:** valet and street. **Cards:** AX, CB, DC, DS, JC, MC, VI.

♿M 🍸

JOE ALLEN **Lunch:** $6-$20 **Dinner:** $10-$25 **Phone:** 305/531-7007 ④

◆◆ American

Location: Just n of Dade Blvd. 1787 Purdy Ave 33139. **Hours:** 11:30 am-11:30 pm. Closed: 12/25. **Reservations:** suggested. **Features:** Although meatloaf is a specialty, many patrons prefer something less mainstream, such as Norwegian salmon or New Zealand rack of lamb. Dressy casual; cocktails. **Parking:** street. **Cards:** MC, VI.

🍸

JOE'S STONE CRAB RESTAURANT Menu on aaa.com **Lunch:** $5-$60 **Dinner:** $5-$60 **Phone:** 305/673-0365 (62)

AAA

◆◆◆ Seafood

Location: 6 blks s of SR A1A. 11 Washington Ave 33139. **Hours:** 11:30 am-2 & 5-10 pm, Fri & Sat-11 pm, Sun 4 pm-10 pm, Mon 5 pm-10 pm; seasonal hours may vary. Closed: 11/23. **Features:** As the restaurant's name implies, the stone crab is mighty popular here. But then again, so is the homemade Key lime pie. Owned by the same family since the early 1900s, the popular eatery offers generous portions of delectable food. Dressy casual; cocktails. **Parking:** on-site and valet. **Cards:** AX, DC, DS, MC, VI. **Classic**

🍸

KIM'S CHINESE RESTAURANT **Lunch:** $5-$16 **Dinner:** $5-$16 **Phone:** 305/672-8822 ⑳

◆◆ Chinese

Location: Jct Lincoln Rd and West Ave; between 16th and 17th sts. 1245 Lincoln Rd 33139. **Hours:** 11:30 am-10 pm, Sun from 1 pm. Closed: 11/23. **Features:** More than 24 traditional Chinese combination platters share menu space with Mandarin, Szechuan and vegetarian entrees. Casual dress; beer & wine only. **Parking:** street. **Cards:** AX, MC, VI.

LA FACTORIA **Lunch:** $9-$20 **Dinner:** $9-$27 **Phone:** 305/695-0044 (59)

◆◆ Deli/Subs Sandwiches

Location: Jct of 1st St. 124 Collins Ave 33139. **Hours:** 11 am-1 am, Fri-Sun to 6 am. **Reservations:** suggested. **Features:** This factory is not just churning out the same old things. A Mediterranean atmosphere envelops diners, who peruse a casual menu of sandwiches, salads, wraps, burgers, soups and pasta. Casual dress; cocktails. **Parking:** valet and street. **Cards:** AX, MC, VI.

⧅

LA LUPA DI ROMA **Dinner:** $12-$30 **Phone:** 305/532-6657 ㉓

◆◆ Italian

Location: Just w of Pennsylvania Ave; in Lincoln Road Mall area. 610 Lincoln Rd 33139. **Hours:** 4 pm-10 pm. **Features:** Dining here is akin to dining in an Italian family kitchen. Simply prepared dishes are the fare du jour. Guests can dine in the small restaurant or experience the international flair of the "piazza" out front on Lincoln Mall. Friendly and unhurried service enables diners to fully enjoy the dining experience. Casual dress; beer & wine only. **Parking:** street. **Cards:** AX, DS, MC, VI.

⧅

LA SPIAGGIA RISTORANTE **Lunch:** $5-$8 **Dinner:** $7-$18 **Phone:** 305/532-3866 ⑩

◆◆ Italian

Location: SR A1A and 35th St; in Claridge Hotel. 3500 Collins Ave 33139. **Hours:** 7 am-11:30 pm. **Reservations:** accepted. **Features:** Italian and Mediterranean-influenced cuisine is served in the tiny dining room inside the Claridge Hotel. Casual dress; cocktails. **Parking:** valet. **Cards:** AX, MC, VI.

LAS VACAS GORDAS **Lunch:** $10-$17 **Dinner:** $10-$17 **Phone:** 305/867-1717 ①

◆◆ Argentine

Location: 0.5 mi w of Collins Ave. 933 Normandy Dr 33141. **Hours:** noon-midnight, Sat from 1:30, Sun 1:30 pm-11 pm. **Reservations:** not accepted. **Features:** The meaning of Las Vacas Gordas—"the fat cows"—helps illustrate the Argentine steakhouse's sense of humor. This place doubles as a sidewalk cafe. Tables are small, the decor is simple, and it's always crowded. Meat comes straight from the grill with no frills, just great taste. Casual dress. **Parking:** on-site. **Cards:** MC, VI.

LEMON TWIST **Dinner:** $9-$18 **Phone:** 305/868-2075 ⑤

◆◆◆ Mediterranean

Location: Just e of Normandy Fountain. 908 71st St 33141. **Hours:** 5:30 pm-midnight. Closed: 7/4, 11/23, 12/25; also Mon & weekend of 7/4. **Reservations:** suggested. **Features:** The bistro is slightly off the beaten path of South Beach but still reflects the chic panache. Complimentary marinated olives and warm baguettes stimulate the appetite. Great for sharing is the charcuterie, a type of antipasto plate with grilled vegetables, olives, cheeses and select cold cuts. The broad entree offerings include leg of lamb, pasta dishes and ahi tuna. Staying for dessert—with a choice of tiramisu, chocolate mousse, flan and profiteroles—is a must. Casual dress; cocktails. **Parking:** on-site. **Cards:** AX, MC, VI.

🍸

LES 2 FONTAINES **Lunch:** $7-$31 **Dinner:** $9-$31 **Phone:** 305/672-7878 ㊶

◆◆ Seafood

Location: E of jct SR A1A (Collins Ave) and 12th St; in Hotel Ocean. 1230 Ocean Dr 33139. **Hours:** 7:30 am-11:30 pm, Fri & Sat-1 am. **Reservations:** suggested. **Features:** Bouillabaisse is the specialty at the moderately upscale restaurant, where diners also can sample well-prepared seafood and meat entrees. Meals can be enjoyed outside on the sidewalk or patio, or inside in one of the cozy dining rooms. Dressy casual; cocktails. **Parking:** on-site (fee) and valet. **Cards:** AX, CB, DC, DS, JC, MC, VI.

♿M 🍸 ⧅

(See maps and indexes starting on p. 545, 548)

LINCOLN ROAD CAFE
Lunch: $4-$8   Dinner: $6-$10   Phone: 305/538-8066   (17)
Cuban
Location: Between N Michigan and Jefferson aves; in Lincoln Road Mall. 943 Lincoln Rd 33139. **Hours:** 8 am-midnight. **Reservations:** accepted. **Features:** Although this eatery is unpretentious, the food is nicely prepared and flavorful. Menu selections include a variety of meat, chiken and seafood, which are cooked in a home-style fashion. Both indoor and outdoor seating areas are available. Casual dress; beer & wine only.
Parking: street.

LITTLE MUSHROOM BAR & CAFE
Lunch: $8-$16   Dinner: $8-$24   Phone: 305/695-9669   (8)
Deli/Subs
Sandwiches
MC, VI.
Location: Between Drexel and Washington sts. 445 Lincoln Rd 33139. **Hours:** 10 am-midnight. **Reservations:** accepted. **Features:** A healthy choice for a quick bite to eat, the cafe prepares a wide selection of sandwiches, such as smoked turkey, grilled chicken, roast beef and veggie. Wraps are especially satisfying, and guests also have the option of creating their own salad, sandwich or cooked-to-order individual pizza. Casual dress; beer & wine only. **Parking:** street. **Cards:** AX, CB, DC, DS, JC,

MAMA VIEJA RESTAURANT & NIGHT CLUB
Lunch: $6-$10   Dinner: $7-$20   Phone: 305/538-2400   (1)
Colombian
Location: Just w of SR A1A (Collins Ave). 235 23rd St 33139. **Hours:** noon-11 pm, Fri & Sat-5 am. Closed: 12/25; also Tues. **Reservations:** accepted. **Features:** A warm, family atmosphere embraces diners in this little slice of Colombia. The architecture and decor combine to reflect the roots of South America, as do the well-prepared dishes of seafood, pasta and steaks, such as the bandeja paisa. Casual dress; cocktails. entertainment. **Parking:** street. **Cards:** AX, DC, DS, MC, VI.

MARK'S SOUTH BEACH
Dinner: $26-$42   Phone: 305/604-9050   (45)
New World
Location: SR A1A, corner of 11th St and Collins Ave; in Nash Hotel. 1120 Collins Ave 33136. **Hours:** noon-3 & 7-11 pm, Fri & Sat-11:30 pm. **Reservations:** suggested. **Features:** Worldly influences, techniques and ingredients lend flavor to dishes of new American cuisine. Excellent preparation and presentation characterize meat, seafood and pasta entrees. The atmosphere is stylish and sophisticated both in the dining room and in the terrace area near the pools. Dressy casual; cocktails. **Parking:** valet. **Cards:** AX, DC, MC, VI.

METRO
Lunch: $7-$20   Dinner: $27-$34   Phone: 305/672-7217   (48)
Asian
Location: From MacArthur Cswy/US 41 to 5th St, then n; in Hotel Astor. 956 Washington Ave 33139. **Hours:** 7:30-11 am, 11:30-2:30 & 7-midnight, Fri & Sat-1 am. **Reservations:** accepted. **Features:** Located in a trendy, deco-style hotel, the restaurant serves lovely presentations of delicious and inventive Asian-fusion cuisine in a gardenlike setting. Dressy casual; cocktails. **Parking:** street. **Cards:** AX, DC, MC, VI.

NEMO RESTAURANT
Lunch: $8-$14   Dinner: $18-$28   Phone: 305/532-4550   (61)
New World
Location: Jct 1st St. 100 Collins Ave 33139. **Hours:** noon-3 & 7-midnight, Sun 11 am-3 & 6-11 pm. **Reservations:** suggested. **Features:** Trendy and distinctive, the eatery features Asian-influenced dishes prepared with the utmost care and expertise. A nice wine list invites diners to peruse. Cocktails. **Parking:** valet and street. **Cards:** AX, MC, VI.

NEWS CAFE
Menu on aaa.com   Lunch: $12-$20   Dinner: $12-$25   Phone: 305/538-6397   (53)
American
Location: I-95 to I-395 E to Ocean Dr, 0.3 mi n. 800 Ocean Dr 33139. **Hours:** 24 hours. **Reservations:** not accepted. **Features:** The cafe, which offers indoor and outdoor seating, is a great spot to relax and enjoy a cappuccino or other coffee while reading a favorite newspaper. Such desserts as chocolate fondue with pastries and fruit are can't-go-wrong choices. Those who prefer heartier fare might opt for a Middle Eastern dish, specialty salad or beef, pork or chicken preparation. Casual dress; cocktails. **Parking:** street. **Cards:** AX, DC, DS, MC, VI.

NEXXT CAFE
Lunch: $6-$13   Dinner: $8-$24   Phone: 305/532-6643   (25)
International
Location: Between Euclid and Meridian aves; in Lincoln Road Mall area. 700 Lincoln Rd 33139. **Hours:** 11:30 am-11 pm, Fri & Sat-11:30 pm. **Features:** An extensive and varied menu as well as tempting desserts await you at this popular and busy restaurant. Fresh salads, pastas, sandwiches and Angus beef main entrees are available, and over 20 decadent desserts tempt you for the grand finale. Casual dress; cocktails. **Parking:** street. **Cards:** AX, MC, VI.

NOBU MIAMI BEACH
Dinner: $16-$38   Phone: 305/695-3100   (3)
Japanese
Location: On SR A1A (Collins Ave), just s of 20th St; in The Shore Club South Beach. 1901 Collins Ave 33139. **Hours:** 6 pm-midnight, Fri & Sat-1 am, Sun-11 pm. **Reservations:** accepted. **Features:** The trendy, upbeat spot treats diners' taste buds to modern Japanese cuisine. The chef's Peruvian influence infuses well-prepared dishes. In addition to an extensive wine list, the restaurant offers a selection of sake. Dressy casual; cocktails. **Parking:** valet. **Cards:** AX, CB, DC, MC, VI.

NOVECENTO
Lunch: $7-$21   Dinner: $12-$25   Phone: 305/531-0900   (47)
Argentine
Location: Corner of Alton Rd and 11th St. 1080 Alton Rd 33139. **Hours:** 11 am-5 & 6-midnight, Sat & Sun 10 am-4 & 6-midnight. **Reservations:** accepted. **Features:** The Argentinian restaurant features appetizers such as empanadas, fried calamari and pan roasted sweet breads, and that's just the beginning. Pastas and fresh fish offerings as well as lamb and beef are just a few main entrees on the menu. The chocolate torte is a great ending for your meal. Casual dress; cocktails. **Parking:** on-site. **Cards:** AX, DC, DS, MC, VI.

OASIS CAFE
Lunch: $6-$10   Dinner: $6-$10   Phone: 305/674-7676   (9)
Mediterranean
Location: Jct Alton Rd and 41st St. 976 41st St 33140. **Hours:** 10:30 am-10 pm, Sun from 5 pm. **Features:** Diners can choose among Mediterranean, Middle Eastern and vegetarian selections while enjoying the soft jazz that plays in the background of the cozy eatery. Casual dress; beer & wine only. **Parking:** street. **Cards:** AX, DC, MC, VI.

(See maps and indexes starting on p. 545, 548)

ONE-NINETY RESTAURANT
Dinner: $18-$33   **Phone:** 305/913-1071   ⑥
New World
Location: From Collins Ave (SR A1A), w on Lincoln Mall Rd, just n. 1650 James Ave 33139. **Hours:** 6 pm-midnight. Closed: 1/1, 11/23, 12/25; also Mon. **Reservations:** suggested. **Features:** The chef creates an exciting array of dishes by combining the best elements of culinary techniques and ingredients from several regions. The decor is very avante garde and artsy, attracting an eclectic crowd that come not only for the food but for the after-hours live music as well. Casual dress; cocktails. **Parking:** street. **Cards:** AX, DS, MC, VI.

OSTERIA DEL TEATRO
Dinner: $16-$42   **Phone:** 305/538-7850   ㉟
Italian
Location: Jct 13th St. 1443 Washington Ave 33139. **Hours:** 6 pm-11 pm, Fri & Sat-midnight. Closed: 1/1, 5/29, 12/24, 12/25; also Sun & week of Memorial Day. **Reservations:** required. **Features:** Patrons are in for a treat at the popular establishment, which has been in business in the area since 1988. The menu lists the best in Northern Italian cuisine. Elegance in its theme, with a touch of flair and trendiness to the decor and service that is top-notch, makes this a spot to try. Casual dress; beer & wine only. **Parking:** valet and street. **Cards:** AX, CB, DC, MC, VI.

PACIFIC TIME
Dinner: $17-$32   **Phone:** 305/534-5979   ⑩
Asian
Location: Between Jefferson and Michigan aves; in Lincoln Road Pedestrian Mall. 915 Lincoln Rd 33139. **Hours:** 6 pm-11 pm, Fri & Sat-11:30 pm. Closed: 11/23, 12/25. **Reservations:** suggested. **Features:** California Pacific Rim cuisine is served in a bustling environment. The chef, who is a master of seafood preparation, presents superb entrees in an attractive, artful and innovative way. Casual dress; cocktails. **Parking:** street. **Cards:** AX, MC, VI.   🅼 🍸

PAESANO'S RISTORANTE
Lunch: $9-$12   **Dinner:** $12-$25   **Phone:** 305/672-2099   ㊿②
Italian
Location: Between 7th and 8th sts; on corner of 8th St. 764 Washington Ave 33139. **Hours:** noon-midnight, Fri & Sat-1 am. **Reservations:** accepted. **Features:** The restaurant's menu has a large variety of traditional and creative meat, pasta and seafood dishes. The knowledgeable and accommodating staff let guests set the pace; dining is comfortable, casual and relaxed, and the restaurant offers complimentary limo service. Dressy casual. **Parking:** street. **Cards:** AX, DC, DS, MC, VI.   🅼

PARRILLADA ARGENTINA
Dinner: $10-$13   **Phone:** 305/532-0102   ㉜
Argentine
Location: Between 15th and 16th sts. 1533 Washington Ave 33139. **Hours:** 5 pm-midnight. **Features:** This place is ideal for a quiet, cozy dining experience. Hearty menu offerings include tasty Russian salad with prosciutto, grilled salmon, Argentinean barbecue and filet mignon. Desserts shouldn't be overlooked. Casual dress. **Parking:** no self-parking. **Cards:** AX, CB, DC, DS, MC, VI.

PLAYWRIGHT IRISH PUB & RESTAURANT
Lunch: $11-$16   **Dinner:** $18-$22   **Phone:** 305/534-0667   ㊴
Irish
Location: Corner of 13th St and Washington Ave. 1265 Washington Ave 33109. **Hours:** 11 am-midnight. **Features:** More than a bar, this is a comfortable, cozy yet classy pub that sometimes features live music. Besides the classic Irish dishes like beef stew, fish and chips, corn beef and cabbage and shepherd's pie there are a range of appetizers and salads available. Casual dress; cocktails. **Parking:** on-site (fee). **Cards:** AX, DC, MC, VI.   🛇

PUERTO SAGUA
Lunch: $6-$20   **Dinner:** $6-$20   **Phone:** 305/673-1115   ㊼
Cuban
Location: Jct 7th St. 700 Collins Ave 33139. **Hours:** 7:30 am-2 am. **Features:** Tourists and locals alike flock to the family-run restaurant for Cuban dishes. The decor may be simple, but the flavors are complex. Choose a seat in the dining room or at the counter. Casual dress; beer & wine only. **Parking:** street. **Cards:** AX, DC, MC, VI.

RISTORANTI Il SOLE
Lunch: $9-$15   **Dinner:** $12-$26   **Phone:** 305/673-1858   ㉔
Italian
Location: Between Meridian and Pennsylvania aves. 626 Lincoln Rd 33139. **Hours:** noon-midnight, Fri & Sat-1 am. **Reservations:** accepted. **Features:** People-watchers can sit back and relax while enjoying dinner and a favorite cocktail outdoors under the stars. Dressy casual; cocktails. **Parking:** no self-parking. **Cards:** AX, MC, VI.   🍸 🛇

ROSINELLA
Lunch: $6-$26   **Dinner:** $6-$26   **Phone:** 305/672-8777   ⑪
Italian
Location: Between Pennsylvania and Drexel aves; in Lincoln Road Mall area. 525 Lincoln Rd 33139. **Hours:** 11:30 am-midnight, Fri & Sat-1 am. **Features:** The Rosinelli family owns and operates this place, which specializes in Roman Italian cuisine. Pizza, panini and pasta dishes figure prominently on the menu, which also includes many daily specials. Outdoor seating is available. Casual dress; cocktails. **Parking:** street. **Cards:** AX, DC, MC, VI.

RUEN THAI AND SUSHI BAR
Dinner: $10-$28   **Phone:** 305/534-1504   ㊾
Thai
Location: Between 9th and 10th sts. 947 Washington Ave 33139. **Hours:** 5:30 pm-midnight, Fri & Sat-1 am. Closed: 11/23, 12/25. **Reservations:** accepted. **Features:** Lavish presentations of Thai and Japanese cuisine feature miniature hibachis to cook skewered meat kebabs and orchids to brighten the plate. Carved teak tables and wall accents lend to a sophisticated and exotic atmosphere. The multipage menu, which lists dishes ranging from vegetarian plates to beef, fowl and fish preparations, ensures something for everyone. Casual dress; beer & wine only. **Parking:** on-site. **Cards:** AX, MC, VI.   🅼 🛇

RUMI RESTAURANT & LOUNGE
Dinner: $25-$35   **Phone:** 305/672-4353   ⑲
Nouvelle Caribbean
Location: Between James and Washington aves; in Lincoln Road Mall. 330 Lincoln Rd 33139. **Hours:** 7 pm-midnight. Closed: 12/25; also Sun, Mon & Wed. **Reservations:** required. **Features:** A recent South Beach hit is this trendy restaurant where, after dinner, the nightclub atmosphere escalates and continues into the wee hours. The menu features mostly Caribbean fare but also has culinary influenes from Latin America and Asia. Sashimi grade tuna, steamed mussels in a spiced rum sauce, roasted duck breast and jerked pork are just a few of the favorites. Dressy casual; cocktails. **Parking:** valet. **Cards:** AX, MC, VI.

(See maps and indexes starting on p. 545, 548)

SAPORI DI ROMA RISTORANTE ITALIANO &
PIZZERIA   Dinner: $9-$20   Phone: 305/868-7001   4

Italian

Location: Jct 71st St. 6984 Collins Ave 33141. **Hours:** 4 pm-11 pm, Fri & Sat-11:30 pm. **Features:** The popular eatery prepares many homemade pastas and desserts. The welcoming wait staff is ready to please and puts a lot of heart into serving. Those who like Italian food and a casual dining experience are likely to enjoy this spot. Representative of the traditional fare are many pasta dishes, as well as several meat, fish, poultry and pizza choices. Casual dress; cocktails. **Parking:** street. **Cards:** AX, DC, DS, MC, VI.

SHOJI SUSHI   Lunch: $9-$25   Dinner: $9-$25   Phone: 305/532-4245   60

Sushi

Location: Between 1st and 2nd sts. 100 Collins Ave 33139. **Hours:** noon-3 & 6-midnight, Fri-1 am, Sat & Sun 6 pm-1 am. **Reservations:** accepted. **Features:** The dining room is a blend of subdued color tones and sedate decor, setting the stage for a comfortable and relaxed experience. Guests are presented with a warm, moist cloth to refresh themselves as skilled chefs prepare a diverse menu of sushi, sushi rolls and sashimi. Other menu selections focus mainly on seafood although there is a limited number of vegetarian, skirt steak and chicken items. Dressy casual; cocktails. **Parking:** street. **Cards:** AX, DC, MC, VI.

SMITH & WOLLENSKY STEAK & CHOP HOUSE   Lunch: $19-$23   Dinner: $23-$39   Phone: 305/673-2800   63

Traditional Steak
House

Location: At Washington Ave and Biscayne St; behind tall condo building; in South Pointe Park. 1 Washington Ave 33139. **Hours:** noon-1:30 am. **Reservations:** suggested. **Features:** At the tip of South Beach and the entrance to Port Miami, the restaurant offers a menu of aged prime beef, prepared to order, prime rib, chops and fresh fish—all served with ample side dishes. The friendly, comfortable place provides a large, award-winning wine list. Dressy casual; cocktails. **Parking:** valet. **Cards:** AX, DC, DS, MC, VI.

SPIGA RISTORANTE ITALIANO   Dinner: $14-$25   Phone: 305/534-0079   40

Italian

Location: Between 11th St and Espanola Way. 1228 Collins Ave 33139. **Hours:** 6 pm-11 pm, Fri & Sat-midnight. **Reservations:** suggested. **Features:** The high-energy trattoria serves home-style Italian fare. Begin with an antipasto, such as prosciutto with melon, sauteed mussels in white wine or antipasto misto, a sampling of tasty treats ideal for sharing. All pastas, including tagliatelle, gnocchi and pappardelle, are homemade. Other favorites are such fish choices as salmon and red snapper, as well as veal scaloppine and New York sirloin. Save room for a rich dessert, such as tiramisu, banana strudel or creme brulee. Casual dress. **Parking:** on-site and street. **Cards:** AX, CB, DC, DS, JC, MC, VI.

SPRIS   Lunch: $7-$15   Dinner: $7-$15   Phone: 305/673-2020   16

Italian

Location: Between Meridian and Jefferson aves; in Lincoln Road Mall area. 731 Lincoln Rd 33139. **Hours:** noon-1 am. Closed: 11/23. **Features:** Brick-oven pizzas are great, salads are huge, and calzones are stuffed full. Guests can sit in the cute Italian sidewalk cafe area or eat inside amid scenes from Italy. Try a Spris. Casual dress; beer & wine only. **Parking:** on-site (fee) and street. **Cards:** AX, MC, VI.

SUSHI SAIGON   Lunch: $10-$15   Dinner: $12-$20   Phone: 305/604-0599   43

Asian

Location: Between 11th and 12th sts. 1131 Washington Ave 33139. **Hours:** noon-3 & 4:30-11 pm, Fri-midnight, Sat noon-midnight, Sun noon-11 pm. **Reservations:** accepted. **Features:** The smartly-designed restaurant with a cordial Asian staff offers dishes from Thailand, Japan and Vietnam. Of course there is the ever-popular Vietnamese national dish, Pho, which comes in a variety of preparation styles. A meal in itself, the green papaya salad includes chicken, shrimp and pork. There is a full sushi and sashimi menu as well as tempura, yaki soba and teriyaki dishes to enjoy. Save room for the tartufo, an ice cream truffle with a chocolate coating. Casual dress; beer & wine only. **Parking:** street. **Cards:** AX, MC, VI.

SUSHI SAMBA DROMO   Lunch: $9-$30   Dinner: $10-$39   Phone: 305/673-5337   21

Sushi

Location: Corner of Pennsylvania Ave; in Lincoln Road Mall. 600 Lincoln Rd 33139. **Hours:** noon-midnight, Fri & Sat-2 am; Sunday brunch. **Reservations:** accepted. **Features:** The restaurant's cuisine blends Japanese, Brazilian and Peruvian cultures. The dining room combines festive and subdued colors with modern deco touches to create an upbeat, yet casual, experience. Samba music plays in the background as skilled chefs prepare a wide variety of sushi and seviche. Casual dress; cocktails. **Parking:** street. **Cards:** AX, MC, VI.

TALULA   Lunch: $7-$20   Dinner: $8-$28   Phone: 305/672-0778   2

American

Location: Corner of US 1 (Collins Ave) and 23rd St, just w. 210 23rd St 33138. **Hours:** noon-2:30 & 6:30-10:30 pm, Fri-11:30 pm, Sat 6:30 pm-11:30 pm, Sun 6 pm-10 pm. Closed major holidays; also Mon. **Reservations:** suggested. **Features:** The concept is American contemporary cuisine, and the experience is one to be remembered. The dining room is casually upscale, while the garden area nurtures a romantic air. On the menu are fresh local seafood and meat items prepared with Italian, Southwestern and island influences. Presentations are executed to amaze. Dressy casual; cocktails. **Parking:** on-site (fee) and street. **Cards:** AX, DC, DS, MC, VI.

TANTRA   Dinner: $30-$90   Phone: 305/672-4765   34

International

Location: Corner of 14th St and Pennsylvania Ave. 1445 Pennsylvania Ave 33139. **Hours:** 7 pm-midnight, Fri & Sat-1 am. **Reservations:** suggested. **Features:** All of your senses will be treated in this adult-oriented restaurant, from the soft grass under your feet to the culinary ecstasy that awaits your dining pleasure. Entrees of ginger kissed salmon, aromatic ossobuco and grilled filet mignon with a Cuban coffee sauce are just a few of the delights that await you. Creme Brulee is a great ending to your dining experience. Casual dress; cocktails. **Parking:** on-site (fee). **Cards:** AX, CB, DC, DS, JC, MC, VI.

(See maps and indexes starting on p. 545, 548)

TIRAMESU **Lunch:** $8-$15 **Dinner:** $10-$32 **Phone:** 305/532-4538 (15)

◆◆

Italian

Location: Between Meridian and Euclid aves; in Lincoln Road Mall. 721 Lincoln Rd 33139. **Hours:** noon-4 & 5:30-midnight, Fri & Sat-1 am, Sun noon-midnight. Closed: 11/23. **Features:** The popular restaurant prepares Italian dishes in a crowded, busy and electric environment. Casual dress; cocktails. **Parking:** street. **Cards:** AX, DC, DS, MC, VI.

TOUCH RESTAURANT **Dinner:** $14-$32 **Phone:** 305/532-8003 (28)

◆◆◆

Regional American

Location: Between Jefferson and Michigan aves; in Lincoln Road Mall. 910 Lincoln Rd 33139. **Hours:** 7 pm-midnight, Fri & Sat-2 am. **Reservations:** suggested. **Features:** A menu of mouthwatering delights includes margarita salmon, herb-encrusted Chilean sea bass and cinnamon smoked duck. High-energy entertainment and an elegant atmosphere contribute to a memorable evening. Casual dress; cocktails. **Parking:** street. **Cards:** AX, DS, MC, VI. 🍸

TUSCAN STEAK **Dinner:** $27-$68 **Phone:** 305/534-2233 (56)

◆◆◆

Steak & Seafood

Location: Jct 5th St and Washington Ave. 433 Washington Ave 33139. **Hours:** 6 pm-11 pm, Fri & Sat-midnight. Closed: 11/23. **Reservations:** suggested. **Features:** Entrees at the upscale steakhouse are served family-style, with generous portions designed for sharing. Casual dress; cocktails. **Parking:** valet. **Cards:** AX, DC, MC, VI.

TWELVE TWENTY **Dinner:** $20-$35 **Phone:** 305/604-5070 (42)

◆◆◆

Provincial American

Location: E of jct SR A1A (Collins Ave) and 12th St; in The Tides Hotel. 1220 Ocean Dr 33139. **Hours:** 7 pm-11 pm, Fri & Sat-midnight. **Reservations:** suggested. **Features:** Light French cuisine is prepared with a Mediterranean flair. Distinctive presentations use fresh seafood and meat. The bar area is neat and comfortable. Dressy casual; cocktails; entertainment. **Parking:** valet and street. **Cards:** AX, DC, DS, MC, VI. ♿M 🍸

VAN DYKE CAFE **Lunch:** $12-$18 **Dinner:** $12-$25 **Phone:** 305/534-3600 (26)

◆◆

Continental

Location: Jct of Jefferson Ave. 846 Lincoln Rd 33139. **Hours:** 8 am-2 am. **Reservations:** not accepted. **Features:** Located on a trendy avenue, the eatery offers deli and comfort food; upstairs and downstairs dining are available and jazz is played later at night. Casual dress; cocktails; entertainment. **Parking:** street. **Cards:** AX, DC, DS, MC, VI. 🚭

VIX **Lunch:** $18-$30 **Dinner:** $26-$43 **Phone:** 305/428-1234 (44)

◆◆◆◆

Regional New World

Location: E of SR A1A (Collins Ave), at 11th St and Ocean Dr; in Hotel Victor. 1144 Ocean Dr 33139. **Hours:** 7 am-11, noon-3 & 7-midnight. **Reservations:** required. **Features:** Enter the chic room and let your taste buds explore the world. The chef has selected herbs and spices from around the world; he then combines these with fresh seafood from various regoins of the globe. The menu also offers meat and pasta items and the wine list is expansive and complements the menu. Dressy casual; cocktails. **Parking:** valet. **Cards:** AX, CB, DC, DS, JC, MC, VI. ♿M 🍸

WISH **Lunch:** $6-$13 **Dinner:** $20-$33 **Phone:** 305/674-9474 (51)

AAA

◆◆◆◆

Northern American

Location: On SR A1A (Collins Ave) and 8th St; in The Hotel. 801 Collins Ave 33139. **Hours:** 7 am-3 & 6-11 pm, Fri-Sun to midnight. Closed: Mon. **Reservations:** suggested. **Features:** American fusion dishes meld Asian, Italian and French influences. The menu includes beef, poultry, fresh fish and some vegetarian appetizers and entrees. Desserts are both beautiful and sweetly satisfying. An Art Deco flair punctuates the dining room and bar. The outside dining area features a large fountain and is almost completely enclosed by foliage. Dressy casual; cocktails. **Parking:** on-site (fee) and valet. **Cards:** AX, CB, DC, DS, MC, VI. 🍸 🚭

WORLD RESOURCE CAFE **Lunch:** $7-$15 **Dinner:** $15-$45 **Phone:** 305/535-8987 (12)

◆◆

Asian

Location: Between Euclid and Meridian aves; in Lincoln Road Mall. 719 Lincoln Rd 33139. **Hours:** noon-11 pm, Fri & Sat-midnight. Closed: 11/23, 12/25. **Features:** The menu at the busy cafe covers several pages of sushi and Asian cuisine. Outdoor seating is available. Casual dress; cocktails. **Parking:** street. **Cards:** AX, DC, MC, VI. 🚭

YEUNG'S CHINESE **Lunch:** $5-$10 **Dinner:** $8-$40 **Phone:** 305/672-1114 (8)

◆◆

Chinese

Location: Corner of 41st St and Garden Ave. 954 41st St 33139. **Hours:** 11:30 am-10 pm, Fri & Sat-11 pm, Sun 3 pm-10 pm. **Reservations:** suggested. **Features:** Hungry guests can stuff themselves with piping-hot salt-and-pepper flounder, crystal grouper, soft-shell crab with cellophane noodles or T-bone steak kew. Casual dress; beer & wine only. **Parking:** street. **Cards:** AX, DS, MC, VI.

YUCA RESTAURANT **Lunch:** $6-$14 **Dinner:** $7-$40 **Phone:** 305/532-9822 (9)

◆◆◆

Cuban

Location: In Lincoln Road Mall. 501 Lincoln Rd 33139. **Hours:** noon-3 & 4-11 pm, Fri & Sat-midnight, Sun-10 pm. Closed: 1/1, 11/23, 12/25. **Reservations:** accepted. **Features:** Expect cutting-edge Cuban entrees with a more global appeal. Gourmet items such as plantain-coated dolphin, black bean soup and yucca filled with a wild mushroom picadillo will stir the palate. Try the dessert of coconut custard served in the shell. Dressy casual; cocktails. **Parking:** on-site. **Cards:** AX, DC, MC, VI. ♿M

The Miami-Miami Beach Vicinity

AVENTURA pop. 25,267   (See map and index starting on p. 545)

—— WHERE TO STAY ——

COURTYARD BY MARRIOTT AVENTURA MALL   *Book at aaa.com*

Phone: (305)937-0805   **22**

1/1-4/22	1P: $152-$169	2P: $152-$169
12/1-12/31	1P: $143-$159	2P: $143-$159
10/1-11/30	1P: $125-$139	2P: $125-$139
4/23-9/30	1P: $107-$119	2P: $107-$119

Small-scale Hotel **Location:** Just e of US 1 at NE 191st and 28th Ave, just se of SR 856. Near the Aventura Mall. 2825 NE 191 St 33180. **Fax:** 305/937-0806. **Facility:** 166 units. 161 one-bedroom standard units, some with whirlpools. 5 one-bedroom suites ($159-$199). 5 stories, interior corridors. *Bath:* combo or shower only. **Parking:** on-site. **Amenities:** high-speed Internet, dual phone lines, voice mail, irons, hair dryers. **Dining:** 6:30-10:30 am, Sat & Sun 7-11 am. **Pool(s):** heated outdoor. **Leisure Activities:** whirlpool, exercise room. **Guest Services:** valet and coin laundry. **Business Services:** meeting rooms, fax (fee). **Cards:** AX, DC, DS, JC, MC, VI. **Special Amenities:** free newspaper and early check-in/late check-out. *(See color ad below)*

SOME UNITS

    /
FEE FEE

THE FAIRMONT TURNBERRY ISLE RESORT & CLUB   *Book at aaa.com*

Phone: (305)932-6200   **21**

12/1-4/30	1P: $350-$4200	2P: $350-$4200	XP: $50	D18
5/1-5/30 & 9/29-11/30	1P: $269-$4200	2P: $269-$4200	XP: $50	D18
5/31-9/28	1P: $143-$2100	2P: $143-$2100	XP: $50	D18

Resort **Location:** 0.5 mi w of SR A1A via SR 856; from US 1 at NE 199th St and Biscayne Blvd. 19999 W Country Club Dr Large-scale Hotel 33180. **Fax:** 305/933-6554. **Facility:** A gate marks the entrance to this service-oriented, Mediterranean-style resort offering golf, tennis and fine dining. 392 units. 366 one-bedroom standard units, some with whirlpools. 26 one-bedroom suites with whirlpools, some with kitchens. 1-7 stories, interior/exterior corridors. **Parking:** valet. **Terms:** check-in 4 pm, 3 day cancellation notice-fee imposed, [BP] meal plan available, package plans, $11 service charge, small pets only. **Amenities:** dual phone lines, voice mail, safes, honor bars, irons, hair dryers. **Fee:** video games, high-speed Internet. *Some:* DVD players, CD players. **Dining:** 5 restaurants, 7 am-midnight; guests only, cocktails, entertainment. **Pool(s):** 2 heated outdoor. **Leisure Activities:** saunas, steamrooms, rental sailboats, private beach club, recreation programs, jogging, spa. **Fee:** windsurfing, marina, charter fishing, golf-36 holes, 11 lighted tennis courts. **Guest Services:** gift shop, valet laundry, area transportation-resort facilities, beach & mall. **Business Services:** conference facilities, business center. **Cards:** AX, DC, DS, MC, VI.

SOME UNITS

(See map and index starting on p. 545)

RESIDENCE INN BY MARRIOTT-AVENTURA MALL   *Book at aaa.com*   Phone: 786/528-1001   ⓴

12/23-4/22	1P: $119-$409	2P: $119-$409
12/1-12/22 & 10/1-11/30	1P: $99-$299	2P: $99-$299
4/23-9/30	1P: $89-$279	2P: $89-$279

Small-scale Hotel   **Location:** 0.5 mi w of SR A1A via SR 856; from US 1 at NE 199th St and Biscayne Blvd. Next to Aventura Mall. 19900 W Country Club Dr 33180. Fax: 786/528-1002. **Facility:** 191 units. 60 one-bedroom standard units with kitchens. 96 one- and 35 two-bedroom suites. 9 stories, interior corridors. *Bath:* combo or shower only. **Parking:** on-site. **Terms:** cancellation fee imposed, [BP] meal plan available, package plans, small pets only ($75 extra charge). **Amenities:** high-speed Internet, dual phone lines, voice mail, safes, irons, hair dryers. **Pool(s):** heated outdoor. **Leisure Activities:** whirlpool, exercise room. **Guest Services:** valet and coin laundry. **Business Services:** meeting rooms, fax (fee). **Cards:** AX, DC, DS, MC, VI.
(See color ad p 593)

SOME UNITS

(ASK) (SD) (🐕) (TI+) (&M) (☂) (🏊) (🍴) (💪) (DATA PORT) (🖥) (🖨) (💻) / (✕) /
FEE

——— WHERE TO DINE ———

THE BAMBOO CLUB ASIAN BISTRO   **Lunch:** $9-$13   **Dinner:** $9-$19   Phone: 305/466-7100   ⑬

Asian   **Location:** Just n of Ives Dairy Rd; in Aventura Mall; between Sears and Bloomingdales. 19501 Biscayne Blvd 33180. **Hours:** 11:30 am-10 pm. **Features:** As the name implies, the menu dabbles in influences from all of the Western Asian countries. Lending to the clublike atmosphere are high ceilings and noises from the kitchen area. Florida's tropical air can be enjoyed outdoors. Casual dress; cocktails. **Parking:** on-site. **Cards:** AX, CB, DC, DS, JC, MC, VI.

(&M) (Y)

CHEF ALLEN'S   **Dinner:** $26-$38   Phone: 305/935-2900   ⑭

American   **Location:** Just e of US 1 at NE 191st St and NE 28th Ave, just se of jct SR 856. 19088 NE 29th Ave 33180. **Hours:** 6 pm-10:30 pm, Fri & Sat-11 pm. Closed: 7/4; also Super Bowl Sun. **Reservations:** suggested. **Features:** Innovative New World cuisine is excellently presented in an Art Deco dining room. Watch the cook whip up your meal through the glass-enclosed "al vista" kitchen. A very extensive wine list and professional service add the finishing touch to a great meal. Dressy casual; cocktails. **Parking:** on-site and valet. **Cards:** AX, DC, MC, VI.

(&M)

BAL HARBOUR pop. 3,305   (See map and index starting on p. 545)

——— WHERE TO STAY ———

SHERATON BAL HARBOUR BEACH RESORT   *Book at aaa.com*   Phone: (305)865-7511   ㉝

(AAA) (SAVE)

12/15-4/30	1P: $399-$499	2P: $399-$499	XP: $25 F18
12/1-12/14 & 5/1-5/31	1P: $309-$369	2P: $309-$369	XP: $25 F18

Large-scale Hotel   **Location:** Oceanfront. On SR A1A, just n on SR 922. 9701 Collins Ave 33154. Fax: 305/864-2601. **Facility:** Tropical trees, flowering plants and a waterfall pool enhance the manicured grounds of this resort offering on-site shopping. 645 units. 602 one-bedroom standard units. 26 one-, 16 two- and 1 three-bedroom suites ($675-$2000), some with whirlpools. 2-16 stories, interior corridors. *Bath:* combo or shower only. **Parking:** valet. **Terms:** open 12/1-5/31, 3 day cancellation notice-fee imposed, package plans, $12 service charge, pets ($75 deposit). **Amenities:** dual phone lines, voice mail, safes, honor bars, irons, hair dryers. *Fee:* video games, high-speed Internet. *Some:* DVD players, CD players, fax. **Dining:** 3 restaurants, 6 am-10 pm, cocktails. **Pool(s):** 2 heated outdoor, wading. **Leisure Activities:** sauna, whirlpools, waterslide, limited beach access, rental paddleboats, landscaped heated river swimming pool with lagoons and cave, 2 lighted tennis courts, childrens summer camp, jogging, spa, personal fitness trainers. *Fee:* sailboats, windsurfing, scuba diving, snorkeling, charter fishing, jet skis. **Guest Services:** gift shop, valet laundry. **Business Services:** conference facilities, business center. **Cards:** AX, CB, DC, DS, JC, MC, VI. **Special Amenities:** free newspaper.
(See color ad p 8)

SOME UNITS

(SD) (🐕) (TI) (24ᴴ) (Y) (🍴) (&) (☂) (🚤) (🐴) (✕) (💪) (DATA PORT) (💻) / (✕) (VCR) (🖥) /
FEE   FEE   FEE

——— WHERE TO DINE ———

BAL HARBOUR BISTRO   *Menu on aaa.com*   **Lunch:** $9-$25   **Dinner:** $9-$25   Phone: 305/861-4544   ㉛

(AAA)

Continental   **Location:** On SR A1A, just n of SR 922; in Bal Harbour Shops, next to Sak's. 9700 Collins Ave 33154. **Hours:** 9 am-10 pm. Closed: 11/23, 12/25. **Reservations:** accepted. **Features:** The restaurant is surrounded by designer shops. Some of the tables are out in the mall with a canopy of trees and the sky, while inside the restaurant provides a bistro feel. A diverse menu with light fare, from salads and sandwiches to fresh seafoods, pastas, and meat items. Dressy casual; cocktails; entertainment. **Parking:** on-site (fee). **Cards:** AX, DC, MC, VI.

(Y) (🍸)

CARPACCIO   **Lunch:** $8-$15   **Dinner:** $14-$21   Phone: 305/867-7777   ㉚

Italian   **Location:** On SR A1A, just n of SR 922; in Bal Harbour Shops. 9700 Collins Ave 33154. **Hours:** 11:30 am-11 pm. Closed: 11/23, 12/25. **Reservations:** suggested, dinner. **Features:** Diners can eat inside the cozy bistro or outside, where people-watching is a popular pastime. Foods are fresh and feature local seafood and pasta. Meat items, too, are prepared with an Italian flair. Casual dress; cocktails. **Parking:** on-site (fee). **Cards:** AX, DC, MC, VI.

(Y) (🍸)

BAY HARBOR ISLANDS   (See map and index starting on p. 545)

——— WHERE TO DINE ———

CAFFE DAVINCI   *Menu on aaa.com*   **Lunch:** $9-$20   **Dinner:** $13-$30   Phone: 305/861-8166   ㉗

Italian   **Location:** Just w of Collins/Harding aves; corner of E Bay Harbor Dr and Kane Concourse. 1009 Kane Concourse 33154. **Hours:** 11:30 am-2:30 & 5:30-10:30 pm, Fri-11:30 pm, Sat 5:30 pm-11:30 pm, Sun 5:30 pm-10:30 pm. **Reservations:** accepted. **Features:** This cute, cozy cafe serves up big satisfaction when it comes to Italian food; when you walk out you will feel like you have been on a trip to Italy. Casual dress; cocktails. **Parking:** valet and street. **Cards:** AX, MC, VI.

(&M)

COCONUT GROVE   (See map and index starting on p. 534)

──── WHERE TO STAY ────

THE DOUBLETREE HOTEL AT COCONUT GROVE   *Book at aaa.com*   **Phone:** 305/858-2500   **46**

Property failed to provide current rates

Small-scale Hotel   **Location:** Jct Darwin St. Located facing the marina. 2649 S Bayshore Dr 33133. Fax: 305/858-5776. **Facility:** 196 units. 176 one-bedroom standard units. 20 one-bedroom suites. 20 stories, interior corridors. *Bath:* combo or shower only. **Parking:** valet. **Amenities:** video games (fee), high-speed Internet, dual phone lines, voice mail, irons, hair dryers. **Pool(s):** heated outdoor. **Leisure Activities:** 2 lighted tennis courts, exercise room. **Guest Services:** valet laundry, area transportation. **Business Services:** meeting rooms, business center.

SOME UNITS

HAMPTON INN-COCONUT GROVE/CORAL GABLES   *Book at aaa.com*   **Phone:** 305/448-2800   **45**

Property failed to provide current rates

Small-scale Hotel   **Location:** Just e of US 1. 2800 SW 28th Terrace 33133. Fax: 305/442-8655. **Facility:** 136 one-bedroom standard units. 6 stories, interior corridors. *Bath:* combo or shower only. **Parking:** on-site. **Amenities:** video games (fee), high-speed Internet, voice mail, irons, hair dryers. **Pool(s):** outdoor. **Leisure Activities:** whirlpool, exercise room. **Guest Services:** valet and coin laundry. **Business Services:** meeting rooms, fax (fee).

SOME UNITS
FEE

MAYFAIR HOTEL & SPA   *Book at aaa.com*   **Phone:** (305)441-0000   **50**

12/1-3/31 & 10/1-11/30	1P: $209-$389
4/1-9/30	1P: $99-$239

Small-scale Hotel   **Location:** At Florida Ave and Virginia St; center. Adjoins May Fair Shops. 3000 Florida Ave 33133. Fax: 305/447-9173. **Facility:** Tiled fountains enhance this hotel built around a ground-floor shopping mall; suites feature individualized decor. 179 units. 153 one-bedroom standard units. 26 one-bedroom suites. 5 stories, interior/exterior corridors. *Bath:* combo or shower only. **Parking:** valet. **Terms:** check-in 4 pm, cancellation fee imposed, [AP], [BP], [CP], [ECP] & [MAP] meal plans available, package plans, small pets only. **Amenities:** DVD players, video games (fee), CD players, high-speed Internet, dual phone lines, voice mail, safes, honor bars, irons, hair dryers. **Dining:** 7 am-11 pm, entertainment. **Pool(s):** heated outdoor, wading. **Leisure Activities:** whirlpool, spa. **Guest Services:** valet laundry. **Business Services:** meeting rooms. **Cards:** MC, VI. *(See color ad below)*

SOME UNITS
FEE

RESIDENCE INN BY MARRIOTT   *Book at aaa.com*   **Phone:** (305)285-9303   **48**

12/1-3/31	2P: $172-$229
10/1-11/30	2P: $142-$229
4/1-9/30	2P: $123-$170

Small-scale Hotel   **Location:** S Bayshore Dr, w on SW 27th Ave/Cornelia Dr, then s; in CocoWalk and May Fair Shops. 2835 Tigertail Ave 33133. Fax: 305/285-9672. **Facility:** 140 units. 32 one-bedroom standard units with efficiencies. 67 one- and 41 two-bedroom suites, some with efficiencies or kitchens. 3-5 stories, exterior corridors. *Bath:* combo or shower only. **Parking:** on-site (fee). **Terms:** small pets only ($75 fee, $10 extra charge). **Amenities:** high-speed Internet, dual phone lines, voice mail, irons, hair dryers. **Pool(s):** 2 outdoor. **Leisure Activities:** exercise room. **Guest Services:** complimentary evening beverages: Mon-Thurs, valet and coin laundry. **Business Services:** meeting rooms. **Cards:** AX, CB, DC, DS, JC, MC, VI.

SOME UNITS
FEE

THE RITZ-CARLTON COCONUT GROVE, MIAMI   *Book at aaa.com*   **Phone:** (305)644-4680   **47**

12/1-4/30	1P: $299-$459
5/1-5/31 & 10/3-11/30	1P: $259-$399
6/1-10/2	1P: $179-$249

Large-scale Hotel   **Location:** Bayshore Dr, just w. 3300 SW 27th Ave 33133. Fax: 305/644-4681. **Facility:** Located near Biscayne Bay, this hotel is close to the CocoWalk shopping and dining complex and the May Fair Shops. 115 units. 97 one-bedroom standard units. 18 one-bedroom suites. 2-8 stories, interior corridors. *Bath:* combo or shower only. **Parking:** valet. **Terms:** cancellation fee imposed, package plans, small pets only ($500 deposit). **Amenities:** DVD players, CD players, dual phone lines, voice mail, safes, honor bars, irons, hair dryers. **Fee:** video games, high-speed Internet. **Dining:** Bizcaya, see separate listing. **Pool(s):** heated outdoor. **Leisure Activities:** spa. **Guest Services:** valet laundry. **Business Services:** meeting rooms, business center. **Cards:** AX, CB, DC, DS, JC, MC, VI.

SOME UNITS
FEE

(See map and index starting on p. 534)

SONESTA HOTEL & SUITES COCONUT GROVE   *Book at aaa.com*   Phone: (305)529-2828   **51**

12/31-4/30	1P: $159-$1039	2P: $159-$1039	XP: $35 F17
10/1-11/30	1P: $149-$1019	2P: $149-$1019	XP: $35 F17
12/1-12/30 & 5/1-9/30	1P: $139-$1009	2P: $139-$1009	XP: $35 F17

Large-scale Hotel   **Location:** Just w of S Bayshore Dr; just e of jct Main Hwy and Grand Ave; in CocoWalk and May Fair Shops. 2889 McFarlane Rd 33133. Fax: 305/529-2008. **Facility:** 220 units. 174 one-bedroom standard units, some with kitchens. 38 one- and 8 two-bedroom suites ($229-$1039) with kitchens, some with whirlpools. 23 stories, interior corridors. **Bath:** combo or shower only. **Parking:** valet. **Terms:** cancellation fee imposed, package plans. **Amenities:** CD players, dual phone lines, voice mail, safes, honor bars, irons, hair dryers. **Fee:** video games, high-speed Internet. **Dining:** Tara Steak & Lobster House, see separate listing. **Pool(s):** small heated outdoor. **Leisure Activities:** sauna, whirlpool, steamroom, exercise room. **Guest Services:** valet and coin laundry, area transportation. **Business Services:** meeting rooms, business center. **Cards:** AX, CB, DC, DS, JC, MC, VI.

SOME UNITS

(ASK) (S🔊) (♉️) (Y) (≈) (✕) (🐾) (DATA PORT) (💻) / (✕) (VCR) (🔋) (🖼️) /
                                                                FEE   FEE

WYNDHAM GRAND BAY-COCONUT GROVE   *Book at aaa.com*   Phone: (305)858-9600   **49**

(AAA) (SAVE)

10/1-11/30	1P: $229	2P: $239	XP: $10 F18
12/1-4/29	1P: $219	2P: $219	XP: $10 F18
4/30-9/30	1P: $179	2P: $189	XP: $10 F18

Small-scale Hotel   **Location:** On Water Front Dr. Located facing Dinner Key Marina. 2669 S Bayshore Dr 33133. Fax: 305/859-2026. **Facility:** Flowering plants cascading over each balcony form a striking accent at this hotel where many rooms offer a view of the bay. 177 units. 156 one-bedroom standard units. 21 one-bedroom suites ($199-$979), some with whirlpools. 12 stories, interior corridors. **Bath:** combo or shower only. **Parking:** valet. **Amenities:** CD players, dual phone lines, voice mail, fax, safes, honor bars, irons, hair dryers. **Fee:** video games, high-speed Internet. **Dining:** 7-11 am, 11:30-3 & 6-10:30 pm, Fri & Sat-11:30 pm; Sunday brunch 11 am-3 pm, entertainment. **Pool(s):** heated outdoor. **Leisure Activities:** saunas, whirlpool, beach privileges at Key Biscayne Resort, exercise room. **Fee:** massage. **Guest Services:** gift shop, valet laundry, beauty salon. **Business Services:** conference facilities, business center. **Cards:** AX, DC, DS, MC, VI. **Special Amenities:** free newspaper and early check-in/late check-out.

SOME UNITS

(♉️) (24) (Y) (🏋️M) (👂) (≈) (✕) (🐾) (DATA PORT) (💻) / (✕) (VCR) /
                                                                FEE

——— WHERE TO DINE ———

ANOKHA FINE INDIAN CUISINE   Dinner: $11-$31   Phone: 786/552-1030   **80**

Indian   **Location:** Jct Grand Ave. 3195 Commodore Plaza 33133. **Hours:** 6 pm-10:30 pm, Thurs-Sat to 11:30 pm. Closed major holidays; also Mon. **Features:** The popular eatery serves noteworthy Indian food. Blended spices are used in the preparation of varying entrees, including such vegetarian choices as eggplant curry and potato croquettes stuffed with nuts and cheese. Those who prefer meat in their food might opt for minced lamb, marinated lobster, ground lamb and any number of other mouthwatering suggestions. Casual dress. **Parking:** on-site (fee). **Cards:** AX, DC, DS, MC, VI.

BALEEN   Lunch: $9-$18   Dinner: $19-$40   Phone: 305/857-5007   **67**

Seafood   **Location:** From Bayshore Dr, e on Fair Isle across bridge to Grove Isle; in Grove Isle Resort. 4 Grove Isle 33133. **Hours:** 7 am-3 & 7-10 pm, Fri & Sat-11 pm. **Reservations:** suggested. **Features:** The romantic restaurant offers two seating areas: outside tables that afford beautiful views of the bay and the stars and a classic inside room that exudes a golden glow. The food—thoughtfully prepared and artfully presented—will not disappoint. The diverse menu incorporates plenty of seafood choices and land foods. Dressy casual; cocktails; entertainment. **Parking:** valet. **Cards:** AX, DC, DS, MC, VI.   (🏋️M) (Y)

BERRIES AT THE GROVE   Lunch: $4-$10   Dinner: $7-$22   Phone: 305/448-2111   **65**

American   **Location:** Just e of US 1. 2884 SW 27th Ave 33133. **Hours:** 7 am-10:30 pm, Fri & Sat-11:30 pm, Sun-10 pm. Closed: 11/23, 12/25. **Features:** Sandwiches, wraps, salads and fresh fruit smoothies can be enjoyed in the relaxed back-deck atmosphere. Casual dress; cocktails. **Parking:** on-site and street. **Cards:** AX, MC, VI.

BIZCAYA   Lunch: $12-$25   Dinner: $18-$35   Phone: 305/644-4680   **70**

Continental   **Location:** Bayshore Dr, just w; in The Ritz-Carlton Coconut Grove, Miami. 3300 SW 27th Ave 33133. **Hours:** 7 am-11, 11:30-2:30 & 6-11 pm. **Reservations:** suggested. **Features:** The restaurant combines elements of a classic steakhouse with European grilling styles. The dining room nurtures a comfortable atmosphere, with rich wood tones and a cascading waterfall outside on the terrace. Dressy casual; cocktails. **Parking:** valet. **Cards:** AX, CB, DC, DS, JC, MC, VI.   (🏋️M) (Y)

CAFE MED   Lunch: $7-$23   Dinner: $7-$23   Phone: 305/443-1770   **74**

Italian   **Location:** At Florida Ave and Virginia St; in CocoWalk. 3015 Grand Ave 33133. **Hours:** 11 am-midnight, Fri & Sat-1 am. **Reservations:** suggested. **Features:** At the entrance of Coco Walk, the Italian restaurant serves pizza, baked pasta, specialty sandwiches and some meat and seafood dishes. Outdoor seating is available. Casual dress; cocktails. **Parking:** on-site (fee). **Cards:** AX, DC, DS, MC, VI.

CAFE' TU TU TANGO   Lunch: $4-$8   Dinner: $5-$9   Phone: 305/529-2222   **73**

International   **Location:** Corner of Grand Ave, Virginia St and McFarlane Rd; at CocoWalk. 3015 Grand Ave #250 33133. **Hours:** 11:30 am-midnight, Thurs-1 am, Fri & Sat-2 am. **Features:** Food and art combine at this cafe. Creations by local painters adorn the walls and guests may watch artists work while enjoying selections off the tapas-style menu. Casual dress; cocktails. **Parking:** on-site (fee). **Cards:** AX, DC, MC, VI.   (Y)

CHART HOUSE   Dinner: $19-$40   Phone: 305/856-9741   **71**

American   **Location:** From jct 27th Ave, just e on S Bayshore Dr. 3371 Pan American Dr 33133. **Hours:** 5 pm-10 pm. **Features:** Directly on the water, the restaurant offers a great view of the waterway and its many yachts. Examples of the fabulous food include prime rib, filet mignon, tomato-basil chicken and varied fresh fish and seafood dishes. The ever-popular hot chocolate lava cake—prepared with Godiva chocolate liqueur, vanilla ice cream, warm chocolate sauce and Heath bar crunch—is a mouthwatering way to finish the meal. Dressy casual; cocktails. **Parking:** valet. **Cards:** MC, VI.   (🏋️M) (Y)

(See map and index starting on p. 534)

THE CHEESECAKE FACTORY
◆◆◆ American

Lunch: $7-$26 **Dinner:** $7-$26 **Phone:** 305/447-9898 [75]
Location: Jct Grand Ave and McFarlane Rd at CocoWalk. 3015 Grand Ave 33133. **Hours:** 11:30 am-midnight, Sun 11 am-11:30 pm. **Closed:** 11/23, 12/25. **Features:** A display case of mouthwatering cheesecakes is the first thing visitors see as they walk through the door. The extensive menu incorporates many types of cuisine, including Asian, Italian, Greek and Spanish. It goes without saying that saving room for dessert is a must. Casual dress; cocktails. **Parking:** street. **Cards:** AX, CB, DC, DS, MC, VI.

COZZOLIS PIZZA CAFE
◆ Italian

Lunch: $3-$22 **Dinner:** $3-$22 **Phone:** 305/567-0080 [83]
Location: Jct Main Hwy and McFarlane Rd, just s. 3421 Main Hwy 33133. **Hours:** 10 am-3 am.
Features: Submarine sandwiches, pizza, lasagna, ziti and spaghetti can be ordered on the go for those in need of a quick bite. Casual dress. **Parking:** street. **Cards:** MC, VI.

DON QUIXOTE
◆◆◆ Spanish

Lunch: $13-$20 **Dinner:** $13-$20 **Phone:** 305/648-0971 [85]
Location: Center. 3148 Commodore Plaza 33133. **Hours:** noon-11 pm. **Closed:** 12/25.
Features: Guests can order from the menu or pick and choose from the 50-item buffet. Six daily paella specials are offered along with steaks, seafood and desserts. Dressy casual; cocktails. **Parking:** on-site (fee). **Cards:** AX, DC, MC, VI.

FEELINGS CAFE
◆◆ Colombian

Dinner: $7-$15 **Phone:** 305/443-8040 [89]
Location: Center. 3112 Commodore Plaza 33133. **Hours:** 5 pm-midnight. **Features:** Back in the corridor and up the stairs, the cafe is a bit hard to find, but the search is worth the effort. Diners can feast on bandeja paisa with grilled beef, chicken, sausage, creamed potatoes or Colombian tamales or empanadas served steaming hot with chili sauce. Casual dress; cocktails. **Parking:** on-site (fee). **Cards:** AX, MC, VI.

FLANIGAN'S
◆◆◆ American

Lunch: $7-$15 **Dinner:** $7-$23 **Phone:** 305/446-1114 [68]
Location: US 1, just s on SW 27th Ave (Unity Blvd), then just w. 2721 Bird Ave 33133. **Hours:** 11 am-3 am. **Closed:** 11/23, 12/25. **Features:** The dining room displays lots of pictures of the catches of fish and many of the owner himself. On the menu is a wide variety of fresh seafood, as well as the well-known baby back ribs. Casual dress; cocktails. **Parking:** on-site. **Cards:** MC, VI.

GREEN STREET CAFE
◆◆◆ Italian

Lunch: $10-$18 **Dinner:** $10-$18 **Phone:** 305/567-0662 [91]
Location: Corner of Main Hwy and Commodore Plaza. 3110 Commodore Plaza 33133. **Hours:** 7:30 am-10:45 pm, Fri & Sat-11:45 pm. **Closed:** 12/25. **Features:** People-watchers find tables on the walkway ideal. The menu boasts such selections as orange brule, brie and fruit plate, burgers, pastas, salmon and veal. Casual dress; cocktails. **Parking:** on-site (fee). **Cards:** AX, DC, MC, VI.

JOHNNY ROCKETS
◆ American

Lunch: $4-$12 **Dinner:** $4-$12 **Phone:** 305/444-1000 [77]
Location: Jct McFarlane Rd and Main Hwy. 3040 Grand Ave 33133. **Hours:** 11 am-midnight, Thurs-Sat to 2 am.
Features: Burgers, hot dogs, grilled cheese and hot fudge sundaes are a few favorites on a menu the whole family will enjoy. Casual dress. **Parking:** street. **Cards:** AX, MC, VI.

LAS CULEBRINAS IN THE GROVE RESTAURANT
◆◆ Spanish

Lunch: $6-$28 **Dinner:** $8-$28 **Phone:** 305/448-4090 [66]
Location: From US 1, just e. 2890 SW 27th Ave 33133. **Hours:** 11:30 am-11 pm, Fri & Sat-midnight.
Reservations: accepted. **Features:** The neat little bistro-like place is swathed in soft colors, primarily brown. Guests can unwind in the upper-level area or the bar. In addition to many tapas selections, the menu lists varied main courses. This is a fun place to eat. Dressy casual; cocktails. **Parking:** on-site and street. **Cards:** AX, DC, MC, VI.

LE BOUCHON DU GROVE
◆◆◆ French

Lunch: $9-$15 **Dinner:** $18-$26 **Phone:** 305/448-6060 [82]
Location: Center. 3430 Main Hwy 33133. **Hours:** 10 am-3 & 5-11 pm, Fri-midnight, Sat 8 am-3 & 5-midnight, Sun 8 am-3 & 5-11 pm. **Reservations:** suggested. **Features:** A French flair punctuates offerings of international cuisine. The popular restaurant is in the heart of Coconut Grove. Casual dress; cocktails. **Parking:** street. **Cards:** AX, MC, VI.

LE MOULIN DU GROVE
◆◆◆ French

Lunch: $9-$16 **Dinner:** $9-$16 **Phone:** 305/774-1111 [86]
Location: Center of town. 3425 Main Hwy 33133. **Hours:** 7:30 am-11 pm, Fri & Sat-1 am.
Reservations: accepted. **Features:** An extensive menu of crepes, extravagant salads, fresh fish and delightful desserts are only the beginning at this French bistro. Speciality entrees of poulet Basquaise, boeuf en daube a la Provencla or duck a l'orange are only some of the great entrees that await your dining pleasure. Casual dress; beer & wine only. **Parking:** on-site. **Cards:** AX, CB, DC, DS, JC, MC, VI.

MAMBO CAFE
◆◆ Cuban

Lunch: $10-$18 **Dinner:** $10-$18 **Phone:** 305/448-2768 [90]
Location: Jct Main Hwy. 3105 Commodore Plaza 33133. **Hours:** 10 am-midnight, Sun from 8 am. **Features:** In the heart of the trendy Coconut Grove shopping area is the cozy bistro, which offers only sidewalk seating. The trendy spot is perfect for people-watching. The food is great, and the service is inviting. Casual dress. **Parking:** on-site (fee). **Cards:** AX, DC, MC, VI.

MEZZANOTTE IN THE GROVE
◆◆◆ Italian

Lunch: $9-$16 **Dinner:** $15-$26 **Phone:** 305/448-7677 [76]
Location: At Mary and Florida sts; center; adjacent to May Fair Shops. 3390 Mary St 33133. **Hours:** noon-3 & 6-11 pm, Sat & Sun 6 pm-midnight. **Reservations:** suggested. **Features:** A popular, upscale bistro, it serves pizza, pasta, grilled meat and fish all cooked to perfection. An impressive seafood salad comes with shrimp and squid on a bed of arugula. Veal-stuffed tortellini smothered in cheese sauce makes a delightful entree. Dressy casual; cocktails. **Parking:** on-site (fee). **Cards:** AX, DC, DS, MC, VI.

(See map and index starting on p. 534)

MR. MOE'S　　　　　　　**Lunch: $7-$22**　　　　**Dinner: $7-$22**　　　**Phone: 305/442-1114**　　87
▼▼ ▼▼　　**Location:** In Commodore Plaza. 3131 Commodore Plaza 33133. **Hours:** 11:30 am-5 am. Closed: 12/25.
American　　**Features:** In the vibrant downtown area, the restaurant has a dining room reminiscent of a rustic Western mountain lodge constructed of logs and stone and decorated with mounted animal heads, pelts, antlers and pictures and items related to hunting and trapping. Many TVs around the room show sporting events. Although the specialty is barbecue, the menu also lists burgers, sandwiches and a few other entrees. Casual dress; cocktails. **Parking:** street. **Cards:** AX, MC, VI.

MONTY'S RAW BAR　　　**Lunch: $10-$19**　　　**Dinner: $10-$19**　　**Phone: 305/856-3992**　　69
▼▼ ▼▼　　**Location:** Jct S Bayshore Dr and Aviation Ave. 2550 S Bayshore Dr 33133. **Hours:** 11:30 am-midnight, Fri & Sat-2
Seafood　　am. **Features:** Patrons can enjoy a relaxing meal on the deck overlooking the waterway and boats. A favorite is coconut shrimp with marmalade sauce with a piece of the award-winning Key lime pie. Casual dress; cocktails. **Parking:** on-site (fee). **Cards:** AX, MC, VI.

NEW YORK ROMA PIZZA & PASTA　　**Lunch: $2-$7**　　**Dinner: $2-$7**　　**Phone: 305/476-6018**　　79
▼　　**Location:** Jct McFarlane Rd and Grand Ave. 2985 McFarlane Rd 33133. **Hours:** 10 am-4 am, Thurs-Sat to 6 am.
Italian　　**Features:** Strombolis, calzones and pizza by the slice or pie are the choices at the quick-serve eatery in the always busy CocoWalk area. Casual dress. **Parking:** street. **Cards:** MC, VI.

OASIS INTERNET CAFE　　**Lunch: $4-$10**　　**Dinner: $4-$10**　　**Phone: 305/446-6565**　　84
▼　　**Location:** Jct McFarlane Rd and Grand Ave. 2977 McFarlane Rd 100A 33133. **Hours:** 8 am-10 pm, Fri & Sat-
American　　midnight. **Features:** While surfing the net, cafe patrons can dine on omelets, sandwiches, wraps, salads, pizza, smoothies and milkshakes. Casual dress. **Parking:** street. **Cards:** MC, VI.

RED LANTERN CHINESE RESTAURANT　　**Lunch: $6-$8**　　**Dinner: $10-$28**　　**Phone: 305/529-9998**　　81
▼▼ ▼▼　　**Location:** Just n of jct Main Hwy. 3176 Commodore Plaza 33133. **Hours:** 11:30 am-11 pm, Fri-midnight, Sat 4 pm-
Chinese　　midnight, Sun 5 pm-11 pm. Closed: 11/23. **Reservations:** suggested. **Features:** A touch of fine-dining flair punches up the atmosphere in the nice Chinese restaurant. Guests enjoy a cozy, intimate experience. On the extensive menu are such items as Cantonese-style fried chicken, kung pao chicken, steamed snapper, pan-fried flounder, Peking-style pork chops, tofu, clay pots and rice or noodle dishes. Dressy casual; beer & wine only. **Parking:** street. **Cards:** AX, DC, DS, MC, VI.

SANDBAR GRILL　　　**Lunch: $8-$13**　　　**Dinner: $8-$13**　　**Phone: 305/444-5270**　　78
▼　　**Location:** Jct Main and Commodore Plaza. 3064 Grand Ave 33133. **Hours:** 11 am-3 am, Sat & Sun from 10 am;
Seafood　　Saturday & Sunday brunch. **Features:** The restaurant sustains a rustic atmosphere. The menu lists everything from shrimp wraps and tacos to egg rolls and burgers. Casual dress; cocktails. **Parking:** on-site (fee). **Cards:** AX, DC, MC, VI.

SCOTTY'S LANDING　　**Lunch: $6-$14**　　　**Dinner: $7-$24**　　**Phone: 305/854-2626**　　72
▼　　**Location:** Jct SW 27th Ave and S Bayshore Dr, just n. 3381 Pan American Dr 33133. **Hours:** 11 am-10 pm, Fri &
Seafood　　Sat-11 pm. Closed major holidays. **Features:** A favorite gathering spot for locals, the open-air restaurant affords views of the bay and marina. Fresh seafood served quick and to the diner's liking is a staple. Casual dress; cocktails. **Parking:** on-site. **Cards:** MC, VI.

SENOR FROG'S　　　**Lunch: $12-$18**　　**Dinner: $12-$18**　　**Phone: 305/448-0999**　　92
▼▼ ▼▼　　**Location:** Center. 3480 Main Hwy 33133. **Hours:** 11:30 am-1 am, Thurs-Sat to 2 am. **Features:** The family-
Mexican　　owned eatery has been operating continuously for 21 years. Huge portions of such Mexican favorites as fajitas, enchiladas, tacos, nachos and quesadillas satisfy patrons. Casual dress; cocktails. **Parking:** on-site (fee). **Cards:** AX, DC, MC, VI.

TARA STEAK & LOBSTER HOUSE　　　**Dinner: $21-$51**　　　**Phone: 305/444-6244**　　88
▼▼ ▼▼　　**Location:** Just w of Bayshore Dr; just e of jct Main Hwy and Grand Ave; in Sonesta Hotel & Suites Coconut Grove.
Steak & Seafood　　2889 McFarlane Rd 33133. **Hours:** 5 pm-10 pm. **Reservations:** suggested. **Features:** Come and experience Tara's aged steaks and her fresh lobster; she even has her own steak sauce if you want. The decor is that of a steakhouse with wood tones and limited art. Casual dress; cocktails. **Parking:** valet. **Cards:** AX, MC, VI.

TUSCANY CAFE　　　**Lunch: $10-$20**　　**Dinner: $10-$20**　　**Phone: 305/445-0022**　　93
▼▼ ▼▼　　**Location:** Just w of jct Commodore Plaza. 3484 Main Hwy 33133. **Hours:** 11:30 am-midnight, Fri & Sat-1 am.
Italian　　**Features:** In the fashionable Coconut Grove area of shops and boutiques, the wonderful Italian eatery has cozy surroundings that replicate an Italian villa setting. Indoor and outdoor seating is available. Menu items include many traditional dishes, such as zuppa di pesce, chicken parmigiana and homemade jumbo ravioli. Among other specialty items are grilled salmon, stuffed Florida lobster and rack of lamb. Casual dress; cocktails. **Parking:** on-site (fee). **Cards:** AX, MC, VI.

CORAL GABLES pop. 42,249   (See map and index starting on p. 534)

——— WHERE TO STAY ———

THE BILTMORE HOTEL CORAL GABLES   *Book at aaa.com*   Phone: (305)445-1926   **41**

1/1-3/31	1P: $306-$369	2P: $306-$369	XP: $20 F18
4/1-5/31	1P: $270-$333	2P: $270-$333	XP: $20 F18
12/1-12/31	1P: $270-$297	2P: $270-$297	XP: $20 F18
6/1-11/30	1P: $234-$297	2P: $234-$297	XP: $20 F18

Classic Historic
Large-scale Hotel

Location: 1 mi w of Le Jeune Rd. Located in a residential area. 1200 Anastasia Ave 33134. Fax: 305/913-3159. **Facility:** This 1920s-era hotel with Spanish Revival architecture and Moorish and Italian accents features hand-painted fresco ceilings in the lobby. 276 units. 241 one-bedroom standard units. 32 one-, 2 two- and 1 three-bedroom suites, some with whirlpools. 2-15 stories, interior corridors. *Bath:* combo or shower only. **Parking:** on-site and valet. **Terms:** package plans, $9 service charge. **Amenities:** dual phone lines, voice mail, safes, honor bars, irons, hair dryers. *Fee:* video games, high-speed Internet. *Some:* CD players. **Dining:** Palme d'Or, see separate listing. **Pool(s):** heated outdoor. **Leisure Activities:** saunas, steamrooms, rental bicycles, jogging, spa. *Fee:* golf-18 holes, 10 lighted tennis courts. **Guest Services:** gift shop, valet laundry, area transportation. **Business Services:** conference facilities, business center. **Cards:** AX, CB, DC, DS, JC, MC, VI.

SOME UNITS

HOLIDAY INN CORAL GABLES BUSINESS DISTRICT   *Book at aaa.com*   Phone: (305)443-2301   **38**

1/1-4/30	1P: $139	2P: $149	XP: $10 F16
5/1-9/30	1P: $119	2P: $129	XP: $10 F16
12/1-12/31 & 10/1-11/30	1P: $109	2P: $109	XP: $10 F16

Large-scale Hotel

Location: On SR 953 (Le Jeune Rd), 0.8 mi s of jct US 41. 2051 Le Jeune Rd 33134. Fax: 305/446-6827. **Facility:** 168 one-bedroom standard units. 6 stories, interior corridors. *Bath:* combo or shower only. **Parking:** on-site (fee). **Terms:** cancellation fee imposed, 13% service charge. **Amenities:** high-speed Internet, voice mail, irons, hair dryers. **Pool(s):** outdoor. **Leisure Activities:** exercise room. **Guest Services:** gift shop, valet and coin laundry. **Business Services:** meeting rooms, fax (fee). **Cards:** AX, CB, DC, DS, MC, VI. *(See color ad below)*

SOME UNITS   FEE   FEE

HOLIDAY INN UNIVERSITY OF MIAMI   *Book at aaa.com*   Phone: (305)667-5611   **42**

All Year   1P: $109-$189   2P: $109-$189

Small-scale Hotel   **Location:** On US 1. Located across from the University of Miami campus. 1350 S Dixie Hwy 33146. Fax: 305/669-3153. **Facility:** 155 one-bedroom standard units. 3 stories, interior corridors. *Bath:* combo or shower only. **Parking:** on-site. **Terms:** 3 day cancellation notice, [AP], [BP], [CP], [ECP] & [MAP] meal plans available. **Amenities:** video games (fee), dual phone lines, voice mail, irons, hair dryers. **Pool(s):** outdoor. **Leisure Activities:** limited exercise equipment. **Guest Services:** valet and coin laundry. **Business Services:** meeting rooms, business center. **Cards:** AX, CB, DC, DS, JC, MC, VI.

SOME UNITS   FEE   FEE

(See map and index starting on p. 534)

HYATT REGENCY CORAL GABLES   *Book at aaa.com*   **Phone:** (305)441-1234   **39**

[AAA] [SAVE]

12/1-5/14 & 9/18-11/30	1P: $159-$325	2P: $159-$325	XP: $25 F18
5/15-9/17	1P: $125-$249	2P: $125-$249	XP: $25 F18

Location: At Alhambra Plaza and Douglas Rd; downtown. 50 Alhambra Plaza 33134. Fax: 305/441-0520.
Facility: Offering large rooms, some with balconies, the hotel is decorated in a Spanish style. 242 units. 231
Large-scale Hotel one-bedroom standard units. 6 one- and 5 two-bedroom suites, some with whirlpools. 14 stories, interior
corridors. *Bath:* combo or shower only. **Parking:** on-site (fee) and valet. **Terms:** cancellation fee imposed.
Amenities: high-speed Internet (fee), dual phone lines, voice mail, safes, honor bars, irons, hair dryers. *Some:* DVD players,
CD players. **Dining:** 6 am-3 & 6-11 pm, cocktails, nightclub. **Pool(s):** heated outdoor. **Leisure Activities:** saunas, whirlpool,
steamrooms, exercise room. **Guest Services:** gift shop, valet laundry. **Business Services:** conference facilities, business
center. **Cards:** AX, CB, DC, DS, JC, MC, VI.

SOME UNITS

[icons] / [icons] FEE

OMNI COLONNADE HOTEL   *Book at aaa.com*   **Phone:** (305)441-2600   **40**

12/1-4/15	1P: $199-$359	2P: $199-$349	XP: $20 F17
10/1-11/30	1P: $189-$349	2P: $189-$349	XP: $20 F17
4/16-6/15	1P: $179-$339	2P: $179-$339	XP: $20 F17
6/16-9/30	1P: $109-$269	2P: $109-$269	XP: $20 F17

Large-scale Hotel

Location: At Aragon Ave and Ponce de Leon Blvd; downtown. 180 Aragon Ave 33134. Fax: 305/445-3929. **Facility:** Pink and green
marble, mahogany trim and hand-blown glass chandeliers impart a luxurious feel to this hotel built around a restored 1926
rotunda. 140 one-bedroom standard units. 17 one-bedroom suites. 7 stories, interior corridors. **Parking:** on-site and
valet. **Terms:** [BP] meal plan available, package plans. **Amenities:** high-speed Internet, dual phone lines, voice mail, fax, honor
bars, irons, hair dryers. *Some:* CD players, safes. **Dining:** Tula, see separate listing. **Pool(s):** heated outdoor. **Leisure
Activities:** whirlpool, exercise room. **Guest Services:** gift shop, valet laundry. **Business Services:** conference facilities,
business center. **Cards:** AX, CB, DC, DS, JC, MC, VI.

SOME UNITS

[icons] / [icons] /

———— **WHERE TO DINE** ————

ARCHIE'S GOURMET PIZZA   **Lunch:** $8-$10   **Dinner:** $8-$12   **Phone:** 305/444-1557   **47**

Location: Just e of Ponce de Leon Blvd. 166 Giralda Ave 33134. **Hours:** noon-11 pm, Fri-12:30 pm, Sat-midnight.
Closed major holidays. **Reservations:** not accepted. **Features:** The brick oven is in the back, but is the
center focus for the gourmet pizzas. Also on the menu are large salads and many varieties of pasta. A
Pizza stylish, informal atmosphere complements the aromas. Casual dress; cocktails. **Parking:** street. **Cards:** AX,
MC, VI.

CAFFE ABBRACCI   **Lunch:** $9-$15   **Dinner:** $14-$28   **Phone:** 305/441-0700   **52**

Location: At Aragon Ave and Salzedo; just e of SR 953 (Le Jeune Rd); downtown. 318 Aragon Ave 33134.
Hours: 11:30 am-3 & 6-midnight, Sat from 6 pm, Sun 6 pm-11 pm. **Reservations:** suggested.
Features: Exquisitely prepared Venetian specialties are served in an elegant yet casually decorated dining
Northern room with a wonderful, fun ambience. The owner supervises the entire operation so rest assured you will
Italian enjoy a well-prepared, delicious dinner. Dressy casual; cocktails. **Parking:** valet. **Cards:** AX, CB, DC,
MC, VI.

CAFFE ITALIA   **Lunch:** $7-$11   **Dinner:** $7-$14   **Phone:** 305/441-1199   **39**

Location: Corner of SW 8th St and 38th Ave. 3800 SW 8th St 33134. **Hours:** 11 am-10 pm. Closed major
holidays. **Features:** Specialty dishes of veal and chicken as well as freshly made pasta and pizza are the
Italian main offerings at the cafe. Tasty salads and desserts complete the menu. Casual dress; beer & wine only.
Parking: on-site. **Cards:** AX, CB, DC, DS, MC, VI.

CARMEN THE RESTAURANT   **Lunch:** $9-$18   **Dinner:** $22-$43   **Phone:** 305/913-1944   **55**

Location: From Le Jeune Rd/SW 42nd Ave, 0.4 mi w; in David William Hotel. 700 Biltmore Way 33134. **Hours:** noon-
2 & 6-10 pm, Fri-11 pm, Sat 6 pm-11 pm, Sun 6 pm-10 pm. **Reservations:** required. **Features:** Guests
settle into the elegant setting to savor creative New American fusion food prepared with a Latin influence.
Latino Carmen puts her twist on some Puerto Rican dishes. Dressy casual; cocktails. **Parking:** valet and street.
Cards: AX, DC, DS, MC, VI.

CHISPA   **Lunch:** $9-$17   **Dinner:** $17-$34   **Phone:** 305/648-2600   **59**

Location: US 1 (Dixie Hwy), n on Ponce De Leon Blvd, then just w. 225 Altrara Ave 33146. **Hours:** 11:30 am-3:30 &
5:30-10:30 pm, Fri-11:30 pm, Sat 5:30 pm-11:30 pm, Sun noon-10:30 pm. Closed: 1/1, 12/25.
Features: The decor is bright and fun in the bustling dining room. The large menu, which delicately
Latino balances Spanish and Cuban dishes, lists seviches, flatbreads, empanadas and meat and seafood dishes,
all with excellent taste and presentation. Dressy casual; cocktails. **Parking:** valet and street. **Cards:** AX, DC, DS, MC, VI.

CHRISTY'S   **Lunch:** $9-$15   **Dinner:** $18-$35   **Phone:** 305/446-1400   **57**

Location: Corner of Ponce de Leon Blvd and Malaga; downtown. 3101 Ponce de Leon Blvd 33134. **Hours:** 11:30 am-
10 pm, Fri-11 pm, Sat 5 pm-11 pm, Sun 5 pm-10 pm. **Reservations:** suggested. **Features:** This classic
steakhouse features dry-aged prime rib and other beef specialties. Red walls with mahogany trim and brass
Steak House wall sconces add to the gentlemen's club atmosphere. Nicknamed "The Powerhouse," it is an excellent
meeting place for professionals. Semi-formal attire; cocktails. **Parking:** on-site. **Cards:** AX, DC, DS, MC, VI.

FRANCESCO RESTAURANT   **Lunch:** $7-$15   **Dinner:** $15-$26   **Phone:** 305/446-1600   **41**

Location: Just w of Ponce de Leon Blvd. 325 Alcazar Ave 33134. **Hours:** noon-3 & 6-10 pm, Sat 1 pm-10 pm,
Sun 1 pm-9 pm. Closed: 1/1, 12/24, 12/25; also Mon. **Reservations:** required. **Features:** Peruvian cuisine
is the major feature, but patrons might catch an Italian special, too. Those who are troubled about what to
Peruvian order can order the tasting menu, which dabbles in the freshest of seafood and meats. Dressy casual; beer
& wine only. **Parking:** valet and street. **Cards:** AX, DC, DS, MC, VI.

(See map and index starting on p. 534)

GABLES DINER Lunch: $9-$16 Dinner: $9-$22 Phone: 305/567-0330 (49)

American

Location: Corner of Aragon and Galiano St. 2320 Galiano St 33134. **Hours:** 8 am-10:30 pm, Fri & Sat-11:30 pm. **Features:** A flair characterizes such comfort foods as the signature turkey loaf. The black and white floor is reminiscent of a diner, and paned windows look out onto the street. Blue-plate specials are prepared daily. Casual dress; cocktails. **Parking:** street. **Cards:** AX, DC, MC, VI.

HOUSTON'S Lunch: $9-$34 Dinner: $9-$34 Phone: 305/529-0141 (53)

American

Location: Corner of Coral Way (Miracle Mile) and Ponce de Leon Blvd. 201 Miracle Mile 33134. **Hours:** 11:30 am-11 pm, Fri & Sat-midnight, Sun & Mon-10 pm. **Features:** This popular, spacious restaurant features leather booths and an open kitchen. On the menu you will find tasty burgers, steaks and salads. Portions are large, the fresh grilled fish selection changes daily, and there is a small wine list. Casual dress; cocktails. **Parking:** valet. **Cards:** AX, MC, VI.

LA PROVENCE FRENCH BAKERY GOURMET DELI & CAFE Lunch: $4-$9 Dinner: $4-$9 Phone: 305/476-0530 (44)

Bakery/Desserts

Location: Corner of Giralda Ave and Ponce de Leon Blvd. 2300 Ponce de Leon Blvd 33134. **Hours:** 7 am-7 pm, Sun-3 pm. **Features:** The eatery offers several lunch combos that include a sandwich or quiche; baguette, croissant or panini sandwiches and salads are also available, as are authentic, delectable items from the bakery case. Counter seating looks out onto the street scene. Casual dress. **Parking:** street. **Cards:** MC, VI.

MISS SAIGON BISTRO Lunch: $11-$19 Dinner: $15-$29 Phone: 305/446-8006 (45)

Vietnamese

Location: Center; between Ponce de Leon Blvd and Galliano St. 148 Giralda Ave 33134. **Hours:** 11:30 am-3 & 5:30-10 pm, Fri-11 pm, Sat 5:30 pm-11 pm, Sun 5:30 pm-10 pm. Closed: 12/25. **Reservations:** suggested. **Features:** The Nguyen family operates one of the newest Vietnamese restaurants in the Miami metro area. Staff members donning aodias, the traditional long gowns of Vietnam, serve home-style Vietnamese dishes in the charming dining room. Some favorite choices include lemon grass crispy fish and caramelized ribs. More than a dozen types of pho, hearty flavored soup, represent various parts of Vietnam. Casual dress; cocktails. **Parking:** on-site (fee) and valet. **Cards:** DS, MC, VI.

MOON Lunch: $9-$12 Dinner: $8-$30 Phone: 305/668-9890 (62)

Asian

Location: Just off Village of Merrick Park. 1118 S Dixie Hwy 33146. **Hours:** 11:30 am-3 & 5-11 pm, Sat & Sun 11:30 am-11 pm. **Reservations:** accepted. **Features:** The trendy eatery offers dependable spicy fare, all properly flavored. Casual dress; cocktails. **Parking:** on-site. **Cards:** AX, MC, VI.

MYLOS RESTAURANT & BAR Lunch: $6-$10 Dinner: $10-$25 Phone: 305/461-0403 (40)

Greek

Location: Corner of Antilla and Ponce de Leon Blvd. 1111 Ponce de Leon Blvd 33134. **Hours:** 7 am-11:30 pm. **Reservations:** suggested, weekends. **Features:** Appetizers and entrees like taramosalata, stuffed vine leaves, octopus and moussaka gives you an authentic taste of Greece. Also offered are grilled whole snapper, Greek sausage, whole lobster, steak, lamb chops and shrimp. Dressy casual; cocktails; entertainment. **Parking:** street. **Cards:** AX, MC, VI.

NORMAN'S Dinner: $26-$39 Phone: 305/446-6767 (56)

Regional New World

Location: 3 blks s of Miracle Mile; just w of Douglas Rd. 21 Almeria Ave 33134. **Hours:** 6 pm-10 pm, Fri & Sat-10:30 pm. Closed major holidays; also Sun. **Reservations:** suggested. **Features:** New World cuisine blends cooking styles from Latin American, Caribbean and Asian cultures. Enjoy a Vietnamese spring roll stuffed with tuna, carrots and cabbage while relaxing in a Spanish-style decor complete with wrought iron fixtures. Dressy casual; cocktails. **Parking:** valet. **Cards:** AX, CB, DC, MC, VI.

ORTANIQUE ON THE MILE Lunch: $7-$15 Dinner: $15-$32 Phone: 305/446-7710 (54)

Caribbean

Location: Between SR 953 (Le Jeune Rd) and Ponce de Leon Blvd; next to theater. 278 Miracle Mile 33134. **Hours:** 11:30 am-2:30 & 6-10 pm, Wed-Fri to 11 pm, Sat 6 pm-11 pm, Sun 5:30 pm-9:30 pm. Closed major holidays. **Reservations:** suggested. **Features:** It's like eating in a Jamaican courtyard, as terraces with draped curtains and warm colors make the atmosphere. Preparations of New World Caribbean cuisine are spiced to varying degrees. Seafood and meat entrees are flavorful and artfully presented. Dressy casual; cocktails. **Parking:** valet. **Cards:** AX, DC, MC, VI.

PALME D'OR Dinner: $20-$40 Phone: 305/445-1926 (58)

French

Location: 1 mi w of Le Jeune Rd; in The Biltmore Hotel Coral Gables. 1200 Anastasia Ave 33134. **Hours:** 6 pm-10 pm, Fri & Sat-11 pm. Closed: Sun & Mon. **Reservations:** required. **Features:** Chef Phillip Ruiz and his staff prepare an outstanding version of modern French cuisine. His creations are distinctive and the flavors memorable from the first course to the last. An attentive, knowledgeable team provides service. Occupying a renowned hotel, the dining room is one of elegance, with frescoed ceilings and crystal chandeliers. Dressy casual; cocktails; entertainment. **Parking:** on-site and valet. **Cards:** AX, CB, DC, DS, MC, VI.

THE PALM RESTAURANT Lunch: $10-$21 Dinner: $18-$66 Phone: 786/552-7256 (61)

Steak House

Location: Corner of Ruiz Ave and Ponce de Leon Blvd, 1 blk n of S Dixie Hwy; across from Village of Merrick Shopping Center. 4425 Ponce de Leon Blvd 33146. **Hours:** 11:30 am-3 & 5-11 pm, Sat from 5 pm, Sun 5 pm-10 pm. Closed: 1/1, 12/25. **Reservations:** required. **Features:** Known for their prime, tender steaks and oversize Nova Scotia lobsters, this restaurant also offers some Italian specialties in big portions using fresh ingredients. The service is warm and exceptional, caricatures of celebrities, politicians and loyal customers adorn the walls, and an extensive wine list is available. Dressy casual; cocktails. **Parking:** on-site (fee) and valet. **Cards:** AX, DC, DS, MC, VI.

(See map and index starting on p. 534)

PUCHETTA RESTAURANT   **Lunch:** $10-$14   **Dinner:** $11-$25   **Phone:** 305/444-4553   46
Italian
Location: Just e of Ponce de Leon Blvd. 160 Giralda Ave 33134. **Hours:** 11:30 am-3 & 6:30-10:30 pm, Fri-11:30 pm, Sat 6 pm-11:30 pm. Closed major holidays; also Sun. **Reservations:** suggested. **Features:** Divine house-made pastas are served at this cozy bistro, along with risottos, chicken, fish and grilled steaks; servers offer cordial, professional service. Cocktails. **Parking:** valet. **Cards:** AX, CB, DC, DS, MC, VI.

RESTAURANT ST. MICHEL   **Lunch:** $7-$20   **Dinner:** $15-$33   **Phone:** 305/446-6572   42
American
Location: At Alcazar Ave and Ponce de Leon Blvd; downtown. 162 Alcazar Ave 33134. **Hours:** 7 am-9:30 & 11-10:30 pm, Fri-11:30 pm, Sat 11 am-11:30 pm, Sun 11 am-10:30 pm. **Reservations:** suggested. **Features:** Art Deco and European influences intermingle in the intimate dining room of the 1926 hotel. Glowing pink lights and fancy chandeliers contribute to an air of romance. Savor the Maryland crab cakes and the yellowtail snapper with tropical fruit salsa. Cocktails; entertainment. **Parking:** street. **Cards:** AX, DC, MC, VI.

SPRIS   **Lunch:** $7-$15   **Dinner:** $7-$15   **Phone:** 305/444-3388   48
Northern Italian
Location: Just s of Giralda Ave; between Aragon and Giralda aves. 2305 Ponce de Leon Blvd 33134. **Hours:** 11:30 am-11 pm, Fri & Sat-midnight. Closed: 11/23, 12/25. **Features:** Brick-oven pizzas are great, salads are huge, and calzones are stuffed full. Guests can sit in the cute Italian sidewalk cafe area or eat inside amid scenes from Italy. Casual dress; cocktails. **Parking:** street. **Cards:** AX, MC, VI.

SUSHI MAKI   **Lunch:** $6-$12   **Dinner:** $8-$18   **Phone:** 305/443-1884   50
Sushi
Location: Jct Ponce de Leon Blvd and Aragon Ave. 2334 Ponce de Leon Blvd 33134. **Hours:** 11 am-10 pm. **Features:** Modern Asian cuisine is served at this restaurant. Sit and dine at the sushi bar to watch the traditional raw rolls and specialty cooked rolls being prepared. Hot and cold appetizers available; specialty platters include single, double or triple boats that are attractive, loaded with a variety sushi and great for sharing. Casual dress; beer & wine only. **Parking:** street. **Cards:** AX, MC, VI.

TAMBO RESTAURANT & LOUNGE   **Lunch:** $17-$23   **Dinner:** $25-$34   **Phone:** 305/476-9025   43
Peruvian
Location: Corner of Salzedo St and Giralda Ave; just e of Le Jeune/42nd Ave; downtown. 275 Giralda Ave 33134. **Hours:** 11:30 am-10 pm, Sat 6 pm-11 pm. Closed major holidays; also Sun. **Reservations:** suggested. **Features:** Savor the Asian-Latino flavors in the chic design of this restaurant that provides warm and attentive service. Referred to as Nikkei cuisine, it is highlighted by offering the bountiful flavors of the sea. Here, east meets west and combines the best aspects of ceviche and sushi. After dinner, linger over the superb quartet of creme brulees for dessert. Dressy casual; cocktails. **Parking:** on-site. **Cards:** AX, DS, MC, VI.

TULA   **Lunch:** $8-$15   **Dinner:** $13-$27   **Phone:** 305/569-6511   51
Italian
Location: At Aragon Ave and Ponce de Leon Blvd; downtown; in Omni Colonnade Hotel. 180 Aragon Ave 33143. **Hours:** 6:30 am-10 pm, Fri & Sat-11 pm. **Reservations:** suggested. **Features:** The softly colored dining room nurtures a bustling atmosphere. Tuscan cuisine is served by friendly, attentive staffers. Sidewalk seating is an option. Dressy casual; cocktails. **Parking:** valet. **Cards:** AX, CB, DC, DS, JC, MC, VI.

The following restaurants have not been evaluated by AAA but are listed for your information only.

THE HEIGHTS   **Phone:** 305/461-1774
[fyi]   Not evaluated. **Location:** Just s of The Miracle Mile. 2530 Ponce de Leon Blvd. **Features:** Creative blending of Southwest and Asian cuisine. Excellent combinations of flavors and ingredients; expensive.

PASCAL'S ON PONCE   **Phone:** 305/444-2024
[fyi]   Not evaluated. **Location:** Just s of the Miracle Mile. 2611 Ponce de Leon Blvd 33134. **Features:** Chef Oudin puts his own twist on French cuisine in a cozy bistro-like setting.

CUTLER RIDGE pop. 24,781

--- **WHERE TO STAY** ---

BAYMONT INN & SUITES MIAMI-CUTLER RIDGE   *Book at aaa.com*   **Phone:** (305)278-0001
Small-scale Hotel
All Year   1P: $79-$109   XP: $7   F18
Location: Florida Tpke, exit 12 (US 1), northwest corner. 10821 Caribbean Blvd 33189. Fax: 305/278-0222. **Facility:** 103 units. 100 one-bedroom standard units. 3 one-bedroom suites. 4 stories, interior corridors. *Bath:* combo or shower only. **Parking:** on-site. **Terms:** [ECP] meal plan available, small pets only ($50 deposit). **Amenities:** video games (fee), voice mail, irons, hair dryers. **Pool(s):** outdoor. **Guest Services:** valet and coin laundry. **Business Services:** fax (fee). **Cards:** AX, CB, DC, DS, MC, VI. **Special Amenities:** free expanded continental breakfast and free local telephone calls. *(See color ad p 560)*   SOME UNITS

FEE

BEST WESTERN FLORIDIAN HOTEL

Book at aaa.com

Phone: (305)253-9960

12/1-3/31 [ECP]	1P: $89-$125	2P: $89-$129	XP: $10	F
4/1-11/30 [ECP]	1P: $79-$100	2P: $79-$100	XP: $10	F

Location: Florida Tpke, exit 12 (US 1), then w. 10775 Caribbean Blvd 33189. Fax: 305/234-9050. **Facility:** 150 units. 140 one-bedroom standard units. 10 one-bedroom suites ($119-$259) with efficiencies. 6 stories,
Small-scale Hotel exterior corridors. *Bath:* combo or shower only. **Parking:** on-site. **Terms:** cancellation fee imposed, small pets only ($45 deposit, $15 extra charge). **Amenities:** high-speed Internet, voice mail, safes, irons, hair dryers. **Dining:** 7 am-10 pm, cocktails. **Pool(s):** heated outdoor. **Leisure Activities:** limited exercise equipment. **Guest Services:** valet and coin laundry. **Business Services:** meeting rooms, business center. **Cards:** AX, CB, DC, DS, MC, VI. **Special Amenities:** free expanded continental breakfast and early check-in/late check-out.

FLORIDA CITY pop. 7,843

------ WHERE TO STAY ------

BEST WESTERN FLORIDA CITY "GATEWAY TO THE KEYS"

Book at aaa.com

Phone: (305)246-5100

12/21-4/30 [ECP]	1P: $95-$259	2P: $95-$259	XP: $10	F17
12/1-12/20 & 5/1-11/30 [ECP]	1P: $75-$259	2P: $75-$259	XP: $10	F17

Location: On US 1, 0.8 mi s of Florida Tpke terminus. 411 S Krome Ave 33034. Fax: 305/242-0056. **Facility:** Smoke free premises. 114 one-bedroom standard units. 2 stories (no elevator), exterior corridors.
Motel *Bath:* combo or shower only. **Parking:** on-site. **Terms:** 30 day cancellation notice. **Amenities:** high-speed Internet, voice mail, irons, hair dryers. **Pool(s):** outdoor. **Leisure Activities:** whirlpool. **Guest Services:** coin laundry. **Business Services:** meeting rooms, fax (fee). **Cards:** AX, CB, DC, DS, MC, VI. **Special Amenities:** free expanded continental breakfast and free local telephone calls.

BUDGET HOST INN

Phone: (305)248-2741

12/26-3/31 [CP]	1P: $79-$110	2P: $79-$110	XP: $5	F12
12/1-12/25 & 4/1-11/30 [CP]	1P: $45-$54	2P: $45-$54	XP: $5	F12

Location: SR 997, just w of US 1; 0.5 mi s of Homestead. 815 N Krome Ave 33034. Fax: 305/246-1884. **Facility:** 45 one-bedroom standard units. 1 story, exterior corridors. **Parking:** on-site. **Terms:** weekly rates available.
Motel **Pool(s):** outdoor. **Guest Services:** coin laundry. **Cards:** AX, CB, DC, DS, MC, VI. **Special Amenities:** free continental breakfast.

COMFORT INN

Book at aaa.com

Phone: (305)248-4009

All Year	1P: $59-$279	2P: $59-$279	XP: $10	F17

Location: On US 1, 0.8 mi s of Florida Tpke terminus. 333 SE 1st Ave 33034. Fax: 305/248-7935. **Facility:** 123 one-bedroom standard units. 2 stories (no elevator), interior/exterior corridors. *Bath:* combo or shower only.
Motel **Parking:** on-site. **Terms:** cancellation fee imposed, weekly rates available, [ECP] meal plan available. **Amenities:** voice mail, safes, irons, hair dryers. *Some:* high-speed Internet. **Pool(s):** outdoor. **Guest Services:** coin laundry. **Cards:** AX, CB, DC, DS, MC, VI. **Special Amenities:** free expanded continental breakfast and free newspaper.

CORAL ROC MOTEL

Phone: (305)246-2888

12/24-3/31 [CP]	1P: $39-$99	2P: $45-$129	XP: $5	F12
4/1-11/30	1P: $30-$65	2P: $32-$99	XP: $5	F12
12/1-12/23	1P: $30-$69	2P: $32-$89	XP: $5	F12

Location: On SR 997; just w of US 1; 0.5 mi s of Homestead. 1100 N Krome Ave 33034. Fax: 305/242-1580. **Facility:** 17 one-bedroom standard units, some with efficiencies (no utensils). 1 story, exterior corridors.
Motel **Parking:** on-site. **Terms:** 3 night minimum stay - seasonal, 3 day cancellation notice, weekly rates available, [CP] meal plan available, package plans, small pets only ($50 deposit). **Pool(s):** small outdoor. **Guest Services:** coin laundry. **Cards:** AX, DC, DS, MC, VI. **Special Amenities:** free local telephone calls and preferred room (subject to availability with advance reservations).

ECONO LODGE

Book at aaa.com

Phone: (305)248-9300

All Year	1P: $40-$155	2P: $45-$175	XP: $10	F10

Location: US 1 at Florida Tpke, exit 1. 553 NE 1st Ave 33034. Fax: 305/245-2753. **Facility:** 42 one-bedroom standard units. 2 stories, interior corridors. *Bath:* combo or shower only. **Parking:** on-site. **Terms:** [CP] meal
Small-scale Hotel plan available, package plans. **Amenities:** hair dryers. **Pool(s):** small outdoor. **Guest Services:** valet and coin laundry. **Business Services:** meeting rooms. **Cards:** AX, DC, DS, MC, VI.

FAIRWAY INN

Phone: (305)248-4202

12/20-3/31	1P: $79-$149	2P: $79-$149	XP: $5	F15
12/1-12/19 & 4/1-11/30	1P: $45-$59	2P: $45-$59	XP: $5	F15

Location: On US 1, 0.7 mi s of Florida Tpke terminus. 100 SE 1st Ave 33034. Fax: 305/245-8578. **Facility:** 160 one-bedroom standard units. 2 stories (no elevator), exterior corridors. **Parking:** on-site. **Amenities:** voice
Motel mail, safes. **Pool(s):** outdoor. **Business Services:** fax (fee). **Cards:** AX, CB, DC, DS, JC, MC, VI. **Special Amenities:** free continental breakfast and early check-in/late check-out.

HAMPTON INN   *Book at aaa.com*   Phone: (305)247-8833

▼▼▼
                12/1-4/30   1P: $114-$124   2P: $114-$124
                5/1-11/30   1P: $84-$99   2P: $84-$99
Motel   **Location:** On US 1, 0.3 mi s of Florida Tpke terminus. 124 E Palm Dr 33034. Fax: 305/247-6456. **Facility:** 123
one-bedroom standard units. 2 stories (no elevator), exterior corridors. **Parking:** on-site. **Terms:** small pets
only. **Amenities:** high-speed Internet, voice mail, irons, hair dryers. **Pool(s):** outdoor. **Guest Services:** valet laundry.
Cards: AX, CB, DC, DS, MC, VI.

SOME UNITS
(ASK) (S/D) (🛏) (📶+) (⏰) (🍽) (📷) (DATA PORT) (💻) /(✕) (🔒) (🖨) /

HOLIDAY INN EXPRESS   Phone: 305/247-3414
(fyi)   All Year   1P: $89-$259   2P: $89-$259   XP: $10   F16
                Too new to rate, opening scheduled for July 2005. **Location:** On US 1, 0.7 mi s of Florida Tpke. 35200 S Dixie
Small-scale Hotel Hwy 33024. **Amenities:** 120 units, coffeemakers, microwaves, refrigerators. **Terms:** cancellation fee
imposed. **Cards:** AX, DC, DS, MC, VI.

KNIGHTS INN   *Book at aaa.com*   Phone: (305)247-6633

(AAA) (SAVE)
                12/20-3/31 [CP]   1P: $79-$110   2P: $79-$110   XP: $5   F12
▼▼▼▼   12/1-12/19 & 4/1-11/30 [CP]   1P: $44-$54   2P: $44-$54   XP: $5   F12
Motel   **Location:** US 1, just n of Florida Tpke terminus, exit 1. 1223 NE 1st Ave 33034. Fax: 305/247-7515. **Facility:** 48
units. 40 one-bedroom standard units. 8 one-bedroom suites. 1-2 stories (no elevator), exterior corridors.
Parking: on-site. **Pool(s):** outdoor. **Guest Services:** coin laundry. **Cards:** AX, CB, DC, DS, MC, VI.
Special Amenities: free continental breakfast.

SOME UNITS
(S/D) (📷) (🍽) (📶+) (🔒) /(✕) (🖨) /

SUPER 8 MOTEL   Phone: (305)245-0311

(AAA) (SAVE)
                12/20-3/31   1P: $79-$149   2P: $79-$149   XP: $5   F
▼▼▼▼   12/1-12/19 & 4/1-11/30   1P: $45-$59   2P: $45-$59   XP: $5   F
Motel   **Location:** SR 997, just w of US 1; 0.5 mi s of Homestead. 1202 N Krome Ave 33034. Fax: 305/247-9136.
Facility: 52 one-bedroom standard units. 1 story, exterior corridors. **Parking:** on-site. **Terms:** [CP] meal
plan available. **Amenities:** safes. **Pool(s):** small outdoor. **Guest Services:** coin laundry. **Cards:** AX, CB,
DC, DS, MC, VI. **Special Amenities:** early check-in/late check-out and free room upgrade (subject to
availability with advance reservations).

SOME UNITS
(S/D) (📶+) (📷) (🍽) (📷) (DATA PORT) /(✕) (🔒) /

-------- **WHERE TO DINE** --------

THE CAPRI RESTAURANT   Lunch: $10-$15   Dinner: $10-$40   Phone: 305/247-1544
▼▼▼ ◆◆◆   **Location:** On SR 997, just w of US 1. 935 N Krome Ave 33030. **Hours:** 11 am-10 pm, Fri & Sat-11 pm. Closed:
                12/25; also Sun. **Reservations:** accepted. **Features:** Fair prices and Italian favorites highlight this menu.
Italian   Fresh local seafood and pasta dishes are served in a pair of dining rooms, one casual and one semi-formal.
                Dark wood paneled walls and red and white tablecloths set the ambience for this meal. Dressy casual;
cocktails. **Parking:** on-site. **Cards:** AX, DS, MC, VI.

MUTINEER RESTAURANT   *Menu on aaa.com*   Lunch: $5-$20   Dinner: $12-$22   Phone: 305/245-3377
(AAA)   **Location:** On US 1, 0.3 mi s of Florida Tpke terminus. 11 SE 1st Ave 33034. **Hours:** 11 am-10 pm.
▼▼▼▼   **Features:** Wooden beams, nautical artifacts and a theme that revolves around pirate boats all set the tone
                in this cozy restaurant. The stuffed grouper filled with crabmeat, broiled and coated in sauce is a menu
Steak & Seafood favorite. A band performs on weekends. Casual dress; cocktails. **Parking:** on-site. **Cards:** AX, DC, DS,
MC, VI.

(🍸)

ROSITA'S RESTAURANTE   Lunch: $5-$9   Dinner: $5-$9   Phone: 305/246-3114
▼▼▼   **Location:** From end of Florida Tpke/US 1, just w. 199 W Palm Dr 33034. **Hours:** 8:30 am-9 pm. **Features:** The
                atmosphere is casual but the Mexican food is serious; you won't find this home-style Mexican cooking
Mexican   anywhere else around town. Get your favorite burritos, tamales, enchiladas and, yes, tacos. Casual dress;
                beer only. **Parking:** street. **Cards:** MC, VI.

SONNY'S REAL PIT BAR-B-Q   Lunch: $6-$12   Dinner: $6-$12   Phone: 305/245-8585
▼▼   **Location:** US 1, just n of Florida Tpke terminus, exit 1. 33505 S Dixie Hwy 33034. **Hours:** 11 am-10 pm.
                Features: Barbecue chicken, ribs and pulled pork are done right: slowly cooked over a hardwood fire then
Barbecue   coated in sauce. Also tempting are smoked turkey, fried catfish and charbroiled chicken. A casual family
                atmosphere surrounds patrons. Casual dress. **Parking:** on-site. **Cards:** MC, VI.

HIALEAH pop. 226,419 (See maps and indexes starting on p. 534, 542)

-------- **WHERE TO STAY** --------

DAYS INN MIAMI LAKES/WESTLAND MALL   *Book at aaa.com*   Phone: (305)823-2121   [35]

(AAA) (SAVE)
                12/26-11/30   1P: $84-$94   2P: $84-$94   XP: $10   F
▼▼▼▼   12/1-12/25   1P: $75-$85   2P: $75-$85   XP: $10   F
                Location: SR 826 (Palmetto Expwy), exit NW 103rd St, just e. 1950 W 49th St 33012. Fax: 305/362-4562.
Small-scale Hotel **Facility:** 83 one-bedroom standard units. 4 stories, interior corridors. **Bath:** combo or shower only. **Parking:**
on-site. **Terms:** small pets only ($25 extra charge). **Amenities:** voice mail, safes (fee), irons, hair dryers.
Leisure Activities: pool privileges. **Guest Services:** valet laundry, airport transportation-Miami International
Airport, area transportation-Port of Miami. **Business Services:** fax (fee). **Cards:** AX, CB, DC, DS, JC, MC, VI.
Special Amenities: free newspaper and early check-in/late check-out.

SOME UNITS
(S/D) (✈) (🛏) (📶+) (📷) (DATA PORT) (💻) /(✕) (🔒) /
FEE   FEE FEE

(See maps and indexes starting on p. 534, 542)

HOLIDAY INN EXPRESS HOTEL & SUITES   *Book at aaa.com*   **Phone: 305/362-7777**   33

(AAA) (SAVE)   All Year   2P: $69-$129

Small-scale Hotel   **Location:** Jct SR 826 (Palmetto Expwy) and NW 122nd St, exit NW 138th and W 68th sts, then w on NW 122nd St. 6650 W 20th Ave 33016. Fax: 305/826-8107. **Facility:** 144 units. 80 one-bedroom standard units. 64 one-bedroom suites ($79-$129), some with whirlpools. 5 stories, interior corridors. *Bath:* combo or shower only. **Parking:** on-site. **Amenities:** video games (fee), dual phone lines, voice mail, irons, hair dryers. **Pool(s):** outdoor. **Leisure Activities:** limited exercise equipment. **Guest Services:** valet and coin laundry. **Business Services:** meeting rooms, business center. **Cards:** AX, CB, DC, DS, JC, MC, VI.

SOME UNITS

RAMADA INN-MIAMI AIRPORT NORTH   *Book at aaa.com*   **Phone: (305)823-2000**   34

(AAA) (SAVE)   1/1-11/30   1P: $99-$119   2P: $99-$119   XP: $10   F
            12/1-12/31   1P: $65-$85   2P: $65-$85   XP: $10   F

Small-scale Hotel   **Location:** SR 826 (Palmetto Expwy), exit NW 103rd St, just e. 1950 W 49th St 33012. Fax: 305/362-4562. **Facility:** 171 one-bedroom standard units. 4 stories, interior corridors. *Bath:* combo or shower only. **Parking:** on-site. **Terms:** small pets only ($25 extra charge). **Amenities:** voice mail, safes (fee), irons, hair dryers. **Dining:** 6 am-2 & 5-10 pm, cocktails. **Pool(s):** outdoor, wading. **Guest Services:** gift shop, valet and coin laundry, airport transportation-Miami International Airport, area transportation-Port of Miami. **Business Services:** meeting rooms, fax (fee). **Cards:** AX, CB, DC, DS, JC, MC, VI. **Special Amenities:** free newspaper and early check-in/late check-out.

SOME UNITS

FEE   FEE FEE

———— WHERE TO DINE ————

———— The following restaurant has not been evaluated by AAA but is listed for your information only. ————

FLANIGAN'S SEAFOOD BAR & GRILL   **Phone: 305/821-0993**

(fyi)   Not evaluated. **Location:** 1550 W 84th St 33018. **Features:** The family-friendly restaurant is known for its baby back ribs, burgers and seafood.

HIALEAH GARDENS pop. 7,700   (See map and index starting on p. 534)

———— WHERE TO STAY ————

HOWARD JOHNSON PLAZA HOTEL & CONFERENCE CENTER-MIAMI AIRPORT   *Book at aaa.com*   **Phone: (305)825-1000**   30

(AAA) (SAVE)   12/1-4/16   1P: $109-$199   2P: $109-$199   XP: $10   F17
            4/17-11/30   1P: $99   2P: $109-$199   XP: $10   F17

Large-scale Hotel   **Location:** SR 826 (Palmetto Expwy), exit NW 103rd St, just w. 7707 NW 103rd St 33016. Fax: 305/556-6785. **Facility:** 259 units. 258 one-bedroom standard units, some with efficiencies. 1 one-bedroom suite ($139-$249). 10 stories, interior corridors. *Bath:* combo or shower only. **Parking:** on-site. **Terms:** cancellation fee imposed, [AP] & [BP] meal plans available, small pets only ($100 fee). **Amenities:** high-speed Internet, voice mail, safes (fee), irons, hair dryers. **Dining:** 7 am-10 pm, cocktails. **Pool(s):** heated outdoor. **Leisure Activities:** whirlpool, lighted tennis court, limited exercise equipment. **Guest Services:** sundries, valet laundry, airport transportation-Miami International Airport. **Business Services:** meeting rooms, business center. **Cards:** AX, CB, DC, DS, MC, VI. **Special Amenities:** free continental breakfast and free local telephone calls.

SOME UNITS

FEE

HOMESTEAD pop. 31,909

———— WHERE TO STAY ————

DAYS INN HOMESTEAD   *Book at aaa.com*   **Phone: (305)245-1260**

(diamonds)   12/26-4/14   1P: $79-$99   2P: $99-$139   XP: $10   D18
            12/1-12/25 & 4/15-11/30   1P: $65-$75   2P: $75-$99   XP: $10   D18

Motel   **Location:** US 1, 1.2 mi n of Florida Tpke, jct 320 St SW and US 1. Located at the edge of the business district. 51 S Homestead Blvd 33030. Fax: 305/247-0939. **Facility:** 109 one-bedroom standard units. 2 stories (no elevator), exterior corridors. *Bath:* combo or shower only. **Parking:** on-site. **Terms:** 3 day cancellation notice-fee imposed, [ECP] meal plan available, pets ($7 extra charge). **Amenities:** high-speed Internet, safes (fee), hair dryers. **Pool(s):** outdoor. **Guest Services:** valet and coin laundry. **Business Services:** fax (fee). **Cards:** AX, CB, DC, DS, JC, MC, VI.

SOME UNITS

(ASK)

FEE

EVERGLADES MOTEL   **Phone: (305)247-4117**

(AAA) (SAVE)   12/24-3/31 [CP]   1P: $39-$79   2P: $44-$109   XP: $5   F12
            12/1-12/23 [CP]   1P: $32-$45   2P: $32-$59   XP: $5   F12
            4/1-11/30   1P: $32-$45   2P: $32-$59   XP: $5   F12

Motel   **Location:** Just w of US 1; between Lucy and 6th sts; on SR 997, 0.5 mi s of center of town. 605 S Krome Ave 33030. **Facility:** 14 one-bedroom standard units. 1 story, exterior corridors. *Bath:* combo or shower only. **Parking:** on-site. **Terms:** package plans, small pets only ($5 extra charge). **Pool(s):** small outdoor. **Guest Services:** coin laundry. **Cards:** AX, DC, DS, MC, VI. **Special Amenities:** free local telephone calls and preferred room (subject to availability with advance reservations).

SOME UNITS

FEE   FEE

REDLAND HOTEL "AN HISTORIC INN"   Phone: 305/246-1904
▽▽△▽▽▽   12/1-5/31 & 10/1-11/30   1P: $89-$99   2P: $89-$99   XP: $10   F10
                6/1-9/30   1P: $69-$89   2P: $69-$89   XP: $10   F10
Historic   **Location:** Florida Tpke, exit 2, 1.9 mi w on Campbell Dr, then 0.6 mi s. 5 S Flagler Ave 33030. Fax: 305/246-9600.
Small-scale Hotel **Facility:** Built in 1904, the property has been renovated to that time in its lobby and cafe. The rooms offer a
modern feel to them with a touch of the past. Designated smoking area. 13 one-bedroom standard units. 2
stories (no elevator), interior corridors. *Bath:* shower only. **Parking:** on-site. **Terms:** cancellation fee imposed, weekly rates
available. **Amenities:** high-speed Internet, irons. **Guest Services:** valet laundry. **Business Services:** meeting rooms, fax (fee).
Cards: DS, MC, VI.

ASK S⬤ 🍴 ✕ VCR 🎥

─────── **WHERE TO DINE** ───────

EL TORO TACO   **Lunch:** $4-$11   **Dinner:** $5-$11   Phone: 305/245-8182
▽△▽   **Location:** Corner of Mowry Dr and SW 177 Ave. 1 S Krome Ave 33030. **Hours:** 11 am-9 pm, Fri & Sat 10 am-10
              pm, Sun 10 am-9 pm. Closed: Mon. **Features:** Enchiladas, burritos and fajitas are served up mild style in
Mexican   this warm and cozy family-owned restaurant, where everything is made from scratch. Take in the fresh air in
              the outdoor courtyard or dine inside. You're welcome to brown bag your own beer. Casual dress. **Parking:**
street. **Cards:** AX, DS, MC, VI.

WHITE LION CAFE   **Lunch:** $8-$12   **Dinner:** $8-$16   Phone: 305/248-1076
▽△▽ ▽△▽   **Location:** From Krome Ave, just w. 146 NW 7th St 33030. **Hours:** 11 am-4 & 5-9:30 pm, Mon-4 pm. Closed: Sun.
              Features: A comfy place to eat, the cafe has dining rooms that mix various types of antiques with some
American   modern pieces. The menu lines up a mix of comfort foods and some fresh local fish. Good desserts, which
MC, VI.   are made on site, are worth a splurge. Casual dress; beer & wine only. **Parking:** on-site. **Cards:** DS,

🍸

KENDALL pop. 75,226   (See map and index starting on p. 534)

─────── **WHERE TO STAY** ───────

AMERISUITES (MIAMI/KENDALL)   *Book at aaa.com*   Phone: (305)279-8688   62
Ⓐ SAVE   1/1-4/15 [ECP]   1P: $129-$179   2P: $139-$189   XP: $10   F18
              12/1-12/31 & 4/16-11/30 [ECP] 1P: $109-$159   2P: $119-$169   XP: $10   F18
▽▽△▽▽   **Location:** Florida Tpke, exit 20 (SW 88th/Kendall Dr), just e on SR 94, then 0.3 mi s. Located across from a shopping
Small-scale Hotel mall. 11520 SW 88th St 33176. Fax: 305/279-7907. **Facility:** 67 one-bedroom standard units. 5 stories, interior
corridors. *Bath:* combo or shower only. **Parking:** on-site. **Terms:** small pets only ($10 extra charge).
              Amenities: voice mail, safes (fee), irons, hair dryers. *Some:* dual phone lines. **Pool(s):** heated outdoor.
Guest Services: valet and coin laundry. **Business Services:** meeting rooms, fax (fee). **Cards:** AX, DC, DS, MC, VI.
Special Amenities: free full breakfast.
                                                                                                  SOME UNITS
S⬤ 🐾 🍴 ♿M 🛢 🌀 🛏 🛗 VCR 🎥 DATA PORT 🔌 📺 💳 / ✕ /
  FEE

WELLESLEY INN (MIAMI/KENDALL)   *Book at aaa.com*   Phone: (305)270-0359   61
Ⓐ SAVE   1/1-4/15 [ECP]   1P: $116-$146   2P: $116-$146
              4/16-11/30 [ECP]   1P: $101-$131   2P: $101-$131
▽▽△▽▽   12/1-12/31 [ECP]   1P: $96-$126   2P: $96-$126
Small-scale Hotel **Location:** Florida Tpke, exit 20, SW 88th (Kendall Dr), 0.3 mi e on SR 94, then 0.3 mi n on SW 117th Ave. Adjoins Town
and Country Mall. 11750 Mills Dr 33183. **Facility:** 106 units. 3 one-bedroom standard
units. 3 one-bedroom suites. 4 stories, interior corridors. **Parking:** on-site. **Terms:** small pets only.
Amenities: high-speed Internet, voice mail, irons, hair dryers. *Fee:* video games, safes. *Some:* dual phone lines. **Pool(s):**
heated outdoor. **Guest Services:** valet laundry. **Business Services:** fax (fee). **Cards:** AX, DS, MC, VI. **Special Amenities:**
free expanded continental breakfast and free newspaper.
                                                                                                  SOME UNITS
S⬤ 🐾 🍴 ♿M 🛢 🌀 🛏 🛗 🎥 DATA PORT 🔌 📺 💳 / ✕ /

─────── **WHERE TO DINE** ───────

GIL CAPA'S BISTRO   **Dinner:** $8-$16   Phone: 305/273-1102   119
▽△▽ ▽   **Location:** Jct SW 113th Pl and SW 107th St. 10712 SW 113th Pl 33176. **Hours:** 5:30 pm-10 pm. Closed major
Italian   holidays; also Mon. **Reservations:** suggested. **Features:** Health-conscious diners take note: You can enjoy
              low-fat adaptations of old-style, Southern Italian dishes like sausage with peppers, eggplant parmigiana,
              steak pizzaiola, veal Marsala and lasagna in this small, cozy neighborhood eatery. Dressy casual; beer &
wine only. **Parking:** on-site. **Cards:** AX, DC, DS, MC, VI.

LA CARRETA   **Lunch:** $6-$22   **Dinner:** $6-$22   Phone: 305/596-5973   118
▽△▽ ▽   **Location:** Just w of 117th Ave and SW 88th St; across from Town and Country Center in Kendall. 11740 SW 88th St
Cuban   33186. **Hours:** 8 am-1 am, Fri & Sat-2 am. Closed: 12/25. **Features:** Colorful artwork and murals adorn the
              walls at this local chain restaurant that efficiently serves a variety of traditional Cuban dishes. Casual dress;
cocktails. **Parking:** on-site. **Cards:** DS, MC, VI.

KEY BISCAYNE pop. 10,507   (See map and index starting on p. 534)

―――――― WHERE TO STAY ――――――

THE RITZ-CARLTON, KEY BISCAYNE   *Book at aaa.com*   Phone: (305)365-4500   55

	1P: $429-$1599	2P: $429-$1599	XP: $25	F18
12/1-1/5				
1/6-5/1	1P: $529-$1499	2P: $529-$1499	XP: $25	F18
5/2-11/30	1P: $199-$679	2P: $199-$679	XP: $25	F18

Resort
Large-scale Hotel   **Location:** Oceanfront. Crandon Blvd, jct e. 455 Grand Bay Dr 33149. Fax: 305/365-4505. **Facility:** In a quiet location just steps away from the Atlantic Ocean, this hotel features soft colors and fine appointments in each room. 402 units. 325 one-bedroom standard units, some with efficiencies. 44 one- and 33 two-bedroom suites, some with kitchens and/or whirlpools. 14 stories, interior corridors. *Bath:* combo or shower only. **Parking:** valet. **Terms:** 7 day cancellation notice-fee imposed, package plans, small pets only ($100 fee). **Amenities:** CD players, dual phone lines, voice mail, safes, honor bars, irons, hair dryers. *Fee:* video games, high-speed Internet. *Some:* DVD players. **Dining:** Cioppino, see separate listing. **Pool(s):** 2 heated outdoor, wading. **Leisure Activities:** saunas, whirlpools, steamrooms, limited beach access, recreation programs, jogging, playground, spa, sports court, basketball, volleyball. *Fee:* 11 lighted tennis courts, bicycles. **Guest Services:** gift shop, valet laundry, area transportation. **Business Services:** conference facilities, business center. **Cards:** AX, DC, DS, MC, VI.

SOME UNITS

🐕 🍴 24⃣ 📺 🏋 🏊 🛥 ✕ ⌧ 📹 ⁄ DATA PORT ⁄ VCR 🔌 🖥 ⁄
FEE

SONESTA BEACH RESORT KEY BISCAYNE   *Book at aaa.com*   Phone: (305)361-2021   54

12/1-5/1	1P: $239-$459	2P: $239-$459	XP: $35	F12
5/2-5/31	1P: $249-$350	2P: $249-$350	XP: $35	F12
6/1-8/31	1P: $169-$339	2P: $169-$339	XP: $35	F12

Resort
Large-scale Hotel   **Location:** 0.3 mi e of Crandon Blvd via Sonesta Dr. Located in a quiet area. 350 Ocean Dr 33149. Fax: 305/361-3096. **Facility:** Water views are abundant at this hotel where tropical trees and flowering plants lend an island ambience. 292 units. 280 one-bedroom standard units. 8 one- and 4 two-bedroom suites ($349-$1349). 8 stories, interior corridors. *Bath:* combo or shower only. **Parking:** valet. **Terms:** open 12/1-8/31, check-in 4 pm, 3 day cancellation notice-fee imposed, package plans, $15 service charge. **Amenities:** video games (fee), CD players, high-speed Internet, dual phone lines, voice mail, safes, honor bars, irons, hair dryers. **Dining:** Purple Dolphin, Two Dragons Restaurant, see separate listings. **Pool(s):** heated outdoor. **Leisure Activities:** saunas, whirlpools, steamroom, 9 tennis courts (3 lighted), recreation programs, playground, spa, sports court. *Fee:* sailboats, windsurfing, charter fishing, bicycles. **Guest Services:** gift shop, valet laundry, area transportation. **Business Services:** conference facilities, business center. **Cards:** AX, CB, DC, DS, JC, MC, VI. *(See color ad p 541)*

SOME UNITS

ASK 🔊 🍴 📺 🏋 ♿ 🛗 ♨ 🛥 ✕ VCR 🎥 DATA PORT 💻 ⁄ ✕ 🔌 ⁄

―――――― WHERE TO DINE ――――――

AD GUSTUM   Lunch: $6-$12   Dinner: $6-$12   Phone: 305/365-9333   100
Greek
Location: 1.4 mi e of bridge, jct Harbor Dr. 180 Crandon Blvd 33149. **Hours:** 7 am-10 pm, Fri & Sat-10:30 pm. **Features:** The gourmet delicatessen serves homemade Greek favorites, including salads, sandwiches and pasta. Casual dress; beer & wine only. **Parking:** on-site. **Cards:** MC, VI.

CHIEF'S SEAFOOD MARKET & SUSHI BAR   Lunch: $9-$12   Dinner: $15-$28   Phone: 305/361-2499   104
Sushi
Location: Corner of East Dr; between East Dr and Key Biscayne Blvd; in Eckerd's Shopping Plaza. 328 Crandon Blvd, Suite 124 33149. **Hours:** 11:30 am-9:45 pm. Closed: 12/25. **Features:** Service is prompt and efficient in the indoor and al fresco seating areas. Start with a soup, such as miso or udon noodle, or an appetite-whetting appetizer, such as wakame, a seaweed salad, or gyoza, pan-fried pork dumplings. Main course sushi and sashimi combinations of 11, 14, 16 or 20 pieces are popular, as are the boats of sushi and sashimi for two, three or four people. Specially priced lunch specials are offered. Casual dress; beer & wine only. **Parking:** on-site. **Cards:** MC, VI.

CIOPPINO   Lunch: $12-$26   Dinner: $27-$43   Phone: 305/365-4500   108
Italian
Location: Crandon Blvd, just e; in The Ritz-Carlton, Key Biscayne. 455 Grand Bay Dr 33149. **Hours:** 7-11 am & 11:30-3 & 6-10 pm. **Reservations:** suggested. **Features:** The chef's seafood and meat courses merge Mediterranean and Spanish cuisines. Adding to the subtle atmosphere are tables that afford views of the courtyard or open kitchen area. Dressy casual; cocktails; entertainment. **Parking:** valet. **Cards:** AX, CB, DC, DS, JC, MC, VI.

♿ 🍴

LA CARRETA   Lunch: $8-$12   Dinner: $14-$25   Phone: 305/365-1177   98
Cuban
Location: Center; just n of Harbour Dr/Ocean Ln. 12 Crandon Blvd 33149. **Hours:** 7 am-midnight. Closed: 12/24, 12/25. **Features:** Part of a small Miami area chain, the three-meal-a-day eatery presents an extensive menu of beef, chicken, pork and seafood preparations. Hungry diners might try the Cuban sampler for fried pork, shredded beef, tamale, ham croquette, plantains, yuca, rice and beans. Also offered is a large selection of sandwiches and a 17-item dessert menu that ranges from rice pudding to coconut custard, tres leches and cheesecake. Casual dress; cocktails. **Parking:** on-site. **Cards:** AX, CB, DC, DS, JC, MC, VI.

LA PIAZETTA   Dinner: $12-$20   Phone: 305/361-8916   102
Italian
Location: SR 913; in The Square Shopping Center. 260 Crandon Blvd, Suite 20-22 33149. **Hours:** 5 pm-11 pm. Closed: 11/23, 12/25. **Features:** Patrons can sample veal, chicken, seafood and pasta entrees at the casual Italian bistro. Casual dress; cocktails. **Parking:** on-site. **Cards:** AX, DS, MC, VI.

LE CROISIC   Dinner: $15-$25   Phone: 305/361-5888   101
French
Location: 1.4 mi e of the bridge; jct Harbor Dr. 180 Crandon Blvd, Suite 117 33149. **Hours:** 6 pm-11 pm. **Reservations:** suggested. **Features:** Tucked away at the end of a small building, the French jewel is well worth searching out. The atmosphere is welcoming and cozy, the food delectable and the wine affordable. Casual dress; beer & wine only. **Parking:** on-site. **Cards:** AX, MC, VI.

(See map and index starting on p. 534)

LINDA B STEAK HOUSE   **Dinner: $17-$30**   **Phone: 305/361-1111**   103
▼▼▼▼
Location: On SR 913, about middle of the island. 320 Crandon Blvd 33149. **Reservations:** required. **Features:** Angus beef, fresh seafood and pasta. A wonderful wine list; all
Steak & Seafood   in an elegant dining room. Dressy casual; cocktails. **Parking:** on-site. **Cards:** AX, MC, VI.

THE OASIS   **Lunch: $3-$10**   **Dinner: $3-$10**   **Phone: 305/361-5709**   99
▼
Location: Jct of Harbor Dr and Crandon Blvd, just w. 19 Harbor Dr 33149. **Hours:** 6 am-9 pm. Closed: 12/25.
Cuban   **Features:** This hole-in-the-wall eatery offers hearty portions, and a Cuban sandwich that even Fidel would love. Casual dress; beer only. **Parking:** on-site. **Cards:** MC, VI.

PURPLE DOLPHIN   **Lunch: $17-$20**   **Dinner: $21-$28**   **Phone: 305/361-2021**   106
▼▼▼ ▼▼▼
Location: 0.3 mi e of Crandon Blvd via Sonesta Dr; in Sonesta Beach Resort Key Biscayne. 350 Ocean Dr 33149.
Seafood   **Hours:** 7 am-11, noon-3 & 6-10:30 pm. **Reservations:** accepted. **Features:** Delightful presentations and well-prepared cuisine are featured at the upscale, intimate bistro. Servers are attentive and personable. Dressy casual; cocktails. **Parking:** valet. **Cards:** AX, DC, DS, MC, VI.

RUSTY PELICAN   **Lunch: $5-$12**   **Dinner: $16-$30**   **Phone: 305/361-3818**   96
AAA
▼▼▼▼
Location: At end of bridge, entrance via marina. 3201 Rickenbacker Cswy 33149. **Hours:** 11:30 am-11 pm, Fri & Sat-midnight, Sun 10:30 am-3 & 5-11 pm. **Reservations:** suggested. **Features:** The nautically appointed family restaurant offers views of the bay and downtown area. Attractive dining rooms, gracious
Seafood   service and a varied menu with many fresh seafood entrees are highlights. Valet parking is available after 5 p.m. Cocktails. **Parking:** valet. **Cards:** AX, CB, DC, DS, MC, VI.

SUNDAYS ON THE BAY   **Lunch: $10-$20**   **Dinner: $10-$20**   **Phone: 305/361-6777**   97
▼▼▼ ▼▼▼
Location: Just s of end of bridge. 5420 Crandon Blvd 33149. **Hours:** 11:30 am-11:30 pm, Fri & Sat-1 am, Sun
Seafood   10:30 am-11 pm. **Reservations:** accepted. **Features:** A longtime favorite, the restaurant offers a good variety of sea fare; the ceviche is a real treat. While the decor is somewhat dated, the lovely setting overlooking the bay more than makes up for it. Casual dress; cocktails. **Parking:** on-site. **Cards:** AX, CB, DC, DS, JC, MC, VI.

SUSHI SIAM   **Lunch: $14-$19**   **Dinner: $22-$35**   **Phone: 305/361-7768**   109
▼▼▼ ▼▼▼
Location: Just s of jct Crandon and McIntyre sts. 632 Crandon Blvd 33149. **Hours:** 11:30 am-3 & 5-11 pm, Sat &
Asian   Sun from 1 pm. **Reservations:** accepted. **Features:** Asian decor is pleasingly appointed in the restaurant, which serves both Thai and Japanese cuisine. On the Japanese side of the spectrum are sushi and sashimi, as well as teriyaki, tempura, soba and udon noodle dinners. The spiciness of Thai cuisine comes alive in house specialties of frog legs, fish curry and pork pad thai. Flavorful soups are not to be missed. Casual dress; beer & wine only. **Parking:** on-site. **Cards:** AX, CB, DC, DS, JC, MC, VI.

TANGO GRILL   **Lunch: $12-$23**   **Dinner: $12-$23**   **Phone: 305/361-1133**   105
▼▼▼ ▼▼▼
Location: On SR 913; about middle of the island; in Key Biscayne Galleria. 328 Crandon Blvd 33149. **Hours:** 11 am-
Argentine   10:30 pm. **Reservations:** suggested. **Features:** In a shopping plaza, the little restaurant prepares both traditional and Argentinean dishes. The dining room is decorated primarily in a hacienda style. Guests can side inside or on the covered sidewalk area. In addition to appetizers and salads, menu entree selections include beef, sausage, chicken, sweetbreads and pasta. Casual dress; beer & wine only. **Parking:** on-site. **Cards:** MC, VI.

TWO DRAGONS RESTAURANT   **Dinner: $14-$25**   **Phone: 305/365-1913**   107
▼▼▼▼
Location: 0.3 mi e of Crandon Blvd via Sonesta Dr; in Sonesta Beach Resort Key Biscayne. 350 Ocean Dr 33149.
Chinese   **Hours:** 5 pm-11 pm. Closed: 11/23. **Reservations:** accepted. **Features:** Oriental decor elements include parasols hanging upside-down from the ceiling and beaded curtains accenting interior booths. The menu lists upscale and traditional selections of Japanese, Chinese and Thai cuisine, as well as sushi. Service is relaxed yet attentive and skilled. Dressy casual; cocktails. **Parking:** valet. **Cards:** AX, DS, MC, VI.

MIAMI LAKES pop. 22,676   (See map and index starting on p. 534)

——— **WHERE TO STAY** ———

COURTYARD BY MARRIOTT-MIAMI LAKES   *Book at aaa.com*   **Phone: (305)556-6665**   23
AAA (SAVE)

12/1-4/16	1P: $139-$209
10/1-11/30	1P: $139-$199
4/17-5/31	1P: $129-$179
6/1-9/30	1P: $119-$159

▼▼▼▼
Small-scale Hotel   **Location:** Nw on service road; jct SR 826 (Palmetto Expwy), exit 154th St. 15700 NW 77th Ct 33016. Fax: 305/556-0282. **Facility:** 151 units. 139 one-bedroom standard units. 12 one-bedroom suites. 4 stories, interior corridors. *Bath:* combo or shower only. **Parking:** on-site. **Terms:** [BP] meal plan available. **Amenities:** high-speed Internet, dual phone lines, voice mail, irons, hair dryers. **Dining:** 6-10 am, Sat & Sun 7 am-noon. **Pool(s):** heated outdoor. **Leisure Activities:** whirlpool, exercise room. **Guest Services:** valet and coin laundry. **Business Services:** meeting rooms, fax (fee). **Cards:** AX, DC, DS, JC, MC, VI. **Special Amenities:** free newspaper.

SOME UNITS

DON SHULA'S GOLF CLUB   *Book at aaa.com*   **Phone: (305)821-1150**   27
▼▼▼▼

1/1-4/30	1P: $159-$165	2P: $159-$165	XP: $10 F13
10/1-11/30	1P: $129-$135	2P: $129-$135	XP: $10 F13
12/1-12/31 & 5/1-9/30	1P: $119-$129	2P: $119-$129	XP: $10 F13

Resort
Small-scale Hotel   **Location:** From SR 826 (Palmetto Expwy), exit NW 154 St, just e. 7601 Miami Lakes Dr 33014. Fax: 305/820-8094. **Facility:** The spacious and comfortable rooms are located in the clubhouse building, which is surrounded by the course. 84 units. 68 one-bedroom standard units. 16 one-bedroom suites. 3 stories, interior corridors. **Parking:** on-site and valet. **Terms:** cancellation fee imposed, [AP], [BP] & [CP] meal plans available, package plans. **Amenities:** voice mail, irons, hair dryers. *Fee:* video games, high-speed Internet. **Dining:** Shula's Steakhouse, see separate listing. **Pool(s):** outdoor. **Leisure Activities:** *Fee:* golf-18 holes. **Guest Services:** gift shop, valet and coin laundry, area transportation. **Business Services:** meeting rooms, business center. **Cards:** AX, DC, MC, VI.

SOME UNITS

(See map and index starting on p. 534)

DON SHULA'S HOTEL   *Book at aaa.com*   Phone: (305)821-1150   26

	1/1-4/30	1P: $179-$209	2P: $179-$209	XP: $10	F13
	10/1-11/30	1P: $145-$165	2P: $145-$165	XP: $10	F13
	12/1-12/31	1P: $145-$159	2P: $145-$159	XP: $10	F13
Large-scale Hotel	5/1-9/30	1P: $135-$155	2P: $135-$155	XP: $10	F13

Location: From SR 826 (Palmetto Expwy), exit NW 154th St, 0.4 mi e to Fairway Dr, s on Miami Lakeway N, then e. 6842 Main St 33014. Fax: 305/820-8094. **Facility:** 205 units. 200 one-bedroom standard units. 5 one-bedroom suites. 3 stories, interior corridors. **Bath:** combo or shower only. **Parking:** on-site and valet. **Terms:** cancellation fee imposed, [AP], [BP] & [CP] meal plans available, package plans. **Amenities:** dual phone lines, voice mail, irons, hair dryers. **Fee:** video games, high-speed Internet. *Some:* safes. **Dining:** Shula's Steak 2, see separate listing. **Pool(s):** outdoor. **Leisure Activities:** whirlpool, jogging, basketball. **Fee:** 9 lighted tennis courts, racquetball courts, massage, professional health programs. **Guest Services:** gift shop, valet laundry, area transportation. **Business Services:** conference facilities, business center. **Cards:** AX, DC, MC, VI.

(ASK) (SOME UNITS) ... FEE

TOWNEPLACE SUITES BY MARRIOTT   *Book at aaa.com*   Phone: (305)512-9191   25

	12/1-3/30	1P: $124-$144
	10/1-11/30	1P: $114-$134
Small-scale Hotel	3/31-9/30	1P: $104-$124

Location: SR 826 (Palmetto Expwy), exit 154th St, 0.4 mi w. 8079 NW 154th St 33016. Fax: 305/512-1284. **Facility:** 95 units. 69 one-bedroom standard units with kitchens. 4 one- and 22 two-bedroom suites ($134-$184) with kitchens. 2-3 stories, interior corridors. **Bath:** combo or shower only. **Parking:** on-site. **Terms:** cancellation fee imposed, pets ($75 fee). **Amenities:** high-speed Internet, dual phone lines, voice mail, irons, hair dryers. **Pool(s):** outdoor. **Leisure Activities:** limited exercise equipment. **Guest Services:** valet and coin laundry. **Business Services:** fax. **Cards:** AX, DC, DS, MC, VI.

(ASK) (SOME UNITS) FEE

WELLESLEY INN (MIAMI LAKES)   *Book at aaa.com*   Phone: (305)821-8274   24

	1/1-4/16	1P: $139-$169
	12/1-12/31	1P: $119-$159
Small-scale Hotel	4/17-11/30	1P: $89-$109

Location: Jct SR 826 (Palmetto Expwy), just w. 7925 NW 154th St 33016. Fax: 305/828-2257. **Facility:** 98 one-bedroom standard units. 4 stories, interior corridors. **Bath:** combo or shower only. **Parking:** on-site. **Terms:** small pets only ($10 extra charge). **Amenities:** voice mail, irons, hair dryers. **Fee:** video games, high-speed Internet. **Pool(s):** heated outdoor. **Guest Services:** valet and coin laundry. **Business Services:** fax (fee). **Cards:** AX, DC, DS, MC, VI.

(SOME UNITS) FEE

─────── WHERE TO DINE ───────

SHULA'S STEAK 2   Lunch: $6-$30   Dinner: $6-$30   Phone: 305/820-8047   32

American

Location: From SR 826 (Palmetto Expwy), exit NW 154th St, 0.4 mi e to Fairway Dr, s on Miami Lakeway N, then e; in Don Shula's Hotel. 6842 Main St 33014. **Hours:** 6:30 am-10:30 & 11:30-midnight, Sun 6:30-10 am, 10:30-2:30 & 3-11 pm. **Reservations:** suggested. **Features:** Energy swells on game nights at this lively steakhouse, which is packed with authentic sports memorabilia. There's nothing better on the menu than the succulent steaks, which are hearty and prepared to diners' specifications. Casual dress; cocktails; entertainment. **Parking:** on-site and valet. **Cards:** AX, DC, MC, VI.

SHULA'S STEAKHOUSE   Lunch: $8-$24   Dinner: $18-$50   Phone: 305/820-8102   33

Steak House

Location: From SR 826 (Palmetto Expwy), exit NW 154 St, just e; in Don Shula's Golf Club. 7601 Miami Lakes Dr/154th St 33014. **Hours:** 11:30 am-2:30 & 6-11 pm. Closed: for lunch Sat & Sun. **Reservations:** suggested. **Features:** Comfortable and clublike, the dining room is decorated with Dolphins football memorabilia. Finish off the 48-ounce porterhouse steak and be recognized on a plaque. The lamb chops and seafood are good, too, as is the to-die-for seven-layer chocolate cake. The dinner menu is also available at lunch. Dressy casual; cocktails. **Parking:** on-site and valet. **Cards:** AX, CB, DC, MC, VI.

MIAMI SPRINGS pop. 13,712   (See maps and indexes starting on p. 534, 542)

─────── WHERE TO STAY ───────

BAYMONT INN & SUITES MIAMI-AIRPORT   *Book at aaa.com*   Phone: (305)871-1777   39

	1/1-4/30	1P: $119-$149	XP: $7	F18
	5/1-11/30	1P: $79-$99	XP: $7	F18
Small-scale Hotel	12/1-12/31	1P: $75-$85	XP: $7	F18

Location: SR 953 (Le Jeune Rd) at jct SR 112. 3501 NW Le Jeune Rd 33142. Fax: 305/871-8080. **Facility:** 145 units. 140 one-bedroom standard units. 5 one-bedroom suites. 4 stories, interior corridors. **Bath:** combo or shower only. **Parking:** on-site. **Terms:** [ECP] meal plan available, small pets only. **Amenities:** video games (fee), dual phone lines, voice mail, irons, hair dryers. **Pool(s):** outdoor. **Guest Services:** valet and coin laundry. **Business Services:** meeting rooms, fax (fee). **Cards:** AX, CB, DC, DS, MC, VI. *(See color ad p 560)*

(ASK) (SOME UNITS)

(See maps and indexes starting on p. 534, 542)

COMFORT INN & SUITES-MIAMI INTERNATIONAL
AIRPORT   *Book at aaa.com*

◇◇◇ (SAVE)
◇◇◇◇◇

			Phone: (305)871-6000	37
12/1-4/30 [ECP]	1P: $129-$249	2P: $139-$259	XP: $10	F18
5/1-11/30 [ECP]	1P: $99-$139	2P: $109-$149	XP: $10	F18

Location: Between Le Jeune Rd and SR 826 (Palmetto Expwy). 5301 NW 36th St 33166. Fax: 305/871-4971. **Facility:** 274 units. 259 one-bedroom standard units. 13 one- and 2 two-bedroom suites ($119-$299). 2-11 stories, interior corridors. *Bath:* combo or shower only. **Parking:** on-site. **Terms:** package plans, small pets only ($25 fee). **Amenities:** voice mail, irons, hair dryers. *Fee:* video games, safes. *Some:* high-speed Internet. **Dining:** 11 am-midnight. **Pool(s):** heated outdoor. **Leisure Activities:** tennis court, racquetball court, exercise room, volleyball. *Fee:* golf privileges. **Guest Services:** gift shop, valet and coin laundry, airport transportation-Miami International Airport, area transportation (fee)-Port of Miami. *Fee:* beauty salon. **Business Services:** meeting rooms, business center. **Cards:** AX, CB, DC, DS, JC, MC, VI. **Special Amenities:** early check-in/late check-out. *(See color ad p 552)*

SOME UNITS

Small-scale Hotel

[S] ✈ 🅿️ 🍽 🍸 🗄 🏊 ⊠ 📷 [DATA PORT] 💻 / ⊠ 📱 🖥 /
FEE

DAYS INN MIAMI AIRPORT NORTH   *Book at aaa.com*

◇◇◇◇◇

			Phone: (305)888-3661	35
10/1-11/30	1P: $65-$99	2P: $75-$139		
12/1-4/15	1P: $65-$99	2P: $75-$129		
4/16-9/30	1P: $55-$99	2P: $65-$119		

Small-scale Hotel   **Location:** Between Le Jeune Rd and SR 826 (Palmetto Expwy) NW 36th St 33166. Fax: 305/887-1194. **Facility:** 145 one-bedroom standard units. 1-2 stories (no elevator), interior/exterior corridors. *Bath:* combo or shower only. **Parking:** on-site. **Terms:** 3 day cancellation notice, weekly rates available. **Amenities:** voice mail, hair dryers, *Some:* irons. **Pool(s):** outdoor. **Guest Services:** coin laundry, area transportation. **Business Services:** fax (fee). **Cards:** AX, CB, DC, DS, JC, MC, VI.

SOME UNITS

(ASK) [S] ✈ 🍽 🍸 🏊 📷 / ⊠ 📱 🖥 /

EMBASSY SUITES MIAMI INTERNATIONAL
AIRPORT   *Book at aaa.com*

◇◇◇◇◇

			Phone: (305)634-5000	38
1/1-4/30 [BP]	1P: $119-$229	2P: $119-$229	XP: $10	F18
12/1-12/31 & 10/1-11/30 [BP]	1P: $129-$139	2P: $129-$139	XP: $10	F18
5/1-9/30 [BP]	1P: $109-$139	2P: $109-$139	XP: $10	F18

Large-scale Hotel   **Location:** Jct SR 112 and 953 (Le Jeune Rd). 3974 NW South River Dr 33142 (3974 MW South River Dr, MIAMI). Fax: 305/635-9499. **Facility:** 316 one-bedroom suites. 10 stories, interior corridors. *Bath:* combo or shower only. **Parking:** on-site (fee). **Terms:** cancellation fee imposed, package plans. **Amenities:** dual phone lines, voice mail, irons, hair dryers. *Fee:* video games, high-speed Internet. **Pool(s):** heated outdoor. **Leisure Activities:** whirlpool, exercise room. **Guest Services:** gift shop, complimentary evening beverages, valet and coin laundry. **Business Services:** meeting rooms, business center. **Cards:** AX, CB, DC, DS, JC, MC, VI.

SOME UNITS

✈ 🍽 🍸 🎿 🗄 🏊 📷 [DATA PORT] 📱 🖥 💻 / ⊠ [VCR] /

Ask Us About
Our Special AAA
Discount Rates

(See maps and indexes starting on p. 534, 542)

HOLIDAY INN EXPRESS MIAMI INTERNATIONAL
AIRPORT *Book at aaa.com* Phone: (305)887-2153 [36]

AAA SAVE

1/1-4/30	1P: $179-$189	2P: $189-$199	XP: $10	F21
12/1-12/31	1P: $169-$179	2P: $179-$189	XP: $10	F21
5/1-11/30	1P: $159-$169	2P: $169-$179	XP: $10	F21

Small-scale Hotel **Location:** Between Le Jeune Rd and SR 826 (Palmetto Expwy). 5125 NW 36th St 33166. Fax: 305/887-3559. **Facility:** 110 one-bedroom standard units. 6 stories, interior corridors. *Bath:* combo or shower only. **Parking:** on-site. **Terms:** cancellation fee imposed, package plans, small pets only ($25 fee). **Amenities:** video games (fee), voice mail, safes, irons, hair dryers. **Guest Services:** valet and coin laundry, airport transportation-Miami International Airport, area transportation (fee)-Port of Miami. **Business Services:** fax (fee). **Cards:** AX, CB, DC, DS, JC, MC, VI. **Special Amenities:** early check-in/late check-out. *(See color ad p 553)*

SOME UNITS

HOLIDAY INN-MIAMI INTERNATIONAL AIRPORT *Book at aaa.com* Phone: (305)885-1941 [32]

AAA SAVE

12/23-4/16	1P: $139-$199
12/1-12/22 & 4/17-11/30	1P: $119-$179

Small-scale Hotel **Location:** Le Jeune Rd, jct NW 36th St and SR 112. 1111 S Royal Poinciana Blvd 33166. Fax: 305/884-1881. **Facility:** 219 one-bedroom standard units. 9 stories, interior corridors. *Bath:* combo or shower only. **Parking:** on-site. **Terms:** cancellation fee imposed, [AP] & [BP] meal plans available, package plans. **Amenities:** video games (fee), voice mail, irons, hair dryers. **Dining:** 6:30 am-2 & 5:30-11 pm, cocktails. **Pool(s):** outdoor. **Leisure Activities:** exercise room. **Guest Services:** gift shop, valet and coin laundry, airport transportation-Miami International Airport, area transportation-Port of Miami. **Business Services:** meeting rooms, fax (fee). **Cards:** AX, DC, DS, MC, VI. **Special Amenities:** free newspaper. *(See color ad p 610)*

SOME UNITS

HOMESTEAD STUDIO SUITES
HOTEL-MIAMI/AIRPORT/MIAMI SPRINGS *Book at aaa.com* Phone: (305)870-0448 [34]

1/2-4/15	1P: $79-$104	2P: $84-$109	XP: $5	F17
12/1-1/1 & 4/16-11/30	1P: $69-$89	2P: $74-$94	XP: $5	F17

Small-scale Hotel **Location:** I-95 to SR 112 W, exit NW 36th St, then w, right on Palmetto Dr, then w; between Le Jeune Rd and SR 826 (Palmetto Expwy); behind Clarion Hotel. 101 Fairway Dr 33166. Fax: 305/871-5044. **Facility:** 103 units. 81 one-bedroom standard units with efficiencies. 22 one-bedroom suites with efficiencies. 3 stories, interior corridors. *Bath:* combo or shower only. **Parking:** on-site. **Terms:** small pets only ($25 fee). **Amenities:** dual phone lines, voice mail, irons, hair dryers. *Fee:* video games, high-speed Internet. **Pool(s):** outdoor. **Leisure Activities:** tennis court, limited exercise equipment. **Guest Services:** valet and coin laundry, area transportation. **Business Services:** fax (fee). **Cards:** AX, DC, DS, MC, VI.

SOME UNITS

RED ROOF INN MIAMI AIRPORT *Book at aaa.com* Phone: (305)871-4221 [40]

12/1-12/31	1P: $80-$100	2P: $85-$100	XP: $5	F18
1/1-4/29	1P: $79-$95	2P: $84-$95	XP: $5	F18
9/30-11/30	1P: $74-$95	2P: $79-$95	XP: $5	F18
4/30-9/29	1P: $58-$79	2P: $63-$79	XP: $5	F18

Small-scale Hotel **Location:** On SR 953 at SR 112; 0.5 mi n of airport entrance. 3401 NW Le Jeune Rd 33142. Fax: 305/871-3933. **Facility:** 200 one-bedroom standard units. 4-5 stories, interior corridors. *Bath:* combo or shower only. **Parking:** on-site. **Terms:** small pets only. **Amenities:** video games (fee), high-speed Internet, voice mail. **Pool(s):** outdoor. **Guest Services:** valet and coin laundry, area transportation. **Business Services:** meeting rooms. **Cards:** AX, CB, DC, DS, MC, VI.

SOME UNITS

SLEEP INN-MIAMI AIRPORT *Book at aaa.com* Phone: (305)871-7553 [33]

AAA SAVE

2/1-4/30	1P: $109-$169	2P: $109-$169	XP: $10	F18
12/1-1/31 & 5/1-11/30	1P: $89-$139	2P: $89-$139	XP: $10	F18

Small-scale Hotel **Location:** I-95 to SR 112 W, exit NW 36th St, then w, right on Palmetto Dr, then w; between Le Jeune Rd and SR 826 (Palmetto Expwy). Located behind Comfort Inn & Suites. 105 Fairway Dr 33166. Fax: 305/871-5441. **Facility:** 119 one-bedroom standard units. 3 stories, interior corridors. *Bath:* shower only. **Parking:** on-site. **Terms:** small pets only ($25 fee). **Amenities:** voice mail, irons, hair dryers. *Fee:* video games, safes. **Pool(s):** heated outdoor. **Leisure Activities:** barbecue grills, volleyball. **Guest Services:** valet and coin laundry, airport transportation-Miami International Airport, area transportation (fee)-Port of Miami. **Business Services:** fax (fee). **Cards:** AX, CB, DC, DS, JC, MC, VI. **Special Amenities:** early check-in/late check-out. *(See color ad p 552)*

SOME UNITS

———— WHERE TO DINE ————

BANGKOK SUSHI
Lunch: $6-$17 **Dinner:** $8-$17 Phone: 305-863-8822 [12]

Thai

Location: Just w of traffic circle. 7 Westward Dr 33166. **Hours:** 11:30 am-3 & 5-10 pm. Closed major holidays; also Sun. **Features:** The small, tight dining room has a low-key Oriental theme. On the menu are well-prepared and flavorful Thai and Japanese dishes, including freshly made sushi. Casual dress; beer & wine only. **Parking:** no self-parking. **Cards:** AX, MC, VI.

BASILICO
Lunch: $6-$9 **Dinner:** $10-$15 Phone: 305/871-3585 [22]

Italian

Location: Between SR 953 (Le Jeune Rd) and SR 826 (Palmetto Expwy). 5879 NW 36th St 33166. **Hours:** 11:30 am-3 & 6-10 pm, Fri & Sat-11 pm. Closed major holidays; also Sun. **Features:** Warm colors and some upscale treatments help create an intimate atmosphere in the small dining room. The chef's traditional pasta, meat and seafood dishes are flavorful. The attentive and professional staff helps promote an enjoyable dining experience. Casual dress; beer & wine only. **Parking:** on-site. **Cards:** AX, DC, MC, VI.

(See maps and indexes starting on p. 534, 542)

CISCO'S CAFE
▼▼ ▼▼
Mexican
DS, MC, VI.

Lunch: $5-$16   **Dinner:** $8-$16   **Phone:** 305/871-2764   ㉓
Location: Jct SR 826 (Palmetto Expwy) and NW 36th St, 1.6 mi e. 5911 NW 36th St 33166. **Hours:** 11:30 am-10 pm, Fri & Sat-11 pm, Sun 3 pm-10 pm. **Reservations:** accepted. **Features:** Examples of the traditional Mexican fare include huge fajita dishes sold by the pound or half-pound. Lunch patrons can sample from a buffet with a multitude of freshly prepared items. Casual dress; cocktails. **Parking:** on-site. **Cards:** AX, DC,

COZY CORNER
▼
American

Lunch: $4-$8   **Dinner:** $6-$9   **Phone:** 305/884-1880   ⑱
Location: 1 blk off the traffic circle. 90 Westward Dr 33166. **Hours:** 5 am-9 pm, Sat from 6 am, Sun 6 am-3 pm. Closed: 11/23, 12/25. **Features:** The eatery has the look and feel of a small-town diner, as well as both booth and counter seating. The menu lists home-style comfort foods and sandwiches that are nicely prepared and flavorful. Casual dress. **Parking:** on-site. **Cards:** AX, DC, MC, VI.

GARDEN RESTAURANT
▼▼ ▼▼
Italian

Lunch: $7-$15   **Dinner:** $7-$15   **Phone:** 305/884-6544   ⑬
Location: Jct Curtiss Pkwy, just sw. 17 Westward Dr 33166. **Hours:** 11 am-3 & 5-10 pm, Sat from 5 pm. Closed: 11/23, 12/25; also Sun. **Features:** Diners can sample pasta, chicken, seafood and vegetarian dishes in the cozy Italian bistro. Casual dress; entertainment. **Parking:** street. **Cards:** DS, MC, VI.

HARVEST MOON BISTRO
▼▼
American

Lunch: $4-$7   **Phone:** 305/863-0707   ⑰
Location: On the traffic circle. 102 Curtiss Pkwy 33166. **Hours:** 9 am-5 pm, Sat from 11 am. Closed: 1/1, 12/25; also Sun. **Features:** Guests order and pay inside, then sit outside on the patio to dine and relax. This small operation specializes in salads, sandwiches, melts and wraps, as well as vitamin juices and a variety of fruit smoothies. Casual dress. **Parking:** no self-parking.

HOLLEMAN'S
▼▼ ▼▼
Steak & Seafood
cocktails. **Parking:** on-site. **Cards:** CB, DC, DS, MC, VI.

Lunch: $6-$14   **Dinner:** $12-$26   **Phone:** 305/888-8097   ⑪
Location: Just n of traffic circle. 1 Curtiss Pkwy 33166. **Hours:** 11 am-10 pm, Fri-11 pm, Sat 5 pm-11 pm, Sun 5 pm-10 pm. Closed: 11/23, 12/25. **Reservations:** accepted. **Features:** For more than 20 years, the casual restaurant has been a fixture on the area's dining scene. In addition to hand-cut, charbroiled steaks and fresh seafood prepared in varied styles, the menu lists ribs, frog legs, chicken and pasta. Casual dress;

PATIO TIPICO
▼
Latino

Lunch: $3-$25   **Dinner:** $3-$25   **Phone:** 305/805-0855   ㉑
Location: Corner of Forest Dr; n of airport. 4591 NW 36th St 33166. **Hours:** 8 am-11:30 pm, Fri & Sat-2 am. **Features:** Although quaint and simple, this restaurant offers tasty Latino fare for the more adventurous diner. Casual dress; cocktails. **Parking:** on-site. **Cards:** AX, CB, DC, DS, JC, MC, VI.

PERU PLACE
▼▼ ▼▼
Peruvian

Lunch: $5-$7   **Dinner:** $6-$12   **Phone:** 305/863-7233   ⑳
Location: Between Le Jeune Rd and SR 826 (Palmetto Expwy). 4579 NW 36 St 33166. **Hours:** 10:30 am-10 pm, Fri & Sat-11 pm. **Features:** The true Peruvian restaurant specializes in seafood, including seviche, parihuelas or choritos. Patrons get their fill for a moderate price. Casual dress; beer & wine only. **Parking:** on-site. **Cards:** DS, MC, VI.

THAI PALACE
▼▼ ▼▼
Thai
Casual dress; beer & wine only. **Parking:** on-site. **Cards:** AX, MC, VI.

Lunch: $6-$8   **Dinner:** $9-$17   **Phone:** 305/887-4558   ⑲
Location: Jct SR 953 (SE 8th Ave) and NW 36th St, just w. 4441 NW 36th St 33166. **Hours:** 11:30 am-3 & 4:30-10 pm, Sat & Sun from 4:30 pm. Closed major holidays. **Reservations:** accepted. **Features:** Thai and Japanese cuisine features prominently on the lengthy menu, which includes a selection of vegetarian dishes and sushi. Among daily lunch specials is a tasty and filling three-course meal, which is reasonably priced.

THAI RAMA SUSHI
▼▼ ▼▼
Thai
beer & wine only. **Parking:** street. **Cards:** DC, DS, MC, VI.

Lunch: $6-$15   **Dinner:** $8-$15   **Phone:** 305/884-4390   ⑭
Location: On the traffic circle. 61 Curtiss Pkwy 33166. **Hours:** 11:30 am-2:30 & 5-10 pm. Closed: 11/23, 12/25; also Sun. **Features:** Although the restaurant specializes in freshly made sushi, it also serves Thai and Japanese dishes. Food is well-prepared and flavorful, with many items prepared in house. The dining room is decorated in a subdued Oriental theme, with woods, wall hangings and decorative items. Casual dress;

TREATS CAFE
▼▼ ▼▼
American

Lunch: $5-$7   **Dinner:** $8-$12   **Phone:** 305/883-2233   ⑯
Location: Just w of traffic circle. 261 Westward Dr 33166. **Hours:** 11 am-7 pm. Closed: Sat & Sun. **Features:** Specialty sandwiches made fresh on order pair well with a thick shake made from real ice cream. Among dinner options are baby back ribs, London broil, pork Marsala and dolphin fillet. Casual dress. **Parking:** street.

WESTWARD CAFE
▼
American

Lunch: $3-$8   **Phone:** 305/888-8550   ⑮
Location: Jct Curtiss Pkwy traffic circle, just sw. 195 Westwood Dr 33166. **Hours:** 7 am-3 pm. Closed: 11/23, 12/25. **Features:** The small storefront delicatessen's menu covers breakfast fare, as well as a lengthy list of sandwiches and hot entrees for lunch. Casual dress. **Parking:** street. **Cards:** MC, VI.

NORTH BAY VILLAGE pop. 6,733 (See maps and indexes starting on p. 534, 545)

———— WHERE TO STAY ————

BEST WESTERN ON THE BAY INN & MARINA *Book at aaa.com* Phone: (305)865-7100 36

	12/20-2/20 [CP]	1P: $74-$114	2P: $74-$114	XP: $5	F12
	12/1-12/19 & 2/21-11/30 [CP]	1P: $64-$104	2P: $69-$109	XP: $5	F12

Location: 2 mi w of SR A1A (Collins Ave). 1819 79th St Cswy 33141. **Fax:** 305/868-3483. **Facility:** 116 one-bedroom standard units. 5 stories, exterior corridors. **Parking:** on-site. **Terms:** 3 night minimum stay - seasonal, 3 day cancellation notice. **Amenities:** voice mail, safes, irons, hair dryers. *Some:* high-speed Internet. **Dining:** 11 am-1 am, cocktails. **Pool(s):** heated outdoor. **Leisure Activities:** *Fee:* boat dock. **Guest Services:** coin laundry. **Business Services:** meeting rooms, fax (fee). **Cards:** AX, CB, DC, DS, JC, MC, VI. **Special Amenities:** free continental breakfast and free local telephone calls. *(See color ad p 572)*

SOME UNITS

———— WHERE TO DINE ————

THE CRAB HOUSE SEAFOOD RESTAURANT **Lunch:** $7-$13 **Dinner:** $12-$39 **Phone:** 305/868-7085 36

Seafood

Location: 2.1 mi w of SR A1A (Collins Ave). 1551 79th St Cswy 33141. **Hours:** 11:30 am-11 pm. **Features:** The atmosphere is boisterous and fun amid the hanging fish, crabs and plants that contribute to an unmistakable nautical feel. The all-you-can-eat seafood bar is always a popular choice, but don't rule out the Alaskan trio and several varieties of shrimp. Casual dress; cocktails. **Parking:** on-site. **Cards:** AX, CB, DC, DS, MC, VI.

OGGI CAFFE RISTORANTE ITALIANO **Lunch:** $8-$18 **Dinner:** $14-$36 **Phone:** 305/866-1238 37

Italian

Location: 2 mi w of SR A1A (Collins Ave). 1740 79th St Cswy 33141. **Hours:** 11:30 am-2:30 & 6-11 pm. **Reservations:** accepted. **Features:** This cute, cozy cafe serves up big satisfaction when it comes to Italian food; when you walk out you will feel like you have been on a trip to Italy. Dressy casual; beer & wine only. **Parking:** on-site. **Cards:** AX, MC, VI.

NORTH MIAMI pop. 59,880 (See map and index starting on p. 534)

———— WHERE TO STAY ————

BEST WESTERN WINDSOR INN Phone: 305/891-7350 20

All Year 1P: $90-$189

Small-scale Hotel

Location: I-95, exit 10A, 2.8 mi e; on US 1 at NE 125th St and Broad Cswy. 12210 Biscayne Blvd 33181. **Fax:** 305/891-6322. **Facility:** 98 one-bedroom standard units. 5 stories, interior corridors. *Bath:* combo or shower only. **Parking:** on-site. **Terms:** cancellation fee imposed. **Amenities:** high-speed Internet, voice mail, irons, hair dryers. **Pool(s):** outdoor, wading. **Guest Services:** valet laundry. **Business Services:** meeting rooms, fax (fee). **Cards:** AX, CB, DC, DS, JC, MC, VI.

SOME UNITS

GOLDEN GLADES INN & CONFERENCE CENTER Phone: (305)945-2621 19

All Year 1P: $89-$109 2P: $99-$119 XP: $10 F18

Small-scale Hotel

Location: I-95, exit 12C (SR 826); just e of Florida Tpke terminus and Palmetto Expwy. 16500 NW 2nd Ave 33169. **Fax:** 305/945-3317. **Facility:** 141 one-bedroom standard units. 4 stories, interior/exterior corridors. **Parking:** on-site. **Terms:** check-in 4 pm, 3 day cancellation notice-fee imposed. **Amenities:** voice mail, safes, irons, hair dryers. **Pool(s):** outdoor. **Leisure Activities:** exercise room. **Guest Services:** coin laundry. **Business Services:** meeting rooms, fax (fee). **Cards:** AX, CB, DC, DS, MC, VI.

SOME UNITS

HOLIDAY INN NORTH MIAMI GOLDEN GLADES *Book at aaa.com* Phone: 305/949-1441 18

All Year 1P: $129-$159 2P: $129-$159 XP: $10 F18

Large-scale Hotel

Location: I-95, exit 12C (SR 826), just e of I-95, Florida Tpke terminus and Palmetto Expwy. 148 NW 167th St 33169. **Fax:** 305/956-9693. **Facility:** 163 one-bedroom standard units. 7 stories, interior corridors. *Bath:* combo or shower only. **Parking:** on-site. **Terms:** 2 night minimum stay - weekends, [AP] meal plan available. **Amenities:** voice mail, safes, irons, hair dryers. **Dining:** 7 am-1 pm & 5-10 pm, cocktails. **Pool(s):** outdoor, wading. **Leisure Activities:** limited exercise equipment. **Guest Services:** valet and coin laundry. **Business Services:** meeting rooms, administrative services, fax (fee). **Cards:** AX, DC, DS, MC, VI. **Special Amenities:** free newspaper.

SOME UNITS

NORTH MIAMI BEACH pop. 40,786 (See map and index starting on p. 545)

———— WHERE TO DINE ————

FUDDRUCKERS WORLD'S GREATEST HAMBURGER **Lunch:** $5-$13 **Dinner:** $5-$13 **Phone:** 305/933-3572 23

American

Location: On US 1/Biscayne Blvd; just s of Miami Gardens Dr; in Aventura Plaza. 17985 Biscayne Blvd 33160. **Hours:** 11 am-11 pm, Fri & Sat-midnight. **Features:** This is where size matters: the eatery offers average burgers and real big burgers, along with a fixin's bar for your burger or sandwich so you can make it bigger or petite. A great place for burgers and fun, they have a video game area for the little kids and the big kids as well. Casual dress; cocktails. **Parking:** on-site. **Cards:** AX, DS, MC, VI.

(See map and index starting on p. 545)

TUNA'S WATERFRONT GRILLE **Lunch:** $8-$16   **Dinner:** $15-$28   **Phone:** 305/945-2567   [24]

Seafood

DS, MC, VI.

Location: 0.6 mi n of SR 826. 17201 Biscayne Blvd 33160. **Hours:** 11:30 am-2 am. **Reservations:** suggested **Features:** Dock your boat and enjoy live Maine lobster and an assortment of fresh seafood. Each mea starts with a bowl of coleslaw in a honey mustard dressing. Pleasant service and an on-site seafood marke make this dockside dining experience special. Casual dress; cocktails. **Parking:** on-site. **Cards:** AX, DC

SOUTH MIAMI pop. 10,741   (See map and index starting on p. 534)

———— **WHERE TO STAY** ————

BEST WESTERN SOUTH MIAMI   *Book at aaa.com*   **Phone:** (305)667-6664   [58]

AAA SAVE

Small-scale Hotel

12/1-4/21	1P: $130-$149	2P: $130-$149
10/1-11/30	1P: $119-$139	2P: $119-$139
4/22-9/30	1P: $109-$119	2P: $109-$119

Location: Off US 1, w on SW 72nd St, n on 59th Pl, then w. 5959 SW 71st St 33143. Fax: 305/667-5424 **Facility:** 117 one-bedroom standard units. 4 stories, interior corridors. *Bath:* combo or shower only **Parking:** on-site (fee). **Terms:** 7 day cancellation notice-fee imposed. **Amenities:** voice mail, safes (fee) irons, hair dryers. **Dining:** 6:30 am-10:30 pm, cocktails. **Pool(s):** outdoor. **Leisure Activities:** exercise room. **Guest Services** airport transportation-Miami International Airport, area transportation-Port of Miami. **Business Services:** meeting rooms, fax (fee). **Cards:** AX, CB, DC, DS, MC, VI. **Special Amenities:** free local telephone calls and free newspaper. *(See color ad below)*

SOME UNITS

———— **WHERE TO DINE** ————

BLU - LA PIZZERIA DEL SOLE   **Lunch:** $8-$14   **Dinner:** $8-$14   **Phone:** 305/666-9285   [114]

Italian

Location: Just se of US 1, exit Sunset Dr. 7201 SW 59th Ave 33143. **Hours:** 11:30 am-11 pm, Fri & Sat-midnight Closed: 11/23; also for lunch 12/25. **Reservations:** not accepted. **Features:** The house specialty at this casual and bustling eatery is thin crust pizzas cooked on a wood-burning fire. Indoor or terrrace dining is available. Casual dress; cocktails. **Parking:** valet. **Cards:** AX, CB, DC, DS, JC, MC, VI.

KHOURY'S   **Lunch:** $4-$12   **Dinner:** $11-$23   **Phone:** 305/662-7707   [115]

Lebanese

Cards: AX, DC, MC, VI.

Location: Just e off US 1. 5887 SW 73rd St 33143. **Hours:** 11 am-10 pm, Fri & Sat-11 pm, Sun 1 pm-10 pm **Features:** This family-owned establishment is a great spot for authentic Lebanese cuisine prepared with the freshest ingredients. Baba ghanouj, crusty falafel, skewered lamb grilled over charcoal and kafta kebab are among the wonderfully executed and delicious choices. Casual dress; beer & wine only. **Parking:**

PICNIC'S AT ALLEN'S DRUGS   **Lunch:** $7-$8   **Dinner:** $7-$8   **Phone:** 305/665-6964   [112]

American

Cards: MC, VI.

Location: Corner of SW 57th Ave and Bird Rd (SW 40th St). 4000 Red Rd 33155. **Hours:** 6 am-8 pm, Sat-5 pm Sun-3 pm. Closed: 11/23, 12/25. **Reservations:** not accepted. **Features:** This vintage 50s style diner located in one end of a drugstore, serves up chili dogs, burgers, roasted turkey sandwiches, soups, salads and cheese melts; quench your thirst with an ice cream soda or malt. Casual dress. **Parking:** on-site

TRATTORIA SOLE   **Lunch:** $8-$16   **Dinner:** $11-$23   **Phone:** 305/666-9392   [113]

AAA

Italian

Location: Just se of US 1. 5894 Sunset Dr 33143. **Hours:** noon-3 & 6-10:30 pm, Fri & Sat-11:30 pm, Sun 6 pm 10:30 pm. Closed: 11/23; also for lunch 12/25. **Reservations:** accepted. **Features:** This chic and stylish restaurant serves up authentic Italian cuisine, including a variety of carefully prepared pastas, meat and grilled fish dishes. Casual dress; cocktails. **Parking:** valet. **Cards:** AX, CB, DC, DS, JC, MC, VI.

SUNNY ISLES BEACH pop. 15,315   (See map and index starting on p. 545)

──── WHERE TO STAY ────

ACQUALINA, A ROSEWOOD RESORT   **Phone:** 305/918-8000

	(fyi)	12/1-4/29	1P: $675-$5000	2P: $675-$5000	XP: $50	F16
		4/30-5/27 & 10/1-11/30	1P: $525-$5000	2P: $525-$5000	XP: $50	F16
Large-scale Hotel		5/28-9/30	1P: $425-$5000	2P: $425-$5000	XP: $50	F16

Too new to rate, opening scheduled for November 2005. **Location:** Oceanfront. On SR A1A (Collins Ave); corner of 178th St. 17875 Collins Ave 33160. Fax: 305/918-8100. **Amenities:** 97 units, pets, restaurant, microwaves, refrigerators, pool, exercise facilities. **Terms:** check-in 4 pm, 14 day cancellation notice-fee imposed. **Cards:** AX, DC, DS, MC, VI.

BEST WESTERN THUNDERBIRD BEACH RESORT   *Book at aaa.com*   **Phone:** (305)931-7700   **26**

AAA (SAVE)	12/23-4/30	1P: $109-$129	2P: $109-$129	XP: $10	F
▼▼▼	12/1-12/22 & 7/1-11/30	1P: $89-$99	2P: $89-$99	XP: $10	F
	5/1-6/30	1P: $79-$89	2P: $79-$89	XP: $10	F

Small-scale Hotel **Location:** Oceanfront. On SR A1A (Collins Ave), just s of SR 856. 18401 Collins Ave 33160. Fax: 305/932-7521. **Facility:** 180 one-bedroom standard units, some with efficiencies. 4 stories, interior corridors. *Bath:* combo or shower only. **Parking:** on-site (fee) and valet. **Terms:** cancellation fee imposed, $6 service charge. **Amenities:** high-speed Internet, voice mail, safes (fee), irons, hair dryers. **Dining:** 2 restaurants, 7 am-11 pm, cocktails, nightclub, entertainment. **Pool(s):** heated outdoor, wading. **Leisure Activities:** whirlpool, limited beach access, recreation programs in winter, exercise room, shuffleboard, volleyball. **Guest Services:** gift shop, valet and coin laundry, area transportation-South Beach, Bal Harbour Aventura Mall. **Business Services:** meeting rooms, fax (fee). **Cards:** AX, DC, DS, MC, VI. **Special Amenities: free local telephone calls and free newspaper.**

SOME UNITS

[icons]

DOUBLETREE OCEAN POINT RESORT &
SPA-MIAMI BEACH NORTH   *Book at aaa.com*   **Phone:** (786)528-2500   **29**

	12/25-4/20	1P: $189-$479	2P: $189-$479	XP: $20	F18
	4/21-11/30	1P: $109-$369	2P: $109-$369	XP: $20	F18
Large-scale Hotel	12/1-12/24	1P: $119-$349	2P: $119-$349	XP: $20	F18

Location: Oceanfront. On SR A1A (Collins Ave), just n of 172nd Ave. 17375 Collins Ave 33160. Fax: 786/528-2536. **Facility:** 152 units. 39 one-bedroom standard units. 73 one- and 40 two-bedroom suites with kitchens and whirlpools. 6-27 stories, interior corridors. *Bath:* combo or shower only. **Parking:** valet. **Terms:** check-in 4 pm, 3 day cancellation notice-fee imposed, package plans. **Amenities:** dual phone lines, voice mail, safes, irons, hair dryers. *Fee:* video library, high-speed Internet. *Some:* CD players. **Pool(s):** heated outdoor. **Leisure Activities:** saunas, whirlpools, steamrooms, lifeguard on duty, limited beach access, rental paddleboats, rental sailboats, spa, volleyball. **Guest Services:** gift shop, valet and coin laundry. **Business Services:** meeting rooms, business center. **Cards:** AX, CB, DC, DS, JC, MC, VI.

SOME UNITS

[icons]   FEE

(See map and index starting on p. 545)

MARCO POLO BEACH RESORT, A RAMADA PLAZA *Book at aaa.com*   Phone: (305)932-2233   25
12/21-3/31	1P: $129-$299	2P: $129-$299	XP: $25	F17
12/1-12/20 & 4/1-11/30	1P: $69-$199	2P: $69-$199	XP: $25	F17

Location: Oceanfront. SR A1A at 192nd St. 19201 Collins Ave 33160. Fax: 305/935-5009. **Facility:** 247 one-bedroom standard units, some with efficiencies. 12 stories, interior corridors. **Parking:** valet. **Terms:** [AP] meal plan available, package plans. **Amenities:** voice mail, safes, irons, hair dryers. **Pool(s):** heated outdoor, wading. **Leisure Activities:** sauna, steamroom, limited beach access, exercise room, spa, shuffleboard, volleyball. **Guest Services:** gift shop, valet and coin laundry. **Business Services:** meeting rooms, business center. **Cards:** AX, CB, DC, DS, MC, VI.

SOME UNITS

NEWPORT BEACHSIDE HOTEL & RESORT   Phone: (305)949-1300   30
12/16-4/15	1P: $139-$325	2P: $139-$325	XP: $10	F18
12/1-12/15 & 4/16-11/30	1P: $99-$249	2P: $99-$249	XP: $10	F18

Location: Oceanfront. SR A1A, jct SR 826 and Sunny Isles Blvd. 16701 Collins Ave 33160. Fax: 305/947-5873. **Facility:** 300 units. 78 one-bedroom standard units, some with whirlpools. 138 one- and 84 two-bedroom suites with whirlpools. 12 stories, interior corridors. *Bath:* combo or shower only. **Terms:** [AP], [BP], [CP] & [MAP] meal plans available, $5 service charge, small pets only. **Amenities:** voice mail, safes, irons, hair dryers. **Dining:** 4 restaurants, 7 am-2 am, cocktails. **Pool(s):** heated outdoor, wading. **Leisure Activities:** whirlpool, fishing, fishing pier, recreation programs, playground, exercise room, volleyball. *Fee:* scuba diving, snorkeling, charter fishing, massage, game room. **Guest Services:** gift shop, coin laundry. **Business Services:** meeting rooms, fax (fee). **Cards:** AX, CB, DC, DS, MC, VI. *(See color ad p 580)*

SOME UNITS

TRAVELODGE MONACO OCEANFRONT RESORT   *Book at aaa.com*   Phone: (305)932-2100   28
12/23-4/30	1P: $109-$129	2P: $109-$129	XP: $10	F
12/1-12/22 & 5/1-11/30	1P: $79-$89	2P: $79-$89	XP: $10	F

Location: Oceanfront. SR A1A at 175th St. 17501 Collins Ave 33160. Fax: 305/931-5519. **Facility:** 110 units. 109 one-bedroom standard units. 1 one-bedroom suite. 2 stories (no elevator), interior/exterior corridors. *Bath:* combo or shower only. **Parking:** on-site (fee). **Terms:** cancellation fee imposed, $6 service charge. **Amenities:** safes (fee), hair dryers. **Dining:** 7 am-2 & 5-10 pm, cocktails, entertainment. **Pool(s):** heated outdoor, wading. **Leisure Activities:** limited beach access, recreation programs, horseshoes, shuffleboard. *Fee:* game room. **Guest Services:** coin laundry. **Cards:** AX, DC, DS, MC, VI. **Special Amenities:** free local telephone calls and free newspaper. *(See color ad p 577)*

SOME UNITS

TRUMP INTERNATIONAL SONESTA BEACH RESORT *Book at aaa.com*   Phone: (305)692-5600   27
12/1-4/30	1P: $325-$850
5/1-6/12 & 10/1-11/30	1P: $269-$650
6/13-9/30	1P: $199-$539

Location: Oceanfront. On SR A1A, just s of The William Lehman Cswy. 18001 Collins Ave 33160. Fax: 305/692-5601. **Facility:** The resort's circular structure towers above its beachfront location, while the rooms offer views of the ocean and some of the Intracoastal Waterway. 390 units. 319 one-bedroom standard units, some with whirlpools. 34 one- and 37 two-bedroom suites ($350-$1050) with whirlpools. 5-30 stories, interior corridors. *Bath:* combo or shower only. **Parking:** valet. **Terms:** check-in 4 pm, 3 day cancellation notice-fee imposed, weekly rates available, package plans, $15 service charge, small pets only ($150 deposit). **Amenities:** video games (fee), CD players, high-speed Internet, dual phone lines, voice mail, safes, honor bars, irons, hair dryers. **Dining:** 7 am-10 pm, cocktails, also, Neomi's Grill, see separate listing, entertainment. **Pool(s):** heated outdoor. **Leisure Activities:** whirlpools, spa, volleyball. *Fee:* beach water sports, game room. **Guest Services:** gift shop, valet laundry, area transportation-South Beach, Aventura Mall & Galleria at Bal Harbour. **Business Services:** conference facilities, business center. **Cards:** AX, CB, DC, DS, MC, VI.

SOME UNITS

——— WHERE TO DINE ———

EMERALD COAST   Lunch: $8-$11   Dinner: $14-$18   Phone: 305/787-1530   20

Chinese

Location: On SR A1A; in RK Center South. 16850 Collins Ave 33160. **Hours:** 11:30 am-3 & 4:30-9:30 pm, Fri-10:30 pm, Sat noon-2 & 4-10:30 pm, Sun noon-2:30 & 4-9:30 pm. **Reservations:** accepted. **Features:** The Chinese buffet lays out more than 100 tasty food items on several island stations. Most favorites are represented, as are such choices as crab legs, carved and sushi rolls and many desserts. Casual dress; cocktails. **Parking:** on-site. **Cards:** AX, DC, MC, VI.

JERRY'S FAMOUS DELI   Lunch: $6-$36   Dinner: $6-$36   Phone: 305/532-8030   19

Deli/Subs Sandwiches

Location: On SR A1A, just s of 172nd St; just s of SR 826. 1450 Collins Ave 33139. **Hours:** 24 hours. **Reservations:** not accepted. **Features:** The eatery has been around for generations. The huge menu comprises traditional Jewish delicatessen items. Guests can sit and eat pickles, have a tall sandwich or succumb to temptation in the form of the bakery items. Casual dress; cocktails. **Parking:** valet. **Cards:** AX, MC, VI.

NEOMI'S GRILL   Lunch: $8-$18   Dinner: $8-$30   Phone: 305/692-5770   17

American

Location: On SR A1A; at The William Lehman Cswy; in Trump International Sonesta Beach Resort. 18001 Collins Ave 33160. **Hours:** 7 am-10 pm. **Reservations:** suggested. **Features:** The dining room's colors with an ocean view as a backdrop make for an artful presentation, which is also reflected in the astoundingly creative presentation of the food. Dressy casual; cocktails. **Parking:** valet. **Cards:** AX, CB, DC, DS, JC, MC, VI.

(See map and index starting on p. 545)

TIMO   **Lunch:** $9-$25   **Dinner:** $12-$26   **Phone:** 305/936-1008   ⑱

Mediterranean

Location: On SR A1A (Collins Ave), 0.9 mi s of SR 856 (William Lehman Cswy); in K K Beach Place Plaza. 17624 Collins Ave 33160. **Hours:** 11:30 am-3 & 6-11 pm. **Reservations:** required. **Features:** Simultaneously abuzz and soothing, the dining room employs the use of wood tones and lighting. The chef/owner puts together a menu that features a wide region of the Mediterranean coast. His seafood selections depend on what the waters provide him, but snapper, swordfish and grouper are mainstays. He prepares sweetbreads in his own personal way, as is the case with everything on the menu. A complementing wine list is available. Dressy casual; cocktails. **Parking:** on-site and valet. **Cards:** AX, MC, VI.

SURFSIDE pop. 4,909   (See map and index starting on p. 545)

──── WHERE TO STAY ────

BEST WESTERN OCEANFRONT RESORT   **Phone:** (305)864-2232

6/21-9/4	1P: $159-$199	2P: $159-$199	XP: $10 F17
12/1-4/21	1P: $149-$199	2P: $149-$199	XP: $10 F17
4/22-6/20 & 9/5-11/30	1P: $129-$199	2P: $129-$199	XP: $10 F17

Motel

Location: Oceanfront. On SR A1A (Collins Ave), just s of SR 922. 9365 Collins Ave 33154. Fax: 305/864-3045. **Facility:** 93 units. 33 one-bedroom standard units with kitchens. 60 one-bedroom suites with kitchens. 3 stories (no elevator), exterior corridors. *Bath:* combo or shower only. **Parking:** on-site. **Terms:** 3 day cancellation notice, weekly rates available, [ECP] meal plan available, package plans. **Amenities:** voice mail, irons, hair dryers. *Some:* high-speed Internet. **Pool(s):** outdoor, heated outdoor. **Leisure Activities:** limited beach access. **Guest Services:** valet laundry. **Business Services:** fax (fee). **Cards:** AX, CB, DC, DS, MC, VI. **Special Amenities:** free expanded continental breakfast and free newspaper. *(See color ad p 571)*

SOME UNITS

──── WHERE TO DINE ────

SUSHI REPUBLIC   **Lunch:** $5-$21   **Dinner:** $5-$21   **Phone:** 305/867-8036   ㉞

Japanese

Location: 1 blk w of Collins Ave; across from Bal Harbour Shops. 9583 Harding Ave 33154. **Hours:** noon-3 & 6-10 pm, Fri-11 pm, Sat 6 pm-11 pm, Sun 5:30 pm-10 pm. Closed major holidays; also Mon. **Features:** With eye-appealing presentation, this small restaurant serves very fresh sushi; take-out is available and is quite popular. Casual dress; beer & wine only. **Parking:** street. **Cards:** AX, MC, VI.

Miami Beach / © Rose Hartman / Corbis

This ends listings for the Miami-Miami Beach Vicinity.
The following page resumes the alphabetical listings of cities in Florida.

MIAMI LAKES —See Miami-Miami Beach p. 608.

MIAMI SPRINGS —See Miami-Miami Beach p. 609.

MICANOPY pop. 653

———— WHERE TO STAY ————

HERLONG MANSION BED & BREAKFAST INN
Phone: 352/466-3322
All Year [BP]   1P: $89-$189   2P: $89-$189   XP: $20   F8
Historic Bed & Breakfast
Location: Just n on US 441; downtown. 402 NE Cholokka Blvd 32667 (PO Box 667). **Facility:** Built in the Cracker style in 1840 and later converted to Greek Revival, this manor features high ceilings, mahogany inlaid floors and oak woodwork. Designated smoking area. 11 units. 9 one-bedroom standard units. 2 cottages ($209-$269). 3 stories (no elevator), interior/exterior corridors. *Bath:* combo or shower only. **Parking:** on-site.
Terms: 7 day cancellation notice-fee imposed, package plans. **Amenities:** *Some:* CD players, hair dryers. **Business Services:** meeting rooms, fax. **Cards:** AX, DS, MC, VI.

SOME UNITS
(ASK) ✕ 🐾 📞 / 📺 VCR 🔌 💻 /

MIDWAY pop. 1,446

———— WHERE TO STAY ————

HOWARD JOHNSON EXPRESS INN   *Book at aaa.com*
Phone: (850)574-8888
All Year   1P: $59-$119   2P: $59-$119   F16
Motel
Location: I-10, exit 192, just n. 56 Fortune Blvd 32343. Fax: 850/574-5011. **Facility:** 49 one-bedroom standard units, some with whirlpools. 2 stories, exterior corridors. *Bath:* combo or shower only. **Parking:** on-site. **Terms:** 7 day cancellation notice, [ECP] meal plan available. **Amenities:** voice mail, irons, hair dryers.
Leisure Activities: exercise room. **Business Services:** fax (fee). **Cards:** AX, CB, DC, DS, MC, VI.

SOME UNITS
(ASK) (S/D) (&M) (&) 🐾 DATA PORT 🔌 📠 💻 / ✕

MILTON pop. 7,200

———— WHERE TO STAY ————

COMFORT INN   *Book at aaa.com*
Phone: (850)623-1511
5/2-9/10 [CP]   1P: $109-$149   2P: $109-$149   XP: $8   F18
3/1-5/1 & 9/11-11/30 [CP]   1P: $79-$109   2P: $79-$109   XP: $8   F18
12/1-2/28 [CP]   1P: $59-$89   2P: $59-$89   XP: $8   F18
Small-scale Hotel
Location: I-10, exit 31, just s. 4962 S Hwy 87 32583. Fax: 850/626-6960. **Facility:** 66 one-bedroom standard units, some with whirlpools. 2 stories, interior corridors. *Bath:* combo or shower only. **Parking:** on-site. **Terms:** pets ($10 extra charge). **Amenities:** irons, hair dryers. **Pool(s):** outdoor. **Guest Services:** coin laundry. **Cards:** AX, CB, DC, DS, JC, MC, VI. **Special Amenities:** free continental breakfast and free local telephone calls.

SOME UNITS
(S/D) 🛏 🐾 🐾 DATA PORT 🔌 📠 💻 / ✕
FEE

HOLIDAY INN EXPRESS HOTEL & SUITES   *Book at aaa.com*
Phone: (850)626-9060
All Year   1P: $90-$160   XP: $10   F
Small-scale Hotel
Location: I-10, exit 31, just n. 8510 Keshav Taylor Dr 32583. Fax: 850/626-8989. **Facility:** 64 units. 60 one-bedroom standard units. 4 one-bedroom suites ($100-$160), some with whirlpools. 3 stories, interior corridors. *Bath:* combo or shower only. **Parking:** on-site. **Terms:** 3 day cancellation notice, package plans. **Amenities:** dual phone lines, voice mail, irons, hair dryers. **Pool(s):** outdoor. **Leisure Activities:** exercise room. **Guest Services:** coin laundry. **Business Services:** meeting rooms. **Cards:** AX, DC, DS, MC, VI.

SOME UNITS
(ASK) (S/D) (🍴) 🐾 🐾 DATA PORT 🔌 📠 💻 / ✕ VCR
FEE

RED ROOF INN & SUITES   *Book at aaa.com*
Phone: 850/995-6100
All Year [CP]   1P: $84-$105   2P: $89-$110   XP: $5   F18
Small-scale Hotel
Location: I-10, exit 22, just s. 2672 Avalon Blvd 32583. Fax: 850/994-1214. **Facility:** 70 units. 62 one-bedroom standard units. 8 one-bedroom suites. 3 stories, interior corridors. *Bath:* some combo or shower only. **Parking:** on-site. **Terms:** 3 day cancellation notice. **Amenities:** hair dryers. *Some:* irons. **Pool(s):** small outdoor. **Guest Services:** coin laundry. **Business Services:** meeting rooms. **Cards:** AX, DC, DS, MC, VI.

SOME UNITS
(ASK) (S/D) 🛏 (🍴) (&M) (&) 🐾 🐾 DATA PORT / ✕ 🔌 📠 💻 /

MIRAMAR —See Fort Lauderdale p. 416.

MONTICELLO pop. 2,533

——— WHERE TO STAY ———

DAYS INN
Motel

8/31-11/30 [CP]	1P: $55-$125	2P: $60-$135	XP: $10	D17
12/1-8/30 [CP]	1P: $55-$90	2P: $60-$95	XP: $8	D17

Phone: (850)997-5988

Location: I-10, exit 225, just s on US 19. 44 Woodworth Dr 32336. **Facility:** 36 one-bedroom standard units. 2 stories, exterior corridors. **Parking:** on-site. **Terms:** check-in 4 pm, 3 day cancellation notice-fee imposed, weekly rates available. **Pool(s):** outdoor. **Cards:** AX, DC, DS, MC, VI.

MOSSY HEAD

——— WHERE TO STAY ———

RAMADA LIMITED
Small-scale Hotel

All Year [CP]	1P: $54-$59	2P: $54-$59	XP: $10	F12

Phone: 850/951-9780

Location: I-10, exit 70, just s. Located at a truck stop. 326 Green Acres Dr 32435 (328 Green Acres Dr, DE FUNIAK SPRINGS). Fax: 850/951-9786. **Facility:** 48 one-bedroom standard units. 2 stories, exterior corridors. *Bath:* combo or shower only. **Parking:** on-site. **Terms:** pets ($25 fee). **Amenities:** irons, hair dryers. **Leisure Activities:** *Fee:* game room. **Guest Services:** coin laundry. **Business Services:** fax (fee). **Cards:** AX, DS, MC, VI.

SOME UNITS

FEE

MOUNT DORA —*See Orlando p. 829.*

MULBERRY pop. 3,230

——— WHERE TO STAY ———

SUPER 8 MOTEL-MULBERRY
Small-scale Hotel

All Year	1P: $62-$70	XP: $5	D12

Phone: (863)425-2500

Location: On SR 60, 1.4 mi e of jct SR 37. 2525 SR 60 E 33860. Fax: 863/869-9354. **Facility:** 64 one-bedroom standard units, some with efficiencies (no utensils) and/or whirlpools. 2 stories, interior corridors. *Bath:* combo or shower only. **Parking:** on-site. **Terms:** cancellation fee imposed, weekly rates available, package plans. **Amenities:** *Some:* hair dryers. **Pool(s):** small outdoor. **Leisure Activities:** limited exercise equipment. **Business Services:** meeting rooms, fax (fee). **Cards:** AX, DC, DS, MC, VI. **Special Amenities:** free continental breakfast and free local telephone calls.

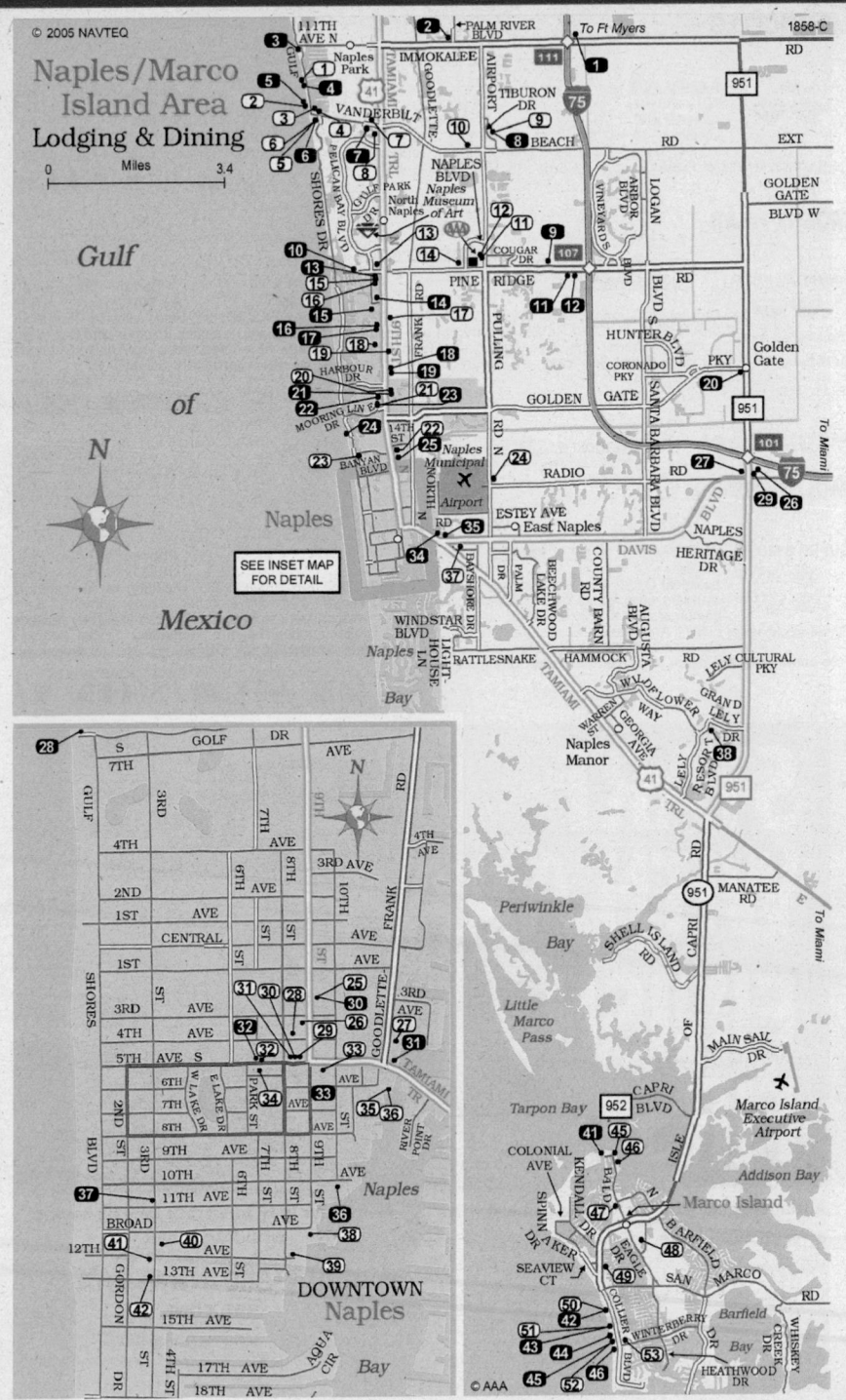

Naples/Marco Island Area

This index helps you "spot" where approved accommodations and restaurants are located on the corresponding detailed maps. Lodging rate ranges are for comparison only and show the property's high season; rates are per night, unless only weekly (W) rates are available. Restaurant rate range is for dinner, unless only lunch (L) is served. Turn to the listing page for more detailed rate information and consult display ads for special promotions.

Spotter/Map Page Number	OA	NAPLES - Lodgings	Diamond Rating	Rate Range High Season	Listing Page
1 / p. 620		Hampton Inn/Naples I-75	◆◆◆	$69-$199	630
2 / p. 620	AAA	The Fairways Resort	◆◆	$110-$240 SAVE	629
3 / p. 620		Vanderbilt Inn Naples - see color ad p 636	◆◆◆	$115-$390	636
4 / p. 620		LaPlaya Beach & Golf Resort	◆◆◆◆	$559-$799	632
5 / p. 620		Vanderbilt Beach Resort	◆◆	$176-$298	636
6 / p. 620	AAA	The Ritz-Carlton, Naples	◆◆◆◆◆	$319-$889 SAVE	635
7 / p. 620		Inn at Pelican Bay - see color ad p 632	◆◆◆	$188-$260	631
8 / p. 620	AAA	The Ritz-Carlton Golf Resort	◆◆◆◆◆	$229-$619 SAVE	635
9 / p. 620	AAA	The Hawthorn Suites of Naples	◆◆◆	$179-$269 SAVE	630
10 / p. 620	AAA	The Registry Resort & Club - see color ad p 634	◆◆◆•◆	$389-$969 SAVE	634
11 / p. 620	AAA	Spinnaker Inn of Naples	◆	$79-$86 SAVE	635
12 / p. 620		Best Western Naples Plaza	◆◆◆	$129-$199	626
13 / p. 620	AAA	Hilton Naples - see color ad p 624	◆◆◆◆	$209-$259 SAVE	630
14 / p. 620		Staybridge Suites by Holiday Inn	◆◆◆	$210-$280	635
15 / p. 620	AAA	Park Shore Resort - see color ad p 626	◆◆◆	$216-$270 SAVE	633
16 / p. 620		Residence Inn by Marriott, Naples	◆◆◆	$199-$329	635
17 / p. 620	AAA	Quality Inn & Suites	◆◆◆	$159-$299 SAVE	633
18 / p. 620		Courtyard by Marriott - see color ad p 628	◆◆◆	$69-$179	628
19 / p. 620		Hampton Inn Naples Central	◆◆◆	$179-$209	630
20 / p. 620		Quality Inn & Suites Golf Resort	◆◆	$149-$179	633
21 / p. 620		Stoney's Courtyard Inn	◆◆	Failed to provide	635
22 / p. 620	AAA	Gulfcoast Inn - see color ad p 629	◆◆	$100-$140 SAVE	629
23 / p. 620	AAA	Best Western Naples Inn & Suites - see color ad p 627	◆◆◆	$129-$229 SAVE	626
24 / p. 620	AAA	Edgewater Beach Hotel & Club	◆◆◆	$335-$1500 SAVE	629
25 / p. 620	AAA	Holiday Inn - see color ad p 630	◆◆◆	$139-$189 SAVE	631
26 / p. 620		Comfort Inn & Suites	◆◆◆	$129-$179	628
27 / p. 620	AAA	Baymont Inn & Suites Naples	◆◆◆	$139-$169 SAVE	625
28 / p. 620	AAA	The Naples Beach Hotel & Golf Club - see color ad p 633	◆◆◆	$265-$485 SAVE	633
29 / p. 620		Holiday Inn Express in Naples	◆◆◆	Failed to provide	631
30 / p. 620	AAA	Bellasera Hotel - see color ad p 626	◆◆◆◆	$310-$510 SAVE	626
31 / p. 620	AAA	Bayfront Inn on Fifth - see color ad p 625	◆◆◆	$210-$695 SAVE	624
32 / p. 620		The Inn on Fifth - see color ad p 632	◆◆◆	$270-$400	632
33 / p. 620		Trianon Old Naples	◆◆◆	$239-$600	636

Spotter/Map Page Number	OA	**NAPLES - Lodgings (continued)**	Diamond Rating	Rate Range High Season	Listing Page
34 / p. 620	AAA	**Wellesley Inn (Naples)**	◈◈	$139-$199 [SAVE]	636
35 / p. 620		Red Roof Inn	◈◈	$80-$90	634
36 / p. 620	AAA	**Charter Club Resort of Naples Bay -** see color ad p 771	◈◈◈	$259-$349 [SAVE]	627
37 / p. 620		Inn by the Sea	◈◈◈	$149-$169	631
38 / p. 620	AAA	**GreenLinks Golf Resort -** see color ad p 626	◈◈◈	$270-$360 [SAVE]	629
		NAPLES - Restaurants			
1 / p. 620	AAA	**Baleen**	◈◈◈◈	$27-$32	637
2 / p. 620		The Turtle Club	◈◈	$16-$30	640
3 / p. 620	AAA	**SeaWitch Restaurant & Lounge**	◈◈	$14-$22	639
4 / p. 620		Da Ru Ma	◈◈	$17-$35	638
5 / p. 620		The Grill	◈◈◈◈	$30-$48	638
6 / p. 620		Artisans in The Dining Room	◈◈◈◈◈	$65-$85	637
7 / p. 620		Bha! Bha! A Persian Bistro	◈◈◈	$14-$23	637
8 / p. 620		Fleming's	◈◈◈	$21-$36	638
9 / p. 620		Lemonia	◈◈◈	$24-$35	638
10 / p. 620		Sanibel Steakhouse	◈◈◈	$20-$40	639
11 / p. 620	AAA	**Skillets Sunrise**	◈	$5-$9(L)	640
12 / p. 620		Streamer's Restaurant	◈	$8-$18	640
13 / p. 620		Aqua Grill	◈◈◈	$15-$30	637
14 / p. 620		Noodles Italian Cafe'	◈◈	$10-$20	639
15 / p. 620	AAA	**Shula's Steak House -** see color ad p 624	◈◈◈	$14-$30	640
16 / p. 620	AAA	**Flacos Mexican Specialties & SteakHouse**	◈◈	$6-$20	638
17 / p. 620	AAA	**Skillets of Naples**	◈	$5-$9(L)	640
18 / p. 620	AAA	**USS Nemo**	◈◈◈	$15-$39	640
19 / p. 620		Mel's Diner Naples	◈	$5-$12	638
20 / p. 620	AAA	**Andre's Steakhouse**	◈◈	$18-$34	637
21 / p. 620		Chardonnay	◈◈◈◈	$23-$35	637
22 / p. 620		Pippin's	◈◈	$16-$28	639
23 / p. 620		First Watch	◈	$4-$7(L)	638
24 / p. 620		Michelbob's	◈	$10-$24	639
25 / p. 620		ZiZi Restaurant & Lounge	◈◈◈	$10-$34	640
26 / p. 620		Lindburgers	◈	$6-$10	638
27 / p. 620		Il Bellagio	◈◈◈	$12-$24	638
28 / p. 620		Ristorante Ciao	◈◈◈	$18-$30	639
29 / p. 620		Pazzo Italian Cafe	◈◈◈	$17-$25	639
30 / p. 620		Chops City Grill	◈◈◈	$18-$34	637
31 / p. 620		Bistro 821	◈◈◈	$16-$29	637

Spotter/Map Page Number	OA	**NAPLES** - Restaurants (continued)	Diamond Rating	Rate Range High Season	Listing Page
㉜ / p. 620		Yabba Island Grill	◆◆◆	$16-$26	640
㉝ / p. 620	AAA	**St. George & the Dragon**	◆◆◆	$15-$30	639
㉞ / p. 620		Vergina	◆◆◆	$15-$27	640
㉟ / p. 620		Pier 41 Restaurant	◆◆	$12-$22	639
㊱ / p. 620	AAA	**Riverwalk Fish & Ale House**	◆◆	$8-$22	639
㊲ / p. 620		The English Pub	◆◆	$10-$16	638
㊳ / p. 620	AAA	**The Boathouse**	◆◆	$10-$24	637
㊴ / p. 620	AAA	**Dock at Crayton Cove**	◆◆	$5-$20	638
㊵ / p. 620		Campiello Ristorante	◆◆◆	$16-$29	637
㊶ / p. 620		Tommy Bahama's	◆◆	$17-$29	640
㊷ / p. 620		Ridgway Bar & Grill	◆◆	$14-$35	639
		MARCO ISLAND - Lodgings			
㊶ / p. 620		Olde Marco Island Inn & Suites	◆◆◆	$199-$229	523
㊷ / p. 620		Marco Island Marriott Resort, Golf Club & Spa	◆◆◆◆	$295-$660	522
㊸ / p. 620	AAA	**Marco Beach Ocean Resort**	◆◆◆◆	$429-$1200 SAVE	522
㊹ / p. 620		The Surf Club of Marco	◆◆◆	$1400-$1625(W)	523
㊺ / p. 620	AAA	**Hilton Marco Island Beach Resort**	◆◆◆◆	$209-$399 SAVE	522
㊻ / p. 620		Radisson Suite Beach Resort on Marco Island - see color ad p 522	◆◆◆	$269-$299	523
		MARCO ISLAND - Restaurants			
㊺ / p. 620		Snook Inn	◆	$8-$25	524
㊻ / p. 620	AAA	**Marek's Collier House Restaurant**	◆◆◆	$23-$27	523
㊼ / p. 620		Arturo's Ristorante Italiano	◆◆◆	$13-$35	523
㊽ / p. 620		Sushi, Blues & Steaks	◆◆◆	$6-$44	524
㊾ / p. 620		Verdi's - An American Bistro	◆◆◆	$17-$28	524
㊿ / p. 620		Kurrents	◆◆◆	$22-$38	523
(51) / p. 620		Sale e Pepe	◆◆◆◆	$22-$34	523
(52) / p. 620		Sandcastles	◆◆◆	$18-$26	524
(53) / p. 620		Konrad's Seafood & Grille Room	◆◆	$13-$38	523

NAPLES pop. 20,976 (See map and index starting on p. 620)

――――― WHERE TO STAY ―――――

BAYFRONT INN ON FIFTH

Phone: (239)649-5800 **31**

	1P: $210-$695	2P: $210-$695	XP: $10	F18
12/1-4/16	1P: $210-$695	2P: $210-$695	XP: $10	F18
4/17-5/31	1P: $155-$395	2P: $155-$395	XP: $10	F18
10/1-11/30	1P: $135-$395	2P: $135-$395	XP: $10	F18
6/1-9/30	1P: $95-$295	2P: $95-$295	XP: $10	F18

Small-scale Hotel **Location:** I-75, exit 101, 6.5 mi w on SR 84, then just n on US 41 (Tamiami Tr) to Goodlette Frank Rd; in Bayfront Area. 1221 5th Ave S 34102. Fax: 239/649-0523. **Facility:** 99 one-bedroom standard units. 4 stories, interior corridors. **Parking:** on-site. **Terms:** [ECP] meal plan available, package plans. **Amenities:** high-speed Internet, voice mail, irons, hair dryers. **Dining:** 11 am-9 pm, cocktails. **Pool(s):** heated outdoor. **Leisure Activities:** whirlpool, rental boats. *Fee:* charter fishing. **Guest Services:** gift shop, coin laundry. **Business Services:** meeting rooms, fax (fee). **Cards:** AX, CB, DC, DS, JC, MC, VI. **Special Amenities:** free expanded continental breakfast and free local telephone calls.
(See color ad p 625)

FEE

TAKE ME TO A

GREAT GETAWAY.

TAKE ME TO THE HILTON.™

Located within walking distance of Waterside shops, art galleries and exhibition halls. We offer complimentary shuttle service to Gulf beaches located just three blocks from our hotel. For dining, we are home to Shula's Steak House, one of America's top 5 steak houses. Just make advance reservations with a call to Hilton's dedicated AAA number at **1-800-916-2221** or your local AAA travel office. Visit us online at **hilton.com**.

Shula's STEAK HOUSE
Five Diamond Award

Hilton HHonors

5111 Tamiami Trail North
Naples, FL 34103
239-430-4900

Hilton
Naples & Towers

(See map and index starting on p. 620)

BAYMONT INN & SUITES NAPLES   *Book at aaa.com*   Phone: (239)352-8400   **27**

1/16-4/30	1P: $139-$169	XP: $7	F18
5/1-11/30	1P: $75-$85	XP: $7	F18
12/1-1/15	1P: $69-$79	XP: $7	F18

Small-scale Hotel **Location:** I-75, exit 101, just w. 185 Bedzel Cir 34104. Fax: 239/352-8401. **Facility:** 103 units. 100 one-bedroom standard units. 3 one-bedroom suites. 4 stories, interior corridors. *Bath:* combo or shower only. **Parking:** on-site. **Terms:** [ECP] meal plan available, small pets only (in smoking units). **Amenities:** video games (fee), voice mail, irons, hair dryers. **Pool(s):** heated outdoor. **Guest Services:** valet and coin laundry. **Business Services:** fax (fee). **Cards:** AX, CB, DC, DS, MC, VI. **Special Amenities:** free expanded continental breakfast and free local telephone calls.

SOME UNITS
FEE FEE

(See map and index starting on p. 620)

BELLASERA HOTEL *Book at aaa.com* Phone: (239)649-7333 **30**

AAA SAVE

2/10-4/22	1P: $310-$510	2P: $310-$510
12/1-1/1	1P: $155-$475	2P: $155-$475
1/2-2/9	1P: $220-$350	2P: $220-$350
4/23-11/30	1P: $175-$270	2P: $175-$270

Small-scale Hotel **Location:** I-75, exit 107, 3.8 mi w on CR 896 (Pine Ridge Rd), then 4.5 mi s on US 41 (Tamiami Tr). 221 9th St S 34102. Fax: 239/649-6233. **Facility:** The splashing sounds of a large fountain give this property's pool area a relaxing ambience, while spacious rooms offer luxury and comfort. Designated smoking area. 100 units. 10 one-bedroom standard units with whirlpools. 30 one-, 48 two- and 12 three-bedroom suites with kitchens. 3 stories, interior/exterior corridors. *Bath:* combo or shower only. **Parking:** on-site and valet. **Terms:** 7 day cancellation notice. **Amenities:** DVD players, video games (fee), CD players, high-speed Internet, dual phone lines, voice mail, irons, hair dryers. **Dining:** ZiZi Restaurant & Lounge, see separate listing. **Pool(s):** heated outdoor. **Leisure Activities:** whirlpool, exercise room. **Guest Services:** gift shop, valet laundry, area transportation-Laudermilk Park Beach. **Business Services:** conference facilities, business center. **Cards:** AX, DC, DS, MC, VI. **Special Amenities:** free newspaper. *(See color ad below)*

SOME UNITS

BEST WESTERN NAPLES INN & SUITES *Book at aaa.com* Phone: (239)261-1148 **23**

AAA SAVE

12/23-3/31 [ECP]	1P: $129-$229	2P: $129-$229	XP: $10	F18
4/1-4/16 [ECP]	1P: $109-$149	2P: $109-$149	XP: $10	F18
12/1-12/22 & 4/17-11/30 [ECP]	1P: $69-$129	2P: $69-$129	XP: $10	F18

Motel **Location:** I-75, exit 107, 3.8 mi w on CR 896 to US 41 (Tamiami Tr), then 2.5 mi s; corner of US 41 and Mooringline Dr. 2329 9th St N 34103. Fax: 239/262-4684. **Facility:** 110 units. 80 one-bedroom standard units. 24 one- and 6 two-bedroom suites ($89-$239) with kitchens. 2-4 stories, exterior corridors. **Parking:** on-site. **Terms:** 3 day cancellation notice-fee imposed. **Amenities:** video library, DVD players, CD players, high-speed Internet, voice mail, safes, irons, hair dryers. **Dining:** Chardonnay, see separate listing. **Pool(s):** 2 heated outdoor. **Leisure Activities:** whirlpools, miniature golf. **Guest Services:** valet and coin laundry. **Cards:** AX, DC, DS, MC, VI. **Special Amenities:** free expanded continental breakfast and free local telephone calls. *(See color ad p 627)*

BEST WESTERN NAPLES PLAZA *Book at aaa.com* Phone: (239)643-6655 **12**

2/1-2/28 [ECP]	1P: $129-$199	2P: $129-$199
12/26-1/31 [ECP]	1P: $109-$149	2P: $109-$149
3/1-11/30 [ECP]	1P: $69-$149	2P: $69-$149
12/1-12/25 [ECP]	1P: $69-$119	2P: $69-$119

Small-scale Hotel **Location:** I-75, exit 107, just w. 6400 Dudley Dr 34105. Fax: 239/643-4063. **Facility:** 240 units. 209 one-bedroom standard units, some with efficiencies. 31 one-bedroom suites with kitchens. 4 stories, interior corridors. *Bath:* combo or shower only. **Parking:** on-site. **Amenities:** voice mail, irons, hair dryers. *Some:* high-speed Internet. **Pool(s):** heated outdoor. **Leisure Activities:** whirlpool, exercise room. **Guest Services:** valet and coin laundry. **Business Services:** meeting rooms, fax (fee). **Cards:** AX, CB, DC, DS, MC, VI.

SOME UNITS

See map and index starting on p. 620)

HARTER CLUB RESORT OF NAPLES BAY   *Book at aaa.com*   Phone: (239)261-5559

12/17-4/21	2P: $259-$349
4/22-11/30	2P: $149-$179
12/1-12/16	2P: $139-$159

Condominium   **Location:** I-75, exit 101, at 10th St. Located on the bay. 1000 10th Ave S 34102. Fax: 239/261-6782. **Facility:** Located just at the edge of the town's historic district, the hotel offers large guest rooms, all featuring private screened lanais with bay views. 33 two-bedroom suites with kitchens. 3 stories (no evator), exterior corridors. **Parking:** on-site. **Terms:** office hours 8 am-6 pm, check-in 4 pm, 15 day cancellation notice-fee mposed. **Amenities:** video library, DVD players, CD players, voice mail, irons, hair dryers. **Dining:** 10 am-8 pm. **Pool(s):** eated outdoor, wading. **Leisure Activities:** whirlpool, boat dock, fishing, beach chairs, towels, umbrellas, fishing equipment, ecreation programs, club room, gas barbecue grills, picnic area, board games, bicycles. *Fee:* personal watercraft. **Guest ervices:** complimentary laundry. **Business Services:** fax (fee). **Cards:** AX, DC, DS, MC, VI. **Special Amenities:** free local elephone calls and preferred room (subject to availability with advance reservations).** *(See color ad p 771)*

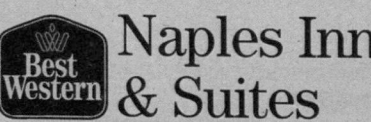

(See map and index starting on p. 620)

COMFORT INN & SUITES *Book at aaa.com* Phone: (239)353-9500 **2**

▽▽▽ ▽▽▽
1/20-4/15	1P: $129-$179	2P: $129-$179
12/17-1/19	1P: $109-$144	2P: $109-$144
12/1-12/16 & 4/16-11/30	1P: $69-$109	2P: $69-$109

Small-scale Hotel **Location:** I-75, exit 101, just w. 3860 Tollgate Blvd 34114. **Fax:** 239/353-0035. **Facility:** 197 one-bedroo standard units, some with efficiencies and/or whirlpools. 4 stories, interior/exterior corridors. *Bath:* combo or shower onl **Parking:** on-site. **Terms:** check-in 4 pm, cancellation fee imposed, [ECP] meal plan available. **Amenities:** irons, hair dryer **Pool(s):** heated outdoor. **Fee:** game room. **Guest Services:** gift shop, valet and coin laundr **Business Services:** meeting rooms, fax (fee). **Cards:** AX, CB, DC, DS, JC, MC, VI.

SOME UNITS

(ASK) (S⊘) (📶) (Y) (🛁) (🐾) (🏊) (DATA PORT) (🔒) (💻) / (✕) (🍽)

COURTYARD BY MARRIOTT Phone: (239)434-8700 **1**

▽▽▽ ▽▽▽
All Year 1P: $69-$179 2P: $69-$179 XP: $10 F▽

Small-scale Hotel **Location:** I-75, exit 107, 3.8 mi w on CR 896 (Pine Ridge Rd), then 1.8 mi s. Located in a quiet area. 3250 Tamiami N (US 41) 34103. **Fax:** 239/434-7787. **Facility:** 102 units. 98 one-bedroom standard units. 4 one-bedroo suites. 4 stories, interior corridors. *Bath:* combo or shower only. **Parking:** on-site. **Terms:** 3 day cancellatio notice-fee imposed, package plans. **Amenities:** high-speed Internet, voice mail, irons, hair dryers. *Some:* dual phone line **Pool(s):** heated outdoor. **Leisure Activities:** whirlpool, exercise room. **Guest Services:** valet and coin laundry. **Busines Services:** meeting rooms, fax (fee). **Cards:** AX, CB, DC, DS, JC, MC, VI. *(See color ad below)*

SOME UNITS

(ASK) (S⊘) (📶) (&M) (🛁) (🏊) (🎮) (DATA PORT) (💻) / (✕) (🔒) (🍽)

DOUBLETREE GUEST SUITES NAPLES *Book at aaa.com* Phone: 239/593-873

▽▽▽ ▽▽▽
Property failed to provide current rates

Small-scale Hotel **Location:** I-75, exit 111, 3.3 mi w on Naples-Immokalee Rd to US 41 (Tamiami Tr), then just n. 12200 Tamiami Tr 34110. **Fax:** 239/593-8734. **Facility:** 101 one-bedroom suites, some with whirlpools. 3 stories, interi corridors. *Bath:* combo or shower only. **Parking:** on-site. **Amenities:** video games (fee), high-spee Internet, dual phone lines, voice mail, irons, hair dryers. **Pool(s):** heated outdoor. **Leisure Activities:** whirlpool, exercise roor **Guest Services:** gift shop, valet laundry. **Business Services:** meeting rooms, business center. *(See color ad below)*

SOME UNIT

(📶) (Y) (&M) (🛁) (🐾) (🏊) (🎮) (DATA PORT) (🔒) (💻) / (✕) /

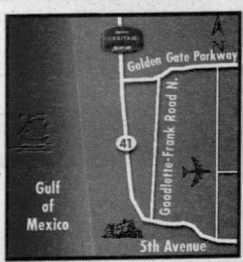

NAPLES, FL
COURTYARD Marriott
10% OFF PUBLISHED RATE
Located in the heart of Naples
Minutes from downtown, beaches, & golf courses
On-site restaurant · Outdoor pool and whirlpool
Fitness room · Free parking
Free high-speed wireless Internet access

For Reservations call 239-434-8700 or 1-877-301-8485
www.naplescourtyard.com, 3250 US 41 North, Naples, FL 34103

PARADISE FOUND
Winner of Hilton's Connie Award for #1 Doubletree, 2001, 2003 & 2004

15% Off
published rates
valid 6/1/06 - 10/31/06
excludes holidays, subject to availability

DOUBLETREE GUEST SUITES
NAPLES
Free High Speed Internet!

Doubletree Guest Suites Naples 12200 Tamiami Trail North, Naples, FL 34110
1-800-222-TREE • 239-593-8733 • www.naplessuites.doubletree.com

Points&Miles Make every stay more rewarding with Hilton HHonors®, the only rewards program to offer both hotel points and airline miles for the same stay. To join, please visit us at www.hiltonhonors.com. ©2004 Hilton

(See map and index starting on p. 620)

EDGEWATER BEACH HOTEL & CLUB *Book at aaa.com*

Phone: (239)403-2000 **24**

12/1-4/30	1P: $335-$1500
5/1-5/29	1P: $249-$1500
10/6-11/30	1P: $190-$895
5/30-10/5	1P: $165-$895

AAA SAVE

Large-scale Hotel Location: I-75, exit 107, 5 mi w on Pine Ridge Rd, then 2.3 mi s on US 41 (Tamiami Tr). 1901 Gulf Shore Blvd N 34102 (475 Slagate Dr, 34103). Fax: 239/403-2100. **Facility:** This waterfront hotel offers one- and two-bedroom units with living rooms, some featuring balconies and individual exterior entrances. Smoke free premises. 126 units. 97 one- and 29 two-bedroom suites. 1-7 stories, interior/exterior corridors. *Bath:* combo or shower only. **Parking:** on-site and valet. **Terms:** 14 day cancellation notice, 7 day 5/1-11/30. **Amenities:** CD players, voice mail, safes, irons, hair dryers. *Fee:* video games, high-speed Internet. *Some:* fax. **Dining:** 2 restaurants, 7 am-2 & 6-10 pm, Fri & Sat-11 pm; hotel guests only, cocktails. **Pool(s):** heated outdoor. **Leisure Activities:** limited beach access, rental sailboats, golf instruction, tennis privileges, exercise room. *Fee:* windsurfing, golf-18 holes, bicycles, massage. **Guest Services:** gift shop, valet laundry. **Business Services:** meeting rooms, fax. **Cards:** AX, CB, DC, DS, MC, VI.

SOME UNITS

(icons) / VCR / FEE

THE FAIRWAYS RESORT

Phone: (239)597-8181 **2**

12/1-4/16 [CP]	1P: $110-$240	2P: $110-$240	XP: $10 F
4/17-11/30 [CP]	1P: $65-$145	2P: $65-$145	XP: $10 F

AAA SAVE

Motel Location: I-75, exit 111, 2.2 mi w on CR 846. 103 Palm River Blvd 34110. Fax: 239/597-5413. **Facility:** 46 units. 45 one-bedroom standard units, some with kitchens. 1 two-bedroom suite with kitchen. 2 stories (no elevator), exterior corridors. **Parking:** on-site. **Terms:** office hours 7 am-10 pm, 3 day cancellation notice-fee imposed, weekly rates available, [ECP] meal plan available, small pets only ($25 fee). **Amenities:** *Some:* irons, hair dryers. **Pool(s):** heated outdoor. **Leisure Activities:** whirlpool, barbecue gas grills, pavilion, shuffleboard. **Guest Services:** coin laundry. **Business Services:** meeting rooms, fax (fee). **Cards:** AX, DC, MC, VI. **Special Amenities:** free continental breakfast and free local telephone calls.

(icons) FEE

GREENLINKS GOLF RESORT *Book at aaa.com*

Phone: (239)732-9920 **38**

2/10-4/22	1P: $270-$360	2P: $270-$360	
12/1-1/1	1P: $130-$330	2P: $130-$330	
1/2-2/9	1P: $230-$300	2P: $230-$300	
4/23-11/30	1P: $150-$195	2P: $150-$195	

AAA SAVE

Resort Condominium Location: I-75, exit 101, 4.9 mi s on SR 951 to entrance of Lely Resort, then 0.9 mi w. 7990 Mahogany Run Ln 34113. Fax: 239/732-5561. **Facility:** Spacious two- and three-bedroom units are nicely furnished; the golf course surrounds the complex. Designated smoking area. 86 units. 56 two- and 30 three-bedroom suites with kitchens. 2 stories (no elevator), exterior corridors. **Parking:** on-site. **Terms:** office hours 8 am-10 pm, 14 day cancellation notice, package plans. **Amenities:** dual phone lines, voice mail, irons, hair dryers. *Some:* DVD players, high-speed Internet. **Pool(s):** heated outdoor. **Leisure Activities:** whirlpool, 2 tennis courts, exercise room. *Fee:* golf-36 holes, golf & tennis instruction. **Guest Services:** complimentary laundry. **Business Services:** fax (fee). **Cards:** AX, DS, MC, VI. **Special Amenities:** free newspaper. *(See color ad p 626)*

SOME UNITS

(icons) / VCR /

GULFCOAST INN *Book at aaa.com*

Phone: (239)261-6046 **22**

12/22-4/20 [CP]	1P: $100-$130	2P: $130-$140
12/1-12/21 & 4/21-11/30 [CP]	1P: $60-$70	2P: $65-$80

AAA SAVE

Motel Location: I-75, exit 107, 3.8 mi w on CR 896, then 2.5 mi s on US 41 (Tamiami Tr); between 26th Ave N and Harbour Dr. 2555 Tamiami Tr N (US 41) 34103. Fax: 239/261-5742. **Facility:** 85 one-bedroom standard units. 2 stories (no elevator), exterior corridors. **Parking:** on-site. **Terms:** cancellation fee imposed, [AP] meal plan available, package plans. **Amenities:** high-speed Internet, voice mail, safes, irons, hair dryers. **Pool(s):** heated outdoor. **Leisure Activities:** shuffleboard, game room. **Guest Services:** valet and coin laundry. **Business Services:** meeting rooms, fax (fee). **Cards:** AX, CB, DC, DS, MC, VI. *(See color ad below)*

SOME UNITS

(icons) / (icons) /

(See map and index starting on p. 620)

HAMPTON INN NAPLES CENTRAL *Book at aaa.com* Phone: (239)261-8000 **19**

▼▼▼▼

Motel

	1P: $179-$209	2P: $179-$209
12/1-4/15 [BP]	1P: $179-$209	2P: $179-$209
11/1-11/30 [BP]	1P: $99-$159	2P: $99-$159
4/16-10/31 [BP]	1P: $59-$99	2P: $59-$99

Location: I-75, exit 107, 3.8 mi w on CR 896 (Pine Ridge Rd), then 1.8 mi s on US 41 (Tamiami Tr). 3210 Tamiami Tr N (US 41) 34103. Fax: 239/261-7802. **Facility:** 107 units. 105 one-bedroom standard units. 2 one-bedroom suites. 4 stories, interior corridors. **Parking:** on-site. **Terms:** cancellation fee imposed. **Amenities:** video games, high-speed Internet, voice mail, irons, hair dryers. **Pool(s):** heated outdoor. **Guest Services:** valet laundry. **Business Services:** meeting rooms, fax (fee). **Cards:** AX, CB, DC, DS, JC, MC, VI.

SOME UNITS

(ASK) (SD) (T) (&M) ⊘ ⊇ (♦) (DATA PORT) 🖵 / (✕) 🔋 🖿 /

HAMPTON INN/NAPLES I-75 *Book at aaa.com* Phone: (239)596-1299 **1**

▼▼▼

Small-scale Hotel

12/19-4/18 [ECP]	1P: $69-$199	2P: $69-$199
11/1-11/30 [ECP]	1P: $69-$139	2P: $69-$139
12/1-12/18 [ECP]	1P: $69-$119	2P: $69-$119

Location: I-75, exit 111, just e, then n. 2630 Northbrooke Plaza Dr 34119. Fax: 239/596-0808. **Facility:** 91 one-bedroom standard units. 3 stories, interior corridors. **Bath:** combo or shower only. **Parking:** on-site. **Terms:** cancellation fee imposed, [BP] meal plan available. **Amenities:** video games (fee), high-speed Internet, dual phone lines, voice mail, irons, hair dryers. **Pool(s):** heated outdoor. **Guest Services:** valet laundry. **Business Services:** meeting rooms, PC, fax (fee). **Cards:** AX, CB, DC, DS, MC, VI.

SOME UNITS

(ASK) (T) (&M) (&) ⊘ ⊇ (♦) (♦) (DATA PORT) 🖵 / (✕) 🔋 /
FEE

THE HAWTHORN SUITES OF NAPLES *Book at aaa.com* Phone: 239/593-1300 **9**

(AAA) (SAVE)
▼▼▼▼

Small-scale Hotel

1/5-4/23 [BP]	1P: $179-$269	2P: $179-$269
12/1-1/4 [BP]	1P: $152-$242	2P: $162-$242
11/1-11/30 [BP]	1P: $98-$170	2P: $98-$180
4/24-10/31 [BP]	1P: $89-$161	2P: $89-$171

Location: I-75, exit 107, 0.7 mi w. 3557 Pine Ridge Rd 34109. Fax: 239/593-1301. **Facility:** 82 units. 40 one-bedroom standard units with efficiencies. 30 one- and 12 two-bedroom suites with kitchens. 3 stories, interior corridors. **Bath:** combo or shower only. **Parking:** on-site. **Terms:** cancellation fee imposed, weekly rates available, package plans, small pets only ($125 fee). **Amenities:** dual phone lines, voice mail, irons, hair dryers. **Fee:** video library, high-speed Internet. **Pool(s):** heated outdoor. **Leisure Activities:** whirlpool, putting green, barbecue grill, exercise room, basketball. **Guest Services:** sundries, complimentary evening beverages: Mon-Thurs, valet and coin laundry. **Business Services:** meeting rooms, PC, fax (fee). **Cards:** AX, CB, DC, DS, MC, VI. **Special Amenities:** free full breakfast and free local telephone calls.

SOME UNITS

(SD) (🛏) (T) (&M) (&) ⊘ ⊇ (✕) (VCR) (♦) (DATA PORT) 🔋 🖿 🖵 / (✕) /
FEE

HILTON NAPLES *Book at aaa.com* Phone: (239)430-4900 **13**

(AAA) (SAVE)
▼▼▼▼▼

Large-scale Hotel

1/2-4/1	1P: $209	2P: $259
12/1-1/1	1P: $159	2P: $179
10/1-11/30	1P: $149	2P: $179
4/2-9/30	1P: $119	2P: $159

Location: US 41 (Tamiami Tr), just sw of jct Pine Ridge Rd. 5111 Tamiami Tr 34103. Fax: 239/430-4901. **Facility:** Large pillars, ironwork and Mediterranean-style archways enhance the lobby of this upscale property. 191 units. 180 one-bedroom standard units. 9 one- and 2 two-bedroom suites ($199). 4 stories, interior corridors. **Bath:** combo or shower only. **Parking:** on-site and valet. **Terms:** 3 day cancellation notice-fee imposed, weekly rates available, [AP] meal plan available. **Amenities:** high-speed Internet, dual phone lines, voice mail, irons, hair dryers. **Dining:** 6:30 am-11 pm, also, Shula's Steak House, see separate listing. **Pool(s):** heated outdoor. **Leisure Activities:** whirlpool, bicycles, exercise room, basketball. **Guest Services:** gift shop, valet laundry, airport transportation-Naples Airport, area transportation-within 5 mi. **Business Services:** conference facilities, business center. **Cards:** AX, CB, DC, DS, MC, VI. **Special Amenities:** free newspaper. *(See color ad p 624)*

SOME UNITS

(SD) (✈) (T) (Y) (&M) (&) ⊘ ⊇ (✕) (♦) (DATA PORT) 🔋 🖵 / (✕) 🖿 /

(See map and index starting on p. 620)

HOLIDAY INN ***Book at aaa.com*** Phone: (239)263-3434 [25]

1/20-4/8	1P: $139-$189	2P: $139-$189
4/9-4/30	1P: $109-$149	2P: $109-$149
12/1-1/19	1P: $89-$139	2P: $89-$139
5/1-11/30	1P: $74-$109	2P: $74-$109

Motel

Location: I-75, exit 107, 3.8 mi w on CR 896, then 3.8 mi s on US 41 (Tamiami Tr). 1100 Tamiami Tr N 34102. Fax: 239/261-3809. **Facility:** 137 one-bedroom standard units. 2 stories (no elevator), exterior corridors. *Bath:* combo or shower only. **Parking:** on-site. **Terms:** package plans, small pets only ($20 fee, in limited units). **Amenities:** high-speed Internet, voice mail, irons, hair dryers. **Dining:** 7 am-10 & 5-10 pm, Fri & Sat-midnight, cocktails. **Pool(s):** heated outdoor. **Leisure Activities:** exercise room. **Guest Services:** valet laundry. **Business Services:** meeting rooms, fax (fee). **Cards:** AX, CB, DC, DS, JC, MC, VI. **Special Amenities:** free local telephone calls and free newspaper. *(See color ad p 630)*

SOME UNITS

HOLIDAY INN EXPRESS IN NAPLES ***Book at aaa.com*** Phone: 239/348-1700 [29]

Property failed to provide current rates

Small-scale Hotel

Location: I-75, exit 101, just s to Davis, then just e. 3837 Toll Gate Blvd 34114. Fax: 239/348-1704. **Facility:** 68 one-bedroom standard units, some with efficiencies. 3 stories, interior corridors. *Bath:* combo or shower only. **Parking:** on-site. **Amenities:** voice mail, irons, hair dryers. **Pool(s):** heated outdoor. **Leisure Activities:** whirlpool. **Guest Services:** coin laundry. **Business Services:** meeting rooms, fax (fee).

SOME UNITS

INN AT PELICAN BAY ***Book at aaa.com*** Phone: (239)597-8777 [7]

12/1-4/15	1P: $188-$260	2P: $188-$260	XP: $20	F16
10/1-11/30	1P: $125-$179	2P: $125-$179	XP: $20	F16
4/16-5/31	1P: $107-$161	2P: $107-$161	XP: $20	F16
6/1-9/30	1P: $80-$104	2P: $80-$104	XP: $20	F16

Small-scale Hotel

Location: Just w of jct US 41 (Tamiami Tr); 0.7 mi e of Vanderbilt Beach; north end of town. 800 Vanderbilt Beach Rd 34108. Fax: 239/597-8012. **Facility:** Designated smoking area. 100 one-bedroom standard units, some with whirlpools. 6 stories, interior corridors. *Bath:* combo or shower only. **Parking:** on-site. **Terms:** 3 day cancellation notice, package plans. **Amenities:** video games (fee), voice mail, safes, irons, hair dryers. *Some:* high-speed Internet. **Pool(s):** heated outdoor. **Leisure Activities:** whirlpool, exercise room. **Guest Services:** valet laundry. **Business Services:** meeting rooms, fax (fee). **Cards:** AX, DC, DS, MC, VI. *(See color ad p 632)*

SOME UNITS

INN BY THE SEA Phone: (239)649-4124 [37]

12/14-4/18 [ECP]	1P: $149-$169	2P: $149-$169
12/1-12/13 & 4/19-11/30 [ECP]	1P: $94-$104	2P: $94-$104

Bed & Breakfast

Location: I-75, exit 101, corner of 11th Ave S and 3rd St S; in Old Naples area. 287 11th Ave S 34102-7022. Fax: 239/434-2842. **Facility:** This sunny, 1937 guest house features polished-pine floors and rooms themed to area islands; the staff speaks several languages. Smoke free premises. 6 units. 3 one-bedroom standard units. 2 one-bedroom suites ($114-$189). 1 cottage ($150-$225). 2 stories (no elevator), interior corridors. *Bath:* combo or shower only. **Parking:** on-site. **Leisure Activities:** bicycles. **Cards:** AX, CB, DC, DS, MC, VI.

SOME UNITS

UPGRADE YOUR VACATION.

Enjoy deluxe accommodations with significant savings exclusively for AAA members. Situated along the Gulf of Mexico and the pristine Estero Bay, the luxurious Hyatt Regency Coconut Point Resort & Spa is surrounded by lavish gardens, a championship golf course and elegant water features. This is not your typical hotel story. This is the Hyatt Touch.™ For reservations call 800 55 HYATT or visit **coconutpoint.hyatt.com**.

HYATT
R E G E N C Y
COCONUT POINT
RESORT AND SPA – NAPLES COAST
BONITA SPRINGS, FLORIDA

(See map and index starting on p. 620)

THE INN ON FIFTH · Book at aaa.com · Phone: (239)403-8777 · **32**

12/1-4/15	1P: $270-$400	2P: $270-$400	XP: $10	F16
4/16-5/31 & 10/1-11/30	1P: $190-$290	2P: $190-$290	XP: $10	F16
6/1-9/30	1P: $150-$260	2P: $150-$260	XP: $10	F16

Small-scale Hotel **Location:** Just w of jct US 41 (Tamiami Tr); downtown; in Old Naples area. 699 5th Ave S 34102. Fax: 239/403-8778. **Facility:** Smoke free premises. 87 units. 76 one-bedroom standard units. 11 one-bedroom suites, some with whirlpools. 3 stories, interior corridors. *Bath:* combo or shower only. **Parking:** on-site and valet. **Terms:** 7 day cancellation notice, package plans. **Amenities:** high-speed Internet (fee), dual phone lines, voice mail, safes, irons, hair dryers. **Pool(s):** heated outdoor. **Leisure Activities:** whirlpool, exercise room, spa. **Guest Services:** valet laundry. **Business Services:** meeting rooms, fax (fee). **Cards:** AX, DC, DS, MC, VI. *(See color ad below)*

SOME UNITS

ASK ⓈⒹ 🍴 🍸 🏋 🎱 ✕ ✕ DATA PORT ▭ / 🛏 FEE

LAPLAYA BEACH & GOLF RESORT · Book at aaa.com · Phone: (239)597-3123 · **4**

12/1-4/30	1P: $559-$799	2P: $559-$799	XP: $30	F18
5/1-5/29 & 10/1-11/30	1P: $379-$519	2P: $379-$519	XP: $30	F18
5/30-9/30	1P: $269-$389	2P: $269-$389	XP: $30	F18

Resort **Location:** Oceanfront. North end of town; US 41 (Tamiami Tr), 1.3 mi w on Vanderbilt Beach Rd (SR 862), then 0.5 mi Large-scale Hotel n. 9891 Gulf Shore Dr 34108. Fax: 239/597-6278. **Facility:** Tropical elegance describes this resort, with its white sandy beaches and lushly landscaped pool areas; guest rooms are well-appointed. Smoke free premises. 189 units. 180 one-bedroom standard units, some with whirlpools. 9 one-bedroom suites ($449-$1475), some with whirlpools. 1-15 stories, interior/exterior corridors. *Bath:* combo or shower only. **Parking:** valet. **Terms:** check-in 4 pm, 2-3 night minimum stay - seasonal, 14 day cancellation notice-fee imposed, package plans, $17 service charge, small pets only ($25 extra charge). **Amenities:** video games (fee), CD players, high-speed Internet, dual phone lines, voice mail, safes, honor bars, irons, hair dryers. **Dining:** Baleen, see separate listing. **Pool(s):** 2 heated outdoor, 2 small heated outdoor. **Leisure Activities:** whirlpool, rental paddleboats, boat dock, recreation programs, spa. *Fee:* sailboats, golf-18 holes, bicycles, fitness instruction. **Guest Services:** gift shop, valet laundry. **Business Services:** conference facilities, business center. **Cards:** AX, CB, DC, DS, JC, MC, VI.

ASK 🛏 🍴 🍸 🏋 👶 🎱 🐾 ✕ ✕ 🎥 DATA PORT ▭ FEE

(See map and index starting on p. 620)

THE NAPLES BEACH HOTEL & GOLF CLUB

Book at aaa.com   Phone: (239)261-2222   **28**

AAA SAVE

12/1-4/16	1P: $265-$485	2P: $265-$485	XP: $15 F17
4/17-5/29 & 9/25-11/30	1P: $185-$375	2P: $185-$375	XP: $15 F17
5/30-9/24	1P: $145-$260	2P: $145-$260	XP: $15 F17

Resort
Large-scale Hotel

Location: I-75, exit 101, 1 mi n via US 41 (Tamiami Tr), then 0.7 mi w on 7th Ave N. 851 Gulf Shore Blvd N 34102. Fax: 239/261-7380. **Facility:** Photographs by local artists decorate guest rooms in this traditional destination resort; a private orchid collection includes some 5,000 plants. 318 units. 277 one-bedroom standard units. 41 one-bedroom suites. 2-9 stories, interior/exterior corridors. *Bath:* combo or shower only. **Parking:** on-site and valet. **Terms:** check-in 4 pm, 8 day cancellation notice-fee imposed. **Amenities:** high-speed Internet (fee), voice mail, safes, irons, hair dryers. **Dining:** 4 restaurants, 7 am-midnight, cocktails, entertainment. **Pool(s):** heated outdoor. **Leisure Activities:** limited beach access, rental paddleboats, recreation programs, rental bicycles, exercise room, spa, volleyball. *Fee:* sailboats, beach chairs, beach towels, umbrellas, golf-18 holes, 6 tennis courts. **Guest Services:** gift shop, valet laundry. **Business Services:** conference facilities, business center. **Cards:** AX, DC, DS, MC, VI. *(See color ad below)*

SOME UNITS

FEE

PARK SHORE RESORT

Book at aaa.com   Phone: (239)263-2222   **15**

AAA SAVE

2/10-4/22	1P: $216-$270
12/23-2/9	1P: $188-$235
4/23-11/30	1P: $120-$150
12/1-12/22	1P: $104-$130

Condominium   **Location:** I-75, exit 107, just w of jct US 41 (Tamiami Tr) via Island Club Loop. 600 Neapolitan Way 34103. Fax: 239/263-0946. **Facility:** A small pond surrounds the tropically landscaped grounds of this hotel that is next to a shopping mall. 62 units. 9 one- and 53 two-bedroom suites with kitchens. 2-4 stories, exterior corridors. **Parking:** on-site. **Terms:** office hours 7 am-11 pm, 3 day cancellation notice, in season, package plans. **Amenities:** voice mail, irons, hair dryers. **Dining:** 11:30 am-9 pm; seasonal hours vary, cocktails. **Pool(s):** heated outdoor. **Leisure Activities:** whirlpool, sun deck, 4 tennis courts, racquetball courts, recreation programs, gas barbecue grills, picnic table & gazebo area, basketball, shuffleboard, volleyball. **Guest Services:** valet and coin laundry, area transportation-beach. **Business Services:** fax (fee). **Cards:** AX, DC, DS, MC, VI. *(See color ad p 626)*

SOME UNITS

QUALITY INN & SUITES

Book at aaa.com   Phone: (239)649-5500   **17**

AAA SAVE

2/1-4/30	1P: $159-$299	2P: $159-$299	XP: $10 F18
12/1-1/31 & 5/1-11/30	1P: $89-$229	2P: $89-$229	XP: $10 F18

Location: I-75, exit 107, 3.5 mi n on US 41, then just n of Park Shore Dr. 4055 Tamiami Tr N 34103. Fax: 239/430-0422. **Facility:** 99 units. 63 one-bedroom standard units. 36 one-bedroom suites. 5 stories,
Small-scale Hotel   interior corridors. *Bath:* combo or shower only. **Parking:** on-site. **Terms:** package plans, small pets only ($25 fee, $5 extra charge). **Amenities:** dual phone lines, voice mail, irons, hair dryers. *Fee:* video library, safes. **Pool(s):** heated outdoor. **Leisure Activities:** exercise room. **Guest Services:** valet and coin laundry. **Business Services:** meeting rooms, business center. **Cards:** AX, CB, DC, DS, JC, MC, VI. **Special Amenities:** free continental breakfast and free local telephone calls.

SOME UNITS
FEE

QUALITY INN & SUITES GOLF RESORT

Book at aaa.com   Phone: (239)455-1010   **20**

2/1-4/15	1P: $149-$179	2P: $149-$179	XP: $10 F18
12/21-1/31	1P: $109-$129	2P: $109-$129	XP: $10 F18
12/1-12/20	1P: $99-$119	2P: $99-$119	XP: $10 F18
4/16-11/30	1P: $89-$119	2P: $89-$119	XP: $10 F18

Resort
Small-scale Hotel

Location: I-75, exit 101, 1.6 mi n via SR 951 (Isle of Capri Rd). 4100 Golden Gate Pkwy 34116. Fax: 239/455-4038. **Facility:** On golf course. 153 units. 121 one-bedroom standard units, some with efficiencies. 24 one- and 8 two-bedroom suites ($135-$345) with kitchens, some with whirlpools. 1-4 stories, interior/exterior corridors. **Parking:** on-site. **Terms:** cancellation fee imposed, package plans. **Amenities:** irons, hair dryers. **Pool(s):** heated outdoor. **Leisure Activities:** whirlpool, 2 tennis courts, shuffleboard. *Fee:* golf-18 holes. **Guest Services:** valet laundry. **Business Services:** meeting rooms, fax (fee). **Cards:** AX, CB, DC, DS, JC, MC, VI.

SOME UNITS

(See map and index starting on p. 620)

RED ROOF INN   *Book at aaa.com*   Phone: (239)774-3117   ③⑤

◇◇ ◇◇
	1/29-4/1	1P: $80-$90	2P: $80-$90
Motel	12/1-1/28	1P: $70-$80	2P: $70-$80
	4/2-11/30	1P: $50-$60	2P: $50-$60

Location: I-75, exit 101, 6.5 mi w on SR 84; just e of jct US 41 (Tamiami Tr). 1925 Davis Blvd 34104. Fax: 239/775-5333. **Facility:** 157 units. 127 one-bedroom standard units. 30 one-bedroom suites with kitchens. 3 stories, exterior corridors. *Bath:* combo or shower only. **Parking:** on-site. **Terms:** check-in 4 pm, small pets only. **Amenities:** video games (fee), voice mail. **Pool(s):** heated outdoor. **Leisure Activities:** whirlpool. **Guest Services:** coin laundry. **Business Services:** fax (fee). **Cards:** AX, CB, DC, DS, MC, VI.

SOME UNITS

🐕 🍴 🖥 🏊 🎥 📶 / ✕ 🛏 📠 🖥 /

THE REGISTRY RESORT & CLUB   *Book at aaa.com*   Phone: (239)597-3232   ①⓪

AAA SAVE
| | 12/1-4/30 [ECP] | 1P: $389-$969 | 2P: $389-$969 | XP: $25 | F17 |
| | 5/1-5/29 & 10/6-11/30 [ECP] | 1P: $279-$719 | 2P: $279-$719 | XP: $25 | F17 |
◇◇ ◇◇ | 5/30-10/5 [ECP] | 1P: $179-$629 | 2P: $179-$629 | XP: $25 | F17 |

Resort
Large-scale Hotel

Location: I-75, exit 107, north end of town; 0.5 mi w of US 41 (Tamiami Tr) via CR 896 (Pine Ridge/Seagate Blvd). 475 Seagate Dr 34103. Fax: 239/594-6777. **Facility:** Italian marble adds a luxurious touch to the public areas of this high-rise; a trolley carries guests over a protected mangrove lagoon to the beach. 474 units. 395 one-bedroom standard units. 79 one-bedroom suites ($969-$1600), some with whirlpools. 1-18 stories, interior/exterior corridors. *Bath:* combo or shower only. **Parking:** on-site and valet. **Terms:** 14 day cancellation notice, 7 day 5/1-11/30-fee imposed, package plans, $20 service charge. **Amenities:** CD players, dual phone lines, voice mail, safes, honor bars, irons, hair dryers. *Fee:* video games, high-speed Internet. *Some:* DVD players. **Dining:** 6 restaurants, 7 am-11 pm; Sunday brunch, cocktails, nightclub, entertainment. **Pool(s):** 5 heated outdoor. **Leisure Activities:** whirlpools, beach access, rental sailboats, fishing, golf & tennis instruction, recreation programs, access to nature preserve, rental bicycles, basketball. *Fee:* canoes, windsurfing, aqua bikes, catamarans, sea kayaks, golf-18 holes, 15 tennis courts (5 lighted), massage. **Guest Services:** gift shop, valet laundry, area transportation (fee). **Business Services:** conference facilities, business center. **Cards:** AX, CB, DC, DS, MC, VI. **Special Amenities:** free expanded continental breakfast. *(See color ad below)*

SOME UNITS

🅂 🆔 ✈ 🍴 24 🍽 🛗 🅜 🖥 🐾 🏊 🚹 ✕ 🎥 📶 🖥 / ✕ VCR 🛏 📠 /
      FEE   FEE   FEE FEE

(See map and index starting on p. 620)

RESIDENCE INN BY MARRIOTT, NAPLES *Book at aaa.com* Phone: (239)659-1300 **16**

2/1-4/30 [BP]	1P: $199-$329	2P: $199-$329
12/21-1/31 [BP]	1P: $159-$309	2P: $159-$309
5/1-11/30 [BP]	1P: $89-$179	2P: $89-$179
12/1-12/20 [BP]	1P: $99-$159	2P: $99-$159

Small-scale Hotel

Location: I-75, exit 107, 3.8 mi w on CR 896 (Pine Ridge Rd), then 1 mi s on US 41 (Tamiami Tr). 4075 Tamiami Tr N 34103. Fax: 239/659-2300. **Facility:** 120 units. 39 one-bedroom standard units with efficiencies. 52 one- and 29 two-bedroom suites with kitchens. 3 stories, interior corridors. *Bath:* combo or shower only. **Parking:** on-site. **Terms:** cancellation fee imposed, weekly rates available, pets ($75 fee, $3 extra charge). **Amenities:** high-speed Internet, dual phone lines, voice mail, irons, hair dryers. **Pool(s):** heated outdoor. **Leisure Activities:** whirlpool, exercise room, sports court. **Guest Services:** complimentary evening beverages: Mon-Thurs, valet and coin laundry, area transportation. **Business Services:** meeting rooms, fax (fee). **Cards:** AX, CB, DC, DS, JC, MC, VI.

THE RITZ-CARLTON GOLF RESORT *Book at aaa.com* Phone: (239)593-2000 **8**

AAA **SAVE**

All Year   1P: $229-$619   2P: $229-$619

Location: I-75, exit 111, 1.6 mi w on CR 846 (Immokalee Rd); 1.3 mi s on CR 31 (Airport-Pulling Rd), just e. 2600 Tiburon Dr 34109. Fax: 239/593-6691. **Facility:** Luxurious rooms, attentive service and 36 holes of golf are among the resort's many offerings. 295 units. 255 one-bedroom standard units. 30 one-, 9 two- and 1 three-bedroom suites ($399-$3000), some with whirlpools. 7 stories, interior corridors. *Bath:* combo or shower only. **Parking:** on-site (fee) and valet. **Terms:** check-in 4 pm, 7 day cancellation notice, 14 day 12/1-4/30-fee imposed. **Amenities:** video library, CD players, dual phone lines, voice mail, safes, honor bars, irons, hair dryers. *Fee:* video games, high-speed Internet. *Some:* DVD players, fax. **Dining:** 6:30 am-10 pm, cocktails, also, Lemonia, see separate listing, entertainment. **Pool(s):** heated outdoor. **Leisure Activities:** sauna, whirlpool, steamroom, water aerobic classes, golf instruction, driving range, tennis instructions, billiards, card room, Ritz Kids Club, playground. *Fee:* swimming lessons, golf-36 holes, 4 tennis courts (2 lighted), tennis equipment, bicycles, massage. **Guest Services:** gift shop, valet laundry, area transportation-Ritz-Carlton, Naples spa & facilities, beach & within 4 mi. **Business Services:** conference facilities, business center. **Cards:** AX, DC, DS, MC, VI. **Special Amenities:** free newspaper.

Large-scale Hotel

THE RITZ-CARLTON, NAPLES *Book at aaa.com* Phone: (239)598-3300 **6**

AAA **SAVE**

All Year   1P: $319-$889   2P: $319-$889

Resort
Large-scale Hotel

Location: Oceanfront. US 41 (Tamiami Tr), 1.3 mi w on CR 846 (Vanderbilt Beach Rd). 280 Vanderbilt Beach Rd 34108. Fax: 239/598-6690. **Facility:** Artwork and antiques add Old World elegance to the public areas of this hotel on the gulf; many guest rooms have water views and some have balconies. 450 units. 415 one-bedroom standard units. 32 one- and 3 two-bedroom suites ($629-$4499). 13 stories, interior corridors. *Bath:* some combo or shower only. **Parking:** on-site (fee) and valet. **Terms:** check-in 4 pm, 7 day cancellation notice, 14 day 12/1-4/30-fee imposed. **Amenities:** video library, DVD players, CD players, dual phone lines, voice mail, safes, honor bars, irons, hair dryers. *Fee:* video games, high-speed Internet. **Dining:** 3 restaurants, 6:30 am-10 pm, cocktails, also, Artisans in The Dining Room, The Grill, see separate listings, nightclub, entertainment. **Pool(s):** 2 heated outdoor. **Leisure Activities:** saunas, whirlpools, steamrooms, seasonal beach pavilion, recreation programs, cooking & wellness programs, Ritz Kids Club, jogging, spa, aerobics. *Fee:* sailboats, boogie boards, catamarans, kayaks, rhino boats, skis, suncats, golf & tennis instruction, 4 lighted tennis courts, bicycles. **Guest Services:** gift shop, valet laundry, area transportation-The Ritz-Carlton Golf Resort. **Business Services:** conference facilities, business center. **Cards:** AX, DC, DS, MC, VI.

SPINNAKER INN OF NAPLES Phone: (239)434-0444 **11**

AAA **SAVE**

2/1-4/15	1P: $79-$86	2P: $79-$86	XP: $6	F16
12/21-1/31	1P: $60-$76	2P: $60-$76	XP: $6	F16
12/1-12/20 & 4/16-11/30	1P: $46-$52	2P: $46-$52	XP: $6	F16

Motel

Location: I-75, exit 107, just w. 6600 Dudley Dr 34105. Fax: 239/434-0414. **Facility:** 110 one-bedroom standard units, some with efficiencies. 1 story, exterior corridors. *Bath:* combo or shower only. **Parking:** on-site. **Terms:** cancellation fee imposed, weekly rates available, small pets only ($10 extra charge). **Pool(s):** small outdoor. **Guest Services:** valet laundry. **Cards:** DC, DS, MC, VI. **Special Amenities:** early check-in/late check-out.

STAYBRIDGE SUITES BY HOLIDAY INN *Book at aaa.com* Phone: (239)643-8002 **14**

2/1-3/31 [CP]	1P: $210-$280	2P: $210-$280
12/21-1/31 [CP]	1P: $160-$250	2P: $160-$250
12/1-12/20 & 4/1-11/30 [CP]	1P: $130-$180	2P: $130-$180

Small-scale Hotel

Location: I-75, exit 107, 3.8 mi w on Pine Ridge Rd to US 41 (Tamiami Tr), then just s. 4805 Tamiami Tr N 34103. Fax: 239/643-8069. **Facility:** 122 units. 68 one-bedroom standard units with efficiencies. 46 one- and 8 two-bedroom suites with kitchens. 4 stories, interior corridors. *Bath:* combo or shower only. **Parking:** on-site. **Terms:** 3 day cancellation notice, 1/1-3/31-fee imposed, pets ($75 fee). **Amenities:** video library (fee), high-speed Internet, dual phone lines, voice mail, irons, hair dryers. **Pool(s):** heated outdoor. **Leisure Activities:** whirlpool, exercise room. **Guest Services:** sundries, complimentary evening beverages: Tues-Thurs, complimentary laundry. **Business Services:** meeting rooms, business center. **Cards:** AX, DC, DS, MC, VI.

STONEY'S COURTYARD INN Phone: 239/261-3870 **21**

Property failed to provide current rates

Motel

Location: I-75, exit 107, 3.8 mi w on CR 896, then s on US 41 (Tamiami Tr). 2630 9th St (N Tamiami Tr) 34103. Fax: 239/261-4932. **Facility:** 76 units. 72 one-bedroom standard units. 4 one-bedroom suites. 2 stories (no elevator), exterior corridors. **Parking:** on-site. **Amenities:** voice mail. *Some: Fee:* safes. **Pool(s):** heated outdoor. **Leisure Activities:** shuffleboard. **Guest Services:** coin laundry.

(See map and index starting on p. 620)

TRIANON OLD NAPLES   *Book at aaa.com*

Phone: (239)435-9600   **33**

◇◇◇◇

12/1-4/30	1P: $239-$600	2P: $239-$600	XP: $10	F
10/1-11/30	1P: $150-$500	2P: $150-$500	XP: $10	F
5/1-9/30	1P: $100-$400	2P: $100-$400	XP: $10	F

Small-scale Hotel   **Location:** Just s of jct US 41 (Tamiami Tr); downtown; in Old Naples area. 955 7th Ave S 34102. Fax: 239/261-0025. **Facility:** 58 units. 55 one-bedroom standard units. 3 one-bedroom suites. 3 stories, interior corridors. **Bath:** combo or shower only. **Parking:** on-site. **Terms:** cancellation fee imposed. **Amenities:** dual phone lines, voice mail, safes, irons, hair dryers. **Pool(s):** heated outdoor. **Guest Services:** valet laundry. **Business Services:** meeting rooms, fax (fee). **Cards:** AX, DC, DS, MC, VI.

SOME UNITS

(ASK) (S/D) (🛏) (⊣) (Y) (🖙) (🏊) (🚶) (🎥) (DATA PORT) (💻) / (✕) (VCR) (🔌) /
            FEE   FEE

VANDERBILT BEACH RESORT

Phone: 239/597-3144   **5**

◇◇◇◇

2/1-4/30	1P: $176-$298	2P: $176-$298	XP: $10	D17
12/1-1/31	1P: $146-$253	2P: $146-$253	XP: $10	D17
5/1-11/30	1P: $104-$195	2P: $104-$195	XP: $6	D17

Motel   **Location:** Oceanfront. I-75, exit 111, north end of town; 1.5 mi w of US 41 (Tamiami Tr) via Vanderbilt Beach Rd (SR 862), then just n. 9225 Gulfshore Dr N 34108. Fax: 239/597-2199. **Facility:** Smoke free premises. 20 units. 10 one-bedroom standard units with efficiencies. 10 one-bedroom suites with efficiencies. 2 stories (no elevator), exterior corridors. **Parking:** on-site. **Terms:** office hours 7 am-10 pm, 14 day cancellation notice, 9% service charge. **Amenities:** video library (fee), voice mail. *Some:* DVD players (fee). **Dining:** The Turtle Club, see separate listing. **Pool(s):** heated outdoor. **Leisure Activities:** boat dock, tennis court. **Guest Services:** coin laundry. **Cards:** AX, MC, VI.

SOME UNITS

(🛏) (Y) (🏊) (✕) (🔌) (📶) (💻) / (VCR) /
                                        FEE

VANDERBILT INN NAPLES   *Book at aaa.com*

Phone: (239)597-3151   **3**

◇◇◇◇

All Year	1P: $115-$390	2P: $115-$390	XP: $10	F17

Motel   **Location:** I-75, exit 111, north end of town; 1.5 mi w of US 41 (Tamiami Tr) via SR 846 (Immokalee Rd). Located next to Delnor-Wiggins Pass State Recreation Area. 11000 Gulf Shore Dr N 34108. Fax: 239/597-3099. **Facility:** 147 one-bedroom standard units, some with efficiencies. 2 stories (no elevator), exterior corridors. **Parking:** on-site. **Terms:** 3 day cancellation notice-fee imposed, weekly rates available. **Amenities:** voice mail, safes, irons, hair dryers. **Pool(s):** heated outdoor. **Leisure Activities:** whirlpool, rental boats, rental sailboats. *Fee:* windsurfing. **Guest Services:** gift shop, coin laundry. **Business Services:** meeting rooms, business center. **Cards:** AX, CB, DC, DS, MC, VI. *(See color ad below)*

SOME UNITS

(ASK) (S/D) (🛏) (Y) (🏊) (✕) (🎥) (DATA PORT) (🔌) / (✕) (📶) (💻) /

WELLESLEY INN (NAPLES)   *Book at aaa.com*

Phone: 239/793-4646   **34**

(AAA) (SAVE)
◇◇◇

Small-scale Hotel   **Location:** I-75, exit 101, 6.5 mi w on SR 84. 1555 5th Ave S 34102. Fax: 239/793-5248. **Facility:** 104 one-bedroom standard units. 3 stories, interior corridors. **Bath:** combo or shower only. **Parking:** on-site. **Terms:** cancellation fee imposed, weekly rates available, small pets only. **Amenities:** voice mail, irons, hair dryers. *Fee:* video games, high-speed Internet, safes. **Pool(s):** heated outdoor. **Guest Services:** valet laundry. **Business Services:** fax (fee). **Cards:** AX, DC, DS, MC, VI.

All Year [CP]	1P: $139-$199	2P: $139-$199	XP: $10 F17

SOME UNITS

(🛏) (⊣) (🖙) (🎥) (🏊) (🚶) (🎥) (DATA PORT) (🔌) (📶) (💻) / (✕) /

(See map and index starting on p. 620)

──────── **WHERE TO DINE** ────────

ANDRE'S STEAKHOUSE

ⒶⒶⒶ
◇◇ ◇◇
Steak House

Dinner: $18-$34   **Phone: 239/263-5851**   ⓴

Location: I-75, exit 107, 3.8 mi w on Pine Ridge Rd (SR 896), then 2 mi s. 2800 N Tamiami Tr 34103. **Hours:** 5 pm-9 pm. **Closed:** 1/1, 11/23, 12/24, 12/25; also Super Bowl Sun. **Reservations:** suggested. **Features:** The restaurant is known for its aged steaks and big side dishes, but if seafood is on the agenda, that also can be taken care of. Casual dress. **Parking:** on-site. **Cards:** AX, DC, DS, MC, VI.

AQUA GRILL

◇▽◇▽◇▽
International

Lunch: $12-$25   **Dinner: $15-$30**   **Phone: 239/254-1234**   ⓭

Location: I-75, exit 107, north end of town; 0.5 mi w of US 41 via CR 896 (Pine Ridge/Seagate Blvd); in Waterside Shops. 5435 Tamiami Trail N 34108. **Hours:** 11:30 am-2:30 & 5-10 pm. **Reservations:** accepted. **Features:** Not far from the blue water of the Gulf you will find a unique dining experience at this upscale grill, which offers a well-rounded menu, but the seafood recipes are the focus. Dressy casual; cocktails. **Parking:** on-site. **Cards:** AX, DS, MC, VI.

ARTISANS IN THE DINING ROOM

◇▽◇▽◇▽◇▽
French

Dinner: $65-$85   **Phone: 239/598-6644**   ⑥

Location: US 41 (Tamiami Tr), 1.3 mi w on CR 846 (Vanderbilt Beach Rd); in The Ritz-Carlton, Naples. 280 Vanderbilt Beach Rd 34108. **Hours:** Open 12/1-7/31 & 9/1-11/30; 6 pm-10 pm. **Closed:** Sun & Mon. **Reservations:** suggested. **Features:** This is beautifully staged, classic dining with a gracious ambience that is rarely found. Appreciate skilled preparation of fresh seafood and other specialties; peruse the outstanding international wine list; and enjoy outdoor dining when weather permits. Semi-formal attire; cocktails; entertainment. **Parking:** valet. **Cards:** AX, CB, DC, DS, JC, MC, VI.

BALEEN

ⒶⒶⒶ
◇▽◇▽◇▽
Regional
Seafood

Lunch: $8-$18   **Dinner: $27-$32**   **Phone: 239/598-5707**   ①

Location: North end of town; US 41 (Tamiami Tr), 1.3 mi w on Vanderbilt Beach Rd (SR 862), then 0.5 mi n; in LaPlaya Beach & Golf Resort. 9891 Gulf Shore Dr 34108. **Hours:** 7 am-11, 11:30-5 & 6-10 pm. **Reservations:** suggested. **Features:** The room offers two settings: the formal inside, where the atmosphere is casually elegant, and the cozy patio, where sunset views are breathtaking. The chef labels the food as "eclectic seafood house." Pacific Rim accents punctuate fresh seafood and aged meats. Dressy casual; cocktails; entertainment. **Parking:** valet. **Cards:** AX, CB, DC, DS, JC, MC, VI.

Ⓨ

BHA! BHA! A PERSIAN BISTRO

◇▽◇▽◇▽
Persian

Lunch: $7-$15   **Dinner: $14-$23**   **Phone: 239/594-5557**   ⑦

Location: Corner of US 41 (Tamiami Tr) and Vanderbilt Beach Rd; in Pavilion Shopping Center. 847 Vanderbilt Beach Rd 34108. **Hours:** 11:30 am-3 & 5-10 pm, Sat 11:30 am-2:30 & 5-10 pm, Sun-9 pm. **Closed:** 1/1, 11/23, 12/25; also Mon. **Features:** Bordered by shops, this dining oasis offers both indoor and outdoor seating. Diners can feast on such creatively prepared delights as fresh seafood couscous or paella, mango-grilled shrimp and succulent lamb, beef or chicken dishes. Save room for dessert with Turkish coffee. Casual dress; beer & wine only. **Parking:** on-site. **Cards:** AX, MC, VI.

BISTRO 821

◇▽◇▽◇▽
Continental

Dinner: $16-$29   **Phone: 239/261-5821**   ㉛

Location: US 41 (Tamiami Tr), just w. 821 Fifth Ave S 34102. **Hours:** 5 pm-10 pm, Fri & Sat-1 am. **Closed:** 12/25. **Reservations:** required. **Features:** The room is aglow with amber walls, candles and angled, wall-mounted mirrors. The food is exciting and on the worldly side of the page with various fresh seafood preparations. Meat and pasta items are also available with the chef's special twist. Dressy casual; cocktails. **Parking:** street. **Cards:** AX, CB, DC, MC, VI.

♿Ⓜ Ⓨ

THE BOATHOUSE

ⒶⒶⒶ
◇▽ ◇▽
American

Menu on aaa.com   **Lunch: $7-$17**   **Dinner: $10-$24**   **Phone: 239/643-2235**   ㊳

Location: US 41 S to 9th St S. 990 Broad Ave S 34102. **Hours:** 11:30 am-10 pm. **Closed:** 12/25. **Reservations:** accepted. **Features:** Right at the water's edge close to downtown, the casual, nautically themed restaurant offers incredible waterfront views. The lively and fun atmosphere—created in part by an outer appearance that resembles an old-time ship's store—has wide appeal. Casual dress; cocktails. **Parking:** on-site. **Cards:** AX, DS, MC, VI.

CAMPIELLO RISTORANTE

◇▽◇▽◇▽
Northern
Italian

Lunch: $9-$14   **Dinner: $16-$29**   **Phone: 239/435-1166**   ㊵

Location: Jct 12th Ave S and Broad Ave; in historic district. 1177 3rd St S 34102. **Hours:** 11:30 am-2:30 & 5:30-10 pm, Fri & Sat-11 pm, Sun noon-10 pm. **Closed:** 11/23, 12/25. **Reservations:** required. **Features:** Sitting outside in the courtyard or in the open-air-like dining room, diners are tempted by thoughtfully prepared offerings of Northern Italian cuisine. Dressy casual; cocktails; entertainment. **Parking:** street. **Cards:** AX, DS, MC, VI. **Historic**

Ⓨ

CHARDONNAY

◇▽◇▽ ◇▽◇▽
French

Dinner: $23-$35   **Phone: 239/261-1744**   ㉑

Location: I-75, exit 107, 3.8 mi w on CR 896 to US 41 (Tamiami Trail), then 2.5 mi s; corner of US 41 and Mooringline Dr; in Best Western Naples Inn & Suites. 2331 Tamiami Tr N (US 41) 34103. **Hours:** 5:30 pm-10 pm. **Closed:** 1/1; also Sun. **Reservations:** suggested. **Features:** Lovely country French decor characterizes this spacious restaurant, which offers several dining sections with decorative lighting and frosted-glass dividers. Creatively prepared and presented entrees include such delights as duck pate, escargot, salmon mousse, filet of sole, red snapper and prime cuts of meat. For dessert, savor the sumptuous creme brulee or souffle. There is a portico for rainy days. Dressy casual; cocktails. **Parking:** on-site and valet. **Cards:** AX, DC, MC, VI.

Ⓨ

CHOPS CITY GRILL

◇▽◇▽◇▽
Steak & Seafood

Dinner: $18-$34   **Phone: 239/262-4677**   ㉚

Location: Just w of US 41 (Tamiami Trail). 837 5th Ave S 34102. **Reservations:** required. **Features:** The menu offers chops, aged steaks, seafood and sushi, all creatively presented. The room is cozy and alive, a great combination for a night out. Dressy casual; cocktails. **Parking:** street. **Cards:** AX, MC, VI.

♿Ⓜ Ⓨ

(See map and index starting on p. 620)

DA RU MA
▼▼▼
Japanese

Dinner: $17–$35   Phone: 239/591-1200   **④**

Location: 1 mi w of US 41 on CR 862 (Vanderbilt Beach Rd). 241 Center St N 34108. **Hours:** 5 pm-10 pm. Closed: 11/23; also Super Bowl Sun. **Reservations:** suggested. **Features:** With hibachi-style steak and seafood and fresh sushi, this restaurant appeals to those looking for a more adventurous dining experience. Fresh, flavorful ingredients and artistic compositions lend themselves perfectly to the exotic delicacies offered. Dressy casual; cocktails; entertainment. **Parking:** on-site. **Cards:** AX, DS, MC, VI.

DOCK AT CRAYTON COVE
ⒶⒶⒶ
▼▼ ▼▼
Seafood

Lunch: $5–$20   Dinner: $5–$20   Phone: 239/263-9940   **㊴**

Location: 8th St S to 12th Ave S, e to bay. 845 12th Ave S at Naples Bay 34102. **Hours:** 11 am-midnight. Closed: 11/23. **Features:** Diners can whet their appetites with gentle breezes and a splendid postcard view of City Dock and Naples Bay, then indulge in creative, Caribbean-style preparations, such as fresh Bahamian conch fritters, or the simple yet tasty fish and chips, burgers or sandwiches. The raw bar is a nice option from 3 pm to 6 pm. Casual dress; cocktails. **Parking:** on-site. **Cards:** AX, DS, MC, VI.

THE ENGLISH PUB
▼▼ ▼▼
English

Lunch: $7–$11   Dinner: $10–$16   Phone: 239/774-2408   **㊲**

Location: I-75, exit 101, 1.5 mi s on US 41 (Tamiami Tr) to Commercial Dr, then e. 2408 Linwood Ave 34112. **Hours:** 11 am-9:30 pm, Sat from noon. **Features:** Authentic English pub food—fish 'n' chips, steak and kidney pie, bangers and mash, and shepherd's pie—is served in a nice, Tudor-style dining room. A wide selection of British beers on tap is available for washing down a hearty meal. Dining may end at 9:30 pm, but the pub stays open until midnight weekdays and 2 am weekends. Casual dress; cocktails. **Parking:** on-site. **Cards:** AX, DC, DS, MC, VI.

FIRST WATCH
▼▼
American

Lunch: $4–$7   Phone: 239/434-0005   **㉓**

Location: 2.3 mi n on US 41 (Tamiami Tr), 1.2 mi sw via Mooringline Dr. 225 Banyan Blvd 34102. **Hours:** 7 am-2:30 pm. Closed: 11/23, 12/25. **Features:** This incredibly popular diner offers breakfast, brunch and lunch. Fresh air in the courtyard dining area makes the eggs, omelets, pancakes, waffles, soups and salads that much more inviting. Casual dress. **Parking:** on-site. **Cards:** AX, DS, MC, VI.

FLACOS MEXICAN SPECIALTIES & STEAKHOUSE
ⒶⒶⒶ
▼▼ ▼▼ ▼▼
Mexican

Lunch: $5–$12   Dinner: $6–$20   Phone: 239/261-7672   **⑯**

Location: Just s of Pine Ridge Rd; in Bank of Naples Plaza. 4947 Tamiami Tr N 34103. **Hours:** 11 am-3 & 5-10:30 pm, Sat & Sun noon-10:30 pm. Closed: 11/23, 12/25. **Features:** Artifacts and soft lighting lend to the coziness of the dining room, where patrons unwind over good food. The menu blends traditional favorites and vegetarian selections. Casual dress; cocktails. **Parking:** on-site. **Cards:** AX, CB, DC, DS, JC, MC, VI.

FLEMING'S
▼▼ ▼▼
Steak House

Dinner: $21–$36   Phone: 239/598-2424   **⑧**

Location: On US 41, just s of Vanderbilt Beach Rd. 8985 Tamiami Tr N 34108. **Hours:** 4 pm-10 pm, Fri & Sat-11 pm. Sun-9 pm. Closed: 11/23, 12/25. **Reservations:** suggested. **Features:** High-quality aged prime beef is served in ample portions. The professional staff is well versed in preparation and ingredients. Guests can anticipate a memorable dining experience. Dressy casual; cocktails. **Parking:** on-site and valet. **Cards:** AX, DC, DS, MC, VI.

THE GRILL
▼▼ ▼▼ ▼▼
American

Dinner: $30–$48   Phone: 239/598-6644   **⑤**

Location: US 41 (Tamiami Tr), 1.3 mi w on CR 846 (Vanderbilt Beach Rd); in The Ritz-Carlton, Naples. 280 Vanderbilt Beach Rd 34108. **Hours:** 6 pm-10 pm. **Reservations:** suggested. **Features:** Intimate, formal dining in a peaceful, club-like atmosphere is enhanced by warm wood, original art and rich fabrics. A variety of steak and seafood is artfully presented and meticulously prepared. Choose the perfect vintage from a comprehensive wine list. Semi-formal attire; cocktails; entertainment. **Parking:** valet. **Cards:** AX, CB, DC, DS, JC, MC, VI.

IL BELLAGIO
▼▼ ▼▼ ▼▼
Italian

Lunch: $8–$15   Dinner: $12–$24   Phone: 239/430-7020   **㉗**

Location: US 41 S (Tamiami Tr S), just e on Goodlette Frank Rd, then s. 492 Bayfront Pl 34102. **Hours:** 11:30 am-3 & 5-11 pm. Closed: 11/23, 12/25. **Reservations:** suggested. **Features:** The dining patio overlooks a small lit lake, while the indoors dining area has the feel of a palace. Food is artfully presented and carefully prepared so diners feel as though they are in Italy. The large menu incorporates all of the expected favorites and more. Dressy casual; cocktails. **Parking:** on-site and valet. **Cards:** AX, CB, DC, DS, JC, MC, VI.

LEMONIA
▼▼ ▼▼ ▼▼
Regional Italian

Lunch: $10–$20   Dinner: $24–$35   Phone: 239/593-2000   **⑨**

Location: I-75, exit 111, 1.6 mi w on CR 846 (Immokalee Rd); 1.3 mi s on CR 31 (Airport-Pulling Rd), just e; in The Ritz-Carlton Golf Resort. 2600 Tiburon Dr 34109. **Hours:** 6:30 am-9 pm, Fri & Sat-10 pm; Sunday brunch. **Reservations:** suggested. **Features:** The atmosphere is soft, the food is Italian, and the service is smooth. From the rotunda in the center of the room, the dining area spreads out onto the patio, which affords views of the golf course. The foods have wonderful aromas and flavors. Dressy casual; cocktails; entertainment. **Parking:** on-site (fee) and valet. **Cards:** AX, CB, DC, DS, JC, MC, VI.

LINDBURGERS
▼▼
American

Lunch: $6–$10   Dinner: $6–$10   Phone: 239/262-1127   **㉖**

Location: On US 41 (Tamiami Tr) and 3rd Ave S. 330 Tamiami Tr S 34102. **Hours:** 11 am-9 pm. Closed major holidays; also Sun. **Features:** The relaxed restaurant may not have sold 50 million burgers, but it lines up more than 50 combinations of burgers. Also on the menu are hot dogs and hot and cold sandwiches. Casual dress; beer & wine only. **Parking:** on-site. **Cards:** AX, DS, MC, VI.

MEL'S DINER NAPLES
▼▼
American

Lunch: $5–$12   Dinner: $5–$12   Phone: 239/643-9898   **⑲**

Location: On US 41, 3.5 mi s of Pine Ridge Rd. 3650 Tamiami Tr 34103. **Hours:** 6:30 am-10 pm. Closed: 12/25. **Features:** American comfort foods—from sandwiches to burgers to ribs—are served in a comfortable setting. Casual dress; beer & wine only. **Parking:** on-site. **Cards:** AX, DS, MC, VI.

(See map and index starting on p. 620)

MICHELBOB'S

American

Lunch: $5-$13 **Dinner:** $10-$24 **Phone:** 239/643-2877 ﹝24﹞
Location: I-75, exit 107, 2 mi w on Pine Ridge Rd (CR 896), then 4 mi s on Airport-Pulling Rd (CR 31). 371 Airport Rd N 34104. **Hours:** Open 12/1-8/31 & 10/1-11/30; 11 am-9 pm, Sat from 4 pm, Sun 4 pm-8 pm. Closed: 11/23, 12/25; also 2 weeks in May. **Features:** Return to the 50s in this comfortable family dining room decorated with period memorabilia. The menu offers basic ribs and chicken selections with fries, coleslaw and homemade baked beans. Friendly and attentive service makes this a popular stop. Casual dress; cocktails. **Parking:** on-site. **Cards:** AX, DC, DS, MC, VI.

NOODLES ITALIAN CAFE'

Italian

Lunch: $6-$10 **Dinner:** $10-$20 **Phone:** 239/592-0050 ﹝14﹞
Location: I-75, exit 107, 2.5 mi w on Pine Ridge Rd/CR 896; in Mission Square. 1585 Pine Ridge Rd, Suite 5 34109. **Hours:** 11 am-10 pm, Sun from 4 pm. Closed: 11/23. **Reservations:** accepted. **Features:** The casual spot lets guests sample both Mediterranean and classic Italian cuisine, including freshly made pastas. Also on the menu are some American standbys. Casual dress; beer & wine only. **Parking:** on-site. **Cards:** AX, CB, DC, DS, JC, MC, VI.

PAZZO ITALIAN CAFE

Italian

Dinner: $17-$25 **Phone:** 239/434-8494 ﹝29﹞
Location: Just w of US 41 (Tamiami Tr). 853 5th Ave S 34102. **Hours:** 5:30 pm-10 pm. Closed: 11/23. **Reservations:** required. **Features:** The cafe serves creative Italian cuisine using fresh local seafood and pastas. Dine inside and experience the imaginative dining room, or eat outside along the sidewalk. Dressy casual; cocktails. **Parking:** street. **Cards:** AX, DS, MC, VI.

PIER 41 RESTAURANT

American

Lunch: $7-$12 **Dinner:** $12-$22 **Phone:** 239/649-5858 ﹝35﹞
Location: Jct US 41 (Tamiami Tr) and Goodbelt Rd; in Tin City complex. 1200 5th Ave S 34102. **Hours:** 11 am-10 pm, Fri & Sat-10:30 pm; Sunday brunch 10 am-3 pm. **Features:** The restaurant treats guests to views of the water from many tables, including those with dockside seating. The menu includes choices from both land and sea, with some local catches. Casual dress; cocktails. **Parking:** on-site. **Cards:** AX, DS, MC, VI.

PIPPIN'S

Steak & Seafood

Dinner: $16-$28 **Phone:** 239/262-2880 ﹝22﹞
Location: 1.5 mi n on US 41 (Tamiami Tr). 1390 US 41 N 34102. **Hours:** 4:30 pm-10 pm. Closed: 11/23; also Super Bowl Sun. **Reservations:** suggested. **Features:** A casual interior design features a huge saltwater aquarium as the centerpiece. A friendly and efficient staff serves up tasty meals like a generously portioned yellowfin tuna cooked to taste. A modest dessert selection is offered for meal's end. Casual dress; cocktails. **Parking:** on-site. **Cards:** AX, CB, DC, DS, MC, VI.

RIDGWAY BAR & GRILL

Continental

Lunch: $8-$14 **Dinner:** $14-$35 **Phone:** 239/262-5500 ﹝42﹞
Location: On 13th Ave; between 2nd and 3rd sts S. 1300 3rd St S 34102. **Hours:** 11:30 am-10 pm. **Reservations:** suggested. **Features:** In Old Naples, this spacious restaurant blends Italian, Mediterranean, American and Asian cuisine. Guests can sit inside or outside on the patio, which is a prime spot for people-watching in the exclusive shopping area. Lump crab cakes and fresh peach-berry cobbler shouldn't be missed. Casual dress; cocktails; entertainment. **Parking:** on-site. **Cards:** AX, DC, DS, MC, VI.

RISTORANTE CIAO

Northern Italian

Dinner: $18-$30 **Phone:** 239/263-3889 ﹝28﹞
Location: Just w of US 41 (Tamiami Tr). 835 4th Ave S 34102. **Hours:** 5:30 pm-9 pm, Fri & Sat-10 pm. Closed: 4/16, 11/23, 12/25; also Sun. **Reservations:** suggested. **Features:** European elegance is in the details: from Italian tenor music to fresh roses on the tables. The owner/chef creates lush preparations such as fettuccine ciao with lobster and mushrooms in a rich cream sauce over pasta. Servers provide knowledgeable and competent assistance, but the style remains relaxed. Try the chef's evening specials. Dressy casual; beer & wine only. **Parking:** on-site. **Cards:** AX, DC, DS, MC, VI.

RIVERWALK FISH & ALE HOUSE

Seafood

Lunch: $8-$22 **Dinner:** $8-$22 **Phone:** 239/263-2734 ﹝36﹞
Location: Jct US 41 (Tamiami Tr) and Goodlett Rd; in Tin City Complex. 1200 5th Ave S 34102. **Hours:** 11 am-11 pm. Closed: 11/23, 12/25. **Features:** This bustling, open-air restaurant offers waterfront dining with a rustic nautical theme. Casual attire is the order of the day. Well-prepared seafood—such as flavorful, filling grouper and chips—is the specialty. Casual dress; cocktails. **Parking:** on-site. **Cards:** AX, DS, MC, VI.

ST. GEORGE & THE DRAGON

Steak & Seafood

Menu on aaa.com **Lunch:** $6-$17 **Dinner:** $15-$30 **Phone:** 239/262-6546 ﹝33﹞
Location: On US 41 (Tamiami Tr); downtown. 936 5th Ave S 34102. **Hours:** 11 am-10 pm, Sun 5 pm-9 pm. Closed: 12/25; also Sun 4/1-12/31. **Features:** Family-operated since 1969, this local favorite presents a menu featuring fresh seafood, prime steak and the ever-popular fish and chips. Dining sections are decorated in a delightful nautical theme with soft lighting, hand-carved beams and brass accents. Semi-formal attire; cocktails. **Parking:** on-site. **Cards:** AX, DC, MC, VI.

SANIBEL STEAKHOUSE

Steak House

Dinner: $20-$40 **Phone:** 239/597-7832 ﹝10﹞
Location: 1.9 mi e of US 41 (Tamiami Tr N) on Vanderbilt Beach Rd; in Vanderbilt Galleria Shops. 8990 Fontana del Sol 34109. **Hours:** 5 pm-11 pm. **Reservations:** suggested. **Features:** The classy and casual steakhouse prepares large aged steaks and fresh seafood. Guests can eat inside in a soothing, comfortable setting or outside on the patio. Dressy casual; cocktails. **Parking:** on-site and valet. **Cards:** AX, CB, DC, DS, JC, MC, VI.

SEAWITCH RESTAURANT & LOUNGE

Seafood

Lunch: $6-$10 **Dinner:** $14-$22 **Phone:** 239/566-1514 ﹝3﹞
Location: North end of town; 1.5 mi w of US 41 via Vanderbilt Beach Dr (SR 862), just n on Gulfshore Dr, then just e. 179 Southbay Dr 34108. **Hours:** 5 pm-9:30 pm; also 11:30 am-2:30 pm 11/1-4/30. Closed: 11/23; also Super Bowl Sun. **Features:** A laid-back dining experience is what diners can expect at this waterfront restaurant. Whether grilled, baked, fried or blackened, the yellowtail snapper rarely misses the mark. A few meat items are offered for landlubbers. Casual dress; cocktails. **Parking:** on-site. **Cards:** AX, DC, DS, MC, VI.

(See map and index starting on p. 620)

SHULA'S STEAK HOUSE   Lunch: $9-$18   Dinner: $14-$30   Phone: 239/430-4999   ⑮
AAA
◈◈◈◈◈
Steak & Seafood *(See color ad p 624)*
Location: US 41 (Tamiami Tr), just sw of jct Pine Ridge Rd; in Hilton Naples. 5111 Tamiami Tr 34103. **Hours:** 11:30 am-10 pm. **Reservations:** accepted. **Features:** Pictures of "the coach" and his team adorn the dining room walls. Representative of steakhouse fare are hearty Angus steaks and large lobsters and other seafood offerings. Dressy casual; cocktails. **Parking:** on-site. **Cards:** AX, CB, DC, DS, JC, MC, VI.

SKILLETS OF NAPLES   *Menu on aaa.com*   Lunch: $5-$9   Phone: 239/262-3788   ⑰
AAA
◈
American
Location: I-75, exit 107, 3.8 mi w on CR 896 (Pine Ridge Rd), then 0.4 mi s; in Heron Place Plaza. 4170 Tamiami Tr N 34103. **Hours:** 7 am-2:30 pm. **Closed:** 11/23, 12/25. **Features:** Breakfast and lunch all of the time. A large selection of omelets and other egg specialties. A wide variety of pancakes, blintzs, and waffles. If sandwiches are your choice, there is a large selection to choose from. Casual dress. **Parking:** on-site. **Cards:** AX, MC, VI.

SKILLETS SUNRISE   *Menu on aaa.com*   Lunch: $5-$9   Phone: 239/566-1999   ⑪
AAA
◈
American
Location: I-75, exit 107, 2 mi w; from US 41 (Tamiami Trail N) 2 mi e; in the Bed, Bath & Beyond Plaza. 5461 Airport Rd N 34109. **Hours:** 7 am-2:30 pm. **Closed:** 11/23, 12/25. **Features:** Breakfast and lunch are served all the time. Offerings range from omelets and other egg specialties to pancakes, blintzes and waffles to a large selection of sandwiches. Casual dress. **Parking:** on-site. **Cards:** AX, MC, VI.

STREAMER'S RESTAURANT   Lunch: $8-$12   Dinner: $8-$18   Phone: 239/593-3388   ⑫
◈
Seafood
Location: I-75, exit 107, 2 mi w; US 41 (Tamiami Tr N), 2 mi e; in Bed, Bath & Beyond Plaza. 5317 Airport Pulling Rd 34109. **Hours:** 11 am-9 pm. Closed major holidays; also Sun. **Features:** Although the atmosphere is casual, the restaurant is serious about its seafood, which is grilled, steamed or fried. And, yes, even the lobster can be fried. Get to this place early before it runs out of the specialty lobster rolls. The only land food is on the children's menu. Casual dress; beer & wine only. **Parking:** on-site. **Cards:** MC, VI.

TOMMY BAHAMA'S   Lunch: $8-$12   Dinner: $17-$29   Phone: 239/643-6889   ㊶
◈◈◈ ◈
Caribbean
Location: Jct 12th Ave S; in historic district. 1220 3rd St S 34102. **Hours:** 11 am-11 pm. **Closed:** 11/23, 12/25. **Features:** A tropical Bahamian theme punctuates this upbeat restaurant in the heart of Old Naples. Live music and a large outdoor patio help set the stage for a relaxed, fun time. A creative menu, large portions and colorful, Caribbean-influenced presentations complete the picture. Casual dress; cocktails. **Parking:** on-site. **Cards:** AX, MC, VI.

THE TURTLE CLUB   Lunch: $6-$16   Dinner: $16-$30   Phone: 239/592-6557   ②
◈◈◈
Seafood
Location: I-75, exit 111, north end of town; 1.5 mi w of US 41 (Tamiami Tr) via Vanderbilt Beach Rd (SR 862), then just n; in Vanderbilt Beach Resort. 9225 Gulfshore Dr N 34108. **Hours:** 11:30 am-3 & 5-9 pm, Fri & Sat-10 pm. **Closed:** 12/25. **Reservations:** required. **Features:** Eat on the beach and hear the surf, or dine inside with a decor reflecting local memories. The seafood is fresh and is prepared with the chef's own twist. Dressy casual; cocktails. **Parking:** valet. **Cards:** AX, CB, DC, MC, VI.

USS NEMO   Lunch: $7-$15   Dinner: $15-$39   Phone: 239/261-6366   ⑱
AAA
◈◈◈ ◈
Asian
Location: 1.4 mi s of Pine Ridge Rd; in small plaza. 3745 Tamiami Tr N 34103. **Hours:** 11:30 am-2 & 5-9:30 pm, Fri-10 pm, Sat 5 pm-10 pm, Sun 5 pm-9:30 pm. **Reservations:** required. **Features:** The restaurant is little on the outside but huge on the inside. Sauce and garnish combinations result in remarkable food. On the menu are fresh seafood and meat, such as steak and lamb. The decor has a nautical theme, but guests must use their imagination, as the chef does with the food. Casual dress; beer & wine only. **Parking:** on-site. **Cards:** AX, DS, MC, VI.

VERGINA   Lunch: $9-$19   Dinner: $15-$27   Phone: 239/659-7008   ㉞
◈◈◈◈
Italian
Location: Just s of US 41 (Tamiami Tr). 700 Fifth Ave S 34102. **Hours:** 11:30 am-4 & 5-11 pm, Sun 5 pm-10 pm. **Closed:** 12/25. **Reservations:** suggested. **Features:** Like in Italy, diners can eat on the sidewalk, in a romantic little courtyard or inside a softly lit room. Foods are big in taste and portions. There is always a fresh seafood dish, as well as traditional favorites. Dressy casual; cocktails. **Parking:** street. **Cards:** AX, MC, VI.

YABBA ISLAND GRILL   Dinner: $16-$26   Phone: 239/262-5787   ㉜
◈◈◈
Caribbean
Location: Just w of US 41 (Tamiami Tr). 711 5th Ave S 34102. **Hours:** 5 pm-10 pm, Fri & Sat-1 am. **Closed:** 11/23, 12/25; also Super Bowl Sun. **Reservations:** accepted. **Features:** The restaurant's flavors, foods and room colors bring the islands to Naples. Try Bahamian conch chowder, Barbados-style baby back ribs or lobster stir-fry, or go light with a tropical salad. Casual dress; cocktails. **Parking:** street. **Cards:** AX, CB, DC, DS, JC, MC, VI.

ZIZI RESTAURANT & LOUNGE   Lunch: $7-$13   Dinner: $10-$34   Phone: 239/649-7333   ㉕
◈◈◈◈
Italian
Location: I-75, exit 107, 3.8 mi w on CR 896 (Pine Ridge Rd), then 4.5 mi s on US 41 (Tamiami Tr); in Bellasera Hotel. 221 9th St S 34102. **Hours:** 7 am-11 pm. **Reservations:** suggested. **Features:** Guests can request seating in the cozy inside dining area or on the patio. Tuscan-style preparations are created from pasta, risotto, meat and some fresh seafood. Casual dress; cocktails. **Parking:** on-site and valet. **Cards:** AX, DS, MC, VI.

NAVARRE

―――――― WHERE TO STAY ――――――

BEST WESTERN NAVARRE   *Book at aaa.com*

Phone: (850)939-9400

5/1-9/6 [CP]	1P: $99-$129	2P: $99-$129	XP: $10	F18
12/1-4/30 & 9/7-11/30 [CP]	1P: $69-$99	2P: $69-$99	XP: $10	F18

Small-scale Hotel

Location: US 98, just e on Navarre Beach Bridge. 8697 Navarre Pkwy 32566. Fax: 850/939-4040. **Facility:** 69 one-bedroom standard units. 3 stories, exterior corridors. **Parking:** on-site. **Amenities:** irons, hair dryers. *Some:* high-speed Internet. **Pool(s):** heated outdoor. **Leisure Activities:** fishing. **Guest Services:** coin laundry. **Business Services:** meeting rooms. **Cards:** AX, CB, DC, DS, JC, MC, VI. **Special Amenities:** free continental breakfast and free local telephone calls.

SOME UNITS

COMFORT INN & CONFERENCE CENTER   *Book at aaa.com*

Phone: 850/939-1761

6/1-8/7	1P: $109-$139	2P: $109-$139	XP: $8	F18
3/1-5/31	1P: $79-$109	2P: $79-$109	XP: $8	F18
12/1-2/28 & 8/8-11/30	1P: $69-$79	2P: $69-$79	XP: $8	F18

Small-scale Hotel

Location: US 98, 0.3 mi e of Navarre Beach Bridge. 8700 Navarre Pkwy 32566. Fax: 850/939-2084. **Facility:** 63 one-bedroom standard units. 2 stories, exterior corridors. **Parking:** on-site. **Terms:** cancellation fee imposed. **Amenities:** irons, hair dryers. **Pool(s):** outdoor. **Guest Services:** coin laundry. **Business Services:** conference facilities. **Cards:** AX, DC, DS, JC, MC, VI.

SOME UNITS

NEPTUNE BEACH —*See Jacksonville p. 500.*

NEW PORT RICHEY —*See Tampa Bay p. 1028.*

NEW SMYRNA BEACH pop. 20,048

―――――― WHERE TO STAY ――――――

BUENA VISTA INN

Phone: 386-428-5565

All Year	1P: $65-$95		XP: $12	F12

Motel

Location: 2 mi e on SR Business Rt 44, at west end of North Causeway Bridge. 500 N Causeway 32169. Fax: 386/428-5565. **Facility:** 8 units. 3 one-bedroom standard units. 5 one-bedroom suites with kitchens. 1 story, exterior corridors. *Bath:* combo or shower only. **Parking:** on-site. **Terms:** office hours 9 am-8 pm, 1-2 night minimum stay, 14 day cancellation notice-fee imposed, package plans, pets ($5-$10 extra charge). **Amenities:** video library. *Some:* DVD players, irons. **Leisure Activities:** boat dock, fishing, bicycles. **Guest Services:** coin laundry. **Cards:** MC, VI.

SOME UNITS

FEE

COASTAL WATERS INN

Phone: (386)428-3800

All Year	1P: $79-$230	2P: $79-$230	XP: $9	F12

Small-scale Hotel

Location: SR A1A; 3.4 mi s of SR 44. 3509 S Atlantic Ave 32169. Fax: 386/423-5002. **Facility:** Smoke free premises. 40 units. 8 one-bedroom standard units. 32 one-bedroom suites with kitchens. 2-3 stories (no elevator), exterior corridors. *Bath:* combo or shower only. **Parking:** on-site. **Terms:** 4 day cancellation notice, weekly rates available. **Amenities:** irons, hair dryers. **Pool(s):** outdoor, wading. **Business Services:** fax (fee). **Cards:** DS, MC, VI.

SOME UNITS

HOLIDAY INN HOTEL & SUITES

Phone: (386)426-0020

All Year	1P: $126-$375	2P: $126-$375	XP: $10	F18

Small-scale Hotel

Location: SR A1A, s of SR 44. 1401 S Atlantic Ave 32169. Fax: 386/423-3977. **Facility:** 102 units. 20 one-bedroom standard units with efficiencies. 76 one- and 6 two-bedroom suites with kitchens. 8 stories, interior corridors. *Bath:* combo or shower only. **Parking:** on-site. **Terms:** check-in 4 pm, 3-7 night minimum stay - seasonal, cancellation fee imposed, [AP] meal plan available. **Amenities:** dual phone lines, voice mail, irons, hair dryers. **Dining:** 7 am-11 & 5-8 pm, wine/beer only. **Pool(s):** outdoor. **Leisure Activities:** limited exercise equipment. **Guest Services:** valet and coin laundry. **Business Services:** fax. **Cards:** AX, CB, DC, DS, JC, MC, VI.

SOME UNITS

NIGHT SWAN INTRACOASTAL BED & BREAKFAST   *Book at aaa.com*

Phone: (386)423-4940

All Year [BP]	1P: $100-$200	2P: $100-$200	XP: $20	F

Bed & Breakfast

Location: Just s of SR 44 Intracoastal Waterway bridge; west side of Intracoastal Waterway. 512 S Riverside Dr 32168. Fax: 386/427-2814. **Facility:** Offering a private dock for boat access, this early 1900s home imbued with Old-Florida character overlooks the Indian River. Smoke free premises. 15 units. 10 one-bedroom standard units, some with whirlpools. 3 one-bedroom suites ($150-$200) with whirlpools. 2 cottages ($150-$175). 2-3 stories (no elevator), interior/exterior corridors. *Bath:* combo or shower only. **Parking:** on-site. **Terms:** 3 day cancellation notice-fee imposed, package plans, pets (in designated unit). **Amenities:** irons, hair dryers. *Some:* DVD players. **Leisure Activities:** boat dock. *Fee:* bicycles. **Guest Services:** coin laundry, area transportation-local marinas. **Business Services:** meeting rooms, PC, fax (fee). **Cards:** AX, DC, DS, MC, VI. **Special Amenities:** free full breakfast and free local telephone calls.

SOME UNITS

FEE

RIVERVIEW HOTEL

Phone: (386)428-5858

AAA SAVE ▽▽▽▽

Country Inn

All Year [ECP]   1P: $110-$1085   2P: $110-$1085   XP: $10 **Location:** East end of North Causeway Bridge. 103 Flagler Ave 32169. Fax: 386/423-8927. **Facility:** This restored 1885 building on the Intracoastal Waterway with easy access to a dock features natural-tone wood on the walls, ceilings and floors. 20 units. 17 one-bedroom standard units. 1 one-bedroom suite. 1 vacation home and 1 cottage. 3 stories (no elevator), interior/exterior corridors. **Bath:** combo or shower only. **Parking:** on-site. **Terms:** weekly rates available. **Amenities:** *Some:* safes, irons. **Dining:** Riverview Restaurant, see separate listing. **Pool(s):** heated outdoor. **Leisure Activities:** boat dock, bicycles, spa. **Guest Services:** gift shop, valet laundry. **Cards:** AX, DC, DS, MC, VI. **Special Amenities:** free expanded continental breakfast.

SOME UNITS

SMYRNA MOTEL

Phone: 386-428-2495

AAA SAVE ▽▽▽

Motel

12/1-4/30   1P: $55-$75   2P: $65-$85   XP: $10   F5
5/1-11/30   1P: $45-$65   2P: $55-$75   XP: $10   F5
Location: 1.2 mi n on US 1. 1050 N Dixie Frwy 32168. **Facility:** 10 one-bedroom standard units. 1 story, exterior corridors. **Bath:** shower only. **Parking:** on-site. **Terms:** office hours 9 am-10 pm, 14 day cancellation notice. **Cards:** AX, MC, VI. **Special Amenities:** free local telephone calls.

SOME UNITS

——— WHERE TO DINE ———

BEACH BUNS CAFE & BAKERY

Lunch: $3-$7   Phone: 386/428-7700

▽▽▽

American

Parking: street.

Location: Just e of Peninsula Ave. 300 Flagler Ave 32169. **Hours:** 8 am-3 pm, Sun 9 am-2 pm. **Features:** Among freshly made entrees is the popular Irish potato soup. Sandwiches are made on homemade breads made the old-fashioned way with certified organic flours, spice and local honey. Sweet temptations include homemade pastries, lemon pound cake, macaroons, cookies, pecan tarts and tea breads. Casual dress.

CHASES

Lunch: $6-$9   Dinner: $12-$18   Phone: 386/423-8787

▽▽▽

Steak & Seafood

Location: SR A1A, 3.3 mi s of SR 44. 3401 S Atlantic Blvd 32169. **Hours:** 11 am-10 pm. Closed: 12/25. **Features:** A scenic oceanfront location offers both indoor and outdoor dining. The menu is traditional fare which includes tasty burgers, homemade soup, creative salads and seafood or landlubber entrees. Casual dress; cocktails; entertainment. **Parking:** on-site. **Cards:** AX, DS, MC, VI.

THE DELI TOUCH

Lunch: $3-$6   Phone: 386/424-9878

▽▽▽

American

Location: Center. 135 Canal St 32168. **Hours:** 7 am-3 pm, Sun-2 pm. **Features:** The cafe atmosphere has fast paced service to keep up with the downtown crowd. Breakfast foods are served in addition to fresh homemade sandwiches. Pick up some sliced meat by the pound on your way home. Casual dress; beer & wine only. **Parking:** street.

HEAVENLY SANDWICHES & SMOOTHIES

Lunch: $6-$9   Dinner: $6-$9   Phone: 386/427-7475

▽▽▽

American

Location: East end of North Causeway Bridge. 115 Flagler Ave 32169. **Hours:** 9 am-8 pm. Closed: 11/23, 12/25. **Reservations:** not accepted. **Features:** Not far from the beach is an opportunity for a healthy meal. Choose from an assortment of sandwiches, wraps, roll ups and gourmet salads. Then top that off with a healthy smoothie that will energize you. Casual dress. **Parking:** on-site. **Cards:** AX, DS, MC, VI.

JB'S FISH CAMP

Lunch: $9-$20   Dinner: $9-$20   Phone: 386/427-5747

▽▽

Seafood

Parking: on-site. **Cards:** AX, DS, MC, VI.

Location: SR A1A, 8.5 mi s of SR 44 on the Indian River. 859 Pompano Ave 32169. **Hours:** 11:30 am-9:30 pm, Fri & Sat-10 pm. Closed: 11/23, 12/25. **Features:** A docking place for hopeful fishermen, this rustic, Florida-style restaurant resembles an old shack but offers delicious local oysters and fresh river clams right off the boat. A popular local spot, it is perfect for a good meal after a day at the beach. Casual dress; cocktails.

NEW SMYRNA STEAKHOUSE

Lunch: $6-$25   Dinner: $6-$25   Phone: 386/424-9696

▽▽ ▽▽

Steak House

Location: SR A1A, 1 mi e of Intracoastal Waterway Bridge. 723 E 3rd Ave 32169. **Hours:** 11:30 am-10 pm, Fri & Sat-11 pm. Closed: 11/23, 12/25. **Features:** Lending to the feel of the rustic steakhouse are dark wood accents, steer heads, saddles and other Western items on the walls. Casual dress; cocktails. **Parking:** on-site. **Cards:** AX, DS, MC, VI.

NORWOOD'S SEAFOOD RESTAURANT

Lunch: $6-$9   Dinner: $6-$29   Phone: 386/428-4621

▽▽ ▽▽

Seafood

MC, VI.

Location: SR 44, 1 mi e of Intracoastal Waterway Bridge. 400 2nd Ave 32169. **Hours:** 11:30 am-9:30 pm. Closed: 12/25. **Features:** Ease into this very popular, very comfortable restaurant. Early bird specials offer the best bargain, with a variety of fresh seafood and beef dishes and an extensive wine list. Try the coconut shrimp served with a tangy, sweet-and-sour sauce. Casual dress; cocktails. **Parking:** on-site. **Cards:** AX, DC, DS,

PATIO RESTAURANT

Lunch: $4-$6   Dinner: $7-$16   Phone: 386/423-8355

▽▽ ▽▽

American

Location: On US 1; downtown. 626 N Dixie Frwy 32168. **Hours:** 11 am-2:30 & 4:30-9 pm, Sat from 4:30 pm. Closed: 12/25; also Sun. **Reservations:** suggested. **Features:** Step into a quaint, romantic world of classical music, wrought iron gates and gardens of night-blooming jasmine. Gourmet dining in an intimate setting showcases an award-winning menu with seafood, a lovely vegetarian entree and a portobello-stuffed filet. Casual dress; beer & wine only. **Parking:** on-site. **Cards:** AX, CB, DC, DS, MC, VI.

PJ'S SEA SHACK

Lunch: $7-$12   Dinner: $14-$20   Phone: 386/428-8850

▽▽ ▽▽

Seafood

Location: SR 44, 1 mi e of Intracoastal Waterway Bridge. 491 3rd Ave 32169. **Hours:** 11:30 am-10 pm, Fri-11 pm, Sat 4 pm-11 pm, Sun 4 pm-10 pm. **Features:** A large crab greets you at the door to introduce you to the colorful, whimsical decor of this restaurant, which offers a variety of sandwiches and wraps for lunch. Casual dress. **Parking:** on-site. **Cards:** AX, MC, VI.

RIVERVIEW RESTAURANT Lunch: $5-$7 Dinner: $14-$23 Phone: 386/428-1865

WWWW **Location:** East end of North Causeway Bridge; in Riverview Hotel. 101 Flagler Ave 32169. **Hours:** 11:30 am-3 &
4:30-10 pm, Sun 10:30 am-3 & 5-10 pm. Closed: Super Bowl Sun. **Reservations:** suggested.
Seafood **Features:** Located in a restored brick building, guests enjoy riverview dining from an inside window or the
undercover deck dining. The creative menu offers fresh fish and shellfish, pasta and chicken. A pastry chef
prepares sinful desserts. Casual dress; cocktails. **Parking:** on-site. **Cards:** AX, DC, DS, MC, VI.

NICEVILLE pop. 11,684

———— **WHERE TO STAY** ————

HAMPTON INN-NICEVILLE/EGLIN AFB Book at aaa.com

WWWW All Year [ECP] 1P: $70-$150 2P: $70-$150 Phone: (850)897-4675
Location: 2 mi e on SR 20. 4400 Ansley Dr 32578. Fax: 850/897-4837. **Facility:** 56 one-bedroom standard units.
Small-scale Hotel 3 stories, interior corridors. *Bath:* combo or shower only. **Parking:** on-site. **Terms:** cancellation fee imposed.
Amenities: high-speed Internet, voice mail, irons, hair dryers. **Pool(s):** outdoor. **Leisure**
Activities: exercise room. **Cards:** AX, CB, DC, DS, MC, VI.

SOME UNITS
(ASK) (S) 🏊 📷 (DATA PORT) 🔌 📠 💻 / ✕ /

HOLIDAY INN EXPRESS Book at aaa.com

WWWW All Year 1P: $99 Phone: (850)678-9131
Location: SR 85, just se on jct SR 20. 106 Bayshore Dr 32578. Fax: 850/678-9272. **Facility:** 89 one-bedroom
Small-scale Hotel standard units, some with efficiencies. 2 stories, interior corridors. *Bath:* combo or shower only. **Parking:** on-
site. **Amenities:** dual phone lines, voice mail, irons, hair dryers. **Pool(s):** outdoor. **Guest Services:** valet
laundry. **Business Services:** meeting rooms, PC. **Cards:** AX, DC, DS, MC, VI.

SOME UNITS
(ASK) (S) 🍽 ♿ 🏊 🛁 📷 📶 (DATA PORT) 🔌 📠 💻 / ✕ /

NOKOMIS pop. 3,334

———— **WHERE TO DINE** ————

PELICAN ALLEY Lunch: $7-$12 Dinner: $9-$18 Phone: 941/485-1893

WW **Location:** US 41, 1 mi w on Albee Rd at the south bridge to Casey Key. 1009 W Albee Rd 34275. **Hours:** 11:30 am-
10 pm. Closed: 4/16, 11/23, 12/25. **Features:** Cozy and casual, the restaurant is a popular place to watch
Seafood traffic on the Intracoastal Waterway. The big draw here is fresh seafood, including the chowder for which
this place is known. It is delectably flavored with substantial chunks of seafood. Casual dress; cocktails.
Parking: on-site. **Cards:** AX, CB, DC, DS, MC, VI.

SALTWATER CAFE Lunch: $6-$16 Dinner: $16-$37 Phone: 941/488-3775

WWWW WWWW **Location:** On US 41 jct Laurel Rd; in Nokomis Village. 1071 Tamiami Tr N 34275. **Hours:** 11:30 am-10 pm, Fri &
Sat-10:30 pm; Sunday brunch. Closed: 12/25. **Reservations:** accepted. **Features:** The multipage menu
Seafood includes such appetizers as fresh oysters, frog legs and middleneck clams and such entrees as crab and
steam pot dishes, other fresh fish and seafood items, pasta, burgers and sandwiches. Also offered are all-
you-can-eat specials, soups and salads. The extensive wine list incorporates hundreds of choices. Numerous wines from Italy,
Spain, Germany, Australia, New Zealand, Chile, South Africa, Japan, Switzerland, California and Florida are represented.
Casual dress; cocktails. **Parking:** on-site. **Cards:** AX, CB, DC, DS, JC, MC, VI.

♿M Y

NORTH BAY VILLAGE —See Miami-Miami Beach p. 613.

NORTH FORT MYERS pop. 40,214   (See map and index starting on p. 428)—See also FORT
MYERS.

———— **WHERE TO STAY** ————

CACTUS MOTEL Phone: 239/995-2456 **28**

W 12/1-4/30 1P: $69-$120 2P: $69-$120 XP: $15 F10
5/1-11/30 1P: $59-$79 2P: $59-$79 XP: $10 F10
Motel **Location:** On Business Rt US 41, just s of jct Bayshore/Pine Island Rd. 1677 N Tamiami Tr (Bus 41) 33903.
Facility: 12 one-bedroom standard units, some with kitchens. 1 story, exterior corridors. **Parking:** on-site.
Terms: 30 day cancellation notice-fee imposed, weekly rates available. **Amenities:** voice mail. *Some:* irons, hair dryers.
Leisure Activities: shuffleboard. **Cards:** DS, MC, VI.

SOME UNITS
🍽 / ✕ 🔌 📠 /

ECONO LODGE Book at aaa.com Phone: (239)995-0571 **29**

(AAA) (SAVE) 12/1-3/27 [CP] 1P: $95-$145 2P: $95-$145 XP: $5 F18
3/28-11/30 [CP] 1P: $49-$95 2P: $49-$95 XP: $5 F18
WWWW **Location:** On US 41, 1.1 mi n of Caloosahatchee Bridge. 13301 N Cleveland Ave 33903. Fax: 239/995-9143.
Motel **Facility:** 48 one-bedroom standard units. 2 stories (no elevator), exterior corridors. **Parking:** on-site.
Terms: package plans, small pets only ($5 extra charge). **Pool(s):** heated outdoor. **Leisure**
Activities: barbecue grill. **Guest Services:** coin laundry. **Business Services:** fax (fee). **Cards:** AX, DS,
MC, VI. **Special Amenities:** free continental breakfast and free local telephone calls.

SOME UNITS
(S) 🛏 🍽 🏊 📷 (DATA PORT) 🔌 📠 / ✕ 💻 /
FEE

(See map and index starting on p. 428)

HOWARD JOHNSON EXPRESS INN   *Book at aaa.com*   Phone: 239/656-4000   30

	3/1-3/31	1P: $159-$209	2P: $159-$209	XP: $10	F18
Motel	1/16-2/28	1P: $109-$149	2P: $109-$149	XP: $10	F18
	12/1-1/15	1P: $79-$109	2P: $79-$109	XP: $10	F18
	4/1-11/30	1P: $49-$79	2P: $49-$79	XP: $10	F18

Location: On US 41, 1 mi n of Caloosahatchee Bridge; jct North Key Dr. 13000 N Cleveland Ave 33903. Fax: 239/656-1612. **Facility:** 120 one-bedroom standard units. 2 stories, exterior corridors. **Parking:** on-site. **Terms:** 2-3 night minimum stay - seasonal, 3 day cancellation notice-fee imposed, package plans, pets ($10 extra charge). **Amenities:** high-speed Internet, voice mail, safes (fee), irons, hair dryers. **Pool(s):** outdoor. **Guest Services:** coin laundry. **Business Services:** meeting rooms, fax (fee). **Cards:** AX, CB, DC, DS, JC, MC, VI.

SOME UNITS

WHERE TO DINE

HURRICANE HARRY'S   Lunch: $8-$12   Dinner: $8-$17   Phone: 239/997-8300   12

American

Location: Just w of US 41 via Hancock Bridge Pkwy. 3448 Marinatown Ln 33903. **Hours:** 11 am-10 pm. Closed major holidays. **Features:** The casual eatery offers food that is nicely prepared with a decent selection to please most palates. This restaurant becomes livelier in the evening, resembling a bar atmosphere. Casual dress; cocktails. **Parking:** on-site. **Cards:** AX, DC, DS, MC, VI.

LAND & SEA FAMILY RESTAURANT   Lunch: $5-$20   Dinner: $5-$20   Phone: 239/656-3030   13

American

Location: On US 41, 1 mi n of Caloosahatchee Bridge; jct North Key Dr. 13121 Cleveland Ave 33903. **Hours:** 6:30 am-9 pm. **Features:** The large family diner serves a great selection of comfort foods, such as fried catfish, chicken fingers, mashed potatoes and country-fried steak. Expect good value and ample portions at reasonable prices. Casual dress; cocktails. **Parking:** on-site. **Cards:** AX, CB, DC, DS, MC, VI.

NORTH MIAMI —See Miami-Miami Beach p. 613.

NORTH MIAMI BEACH —See Miami-Miami Beach p. 613.

NORTH PALM BEACH pop. 12,064   (See map and index starting on p. 843)—See also PALM BEACH.

WHERE TO STAY

SUPER 8 MOTEL   *Book at aaa.com*   Phone: 561/848-1424   34

	1/21-4/20	1P: $119-$199	2P: $119-$199	XP: $10	F
	12/21-1/20	1P: $99-$149	2P: $99-$149	XP: $10	F
Motel	12/1-12/20 & 4/21-11/30	1P: $79-$99	2P: $79-$99	XP: $10	F

Location: 1.3 mi s of PGA Blvd (SR 786). 757 US Hwy 1 33408. Fax: 561/840-8959. **Facility:** 100 one-bedroom standard units. 2 stories (no elevator), exterior corridors. **Bath:** combo or shower only. **Parking:** on-site. **Terms:** check-in 4 pm, 5 day cancellation notice. **Pool(s):** outdoor. **Guest Services:** coin laundry. **Cards:** AX, DS, MC, VI. **Special Amenities:** free continental breakfast and early check-in/late check-out.

SOME UNITS

WHERE TO DINE

PANAMA HATTIE'S   *Menu on aaa.com*   Lunch: $6-$13   Dinner: $9-$33   Phone: 561/627-1545   29

Seafood

Location: I-95, exit 79 AB (SR 786/PGA Blvd), 2.7 mi e to Ellison Wilson Rd, then s. 11511 Ellison Wilson Rd 33408. **Hours:** 11 am-10 pm, Fri & Sat-11 pm; Sunday brunch. Closed: 12/25. **Reservations:** suggested. **Features:** Guests can park their car or dock their boat before stopping in this great place to relax. Seating inside or dockside can be requested. Fresh seafood makes up the majority of the menu, but some land food items are among choices. Casual dress; cocktails; entertainment. **Parking:** on-site and valet. **Cards:** AX, DC, MC, VI.

NORTH PORT pop. 22,797

WHERE TO DINE

OLDE WORLD RESTAURANT & LOUNGE   Lunch: $5-$18   Dinner: $5-$18   Phone: 941/426-1155

American

Location: On US 41, just s of North Port Blvd; center. 14415 S Tamiami Tr 34287. **Hours:** 7 am-10 pm. Closed: 1/1, 12/25. **Reservations:** suggested. **Features:** Friendly and casual, the relaxed restaurant boasts a bubbly service staff and all-day breakfast. Browse the varied menu for burgers, filet mignon, stuffed flounder and the three-layer chocolate fantasy, which incorporates seven decadent types of chocolate. Casual dress; cocktails. **Parking:** on-site. **Cards:** AX, DS, MC, VI.

NORTH REDINGTON BEACH —See Tampa Bay p. 1029.

OCALA pop. 45,943

―――― **WHERE TO STAY** ――――

BEST WESTERN OCALA PARK CENTRE   *Book at aaa.com*

AAA SAVE

Small-scale Hotel

All Year [CP] 1P: $59-$129 2P: $59-$129 XP: $7 F17
Phone: (352)237-4848
Location: I-75, exit 350, just w on SR 200; in Park Centre. 3701 SW 38th Ave 34474. Fax: 352/237-2281. **Facility:** 138 units. 137 one-bedroom standard units. 1 one-bedroom suite with kitchen. 4 stories, interior corridors. **Parking:** on-site. **Amenities:** irons, hair dryers. *Some:* high-speed Internet. **Pool(s):** heated outdoor. **Leisure Activities:** whirlpool. **Guest Services:** coin laundry. **Business Services:** meeting rooms, fax. **Cards:** AX, CB, DC, DS, JC, MC, VI. **Special Amenities:** free continental breakfast and free local telephone calls.

SOME UNITS

BUDGET HOST INN

AAA SAVE

Motel

12/1-4/14 [CP] 1P: $42-$82 2P: $52-$92 XP: $10 F
4/15-11/30 [CP] 1P: $35-$75 2P: $45-$85 XP: $10 F
Phone: (352)732-6940
Location: I-75, exit 354, 0.3 mi n on US 27. 4013 NW Bonnie Heath Blvd 34482. Fax: 352/629-8048. **Facility:** 21 one-bedroom standard units. 1 story, exterior corridors. *Bath:* combo or shower only. **Parking:** on-site. **Terms:** pets ($4-$6 extra charge). **Business Services:** fax (fee). **Cards:** AX, DS, MC, VI. **Special Amenities:** free continental breakfast and early check-in/late check-out.

SOME UNITS
FEE

COMFORT INN   *Book at aaa.com*

AAA SAVE

Small-scale Hotel

12/1-3/31 [ECP] 1P: $75-$130 2P: $75-$130 XP: $5 F18
4/1-11/30 [ECP] 1P: $65-$95 2P: $65-$95 XP: $5 F18
Phone: (352)629-8850
Location: I-75, exit 352, just w on SR 40. 4040 W Silver Springs Blvd 34482. Fax: 352/732-0831. **Facility:** 132 units. 128 one-bedroom standard units. 4 one-bedroom suites ($99-$175), some with whirlpools. 2 stories, exterior corridors. **Parking:** on-site. **Terms:** cancellation fee imposed, small pets only ($5 extra charge). **Amenities:** irons, hair dryers. **Dining:** 6 am-3 & 5-9 pm, Sat from 7 am. **Pool(s):** outdoor. **Guest Services:** coin laundry. **Business Services:** meeting rooms, fax (fee). **Cards:** AX, CB, DC, DS, JC, MC, VI. **Special Amenities:** free expanded continental breakfast and free local telephone calls.

SOME UNITS
FEE   FEE FEE

COUNTRY INN & SUITES   *Book at aaa.com*

Small-scale Hotel

1/1-3/31 [ECP] 1P: $119
4/1-4/30 [ECP] 1P: $109
12/1-12/31 & 5/1-11/30 [ECP] 1P: $99
Phone: (352)237-0715
Location: I-75, exit 350, just e. 3720 SW College Rd 34474. Fax: 352/237-3615. **Facility:** Smoke free premises. 59 units. 48 one-bedroom standard units, some with whirlpools. 11 one-bedroom suites ($139-$249), some with whirlpools. 5 stories, interior corridors. *Bath:* combo or shower only. **Parking:** on-site. **Amenities:** high-speed Internet, dual phone lines, voice mail, irons, hair dryers. **Pool(s):** heated indoor. **Leisure Activities:** whirlpool, exercise room. **Guest Services:** coin laundry. **Business Services:** meeting rooms, business center. **Cards:** AX, CB, DC, DS, JC, MC, VI.

SOME UNITS
FEE

COURTYARD BY MARRIOTT   *Book at aaa.com*

AAA SAVE

Small-scale Hotel

12/26-5/1 [BP] 1P: $119-$159 2P: $119-$159
12/1-12/25 & 5/2-11/30 [BP] 1P: $109-$139 2P: $109-$139
Phone: (352)237-8000
Location: I-75, exit 350, just w on SR 200; in Park Centre. 3712 SW 38th Ave 34474. Fax: 352/237-0580. **Facility:** 175 units. 167 one-bedroom standard units. 8 one-bedroom suites, some with whirlpools. 3 stories, interior corridors. *Bath:* combo or shower only. **Parking:** on-site. **Amenities:** video games, high-speed Internet, voice mail, irons, hair dryers. **Dining:** 6:30-10:30 am, cocktails. **Pool(s):** heated outdoor. **Leisure Activities:** whirlpool, exercise room. **Guest Services:** valet and coin laundry. **Business Services:** meeting rooms, fax. **Cards:** AX, DS, MC, VI. **Special Amenities:** free local telephone calls and free newspaper.

SOME UNITS
FEE

DAYS INN   *Book at aaa.com*

Small-scale Hotel

All Year 1P: $49-$95 2P: $49-$95 XP: $5 F18
Phone: (352)629-0091
Location: I-75, exit 352, just e. 3620 W Silver Springs Blvd 34475. Fax: 352/867-8399. **Facility:** 100 one-bedroom standard units. 2 stories (no elevator), interior/exterior corridors. *Bath:* combo or shower only. **Parking:** on-site. **Terms:** pets ($10 extra charge). **Amenities:** hair dryers. **Pool(s):** outdoor. **Leisure Activities:** shuffleboard, volleyball. **Guest Services:** valet and coin laundry. **Cards:** AX, CB, DC, DS, JC, MC, VI.

SOME UNITS
FEE

DAYS INN   *Book at aaa.com*

AAA SAVE

Small-scale Hotel

All Year 1P: $65-$150 2P: $65-$150 XP: $5 F17
Phone: 352/629-7041
Location: I-75, exit 354, just n on US 27. 3811 NW Bonnie Heath Blvd 34482. Fax: 352/629-1026. **Facility:** 65 one-bedroom standard units, some with whirlpools. 2 stories, interior/exterior corridors. **Parking:** on-site. **Terms:** pets ($5 extra charge). **Amenities:** hair dryers. **Pool(s):** outdoor. **Leisure Activities:** playground. **Guest Services:** coin laundry. **Business Services:** fax. **Cards:** AX, CB, DC, DS, JC, MC, VI. **Special Amenities:** free full breakfast and free local telephone calls.

SOME UNITS
FEE

FAIRFIELD INN BY MARRIOTT   *Book at aaa.com*   Phone: 352/861-8400

AAA SAVE

	12/26-4/15	1P: $107-$139	2P: $107-$139
	10/1-11/30	1P: $111-$128	2P: $111-$128
	12/1-12/25 & 4/16-9/30	1P: $103-$121	2P: $103-$121

Location: I-75, exit 350, just w on SR 200. 4101 SW 38th Ct 34474. Fax: 352/861-8401. **Facility:** 97 one-bedroom
Small-scale Hotel standard units, some with whirlpools. 3 stories, interior corridors. *Bath:* combo or shower only. **Parking:** on-site. **Terms:** [CP] & [ECP] meal plans available, package plans. **Amenities:** high-speed Internet, dual phone lines, voice mail, irons, hair dryers. **Pool(s):** heated outdoor. **Leisure Activities:** whirlpool, exercise room. **Guest Services:** valet and coin laundry. **Business Services:** fax. **Cards:** AX, CB, DC, DS, JC, MC, VI. **Special Amenities:** free expanded continental breakfast and free local telephone calls.

SOME UNITS

HAMPTON INN OCALA   *Book at aaa.com*   Phone: (352)854-3200

| | All Year [ECP] | 1P: $109-$169 | 2P: $114-$174 | F18 |

Location: I-75, exit 350, 0.4 mi e on SR 200. 3434 SW College Rd 34474. Fax: 352/854-5633. **Facility:** 152 units. 148 one-bedroom standard units, some with whirlpools. 4 one-bedroom suites. 3 stories, exterior corridors.
Small-scale Hotel **Parking:** on-site. **Amenities:** high-speed Internet, voice mail, irons, hair dryers. **Pool(s):** heated outdoor. **Leisure Activities:** exercise room. **Guest Services:** valet and coin laundry. **Business Services:** meeting rooms, fax. **Cards:** AX, DC, DS, MC, VI.

SOME UNITS

FEE

HILTON OCALA   *Book at aaa.com*   Phone: (352)854-1400

| | 1/9-4/30 & 8/30-11/30 | 1P: $119-$229 | 2P: $119-$229 | XP: $10 | F18 |
| | 12/1-1/8 & 5/1-8/29 | 1P: $109-$199 | 2P: $109-$199 | XP: $10 | F18 |

Location: I-75, exit 350, 0.3 mi e on SR 200. 3600 SW 36th Ave 34474. Fax: 352/854-4010. **Facility:** 197 units.
Large-scale Hotel 192 one-bedroom standard units. 5 one-bedroom suites ($229-$429), some with whirlpools. 9 stories, interior corridors. **Parking:** on-site. **Terms:** cancellation fee imposed, package plans, small pets only. **Amenities:** high-speed Internet, dual phone lines, voice mail, irons, hair dryers. **Dining:** Arthur's, see separate listing. **Pool(s):** heated outdoor. **Leisure Activities:** whirlpool, 2 lighted tennis courts, exercise room, volleyball. **Guest Services:** valet laundry. **Business Services:** meeting rooms, business center. **Cards:** AX, CB, DC, DS, JC, MC, VI. *(See color ad below)*

SOME UNITS

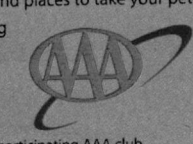

HOLIDAY INN EXPRESS   *Book at aaa.com*

Phone: (352)629-7300

All Year   1P: $95-$145   2P: $95-$145

Small-scale Hotel

Location: 0.8 mi s on US 27, 301 and 441; just s of SR 200. 1212 S Pine Ave 34474. Fax: 352/629-3331. **Facility:** 55 one-bedroom standard units, some with whirlpools. 3 stories, interior corridors. *Bath:* combo or shower only. **Parking:** on-site. **Amenities:** high-speed Internet, dual phone lines, voice mail, irons, hair dryers. **Pool(s):** outdoor. **Guest Services:** valet and coin laundry. **Business Services:** meeting rooms, fax. **Cards:** AX, DC, DS, MC, VI.

SOME UNITS

HOWARD JOHNSON INN   *Book at aaa.com*

Phone: (352)629-7021

1/28-3/31   1P: $50-$150   2P: $60-$200   XP: $10   F12
12/1-1/27 & 4/1-11/30   1P: $40-$90   2P: $50-$130   XP: $10   F12

Motel

Location: I-75, exit 354, just w. 3951 NW Bonnie Heath Blvd 34482. Fax: 352/629-0510. **Facility:** 125 one-bedroom standard units, some with whirlpools. 3 stories (no elevator), exterior corridors. **Parking:** on-site. **Terms:** cancellation fee imposed, weekly rates available, [AP], [BP], [CP] & [MAP] meal plans available, package plans, pets ($10 extra charge). **Amenities:** high-speed Internet, voice mail, irons, hair dryers. **Dining:** 6 am-noon & 5-9:30 pm, wine/beer only. **Pool(s):** heated outdoor. **Leisure Activities:** whirlpool, miniature golf, exercise room. **Guest Services:** coin laundry. **Business Services:** meeting rooms, business center. **Cards:** AX, CB, DC, DS, MC, VI. **Special Amenities:** free newspaper and early check-in/late check-out. *(See color ad below)*

SOME UNITS
FEE   FEE   FEE

LA QUINTA INN & SUITES OCALA   *Book at aaa.com*

Phone: (352)861-1137

1/1-5/4   1P: $135-$155   XP: $7   F18
5/5-11/30   1P: $99-$109   XP: $7   F18
12/1-12/31   1P: $92-$102   XP: $7   F18

Small-scale Hotel

Location: I-75, exit 350, just e on SR 200. 3530 SW 36th Ave 34474. Fax: 352/861-1157. **Facility:** 117 units. 111 one-bedroom standard units. 6 one-bedroom suites ($129-$190). 6 stories, interior corridors. *Bath:* combo or shower only. **Parking:** on-site. **Terms:** [ECP] meal plan available, small pets only. **Amenities:** video games, high-speed Internet, voice mail, irons, hair dryers. *Some:* dual phone lines. **Pool(s):** heated outdoor. **Leisure Activities:** whirlpool, exercise room. **Guest Services:** valet and coin laundry. **Business Services:** meeting rooms, business center. **Cards:** AX, CB, DC, DS, MC, VI. **Special Amenities:** free expanded continental breakfast and free local telephone calls.

SOME UNITS

MICROTEL SUITES   *Book at aaa.com*

Phone: (352)307-1166

1/15-3/31 [CP]   1P: $49-$89   2P: $49-$89   XP: $5   F18
12/1-1/14 & 4/1-11/30 [CP]   1P: $49-$69   2P: $49-$69   XP: $5   F18

Small-scale Hotel

Location: I-75, exit 341, just e. 1770 SW 134th St 34473. Fax: 352/307-1086. **Facility:** 63 one-bedroom standard units, some with whirlpools. 3 stories, interior corridors. *Bath:* combo or shower only. **Parking:** on-site. **Amenities:** irons. *Some:* hair dryers. **Pool(s):** outdoor. **Guest Services:** coin laundry. **Business Services:** meeting rooms. **Cards:** AX, DC, DS, MC, VI. **Special Amenities:** free continental breakfast and free local telephone calls.

SOME UNITS
FEE

QUALITY INN OCALA HOTEL AND CONFERENCE CENTER *Book at aaa.com*

Phone: (352)629-0381

AAA SAVE

Small-scale Hotel

1/31-5/2	1P: $69-$129	2P: $69-$129
5/3-11/30	1P: $49-$99	2P: $49-$99
12/1-1/30	1P: $49-$89	2P: $49-$89

Location: I-75, exit 352, just e on SR 40. 3621 W Silver Springs Blvd 34475. **Fax:** 352/629-8813. **Facility:** 256 one-bedroom standard units. 2 stories, exterior corridors. **Parking:** on-site. **Terms:** small pets only ($20 fee). **Amenities:** irons, hair dryers. **Dining:** 6 am-10 & 5-9 pm, cocktails. **Pool(s):** outdoor, wading. **Leisure Activities:** exercise room. **Guest Services:** valet and coin laundry. **Business Services:** meeting rooms, fax. **Cards:** AX, CB, DC, DS, MC, VI.

SOME UNITS

RED ROOF INN & SUITES *Book at aaa.com*

Phone: (352)732-4590

AAA SAVE

Small-scale Hotel

All Year — 1P: $60-$90 — 2P: $60-$90 — XP: $5 — F18

Location: I-75, exit 352, just w. 120 NW 40th Ave 34482. **Fax:** 352/732-4598. **Facility:** 62 one-bedroom standard units, some with whirlpools. 3 stories, interior corridors. *Bath:* combo or shower only. **Parking:** on-site. **Terms:** small pets only. **Amenities:** voice mail, irons, hair dryers. **Pool(s):** outdoor. **Leisure Activities:** exercise room. **Guest Services:** coin laundry. **Business Services:** meeting rooms, fax (fee). **Cards:** AX, CB, DC, DS, MC, VI. **Special Amenities:** free expanded continental breakfast and free local telephone calls.

SOME UNITS

SEVEN SISTERS INN

Phone: (352)867-1170

Historic Bed & Breakfast

All Year [BP] — 2P: $119-$279 — XP: $50

Location: Just s of jct SR 40 on SE Winona Ave; in downtown historic district. Located in a residential area. 820 SE Fort King St 34471. **Fax:** 352/867-5266. **Facility:** Built in 1888 in the Queen Anne style, this home offers rooms of varied shapes and sizes furnished with canopied or wrought iron beds. Designated smoking area. 14 units. 11 one- and 2 two-bedroom standard units, some with whirlpools. 1 one-bedroom suite. 3 stories (no elevator), interior corridors. *Bath:* combo or shower only. **Parking:** on-site. **Terms:** age restrictions may apply, 7 day cancellation notice, package plans, small pets only ($35 fee). **Amenities:** video library, DVD players, CD players, hair dryers. *Some:* irons. **Leisure Activities:** bicycles. **Guest Services:** gift shop, complimentary evening beverages. **Business Services:** meeting rooms, PC, fax. **Cards:** AX, DS, MC, VI.

SLEEP INN & SUITES *Book at aaa.com*

Phone: (352)347-8383

Small-scale Hotel

| 12/1-4/5 [CP] | 1P: $100-$200 | 2P: $125-$250 | XP: $15 | D12 |
| 4/6-11/30 [CP] | 1P: $60-$125 | 2P: $75-$175 | XP: $15 | D12 |

Location: I-75, exit 341, just e. 13600 SW 17th Ct 34473. **Fax:** 352/347-7830. **Facility:** Smoke free premises. 74 one-bedroom standard units. 3 stories, interior corridors. *Bath:* combo or shower only. **Parking:** on-site. **Terms:** 1-3 night minimum stay - seasonal and/or weekends, package plans. **Amenities:** high-speed Internet, voice mail, irons, hair dryers. **Pool(s):** small outdoor. **Leisure Activities:** exercise room. **Guest Services:** coin laundry. **Business Services:** business center. **Cards:** AX, CB, DC, DS, JC, MC, VI.

STEINBRENNER'S RAMADA INN & CONFERENCE CENTER *Book at aaa.com*

Phone: (352)732-3131

AAA SAVE

Small-scale Hotel

All Year — 2P: $79-$139 — XP: $10 — F18

Location: I-75, exit 354, just w. 3810 NW Bonnie Heath Blvd 34482. **Fax:** 352/732-3821. **Facility:** 124 units. 123 one-bedroom standard units. 1 one-bedroom suite ($125-$250). 2 stories, exterior corridors. *Bath:* combo or shower only. **Parking:** on-site. **Terms:** cancellation fee imposed, weekly rates available, [AP], [BP] & [CP] meal plans available, pets ($20 fee). **Amenities:** voice mail, irons, hair dryers. **Dining:** 6:30 am-11 pm, cocktails. **Pool(s):** heated outdoor. **Leisure Activities:** whirlpool, playground, exercise room. **Guest Services:** valet and coin laundry. **Business Services:** meeting rooms, fax. **Cards:** AX, DC, DS, MC, VI. **Special Amenities:** free newspaper and preferred room (subject to availability with advance reservations).

SOME UNITS

——— WHERE TO DINE ———

AMRIT PALACE INDIAN RESTAURANT

Lunch: $6-$16 **Dinner:** $10-$16 **Phone:** 352/873-8500

Indian

Location: I-75, exit 350, 1.6 mi ne on SR 200. 2635 SW College Rd 34474. **Hours:** 11:30 am-9:30 pm, Fri & Sat 10:30 pm, Sun 5 pm-9:30 pm. **Features:** This restaurant offers a wide range of traditional Indian preparations, including chutney, achar, curry, lamb, chicken, seafood, biryani rice, vegetarian specialties and several specialty breads. Many items are cooked in a tandoor oven. Casual dress; beer & wine only. **Parking:** on-site. **Cards:** AX, MC, VI.

ARTHUR'S

Dinner: $14-$27 **Phone:** 352/854-1400

Regional Steak & Seafood

Location: I-75, exit 350, 0.3 mi e on SR 200; in Hilton Ocala. 3600 SW 36th Ave 34474. **Hours:** 4:30 pm-10 pm. **Reservations:** suggested, in winter. **Features:** Noted for lobster bisque, the menu also offers tempting steak dishes. The grouper, covered in an herbed nut crust, gives new a twist to an old theme. Large windows overlook a courtyard, and fine linen tablecloths and napkins add an air of sophistication. Casual dress; cocktails. **Parking:** on-site. **Cards:** AX, CB, DC, DS, MC, VI.

BELLA LUNA CAFE

Lunch: $5-$9 **Dinner:** $9-$20 **Phone:** 352/237-9155

Italian

Location: I-75, exit 350, 0.4 mi e on SR 200. 3425 SW College Rd 34474. **Hours:** 11 am-11 pm, Fri-11 pm, Sat 3 pm-11 pm; Sunday brunch. **Closed:** 11/23, 12/25. **Reservations:** suggested, weekends. **Features:** Fine dining in an elegant, romantic setting boasts an excellent variety of entrees with unique combinations certain to inspire a return visit. The chicken and spinach served on a bed of pasta is generously portioned as well as flavorful. Dressy casual; cocktails. **Parking:** valet. **Cards:** AX, DC, DS, MC, VI.

BISTRO MEDITERRANEAN GRILL

Italian

Lunch: $6-$10 **Dinner:** $7-$16 **Phone:** 352/873-7876
Location: I-75, exit 350, 0.4 mi e. 3500 SW College Rd, Suite 400 34474. **Hours:** 11 am-9 pm, Fri & Sat-10 pm. Closed: 11/23. **Reservations:** accepted. **Features:** The trendy bistro offers classic pasta specialties like penne primavera and fettuccini alfredo or sandwiches like reuben, french onion and rustic tuscan. Among the salad selections are Caesar, Grecian and steak, while soups include roasted eggplant and sundried tomatoes or zuppa di giorno. Casual dress; cocktails. **Parking:** on-site. **Cards:** AX, MC, VI.

BRANDING IRON OF OCALA

Steak & Seafood

Dinner: $9-$17 **Phone:** 352/351-9111
Location: Jct 42nd St. 4201 NE Jacksonville Rd 34479. **Hours:** 4 pm-10 pm. Closed: 1/1; also Mon & Tues. **Reservations:** accepted. **Features:** Try fried mushrooms for starters, an ultimate prime rib sandwich as an entree and a piece of homemade cheesecake as a meal-ender. Casual dress; cocktails. **Parking:** on-site. **Cards:** AX, MC, VI.

CARMICHAEL'S RESTAURANT

American

Lunch: $6-$12 **Dinner:** $6-$17 **Phone:** 352/622-3636
Location: On SR 40, 3 mi e of jct US 27/301/441. 3105 NE Silver Springs Blvd 34470. **Hours:** 6:30 am-8:30 pm. **Reservations:** suggested. **Features:** An array of made-from-scratch specialties are the attraction in this dining room. Friendly and attentive servers welcome you to a warm, wood-accented interior. Choose from a good selection of well-prepared fish, meat, chicken and pasta dishes. Casual dress; cocktails. **Parking:** on-site. **Cards:** AX, MC, VI.

CHINA EXPRESS

Chinese

Lunch: $4-$10 **Dinner:** $4-$10 **Phone:** 352/236-2088
Location: SR 40, 1 mi w of Silver Springs attraction; in the Shoppes Silver Springs. 4901 E Silver Springs Blvd 34470. **Hours:** 10:30 am-10 pm, Fri & Sat-11 pm, Sun 11:30 am-10 pm. **Features:** Offering quick-serve Chinese food to-go, the eatery has no frills but plenty of food for a good price. Casual dress. **Parking:** on-site. **Cards:** MC, VI.

THE COPPER POT

American

Lunch: $6-$13 **Dinner:** $8-$20 **Phone:** 352/369-3636
Location: 1.5 mi s of jct Pine Ave; in Ocala Shopping Center. 2109-102 E Silver Springs Blvd 34470. **Hours:** 11 am-10 pm. **Features:** A local favorite for lunch, this eatery offers quick lunches at a reasonable price. Dressy casual; wine only. **Parking:** on-site. **Cards:** AX, CB, DC, DS, JC, MC, VI.

EL TAXCO

Mexican

Lunch: $7-$12 **Dinner:** $9-$20 **Phone:** 352/438-0075
Location: On SR 40, 1 mi w of Silver Springs attraction. 4901 E Silver Springs Blvd 34470. **Hours:** 10 am-9 pm. **Features:** The menu offers a wide range of authentic Mexican dishes in a festive, colorful environment. Casual dress; cocktails. **Parking:** on-site. **Cards:** AX, CB, DC, DS, JC, MC, VI.

FELIX'S

American

Lunch: $6-$12 **Dinner:** $8-$24 **Phone:** 352/629-0339
Location: 0.5 mi e of downtown. 917 E Silver Springs Blvd 34470. **Hours:** 11 am-2:30 & 4:30-10 pm, Sat from 4:30 pm. Closed major holidays; also Sun & Mon. **Reservations:** suggested. **Features:** Housed in a historic building painted pink, the restaurant is easy to locate even on rainy days. Well known around town for their desserts, they also offer tasty main course meals like grilled rack of lamb and Chilean sea bass. A petite portions menu and vegetarian dishes are also available. Dressy casual; cocktails. **Parking:** on-site. **Cards:** AX, CB, DC, DS, JC, MC, VI.

FRED FLEMING'S FAMOUS BAR-B-QUE

Barbecue

Lunch: $6-$17 **Dinner:** $6-$17 **Phone:** 352/861-8300
Location: I-75, exit 350, 2 mi e. 2415 SW College Rd 34474. **Hours:** 11 am-10 pm, Fri & Sat-11 pm. Closed: 11/23, 12/25. **Features:** Create your own combo with your choice of beef, chicken, catfish, sausage, pork or ribs. Sandwiches, wraps and burgers also available. Desserts include carrot cake, sugar crusted cobbler and coconut cake. Casual dress; beer & wine only. **Parking:** on-site. **Cards:** AX, DS, MC, VI.

HARRY'S SEAFOOD BAR & GRILLE

American

Lunch: $5-$7 **Dinner:** $5-$18 **Phone:** 352/840-0900
Location: Just e on SR 40 from jct US 27/301/441. 24 SE First Ave 34471. **Hours:** 11 am-10 pm, Fri & Sat-11 pm, Sun-9 pm. Closed: 11/23, 12/25. **Features:** Expect tasty, well-presented food in a bustling, laid-back atmosphere. the menu features great variety highlighted with a few Cajun choices. Peruse the ample appetizer section or order a meal of steak, chicken or seafood. Casual dress; cocktails. **Parking:** on-site. **Cards:** AX, DC, DS, MC, VI.

HORSE & HOUNDS RESTAURANT

Steak & Seafood

Lunch: $6-$15 **Dinner:** $15-$21 **Phone:** 352/620-2500
Location: I-75, exit 354, 4.5 mi w. 6998 NW Hwy 27 34482. **Hours:** 11 am-9 pm, Fri & Sat-10 pm. Closed: 1/1, 12/24, 12/25. **Reservations:** accepted. **Features:** The hunting motif provides the appropriate ambience for the venison and bison specialties. The sweet potato souffle is a unique palate surprise. Casual dress; cocktails. **Parking:** on-site. **Cards:** AX, CB, DC, DS, JC, MC, VI.

HUCKLEBERRY FINN'S RESTAURANTS & COUNTRY STORE

Southern

Lunch: $5-$7 **Phone:** 352/402-0776
Location: I-75, exit 354, just w. 3821 NW Blitchton Rd 34482. **Hours:** 7 am-3 pm. Closed major holidays. **Features:** Good selection of homestyle food at a good price. Quaint gift shop at entrance. Casual dress; cocktails. **Parking:** on-site. **Cards:** AX, DS, MC, VI.

LORENZO'S PIZZA & PASTA

Italian

Lunch: $6-$15 **Dinner:** $6-$15 **Phone:** 352/690-7220
Location: I-75, exit 354, 1.2 mi w. 4953 N Hwy 27 34482. **Hours:** 11 am-9 pm, Fri & Sat-10 pm, Sun 4 pm-10 pm. Closed major holidays. **Features:** Pizza is a specialty, but the pasta dishes shouldn't be overlooked. Mussels, shrimp, scampi, gnocchi, ravioli and manicotti are among selections. Casual dress; beer & wine only. **Parking:** on-site. **Cards:** AX, MC, VI.

SONNY'S REAL PIT BBQ
Barbecue

Lunch: $6-$9   **Dinner:** $6-$15   **Phone:** 352/245-5595
Location: I-75, exit 341, just e. 1794 SW CR 484 34473. **Hours:** 11 am-9:30 pm, Fri & Sat-10 pm. **Features:** The country themed restaurant offers slow-cooked barbecue, daily all-you-can-eat specials and a salad bar. Casual dress; beer only. **Parking:** on-site. **Cards:** AX, DS, MC, VI.

SONNY'S REAL PIT BBQ
Barbecue

Lunch: $6-$9   **Dinner:** $6-$15   **Phone:** 352/236-1012
Location: On SR 40, 1 mi w of Silver Springs attraction. 4102 E Silver Springs Blvd 34470. **Hours:** 11 am-9:30 pm, Fri & Sat-10 pm. **Features:** The country themed restaurant offers slow-cooked barbecue, daily all-you-can-eat specials and a salad bar. Casual dress; beer only. **Parking:** on-site. **Cards:** AX, DS, MC, VI.

THAI RUBY
Thai

Lunch: $4-$10   **Dinner:** $9-$23   **Phone:** 352/237-4949
Location: I-75, exit 350, 0.7 mi e. 3131 SW College Rd 34474. **Hours:** 11 am-3 & 4:30-10 pm. Closed: 11/23, 12/25. **Reservations:** accepted. **Features:** Thailand's unique culinary offerings are showcased like precious stones. Specialties include Two Friends Panang - an award-winning dish with prawns, chicken and fresh asparagus - and Shrimp Bean Thread, shrimp with clear noodles in brown sauce. Macrobiotic and vegetarian menus are available. Casual dress; beer & wine only. **Parking:** on-site. **Cards:** DS, MC, VI.

TONY'S SUSHI JAPANESE STEAKHOUSE
Japanese

Lunch: $7-$25   **Dinner:** $7-$25   **Phone:** 352/237-3151
Location: I-75, exit 354, 0.7 mi e on SR 200. 3405 SW College Rd #103 34474. **Hours:** 11 am-10 pm, Fri & Sat-11 pm, Sun 3 pm-10 pm. Closed: 7/4, 9/4, 11/23. **Reservations:** accepted. **Features:** Made-to-order sushi dishes, as well as a long list of specialty rolls, are worth trying. Sashimi and sushi combination platters also are available. Casual dress; cocktails. **Parking:** on-site. **Cards:** AX, CB, DC, DS, JC, MC, VI.

OCOEE —See Orlando p. 831.

OKEECHOBEE pop. 5,376

——— **WHERE TO STAY** ———

BUDGET INN
Motel

Phone: 863/763-3185

	1P: $89-$145	2P: $89-$145	XP: $10	F15
1/1-4/30				
12/1-12/31	1P: $89-$125	2P: $89-$125	XP: $10	F15
5/1-11/30	1P: $69-$125	2P: $69-$125	XP: $10	F15

Location: US 98 and 441, just s of jct SR 70. 201 S Parrott Ave (US 441) 34974. **Fax:** 863/763-3185. **Facility:** 24 one-bedroom standard units. 1 story, exterior corridors. *Bath:* combo or shower only. **Parking:** on-site. **Terms:** 3-5 night minimum stay, [CP] meal plan available, small pets only ($20 extra charge). **Pool(s):** outdoor. **Cards:** AX, DS, MC, VI. **Special Amenities: free continental breakfast and free local telephone calls.**

SOME UNITS

ECONOMY INN
Motel

Phone: 863/763-1148

1/1-4/15	1P: $119-$149	2P: $129-$169	XP: $10	F12
12/1-12/31 & 4/16-11/30	1P: $79-$119	2P: $89-$129	XP: $10	F12

Location: US 441, 0.3 mi n of jct SR 70. 507 N Parrott Ave 34972. **Fax:** 863/763-1149. **Facility:** 24 one-bedroom standard units. 1 story, exterior corridors. *Bath:* shower only. **Parking:** on-site. **Terms:** 3 day cancellation notice, small pets only ($10 extra charge). **Cards:** AX, DS, MC, VI. **Special Amenities: free local telephone calls and preferred room (subject to availability with advance reservations).**

SOME UNITS

HOLIDAY INN EXPRESS   *Book at aaa.com*
Small-scale Hotel

Phone: 863/357-3529

1/1-4/30	1P: $125-$299	2P: $129-$299	XP: $10	F17
12/1-12/31	1P: $99-$145	2P: $99-$145	XP: $10	F17
5/1-11/30	1P: $89-$145	2P: $89-$145	XP: $10	F17

Location: US 98 and 441, 3 mi s of jct SR 70; 0.3 mi n of Lake Okeechobee and jct SR 78. 3975 Hwy 441 S 34974. **Fax:** 863/357-3529. **Facility:** 43 one-bedroom standard units, some with whirlpools. 2 stories, exterior corridors. **Parking:** on-site. **Terms:** 3-5 night minimum stay, cancellation fee imposed, [ECP] meal plan available. **Amenities:** voice mail, irons, hair dryers. **Pool(s):** outdoor. **Guest Services:** valet and coin laundry. **Cards:** AX, CB, DC, DS, MC, VI.

SOME UNITS

——— **WHERE TO DINE** ———

LIGHTSEY'S SEAFOOD RESTAURANT
Seafood

Lunch: $4-$13   **Dinner:** $7-$32   **Phone:** 863/763-4276
Location: SR 78, 4.5 mi sw of jct US 98 and 441; in Okeetanti Recreational Area. 10435 Hwy 78 W 34974. **Hours:** 11 am-9 pm, Fri & Sat-10 pm. Closed: 4/16, 11/23, 12/25. **Reservations:** accepted. **Features:** The restaurant gleans its character from the many fish tanks, animal mounts and huge bay windows that overlook the marina. Cooter fritters (turtle), catnips (catfish), alligator and frog legs are among the down-to-earth selections. Casual dress; cocktails. **Parking:** on-site. **Cards:** AX, DS, MC, VI.

R.J. GATOR'S
American

Lunch: $4-$15   **Dinner:** $6-$21   **Phone:** 863/763-2800
Location: US 98 and 441, 1.5 mi s of SR 70. 102 SW 14th St 34974. **Hours:** 11 am-10 pm, Fri & Sat-11 pm. Closed major holidays. **Features:** Multiple televisions and video games are a few ways to keep entertained while you wait for wings, ribs, seafood specials or a specialty sandwich. Casual dress; cocktails. **Parking:** on-site. **Cards:** AX, DS, MC, VI.

OLDSMAR —See Tampa Bay p. 1030.

OLD TOWN

------ **WHERE TO STAY** ------

SUWANEE GABLES MOTEL

AAA SAVE

◆◆◆

Motel

All Year   1P: $69-$79   2P: $79-$99   XP: $10   D14   Phone: 352/542-7752
Location: US 19, 98 and 27A; 2 mi s of jct SR 349. 27659 SE Hwy 19, Alt 27 32680. Fax: 352/542-9212. **Facility:** 22 units. 18 one-bedroom standard units. 1 one-bedroom suite ($189-$209). 3 cottages ($198-$396). 1 story, exterior corridors. **Parking:** on-site. **Terms:** 3-4 night minimum stay - seasonal, 7 day cancellation notice-fee imposed, small pets only ($8 extra charge). **Pool(s):** outdoor. **Leisure Activities:** Fee: boat dock. **Guest Services:** coin laundry. **Cards:** AX, DS, MC, VI.

ORANGE CITY pop. 6,604

------ **WHERE TO STAY** ------

COMFORT INN   *Book at aaa.com*

AAA SAVE

◆◆◆

Motel

All Year [ECP]   1P: $75-$225   2P: $75-$225   XP: $10   F18   Phone: (386)775-7444
Location: I-4, exit 114, 2.8 mi w on SR 472, then 2 mi s on US 17-92. Located in a commercial area. 445 S Volusia Ave 32763. Fax: 386/775-9887. **Facility:** 60 one-bedroom standard units. 2 stories (no elevator), exterior corridors. **Parking:** on-site. **Terms:** 3-4 night minimum stay - seasonal, 30 day cancellation notice, pets ($25 deposit, $10 extra charge). **Amenities:** voice mail, safes (fee), irons, hair dryers. **Pool(s):** outdoor. **Leisure Activities:** exercise room. **Cards:** AX, CB, DC, DS, JC, MC, VI. **Special Amenities:** free expanded continental breakfast and free local telephone calls.

COUNTRY INN & SUITES BY CARLSON   *Book at aaa.com*

AAA SAVE

◆◆◆

Small-scale Hotel

All Year [ECP]   1P: $79-$109   2P: $79-$109   XP: $10   F17   Phone: (386)917-0004
Location: I-4, exit 111 westbound, just w; exit 111B eastbound. 1330 Saxon Blvd 32763. Fax: 386/917-0005. **Facility:** 116 units. 96 one-bedroom standard units. 20 one-bedroom suites ($109-$279) with whirlpools. 5 stories, interior corridors. **Bath:** combo or shower only. **Parking:** on-site. **Amenities:** high-speed Internet, dual phone lines, voice mail, irons, hair dryers. **Pool(s):** heated outdoor. **Leisure Activities:** whirlpool, exercise room. **Guest Services:** valet and coin laundry. **Business Services:** meeting rooms. **Cards:** AX, DC, DS, MC, VI.

DAYS INN   *Book at aaa.com*

AAA SAVE

◆◆◆

Motel

All Year   1P: $65-$225   2P: $65-$225   XP: $10   F18   Phone: (386)775-4522
Location: I-4, exit 114, 2.8 mi w on SR 472, then 0.3 mi s on US 17-92. 2501 N Volusia Ave 32763. Fax: 386/775-0919. **Facility:** 37 one-bedroom standard units, some with efficiencies (utensils extra charge). 1-2 stories (no elevator), exterior corridors. **Parking:** on-site. **Terms:** 1-3 night minimum stay - seasonal, 7 day cancellation notice, weekly rates available, [CP] meal plan available, package plans. **Amenities:** hair dryers. **Pool(s):** outdoor. **Leisure Activities:** barbecue pit. **Cards:** AX, DS, MC, VI. **Special Amenities:** free expanded continental breakfast and free newspaper.

------ **WHERE TO DINE** ------

STACEY'S HOMESTYLE BUFFET   **Lunch:** $7   **Dinner:** $9   Phone: 386/775-9590

◆

American

Location: Jct US 17-92 and Enterprize Rd; in Four Towns Plaza. 2404 S Volusia Ave 32763. **Hours:** 11 am-8 pm. **Features:** As the restaurant's name suggests, an all-you-can-eat buffet offers a wide variety of comfort foods prepared in a homestyle manner; in addition to entrees and side dishes there are salads and breads, as well as a wide selection of desserts. The atmosphere and surroundings are very casual and informal. Casual dress. **Parking:** on-site. **Cards:** DS, MC, VI.

ORANGE PARK —*See Jacksonville p. 501.*

Destination Orlando
pop. 185,951

There's much more to Orlando than theme parks. Mother Nature has blessed central Florida with an abundance of sunshine—and locals love to take advantage of it.

Airboating, Greater Orlando Area. Shallow water and a desire for speed have made airboats a popular way to visit the less-dry regions of Central Florida.

Recreational opportunities abound—frolicking in the waters of a nearby lake or river, hiking or bicycling along plentiful trails, golfing at one of the area's plush resorts. Still, others maintain that sufficient exercise can be obtained by walking from store to store.

Kissimmee - St. Cloud CVB

Silver Spurs Rodeo, Kissimmee. The former cow town harkens back to its origins with heritage events. (See mention page 165)

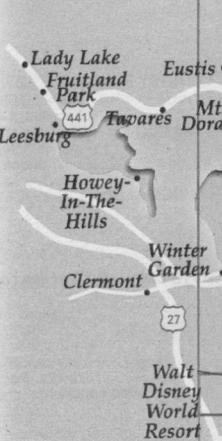

See Orlando South
map page 666

Places included in this AAA Destination City:

© Gibson Stock Photography

*Swan boats in
Lake Eola Park, Orlando.*
How do you get these
Ugly Ducklings to swim?
Pedal, pedal, pedal. (See
listing page 154)

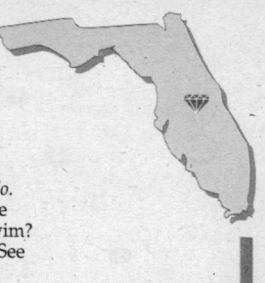

See Orlando map
page 656

© Henry P. Leu Gardens

To Astor

Heathrow

Sanford
Lake Mary

Longwood
Fern Park
Maitland
Apopka
Casselberry
Altamonte
Springs
Winter Springs
Oviedo

Winter Park

Ocoee

See Orlando
Downtown
map page
654

Lake
Buena
Vista
Orlando

Kissimmee

Celebration

St. Cloud

Davenport

*Harry P. Leu Gardens,
Orlando.*
Rest in the shade on
a humid summer
afternoon among this
garden's ornamental
grasses and foliage. (See
listing page 150)

Dining out, Greater Orlando.
With more than 4,300 restaurants
in the Orlando vicinity, you'll
have no problem finding one to
suit your tastes.

© Old Town, Kissimmee

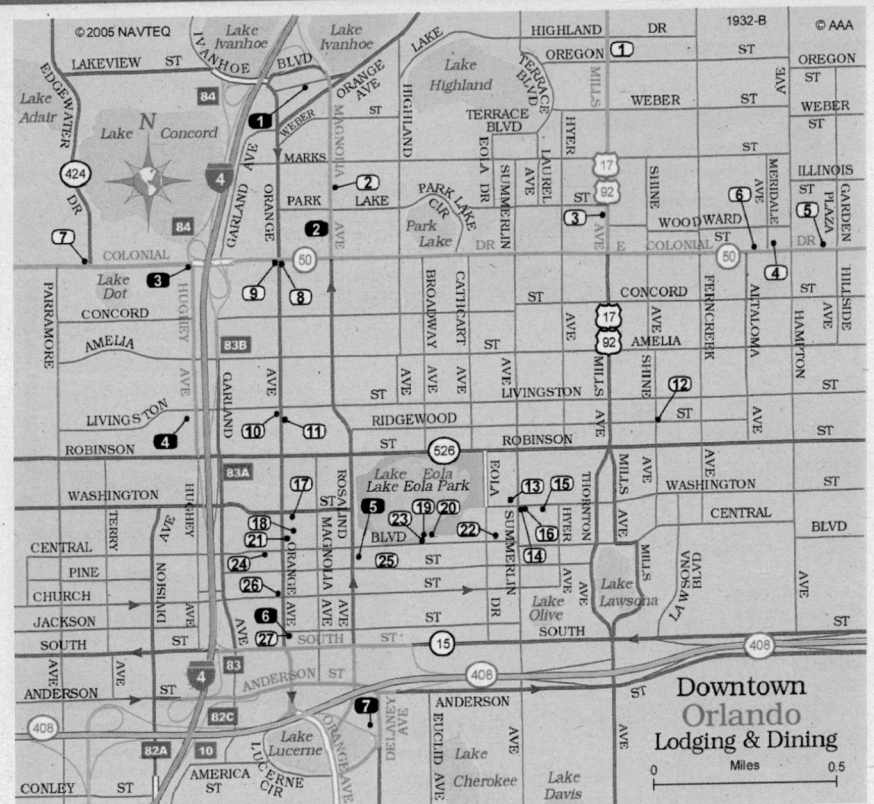

Downtown Orlando

This index helps you "spot" where approved accommodations and restaurants are located on the corresponding detailed maps. Lodging rate ranges are for comparison only and show the property's high season; rates are per night, unless only weekly (W) rates are available. Restaurant rate range is for dinner, unless only lunch (L) is served. Turn to the listing page for more detailed rate information and consult display ads for special promotions.

Spotter/Map Page Number	OA	**DOWNTOWN ORLANDO - Lodgings**	Diamond Rating	Rate Range High Season	Listing Page
1 / below		Radisson Plaza Hotel Orlando	▽▽▽	$179-$259	688
2 / below		Courtyard by Marriott - Downtown Orlando - see color ad p 687	▽▽▽	$98-$149	687
3 / below		Americas Best Value Inn	▽▽▽	Failed to provide	687
4 / below		Orlando Marriott Downtown - see color ad p 687	▽▽▽	$107-$180	688
5 / below		Embassy Suites Orlando Downtown	▽▽▽	$120-$250	688
6 / below	AAA	**Westin Grand Bohemian**	▽▽▽▽	$239-$439 SAVE	689
7 / below		The Courtyard at Lake Lucerne	▽▽▽	$115-$225	687
		DOWNTOWN ORLANDO - Restaurants			
① / below		Chinatown	▽▽	$7-$20	689
② / below		Cafe Trastevere	▽▽	$10-$21	689
③ / below		Pho 88	▽	$7-$12	691
④ / below		Chan's Chinese Cuisine	▽▽	$6-$30	689

Spotter/Map Page Number	OA	DOWNTOWN ORLANDO - Restaurants (continued)	Diamond Rating	Rate Range High Season	Listing Page
⑤ / p. 654		Thai House	◈◈	$7-$13	691
⑥ / p. 654		Vega's Cafe	◈	$4-$5(L)	691
⑦ / p. 654		O-Boys Bar-B-Q	◈	$4-$12	690
⑧ / p. 654		New York Deli	◈	$3-$7	690
⑨ / p. 654		Mama B's Giant Subs	◈	$3-$7(L)	690
⑩ / p. 654	AAA	**Manuel's on the 28th**	◈◈◈◈	$28-$36	690
⑪ / p. 654		N.Y.P.D. Pizza & Delicatessen	◈	$6-$17	690
⑫ / p. 654		Bravissimo Italian Cafe	◈◈	$4-$11	689
⑬ / p. 654		Anthony's Pizzeria Restaurant	◈◈	$5-$12	689
⑭ / p. 654		The Coffee House of Thornton Park	◈	$3-$5(L)	689
⑮ / p. 654		Dexter's of Thornton Park	◈◈	$10-$25	689
⑯ / p. 654		Wildside Restaurant	◈◈	$8-$18	691
⑰ / p. 654		Sushi Hatsu	◈◈	$9-$19	691
⑱ / p. 654		The Globe	◈◈	$8-$16	689
⑲ / p. 654		Metro Espresso Pizza Cafe	◈	$5-$15	690
⑳ / p. 654		Lee's Lakeside Restaurant	◈◈	$19-$29	690
㉑ / p. 654		Wall Street Cantina	◈	$7-$14	691
㉒ / p. 654		Hue	◈◈◈	$13-$26	690
㉓ / p. 654		Lake Eola Yacht Club (LEYC)	◈◈	$8-$22	690
㉔ / p. 654		Kate O'Brien's Irish Pub & Restaurant	◈	$8-$15	690
㉕ / p. 654		Sam Snead's Downtown	◈◈	$8-$28	691
㉖ / p. 654		Kres ChopHouse	◈◈◈	$10-$32	690
㉗ / p. 654	AAA	**The Boheme**	◈◈◈◈	$19-$32	689

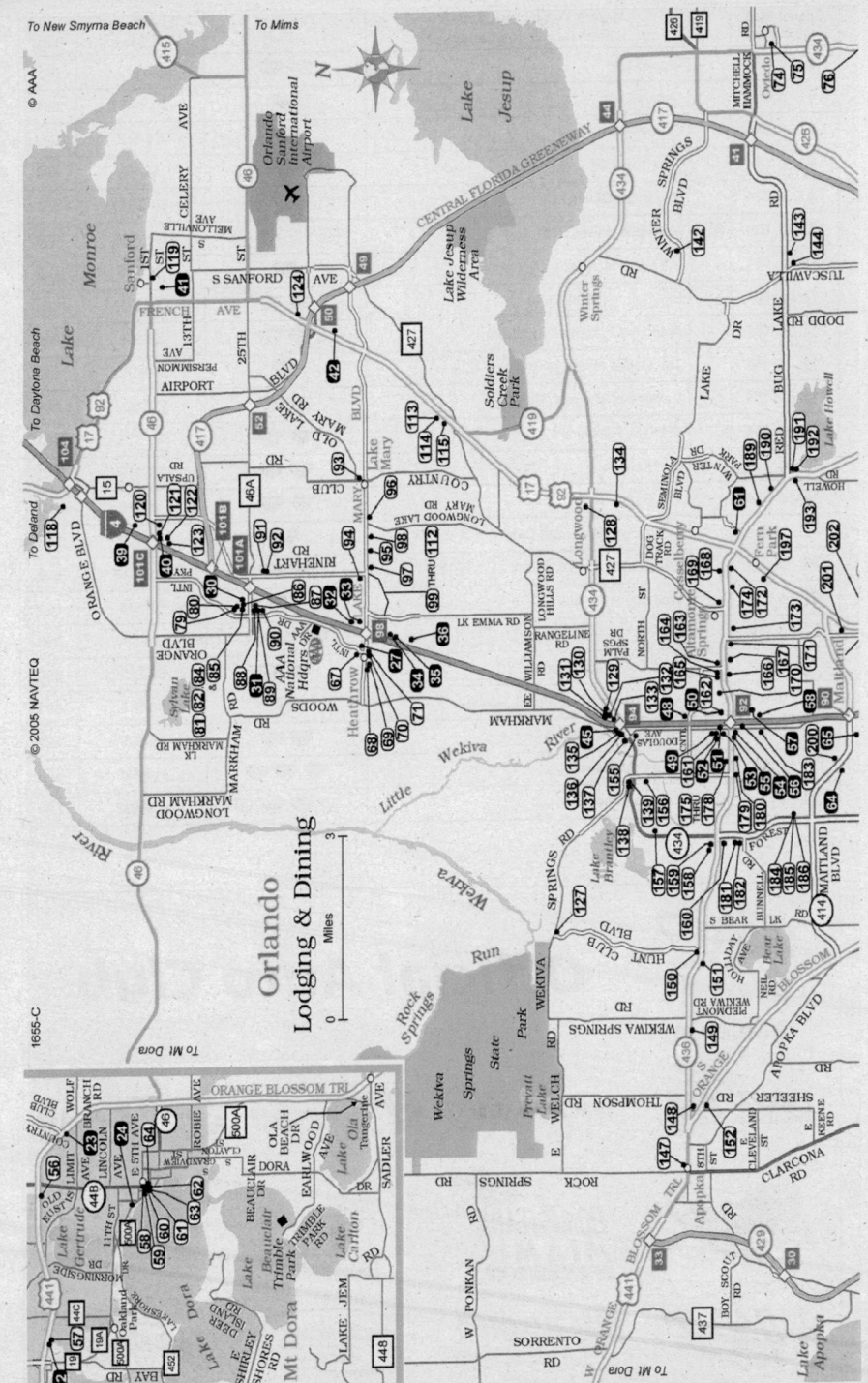

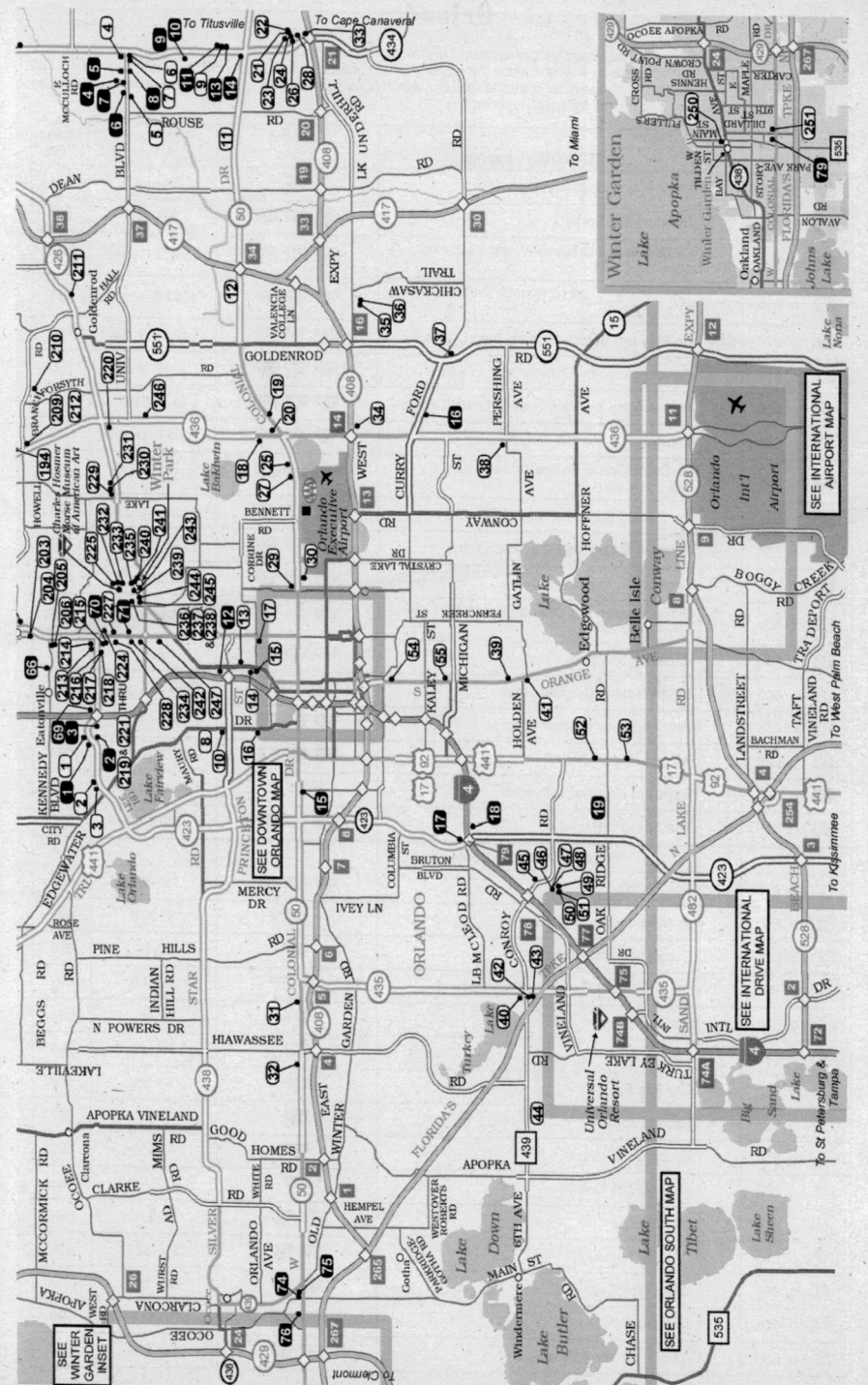

Orlando

This index helps you "spot" where approved accommodations and restaurants are located on the corresponding detailed maps. Lodging rate ranges are for comparison only and show the property's high season; rates are per night, unless only weekly (W) rates are available. Restaurant rate range is for dinner, unless only lunch (L) is served. Turn to the listing page for more detailed rate information and consult display ads for special promotions.

Spotter/Map Page Number	OA	ORLANDO - Lodgings	Diamond Rating	Rate Range High Season	Listing Page
1 / p. 656		Motel 6 Orlando-Winter Park #791	◆	$41-$57	694
2 / p. 656	AAA	**Comfort Inn-North**	◆◆◆	$69 SAVE	691
3 / p. 656	AAA	**La Quinta Inn Orlando-Winter Park -** see color ad p 694	◆◆◆	$59-$249 SAVE	694
4 / p. 656		TownePlace Suites by Marriott Orlando East/UCF	◆◆◆	Failed to provide	695
5 / p. 656	AAA	**Holiday Inn Select-Orlando East-UCF Area**	◆◆◆	$89-$169 SAVE	693
6 / p. 656		Residence Inn by Marriott/Orlando East	◆◆◆	$159-$209	695
7 / p. 656		Hampton Inn & Suites/Orlando East-UCF Area	◆◆◆	$109-$129	693
8 / p. 656		Courtyard by Marriott @ UCF	◆◆◆	Failed to provide	693
9 / p. 656	AAA	**La Quinta Inn & Suites Orlando (U.C.F.) -** see color ad p 721	◆◆◆	$79-$95 SAVE	694
10 / p. 656		Homewood Suites by Hilton UCF	◆◆◆	Failed to provide	694
11 / p. 656	AAA	**Comfort Suites UCF-Research Park**	◆◆◆	$99-$199 SAVE	692
12 / p. 656	AAA	**Comfort Suites Downtown**	◆◆◆	$109-$139 SAVE	692
13 / p. 656	AAA	**Hilton Garden Inn Orlando East/UCF -** see color ad p 693	◆◆◆	$110-$250 SAVE	693
14 / p. 656		Radisson University Hotel	◆◆◆	$99	694
15 / p. 656	AAA	**Best Western Orlando West**	◆◆	$59-$125 SAVE	691
16 / p. 656		Ventura Resort Rentals Orlando	◆◆◆	$64-$152	695
17 / p. 656		Ramada Plaza Orlando	◆◆◆	$109-$129	694
18 / p. 656	AAA	**Days Inn North of Universal**	◆◆	$40-$150 SAVE	693
19 / p. 656		The Seasons Resort	◆◆◆	$89-$338	695
		ORLANDO - Restaurants			
(1) / p. 656		Del Frisco's	◆◆◆	$50-$75	696
(2) / p. 656		Jo Ming Garden	◆	$8-$16	697
(3) / p. 656		Cuban Sandwiches To Go	◆	$3-$6	696
(4) / p. 656		Giovanni's Italian Restaurant & Pizzeria	◆◆	$6-$19	697
(5) / p. 656		Backyard Burger	◆	$5-$8	695
(6) / p. 656		Falafel Cafe	◆	$5-$10	696
(7) / p. 656		The Pita Pit	◆	$4-$6	699
(8) / p. 656		Habana Joe's	◆	$5-$8	697
(9) / p. 656		Bubbalou's Bodacious BBQ	◆	$4-$10	696
(10) / p. 656		College Park Cafe	◆	$3-$7(L)	696
(11) / p. 656		Maria Bonita	◆◆	$5-$12	698
(12) / p. 656		Olympia Restaurant	◆◆	$10-$22	698
(13) / p. 656		White Wolf Cafe	◆◆	$10-$23	700
(14) / p. 656		Tiramisu Cafe	◆◆	$8-$14	699
(15) / p. 656		Gargi's at Lake Ivanhoe	◆◆	$11-$23	697

Spotter/Map Page Number	OA	ORLANDO - Restaurants (continued)	Diamond Rating	Rate Range High Season	Listing Page
16 / p. 656		Shakers American Cafe	◈	$3-$8(L)	699
17 / p. 656		Kim Long Vietnamese Cuisine	◈◈	$6-$12	697
18 / p. 656		Royal Thai	◈◈	$6-$12	699
19 / p. 656		Patio Cafe Restaurant	◈	$3-$11	698
20 / p. 656		High Tide Harry's	◈◈	$8-$30	697
21 / p. 656		Crispers	◈	$4-$8	696
22 / p. 656		Johnny Rockets	◈	$3-$8	697
23 / p. 656		California Pizza Kitchen	◈◈	$7-$26	696
24 / p. 656		Toojay's Original Gourmet Deli	◈◈	$5-$10	700
25 / p. 656	▲▲▲	**Hot Dog Heaven**	◈	$2-$6	697
26 / p. 656		Amigo's Original Tex-Mex Restaurant & Cantina	◈◈	$5-$23	695
27 / p. 656		Straub's Fine Seafood Restaurant	◈◈	$12-$29	699
28 / p. 656		Panera Bread	◈	$3-$6	698
29 / p. 656		Soprano's Ristorante & Pizzeria	◈	$8-$18	699
30 / p. 656		BAJA Burrito Kitchen	◈	$4-$8	695
31 / p. 656		Sonny's Real Pit BBQ	◈◈	$8-$15	699
32 / p. 656		Smokey Bones Bar-B-Q and Sports Bar	◈◈	$9-$16	699
33 / p. 656		Smokey Bones	◈◈	$5-$18	699
34 / p. 656		Choo-Choo Churros Argentinean Restaurant & Steakhouse	◈	$12-$20	696
35 / p. 656		Amalfi Italian Restaurant	◈◈	$6-$19	695
36 / p. 656		Margarita's Grill	◈◈	$8-$17	698
37 / p. 656		Jack and Mary's	◈	$4-$8(L)	697
38 / p. 656		Brooklyn Pizza	◈	$6-$25	696
39 / p. 656		Julie's Waterfront	◈	$5-$19	697
40 / p. 656		Le Peep Restaurant	◈◈	$3-$9(L)	698
41 / p. 656		Le Coq au Vin	◈◈◈	$16-$29	698
42 / p. 656		Bubbaloo's Bodacious Bar-B-Que	◈	$4-$15	696
43 / p. 656		P.R.'s Mexican Restaurant	◈	$5-$16	699
44 / p. 656		Stonewood Tavern and Grill	◈◈◈	$8-$27	699
45 / p. 656		Mimi's Cafe	◈◈	$4-$16	698
46 / p. 656		McCormick & Schmick's	◈◈◈	$5-$16	698
47 / p. 656		P.F. Chang's China Bistro	◈◈◈	$10-$25	699
48 / p. 656		The Cheesecake Factory	◈◈◈	$5-$27	696
49 / p. 656		Brio Tuscan Grille	◈◈◈	$8-$23	695
50 / p. 656		Jonny Rockets	◈	$4-$10	697
51 / p. 656		Panera Bread	◈	$4-$8	698
52 / p. 656		Gain's German Restaurant	◈◈	$11-$18	697
53 / p. 656		Charley's Steak House	◈◈◈	$15-$50	696
54 / p. 656		Mama B's	◈	$3-$7(L)	698

Spotter/Map Page Number	OA	**ORLANDO** - Restaurants (continued)	Diamond Rating	Rate Range High Season	Listing Page
(55) / p. 656		Numero Uno	◆◆	$8-$25	698
		MOUNT DORA - Lodgings			
(22) / p. 656	AAA	**Comfort Inn and Suites**	◆◆	$70-$130 SAVE	829
(23) / p. 656	AAA	**Hampton Inn**	◆◆◆	$89-$129 SAVE	830
(24) / p. 656		Darst Victorian Manor	◆◆◆◆	$150-$250	830
		MOUNT DORA - Restaurants			
(56) / p. 656		Dixie Crossroads	◆◆	$8-$22	830
(57) / p. 656		Cafe Stella	◆◆	$9-$18	830
(58) / p. 656		5th Ave Cafe & Market	◆◆	$6-$18	830
(59) / p. 656		Cecile's French Corner Cafe	◆◆	$5-$17	830
(60) / p. 656		The Frosty Mug	◆◆	$12-$22	830
(61) / p. 656		The Windsor Rose English Tea Room	◆◆	$6-$18	831
(62) / p. 656		Palm Tree Grill	◆◆	$10-$22	831
(63) / p. 656	AAA	**The Gables Restaurant**	◆◆	$15-$27	830
(64) / p. 656		The Goblin Market	◆◆◆	$16-$28	830
		HEATHROW - Lodgings			
(27) / p. 656		Courtyard by Marriott	◆◆◆	Failed to provide	754
		HEATHROW - Restaurants			
(67) / p. 656	AAA	**Luigino's**	◆◆◆	$15-$35	754
(68) / p. 656		Peach Valley Cafe	◆◆	$3-$12(L)	754
(69) / p. 656		Panera Bread Co	◆	$5-$7	754
(70) / p. 656		Stonewood Grill & Tavern	◆◆◆	$9-$29	754
(71) / p. 656		Mammolito's Pizza & Pasta	◆◆	$9-$18	754
		LAKE MARY - Lodgings			
(30) / p. 656		Hampton Inn & Suites at Colonial TownPark	◆◆◆	$109-$179	821
(31) / p. 656	AAA	**Orlando Marriott Lake Mary** - see color ad p 821	◆◆◆	$99-$229 SAVE	822
(32) / p. 656	AAA	**Hilton Garden Inn Lake Mary**	◆◆◆	$69-$199 SAVE	821
(33) / p. 656	AAA	**Homewood Suites by Hilton** - see color ad p 821	◆◆◆	$99-$149 SAVE	822
(34) / p. 656		Homestead Studio Suites-Orlando/Lake Mary	◆◆◆	$44-$79	822
(35) / p. 656	AAA	**La Quinta Inn & Suites Orlando (Lake Mary)** - see color ad p 721	◆◆◆	$89-$109 SAVE	822
(36) / p. 656		Candlewood Suites Lake Mary-Heathrow	◆◆◆	$69-$139	821
		LAKE MARY - Restaurants			
(79) / p. 656		Papa Joe's Pizza Colonial Town Park	◆◆	$9-$17	825
(80) / p. 656	AAA	**Amura**	◆◆◆	$8-$32	822
(81) / p. 656		Dexter's of Lake Mary	◆◆◆	$10-$25	823
(82) / p. 656		The Coffee Cafe	◆	$4-$9	823
(84) / p. 656		McAlister's Deli	◆	$5-$7	824
(85) / p. 656		Mama Fu's Asian House	◆	$4-$10	824
(86) / p. 656		Crispers	◆	$3-$8	823

Spotter/Map Page Number	OA	**LAKE MARY** - Restaurants (continued)	Diamond Rating	Rate Range High Season	Listing Page
87 / p. 656		Harvey's Bistro	◆◆◆	$9-$29	824
88 / p. 656		Moe's Southwest Grill	◆	$3-$8	824
89 / p. 656		Bistro 1501	◆◆◆	$15-$23	822
90 / p. 656		Jinja Asia Cafe	◆◆◆	$5-$17	824
91 / p. 656		Lee's Palace	◆◆	$5-$15	824
92 / p. 656		Giovanni's Italian Restaurant & Pizzeria	◆◆	$9-$18	823
93 / p. 656		Dalli's Pizzeria	◆	$5-$19	823
94 / p. 656		Coconuts Cuban Cafe & Deli	◆	$4-$7	823
95 / p. 656		Appleton's Cafe	◆◆	$8-$17	822
96 / p. 656		Tijuana Flats	◆	$4-$8	825
97 / p. 656		Taste of China	◆◆	$8-$11	825
98 / p. 656		Mamma Lou's	◆	$5-$11	824
99 / p. 656		Golden China Buffet	◆◆	$10-$13	824
100 / p. 656		Gator's Dockside	◆◆	$5-$17	823
101 / p. 656		Caffe Positano	◆◆◆	$6-$18	823
102 / p. 656		Keller's Real Smoked Bar-B-Q	◆	$3-$12	824
103 / p. 656		Atlanta Bread Company	◆	$4-$7	822
104 / p. 656		Osaka Japanese Steak House	◆◆	$8-$24	824
105 / p. 656		Papa Joe's	◆◆	$7-$15	825
106 / p. 656		Chengs	◆◆	$6-$21	823
107 / p. 656	AAA	**Thai Corner Restaurant**	◆◆	$7-$15	825
108 / p. 656		Firehouse Subs	◆	$5-$7	823
109 / p. 656		Tropical Smoothie Cafe	◆	$4-$7	825
110 / p. 656		Tony's Original Wings & Grill	◆	$4-$11	825
111 / p. 656		India Village	◆◆	$6-$13	824
112 / p. 656		Toojay's Original Gourmet Deli	◆◆	$5-$10	825
113 / p. 656		China Cook	◆	$5-$11	823
114 / p. 656		Vivona's II of Lake Mary	◆◆	$7-$14	825
115 / p. 656		Westshore Pizza	◆	$6-$21	825
		SANFORD - Lodgings			
39 / p. 656	AAA	**Comfort Inn & Suites North Orlando** - see color ad p 832	◆◆◆	$69-$259 [SAVE]	832
40 / p. 656		SpringHill Suites by Marriott	◆◆◆	$109-$179	832
41 / p. 656		The Higgins House Bed & Breakfast	◆◆◆	Failed to provide	832
42 / p. 656		Holiday Inn Express-Sanford/Lake Mary	◆◆◆	$89-$175	832
		SANFORD - Restaurants			
118 / p. 656		Otter's Riverside Restaurant	◆◆	$9-$25	833
119 / p. 656		Da Vinci, A Dining Place	◆◆	$14-$26	833
120 / p. 656		Joe's Crab Shack	◆◆	$9-$25	833
121 / p. 656		Hops Grillhouse & Brewery	◆◆	$4-$23	833
122 / p. 656		Tony's New York Pizza & Restaurant	◆◆	$6-$19	833

Spotter/Map Page Number	OA	SANFORD - Restaurants (continued)	Diamond Rating	Rate Range High Season	Listing Page
123 / p. 656		Sanford Ale House	◆◆	$4-$16	833
124 / p. 656		Sergio's Italian Restaurant	◆◆	$7-$24	833
		LONGWOOD - Lodgings			
45 / p. 656		Comfort Inn & Conference Center	◆◆◆	$79-$149	827
		LONGWOOD - Restaurants			
127 / p. 656		Anthony's New York Pizza & Pasta	◆◆	$5-$18	827
128 / p. 656		Korea House	◆	$13-$20	828
129 / p. 656		Bonefish Grill	◆◆◆	$13-$21	827
130 / p. 656		Journey's	◆◆◆	$14-$32	828
131 / p. 656		Crispers	◆	$5-$9	827
132 / p. 656		Calypso Grille	◆◆	$6-$15	827
133 / p. 656		Volcanos Coffee Bar	◆	$4-$6	828
134 / p. 656		Enzo's Restaurant On The Lake	◆◆◆	$20-$38	827
135 / p. 656		Melting Pot	◆◆	$12-$39	828
136 / p. 656	◉◉◉	**Imperial Dynasty Chinese Restaurant & Lounge**	◆◆	$6-$30	828
137 / p. 656		Markham's Sports Bar & Grill	◆◆	$8-$18	828
138 / p. 656		First Watch	◆◆	$5-$7(L)	827
139 / p. 656		Mykonos	◆◆	$9-$18	828
		ALTAMONTE SPRINGS - Lodgings			
48 / p. 656		Candlewood Suites	◆◆◆	$79-$99	743
49 / p. 656		Residence Inn by Marriott	◆◆◆	$89-$289	744
50 / p. 656	◉◉◉	**Embassy Suites Orlando North**	◆◆◆	$120-$220 [SAVE]	743
51 / p. 656		Hampton Inn	◆◆◆	$71-$159	743
52 / p. 656	◉◉◉	**Best Western Altamonte Springs**	◆◆◆	$69-$129 [SAVE]	743
53 / p. 656		SpringHill Suites by Marriott Orlando/Altamonte Springs	◆◆◆	$99-$129	744
54 / p. 656	◉◉◉	**Holiday Inn Orlando North/Altamonte Springs** - see color ad p 744	◆◆◆	$72-$109 [SAVE]	744
55 / p. 656	◉◉◉	**Days Inn Altamonte Springs**	◆◆◆	$50-$150 [SAVE]	743
56 / p. 656	◉◉◉	**Quality Inn North**	◆◆	$59-$99 [SAVE]	744
57 / p. 656		Homestead Studio Suites Hotel-Orlando/Altamonte Springs	◆◆◆	$44-$69	744
58 / p. 656		Hilton Orlando/Altamonte Springs	◆◆◆	$160	743
		ALTAMONTE SPRINGS - Restaurants			
155 / p. 656		August Moon Chinese Restaurant & Sushi Bar	◆◆	$7-$16	745
156 / p. 656		China Gate Restaurant	◆◆	$8-$14	745
157 / p. 656		Baja Burrito Kitchen	◆	$4-$8	745
158 / p. 656		Crazy Buffet	◆◆	$18-$20	746
159 / p. 656		Don Pepe's Cuban Cafe	◆◆	$9-$20	746
160 / p. 656		El Charro Mexican Restaurant	◆◆	$7-$12	746
161 / p. 656		Bangkok Restaurant	◆◆	$7-$12	745
162 / p. 656		Omaha Steakhouse	◆◆◆	$13-$33	747

Spotter/Map Page Number	OA	ALTAMONTE SPRINGS - Restaurants (continued)	Diamond Rating	Rate Range High Season	Listing Page
163 / p. 656		Mimi's Cafe	◆◆	$5-$16	746
164 / p. 656		Bahama Breeze	◆◆◆	$7-$24	745
165 / p. 656		Altamonte Ale House & Raw Bar	◆◆	$4-$14	745
166 / p. 656	AAA	**Eastern Pearl Chinese Restaurant**	◆◆◆	$7-$28	746
167 / p. 656		Straub's Fine Seafood	◆◆	$12-$29	747
168 / p. 656	AAA	**Amira's**	◆	$5-$11	745
169 / p. 656		Bubbalou's Bodacious B-B-Q	◆	$3-$12	745
170 / p. 656		Jason's Deli	◆	$5-$10	746
171 / p. 656		Panera Bread	◆	$3-$6	747
172 / p. 656		Uncle Jones Bar-B-Que	◆	$3-$10	747
173 / p. 656		Sam Seltzer's Steakhouse	◆◆	$10-$20	747
174 / p. 656		Athena Greek Cafe	◆◆	$4-$8	745
175 / p. 656		Amigos	◆◆	$7-$12	745
176 / p. 656		Kohinoor Indian Restaurant	◆◆	$8-$17	746
177 / p. 656		First Watch	◆◆	$4-$8(L)	746
178 / p. 656		Lawless Cafe & Deli	◆	$4-$8	746
179 / p. 656		Sweet Tomatoes	◆	$8-$13	747
180 / p. 656		Chipotle	◆	$4-$6	745
181 / p. 656		Panera Bread	◆	$3-$8	747
182 / p. 656		Backyard Burger	◆	$3-$6	745
183 / p. 656	AAA	**Maison & Jardin Restaurant**	◆◆◆◆	$22-$38	746
184 / p. 656		Moe's Southwest Grill	◆	$2-$8	746
185 / p. 656		Yum Yum Asia Cafe	◆	$4-$15	747
186 / p. 656		Papa Anthony's Pizza	◆	$8-$12	747
		CASSELBERRY - Lodgings			
61 / p. 656		Suburban Lodge	◆◆	$80-$180	748
		CASSELBERRY - Restaurants			
189 / p. 656		Cypriana Restaurant	◆◆	$8-$17	748
190 / p. 656		Rolando's Cuban Restaurant	◆◆	$7-$24	749
191 / p. 656		Italian Village Pizza	◆	$5-$17	748
192 / p. 656		Colorado Fondue Company	◆◆	$11-$19	748
193 / p. 656		Aladdin's Cafe	◆	$7-$19	748
194 / p. 656		Smokey Bones BBQ	◆◆	$5-$21	749
		MAITLAND - Lodgings			
64 / p. 656		Courtyard by Marriott Orlando/Maitland	◆◆◆	$79-$149	828
65 / p. 656	AAA	**Homewood Suites by Hilton Orlando North**	◆◆◆	$89-$339 [SAVE]	828
66 / p. 656		Thurston House	◆◆◆	$150-$170	829
		MAITLAND - Restaurants			
200 / p. 656		Sam Snead's	◆◆	$6-$22	829
201 / p. 656		Kappy's	◆	$2-$5	829

Spotter/Map Page Number	OA	MAITLAND - Restaurants (continued)	Diamond Rating	Rate Range High Season	Listing Page
(202) / p. 656		Melting Pot	◈◈	$15-$30	829
(203) / p. 656	AAA	**Antonio's La Fiamma**	◈◈	$6-$20	829
(204) / p. 656	AAA	**Antonio's La Fiamma Ristorante**	◈◈◈	$12-$37	829
(205) / p. 656		Fast Eddie's Famous Hamburgers	◈	$2-$5	829
(206) / p. 656		First Watch	◈◈	$4-$10(L)	829
		WINTER PARK - Lodgings			
(69) / p. 656	AAA	**Park Inn Orlando/Winter Park**	◈◈	$59-$79 [SAVE]	835
(70) / p. 656	AAA	**Ramada Inn**	◈◈	$50-$80 [SAVE]	835
(71) / p. 656	AAA	**Best Western Mt. Vernon Inn** - see color ad p 834	◈◈◈	$84-$119 [SAVE]	834
		WINTER PARK - Restaurants			
(209) / p. 656		Greek Flame Taverna	◈◈	$5-$20	837
(210) / p. 656		Chef Henry's Cafe	◈◈	$14-$22	836
(211) / p. 656		Saikyo Sushi Bar and Grill	◈◈	$17	838
(212) / p. 656		Old Germany Restaurant	◈◈	$6-$24	837
(213) / p. 656		Bubbalou's Bodacious Bar-b-que	◈	$4-$13	836
(214) / p. 656		Fuji Sushi	◈◈	$11-$25	837
(215) / p. 656		Fleming's Prime Steakhouse & Wine Bar	◈◈◈	$21-$36	836
(216) / p. 656		El Potro Mexican Restaurant	◈	$6-$13	836
(217) / p. 656		Daily Express Deli & Grill	◈	$3-$6(L)	836
(218) / p. 656		A Taste of Jamaica Restaurant	◈	$3-$7(L)	835
(219) / p. 656		Siam Garden	◈◈	$10-$21	838
(220) / p. 656		Amigos	◈◈	$7-$12	835
(221) / p. 656		Ruth's Chris Steak House	◈◈◈	$18-$40	838
(222) / p. 656		Seito Sushi	◈◈	$7-$18	838
(223) / p. 656		Cheesecake Factory	◈◈◈	$8-$25	836
(224) / p. 656		Brio Tuscan Grille	◈◈	$10-$24	836
(225) / p. 656		Brandywine's Delicatessen	◈	$3-$7(L)	835
(227) / p. 656		Crispers	◈	$4-$9	836
(228) / p. 656		P. F. Chang's China Bistro	◈◈◈	$7-$17	837
(229) / p. 656		Tijuana Flats	◈	$4-$9	838
(230) / p. 656		Giovanni's Italian Restaurant & Pizzeria	◈◈	$8-$19	837
(231) / p. 656		Jum-Bo	◈◈	$9-$15	837
(232) / p. 656		Chapters Cafe & Bookshop Inc	◈◈	$9-$15	836
(233) / p. 656		Briar Patch	◈◈	$6-$14	835
(234) / p. 656		Houston's	◈◈◈	$12-$28	837
(235) / p. 656		Pannullo's Italian Restaurant	◈◈	$9-$17	837
(236) / p. 656		Hot Olives	◈◈	$8-$19	837

Spotter/Map Page Number	OA	WINTER PARK - Restaurants (continued)	Diamond Rating	Rate Range High Season	Listing Page
⟨237⟩ / p. 656		Chez Vincent	◈◈◈	$18-$26	836
⟨238⟩ / p. 656		Dexter's of Winter Park	◈◈◈	$10-$25	836
⟨239⟩ / p. 656	AAA	**Park Plaza Gardens**	◈◈◈	$21-$30	837
⟨240⟩ / p. 656		Powerhouse Cafe	◈	$6-$10	838
⟨241⟩ / p. 656	AAA	**Allegria Wine Bar & Cucina**	◈◈◈	$11-$30	835
⟨242⟩ / p. 656		Black Bean Deli	◈	$6-$10	835
⟨243⟩ / p. 656		Shiki Japanese Cuisine	◈◈	$12-$29	838
⟨244⟩ / p. 656		Bakely's Restaurant & Bake Shop	◈	$4-$9(L)	835
⟨245⟩ / p. 656		PR's Mexican Restaurant	◈	$8-$18	838
⟨246⟩ / p. 656		Orlando Ale House	◈◈	$4-$14	837
⟨247⟩ / p. 656		Moe's Southwest Grill	◈	$3-$9	837
		OCOEE - Lodgings			
⟨74⟩ / p. 656		Courtyard by Marriott Orlando Ocoee	◈◈◈	$109-$149	831
⟨75⟩ / p. 656		Best Western Turnpike West-Orlando	◈◈◈	$69-$94	831
⟨76⟩ / p. 656		Red Roof Inn Orlando West	◈◈	$59-$84	831
		OVIEDO - Restaurants			
⟨74⟩ / p. 656		Bajo El Puente	◈	$4-$11	831
⟨75⟩ / p. 656		D'Amici Italian Grill & Pizzeria	◈◈	$6-$16	831
⟨76⟩ / p. 656		Big Daddy's Pizza	◈	$3-$17	831
		WINTER SPRINGS - Restaurants			
⟨142⟩ / p. 656		Tuscany's	◈◈	$8-$19	838
⟨143⟩ / p. 656		Athens Cafe	◈◈	$4-$16	838
⟨144⟩ / p. 656		369 Chinese Restaurant	◈◈	$8-$22	838
		APOPKA - Restaurants			
⟨147⟩ / p. 656	AAA	**Catfish Place of Apopka**	◈◈	$7-$16	747
⟨148⟩ / p. 656		Mi Tierra Restaurant	◈	$6-$13	748
⟨149⟩ / p. 656		Sonny's Real Pit BBQ	◈◈	$6-$15	748
⟨150⟩ / p. 656		Scampi's Italian Eatery	◈◈	$5-$17	748
⟨151⟩ / p. 656		Caffe' Positano	◈◈	$10-$30	747
⟨152⟩ / p. 656		Roma Ristorante Italiano	◈◈	$10-$20	748
		FERN PARK - Restaurant			
⟨197⟩ / p. 656		New York Pizza & Restaurant	◈	$6-$19	753
		WINTER GARDEN - Restaurants			
⟨250⟩ / p. 656		Choctaw Willy's	◈	$3-$17	834
⟨251⟩ / p. 656		Taquitos Jalisco	◈◈	$5-$14	834

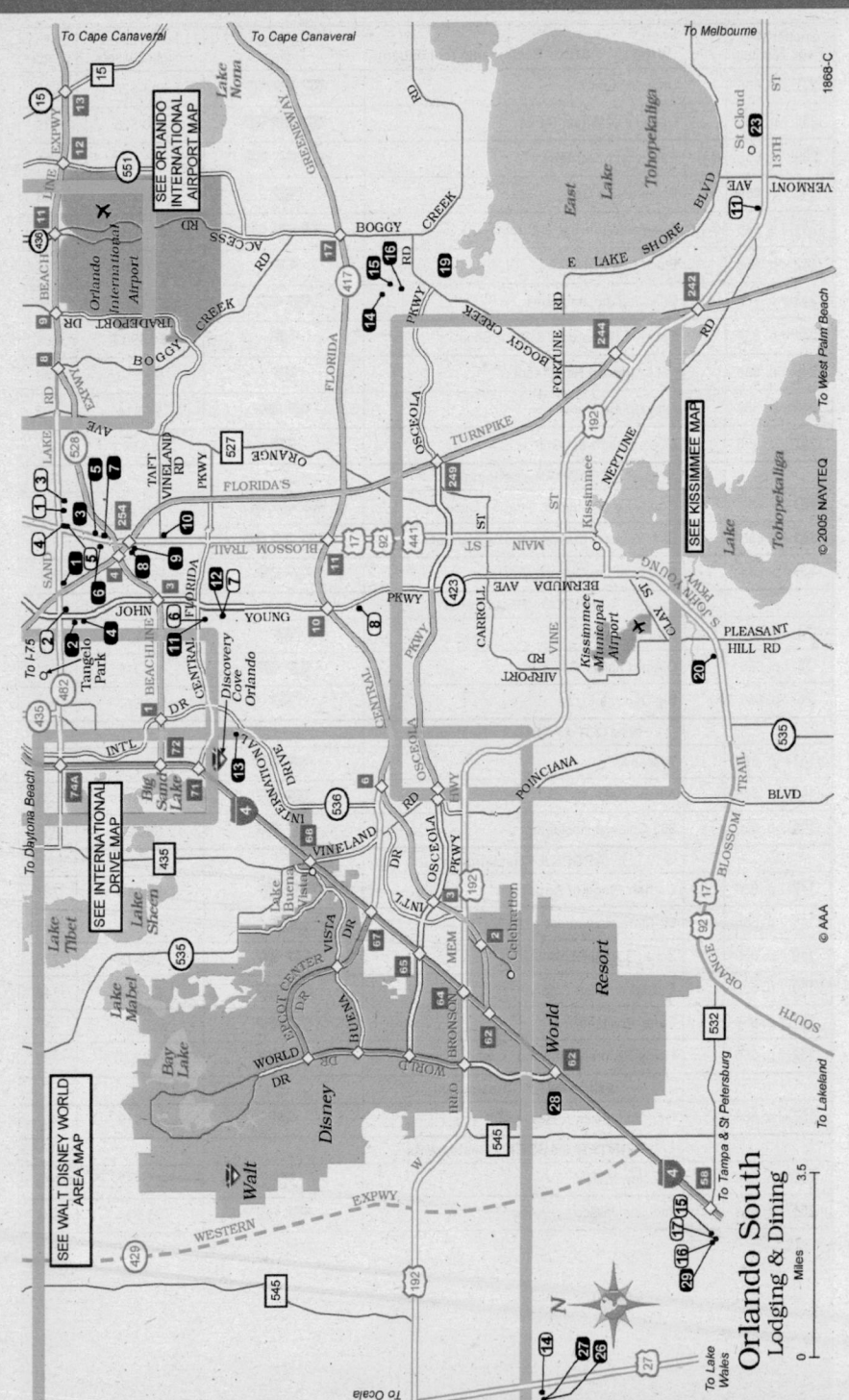

Orlando South
Lodging & Dining

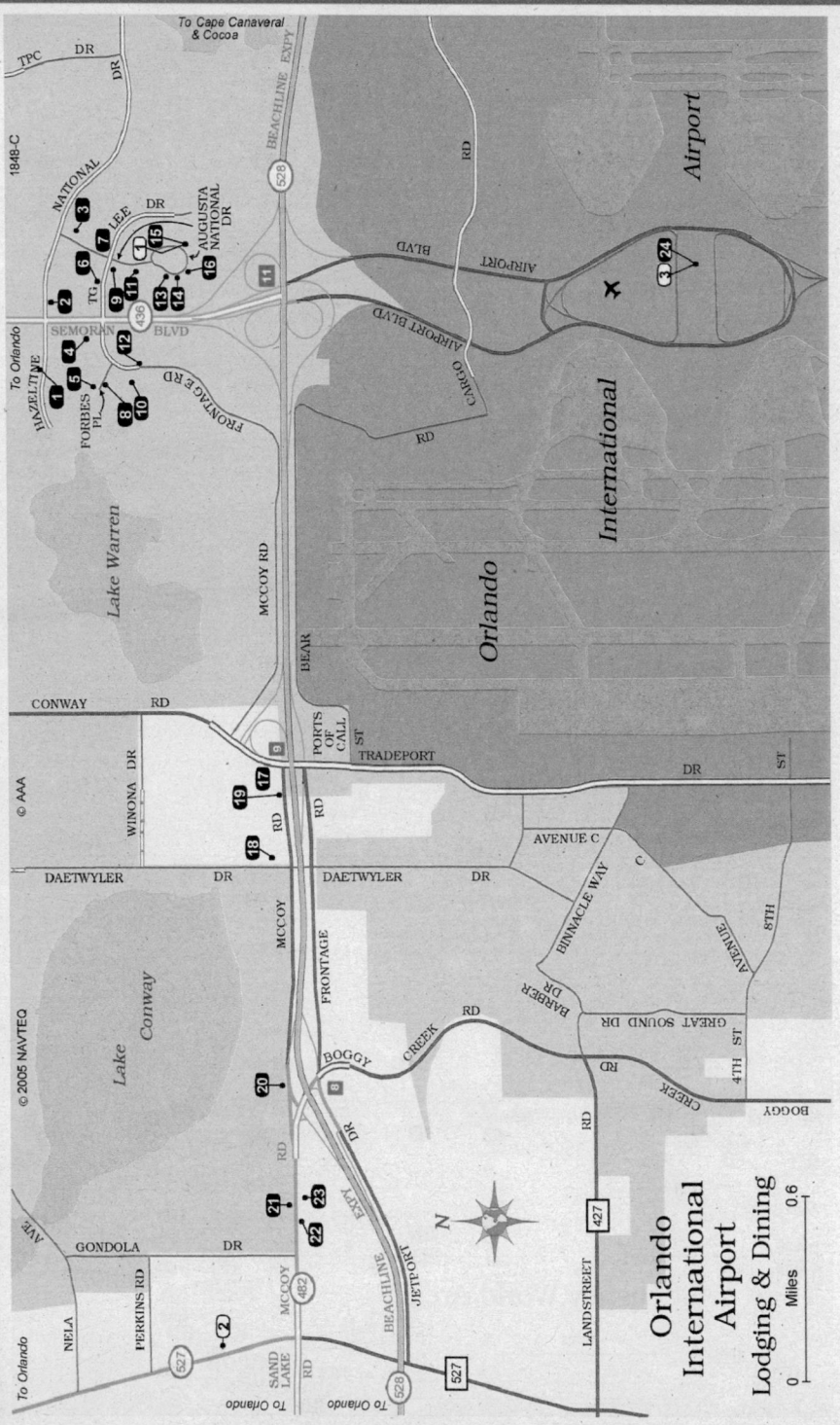

Orlando International
Airport
Lodging & Dining

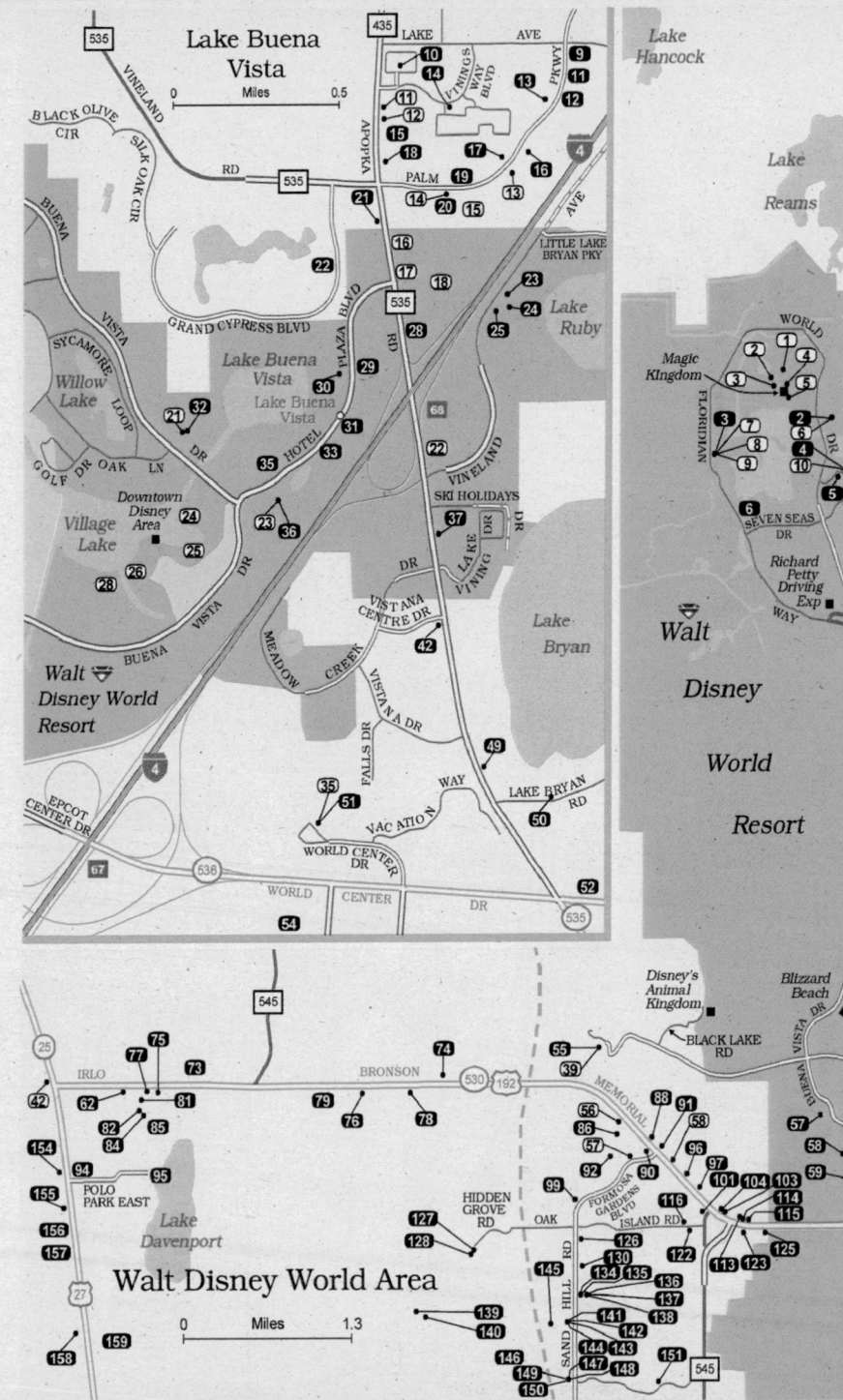

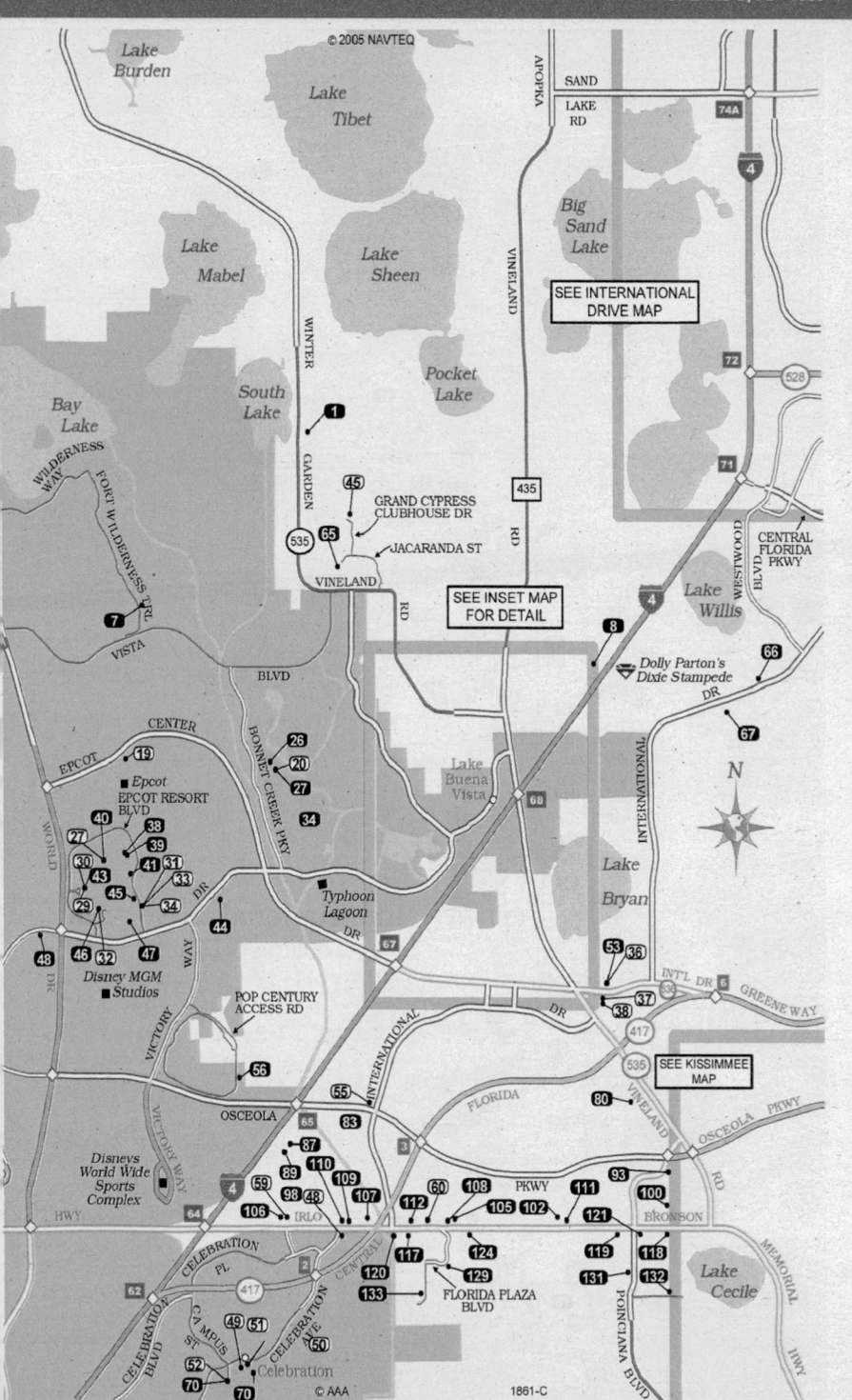

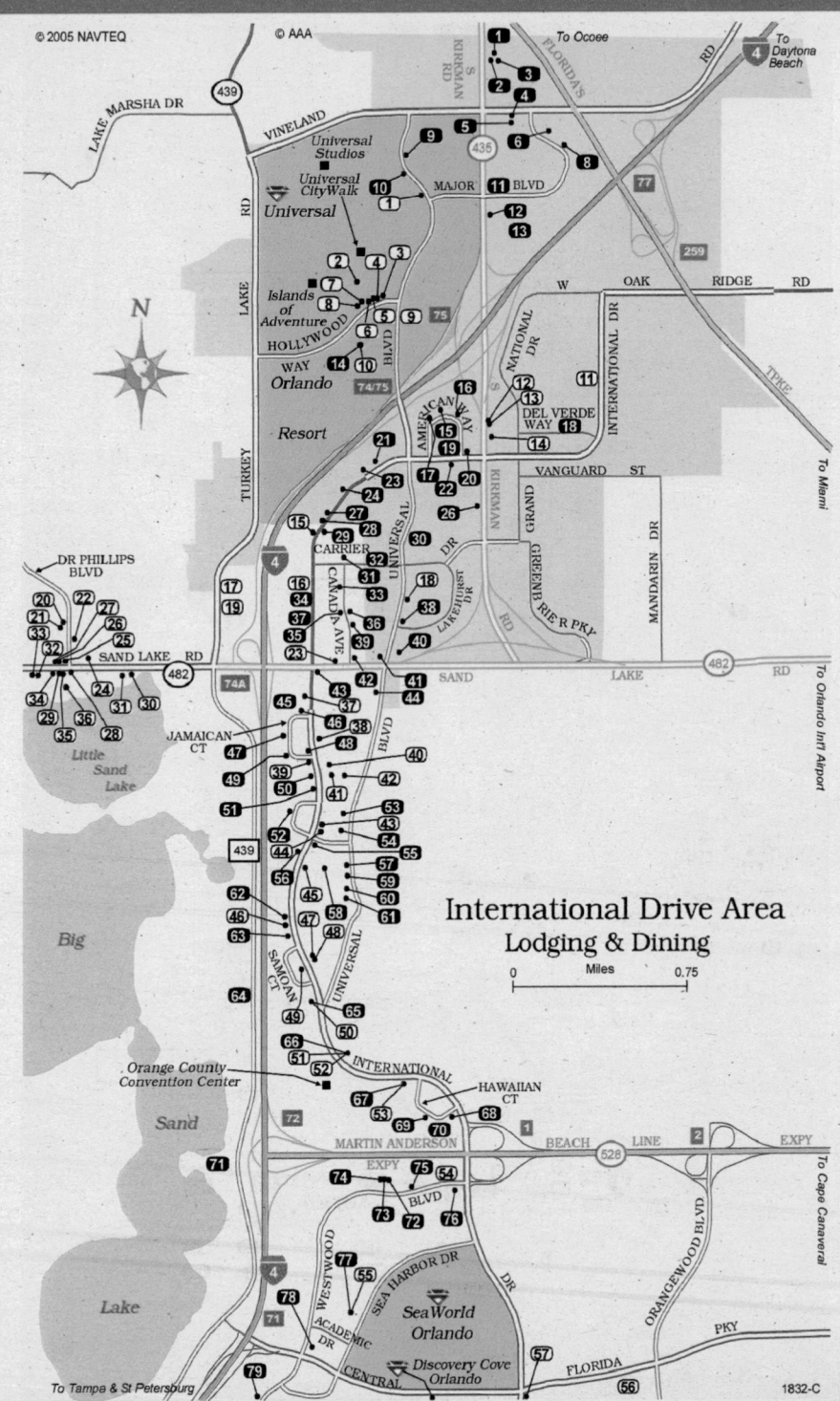

© 2005 NAVTEQ

© AAA

International Drive Area
Lodging & Dining

0   Miles   0.75

1832-C

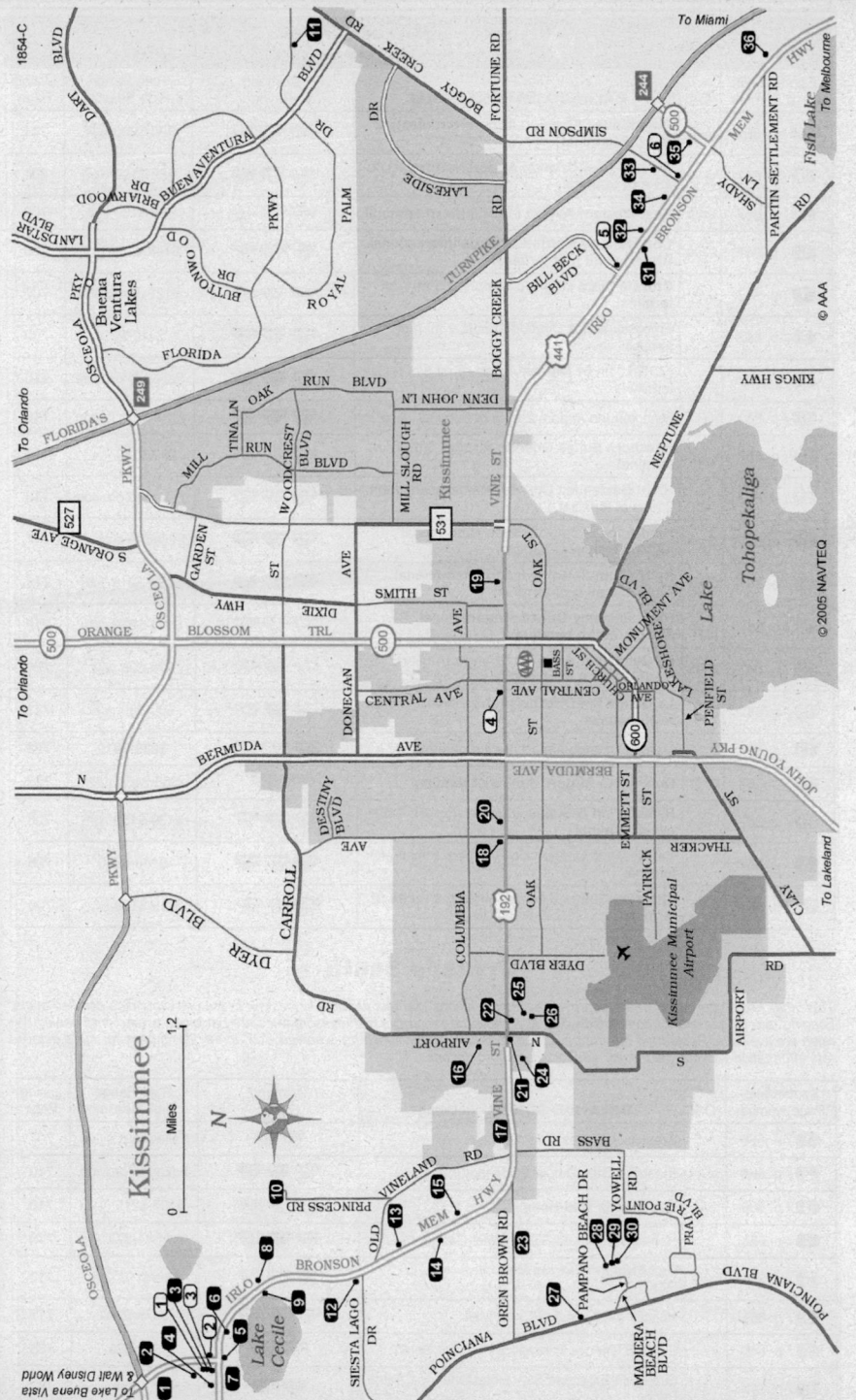

✈ Airport Accommodations

Spotter/Map Page Number	OA	ORLANDO INTERNATIONAL	Diamond Rating	Rate Range High Season	Listing Page
14 / p. 667	AAA	AmeriSuites (Orlando Airport/Northeast), 2 mi n of terminal	◇◇◇	$90-$200 SAVE	701
5 / p. 667	AAA	AmeriSuites (Orlando Airport/Northwest), 2 mi n of terminal	◇◇◇	$89-$199 SAVE	701
23 / p. 667	AAA	Best Western Airport Inn, 4.5 nw of terminal	◇◇◇	$89-$109 SAVE	702
12 / p. 667	AAA	Courtyard by Marriott Orlando International Airport, 2 mi n of terminal	◇◇◇	$149-$189 SAVE	706
1 / p. 667	AAA	Crowne Plaza Orlando Airport, 2.5 mi n of terminal	◇◇◇	$129-$144 SAVE	707
7 / p. 667		Embassy Suites Orlando Airport, 2 mi n of terminal	◇◇◇	$110-$219	709
3 / p. 667		Fairfield Inn by Marriott-Airport, 2 mi n of terminal	◇◇◇	Failed to provide	710
6 / p. 667		Hampton Inn Airport, 2 mi n of terminal	◇◇◇	Failed to provide	710
13 / p. 667	AAA	Hawthorn Suites Orlando Airport, 2 mi n of terminal	◇◇◇	$99-$149 SAVE	714
11 / p. 667		Hilton Garden Inn Orlando International Airport, 2 mi n of terminal	◇◇◇	Failed to provide	716
17 / p. 667		Holiday Inn Express Orlando International Airport, 2 mi nw of terminal	◇◇◇	Failed to provide	717
9 / p. 667	AAA	Holiday Inn Select Orlando International Airport, 2 mi n of terminal	◇◇◇	$169-$219 SAVE	718
24 / p. 667	AAA	Hyatt Regency Orlando International Airport, at the terminal	◇◇◇	$145-$239 SAVE	719
10 / p. 667	AAA	La Quinta Inn & Suites Orlando (Airport North), 2 mi n of terminal	◇◇◇	$79-$95 SAVE	721
18 / p. 667	AAA	La Quinta Inn Orlando (Airport West), 3.5 mi w of terminal	◇◇◇	$69-$89 SAVE	721
15 / p. 667		Marriott Orlando Airport, 2 mi n of terminal	◇◇◇	$289-$319	722
20 / p. 667	AAA	Quality Inn Airport, 3 mi w of terminal	◇◇	$65-$180 SAVE	723
21 / p. 667	AAA	Ramada Inn & Suites Orlando Airport, 4 mi nw of terminal	◇◇◇	$139-$159 SAVE	726
4 / p. 667		Renaissance Orlando Hotel-Airport, 2 mi n of terminal	◇◇◇	$159-$250	728
16 / p. 667	AAA	Sheraton Suites Orlando Airport, 2 mi ne of terminal	◇◇◇	$119-$179 SAVE	730

Orlando South

This index helps you "spot" where approved accommodations and restaurants are located on the corresponding detailed maps. Lodging rate ranges are for comparison only and show the property's high season; rates are per night, unless only weekly (W) rates are available. Restaurant rate range is for dinner, unless only lunch (L) is served. Turn to the listing page for more detailed rate information and consult display ads for special promotions.

Spotter/Map Page Number	OA	ORLANDO SOUTH - Lodgings	Diamond Rating	Rate Range High Season	Listing Page
1 / p. 666		Crestwood Suites Orlando	◇◇	Failed to provide	707
2 / p. 666		Extended Stay Deluxe (Orlando/Southpark)	◇◇◇	Failed to provide	710
3 / p. 666	AAA	The Florida Mall Hotel	◇◇◇	$107-$219 SAVE	710
4 / p. 666		Homestead Studio Suites Hotel-Orlando/South	◇◇◇	$44-$74	718
5 / p. 666	AAA	Hampton Inn-Florida Mall - see color ad p 693	◇◇◇	$89-$119 SAVE	712
6 / p. 666		Holiday Inn Express Florida Mall	◇◇	$175-$200	717
7 / p. 666		Super 8 Orlando International Airport South	◇◇	$59-$89	733
8 / p. 666		Suburban Extended Stay Hotel-Orlando Central Park	◇◇	Failed to provide	733

Spotter/Map Page Number	OA	ORLANDO SOUTH - Lodgings (continued)	Diamond Rating	Rate Range High Season	Listing Page
9 / p. 666	ⒶⒶⒶ	**Baymont Inn & Suites Orlando South**	◈◈◈	$85-$105 [SAVE]	701
10 / p. 666	ⒶⒶⒶ	**Holiday Homes of Orlando** - see color ad p 716	◈◈◈	$99-$269 [SAVE]	716
11 / p. 666		JW Marriott Orlando, Grande Lakes	◈◈◈◈	$459-$949	719
12 / p. 666	ⒶⒶⒶ	**The Ritz-Carlton Orlando, Grande Lakes**	◈◈◈◈◈	$499-$999 [SAVE]	729
13 / p. 666	ⒶⒶⒶ	**Parc Corniche Condominium Suite Hotel**	◈◈◈	$89-$199 [SAVE]	723
14 / p. 666		Sand Point-American Vacation Homes - see color ad p 756	◈◈◈	$89-$289	730
15 / p. 666		Summerfield Villas-American Vacation Homes - see color ad p 756	◈◈◈	$89-$289	733
16 / p. 666		Keystone-American Vacation Homes - see color ad p 756	◈◈◈	$89-$289	720
		ORLANDO SOUTH - Restaurants			
① / p. 666		Smokey Bones Barbeque & Grill	◈◈	$5-$21	741
② / p. 666		Jockamo's New Orleans Kitchen	◈	$4-$12	738
③ / p. 666		Panera Bread	◈	$3-$8	740
④ / p. 666		California Pizza Kitchen	◈◈	$5-$17	737
⑤ / p. 666		Boston Lobster Feast	◈	$12-$30	736
⑥ / p. 666		Primo	◈◈◈◈	$21-$35	740
⑦ / p. 666		Norman's	◈◈◈◈	$26-$38	739
⑧ / p. 666		La Piaza Italian Restaurant	◈◈	$7-$17	739
		KISSIMMEE - Lodgings			
19 / p. 666		Jade East Town Homes-Alexander Holiday Homes - see color ad p 769	◈◈◈	$65-$115	773
20 / p. 666		Wonderland Inn	◈◈◈	$79-$159	788
		ST. CLOUD - Lodgings			
23 / p. 666	ⒶⒶⒶ	**Budget Inn of St Cloud**	◈◈	$35-$90 [SAVE]	831
		ST. CLOUD - Restaurant			
⑪ / p. 666		Fat Boy's Bar-B-Que	◈	$3-$12	832
		DAVENPORT - Lodgings			
26 / p. 666		Regal Palms Resort at Highlands Reserve	◈◈◈	$149-$239	752
27 / p. 666	ⒶⒶⒶ	**Regal Palms Resort at Highlands Reserve -** see color ad p 727	◈◈◈	$119-$199 [SAVE]	751
28 / p. 666		The Sanctuary-American Vacation Homes - see color ad p 756	◈◈◈	$89-$289	752
29 / p. 666	ⒶⒶⒶ	**Omni Orlando Resort at ChampionsGate**	◈◈◈◈	$189-$269 [SAVE]	751
		DAVENPORT - Restaurants			
⑭ / p. 666		Mia Pizza Pasta Kitchen	◈	$3-$16	753
⑮ / p. 666		Pepperon' Pizzeria & Restaurant	◈◈	$7-$25	753
⑯ / p. 666		Zen	◈◈◈	$8-$37	753
⑰ / p. 666		La Crepe Restaurant	◈◈	$8-$16	753

Orlando International Airport

This index helps you "spot" where approved accommodations and restaurants are located on the corresponding detailed maps. Lodging rate ranges are for comparison only and show the property's high season; rates are per night, unless only weekly (W) rates are available. Restaurant rate range is for dinner, unless only lunch (L) is served. Turn to the listing page for more detailed rate information and consult display ads for special promotions.

Spotter/Map Page Number	OA	ORLANDO SOUTH - Lodgings	Diamond Rating	Rate Range High Season	Listing Page
1 / p. 667	AAA	Crowne Plaza Orlando Airport	▽▽▽	$129-$144 SAVE	707
2 / p. 667		Wingate Inn @ Orlando International Airport	▽▽▽	$99-$165	735
3 / p. 667		Fairfield Inn by Marriott-Airport	▽▽	Failed to provide	710
4 / p. 667		Renaissance Orlando Hotel-Airport - see color ad p 728	▽▽	$159-$250	728
5 / p. 667	AAA	AmeriSuites (Orlando Airport/Northwest)	▽▽▽	$89-$199 SAVE	701
6 / p. 667		Hampton Inn Airport	▽▽▽	Failed to provide	710
7 / p. 667		Embassy Suites Orlando Airport	▽▽▽	$110-$219	709
8 / p. 667		Country Inn & Suites by Carlson-Orlando International Airport	▽▽▽	$100-$149	706
9 / p. 667	AAA	Holiday Inn Select Orlando International Airport	▽▽▽	$169-$219 SAVE	718
10 / p. 667	AAA	La Quinta Inn & Suites Orlando (Airport North) - see color ad p 721	▽▽▽	$79-$95 SAVE	721
11 / p. 667		Hilton Garden Inn Orlando International Airport	▽▽▽	Failed to provide	716
12 / p. 667	AAA	Courtyard by Marriott Orlando International Airport	▽▽▽	$149-$189 SAVE	706
13 / p. 667	AAA	Hawthorn Suites Orlando Airport - see color ad p 714	▽▽▽	$99-$149 SAVE	714
14 / p. 667	AAA	AmeriSuites (Orlando Airport/Northeast)	▽▽▽	$90-$200 SAVE	701
15 / p. 667		Marriott Orlando Airport - see color ad p 722	▽▽▽	$289-$319	722
16 / p. 667	AAA	Sheraton Suites Orlando Airport	▽▽▽	$119-$179 SAVE	730
17 / p. 667		Holiday Inn Express Orlando International Airport	▽▽▽	Failed to provide	717
18 / p. 667	AAA	La Quinta Inn Orlando (Airport West) - see color ad p 721	▽▽▽	$69-$89 SAVE	721
19 / p. 667	AAA	Clarion Hotel & Conference Center-Orlando International Airport	▽▽▽	$89-$149 SAVE	702
20 / p. 667	AAA	Quality Inn Airport	▽▽	$65-$180 SAVE	723
21 / p. 667	AAA	Ramada Inn & Suites Orlando Airport - see color ad p 726	▽▽▽	$139-$159 SAVE	726
22 / p. 667	AAA	Sleep Inn & Suites Orlando International Airport	▽▽	$70-$150 SAVE	731
23 / p. 667	AAA	Best Western Airport Inn	▽▽▽	$89-$109 SAVE	702
24 / p. 667	AAA	Hyatt Regency Orlando International Airport - see color ad p 811	▽▽▽	$145-$239 SAVE	719
		ORLANDO SOUTH - Restaurants			
1 / p. 667		Murphy's Chop House	▽▽▽	$16-$29	739
2 / p. 667		Bauern Stube Authentic German Restaurant	▽▽	$6-$18	736
3 / p. 667		Hemisphere	▽▽▽	$18-$31	738

Walt Disney World

This index helps you "spot" where approved accommodations and restaurants are located on the corresponding detailed maps. Lodging rate ranges are for comparison only and show the property's high season; rates are per night, unless only weekly (W) rates are available. Restaurant rate range is for dinner, unless only lunch (L) is served. Turn to the listing page for more detailed rate information and consult display ads for special promotions.

Spotter/Map Page Number	OA	LAKE BUENA VISTA - Lodgings	Diamond Rating	Rate Range High Season	Listing Page
❶ / p. 668		PerriHouse Bed & Breakfast Inn	◈◈◈		812
❷ / p. 668	AAA	Disney's Contemporary Resort - see color ad starting on p 795	◈◈◈	$244-$695	801
❸ / p. 668	AAA	Disney's Grand Floridian Resort & Spa - see color ad starting on p 795	◈◈◈◈	$349-$870	802
❹ / p. 668	AAA	The Villas at Disney's Wilderness Lodge - see color ad starting on p 795	◈◈◈	$284-$1015	814
❺ / p. 668	AAA	Disney's Wilderness Lodge - see color ad starting on p 795	◈◈◈	$199-$505	803
❻ / p. 668	AAA	Disney's Polynesian Resort - see color ad starting on p 795	◈◈◈	$304-$720	802
❼ / p. 668	AAA	Disney's Fort Wilderness Resort Campground - see color ad starting on p 795		$234-$339	801
❽ / p. 668		Embassy Suites Hotel-Lake Buena Vista Resort - see color ad p 805	◈◈◈	$109-$229	804
❾ / p. 668		Extended Stay Deluxe	◈◈◈	$95-$149	805
❿ / p. 668	AAA	Staybridge Suites/Lake Buena Vista - see color ad p 814	◈◈◈	$129-$269 SAVE	814
⓫ / p. 668	AAA	Hampton Inn Lake Buena Vista - see color ad p 693	◈◈◈	$59-$169 SAVE	806
⓬ / p. 668	AAA	Homewood Suites Hotel By Hilton-Lake Buena Vista - see color ad p 693	◈◈◈	$99-$169 SAVE	809
⓭ / p. 668	AAA	Hawthorn Suites Hotel Lake Buena Vista - see color ad p 693	◈◈◈	$139-$179 SAVE	806
⓮ / p. 668	AAA	Westgate Blue Tree at Lake Buena Vista - see color ad p 734	◈◈◈	$89-$189 SAVE	815
⓯ / p. 668	AAA	Country Inn & Suites By Carlson - see color ad p 793, p 793, p 692	◈◈◈	$80-$98 SAVE	793
⓰ / p. 668	AAA	Comfort Inn Lake Buena Vista	◈◈	$59-$89 SAVE	791
⓱ / p. 668	AAA	Celebrity Resorts Lake Buena Vista	◈◈◈	$137-$245 SAVE	791
⓲ / p. 668	AAA	Sheraton Safari Hotel - see color ad p 813	◈◈◈	$139-$249 SAVE	812
⓳ / p. 668	AAA	Courtyard by Marriott Lake Buena Vista @ Vista Centre - see color ad p 794	◈◈◈	$119-$139 SAVE	794
⓴ / p. 668		Radisson Inn Lake Buena Vista	◈◈◈	$79-$159	812
㉑ / p. 668	AAA	Doubletree Club Hotel Lake Buena Vista - see color ad p 804	◈◈◈	$89-$149 SAVE	804
㉒ / p. 668	AAA	Hyatt Regency Grand Cypress - see color ad p 811	◈◈◈◈	$255-$385 SAVE	810
㉓ / p. 668	AAA	Fairfield Inn at Marriott Village - see color ad p 805	◈◈◈	$65-$116 SAVE	805
㉔ / p. 668	AAA	Courtyard by Marriott at Marriott Village	◈◈◈	$79-$129 SAVE	794
㉕ / p. 668	AAA	SpringHill Suites at The Marriott Village - see color ad p 813	◈◈◈	$79-$129 SAVE	814
㉖ / p. 668	AAA	Disney's Port Orleans-French Quarter Resort	◈◈◈	$134-$209	803
㉗ / p. 668	AAA	Disney's Port Orleans-Riverside Resort - see color ad starting on p 795	◈◈◈	$134-$209	803
㉘ / p. 668	AAA	Days Inn Lake Buena Vista Hotel	◈◈	$69-$129 SAVE	794
㉙ / p. 668		DoubleTree Guest Suites in the Walt Disney World Resort	◈◈◈	$159-$299	804

Spotter/Map Page Number	OA	**LAKE BUENA VISTA** - Lodgings (continued)	Diamond Rating	Rate Range High Season	Listing Page
30 / p. 668	AAA	Best Western Lake Buena Vista Resort Hotel in the Walt Disney World Resorts - see color ad p 780	◇◇◇	$79-$199 SAVE	791
31 / p. 668	AAA	Hotel Royal Plaza in the Disney World Resort - see color ad p 809	◇◇◇	$85-$215 SAVE	809
32 / p. 668	AAA	Wyndham Palace Resort & Spa in the WALT DISNEY WORLD (R) Resort	◇◇◇	$169-$219 SAVE	815
33 / p. 668	AAA	Holiday Inn-in the Walt Disney World Resort - see color ad p 807	fyi	$139-$179 SAVE	807
34 / p. 668	AAA	Disney's Old Key West Resort - see color ad starting on p 795	◇◇◇	$259-$805	802
35 / p. 668	AAA	Grosvenor Resort at Walt Disney World Resort - see color ad p 806	◇◇◇	$89-$145 SAVE	806
36 / p. 668	AAA	Hilton in the Walt Disney World Resort	◇◇◇◇	$99-$299 SAVE	807
37 / p. 668	AAA	Holiday Inn-SunSpree Resort-Lake Buena Vista - see color ad p 808	◇◇◇	$89-$129 SAVE	808
38 / p. 668	AAA	Disney's Beach Club Resort - see color ad starting on p 795	◇◇◇◇	$294-$675	800
39 / p. 668	AAA	Disney's Beach Club Villas - see color ad starting on p 795	◇◇◇◇	$294-$1040	800
40 / p. 668	AAA	Disney's Yacht Club Resort - see color ad starting on p 795	◇◇◇◇	$294-$680	803
41 / p. 668	AAA	Disney's Saratoga Springs Resort & Spa - see color ad starting on p 795	◇◇◇	$259-$805	803
42 / p. 668		Sheraton's Vistana Resort - see color ad p 8, p 688	◇◇◇	$259	813
43 / p. 668	AAA	Walt Disney World Dolphin - see color ad p 8	◇◇◇◇	$339-$499 SAVE	815
44 / p. 668	AAA	Disney's Caribbean Beach Resort - see color ad starting on p 795	◇◇◇	$134-$209	801
45 / p. 668	AAA	Disney's BoardWalk Villas - see color ad starting on p 795	◇◇◇◇	$294-$1040	801
46 / p. 668	AAA	Walt Disney World Swan - see color ad p 8	◇◇◇◇	$339-$499 SAVE	815
47 / p. 668	AAA	Disney's BoardWalk Resort - see color ad starting on p 795	◇◇◇◇	$294-$690	800
48 / p. 668	AAA	Disney's Coronado Springs Resort - see color ad starting on p 795	◇◇◇	$134-$209	801
49 / p. 668	AAA	Bryan's Spanish Cove	◇◇◇	$159-$219 SAVE	791
50 / p. 668		Embassy Vacation Resort Grand Beach	◇◇◇	$225-$285	804
51 / p. 668	AAA	Orlando World Center Marriott Resort & Convention Center - see color ad p 812	◇◇◇	$219-$329 SAVE	812
52 / p. 668	AAA	Buena Vista Suites - see color ad p 792	◇◇◇	$119-$159 SAVE	791
53 / p. 668	AAA	Caribe Royale All-Suites Resort and Convention Center - see color ad p 792	◇◇◇	$159-$249 SAVE	791
54 / p. 668	AAA	Nickelodeon Family Suites by Holiday Inn - see color ad p 810	◇◇◇	$160-$275 SAVE	810
55 / p. 668	AAA	Disney's Animal Kingdom Lodge - see color ad starting on p 795	◇◇◇	$199-$620	800
56 / p. 668	AAA	Disney's Pop Century Resort - see color ad starting on p 795	◇◇	$77-$131	802
57 / p. 668	AAA	Disney's All-Star Sports - see color ad starting on p 795	◇◇	$77-$131	800
58 / p. 668	AAA	Disney's All-Star Music - see color ad starting on p 795	◇◇	$77-$131	799
59 / p. 668	AAA	Disney's All-Star Movies Resort - see color ad starting on p 795	◇◇	$77-$131	794
		LAKE BUENA VISTA - Restaurants			
1 / p. 668		Cinderella's Royal Table	◇◇	$19-$26	816
2 / p. 668		Liberty Tree Tavern	◇◇	$11-$23	817

Spotter/Map Page Number	OA	LAKE BUENA VISTA - Restaurants (continued)	Diamond Rating	Rate Range High Season	Listing Page
③ / p. 668		The Crystal Palace	◆	$10-$27	816
④ / p. 668		The Plaza Restaurant	◆	$5-$10	818
⑤ / p. 668		Tony's Town Square Restaurant	◆◆	$17-$22	819
⑥ / p. 668		California Grill	◆◆◆	$20-$35	816
⑦ / p. 668		Narcoosee's	◆◆	$25-$39	818
⑧ / p. 668		Victoria & Albert's	◆◆◆◆◆	$85-$100	819
⑨ / p. 668		Citricos	◆◆◆	$19-$32	816
⑩ / p. 668		Artist Point	◆◆◆	$24-$34	815
⑪ / p. 668		Giordano's Italian Restaurant & Pizzeria	◆◆	$6-$20	817
⑫ / p. 668		New York China Buffet	◆	$5-$12	818
⑬ / p. 668		Crab House Seafood Restaurant	◆◆	$14-$25	816
⑭ / p. 668		Havana's Cafe	◆◆	$5-$18	817
⑮ / p. 668		India Palace	◆◆	$11-$16	817
⑯ / p. 668		Black Angus Steakhouse	◆◆	$6-$30	816
⑰ / p. 668		dakshin	◆◆◆	$12-$20	816
⑱ / p. 668		Pebbles/Island Grill	◆◆	$8-$28	818
⑲ / p. 668		Restaurant Marrakesh	◆◆	$16-$25	818
⑳ / p. 668		Boatwright's Dining Hall	◆◆	$12-$24	816
㉑ / p. 668		Arthur's 27	◆◆◆	$31-$39	815
㉒ / p. 668		Bahama Breeze	◆◆◆	$6-$24	816
㉓ / p. 668		Finn's Grill	◆◆	$19-$26	817
㉔ / p. 668		Rain Forest Cafe	◆◆	$10-$23	818
㉕ / p. 668		Fulton's Crab House	◆◆	$16-$47	817
㉖ / p. 668		Portobello Yacht Club	◆◆	$15-$32	818
㉗ / p. 668		Yachtsman's Steak House	◆◆◆	$23-$51	819
㉘ / p. 668		Bongos Cuban Cafe	◆◆	$12-$26	816
㉙ / p. 668		Todd English's Bluezoo	◆◆◆◆	$18-$54	819
㉚ / p. 668		Shula's Steak House	◆◆◆	$22-$68	818
㉛ / p. 668		ESPN Club	◆◆	$8-$16	817
㉜ / p. 668		Palio	◆◆◆	$17-$32	818
㉝ / p. 668		Spoodles	◆◆	$14-$26	818
㉞ / p. 668		Flying Fish Cafe	◆◆◆	$18-$36	817
㉟ / p. 668		Hawk's Landing Steakhouse & Grille	◆◆◆	$14-$40	817
㊱ / p. 668	◬	**The Venetian Room**	◆◆◆◆	$29-$36	819
㊲ / p. 668		Asian Harbor	◆◆◆	$15-$30	816
㊳ / p. 668		Gourmeto's NY Pizza	◆	$3-$13	817
㊴ / p. 668		Jiko	◆◆◆	$18-$30	817
		CLERMONT - Lodgings			
㊷ / p. 668	◬	**Highlands Reserve-Best Western IPG Florida Vacation Homes**	◆◆◆	$175-$375 [SAVE]	750

Spotter/Map Page Number	OA	CLERMONT - Restaurant	Diamond Rating	Rate Range High Season	Listing Page
42 / p. 668		Santiago's Mexican Restaurant	◆◆	$7-$17	750
		ORLANDO SOUTH - Lodgings			
65 / p. 668	AAA	**The Villas of Grand Cypress**	◆◆◆◆	$400-$2000 SAVE	734
66 / p. 668	AAA	**Crowne Plaza Resort Orlando** - see color ad p 707	◆◆◆	$140-$229 SAVE	707
67 / p. 668		Sheraton Vistana Villages - see color ad p 8, p 688	◆◆◆	$304	730
		ORLANDO SOUTH - Restaurant			
45 / p. 668		The Black Swan	◆◆◆◆	$25-$40	736
		CELEBRATION - Lodgings			
70 / p. 668	AAA	**Celebration Hotel**	◆◆◆◆	$269-$459 SAVE	749
		CELEBRATION - Restaurants			
48 / p. 668		Joe's Crab Shack	◆◆	$4-$18	749
49 / p. 668		Cafe D'Antonio	◆◆◆	$12-$34	749
50 / p. 668		Market Street Cafe	◆◆	$6-$15	749
51 / p. 668		Columbia Restaurant	◆◆◆	$14-$23	749
52 / p. 668		Plantation Room	◆◆◆◆	$18-$32	749
		KISSIMMEE - Lodgings			
73 / p. 668	AAA	**Liki Tiki Village-A Club Navigo Resort** - see color ad p 771	◆◆◆	$99-$399 SAVE	775
74 / p. 668		Orange Lake Resort & Country Club	◆◆◆	Failed to provide	777
75 / p. 668	AAA	**Westgate Inn**	◆◆	$39-$65 SAVE	787
76 / p. 668	AAA	**Howard Johnson Maingate Resort West** - see color ad p 769	◆◆	$69-$129 SAVE	769
77 / p. 668	AAA	**Comfort Inn-Maingate West** - see color ad p 759	◆◆	$39-$149 SAVE	759
78 / p. 668	AAA	**Sleep Inn Maingate**	◆◆	$59-$89 SAVE	783
79 / p. 668	AAA	**ResortQuest Orlando Vacation Homes**	◆◆◆	$128-$415 SAVE	782
80 / p. 668	AAA	**La Quinta Inn & Suites Kissimmee (Orlando Maingate)** - see color ad p 775	◆◆◆	$99-$179 SAVE	774
81 / p. 668		Oak Island-Alexander Holiday Houses - see color ad p 769	◆◆◆	$135-$195	777
82 / p. 668		Rolling Hills-Alexander Holiday Homes - see color ad p 769	◆◆◆	$100-$245	782
83 / p. 668	AAA	**Gaylord Palms Resort** - see color ad p 765	◆◆◆◆	$199-$439 SAVE	764
84 / p. 668		Rolling Hills-Regent Vacations & Management	◆◆◆	$99-$300	783
85 / p. 668		Sunset Lakes-Alexander Holiday Homes - see color ad p 769	◆◆◆	$100-$245	784
86 / p. 668	AAA	**Comfort Suites MainGate Resort** - see color ad p 760	◆◆◆	$59-$150 SAVE	760
87 / p. 668	AAA	**Hampton Inn-Maingate East**	◆◆◆	$89-$119 SAVE	764
88 / p. 668	AAA	**Quality Inn Main Gate West**	◆◆	$39-$169 SAVE	778
89 / p. 668		The Palms Hotel and Villas	◆◆◆	$94-$140	777
90 / p. 668		Rolling Hills-Orlando's Key Vacation Homes	◆◆◆	$150-$192	782
91 / p. 668	AAA	**Best Western Lakeside** - see color ad p 757	◆◆◆	$59-$129 SAVE	757
92 / p. 668	AAA	**Acadia Estates-All Star Vacation Homes** - see color ad p 755	◆◆◆	$2093-$3300(W) SAVE	754
93 / p. 668	AAA	**Country Inn & Suites at Calypso Cay** - see color ad p 760	◆◆◆	$99-$179 SAVE	760

Spotter/Map Page Number	OA	KISSIMMEE - Lodgings (continued)	Diamond Rating	Rate Range High Season	Listing Page
94 / p. 668	AAA	Hampton Lakes-The Florida Store	◆◆◆	$90-$270 SAVE	766
95 / p. 668		Lindfields-Alexander Holiday Homes - see color ad p 769	◆◆◆	$100-$215	775
96 / p. 668	AAA	Clarion Hotel Maingate - see color ad p 758	◆◆◆	$69-$119 SAVE	758
97 / p. 668	AAA	Holiday Inn Maingate West	◆◆◆	$59-$129 SAVE	766
98 / p. 668	AAA	Parkway International Resort - see color ad p 771	◆◆◆	$149-$219 SAVE	777
99 / p. 668		Ventura Resort Rentals-Kissimmee	◆◆◆	$83-$196	786
100 / p. 668	AAA	Fantasy World Club Villas	◆◆◆	$99-$195 SAVE	763
101 / p. 668	AAA	Westgate Towers - see color ad p 734	◆◆◆	$79-$259 SAVE	787
102 / p. 668	AAA	Travelodge Suites Kissimmee East Gate Orange - see color ad p 787	◆◆	$39-$200 SAVE	786
103 / p. 668	AAA	Radisson Resort WorldGate	◆◆◆	$109-$159 SAVE	779
104 / p. 668	AAA	Hampton Inn Main Gate West - see color ad p 693	◆◆◆	$79-$109 SAVE	764
105 / p. 668	AAA	Travelodge Hotel Maingate East - see color ad p 780	◆◆	$49-$129 SAVE	785
106 / p. 668	AAA	Radisson Resort Parkway - see color ad p 779	◆◆◆	$79-$129 SAVE	779
107 / p. 668		Rodeway Inn Maingate - see color ad p 782	◆◆	$35-$90	782
108 / p. 668		Motel 6 - #0464	◆	$33-$49	776
109 / p. 668	AAA	Howard Johnson Maingate East	◆◆	$47-$100 SAVE	768
110 / p. 668		County Hearth Inn & Suites	◆◆	$49-$79	760
111 / p. 668	AAA	Masters Inn-Kissimmee	◆◆	$49-$59 SAVE	776
112 / p. 668	AAA	Super 8 Motel Maingate	◆◆	$35-$89 SAVE	785
113 / p. 668	AAA	AmeriHost Resort	◆◆◆	$99 SAVE	755
114 / p. 668	AAA	Knights Inn-Maingate - see color ad p 773	◆	$35-$89 SAVE	773
115 / p. 668		Motel 6 - #0436	◆	$33-$49	776
116 / p. 668	AAA	Orbit One Vacation Villas - see color ad p 771	◆◆◆	$89-$179 SAVE	777
117 / p. 668	AAA	Days Inn Maingate East - see color ad p 762	◆◆	$59-$129 SAVE	762
118 / p. 668	AAA	Sun Inn & Suites	◆◆	$40-$95 SAVE	784
119 / p. 668	AAA	Baymont Inn Orlando-Kissimmee	◆◆◆	$79-$99 SAVE	757
120 / p. 668	AAA	Quality Suites Maingate East - see color ad p 799	◆◆◆	$99-$299 SAVE	779
121 / p. 668	AAA	Ramada Inn Resort Eastgate - see color ad p 780	◆◆	$49-$129 SAVE	781
122 / p. 668	AAA	Masters Inn-Main Gate	◆◆	$39-$150 SAVE	776
123 / p. 668	AAA	Ramada Plaza Hotel and Inn Gateway - see color ad p 781	◆◆◆	$69-$119 SAVE	781
124 / p. 668	AAA	Seralago Hotel & Suites Main Gate East	◆◆◆	$69-$99 SAVE	783
125 / p. 668	AAA	Holiday Inn-Nikki Bird Resort-Maingate	◆◆◆	$119-$149 SAVE	766
126 / p. 668	AAA	Formosa Gardens Estates - All Star Vacation Homes - see color ad p 755	◆◆◆	$1700-$3500(W) SAVE	764
127 / p. 668		Emerald Island-Orlando's Key Vacation Homes	◆◆◆	$110-$190	762
128 / p. 668	AAA	Emerald Island Resort-Holiday Resort Management	◆◆◆	$115-$240 SAVE	763
129 / p. 668	AAA	Comfort Suites Maingate East - see color ad p 759	◆◆◆	$69-$175 SAVE	759

Spotter/Map Page Number	OA	KISSIMMEE - Lodgings (continued)	Diamond Rating	Rate Range High Season	Listing Page
130 / p. 668		Formosa Garden Estates - The Kissimmee Rental Company	◇◇◇	$80-$450	763
131 / p. 668	AAA	**Celebrity Resorts**	◇◇◇	$113-$245 SAVE	758
132 / p. 668	AAA	**Star Island Resort & Club** - see color ad p 784	◇◇◇	$179-$295 SAVE	784
133 / p. 668		Tropical Palms Resort	◇◇	$61-$149	786
134 / p. 668	AAA	**Indian Creek-Orlando's Key Vacation Homes**	◇◇◇	$95-$270 SAVE	770
135 / p. 668		Indian Creek-The Florida Store	◇◇◇	Failed to provide	770
136 / p. 668		Regency Vacations & Management	◇◇◇	$75-$299	782
137 / p. 668		Indian Creek-Premier Vacation Homes	◇◇◇	$129-$279	770
138 / p. 668		Indian Creek-Alexander Holiday Homes - see color ad p 769	◇◇◇	$100-$215	770
139 / p. 668		Emerald Island - The Kissimmee Rental Company	◇◇◇	$80-$450	763
140 / p. 668		Emerald Island - Loyalty Homes	◇◇◇	$89-$390	762
141 / p. 668		Indian Ridge-Alexander Holiday Homes - see color ad p 769	◇◇◇	$100-$215	770
142 / p. 668		Indian Ridge Oaks-Premier Vacation Homes	◇◇◇	$129-$279	772
143 / p. 668	AAA	**Indian Ridge-Loyalty Homes** - see color ad p 771	◇◇◇	$89-$395 SAVE	771
144 / p. 668		Indian Ridge Oaks-Loyalty Homes	◇◇◇	$89-$390	772
145 / p. 668		Indian Creek-American Vacation Homes	◇◇◇	$89-$289	770
146 / p. 668		Indian Creek - The Kissimmee Rental Company	◇◇◇	$80-$450	770
147 / p. 668		Windsor Palms - Orlando's Key Vacation Homes	◇◇◇	$120-$145	787
148 / p. 668		Windsor Palms-Premier Vacation Homes	◇◇◇	$129-$279	788
149 / p. 668		Windsor Palms-Regent Vacations & Management	◇◇◇	$99-$300	788
150 / p. 668		Windsor Palms - The Kissimmee Rental Company	◇◇◇	$80-$450	788
151 / p. 668	AAA	**Wyndham Palms Resort & Country Club** - see color ad p 788	◇◇◇	$162-$207 SAVE	789
		KISSIMMEE - Restaurants			
55 / p. 668	AAA	**Sunset Sam's Restaurant**	◇◇	$19-$29	790
56 / p. 668		Giordano's	◇◇	$7-$18	789
57 / p. 668		Taste of China	◇◇	$7-$21	790
58 / p. 668		Key W. Kool's Open Pit Grill	◇◇	$15-$52	789
59 / p. 668		Fioni's Italian Restaurant & Grill	◇◇	$8-$23	789
60 / p. 668		Pacino's Italian Ristorante	◇◇	$10-$28	789
		DAVENPORT - Lodgings			
154 / p. 668		Westridge-American Vacation Homes - see color ad p 756	◇◇◇	$89-$289	753
155 / p. 668		Southern Dunes-The Florida Store	◇◇◇	Failed to provide	752
156 / p. 668		Esprit-Premier Vacation Homes	◇◇◇	$129-$279	751
157 / p. 668		Calabay Parc-The Florida Store	◇◇◇	Failed to provide	751
158 / p. 668		Greater Groves-Premier Vacation Homes	◇◇◇	$129-$279	751
159 / p. 668		Vistapark Resort	◇◇◇	$189-$439	752

International Drive Area

This index helps you "spot" where approved accommodations and restaurants are located on the corresponding detailed maps. Lodging rate ranges are for comparison only and show the property's high season; rates are per night, unless only weekly (W) rates are available. Restaurant rate range is for dinner, unless only lunch (L) is served. Turn to the listing page for more detailed rate information and consult display ads for special promotions.

Spotter/Map Page Number	OA	**ORLANDO SOUTH** - Lodgings	Diamond Rating	Rate Range High Season	Listing Page
❶ / p. 670	AAA	**Quality Inn & Suites-Universal Orlando**	▽ ▽ ▽	$50-$129 SAVE	723
❷ / p. 670	AAA	**Wingate Inn/Universal Studios**	▽ ▽ ▽	$79-$149 SAVE	735
❸ / p. 670	AAA	**Hampton Inn at Universal Studios** - see color ad p 693	▽ ▽ ▽	$79-$179 SAVE	712
❹ / p. 670		Fairfield Inn & Suites at Universal Studios Orlando - see color ad p 693	▽ ▽ ▽	$79-$119	710
❺ / p. 670		Best Western Universal Inn	▽ ▽	Failed to provide	702
❻ / p. 670		Sleep Inn and Suites	▽ ▽	Failed to provide	731
❽ / p. 670		Comfort Suites	▽ ▽ ▽	$79-$199	704
❾ / p. 670	AAA	**Universal's Portofino Bay Hotel, A Loews Hotel**	▽ ▽ ▽ ▽	$309-$488 SAVE	733
❿ / p. 670	AAA	**Universal's Hard Rock Hotel, A Loews Hotel**	▽ ▽ ▽ ▽	$277-$466 SAVE	733
⓫ / p. 670		DoubleTree Hotel at the Entrance to Universal Orlando - see color ad p 709	▽ ▽ ▽	Failed to provide	709
⓬ / p. 670	AAA	**Holiday Inn & Suites At Universal Orlando** - see color ad p 717	▽ ▽ ▽	$89-$169 SAVE	717
⓭ / p. 670	AAA	**AmeriSuites (Orlando/Universal)**	▽ ▽ ▽	$139-$179 SAVE	701
⓮ / p. 670	AAA	**Universal's Royal Pacific Resort, A Loews Hotel**	▽ ▽ ▽	$245-$428 SAVE	734
⓯ / p. 670		Homewood Suites by Hilton-Nearest to Universal	▽ ▽ ▽	$109-$209	718
⓰ / p. 670		Hilton Garden Inn-International Dr North/Universal Studios	▽ ▽ ▽	$119-$199	715
⓱ / p. 670		Motel 6 Orlando-International Drive #1079	▽ ▽	$45-$61	723
⓳ / p. 670	AAA	**Sheraton Studio City Hotel**	▽ ▽ ▽	$79-$299 SAVE	730
⓴ / p. 670	AAA	**Red Horse Inn**	▽ ▽	$59-$119 SAVE	726
㉑ / p. 670	AAA	**Best Western Movieland Orlando** - see color ad p 702	▽ ▽ ▽	$65-$125 SAVE	702
㉒ / p. 670		Americas Best Value Inn & Suites	▽ ▽ ▽	$59-$99	700
㉓ / p. 670		I-Drive Inn	▽ ▽	Failed to provide	719
㉔ / p. 670		Rodeway Inn International	▽ ▽	$49-$95	729
㉖ / p. 670		Hampton Inn-South of Universal Studios - see color ad p 713	▽ ▽ ▽	Failed to provide	713
㉗ / p. 670		Holiday Inn-International Drive Resort	▽ ▽ ▽	$119-$159	717
㉘ / p. 670		Howard Johnson Inn-International Drive	▽ ▽	$89-$125	718
㉙ / p. 670		Ramada Inn International Drive Lakefront	▽ ▽ ▽	$69-$129	726
㉚ / p. 670	AAA	**Clarion Hotel Universal** - see color ad p 703	▽ ▽ ▽	$79-$129 SAVE	703
㉜ / p. 670	AAA	**Westgate Palace** - see color ad p 734	▽ ▽ ▽	$139-$209 SAVE	735

Spotter/Map Page Number	OA	**ORLANDO SOUTH** - Lodgings (continued)	Diamond Rating	Rate Range High Season	Listing Page
33 / p. 670	AAA	**Quality Suites Universal Orlando** - see color ad p 725	◇◇◇	$79-$129 [SAVE]	724
34 / p. 670	AAA	**Hampton Inn & Suites** - see color ad p 712	◇◇◇	$89-$154 [SAVE]	712
35 / p. 670	AAA	**Microtel Inn & Suites**	◇◇	$49-$69 [SAVE]	723
36 / p. 670		Fairfield Inn & Suites by Marriott-International Cove	◇◇◇	$77-$119	710
37 / p. 670		Quality Inn International	◇◇	$59-$99	724
38 / p. 670	AAA	**Country Inn & Suites International Drive**	◇◇◇	$69-$139 [SAVE]	706
39 / p. 670	AAA	**Hawthorn Suites Universal Orlando** - see color ad p 715	◇◇◇	$79-$149 [SAVE]	715
40 / p. 670		Comfort Inn Universal Studios - see color ad p 705	◇◇◇	Failed to provide	704
41 / p. 670	AAA	**Crowne Plaza Universal** - see color ad p 708	◇◇◇	$189-$269 [SAVE]	708
42 / p. 670	AAA	**Residence Inn by Marriott-Orlando International Dr**	◇◇◇	$119-$229 [SAVE]	729
43 / p. 670	AAA	**Wyndham Orlando Resort**	◇◇◇	$129-$195 [SAVE]	735
44 / p. 670	AAA	**Holiday Inn Hotel & Suites/Orlando/Orange County Convention Center** - see color ad p 693	◇◇◇	$99-$179 [SAVE]	717
45 / p. 670	AAA	**Comfort Inn International**	◇◇◇	$59-$149 [SAVE]	704
46 / p. 670	AAA	**Masters Inn International Drive**	◇◇	$49-$120 [SAVE]	723
47 / p. 670	AAA	**Inn of America**	◇◇	$89-$139 [SAVE]	719
48 / p. 670	AAA	**Embassy Suites International Drive/Jamaican Ct**	◇◇◇	$129-$229 [SAVE]	709
49 / p. 670	AAA	**La Quinta Inn Orlando (International Drive)** - see color ad p 721	◇◇◇	$110-$125 [SAVE]	722
50 / p. 670	AAA	**Radisson Barcelo Resort** - see color ad p 725	◇◇◇	$89-$129 [SAVE]	725
51 / p. 670	AAA	**Staybridge Suites-Orlando/International Drive** - see color ad p 814	◇◇◇	$129-$269 [SAVE]	732
52 / p. 670	AAA	**Courtyard by Marriott, International Drive**	◇◇◇	$109-$209 [SAVE]	706
53 / p. 670	AAA	**La Quinta Inn & Suites Orlando (Convention Center)** - see color ad p 721	◇◇◇	$89-$109 [SAVE]	721
54 / p. 670	AAA	**DoubleTree Castle Hotel** - see color ad p 708	◇◇◇	$100-$230 [SAVE]	708
55 / p. 670	AAA	**AmeriSuites (Orlando/Convention Center)**	◇◇◇	$89-$149 [SAVE]	701
56 / p. 670	AAA	**Best Western Plaza International** - see color ad p 702	◇◇◇	$65-$125 [SAVE]	702
57 / p. 670		Extended Stay Deluxe	◇◇◇	$95-$149	710
58 / p. 670	AAA	**Homewood Suites by Hilton** - see color ad p 718	◇◇◇	$139-$199 [SAVE]	718
59 / p. 670		Residence Inn by Marriott Orlando Convention Center	◇◇◇	Failed to provide	728
60 / p. 670		SpringHill Suites by Marriott-Orlando Conv Ctr/International Drive Area - see color ad p 732	◇◇◇	Failed to provide	732
61 / p. 670	AAA	**Hampton Inn-Convention Center**	◇◇◇	$79-$159 [SAVE]	712
62 / p. 670		Embassy Suites Hotel Orlando International Dr/C.C. - see color ad p 805	◇◇◇	$129-$289	709
63 / p. 670		Quality Inn Plaza	◇◇	$59-$99	724

Spotter/Map Page Number	OA	ORLANDO SOUTH - Lodgings (continued)	Diamond Rating	Rate Range High Season	Listing Page
64 / p. 670	AAA	**Comfort Suites Orlando** - see color ad p 704	▽▽▽	$109-$129 [SAVE]	706
65 / p. 670		Rosen Plaza	▽▽▽	$299	730
66 / p. 670	AAA	**The Peabody Orlando**	▽▽▽▽	$400-$1725 [SAVE]	723
67 / p. 670		Rosen Centre Hotel	▽▽▽	$99-$350	730
68 / p. 670	AAA	**Days Inn-Convention Center/North of Sea World**	▽▽	$99 [SAVE]	708
69 / p. 670		Red Roof Inn Convention Center	▽▽	$46-$100	726
70 / p. 670	AAA	**Howard Johnson Plaza Hotel & Suites/International Dr South** - see color ad p 686	▽▽▽	$69-$139 [SAVE]	719
71 / p. 670	AAA	**Westgate Lakes Resort & Spa** - see color ad p 734	▽▽▽	$79-$149 [SAVE]	735
72 / p. 670		StudioPlus-Orlando Convention Center/Sea World/Disney Area	▽▽	Failed to provide	732
73 / p. 670		Hawthorn Suites Orlando - see color ad p 713	▽▽▽	$79-$189	713
74 / p. 670		Extended StayAmerica-Orlando Convention Center/Sea World/Disney Area	▽▽	Failed to provide	709
75 / p. 670	AAA	**Sleep Inn-Convention Center**	▽▽	$75-$95 [SAVE]	731
76 / p. 670		Sheraton World Resort - see color ad p 731	▽▽▽	$239-$310	731
77 / p. 670	AAA	**Renaissance Orlando Resort at SeaWorld**	▽▽▽▽	$119-$329 [SAVE]	728
78 / p. 670	AAA	**Hilton Garden Inn Orlando at SeaWorld International Center** - see color ad p 716	▽▽▽	$109-$189 [SAVE]	715
79 / p. 670	AAA	**Residence Inn by Marriott SeaWorld International Center** - see color ad p 729	▽▽▽	$79-$145 [SAVE]	729
		ORLANDO SOUTH - Restaurants			
1 / p. 670		The Kitchen	▽▽▽	$8-$33	739
2 / p. 670		Latin Quarter	▽▽	$13-$30	739
3 / p. 670		Bob Marley-A Tribute to Freedom	▽▽	$4-$11	736
4 / p. 670		Emeril's Restaurant Orlando	▽▽▽	$24-$40	738
5 / p. 670		Pastamore'	▽▽	$9-$27	740
6 / p. 670		Pat O'Brien's	▽	$7-$12	740
7 / p. 670	AAA	**NASCAR Cafe**	▽▽	$7-$19	739
8 / p. 670		Palm Restaurant	▽▽▽	$15-$34	740
9 / p. 670		Jimmy Buffett's Margaritaville	▽▽	$8-$19	738
10 / p. 670		Tchoup Chop	▽▽▽	$20-$34	741
11 / p. 670		Texas Brazil Churrascaria	▽▽▽	$23-$40	741
12 / p. 670		Sweet Tomatoes	▽	$9	741
13 / p. 670		Kanpai	▽▽	$11-$35	738
14 / p. 670		Red Bamboo Thai Restaurant	▽▽▽	$11-$21	741
15 / p. 670	AAA	**Shamiana**	▽	$9-$15	741
16 / p. 670		Orlando's Wild Jacks	▽▽	$10-$22	740
17 / p. 670		Memories of India	▽▽	$8-$18	739

Spotter/Map Page Number	OA	ORLANDO SOUTH - Restaurants (continued)	Diamond Rating	Rate Range High Season	Listing Page
18 / p. 670	AAA	**Siam Orchid**	◆◆◆	$10-$22	741
19 / p. 670		1-6-8 Restaurant	◆◆	$6-$22	735
20 / p. 670		Pup's	◆	$3-$6	740
21 / p. 670		TooJay's Original Gourmet Deli	◆◆	$6-$11	742
22 / p. 670		Chatham's Place	◆◆◆	$20-$38	737
23 / p. 670		FishBones	◆◆	$13-$40	738
24 / p. 670		Antonio's Sand Lake	◆◆◆	$12-$35	736
25 / p. 670		Moon Fish	◆◆◆	$13-$30	739
26 / p. 670		Moe's Southwest Grill	◆	$3-$9	739
27 / p. 670		Tropical Smoothie Cafe	◆	$3-$7	742
28 / p. 670		First Watch	◆◆	$4-$10	738
29 / p. 670		Carrino's Lakefront Restaurant	◆◆	$10-$18	737
30 / p. 670		Samba Room	◆◆◆	$13-$28	741
31 / p. 670		Timpano Italian Chophouse	◆◆◆	$16-$30	742
32 / p. 670		Panera Bread	◆	$4-$9	740
33 / p. 670		Bonefish Grill	◆◆◆	$12-$18	736
34 / p. 670		Roy's	◆◆◆	$18-$30	741
35 / p. 670		Cedar's Restaurant	◆◆	$9-$26	737
36 / p. 670		Seasons 52	◆◆◆	$10-$20	741
37 / p. 670		Aussi Steak House Orlando	◆◆	$12-$25	736
38 / p. 670		Charley's Steak House	◆◆◆	$13-$35	737
39 / p. 670		Ran-Getsu of Tokyo	◆◆	$14-$50	740
40 / p. 670		Hanamizuki Japanese Restaurant	◆◆	$9-$70	738
41 / p. 670		Bergamo's Italian Restaurant	◆◆◆	$15-$35	736
42 / p. 670		The Butcher Shop Steak House	◆◆	$18-$34	737
43 / p. 670		Cafe Tu Tu Tango	◆◆	$4-$20	737
44 / p. 670		Vito's Chop House	◆◆◆	$14-$33	742
45 / p. 670		Bahama Breeze	◆◆◆	$8-$24	736
46 / p. 670		Race Rock Supercharged Restaurant	◆◆	$6-$17	740
47 / p. 670		Pac-Man Cafe at XS Orlando	◆◆◆	$6-$19	740
48 / p. 670		Adobe Gila's	◆	$10-$18	735
49 / p. 670		Ming Court	◆◆◆	$12-$30	739
50 / p. 670	AAA	**Jack's Place**	◆◆◆	$16-$28	738
51 / p. 670		Capriccio Grill	◆◆◆	$18-$38	737
52 / p. 670		Dux	◆◆◆◆	$25-$42	737
53 / p. 670	AAA	**Everglades Restaurant**	◆◆◆	$17-$30	738

Spotter/Map Page Number	OA	ORLANDO SOUTH - Restaurants (continued)	Diamond Rating	Rate Range High Season	Listing Page
54 / p. 670	AAA	Ciao Italia Ristorante Italiano	▽▽▽	$15-$30	737
55 / p. 670		Atlantis	▽▽▽▽	$27-$35	736
56 / p. 670		Famas Pizza & Pasta	▽	$5-$17	738
57 / p. 670		Thai Thani Restaurant	▽▽▽	$12-$20	741

Kissimmee

This index helps you "spot" where approved accommodations and restaurants are located on the corresponding detailed maps. Lodging rate ranges are for comparison only and show the property's high season; rates are per night, unless only weekly (W) rates are available. Restaurant rate range is for dinner, unless only lunch (L) is served. Turn to the listing page for more detailed rate information and consult display ads for special promotions.

Spotter/Map Page Number	OA	KISSIMMEE - Lodgings	Diamond Rating	Rate Range High Season	Listing Page
1 / p. 671	AAA	AmeriSuites (Orlando/Lake Buena Vista South) - see color ad p 756	▽▽▽	$114-$184 SAVE	756
2 / p. 671		Red Roof Inn	▽▽	$40-$85 SAVE	781
3 / p. 671	AAA	Holiday Villas - see color ad p 767	▽▽▽	$149-$219 SAVE	766
4 / p. 671	AAA	Howard Johnson Enchantedland Hotel - see color ad p 767	▽▽	$49-$125 SAVE	766
5 / p. 671		Golden Link Motel	▽▽	$34-$69	764
6 / p. 671	AAA	Howard Johnson Express Inn & Suites Lakefront Park - see color ad p 768	▽	$39-$150 SAVE	768
7 / p. 671	AAA	Quality Inn & Suites Eastgate - see color ad p 778	▽▽	$39-$200 SAVE	778
8 / p. 671		DoubleTree Resort Orlando Villas at Maingate	▽▽▽	$109-$269	762
9 / p. 671	AAA	MainStay Suites Maingate - see color ad p 776	▽▽▽	$99-$129 SAVE	776
10 / p. 671		The Hamlets - The Kissimmee Rental Company	▽▽	$80-$450	764
11 / p. 671		Lago Vista Resort	▽▽	$75-$100	773
12 / p. 671	AAA	Travelodge Suites Maingate - see color ad p 773	▽▽	$44-$129 SAVE	786
13 / p. 671	AAA	Record (Parkside) Inn & Suites	▽▽	$45-$85 SAVE	781
14 / p. 671	AAA	Four Winds Motel	▽▽	$49-$75 SAVE	764
15 / p. 671	AAA	Rodeway Inn Eastgate	▽▽	$49-$109 SAVE	782
16 / p. 671	AAA	Oak Plantation Resort	▽▽	$89-$127 SAVE	777
17 / p. 671	AAA	Howard Johnson Express Inn Parkside	▽▽	$39-$59 SAVE	768
18 / p. 671		Ramada Inn Kissimmee Downtown	▽▽▽	$40-$198	780
19 / p. 671		Flamingo Inn - see color ad p 763	▽▽	$29-$39	763
20 / p. 671	AAA	Super 8 Motel Suites	▽▽	$45-$59 SAVE	785
21 / p. 671	AAA	Days Inn 192 Orlando-Kissimmee - see color ad p 761	▽▽	$35-$150 SAVE	761
22 / p. 671	AAA	Best Western Maingate East Hotel & Suites	▽▽▽	$89-$169 SAVE	758
23 / p. 671		Lake Berkley - The Kissimmee Rental Company	▽▽▽	$80-$450	774
24 / p. 671		Maingate Inn	fyi	Failed to provide	775

Spotter/Map Page Number	OA	KISSIMMEE - Lodgings (continued)	Diamond Rating	Rate Range High Season	Listing Page
25 / p. 671		Sunset Lakes-Premier Vacation Homes	◈◈◈	$129-$279	785
26 / p. 671		Indian Point-Premier Vacation Homes	◈◈◈	$129-$279	770
27 / p. 671		Eagle Pointe - The Kissimmee Rental Company	◈◈	$80-$450	762
28 / p. 671		Terra Verde-American Vacation Homes	◈◈◈	$89-$289	785
29 / p. 671		Terra Verde - The Kissimmee Rental Company	◈◈◈	$80-$450	785
30 / p. 671	AAA	**Terra Verde Resort- Holiday Resort Management -** see color ad p 693	◈◈◈	$125-$250 SAVE	785
31 / p. 671	AAA	**Quality Inn Conference Center**	◈◈	$49-$139 SAVE	778
32 / p. 671		Days Inn-Kissimmee	◈◈	Failed to provide	761
34 / p. 671	AAA	**Best Western Heritage Park**	◈◈◈	$69-$99 SAVE	757
35 / p. 671	AAA	**Travelodge Kissimmee Heritage Park -** see color ad p 786	◈◈	$59-$129 SAVE	786
36 / p. 671	AAA	**Regency Express Inn & Suites**	◈◈	$79 SAVE	781
		KISSIMMEE - Restaurants			
1 / p. 671		Flippers Pizzeria	◈	$5-$18	789
2 / p. 671		Smokey Bones	◈◈	$6-$18	789
3 / p. 671		Cattleman's Steak House	◈◈	$7-$29	789
4 / p. 671		Puerto Rico Cafe	◈◈	$6-$25	789
5 / p. 671		Serrone's Pizzeria	◈	$5-$17	789
6 / p. 671		Olde Cuba Restaurant	◈◈	$5-$17	789

DOWNTOWN ORLANDO   (See map and index starting on p. 654)

──────── WHERE TO STAY ────────

AMERICAS BEST VALUE INN   *Book at aaa.com*   **Phone:** 407/996-0100   **3**

▼▼◇◇▼   Property failed to provide current rates

Small-scale Hotel   **Location:** I-4, exit 84, just w on SR 50. 304 W Colonial Dr 32801. Fax: 407/996-0103. **Facility:** 276 units. 275 one-bedroom standard units. 1 two-bedroom suite with whirlpool. 14 stories, interior corridors. *Bath:* combo or shower only. **Parking:** on-site. **Amenities:** voice mail, safes, irons, hair dryers. *Some:* CD players. **Pool(s):** heated outdoor. **Leisure Activities:** exercise room. **Guest Services:** gift shop, coin laundry. **Business Services:** meeting rooms, fax.

SOME UNITS

THE COURTYARD AT LAKE LUCERNE   *Book at aaa.com*   **Phone:** (407)648-5188   **7**

▼▼◇◇▼   All Year   1P: $115-$225   2P: $115-$225   XP: $15   F10

Historic Country Inn   **Location:** I-4, exit Anderson St, 0.5 mi e to Delany, then 0.5 mi s; end of Orange Ave off-ramp SR 408 eastbound. 211 N Lucerne Cir 32801. Fax: 407/246-1368. **Facility:** The Courtyard at Lake Lucerne is a collection of four buildings from varied architectural periods, each furnished accordingly. 30 units. 15 one-bedroom standard units, some with whirlpools. 15 one-bedroom suites ($115-$225). 2-3 stories, interior/exterior corridors. **Parking:** on-site. **Terms:** 7 day cancellation notice-fee imposed. **Amenities:** hair dryers. *Some:* irons. **Guest Services:** complimentary evening beverages. **Business Services:** meeting rooms, fax (fee). **Cards:** AX, DC, DS, MC, VI.

SOME UNITS

COURTYARD BY MARRIOTT - DOWNTOWN ORLANDO   *Book at aaa.com*   **Phone:** (407)996-1000   **2**

▼▼◇◇▼   All Year   1P: $98-$149   2P: $98-$149

Small-scale Hotel   **Location:** I-4, exit 83B, just e; just n of SR 50 (Colonial Dr). 730 N Magnolia Ave 32803. Fax: 407/996-1001. **Facility:** 200 units. 189 one-bedroom standard units, some with whirlpools. 11 one-bedroom suites. 6 stories, interior corridors. *Bath:* combo or shower only. **Parking:** on-site. **Amenities:** video games, high-speed Internet, dual phone lines, voice mail, irons, hair dryers. **Pool(s):** heated outdoor. **Leisure Activities:** whirlpool, exercise room. **Guest Services:** complimentary laundry. **Business Services:** meeting rooms, fax (fee). **Cards:** AX, CB, DC, DS, JC, MC, VI. *(See color ad below)*

SOME UNITS

(See map and index starting on p. 654)

EMBASSY SUITES ORLANDO DOWNTOWN   *Book at aaa.com*   Phone: 407/841-1000 **5**
All Year   1P: $120-$250   2P: $120-$250   XP: $15   F18
Location: I-4, exit 82C, 0.3 mi e on Anderson St, then 0.3 mi n on Rosalind Ave. 191 E Pine St 32801.
Small-scale Hotel   Fax: 407/841-0010. **Facility:** 167 one-bedroom suites, some with whirlpools. 7 stories, interior corridors.
Bath: combo or shower only. **Parking:** on-site (fee) and valet. **Terms:** check-in 4 pm, package plans.
Amenities: video games (fee), high-speed Internet, dual phone lines, voice mail, irons, hair dryers. **Pool(s):** heated outdoor.
Leisure Activities: whirlpool, exercise room. **Guest Services:** gift shop, complimentary evening beverages, valet and coin
laundry. **Business Services:** conference facilities, business center. **Cards:** AX, DC, DS, MC, VI.

SOME UNITS
(ASK) 🍴 🍸 📶 🏊 📹 🖥 🖨 💻 / 🗙 /

ORLANDO MARRIOTT DOWNTOWN   *Book at aaa.com*   Phone: (407)843-6664 **4**
All Year   1P: $107-$180   2P: $107-$180   XP: $15   F17
Location: I-4, exit 84 (Colonial Dr) westbound; exit 40 (Robinson St) eastbound, just w at jct Livingston and Hughey sts.
Small-scale Hotel   Located opposite T.D. Waterhouse Centre & Bob Carr Arts Center. 400 W Livingston St 32801. Fax: 407/648-5414.
Facility: 290 units. 282 one-bedroom standard units. 8 one-bedroom suites, some with whirlpools. 15
stories, interior corridors. **Parking:** on-site (fee) and valet. **Terms:** cancellation fee imposed, package plans. **Amenities:** high-
speed Internet (fee), dual phone lines, voice mail, irons, hair dryers. **Pool(s):** heated outdoor. **Leisure Activities:** whirlpool,
exercise room. **Guest Services:** gift shop, valet laundry. **Business Services:** conference facilities, business center. **Cards:** AX,
CB, DC, DS, JC, MC, VI. *(See color ad p 687)*

SOME UNITS
(ASK) 🅂 🍴 🍸 🛗 📶 🏊 📹 🖥 💻 / 🗙 🖨 /
FEE

RADISSON PLAZA HOTEL ORLANDO   Phone: (407)425-4455 **1**
All Year   1P: $179-$259   2P: $179-$259
Location: I-4, exit Ivanhoe Blvd. 60 Ivanhoe Blvd 32804. Fax: 407/843-0262. **Facility:** 337 one-bedroom
standard units, some with whirlpools. 15 stories, interior corridors. **Parking:** on-site (fee) and valet.
Small-scale Hotel   **Terms:** cancellation fee imposed, [BP] meal plan available, package plans. **Amenities:** video games (fee),
dual phone lines, voice mail, irons, hair dryers. **Pool(s):** heated outdoor. **Leisure Activities:** whirlpool, 2 lighted tennis courts,
exercise room, basketball. *Fee:* massage. **Guest Services:** gift shop, valet laundry. **Business Services:** conference facilities,
business center. **Cards:** AX, CB, DC, DS, JC, MC, VI.

SOME UNITS
(ASK) 🍴 24🍴 🍸 📶 🏊 🗙 📹 🖥 💻 / 🗙 🖨 /

(See map and index starting on p. 654)

WESTIN GRAND BOHEMIAN   *Book at aaa.com*   Phone: (407)313-9000   **6**

AAA SAVE
▼▼▼ ▼▼▼
Large-scale Hotel

All Year   1P: $239-$439   2P: $239-$439   XP: $25   F18
Location: Downtown. 325 S Orange Ave 32801. Fax: 407/313-9001. **Facility:** In addition to a rare Imperial Grand Bosendorfer piano, the hotel showcases many classic and contemporary works of art. 250 units. 214 one-bedroom standard units. 36 one-bedroom suites ($349-$549), some with whirlpools. 14 stories, interior corridors. *Bath:* combo or shower only. **Parking:** on-site (fee) and valet. **Terms:** cancellation fee imposed, small pets only ($100 fee). **Amenities:** CD players, dual phone lines, voice mail, safes, honor bars, irons, hair dryers. *Fee:* video games, high-speed Internet. **Dining:** 24 hours, also, The Boheme, see separate listing. **Pool(s):** heated outdoor. **Leisure Activities:** whirlpool, exercise room. *Fee:* massage. **Guest Services:** gift shop, valet laundry. **Business Services:** conference facilities, business center. **Cards:** AX, DC, DS, MC, VI. **Special Amenities:** free newspaper.

SOME UNITS

🐕 🍴 24⃣ 🍸 ⛨M 🖐 ⬚ 🏊 ✕ 🎦 DATA PORT 📺 / ✕ /
FEE

——— WHERE TO DINE ———

ANTHONY'S PIZZERIA RESTAURANT   Lunch: $5-$10   Dinner: $5-$12   Phone: 407/648-0009   **13**

▼▼▼ ▼▼▼
Italian

Location: I-4, exit 83B/84, 0.3 mi on SR 50, then s. 100 N Summerlin Ave 32801. **Hours:** 11 am-10 pm, Fri & Sat-11 pm, Sun noon-10 pm. Closed major holidays. **Features:** Near Thornton Park, the pizzeria has some outdoor seating that's great for people-watching. The menu centers on pizza slices, pies, pasta and traditional dishes. Casual dress; beer & wine only. **Parking:** on-site. **Cards:** AX, DS, MC, VI.

THE BOHEME   *Menu on aaa.com*   Lunch: $8-$16   Dinner: $19-$32   Phone: 407/313-9000   **27**

AAA
▼▼▼ ▼▼▼
Continental

Location: Downtown; in Westin Grand Bohemian. 325 S Orange Ave 32801. **Hours:** 6 am-10:30 pm, Fri & Sat-11:30 pm. **Reservations:** suggested. **Features:** The restaurant lists mildly eclectic and diverse selections on its menu. Nouvelle American cuisine reflects French and Pacific Rim influences. Casual dress; cocktails. **Parking:** on-site (fee) and valet. **Cards:** AX, DC, DS, MC, VI.

⛨M 🍸

BRAVISSIMO ITALIAN CAFE   Lunch: $4-$8   Dinner: $4-$11   Phone: 407/898-7333   **12**

▼▼▼ ▼▼▼
Italian

Location: I-4, exit 83C (Colonial Dr), 1 mi e, 0.7 mi s on Mills Ave, just e on Livingston St, then just s. 337 N Shine Ave 32803. **Hours:** 11 am-10 pm, Fri-11 pm, Sat 4:30-11 pm, Sun 4:30 pm-9:30 pm. Closed: 7/4, 11/23, 12/25. **Reservations:** suggested. **Features:** Hidden in a downtown residential area, the intimate cafe presents a menu of scrumptious pasta, chicken dishes and pizza. Zesty tomato and light cream sauces satisfy the palate without overwhelming the tummy. Casual dress; beer & wine only. **Parking:** on-site. **Cards:** AX, MC, VI.

CAFE TRASTEVERE   Lunch: $10-$21   Dinner: $10-$21   Phone: 407/839-0235   **2**

▼▼▼ ▼▼▼
Italian

Location: Just n of jct Colonial Dr (SR 50); downtown. 825 N Magnolia Ave 32803. **Hours:** 11:30 am-10 pm, Fri-11 pm, Sat 5 pm-11 pm. Closed: 12/25; also Sun. **Features:** Patrons can savor an intimate dinner or take in a power lunch at the little cafe. The service staff is friendly and attentive, and the food is fresh. Those who love Italian food are in for a treat. Dressy casual; cocktails. **Parking:** on-site. **Cards:** AX, DS, MC, VI.

🍸

CHAN'S CHINESE CUISINE   Lunch: $4-$8   Dinner: $6-$30   Phone: 407/896-0093   **4**

▼▼▼ ▼▼▼
Chinese

Location: I-4, exit 83B, 1.5 mi e on SR 50. 1901 E Colonial Dr 32803. **Hours:** 10 am-11 pm. **Features:** Feast on a far-ranging menu of dim sum and Hong Kong-style dinners. Delectable dishes include fried chicken with ginger sauce and stir-fried jumbo shrimp with honey walnut sauce. Traditional Chinese paintings and curios create a serene setting. Casual dress; cocktails. **Parking:** on-site. **Cards:** AX, MC, VI.

CHINATOWN   Lunch: $5-$8   Dinner: $7-$20   Phone: 407/896-9383   **1**

▼▼▼ ▼▼▼
Chinese

Location: I-4, exit 83B (US 17-92) and SR 50 (Colonial Dr), 1 mi e on SR 50 (Colonial Dr), then 0.5 mi n. 1103 N Mills Ave 32803. **Hours:** 11 am-10:30 pm. **Reservations:** suggested. **Features:** If seafood is the craving, none is any fresher than that found in the tanks in the market adjacent to the family-operated restaurant. En route to the cozy dining room, guests walk past the koi pond and fountain. The chef prepares selections to order, or diners may choose from among tasty traditional menu items. Casual dress; beer & wine only. **Parking:** on-site. **Cards:** AX, DC, MC, VI.

THE COFFEE HOUSE OF THORNTON PARK   Lunch: $3-$5   Phone: 407/426-8989   **14**

▼▼▼
American

Location: I-4, exit 82B (SR 50/Colonial Dr), 0.8 mi e, 0.6 mi s on Summerlin, then e. 712 E Washington St 32801. **Hours:** 8 am-4 pm. Closed major holidays; also Mon. **Features:** In the trendy Thornton Park area, the quaint café serves a variety of sweets and sandwiches and boasts a wonderful espresso bar. Casual dress. **Parking:** on-site. **Cards:** MC, VI.

DEXTER'S OF THORNTON PARK   Lunch: $6-$12   Dinner: $10-$25   Phone: 407/648-2777   **15**

▼▼▼ ▼▼▼
Nouvelle American

Location: I-4, exit Robinson St, 0.7 mi e, just s on Eola, then just e; 0.3 mi e of Lake Eola Park. 808 E Washington St 32801. **Hours:** 11 am-10 pm, Fri & Sat-11 pm; Sunday brunch. Closed major holidays. **Reservations:** accepted. **Features:** This eclectic neighborhood meeting place serves a variety of creative soups, pastas, salads and entrees. Some may be content to have a glass of wine and a platter of gourmet cheese with fresh bread and fruit, but don't stop there. The food is wonderful. Casual dress; cocktails. **Parking:** on-site. **Cards:** AX, DC, DS, MC, VI.

THE GLOBE   Lunch: $6-$12   Dinner: $8-$16   Phone: 407/849-9904   **18**

▼▼▼ ▼▼▼
American

Location: Between Orange and Garland aves; downtown. 25 Wall St Plaza 32801. **Hours:** 11 am-11 pm. **Reservations:** accepted. **Features:** This tragically hip and trendy eatery is just off Heritage Square Park and is open from breakfast through the late night hours. The menu features unique twists on classic dishes from around the globe. Cocktails. **Parking:** on-site. **Cards:** AX, MC, VI.

(See map and index starting on p. 654)

HUE

Lunch: $13-$19   Dinner: $13-$26   Phone: 407/849-1800   [22]

Continental

Location: I-4, exit 41, 0.5 mi e to Summerlin Ave, then just s. 629 E Central Blvd 32801. **Hours:** 11:30 am-11 pm, Thurs-Sat to midnight. Closed major holidays. **Features:** The trendy downtown restaurant has become a popular place to celebrate special occasions or just people-watch from the patio. Asian cuisine prepared with a Continental flair is the specialty, and menu items change daily. The upscale atmosphere and creatively prepared dishes make this a wonderful spot. Casual dress; cocktails. **Parking:** on-site (fee). **Cards:** AX, DC, DS, MC, VI.

KATE O'BRIEN'S IRISH PUB & RESTAURANT

Lunch: $8-$15   Dinner: $8-$15   Phone: 407/649-7646   [24]

Irish

Location: Just w of jct Orange Ave; downtown. 42 W Central Blvd 32801. **Hours:** 11:30 am-7 pm. **Features:** Diners can taste good Irish food, such as shepherd's pie, or typical American fare along the lines of burgers and wings in the casual pub-style establishment. What the restaurant lacks in basic decor, it makes up for with friendly service and quality food. Casual dress; cocktails. **Parking:** street.
Cards: MC, VI.

KRES CHOPHOUSE

Lunch: $6-$17   Dinner: $10-$32   Phone: 407/447-7950   [26]

Steak & Seafood

Location: I-4, exit 82C; in Church Street Station. 17 W Church St 32801. **Hours:** 11:30 am-4 & 5-11 pm. Closed major holidays. **Reservations:** suggested, weekends. **Features:** Located in the heart of downtown this popular restaurant draws large crowds at lunch and dinner. A sophisicated atmosphere lures patrons in to enjoy a wonderful dining experience; steak and seafood dishes are popular choices. Casual dress; cocktails. **Parking:** street. **Cards:** AX, DS, MC, VI.

LAKE EOLA YACHT CLUB (LEYC)

Lunch: $8-$10   Dinner: $8-$22   Phone: 407/841-0033   [23]

American

Location: On southside of Lake Eola between Osceola and Rosalind aves. 407 E Central Blvd 32801. **Hours:** 11 am-10 pm, Fri & Sat-11 pm, Sun-9 pm. **Reservations:** suggested. **Features:** The diner-like menu belies the extreme pleasures concocted by the chef. Each dish is a delight to both the eye and the palate. Dine al fresco on the lake and enjoy the view of the city and fountain. Reasonably priced glasses of wine and starters, such as the spinach dip or cheese fondue, enhance the experience. No entree should be overlooked, but the seafood dishes stand out in this crowd. Casual dress; cocktails. **Parking:** on-site and street. **Cards:** AX, DS, MC, VI.

LEE'S LAKESIDE RESTAURANT

Dinner: $19-$29   Phone: 407/841-1565   [20]

American

Location: On Lake Eola at Central Blvd and Osceola Ave. 431 E Central Blvd 32801. **Hours:** 5 pm-close, Sun from 11 am; Sunday brunch. Closed: Mon. **Reservations:** suggested. **Features:** From large bay windows, look out at the Lake Eola fountain and the downtown skyline. Tasty and well-presented dishes, such as tenderloin stuffed with crabmeat and pina colada muffins, and attentive service are trademarks of the elegant restaurant. Patio dining is available. Casual dress; cocktails; entertainment. **Parking:** on-site. **Cards:** AX, CB, DC, DS, MC, VI.

MAMA B'S GIANT SUBS

Lunch: $3-$7   Phone: 407/422-7353   [9]

American

Location: I-4, exit 83B/84, just e, jct Colonial Dr (SR 50). 692 N Orange Ave 32801. **Hours:** 8:30 am-4 pm, Sat 9 am-3 pm. Closed major holidays; also Sun. **Features:** The fast-paced shop, in which 27 varieties of subs are prepared, plays host to most of downtown during lunchtime. Also served are sandwiches, salads and chips. Casual dress. **Parking:** on-site.

MANUEL'S ON THE 28TH

Dinner: $28-$36   Phone: 407/246-6580   [10]

International

Location: Orange Ave and E Livingston St; on 28th floor of Bank of America Building. 390 N Orange Ave, Suite 2800 32801. **Hours:** 6 pm-10 pm. Closed: 11/23, 12/25; also Sun & Mon. **Reservations:** suggested. **Features:** A candlelit setting on the 28th floor offers unparalleled views of downtown. The seasonally changing menu lists memorable dishes prepared with an international flair. While the chef specializes in the use of exotic meats, the fare also includes tamer selections. The signature duck confit appetizer is a perennial favorite. Semi-formal attire; cocktails. **Parking:** on-site (fee). **Cards:** AX, DC, DS, MC, VI.

METRO ESPRESSO PIZZA CAFE

Lunch: $5-$15   Dinner: $5-$15   Phone: 407/422-5282   [19]

Italian

Location: At Central Blvd and Osceola Ave. 417 E Central Blvd 32801. **Hours:** 11 am-10 pm, Fri & Sat-11 pm. Closed: 1/1, 11/23, 12/25; also Sun. **Features:** Minutes from Lake Eola in the trendy downtown area, the cafe presents a menu of made-to-order food, including specialty pizzas, sandwiches and salads. Diners can take a few minutes out of their day to enjoy the relaxing atmosphere. Casual dress. **Parking:** street.
Cards: AX, MC, VI.

NEW YORK DELI

Lunch: $3-$7   Dinner: $3-$7   Phone: 407/649-4900   [8]

American

Location: I-4, exit 83B, 0.3 mi e. 693 N Orange Ave 32801. **Hours:** 9 am-5 pm. Closed major holidays; also Sun. **Features:** The busy, quick-serve, downtown delicatessen serves a variety of subs and sandwiches for people on the go. Limited seating is available. Casual dress. **Parking:** on-site. **Cards:** VI.

N.Y.P.D. PIZZA & DELICATESSEN

Lunch: $6-$17   Dinner: $6-$17   Phone: 407/872-6973   [11]

Italian

Location: Downtown. 373 N Orange Ave 32801. **Hours:** 11 am-3 pm, Fri-9 pm. Closed major holidays; also Sat & Sun. **Features:** Once a favorite hangout of many 'N Sync members, the restaurant prepares brick-oven rolls, hand-tossed pizza, gourmet hot heroes and baked pasta selections. On the wall are pictures of famous people, some local and some who just stopped by. Eat-in and carry-out service are available. Casual dress. **Parking:** street. **Cards:** AX, MC, VI.

O-BOYS BAR-B-Q

Lunch: $4-$12   Dinner: $4-$12   Phone: 407/425-6269   [7]

Barbecue

Location: I-4, exit 84, just w. 601 W Colonial Dr 32801. **Hours:** 11 am-9 pm, Fri & Sat-10 pm. Closed major holidays; also Sun. **Features:** Tasty barbecue is slowly smoked over hickory in house and basted with "secret" sauce. Begin with deep-fried corn nuggets, then choose from among barbecue sandwiches, platters or combination plates. Lunchtime at the quick-serve restaurant is busy, as is the period before any event at nearby TD Waterhouse Centre. Casual dress; cocktails. **Parking:** on-site. **Cards:** AX, DC, DS, MC, VI.

(See map and index starting on p. 654)

PHO 88   **Lunch:** $5-$10   **Dinner:** $7-$12   **Phone:** 407/897-3488 ③

▼

Vietnamese

Location: I-4, exit 84, 3 mi e on SR 50, then just n on US 17-92 and SR 15. 730 N Mills Ave 32803. **Hours:** 10 am-10 pm. **Reservations:** accepted. **Features:** In Orlando's version of Little Saigon, the spacious diner employs quick, smartly attired waiters. The menu lists a whopping 143 items, including numerous combinations and sizes of pho, a well-known, meal-in-itself soup that is the Vietnamese national dish. Healthy drinks, exotic fruit juices and unusually flavored puddings complement the meal. Casual dress; beer & wine only. **Parking:** on-site. **Cards:** AX, MC, VI.

SAM SNEAD'S DOWNTOWN   **Lunch:** $6-$15   **Dinner:** $8-$28   **Phone:** 407/999-0109 ㉕

▼▼ ▼▼

American

DS, MC, VI.

Location: Jct Pine and Robinson sts, just e. 301 E Pine St 32801. **Hours:** 11:30 am-11 pm. Closed: 12/25. **Reservations:** suggested. **Features:** Golf memorabilia mixes with deep mahogany and rich green accents and wood floors to create a comfortable gathering spot for business or social lunches and dinners. Steak and seafood are at the heart of the dinner menu. Casual dress; cocktails. **Parking:** street. **Cards:** AX, DC,

SUSHI HATSU   **Lunch:** $6-$9   **Dinner:** $9-$19   **Phone:** 407/422-1551 ⑰

▼ ▼

Ethnic

Location: Between Magnolia and Orange aves. 24 E Washington St 32801. **Hours:** 11 am-2:30 & 5-10 pm, Fri & Sat-11 pm. Closed: 1/1, 11/23, 12/25; also Sun. **Reservations:** accepted, Mon-Fri. **Features:** A few Korean dishes are found among sushi and other Japanese items on the menu. Try the bibimbap — small chunks of beef, shredded vegetables and a fried egg, drizzled with a spicy sauce and served over rice. Quick and helpful service makes dinner easy. Casual dress; beer & wine only. **Parking:** on-site. **Cards:** AX, DC, MC, VI.

THAI HOUSE   **Lunch:** $6-$7   **Dinner:** $7-$13   **Phone:** 407/898-0820 ⑤

▼ ▼

Thai

Location: I-4, exit 83C, 1.8 mi e. 2117 E Colonial Dr 32803. **Hours:** 11 am-2 & 5-9:30 pm, Fri-10 pm, Sat 5 pm-10 pm, Sun 5 pm-9 pm. **Features:** Efficiency and dependability are hallmarks of the local Thai favorite. Be prepared for a wait on weekends. Popular items include seafood combinations and curries. Casual dress; beer & wine only. **Parking:** on-site. **Cards:** AX, DS, MC, VI.

VEGA'S CAFE   **Lunch:** $4-$5   **Phone:** 407/898-5196 ⑥

▼

Cuban

Location: I-4, exit 83B/84, 1.4 mi e on SR 50. 1835 E Colonial Dr 32801. **Hours:** 10 am-5 pm, Sat-4 pm. Closed major holidays; also Sun. **Features:** The converted filling station has been serving the downtown area since 1976. On the menu are Cuban sandwiches, black beans and rice, garbanzo soup and flan. Seating is limited, as are the menu offerings. Casual dress. **Parking:** on-site.

WALL STREET CANTINA   **Lunch:** $7-$14   **Dinner:** $7-$14   **Phone:** 407/420-1515 ㉑

▼

Mexican

Location: At Wall Street Plaza; downtown. 19 N Orange Ave 32801. **Hours:** 11 am-11 pm. Closed: 12/25. **Features:** Central to shops and pubs, the restaurant offers guests indoor or patio seating. This place is more geared toward the nighttime crowd. Casual dress; cocktails. **Parking:** on-site (fee). **Cards:** AX, DS, MC, VI.

Ⓨ

WILDSIDE RESTAURANT   **Lunch:** $7-$13   **Dinner:** $8-$18   **Phone:** 407/872-8665 ⑯

▼▼ ▼▼

Barbecue

Location: I-4, exit 82B (US 17/92 and SR 50/Colonial Dr), 0.8 mi e on SR 50, then 0.6 mi s on Summerlin Ave; in Thornton Park district. 700 E Washington St 32810. **Hours:** 11 am-10:30 pm, Fri & Sat-11:30 pm. Closed: 11/23, 12/25. **Features:** Those who follow their nose while strolling Lake Eola will be led directly to the pork and beef on the smoker at Wildfire. While savoring tasty ribs or sandwiches from the open patio, guests can check out the comings and goings in trendy Thornton Park. With TVs and music, this is a great place to hang out. Casual dress; cocktails. **Parking:** on-site. **Cards:** AX, DC, DS, MC, VI.

ORLANDO pop. 185,951   (See map and index starting on p. 656)

———— **WHERE TO STAY** ————

BEST WESTERN ORLANDO WEST   *Book at aaa.com*   **Phone:** (407)841-8600 ⑮

AAA SAVE

▼ ▼

Small-scale Hotel

All Year	1P: $59-$125	2P: $59-$125	XP: $10 F12

Location: I-4, exit 84, 1.5 mi w on SR 50; 0.4 mi e of SR 423. 2014 W Colonial Ave 32804. Fax: 407/843-7080. **Facility:** 109 one-bedroom standard units, some with efficiencies. 2 stories, interior corridors. *Bath:* combo or shower only. **Parking:** on-site. **Terms:** 14 day cancellation notice-fee imposed, [AP] & [BP] meal plans available, small pets only ($25 deposit, $5 extra charge). **Amenities:** voice mail, safes (fee), irons, hair dryers. *Some:* high-speed Internet. **Dining:** 7 am-2:30 pm, Sat & Sun-noon. **Pool(s):** outdoor. **Guest Services:** valet and coin laundry. **Business Services:** meeting rooms, fax (fee). **Cards:** AX, DC, DS, MC, VI. **Special Amenities: free local telephone calls.**

SOME UNITS

🅢🄳 🐾 🍴 Ⓨ 📶 🛗 📡 ▢ / ✕ 📶 📺 /   FEE   FEE   FEE

COMFORT INN-NORTH   *Book at aaa.com*   **Phone:** (407)629-4000 ②

AAA SAVE

▼▼▼ ▼▼▼

Small-scale Hotel

2/1-3/31 [CP]	1P: $69	2P: $69	XP: $5 F17
12/1-1/31 & 4/1-11/30 [CP]	1P: $63	2P: $63	XP: $5 F17

Location: I-4, exit 88, 0.4 mi w on SR 423. 830 Lee Rd 32810. Fax: 407/645-2809. **Facility:** 145 one-bedroom standard units. 5 stories, interior corridors. **Parking:** on-site. **Terms:** cancellation fee imposed, small pets only ($25 fee, $10 extra charge). **Amenities:** voice mail, irons, hair dryers. *Fee:* video games, safes. **Pool(s):** heated outdoor. **Leisure Activities:** sauna, whirlpool. *Fee:* game room. **Guest Services:** valet and coin laundry. **Business Services:** meeting rooms, fax (fee). **Cards:** AX, DC, DS, MC, VI. **Special Amenities: free continental breakfast and free local telephone calls.**

SOME UNITS

🅢🄳 🐾 🍴 📡 🛗 📶 ✕ 📺 📡 🛗 📺 / ✕ /
  FEE

(See map and index starting on p. 656)

COMFORT SUITES DOWNTOWN   *Book at aaa.com*   Phone: (407)228-4007   **12**

(AAA) [SAVE]

| 12/1-5/31 & 9/15-11/30 | 1P: $109-$139 | 2P: $109-$139 |
| 6/1-9/14 | 1P: $89 | 2P: $119 |

Location: I-4, exit 85, just e on Princeton, then just n. 2416 N Orange Ave 32804. Fax: 407/228-3820. **Facility:** 77 units. 73 one-bedroom standard units, some with efficiencies. 4 one-bedroom suites with efficiencies and whirlpools. 3 stories, interior corridors. *Bath:* combo or shower only. **Parking:** on-site. **Terms:** check-in 4 pm, [CP] meal plan available. **Amenities:** voice mail, irons, hair dryers. **Pool(s):** heated outdoor. **Leisure Activities:** whirlpool. **Guest Services:** valet and coin laundry, area transportation-Florida Hospital. **Business Services:** meeting rooms, business center. **Cards:** AX, CB, DC, DS, JC, MC, VI. **Special Amenities:** free local telephone calls and free newspaper.

Small-scale Hotel

SOME UNITS

[icons] FEE

COMFORT SUITES UCF-RESEARCH PARK   *Book at aaa.com*   Phone: (407)737-7303   **11**

(AAA) [SAVE]

| 12/1-10/26 [ECP] | 1P: $99-$199 | 2P: $99-$199 | XP: $10 | F12 |
| 10/27-11/30 [ECP] | 1P: $89-$169 | 2P: $89-$169 | XP: $10 | F12 |

Location: On SR 434 (Alafaya Tr); 1.6 mi n of SR 408, exit 21; 0.4 mi n of SR 50. 12101 Challenger Pkwy 32826. Fax: 407/737-7304. **Facility:** 70 one-bedroom standard units, some with whirlpools. 3 stories, interior corridors. *Bath:* combo or shower only. **Parking:** on-site. **Terms:** 2-3 night minimum stay - seasonal and/or weekends, 14 day cancellation notice-fee imposed. **Amenities:** high-speed Internet, dual phone lines, voice mail, irons, hair dryers. **Pool(s):** outdoor. **Leisure Activities:** exercise room. **Guest Services:** valet and coin laundry. **Business Services:** meeting rooms, business center. **Cards:** AX, DC, DS, MC, VI. **Special Amenities:** free expanded continental breakfast and free local telephone calls.

Small-scale Hotel

SOME UNITS

[icons]

(See map and index starting on p. 656)

COURTYARD BY MARRIOTT @ UCF   *Book at aaa.com*   Phone: 407/277-7676   **8**
Property failed to provide current rates
Small-scale Hotel   **Location:** On University Blvd, 2.2 mi e of SR 417, exit 32A; just w of SR 434 (Alafaya Tr). Located at Collegiate Square. 12000 Collegiate Way 32817. Fax: 407/277-5710. **Facility:** 123 units. 119 one-bedroom standard units. 4 one-bedroom suites. 4 stories, interior corridors. *Bath:* combo or shower only. **Parking:** on-site. **Amenities:** high-speed Internet (fee), voice mail, irons, hair dryers. **Pool(s):** heated outdoor. **Leisure Activities:** whirlpool, exercise room. **Guest Services:** valet and coin laundry. **Business Services:** meeting rooms, fax (fee).

SOME UNITS

DAYS INN NORTH OF UNIVERSAL   *Book at aaa.com*   Phone: (407)841-3731   **18**
All Year   1P: $40-$150   2P: $40-$150
Small-scale Hotel   **Location:** I-4, exit 79, just e. 2500 W 33rd St 32839. Fax: 407/841-0642. **Facility:** 200 one-bedroom standard units. 4 stories, exterior corridors. *Bath:* combo or shower only. **Parking:** on-site. **Terms:** $2 service charge, pets ($10 extra charge). **Amenities:** irons, hair dryers. **Dining:** 2 pm-1 am, Sat & Sun from noon, cocktails. **Pool(s):** outdoor. **Guest Services:** valet and coin laundry. **Business Services:** fax (fee). **Cards:** AX, CB, DC, DS, MC, VI. **Special Amenities:** free newspaper and early check-in/late check-out.

SOME UNITS
FEE

HAMPTON INN & SUITES/ORLANDO EAST-UCF
AREA   *Book at aaa.com*   Phone: (407)282-0029   **7**
All Year [ECP]   1P: $109-$129   2P: $109-$129
Small-scale Hotel   **Location:** 2.2 mi e of SR 417 on University Blvd, just n; in Quadrangle Office Park. 3450 Quadrangle Blvd 32817. Fax: 407/206-3001. **Facility:** 110 units. 76 one-bedroom standard units. 34 one-bedroom suites ($139-$159) with efficiencies. 3 stories, interior corridors. *Bath:* combo or shower only. **Parking:** on-site. **Amenities:** high-speed Internet, dual phone lines, voice mail, irons, hair dryers. *Some:* CD players. **Pool(s):** heated outdoor. **Leisure Activities:** whirlpool, exercise room. **Guest Services:** complimentary evening beverages: Wed, valet and coin laundry. **Business Services:** meeting rooms, fax (fee). **Cards:** AX, DC, DS, MC, VI.

SOME UNITS

HILTON GARDEN INN ORLANDO EAST/UCF   *Book at aaa.com*   Phone: (407)992-5000   **13**
All Year   1P: $110-$250   2P: $110-$250   XP: $10   F
Small-scale Hotel   **Location:** Just n of SR 50; 1.4 mi n of SR 408 (East-West Expwy). 1959 N Alafaya Tr 32826. Fax: 407/992-7000. **Facility:** 122 units. 116 one-bedroom standard units. 6 one-bedroom suites. 3 stories, interior corridors. *Bath:* combo or shower only. **Parking:** on-site. **Terms:** cancellation fee imposed, [BP] & [CP] meal plans available, package plans. **Amenities:** video games (fee), high-speed Internet, dual phone lines, voice mail, irons, hair dryers. **Dining:** 6 am-11 & 5-10 pm, cocktails. **Pool(s):** heated outdoor. **Leisure Activities:** whirlpool, exercise room. **Guest Services:** valet and coin laundry. **Business Services:** meeting rooms, business center. **Cards:** AX, CB, DC, DS, JC, MC, VI. *(See color ad below)*

SOME UNITS

HOLIDAY INN SELECT-ORLANDO EAST-UCF AREA   *Book at aaa.com*   Phone: (407)275-9000   **5**
1/16-4/30   1P: $89-$169
12/1-1/15 & 5/1-11/30   1P: $75-$159
Small-scale Hotel   **Location:** 2.4 mi e of SR 417 on University Blvd, just n. 12125 High Tech Ave 32817. Fax: 407/381-0019. **Facility:** 246 one-bedroom standard units. 6 stories, interior corridors. **Parking:** on-site. **Terms:** cancellation fee imposed, package plans. **Amenities:** voice mail, irons, hair dryers. *Some:* CD players, dual phone lines. **Dining:** 6 am-11 pm, cocktails. **Pool(s):** outdoor. **Leisure Activities:** sauna, whirlpool, jogging, exercise room, volleyball. **Guest Services:** valet laundry, area transportation-within 5 mi. **Business Services:** meeting rooms, business center. **Cards:** AX, CB, DC, DS, JC, MC, VI. **Special Amenities:** free newspaper and early check-in/late check-out.

SOME UNITS
FEE   FEE FEE

(See map and index starting on p. 656)

HOMEWOOD SUITES BY HILTON UCF   *Book at aaa.com*   Phone: 407/282-0067   **10**
Property failed to provide current rates
Small-scale Hotel   **Location:** 2.1 mi n of SR 50. 3028 N Alafaya Tr 32826. **Facility:** 99 units. 94 one- and 5 two-bedroom suites. 4 stories, interior corridors. *Bath:* combo or shower only. **Parking:** on-site. **Amenities:** high-speed Internet, dual phone lines, voice mail, irons, hair dryers. **Pool(s):** heated outdoor. **Leisure Activities:** exercise room. **Guest Services:** coin laundry. **Business Services:** business center.

SOME UNITS

LA QUINTA INN & SUITES ORLANDO (U.C.F.)   *Book at aaa.com*   Phone: (407)737-6075   **9**
(AAA) [SAVE]   All Year   1P: $79-$95   XP: $7   F18
Location: Just se of jct University Blvd and SR 434 (Alafaya Tr). 11805 Research Pkwy 32826. Fax: 407/737-7562. **Facility:** 130 units. 123 one-bedroom standard units. 7 one-bedroom suites ($115-$130). 6 stories, interior corridors. *Bath:* combo or shower only. **Parking:** on-site. **Terms:** [ECP] meal plan available, small pets only.
Small-scale Hotel   **Amenities:** voice mail, irons, hair dryers. *Fee:* video games, high-speed Internet. *Some:* dual phone lines. **Pool(s):** heated outdoor. **Leisure Activities:** whirlpool, exercise room. **Guest Services:** valet and coin laundry. **Business Services:** meeting rooms, fax (fee). **Cards:** AX, CB, DC, DS, MC, VI. **Special Amenities:** free expanded continental breakfast and free local telephone calls. *(See color ad p 721)*

SOME UNITS

LA QUINTA INN ORLANDO-WINTER PARK   *Book at aaa.com*   Phone: (407)645-5600   **3**
(AAA) [SAVE]   All Year [ECP]   1P: $59-$199   2P: $69-$249
Location: I-4, exit 88 (Lee Rd), just w on SR 438. 626 Lee Rd 32810. Fax: 407/740-7912. **Facility:** 200 one-bedroom standard units, some with whirlpools. 5 stories, interior corridors. *Bath:* combo or shower only. **Parking:** on-site. **Terms:** [AP] meal plan available. **Amenities:** high-speed Internet, dual phone lines, voice
Small-scale Hotel   mail, irons, hair dryers. **Dining:** 6 am-8 pm. **Pool(s):** outdoor. **Leisure Activities:** exercise room. **Guest Services:** valet and coin laundry. **Business Services:** meeting rooms, fax (fee). **Cards:** AX, CB, DC, DS, JC, MC, VI. **Special Amenities:** free expanded continental breakfast and free local telephone calls.
(See color ad below)

SOME UNITS

MOTEL 6 ORLANDO-WINTER PARK #791   *Book at aaa.com*   Phone: 407/647-1444   **1**
   1/1-5/29   1P: $41-$51   2P: $47-$57   XP: $3   F17
   12/1-12/31 & 5/30-11/30   1P: $39-$49   2P: $45-$55   XP: $3   F17
Motel   **Location:** I-4, exit 88, 0.5 mi w on SR 423 (Lee Rd). 5300 Adanson Rd 32810 (14651 Dallas Pkwy, #500, DALLAS, TX, 75254). Fax: 407/647-1016. **Facility:** 121 one-bedroom standard units. 2 stories, exterior corridors. *Bath:* combo or shower only. **Parking:** on-site. **Pool(s):** heated outdoor. **Guest Services:** coin laundry. **Business Services:** fax (fee). **Cards:** AX, CB, DC, DS, MC, VI.

RADISSON UNIVERSITY HOTEL   *Book at aaa.com*   Phone: (407)658-9008   **14**
   1/1-3/31   1P: $99   2P: $99
   4/1-11/30   1P: $95   2P: $95
   12/1-12/31   1P: $89   2P: $89
Small-scale Hotel   **Location:** 1 mi n of SR 408 (East-West Expwy); 0.3 mi n of SR 50; 3.8 mi e of jct SR 50 and 417. 1724 Alafaya Tr 32826. Fax: 407/381-5456. **Facility:** 149 one-bedroom standard units. 7 stories, interior corridors. *Bath:* combo or shower only. **Parking:** on-site. **Terms:** 3 day cancellation notice-fee imposed, [AP], [BP] & [CP] meal plans available. **Amenities:** video games (fee), dual phone lines, voice mail, irons, hair dryers. **Pool(s):** outdoor. **Leisure Activities:** exercise room. **Guest Services:** valet laundry, area transportation. **Business Services:** meeting rooms, fax (fee). **Cards:** AX, CB, DC, DS, MC, VI.

SOME UNITS

RAMADA PLAZA ORLANDO   *Book at aaa.com*   Phone: (407)841-6450   **17**
   All Year   1P: $109   2P: $129   XP: $10   D17
Small-scale Hotel   **Location:** I-4, exit 32, just nw. 3155 S John Young Pkwy 32805. Fax: 407/841-4186. **Facility:** 205 one-bedroom standard units. 5 stories, interior/exterior corridors. *Bath:* combo or shower only. **Parking:** on-site. **Terms:** cancellation fee imposed. **Amenities:** video games, voice mail, safes, irons, hair dryers. **Pool(s):** heated outdoor, wading. **Leisure Activities:** whirlpool, playground, exercise room. *Fee:* massage, game room. **Guest Services:** gift shop, valet and coin laundry. **Business Services:** meeting rooms, business center. **Cards:** AX, DC, DS, MC, VI.

SOME UNITS

(See map and index starting on p. 656)

RESIDENCE INN BY MARRIOTT/ORLANDO EAST   *Book at aaa.com*   Phone: (407)513-9000 **6**
WWW   All Year   1P: $159-$209   2P: $159-$209
Location: 2.2 mi e of SR 417 on University Blvd; just w of SR 434 (Alafaya Tr). 11651 University Blvd 32817.
Small-scale Hotel   Fax: 407/513-9001. **Facility:** 99 units. 36 one-bedroom standard units with kitchens. 39 one- and 24 two-bedroom suites with kitchens. 4 stories, interior corridors. *Bath:* combo or shower only. **Parking:** on-site.
Terms: cancellation fee imposed, pets ($25 extra charge). **Amenities:** high-speed Internet (fee), dual phone lines, voice mail, irons, hair dryers. **Pool(s):** heated outdoor. **Leisure Activities:** whirlpool, exercise room, sports court. **Guest Services:** complimentary evening beverages: Mon-Thurs, valet and coin laundry. **Business Services:** meeting rooms, fax (fee).
Cards: AX, DC, DS, MC, VI.

THE SEASONS RESORT   Phone: 407/851-2278 **19**
WWW   All Year   1P: $89-$338   2P: $89-$338
Location: I-4, exit 79, 2.6 mi s on SR 423 (John Young Pkwy), 0.3 mi e on Oak Ridge Rd, then just n. 5736 S Texas
Condominium   Ave 32839. Fax: 407/438-1362. **Facility:** The resort's spacious apartments include kitchens, dishwashers and washer/dryers. 24 two-bedroom standard units with kitchens. 2 stories, exterior corridors. **Parking:** on-site. **Terms:** check-in 4 pm, 3 night minimum stay, 14 day cancellation notice-fee imposed, weekly rates available. **Amenities:** video library (fee), safes, irons, hair dryers. **Pool(s):** heated outdoor, wading. **Leisure Activities:** sauna, whirlpool, racquetball court, playground, exercise room. *Fee:* game room. **Guest Services:** complimentary laundry. **Business Services:** fax (fee). **Cards:** AX, DS, MC, VI.

TOWNEPLACE SUITES BY MARRIOTT ORLANDO
EAST/UCF   *Book at aaa.com*   Phone: 407/243-6100 **4**
WWW   Property failed to provide current rates
Location: 2.2 mi e of SR 417 on University Blvd. 11801 High Tech Ave 32817. Fax: 407/243-6111. **Facility:** 105
Small-scale Hotel   units. 72 one-bedroom standard units with kitchens. 11 one- and 22 two-bedroom suites with kitchens. 5 stories, interior corridors. *Bath:* combo or shower only. **Parking:** on-site. **Terms:** pets ($75 fee).
Amenities: high-speed Internet, dual phone lines, voice mail, irons, hair dryers. **Pool(s):** heated outdoor. **Leisure Activities:** exercise room. **Guest Services:** valet and coin laundry. **Business Services:** business center.

VENTURA RESORT RENTALS ORLANDO   Phone: (407)273-8770 **16**
WWW   All Year   2P: $64-$152
Location: 0.6 mi e of SR 436. Located in a gated community. 5946 Curry Ford Rd 32822. Fax: 407/658-6530.
Condominium   **Facility:** These rental condominiums and houses are in a golf community; registration is off site. 200 units. 30 one-, 87 two- and 31 three-bedroom suites. 52 vacation homes ($94-$183). 1-2 stories, exterior corridors. **Parking:** on-site. **Terms:** 7 night minimum stay - seasonal and/or weekends, 91 day cancellation notice-fee imposed, weekly rates available, $55 service charge, small pets only ($100 fee, $100 deposit). **Amenities:** irons. *Some:* DVD players (fee). **Pool(s):** 17 outdoor. **Leisure Activities:** 4 lighted tennis courts, playground, basketball, shuffleboard. **Guest Services:** complimentary laundry. **Business Services:** fax (fee). **Cards:** AX, DS, MC, VI.

───── **WHERE TO DINE** ─────

AMALFI ITALIAN RESTAURANT   Lunch: $6-$12   Dinner: $6-$19   Phone: 407/282-6283 **35**
WWW   **Location:** Jct Chickasaw Tr and Lake Underhill Rd; in Rio Pinar Plaza. 523 S Chickasaw Tr 32825. **Hours:** 11 am-9:30 pm, Sat 5 pm-10:30 pm. Closed major holidays; also Sun. **Features:** The family-owned-and-operated
Italian   restaurant's traditional favorites include flounder Florentine, veal cutlets, chicken parmigiana and lasagna. Casual dress; cocktails. **Parking:** on-site. **Cards:** AX, DC, DS, MC, VI.

AMIGO'S ORIGINAL TEX-MEX RESTAURANT &
CANTINA   Lunch: $5-$16   Dinner: $5-$23   Phone: 407/823-7138 **26**
WWW   **Location:** 0.3 mi s of jct SR 50 and 434; in Waterford Lakes Shopping Plaza. 749 N Alafaya Tr 32828. **Hours:** 11 am-10 pm. Closed major holidays. **Features:** In Waterford Lakes Shopping Plaza, the restaurant presents a
Mexican   menu of simple and straightforward Tex-Mex dishes. Prices are reasonable. Casual dress; cocktails. **Parking:** on-site. **Cards:** AX, CB, DC, DS, JC, MC, VI.

BACKYARD BURGER   Lunch: $5-$8   Dinner: $5-$8   Phone: 407/736-0040 **5**
WW   **Location:** Just e of Rouse Rd. 11556 University Blvd 32817. **Hours:** 10:30 pm-10 pm. **Features:** Patrons select from several unusual burgers and chicken sandwiches. Hawaiian chicken has a sliced pineapple ring, while
American   the black jack burger has Cajun seasoning and coleslaw. Casual dress. **Parking:** on-site. **Cards:** MC, VI.

BAJA BURRITO KITCHEN   Lunch: $4-$8   Dinner: $4-$8   Phone: 407/895-6112 **30**
W   **Location:** Just s of SR 50; 2 mi e of I-4, exit 83B; in Colonial Market Center. 2716 E Colonial Dr 32803. **Hours:** 11 am-10 pm. Closed: 4/16, 11/23, 12/25. **Features:** This fast-food shop located in a shopping complex serves
American   good, freshly prepared Tex-Mex dishes. A salsa bar offers a variety of tasty toppings from fresh tomatoes to hot habanero salsa and chopped cilantro. Enjoy a nice made-to-order meal served up fast. Casual dress; beer & wine only. **Parking:** on-site. **Cards:** AX, DC, DS, MC, VI.

BRIO TUSCAN GRILLE   Lunch: $8-$15   Dinner: $8-$23   Phone: 407/351-8909 **49**
WWW   **Location:** I-4, exit 78, just e on Conroy Rd; at The Mall of Millenia. **Hours:** 11 am-10 pm, Fri & Sat-11 pm, Sun-9 pm. Closed major holidays. **Features:** The menu comprises upscale Tuscan fare. The large, airy dining
Italian   room and extensive menu contribute to a comfortable, sophisticated and filling dining experience. Both lunch and dinner service offer all the attentiveness a diner expects, and the food is superlative. From the garlic, spinach and artichoke dip starter to chicken, veal, seafood or pasta entrees, there's enough of a selection for everyone. Casual dress; cocktails. **Parking:** on-site. **Cards:** AX, DS, MC, VI.

(See map and index starting on p. 656)

BROOKLYN PIZZA
Italian

Lunch: $6-$25   **Dinner:** $6-$25   **Phone:** 407/282-0110   38

Location: Just w of jct SR 436. 5681 Pershing Ave 32822. **Hours:** 11 am-10 pm, Fri & Sat-11 pm, Sun noon-9:30 pm. **Features:** The basic eatery prepares fabulous New York-style pizzas, as well as calzones and the Brooklyn Bridge Italian combination plate, which leaves bellies full and happy. Tiramisu is a fabulous choice among the homemade desserts. Casual dress; beer & wine only. **Parking:** on-site. **Cards:** MC, VI.

BUBBALOO'S BODACIOUS BAR-B-QUE
Barbecue

Lunch: $4-$15   **Dinner:** $4-$15   **Phone:** 407/295-1212   42

Location: I-4, exit 75B, 1.5 mi e on Kirkman Rd; jct of Conroy and Kirkman rds. 5818 Conroy Rd 32835. **Hours:** 10 am-9:30 pm, Fri & Sat-10:30 pm, Sun 11 am-9 pm. Closed major holidays. **Features:** Famous for its barbecue and quick-serve lunch and dinner specials, the eatery is a hot spot for fun family dining at a great value. Casual dress; beer only. **Parking:** on-site. **Cards:** MC, VI.

BUBBALOU'S BODACIOUS BBQ
Barbecue

Lunch: $4-$10   **Dinner:** $4-$10   **Phone:** 407/423-1212   9

Location: Just n of SR 50; 1.4 mi n of SR 408 (East-West Expwy). 12100 Challenger Pkwy 32826. **Hours:** 10 am-9 pm, Fri & Sat-10 pm, Sun 11 am-9 pm. **Features:** Famous for its barbecue and quick-serve lunch and dinner specials, the eatery is a hot spot for fun family dining at a great value. Casual dress; beer & wine only. **Parking:** on-site. **Cards:** MC, VI.

CALIFORNIA PIZZA KITCHEN
Italian

Lunch: $7-$26   **Dinner:** $7-$26   **Phone:** 407/384-5689   23

Location: 0.3 mi s of jct SR 50 and 434 (Alafaya Tr); in Waterford Lakes Shopping Plaza. 695 N Alafaya Tr 32828. **Hours:** 11 am-10 pm, Fri & Sat-11 pm. Closed: 11/23, 12/25. **Features:** Gourmet pizzas, such as barbecue chicken and Gorgonzola cheese and pear, contribute to a mouthwatering selection. Desserts are worth the splurge. Casual dress; cocktails. **Parking:** on-site. **Cards:** AX, DS, MC, VI.

CHARLEY'S STEAK HOUSE
Steak House

Dinner: $15-$50   **Phone:** 407/851-7130   53

Location: US 17-92 and 441, 3.8 mi s of jct I-4, exit 80. 6107 S Orange Blossom Tr 32809. **Hours:** 4:30 pm-10 pm, Fri & Sat-11 pm. Closed: 11/23, 12/25. **Reservations:** suggested. **Features:** Specializing in aged steak, chops and chicken grilled over an open flame of oak and orange woods, the casually elegant restaurant offers ample portions and an impressive wine list. Desserts are huge in taste and size, a great value and enough for two. Dressy casual; cocktails. **Parking:** on-site. **Cards:** AX, MC, VI.   🍸

THE CHEESECAKE FACTORY
American

Lunch: $5-$27   **Dinner:** $5-$27   **Phone:** 407/226-0333   48

Location: I-4, exit 78, just e; in Mall at Millenia. 4200 Conroy Rd, SP A148 32839. **Hours:** 11 am-11 pm, Fri & Sat-12:30 am. Closed major holidays. **Features:** Located in a busy shopping mall, this eatery is most noted for its large portions and varieties of homemade cheesecake. The menu's many pages list numerous types of cuisines. Casual dress; cocktails. **Parking:** on-site. **Cards:** AX, DS, MC, VI.

CHOO-CHOO CHURROS ARGENTINEAN RESTAURANT & STEAKHOUSE
Argentine

Dinner: $12-$20   **Phone:** 407/382-6001   34

Location: I-4, exit 82, 3.3 mi e on SR 408 (East-West Expwy); exit 14 (SR 436/Semoran Blvd/International Airport), just s. 5810 Lake Underhill Rd 32807. **Hours:** 5 pm-midnight, Sun 2 pm-10 pm. Closed: 12/25; also Mon & Tues. **Reservations:** accepted. **Features:** The small, intimate eatery caters to the devout carnivore. Huge portions of churrasco, the classic Argentinean steak, are accompanied by garlicky chimichurri sauce. Among other specialties are varied sausages, beef short ribs and grilled sweetbreads. The bilingual staff is pleasantly accommodating. Casual dress; beer & wine only. **Parking:** on-site. **Cards:** AX, CB, DC, MC, VI.

COLLEGE PARK CAFE
American

Lunch: $3-$7   **Phone:** 407/420-9892   10

Location: I-4, exit 85, 1 mi w. 2304 Edgewater Dr 32804. **Hours:** 6 am-3 pm, Sun 7 am-2 pm. Closed major holidays. **Features:** The simple, no-fuss diner's menu offers great value and traditional favorites such as burgers, hot lunches and sandwiches. For breakfast, patrons can try omelets, French toast and pancakes. Casual dress. **Parking:** street.

CRISPERS
American

Lunch: $4-$8   **Dinner:** $4-$8   **Phone:** 407/482-4727   21

Location: 0.3 mi s of jct SR 50 and SR 434 (Alafaya Tr); in Waterford Lakes Shopping Center. 557 N Alafaya Tr 32828. **Hours:** 10:30 am-9 pm, Fri & Sat-10 pm, Sun 11 am-8 pm. **Features:** A healthy alternative for lunch or dinner, the restaurant prepares towering specialty sandwiches on warm, fresh homemade bread. Salad selections with combinations of meats, fruit and cheese are just as tempting. Casual dress. **Parking:** on-site. **Cards:** MC, VI.

CUBAN SANDWICHES TO GO
Cuban

Lunch: $3-$6   **Dinner:** $3-$6   **Phone:** 407/578-8888   3

Location: Just e of Edgewater Dr. 1605 Lee Rd 32810. **Hours:** 10 am-6 pm, Fri 11 am-7 pm, Sat 10 am-7 pm. **Features:** These Cuban sandwiches are the real deal; don't forget the black beans and rice or the fruit soda. Casual dress. **Parking:** on-site.   🏧

DEL FRISCO'S
Steak House

Dinner: $50-$75   **Phone:** 407/645-4443   1

Location: I-4, exit 88, just w. 729 Lee Rd 32810. **Hours:** 5 pm-10 pm, Fri & Sat-11 pm. Closed major holidays; also Sun. **Reservations:** suggested. **Features:** With a clubby atmosphere and a guest list that has included celebrity diners, the restaurant is a longstanding local favorite for USDA prime beef, which is aged, never frozen and cut to order. Among favorites are filet mignon, the 16-ounce bone-in rib-eye and the 24-ounce porterhouse and lobster. In addition to an excellent wine list, guests can order from an extensive selection of single-malt scotches, fine cognacs and Armagnacs. Save room for bread pudding and Mandarin orange cake. Dressy casual; cocktails. **Parking:** on-site and valet. **Cards:** AX, DC, DS, MC, VI.   🍸

FALAFEL CAFE
Middle Eastern

Lunch: $5-$10   **Dinner:** $5-$10   **Phone:** 407/382-6600   6

Location: Just w of SR 434 (Alafaya Tr), just s of University Blvd; in Collegiate Sq. 12140 Collegiate Way 32817. **Hours:** 11 am-8 pm. Closed major holidays; also Sat & Sun. **Features:** Near the University of Central Florida, the cafe is a popular spot for students. Kebabs, pitas, falafel, salads and sandwiches are on the menu. Casual dress. **Parking:** on-site. **Cards:** AX, DS, MC, VI.   ♿M

(See map and index starting on p. 656)

GAIN'S GERMAN RESTAURANT   Lunch: $7-$8   Dinner: $11-$18   Phone: 407/438-8997   52
German
Location: I-4, exit 80, 1.8 mi s; on US 17-92 and 441. 5731 S Orange Blossom Tr 32809. **Hours:** 11:30 am-2:30 & 4:30-9 pm, Fri-10 pm, Sat 4:30 pm-10 pm, Sun 4:30 pm-9 pm. Closed: 7/4, 11/23, 12/24, 12/25; also Mon & Super Bowl Sun. **Reservations:** accepted. **Features:** Featuring authentic German cuisine and a homey decor, the pleasant little restaurant also serves a good selection of German draft and bottled beer. Casual dress; beer & wine only. **Parking:** on-site. **Cards:** AX, DC, DS, MC, VI.

GARGI'S AT LAKE IVANHOE   Lunch: $5-$9   Dinner: $11-$23   Phone: 407-894-7907   15
Italian
Location: I-4, exit 85 (Princeton St), 0.8 mi se. 1414 N Orange Ave 32804. **Hours:** 11:30 am-3 & 5-9 pm, Fri & Sat-11 pm. Closed major holidays. **Reservations:** accepted. **Features:** Good cuisine is served in a small, intimate restaurant that maintains the feel of a New York-style neighborhood eatery. A busy lunch crowd from nearby downtown keeps this place hopping. Wonderful eggplant and a rich cheesecake are menu highlights. Casual dress; beer & wine only. **Parking:** street. **Cards:** AX, DS, MC, VI.

GIOVANNI'S ITALIAN RESTAURANT & PIZZERIA   Lunch: $6-$19   Dinner: $6-$19   Phone: 407/359-5900   4
Italian
Location: 0.5 mi n of jct University Blvd; in University Palms Shopping Plaza. 4250 Alafaya Tr 32765. **Hours:** 11 am-10 pm, Fri & Sat-11 pm, Sun noon-10 pm. **Features:** Pizzas are a specialty here, but the extensive menu of traditional Italian favorites cannot be ignored. Ravioli, lasagna, chicken Marsala, seafood and pasta dishes are just a few tantalizing options. Casual dress; beer & wine only. **Parking:** on-site. **Cards:** AX, DC, DS, MC, VI.

HABANA JOE'S   Lunch: $5-$8   Dinner: $5-$8   Phone: 407/246-0609   8
Cuban
Location: I-4, exit 85, 1 mi w, then 0.3 mi n. 2912 Edgewater Dr 32804. **Hours:** 9:30 am-5 pm. Closed major holidays; also Sun. **Features:** The cafe serves made-to-order sandwiches, salads and traditional Cuban side dishes. Tropical juices, Mojitos, sangria and Spanish wines are a few of the beverage choices. Casual dress; beer & wine only. **Parking:** on-site. **Cards:** MC, VI.

HIGH TIDE HARRY'S   Lunch: $5-$10   Dinner: $8-$30   Phone: 407/273-4422   20
Seafood
Location: Just n on SR 436 from jct SR 50. 925 N Semoran Blvd 32807. **Hours:** 11 am-10 pm, Fri & Sat-11 pm. Closed: 11/23, 12/25. **Features:** This laid-back eatery features a fishing motif. Quality seafood includes all-you-can-eat dinner specials Sun-Thurs. Expect simple presentation at affordable prices. An excellent selection of microbrewed beer is offered with two-for-one specials on Wednesday nights. Casual dress; cocktails. **Parking:** on-site. **Cards:** AX, CB, DC, DS, JC, MC, VI.

HOT DOG HEAVEN   *Menu on aaa.com*   Lunch: $2-$6   Dinner: $2-$6   Phone: 407/282-5746   25
American
Location: SR 50, just w of jct SR 436. 5355 E Colonial Dr 32807. **Hours:** 11 am-6 pm. Closed major holidays. **Reservations:** not accepted. **Features:** Authentic Chicago hot dogs and hand-dipped ice cream are served in a pristine '50s-style cafeteria. Pile on the sauerkraut or choose a chili-cheese combo. A lunch-time favorite, it offers outside seating when crowded. Look for the landmark hot dog sign. Casual dress. **Parking:** on-site. **Cards:** MC, VI.

JACK AND MARY'S   Lunch: $4-$8   Phone: 407/281-1113   37
American
Location: Just s of jct SR 552 and 551; in Curry Ford Shopping Center. 2323 S Goldenrod Rd 32822. **Hours:** 5 am-2 pm, Sun from 7 am. Closed: 11/23, 12/25. **Features:** Locals love the tiny diner, where award-winning breakfasts are available all day. Lunches include classic fare with Southern flavor, such as meatloaf and country fried steak. Casual dress. **Parking:** on-site.

JOHNNY ROCKETS   Lunch: $3-$8   Dinner: $3-$8   Phone: 407/381-9010   22
American
Location: 0.3 mi s of jct SR 50 and SR 434 (Alafaya Tr); in Waterford Lakes Shopping Center. 551 N Alafaya Tr 32828. **Hours:** 11 am-9:30 pm, Fri & Sat-11 pm, Sun-9 pm. Closed major holidays. **Features:** Burgers, hot dogs, grilled cheese and hot fudge sundaes are a few favorites on a menu the whole family will enjoy. Casual dress. **Parking:** on-site. **Cards:** AX, DS, MC, VI.

JO MING GARDEN   Lunch: $5-$9   Dinner: $8-$16   Phone: 407/298-7668   2
Chinese
Location: I-4, exit 46, 0.6 mi w. 1551 Lee Rd 32810. **Hours:** 11:30 am-10 pm. **Features:** Traditional Chinese food of Cantonese, Szechuan and Mandarin origins is offered, as well as many vegetarian selections. Casual dress; cocktails. **Parking:** on-site. **Cards:** MC, VI.

JONNY ROCKETS   Lunch: $4-$10   Dinner: $4-$10   Phone: 407/903-1006   50
American
Location: I-4, exit 78, just e; in Mall at Millenia. 4200 Conroy Rd 32839. **Hours:** 10 am-9 pm, Sun 11 am-7 pm. Closed major holidays. **Features:** Burgers, hot dogs, grilled cheese and hot fudge sundaes are a few favorites on a menu the whole family will enjoy. Casual dress. **Parking:** on-site. **Cards:** MC, VI.

JULIE'S WATERFRONT   Lunch: $5-$12   Dinner: $5-$19   Phone: 407/240-2557   39
Seafood
Location: I-4, exit 81A, 1 mi e on Michigan St, then 2.5 mi s. 4201 S Orange Ave 32806. **Hours:** 11 am-10 pm, Sat from 8 am, Sun 8 am-9 pm, Mon 11 am-9 pm. Closed major holidays. **Features:** The mood is casual and relaxed both in the small dining room and on the rustic covered deck, which overlooks the lake. Casual dress. **Parking:** on-site. **Cards:** AX, DS, MC, VI.

KIM LONG VIETNAMESE CUISINE   Lunch: $6-$12   Dinner: $6-$12   Phone: 407/228-0031   17
Vietnamese
Location: 0.5 mi n of SR 50. 1326 N Mills Ave 32803. **Hours:** 10 am-9 pm. Closed: Sun. **Features:** There are 155 menu choices at the downtown Vietnamese eatery. Rice platters, fried rice and vegetarian dishes are a few of the food selections. Casual dress; beer & wine only. **Parking:** on-site. **Cards:** AX, MC, VI.

(See map and index starting on p. 656)

LE COQ AU VIN **Lunch:** $12-$14 **Dinner:** $16-$29 **Phone:** 407/851-6980 ㊶

French

Location: I-4, exit 81A, 2.3 mi se. 4800 S Orange Ave 32806. **Hours:** 11:30 am-2 & 5:30-10 pm, Sat from 5:30 pm, Sun 5 pm-9 pm. Closed major holidays; also Mon. **Reservations:** suggested. **Features:** The simple setting is reminiscent of a cozy, country cottage. While the candlelight dinner setting appears elegant, the local clientele has come to expect a refined, but more casual, dining experience. The menu provides an interesting blend of country and cosmopolitan fare. Favorites include escargot, onion and herb-seasoned rack of lamb, coq au vin, duck a L'Orange and creme brulee with seasonal berries. Light eaters can request half portions of all entrees. Dressy casual; beer & wine only. **Parking:** on-site. **Cards:** AX, DC, DS, MC, VI.

LE PEEP RESTAURANT **Lunch:** $3-$9 **Phone:** 407/291-4580 ㊵

American

Location: I-4, exit 75B, 1.5 mi e on Kirkman Rd; jct Conroy and Kirkman rds; in Oaks Shopping Plaza. 4666 S Kirkman Rd 32811. **Hours:** 6:30 am-2 pm, Sat & Sun 7 am-2:30 pm. Closed major holidays. **Features:** A hot spot for breakfast and brunch, the fast-paced restaurant serves eggs Benedict, skillet dishes, omelets, crepes and pancakes made any way desired. Come here hungry. Casual dress. **Parking:** on-site. **Cards:** AX, DS, MC, VI.

MAMA B'S **Lunch:** $3-$7 **Phone:** 407/839-3633 (54)

American

Location: Just s of Gore St; downtown. 1101 S Orange Ave 32806. **Hours:** 8:30 am-4 pm. Closed major holidays. **Features:** This fast-paced sub shop, in which 27 varieties of subs are prepared, plays host to many in downtown during lunchtime. Sandwiches, salads and chips are all available as well. Casual dress. **Parking:** on-site.

MARGARITA'S GRILL **Lunch:** $6-$12 **Dinner:** $8-$17 **Phone:** 407/380-2600 ㊱

Mexican

Location: Jct Chickasaw Tr and Lake Underhill Rd; in Rio Pinar Plaza. 587 S Chickasaw Tr 32825. **Hours:** 11 am-3 & 5-9 pm, Fri & Sat 11 am-10 pm, Sun noon-8 pm. Closed major holidays; also Mon. **Features:** The interior is decorated to make diners feel they are eating on an outdoor patio. All dishes are made to order, so expect a bit of a wait. Fajitas and the taco platter are popular choices. Casual dress; cocktails. **Parking:** on-site. **Cards:** AX, MC, VI.

MARIA BONITA **Lunch:** $5-$9 **Dinner:** $5-$12 **Phone:** 407/282-1411 ⑪

Mexican

Location: Just w of SR 434. 10615 E Colonial Dr 32817. **Hours:** 11 am-10 pm, Fri & Sat-11 pm. Closed: 1/1, 12/25. **Features:** Freshly made flaky tortilla chips and salsa are your introduction to this restaurant; the menu is loaded with Mexican fare that is made to order and is well worth the time and effort. Casual dress; cocktails. **Parking:** on-site. **Cards:** AX, DS, MC, VI.

MCCORMICK & SCHMICK'S **Lunch:** $5-$16 **Dinner:** $5-$16 **Phone:** 407/226-6515 ㊻

Seafood

Location: I-4, exit 78, just e, in Mall of Millenia. 4200 Conroy Rd 32839. **Hours:** 11 am-11 pm, Fri & Sat-midnight, Sun-10 pm. Closed major holidays. **Features:** At the top of the menu is a list of fresh fish and what states they are brought in from. Seafood lovers will enjoy the variety of dishes and the creative ways they are prepared. Casual dress; cocktails. **Parking:** on-site. **Cards:** AX, MC, VI.

MIMI'S CAFE **Lunch:** $4-$16 **Dinner:** $4-$16 **Phone:** 407/370-0333 ㊺

American

Location: I-4, exit 78, just e on Conroy Rd. 4175 Millenia Blvd 32839. **Hours:** 7 am-11 pm. Closed: 12/25. **Features:** Breakfast, lunch and dinner are offered throughout the day at this eclectic and popular eatery. With New Orleans inspired decor and a menu that features something for everyone, finding a favorite dish should be no problem. Casual dress; cocktails. **Parking:** on-site. **Cards:** AX, DS, MC, VI.

NUMERO UNO **Lunch:** $4-$7 **Dinner:** $8-$25 **Phone:** 407/841-3840 (55)

Cuban

Location: I-4, exit 81 (Michigan Ave), 1 mi e, then just n. 2499 S Orange Ave 32806. **Hours:** 11 am-3 & 5-9:30 pm, Fri-10 pm, Sat noon-10 pm. Closed major holidays; also Sun. **Features:** Since 1978, the small, family-run restaurant has offered delicious Cuban dishes at reasonable prices. The lengthy menu features spicy beef and pork, arroz con pollo and other palate-tempting traditional fare. Casual dress; beer & wine only. **Parking:** on-site. **Cards:** AX, DS, MC, VI.

OLYMPIA RESTAURANT **Dinner:** $10-$22 **Phone:** 407/273-7836 ⑫

Greek

Location: SR 417, exit 34 (Colonial Dr), just w. 8505 E Colonial Dr 32817. **Hours:** 5 pm-10 pm, Fri & Sat-2 am. Closed major holidays; also Mon. **Features:** The diners and staff, including belly dancers, combine to create a festive atmosphere. Don't miss the tasty cuisine, which features classics such as moussaka, gyros and grilled seafood. Casual dress; cocktails. **Parking:** on-site. **Cards:** AX, CB, DC, DS, MC, VI.

PANERA BREAD **Lunch:** $4-$8 **Dinner:** $4-$8 **Phone:** 407/248-0811 (51)

American

Location: I-4, exit 78, just e; in Mall at Millenia. 4200 Conroy Rd, #253 32839. **Hours:** 7 am-9 pm, Sun 9 am-7 pm. Closed major holidays. **Features:** Located in a shopping area, the restaurant is a great place for healthy sandwiches and homemade soups served in large bread bowls. Numerous varieties of freshly baked breads and bagels make this a popular stop for breakfast. Casual dress. **Parking:** on-site. **Cards:** AX, DS, MC, VI.

PANERA BREAD **Lunch:** $3-$6 **Dinner:** $3-$6 **Phone:** 407/737-3011 ㉘

American

Location: 0.3 mi s of jct Colonial Dr and SR 434. 473 N Alafaya Tr 32828. **Hours:** 6:30 am-9:30 pm, Sun 6 am-8:30 pm. Closed: 12/25. **Features:** Diners order and pick up their soup, salad or "upscale" sandwich at the counter in this casual eatery and bakery, a popular place for a quick bite during or after shopping or a weekend outing with the family. Simple, comfortable tables are offered for eating in, but carry out is another option. Casual dress. **Parking:** on-site. **Cards:** AX, MC, VI.

PATIO CAFE RESTAURANT **Lunch:** $3-$11 **Dinner:** $3-$11 **Phone:** 407/281-4700 ⑲

Cuban

Location: Jct SR 417 and 50, 2 mi w. 6096 E Colonial Dr 32807. **Hours:** 7 am-7 pm. Closed major holidays. **Features:** In a shopping plaza, the quaint cafe prepares Cuban and Spanish food. Cuban sandwiches, flank steaks, rice and beans and plantains are among mouthwatering menu items. Casual dress. **Parking:** on-site. **Cards:** MC, VI.

(See map and index starting on p. 656)

P.F. CHANG'S CHINA BISTRO
Chinese
MC, VI.
Lunch: $7-$22   **Dinner:** $10-$25   **Phone:** 407/345-2888   **47**
Location: I-4, exit 78, just e; in Mall at Millenia. 4200 Conroy Rd, #A144 32839. **Hours:** 11 am-11 pm, Fri & Sat-midnight. Closed major holidays. **Features:** In a busy shopping mall, the eatery nurtures a wonderful atmosphere for dining. Dim lighting enhances the warm gold and wood tones that surround the dining room, where Chinese favorites are served with flair. Casual dress; cocktails. **Parking:** on-site. **Cards:** AX, DS,

THE PITA PIT
American
Lunch: $4-$6   **Dinner:** $4-$6   **Phone:** 407/380-2333   **7**
Location: On University Blvd, 2.2 mi e of SR 417, exit 32A; just w of SR 434 (Alafaya Tr); at Collegiate Square. 12140 Collegiate Way 32817. **Hours:** 11 am-3 am, Sun-11 pm. Closed major holidays. **Features:** The eatery wraps healthy ingredients in a variety of pitas. Chicken Caesar, steak, chicken, club and roast beef pitas are favorites. Casual dress. **Parking:** on-site. **Cards:** MC, VI.

P.R.'S MEXICAN RESTAURANT
Mexican
Lunch: $5-$16   **Dinner:** $5-$16   **Phone:** 407/293-8226   **43**
Location: I-4, exit 75B, 1.5 mi e; jct of Conroy and Kirkman rds. 4750 S Kirkman Rd 32803. **Hours:** 11 am-10 pm, Fri & Sat-11 pm. Closed major holidays. **Features:** The casual eatery has been a favorite among the locals for decades. The menu features Tex-Mex cuisine with all the standard favorites. Casual dress; cocktails. **Parking:** on-site. **Cards:** AX, MC, VI.

ROYAL THAI
Thai
Lunch: $6-$8   **Dinner:** $6-$12   **Phone:** 407/275-0776   **18**
Location: Jct Old Cheney Hwy and Semoran Blvd. 1202 N Semoran Blvd 32807. **Hours:** 11 am-2 & 5-9:30 pm, Fri-10 pm. Closed major holidays. **Features:** More than 75 options of Thai noodles, yum (salads), soups, seafood and curries await guests of the popular restaurant. Thai curries are prepared with delicious coconut milk, and the many variations of seafood and noodles are sure to satisfy. Most flavorful are the four types of duck and the many ginger recipes. Casual dress; beer & wine only. **Parking:** on-site. **Cards:** AX, DC, DS, MC, VI.

SHAKERS AMERICAN CAFE
American
Lunch: $3-$8   **Phone:** 407/422-3534   **16**
Location: I-4, exit 85, 1 mi w, then 0.4 mi s. 1308 Edgewater Dr 32804. **Hours:** 7 am-3 pm, Sat-2 pm. Closed major holidays; also Sun. **Features:** The cafe is busy during the lunchtime rush. Seating is limited, and the decor is simple, but the unusual sandwiches, gourmet salads and homemade desserts are well worth the wait in line. Casual dress. **Parking:** on-site. **Cards:** MC, VI.

SMOKEY BONES
Barbecue
Lunch: $5-$18   **Dinner:** $5-$18   **Phone:** 407/249-2009   **33**
Location: 0.4 mi s of jct SR 50 and 434 (Alafaya Tr); in Waterford Lakes Shopping Center. 303 N Alafaya Tr 32826. **Hours:** 11 am-10 pm, Fri & Sat-11 pm. **Features:** Hand-pulled pork, beef brisket and smoked turkey are among meats that are slow-smoked over aged hickory. Combination platters offer a bit of everything. Steaks, sandwiches, salads and burgers are among other options. The bag of doughnuts dessert is a specialty. Casual dress; cocktails. **Parking:** on-site. **Cards:** AX, DS, MC, VI.

SMOKEY BONES BAR-B-Q AND SPORTS BAR
Barbecue
Lunch: $5-$12   **Dinner:** $9-$16   **Phone:** 407/293-3330   **32**
Location: Just w of Hiawassee Blvd. 7225 W Colonial Dr 32818. **Hours:** 11 am-10 pm, Fri & Sat-11 pm. Closed: 11/23, 12/25. **Features:** Famous for its barbecue and quick-serve lunch and dinner specials, the eatery is a hot spot for fun family dining. The food is a great value. Casual dress; cocktails. **Parking:** on-site. **Cards:** AX, CB, DC, DS, JC, MC, VI.

SONNY'S REAL PIT BBQ
Barbecue
Lunch: $6-$10   **Dinner:** $8-$15   **Phone:** 407/291-6791   **31**
Location: Jct Kirkman Rd. 5967 W Colonial Dr 32808. **Hours:** 11 am-9:30 pm, Fri & Sat-10 pm. Closed: 9/4, 11/23. **Features:** The country-themed restaurant offers slow-cooked barbecue, daily all-you-can-eat specials and a salad bar. Casual dress; beer only. **Parking:** on-site. **Cards:** AX, DS, MC, VI.

SOPRANO'S RISTORANTE & PIZZERIA
Italian
Cards: AX, DC, DS, MC, VI.
Lunch: $5-$15   **Dinner:** $8-$18   **Phone:** 407/898-5808   **29**
Location: I-4, exit 83B/84, 1.8 mi e on SR 50; in Cogtown Shopping Center. 2425 E Colonial Dr 33801. **Hours:** 11 am-10 pm, Fri & Sat-11 pm. **Features:** The walls of the family restaurant are covered with scenes of New York City, the Sopranos cast and baseball memorabilia. Italian favorites, such as chicken parmigiana, veal Marsala, gourmet pizza, calzones and salads, are made to order. Casual dress; beer only. **Parking:** on-site.

STONEWOOD TAVERN AND GRILL
Steak House
Parking: on-site. Cards: AX, DC, DS, MC, VI.
Dinner: $8-$27   **Phone:** 407/297-8682   **44**
Location: 3 mi w on Conroy Rd. 5078 Dr. Phillips Blvd 32819. **Hours:** 5 pm-10 pm, Sat 4 pm-11 pm, Sun noon-9 pm. Closed: 11/23, 12/25. **Features:** Enjoy an array of well-prepared dishes, including filet mignon, rack of lamb and grilled scallops. The dining room is comfortably appointed, with the decor reflecting a beautiful use of stone, wood and earth tones. Servers are knowledgeable and attentive. Dressy casual; cocktails.

STRAUB'S FINE SEAFOOD RESTAURANT
Seafood
cocktails. Parking: on-site. Cards: AX, CB, DC, DS, MC, VI.
Dinner: $12-$29   **Phone:** 407/273-9330   **27**
Location: I-4, exit 83B, 3.8 mi e on SR 50. 5101 E Colonial Dr 32803. **Hours:** 4:30 pm-10 pm, Sun-9 pm. Closed: 11/23, 12/25. **Reservations:** suggested. **Features:** Here you will find seafood prepared in a wide range of styles: traditional, blackened, broiled, baked or mesquite-grilled. The salmon is marinated in Straub's own special sauce. You may also choose pasta dishes and a limited selection of beef and chicken. Casual dress;

TIRAMISU CAFE
Italian
Lunch: $5-$10   **Dinner:** $8-$14   **Phone:** 407/228-0303   **14**
Location: Jct N Orange Ave and Ivanhoe St. 1600 N Orange Ave 32803. **Hours:** 11 am-3 & 5-9 pm, Mon-3 pm, Fri & Sat 11 am-10 pm. Closed major holidays; also Sun. **Features:** In a popular downtown antique district, the eatery entertains patrons with live music three nights a week. Included among the outstanding dishes are such specialty sandwiches as the capri, which is made with buffalo mozzarella and tomato on focaccia bread, and entrees including lobster ravioli, veal Ivanhoe and chicken Siciliano. Chocolate devastation cake is to die for. Outdoor seating is an option. Casual dress; cocktails. **Parking:** on-site. **Cards:** AX, DS, MC, VI.

(See map and index starting on p. 656)

TOOJAY'S ORIGINAL GOURMET DELI   **Lunch:** $5-$10   **Dinner:** $5-$10   **Phone:** 407/249-9475   ㉔
♦♦ ♦♦   **Location:** 0.3 mi s at jct SR 50 and 434; in Waterford Lakes Towne Center. 715 N Alafaya Tr 32828. **Hours:** 8 am-9
American   pm, Fri & Sat-10 pm. Closed: 11/23, 12/25. **Features:** The quick-serve delicatessen offers take-out or dine-
                 in service. A large case displays homemade salads and desserts. Diners also can choose from a large
MC, VI.   selection of sandwiches and entrees. Casual dress; beer & wine only. **Parking:** on-site. **Cards:** AX, DC, DS,

WHITE WOLF CAFE   **Lunch:** $7-$10   **Dinner:** $10-$23   **Phone:** 407/895-9911   ⑬
♦♦ ♦♦   **Location:** I-4, exit 85, just e, then just s. 1829 N Orange Ave 32804. **Hours:** 11 am-4 pm, Tues-Thurs to 10 pm, Fri
American   & Sat-11 pm. Closed major holidays; also Sun. **Reservations:** accepted. **Features:** A good selection of
                 many types of creative cuisine, including many healthy choices, is on offer at White Wolf Cafe. Also featured
MC, VI.   are a soda fountain and an espresso bar. Casual dress; beer & wine only. **Parking:** street. **Cards:** AX,

——————   ***The following restaurant has not been evaluated by AAA***   ——————
but is listed for your information only.

JOHNSON'S DINER   **Phone:** 407/841-0717
fyi   Not evaluated. **Location:** I-4, exit 41, 1 mi sw, jct Robinson St and Parramore Ave. 692 W Robinson St 32801.
             Features: Although the menu changes daily, some things—such as stew beef, smothered pork chops,
Delmonico steak, peach cobbler and sweet potato pie—are always available.

ORLANDO SOUTH   (See maps and indexes p. 666-672, 667-674, 668-678, 670-682)

——————   **WHERE TO STAY**   ——————

AMERICAS BEST VALUE INN & SUITES   **Phone:** (407)351-4410   ㉒
♦♦♦♦   All Year   1P: $59-$99   2P: $59-$99
                 Location: I-4, exit 75A, just s on (SR 435 (Kirkman Rd), then just w. 5858 International Dr 32819. Fax: 407/351-2481.
Small-scale Hotel **Facility:** 241 units. 226 one-bedroom standard units. 15 one-bedroom suites ($99-$129). 2-4 stories,
                 exterior corridors. *Bath:* combo or shower only. **Parking:** on-site. **Terms:** check-in 4 pm, $4 service charge,
small pets only ($50 deposit, $10 extra charge). **Amenities:** voice mail, safes, irons, hair dryers. **Pool(s):** outdoor. **Leisure
Activities:** *Fee:* game room. **Guest Services:** coin laundry, area transportation. **Business Services:** meeting rooms, fax (fee).
Cards: AX, MC, VI.

SOME UNITS
(ASK) (S♦) 🛏 (▯+) (🍸) (♿) (🐾) 🏊 (DATA PORT) (▯) / (✕) (▮) (▣) /
FEE

(See maps and indexes p. 666-672, 667-674, 668-678, 670-682)

AMERISUITES (ORLANDO AIRPORT/NORTHEAST)   *Book at aaa.com*   **Phone: (407)240-3939**   **14**
All Year [ECP]   1P: $90-$200   XP: $10   F
Location: SR 528 (Bee Line Expwy), exit 11, 0.5 mi n on SR 436, just e on TG Lee Blvd, then just s. 7500 Augusta National Dr 32822. Fax: 407/240-3920. **Facility:** 128 one-bedroom standard units. 4 stories, interior corridors. *Bath:* combo or shower only. **Parking:** on-site. **Terms:** [AP], [BP], [CP] & [MAP] meal plans available, **Small-scale Hotel** package plans, small pets only ($10 fee). **Amenities:** voice mail, safes, irons, hair dryers. *Fee:* video games, high-speed Internet. *Some:* dual phone lines. **Pool(s):** heated outdoor. **Leisure Activities:** exercise room. **Guest Services:** complimentary evening beverages: Wed, valet and coin laundry, area transportation-within 2 mi. **Business Services:** meeting rooms, fax (fee). **Cards:** AX, CB, DC, DS, MC, VI. **Special Amenities:** free full breakfast.

SOME UNITS

AMERISUITES (ORLANDO AIRPORT/NORTHWEST)   *Book at aaa.com*   **Phone: (407)816-7800**   **5**
All Year [ECP]   1P: $89-$199   XP: $10   F
Location: SR 528 (Bee Line Expwy), exit 11, 0.5 mi n on SR 436, then just w. 5435 Forbes Pl 32812. Fax: 407/816-0050. **Facility:** 135 one-bedroom standard units. 6 stories, interior corridors. *Bath:* combo or shower only. **Parking:** on-site. **Terms:** package plans, small pets only ($10 fee). **Amenities:** video games **Small-scale Hotel** (fee), high-speed Internet, dual phone lines, voice mail, irons, hair dryers. **Pool(s):** heated outdoor. **Leisure Activities:** exercise room. **Guest Services:** valet and coin laundry, area transportation-within 2 mi. **Business Services:** meeting rooms, fax (fee). **Cards:** AX, CB, DC, DS, MC, VI. **Special Amenities:** free full breakfast.

SOME UNITS

AMERISUITES (ORLANDO/CONVENTION CENTER)   *Book at aaa.com*   **Phone: (407)370-4720**   **55**
All Year   1P: $89-$149   2P: $89-$149   XP: $10   F
Location: I-4, exit 74A, just e, then 0.7 mi s of SR 482 (Sand Lake Rd). 8741 International Dr 32819. Fax: 407/370-4721. **Facility:** 152 one-bedroom standard units. 7 stories, interior corridors. *Bath:* combo or shower only. **Parking:** on-site. **Terms:** cancellation fee imposed, small pets only ($10 fee). **Small-scale Hotel** **Amenities:** voice mail, irons, hair dryers. *Fee:* video games, high-speed Internet. *Some:* dual phone lines. **Pool(s):** heated outdoor. **Leisure Activities:** exercise room. **Guest Services:** valet and coin laundry. **Business Services:** meeting rooms, fax (fee). **Cards:** AX, DC, DS, MC, VI. **Special Amenities:** free full breakfast.

SOME UNITS

AMERISUITES (ORLANDO/UNIVERSAL)   *Book at aaa.com*   **Phone: (407)351-0627**   **13**
All Year [ECP]   1P: $139-$179   2P: $139-$179   XP: $10   F18
Location: I-4, exit 75B, 0.6 mi ne. 5895 Caravan Ct 32819. Fax: 407/351-3317. **Facility:** 151 one-bedroom standard units. 7 stories, interior corridors. *Bath:* combo or shower only. **Parking:** on-site. **Terms:** pets ($10 fee). **Amenities:** video games, voice mail, irons, hair dryers. *Fee:* high-speed Internet, safes. *Some:* dual **Small-scale Hotel** phone lines. **Pool(s):** heated outdoor. **Leisure Activities:** exercise room. **Guest Services:** valet and coin laundry, airport transportation (fee)-Orlando International Airport, area transportation-major attractions. **Business Services:** meeting rooms, fax (fee). **Cards:** AX, CB, DC, DS, JC, MC, VI. **Special Amenities:** free full breakfast.

SOME UNITS

BAYMONT INN & SUITES ORLANDO SOUTH   *Book at aaa.com*   **Phone: (407)240-0500**   **9**
All Year   1P: $85-$105   XP: $7   F18
Location: US 17-92 and 441, just s of SR 528 (Bee Line Expwy); off Florida Tpke, exit 254. 2051 Consulate Dr 32837. Fax: 407/240-5194. **Facility:** 124 units. 121 one-bedroom standard units. 3 one-bedroom suites with whirlpools. 3 stories, interior corridors. *Bath:* combo or shower only. **Parking:** on-site. **Terms:** [ECP] meal **Small-scale Hotel** plan available, small pets only. **Amenities:** video games (fee), voice mail, irons, hair dryers. **Pool(s):** outdoor. **Guest Services:** valet and coin laundry. **Business Services:** meeting rooms, fax (fee). **Cards:** AX, CB, DC, DS, MC, VI. **Special Amenities:** free expanded continental breakfast and free local telephone calls.

SOME UNITS

(See maps and indexes p. 666-673, 667-674, 668-678, 670-685)

BEST WESTERN AIRPORT INN — *Book at aaa.com* — Phone: (407)581-2800 — 23

AAA SAVE WWW — Small-scale Hotel

12/1-4/15 [ECP]	1P: $89-$109	2P: $89-$109	XP: $10	F18
4/16-11/30 [ECP]	1P: $79-$99	2P: $79-$99	XP: $10	F18

Location: SR 528 (Bee Line Expwy), exit 8, just w. 1850 McCoy Rd 32809 (8101 Aircenter Ct, ORLANDO). Fax: 407/581-2810. **Facility:** 95 one-bedroom standard units. 5 stories, interior corridors. *Bath:* combo or shower only. **Parking:** on-site. **Terms:** cancellation fee imposed, $2 service charge. **Amenities:** safes (fee), irons, hair dryers. **Pool(s):** outdoor. **Leisure Activities:** exercise room. **Guest Services:** coin laundry, area transportation (fee). **Business Services:** fax (fee). **Cards:** AX, CB, DC, DS, JC, MC, VI. **Special Amenities:** free expanded continental breakfast and free local telephone calls.

SOME UNITS
⚟🖂 ✈ 🍽️ ⅗M 📺 🎦 ✈ 🎥 DATA PORT 💻 / ✕ 📠 🖨️ /

BEST WESTERN MOVIELAND ORLANDO — *Book at aaa.com* — Phone: (407)351-3900 — 21

AAA SAVE WWW — Small-scale Hotel

All Year	1P: $65-$125	2P: $65-$125	XP: $10	F17

Location: I-4, exit 74A, 1.5 mi n of SR 482 (Sand Lake Rd). Located across from Wet'n Wild. 6233 International Dr 32819. Fax: 407/363-5119. **Facility:** 261 units. 258 one-bedroom standard units, some with whirlpools. 3 one-bedroom suites with whirlpools. 4 stories, interior corridors. *Bath:* combo or shower only. **Parking:** on-site. **Terms:** cancellation fee imposed, $3 service charge. **Amenities:** voice mail, safes (fee), irons, hair dryers. **Dining:** 7:30 am-11 pm. **Pool(s):** heated outdoor. **Leisure Activities:** limited exercise equipment. *Fee:* game room. **Guest Services:** gift shop, valet and coin laundry, area transportation-Universal & Sea World. **Business Services:** meeting rooms, fax (fee). **Cards:** AX, CB, DC, DS, MC, VI. **Special Amenities:** free room upgrade (subject to availability with advance reservations). *(See color ad below)*

SOME UNITS
⚟🖂 🍽️ 📺 🎦 ✈ 🎥 DATA PORT 💻 / ✕ 📠 🖨️ /
FEE

BEST WESTERN PLAZA INTERNATIONAL — *Book at aaa.com* — Phone: (407)345-8195 — 56

AAA SAVE WWW — Small-scale Hotel

All Year	1P: $65-$125	2P: $65-$125	XP: $10	F17

Location: I-4, exit 74A, just e on SR 482 (Sand Lake Rd), then 0.8 mi s. 8738 International Dr 32819. Fax: 407/345-0417. **Facility:** 672 units. 568 one-bedroom standard units, some with efficiencies and/or whirlpools. 104 one-bedroom suites. 4 stories, interior/exterior corridors. *Bath:* combo or shower only. **Parking:** on-site. **Terms:** check-in 4 pm, cancellation fee imposed, $3 service charge. **Amenities:** voice mail, irons, hair dryers. *Fee:* video games, safes. *Some:* high-speed Internet. **Dining:** 8 am-midnight. **Pool(s):** heated outdoor, wading. **Leisure Activities:** whirlpool. *Fee:* game room. **Guest Services:** gift shop, valet and coin laundry, area transportation-major attractions. **Business Services:** fax (fee). **Cards:** AX, CB, DC, DS, MC, VI. **Special Amenities:** free room upgrade (subject to availability with advance reservations). *(See color ad below)*

SOME UNITS
⚟🖂 🍽️ 📺 🎦 ✈ ⊞ 🎥 DATA PORT 💻 / ✕ 📠 🖨️ /

BEST WESTERN UNIVERSAL INN — *Book at aaa.com* — Phone: 407/226-9119 — 5

WWW — Small-scale Hotel

Property failed to provide current rates

Location: I-4, exit 75B, 0.5 mi n, then just e. 5618 Vineland Rd 32819. Fax: 407/370-2448. **Facility:** 70 one-bedroom standard units. 3 stories, interior corridors. *Bath:* combo or shower only. **Parking:** on-site. **Amenities:** high-speed Internet, voice mail, safes (fee), irons, hair dryers. **Pool(s):** outdoor. **Guest Services:** coin laundry. **Business Services:** fax (fee).

SOME UNITS
🍽️ ⅗M 📺 🎦 ✈ 🎥 DATA PORT 💻 / ✕ 📠 🖨️ /

CLARION HOTEL & CONFERENCE CENTER-ORLANDO INTERNATIONAL AIRPORT — *Book at aaa.com* — Phone: (407)859-2711 — 19

AAA SAVE WWWW — Small-scale Hotel

12/1-4/30 [ECP]	1P: $89-$149	2P: $89-$149	
5/1-11/30 [ECP]	1P: $79-$119	2P: $79-$119	

Location: On SR 528 (Bee Line Expwy), exit 9, just w. 3835 McCoy Rd 32812. Fax: 407/313-5900. **Facility:** 204 units. 200 one-bedroom standard units. 4 one-bedroom suites. 2-4 stories, interior/exterior corridors. *Bath:* combo or shower only. **Parking:** on-site. **Terms:** $3 service charge. **Dining:** 6-10 am, 11-2 & 5-10 pm, cocktails. **Pool(s):** heated outdoor, wading. **Leisure Activities:** whirlpool, exercise room. **Guest Services:** gift shop, valet and coin laundry, area transportation-within 5 mi. **Business Services:** conference facilities, fax (fee). **Cards:** AX, DC, DS, MC, VI. **Special Amenities:** free expanded continental breakfast and free local telephone calls.

SOME UNITS
⚟🖂 ✈ 🍽️ 📺 📺 🎦 ✈ 🎥 DATA PORT 💻 / ✕ /

ACCOMMODATIONS
FOR EVERY OCCASION.

On the road, you can count on Carlson hotels to offer the choices
and locations to fit your every need. From full service to economy
hotels, our amenities provide the perfect end to every travel day.
Four brands. One promise. Total satisfaction.

For reservations or information call or visit us online.

800-333-3333
www.radisson.com

800-814-7000
www.parkplaza.com

800-456-4000
www.countryinns.com

800-670-7275
www.parkinn.com

MEMBERS OF THE CARLSON FAMILY OF BRANDS.

A LOCATION FOR EVERY DESTINATION.

Stay Your Own Way[SM] with a full complement of services and amenities. Sleep Number® beds, exclusively at Radisson Hotels & Resorts, let you adjust the mattress firmness at the touch of a button. And you can check in online at your convenience up to seven days in advance with Express Yourself.[SM]

Park Plaza Hotels & Resorts offer excellent service at an outstanding value. With meeting facilities, room service, restaurants, a helpful staff and comfortable rooms, we're totally dedicated to accommodating our guests' every need.

Country Inns & Suites By Carlson provides a warm, inviting stay at an affordable price. Clean rooms, a cozy lobby fireplace, friendly staff and complimentary breakfast all help us earn some of the highest satisfaction ratings in the industry. And our 330 worldwide locations are always right on your way– with easy freeway and interstate access.

Park Inn offers comfortable rooms, a worry-free place to relax and recharge, a helpful staff, and a complimentary breakfast. Every visit, every location, guests can count on Park Inn to be simply, more satisfying.

(See maps and indexes p. 666-673, 667-674, 668-678, 670-685)

CLARION HOTEL UNIVERSAL   *Book at aaa.com*   **Phone:** (407)351-5009

 [SAVE]   All Year   1P: $79-$129   2P: $79-$129

Location: I-4, exit 75A, just e of International Dr. Located adjacent to Wet'n Wild. 7299 Universal Blvd 32819.
Large-scale Hotel   Fax: 407/352-7277. **Facility:** 298 one-bedroom standard units. 7-8 stories, interior corridors. *Bath:* combo or
shower only. **Parking:** on-site. **Terms:** check-in 4 pm, package plans, $3 service charge. **Amenities:** voice
mail, irons, hair dryers. *Fee:* video games, safes. **Dining:** 2 restaurants, 7 am-11 & 5-10 pm, cocktails.
Pool(s): heated outdoor. **Leisure Activities:** whirlpools, lighted tennis court, basketball. *Fee:* game room.
Guest Services: valet and coin laundry, area transportation-major attractions. **Business Services:** meeting rooms, fax (fee).
Cards: AX, CB, DC, DS, MC, VI. *(See color ad below)*   SOME UNITS

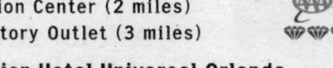

(See maps and indexes p. 666-673, 667-674, 668-678, 670-685)

COMFORT INN INTERNATIONAL   *Book at aaa.com*   Phone: (407)313-4000   49

AAA SAVE   All Year   1P: $59-$149   2P: $59-$149   XP: $5   F1

Location: I-4, exit 74A, just e on SR 482 (Sand Lake Rd), then just s. 8134 International Dr 32819. Fax: 407/313-4001. **Facility:** 112 one-bedroom standard units. 6 stories, interior corridors. *Bath:* combo o shower only. **Parking:** on-site. **Terms:** $3 service charge. **Amenities:** high-speed Internet (fee), voice mail

Small-scale Hotel   safes, irons, hair dryers. **Pool(s):** outdoor. **Guest Services:** gift shop, coin laundry, area transportation major attractions. **Business Services:** fax (fee). **Cards:** AX, DC, DS, MC, VI. **Special Amenities:** fre

continental breakfast and free local telephone calls.

SOME UNITS

[icons]

COMFORT INN UNIVERSAL STUDIOS   *Book at aaa.com*   Phone: 407/363-7886   40

Property failed to provide current rates

Location: I-4, exit 74A, 0.3 mi e on SR 482 (Sand Lake Rd), at Universal Blvd. 6101 Sand Lake Rd 32819.

Small-scale Hotel   Fax: 407/345-0670. **Facility:** 334 one-bedroom standard units. 4 stories, exterior corridors. *Bath:* combo o shower only. **Parking:** on-site. **Terms:** pets ($10 fee). **Amenities:** video games, high-speed Internet (fee)

voice mail, irons, hair dryers. **Pool(s):** outdoor, wading. **Leisure Activities:** exercise room. *Fee:* game room. **Guest Services** gift shop, valet and coin laundry, area transportation. **Business Services:** meeting rooms, fax (fee). *(See color ad p 705)*

SOME UNITS

[icons]

COMFORT SUITES   *Book at aaa.com*   Phone: (407)363-1967   8

All Year [ECP]   1P: $79-$199   XP: $10   F18

Location: I-4, exit 75B, 1 mi n on SR 435 (Kirkman Rd), then e. 5617 Major Blvd 32819. Fax: 407/363-6873

Small-scale Hotel   **Facility:** 101 one-bedroom standard units. 4 stories, interior corridors. *Bath:* combo or shower only. **Parking:** on-site. **Terms:** cancellation fee imposed. **Amenities:** video games (fee), voice mail, irons, hai dryers. **Pool(s):** heated outdoor. **Leisure Activities:** whirlpool, exercise room. **Guest Services:** valet and coin laundry **Business Services:** meeting rooms, fax (fee). **Cards:** AX, CB, DC, DS, MC, VI.

[icons]

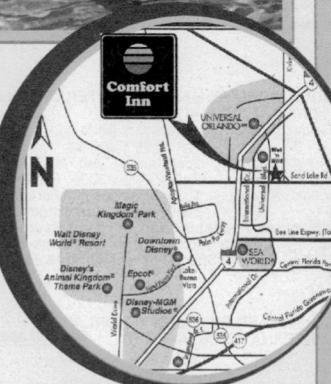

(See maps and indexes p. 666-673, 667-674, 668-678, 670-685)

COMFORT SUITES ORLANDO   *Book at aaa.com*   Phone: (407)351-5050   **64**

(AAA) (SAVE)

12/24-4/30 [ECP]	1P: $109-$129	2P: $109-$129
7/1-11/30 [ECP]	1P: $89-$129	2P: $89-$129
5/1-6/30 [ECP]	1P: $79-$109	2P: $79-$109
12/1-12/23 [ECP]	1P: $69-$99	2P: $69-$99

Small-scale Hotel **Location:** I-4, exit 74A, just w on SR 482 (Sand Lake Rd), then 1.5 mi s. 9350 Turkey Lake Rd 32819. Fax: 407/363-7953. **Facility:** 214 one-bedroom standard units. 3 stories, exterior corridors. *Bath:* combo or shower only. **Parking:** on-site. **Terms:** package plans, $3 service charge, pets ($10 fee). **Amenities:** high-speed Internet, voice mail, irons, hair dryers. *Fee:* video games, safes. **Pool(s):** heated outdoor, wading. **Leisure Activities:** whirlpool, game room. **Guest Services:** sundries, valet and coin laundry, area transportation-major attractions. **Business Services:** fax (fee). **Cards:** AX, DC, DS, MC, VI. **Special Amenities:** free expanded continental breakfast and free newspaper. *(See color ad p 704)*

SOME UNITS

🆂🅳 ➡ 🐾 🔥M 🛋 🎧 🏊 🎦 DATA PORT 🍴 🖥 💻 / ⊠

FEE   FEE

COUNTRY INN & SUITES BY CARLSON-ORLANDO INTERNATIONAL AIRPORT   *Book at aaa.com*   Phone: 407/856-8896   **8**

| All Year [ECP] | 1P: $100-$149 | 2P: $100-$149 |

Small-scale Hotel **Location:** SR 528 (Bee Line Expwy), exit 11, 0.6 mi n on SR 436, then just w. 5440 Forbes Pl 32812. Fax: 407/857-7456. **Facility:** 136 units. 100 one-bedroom standard units, some with whirlpools. 36 one-bedroom suites. 6 stories, interior corridors. *Bath:* combo or shower only. **Parking:** on-site. **Amenities:** high-speed Internet, voice mail, irons, hair dryers. **Pool(s):** heated outdoor. **Leisure Activities:** whirlpool, exercise room. **Guest Services:** valet and coin laundry. **Business Services:** meeting rooms, fax (fee). **Cards:** AX, DC, DS, MC, VI.

SOME UNITS

ASK 🆂🅳 ➡ 🍴 🎧 🏊 🎦 DATA PORT 💻 / ⊠ 🍴 🖥 /

COUNTRY INN & SUITES INTERNATIONAL DRIVE   *Book at aaa.com*   Phone: (407)313-4200   **38**

(AAA) (SAVE)

| All Year [ECP] | 1P: $69-$139 | 2P: $69-$139 | XP: $5 | F18 |

Location: I-4, exit 74A, just e on SR 482 (Sand Lake Rd), then just n. 7701 Universal Blvd 32819. Fax: 407/313-4201. **Facility:** 170 units. 122 one-bedroom standard units, some with whirlpools. 48 one-bedroom suites. 5 stories, interior corridors. *Bath:* combo or shower only. **Parking:** on-site. **Amenities:** high-speed Internet, voice mail, safes, irons, hair dryers. **Pool(s):** outdoor. **Leisure Activities:** exercise room. **Guest Services:** valet laundry, area transportation-Disney. **Business Services:** meeting rooms, fax (fee). **Cards:** AX, DC, DS, MC, VI. **Special Amenities:** free expanded continental breakfast. *(See color ad below)*

SOME UNITS

🆂🅳 🍴 🔥M 🛋 🎧 🏊 🎦 DATA PORT 💻 / ⊠ 🍴 🖥 /

COURTYARD BY MARRIOTT, INTERNATIONAL DRIVE   *Book at aaa.com*   Phone: (407)351-2244   **52**

(AAA) (SAVE)

| 12/26-4/22 & 9/6-11/30 | 1P: $109-$209 | 2P: $109-$209 |
| 12/1-12/25 & 4/23-9/5 | 1P: $99-$189 | 2P: $99-$189 |

Location: I-4, exit 74A, just e on Sand Lake Rd, then just s on International Dr. 8600 Austrian Ct 32819. Fax: 407/351-3306. **Facility:** 151 units. 140 one-bedroom standard units. 11 one-bedroom suites ($149-$329). 4 stories, interior corridors. *Bath:* combo or shower only. **Parking:** on-site. **Terms:** [AP] & [BP] meal plans available, package plans. **Amenities:** high-speed Internet, dual phone lines, voice mail, safes, irons, hair dryers. **Pool(s):** heated outdoor. **Leisure Activities:** whirlpool, exercise room. **Guest Services:** sundries, valet and coin laundry, area transportation-area attractions & within 2 mi. **Business Services:** meeting rooms, business center. **Cards:** AX, DC, DS, MC, VI. **Special Amenities:** free newspaper.

SOME UNITS

🆂🅳 🍴 🔥M 🛋 🎧 🏊 🎦 DATA PORT 💻 / ⊠ 🍴 🖥 /

COURTYARD BY MARRIOTT ORLANDO INTERNATIONAL AIRPORT   *Book at aaa.com*   Phone: (407)240-7200   **12**

(AAA) (SAVE)

| 12/1-5/31 & 10/1-11/30 | 1P: $149-$189 |
| 6/1-9/30 | 1P: $109-$129 |

Location: SR 436, 0.3 mi n of SR 528 (Bee Line Expwy). 7155 N Frontage Rd 32812. Fax: 407/240-8962. **Facility:** 149 units. 138 one-bedroom standard units. 11 one-bedroom suites. 3 stories, interior corridors. Small-scale Hotel *Bath:* combo or shower only. **Parking:** on-site. **Terms:** package plans. **Amenities:** high-speed Internet, dual phone lines, voice mail, irons, hair dryers. **Dining:** 6-11 am. **Pool(s):** heated outdoor. **Leisure Activities:** whirlpool, exercise room. **Guest Services:** sundries, valet and coin laundry. **Business Services:** meeting rooms, business center. **Cards:** AX, CB, DC, DS, JC, MC, VI. **Special Amenities:** free newspaper.

SOME UNITS

🆂🅳 ➡ 🍴 🔥M 🛋 🎧 🏊 🎦 DATA PORT 💻 / ⊠ 🍴 🖥 /

(See maps and indexes p. 666-673, 667-674, 668-678, 670-685)

CRESTWOOD SUITES ORLANDO   *Book at aaa.com*   Phone: 407/587-1800   **1**

Property failed to provide current rates

▼▼ ▼▼
Small-scale Hotel
Location: I-4, exit 79, 4.3 mi s on SR 423 (John Young Pkwy), then 0.6 mi e on SR 482 (Sand Lake Rd). 8010 Presidents Dr 32809. Fax: 407/888-8578. **Facility:** 144 units. 120 one-bedroom standard units. 24 one-bedroom suites with kitchens. 3 stories, interior corridors. *Bath:* combo or shower only. **Parking:** on-site.
Amenities: voice mail, irons. **Guest Services:** coin laundry. **Business Services:** fax (fee).

SOME UNITS

CROWNE PLAZA ORLANDO AIRPORT   *Book at aaa.com*   Phone: (407)856-0100   **1**

AAA SAVE
▼▼ ◆◆
Large-scale Hotel
All Year   1P: $129-$144   2P: $129-$144
Location: SR 528 (Bee Line Expwy), exit 11, 0.8 mi n on SR 436, then just w. 5555 Hazeltine National Dr 32812. Fax: 407/855-7991. **Facility:** 353 units. 352 one-bedroom standard units. 1 one-bedroom suite. 10 stories, interior corridors. *Bath:* combo or shower only. **Amenities:** high-speed Internet (fee), dual phone lines, voice mail, irons, hair dryers. **Dining:** 6 am-midnight, cocktails. **Pool(s):** heated outdoor. **Leisure Activities:** whirlpool, exercise room. **Guest Services:** gift shop, valet laundry, area transportation-within 3 mi. **Business Services:** conference facilities, business center. **Cards:** AX, CB, DC, DS, MC, VI.

SOME UNITS

FEE FEE FEE

CROWNE PLAZA RESORT ORLANDO   *Book at aaa.com*   Phone: (407)239-1222   **66**

AAA SAVE
▼▼ ◆◆
Small-scale Hotel
All Year   1P: $140-$229   2P: $140-$229
Location: I-4, exit 72, just e on SR 528 (Bee Line Expwy) to exit 1, then 2.7 mi s. 12000 International Dr 32821. Fax: 407/239-1190. **Facility:** 101 units. 97 one-bedroom standard units. 4 one-bedroom suites. 5 stories, interior corridors. *Bath:* combo or shower only. **Parking:** on-site. **Terms:** cancellation fee imposed, package plans, $8 service charge. **Amenities:** video games, CD players, high-speed Internet (fee), dual phone lines, voice mail, safes, irons, hair dryers. **Dining:** 7 am-11 pm, cocktails. **Pool(s):** 2 heated outdoor, wading. **Leisure Activities:** whirlpools, lighted tennis court, playground, exercise room, volleyball. *Fee:* game room. **Guest Services:** gift shop, valet and coin laundry, area transportation (fee). **Business Services:** meeting rooms, business center. **Cards:** AX, CB, DC, DS, MC, VI. *(See color ad below)*

SOME UNITS

(See maps and indexes p. 666-673, 667-674, 668-678, 670-685)

CROWNE PLAZA UNIVERSAL   *Book at aaa.com*   Phone: (407)355-0550   **41**

(AAA) (SAVE)   12/1-4/16 & 10/1-11/30   1P: $189-$269   2P: $189-$269   XP: $20   F12

          4/17-9/30   1P: $129-$189   2P: $129-$189   XP: $20   F12

▽▽▽▽   **Location:** I-4, exit 29, 0.5 mi e on SR 482 (Sand Lake Rd), then just n. 7800 Universal Blvd 32819. Fax: 407/355-0504. **Facility:** 400 one-bedroom standard units. 15 stories, interior corridors. *Bath:* combo or

Small-scale Hotel   shower only. **Parking:** on-site. **Terms:** check-in 4 pm, 3 day cancellation notice, [AP] meal plan available. **Amenities:** CD players, dual phone lines, voice mail, safes, irons, hair dryers. *Fee:* video games, high-speed Internet. **Dining:** 2 restaurants, 6:30 am-11 pm, cocktails. **Pool(s):** heated outdoor. **Leisure Activities:** whirlpool, exercise room. *Fee:* game room. **Guest Services:** gift shop, valet and coin laundry, area transportation-major attractions. **Business Services:** conference facilities, business center. **Cards:** AX, CB, DC, DS, JC, MC, VI. **Special Amenities:** early check-in/late check-out and free room upgrade (subject to availability with advance reservations). *(See color ad below)*

SOME UNITS

⑤ⓓ 🍴 🍸 ⓒⓜ 🛗 🎿 🏊 🖨 📶 ☕ / ✕ 🛗 /

DAYS INN-CONVENTION CENTER/NORTH OF SEA WORLD   *Book at aaa.com*   Phone: (407)352-8700   **68**

(AAA) (SAVE)   All Year   1P: $99   2P: $99

      Location: I-4, exit 72, just e to International Dr; SR 528 (Bee Line Expwy), exit 1, just n. 9990 International Dr 32819. Fax: 407/363-3965. **Facility:** 220 one-bedroom standard units. 4 stories, exterior corridors. *Bath:* combo or

▽▽▽▽   shower only. **Parking:** on-site. **Terms:** check-in 4 pm, cancellation fee imposed. **Amenities:** voice mail,

Small-scale Hotel   safes, hair dryers. *Some:* irons. **Dining:** 6 am-11 pm, wine/beer only. **Pool(s):** outdoor. **Leisure Activities:** playground. **Guest Services:** valet and coin laundry. **Business Services:** fax (fee). **Cards:** AX, DC, DS, MC, VI.

SOME UNITS

⑤ⓓ 🍴 ⓒⓜ 🛗 🎿 🏊 🖨 📶 / ✕ 🛗 🛗 /

                                                          FEE   FEE

DOUBLETREE CASTLE HOTEL   *Book at aaa.com*   Phone: (407)345-1511   **54**

(AAA) (SAVE)   All Year   1P: $100-$230   2P: $100-$230   XP: $15   F17

▽▽▽▽   **Location:** I-4, exit 74A, 1 mi se, just e of International Dr; 0.5 mi s of SR 482 (Sand Lake Rd). 8629 International Dr 32819. Fax: 407/248-8181. **Facility:** 216 one-bedroom standard units. 9 stories, interior corridors. *Bath:* combo or shower only. **Parking:** on-site. **Terms:** check-in 4 pm, 3 day cancellation notice-fee imposed, [BP]

Small-scale Hotel   meal plan available, $5 service charge. **Amenities:** voice mail, safes, irons, hair dryers. *Fee:* video games, high-speed Internet. **Dining:** 6:30-10:30 am, also, Cafe Tu Tu Tango, Vito's Chop House, see separate listings. **Pool(s):** heated outdoor. **Leisure Activities:** whirlpool, exercise room. **Guest Services:** valet and coin laundry, area transportation-major attractions. **Business Services:** meeting rooms, fax (fee). **Cards:** AX, DS, MC, VI. **Special Amenities:** early check-in/late check-out and preferred room (subject to availability with advance reservations). *(See color ad below)*

SOME UNITS

🍴 🍸 ⓒⓜ 🛗 🎿 🏊 🖨 📶 🛗 ☕ / ✕ 🛗 /

(See maps and indexes p. 666-673, 667-674, 668-678, 670-685)

DOUBLETREE HOTEL AT THE ENTRANCE TO
UNIVERSAL ORLANDO   *Book at aaa.com*   Phone: 407/351-1000   **11**

Property failed to provide current rates

Location: I-4, exit 75B, 0.7 mi n on SR 435 (Kirkman Rd). Located opposite the main entrance to Universal Studios. 5780 Major Blvd 32819. Fax: 407/363-0106. **Facility:** 742 units. 738 one-bedroom standard units. 4 two-bedroom suites. 18 stories, interior corridors. *Bath:* combo or shower only. **Parking:** on-site. **Terms:** check-in 4 pm. **Amenities:** voice mail, irons, hair dryers. *Fee:* video games, high-speed Internet, safes. **Pool(s):** heated outdoor, wading. **Leisure Activities:** whirlpool, exercise room. **Guest Services:** gift shop, valet and coin laundry, area transportation, beauty salon. **Business Services:** conference facilities, business center. *(See color ad below)*

Small-scale Hotel

SOME UNITS

EMBASSY SUITES HOTEL ORLANDO
INTERNATIONAL DR/C.C.   *Book at aaa.com*   Phone: (407)352-1400   **62**

All Year [BP]   1P: $129-$289   2P: $129-$289   XP: $10   F17

Facility: 244 units. 243 one- and 1 two-bedroom suites. 8 stories, interior corridors. *Bath:* combo or shower only. **Parking:** on-site. **Terms:** check-in 4 pm, 3 day cancellation notice-fee imposed, package plans. **Amenities:** dual phone lines, voice mail, irons, hair dryers. *Fee:* video games, high-speed Internet. *Some:* CD players. **Pool(s):** heated outdoor, heated indoor, wading. **Leisure Activities:** sauna, whirlpools, steamroom, exercise room. *Fee:* game room. **Guest Services:** gift shop, complimentary evening beverages, valet and coin laundry, area transportation. **Business Services:** meeting rooms, business center. **Cards:** AX, CB, DC, DS, MC, VI. *(See color ad p 805)*

Large-scale Hotel

SOME UNITS

EMBASSY SUITES INTERNATIONAL
DRIVE/JAMAICAN CT   *Book at aaa.com*   Phone: (407)345-8250   **48**

All Year [BP]   1P: $129-$229   2P: $129-$229   XP: $10   F18

Location: I-4, exit 74A, just e on Sand Lake Rd, then just s on International Dr. 8250 Jamaican Ct 32819. Fax: 407/352-1463. **Facility:** 246 one-bedroom suites. 8 stories, interior corridors. *Bath:* combo or shower only. **Parking:** on-site. **Terms:** 3 day cancellation notice-fee imposed, package plans. **Amenities:** high-speed Internet, dual phone lines, voice mail, safes, irons, hair dryers. **Pool(s):** indoor/outdoor. **Leisure Activities:** sauna, whirlpool, exercise room. **Guest Services:** gift shop, complimentary evening beverages, valet and coin laundry, area transportation-major attractions. **Business Services:** meeting rooms, business center. **Cards:** AX, CB, DC, DS, JC, MC, VI. **Special Amenities:** free full breakfast and free newspaper.

Small-scale Hotel

SOME UNITS

EMBASSY SUITES ORLANDO AIRPORT   *Book at aaa.com*   Phone: (407)888-9339   **7**

All Year [BP]   1P: $110-$219   2P: $110-$219   XP: $15   F18

Location: SR 528 (Bee Line Expwy), exit 11, 0.5 mi n on SR 436, then just e. 5835 TG Lee Blvd 32822. Fax: 407/856-5956. **Facility:** 174 one-bedroom suites. 7 stories, interior corridors. *Bath:* combo or shower only. **Parking:** on-site. **Terms:** check-in 4 pm. **Amenities:** dual phone lines, voice mail, irons, hair dryers. *Fee:* video games, high-speed Internet. **Pool(s):** heated outdoor. **Leisure Activities:** whirlpool, exercise room. *Fee:* game room. **Guest Services:** gift shop, complimentary evening beverages, valet and coin laundry. **Business Services:** meeting rooms, fax (fee). **Cards:** AX, DC, DS, MC, VI.

Small-scale Hotel

SOME UNITS

EXTENDED STAYAMERICA-ORLANDO
CONVENTION CENTER/SEA WORLD/DISNEY AREA   *Book at aaa.com*   Phone: 407/352-3454   **74**

Property failed to provide current rates

Location: I-4, exit 72, just e on SR 528 (Bee Line Expwy) to exit 1 (International Dr), just s, then just w. 6451 Westwood Blvd 32821. Fax: 407/352-1708. **Facility:** 119 one-bedroom standard units. 3 stories, interior corridors. *Bath:* combo or shower only. **Parking:** on-site. **Terms:** small pets only ($25 fee). **Amenities:** voice mail, irons. **Guest Services:** coin laundry. **Business Services:** fax (fee).

Small-scale Hotel

SOME UNITS

(See maps and indexes p. 666-673, 667-674, 668-678, 670-685)

EXTENDED STAY DELUXE *Book at aaa.com* Phone: (407)903-1500 **57**

▼▼▼ All Year [ECP] 1P: $95-$149 2P: $95-$149
Location: I-4, exit 74A, 0.5 mi e on SR 482 (Sand Lake Rd), then 0.7 mi s. 8750 Universal Blvd 32819.
Small-scale Hotel Fax: 407/903-1555. **Facility:** 137 one-bedroom standard units with efficiencies. 3 stories, interior corridors.
Bath: combo or shower only. **Parking:** on-site. **Terms:** check-in 4 pm. **Amenities:** dual phone lines, voice
mail, irons, hair dryers. *Fee:* video library, high-speed Internet, safes. **Pool(s):** heated outdoor. **Leisure Activities:** whirlpool,
exercise room. *Fee:* game room. **Guest Services:** valet and coin laundry, area transportation. **Business Services:** fax (fee).
Cards: AX, CB, DC, DS, JC, MC, VI.

SOME UNITS
(ASK) (SO) (†¦+) ✦ (&M) (&) (⌂) (⊃) (✕) (VCR) (✻) (DATA PORT) (▤) (⬚) (▣) / (✕) /

EXTENDED STAY DELUXE Phone: 407/248-8010 **2**
(ORLANDO/SOUTHPARK) *Book at aaa.com*
Property failed to provide current rates
▼▼▼ Location: Just sw of jct SR 423 (John Young Pkwy) and 482 (Sand Lake Rd). 8687 Commodity Cir 32819.
Small-scale Hotel Fax: 407/248-9940. **Facility:** 129 one-bedroom standard units with efficiencies. 9 one-bedroom
suites with efficiencies. 3 stories, interior corridors. *Bath:* combo or shower only. **Parking:** on-site.
Terms: small pets only ($10 fee). **Amenities:** dual phone lines, voice mail, irons, hair dryers. *Fee:* video games, high-speed
Internet. **Pool(s):** outdoor. **Leisure Activities:** exercise room. **Guest Services:** valet and coin laundry. **Business Services:**
meeting rooms, fax.

SOME UNITS
(☝) (&) (⌂) (⊃) (✻) (DATA PORT) (▤) (⬚) (▣) / (✕) (VCR) /
FEE   FEE

FAIRFIELD INN & SUITES AT UNIVERSAL STUDIOS
ORLANDO *Book at aaa.com* Phone: 407/581-5600 **4**
▼▼▼ 12/1-4/15 & 11/1-11/30 [ECP] 1P: $79-$119 2P: $79-$119
6/1-10/31 [ECP] 1P: $79-$109 2P: $79-$109
4/16-5/31 [ECP] 1P: $79-$99 2P: $79-$99
Small-scale Hotel Location: I-4, exit 75B, 1 mi n on SR 435 (Kirkman Rd), then just e. 5614 Vineland Rd 32819. Fax: 407/581-5601.
Facility: 116 one-bedroom standard units. 6 stories, interior corridors. *Bath:* combo or shower only. **Parking:** on-site.
Amenities: high-speed Internet, voice mail, irons, hair dryers. *Some:* dual phone lines. **Pool(s):** outdoor. **Leisure
Activities:** whirlpool, exercise room. **Guest Services:** valet and coin laundry. **Business Services:** fax (fee). **Cards:** AX, CB,
DC, DS, JC, MC, VI. *(See color ad p 693)*

SOME UNITS
(ASK) (SO) (&) (⌂) (⊃) (✻) (DATA PORT) (▣) / (✕) (▤) (⬚) /

FAIRFIELD INN & SUITES BY
MARRIOTT-INTERNATIONAL COVE *Book at aaa.com* Phone: (407)351-7000 **36**
▼▼▼ All Year 1P: $77-$119 2P: $77-$119
Location: I-4, exit 74A, just e on SR 482 (Sand Lake Rd), then left. 7495 Canada Ave 32819. Fax: 407/351-0052.
Facility: 200 one-bedroom standard units. 5 stories, interior corridors. *Bath:* combo or shower only.
Small-scale Hotel **Parking:** on-site. **Terms:** [ECP] meal plan available. **Amenities:** voice mail, irons, hair dryers. *Some:* CD
players. **Pool(s):** heated outdoor. **Leisure Activities:** whirlpool, exercise room. *Fee:* game room. **Guest Services:** sundries,
valet and coin laundry, area transportation. **Business Services:** fax (fee). **Cards:** AX, CB, DC, DS, JC, MC, VI.

SOME UNITS
(ASK) (†¦+) (&M) (&) (⌂) (⊃) (✕) (✻) (DATA PORT) (▣) / (✕) (▤) (⬚) /

FAIRFIELD INN BY MARRIOTT-AIRPORT *Book at aaa.com* Phone: 407/888-2666 **3**
Property failed to provide current rates
▼▼▼ Location: SR 528 (Bee Line Expwy), exit 11, 0.5 mi n on SR 436, then just e. 7100 Augusta National Dr 32822.
Fax: 407/888-8464. **Facility:** 139 one-bedroom standard units, some with whirlpools. 4 stories, interior corridors.
Small-scale Hotel *Bath:* combo or shower only. **Parking:** on-site. **Amenities:** high-speed Internet, voice mail, irons,
hair dryers. **Pool(s):** heated outdoor. **Leisure Activities:** whirlpool, exercise room. **Guest Services:** valet and coin laundry.
Business Services: meeting rooms, fax (fee).

SOME UNITS
(✈) (†¦+) (&) (⌂) (⊃) (✻) (DATA PORT) / (✕) (▤) (⬚) /

THE FLORIDA MALL HOTEL *Book at aaa.com* Phone: (407)859-1500 **3**
(AAA) (SAVE) All Year 1P: $107-$209 2P: $117-$219 XP: $15 F18
Location: Just s of jct Sand Lake Rd and S Orange Blossom Tr; south end of the Florida Mall. 1500 Sand Lake Rd
▼▼▼ 32809. Fax: 407/855-1585. **Facility:** 510 units. 508 one-bedroom standard units. 2 one-bedroom suites with
whirlpools. 11 stories, interior corridors. *Bath:* combo or shower only. **Parking:** on-site and valet.
Large-scale Hotel **Amenities:** video games (fee), dual phone lines, voice mail, irons, hair dryers. **Dining:** 6 am-11 pm,
cocktails. **Pool(s):** heated outdoor. **Leisure Activities:** whirlpool, exercise room. **Guest Services:** gift shop,
valet laundry. **Business Services:** conference facilities, business center. **Cards:** AX, CB, DC, DS, MC, VI.

SOME UNITS
(SO) (†¦) (Y) (&M) (&) (⌂) (⊃) (✻) (DATA PORT) (▣) / (✕) (▤) /

HAMPTON INN AIRPORT *Book at aaa.com* Phone: 407/888-2995 **6**
Property failed to provide current rates
▼▼▼ Location: SR 528 (Bee Line Expwy), exit 11, 0.5 mi n on SR 436, then just e. 5767 TG Lee Blvd 32822.
Fax: 407/888-2418. **Facility:** 123 one-bedroom standard units. 7 stories, interior corridors. *Bath:* combo or
Small-scale Hotel shower only. **Parking:** on-site. **Amenities:** high-speed Internet, voice mail, irons, hair dryers. **Pool(s):**
outdoor. **Leisure Activities:** limited exercise equipment. **Guest Services:** valet and coin laundry. **Business Services:** meeting
rooms, fax (fee).

SOME UNITS
(✈) (†¦+) (&M) (&) (⌂) (⊃) (✻) (DATA PORT) (▤) (⬚) (▣) / (✕) /

(See maps and indexes p. 666-672, 667-674, 668-678, 670-682)

HAMPTON INN & SUITES   *Book at aaa.com*   **Phone:** (407)313-3030   34

(AAA) (SAVE)   All Year   1P: $89-$149   2P: $94-$154
▼▼▼▼   **Location:** I-4, exit 74A, e on Sand Lake Rd, then just n. 7448 International Dr 32819. **Fax:** 407/313-3031. **Facility:** 108 one-bedroom standard units. 6 stories, interior corridors. *Bath:* combo or shower only. **Parking:** on-site.
Amenities: video games (fee), high-speed Internet, dual phone lines, voice mail, irons, hair dryers. **Pool(s):**
Small-scale Hotel   heated outdoor. **Leisure Activities:** exercise room. *Fee:* game room. **Guest Services:** valet and coin laundry.
Business Services: meeting rooms, fax (fee). **Cards:** AX, CB, DC, DS, MC, VI. **Special Amenities:** free
expanded continental breakfast and free local telephone calls. *(See color ad below)*

SOME UNITS

[icons] / ⊠ /

HAMPTON INN AT UNIVERSAL STUDIOS   *Book at aaa.com*   **Phone:** (407)351-6716   3

(AAA) (SAVE)   All Year [BP]   1P: $79-$179   2P: $79-$179
▼▼▼▼   **Location:** I-4, exit 75B, 1 mi n on SR 435 (Kirkman Rd), then just e. 5621 Windhover Dr 32819. **Fax:** 407/363-1711.
Facility: 120 one-bedroom standard units. 5 stories, interior corridors. *Bath:* combo or shower only. **Parking:**
on-site. **Terms:** check-in 4 pm, cancellation fee imposed. **Amenities:** high-speed Internet, voice mail, irons,
Small-scale Hotel   hair dryers. **Pool(s):** outdoor. **Leisure Activities:** *Fee:* game room. **Guest Services:** valet laundry, area
transportation-major attractions. **Business Services:** meeting rooms, fax. **Cards:** AX, DC, DS, MC, VI.
Special Amenities: free full breakfast and free local telephone calls. *(See color ad p 693)*

SOME UNITS

[icons] / ⊠ [icons] /

FEE FEE

HAMPTON INN-CONVENTION CENTER   *Book at aaa.com*   **Phone:** (407)354-4447   61

(AAA) (SAVE)   All Year [BP]   1P: $79-$159   2P: $79-$159
▼▼▼▼   **Location:** I-4, exit 74A, 0.5 mi e on SR 482 (Sand Lake Rd), then 0.9 mi s. 8900 Universal Blvd 32819.
Fax: 407/354-3031. **Facility:** 170 one-bedroom standard units. 7 stories, interior corridors. *Bath:* combo or
shower only. **Parking:** on-site. **Terms:** cancellation fee imposed, package plans. **Amenities:** video games (fee),
Small-scale Hotel   high-speed Internet, dual phone lines, voice mail, irons, hair dryers. **Pool(s):** heated outdoor. **Leisure
Activities:** exercise room. **Guest Services:** valet and coin laundry. **Business Services:** meeting rooms, PC,
fax (fee). **Cards:** AX, CB, DC, DS, JC, MC, VI. **Special Amenities: free full breakfast and free newspaper.**

SOME UNITS

[icons] / ⊠ [icons] /

FEE   FEE FEE

HAMPTON INN-FLORIDA MALL   *Book at aaa.com*   **Phone:** (407)859-4100   5

(AAA) (SAVE)   All Year [BP]   1P: $89-$119   2P: $89-$119
▼▼▼▼   **Location:** On US 17-92 and 441, 0.5 mi n of Florida Tpke, exit 254. 8601 S Orange Blossom Tr 32809.
Fax: 407/240-4736. **Facility:** 128 one-bedroom standard units. 2 stories, interior corridors. *Bath:* combo or
shower only. **Parking:** on-site. **Amenities:** dual phone lines, voice mail, irons, hair dryers. **Pool(s):** outdoor.
Small-scale Hotel   **Guest Services:** valet and coin laundry. **Business Services:** meeting rooms, fax. **Cards:** AX, CB, DC, DS, JC,
MC, VI. **Special Amenities: free full breakfast and free local telephone calls.** *(See color ad p 693)*

SOME UNITS

[icons] / ⊠ [icons] /

FEE

(See maps and indexes p. 666-673, 667-674, 668-678, 670-685)

HAMPTON INN-SOUTH OF UNIVERSAL STUDIOS   *Book at aaa.com*   Phone: 407/345-1112   26
▼▼▼▼   Property failed to provide current rates
Small-scale Hotel   **Location:** I-4, exit 75B, 0.8 mi s on SR 435 (Kirkman Rd). 7110 S Kirkman Rd 32819. Fax: 407/352-6591. **Facility:** 170 units. 169 one-bedroom standard units, some with whirlpools. 1 one-bedroom suite. 8 stories, interior corridors. *Bath:* combo or shower only. **Parking:** on-site. **Amenities:** high-speed Internet, voice mail, irons, hair dryers. **Pool(s):** outdoor, wading. **Leisure Activities:** exercise room. *Fee:* game room. **Business Services:** meeting rooms, fax (fee). *(See color ad below)*

SOME UNITS

🛗➕ &M 🔆 📶 ⇔ 📺 DATAPORT 🖥 📠 💻 /✕/

HAWTHORN SUITES ORLANDO   *Book at aaa.com*   Phone: (407)351-6600   73
▼▼▼▼   All Year [BP]   1P: $79-$189   2P: $79-$189
Small-scale Hotel   **Location:** I-4, exit 72, just e on SR 528 (Bee Line Expwy) to exit 1, then just s. 6435 Westwood Blvd 32821. Fax: 407/351-1977. **Facility:** 150 units. 30 one-bedroom standard units. 120 one-bedroom suites with kitchens. 5 stories, interior corridors. **Parking:** on-site. **Terms:** check-in 4 pm, cancellation fee imposed. **Amenities:** video library (fee), video games, voice mail, irons, hair dryers. **Pool(s):** heated outdoor, wading. **Leisure Activities:** whirlpool, playground, exercise room. *Fee:* game room. **Guest Services:** gift shop, valet and coin laundry, area transportation. **Business Services:** meeting rooms, fax (fee). **Cards:** AX, DC, DS, MC, VI. *(See color ad below)*

SOME UNITS

ASK S/D 🛗➕ 📶 ⇔ ✕ VCR 📺 DATAPORT 🖥 📠 💻 /✕/

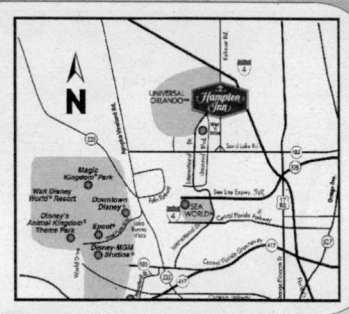

(See maps and indexes p. 666-673, 667-674, 668-678, 670-685)

HAWTHORN SUITES ORLANDO AIRPORT   *Book at aaa.com*   Phone: (407)438-2121 **13**

	1/1-4/30	1P: $99-$149	2P: $99-$149
	5/1-11/30	1P: $95-$139	2P: $95-$139
	12/1-12/31	1P: $89-$129	2P: $89-$129

Small-scale Hotel **Location:** SR 528 (Bee Line Expwy), exit 11, 0.5 mi n on SR 436, just e, then just s. 7450 Augusta National Dr 32822. **Fax:** 407/438-2275. **Facility:** 135 units. 129 one- and 6 two-bedroom suites, some with efficiencies or kitchens. 3 stories, interior corridors. *Bath:* combo or shower only. **Parking:** on-site. **Terms:** cancellation fee imposed, pets ($50 extra charge). **Amenities:** CD players, high-speed Internet, dual phone lines, voice mail, fax, safes, irons, hair dryers. **Pool(s):** heated outdoor. **Leisure Activities:** whirlpool, exercise room, sports court, basketball, volleyball. **Guest Services:** sundries, complimentary evening beverages, valet and coin laundry, area transportation-within 2 mi. **Business Services:** meeting rooms, business center. **Cards:** AX, CB, DC, DS, JC, MC, VI. **Special Amenities:** free full breakfast and early check-in/late check-out. *(See color ad below)*

SOME UNITS

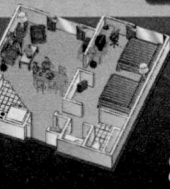

(See maps and indexes p. 666-673, 667-674, 668-678, 670-685)

HAWTHORN SUITES UNIVERSAL ORLANDO *Book at aaa.com* Phone: (407)581-2151 **39**

(AAA) (SAVE) All Year [BP] 1P: $79-$149 2P: $79-$149

▼▼▼ **Location:** Just e of jct Sand Lake Rd and International Dr. 7601 Canada Dr 32819. Fax: 407/581-2152. **Facility:** 143 units. 133 one- and 10 two-bedroom suites with kitchens. 6 stories, interior corridors. *Bath:* combo or shower only. **Parking:** on-site. **Terms:** cancellation fee imposed, package plans. **Amenities:** CD

Small-scale Hotel players, high-speed Internet (fee), dual phone lines, voice mail, safes, irons, hair dryers. **Pool(s):** heated outdoor. **Leisure Activities:** whirlpool, gas grills, exercise room, sports court. *Fee:* game room. **Guest Services:** complimentary evening beverages, valet and coin laundry, area transportation-major attractions. **Business Services:** meeting rooms, fax (fee). **Cards:** AX, CB, DC, DS, MC, VI. **Special Amenities:** free full breakfast and free local telephone calls. *(See color ad below)*

SOME UNITS

**HILTON GARDEN INN-INTERNATIONAL DR
NORTH/UNIVERSAL STUDIOS** *Book at aaa.com* Phone: (407)363-9332 **16**

▼▼▼ 12/22-4/23 1P: $119-$199 2P: $119-$199 XP: $10 F18
4/24-11/30 1P: $89-$169 2P: $89-$169 XP: $10 F18
Small-scale Hotel 12/1-12/21 1P: $89-$149 2P: $89-$149 XP: $10 F18

Location: I-4, exit 75A, just w of SR 435, then just n. 6623 Hospitality Way 32819. Fax: 407/363-9335. **Facility:** 158 one-bedroom standard units. 6 stories, interior corridors. *Bath:* combo or shower only. **Parking:** on-site. **Terms:** 2-6 night minimum stay - seasonal and/or weekends, cancellation fee imposed, [BP] meal plan available, package plans. **Amenities:** dual phone lines, voice mail, irons, hair dryers. *Fee:* video games, high-speed Internet. **Pool(s):** heated outdoor. **Leisure Activities:** whirlpool, putting green, exercise room, game room. **Guest Services:** sundries, valet and coin laundry, area transportation. **Business Services:** meeting rooms, business center. **Cards:** AX, CB, DC, DS, JC, MC, VI.

SOME UNITS

**HILTON GARDEN INN ORLANDO AT SEAWORLD
INTERNATIONAL CENTER** *Book at aaa.com* Phone: (407)354-1500 **78**

(AAA) (SAVE) All Year 1P: $109-$189 2P: $109-$189 XP: $10 F17

▼▼▼ **Location:** I-4, exit 72, 1 mi e to International Dr, then 0.4 mi w. 6850 Westwood Blvd 32821. Fax: 407/354-1528. **Facility:** 233 units. 226 one-bedroom standard units. 7 one-bedroom suites. 8 stories, interior corridors.

Small-scale Hotel *Bath:* combo or shower only. **Parking:** on-site. **Terms:** check-in 4 pm, cancellation fee imposed, package plans. **Amenities:** video games (fee), high-speed Internet, dual phone lines, voice mail, irons, hair dryers. **Dining:** 6:30 am-10:30 pm, cocktails. **Pool(s):** heated outdoor. **Leisure Activities:** whirlpool, exercise room. **Guest Services:** sundries, valet and coin laundry, area transportation-major attractions. **Business Services:** meeting rooms, business center. **Cards:** AX, CB, DC, DS, JC, MC, VI. *(See color ad p 716)*

SOME UNITS

(See maps and indexes p. 666-673, 667-674, 668-678, 670-685)

HILTON GARDEN INN ORLANDO INTERNATIONAL AIRPORT *Book at aaa.com*   **Phone:** 407/240-3725   **11**

▼▼▼   Property failed to provide current rates
Location: SR 528 (Bee Line Expwy), exit 11, 0.5 mi n on SR 436, just e, then just s. 7300 Augusta National Dr 32822.
Small-scale Hotel   Fax: 407/240-3825. **Facility:** 132 units. 129 one-bedroom standard units, some with whirlpools. 3 one-bedroom suites. 4 stories, interior corridors. *Bath:* combo or shower only. **Parking:** on-site.
Amenities: video games (fee), high-speed Internet, dual phone lines, voice mail, irons, hair dryers. **Pool(s):** outdoor. **Leisure Activities:** exercise room. **Guest Services:** valet and coin laundry. **Business Services:** meeting rooms, business center.
SOME UNITS

HOLIDAY HOMES OF ORLANDO   **Phone:** (407)240-5527   **10**

(AAA) (SAVE)   All Year   1P: $99-$269   2P: $99-$269
▼▼▼   **Location:** 0.5 mi s of jct Florida Tpke, exit 254, then e on Taft-Vineland; in Cypress Park Plaza Business Park. 9521 S
Vacation Home   Orange Blossom Trail, Suite 103 32837. Fax: 407/240-5530. **Facility:** This property offers professionally decorated homes with full kitchens near shops and attractions. 75 vacation homes with pools. 1-2 stories, exterior corridors. **Parking:** on-site. **Terms:** check-in 4 pm, 4 night minimum stay, 30 day cancellation notice-fee imposed, weekly rates available. **Amenities:** irons. **Guest Services:** complimentary laundry.
Business Services: fax (fee). **Cards:** MC, VI. **Special Amenities:** free local telephone calls. *(See color ad below)*

(See maps and indexes p. 666-673, 667-674, 668-678, 670-685)

HOLIDAY INN & SUITES AT UNIVERSAL ORLANDO   *Book at aaa.com*   Phone: (407)351-3333   12

(AAA) [SAVE]

▽▽▽▽

Small-scale Hotel

All Year   1P: $89-$169   2P: $89-$169
Location: I-4, exit 75B, 0.5 mi n on SR 435 (Kirkman Rd). 5905 S Kirkman Rd 32819. Fax: 407/351-3577. **Facility:** 390 units. 257 one-bedroom standard units. 94 one- and 39 two-bedroom suites ($119-$239). 10 stories, interior corridors. *Bath:* combo or shower only. **Parking:** on-site. **Terms:** check-in 4 pm, 3 day cancellation notice-fee imposed, package plans, pets ($50 fee). **Amenities:** video games, high-speed Internet, voice mail, irons, hair dryers. *Some:* dual phone lines, safes (fee). **Dining:** 6:30 am-11 pm, cocktails. **Pool(s):** heated outdoor, wading. **Leisure Activities:** exercise room. *Fee:* game room. **Guest Services:** gift shop, valet and coin laundry, area transportation-selected attractions. **Business Services:** meeting rooms, business center. **Cards:** AX, CB, DC, DS, VI. *(See color ad below)*

SOME UNITS

[icons] [SD] [🐾] [🍽] [Y] [👤M] [🎬] [📷] [🏊] [👔] [DATA PORT] [💻] / [✕] [🔌] [🍽] /
FEE

HOLIDAY INN EXPRESS FLORIDA MALL   *Book at aaa.com*   Phone: (407)851-8200   6

▽▽▽▽

Small-scale Hotel

All Year   1P: $175-$200
Location: Florida Tpke, exit 254, just n. 8820 S Orange Blossom Tr 32809. Fax: 407/855-7153. **Facility:** 162 units. 137 one-bedroom standard units. 25 one-bedroom suites ($200-$250). 2 stories (no elevator), interior corridors. *Bath:* combo or shower only. **Parking:** on-site. **Terms:** 2-7 night minimum stay - seasonal, cancellation fee imposed, [ECP] meal plan available, package plans. **Amenities:** high-speed Internet, dual phone lines, voice mail, irons, hair dryers. **Pool(s):** outdoor, wading. **Leisure Activities:** exercise room. **Guest Services:** valet and coin laundry, area transportation (fee). **Business Services:** meeting rooms. **Cards:** AX, DC, DS, MC, VI.

SOME UNITS

[ASK] [SD] [✈] [🍽] [👤M] [🎬] [📷] [🏊] [👔] [DATA PORT] [🔌] [🍽] [💻] / [✕] /

HOLIDAY INN EXPRESS ORLANDO
INTERNATIONAL AIRPORT   *Book at aaa.com*   Phone: 407/581-7900   17

▽▽▽

Small-scale Hotel

Property failed to provide current rates

Location: SR 528 (Bee Line Expwy), exit 9, just n. 7900 Conway Rd 32812. Fax: 407/581-7901. **Facility:** 107 one-bedroom standard units, some with efficiencies. 4 stories, interior corridors. *Bath:* combo or shower only. **Parking:** on-site. **Amenities:** high-speed Internet, voice mail, irons, hair dryers. **Pool(s):** outdoor. **Leisure Activities:** limited exercise equipment. **Guest Services:** valet laundry. **Business Services:** meeting rooms, business center.

SOME UNITS

[✈] [👤M] [🎬] [📷] [🏊] [👔] [DATA PORT] [🔌] [🍽] [💻] / [✕] /

HOLIDAY INN HOTEL &
SUITES/ORLANDO/ORANGE COUNTY CONVENTION CENTER   *Book at aaa.com*   Phone: (407)581-9001   44

(AAA) [SAVE]

▽▽▽▽

Small-scale Hotel

All Year   1P: $99-$179   2P: $99-$179
Location: I-4, exit 74A, 0.5 mi e on SR 482 (Sand Lake Rd), then just s; exit 29A westbound. 8214 Universal Blvd 32819. Fax: 407/581-9002. **Facility:** 150 units. 115 one-bedroom standard units. 35 one-bedroom suites with kitchens. 6 stories, interior corridors. *Bath:* combo or shower only. **Parking:** on-site. **Terms:** cancellation fee imposed, [BP] meal plan available, $3 service charge. **Amenities:** high-speed Internet, dual phone lines, voice mail, irons, hair dryers. **Dining:** 6 am-9:30 & 5-10 pm, cocktails. **Pool(s):** outdoor. **Leisure Activities:** whirlpool, exercise room. **Guest Services:** valet and coin laundry. **Business Services:** meeting rooms, business center. **Cards:** AX, CB, DC, DS, MC, VI. **Special Amenities:** free local telephone calls. *(See color ad p 693)*

SOME UNITS

[SD] [✈] [🍽] [Y] [👤M] [🎬] [📷] [🏊] [👔] [DATA PORT] [🔌] [💻] / [✕] /
FEE

HOLIDAY INN-INTERNATIONAL DRIVE RESORT   *Book at aaa.com*   Phone: (407)351-3500   27

▽▽▽▽

Small-scale Hotel

12/24-4/15	1P: $119-$159	2P: $119-$159	XP: $10	F18
4/16-11/30	1P: $99-$149	2P: $99-$149	XP: $10	F18
12/1-12/23	1P: $89-$129	2P: $89-$129	XP: $10	F18

Location: I-4, exit 74A, just e on SR 482 (Sand Lake Rd), then 0.5 mi n. 6515 International Dr 32819. Fax: 407/351-5727. **Facility:** 652 units. 646 one-bedroom standard units. 6 one-bedroom suites, some with efficiencies (no utensils). 2-12 stories, interior/exterior corridors. *Bath:* combo or shower only. **Parking:** on-site. **Terms:** check-in 4 pm, cancellation fee imposed, [AP], [BP] & [CP] meal plans available, $4 service charge, pets ($25 fee, $75 deposit). **Amenities:** video games (fee), voice mail, safes, irons, hair dryers. *Some:* fax. **Pool(s):** heated outdoor, wading. **Leisure Activities:** whirlpool, exercise room, shuffleboard, volleyball. **Guest Services:** gift shop, valet and coin laundry, area transportation. **Business Services:** conference facilities, business center. **Cards:** AX, CB, DC, DS, JC, MC, VI.

SOME UNITS

[ASK] [🐾] [🍽] [Y] [👤M] [🎬] [📷] [🏊] [✕] [👔] [DATA PORT] [🔌] [🍽] [💻] / [✕] /
FEE

(See maps and indexes p. 666-673, 667-674, 668-678, 670-685)

HOLIDAY INN SELECT ORLANDO INTERNATIONAL
AIRPORT *Book at aaa.com*   **Phone:** (407)851-6400   **9**

1/1-4/30	1P: $169-$219	2P: $169-$219
12/1-12/31	1P: $159-$199	2P: $159-$199
10/1-11/30	1P: $139-$189	2P: $139-$189
5/1-9/30	1P: $129-$169	2P: $129-$169

Small-scale Hotel **Location:** SR 528 (Bee Line Expwy), exit 11, 0.5 mi n on SR 436, then just e. 5750 TG Lee Blvd 32822. **Fax:** 407/240-3717. **Facility:** 288 one-bedroom standard units. 7 stories, interior corridors. *Bath:* combo or shower only. **Parking:** on-site. **Terms:** [BP] meal plan available. **Amenities:** video games (fee), high-speed Internet, voice mail, irons, hair dryers. **Dining:** 6 am-11 pm, cocktails. **Pool(s):** heated outdoor. **Leisure Activities:** saunas, whirlpool, 2 lighted tennis courts, exercise room, basketball, volleyball. **Guest Services:** gift shop, valet and coin laundry, area transportation-within 3 mi. **Business Services:** conference facilities, business center. **Cards:** AX, CB, DC, DS, JC, MC, VI. **Special Amenities:** free newspaper.

SOME UNITS
🛬 🍴 🍸 🔊M 🅿 ⊘ ⇄ 🖨 🎥 📠 ▣ / ⊠ 📧 / FEE

HOMESTEAD STUDIO SUITES
HOTEL-ORLANDO/SOUTH *Book at aaa.com*   **Phone:** (407)352-5577   **4**

All Year	1P: $44-$69	2P: $49-$74 XP: $5 F17

Location: Just sw of jct SR 423 (John Young Pkwy) and 482 (Sand Lake Rd). 4101 Equity Row 32819.
Small-scale Hotel **Fax:** 407/352-2029. **Facility:** 135 one-bedroom standard units with efficiencies. 3 stories, interior corridors. *Bath:* combo or shower only. **Parking:** on-site. **Terms:** pets ($75 fee). **Amenities:** high-speed Internet (fee), voice mail, irons. **Pool(s):** heated outdoor. **Guest Services:** valet and coin laundry. **Business Services:** fax (fee). **Cards:** AX, DC, DS, MC, VI.

SOME UNITS
ASK 🔊D 🐾 🔊M 🅿 ⊘ ⇄ 🛠 🎥 📠 ▣ 📧 ▣ / ⊠ / FEE

HOMEWOOD SUITES BY HILTON *Book at aaa.com*   **Phone:** (407)248-2232   **58**

All Year [BP]	1P: $139-$199	2P: $139-$199 XP: $10 F18

Location: I-4, exit 74A, just e on SR 482 (Sand Lake Rd), then 0.5 mi s. 8745 International Dr 32819. **Fax:** 407/248-6552. **Facility:** 252 units. 231 one- and 21 two-bedroom suites with efficiencies. 6 stories, interior corridors. *Bath:* combo or shower only. **Parking:** on-site. **Terms:** check-in 4 pm, cancellation fee imposed, package plans. **Amenities:** high-speed Internet, dual phone lines, voice mail, irons, hair dryers. *Fee:* video games, safes. **Pool(s):** heated outdoor. **Leisure Activities:** whirlpool, exercise room. *Fee:* game room. **Guest Services:** complimentary evening beverages: Mon-Thurs, valet and coin laundry, area transportation-major attractions. **Business Services:** meeting rooms, business center. **Cards:** AX, CB, DC, DS, JC, MC, VI. **Special Amenities:** free full breakfast and free newspaper. *(See color ad below)*

SOME UNITS
🔊D 🍴 🔊M 🅿 ⊘ ⇄ 🛠 VCR 🎥 📠 📧 ▣ / ⊠ /

HOMEWOOD SUITES BY HILTON-NEAREST TO
UNIVERSAL *Book at aaa.com*   **Phone:** (407)226-0669   **15**

All Year	1P: $109-$209	2P: $109-$209

Location: I-4, exit 75A, just w of SR 435, then just n. 6624 Hospitality Way 32819. **Fax:** 407/226-0353. **Facility:** 122 one-bedroom suites with kitchens. 5 stories, interior corridors. *Bath:* combo or shower only. **Parking:** on-site. **Terms:** cancellation fee imposed, [BP] meal plan available. **Amenities:** video games (fee), high-speed Internet, dual phone lines, voice mail, irons, hair dryers. **Pool(s):** heated outdoor. **Leisure Activities:** whirlpool, exercise room, sports court. *Fee:* game room. **Guest Services:** sundries, complimentary evening beverages: Mon-Thurs, valet and coin laundry, area transportation. **Business Services:** meeting rooms, business center. **Cards:** AX, CB, DC, DS, JC, MC, VI.

SOME UNITS
ASK 🔊D 🛬 ⊘ ⇄ 🛠 📠 📧 ▣ ▣ / ⊠ /
FEE

HOWARD JOHNSON INN-INTERNATIONAL DRIVE   *Book at aaa.com*   **Phone:** (407)351-2900   **28**

All Year	1P: $89-$125	XP: $10 F

Location: I-4, exit 74A, just e on SR 482 (Sand Lake Rd), then 0.4 mi n. 6603 International Dr 32819. **Fax:** 407/352-2738. **Facility:** 165 units. 159 one-bedroom standard units. 6 one-bedroom suites ($125). 3 stories, exterior corridors. **Parking:** on-site. **Terms:** package plans, $2 service charge, pets (dogs only, $100 deposit). **Amenities:** voice mail, safes, irons, hair dryers. **Pool(s):** outdoor, wading. **Leisure Activities:** exercise room, game room. **Guest Services:** valet and coin laundry, area transportation. **Business Services:** fax (fee). **Cards:** AX, DS, MC, VI.

SOME UNITS
ASK 🐾 ⊘ ⇄ 🎥 📠 ▣ / ⊠ 📧 /
FEE

(See maps and indexes p. 666-673, 667-674, 668-678, 670-685)

HOWARD JOHNSON PLAZA HOTEL & SUITES/INTERNATIONAL DR SOUTH   *Book at aaa.com*

Phone: (407)351-5100   **70**

AAA SAVE

12/1-4/22 & 7/1-8/19 [ECP]	1P: $69-$139	2P: $69-$139	XP: $10	F18
4/23-6/30 & 8/20-11/30 [ECP]	1P: $59-$129	2P: $59-$129	XP: $10	F18

Location: I-4, exit 72, just e to International Dr; SR 528 (Bee Line Expwy), exit 1, just n. 9956 Hawaiian Ct 32819.
Small-scale Hotel Fax: 407/352-7188. **Facility:** 223 units. 175 one-bedroom standard units, some with whirlpools. 48 one-bedroom suites ($99-$189). 2 stories, interior corridors. *Bath:* combo or shower only. **Parking:** on-site.
Terms: check-in 4 pm, 3 day cancellation notice-fee imposed. **Amenities:** voice mail, irons, hair dryers.
Fee: video games, safes. **Pool(s):** outdoor. **Leisure Activities:** whirlpool, exercise room. *Fee:* game room. **Guest Services:** valet and coin laundry, area transportation-major attractions. **Business Services:** meeting rooms, fax (fee). **Cards:** AX, CB, DC, DS, JC, MC, VI. **Special Amenities:** free expanded continental breakfast and free newspaper. *(See color ad p 686)*

SOME UNITS

[icons] 🔊 🍴 🛗 ♿ 🅿 🏊 ✕ 📹 DATA PORT 💻 / ✕ 🧊 📠 /

HYATT REGENCY ORLANDO INTERNATIONAL AIRPORT   *Book at aaa.com*

Phone: (407)825-1234   **24**

AAA SAVE

All Year	1P: $145-$239	2P: $145-$239	XP: $25	F18

Location: At Orlando International Airport (Terminal A). 9300 Airport Blvd 32827. Fax: 407/856-1672. **Facility:** 446
Large-scale Hotel units. 431 one-bedroom standard units. 15 one-bedroom suites, some with whirlpools. 10 stories, interior corridors. *Bath:* combo or shower only. **Parking:** on-site (fee) and valet. **Terms:** check-in 4 pm, cancellation fee imposed. **Amenities:** video games (fee), voice mail, irons, hair dryers. *Some:* CD players, high-speed Internet, dual phone lines. **Dining:** 2 restaurants, 24 hours, cocktails, also, Hemisphere, see separate listing. **Pool(s):** heated outdoor. **Leisure Activities:** jogging, exercise room, spa. *Fee:* game room. **Guest Services:** gift shop, valet laundry. **Business Services:** conference facilities, business center. **Cards:** AX, CB, DC, DS, JC, MC, VI. *(See color ad p 811)*

SOME UNITS

[icons] 🍴 24 🍴 🛗 🏊 ✕ 📹 DATA PORT 🧊 💻 / ✕ 📠 /

I-DRIVE INN

Phone: 407/351-4430   **23**

Property failed to provide current rates
Location: I-4, exit 74A, just e on SR 482 (Sand Lake Rd), then 0.7 mi n. 6323 International Dr 32819.
Small-scale Hotel Fax: 407/345-0742. **Facility:** 218 one-bedroom standard units. 2 stories, interior corridors. *Bath:* combo or shower only. **Parking:** on-site. **Terms:** check-in 4 pm, small pets only ($75 fee, $50 deposit).
Amenities: safes, irons, hair dryers. *Some:* high-speed Internet. **Pool(s):** heated outdoor. **Leisure Activities:** *Fee:* game room.
Guest Services: valet and coin laundry, area transportation. **Business Services:** fax (fee).

SOME UNITS

[icons] 🐾 🍴 🛗 ♿ 🅿 🏊 📹 DATA PORT / ✕ 🧊 📠 💻 /
FEE

INN OF AMERICA   *Book at aaa.com*

Phone: (407)363-1944   **47**

AAA SAVE

2/1-4/30 & 10/1-11/30	1P: $89-$139	2P: $89-$139
12/1-1/31	1P: $79-$139	2P: $79-$139
5/1-9/30	1P: $69-$109	2P: $69-$109

Location: I-4, exit 74A, just e on Sand Lake Rd, then just s on International Dr. 8342 Jamaican Ct 32819.
Small-scale Hotel Fax: 407/363-4844. **Facility:** 135 one-bedroom standard units. 3 stories, interior/exterior corridors. **Parking:** on-site. **Amenities:** high-speed Internet, safes, irons, hair dryers. **Pool(s):** heated outdoor. **Guest Services:** valet laundry. **Business Services:** fax (fee). **Cards:** AX, DC, DS, MC, VI. **Special Amenities:** free continental breakfast and free local telephone calls.

SOME UNITS

[icons] 🍴 🛗 📹 🏊 🛁 📹 DATA PORT / ✕ 🧊 📠 /

JW MARRIOTT ORLANDO, GRANDE LAKES   *Book at aaa.com*

Phone: (407)206-2300   **11**

12/1-4/20	1P: $459-$949
4/21-5/24 & 9/5-11/30	1P: $359-$749
Large-scale Hotel 5/25-9/4	1P: $249-$649

Location: I-4, exit 72, just e on SR 528 (Bee Line Expwy) to exit 1, 1.8 mi s on International Dr, then 1.3 mi e. 4040 Central Florida Pkwy 32837. Fax: 407/206-2301. **Facility:** Formal gardens and manicured walkways surround the hotel while a tranquil Spanish fountain is the focal point of the lobby. 998 units. 932 one-bedroom standard units. 66 one-bedroom suites ($459-$5999). 26 stories, interior corridors. *Bath:* combo or shower only. **Parking:** on-site (fee) and valet. **Terms:** cancellation fee imposed, package plans. **Amenities:** video games, CD players, high-speed Internet (fee), dual phone lines, voice mail, safes, honor bars, irons, hair dryers. *Some:* DVD players. **Dining:** Primo, see separate listing. **Pool(s):** heated outdoor, wading. **Leisure Activities:** 6 lighted tennis courts, recreation programs in summer, playground, exercise room, spa, basketball. *Fee:* golf-18 holes, game room. **Guest Services:** gift shop, valet and coin laundry, area transportation. **Business Services:** conference facilities, business center. **Cards:** AX, CB, DC, DS, JC, MC, VI.

SOME UNITS

[icons] ASK 🔊 🍴 24 🍴 🍴 🛗 📹 🏊 ✕ DATA PORT 💻 / ✕ /

(See maps and indexes p. 666-673, 667-674, 668-678, 670-685)

KEYSTONE-AMERICAN VACATION HOMES   **Phone:** (407)396-2880   🔟

All Year   2P: $89-$289

Condominium   **Location:** Florida Tpke, exit 244, 2.1 mi w on US 192. 2983 Vineland Rd 34746. Fax: 407/397-4132. **Facility:** Most of the three- to five-bedroom condos and homes have been individually decorated; homes have pools and condo units have access to a community pool. 7 units. 1 two- and 6 three-bedroom suites. 1-2 stories, exterior corridors. **Parking:** on-site. **Terms:** check-in 4 pm, 5 night minimum stay - seasonal, 30 day cancellation notice, 14 day off season-fee imposed, package plans, 7% service charge. **Amenities:** irons. **Leisure Activities:** playground. **Guest Services:** complimentary laundry. **Business Services:** fax (fee). **Cards:** AX, DC, MC, VI. *(See color ad p 756)*

(See maps and indexes p. 666-673, 667-674, 668-678, 670-685)

LA QUINTA INN & SUITES ORLANDO (AIRPORT NORTH) *Book at aaa.com*

Phone: (407)240-5000  **10**

(AAA) SAVE
Small-scale Hotel

All Year 1P: $79-$95 XP: $7 F18
Location: SR 528 (Bee Line Expwy), exit 11, 0.5 mi n on SR 436, then just w. 7160 N Frontage Rd 32812. **Fax:** 407/240-5261. **Facility:** 148 units. 143 one-bedroom standard units. 5 one-bedroom suites ($115-$130). 5 stories, interior corridors. *Bath:* combo or shower only. **Parking:** on-site. **Terms:** [ECP] meal plan available, small pets only. **Amenities:** dual phone lines, voice mail, irons, hair dryers. *Fee:* video games, high-speed Internet. **Pool(s):** heated outdoor. **Leisure Activities:** whirlpool, exercise room. **Guest Services:** valet and coin laundry. **Business Services:** meeting rooms, fax (fee). **Cards:** AX, CB, DC, DS, MC, VI. **Special Amenities:** free expanded continental breakfast and free local telephone calls. *(See color ad below)*

SOME UNITS

LA QUINTA INN & SUITES ORLANDO (CONVENTION CENTER) *Book at aaa.com*

Phone: (407)345-1365 **53**

(AAA) SAVE
Small-scale Hotel

All Year 1P: $89-$109 XP: $7 F18
Location: I-4, exit 74A, 0.5 mi e on SR 482 (Sand Lake Rd), then 0.5 mi s. 8504 Universal Blvd 32819. **Fax:** 407/345-5586. **Facility:** 184 units. 169 one-bedroom standard units. 15 one-bedroom suites ($125-$145). 7 stories, interior corridors. *Bath:* combo or shower only. **Parking:** on-site. **Terms:** [ECP] meal plan available, small pets only. **Amenities:** voice mail, irons, hair dryers. *Fee:* video games, high-speed Internet. **Pool(s):** heated outdoor. **Leisure Activities:** whirlpool, exercise room. **Guest Services:** coin laundry. **Business Services:** meeting rooms, fax (fee). **Cards:** AX, CB, DC, DS, MC, VI. **Special Amenities:** free expanded continental breakfast and free local telephone calls. *(See color ad below)*

SOME UNITS

LA QUINTA INN ORLANDO (AIRPORT WEST) *Book at aaa.com*

Phone: (407)857-9215 **18**

(AAA) SAVE
Small-scale Hotel

All Year 1P: $69-$89 XP: $7 F18
Location: SR 528 (Bee Line Expwy), exit 9 (Tradeport), via McCoy Rd. 7931 Daetwyler Dr 32812. **Fax:** 407/857-0877. **Facility:** 130 one-bedroom standard units. 3 stories, exterior corridors. *Bath:* combo or shower only. **Parking:** on-site. **Terms:** [ECP] meal plan available. **Amenities:** video games (fee), voice mail, irons, hair dryers. **Pool(s):** heated outdoor. **Guest Services:** coin laundry, area transportation-within 1 mi. **Business Services:** meeting rooms, fax (fee). **Cards:** AX, CB, DC, DS, MC, VI. **Special Amenities:** free expanded continental breakfast and free local telephone calls. *(See color ad below)*

(See maps and indexes p. 666-673, 667-674, 668-678, 670-685)

LA QUINTA INN ORLANDO (INTERNATIONAL DRIVE) *Book at aaa.com*

Phone: (407)351-1660 **49**

2/1-4/30	1P: $110-$125		XP: $7 F18
12/1-1/31 & 5/1-11/30	1P: $75-$85		XP: $7 F18

Small-scale Hotel

Location: I-4, exit 74A, just e on SR 482 (Sand Lake Rd), then just s on International Dr. 8300 Jamaican Ct 32819. Fax: 407/351-9264. **Facility:** 200 one-bedroom standard units. 4 stories, exterior corridors. **Bath:** combo or shower only. **Parking:** on-site. **Terms:** [ECP] meal plan available. **Amenities:** video games, high-speed Internet (fee), voice mail, irons, hair dryers. **Pool(s):** heated outdoor, wading. **Leisure Activities:** whirlpool, putting green. *Fee:* game room. **Guest Services:** valet and coin laundry. **Business Services:** fax (fee). **Cards:** AX, CB, DC, DS, MC, VI. **Special Amenities:** free expanded continental breakfast and free local telephone calls.
(See color ad p 721)

SOME UNITS

🛏️ 🍽️ 🄼 ⬚ 🏊 🐾 ⬚ ⊠ 📷 📠 🖥️ / ⊠ 🛢️ 🖨️ /
FEE

MARRIOTT ORLANDO AIRPORT *Book at aaa.com*

Phone: (407)851-9000 **15**

1/8-4/30	1P: $289-$319	2P: $289-$319	
12/1-1/7 & 9/10-11/30	1P: $259-$289	2P: $259-$289	
4/16-9/9	1P: $239-$269	2P: $239-$269	

Large-scale Hotel

Location: SR 528 (Bee Line Expwy), exit 11, 0.5 mi n on SR 436, just e, then s. 7499 Augusta National Dr 32822. Fax: 407/857-6211. **Facility:** 484 one-bedroom standard units. 9 stories, interior corridors. *Bath:* combo or shower only. **Parking:** on-site and valet. **Terms:** cancellation fee imposed. **Amenities:** dual phone lines, voice mail, irons, hair dryers. *Fee:* video games, high-speed Internet. **Dining:** Murphy's Chop House, see separate listing. **Pool(s):** heated indoor/outdoor, wading. **Leisure Activities:** saunas, whirlpool, 2 lighted tennis courts, basketball, volleyball. *Fee:* massage. **Guest Services:** gift shop, valet and coin laundry. **Business Services:** conference facilities, business center. **Cards:** AX, DC, DS, MC, VI.
(See color ad below)

SOME UNITS

ⓈⒹ ✈️ 🍽️ 24 🍽️ ⬚ 🐾 ⬚ ⊠ 📷 📠 🖥️ / ⊠ 🛢️ /

(See maps and indexes p. 666-673, 667-674, 668-678, 670-685)

MASTERS INN INTERNATIONAL DRIVE *Book at aaa.com* **Phone:** (407)345-1172 **46**

All Year [CP] 1P: $49-$120 2P: $49-$120
Location: I-4, exit 74A, e on SR 482 (Sand Lake Rd), then just s on International Dr. 8222 Jamaican Ct 32819. Fax: 407/352-2801. **Facility:** 120 one-bedroom standard units. 4 stories, exterior corridors. **Parking:** on-site. **Terms:** check-in 4 pm, 3 day cancellation notice-fee imposed, small pets only ($20 fee).
Small-scale Hotel **Amenities:** voice mail, safes (fee), irons, hair dryers. **Pool(s):** heated outdoor. **Guest Services:** coin laundry. **Business Services:** fax (fee). **Cards:** AX, DC, DS, MC, VI. **Special Amenities:** free continental breakfast and free local telephone calls.

SOME UNITS

MICROTEL INN & SUITES *Book at aaa.com* **Phone:** (407)226-9887 **35**

All Year 1P: $49-$69 2P: $49-$69
Location: I-4, exit 74A, just e on SR 482 (Sand Lake Rd), then n. 7531 Canada Ave 32819. Fax: 407/226-9877. **Facility:** 130 one-bedroom standard units. 3 stories, interior corridors. *Bath:* combo or shower only. **Parking:** on-site. **Terms:** pets ($25 fee). **Amenities:** safes (fee), irons. **Pool(s):** outdoor. **Guest Services:**
Small-scale Hotel valet laundry. **Business Services:** fax (fee). **Cards:** AX, DS, MC, VI. **Special Amenities:** free continental breakfast and free local telephone calls.

SOME UNITS

MOTEL 6 ORLANDO-INTERNATIONAL DRIVE #1079 *Book at aaa.com* **Phone:** 407/351-6500 **17**

1/1-3/27	1P: $45-$55	2P: $51-$61	XP: $3	F17
3/28-5/26	1P: $41-$51	2P: $47-$57	XP: $3	F17
12/1-12/31 & 5/27-11/30	1P: $39-$49	2P: $45-$55	XP: $3	F17

Small-scale Hotel **Location:** I-4, exit 75A, just w of SR 435, then just n. 5909 American Way 32819. Fax: 407/352-5481. **Facility:** 148 one-bedroom standard units. 3 stories, interior corridors. *Bath:* combo or shower only. **Parking:** on-site. **Pool(s):** heated outdoor. **Guest Services:** coin laundry. **Business Services:** fax (fee). **Cards:** AX, CB, DC, DS, MC, VI.

SOME UNITS

PARC CORNICHE CONDOMINIUM SUITE HOTEL *Book at aaa.com* **Phone:** (407)239-7100 **13**

All Year 1P: $89-$199 2P: $89-$199
Location: I-4, exit 72, just e on SR 528 (Bee Line Expwy) to exit 1, then 1.7 mi s on International Dr. Located in a quiet area. 6300 Parc Corniche Dr 32821. Fax: 407/239-8501. **Facility:** Bordered by a golf course, this property offers condominium-style units, all with private porches. Designated smoking area. 210 units. 90 one- and
Condominium 120 two-bedroom suites with kitchens. 3 stories, exterior corridors. **Parking:** on-site. **Terms:** check-in 4 pm, 3 day cancellation notice, package plans. **Amenities:** voice mail, safes, irons. **Dining:** 5 pm-10 pm, cocktails. **Pool(s):** heated outdoor, wading. **Leisure Activities:** whirlpool, playground, exercise room. *Fee:* golf privileges, game room. **Guest Services:** gift shop, valet and coin laundry, area transportation-selected attractions. **Business Services:** meeting rooms, fax (fee). **Cards:** AX, DC, DS, MC, VI. **Special Amenities:** free expanded continental breakfast.

THE PEABODY ORLANDO *Book at aaa.com* **Phone:** (407)352-4000 **66**

1/1-11/30	1P: $400-$1725	2P: $400-$1725	XP: $15	F18
12/1-12/31	1P: $395-$1700	2P: $395-$1700	XP: $15	F18

Location: 0.5 mi n of SR 528 (Bee Line Expwy). Located opposite the Orange County Convention Center. 9801 International Dr 32819. Fax: 407/351-9177. **Facility:** This service-oriented hotel featuring marble-accented
Large-scale Hotel public spaces is known for the resident ducks that parade twice daily through its lobby. 891 units. 872 one-bedroom standard units. 19 one-bedroom suites, some with whirlpools. 27 stories, interior corridors. *Bath:* combo or shower only. **Parking:** on-site (fee) and valet. **Terms:** 3 day cancellation notice-fee imposed, package plans, $7 service charge. **Amenities:** dual phone lines, voice mail, safes, honor bars, irons, hair dryers. *Fee:* video games, high-speed Internet. *Some:* CD players. **Dining:** 3 restaurants, 24 hours, cocktails, also, Capriccio Grill, Dux, see separate listings, entertainment. **Pool(s):** heated outdoor, wading. **Leisure Activities:** saunas, whirlpools, steamrooms, 4 lighted tennis courts. *Fee:* cabanas, tennis instruction, massage, game room. **Guest Services:** gift shop, valet laundry, area transportation (fee)-Disney, beauty salon, tanning facilities. **Business Services:** conference facilities, business center. **Cards:** AX, DC, DS, JC, MC, VI. Affiliated with A Preferred Hotel.

SOME UNITS

QUALITY INN AIRPORT *Book at aaa.com* **Phone:** (407)856-4663 **20**
F21

All Year [CP] 1P: $65-$160 2P: $65-$180 XP: $5
Location: SR 482 (Sand Lake Rd) at SR 528 (Bee Line Expwy). 2601 McCoy Rd 32809. Fax: 407/856-4663. **Facility:** 98 one-bedroom standard units. 2 stories, exterior corridors. **Parking:** on-site. **Amenities:** safes (fee), irons, hair dryers. **Pool(s):** outdoor. **Leisure Activities:** limited exercise equipment. *Fee:* game room.
Small-scale Hotel **Guest Services:** complimentary evening beverages: Mon-Sat, coin laundry. **Business Services:** fax (fee). **Cards:** AX, CB, DC, DS, JC, MC, VI. **Special Amenities:** free continental breakfast and free local telephone calls.

SOME UNITS

QUALITY INN & SUITES-UNIVERSAL ORLANDO *Book at aaa.com* **Phone:** (407)370-5100 **1**

All Year 1P: $50-$129 2P: $50-$129
Location: I-4, exit 75B, 1 mi n on SR 435 (Kirkman Rd), then just e. 5635 Windhover Dr 32819. Fax: 407/370-2026. **Facility:** 104 units. 93 one-bedroom standard units. 11 one-bedroom suites. 4 stories, interior corridors. *Bath:* combo or shower only. **Parking:** on-site. **Terms:** cancellation fee imposed, package plans.
Small-scale Hotel **Amenities:** voice mail, safes (fee), irons, hair dryers. **Pool(s):** heated outdoor. **Guest Services:** valet and coin laundry, area transportation-Universal. **Business Services:** fax (fee). **Cards:** AX, CB, DC, DS, JC, MC, VI. **Special Amenities:** free continental breakfast and free local telephone calls.

SOME UNITS

(See maps and indexes p. 666-673, 667-674, 668-678, 670-685)

QUALITY INN INTERNATIONAL   *Book at aaa.com*   Phone: (407)996-1600   **37**

◆◆ ◆◆   All Year   1P: $59-$99

Small-scale Hotel   **Location:** I-4, exit 74A, just e on SR 482 (Sand Lake Rd), then just n. 7600 International Dr 32819. Fax: 407/996-5328. **Facility:** 728 one-bedroom standard units. 2-6 stories, exterior corridors. *Bath:* combo or shower only. **Parking:** on-site. **Terms:** $2 service charge, pets ($10 extra charge). **Amenities:** voice mail, safes, irons, hair dryers. **Pool(s):** 2 heated outdoor, wading. **Leisure Activities:** *Fee:* game room. **Guest Services:** gift shop, valet and coin laundry, area transportation. **Business Services:** business center. **Cards:** AX, CB, DC, DS, JC, MC, VI.

SOME UNITS

(ASK) [SD] [🛏] [🍴] [🍸] [&M] [👜] [∅] [🏊] [👫] FEE [📹] [DATA PORT] [🔌] [📺] [💻] / [✕] /

QUALITY INN PLAZA   *Book at aaa.com*   Phone: (407)996-8585   **63**

◆◆ ◆◆   All Year   1P: $59-$99   2P: $59-$99   XP: $5   F18

Small-scale Hotel   **Location:** I-4, exit 74A, just e on SR 482 (Sand Lake Rd), then 1 mi s. 9000 International Dr 32819. Fax: 407/996-6839. **Facility:** 1020 one-bedroom standard units. 4-10 stories, exterior corridors. *Bath:* combo or shower only. **Parking:** on-site. **Terms:** package plans, $2 service charge, pets ($10 extra charge). **Amenities:** video games (fee), voice mail, safes, irons, hair dryers. **Pool(s):** outdoor, 2 heated outdoor. **Leisure Activities:** playground. *Fee:* game room. **Guest Services:** gift shop, valet and coin laundry, area transportation (fee). **Business Services:** meeting rooms, business center. **Cards:** AX, CB, DC, DS, JC, MC, VI.

SOME UNITS

(ASK) [SD] [🛏] FEE [🐾] FEE [🍴] [🍸] [&M] [👜] [∅] [🏊] [👫] FEE [📹] [🔌] [📺] [💻] / [✕] [DATA PORT] /

QUALITY SUITES UNIVERSAL ORLANDO   *Book at aaa.com*   Phone: (407)363-0332   **33**

(AAA) [SAVE]   All Year [BP]   1P: $79-$129   2P: $79-$129

◆◆ ◆◆   **Location:** I-4, exit 74A, just e on SR 482 (Sand Lake Rd), then just n. 7400 Canada Ave 32819. Fax: 407/352-2598.

Small-scale Hotel   **Facility:** 154 one-bedroom suites. 7 stories, exterior corridors. *Bath:* combo or shower only. **Parking:** on-site. **Terms:** 3 day cancellation notice. **Amenities:** CD players, high-speed Internet, voice mail, safes, irons, hair dryers. **Pool(s):** heated outdoor. **Leisure Activities:** whirlpool, playground, exercise room. *Fee:* game room. **Guest Services:** gift shop, complimentary evening beverages, valet and coin laundry, area transportation-major attractions. **Business Services:** meeting rooms, fax (fee). **Cards:** AX, DC, DS, MC, VI. **Special Amenities:** free full breakfast and free local telephone calls. (See color ad p 725)

SOME UNITS

[SD] [🛏] [∅] [🏊] [✕] [📹] [DATA PORT] [🔌] [📺] [💻] / [✕] /

(See maps and indexes p. 666-673, 667-674, 668-678, 670-685)

RADISSON BARCELO RESORT   *Book at aaa.com*   Phone: (407)345-0505 ⑤⓪

(AAA) (SAVE)   12/1-4/23 & 6/16-8/12   1P: $89-$129
VVVV   4/24-6/15 & 8/13-11/30   1P: $69-$109
Small-scale Hotel   **Location:** I-4, exit 74A, just e on SR 482 (Sand Lake Rd), then just s. 8444 International Dr 32819. **Fax:** 407/581-2022. **Facility:** 522 one-bedroom standard units. 5-7 stories, interior/exterior corridors. **Bath:** combo or shower only. **Parking:** on-site. **Terms:** check-in 4 pm, 3 day cancellation notice. **Amenities:** voice mail, safes, irons, hair dryers. *Some:* video games (fee), dual phone lines. **Dining:** 2 restaurants, 6:30 am-11 pm, cocktails. **Pool(s):** heated outdoor. **Leisure Activities:** whirlpool, lighted tennis court, bocci, playground, horseshoes, volleyball. *Fee:* game room. **Guest Services:** gift shop, valet and coin laundry, area transportation-major attractions. **Business Services:** meeting rooms. *Fee:* administrative services, fax. **Cards:** AX, DC, DS, MC, VI. **Special Amenities:** free newspaper and preferred room (subject to availability with advance reservations). *(See color ad below)*

SOME UNITS

🆓 ✈️ 🍴 🍽️ 👤 📷 🏊 🐾 🚲 ✂️ 📹 📶 📞 💻 / ✖️ 📠 /
FEE

(See maps and indexes p. 666-673, 667-674, 668-678, 670-685)

RAMADA INN & SUITES ORLANDO AIRPORT   *Book at aaa.com*   Phone: (407)851-1113   **21**
All Year   1P: $139-$159   2P: $139-$159   XP: $10   F21
Location: SR 482 (Sand Lake Rd), just w of jct SR 528 (Bee Line Expwy). 1853 McCoy Rd 32809. Fax: 407/438-5883. **Facility:** 168 units. 114 one-bedroom standard units. 54 one-bedroom suites ($159-$179). 3 stories, interior/exterior corridors. *Bath:* combo or shower only. **Parking:** on-site. **Terms:** [BP] meal
Small-scale Hotel   plan available. **Amenities:** voice mail, irons, hair dryers. *Some:* CD players, dual phone lines, safes. **Pool(s):** heated outdoor. **Leisure Activities:** whirlpool, exercise room. **Guest Services:** sundries, complimentary evening beverages, valet and coin laundry, area transportation-within 1 mi. **Business Services:** meeting rooms, business center. **Cards:** AX, CB, DC, DS, JC, MC, VI. **Special Amenities: free full breakfast and free local telephone calls.** *(See color ad below)*

SOME UNITS

RAMADA INN INTERNATIONAL DRIVE LAKEFRONT   *Book at aaa.com*   Phone: (407)345-5340   **29**
All Year [CP]   1P: $69-$129   2P: $69-$129
Location: I-4, exit 75A, 0.8 mi s. 6500 International Dr 32819. Fax: 407/363-0976. **Facility:** 164 one-bedroom standard units. 12 stories, exterior corridors. *Bath:* combo or shower only. **Parking:** on-site. **Terms:** check-in
Small-scale Hotel   4 pm. **Amenities:** dual phone lines, voice mail, safes (fee), irons, hair dryers. **Pool(s):** heated outdoor.
Leisure Activities: *Fee:* game room. **Guest Services:** valet and coin laundry. **Business Services:** fax (fee). **Cards:** AX, DC, DS, MC, VI.

RED HORSE INN   *Book at aaa.com*   Phone: (407)351-4100   **20**
All Year [ECP]   1P: $59-$119   2P: $59-$119
Location: I-4, exit 75A, just w. 5825 International Dr 32819. Fax: 407/996-4599. **Facility:** 159 one-bedroom standard units. 2 stories, exterior corridors. *Bath:* combo or shower only. **Parking:** on-site. **Terms:** check-in
Small-scale Hotel   4 pm, 3 day cancellation notice-fee imposed, package plans, $5 service charge, small pets only ($10 extra charge). **Amenities:** voice mail, safes (fee), irons, hair dryers. **Pool(s):** heated outdoor, wading. **Leisure Activities:** shuffleboard. **Guest Services:** coin laundry. **Business Services:** meeting rooms, fax (fee). **Cards:** AX, CB, DC, DS, JC, MC, VI. **Special Amenities: free expanded continental breakfast and free local telephone calls.**

SOME UNITS
FEE   FEE   FEE

RED ROOF INN CONVENTION CENTER   *Book at aaa.com*   Phone: (407)352-1507   **69**
All Year   1P: $46-$100   2P: $46-$100
Location: I-4, exit 72, 0.9 mi e on SR 528 (Bee Line Expwy) to exit 1, then just n. 9922 Hawaiian Ct 32819. Fax: 407/352-5550. **Facility:** 134 one-bedroom standard units. 2 stories, exterior corridors. *Bath:* combo or
Small-scale Hotel   shower only. **Parking:** on-site. **Amenities:** video games (fee), voice mail. **Pool(s):** small outdoor. **Leisure Activities:** whirlpool. **Guest Services:** valet and coin laundry. **Business Services:** fax (fee). **Cards:** AX, CB, DC, DS, MC, VI.

SOME UNITS

(See maps and indexes p. 666-673, 667-674, 668-678, 670-685)

RENAISSANCE ORLANDO HOTEL-AIRPORT *Book at aaa.com* Phone: (407)240-1000 **4**

▼▼▼ 12/1-4/13 1P: $159-$250
9/1-11/30 1P: $150-$250
Large-scale Hotel 4/14-6/29 1P: $149-$200
6/30-8/31 1P: $130-$200

Location: On SR 436; just n of SR 528 (Bee Line Expwy). 5445 Forbes Pl 32812. Fax: 407/240-1005. **Facility:** 298 units. 297 one-bedroom standard units. 1 one-bedroom suite. 9 stories, interior corridors. *Bath:* combo or shower only. **Parking:** on-site and valet. **Terms:** cancellation fee imposed, package plans. **Amenities:** dual phone lines, voice mail, irons, hair dryers. *Fee:* video games, high-speed Internet. *Some:* CD players. **Pool(s):** heated outdoor. **Leisure Activities:** sauna, whirlpool, exercise room. *Fee:* massage. **Guest Services:** valet laundry. **Business Services:** conference facilities, business center. **Cards:** AX, CB, DC, DS, JC, MC, VI. *(See color ad below)*

SOME UNITS

(ASK) (S📶) 🚲 [Y1] [24🕐] [Y] [≜M] [📶] [🔲] [⚓] [✕] [🎬] [DATA PORT] [▣] / [✕] [📱] [⊟] /

RENAISSANCE ORLANDO RESORT AT SEAWORLD *Book at aaa.com* Phone: (407)351-5555 **77**

(AAA) (SAVE) All Year 1P: $119-$329 2P: $119-$329
▼▼▼▼ **Location:** I-4, exit 72, just e on Central Florida Pkwy, then 0.3 mi n or 0.7 mi w of International Dr. Located across from Sea World. 6677 Sea Harbor Dr 32821-8092. Fax: 407/351-9991. **Facility:** The atrium lobby of this convention hotel features an aviary and a waterfall pond stocked with fish. 778 units. 777 one-bedroom standard units.
Resort 1 one-bedroom suite ($279-$1999) with whirlpool. 10 stories, interior corridors. *Bath:* combo or shower only.
Large-scale Hotel **Parking:** on-site and valet. **Terms:** [BP] meal plan available, package plans. **Amenities:** dual phone lines, voice mail, safes, honor bars, irons, hair dryers. *Fee:* video games, high-speed Internet. **Dining:** 4 restaurants, 24 hours, cocktails, also, Atlantis, see separate listing, entertainment. **Pool(s):** heated outdoor, wading. **Leisure Activities:** sauna, whirlpool, steamroom, 3 lighted tennis courts, jogging, playground, basketball, volleyball. *Fee:* golf privileges, tennis instruction & equipment, massage, game room. **Guest Services:** gift shop, valet laundry, area transportation (fee)-major attractions, beauty salon. **Business Services:** conference facilities, business center. **Cards:** AX, CB, DC, DS, JC, MC, VI. **Special Amenities:** free newspaper and early check-in/late check-out.

SOME UNITS

[S📶] 🚲 [Y1] [24🕐] [Y] [≜M] [📶] [🔲] [⚓] [🎬] [✕] [🎬] [DATA PORT] / [✕] [📱] /
FEE FEE

RESIDENCE INN BY MARRIOTT ORLANDO CONVENTION CENTER *Book at aaa.com* Phone: 407/226-0288 **59**

▼▼▼ Property failed to provide current rates
Location: I-4, exit 74A, 0.5 mi e on SR 482 (Sand Lake Rd), then 0.8 mi s. 8800 Universal Blvd 32819.
Small-scale Hotel Fax: 407/226-9979. **Facility:** 124 units. 23 one-bedroom standard units with kitchens. 67 one- and 34 two-bedroom suites with kitchens. 5 stories, interior corridors. *Bath:* combo or shower only. **Parking:** on-site.
Terms: check-in 4 pm, small pets only ($75 fee, $75 deposit). **Amenities:** video library (fee), high-speed Internet, dual phone lines, voice mail, irons, hair dryers. **Pool(s):** heated outdoor. **Leisure Activities:** whirlpool, exercise room, sports court. *Fee:* game room. **Guest Services:** complimentary evening beverages: Mon-Thurs, valet and coin laundry, area transportation. **Business Services:** meeting rooms, fax (fee).

SOME UNITS

[🛏] [Y1+] [≜M] [📶] [🔲] [⚓] [✕] [VCR] [🎬] [DATA PORT] [📱] [🍽] [⊟] / [✕] /
FEE

(See maps and indexes p. 666-673, 667-674, 668-678, 670-685)

RESIDENCE INN BY MARRIOTT-ORLANDO
INTERNATIONAL DR   Book at aaa.com

Phone: (407)345-0117   42

(AAA) [SAVE]
◇◇◇◇

Small-scale Hotel

All Year [BP]   1P: $119-$229
Location: I-4, exit 74A, just e on SR 482 (Sand Lake Rd). 7975 Canada Ave 32819. Fax: 407/352-2689. **Facility:** 176 units. 132 one-bedroom standard units with kitchens. 44 two-bedroom suites with kitchens. 2 stories, exterior corridors. *Bath:* combo or shower only. **Parking:** on-site. **Terms:** check-in 4 pm, cancellation fee imposed, package plans, 5% service charge, small pets only ($75 fee). **Amenities:** video games (fee), high-speed Internet, voice mail, safes, irons, hair dryers. *Some:* CD players. **Pool(s):** heated outdoor. **Leisure Activities:** whirlpool, poolside gas grills, exercise room, sports court, volleyball. **Guest Services:** complimentary evening beverages: Mon-Thurs, valet and coin laundry, area transportation-Universal & SeaWorld. **Business Services:** meeting rooms, business center. **Cards:** AX, CB, DC, DS, JC, MC, VI. **Special Amenities:** free full breakfast and free newspaper.

SOME UNITS

[icons] FEE

RESIDENCE INN BY MARRIOTT SEAWORLD
INTERNATIONAL CENTER   Book at aaa.com

Phone: (407)313-3600   79

(AAA) [SAVE]
◇◇◇◇

Small-scale Hotel

All Year [BP]   1P: $79-$145   2P: $79-$145
Location: I-4, exit 72. 11000 Westwood Blvd 32821. Fax: 407/313-3611. **Facility:** 350 units. 154 one-bedroom standard units with kitchens. 143 one- and 53 two-bedroom suites with kitchens. 6 stories, interior corridors. *Bath:* combo or shower only. **Parking:** on-site. **Terms:** check-in 4 pm, cancellation fee imposed, package plans, pets ($150 fee). **Amenities:** video games (fee), high-speed Internet, dual phone lines, voice mail, irons, hair dryers. **Dining:** noon-11 pm. **Pool(s):** heated outdoor. **Leisure Activities:** whirlpool, barbecue grills, playground, exercise room, sports court, volleyball. *Fee:* game room. **Guest Services:** gift shop, complimentary evening beverages: Mon-Thurs, valet and coin laundry, area transportation-major attractions. **Business Services:** meeting rooms, business center. **Cards:** AX, CB, DC, DS, JC, MC, VI. **Special Amenities:** free full breakfast and free newspaper.
(See color ad below)

SOME UNITS

[icons] FEE

THE RITZ-CARLTON ORLANDO, GRANDE LAKES   Book at aaa.com

Phone: (407)206-2400   12

(AAA) [SAVE]
◇◇◇◇◇

Large-scale Hotel

12/1-4/20   1P: $499-$999   2P: $499-$999
4/21-5/24 & 9/5-11/30   1P: $399-$799   2P: $399-$799
5/25-9/4   1P: $269-$699   2P: $269-$699
Location: I-4, exit 72, just e on SR 528 (Bee Line Expwy) to exit 1, 0.8 mi s on International Dr, then 1.3 mi e. 4012 Central Florida Pkwy 32837. Fax: 407/206-2401. **Facility:** Manicured grounds and tropical greenery decorate the perimeter of this elegant structure, which offers numerous facilities for guest use. Designated smoking area. 584 units. 522 one-bedroom standard units. 62 one-bedroom suites ($499-$6000). 14 stories, interior corridors. *Bath:* combo or shower only. **Parking:** valet. **Terms:** 14 day cancellation notice-fee imposed, package plans. **Amenities:** CD players, dual phone lines, voice mail, safes, honor bars, irons, hair dryers. *Fee:* video games, high-speed Internet. *Some:* DVD players. **Dining:** 5 restaurants, 24 hours, cocktails, also, Norman's, see separate listing. **Pool(s):** heated outdoor, wading. **Leisure Activities:** sauna, steamroom, 3 lighted tennis courts, recreation programs, jogging, playground, exercise room, spa, bocci, outdoor chess board, surry bikes. *Fee:* golf-18 holes, game room. **Guest Services:** valet laundry. **Business Services:** conference facilities, business center. **Cards:** AX, CB, DC, DS, JC, MC, VI. **Special Amenities:** free newspaper.

SOME UNITS

[icons] FEE   FEE

RODEWAY INN INTERNATIONAL   Book at aaa.com

Phone: (407)996-4444   24

◇◇◇◇
◇◇

Small-scale Hotel

All Year   1P: $49-$95   2P: $49-$95
Location: I-4, exit 74A, just e on SR 482 (Sand Lake Rd), then 0.7 mi n. 6327 International Dr 32819. Fax: 407/996-5806. **Facility:** 315 one-bedroom standard units. 4-9 stories, interior/exterior corridors. *Bath:* combo or shower only. **Parking:** on-site. **Terms:** [BP] meal plan available, $2 service charge, pets ($10 extra charge). **Amenities:** video library (fee), voice mail, safes, hair dryers. **Pool(s):** heated outdoor. **Leisure Activities:** *Fee:* game room. **Guest Services:** gift shop, valet and coin laundry, area transportation. **Business Services:** fax (fee). **Cards:** AX, DC, DS, MC, VI.

SOME UNITS

[icons] FEE

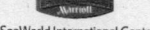

(See maps and indexes p. 666-673, 667-674, 668-678, 670-685)

ROSEN CENTRE HOTEL   *Book at aaa.com*   Phone: (407)996-9840   67
◎◎◎◎   All Year   1P: $99-$350   2P: $99-$350   XP: $20   F18
Small-scale Hotel   **Location:** I-4, exit 72, just e on SR 528 (Bee Line Expwy) to exit 1 (International Dr), then just n. Located next to the
convention center. 9840 International Dr 32819. Fax: 407/996-3169. **Facility:** 1334 one-bedroom standard units,
some with whirlpools. 24 stories, interior corridors. *Bath:* combo or shower only. **Parking:** on-site and valet.
Terms: 5 day cancellation notice-fee imposed, [AP] meal plan available. **Amenities:** high-speed Internet (fee), voice mail,
safes, irons, hair dryers. *Some:* CD players. **Dining:** Everglades Restaurant, see separate listing. **Pool(s):** heated outdoor,
wading. **Leisure Activities:** whirlpools. *Fee:* 2 lighted tennis courts, massage. **Guest Services:** gift shop, valet and coin
laundry, area transportation (fee), beauty salon. **Business Services:** conference facilities, business center. **Cards:** AX, CB, DC,
DS, JC, MC, VI.

SOME UNITS

ROSEN PLAZA   *Book at aaa.com*   Phone: (407)996-9700   65
◎◎◎◎   1/11-6/12 & 9/10-11/30   1P: $299   2P: $299   XP: $20   F17
               12/1-1/10   1P: $199   2P: $199   XP: $20   F17
Small-scale Hotel 6/13-9/9   1P: $149   2P: $149   XP: $20   F17
Location: I-4, exit 72, just n; SR 528 (Bee Line Expwy), exit 1, then just n. 9700 International Dr 32819.
Fax: 407/354-5774. **Facility:** 800 units. 786 one-bedroom standard units. 14 one-bedroom suites ($399-$1250). 14 stories,
interior corridors. *Bath:* combo or shower or tub only. **Parking:** on-site and valet. **Terms:** 5 day cancellation notice-fee imposed.
Amenities: video games, high-speed Internet, voice mail, safes, irons, hair dryers. **Dining:** Jack's Place, see separate listing.
Pool(s): heated outdoor. **Leisure Activities:** whirlpool, exercise room. *Fee:* game room. **Guest Services:** gift shop, valet and
coin laundry, area transportation (fee). **Business Services:** conference facilities, business center. **Cards:** AX, CB, DC, DS, JC,
MC, VI.

SOME UNITS

SAND POINT-AMERICAN VACATION HOMES   Phone: (407)396-2880   14
◎◎◎   All Year   2P: $89-$289
Vacation Home **Location:** Florida Tpke, exit 244, 2.1 mi w on US 192. 2983 Vineland Rd 34746. Fax: 407/397-4132. **Facility:** Most
of the 3- to 5-bedroom condos and homes have been individually decorated; homes have pools and condo
units have access to a community pool. 7 vacation homes with pools. 1-2 stories, exterior corridors.
Parking: on-site. **Terms:** check-in 4 pm, 5 night minimum stay - seasonal, 30 day cancellation notice, 14 day off season-fee
imposed, package plans, 7% service charge. **Amenities:** irons. **Guest Services:** complimentary laundry. **Business Services:**
fax (fee). **Cards:** AX, DC, MC, VI. *(See color ad p 756)*

SHERATON STUDIO CITY HOTEL   *Book at aaa.com*   Phone: (407)351-2100   19
◎◎◎ SAVE   All Year   1P: $79-$299   2P: $79-$299   XP: $10   F17
◎◎◎   **Location:** I-4, exit 75A, just w of SR 435 (Kirkman Rd). 5905 International Dr 32819. Fax: 407/248-0266.
Facility: 302 one-bedroom standard units. 21 stories, interior corridors. *Bath:* combo or shower only.
Small-scale Hotel **Parking:** on-site. **Terms:** 3 day cancellation notice, [BP] & [CP] meal plans available, package plans, $5
service charge, pets ($25 fee). **Amenities:** voice mail, safes, irons, hair dryers. *Fee:* video games, high-
speed Internet. *Some:* fax. **Dining:** 6:30 am-10:30 & 11:30-11 pm, cocktails. **Pool(s):** heated outdoor,
wading. **Leisure Activities:** exercise room. *Fee:* massage, game room. **Guest Services:** gift shop, valet and coin laundry, area
transportation-major attractions. **Business Services:** conference facilities, business center. **Cards:** AX, CB, DC, DS, JC,
MC, VI. **Special Amenities:** free local telephone calls and free newspaper.

SOME UNITS

SHERATON SUITES ORLANDO AIRPORT   *Book at aaa.com*   Phone: (407)240-5555   16
◎◎◎ SAVE   1/8-4/30 & 10/1-11/30   1P: $119-$179   2P: $119-$179   XP: $10   F17
◎◎◎   12/1-1/7 & 5/1-9/30   1P: $99-$139   2P: $99-$139   XP: $10   F17
Location: 2 mi n of airport terminal via SR 436 and TG Lee Blvd. 7550 Augusta National Dr 32822.
Fax: 407/240-1300. **Facility:** 150 one-bedroom suites. 3 stories, interior corridors. *Bath:* combo or shower
Small-scale Hotel only. **Parking:** on-site. **Terms:** cancellation fee imposed, pets ($150 deposit). **Amenities:** dual phone lines,
voice mail, irons, hair dryers. *Fee:* video games, high-speed Internet. *Some:* fax. **Dining:** 6:30 am-10:30
pm, cocktails. **Pool(s):** heated indoor/outdoor. **Leisure Activities:** whirlpool, exercise room. **Guest Services:** gift shop, valet
and coin laundry, area transportation-within 2 mi. **Business Services:** meeting rooms, fax (fee). **Cards:** AX, DS, JC,
MC, VI. **Special Amenities:** free newspaper.

SOME UNITS

SHERATON VISTANA VILLAGES   *Book at aaa.com*   Phone: (407)238-5000   67
◎◎◎   All Year   2P: $304
◎◎◎   **Location:** Between SR 535 and Central Florida Pkwy. 12401 International Dr 32821. Fax: 407/238-5005.
Condominium   **Facility:** The spacious condos are surrounded by lush landscaping and an attractive pool area, and are a
short drive from shopping, dining and attractions. 360 units. 150 one- and 210 two-bedroom suites with
kitchens and whirlpools. 5 stories, exterior corridors. *Bath:* combo or shower only. **Parking:** on-site. **Terms:** check-in 4 pm, 3
day cancellation notice-fee imposed. **Amenities:** video library (fee), voice mail, safes, irons, hair dryers. *Some:* CD players.
Pool(s): 2 heated outdoor. **Leisure Activities:** sauna, whirlpools, steamroom, 2 lighted tennis courts, recreation programs,
jogging, playground, exercise room, basketball, shuffleboard, volleyball. *Fee:* massage, game room. **Guest Services:**
complimentary laundry, area transportation. *Fee:* tanning facility. **Business Services:** fax (fee). **Cards:** AX, DC, DS, MC, VI.
(See color ad p 8 & p 688)

(See maps and indexes p. 666-673, 667-674, 668-678, 670-685)

SHERATON WORLD RESORT   *Book at aaa.com*   Phone: (407)352-1100   76
▼▼▼▼   All Year   1P: $239-$299   2P: $259-$310   XP: $20
Location: I-4, exit 72, just s on International Dr; SR 528 (Bee Line Expwy), exit 1, just e. 10100 International Dr 32821.
Large-scale Hotel   Fax: 407/352-3679. Facility: 1102 one-bedroom standard units. 2-16 stories, interior/exterior corridors. *Bath:* some combo or shower only. Parking: on-site. Terms: 3 day cancellation notice-fee imposed, package plans, small pets only ($50 deposit). Amenities: video games, dual phone lines, voice mail, irons, hair dryers. *Some:* fax, safes. Pool(s): 3 heated outdoor, 2 wading. Leisure Activities: whirlpool, miniature golf, playground, exercise room. *Fee:* massage, game room. Guest Services: gift shop, valet and coin laundry, area transportation, beauty salon. Business Services: conference facilities, business center. Cards: AX, DS, MC, VI. *(See color ad below)*

SOME UNITS

(ASK) (SD) 🐾 🍴 🍽 🛗 📶 🖼 🛢 🛩 🚫 🎥 (DATA PORT) 🔋 💻 / 🚫 📺
FEE

SLEEP INN AND SUITES   *Book at aaa.com*   Phone: 407/363-1333   6
▼▼▼   Property failed to provide current rates
Location: I-4, exit 75B, just n, then just e. 5605 Major Blvd 32819. Fax: 407/363-4510. Facility: 196 one-bedroom
Small-scale Hotel   standard units. 11 stories, interior corridors. *Bath:* combo or shower only. Parking: on-site. Amenities: video games (fee), voice mail. *Some:* irons, hair dryers. Pool(s): heated outdoor. Leisure Activities: exercise room. *Fee:* game room. Guest Services: valet and coin laundry, area transportation. Business Services: meeting rooms, fax (fee).

SOME UNITS

🖼 🛩 🎥 (DATA PORT) / 🚫 🔋 📺 💻 /

SLEEP INN & SUITES ORLANDO INTERNATIONAL
AIRPORT   *Book at aaa.com*   Phone: (407)855-4447   22
(AAA) (SAVE)   All Year   1P: $70-$150   2P: $70-$150   XP: $10   F18
▼▼▼   Location: SR 528 (Bee Line Expwy), exit 8, just w. 1700 McCoy Rd 32809. Fax: 407/856-9350. Facility: 74 one-
bedroom standard units, some with whirlpools. 3 stories, interior corridors. *Bath:* combo or shower only.
Small-scale Hotel   Parking: on-site. Terms: cancellation fee imposed, [CP] meal plan available, $2 service charge.
Amenities: high-speed Internet, safes (fee), irons, hair dryers. Pool(s): outdoor. Leisure Activities: whirlpool, limited exercise equipment. Guest Services: valet and coin laundry. Business Services: meeting rooms, business center. Cards: AX, CB, DC, DS, JC, MC, VI. Special Amenities: free continental breakfast and free local telephone calls.

SOME UNITS

(SD) ✈ 🍴 🖼 🛩 🎥 (DATA PORT) / 🚫 🔋 📺 /

SLEEP INN-CONVENTION CENTER   *Book at aaa.com*   Phone: (407)313-4100   75
(AAA) (SAVE)   12/25-4/30 & 10/1-11/30   1P: $75-$95   2P: $75-$95
▼▼▼   12/1-12/24 & 5/1-9/30   1P: $70-$80   2P: $70-$80
Location: I-4, exit 72, just e on SR 528 (Bee Line Expwy) to exit 1 (International Dr), just s, then just w. 6301 Westwood Blvd 32821. Fax: 407/313-4101. Facility: 94 one-bedroom standard units. 4 stories, interior corridors. *Bath:*
Small-scale Hotel   combo or shower only. Parking: on-site. Terms: package plans, $3 service charge. Amenities: safes, irons, hair dryers. Pool(s): outdoor. Guest Services: valet and coin laundry, area transportation-Disney. Business Services: fax. Cards: AX, CB, DC, DS, MC, VI. Special Amenities: free expanded continental breakfast and free newspaper.

SOME UNITS

(SD) 🍴 🛗 🖼 🛢 🛩 🚫 🎥 (DATA PORT) / 🔋 /
FEE

(See maps and indexes p. 666-673, 667-674, 668-678, 670-685)

SPRINGHILL SUITES BY MARRIOTT-ORLANDO
CONV CTR/INTERNATIONAL DRIVE AREA   **Book at aaa.com**   **Phone:** 407/345-9073   60
Property failed to provide current rates
Location: I-4, exit 74A, 0.5 mi e on SR 482 (Sand Lake Rd), then 0.8 mi s. 8840 Universal Blvd 32819.
Small-scale Hotel Fax: 407/345-9075. **Facility:** 167 one-bedroom standard units. 7 stories, interior corridors. *Bath:* combo or shower only. **Parking:** on-site. **Amenities:** high-speed Internet (fee), dual phone lines, voice mail, irons, hair dryers. **Pool(s):** heated outdoor, wading. **Leisure Activities:** exercise room. *Fee:* game room. **Guest Services:** valet and coin laundry, area transportation. **Business Services:** business center. *(See color ad below)*

SOME UNITS

STAYBRIDGE SUITES-ORLANDO/INTERNATIONAL
DRIVE   **Book at aaa.com**   **Phone:** (407)352-2400   51
All Year   1P: $129-$219   2P: $149-$269
Location: I-4, exit 74A, just e on SR 482 (Sand Lake Rd), then just s. 8480 International Dr 32819.
Fax: 407/352-4631. **Facility:** 146 units. 42 one- and 104 two-bedroom suites with kitchens. 5 stories, exterior corridors. **Parking:** on-site, package plans. **Amenities:** video library (fee), DVD players, CD players, high-speed Internet,
Small-scale Hotel voice mail, safes, irons, hair dryers. *Some:* dual phone lines. **Pool(s):** heated outdoor, wading. **Leisure Activities:** whirlpool, exercise room. *Fee:* game room. **Guest Services:** gift shop, valet and coin laundry. **Business Services:** meeting rooms, business center. **Cards:** AX, DC, DS, MC, VI. **Special Amenities:** free expanded continental breakfast and free newspaper. *(See color ad p 814)*

SOME UNITS

STUDIOPLUS-ORLANDO CONVENTION
CENTER/SEA WORLD/DISNEY AREA   **Book at aaa.com**   **Phone:** 407/351-1982   72
Property failed to provide current rates
Location: I-4, exit 72, just e on SR 528 (Bee Line Expwy) to exit 1 (International Dr), just s, then just w. 6443 Westwood
Small-scale Hotel Blvd 32821. Fax: 407/351-1719. **Facility:** 113 one-bedroom standard units. 4 stories, interior corridors. *Bath:* combo or shower only. **Parking:** on-site. **Terms:** pets ($25 fee). **Amenities:** voice mail, irons. **Pool(s):** outdoor. **Leisure Activities:** exercise room. **Guest Services:** coin laundry. **Business Services:** fax (fee).

SOME UNITS
FEE

(See maps and indexes p. 666-673, 667-674, 668-678, 670-685)

SUBURBAN EXTENDED STAY HOTEL-ORLANDO
CENTRAL PARK   *Book at aaa.com*

Phone: 407/251-1110   **8**

Property failed to provide current rates

▼▼ ▼▼
Small-scale Hotel

Location: Just s of SR 528 (Bee Line Expwy), exit 4; just w of US 17-92 and 441; just s of Florida Tpke, exit 244. 9435 Delegates Dr 32837. Fax: 407/855-3625. **Facility:** 144 one-bedroom standard units with efficiencies. 3 stories, exterior corridors. *Bath:* combo or shower only. **Parking:** on-site. **Terms:** office hours 8 am-11 pm. **Amenities:** voice mail. **Pool(s):** heated outdoor. **Guest Services:** coin laundry.

SOME UNITS

`[icons]`

SUMMERFIELD VILLAS-AMERICAN VACATION
HOMES

Phone: (407)396-2880   **15**

All Year   2P: $89-$289

▼▼▼▼
Condominium

Location: Florida Tpke, exit 244, 2.1 mi w on US 192. 2983 Vineland Rd 34746. Fax: 407/397-4132. **Facility:** Most of the three- to five-bedroom condos and homes have been individually decorated; homes have pools and condo units have access to a community pool. 22 three-bedroom suites. 1-2 stories, exterior corridors. **Parking:** on-site. **Terms:** check-in 4 pm, 5 night minimum stay - seasonal, 30 day cancellation notice, 14 day off season-fee imposed, package plans, 7% service charge. **Amenities:** irons. **Leisure Activities:** playground. **Guest Services:** complimentary laundry. **Business Services:** fax (fee). **Cards:** AX, DC, MC, VI. *(See color ad p 756)*

`[icons]`

SUPER 8 ORLANDO INTERNATIONAL AIRPORT
SOUTH   *Book at aaa.com*

Phone: (407)240-8400   **7**

12/1-4/22 & 6/18-11/30 [CP]	1P: $59-$89	2P: $59-$89
4/23-6/17 [CP]	1P: $49-$79	2P: $49-$79

▼▼ ▼▼
Small-scale Hotel

Location: Just e of Landstreet Rd and S Orange Blossom Tr; Florida Tpke, exit 254, just n. 1850 Landstreet Rd 32809. Fax: 407/240-8832. **Facility:** 132 one-bedroom standard units. 3 stories, interior/exterior corridors. *Bath:* combo or shower only. **Parking:** on-site. **Terms:** cancellation fee imposed. **Amenities:** irons, hair dryers. **Pool(s):** heated outdoor. **Guest Services:** valet laundry. **Business Services:** fax (fee). **Cards:** AX, DC, DS, MC, VI.

SOME UNITS

`[icons]`

UNIVERSAL'S HARD ROCK HOTEL, A LOEWS
HOTEL   *Book at aaa.com*

Phone: (407)503-2000   **10**

2/10-8/19	1P: $277-$466	2P: $277-$466	XP: $25	F17
10/2-11/30	1P: $260-$384	2P: $260-$384	XP: $25	F17
8/20-10/1	1P: $240-$351	2P: $240-$351	XP: $25	F17
12/1-2/9	1P: $229-$351	2P: $229-$351	XP: $25	F17

Resort
Large-scale Hotel

Location: I-4, exit 75A, 1 mi n, follow signs. 5800 Universal Blvd 32819 (1000 Universal Studios Plaza, ORLANDO). Fax: 407/503-2010. **Facility:** Lush landscaping surrounds this hotel designed in a California-Mission style; it is walking distance to Universal Studios and CityWalk. 650 units. 630 one-bedroom standard units. 20 one-bedroom suites ($489-$2040), some with whirlpools. 7 stories, interior corridors. *Bath:* combo or shower only. **Parking:** on-site (fee) and valet. **Terms:** check-in 4 pm, 5 day cancellation notice-fee imposed, pets ($25 fee). **Amenities:** CD players, dual phone lines, voice mail, safes, honor bars, irons, hair dryers, high-speed Internet. *Some:* fax. *Fee:* DVD players. **Dining:** 2 restaurants, 24 hours, cocktails, also, The Kitchen, Palm Restaurant, see separate listings. **Pool(s):** heated outdoor, wading. **Leisure Activities:** whirlpools, waterslide, recreation programs, jogging, playground, exercise room, shuffleboard, volleyball. *Fee:* scooters, massage, game room. **Guest Services:** gift shop, valet and coin laundry, area transportation-Universal Studios. **Business Services:** conference facilities, business center. **Cards:** AX, CB, DC, DS, JC, MC, VI. Affiliated with Loews Hotels.

SOME UNITS

`[icons]` FEE FEE   FEE FEE FEE

UNIVERSAL'S PORTOFINO BAY HOTEL, A LOEWS
HOTEL   *Book at aaa.com*

Phone: (407)503-1000   **9**

2/10-8/19	1P: $309-$488	2P: $309-$488	XP: $25	F17
10/2-11/30	1P: $299-$422	2P: $299-$422	XP: $25	F17
8/20-10/1	1P: $279-$389	2P: $279-$389	XP: $25	F17
12/1-2/9	1P: $264-$389	2P: $264-$389	XP: $25	F17

Resort
Large-scale Hotel

Location: I-4, exit 74B westbound; exit 75A eastbound, 1 mi n, follow signs. Located at Universal Studios. 5601 Universal Blvd 32819 (1000 Universal Studios Plaza, ORLANDO). Fax: 407/503-1010. **Facility:** Styled after a small town on the Italian Riviera, the property includes a miniature bay, gardens, piazzas and several pools. 750 units. 706 one-bedroom standard units. 44 one-bedroom suites ($459-$2400), some with whirlpools. 6 stories, interior corridors. *Bath:* combo or shower only. **Parking:** on-site. **Terms:** check-in 4 pm, 5 day cancellation notice-fee imposed. **Amenities:** DVD players, CD players, dual phone lines, voice mail, safes, honor bars, irons, hair dryers. *Fee:* high-speed Internet. **Dining:** 7 restaurants, 24 hours, cocktails, entertainment. **Pool(s):** 3 heated outdoor, wading. **Leisure Activities:** whirlpools, waterslide, beach & pool activities, water taxi, recreation programs, bocci, pool tables, playground, spa. *Fee:* game room. **Guest Services:** gift shop, valet laundry, area transportation-Universal attractions, beauty salon. **Business Services:** conference facilities, business center. **Cards:** AX, CB, DC, DS, JC, MC, VI.

SOME UNITS

`[icons]` FEE   FEE

(See maps and indexes p. 666-673, 667-674, 668-678, 670-685)

UNIVERSAL'S ROYAL PACIFIC RESORT, A LOEWS
HOTEL *Book at aaa.com* Phone: (407)503-3000 **14**

AAA (SAVE)

	2/10-8/19	1P: $245-$428	2P: $245-$428	XP: $25	F17
	10/2-11/30	1P: $235-$351	2P: $235-$351	XP: $25	F17
	8/20-10/1	1P: $209-$329	2P: $209-$329	XP: $25	F17
	12/1-2/9	1P: $199-$329	2P: $199-$329	XP: $25	F17

Resort Large-scale Hotel **Location:** I-4, exit 74B, just n. 6300 Hollywood Way 32819 (1000 Universal Studios Plaza, ORLANDO). Fax: 407/503-3010. **Facility:** With its tropical gardens, towering palms and soothing water features, this South Pacific-themed hotel immerses guests in an island ambience. 1000 units. 949 one-bedroom standard units. 51 one-bedroom suites ($325-$1875), some with whirlpools. 7 stories, interior corridors. *Bath:* combo or shower only. **Parking:** on-site (fee) and valet. **Terms:** check-in 4 pm, 5 day cancellation notice-fee imposed, pets ($25 fee). **Amenities:** dual phone lines, voice mail, safes, honor bars, irons, hair dryers. *Fee:* video games, high-speed Internet. *Some:* DVD players. **Dining:** 5 restaurants, 24 hours, cocktails, also, Tchoup Chop, see separate listing. **Pool(s):** heated outdoor, wading. **Leisure Activities:** whirlpools, cabanas, sand castle play area, recreation programs, croquet, shuffleboard, volleyball. *Fee:* massage, game room. **Guest Services:** gift shop, valet and coin laundry, area transportation-water taxi to Universal properties. **Business Services:** conference facilities, business center. **Cards:** AX, CB, DC, DS, JC, MC, VI.

SOME UNITS

[icons] FEE FEE FEE FEE

THE VILLAS OF GRAND CYPRESS
Book at aaa.com Phone: (407)239-4700 **65**

AAA (SAVE)

	1/9-5/13	1P: $400-$2000	2P: $400-$2000
	12/1-1/8 & 10/1-11/30	1P: $300-$1560	2P: $300-$1560
	5/14-9/30	1P: $215-$980	2P: $215-$980

Small-scale Hotel **Location:** I-4, exit 68, 2.3 mi nw on SR 535. 1 N Jacaranda 32836. Fax: 407/239-7219. **Facility:** This golf course property offers extensive recreational facilities; some guest rooms include a fireplace. 121 units. 73 one-bedroom standard units, some with whirlpools. 23 one- and 25 two-bedroom suites with kitchens, some with whirlpools. 2 stories, exterior corridors. *Bath:* combo or shower only. **Parking:** on-site. **Terms:** check-in 4 pm, 3 day cancellation notice, [AP] meal plan available, package plans, $12 service charge. **Amenities:** video library, CD players, high-speed Internet, dual phone lines, voice mail, safes, honor bars, irons, hair dryers. **Dining:** 3 restaurants, 24 hours, cocktails, also, The Black Swan, see separate listing, entertainment. **Pool(s):** heated outdoor. **Leisure Activities:** whirlpools, paddleboats, 12 tennis courts (3 lighted), recreation programs, equestrian center, bicycles, jogging, playground. *Fee:* golf-45 holes, massage. **Guest Services:** gift shop, valet laundry, area transportation-Disney. **Business Services:** meeting rooms, business center. **Cards:** AX, CB, DC, DS, JC, MC, VI. **Special Amenities:** free local telephone calls and free newspaper.

SOME UNITS

[icons] VCR DATA PORT

(See maps and indexes p. 666-673, 667-674, 668-678, 670-685)

WESTGATE LAKES RESORT & SPA   *Book at aaa.com*   Phone: (407)345-0000   71

(AAA) (SAVE)
◇◇◇◇ ◇◇◇
Resort
Condominium

All Year   1P: $79-$149
Location: I-4, exit 74A, 0.3 mi w on SR 482 (Sand Lake Rd), then 2.5 mi s. 10000 Turkey Lake Rd 32819 (2801 Professional Pkwy, OCOEE, 34761). Fax: 407/355-2979. **Facility:** The property offers one- and two-bedroom villas, some with lake views; numerous on-site activities are available. 1608 units. 762 one-bedroom standard units with whirlpools. 846 two-bedroom suites ($159-$419) with whirlpools, some with kitchens. 6 stories, exterior corridors. **Bath:** combo or tub only. **Parking:** on-site. **Terms:** check-in 4 pm, 7 day cancellation notice. **Amenities:** video library (fee), CD players, voice mail, safes, irons, hair dryers. **Dining:** 2 restaurants, 6:30 am-10 pm, Fri & Sat-11 pm, cocktails. **Pool(s):** 7 heated outdoor, 7 wading. **Leisure Activities:** whirlpools, rental canoes, rental paddleboats, rental sailboats, marina, fishing, 2 lighted tennis courts, recreation programs, rental bicycles, jogging, playground, spa, basketball, horseshoes, shuffleboard, volleyball. **Fee:** miniature golf, game room. **Guest Services:** gift shop, complimentary laundry. **Business Services:** meeting rooms, fax (fee). **Cards:** AX, DC, DS, MC, VI. *(See color ad p 734)*

SOME UNITS
🍽 🍸 🛗 🎣 🏊 🛠 ✕ 🎦 [DATA PORT] 🔌 💼 📺 / ✕ / [VCR]

WESTGATE PALACE   *Book at aaa.com*   Phone: (407)996-6000   32

(AAA) (SAVE)
◇◇◇◇ ◇◇◇
Condominium

All Year   1P: $139-$209   2P: $139-$209
Location: I-4, exit 74A, just e on SR 482 (Sand Lake Rd), 0.6 mi n on International Dr, then just e. 6137 Carrier Dr 32819 (2801 Professional Pkwy, OCOEE, 34761). Fax: 407/355-2979. **Facility:** Spacious condominium accommodations and numerous on-site activities keep guests entertained; restaurants and shops are close by. 202 two-bedroom suites with kitchens and whirlpools. 19 stories, interior corridors. **Parking:** on-site. **Terms:** check-in 4 pm, 7 day cancellation notice. **Amenities:** DVD players, CD players, voice mail, safes, irons, hair dryers. **Pool(s):** heated outdoor, wading. **Leisure Activities:** steamroom, fishing, sports court. **Fee:** game room. **Guest Services:** complimentary laundry. **Business Services:** fax (fee). **Cards:** AX, DC, DS, MC, VI. *(See color ad p 734)*

🎣 🏊 ✕ ✕ 🎦 [DATA PORT] 🔌 💼 📺

WINGATE INN @ ORLANDO INTERNATIONAL AIRPORT   *Book at aaa.com*   Phone: (407)826-5258   2

◇◇◇◇
Small-scale Hotel

1/12-4/20 [BP]   1P: $99-$165   2P: $99-$165   XP: $15   F12
12/1-1/11 & 4/21-11/30 [BP]   1P: $79-$129   2P: $79-$129   XP: $15   F12
Location: SR 528 (Bee Line Expwy), exit 11, 0.8 mi n on SR 436, then just e. 5750 Hazeltine National Dr 32822. Fax: 407/826-5206. **Facility:** 101 units. 93 one-bedroom standard units. 8 one-bedroom suites ($99-$219), some with whirlpools. 5 stories, interior corridors. **Bath:** combo or shower only. **Parking:** on-site. **Terms:** check-in 4 pm, cancellation fee imposed. **Amenities:** video games (fee), high-speed Internet, dual phone lines, voice mail, safes, irons, hair dryers. **Pool(s):** outdoor. **Leisure Activities:** whirlpool, exercise room. **Guest Services:** sundries, valet and coin laundry. **Business Services:** meeting rooms, business center. **Cards:** AX, DC, DS, MC, VI.

SOME UNITS
(ASK) [S/D] 🔄 🎣 🏊 🎦 [DATA PORT] 🔌 💼 📺 / ✕ /

WINGATE INN/UNIVERSAL STUDIOS   *Book at aaa.com*   Phone: (407)226-0900   2

(AAA) (SAVE)
◇◇◇◇
Small-scale Hotel

All Year [ECP]   1P: $79-$149   2P: $79-$149
Location: Jct SR 435 (Kirkman Rd) and I-4, exit 75B, 1 mi n, then just e. 5661 Windhover Dr 32819. Fax: 407/226-0920. **Facility:** 100 units. 99 one-bedroom standard units. 1 one-bedroom suite. 4 stories, interior corridors. **Bath:** combo or shower only. **Parking:** on-site. **Terms:** [BP] meal plan available. **Amenities:** video games (fee), high-speed Internet, dual phone lines, voice mail, safes, irons, hair dryers. **Pool(s):** outdoor. **Leisure Activities:** whirlpool, exercise room. **Guest Services:** valet and coin laundry, area transportation-Universal. **Business Services:** meeting rooms, business center. **Cards:** AX, CB, DC, DS, MC, VI.

SOME UNITS
[S/D] 🔄 🍴 🏋 🎣 🏊 🎦 [DATA PORT] 🔌 💼 📺 / ✕ /

WYNDHAM ORLANDO RESORT   *Book at aaa.com*   Phone: (407)351-2420   43

(AAA) (SAVE)
◇◇◇◇
Large-scale Hotel

All Year   1P: $129-$195   2P: $129-$195   XP: $10   F18
Location: I-4, exit 74A, just e on SR 482 (Sand Lake Rd). 8001 International Dr 32819. Fax: 407/345-5611. **Facility:** 1052 units. 1046 one-bedroom standard units. 6 one-bedroom suites ($169-$235), some with whirlpools. 2 stories, interior/exterior corridors. **Bath:** combo or shower only. **Parking:** on-site. **Terms:** check-in 4 pm, 3 day cancellation notice, 8% service charge, small pets only ($50 extra charge). **Amenities:** dual phone lines, voice mail, safes, irons, hair dryers. **Fee:** video games, high-speed Internet. **Dining:** 3 restaurants, 6:30 am-midnight, cocktails. **Pool(s):** 3 heated outdoor, 2 wading. **Leisure Activities:** saunas, whirlpool, steamrooms, recreation programs, jogging, playground. **Fee:** massage, game room. **Guest Services:** gift shop, valet and coin laundry, area transportation-major attractions. **Business Services:** conference facilities, business center. **Cards:** AX, CB, DC, DS, JC, MC, VI.

SOME UNITS
🛏 🍽 🍸 🏋 🎣 🏊 🛠 ✕ 🎦 [DATA PORT] 📺 / ✕ /
FEE   FEE

WHERE TO DINE

1-6-8 RESTAURANT   Lunch: $5-$9   Dinner: $6-$22   Phone: 407-363-1688   19

◇◇◇◇ ◇◇◇
Chinese

Location: I-4, exit 74A, just w on SR 482 (Sand Lake Rd), then just n; in Bayhill Shopping Center. 7721 Turkey Lake Rd 32819. **Hours:** 11:30 am-10:30 pm, Fri & Sat-11 pm. Closed: 11/23, 12/25. **Features:** More than 40 daily lunch specials featuring Mandarin and Szechuan cuisine attract the local business crowd. Spotless and clean with pleasant, congenial service, this dining room displays lovely decorator touches. Casual dress; beer & wine only. **Parking:** on-site. **Cards:** AX, MC, VI.

ADOBE GILA'S   Lunch: $8-$12   Dinner: $10-$18   Phone: 407-903-1477   48

◇◇◇
Mexican

Location: I-4, exit 74A, 1 mi e on SR 482 (Sand Lake Rd), then 1.5 mi s; in Pointe Orlando. 9101 International Dr, Suite 2200 32819. **Hours:** 11:30 am-11 pm. **Features:** It's fiesta time at the Mexican-style cantina, where cooks dish up tamales, burritos, enchiladas and quesadillas, all hot and hearty and meant to be washed down with one of the more than 75 varieties of obligatory margaritas. Guests can groove to the tunes of the late-night band Wednesday through Saturday. Casual dress; cocktails. **Parking:** on-site (fee). **Cards:** AX, MC, VI.

(See maps and indexes p. 666-673, 667-674, 668-678, 670-685)

ANTONIO'S SAND LAKE   **Dinner:** $12-$35   **Phone:** 407/363-9191   24
Italian
Location: I-4, exit 74A (Sand Lake Rd), 1 mi w; in Fountains Plaza. 7559 W Sand Lake Rd 32819. **Hours:** 5 pm-10 pm. Closed major holidays; also Sun. **Reservations:** suggested. **Features:** Lending to the Tuscan atmosphere are gothic and barrel-vault ceilings and wood floors. Italian dishes center on fresh fish, black Angus steak, veal, lamb and pork. The bread is freshly baked, and desserts are many. On the wine list are more than 250 selections ranging from rare to popular; a full bar also is available. Casual dress; cocktails. **Parking:** on-site. **Cards:** AX, CB, DC, MC, VI.

ATLANTIS   **Dinner:** $27-$35   **Phone:** 407/351-5555   55
Seafood
Location: I-4, exit 72, just e on Central Florida Pkwy, then 0.3 mi n or 0.7 mi w of International Dr; in Renaissance Orlando Resort at SeaWorld. 6677 Sea Harbor Dr 32821-8092. **Hours:** 6 pm-10 pm. Closed major holidays; also Sun. **Reservations:** suggested. **Features:** Relax in a lovely formal setting complete with crystal chandeliers and hand-painted murals. Fresh, expertly prepared seafood is offered along with lamb and filet mignon. Savor a glass of wine from a very select list. Resort-casual attire is accepted. Dressy casual; cocktails. **Parking:** on-site and valet. **Cards:** AX, CB, DC, DS, JC, MC, VI.

AUSSI STEAK HOUSE ORLANDO   **Dinner:** $12-$25   **Phone:** 407/345-8884   37
American
Location: I-4, exit 74A, just e on SR 482 (Sand Lake Rd), then 0.3 mi s. 8148 International Dr 32819. **Hours:** 4 pm-11 pm. **Reservations:** accepted. **Features:** Featured steaks, lamb and chicken are cooked to your liking. Also, enjoy barbecue from down under as well as the catch of the day. Casual dress; cocktails. **Parking:** on-site. **Cards:** AX, MC, VI.

BAHAMA BREEZE   **Lunch:** $8-$24   **Dinner:** $8-$24   **Phone:** 407/248-2499   45
Caribbean
Location: I-4, exit 74A, 1 mi s. 8849 International Dr 32817. **Hours:** 11 am-1 am, Fri & Sat-1:30 am. Closed 11/23, 12/25. **Features:** Move to an island beat at this popular restaurant featuring Caribbean fare in a tropical decor. Many favorites are offered, including a jerk chicken that gives you a spicy taste of Jamaica. Visit the on-site gift shop for a little after-dinner browsing. Casual dress; cocktails; entertainment. **Parking:** on-site and valet. **Cards:** AX, DC, DS, MC, VI.

BAUERN STUBE AUTHENTIC GERMAN
  RESTAURANT   **Lunch:** $4-$18   **Dinner:** $6-$18   **Phone:** 407/857-8404   2
German
Location: Jct SR 482 (Sand Lake Rd) and Orange Ave. 8015 S Orange Ave 32809. **Hours:** 11 am-2 & 5-close, Fri-11 pm, Sat 5 pm-11 pm. Closed: Sun. **Reservations:** suggested. **Features:** Patrons might think they have embarked on a trip to Germany, as the atmosphere and decor are reminiscent of those seen in 'Heidi.' Home-style recipes of sauerbraten, schnitzel and bratwurst are delightful. Save room for a homemade dessert and a complimentary schnapps at meal end. Casual dress. **Parking:** on-site. **Cards:** AX, DS, MC, VI.

BERGAMO'S ITALIAN RESTAURANT   **Dinner:** $15-$35   **Phone:** 407/352-3805   41
Italian
Location: I-4, exit 74A, just e on SR 482 (Sand Lake Rd), then 0.5 mi s; on west side of Mercado Shopping Village. 8445 International Dr 32819. **Hours:** 5 pm-10 pm. Closed: 11/23, 12/25. **Reservations:** suggested. **Features:** Although the elegent decor might lead you to believe this place is haughty and stiff, you'll quickly notice a more casual and bustling atmosphere pervades. Accomplished vocalists, the servers take turns belting out opera and Broadway tunes at the mic. Casual dress; cocktails; entertainment. **Parking:** on-site. **Cards:** AX, DC, DS, MC, VI.

THE BLACK SWAN   **Dinner:** $25-$40   **Phone:** 407/239-1999   45
Continental
Location: I-4, exit 68, 2.3 mi nw on SR 535; in The Villas of Grand Cypress. 1 N Jacaranda 32819. **Hours:** 6 pm-10 pm. **Reservations:** suggested. **Features:** Piano music plays while an extensive menu is served in a multi-level dining room that overlooks an emerald green golf course. The seared tuna is peppered, sliced thin and tied with orange rind to a tower of scallions. A 16% service charge will be assessed. Semi-formal attire; cocktails; entertainment. **Parking:** on-site. **Cards:** AX, CB, DC, DS, JC, MC, VI.

BOB MARLEY-A TRIBUTE TO FREEDOM   **Dinner:** $4-$11   **Phone:** 407/224-2262   3
Jamaican
Location: I-4, exit 74B; in Universal Studios CityWalk. Universal Studios 32835. **Hours:** 4 pm-2 am. **Features:** This themed restaurant not only features light Jamaican fare but also memorabilia from the legendary musician's life. Continuous concerts are shown on numerous televisions scattered throughout the restaurant. Casual dress; cocktails; entertainment. **Parking:** on-site (fee). **Cards:** AX, DS, MC, VI.

BONEFISH GRILL   **Dinner:** $12-$18   **Phone:** 407/355-7707   33
Seafood
Location: I-4, exit 74A, just w. 7830 W Sand Lake Rd 32819. **Hours:** 4 pm-10:30 pm, Fri & Sat-11:30 pm, Sun-10 pm. Closed: 11/23, 12/25. **Features:** In a shopping plaza, the popular restaurant creatively prepares fresh seafood over a wood-burning grill. Among choices are Chilean sea bass, ahi, tuna and rainbow trout, to name a few. Casual dress; cocktails. **Parking:** on-site. **Cards:** AX, DS, MC, VI.

BOSTON LOBSTER FEAST   **Dinner:** $12-$30   **Phone:** 407/438-0607   5
Seafood
Location: Se of jct SR 482 (Sand Lake Rd) and US 17-92 and 441. 8204 Crystal Clear Ln 32809. **Hours:** 4 pm-10 pm, Sat & Sun from 2 pm. **Features:** Famished after a day of shopping at the Florida Mall? This casual, all-you-can-eat Maine lobster buffet may be just what you need. Lobster, crab, beef, salad and soup are among the many selections served in an inventive, nautical atmosphere. Casual dress; cocktails. **Parking:** on-site. **Cards:** AX, DC, DS, MC, VI.

(See maps and indexes p. 666-673, 667-674, 668-678, 670-685)

THE BUTCHER SHOP STEAK HOUSE
Steak House

Dinner: $18-$34   **Phone:** 407/363-9727   42

Location: I-4, exit 74A, just e on SR 482 (Sand Lake Rd), then 0.5 mi s; in Mercado Shopping Village. 8445 International Dr, Suite 140 32819. **Hours:** 5 pm-10 pm, Fri & Sat-11 pm. **Closed:** 11/23, 12/25. **Reservations:** suggested. **Features:** Richly appointed dining rooms decked out in mahogany are the setting for surprisingly informal dining. The menu is primarily charcoal-broiled steak and prime rib ranging in size from an 8-oz filet to a 32-oz bone-in rib eye. A cook-your-own option is featured. Casual dress; cocktails. **Parking:** on-site. **Cards:** AX, DC, DS, MC, VI.

CAFE TU TU TANGO
International

Lunch: $4-$20   **Dinner:** $4-$20   **Phone:** 407/248-2222   43

Location: I-4, exit 74A, 1 mi se, just e of International Dr; 0.5 mi s of SR 482 (Sand Lake Rd); in DoubleTree Castle Hotel. 8625 International Dr 32819. **Hours:** 11:30 am-11 pm, Fri & Sat-2 am. **Closed:** 11/23, 12/25. **Features:** A multi-ethnic menu that reaches into different parts of the world offers a broad variety of exclusively appetizer-sized dishes. Creativity and flair shows in such specialties as Cajun chicken egg rolls, Barcelona stir-fry and tenderloin skewers. View the works of local artists on display throughout the restaurant. Casual dress; cocktails; entertainment. **Parking:** on-site. **Cards:** AX, DS, MC, VI.

CALIFORNIA PIZZA KITCHEN
Italian

Lunch: $5-$17   **Dinner:** $5-$17   **Phone:** 407/248-7887   4

Location: I-4, exit 78, just e; in Mall at Millenia. 4200 Conroy Rd, SP 1590 32839. **Hours:** 11 am-9:30 pm, Fri & Sat-10 pm, Sun 11:30 am-7:30 pm. Closed major holidays. **Features:** Gourmet pizzas, such as barbecue chicken and gorgonzola cheese and pear, contribute to a mouthwatering selection; desserts are worth the splurge. Casual dress; cocktails. **Parking:** on-site. **Cards:** AX, DS, MC, VI.

CAPRICCIO GRILL
Northern Italian

Dinner: $18-$38   **Phone:** 407/345-4540   51

Location: 0.5 mi n of SR 528 (Bee Line Expwy); in The Peabody Orlando. 9801 International Dr 32819. **Hours:** 6 pm-11 pm, Sun also 11 am-2 pm. **Closed:** Mon. **Reservations:** suggested. **Features:** Buzzing with a bustling atmosphere, this upscale, casual eatery features an exhibition kitchen with a wood-burning pizza oven. Sunday champagne brunch is popular and offers an abundance of hearty, delicious choices. Choose from a well-rounded wine list. Dressy casual; cocktails. **Parking:** on-site and valet. **Cards:** AX, CB, DC, DS, JC, MC, VI.

CARRINO'S LAKEFRONT RESTAURANT
Italian

Lunch: $10-$18   **Dinner:** $10-$18   **Phone:** 407/352-8407   29

Location: I-4, exit 74A, just w. 7572 W Sandlake Rd 32819. **Hours:** 11 am-10 pm, Fri & Sat-11 pm, Sun noon-9 pm. Closed major holidays. **Features:** Enjoy a view of the lake while dining on homemade Italian dishes or a specialty pizza. Pizzas are hand-tossed and a wide variety of toppings are offered; baked dishes are also favorites including eggplant, chicken and veal. Outside dining is available. Casual dress; cocktails. **Parking:** on-site. **Cards:** AX, DS, MC, VI.

CEDAR'S RESTAURANT
Lebanese

Lunch: $9-$26   **Dinner:** $9-$26   **Phone:** 407/351-6000   35

Location: I-4, exit 74A, 0.4 mi w. 7732 W Sand Lake Rd 32819. **Hours:** 11:30 am-3 & 5-10 pm, Sat from noon, Sun noon-9 pm. **Features:** Lebanese and Mediterranean dishes make up the busy eatery's menu. Begin with spicy sun-dried beef or grape leaves stuffed with rice, tomato, parsley and onions. Entrees include shish kebab, mixed grill, fish stew and stuffed vegetables, rice and meat. The wine list is extensive. High ceilings contribute to a comfortable atmosphere. Casual dress; cocktails. **Parking:** on-site. **Cards:** AX, DC, DS, MC, VI.

CHARLEY'S STEAK HOUSE
Steak House

Dinner: $13-$35   **Phone:** 407/363-0228   38

Location: I-4, exit 74A, just e on SR 482 (Sand Lake Rd), then 0.3 mi s. 8255 International Dr 32819. **Hours:** 5 pm-10:30 pm, Fri & Sat-11 pm. **Closed:** 11/23, 12/25. **Reservations:** suggested. **Features:** The restaurant specializes in steak, chicken and seafood grilled over an open flame. Five dining rooms with an antique look are available. Peruse the extensive wine list to find the perfect complement to the 20-oz filet mignon or the 52-oz porterhouse steak. Casual dress; cocktails. **Parking:** on-site. **Cards:** AX, MC, VI.

CHATHAM'S PLACE
Continental

Dinner: $20-$38   **Phone:** 407/345-2992   22

Location: I-4, exit 74A, 0.5 mi w; opposite Market Place Shopping Center. 7575 Dr Phillips Blvd 32819. **Hours:** 5:30 pm-10 pm. Closed major holidays. **Reservations:** suggested. **Features:** Relaxed elegance is evoked in the small, intimate dining room where live music is performed nightly and the refined menu boasts a selection of entrees ranging from rack of lamb to fresh blackened grouper with a pecan butter crust. Dressy casual; cocktails; entertainment. **Parking:** on-site. **Cards:** AX, DC, DS, MC, VI.

CHRISTINI'S RISTORANTE ITALIANO
Italian

Dinner: $18-$39   **Phone:** 407/345-8770

Location: I-4, exit 74A, 0.5 mi w; in Marketplace Shopping Center. 7600 Dr Phillips Blvd 32819. **Hours:** 6 pm-midnight. Closed major holidays. **Reservations:** suggested. **Features:** Famous for their 26 ounce veal chop, the restaurant also makes their own fresh pasta. Menu selections include shrimp diablo, veal with four cheeses and calamari. Italian art and a strolling accordionist add charm to a friendly, though bustling atmosphere. Semi-formal attire; cocktails. **Parking:** on-site. **Cards:** AX, CB, DC, MC, VI.

CIAO ITALIA RISTORANTE ITALIANO
AAA
Italian

Dinner: $15-$30   **Phone:** 407/354-0770   54

Location: SR 528 (Bee Line Expwy), exit 1, just e; in International Towne Center. 6149 Westwood Blvd 32821. **Hours:** 5 pm-11 pm. **Features:** This Italian bistro is located within a strip mall. Their walls have decorative tiles, the dishes are prepared using the freshest of ingredients, and the friendly wait staff is happy to offer suggestions. Casual dress; cocktails. **Parking:** on-site. **Cards:** AX, DC, DS, MC, VI.

DUX

Continental

Dinner: $25-$42   **Phone:** 407/345-4540   52

Location: 0.5 mi n of SR 528 (Bee Line Expwy); opposite Orange County Convention Center; in The Peabody Orlando. 9801 International Dr 32819. **Hours:** Open 12/1-7/31 & 9/1-11/30; 6 pm-10 pm, Fri & Sat-11 pm. **Closed:** Sun. **Reservations:** suggested. **Features:** An intimate, elegant dining room and refined service set the scene for traditional cuisine with a creative, international spin. The menu changes seasonally and features dishes like skewered beef in a spicy, tangy sauce. Gentlemen's jackets are suggested. Semi-formal attire; cocktails. **Parking:** on-site. **Cards:** AX, CB, DC, DS, JC, MC, VI.

(See maps and indexes p. 666-673, 667-674, 668-678, 670-685)

EMERIL'S RESTAURANT ORLANDO   **Lunch:** $18-$22   **Dinner:** $24-$40   **Phone:** 407/224-2424   ④

Creole

Location: In Universal Studios CityWalk. 6000 Universal Blvd, S-702 32819. **Hours:** 11:30 am-2 & 5:30-10 pm, Fri & Sat-11 pm. **Reservations:** suggested. **Features:** You will find a wonderful mix of Old World, Louisiana cooking with the style of today's modern kitchen. From oven-baked pizza to rack of lamb to ham crusted snapper, all dishes are fabulously well-prepared and graciously served in a New Vogue setting. Dressy casual; cocktails. **Parking:** on-site (fee) and valet. **Cards:** AX, CB, DC, DS, JC, MC, VI.

EVERGLADES RESTAURANT   **Dinner:** $17-$30   **Phone:** 407/996-9840   ㊾

Regional American

Location: I-4, exit 72, just e on SR 528 (Bee Line Expwy) to exit 1 (International Dr), then just n; in Rosen Centre Hotel. 9840 International Dr 32819. **Hours:** 5:30 pm-10 pm. **Reservations:** suggested. **Features:** Diners here can unwind in an artfully created atmosphere among images of the flora and fauna of Florida. Flashes of color and motion coming from the large aquarium entice patrons to relax. On the adventurous menu are such choices as Alligator Bay chowder, sauteed wild boar medallions, venison pepper steak and tenderloin of buffalo. Those who prefer to stay closer to home can opt for one of the many fresh seafood or beef entrees. An 18 percent gratuity is added automatically to the bill. Casual dress; cocktails. **Parking:** on-site and valet. **Cards:** AX, DC, DS, JC, MC, VI.

FAMAS PIZZA & PASTA   **Lunch:** $5-$17   **Dinner:** $5-$17   **Phone:** 407/239-1500   ㊽

Italian

Location: I-4, exit 72, 2 mi e; in shopping plaza. 5478 Central Florida Pkwy 32821. **Hours:** 11 am-2 am. Closed major holidays. **Features:** The quaint, simple eatery serves hearty Italian food. Some imported pastas, oils and seasonings can be purchased. Casual dress. **Parking:** on-site. **Cards:** AX, MC, VI.

FIRST WATCH   **Lunch:** $4-$10   **Dinner:** $4-$10   **Phone:** 407/363-5622   ㉘

American

Location: I-4, exit 74A, just w. 7500 Sand Lake Rd 32819. **Hours:** 7 am-2:30 pm. Closed major holidays. **Features:** One of a dozen like it in Florida, it serves breakfast, brunch and lunch with traditional omelettes, pancakes, waffles and crepes. Great salads and sandwiches are accompanied by fresh fruits and muffins. Attentive and accurate service brings patrons back. Casual dress. **Parking:** on-site. **Cards:** AX, MC, VI.

FISHBONES   **Dinner:** $13-$40   **Phone:** 407/352-0135   ㉓

Seafood

Location: I-4, exit 74A, 0.3 mi e on SR 482 (Sand Lake Rd). 6707 Sand Lake Rd 32819. **Hours:** 5 pm-10:30 pm, Fri & Sat-11 pm. Closed: 11/23, 12/25. **Reservations:** suggested. **Features:** Nine dining rooms cast off a nautical personality, with plenty of wood, fishing poles and a big saltwater fish tank. Fresh fish cooked over an open citrus and oak flame, pan-seared sesame tuna and crab-stuffed filet mignon are all good choices. Casual dress; cocktails. **Parking:** on-site. **Cards:** AX, MC, VI.

HANAMIZUKI JAPANESE RESTAURANT   **Lunch:** $6-$25   **Dinner:** $9-$70   **Phone:** 407/363-7200   ㊵

Japanese

Location: 0.5 mi s of jct Universal Blvd; in Goodings Plaza. 8255 International Dr, Suite 136 32819. **Hours:** 11:30 am-2 & 5-10:30 pm. Closed: Sun. **Reservations:** suggested. **Features:** The trendy restaurant offers some excellent Japanese food, including sushi and salmon teriyaki. The wait staff is attentive and set on sending diners away happy. Dressy casual; beer & wine only. **Parking:** on-site. **Cards:** AX, DC, DS, JC, MC, VI.

HEMISPHERE   **Dinner:** $18-$31   **Phone:** 407/825-1234   ③

Continental

Location: At Orlando International Airport (Terminal A); in Hyatt Regency Orlando International Airport. 9300 Airport Blvd 32827. **Hours:** 6:30 am-11:30 & 5-10 pm, Sat & Sun-noon. **Reservations:** suggested. **Features:** Watch planes depart while enjoying a delightful meal in this rich, airy 9th floor dining room overlooking a terminal and runway. A tasteful decor and delicious food are the strong points. Be sure to make a reservation as this restaurant is quite popular. Casual dress; cocktails. **Parking:** valet. **Cards:** AX, CB, DC, DS, JC, MC, VI.

JACK'S PLACE   **Dinner:** $16-$28   **Phone:** 407/996-9700   ㊿

Steak & Seafood

Location: I-4, exit 72, just n; SR 528 (Bee Line Expwy), exit 1, then just n; in Rosen Plaza. 9700 International Dr 32819. **Hours:** 5:30 pm-11 pm. **Reservations:** suggested. **Features:** A casually elegant decor features a collection of autographed celebrity caricatures. Excellent cuisine is skillfully prepared, and offered along with list of daily specials. Please note, a service charge of 18 percent is automatically added to the check. Casual dress; cocktails. **Parking:** on-site and valet. **Cards:** AX, DC, DS, JC, MC, VI.

JIMMY BUFFETT'S MARGARITAVILLE   **Lunch:** $8-$19   **Dinner:** $8-$19   **Phone:** 407/224-2155   ⑨

American

Location: In Universal Studios CityWalk. 6000 Universal Blvd, S-704 32819. **Hours:** 11 am-2 am. **Reservations:** not accepted. **Features:** Kick back with a margarita and feast on cheeseburgers in paradise. Island trinkets and twinkling lights decorate a two-story dining room where favorite Buffett tunes are played to set the perfect lazy-day-at-the-beach mood. A must for devoted parrotheads. Casual dress; cocktails. **Parking:** on-site (fee) and valet. **Cards:** AX, DC, DS, MC, VI.

JOCKAMO'S NEW ORLEANS KITCHEN   **Lunch:** $4-$12   **Dinner:** $4-$12   **Phone:** 407/226-2848   ②

Creole

Location: Jct Sand Lake Rd and John Young Pkwy, just e. 3042 Sand Lake Rd 32819. **Hours:** 11 am-9 pm. Closed major holidays; also Sun. **Features:** For a taste of New Orleans visit this eatery and experience crawfish etouffee, jambalaya, crawgator or a giant muffuletta sandwich; beers from Louisiana are also featured. Casual dress; beer & wine only. **Parking:** on-site. **Cards:** AX, DC, DS, MC, VI.

KANPAI   **Lunch:** $6-$13   **Dinner:** $11-$35   **Phone:** 407/352-4811   ⑬

Japanese

Location: I-4, exit 75A, just s on SR 435 (Kirkman Rd), then just e; in International Festival Plaza. 6687 S Kirkman Rd 32819. **Hours:** 11:30 am-2 & 5-10 pm. Closed major holidays. **Features:** This Japanese steak house features teppanyaki style Japanese cuisine prepared at the guests' table. There is also a separate sushi bar and lounge; the sushi menu consists of over 40 sushi rolls and fresh nigiri. Casual dress; cocktails. **Parking:** on-site. **Cards:** AX, CB, DC, DS, JC, MC, VI.

(See maps and indexes p. 666-673, 667-674, 668-678, 670-685)

THE KITCHEN
▼▼▼▼
American

Lunch: $8-$21 **Dinner:** $8-$33 **Phone:** 407/503-2430 ①
Location: I-4, exit 75A, 1 mi n, follow signs; in Universal's Hard Rock, A Loews Hotel. 5800 Universal Blvd 32819. **Hours:** 7 am-11 pm. **Reservations:** suggested. **Features:** Visiting rock stars have been known to cook their favorite dishes in the open exhibition kitchen at this fun eatery. The menu offers seared ahi tuna, mac and cheese, meatloaf, cedar plank salmon and jumbo crab cakes. Casual dress; cocktails. **Parking:** on-site (fee) and valet. **Cards:** AX, CB, DC, MC, VI.

LA PIAZA ITALIAN RESTAURANT
▼▼▼
Italian

Lunch: $5-$9 **Dinner:** $7-$17 **Phone:** 407/855-1170 ⑧
Location: SR 417, exit 10, 1 mi s on John Young Pkwy; in Colonial Hunter Creek Promenade Shopping Mall. 4060 Town Center Blvd 32837. **Hours:** 11:30 am-9:30 pm, Fri & Sat-10:30 pm. Closed major holidays; also Mon. **Reservations:** accepted. **Features:** Decorated to resemble the patio of an Italian villa, this restaurant offers delicious food and gracious service. The menu features reliable Italian fare, such as pizza, pasta and sandwiches. Simple food preparations make this a pleasant place for lunch or a casual supper. Dressy casual; cocktails. **Parking:** on-site. **Cards:** AX, DC, DS, MC, VI.

LATIN QUARTER
▼▼▼
Latino

Lunch: $7-$25 **Dinner:** $13-$30 **Phone:** 407/224-2800 ②
Location: I-4, exit 74B; in Universal Studios CityWalk. 6000 Universal CityWalk S-606 32835. **Hours:** 5 pm-11 pm, Fri-Sun from noon. **Features:** Contributing to the elegant, lively and earthy decor are colorful mosaic tile, strobe lighting and fine table settings. Menu items are light, creative and artistic, combining distinct flavorings with pork, lamb, chicken and beef. This place is great for a good meal and all-night dancing. Casual dress; cocktails. **Parking:** on-site (fee). **Cards:** AX, MC, VI.

MEMORIES OF INDIA
▼▼▼ ▼▼▼
Indian

Lunch: $6-$9 **Dinner:** $8-$18 **Phone:** 407/370-3277 ⑰
Location: I-4, exit 74A (Turkey Lake Rd), just w, then just n; in Bay Hill Plaza. 7625 Turkey Lake Rd 32819. **Hours:** 11:30 am-2:30 & 5:30-10 pm, Fri & Sat-10:30 pm, Sun-9 pm. Closed: 9/4. **Reservations:** required. **Features:** Wondrous tastes await diners in a delightful, intimate setting. Tucked in a shopping plaza near the entrance to Universal Studios, the restaurant is worth a trip. The scent of chicken and shrimp cooking in the clay tandoor oven whets appetites of entering diners. Dishes represent many regions of India, and the chef/owner lets guests share their preference for spiciness. Food is flavored with the freshest herbs. Casual dress; beer & wine only. **Parking:** on-site. **Cards:** AX, DS, MC, VI.

MING COURT
▼▼▼ ▼▼▼
Chinese

Lunch: $5-$10 **Dinner:** $12-$30 **Phone:** 407/351-9988 ㊾
Location: 0.8 mi n of SR 528 (Bee Line Expwy); 1 mi s of SR 482 (Sand Lake Rd). 9188 International Dr 32819. **Hours:** 11 am-2:30 & 4:30-11:30 pm. **Reservations:** suggested. **Features:** A 250-foot dragon will greet you as you enter the courtyard of this elegant Oriental restaurant. Gourmet regional specialties served in split-level dining rooms have a nouvelle flair, including the Szechuan Flaming Wok, sushi bar and daily Dim Sum lunch. Dressy casual; cocktails; entertainment. **Parking:** on-site. **Cards:** AX, CB, DC, DS, JC, MC, VI.

MOE'S SOUTHWEST GRILL
▼▼▼
Mexican

Lunch: $3-$9 **Dinner:** $3-$9 **Phone:** 407/264-9903 ㉖
Location: I-4, exit 74A (Sand Lake Rd), 0.4 mi w. 7541-D W Sand Lake Rd 32819. **Hours:** 11 am-10 pm. Closed major holidays. **Features:** With locations in several states, the casual eatery serves Mexican food in huge portions; guests drop in for friendly service and fresh food at great prices. Casual dress; beer only. **Parking:** on-site. **Cards:** AX, DS, MC, VI.

MOON FISH
▼▼▼
Seafood

Dinner: $13-$30 **Phone:** 407/363-7262 ㉕
Location: I-4, exit 74A (Sand Lake Rd), 1 mi w; in Fountains Plaza. 7525 W Sand Lake Rd 32819. **Hours:** 5 pm-10:30 pm, Fri & Sat-11 pm. Closed major holidays. **Reservations:** accepted. **Features:** The award-winning restaurant presents a menu of distinctive fish-centered fusion cuisine: sushi, sashimi and a raw bar offering an array of choices from oysters to duck carpaccio. Semi-formal attire; cocktails. **Parking:** on-site. **Cards:** AX, MC, VI.

MURPHY'S CHOP HOUSE
▼▼▼
Steak House

Dinner: $16-$29 **Phone:** 407/851-9000 ①
Location: SR 528 (Bee Line Expwy), exit 11, 0.5 mi n on SR 436, just e, then s; in Marriott Orlando Airport. 7499 Augusta National Dr 32822. **Hours:** 5 pm-10 pm. Closed: Sun. **Reservations:** suggested. **Features:** This mainly Chicago-style chop house also offers seafood dishes such as tuna fillet coated with sesame seeds or horseradish-encrusted red snapper. In the center of a mid-rise hotel just north of Orlando International Airport, the setting is classic, complete with hardwood floors and brass accents. Casual dress; cocktails. **Parking:** valet. **Cards:** AX, DC, DS, JC, MC, VI.

NASCAR CAFE
AAA
▼▼▼ ▼▼
American

Lunch: $7-$19 **Dinner:** $7-$19 **Phone:** 407/224-7223 ⑦
Location: I-4, exit 74B; in Universal Studios CityWalk. 6000 Universal CityWalk 32819. **Hours:** 11 am-10 pm. **Features:** Cars displayed out front are only the beginning of this auto racing adventure. Forget dieting! The portions of burgers, steaks, barbecue ribs and chicken are huge. A gift shop and arcade games make this more than your usual burger joint. Casual dress; cocktails. **Parking:** on-site (fee). **Cards:** AX, DC, DS, MC, VI.

NORMAN'S
▼▼▼ ▼▼▼
Continental

Dinner: $26-$38 **Phone:** 407/393-4333 ⑦
Location: I-4, exit 72, just e on SR 528 (Bee Line Expwy) to exit 1, 0.8 mi s on International Dr, then 1.3 mi e; in The Ritz-Carlton Orlando, Grande Lakes. 4012 Central Florida Pkwy 32837. **Hours:** 6 pm-10 pm, Fri & Sat-10:30 pm. **Reservations:** suggested. **Features:** Chef Norman Van Aken's New World cuisine fuses Latin and Caribbean flavors with traditional European preparation techniques. Among delightful and imaginative creations are jumbo shrimp stuffed with yuca and sour orange sauce; serrano-wrapped roasted loin of Hawaiian tuna; and chocolate cake en cotte. Sophisticated and warm, the dining room decor is reminiscent of a Colonial Italian palazzo. Casual dress; cocktails. **Parking:** valet. **Cards:** AX, MC, VI.

(See maps and indexes p. 666-673, 667-674, 668-678, 670-685)

ORLANDO'S WILD JACKS — Dinner: $10-$22 — Phone: 407/352-4407 — 16
American
Location: 0.3 mi n of SR 482 (Sand Lake Rd); 0.5 mi ne of I-4, exit 74A. 7364 International Dr 32819. **Hours:** 4 pm-11 pm, Fri & Sat 5 pm-11:30 pm. **Reservations:** accepted. **Features:** A unique experience, the restaurant features a charcoal grill and flavors indicative of Florida, as well as American microbrews and a selection of wines that compliment the fresh grilled tastes of the eatery. Casual dress; cocktails. **Parking:** on-site.
Cards: AX, CB, DS, MC, VI.

PAC-MAN CAFE AT XS ORLANDO — Lunch: $6-$19 — Dinner: $6-$19 — Phone: 407/226-8922 — 47
International
Location: I-4, exit 74A, 1 mi e on SR 482 (Sand Lake Rd), 1.5 mi s; in Pointe Orlando. 9101 International Dr, Suite 2400 32819. **Hours:** noon-10 pm, Fri & Sat-11 pm. **Reservations:** accepted. **Features:** Fun, entertainment and gourmet cuisine are spread over three floors: the top, which offers rooftop dancing and live bands; the second, stocked with the latest in virtual reality and interactive games; and the ground, which opens to a modish, swanky dining room surging with coolness. Trendy dishes give a twist on traditional favorites, such as chicken and ribs, lasagna, jambalaya and macadamia-encrusted mahi mahi. Among other choices are Cuban sandwiches and brick oven gourmet pizzas. Dressy casual; cocktails. **Parking:** on-site (fee). **Cards:** AX, DC, DS, MC, VI.

PALM RESTAURANT — Dinner: $15-$34 — Phone: 407/503-7256 — 8
American
Location: I-4, exit 75A, 1 mi n, follow signs; in Universal's Hard Rock Hotel, A Loews Hotel. 5800 Universal Blvd 32819. **Hours:** 5 pm-11 pm. **Reservations:** suggested. **Features:** At this classic, bustling steakhouse, diners are treated to superb steaks and chops in flavorful and ample cuts, along with a variety of pasta, poultry and seafood dishes. Dressy casual; cocktails. **Parking:** valet. **Cards:** AX, CB, DC, MC, VI.

PANERA BREAD — Lunch: $3-$8 — Dinner: $3-$8 — Phone: 407/856-6706 — 3
American
Location: Jct Sand Lake Rd and Orange Blossom Tr, just e; located outside of the Florida Mall. 1117 Florida Mall Ave 32809. **Hours:** 7 am-9 pm, Sun from 8:30 am. Closed major holidays. **Features:** Located in a shopping area, the restaurant is a great place for healthy sandwiches and homemade soups served in large bread bowls. Numerous varieties of freshly baked breads and bagels make this a popular stop for breakfast. Casual dress. **Parking:** on-site. **Cards:** AX, DS, MC, VI.

PANERA BREAD — Lunch: $4-$9 — Dinner: $4-$9 — Phone: 407/226-6992 — 32
American
Location: I-4, exit 74A, just w. 7826 W Sand Lake Rd 32819. **Hours:** 6:30 am-9:30 pm, Sun 7 am-8:30 pm. Closed: 11/23, 12/25. **Features:** In a shopping area, the restaurant is a great place for healthy sandwiches and homemade soups served in large bread bowls. Numerous varieties of freshly baked breads and bagels make this a popular stop for breakfast. Casual dress. **Parking:** on-site. **Cards:** AX, DS, MC, VI.

PASTAMORE' — Lunch: $6-$13 — Dinner: $9-$27 — Phone: 407/224-2244 — 5
Italian
Location: In Universal Studios CityWalk. 6000 Universal Blvd, S-700 32819. **Hours:** 7 am-1 & 5-10:30 pm, Fri & Sat-midnight. **Features:** One of Universal Studio's favorites, it offers wonderful pastries and coffee served in a sidewalk cafe or inside a spacious dining room. A menu of veal, chicken, pizza and homemade pasta is highlighted by cheese-covered tomatoes soaked in oil and basil. Casual dress; cocktails. **Parking:** on-site (fee). **Cards:** AX, CB, DC, DS, JC, MC, VI.

PAT O'BRIEN'S — Dinner: $7-$12 — Phone: 407/224-2106 — 6
Creole
Location: In Universal Studios CityWalk. 6000 Universal Blvd, S-723 32819. **Hours:** 4 pm-1 am. **Reservations:** accepted. **Features:** This exact replica of the famous New Orleans bar offers nightly entertainment, a courtyard and three bars. A clean-cut deli delivers dishes mixed with spicy Cajun and Creole specialties. Don't miss the better-than-Grandma's creamy bread pudding. Casual dress; cocktails; entertainment. **Parking:** on-site (fee). **Cards:** AX, DS, MC, VI.

PRIMO — Dinner: $21-$35 — Phone: 407/393-4444 — 6
Italian
Location: I-4, exit 72, just e on SR 528 (Bee Line Expwy) to exit 1, 1.8 mi s on International Dr, then 1.3 mi e; in JW Marriott Orlando, Grande Lakes. 4040 Central Florida Pkwy 32837. **Hours:** 5:30 pm-11 pm. **Reservations:** suggested. **Features:** The restaurant is the creation of Chef Melissa Kelly, who pairs contemporary Italian cuisine with fresh local ingredients. The combination leads to such imaginative menu creations as island creek oysters Rockefeller with spinach, Pernod and fennel or lobster on hand-made pansotti stuffed with butternut squash and toasted pumpkin-seed sauce. For dessert, try caramelized banana cream Napoleon with vanilla rum cream and macadamia nut brittle. Casual dress; cocktails. **Parking:** on-site. **Cards:** AX, DC, DS, MC, VI.

PUP'S — Lunch: $3-$6 — Dinner: $3-$6 — Phone: 407/351-5151 — 20
American
Location: I-4, exit 74A, 0.4 mi w. 7600 Dr. Phillips Blvd, Suite 108 32819. **Hours:** 11 am-8 pm, Sun-6 pm. **Features:** This specialty restaurant offers relish covered hot dogs, exotic hot dogs, traditionally topped hot dogs and kraut or chili smothered hot dogs. Italian sausage and some wraps are also offered. Casual dress; beer only. **Parking:** on-site. **Cards:** MC, VI.

RACE ROCK SUPERCHARGED RESTAURANT — Lunch: $6-$17 — Dinner: $6-$17 — Phone: 407/248-9876 — 46
American
Location: I-4, exit 74A, 1 mi s. 8986 International Dr 32819. **Hours:** 11:30 am-11 pm. **Reservations:** not accepted. **Features:** This loud and lively racing-themed restaurant displays an impressive collection of authentic racing memorabilia. Tasty offerings include burgers, sandwiches, pasta and some gourmet items. Fast, friendly service makes this a favorable pit stop. Casual dress; cocktails. **Parking:** on-site. **Cards:** AX, DS, MC, VI.

RAN-GETSU OF TOKYO — Dinner: $14-$50 — Phone: 407/345-0044 — 39
Japanese
Location: I-4, exit 74A, 0.3 mi s of SR 482 (Sand Lake Rd), then just se. 8400 International Dr 32819. **Hours:** 5 pm-11:30 pm. **Reservations:** suggested. **Features:** Located near local attractions, the restaurant serves authentic Japanese cuisine in a nice, cozy setting. Order from the sushi bar, or try the Shabu-Shabu, a sirloin and vegetable dinner for two cooked right at the table. Traditional drum shows on weekends. Casual dress; cocktails. **Parking:** on-site. **Cards:** AX, CB, DC, DS, JC, MC, VI.

(See maps and indexes p. 666-673, 667-674, 668-678, 670-685)

RED BAMBOO THAI RESTAURANT   **Lunch:** $4-$7   **Dinner:** $11-$21   **Phone:** 407/226-8997   ⑭
Thai
Location: I-4, exit 75A westbound (left side), just s, then e; in International Festival Plaza. 6803 S Kirkman Rd 32819. **Hours:** 11 am-2:30 & 5-10 pm, Sat & Sun noon-10 pm. Closed: Mon. **Reservations:** accepted. **Features:** No need to travel to Asia to indulge in the finest delights of dining; this friendly estalishment is an escape into a culinary experience most only dream about. Enjoy authentic Asian delights in a comtemporary setting. Casual dress; cocktails. **Parking:** on-site. **Cards:** AX, MC, VI.

ROY'S   **Dinner:** $18-$30   **Phone:** 407/352-4844   ㉞
Seafood
Location: I-4, exit 74A, 0.8 mi w. 7760 W Sand Lake Rd 32819. **Hours:** 5:30 pm-10 pm, Fri & Sat-10:30 pm. Closed: 11/23, 12/25. **Reservations:** accepted, recommended on weekends. **Features:** From greetings of "aloha" to departing, guests enjoy a warm, satisfying dining experience. The open surroundings blend traditional concepts with wood accents to create a comfortable, casual setting. Well-trained, friendly staff are knowledgeable and skilled in attending to guests' needs. The menu changes daily, always offering a varied selection of Hawaiian and Pacific seafood, highlighted by highly creative sauces. Dressy casual; cocktails. **Parking:** on-site and valet. **Cards:** AX, DC, DS, MC, VI.

SAMBA ROOM   **Lunch:** $9-$16   **Dinner:** $13-$28   **Phone:** 407/226-0550   ㉚
Cuban
Location: I-4, exit 74A, 0.4 mi w. 7468 W Sand Lake Rd 32819. **Hours:** 11:30 am-10 pm, Fri-midnight, Sat 4 pm-midnight, Sun 4 pm-10 pm. Closed: 11/23, 12/25. **Reservations:** suggested. **Features:** Guests unwind in a relaxing atmosphere to ponder a menu of Spanish and Cuban food. Mango-barbecued ribs and plantain-crusted mahi mahi are a few favorites. After dinner, move into the dance club, where a live band plays Latin music. Casual dress; cocktails. **Parking:** on-site. **Cards:** AX, DC, DS, MC, VI.

SEASONS 52   **Dinner:** $10-$20   **Phone:** 407/354-5212   ㊱
American
Location: I-4, exit 74A, just w. 7700 Sand Lake Rd 32819. **Hours:** 4:30 pm-11 pm. Closed major holidays. **Features:** Named for the number of weeks in a year, the restaurant focuses on making the freshest, best-tasting products available each week. All entrees have less than 475 calories. Try herb ricotta ravioli or ahi tuna steak, and save room for carrot cake with rum-raisin sauce. Casual dress; cocktails. **Parking:** on-site. **Cards:** AX, CB, DC, DS, JC, MC, VI.

SHAMIANA   **Lunch:** $4-$9   **Dinner:** $9-$15   **Phone:** 407/354-1160   ⑮
ⓐⓐⓐ
East Indian
Location: I-4, exit 74A, just n; in small shopping plaza. 7040 International Dr 32819. **Hours:** 11:30 am-2:30 & 5-11 pm, Sat from 5 pm. Closed: 7/4, 11/23; also 12/24. **Reservations:** suggested. **Features:** A far-ranging menu offers popular East Indian fare as well as Tandoori selections. Spicy flavors can be adjusted to suit the tastes of the uninitiated. Vegetarian dishes are available, and a wonderful flat bread is served with the meal. Beer & wine only. **Parking:** on-site. **Cards:** AX, DC, DS, MC, VI.

SIAM ORCHID   **Lunch:** $7-$10   **Dinner:** $10-$22   **Phone:** 407/351-0821   ⑱
ⓐⓐⓐ
Thai
Location: I-4, exit 74A, 0.5 mi e on SR 482 (Sand Lake Rd), then 0.3 mi n. 7575 Universal Blvd 32819. **Hours:** 11 am-2 & 5-11 pm, Sat & Sun from 5 pm. Closed major holidays. **Reservations:** suggested, weekends. **Features:** Fine khundoke or Thai-style dining can be enjoyed in a subdued, relaxing atmosphere. The focus is on Thai and other Oriental specialties, including Pad Thai pot pie filled with rice, noodles, vegetables, shrimp and crab meat. Another classic dish is whole snapper. Casual dress; cocktails. **Parking:** on-site. **Cards:** AX, CB, DS, MC, VI.

SMOKEY BONES BARBEQUE & GRILL   **Lunch:** $5-$21   **Dinner:** $5-$21   **Phone:** 407/850-5010   ①
Barbecue
Location: Jct Sand Lake Rd and Orange Blossom Trail, just e; north side of Florida Mall. 8016 Golden Sky Ln 32809. **Hours:** 11 am-10 pm, Fri & Sat-11 pm. Closed major holidays. **Features:** The menu features barbecue that is slowly smoked over aged hickory. barbecue platters with hand-pulled pork, beef brisket or smoked turkey are available in addition to combo platters that offer a bit of everything. Steaks, sandwiches, salad and burgers are also available. Casual dress; cocktails. **Parking:** on-site. **Cards:** AX, DS, MC, VI.

SWEET TOMATOES   **Lunch:** $7   **Dinner:** $9   **Phone:** 407/363-1616   ⑫
American
Location: I-4, exit 75A (SR 435 S), 0.6 mi s; corner of International Dr and Kirkman Rd. 6877 S Kirkman Rd 32819. **Hours:** 10:30 am-9 pm, Fri & Sat-10 pm. Closed major holidays. **Reservations:** not accepted. **Features:** The all-you-can-eat salad and soup buffet lines up freshly cut produce, specialty prepared salads, homemade soups, pasta, breads and more. Casual dress. **Parking:** on-site. **Cards:** AX, MC, VI.

TCHOUP CHOP   **Lunch:** $13-$24   **Dinner:** $20-$34   **Phone:** 407/503-2467   ⑩
Polynesian
Location: I-4, exit 74B, just n; in Universal's Royal Pacific Resort, A Loews Hotel. 6300 Hollywood Way 32819. **Hours:** 11:30 am-2 & 5:30-10 pm, Fri & Sat-11 pm. **Features:** Wonderful menu creations are inspired by Polynesian, Asian and some New Orleans Cajun cuisine. A wall of water, a reflection pool and two massive colored-glass chandeliers lend to the feel of an Asian-Pacific wonderland. Inspired dishes wake up the taste buds. Casual dress; cocktails. **Parking:** on-site (fee) and valet. **Cards:** AX, DS, MC, VI.

TEXAS BRAZIL CHURRASCARIA   **Dinner:** $23-$40   **Phone:** 407/355-0355   ⑪
Brazilian
Location: I-4, exit 75A, 1.4 mi e. 5259 International Dr 32819. **Hours:** 5 pm-10 pm, Fri-11 pm, Sat 4 pm-10:30 pm, Sun noon-9:30 pm. Closed: 12/25. **Reservations:** suggested. **Features:** With the flip of a "Stop/Go" disk at your table, you control the Gaucho-costumed carvers parading fire-roasted cuts of Angus beef, pork, chicken, lamb and Brazilian sausage around the dining room for your enjoyment. But beware: the 40-item salad bar might take a bite out of your appetite with its enticing array of appetizers, salads, soups and extras. While the decor is upscale, the ambiance is conducive to dining in shorts or in a suit, with other adults or with children. Casual dress; cocktails. **Parking:** on-site and valet. **Cards:** AX, DC, DS, MC, VI.

THAI THANI RESTAURANT   **Lunch:** $6-$10   **Dinner:** $12-$20   **Phone:** 407/239-9733   ㊷
Thai
Location: Jct International Dr and Central Florida Pkwy. 11025 S International Dr 32821. **Hours:** 11:30 am-11 pm. **Features:** Ornate decor featuring gold leaf and thick mahogany carved woods surrounds the dining room. Among Asian delights on the expansive menu are preparations of prawns, duck and fried rice and noodles. Casual dress; cocktails. **Parking:** on-site. **Cards:** AX, DC, DS, MC, VI.

(See maps and indexes p. 666-673, 667-674, 668-678, 670-685)

TIMPANO ITALIAN CHOPHOUSE   **Lunch:** $8-$20   **Dinner:** $16-$30   **Phone:** 407/248-0429   31

Italian

Location: I-4, exit 29, just w on SR 482 (Sand Lake Rd). 7488 W Sand Lake Rd 32819. **Hours:** 11 am-11 pm, Sat & Sun from noon. Closed: 12/25. **Reservations:** suggested. **Features:** Chicken, chops and veal prepared with Italian flare and seasoned to perfection are highlights on this unique menu. Casual dress; cocktails. **Parking:** on-site. **Cards:** AX, CB, DC, DS, JC, MC, VI.

TOOJAY'S ORIGINAL GOURMET DELI   **Lunch:** $6-$11   **Dinner:** $6-$11   **Phone:** 407/355-0340   21

American

Location: I-4, exit 74A, 0.4 mi w; in Dr Phillips Market Place. 7600 Dr Phillips Blvd 32819. **Hours:** 8 am-9 pm, Fri & Sat-10 pm. Closed: 11/23, 12/25. **Features:** Healthy selections are served at lunch and dinner. Salads, soups, light fare, burgers and classic delicatessen combination plates are a few of the menu highlights. Casual dress; beer & wine only. **Parking:** on-site. **Cards:** AX, CB, DC, DS, JC, MC, VI.

TROPICAL SMOOTHIE CAFE   **Lunch:** $3-$7   **Dinner:** $3-$7   **Phone:** 407/248-0707   27

American
Cards: MC, VI.

Location: I-4, exit 74A (Sand Lake Rd), 0.4 mi w. 7561 W Sand Lake Rd 32819. **Hours:** 8:30 am-8 pm, Sun 11 am-6 pm. Closed major holidays. **Features:** Patrons can top off a tasty gourmet wrap or a made-to-order sandwich with a tropical smoothie. Many other smoothie varieties also are available. In a busy commercial shopping center, the eatery is a fast alternative for lunch or dinner. Casual dress. **Parking:** on-site.

VITO'S CHOP HOUSE   **Dinner:** $14-$33   **Phone:** 407/354-2467   44

Steak House

Location: I-4, exit 74A, 1 mi se, just e of International Dr; 0.5 mi s of SR 482 (Sand Lake Rd); in DoubleTree Castle Hotel. 8633 International Dr 32821. **Hours:** 5 pm-10:30 pm, Fri & Sat-11 pm. Closed: 11/23, 12/25. **Reservations:** accepted. **Features:** Decorated in a comfortably masculine style, the classy operation reflects touches of Tuscany. Ample portions of doubly thick veal chops, tender all the way through, are nicely complemented by an expansive wine list. For dessert, pucker up for the luscious key lime pie. Dressy casual; cocktails. **Parking:** on-site. **Cards:** AX, MC, VI.

---

*The following restaurants have not been evaluated by AAA
but are listed for your information only.*

CITYJAZZ   **Phone:** 407/224-2189
fyi

Not evaluated. Location: I-4, exit 74B; in Universal Studios CityWalk. Universal Studios. **Features:** Best jazz Orlando has to offer! Light menu offers appetizers, drinks, coffees and cigars. Open nightly.

DAN MARINO'S TOWN TAVERN   **Phone:** 407/363-1013
fyi

Not evaluated. Location: I-4, exit 74A (Sand Lake Rd), just e, then 1.1 mi s; in Pointe Orlando. 9101 International Dr, Suite 1300 32819. **Features:** Launched by legendary Miami Dolphins football quarterback Dan Marino, the upscale-looking sports eatery offers televisions with sports broadcasts, lots of polished hardwood, large portions, a full bar and a children's menu.

VINES GRILLE & WINE BAR   **Phone:** 407/351-1227
fyi

Not evaluated. Location: I-4, exit 74A (Sand Lake Rd), 1 mi w; in Fontains Plaza. 7563 W Sand Lake Rd 32819. **Features:** The restaurant specializes in aged steaks and fresh seafood, which are paired with a wine list that includes 40 by-the-glass choices and a bar where more than 50 types of martinis are prepared. Wine connoisseurs appreciate the wine list, which is actually an extensive compilation of descriptions, tasting notes, photos of wine labels and ratings from premier wine magazines. Selections come from around the world with a strong emphasis on California.

The Orlando Vicinity

ALTAMONTE SPRINGS pop. 41,200 (See map and index starting on p. 656)

──────── WHERE TO STAY ────────

BEST WESTERN ALTAMONTE SPRINGS   Book at aaa.com
52
AAA SAVE
All Year   1P: $69-$129   2P: $69-$129   Phone: (407)862-8200
                                                            XP: $10   F17
Small-scale Hotel
Location: I-4, exit 92, just nw. 150 Douglas Ave 32714. **Fax:** 407/862-5750. **Facility:** 144 one-bedroom standard units. 3 stories, exterior corridors. *Bath:* combo or shower only. **Parking:** on-site. **Amenities:** voice mail, irons, hair dryers. *Some:* high-speed Internet. **Pool(s):** outdoor. **Leisure Activities:** exercise room. **Guest Services:** valet and coin laundry. **Business Services:** meeting rooms, fax (fee). **Cards:** AX, DS, MC, VI. **Special Amenities:** free expanded continental breakfast and free local telephone calls.

SOME UNITS

CANDLEWOOD SUITES   Book at aaa.com
48
All Year   1P: $79-$99   2P: $79-$99   Phone: (407)767-5757
Small-scale Hotel
Location: I-4, exit 92, just w to Douglas Ave, 0.8 mi n to Central Pkwy, then just e. 644 Raymond Ave 32701. **Fax:** 407/767-0097. **Facility:** 122 units. 98 one-bedroom standard units with efficiencies. 24 one-bedroom suites ($99-$119) with efficiencies. 3 stories, interior corridors. *Bath:* combo or shower only. **Parking:** on-site. **Terms:** small pets only ($75-$150 fee). **Amenities:** video library, CD players, dual phone lines, voice mail, irons, hair dryers. **Pool(s):** heated outdoor. **Leisure Activities:** exercise room. **Guest Services:** complimentary laundry. **Business Services:** fax. **Cards:** AX, CB, DC, DS, JC, MC, VI.

SOME UNITS
FEE

DAYS INN ALTAMONTE SPRINGS   Book at aaa.com
55
AAA SAVE
All Year   1P: $50-$150   2P: $50-$150   Phone: (407)788-1411
                                                            XP: $5
Motel
Location: I-4, exit 92, 0.3 mi w on SR 436, then just s. 150 S Westmonte Dr 32714. **Fax:** 407/788-6472. **Facility:** 115 units. 105 one-bedroom standard units. 10 one-bedroom suites. 2 stories, exterior corridors. *Bath:* combo or shower only. **Parking:** on-site. **Terms:** 3 day cancellation notice, [ECP] meal plan available, package plans, pets ($10 fee). **Amenities:** video games (fee), voice mail, irons, hair dryers. **Pool(s):** heated outdoor. **Business Services:** meeting rooms, fax (fee). **Cards:** AX, DS, MC, VI. **Special Amenities:** free expanded continental breakfast.

SOME UNITS
FEE

EMBASSY SUITES ORLANDO NORTH   Book at aaa.com
50
AAA SAVE
All Year [BP]   1P: $120-$220   2P: $120-$220   Phone: (407)834-2400
                                                            XP: $15   F18
Small-scale Hotel
Location: I-4, exit 92, 0.3 mi e on SR 436, then just n on North Lake Blvd. 225 E Altamonte Dr 32701. **Fax:** 407/834-2117. **Facility:** 277 one-bedroom suites. 4-7 stories, interior corridors. *Bath:* combo or shower only. **Parking:** on-site. **Terms:** check-in 4 pm, cancellation fee imposed, pets ($20 extra charge). **Amenities:** video games (fee), dual phone lines, voice mail, irons, hair dryers. *Some:* high-speed Internet (fee). **Dining:** 6:30 am-9 & 11-11 pm, Sat & Sun 7 am-10:30 & 11-11 pm, cocktails. **Pool(s):** heated indoor. **Leisure Activities:** sauna, whirlpool, steamroom, jogging, exercise room. **Guest Services:** gift shop, complimentary evening beverages, valet and coin laundry, area transportation-within 3 mi. **Business Services:** conference facilities, business center. **Cards:** AX, CB, DC, DS, JC, MC, VI. **Special Amenities:** free full breakfast and free newspaper.

SOME UNITS
FEE

HAMPTON INN   Book at aaa.com
51
12/1-5/18   1P: $71-$159   Phone: (407)869-9000
9/14-11/30   1P: $71-$97
5/19-9/13   1P: $69-$95
Small-scale Hotel
Location: I-4, exit 92, just nw. 151 N Douglas Ave 32714. **Fax:** 407/788-6746. **Facility:** 210 one-bedroom standard units. 2 stories, exterior corridors. *Bath:* combo or shower only. **Parking:** on-site. **Terms:** cancellation fee imposed. **Amenities:** high-speed Internet, voice mail, irons, hair dryers. **Pool(s):** heated outdoor. **Leisure Activities:** whirlpool, exercise room. **Guest Services:** complimentary evening beverages, valet and coin laundry. **Business Services:** meeting rooms, business center. **Cards:** AX, CB, DC, DS, MC, VI.

SOME UNITS

HILTON ORLANDO/ALTAMONTE SPRINGS   Book at aaa.com
58
All Year   1P: $160   2P: $160   Phone: 407/830-1985
                                                            XP: $10
Small-scale Hotel
Location: I-4, exit 92, just e on SR 436, then 0.5 mi s. 350 S North Lake Blvd 32701. **Fax:** 407/331-2911. **Facility:** 322 units. 317 one-bedroom standard units. 5 one-bedroom suites. 8 stories, interior corridors. *Bath:* combo or shower only. **Parking:** on-site. **Terms:** package plans. **Amenities:** video games (fee), dual phone lines, voice mail, irons, hair dryers. *Some: Fee:* high-speed Internet. **Pool(s):** heated outdoor. **Leisure Activities:** whirlpool, exercise room. **Guest Services:** gift shop, valet laundry, area transportation. **Business Services:** conference facilities. *Fee:* administrative services, fax. **Cards:** AX, DC, DS, MC, VI.

SOME UNITS
FEE FEE

(See map and index starting on p. 656)

HOLIDAY INN ORLANDO NORTH/ALTAMONTE SPRINGS *Book at aaa.com*

Phone: (407)862-4455 54

All Year   1P: $72-$109   2P: $72-$109   XP: $10   F17

Small-scale Hotel

Location: I-4, exit 92, just sw. 230 W SR 436 32714. Fax: 407/682-5982. **Facility:** 263 one-bedroom standard units, some with whirlpools. 3-4 stories, interior/exterior corridors. *Bath:* combo or shower only. **Parking:** on-site. **Terms:** check-in 4 pm, 7 day cancellation notice, package plans, pets ($40 fee). **Amenities:** video games (fee), high-speed Internet, voice mail, irons, hair dryers. **Dining:** 6 am-2 & 5-10 pm, cocktails. **Pool(s):** outdoor. **Leisure Activities:** exercise room. **Guest Services:** valet and coin laundry, area transportation-within 3 mi. **Business Services:** conference facilities, business center. **Cards:** AX, CB, DC, DS, MC, VI. **Special Amenities:** free newspaper and preferred room (subject to availability with advance reservations).
(See color ad below)

SOME UNITS

HOMESTEAD STUDIO SUITES HOTEL-ORLANDO/ALTAMONTE SPRINGS *Book at aaa.com*

Phone: (407)332-9300 57

All Year   1P: $44-$64   2P: $49-$69   XP: $5   F17

Small-scale Hotel

Location: I-4, exit 92, just e, then 0.3 mi s. 302 S North Lake Blvd 32701. Fax: 407/332-9330. **Facility:** 135 one-bedroom standard units with efficiencies. 3 stories, interior corridors. *Bath:* combo or shower only. **Parking:** on-site. **Terms:** pets ($75 extra charge). **Amenities:** voice mail, irons. **Guest Services:** valet and coin laundry. **Business Services:** fax (fee). **Cards:** AX, DC, DS, MC, VI.

SOME UNITS

QUALITY INN NORTH *Book at aaa.com*

Phone: (407)862-2800 56

2/1-4/15 [ECP]   1P: $59-$89   2P: $65-$99
12/16-1/31 [ECP]   1P: $55-$75   2P: $59-$79
12/1-12/15 & 4/16-11/30 [ECP]   1P: $49-$65   2P: $52-$69

Small-scale Hotel

Location: I-4, exit 92, just s. 235 S Wymore Rd 32714. Fax: 407/862-7982. **Facility:** 167 units. 157 one-bedroom standard units. 10 one-bedroom suites ($89-$149) with kitchens (no utensils). 3 stories, exterior corridors. *Bath:* combo or shower only. **Parking:** on-site. **Amenities:** voice mail, safes (fee), irons, hair dryers. **Pool(s):** outdoor. **Guest Services:** complimentary evening beverages: Mon-Fri, coin laundry. **Cards:** AX, CB, DC, DS, MC, VI. **Special Amenities:** free expanded continental breakfast and free local telephone calls.

SOME UNITS

RESIDENCE INN BY MARRIOTT *Book at aaa.com*

Phone: (407)788-7991 49

All Year [BP]   1P: $89-$289

Small-scale Hotel

Location: I-4, exit 92, just w on SR 436, then just n. 270 Douglas Ave 32714. Fax: 407/869-5468. **Facility:** 128 units. 96 one-bedroom standard units with kitchens. 32 two-bedroom suites with kitchens. 2 stories, exterior corridors. *Bath:* combo or shower only. **Parking:** on-site. **Terms:** cancellation fee imposed, pets ($75 fee). **Amenities:** high-speed Internet, voice mail, irons, hair dryers. **Pool(s):** heated outdoor. **Leisure Activities:** whirlpools, sports court. **Guest Services:** complimentary evening beverages: Mon-Thurs, valet and coin laundry. **Business Services:** meeting rooms, fax (fee). **Cards:** AX, DC, DS, MC, VI.

SOME UNITS

SPRINGHILL SUITES BY MARRIOTT ORLANDO/ALTAMONTE SPRINGS *Book at aaa.com*

Phone: (407)865-6400 53

12/1-2/19   1P: $99-$129   2P: $99-$129
2/20-11/30   1P: $129   2P: $129

Small-scale Hotel

Location: I-4, exit 92, just w. 205 W Hwy 436 32714. Fax: 407/865-6773. **Facility:** 91 one-bedroom standard units. 4 stories, interior corridors. *Bath:* combo or shower only. **Parking:** on-site. **Terms:** weekly rates available, package plans. **Amenities:** high-speed Internet, dual phone lines, voice mail, irons, hair dryers. **Pool(s):** heated indoor. **Leisure Activities:** whirlpool, exercise room. **Guest Services:** valet and coin laundry. **Business Services:** meeting rooms. **Cards:** AX, DC, DS, JC, MC, VI.

SOME UNITS

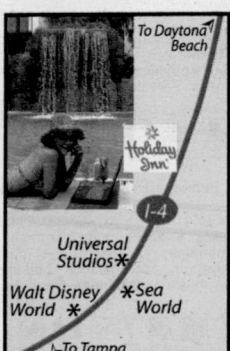

(See map and index starting on p. 656)

———— WHERE TO DINE ————

ALTAMONTE ALE HOUSE & RAW BAR
Lunch: $4–$14   **Dinner:** $4–$14   **Phone:** 407/331-6611   (165)
American
Location: I-4, exit 92, 1.5 mi e. 477 E Altamonte Dr 32701. **Hours:** 11 am-2 am. Closed major holidays. **Features:** Enjoy selections of clams on the half shell, oysters and peel and eat shrimp from the raw bar or choose an 8 oz. filet, baby back ribs or chicken parmesan from the appetizing menu. Casual dress; cocktails. **Parking:** on-site. **Cards:** AX, DS, MC, VI.

AMIGOS
Lunch: $6–$8   **Dinner:** $7–$12   **Phone:** 407/774-4334   (175)
Tex-Mex
Location: I-4, exit 92, 0.5 mi w; just n of SR 436. 120 N Westmonte Dr 32714. **Hours:** 11 am-9:30 pm, Fri & Sat-10 pm, Sun & Mon-9 pm. Closed major holidays. **Features:** Very popular on weekends, this Tex-Mex style of dining is enjoyed in an establishment decorated with license plates and Mexican curios. Your favorite Tex-Mex entrees overflow the plates, so grab a pitcher of margaritas, and settle down to a hearty meal. Casual dress; cocktails. **Parking:** on-site. **Cards:** AX, DC, MC, VI.

AMIRA'S
Lunch: $5–$8   **Dinner:** $5–$11   **Phone:** 407/831-0999   (168)
Kosher
Location: Between CR 427 and US 17-92, on SR 436. 1349 E Altamonte Dr 32701. **Hours:** 7 am-5 pm, Mon-2 pm, Sun 8 am-7 pm. Closed: Sat, Jewish holidays & Passover week. **Features:** This New York-style kosher deli with an adjoining market serves a wide range of deli sandwiches, plus specialties such as falafel, hummus, chopped liver and stuffed cabbage rolls. Although the decor is plain, the food more than makes up for it. The restaurant is popular enough with the locals that servers are likely to call many patrons by name. Casual dress; beer & wine only. **Parking:** on-site. **Cards:** AX, DS, MC, VI.

ATHENA GREEK CAFE
Lunch: $4–$8   **Dinner:** $4–$8   **Phone:** 407/830-0707   (174)
Greek
Location: Between CR 427 and US 17-92 on SR 436. 1140 E Altamonte Dr 32701. **Hours:** 7 am-8:30 pm. Closed major holidays; also Sun. **Features:** Specializing in Greek and American dishes, the restaurant makes it possible to order a steak and cheese submarine sandwich with a serving of pastitsio, a baked dish of macaroni, beef and cheese. Also served are rotisserie chicken, children's dishes and vegetarian selections. Lunchtime is busy, so come early or prepare to wait. Casual dress. **Parking:** on-site. **Cards:** AX, DC, DS, MC, VI.

AUGUST MOON CHINESE RESTAURANT & SUSHI BAR
Lunch: $4–$7   **Dinner:** $7–$16   **Phone:** 407/788-9388   (155)
Chinese
Location: I-4, exit 94, 0.4 mi w; in Spring Center. 1185 Spring Center Blvd S 32714. **Hours:** 11:30 am-10 pm, Fri-10:30 pm, Sat noon-10:30 pm, Sun noon-9:30 pm. Closed major holidays. **Features:** A tranquil stream filled with koi winds its way through the restaurant. Traditional favorites share menu space with vegetarian dishes and lighter fare. Don't pass up the gourmet specialties section on the menu. Guests must cross a small footbridge to reach some tables. The staff is attentive and accommodating. Casual dress; cocktails. **Parking:** on-site. **Cards:** AX, DC, DS, MC, VI.

BACKYARD BURGER
Lunch: $3–$6   **Dinner:** $3–$6   **Phone:** 407/862-0660   (182)
American
Location: Jct SR 436 and 434, 0.3 mi s. 290 S SR 434 32714. **Hours:** 10 am-10 pm, Fri & Sat-11 pm. Closed major holidays. **Features:** Super popular and super fun: if you are looking for a fast bite take the drive-thru, otherwise enjoy the biggest burgers in town on the outdoor patio. Casual dress. **Parking:** on-site. **Cards:** AX, DS, MC, VI.

BAHAMA BREEZE
Lunch: $7–$24   **Dinner:** $7–$24   **Phone:** 407/831-2929   (164)
Caribbean
Location: I-4, exit 92, 1.5 mi e. 499 E Altamonte Dr 32701. **Hours:** 11 am-11:30 pm, Thurs-Sat to 12:30 am, Sun-10:30 pm. Closed: 11/23, 12/25. **Features:** Capturing the sights, sounds and sensations of the Caribbean, Bahama Breeze caters to those seeking an exciting evening out. In addition to delicious food such as fresh mahi-mahi and Key lime pie, there is a full bar, retail shop and live entertainment. Casual dress; cocktails; entertainment. **Parking:** on-site. **Cards:** AX, CB, DC, DS, MC, VI.

BAJA BURRITO KITCHEN
Lunch: $4–$8   **Dinner:** $4–$8   **Phone:** 407/788-2252   (157)
Mexican
Location: 1 mi n of jct SR 434 and 436; in Jamestown Place Mall. 931 N SR 434 32714. **Hours:** 11 am-10 pm, Sun 11:30 am-9 pm. Closed: 11/23, 12/25. **Features:** A salsa bar offers an impressive array of fresh choices, from basic chopped tomatoes to very hot habanero salsa. Fast, walk-up counter service provides good food made to order at this friendly shop tucked into a strip mall. Casual dress; beer & wine only. **Parking:** on-site.

BANGKOK RESTAURANT
Lunch: $4–$7   **Dinner:** $7–$12   **Phone:** 407/788-2685   (161)
Thai
Location: I-4, exit 92; just w; just n of jct SR 436 and Douglas Ave. 260 Douglas Ave 32714. **Hours:** 11 am-3 & 5-10 pm, Sat & Sun 5 pm. **Features:** Reasonably priced Thai cuisine is colorfully presented and may be ordered in hot, spicy or mild varieties. The menu is varied, offering beef, pork, chicken, seafood and vegetables in authentic preparations. In keeping with the Thai tradition of hospitality, service is friendly and attentive. Convenient to commercial areas, the location is a plus. Casual dress; cocktails. **Parking:** on-site. **Cards:** AX, DS, MC, VI.

BUBBALOU'S BODACIOUS B-B-Q
Lunch: $3–$12   **Dinner:** $3–$12   **Phone:** 407/478-1212   (169)
American
Location: Between CR 427 and US 17-92, on SR 436. 1049 E Altamonte Dr 32701. **Hours:** 10 am-9:30 pm, Fri & Sat-10:30 pm, Sun 11 am-9:30 pm. Closed major holidays. **Features:** Famous for its barbecue and quick-serve lunch and dinner specials, the eatery is a hot spot for fun family dining at a great value. Casual dress; beer only. **Parking:** on-site. **Cards:** AX, DC, DS, MC, VI.

CHINA GATE RESTAURANT
Lunch: $8–$14   **Dinner:** $8–$14   **Phone:** 407/774-5445   (156)
Chinese
Location: I-4, exit 49, 1 mi w on SR 434; in Winn Dixie Shopping Plaza. 1062 Montgomery Rd 32714. **Hours:** 11:30 am-10 pm. Closed major holidays. **Features:** Popular for takeout or dining in, the eatery presents a sampling of Chinese cuisine that includes the bo bo platter, seven stars around the moon and vegetarian dishes. Portions are ample. Casual dress. **Parking:** on-site. **Cards:** MC, VI.

CHIPOTLE
Lunch: $4–$6   **Dinner:** $4–$6   **Phone:** 407/682-2747   (180)
Mexican
Location: I-4, exit 92, 0.3 mi w. 400 SR 436 32714. **Hours:** 11 am-11 pm. **Features:** Create your own burrito and taco as you proceed down an assembly line of fillings and toppings; a variety of hot and mild sauces are offered to top off your meal. Casual dress. **Parking:** on-site. **Cards:** MC, VI.

(See map and index starting on p. 656)

CRAZY BUFFET
Lunch: $10-$16   **Dinner:** $18-$20   **Phone:** 407/869-1233   (158)
♦♦ ♦♦
Asian
Location: Jct SR 434 and 436. 945 W SR 436, Unit 1179 32714. **Hours:** 11:30 am-2:30 & 5-9 pm, Fri-10 pm, Sat noon-4 & 5-10 pm, Sun noon-4 & 5-9 pm. Closed: 11/23. **Features:** The huge buffet lines up a wide variety of Japanese, Korean, Chinese and Thai offerings. Included are a separate sushi bar and hibachi cooking grill. Dinners and weekend brunches often include more specialty dishes, such as Peking duck, crab legs and steak. Live entertainment adds to the casual atmosphere. Expect a wait on weekends. Casual dress; cocktails. **Parking:** on-site. **Cards:** AX, MC, VI.

DON PEPE'S CUBAN CAFE
Dinner: $9-$20   **Phone:** 407/682-6834   (159)
♦♦ ♦♦
Cuban
Location: Jct SR 434 and 436; in K-Mart Plaza. 937 W SR 436, Suite 1095 32714. **Hours:** 4 pm-10 pm, Fri & Sat-11 pm, Sun 1 pm-9 pm. Closed major holidays. **Reservations:** suggested. **Features:** Family-owned and operated, the lively cafe serves home-style cooking in a warm, fun and festive atmosphere. Representative of tasty menu fare are garbanzo soups, Cuban Rican nachos, paella and the Cuban classic. Musicians and dancers perform on the weekends. Casual dress; cocktails. **Parking:** on-site. **Cards:** AX, DC, DS, MC, VI.

EASTERN PEARL CHINESE RESTAURANT
AAA
Lunch: $5-$28   **Dinner:** $7-$28   **Phone:** 407/339-8877   (166)
♦♦♦ ♦♦♦
Chinese
Location: I-4, exit 92, 0.7 mi e on SR 436. 478 E Altamonte Dr, Suite 102 32701. **Hours:** 11:30 am-2:30 & 4:30-9 pm, Tues-Thurs to 9:30 pm, Fri-10 pm, Sat noon-10 pm, Sun noon-9 pm. Closed: 11/23. **Reservations:** suggested. **Features:** Imaginative, superbly prepared food is presented in a busy, yet refined, atmosphere. A distinctive wall fountain enhances a feel of tranquility. Dressy casual; cocktails. **Parking:** on-site. **Cards:** AX, DS, MC, VI.

EL CHARRO MEXICAN RESTAURANT
Lunch: $5-$8   **Dinner:** $7-$12   **Phone:** 407/682-5156   (160)
♦♦ ♦♦
Mexican
Location: Just w of jct SR 434. 946 W SR 436 32714. **Hours:** 11-10 pm, Fri & Sat-11 pm. **Features:** Colorful walls and traditional Mexican decorations provide a warm atmosphere for diners. The menu focuses on traditional choices. Casual dress; cocktails. **Parking:** on-site. **Cards:** AX, DS, MC, VI.

FIRST WATCH
Lunch: $4-$8   **Phone:** 407/682-2315   (177)
♦♦ ♦♦
American
Location: I-4, exit 92, just nw; in Ethan Allen Plaza. 249 W SR 436 32714. **Hours:** 7 am-2:30 pm. Closed: 11/23, 12/25. **Features:** This eatery serves breakfast and lunch, from traditional eggs and omelets to waffles and crepes. Pancakes fill the entire plate and are topped with fresh fruits and syrup. Great salad, soups and sandwiches are featured to satisfy the busy lunch crowd. Casual dress. **Parking:** on-site. **Cards:** AX, DS, MC, VI.

JASON'S DELI
Lunch: $5-$10   **Dinner:** $5-$10   **Phone:** 407/830-0699   (170)
♦♦
Deli/Subs Sandwiches
Location: I-4, exit 92, 1.2 mi e. 303 E Altamonte Dr, Suite 1350 32701. **Hours:** 10 am-10 pm. Closed major holidays. **Features:** Soups, salads, wraps, muffulettas, submarine sandwiches and super spuds make up the menu. Healthy selections are specially marked, and vegetarian dishes are available. Busy at lunchtime, the cafeteria-style eatery is in a shopping plaza. Casual dress. **Parking:** on-site. **Cards:** AX, MC, VI.

KOHINOOR INDIAN RESTAURANT
Lunch: $9   **Dinner:** $8-$17   **Phone:** 407/788-6004   (176)
♦♦ ♦♦
Indian
Location: I-4, exit 92, 0.3 mi w; in Ethan Allen Plaza. 249 W SR 436 32714. **Hours:** 11:30 am-2:30 & 5-10 pm, Fri & Sat-11 pm. Closed: Mon. **Reservations:** accepted. **Features:** Partake of expertly prepared Indian cuisine made with fine ingredients and fresh spices. The mixed tandoori platter offers a chance to sample all the meats cooked in the tandoor oven. Freshly made mango ice cream for dessert makes this a worthy venture. Korma dishes are the specialty. Dressy casual; beer & wine only. **Parking:** on-site. **Cards:** AX, DS, MC, VI.

LAWLESS CAFE & DELI
Lunch: $4-$8   **Dinner:** $4-$8   **Phone:** 407/774-8827   (178)
♦♦
American
Location: I-4, exit 92, 1 mi w. 445 W SR 436, Suite 1033 32714. **Hours:** 10:30 am-7 pm. Closed major holidays; also Sun. **Features:** Subs, sandwiches, and salads are on the menu at this quick-serve deli. Choices of subs include roast beef, salami, chicken Salad, and a vegetarian three cheese sandwich. Seating is very limited and carry-out is preferred. Casual dress. **Parking:** on-site. **Cards:** MC, VI.

MAISON & JARDIN RESTAURANT
Menu on aaa.com   **Dinner:** $22-$38   **Phone:** 407/862-4410   (183)
AAA
♦♦♦ ♦♦♦
Continental
Location: I-4, exit 92, just w on SR 436, then 0.5 mi s. 430 S Wymore Rd 32714. **Hours:** 6 pm-10 pm. Closed major holidays; also Sun & Mon. **Reservations:** suggested. **Features:** Expect an elegant, candlelit meal in a secluded Mediterranean villa and service that caters to your every whim. A variety of fresh seafood, prime beef, veal, lamb and wild game is prepared with a French-Continental flair. The wine list is extensive. Semi-formal attire; cocktails. **Parking:** on-site. **Cards:** AX, CB, DC, DS, JC, MC, VI.

MIMI'S CAFE
Lunch: $5-$16   **Dinner:** $5-$16   **Phone:** 407/331-7300   (163)
♦♦ ♦♦
American
Location: I-4, exit 92, 1.4 mi e on SR 436. 525 E Altamonte Dr 32701. **Hours:** 7 am-11 pm. Closed major holidays. **Features:** Breakfast, lunch and dinner are offered throughout the day at this eclectic and popular eatery. With New Orleans inspired decor and a menu that features something for everyone, finding a favorite dish should be no problem. Casual dress; cocktails. **Parking:** on-site. **Cards:** AX, DS, MC, VI.

MOE'S SOUTHWEST GRILL
Lunch: $2-$8   **Dinner:** $2-$8   **Phone:** 407/253-2120   (184)
♦♦
American
Location: Jct Maitland Blvd and SR 434; in Gateway Crossings Shopping Center. 851 SR 434 32714. **Hours:** 11 am-10 pm, Sun-9 pm. Closed major holidays. **Features:** With locations in several states, the casual eatery serves Mexican food in huge portions. Guests drop in for friendly service and fresh food at great prices. Casual dress; beer only. **Parking:** on-site. **Cards:** MC, VI.

(See map and index starting on p. 656)

OMAHA STEAKHOUSE   Lunch: $13-$33   Dinner: $13-$33   Phone: 407/834-2400   (162)
▼▼▼▼
Steak House
Location: I-4, exit 92, 0.3 mi e on SR 436, just n on North Lake Blvd. 225 E Altamonte Dr 32701. **Hours:** 11:30 am-11 pm. **Reservations:** accepted. **Features:** Serving steak any way you like it, the restaurant rewards frequent visitors with their own knife on the wall with their name on it. Dressy casual; cocktails. **Parking:** on-site. **Cards:** AX, DS, MC, VI.

PANERA BREAD   Lunch: $3-$8   Dinner: $3-$8   Phone: 407/831-3741   (181)
▼▼▼
American
Location: Jct SR 434 and 436, just s. 200 S SR 434 32826. **Hours:** 7 am-9 pm, Sun from 8:30 am. Closed major holidays. **Features:** Located in a shopping area, the restaurant is a great place for healthy sandwiches and homemade soups served in large bread bowls. Numerous varieties of freshly baked breads and bagels make this a popular stop for breakfast. Casual dress. **Parking:** on-site. **Cards:** AX, DS, MC, VI.

PANERA BREAD   Lunch: $3-$6   Dinner: $3-$6   Phone: 407/332-7600   (171)
▼▼▼
American
Location: I-4, exit 92, 1.3 mi e. 696 E Altamonte Dr 32701. **Hours:** 6:30 am-9:30 pm, Sun 7 am-8:30 pm. Closed: 12/25. **Features:** Diners order and pick up their soup, salad or "upscale" sandwich at the counter in this casual eatery and bakery, a popular place for a quick bite during or after shopping or a weekend outing with the family. Simple, comfortable tables are offered for eating in, but carry out is another option. Casual dress. **Parking:** on-site. **Cards:** AX, MC, VI.   [&M]

PAPA ANTHONY'S PIZZA   Lunch: $5-$11   Dinner: $8-$12   Phone: 407/296-3066   (186)
▼▼▼
Italian
Location: Jct Maitland Ave and SR 434; in Gateway Crossings Shopping Center. 851 S SR 434, #101 32714. **Hours:** 11 am-9:30 pm, Fri & Sat-10 pm, Sun noon-9 pm. Closed: 11/23, 12/25. **Reservations:** not accepted. **Features:** Pizza, pasta, submarine sandwiches, homemade soups and salads are popular with the lunchtime patrons who frequent the eatery. Casual dress; beer & wine only. **Parking:** on-site. **Cards:** AX, DC, DS, MC, VI.   [&M]

SAM SELTZER'S STEAKHOUSE   Lunch: $10-$20   Dinner: $10-$20   Phone: 407/332-7267   (173)
▼▼▼ ▼▼▼
Steak House
Location: I-4, exit 92, 1.3 mi e. 800 E Altamonte Dr 32701. **Hours:** 11:30 am-10 pm, Fri-11 pm, Sat noon-11:30 pm, Sun noon-10 pm. Closed: 11/23, 12/25. **Features:** The American steakhouse offers a full menu of steaks and seafood. The decor is traditional, featuring dark wood tones. Casual dress; cocktails. **Parking:** on-site. **Cards:** AX, CB, DC, DS, JC, MC, VI.   [&M] [◣]

STRAUB'S FINE SEAFOOD   Lunch: $7-$11   Dinner: $12-$29   Phone: 407/831-2250   (167)
▼▼▼ ▼▼▼
Seafood
Location: I-4, exit 92, 0.8 mi e on SR 436. 512 E Altamonte Dr 32701. **Hours:** 11 am-10 pm, Fri-11 pm, Sat 4:30 pm-11 pm, Sun 4:30 pm-10 pm. Closed: 11/23, 12/25; also Super Bowl Sun. **Reservations:** suggested. **Features:** Mesquite-grilled and Cajun seafood entrees are highlights on a menu that offers a wide selection of fresh seasonal seafood. Beef, chicken and pasta dishes also are available. Service is friendly and efficient, and the ambience is casual. Dressy casual; cocktails. **Parking:** on-site. **Cards:** AX, DC, DS, MC, VI.

SWEET TOMATOES   Lunch: $8-$13   Dinner: $8-$13   Phone: 407/869-5550   (179)
▼▼▼
American
Location: I-4, exit 92 (SR 436/Semoran Blvd), just w. 474 W SR 436 32714. **Hours:** 11 am-9 pm, Fri & Sat-10 pm. Closed major holidays. **Reservations:** not accepted. **Features:** The all-you-can-eat salad and soup buffet serves up freshly cut produce, specialty prepared salads, homemade soups, pasta, breads and more. Casual dress. **Parking:** on-site. **Cards:** AX, MC, VI.

UNCLE JONES BAR-B-QUE   Lunch: $3-$10   Dinner: $3-$10   Phone: 407/260-2425   (172)
▼▼▼
Barbecue
Location: Between CR 427 and US 17-92 on SR 436. 1370 E Altamonte Blvd 32701. **Hours:** 11 am-9 pm, Fri & Sat-10 pm. Closed major holidays. **Features:** In a run-down red house along SR 436, the family-owned barbecue restaurant may be small and the menu limited, but the pork, beef, chicken and rib platters have guests lining up for seconds. Barbecue meats also are sold by the pound. Casual dress. **Parking:** on-site. **Cards:** MC, VI.

YUM YUM ASIA CAFE   Lunch: $4-$9   Dinner: $4-$15   Phone: 407/522-8818   (185)
▼▼▼
Chinese
Location: Jct Maitland Ave and SR 434; in Gateway Crossings Shopping Center. 851 S SR 434, #1120 32714. **Hours:** 11 am-9:30 pm, Fri & Sat-10 pm, Sun noon-9 pm. Closed: 11/23, 12/25. **Features:** Popular with the lunchtime crowd, the cafe presents an expansive menu of just about any Asian favorites. Seating is limited, and take-out is offered. Casual dress. **Parking:** on-site. **Cards:** AX, DC, DS, MC, VI.

APOPKA pop. 26,642 (See map and index starting on p. 656)

——— **WHERE TO DINE** ———

CAFFE' POSITANO   Lunch: $5-$15   Dinner: $10-$30   Phone: 407/774-8080   (151)
▼▼▼ ▼▼▼
Italian
Location: Just w of Hunt Club Blvd. 3030 E Semoran Blvd 32703. **Hours:** 11 am-10:30 pm, Fri & Sat-11 pm, Sun noon-10:30 pm. Closed: 11/23, 12/25. **Reservations:** accepted. **Features:** The cafe is a local favorite, and serves good, authentic Italian fare at a reasonable price; the New York cheesecake is a specialty. Casual dress; cocktails. **Parking:** on-site. **Cards:** AX, DS, MC, VI.

CATFISH PLACE OF APOPKA   *Menu on aaa.com*   Lunch: $5-$8   Dinner: $7-$16   Phone: 407/889-7980   (147)
(AAA)
▼▼▼
Steak & Seafood
Location: US 441 and Forest Ave; across from Chamber of Commerce. 311 S Forest Ave 32703. **Hours:** 11 am-9 pm, Fri & Sat-10 pm. Closed: Sun & Mon. **Features:** Sample crispy fried catfish at this aptly named, fish camp-style favorite. A simple menu features well-seasoned, boneless or fingerling catfish, chunky clam chowder, creamy coleslaw and crunchy hush puppies. Take out dinners are available. Casual dress; beer & wine only. **Parking:** on-site. **Cards:** DS, MC, VI.

(See map and index starting on p. 656)

MI TIERRA RESTAURANT   **Lunch:** $6-$13   **Dinner:** $6-$13   **Phone:** 407/889-8898   148

Mexican

Location: Just e of jct US 441. 899 Semoran Blvd 32703. **Hours:** 11 am-9 pm. **Features:** Everything is authentic about the Mexican cuisine served at this local favorite. Recipes from Puerto Vallarta, Jalisco and Nayarit fill the menu. House specialties include mahi mahi, red snapper and shrimp prepared in your choice of sauce. Casual dress; cocktails. **Parking:** on-site. **Cards:** AX, MC, VI.

ROMA RISTORANTE ITALIANO   **Lunch:** $7-$10   **Dinner:** $10-$20   **Phone:** 407/886-2360   152

Italian

Location: 0.8 mi s of jct SR 436. 730 Orange Blossom Tr 32703. **Hours:** 11:30 am-2 & 4:30-10 pm, Sat from 4:30 pm. Closed major holidays; also 12/24. **Reservations:** accepted. **Features:** The family operated restaurant features recipes passed down through the generations. Their motto states "If you want genuine, home-made Italian food, you can fly to Italy or drive to Roma's". Casual dress; beer & wine only. **Parking:** on-site. **Cards:** AX, DC, DS, MC, VI.

SCAMPI'S ITALIAN EATERY   **Lunch:** $5-$17   **Dinner:** $5-$17   **Phone:** 407/774-0977   150

Italian

Location: Jct SR 436 and Hunt Club Blvd. 614 Hunt Club Blvd 32703. **Hours:** 11 am-10 pm, Fri-11 pm, Sun 4 pm-9 pm. Closed major holidays. **Features:** The busy eatery emphasizes create-your-own pasta dishes. Patrons mix homemade sauces with beef, poultry or seafood and various kinds of homemade pasta. Save room for one of the wonderful desserts. Casual dress; beer & wine only. **Parking:** on-site. **Cards:** MC, VI.

SONNY'S REAL PIT BBQ   **Lunch:** $6-$9   **Dinner:** $6-$15   **Phone:** 407/814-8888   149

Barbecue

Location: Jct Wekiva Springs Rd. 2210 E Semoran Blvd 32703. **Hours:** 11 am-9:30 pm, Fri & Sat-10 pm. **Features:** Fresh smoked and barbecued meats are the main focus of the country-style eatery. Diners help themselves at the salad bar and shouldn't forget to ask about dessert. Casual dress; beer only. **Parking:** on-site. **Cards:** AX, DS, MC, VI.

ASTOR pop. 1,487

——— **WHERE TO STAY** ———

ASTOR BRIDGE MARINA   **Phone:** 386-749-4407

Motel

All Year   1P: $125-$745   2P: $125-$745

Location: East side of St. John's River Bridge. 1575 W Hwy 40 32102. **Fax:** 386/749-4408. **Facility:** 10 units. 4 one-bedroom standard units. 6 one-bedroom suites with kitchens. 1 story, exterior corridors. *Bath:* shower only. **Parking:** on-site. **Terms:** office hours 7 am-6 pm. **Dining:** 11 am-9 pm, Wed from 4 pm; closed Tues. **Leisure Activities:** marina, pontoon rental. *Fee:* boats. **Cards:** MC, VI.

SOME UNITS

CASSELBERRY pop. 22,629   (See map and index starting on p. 656)

——— **WHERE TO STAY** ———

SUBURBAN LODGE   *Book at aaa.com*   **Phone:** (407)265-7699   61

Small-scale Hotel

All Year   1P: $80-$160   2P: $90-$180

Location: Just e of jct SR 436 and US 17-92. 210 N Oxford Rd 32707. **Fax:** 407/265-0291. **Facility:** 144 one-bedroom standard units with efficiencies. 3 stories, exterior corridors. *Bath:* combo or shower only. **Parking:** on-site. **Terms:** cancellation fee imposed, weekly rates available. **Amenities:** voice mail. **Guest Services:** coin laundry. **Business Services:** fax (fee). **Cards:** AX, DC, DS, MC, VI.

SOME UNITS

——— **WHERE TO DINE** ———

ALADDIN'S CAFE   **Lunch:** $7-$11   **Dinner:** $7-$19   **Phone:** 407/331-0488   193

Ethnic

Location: On SR 436, 1 mi se of US 17-92. 1015 E Semoran Blvd 32707. **Hours:** 11 am-9:30 pm, Fri-11 pm. Closed major holidays; also Sun. **Reservations:** suggested. **Features:** Freshly made kabobs with rice, tabbouleh, falafel and baklava are among the samplings of traditional Middle Eastern cuisine, primarily of the Lebanese persuasion, served at this small and cozy restaurant. The dinner buffet is especially popular. Casual dress. **Parking:** on-site. **Cards:** AX, DC, DS, MC, VI.

COLORADO FONDUE COMPANY   **Dinner:** $11-$19   **Phone:** 407/767-8232   192

Fondue

Location: SR 436 and Red Bug Lake Rd; in Greater Market Plaza. 1016 E Semoran Blvd 32707. **Hours:** 5:30 pm-9:30 pm, Fri & Sat 5 pm-10:30 pm, Sun 5 pm-9 pm. Closed: 1/1, 11/23, 12/25. **Reservations:** suggested. **Features:** Touches such as grapevine-shaped wine racks set a romantic tone in the fondue restaurant. Raw meat, seafood and vegetables are laid before diners, who then cook them at the table in hot liquids or on a hot rock. Those who are new to this style of dining should try the combination platter, a good introduction to the variety of methods and results. Dressy casual; beer & wine only. **Parking:** on-site. **Cards:** AX, DC, DS, MC, VI.

CYPRIANA RESTAURANT   **Lunch:** $6-$11   **Dinner:** $8-$17   **Phone:** 407/834-8088   189

Greek

Location: On SR 436, just n of Red Bug Lake Rd. 505 Semoran Blvd 32707. **Hours:** 11 am-10 pm. Closed: 7/4, 11/23, 12/25; also Sun. **Reservations:** accepted. **Features:** The traditional moussaka of potatoes and eggplant layered with meat sauce is a wonderful example of the good, authentic Greek food in this bustling atmosphere. Also on the menu are combination dinners and gyros. Tables and seating can be a bit crowded. Casual dress; beer & wine only. **Parking:** on-site. **Cards:** AX, DS, MC, VI.

ITALIAN VILLAGE PIZZA   **Lunch:** $5-$17   **Dinner:** $5-$17   **Phone:** 407/331-9090   191

Italian

Location: SR 436 and Red Bug Lake Rd; in The Greater Market Place. 1014 Semoran Blvd 32707. **Hours:** 10 am-10 pm, Fri & Sat-11 pm, Sun 11 am-10 pm. Closed: 11/23, 12/25. **Features:** Pizza is the specialty, but the menu also lists submarine sandwiches, wings, seafood, eggplant and variety of salads. Seating is limited, and take-out is available. Casual dress. **Parking:** on-site. **Cards:** AX, DS, MC, VI.

(See map and index starting on p. 656)

ROLANDO'S CUBAN RESTAURANT — Lunch: $4-$10   Dinner: $7-$24   Phone: 407/767-9677   (190)
♦♦♦♦
Cuban
Location: On SR 436, 1.3 mi se of US 17-92. 870 N Semoran Blvd 32707. **Hours:** 11 am-9 pm, Fri-10 pm, Sat noon-10 pm, Sun noon-8:30 pm. Closed: 1/1, 11/23, 12/25. **Features:** Simple textured walls and basic decor belie the sumptuous offerings of this casual establishment. Try the Cuban sandwich or picadillo for lunch, or take advantage of an extensive dinner menu that tempts with tamales, fried eggplant and sweet plantains. Casual dress; beer & wine only. **Cards:** AX, DC, DS, MC, VI.

SMOKEY BONES BBQ — Lunch: $5-$21   Dinner: $5-$21   Phone: 407/673-4901   (194)
♦♦♦♦
Barbecue
Location: Jct SR 436 and Howell Branch Rd. 1430 SR 436 32707. **Hours:** 11 am-10 pm, Fri & Sat-11 pm. Closed major holidays. **Features:** The menu features barbecue that is slowly smoked over aged hickory. Barbecue platters with hand-pulled pork, beef brisket or smoked turkey are available in addition to combo platters that offer a bit of everything. Steaks, sandwiches, salad and burgers are also available. Casual dress; cocktails. **Parking:** on-site. **Cards:** AX, DS, MC, VI.

CELEBRATION pop. 2,736 (See map and index starting on p. 668)

——— WHERE TO STAY ———

CELEBRATION HOTEL — *Book at aaa.com*   Phone: (407)566-6000   (70)
AAA SAVE
♦♦♦♦ ♦♦♦♦
Small-scale Hotel

12/1-5/31 & 10/1-11/30	1P: $269-$459	XP: $20 F17
6/1-9/30	1P: $219-$399	XP: $20 F17

Location: I-4, exit 64A, 0.8 mi w to Celebration Ave, then s to Village Center, off Front St. 700 Bloom St 34747. **Fax:** 407/566-6001. **Facility:** The village of Celebration is the backdrop of this lakeside hotel. 115 units. 109 one-bedroom standard units. 6 one-bedroom suites. 3 stories, interior corridors. *Bath:* combo or shower only. **Parking:** on-site (fee). **Terms:** check-in 4 pm, 3 day cancellation notice-fee imposed, $10 service charge. **Amenities:** video games, high-speed Internet, dual phone lines, voice mail, safes, honor bars, irons, hair dryers. **Dining:** Plantation Room, see separate listing. **Pool(s):** heated outdoor. **Leisure Activities:** whirlpool, paddleboats, jogging, exercise room. *Fee:* massage. **Guest Services:** valet laundry, area transportation-Disney & within Celebration. **Business Services:** meeting rooms. *Fee:* administrative services, fax. **Cards:** AX, CB, DC, DS, MC, VI.

SOME UNITS

——— WHERE TO DINE ———

CAFE D'ANTONIO — Lunch: $5-$14   Dinner: $12-$34   Phone: 407/566-2233   (49)
♦♦♦
Regional
Italian
Location: I-4, exit 64A, 0.7 mi e on US 192, then 1.3 mi s on Celebration Ave; 1 blk e of Celebration Ave; at corner of Front and Market sts. 691 Front St, Suite 110 34747. **Hours:** 11:30 am-3 & 5-10 pm, Sat 11:30 am-10 pm, Sun noon-9 pm. Closed major holidays. **Reservations:** suggested. **Features:** On the ground floor of a building in the heart of downtown, the cafe overlooks the water. Diners can eat indoors or al fresco on the front veranda or in the side alley. Both outdoor areas are covered, and the veranda can be enclosed with vinyl curtains in inclement weather. Fresh ingredients are used in the preparation of multiregional Italian cuisine, and some meals are prepared in a wood-fired oven. Casual dress; cocktails. **Parking:** on-site and street. **Cards:** AX, CB, DC, DS, MC, VI.

COLUMBIA RESTAURANT — Lunch: $6-$23   Dinner: $14-$23   Phone: 407/566-1505   (51)
♦♦♦
Cuban
Location: Jct SR 417 and Campus St, 1 mi s, then just e. 649 Front St 34747. **Hours:** 11:30 am-10:30 pm. **Reservations:** suggested. **Features:** The restaurant hails the oldest Spanish restaurant pedigree in all of Florida. Established in 1905 in Ybor City, it carries on all of its original traditions such as the "1905" salad, which is prepared tableside and should not be missed; the seemingly simple concoction tastes incredibly good. That should be followed with Cuban black bean soup and any of the many superlative entrees, and finished with a slice of Godiva Chocolate Cake. Casual dress; cocktails. **Parking:** on-site. **Cards:** AX, DC, DS, MC, VI.

JOE'S CRAB SHACK — Lunch: $4-$18   Dinner: $4-$18   Phone: 321/939-6880   (48)
♦♦
Seafood
Location: I-4, exit 64A, 0.4 mi e. 10 Blake Blvd 34747. **Hours:** 11 am-10 pm, Fri & Sat-11 pm. Closed major holidays. **Features:** Just off the interstate, the whimsically decorated restaurant is a fun place to enjoy seafood favorites. Casual dress; cocktails. **Parking:** on-site. **Cards:** AX, MC, VI.

MARKET STREET CAFE — Lunch: $6-$15   Dinner: $6-$15   Phone: 407/566-1144   (50)
♦♦
American
Location: Downtown. 701 Front St, Suite 110 34747. **Hours:** 8 am-10 pm. Closed: 11/23, 12/25. **Features:** In the middle of downtown, the retro diner prepares such favorites as meat loaf, turkey, specialty burgers, sandwiches and prime rib dinners. Ice cream floats, shakes, homemade strawberry shortcake and temptations from the coffee bar end a meal nicely. Breakfast also is served. Casual dress; beer & wine only. **Parking:** street. **Cards:** AX, DC, DS, MC, VI.

PLANTATION ROOM — Lunch: $8-$15   Dinner: $18-$32   Phone: 407/566-6000   (52)
♦♦♦♦
Continental
Location: I-4, exit 64A, 0.8 mi w to Celebration Ave, then s to Village Center, off Front St; in Celebration Hotel. 700 Bloom St 34747. **Hours:** 7 am-10:30 & 6-10 pm; Sunday brunch 11 am-3 pm. **Features:** At the end of the day nothing could be more relaxing than a meal at the Plantation Room. The chef creates exciting menu selections that make choosing just one seem impossible. The jumbo crab cakes with mango fruit salsa, seared breast of duck in port wine and the infamous bananas foster are just a sample of what awaits you. Casual dress; cocktails. **Parking:** on-site. **Cards:** AX, CB, DC, DS, JC, MC, VI.

CLERMONT pop. 9,333 (See map and index starting on p. 668)

——— WHERE TO STAY ———

FLORIDA PINES-THE FLORIDA STORE — Phone: 407/846-1722
♦♦♦♦
Vacation Home
Property failed to provide current rates
Location: I-4, exit 68, 3.5 mi s on SR 535, then 3.8 mi e on US 192. 3479 W Vine St 34741. **Fax:** 407/846-7680. **Facility:** Located near shopping, dining and the attractions, the spacious four- to six-bedroom homes offer heated, screened-in pools. 6 vacation homes with pools. 1-2 stories, exterior corridors. **Parking:** on-site. **Terms:** check-in 4 pm, pets ($100 fee). **Amenities:** DVD players (fee), CD players, irons, hair dryers. **Guest Services:** complimentary laundry. **Business Services:** fax (fee).

(See map and index starting on p. 668)

GREATER GROVES-AWARD VACATION HOMES
Phone: (352)243-8669

Vacation Home

All Year   2P: $150-$250
Location: Jct US 192 and 27, 2 mi n; in Greater Groves Subdivision. 2303 Hamlin Tr 34714. Fax: 352/241-0960. **Facility:** All homes are professionally decorated, have a private screened in pool and offer up to five bedrooms. 48 vacation homes with pools. 1 story, exterior corridors. **Parking:** on-site. **Terms:** check-in 4 pm, 3-7 night minimum stay - seasonal, 31 day cancellation notice-fee imposed, package plans, $25 service charge. **Amenities:** voice mail, safes, irons, hair dryers. **Leisure Activities:** whirlpools, community recreation area. **Guest Services:** complimentary laundry. **Business Services:** fax (fee). **Cards:** AX, DS, MC, VI. **Special Amenities:** free local telephone calls and early check-in/late check-out.

HIGHLANDS RESERVE-BEST WESTERN IPG
FLORIDA VACATION HOMES   *Book at aaa.com*
Phone: (863)547-1057   62

Vacation Home

All Year   1P: $175-$375   2P: $175-$375
Location: 0.5 mi e of jct US 27 and 192. 9550 W US Highway 192 34711. Fax: 863/547-1059. **Facility:** The conveniently located executive homes feature three- to six-bedrooms, screened pool and patio and spacious living areas. 50 vacation homes with pools. 1-2 stories, exterior corridors. **Parking:** on-site. **Terms:** check-in 4 pm, 7 day cancellation notice-fee imposed. **Amenities:** voice mail, irons, hair dryers. **Guest Services:** complimentary laundry, area transportation-major attractions. **Business Services:** fax (fee). **Cards:** AX, DS, MC, VI. **Special Amenities:** free local telephone calls and free room upgrade (subject to availability with advance reservations).

HOLIDAY INN EXPRESS   *Book at aaa.com*
Phone: (352)243-7878

Small-scale Hotel

All Year [ECP]   1P: $90-$100
Location: Just s of SR 50. 1810 S US Hwy 27 34711. Fax: 352/243-7882. **Facility:** 70 units. 69 one-bedroom standard units, some with whirlpools. 1 one-bedroom suite ($110-$150) with kitchen (no utensils). 3 stories, interior corridors. *Bath:* combo or shower only. **Parking:** on-site. **Amenities:** high-speed Internet, dual phone lines, voice mail, irons, hair dryers. **Pool(s):** outdoor. **Guest Services:** valet and coin laundry. **Business Services:** meeting rooms, fax (fee). **Cards:** AX, DC, DS, MC, VI.

SOME UNITS

HOLIDAY INN EXPRESS & SUITES WEST OF
THEME PARKS   *Book at aaa.com*
Phone: (407)239-8315

Small-scale Hotel

All Year [ECP]   1P: $89-$149   2P: $89-$149
Location: I-4, exit 64B, 7.2 mi w on US 192; 0.5 mi e of jct US 27. 105 Summer Bay Blvd 34711. Fax: 407/239-8297. **Facility:** 155 one-bedroom standard units. 4 stories, interior corridors. *Bath:* combo or shower only. **Parking:** on-site. **Terms:** $2 service charge. **Amenities:** video games (fee), dual phone lines, voice mail, irons, hair dryers. **Pool(s):** heated outdoor. **Leisure Activities:** exercise room. *Fee:* game room. **Guest Services:** valet and coin laundry. **Business Services:** meeting rooms, fax (fee). **Cards:** AX, DC, DS, MC, VI. *(See color ad p 808)*

SOME UNITS

ORANGE TREE-AWARD VACATION HOMES
Phone: (352)243-8669

Vacation Home

All Year   2P: $150-$250
Location: Jct US 192 and 27, 2 mi n; in Greater Groves Subdivision. 2303 Hamlin Tr 34714. Fax: 352/241-0960. **Facility:** All homes are professionally decorated, have a private screened in pool and offer up to five bedrooms. 60 vacation homes with pools. 1 story, exterior corridors. **Parking:** on-site. **Terms:** check-in 4 pm, 3-7 night minimum stay - seasonal, 31 day cancellation notice-fee imposed, package plans, $25 service charge. **Amenities:** voice mail, safes, irons, hair dryers. *Some:* DVD players. **Leisure Activities:** whirlpools, community recreation center, soccer field. **Guest Services:** complimentary laundry. **Business Services:** fax (fee). **Cards:** AX, DS, MC, VI. **Special Amenities:** free local telephone calls and early check-in/late check-out. *(See color ad p 720)*

------- **WHERE TO DINE** -------

RANDY'S RESTAURANT
Lunch: $4-$14   **Dinner:** $4-$14   Phone: 352/394-6805

American

Location: Jct US 192 and 27, 1 mi n on US 27. 1213 Hwy 27 S 34711. **Hours:** 8 am-10 pm, Sun-9 pm. Closed major holidays. **Features:** This menu features home cooked favorites such as meatloaf, pot roast, hot sandwiches and burgers. Casual dress; cocktails. **Parking:** on-site. **Cards:** MC, VI.

SANTIAGO'S MEXICAN RESTAURANT
Lunch: $6-$17   **Dinner:** $7-$17   Phone: 352/243-9986   42

Mexican

Location: Just n of SR 50; in the Citrus Tower. 139 N Hwy 27 34711. **Hours:** 11 am-3 & 5-9 pm, Fri & Sat 11 am-10 pm, Sun noon-8 pm. Closed: 1/1, 4/16, 12/25. **Features:** If your curiosity takes you to the top of the Citrus Tower, you can satisfy your hunger in the same building when you get your feet back on the ground. Many Mexican specialties are on the menu. Casual dress; cocktails. **Parking:** on-site. **Cards:** AX, DS, MC, VI.

DAVENPORT pop. 1,924 (See maps and indexes starting on p. 666, 668)

------- **WHERE TO STAY** -------

BEST WESTERN MAINGATE SOUTH   *Book at aaa.com*
Phone: (863)424-2596

Small-scale Hotel

12/1-1/2 & 2/16-4/24	1P: $89	2P: $89
1/3-2/15 & 4/25-11/30	1P: $69	2P: $69

Location: I-4, exit 55, just s on US 27. 2425 Frontage Rd 33837. Fax: 863/420-8717. **Facility:** 113 units. 104 one-bedroom standard units. 9 one-bedroom suites. 2 stories, exterior corridors. **Parking:** on-site. **Terms:** [CP] meal plan available, small pets only ($10 extra-charge). **Amenities:** irons, hair dryers. **Pool(s):** heated outdoor. **Leisure Activities:** whirlpool. **Guest Services:** gift shop, coin laundry, area transportation-Disney. **Business Services:** fax (fee). **Cards:** AX, DC, DS, MC, VI. **Special Amenities:** free continental breakfast and free newspaper. *(See color ad p 701)*

SOME UNITS

(See maps and indexes starting on p. 666, 668)

CALABAY PARC-THE FLORIDA STORE

Phone: 407/846-1722   **157**

Vacation Home

Property failed to provide current rates

Location: I-4, exit 68, 3.5 mi s on SR 535, then 3.8 mi e on US 192. 3479 W Vine St 34741. Fax: 407/846-7680. **Facility:** Located near shopping, dining and the attractions, the spacious four- to six-bedroom homes offer heated, screened-in pools. 3 vacation homes with pools. 1-2 stories, exterior corridors. **Parking:** on-site. **Terms:** check-in 4 pm, pets ($100 fee). **Amenities:** DVD players, CD players, irons, hair dryers. **Guest Services:** complimentary laundry. **Business Services:** fax (fee).

ESPRIT-PREMIER VACATION HOMES

Phone: (407)396-2401   **156**

All Year   1P: $129-$279

Vacation Home

Location: I-4, exit 68, 2.5 mi e on SR 535 (Apopka-Vineland Rd). 3160 Vineland Rd, Suite 1 34746. Fax: 407/396-0113. **Facility:** All homes are professionally decorated, have a private screened-in pool and offer up to five bedrooms. 26 vacation homes with pools. 1 story, exterior corridors. **Parking:** on-site. **Terms:** off-site registration, check-in 4 pm, 4 night minimum stay, 30 day cancellation notice-fee imposed. **Amenities:** irons, hair dryers. **Guest Services:** complimentary laundry. **Business Services:** fax (fee). **Cards:** AX, DS, MC, VI.

GREATER GROVES-PREMIER VACATION HOMES

Phone: (407)396-2401   **158**

All Year   1P: $129-$279

Vacation Home

Location: I-4, exit 68, 2.5 mi e on SR 535 (Apopka-Vineland Rd). 3160 Vineland Rd, Suite 1 34746. Fax: 407/396-0113. **Facility:** All homes are professionally decorated, have a private screened in pool and offer up to five bedrooms. 14 vacation homes with pools. 1 story, exterior corridors. **Parking:** on-site. **Terms:** off-site registration, check-in 4 pm, 4 night minimum stay, 30 day cancellation notice-fee imposed. **Amenities:** irons, hair dryers. **Guest Services:** complimentary laundry. **Business Services:** fax (fee). **Cards:** AX, DS, MC, VI.

HAMPTON INN ORLANDO-S OF WALT DISNEY RESORT

Phone: 863/420-9898

Small-scale Hotel

Property failed to provide current rates

Location: I-4, exit 55, just nw. 44117 Hwy 27 33897. Fax: 863/420-9797. **Facility:** 83 one-bedroom standard units. 5 stories, interior corridors. *Bath:* combo or shower only. **Parking:** on-site. **Terms:** small pets only ($25 fee, $10 extra charge). **Amenities:** voice mail, irons, hair dryers. *Fee:* video games, high-speed Internet. **Pool(s):** heated outdoor. **Leisure Activities:** whirlpool, exercise room. **Guest Services:** coin laundry. **Business Services:** meeting rooms, fax (fee).

SOME UNITS

HOLIDAY INN EXPRESS HOTEL & SUITES

Book at aaa.com

Phone: (863)424-2120

All Year   1P: $89-$165   2P: $89-$165

Small-scale Hotel

Location: I-4, exit 55, just s. 43824 Hwy 27 33837. Fax: 863/424-5317. **Facility:** 104 one-bedroom standard units. 2 stories, interior corridors. *Bath:* combo or shower only. **Parking:** on-site. **Terms:** cancellation fee imposed. **Amenities:** high-speed Internet, voice mail, safes, irons, hair dryers. **Pool(s):** heated outdoor, wading. **Guest Services:** valet and coin laundry. **Business Services:** meeting rooms, fax (fee). **Cards:** AX, CB, DS, MC, VI.

SOME UNITS

OMNI ORLANDO RESORT AT CHAMPIONSGATE

Phone: 407/390-6664   **29**

All Year   1P: $189-$269   XP: $30   F18

Resort
Large-scale Hotel

Location: I-4, exit 58, 0.3 mi w. 1500 Masters Blvd 33896. Fax: 407/390-6600. **Facility:** Luxury accommodations for leisure or business travelers: extensive resort activities include two Greg Norman golf courses and a full service spa. 730 units. 717 one-bedroom standard units. 13 one-bedroom suites, some with whirlpools. 16 stories, interior corridors. *Bath:* combo or shower only. **Parking:** on-site and valet. **Terms:** 3 day cancellation notice, $10 service charge, pets ($50 fee). **Amenities:** high-speed Internet, dual phone lines, voice mail, safes, honor bars, irons, hair dryers. **Dining:** 5 restaurants, 24 hours, cocktails, also, Zen, see separate listing. **Pool(s):** 2 heated outdoor. **Leisure Activities:** whirlpools, waterslide, 9-hole par 3, 2 lighted tennis courts, recreation programs, lazy river water ride, interactive water feature, jogging, playground, spa, basketball, volleyball. *Fee:* golf-36 holes, game room. **Guest Services:** gift shop, valet laundry, airport transportation (fee)-Orlando International Airport. **Business Services:** conference facilities, business center. **Cards:** AX, CB, DC, DS, JC, MC, VI. **Special Amenities:** free local telephone calls and free newspaper.

SOME UNITS

REGAL PALMS RESORT AT HIGHLANDS RESERVE

Phone: (863)424-8411   **27**

All Year   1P: $119-$199

Condominium

Location: Jct US 192 and 27, 1 mi s. 2700 Sand Mine Rd 33897. Fax: 863/420-6552. **Facility:** Townhomes are available for vacation rentals; clubhouse amenities such as a pool, restauant and exercise room are available. 214 three-bedroom suites with kitchens. 2 stories, exterior corridors. **Parking:** on-site. **Terms:** check-in 4 pm, 3 day cancellation notice-fee imposed, [CP] meal plan available, package plans, pets ($500 fee). **Amenities:** voice mail, irons, hair dryers. *Some:* DVD players (fee), CD players. **Dining:** 11:30 am-11 pm, cocktails. **Pool(s):** 2 heated outdoor, wading. **Leisure Activities:** whirlpools, waterslide, 4 lighted tennis courts. *Fee:* golf-18 holes, game room. **Guest Services:** complimentary laundry, area transportation-major attractions. **Business Services:** meeting rooms, business center. **Cards:** AX, DS, MC, VI. **Special Amenities:** free continental breakfast and free local telephone calls. *(See color ad p 727)*

SOME UNITS

(See maps and indexes starting on p. 666, 668)

REGAL PALMS RESORT AT HIGHLANDS RESERVE   *Book at aaa.com*   Phone: (863)424-8411   **26**

▼▼▼▼ All Year   2P: $149-$239
Vacation Home   **Location:** On US 192, 1 mi e of US 27. 2700 Sand Mine Rd 33897. Fax: 863/420-6652. **Facility:** All homes are professionally decorated, have a private screened in pool and offer up to five bedrooms. 200 vacation homes ($149-$239) with pools. 1 story, exterior corridors. **Parking:** on-site. **Terms:** check-in 4 pm, 3 night minimum stay, 3 day cancellation notice-fee imposed, [CP] meal plan available, package plans, pets ($500 fee). **Amenities:** video library (fee), voice mail, safes, irons, hair dryers. *Some:* CD players. **Leisure Activities:** playground, basketball, volleyball. *Fee:* golf-18 holes. **Guest Services:** complimentary laundry. **Business Services:** fax (fee). **Cards:** AX, DS, MC, VI.

SOME UNITS
[ASK] [S🐾] [🛏] [🏊] [✕] [DATA PORT] [🛢] [🖥] [💻] / [VCR] /
         FEE   FEE

THE SANCTUARY-AMERICAN VACATION HOMES   Phone: (407)396-2880   **28**

▼▼▼ All Year   2P: $89-$289
Vacation Home   **Location:** Florida Tpke, exit 244, 2.1 mi w on US 192. (2983 Vineland Rd, KISSIMMEE, 34746). Fax: 407/397-4132. **Facility:** Most of the 3- to 5-bedroom condos and homes have been individually decorated; homes have pools and condo units have access to a community pool. 13 vacation homes with pools. 1-2 stories, exterior corridors. **Parking:** on-site. **Terms:** check-in 4 pm, 5 night minimum stay - seasonal, 30 day cancellation notice, 14 day off season-fee imposed, package plans, 7% service charge. **Amenities:** irons. **Guest Services:** complimentary laundry. **Business Services:** fax (fee). **Cards:** AX, DC, MC, VI. *(See color ad p 756)*

[ASK] [S🐾] [🏊] [✕] [VCR] [DATA PORT] [🛢] [🖥] [💻]
                                      FEE

THE SANCTUARY AT WEST HAVEN - THE KISSIMMEE RENTAL COMPANY   Phone: 407/396-4047

▼▼▼ All Year   1P: $80-$450   2P: $80-$450
Vacation Home   **Location:** I-4, exit 68, 3 mi s on SR 535, then 1.5 mi w on US 192; in shopping plaza. 421 Bal Moral Dr 33896 (5287 W Irlo Bronson Hwy, KISSIMMEE, 34746). Fax: 407/397-4265. **Facility:** Only a short drive from the attractions, dining and shopping, these 3- to 5-bedroom homes offer multiple baths and a screened-in, private pool area. 5 vacation homes with pools. 1-2 stories, exterior corridors. **Parking:** on-site. **Terms:** check-in 4 pm, 3 night minimum stay - seasonal, 60 day cancellation notice-fee imposed. **Amenities:** DVD players, CD players, irons, hair dryers. **Guest Services:** complimentary laundry. **Business Services:** fax (fee). **Cards:** AX, DS, MC, VI.

[ASK] [🏊] [✕] [DATA PORT] [🛢] [🖥] [💻]

SOUTHERN DUNES-THE FLORIDA STORE   Phone: 407/846-1722   **155**

▼▼▼ Property failed to provide current rates
Vacation Home   **Location:** I-4, exit 68, 3.5 mi s on SR 535, then 3.8 mi e on US 192. 3479 W Vine St 34741. Fax: 407/846-7680. **Facility:** Located near shopping, dining and the attractions, the spacious four- to six-bedroom homes offer heated, screened-in pools. 34 vacation homes with pools. 1-2 stories, exterior corridors. **Parking:** on-site. **Terms:** check-in 4 pm, pets ($100 fee). **Amenities:** DVD players (fee), CD players, irons, hair dryers. **Leisure Activities:** 2 tennis courts, playground, exercise room. **Business Services:** fax (fee).

[🛏] [🍴] [🏊] [✕] [✕] [VCR] [🛢] [🖥] [💻]
         FEE

SUPER 8 MOTEL MAINGATE SOUTH   *Book at aaa.com*   Phone: 863/420-8888

▼▼ Property failed to provide current rates
Small-scale Hotel   **Location:** I-4, exit 55, 0.5 mi n. 44199 Hwy 27 33897. Fax: 863/424-6602. **Facility:** 154 one-bedroom standard units. 2 stories, exterior corridors. *Bath:* combo or shower only. **Parking:** on-site. **Terms:** pets ($10 extra charge). **Amenities:** hair dryers. **Pool(s):** heated outdoor. **Leisure Activities:** playground. **Guest Services:** coin laundry. **Business Services:** fax (fee).

SOME UNITS
[🛏] [🍴] [♿] [🐾] [🏊] [🎦] [DATA PORT] / [✕] [🛢] [🖥] [💻] /
         FEE

THOUSAND OAKS - PRESTIGE VACATION HOMES   Phone: (863)424-7400

(AAA) [SAVE]
▼▼▼▼
Vacation Home   All Year   1P: $106-$286
Location: I-4, exit 58, 1.5 mi e on CR 532, 1 mi s on CR 545, then 1.2 mi e on CR 54. Located in a residential area. 101 Thousand Oaks Blvd 33896. Fax: 863/424-7500. **Facility:** This property is a subdivision of three- to five-bedroom rental houses, each with a landscaped yard and screened-in pool. 68 vacation homes with pools. 1 story, exterior corridors. **Parking:** on-site. **Terms:** check-in 4 pm, 3 night minimum stay, cancellation fee imposed, package plans. **Amenities:** voice mail, safes, irons, hair dryers. **Guest Services:** complimentary laundry. **Business Services:** fax (fee). **Cards:** AX, DS, MC, VI. **Special Amenities:** free local telephone calls.
(See color ad p 724)

[S🐾] [🏊] [VCR] [🎦] [DATA PORT] [🛢] [🖥] [💻]

VISTAPARK RESORT   Phone: (863)420-1999   **159**

▼▼▼ All Year   1P: $189-$439
Vacation Home   **Location:** Jct US 192 and 27, 2 mi s on US 27 to Florence Villa Grove Rd, then e. 2025 Florence Villa Grove Rd 33897. Fax: 863/420-9669. **Facility:** These rental homes are all professionally decorated, have screened pools and three to five bedrooms; shops, attractions and restaurants are nearby. 60 vacation homes with pools, some with whirlpools. 1-2 stories, exterior corridors. *Bath:* combo or shower only. **Parking:** on-site. **Terms:** check-in 4 pm, 3 night minimum stay, 30 day cancellation notice-fee imposed. **Amenities:** CD players, voice mail, irons, hair dryers. **Leisure Activities:** tennis court, playground, basketball. **Guest Services:** complimentary laundry. **Business Services:** fax (fee). **Cards:** AX, DC, DS, MC, VI.

[ASK] [🏊] [✕] [✕] [DATA PORT] [🛢] [🖥] [💻]

(See maps and indexes starting on p. 666, 668)

WESTRIDGE-AMERICAN VACATION HOMES   Phone: (407)396-2880   [154]

Vacation Home

All Year   2P: $89-$289
Location: Florida Tpke, exit 244, 2.1 mi w on US 192. (2983 Vineland Rd, KISSIMMEE, 34746). Fax: 407/397-4132. **Facility:** Most of the three- to five-bedroom condos and homes have been individually decorated; homes have pools and condo units have access to a community pool. 10 vacation homes with pools. 1-2 stories, exterior corridors. **Parking:** on-site. **Terms:** check-in 4 pm, 5 night minimum stay - seasonal, 30 day cancellation notice, 14 day off season-fee imposed, package plans, 7% service charge. **Amenities:** irons. **Leisure Activities:** playground. **Guest Services:** complimentary laundry. **Business Services:** fax (fee). **Cards:** AX, DC, MC, VI. *(See color ad p 756)*

——— **WHERE TO DINE** ———

LA CREPE RESTAURANT   Lunch: $5-$10   Dinner: $8-$16   Phone: 407-397-2020   [17]

French

Location: I-4, exit 58, 0.3 mi w; in ChampionsGate. 8289 Champions Gate Blvd 33896. **Hours:** 11 am-9:30 pm. Closed: 11/23. **Features:** The menu features a variety of crepes made to order; choose to fill a crepe with ham and cheese and bechamel sauce or sea scallops sauteed in garlic and butter. Save room for the dessert crepes that can be filled with ice cream and fruit. Casual dress; beer & wine only. **Parking:** on-site. **Cards:** AX, DS, MC, VI.

MIA PIZZA PASTA KITCHEN   Lunch: $3-$16   Dinner: $3-$16   Phone: 863/420-3336   [14]

Italian

Location: Jct US 192 and 27, 2.3 mi s on US 27. 2440 Sand Mine Rd 33897. **Hours:** 11:30 am-9:30 pm, Sun from 4 pm. Closed major holidays. **Features:** This restaurant has a limited menu, is mainly take out and offers pizza and a few select appetizers. Casual dress. **Parking:** on-site. **Cards:** MC, VI.

NEW YORK PIZZA WORLD   Lunch: $4-$17   Dinner: $4-$17   Phone: 863/424-0840

Italian

Location: I-4, exit 23, just nw. 44294 Hwy 27 33897. **Hours:** 11:30 am-10:30 pm. Closed: 11/23. **Features:** Although pizza is the specialty, hot heroes, cold submarine sandwiches and pasta dishes also are options. Casual dress; beer & wine only. **Parking:** on-site. **Cards:** AX, DC, DS, MC, VI.

PEPPERON' PIZZERIA & RESTAURANT   Lunch: $5-$15   Dinner: $7-$25   Phone: 407/397-7499   [15]

Italian

Location: I-4, exit 58, just w; in ChampionsGate. 8293 Champions Gate Blvd 33896. **Hours:** 10 am-10 pm. Closed major holidays. **Features:** Patrons enjoy hand-tossed gourmet pizza, calzones and homemade pasta dishes at the quaint eatery. Eggplant, veal and chicken dishes also are on the menu. Casual dress; cocktails. **Parking:** on-site. **Cards:** AX, DS, MC, VI.

ZEN   Dinner: $8-$37   Phone: 407/390-6664   [16]

Japanese

Location: I-4, exit 58, 0.3 mi w; in Omni Orlando Resort at ChampionsGate. 1500 Masters Blvd 33896. **Hours:** 6 pm-10 pm. Closed: Mon. **Reservations:** suggested. **Features:** The restaurant's relaxing and cozy atmosphere that enhances the "Zen experience"; Pan-Asian dishes are featured as well as a saki and sushi bar. Begin with crispy chicken wings stuffed with noodles and vegetables or a sweet potato tempura with Thai sauce; follow that with General Tao's chicken, Szechwan beef or sauteed shrimp with glazed walnuts and a chili pepper sauce. Casual dress; cocktails. **Parking:** on-site. **Cards:** AX, CB, DC, DS, JC, MC, VI.

EUSTIS pop. 15,106

——— **WHERE TO DINE** ———

CRISPERS   Lunch: $5-$9   Dinner: $5-$9   Phone: 352/483-0656

American

Location: On US 441; in Eustis Village. 2884 David Walker Rd 32726. **Hours:** 10:30 am-9 pm, Sun 11 am-8 pm. Closed major holidays. **Features:** A healthy alternative for lunch or dinner, the restaurant prepares towering specialty sandwiches on warm, fresh homemade bread. Salad selections with combinations of meats, fruit and cheese are just as tempting. Varied coffees go well with freshly baked cakes and brownies. Casual dress. **Parking:** on-site. **Cards:** AX, DS, MC, VI.

GATOR'S DOCKSIDE   Lunch: $5-$15   Dinner: $5-$15   Phone: 352/357-1255

American

Location: On US 441; in Eustis Village. 15241 US Hwy 441 32726. **Hours:** 11 am-midnight. Closed: 11/23, 12/25. **Features:** Multiple large screen televisions broadcasting major sporting events, pool tables, and video games are a few ways to keep entertained while you wait for wings, ribs, seafood specials or a specialty sandwich. Casual dress; cocktails. **Parking:** on-site. **Cards:** AX, DS, MC, VI.

FERN PARK pop. 8,318   (See map and index starting on p. 656)

——— **WHERE TO DINE** ———

NEW YORK PIZZA & RESTAURANT   Lunch: $6-$19   Dinner: $6-$19   Phone: 407/830-8585   [197]

Italian

Location: On US 17-92, 1 mi s of SR 436; in Main Street Square Shopping Plaza. 7800 S US Hwy 17-92 32730. **Hours:** 11 am-10 pm, Fri & Sat-11 pm. Closed: Sun. **Features:** Limited seating contributes to a busy lunchtime. Antipasto salads, stromboli, submarine sandwiches and baked Italian favorites make up the bulk of the menu. Take-out service is available. Casual dress. **Parking:** on-site. **Cards:** MC, VI.

FRUITLAND PARK pop. 3,186

——— **WHERE TO DINE** ———

CAROUSEL BAKERY BAGELS & DELI   Lunch: $4-$6   Phone: 352/365-6900

American

Location: On US 27 N. 3430 US Hwy 27 34731. **Hours:** 6 am-3 pm. Closed major holidays; also Mon. **Features:** Homemade sandwiches are made to order, and varied muffins, cakes, cookies and bagels are baked daily. On US 27 just a few miles from Lady Lake, this place stays busy when it's open, which is only for breakfast and lunch. Pastries are awesome. Casual dress. **Parking:** on-site.

HEATHROW pop. 4,068 (See map and index starting on p. 656)

——— WHERE TO STAY ———

COURTYARD BY MARRIOTT   *Book at aaa.com*   Property failed to provide current rates   **Phone:** 407/444-1000   27

▼▼▼   **Location:** I-4, exit 98, just nw. 135 International Pkwy 32746. **Fax:** 407/444-5921. **Facility:** 83 units. 77 one-bedroom standard units. 6 one-bedroom suites. 3 stories, interior corridors. **Bath:** combo or shower only.
Small-scale Hotel   **Parking:** on-site. **Amenities:** high-speed Internet, voice mail, irons, hair dryers. **Pool(s):** heated outdoor. **Leisure Activities:** whirlpool, exercise room. **Guest Services:** valet and coin laundry. **Business Services:** meeting rooms, business center.

SOME UNITS

🍽 🍸 🕎 ♿ 👂 🛥 📷 DATA PORT 🖥 / ✕ VCR 🔌 🖨 /

——— WHERE TO DINE ———

LUIGINO'S   **Lunch:** $7-$16   **Dinner:** $15-$35   **Phone:** 407/333-2847   67

AAA   **Location:** I-4, exit 98, 0.5 mi w; in Heathrow Shops. 120 International Pkwy, Suite 140 32746. **Hours:** 11:30 am-9:30 pm, Fri-10:30 pm, Sat 4:30 pm-10:30 pm, Sun 4:30 pm-9:30 pm. **Closed:** 11/23, 12/25.
▼▼▼   **Reservations:** suggested. **Features:** Located in a fairly upscale shopping plaza, this restaurant offers two
Italian   distinctly different dining rooms. One offers excellent views of the adjacent private golf course while the other offers a dark, masculine setting. While the menu is predominantly Italian, there is also a selection of high-quality Midwestern steaks. Make sure to start off your dining experience with the bruschetta with a nice variety of pasta and entree selections, everyone will find something they enjoy. Dressy casual; cocktails. **Parking:** valet. **Cards:** AX, DC, DS, MC, VI.   🍸

MAMMOLITO'S PIZZA & PASTA   **Lunch:** $6-$14   **Dinner:** $9-$18   **Phone:** 407/333-9920   71

▼▼   **Location:** I-4, exit 98, just w. 1210 S International Pkwy 32746. **Hours:** 11 am-9 pm, Sun from noon. Closed major holidays. **Features:** This Italian eatery offers a variety of pizza creations, calzones, oven baked pasta and
Italian   specialty dishes with veal, chicken and seafood. Casual dress; beer & wine only. **Parking:** on-site. **Cards:** AX, MC, VI.

PANERA BREAD CO   **Lunch:** $5-$7   **Dinner:** $5-$7   **Phone:** 407/804-8340   69

▼   **Location:** I-4, exit 98, just w; in Shoppes at Oakmont. 1210 International Pkwy, Suite 110 32746. **Hours:** 6:30 am-9:30 pm, Sun 7 am-8:30 pm. **Closed:** 11/23, 12/25. **Features:** In a shopping area, the restaurant is a great
American   place for healthy sandwiches and homemade soups served in a large bread bowl. Numerous varieties of freshly baked breads and bagels make this a popular stop for breakfast. Outdoor seating is available. Casual dress. **Parking:** on-site. **Cards:** AX, DS, MC, VI.

PEACH VALLEY CAFE   **Lunch:** $3-$12   **Phone:** 407/833-9440   68

▼▼   **Location:** I-4, exit 98, just w; in Shoppes at Oakmont. 1210 S International Pkwy 32746. **Hours:** 7 am-2:30 pm. **Closed:** 11/23, 12/25. **Features:** Only open for breakfast and lunch, the cafe prepares eggs Benedict,
American   waffles, pancakes and sandwich platters of chicken salad, burgers and clubs. Casual dress. **Parking:** on-site. **Cards:** AX, DC, DS, MC, VI.

STONEWOOD GRILL & TAVERN   **Dinner:** $9-$29   **Phone:** 407/333-3292   70

▼▼▼   **Location:** I-4, exit 98, just w; in Shoppes at Oakmont. 1210 International Pkwy S 32746. **Hours:** 4 pm-10 pm, Fri & Sat-11 pm. **Closed:** 11/23, 12/25. **Features:** Enjoy an array of well-prepared dishes, including filet mignon,
Steak & Seafood   rack of lamb and grilled scallops. The dining room is comfortably appointed, with the decor reflecting a beautiful use of stone, wood and earth tones. Servers are knowledgeable and attentive. Casual dress; cocktails. **Parking:** on-site. **Cards:** AX, CB, DC, DS, MC, VI.   🍸

HOWEY-IN-THE-HILLS pop. 956

——— WHERE TO STAY ———

MISSION INN GOLF & TENNIS RESORT   **Phone:** (352)324-3101

▼▼▼   All Year   1P: $155-$760   2P: $155-$760   XP: $15   F16
   Location: On CR 48, jct SR 19. Located in a quiet rural area. 10400 CR 48 34737. **Fax:** 352/324-2636. **Facility:** Set
Resort   on lush grounds, the resort offers screened patios or balconies with most rooms; a professionally
Large-scale Hotel   maintained golf course is featured. 196 units. 169 one-bedroom standard units. 6 one-, 12 two- and 9 three-bedroom suites, some with kitchens and/or whirlpools. 1-4 stories, interior/exterior corridors. **Bath:** combo or shower only. **Parking:** on-site. **Terms:** check-in 4 pm, 15 day cancellation notice-fee imposed, [BP] & [CP] meal plans available, package plans. **Amenities:** voice mail, irons, hair dryers. *Some:* high-speed Internet. **Pool(s):** outdoor, heated outdoor. **Leisure Activities:** whirlpools, rental boats, rental bicycles, jogging, playground, exercise room, shuffleboard, volleyball. *Fee:* sailboats, marina, golf-36 holes, 8 tennis courts (6 lighted), massage. **Guest Services:** gift shop, valet and coin laundry, area transportation (fee). **Business Services:** meeting rooms, business center. **Cards:** AX, DC, MC, VI.

SOME UNITS

ASK 🍽 24🍽 🍸 🏋 💪 🕎 🛥 ✕ 🐟 DATA PORT 🖥 / ✕ VCR 🔌 🖨 /
FEE   FEE

KISSIMMEE pop. 47,814   (See maps and indexes p. 666-673, 668-680, 671-686)

——— WHERE TO STAY ———

ACADIA ESTATES-ALL STAR VACATION HOMES   Phone: (407)997-0733   **92**

(AAA) (SAVE)   All Year Wkly   1P: $2093-$3300   2P: $2093-$3300

▼▼▼▼   **Location:** I-4, exit 64B, 2.3 mi w to Formosa Garden Blvd, then 0.5 mi s. 7822 W Irlo Bronson Hwy 34747.
Vacation Home   **Fax:** 407/997-1370. **Facility:** Professionally decorated estate homes are offered; some include garages converted to game rooms. 29 vacation homes with pools. 2 stories, exterior corridors. **Parking:** on-site.
Terms: check-in 4 pm, 4 night minimum stay, cancellation fee imposed, daily rates available.
Amenities: DVD players, video games, CD players, high-speed Internet, voice mail, irons, hair dryers.
Leisure Activities: whirlpools. **Guest Services:** complimentary laundry. **Business Services:** fax (fee). **Cards:** AX, DS, MC, VI.
Special Amenities: free local telephone calls. *(See color ad below)*   🅂Ⓓ 🖉 ⤢ ✕ (VCR) (DATA PORT) 🖥 🖼 🖵

ALHAMBRA RESORT   Phone: 407/933-0700

▼▼▼▼   All Year   1P: $100-$120
Condominium   **Location:** 13 mi s on Poinciana Blvd from jct US 192, 1 mi w. 500 E Cypress Pkwy 34759. Fax: 407/870-5412.
Facility: Amenities include screened patios or balconies, oversize bathtubs and in-room laundry equipment.
112 units. 56 one-bedroom standard units. 56 one-bedroom suites ($120-$160) with kitchens. 2 stories,
exterior corridors. **Parking:** on-site. **Terms:** check-in 4 pm, 14 day cancellation notice-fee imposed. **Amenities:** voice mail,
irons. **Pool(s):** heated outdoor, wading. **Leisure Activities:** lighted tennis court, playground. **Business Services:** meeting
rooms, fax (fee). **Cards:** AX, DS, MC, VI.

SOME UNITS

(ASK) (🍴) 🖉 ⤢ 🎦 🖥 🖼 🖵 / ✕ /

AMERIHOST RESORT   *Book at aaa.com*   Phone: (407)396-6000   **113**

(AAA) (SAVE)   All Year   1P: $99   2P: $99   XP: $10   F17

▼▼▼▼   **Location:** I-4, exit 64B, 2.6 mi w on US 192; 1.3 mi w of Disney World main gate. 7491 W Irlo Bronson Memorial Hwy
34747. Fax: 407/396-2895. **Facility:** 442 one-bedroom standard units. 4 stories, interior corridors. *Bath:*
Small-scale Hotel   combo or shower only. **Parking:** on-site. **Terms:** cancellation fee imposed, [BP] meal plan available.
Amenities: voice mail, irons, hair dryers. *Fee:* video games, safes. **Dining:** 7 am-midnight, cocktails,
entertainment. **Pool(s):** heated outdoor, heated indoor. **Leisure Activities:** whirlpool, recreation programs in
summer, exercise room. **Guest Services:** gift shop, valet and coin laundry, area transportation-major attractions. **Business
Services:** meeting rooms, fax (fee). **Cards:** AX, CB, DC, DS, MC, VI. **Special Amenities:** free local telephone calls and free
newspaper.

SOME UNITS

🅂Ⓓ 🚱 🍴 🍸 🖉 ⤢ ✕ 🎦 (DATA PORT) 🖥 🖵 / ✕ /
FEE

(See maps and indexes p. 666-673, 668-680, 671-686)

AMERISUITES (ORLANDO/LAKE BUENA VISTA SOUTH) *Book at aaa.com*

Phone: (407)997-1300   ❶

1/1-8/12 [CP]	1P: $114-$184	2P: $114-$184	XP: $5	F17
12/1-12/31 [CP]	1P: $99-$169	2P: $99-$169	XP: $5	F17
8/13-11/30 [CP]	1P: $99-$154	2P: $99-$154	XP: $5	F17

Small-scale Hotel

Location: I-4, exit 68, 3 mi s on SR 535. 4991 Calypso Cay Way 34746. Fax: 407/997-1301. **Facility:** 151 one-bedroom standard units. 6 stories, interior corridors. *Bath:* combo or shower only. **Parking:** on-site. **Terms:** check-in 4 pm, cancellation fee imposed, pets ($25 fee). **Amenities:** video games (fee), dual phone lines, voice mail, irons, hair dryers. **Pool(s):** heated outdoor. **Leisure Activities:** whirlpool, miniature golf, playground, exercise room, volleyball, game room. **Guest Services:** valet and coin laundry, area transportation-major attractions. **Business Services:** meeting rooms, fax (fee). **Cards:** AX, DC, DS, MC, VI. **Special Amenities:** free continental breakfast and free newspaper. *(See color ad below)*

SOME UNITS

FEE

(See maps and indexes p. 666-673, 668-680, 671-686)

BAYMONT INN ORLANDO-KISSIMMEE *Book at aaa.com* Phone: (407)787-3555 [119]
(AAA) [SAVE] 12/26-11/30 [ECP] 1P: $79-$99 2P: $79-$99 XP: $10 F16
12/1-12/25 [ECP] 1P: $69-$89 2P: $69-$89 XP: $10 F16
Location: I-4, exit 64A, 2 mi e on US 192. 5196 W Irlo Bronson Memorial Hwy 34746. Fax: 407/787-0700.
Facility: 64 one-bedroom standard units, some with whirlpools. 4 stories, interior corridors. *Bath:* combo or
Small-scale Hotel shower only. **Parking:** on-site. **Terms:** check-in 4 pm, cancellation fee imposed. **Amenities:** high-speed
Internet, dual phone lines, voice mail, irons, hair dryers. *Fee:* video library, video games. **Pool(s):** outdoor. **Leisure Activities:** whirlpool. **Guest Services:** valet and coin laundry. **Business Services:** fax (fee). **Cards:** AX, CB, DC, DS,
JC, MC, VI. **Special Amenities:** free expanded continental breakfast and free local telephone calls.

SOME UNITS
[icons]

BEST WESTERN HERITAGE PARK *Book at aaa.com* Phone: (407)846-4646 [34]
(AAA) [SAVE] All Year 1P: $69-$99 2P: $69-$99
Location: US 192 and 441 at Florida Tpke, exit 244, 0.3 mi w. 2145 E Irlo Bronson Memorial Hwy 34744.
Fax: 407/932-2467. **Facility:** 146 one-bedroom standard units. 2 stories (no elevator), exterior corridors.
Bath: combo or shower only. **Parking:** on-site. **Amenities:** voice mail, safes, irons, hair dryers. *Some:* high-
Small-scale Hotel speed Internet. **Pool(s):** outdoor. **Leisure Activities:** *Fee:* game room. **Guest Services:** coin laundry.
Business Services: meeting rooms, fax (fee). **Cards:** AX, CB, DC, DS, MC, VI. **Special Amenities:** free
continental breakfast and early check-in/late check-out.

SOME UNITS
[icons]

BEST WESTERN LAKESIDE *Book at aaa.com* Phone: (407)396-2222 [91]
(AAA) [SAVE] All Year 1P: $59-$129 XP: $10 F18
Location: I-4, exit 64B westbound on US 192; exit 64A eastbound, 3 mi w; 1.8 mi w of Disney World main gate. 7769 W
Irlo Bronson Memorial Hwy 34747-1750. Fax: 407/396-7087. **Facility:** 651 one-bedroom standard units. 2
stories (no elevator), exterior corridors. *Bath:* combo or shower only. **Parking:** on-site. **Terms:** cancellation
Large-scale Hotel fee imposed, $4 service charge. **Amenities:** dual phone lines, voice mail, irons, hair dryers. *Fee:* video
games, safes. **Dining:** 2 restaurants, 6 am-11:30 & 5-11 pm, cocktails. **Pool(s):** 3 heated outdoor, 2 wading.
Leisure Activities: miniature golf, playground, exercise room. *Fee:* game room. **Guest Services:** gift shop, valet and coin
laundry, area transportation-major attractions. **Business Services:** meeting rooms, business center. **Cards:** AX, CB, DC, DS,
JC, MC, VI. *(See color ad below)*

SOME UNITS
[icons]

(See maps and indexes p. 666-673, 668-680, 671-686)

BEST WESTERN MAINGATE EAST HOTEL & SUITES *Book at aaa.com*

Phone: (407)870-2000 [22]

6/2-11/30	2P: $89-$169	XP: $10	F17
1/3-6/1	2P: $89-$159	XP: $10	F17
12/1-1/2	2P: $99-$149	XP: $10	F17

Small-scale Hotel   **Location:** I-4, exit 64A, 7 mi e on US 192. 4018 W Vine St 34741. Fax: 407/870-2010. **Facility:** 223 one-bedroom standard units. 3-5 stories, exterior corridors. **Parking:** on-site. **Terms:** cancellation fee imposed, $5 service charge, pets ($50 fee). **Amenities:** high-speed Internet, dual phone lines, voice mail, safes, irons, hair dryers. **Pool(s):** heated outdoor, wading. **Leisure Activities:** whirlpool, exercise room. *Fee:* game room. **Guest Services:** valet and coin laundry, area transportation-Disney. **Business Services:** meeting rooms, fax (fee). **Cards:** AX, DC, DS, MC, VI. **Special Amenities:** free local telephone calls and free newspaper.

SOME UNITS

🅂ⅅ 🐾 🎦 🏊 ✕ 🎬 DATA PORT 💻 / ✕ 🖥 /
FEE   FEE

CELEBRITY RESORTS *Book at aaa.com*

Phone: (407)997-5000 [131]

12/1-1/3 & 4/3-9/20	1P: $113-$245	2P: $113-$245
1/4-4/2	1P: $89-$245	2P: $89-$245
9/21-11/30	1P: $81-$245	2P: $81-$245

Condominium   **Location:** I-4, exit 64A, 2.8 mi e on US 192, then just s. Located in a gated property. 2800 N Poinciana Blvd 34746. Fax: 407/997-5225. **Facility:** Buffered by a gated entry, this spacious property offers varied apartment-style lodging; it is convenient to shopping and restaurants. 311 units. 226 one- and 85 two-bedroom suites, some with kitchens and/or whirlpools. 2-3 stories, exterior corridors. **Parking:** on-site. **Terms:** check-in 4 pm, 3 day cancellation notice. **Amenities:** video library (fee), voice mail, safes. *Some:* irons, hair dryers. **Pool(s):** outdoor, 3 heated outdoor, wading. **Leisure Activities:** saunas, whirlpools, 6 tennis courts (4 lighted), racquetball courts, recreation programs, recreation area in spa section, bicycles, exercise room, basketball, shuffleboard, volleyball. *Fee:* game room. **Guest Services:** gift shop, complimentary laundry, area transportation (fee)-Disney. **Business Services:** meeting rooms, fax (fee). **Cards:** AX, DS, MC, VI.

SOME UNITS

🅂ⅅ 🍽 🎦 🏊 ✕ VCR 🎬 DATA PORT 🗄 📠 💻 / ✕ /

CLARION HOTEL MAINGATE *Book at aaa.com*

Phone: (407)396-4000 [96]

All Year	1P: $69-$119	2P: $69-$119

Small-scale Hotel   **Location:** I-4, exit 64B, 2.9 mi w on US 192, then 1.7 mi w of Disney World main gate. 7675 W Irlo Bronson Memorial Hwy 34747. Fax: 407/396-0714. **Facility:** 198 one-bedroom standard units. 5 stories, interior corridors. *Bath:* combo or shower only. **Parking:** on-site. **Terms:** cancellation fee imposed. **Amenities:** voice mail, safes (fee), irons, hair dryers. **Dining:** 7 am-11 & 5-11 pm. **Pool(s):** heated outdoor, wading. **Leisure Activities:** whirlpool, exercise room. *Fee:* game room. **Guest Services:** gift shop, valet and coin laundry, area transportation-major attractions & outlet malls. **Business Services:** meeting rooms, fax (fee). **Cards:** AX, DC, DS, MC, VI. *(See color ad below)*

SOME UNITS

🅂ⅅ 🍴 🍽 🏋 🔥M 📶 🎦 🏊 ✕ 🎬 DATA PORT 💻 / ✕ 🖥 /

CLEAR CREEK-THE FLORIDA STORE

Phone: 407/846-1722

Property failed to provide current rates

Vacation Home   **Location:** I-4, exit 68, 3.5 mi s on SR 535, then 3.8 mi e on US 192. 3479 W Vine St 34741. Fax: 407/846-7680. **Facility:** Located near shopping, dining and the attractions, the spacious four- to six-bedroom homes offer heated, screened-in pools. 7 vacation homes with pools. 1-2 stories, exterior corridors. **Parking:** on-site. **Terms:** check-in 4 pm, pets ($100 fee). **Amenities:** DVD players (fee), CD players, irons, hair dryers. **Guest Services:** complimentary laundry. **Business Services:** fax (fee).

🐾 🏊 ✕ VCR 🗄 📠 💻
FEE

Location, Location, Location!

Newly Renovated Lobby

For Reservations call: 800.568.3352
or visit www.clarionhotelmaingate.com
Save 10% off published AAA rates (ask for offer: S3A)
2 for 1 Drink Coupon at Check-in

Clarion Hotel Maingate
7675 W. Irlo Bronson Memorial Hwy.
Mile Marker #5
Kissimmee, FL 34747
T: 407.396.4000

- **198 Interior Corridor Rooms**
- Only 1.5 mi to Disney's Maingate
- Free Scheduled Shuttle to Disney's Theme Parks, Universal, SeaWorld & LBV Mall
- Kids Eat Breakfast Free Program
- Disney's Magic Your Way Tickets Available
- Heated Pool, Tiki Bar & Grille, Hot Tub, Kids Pool
- Gift Shop, Game Room, Fitness Room & Meeting Facilities
- In-Room Color TV w/HBO, Data Ports, Voice Mail, Safe, Iron/Board, Hairdryer, Coffeemaker
- High Speed Internet Access

Clarion Hotel
BY CHOICE HOTELS

(See maps and indexes p. 666-673, 668-680, 671-686)

COMFORT INN-MAINGATE WEST   *Book at aaa.com*   Phone: (863)424-8420   **77**
AAA SAVE   All Year [CP]   1P: $39-$149   2P: $39-$149   XP: $10   F18
Location: I-4, exit 64B, 7.3 mi w; 0.7 mi e of jct US 27. 9330 W Hwy 192 34711 (PO Box 691484, ORLANDO, 32869).
Fax: 863/424-9670. **Facility:** Smoke free premises. 73 one-bedroom standard units. 2 stories, exterior corridors. *Bath:* combo or shower only. **Parking:** on-site. **Terms:** check-in 4 pm. **Amenities:** voice mail,
Small-scale Hotel   irons, hair dryers. **Pool(s):** outdoor. **Cards:** AX, CB, DC, DS, JC, MC, VI. **Special Amenities:** free continental breakfast and free local telephone calls. *(See color ad below)*

COMFORT SUITES MAINGATE EAST   *Book at aaa.com*   Phone: (407)397-7848   **129**
AAA SAVE   All Year [ECP]   1P: $69-$175   2P: $69-$175   XP: $10   F
Location: I-4, exit 64A, 1.7 mi e on US 192, then just s. 2775 Florida Plaza Blvd 34746. Fax: 407/396-7045.
Facility: 198 one-bedroom standard units, some with whirlpools. 7 stories, interior corridors. *Bath:* combo or shower only. **Parking:** on-site. **Terms:** package plans, $2 service charge. **Amenities:** high-speed Internet,
Small-scale Hotel   dual phone lines, voice mail, safes, irons, hair dryers. **Pool(s):** heated outdoor, wading. **Leisure Activities:** whirlpool, exercise room. *Fee:* game room. **Guest Services:** gift shop, valet and coin laundry,
area transportation-major attractions. **Business Services:** meeting rooms, business center. **Cards:** AX, CB, DC, DS, JC, MC, VI. **Special Amenities:** free expanded continental breakfast. *(See color ad below)*   SOME UNITS

(See maps and indexes p. 666-673, 668-680, 671-686)

COMFORT SUITES MAINGATE RESORT *Book at aaa.com*   Phone: (407)390-9888   86

All Year   **Location:** I-4, exit 64B, 3.5 mi w on US 192. 7888 W Irlo Bronson Memorial Hwy 34747. Fax: 407/390-0981. **Facility:** 150 units. 149 one-bedroom standard units. 1 one-bedroom suite with efficiency and whirlpool. 3 stories, exterior corridors. *Bath:* combo or shower only. **Parking:** on-site. **Terms:** check-in 4 pm, cancellation fee imposed, [ECP] meal plan available, $2 service charge. **Amenities:** voice mail, safes (fee), irons, hair dryers. **Pool(s):** heated outdoor, wading. **Leisure Activities:** whirlpool. *Fee:* game room. **Guest Services:** gift shop, valet and coin laundry, area transportation-major attractions. **Business Services:** meeting rooms, fax (fee). **Cards:** AX, DC, DS, MC, VI. **Special Amenities:** free expanded continental breakfast and free local telephone calls.
(See color ad below)

SOME UNITS

       / ✕ /

COUNTRY INN & SUITES AT CALYPSO CAY *Book at aaa.com*   Phone: (407)997-1400   93

2/17-8/12 [CP]	1P: $99-$179	2P: $99-$179	XP: $5	F17
12/1-12/31 [CP]	1P: $99-$164	2P: $99-$164	XP: $5	F17
1/1-2/16 & 8/13-11/30 [CP]	1P: $99-$154	2P: $99-$154	XP: $5	F17

Location: I-4, exit 68, 3 mi s on SR 535; just s of Osceola Pkwy; just n of US 192. 5001 Calypso Cay Way 34746. Fax: 407/997-1401. **Facility:** 162 units. 114 one-bedroom standard units. 48 one-bedroom suites ($119-$199). 7 stories, interior corridors. *Bath:* combo or shower only. **Parking:** on-site. **Terms:** check-in 4 pm, cancellation fee imposed, pets ($25 extra charge). **Amenities:** video games (fee), dual phone lines, voice mail, irons, hair dryers. **Pool(s):** heated outdoor, whirlpool, miniature golf, playground, exercise room, volleyball. *Fee:* massage, game room. **Guest Services:** sundries, valet laundry, area transportation-major attractions. **Business Services:** meeting rooms, fax (fee). **Cards:** AX, DC, DS, MC, VI. **Special Amenities:** free continental breakfast and free local telephone calls. *(See color ad below)*

SOME UNITS

FEE / ✕ /

COUNTY HEARTH INN & SUITES *Book at aaa.com*   Phone: (407)396-6100   110

12/23-8/15	1P: $49-$79	2P: $49-$79	XP: $10	F
12/1-12/22 & 8/16-11/30	1P: $39-$59	2P: $39-$59	XP: $10	F

Location: I-4, exit 64A, 1 mi e on US 192; between MM 8 and 9. Located next to a water park. 6075 W Irlo Bronson Memorial Hwy 34747. Fax: 407/396-6965. **Facility:** 176 units. 160 one-bedroom standard units. 16 one-bedroom suites. 4 stories, exterior corridors. *Bath:* combo or shower only. **Parking:** on-site. **Terms:** check-in 4 pm, [CP] meal plan available, package plans, pets ($10 fee, $150 deposit). **Amenities:** voice mail, safes, irons, hair dryers. **Pool(s):** heated outdoor. **Leisure Activities:** whirlpool, playground. *Fee:* game room. **Guest Services:** gift shop, coin laundry. **Business Services:** fax (fee). **Cards:** AX, CB, DC, DS, JC, MC, VI.

SOME UNITS

ASK FEE / ✕ /

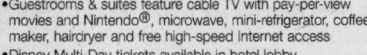

(See maps and indexes p. 666-673, 668-680, 671-686)

DAYS INN 192 ORLANDO-KISSIMMEE   *Book at aaa.com*   Phone: (407)846-4714   21

(AAA) (SAVE)   All Year   1P: $35-$150   2P: $35-$150   XP: $10   F

Location: US 192, 3 mi w of jct US 17-92. 4104 W Irlo Bronson Memorial Hwy 34741. Fax: 407/932-2699.
Facility: 174 one-bedroom standard units. 3 stories, exterior corridors. **Parking:** on-site.
Terms: cancellation fee imposed. **Amenities:** safes (fee), hair dryers. **Pool(s):** heated outdoor. **Leisure**

Small-scale Hotel **Activities:** *Fee:* game room. **Guest Services:** coin laundry, area transportation-major attractions. **Business Services:** fax (fee). **Cards:** AX, CB, DC, DS, MC, VI. **Special Amenities:** free expanded continental breakfast and free newspaper. *(See color ad below)*

SOME UNITS

(icons) / (icons) /

DAYS INN-KISSIMMEE   *Book at aaa.com*   Phone: 407/846-7136   32

Property failed to provide current rates

Location: Florida Tpke, exit 244, 0.3 mi w on US 192. 2095 E Irlo Bronson Memorial Hwy 34744. Fax: 407/846-8423.

Small-scale Hotel **Facility:** 118 one-bedroom standard units. 2 stories (no elevator), exterior corridors. **Parking:** on-site. **Terms:** pets ($20 extra charge). **Amenities:** safes (fee), hair dryers. **Pool(s):** outdoor. **Guest Services:** coin laundry. **Business Services:** fax (fee).

SOME UNITS

(icons) FEE / (icons) FEE FEE /

(See maps and indexes p. 666-673, 668-680, 671-686)

DAYS INN MAINGATE EAST   *Book at aaa.com*   **Phone: (407)396-7969**   117

(AAA) (SAVE)   All Year   1P: $59-$129   2P: $59-$129
▼▼▼   **Location:** I-4, exit 64A, 1 mi w on US 192. 5840 W Irlo Bronson Memorial Hwy 34746. **Fax:** 407/396-8103.
Small-scale Hotel   **Facility:** 404 one-bedroom standard units. 3 stories, exterior corridors. *Bath:* combo or shower only. $3 service charge, pets ($10 extra charge, in limited units). **Amenities:** high-speed Internet, voice mail, irons, hair dryers. *Fee:* video games, safes. **Dining:** 2 restaurants, 7 am-10 pm. **Pool(s):** heated outdoor.
Leisure Activities: playground. *Fee:* game room. **Guest Services:** valet and coin laundry, area transportation-major attractions. **Business Services:** fax (fee). **Cards:** AX, CB, DC, DS, MC, VI. **Special Amenities:** free newspaper and early check-in/late check-out. *(See color ad below)*

SOME UNITS
[⊙D] [📞] [¶¶] [👤] [📷] [🏊] [🎥] [DATA PORT] [💻] / [⊠] [🔌] [🛗] /
  FEE   FEE FEE

DOUBLETREE RESORT ORLANDO VILLAS AT
  MAINGATE   *Book at aaa.com*   **Phone: (407)397-0555**   8
▼▼▼   6/16-8/20   1P: $109-$249   2P: $119-$269   XP: $5   F18
           4/1-6/15   1P: $85-$209   2P: $95-$249   XP: $5   F18
Small-scale Hotel   12/1-3/31   1P: $89-$199   2P: $99-$239   XP: $5   F18
           8/21-11/30   1P: $85-$199   2P: $95-$209   XP: $5   F18
Location: On US 192 at MM 12; 4.8 mi w of jct US 17-92 and 441; 0.5 mi e of jct SR 535. 4787 W Irlo Bronson Memorial Hwy 34746. **Fax:** 407/397-0553. **Facility:** 150 units. 20 one-, 80 two- and 50 three-bedroom suites with kitchens. 2 stories (no elevator), exterior corridors. **Parking:** on-site. **Terms:** 3 day cancellation notice-fee imposed, [AP], [BP] & [CP] meal plans available. **Amenities:** voice mail, irons, hair dryers. *Some:* high-speed Internet. **Pool(s):** heated outdoor, wading. **Leisure Activities:** whirlpool, lighted tennis court, playground, exercise room, basketball. *Fee:* game room. **Guest Services:** gift shop, coin laundry, area transportation. **Business Services:** meeting rooms. *Fee:* PC, fax. **Cards:** AX, DC, DS, MC, VI.

SOME UNITS
[ASK] [⊙D] [¶¶] [📷] [🏊] [⊠] [🎥] [DATA PORT] [🔌] [🛗] [💻] / [⊠] /

EAGLE POINTE - THE KISSIMMEE RENTAL
  COMPANY   **Phone: 407/396-4047**   27
▼▼▼   All Year   1P: $80-$450   2P: $80-$450
Vacation Home   **Location:** I-4, exit 68, 3 mi s of SR 535, then 1.5 w on US 192; in shopping plaza. 4648 Eagle Peak Dr 34746 (5287 W Irlo Bronson Hwy). **Fax:** 407/397-4265. **Facility:** 15 vacation homes with pools. 1-2 stories, exterior corridors. **Parking:** on-site. **Terms:** check-in 4 pm, 3 night minimum stay - seasonal, 60 day cancellation notice-fee imposed. **Amenities:** DVD players, CD players, irons, hair dryers. **Leisure Activities:** playground. **Guest Services:** complimentary laundry. **Business Services:** fax (fee). **Cards:** AX, DS, MC, VI.

[ASK] [🏊] [⊠] [🔌] [🛗] [💻]

EMERALD ISLAND - LOYALTY HOMES   **Phone: 407/397-7475**   140
▼▼▼   All Year   1P: $89-$390
Vacation Home   **Location:** I-4, exit 25B, 4 mi w on US 192, 1.5 mi s on Old Lake Wilson Rd, then 0.5 mi w. 8543 La Isla Dr 34747 (1579 Oak Hill Tr). **Facility:** Townhomes and private homes are available for vacation rentals; clubhouse amenities such as a pool and exercise room are available. 6 vacation homes, some with pools. 1-2 stories, exterior corridors. **Parking:** on-site. **Terms:** check-in 4 pm, 3 night minimum stay, 60 day cancellation notice, weekly rates available. **Amenities:** irons, hair dryers. **Guest Services:** complimentary laundry. **Business Services:** fax (fee). **Cards:** AX, MC, VI.

[🏊] [⊠] [DATA PORT] [🔌] [🛗] [💻]

EMERALD ISLAND-ORLANDO'S KEY VACATION
  HOMES   **Phone: (407)997-7789**   127
▼▼▼   All Year   1P: $110-$190   2P: $110-$190
Vacation Home   **Location:** I-4, exit 64B, 3 mi w to Formosa Gardens Blvd, then 0.8 mi s. Located in residential area. 7802 W Irlo Bronson Hwy 34737. **Fax:** 407/997-2742. **Facility:** A gated entry into a community of 3-5 bedroom homes and 2-3 bedroom townhomes, all with contemporary decor; a large community center is offered. Designated smoking area. 4 vacation homes with pools. 1-2 stories, exterior corridors. **Parking:** on-site. **Terms:** check-in 4 pm, 3 night minimum stay, cancellation fee imposed, weekly rates available, package plans. **Amenities:** safes, irons. **Leisure Activities:** whirlpools. **Guest Services:** complimentary laundry. **Business Services:** fax (fee). **Cards:** AX, DS, MC, VI.

[ASK] [⊙D] [🏊] [⊠] [VCR] [DATA PORT] [🔌] [🛗] [💻]

(See maps and indexes p. 666-673, 668-680, 671-686)

EMERALD ISLAND RESORT-HOLIDAY RESORT MANAGEMENT

Condominium

Phone: (407)396-9444 **128**

All Year 1P: $115-$240

Location: I-4, exit 64B, 2.3 mi w on US 192 to Formosa Garden Blvd, 0.5 mi s to Funnie Steed Rd, then 5 mi w to entrance. 2751 Emerald Island Blvd 34741. Fax: 407/787-3965. **Facility:** Townhomes and private homes are available for vacation rentals; clubhouse amenities such as a pool and exercise room are available. 85 units. 60 three-bedroom suites with kitchens. 25 vacation homes. 2 stories, exterior corridors. **Parking:** on-site. **Terms:** 3 night minimum stay. **Amenities:** irons, hair dryers. **Pool(s):** 25 heated outdoor. **Leisure Activities:** steamroom, playground, exercise room. **Fee:** game room. **Guest Services:** complimentary laundry. **Business Services:** fax (fee). **Cards:** AX, CB, DC, DS, MC, VI.

EMERALD ISLAND - THE KISSIMMEE RENTAL COMPANY

Vacation Home

Phone: 407/396-4047 **139**

All Year 1P: $80-$450 2P: $80-$450

Location: I-4, exit 68, 3 mi s on SR 535, then 1.5 mi w on US 192; in shopping plaza. 8561 La Isla Dr 34747 (5287 W Irlo Bronson Hwy, 34746). Fax: 407/397-4265. **Facility:** Townhomes and private homes are available for vacation rentals; clubhouse amenities such as a pool and exercise room are available. 9 units. 4 three-bedroom suites. 5 vacation homes. 1-2 stories, exterior corridors. **Parking:** on-site. **Terms:** check-in 4 pm, 3 night minimum stay - seasonal, 60 day cancellation notice-fee imposed. **Amenities:** DVD players, CD players, irons, hair dryers. **Pool(s):** 5 heated outdoor. **Leisure Activities:** whirlpools, playground, exercise room. **Guest Services:** complimentary laundry. **Business Services:** fax (fee). **Cards:** AX, DS, MC, VI.

FANTASY WORLD CLUB VILLAS *Book at aaa.com*

Condominium

Phone: 407/396-1808 **100**

All Year 1P: $99-$195 2P: $99-$195

Location: I-4, exit 64A, 3.5 mi e on US 192 and just n; at MM 11. 5005 Kyngs Heath Rd 34746. Fax: 407/396-6737. **Facility:** Most guest units are grouped around cul-de-sacs on this property's manicured grounds. 334 two-bedroom suites with kitchens, some with whirlpools. 2-4 stories, exterior corridors. **Parking:** on-site. **Terms:** check-in 4 pm, cancellation fee imposed, small pets only ($30 extra charge). **Amenities:** video library (fee), voice mail, irons, hair dryers. *Some:* safes. **Pool(s):** 2 outdoor, 2 heated outdoor. **Leisure Activities:** whirlpool, 5 lighted tennis courts, playground, basketball. *Fee:* tennis equipment, game room. **Guest Services:** gift shop, coin laundry, area transportation-major attractions. **Business Services:** fax (fee). **Cards:** AX, DC, DS, MC, VI.

SOME UNITS

FLAMINGO INN *Book at aaa.com*

Motel

Phone: (407)846-1935 **19**

All Year 1P: $29-$39 2P: $29-$39

Location: 0.3 mi e of jct US 441 and 192 on US 192. 801 E Vine St 34744. Fax: 407/846-7225. **Facility:** 40 one-bedroom standard units. 2 stories (no elevator), exterior corridors. *Bath:* combo or shower only. **Parking:** on-site. **Terms:** 3 day cancellation notice, small pets only ($8 extra charge). **Pool(s):** outdoor. **Business Services:** fax (fee). **Cards:** AX, DS, MC, VI. *(See color ad below)*

SOME UNITS

FORMOSA GARDEN ESTATES - THE KISSIMMEE RENTAL COMPANY

Vacation Home

Phone: 407/396-4047 **130**

All Year 1P: $80-$450 2P: $80-$450

Location: I-4, exit 68, 3 mi s on SR 535, then 1.5 mi w on US 192; in shopping plaza. 7978 Sea Pearl Ct 34747 (5287 W Irlo Bronson Hwy, 34746). Fax: 407/397-4265. **Facility:** Professionally decorated and designed estate homes are offered; some include garages converted to game rooms. 4 vacation homes with pools. 1-2 stories, exterior corridors. **Parking:** on-site. **Terms:** check-in 4 pm, 3 night minimum stay - seasonal, 60 day cancellation notice-fee imposed. **Amenities:** DVD players, CD players, irons, hair dryers. **Leisure Activities:** whirlpools, game room. **Guest Services:** complimentary laundry. **Business Services:** fax (fee). **Cards:** AX, DS, MC, VI.

(See maps and indexes p. 666-673, 668-680, 671-686)

FORMOSA GARDENS ESTATES - ALL STAR VACATION HOMES
Phone: (407)997-0733 **126**

AAA SAVE

▼▼▼▼

Vacation Home

All Year Wkly   1P: $1700-$3500   2P: $1700-$3500
Location: I-4, exit 64B, 2.3 mi w to Formosa Garden Blvd, then 0.5 mi s. 7822 W Irlo Bronson Hwy 34747. **Fax:** 407/997-1370. **Facility:** Professionally decorated estate homes are offered; some include garages converted to game rooms. 13 vacation homes with pools. 1-2 stories, exterior corridors. **Parking:** on-site. **Terms:** check-in 4 pm, 4 night minimum stay, cancellation fee imposed, daily rates available. **Amenities:** DVD players, video games, CD players, high-speed Internet, voice mail, irons, hair dryers. **Leisure Activities:** whirlpools. **Guest Services:** complimentary laundry. **Business Services:** fax (fee). **Cards:** AX, DS, MC, VI. **Special Amenities:** free local telephone calls. *(See color ad p 755)*

[icons]

FOUR WINDS MOTEL   *Book at aaa.com*
Phone: 407/396-4011 **14**

AAA SAVE

▼▼▼▼

Motel

12/21-4/25	1P: $49-$69	2P: $55-$75	XP: $10	D18
4/26-8/31	1P: $45-$65	2P: $50-$70	XP: $10	D18
12/1-12/20 & 9/1-11/30	1P: $35-$45	2P: $35-$45	XP: $10	D18

Location: US 192, 3.8 mi w of jct US 17-92 and 441; 1.3 mi e of SR 535. 4596 W Irlo Bronson Memorial Hwy 34746. **Fax:** 407/396-0409. **Facility:** 48 one-bedroom standard units. 2 stories (no elevator), exterior corridors. **Parking:** on-site. **Terms:** 3 day cancellation notice, weekly rates available. **Amenities:** safes (fee). **Pool(s):** outdoor. **Guest Services:** coin laundry. **Cards:** AX, DS, MC, VI. **Special Amenities:** early check-in/late check-out and preferred room (subject to availability with advance reservations).

SOME UNITS
[icons] FEE FEE

GAYLORD PALMS RESORT   *Book at aaa.com*
Phone: (407)586-0000 **83**

AAA SAVE

▼▼▼ ▼▼▼

Large-scale Hotel

All Year   1P: $199-$439   2P: $199-$439   XP: $20   F17
Location: SR 417, exit 3 (Osceola Pkwy); I-4 to exit 65 (Osceola Pkwy), just e. 3200 International Dr 34746. **Fax:** 407/586-0199. **Facility:** The impressive lobby houses large rock formations with streams running through it, and all rooms have balconies that face the interior atrium. 1406 units. 1291 one-bedroom standard units. 115 one-bedroom suites ($625-$2700), some with whirlpools. 9 stories, interior corridors. *Bath:* combo or shower only. **Parking:** on-site (fee) and valet. **Terms:** 3 day cancellation notice-fee imposed, $10 service charge. **Amenities:** video games (fee), CD players, high-speed Internet, dual phone lines, voice mail, safes, irons, hair dryers. **Dining:** 5 restaurants, 24 hours, cocktails, also, Sunset Sam's Restaurant, see separate listing. **Pool(s):** heated outdoor, wading. **Leisure Activities:** whirlpools, recreation programs, bocci, croquet, spa, shuffleboard, volleyball. *Fee:* golf-9 holes, game room. **Guest Services:** gift shop, valet and coin laundry, area transportation-major attractions. **Business Services:** conference facilities, business center. **Cards:** AX, CB, DC, DS, JC, MC, VI. *(See color ad p 765)*

SOME UNITS
[icons] FEE

GOLDEN LINK MOTEL
Phone: (407)396-0555 **5**

▼▼▼ ▼▼▼

Motel

12/1-4/30	1P: $34-$69	2P: $34-$69	XP: $3	D18
5/1-11/30	1P: $34-$49	2P: $34-$49	XP: $3	D18

Location: I-4, exit 64A, 3.7 mi e on US 192; jct SR 535. 4914 W Irlo Bronson Memorial Hwy (Hwy 192) 34746. **Facility:** 84 one-bedroom standard units. 2 stories (no elevator), exterior corridors. *Bath:* combo or shower only. **Parking:** on-site. **Amenities:** safes (fee). **Pool(s):** heated outdoor. **Leisure Activities:** *Fee:* waterskiing. **Guest Services:** coin laundry. **Business Services:** fax (fee). **Cards:** AX, DS, MC, VI.

SOME UNITS
[icons] FEE FEE

THE HAMLETS - THE KISSIMMEE RENTAL COMPANY
Phone: 407/396-4047 **10**

▼▼▼ ▼▼

Vacation Home

All Year   1P: $80-$450   2P: $80-$450
Location: I-4, exit 68, 3 mi s on SR 535, then 1.5 mi w on US 192; in shopping plaza. 2539 Hamlet Ln 34746 (5287 W Irlo Bronson Hwy). **Fax:** 407/397-4265. **Facility:** 5 vacation homes with pools. 1-2 stories, exterior corridors. **Parking:** on-site. **Terms:** check-in 4 pm, 3 night minimum stay, cancellation 60 day cancellation notice-fee imposed. **Amenities:** DVD players, CD players, irons, hair dryers. **Leisure Activities:** whirlpools. **Guest Services:** complimentary laundry. **Business Services:** fax (fee). **Cards:** AX, DS, MC, VI.

[icons]

HAMPTON INN-MAINGATE EAST   *Book at aaa.com*
Phone: (407)396-8484 **87**

AAA SAVE

▼▼▼▼

Small-scale Hotel

2/17-4/22 [ECP]	1P: $89-$119	2P: $89-$119	XP: $10	F18
12/1-2/16 & 4/23-11/30 [ECP]	1P: $69-$99	2P: $69-$99	XP: $10	F18

Location: I-4, exit 64A, 0.3 mi e on US 192, then 0.5 mi n. 3104 Parkway Blvd 34747. **Fax:** 407/396-7344. **Facility:** 163 one-bedroom standard units. 4 stories, interior corridors. **Parking:** on-site. **Amenities:** high-speed Internet, voice mail, safes (fee), irons, hair dryers. **Pool(s):** heated outdoor. **Leisure Activities:** exercise room privileges, sports court. **Guest Services:** valet and coin laundry, area transportation-Disney. **Business Services:** meeting rooms. **Cards:** AX, CB, DC, DS, JC, MC, VI.

SOME UNITS
[icons] FEE FEE

HAMPTON INN MAIN GATE WEST   *Book at aaa.com*
Phone: (407)396-6300 **104**

AAA SAVE

▼▼▼▼

Small-scale Hotel

12/21-8/13	1P: $79-$109	2P: $79-$109	
12/1-12/20 & 8/14-11/30	1P: $69-$79	2P: $69-$79	

Location: I-4, exit 64B, 2.5 mi w on US 192. 3000 Main Gate Ln 34747. **Fax:** 407/396-8989. **Facility:** 118 one-bedroom standard units. 5 stories, interior corridors. *Bath:* combo or shower only. **Parking:** on-site. **Terms:** cancellation fee imposed. **Amenities:** high-speed Internet, dual phone lines, voice mail, irons, hair dryers. **Pool(s):** outdoor. **Guest Services:** valet laundry, area transportation-Disney. **Business Services:** fax (fee). **Cards:** AX, DC, DS, MC, VI. **Special Amenities:** free expanded continental breakfast and free local telephone calls. *(See color ad p 693)*

SOME UNITS
[icons] /[icon]/

(See maps and indexes p. 666-673, 668-680, 671-686)

HAMPTON LAKES-THE FLORIDA STORE

Phone: (407)846-1722 [94]

AAA SAVE
▽▽▽▽
Vacation Home

All Year   1P: $90-$270   2P: $90-$270
Location: I-4, exit 68, 3.5 mi s on SR 535, then 3.8 mi e on US 192. 3479 W Vine St 34741. Fax: 407/846-7680. **Facility:** Located near shopping, dining and the attractions, the spacious four- to six-bedroom homes offer heated, screened-in pools. 7 vacation homes with pools. 1-2 stories, exterior corridors. **Parking:** on-site. **Terms:** check-in 4 pm, 30 day cancellation notice, weekly rates available, pets ($100 fee). **Amenities:** DVD players (fee), CD players, irons, hair dryers. **Guest Services:** complimentary laundry. **Business Services:** fax (fee). **Cards:** AX, DS, MC, VI.

🅂🅳 🐾 🈂️ ✕ 📼 🔲 🍽️ 🖥️
FEE

HOLIDAY INN MAINGATE WEST   *Book at aaa.com*

Phone: (407)396-1100 [97]

AAA SAVE
▽▽▽▽
Small-scale Hotel

3/10-6/15   1P: $59-$129   2P: $59-$129
6/16-8/12   1P: $59-$109   2P: $59-$109
12/1-3/9   1P: $49-$109   2P: $49-$109
8/13-11/30   1P: $49-$99   2P: $49-$99
Location: I-4, exit 64B, 2.9 mi w on US 192, then just n; 1 mi w of Disney World main gate access road. 7601 Black Lake Rd 34747. Fax: 407/396-0689. **Facility:** 295 one-bedroom standard units. 6 stories, exterior corridors. *Bath:* combo or shower only. **Parking:** on-site. **Terms:** check-in 4 pm, [BP] & [CP] meal plans available, package plans, $3 service charge. **Amenities:** high-speed Internet, safes (fee), irons, hair dryers. *Some:* video games, CD players. **Dining:** 7 am-11 & 5-10 pm, cocktails. **Pool(s):** heated outdoor, wading. **Leisure Activities:** exercise room, volleyball. *Fee:* game room. **Guest Services:** gift shop, valet and coin laundry, area transportation-Disney. **Business Services:** meeting rooms, fax (fee). **Cards:** AX, CB, DC, DS, MC, VI. **Special Amenities:** free newspaper and early check-in/late check-out.

🅂🅳 ⊞ 🍽️ 🍸 🛋️ 🏊 ✕ 🐾 📶 🔲 🍽️ 🖥️ / ✕ 📼 /
FEE   SOME UNITS

HOLIDAY INN-NIKKI BIRD RESORT-MAINGATE   *Book at aaa.com*

Phone: (407)396-7300 [125]

AAA SAVE
▽▽▽▽
Small-scale Hotel

12/19-1/4   1P: $119-$149
12/1-12/18 & 1/5-11/30   1P: $99-$129
Location: I-4, exit 64B, 2.3 mi w on US 192; 1 mi w of Disney World main gate. 7300 W Irlo Bronson Memorial Hwy 34747. Fax: 407/396-7555. **Facility:** 530 one-bedroom standard units. 2 stories (no elevator), exterior corridors. *Bath:* combo or shower only. **Parking:** on-site. **Terms:** check-in 4 pm, cancellation fee imposed, $4 service charge. **Amenities:** video games (fee), voice mail, safes, irons, hair dryers. *Some:* CD players, high-speed Internet. **Dining:** 2 restaurants, 6:30 am-11 pm, cocktails. **Pool(s):** 3 heated outdoor, 2 wading. **Leisure Activities:** whirlpools, 3 lighted tennis courts, playground, exercise room, basketball, horseshoes, volleyball. **Guest Services:** gift shop, valet and coin laundry, area transportation-Disney. **Business Services:** meeting rooms, fax. **Cards:** AX, CB, DC, DS, JC, MC, VI. **Special Amenities:** free newspaper.

🅂🅳 ⊞ 🍽️ 🍸 🏋️ 👤M ♿ 🏊 ✕ 🐾 📶 🔲 🍽️ 🖥️ / ✕ 📼 /
FEE   SOME UNITS

HOLIDAY VILLAS   *Book at aaa.com*

Phone: (407)397-0700 [3]

AAA SAVE
▽▽▽▽
Condominium

12/1-1/1   1P: $149-$199   2P: $159-$219
1/2-8/24   1P: $149-$179   2P: $159-$189
8/25-11/30   1P: $149-$159   2P: $149-$159
Location: I-4, exit 64A, 2.8 mi e on US 192; northwest corner of US 192 and SR 535; between MM 11 and 12. Located adjacent to the International Promenade Shopping Plaza. 2928 Vineland Rd 34746. Fax: 407/397-0566. **Facility:** The property's three complexes feature guest units and recreational facilities on manicured grounds. 225 units. 100 two- and 125 three-bedroom suites with kitchens. 2 stories, exterior corridors. **Parking:** on-site. **Terms:** check-in 4 pm, 3 day cancellation notice-fee imposed, package plans. **Amenities:** irons. *Fee:* video library, safes. **Pool(s):** heated outdoor. **Leisure Activities:** sauna, whirlpool, lighted tennis court, playground, exercise room. *Fee:* game room. **Guest Services:** area transportation-Disney. **Business Services:** fax (fee). **Cards:** AX, DS, MC, VI. *(See color ad p 767)*

🅂🅳 🍽️ 🏊 ✕ 📼 📹 📶 🔲 🍽️ 🖥️ / ✕ /
SOME UNITS

HOWARD JOHNSON ENCHANTEDLAND HOTEL   *Book at aaa.com*

Phone: (407)396-4343 [4]

AAA
▽▽
Small-scale Hotel

All Year   1P: $49-$125   2P: $49-$125
Location: I-4, exit 64A, 3.2 mi e on US 192. 4985 W Irlo Bronson Memorial Hwy 34746. Fax: 407/396-8998. **Facility:** 158 one-bedroom standard units, some with whirlpools. 2 stories (no elevator), exterior corridors. *Bath:* combo or shower only. **Parking:** on-site. **Terms:** cancellation fee imposed, [BP] meal plan available, pets ($10 extra charge, in limited units). **Amenities:** video library, voice mail, safes (fee), irons, hair dryers. **Dining:** 7-10 am. **Pool(s):** heated outdoor. **Leisure Activities:** whirlpool. *Fee:* children's adventure club, game room. **Guest Services:** sundries, valet and coin laundry, area transportation-major attractions. **Business Services:** fax (fee). **Cards:** AX, CB, DC, DS, JC, MC, VI. **Special Amenities:** free full breakfast and free newspaper. *(See color ad p 767)*

🅂🅳 📶 🍽️ ♿ 🏊 ✕ 📼 📹 📶 🖥️ / ✕ 📼 🔲 🍽️ /
FEE   SOME UNITS

(See maps and indexes p. 666-673, 668-680, 671-686)

HOWARD JOHNSON EXPRESS INN & SUITES
LAKEFRONT PARK   *Book at aaa.com*   Phone: (407)396-4762   **6**
(AAA) [SAVE]   All Year [CP]   1P: $39-$150   2P: $39-$150   XP: $5   F12
            Location: I-4, exit 64A, 3.9 mi e on US 192; jct SR 535, just e. 4836 W Irlo Bronson Memorial Hwy 34746.
            Fax: 407/396-4866. **Facility:** 131 units. 89 one-bedroom standard units, some with whirlpools. 42 one-
            bedroom suites ($59-$200) with kitchens. 2 stories (no elevator), exterior corridors. *Bath:* combo or shower
Small-scale Hotel only. **Parking:** on-site. **Amenities:** safes (fee), irons, hair dryers. **Pool(s):** heated outdoor, wading. **Leisure**
            Activities: whirlpool, boat dock, fishing, covered picnic pavilion, playground. *Fee:* game room. **Guest**
Services: coin laundry, area transportation-Disney. **Business Services:** fax (fee). **Cards:** AX, DS, MC, VI. **Special Amenities:**
free continental breakfast and free newspaper. *(See color ad below)*

SOME UNITS

[icons]

HOWARD JOHNSON EXPRESS INN PARKSIDE   *Book at aaa.com*   Phone: (407)396-7100   **17**
(AAA) [SAVE]   All Year [ECP]   1P: $39-$59   2P: $39-$59
            Location: I-4, exit 64A, 3.5 mi w of jct US 17-92 and 441. 4311 W Vine St/W Hwy 192 34746-6315.
◆◆◆   Fax: 407/239-2636. **Facility:** 170 one-bedroom standard units. 2-3 stories, exterior corridors. **Parking:** on-
Small-scale Hotel site. **Terms:** check-in 4 pm, 7 day cancellation notice, $2 service charge, small pets only ($10 extra charge).
            Amenities: voice mail, irons, hair dryers. *Some:* safes. **Pool(s):** heated outdoor, wading. **Guest Services:**
            coin laundry. **Business Services:** fax (fee). **Cards:** AX, DS, MC, VI. **Special Amenities:** free expanded
continental breakfast and preferred room (subject to availability with advance reservations).

SOME UNITS

[icons] FEE   FEE   FEE FEE

HOWARD JOHNSON MAINGATE EAST   *Book at aaa.com*   Phone: (407)396-1748   **109**
(AAA) [SAVE]   All Year   1P: $47-$100   2P: $47-$100   XP: $10   F17
◆◆◆ ◆◆◆   Location: I-4, exit 64A, 1 mi e. 6051 W Irlo Bronson Memorial Hwy 34747. Fax: 407/396-4835. **Facility:** 367 units.
            359 one-bedroom standard units, some with kitchens and/or whirlpools. 8 one-bedroom suites. 2-3 stories,
            interior/exterior corridors. *Bath:* combo or shower only. **Parking:** on-site. **Terms:** check-in 4 pm, 7 day
Small-scale Hotel cancellation notice-fee imposed, $3 service charge. **Amenities:** voice mail. *Fee:* video games, safes.
            Pool(s): heated outdoor, wading. **Leisure Activities:** whirlpool. *Fee:* game room. **Guest Services:** gift
shop, coin laundry, area transportation-Disney. **Business Services:** fax (fee). **Cards:** AX, CB, DC, DS, MC, VI.
Special Amenities: free newspaper and free room upgrade (subject to availability with advance reservations).

SOME UNITS

[icons]

(See maps and indexes p. 666-673, 668-680, 671-686)

HOWARD JOHNSON MAINGATE RESORT WEST   *Book at aaa.com*   Phone: (407)396-4500   **76**

(AAA) (SAVE)

12/17-12/31	1P: $69-$129	2P: $69-$129
2/16-11/30	1P: $42-$109	2P: $42-$109
12/1-12/16	1P: $42-$59	2P: $42-$59
1/1-2/15	1P: $39-$59	2P: $39-$59

Small-scale Hotel Location: I-4, exit 64B, 5.6 mi w on SR 192. 8660 W Irlo Bronson Memorial Hwy 34747. Fax: 407/997-4500. **Facility:** 435 units. 434 one-bedroom standard units. 1 one-bedroom suite. 2 stories, exterior corridors. *Bath:* combo or shower only. **Parking:** on-site. **Terms:** cancellation fee imposed, weekly rates available, package plans, $3 service charge, pets ($25 fee). **Amenities:** voice mail, safes (fee), irons, hair dryers. **Dining:** 2 restaurants, 7 am-10 pm, cocktails. **Pool(s):** 2 outdoor, heated outdoor, wading. **Leisure Activities:** whirlpool, 2 lighted tennis courts, playground, limited exercise equipment, basketball, shuffleboard, volleyball. *Fee:* game room. **Guest Services:** valet and coin laundry, area transportation-Disney. **Business Services:** meeting rooms, fax. **Cards:** AX, CB, DC, DS, MC, VI. *(See color ad below)*

SOME UNITS

(symbols) FEE   /   FEE

(See maps and indexes p. 666-673, 668-680, 671-686)

INDIAN CREEK-ALEXANDER HOLIDAY HOMES
Phone: (407)932-3683   **138**

▼▼▼   12/19-11/30   1P: $100-$215   2P: $100-$215
12/1-12/18   1P: $100-$155   2P: $100-$155
Vacation Home   **Location:** Jct US 192 and SR 423 (John Young Pkwy), 0.3 mi s. 1400 W Oak St, Suite J 34741. Fax: 407/870-2060. **Facility:** Each of the variety of homes and town homes with different room configurations features a private pool or a community pool and recreation center. 23 vacation homes with pools. 1-2 stories, exterior corridors. **Parking:** on-site. **Terms:** check-in 4 pm, 3 night minimum stay, cancellation fee imposed. **Amenities:** irons. **Guest Services:** complimentary laundry. **Business Services:** fax (fee). **Cards:** AX, DS, MC, VI. *(See color ad p 769)*   (ASK) 🔄 (VCR) (DATA PORT) 🛁 🖥 🖥

INDIAN CREEK-AMERICAN VACATION HOMES
Phone: (407)396-2880   **145**

▼▼▼   All Year   2P: $89-$289
Location: I-4, exit 68, 3.4 mi s on SR 535 (Apopka-Vineland Rd). 8009 Bow Creek Rd 34746 (2983 Vineland Rd).
Vacation Home   Fax: 407/397-4132. **Facility:** Located within minutes of shops and restaurants, the houses have three to six bedrooms available, all with screened-in pools and two car garages. 10 vacation homes with pools. 1-2 stories, exterior corridors. **Parking:** on-site. **Terms:** check-in 4 pm, 5 night minimum stay - seasonal, 30 day cancellation notice, 14 day off season-fee imposed, package plans, 7% service charge. **Amenities:** DVD players (fee), CD players, irons, hair dryers. *Some:* video games. **Guest Services:** complimentary laundry. **Business Services:** fax (fee). **Cards:** AX, DC, MC, VI.   (ASK) 🔄 ✕ (DATA PORT) 🛁 🖥 🖥

INDIAN CREEK-ORLANDO'S KEY VACATION HOMES
Phone: (407)997-7789   **134**

(AAA) (SAVE)   12/1-1/5 & 6/16-8/31   1P: $95-$270   2P: $95-$270
1/6-6/15 & 9/1-11/30   1P: $90-$250   2P: $90-$250
▼▼▼   **Location:** I-4, exit 64B, 3 mi w to Formosa Gardens Blvd, then 0.8 mi s. Located in a residential area. 7802 W Irlo Bronson Memorial Hwy 34747. Fax: 407/997-2742. **Facility:** Houses with three to six bedrooms are available;
Vacation Home   all have screened-in pools and two-car garages and are near shops and restaurants. Designated smoking area. 20 vacation homes with pools. 1-2 stories, exterior corridors. **Parking:** on-site. **Terms:** check-in 4 pm, 3 night minimum stay, 30 day cancellation notice-fee imposed, weekly rates available. **Amenities:** safes, irons. *Some:* CD players. **Leisure Activities:** whirlpools. **Guest Services:** complimentary laundry. **Business Services:** fax (fee). **Cards:** AX, DS, MC, VI. **Special Amenities:** free local telephone calls.   🔄 ✕ (VCR) (DATA PORT) 🛁 🖥 🖥

INDIAN CREEK-PREMIER VACATION HOMES
Phone: (407)396-2401   **137**

▼▼▼   All Year   1P: $129-$279
Location: I-4, exit 68, 2.5 mi e on SR 535 (Apopka-Vineland Rd). 3160 Vineland Rd, Suite 1 34746.
Vacation Home   Fax: 407/396-0113. **Facility:** All homes are professionally decorated, have a private screened-in pool and offer up to five bedrooms. 20 vacation homes with pools. Exterior corridors. **Parking:** on-site. **Terms:** off-site registration, check-in 4 pm, 4 night minimum stay, 30 day cancellation notice-fee imposed. **Amenities:** irons, hair dryers. **Guest Services:** complimentary laundry. **Business Services:** fax (fee). **Cards:** AX, DS, MC, VI.   (ASK) 🔄 ✕ (DATA PORT) 🛁 🖥

INDIAN CREEK-THE FLORIDA STORE
Phone: 407/846-1722   **135**

▼▼▼   Property failed to provide current rates
Location: I-4, exit 68, 3.5 mi s on SR 535, then 3.8 mi e on US 192. 3479 W Vine St 34741. Fax: 407/846-7680.
Vacation Home   **Facility:** Located near shopping, dining and the attractions, the spacious four- to six-bedroom homes offer heated, screened-in pools. 3 vacation homes with pools. 1-2 stories, exterior corridors. **Parking:** on-site. **Terms:** check-in 4 pm, pets ($100 fee). **Amenities:** DVD players (fee), CD players, irons, hair dryers. **Guest Services:** complimentary laundry. **Business Services:** fax (fee).   🐾 🔄 ✕ (VCR) 🛁 🖥
FEE

INDIAN CREEK - THE KISSIMMEE RENTAL COMPANY
Phone: 407/396-4047   **146**

▼▼▼   All Year   1P: $80-$450   2P: $80-$450
Location: I-4, exit 68, 3 mi s on SR 535, then 1.5 mi w on US 192; in shopping plaza. 8092 Santee Dr 34746 (5287 W
Vacation Home   Irlo Bronson Hwy). Fax: 407/397-4265. **Facility:** Located within minutes of shops and restaurants, the houses have three to six bedrooms available, all with screened-in pools and two car garages. 9 vacation homes with pools. 1-2 stories, exterior corridors. **Parking:** on-site. **Terms:** check-in 4 pm, 3 night minimum stay - seasonal, 60 day cancellation notice-fee imposed. **Amenities:** DVD players, CD players, irons, hair dryers. **Guest Services:** complimentary laundry. **Business Services:** fax (fee). **Cards:** AX, DS, MC, VI.   (ASK) 🔄 ✕ (DATA PORT) 🛁 🖥 🖥

INDIAN POINT-PREMIER VACATION HOMES
Phone: (407)396-2401   **26**

▼▼▼   All Year   1P: $129-$279
Location: I-4, exit 68, 2.5 mi e on SR 535 (Apopka-Vineland Rd). 3160 Vineland Rd, Suite 1 34746.
Vacation Home   Fax: 407/396-0113. **Facility:** All homes are professionally decorated, have a private screened-in pool and offer up to five bedrooms. 11 vacation homes with pools. 1 story, exterior corridors. **Parking:** on-site. **Terms:** off-site registration, check-in 4 pm, 4 night minimum stay, 30 day cancellation notice-fee imposed. **Amenities:** irons, hair dryers. **Guest Services:** complimentary laundry. **Business Services:** fax (fee). **Cards:** AX, DS, MC, VI.   (ASK) 🔄 ✕ (DATA PORT) 🛁 🖥 🖥

INDIAN RIDGE-ALEXANDER HOLIDAY HOMES
Phone: (407)932-3683   **141**

▼▼▼   12/19-11/30   1P: $100-$215   2P: $100-$215
12/1-12/18   1P: $100-$155   2P: $100-$155
Vacation Home   **Location:** Jct US 192 and SR 423 (John Young Pkwy), 0.3 mi s. 1400 W Oak St, Suite J 34741. Fax: 407/870-2060. **Facility:** Each of the variety of homes and town homes with different room configurations features a private pool or a community pool and recreation center. 47 vacation homes with pools. 1-2 stories, exterior corridors. **Parking:** on-site. **Terms:** check-in 4 pm, cancellation fee imposed. **Amenities:** irons, hair dryers. **Guest Services:** complimentary laundry. **Business Services:** fax (fee). **Cards:** AX, DS, MC, VI. *(See color ad p 769)*   (ASK) 🔄 (VCR) (DATA PORT) 🛁 🖥 🖥

(See maps and indexes p. 666-673, 668-680, 671-686)

INDIAN RIDGE-LOYALTY HOMES   Phone: (407)397-7475   143

Vacation Home

All Year   2P: $89-$395

Location: I-4, exit 25B, 4 mi w on US 192, 1.5 mi s on Old Lake Wilson Rd, then 0.5 mi n. 1579 Oak Hill Tr 34747. Fax: 407/397-7018. **Facility:** All homes—some featuring game rooms and arcade machines—are individually decorated by owners, and have heated pools. 9 vacation homes with pools. 1 story, exterior corridors. **Parking:** on-site. **Terms:** check-in 4 pm, 3 night minimum stay, 60 day cancellation notice, weekly rates available. **Amenities:** DVD players, voice mail, irons, hair dryers. **Guest Services:** complimentary laundry. **Business Services:** fax (fee). **Cards:** AX, MC, VI. **Special Amenities:** free local telephone calls and early check-in/late check-out. *(See color ad below)*

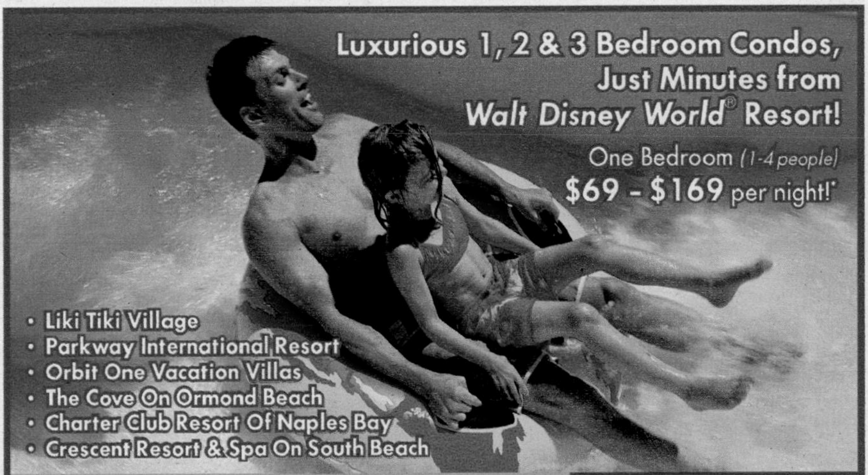

(See maps and indexes p. 666-673, 668-680, 671-686)

INDIAN RIDGE OAKS-LOYALTY HOMES   **Phone: (407)397-7475**   144

▽▽▽▽▽   All Year   1P: $89-$390
Vacation Home   **Location:** I-4, exit 25B, 4 mi w on US 192, 1.5 mi s on Old Lake Wilson Rd, then 0.5 mi w. 1579 Oak Hill Tr 34747.
Fax: 407/397-7018. **Facility:** All homes—some featuring game rooms and arcade machines—are individually decorated by owners, and have heated pools. 28 vacation homes with pools. 1 story, exterior corridors. **Parking:** on-site. **Terms:** check-in 4 pm, 3 night minimum stay, 60 day cancellation notice, weekly rates available. **Amenities:** DVD players, video games, voice mail, irons, hair dryers. **Leisure Activities:** whirlpools, lighted tennis court, playground. **Guest Services:** complimentary laundry. **Business Services:** fax (fee). **Cards:** AX, MC, VI.

(ASK) (S/D) (☞) (✕) (☒) (VCR) (DATA PORT) (🔒) (🖥) (🖨)

INDIAN RIDGE OAKS-PREMIER VACATION HOMES   **Phone: (407)396-2401**   142

▽▽▽▽▽   All Year   1P: $129-$279
Vacation Home   **Location:** I-4, exit 68, 2.5 mi e on SR 535 (Apopka-Vineland Rd). 3160 Vineland Rd, Suite 1 34746.
Fax: 407/396-0113. **Facility:** All homes are professionally decorated, have a private screened-in pool and offer up to five bedrooms. 57 vacation homes with pools. Exterior corridors. **Parking:** on-site. **Terms:** off-site registration, check-in 4 pm, 4 night minimum stay, 30 day cancellation notice-fee imposed. **Amenities:** irons, hair dryers. **Guest Services:** complimentary laundry. **Business Services:** fax (fee). **Cards:** AX, DS, MC, VI.

(ASK) (☞) (✕) (DATA PORT) (🔒) (🖥) (🖨)

A week in the right place will last forever.

Stay in Kissimmee and you get more giggles, more moments, more togetherness. You get more dining options, more affordable next-door access to Orlando's theme parks. Get "more" from your Central Florida vacation - get your Book of Dreams vacation planner at **FloridaKiss.com** or **800.333.KISS** today.

Make More Dreams Come True.

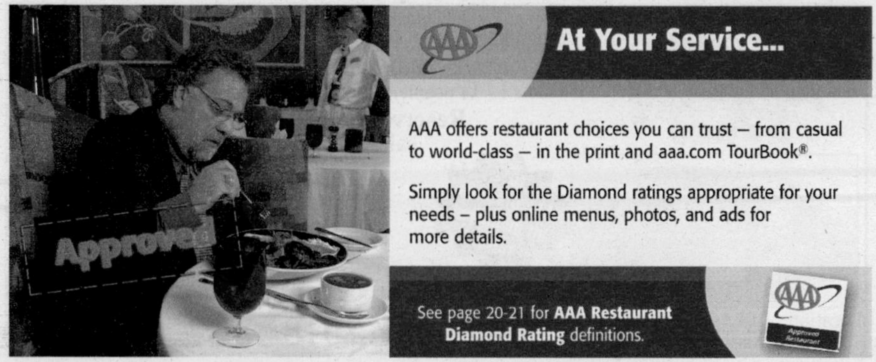

(See maps and indexes p. 666-673, 668-680, 671-686)

JADE EAST TOWN HOMES-ALEXANDER HOLIDAY HOMES
Phone: (407)932-3683 **19**

▼▼▼
Condominium

12/19-11/30	1P: $65-$115	2P: $65-$115
12/1-12/18	1P: $65-$75	2P: $65-$75

Location: Jct US 192 and SR 423 (John Young Pkwy), 0.3 mi s. 1400 W Oak St, Suite H 34741. Fax: 407/870-2060. **Facility:** Each of the variety of homes and town homes with different room configurations features a private pool or a community pool and recreation center. 27 units. 3 two- and 24 three-bedroom suites with kitchens. 1 story, exterior corridors. **Parking:** on-site. **Terms:** check-in 4 pm, 3 night minimum stay, cancellation fee imposed. **Amenities:** irons, hair dryers. **Pool(s):** outdoor. **Guest Services:** complimentary laundry. **Business Services:** fax (fee). **Cards:** AX, DS, MC, VI. *(See color ad p 769)*

(ASK) (VCR) (DATA PORT) [icons]

KNIGHTS INN-MAINGATE   *Book at aaa.com*
Phone: (407)396-4200 **114**

AAA (SAVE)
◆◆◆
Motel

All Year [CP]	1P: $35-$89	2P: $35-$89

Location: I-4, exit 64B, 2.3 mi w on US 192; 1 mi w of Disney World main gate. 7475 W Irlo Bronson Memorial Hwy 34746. Fax: 407/396-8838. **Facility:** 120 units. 119 one-bedroom standard units, some with efficiencies (no utensils). 1 two-bedroom suite with kitchen. 1 story, exterior corridors. **Parking:** on-site. **Terms:** $2 service charge. **Amenities:** safes (fee). **Pool(s):** outdoor. **Guest Services:** coin laundry, area transportation-major attractions. **Cards:** AX, DC, DS, MC, VI. **Special Amenities: free continental breakfast and free local telephone calls.** *(See color ad below)*

SOME UNITS
[icons] / [icons] /

LAGO VISTA RESORT
Phone: (407)348-5246 **11**

▼▼▼
Condominium

All Year	1P: $75-$100	2P: $75-$100

Location: Florida Tpke, exit 249 (Osceola Pkwy), 1.1 mi e to Buenaventura Blvd, 1.7 mi s to Royal Plam Dr, then 0.4 mi w. 180 Royal Palm Dr 34743. Fax: 407/348-5083. **Facility:** 40 two-bedroom suites with kitchens. 2 stories (no elevator), exterior corridors. **Parking:** on-site. **Terms:** check-in 4 pm, 3 night minimum stay, 14 day cancellation notice-fee imposed, weekly rates available. **Amenities:** video library (fee), voice mail, hair dryers. **Pool(s):** heated outdoor. **Leisure Activities:** sauna, playground, exercise room, shuffleboard, volleyball. **Business Services:** fax (fee). **Cards:** AX, DS, MC, VI.

SOME UNITS
(ASK) [icons] / (VCR) FEE

(See maps and indexes p. 666-673, 668-680, 671-686)

LAKE BERKLEY - THE KISSIMMEE RENTAL COMPANY

Phone: 407/396-4047 **23**

▼▼▼ All Year 1P: $80-$450 2P: $80-$450

Vacation Home **Location:** I-4, exit 68, 3 mi s on SR 535, then 1.5 mi w on US 192; in shopping plaza. 1040 Lake Berkley Dr 34746 (5287 W Irlo Bronson Hwy). Fax: 407/397-4265. **Facility:** All homes are professionally decorated; some have a private screened-in pool and offer 3-5 bedrooms. 7 units. 2 three-bedroom suites. 5 vacation homes. 1-2 stories, exterior corridors. **Parking:** on-site. **Terms:** check-in 4 pm, 3 night minimum stay - seasonal, 60 day cancellation notice-fee imposed. **Amenities:** DVD players, CD players, irons, hair dryers. **Pool(s):** 5 heated outdoor. **Leisure Activities:** whirlpools. **Guest Services:** complimentary laundry. **Business Services:** fax (fee). **Cards:** AX, DS, MC, VI.

(ASK) 🍽️ ✕ DATA PORT 🛏️ 🖥️ 💻

LAKE MARION RESORT COMMUNITY *Book at aaa.com* Phone: 863/427-3911

(AAA) (SAVE) 12/1-3/31 & 6/1-8/14 [BP] 1P: $88-$158 2P: $88-$158
8/15-11/30 [BP] 1P: $70-$158 2P: $70-$158
▼▼ ▼▼ 4/1-5/31 [BP] 1P: $70-$105 2P: $70-$105
Condominium **Location:** 687 Lake Marion Golf Dr 34759. Fax: 863/427-3913. **Facility:** 80 units. 24 two- and 56 three-bedroom suites with kitchens. 1 story, exterior corridors. **Parking:** on-site. **Terms:** 3 day cancellation notice. **Amenities:** irons. **Pool(s):** heated outdoor. **Leisure Activities:** fishing, 2 lighted tennis courts, club house, jogging, playground, exercise room, basketball, shuffleboard, volleyball. **Guest Services:** complimentary laundry. **Business Services:** fax (fee). **Cards:** DS, MC, VI. *(See color ad below)* SOME UNITS

🛏️ 🍽️ ✕ DATA PORT 🛏️ 🖥️ 💻 / ✕ /

LA QUINTA INN & SUITES KISSIMMEE (ORLANDO MAINGATE) *Book at aaa.com* Phone: (407)997-1700 **80**

(AAA) (SAVE) 2/17-8/12 [CP] 1P: $99-$179 2P: $99-$179 XP: $5 F17
12/1-12/31 [CP] 1P: $99-$164 2P: $99-$164 XP: $5 F17
▼▼ ▼▼ 1/1-2/16 & 8/13-11/30 [CP] 1P: $99-$154 2P: $99-$154 XP: $5 F17
Small-scale Hotel **Location:** I-4, exit 68, s on SR 535, then just e. 3484 Polynesian Isle Blvd 34746. Fax: 407/997-1701. **Facility:** 148 units. 132 one-bedroom standard units. 16 one-bedroom suites ($119-$199). 4 stories, interior corridors. **Bath:** combo or shower only. **Parking:** on-site. **Terms:** cancellation fee imposed, small pets only ($25 fee). **Amenities:** video games (fee), dual phone lines, voice mail, irons, hair dryers. **Pool(s):** heated outdoor. **Leisure Activities:** whirlpool, privileges at Calypso Cay Resort, playground, exercise room. *Fee:* game room. **Guest Services:** sundries, valet and coin laundry, area transportation-Lake Buena Vista outlet stores & major attractions. **Business Services:** meeting rooms, fax (fee). **Cards:** AX, DC, DS, MC, VI. **Special Amenities:** free continental breakfast and free local telephone calls. *(See color ad p 775)* SOME UNITS

[S/D] 🛏️ 🐾 🍽️ ✕ 📶 DATA PORT 🛏️ 🖥️ 💻 / ✕ /
FEE

(See maps and indexes p. 666-673, 668-680, 671-686)

LIKI TIKI VILLAGE-A CLUB NAVIGO RESORT   *Book at aaa.com*   Phone: (407)239-5000   **73**
AAA SAVE   All Year   1P: $99-$399   2P: $99-$399
Condominium   **Location:** I-4, exit 64B, 7 mi w on US 192; 1 mi e of jct US 27. 17777 Bali Blvd 34787. Fax: 407/857-2698. **Facility:** The property's lodgings range in size and setting but all include a screened patio or open balcony. 558 units. 283 one- and 275 two-bedroom suites with kitchens, some with whirlpools. 2-5 stories, exterior corridors. *Bath:* combo or shower only. **Parking:** on-site. **Terms:** check-in 4 pm, 15 day cancellation notice-fee imposed. **Amenities:** video library (fee), voice mail, safes, irons, hair dryers. *Some:* DVD players, CD players. **Pool(s):** 2 heated outdoor. **Leisure Activities:** saunas, whirlpools, waterslide, paddleboats, fishing, bumper boats, lagoon water island, wave pool, 2 lighted tennis courts, bicycles, playground, exercise room, fitness trail, basketball, volleyball. *Fee:* miniature golf, game room. **Guest Services:** gift shop, complimentary laundry, area transportation-major attractions. **Business Services:** meeting rooms, fax (fee). **Cards:** AX, DC, DS, MC, VI. *(See color ad p 771)*

FEE

LINDFIELDS-ALEXANDER HOLIDAY HOMES   Phone: (407)932-3683   **95**
    12/19-11/30   1P: $100-$215   2P: $100-$215
    12/1-12/18   1P: $100-$155   2P: $100-$155
Vacation Home   **Location:** Jct US 192 and SR 423 (John Young Pkwy), 0.3 mi s. 1400 W Oak St, Suite J 34741. Fax: 407/870-2060. **Facility:** Each of the variety of homes and town homes with different room configurations features a private pool or a community pool and recreation center. 41 units. 4 three-bedroom suites. 37 vacation homes. 1-2 stories, exterior corridors. **Parking:** on-site. **Terms:** check-in 4 pm, 3 night minimum stay - seasonal, cancellation fee imposed. **Amenities:** irons, hair dryers. **Pool(s):** 35 outdoor. **Guest Services:** complimentary laundry. **Business Services:** fax (fee). **Cards:** AX, DS, MC, VI. *(See color ad p 769)*

ASK

MAINGATE INN   Phone: 407/870-7374   **24**
[fyi]   Property failed to provide current rates
Small-scale Hotel   Under major renovation, scheduled to be completed May 2005. **Last rated:** ▼▼ **Location:** US 192, 2.8 mi w of jct US 17-92 and 441. 4156 W Vine St 34741. Fax: 407/870-2154. **Facility:** 131 one-bedroom standard units. 3 stories, exterior corridors. **Parking:** on-site. **Amenities:** irons, hair dryers. *Some: Fee:* safes. **Pool(s):** outdoor. **Guest Services:** coin laundry. **Business Services:** fax (fee).

SOME UNITS
   /
FEE   FEE

(See maps and indexes p. 666-673, 668-680, 671-686)

MAINSTAY SUITES MAINGATE *Book at aaa.com* Phone: (407)396-2056 **9**

2/10-4/22 [ECP]	1P: $99-$129	2P: $99-$129
4/23-8/26 [ECP]	1P: $89-$129	2P: $89-$129
12/1-2/9 [ECP]	1P: $79-$129	2P: $79-$129
8/27-11/30 [ECP]	1P: $79-$109	2P: $79-$109

Small-scale Hotel **Location:** I-4, exit 64A, 4 mi e on US 192; 4.8 mi w of jct US 17-92 and 441. 4786 W Irlo Bronson Memorial Hwy 34746. Fax: 407/396-2909. **Facility:** 144 one-bedroom suites ($109-$159) with kitchens. 2 stories (no elevator), exterior corridors. **Parking:** on-site. **Terms:** check-in 4 pm, package plans, $5 service charge, small pets only ($10 extra charge). **Amenities:** high-speed Internet, voice mail, safes (fee), irons, hair dryers. **Pool(s):** heated outdoor. **Leisure Activities:** whirlpool, boat dock, fishing, recreational dock, small picnic area with grills, playground, sports court, basketball. *Fee:* personal watercraft. **Guest Services:** valet and coin laundry, area transportation-Disney. **Business Services:** meeting rooms, fax (fee). **Cards:** AX, CB, DC, DS, JC, MC, VI. **Special Amenities: free expanded continental breakfast and free newspaper.** *(See color ad below)*

SOME UNITS

MASTERS INN-KISSIMMEE *Book at aaa.com* Phone: (407)396-4020 **111**

12/1-3/31	1P: $49-$59	XP: $4 F17
4/1-11/30	1P: $39-$49	XP: $4 F17

Location: I-4, exit 25, 2.5 mi e on US 192. 5367 W Irlo Bronson Memorial Hwy 34746. Fax: 407/396-5450. **Facility:** 186 units. 180 one-bedroom standard units. 6 one-bedroom suites ($70-$80). 2 stories, exterior Small-scale Hotel corridors. **Parking:** on-site. **Terms:** check-in 4 pm, 3 day cancellation notice-fee imposed, small pets only ($20 extra charge). **Amenities:** safes (fee). **Pool(s):** heated outdoor. **Guest Services:** coin laundry. **Business Services:** fax (fee). **Cards:** AX, CB, DC, DS, MC, VI. **Special Amenities: free continental breakfast and free local telephone calls.**

SOME UNITS

MASTERS INN-MAIN GATE *Book at aaa.com* Phone: (407)396-7743 **122**

All Year [CP] 1P: $39-$150 2P: $39-$150

Location: I-4, exit 25, 2.5 mi w on US 192; 1 mi w of Disney World main gate. 2945 Entry Point Blvd 34747. Fax: 407/396-6307. **Facility:** 116 one-bedroom standard units. 3 stories, exterior corridors. **Parking:** on-site. **Terms:** check-in 4 pm, 3 day cancellation notice-fee imposed, small pets only ($20 fee). **Amenities:** safes Small-scale Hotel (fee). **Pool(s):** heated outdoor. **Guest Services:** coin laundry. **Business Services:** fax (fee). **Cards:** AX, CB, DC, DS, MC, VI. **Special Amenities: free continental breakfast and free local telephone calls.**

SOME UNITS

MOTEL 6 - #0436 *Book at aaa.com* Phone: 407/396-6422 **115**

All Year 1P: $33-$43 2P: $39-$49 XP: $3 F17

Location: I-4, exit 64B, 1.3 mi w on US 192. 7455 W Irlo Bronson Memorial Hwy 34747. Fax: 407/396-0720. Small-scale Hotel **Facility:** 148 one-bedroom standard units. 2 stories, exterior corridors. *Bath:* combo or shower only. **Parking:** on-site. **Pool(s):** outdoor. **Guest Services:** coin laundry. **Business Services:** fax (fee). **Cards:** AX, CB, DC, DS, MC, VI.

SOME UNITS

MOTEL 6 - #0464 *Book at aaa.com* Phone: 407/396-6333 **108**

All Year 1P: $33-$43 2P: $39-$49 XP: $3 F17

Location: I-4, exit 64A, 2 mi e. 5731 W Hwy 192 34746. Fax: 407/396-7715. **Facility:** 347 one-bedroom standard Motel units. 2 stories, exterior corridors. *Bath:* combo or shower only. **Parking:** on-site. **Terms:** small pets only. **Pool(s):** 2 heated outdoor. **Guest Services:** coin laundry. **Cards:** AX, CB, DC, DS, MC, VI.

SOME UNITS

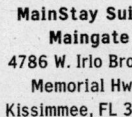

(See maps and indexes p. 666-673, 668-680, 671-686)

OAK ISLAND-ALEXANDER HOLIDAY HOUSES
Phone: (407)932-3683 **81**

| | 12/19-11/30 | 1P: $135-$195 | 2P: $135-$195 |
| | 12/1-12/18 | 1P: $135-$155 | 2P: $135-$155 |

Vacation Home **Location:** Jct US 192 and SR 423 (John Young Pkwy), 0.3 mi s. 1400 W Oak St, Suite J 34741. Fax: 407/870-2060. **Facility:** Each of the variety of homes and town homes with different room configurations features a private pool or a community pool and recreation center. 24 vacation homes with pools. 1-2 stories, exterior corridors. **Parking:** on-site. **Terms:** check-in 4 pm, 3 night minimum stay, cancellation fee imposed. **Amenities:** irons, hair dryers. **Guest Services:** complimentary laundry. **Business Services:** fax (fee). **Cards:** AX, DS, MC, VI. *(See color ad p 769)*

`ASK` `VCR` `DATA PORT`

OAK PLANTATION RESORT   *Book at aaa.com*
Phone: 407/847-8200 **16**

(AAA) (SAVE)   All Year   1P: $89-$127

Condominium **Location:** Just n of jct US 192 and Hoagland Blvd. Located in a gated community. 4090 Enchanted Oaks Cir 34741. Fax: 407/847-7948. **Facility:** Lovely setting in wooded area. 242 units. 167 one- and 75 two-bedroom suites with kitchens. 2-3 stories (no elevator), exterior corridors. **Parking:** on-site. **Terms:** check-in 4 pm, 2-3 night minimum stay, cancellation notice-fee imposed. **Amenities:** video library (fee), voice mail, safes, irons, hair dryers. **Pool(s):** 2 heated outdoor, wading. **Leisure Activities:** whirlpool, lighted tennis court, grills, table tennis on pool deck, jogging, playground, exercise room, basketball, volleyball. *Fee:* game room. **Guest Services:** complimentary laundry, area transportation (fee)-Disney. **Business Services:** fax (fee). **Cards:** AX, DS, MC, VI.

SOME UNITS

`S/D` `VCR` `DATA PORT`

ORANGE LAKE RESORT & COUNTRY CLUB
Phone: 407/239-0000 **74**

Property failed to provide current rates

Resort Small-scale Hotel **Location:** I-4, exit 64B, 5 mi w on US 192; 3.5 mi e of US 27. 8505 W Irlo Bronson Memorial Hwy 34747. Fax: 407/239-5119. **Facility:** This 1,200-unit time-share complex on manicured grounds includes single-room efficiencies and two- and three-bedroom villas and mid-rise units. 105 units. 25 one-bedroom standard units. 65 two- and 15 three-bedroom suites with kitchens, some with whirlpools. 1-6 stories, interior/exterior corridors. **Parking:** on-site. **Terms:** check-in 4 pm. **Amenities:** video library (fee), voice mail, irons, hair dryers. **Pool(s):** 6 heated outdoor, 2 wading. **Leisure Activities:** whirlpools, waterslide, rental boats, rental canoes, rental paddleboats, 12 lighted tennis courts, racquetball courts, recreation programs, playground, exercise room, basketball, shuffleboard, volleyball. *Fee:* waterskiing, fishing, golf-90 holes, miniature golf, game room. **Guest Services:** gift shop, complimentary laundry, area transportation (fee). **Business Services:** meeting rooms, fax (fee).

SOME UNITS

`FEE` `VCR` `DATA PORT`

ORANGE TREE-AMERICAN VACATION HOMES
Phone: (407)396-2880

All Year   2P: $89-$289

Vacation Home **Location:** Florida Tpke, exit 244, 2.1 mi w on US 192. 2983 Vineland Rd 34746. Fax: 407/397-4132. **Facility:** Most of the 3- to 5-bedroom condos and homes have been individually decorated; homes have pools and condo units have access to a community pool. 14 vacation homes with pools. 1 story, exterior corridors. **Parking:** on-site. **Terms:** check-in 4 pm, 5 night minimum stay - seasonal, 30 day cancellation notice, 14 day off season-fee imposed, package plans, 7% service charge. **Amenities:** irons. **Guest Services:** complimentary laundry. **Business Services:** fax (fee). **Cards:** AX, DC, MC, VI. *(See color ad p 756)*

`ASK` `S/D` `VCR` `DATA PORT` `FEE`

ORBIT ONE VACATION VILLAS   *Book at aaa.com*
Phone: (407)396-1300 **116**

(AAA) (SAVE)   All Year   1P: $89-$179   2P: $89-$179

Condominium **Location:** I-4, exit 64B, 2.5 mi w on US 192. 2950 Entry Point Blvd 34747. Fax: 407/857-2698. **Facility:** This property offers two-bedroom, two-bathroom housekeeping units with many homelike amenities. 116 two-bedroom suites with kitchens and whirlpools. 2-3 stories (no elevator), exterior corridors. **Parking:** on-site. **Terms:** check-in 4 pm, 15 day cancellation notice-fee imposed. **Amenities:** video library (fee), CD players, voice mail, safes, irons, hair dryers. **Pool(s):** 2 heated outdoor, wading. **Leisure Activities:** sauna, whirlpool, putting green, 2 lighted tennis courts, racquetball court, playground, exercise room, basketball, horseshoes, shuffleboard, volleyball. *Fee:* game room. **Guest Services:** complimentary laundry. **Business Services:** fax (fee). **Cards:** AX, CB, DC, DS, MC, VI. **Special Amenities:** preferred room (subject to availability with advance reservations). *(See color ad p 771)*

`S/D` `VCR` `DATA PORT`

THE PALMS HOTEL AND VILLAS   *Book at aaa.com*
Phone: (407)396-2229 **89**

| | 2/17-4/22 & 4/23-8/20 | 1P: $94-$130 | 2P: $104-$140 | XP: $10 | D18 |
| | 12/1-2/16 & 8/21-11/30 | 1P: $77-$120 | 2P: $87-$130 | XP: $10 | D18 |

Small-scale Hotel **Location:** I-4, exit 64A, 0.3 mi e on US 192, then 0.5 mi n. 3100 Parkway Blvd 34747. Fax: 407/396-4833. **Facility:** 156 units. 147 one- and 9 two-bedroom suites with efficiencies. 2-3 stories, interior/exterior corridors. **Parking:** on-site. **Terms:** 3 day cancellation notice, pets ($100 fee). **Amenities:** video games, voice mail, irons, hair dryers. **Pool(s):** heated outdoor, wading. **Leisure Activities:** whirlpool, playground, exercise room, sports court, basketball. *Fee:* game room. **Guest Services:** gift shop, complimentary evening beverages: Mon-Thurs, valet and coin laundry, area transportation. **Business Services:** meeting rooms, fax (fee). **Cards:** AX, CB, DC, DS, JC, MC, VI.

SOME UNITS

`ASK` `S/D` `DATA PORT` `FEE`

PARKWAY INTERNATIONAL RESORT
Phone: (407)396-6600 **98**

(AAA) (SAVE)   All Year   1P: $149-$219   2P: $149-$219

Condominium **Location:** I-4, exit 64A, 0.3 mi e on US 192, then just n. 6200 Safari Tr 34746. Fax: 407/396-6165. **Facility:** These safari-themed condominiums come fully equipped; recreational facilities are on site. 144 two-bedroom suites with kitchens and whirlpools. 3 stories (no elevator), exterior corridors. **Parking:** on-site. **Terms:** check-in 4 pm, 3 night minimum stay - seasonal, 15 day cancellation notice-fee imposed, package plans. **Amenities:** video library (fee), CD players, voice mail, safes, irons, hair dryers. **Pool(s):** heated outdoor, wading. **Leisure Activities:** whirlpool, lighted tennis court, recreation programs, playground, exercise room, basketball, shuffleboard. *Fee:* game room. **Guest Services:** complimentary laundry, area transportation (fee)-Disney. **Business Services:** fax (fee). **Cards:** AX, CB, DC, DS, MC, VI. *(See color ad p 771)*

`S/D` `VCR` `DATA PORT` `FEE`

(See maps and indexes p. 666-673, 668-680, 671-686)

QUALITY INN & SUITES EASTGATE
Book at aaa.com
Phone: (407)396-1376 **7**

(AAA) (SAVE)
All Year [ECP] 1P: $39-$200 2P: $39-$200 XP: $5 F12
Location: I-4, exit 64A, 3.5 mi e on US 192. 4960 W Irlo Bronson Memorial Hwy 34746. Fax: 407/396-0716. **Facility:** 176 one-bedroom standard units. 2 stories (no elevator), exterior corridors. **Parking:** on-site. **Amenities:** irons, hair dryers. **Pool(s):** outdoor. **Leisure Activities:** whirlpool, playground. **Business Services:**
Small-scale Hotel valet and coin laundry, area transportation-Disney. **Business Services:** fax (fee). **Cards:** AX, CB, DC, DS, MC, VI. **Special Amenities:** free expanded continental breakfast and free newspaper.

(See color ad below)

SOME UNITS
🅂🄳 🍴 🏊 🎥 📠 💻 / ✕ 🔌 📺

QUALITY INN CONFERENCE CENTER
Book at aaa.com
Phone: (407)846-4545 **31**

(AAA) (SAVE)
12/22-4/9 1P: $49-$139 2P: $49-$139
4/10-11/30 1P: $49-$109 2P: $49-$109
12/1-12/21 1P: $49-$79 2P: $49-$79
Location: Florida Tpke, exit 244, 1 mi w on US 192. 2050 E Irlo Bronson Memorial Hwy 34744. Fax: 407/932-2268.
Small-scale Hotel **Facility:** 151 units. 150 one-bedroom standard units. 1 one-bedroom suite. 2 stories (no elevator), exterior corridors. *Bath:* combo or shower only. **Parking:** on-site. **Amenities:** voice mail, irons, hair dryers. **Dining:** 5 pm-9 pm; closed Sun. **Pool(s):** outdoor. **Leisure Activities:** playground, exercise room. *Fee:* game room. **Guest Services:** coin laundry. **Business Services:** meeting rooms, fax (fee). **Cards:** AX, CB, DC, DS, MC, VI. **Special Amenities:** free local telephone calls and free newspaper.

SOME UNITS
🅂🄳 🍴 ♿ 👂 🏊 ✕ 🎥 📠 💻 / ✕ 🔌 📺
FEE FEE

QUALITY INN MAIN GATE WEST
Book at aaa.com
Phone: (407)396-1828 **88**

(AAA) (SAVE)
All Year 1P: $39-$149 2P: $45-$169 XP: $5 F16
Location: I-4, exit 64B, 3 mi w on US 192; 2 mi w of Disney World main gate. 7785 W Irlo Bronson Memorial Hwy 34747. Fax: 407/396-1305. **Facility:** 198 one-bedroom standard units, some with efficiencies. 3 stories, exterior corridors. *Bath:* combo or shower only. **Parking:** on-site. **Terms:** [CP] meal plan available. Small-scale Hotel **Amenities:** safes (fee), irons, hair dryers. **Pool(s):** heated outdoor. **Leisure Activities:** playground. *Fee:* game room. **Guest Services:** gift shop, coin laundry, area transportation-major attractions & Premier Outlets. **Cards:** AX, CB, DC, DS, MC, VI. **Special Amenities:** free continental breakfast and free local telephone calls.

SOME UNITS
🅂🄳 🍴 ♿M ♿ 👂 🏊 🎥 📠 💻 / ✕ 🔌 📺
FEE FEE

(See maps and indexes p. 666-673, 668-680, 671-686)

QUALITY SUITES MAINGATE EAST   *Book at aaa.com*   Phone: (407)396-8040   120

(AAA) (SAVE)
♦♦♦
12/1-4/22	1P: $99-$299	2P: $99-$299
6/16-9/3	1P: $109-$259	2P: $109-$259
4/23-6/15	1P: $94-$189	2P: $94-$189
9/4-11/30	1P: $89-$179	2P: $89-$179

Small-scale Hotel **Location:** I-4, exit 64A, 1 mi e on US 192. 5876 W Irlo Bronson Memorial Hwy 34746. Fax: 407/396-6766. **Facility:** Smoke free premises. 225 units. 113 one- and 112 two-bedroom suites with efficiencies. 5 stories, exterior corridors. *Bath:* combo or shower only. **Parking:** on-site. **Terms:** check-in 4 pm, 3 day cancellation notice-fee imposed, pets ($20 extra charge, im limited units). **Amenities:** dual phone lines, voice mail, irons, hair dryers. *Fee:* video games, safes. **Pool(s):** heated outdoor, wading. **Leisure Activities:** whirlpool, playground. *Fee:* game room. **Guest Services:** gift shop, complimentary evening beverages, valet and coin laundry, area transportation-Disney. **Business Services:** fax (fee). **Cards:** AX, CB, DC, DS, JC, MC, VI. **Special Amenities: free expanded continental breakfast and free local telephone calls.** *(See color ad p 799)*

RADISSON RESORT PARKWAY   *Book at aaa.com*   Phone: (407)396-7000   106

(AAA) (SAVE)   All Year [BP]   1P: $79-$129   2P: $79-$129
♦♦♦   **Location:** I-4, exit 64A, 0.3 mi e on US 192, then just n. 2900 Parkway Blvd 34747. Fax: 407/396-6792. **Facility:** 718 one-bedroom standard units. 3-8 stories, interior corridors. *Bath:* combo or shower only.
Large-scale Hotel safes, honor bars, irons, hair dryers. **Dining:** 2 restaurants, 6:30 am-12:30 am, cocktails. **Pool(s):** outdoor, heated outdoor, wading. **Leisure Activities:** sauna, waterslide, 2 lighted tennis courts, playground, exercise room, volleyball. *Fee:* game room. **Guest Services:** gift shop, valet and coin laundry, area transportation-major attractions. **Business Services:** conference facilities, business center. **Cards:** AX, CB, DC, DS, JC, MC, VI. **Special Amenities: free newspaper.** *(See color ad below)*

RADISSON RESORT WORLDGATE   *Book at aaa.com*   Phone: (407)396-1400   103

(AAA) (SAVE)
♦♦♦
| 12/1-1/2 | 1P: $109-$159 | 2P: $109-$159 |
| 1/3-11/30 | 1P: $89-$129 | 2P: $89-$129 |

Large-scale Hotel **Location:** US 192, 2.8 mi w of I-4, 1 mi w of Disney World main gate access road. 3011 Maingate Ln 34747. Fax: 407/396-0660. **Facility:** 566 one-bedroom standard units. 7 stories, interior corridors. *Bath:* combo or shower only. **Parking:** on-site. **Terms:** check-in 4 pm, 3 day cancellation notice, package plans, pets ($75 extra charge, with prior approval). **Amenities:** dual phone lines, voice mail, safes, irons, hair dryers. *Fee:* video library, video games. **Dining:** 7 am-midnight, cocktails. **Pool(s):** 2 heated outdoor, wading. **Leisure Activities:** whirlpool, 2 lighted tennis courts, exercise room, basketball. *Fee:* game room. **Guest Services:** gift shop, valet and coin laundry, area transportation-major attractions. **Business Services:** conference facilities, business center. **Cards:** AX, CB, DC, DS, JC, MC, VI. **Special Amenities: free newspaper and preferred room (subject to availability with advance reservations).**

(See maps and indexes p. 666-673, 668-680, 671-686)

RAMADA INN KISSIMMEE DOWNTOWN   *Book at aaa.com*   Phone: (407)846-2713   **18**

All Year   1P: $40-$100   2P: $160-$198

Small-scale Hotel

Location: I-4, exit 64A, 8 mi e on US 192; 1.4 mi w of jct US 17-92 and 441. 2009 W Vine St 34741. **Fax:** 407/846-8695. **Facility:** 200 one-bedroom standard units. 3-4 stories, exterior corridors. *Bath:* combo or shower only. **Parking:** on-site. **Terms:** check-in 4 pm. **Amenities:** voice mail, safes, irons, hair dryers. **Pool(s):** outdoor, heated outdoor, wading. **Leisure Activities:** whirlpool, lighted tennis court, playground, exercise room. *Fee:* game room. **Guest Services:** gift shop, valet and coin laundry. **Business Services:** meeting rooms, fax (fee). **Cards:** AX, CB, DC, DS, JC, MC, VI.

SOME UNITS

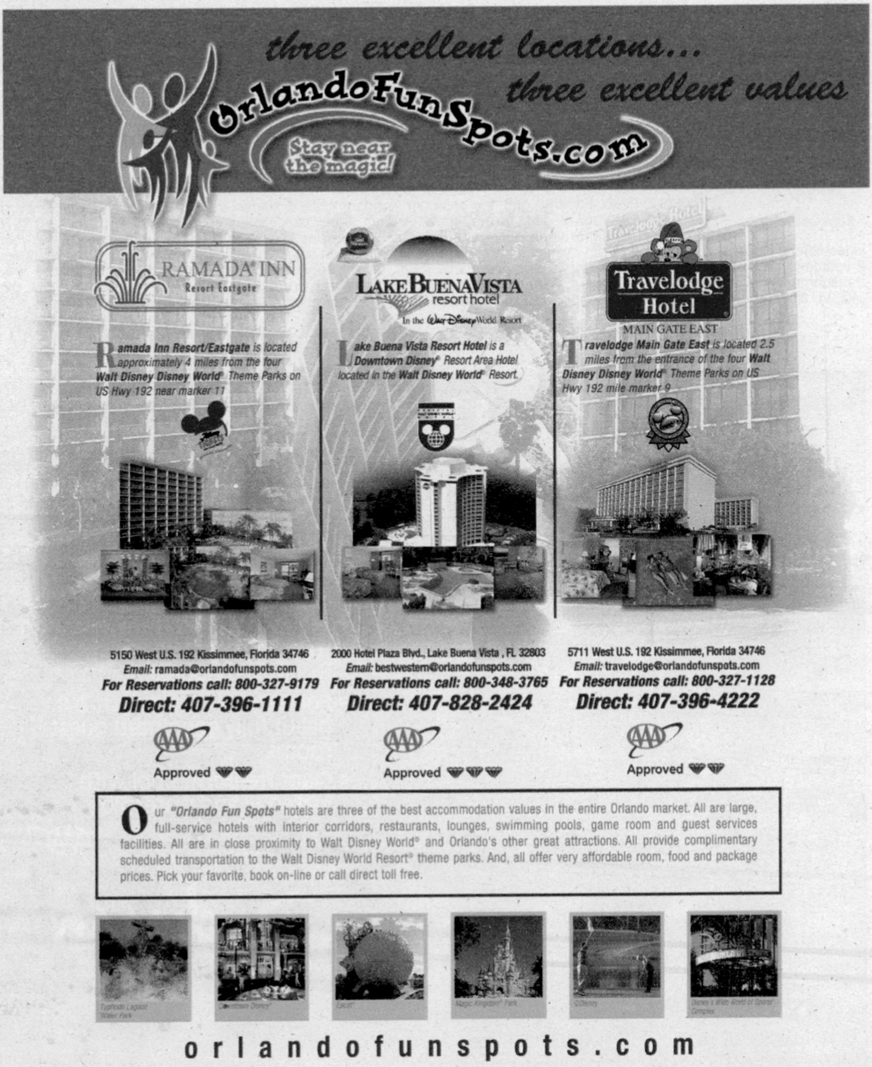

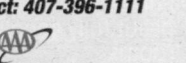

(See maps and indexes p. 666-673, 668-680, 671-686)

RAMADA INN RESORT EASTGATE *Book at aaa.com* Phone: (407)396-1111 [121]
AAA SAVE All Year 1P: $49-$129 2P: $49-$129
Location: I-4, exit 64A, 2.8 mi e on US 192. 5150 W Irlo Bronson Memorial Hwy 34746. Fax: 407/396-1607.
Facility: 402 one-bedroom standard units, some with efficiencies. 4-10 stories, interior corridors. *Bath:* combo or shower only. **Parking:** on-site. **Terms:** check-in 4 pm, cancellation fee imposed, package plans,
Small-scale Hotel $3 service charge, small pets only ($25 fee). **Amenities:** voice mail, irons, hair dryers. *Fee:* video games, safes. **Dining:** 7 am-11 & 4-10 pm, cocktails. **Pool(s):** heated outdoor, wading. **Leisure**
Activities: whirlpool, 2 lighted tennis courts, playground, basketball, shuffleboard, volleyball. *Fee:* game room. **Guest Services:** gift shop, valet and coin laundry, area transportation-Disney. **Business Services:** meeting rooms, fax (fee). **Cards:** AX, DC, DS, MC, VI. **Special Amenities:** free continental breakfast and free newspaper. *(See color ad p 780)*

SOME UNITS

RAMADA PLAZA HOTEL AND INN GATEWAY *Book at aaa.com* Phone: (407)396-4400 [123]
AAA SAVE All Year 1P: $69-$119
Location: I-4, exit 64B, 2.3 mi w on US 192; 1 mi w of Disney World main gate. 7470 W Irlo Bronson Memorial Hwy
34747. Fax: 407/397-4481. **Facility:** 500 one-bedroom standard units. 2-8 stories, interior/exterior corridors.
Bath: combo or shower only. **Parking:** on-site. **Terms:** check-in 4 pm, small pets only ($10 extra
Large-scale Hotel charge). **Amenities:** voice mail, irons, hair dryers. **Dining:** 2 restaurants, 7 am-11 pm, cocktails. **Pool(s):** outdoor, heated outdoor. **Leisure Activities:** putting green, exercise room, basketball, shuffleboard. *Fee:*
game room. **Guest Services:** gift shop, valet and coin laundry, area transportation-Disney. **Business Services:** meeting rooms, business center. **Cards:** AX, CB, DC, DS, JC, MC, VI. **Special Amenities:** free newspaper. *(See color ad below)*

SOME UNITS

RECORD (PARKSIDE) INN & SUITES *Book at aaa.com* Phone: (407)396-8400 [13]
AAA SAVE 12/1-4/26 1P: $45-$49 2P: $59-$85 XP: $7 F
8/17-11/30 1P: $30-$45 2P: $35-$85 XP: $7 F
6/27-8/16 1P: $32-$44 2P: $35-$65 XP: $10 F
4/27-6/26 1P: $28-$39 2P: $32-$42 XP: $6 F
Motel **Location:** US 192, 4.2 mi w of jct US 17-92 and 441. 4651 W Irlo Bronson Memorial Hwy 34746. Fax: 407/396-8415.
Facility: 57 one-bedroom standard units, some with efficiencies. 1-2 stories (no elevator), interior corridors.
Parking: on-site. **Terms:** office hours 7 am-midnight, 3-7 night minimum stay - seasonal, 3 day cancellation notice-fee imposed,
13% service charge. **Amenities:** high-speed Internet, hair dryers. **Pool(s):** heated outdoor. **Leisure Activities:** picnic grill area.
Guest Services: coin laundry. **Business Services:** fax (fee). **Cards:** AX, CB, DC, DS, JC, MC, VI. **Special Amenities:** free
continental breakfast and early check-in/late check-out.

SOME UNITS

RED ROOF INN *Book at aaa.com* Phone: (407)396-0065 [2]
AAA SAVE All Year 1P: $40-$85 2P: $40-$85
Location: I-4, exit 64A, 3.6 mi e on US 192; jct SR 535. 4970 Kyngs Heath Rd 34746. Fax: 407/396-0245.
Facility: 102 one-bedroom standard units. 3 stories, exterior corridors. **Parking:** on-site. **Terms:** small pets
only. **Amenities:** video games (fee), voice mail. **Pool(s):** heated outdoor. **Leisure Activities:** whirlpool.
Small-scale Hotel **Guest Services:** coin laundry, area transportation-major attractions. **Business Services:** fax (fee).
Cards: AX, CB, DC, DS, MC, VI. **Special Amenities:** free continental breakfast and free local telephone
calls.

SOME UNITS

REGENCY EXPRESS INN & SUITES Phone: (407)933-2400 [36]
AAA SAVE All Year 1P: $79 2P: $79 XP: $10 F
Location: I-4, exit 64A on US 192; 1.5 mi w of jct US 17/92/441. 2407 W Irlo Bronson Memorial Hwy 34741.
Fax: 407/933-1474. **Facility:** 131 one-bedroom standard units, some with efficiencies. 2 stories (no
elevator), exterior corridors. **Parking:** on-site. **Terms:** package plans, $3 service charge. **Amenities:** voice
Small-scale Hotel mail, safes, irons. **Pool(s):** outdoor. **Leisure Activities:** exercise room. *Fee:* game room. **Guest Services:**
valet and coin laundry, area transportation (fee)-major attactions. **Business Services:** meeting rooms, fax.
Cards: AX, DC, DS, MC, VI. **Special Amenities:** free expanded continental breakfast and early check-in/late check-out.

SOME UNITS

(See maps and indexes p. 666-673, 668-680, 671-686)

REGENCY VACATIONS & MANAGEMENT

Phone: (407)397-9333 **136**

Vacation Home

All Year　　　　1P: $75-$299　　　2P: $75-$299
Location: I-4, exit 64B, 3.1 mi w on US 192. 7801 W Irlo Bronson Hwy 34747. Fax: 407/397-7881. **Facility:** All homes are professionally decorated, have a private screened-in pool and offer up to five bedrooms. 5 vacation homes with pools. Exterior corridors. **Parking:** on-site. **Terms:** off-site registration, check-in 4 pm, 56 day cancellation notice-fee imposed, weekly rates available, $25 service charge. **Amenities:** irons, hair dryers. **Guest Services:** complimentary laundry. **Business Services:** fax (fee). **Cards:** AX, MC, VI.

(ASK) (SD) ⬟ ✕ ⬟ ⬟ ⬟

RESORTQUEST ORLANDO VACATION HOMES　　*Book at aaa.com*

Phone: (407)396-2262 **79**

(AAA) (SAVE)

Vacation Home

All Year　　　　1P: $128-$415　　　2P: $128-$415
Location: I-4, exit 64B, 6 mi w on US 192, then just s; 2 mi e of US 27. 7799 Styles Blvd 34747. Fax: 407/396-1588. **Facility:** These homes each have an entertainment center, intercom system, full kitchen and washer/dryer. 16 vacation homes with pools. 1-2 stories (no elevator), exterior corridors. **Parking:** on-site. **Terms:** office hours 8 am-10 pm, check-in 4 pm, 3-5 night minimum stay - seasonal, 30 day cancellation notice-fee imposed. **Amenities:** CD players, voice mail, irons, hair dryers. **Leisure Activities:** whirlpools, lighted tennis court. **Guest Services:** complimentary laundry. **Business Services:** fax (fee). **Cards:** AX, DS, MC, VI. **Special Amenities:** free local telephone calls.

(SD) ⬟ ✕ (VCR) ⬟ ⬟ ⬟

RODEWAY INN EASTGATE　　　*Book at aaa.com*

Phone: (407)396-1212 **15**

(AAA) (SAVE)

Motel

12/1-3/30	1P: $49-$99	2P: $59-$109	XP: $10	F16
7/1-9/15	1P: $55-$85	2P: $65-$95	XP: $10	F16
3/31-6/30	1P: $39-$59	2P: $49-$69	XP: $10	F16
9/16-11/30	1P: $45-$65	2P: $55-$65	XP: $10	F16

Location: I-4, exit 68, 4 mi s on SR 535, then 3 mi e. 4559 W Hwy 192 34746. Fax: 407/396-7926. **Facility:** 113 one-bedroom standard units. 2 stories, exterior corridors. **Parking:** on-site. **Terms:** package plans. **Amenities:** hair dryers. **Pool(s):** outdoor. **Guest Services:** coin laundry. **Business Services:** fax (fee). **Cards:** AX, DS, MC, VI. **Special Amenities:** free continental breakfast and free local telephone calls.

SOME UNITS

(SD) (⫸) ⬟ (▣) (DATA PORT) ⬟ ⬟ / ✕ ⬟ /

RODEWAY INN MAINGATE　　*Book at aaa.com*

Phone: (407)396-4300 **107**

Small-scale Hotel

All Year　　　　1P: $35-$90　　　2P: $35-$90　　　XP: $10　　F17
Location: I-4, exit 64A, 1 mi e. 5995 W Irlo Bronson Memorial Hwy 34747. Fax: 407/589-1240. **Facility:** 200 one-bedroom standard units, some with kitchens. 2 stories, exterior corridors. **Bath:** combo or shower only. **Parking:** on-site. **Terms:** check-in 4 pm, 7 day cancellation notice-fee imposed, $3 service charge, pets ($10 fee, $50 deposit). **Amenities:** voice mail, safes (fee). **Pool(s):** heated outdoor. **Guest Services:** gift shop, coin laundry. **Business Services:** meeting rooms, fax (fee). **Cards:** AX, CB, DC, DS, MC, VI. *(See color ad below)*

SOME UNITS

(ASK) (SD) (▤) (⫸) (♿) (▣) ⬟ (DATA PORT) ⬟ / ✕ ⬟ /
FEE　　　　　　　　　　　　　　　　　　　　FEE　FEE

ROLLING HILLS-ALEXANDER HOLIDAY HOMES

Phone: (407)932-3683 **82**

Vacation Home

12/19-11/30	1P: $100-$245	2P: $100-$245
12/1-12/18	1P: $100-$175	2P: $100-$175

Location: Jct US 192 and SR 423 (John Young Pkwy), 0.3 mi s. 1400 W Oak St, Suite J 34741. Fax: 407/870-2060. **Facility:** Each of the variety of homes and town homes with different room configurations features a private pool or a community pool and recreation center. 24 vacation homes with pools. 1-2 stories, exterior corridors. **Parking:** on-site. **Terms:** check-in 4 pm, 3 night minimum stay, cancellation fee imposed. **Amenities:** irons, hair dryers. **Guest Services:** complimentary laundry. **Business Services:** fax (fee). **Cards:** AX, DS, MC, VI. *(See color ad p 769)*

(ASK) ⬟ (VCR) (DATA PORT) ⬟ ⬟ ⬟

ROLLING HILLS-ORLANDO'S KEY VACATION HOMES

Phone: (407)997-7789 **90**

Vacation Home

All Year　　　　1P: $150-$192
Location: I-4, exit 64B, 3 mi w to Formosa Gardens Blvd, then 0.8 mi s. Located in residential area. 7802 W Irlo Bronson Memorial Hwy 34747. Fax: 407/997-2742. **Facility:** Executive homes with three to six bedrooms, screened in pool and two car garage are available from this rental agency; phone for office location. Designated smoking area. 6 vacation homes with pools. 1-2 stories, exterior corridors. **Parking:** on-site. **Terms:** check-in 4 pm, 3 night minimum stay, weekly rates available, package plans. **Amenities:** safes, irons. **Leisure Activities:** whirlpools. **Guest Services:** complimentary laundry. **Business Services:** fax (fee). **Cards:** AX, DS, MC, VI.

(ASK) (SD) ⬟ ✕ (VCR) (DATA PORT) ⬟ ⬟ ⬟

(See maps and indexes p. 666-673, 668-680, 671-686)

ROLLING HILLS-REGENT VACATIONS & MANAGEMENT

▼▼▼▼   All Year   1P: $99-$300   2P: $99-$300   **Phone: (407)397-9333**   [84]

Vacation Home   **Location:** I-4, exit 64B, 3.1 mi w on US 192. 7801 W Irlo Bronson Memorial Hwy 34747. Fax: 407/397-7881. **Facility:** All homes are professionally decorated, have a private screened-in pool and offer up to five bedrooms. 7 vacation homes ($99-$300) with pools. 1-2 stories, exterior corridors. **Parking:** on-site. **Terms:** off-site registration, check-in 4 pm, 56 day cancellation notice, weekly rates available. **Amenities:** irons, hair dryers. **Guest Services:** complimentary laundry. **Business Services:** fax (fee). **Cards:** AX, DS, MC, VI.

(ASK) (SD) 🗲 ✕ 📶 🖼 🖵

SERALAGO HOTEL & SUITES MAIN GATE EAST   *Book at aaa.com*   **Phone: (407)396-4488**   [124]

(AAA) (SAVE)   12/23-8/17   1P: $69-$99   2P: $69-$99
▼▼▼▼   12/1-12/22 & 8/18-11/30   1P: $59-$89   2P: $59-$89

Small-scale Hotel   **Location:** I-4, exit 64A; between MM 9 and 10. 5678 W Irlo Bronson Memorial Hwy 34746. Fax: 407/396-8915. **Facility:** 614 one-bedroom standard units, some with whirlpools. 2 stories, exterior corridors. *Bath:* combo or shower only. **Parking:** on-site. **Terms:** check-in 4 pm, cancellation fee imposed, [BP] & [CP] meal plans available, package plans, small pets only ($10 fee). **Amenities:** video library (fee), voice mail, irons, hair dryers. *Some:* video games, CD players. **Dining:** 6:30 am-11 & 6-midnight, cocktails. **Pool(s):** 2 heated outdoor, wading. **Leisure Activities:** whirlpools, 2 lighted tennis courts, playground, exercise room, basketball, volleyball. *Fee:* game room. **Guest Services:** gift shop, valet and coin laundry, area transportation-Disney. **Business Services:** meeting rooms, fax (fee). **Cards:** AX, CB, DC, DS, MC, VI. **Special Amenities:** early check-in/late check-out and preferred room (subject to availability with advance reservations).

(SD) 🛏 🍴 🍸 🖥 📶 🗲 ✕ (VCR) (DATA PORT) 🖼 🖵   SOME UNITS /✕/

SLEEP INN MAINGATE   *Book at aaa.com*   **Phone: (407)396-1600**   [78]

(AAA) (SAVE)   All Year [ECP]   1P: $59-$89   2P: $59-$89
▼▼▼▼

Small-scale Hotel   **Location:** On US 192, 2.7 mi e of jct US 27; I-4, exit 64B, 5.3 mi w. 8536 W Irlo Bronson Memorial Hwy 34747. Fax: 407/396-1971. **Facility:** Smoke free premises. 104 one-bedroom standard units. 3 stories, interior corridors. *Bath:* shower only. **Parking:** on-site. **Terms:** package plans. **Amenities:** high-speed Internet, safes (fee), irons, hair dryers. **Pool(s):** outdoor. **Guest Services:** coin laundry, area transportation-major attractions. **Business Services:** fax (fee). **Cards:** AX, DS, MC, VI. **Special Amenities:** free expanded continental breakfast and early check-in/late check-out.

(SD) 📶 🖥 🗲 ✕ 📷 (DATA PORT) 🖼 🖵

(See maps and indexes p. 666-673, 668-680, 671-686)

STAR ISLAND RESORT & CLUB   *Book at aaa.com*   Phone: (407)997-8000   [132]

AAA SAVE
◇◇◇

Resort
Large-scale Hotel

12/1-1/3 & 2/2-4/29   1P: $179-$295
1/4-2/1 & 4/30-11/30   1P: $137-$235
Location: I-4, exit 64A, 3.5 mi e on US 192, then 0.5 mi s at MM 11. Located in a gated property. 5000 Avenue of the Stars 34746. Fax: 407/997-7883. **Facility:** Landscaped grounds complete the Mediterranean-style design of this golf, tennis and spa resort buffered by a gated entry. 456 two-bedroom suites with kitchens and whirlpools. 3-6 stories, exterior corridors. *Bath:* combo or shower only. **Parking:** on-site. **Terms:** check-in 4 pm. **Amenities:** video library (fee), CD players, voice mail, safes, irons, hair dryers. **Dining:** noon-10 pm, Sun from 1 pm. **Pool(s):** 2 heated outdoor. **Leisure Activities:** saunas, whirlpools, steamrooms, driving range, 9 lighted tennis courts, recreation programs, playground, spa, sports court. *Fee:* paddleboats, personal watercraft, putting green, tennis lessons; some complimentary tennis clinics, game room. **Guest Services:** sundries, valet and coin laundry. **Business Services:** fax (fee). **Cards:** AX, DC, DS, MC, VI. *(See color ad below)*

FEE

SUN INN & SUITES   Phone: (407)396-2673   [118]

AAA SAVE
◇◇

Motel

12/22-9/3   1P: $40-$60   2P: $50-$95   XP: $10   D9
12/1-12/21 & 9/4-11/30   1P: $28-$38   2P: $35-$40   XP: $10   D9
Location: I-4, exit 64A, 3.3 mi e on US 192. 5020 W Hwy 192 34746. Fax: 407/396-0878. **Facility:** 106 one-bedroom standard units, some with efficiencies. 2 stories (no elevator), exterior corridors. **Parking:** on-site. **Terms:** 2 night minimum stay - seasonal, $3 service charge. **Amenities:** hair dryers. **Pool(s):** heated outdoor. **Guest Services:** coin laundry. **Business Services:** fax (fee). **Cards:** AX, DS, MC, VI.

SOME UNITS

SUNSET LAKES-ALEXANDER HOLIDAY HOMES   Phone: (407)932-3683   [85]

◇◇◇

Vacation Home

12/19-11/30   1P: $100-$245   2P: $100-$245
12/1-12/18   1P: $100-$175   2P: $100-$175
Location: Jct US 192 and SR 423 (John Young Pkwy), 0.3 mi s. 1400 W Oak St, Suite J 34741. Fax: 407/870-2060. **Facility:** Each of the variety of homes and town homes with different room configurations features a private pool or a community pool and recreation center. 25 vacation homes with pools. 1-2 stories, exterior corridors. **Parking:** on-site. **Terms:** check-in 4 pm, 3 night minimum stay - seasonal, cancellation fee imposed. **Amenities:** irons, hair dryers. **Guest Services:** complimentary laundry. **Business Services:** fax (fee). **Cards:** AX, DS, MC, VI. *(See color ad p 769)*

(See maps and indexes p. 666-673, 668-680, 671-686)

SUNSET LAKES-PREMIER VACATION HOMES

All Year   1P: $129-$279   Phone: (407)396-2401   **25**

Vacation Home   **Location:** I-4, exit 68, 2.5 mi e on SR 535 (Apopka-Vineland Rd). 3160 Vineland Rd, Suite 1 34746. **Fax:** 407/396-0113. **Facility:** All homes are professionally decorated, have a private screened in pool and offer up to five bedrooms. 7 vacation homes with pools. Exterior corridors. **Parking:** on-site. **Terms:** off-site registration, check-in 4 pm, 4 night minimum stay, 30 day cancellation notice-fee imposed. **Amenities:** irons, hair dryers. **Guest Services:** complimentary laundry. **Business Services:** fax (fee). **Cards:** AX, DS, MC, VI.

(ASK) (⤢) (✕) (DATA PORT) (🔌) (🛏) (📺)

SUPER 8 MOTEL MAINGATE   *Book at aaa.com*

(AAA) (SAVE)   All Year [CP]   2P: $35-$89   Phone: (407)396-8883   **112**

Small-scale Hotel   **Location:** I-4, exit 64A, 1.5 mi e on US 192. 5875 W Irlo Bronson Hwy 34746. **Fax:** 407/396-8907. **Facility:** 60 one-bedroom standard units. 2 stories (no elevator), exterior corridors. **Parking:** on-site. **Terms:** cancellation fee imposed. **Pool(s):** outdoor. **Guest Services:** coin laundry. **Business Services:** fax (fee). **Cards:** AX, DS, MC, VI. **Special Amenities:** free continental breakfast and early check-in/late check-out.

SOME UNITS
(S🐕) (🛗) (🌀) (⤢) (📺) (DATA PORT) (✕) (🔌) (📺) /

SUPER 8 MOTEL SUITES   *Book at aaa.com*

(AAA) (SAVE)   12/1-4/8 & 6/16-8/19   1P: $45-$59   2P: $45-$59   Phone: (407)847-6121   **20**
               4/9-6/15 & 8/20-11/30   1P: $35-$49   2P: $35-$49

Motel   **Location:** I-4, exit 64A, 8 mi e on US 192; 1.3 mi w of jct US 17-92 and 441. 1815 W Vine St 34741. **Fax:** 407/847-0728. **Facility:** 123 units. 83 one-bedroom standard units. 40 two-bedroom suites ($65-$99) with efficiencies. 2 stories (no elevator), exterior corridors. **Parking:** on-site. **Terms:** cancellation fee imposed, [CP] meal plan available. **Pool(s):** outdoor. **Business Services:** fax (fee). **Cards:** AX, CB, DC, DS, JC, MC, VI. **Special Amenities:** free continental breakfast.

SOME UNITS
(S🐕) (🛗) (⤢) (📺) (🔌) (📺) /(✕)/

TERRA VERDE-AMERICAN VACATION HOMES

All Year   2P: $89-$289   Phone: (407)396-2880   **28**

Vacation Home   **Location:** I-4, exit 68, 3.4 mi s on SR 535 (Apopka-Vineland Rd). 155 Barefoot Beach Rd 34746 (2983 Vineland Rd). **Fax:** 407/397-4132. **Facility:** Townhomes and private homes are available for vacation rentals; clubhouse amenities include a pool, exercise room and spa facilities. 15 units. 8 three-bedroom suites. 7 vacation homes. 1-2 stories, exterior corridors. **Parking:** on-site. **Terms:** check-in 4 pm, 5 night minimum stay - seasonal, 30 day cancellation notice, 14 day off season-fee imposed, 7% service charge. **Amenities:** irons, hair dryers. *Some:* video games. **Pool(s):** 7 heated outdoor, 8 wading. **Leisure Activities:** exercise room. **Guest Services:** complimentary laundry. **Business Services:** fax (fee). **Cards:** AX, DC, MC, VI.

(ASK) (S🐕) (⤢) (✕) (VCR FEE) (DATA PORT) (🔌) (📺) (📺)

TERRA VERDE RESORT- HOLIDAY RESORT MANAGEMENT

(AAA) (SAVE)   All Year   1P: $125-$250   Phone: (407)396-2327   **30**

Vacation Home   **Location:** I-4, exit 64A, 2.8 mi e on US 192 to Poinciana Blvd, then 2.4 mi s. 109 Madiera Beach Blvd 34746. **Fax:** 407/396-8265. **Facility:** Townhomes and private homes are available for vacation rentals; clubhouse amenities include a pool, exercise room and spa facilities. 50 units. 15 two-bedroom suites with kitchens, some with whirlpools. 35 vacation homes, some with whirlpools. 1-2 stories, exterior corridors. **Parking:** on-site. **Terms:** check-in 4 pm, 3 night minimum stay. **Amenities:** DVD players, CD players, irons, hair dryers. **Dining:** 2 pm-10 pm. **Pool(s):** 16 heated outdoor. **Leisure Activities:** sauna, whirlpools, fishing, jogging, playground, exercise room, spa, basketball, volleyball. *Fee:* game room. **Guest Services:** complimentary laundry. *Fee:* airport transportation-Orlando International Airport, area transportation-major attractions. **Business Services:** meeting rooms, business center. **Cards:** AX, CB, DC, DS, MC, VI. *(See color ad p 693)*

(S🐕) (✈ FEE) (🛗) (⤢) (✕) (✕) (DATA PORT) (🔌) (📺) (📺)

TERRA VERDE - THE KISSIMMEE RENTAL COMPANY

All Year   1P: $80-$450   2P: $80-$450   Phone: 407/396-4047   **29**

Vacation Home   **Location:** I-4, exit 68, 3 mi s on SR 535, then 1.5 mi w on US 192; in shopping plaza. 146 Madiera Beach Blvd 34746 (5287 W Irlo Bronson Hwy). **Fax:** 407/397-4265. **Facility:** Townhomes and private homes are available for vacation rentals; clubhouse amenities include a pool, exercise room and spa facilities. 7 units. 2 three-bedroom suites. 5 vacation homes. 1-2 stories, exterior corridors. **Parking:** on-site. **Terms:** check-in 4 pm, 3 night minimum stay - seasonal, 60 day cancellation notice-fee imposed. **Amenities:** DVD players, CD players, irons, hair dryers. **Pool(s):** 6 heated outdoor. **Leisure Activities:** whirlpool. **Guest Services:** complimentary laundry. **Cards:** AX, DS, MC, VI.

(ASK) (⤢) (✕) (DATA PORT) (🔌) (📺) (📺)

TRAVELODGE HOTEL MAINGATE EAST   *Book at aaa.com*

(AAA) (SAVE)   All Year   1P: $49-$129   2P: $49-$129   Phone: (407)396-4222   **105**

Small-scale Hotel   **Location:** I-4, exit 64A, 2 mi e on US 192. 5711 W Irlo Bronson Memorial Hwy 34746. **Fax:** 407/396-0570. **Facility:** 446 one-bedroom standard units, some with whirlpools. 8 stories, interior corridors. **Parking:** on-site. **Terms:** check-in 4 pm, cancellation fee imposed, package plans, $3 service charge, small pets only ($25 fee). **Amenities:** voice mail, irons, hair dryers. *Fee:* video games, safes. **Dining:** 7 am-11 pm. **Pool(s):** heated outdoor, wading. **Leisure Activities:** saunas, whirlpool, volleyball. *Fee:* game room. **Guest Services:** gift shop, valet and coin laundry, area transportation-selected attractions. **Business Services:** meeting rooms, fax (fee). **Cards:** AX, DC, DS, MC, VI. **Special Amenities:** free newspaper. *(See color ad p 780)*

SOME UNITS
(S🐕) (🛗) (🛗) (🍴) (🍷) (🌀) (⤢) (✕) (📺) /(✕) (🔌) (📺) /
FEE

(See maps and indexes p. 666-673, 668-680, 671-686)

TRAVELODGE KISSIMMEE HERITAGE PARK *Book at aaa.com* Phone: (407)846-2221 **35**
AAA SAVE All Year [ECP] 1P: $59-$129 2P: $59-$129
Location: US 192 and 441 at Florida Tpke, exit 244. 2261 E Irlo Bronson Memorial Hwy 34744. Fax: 407/846-3785.
Small-scale Hotel **Facility:** 282 one-bedroom standard units, some with efficiencies. 2-3 stories, exterior corridors. *Bath:* combo or shower only. **Parking:** on-site. **Terms:** cancellation fee imposed, $3 service charge, pets ($10 fee). **Amenities:** voice mail, safes (fee), irons, hair dryers. **Pool(s):** outdoor, heated outdoor. **Leisure Activities:** playground, basketball. *Fee:* game room. **Guest Services:** gift shop, coin laundry, area transportation-Disney. **Business Services:** fax (fee). **Cards:** AX, CB, DC, DS, MC, VI. **Special Amenities:** free expanded continental breakfast and free local telephone calls. *(See color ad below)*

TRAVELODGE SUITES KISSIMMEE EAST GATE
ORANGE *Book at aaa.com* Phone: (407)396-7666 **102**
AAA SAVE All Year [CP] 1P: $39-$200 2P: $39-$200 XP: $5 F12
Location: I-4, exit 64A, 2.5 mi e on US 192; between MM 10 and 11. 5399 W Irlo Bronson Memorial Hwy 34746.
Small-scale Hotel Fax: 407/396-0696. **Facility:** 158 units. 156 one-bedroom standard units, some with whirlpools. 2 two-bedroom suites with kitchens, some with whirlpools. 2 stories, exterior corridors. *Bath:* combo or shower only. **Parking:** on-site. **Amenities:** safes, hair dryers. **Pool(s):** heated outdoor. **Leisure Activities:** whirlpool, playground. *Fee:* game room. **Guest Services:** coin laundry, area transportation-Disney. **Business Services:** meeting rooms, fax (fee). **Cards:** AX, CB, DC, DS, MC, VI. **Special Amenities:** free continental breakfast. *(See color ad p 787)*

TRAVELODGE SUITES MAINGATE *Book at aaa.com* Phone: (407)396-1780 **12**
AAA SAVE All Year [CP] 1P: $44-$129 2P: $44-$129
Location: I-4, exit 64A, 4.8 mi e on US 192; 1.3 mi e of SR 535. 4694 W Irlo Bronson Memorial Hwy 34746.
Small-scale Hotel Fax: 407/846-1095. **Facility:** 131 one-bedroom standard units. 2 stories (no elevator), exterior corridors. *Bath:* combo or shower only. **Parking:** on-site. **Terms:** $2 service charge. **Amenities:** voice mail, safes (fee), hair dryers. *Some:* irons. **Pool(s):** outdoor. **Guest Services:** coin laundry, area transportation-major attractions. **Business Services:** fax (fee). **Cards:** AX, DC, DS, MC, VI. **Special Amenities:** free continental breakfast and free local telephone calls. *(See color ad p 773)*

TROPICAL PALMS RESORT *Book at aaa.com* Phone: (407)396-4595 **133**
All Year 2P: $61-$149
Cabin Location: I-4, exit 64A, 1.2 mi e on US 192, then 0.5 mi s at MM 9. 2650 Holiday Tr 34746. Fax: 407/396-8938. **Facility:** 138 cabins. 1 story, exterior corridors. **Parking:** on-site. **Terms:** check-in 4 pm, cancellation fee imposed, 13% service charge. **Pool(s):** heated outdoor, wading. **Leisure Activities:** fishing, playground, basketball, horseshoes, shuffleboard, volleyball. **Guest Services:** gift shop, coin laundry, area transportation (fee). **Business Services:** meeting rooms, fax (fee). **Cards:** AX, DC, MC, VI.

VENTURA RESORT RENTALS-KISSIMMEE Phone: (407)273-8770 **99**
All Year 1P: $83-$196 2P: $83-$196
Vacation Home Location: 0.6 mi e of SR 436. 5946 Curry Ford Rd 32822. Fax: 407/658-6530. **Facility:** This property offers a range of off-site lodgings including detached houses with pools. 143 units. 13 two- and 77 three-bedroom suites, some with kitchens. 53 vacation homes ($139-$259). 1-2 stories, exterior corridors. **Parking:** on-site. **Terms:** 3 night minimum stay, 91 day cancellation notice-fee imposed, weekly rates available, $60 service charge, small pets only ($100 fee, $100 deposit). **Amenities:** irons. *Some:* DVD players (fee), CD players. **Pool(s):** 56 outdoor. **Guest Services:** complimentary laundry. **Business Services:** fax (fee). **Cards:** AX, DS, MC, VI.

(See maps and indexes p. 666-673, 668-680, 671-686)

WESTGATE INN

Small-scale Hotel

Phone: (863)424-2621 **75**

All Year [CP]   2P: $39-$65   XP: $10
Location: I-4, exit 64B, 6 mi w. 9200 W US Hwy 192 34741. Fax: 863/424-4630. **Facility:** 198 one-bedroom standard units. 2 stories (no elevator), exterior corridors. **Parking:** on-site. **Terms:** package plans, $3 service charge, pets ($15 fee). **Amenities:** *Some:* irons, hair dryers. **Pool(s):** heated outdoor. **Leisure Activities:** *Fee:* game room. **Guest Services:** coin laundry, area transportation-Disney. **Business Services:** meeting rooms, fax (fee). **Cards:** AX, DC, DS, MC, VI. **Special Amenities:** free continental breakfast and preferred room (subject to availability with advance reservations).

SOME UNITS

⬤⬤ ⬤⬤ ⬤⬤ ⬤⬤ ⬤⬤ ⬤⬤ / ⬤⬤ ⬤⬤ ⬤⬤ ⬤⬤ /
FEE

WESTGATE TOWERS   *Book at aaa.com*

Condominium

Phone: (407)396-2500 **101**

All Year   1P: $79-$259   2P: $79-$259
Location: I-4, exit 64B, 2.5 mi w on US 192, jct SR 545; 1 mi w of Disney World main gate. 7600 W Irlo Bronson Memorial Hwy 34747 (2801 Professional Pkwy, OCOEE, 34761). Fax: 407/355-2979. **Facility:** A barbecue and welcome party are held weekly at this property; spacious accommodations and numerous on-site activities keep guests entertained. 268 units. 124 one- and 144 two-bedroom suites with kitchens. 3-5 stories, interior corridors. **Parking:** on-site. **Terms:** check-in 4 pm, 7 day cancellation notice. **Amenities:** video library (fee), voice mail, safes, hair dryers. *Some:* irons. **Pool(s):** 3 heated outdoor, 2 wading. **Leisure Activities:** whirlpools, exercise room. **Guest Services:** complimentary laundry. **Business Services:** fax (fee). **Cards:** AX, DC, DS, MC, VI. *(See color ad p 734)*

⬤⬤ ⬤⬤ ⬤⬤ ⬤⬤ ⬤⬤ ⬤⬤ ⬤⬤ ⬤⬤ ⬤⬤

WINDSOR PALMS - ORLANDO'S KEY VACATION HOMES

Vacation Home

Phone: (407)997-7789 **147**

All Year   1P: $120-$145
Location: I-4, exit 64B, 3 mi w to Formosa Gardens Blvd, then 0.8 mi s. Located in a residential area. 7802 W Irlo Bronson Memorial Hwy 34747. Fax: 407/997-2742. **Facility:** Executive homes with three to six bedrooms, screened in pool and two car garage are available from this rental agency; phone for office location. Designated smoking area. 12 vacation homes with pools. 1-2 stories, exterior corridors. **Parking:** on-site. **Terms:** check-in 4 pm, 3 night minimum stay, cancellation fee imposed, weekly rates available, package plans. **Amenities:** safes, irons. **Leisure Activities:** whirlpools. **Guest Services:** complimentary laundry. **Business Services:** fax (fee). **Cards:** AX, DS, MC, VI.

ⒶⓈⓀ ⬤⬤ ⬤⬤ ⬤⬤ ⬤⬤ ⬤⬤ ⬤⬤ ⬤⬤ ⬤⬤

(See maps and indexes p. 666-673, 668-680, 671-686)

WINDSOR PALMS-PREMIER VACATION HOMES

Phone: (407)396-2401 [148]

▼▼▼▼

Vacation Home

All Year · 1P: $129-$279

Location: I-4, exit 68, 2.5 mi e on SR 535 (Apopka-Vineland Rd). 3160 Vineland Rd, Suite 1 34746. Fax: 407/396-0113. **Facility:** All homes are professionally decorated, have a private screened-in pool and offer up to five bedrooms. 19 vacation homes, some with pools. Exterior corridors. **Parking:** on-site. **Terms:** off-site registration, check-in 4 pm, 4 night minimum stay, 30 day cancellation notice-fee imposed. **Amenities:** irons, hair dryers. **Guest Services:** complimentary laundry. **Business Services:** fax (fee). **Cards:** AX, DS, MC, VI.

SOME UNITS

(A$K) 🏊 (DATA PORT) 🛏 🖨 🖥 / ⊠ /

WINDSOR PALMS-REGENT VACATIONS & MANAGEMENT

Phone: 407/397-9868 [149]

▼▼▼▼

Vacation Home

All Year · 2P: $99-$300

Location: I-4, exit 64B, 3.1 mi w on US 192. 7801 W Irlo Bronson Memorial Hwy 34747. Fax: 407/397-7881. **Facility:** All homes are professionally decorated, have a private screened-in pool and offer up to five bedrooms. 7 vacation homes with pools. 1 story, exterior corridors. **Parking:** on-site. **Terms:** off-site registration, check-in 4 pm, 56 day cancellation notice. **Amenities:** irons, hair dryers. **Guest Services:** complimentary laundry. **Business Services:** fax (fee). **Cards:** AX, DS, MC, VI.

🏊 ⊠ 🛏 🖨 🖥

WINDSOR PALMS - THE KISSIMMEE RENTAL COMPANY

Phone: 407/396-4047 [150]

▼▼▼▼

Vacation Home

All Year · 1P: $80-$450 · 2P: $80-$450

Location: I-4, exit 68, 3 mi s on SR 535, then 1.5 mi w on US 192; in shopping plaza. 2304 Silver Palm Dr 34747 (5287 W Irlo Bronson Hwy, 34746). Fax: 407/397-4265. **Facility:** All homes are professionally decorated, have a private screened-in pool and offer up to five bedrooms. 8 units. 1 two- and 3 three-bedroom suites. 4 vacation homes. 1-2 stories, exterior corridors. **Parking:** on-site. **Terms:** check-in 4 pm, 3 night minimum stay - seasonal, 60 day cancellation notice-fee imposed. **Amenities:** DVD players, CD players, irons, hair dryers. **Pool(s):** 4 heated outdoor. **Leisure Activities:** whirlpools. **Guest Services:** complimentary laundry. **Business Services:** fax (fee). **Cards:** AX, DS, MC, VI.

(A$K) 🏊 ⊠ (DATA PORT) 🛏 🖨 🖥

WONDERLAND INN

Phone: (407)847-2477 [20]

▼▼▼▼

Motel

All Year [BP] · 1P: $79-$159 · 2P: $79-$159

Location: US 192, 3 mi s on US 17-92 (John Young Pkwy/Bermuda Ave). 3601 S Orange Blossom Tr 34741. Fax: 407/847-4099. **Facility:** Designated smoking area. 10 one-bedroom standard units, some with efficiencies and/or whirlpools. 1 story, exterior corridors. **Bath:** combo or shower only. **Parking:** on-site. **Terms:** 30 day cancellation notice-fee imposed, package plans. **Amenities:** voice mail, hair dryers. **Leisure Activities:** Fee: massage. **Guest Services:** complimentary evening beverages. **Business Services:** fax (fee). **Cards:** AX, DS, MC, VI.

SOME UNITS

(A$K) (S🛡) ⊠ 🍽 🛏 🖥 / 🖨 /

(See maps and indexes p. 666-673, 668-680, 671-686)

WYNDHAM PALMS RESORT & COUNTRY CLUB   *Book at aaa.com*   **Phone:** (407)226-9501   **151**
(AAA) (SAVE)   All Year   1P: $162-$207   2P: $162-$207
◆◆◆◆   **Location:** I-4, exit 64B, 2.4 mi w on US 192, then 1.2 mi s on Old Lake Wilson Rd. Located in a rural area. 7900 Palms
Condominium   Pkwy 34747. Fax: 407/226-9505. **Facility:** Set on 633 acres, the property offers modern villas in a peaceful
setting. 360 units. 194 one- and 166 two-bedroom suites ($162-$351) with whirlpools, some with efficiencies
or kitchens. 3-4 stories, exterior corridors. **Parking:** on-site. **Terms:** check-in 4 pm, 3 day cancellation
notice. **Amenities:** video library (fee), voice mail, safes, irons. **Pool(s):** 3 heated outdoor, 2 wading. **Leisure
Activities:** miniature golf, 2 lighted tennis courts, recreation programs, bicycles, playground, basketball. *Fee:* golf-18 holes,
game room. **Guest Services:** gift shop, complimentary laundry, area transportation (fee)-Disney. **Cards:** AX, DC, DS, MC, VI.
(See color ad p 788)

———— **WHERE TO DINE** ————

CATTLEMAN'S STEAK HOUSE   **Dinner:** $7-$29   **Phone:** 407/397-1888   ③
◆◆ ◆◆   **Location:** Jct SR 535 and US 192. 2948 Vineland Rd 34746. **Hours:** 4 pm-11 pm. **Features:** On the menu at the
American   Western-themed eatery are fresh hand-cut meats and barbecue combination platters. Guests also can
linger over the large salad bar. Casual dress; cocktails. **Parking:** on-site. **Cards:** AX, MC, VI.

FIONI'S ITALIAN RESTAURANT & GRILL   **Lunch:** $7-$15   **Dinner:** $8-$23   **Phone:** 407/397-1485   ㊳
◆◆ ◆◆   **Location:** I-4, exit 64A, just e on US 192, then n. 2901 Parkway Blvd, Suite B-12 34747. **Hours:** 11 am-11 pm.
Italian   **Features:** In a busy shopping plaza just off the interstate, the eatery is a good place to grab a hearty dinner.
Manicotti, lasagna, chicken Marsala and seafood fettuccine are a few tempting selections. Casual dress;
cocktails. **Parking:** on-site. **Cards:** MC, VI.

FLIPPERS PIZZERIA   **Lunch:** $5-$18   **Dinner:** $5-$18   **Phone:** 407/396-1202   ①
◆◆   **Location:** Jct SR 535 and US 192. 2934 Vineland Rd 34746. **Hours:** 11 am-midnight. **Features:** In a busy
Italian   shopping plaza, the pizzeria prepares hand-tossed pizzas, calzones and submarine sandwiches. Because
seating is limited, takeout is a popular alternative. Casual dress; beer & wine only. **Parking:** on-site.
Cards: MC, VI.

GIORDANO'S   **Lunch:** $6-$8   **Dinner:** $7-$18   **Phone:** 407/397-0044   ㊾
◆◆ ◆◆   **Location:** I-4, exit 64, 3.5 mi w on US 192; in Formosa Garden Shopping Center. 7866 W Irlo Bronson Memorial Hwy
Italian   34746. **Hours:** 11 am-midnight. **Features:** Chicago-style stuffed pizza is the specialty of the house with
home delivery an option. A friendly, casual atmosphere with traditional Italian dishes is offered here. Feast
on the pizza, but don't skip dessert at this family-oriented restaurant. Casual dress; cocktails. **Parking:** on-
site. **Cards:** AX, CB, DC, MC, VI.

KEY W. KOOL'S OPEN PIT GRILL   **Dinner:** $15-$52   **Phone:** 407/396-1166   ㊲
◆◆ ◆◆   **Location:** I-4, exit 64, 2.8 mi w. 7725 W US 192 34746. **Hours:** 4 pm-11 pm. **Reservations:** suggested, after 8
Steak House   pm. **Features:** After waiting in hot lines at the attractions, cool off in this casual, comfortable eatery that
specializes in steak and seafood. Start with a fresh salad, then choose from a host of grilled items. The
DS, MC, VI.   dessert tray tempts with a variety of confections. Casual dress; cocktails. **Parking:** on-site. **Cards:** AX, DC,

OLDE CUBA RESTAURANT   **Lunch:** $5-$17   **Dinner:** $5-$17   **Phone:** 407/518-0510   ⑥
◆◆ ◆◆   **Location:** Florida Tpke, exit 244, just w. 2215 E Hwy 192 34744. **Hours:** 11:30 am-9 pm, Fri & Sat-10 pm. Closed
Cuban   major holidays; also Tues. **Features:** The restaurant serves traditional Cuban cuisine. Begin the meal with
shredded flank steak, fried pork or chicken and mojo criollo, and end with delicious flan. Also on the menu
are empanadas, fried plantains, tostones and Cuban sandwiches. Casual dress; cocktails. **Parking:** on-site.
Cards: AX, DS, MC, VI.

PACINO'S ITALIAN RISTORANTE   **Lunch:** $7-$16   **Dinner:** $10-$28   **Phone:** 407/396-8022   ㊿
◆◆ ◆◆   **Location:** I-4, exit 64A, 1.7 mi e on US 192; just e of MM 9. 5795 W Hwy 192 34746. **Hours:** 11 am-11 pm, Sun
Italian   from noon. **Reservations:** accepted. **Features:** Owned and operated by an Italian family, the red-brick
trattoria features hand-cut steaks, individual pizzas and southern Italian selections prepared with homemade
pasta. Casual dress; cocktails. **Parking:** on-site. **Cards:** AX, DC, DS, MC, VI.

PUERTO RICO CAFE   **Lunch:** $6-$25   **Dinner:** $6-$25   **Phone:** 407/847-6399   ④
◆◆ ◆◆   **Location:** On US 192, between John Young Pkwy (SR 423) and Orange Blossom Tr (US 17-92/441). 507 W Vine St
Regional Spanish   (US 192) 34741. **Hours:** 10 am-10 pm, Fri & Sat-midnight. **Features:** Diners choose among Cuban and
Spanish traditional dishes while relaxing in a comfortable, homey atmosphere. Casual dress; cocktails.
Parking: on-site. **Cards:** AX, DS, MC, VI.

SERRONE'S PIZZERIA   **Lunch:** $5-$17   **Dinner:** $5-$17   **Phone:** 407/343-6031   ⑤
◆◆   **Location:** Florida Tpke, exit 244, 2 mi w. 1943 E Irlo Bronson Memorial Hwy 34744. **Hours:** 10 am-10 pm, Fri &
Italian   Sat-11 pm, Sun noon-9 pm. Closed major holidays. **Features:** Specializing in pizza, this eatery also offers
hot and cold subs, salads, pasta and casserole dishes. Casual dress. **Parking:** on-site. **Cards:** AX,
MC, VI.

SMOKEY BONES   **Lunch:** $6-$18   **Dinner:** $6-$18   **Phone:** 407/397-7102   ②
◆◆ ◆◆   **Location:** Jct SR 535 and US 192. 2911 Vineland Rd 34746. **Hours:** 11 am-11 pm. Closed major holidays.
Barbecue   **Features:** The menu features barbecue that is slowly smoked over aged hickory. barbecue platters with
hand-pulled pork, beef brisket or smoked turkey are available in addition to combo platters that offer a bit of
everything. Steaks, sandwiches, salad and burgers are also available. Casual dress; cocktails. **Parking:** on-
site. **Cards:** AX, DS, MC, VI.

(See maps and indexes p. 666-673, 668-680, 671-686)

SUNSET SAM'S RESTAURANT   **Lunch:** $10-$17   **Dinner:** $19-$29   **Phone:** 407/586-0000   55

Caribbean

Location: SR 417, exit 3 (Osceola Pkwy); I-4 to exit 65 (Osceola Pkwy), just e; in Gaylord Palms Resort. 3200 International Dr 34746. **Hours:** 11:30 am-11 pm. **Reservations:** suggested. **Features:** Focusing on fresh seafood, the casual restaurant features creative Floridian and Caribbean cuisine. The decor centers on the towering mast of a 60-foot sailboat. Casual dress; cocktails. **Parking:** on-site and valet. **Cards:** AX, DS, MC, VI.

TASTE OF CHINA   **Lunch:** $4-$8   **Dinner:** $7-$21   **Phone:** 407/397-9911   57

Chinese

Location: I-4, exit 64, 3.5 mi w on US 192; in Formosa Garden Shopping Center. 7832 W Hwy 192 34747. **Hours:** 11:30 am-9 pm. **Features:** Traditional Chinese favorites—more than 110 of them—make up the quaint eatery's menu. Among choices are sizzling plates, vegetable dishes and seafood specialties. Casual dress; beer & wine only. **Parking:** on-site. **Cards:** MC, VI.

LADY LAKE pop. 11,828

———— **WHERE TO STAY** ————

COMFORT SUITES   *Book at aaa.com*   **Phone:** (352)259-6578

[AAA] [SAVE]

Small-scale Hotel

All Year   1P: $99-$150

Location: Just n on US 441. 1202 Avenida Central N 32159. Fax: 352/205-7699. **Facility:** 80 one-bedroom standard units, some with whirlpools. 3 stories, interior corridors. *Bath:* combo or shower only. **Parking:** on-site. **Terms:** [CP] meal plan available, pets ($35 fee). **Amenities:** high-speed Internet, dual phone lines, voice mail, irons, hair dryers. **Pool(s):** heated outdoor. **Leisure Activities:** exercise room. **Guest Services:** coin laundry. **Business Services:** meeting rooms, fax. **Cards:** AX, DC, DS, MC, VI. **Special Amenities:** free expanded continental breakfast and free local telephone calls.

SOME UNITS
🚭 🖥 🛏 🎥 DATA PORT 🔒 📷 🛗 / ✕
FEE

HAMPTON INN & SUITES-LADY LAKE/THE VILLAGES   **Phone:** 352/259-8246

[fyi]

Small-scale Hotel

1/1-4/30 [ECP]	1P: $119-$129	2P: $119-$129
12/1-12/31 & 10/1-11/30 [ECP]	1P: $109-$119	2P: $109-$119
5/1-9/30 [ECP]	1P: $99-$109	2P: $99-$109

Too new to rate, opening scheduled for August 2005. **Location:** I-75, exit 329 (SR 44/Wildwood), e to Wildwood, n on US 301 to Oxford, then e on CR 466. 11727 NE 63rd Dr 32162. **Amenities:** 82 units, coffeemakers, microwaves, refrigerators, pool. **Terms:** cancellation fee imposed. **Cards:** AX, DC, DS, MC, VI.

HOLIDAY INN EXPRESS HOTEL & SUITES   *Book at aaa.com*   **Phone:** 352/750-3888

[AAA] [SAVE]

Small-scale Hotel

All Year   1P: $94-$98   XP: $5

Location: Just n on US 441. 1205 Avenida Central N 32159. Fax: 352/750-2779. **Facility:** 80 one-bedroom standard units. 3 stories, interior corridors. *Bath:* combo or shower only. **Parking:** on-site. **Terms:** small pets only ($25 fee). **Amenities:** high-speed Internet, dual phone lines, voice mail, irons, hair dryers. **Pool(s):** heated outdoor. **Leisure Activities:** exercise room. **Guest Services:** coin laundry. **Business Services:** meeting rooms, fax (fee). **Cards:** AX, DC, DS, MC, VI.

SOME UNITS
[ASK] 🚭 🛏 🍴 🛗 DATA PORT 🛗 / ✕ 🔒 📷 /
FEE

MICROTEL INN & SUITES   *Book at aaa.com*   **Phone:** 352/259-0184

Small-scale Hotel

1/1-4/30 [CP]	1P: $69-$89	2P: $69-$89	XP: $5 F16
12/1-12/31 & 10/1-11/30 [CP]	1P: $65-$85	2P: $65-$85	XP: $5 F16
5/1-9/30 [CP]	1P: $59-$79	2P: $59-$79	XP: $5 F16

Location: 1 mi s. 850 US 27/441 32159. Fax: 352/259-8656. **Facility:** Designated smoking area. 80 one-bedroom standard units. 3 stories, interior corridors. *Bath:* combo or shower only. **Parking:** on-site. **Terms:** cancellation fee imposed. **Amenities:** voice mail, irons, hair dryers. **Pool(s):** outdoor. **Business Services:** meeting rooms, fax (fee). **Cards:** AX, CB, DC, DS, JC, MC, VI.

SOME UNITS
[ASK] 🍴 🛏 ✕ 🎥 DATA PORT 🛗 / 🔒 🛗 /

SHAMROCK THISTLE & CROWN   **Phone:** (352)821-1887

Bed & Breakfast

10/1-11/30 [BP]	1P: $85-$200	2P: $95-$210	XP: $15
12/23-4/29 [BP]	1P: $88-$195	2P: $98-$205	XP: $15
12/1-12/22 [BP]	1P: $80-$190	2P: $90-$200	XP: $15
4/30-9/30 [BP]	1P: $82-$180	2P: $92-$190	XP: $15

Location: US 27/441, 2.8 mi e. 12971 SE CR 42 32195 (PO Box 624, WEIRSDALE). Fax: 352/821-1886. **Facility:** This 1887 home with a quaint front porch offers a retreatlike ambience; some rooms have a fireplace. Smoke free premises. 7 units. 6 one-bedroom standard units, some with whirlpools. 1 cottage ($169-$210) with whirlpool. 3 stories, interior corridors. *Bath:* combo or shower only. **Parking:** on-site. **Terms:** 2 night minimum stay - seasonal, age restrictions may apply, 7 day cancellation notice-fee imposed. **Amenities:** irons, hair dryers. *Some:* CD players. **Pool(s):** heated outdoor. **Business Services:** fax (fee). **Cards:** DC, MC, VI.

SOME UNITS
🛏 ✕ [VCR] 🎥 🛗 / DATA PORT 🔒

———— **WHERE TO DINE** ————

BILLY'S CAFE   **Lunch:** $3-$6   **Phone:** 352/259-8988

American

Location: Just n of center. 13752 Hwy 441 32195. **Hours:** 7 am-2 pm. **Features:** Popular and bustling for breakfast and lunch, the cafe specializes in pancakes, waffles and french toast. Casual dress. **Parking:** on-site.

THE LEGACY RESTAURANT AT THE NANCY LOPEZ COUNTRY CLUB   **Lunch:** $7-$14   **Dinner:** $7-$22   **Phone:** 352/753-1475

American

Location: US 27/441, 1.5 mi w, then 0.3 mi s. 8455 SE 172nd Ln 32162. **Hours:** 11 am-3 & 4-9 pm, Fri & Sat-9:30 pm, Sun noon-9 pm. **Closed:** 12/25. **Features:** After you finish the back nine enter the country club restaurant of famed golfer Nancy Lopez where you can sample anything from a simple sandwich to blue crab and artichoke on bowtie pasta. Casual dress; cocktails. **Parking:** on-site. **Cards:** MC, VI.

LAKE BUENA VISTA pop. 16 (See map and index starting on p. 668)

———— WHERE TO STAY ————

BEST WESTERN LAKE BUENA VISTA RESORT
HOTEL IN THE WALT DISNEY WORLD RESORTS *Book at aaa.com* Phone: (407)828-2424 30

(AAA) (SAVE)
▽▽▽▽

Small-scale Hotel

All Year 1P: $79-$199 2P: $79-$199
Location: I-4, exit 68. 2000 Hotel Plaza Blvd 32830 (PO Box 22205). Fax: 407/828-1985. **Facility:** 325 units. 321 one-bedroom standard units. 4 one-bedroom suites ($299-$399) with whirlpools. 18 stories, interior corridors. *Bath:* combo or shower only. **Parking:** on-site. **Terms:** [BP] & [CP] meal plans available, package plans, $6 service charge. **Amenities:** video games (fee), voice mail, safes, irons, hair dryers. **Dining:** 2 restaurants, 7 am-11 pm, cocktails. **Pool(s):** heated outdoor, wading. **Leisure Activities:** golf & tennis privileges, playground, exercise room. *Fee:* game room. **Guest Services:** gift shop, valet and coin laundry, area transportation-Disney. **Business Services:** meeting rooms, business center. **Cards:** AX, CB, DC, DS, JC, MC, VI. **Special Amenities:** free local telephone calls and free room upgrade (subject to availability with advance reservations). *(See color ad p 780)*

SOME UNITS
[S/D] [🛏] [⟟] [Ⓨ] [♿] [⚓] [⊗] [📷] [DATA PORT] [💻] [/] [✕] [🛄] [📷] /

BRYAN'S SPANISH COVE Phone: (407)239-4222 49

(AAA) (SAVE)
▽▽▽▽

Condominium

All Year 1P: $159-$219 2P: $159-$219
Location: I-4, exit 68, 1 mi s. 13875 SR 535 32821. Fax: 407/239-1886. **Facility:** This Spanish-style hotel is on spring-fed Lake Bryan and within minutes of Walt Disney World, Sea World, Universal Studios and more. 44 two-bedroom suites with kitchens and whirlpools. 2 stories, exterior corridors. **Parking:** on-site. **Terms:** check-in 4 pm, 15 day cancellation notice-fee imposed. **Amenities:** video library (fee), voice mail, safes, irons, hair dryers. **Pool(s):** small heated outdoor. **Leisure Activities:** whirlpool, boating, canoeing, paddleboats, boat dock, fishing, playground. **Guest Services:** complimentary laundry. **Business Services:** fax (fee). **Cards:** AX, CB, DC, DS, MC, VI.

[S/D] [⚓] [⊗] [VCR] [🛄] [📷]

BUENA VISTA SUITES *Book at aaa.com* Phone: (407)239-8588 52

(AAA) (SAVE)
▽▽▽▽

Small-scale Hotel

12/23-9/1 [BP] 1P: $119-$159 2P: $119-$159
9/2-11/30 [BP] 1P: $109-$149 2P: $109-$149
12/1-12/22 [BP] 1P: $109-$139 2P: $109-$139
Location: I-4, exit 67, 1.3 mi e; jct SR 535 and 536. 8203 World Center Dr 32821. Fax: 407/239-1401. **Facility:** 280 one-bedroom suites, some with whirlpools. 7 stories, interior corridors. *Bath:* combo or shower only. **Parking:** on-site. **Terms:** cancellation fee imposed, package plans, small pets only ($50 deposit, $10 extra charge). **Amenities:** video games, voice mail, safes (fee), irons, hair dryers. **Dining:** noon-10 pm. **Pool(s):** heated outdoor. **Leisure Activities:** whirlpool, 2 lighted tennis courts, exercise room. *Fee:* game room. **Guest Services:** gift shop, valet and coin laundry, area transportation-Disney. **Business Services:** meeting rooms, fax (fee). **Cards:** AX, CB, DC, DS, JC, MC, VI. **Special Amenities:** free full breakfast. *(See color ad p 792)*

SOME UNITS
[S/D] [🛏] [⟟] [Ⓨ] [♿] [⚓] [⊗] [📷] [DATA PORT] [🛄] [📷] [💻] [/] [✕] /
    FEE FEE

CARIBE ROYALE ALL-SUITES RESORT AND
CONVENTION CENTER *Book at aaa.com* Phone: (407)238-8000 53

(AAA) (SAVE)
▽▽▽▽

Large-scale Hotel

1/15-4/30 1P: $159-$249
12/1-1/14 1P: $109-$229
10/1-11/30 1P: $109-$209
5/1-9/30 1P: $109-$179
Location: I-4, exit 68, 1.2 mi s on SR 535, then 0.3 mi e. 8101 World Center Dr 32830. Fax: 407/238-8050. **Facility:** 1338 units. 1218 one- and 120 two-bedroom suites ($229-$359), some with kitchens. 4-10 stories, interior/exterior corridors. *Bath:* combo or shower only. **Parking:** on-site. **Terms:** 2 night minimum stay - seasonal, 3 day cancellation notice-fee imposed, package plans. **Amenities:** video games, voice mail, irons, hair dryers. *Fee:* high-speed Internet, safes. *Some:* CD players, honor bars. **Dining:** 4 restaurants, 24 hours, cocktails, also, The Venetian Room, see separate listing. **Pool(s):** 2 heated outdoor, wading. **Leisure Activities:** whirlpools, waterslide, 2 lighted tennis courts, playground, exercise room, weight training room. *Fee:* game room. **Guest Services:** gift shop, valet and coin laundry, area transportation-Disney. **Business Services:** conference facilities, business center. **Cards:** AX, CB, DC, DS, JC, MC, VI. **Special Amenities:** free newspaper. *(See color ad p 792)*

SOME UNITS
[S/D] [🛏] [Ⓨ] [&M] [♿] [⚓] [⊗] [📷] [DATA PORT] [📷] [💻] [/] [✕] [VCR] [🛄] /

CELEBRITY RESORTS LAKE BUENA VISTA *Book at aaa.com* Phone: (407)238-1700 17

(AAA) (SAVE)
▽▽▽▽

Condominium

All Year 1P: $137-$245
Location: I-4, exit 68, 0.6 mi n on SR 535, then 0.4 mi e. 8451 Palm Pkwy 32836 (2800 N Poinciana Blvd, KISSIMMEE, 34746). Fax: 407/238-0255. **Facility:** Close to attractions, shopping, and restaurants, the resort offers all different sizes of suites to suit one or many. 120 one-bedroom suites, some with whirlpools. 2 stories, exterior corridors. **Parking:** on-site. **Terms:** check-in 4 pm, 3 day cancellation notice. **Amenities:** video library (fee), voice mail, safes, irons, hair dryers. **Pool(s):** heated outdoor. **Leisure Activities:** 2 lighted tennis courts, playground, exercise room, basketball, volleyball. *Fee:* game room. **Guest Services:** coin laundry. **Business Services:** fax (fee). **Cards:** AX, DS, MC, VI.

[S/D] [⚓] [⊗] [VCR] [📷] [DATA PORT] [🛄] [📷] [💻]

COMFORT INN LAKE BUENA VISTA *Book at aaa.com* Phone: (407)996-7300 16

(AAA) (SAVE)
▽▽▽▽

Small-scale Hotel

All Year [CP] 1P: $59-$89 2P: $59-$89
Location: I-4, exit 68, 0.6 mi n on SR 535, then 0.5 mi e. 8442 Palm Pkwy 32836. Fax: 407/996-7301. **Facility:** 640 one-bedroom standard units. 5 stories, exterior corridors. *Bath:* combo or shower only. **Parking:** on-site. **Terms:** [BP] meal plan available, package plans, $3 service charge, small pets only ($10 extra charge). **Amenities:** high-speed Internet, voice mail, safes, irons, hair dryers. **Dining:** 6 am-midnight, cocktails. **Pool(s):** 2 heated outdoor. **Leisure Activities:** playground. *Fee:* game room. **Guest Services:** gift shop, valet and coin laundry. **Business Services:** fax (fee). **Cards:** AX, CB, DC, DS, JC, MC, VI. **Special Amenities:** free continental breakfast and free local telephone calls.

SOME UNITS
[S/D] [🐾] [⟟] [Ⓨ] [&M] [♿] [⚓] [📷] [DATA PORT] [🛄] [📷] [💻] [/] [✕] [VCR] /
    FEE

THERE IS AN OASIS IN ORLANDO UNLIKE ANY OTHER.

CARIBE ROYALE ORLANDO
ALL-SUITES RESORT & CONVENTION CENTER

- 1,218 SPACIOUS TWO ROOM SUITES
- 120 TWO-BEDROOM VILLAS
- A REFRESHING 250,000-GALLON FREE-FORM SWIMMING POOL FEATURING WATERFALLS AND A 75-FOOT WATER SLIDE
- COMPLIMENTARY SCHEDULED TRANSPORTATION TO WALT DISNEY WORLD® RESORT
- RESTAURANTS ON-SITE OFFERING FINE DINING TO CASUAL FARE
- FITNESS FACILITY AND TWO LIGHTED TENNIS COURTS
- CONVENIENT TO MAJOR ATTRACTIONS AND WORLD-CLASS SHOPPING

Call 407-238-8000 or visit
www.cariberoyale.com

Buena Vista Suites
ALL-SUITES HOTEL

- FREE FULL AMERICAN BREAKFAST BUFFET DAILY
- 280 SPACIOUS TWO-ROOM SUITES
- COMPLIMENTARY SCHEDULED TRANSPORTATION TO WALT DISNEY WORLD® RESORT
- HEATED POOL, WHIRLPOOL, EXERCISE ROOM AND TENNIS COURTS
- CONVENIENT TO MAJOR ATTRACTIONS AND WORLD-CLASS SHOPPING

Call 407-239-8588 or visit
www.BuenaVistaSuites.com

Approved ▼▼▼

Approved ▼▼▼

(See map and index starting on p. 668)

COUNTRY INN & SUITES BY CARLSON *Book at aaa.com* Phone: (407)239-1115 **15**

All Year [ECP] 1P: $80-$98 2P: $80-$98
Location: I-4, exit 68, 0.6 mi n. 12191 S Apopka-Vineland Rd 32836. Fax: 407/239-8882. **Facility:** 170 units. 160 one-bedroom standard units, some with whirlpools. 10 one-bedroom suites. 5 stories, interior corridors. *Bath:* combo or shower only. **Parking:** on-site. **Terms:** cancellation fee imposed, package plans. **Amenities:** video library, high-speed Internet, voice mail, irons, hair dryers. *Some:* video games. **Pool(s):** heated outdoor. **Leisure Activities:** exercise room. *Fee:* game room. **Guest Services:** gift shop, valet and coin laundry, area transportation-Disney. **Business Services:** meeting rooms, fax (fee). **Cards:** AX, CB, DC, DS, JC, MC, VI. **Special Amenities:** free expanded continental breakfast. *(See color ads below, & p 692)*

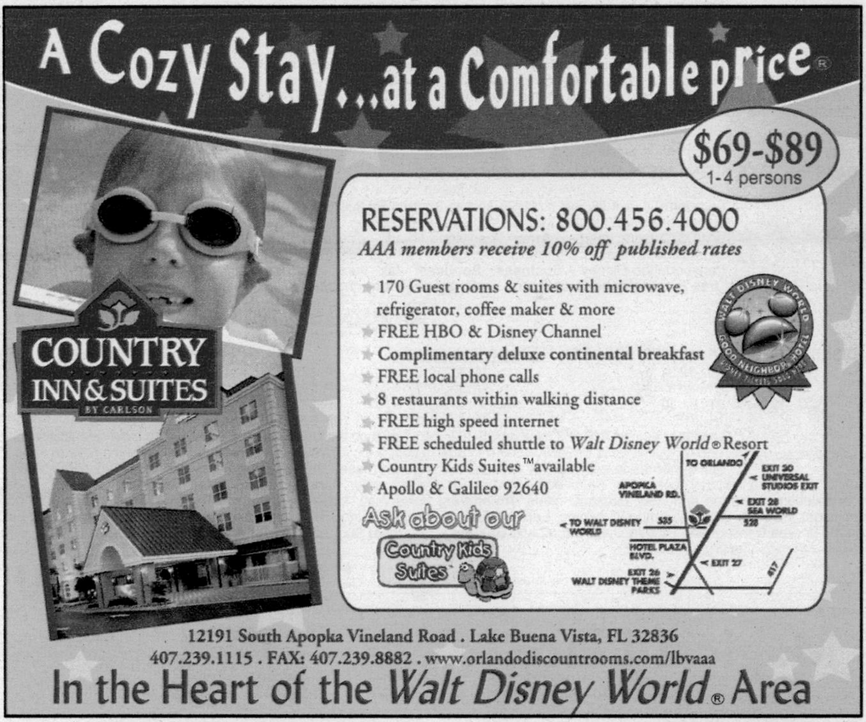

Small-scale Hotel

SOME UNITS

(See map and index starting on p. 668)

COURTYARD BY MARRIOTT AT MARRIOTT VILLAGE
Book at aaa.com

Phone: (407)938-9001 **24**

AAA SAVE

Small-scale Hotel

All Year 1P: $79-$129 2P: $79-$129
Location: I-4, exit 68, just e on SR 535 to Vineland Ave, then n. 8623 Vineland Ave 32821. **Fax:** 407/938-9002. **Facility:** 312 one-bedroom standard units, some with whirlpools. 5 stories, interior corridors. *Bath:* combo or shower only. **Parking:** on-site. **Terms:** cancellation fee imposed, [AP] meal plan available, package plans. **Amenities:** video games, high-speed Internet, dual phone lines, voice mail, irons, hair dryers. **Dining:** 6 am-11 pm. **Pool(s):** heated indoor/outdoor. **Leisure Activities:** whirlpools, exercise room. *Fee:* game room. **Guest Services:** gift shop, valet and coin laundry. **Business Services:** conference facilities, business center. **Cards:** AX, CB, DC, DS, JC, MC, VI. **Special Amenities:** free newspaper.

SOME UNITS

COURTYARD BY MARRIOTT LAKE BUENA VISTA @ VISTA CENTRE
Book at aaa.com

Phone: (407)239-6900 **19**

AAA SAVE

Small-scale Hotel

All Year 1P: $119-$139 2P: $119-$139
Location: I-4, exit 68, 0.6 mi n on SR 535, then 0.3 mi e. 8501 Palm Pkwy 32830. **Fax:** 407/239-1287. **Facility:** 308 units. 222 one-bedroom standard units. 86 one-bedroom suites. 3 stories, interior/exterior corridors. *Bath:* combo or shower only. **Parking:** on-site. **Terms:** check-in 4 pm, cancellation fee imposed, [AP], [BP] & [CP] meal plans available. **Amenities:** high-speed Internet, dual phone lines, voice mail, safes, irons, hair dryers. **Dining:** 6:30-11 am. **Pool(s):** 2 heated outdoor, wading. **Leisure Activities:** whirlpool, playground, exercise room, shuffleboard. *Fee:* game room. **Guest Services:** gift shop, valet and coin laundry, area transportation-Disney & Premium Outlet Store. **Business Services:** meeting rooms, business center. **Cards:** AX, DC, DS, JC, MC, VI. **Special Amenities:** free local telephone calls and free newspaper. *(See color ad below)*

SOME UNITS

DAYS INN LAKE BUENA VISTA HOTEL
Book at aaa.com

Phone: (407)239-4441 **28**

AAA SAVE

Small-scale Hotel

All Year 1P: $69-$129 2P: $69-$129 XP: $10 F12
Location: I-4, exit 68, just n. 12799 Apopka-Vineland Rd 32836. **Fax:** 407/239-0325. **Facility:** 203 one-bedroom standard units. 8 stories, interior corridors. *Bath:* combo or shower only. **Parking:** on-site. **Terms:** small pets only ($10 extra charge). **Amenities:** video library, voice mail, hair dryers. *Some:* irons. **Pool(s):** outdoor. **Leisure Activities:** playground. *Fee:* game room. **Guest Services:** gift shop, valet and coin laundry, area transportation-Disney. **Business Services:** fax (fee). **Cards:** AX, CB, DC, DS, JC, MC, VI. **Special Amenities:** free local telephone calls and early check-in/late check-out.

SOME UNITS

DISNEY'S ALL-STAR MOVIES RESORT
Book at aaa.com

Phone: (407)939-7000 **59**

AAA

Resort
Large-scale Hotel

12/1-12/31	1P: $77-$131	2P: $77-$131	XP: $10 F17
2/16-8/26	1P: $99-$127	2P: $99-$127	XP: $10 F17
8/27-11/30	1P: $79-$111	2P: $79-$111	XP: $10 F17
1/1-2/15	1P: $79-$91	2P: $79-$91	XP: $10 F17

Location: I-4, exit 64B, 1.3 mi w on US 192, then 1 mi n on World Dr; just w of Disney World main gate access road. 1991 W Buena Vista Dr 32830-1000 (PO Box 10,000). **Fax:** 407/939-7111. **Facility:** From talking toys to spotted dogs, themes in each of this resort's buildings are based on Disney movies. 1920 one-bedroom standard units. 3 stories, exterior corridors. *Bath:* some combo or shower only. **Parking:** on-site. **Terms:** check-in 4 pm, 6 day cancellation notice-fee imposed, package plans. **Amenities:** voice mail, safes, irons. *Some:* hair dryers. **Dining:** 6:30 am-midnight. **Pool(s):** 2 heated outdoor, wading. **Leisure Activities:** playground. *Fee:* game room. **Guest Services:** gift shop, coin laundry, area transportation-within Disney complex. **Business Services:** fax (fee). **Cards:** AX, DC, DS, JC, MC, VI. *(See color ad starting on p 795)*

SOME UNITS

Walt Disney World
Resort Guide

Staying at a select *Walt Disney World* Resort hotel is even more fantastic during the *Happiest Celebration On Earth* because you'll enjoy greater *Disney Resort* Guest benefits than ever!

Disney's Pop Century Resort–Value Resort

Disney Value Resorts The most affordable way to enjoy Disney magic! Adorned with whimsical, larger-than-life icons, these Resorts are big on everything but price.

Disney Moderate Resorts The perfect combination of magical Disney theming, value and amenities including incredible pools plus family restaurants and food courts.

Disney Deluxe Resorts These magnificent Resorts are famed for the highest level of personal service and meticulous detail.

Disney Vacation Club Resorts Enjoy all the comforts of home including fully equipped kitchens or kitchenettes and separate bedrooms to accommodate up to twelve Guests.
The number of rooms available is very limited, in part due to membership usage.

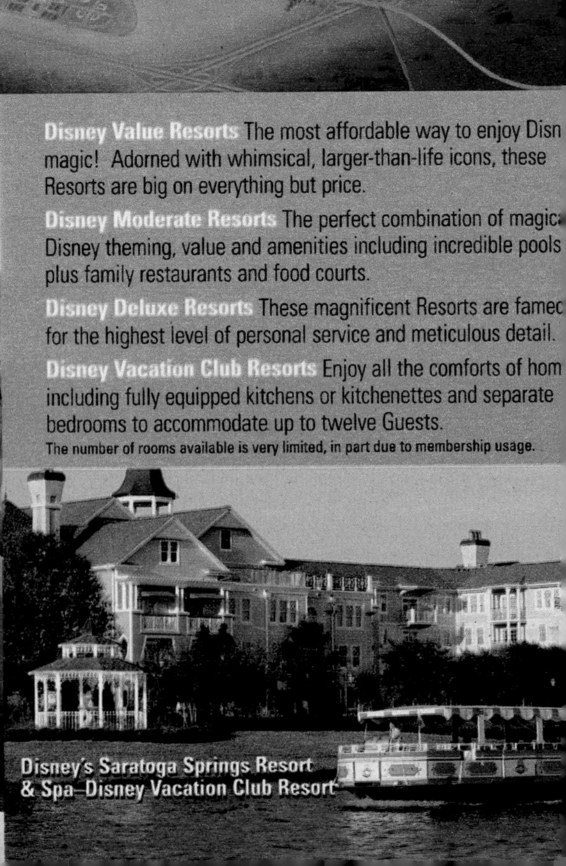

Disney's Saratoga Springs Resort & Spa–Disney Vacation Club Resort

Disney's Port Orleans Resort–French Quarter–Moderate Resort

Disney's Animal Kingdom Lodge–Deluxe Resort

Disney Value Resorts

1. Disney's All-Star Sports Resort
2. Disney's All-Star Music Resort
3. Disney's All-Star Movies Resort
4. Disney's Pop Century Resort

Disney Moderate Resorts

5. Disney's Caribbean Beach Resort
6. Disney's Coronado Springs Resort
7. Disney's Port Orleans Resort - Riverside
8. Disney's Port Orleans Resort - French Quarter

Disney Deluxe Resorts

9. Disney's Grand Floridian Resort & Spa
10. Disney's Contemporary Resort
11. Disney's Polynesian Resort
12. Disney's Wilderness Lodge
13. Disney's Yacht Club Resort
14. Disney's Beach Club Resort
15. Disney's BoardWalk Inn
16. Disney's Animal Kingdom Lodge

Disney Vacation Club Resorts

17. Disney's Old Key West Resort
18. Disney's BoardWalk Villas
19. The Villas at Disney's Wilderness Lodge
20. Disney's Beach Club Villas
21. Disney's Saratoga Springs Resort & Spa

22. Disney's Fort Wilderness Resort & Campground

See the LODGING section of this TourBook for more information on select *Walt Disney World* Resort hotels.

Disney Resort Guest benefits are greater than ever!

There's nothing like being a Guest at select *Walt Disney World* Resort hotels. You'll enjoy these special benefits along the way:

● NEW! Disney's Magical Express Service
This brand-new benefit is complimentary during the *Happiest Celebration On Earth*. Motor coaches pick you up at Orlando International Airport while your checked bags are picked up* and taken from the plane to your room. And when your vacation's over, you and your bags are taken back to Orlando International Airport. Book at least 10 days in advance.
*Pet carriers not included.

● NEW! Disney Dining Plan
By purchasing the *Magic Your Way* Package Plus Dining, you have a convenient and affordable way to enjoy meals and snacks, including Character Dining, at over 100 select restaurants throughout *Walt Disney World* Resort. Visit disneyworld.com/dineplan or call your AAA Travel professional for included restaurants.

● ENHANCED! Extra Magic Hours Benefit
Each day one of the Theme Parks opens an hour early or stays open up to 3 hours after Park closing so you can experience select attractions. Valid Theme Park ticket and Resort I.D. required.

AAA Vacations Packages put it all together!

Packages include a *Disney Resort* stay, tickets, and EXCLUSIVE benefits. Call or visit your local AAA Travel office today. They can help with all your travel needs. Save on select *Disney Resort* accommodations with the AAA Disney *Magic Moments* Savings plan (based on availability).

AAA Vacations benefits include:
● EXCLUSIVE - *AAA Vacations* Diamond Card, entitling you to special savings and values on meals, merchandise and recreation at participating Disney locations.

● EXCLUSIVE - *AAA VIP Lounge* in the *Magic Kingdom* Park, a great place to unwind and enjoy a complimentary soft drink (subject to change, voucher required).

● EXCLUSIVE - *AAA Diamond Parking* - Preferred Parking in special AAA spaces at all four *Walt Disney World* Theme Parks (subject to availability, voucher required, some block-out dates apply).

Call your AAA Travel office today and make your Disney dreams come true!

©Disney 4058025CMC0107

(See map and index starting on p. 668)

DISNEY'S ALL-STAR MUSIC — *Book at aaa.com*

AAA
◇◇◇◇

				Phone: (407)939-6000	**58**
12/1-12/31	1P: $77-$131	2P: $77-$131	XP: $10		F17
2/16-8/26	1P: $99-$127	2P: $99-$127	XP: $10		F17
8/27-11/30	1P: $79-$111	2P: $79-$111	XP: $10		F17
1/1-2/15	1P: $79-$91	2P: $79-$91	XP: $10		F17

Resort
Large-scale Hotel

Location: Just w of Disney World main gate access road (World Dr); 1 mi n of US 192. 1801 W Buena Vista Dr 32830-1000 (PO Box 10,000). Fax: 407/939-7222. **Facility:** Music is the theme and images of standout performers are everywhere at this property dedicated to lyrics and legends. 1920 one-bedroom standard units. 3 stories, exterior corridors. *Bath:* combo or shower only. **Parking:** on-site. **Terms:** 6 day cancellation notice-fee imposed, package plans. **Amenities:** voice mail, safes, irons. **Dining:** 6:30 am-midnight. **Pool(s):** 2 heated outdoor, wading. **Leisure Activities:** playground. *Fee:* game room. **Guest Services:** gift shop, valet and coin laundry, area transportation-within Disney complex. **Business Services:** fax. **Cards:** AX, DC, DS, JC, MC, VI. *(See color ad starting on p 795)*

SOME UNITS

(See map and index starting on p. 668)

DISNEY'S ALL-STAR SPORTS — Book at aaa.com
Phone: (407)939-5000 **57**

12/1-12/31	1P: $77-$131	2P: $77-$131	XP: $10 F17
2/16-8/26	1P: $99-$127	2P: $99-$127	XP: $10 F17
8/27-11/30	1P: $79-$111	2P: $79-$111	XP: $10 F17
1/1-2/15	1P: $79-$91	2P: $79-$91	XP: $10 F17

Resort
Large-scale Hotel
Location: Just w of Disney World main gate access road (World Dr); 1 mi n of US 192. 1701 W Buena Vista Dr 32830-1000 (PO Box 10,000). Fax: 407/939-7333. **Facility:** Larger-than-life sports icons decorate stairways, vending areas and courtyards at this athletics-themed property. 1920 one-bedroom standard units. 3 stories, exterior corridors. *Bath:* combo or shower only. **Parking:** on-site. **Terms:** 6 day cancellation notice-fee imposed, package plans. **Amenities:** voice mail, safes, irons. **Dining:** 6:30 am-midnight. **Pool(s):** 2 heated outdoor, wading. **Leisure Activities:** jogging, playground. *Fee:* game room. **Guest Services:** gift shop, valet and coin laundry, area transportation-within Disney complex. **Business Services:** meeting rooms, fax (fee). **Cards:** AX, DC, DS, JC, MC, VI. *(See color ad starting on p 795)*

SOME UNITS

DISNEY'S ANIMAL KINGDOM LODGE — Book at aaa.com
Phone: (407)938-3000 **55**

12/1-12/31	1P: $199-$620	2P: $199-$620	XP: $25 F17
2/16-7/4	1P: $249-$555	2P: $249-$555	XP: $25 F17
7/5-11/30	1P: $205-$490	2P: $205-$490	XP: $25 F17
1/1-2/15	1P: $205-$435	2P: $205-$435	XP: $25 F17

Resort
Large-scale Hotel
Location: I-4, exit 64 or 65; n of US 192 on World Dr, follow signs. 2901 Osceola Pkwy 32830. Fax: 407/938-4799. **Facility:** This wonderful re-creation of an African Kraal, or village, invites guests to experience African wildlife and culture all under one roof. 1293 units. 1274 one-bedroom standard units. 5 one- and 14 two-bedroom suites ($655-$2585), some with whirlpools. 5 stories, interior corridors. *Bath:* combo or shower only. **Parking:** on-site and valet. **Terms:** 6 day cancellation notice-fee imposed, package plans. **Amenities:** voice mail, safes, irons, hair dryers. *Some:* DVD players, CD players, dual phone lines. **Dining:** 3 restaurants, 6 am-midnight, cocktails, also, Jiko, see separate listing. **Pool(s):** heated outdoor, wading. **Leisure Activities:** saunas, whirlpools, steamrooms, waterslide, playground, exercise room. *Fee:* massage, game room. **Guest Services:** gift shop, valet and coin laundry, area transportation-within Disney complex. **Business Services:** fax (fee). **Cards:** AX, DC, DS, JC, MC, VI. *(See color ad starting on p 795)*

SOME UNITS

DISNEY'S BEACH CLUB RESORT — Book at aaa.com
Phone: (407)934-8000 **38**

12/1-12/31	1P: $294-$675	2P: $294-$675	XP: $25 F17
2/16-7/4	1P: $345-$615	2P: $345-$615	XP: $25 F17
7/5-11/30	1P: $305-$540	2P: $305-$540	XP: $25 F17
1/1-2/15	1P: $305-$475	2P: $305-$475	XP: $25 F17

Resort
Large-scale Hotel
Location: I-4, exit 67, follow signs to Disney's Epcot Park; in Walt Disney World. 1700 Epcot Resorts Blvd 32830 (PO Box 10,000). Fax: 407/934-3450. **Facility:** The resort sports a New England yachting and beach theme and includes a lagoon-style pool featuring various water and sand activity areas. 583 units. 567 one-bedroom standard units. 9 one- and 7 two-bedroom suites ($500-$2220). 5 stories, interior corridors. *Bath:* combo or shower only. **Parking:** on-site and valet. **Terms:** 6 day cancellation notice-fee imposed. **Amenities:** high-speed Internet (fee), voice mail, safes, honor bars, irons, hair dryers. *Some:* DVD players, dual phone lines. **Dining:** shared food & beverage facilities with Disney's Yacht Club Resort. **Leisure Activities:** shared leisure activities and recreational facilities with Disney's Yacht Club Resort. **Guest Services:** gift shop, valet and coin laundry, area transportation-within Disney complex, beauty salon. **Business Services:** conference facilities, fax (fee). **Cards:** AX, DC, DS, JC, MC, VI. *(See color ad starting on p 795)*

SOME UNITS

DISNEY'S BEACH CLUB VILLAS — Book at aaa.com
Phone: (407)934-8000 **39**

12/1-12/31	1P: $294-$1040	2P: $294-$1040
2/16-7/4	1P: $345-$945	2P: $345-$945
7/5-11/30	1P: $305-$745	2P: $305-$745
1/1-2/15	1P: $305-$575	2P: $305-$575

Resort
Large-scale Hotel
Location: I-4, exit 67, follow signs to Disney's Epcot Park; in Walt Disney World. 1700 Epcot Resorts Blvd 32830 (PO Box 10000). Fax: 407/934-3450. **Facility:** The resort sports a New England yachting and beach theme and includes a lagoon-style pool featuring various water and sand activity areas. 282 units. 110 one-bedroom standard units with efficiencies. 94 one- and 78 two-bedroom suites with kitchens and whirlpools. 5 stories, interior corridors. *Bath:* combo or shower only. **Parking:** on-site and valet. **Terms:** check-in 4 pm, 6 day cancellation notice-fee imposed, package plans. **Amenities:** high-speed Internet (fee), voice mail, safes, irons, hair dryers. *Some:* DVD players. **Dining:** shared food and beverage facilities with Disney's Yacht Club and Beach Club Resorts. **Leisure Activities:** shared leisure activities and recreational facilities with Disney's Yacht Club and Beach Club Resorts. **Guest Services:** area transportation-within Disney complex. **Cards:** AX, DC, DS, JC, MC, VI. *(See color ad starting on p 795)*

DISNEY'S BOARDWALK RESORT — Book at aaa.com
Phone: (407)939-5100 **47**

12/1-12/31	1P: $294-$690	2P: $294-$690	XP: $25 F17
2/16-7/4	1P: $345-$645	2P: $345-$645	XP: $25 F17
7/5-11/30	1P: $305-$585	2P: $305-$585	XP: $25 F17
1/1-2/15	1P: $305-$540	2P: $305-$540	XP: $25 F17

Resort
Large-scale Hotel
Location: 0.5 mi e of Disney World main gate access road; 2 mi n of US 192; in Walt Disney World. 2101 N Epcot Resorts Blvd 32830 (PO Box 10,000). Fax: 407/939-5150. **Facility:** Inn or villa units are available at this resort where the fixtures, furniture and finishes reflect the styles of the 1920s and '30s. 372 units. 366 one-bedroom standard units. 6 one-bedroom suites ($575-$2460). 3 stories, interior/exterior corridors. *Bath:* combo or shower only. **Parking:** on-site and valet. **Terms:** 6 day cancellation notice-fee imposed, package plans. **Amenities:** high-speed Internet (fee), dual phone lines, voice mail, safes, irons, hair dryers. *Some:* DVD players. **Dining:** 4 restaurants, 7 am-midnight, cocktails, also, Flying Fish Cafe, Spoodles, see separate listings. **Pool(s):** 3 heated outdoor, wading. **Leisure Activities:** sauna, whirlpools, 2 lighted tennis courts, jogging, playground. *Fee:* bicycles, massage, game room. **Guest Services:** gift shop, coin laundry, airport transportation (fee)-Orlando International Airport, area transportation-within Disney complex. **Business Services:** conference facilities, business center. **Cards:** AX, DC, DS, JC, MC, VI. *(See color ad starting on p 795)*

SOME UNITS

(See map and index starting on p. 668)

DISNEY'S BOARDWALK VILLAS   *Book at aaa.com*   Phone: (407)939-5100   **45**

12/1-12/31	1P: $294-$1040	2P: $294-$1040	
2/16-7/4	1P: $345-$945	2P: $345-$945	
7/5-11/30	1P: $305-$745	2P: $305-$745	
1/1-2/15	1P: $305-$575	2P: $305-$575	

Resort **Location:** 0.5 mi e of Disney World Maingate access road; 2 mi n of US 192; in Walt Disney World. 2101 N Epcot
Large-scale Hotel Resorts Blvd 32830 (PO Box 10,000). Fax: 407/939-5150. **Facility:** The villa units are designed where the fixtures, furniture and finishes reflect the styles of the 1920s and '30s. 253 one-bedroom standard units with efficiencies. 273 one- and 7 three-bedroom suites ($1395-$2020). 5 stories, interior/exterior corridors. **Parking:** on-site and valet. **Terms:** check-in 4 pm, 6 day cancellation notice-fee imposed, package plans. **Amenities:** high-speed Internet, voice mail, safes, irons, hair dryers. *Some:* DVD players, CD players, dual phone lines. **Dining:** shared food and beverage facilities with Disney. **Pool(s):** wading. **Leisure Activities:** saunas, recreation programs, shared leisure activities and recreational facilities with Disney, jogging, playground. *Fee:* bicycles, massage. **Guest Services:** gift shop, complimentary laundry, area transportation-within Disney complex. **Business Services:** conference facilities, business center. **Cards:** AX, DC, DS, JC, MC, VI. *(See color ad starting on p 795)*

SOME UNITS

DISNEY'S CARIBBEAN BEACH RESORT   *Book at aaa.com*   Phone: (407)934-3400   **44**

12/1-12/31	1P: $134-$209	2P: $134-$209	XP: $15	F17
2/16-8/26	1P: $155-$199	2P: $155-$199	XP: $15	F17
8/27-11/30	1P: $139-$175	2P: $139-$175	XP: $15	F17
1/1-2/15	1P: $139-$155	2P: $139-$155	XP: $15	F17

Small-scale Hotel **Location:** I-4, exit 67, 1.5 mi e of Disney World main gate access road; 2 mi n of US 192. 900 Cayman Way 32830 (PO Box 10,000). Fax: 407/934-3288. **Facility:** 2112 one-bedroom standard units. 2 stories, exterior corridors. *Bath:* combo or shower only. **Parking:** on-site. **Terms:** 6 day cancellation notice-fee imposed, package plans. **Amenities:** voice mail, safes, irons, hair dryers. **Dining:** 6:30 am-11 pm, cocktails. **Pool(s):** 7 heated outdoor, wading. **Leisure Activities:** whirlpool, rental boats, rental paddleboats, rental sailboats, dock, boat dock, children's recreation island, rental bicycles, jogging, playground, volleyball. *Fee:* waterskiing, pontoon boats, water mice, game room. **Guest Services:** gift shop, valet and coin laundry, area transportation-within Disney complex. **Business Services:** fax (fee). **Cards:** AX, DC, DS, JC, MC, VI. *(See color ad starting on p 795)*

SOME UNITS

DISNEY'S CONTEMPORARY RESORT   *Book at aaa.com*   Phone: (407)824-1000   **2**

12/1-12/31	1P: $244-$695	2P: $244-$695	XP: $25	F17
2/16-7/4	1P: $279-$645	2P: $279-$645	XP: $25	F17
7/5-11/30	1P: $249-$575	2P: $249-$575	XP: $25	F17
1/1-2/15	1P: $249-$515	2P: $249-$515	XP: $25	F17

Resort **Location:** I-4, exit 67, follow signs to Disney's Magic Kingdom; in Walt Disney World. 4600 N World Dr 32830 (PO Box
Large-scale Hotel 10,000). Fax: 407/824-3539. **Facility:** A soaring structure, the resort features a monorail line traversing the building; public areas and guest rooms have contemporary decor. 997 one-bedroom standard units. 6 one- and 5 two-bedroom suites ($820-$2530). 3-15 stories, interior corridors. *Bath:* combo or shower only. **Parking:** on-site and valet. **Terms:** 6 day cancellation notice-fee imposed, package plans, no pets allowed (owner kennel available). **Amenities:** high-speed Internet (fee), voice mail, safes, irons, hair dryers. *Some:* CD players, fax. **Dining:** 5 restaurants, 24 hours, cocktails, also, California Grill, see separate listing. **Pool(s):** 2 heated outdoor. **Leisure Activities:** sauna, whirlpools, waterslide, rental boats, rental sailboats, recreation programs, jogging, playground, basketball, volleyball. *Fee:* waterskiing, parasailing, water mice, golf-99 holes, 6 lighted tennis courts, tennis instruction, massage, game room. **Guest Services:** gift shop, valet and coin laundry, area transportation-within Disney complex. *Fee:* beauty salon, tanning facilities. **Business Services:** conference facilities, business center. **Cards:** AX, DC, DS, JC, MC, VI. *(See color ad starting on p 795)*

SOME UNITS

DISNEY'S CORONADO SPRINGS RESORT   *Book at aaa.com*   Phone: (407)939-1000   **48**

12/1-12/31	1P: $134-$209	2P: $134-$209	XP: $15	F17
2/16-8/26	1P: $155-$199	2P: $155-$199	XP: $15	F17
8/27-11/30	1P: $139-$175	2P: $139-$175	XP: $15	F17
1/1-2/15	1P: $139-$155	2P: $139-$155	XP: $15	F17

Resort **Location:** I-4, exit 67, just nw, follow signs to Disney's Animal Kingdom Park. 1000 W Buena Vista Blvd 32830 (PO Box
Large-scale Hotel 10,000). Fax: 407/939-1001. **Facility:** Water activities, as well as dining and shopping, provide diversions at this resort where landscaping and decor set a Southwestern theme. Designated smoking area. 1921 units. 1875 one-bedroom standard units. 46 one-bedroom suites ($300-$1170), some with whirlpools. 2-4 stories, exterior corridors. *Bath:* combo or shower only. **Parking:** on-site. **Terms:** 6 day cancellation notice-fee imposed, package plans. **Amenities:** high-speed Internet (fee), voice mail, safes, irons, hair dryers. *Some:* fax. **Dining:** 2 restaurants, 7 am-11 pm, cocktails. **Pool(s):** 4 heated outdoor, wading. **Leisure Activities:** sauna, whirlpool, waterslide, rental paddleboats, rental bicycles, playground, volleyball. *Fee:* pontoon boats, surrey bikes, water mice, massage, game room. **Guest Services:** gift shop, valet and coin laundry, area transportation-within Disney complex. **Business Services:** conference facilities, business center. **Cards:** AX, DC, DS, JC, MC, VI. *(See color ad starting on p 795)*

DISNEY'S FORT WILDERNESS RESORT
CAMPGROUND   *Book at aaa.com*   Phone: (407)824-2900   **7**

12/1-12/31	1P: $234-$339	2P: $234-$339	XP: $5	F17
2/16-7/4	1P: $279-$319	2P: $279-$319	XP: $5	F17
7/5-11/30	1P: $239-$279	2P: $239-$279	XP: $5	F17
1/1-2/15	1P: $239	2P: $239	XP: $5	F17

Cabin **Location:** Off US 192; in Walt Disney World. 4510 N Fort Wilderness Tr 32830-1000. Fax: 407/824-3508.
Facility: The property features cabins in a wooded campground setting, all with grills and picnic tables; transportation is offered to Walt Disney World. 409 cabins. 1 story, exterior corridors. *Bath:* combo or shower only. **Parking:** on-site. **Terms:** 6 day cancellation notice-fee imposed, package plans. **Amenities:** high-speed Internet (fee), voice mail, safes, irons, hair dryers. **Dining:** 7:30 am-11, noon-3:30 & 4:30-10 pm, cocktails. **Pool(s):** 2 heated outdoor, wading. **Leisure Activities:** rental canoes, rental paddleboats, fishing, 2 lighted tennis courts, recreation programs, hay rides, nightly campfire & Disney movie, petting farm, tetherball, carriage rides, jogging, playground, basketball, horseshoes, shuffleboard, volleyball. *Fee:* fishing equipment, bicycles, horseback riding, game room. **Guest Services:** valet and coin laundry, area transportation-within Disney complex. **Business Services:** fax (fee). **Cards:** AX, DC, DS, JC, MC, VI. *(See color ad starting on p 795)*

SOME UNITS

(See map and index starting on p. 668)

DISNEY'S GRAND FLORIDIAN RESORT & SPA

Book at aaa.com   **Phone: (407)824-3000**   **3**

12/1-12/31	1P: $349-$870	2P: $349-$870	XP: $25	F17
2/16-7/4	1P: $405-$805	2P: $405-$805	XP: $25	F17
7/5-11/30	1P: $359-$715	2P: $359-$715	XP: $25	F17
1/1-2/15	1P: $359-$630	2P: $359-$630	XP: $25	F17

Resort   **Location:** 8 mi nw of jct I-4 and US 192. 4401 Grand Floridian Way 32830 (PO Box 10,000). Fax: 407/824-3186.
Large-scale Hotel   **Facility:** Cypress and magnolia trees and manicured lawns surround white, frame buildings at this resort which merges Victorian and old-Florida styles. 867 units. 843 one-bedroom standard units. 8 one- and 16 two-bedroom suites ($940-$2600) with whirlpools. 4-5 stories, interior corridors. *Bath:* combo or shower only. **Parking:** on-site and valet. **Terms:** 6 day cancellation notice-fee imposed, no pets allowed (kennel on property). **Amenities:** video library, CD players, high-speed Internet (fee), voice mail, safes, honor bars, irons, hair dryers. *Some:* DVD players. **Dining:** 5 restaurants, 24 hours, cocktails, also, Citricos, Narcoosee's, Victoria & Albert's, see separate listings, entertainment. **Pool(s):** heated outdoor, small heated outdoor. **Leisure Activities:** saunas, whirlpools, rental boats, rental sailboats, recreation programs, croquet, jogging, playground, spa, volleyball. *Fee:* charter fishing, pontoon boats, yacht, golf-99 holes, 2 lighted tennis courts, tennis instruction, game room. **Guest Services:** gift shop, valet and coin laundry, area transportation-within Disney complex. **Business Services:** conference facilities, business center. **Cards:** AX, DC, DS, JC, MC, VI. *(See color ad starting on p 795)*

SOME UNITS

DISNEY'S OLD KEY WEST RESORT

Book at aaa.com   **Phone: (407)827-7700**   **34**

12/1-12/31	1P: $259-$805	2P: $259-$805
2/16-7/4	1P: $299-$720	2P: $299-$720
7/5-11/30	1P: $269-$590	2P: $269-$590
1/1-2/15	1P: $269-$500	2P: $269-$500

Condominium   **Location:** I-4, exit 67, 2 mi nw on SR 536 and Bennet Creek Pkwy. 1510 N Cove Rd 32830 (PO Box 10,000). Fax: 407/827-1192. **Facility:** The property's bright, airy buildings are pastel-painted with decorative gingerbread trim; one-, two- and three-bedroom condo-style units are offered. 761 units. 230 one-bedroom standard units. 230 one-, 274 two- and 27 three-bedroom suites ($1100-$1545) with kitchens and whirlpools. 2-3 stories (no elevator), exterior corridors. *Bath:* some combo or shower only. **Parking:** on-site. **Terms:** check-in 4 pm, 6 day cancellation notice-fee imposed, package plans. **Amenities:** voice mail, irons, hair dryers. *Fee:* video library, high-speed Internet. *Some:* DVD players, safes. **Dining:** 7:30 am-10:30 & 11-11 pm, cocktails. **Pool(s):** 4 heated outdoor, wading. **Leisure Activities:** sauna, whirlpools, waterslide, rental boats, rental paddleboats, 3 tennis courts (2 lighted), recreation programs, rental bicycles, jogging, playground, exercise room, basketball, shuffleboard, volleyball. *Fee:* fishing, canopy boats, pontoon boats, water mice boats, tennis equipment, massage, game room. **Guest Services:** gift shop, complimentary laundry, area transportation-within Disney complex. **Business Services:** fax (fee). **Cards:** AX, DC, DS, JC, MC, VI. *(See color ad starting on p 795)*

SOME UNITS

DISNEY'S POLYNESIAN RESORT

Book at aaa.com   **Phone: (407)824-2000**   **6**

12/1-12/31	1P: $304-$720	2P: $304-$720	XP: $25	F17
2/16-7/4	1P: $369-$710	2P: $369-$710	XP: $25	F17
7/5-11/30	1P: $315-$625	2P: $315-$625	XP: $25	F17
1/1-2/15	1P: $315-$550	2P: $315-$550	XP: $25	F17

Resort   **Location:** I-4, exit 67, nw and follow signs to Disney's Magic Kingdom; in Walt Disney World. 1600 Seven Seas Dr
Large-scale Hotel   32830 (PO Box 10,000). Fax: 407/824-3174. **Facility:** A lagoon anchors this sprawling 11-building complex that's just a monorail ride away from attractions. 847 units. 842 one-bedroom standard units. 1 one- and 4 two-bedroom suites ($550-$2640). 2-3 stories, interior corridors. *Bath:* combo or shower only. **Parking:** on-site and valet. **Terms:** 6 day cancellation notice-fee imposed, package plans. **Amenities:** voice mail, safes, irons, hair dryers. *Some:* CD players, dual phone lines. **Dining:** 4 restaurants, 6:30 am-11 pm, cocktails. **Pool(s):** heated outdoor, wading. **Leisure Activities:** waterslide, rental boats, rental sailboats, racquetball court, recreation programs, 1.5 mi paved walking trail. *Fee:* fishing, charter fishing, personal watercraft, pontoon boats, specialty cruises, water mice, golf-99 holes, bicycles, massage, game room. **Guest Services:** gift shop, valet and coin laundry, area transportation-within Disney complex. **Business Services:** fax (fee). **Cards:** AX, DC, DS, JC, MC, VI. *(See color ad starting on p 795)*

SOME UNITS

DISNEY'S POP CENTURY RESORT

Book at aaa.com   **Phone: (407)938-4000**   **56**

12/1-12/31	1P: $77-$131	2P: $77-$131	XP: $10	F17
2/16-8/26	1P: $99-$127	2P: $99-$127	XP: $10	F17
8/27-11/30	1P: $79-$111	2P: $79-$111	XP: $10	F17
1/1-2/15	1P: $79-$91	2P: $79-$91	XP: $10	F17

Resort   **Location:** Just w of Disney World main gate access road (World Dr); 1 mi n of US 192. 1050 Century Dr 32830 (PO
Large-scale Hotel   Box 10,000). Fax: 407/938-4040. **Facility:** In Disney's Wide World of Sports complex this 2880-room resort replicates memorabilia from the 1950s to the 1980s in massive forms around the resort. 2880 one-bedroom standard units. 4 stories, exterior corridors. *Bath:* some shower only. **Parking:** on-site. **Terms:** 6 day cancellation notice-fee imposed, package plans. **Amenities:** voice mail, safes, irons. **Pool(s):** 3 heated outdoor, wading. **Leisure Activities:** jogging, playground. *Fee:* game room. **Guest Services:** valet and coin laundry, area transportation. **Business Services:** fax (fee). **Cards:** AX, DC, DS, JC, MC, VI. *(See color ad starting on p 795)*

SOME UNITS

(See map and index starting on p. 668)

DISNEY'S PORT ORLEANS-FRENCH QUARTER
RESORT *Book at aaa.com* Phone: (407)934-5000 **26**

12/1-12/31	1P: $134-$209	2P: $134-$209	XP: $15 F17
2/16-8/26	1P: $155-$199	2P: $155-$199	XP: $15 F17
8/27-11/30	1P: $139-$175	2P: $139-$175	XP: $15 F17
1/1-2/15	1P: $139-$155	2P: $139-$155	XP: $15 F17

Resort
Large-scale Hotel

Location: I-4, exit 67, just nw, follow signs to Downtown Disney. 2201 Orleans Dr 32830 (PO Box 10,000). Fax: 407/934-5353. **Facility:** Pale-colored stucco and black wrought iron adorn this French Quarter-themed resort; rooms overlook landscaped courtyards, the pool area or a river. 1008 one-bedroom standard units. 3 stories, exterior corridors. *Bath:* combo or shower only. **Parking:** on-site. **Terms:** 6 day cancellation notice-fee imposed. **Amenities:** voice mail, safes, irons, hair dryers. **Pool(s):** heated outdoor, wading. **Leisure Activities:** whirlpool, waterslide, rental boats, playground. *Fee:* game room. **Guest Services:** gift shop, coin laundry, area transportation. **Business Services:** fax (fee). **Cards:** AX, DC, DS, JC, MC, VI.

DISNEY'S PORT ORLEANS-RIVERSIDE RESORT *Book at aaa.com* Phone: (407)934-6000 **27**

12/1-12/31	1P: $134-$209	2P: $134-$209	XP: $15 F17
2/16-8/26	1P: $155-$199	2P: $155-$199	XP: $15 F17
8/27-11/30	1P: $139-$175	2P: $139-$175	XP: $15 F17
1/1-2/15	1P: $139-$155	2P: $139-$155	XP: $15 F17

Resort
Large-scale Hotel

Location: I-4, exit 67, just nw, follow signs to Downtown Disney. 1251 Riverside Dr 32830 (PO Box 10,000). Fax: 407/934-5777. **Facility:** A gated entry buffers this antebellum-style resort's 350 acres of manicured grounds; a canal system provides boat transportation to attractions. 2048 one-bedroom standard units. 2-3 stories, exterior corridors. *Bath:* combo or shower only. **Parking:** on-site. **Terms:** 6 day cancellation notice-fee imposed, package plans. **Amenities:** voice mail, safes, irons, hair dryers. **Dining:** 6 am-midnight, cocktails, also, Boatwright's Dining Hall, see separate listing, entertainment. **Pool(s):** 7 heated outdoor, wading. **Leisure Activities:** whirlpool, waterslide, rental paddleboats, rental bicycles, playground. *Fee:* game room. **Guest Services:** gift shop, valet and coin laundry, area transportation-within Disney complex. **Business Services:** fax (fee). **Cards:** AX, DC, DS, JC, MC, VI.
(See color ad starting on p 795)

DISNEY'S SARATOGA SPRINGS RESORT & SPA *Book at aaa.com* Phone: (407)827-1100 **41**

12/1-12/31	1P: $259-$805	2P: $259-$805
2/16-7/4	1P: $299-$720	2P: $299-$720
7/5-11/30	1P: $269-$590	2P: $269-$590
1/1-2/15	1P: $269-$500	2P: $269-$500

Resort
Large-scale Hotel

Location: I-4, exit 67, to Community Dr to Broadway. 1960 Broadway 32830 (PO Box 10,000). **Facility:** Located in the Downtown Disney area, these vacation villas are modeled around the Victorian architecture of Saratoga Springs, NY. 350 units. 120 one-bedroom standard units with kitchens. 120 one-, 100 two- and 10 three-bedroom suites ($1100-$1545) with kitchens. 4 stories, exterior corridors. *Bath:* combo or shower only. **Parking:** on-site. **Terms:** check-in 4 pm, 6 day cancellation notice-fee imposed, package plans. **Amenities:** voice mail, safes, irons, hair dryers. *Fee:* video library, high-speed Internet. *Some:* DVD players, CD players. **Pool(s):** 2 heated outdoor. **Leisure Activities:** whirlpools, waterslide, 2 lighted tennis courts, recreation programs, rental bicycles, jogging, playground, spa, basketball, shuffleboard. *Fee:* golf-18 holes, game room. **Guest Services:** gift shop, complimentary laundry, area transportation. **Business Services:** fax (fee). **Cards:** AX, DC, DS, JC, MC, VI. *(See color ad starting on p 795)*

DISNEY'S WILDERNESS LODGE *Book at aaa.com* Phone: (407)824-3200 **5**

12/1-12/31	1P: $199-$505	2P: $199-$505	XP: $25 F17
2/16-7/4	1P: $249-$455	2P: $249-$455	XP: $25 F17
7/5-11/30	1P: $205-$405	2P: $205-$405	XP: $25 F17
1/1-2/15	1P: $205-$370	2P: $205-$370	XP: $25 F17

Resort
Large-scale Hotel

Location: I-4, exit 67, follow signs to Disney's Magic Kingdom; in Walt Disney World. 901 W Timberline Dr 32830 (PO Box 10,000). Fax: 407/824-3232. **Facility:** Set on the edge of a forest of cypress and slash pine, this rustic lodge is fashioned after an inn at Yellowstone National Park. 765 units. 738 one-bedroom standard units. 27 one-bedroom suites ($380-$1250). 7 stories, interior corridors. *Bath:* combo or shower only. **Parking:** on-site (fee) and valet. **Terms:** 6 day cancellation notice-fee imposed, package plans. **Amenities:** voice mail, safes, irons, hair dryers. *Some:* DVD players, CD players. **Dining:** 2 restaurants, 7 am-midnight, cocktails, also, Artist Point, see separate listing. **Pool(s):** 2 heated outdoor, 2 wading. **Leisure Activities:** whirlpools, waterslide, rental boats, rental canoes, recreation programs, rental bicycles, hiking trails, jogging, playground, volleyball. *Fee:* marina, waterskiing, fishing, float boats, water mice, massage, game room. **Guest Services:** gift shop, coin laundry, area transportation-within Disney complex. **Business Services:** business center. **Cards:** AX, DC, DS, JC, MC, VI. *(See color ad starting on p 795)*

DISNEY'S YACHT CLUB RESORT *Book at aaa.com* Phone: (407)934-7000 **40**

12/1-12/31	1P: $294-$680	2P: $294-$680	XP: $25 F17
2/16-7/4	1P: $345-$635	2P: $345-$635	XP: $25 F17
7/5-11/30	1P: $305-$560	2P: $305-$560	XP: $25 F17
1/1-2/15	1P: $305-$500	2P: $305-$500	XP: $25 F17

Resort
Large-scale Hotel

Location: I-4, exit 67, follow signs to Disney's Epcot Resort; in Walt Disney World. 1700 Epcot Resorts Blvd 32830 (PO Box 10,000). Fax: 407/934-3450. **Facility:** The resort sports a New England yachting theme and includes a lagoon-style pool featuring various water and sand activity areas. 630 units. 619 one-bedroom standard units. 9 one- and 2 two-bedroom suites ($555-$2440). 5 stories, interior corridors. *Bath:* combo or shower only. **Parking:** on-site and valet. **Terms:** 6 day cancellation notice-fee imposed, package plans. **Amenities:** high-speed Internet (fee), voice mail, safes, honor bars, irons, hair dryers. *Some:* DVD players, dual phone lines. **Dining:** 3 restaurants, 24 hours, cocktails, also, Yachtsman's Steak House, see separate listing. **Pool(s):** heated outdoor, wading. **Leisure Activities:** sauna, whirlpools, waterslide, rental boats, water mice, lighted tennis court, tennis equipment, recreation programs, croquet, jogging, playground, volleyball. *Fee:* fishing, massage, game room. **Guest Services:** gift shop, valet laundry, area transportation-within Disney complex, beauty salon. **Business Services:** conference facilities, fax (fee). **Cards:** AX, DC, DS, JC, MC, VI.
(See color ad starting on p 795)

(See map and index starting on p. 668)

DOUBLETREE CLUB HOTEL LAKE BUENA VISTA   *Book at aaa.com*   Phone: (407)239-4646   **21**

AAA (SAVE)   All Year   1P: $89-$149   2P: $89-$149   XP: $15   F18

▼▼▼▼   **Location:** I-4, exit 68, 0.4 mi n on SR 535. Located in a busy commercial frontage district. 12490 Apopka-Vineland Rd 32836. Fax: 407/239-8469. **Facility:** 246 units. 242 one-bedroom standard units. 4 one-bedroom suites. 7 stories, interior corridors. *Bath:* combo or shower only. **Parking:** on-site. **Terms:** check-in 4 pm, package plans. **Amenities:** voice mail, irons, hair dryers. *Fee:* video games, safes. **Dining:** 7 am-11 pm, cocktails. **Pool(s):** heated outdoor, wading. **Leisure Activities:** whirlpool, exercise room. *Fee:* game room. **Guest Services:** gift shop, valet and coin laundry, area transportation-Disney. **Business Services:** meeting rooms, business center. **Cards:** AX, CB, DC, DS, JC, MC, VI. **Special Amenities:** free newspaper. *(See color ad below)*

Small-scale Hotel

SOME UNITS

🍴 🍸 🔔 &M 🛋 ⊘ ≋ ✖ 📹 DATA PORT 💻 / ✖ 🔌 🖨 /
FEE   FEE

DOUBLETREE GUEST SUITES IN THE WALT DISNEY WORLD RESORT   *Book at aaa.com*   Phone: (407)934-1000   **29**

▼▼▼▼   12/1-4/6   1P: $159-$299   2P: $159-$299   XP: $20   F17
4/7-8/12   1P: $139-$299   2P: $139-$299   XP: $20   F17
10/1-11/30   1P: $139-$239   2P: $139-$239   XP: $20   F17
8/13-9/30   1P: $99-$159   2P: $99-$159   XP: $20   F17

Small-scale Hotel

Location: I-4, exit 68. 2305 Hotel Plaza Blvd 32830. Fax: 407/934-1015. **Facility:** 229 units. 224 one- and 5 two-bedroom suites. 7 stories, interior corridors. *Bath:* combo or shower only. **Parking:** on-site. **Terms:** check-in 4 pm, 3 day cancellation notice-fee imposed, package plans. **Amenities:** voice mail, irons, hair dryers. *Fee:* video games, high-speed Internet, safes. **Pool(s):** heated outdoor, wading. **Leisure Activities:** whirlpool, 2 lighted tennis courts, playground, exercise room, volleyball. *Fee:* game room. **Guest Services:** sundries, valet and coin laundry, area transportation. **Business Services:** meeting rooms, business center. **Cards:** AX, CB, DC, DS, JC, MC, VI.

SOME UNITS

🍴 🍸 &M 🛋 ⊘ ≋ ✖ 📹 DATA PORT 🔌 🖨 💻 / ✖ /

EMBASSY SUITES HOTEL-LAKE BUENA VISTA RESORT   *Book at aaa.com*   Phone: (407)239-1144   **8**

▼▼▼▼   All Year   1P: $109-$229   2P: $109-$229   XP: $15   F18

Small-scale Hotel   **Location:** I-4, exit 68, 0.6 mi n on SR 535, 1 mi e on Palm Pkwy, then just se. 8100 Lake Ave 32836. Fax: 407/239-1718. **Facility:** 333 one-bedroom suites ($109-$229). 5-6 stories, interior/exterior corridors. *Bath:* combo or shower only. **Parking:** on-site and valet. **Terms:** check-in 4 pm, 3 day cancellation notice-fee imposed, package plans, small pets only ($25 extra charge). **Amenities:** video games (fee), dual phone lines, voice mail, safes, irons, hair dryers. **Pool(s):** heated indoor/outdoor, wading. **Leisure Activities:** sauna, whirlpool, lighted tennis court, jogging, playground, exercise room, basketball, volleyball. *Fee:* game room. **Guest Services:** gift shop, complimentary evening beverages, valet and coin laundry, area transportation. **Business Services:** meeting rooms, business center. **Cards:** AX, CB, DC, DS, JC, MC, VI. *(See color ad p 805)*

SOME UNITS

ASK 🐾 🍴 🍸 &M 🛋 ⊘ ≋ ✖ 📹 DATA PORT 🔌 🖨 💻 / ✖ VCR /
FEE   FEE

EMBASSY VACATION RESORT GRAND BEACH   *Book at aaa.com*   Phone: (407)238-2500   **50**

▼▼▼▼   All Year   1P: $225-$285   2P: $225-$285

Small-scale Hotel   **Location:** I-4, exit 68, 1.1 mi s. 8317 Lake Bryan Beach Blvd 32821. Fax: 407/238-1825. **Facility:** 216 units. 30 one-, 30 two- and 156 three-bedroom suites, some with efficiencies, kitchens and/or whirlpools. 5 stories, interior corridors. *Bath:* combo or shower only. **Parking:** on-site. **Terms:** check-in 4 pm, cancellation fee imposed. **Amenities:** voice mail, irons, hair dryers. **Pool(s):** 2 heated outdoor, wading. **Leisure Activities:** whirlpool, exercise room, sports court, volleyball. *Fee:* boats, canoes, paddleboats, game room. **Guest Services:** sundries, complimentary laundry. **Business Services:** fax (fee). **Cards:** AX, DS, MC, VI.

ASK 🔊 📶 &M 🛋 ⊘ ≋ ✖ VCR 📹 🔌 🖨 💻

(See map and index starting on p. 668)

EXTENDED STAY DELUXE   *Book at aaa.com*   Phone: (407)239-4300  **9**
All Year [ECP]   1P: $95-$149   2P: $95-$149
Location: I-4, exit 68, 0.6 mi n on SR 535, then 0.7 mi e. 8100 Palm Pkwy 32836. Fax: 407/239-4446. **Facility:** 124 one-bedroom standard units with efficiencies. 3 stories, interior corridors. *Bath:* combo or shower only.
Small-scale Hotel   **Parking:** on-site. **Terms:** check-in 4 pm. **Amenities:** dual phone lines, voice mail, irons, hair dryers. *Fee:* video library, high-speed Internet, safes. **Pool(s):** heated outdoor. **Leisure Activities:** whirlpool, exercise room. *Fee:* game room. **Guest Services:** valet and coin laundry, area transportation. **Business Services:** fax (fee). **Cards:** AX, CB, DC, DS, JC, MC, VI.

SOME UNITS

FAIRFIELD INN AT MARRIOTT VILLAGE   *Book at aaa.com*   Phone: (407)938-9001 **23**
All Year [CP]   1P: $65-$116   2P: $65-$116
Location: I-4, exit 68, e on SR 535 to Vineland Ave. 8623 Vineland Ave 32821. Fax: 407/938-9002. **Facility:** 388 one-bedroom standard units. 5 stories, interior corridors. *Bath:* combo or shower only. **Parking:** on-site.
Terms: cancellation fee imposed, package plans. **Amenities:** video games (fee), dual phone lines, voice
Small-scale Hotel   mail, irons, hair dryers. **Pool(s):** heated outdoor. **Leisure Activities:** whirlpool, exercise room. *Fee:* game room. **Guest Services:** valet and coin laundry. **Business Services:** fax (fee). **Cards:** AX, CB, DC, DS, JC, MC, VI. **Special Amenities:** free continental breakfast and free local telephone calls. *(See color ad below)*

SOME UNITS

(See map and index starting on p. 668)

GROSVENOR RESORT AT WALT DISNEY WORLD
RESORT *Book at aaa.com*   Phone: (407)828-4444 **35**

12/22-4/22	1P: $89-$145	2P: $89-$145	XP: $18 F18
4/23-11/30	1P: $79-$125	2P: $79-$125	XP: $18 F18
12/1-12/21	1P: $69-$89	2P: $69-$89	XP: $18 F18

Location: I-4, exit 68. Located opposite Disney Marketplace. 1850 Hotel Plaza Blvd 32830. Fax: 407/828-8192.
Large-scale Hotel **Facility:** 626 one-bedroom standard units. 5-19 stories, interior/exterior corridors. *Bath:* combo or shower only. **Parking:** on-site. **Terms:** 5 day cancellation notice-fee imposed, [AP], [BP] & [CP] meal plans available, package plans, 5% service charge. **Amenities:** video games, voice mail, irons, hair dryers. *Fee:* video library, safes. **Dining:** 3 restaurants, 24 hours, cocktails. **Pool(s):** 2 heated outdoor, wading. **Leisure Activities:** whirlpool, 2 lighted tennis courts, playground, exercise room, sports court, shuffleboard, volleyball. *Fee:* tennis equipment, game room. **Guest Services:** gift shop, valet and coin laundry, area transportation-Disney. **Business Services:** conference facilities, business center. **Cards:** AX, CB, DC, JC, MC, VI. *(See color ad below)*

SOME UNITS

HAMPTON INN LAKE BUENA VISTA *Book at aaa.com*   Phone: (407)465-8150 **11**

All Year [BP]	1P: $59-$169	2P: $59-$169

Location: I-4, exit 68, 0.6 mi n on SR 535, then 0.6 mi e. 8150 Palm Pkwy 32836. Fax: 407/465-0150. **Facility:** 147 one-bedroom standard units. 5 stories, interior corridors. *Bath:* combo or shower only. **Parking:** on-site.
Small-scale Hotel dryers. **Pool(s):** small outdoor. **Leisure Activities:** whirlpool, exercise room. **Guest Services:** valet laundry, area transportation-Disney. **Business Services:** fax (fee). **Cards:** AX, DC, DS, MC, VI. **Special Amenities:** free full breakfast and free local telephone calls. *(See color ad p 693 & p 712)*

SOME UNITS

HAWTHORN SUITES HOTEL LAKE BUENA VISTA *Book at aaa.com*   Phone: (407)597-5000 **13**

2/10-4/22	1P: $139-$179	2P: $139-$179
12/1-2/9 & 4/23-8/19	1P: $109-$179	2P: $109-$179
8/20-11/30	1P: $99-$159	2P: $99-$159

Location: I-4, exit 68, 0.6 mi n on SR 535, then 0.8 mi e. 8303 Palm Pkwy 32836. Fax: 407/597-6000. **Facility:** 120 units. 8 stories, interior corridors. **Terms:** cancellation fee imposed. **Amenities:** video games (fee), dual phone lines, voice mail, irons, hair dryers. **Pool(s):** outdoor. **Leisure Activities:** whirlpool, exercise room, basketball. **Guest Services:** gift shop, complimentary evening beverages: Mon-Thurs, valet and coin laundry, area transportation-Disney. **Business Services:** meeting rooms, fax (fee). **Cards:** AX, DS, MC, VI. **Special Amenities:** free full breakfast.
(See color ad p 693)

SOME UNITS

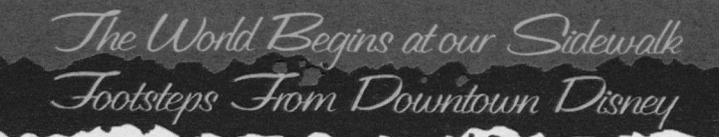

(See map and index starting on p. 668)

HILTON IN THE WALT DISNEY WORLD RESORT

Book at aaa.com

Phone: (407)827-4000

 SAVE   All Year   1P: $99-$299   2P: $109-$299   XP: $20   F18
Location: I-4, exit 68. 1751 Hotel Plaza Blvd 32830 (PO Box 22781). Fax: 407/827-3890. **Facility:** Close to tourist attractions, shopping and restaurants, this full-service hotel offers many conveniences. 814 units. 813 one-bedroom standard units. 1 two-bedroom suite with efficiency. 10 stories, interior corridors. *Bath:* combo or shower only. **Parking:** on-site. **Terms:** 5 day cancellation notice-fee imposed, package plans.
Large-scale Hotel   **Amenities:** dual phone lines, voice mail, safes, honor bars, irons, hair dryers. *Fee:* video games, high-speed Internet. *Some:* DVD players, CD players. **Dining:** 4 restaurants, 24 hours, cocktails, also, Finn's Grill, see separate listing, entertainment. **Pool(s):** 2 heated outdoor, wading. **Leisure Activities:** whirlpools, recreation programs. *Fee:* massage, game room. **Guest Services:** gift shop, valet and coin laundry, area transportation-within Disney complex. **Business Services:** conference facilities, business center. **Cards:** AX, CB, DC, DS, JC, MC, VI. **Special Amenities:** free newspaper.

HOLIDAY INN-IN THE WALT DISNEY WORLD RESORT

Phone: (407)828-8888   33

 SAVE   1/2-4/30   1P: $139-$179
[fyi]   12/1-1/1   1P: $129-$179
   10/1-11/30   1P: $119-$159
   5/1-9/30   1P: $89-$139
Small-scale Hotel   Under major renovation, scheduled to be completed June 2005. **Last rated:** Location: I-4, exit 68, just n. 1805 Hotel Plaza Blvd 32830 (PO Box 22204). Fax: 407/827-4623. **Facility:** 323 one-bedroom standard units. 6-14 stories, interior corridors. *Bath:* combo or shower only. **Parking:** on-site. **Terms:** check-in 4 pm, cancellation fee imposed, package plans. **Amenities:** video games, high-speed Internet (fee), voice mail, safes, irons, hair dryers. **Dining:** 2 restaurants, 6:30 am-midnight, cocktails. **Pool(s):** 2 heated outdoor, wading. **Leisure Activities:** whirlpool, playground, exercise room. *Fee:* game room. **Guest Services:** gift shop, valet and coin laundry, area transportation-major attractions. **Business Services:** meeting rooms, fax (fee). **Cards:** AX, DC, DS, MC, VI. **Special Amenities:** free newspaper and free room upgrade (subject to availability with advance reservations). *(See color ad below)*

(See map and index starting on p. 668)

HOLIDAY INN-SUNSPREE RESORT-LAKE BUENA VISTA *Book at aaa.com*

AAA SAVE	4/7-8/18	1P: $89-$129	2P: $89-$129
	12/1-4/6 & 8/19-11/30	1P: $79-$109	2P: $79-$109

Phone: (407)239-4500   **37**
XP: $10   F17
XP: $10   F17

Large-scale Hotel

Location: I-4, exit 68, 0.3 mi se. 13351 SR 535 32821. Fax: 407/239-8463. **Facility:** 507 one-bedroom standard units. 6 stories, exterior corridors. *Bath:* combo or shower only. **Parking:** on-site. **Terms:** check-in 4 pm, [AP] meal plan available, $5 service charge, small pets only ($25 fee). **Amenities:** video library (fee), high-speed Internet, voice mail, safes, irons, hair dryers. *Some:* video games (fee). **Dining:** 7 am-11 pm, cocktails. **Pool(s):** heated outdoor, wading. **Leisure Activities:** whirlpools, recreation programs, family movie theater, playground, exercise room, basketball. *Fee:* game room. **Guest Services:** gift shop, valet and coin laundry, area transportation-Disney. **Business Services:** meeting rooms, fax (fee). **Cards:** AX, CB, DC, DS, JC, MC, VI. **Special Amenities:** free local telephone calls and free newspaper. *(See color ad below)*

SOME UNITS

(See map and index starting on p. 668)

HOMEWOOD SUITES HOTEL BY HILTON-LAKE BUENA VISTA *Book at aaa.com*   Phone: (407)465-8200 **12**

(AAA) (SAVE)
▼▼▼

All Year [BP]   1P: $99-$169
Location: I-4, exit 68, 0.6 mi n on SR 535, then 0.5 mi e. 8200 Palm Pkwy 32836. Fax: 407/465-0200. **Facility:** 123 units. 120 one- and 3 two-bedroom suites ($99-$169) with kitchens. 4 stories, interior corridors. *Bath:* combo or shower only. **Parking:** on-site. **Amenities:** high-speed Internet, dual phone lines, voice mail, irons, hair dryers. **Pool(s):** outdoor. **Leisure Activities:** whirlpool, grills, jogging, exercise room. *Fee:* game room. **Guest Services:** gift shop, complimentary evening beverages: Mon-Thurs, valet and coin laundry, area transportation-Disney. **Business Services:** meeting rooms, business center. **Cards:** AX, DC, DS, MC, VI. **Special Amenities: free full breakfast and free local telephone calls.** *(See color ad p 693)*

Small-scale Hotel

SOME UNITS

 (icon row)

HOTEL ROYAL PLAZA IN THE DISNEY WORLD RESORT *Book at aaa.com*   Phone: (407)828-2828 **31**

(AAA) (SAVE)
▼▼▼

All Year   1P: $85-$215   2P: $85-$215
Location: Sw jct I-4 and SR 535. Located in Disney World Village. 1905 Hotel Plaza Blvd 32830. Fax: 407/827-6338. **Facility:** 394 units. 371 one-bedroom standard units, some with whirlpools. 23 one-bedroom suites with whirlpools. 2-16 stories, interior corridors. *Bath:* combo or shower only. **Parking:** on-site and valet. **Terms:** check-in 4 pm, 3 day cancellation notice-fee imposed, package plans, $8 service charge. **Amenities:** video games (fee), voice mail, safes, honor bars, irons, hair dryers. *Some:* high-speed Internet, dual phone lines. **Dining:** 6:30 am-11 pm, cocktails. **Pool(s):** heated outdoor. **Leisure Activities:** whirlpool, 4 lighted tennis courts, exercise room. **Guest Services:** gift shop, valet and coin laundry, area transportation-Disney. **Business Services:** meeting rooms, business center. **Cards:** AX, CB, DC, DS, JC, MC, VI. *(See color ad below)*

Large-scale Hotel

SOME UNITS

FEE

 (icon row)

(See map and index starting on p. 668)

HYATT REGENCY GRAND CYPRESS *Book at aaa.com*   Phone: (407)239-1234   **22**

12/1-5/31 & 10/1-11/30	1P: $255-$385	2P: $255-$385	XP: $25	F18
6/1-9/30	1P: $199-$295	2P: $199-$295	XP: $25	F18

Location: I-4, exit 68, just w on SR 535; near entrance to Walt Disney World Village. 1 Grand Cypress Blvd 32836. Fax: 407/239-3800. **Facility:** A dramatic atrium lobby is featured at this property offering fine facilities and

Resort extensive landscaped grounds; activities include golf and horseback riding. 750 units. 745 one-bedroom

Large-scale Hotel standard units. 5 one-bedroom suites. 18 stories, interior corridors. *Bath:* combo or shower only. **Parking:** on-site and valet. **Terms:** check-in 4 pm, 3 day cancellation notice-fee imposed, $13 service charge. **Amenities:** video games, high-speed Internet, dual phone lines, voice mail, safes, honor bars, irons, hair dryers. **Dining:** 3 restaurants, 24 hours, cocktails, entertainment. **Pool(s):** 2 outdoor, heated outdoor. **Leisure Activities:** saunas, whirlpools, rental boats, rental canoes, rental paddleboats, rental sailboats, racquetball courts, recreation programs, rental bicycles, playground, basketball, volleyball. *Fee:* golf-45 holes, 12 tennis courts (5 lighted), horseback riding, game room. **Guest Services:** gift shop, valet laundry, area transportation-major attractions. **Business Services:** conference facilities, business center. **Cards:** AX, CB, DC, DS, JC, MC, VI. *(See color ad p 811)*

SOME UNITS

NICKELODEON FAMILY SUITES BY HOLIDAY INN *Book at aaa.com*   Phone: (407)387-5437   **54**

All Year	1P: $160-$275	2P: $160-$275

Location: I-4, exit 67, 0.5 mi e on SR 536. 14500 Continental Gateway 32821. Fax: 407/387-1489. **Facility:** 789 units. 85 one-, 693 two- and 11 three-bedroom suites ($160-$275), some with kitchens and/or whirlpools. 6 stories, exterior corridors. *Bath:* combo or shower only. **Parking:** on-site. **Terms:** check-in 4 pm, 3 day

Large-scale Hotel cancellation notice-fee imposed. **Amenities:** high-speed Internet, dual phone lines, voice mail, safes, irons, hair dryers. *Fee:* video library, video games. *Some:* CD players. **Dining:** 6:30 am-midnight. **Pool(s):** 2 heated outdoor. **Leisure Activities:** whirlpools, waterslide, recreation programs, kiddie train, playground, exercise room, shuffleboard. *Fee:* game room. **Guest Services:** gift shop, valet and coin laundry, area transportation-Disney. **Business Services:** meeting rooms, business center. **Cards:** AX, CB, DC, DS, JC, MC, VI. *(See color ad below)*

SOME UNITS

THREE LETTERS.
FOUR DIAMONDS.
ONE AMAZING DISCOUNT.

With Disney next door, Jack Nicklaus-designed golf, tropical pools and lagoons, tennis courts and an equestrian center, the Hyatt Regency Grand Cypress is Orlando's 4-diamond family paradise. Call and request our special AAA rate, show your AAA card when you check in and enjoy the perfect family vacation for less. This is not your typical hotel story. This is the Hyatt touch. Call 800-55 HYATT or visit **hyattgrandcypress.com** for more information.

One Grand Cypress Boulevard
Orlando, FL

UPGRADE YOUR VACATION.

Enjoy deluxe accommodations with significant savings exclusively for AAA members. Located inside the main terminal of the Orlando International Airport, the Hyatt Regency provides the most convenient location for leisure and business travelers. With airline gates just five minutes from your door and wireless high-speed Internet, the hotel is ideal for frequent travelers and cruise passengers. Simply request the AAA member rate and present your card at check-in. This is not your typical hotel story. This is the Hyatt Touch.™ For reservations call 800 532 1496 or visit **orlandoairport.hyatt.com**.

(See map and index starting on p. 668)

ORLANDO WORLD CENTER MARRIOTT RESORT & CONVENTION CENTER   *Book at aaa.com*
Phone: 407/239-4200   **51**

(AAA) (SAVE)
▼▼▼▼

	9/5-11/30	1P: $219-$329	2P: $219-$329
	1/5-4/9	1P: $199-$329	2P: $199-$329
	12/1-1/4	1P: $169-$299	2P: $169-$299
	4/10-9/4	1P: $199-$259	2P: $199-$259

Resort
Large-scale Hotel

Location: I-4, exit 67, 0.5 mi e on SR 536. 8701 World Center Dr 32821. Fax: 407/238-8777. **Facility:** A full-service spa is a highlight at this hotel, which features expansive grounds and a range of accommodations spread over several sections. 2000 units. 1954 one-bedroom standard units, some with whirlpools. 46 one-bedroom suites. 28 stories, interior corridors. *Bath:* combo or shower only. **Parking:** on-site and valet. **Terms:** check-in 4 pm, cancellation fee imposed, package plans. **Amenities:** dual phone lines, voice mail, safes, honor bars, irons, hair dryers. *Fee:* video library, video games, high-speed Internet. **Dining:** 7 restaurants, 24 hours, cocktails, entertainment. **Pool(s):** 3 heated outdoor, heated indoor, 2 wading. **Leisure Activities:** saunas, whirlpools, steamrooms, 4 lighted tennis courts, recreation programs, playground, exercise room, spa, sports court, basketball, volleyball. *Fee:* golf-18 holes, golf and tennis instruction & equipment, driving range, game room. **Guest Services:** gift shop, valet and coin laundry, area transportation (fee)-major attractions. **Business Services:** conference facilities, business center. **Cards:** AX, CB, DC, DS, JC, MC, VI. *(See color ad below)*

SOME UNITS

[icons] ✈ 🍴 24 ⓘ &M 🛗 🕐 🏊 ✕ 📷 DATA PORT 🖥 / ✕ VCR 📠 /
FEE   FEE

PERRIHOUSE BED & BREAKFAST INN
Phone: (407)876-4830   **1**

▼▼▼

| | All Year | 1P: $89 | 2P: $149 |

Bed & Breakfast

Location: I-4, exit 68, 3.4 mi n on SR 535. Located adjacent to the Grand Cypress Equestrian Center. 10417 Vista Oaks Ct 32836. Fax: 407/909-1294. **Facility:** A natural setting is the backdrop for this modern home where each guest unit has an exterior entrance as well as a doorway to the common area. Smoke free premises. 8 one-bedroom standard units. 1 story, interior/exterior corridors. **Parking:** on-site. **Terms:** 3 day cancellation notice, [ECP] meal plan available, package plans. **Amenities:** CD players, voice mail, hair dryers. **Pool(s):** outdoor. **Leisure Activities:** whirlpool. **Business Services:** fax (fee). **Cards:** AX, CB, DS, MC, VI.

ASK S/D 🏊 ✕ VCR

RADISSON INN LAKE BUENA VISTA   *Book at aaa.com*
Phone: (407)239-8400   **20**

▼▼▼

| | All Year | 1P: $79-$159 | 2P: $79-$159 |

Small-scale Hotel

Location: I-4, exit 68, 0.5 mi n on CR 535, then 0.3 mi e. 8686 Palm Pkwy 32836. Fax: 407/239-8025. **Facility:** 200 one-bedroom standard units. 7 stories, interior corridors. *Bath:* combo or shower only. **Parking:** on-site. **Terms:** cancellation fee imposed. **Amenities:** dual phone lines, voice mail, irons, hair dryers. *Fee:* video library, high-speed Internet. **Pool(s):** heated outdoor. **Leisure Activities:** whirlpool, waterslide, playground, exercise room. *Fee:* game room. **Guest Services:** gift shop, valet laundry, area transportation. **Business Services:** fax (fee). **Cards:** AX, DC, DS, MC, VI.

SOME UNITS

ASK S/D 🍴 🍸 🕐 🏊 ✕ DATA PORT 🖥 / ✕ 📠 /

SHERATON SAFARI HOTEL   *Book at aaa.com*
Phone: (407)239-0444   **18**

(AAA) (SAVE)
▼▼▼

	2/17-4/22	1P: $139-$249	2P: $139-$249
	9/29-11/30	1P: $119-$229	2P: $119-$229
	12/1-2/16	1P: $119-$199	2P: $119-$199
	4/23-9/28	1P: $109-$199	2P: $109-$199

Small-scale Hotel

Location: I-4, exit 68, 0.5 mi n on SR 535. 12205 Apopka-Vineland Rd 32836. Fax: 407/239-1778. **Facility:** 489 units. 393 one-bedroom standard units. 96 one-bedroom suites ($159-$279), some with kitchens. 6 stories, interior/exterior corridors. *Bath:* combo or shower only. **Parking:** on-site. **Terms:** 3 day cancellation notice-fee imposed. **Amenities:** dual phone lines, voice mail, irons, hair dryers. *Fee:* video games, high-speed Internet, safes. **Dining:** 6:30 am-10 pm, cocktails. **Pool(s):** heated outdoor, wading. **Leisure Activities:** whirlpool, waterslide, playground, exercise room. *Fee:* game room. **Guest Services:** gift shop, valet and coin laundry, area transportation-Disney. **Business Services:** conference facilities, business center. **Cards:** AX, DC, DS, JC, MC, VI. *(See color ad p 813)*

SOME UNITS

S/D 🛏 🍴 🍸 &M 🛗 🕐 🏊 ✕ VCR 🎬 DATA PORT 🖥 / ✕ 📠 🖨 /

(See map and index starting on p. 668)

SHERATON'S VISTANA RESORT   **Book at aaa.com**   Phone: (407)239-3100   **42**

▼▼▼▼ All Year   2P: $259
       Location: I-4, exit 68, 0.6 mi s. 8800 Vistana Centre Dr 32821. Fax: 407/239-3111. **Facility:** This extensive
Condominium complex is near major attractions; all units have washer/dryers. 200 units. 100 one- and 100 two-bedroom
       suites with kitchens, some with whirlpools. 3-5 stories, exterior corridors. *Bath:* combo or shower only.
Parking: on-site. **Terms:** check-in 4 pm, 3 day cancellation notice-fee imposed. **Amenities:** video library (fee), voice mail, irons,
hair dryers. *Some:* CD players. **Pool(s):** 7 heated outdoor, 6 wading. **Leisure Activities:** saunas, whirlpools, steamrooms, 13
lighted tennis courts, recreation programs, rental bicycles, jogging, playground, basketball, shuffleboard, volleyball. *Fee:*
miniature golf, massage, game room. **Guest Services:** gift shop, complimentary laundry, area transportation. **Business
Services:** business center. **Cards:** AX, DC, DS, MC, VI. *(See color ad p 8 & p 688)*

(See map and index starting on p. 668)

SPRINGHILL SUITES AT THE MARRIOTT VILLAGE *Book at aaa.com* **Phone:** (407)938-9001 **25**

All Year [ECP] 1P: $79-$129 2P: $79-$129
Location: I-4, exit 68, just e, then n on SR 535. 8623 Vineland Ave 32821. Fax: 407/938-9002. **Facility:** 400 one-bedroom suites. 5 stories, interior corridors. *Bath:* combo or shower only. **Parking:** on-site. **Terms:** cancellation fee imposed, package plans. **Amenities:** video games, high-speed Internet, dual phone lines, voice mail, irons, hair dryers. **Pool(s):** heated outdoor. **Leisure Activities:** whirlpool, exercise room.
Small-scale Hotel
Guest Services: valet and coin laundry. **Business Services:** meeting rooms, fax (fee). **Cards:** AX, CB, DC, DS, JC, MC, VI. **Special Amenities: free expanded continental breakfast and free local telephone calls.**
(See color ad p 813)

SOME UNITS

STAYBRIDGE SUITES/LAKE BUENA VISTA *Book at aaa.com* **Phone:** (407)238-0777 **10**

All Year 1P: $129-$219 2P: $149-$269
Location: I-4, exit 68, 0.8 mi n. 8751 Suiteside Dr 32836. Fax: 407/238-2640. **Facility:** 150 units. 47 one- and 103 two-bedroom suites, some with efficiencies or kitchens. 3 stories (no elevator), interior/exterior corridors. *Bath:* combo or shower only. **Parking:** on-site. **Terms:** check-in 4 pm, 3 day cancellation notice-fee imposed. [ECP] meal plan available, package plans. **Amenities:** voice mail, irons,
Small-scale Hotel
hair dryers. *Fee:* video library, high-speed Internet, safes. *Some:* dual phone lines. **Pool(s):** heated outdoor, wading. **Leisure Activities:** whirlpool, exercise room. *Fee:* game room. **Guest Services:** gift shop, valet and coin laundry, area transportation-Disney. **Business Services:** meeting rooms, fax (fee). **Cards:** AX, DC, DS, MC, VI. **Special Amenities: free expanded continental breakfast and free newspaper.** *(See color ad below)*

SOME UNITS

THE VILLAS AT DISNEY'S WILDERNESS LODGE *Book at aaa.com* **Phone:** (407)824-3200 **4**

12/1-12/31	1P: $284-$1015	2P: $284-$1015
2/16-7/4	1P: $335-$890	2P: $335-$890
7/5-11/30	1P: $295-$735	2P: $295-$735
1/1-2/15	1P: $295-$570	2P: $295-$570

Resort
Large-scale Hotel
Location: I-4, exit 67, follow signs to Disney's Magic Kingdom Park; in Walt Disney World. 901 W Timberline Dr 32830 (PO Box 10000). Fax: 407/824-3232. **Facility:** Set on the edge of a forest of cypress and slash pine, this resort is inspired by Yellowstone National Park. 181 units. 65 one-bedroom standard units with efficiencies. 72 one- and 44 two-bedroom suites with kitchens and whirlpools. 5 stories, interior corridors. *Bath:* combo or shower only. **Parking:** on-site and valet. **Terms:** check-in 4 pm, 6 day cancellation notice-fee imposed, package plans. **Amenities:** high-speed Internet (fee), voice mail, safes, irons, hair dryers. **Dining:** Shares food & beverage facilities with Disney's Wilderness Lodge. **Leisure Activities:** shared leisure activities and recreational facilities with Disney's Wilderness Lodge. **Guest Services:** gift shop, complimentary laundry, area transportation-within Disney complex. **Business Services:** business center. **Cards:** AX, DC, DS, JC, MC, VI. *(See color ad starting on p 795)*

SOME UNITS

FEE

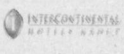

(See map and index starting on p. 668)

WALT DISNEY WORLD DOLPHIN   *Book at aaa.com*   Phone: (407)934-4000   43

(AAA) **(SAVE)**

Resort
Large-scale Hotel

All Year   1P: $339-$499   2P: $339-$499   XP: $25   F
Location: I-4, exit 67, follow Epcot Resort area signs; 0.3 mi e of Walt Disney World Resort; 2 mi n of US 192. 1500 Epcot Resorts Blvd 32830 (PO Box 22786). Fax: 407/934-4884. **Facility:** Extensive seaside theme. "Entertainment" architecture. 1509 units. 1373 one-bedroom standard units. 136 one-bedroom suites. 25 stories, interior corridors. *Bath:* combo or shower only. **Parking:** on-site (fee) and valet. **Terms:** 5 day cancellation notice-fee imposed, $10 service charge. **Amenities:** dual phone lines, voice mail, safes, honor bars, irons, hair dryers. *Fee:* video games, high-speed Internet. **Dining:** 6 restaurants, 24 hours, cocktails, also, Shula's Steak House, Todd English's Bluezoo, see separate listings, entertainment. **Pool(s):** 2 outdoor, heated outdoor, wading. **Leisure Activities:** saunas, whirlpools, recreation programs, playground, exercise room, spa, basketball, volleyball. *Fee:* paddleboats, game room. **Guest Services:** gift shop, valet and coin laundry, area transportation-within Disney complex. **Business Services:** conference facilities, business center. **Cards:** AX, CB, DC, DS, JC, MC, VI. *(See color ad p 8)*

SOME UNITS

WALT DISNEY WORLD SWAN   *Book at aaa.com*   Phone: (407)934-3000   46

(AAA) **(SAVE)**

Resort
Large-scale Hotel

All Year   1P: $339-$499   2P: $339-$499   XP: $25   F
Location: I-4, exit 67, follow Epcot Resort area signs; 0.3 mi e of Walt Disney World Resort main gate access road; 2 mi n of US 192. 1200 Epcot Resorts Blvd 32830. Fax: 407/934-4884. **Facility:** The hotel complex, which includes a glass pyramid surrounded by pastel masonry buildings, offers numerous restaurants and meeting facilities. 756 units. 701 one-bedroom standard units. 55 one-bedroom suites, some with whirlpools. 12 stories, interior corridors. *Bath:* combo or shower only. **Parking:** on-site (fee) and valet. **Terms:** 5 day cancellation notice-fee imposed, $10 service charge. **Amenities:** dual phone lines, voice mail, safes, honor bars, irons, hair dryers. *Fee:* video games, high-speed Internet. **Dining:** 5 restaurants, 24 hours, cocktails, also, Palio, see separate listing. **Pool(s):** heated outdoor. **Leisure Activities:** whirlpool, exercise room, basketball. *Fee:* massage, game room. **Guest Services:** gift shop, valet laundry, area transportation-within Disney complex. **Business Services:** conference facilities, business center. **Cards:** AX, CB, DC, DS, JC, MC, VI. *(See color ad p 8)*

SOME UNITS

WESTGATE BLUE TREE AT LAKE BUENA VISTA   *Book at aaa.com*   Phone: 407/597-2200   14

(AAA) **(SAVE)**

Small-scale Hotel

All Year   1P: $89-$189
Location: I-4, exit 68, 0.5 mi n on SR 535, just n on Apopka-Vineland Rd, then just e on Vining's Way Blvd. 12007 Cypress Run Rd 32836. Fax: 407/355-2979. **Facility:** 394 units. 104 one- and 290 two-bedroom suites ($159-$279) with kitchens, some with whirlpools. 3 stories (no elevator). Exterior corridors. **Parking:** on-site. **Terms:** check-in 4 pm, 7 day cancellation notice, pets ($50 deposit, limit 1). **Amenities:** video library (fee), voice mail, irons, hair dryers. **Pool(s):** 2 outdoor, 2 heated outdoor, wading. **Leisure Activities:** whirlpools, miniature golf, lighted tennis court, recreation programs, ping pong, exercise room, basketball, horseshoes, shuffleboard, volleyball. *Fee:* game room. **Guest Services:** coin laundry. **Business Services:** fax (fee). **Cards:** AX, DC, DS, MC, VI. *(See color ad p 734)*

WYNDHAM PALACE RESORT & SPA IN THE WALT DISNEY WORLD (R) RESORT   *Book at aaa.com*   Phone: (407)827-2727   32

(AAA) **(SAVE)**

Large-scale Hotel

1/1-4/22	1P: $169-$219	2P: $169-$219	XP: $10	F17
10/4-11/30	1P: $149-$189	2P: $149-$189	XP: $10	F17
4/23-10/3	1P: $119-$159	2P: $119-$159	XP: $10	F17
12/1-12/31	1P: $119-$149	2P: $119-$149	XP: $10	F17

Location: I-4, exit 68, just n on SR 535 to Hotel Plaza Blvd (Walt Disney World Resort), 0.7 mi sw, then just nw. 1900 Buena Vista Dr 32830. Fax: 407/827-6034. **Facility:** 1012 units. 884 one-bedroom standard units, some with whirlpools. 128 one-bedroom suites ($179-$299), some with whirlpools. 6-27 stories, interior corridors. *Bath:* combo or shower only. **Parking:** on-site and valet. **Terms:** 3 day cancellation notice, $10 service charge. **Amenities:** dual phone lines, voice mail, safes, honor bars, irons, hair dryers. *Fee:* video games, high-speed Internet. **Dining:** 3 restaurants, 24 hours, cocktails, also, Arthur's 27, see separate listing, nightclub, entertainment. **Pool(s):** 3 heated outdoor, wading. **Leisure Activities:** saunas, whirlpools, lighted tennis court, spa, volleyball. *Fee:* game room. **Guest Services:** gift shop, valet and coin laundry, area transportation-Disney. **Business Services:** conference facilities, business center. **Cards:** AX, CB, DC, DS, JC, MC, VI.

SOME UNITS

-------- **WHERE TO DINE** --------

ARTIST POINT   Dinner: $24-$34   Phone: 407/939-3463   10

Regional American

Location: I-4, exit 67, follow signs to Disney's Magic Kingdom; in Walt Disney World; in Disney's Wilderness Lodge. 901 W Timberline Dr 32830. **Hours:** 5:30 pm-10 pm. **Reservations:** suggested. **Features:** Bring the kids to the character breakfast and enjoy folksy service in a lodge setting. A selection of Northwestern steak and seafood favorites and vegetarian dishes are cooked over an open hardwood fire. Fresh ingredients and homemade desserts make this a delicious find. Casual dress; cocktails. **Parking:** valet. **Cards:** AX, DC, DS, JC, MC, VI.

(See map and index starting on p. 668)

ASIAN HARBOR

Asian

Lunch: $6-$10   **Dinner:** $15-$30   **Phone:** 407/238-9998   ③⑦
Location: I-4, exit 67, 1.4 mi e, jct SR 535 and 536. 8216A World Center Dr 32821. **Hours:** 11:30 am-11 pm. **Features:** In a small shopping plaza, the Asian restaurant has combination platters and two-person dinners that feature the best of menu selections. Casual dress; cocktails. **Parking:** on-site. **Cards:** AX, CB, DC, DS, JC, MC, VI.

BAHAMA BREEZE

Caribbean

Lunch: $6-$24   **Dinner:** $6-$24   **Phone:** 407/938-9010   ㉒
Location: I-4, exit 68, 0.3 mi e. 8735 Vineland Ave 32821. **Hours:** 11 am-1 am, Fri & Sat-1:30 am. Closed: 11/23, 12/25. **Features:** Catering to those who seek an exciting evening out, the restaurant captures the sights, sounds and sensations of the Caribbean. Such delicious food as fresh mahi mahi and Key lime pie is served. A full bar and live entertainment add to the atmosphere. Casual dress; cocktails. **Parking:** on-site. **Cards:** AX, CB, DC, DS, JC, MC, VI.

⏛

BLACK ANGUS STEAKHOUSE

Steak House

Lunch: $6-$30   **Dinner:** $6-$30   **Phone:** 407/239-4414   ⑯
Location: I-4, exit 68 (SR 535), 0.5 mi n. 12399 SR 535 32836. **Hours:** 11 am-11 pm. Closed major holidays. **Features:** Besides USDA Prime or Choice beef cuts, the Disney-area steakhouse tempts guests with a large selection of fresh seafood. Casual dress; cocktails. **Parking:** on-site. **Cards:** AX, MC, VI.

⏛ ◥

BOATWRIGHT'S DINING HALL

South American

Dinner: $12-$24   **Phone:** 407/934-5422   ⑳
Location: I-4, exit 67, just nw, follow signs to Downtown Disney; in Disney's Port Orleans-Riverside Resort. 1251 Riverside Dr 32830. **Hours:** 7 am-11:30 & 5-10 pm. **Reservations:** suggested. **Features:** Traditional and unique American, Southern and Cajun specialties are offered in Dixie Landing's restored boat building warehouse along the Sassagoula River. Boat transportation to and from Downtown Disney and Pleasure Island is available. Casual dress; cocktails; entertainment. **Parking:** on-site. **Cards:** AX, DC, DS, MC, VI.

♿ ⏛

BONGOS CUBAN CAFE

Cuban

Lunch: $9-$20   **Dinner:** $12-$26   **Phone:** 407/828-0999   ㉘
Location: In Downtown Disney. 1498 E Buena Vista Dr 32830. **Hours:** 11 am-11 pm. **Features:** In an old Havana setting, the restaurant displays the flair of traditionally Cuban South Beach. On the menu is an enticing mix of soups and sandwiches as well as chicken, pork and beef preparations. A favorite is churrasco, a skirt steak marinated in a Cuban sauce. Casual dress; cocktails. **Parking:** on-site. **Cards:** AX, MC, VI.

♿ ⏛

CALIFORNIA GRILL

Regional American

Dinner: $20-$35   **Phone:** 407/824-1576   ⑥
Location: I-4, exit 67, follow signs to Disney's Magic Kingdom; in Walt Disney World; in Disney's Contemporary Resort. 4600 W World Dr 32830. **Hours:** 5:30 pm-10 pm. **Reservations:** suggested. **Features:** This is a full service, fine dining restaurant appealing to adults, particularly those with an appetite for innovative concepts in food. The menu is revised weekly but it consistently offers sophisticated, cutting edge California dishes with Pacific Rim influences throughout. House specialties include flatbread appetizers baked in a brick oven, sushi, sashimi and some vegetarian dishes. The wine list is primarily California vintages. Casual dress; cocktails. **Parking:** on-site. **Cards:** AX, DC, DS, JC, MC, VI.

♿ ⏛

CINDERELLA'S ROYAL TABLE

American

Lunch: $11-$16   **Dinner:** $19-$26   **Phone:** 407/939-3463   ①
Location: In Walt Disney World's Magic Kingdom. **Hours:** 8-10 am, 11:30-2:55 & 4-9 pm; closing hours may vary. **Reservations:** required. **Features:** Diners can experience the grandeur of royalty from a setting inside the legendary Cinderella's castle. The menu features prime rib, beef pie, roast chicken, barbecue and other comfort foods. Particularly popular for its Disney character breakfast, the eatery is a favorite dining spot in the Magic Kingdom. Casual dress. **Parking:** on-site (fee). **Cards:** AX, DS, MC, VI.

CITRICOS

Nouvelle French

Dinner: $19-$32   **Phone:** 407/939-3463   ⑨
Location: 8 mi nw of jct I-4 and US 192; in Disney's Grand Floridian Resort & Spa. 4401 Grand Floridian Way 32830. **Hours:** 5:30 pm-10 pm. Closed: Mon & Tues. **Reservations:** accepted. **Features:** Wonderful open kitchen with fusion of French and Mediterranean styles of cooking and decor, soft lighting and warm service top off the evening. Entrees range from seafood to roast leg of lamb and duck. A chef's vegetarian special and wine pairing is available. Dressy casual; cocktails. **Parking:** on-site. **Cards:** AX, CB, DC, DS, JC, MC, VI.

♿ ⏛

CRAB HOUSE SEAFOOD RESTAURANT

Seafood

Lunch: $9-$22   **Dinner:** $14-$25   **Phone:** 407/239-1888   ⑬
Location: I-4, exit 68, 0.5 mi n off SR 535; in Vista Center. 8496 Palm Pkwy 32836. **Hours:** 11:30 am-11 pm. **Features:** Featuring casual family dining amid a nautical decor, this is the place for an abundance of crab and other seafood choices. For a fresh taste of the ocean, try the shrimp scampi with rice pilaf. A self-serve salad bar completes a delicious meal. Casual dress; cocktails. **Parking:** on-site. **Cards:** AX, CB, DC, DS, JC, MC, VI.

⏛

THE CRYSTAL PALACE

American

Lunch: $9-$19   **Dinner:** $10-$27   **Phone:** 407/939-3463   ③
Location: In Walt Disney World's Magic Kingdom. **Hours:** 8:05-10:30 am, 11:30-2:45 & 4-9 pm; closing hours may vary. **Features:** Left of Main Street USA, this stunning, beautifully designed glass palace features a family-oriented all-you-can-eat buffet. Salad, pasta and dessert bars compliment entree selections of freshly roasted and carved meat. Disney characters appear. Casual dress. **Parking:** on-site (fee). **Cards:** AX, DC, DS, JC, MC, VI.

DAKSHIN

South Indian

Lunch: $7-$12   **Dinner:** $12-$20   **Phone:** 407/827-9080   ⑰
Location: I-4, exit 68 (SR 535), 0.3 mi n; in Crossroads Shopping Center. 12541 SR 535 32836. **Hours:** 11:30 am-2:30 & 5:30-11 pm. Closed major holidays. **Features:** To provide the best in Indian tastes, the restaurant trains its chefs in the kitchens of traditional homes and procures ingredients from original sources. Cuisines from the Tamilias of Tamil Nadu, the Malayalees of Kerala, the Bunts of Mangalore, the Portuguese of Goa and the East Indians of Mumbai are represented. Examples of menu selections include aloo paratha, dosai, uttapam, biryani, masala dosai, chicken tikka masala, cutlets and bhonda. Casual dress; beer & wine only. **Parking:** on-site. **Cards:** AX, DS, MC, VI.

♿

(See map and index starting on p. 668)

ESPN CLUB
◆◆◆
American
| Lunch: $8-$16 | Dinner: $8-$16 | Phone: 407/939-1177 | **31** |

Location: On Disney's Boardwalk. 2101 N Epcot Resorts Blvd 32830. **Hours:** 11:30 am-1 am, Fri & Sat-2 am. **Features:** With more than 100 video monitors and the tasty finger foods that go with them, sports fans will be in paradise. The signature "Red Wings" are huge and fiery hot, while the "Slider Burger" is cooked to perfection. Expect a wait during Monday Night Football. Casual dress; cocktails. **Parking:** on-site and valet.
Cards: AX, CB, DC, DS, JC, MC, VI.

FINN'S GRILL
◆◆◆
American
| Dinner: $19-$26 | Phone: 407/827-4000 | **23** |

Location: I-4, exit 68; in Hilton in the Walt Disney World Resort. 1751 Hotel Plaza Blvd 32830. **Hours:** 5:30 pm-11 pm. **Reservations:** suggested. **Features:** Kick back in an upbeat Key West atmosphere, and choose from a variety of seafood, black Angus steak, pasta and salad choices served by a professional staff. The hearty, spicy Cajun gumbo shouldn't be missed. Come in on Saturday for the excellent seafood buffet. Dressy casual; cocktails. **Parking:** on-site and valet. **Cards:** AX, CB, DC, DS, JC, MC, VI.

FLYING FISH CAFE
◆◆◆
Seafood
| Dinner: $18-$36 | Phone: 407/939-3463 | **34** |

Location: 0.5 mi e of Disney World main gate access road; 2 mi n of US 192; in Walt Disney World; in Disney's BoardWalk Resort. 2101 N Epcot Resort Blvd 32830. **Hours:** 5:30 pm-10 pm, Fri & Sat-10:30 pm. **Reservations:** suggested. **Features:** Casual dining in an eclectic decor offers fresh, seasonal specialties served from a cutting-edge open kitchen. The lobster appetizer is creatively produced. Stroll around the boardwalk after dinner to walk off those extra calories from dessert. Casual dress; cocktails. **Parking:** valet. **Cards:** AX, CB, DC, DS, JC, MC, VI.

FULTON'S CRAB HOUSE
◆◆◆
Seafood
| Lunch: $10-$18 | Dinner: $16-$47 | Phone: 407/934-2628 | **25** |

Location: Downtown Disney; between Pleasure Island and Disney Village Marketplace. 1670 Buena Vista Dr 32819. **Hours:** 11:30 am-4 & 5-11 pm. **Reservations:** suggested. **Features:** Exceptionally fresh and expertly prepared seafood is the highlight of a menu that changes daily. Alaskan king crab is a house specialty. If you experience a wait, you can enjoy a drink and savor the appetizers outside on the patio deck. Dressy casual; cocktails. **Parking:** on-site. **Cards:** AX, CB, DC, DS, JC, MC, VI.

GIORDANO'S ITALIAN RESTAURANT & PIZZERIA
◆◆◆
Italian
| Lunch: $6-$20 | Dinner: $6-$20 | Phone: 407/239-8900 | **11** |

Location: I-4, exit 68, 0.7 mi n; in Shops of Buena Vista. 12151 S Apopka Vineland Rd 32819. **Hours:** 11 am-midnight. **Features:** Chicago-style stuffed pizza is the specialty, and home delivery is an option. Traditional Italian dishes make up most of the rest of the menu. The atmosphere is friendly and casual in the family-oriented eatery. Don't skip dessert. Casual dress; cocktails. **Parking:** on-site. **Cards:** AX, DC, MC, VI.

GOURMETO'S NY PIZZA
◆
Italian
| Dinner: $3-$13 | Phone: 407/465-1818 | **38** |

Location: I-4, exit 67, 1.3 mi e; jct SR 535 and 536. 12748 SR 535 32836. **Hours:** 4 pm-4 am. Closed major holidays. **Features:** The takeout pizzeria stands apart from others in that the menu lists not only pizza and calzones but also wines, imported beers and cigars. No tables are available. Casual dress; beer & wine only. **Parking:** on-site. **Cards:** MC, VI.

HAVANA'S CAFE
◆◆
Caribbean
| Lunch: $5-$18 | Dinner: $5-$18 | Phone: 407/238-5333 | **14** |

Location: I-4, exit 68, 0.6 mi n on SR 535, then just e. 8544 Palm Pkwy 32836. **Hours:** 11 am-11 pm. Closed major holidays. **Features:** Located near the attractions and shopping, this eatery features authentic Cuban and International cuisine. Casual dress; beer & wine only. **Parking:** on-site. **Cards:** AX, MC, VI.

HAWK'S LANDING STEAKHOUSE & GRILLE
◆◆◆
Steak House
| Dinner: $14-$40 | Phone: 407/238-8829 | **35** |

Location: I-4, exit 67, 0.5 mi e on SR 536; in Orlando World Center Marriott Resort & Convention Center. 8701 World Center Dr 32821. **Hours:** 6 pm-10 pm. Closed major holidays. **Reservations:** required. **Features:** One of 10 restaurants in what is said to be the world's largest Marriott, the contemporary steakhouse overlooks a golf course. Diners can sample the finest cuts of USDA Prime beef and the freshest seafood. Semi-formal attire; cocktails. **Parking:** on-site and valet. **Cards:** AX, DC, DS, MC, VI.

INDIA PALACE
◆◆
Indian
| Lunch: $8-$16 | Dinner: $11-$16 | Phone: 407/238-2322 | **15** |

Location: I-4, exit 68, 0.5 mi n on SR 535, then 0.3 mi e; in The Shoppes at Vista Center. 8530 Palm Pkwy 32836. **Hours:** 11:30 am-2:30 & 5-11 pm, Mon from 5 pm. **Features:** Guests are invited to choose from an extensive menu of well-prepared, authentic dishes spiced to the requested level; choices include chicken, lamb and seafood specialties as well as a selection of vegetarian and rice dishes. Staff are knowledgeable about menu preparations and attentive to the guest; the casual and relaxed dining combines with prepared-to-order cuisine for a pleasurable experience. A lunch buffet is offered Tuesday through Sunday. Casual dress; beer & wine only. **Parking:** on-site. **Cards:** AX, DC, DS, MC, VI.

JIKO
◆◆◆ ◆◆◆
African
| Dinner: $18-$30 | Phone: 407/938-3000 | **39** |

Location: I-4, exit 64 or 65; n of US 192 on World Dr, follow signs; in Disney's Animal Kingdom Lodge. 2901 Osceola Pkwy 32820. **Hours:** 5:30 pm-11 pm. **Reservations:** suggested. **Features:** As African music plays in the background, a polished and knowledgeable staff attends to guests' dining needs. A highly skilled culinary staff prepares impressive and colorful offerings. The restaurant defines its food as traditional African dishes with influences from other cultures to create a cuisine described as New African. Casual dress; cocktails. **Parking:** on-site and valet. **Cards:** AX, DS, MC, VI.

LIBERTY TREE TAVERN
◆◆
American
| Lunch: $5-$15 | Dinner: $11-$23 | Phone: 407/939-3463 | **2** |

Location: In Walt Disney World's Magic Kingdom. **Hours:** call for hours. **Reservations:** suggested. **Features:** This colonial style eatery, located in Liberty Square features nightly Disney character dinners. Menu is fixed price offering a hearty selection of regal foods including salad, entree and beverage. Fresh baked desserts are extra. Casual dress. **Parking:** on-site (fee). **Cards:** AX, DS, MC, VI.

(See map and index starting on p. 668)

NARCOOSEE'S — **Dinner:** $25-$39 — **Phone:** 407/939-3463 (7)

Spanish

Location: 8 mi nw of jct I-4 and US 192; in Disney's Grand Floridian Resort & Spa. 4401 Floridian Way 32830. **Hours:** 5:30 pm-10 pm. **Reservations:** accepted. **Features:** In a lovely location on the water, the octagonal building is notable for its rotunda depicting a sea mural as well as innovative samplings of grilled salmon, tuna, chops and filets. The wine list is matched daily, and desserts should never be overlooked. Casual dress; cocktails. **Parking:** valet. **Cards:** AX, CB, DC, DS, JC, MC, VI.

NEW YORK CHINA BUFFET — **Lunch:** $5-$11 — **Dinner:** $5-$12 — **Phone:** 407/238-9198 (12)

Chinese

Location: I-4, exit 68, 0.7 mi n. 12173 S Apopka-Vineland Rd 32836. **Hours:** 11 am-10:30 pm. **Features:** In a small shopping plaza, the restaurant lays out more than 200 items on its extensive buffet. Although most choices are of Chinese cuisine, other Japanese and American selections can be sampled, as can Mongolian barbecue and sushi bar creations. Casual dress. **Parking:** on-site. **Cards:** AX, CB, DC, DS, JC, MC, VI.

PALIO — **Dinner:** $17-$32 — **Phone:** 407/939-3463 (32)

Northern Italian

Location: I-4, exit 67, follow Epcot Resort area signs; 0.3 mi e of Walt Disney World Resort main gate access road; 2 mi n of US 192; in Walt Disney World Swan. 1200 Epcot Resorts Blvd 32830-2786. **Hours:** 6 pm-11 pm. **Reservations:** suggested. **Features:** Dinner at this full service, fine dining restaurant starts with tempting antipasto including carpaccio, bruschetta, and porcini risotto. The restaurant also serves a variety of seafood, veal and pasta entrees. Hearty Northern Italian dishes are the backbone of the menu: osso buco with saffron risotto, piccata alla Milanese and a beef filet with polenta and shallots. The decor is taken from the Palio Horse Race in Siena and includes colorful flags from the city. Casual dress; cocktails; entertainment. **Parking:** valet. **Cards:** AX, CB, DC, DS, JC, MC, VI.

PEBBLES/ISLAND GRILL — **Lunch:** $8-$28 — **Dinner:** $8-$28 — **Phone:** 407/827-1111 (18)

American

Location: I-4, exit 68, 0.3 mi n; in Crossroads Shopping Center. 12551 SR 535 32836. **Hours:** 11 am-10 pm, Fri-11 pm, Sat 4 pm-11 pm, Sun 4 pm-10 pm. Closed: 11/23, 12/25. **Features:** This is a casual gourmet dining adventure. The homemade soups and salads are fresh and spicy. Well-seasoned seafood, duck, lamb, beef and pasta specialties round out this menu. A tiki bar and patio provide a nice setting for outdoor dining. Casual dress; cocktails. **Parking:** on-site. **Cards:** AX, CB, DC, DS, MC, VI.

THE PLAZA RESTAURANT — **Lunch:** $5-$10 — **Dinner:** $5-$10 — **Phone:** 407/939-3463 (4)

American

Location: In Walt Disney World's Magic Kingdom. **Hours:** 11 am-2:55 & 3-close; hours vary with park closing. **Reservations:** suggested. **Features:** This old-time southern soda fountain is located to the right of Mainstreet USA in the heart of the Magic Kingdom. The menu offers burgers, fries, deli sandwiches and sundaes. Reservations are suggested for both lunch and dinner. Casual dress. **Parking:** on-site (fee). **Cards:** AX, DS, MC, VI.

PORTOBELLO YACHT CLUB — **Dinner:** $15-$32 — **Phone:** 407/934-8888 (26)

Regional Italian

Location: At Downtown Disney. 1650 E Buena Vista Dr 32830. **Hours:** 5 pm-11 pm. **Features:** The lively, inviting atmosphere is perfect for tourists in the Lake Buena Vista area. The chef presents special creations nightly featuring fresh seafood. The dining room affords a lovely lakeside view, or enjoy it with fresh air on the outdoor deck. Casual dress; cocktails. **Parking:** on-site. **Cards:** AX, CB, DC, DS, JC, MC, VI.

RAIN FOREST CAFE — **Lunch:** $9-$17 — **Dinner:** $10-$23 — **Phone:** 407/827-8500 (24)

American

Location: In Disney Marketplace. 1800 E Buena Vista Dr 32830. **Hours:** 11:30 am-11 pm, Fri & Sat-11:30 pm. **Reservations:** accepted. **Features:** A lively atmosphere of a simulated rain forest with dripping water, plants, trees, birds, elephants and fish tanks will keep the kids busy, then comes the storm! Finger food, pasta, frozen drinks and great dessert are offered. Casual dress; cocktails. **Parking:** on-site. **Cards:** AX, CB, DC, DS, MC, VI.

RESTAURANT MARRAKESH — **Lunch:** $10-$17 — **Dinner:** $16-$25 — **Phone:** 407/939-3463 (19)

Moroccan

Location: In Walt Disney World Resort Epcot; in Morocco Pavilion. **Hours:** noon-3:45 & 4:30-9 pm; closing hours vary with park closing. **Features:** Enjoy Moroccan cuisine in a recreation of a royal palace with mosaic tile work and inlaid ceilings. Selections include couscous and shish-kabob. Belly dancers and musicians perform regularly throughout the day. Casual dress; cocktails. **Parking:** on-site (fee). **Cards:** AX, DC, DS, JC, MC, VI.

SHULA'S STEAK HOUSE — **Dinner:** $22-$68 — **Phone:** 407/934-1362 (30)

Steak House

Location: I-4, exit 67, follow Epcot Resort area signs; 0.3 mi e of Walt Disney World Resort; 2 mi n of US 192; in Walt Disney World Dolphin. 1500 Epcot Resorts Blvd 32830. **Hours:** 5 pm-11 pm. **Reservations:** suggested. **Features:** The high-end eatery is nestled in the impressive public areas of the Walt Disney World Swan Hotel. The theme revolves around Don Shula and the Miami Dolphins' perfect football season of years past. Patrons dine on oversized portions of lamb, certified Angus beef and fresh seafood, including three- to five-pound Maine lobsters. Upscale decor marks the casual atmosphere. Dressy casual; cocktails. **Parking:** on-site and valet. **Cards:** AX, CB, DC, MC, VI.

SPOODLES — **Dinner:** $14-$26 — **Phone:** 407/939-3463 (33)

Mediterranean

Location: 0.5 mi e of Disney World main gate access road; 2 mi n of US 192; in Walt Disney World; in Disney's BoardWalk Resort. 2101 N Epcot Resorts Blvd 32830. **Hours:** 7:30 am-11 & 5-9:50 pm. **Reservations:** accepted. **Features:** Mediterranean fare is the highlight of the menu at this fast-paced eatery. Affable and knowledgeable servers present a variety of creative pasta dishes, as well as chicken and seafood preparations. The wine bar is a nice spot in which to unwind. Casual dress; cocktails. **Parking:** valet. **Cards:** AX, DC, DS, JC, MC, VI.

(See map and index starting on p. 668)

TODD ENGLISH'S BLUEZOO **Dinner: $18-$54** **Phone:** 407/934-4644 (29)
♦♦♦ ♦♦♦ **Location:** I-4, exit 67, follow Epcot Resort area signs; 0.3 mi e of Walt Disney World Resort; 2 mi n of US 192; in Walt
Seafood Disney World Dolphin. 1500 Epcot Resorts Blvd 32830. **Hours:** 5 pm-11 pm. **Reservations:** suggested.
Features: Fresh seafood is selected from the waters of the Atlantic seaboard, the Pacific Northwest and
Prince Edward Island. Daily fresh catches, clams, oysters, chilled lobster tail and stone crab tempt the
seafood lover in such entrees as miso-glazed Chilean sea bass, Cantonese lobster and yellowfin tuna steaks. Mouthwatering
desserts should not be missed. Dressy casual; cocktails. **Parking:** valet. **Cards:** AX, CB, DC, DS, JC, MC, VI.

TONY'S TOWN SQUARE RESTAURANT **Lunch: $10-$15** **Dinner: $17-$22** **Phone:** 407/939-3463 (5)
♦♦ ♦♦ **Location:** In Walt Disney World's Magic Kingdom. **Hours:** 8:05 am-10:15, noon-3 & 4-9 pm; closing hours may
Italian vary. **Reservations:** suggested. **Features:** A first stop on Mainstreet USA, this popular outtake from
Disney's Lady and the Tramp offers an Italian-influenced menu including large portions of pasta, salad,
panini and various specialty entrees. Indoor and outdoor patio dining available. Casual dress. **Parking:** on-
site (fee). **Cards:** AX, DS, MC, VI.

THE VENETIAN ROOM **Dinner: $29-$36** **Phone:** 407/238-8060 (36)
ⓐⓐⓐ **Location:** I-4, exit 68, 1.2 mi s on SR 535, then 0.3 mi e; in Caribe Royale All-Suites Resort and Convention Center.
8101 World Center Dr 32821. **Hours:** 6 pm-10 pm. Closed: Sun & Mon. **Reservations:** suggested.
♦♦♦ ♦♦♦ **Features:** Decorated with rich woods, carved frosted glass, impressive chandeliers and classic red accents,
Continental the intimate dining room creates an atmosphere of warmth and sophistication that enhances the dining
experience. Menu selections include lump crab cake with pommerey mustard butter sauce, lobster bisque,
roasted rack of lamb, braised veal chop and Maine lobster. Save room for dessert. Cocktails. **Parking:** on-
site and valet. **Cards:** AX, CB, DC, DS, JC, MC, VI.

VICTORIA & ALBERT'S **Dinner: $85-$100** **Phone:** 407/939-3463 (8)
♦♦♦♦ ♦♦♦♦ **Location:** 8 mi nw of jct I-4 and US 192; in Disney's Grand Floridian Resort & Spa. 4401 Grand Floridian Way 32830.
Hours: seatings at 5:45 pm-6:30 & 9-9:45 pm; 6:30 pm-8 pm, Fri & Sat 5:45 pm-6:30 & 9-9:45 pm 7/1-8/31.
American **Reservations:** required. **Features:** Hidden within the Grand Floridian Resort, this is Disney's best
restaurant. Intimate surroundings complement personalized service from your attendants, Victoria and
Albert. The dinner menu offers an ever-changing six-course culinary adventure. The chef creates meticulous and incredibly
delicious world-class contemporary cuisine, reflecting both American and International influences. The coffee presentation is
extraordinary and the souffles are to die for. Formal attire; cocktails; entertainment. **Parking:** on-site and valet. **Cards:** AX, CB,
DC, DS, JC, MC, VI.

YACHTSMAN'S STEAK HOUSE **Dinner: $23-$51** **Phone:** 407/939-3463 (27)
♦♦♦ **Location:** I-4, exit 67, follow signs to Disney's Epcot Resort; in Walt Disney World; in Disney's Yacht Club Resort. 1700
Steak House Epcot Resorts Blvd 32830. **Hours:** 5:30 pm-9:45 pm. **Reservations:** suggested. **Features:** A spacious wood-
beamed dining room is the setting for guests to enjoy choice, dry-aged steaks cut daily and cooked over a
wood-burning grill. Various fresh seafood selections, lighter creative vegetarian menu offerings and a
creative assortment of unique dessert creations are also offered. Casual dress; cocktails. **Parking:** on-site and valet.
Cards: AX, CB, DC, DS, JC, MC, VI.

─────── *The following restaurants have not been evaluated by AAA* ───────
but are listed for your information only.

AKERSHUS **Phone:** 407/939-3463
[fyi] Not evaluated. **Location:** In Walt Disney World's Epcot Center. Norway, World Showcase 32830. **Features:** 40 plus
item selection of Scandinavian cuisine, including seafood and smoked meat. The restaurant is modeled
after a medieval Norwegian castle.

ALFREDO'S **Phone:** 407/939-3463
[fyi] Not evaluated. **Location:** In Walt Disney World's Epcot Center. Italy, World Showcase 32830. **Features:** Dark and
rich decor accents the Italian piazza murals. Traditional Italian cuisine; selection of Italian wines.

BIERGARTEN **Phone:** 407/939-3463
[fyi] Not evaluated. **Location:** In Walt Disney World's Epcot Center. Germany, World Showcase 32830. **Features:** All-
you-can-eat buffet featuring assorted sausage, cabbage, spaetzle, strudel, etc.

BOULANGERIE PATISSERIE **Phone:** 407/939-3463
[fyi] Not evaluated. **Location:** In Walt Disney World's Epcot Center. France, World Showcase 32830. **Features:** Counter
service. Specialties include French pastry, quiche and coffee.

CHEFS DE FRANCE **Phone:** 407/939-3463
[fyi] Not evaluated. **Location:** In Walt Disney World's Epcot Center. France, World Showcase 32830. **Features:** Creative
menu of French cuisine, served in a more formal surrounding. Varied wine selections; exceptional pastries
and desserts.

THE CORAL REEF **Phone:** 407/939-3463
[fyi] Not evaluated. **Location:** In Walt Disney World's Epcot Center. Living Seas, Future World 32830.
Features: Seafood offerings; menu varies seasonally. Tiered dining room offers view of the marine life
tank.

THE GARDEN GRILL **Phone:** 407/939-3463
[fyi] Not evaluated. **Location:** In Walt Disney World's Epcot Center. The Land, Future World 32830. **Features:** Character
meals at breakfast and lunch. Dining room revolves through scenes in nature. Meals served family style,
with some vegetables grown on-site.

(See map and index starting on p. 668)

HOLLYWOOD AND VINE CAFE OF STARS

[fyi] Not evaluated. **Location:** In Walt Disney World's MGM Studios. **Features:** Recreates a 40's-50's diner, with stainless steel and deco touches. Serve yourself buffet offering traditional American fare. Moderately priced.

Phone: 407/939-3463

THE HOLLYWOOD BROWN DERBY

[fyi] Not evaluated. **Location:** In Walt Disney World's MGM Studios. Hollywood Blvd 32830. **Features:** Recreation of the original Brown Derby, including caricatures of stars. American cuisine. Moderately priced.

Phone: 407/939-3463

LE CELLIER STEAK HOUSE

[fyi] Not evaluated. **Location:** In Walt Disney World's Epcot Center. Canada, World Showcase 32830. **Features:** "Canadian" foods served in the wine cellar (lower level) of a replica of a Canadian national historic hotel.

Phone: 407/939-3463

MAMA MELROSE'S

[fyi] Not evaluated. **Location:** In Walt Disney World's MGM Studios. **Features:** Recreating the look of a neighborhood restaurant. Traditional pasta selections and seafood specialties. Moderately priced.

Phone: 407/939-3463

MITSUKOSHI TEPPANYAKI

[fyi] Not evaluated. **Location:** In Walt Disney World's Epcot Center. Japan, World Showcase 32830. **Features:** Grilled meat, seafood and chicken prepared at your teppanyaki table. Be entertained as you watch your chef prepare your meal. Touches of traditional Japanese decor. Sushi available.

Phone: 407/939-3463

NINE DRAGONS

[fyi] Not evaluated. **Location:** In Walt Disney World's Epcot Center. China, World Showcase 32830. **Features:** Menu selections include Mandarin, Cantonese and Szechuan items. Dining room rich in Oriental decor.

Phone: 407/939-3463

PRIME TIME CAFE

[fyi] Not evaluated. **Location:** In Walt Disney World's MGM Studios. **Features:** Fun atmosphere. Decor reminiscent of a 50's TV sitcom kitchen. Home-type specialties and soda fountain drinks. Moderately priced.

Phone: 407/939-3463

ROSE AND CROWN

[fyi] Not evaluated. **Location:** In Walt Disney World's Epcot Center. UK, World Showcase 32830. **Features:** Limited menu selection of traditional English pub fare. Selections of British beer and ale. Rustic dining room and outdoor patio seating.

Phone: 407/939-3463

SAN ANGEL INN

[fyi] Not evaluated. **Location:** In Walt Disney World's Epcot Center. Mexico, World Showcase 32830. **Features:** Selection of traditional Mexican offerings with some creative combinations. Standard, commercial type Mexican decor; dim lighting.

Phone: 407/939-3463

SCI-FI DINE-IN THEATRE

[fyi] Not evaluated. **Location:** In Walt Disney World's MGM Studios. Backlot 32830. **Features:** Dine in a 50's style replica car at the drive-in theater while watching clips of sci-fi films. Traditional American menu selections. Moderate prices.

Phone: 407/939-3463

LAKE MARY pop. 11,458   (See map and index starting on p. 656)

──────── **WHERE TO STAY** ────────

CANDLEWOOD SUITES LAKE MARY-HEATHROW   *Book at aaa.com*   Phone: (407)585-3000   **36**
All Year   1P: $69-$139
Location: I-4, exit 98, just e to Lake Emma Rd. 0.5 mi s to Greenwood Blvd, then 0.6 mi w. 1130 Greenwood Blvd
Small-scale Hotel   32746. Fax: 407/585-3030. **Facility:** 123 units. 99 one-bedroom standard units. 24 one-bedroom suites. 4
stories, interior corridors. *Bath:* combo or shower only. **Parking:** on-site. **Terms:** pets ($75 fee).
Amenities: DVD players, high-speed Internet, dual phone lines, voice mail, irons, hair dryers. **Pool(s):** heated outdoor. **Leisure
Activities:** exercise room. **Guest Services:** sundries, complimentary laundry. **Business Services:** meeting rooms, fax (fee).
Cards: AX, CB, DC, DS, JC, MC, VI.
SOME UNITS

HAMPTON INN & SUITES AT COLONIAL TOWNPARK   *Book at aaa.com*   Phone: 407/995-9000   **30**
All Year [ECP]   1P: $109-$179   2P: $109-$179
Location: I-4, exit 101A, just w to Colonial Center Pkwy, then just n. 850 Village Oak Ln 32746. Fax: 407/995-9001.
Small-scale Hotel   **Facility:** 131 units. 130 one-bedroom standard units. 1 one-bedroom suite ($119-$229). 5 stories, interior
corridors. *Bath:* combo or shower only. **Parking:** on-site. **Amenities:** video library, high-speed Internet, dual
phone lines, voice mail, irons, hair dryers. *Some:* DVD players, CD players. **Pool(s):** heated outdoor. **Leisure
Activities:** whirlpool, bicycles, jogging, exercise room. **Guest Services:** sundries, valet and coin laundry. **Business Services:**
meeting rooms, fax (fee). **Cards:** AX, CB, DC, DS, JC, MC, VI.
SOME UNITS

HILTON GARDEN INN LAKE MARY   *Book at aaa.com*   Phone: (407)531-9900   **32**
All Year   1P: $69-$199   2P: $69-$199
Location: I-4, exit 98, just ne via Lake Mary Blvd and Primera. 705 Currency Cir 32746. Fax: 407/531-1144.
Facility: 123 units. 122 one-bedroom standard units, some with whirlpools. 1 one-bedroom suite with
whirlpool. 3 stories, interior corridors. *Bath:* combo or shower only. **Parking:** on-site. **Terms:** [BP] meal plan
Small-scale Hotel   available. **Amenities:** dual phone lines, voice mail, irons, hair dryers. *Fee:* video games, high-speed
Internet. **Pool(s):** heated outdoor. **Leisure Activities:** whirlpool, exercise room. **Guest Services:** valet and
coin laundry. **Business Services:** meeting rooms, business center. **Cards:** AX, CB, DC, DS, JC, MC, VI. **Special Amenities:**
free newspaper and early check-in/late check-out.
SOME UNITS

(See map and index starting on p. 656)

HOMESTEAD STUDIO SUITES-ORLANDO/LAKE MARY *Book at aaa.com*
All Year   1P: $44-$74   2P: $49-$79   Phone: (407)829-2332   **34**
          XP: $5   F17
Location: I-4, exit 98, 0.5 mi s on Lake Emma Rd; in Commerce Park. 1040 Greenwood Blvd 32746.
Small-scale Hotel   **Fax:** 407/829-4436. **Facility:** 100 units. 76 one-bedroom standard units with efficiencies. 24 one-bedroom suites with efficiencies. 3 stories, interior corridors. *Bath:* combo or shower only. **Parking:** on-site.
Terms: small pets only ($25-$75 fee). **Amenities:** dual phone lines, voice mail, irons, hair dryers. *Fee:* video games, high-speed Internet. **Pool(s):** outdoor. **Leisure Activities:** exercise room. **Guest Services:** coin laundry. **Business Services:** meeting rooms. **Cards:** AX, DC, DS, MC, VI.

SOME UNITS

HOMEWOOD SUITES BY HILTON *Book at aaa.com*
All Year [BP]   1P: $99-$149   Phone: (407)805-9111   **33**
          XP: $10   F
Location: I-4, exit 98, just ne via Lake Mary Blvd and Primera. 755 Currency Cir 32746. **Fax:** 407/805-0236.
Facility: 112 units. 105 one- and 7 two-bedroom suites with kitchens. 5 stories, interior corridors. *Bath:* combo or shower only. **Parking:** on-site. **Terms:** cancellation fee imposed, 4% service charge.
Small-scale Hotel   **Amenities:** video games (fee), high-speed Internet, dual phone lines, voice mail, irons, hair dryers. **Pool(s):** outdoor. **Leisure Activities:** grills, exercise room. **Guest Services:** sundries, complimentary evening beverages: Mon-Thurs, valet and coin laundry. **Business Services:** meeting rooms, business center. **Cards:** AX, CB, DC, DS, JC, MC, VI. **Special Amenities:** free newspaper. *(See color ad p 821)*

SOME UNITS
FEE

LA QUINTA INN & SUITES ORLANDO (LAKE MARY) *Book at aaa.com*
All Year   1P: $89-$109   Phone: (407)805-9901   **35**
          XP: $7   F18
Location: I-4, exit 98, just se via Lake Mary Blvd. 1060 Greenwood Blvd 32746. **Fax:** 407/805-9968. **Facility:** 128 units. 123 one-bedroom standard units. 5 one-bedroom suites ($125-$145). 5 stories, interior corridors.
Bath: combo or shower only. **Parking:** on-site. **Terms:** [ECP] meal plan available, small pets only.
Small-scale Hotel   **Amenities:** video games (fee), high-speed Internet, voice mail, irons, hair dryers. *Some:* dual phone lines. **Pool(s):** heated outdoor. **Leisure Activities:** whirlpool, exercise room. **Guest Services:** valet and coin laundry, airport transportation-Sanford-Orlando International Airport, area transportation-within 10 mi. **Business Services:** meeting rooms, fax (fee). **Cards:** AX, CB, DC, DS, MC, VI. **Special Amenities:** free expanded continental breakfast and free local telephone calls. *(See color ad p 721)*

SOME UNITS

ORLANDO MARRIOTT LAKE MARY *Book at aaa.com*
All Year   1P: $99-$199   2P: $99-$229   Phone: (407)995-1100   **31**
Location: I-4, exit 101A, just w. 1501 International Pkwy 32746. **Fax:** 407/995-1150. **Facility:** 304 units. 299 one-bedroom standard units. 5 one-bedroom suites ($299-$499). 10 stories, interior corridors. *Bath:* combo or shower only. **Parking:** on-site. **Amenities:** video games (fee), high-speed Internet, dual phone lines, voice mail, irons, hair dryers. **Dining:** 6:30 am-11 pm, cocktails. **Pool(s):** heated outdoor. **Leisure**
Small-scale Hotel   **Activities:** whirlpool, exercise room. **Guest Services:** gift shop, valet and coin laundry. **Business Services:** conference facilities, business center. **Cards:** AX, CB, DC, DS, JC, MC, VI. **Special Amenities:** free newspaper.
(See color ad p 821)

SOME UNITS
FEE

────── **WHERE TO DINE** ──────

AMURA
Japanese
Lunch: $8-$12   Dinner: $8-$32   Phone: 407/936-6001   **80**
Location: I-4, exit 101A (SR 46A), 0.5 mi w, then just n; in Colonial TownPark. 950 Market Promenade Ave 32746.
Hours: 11 am-3 & 5-10:30 pm, Thurs-Sat to 11 pm. Closed major holidays. **Reservations:** not accepted.
Features: A top pick for sushi and Japanese cuisine, the eatery prepares a wide variety, including several wonderful rolls. Among other good choices are the bagel roll, with smoked salmon and cream cheese; the asparagus roll; and octopus. For those leery of sushi, there is a full Japanese menu. Casual dress; cocktails. **Parking:** on-site. **Cards:** AX, MC, VI.

APPLETON'S CAFE
American
DS, MC, VI.
Lunch: $5-$7   Dinner: $8-$17   Phone: 407/323-7663   **95**
Location: I-4, exit 98, 1.3 mi e; in Driftwood Village. 3575 W Lake Mary Blvd 32746. **Hours:** 7 am-3 pm, Fri & Sat also 5 pm-9 pm. Closed: Mon. **Features:** The friendly neighborhood restaurant serves large portions of meat loaf, Southern fried chicken, prime rib and baked ham. All desserts, including the three-layer Jack Daniels chocolate cake, are made on site. Casual dress; beer & wine only. **Parking:** on-site. **Cards:** AX,

ATLANTA BREAD COMPANY
American
Lunch: $4-$7   Dinner: $4-$7   Phone: 407/804-0105   **103**
Location: I-4, exit 98, 1 mi e on Lake Mary Blvd, then just s. 864 S Sun Dr 32746. **Hours:** 6:30 am-10 pm, Sun 7 am-9 pm. Closed major holidays. **Features:** The menu offers a variety of sandwiches, salads, pizza, pasta, omelettes and a large array of cookies, cakes and pies. Casual dress. **Parking:** on-site. **Cards:** AX, MC, VI.

BISTRO 1501
American
Lunch: $6-$11   Dinner: $15-$23   Phone: 407/995-7053   **89**
Location: I-4, exit 101A, just n on CR 46A. 1501 International Pkwy 32746. **Hours:** 6:30-10:30 am, 11-2 & 5-10 pm, Fri-11 pm, Sat 7-10:30 am, 11-2 & 5-11 pm, Sun 7-10 am, 11-3 & 5-10 pm. Closed: for dinner 12/25.
Reservations: accepted. **Features:** Locals and others flock to the Friday night seafood buffet, which is chock full of the sea's bounty of salmon, shrimp and fresh catches of the day. Dishes from the menu include filet mignon and New Zealand lamb. Desserts for which this place is known include mouthwatering crepes and Snickers pie. Casual dress; cocktails. **Parking:** on-site. **Cards:** AX, CB, DC, DS, MC, VI.

(See map and index starting on p. 656)

CAFFE POSITANO
▼▼▼▼
Italian
Lunch: $6-$18   Dinner: $6-$18   Phone: 407/833-9377   [101]
Location: I-4, exit 98, just e, then s; in Lake Mary Center. 3837 Lake Emma Rd 32746. **Hours:** 11 am-10:30 pm, Fri & Sat-11 pm, Sun from noon. Closed: 11/23, 12/25. **Features:** This modest Italian eatery is tucked away in Lake Mary Center. Order cautiously as the chef serves up large portions of contemporary homemade fare. If you are feeling full, try the dessert sampler serving four to five people at a real value. Subs, pizza and calzones are also available. Casual dress; cocktails. **Parking:** on-site. **Cards:** AX, CB, DC, DS, JC, MC, VI.

CHENGS
▼▼ ▼▼
Chinese
Lunch: $5-$7   Dinner: $6-$21   Phone: 407/333-0099   [106]
Location: I-4, exit 98, 0.5 mi e; in Lake Mary Center. 3705 Lake Emma Rd 32746. **Hours:** 11 am-10 pm, Fri-11 pm, Sat 11:30 am-10:30 pm. Closed major holidays. **Features:** Cantonese, Mandarin, Szechuan and Hunan are all offered at this modest, informal restaurant. You will find many delicious selections at the popular lunch buffet served every weekday, or taste such specialties as Rainbow Delight or General Teau chicken. Casual dress; beer & wine only. **Parking:** on-site. **Cards:** AX, DC, MC, VI.   [⬧]

CHINA COOK
▼
Chinese
Lunch: $4-$6   Dinner: $5-$11   Phone: 407/688-4352   [113]
Location: Jct US 17-92 and Weldon Blvd. 601 Weldon Blvd, Suite 113 32746. **Hours:** 11 am-10 pm, Sat-11 pm, Sun noon-9:30 pm. **Features:** Guests order take-out from the eatery, which serves fried rice, lo mein, mu shu, egg foo yong and sweet and sour dishes. Casual dress. **Parking:** on-site. **Cards:** AX, MC, VI.

COCONUTS CUBAN CAFE & DELI
▼
Caribbean
Lunch: $4-$7   Dinner: $4-$7   Phone: 407/804-5161   [94]
Location: I-4, exit 98, 0.7 mi e. 4044 W Lake Mary Blvd 32746. **Hours:** 10:30 am-4 pm, Fri & Sat-8 pm. Closed major holidays. **Features:** The quick-serve eatery prepares Cuban sandwiches, roasted pork, meatballs, croquetas, stuffed potatoes, tostones and maduros. Casual dress. **Parking:** on-site. **Cards:** AX, MC, VI.

THE COFFEE CAFE
▼
American
Lunch: $4-$9   Dinner: $4-$9   Phone: 407/833-0446   [82]
Location: I-4, exit 101A, just w, then n; in Colonial TownPark. 1145 TownPark Ave, Suite 1221 32746. **Hours:** 6:30 am-11 pm, Fri-midnight, Sat 7 am-midnight. Closed major holidays; also Sun. **Features:** A menu of lighter fare complements the varied espresso specialties and tea, chai and hot chocolate drinks. Pastries, cookies and dessert bars satisfy the sweet tooth. Casual dress. **Parking:** on-site. **Cards:** AX, DC, DS, MC, VI.

CRISPERS
▼
American
Lunch: $3-$8   Dinner: $3-$8   Phone: 407/833-0901   [86]
Location: I-4, exit 101A, just w; in Colonial TownPark. 1120 Town Park Ave 32746. **Hours:** 10:30 am-9 pm, Fri & Sat-10 pm, Sun-8 pm. Closed major holidays. **Features:** A healthy alternative for lunch or dinner, the restaurant prepares towering specialty sandwiches on warm, fresh homemade bread. Salad selections with combinations of meats, fruit and cheese are just as tempting. Casual dress. **Parking:** on-site. **Cards:** AX, DS, MC, VI.

DALLI'S PIZZERIA
▼
Italian
Lunch: $5-$15   Dinner: $5-$19   Phone: 407/302-2707   [93]
Location: Jct N Country Club Rd and Lake Mary Blvd. 101 N Country Club Rd #111 32746. **Hours:** 11 am-10 pm. Closed major holidays; also Sun. **Features:** Hot and cold subs, pasta dishes and pizzas are at the heart of the menu in the fast-paced eatery, which is particularly busy on weekends. Seating is limited. Casual dress; beer & wine only. **Parking:** on-site. **Cards:** MC, VI.

DEXTER'S OF LAKE MARY
▼▼▼▼
American
Lunch: $6-$12   Dinner: $10-$25   Phone: 407/805-3090   [81]
Location: I-4, exit 101A, just w; in Colonial TownPark. 950 Market Promenade Ave, Suite 1201 32746. **Hours:** 11 am-10 pm, Fri & Sat-11 pm; Sunday brunch. Closed major holidays. **Reservations:** accepted. **Features:** Many wine connoisseurs frequent the establishment for its interesting selection of wines. Food is trendy yet simple. Outdoor seating is an option. Casual dress; cocktails. **Parking:** on-site. **Cards:** AX, DC, DS, MC, VI.

FIREHOUSE SUBS
▼
American
Lunch: $5-$7   Dinner: $5-$7   Phone: 407/833-8447   [108]
Location: I-4, exit 98, 0.5 mi e; in Lake Mary Center. 3579 Lake Emma Rd 32746. **Hours:** 10:30 am-9 pm, Fri & Sat-10 pm. Closed: 11/23, 12/25. **Features:** Hot and cold submarine sandwiches, in addition to specialty subs, are named after fire station items. Casual dress. **Parking:** on-site. **Cards:** AX, DS, MC, VI.

GATOR'S DOCKSIDE
▼▼ ▼▼
American
Lunch: $5-$17   Dinner: $5-$17   Phone: 407/330-2557   [100]
Location: I-4, exit 98, 1 mi e. 4349 W Lake Mary Blvd 32746. **Hours:** 11 am-11 pm. Closed major holidays. **Features:** Multiple large screen televisions broadcasting major sporting events, pool tables, and video games are a few ways to keep entertained while you wait for wings, ribs, seafood specials or a specialty sandwich. Casual dress; cocktails. **Parking:** on-site. **Cards:** AX, DS, MC, VI.

GIOVANNI'S ITALIAN RESTAURANT & PIZZERIA
▼▼ ▼▼
Italian
Lunch: $6-$9   Dinner: $9-$18   Phone: 407/330-4350   [92]
Location: I-4, exit 101A, just e, then 0.3 mi s; in Publix Shopping Plaza. 875 Rinehart Rd 32746. **Hours:** 11 am-10 pm, Fri & Sat-11 pm, Sun noon-10 pm. Closed: 4/16, 11/23, 12/25; also for lunch Memorial Day, Labor Day, July 4th & New Year's Day. **Features:** Although pizza is the specialty at the shopping plaza eatery, and extensive menu of traditional Italian favorites cannot be ignored. Ravioli, lasagna, chicken Marsala and seafood dishes are just a few tantalizing options. The family-owned-and-operated spot is often busy for lunch and dinner. Casual dress; cocktails. **Parking:** on-site. **Cards:** AX, DS, MC, VI.   [🍸]

(See map and index starting on p. 656)

GOLDEN CHINA BUFFET
Chinese

Lunch: $6-$13 **Dinner:** $10-$13 **Phone:** 407/321-5858 (99)
Location: I-4, exit 98, 1 mi e. 4225 W Lake Mary Blvd 32746. **Hours:** 11 am-3 & 4-10:30 pm, Fri & Sat-11 pm. Closed: 11/23. **Reservations:** accepted. **Features:** Known for abundant food at a reasonable price, the buffet features more than 100 Chinese and traditional American selections. In a busy shopping plaza, this place is almost always packed for lunch. Casual dress. **Parking:** on-site. **Cards:** AX, DS, MC, VI.

HARVEY'S BISTRO
Continental

Lunch: $9-$29 **Dinner:** $9-$29 **Phone:** 407/936-1267 (87)
Location: I-4, exit 101A, just w. 7025 CR 46A, #1001 32746. **Hours:** 4 pm-11 pm, Sun 11 am-9 pm. Closed major holidays. **Features:** The atmosphere in this bistro is comfortable and sleek. The metal sculpture of the restaurant's logo tops the lounge area and is bound to inspire discussions. The menu offers lobster bisque and wild mushroom and brie baguette for starters, followed by entrees that include herb crusted scallops and papardelle pomodoro with lump crab. Leave room for the house specialty dessert, Harvey's carrot cake. Casual dress; cocktails. **Parking:** on-site. **Cards:** AX, DS, MC, VI.

INDIA VILLAGE
Indian

Lunch: $6-$13 **Dinner:** $6-$13 **Phone:** 407/333-0003 (111)
Location: I-4, exit 98, just e, then just s. 3577-111 Lake Emma Rd 32746. **Hours:** 11 am-3 & 4-9 pm, Fri & Sat-10 pm. Closed major holidays; also Sun. **Features:** Nestled in a corner of the hustle and bustle of coming and going is a retreat in adventurous Indian dining. Come at lunch and enjoy a buffet spread with many selections that change daily. The chef/owner is more than willing to take time with guests and give onsite instruction. On cool days enjoy sitting on the sidewalk. Casual dress; beer & wine only. **Parking:** on-site. **Cards:** AX, MC, VI.

JINJA ASIA CAFE
Asian

Lunch: $5-$17 **Dinner:** $5-$17 **Phone:** 407/936-9990 (90)
Location: I-4, exit 101A (CR 46A), 0.5 mi w; in Park Plaza. 1541 International Pkwy 32746. **Hours:** 11 am-10 pm, Fri & Sat-11 pm. Closed: 1/1, 11/23, 12/25. **Reservations:** not accepted. **Features:** The modern, casual restaurant serves fresh, flavorful dishes from six Asian countries: Japan, China, Thailand, Vietnam, Malaysia and Singapore. Recipes use the most authentic ingredients available, and the chefs have adapted the recipes for American tastes. Casual dress; cocktails. **Parking:** on-site. **Cards:** AX, MC, VI.

KELLER'S REAL SMOKED BAR-B-Q
American

Lunch: $3-$8 **Dinner:** $3-$12 **Phone:** 407/333-1444 (102)
Location: I-4, exit 98, 0.5 mi e; in Lake Mary Center. 3893 Lake Emma Rd 32746. **Hours:** 11 am-9 pm, Fri & Sat-10 pm. Closed major holidays; also Sun. **Features:** Tables fill quickly at the popular, no-frills barbecue restaurant. Recipes handed down from generation to generation ensure that quality, mouthwatering barbecue is served all the time, every time. Dinner platters—including the chicken and rib combination plate, three-meat platter and the sampler—allow for a taste of the most popular items. Casual dress; beer & wine only. **Parking:** on-site. **Cards:** AX, MC, VI.

LEE'S PALACE
Chinese

Lunch: $5-$10 **Dinner:** $5-$15 **Phone:** 407/330-0013 (91)
Location: I-4, exit 101A, 0.3 mi e to Rinehart Rd, then just s; in Publix Shopping Plaza. 841 Rinehart Rd 32746. **Hours:** 11 am-10 pm, Sat & Sun from noon. Closed major holidays. **Features:** The bustling eatery prepares an extensive menu of Japanese and Chinese food. Combination platters, seafood, sushi and sashimi are among choices. Seating is limited in the cozy dining room. Casual dress; beer & wine only. **Parking:** on-site. **Cards:** AX, DS, MC, VI.

MAMA FU'S ASIAN HOUSE
Asian

Lunch: $4-$10 **Dinner:** $4-$10 **Phone:** 407/804-9092 (85)
Location: I-4, exit 101A, just w, then n; in Colonial TownPark. 1125 Colonial Town Park 32746. **Hours:** 11 am-9:30 pm, Thurs-Sat to 10 pm. Closed: 11/23, 12/25. **Features:** Fresh, hot, and woking! Mama Fu's dishes out authentic Asian cuisine with flair. Enjoy sesame crusted ahi tuna or pot stickers for a starter. Favorites of the house include red Thai curry prepared with coconut and Thai basil, as well as peanut soy chicken salad whisked to your table directly from the wok. Seating is available inside or outside under a covered awning. Beer & wine only. **Parking:** on-site. **Cards:** AX, CB, DC, DS, MC, VI.

MAMMA LOU'S
Italian

Lunch: $5-$11 **Dinner:** $5-$11 **Phone:** 407/302-0555 (98)
Location: I-4, exit 98, 2 mi e; between Lake Mary Post Office and Discount Auto Parts. 118 Middle St 32746. **Hours:** 10 am-6 pm, Sat-5 pm. Closed major holidays; also Sun & Mon. **Features:** Among homemade delicatessen items are pastas, sauces, made-to-order sandwiches and salads. There is no seating. Pastas and sauces also can be taken home. Imported Italian ingredients also are available. Casual dress. **Parking:** on-site. **Cards:** AX, DC, DS, MC, VI.

MCALISTER'S DELI
American

Lunch: $5-$7 **Dinner:** $5-$7 **Phone:** 407/805-3232 (84)
Location: I-4, exit 101A, just w, then n; in Colonial TownPark. 950 Market Promenade Ave 32746. **Hours:** 10:30 am-9 pm, Fri & Sat-10:30 pm. Closed: 11/23, 12/25. **Features:** A great spot to stop for a quick bite or to linger over a meal. Enjoy freshly made sandwhiches and salads. Casual dress. **Parking:** on-site. **Cards:** AX, DS, MC, VI.

MOE'S SOUTHWEST GRILL
Mexican

Lunch: $3-$8 **Dinner:** $3-$8 **Phone:** 407/833-0050 (88)
Location: I-4, exit 101A, just w, then s; in Park Plaza Shopping Center. 7025 CR 46A, Suite 1111 32746. **Hours:** 11 am-10 pm. Closed: 11/23, 12/25. **Features:** Welcome to Moe's! Not only is the food entertaining but the staff and decor will also delight you. Friendly cooks dish out standard favorites cooked to your liking including burritos, quesadillas and fajitas. The walls are adorned with eclectic portraits of popular musicians. Sit inside or enjoy a spot in the sun on the patio. Beer only. **Parking:** on-site. **Cards:** AX, CB, DC, DS, JC, MC, VI.

OSAKA JAPANESE STEAK HOUSE
Japanese

Lunch: $6-$10 **Dinner:** $8-$24 **Phone:** 407/333-2419 (104)
Location: I-4, exit 98, just e; in Lake Mary Center; by movie cinema. 3847 Lake Emma Rd 32746. **Hours:** 11:30 am-2:30 & 5-9:30 pm, Sat & Sun from 5 pm. Closed: Mon. **Features:** Combination platters with chicken and steak, steak and shrimp or chicken and shrimp—in addition to an expansive sushi menu—make the steakhouse popular. Chefs prepare dinner right at the table. Casual dress; cocktails. **Parking:** on-site. **Cards:** AX, CB, DC, DS, JC, MC, VI.

(See map and index starting on p. 656)

PAPA JOE'S
♦♦♦ ♦♦♦
Italian
Lunch: $7-$15   **Dinner:** $7-$15   **Phone:** 407/323-9222   [105]
Location: I-4, exit 98, 1 mi e. 4205 Lake Mary Blvd 32746. **Hours:** 11 am-10 pm, Sat-11 pm, Sun noon-10 pm. Closed major holidays. **Features:** This family pizzeria is located in a shopping plaza and is always busy; the menu highlights specialty and gourmet pies as well as traditional Italian favorites. Casual dress; beer & wine only. **Parking:** on-site. **Cards:** AX, DS, MC, VI.

PAPA JOE'S PIZZA COLONIAL TOWN PARK
♦♦♦ ♦♦♦
Italian
Lunch: $5-$10   **Dinner:** $9-$17   **Phone:** 407/936-3300   [79]
Location: I-4, exit 101A, just w; in Colonial TownPark. 960 Colonial Town Park 32746. **Hours:** 10 am-10 pm, Fri & Sat-11 pm, Sun 11 am-10 pm. Closed: 4/16, 11/23, 12/25. **Reservations:** not accepted. **Features:** Next door to a movie theater, the family pizzeria is busy before and after show times. The menu highlights specialty and gourmet pies. Casual dress; beer & wine only. **Parking:** on-site. **Cards:** AX, DC, DS, MC, VI.

TASTE OF CHINA
♦♦♦ ♦♦♦
Chinese
Lunch: $5-$6   **Dinner:** $8-$11   **Phone:** 407/328-9998   [97]
Location: I-4, exit 98, 1 mi e; in Lake Mary Village Shops. 3801 W Lake Mary Blvd 32746. **Hours:** 11 am-10 pm, Fri-11 pm, Sat & Sun 4 pm-10 pm. Closed: 11/23, 12/25. **Features:** Combination platters for one, vegetarian delights and family dinners are a few of the many ways the restaurant caters to individuals and families alike. Among seafood offerings are Hunan shrimp, five-flavored shrimp and kung pao. The staff is happy and friendly. Casual dress. **Parking:** on-site. **Cards:** MC, VI.

THAI CORNER RESTAURANT

♦♦♦ ♦♦♦
Thai
Lunch: $6-$8   **Dinner:** $7-$15   **Phone:** 407/833-8066   [107]
Location: I-4, exit 98, 0.4 mi e; in Shoppes at Lake Mary. 3589 Lake Emma Rd 32746. **Hours:** 11 am-2:30 & 5-9 pm, Fri-10 pm, Sat 5 pm-10 pm. Closed: Sun. **Features:** Guests can unwind in a casual atmosphere and sample noodles, fried rice, sweet and sour preparations and red, green and yellow curry dishes. The menu also lists vegetarian selections. Casual dress; cocktails. **Parking:** on-site. **Cards:** MC, VI.

TIJUANA FLATS
♦♦♦
Tex-Mex
Lunch: $4-$8   **Dinner:** $4-$8   **Phone:** 407/328-0907   [96]
Location: I-4, exit 98, 1.7 mi e; next to Dockside Imports. 3005 W Lake Mary Blvd 32746. **Hours:** 11 am-9 pm. Closed major holidays. **Features:** The quick-serve Tex-Mex eatery sets up a distinctive "hot sauce bar" to accompany its burritos, chimichangas, tacos and enchiladas. Guests can expect a line out the door at lunch. Casual dress; beer only. **Parking:** on-site. **Cards:** MC, VI.

TONY'S ORIGINAL WINGS & GRILL
♦♦♦
American
MC, VI.
Lunch: $4-$11   **Dinner:** $4-$11   **Phone:** 407/333-4656   [110]
Location: I-4, exit 98, just e; in Lake Mary Center. 3689 Lake Emma Rd 32746. **Hours:** 11 am-9:30 pm, Thurs-Sat to 10:30 pm. Closed major holidays. **Features:** No-nonsense wings and things make up the restaurant's menu. The mood is fast and friendly. Homemade French fries with the customary malt vinegar are featured with draft beer, sandwiches and sports on the TV. Casual dress; cocktails. **Parking:** on-site. **Cards:** AX, DS, 🍸

TOOJAY'S ORIGINAL GOURMET DELI
♦♦♦ ♦♦♦
American
MC, VI.
Lunch: $5-$10   **Dinner:** $5-$10   **Phone:** 407/833-0848   [112]
Location: I-4, exit 98, just e to Lake Emma Rd, then just s. 3577 Lake Emma Rd 32746. **Hours:** 8 am-9 pm, Fri & Sat-10 pm. Closed: 11/23, 12/25. **Features:** The quick-serve delicatessen offers take-out or dine-in options. A large display case showcases homemade salads and desserts. Diners also can choose from a large selection of sandwiches and entrees. Casual dress; cocktails. **Parking:** on-site. **Cards:** AX, DC, DS,

TROPICAL SMOOTHIE CAFE
♦♦♦
American
Casual dress. **Parking:** on-site. **Cards:** AX, DS, MC, VI.
Lunch: $4-$7   **Dinner:** $4-$7   **Phone:** 407/942-0050   [109]
Location: I-4, exit 98, 0.5 mi e; in Lake Mary Center. 3785 Lake Emma Rd 32746. **Hours:** 8 am-10 pm, Sat from 10 am, Sun 11 am-8 pm. Closed major holidays. **Features:** Patrons can top off a tasty gourmet wrap or a made-to-order sandwich with a tropical smoothie. Many other smoothie varieties also are available. In a busy commercial shopping center, the eatery is a fast alternative for lunch or dinner. Seating is limited.

VIVONA'S II OF LAKE MARY
♦♦♦ ♦♦♦
Italian
Cards: MC, VI.
Lunch: $7-$14   **Dinner:** $7-$14   **Phone:** 407/330-2040   [114]
Location: Jct US 17-92 and Weldon Blvd. 601 Weldon Blvd, #117 32746. **Hours:** 10 am-10 pm, Sun noon-9 pm. Closed major holidays. **Features:** Among choices at the family-run restaurant are homemade pasta dishes, pizza and hot and cold submarine sandwiches. For breakfast, try pizza with eggs, mozzarella cheese, peppers, mushrooms and a choice of meat. Casual dress; beer & wine only. **Parking:** on-site.

WESTSHORE PIZZA
♦♦♦
Italian
on-site. **Cards:** AX, DS, MC, VI.
Lunch: $5-$15   **Dinner:** $6-$21   **Phone:** 407/324-0110   [115]
Location: Jct US 17-92 and Weldon Blvd; in Victoria Square Shopping Center. 3590 US Hwy 17-92 32746. **Hours:** 11 am-10 pm. Closed major holidays. **Features:** The family restaurant's menu will please most anyone. In addition to specialty pizzas, diners can order baked pasta, eggplant dishes, salads and submarine sandwiches. A children's menu and take-out service are options. Casual dress; beer & wine only. **Parking:**

LEESBURG pop. 15,956

―――― WHERE TO STAY ――――

DAYS INN LEESBURG *Book at aaa.com*   Phone: (352)787-3131
AAA SAVE   12/1-4/30   1P: $75-$135   2P: $75-$135
            5/1-11/30   1P: $75-$110   2P: $75-$110
            Location: US 441, 0.5 mi s of jct US 27. 1115 W North Blvd 34748. Fax: 352/365-1497. **Facility:** 61 one-bedroom
Small-scale Hotel standard units, some with efficiencies (no utensils). 2 stories, exterior corridors. **Parking:** on-site. **Terms:** 3
            day cancellation notice, [CP] meal plan available. **Amenities:** hair dryers. **Pool(s):** heated outdoor. **Guest
            Services:** coin laundry. **Cards:** AX, DC, DS, MC, VI. **Special Amenities:** free continental breakfast and
free local telephone calls. *(See color ad below)*

SOME UNITS

GUESTHOUSE INTERNATIONAL INN & SUITES *Book at aaa.com*   Phone: (352)787-1210
AAA SAVE   All Year   1P: $49-$99
            Location: Jct US 27 and 441. 1308 N 14th St 34748. Fax: 352/365-0163. **Facility:** 129 units. 117 one-bedroom
            standard units. 12 one-bedroom suites. 2 stories, exterior corridors. **Parking:** on-site. **Terms:** cancellation
Small-scale Hotel fee imposed, package plans, pets ($15 fee). **Amenities:** voice mail, safes (fee). **Pool(s):** heated outdoor.
            Guest Services: coin laundry. **Business Services:** meeting rooms, fax (fee). **Cards:** AX, CB, DC, DS,
            MC, VI. **Special Amenities:** free expanded continental breakfast and free local telephone calls.

SOME UNITS

FEE

MICROTEL INN & SUITES *Book at aaa.com*   Phone: (352)315-1234
AAA SAVE   1/15-3/31   1P: $59-$99   2P: $59-$99   XP: $5   F18
            12/1-1/14 & 4/1-11/30 1P: $49-$74   2P: $49-$74   XP: $5   F18
            Location: 4 mi e of US 27. 9700 US Hwy 441 34788. Fax: 352/315-1027. **Facility:** 81 one-bedroom standard
            units. 3 stories, interior corridors. *Bath:* combo or shower only. **Parking:** on-site. **Amenities:** dual phone
Small-scale Hotel lines, irons. *Some:* hair dryers. **Pool(s):** outdoor. **Business Services:** meeting rooms, fax (fee). **Cards:** AX,
            CB, DC, DS, MC, VI. **Special Amenities:** free continental breakfast and free local telephone calls.

SOME UNITS

SLEEP INN *Book at aaa.com*   Phone: (352)326-9002
AAA SAVE   All Year   1P: $50-$129   2P: $50-$129   XP: $10   F10
            Location: On US 27 N. 2476 N Citrus Blvd, Hwy 27 34748. Fax: 352/326-8668. **Facility:** 66 one-bedroom
            standard units. 4 stories, interior corridors. *Bath:* combo or shower only. **Parking:** on-site.
            Terms: cancellation fee imposed, [ECP] meal plan available. **Amenities:** high-speed Internet, dual phone
Small-scale Hotel lines, voice mail, hair dryers. **Pool(s):** outdoor. **Leisure Activities:** exercise room. **Guest Services:** coin
            laundry. **Business Services:** meeting rooms, fax (fee). **Cards:** AX, CB, DC, DS, JC, MC, VI.
Special Amenities: free expanded continental breakfast and free local telephone calls.

SOME UNITS

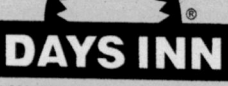
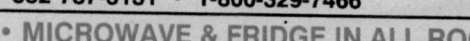

SUPER 8 MOTEL · *Book at aaa.com*
AAA · SAVE
Small-scale Hotel

12/1-4/25	1P: $50-$100	2P: $50-$106	XP: $6 · F12
4/26-11/30	1P: $30-$55	2P: $36-$61	XP: $6 · F12

Phone: (352)787-6363

Location: Jct US 27 and 441. 1392 North Blvd W 34748. **Fax:** 352/787-6363. **Facility:** 50 one-bedroom standard units. 3 stories, interior corridors. **Parking:** on-site. **Terms:** [ECP] meal plan available, small pets only ($10 fee). **Amenities:** safes (fee). **Pool(s):** outdoor. **Business Services:** fax (fee). **Cards:** AX, CB, DC, DS, JC, MC, VI. **Special Amenities:** free expanded continental breakfast and free local telephone calls.

SOME UNITS

----- **WHERE TO DINE** -----

TAKIS PIZZA RESTAURANT
Greek

Lunch: $3-$14   **Dinner:** $3-$14   **Phone:** 352/787-2344
Location: On US 441. 1324 W North Blvd 34748. **Hours:** 11 am-3 & 5-10 pm. Closed major holidays. **Reservations:** accepted. **Features:** The menu combines the best of both Greek and Italian cuisine. Guests can choose from such options as moussaka, souvlaki, gyros, baked manicotti, eggplant parmigiana and spaghetti. Two appetizer favorites are cheese bread and pita with tzatziki. Other options include combination platters, submarine sandwiches, pitas, salads and children's choices. Casual dress; cocktails. **Parking:** on-site. **Cards:** AX, DS, MC, VI.

VIC'S EMBERS
American

Dinner: $12-$22   **Phone:** 352/728-8989
Location: On US 441, 4.4 mi se of jct US 27. 7940 US 441 34788. **Hours:** 4:30 pm-10 pm, Fri & Sat-11 pm, Sun 11:30 am-2:30 & 4-9:30 pm. Closed major holidays. **Features:** This casual, somewhat elegant eatery boasts a pleasant atmosphere and some tableside preparations. Watch the planes fly into Leesburg Airport and order the Polynesian salmon heaped with vegetables and garlic mashed potatoes. Casual dress; cocktails; entertainment. **Parking:** valet. **Cards:** MC, VI.

LONGWOOD pop. 13,745   (See map and index starting on p. 656)

----- **WHERE TO STAY** -----

COMFORT INN & CONFERENCE CENTER · *Book at aaa.com*
Small-scale Hotel

All Year [CP]	1P: $79-$149	2P: $79-$149	XP: $10 · F17

Phone: (407)862-4000   **45**

Location: I-4, just nw. 2025 W SR 434 32779. **Fax:** 407/862-3530. **Facility:** 194 units. 193 one-bedroom standard units. 1 one-bedroom suite ($129-$199). 2 stories, exterior corridors. *Bath:* combo or shower only. **Parking:** on-site. **Terms:** [BP] meal plan available, package plans, pets ($10 fee). **Amenities:** voice mail, irons, hair dryers. **Pool(s):** outdoor. **Leisure Activities:** exercise room. **Guest Services:** coin laundry. **Business Services:** meeting rooms, fax (fee). **Cards:** AX, CB, DC, DS, MC, VI.

SOME UNITS

----- **WHERE TO DINE** -----

ANTHONY'S NEW YORK PIZZA & PASTA
Italian

Lunch: $5-$18   **Dinner:** $5-$18   **Phone:** 407-774-7878   **127**
Location: Jct Hunt Club and Wekiva Springs rds. 3907 Wekiva Springs Rd 32779. **Hours:** 10 am-10 pm, Fri & Sat-11 pm. Closed major holidays. **Features:** Located in a shopping plaza, this eatery's menu centers on pizza slices, pies, pasta and traditional dishes. Casual dress; beer & wine only. **Parking:** on-site. **Cards:** AX, DS, MC, VI.

BONEFISH GRILL
Seafood

Dinner: $13-$21   **Phone:** 407/331-4256   **129**
Location: I-4, exit 94, just e. 1761 W SR 434 32750. **Hours:** 4 pm-10:30 pm, Fri & Sat-11:30 pm, Sun-10 pm. Closed: 11/23, 12/25. **Reservations:** accepted. **Features:** In a shopping plaza, the popular restaurant creatively prepares fresh seafood over a wood-burning grill. Among choices are Chilean sea bass, ahi, tuna and rainbow trout, to name a few. Dressy casual; cocktails. **Parking:** on-site. **Cards:** AX, DC, MC, VI.

CALYPSO GRILLE
Caribbean

Lunch: $6-$15   **Dinner:** $6-$15   **Phone:** 407/332-0176   **132**
Location: I-4, exit 94, just e; located in Longwood Village. 1891 W SR 434 32750. **Hours:** 11 am-3 & 5-8:30 pm, Fri & Sat-9 pm. Closed major holidays; also Sun. **Features:** Eat under a swirling bamboo fan surrounded by the colors of the Caribbean. This eatery adds island seasonings to dishes such as grilled grouper with a mango salsa, Trinidad fricassee stew chicken (bone in), and grilled jerk chicken. Red beans and plantains accompany most dishes. Casual dress; beer & wine only. **Parking:** on-site. **Cards:** AX, DS, MC, VI.

CRISPERS
American

Lunch: $5-$9   **Dinner:** $5-$9   **Phone:** 407/834-4191   **131**
Location: I-4, exit 94, just e; in Shoppes of Longwood Village. 1869 W SR 434 32750. **Hours:** 10:30 am-9 pm, Sun 11 am-8 pm. Closed major holidays. **Features:** A healthy alternative for lunch or dinner, the restaurant prepares towering specialty sandwiches on warm, fresh homemade bread. Salad selections with combinations of meats, fruit and cheese are just as tempting. The varied coffees go well with freshly baked cakes and brownies. Casual dress. **Parking:** on-site. **Cards:** MC, VI.

ENZO'S RESTAURANT ON THE LAKE
Italian

Dinner: $20-$38   **Phone:** 407/834-9872   **134**
Location: 0.5 mi s of SR 434. 1130 S Hwy 17-92 32750. **Hours:** 6 pm-10 pm, Fri also 11:30 am-2:30 pm. Closed: 1/1, 12/25; also Sun. **Reservations:** suggested. **Features:** Elegant trattoria ambience is found in a converted house on Lake Fairy. Go early for the sunsets since dinner is a very busy time. Excellent house pastas, fresh veal and fish specialties are served with finesse. The tiramisu is rich with flavor. Dressy casual; cocktails. **Parking:** on-site and valet. **Cards:** AX, DC, DS, MC, VI.

FIRST WATCH
American

Lunch: $5-$7   **Phone:** 407/774-1830   **138**
Location: Jct Wekiva Springs Rd. 2454 W SR 434 32779. **Hours:** 7 am-2:30 pm. Closed: 11/23, 12/25. **Features:** One of a dozen like it in Florida, it serves breakfast, brunch and lunch with traditional omelets, pancakes, waffles and crepes. Great salads and sandwiches are accompanied by fresh fruits and muffins. Attentive and accurate service brings patrons back. Casual dress. **Parking:** on-site. **Cards:** AX, DS, MC, VI.

(See map and index starting on p. 656)

IMPERIAL DYNASTY CHINESE RESTAURANT & LOUNGE

AAA ▽▽▽ Chinese

Lunch: $6-$8   **Dinner:** $6-$30   **Phone:** 407/786-2266 136
Location: I-4, exit 94, just w. 2045 W SR 434 32779. **Hours:** 11 am-9:30 pm, Fri-10:30 pm, Sun noon-9:30 pm. Closed: 11/23; also for lunch Easter & 7/4. **Reservations:** suggested. **Features:** Traditional sure-to-please favorites—preparations of beef, chicken, fish, pork and vegetables—are served at the eatery. Dishes are prepared with minimal salt and no MSG. Casual dress; cocktails. **Parking:** on-site. **Cards:** AX, DC, DS, MC, VI.

JOURNEY'S

▽▽▽ Continental

Lunch: $7-$11   **Dinner:** $14-$32   **Phone:** 407/629-2221 130
Location: I-4, exit 94, just e; in Longwood Village Shopping Center. 1831 W SR 434 32750. **Hours:** 11:30 am-2 & 5:30-10 pm. Closed major holidays. **Reservations:** suggested, weekends. **Features:** World-inspired cuisine is the highlight of this "off the beaten path" restaurant. Select from entrees of ahi tuna, maple leaf farm roasted duck, braised New Zealand lamb rack or a 32 oz. "Cowboy Steak" bone-in ribeye. Desserts are a must for anyone with a sweet tooth. Casual dress; cocktails. **Parking:** on-site. **Cards:** AX, DS, MC, VI.

KOREA HOUSE

▽▽ Korean

Lunch: $9-$15   **Dinner:** $13-$20   **Phone:** 407/767-5918 128
Location: I-4, exit 94, 1.6 mi e on SR 434 towards Longwood/Winter Springs; next to Winn Dixie. 977 W SR 434 32750. **Hours:** 11:30 am-10 pm, Sun 4 pm-10 pm. **Reservations:** accepted. **Features:** The modest Korean-style diner serves various preparations of beef, fish and pork. Adventurous diners may want to try black goat (young yang tang). Most meals are accompanied by an array of pickled and fermented vegetables, such as kimchee. Casual dress; beer & wine only. **Parking:** on-site. **Cards:** AX, DS, MC, VI.

MARKHAM'S SPORTS BAR & GRILL

▽▽ American

Lunch: $8-$18   **Dinner:** $8-$18   **Phone:** 407/774-8868 137
Location: I-4, exit 94, just w; jct SR 434 and Markham Woods Rd. 108 Markham Woods Rd 32779. **Hours:** 11 am-2 am, Sun-11 pm. Closed major holidays. **Features:** Sports-themed murals are painted on every wall of the neighborhood restaurant. Guests can choose to sit outside to enjoy their burgers, steaks and seafood selections. Casual dress; cocktails. **Parking:** on-site. **Cards:** AX, MC, VI.

MELTING POT

▽▽ Fondue

Dinner: $12-$39   **Phone:** 407/862-8773 135
Location: I-4, exit 94, just w. 1200 Douglas Ave 32779. **Hours:** 5:30 pm-9:30 pm, Fri & Sat-10:30 pm. Closed major holidays. **Reservations:** suggested. **Features:** The moderately upscale restaurant is known for tableside fondue preparations. Combination platters allow for a variety of meats, seafood and poultry to be cooked using different oils and batters. White- or dark-chocolate fondue is a treat on various fruits and cake. Casual dress; cocktails. **Parking:** on-site. **Cards:** AX, CB, DC, DS, JC, MC, VI.

MYKONOS

▽▽ Greek

Lunch: $5-$8   **Dinner:** $9-$18   **Phone:** 407/788-9095 139
Location: I-4, exit 94, 1 mi w on SR 434; in Albertson's Shopping Plaza. 2401 W SR 434 32779. **Hours:** 11 am-10 pm. Closed major holidays; also Sun. **Features:** Authentic Greek dishes served to you while you are surrounded by the scenic landscape of Mykonos. Begin with the flamming saganaki, continue with the mousaka, and finish with ever so tempting baklava. Casual dress; beer & wine only. **Parking:** on-site. **Cards:** AX, DC, MC, VI.

VOLCANOS COFFEE BAR

▽ American

Lunch: $4-$6   **Dinner:** $4-$6   **Phone:** 407/260-8845 133
Location: I-4, exit 94, just e; located in Longwood Village. 1897 W SR 434 32750. **Hours:** 6 am-9 pm, Fri & Sat-10 pm. Closed major holidays. **Features:** Baked goods and panini sandwiches are on the menu but coffee and espresso driks are the specialty. An extensive menu of classic, signature and frozen espresso drinks are available; fruit smoothies are also an option. Casual dress. **Parking:** on-site. **Cards:** MC, VI.

MAITLAND pop. 12,019 (See map and index starting on p. 656)

——— WHERE TO STAY ———

COURTYARD BY MARRIOTT ORLANDO/MAITLAND

▽▽▽ Small-scale Hotel

Book at aaa.com   **Phone:** (407)659-9100 64
1/1-5/31   1P: $79-$149
12/1-12/31 & 6/1-11/30   1P: $69-$119
Location: I-4, exit 90B, 0.5 mi w, just s on Keller Rd, then just w. 1750 Pembrook Dr 32810. **Fax:** 407/659-9101. **Facility:** 112 units. 108 one-bedroom standard units, some with whirlpools. 4 one-bedroom suites ($69-$169). 4 stories, interior corridors. **Bath:** combo or shower only. **Parking:** on-site. **Terms:** package plans. **Amenities:** high-speed Internet, dual phone lines, voice mail, irons, hair dryers. **Pool(s):** heated outdoor. **Leisure Activities:** whirlpool, exercise room. **Guest Services:** valet and coin laundry. **Business Services:** meeting rooms, PC, fax. **Cards:** AX, DC, DS, JC, MC, VI.

SOME UNITS
(ASK) (SD) ⊓ Ⓨ ⌖M ⊡ ⊘ ⊷ ✦ DATA/PORT ⊡ / ⊠ ⊟ ⊡ /

HOMEWOOD SUITES BY HILTON ORLANDO NORTH

AAA (SAVE) ▽▽▽ Small-scale Hotel

Book at aaa.com   **Phone:** (407)875-8777 65
All Year [BP]   1P: $89-$329   2P: $99-$339   XP: $15   F18
Location: I-4, exit 90, just w, then just s on Lake Destiny. 290 Southhall Ln 32751. **Fax:** 407/875-8812. **Facility:** 143 units. 138 one- and 5 two-bedroom suites with efficiencies. 6 stories, interior corridors. **Bath:** combo or shower only. **Parking:** on-site. **Terms:** check-in 4 pm, package plans, pets ($75 fee). **Amenities:** video library, video games (fee), high-speed Internet, dual phone lines, voice mail, irons, hair dryers. **Pool(s):** outdoor. **Leisure Activities:** exercise room. **Guest Services:** complimentary evening beverages: Mon-Thurs, valet and coin laundry, area transportation-within 7 mi. **Business Services:** meeting rooms, business center. **Cards:** AX, DC; DS, MC, VI. **Special Amenities:** free full breakfast and free newspaper.

SOME UNITS
(SD) (ⓕ) ⊓+ ⌖M ⊡ ⊘ ⊷ (VCR) ✦ DATA/PORT ⊟ ⊡ ⊡ / ⊠ /
FEE

(See map and index starting on p. 656)

THURSTON HOUSE   Phone: (407)539-1911 66

▼▼▼▼   All Year   1P: $150-$170   2P: $150-$170
            Location: 0.5 mi w of US 17-92. 851 Lake Ave 32751. Fax: 407/539-0365. **Facility:** A swing and rocking chairs
Bed & Breakfast   invite lingering on the screened porch of this 1885 Queen Anne house; a parlor has cable TV and a
            fireplace. Designated smoking area. 4 one-bedroom standard units. 2 stories, interior corridors. *Bath:* combo
or shower only. **Parking:** on-site. **Terms:** age restrictions may apply, 5 day cancellation notice. **Amenities:** video library, CD
players, voice mail, irons, hair dryers. **Guest Services:** complimentary evening beverages. **Cards:** AX, MC, VI.

SOME UNITS
(A$K) (S⃝) (✕) (DATA PORT) / (VCR) /

─────── **WHERE TO DINE** ───────

ANTONIO'S LA FIAMMA   **Lunch:** $6-$15   **Dinner:** $6-$20   **Phone:** 407/645-5523 203
(AAA)   **Location:** On US 17-92, 1.3 mi n of jct SR 423 (Lee Rd). 611 S Orlando Ave 32751. **Hours:** 11 am-10 pm, Sun
▼▼ ▼▼   noon-9 pm. Closed major holidays. **Features:** The bustling eatery is surrounded by hundreds of bottles of
            wine and imported pasta, tea and chocolate. Locals flock here for sandwiches, salads, homemade ravioli
Italian   and fettuccine. Casual dress; cocktails. **Parking:** on-site. **Cards:** AX, CB, DS, MC, VI.

ANTONIO'S LA FIAMMA RISTORANTE   *Menu on aaa.com*   **Lunch:** $5-$14
                                                                Phone: 407/645-5523 204
                                       Dinner: $12-$37
(AAA)   **Location:** On US 17-92, 1.3 mi n of jct SR 423 (Lee Rd). 611 S Orlando Ave 32751. **Hours:** 11 am-2:30 & 5-10 pm,
▼▼▼▼   Sat from 5 pm. Closed major holidays; also Sun. **Reservations:** suggested. **Features:** The second floor
            dining room of the energetic and elegant restaurant overlooks Lake Lily. Wood-fired ovens contribute to the
Italian   rich flavors of gourmet creations of chicken, fish and beef. Be sure to try their version of that classic dessert,
            tiramisu. The first-floor delicatessen has a feel all its own. Dressy casual; cocktails. **Parking:** on-site.
            Cards: AX, CB, DC, DS, MC, VI.
                                                                                            (Y)

FAST EDDIE'S FAMOUS HAMBURGERS   **Lunch:** $2-$5   **Dinner:** $2-$5   **Phone:** 407/644-3334 205
▼▼   **Location:** 1 mi s on US 17-92. 118 Lake Ave 32751. **Hours:** 10:30 am-7 pm. Closed major holidays; also Sun.
            Features: The eatery specializes in quick-serve hamburgers that are made fresh while you wait; tasty chili
American   tops off your meal. Casual dress. **Parking:** on-site.
                                                                                            (K⃝)

FIRST WATCH   **Lunch:** $4-$10   **Phone:** 407/740-7437 206
▼▼▼▼   **Location:** 0.4 mi s of Maitland Ave. 1221 S Orlando Ave 32751. **Hours:** 7 am-2:30 pm. **Features:** Breakfast is the
            most important meal of the day and this is the place to get any of your favorites; bring the whole gang.
American   Casual dress. **Parking:** on-site. **Cards:** AX, DS, MC, VI.

KAPPY'S   **Lunch:** $2-$5   **Dinner:** $2-$5   **Phone:** 407/647-9099 201
▼▼   **Location:** On US 17-92, 2 mi n of jct SR 423 (Lee Rd). 501 N Orlando Ave 32751. **Hours:** 10:30 am-9 pm, Sun 11
            am-4 pm. Closed major holidays. **Reservations:** not accepted. **Features:** Along busy US 17/92, the popular
American   lunchtime restaurant has a small indoor counter for sitting and several picnic tables outside. Hamburgers,
            Philadelphia cheese steak, chicken Philly subs and a few sandwiches are featured on the menu. Casual
dress. **Parking:** on-site. **Cards:** MC, VI.
                                                                                            (K⃝)

MELTING POT   **Dinner:** $15-$30   **Phone:** 407/628-1134 202
▼▼▼▼   **Location:** Jct US 17-92 and Horatio Ave, just e. 500 E Horatio Ave 32751. **Hours:** 5:30 pm-9:45 pm, Fri-10:45 pm,
            Sat 5 pm-10:45 pm, Sun 5 pm-9:45 pm. Closed major holidays. **Reservations:** suggested.
Fondue   **Features:** Guests should arrive at the eatery hungry. Tableside preparation and "cook-it-yourself"
            combination platters are just the beginning of a wonderful dining experience. Mouthwatering white chocolate
amaretto fondue with an array of fresh fruits tops off a fun-filled evening. This is a great place for special occasions. Casual
dress; cocktails. **Parking:** on-site. **Cards:** AX, DC, DS, MC, VI.

SAM SNEAD'S   **Lunch:** $5-$12   **Dinner:** $6-$22   **Phone:** 407/622-8800 200
▼▼▼▼   **Location:** I-4, exit 90, just w. 1801 Maitland Blvd 32810. **Hours:** 11 am-11 pm, Sat from 4 pm. Closed major
            holidays; also Sun. **Features:** Golf memorabilia mixes with deep mahogany and rich green accents and
American   wood floors to create a comfortable gathering spot for business or social lunches and dinners. Casual dress;
            cocktails. **Parking:** on-site. **Cards:** AX, DC, DS, MC, VI.
                                                                                            (Y)

MOUNT DORA pop. 9,418 (See map and index starting on p. 656)

─────── **WHERE TO STAY** ───────

COMFORT INN AND SUITES   *Book at aaa.com*   **Phone:** (352)383-3400 22
(AAA) (SAVE)   All Year   1P: $70-$130
▼▼▼▼   **Location:** Just s of southern jct SR 19. 16630 Hwy 441 W 32757. Fax: 352/383-8499. **Facility:** 89 units. 62 one-
            bedroom standard units, some with whirlpools. 27 one-bedroom suites ($90-$150). 2 stories, exterior
            corridors. *Bath:* combo or shower only. **Parking:** on-site. **Terms:** cancellation fee imposed, [CP] meal plan
Small-scale Hotel   available. **Amenities:** irons, hair dryers. **Pool(s):** outdoor. **Leisure Activities:** whirlpool, fishing. **Guest
            Services:** coin laundry. **Cards:** AX, CB, DC, DS, JC, MC, VI. **Special Amenities:** free continental
breakfast and free local telephone calls.

SOME UNITS
(S⃝) (¶↑) (🏊) (🚲) (🏋) (DATA PORT) (🔒) (📷) (💻) / (✕) /

(See map and index starting on p. 656)

DARST VICTORIAN MANOR   Phone: (352)383-4050 [24]

| | 12/1-5/31 & 10/1-11/30 [BP] | 1P: $150-$240 | 2P: $160-$250 | XP: $25 |
| | 6/1-9/30 [BP] | 1P: $140-$240 | 2P: $150-$250 | XP: $25 |

Bed & Breakfast   **Location:** On CR 441 (Old US 441), 0.3 mi w. 495 Old Hwy 441 32757. **Fax:** 352/383-7653. **Facility:** This reproduction of a late-1800s, Queen Anne-style home overlooks Lake Dora; check-in time is 3-6 p.m. Smoke free premises. 5 units. 3 one-bedroom standard units. 2 one-bedroom suites ($205-$250). 3 stories (no elevator), interior corridors. *Bath:* combo or shower only. **Parking:** on-site. **Terms:** 2 night minimum stay, age restrictions may apply, 7 day cancellation notice-fee imposed. **Amenities:** irons, hair dryers. **Leisure Activities:** whirlpool. *Fee:* massage. **Cards:** AX, DS, MC, VI.

[icons]

HAMPTON INN   *Book at aaa.com*   Phone: (352)383-4267 [23]
(AAA) (SAVE)

| | 12/1-3/31 [BP] | 1P: $89-$129 | 2P: $89-$129 |
| | 4/1-11/30 [BP] | 1P: $79-$129 | 2P: $79-$129 |

Small-scale Hotel   **Location:** 1.6 mi n of jct SR 46 and US 441. 19700 US Hwy 441 32757. **Fax:** 352/383-4114. **Facility:** 62 one-bedroom standard units. 3 stories, interior corridors. *Bath:* combo or shower only. **Parking:** on-site. **Terms:** 3 day cancellation notice, package plans. **Amenities:** high-speed Internet, dual phone lines, voice mail, irons, hair dryers. **Pool(s):** outdoor. **Leisure Activities:** whirlpool, exercise room. **Guest Services:** coin laundry. **Business Services:** meeting rooms, fax. **Cards:** AX, CB, DC, DS, JC, MC, VI. **Special Amenities:** free local telephone calls and free newspaper.

SOME UNITS
[icons] / X /

─────── **WHERE TO DINE** ───────

5TH AVE CAFE & MARKET   **Lunch:** $6-$12   **Dinner:** $6-$18   Phone: 352/383-0090 [58]

Location: Between N Donnelly and Baker sts; downtown. 116 E Fifth Ave 32757. **Hours:** 9 am-9 pm, Sun 10 am-3 pm. Closed: 11/23, 12/25; also Mon. **Features:** If you are looking for fresh, wholesome and organic, come and relax in this sunny dining room next to the small organic market and enjoy a variety of made-to-order delights highlighting organically grown dishes. Casual dress; beer & wine only. **Parking:** street. **Cards:** AX, MC, VI.

American

CAFE STELLA   **Lunch:** $6-$10   **Dinner:** $9-$18   Phone: 352/385-1888 [57]

Location: On US 441, 0.5 mi s of south jct of SR 19. 4931 Lake Park Ct 32757. **Hours:** 11 am-9:30 pm, Fri & Sat-10 pm. Closed: 12/25. **Reservations:** accepted. **Features:** The special touches of the dining room's inviting decor help set the mood for relaxed, enjoyable dining. The menu features traditional and creative Italian favorites that are made in-house. Selections include chicken, veal, seafood, pasta, pizzas and subs. In addition to the menu, an Italian lunch buffet is available Monday through Saturday. Casual dress; beer & wine only. **Parking:** on-site. **Cards:** AX, DS, MC, VI.

Italian

[icon M]

CECILE'S FRENCH CORNER CAFE   **Lunch:** $5-$17   **Dinner:** $5-$17   Phone: 352/383-7100 [59]

Location: Downtown. 237 W 4th Ave 32757. **Hours:** 10 am-5 pm, Fri & Sat-11 pm, Sun-8 pm. Closed major holidays. **Reservations:** accepted. **Features:** Located in downtown area within walking distance of many shops and galleries, this cafe serves wonderful salads and sandwiches. Casual dress; beer & wine only. **Parking:** street. **Cards:** AX, MC, VI.

French

DIXIE CROSSROADS   **Lunch:** $8-$22   **Dinner:** $8-$22   Phone: 352/385-0774 [56]

Location: 3 mi n of jct SR 46 and US 441. 18660 US Hwy 441 32757. **Hours:** 11:30 am-9 pm. Closed major holidays. **Features:** On the menu are fresh seafood items prepared any way the guest wants it, in addition to steak, prime rib and chicken selections. Among popular choices are Canadian lobster tail, Icelandic cod, salmon, fried shrimp, oysters and alligator. A sister restaurant is in Titusville. Casual dress; cocktails. **Parking:** on-site. **Cards:** AX, MC, VI.

Seafood

THE FROSTY MUG   **Lunch:** $8-$12   **Dinner:** $12-$22   Phone: 352/383-1696 [60]

Location: Downtown; in cellar of Renaissance Building. 411 N Donnelly St 32757. **Hours:** 11 am-9:30 pm, Fri & Sat-10:30 pm. Closed: 11/23, 12/25. **Reservations:** accepted. **Features:** In the cellar of a building in the historic shopping district of Mount Dora, the pub presents a European menu with such choices as fish and chips, schnitzel and chicken Reykjavik. Beverages include varied wines, as well as 50 imported and domestic beers, ranging from Bass and Harp to Hacker-Pschorr and Ringnes. Locals love to hang out at the friendly spot, which employs pleasant servers. Casual dress; beer & wine only; entertainment. **Parking:** on-site. **Cards:** AX, CB, DC, DS, JC, MC, VI.

Norwegian

THE GABLES RESTAURANT   **Lunch:** $7-$12   **Dinner:** $15-$27   Phone: 352/383-8993 [63]
(AAA)

Location: Just s of old US 441; opposite Chamber of Commerce. 322 Alexander St 32757. **Hours:** 11 am-2:30 & 5-8:30 pm, Fri-9 pm, Sat 11 am-3 & 5-9 pm, Sun 11 am-3 & 5-8:30 pm. Closed: 1/1, 12/25. **Reservations:** suggested. **Features:** A country garden setting includes limited dining on the front porch. International offerings feature beef, poultry and seafood selections. Consistent servers bring dishes like turkey chili made with fresh vegetables and a rich peanut butter pie. Casual dress; cocktails. **Parking:** street. **Cards:** AX, MC, VI.

American

[icon]

THE GOBLIN MARKET   **Lunch:** $5-$14   **Dinner:** $16-$28   Phone: 352/735-0059 [64]

Location: On the alley between 4th and 5th aves. 330 Dora Drawdy Ln 32757. **Hours:** 11 am-3 & 5-9 pm, Fri & Sat-10 pm, Sun noon-4 pm. Closed major holidays; also 12/24 & Mon. **Reservations:** suggested. **Features:** After a day visiting the town's antique shops, diners can gather with their friends to relax in the peaceful intimacy of this centrally located, "back alley" restaurant. Offered is a selection of well-prepared and artfully presented dishes, including entrees of beef, pork, lamb, poultry and seafood. The Chesapeake Bay crab cakes are a popular starter. An often-requested entree is a signature dish: potato-crusted black grouper. Dressy casual; cocktails. **Parking:** street. **Cards:** AX, DS, MC, VI.

American

[icon]

(See map and index starting on p. 656)

PALM TREE GRILL   Lunch: $6-$10   Dinner: $10-$22   Phone: 352/735-1936   **62**

Italian   **Location:** Center of downtown. 351 N Donnelly 32757. **Hours:** 11 am-9 pm, Fri & Sat-9:30 pm, Sun-8 pm. Closed major holidays. **Features:** Near shops in the historic downtown area, the restaurant serves traditional favorites in a patio-type setting. The menu includes a nice selection of seafood and beef dishes. Casual dress; cocktails. **Parking:** street. **Cards:** AX, DC, DS, MC, VI.

THE WINDSOR ROSE ENGLISH TEA ROOM   Lunch: $6-$8   Dinner: $6-$18   Phone: 352/735-2551   **61**

English   **Location:** Downtown. 144 W 4th Ave 32757. **Hours:** 10 am-5 pm. Closed major holidays. **Features:** Traditional English tea served in beautifully maintained garden setting. Casual dress; beer only. **Parking:** street. **Cards:** AX, DS, MC, VI.

OCOEE pop. 24,391 (See map and index starting on p. 656)

——— WHERE TO STAY ———

BEST WESTERN TURNPIKE WEST-ORLANDO   *Book at aaa.com*   Phone: (407)656-5050   **75**

Small-scale Hotel   All Year   1P: $69-$94

Location: I-4, exit 84, 10 mi w on SR 50; 0.5 mi e of Florida Tpke, exit 267B. 10945 W Colonial Dr 34761. Fax: 407/877-9346. **Facility:** 110 one-bedroom standard units. 2-3 stories, exterior corridors. **Parking:** on-site. **Terms:** small pets only. **Amenities:** video games (fee), voice mail, irons, hair dryers. *Some:* high-speed Internet, dual phone lines. **Pool(s):** outdoor. **Leisure Activities:** whirlpool. **Guest Services:** valet and coin laundry. **Business Services:** meeting rooms, fax. **Cards:** AX, CB, DC, DS, MC, VI.

COURTYARD BY MARRIOTT ORLANDO OCOEE   *Book at aaa.com*   Phone: 407/573-1010   **74**

Small-scale Hotel   2/5-11/30   1P: $109-$149   2P: $109-$149
          12/1-2/4   1P: $99-$139   2P: $99-$139

Location: I-4, exit 84, 10 mi w on SR 50; 0.5 mi e of Florida Tpke, exit 267B. 10971 W Colonial Dr 34761. Fax: 407/993-1010. **Facility:** 80 units. 77 one-bedroom standard units. 3 one-bedroom suites. 3 stories, interior corridors. *Bath:* combo or shower only. **Terms:** 2-7 night minimum stay - seasonal, 7 day cancellation notice, [BP] meal plan available. **Amenities:** high-speed Internet, voice mail, irons, hair dryers. **Pool(s):** heated outdoor. **Leisure Activities:** whirlpool, exercise room. **Guest Services:** sundries, valet and coin laundry. **Business Services:** meeting rooms, business center. **Cards:** AX, DC, DS, MC, VI.

RED ROOF INN ORLANDO WEST   *Book at aaa.com*   Phone: (407)347-0140   **76**

Small-scale Hotel   All Year   1P: $59-$84

Location: I-4, exit 84, 10 mi w on SR 50; 0.6 mi e of Florida Tpke, exit 267. 11241 W Colonial Dr 34761 (10945 W Colonial Dr). Fax: 407/347-0149. **Facility:** 83 one-bedroom standard units. 3 stories, interior corridors. *Bath:* combo or shower only. **Parking:** on-site. **Amenities:** high-speed Internet, voice mail. **Pool(s):** small heated outdoor. **Guest Services:** coin laundry. **Business Services:** meeting rooms, fax (fee). **Cards:** AX, CB, DC, DS, MC, VI.

OVIEDO pop. 26,316 (See map and index starting on p. 656)

——— WHERE TO DINE ———

BAJO EL PUENTE   Lunch: $4-$11   Dinner: $4-$11   Phone: 407/706-0239   **74**

Spanish   **Location:** Jct SR 434 and Alafaya Woods Blvd, 0.3 mi s of Mitchell Hammock Rd. 7 Alafaya Woods, Suite 300 Blvd 32765. **Hours:** 8 am-9 pm. Closed major holidays; also Sun. **Features:** Meals are made in advance and presented in a heated display case. Choose from chicken or beef stew, skirt steak or mofongo de camarones. Cuban sandwiches, tostones and empanadas also are on the menu. Casual dress. **Parking:** on-site.

BIG DADDY'S PIZZA   Lunch: $3-$17   Dinner: $3-$17   Phone: 407/658-2443   **76**

Italian   **Location:** 0.6 mi n of jct University Blvd. 3050 Alafaya Tr 32765. **Hours:** 11 am-10 pm, Fri & Sat-midnight, Sun noon-11 pm. Closed major holidays. **Features:** Pizza and wings are favorites. Because seating is limited, take-out is a popular option. Casual dress; beer only. **Parking:** on-site. **Cards:** AX, MC, VI.

D'AMICI ITALIAN GRILL & PIZZERIA   Lunch: $6-$16   Dinner: $6-$16   Phone: 407/706-0217   **75**

Italian   **Location:** Jct of SR 434 and Alafaya Woods Blvd, 0.3 mi s of Mitchell Hammock Rd. 7 Alafaya Woods Blvd, Suite 1000 32765. **Hours:** 11 am-10 pm, Fri-11 pm, Sat 4 pm-10 pm, Sun 4 pm-9 pm. Closed major holidays. **Features:** Patrons enjoy hand-tossed gourmet pizza, calzones and homemade pasta dishes at the quaint eatery. Eggplant, veal and chicken dishes also are on the menu. Casual dress; beer & wine only. **Parking:** on-site. **Cards:** AX, MC, VI.

ST. CLOUD pop. 20,074 (See map and index starting on p. 666)

——— WHERE TO STAY ———

BUDGET INN OF ST CLOUD   Phone: (407)892-2858   **23**

Motel   All Year   1P: $35-$90   2P: $45-$90   XP: $5   D5

Location: On US 192, 0.5 mi e of The Water Tower, 2 mi w of jct CR 15. 602 13th St 34769. Fax: 407/892-8063. **Facility:** 17 one-bedroom standard units, some with kitchens. 1 story, exterior corridors. *Bath:* combo or shower only. **Parking:** on-site. **Terms:** 3 day cancellation notice, weekly rates available, pets ($10 fee, with prior approval). **Amenities:** hair dryers. **Business Services:** fax (fee). **Cards:** AX, DS, MC, VI.

(See map and index starting on p. 666)

──────── WHERE TO DINE ────────

FAT BOY'S BAR-B-QUE   **Lunch:** $3-$12   **Dinner:** $3-$12   **Phone:** 407/892-4400   ⑪

Barbecue

Location: Jct Florida Tpke and US 192, 4 mi e on US 192. 2912 13th St 34769. **Hours:** 8 am-9 pm. Closed major holidays. **Features:** Tasty barbecue is slowly smoked in-house over hickory and basted with "secret" sauce. Begin with deep-fried corn nuggets, then choose from among barbecue sandwiches, platters or combination plates. Lunchtime at the quick-serve restaurant is busy, as is the period before any event at nearby arena. Casual dress; beer only. **Parking:** on-site. **Cards:** AX, DS, MC, VI.

SANFORD pop. 38,291   (See map and index starting on p. 656)

──────── WHERE TO STAY ────────

COMFORT INN & SUITES NORTH ORLANDO   *Book at aaa.com*   **Phone:** (407)585-1580   ㊴

Small-scale Hotel

All Year   1P: $69-$259
Location: I-4, exit 101C, just e, just n on Hickman Dr, then just w. 590 Ava Ct 32771. **Fax:** 407/585-1599. **Facility:** 107 units. 104 one-bedroom standard units. 3 one-bedroom suites. 4 stories, interior corridors. *Bath:* combo or shower only. **Parking:** on-site. **Amenities:** high-speed Internet, dual phone lines, voice mail, irons, hair dryers. **Pool(s):** heated outdoor. **Leisure Activities:** exercise room. **Guest Services:** coin laundry. **Business Services:** meeting rooms, business center. **Cards:** AX, CB, DC, DS, JC, MC, VI.
Special Amenities: free expanded continental breakfast and free local telephone calls. *(See color ad below)*

   SOME UNITS

THE HIGGINS HOUSE BED & BREAKFAST   **Phone:** 407/324-9238   ㊶

Historic Bed & Breakfast

Property failed to provide current rates
Location: Just s of 1st St; in historic district. 420 S Oak Ave 32771. **Fax:** 407/324-2024. **Facility:** Built circa 1894, this small historic inn has been restored; its Victorian ambience provides for a peaceful stay just 5 minutes from I-4. Smoke free premises. 3 one-bedroom standard units. 1-2 stories, interior corridors. **Parking:** street. **Amenities:** high-speed Internet, hair dryers. **Leisure Activities:** bicycles. **Guest Services:** complimentary evening beverages. **Business Services:** fax.

HOLIDAY INN EXPRESS-SANFORD/LAKE MARY   **Phone:** (407)320-0845   ㊷

Small-scale Hotel

All Year   1P: $89-$175   2P: $89-$175
Location: I-4, exit 98, e on Lake Mary Blvd, then 0.5 mi n on US 17-92. 3401 S Orlando Dr 32773. **Fax:** 407/328-6306. **Facility:** 72 units. 69 one-bedroom standard units, some with whirlpools. 3 one-bedroom suites ($119-$175) with whirlpools. 4 stories, interior corridors. *Bath:* combo or shower only. **Parking:** on-site. **Terms:** cancellation fee imposed. **Amenities:** dual phone lines, voice mail, irons, hair dryers. **Pool(s):** outdoor. **Guest Services:** valet laundry. **Business Services:** meeting rooms, fax (fee). **Cards:** AX, CB, DC, DS, MC, VI.

                                                                                              SOME UNITS

SPRINGHILL SUITES BY MARRIOTT   *Book at aaa.com*   **Phone:** 407/995-1000   ㊵

Small-scale Hotel

All Year   1P: $109-$159   2P: $119-$179
Location: I-4, exit 101C, just se. Located in a commercial area. 201 N Towne Rd 32771. **Fax:** 407/995-5921. **Facility:** 105 one-bedroom standard units, some with whirlpools. 5 stories, interior corridors. *Bath:* combo or shower only. **Parking:** on-site. **Terms:** [ECP] meal plan available. **Amenities:** high-speed Internet, dual phone lines, voice mail, irons, hair dryers. **Pool(s):** outdoor. **Leisure Activities:** whirlpool, exercise room. **Guest Services:** valet and coin laundry. **Business Services:** meeting rooms, business center. **Cards:** AX, DC, DS, JC, MC, VI.

                                                                                              SOME UNITS

(See map and index starting on p. 656)

———— WHERE TO DINE ————

DA VINCI, A DINING PLACE   Lunch: $5-$12   Dinner: $14-$26   Phone: 407/323-1388   119
Italian
Location: I-4, exit 101, 5 mi e on SR 46; jct US 17-92, just e on 1st St. 107 Magnolia Ave 32771. **Hours:** 11:30 am-2 & 5:30-10 pm. Closed major holidays; also Sun. **Reservations:** suggested. **Features:** Near a shopping area in the historic downtown district, the restaurant serves large portions to ensure diners don't walk away hungry. Combinations of seafood, meat and pasta are creatively prepared to please the taste buds, and desserts should not be forgotten. Casual dress; cocktails. **Parking:** street. **Cards:** AX, MC, VI.

HOPS GRILLHOUSE & BREWERY   Lunch: $4-$23   Dinner: $4-$23   Phone: 407/320-8158   121
American
Location: I-4, exit 101C, just se. 111 Oregon Ave 32771. **Hours:** 11 am-10 pm, Fri & Sat-11 pm. **Features:** Specially brewed beers, brewmaster steaks and hot honey muffin croissants are a few of the mouthwatering choices available on the menu. Casual dress; cocktails. **Parking:** on-site. **Cards:** AX, CB, DC, DS, JC, MC, VI.

JOE'S CRAB SHACK   Lunch: $7-$9   Dinner: $9-$25   Phone: 407/323-0934   120
Seafood
Location: I-4, exit 104, just e. 4659 W First St 32771. **Hours:** 11 am-10 pm, Fri & Sat-11 pm. Closed: 11/23, 12/25. **Features:** Just off the interstate, the whimsically decorated restaurant is a fun place to enjoy seafood favorites. A playground for the kids can be found out back. **Parking:** on-site. **Cards:** AX, CB, DC, DS, JC, MC, VI.

OTTER'S RIVERSIDE RESTAURANT   Lunch: $6-$9   Dinner: $9-$25   Phone: 407/323-3991   118
Steak & Seafood
Location: I-4, exit 104; in "Port of Sanford". 4380 Carraway Pl 32771. **Hours:** 11 am-9 pm, Wed & Thurs-10 pm, Fri & Sat-11 pm, Sun 10 am-9 pm. Closed: 11/23, 12/25. **Features:** At this very popular spot, you may dine on an enclosed patio while the kids splash and play in the swimming pool. A view of the marina sets the mood for feasting on all-you-can-eat crab legs, or partake of the champagne brunch buffet on Sundays. Casual dress; cocktails. **Parking:** on-site. **Cards:** AX, CB, DC, DS, MC, VI.   ▣

SANFORD ALE HOUSE   Lunch: $4-$16   Dinner: $4-$16   Phone: 407/328-7037   123
American
Location: I-4, exit 101C, just se. 50 Town Center Cir 32771. **Hours:** 11 am-1:30 am. Closed major holidays. **Features:** Enjoy selections of clams on the half shell, oysters and peel and eat shrimp from the raw bar or choose an 8 oz. filet, baby back ribs or chicken parmesan from the appetizing menu. Casual dress; cocktails. **Parking:** on-site. **Cards:** AX, CB, DC, DS, JC, MC, VI.

SERGIO'S ITALIAN RESTAURANT   Lunch: $5-$8   Dinner: $7-$24   Phone: 407/323-4040   124
Italian
Location: 0.5 mi n of Airport Blvd on US 17-92. 2895 Orlando Dr 32773. **Hours:** 11 am-10 pm. Closed: 11/23, 12/25; also Sun. **Reservations:** accepted. **Features:** On the restaurant's menu is a traditional selection of well-prepared and moderately priced items. Families are welcomed in the straightforward and relaxed environment. Tables are well-spaced. Casual dress; cocktails. **Parking:** on-site. **Cards:** AX, CB, DC, DS, MC, VI.   ▣ ▣

TONY'S NEW YORK PIZZA & RESTAURANT   Lunch: $6-$15   Dinner: $6-$19   Phone: 407/321-7575   122
Italian
Location: I-4, exit 101C, just e to Mall Blvd. 312 N Entrance Rd 32771. **Hours:** 11 am-9 pm, Fri & Sat-10 pm. Closed major holidays. **Features:** Hand tossed pizza and traditional Italian favorites are featured on this expansive menu. Casual dress; beer & wine only. **Parking:** on-site. **Cards:** AX, DS, MC, VI.

TAVARES pop. 9,700

———— WHERE TO STAY ————

BUDGET INN   Phone: (352)343-4666
Motel
All Year   1P: $49-$59   2P: $49-$59   XP: $10   D12
Location: On US 441, 0.3 mi e of jct SR 19 S. 101 W Burleigh Blvd 32778-2498. Fax: 352/742-2717. **Facility:** 40 one-bedroom standard units, some with efficiencies. 2 stories, exterior corridors. **Parking:** on-site. **Terms:** 7 day cancellation notice, weekly rates available, package plans, small pets only ($8 fee). **Pool(s):** outdoor.
Cards: AX, DS, MC, VI.

SOME UNITS
(ASK) [S/D] [🛏] [🍴] [🏊] [✕] [📶] [📠] / [✕] /
FEE

HOLIDAY INN EXPRESS HOTEL & SUITES   *Book at aaa.com*   Phone: (352)742-1600
Small-scale Hotel
1/7-4/30 & 9/1-11/30   1P: $89-$199   2P: $99-$220
5/1-8/31   1P: $77-$200   2P: $87-$210
12/1-1/6   1P: $77-$189   2P: $88-$199
Location: On US 441, 2 mi w of US 19. 3601 W Burleigh Blvd 32778. Fax: 352/742-1662. **Facility:** 73 units. 71 one-bedroom standard units, some with whirlpools. 2 one-bedroom suites ($88-$379) with whirlpools. 3 stories, interior corridors. *Bath:* combo or shower only. **Parking:** on-site. **Terms:** cancellation fee imposed, [BP] meal plan available. **Amenities:** high-speed Internet, voice mail, irons, hair dryers. **Pool(s):** heated outdoor. **Leisure Activities:** exercise room. **Guest Services:** valet laundry. **Business Services:** meeting rooms, fax (fee). **Cards:** AX, CB, DC, DS, MC, VI.

SOME UNITS
(ASK) [S/D] [♿] [🔷] [🏊] [✕] [DATA PORT] [📶] / [✕] [📠] [📺] /

———— WHERE TO DINE ————

AMIGOS ORIGINAL TEX-MEX RESTAURANT   Lunch: $5-$12   Dinner: $7-$12   Phone: 352/253-1045
Tex-Mex
Location: SR 436 N to US 441 N; approximately 20 mi to Tavares. 901 Lakeshore Blvd 32778. **Hours:** 11 am-9 pm, Fri & Sat-10 pm. Closed: 1/1, 11/23, 12/25. **Features:** The staff moves at a bustling pace to deliver oversized burritos and platefuls of tacos. Casual surroundings and popular Tex-Mex dishes are offered for the whole family. Dine indoors or on the outdoor deck, with a good view of the lake. Casual dress; cocktails. **Parking:** on-site. **Cards:** AX, DC, MC, VI.

ANGELO'S

▼▼▼ ▼▼▼
Italian

Lunch: $5-$12   **Dinner:** $7-$15   **Phone:** 352/343-2757
Location: On US 441, 1.5 mi w of SR 19. 2270 Vindale Rd 32778. **Hours:** 11 am-10 pm, Sun-8 pm. Closed: Mon. **Features:** The eatery features baked Italian dishes such as gnocchi, manicotti, lasagna, stuffed shells, and cannelloni. Seafood dishes include linguini with clams, shrimp scampi and snapper Mediterraneo. Casual dress; cocktails. **Parking:** on-site. **Cards:** AX, DS, MC, VI.

DEAD RIVER VIC'S

▼▼▼ ▼▼▼
Steak & Seafood
MC, VI.

Lunch: $7-$10   **Dinner:** $7-$20   **Phone:** 352/742-5000
Location: On US 441, 2 mi w of SR 19. 3351 W Burleigh Blvd 32778. **Hours:** 11 am-10 pm, Fri & Sat-11 pm. **Features:** Golf carts will ferry you from the parking lot to this lovely, waterfront restaurant with outdoor seating, a gift shop and boat slips. Fresh seafood, chicken and ribs are featured, and the banana muffin with caramel ice cream will make your mouth water. Casual dress; cocktails. **Parking:** on-site. **Cards:** DS,

WINTER GARDEN pop. 14,351   (See map and index starting on p. 656)

─── **WHERE TO STAY** ───

ORANGE COUNTY NATIONAL GOLF CENTER AND LODGE

(AAA) [SAVE]

▼▼▼ ▼▼
Small-scale Hotel

Phone: 407/656-2626

| 1/1-11/30 | 1P: $85-$107 | 2P: $85-$107 |
| 12/1-12/31 | 1P: $79-$107 | 2P: $79-$107 |

Location: US 192, 6.8 mi n on CR 545. 16301 Phil Ritson Way 34787. **Fax:** 407/656-4045. **Facility:** 46 one-bedroom standard units. 1 story, exterior corridors. *Bath:* combo or shower only. **Parking:** on-site. **Terms:** 7 day cancellation notice, package plans. **Amenities:** voice mail, irons, hair dryers. **Dining:** 6:30 am-7 pm, cocktails. **Leisure Activities:** *Fee:* golf-45 holes, massage. **Guest Services:** gift shop. **Business Services:** meeting rooms, fax (fee). **Cards:** AX, DC, DS, MC, VI. **Special Amenities:** free full breakfast.

─── **WHERE TO DINE** ───

CHOCTAW WILLY'S

▼
Barbecue

Lunch: $3-$17   **Dinner:** $3-$17   **Phone:** 407/905-9917   (250)
Location: Downtown. 99 W Plant St 34787. **Hours:** 11 am-9 pm. Closed major holidays; also Sun. **Features:** Mouth-watering barbecue baby back ribs, pork, chicken, and beef are all served as a plate or a platter, and numerous tasty sides are offered. The homemade cobbler is worth saving room for. Casual dress. **Parking:** on-site. **Cards:** AX, DS, MC, VI.

TAQUITOS JALISCO

▼▼▼ ▼▼
Mexican

Lunch: $3-$9   **Dinner:** $5-$14   **Phone:** 407/654-0363   (251)
Location: In Tri-City Shopping Center. 1041 S Dillard St 34787. **Hours:** 11 am-9 pm, Fri-10 pm, Sat-9:30 pm. Closed: 11/23; also Mon. **Reservations:** accepted. **Features:** A friendly staff serves cuisine with fresh ingredients, lots of heat and lots of flavor. Entrees are presented with a colorful flair and prepared from authentic recipes. A modest place with only a few tables and chairs, it is important to arrive early. Casual dress; beer & wine only. **Parking:** on-site. **Cards:** AX, DS, MC, VI.

WINTER PARK pop. 24,090   (See map and index starting on p. 656)

─── **WHERE TO STAY** ───

BEST WESTERN MT. VERNON INN

(AAA) [SAVE]

▼▼▼ ▼▼
Small-scale Hotel

Book at aaa.com   **Phone:** (407)647-1166   [71]

| 12/25-11/30 | 1P: $84-$119 | 2P: $84-$119 | XP: $10 | F18 |
| 12/1-12/24 | 1P: $79-$114 | 2P: $79-$114 | XP: $10 | F18 |

Location: I-4, exit 87 (Fairbanks Ave), 1 mi e, then 0.3 mi n on US 17-92. Located opposite the Winter Park Civic Center. 110 S Orlando Ave 32789-3698. **Fax:** 407/647-8011. **Facility:** 144 one-bedroom standard units. 2 stories, interior/exterior corridors. *Bath:* combo or shower only. **Parking:** on-site. **Terms:** 3 day cancellation notice. **Amenities:** voice mail, irons, hair dryers. *Some:* high-speed Internet, dual phone lines. **Dining:** 7 am-2 pm, entertainment. **Pool(s):** outdoor. **Leisure Activities:** jogging. *Fee:* tennis privileges. **Guest Services:** valet laundry. **Business Services:** conference facilities, fax. **Cards:** AX, CB, DC, DS, JC, MC, VI. **Special Amenities:** early check-in/late check-out and preferred room (subject to availability with advance reservations). *(See color ad below)*

SOME UNITS

(See map and index starting on p. 656)

PARK INN ORLANDO/WINTER PARK　*Book at aaa.com*　　Phone: (407)539-1955　69
　AAA SAVE　All Year [ECP]　1P: $59-$79　2P: $59-$79　XP: $10　F12
　　Location: I-4, exit 88, just ne. 951 Wymore Rd 32789. Fax: 407/539-0705. Facility: 133 one-bedroom standard units. 3 stories, interior/exterior corridors. Parking: on-site. Amenities: high-speed Internet, voice mail, irons, hair dryers. Pool(s): heated outdoor. Guest Services: coin laundry. Cards: AX, CB, DC, DS, JC,
Small-scale Hotel　MC, VI. Special Amenities: free expanded continental breakfast and early check-in/late check-out.
SOME UNITS
FEE FEE

RAMADA INN　*Book at aaa.com*　　Phone: (407)644-8000　70
　AAA SAVE　All Year　1P: $50-$70　2P: $60-$80　XP: $10　D17
　　Location: I-4, exit 88, 1 mi e on Lee Rd, then just s. 901 N Orlando Ave 32789. Fax: 407/644-0032. Facility: 99 one-bedroom standard units. 2 stories, exterior corridors. Parking: on-site. Terms: [CP] meal plan available. Amenities: irons, hair dryers. Pool(s): outdoor. Guest Services: coin laundry. Business Services: fax
Motel　(fee). Cards: AX, CB, DC, DS, MC, VI. Special Amenities: free continental breakfast and free newspaper.
SOME UNITS

—— WHERE TO DINE ——

ALLEGRIA WINE BAR & CUCINA　Lunch: $8-$15　Dinner: $11-$30　Phone: 407/628-1641　241
　AAA　Location: Fairbanks Ave, just n on Park Ave, then just e. 115 E Lyman Ave 32789. Hours: 11 am-10 pm. Closed: 12/25. Reservations: accepted. Features: An Italian atmosphere, muted colors and wonderful aromas give personality to the cozy eatery. Daily changing offerings of antipasto are a must. Also on the menu are fresh pastas, seafood items and meats. Dressy casual; beer & wine only. Parking: street. Cards: AX, CB, DC,
Italian　DS, MC, VI.

AMIGOS　Lunch: $5-$12　Dinner: $7-$12　Phone: 407/657-8111　220
　　Location: Jct Aloma Ave and SR 436; just sw. 494 N Semoran Blvd 32792. Hours: 11 am-9:30 pm, Fri & Sat-10 pm, Sun-9 pm. Closed major holidays. Features: The staff moves at a bustling pace to deliver oversized
Tex-Mex　burritos and platefuls of tacos. Casual surroundings and popular Tex-Mex dishes are offered for the whole family. Order the fajitas for a sizzling, hot sensation. Casual dress; cocktails. Parking: on-site. Cards: AX,
DC, DS, MC, VI.

A TASTE OF JAMAICA RESTAURANT　Lunch: $3-$7　Phone: 407/539-0671　218
　　Location: I-4, exit 88, 0.6 mi e; jct US 17-92 and Lee Rd; in shopping plaza. 501 N Orlando Ave 32789. Hours: 11 am-6 pm. Closed major holidays; also Sat & Sun. Features: Examples of items on the Caribbean menu are
Caribbean　curried stewed chicken, Guyanese Chinese chow mein and Dhalpouri roti with either potato, vegetable, chicken or beef. Homemade ice cream is offered for dessert. Casual dress. Parking: on-site.
Cards: MC, VI.

BAKELY'S RESTAURANT & BAKE SHOP　Lunch: $4-$9　Phone: 407/645-5767　244
　　Location: Just w of Rollins College and jct Park and Fairbanks aves. 345 W Fairbanks Ave 32789. Hours: 6:30 am-4 pm. Closed major holidays. Features: Diners can eat breakfast, lunch or dinner at any time of the day at
American　this spot along Fairbanks Avenue. Omelets, sandwiches, burgers and hand-dipped milkshakes will tempt the taste buds, as do the yummy homemade muffins, pies and cakes. Casual dress; beer & wine only. Parking:
on-site. Cards: AX, MC, VI.

BLACK BEAN DELI　Lunch: $6-$10　Dinner: $6-$10　Phone: 407/628-0294　242
　　Location: I-4, exit 87, 1.2 mi e on SR 426/Fairbanks Ave, then just n on US 17-92/SR 15/SR 600; in Ranch Mall Shopping Plaza. 325 S Orlando Ave 32789. Hours: 11 am-8 pm. Closed major holidays; also Sat & Sun.
Cuban　Features: A hole-in-the-wall kind of place, the family-owned take-out eatery specializes in filling six- and nine-inch Cuban sandwiches. Later in the afternoon, guests can satisfy their hearty cravings with tamales and baked chicken platters. Save room for the silky flan de queso. Casual dress. Parking: on-site. Cards: MC, VI.

BRANDYWINE'S DELICATESSEN　Lunch: $3-$7　Phone: 407/647-0055　225
　　Location: Just n of Morse Blvd. 505 N Park Ave 32789. Hours: 8 am-6 pm, Sat & Sun 9 am-5 pm. Closed major holidays. Reservations: not accepted. Features: The deli is popular with the locals and offers hearty
American　sandwiches served with few frills but plenty of taste. Casual dress; beer & wine only. Parking: on-site. Cards: AX, MC, VI.

BRIAR PATCH　Lunch: $6-$14　Dinner: $6-$14　Phone: 407/645-4566　233
　　Location: I-4, exit 87, 2 mi e, then 0.5 mi n. 252 N Park Ave 32789. Hours: 7 am-6 pm, Sun 8 am-5 pm. Closed: 11/23, 12/25. Reservations: accepted. Features: Breakfast, lunch and dinner all are dished up at the
American　country-style eatery. Freshly prepared dishes can be followed by delicious desserts. The all-around experience is enjoyable. Casual dress; beer & wine only. Parking: street. Cards: AX, MC, VI.

(See map and index starting on p. 656)

BRIO TUSCAN GRILLE   **Lunch:** $9-$20   **Dinner:** $10-$24   **Phone:** 407/622-5611   (224)

Regional Italian

Location: Jct SR 423/US 17-92, just s on US 17-92; in Winter Park Village. 480 N Orlando Ave 32789. **Hours:** 11 am-10 pm, Fri & Sat-midnight. Closed major holidays. **Reservations:** suggested. **Features:** Enjoy upscale Tuscan Italian at its finest. The large airy dining room and extensive menu make for a comfortable, sophisticated and filling dining experience. Both lunch and dinner offer all the attentiveness a diner expects and the food is superlative. From the garlic, spinach, and artichoke dip starter to the chicken, veal, seafood or pasta entrees, there's enough of a selection for everyone. Casual dress; cocktails. **Parking:** on-site. **Cards:** AX, DS, MC, VI.

BUBBALOU'S BODACIOUS BAR-B-QUE   **Lunch:** $4-$13   **Dinner:** $4-$13   **Phone:** 407/628-1212   (213)

Barbecue

Location: I-4, exit 88, 0.5 mi e. 1471 Lee Rd 32789. **Hours:** 10 am-9:30 pm, Fri-10:30 pm, Sun 11 am-8 pm. Closed: 11/23, 12/25. **Features:** Barbecue sandwiches and meats. Limited inside dining. Counter service. Inexpensive. Casual dress. **Parking:** on-site. **Cards:** AX, DS, MC, VI.

CHAPTERS CAFE & BOOKSHOP INC   **Lunch:** $6-$11   **Dinner:** $9-$15   **Phone:** 407/246-1546   (232)

American

Location: I-4, exit 85. 358 N Park Ave 32789. **Hours:** 11 am-9 pm, Fri & Sat-11 pm. Closed: 1/1, 4/16, 12/25. **Features:** Exceptional service and elegant decor—not to mention the infamous steaks sizzling in butter—make for a memorable dining experience. Casual dress; beer & wine only. **Parking:** on-site. **Cards:** AX, MC, VI.

CHEESECAKE FACTORY   **Lunch:** $8-$25   **Dinner:** $8-$25   **Phone:** 407/644-4220   (223)

American

Location: Just e of US 17-92; just s of jct US 17-92 and Lee Rd; in Winter Park Village Shops. 520 N Orlando Ave #110 32789. **Hours:** 11:30 am-11 pm, Fri & Sat-midnight, Sun 10 am-11 pm. Closed: 11/23, 12/25. **Features:** In a busy shopping plaza, the eatery is most-noted for its large portions and varieties of homemade cheesecake. The menu's many pages list numerous types of cuisines. Casual dress; cocktails. **Parking:** on-site. **Cards:** AX, CB, DC, DS, JC, MC, VI.

CHEF HENRY'S CAFE   **Dinner:** $14-$22   **Phone:** 407/657-2230   (210)

Continental

Location: I-4, exit 92, 5.5 mi se on SR 436, then 0.7 mi n. 3716 Howell Branch Rd 32792. **Hours:** 5 pm-9 pm. Closed: 1/1, 11/23, 12/24, 12/25; also Sun & Mon. **Reservations:** suggested. **Features:** Diners who choose the family-operated cafe are in for a treat of European cuisine that blends the best of Polish, German and Hungarian cuisine, as well as the creativity of Chef Henrich Brestowski. The homey decor has some elegant touches. Any one of the variety of pork or veal schnitzel preparations is tempting. Fish paprikash, served in a puff pastry shell, and Hungarian goulash with spaetzle are house specialties. Save room for an award-winning strudel. Dressy casual; beer & wine only. **Parking:** on-site. **Cards:** AX, DC, DS, MC, VI.

CHEZ VINCENT   **Lunch:** $5-$16   **Dinner:** $18-$26   **Phone:** 407/599-2929   (237)

French

Location: 0.3 mi n on Pennsylvania Ave, just e. 533 W New England Ave 32789. **Hours:** 11:30 am-2 & 6-10 pm. Closed: 12/25. **Reservations:** accepted. **Features:** The restaurant features an intimate dining room that accomodates romantic dining as well as casual friends, and a well-rounded menu sure to please even the most discriminating palates. Dressy casual; cocktails. **Parking:** on-site. **Cards:** AX, MC, VI.

CRISPERS   **Lunch:** $4-$9   **Dinner:** $4-$9   **Phone:** 407/622-4403   (227)

Deli/Subs
Sandwiches

Location: Just e of US 17-92; just s of jct US 17-92 and Lee Rd; in Winter Park Village Shops. 480 N Orlando Ave 32789. **Hours:** 10:30 am-9 pm, Fri & Sat-10 pm. **Features:** A healthy alternative for lunch or dinner, the restaurant prepares towering specialty sandwiches on warm, fresh homemade bread. Salad selections with combinations of meats, fruit and cheese are just as tempting. Varied coffees go well with freshly baked cakes and brownies. Casual dress. **Parking:** on-site. **Cards:** AX, MC, VI.

DAILY EXPRESS DELI & GRILL   **Lunch:** $3-$6   **Phone:** 407/644-6282   (217)

Deli/Subs
Sandwiches

Location: I-4, exit 88, 0.6 mi e; jct US 17-92 and Lee Rd; in shopping plaza. 501 N Orlando Ave, Suite 231 32789. **Hours:** 6:30 am-2:30 pm, Sat 8 am-2 pm. Closed major holidays; also Sun. **Features:** Serving only breakfast and lunch, the busy eatery is always hopping. Breakfast specials include French toast, eggs any style and croissant sandwiches. At the heart of the lunch menu are submarine sandwiches, burgers and salads. Casual dress. **Parking:** on-site. **Cards:** MC, VI.

DEXTER'S OF WINTER PARK   **Lunch:** $6-$12   **Dinner:** $10-$25   **Phone:** 407/629-1150   (238)

American

Location: I-4, exit 87, 0.7 mi e on Fairbanks Ave, 0.3 mi n to Morse Blvd, just e to Pennsylvania Ave, then just s. 558 W New England Ave, Suite 100 32789. **Hours:** 11 am-10 pm, Fri & Sat-11 pm; Sunday brunch. Closed major holidays. **Reservations:** accepted. **Features:** Located just three blocks off prominent Park Avenue, this eatery features a rotating art collection hung on every wall. Many wine connoisseurs frequent this establishment for the interesting selection of wines available. The food is trendy yet simple. Eggplant pie and stuffed meatloaf are local favorites. Casual dress. **Parking:** on-site. **Cards:** AX, DC, DS, MC, VI.

EL POTRO MEXICAN RESTAURANT   **Lunch:** $4-$8   **Dinner:** $6-$13   **Phone:** 407/975-9132   (216)

Mexican

Location: Just w of Orlando Ave, off Orange Ave; in shopping center. 501 N Orlando Ave, Suite 217 32789. **Hours:** 11 am-10 pm, Fri & Sat-10:30 pm, Sun-9 pm. **Reservations:** accepted. **Features:** The lunch buffet is full of all-time favorites, but guests also can choose from many combination platters. Local favorites include quesadillas, tostados and banana chimichangas. Mexican music and a friendly staff make the meal experience complete. Casual dress; beer & wine only. **Parking:** on-site. **Cards:** AX, DC, DS, MC, VI.

FLEMING'S PRIME STEAKHOUSE & WINE BAR   **Dinner:** $21-$36   **Phone:** 407/669-9463   (215)

American

Location: On US 17-92 at Lee Rd. 933 N Orlando Ave 32789. **Hours:** 5 pm-10 pm, Fri & Sat 4:30 pm-11 pm, Sun 4 pm-9 pm. Closed: 11/23, 12/25. **Reservations:** suggested. **Features:** This upscale steak and chop house features aged USDA Prime corn-fed beef; pork, lamb and veal chops; chicken and a variety of seafood dishes. The side dishes are meant for sharing and all the sauces and desserts are made in-house daily. If you have a hankering for prime rib, it is available but only on Sundays. Tthe extensive selection of wines available by the glass is a very nice feature. Dressy casual; cocktails. **Parking:** on-site and valet. **Cards:** AX, DC, DS, MC, VI.

(See map and index starting on p. 656)

FUJI SUSHI
Sushi
Lunch: $8-$12   **Dinner:** $11-$25   **Phone:** 407/645-1299   (214)
Location: I-4, exit 88 (Lee Rd), 1 mi e. 1449 Lee Rd 32789. **Hours:** 11:30 am-2:30 & 5-10 pm, Fri & Sat 5 pm-11 pm, Sun 5 pm-9:30 pm. Closed major holidays. **Reservations:** suggested, recommended for Friday & Saturday. **Features:** The popular spot entices those in search of Japanese fare, seafood and sushi. Selections include crab and asparagus rolls, eel and cucumber rolls, fish broth, seaweed salads and fried squid. Beer and wine are served. Casual dress; beer & wine only. **Parking:** on-site. **Cards:** AX, DC, DS, MC, VI.

GIOVANNI'S ITALIAN RESTAURANT & PIZZERIA
Italian
Lunch: $8-$19   **Dinner:** $8-$19   **Phone:** 407/673-8800   (230)
Location: Jct SR 436 and Aloma Ave, 0.4 mi w; in Winter Park Corners Shopping Center. 1915 Aloma Ave 32792. **Hours:** 11 am-10 pm, Fri & Sat-11 pm, Sun noon-10 pm. Closed major holidays. **Features:** Although pizza is the specialty at the shopping plaza eatery, the extensive menu of traditional Italian favorites cannot be ignored. Ravioli, lasagna, chicken Marsala and seafood dishes are just a few tantalizing options. The family-owned-and-operated spot is one of four such locations. Casual dress; beer & wine only. **Parking:** on-site. **Cards:** AX, MC, VI.

GREEK FLAME TAVERNA
Greek
Lunch: $4-$10   **Dinner:** $5-$20   **Phone:** 407/678-2388   (209)
Location: Just s of Howell Branch Rd. 1560 N SR 436 32792. **Hours:** 11 am-9 pm, Fri & Sat-10 pm. Closed holidays; also Sun. **Reservations:** accepted. **Features:** Authentic Greek recipes are made to order and accompanied by Greek music and ambience. Casual dress; beer & wine only. **Parking:** on-site. **Cards:** AX, DS, MC, VI.

HOT OLIVES
American
Lunch: $6-$15   **Dinner:** $8-$19   **Phone:** 407/629-1030   (236)
Location: Just n of SR 424A (W Fairbanks Ave); between S Pennsylvania and S New York aves; in Hannibal Square section. 463 W New England Ave 32789. **Hours:** 11 am-9:30 pm, Fri & Sat-10 pm. Closed major holidays; also Sun. **Reservations:** suggested. **Features:** Voted one of the best outdoor dining facilities in the Orlando area, the restaurant offers a full menu of creatively cooked dishes and offers an airy garden patio or cozy dining room to enjoy the selected fare. Service is very good and the menu selection will appeal to any diner. Casual dress; beer & wine only. **Parking:** street. **Cards:** AX, DS, MC, VI.

HOUSTON'S
American
Lunch: $12-$28   **Dinner:** $12-$28   **Phone:** 407/740-4005   (234)
Location: I-4, exit 87, 1 mi e on SR 426, then just n on US 17/92. 215 S Orlando Ave 32789. **Hours:** 11 am-11 pm, Sun-10 pm. Closed major holidays. **Reservations:** not accepted. **Features:** Although Houston's is known for being the place for hip young professionals to have happy hour after work, it also has good food and a spectacular view. Among food selections are prime rib, grilled salmon, roasted chicken and delicious steaks. Casual dress; cocktails. **Parking:** on-site. **Cards:** AX, MC, VI.

JUM-BO
Chinese
Lunch: $5-$9   **Dinner:** $9-$15   **Phone:** 407/657-8878   (231)
Location: 1.5 mi w of jct SR 436 at Lakemont Ave. 1967 Aloma Ave 32792. **Hours:** 11:30 am-10 pm, Fri-11 pm, Sat noon-11 pm, Sun 4 pm-10 pm. Closed: 11/23, 12/25. **Features:** A family operation since 1988, the casual restaurant serves traditional cuisine. Whether in the dining room or on the sidewalk patio, guests can savor the chef's tasty creations. Casual dress; beer & wine only. **Parking:** on-site. **Cards:** AX, DS, MC, VI.

MOE'S SOUTHWEST GRILL
Mexican
Lunch: $3-$9   **Dinner:** $3-$9   **Phone:** 407/629-4500   (247)
Location: Just s of jct Fairbanks Ave; in Winter Park Business Center. 847 S Orlando Ave 32789. **Hours:** 11 am-10 pm. Closed: 11/23, 12/25. **Features:** With locations in several states, the casual eatery serves Mexican food in huge portions. Guests drop in for friendly service and fresh food at great prices. Casual dress; beer & wine only. **Parking:** on-site. **Cards:** AX, DS, MC, VI.

OLD GERMANY RESTAURANT
German
Lunch: $4-$11   **Dinner:** $6-$24   **Phone:** 407/657-6800   (212)
Location: 0.5 mi n of Aloma Ave. 2054 N SR 436 32792. **Hours:** noon-10 pm, Fri & Sat-1 am. Closed: 11/23, 12/25. **Reservations:** accepted. **Features:** Atmosphere is everything: German memorabilia adorns the walls and a clothesline hangs from the ceiling. Casual dress; cocktails. **Parking:** on-site. **Cards:** AX, DS, MC, VI.

ORLANDO ALE HOUSE
American
Lunch: $4-$14   **Dinner:** $4-$14   **Phone:** 407/671-1011   (246)
Location: Jct SR 436 and University Blvd, just e. 101 University Park Dr 32792. **Hours:** 11 am-2 am. Closed major holidays. **Features:** Enjoy selections of clams on the half shell, oysters and peel and eat shrimp from the raw bar or choose an 8 oz. filet, baby back ribs or chicken parmesan from the appetizing menu. Casual dress; cocktails. **Parking:** on-site. **Cards:** AX, DS, MC, VI.

PANNULLO'S ITALIAN RESTAURANT
Italian
Lunch: $5-$9   **Dinner:** $9-$17   **Phone:** 407/629-7270   (235)
Location: Just s of New England Ave; center. 216 Park Ave S 32789. **Hours:** 11 am-10 pm, Fri & Sat-11 pm, Sun noon-10 pm. Closed: 11/23, 12/25. **Features:** Diners with a hankering for a generous portion of spaghetti with marinara or a delicious East Coast-style pizza should set their sights here. As shoppers stroll Park Avenue, patrons take advantage of leisurely patio dining. Casual dress; beer & wine only. **Parking:** street. **Cards:** AX, DC, DS, MC, VI.

PARK PLAZA GARDENS
Continental
Lunch: $6-$18   **Dinner:** $21-$30   **Phone:** 407/645-2475   (239)
Location: Center; jct Park Ave S and New England Ave. 319 Park Ave S 32789. **Hours:** 11:30 am-10 pm, Sun from 11 am; Sunday brunch. Closed: 1/1, 7/4, 12/25. **Reservations:** suggested. **Features:** A glass-enclosed garden filled with lush plants brings the outdoors indoors. You will find impeccable service with great attention to detail. Beef, seafood and pork are featured with lighter fair available in the lounge between lunch and dinner. Semi-formal attire; cocktails. **Parking:** street. **Cards:** AX, CB, DC, DS, MC, VI.

P. F. CHANG'S CHINA BISTRO
Chinese
Lunch: $7-$17   **Dinner:** $7-$17   **Phone:** 407/622-0188   (228)
Location: On US 17-92, just s of jct Lee Rd; in Winter Park Village Shops. 436 N Orlando Ave 32789. **Hours:** 11 am-11 pm, Fri & Sat-midnight, Sun-10 pm. Closed: 11/23, 12/25. **Features:** In a busy shopping area, the eatery nurtures a wonderful atmosphere for dining. Dim lighting enhances the warm gold and wood tones that surround the dining room. Chinese favorites are served with flair. Casual dress; cocktails. **Parking:** on-site. **Cards:** AX, CB, DC, DS, JC, MC, VI.

(See map and index starting on p. 656)

POWERHOUSE CAFE   **Lunch:** $6-$10   **Dinner:** $6-$10   **Phone:** 407/645-3616   240
Deli/Subs
Sandwiches
Location: Corner of S Park and E Lyman aves. 111 E Lyman Ave 32789. **Hours:** 9 am-7 pm, Sat 10 am-5 pm, Sun 9 am-5 pm. Closed major holidays. **Features:** Nestled in the heart of town, this little sandwich shop offers healthy sandwiches and wraps. Soups are also a specialty here, made fresh daily. Casual dress. **Parking:** street. **Cards:** MC, VI.

PR'S MEXICAN RESTAURANT   **Lunch:** $6-$12   **Dinner:** $8-$18   **Phone:** 407/645-2225   245
Mexican
Location: I-4, exit 87, 1.7 mi e; jct Fairbanks Ave and US 17-92, 0.8 mi e. 499 W Fairbanks Ave 32789. **Hours:** 11 am-10 pm, Fri & Sat-11 pm. Closed major holidays. **Features:** The casual eatery has been a favorite among the locals for decades. The menu features Tex-Mex cuisine with all the standard favorites. Casual dress; cocktails. **Parking:** on-site. **Cards:** AX, MC, VI.

RUTH'S CHRIS STEAK HOUSE   **Dinner:** $18-$40   **Phone:** 407/622-2444   221
Steak House
Location: Just e of SR 17-92. 610 N Orlando Ave 32789. **Hours:** 5 pm-10 pm, Sun-9 pm. Closed: 11/23, 12/25; also Super Bowl Sun. **Reservations:** accepted. **Features:** An elegant, intimate atmosphere coupled with impeccable service and a menu of Angus beef prepared and seasoned to melt in the mouth make this a popular steakhouse. Dressy casual; cocktails. **Parking:** valet. **Cards:** AX, CB, DC, DS, JC, MC, VI.

SAIKYO SUSHI BAR AND GRILL   **Lunch:** $5   **Dinner:** $17   **Phone:** 407/673-8294   211
Japanese
Location: 2.5 mi ne. 2522 Aloma Ave 32792. **Hours:** 11:30 am-3 & 5-10 pm. Closed: 11/23, 12/25. **Features:** The staff serves delectable food for the serious diner. Presentations are colorful, and portions are ample. Fresh sushi is wonderful. Casual dress; cocktails. **Parking:** on-site. **Cards:** AX, DS, MC, VI.

SEITO SUSHI   **Lunch:** $6-$15   **Dinner:** $7-$18   **Phone:** 407/644-5050   222
Japanese
Location: I-4, exit 88, 1 mi e on Lee Rd, then 0.5 mi s; in Winter Park Village. 510 N Orlando Ave #104 32789. **Hours:** 11:30 am-2:30 & 5-10 pm, Fri-11 pm, Sat & Sun noon-10 pm. Closed major holidays. **Features:** Guests seated at the sushi bar are impressed to watch the chef create dinner. Delectable sushi and tempura are presented creatively to those seated indoors or at the sidewalk tables. Casual dress; beer & wine only. **Parking:** street. **Cards:** AX, DC, DS, MC, VI.

SHIKI JAPANESE CUISINE   **Dinner:** $12-$29   **Phone:** 407/740-8018   243
Japanese
Location: I-4, exit 87, 2 mi e to S Park Ave, then just n. 525 S Park Ave 32789. **Hours:** 5:30 pm-9:30 pm, Tues-Thurs to 10 pm, Fri & Sat-11 pm, Sun-10 pm. Closed major holidays. **Reservations:** accepted. **Features:** Catering to a loyal local following, the restaurant offers a wide array of Japanese dishes, including some of the freshest sushi around. Service is friendly. Casual dress; cocktails. **Parking:** street. **Cards:** AX, MC, VI.

SIAM GARDEN   **Lunch:** $8-$11   **Dinner:** $10-$21   **Phone:** 407/599-7443   219
Thai
Location: Just e of US 17-92; across from Winter Park Village Shops. 1111 Webster Ave 32789. **Hours:** 11 am-2:30 & 5-10 pm, Sat & Sun from 5 pm. Closed: 11/23, 12/25. **Features:** Full-bodied and flavorful soups are a wonderful lead in to such preparations as savory Pad Thai, a mixture of flat noodles stir-fried with shrimp, scallions, egg and paprika. Casual dress; beer & wine only. **Parking:** on-site. **Cards:** AX, DS, MC, VI.

TIJUANA FLATS   **Lunch:** $4-$9   **Dinner:** $4-$9   **Phone:** 407/679-2132   229
Mexican
Location: Jct SR 436 and Aloma Ave, 0.4 mi w; in Winter Park Corners Shopping Center. 1955 Aloma Ave 32789. **Hours:** 11 am-10 pm, Fri-10:30 pm, Sun-9 pm. Closed major holidays. **Features:** The quick-serve Tex-Mex eatery sets up a distinctive "hot sauce bar" to accompany its burritos, chimichangas, tacos and enchiladas. Guests can expect a line out the door at lunch. Beer and sangria are available. Casual dress; beer & wine only. **Parking:** on-site. **Cards:** MC, VI.

WINTER SPRINGS pop. 31,666   (See map and index starting on p. 656)

—— WHERE TO DINE ——

369 CHINESE RESTAURANT   **Lunch:** $4-$16   **Dinner:** $8-$22   **Phone:** 407/695-3699   144
Chinese
Location: SR 417, exit 49 (Red Bug Lake Rd), 1 mi w; in The Promenade at Tuskawilla. 1425 Tuskawilla Rd, Unit 161 32708. **Hours:** 11:30 am-9:30 pm, Fri & Sat-10:30 pm. **Features:** Fresh seafood and garden-fresh vegetables go into the restaurant's culinary delights. The service staff is professional. Casual dress; cocktails. **Parking:** on-site. **Cards:** AX, MC, VI.

ATHENS CAFE   **Lunch:** $4-$16   **Dinner:** $4-$16   **Phone:** 407/696-4282   143
Greek
Location: SR 417, exit 49 (Red Bug Lake Rd), 1 mi w; in Promenade at Tuskawilla. 5965 Red Bug Lake Rd, Suite 137 32708. **Hours:** 11 am-9:30 pm, Fri & Sat-10 pm, Sun 8:30 am-2:30 pm; Sunday brunch. Closed: 12/25. **Features:** Mouthwatering rotisserie chicken and the signature spinach pie are a few tantalizing items on the menu. Casual dress. **Parking:** on-site. **Cards:** AX, DS, MC, VI.

TUSCANY'S   **Dinner:** $8-$19   **Phone:** 407/366-3375   142
Italian
JC, MC, VI.
Location: SR 417, exit 44, 2.2 mi w on SR 434, 1.5 mi s on Tuskawilla Rd, then 0.9 mi e. 1301 Winter Springs Blvd 32708. **Hours:** 5 pm-10 pm, Sun-9 pm. Closed: 1/1, 12/25; also Mon. **Features:** Great for family gatherings or get togethers, the restaurant offers Italian dishes made to order and well worth the wait. Be sure to save room for the variety of desserts offered. Casual dress; cocktails. **Parking:** on-site. **Cards:** AX, CB, DC, DS,

The previous listings were for the Orlando Vicinity.
This page resumes the alphabetical listings of cities in Florida.

ORMOND BEACH pop. 36,301 (See map and index starting on p. 285)

―――――― WHERE TO STAY ――――――

BEST WESTERN MAINSAIL INN AND SUITES *Book at aaa.com*   Phone: (386)677-2131   **35**

4/1-7/31	1P: $90-$400	2P: $95-$420	XP: $10	F17
12/1-3/31	1P: $80-$375	2P: $85-$400	XP: $10	F17
8/1-10/1	1P: $65-$350	2P: $75-$360	XP: $10	F17
10/2-11/30	1P: $59-$275	2P: $69-$285	XP: $10	F17

Motel   **Location:** On SR A1A, 0.5 mi s of SR 40. 281 S Atlantic Ave 32176. Fax: 386/676-0323. **Facility:** 44 units. 33 one-bedroom standard units, some with efficiencies or kitchens. 8 one- and 2 two-bedroom suites ($130-$400), some with kitchens and/or whirlpools. 4 stories, interior/exterior corridors. *Bath:* combo or shower only. **Parking:** on-site. **Terms:** 3-7 night minimum stay - seasonal and/or weekends, age restrictions may apply, 30 day cancellation notice-fee imposed, [CP] meal plan available, package plans. **Amenities:** voice mail, safes, irons, hair dryers. **Pool(s):** outdoor, wading. **Guest Services:** valet and coin laundry. **Cards:** AX, CB, DC, DS, MC, VI. **Special Amenities:** free continental breakfast and free newspaper. *(See color ad p 292)*

SOME UNITS

COMFORT INN INTERSTATE   *Book at aaa.com*   Phone: 386/672-8621   **33**

	1P	XP	
All Year	1P: $250	XP: $10	F13

Small-scale Hotel   **Location:** I-95, exit 273, just e. 1567 N US 1 32174. Fax: 386/672-7735. **Facility:** 70 one-bedroom standard units. 2 stories, exterior corridors. **Parking:** on-site. **Terms:** 2-3 night minimum stay - seasonal, 7 day cancellation notice, package plans. **Amenities:** irons, hair dryers. **Pool(s):** outdoor. **Guest Services:** coin laundry. **Cards:** AX, DS, MC, VI. **Special Amenities:** free continental breakfast and free local telephone calls.

SOME UNITS

COMFORT INN ON THE BEACH   *Book at aaa.com*   Phone: (386)677-8550   **38**

12/1-3/14 & 7/1-8/31	1P: $95-$225	2P: $95-$225	XP: $10	F18
3/15-6/30	1P: $110-$125	2P: $110-$125	XP: $10	F18
9/1-11/30	1P: $85-$100	2P: $85-$100	XP: $10	F18

Motel   **Location:** On SR A1A, 1 mi s of jct SR 40. 507 S Atlantic Ave 32176. Fax: 386/673-6260. **Facility:** 47 units. 44 one-bedroom standard units, some with efficiencies. 3 one-bedroom suites with efficiencies. 4 stories, exterior corridors. **Parking:** on-site. **Terms:** 10 day cancellation notice, weekly rates available, [CP] meal plan available, small pets only ($10 extra charge). **Amenities:** voice mail, safes (fee), irons, hair dryers. **Pool(s):** outdoor, wading. **Business Services:** fax (fee). **Cards:** AX, CB, DC, DS, MC, VI. **Special Amenities:** free continental breakfast.

SOME UNITS
FEE

CORAL BEACH MOTEL   Phone: (386)677-4712   **40**

4/18-8/8	1P: $65-$350	2P: $65-$350	XP: $10	F16
2/1-4/17	1P: $60-$350	2P: $60-$350	XP: $10	F16
8/9-11/30	1P: $60-$325	2P: $60-$325	XP: $10	F16
12/1-1/31	1P: $55-$140	2P: $55-$140	XP: $10	F16

Small-scale Hotel   **Location:** On SR A1A, 1.5 mi s of SR 40. 711 S Atlantic Ave 32176. Fax: 386/523-1000. **Facility:** 97 units. 78 one- and 17 two-bedroom standard units, some with efficiencies. 2 two-bedroom suites with efficiencies. 7 stories, interior/exterior corridors. *Bath:* combo or shower only. **Parking:** on-site. **Terms:** 10 day cancellation notice. **Amenities:** hair dryers. **Pool(s):** outdoor, heated indoor. **Leisure Activities:** shuffleboard. *Fee:* game room. **Guest Services:** coin laundry. **Cards:** AX, DC, DS, MC, VI.

SOME UNITS

THE COVE ON ORMOND BEACH A CLUB NAVIGO RESORT   *Book at aaa.com*   Phone: (386)677-1446   **34**

	1P	2P
All Year	1P: $79-$299	2P: $79-$299

Condominium   **Location:** Just s of jct SR 40. 145 S Atlantic Ave 32176. Fax: 386/677-2834. **Facility:** This beachfront resort offers condominium-style units that are fully equipped with homelike amenities. 54 units. 6 one-bedroom standard units with efficiencies. 30 one- and 18 two-bedroom suites ($79-$299) with efficiencies. 7 stories, interior corridors. *Bath:* combo or shower only. **Parking:** on-site. **Terms:** check-in 4 pm, 2 night minimum stay - seasonal, 15 day cancellation notice-fee imposed, package plans. **Amenities:** video library (fee), voice mail, irons, hair dryers. **Pool(s):** heated outdoor. **Leisure Activities:** playground, exercise room, game room. **Guest Services:** coin laundry. **Business Services:** meeting rooms. **Cards:** AX, CB, DC, DS, MC, VI. *(See color ad p 771)*

SOME UNITS

DRIFTWOOD BEACH MOTEL   Phone: (386)677-1331   **39**

All Year	1P: $45-$175	2P: $45-$175	XP: $7	F15.

Motel   **Location:** On SR A1A, 1.5 mi s of jct SR 40. 657 S Atlantic Ave 32176. Fax: 386/677-0625. **Facility:** 44 units. 38 one-bedroom standard units, some with efficiencies. 4 one- and 2 two-bedroom suites ($110-$375) with efficiencies. 2-3 stories (no elevator), exterior corridors. *Bath:* combo or shower only. **Parking:** on-site. **Terms:** 14 day cancellation notice-fee imposed. **Pool(s):** heated outdoor. **Leisure Activities:** shuffleboard. **Guest Services:** coin laundry. **Business Services:** fax (fee). **Cards:** DS, MC, VI. **Special Amenities:** free newspaper and preferred room (subject to availability with advance reservations). *(See color ad p 295)*

SOME UNITS

(See map and index starting on p. 285)

ECONO LODGE ON THE BEACH — *Book at aaa.com* — Phone: (386)672-2651 — **36**

	12/1-3/14 & 7/1-8/31	1P: $95-$225	2P: $95-$225	XP: $10	F18
	3/15-6/30	1P: $110-$125	2P: $110-$125	XP: $10	F18
Motel	9/1-11/30	1P: $85-$100	2P: $85-$100	XP: $10	F18

Location: On SR A1A, 0.5 mi s of SR 40. 295 S Atlantic Ave 32176. Fax: 386/672-4491. **Facility:** 57 one-bedroom standard units, some with efficiencies. 4 stories, exterior corridors. **Parking:** on-site. **Terms:** 10 day cancellation notice, weekly rates available, package plans. **Amenities:** safes (fee), irons, hair dryers. **Pool(s):** heated outdoor, wading. **Guest Services:** coin laundry. **Cards:** AX, CB, DC, DS, MC, VI.

SOME UNITS

HAMPTON INN ORMOND BEACH — *Book at aaa.com* — Phone: (386)677-9999 — **41**

All Year [ECP] — 1P: $84-$255 — 2P: $94-$255

Small-scale Hotel — **Location:** I-95, exit 268, just w. 155 Interchange Blvd 32174. Fax: 386/677-0663. **Facility:** 84 one-bedroom standard units, some with whirlpools. 4 stories, interior corridors. *Bath:* combo or shower only. **Parking:** on-site. **Terms:** check-in 4 pm, 5 night minimum stay - seasonal. **Amenities:** voice mail, irons, hair dryers. **Pool(s):** outdoor. **Leisure Activities:** exercise room. **Guest Services:** valet and coin laundry. **Business Services:** meeting rooms. **Cards:** AX, CB, DC, DS, JC, MC, VI.

SOME UNITS

JAMESON INN — *Book at aaa.com* — Phone: (386)672-3675 — **42**

All Year [ECP] — 1P: $54-$104

Location: I-95, exit 268, just w, then just s. 175 Interchange Blvd 32174. Fax: 386/672-0453. **Facility:** 66 units. 64 Small-scale Hotel one-bedroom standard units. 2 one-bedroom suites. 3 stories, interior corridors. *Bath:* combo or shower only. **Parking:** on-site. **Terms:** cancellation fee imposed, small pets only. **Amenities:** voice mail, irons, hair dryers. **Pool(s):** outdoor. **Leisure Activities:** exercise room. **Guest Services:** valet laundry. **Business Services:** meeting rooms. **Cards:** AX, CB, DC, DS, MC, VI.

SOME UNITS

SLEEP INN — *Book at aaa.com* — Phone: (386)673-6030 — **43**

All Year — 1P: $75-$200 — 2P: $75-$200 — XP: $5 — F18

Small-scale Hotel — **Location:** I-95, exit 268, just e. 170 Williamson Blvd 32174. Fax: 386/673-7017. **Facility:** 83 one-bedroom standard units. 3 stories, interior corridors. *Bath:* shower only. **Parking:** on-site. **Amenities:** *Some:* irons, hair dryers. **Pool(s):** outdoor. **Guest Services:** coin laundry. **Cards:** AX, CB, DC, DS, JC, MC, VI.

SOME UNITS

SYMPHONY BEACH CLUB — Phone: 386/672-7373 — **37**

All Year — 1P: $59-$95 — 2P: $59-$95 — XP: $10

Location: On SR A1A, 0.8 mi s of jct SR 40. 453 S Atlantic Ave 32176. Fax: 386/673-1174. **Facility:** 30 units. 28 Condominium one-bedroom standard units with efficiencies. 2 one-bedroom suites with efficiencies. 4 stories, exterior corridors. **Parking:** on-site. **Terms:** 30 day cancellation notice-fee imposed, weekly rates available. **Pool(s):** heated outdoor. **Leisure Activities:** limited exercise equipment. **Guest Services:** coin laundry. **Cards:** DS, MC, VI.

SOME UNITS

——— WHERE TO DINE ———

BARRY'S PATIO BAR & GRILL — Lunch: $5-$12 — Dinner: $5-$12 — Phone: 386/676-2090 — **20**

American — **Location:** I-95, exit 89, 2.5 mi s. 241 N US 1 32174. **Hours:** 11 am-2 am, Sun-Tues to 8 pm. Closed major holidays. **Features:** The sports bar extends a warm welcome to patrons who stop in for good food. The six-ounce filet sandwich is excellent. Casual dress; cocktails. **Parking:** on-site. **Cards:** MC, VI.

BILLY'S TAP ROOM & GRILL — Lunch: $6-$15 — Dinner: $9-$22 — Phone: 386/672-1910 — **19**

Location: 0.3 mi w of SR A1A. 58 E Granada Blvd 32176. **Hours:** 11:30 am-10 pm. Closed: 11/23, 12/25. **Reservations:** suggested. **Features:** The English pub-style neighborhood restaurant exudes a 1920s feel. Warm congeniality and consistently high-quality food lend to the appeal. Casual dress; cocktails. **Parking:** street. **Cards:** AX, MC, VI.

American

CHARLIE HORSE RESTAURANT — Lunch: $5-$8 — Dinner: $6-$19 — Phone: 386/672-4347 — **23**

Location: Jct SR 40, 1.5 mi s. 810 S Atlantic Ave 32176. **Hours:** 11 am-11 pm. Closed: 12/25. **Reservations:** not American accepted. **Features:** The casual family restaurant is popular with locals and out-of-towners alike. Preparations from steaks to burgers are served. Guests can watch one of the many TVs or play video games with the kids. Casual dress; beer & wine only. **Parking:** on-site. **Cards:** MC, VI.

DUSTIN'S BAR-B-Q — Lunch: $6-$8 — Dinner: $8-$13 — Phone: 386/677-5292 — **25**

Location: I-95, exit 268 (SR 40), 0.5 mi e. 1320 W Granada Blvd 32174. **Hours:** 11 am-9 pm. Closed: 11/23, Barbecue 12/25. **Features:** Barbecue and smoked meats highlight the menu at the casual eatery. Guests choose their own sauce from the selection on the table. The atmosphere and service are informal. Casual dress; beer only. **Parking:** on-site. **Cards:** DS, MC, VI.

(See map and index starting on p. 285)

ENGLISH ROSE TEA ROOM

Lunch: $8-$10 **Phone:** 386/672-7673 ㉑

▽▽ ▽▽
English

Location: On SR A1A, 1.3 mi n on SR 40. 49 W Granada Blvd (Rt 40) 32174. **Hours:** 8 am-4 pm, Sat-3 pm. **Closed:** 12/25; also Sun & Mon. **Reservations:** accepted. **Features:** British and vegetarian foods are among the breakfast, lunch and afternoon tea items served at the cozy tea room. Casual dress. **Parking:** on-site. **Cards:** AX, MC, VI.

JULIAN'S

Dinner: $12-$20 **Phone:** 386/677-6767 ⑰

◢◣◣
▽▽ ▽▽
American

Location: On SR A1A, just s of SR 40. 88 S Atlantic Ave 32176. **Hours:** 4 pm-11 pm. **Reservations:** accepted. **Features:** Vintage decor in a Polynesian motif sets a tropical feel in the casual restaurant. A wall mural of a Hawaiian village brightens the sunken bar. The cordial and knowledgeable wait staff adeptly describe the menu offerings, such as grilled salmon. Casual dress; cocktails; entertainment. **Parking:** on-site. **Cards:** AX, CB, DC, DS, MC, VI.

LA CREPE EN HAUT

Lunch: $11-$20 **Dinner:** $26-$50 **Phone:** 386/673-1999 ⑯

◢◣◣
▽▽▽ ▽▽▽
French

Location: On SR 40, just w of se SR A1A. 142 E Granada Blvd 32176. **Hours:** 11:30 am-2:30 & 5:30-10 pm, Sat & Sun from 5:30 pm. **Closed:** 4/16, 11/23, 12/25; also Mon, 1/1-1/4 & 7/3-7/14. **Reservations:** suggested. **Features:** Expect fine French cuisine offered in a charming dining room. A polished wait staff gives personalized service and extends a warm invitation for a return visit. Excellent veal smothered in a fabulous sauce is colorfully presented with crisp vegetables. Semi-formal attire; cocktails. **Parking:** on-site. **Cards:** AX, MC, VI.

MARIO'S

Dinner: $10-$19 **Phone:** 386/677-2711 ㉔

▽▽ ▽▽
Traditional Italian

Location: On US 1. 521 S Yonge St 32176. **Hours:** 4:30 pm-10 pm, Fri & Sat-11 pm. **Closed:** 11/23, 12/25. **Reservations:** accepted. **Features:** Moderately priced lunch and dinner selections tend toward the traditional at this family-owned Italian restaurant. The menu includes a tasty choice of pastas, salads, pizzas, lasagna and seafood. The atmosphere is casual and comfortable. Casual dress; cocktails. **Parking:** on-site. **Cards:** AX, MC, VI. ▼

ORMOND STEAKHOUSE

Lunch: $6-$15 **Dinner:** $10-$25 **Phone:** 386/671-9992 ㉒

▽▽ ▽▽
Steak House

Location: 0.3 mi n of SR 40; in Trails Shopping Center. 324 N Nova Rd 32174. **Hours:** 11:30 am-10 pm. **Closed:** 12/25. **Features:** The subdued steakhouse has high-backed booths, dark wood accents and a homey atmosphere. Casual dress; cocktails. **Parking:** on-site. **Cards:** AX, DS, MC, VI. ▼

PEACH VALLEY CAFE

Lunch: $5-$7 **Phone:** 386/615-0096 ⑮

▽▽ ▽▽
American

Location: Just w of A1A. 185 E Granada Blvd 32176. **Hours:** 7 am-2:30 pm. **Closed:** 11/23, 12/25. **Features:** Open only for breakfast and lunch, the cafe prepares such dishes as eggs Benedict, waffles, pancakes and sandwich platters of chicken salad, burgers and clubs. Casual dress. **Parking:** on-site. **Cards:** AX, MC, VI.

ROYAL DYNASTY RESTAURANT & LOUNGE

Lunch: $5-$8 **Dinner:** $8-$17 **Phone:** 386/676-2266 ㉖

▽▽
Chinese

Location: Jct Williamson Blvd and SR 40. 1482 W Granada Blvd 32174. **Hours:** 11 am-9:30 pm, Fri & Sat-10:30 pm. **Closed:** 11/23. **Reservations:** accepted. **Features:** Delectable moo shu chicken is prepared right at your table. Lunch combination plates as well as an a la carte menu feature a very good variety of traditional Chinese entrees. Clean and neat service with quality table settings are nice touches. Casual dress; cocktails. **Parking:** on-site. **Cards:** AX, DS, MC, VI. ▼

STONEWOOD GRILL & TAVERN

Dinner: $14-$28 **Phone:** 386/671-1199 ⑱

▽▽▽ ▽▽
American

Location: On SR A1A, just s of SR 40. 100 S Atlantic Ave 32176. **Hours:** 4 pm-10 pm, Fri & Sat-11 pm. **Closed:** 1/1, 11/23, 12/25. **Reservations:** not accepted. **Features:** By the beach, the upscale restaurant has many large windows in the dining room so guests can watch the cars drive by. Flavorful filet mignon is cooked on the oak grill. Expect nice prices for drinks during happy hour. Casual dress; cocktails. **Parking:** on-site. **Cards:** AX, DC, DS, MC, VI. ▼

The following restaurant has not been evaluated by AAA but is listed for your information only.

GENOVESE'S ITALIAN CAFE

Phone: 386/677-3222

[fyi]

Not evaluated. Location: 183 E Granada Blvd 32176. **Features:** In a small strip mall, the casual little cafe is a great place to dine in or take out. Pizza and such dishes as shrimp scampi make up the menu. A good appetite is advised for taking on the healthy portions.

OSPREY pop. 4,143

——— WHERE TO STAY ———

RAMADA INN-SARASOTA SOUTH   *Book at aaa.com*   **Phone:** (941)966-2121

Motel

| | 12/20-11/30 | 1P: $129-$139 | 2P: $129-$139 | XP: $10 |
| | 12/1-12/19 | 1P: $79 | 2P: $79 | XP: $10 |

Location: On US 41, 1.8 mi n of jct SR 681. 1660 S Tamiami Tr 34229. Fax: 941/966-1124. **Facility:** 136 units. 128 one-bedroom standard units. 8 one-bedroom suites, some with kitchens. 2 stories, interior/exterior corridors. **Parking:** on-site. **Terms:** cancellation fee imposed, pets ($25 fee in designated units). **Amenities:** voice mail, irons, hair dryers. **Pool(s):** heated outdoor. **Leisure Activities:** exercise room. **Guest Services:** valet and coin laundry. **Business Services:** meeting rooms, fax. **Cards:** AX, DC, DS, MC, VI. *(See color ad p 914)*

SOME UNITS
FEE

OVIEDO —See Orlando p. 831.

PALATKA pop. 10,033

——— WHERE TO STAY ———

RIVERFRONT INN   **Phone:** (386)328-3481

Small-scale Hotel

| | All Year | | 2P: $70-$249 | XP: $5 |
| | | | | F18 |

Location: On US 17; at foot of St. John's River Bridge. 201 N First St 32177. Fax: 386/329-9907. **Facility:** 130 one-bedroom standard units. 2 stories (no elevator), exterior corridors. **Parking:** on-site. **Terms:** [AP] & [BP] meal plans available, package plans. **Amenities:** voice mail, irons, hair dryers. **Pool(s):** outdoor. **Leisure Activities:** marina, fishing, exercise room. **Guest Services:** valet and coin laundry. **Business Services:** meeting rooms. **Cards:** AX, CB, DC, DS, JC, MC, VI.

SOME UNITS
FEE

PALM BAY pop. 79,413

——— WHERE TO STAY ———

JAMESON INN   *Book at aaa.com*   **Phone:** (321)725-2952

Small-scale Hotel

| | All Year [ECP] | 1P: $54-$104 |

Location: I-95, exit 176. 890 Palm Bay Rd 32905. Fax: 321/768-1759. **Facility:** 67 units. 65 one-bedroom standard units. 2 one-bedroom suites. 3 stories, interior corridors. *Bath:* combo or shower only. **Parking:** on-site. **Terms:** cancellation fee imposed, small pets only ($10 fee). **Amenities:** voice mail, irons, hair dryers. **Pool(s):** outdoor. **Leisure Activities:** exercise room. **Guest Services:** valet laundry. **Business Services:** meeting rooms. **Cards:** AX, CB, DC, DS, MC, VI.

SOME UNITS
FEE

SAFAR INN HOTEL   *Book at aaa.com*   **Phone:** (321)723-8181

Small-scale Hotel

| | All Year | | 2P: $69-$139 |

Location: I-95, exit 176, 2.1 mi e. 1881 Palm Bay Rd NE 32905. Fax: 321/727-7390. **Facility:** 122 units. 120 one-bedroom standard units. 2 one-bedroom suites. 4 stories, interior corridors. **Parking:** on-site. **Amenities:** voice mail, irons, hair dryers. **Pool(s):** outdoor, indoor. **Leisure Activities:** exercise room. **Business Services:** conference facilities, business center. **Cards:** AX, DS, MC, VI.

SOME UNITS

——— WHERE TO DINE ———

BIZZARRO PIZZERIA   **Lunch:** $2-$20   **Dinner:** $2-$20   **Phone:** 321/409-8111

Italian

Location: I-95, exit 173, just w; in Shoppes of Palm Bay. 1150 Malabar Rd #117 32907. **Hours:** 10 am-10 pm, Fri & Sat-11 pm, Sun-9 pm. Closed: 11/23, 12/25. **Features:** Families enjoy dining at the Italian eatery, which specializes in pizza, stuffed pizza and hot submarine sandwiches. Pizza is available by the slice. Salads also make a menu appearance. Casual dress. **Parking:** on-site. **Cards:** MC, VI.

GREEN TEA   **Lunch:** $3-$11   **Dinner:** $3-$11   **Phone:** 321/722-9288

Chinese

Location: I-95, exit 176, 1.9 mi e. 1831 Palm Bay Rd 32905. **Hours:** 11 am-10 pm, Fri & Sat-11 pm, Sun noon-10:30 pm. Closed major holidays. **Features:** The takeout restaurant, which offers walk-up and drive-through service, serves Cantonese-, Hunan- and Szechwan-style food. A few picnic tables are near the takeout window. Casual dress. **Parking:** on-site. **Cards:** MC, VI.

JERKY'S JAMAICAN FOOD   **Lunch:** $4-$10   **Dinner:** $4-$10   **Phone:** 321/728-8107

Jamaican

Location: I-95, exit 176, 1.6 mi e. 1516 Palm Bay Rd NE 32905. **Hours:** 11 am-9 pm, Fri & Sat-10 pm, Sun-6 pm. Closed major holidays. **Features:** Among Jamaican favorites at the small takeout eatery, where all meals must be ordered to go, are curry goat, oxtail, rice and peas. Food can be washed down with ginger beer or an Irish moss drink. Casual dress. **Parking:** on-site. **Cards:** MC, VI.

WAGON WHEEL PIZZA & RESTAURANT   **Lunch:** $5-$18   **Dinner:** $5-$18   **Phone:** 321/724-4769

Italian

Location: I-95, exit 176, 2.1 mi e. 1760 Palm Bay Rd 32905. **Hours:** 11 am-10 pm, Sun noon-9 pm. Closed major holidays. **Features:** Although pizzas are a specialty here, salads and pasta dishes also find space on the menu. Casual dress; beer & wine only. **Parking:** on-site. **Cards:** AX, DC, DS, MC, VI.

WOK ROLL   **Lunch:** $5-$15   **Dinner:** $5-$15   **Phone:** 321/726-8481

Chinese

Location: I-95, exit 173, just w; in Shoppes of Palm Bay. 1150 Malabar Rd SE, Suite 119 32907. **Hours:** 11 am-10 pm, Fri & Sat-11 pm, Sun noon-10 pm. **Features:** Traditional Chinese favorites are served at the to-go restaurant. Among the more than 110 choices are combination plates, vegetable dishes and seafood specialties. Casual dress. **Parking:** on-site. **Cards:** AX, MC, VI.

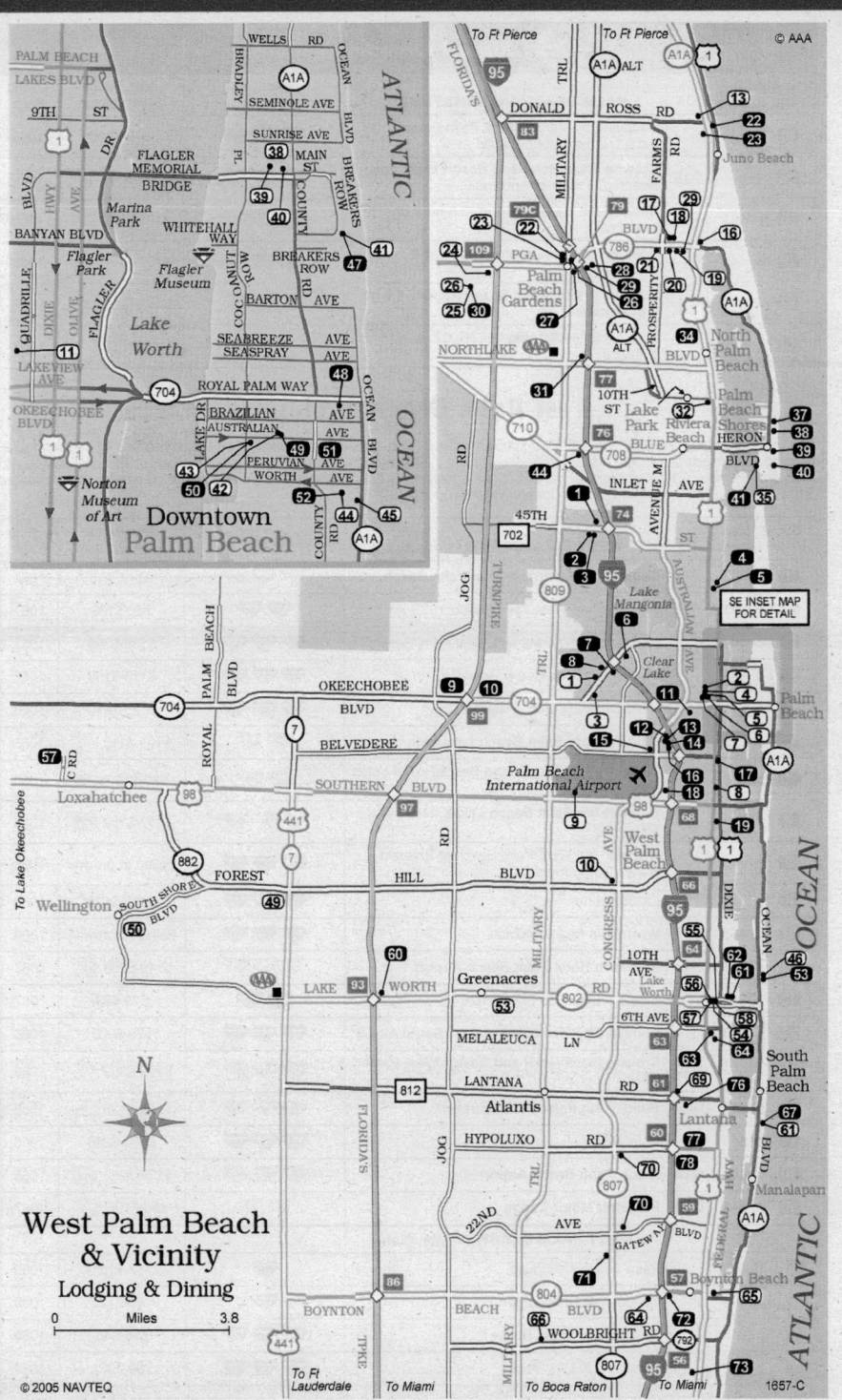

© AAA

Downtown
Palm Beach

West Palm Beach
& Vicinity

Lodging & Dining

0   Miles   3.8

© 2005 NAVTEQ

1657-C

✈ Airport Accommodations

Spotter/Map Page Number	OA	PALM BEACH INTERNATIONAL	Diamond Rating	Rate Range High Season	Listing Page
14 / p. 843		Courtyard by Marriott West Palm Beach Airport, 0.8 mi n of entrance	▽▽▽	$79-$329	1065
15 / p. 843	AAA	Crowne Plaza Hotel and Resort West Palm Beach, 0.3 mi n of entrance	▽▽▽	$209-$309 [SAVE]	1066
18 / p. 843	AAA	Hilton Palm Beach Airport, 0.8 mi s of entrance	▽▽▽	$179-$269 [SAVE]	1066
16 / p. 843	AAA	Holiday Inn Palm Beach Airport, 0.8 mi ne of entrance	▽▽▽	$109-$139 [SAVE]	1066
12 / p. 843	AAA	Radisson Hotel Palm Beach Airport, 0.8 mi n of entrance	▽▽▽	$149-$209 [SAVE]	1067
13 / p. 843		Studio 6 Extended Stay #6026, 0.8 mi n of entrance	▽▽	$79-$93	1067

West Palm Beach & Vicinity

This index helps you "spot" where approved accommodations and restaurants are located on the corresponding detailed maps. Lodging rate ranges are for comparison only and show the property's high season; rates are per night, unless only weekly (W) rates are available. Restaurant rate range is for dinner, unless only lunch (L) is served. Turn to the listing page for more detailed rate information and consult display ads for special promotions.

Spotter/Map Page Number	OA	WEST PALM BEACH - Lodgings	Diamond Rating	Rate Range High Season	Listing Page
1 / p. 843	AAA	Courtyard by Marriott-West Palm Beach	▽▽▽	$249 [SAVE]	1065
2 / p. 843		Red Roof Inn-West Palm Beach	▽▽	$80-$100	1067
3 / p. 843		Residence Inn by Marriott West Palm Beach	▽▽▽	$189-$359	1067
4 / p. 843		Tropical Gardens Bed & Breakfast	▽▽▽	$110-$160	1067
5 / p. 843		Hibiscus House Bed & Breakfast	▽▽▽	$125-$210	1066
6 / p. 843	AAA	Best Western Palm Beach Lakes Inn	▽▽	$105-$110 [SAVE]	1065
7 / p. 843	AAA	Wellesley Inn (West Palm Beach) - see color ad p 1068	▽▽	$89-$159 [SAVE]	1068
8 / p. 843	AAA	Comfort Inn-Palm Beach Lakes - see color ad p 1065	▽▽▽	$119-$159 [SAVE]	1065
9 / p. 843		Hampton Inn West Palm Beach at Emerald Dunes Golf Course	▽▽▽	Failed to provide	1066
10 / p. 843		La Quinta Inn	▽▽▽	$109-$129	1067
11 / p. 843		West Palm Beach Marriott	▽▽▽	Failed to provide	1068
12 / p. 843	AAA	Radisson Hotel Palm Beach Airport	▽▽▽	$149-$209 [SAVE]	1067
13 / p. 843		Studio 6 Extended Stay #6026	▽▽	$79-$93	1067
14 / p. 843		Courtyard by Marriott West Palm Beach Airport	▽▽▽	$79-$329	1065
15 / p. 843	AAA	Crowne Plaza Hotel and Resort West Palm Beach	▽▽▽	$209-$309 [SAVE]	1066
16 / p. 843	AAA	Holiday Inn Palm Beach Airport	▽▽▽	$109-$139 [SAVE]	1066
17 / p. 843		Hotel Biba	▽▽▽	$170-$200	1066
18 / p. 843	AAA	Hilton Palm Beach Airport	▽▽▽	$179-$269 [SAVE]	1066
19 / p. 843	AAA	Parkview Motor Lodge	▽▽	$90-$105 [SAVE]	1067
		WEST PALM BEACH - Restaurants			
1 / p. 843		Palm Beach Ale House	▽	$7-$18	1069
2 / p. 843		Cheeburger Cheeburger	▽	$6-$12	1069
3 / p. 843		Rain Dancer Steak House	▽▽▽	$15-$40	1069
4 / p. 843		Il Bellagio at City Place	▽▽▽	$9-$27	1069

Spotter/Map Page Number	OA	WEST PALM BEACH - Restaurants (continued)	Diamond Rating	Rate Range High Season	Listing Page
⑤ / p. 843		Brewzzi Italian American Bistro & Microbrewery	◆◆◆	$9-$24	1069
⑥ / p. 843		City Cellar Wine Bar & Grill	◆◆◆	$10-$30	1069
⑦ / p. 843		Tsunami Restaurant	◆◆◆	$25-$35	1070
⑧ / p. 843		Pippenella's	◆◆	$10-$19	1069
⑨ / p. 843		391st Bomb Group	◆◆	$12-$29	1069
⑩ / p. 843		Orchids of Siam	◆◆	$10-$19	1069
⑪ / p. 843		Mark's City Place	◆◆	$18-$38	1069
		JUNO BEACH - Lodgings			
㉒ / p. 843		Holiday Inn Express-North Palm Beach	◆◆◆	$99-$169	507
㉓ / p. 843		Hampton Inn Juno Beach	◆◆◆	$159-$299	507
		JUNO BEACH - Restaurant			
⑬ / p. 843		Classico's Italian Restaurant	◆◆	$10-$23	507
		PALM BEACH GARDENS - Lodgings			
㉖ / p. 843	AAA	**DoubleTree Hotel In The Gardens** - see color ad p 850	◆◆◆	$179-$319 [SAVE]	850
㉗ / p. 843		Embassy Suites Hotel	◆◆◆	$259-$309	850
㉘ / p. 843		Hampton Inn	◆◆◆	$189-$249	850
㉙ / p. 843	AAA	**Palm Beach Gardens Marriott**	◆◆◆	$139-$269 [SAVE]	851
㉚ / p. 843	AAA	**PGA National Resort & Spa**	◆◆◆◆	$199-$395 [SAVE]	851
㉛ / p. 843	AAA	**Inn of America**	◆◆	$149-$189 [SAVE]	851
		PALM BEACH GARDENS - Restaurants			
⑯ / p. 843		Bonefish Grill	◆◆◆	$14-$18	851
⑰ / p. 843		Carmine's La Trattoria	◆◆◆	$15-$25	851
⑱ / p. 843		The River House	◆◆◆	$17-$40	852
⑲ / p. 843		Waterway Cafe	◆◆	$8-$28	852
⑳ / p. 843		Carmine's Ocean Grill & Sushi Bar	◆◆◆	$13-$43	852
㉑ / p. 843		No Anchovies! Neighborhood Pastaria	◆◆	$4-$19	852
㉒ / p. 843		Paddy Mac's	◆◆	$9-$19	852
㉓ / p. 843		Cafe Chardonnay	◆◆◆	$20-$38	851
㉔ / p. 843		Ebisu Japanese Restaurant	◆◆	$12-$20	852
㉕ / p. 843		Shula's Steak House	◆◆◆	$30-$50	852
㉖ / p. 843		Arezzo	◆◆◆	$12-$25	851
		NORTH PALM BEACH - Lodgings			
㉞ / p. 843	AAA	**Super 8 Motel**	◆◆	$119-$199 [SAVE]	644
		NORTH PALM BEACH - Restaurant			
㉙ / p. 843	AAA	**Panama Hattie's**	◆◆	$9-$33	644
		PALM BEACH SHORES - Lodgings			
㊲ / p. 843		Hilton Singer Island Oceanfront Resort	◆◆◆	$239-$319	853
㊳ / p. 843	AAA	**Crowne Plaza Oceanfront Singer Island Hotel**	◆◆◆	$159-$259 [SAVE]	853
㊴ / p. 843		Palm Beach Shores Resort and Vacation Villas	◆◆◆	$219-$289	853
㊵ / p. 843	AAA	**Best Western Seaspray Inn** - see color ad p 853	◆◆	$140-$230 [SAVE]	853

Spotter/Map Page Number	OA	PALM BEACH SHORES - Lodgings (continued)	Diamond Rating	Rate Range High Season	Listing Page
41 / p. 843		Sailfish Marina	◆◆	$95-$180	853
		PALM BEACH SHORES - Restaurant			
35 / p. 843		Sailfish Waterfront Dining	◆◆	$15-$27	854
		RIVIERA BEACH - Lodgings			
44 / p. 843		Super 8 Motel West Palm Beach/Riviera Beach	◆◆	$89-$199	873
		PALM BEACH - Lodgings			
47 / p. 843	AAA	**The Breakers**	◆◆◆◆◆	$470-$1200	848
48 / p. 843		Heart of Palm Beach Hotel	◆◆◆	$99-$1000	849
49 / p. 843		Brazilian Court Hotel	◆◆◆◆	$500-$3000	848
50 / p. 843	AAA	**The Chesterfield Hotel**	◆◆◆◆	$250-$1600 SAVE	848
51 / p. 843		Palm Beach Historic Inn	◆◆◆	Failed to provide	849
52 / p. 843	AAA	**The Colony**	◆◆◆◆	$440-$1500 SAVE	848
53 / p. 843	AAA	**The Four Seasons Resort, Palm Beach**	◆◆◆◆	$455-$785 SAVE	848
		PALM BEACH - Restaurants			
38 / p. 843		Echo	◆◆◆	$18-$36	849
39 / p. 843		Chuck & Harold's	◆◆	$8-$24	849
40 / p. 843	AAA	**Testa's Restaurant**	◆◆	$12-$25	850
41 / p. 843	AAA	**L'Escalier**	◆◆◆◆◆	$85-$100	849
42 / p. 843		Cafe Boulud	◆◆◆◆	$18-$36	849
43 / p. 843		The Leopard Room	◆◆◆	$18-$40	849
44 / p. 843	AAA	**Polo Steakhouse**	◆◆◆	$22-$39	849
45 / p. 843		Charley's Crab	◆◆◆	$16-$38	849
46 / p. 843	AAA	**The Restaurant at The Four Seasons**	◆◆◆◆	$29-$36	850
		LOXAHATCHEE - Lodgings			
57 / p. 843		Southern Palm Bed & Breakfast	◆◆◆	$139-$239	521
		LAKE WORTH - Lodgings			
60 / p. 843		Holiday Inn West Palm Beach-Turnpike	◆◆◆	$135-$155	515
61 / p. 843	AAA	**Sabal Palm House B & B Inn**	◆◆◆◆	$155-$250 SAVE	516
62 / p. 843		The Mango Inn Bed and Breakfast	◆◆◆	$140-$300	516
63 / p. 843	AAA	**Lago Motor Inn**	◆◆	$85-$115 SAVE	515
64 / p. 843	AAA	**New Sun Gate Motel**	◆◆	$69-$89 SAVE	516
		LAKE WORTH - Restaurants			
53 / p. 843	AAA	**Bohemian Garden Restaurant**	◆◆	$10-$21	516
54 / p. 843		Rustico Italiano	◆◆	$15	516
55 / p. 843		Dave's Last Resort & Raw Bar	◆◆	$7-$20	516
56 / p. 843		L'Anjou	◆◆◆	$18-$36	516
57 / p. 843		Saito Bangkok	◆◆	$14-$22	517
58 / p. 843		Brogue's Irish Pub	◆◆	$6-$16	516
		MANALAPAN - Lodgings			
67 / p. 843	AAA	**The Ritz-Carlton, Palm Beach**	fyi	$375-$4000 SAVE	521

Spotter/Map Page Number	OA	MANALAPAN - Restaurant	Diamond Rating	Rate Range High Season	Listing Page
61 / p. 843		The Grill	◈◈◈◈	$22-$42	521
		BOYNTON BEACH - Lodgings			
70 / p. 843		Hampton Inn & Suites Boynton Beach	◈◈◈	Failed to provide	260
71 / p. 843		Holiday Inn-Boynton Beach - see color ad p 260	◈◈◈	$139-$149	260
72 / p. 843	AAA	Holiday Inn Express I-95 - see color ad p 261	◈◈	$149-$249 SAVE	261
73 / p. 843	AAA	Atlantic Lodge	◈	$70-$90 SAVE	260
		BOYNTON BEACH - Restaurants			
64 / p. 843	AAA	Mama Jennie's Italian Restaurant	◈◈	$8-$15	262
65 / p. 843		Two Georges Waterfront Grille	◈◈	$14-$30	262
66 / p. 843	AAA	Michael's Sonoma Grille	◈◈◈	$15-$23	262
		LANTANA - Lodgings			
76 / p. 843		Motel 6 Lantana #688	◈	$56-$72	517
77 / p. 843	AAA	Comfort Inn & Suites Lantana/Boynton Beach - see color ad p 260	◈◈◈	$79-$149 SAVE	517
78 / p. 843		Best Western Inn of America	◈◈◈	$99-$169	517
		LANTANA - Restaurants			
69 / p. 843		Riggins Crabhouse	◈◈	$12-$25	517
70 / p. 843		Anchor Inn Restaurant	◈◈	$16-$26	517
		LAKE PARK - Restaurant			
32 / p. 843		Cafe du Park	◈◈◈	$16-$34	514
		WELLINGTON - Restaurants			
49 / p. 843		Smokey Bones	◈◈	$7-$21	1063
50 / p. 843		The Player's Club	◈◈◈	$21-$39	1063

PALM BEACH pop. 10,468 (See map and index starting on p. 843)—
See also NORTH PALM BEACH, PALM BEACH GARDENS, PALM BEACH SHORES & WEST PALM BEACH.

——————— WHERE TO STAY ———————

BRAZILIAN COURT HOTEL *Book at aaa.com*   Phone: (561)655-7740 [49]

	1P: $500-$3000	2P: $500-$3000	XP: $50	F12
12/1-4/30				
5/1-6/30 & 10/1-11/30	1P: $350-$2200	2P: $350-$2200	XP: $50	F12
7/1-9/30	1P: $250-$1100	2P: $250-$1100	XP: $50	F12

Small-scale Hotel **Location:** From Royal Palm Way (SR 204), s on Cocoanut Row, 2 blks to Australian Ave, then just e; corner of Hibiscus and Australian aves. 301 Australian Ave 33480. Fax: 561/655-0801. **Facility:** Designated smoking area. 80 units. 42 one-bedroom standard units with whirlpools. 25 one-, 10 two- and 3 three-bedroom suites. 3 stories, interior corridors. **Parking:** valet and street. **Terms:** 3 day cancellation notice-fee imposed, small pets only ($100 extra charge). **Amenities:** DVD players, video games (fee), high-speed Internet, dual phone lines, voice mail, safes, honor bars, hair dryers. **Dining:** Cafe Boulud, see separate listing. **Pool(s):** heated outdoor. **Leisure Activities:** exercise room, spa. *Fee:* bicycles. **Guest Services:** sundries, valet laundry, area transportation, beauty salon. **Business Services:** meeting rooms, PC, fax (fee). **Cards:** AX, DC, DS, MC, VI.

THE BREAKERS *Book at aaa.com*   Phone: (561)655-6611 [47]

	1P: $470-$1200	2P: $470-$1200	XP: $50	F16
12/1-5/6				
11/1-11/30	1P: $400-$1050	2P: $400-$1050	XP: $50	F16
5/7-10/31	1P: $250-$680	2P: $250-$680	XP: $50	F16

Classic Resort **Location:** On SR A1A, 0.3 mi s of jct Royal Poinciana Way. One S County Rd 33480. Fax: 561/659-8403.
Large-scale Hotel **Facility:** Fine hardwoods enhance the guest rooms of this service-oriented, Italian villa-style hotel built in 1896 by Henry Flagler. Smoke free premises. 560 units. 515 one-bedroom standard units. 45 one-bedroom suites ($450-$4500), some with whirlpools. 5-7 stories, interior corridors. *Bath:* combo or shower only. **Parking:** on-site and valet. **Terms:** check-in 4 pm, 14 day cancellation notice, 7 day off season-fee imposed. **Amenities:** video library, CD players, dual phone lines, voice mail, safes, honor bars, irons, hair dryers. *Fee:* video games, high-speed Internet. **Dining:** 7 restaurants, 7 am-11 pm, cocktails, also, L'Escalier, see separate listing, entertainment. **Pool(s):** 3 heated outdoor, wading. **Leisure Activities:** whirlpool, pool & beach cabana, recreation programs, family entertainment center, rental bicycles, playground, spa. *Fee:* scuba diving, snorkeling, charter fishing, golf-36 holes, golf instruction, 10 lighted tennis courts, tennis intruction, game room. **Guest Services:** gift shop, valet laundry, area transportation (fee), barber shop, beauty salon. **Business Services:** conference facilities, business center. **Cards:** AX, CB, DS, MC, VI. Affiliated with A Preferred Hotel.

SOME UNITS

THE CHESTERFIELD HOTEL   Phone: (561)659-5800 [50]

	1P: $250-$1600		XP: $25	F12
12/1-4/30				
5/1-5/31 & 9/29-11/30	1P: $155-$695		XP: $25	F12
6/1-9/28	1P: $140-$695		XP: $25	F12

Historic **Location:** Just w of SR A1A; at Australian Ave and Cocoanut Row. 363 Cocoanut Row 33480. Fax: 561/659-6707.
Small-scale Hotel **Facility:** This 1926 hotel features a private pool patio, a library and a cigar room; some rooms are compact. 53 units. 42 one-bedroom standard units. 10 one- and 1 two-bedroom suites. 4 stories, interior corridors. **Parking:** valet. **Terms:** 3 day cancellation notice-fee imposed, pets ($50 fee, $100 deposit). **Amenities:** video library, high-speed Internet, dual phone lines, voice mail, safes, irons, hair dryers. *Some:* CD players. **Dining:** The Leopard Room, see separate listing, entertainment. **Pool(s):** heated outdoor. **Leisure Activities:** *Fee:* massage. **Guest Services:** valet laundry. **Business Services:** meeting rooms, business center. **Cards:** AX, DC, DS, MC, VI. **Special Amenities:** free newspaper.

SOME UNITS

THE COLONY *Book at aaa.com*   Phone: (561)655-5430 [52]

	1P: $440-$1500	2P: $440-$1500	XP: $25	F17
12/24-5/7				
12/1-12/23 & 5/8-5/31	1P: $225-$1200	2P: $225-$1200	XP: $25	F17
6/1-11/30	1P: $179-$1000	2P: $179-$1000	XP: $25	F17

Location: On SR A1A, just s of Worth Ave. 155 Hammon Ave 33480. Fax: 561/659-8104. **Facility:** Enjoy luxurious
Small-scale Hotel accommodations and welcoming service at this boutique style establishment, located within walking distance of many shops and dining. 92 units. 71 one-bedroom standard units. 14 one- and 7 two-bedroom suites ($525-$1500), some with kitchens and/or whirlpools. 2-6 stories, interior corridors. *Bath:* combo or shower only. **Parking:** on-site (fee) and valet. **Terms:** check-in 4 pm, 3 day cancellation notice, package plans. **Amenities:** CD players, high-speed Internet, voice mail, safes, irons, hair dryers. *Some:* DVD players. **Dining:** 7 am-10 pm, cocktails, also, Polo Steakhouse, see separate listing, entertainment. **Pool(s):** 2 heated outdoor. **Leisure Activities:** whirlpool, beach access, beach chairs, towels, umbrellas. *Fee:* bicycles, massage. **Guest Services:** valet laundry, area transportation-within 5 mi. **Business Services:** meeting rooms, business center. **Cards:** AX, CB, DC, DS, MC, VI. **Special Amenities:** free newspaper.

SOME UNITS

THE FOUR SEASONS RESORT, PALM BEACH *Book at aaa.com*   Phone: (561)582-2800 [53]

	1P: $455-$785	2P: $455-$785	XP: $30	F17
12/1-5/31				
10/1-11/30	1P: $370-$700	2P: $370-$700	XP: $30	F17
6/1-9/30	1P: $295-$550	2P: $295-$550	XP: $30	F17

Location: SR A1A, 0.3 mi n of jct SR 802. 2800 S Ocean Blvd 33480. Fax: 561/547-1374. **Facility:** An on-site spa,
Large-scale Hotel private beach and fine dining contribute an elegant ambience to this waterfront property. 210 units. 197 one-bedroom standard units. 9 one- and 4 two-bedroom suites ($1900-$3500). 4 stories, interior corridors. *Bath:* combo or shower only. **Parking:** valet. **Terms:** check-in 4 pm, 7 day cancellation notice-fee imposed, package plans, small pets only. **Amenities:** video library, DVD players, CD players, dual phone lines, voice mail, safes, honor bars, irons, hair dryers. *Fee:* video games, high-speed Internet. *Some:* DVD players. **Dining:** 2 restaurants, 7 am-10 pm, Fri & Sat-11 pm, cocktails, also, The Restaurant at The Four Seasons, see separate listing. **Pool(s):** heated outdoor. **Leisure Activities:** saunas, whirlpools, steamrooms, recreation programs, jogging, spa, game room. *Fee:* sailboats, windsurfing, boogie boards, kayaks, personal watercraft, 3 tennis courts, tennis instruction, bicycles. **Guest Services:** gift shop, valet laundry, area transportation. *Fee:* beauty salon. **Business Services:** conference facilities, business center. **Cards:** AX, CB, DC, DS, JC, MC, VI.

SOME UNITS

(See map and index starting on p. 843)

HEART OF PALM BEACH HOTEL   *Book at aaa.com*   Phone: (561)655-5600   **48**

All Year   1P: $99-$1000

Small-scale Hotel
Location: Just e of SR A1A; center. 160 Royal Palm Way 33480. Fax: 561/832-1201. **Facility:** Smoke free premises. 92 one-bedroom standard units. 2-3 stories, interior corridors. **Parking:** on-site and valet. **Terms:** 3 day cancellation notice-fee imposed, small pets only ($100 fee). **Amenities:** high-speed Internet, dual phone lines, voice mail, safes, irons, hair dryers. **Pool(s):** heated outdoor. **Leisure Activities:** spa. **Guest Services:** valet laundry. **Business Services:** meeting rooms. **Cards:** AX, CB, DC, MC, VI.

PALM BEACH HISTORIC INN   Phone: 561/832-4009   **51**

Property failed to provide current rates

Historic Bed
& Breakfast
Location: On SR A1A at Chilian Ave; just n of Worth Ave; center. 365 S County Rd 33480. Fax: 561/832-6255. **Facility:** All guest rooms are on the second floor of this 1921 inn, which includes smoke-free public areas and some on-site parking. Smoke free premises. 13 units. 9 one-bedroom standard units. 4 one-bedroom suites. 2 stories (no elevator), interior corridors. **Parking:** on-site. **Amenities:** video library, voice mail, irons, hair dryers.

———— **WHERE TO DINE** ————

CAFE BOULUD   Lunch: $18-$28   Dinner: $18-$36   Phone: 561-655-6060   **42**

French
Location: From Royal Palm Way (SR 204), s on Cocoanut Row, 2 blks to Australian Ave, then just e; corner of Hibiscus and Australian aves; in Brazilian Court Hotel. 301 Australian Blvd 33480. **Hours:** 7 am-10, noon-2:30 & 5:30-10 pm, Sat & Sun 7 am-11, noon-2:30 & 5:30-10 pm. **Reservations:** required. **Features:** Casual elegance marks the setting for fine contemporary country French food. This place is divided into four sections: La Tradition (French and American dishes), La Saison (seasonal dishes), Le Portager (dishes inspired by the vegetable market) and Le Voyage (world cuisine). The chef combines the finest of local and worldly seafood and meats, produce and spices to create meals that won't soon be forgotten. Dressy casual; cocktails. **Parking:** valet. **Cards:** AX, MC, VI.

CHARLEY'S CRAB   Lunch: $9-$19   Dinner: $16-$38   Phone: 561-659-1500   **45**

Seafood
Location: 0.4 mi s of Royal Palm Way; across from ocean. 456 S Ocean Blvd 33480. **Hours:** 11:30 am-10 pm, Fri & Sat-11 pm, Sun 11 am-10 pm. **Reservations:** suggested, for dinner. **Features:** A snappy chipotle pepper sauce adds intrigue to the spring roll stuffed with crab, alfalfa sprouts and bamboo shoots. A knowledgeable staff helps you select from an extensive menu of fresh seafood. Enjoy cozy ambience with an ocean view from the bar. Dressy casual; cocktails. **Parking:** valet. **Cards:** AX, CB, DC, DS, MC, VI.

CHUCK & HAROLD'S   Lunch: $8-$24   Dinner: $8-$24   Phone: 561-659-1440   **39**

American
Location: 0.3 mi e of Flager Memorial Bridge on SR A1A. 207 Royal Poinciana Way 33480. **Hours:** 11 am-10 pm, Fri-11 pm, Sat & Sun 9 am-10 pm. **Reservations:** suggested. **Features:** Diners here will experience comfort whether they eat inside or at the tables on the sidewalk. The daily-changing menu offers a variety of fresh seafood dishes prepared in many ways, as well as non-seafood selections. Casual dress; cocktails. **Parking:** street. **Cards:** AX, DC, DS, MC, VI.

ECHO   Dinner: $18-$36   Phone: 561-802-4222   **38**

Pacific Rim
Location: SR A1A/Royal Poinciana Way, just n to Sunrise Ave, then just e. 230 Sunrise Ave 33480. **Hours:** 5:30 pm-9:30 pm, Fri & Sat-10 pm. Closed: 1/1, 11/23, 12/25; also Mon & Tues 6/1-10/1. **Reservations:** suggested. **Features:** The sophisticated restaurant serves a medley of Oriental cuisines in an upbeat and trendy dining room. Dressy casual; cocktails. **Parking:** valet. **Cards:** AX, CB, DC, DS, JC, MC, VI.

THE LEOPARD ROOM   Lunch: $9-$12   Dinner: $18-$40   Phone: 561-659-5800   **43**

Continental
Historic
Location: Just w of SR A1A; at Australian Ave and Cocoanut Row; in The Chesterfield Hotel. 363 Cocoanut Row 33480. **Hours:** 7 am-11 pm, Thurs-Sat to 1 am. **Reservations:** suggested. **Features:** The classic room has an artful ceiling. Diverse dishes represent many cuisine styles and incorporate fresh seafood as well as area produce and meats. Dressy casual; cocktails. **Parking:** valet. **Cards:** AX, CB, DC, DS, JC, MC, VI.

L'ESCALIER   Dinner: $85-$100   Phone: 561-655-6611   **41**

French
Location: On SR A1A, 0.3 mi s of jct Royal Poinciana Way; in The Breakers. One S County Rd 33480. **Hours:** 6 pm-10 pm. Closed: Sun & Mon. **Reservations:** suggested. **Features:** The richly decorated dining room displays detailed workmanship, including a handcrafted fresco on the 30-foot-high ceiling. Modern French cuisine is prepared with fresh ingredients and artfully presented to enhance a sumptuous dining occasion. Try the chef's daily presentation of foie gras, followed by a roasted rack and grilled saddle of lamb. Diners looking for a special treat should splurge on the nightly tasting menu. Save room for a sensational dessert. Semi-formal attire; cocktails; entertainment. **Parking:** valet. **Cards:** AX, CB, DC, DS, MC, VI.

POLO STEAKHOUSE   Lunch: $9-$16   Dinner: $22-$39   Phone: 561-655-5430   **44**

Steak & Seafood
Location: On SR A1A, just s of Worth Ave; in The Colony. 155 Hammon Ave 33480. **Hours:** 7 am-10 pm. **Reservations:** suggested. **Features:** In the classic retro hotel dining room, the staff shows that service is as important as the flavorful food. Lunch is always a popular choice on sunny days, when most diners sit poolside at linen-draped tables shaded by wide umbrellas. Key lime pie is a specialty of the house. Dressy casual; cocktails; entertainment. **Parking:** on-site (fee). **Cards:** AX, CB, DC, DS, JC, MC, VI.

(See map and index starting on p. 843)

THE RESTAURANT AT THE FOUR
SEASONS *Menu on aaa.com*   **Dinner:** $29-$36   **Phone:** 561/533-3750   46

Location: SR A1A, 0.3 mi n of jct SR 802; in The Four Seasons Resort, Palm Beach. 2800 S Ocean Blvd 33480.
Hours: 6 pm-10 pm. Closed: Mon, also Tues 5/1-11/15. **Reservations:** suggested. **Features:** Guests are in
for a treat at this top-notch establishment. Dining is an all-around pleasurable experience—from the wait
staff's casually elegant service approach to the tranquil, oceanfront setting to the striking grounds views
from the cozy dining area. The chef transforms ingredients, based on what is seasonally and regionally
available, into sumptuous, mouthwatering dishes. Examples include yellowtail snapper, sea bass or tender
lamb. Decadent desserts put an exclamation mark on the meal. Semi-formal attire; cocktails; entertainment.
Parking: valet. **Cards:** AX, CB, DC, DS, MC, VI.

Regional American

TESTA'S RESTAURANT   **Lunch:** $7-$12   **Dinner:** $12-$25   **Phone:** 561/832-0992   40

Location: 0.3 mi e of Flagler Memorial Bridge on SR A1A. 221 Royal Poinciana Way 33480. **Hours:** 7 am-10 pm.
Closed: 11/23. **Reservations:** accepted. **Features:** Under the same family ownership for more than 80
years, the eatery promises consistency. Seafood, steak and Italian dishes are offered; guests may choose
to dine in the dining room, on a sidewalk terrace or on an open-air patio. Dressy casual; cocktails. **Parking:**
on-site and valet. **Cards:** AX, CB, DC, DS, MC, VI.

Steak & Seafood

PALM BEACH GARDENS pop. 35,058 (See map and index starting on p. 843)—See also PALM BEACH.

———— **WHERE TO STAY** ————

DOUBLETREE HOTEL IN THE GARDENS *Book at aaa.com*   **Phone:** (561)622-2260   26

1/8-3/31	1P: $179-$319	2P: $179-$319	XP: $15	F18
4/1-4/30	1P: $159-$259	2P: $159-$259	XP: $15	F18
12/1-1/7 & 5/1-11/30	1P: $129-$199	2P: $129-$199	XP: $15	F18

Location: I-95, exit 79B northbound; exit 79AB southbound; 1.8 mi e of Florida Tpke. 4431 PGA Blvd 33410.
Large-scale Hotel Fax: 561/624-1043. **Facility:** 279 one-bedroom standard units. 6 stories, interior corridors. *Bath:* combo or
shower only. **Parking:** on-site. **Terms:** [BP] & [CP] meal plans available. **Amenities:** dual phone lines, voice
mail, irons, hair dryers. **Fee:** video games, high-speed Internet. **Dining:** 6:30 am-2 & 5-10 pm, cocktails. **Pool(s):** heated
outdoor. **Leisure Activities:** whirlpool, exercise room. **Guest Services:** valet laundry, area transportation-Gardens Mall.
Business Services: meeting rooms, business center. **Cards:** AX, CB, DC, DS, JC, MC, VI. **Special Amenities:** early check-
in/late check-out. *(See color ad below)*

SOME UNITS

EMBASSY SUITES HOTEL *Book at aaa.com*   **Phone:** (561)622-1000   27

1/1-4/30 [BP]	1P: $259-$309	2P: $259-$309	XP: $10	F17
12/1-12/31 & 11/1-11/30 [BP]	1P: $209-$259	2P: $209-$259	XP: $10	F17
5/1-10/31 [BP]	1P: $149-$199	2P: $149-$199	XP: $10	F17

Small-scale Hotel **Location:** I-95, exit 79AB, 1.8 mi e of Florida Tpke, exit 109. 4350 PGA Blvd 33410. Fax: 561/626-6254.
Facility: 160 one-bedroom suites, some with whirlpools. 10 stories, interior corridors. *Bath:* combo or shower only. **Parking:** on-
site. **Terms:** cancellation fee imposed. **Amenities:** high-speed Internet (fee), dual phone lines, voice mail, irons, hair dryers.
Pool(s): heated outdoor. **Leisure Activities:** sauna, whirlpool, tennis court, jogging, exercise room. **Guest Services:** gift shop,
complimentary evening beverages, valet and coin laundry, area transportation. **Business Services:** meeting rooms, business
center. **Cards:** AX, CB, DC, DS, MC, VI.

SOME UNITS

HAMPTON INN *Book at aaa.com*   **Phone:** 561/625-8880   28

12/1-3/31	1P: $189-$239	2P: $199-$249	
5/1-11/30	1P: $99-$159	2P: $99-$179	
4/1-4/30	1P: $99-$159	2P: $109-$169	

Small-scale Hotel **Location:** I-95, exit 79AB, just se of PGA Blvd; 2 mi e of Florida Turnpike, exit 109. 4001 RCA Blvd 33410.
Fax: 561/625-6766. **Facility:** 116 units. 113 one-bedroom standard units with kitchens. 4 stories, interior
corridors. *Bath:* combo or shower only. **Parking:** on-site. **Terms:** [CP] meal plan available. **Amenities:** video games (fee), high-
speed Internet, dual phone lines, voice mail, irons, hair dryers. **Pool(s):** heated outdoor. **Guest Services:** complimentary
evening beverages: Mon-Thurs, valet and coin laundry. **Business Services:** meeting rooms, business center. **Cards:** AX, CB,
DC, DS, MC, VI.

SOME UNITS

(See map and index starting on p. 843)

INN OF AMERICA   *Book at aaa.com*   Phone: (561)626-4918   **31**

AAA SAVE

1/1-4/30 [CP]	2P: $149-$189	XP: $10	F12
12/1-12/31 [CP]	2P: $99-$169	XP: $10	F12
5/1-11/30 [CP]	2P: $89-$149	XP: $10	F12

Motel   **Location:** I-95, exit 77, just w. 4123 Northlake Blvd 33410. Fax: 561/626-8790. **Facility:** 95 one-bedroom standard units. 3 stories, exterior corridors. *Bath:* combo or shower only. **Parking:** on-site. **Terms:** cancellation fee imposed, pets ($10 fee). **Amenities:** irons, hair dryers. **Pool(s):** heated outdoor. **Guest Services:** coin laundry. **Cards:** AX, DS, MC, VI. **Special Amenities: free continental breakfast and free local telephone calls.**

SOME UNITS

🛏 🐾 🍴 🏊 📷 DATA PORT 🖥 📠 / ✕ /
　　　FEE

PALM BEACH GARDENS MARRIOTT   *Book at aaa.com*   Phone: (561)622-8888   **29**

AAA SAVE

1/1-11/30	1P: $139-$269	2P: $139-$269
12/1-12/31	1P: $179	2P: $179

Large-scale Hotel   **Location:** I-95, exit 79AB southbound; exit 79A northbound; 2 mi e of Florida Tpke, exit 109. 4000 RCA Blvd 33410. Fax: 561/622-0052. **Facility:** 279 one-bedroom standard units. 11 stories, interior corridors. *Bath:* combo or shower only. **Parking:** on-site. **Terms:** check-in 4 pm, package plans. **Amenities:** voice mail, irons, hair dryers. **Dining:** 6:30 am-2 & 5-10 pm, cocktails, nightclub. **Pool(s):** heated outdoor. **Leisure Activities:** sauna, whirlpool, exercise room. **Guest Services:** gift shop, valet and coin laundry, area transportation-Gardens Mall & within 5 mi. **Business Services:** conference facilities, business center. **Cards:** AX, CB, DC, DS, MC, VI. **Special Amenities: early check-in/late check-out and preferred room (subject to availability with advance reservations).**

SOME UNITS

🛏 🅿 🍴 🍸 📷 🗞 🏊 ✕ 🐾 DATA PORT 🖥 / ✕ VCR 🖥 /
　　　　　　　　　　　　　　　　　　FEE FEE

PGA NATIONAL RESORT & SPA   *Book at aaa.com*   Phone: (561)627-2000   **30**

AAA SAVE

12/1-4/16	1P: $199-$395	2P: $199-$395	XP: $15	F17
4/17-5/28 & 10/1-11/30	1P: $199-$299	2P: $199-$299	XP: $15	F17
5/29-9/30	1P: $99-$199	2P: $99-$199	XP: $15	F17

Resort
Large-scale Hotel   **Location:** I-95, exit 79AB, 2 mi w; Florida Tpke, exit 109, just w. Located at PGA National. 400 Ave of the Champions 33418. Fax: 561/622-0261. **Facility:** Two mineral pools are part of this lakefront property's European-style spa; a balcony lounging area overlooks a swimming pool and the golf course. 337 units. 329 one-bedroom standard units. 8 one-bedroom suites. 3-4 stories, interior corridors. *Bath:* combo or shower only. **Parking:** on-site and valet. **Terms:** check-in 4 pm, 14 day cancellation notice, 7 off season-fee imposed, package plans, $11 service charge. **Amenities:** video games (fee), dual phone lines, voice mail, safes, honor bars, irons, hair dryers. **Dining:** 5 restaurants, 6:30 am-midnight; 18% service charge, cocktails, also, Arezzo, Shula's Steak House, see separate listings. **Pool(s):** 2 heated outdoor, wading, lap. **Leisure Activities:** saunas, whirlpools, fishing, golf-90 holes, jogging, spa, basketball, volleyball. *Fee:* 19 tennis courts (12 lighted), racquetball court, golf & tennis instruction, croquet & instruction, bicycles, game room. **Guest Services:** gift shop, valet laundry, area transportation (fee). **Business Services:** conference facilities, business center. **Cards:** AX, CB, DC, DS, JC, MC, VI. **Special Amenities: free newspaper.**

SOME UNITS

🛏 ✈ 🍴 🍸 🏌 🦽 📷 🏊 🐾 ✕ 🐾 DATA PORT 🖥 / ✕ VCR 🖥 /
　　FEE　　　　　　　　　　　　　　　　　　　　　FEE

──────── **WHERE TO DINE** ────────

AREZZO   Dinner: $12-$25   Phone: 561/627-2000   **26**

◆◆◆◆

Italian   **Location:** I-95, exit 79AB, 2 mi w; Florida Tpke, exit 109, just w; in PGA National Resort & Spa. 400 Ave of the Champions 33418. **Hours:** 5:30 pm-10 pm. Closed: Mon. **Reservations:** accepted. **Features:** Tables offer a view of the open kitchen and some of the golf course, and ceilings are copies of Michelangelo's frescoes. The menu builds on comfortable offerings of Northern Italian cuisine. Casual dress; cocktails. **Parking:** on-site and valet. **Cards:** AX, CB, DC, DS, JC, MC, VI.

🍸

BONEFISH GRILL   Dinner: $14-$18   Phone: 561/799-2965   **16**

◆◆◆

American   **Location:** Jct PGA Blvd, northeast corner. 11650 US Hwy 1 33408. **Hours:** 4 pm-10:30 pm, Fri & Sat-11:30 pm, Sun-10 pm. **Reservations:** accepted. **Features:** Fresh fish is the house specialty, and the menu and nightly specials offer a variety of choices. Well-prepared food is cooked to perfection. Service is casual in nature, and the staff is skilled and attentive. Dressy casual; cocktails. **Parking:** valet. **Cards:** AX, DC, DS, MC, VI.

♿M

CAFE CHARDONNAY   Lunch: $8-$15   Dinner: $20-$38   Phone: 561/627-2662   **23**

◆◆◆◆

American   **Location:** I-95, exit 79AB, 0.3 mi w, jct PGA Blvd and Military Tr; in Garden Square Shoppes. 4533 PGA Blvd 33418. **Hours:** 11:30 am-2:30 & 5:30-10 pm, Fri-10:30 pm, Sat 5:30 pm-10:30 pm, Sun 5:30 pm-10 pm. Closed: 11/23, 12/25. **Reservations:** suggested. **Features:** For an inventive meal, step into this bright, colorful, bi-level dining room. The house speciality is macadamia nut crusted yellowtail snapper. An efficient team provides good service and sets the tone for an enjoyable evening out. Dressy casual; cocktails. **Parking:** on-site. **Cards:** AX, DC, DS, MC, VI.

🍸

CARMINE'S LA TRATTORIA   Lunch: $6-$25   Dinner: $15-$25   Phone: 561/775-0186   **17**

◆◆◆

Italian   **Location:** I-95, exit 79AB, 2.3 mi e; from US 1, 0.5 mi w; in the Harbour Financial Center. 2401 PGA Blvd 33410. **Hours:** 11 am-11 pm. Closed: 12/25. **Features:** The restaurant's decor is soothing inside or outside with a view of the marina. They offer veal, seafood, pastas, risottos and, for the lighter side, brick oven pizzas and paninis; do not forget the gourmet market in front. Dressy casual; cocktails. **Parking:** on-site. **Cards:** AX, MC, VI.

♿M

(See map and index starting on p. 843)

CARMINE'S OCEAN GRILL & SUSHI BAR　　**Lunch:** $8-$15　　**Dinner:** $13-$43　　**Phone:** 561/624-1141　　⑳
▼▼▼▼　　**Location:** I-95, exit 79AB, 2.3 mi e, then 0.5 mi w of US 1; corner of Prosperity Farms Rd; behind Barnes & Noble
　　Bookstore. 2460 PGA Blvd 33410. **Hours:** 11 am-11 pm, Fri & Sat-midnight. Closed: 11/23, 12/25.
Seafood　　**Features:** The contemporary setting features fish mobiles hanging from the ceiling, etched glass with fish
scenes between the booths, a bustling lounge area and a sushi bar in the rear. The seafood is fresh daily,
the steaks are Black Angus and the service is prompt and friendly and can expertly advise you on your selections. Dressy
casual; cocktails. **Parking:** on-site. **Cards:** AX, MC, VI.

EBISU JAPANESE RESTAURANT　　**Lunch:** $7-$10　　**Dinner:** $12-$20　　**Phone:** 561/622-4495　　㉔
▼▼▼ ▼▼▼　　**Location:** Just w of jct Florida Tpke, exit 102 (PGA Blvd); 1.7 mi w of jct I-95, exit 57; in Shoppes on the Green
　　Shopping Center. 7100 Fairway Dr 33418. **Hours:** 10:30 am-2 & 5:30-10 pm, Fri-10:30 pm, Sat 5:30 pm-10:30
Japanese　　pm, Sun 5:30 pm-10 pm. Closed: 7/4, 11/23, 12/25. **Reservations:** accepted. **Features:** Beautifully
presented, authentic Japanese cuisine features several styles of preparation, including sushi and sashimi. A
traditional dining room offers both Western and Japanese seating. The owner/chef sends out pickled bean sprouts as an
appetizer. Casual dress; beer & wine only. **Parking:** on-site. **Cards:** AX, MC, VI.

NO ANCHOVIES! NEIGHBORHOOD PASTARIA　　**Lunch:** $3-$11　　**Dinner:** $4-$19　　**Phone:** 561/622-7855　　㉑
▼▼▼ ▼▼▼　　**Location:** 0.5 mi w of jct US 1; at Prosperity Farms Rd; in PGA Plaza. 2650 PGA Blvd 33410. **Hours:** 11:30 am-2:30
　　& 4:30-10 pm. **Features:** The name is a solemn promise. An open kitchen adds to the lively ambience of
Italian　　this modern pastaria. Some of the specialty pasta dishes are prepared in a wood-burning oven along with
tasty pizzas. This is a great value on family favorites. Dressy casual; cocktails. **Parking:** on-site. **Cards:** AX,
MC, VI.

PADDY MAC'S　　**Lunch:** $6-$9　　**Dinner:** $9-$19　　**Phone:** 561/691-4366　　㉒
▼▼▼ ▼▼▼　　**Location:** Jct Military Tr and PGA Blvd; at north end of Garden Square Shoppes; 0.3 mi w of jct I-95, exit 57. 10971 N
　　Military Tr 33410. **Hours:** 11:30 am-3 & 4:30-10 pm, Sun from 4:30 pm. Closed: 5/29, 11/23, 12/25.
Irish　　**Features:** Log fireplaces, Irish paintings and a wood bar evoke the aura of a Dublin pub. Casual and noisy,
the restaurant serves up such entrees as salmon with citrus butter and chicken with apple-honey stuffing.
Entertainers perform on Friday and Saturday nights. Casual dress; cocktails. **Parking:** on-site. **Cards:** AX, DC, DS, MC, VI.

THE RIVER HOUSE　　**Dinner:** $17-$40　　**Phone:** 561/694-1188　　⑱
▼▼▼　　**Location:** 0.5 mi w of jct US 1; at Soverel Harbour. 2373 PGA Blvd 33410. **Hours:** 5 pm-10 pm, Fri & Sat-10:30
　　pm. Closed: 11/23, 12/25. **Reservations:** required, Fri & Sat. **Features:** Bustling and warm, the atmosphere
Steak & Seafood　　of the restaurant lends itself to a pleasant dining experience. Lots of windows offer views of the Intracoastal
Waterway. A sweet fresh fruit chutney accompanies the yellowtail snapper and Chilean sea bass which is
topped with macadamia nuts. Another favorite is the 25 ounce prime rib on the bone. Dressy casual; cocktails. **Parking:** valet.
Cards: AX, DC, DS, MC, VI.

SHULA'S STEAK HOUSE　　**Dinner:** $30-$50　　**Phone:** 561/627-4852　　㉕
▼▼▼　　**Location:** I-95, exit 79AB, 2 mi w; Florida Tpke, exit 109, just w; in PGA National Resort & Spa. 400 Ave of the
　　Champions 33418. **Hours:** 6 pm-9:30 pm, Fri & Sat-10 pm. **Reservations:** suggested. **Features:** Miami's
Steak House　　honored football coach filled his dining room with rich wood and Dolphins' memorabilia. Extra large lobsters
and Angus beef will please the heartiest of appetites. Menu options are listed on a football along with a fine
selection of delicious wines. Dressy casual; cocktails. **Parking:** on-site and valet. **Cards:** AX, CB, DC, DS, JC, MC, VI.

WATERWAY CAFE　　**Lunch:** $8-$15　　**Dinner:** $8-$28　　**Phone:** 561/694-1700　　⑲
▼▼ ▼▼　　**Location:** I-95, exit 79AB, 2.2 mi e, just before the bridge. 2300 PGA Blvd 33410. **Hours:** 11:30 am-10 pm, Fri &
　　Sat-11 pm. Closed: 11/23, 12/25. **Features:** On the Intracoastal Waterway, the restaurant affords water
Seafood　　views from most tables in the dining room and on the patio. The floating bar is a neat feature. Casual dress;
cocktails. **Parking:** on-site. **Cards:** AX, DC, MC, VI.

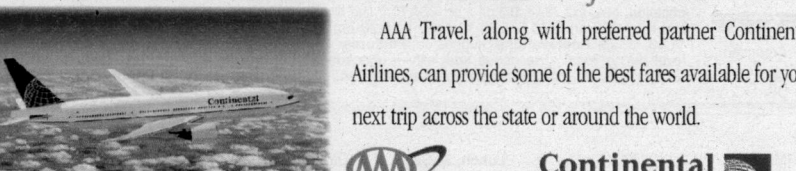

PALM BEACH SHORES pop. 1,269   (See map and index starting on p. 843)—*See also PALM BEACH.*

———— **WHERE TO STAY** ————

BEST WESTERN SEASPRAY INN   *Book at aaa.com*
Phone: (561)844-0233   **40**

12/1-4/28	1P: $140-$230	2P: $150-$230	XP: $10 F18
4/29-11/30	1P: $90-$150	2P: $100-$150	XP: $10 F18

Location: On Singer Island; 0.5 mi s of SR A1A. 123 S Ocean Ave 33404. Fax: 561/844-9885. **Facility:** 50 one-bedroom standard units. 4 stories, interior corridors. **Parking:** on-site. **Terms:** 14 day cancellation notice, pets ($15 extra charge). **Amenities:** safes (fee), irons, hair dryers. **Dining:** 8 am-2:30 & 5:30-9:30 pm, cocktails, entertainment. **Pool(s):** heated outdoor. **Guest Services:** valet laundry. **Cards:** AX, CB, DC, DS, MC, VI. **Special Amenities:** free local telephone calls. *(See color ad below)*

Small-scale Hotel

SOME UNITS
FEE   FEE FEE

CROWNE PLAZA OCEANFRONT SINGER ISLAND HOTEL   *Book at aaa.com*
Phone: (561)842-6171   **38**

All Year	1P: $159-$259	2P: $159-$259	XP: $18 F17

Location: 1.8 mi e, n on SR A1A from jct US 1. 3200 N Ocean Dr 33404. Fax: 561/848-6842. **Facility:** 193 units. 187 one-bedroom standard units. 6 one-bedroom suites. 9 stories, interior corridors. **Bath:** combo or shower only. **Parking:** on-site (fee) and valet. **Terms:** check-in 4 pm, 3 day cancellation notice-fee imposed. **Amenities:** video games (fee), CD players, dual phone lines, voice mail, safes, irons, hair dryers. **Dining:** 6:30 am-11 pm, cocktails. **Pool(s):** heated outdoor. **Leisure Activities:** whirlpool, exercise room. *Fee:* scuba diving, snorkeling, cabana supplies, jet ski, bicycles, massage. **Guest Services:** gift shop, valet and coin laundry. **Business Services:** meeting rooms, business center. **Cards:** AX, CB, DC, DS, JC, MC, VI. **Special Amenities:** free newspaper.

Large-scale Hotel

SOME UNITS

HILTON SINGER ISLAND OCEANFRONT RESORT   *Book at aaa.com*
Phone: (561)848-3888   **37**

12/1-4/30	1P: $239-$319	2P: $239-$319	XP: $15 F18
5/1-11/30	1P: $249-$309	2P: $249-$309	XP: $15 F18

Location: On Singer Island; 1.8 mi n and e on SR A1A from jct US 1. 3700 N Ocean Dr 33404. Fax: 561/848-4299. **Facility:** 223 one-bedroom standard units. 8 stories, interior corridors. **Bath:** combo or shower only. **Parking:** on-site. **Terms:** check-in 4 pm, cancellation fee imposed, [AP], [BP] & [MAP] meal plans available. **Amenities:** video games (fee), voice mail, irons, hair dryers. **Pool(s):** heated outdoor, wading. **Leisure Activities:** whirlpool, exercise room. *Fee:* bicycles, massage. **Guest Services:** gift shop, valet and coin laundry. **Business Services:** meeting rooms, business center. **Cards:** AX, DC, DS, MC, VI.

Large-scale Hotel

SOME UNITS

PALM BEACH SHORES RESORT AND VACATION VILLAS   *Book at aaa.com*
Phone: (561)863-4000   **39**

12/22-5/2	1P: $219-$289	2P: $219-$289	
12/1-12/21 & 5/3-11/30	1P: $119-$189	2P: $119-$189	

Location: On Singer Island; 0.3 mi s of SR A1A. 181 Ocean Ave 33404. Fax: 561/845-3245. **Facility:** 260 units. 250 one- and 10 two-bedroom suites with efficiencies. 6 stories, interior corridors. **Parking:** on-site (fee) and valet. **Terms:** check-in 4 pm, 3 day cancellation notice. **Amenities:** CD players, voice mail, irons, hair dryers. *Fee:* video games, safes. **Pool(s):** heated outdoor, wading. **Leisure Activities:** whirlpool, snorkeling, recreation programs, playground, exercise room. *Fee:* massage, game room. **Guest Services:** gift shop, valet and coin laundry. **Cards:** AX, DS, MC, VI.

Small-scale Hotel

SAILFISH MARINA
Phone: 561/844-1724   **41**

All Year	1P: $95-$180	2P: $95-$180

Location: US 1, 1 mi e, then 0.4 mi s. 98 Lake Dr 33404 (PO Box 10848, 33419). Fax: 561/848-9684. **Facility:** 26 units. 17 one-bedroom standard units, some with efficiencies. 9 one-bedroom suites with kitchens. 1-2 stories, exterior corridors. **Bath:** combo or shower only. **Parking:** on-site. **Terms:** office hours 7 am-9 pm, 3 day cancellation notice-fee imposed, weekly rates available. **Amenities:** *Some:* voice mail. **Dining:** Sailfish Waterfront Dining, see separate listing. **Pool(s):** small heated outdoor. **Leisure Activities:** rental boats, fishing. *Fee:* sailboats, marina, charter fishing, bicycles. **Guest Services:** gift shop, coin laundry. **Business Services:** meeting rooms. **Cards:** AX, MC, VI.

Motel

SOME UNITS

(See map and index starting on p. 843)

———— *The following lodging was either not evaluated or did not* ————
meet AAA rating requirements but is listed for your information only.

MARRIOTT'S OCEAN POINTE   Phone: 561/882-3000
[fyi]   Not evaluated. **Location:** 71 Ocean Ave 33404. Facilities, services, and decor characterize a mid-range property.

———— **WHERE TO DINE** ————

SAILFISH WATERFRONT DINING   **Lunch:** $8-$13   **Dinner:** $15-$27   **Phone:** 561/842-8449   [35]
◆◆◆◆ ◆◆◆◆   **Location:** US 1, 1 mi e, then 0.4 mi s; in Sailfish Marina & Resort. 98 Lake Dr 33404. **Hours:** 7 am-10 pm; to noon
Seafood   12/24. Closed: 11/23, 12/25. **Features:** Fresh seafood and meat dishes are prepared with a special twist.
The open air dining room, overlooking the water, promotes the tropical feel. Casual dress; cocktails.
Parking: on-site and valet. **Cards:** AX, MC, VI.   [&M] [Y]

PALM COAST pop. 32,732

———— **WHERE TO STAY** ————

HAMPTON INN   *Book at aaa.com*   Phone: (386)446-4457
◆◆◆ [SAVE]   All Year   1P: $79-$299   2P: $79-$299
          Location: I-95, exit 289, 0.5 mi se via Old Kings Rd; in Kingswood Center. 5 Kingswood Dr 32137.
◆◆◆◆ ◆◆◆◆   Fax: 386/445-1438. **Facility:** 50 one-bedroom standard units. 2 stories (no elevator), exterior corridors.
Small-scale Hotel   **Parking:** on-site. **Terms:** 7 day cancellation notice-fee imposed. **Amenities:** voice mail, irons, hair dryers.
Pool(s): outdoor. **Leisure Activities:** whirlpool. **Guest Services:** valet laundry. **Cards:** AX, DS, MC, VI.
Special Amenities: free expanded continental breakfast and free local telephone calls.
                                                          SOME UNITS
                    [S/D] [T|+] [⊇] [⌦] [DATA PORT] [▣] / [✕] /

HOLIDAY INN EXPRESS HOTEL & SUITES   *Book at aaa.com*   Phone: (386)439-3939
◆◆◆ [SAVE]   All Year [CP]   1P: $80-$300   2P: $80-$300   XP: $10   F7
          Location: I-95, exit 284 (SR 100), just se. 200 Flagler Plaza Dr 32137. Fax: 386/439-4300. **Facility:** 81 one-
◆◆◆◆ ◆◆◆◆   bedroom standard units. 3 stories, interior corridors. *Bath:* combo or shower only. **Parking:** on-site.
Small-scale Hotel   **Terms:** 2-4 night minimum stay - seasonal, cancellation fee imposed, 10% service charge. **Amenities:** dual
phone lines, voice mail, irons, hair dryers. **Pool(s):** outdoor. **Leisure Activities:** whirlpool. **Guest Services:**
valet and coin laundry. **Business Services:** meeting rooms. **Cards:** AX, CB, DC, DS, JC, MC, VI.
Special Amenities: free continental breakfast and free local telephone calls.   SOME UNITS
                  [S/D] [T|+] [&] [⊘] [⊇] [⌦] [DATA PORT] [▣] / [✕] [⊟] [▣]

MICROTEL INN & SUITES   *Book at aaa.com*   Phone: (386)445-8976
◆◆◆◆ ◆◆◆◆   All Year   1P: $57-$159   2P: $57-$159   XP: $10   F16
          Location: I-95, exit 289, 0.5 mi se via Old Kings Rd. Located in Kingswood Center. 16 Kingswood Dr 32137.
Small-scale Hotel   Fax: 386/445-8977. **Facility:** 83 one-bedroom standard units. 3 stories, interior corridors. *Bath:* combo or
shower only. **Parking:** on-site. **Terms:** 30 day cancellation notice-fee imposed, small pets only ($25 fee).
Amenities: safes (fee). *Some:* irons, hair dryers. **Pool(s):** small outdoor. **Guest Services:** coin laundry. **Cards:** AX, DS,
MC, VI.
                                                          SOME UNITS
          [A$K] [⌂] [T|+] [&M] [&] [⊇] [↔] [⌦] [DATA PORT] / [✕] [⊟] [▣] [▣]
          FEE

OCEAN HAMMOCK RESORT, THE LODGE   *Book at aaa.com*   Phone: (386)445-3000
◆◆◆ [SAVE]   2/1-3/31   1P: $285-$475   2P: $285-$475   XP: $25   F17
          10/1-11/30.   1P: $255-$475   2P: $255-$475   XP: $25   F17
◆◆◆ ◆◆◆◆   4/1-9/30   1P: $245-$450   2P: $245-$450   XP: $25   F17
Resort   12/1-1/31   1P: $199-$385   2P: $199-$385   XP: $25   F17
Small-scale Hotel   **Location:** I-95, exit 289, 4.7 mi e, ne via Palm Coast and Hammock Dunes pkwys, then 0.4 mi e. 105 16th Rd 32137.
Fax: 386/445-9685. **Facility:** Overlooking the ocean, this golf and beach resort has an intimate atmosphere.
Smoke free premises. 20 units. 19 one-bedroom standard units. 1 one-bedroom suite. 3 stories, interior
corridors. *Bath:* combo or shower only. **Parking:** on-site. **Terms:** 3 day cancellation notice-fee imposed, [AP] meal plan
available, package plans, $12 service charge. **Amenities:** CD players, high-speed Internet, dual phone lines, voice mail, safes,
honor bars, irons, hair dryers. **Dining:** Atlantic Grille, see separate listing. **Pool(s):** outdoor, wading. **Leisure
Activities:** whirlpool, exercise room. *Fee:* golf-18 holes. **Guest Services:** valet laundry. **Business Services:** meeting rooms.
Cards: AX, DS, MC, VI.
                                                          SOME UNITS
                    [S/D] [T|] [Y] [⊇] [✕] [✕] [DATA PORT] [▣] / [⊟] /

PALM COAST VILLAS   Phone: (386)445-3525
◆◆◆ [SAVE]   2/1-8/15   1P: $59-$79   2P: $59-$79   XP: $10   F17
          12/1-1/31 & 8/16-11/30   1P: $54-$74   2P: $54-$74   XP: $10   F17
◆◆◆◆ ◆◆◆◆   **Location:** I-95, exit 289, 2.8 mi e to SR A1A, then 1.8 mi n. 5454 N Oceanshore Blvd 32137. Fax: 386/246-4222.
Motel   **Facility:** 28 units. 23 one- and 5 two-bedroom standard units, some with efficiencies. 2 stories, exterior
corridors. *Bath:* combo or shower only. **Parking:** on-site. **Terms:** office hours 8 am-10:30 pm, check-in 4
pm, weekly rates available, small pets only (in designated units). **Amenities:** video library (fee), voice mail.
Some: hair dryers. **Pool(s):** outdoor. **Leisure Activities:** rental bicycles. **Guest Services:** coin laundry. **Cards:** DC, MC, VI.
Special Amenities: free local telephone calls and free newspaper.
                                                          SOME UNITS
                    [S/D] [⌂] [⊇] [⊟] [▣] / [✕] [VCR] [▣]
                                                              FEE

SLEEP INN   **Book at aaa.com**   Phone: (386)446-8180
▼▼▼▼ ▼▼▼▼   All Year   1P: $70-$200   2P: $70-$200   XP: $5   F
           Location: I-95, exit 289, 0.5 mi se via Old Kings Rd; in Kingswood Center. 10 Kingswood Dr 32137.
Small-scale Hotel   Fax: 386/446-4004. **Facility:** 78 one-bedroom standard units. 3 stories, interior corridors. *Bath:* shower only.
           Parking: on-site. **Terms:** 10 day cancellation notice. **Amenities:** hair dryers. *Some:* irons. **Pool(s):** outdoor.
Leisure Activities: whirlpool. **Guest Services:** coin laundry. **Business Services:** meeting rooms. **Cards:** AX, DC, DS,
MC, VI.
                                                                                         SOME UNITS
                        (ASK) (S��) (†↦) (Å M) (Å) (🛏) (👷) (DATA PORT) / (✉) (🛄) (💻) /

─────── **WHERE TO DINE** ───────

ATLANTIC GRILLE   Lunch: $12-$16   Dinner: $18-$28   Phone: 386/447-4600
  ⓐⓐⓐ   **Location:** I-95, exit 289, 4.7 mi e, ne via Palm Coast and Hammock Dunes pkwys, then 0.4 mi e; in Ocean Hammock
           Resort, The Lodge. 105 16th Rd 32137. **Hours:** 6:30 am-2 & 5:30-10 pm. **Reservations:** accepted.
▼▼▼▼ ▼▼▼▼   **Features:** Fresh seafood and steaks highlight the menu. The cuisine is skillfully prepared to order and
  American   artfully presented, providing guests with a fine dining experience. The dining room's refined yet subtle
           upscale decor focuses attention to views of the beach and ocean. Dressy casual; cocktails. **Parking:** on-
           site. **Cards:** AX, DC, DS, MC, VI.   (Å M) (Y)

CARUSO'S ITALIAN CUISINE   Lunch: $5-$14   Dinner: $8-$19   Phone: 386/446-2457
▼▼▼ ▼▼▼   **Location:** I-95, exit 289, just e; in Old Kings Common Shopping Center. 7 Old Kings Rd N, #28 32137. **Hours:** 11 am-
           2 & 4-10 pm, Sun from 4 pm. Closed major holidays. **Reservations:** accepted. **Features:** The extensive
  Italian   Italian menu features traditional selections of chicken parmigiana and cacciatore, spaghetti frutti di mare and
           fettucini alfredo and linguini with clam sauce; lighter fare includes pizza and subs. Casual dress; beer &
wine only. **Parking:** on-site. **Cards:** DS, MC, VI.

COSTA DO SOL   Lunch: $7-$9   Dinner: $10-$17   Phone: 386/447-8806
▼▼▼ ▼▼▼   **Location:** I-95, exit 289, just e to Old Kings Rd, 0.3 mi s to Utility Dr, then just e. 1 Commercial Ct 32137.
           Hours: 11:30 am-9 pm, Fri-10 pm, Sat 1 pm-10 pm, Sun noon-9 pm. Closed: 11/23, 12/25; also Mon.
  Portuguese **Features:** Eastern Mediterranean and American cuisine make up the menu in the unpretentious restaurant.
           Entrees include selections of seafood, beef and pork, with an emphasis on Spanish, Portuguese and Italian
preparations. Much of the nicely prepared food is made on site. The service style is casual and informal. Casual dress; wine
only. **Parking:** on-site. **Cards:** MC, VI.   (Å M)

LA HACIENDA MEXICAN RESTAURANT   Lunch: $5-$7   Dinner: $9-$18   Phone: 386/446-4843
▼▼▼ ▼▼▼   **Location:** I-95, exit 289, 0.5 mi e; in Palm Harbor Shopping Village. 242 Palm Coast Pkwy NE 32137. **Hours:** 11 am-
           10 pm, Sat from noon, Sun noon-9 pm. Closed: 11/23, 12/25. **Reservations:** accepted. **Features:** Popular
  Mexican   with locals for lunch, the restaurant offers generous portions for a nominal price. The menu selections
           include a la carte items, chicken plates, vegetarian plates, seafood and fajitas. Casual dress; cocktails.
Parking: on-site. **Cards:** AX, DS, MC, VI.   (Y)

THE MEETING PLACE   Lunch: $6-$8   Dinner: $9-$15   Phone: 386/445-1310
▼▼▼ ▼▼▼   **Location:** I-95, exit 289, 0.5 mi e; in Palm Harbor Shopping Village. 278 Palm Coast Pkwy 32137. **Hours:** 11 am-3 &
           4-9 pm, Wed-Sat to 10 pm. Closed major holidays. **Features:** A relaxed, casual atmosphere, popular with
  American   the local business crowd, offers the chance to enjoy flavorful entrees like the traditional Reuben sandwich
           served with a New York deli-style pickle. An organized staff expertly attends to your needs. Casual dress;
cocktails. **Parking:** on-site. **Cards:** AX, CB, DC, DS, MC, VI.   (Y)

PALMETTO pop. 12,571   (See map and index starting on p. 904)

─────── **WHERE TO DINE** ───────

A LA MODE ICE CREAM PARLOUR & SANDWICH
  SHOPPE   Lunch: $5-$9   Dinner: $5-$9   Phone: 941/722-6974   51
   ▼▼▼   **Location:** Just s of jct SR 674; downtown. 336 8th Ave W 34221. **Hours:** 11 am-9:30 pm, Fri & Sat-10 pm, Sun-9
           pm. Closed: Mon. **Features:** Guests can take a trip down memory lane in the cozy ice cream parlor and
  American   sandwich shop, set in a restored Victorian home. On the menu are various sandwich and delicatessen
           items, plus dishes such as red beans and rice and the specialty chicken gumbo. Hand-dipped ice cream is a
must for dessert. Casual dress. **Parking:** on-site. **Cards:** MC, VI.

KOJAK'S PALMETTO RIBHOUSE   Lunch: $6-$19   Dinner: $6-$19   Phone: 941/729-8986   50
   ▼▼▼   **Location:** On Business US 41 at jct 17th St W. 1631 8th Ave W 34221. **Hours:** 11 am-9:30 pm, Fri & Sat-10 pm.
           Features: A local favorite since 1978, the restaurant is known for its Oklahoma-style barbecue. It offers
  Barbecue   some great pork spareribs, as well as sandwiches and combination dinners. Casual dress; beer & wine only.
           Parking: on-site. **Cards:** MC, VI.

LEE'S CRAB TRAP 1   Lunch: $8-$14   Dinner: $9-$39   Phone: 941/722-6255   49
▼▼▼▼ ▼▼▼   **Location:** I-75, exit 224, 3 mi w on US 301, then 2.3 mi n; I-275, exit 2, just s. 5611 US 19 N 34221. **Hours:** 11:30
           am-9 pm, Fri & Sat-10 pm. Closed: 11/23, 12/25. **Reservations:** not accepted. **Features:** Stone crabs,
  Seafood   three-crab soup and other rural Florida dishes are served in a very rustic setting. Among the more daring
           selections are the gator and wild boar. Frog legs, scalloped bananas, conch fritters and fresh lobster are all
prepared from scratch. Dressy casual; cocktails. **Parking:** on-site. **Cards:** DS, MC, VI.   (Y) (◣)

PALM HARBOR —See Tampa Bay p. 1030.

PANAMA CITY pop. 36,417

─── WHERE TO STAY ───

BEST WESTERN SUITES *Book at aaa.com* Phone: 850/784-7700

AAA SAVE
▽▽▽▽
Small-scale Hotel

3/1-9/30 [BP]	1P: $80	2P: $80
12/1-2/28 & 10/1-11/30 [BP]	1P: $70	2P: $70

Location: US 98, 1.5 mi ne on US 231, just w on SR 368. 1035 E 23rd St 32405. Fax: 850/763-9095. **Facility:** 50 one-bedroom standard units, some with whirlpools. 2 stories, interior corridors. *Bath:* combo or shower only. **Parking:** on-site. **Amenities:** high-speed Internet, irons, hair dryers. **Pool(s):** outdoor. **Leisure Activities:** exercise room. **Guest Services:** valet laundry. **Business Services:** meeting rooms, fax. **Cards:** AX, CB, DC, DS, MC, VI. **Special Amenities:** free full breakfast and free local telephone calls.

SOME UNITS

COMFORT INN & CONFERENCE CENTER *Book at aaa.com* Phone: (850)769-6969

AAA SAVE
▽▽▽▽
Small-scale Hotel

2/15-9/4	1P: $100	2P: $100	XP: $6	F18
9/5-11/30	1P: $69-$71	2P: $69-$71	XP: $6	F18
12/1-2/14	1P: $67-$69	2P: $67-$69	XP: $6	F18

Location: SR 368, just w of jct US 231. 1013 E 23rd St 32405. Fax: 850/763-4353. **Facility:** 105 one-bedroom standard units. 2 stories, exterior corridors. **Terms:** [CP] meal plan available. **Amenities:** high-speed Internet, voice mail, irons, hair dryers. **Pool(s):** heated outdoor. **Leisure Activities:** picnic area, exercise room, basketball. **Guest Services:** complimentary evening beverages: Mon-Thurs, coin laundry. **Business Services:** conference facilities, fax (fee). **Cards:** AX, CB, DC, DS, JC, MC, VI.

SOME UNITS

COMFORT INN AND SUITES *Book at aaa.com* Phone: (850)763-0101

▽▽▽▽
Small-scale Hotel

2/16-9/15	1P: $89-$180	2P: $99-$190	XP: $10	F12
12/1-2/15 & 9/16-11/30	1P: $69-$100	2P: $79-$125	XP: $10	F12

Location: 4 mi w of jct SR 231. 4128 W US 98 32401. Fax: 850/763-4234. **Facility:** 40 one-bedroom standard units, some with whirlpools. 2 stories, exterior corridors. **Parking:** on-site. **Terms:** 2-4 night minimum stay - seasonal and/or weekends, 3 day cancellation notice. **Amenities:** high-speed Internet, voice mail, irons, hair dryers. **Pool(s):** outdoor. **Guest Services:** coin laundry. **Business Services:** *Fee:* PC, fax. **Cards:** AX, CB, DC, DS, MC, VI.

SOME UNITS

COUNTRY INN & SUITES BY CARLSON PANAMA CITY *Book at aaa.com* Phone: (850)913-0074

▽▽▽▽
Small-scale Hotel

5/2-8/31	1P: $99-$199	2P: $99-$199
3/1-5/1	1P: $109-$139	2P: $109-$139
12/1-2/28 & 9/1-11/30	1P: $89-$99	2P: $89-$99

Location: 0.5 mi w of US 231; just s of 23rd St. 2203 Harrison Ave 32405. Fax: 850/913-9970. **Facility:** 53 units. 47 one-bedroom standard units. 6 one-bedroom suites ($139-$169), some with whirlpools. 2 stories, interior corridors. *Bath:* combo or shower only. **Parking:** on-site. **Terms:** 7 day cancellation notice, [BP] meal plan available. **Amenities:** dual phone lines, voice mail, irons, hair dryers. **Pool(s):** outdoor. **Leisure Activities:** exercise room. **Guest Services:** valet laundry. **Business Services:** meeting rooms, fax. **Cards:** AX, CB, DC, DS, MC, VI.

SOME UNITS

DAYS INN & SUITES *Book at aaa.com* Phone: (850)769-7400

▽▽▽▽
Small-scale Hotel

3/1-9/15 [ECP]	1P: $89-$159	2P: $89-$159	XP: $10	F
12/1-2/28 & 9/16-11/30 [ECP]	1P: $68-$119	2P: $68-$119	XP: $10	F

Location: US 98 E, 2 mi e of jct US 98 E and Transmitter Rd. 435 N Tyndall Pkwy 32404. Fax: 850/769-9558. **Facility:** 52 one-bedroom standard units, some with whirlpools. 2 stories, interior corridors. *Bath:* combo or shower only. **Parking:** on-site. **Amenities:** high-speed Internet, voice mail, irons, hair dryers. **Pool(s):** outdoor. **Business Services:** fax (fee). **Cards:** AX, DC, DS, MC, VI.

SOME UNITS

DAYS INN BAYSIDE Phone: (850)763-4622

AAA SAVE
▽▽▽▽
Small-scale Hotel

2/24-8/6	1P: $79-$115	2P: $85-$125	XP: $7	F12
8/7-10/7	1P: $79-$105	2P: $86-$115	XP: $7	F12
10/8-11/30	1P: $59-$85	2P: $72-$95	XP: $7	F12
12/1-2/23	1P: $55-$85	2P: $72-$95	XP: $7	F12

Location: Business Rt US 98, 0.5 mi w of jct US 231. 711 W Beach Dr 32401. Fax: 850/747-9522. **Facility:** 100 units. 99 one-bedroom standard units. 1 one-bedroom suite ($159-$239). 2 stories, exterior corridors. **Parking:** on-site. **Terms:** cancellation fee imposed, [BP] & [CP] meal plans available, package plans, small pets only ($10 extra charge). **Amenities:** hair dryers. **Dining:** 6:30 am-10 & 5-9 pm, Sat from 7 am; Sun & Mon 7 am-noon off season, cocktails. **Pool(s):** outdoor. **Leisure Activities:** playground, volleyball. **Guest Services:** valet and coin laundry. **Business Services:** meeting rooms, fax (fee). **Cards:** AX, DC, DS, MC, VI. **Special Amenities:** free local telephone calls.

SOME UNITS
FEE

HOLIDAY INN SELECT *Book at aaa.com* Phone: (850)769-0000

▽▽▽▽
Small-scale Hotel

All Year	1P: $99-$109	2P: $99-$109	XP: $10

Location: SR 77, just n of jct US 231. 2001 N Martin Luther King Blvd 32405. Fax: 850/763-3828. **Facility:** 173 one-bedroom standard units. 6 stories, interior corridors. **Parking:** on-site. **Terms:** [AP], [BP], [CP], [ECP] & [MAP] meal plans available. **Amenities:** high-speed Internet, voice mail, irons, hair dryers. **Pool(s):** heated indoor. **Leisure Activities:** saunas, whirlpool, jogging, exercise room. **Guest Services:** valet and coin laundry. **Business Services:** meeting rooms. **Cards:** AX, CB, DC, DS, JC, MC, VI.

SOME UNITS

HOWARD JOHNSON EXPRESS INN *Book at aaa.com* Phone: (850)872-8585

▽▽ ▽▽▽

Motel

3/1-8/31	1P: $110-$199	2P: $125-$199	XP: $6 F17
12/1-2/28 & 9/1-11/30	1P: $55-$125	2P: $65-$125	XP: $6 F17

Location: 0.4 mi w of jct US 231. 301 E 23rd St 32405. Fax: 850/872-8585. **Facility:** 44 one-bedroom standard units. 2 stories, exterior corridors. *Bath:* combo or shower only. **Parking:** on-site. **Terms:** 3-4 night minimum stay - seasonal, cancellation fee imposed, 7% service charge. **Amenities:** voice mail, irons, hair dryers. **Pool(s):** outdoor. **Guest Services:** coin laundry. **Business Services:** fax (fee), **Cards:** AX, CB, DC, DS, MC, VI.

SOME UNITS

(ASK) (SD) (†↓↑) (≈) (✱) (☐) (☞) (▭) / (✕) /

HOWARD JOHNSON INN *Book at aaa.com* Phone: (850)785-0222

▽▽ ▽▽▽

Small-scale Hotel

7/1-8/31	1P: $99-$129
4/8-6/30	1P: $84-$129
12/1-4/7	1P: $54-$89
8/7-11/30	1P: $54-$79

Location: US 98, 0.8 mi e of Hathaway Bridge. 4601 W Hwy 98 32401. Fax: 850/769-3472. **Facility:** 80 one-bedroom standard units. 1-3 stories (no elevator), interior/exterior corridors. **Parking:** on-site. **Terms:** 3 day cancellation notice-fee imposed, [AP] meal plan available, small pets only ($25 fee). **Amenities:** irons, hair dryers. **Pool(s):** outdoor. **Leisure Activities:** boat dock. **Business Services:** meeting rooms, fax. **Cards:** AX, CB, DC, DS, JC, MC, VI.

SOME UNITS

(ASK) (SD) (✈) (🐾) (†↓↑) (Y) (≈) (✱) (DATA PORT) (☐) (☞) (▭) / (✕) /
FEE

LA QUINTA INN & SUITES PANAMA CITY *Book at aaa.com* Phone: (850)914-0022

(AAA) (SAVE)

▽▽▽ ▽▽▽

Small-scale Hotel

3/1-9/10	1P: $108-$128	2P: $115-$135	XP: $7 F18
12/1-2/28 & 9/11-11/30	1P: $95-$115	2P: $102-$122	XP: $7 F18

Location: Jct US 231 and CR 390A. 1030 E 23rd St 32405. Fax: 850/914-0027. **Facility:** 119 units. 113 one-bedroom standard units. 6 one-bedroom suites ($125-$159). 6 stories, interior corridors. *Bath:* combo or shower only. **Parking:** on-site. **Terms:** [ECP] meal plan available, small pets only. **Amenities:** video games, high-speed Internet, voice mail, irons, hair dryers. *Some:* dual phone lines. **Pool(s):** heated outdoor. **Leisure Activities:** whirlpool, exercise room. **Guest Services:** coin laundry. **Business Services:** meeting rooms, fax (fee). **Cards:** AX, CB, DC, DS, MC, VI. **Special Amenities:** free expanded continental breakfast and free local telephone calls.

SOME UNITS

(🐾) (&M) (&) (🐾) (✱) (DATA PORT) (▭) / (✕) (☐) (☞) /

SLEEP INN *Book at aaa.com* Phone: (850)763-7777

▽▽ ▽▽

Small-scale Hotel

2/26-9/15	1P: $60-$190	2P: $60-$190	XP: $10 F18
12/1-2/25 & 9/16-11/30	1P: $50-$70	2P: $50-$70	XP: $5 F18

Location: US 98, 0.5 mi e of Hathaway Bridge. 5126 W Hwy 98 32401. Fax: 850/785-9545. **Facility:** 82 one-bedroom standard units. 2 stories, interior corridors. *Bath:* shower only. **Parking:** on-site. **Terms:** cancellation fee imposed. **Amenities:** irons, hair dryers. **Pool(s):** outdoor. **Business Services:** meeting rooms, fax (fee). **Cards:** AX, CB, DS, MC, VI.

SOME UNITS

(SD) (&M) (🐾) (✱) (DATA PORT) / (✕) (☐) (☞) (▭) /

SUPER 8 MOTEL *Book at aaa.com* Phone: (850)784-1988

▽▽

Motel

All Year	1P: $45-$99	2P: $50-$109	XP: $5 F12

Location: Just n of jct US 98. 207 Hwy 231 N 32405. Fax: 850/763-9154. **Facility:** 60 one-bedroom standard units. 2 stories, interior/exterior corridors. **Parking:** on-site. **Terms:** 2-3 night minimum stay - weekends, [CP] meal plan available, small pets only ($10 extra charge). **Amenities:** safes. **Pool(s):** outdoor. **Business Services:** fax (fee). **Cards:** AX, DC, DS, MC, VI.

SOME UNITS

(ASK) (SD) (🐾) (†↓↑) (🐾) (✱) (☐) (☞) / (✕) /
FEE

——— WHERE TO DINE ———

BLACKBEARD'S RESTAURANT Lunch: $5-$10 Dinner: $10-$25 Phone: 850/770-4040

▽▽▽ ▽▽▽

Seafood

Location: 0.5 mi w of US 231. 1025 W 23rd St 32405. **Hours:** 11 am-9 pm, Fri & Sat-9:30 pm, Sun-8 pm. Closed: 1/1, 11/23, 12/25; also Mon. **Features:** The restaurant is the place to go for barbecue, seafood and steaks. Galley specials include platters for two with shrimp, oysters, scallops, stuffed crab, grouper and hushpuppies. Casual dress; beer & wine only. **Parking:** on-site. **Cards:** AX, MC, VI.

CANOPIES Dinner: $11-$27 Phone: 850/872-8444

▽▽▽ ▽▽▽

Continental

Location: 1 mi e of bridge on US 98. 4423 W Hwy 98 32401. **Hours:** 5 pm-10 pm. Closed: 11/23, 12/25. **Reservations:** suggested. **Features:** Upscale decor with black and white color scheme, featuring black cloth napkins. Signature dessert of white creme brule is excellent. Sophisticated wine selections. Dressy casual; cocktails. **Parking:** on-site. **Cards:** AX, DC, DS, MC, VI.

(Y)

FERRUCCI RISTORANTE Lunch: $5-$8 Dinner: $10-$21 Phone: 850/913-9131

▽▽▽ ▽▽▽

Italian

Location: Downtown. 301 Harrison Ave 32401. **Hours:** 10 am-2 & 5-9:30 pm, Sat from 5 pm. Closed: Sun & Mon. **Reservations:** accepted. **Features:** In a quaint, downtown location, the restaurant offers a sophisticated dining experience that appeals to locals and tourists alike. Dressy casual; cocktails. **Parking:** street. **Cards:** AX, DS, MC, VI.

MOE'S SOUTHWEST GRILL Lunch: $3-$8 Dinner: $3-$8 Phone: 850/522-8606

▽▽

Southwestern

Location: Just w of US 231. 1000 E 23rd St 32405. **Hours:** 11 am-9 pm. Closed: 11/23, 12/25. **Features:** Quick-serve burritos made while you wait and served up with a side of red and blue tortilla chips. Casual dress. **Parking:** on-site. **Cards:** AX, CB, DC, DS, JC, MC, VI.

UNCLE ERNIE'S BAYFRONT GRILL & BREWHOUSE   Lunch: $7-$9   Dinner: $16-$30   Phone: 850/763-8427

Seafood

Location: US 98 S, 0.5 mi w on US 98 Business (Beck St), then just e on 12th Ave. 1151 Bayview Ave 32401. **Hours:** 11 am-10:30 pm. Closed major holidays; also Sun. **Features:** Specializing in inexpensive to moderately priced steaks, seafood and pasta, the restaurant affords nice views of the bay, particularly from the patio. Varied beers are made in the on-premises brewery. Casual dress; cocktails. **Parking:** street.

Cards: AX, DC, DS, MC, VI.

PANAMA CITY BEACH pop. 7,671

―――― WHERE TO STAY ――――

BAY POINT MARRIOTT RESORT   *Book at aaa.com*   **Phone:** 850/236-6000

Property failed to provide current rates

Resort
Large-scale Hotel

Location: US 98, 0.5 mi w of bridge, 2 mi s on CR 3031, then 1.8 mi e on Magnolia Beach Rd, follow signs. 4200 Marriott Dr 32408. Fax: 850/236-6153. **Facility:** A bay and a wildlife sanctuary provide pleasant views from the guest rooms at this 1,100-acre resort; every unit has a patio or balcony. 350 units. 272 one-bedroom standard units. 78 one-bedroom suites, some with whirlpools. 5 stories, interior/exterior corridors. **Parking:** on-site. **Terms:** check-in 4 pm. **Amenities:** video games, high-speed Internet, dual phone lines, voice mail, irons, hair dryers. **Dining:** 30 Degree Blue, see separate listing. **Pool(s):** 3 heated outdoor, heated indoor, wading. **Leisure Activities:** whirlpools, rental boats, rental sailboats, fishing, recreation programs, rental bicycles, playground, exercise room, spa, volleyball. *Fee:* windsurfing, marina, waterskiing, scuba diving, snorkeling, charter fishing, golf-36 holes. **Guest Services:** gift shop, valet laundry, area transportation. **Business Services:** conference facilities, business center.

SOME UNITS

FEE

BEACHBREAK BY THE SEA   **Phone:** (850)234-6644

	5/26-7/29	1P: $139-$209	2P: $139-$209	XP: $20	F17
	3/3-5/25	1P: $109-$179	2P: $109-$179	XP: $20	F17
	7/30-11/30	1P: $45-$159	2P: $45-$159	XP: $20	F17
	12/1-3/2	1P: $45-$99	2P: $45-$99	XP: $20	F17

Small-scale Hotel **Location:** 1.8 mi e of jct SR 79 and US 98. 15405 Front Beach Rd 32413. Fax: 850/234-3882. **Facility:** 96 units. 77 one-bedroom standard units, some with kitchens. 19 one-bedroom suites with kitchens. 4 stories (no elevator), exterior corridors. *Bath:* combo or shower only. **Parking:** on-site. **Terms:** check-in 4 pm, 3 night minimum stay - seasonal and/or weekends, cancellation fee imposed, package plans. **Pool(s):** heated outdoor. **Leisure Activities:** whirlpool. **Guest Services:** coin laundry. **Cards:** AX, DS, MC, VI. *(See color ad below)*

SOME UNITS

BEACHCOMBER BY THE SEA

Book at aaa.com

Phone: (850)233-3600

5/26-7/29	1P: $159-$229	2P: $159-$229	XP: $20	F17
3/3-5/25	1P: $129-$199	2P: $129-$199	XP: $20	F17
7/30-11/30	1P: $49-$179	2P: $49-$179	XP: $20	F17
12/1-3/2	1P: $59-$109	2P: $59-$109	XP: $20	F17

Small-scale Hotel Location: Jct SR 79 and US 98. 17101 Front Beach Rd 32413. **Fax:** 850/233-3622. **Facility:** 96 one-bedroom standard units, some with kitchens and/or whirlpools. 8 stories, exterior corridors. *Bath:* combo or shower only. **Parking:** on-site. **Terms:** check-in 4 pm, 3 night minimum stay - seasonal and/or weekends, cancellation fee imposed, package plans. **Amenities:** irons, hair dryers. **Pool(s):** heated outdoor. **Leisure Activities:** whirlpool. *Fee:* water sports and lounge chairs, game room. **Guest Services:** coin laundry. **Business Services:** meeting rooms, fax (fee). **Cards:** AX, DS, MC, VI. *(See color ad p 858)*

SOME UNITS

BEST WESTERN CASA LOMA

Book at aaa.com

Phone: (850)234-1100

5/21-8/14	1P: $169-$199	2P: $169-$199
3/1-5/20	1P: $139-$199	2P: $139-$199
8/15-11/30	1P: $79-$109	2P: $79-$109
12/1-2/28	1P: $59-$89	2P: $59-$89

Motel Location: US 98A, 3.2 mi sw of jct CR 392. 13615 Front Beach Rd 32413 (PO Box 18049, 32407). **Fax:** 850/234-0864. **Facility:** 101 one-bedroom standard units, some with kitchens. 3 stories (no elevator), exterior corridors. *Bath:* combo or shower only. **Parking:** on-site. **Terms:** check-in 4 pm, 2-4 night minimum stay - seasonal and/or weekends, 3 day cancellation notice-fee imposed, [CP] meal plan available. **Amenities:** irons, hair dryers. **Pool(s):** heated outdoor. **Business Services:** fax. **Cards:** AX, DC, DS, MC, VI. **Special Amenities: free local telephone calls and free room upgrade (subject to availability with advance reservations).**

SOME UNITS

DAYS INN BEACH

Book at aaa.com

Phone: (850)233-3333

2/26-4/30	1P: $189	2P: $189
5/1-9/10	1P: $179	2P: $179
9/11-11/30	1P: $69	2P: $69
12/1-2/25	1P: $59	2P: $59

Small-scale Hotel Location: US 98A, 2.5 mi sw of jct CR 392. 12818 Front Beach Rd 32407. **Fax:** 850/233-9568. **Facility:** 188 one-bedroom standard units, some with kitchens. 7 stories, exterior corridors. **Parking:** on-site. **Terms:** check-in 4 pm, 3 day cancellation notice. **Amenities:** voice mail, irons, hair dryers. **Pool(s):** outdoor. **Leisure Activities:** whirlpool. **Business Services:** fax (fee). **Cards:** AX, CB, DC, DS, MC, VI.

SOME UNITS

EDGEWATER BEACH RESORT

Phone: (850)235-4044

All Year   2P: $79-$1100

Condominium Location: US 98A, 1.3 mi sw of jct CR 392. 11212 Front Beach Rd 32407. **Fax:** 850/233-7591. **Facility:** Golf course or ocean views are available in this property's spacious one- to three-bedroom apartments. 510 one-bedroom standard units. 2-12 stories, exterior corridors. **Parking:** on-site. **Terms:** check-in 4 pm, 3 day cancellation notice-fee imposed, package plans, no pets allowed (owner's pets on premises). **Amenities:** voice mail, irons, hair dryers. **Pool(s):** outdoor, 10 heated outdoor. **Leisure Activities:** whirlpools, rental sailboats, recreation programs, spa, shuffleboard. *Fee:* charter fishing, golf-36 holes, 11 tennis courts (6 lighted). **Guest Services:** gift shop, complimentary laundry. **Business Services:** conference facilities. **Cards:** AX, CB, DC, DS, MC, VI. *(See color ad below)*

SOME UNITS

FEE   FEE

HAMPTON INN AT BAY POINT *Book at aaa.com* Phone: 850/236-8988

Property failed to provide current rates

Location: US 98, 0.5 mi w of bridge, 2.5 mi s on CR 3031. 2909 Thomas Dr 32408. Fax: 850/236-1157. **Facility:** 89 units. 85 one-bedroom standard units. 4 one-bedroom suites with whirlpools. 3 stories, interior corridors. Small-scale Hotel
Bath: combo or shower only. **Parking:** on-site. **Amenities:** video games, high-speed Internet, dual phone lines, voice mail, irons, hair dryers. **Pool(s):** heated outdoor. **Leisure Activities:** whirlpool, exercise room. **Guest Services:** valet laundry. **Business Services:** meeting rooms, fax (fee).

SOME UNITS

HOLIDAY INN SUNSPREE RESORT *Book at aaa.com* Phone: (850)234-1111

2/25-4/22	1P: $199-$299	2P: $199-$299	XP: $20	F19
4/23-9/4	1P: $129-$299	2P: $129-$299	XP: $20	F19
12/1-2/24	1P: $99-$169	2P: $99-$169	XP: $20	F19
9/5-11/30	1P: $109-$159	2P: $109-$159	XP: $20	F19

Large-scale Hotel **Location:** US 98A, 1.1 mi w of jct CR 392. 11127 Front Beach Rd 32407. Fax: 850/235-1907. **Facility:** 341 units. 338 one-bedroom standard units. 2 one- and 1 two-bedroom suites ($400-$1000) with whirlpools. 15 stories, exterior corridors. **Parking:** on-site. **Terms:** check-in 4 pm, 3 day cancellation notice-fee imposed. **Amenities:** high-speed Internet, voice mail, safes, irons, hair dryers. **Dining:** 7 am-11 & 5-10 pm; grill service for lunch in season, cocktails. **Pool(s):** heated outdoor. **Leisure Activities:** sauna, whirlpools, steamroom, recreation programs, playground, exercise room. *Fee:* scuba diving, snorkeling, beach watersports, golf-18 holes, 9 hole par 3, lighted driving range. **Guest Services:** gift shop, valet and coin laundry. **Business Services:** meeting rooms, PC, fax. **Cards:** AX, CB, DC, DS, JC, MC, VI. **Special Amenities:** free local telephone calls and free newspaper. *(See color ad below)*

SOME UNITS

LEGACY BY THE SEA Phone: (850)249-8601

5/26-7/29	1P: $179-$249	2P: $179-$249	XP: $20	F17
3/3-5/25	1P: $149-$219	2P: $149-$219	XP: $20	F17
7/30-11/30	1P: $69-$199	2P: $69-$199	XP: $20	F17
12/1-3/2	1P: $69-$119	2P: $69-$119	XP: $20	F17

Small-scale Hotel **Location:** 2 mi e of jct SR 79 and US 98. 15325 Front Beach Rd 32407. Fax: 850/249-8612. **Facility:** 139 units. 11 one-bedroom standard units, some with whirlpools. 123 one- and 5 two-bedroom suites with kitchens. 14 stories, interior corridors. **Bath:** combo or shower only. **Parking:** on-site. **Terms:** 3 night minimum stay - seasonal and/or weekends, cancellation fee imposed, package plans. **Amenities:** irons, hair dryers. *Some:* DVD players, high-speed Internet. **Pool(s):** heated outdoor. **Leisure Activities:** whirlpool, volleyball. *Fee:* game room. **Guest Services:** coin laundry. **Business Services:** meeting rooms. **Cards:** AX, DS, MC, VI. *(See color ad p 858)*

MOONSPINNER CONDOMINIUM   Phone: 850/234-8900

	5/27-8/4	1P: $220-$330	2P: $220-$330
	3/15-5/26	1P: $145-$240	2P: $145-$240
Condominium	8/5-11/30	1P: $125-$185	2P: $125-$185
	12/1-3/14	1P: $125-$165	2P: $125-$165

Location: Jct US 98, 3.5 mi s on CR 3031, then e. 4425 Thomas Dr 32408. Fax: 850/233-0719. **Facility:** This beachfront property offers individually decorated two- and three-bedroom units. 121 units. 90 two- and 31 three-bedroom suites ($175-$370). 8 stories, exterior corridors. **Parking:** on-site. **Terms:** 3 night minimum stay - weekends, age restrictions may apply, 14 day cancellation notice-fee imposed, $60 service charge, no pets allowed (owner's pets on premises). **Amenities:** irons. *Some:* CD players. **Pool(s):** heated outdoor, wading. **Leisure Activities:** whirlpool, 2 lighted tennis courts, exercise room, basketball, shuffleboard, volleyball. **Fee:** game room. **Guest Services:** complimentary laundry. **Business Services:** meeting rooms, fax (fee). **Cards:** MC, VI.

SOME UNITS

OSPREY RESORT MOTEL   Phone: 850/234-0303

	5/23-8/12	1P: $114-$175	2P: $114-$175	XP: $10	F17
	3/1-5/22	1P: $75-$134	2P: $75-$134	XP: $10	F17
Motel	12/1-2/28 & 8/13-11/30	1P: $60-$124	2P: $60-$124	XP: $10	F17

Location: 2 mi e of jct SR 79 and US 98. 15801 Front Beach Rd 32413. Fax: 850/234-0303. **Facility:** 70 one-bedroom standard units with kitchens. 6 stories, exterior corridors. **Parking:** on-site. **Terms:** 3-5 night minimum stay - seasonal and/or weekends, 14 day cancellation notice-fee imposed. **Amenities:** irons, hair dryers. **Pool(s):** heated outdoor. **Leisure Activities:** whirlpool. **Guest Services:** coin laundry. **Business Services:** fax (fee). **Cards:** AX, MC, VI.

QUALITY INN GULF FRONT   *Book at aaa.com*   Phone: (850)234-6636

	5/26-9/4 [ECP]	1P: $69-$209	2P: $69-$209	XP: $10	F18
	2/25-5/25 [ECP]	1P: $69-$179	2P: $69-$179	XP: $10	F18
	9/5-11/30 [ECP]	1P: $49-$119	2P: $49-$119	XP: $10	F18
	12/1-2/24 [ECP]	1P: $49-$89	2P: $49-$89	XP: $10	F18

Small-scale Hotel **Location:** 2 mi e of jct SR 79 and US 98. 15285 Front Beach Rd 32413. Fax: 850/235-4202. **Facility:** 124 units. 80 one-bedroom standard units. 42 one- and 2 three-bedroom suites with kitchens, some with whirlpools. 4-7 stories, exterior corridors. **Parking:** on-site. **Terms:** check-in 4 pm, 2-3 night minimum stay - seasonal and/or weekends, cancellation fee imposed. **Amenities:** voice mail, irons, hair dryers. **Pool(s):** outdoor. **Leisure Activities:** **Fee:** jet ski, parasailing, rental boats & sailboats in summer. **Guest Services:** coin laundry. **Cards:** AX, CB, DC, DS, JC, MC, VI. **Special Amenities:** free expanded continental breakfast and free local telephone calls. *(See color ad below)*

SOME UNITS

SUNSET INN   Phone: (850)234-7370

	5/25-9/6	1P: $65-$195	2P: $70-$195	XP: $5	F
	3/1-5/24	1P: $55-$195	2P: $60-$195	XP: $5	F
Motel	12/1-2/28 & 9/7-11/30	1P: $45-$120	2P: $50-$120	XP: $5	F

Location: US 98A, 1.5 mi s on Joan Ave, then 0.5 mi e. 8109 Surf Dr 32408. Fax: 850/234-7370. **Facility:** 62 one-bedroom standard units, some with kitchens. 2 stories, exterior corridors. *Bath:* combo or shower only. **Parking:** on-site. **Terms:** 7 day cancellation notice. **Pool(s):** heated outdoor. **Guest Services:** coin laundry. **Business Services:** fax. **Cards:** AX, DS, MC, VI.

────── WHERE TO DINE ──────

30 DEGREE BLUE
Dinner: $17-$26
Phone: 850/236-1115

▼▼▼

New World

Location: US 98, 0.5 mi w of bridge, 2 mi s on CR 3031, then 1.8 mi e on Magnolia Beach Rd, follow signs; in Bay Point Marriott Resort. 3900 Marriott Dr, Suite G 32408. **Hours:** 5:30 pm-9 pm, Fri & Sat-10 pm. Closed: 12/25; also Sun & Mon. **Reservations:** suggested. **Features:** Guests can dine comfortably while gazing out at the bay. Although the menu changes regularly, it always includes the chef's distinctive creations, such as crab mango salad, coconut-encrusted fish and the exquisite coconut creme brulee dessert. Knowledgeable staff members help with wine selections. Dressy casual; cocktails. **Parking:** on-site. **Cards:** AX, CB, DC, DS, JC, MC, VI.

ALL AMERICAN DINER
Lunch: $4-$11
Dinner: $4-$11
Phone: 850/235-2443

◆

American

Location: 3 mi w of jct US 98. 10590 Front Beach Rd 32407. **Hours:** 6 am-10 pm; to midnight in summer. **Features:** '50s style diner. Inexpensive. Casual dress. **Parking:** on-site. **Cards:** MC, VI.

BOAR'S HEAD RESTAURANT
Dinner: $14-$26
Phone: 850/234-6628

AAA
▼▼ ▼▼

Steak & Seafood

Location: 0.3 mi w of jct SR 79, on US 98. 17290 Front Beach Rd 32413. **Hours:** 4:30 pm-9 pm, Fri & Sat-10 pm. Closed: 11/23; also 12/20-12/26. **Features:** This quiet, rustic spot offers many seafood and steak entrees, and appeals to those who recognize good value. The eager-to-please staff aims for professional service. Try fried shrimp served with sweet potatoes, green beans, and a scrumptious dessert. Casual dress; cocktails. **Parking:** on-site. **Cards:** AX, DC, DS, MC, VI.

HAMILTON'S RESTAURANT
Dinner: $13-$24
Phone: 850/234-1255

▼▼ ▼▼

Seafood

Location: Jct Thomas Dr. 5711 N Lagoon Dr 32408. **Hours:** 5 pm-10 pm. **Features:** Taste the zesty flavor of feta cheese in the shrimp Christo entree or the decadent chocolate sweetness of mud pie while you gaze out over the scenic lagoon. Hardwood floors and stained glass windows help to give the restaurant a romantic feel. Casual dress; cocktails. **Parking:** on-site. **Cards:** AX, DS, MC, VI.

JADE GARDEN ORIENTAL RESTAURANT
Lunch: $4-$7
Dinner: $4-$7
Phone: 850/234-1422

▼

Asian

Location: Jct Thomas Dr. 7119 Hwy 98 32407. **Hours:** 10:45 am-8:30 pm, Sat from 1 pm. Closed: 1/1; also Sun. **Features:** Although there is a small dining area, this is predominantly a quick-serve restaurant kept busy by locals. Favorites like bourbon chicken and sweet and sour pork are batch prepared and packaged for take out. Casual dress. **Parking:** on-site. **Cards:** AX, CB, DC, DS, JC, MC, VI.

🚹M

RUTHIE T'S
Dinner: $13-$27
Phone: 850/234-2111

▼▼ ▼▼

American

Location: 1.5 mi e of Joan Ave. 8503 Thomas Dr 32408. **Hours:** 4:30 pm-10 pm. Closed: 1/1, 11/23, 12/25. **Reservations:** accepted. **Features:** Rustic country decor welcomes you to this locally favorite steakhouse. Casual dress; cocktails. **Parking:** on-site. **Cards:** AX, DS, MC, VI.

SALTWATER GRILL
Dinner: $13-$22
Phone: 850/230-2739

▼▼ ▼▼

Seafood

Location: 1.5 mi w of Front Beach Rd. 11040 Hutchison Blvd 32407. **Hours:** 4 pm-10 pm, Fri & Sat-11 pm. **Features:** The great ocean-themed decor includes a large aquarium behind the bar. The menu offers lobster five different ways and many other seafood specialties. Casual dress; cocktails. **Parking:** on-site. **Cards:** MC, VI.

🚹M

TRIPLE "J" STEAKHOUSE
Dinner: $10-$29
Phone: 850/233-9514

▼▼ ▼▼

Steak House

Location: 1 mi s of US 98. 2218 Thomas Dr 32408. **Hours:** 11 am-10 pm, Fri & Sat-11 pm. Closed: 11/23, 12/25. **Features:** Casual dress; cocktails. **Parking:** on-site. **Cards:** AX, DC, DS, MC, VI.

PEMBROKE PINES —See Fort Lauderdale p. 417.

PENSACOLA pop. 56,255

─────── **WHERE TO STAY** ───────

AMERICAS BEST VALUE INN & SUITES   Phone: (850)479-1099
◇◇◇ [SAVE]   3/1-8/31 [ECP]   1P: $69-$89   2P: $69-$89   XP: $5   F18
            12/1-2/28 & 9/1-11/30 [ECP]   1P: $59-$69   2P: $59-$69   XP: $5   F18
▽▽▽▽   **Location:** I-10, exit 13, 0.8 mi n. Located across from West Florida Hospital. 8240 N Davis Hwy 32514.
Small-scale Hotel Fax: 850/479-9320. **Facility:** 143 units. 96 one-bedroom standard units. 47 one-bedroom suites ($79-$99)
            with kitchens, some with whirlpools. 3 stories, interior/exterior corridors. *Bath:* combo or shower only.
            Parking: on-site. **Terms:** pets ($10 extra charge). **Amenities:** irons, hair dryers. **Pool(s):** outdoor. **Guest**
Services: valet laundry. **Business Services:** PC. **Cards:** AX, CB, DC, DS, MC, VI. *(See color ad below)*

SOME UNITS
[S] [D] 🛏️ [†↑↓] �· 🐾 [👤👥] [DATA PORT] ☕ / ✕ [📶] 🖥️ /
FEE

ASHTON INN & SUITES   *Book at aaa.com*   Phone: (850)454-0280
▽▽▽▽   All Year   1P: $75-$99
Small-scale Hotel **Location:** Just n of jct US 98 and SR 295. 4 New Warrington Rd 32506. Fax: 850/454-0250. **Facility:** 71 units. 59
            one-bedroom standard units, some with efficiencies. 12 one-bedroom suites ($85-$120) with efficiencies. 3
            stories, interior corridors. *Bath:* combo or shower only. **Parking:** on-site. **Terms:** pets ($25 fee).
Amenities: high-speed Internet, voice mail, safes, irons, hair dryers. **Pool(s):** heated indoor. **Leisure Activities:** exercise room.
Guest Services: valet and coin laundry. **Business Services:** meeting rooms, PC, fax. **Cards:** AX, DC, DS, MC, VI.

SOME UNITS
[ASK] [S] [D] 🛏️ �· 🐾 📷 [DATA PORT] [📶] 🖥️ / ✕ /
FEE

BEST WESTERN PENSACOLA   Phone: 850-476-7200
▽▽ ▽▽   Property failed to provide current rates
            Location: I-10, exit 10A, 1.3 mi s on US 29. Located at Car City. 6501 Pensacola Blvd 32505. Fax: 850/476-1277.
Small-scale Hotel **Facility:** 120 one-bedroom standard units. 2 stories, exterior corridors. *Bath:* combo or shower only.
            Parking: on-site. **Amenities:** voice mail, irons, hair dryers. **Pool(s):** outdoor. **Leisure Activities:** exercise
room. **Guest Services:** valet and coin laundry. **Business Services:** meeting rooms, fax.

SOME UNITS
✈️ [†↑↓] �· 🏊 🐾 📷 [DATA PORT] ☕ / ✕ [📶] 🖥️ /

COMFORT INN   *Book at aaa.com*   Phone: 850-484-8070
◇◇◇ [SAVE]   All Year   1P: $70-$160   2P: $70-$160   XP: $7   F16
▽▽▽▽   **Location:** I-10, exit 13, just n on SR 291. 8080 N Davis Hwy 32514. Fax: 850/484-3853. **Facility:** 115 one-
            bedroom standard units. 5 stories, interior corridors. *Bath:* some combo or shower only. **Parking:** on-site.
Small-scale Hotel **Terms:** small pets only ($20 extra charge). **Amenities:** voice mail, irons, hair dryers. *Some:* high-speed
            Internet. **Pool(s):** outdoor. **Leisure Activities:** exercise room. **Guest Services:** valet and coin laundry.
            Business Services: meeting rooms, business center. **Cards:** AX, CB, DC, DS, JC, MC, VI.
Special Amenities: free continental breakfast and free newspaper.

SOME UNITS
[S] [D] 🛏️ [†↑↓] �· 📷 [DATA PORT] [📶] 🖥️ / ✕ /
FEE

COMFORT INN-NAS CORRY   *Book at aaa.com*   Phone: (850)455-3233
▽▽▽▽   All Year   1P: $77   2P: $77   XP: $6   F
Small-scale Hotel **Location:** Just n of jct US 98 and SR 295. Located at entrance to Corry Field. 3 New Warrington Rd 32506.
            Fax: 850/453-3445. **Facility:** 101 one-bedroom standard units. 2-3 stories (no elevator), exterior corridors.
            Parking: on-site. **Terms:** check-in 4 pm, 3 day cancellation notice-fee imposed, pets ($25 fee).
Amenities: high-speed Internet, voice mail, irons, hair dryers. **Pool(s):** outdoor. **Guest Services:** valet and coin laundry.
Business Services: meeting rooms, PC, fax. **Cards:** AX, CB, DC, DS, JC, MC, VI.

SOME UNITS
[ASK] ✈️ 🛏️ [†↑↓] [Y] �· 📷 [DATA PORT] [📶] 🖥️ 🖥️ / ✕ /
FEE

COURTYARD BY MARRIOTT　*Book at aaa.com*　　　　　　　Phone: (850)857-7744
▼▼▼▼　All Year　　　　　　　　1P: $99-$189
Small-scale Hotel　Location: I-10, exit 13, 0.5 mi s, then just w. 451 Creighton Rd 32504. Fax: 850/857-0904. **Facility:** 90 units. 87 one-bedroom standard units, some with whirlpools. 3 one-bedroom suites with whirlpools. 3 stories, interior corridors. *Bath:* combo or shower only. **Parking:** on-site. **Terms:** cancellation fee imposed. **Amenities:** voice mail, irons, hair dryers. **Pool(s):** heated indoor. **Leisure Activities:** whirlpool, exercise room. **Guest Services:** valet and coin laundry. **Business Services:** meeting rooms, PC. **Cards:** AX, DC, DS, JC, MC, VI.

SOME UNITS
(ASK) 🍴 ⤳ 🏋 📶 💻 / ⊠ 📶 🖭 /

FAIRFIELD INN BY MARRIOTT　*Book at aaa.com*　　　　　　　Phone: 850/484-8001
▼▼▼　　　　　　　　Property failed to provide current rates
Small-scale Hotel　Location: I-10, exit 13, just s. 7325 N Davis Hwy 32514. Fax: 850/484-6008. **Facility:** 63 one-bedroom standard units. 3 stories, interior corridors. *Bath:* combo or shower only. **Amenities:** irons, hair dryers. **Pool(s):** heated indoor. **Guest Services:** valet laundry.

SOME UNITS
🍴 ♿ ⤳ 📶 🏋 📶 💻 / ⊠ 📶 🖭 /

HOLIDAY INN EXPRESS UNIVERSITY MALL　*Book at aaa.com*　　　　　Phone: 850/477-3333
(AAA) (SAVE)　4/1-8/31　　　　　1P: $79-$89　　　2P: $79-$89
▼▼▼▼　12/1-3/31 & 9/1-11/30　1P: $74-$79　　　2P: $74-$79
Small-scale Hotel　Location: I-10, exit 13, just s. Located at entrance to the University Mall. 7330 Plantation Rd 32504. Fax: 850/477-8163. **Facility:** 122 one-bedroom standard units. 3 stories, exterior corridors. *Bath:* combo or shower only. **Parking:** on-site. **Terms:** cancellation fee imposed. **Amenities:** dual phone lines, voice mail, irons, hair dryers. **Leisure Activities:** pool privileges. **Guest Services:** valet laundry. **Business Services:** meeting rooms. **Cards:** AX, CB, DC, DS, JC, MC, VI.

SOME UNITS
(SD) ♿ 🍴 📶 🏋 📶 💻 / ⊠ /

HOLIDAY INN PENSACOLA-UNIVERSITY MALL　*Book at aaa.com*　　　Phone: 850/474-0100
(AAA) (SAVE)　All Year　　　　　　1P: $70-$80　　　2P: $70-$80　　　XP: $10　　F
▼▼▼　Location: I-10, exit 13, just s; use University Mall entrance. 7200 Plantation Rd 32504. Fax: 850/477-9821. **Facility:** 152 one-bedroom standard units. 3 stories (no elevator), exterior corridors. *Bath:* combo or shower only. **Parking:** on-site. **Terms:** pets ($25 fee). **Amenities:** video games (fee), voice mail, irons, hair dryers. Small-scale Hotel　**Dining:** 6 am-10 & 5-9 pm, cocktails, entertainment. **Pool(s):** outdoor. **Guest Services:** valet and coin laundry. **Business Services:** meeting rooms, fax (fee). **Cards:** AX, CB, DC, DS, MC, VI.

SOME UNITS
✈ ♿ 🍴 🍸 ♿ 📷 ⤳ 📶 🏋 📶 / ⊠ 📶 🖭 /
FEE

LA QUINTA INN PENSACOLA　*Book at aaa.com*　　　　　　　Phone: (850)474-0411
▼▼▼　12/1-9/6　　　　　1P: $83-$93　　　2P: $90-$100　　　XP: $7　　F18
　　9/7-11/30　　　　1P: $69-$79　　　2P: $76-$86　　　XP: $7　　F18
Small-scale Hotel　Location: I-10, exit 13, just n. 7750 N Davis Hwy 32514-7557. Fax: 850/474-1521. **Facility:** 130 units. 128 one-bedroom standard units. 2 one-bedroom suites. 3 stories, exterior corridors. *Bath:* combo or shower only. **Parking:** on-site. **Terms:** [ECP] meal plan available. **Amenities:** video games (fee), voice mail, irons, hair dryers. **Pool(s):** outdoor. **Guest Services:** coin laundry. **Cards:** AX, CB, DC, DS, MC, VI.

SOME UNITS
(ASK) 🐾 🍴 ♿ ⤳ 🏋 💻 / ⊠ 📶 🖭 /

MICROTEL INN & SUITES　*Book at aaa.com*　　　　　　　Phone: (850)941-8902
▼▼▼▼　All Year　　　　　　1P: $49-$109　　　2P: $49-$109　　　XP: $10　　F
Small-scale Hotel　Location: I-10, exit 7, just s. 8001 Lavelle Way 32526. Fax: 850/941-8906. **Facility:** Smoke free premises. 71 one-bedroom standard units. 2 stories, interior corridors. *Bath:* combo or shower only. **Parking:** on-site. **Amenities:** safes. *Some:* irons, hair dryers. **Business Services:** meeting rooms. **Cards:** AX, CB, DC, DS, MC, VI.

SOME UNITS
(ASK) (SD) 🍴 ♿ 📶 ⊠ 🏋 / 📶 🖭 💻 /

MOTEL 6 #1105　*Book at aaa.com*　　　　　　　Phone: 850/474-1060
▼▼▼　1/1-8/6　　　　　1P: $37-$47　　　2P: $43-$53　　　XP: $3　　F17
Motel　12/1-12/31 & 8/7-11/30　1P: $34-$44　　　2P: $40-$50　　　XP: $3　　F17
Location: I-10, exit 13, sw on Mall Rd. 7226 Plantation Rd 32504. Fax: 850/476-5104. **Facility:** 80 one-bedroom standard units. 2 stories, exterior corridors. *Bath:* combo or shower only. **Parking:** on-site. **Terms:** small pets only. **Pool(s):** outdoor. **Guest Services:** coin laundry. **Cards:** AX, CB, DC, DS, MC, VI.

SOME UNITS
(SD) 🐾 🍴 ♿ ⤳ 🏋 📶 / ⊠ /

MOTEL 6 #1183　*Book at aaa.com*　　　　　　　Phone: 850/476-5386
▼▼▼　1/1-11/30　　　　1P: $35-$45　　　2P: $41-$51　　　XP: $3　　F17
Motel　12/1-12/31　　　　1P: $33-$43　　　2P: $39-$49　　　XP: $3　　F17
Location: I-10, exit 13, 0.3 mi n. 7827 N Davis Hwy 32514. Fax: 850/476-7458. **Facility:** 108 one-bedroom standard units. 3 stories, exterior corridors. **Parking:** on-site. **Pool(s):** outdoor. **Cards:** AX, CB, DC, DS, MC, VI.

SOME UNITS
(SD) 🐾 🍴 ♿ ⤳ 🏋 / ⊠ /

QUALITY INN　*Book at aaa.com*　　　　　　　Phone: (850)477-0711
(AAA) (SAVE)　5/1-9/4 [CP]　　　1P: $79　　　2P: $79
　　12/1-4/30 [CP]　　1P: $69　　　2P: $69
▼▼▼　9/5-11/30 [CP]　　1P: $59　　　2P: $59
Small-scale Hotel　Location: I-10, exit 10A, 1.2 mi s on US 29. Located at Car City. 6550 N Pensacola Blvd 32505. Fax: 850/479-1977. **Facility:** 106 units. 103 one-bedroom standard units. 3 one-bedroom suites with whirlpools. 2 stories, interior/exterior corridors. **Parking:** on-site. **Terms:** pets ($25-$50 fee). **Amenities:** voice mail, irons, hair dryers. **Pool(s):** outdoor. **Guest Services:** coin laundry. **Business Services:** meeting rooms, fax (fee). **Cards:** AX, CB, DC, DS, JC, MC, VI. **Special Amenities:** free continental breakfast and free newspaper.

SOME UNITS
(SD) ♿ 🐾 📷 🍴 🏋 💻 / ⊠ 📶 🖭 /
FEE

RAMADA INN BAYVIEW — Book at aaa.com

Phone: (850)477-7155

AAA SAVE

Small-scale Hotel

All Year — 1P: $129 — 2P: $129 — XP: $10 — F18
Location: I-10, exit 17, just s on US 90. 7601 Scenic Hwy 32504. Fax: 850/478-2479. **Facility:** 150 units. 140 one-bedroom standard units. 10 one-bedroom suites ($125-$150). 2 stories, interior corridors. **Parking:** on-site. **Terms:** small pets only ($25 fee, in designated units). **Amenities:** video games (fee), voice mail, irons, hair dryers. **Dining:** 6-10 am, entertainment. **Pool(s):** outdoor. **Leisure Activities:** exercise room. **Guest Services:** valet and coin laundry. **Business Services:** meeting rooms. **Cards:** AX, DC, DS, MC, VI.
Special Amenities: free local telephone calls and free newspaper.

SOME UNITS

RAMADA LIMITED — Book at aaa.com

Phone: (850)944-0333

AAA SAVE

Small-scale Hotel

All Year — 1P: $59-$89 — 2P: $59-$89 — XP: $10 — F17
Location: I-10, exit 7, just s. 8060 Lavalle Way 32526. Fax: 850/941-1961. **Facility:** 93 one-bedroom standard units. 2 stories, exterior corridors. **Parking:** on-site. **Terms:** cancellation fee imposed, [ECP] meal plan available, small pets only ($25 fee, in designated units). **Amenities:** voice mail, safes, irons, hair dryers. **Pool(s):** outdoor. **Guest Services:** coin laundry. **Cards:** AX, CB, DC, DS, JC, MC, VI. **Special Amenities:** free expanded continental breakfast and free local telephone calls.

SOME UNITS

RED ROOF INN — Book at aaa.com

Phone: (850)476-7960

Motel

5/14-9/9 — 1P: $40-$58 — 2P: $46-$58 — XP: $3 — F18
1/1-5/13 & 9/10-11/30 — 1P: $37-$52 — 2P: $43-$58 — XP: $3 — F18
12/1-12/31 — 1P: $40-$50 — 2P: $46-$56 — XP: $3 — F18
Location: I-10, exit 13, just s. Located at entrance to the University Mall. 7340 Plantation Rd 32504. Fax: 850/479-4706. **Facility:** 108 one-bedroom standard units. 2 stories, exterior corridors. **Parking:** on-site. **Terms:** small pets only. **Amenities:** video games (fee), voice mail. **Cards:** AX, CB, DC, DS, MC, VI.

SOME UNITS

RESIDENCE INN BY MARRIOTT — Book at aaa.com

Phone: (850)479-1000

AAA SAVE

Small-scale Hotel

1/1-11/30 [ECP] — 1P: $154-$195 — 2P: $154-$195
12/1-12/31 [ECP] — 1P: $144-$185 — 2P: $144-$185
Location: I-10, exit 13, just s. Located at entrance to the University Mall. 7230 Plantation Rd 32504. Fax: 850/477-3399. **Facility:** 64 units. 60 one- and 4 two-bedroom standard units with kitchens. 2 stories, exterior corridors. **Parking:** on-site. **Terms:** small pets only ($75 fee). **Amenities:** high-speed Internet, voice mail, irons, hair dryers. **Pool(s):** outdoor. **Leisure Activities:** whirlpool, exercise room, sports court. **Guest Services:** sundries, valet and coin laundry. **Business Services:** meeting rooms, PC. **Cards:** AX, CB, DC, DS, JC, MC, VI. **Special Amenities:** free expanded continental breakfast and free newspaper.

SOME UNITS

SLEEP INN — Book at aaa.com

Phone: 850/941-0908

Small-scale Hotel

Property failed to provide current rates
Location: I-10, exit 7, just s. 2591 Wilde Lake Blvd 32526. Fax: 850/941-0760. **Facility:** 77 one-bedroom standard units. 3 stories, interior corridors. *Bath:* combo or shower only. **Parking:** on-site. **Amenities:** high-speed Internet. *Some:* irons, hair dryers. **Pool(s):** outdoor. **Guest Services:** coin laundry. **Business Services:** meeting rooms.

SOME UNITS

------ WHERE TO DINE ------

BONEFISH GRILL

Dinner: $14-$21 — **Phone:** 850/471-2324

Seafood

Location: Jct Airport Rd, just s. 5025 N 12th Ave 32504. **Hours:** 4 pm-10:30 pm, Fri & Sat-11:30 pm, Sun-10 pm. Closed: 11/23, 12/25. **Reservations:** accepted. **Features:** Fresh fish is the specialty of the house and the menu and nightly specials offer a variety from which to choose. The food is well prepared and cooked to perfection; service is casual in nature and staff are skilled and attentive. Dressy casual; cocktails. **Parking:** on-site. **Cards:** AX, DC, DS, MC, VI.

CHINA STAR — Menu on aaa.com

Lunch: $5-$6 — Dinner: $7-$12 — **Phone:** 850/477-6163

Chinese

Location: I-110, exit Brent Ln, 0.8 mi e. 505 E Brent Ln 32503. **Hours:** 11 am-10 pm, Fri & Sat-11 pm. Closed: 11/23. **Features:** Pick and choose from the extensive all-day buffet, or select such Szechuan and Mandarin staples as sweet and sour shrimp, cashew chicken and shrimp with vegetables from the menu. The dining room is roomy and quiet, and the service attentive. Casual dress; cocktails. **Parking:** on-site. **Cards:** AX, DS, MC, VI.

COFFEE CUP

Lunch: $5-$7 — **Phone:** 850/432-7060

American

Location: I-110, exit Cervantes St, 0.5 mi e. 520 E Cervantes St 32501. **Hours:** 6 am-2 pm. Closed: 11/23, 12/25; also Sun. **Features:** The traditional diner offers inexpensive breakfast fare at a reasonable price. Casual dress. **Parking:** on-site. **Cards:** AX, CB, DC, DS, MC, VI.

JACKSON'S

Dinner: $24-$38 — **Phone:** 850/469-9898

American

Location: Downtown, Palafox. 502 S Palafox St 32501. **Hours:** 5:30 pm-9 pm, Fri & Sat-10 pm. Closed major holidays; also Sun. **Reservations:** suggested. **Features:** This historic downtown restaurant provides a selection of prime aged meats, fresh local and Pan-American seafood. Also an extensive selection of wine. Semi-formal attire; cocktails. **Parking:** street. **Cards:** AX, CB, DC, DS, JC, MC, VI.

JAMIE'S FRENCH RESTAURANT   Lunch: $8-$9   Dinner: $18-$30   Phone: 850/434-2911
▽▽▽▽
French   **Location:** Downtown historic district. 424 E Zarragossa 32501. **Hours:** 11:30 am-2 & 5:30-9 pm, Fri & Sat-10 pm. Closed: 11/23, 12/25; also Sun. **Reservations:** accepted. **Features:** In an 1884 cottage, the restaurant offers a menu of Provencal-style French cuisine with an award-winning wine list. Dressy casual; beer & wine only. **Parking:** on-site. **Cards:** AX, MC, VI.

JERRY'S CAJUN CAFE   Lunch: $6-$19   Dinner: $6-$19   Phone: 850/484-6962
▽▽▽ ▽▽▽
Cajun   **Location:** 1.3 mi e on Airport Blvd, then 1 mi n. 6205 N 9th Ave 32504. **Hours:** 11 am-8:30 pm, Fri & Sat-9:30 pm. Closed major holidays; also Sun. **Features:** A bright, cheery New Orleans-style setting and authentic Cajun cuisine combine to satisfy diners. Louisiana specialties such as gumbo, jambalaya, etouffee, muffulettas and po'boys round out the menu. Dishes are seasoned mild or spicy, depending on the guest's preference.
Casual dress; beer & wine only. **Parking:** on-site. **Cards:** AX, DS, MC, VI.

MCGUIRE'S IRISH PUB   Lunch: $7-$11   Dinner: $9-$25   Phone: 850/433-6789
(AAA)
▽▽▽ ▽▽▽
Steak House   **Location:** 0.3 mi e of civic center; downtown. 600 E Gregory St 32502. **Hours:** 11 am-2 am. Closed: 11/23, 12/25. **Features:** Here is a pleasant surprise in a unique wine cellar atmosphere. After a hearty welcome from the staff, start with a chicken, bean and corn eggroll in a delicious avocado sauce; then feast on steak, seafood and an exceptional variety of large hamburgers. Casual dress; cocktails; entertainment. **Parking:** on-site. **Cards:** AX, DC, DS, MC, VI.

MESQUITE CHARLIE'S STEAKS & SEAFOOD   Lunch: $4-$7   Dinner: $9-$20   Phone: 850/434-0498
▽▽▽ ▽▽▽
Steak & Seafood   **Location:** I-110, exit 5, 1.5 mi w on Brent Ln, then 0.8 mi n. 5901 N "W" St 32505. **Hours:** 11 am-10 pm, Fri & Sat-11 pm. Closed: 11/23, 12/25. **Features:** Round up the family and head to this casual restaurant, where the flavor of the West is evident in everything from the charcoal-grilled steaks to the late 1900s decor. Seafood is also a must. Cattle and deer heads, antiques and bronze sculptures convey the mood. Casual dress;
cocktails. **Parking:** on-site. **Cards:** AX, DS, MC, VI.

THE OYSTER BAR   Lunch: $5-$9   Dinner: $8-$20   Phone: 850/455-3925
▽▽▽ ▽▽▽
Seafood   **Location:** 3.5 mi w on US 98. 709 N Navy Blvd 32507. **Hours:** 11 am-10 pm, Fri & Sat-11 pm. Closed: 11/23, 12/25. **Reservations:** not accepted. **Features:** The attractive, well-coordinated decor, which revolves around the sea, enhances your experience in this large and busy restaurant. Seasonal ingredients give the New Orleans-style seafood gumbo a snappy kick. The extensive menu also features steaks. Casual dress;
cocktails. **Parking:** on-site. **Cards:** AX, DC, MC, VI.

SKOPELOS ON THE BAY   Lunch: $9-$14   Dinner: $14-$26   Phone: 850/432-6565
▽▽▽▽
Seafood   **Location:** US 90/Scenic Hwy, continuing e from Cervantes. 670 Scenic Hwy 32503. **Hours:** 5 pm-close, Fri also 11:30 am-2:30 pm, Sun 10:30 am-2 pm. Closed: 1/1, 12/25; also Mon. **Reservations:** accepted. **Features:** Fresh vegetables and seafood are well-prepared and served to you in this bayfront dining room. Local patrons rave about the seafood, lamb, steak and veal choices including the tender roasted lamb accompanied by a traditional green jelly. Dressy casual; cocktails. **Parking:** on-site. **Cards:** AX, DS, MC, VI.

PENSACOLA BEACH

——— WHERE TO STAY ———

BEST WESTERN RESORT PENSACOLA BEACH   *Book at aaa.com*   Phone: (850)934-3300

3/2-9/6 [CP]	1P: $89-$279	2P: $89-$279
9/7-11/13 [CP]	1P: $119-$159	2P: $119-$159
12/1-3/1 & 11/14-11/30 [CP]	1P: $59-$89	2P: $59-$89

Small-scale Hotel   **Location:** 0.5 mi e on SR 399. 16 Via De Luna 32561. **Fax:** 850/934-9780. **Facility:** 123 one-bedroom standard units. 3 stories, exterior corridors. *Bath:* combo or shower only. **Parking:** on-site. **Terms:** 7 day cancellation notice. **Amenities:** voice mail, irons, hair dryers. **Pool(s):** 2 outdoor. **Leisure Activities:** playground, volleyball. **Guest Services:** valet and coin laundry. **Business Services:** meeting rooms. **Cards:** AX, DC, DS, MC, VI. **Special Amenities: free continental breakfast and free room upgrade (subject to availability with advance reservations).**

SOME UNITS

COMFORT INN PENSACOLA BEACH   *Book at aaa.com*   Phone: (850)934-5400

All Year	1P: $85-$250	2P: $85-$250	XP: $10 F18

Small-scale Hotel   **Location:** Just off SR 399. 40 Ft Pickens Rd 32561. **Fax:** 850/932-7210. **Facility:** 100 one-bedroom standard units. 4 stories, exterior corridors. *Bath:* combo or shower only. **Parking:** on-site. **Terms:** [ECP] meal plan available, small pets only ($50 extra charge). **Amenities:** voice mail, irons, hair dryers. **Pool(s):** outdoor.
Guest Services: coin laundry. **Business Services:** meeting rooms. **Cards:** AX, CB, DC, DS, JC, MC, VI.

SOME UNITS

FEE

HILTON GARDEN INN PENSACOLA BEACH   *Book at aaa.com*   Phone: (850)916-2999

5/26-8/5	1P: $199-$309	2P: $199-$309	XP: $10 F18
3/13-5/25	1P: $119-$249	2P: $119-$249	XP: $10 F18
8/6-11/30	1P: $99-$189	2P: $99-$189	XP: $10 F18
12/1-3/12	1P: $89-$169	2P: $89-$169	XP: $10 F18

Large-scale Hotel   **Location:** I-10, exit 12. 12 Via De Luna 32561. **Fax:** 850/934-0891. **Facility:** 181 units. 179 one-bedroom standard units, some with whirlpools. 2 one-bedroom suites. 7 stories, interior corridors. *Bath:* combo or shower only. **Parking:** on-site. **Terms:** check-in 4 pm, 2 night minimum stay - seasonal, 3 day cancellation notice-fee imposed, package plans. **Amenities:** video games (fee), high-speed Internet, dual phone lines, voice mail, irons, hair dryers. **Dining:** 6:30 am-10:30 & 11-10 pm, cocktails. **Pool(s):** heated outdoor, heated indoor, wading. **Leisure Activities:** sauna, whirlpool, recreation programs, exercise room, spa. *Fee:* game room. **Guest Services:** sundries, valet and coin laundry. **Business Services:** conference facilities, business center. **Cards:** AX, DC, DS, MC, VI. *(See color ad p 867)*

SPRINGHILL SUITES

Phone: 850/932-6000

Small-scale Hotel

3/1-8/31 [ECP]	1P: $189-$239
9/1-11/30 [ECP]	1P: $129-$169
2/1-2/28 [ECP]	1P: $99-$139
12/1-1/31 [ECP]	1P: $79-$129

Under major renovation, scheduled to be completed July 2005. **Last rated:** ◯◯◯ **Location:** On SR 399, 0.3 mi e. 24 Via De Luna 32561. Fax: 850/932-6050. **Facility:** 117 units. 115 one-bedroom standard units. 2 two-bedroom suites. 5 stories, interior corridors. *Bath:* combo or shower only. **Parking:** on-site. **Terms:** check-in 4 pm, 2-3 night minimum stay - seasonal and/or weekends, cancellation fee imposed. **Amenities:** high-speed Internet, dual phone lines, voice mail, irons, hair dryers. **Pool(s):** heated outdoor. **Leisure Activities:** whirlpool, exercise room. **Guest Services:** sundries, valet and coin laundry. **Business Services:** meeting rooms, business center. **Cards:** AX, CB, DC, DS, JC, MC, VI.

SOME UNITS

(ASK) (S/D) (†↑) (Y) (≈) (✦) (DATA PORT) (🛏) (🖥) (📼) / (✕) /

Hilton Garden Inn®
Pensacola Beach

Beachfront on the Gulf of Mexico.

In the heart of Pensacola Beach. Stroll to family amusements, watersports, shopping and nightlife; 20 minutes from Pensacola Airport.

- All rooms feature: microwave, fridge, coffeemaker and complimentary high-speed Internet
- H2O Grill with great ocean views; Bonsai Sushi Bar; Latitudes Beach Bar & Grill
- Heated indoor and outdoor pools (including fantasy pool)
- Coin laundry
- Complimentary parking

Everything. Right where you need it.®

stayhgi.com/AAA
1-800-871-5917

*10% DISCOUNT

Hilton HHonors®

——— WHERE TO DINE ———

FLOUNDERS CHOWDER HOUSE   Lunch: $6-$14   Dinner: $6-$21   Phone: 850/932-2003

(AAA)
Location: Just e of Quietwater Beach Boardwalk. 800 Quietwater Beach Rd 32561. **Hours:** 11 am-midnight;
summer hours may vary. Closed: 11/23, 12/25. **Features:** On Santa Rosa Sound, the restaurant is known
for its friendly service and generous portions of such dishes as blackened tuna, stuffed flounder and eye-
watering barbecue shrimp. The three-layer Key lime pie will leave you with serious pucker power. Casual
Steak & Seafood dress; cocktails; entertainment. **Parking:** on-site. **Cards:** AX, CB, DC, DS, MC, VI.

PERRY pop. 6,847

——— WHERE TO STAY ———

BEST BUDGET INN   Phone: (850)584-6231

(AAA) [SAVE]   All Year [CP]   1P: $40-$43   2P: $43-$46   XP: $5   F10
Location: US 19 and 98, 0.4 mi s of jct US 221. 2220 US 19 S 32348. **Fax:** 850/584-3700. **Facility:** 61 one-
bedroom standard units, some with whirlpools. 2 stories, exterior corridors. **Terms:** 2 night
minimum stay - weekends, weekly rates available, pets ($5-$10 extra charge). **Pool(s):** outdoor. **Business
Services:** fax (fee). **Cards:** AX, DS, MC, VI. **Special Amenities: free continental breakfast and free local
telephone calls.**

THE CHAPARRAL INN   Phone: 850/584-2441

(AAA) [SAVE]   All Year   1P: $38-$42   2P: $45-$48   XP: $8   F12
Location: US 19 and 98, 0.3 mi s of jct US 221. 2159 S Byron Butler Pkwy 32347. **Fax:** 850/838-1747. **Facility:** 24
one-bedroom standard units. 1 story, exterior corridors. **Parking:** on-site. **Pool(s):** outdoor. **Business
Services:** fax (fee). **Cards:** AX, DS, MC, VI. **Special Amenities: free local telephone calls and preferred
room (subject to availability with advance reservations).**

HAMPTON INN   Phone: (850)223-3000

All Year   1P: $78-$90   2P: $82-$100
Location: 1 mi s of jct US 221 and 19. 2399 S Byron Butler Pkwy 32348 (PO Box 111). **Fax:** 850/223-2622.
Small-scale Hotel **Facility:** 60 one-bedroom standard units, some with whirlpools. 3 stories, interior corridors. **Bath:** combo or
shower only. **Parking:** on-site. **Amenities:** high-speed Internet, voice mail, irons, hair dryers. *Some:* dual
phone lines. **Pool(s):** outdoor. **Leisure Activities:** exercise room. **Guest Services:** valet and coin laundry. **Business Services:**
meeting rooms, business center. **Cards:** AX, CB, DC, DS, JC, MC, VI.

——— WHERE TO DINE ———

MAMA'S ITALIAN FAMILY RESTAURANT   Lunch: $5-$10   Dinner: $8-$17   Phone: 850/223-1109

Location: 0.7 mi s of jct US 221. 2275 S Byron Butler Pkwy 32348. **Hours:** 11 am-3 & 4-9 pm. Closed major
holidays. **Features:** Expect to be pleasantly surprised by these classic Italian recipes in this small Southern
Italian   town; the menu is loaded with traditional favorites. Casual dress; cocktails. **Parking:** on-site. **Cards:** AX,
MC, VI.

POUNCEY'S RESTAURANT   Lunch: $4-$6   Dinner: $8-$12   Phone: 850/584-9942

Location: US 19 and 98, 0.3 mi s of jct US 221. 2186 S Byron Butler Pkwy 32347. **Hours:** 6 am-10 pm. Closed:
11/23, 12/25. **Features:** Simple but scrumptious describes the menu offerings at this family-style diner. Walk
American   in, seat yourself and enjoy everything from BLT sandwiches and seafood specials to fresh vegetables and
chocolate meringue pie. The dishes leave your taste buds satisfied. Casual dress. **Parking:** on-site.

——— *The following restaurant has not been evaluated by AAA* ———
but is listed for your information only.

POPPA JIM'S SEAFOOD   Phone: 850/838-2109

[fyi]   Not evaluated. **Location:** 2218 Hwy 19 S 32347. **Features:** The restaurant offers great seafood served up by a
local family in tribute to patriarch Poppa Jim.

PINELAND pop. 444

——— WHERE TO DINE ———

CABBAGE KEY RESTAURANT, BAR & INN   Lunch: $6-$11   Dinner: $6-$11   Phone: 239/283-2278

Location: MM 60; in Cabbage Key. **Hours:** 7:30-9 am, 11:30-3 & 6-8:30 pm. **Features:** On the hillside of this
gorgeous tropical island and overlooking Tarpon Bay, the popular spot can be reached only via watercraft.
American   It's well worth the voyage. A fun place to dine, this place is known as the inspiration for Jimmy Buffett's tune,
"Cheeseburger in Paradise". Casual dress; cocktails. **Parking:** on-site. **Cards:** MC, VI.

PINELLAS PARK —*See Tampa Bay p. 1032.*

PLANTATION —*See Fort Lauderdale p. 417.*

PLANT CITY —*See Tampa Bay p. 1032.*

POMPANO BEACH —*See Fort Lauderdale p. 420.*

PONCE INLET pop. 2,513   (See map and index starting on p. 285)

―――――― **WHERE TO DINE** ――――――

**INLET HARBOR MARINA &
RESTAURANT**

AAA

◆◆◆ ◆◆◆

American

Lunch: $6-$9	**Dinner:** $9-$23	**Phone:** 386/767-3266 47

Location: 0.5 mi w of S Atlantic Ave, 4.8 mi s of jct Dunlawton. 133 Inlet Harbor Rd 32127. **Hours:** 11 am-10 pm. Closed: 12/25. **Features:** It's hard to say what's most notable at this waterfront restaurant: the scenic views of birds, boats and the nearby sandbar or the savory flavors that go into the many steak, chicken and seafood dishes. Dine on the deck for maximum ambience. Casual dress; cocktails; entertainment. **Parking:** on-site. **Cards:** AX, DC, DS, MC, VI.

PONTE VEDRA BEACH —*See Jacksonville p. 502.*

PORT CHARLOTTE pop. 46,451

―――――― **WHERE TO STAY** ――――――

DAYS INN OF PORT CHARLOTTE

◆◆◆ ◆◆◆

Small-scale Hotel

Book at aaa.com

Phone: (941)627-8900

2/1-4/8	1P: $109-$149	2P: $109-$149	XP: $10	F18
12/21-1/31	1P: $79-$129	2P: $79-$129	XP: $10	F18
12/1-12/20 & 4/9-11/30	1P: $59-$109	2P: $59-$109	XP: $10	F18

Location: On US 41, just s of jct Toledo Blade Blvd. 1941 Tamiami Tr 33948. Fax: 941/743-8503. **Facility:** 126 one-bedroom standard units. 3 stories, exterior corridors. **Parking:** on-site. **Terms:** check-in 4 pm. **Amenities:** safes (fee), irons, hair dryers. **Pool(s):** heated outdoor. **Guest Services:** coin laundry. **Business Services:** meeting rooms, fax (fee). **Cards:** AX, CB, DC, DS, JC, MC, VI.

SOME UNITS

⟨ASK⟩ 🆂🅳 🍴 ⟨Y⟩ 🤿 🏊 📷 🛢 / ✕ DATA PORT 📠 💻 /

―――――― **WHERE TO DINE** ――――――

CAP'N & THE COWBOY

◆◆◆ ◆◆◆

Steak & Seafood

Lunch: $6-$11	**Dinner:** $11-$22	**Phone:** 941/743-3969

Location: I-75, exit 170, 1.6 mi w on Kings Hwy (SR 769); in Maple Leaf Plaza. 2200 Kings Hwy, Unit 3N 33980. **Hours:** 11 am-9 pm, Fri & Sat-10 pm. Closed major holidays; also Mon. **Features:** A favorite spot of the locals, this laid-back restaurant has a menu of such tasty dishes as coconut fried shrimp, fresh grouper, yellowfin tuna and a signature filet topped with Jack Daniels, mushrooms, onions and Monterey Jack cheese. Casual dress; cocktails. **Parking:** on-site. **Cards:** AX, DS, MC, VI.

CHARLEY'S GRILLED SUBS

◆◆◆

American

Lunch: $5-$7	**Dinner:** $5-$7	**Phone:** 941/766-0005

Location: On US 41, just s of jct SR 776 (El Jobean Rd); in Trents Food Court at Port Charlotte Town Center. 1441 Tamiami Tr 33948. **Hours:** 10 am-9 pm. **Features:** If you're hungry after a day of shopping at the mall, stop by this quick-serve type establishment and grab a yummy Philly cheesesteak or a grilled chicken salad. The service is quick and the food is fresh. Casual dress. **Parking:** on-site. **Cards:** MC, VI.

LA ROMANA CAFE & ITALIAN GRILL

◆◆◆ ◆◆◆

Italian

Lunch: $6-$20	**Dinner:** $6-$20	**Phone:** 941/629-0404

Location: On US 41, just n of jct Easy St. 3591 Tamiami Tr 33952. **Hours:** 11 am-9 pm, Fri & Sat-10 pm. Closed: Sun. **Features:** Enjoy fresh Italian fare at this casual eatery. Anything from their popular gourmet pizzas to their pasta dishes, baked dishes, soups, sandwiches or salads are all a treat, so come hungry. Casual dress. **Parking:** on-site. **Cards:** AX, DS, MC, VI.

SAM'S SUBS & SOUP

◆◆◆

American

Lunch: $4-$8	**Dinner:** $4-$8	**Phone:** 941/743-4649

Location: Jct US 41, 0.8 mi ne on Elkcam Blvd, just n. 21320 Gertrude Ave 33952. **Hours:** 10:30 am-6 pm, Fri-7 pm, Sat noon-3 pm. Closed: Sun. **Features:** Reminiscent of a casual delicatessen, the family-run eatery employs a friendly staff. Lining the menu are soups, salads, finger foods and submarine sandwiches. Hand-dipped ice cream is a favorite. Casual dress. **Parking:** on-site. **Cards:** MC, VI.

WHISKEY CREEK GRILL

◆◆◆ ◆◆◆

Steak & Seafood

Lunch: $6-$21	**Dinner:** $7-$21	**Phone:** 941/766-0045

Location: On US 41, just n of jct Port Charlotte Blvd. 2746 Tamiami Tr 33952. **Hours:** 11 am-10 pm. Closed: 11/23, 12/25. **Features:** A rustic theme gives diners the feel that they have taken a step into the wild, wild West. On the casual dining spot's menu are fire-grilled steaks, oak-grilled ribs and chicken, sizzling fajitas and any number of soups, salads, sandwiches and appetizers. Casual dress; cocktails. **Parking:** on-site. **Cards:** AX, DS, MC, VI.

PORT ORANGE pop. 45,823   (See map and index starting on p. 285)

―――――― **WHERE TO DINE** ――――――

AUNT CATFISH'S ON THE RIVER

◆◆◆ ◆◆◆

American

Lunch: $7-$15	**Dinner:** $9-$29	**Phone:** 386/767-4768 42

Location: On SR A1A, just e of US 1; on the Intracoastal Waterway at west end of Port Orange Bridge Cswy (Dunlawton Ave). 4009 Halifax Dr 32127. **Hours:** 11:30 am-9 pm, Fri & Sat-10 pm, Sun 9 am-9 pm. Closed: 12/25. **Reservations:** suggested. **Features:** Southern hospitality, a waterfront view and a down-home menu complete with grits and catfish can be found at this bustling, casual eatery. Fresh local seafood, chicken, steak, ribs and an extensive salad bar make any wait during peak hours worthwhile. Casual dress; cocktails. **Parking:** on-site. **Cards:** DS, MC, VI.

PORT ORANGE STEAKHOUSE

◆◆◆ ◆◆◆

Steak House

Lunch: $6-$22	**Dinner:** $8-$22	**Phone:** 386/756-2660 44

Location: Jct Dunlawton Ave. 3851 S Nova Rd 32127. **Hours:** 11 am-11 pm. Closed: 11/23, 12/25. **Features:** Lending to the Western feel of the rustic steakhouse are dark wood accents, steer heads and saddles. Casual dress; cocktails. **Parking:** on-site. **Cards:** AX, DS, MC, VI.

(See map and index starting on p. 285)

SORRENTO'S DELI   **Lunch:** $4-$10   **Dinner:** $5-$15   **Phone:** 386/761-2181   ㊸

Deli/Subs
Sandwiches

Location: Jct Dunlawton Ave; in Port Orange Plaza. 4050 S Ridgewood Ave 32137. **Hours:** 11 am-9 pm, Mon-8 pm. Closed: Sun. **Features:** Serving the city since 1972, the Italian restaurant knows how to please the locals. Delicious pizza, baked pasta dishes and freshly made submarine sandwiches keep them coming back. Don't forget about Italian ice for dessert. Casual dress. **Parking:** on-site. **Cards:** MC, VI.

PORT RICHEY —*See Tampa Bay p. 1034.*

PORT ST. LUCIE pop. 88,769

─────────── **WHERE TO STAY** ───────────

BEST WESTERN PORT ST. LUCIE   *Book at aaa.com*   **Phone:** (772)878-7600

AAA SAVE

3/1-3/31 [ECP]	1P: $129-$229	2P: $129-$229	XP: $5	F18
2/1-2/28 [ECP]	1P: $119-$199	2P: $119-$199	XP: $5	F18
12/1-1/31 [ECP]	1P: $89-$149	2P: $89-$149	XP: $5	F18
4/1-11/30 [ECP]	1P: $74-$119	2P: $74-$119	XP: $5	F18

Small-scale Hotel **Location:** 0.5 mi s of Prima Vista Blvd, at Spanish Lakes Blvd. 7900 S US 1 34952. **Fax:** 772/340-0422. **Facility:** 98 one-bedroom standard units. 2 stories, exterior corridors. *Bath:* combo or shower only. **Parking:** on-site. **Terms:** weekly rates available. **Amenities:** video games (fee), irons, hair dryers. **Pool(s):** heated outdoor. **Leisure Activities:** whirlpool. **Guest Services:** coin laundry. **Business Services:** meeting rooms, fax (fee). **Cards:** AX, DC, DS, MC, VI. **Special Amenities:** early check-in/late check-out and free room upgrade (subject to availability with advance reservations).

SOME UNITS

🅂🄳 🛗 📶 🏊 ♿ DATA PORT 🍴 🍽 / ✕ 🖨 /

HAMPTON INN & SUITES PORT ST. LUCIE   *Book at aaa.com*   **Phone:** 772/878-5900

12/1-4/30	1P: $159-$199	2P: $159-$199	XP: $10	F10
5/1-11/30	1P: $119-$159	2P: $119-$159	XP: $10	F10

Small-scale Hotel **Location:** I-95, exit 121, just e. 155 Peacock Blvd 34986. **Fax:** 772/878-9338. **Facility:** 73 one-bedroom standard units, some with whirlpools. 4 stories, interior corridors. *Bath:* combo or shower only. **Parking:** on-site. **Terms:** cancellation fee imposed. **Amenities:** video games (fee), high-speed Internet, dual phone lines, voice mail, irons, hair dryers. **Pool(s):** outdoor. **Leisure Activities:** whirlpool, exercise room. **Guest Services:** gift shop, coin laundry. **Business Services:** meeting rooms, business center. **Cards:** AX, DC, DS, MC, VI.

SOME UNITS

♿ 📶 🏊 📹 DATA PORT 🍴 🖨 🍽 / ✕ /

HOLIDAY INN-PORT ST LUCIE   *Book at aaa.com*   **Phone:** (772)337-2200

2/1-5/31	1P: $169-$229	2P: $169-$229	XP: $10	F19
12/24-1/31	1P: $129-$189	2P: $19-$189	XP: $10	F19
12/1-12/23 & 6/1-11/30	1P: $99-$159	2P: $99-$159	XP: $10	F19

Small-scale Hotel **Location:** US 1, 0.5 mi n of jct SR 716, Port St Lucie Blvd. 10120 S Federal Hwy, Rt 1 34952. **Fax:** 772/335-7872. **Facility:** 142 units. 70 one-bedroom standard units. 72 one-bedroom suites, some with whirlpools. 5 stories, interior corridors. *Bath:* combo or shower only. **Parking:** on-site. **Terms:** cancellation fee imposed, [BP] meal plan available, package plans, pets ($50 fee). **Amenities:** high-speed Internet, dual phone lines, voice mail, irons, hair dryers. **Pool(s):** heated outdoor. **Leisure Activities:** whirlpool, exercise room. **Guest Services:** gift shop, valet and coin laundry. **Business Services:** meeting rooms, business center. **Cards:** AX, CB, DC, DS, MC, VI. *(See color ad below)*

SOME UNITS

ASK 🅂🄳 🛗 🍴 🍷 📶 🏊 📹 DATA PORT 🖨 / ✕ 🍴 🖨 /
       FEE   FEE FEE

MAINSTAY SUITES AT PGA VILLAGE   *Book at aaa.com*   **Phone:** 772/460-8882

Property failed to provide current rates

Small-scale Hotel **Location:** I-95, exit 121, just w. 8501 Champions Way 34953. **Fax:** 772/460-8301. **Facility:** 80 units. 68 one-bedroom standard units, some with efficiencies. 12 one-bedroom suites with kitchens. 2 stories, interior corridors. *Bath:* combo or shower only. **Parking:** on-site. **Amenities:** dual phone lines, voice mail, irons. *Some:* hair dryers. **Pool(s):** outdoor. **Guest Services:** coin laundry. **Business Services:** meeting rooms.

SOME UNITS

♿ 📶 🏊 DATA PORT 🍴 🖨 / ✕ 🖨 /

MICROTEL INN & SUITES
(fyi)
Motel
Under construction, scheduled to open May 2006. **Location:** On US 1, 0.3 mi s of SE Port St. Lucie Blvd. 10734 S US Hwy 1 34952 (1461 Kinetic Rd, LAKE PARK, 33403). Fax: 561/863-9007. **Planned Amenities:** coffeemakers, microwaves, refrigerators, pool.

SHERATON'S PGA VACATION RESORT *Book at aaa.com* **Phone:** (772)460-5700
▼▼▼▼
Condominium
All Year   2P: $300
Location: I-95, exit 121, just w. 8702 Champions Way 34986. Fax: 772/460-5705. **Facility:** The elegantly appointed condos offer multiple bedrooms and full kitchens and are located a short drive from the ocean. 42 units. 24 one- and 18 two-bedroom suites with kitchens, some with whirlpools. 3 stories, exterior corridors.
Parking: on-site. **Terms:** check-in 4 pm, 3 day cancellation notice-fee imposed. **Amenities:** voice mail, safes, irons, hair dryers. *Some:* CD players. **Pool(s):** heated outdoor, wading. **Leisure Activities:** whirlpool, playground. **Guest Services:** complimentary laundry. **Business Services:** fax (fee). **Cards:** AX, DC, DS, MC, VI.

(ASK) (S/D) (¶¶+) (&/M) (⚙) (🐾) (🏊) (VCR) (⚡) (DATA PORT) (🛏) (📺) (💻)

SPRINGHILL SUITES *Book at aaa.com* **Phone:** (772)871-2929
▼▼▼▼
Small-scale Hotel
12/1-4/29   1P: $169
10/1-11/30   1P: $129
4/30-7/29   1P: $124
7/30-9/30   1P: $119
Location: I-95, exit 121, just e on St. Lucie West Blvd, then just n on Peacock Blvd. 2000 NW Courtyard Cir 34986. Fax: 772/871-0016. **Facility:** 105 one-bedroom standard units. 4 stories, interior corridors. *Bath:* combo or shower only. **Parking:** on-site. **Terms:** cancellation fee imposed. **Amenities:** high-speed Internet, dual phone lines, voice mail, irons, hair dryers. **Pool(s):** heated outdoor. **Leisure Activities:** whirlpool, exercise room. **Guest Services:** valet and coin laundry. **Business Services:** meeting rooms, business center. **Cards:** AX, CB, DC, DS, JC, MC, VI. *(See color ad below)* SOME UNITS

(ASK) (S/D) (¶¶+) (&/M) (⚙) (🐾) (🏊) (⚡) (DATA PORT) (🛏) (📺) (💻) / (✕) /

────── **WHERE TO DINE** ──────

LE BRITTANY

Continental

Dinner: $15-$26   Phone: 772/871-2231

Location: Jct US 1 and Prima Vista Blvd; in St. Lucie Shopping Center. 899A Prima Vista Blvd 34952. **Hours:** Open 12/1-8/31 & 10/1-11/30; 4:30 pm-9 pm. Closed: Mon & Tues. **Reservations:** suggested. **Features:** Fine home-style cooking with a French flair is what you'll get in this cozy restaurant. The chef/owner whips up tasty offerings, such as beef and vegetable soup and the scrumptious duck, served with chutney and a carrot-broccoli medley. Casual dress; beer & wine only. **Parking:** on-site. **Cards:** AX, MC, VI.

MCALISTER'S DELI
AAA

Deli/Subs
Sandwiches

Lunch: $4-$8   **Dinner: $4-$8**   Phone: 772/871-1978

Location: I-95, exit 121, just e to Peacock Blvd. 220 NW Peacock Blvd 34986. **Hours:** 10:30 am-10 pm. Closed: 11/23, 12/25. **Features:** Patrons can choose from more than 30 sandwiches and 11 ways to have their extra-large baked potatoes served. Kentucky pie is a sinful favorite from the dessert menu. Casual dress. **Parking:** on-site. **Cards:** MC, VI.

PUNTA GORDA pop. 14,344

────── **WHERE TO STAY** ──────

MARINA INN

Condominium

			Phone: 941/575-4488	
12/1-4/30	1P: $150-$195	2P: $150-$195	XP: $10	F12
5/1-11/30	1P: $89-$99	2P: $89-$99	XP: $10	F12

Location: I-75, exit 161, 11.2 mi w on CR 768/765 (Burnt Store Rd); in The Burnt Store Marina and Country Club. Located in gated area. 3160 Matecumbe Key Rd 33955. Fax: 941/575-2363. **Facility:** 25 units. 22 one- and 3 two-bedroom suites ($195-$275) with kitchens. 3 stories, exterior corridors. **Parking:** on-site. **Terms:** office hours 8 am-5 pm, 3 day cancellation notice-fee imposed, weekly rates available, package plans. **Amenities:** irons. *Some:* CD players. **Pool(s):** heated outdoor. **Leisure Activities:** fishing, rental bicycles. *Fee:* charter fishing. **Guest Services:** coin laundry. **Business Services:** fax (fee). **Cards:** AX, DS, MC, VI.

SOME UNITS
(ASK) (T→) ⊘ ✕ 🖭 🖵 / ✕ (VCR) /

MOTEL 6 #1231

Motel

Book at aaa.com

			Phone: 941/639-9585	
1/28-4/9	1P: $66-$76	2P: $72-$82	XP: $3	F17
1/1-1/27	1P: $54-$64	2P: $60-$70	XP: $3	F17
4/10-11/30	1P: $49-$59	2P: $55-$65	XP: $3	F17
12/1-12/31	1P: $39-$49	2P: $45-$55	XP: $3	F17

Location: I-75, exit 161, just w on CR 768. 9300 Knights Dr 33950. Fax: 941/639-6820. **Facility:** 73 one-bedroom standard units. 1 story, exterior corridors. *Bath:* combo or shower only. **Parking:** on-site. **Terms:** small pets only. **Pool(s):** outdoor. **Guest Services:** coin laundry. **Business Services:** fax (fee). **Cards:** AX, CB, DC, DS, MC, VI.

SOME UNITS
🖭 🐾 (T→) (ⓈM) (🖆) ⊘ (🎥) (DATA PORT) / ✕ 🖵 🖵
FEE FEE

────── **WHERE TO DINE** ──────

CAPTAIN'S TABLE

Seafood

Lunch: $6-$13   **Dinner: $17-$30**   Phone: 941/637-1177

Location: 1.5 mi w of jct Marion Ave; in Fisherman's Village. 1200 W Retta Esplanade 33951-1289. **Hours:** 11 am-9 pm, Fri & Sat-10 pm. Closed: 1/1. **Features:** A lovely, scenic view of Charlotte Harbor and plenty of fresh seafood bring in the locals. The fisherman's platter spills over with whitefish, shrimp, mussels, scallops and fried rice. A lunch and dinner buffet offers seafood and nice crisp salads. Casual dress; cocktails. **Parking:** on-site. **Cards:** AX, DS, MC, VI.

🍸

MAMMA NUNZIA RISTORANTE

Italian

Lunch: $5-$9   **Dinner: $12-$30**   Phone: 941/575-7575

Location: On US 41, 1.2 mi s. 1975 Tamiami Tr 33950. **Hours:** 11 am-10 pm, Sun-9 pm. Closed: 11/23, 12/25. **Reservations:** suggested. **Features:** The cozy restaurant serves genuine cuisine from the Isle of Capri. On a menu of tasty, freshly prepared food are such items as pollo Vesuvio and linguine con calamari. Penne al pesto is excellent. Dressy casual; cocktails; entertainment. **Parking:** on-site. **Cards:** AX, DS, MC, VI.

🍸

PORTABELLOS AT LATITUDES

American

Lunch: $8-$15   **Dinner: $10-$25**   Phone: 941/639-3650

Location: I-75, exit 161, 11.2 mi w on CR 768/765 (Burnt Store Rd); in Burnt Store Marina and Country Club. 3200 Matecumbe Key Rd 33955. **Hours:** 11 am-10 pm, Sun from 10 am. Closed: 12/25. **Features:** A beautiful harbor view of many luxurious boats and yachts is a strong point at this restaurant set back within the grounds of a popular country club. Although service is casual, the chef puts together well-prepared dishes marked by beautiful presentation. Chicken marsala is a delight. Casual dress; cocktails. **Parking:** on-site. **Cards:** AX, DC, DS, MC, VI.

🍸

QUINCY pop. 6,982

────── **WHERE TO STAY** ──────

ALLISON HOUSE INN

Historic Bed
& Breakfast

			Phone: (850)875-2511	
All Year [ECP]	1P: $75-$110	2P: $85-$140	XP: $20	F12

Location: Just e of town center; in historic district. 215 N Madison St 32351. Fax: 850/875-2511. **Facility:** Enjoy granola and biscotti among the homemade foods served to guests at this 1843 Greek Revival home. Smoke free premises. 6 one-bedroom standard units. 2 stories, interior corridors. *Bath:* combo or shower only. **Parking:** on-site. **Terms:** 14 day cancellation notice-fee imposed, small pets only (owner's pet on premises). **Amenities:** hair dryers. **Leisure Activities:** bicycles. **Business Services:** fax. **Cards:** AX, DS, MC, VI.

(ASK) 🖭 🐾 ✕ (DATA PORT)

MCFARLIN HOUSE BED & BREAKFAST INN
Historic Bed & Breakfast
All Year [BP]
1P: $90-$200
XP: $25
Phone: 850/875-2526
Location: Corner of King and Love sts; in historic district. 305 E King St 32351. **Fax:** 850/627-4703. **Facility:** This 1895 Queen Anne Victorian features dramatic woodwork and a grand stairway, both elegantly restored. Designated smoking area. 9 one-bedroom standard units, some with whirlpools. 4 stories (no elevator), interior corridors. **Bath:** combo or shower only. **Parking:** on-site. **Terms:** check-in 4 pm, 2 night minimum stay - weekends, 30 day cancellation notice-fee imposed. **Amenities:** CD players. **Guest Services:** area transportation. **Business Services:** fax. **Cards:** AX, DS, MC, VI.

SOME UNITS

——— WHERE TO DINE ———

LISA & JOE'S CAFE
Cuban
Lunch: $5-$7
Phone: 850/875-1922
Location: Downtown. 114 E Washington St 32351. **Hours:** 10 am-3 pm. **Closed:** Sat & Sun. **Features:** The cafe-style establishment is the talk of the town—a local favorite that may turn out to be yours too. Casual dress. **Parking:** street. **Cards:** MC, VI.

REDINGTON SHORES —See Tampa Bay p. 1034.

RIVERVIEW —See Tampa Bay p. 1034.

RIVIERA BEACH pop. 29,884 (See map and index starting on p. 843)

——— WHERE TO STAY ———

SUPER 8 MOTEL WEST PALM BEACH/RIVIERA BEACH **Book at aaa.com**
Motel

2/1-4/30 [CP]	1P: $89-$199	2P: $89-$199	XP: $5	F16
12/1-1/31 [CP]	1P: $59-$149	2P: $59-$149	XP: $5	F16
5/1-11/30 [CP]	1P: $59-$99	2P: $59-$99	XP: $5	F16

Phone: 561/848-1188 **44**

Location: I-95, exit 76, just w on SR 708. 4112 W Blue Heron Blvd 33404. **Fax:** 561/848-4583. **Facility:** 100 one-bedroom standard units. 2 stories (no elevator), exterior corridors. **Parking:** on-site. **Terms:** 3 day cancellation notice-fee imposed. **Amenities:** voice mail. Some: hair dryers. **Pool(s):** outdoor. **Guest Services:** coin laundry. **Cards:** AX, CB, DC, DS, MC, VI.

SOME UNITS

RUSKIN —See Tampa Bay p. 1035.

SAFETY HARBOR —See Tampa Bay p. 1036.

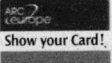

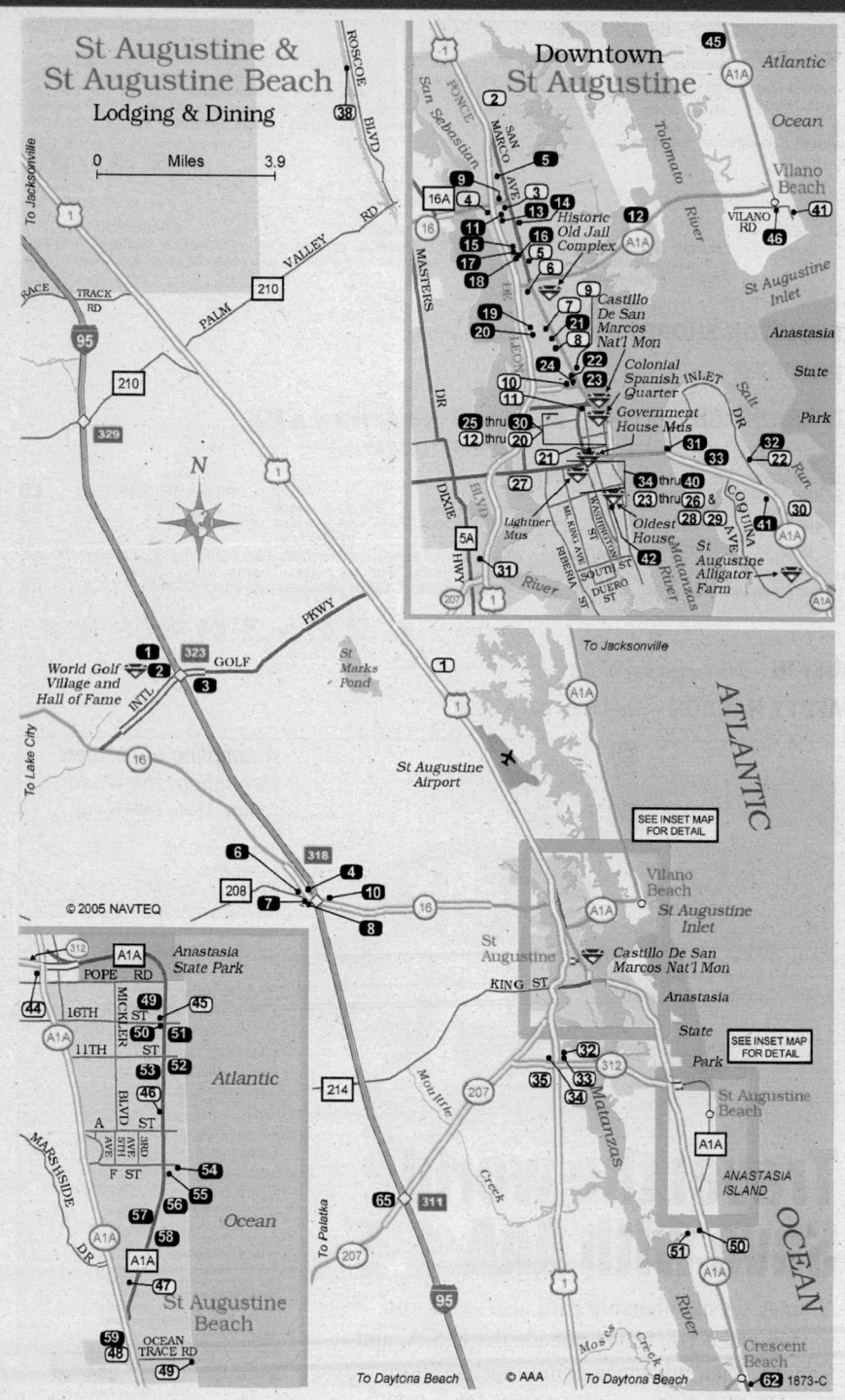

St. Augustine & St. Augustine Beach

This index helps you "spot" where approved accommodations and restaurants are located on the corresponding detailed maps. Lodging rate ranges are for comparison only and show the property's high season; rates are per night, unless only weekly (W) rates are available. Restaurant rate range is for dinner, unless only lunch (L) is served. Turn to the listing page for more detailed rate information and consult display ads for special promotions.

Spotter/Map Page Number	OA	ST. AUGUSTINE - Lodgings	Diamond Rating	Rate Range High Season	Listing Page
1 / p. 874		Grande Villas at World Golf Village	◆◆◆	Failed to provide	882
2 / p. 874	AAA	World Golf Village Renaissance Resort - see color ad p 888	◆◆◆	$129-$499 SAVE	888
3 / p. 874	AAA	Comfort Suites	◆◆◆	$99-$139 SAVE	881
4 / p. 874	AAA	Days Inn-West	◆◆	$59-$199 SAVE	882
5 / p. 874	AAA	Travelodge & Suites	◆◆	$69-$399 SAVE	888
6 / p. 874	AAA	Ramada Limited	◆◆	$79-$109 SAVE	887
7 / p. 874	AAA	Hampton Inn St. Augustine Outlet Center	◆◆◆	$89-$129 SAVE	883
8 / p. 874	AAA	Best Western St. Augustine I-95 - see color ad p 879	◆◆	$59-$150 SAVE	879
9 / p. 874	AAA	Days Inn Historic	◆◆	$56-$199 SAVE	882
10 / p. 874	AAA	Holiday Inn Express	◆◆◆	$92-$185 SAVE	884
11 / p. 874	AAA	Alhambra Inn & Suites/Best Value Inn & Suites	◆◆	$69-$175 SAVE	878
12 / p. 874		The Inn At Camachee Harbor	◆◆	$99-$159	884
13 / p. 874	AAA	Knights Inn	◆	$45-$75 SAVE	884
14 / p. 874	AAA	Country Inn & Suites Downtown Historic District	◆◆◆	$99-$195 SAVE	882
15 / p. 874	AAA	Merida Motel	◆◆	$39-$129 SAVE	887
16 / p. 874	AAA	The Cozy Inn	◆◆	$45-$99 SAVE	882
17 / p. 874		Hampton Inn Historic - see color ad p 883	◆◆◆	$99-$209	883
18 / p. 874	AAA	Best Western Historical Inn - see color ad p 879	◆◆	$69-$160 SAVE	879
19 / p. 874	AAA	Holiday Inn Hotel & Suites-Historic - see color ad p 884	◆◆	$134-$220 SAVE	884
20 / p. 874	AAA	La Quinta Inn St. Augustine - see color ad p 885	◆◆	$59-$150 SAVE	885
21 / p. 874	AAA	Scottish Inns	◆◆	$50-$110 SAVE	887
22 / p. 874		Comfort Suites	◆◆◆	$79-$350	881
23 / p. 874		Castle Garden Bed & Breakfast	◆◆	$79-$199	881
24 / p. 874	AAA	Best Western Spanish Quarters Inn - see color ad p 880	◆◆	$89-$139 SAVE	880
25 / p. 874	AAA	Alexander Homestead Bed & Breakfast	◆◆◆	$129-$229 SAVE	878
26 / p. 874	AAA	Casa de Suenos Bed & Breakfast	◆◆◆	$145-$245 SAVE	880
27 / p. 874	AAA	Centennial House Bed & Breakfast	◆◆◆	$120-$250 SAVE	881
28 / p. 874	AAA	Monterey Inn - see color ad p 886	◆◆	$69-$150 SAVE	887
29 / p. 874	AAA	Casa de la Paz Bayfront Bed & Breakfast	◆◆◆	$150-$300 SAVE	880
30 / p. 874	AAA	Hilton-St. Augustine Historic Bayfront - see color ad p 883	◆◆◆◆	$159-$355 SAVE	883
31 / p. 874	AAA	Edgewater Inn	◆◆	$59-$149 SAVE	882
32 / p. 874		Conch House Marina Resort	◆◆	$100-$350	882
33 / p. 874	AAA	Anastasia Inn	◆◆	$45-$275 SAVE	878
34 / p. 874	AAA	Casa Monica Hotel - see color ad p 881	◆◆◆◆	$179-$309 SAVE	880

Spotter/Map Page Number	OA	ST. AUGUSTINE - Lodgings (continued)	Diamond Rating	Rate Range High Season	Listing Page
35 / p. 874		Casa De Solana Bed & Breakfast Inn	◈◈◈	$129-$259	880
36 / p. 874		Old City House Inn & Restaurant	◈◈◈	Failed to provide	887
37 / p. 874	AAA	**Bayfront Inn** - see color ad p 878	◈◈	$69-$179 SAVE	878
38 / p. 874	AAA	**Peace and Plenty Inn**	◈◈◈	$119-$209 SAVE	887
39 / p. 874	AAA	**Cedar House Inn Victorian B & B**	◈◈◈	$124-$259 SAVE	881
40 / p. 874		Bayfront Westcott House	◈◈◈	$119-$279	879
41 / p. 874	AAA	**Sleep Inn** - see color ad p 888	◈◈	$75-$199 SAVE	888
42 / p. 874	AAA	**St. Francis Inn**	◈◈◈	$119-$239 SAVE	887
		ST. AUGUSTINE - Restaurants			
1 / p. 874		King's Head British Pub	◈	$4-$13	890
2 / p. 874		Schooner's Seafood House	◈	$8-$16	891
3 / p. 874		Cheese Wheel & Sandwich Board	◈	$4-$6(L)	889
4 / p. 874		Marty's Seafood & Steak House	◈◈	$13-$25	891
5 / p. 874		Cafe Spain	◈◈	$5-$18	889
6 / p. 874		Cortesse's Bistro & Flamingo Room	◈◈	$12-$24	890
7 / p. 874		Yahala Mediterranean Cafe	◈	$4-$11	892
8 / p. 874	AAA	**Raintree Restaurant**	◈◈◈	$15-$32	891
9 / p. 874		Le Pavillon	◈◈	$14-$27	891
10 / p. 874		Barnacle Bill's Seafood House	◈◈	$9-$17	889
11 / p. 874		City Gates Cafe	◈	$4-$7(L)	889
12 / p. 874		White Lion Restaurant	◈◈	$7-$14	891
13 / p. 874		Mi Casa	◈	$5-$8	891
14 / p. 874		Acapulco Mexican Restaurant	◈◈	$6-$15	889
15 / p. 874		Florida Cracker Cafe	◈	$8-$15	890
16 / p. 874		Bistro Hypolita	◈◈	$9-$13(L)	889
17 / p. 874		Columbia Restaurant	◈◈	$15-$26	889
18 / p. 874		La Parisienne-Continental Cuisine	◈◈◈	$19-$50	890
19 / p. 874		La Pentola	◈◈	$11-$22	891
20 / p. 874		Tavern on the Bay	◈	$8-$17	891
21 / p. 874		J. J.'s Heritage Cafe	◈	$5-$15	890
22 / p. 874		The Conch House Restaurant and Lounge	◈◈	$17-$25	890
23 / p. 874		A1A Ale Works Brewery and Restaurant	◈◈	$10-$19	889
24 / p. 874		Habana Village Cafe	◈◈	$10-$20	890
25 / p. 874		95 Cordova - see color ad p 881	◈◈◈	$14-$25	889
26 / p. 874		Denoel French Pastry Shop	◈	$7-$9(L)	890
27 / p. 874	AAA	**Theos' Restaurant**	◈	$5-$8(L)	891
28 / p. 874		Old City House Restaurant	◈◈◈	$16-$27	891
29 / p. 874		Cafe Alcazar	◈◈	$7-$10(L)	889
30 / p. 874	AAA	**Gypsy Cab Company**	◈◈	$15-$21	890
31 / p. 874		Azalea's Cafe	◈	$5-$10(L)	889

Spotter/Map Page Number	OA	ST. AUGUSTINE - Restaurants (continued)	Diamond Rating	Rate Range High Season	Listing Page
32 / p. 874	AAA	Creekside Dinery	◆◆	$6-$19	890
33 / p. 874		Sonny's Real Pit Bar-B-Q	◆	$4-$14	891
34 / p. 874		First Wok Chinese Food	◆	$4-$13	890
35 / p. 874		Woody's Bar-B-Q	◆◆	$8-$14	891
		VILANO BEACH - Lodgings			
45 / p. 874	AAA	Ocean Sands Beach Inn - see color ad p 886	◆◆	$49-$149 SAVE	1063
46 / p. 874		Clarion Collection Casa Del Mar	◆◆◆	$179-$269	1062
		VILANO BEACH - Restaurant			
41 / p. 874	AAA	Fiddler's Green	◆◆	$12-$25	1063
		ST. AUGUSTINE BEACH - Lodgings			
49 / p. 874	AAA	Super 8 By The Beach	◆◆	$59-$229 SAVE	894
50 / p. 874		Hilton Garden Inn-St. Augustine Beach	◆◆◆	$99-$229	893
51 / p. 874		Hampton Inn-St. Augustine Beach	◆◆	$109-$229	893
52 / p. 874		Castillo Real Resort Hotel by Clarion Collection	◆◆◆	Failed to provide	892
53 / p. 874	AAA	Days Inn-St. Augustine Beach - see color ad p 893	◆◆	$69-$150 SAVE	892
54 / p. 874	AAA	Beachfront Bed & Breakfast	◆◆◆	$159-$249 SAVE	892
55 / p. 874	AAA	La Fiesta Ocean Inn & Suites - see color ad p 885	◆◆	$100-$300 SAVE	893
56 / p. 874	AAA	Holiday Inn-St Augustine Beach	◆◆	$135-$169 SAVE	893
57 / p. 874	AAA	Comfort Inn at St. Augustine Beach	◆◆	$89-$107 SAVE	892
58 / p. 874		Ramada Limited, at the Beach	◆◆	$69-$109	893
59 / p. 874	AAA	Best Western Ocean Inn	◆◆	$79-$199 SAVE	892
		ST. AUGUSTINE BEACH - Restaurants			
44 / p. 874		Amici Italian Restaurant	◆◆	$10-$18	894
45 / p. 874	AAA	Sunset Grille	◆◆	$9-$20	894
46 / p. 874	AAA	Cafe Atlantico	◆◆◆	$13-$21	894
47 / p. 874		Sea Oats Caffe	◆	$11-$21	894
48 / p. 874		Zaharias Restaurant	◆◆	$11-$20	894
49 / p. 874	AAA	The World Famous Oasis Restaurant & Deck	◆	$4-$14	894
50 / p. 874		Beach Street Cafe	◆	$3-$7(L)	894
51 / p. 874	AAA	Saltwater Cowboys	◆◆	$10-$19	894
		CRESCENT BEACH - Lodgings			
62 / p. 874	AAA	Beacher's Lodge	◆◆	$109-$225 SAVE	282
		ELKTON - Lodgings			
65 / p. 874	AAA	Comfort Inn St. Augustine	◆◆	$79-$109 SAVE	320
		PONTE VEDRA BEACH - Restaurant			
38 / p. 874		Barbara Jean's	◆	$8-$20	506

ST. AUGUSTINE pop. 11,592   (See map and index starting on p. 874)

——— WHERE TO STAY ———

ALEXANDER HOMESTEAD BED & BREAKFAST
Phone: (904)826-4147   **25**

(AAA) (SAVE)

▼▼▼▼

Historic Bed & Breakfast

All Year   1P: $129-$229   2P: $129-$229   XP: $20   F
Location: Just s of Orange St; center. 14 Sevilla St 32084. Fax: 904/823-9503. **Facility:** This Victorian home built in 1888 is decorated with antiques and features wood-burning fireplaces in two guest rooms. Smoke free premises. 5 one-bedroom standard units, some with whirlpools. 2 stories, interior corridors. **Parking:** on-site. **Terms:** age restrictions may apply, 7 day cancellation notice-fee imposed, package plans. **Amenities:** safes, hair dryers. **Leisure Activities:** bicycles. **Guest Services:** complimentary evening beverages. **Business Services:** fax. **Cards:** AX, DC, DS, MC, VI. **Special Amenities:** free full breakfast and free local telephone calls.

ALHAMBRA INN & SUITES/BEST VALUE INN & SUITES   *Book at aaa.com*
Phone: 904/824-2883   **11**

(AAA) (SAVE)

▼▼

Motel

12/1-4/30   1P: $69-$175   2P: $69-$175   XP: $6
5/1-11/30   1P: $59-$175   2P: $59-$175   XP: $6
Location: On US 1, jct SR 16. 2700 N Ponce de Leon Blvd 32084. Fax: 904/825-0976. **Facility:** 77 units. 72 one-bedroom standard units. 5 one-bedroom suites with whirlpools. 2 stories, exterior corridors. *Bath:* combo or shower only. **Parking:** on-site. **Terms:** check-in 4 pm. **Amenities:** video library (fee), irons, hair dryers. **Dining:** 6 am-11 pm. **Pool(s):** outdoor. **Leisure Activities:** whirlpool. **Guest Services:** gift shop. **Business Services:** meeting rooms, fax (fee). **Cards:** AX, DS, MC, VI. **Special Amenities:** free local telephone calls and preferred room (subject to availability with advance reservations).

SOME UNITS
FEE

ANASTASIA INN   *Book at aaa.com*
Phone: 904/825-2879   **33**

(AAA) (SAVE)

▼▼▼▼

Motel

All Year [CP]   1P: $45-$275   2P: $50-$275   XP: $10   F5
Location: On SR A1A, 0.3 mi s of Bridge of Lions. 218 Anastasia Blvd 32080. Fax: 904/825-2724. **Facility:** 23 one-bedroom standard units. 2 stories (no elevator), exterior corridors. *Bath:* combo or shower only. **Parking:** on-site. **Terms:** 3 day cancellation notice-fee imposed. **Amenities:** voice mail. **Pool(s):** small heated outdoor. **Business Services:** fax. **Cards:** AX, DS, MC, VI. **Special Amenities:** free continental breakfast and free local telephone calls.

SOME UNITS

BAYFRONT INN
Phone: (904)824-1681   **37**

(AAA) (SAVE)

▼▼▼▼

Motel

All Year   1P: $69-$179   2P: $69-$179   XP: $7
Location: Just s of SR A1A and Bridge of Lions; center; in historic district. Located in a quiet area. 138 Avenida Menendez 32084. Fax: 904/829-8721. **Facility:** 39 units. 38 one-bedroom standard units. 1 two-bedroom suite ($99-$259). 1-2 stories, exterior corridors. *Bath:* combo or shower only. **Parking:** on-site. **Terms:** 3 day cancellation notice. **Amenities:** voice mail, irons, hair dryers. **Pool(s):** small outdoor. **Leisure Activities:** whirlpool. **Cards:** AX, DS, MC, VI. **Special Amenities:** free continental breakfast and free local telephone calls. *(See color ad below)*

History surrounds your stay at Bayfront Inn. Watch the Matanzas Bay tides rise and fall... watch boats pass through the Bridge of Lions...stroll along the seawall. You are in the heart of historic St. Augustine, with many original buildings, fine shops, restaurants, the old fort and much more. Stay in the Historic Rodriguez House located on the property. This historic, coquina building, documented on a 1764 map, is one of the surviving Spanish structures in St. Augustine, making it one of the oldest buildings in the state of Florida. Enjoy the beauty of St. Augustine in the comfort and charm of Bayfront Inn.

BAYFRONT INN

138 Avenida Menendez • St. Augustine, FL 32084 • (800) 558-3455 • www.bayfrontinn.com

(See map and index starting on p. 874)

BAYFRONT WESTCOTT HOUSE
Historic Bed & Breakfast
All Year [BP]   1P: $119-$279   2P: $119-$279   **Phone: (904)824-4301** **40**
XP: $20   D18
Location: 1 blk s of the Bridge of Lions. 146 Avenida Menendez 32084-5049. Fax: 904/824-1502. **Facility:** Across the street from Matanzas Bay, this property dating from 1890 offers views of the water in a Victorian-style setting. Smoke free premises. 16 one-bedroom standard units, some with whirlpools. 2 stories, interior/exterior corridors. *Bath:* combo or shower only. **Parking:** street. **Terms:** 2 night minimum stay - weekends, 7 day cancellation notice-fee imposed, package plans, pets ($15 extra charge, in designated units). **Amenities:** hair dryers. **Leisure Activities:** bicycles. **Cards:** DS, MC, VI.

(ASK) (S/D) (🛏) (📶) (✕) (DATA PORT)
FEE

BEST WESTERN HISTORICAL INN   *Book at aaa.com*
Small-scale Hotel
All Year [ECP]   1P: $69-$160   2P: $69-$160   **Phone: (904)829-9088** **18**
XP: $10   F18
Location: 0.5 mi s of jct SR 16 and US 1; 6 blks n from historic district. 2010 N Ponce de Leon Blvd 32084. Fax: 904/829-6629. **Facility:** 39 units. 38 one-bedroom standard units. 1 two-bedroom suite with kitchen. 2 stories, exterior corridors. **Parking:** on-site. **Terms:** package plans. **Amenities:** irons, hair dryers. **Pool(s):** outdoor. **Leisure Activities:** whirlpool. *Fee:* historical tours. **Guest Services:** coin laundry. **Cards:** AX, CB, DC, DS, MC, VI. **Special Amenities:** free expanded continental breakfast and free local telephone calls. *(See color ad below)*

SOME UNITS
(S/D) (🏊) (DATA PORT) (📺) / (✕) (🍴) (🔲) /

BEST WESTERN ST. AUGUSTINE I-95   *Book at aaa.com*
Motel
All Year   1P: $59-$125   2P: $59-$150   **Phone: (904)829-1999** **8**
XP: $10   F12
Location: I-95, exit 318, just w. 2445 SR 16 32092. Fax: 904/829-0660. **Facility:** 120 one-bedroom standard units. 2 stories, exterior corridors. *Bath:* combo or shower only. **Parking:** on-site. **Terms:** cancellation fee imposed, pets ($10 extra charge). **Amenities:** voice mail, safes (fee), irons, hair dryers. **Pool(s):** outdoor. **Guest Services:** coin laundry. **Business Services:** fax. **Cards:** AX, CB, DC, DS, MC, VI. **Special Amenities:** free continental breakfast and free local telephone calls. *(See color ad below)*

SOME UNITS
(S/D) (🛏) (📶) (🏊) (📹) (📺) / (✕) /
FEE

(See map and index starting on p. 874)

BEST WESTERN SPANISH QUARTERS INN   *Book at aaa.com*

Phone: (904)824-4457   **24**

AAA **SAVE**
▼▼▼ ▼▼

Motel

All Year   1P: $89-$139   2P: $89-$139   XP: $10   F18
Location: Just w of San Marcos Ave. Located across from visitor's center. 6 Castillo Dr 32084. Fax: 904/829-8330. **Facility:** 40 one-bedroom standard units. 2 stories (no elevator), exterior corridors. **Parking:** on-site. **Terms:** 1-3 night minimum stay - seasonal and/or weekends. **Amenities:** irons, hair dryers. **Pool(s):** outdoor. **Leisure Activities:** whirlpool. **Guest Services:** coin laundry. **Business Services:** fax. **Cards:** AX, CB, DC, DS, MC, VI. **Special Amenities:** free expanded continental breakfast and free local telephone calls. *(See color ad below)*

SOME UNITS

CASA DE LA PAZ BAYFRONT BED & BREAKFAST

Phone: 904/829-2915   **29**

AAA **SAVE**
▼▼▼ ▼▼

Historic Bed
& Breakfast

All Year   1P: $150-$300   2P: $150-$300   XP: $50
Location: 0.3 mi n of Bridge of Lions on SR A1A. 22 Avenida Menendez 32084. Fax: 904/824-6269. **Facility:** A fireplace adds a warm touch to one guest room of this Mediterranean-style home overlooking Matanzas Bay. Smoke free premises. 7 one-bedroom standard units, some with whirlpools. 3 stories (no elevator), interior/exterior corridors. *Bath:* combo or shower only. **Parking:** on-site. **Terms:** office hours 9 am-8 pm, 2-3 night minimum stay - weekends, age restrictions may apply, 7 day cancellation notice-fee imposed, package plans. **Amenities:** irons, hair dryers. **Guest Services:** complimentary evening beverages. **Business Services:** fax. **Cards:** AX, DS, MC, VI. **Special Amenities:** free full breakfast and free local telephone calls.

SOME UNITS

CASA DE SOLANA BED & BREAKFAST INN   *Book at aaa.com*

Phone: (904)824-3555   **35**

▼▼▼ ▼▼

Historic Bed
& Breakfast

All Year [BP]   1P: $129-$259   2P: $129-$259   XP: $20
Location: Aviles St at Cadiz St; in historic district. 21 Aviles St 32084. Fax: 904/824-3316. **Facility:** This Spanish Colonial house overlooking a courtyard features sleeping quarters and a parlor in most units. Smoke free premises. 10 units. 9 one-bedroom standard units, some with whirlpools. 1 one-bedroom suite ($169-$249) with whirlpool. 3 stories (no elevator), interior corridors. **Parking:** street. **Terms:** age restrictions may apply, 7 day cancellation notice-fee imposed. **Amenities:** high-speed Internet, voice mail, irons, hair dryers. **Leisure Activities:** bicycles. **Guest Services:** complimentary evening beverages. **Business Services:** fax. **Cards:** AX, CB, DS, MC, VI.

SOME UNITS

CASA DE SUENOS BED & BREAKFAST

Phone: (904)824-0887   **26**

AAA **SAVE**
▼▼▼ ▼▼

Historic Bed
& Breakfast

All Year   2P: $145-$245   XP: $15
Location: Corner of Saragossa St; in historic district. 20 Cordova St 32084. Fax: 877/899-7884. **Facility:** Tastefully decorated units. Smoke free premises. 5 one-bedroom standard units, some with whirlpools. 2 stories, interior/exterior corridors. *Bath:* combo or shower only. **Parking:** on-site. **Terms:** age restrictions may apply, 14 day cancellation notice-fee imposed, package plans. **Amenities:** video library, CD players, hair dryers. *Some:* irons. **Guest Services:** complimentary evening beverages: weekends. **Business Services:** fax. **Cards:** AX, DS, MC, VI. **Special Amenities:** free full breakfast and free local telephone calls.

SOME UNITS

CASA MONICA HOTEL   *Book at aaa.com*

Phone: (904)827-1888   **34**

AAA **SAVE**
▼▼▼ ▼▼

Historic
Large-scale Hotel

12/1-5/31 & 10/1-11/30   1P: $179-$309   2P: $179-$309   XP: $15   F17
6/1-9/30   1P: $169-$309   2P: $169-$309   XP: $15   F17
Location: Downtown; across from Lightner Museum and Flagler College. 95 Cordova St 32084. Fax: 904/819-6065. **Facility:** This boutique hotel, built in 1888, offers cozy guest units with Spanish-style furnishings and dramatic public areas. Smoke free premises. 138 units. 126 one-bedroom standard units. 12 one-bedroom suites ($339-$609), some with whirlpools. 5 stories (no elevator), interior corridors. *Bath:* combo or shower only. **Parking:** valet and street. **Terms:** check-in 4 pm, 2 night minimum stay - weekends, 3 day cancellation notice, [BP] meal plan available, package plans, $10 service charge. **Amenities:** video games (fee), high-speed Internet, dual phone lines, voice mail, safes, irons, hair dryers. **Dining:** 6 am-11 pm, also, 95 Cordova, see separate listing. **Pool(s):** heated outdoor. **Leisure Activities:** whirlpool, exercise room. *Fee:* golf privileges, beach club access, bicycles. **Guest Services:** gift shop, valet laundry. **Business Services:** meeting rooms, business center. **Cards:** AX, DC, DS, JC, MC, VI. *(See color ad p 881)*

SOME UNITS

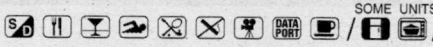

(See map and index starting on p. 874)

CASTLE GARDEN BED & BREAKFAST
Phone: (904)829-3839 · **23** · D18

Historic Bed & Breakfast

All Year [BP] · 1P: $79-$199 · 2P: $79-$199 · XP: $20

Location: Center of downtown. Located opposite Ripley's Believe It or Not Museum. 15 Shenandoah St 32084. Fax: 904/829-9049. **Facility:** This late 1800s building was once the carriage house for a mansion across the street. Smoke free premises. 6 one-bedroom standard units, some with whirlpools. 2 stories, interior corridors. *Bath:* combo or shower only. **Parking:** on-site. **Terms:** 2-3 night minimum stay - weekends, age restrictions may apply, 7 day cancellation notice-fee imposed. **Leisure Activities:** bicycles. **Business Services:** PC, fax. **Cards:** AX, DS, MC, VI.

CEDAR HOUSE INN VICTORIAN B & B
Phone: (904)829-0079 · **39**

AAA SAVE · *Historic Bed & Breakfast*

All Year [BP] · 1P: $124-$254 · 2P: $129-$259 · XP: $35

Location: Jct King St, just s on Granda St, then just w. 79 Cedar St 32084-4311. Fax: 904/825-0916. **Facility:** In a quiet neighborhood, near shops, museums and restaurants, this 1893 restored Victorian home is tastefully decorated with family antiques. Smoke free premises. 6 one-bedroom standard units, some with whirlpools. 2 stories, interior/exterior corridors. **Parking:** on-site. **Terms:** age restrictions may apply, 14 day cancellation notice-fee imposed, package plans. **Amenities:** video library, CD players, high-speed Internet, voice mail, irons, hair dryers. **Leisure Activities:** whirlpool, bicycles. **Guest Services:** complimentary evening beverages. **Business Services:** business center. **Cards:** AX, DS, MC, VI. **Special Amenities:** free full breakfast and free local telephone calls.

CENTENNIAL HOUSE BED & BREAKFAST
Phone: 904/810-2218 · **27**

AAA SAVE · *Bed & Breakfast*

12/1-12/22 & 12/26-11/30 [BP] · 1P: $120-$250 · 2P: $120-$250 · XP: $25

Location: Corner of Saragossa St; in historic district. 26 Cordova St 32084. Fax: 904/810-1930. **Facility:** Fireplaces enhance the ambience of some of this upscale B&B's comfortable accommodations. Smoke free premises. 8 one-bedroom standard units, some with whirlpools. 2 stories, interior/exterior corridors. *Bath:* combo or shower only. **Parking:** on-site. **Terms:** open & 12/1-12/22 & 12/26-11/30, 2-4 night minimum stay - seasonal and/or weekends, age restrictions may apply, 7 day cancellation notice-fee imposed. **Amenities:** video library, high-speed Internet, hair dryers. *Some:* irons. **Leisure Activities:** *Fee:* massage. **Guest Services:** complimentary evening beverages. **Business Services:** fax. **Cards:** MC, VI. **Special Amenities:** free full breakfast and free local telephone calls.

COMFORT SUITES
Book at aaa.com · Phone: (904)829-2292 · **22**

Small-scale Hotel

All Year · 1P: $79-$350 · 2P: $79-$350

Location: 1 mi n of Bridge of Lions. 42 San Marco Ave 32084. Fax: 904/584-0004. **Facility:** 50 one-bedroom standard units, some with whirlpools. 4 stories, interior corridors. *Bath:* combo or shower only. **Parking:** on-site. **Terms:** check-in 4 pm, 1-3 night minimum stay - seasonal and/or weekends. **Amenities:** voice mail, irons, hair dryers. **Pool(s):** small outdoor. **Leisure Activities:** whirlpool, exercise room. **Guest Services:** coin laundry. **Cards:** AX, CB, DC, DS, JC, MC, VI.

COMFORT SUITES
Book at aaa.com · Phone: (904)940-9500 · **3**

AAA SAVE · *Small-scale Hotel*

2/1-4/30 [ECP] · 1P: $99-$139 · 2P: $99-$139 · XP: $10 · F18
12/1-1/31 & 5/1-11/30 [ECP] · 1P: $89-$109 · 2P: $89-$109 · XP: $10 · F18

Location: I-95, exit 323, just e, then just s. 475 Commerce Lake Dr 32095. Fax: 904/940-9600. **Facility:** 162 units. 160 one-bedroom standard units, some with whirlpools. 2 one-bedroom suites. 6 stories, interior corridors. *Bath:* combo or shower only. **Parking:** on-site. **Amenities:** voice mail, irons, hair dryers. *Fee:* video games, high-speed Internet, safes. **Pool(s):** outdoor, heated indoor. **Leisure Activities:** whirlpool, exercise room. *Fee:* golf privileges. **Guest Services:** sundries, valet and coin laundry. **Business Services:** meeting rooms, PC. **Cards:** AX, DC, DS, JC, MC, VI. **Special Amenities:** free expanded continental breakfast and free local telephone calls.

(See map and index starting on p. 874)

CONCH HOUSE MARINA RESORT
▼▼ ▼▼
Small-scale Hotel

Phone: 904/829-8646 **32**

All Year   2P: $100-$350   XP: $10   F10
Location: 0.7 mi s of Bridge of Lions on SR A1A, 0.3 mi n. 57 Comares Ave 32084. Fax: 904/829-5414. **Facility:** 16 units. 8 one-bedroom standard units. 6 one- and 2 two-bedroom suites ($150-$400), some with kitchens. 1 story, exterior corridors. *Bath:* combo or shower only. **Parking:** on-site. **Terms:** 7 day cancellation notice, pets ($50 fee, in designated units). **Amenities:** hair dryers. **Dining:** The Conch House Restaurant and Lounge, see separate listing. **Pool(s):** outdoor. **Leisure Activities:** fishing. *Fee:* boats, sailboats, windsurfing, marina, scuba diving, charter fishing. **Guest Services:** gift shop, coin laundry. **Cards:** AX, DS, MC, VI.

SOME UNITS
(ASK) (S/D) 🐾 🍴 🏊 ✕ 📞 ☕ / 🛢 🖼 /
FEE

COUNTRY INN & SUITES
[fyi]
Small-scale Hotel

Phone: 904/824-0355

All Year   1P: $84-$160   2P: $84-$160
Too new to rate. **Location:** I-95, exit 318, just e. 2367 SR 16 32095. Fax: 904/824-0395. **Amenities:** 54 units, coffeemakers, pool. **Cards:** AX, DS, MC, VI.

COUNTRY INN & SUITES DOWNTOWN HISTORIC
DISTRICT   *Book at aaa.com*
(AAA) (SAVE)
▼▼▼▼
Small-scale Hotel

Phone: (904)827-1766 **14**

12/1-7/31	1P: $99-$195	2P: $99-$195	XP: $10	F18
8/1-11/30	1P: $84-$195	2P: $84-$195	XP: $10	F18

Location: Jct SR 16, just s. 231 San Marco Ave 32084. Fax: 904/827-1772. **Facility:** 54 units. 45 one-bedroom standard units, some with whirlpools. 9 one-bedroom suites ($129-$195). 3 stories; interior corridors. *Bath:* combo or shower only. **Parking:** on-site. **Terms:** cancellation fee imposed, [CP] meal plan available, package plans. **Amenities:** voice mail, irons, hair dryers. **Pool(s):** heated outdoor. **Leisure Activities:** whirlpool, exercise room. **Guest Services:** coin laundry. **Business Services:** business center. **Cards:** AX, CB, DC, DS, MC, VI. **Special Amenities:** free local telephone calls and early check-in/late check-out.

SOME UNITS
(S/D) (&) 🏊 📹 ☕ / ✕ 🛢 🖼 /

THE COZY INN
(AAA) (SAVE)
◇◇ ◇
Motel

Phone: (904)824-2449 **16**

All Year   1P: $45-$89   2P: $49-$99
Location: 0.3 mi s of jct SR 16. 202 San Marco Ave 32084. Fax: 904/819-0655. **Facility:** 19 units. 8 one-bedroom standard units. 11 one-bedroom suites ($99-$250) with kitchens, some with whirlpools. 2 stories, exterior corridors. *Bath:* combo or shower only. **Parking:** on-site. **Terms:** weekly rates available, package plans, small pets only ($25 fee, $100 deposit). **Amenities:** voice mail, irons. *Some:* hair dryers. **Business Services:** fax. **Cards:** AX, DS, MC, VI. **Special Amenities:** free local telephone calls.

SOME UNITS
(S/D) 🐾 🍴 📹 (DATA PORT) 🛢 🖼 ☕ / ✕ /
FEE

DAYS INN HISTORIC
(AAA) (SAVE)
▼▼
Small-scale Hotel

Book at aaa.com   **Phone:** (904)829-6581 **9**

All Year   1P: $56-$199   2P: $56-$199   XP: $5   F13
Location: US 1 at SR 16; in historic district. Located next to sightseeing-tram departure. 2800 N Ponce de Leon Blvd 32084. Fax: 904/824-0135. **Facility:** 124 one-bedroom standard units. 2 stories, exterior corridors. **Parking:** on-site. **Terms:** [AP], [BP], [CP], [ECP] & [MAP] meal plans available, package plans, small pets only (no cats, $10 extra charge, in designated units). **Amenities:** hair dryers. *Some:* hair dryers. **Dining:** 6-11:30 am. **Pool(s):** outdoor. **Leisure Activities:** gazebo, picnic tables. **Guest Services:** sundries, coin laundry, airport transportation-St. Augustine Airport. **Business Services:** fax (fee). **Cards:** AX, CB, DC, DS, JC, MC, VI. **Special Amenities:** free newspaper and early check-in/late check-out.

SOME UNITS
(S/D) ✈ 🐾 🍴 🍳 🏊 ♿ 📹 (DATA PORT) / ✕ 🛢 🖼 /
FEE

DAYS INN-WEST
(AAA) (SAVE)
▼▼
Small-scale Hotel

Book at aaa.com   **Phone:** (904)824-4341 **4**

All Year   1P: $59-$199   2P: $59-$199
Location: I-95, exit 318, just w. Located adjacent to an outlet mall. 2560 SR 16 32092. Fax: 904/824-1158. **Facility:** 120 one-bedroom standard units. 2 stories, exterior corridors. **Parking:** on-site. **Terms:** 3-4 night minimum stay - weekends, 14 day cancellation notice-fee imposed, weekly rates available, [AP] meal plan available, pets (small dogs only, $10 extra charge). **Amenities:** high-speed Internet, hair dryers. **Pool(s):** outdoor. **Guest Services:** coin laundry. **Business Services:** fax (fee). **Cards:** AX, DS, MC, VI. **Special Amenities:** free newspaper and early check-in/late check-out.

SOME UNITS
(S/D) 🐾 🏊 📹 (DATA PORT) ☕ / ✕ 🛢 🖼 /
FEE

EDGEWATER INN
(AAA) (SAVE)
▼▼
Motel

Phone: (904)825-2697 **31**

All Year   1P: $59-$149   2P: $59-$149   XP: $7
Location: On SR A1A, just s of Bridge of Lions. 2 St. Augustine Blvd 32080. Fax: 904/824-0436. **Facility:** Smoke free premises. 20 one-bedroom standard units. 1 story, exterior corridors. *Bath:* combo or shower only. **Parking:** on-site. **Terms:** cancellation fee imposed. **Amenities:** voice mail, hair dryers. **Pool(s):** outdoor. **Business Services:** fax (fee). **Cards:** AX, DS, MC, VI. **Special Amenities:** free continental breakfast and free local telephone calls.

🍴 🏊 ✕ (DATA PORT) ☕

GRANDE VILLAS AT WORLD GOLF VILLAGE
▼◇◇▼
Condominium

Book at aaa.com   **Phone:** 904/940-2000 **1**

Property failed to provide current rates
Location: I-95, exit 323, just w to WGV Blvd, 1.3 mi n, then just s. 100 Front Nine Dr 32092. Fax: 904/940-2092. **Facility:** Lovely grounds complement well-equipped condominiums; walk to the Golf Hall of Fame or enjoy prestigious golf courses designed by the masters. 134 units. 104 one- and 30 two-bedroom standard units with kitchens, some with whirlpools. 5 stories, exterior corridors. *Bath:* combo or shower only. **Parking:** on-site. **Terms:** check-in 4 pm. **Amenities:** video library (fee), CD players, voice mail, safes, irons, hair dryers. **Pool(s):** heated outdoor, wading. **Leisure Activities:** whirlpool, 2 lighted tennis courts, recreation programs, playground, exercise room, basketball, volleyball. *Fee:* golf-36 holes, game room. **Guest Services:** sundries, complimentary laundry. **Business Services:** fax (fee).

♿ 🏊 ✕ (VCR) 📹 (DATA PORT) 🛢 🖼 ☕

(See map and index starting on p. 874)

HAMPTON INN HISTORIC   *Book at aaa.com*   Phone: (904)829-1996   **17**

◆◆◆◆◆   All Year [BP]   1P: $99-$199   2P: $109-$209
Small-scale Hotel   **Location:** On US 1, 0.3 mi s of jct SR 16. 2050 N Ponce de Leon Blvd 32084. Fax: 904/829-1988. **Facility:** 52 one-bedroom standard units, some with whirlpools. 3 stories, interior corridors. *Bath:* combo or shower only. **Parking:** on-site. **Terms:** package plans. **Amenities:** high-speed Internet, voice mail, irons, hair dryers. **Pool(s):** outdoor. **Leisure Activities:** whirlpool, exercise room. **Business Services:** fax. **Cards:** AX, CB, DC, DS, MC, VI. *(See color ad below)*

SOME UNITS

[ASK] [S/D] [GM] [icons] [DATA PORT] / [X] [icons] /

HAMPTON INN ST. AUGUSTINE OUTLET CENTER   *Book at aaa.com*   Phone: (904)824-4422   **7**

[AAA] [SAVE]   12/1-4/30 [BP]   1P: $89-$129   2P: $89-$129
◆◆◆   5/1-8/31 [BP]   1P: $84-$119   2P: $84-$119
Small-scale Hotel   9/1-11/30 [BP]   1P: $79-$119   2P: $79-$119
Location: I-95, exit 318, just w to CR 208, then s. 2525 CR 208 32092. Fax: 904/824-4400. **Facility:** 67 one-bedroom standard units. 4 stories, interior corridors. *Bath:* combo or shower only. **Parking:** on-site. **Amenities:** voice mail, irons, hair dryers. **Pool(s):** outdoor. **Leisure Activities:** whirlpool. **Guest Services:** coin laundry. **Business Services:** fax. **Cards:** AX, CB, DC, DS, MC, VI. **Special Amenities:** free full breakfast and free local telephone calls.

SOME UNITS

[S/D] [icons] [GM] [icons] [DATA PORT] / [X] /

HILTON-ST. AUGUSTINE HISTORIC BAYFRONT   *Book at aaa.com*   Phone: (904)829-2277   **30**

[AAA] [SAVE]   5/2-9/6   1P: $159-$355   2P: $159-$355   XP: $10   F18
◆◆◆◆   12/1-5/1   1P: $139-$355   2P: $139-$355   XP: $10   F18
◆◆◆◆   9/7-11/30   1P: $129-$355   2P: $129-$355   XP: $10   F18
Small-scale Hotel   **Location:** US 1 business route and SR A1A; center in historic district. 32 Avenida Menendez 32084. Fax: 904/826-2005. **Facility:** In the Spanish Quarter, this hotel resembles a small village of several buildings all connected on the outside, and a boutique hotel on the inside. Smoke free premises. 72 one-bedroom standard units, some with whirlpools. 2 stories, interior corridors. **Parking:** valet. **Terms:** check-in 4 pm, 3 day cancellation notice-fee imposed, package plans. **Amenities:** video games (fee), high-speed Internet, dual phone lines, voice mail, safes, irons, hair dryers. **Dining:** 6:30 am-10 pm, cocktails. **Pool(s):** outdoor. **Leisure Activities:** exercise room. **Guest Services:** gift shop, valet and coin laundry. **Business Services:** meeting rooms. **Cards:** AX, CB, DC, DS, MC, VI. **Special Amenities:** free local telephone calls and free newspaper. *(See color ad below)*

[icons] [DATA PORT] [icons]

(See map and index starting on p. 874)

HOLIDAY INN EXPRESS

Book at aaa.com

Phone: (904)823-8636 🔟

AAA SAVE

| | 2/1-3/31 | 1P: $92-$185 | 2P: $92-$185 | XP: $10 | F16 |
| | 12/1-1/31 & 4/1-11/30 | 1P: $82-$185 | 2P: $82-$185 | XP: $10 | F16 |

Motel

Location: I-95, exit 318, just e. 2310 SR 16 32095. Fax: 904/823-8728. **Facility:** 50 one-bedroom standard units, some with whirlpools. 2 stories, exterior corridors. **Parking:** on-site. **Terms:** 4 night minimum stay - seasonal. **Amenities:** high-speed Internet, voice mail, irons, hair dryers. **Pool(s):** outdoor. **Guest Services:** valet and coin laundry. **Business Services:** fax (fee). **Cards:** AX, CB, DC, DS, JC, MC, VI. **Special Amenities:** free expanded continental breakfast and free local telephone calls.

SOME UNITS

HOLIDAY INN HOTEL & SUITES-HISTORIC

Book at aaa.com

Phone: (904)494-2100 🔟9️⃣

AAA SAVE

	2/17-8/6	1P: $134-$220	2P: $134-$220
	8/7-11/30	1P: $104-$200	2P: $104-$200
	12/1-2/16	1P: $104-$165	2P: $104-$165

Small-scale Hotel

Location: 0.7 mi s of jct SR 16. 1302 N Ponce de Leon Blvd 32084. Fax: 904/494-2101. **Facility:** 121 units. 99 one-bedroom standard units, some with whirlpools. 22 one-bedroom suites. 4 stories, interior corridors. *Bath:* combo or shower only. **Parking:** on-site. **Terms:** check-in 4 pm, $2 service charge. **Amenities:** high-speed Internet, dual phone lines, voice mail, irons, hair dryers. **Dining:** 7 am-11 & 5-10 pm, cocktails. **Pool(s):** outdoor. **Leisure Activities:** whirlpool, exercise room. **Guest Services:** valet and coin laundry. **Business Services:** meeting rooms, fax (fee). **Cards:** AX, CB, DC, DS, MC, VI. **Special Amenities:** free local telephone calls and free newspaper. *(See color ad below)*

SOME UNITS

THE INN AT CAMACHEE HARBOR

Phone: 904/825-0003 🔟2️⃣

| | All Year | 1P: $99-$159 |

Small-scale Hotel

Location: On Intracoastal Waterway at west side of Usine Bridge; 1 mi e of jct N SR A1A and San Marco Blvd. 201 Yacht Club Dr 32084. Fax: 904/825-0048. **Facility:** 19 units. 14 one-bedroom standard units, some with whirlpools. 5 one-bedroom suites ($149-$159), some with kitchens. 2 stories (no elevator), interior/exterior corridors. *Bath:* combo or shower only. **Parking:** on-site. **Terms:** 3 day cancellation notice, package plans, $10 service charge, pets ($15 extra charge, in designated units). **Amenities:** voice mail, hair dryers. *Some:* DVD players, CD players, irons. **Leisure Activities:** in-room workout equipment. *Fee:* sailboats, boat dock, fishing, charter fishing. **Guest Services:** coin laundry, area transportation (fee). **Business Services:** meeting rooms. **Cards:** AX, DS, MC, VI.

SOME UNITS

FEE

KNIGHTS INN

Book at aaa.com

Phone: (904)824-1341 🔟3️⃣

AAA SAVE

| | All Year | 1P: $45-$65 | 2P: $55-$75 | XP: $10 | F3 |

Motel

Location: Jct SR 16, just s on US 1. 2500 N Ponce de Leon Blvd 32084. Fax: 904/823-9850. **Facility:** 31 one-bedroom standard units. 2 stories (no elevator), exterior corridors. **Parking:** on-site. **Terms:** cancellation fee imposed, package plans. **Pool(s):** small outdoor. **Business Services:** fax. **Cards:** AX, DS, MC, VI. **Special Amenities:** early check-in/late check-out and free room upgrade (subject to availability with advance reservations).

SOME UNITS

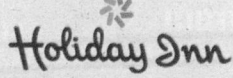

(See map and index starting on p. 874)

LA QUINTA INN ST. AUGUSTINE *Book at aaa.com* Phone: (904)824-3383 ⑳

| | 12/1-9/4 | 1P: $59-$135 | 2P: $59-$150 | XP: $6 | F12 |
| | 9/5-11/30 | 1P: $59-$110 | 2P: $59-$120 | XP: $6 | F12 |

Location: US 1, 1 mi n. 1300 Ponce de Leon Blvd 32084. Fax: 904/829-0668. **Facility:** 115 one-bedroom standard units. 2 stories, exterior corridors. *Bath:* combo or shower only. **Parking:** on-site. **Amenities:** voice mail, safes (fee), irons, hair dryers. **Dining:** 24 hours. **Pool(s):** outdoor. **Guest Services:** valet and coin laundry. **Business Services:** meeting rooms. **Cards:** AX, CB, DC, DS, JC, MC, VI. **Special Amenities:** free local telephone calls and free room upgrade (subject to availability with advance reservations).

Small-scale Hotel

(See color ad below)

SOME UNITS

When You Really Need to Speak Their Language... Let the IDP Speak for You

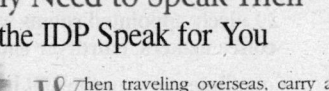

When traveling overseas, carry an **International Driving Permit...** even if you're not planning to drive. Should you need to communicate with foreign authorities, this recognizable form of identification can help you get on your way more quickly. Valid in over 150 countries, the permit contains information translated into ten languages.

Before you travel the world, travel to any AAA office for your International Driving Permit. Bring your valid U.S. driver's license, $10, and two passport-size photos (also available at AAA offices).

Travel With Someone You Trust®

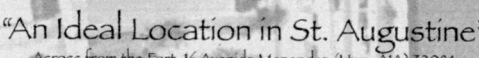

MERIDA MOTEL

Phone: (904)825-2398 **15**

(AAA) (SAVE)

♦♦♦♦

Motel

All Year 1P: $39-$99 2P: $49-$129 XP: $10 D12
Location: Just s of jct US 1 and SR 16. 2150 N Ponce de Leon Blvd 32084. Fax: 904/824-7822. **Facility:** 18 one-bedroom standard units, some with kitchens and/or whirlpools. 2 stories, exterior corridors. **Parking:** on-site. **Terms:** weekly rates available. **Amenities:** *Some:* hair dryers. **Pool(s):** outdoor. **Business Services:** fax. **Cards:** AX, DS, MC, VI. **Special Amenities:** free local telephone calls and free newspaper.

SOME UNITS

MONTEREY INN

Phone: 904/824-4482 **28**

(AAA) (SAVE)

♦♦♦♦

Small-scale Hotel

(See color ad p 886)

All Year 1P: $69-$150 2P: $69-$150 XP: $10 F
Location: US 1 business route and SR A1A; center; in historic district. 16 Avenida Menendez 32084. Fax: 904/829-8854. **Facility:** Smoke free premises. 59 one-bedroom standard units, some with kitchens. 2 stories, exterior corridors. *Bath:* combo or shower only. **Parking:** on-site. **Terms:** 2-3 night minimum stay - seasonal and/or weekends, cancellation fee imposed. **Amenities:** voice mail, hair dryers. **Dining:** 7 am-9 pm. **Pool(s):** outdoor. **Business Services:** fax. **Cards:** AX, CB, DC, DS, JC, MC, VI.

SOME UNITS

OLD CITY HOUSE INN & RESTAURANT

Phone: 904/826-0113 **36**

♦♦♦

Bed & Breakfast

Property failed to provide current rates
Location: Center. Located across from the Lightner Museum. 115 Cordova St 32084. **Facility:** In the Spanish historic district, this 19th-century building offers comfortably decorated guest rooms with an old-world feel. Smoke free premises. 7 one-bedroom standard units, some with whirlpools. 2 stories, exterior corridors. *Bath:* combo or shower only. **Parking:** on-site. **Amenities:** *Some:* CD players. **Dining:** restaurant, see separate listing. **Leisure Activities:** bicycles. **Guest Services:** complimentary evening beverages: Fri & Sat.

PEACE AND PLENTY INN

Phone: (904)829-8209 **38**

(AAA) (SAVE)

♦♦♦♦

Bed & Breakfast

All Year [BP] 1P: $119-$209 2P: $119-$209 XP: $35
Location: Just w of Lightner Museum; just s of King St via Granada St. 87 Cedar St 32084. Fax: 904/829-8209. **Facility:** This restored Victorian from the Henry Flagler era features extensive common areas and picturesque gardens; some rooms have a fireplace. Smoke free premises. 6 one-bedroom standard units with whirlpools, some with kitchens. 2 stories, interior corridors. **Parking:** on-site. **Terms:** age restrictions may apply, 7 day cancellation notice-fee imposed, weekly rates available, package plans, no pets allowed (owner's pets on premises). **Amenities:** irons, hair dryers. **Guest Services:** complimentary evening beverages. **Cards:** AX, DC, DS, MC, VI. **Special Amenities:** free full breakfast and free local telephone calls.

SOME UNITS

RAMADA LIMITED *Book at aaa.com*

Phone: 904/829-5643 **6**

(AAA) (SAVE)

♦♦♦

Motel

1/31-4/30 & 10/1-11/30 [CP] 1P: $79-$109 2P: $79-$109
5/1-9/30 [CP] 1P: $69-$109 2P: $69-$109
12/1-1/30 [CP] 1P: $69-$99 2P: $69-$99
Location: I-95, exit 318, just w. 2535 SR 16 32092. Fax: 904/829-0804. **Facility:** 140 units. 139 one-bedroom standard units. 1 one-bedroom suite. 2 stories, exterior corridors. **Parking:** on-site. **Terms:** small pets only ($15 extra charge). **Amenities:** voice mail, safes, irons, hair dryers. **Pool(s):** outdoor, wading. **Guest Services:** coin laundry. **Business Services:** meeting rooms. **Cards:** AX, DS, MC, VI. **Special Amenities:** free continental breakfast and free local telephone calls.

SOME UNITS

ST. FRANCIS INN *Book at aaa.com*

Phone: (904)824-6068 **42**

(AAA) (SAVE)

♦♦♦♦

Historic Bed
& Breakfast

All Year 1P: $119-$239 2P: $119-$239 XP: $20 D
Location: Just s; in the historic district. 279 St George St 32084. Fax: 904/810-5525. **Facility:** This inn dating to the late 1700s has units in several different buildings and features a courtyard with tropical plants. Smoke free premises. 17 units. 13 one-bedroom standard units, some with whirlpools. 4 one-bedroom suites ($149-$249), some with whirlpools. 3 stories (no elevator), interior/exterior corridors. *Bath:* combo or shower only. **Parking:** on-site. **Terms:** age restrictions may apply, 7 day cancellation notice-fee imposed, package plans, small pets only ($10 extra charge, in designated units). **Amenities:** voice mail, irons, hair dryers. **Pool(s):** small outdoor. **Leisure Activities:** beach accessories, bicycles. **Guest Services:** complimentary evening beverages. **Cards:** AX, CB, DC, DS, MC, VI. **Special Amenities:** free full breakfast and free local telephone calls.

SOME UNITS

SCOTTISH INNS *Book at aaa.com*

Phone: (904)824-2871 **21**

(AAA) (SAVE)

♦♦♦

Motel

All Year 1P: $50-$110 2P: $50-$110 XP: $10 F17
Location: Old Mission and San Marco aves; center. Located across from Mission of Nombre De Dios; on route of train. 110 San Marco Ave 32084. Fax: 904/826-4149. **Facility:** 27 one-bedroom standard units. 1-2 stories (no elevator), exterior corridors. **Parking:** on-site. **Terms:** cancellation fee imposed, small pets only ($10-$20 extra charge). **Pool(s):** outdoor. **Business Services:** fax. **Cards:** AX, DS, MC, VI. **Special Amenities:** free local telephone calls.

SOME UNITS

(See map and index starting on p. 874)

SLEEP INN *Book at aaa.com*   Phone: 904/825-4535 **41**

AAA [SAVE]   6/1-9/10   1P: $75-$199   2P: $75-$199   XP: $10   F16
            2/10-5/31   1P: $69-$199   2P: $69-$199   XP: $10   F16
WWW WWW   12/1-2/9 & 9/11-11/30   1P: $49-$99   2P: $49-$99   XP: $10   F16
Small-scale Hotel **Location:** 1.3 mi s of Bridge of Lions on SR A1A. 601 Anastasia Blvd 32084. Fax: 904/829-8963. **Facility:** 50 one-
bedroom standard units. 2 stories, interior corridors. *Bath:* combo or shower only. **Parking:** on-site.
Amenities: irons, hair dryers. **Pool(s):** outdoor. **Leisure Activities:** whirlpool. **Business Services:** meeting
rooms. **Cards:** AX, DC, DS, MC, VI. *(See color ad below)*

SOME UNITS

TRAVELODGE & SUITES   *Book at aaa.com*   Phone: (904)829-3850 **5**

AAA [SAVE]   All Year   1P: $69-$399   2P: $69-$399   XP: $5   F12
WWW WWW   **Location:** 2 mi n, just off US 1; center. 290 San Marco Ave 32084. Fax: 904/829-0313. **Facility:** 30 one-bedroom
standard units, some with whirlpools. 2 stories (no elevator), exterior corridors. **Parking:** on-site. **Terms:** 2-3
night minimum stay - seasonal, cancellation fee imposed. **Amenities:** safes (fee), irons, hair dryers.
Small-scale Hotel **Pool(s):** outdoor. **Guest Services:** coin laundry, airport transportation-St. Augustine Airport, area
transportation-sightseeing trains. **Business Services:** fax. **Cards:** AX, DC, DS, MC, VI. **Special Amenities:**
free continental breakfast.

SOME UNITS

WORLD GOLF VILLAGE RENAISSANCE RESORT   *Book at aaa.com*   Phone: (904)940-8000 **2**

AAA [SAVE]   2/12-4/15 & 10/1-11/30   1P: $129-$499   2P: $129-$499
            4/16-9/30   1P: $119-$499   2P: $119-$499
WWWWWW   12/1-2/11   1P: $109-$499   2P: $109-$499
Large-scale Hotel **Location:** I-95, exit 323, just w, then 2 mi follow signs. 500 S Legacy Tr 32092. Fax: 904/940-8008. **Facility:** 301
units. 271 one-bedroom standard units. 30 one-bedroom suites, some with whirlpools. 9 stories, interior
corridors. *Bath:* combo or shower only. **Parking:** valet. **Terms:** check-in 4 pm, 3 day cancellation notice-fee
imposed, $15 service charge, small pets only ($50 deposit). **Amenities:** dual phone lines, voice mail, irons, hair dryers. *Fee:*
video games, high-speed Internet. **Dining:** 6 am-10 pm. **Pool(s):** heated outdoor. **Leisure Activities:** sauna, whirlpool, beach
club, 2 lighted tennis courts, billiards, playground, exercise room, basketball, volleyball. *Fee:* golf-36 holes, golf simulator,
bicycles, massage, game room. **Guest Services:** gift shop, valet and coin laundry, area transportation (fee)-within 20 mi.
Business Services: conference facilities, business center. **Cards:** AX, CB, DC, DS, JC, MC, VI. **Special Amenities:** free
newspaper. *(See color ad below)*

SOME UNITS

(See map and index starting on p. 874)

——— WHERE TO DINE ———

95 CORDOVA   **Lunch:** $5-$12   **Dinner:** $14-$25   **Phone:** 904/810-6810   25

American   **Location:** Downtown; across from Lightner Museum and Flagler College; in Casa Monica Hotel. 95 Cordova St 32084. **Hours:** 6:45-10 am, 11-2:30 & 5-10:30 pm, Fri & Sat-11 pm. **Reservations:** suggested. **Features:** Enjoy a special experience in the newly renovated hotel, which dates to 1888. An intriguing wine list with many selections by the glass accompanies an enticing menu of steak, seafood and chicken entrees. Salmon is popular, as is the tangy Key lime pie. Dressy casual; cocktails. **Parking:** valet. **Cards:** AX, DC, DS, JC, MC, VI. **Historic**
(See color ad p 881)

A1A ALE WORKS BREWERY AND RESTAURANT   **Lunch:** $6-$9   **Dinner:** $10-$19   **Phone:** 904/829-2977   23

Caribbean   **Location:** Corner of Avenida Menendez; downtown. 1 King St 32084. **Hours:** 11 am-10:30 pm, Fri & Sat-11:30 pm. Closed: 11/23, 12/25; also for dinner 12/24. **Features:** The second-floor restaurant overlooks the bay and the Bridge of Lions. Examples of New World cuisine include seafood paella and island cavatappi pasta. The brews are renowned. For a quick bite, migrate to the lengthy list of appetizers, which includes calamari, boniachos or "hommus". Casual dress; cocktails. **Parking:** street. **Cards:** AX, DC, DS, MC, VI.

ACAPULCO MEXICAN RESTAURANT   **Lunch:** $4-$9   **Dinner:** $6-$15   **Phone:** 904/808-9933   14

Mexican   **Location:** Downtown. 12 Avenida Menendez 32084. **Hours:** 11 am-10 pm, Fri & Sat-11 pm, Sun-9 pm. Closed: 12/25. **Features:** Standard dishes are served in ample portions. If the wait is long, guests can go upstairs to the bar. The atmosphere is pleasant. Casual dress; cocktails. **Parking:** street. **Cards:** AX, DS, MC, VI.

AZALEA'S CAFE   **Lunch:** $5-$10   **Phone:** 904/824-6465   31

Continental   **Location:** Historic district, s of King St. 4 Aviles St 32084. **Hours:** 10 am-4 pm, Sat & Sun from 9 am. Closed: 4/16, 11/23, 12/25; also Wed, dates may vary 7/5-8/5. **Features:** Watch the horses trot by and enjoy a cozy, friendly cafe with indoor and outdoor seating. The owner/chef has drawn up a health-conscious menu with a host of vegetable selections. Breakfast is served all day, and the desserts are made right in the kitchen. Casual dress; beer & wine only. **Parking:** street. **Cards:** MC, VI.

BARNACLE BILL'S SEAFOOD HOUSE   **Lunch:** $6-$8   **Dinner:** $9-$17   **Phone:** 904/824-3663   10

Seafood   **Location:** Across from visitor's information center. 14 Castillo Dr 32084. **Hours:** 11 am-9 pm. Closed: 11/23, 12/25. **Features:** A St. Augustine tradition since 1981. Lines can be long at this popular laid back restaurant. Enjoy Minorcan clam chowder, Florida gator tail, catfish and grits, or the ever popular shrimp dinner. A good selection of steak and chicken is available for the landlubber. Casual dress; cocktails. **Parking:** on-site. **Cards:** AX, CB, DC, DS, MC, VI.

BISTRO HYPOLITA   **Lunch:** $9-$13   **Phone:** 904/808-8395   16

French   **Location:** In Historic District. 15 Hypolita St 32084. **Hours:** 11 am-4 pm. Closed major holidays; also Mon & Tues. **Reservations:** accepted. **Features:** The bistro offers lunch with a European flair featuring homemade soups, French specialty sandwiches, omelettes and traditional quiches. Casual dress; beer & wine only. **Parking:** street. **Cards:** MC, VI.

CAFE ALCAZAR   **Lunch:** $7-$10   **Phone:** 904/824-7813   29

Continental   **Location:** In Lightner Museum Complex. 25 Granada St 32084. **Hours:** 11:30 am-3 pm. Closed major holidays; also Sun & Mon. **Reservations:** not accepted. **Features:** In the deep end of what was once a huge swimming pool, the elegant cafe exudes a quaint ambience that makes it an ideal place to take your mom. Creativity characterizes the entrees. Top one off with warm oatmeal cookies coated with ice cream. Casual dress; beer & wine only; entertainment. **Parking:** on-site (fee) and street. **Cards:** MC, VI. **Historic**

CAFE SPAIN   **Lunch:** $5-$12   **Dinner:** $5-$18   **Phone:** 904/823-8585   5

Spanish   **Location:** Jct SR A1A, just n on US 1 business route. 193 San Marco Ave 32084. **Hours:** 11 am-midnight. Closed: Wed. **Features:** The casual eatery serves Spanish cuisine in a neighborhood atmosphere. Among choices are tapas, sandwiches and such traditional items as palomilla steak, Castilian picadillo and arroz con pollo. Casual dress; beer & wine only. **Parking:** on-site. **Cards:** MC, VI.

CHEESE WHEEL & SANDWICH BOARD   **Lunch:** $4-$6   **Phone:** 904/824-8286   3

American   **Location:** Just s of jct SR 16. 252 San Marco Ave 32084. **Hours:** 9:30 am-4:30 pm, Sun 10:30 am-2:30 pm. **Features:** This homestyle restaurant offers classic sandwiches and some Southern dishes that will remind you of home. Casual dress. **Parking:** on-site.

CITY GATES CAFE   **Lunch:** $4-$7   **Phone:** 904/825-4547   11

American   **Location:** Corner of Orange and Cordova sts; downtown. 3 Cordova St 32084. **Hours:** 8 am-4 pm. Closed: 11/23, 12/25. **Features:** Diners nosh on breakfast or lunch at the small cafe. The menu lists traditional breakfast fare—such as pancakes, French toast, bacon and eggs—as well as an array of salads, sandwiches and burgers for lunch. Casual dress. **Parking:** street. **Cards:** MC, VI.

COLUMBIA RESTAURANT   **Lunch:** $7-$16   **Dinner:** $15-$26   **Phone:** 904/824-3341   17

Ethnic   **Location:** St. George St at Hypolita St; center. 98 St. George St 32084. **Hours:** 11 am-9 pm, Fri & Sat-10 pm, Sun noon-9 pm. **Reservations:** suggested, for dinner. **Features:** Hearty portions of Cuban and Spanish specialties can be found in this bustling tourist destination in the historical district of St. Augustine. An informal atmosphere includes a violin trio to set the mood, and the outdoor lounge is a popular gathering spot. Parking is limited. Casual dress; cocktails. **Parking:** on-site and street. **Cards:** AX, MC, VI.

(See map and index starting on p. 874)

THE CONCH HOUSE RESTAURANT AND LOUNGE **Lunch:** $7-$16 **Dinner:** $17-$25 **Phone:** 904/829-8646 [22]
Seafood
Location: 0.7 mi s of Bridge of Lions on SR A1A, 0.3 mi n; in Conch House Marina Resort. 57 Comares Ave 32080. **Hours:** 11 am-9 pm, Fri-10 pm, Sat 8 am-10 pm, Sun 8 am-9 pm. Closed: 12/25; also for dinner 12/24. **Reservations:** not accepted. **Features:** Palm-thatched dining huts give diners unusual vantage points from which to gaze out over the Intracoastal Waterway. A Caribbean influence is evident in many dishes, which are presented with colorful garnishes. The tangy Key lime pie is homemade. Casual dress; cocktails. **Parking:** on-site and street. **Cards:** AX, DC, DS, MC, VI.

CORTESSE'S BISTRO & FLAMINGO ROOM **Lunch:** $5-$10 **Dinner:** $12-$24 **Phone:** 904/825-6775 [6]
Continental
Location: Corner of San Marco and San Carlos aves; in historic district. 172 San Marco Ave 32084. **Hours:** 11 am-10 pm, Fri & Sat-11 pm. Closed: 12/25. **Reservations:** suggested, weekends. **Features:** Such culinary treats as sauteed veal with crabmeat are dished up in the late-19th-century house. The Flamingo Room, a martini bar features local musicians, jazz and '40s contemporary music. Works by local artists enliven the walls of the restaurant. Smoking is permitted in the Flamingo Room. Casual dress; cocktails; entertainment. **Parking:** on-site. **Cards:** AX, DS, MC, VI. **Historic**

CREEKSIDE DINERY **Dinner:** $6-$19 **Phone:** 904/829-6113 [32]
Seafood
Location: Just e of US 1; just n of jct SR 312. 160 Nix Boatyard Rd 32084. **Hours:** 5 pm-9 pm, Fri & Sat-10 pm. Closed: 1/1, 11/23, 12/25; also Mon off season. **Features:** Settle into a rocking chair and relax in this quaint, Southern-style atmosphere complete with a jasmine-entwined, columned porch under sheltering oaks and magnolias. Well-chosen spices enliven entrees served with sweet potato compote and Indian corn. Casual dress; cocktails. **Parking:** on-site. **Cards:** AX, DC, DS, MC, VI.

DENOEL FRENCH PASTRY SHOP **Lunch:** $7-$9 **Phone:** 904/829-3974 [26]
French
Location: In historic district; just s of the plaza. 212 Charlotte St 32084. **Hours:** 10 am-5 pm. Closed major holidays; also Mon & Tues. **Reservations:** accepted. **Features:** A local favorite since 1966, this nifty, out-of-the-way place features a bakery that's the real reason to visit. Scrumptious croissants and wonderful pastries are all baked right on the premises. Sandwiches, soups, and salads are also a lunch-time treat. Casual dress. **Parking:** street.

FIRST WOK CHINESE FOOD **Lunch:** $4-$13 **Dinner:** $4-$13 **Phone:** 904/829-1411 [34]
Chinese
Location: On US 1, just nw of jct SR 312; in Seabridge Square. 1835 US 1 S #139 32084. **Hours:** 11 am-10:30 pm, Fri & Sat-11 pm, Sun noon-10 pm. **Features:** Although seating in the casual eatery is limited, the menu is far from it. Among some 135 items are egg foo yong, mu shu, chow mein, lo mein and varied house specialties, including happy family, seafood delight and Gen. Tso's chicken. Casual dress. **Parking:** on-site. **Cards:** MC, VI.

FLORIDA CRACKER CAFE **Lunch:** $6-$12 **Dinner:** $8-$15 **Phone:** 904/829-0397 [15]
American
Location: Center; in historic district. 81 St. George St 32084. **Hours:** 11 am-4 & 5-9 pm, Fri & Sat from 5 pm, Sun 11 am-8 pm. Closed: 11/23, 12/25. **Features:** Guests can take in the Old World charm of historic St. Augustine from the casual dining room, in which the works of community artists are displayed. Seating on the landscaped garden patio also is an option. Casual dress; beer & wine only. **Parking:** on-site. **Cards:** DS, MC, VI.

GYPSY CAB COMPANY **Lunch:** $5-$10 **Dinner:** $15-$21 **Phone:** 904/824-8244 [30]
Ethnic
Location: On SR A1A, 1 mi s of the Bridge of Lions. 828 Anastasia Blvd 32080. **Hours:** 11 am-3 & 4:30-10 pm, Fri & Sat-11 pm, Sun 10:30 am-4 & 4:30-10 pm. Closed: 7/4, 12/25. **Features:** A casual atmosphere with an eclectic decor. The "surprise" menu changes daily, reflecting cuisine from around the world served up in hearty portions. Mainstays include black bean soup and Key lime and peanut butter pies. Come early for specials. Casual dress; cocktails. **Parking:** on-site and street. **Cards:** AX, CB, DC, DS, MC, VI.

HABANA VILLAGE CAFE **Lunch:** $10-$12 **Dinner:** $10-$20 **Phone:** 904/827-1700 [24]
Cuban
Location: Jct SR A1A/US Business Rt 1(Avenida Menendez). 1 King St #103 32084. **Hours:** noon-9 pm. Closed: Tues. **Features:** In the heart of the historic district, the cafe offers seating at windowside tables that afford a view of horse-drawn carriages wandering by or interior tables that are nearer the Latin entertainers known to perform here. Cuban-focused entrees include sweet plantains, chicken with yellow rice and black beans. Flan for dessert is a must-try. Casual dress; cocktails; entertainment. **Parking:** street. **Cards:** MC, VI.

J. J.'S HERITAGE CAFE **Lunch:** $5-$15 **Dinner:** $5-$15 **Phone:** 904/824-2784 [21]
American
Location: Just s of jct Cordova St; in historic district; in Heritage Walk Mall. 61 Treasury St 32084. **Hours:** 11 am-9 pm. **Features:** Diners can enjoy a fresh delicatessen-style sandwich or a yummy bacon cheeseburger at this spot in the heart of the historic district. Those with heartier appetites might try the fresh grouper plate, which is served with French fries, slaw and garlic bread. Casual dress; beer & wine only. **Parking:** on-site (fee). **Cards:** MC, VI.

KING'S HEAD BRITISH PUB **Lunch:** $4-$13 **Dinner:** $4-$13 **Phone:** 904/823-9787 [1]
English
Location: 6 mi n. 6460 US Hwy 1 N 32084. **Hours:** 11:30 am-midnight. Closed: 11/23, 12/25; also Mon. **Features:** Owned and operated by an English chef, the authentic British pub delivers a wide selection of beers and hearty meals. Enjoy Scotch egg, bangers and mash, Cornish pastry or fish and chips. British keepsakes line the walls of the friendly restaurant. Casual dress; beer & wine only. **Parking:** on-site. **Cards:** AX, DC, DS, MC, VI.

LA PARISIENNE-CONTINENTAL CUISINE **Lunch:** $5-$12 **Dinner:** $19-$50 **Phone:** 904/829-0055 [18]
French
Location: Corner of Spanish St. 60 Hypolita St 32084. **Hours:** 11 am-2:30 & 5-close, Sat from 5 pm; Sunday brunch. Closed: 9/7-9/21. **Reservations:** suggested. **Features:** Sesame ahi tuna and a warm spinach salad followed by crispy duck au poivre is a sample of what awaits patrons of the French-inspired restaurant. The chef also has a tasting menu that pairs wines with each course. Casual dress; beer & wine only. **Parking:** street. **Cards:** AX, DS, MC, VI.

(See map and index starting on p. 874)

LA PENTOLA
Continental
ᗯᗯᗯᗯ

Lunch: $7-$18   **Dinner:** $11-$22   **Phone:** 904/824-3282   19
Location: Jct US 1 and SR 207. 58 Charlotte St 32084. **Hours:** 11 am-3 & 5-10 pm, Sun 9 am-3 & 5-9 pm. Closed: Mon. **Reservations:** accepted. **Features:** The restaurant offers creative continental cuisine featuring fresh seafood, wild game and exotic specialties. Casual dress; beer & wine only. **Parking:** on-site. **Cards:** AX, DS, MC, VI.   ⑤M

LE PAVILLON
Continental
ᗯᗯ ᗯᗯ

Lunch: $5-$13   **Dinner:** $14-$27   **Phone:** 904/824-6202   9
Location: 0.8 mi n on SR A1A; just n of Mulberry St. 45 San Marco Ave 32084. **Hours:** 11:30 am-2:30 & 5-10 pm. **Reservations:** suggested, weekends. **Features:** Antiques and fresh flowers set the stage for quiet, intimate dining in an old-style house. A varied menu offers selections ranging from light dining, to more robust entrees like the marinated rack of lamb. Tiramisu is a house specialty. Dressy casual; cocktails. **Parking:** on-site. **Cards:** CB, DC, DS, MC, VI.

MARTY'S SEAFOOD & STEAK HOUSE
American
ᗯᗯ ᗯᗯ

Lunch: $8-$10   **Dinner:** $13-$25   **Phone:** 904/829-8679   4
Location: Southwest corner of US 1 N and SR 16. 2703 Ponce de Leon Blvd 32085. **Hours:** 4 pm-9 pm, Fri-Sun from 11:30 am. Closed: 12/25; also 3rd week in Dec. **Features:** A different fresh-baked bread is offered each day, and seafood selections like the half lobster stuffed with crab meat are enjoyed in a nautical antique decor. If you can save room, indulge in the Key lime pie. A well-trained staff keeps the pace smooth. Casual dress; cocktails. **Parking:** on-site. **Cards:** DS, MC, VI.

MI CASA
American
ᗯᗯ

Lunch: $5-$8   **Dinner:** $5-$8   **Phone:** 904/824-9317   13
Location: Jct Cuna St, just w. 69 St. George St 32084. **Hours:** 11 am-7 pm, Sat-8 pm, Sun-5 pm. Closed: 11/23, 12/25. **Features:** Shoppers can take a break from browsing along St. George Street to enjoy a quick lunch bite in the small dining room or outside on the patio. In addition to burgers, tacos, hot dogs and sandwiches, the menu features vegetarian fare and some ethnic entrees, including lasagna and picadillo. Casual dress; beer & wine only. **Parking:** street.

OLD CITY HOUSE RESTAURANT
American
ᗯᗯᗯᗯ

Lunch: $8-$10   **Dinner:** $16-$27   **Phone:** 904/826-0184   28
Location: Center; in Old City House Inn. 115 Cordova St 32084. **Hours:** 8:30-10 am, 11:30-2 & 5:30-9 pm. Closed: 1/1 & 12/25. **Reservations:** accepted. **Features:** In a 19th-century building in the Spanish historic district, the dining room has an upscale country-inn feel. The cuisine reflects influences ranging from Thailand to the Lowcountry. Ostrich is a signature dish. The talented staff prepares many of the fresh ingredients on the premises. Dressy casual; cocktails. **Parking:** on-site. **Cards:** AX, DC, DS, MC, VI.

RAINTREE RESTAURANT   *Menu on aaa.com*
AAA
ᗯᗯᗯᗯ
Continental

Dinner: $15-$32   **Phone:** 904/824-7211   8
Location: 1 mi n of Bridge of Lions. 102 San Marco Ave 32084. **Hours:** 5 pm-9:30 pm, Sat-10 pm. Closed: 12/25. **Reservations:** suggested. **Features:** A rambling Victorian home with brick courtyards, an aviary and antiques provides the setting for outstanding, creative selections like the lamb chop in a potato basket accompanied by mini zucchini and yellow squash. Be sure to save room for dessert. Casual dress; cocktails. **Parking:** on-site. **Cards:** AX, DC, MC, VI.   ⓨ

SCHOONER'S SEAFOOD HOUSE
Seafood
ᗯᗯ

Lunch: $6-$8   **Dinner:** $8-$16   **Phone:** 904/826-0233   2
Location: Just n of jct San Marco Ave. 3560 N Ponce de Leon Blvd 32084. **Hours:** 11 am-9 pm. **Features:** Fresh seafood is either lightly fried, broiled or grilled. Out-of-the-creek specials center on frog legs, alligator tail and catfish. A children's menu is offered. Casual dress. **Parking:** on-site. **Cards:** AX, MC, VI.

SONNY'S REAL PIT BAR-B-Q
Barbecue
ᗯᗯ

Lunch: $4-$14   **Dinner:** $4-$14   **Phone:** 904/824-3220   33
Location: I-95, exit 318, just w. 1720 US 1 32084. **Hours:** 11 am-9:30 pm, Fri & Sat-10 pm. Closed: 11/23, 12/25. **Features:** Barbecue chicken, ribs and pulled pork are done right: slowly cooked over a hardwood fire then coated in sauce. Also tempting are smoked turkey, fried catfish and charbroiled chicken. A casual family atmosphere surrounds patrons. Casual dress. **Parking:** on-site. **Cards:** AX, MC, VI.

TAVERN ON THE BAY
American
ᗯᗯ

Lunch: $5-$17   **Dinner:** $8-$17   **Phone:** 904/810-1919   20
Location: On bayfront; in historic downtown area. 20 Avenida Menendez 32221. **Hours:** 11:30 am-9 pm, Fri & Sat-10 pm. **Reservations:** accepted. **Features:** Diners can engage in people- or whale-watching at this bayfront establishment. Such menu offerings as gourmet burgers and seafood all are labeled with creative names from jolly old England. The house is famous for its many appetizers, particularly spicy chicken wings. Casual dress; cocktails. **Parking:** on-site (fee). **Cards:** AX, MC, VI.

THEOS' RESTAURANT
AAA
ᗯᗯ
American

Lunch: $5-$8   **Phone:** 904/824-5022   27
Location: Jct US 1 and King St, just e. 169 W King St 32084. **Hours:** 6:30 am-3 pm, Sat-noon. Closed: 11/23, 12/24, 12/25; also Sun. **Features:** A small, attractive spot that is popular with locals, the decor reflects St. Augustine's rich history, with vintage photos and paintings by local artists. Generous portions of pastitso, (Greek lasagna) and homemade bread are highlights of a varied menu. Casual dress. **Parking:** on-site. **Cards:** AX, DS, MC, VI.

WHITE LION RESTAURANT
American
ᗯᗯ ᗯᗯ

Lunch: $7-$14   **Dinner:** $7-$14   **Phone:** 904/829-2388   12
Location: Historic district across street from fort; center. 20 Cuna St 32084. **Hours:** 11 am-9 pm, Sat 11:30 am-10 pm, Sun 11 am-10 pm. Closed: 11/23, 12/25. **Features:** Located in the historic district, White Lion offers indoor and outdoor dining in the tradition of old English taverns. The menu spotlights grilled, blackened and fried seafood, and desserts like Key Lime pie. Florida folk music is featured on weekends. Casual dress; cocktails. **Parking:** street. **Cards:** MC, VI.

WOODY'S BAR-B-Q
Barbecue
ᗯᗯ ᗯᗯ

Lunch: $8-$14   **Dinner:** $8-$14   **Phone:** 904/819-8880   35
Location: On SR 312 W, 0.5 mi w of jct US 1; in Cobblestone Village. 135 Jenkins St 32086. **Hours:** 11 am-9 pm, Fri & Sat-10 pm. **Features:** Hand-carved meats—such as beef, pork, turkey and ribs—are slow-smoked and smothered with one of several barbecue sauces, ranging from original to sweet. Guests can watch sporting events on strategically placed television monitors while enjoying their food. Casual dress; cocktails. **Parking:** on-site. **Cards:** MC, VI.   ⑤M

(See map and index starting on p. 874)

YAHALA MEDITERRANEAN CAFE   **Lunch:** $4-$11   **Dinner:** $4-$11   **Phone:** 904/829-8336   (7)

Mediterranean
Location: 0.8 mi s of SR 16. 120 San Marco Ave 32084. **Hours:** 11 am-10 pm. Closed: 11/23, 12/25. **Reservations:** accepted. **Features:** Middle Eastern food is the name of the game. Among favorites are tabbouleh salads, meat and cheese pies, kebabs and combination plates. Casual dress. **Parking:** on-site. **Cards:** AX, CB, DC, DS, JC, MC, VI.

The following restaurants have not been evaluated by AAA but are listed for your information only.

DREAMSICLE CAFE   **Phone:** 904/829-1005

[fyi] Not evaluated. **Location:** 116 San Marco Ave 32086. **Features:** In the heart of St Augustine, this cafe is serving up all the breakfast favorites at a reasonable price.

LARRY'S GIANT SUBS   **Phone:** 904/823-0090

[fyi] Not evaluated. **Location:** I-95, exit 95, just w. 2450 SR 16, Suite 7 32092. **Features:** Larry's is a deli with big ideas. The big subs are packed with big flavor and plenty of your favorite fixings and condiments.

ST. AUGUSTINE BEACH pop. 4,683   (See map and index starting on p. 874)

———— WHERE TO STAY ————

BEACHFRONT BED & BREAKFAST   **Phone:** (904)461-8727   54

All Year	1P: $159-$249	2P: $159-$249	XP: $40

Bed & Breakfast
Location: Jct SR 312 and A1A, 1 mi e. 1 F St 32080. Fax: 904/471-6779. **Facility:** Breakfast can be taken upstairs with an ocean view at this property, where elegant wood accents contribute to a warm, cottage feel. Smoke free premises. 6 one-bedroom standard units. 2 stories, interior/exterior corridors. *Bath:* combo or shower only. **Parking:** on-site. **Terms:** 2 night minimum stay - weekends, age restrictions may apply, 10 day cancellation notice. **Amenities:** DVD players, CD players. **Pool(s):** outdoor. **Leisure Activities:** whirlpool, beach accessories, bicycles. **Cards:** AX, CB, DC, DS, MC, VI.

SOME UNITS

BEST WESTERN OCEAN INN   *Book at aaa.com*   **Phone:** (904)471-8010   59

2/3-9/9	1P: $79-$199	2P: $79-$199	XP: $10	F17
12/1-2/2 & 9/10-11/30	1P: $69-$159	2P: $69-$159	XP: $10	F17

Small-scale Hotel
Location: 2 mi s of jct SR 312. 3955 A1A S 32080. Fax: 904/460-9124. **Facility:** 34 units. 33 one-bedroom standard units. 1 one-bedroom suite with whirlpool. 2 stories, exterior corridors. **Parking:** on-site. **Amenities:** irons, hair dryers. **Pool(s):** heated outdoor. **Leisure Activities:** beach access. **Guest Services:** coin laundry. **Cards:** AX, CB, DC, DS, MC, VI. **Special Amenities:** early check-in/late check-out and preferred room (subject to availability with advance reservations).

SOME UNITS

CASTILLO REAL RESORT HOTEL BY CLARION COLLECTION   *Book at aaa.com*   **Phone:** 904/471-3505   52

Small-scale Hotel
Property failed to provide current rates
Location: On Business Rt SR A1A, 1.3 mi s of jct SR 312: 530 SR A1A Beach Blvd 32080. Fax: 904/471-6946. **Facility:** 60 one-bedroom standard units, some with whirlpools. 4 stories, interior corridors. *Bath:* combo or shower only. **Parking:** on-site. **Terms:** check-in 4 pm. **Amenities:** DVD players, high-speed Internet, voice mail, irons, hair dryers. **Pool(s):** outdoor. **Leisure Activities:** sauna, whirlpool, steamroom. *Fee:* massage. **Guest Services:** coin laundry.

COMFORT INN AT ST. AUGUSTINE BEACH   *Book at aaa.com*   **Phone:** 904/471-1474   57

2/1-7/31	1P: $89-$107	2P: $89-$107	XP: $10	F18
12/1-1/31	1P: $79-$99	2P: $79-$99	XP: $10	F18
8/1-11/30	1P: $69-$79	2P: $69-$79	XP: $10	F18

Small-scale Hotel
Location: On Business Rt SR A1A, 1.6 mi s of jct SR 312 and A1A. 901 A1A Beach Blvd 32080. Fax: 904/461-9659. **Facility:** 70 one-bedroom standard units, some with whirlpools. 3 stories, exterior corridors. **Parking:** on-site. **Terms:** cancellation fee imposed, pets ($15 extra charge). **Amenities:** voice mail, irons, hair dryers. **Pool(s):** heated outdoor. **Leisure Activities:** whirlpool. **Guest Services:** coin laundry. **Cards:** AX, CB, DC, DS, MC, VI. **Special Amenities:** free continental breakfast and free local telephone calls.

SOME UNITS
FEE

DAYS INN-ST. AUGUSTINE BEACH   **Phone:** (904)461-9990   53

2/3-3/30 [ECP]	1P: $69-$150	2P: $69-$150	XP: $10	F18
3/31-8/31 [ECP]	1P: $59-$150	2P: $59-$150	XP: $10	F18
9/1-11/30 [ECP]	1P: $49-$130	2P: $49-$130	XP: $10	F18
12/1-2/2 [ECP]	1P: $49-$99	2P: $49-$99	XP: $10	F18

Small-scale Hotel
Location: On Business Rt SR A1A, 1.3 mi s of jct SR 312 and A1A. 541 A1A Beach Blvd 32080. Fax: 904/471-4774. **Facility:** 50 units. 48 one-bedroom standard units. 2 one-bedroom suites with whirlpools. 2 stories, exterior corridors. **Parking:** on-site. **Terms:** package plans. **Amenities:** irons, hair dryers. **Pool(s):** outdoor. **Leisure Activities:** whirlpool. **Guest Services:** coin laundry. **Business Services:** fax. **Cards:** AX, CB, DC, DS, MC, VI. **Special Amenities:** free expanded continental breakfast and free local telephone calls. *(See color ad p 893)*

SOME UNITS

(See map and index starting on p. 874)

HAMPTON INN-ST. AUGUSTINE BEACH   *Book at aaa.com*   **Phone:** (904)471-4000   **51**
▼▼ ▼▼   2/2-9/10 [ECP]   1P: $109-$219   2P: $109-$229   XP: $10   F17
12/1-2/1 & 9/11-11/30 [ECP]   1P: $89-$189   2P: $99-$199   XP: $10   F17
Small-scale Hotel   **Location:** On Business Rt SR A1A, 1.3 mi s of jct SR 312 and A1A. 430 A1A Beach Blvd 32080. Fax: 904/471-4888. **Facility:** 100 one-bedroom standard units, some with whirlpools. 4 stories, interior corridors. *Bath:* combo or shower only. **Parking:** on-site. **Terms:** 2-6 night minimum stay - seasonal and/or weekends. **Amenities:** video games (fee), dual phone lines, voice mail, irons, hair dryers. **Pool(s):** outdoor. **Leisure Activities:** whirlpool, exercise room, volleyball. **Guest Services:** coin laundry. **Business Services:** meeting rooms. **Cards:** AX, CB, DC, DS, MC, VI.

SOME UNITS
(ASK) (SD) (TI+) (&) (🏊) (☓) (🎬) (DATA PORT) (💻) / (☓) (🖥) (🖨) /

HILTON GARDEN INN-ST. AUGUSTINE BEACH   *Book at aaa.com*   **Phone:** (904)471-5559   **50**
▼▼ ▼▼   All Year   1P: $99-$229   2P: $99-$229
Location: Jct SR 312 and A1A, 1.2 mi e. 401 A1A Beach Blvd 32084. Fax: 904/471-7146. **Facility:** 83 units. 81 one-bedroom standard units, some with whirlpools. 3 stories, interior corridors. *Bath:* combo or shower only. **Parking:** on-site. **Terms:** cancellation fee imposed, [BP] & [ECP] meal plans available, package plans, 3% service charge. **Amenities:** video games (fee), high-speed Internet, dual phone lines, voice mail, irons, hair dryers. **Pool(s):** outdoor. **Leisure Activities:** whirlpool, exercise room. **Guest Services:** sundries, valet and coin laundry. **Business Services:** meeting rooms, business center. **Cards:** AX, CB, DC, DS, MC, VI.

SOME UNITS
(ASK) (SD) (&) (🏊) (🎬) (DATA PORT) (🖥) (🖨) (💻) / (☓) /

HOLIDAY INN-ST AUGUSTINE BEACH   *Book at aaa.com*   **Phone:** (904)471-2555   **56**
(AAA) (SAVE)   2/1-9/4   1P: $135-$169   2P: $135-$169
▼▼ ▼▼   12/1-1/31 & 9/5-11/30   1P: $114-$149   2P: $114-$149
Small-scale Hotel   **Location:** On Business Rt SR A1A, 1.8 mi s of jct SR 312 and A1A. 860 A1A Beach Blvd 32080. Fax: 904/461-8450. **Facility:** 152 one-bedroom standard units. 5 stories, interior/exterior corridors. *Bath:* combo or shower only. **Parking:** on-site. **Terms:** check-in 4 pm, 2 night minimum stay - seasonal and/or weekends, small pets only ($20 extra charge). **Amenities:** voice mail, irons, hair dryers. **Dining:** 7 am-11:30 & 5-10 pm, Sun 7 am-noon & 5-10 pm, cocktails. **Pool(s):** outdoor. **Leisure Activities:** exercise room. **Guest Services:** valet and coin laundry. **Business Services:** meeting rooms. **Special Amenities:** free newspaper.

SOME UNITS
(🛏) (🍽) (🍸) (&) (🏊) (🎬) (DATA PORT) (💻) / (☓) (🖥) /
FEE   FEE

LA FIESTA OCEAN INN & SUITES   *Book at aaa.com*   **Phone:** (904)471-2220   **55**
(AAA) (SAVE)   2/17-9/4 [ECP]   1P: $100-$300   2P: $100-$300   XP: $10   F11
▼▼ ▼▼   12/1-2/16 & 9/5-11/30 [ECP]   1P: $80-$200   2P: $80-$200   XP: $10   F11
Motel   **Location:** On Business Rt A1A, 1.7 mi s of jct SR 312 and A1A. 810 A1A Beach Blvd 32080. Fax: 904/471-0186. **Facility:** 44 units. 38 one-bedroom standard units, some with whirlpools. 6 one-bedroom suites, some with whirlpools. 2 stories, exterior corridors. *Bath:* combo or shower only. **Parking:** on-site. **Terms:** 2 night minimum stay - seasonal and/or weekends, 7 day cancellation notice, weekly rates available. **Amenities:** hair dryers. *Some:* safes, irons. **Pool(s):** outdoor. **Leisure Activities:** *Fee:* miniature golf. **Guest Services:** coin laundry. **Cards:** AX, CB, DC, DS, MC, VI. **Special Amenities:** free expanded continental breakfast and free newspaper.
(See color ad p 885)

SOME UNITS
(SD) (&) (🏊) (🎬) (DATA PORT) (🖥) (🖨) (💻) / (☓) /

RAMADA LIMITED, AT THE BEACH   *Book at aaa.com*   **Phone:** (904)471-1440   **58**
▼▼ ▼▼   2/1-7/31   1P: $69-$109   2P: $69-$109   XP: $5   F17
8/1-11/30   1P: $59-$89   2P: $59-$89   XP: $5   F17
Small-scale Hotel   12/1-1/31   1P: $59-$79   2P: $59-$79   XP: $5   F17
Location: On Business Rt SR A1A, 2 mi s of jct SR 312 and A1A. 894 A1A Beach Blvd 32084. Fax: 904/471-2922. **Facility:** 38 one-bedroom standard units, some with whirlpools. 3 stories, interior corridors. *Bath:* combo or shower only. **Parking:** on-site. **Terms:** 2 night minimum stay, 30 day cancellation notice-fee imposed, [CP] meal plan available, package plans. **Amenities:** voice mail, irons, hair dryers. **Pool(s):** outdoor. **Guest Services:** coin laundry. **Cards:** AX, DC, DS, MC, VI.

SOME UNITS
(ASK) (SD) (TI+) (&) (🏊) (🎬) (DATA PORT) (💻) / (☓) (🖥) (🖨) /

(See map and index starting on p. 874)

SUPER 8 BY THE BEACH   *Book at aaa.com*   Phone: (904)471-2330   🔲49

AAA SAVE   2/1-3/31 & 6/29-11/30 [CP]   1P: $59-$229   2P: $59-$229
                 12/1-1/31 & 4/1-6/28 [CP]   1P: $49-$129   2P: $49-$129
🔷🔷   **Location:** On Business Rt SR A1A, 1 mi s of jct SR 312 and A1A. 311 A1A Beach Blvd 32080. Fax: 904/471-1018.
Small-scale Hotel **Facility:** 50 one-bedroom standard units. 2 stories, exterior corridors. **Parking:** on-site. **Terms:** pets ($15
                 fee). **Pool(s):** outdoor. **Leisure Activities:** whirlpool. **Guest Services:** coin laundry. **Cards:** AX, CB, DC,
                 DS, JC, MC, VI. **Special Amenities:** free continental breakfast and free local telephone calls.

SOME UNITS

（icons）

———— **WHERE TO DINE** ————

AMICI ITALIAN RESTAURANT   Lunch: $5-$9   Dinner: $10-$18   Phone: 904/461-0102   🔲44
🔷🔷 🔷🔷   **Location:** Corner of SR 312. 1915 B A1A Beach Blvd 32080. **Hours:** 11:30 am-10 pm. Closed: 1/1, 11/23, 12/25.
Italian   **Features:** Sicily is the inspiration for the restaurant's extensive menu, which lists pasta dishes, pizzas and
             calzones as entrees and such homemade desserts as tiramisu and Italian rum cake. Casual dress;
             cocktails. **Parking:** on-site. **Cards:** AX, DC, DS, MC, VI.

BEACH STREET CAFE   Lunch: $3-$7   Phone: 904/461-0500   🔲50
🔷   **Location:** Center. 4285 A1A S 32080. **Hours:** 8 am-4 pm. Closed: 4/16, 11/23, 12/25. **Features:** Breakfast
American   bagels, burritos and pastries complement selections from the coffee bar. At lunchtime, French dip,
           Philadelphia cheese steak and club sandwiches, as well as fresh salads and quiches, are among offerings.
           Casual dress. **Parking:** on-site. **Cards:** AX, MC, VI.

CAFE ATLANTICO   Dinner: $13-$21   Phone: 904/471-7332   🔲46
AAA   **Location:** 0.8 mi s of jct SR 312. 647 A1A Beach Blvd 32080. **Hours:** 5 pm-10 pm. Closed: 4/16, 12/25; also Sun.
🔷🔷🔷   **Reservations:** suggested. **Features:** Crisp, sophisticated decor welcomes guests and brightens the dining
Italian   room, in which original artwork adorns the walls. A range of specialties and delightful desserts tempt diners.
            Dressy casual; beer & wine only. **Parking:** on-site. **Cards:** AX; DC, DS, MC, VI.

SALTWATER COWBOYS   Dinner: $10-$19   Phone: 904/471-2332   🔲51
AAA   **Location:** At the western end of Dondanville Rd; off SR A1A, 0.8 mi s of southern jct SR 3. 299 Dondanville Rd 32080.
🔷🔷🔷   **Hours:** 5 pm-9 pm, Fri & Sat-10 pm. Closed major holidays; also Mon 11/1-1/31. **Features:** Travel down a
Regional   dirt road to a saltwater marsh to find this quaint, waterfront restaurant. A casual atmosphere recaptures the
American   charm of Old Florida, with a menu offering seafood, rib and chicken dishes. Casual dress; cocktails.
            Parking: on-site. **Cards:** AX, DS, MC, VI.

SEA OATS CAFFE   Lunch: $5-$9   Dinner: $11-$21   Phone: 904/471-7350   🔲47
🔷🔷   **Location:** Just n of jct SR A1A; in Anastasia Publix Plaza. 1075 A1A Beach Blvd 32080. **Hours:** 7 am-4 pm, Fri-
American   close. Closed: Mon. **Reservations:** suggested, for dinner. **Features:** Breakfast creations include a variety of
           egg sandwiches and your choice of blueberry, chocolate chip, cheddar cheese, bacon or banana pancakes.
           Casual dress. **Parking:** on-site. **Cards:** AX, DC, DS, MC, VI.

SUNSET GRILLE   Lunch: $5-$9   Dinner: $9-$20   Phone: 904/471-5555   🔲45
AAA   **Location:** On Business Rt A1A, 1.3 mi s of jct SR 312 and A1A. 421 A1A Beach Blvd 32080. **Hours:** 11 am-1 am.
🔷🔷   Closed: 12/25. **Features:** The pink-accented building and sign beckon to passersby. The casual bar and grill
Seafood   is popular with locals and tourists alike. Casual dress; cocktails. **Parking:** on-site. **Cards:** AX, DS, MC, VI.

THE WORLD FAMOUS OASIS
RESTAURANT & DECK   *Menu on aaa.com*   Lunch: $4-$14   Dinner: $4-$14   Phone: 904/471-3424   🔲49
AAA   **Location:** 0.3 mi s of SR A1A at Ocean Trace Rd. 4000 A1A S 32095. **Hours:** Open 12/1-12/4 & 12/28-11/30; 6
🔷   am-midnight. Closed: 11/23. **Features:** Bustling, friendly neighborhood spot. Join the locals for a breakfast
Seafood   of omelets or a salad for lunch. Daily dinner specials feature steak, chicken or fish. The open air deck is a
            great place to unwind after a day on the beach. Casual dress; cocktails; entertainment. **Parking:** on-site.
            Cards: AX, DC, DS, MC, VI.

ZAHARIAS RESTAURANT   Lunch: $7-$9   Dinner: $11-$20   Phone: 904/471-4799   🔲48
🔷🔷 🔷🔷   **Location:** 2 mi s of jct SR 312. 3945 A1A S 32080. **Hours:** 8 am-10 pm. Closed: 12/24.
American   **Reservations:** accepted. **Features:** In addition to seafood, steaks and pasta, enjoy homemade Greek
           specialties such as dolmathes (stuffed grape leaves) and spanakopita (spinach and cheese pie). A few
           Italian specialties are also offered. This well-established family owned and operated restaurant has a
           casual, informal atmosphere and a relaxed service style. Casual dress; cocktails. **Parking:** on-site. **Cards:** AX, DS, MC, VI.

———— *The following restaurant has not been evaluated by AAA* ————
but is listed for your information only.

VERRAZANO PIZZA & SUB   Phone: 904/461-9797
fyi   Not evaluated. **Location:** 1915 A1A Beach Blvd. **Features:** Pizzas made to your liking: piled high or piled low.
           Enjoy the friendliest of service at this happening beach place.

ST. CLOUD —See Orlando p. 831.

ST. MARKS pop. 272

——— WHERE TO STAY ———

SWEET MAGNOLIA INN
▽▽▽▽
Bed & Breakfast
Phone: 850/925-7670
All Year [BP]   1P: $85-$135   2P: $95-$145   XP: $10
Location: Center on CR 363. 803 Port Leon Dr 32355 (PO Box 335). Fax: 850/925-0569. **Facility:** This B&B, built in 1916, is nicely decorated with themed rooms with names like Sake, Safari and Magnolia. Most rooms have queen-sized poster beds. Designated smoking area. 7 one-bedroom standard units, some with whirlpools. 2 stories, interior corridors. *Bath:* combo or shower only. **Parking:** on-site. **Terms:** age restrictions may apply, 7 day cancellation notice. **Leisure Activities:** boat dock, bicycles. **Guest Services:** complimentary laundry, area transportation. **Cards:** AX, CB, DC, DS, JC, MC, VI.

SOME UNITS
(ASK) ⬛ ✕ 🎥 ☎ / VCR /

ST. PETERSBURG —See Tampa Bay p. 961.

ST. PETE BEACH —See Tampa Bay p. 1037.

SANFORD —See Orlando p. 832.

SANIBEL pop. 6,064 (See map and index starting on p. 428)

——— WHERE TO STAY ———

BEST WESTERN SANIBEL ISLAND BEACH RESORT *Book at aaa.com*
AAA (SAVE)
▽▽▽ ▽▽
Motel
Phone: (239)472-1700 [83]
2/10-4/22   1P: $320-$352
12/1-2/9 & 4/23-5/28   1P: $215-$246
5/29-11/30   1P: $184-$199
Location: Oceanfront. From causeway, 2.8 mi w on Periwinkle Way, 0.8 mi s on Tarpon Bay Rd, then 1.3 mi w. 3287 W Gulf Dr 33957. Fax: 239/472-5032. **Facility:** 45 units. 42 one-bedroom standard units, some with efficiencies. 3 two-bedroom suites with kitchens. 2 stories, exterior corridors. **Parking:** on-site. **Terms:** check-in 4 pm, 2-4 night minimum stay - seasonal and/or weekends, 14 day cancellation notice-fee imposed, [CP] meal plan available. **Amenities:** safes, irons, hair dryers. **Pool(s):** heated outdoor. **Leisure Activities:** fishing, tennis court, barbecue grills, picnic area, shell hut beach chairs, bicycles, volleyball. **Guest Services:** valet and coin laundry. **Business Services:** fax. **Cards:** AX, CB, DC, DS, MC, VI. **Special Amenities:** free continental breakfast and free newspaper.

SOME UNITS
(S/D) 🅿 🏊 🏋 ✕ VCR 📷 DATA PORT 🔌 🖥 🖳 / ✕ /

BRENNEN'S TARPON TALE INN
AAA (SAVE)
▽▽▽▽▽
Motel
Phone: (239)472-0939 [68]
2/1-4/30   1P: $139-$209   XP: $30   F10
12/1-1/31 & 5/1-5/31   1P: $109-$149   XP: $30   F10
6/1-11/30   1P: $89-$129   XP: $30   F10
Location: From causeway, 0.9 mi e at jct East Gulf Dr. 367 Periwinkle Way 33957. Fax: 239/472-6202. **Facility:** Designated smoking area. 5 units. 2 one-bedroom standard units, some with efficiencies. 3 one-bedroom suites with kitchens. 1 story, exterior corridors. *Bath:* shower only. **Parking:** on-site. **Terms:** office hours 9 am-3 pm, 35 day cancellation notice-fee imposed. **Amenities:** CD players, irons, hair dryers. *Some:* DVD players. **Leisure Activities:** whirlpool, grill, beach chairs, small lending library, bicycles. **Guest Services:** coin laundry. **Business Services:** PC, fax. **Cards:** DS, MC, VI. **Special Amenities:** free continental breakfast.

(S/D) 🍽 ✕ ✕ VCR 🎥 ☎ 🔌 🖥 🖳

COLONY RESORT
AAA (SAVE)
▽▽▽ ◆◆
Condominium
Phone: (239)472-5151 [69]
2/1-4/30   2P: $175-$210   XP: $15   F12
12/16-1/31   2P: $155-$175   XP: $15   F12
12/1-12/15 & 5/1-11/30   2P: $110-$150   XP: $15   F12
Location: From causeway, 1 mi e. 419 E Gulf Dr 33957. Fax: 239/472-3541. **Facility:** 44 one-bedroom units with kitchens. 1-2 stories, exterior corridors. **Parking:** on-site. **Terms:** office hours 9 am-5 pm, 30 day cancellation notice, package plans. **Amenities:** *Some:* CD players, irons, hair dryers. **Pool(s):** heated outdoor. **Leisure Activities:** beach access, picnic tables, barbecue grills, sun deck. **Guest Services:** coin laundry. **Business Services:** fax (fee). **Cards:** MC, VI. **Special Amenities:** free local telephone calls and free newspaper.

SOME UNITS
(S/D) 🍽 🏊 VCR 🔌 🖥 / ✕ /

HOLIDAY INN SANIBEL ISLAND *Book at aaa.com*
AAA (SAVE)
▽▽▽ ▽▽
Small-scale Hotel
Phone: (239)472-4123 [79]
2/10-4/15   1P: $299-$399   2P: $299-$399
4/16-9/3   1P: $199-$359   2P: $199-$359
9/4-11/30   1P: $169-$329   2P: $169-$329
12/1-2/9   1P: $189-$289   2P: $189-$289
Location: Oceanfront. From causeway, 0.7 mi w on Periwinkle Way, 0.5 mi s on Donax St. 1231 Middle Gulf Dr 33957. Fax: 239/472-0930. **Facility:** 98 units. 97 one-bedroom standard units, some with efficiencies. 1 one-bedroom suite with kitchen. 2 stories, exterior corridors. *Bath:* some combo or shower only. **Parking:** on-site. **Terms:** 3 day cancellation notice-fee imposed, package plans. **Amenities:** video games (fee), high-speed Internet, voice mail, safes, irons, hair dryers. **Dining:** Morgan's Forest, see separate listing. **Pool(s):** heated outdoor. **Leisure Activities:** beach cabanas & chairs, 2 tennis courts, table tennis. **Fee:** bicycles. **Guest Services:** gift shop, valet and coin laundry. **Business Services:** meeting rooms, administrative services, fax. **Cards:** AX, CB, DC, DS, JC, MC, VI. **Special Amenities:** free local telephone calls and free newspaper.

SOME UNITS
(S/D) 🍽 🍸 📶 ⬛ 🅿 🏊 ✕ 🎥 DATA PORT 🔌 🖥 🖳 / ✕ /

(See map and index starting on p. 428)

HURRICANE HOUSE　　　　　　　　　　　　　　　　　　**Phone:** (239)472-1696　84

2/3-4/20 Wkly	2P: $2485
12/1-1/5 Wkly	2P: $1505-$2380
1/6-2/2 Wkly	2P: $1610
4/21-11/30 Wkly	2P: $1505

Condominium

Location: From causeway, 2.8 mi w on Periwinkle Way, 0.8 mi s on Tarpon Bay Rd, then 0.7 mi w. 2939 W Gulf Dr 33957. Fax: 239/472-1718. **Facility:** Set on the Gulf of Mexico, the property offers large condominium units adorned with modern furnishings and many amenities. 15 two-bedroom suites with kitchens and whirlpools. 3 stories, exterior corridors. **Parking:** on-site. **Terms:** 3 night minimum stay, 30 day cancellation notice, 14 day off season-fee imposed, daily rates available. **Amenities:** video library (fee), irons. **Pool(s):** heated outdoor. **Leisure Activities:** whirlpools, tennis court. **Guest Services:** complimentary laundry. **Business Services:** fax (fee). **Cards:** AX, DS, MC, VI.

(ASK) (S🔒) (🍴→) (🏊) (VCR) (🐾) 🖥 🖨

PELICANS ROOST　　　　　　　　　　　　　　　　　　**Phone:** (239)472-2996　78

1/28-4/22 Wkly	1P: $2500
12/1-12/31 Wkly	1P: $1200-$2450
1/1-1/27 Wkly	1P: $1850
4/23-11/30 Wkly	1P: $1300-$1500

Condominium

Location: From causeway, 0.7 mi w on Periwinkle Way, 0.5 mi s. 605 Donax St 33957. Fax: 239/472-0317. **Facility:** Set on the Gulf of Mexico, each condo unit offers all of the amenities of home; enjoy a gorgeous sunset while taking a relaxing walk on the beach. 20 two-bedroom suites with kitchens, some with whirlpools. 4 stories, exterior corridors. **Parking:** on-site. **Terms:** office hours 9 am-5 pm, 7 night minimum stay, 60 day cancellation notice. **Amenities:** CD players, irons. *Some:* DVD players. **Pool(s):** heated outdoor. **Leisure Activities:** fishing, 2 lighted tennis courts, shuffleboard. **Guest Services:** complimentary laundry. **Business Services:** fax (fee). *(See color ad below)*

SOME UNITS

(🍴→) (🏊) (🎾) (VCR) (DATA PORT) 🖥 🖨 /(✕)/

SANDALFOOT CONDOMINIUM　　　　　　　　　　　　　**Phone:** (239)472-2275　71

1/28-4/21 Wkly	2P: $1545-$2395
12/1-1/27 Wkly	2P: $990-$2295
11/19-11/30 Wkly	2P: $1095-$1495
4/22-11/18 Wkly	2P: $990-$1395

Condominium

Location: Oceanfront. From causeway, 0.6 mi e. 671 E Gulf Dr 33957. Fax: 239/472-5135. **Facility:** Set on the Gulf of Mexico, each condo unit offers homelike amenities in a relaxing beach setting. 59 units. 15 one- and 44 two-bedroom suites with kitchens. 3 stories, exterior corridors. *Bath:* combo or shower only. **Parking:** on-site. **Terms:** office hours 9 am-4 pm, 3-7 night minimum stay, 60 day cancellation notice-fee imposed, $40 service charge. **Amenities:** irons, hair dryers. *Some:* DVD players, CD players, voice mail. **Pool(s):** heated outdoor. **Leisure Activities:** tennis court, shuffleboard. *Fee:* bicycles. **Guest Services:** coin laundry. **Business Services:** fax (fee). **Cards:** MC, VI. *(See color ad below)*

(🍴→) (♿) (🏊) (🎾) (VCR) (DATA PORT) 🖥 🖨 📺

(See map and index starting on p. 428)

SANIBEL ARMS WEST CONDOMINIUM Phone: (239)472-1138 72

1/28-11/30 Wkly	2P: $725-$2150
12/17-12/31 Wkly	2P: $1575-$1795
1/1-1/27 Wkly	2P: $1295-$1595
12/1-12/16 Wkly	2P: $725-$1195

Condominium

Location: From causeway, 0.4 mi e. 827 E Gulf Dr 33957. Fax: 239/472-9688. **Facility:** A bike path is featured at this property where each two-bedroom unit has a screened porch. 95 two-bedroom suites with kitchens. 2 stories, exterior corridors. **Parking:** on-site. **Terms:** office hours 8:30 am-4:30 pm, 3 night minimum stay, 60 day cancellation notice-fee imposed, daily rates available. **Amenities:** video library (fee), irons, hair dryers. *Some:* DVD players, CD players. **Pool(s):** heated outdoor. **Leisure Activities:** boat dock, 2 tennis courts, shuffleboard. *Fee:* bicycles. **Guest Services:** valet and coin laundry. **Business Services:** meeting rooms, fax (fee). **Cards:** MC, VI.

SOME UNITS

SANIBEL BEACH CLUB *Book at aaa.com* Phone: 239/472-3382 77

2/11-4/22 Wkly	1P: $2325	2P: $2325
1/28-2/10 Wkly	1P: $1925	2P: $1925
12/1-1/27 Wkly	1P: $1575	2P: $1575
4/23-11/30 Wkly	1P: $1295	2P: $1295

Condominium

Location: From causeway, 0.7 mi w on Periwinkle Way, 0.5 mi s on Donax, then just ne on Middle Gulf Dr. 626 Nerita St 33957. Fax: 239/472-8944. **Facility:** Set on the Gulf of Mexico, each condo unit offers all of the amenities of home; enjoy a gorgeous sunset while taking a relaxing walk on the beach. 31 two-bedroom suites with kitchens. 2 stories, exterior corridors. **Parking:** on-site. **Terms:** 2 night minimum stay, 30 day cancellation notice-fee imposed. **Amenities:** video library, irons. *Some:* hair dryers. **Pool(s):** heated outdoor. **Leisure Activities:** sauna, whirlpool, 2 tennis courts, bicycles, basketball, horseshoes, shuffleboard, volleyball. **Business Services:** fax (fee). **Cards:** AX, CB, DC, DS, JC, MC, VI.

FEE

SANIBEL COTTAGES Phone: (239)472-1868 86

2/3-4/20 Wkly	2P: $2800
12/1-1/5 Wkly	2P: $1820-$2660
1/6-2/2 & 4/21-11/30 Wkly	2P: $1820

Condominium

Location: From causeway, 2.8 mi on Periwinkle Way, 0.8 mi s on Tarpon Bay Rd, then 0.3 mi e. 2341 W Gulf Dr 33957. Fax: 239/472-8711. **Facility:** Set on the Gulf of Mexico, the attractively landscaped property offers large units adorned with modern furnishings and many amenities. 28 two-bedroom suites with kitchens and whirlpools. 3 stories (no elevator), exterior corridors. **Parking:** on-site. **Terms:** 3 night minimum stay, 30 day cancellation notice, 14 day off season-fee imposed, daily rates available. **Amenities:** video library (fee), safes, irons. *Some:* hair dryers. **Pool(s):** heated outdoor. **Leisure Activities:** whirlpool, limited beach access, fishing, 2 tennis courts, shuffleboard, volleyball. **Guest Services:** complimentary laundry. **Business Services:** fax (fee). **Cards:** AX, DS, MC, VI.

(See map and index starting on p. 428)

THE SANIBEL INN *Book at aaa.com* Phone: (239)472-3181 **76**

(AAA) (SAVE)
▼▼▼▼▼

2/10-4/22	1P: $213-$427
12/1-2/9 & 4/23-5/28	1P: $149-$231
5/29-11/30	1P: $116-$217

Small-scale Hotel
Location: From causeway, just w at jct Lindgren Blvd. 937 E Gulf Dr 33957. Fax: 239/472-5234. **Facility:** 92 units. 48 one-bedroom standard units. 20 one- and 24 two-bedroom suites, some with kitchens. 2-3 stories, exterior corridors. *Bath:* combo or shower only. **Parking:** on-site. **Terms:** check-in 4 pm, 14 day cancellation notice-fee imposed, package plans. **Amenities:** voice mail, safes, irons, hair dryers. **Dining:** 7:30 am-11 & 5-midnight, cocktails. **Pool(s):** heated outdoor. **Leisure Activities:** 2 tennis courts, recreation programs, barbecue grills, rental bicycles. *Fee:* kayaks, golf privileges, umbrellas, massage. **Guest Services:** gift shop, valet laundry. **Business Services:** meeting rooms, fax (fee). **Cards:** AX, CB, DC, DS, MC, VI. **Special Amenities:** free local telephone calls and free newspaper. *(See color ad p 899)*

SOME UNITS

(icons) /✕/

SANIBEL MOORINGS *Book at aaa.com* Phone: (239)472-4119 **73**

(AAA) (SAVE)
▼▼▼▼▼

2/4-4/24	1P: $227-$392	2P: $227-$392	XP: $15
1/2-2/3	1P: $198-$356	2P: $198-$356	XP: $15
12/1-1/1	1P: $134-$356	2P: $134-$356	XP: $15
4/25-11/30	1P: $147-$309	2P: $147-$309	XP: $15

Condominium
Location: From causeway, 0.4 mi e. 845 E Gulf Dr 33957 (PO Box 899). Fax: 239/472-8148. **Facility:** Screened porches add appeal to the spacious guest units of this property located in a quiet area. Designated smoking area. 112 units. 16 one-, 87 two- and 9 three-bedroom suites with kitchens. 2 stories, exterior corridors. **Parking:** on-site. **Terms:** office hours 8 am-6 pm, check-in 4:30 pm, 4-7 night minimum stay - seasonal, 30 day cancellation notice-fee imposed. **Amenities:** video library (fee), DVD players, dual phone lines, voice mail, irons, hair dryers. *Some:* video games (fee), CD players. **Pool(s):** 2 heated outdoor, wading. **Leisure Activities:** canoeing, boat dock, fishing, kayaks, 2 tennis courts, barbecue grill area, horticultural tours, lending library, exercise room. *Fee:* bicycles. **Guest Services:** valet and coin laundry. **Business Services:** meeting rooms, business center. **Cards:** MC, VI. *(See color ad below)*

(icons)

SANIBEL SIESTA CONDOMINIUM *Book at aaa.com* Phone: (239)472-4117 **80**

(AAA) (SAVE)
▼▼▼▼▼

12/17-4/19 Wkly	1P: $1456-$2470	2P: $1456-$2470	XP: $15	F6
4/20-11/30 Wkly	1P: $1000-$1360	2P: $1000-$1360	XP: $15	F6
12/1-12/16 Wkly	1P: $957-$1298	2P: $957-$1298	XP: $15	F6

Condominium
Location: Oceanfront. From causeway, 0.7 mi w on Periwinkle Way, 0.5 mi s on Donax St, then just w on Middle Gulf Dr. 1246 Fulgur St 33957. Fax: 239/472-6826. **Facility:** Set on the Gulf of Mexico, each condo unit offers all of the amenities of home; enjoy a gorgeous sunset while taking a relaxing walk on the beach. 57 two-bedroom suites with kitchens. 3 stories, exterior corridors. **Parking:** on-site. **Terms:** 3 night minimum stay - seasonal, 60 day cancellation notice-fee imposed, daily rates available. **Amenities:** voice mail, irons, hair dryers. *Some:* CD players. **Pool(s):** heated outdoor. **Leisure Activities:** fishing, 2 tennis courts, gas grills, shuffleboard. **Guest Services:** coin laundry. **Business Services:** fax (fee). **Cards:** AX, DS, MC, VI. **Special Amenities:** free local telephone calls.

SOME UNITS

(icons) /✕/

SANIBEL'S SONG OF THE SEA, A EUROPEAN-STYLE SEASIDE INN *Book at aaa.com* Phone: (239)472-2220 **74**

(AAA) (SAVE)
▼▼▼▼▼

2/10-4/22 [CP]	1P: $299-$449
12/1-2/9 & 4/23-5/28 [CP]	1P: $219-$319
5/29-11/30 [CP]	1P: $159-$249

Motel
Location: From causeway, just e. 863 E Gulf Dr 33957. Fax: 239/472-8569. **Facility:** Designated smoking area. 30 units. 22 one-bedroom standard units with efficiencies. 8 one-bedroom suites with kitchens. 2 stories, exterior corridors. **Parking:** on-site. **Terms:** office hours 8 am-11 pm, check-in 4 pm, 14 day cancellation notice-fee imposed, package plans. **Amenities:** video library, CD players, voice mail, safes, irons, hair dryers. **Pool(s):** heated outdoor. **Leisure Activities:** whirlpool, gas grill, lending library, bicycles, shuffleboard. *Fee:* golf & tennis privileges, recreational program privileges, massage. **Guest Services:** gift shop, valet and coin laundry. **Business Services:** fax (fee). **Cards:** AX, CB, DC, DS, MC, VI. **Special Amenities:** free continental breakfast and free newspaper. *(See color ad p 899)*

(icons)

(See map and index starting on p. 428)

SEASIDE INN　　*Book at aaa.com*　　　　　　　　　　Phone: (239)472-1400　　70

(AAA) (SAVE)
2/10-4/22 [CP]	1P: $319-$419
12/1-2/9 & 4/23-5/28 [CP]	1P: $239-$339
5/29-11/30 [CP]	1P: $175-$275

Motel　　**Location:** From causeway, 0.7 mi e. 541 E Gulf Dr 33957. Fax: 239/472-6518. **Facility:** Designated smoking area. 32 units. 22 one-bedroom standard units. 2 one-, 1 two- and three-bedroom suites with kitchens. 6 cottages. 1-2 stories, exterior corridors. *Bath:* combo or shower only. **Parking:** on-site. **Terms:** office hours 7:30 am-11 pm, check-in 4 pm, 14 day cancellation notice-fee imposed, package plans. **Amenities:** video library, voice mail, safes, irons, hair dryers. **Pool(s):** heated outdoor. **Leisure Activities:** fishing, gas barbecue grills, beach chairs, pool towels, bicycles, shuffleboard. **Guest Services:** gift shop, coin laundry. **Business Services:** fax (fee). **Cards:** AX, CB, DC, DS, MC, VI. *(See color ad p 899)*

⬛⬛ ⬛⬛ ⬛ ⬛ ⬛ ⬛ ⬛ ⬛ ⬛ ⬛
　　　　　FEE

SHALIMAR COTTAGE & MOTEL　　　　　　　　　　　　Phone: (239)472-1353　　85

(AAA) (SAVE)
2/1-4/30	1P: $265-$345	2P: $265-$345	XP: $20	F12
12/1-1/31	1P: $145-$345	2P: $145-$345	XP: $20	F12
5/1-5/31	1P: $166-$265	2P: $166-$265	XP: $20	F12
6/1-11/30	1P: $145-$245	2P: $145-$245	XP: $20	F12

Motel　　**Location:** From causeway, 2.8 mi w on Periwinkle Way, 0.8 mi s on Tarpon Bay Rd, then 0.5 mi w. 2823 W Gulf Dr 33957 (PO Box 389). Fax: 239/472-6430. **Facility:** 33 units. 20 one-bedroom standard units with kitchens. 2 two-bedroom suites with kitchens. 11 cottages. 1-2 stories, exterior corridors. **Parking:** on-site. **Terms:** 5-7 night minimum stay - seasonal, 45 day cancellation notice-fee imposed, weekly rates available. **Amenities:** video library, voice mail. *Some:* irons, hair dryers. **Pool(s):** heated outdoor. **Leisure Activities:** fishing, gas barbecues, basketball, shuffleboard. *Fee:* bicycles. **Guest Services:** coin laundry. **Business Services:** fax (fee). **Cards:** AX, DS, MC, VI. **Special Amenities:** free local telephone calls and preferred room (subject to availability with advance reservations).

⬛⬛ ⬛⬛ ⬛ ⬛ ⬛ ⬛ ⬛ ⬛

SHELL ISLAND BEACH CLUB　　　　　　　　　　　　Phone: (239)472-4497　　67

2/4-4/21 Wkly	2P: $2450-$2625
12/1-1/6 Wkly	2P: $1435-$2415
1/7-2/3 Wkly	2P: $1505-$1715
4/22-11/30 Wkly	2P: $1470-$1645

Condominium　　**Location:** From causeway, 1.2 mi e. 255 Periwinkle Way 33957. Fax: 239/472-4218. **Facility:** This family-oriented waterfront property has screened terraces and covered parking. 44 two-bedroom suites with kitchens. 3 stories (no elevator), exterior corridors. **Parking:** on-site. **Terms:** office hours 8:30 am-5 pm, 3 night minimum stay, 30 day cancellation notice, 14 day off season-fee imposed, daily rates available. **Amenities:** video library (fee), CD players, irons. *Some:* hair dryers. **Pool(s):** 2 heated outdoor. **Leisure Activities:** sauna, whirlpool, tennis court, bicycles, shuffleboard. **Guest Services:** gift shop, complimentary laundry. **Business Services:** meeting rooms. **Cards:** AX, DS, MC, VI.

(ASK) ⬛⬛ ⬛⬛ ⬛ ⬛ ⬛ ⬛ ⬛ ⬛

SUNDIAL BEACH RESORT　　*Book at aaa.com*　　　　　Phone: (239)472-4151　　81

(AAA) (SAVE)
2/10-4/22	1P: $359-$679
12/1-2/9 & 4/23-5/29	1P: $239-$389
5/30-11/30	1P: $189-$349

Resort
Condominium　　**Location:** Oceanfront. From causeway, 0.7 mi w on Periwinkle Way, s on Donax St to Gulf Dr, then 1 mi nw. 1451 Middle Gulf Dr 33957. Fax: 239/481-4947. **Facility:** This facility, fronting on a mile of beach, offers extensive activities as well as spacious one- or two- and three-bedroom condominium units. 261 units. 112 one- and 149 two-bedroom suites with kitchens. 4 stories, exterior corridors. **Parking:** on-site. **Terms:** check-in 4 pm, 14 day cancellation notice-fee imposed, package plans. **Amenities:** video library (fee), high-speed Internet, voice mail, safes, irons, hair dryers. **Dining:** 3 restaurants, 7 am-11 pm, cocktails, also, Windows on the Water, see separate listing, entertainment. **Pool(s):** 5 heated outdoor. **Leisure Activities:** whirlpool, waterslide, fishing, 12 tennis courts (2 lighted), recreation programs, ecological center, rental bicycles, jogging, playground, exercise room, shuffleboard, volleyball. *Fee:* sailboats, windsurfing, charter fishing, catamaran, kayak, golf privileges, tennis instruction, photographer, massage, game room. **Guest Services:** gift shop, valet and coin laundry. **Business Services:** conference facilities, business center. **Cards:** AX, CB, DC, DS, MC, VI. **Special Amenities:** free local telephone calls and free newspaper. *(See color ad p 899 & p 200)*

　　　　　　　　　　　　　　　　　　　　　　　　　　SOME UNITS
⬛⬛ ⬛ ⬛ ⬛ ⬛ ⬛ ⬛ ⬛ ⬛ ⬛ ⬛ ⬛ ⬛ ⬛ / ⬛ /

TORTUGA BEACH CLUB　　　　　　　　　　　　　　Phone: (239)472-0400　　75

12/1-1/5 Wkly	1P: $2800	2P: $2800
2/3-4/20 Wkly	1P: $2695	2P: $2695
1/6-2/2 Wkly	1P: $1820	2P: $1820
4/21-11/30 Wkly	1P: $1680	2P: $1680

Condominium　　**Location:** From causeway, just w. 959 E Gulf Dr 33957. Fax: 239/472-6540. **Facility:** This family-oriented, waterfront property is near shops and restaurants. 54 two-bedroom suites with kitchens and whirlpools. 3 stories (no elevator), exterior corridors. **Parking:** on-site. **Terms:** office hours 8:30 am-5 pm, 3-7 night minimum stay - seasonal, 60 day cancellation notice, daily rates available. **Amenities:** video library (fee), irons. *Some:* hair dryers. **Pool(s):** heated outdoor. **Leisure Activities:** whirlpool, 4 tennis courts, recreation programs, horseshoes, shuffleboard, volleyball. **Guest Services:** complimentary laundry. **Business Services:** fax (fee). **Cards:** AX, DC, DS, MC, VI.

(ASK) ⬛⬛ ⬛ ⬛ ⬛ ⬛ ⬛ ⬛

WEST WIND INN　　*Book at aaa.com*　　　　　　　　　Phone: (239)472-1541　　82

(AAA) (SAVE)
2/1-4/30	1P: $267-$334	2P: $267-$334	XP: $22	F14
12/21-1/31	1P: $205-$260	2P: $205-$260	XP: $22	F14
5/1-11/30	1P: $164-$222	2P: $164-$222	XP: $22	F14
12/1-12/20	1P: $159-$216	2P: $159-$216	XP: $22	F14

Motel　　**Location:** From causeway, 2.8 mi w on Periwinkle Way, 0.8 mi s on Tarpon Bay Rd, then 1.5 mi w. 3345 W Gulf Dr 33957. Fax: 239/472-8134. **Facility:** 103 units. 102 one-bedroom standard units, some with kitchens. 1 one-bedroom suite ($316-$425) with kitchen. 2 stories, exterior corridors. **Parking:** on-site. **Terms:** 3 day cancellation notice, weekly rates available, package plans. **Amenities:** voice mail, safes, irons, hair dryers. **Dining:** 8 am-2 pm, Fri & Sat 5 pm-9 pm, cocktails. **Pool(s):** heated outdoor, wading. **Leisure Activities:** rental sailboats, windsurfing, fish cleaning facilities, 2 tennis courts, barbecue grills, butterfly garden, croquet, rental bicycles, shuffleboard, volleyball. *Fee:* floats, sun decks, golf privileges. **Guest Services:** gift shop, coin laundry. **Business Services:** meeting rooms, fax (fee). **Cards:** AX, DS, MC, VI. **Special Amenities:** free local telephone calls and free newspaper.

　　　　　　　　　　　　　　　　　　　　　　SOME UNITS
⬛ ⬛ ⬛ ⬛ ⬛ ⬛ ⬛ / ⬛ ⬛ ⬛

(See map and index starting on p. 428)

—— WHERE TO DINE ——

AMY'S OVER EASY CAFE
Lunch: $7-$12 **Phone:** 239-472-2625 66
American
Location: From causeway, 2.8 mi w. 630 Tarpon Bay Rd 33957. **Hours:** 7 am-2:30 pm. Closed: 11/23, 12/25. **Reservations:** not accepted. **Features:** Sporting a chicken and rooster motif, the cute little place lets patrons taste some yummy home cooking. Breakfast and lunch offerings range from the Western omelet for breakfast to the grilled chicken Caesar wrap for lunch. Casual dress; beer & wine only. **Parking:** on-site. **Cards:** DS, MC, VI.

BEACHVIEW STEAKHOUSE & SEAFOOD RESTAURANT
Lunch: $5-$9 **Dinner:** $18-$31 **Phone:** 239-472-4394 61
Steak & Seafood
Location: From causeway, 0.7 mi w on Periwinkle Way, 0.5 mi s on Donax St, then just w in; Beachview Golf Club. 1100 Par View Dr 33957. **Hours:** 11 am-3 & 5-9 pm. Closed: 12/25. **Features:** With its popular golf club setting, the restaurant invites guests to enjoy a casual lunch of a sandwich or burger after a round on the links. Examples of good dinner choices include steaks and Maryland-style crab cakes. Casual dress; cocktails. **Parking:** on-site. **Cards:** AX, DS, MC, VI.

CHEEBURGER CHEEBURGER
Lunch: $5-$12 **Dinner:** $5-$12 **Phone:** 239-472-6111 63
American
Location: From causeway, 2.8 mi w. 2413 Periwinkle Way 33957. **Hours:** 11 am-9 pm. Closed: 11/23, 12/25. **Features:** The fun, family-focused establishment emphasizes '50s decor and, of course, cheeseburgers. Those can who polish off a 20-ounce "pounder" burger can join the "wall of famers." The food is reasonably priced. Casual dress; beer only. **Parking:** on-site. **Cards:** AX, DC, DS, MC, VI.

DOC FORD'S RUM BAR & GRILLE
Lunch: $8-$29 **Dinner:** $8-$29 **Phone:** 239-472-8311 55
American
Location: Sanibel-Captiva Rd at Rabbit Rd. 975 Rabbit Rd 33957. **Hours:** 11 am-10 pm. Closed: 11/23, 12/25. **Features:** The relaxed sports bar prepares a nice selection of appetizers, as well as sandwiches and entrees of seafood, beef, pork, baby back ribs and chicken. Casual dress; cocktails. **Parking:** on-site. **Cards:** AX, DS, MC, VI.

DOLCE VITA RESTAURANT & LOUNGE
Dinner: $17-$27 **Phone:** 239-472-5555 47
Italian
Location: From causeway, 0.7 mi w. 1244 Periwinkle Way 33957. **Hours:** 5:30 pm-10:30 pm. Closed: Super Bowl Sun. **Features:** The restaurant caters to those seeking an intimate fine-dining experience. The professional wait staff serves many creatively presented entrees, such as wild boar and buffalo strip steak. A pianist and singer provide nightly entertainment. Dressy casual; cocktails; entertainment. **Parking:** on-site. **Cards:** AX, DC, DS, MC, VI.

GRAMMA DOT'S
Lunch: $8-$15 **Dinner:** $17-$24 **Phone:** 239-472-8138 43
Seafood
Location: From causeway, 0.8 mi e on Periwinkle Way, just n; at Sanibel Marina. 634 N Yachtman 33957. **Hours:** 11:30 am-7:30 pm. Closed: 12/25; also 3 weeks in September. **Features:** At the Sanibel Marina, the restaurant serves casual lunches of fried grouper or shrimp baskets against a backdrop of trolling yachts and boats. Patrons might see a manatee or any number of fish while strolling along the dock area. Casual dress. **Parking:** on-site. **Cards:** MC, VI.

GULLY'S OF SANIBEL FAMILY RESTAURANT
Lunch: $8-$16 **Dinner:** $8-$16 **Phone:** 239-472-2525 58
American
Location: From causeway, 2 mi w; in Periwinkle Place. 2075 Periwinkle Way 33957. **Hours:** 8 am-8 pm. **Features:** The casual eatery is in a busy strip mall of shops and boutiques. Home cooking is served for breakfast, lunch and dinner. On the extensive menu are numerous soups, salads, sandwiches and dinner items. Casual dress. **Parking:** on-site. **Cards:** AX, DS, MC, VI.

HUNGRY HERON
Lunch: $7-$21 **Dinner:** $7-$21 **Phone:** 239-395-2300 59
American
Location: From causeway, 2.4 mi w on Periwinkle Way, then just n; in Palm Ridge Plaza. 2330 Palm Ridge Rd 33957. **Hours:** 11 am-9 pm, Sat & Sun from 7:30 am. Closed: 12/25. **Features:** Native Florida cuisine, crisp salads and overstuffed sandwiches bring in a loyal crowd of locals. Guests can choose from more than 250 dishes on a menu that includes several homemade desserts. Casual dress; beer & wine only. **Parking:** on-site. **Cards:** AX, CB, DC, DS, JC, MC, VI.

THE ISLAND COW
Lunch: $6-$25 **Dinner:** $6-$25 **Phone:** 239-472-0606 60
American
Location: From causeway, 2.7 mi w. 2163 Periwinkle Way 33957. **Hours:** 7 am-10 pm. **Features:** The nifty eatery mixes nautical appointments with a theme of—can you believe it?—cows. Among at least 100 offerings of what the eatery claims is "udderly great food" are choices ranging from a hearty "cowabunga breakfast" to "Mama's cookin'". Casual dress; beer only. **Parking:** on-site. **Cards:** DS, MC, VI.

THE JACARANDA
Dinner: $17-$35 **Phone:** 239-472-1771 48
American
Location: From causeway, 0.7 mi w. 1223 Periwinkle Way 33957. **Hours:** 5 pm-10 pm. **Reservations:** suggested. **Features:** Known to locals as the "Jac," the popular dining spot offers a casual setting with fine dining touches. In addition to good seafood, offerings include selections from the patio raw bar. On weekends, nightly entertainment might include jazz, top 40 or reggae bands. Dressy casual; cocktails; entertainment. **Parking:** on-site. **Cards:** AX, DC, DS, MC, VI.

LAVIGNA ITALIAN RESTAURANT & GRILLE
Dinner: $9-$29 **Phone:** 239-472-5453 54
Italian
Location: From causeway, 1.7 mi w. 1625 Periwinkle Way 33957. **Hours:** 5 pm-10 pm. Closed: 1/1, 12/25. **Features:** While on the island, guests looking for a more dressy type of dining experience will find this place a must. A professional service staff and nice surroundings enhance a fine meal. From fresh pasta to meat or fish dishes, diners are in for a treat. Dressy casual; cocktails. **Parking:** on-site. **Cards:** AX, DC, DS, MC, VI.

(See map and index starting on p. 428)

LAZY FLAMINGO Lunch: $8-$16 Dinner: $8-$16 Phone: 239/472-5353 42
Seafood
Location: Jct Blind Pass. 6520 C Pine Ave 33957. **Hours:** 11 am-midnight. Closed: 11/23, 12/25.
Features: Fresh seafood lines the popular spot's raw bar, while the menu lists a selection of sandwiches, burgers, salads, wings and other casual fare. Casual dress; cocktails. **Parking:** on-site. **Cards:** AX, DS, MC, VI.

LAZY FLAMINGO SEAFOOD GRILL Lunch: $9-$19 Dinner: $9-$19 Phone: 239/472-6939 44
Seafood
Location: From causeway, 0.3 mi w. 1036 Periwinkle Way 33957. **Hours:** 11:30 am-midnight. Closed: 11/23, 12/25. **Features:** The fun restaurant sports rustic and tropical decor and employs a friendly service staff. Come early for a seat, as this place is popular with the islanders. The menu is seafood-oriented, with such dishes as mesquite-grilled grouper, mussels marinara and peel-and-eat shrimp. Casual dress; beer & wine only. **Parking:** on-site. **Cards:** AX, DS, MC, VI.

MAD HATTER Dinner: $27-$30 Phone: 239/472-0033 41
American
Location: 7.5 mi n from jct Periwinkle Way and Sanibel-Captiva Rd. 6467 Sanibel-Captiva Rd 33957. **Hours:** Open 12/1-8/31 & 10/1-11/30; 5 pm-9:30 pm. Closed: 4/16, 11/23, 12/25; also Super Bowl Sun. **Reservations:** suggested. **Features:** A delightful find, the small, charming dining room offers superior vantage points for viewing sunsets and local wildlife. Service is friendly, unpretentious and informative. The menu features market fresh fish and veal among dishes prepared with care and artistic presentation. Dressy casual; beer & wine only. **Parking:** on-site. **Cards:** AX, DS, MC, VI.

MATZALUNA THE ITALIAN KITCHEN! Dinner: $9-$20 Phone: 239/472-1998 45
Italian
Location: From causeway, 0.6 mi w. 1200 Periwinkle Way 33957. **Hours:** 5 pm-9 pm. Closed: 11/23, 12/25. **Reservations:** not accepted. **Features:** The bustling restaurant offers some of the city's best pizzas, which are made in a wood-fired oven. Also on the menu are pasta, veal, chicken, shrimp and seafood dishes. A popular draw among the many visitors to the island, this place shouldn't be missed. Casual dress; cocktails. **Parking:** on-site. **Cards:** AX, MC, VI.

MCT'S SHRIMP HOUSE & TAVERN Dinner: $14-$26 Phone: 239/472-3161 51
Seafood
Location: From causeway, 1.3 mi w. 1523 Periwinkle Way 33957. **Hours:** 4:45 pm-10 pm. Closed: 11/23, 12/25. **Features:** Seafood and more seafood lines the menu at the casual establishment, which adheres to a rustic/nautical theme. The signature shrimp can be prepared any way from blackened to barbecued to zydeco (or Cajun style). Casual dress; cocktails. **Parking:** on-site. **Cards:** MC, VI.

THE MERMAID KITCHEN & CAKE FACTORY Lunch: $8-$14 Dinner: $9-$23 Phone: 239/472-1242 46
Continental
Location: From causeway, 1.9 mi w. 2055 Periwinkle Way 33957. **Hours:** 11 am-10 pm, Sun-9 pm. Closed: 12/25; also Sun off season. **Reservations:** suggested. **Features:** Mermaids are the theme at this ecclectic restaurant which has literally hundreds of knickknacks, pictures and memorabilia with the mermaid theme strewn about the dining room. Food is fresh and tasty; service is pleasant and welcoming. Casual dress; cocktails. **Parking:** on-site. **Cards:** AX, MC, VI.

MORGAN'S FOREST Dinner: $16-$28 Phone: 239/472-4100 64
American
Location: From causeway, 0.7 mi w on Periwinkle Way, 0.5 mi s on Donax St; in Holiday Inn Sanibel Island. 1231 Middle Gulf Dr 33957. **Hours:** 5 pm-10 pm. **Features:** A reproduction of a tropical rainforest, the setting at this fun eatery incorporates waterfalls, lush foliage and animated birds and animals. On the menu are seafood, poultry, pasta, beef, soup and salad dishes. Casual dress; cocktails. **Parking:** on-site. **Cards:** AX, DC, DS, MC, VI.

RIVIERA RESTAURANT Dinner: $17-$30 Phone: 239/472-1141 69
Italian
Location: From causeway, 2.8 mi w on Periwinkle Way, 0.8 mi s on Tarpon Bay Rd, then 0.4 mi w. 2761 W Gulf Dr 33957. **Hours:** 5:30 pm-10 pm. Closed: Super Bowl Sun. **Reservations:** suggested. **Features:** Northern Italian cuisine is at the heart of the popular dinner spot's menu. In addition to many fresh seafood items, guests can choose from rack of lamb and venison. The piano bar is a favorite diversion. Dressy casual; cocktails; entertainment. **Parking:** on-site and valet. **Cards:** AX, DC, DS, MC, VI.

THE SANIBEL CAFE Lunch: $4-$12 Dinner: $5-$16 Phone: 239/472-5323 56
American
Location: From causeway, 1.8 mi w; in Tahitian Gardens. 2007 Periwinkle Way 33957. **Hours:** 7 am-9 pm. Closed: 12/25. **Features:** In a popular strip mall of shops and boutiques, the casual family-owned-and-operated eatery has been in business since 1984. The extensive menu lists not only lunch and dinner items but breakfast dishes as well. Patrons can find everything from salads and sandwiches to steak fillets. Finish the meal with a slice of homemade Key lime pie. Casual dress; beer & wine only. **Parking:** on-site. **Cards:** MC, VI.

THE SANIBEL GRILL Dinner: $7-$16 Phone: 239/472-4453
American
Location: From causeway, 2.8 mi w on Periwinkle Way, then just n. 703 Tarpon Bay Rd 33957. **Hours:** 4:30 pm-12:30 am. **Reservations:** not accepted. **Features:** Guests can nosh on casual fare while watching sports on television monitors throughout the dining room. On the menu are burgers, sandwiches, salads, pizza and "killer quesadillas". Casual dress; cocktails. **Parking:** on-site. **Cards:** AX, MC, VI.

SANIBEL ISLAND PIZZA & PASTA Lunch: $5-$14 Dinner: $9-$14 Phone: 239/472-1581 53
Italian
Location: From causeway, 1.7 mi w; in Island Tower Plaza. 1619 Periwinkle Way 33957. **Hours:** 11 am-10 pm. **Reservations:** not accepted. **Features:** Popular among locals for its fabulous pizza, the restaurant also prepares pasta, chicken, veal and steak dishes. The setting is extremely casual, but the food is a notch above. Casual dress; beer & wine only. **Parking:** on-site. **Cards:** MC, VI.

(See map and index starting on p. 428)

THE SANIBEL STEAKHOUSE   **Dinner:** $16-$28   **Phone:** 239/472-5700   (49)
Steak House
Location: From causeway, 1.2 mi w. 1473 Periwinkle Way 33957. **Hours:** 5 pm-10 pm. **Features:** Island guests in search of a fine dining experience should pay a visit to this spot, where friendly, professional service and well-prepared food contribute to the appeal. Such entrees as tasty filet mignon are nicely complemented by the wonderful desserts. Casual dress; cocktails. **Parking:** on-site. **Cards:** AX, MC, VI.

SCHNAPPER'S HOTS   **Lunch:** $4-$8   **Dinner:** $4-$8   **Phone:** 239/472-8686   (50)
American
Location: From causeway, 1.3 mi w; in Coral Center. 1528 Periwinkle Way 33957. **Hours:** 11:30 am-10 pm. **Features:** Kids of all ages favor this fun spot for take-out fries and chargrilled hot dogs and burgers. Also on the menu are such items as bratwurst, kielbasa, fish and chips and savory buffalo wings. A dip of chocolate chip mint ice cream is a tasty topper. Casual dress. **Parking:** on-site. **Cards:** AX, DS, MC, VI.

THE SEAFOOD FACTORY   **Lunch:** $7-$14   **Dinner:** $15-$25   **Phone:** 239/472-2323   (65)
Seafood
Location: From causeway, 2.8 mi w. 2499 Periwinkle Way 33957. **Hours:** 11:30 am-10 pm. Closed: 11/23, 12/25. **Features:** Specializing in a wide variety of seafood; you'll enjoy hearty portions at this popular spot on the island. With it's nautical theme and friendly service, you'll be in for a treat here. Casual dress; cocktails. **Parking:** on-site. **Cards:** AX, DC, DS, MC, VI.   ⛾

THISTLE LODGE BEACHFRONT RESTAURANT   **Lunch:** $10-$14   **Dinner:** $15-$25   **Phone:** 239/472-9200   (68)
American
Location: From causeway, 1.3 mi w on Periwinkle Way, 1.3 mi s on Casa Ybel; in Casa Ybel Resort. 2255 W Gulf Dr 33957. **Hours:** 11 am-3 & 4:30-10 pm. **Features:** In a historic Victorian mansion, the restaurant affords gorgeous views of the Gulf of Mexico. Menu selections center on fresh seafood, steak and pasta. Casual dress; entertainment. **Parking:** on-site. **Cards:** MC, VI.   ♿M

THE TIMBERS RESTAURANT & FISH MARKET   **Dinner:** $13-$34   **Phone:** 239/472-3128   (62)
Seafood
Location: From causeway, 2.8 mi w on Periwinkle Way, just n. 703 Tarpon Bay Rd 33957. **Hours:** 5 pm-9 pm. Closed: 7/4; also Super Bowl Sun. **Reservations:** not accepted. **Features:** The menu centers on fresh seafood and beef specialties. Fresh catches, such as tuna, mahi mahi and snapper, are particularly popular. Casual dress; cocktails. **Parking:** on-site. **Cards:** AX, MC, VI.   ⛾

TRADERS STORE & CAFE   **Lunch:** $7-$14   **Dinner:** $14-$26   **Phone:** 239/472-7242   (52)
American
Location: From causeway, 1.1 mi w. 1551 Periwinkle Way 33957. **Hours:** 11 am-3 & 5-9 pm. **Features:** Comprising the menu are such palatable items as grilled shrimp and chicken burritos and poached Atlantic salmon. After enjoying Chef Patnode's creations, diners can browse artifacts from around the world. Casual dress; beer & wine only. **Parking:** on-site. **Cards:** AX, MC, VI.

TWILIGHT CAFE   **Dinner:** $20-$30   **Phone:** 239/472-8818   (57)
American
Location: From causeway, 2.8 mi w on Periwinkle Way, just n; in The Gallery Place. 751 Tarpon Bay Rd 33957. **Hours:** 5:30 pm-9 pm; closing hours may vary. Closed: 11/23, 12/25. **Features:** Works by area artists decorate the dining area, where patrons linger over creative preparations, such as grilled Asian spiced shrimp and medallions of beef in Dianne sauce. Dishes are prepared in the open kitchen. Dressy casual; cocktails. **Parking:** on-site. **Cards:** MC, VI.

WINDOWS ON THE WATER   **Lunch:** $7-$13   **Dinner:** $17-$25   **Phone:** 239/395-6014   (67)
Regional American
Location: From causeway, 0.7 mi w on Periwinkle Way, s on Donax St to Gulf Dr, then 1 mi nw; in Sundial Beach Resort. 1451 Middle Gulf Dr 33957. **Hours:** 7:30-10:30 am, 11:30-4 & 5:30-9:30 pm; Sunday brunch. **Reservations:** suggested. **Features:** In Sundial Beach Resort, the restaurant has a bright, airy dining room that affords views of the Gulf of Mexico. Floridian cuisine consists of fresh local seafood seasoned with Mexican and Caribbean spices. Casual dress; cocktails; entertainment. **Parking:** on-site. **Cards:** AX, CB, DC, DS, MC, VI.   ⛾

SANTA ROSA BEACH

─────── **WHERE TO STAY** ───────

A HIGHLANDS HOUSE BED & BREAKFAST INN   **Phone:** 850/267-0110
Bed & Breakfast
All Year [BP]   2P: $130-$220   XP: $20
Location: US 98, 2 mi s on CR 393, just e. 4193 W Scenic SR 30A 32459. Fax: 850/267-3602. **Facility:** A large porch on the second floor of this B&B allows views of the ocean and sunsets; a boardwalk extends to the beach. Smoke free premises. 8 one-bedroom standard units, some with whirlpools. 2 stories, interior corridors. *Bath:* combo or shower only. **Parking:** on-site. **Terms:** 2 night minimum stay, 3 day cancellation notice-fee imposed. **Amenities:** high-speed Internet, irons. **Leisure Activities:** beach access, bicycles. **Business Services:** fax. **Cards:** AX, DS, MC, VI.

─────── **WHERE TO DINE** ───────

GUGLIELMO'S LA DOLCE VITA   **Dinner:** $15-$35   **Phone:** 850/622-1119
Italian
Location: On US 98. 4942 Hwy 98 W 32459. **Hours:** 5 pm-10 pm. Closed: 11/23, 12/25; also Mon. **Reservations:** accepted. **Features:** The Italian staff serves Northern Italian cuisine that is prepared "a la minute". Casual dress; beer & wine only. **Parking:** on-site. **Cards:** AX, CB, DC, DS, JC, MC, VI.

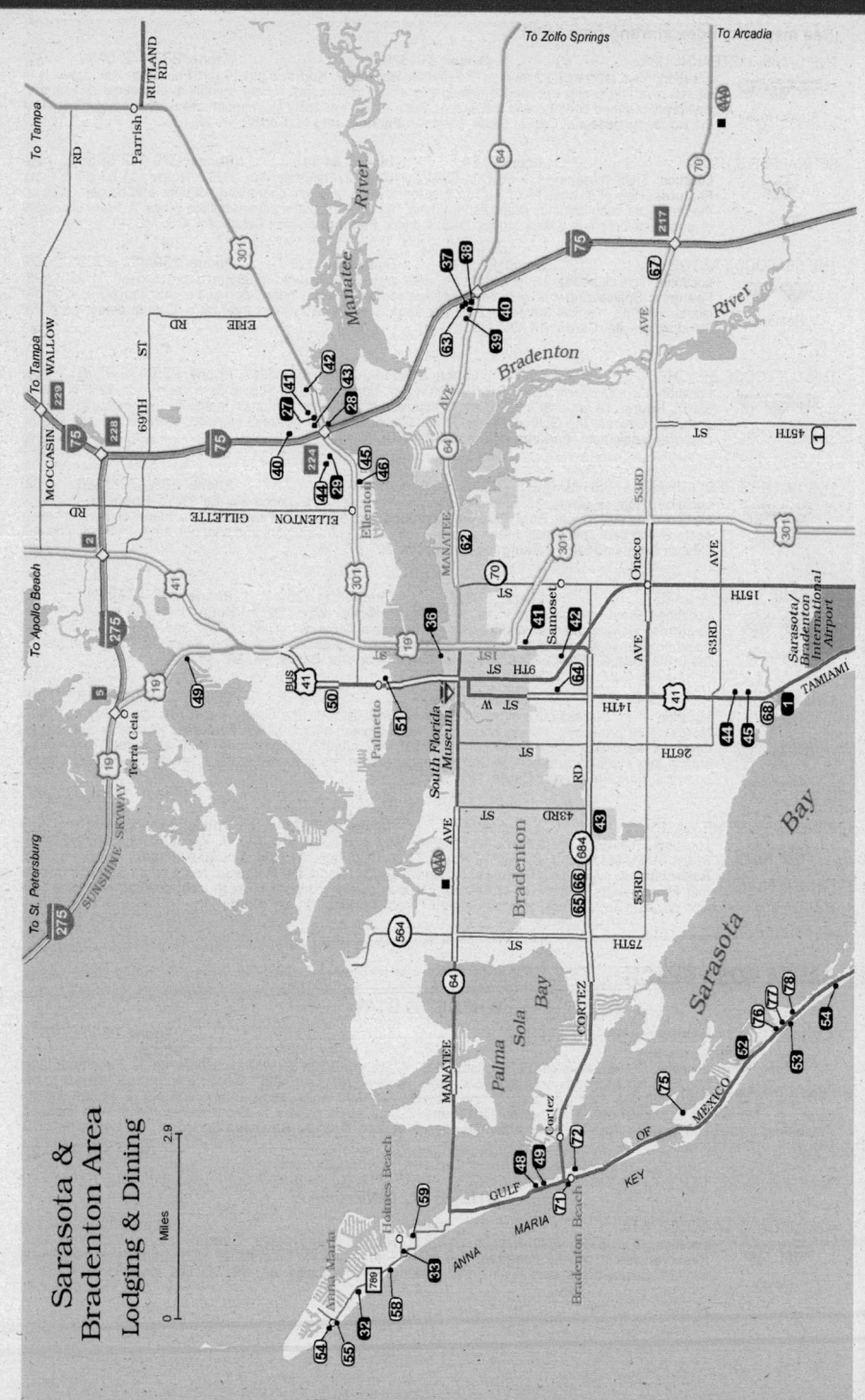

Sarasota & Bradenton Area Lodging & Dining

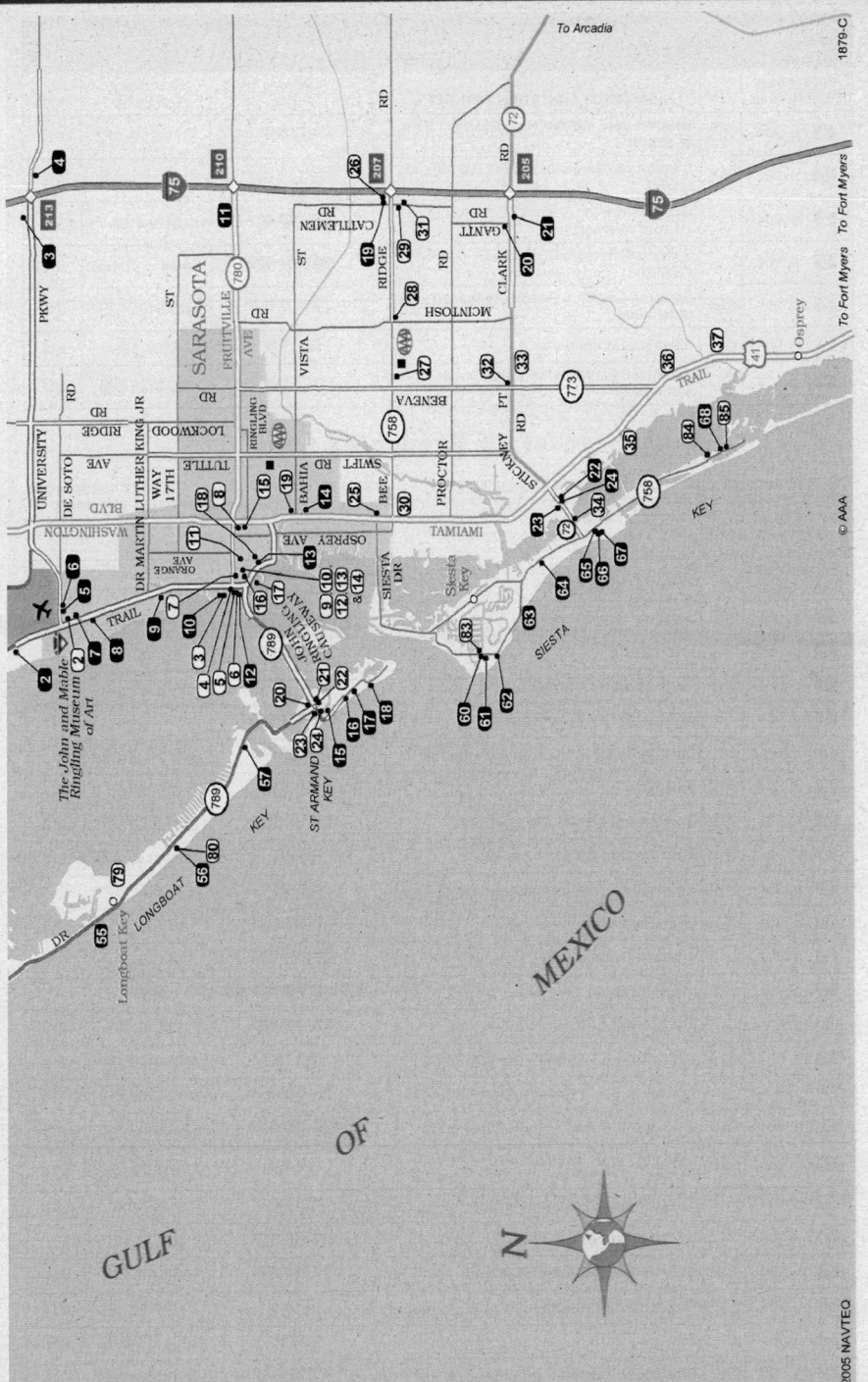

✈ Airport Accommodations

Spotter/Map Page Number	OA	SARASOTA-BRADENTON INT'L	Diamond Rating	Rate Range High Season	Listing Page
8 / p. 904	AAA	Best Western Golden Host Resort, 1.5 mi s of airport	◆◆	$139-$149 SAVE	910
7 / p. 904	AAA	Comfort Inn Sarasota Airport, 0.5 mi s of airport	◆◆◆	$110-$150 SAVE	910
2 / p. 904		Hilton Garden Inn Sarasota-Bradenton Airport, 1.1 mi n of airport	◆◆◆	$179-$199	912
5 / p. 904		Sarasota/Bradenton Courtyard By Marriott, at entrance	◆◆◆	Failed to provide	916
1 / p. 904	AAA	Sarasota Cay Club Resort Marina, 2.7 mi n of terminal	◆◆◆	$89-$189 SAVE	916
6 / p. 904	AAA	Sleep Inn, at entrance	◆◆	$109 SAVE	916
9 / p. 904	AAA	Southland Inn Motel and Apartments, 2.7 mi s of airport	◆◆	$59-$149 SAVE	917

Sarasota & Bradenton Area

This index helps you "spot" where approved accommodations and restaurants are located on the corresponding detailed maps. Lodging rate ranges are for comparison only and show the property's high season; rates are per night, unless only weekly (W) rates are available. Restaurant rate range is for dinner, unless only lunch (L) is served. Turn to the listing page for more detailed rate information and consult display ads for special promotions.

Spotter/Map Page Number	OA	SARASOTA - Lodgings	Diamond Rating	Rate Range High Season	Listing Page
1 / p. 904	AAA	Sarasota Cay Club Resort Marina	◆◆◆	$89-$189 SAVE	916
2 / p. 904		Hilton Garden Inn Sarasota-Bradenton Airport	◆◆◆	$179-$199	912
3 / p. 904	AAA	Comfort Suites University Park	◆◆◆	$99-$189 SAVE	911
4 / p. 904		Holiday Inn Lakewood Ranch	◆◆◆	$149-$189	912
5 / p. 904		Sarasota/Bradenton Courtyard By Marriott	◆◆◆	Failed to provide	916
6 / p. 904	AAA	Sleep Inn	◆◆	$109 SAVE	916
7 / p. 904	AAA	Comfort Inn Sarasota Airport	◆◆◆	$110-$150 SAVE	910
8 / p. 904	AAA	Best Western Golden Host Resort	◆◆	$139-$149 SAVE	910
9 / p. 904	AAA	Southland Inn Motel and Apartments	◆◆	$59-$149 SAVE	917
10 / p. 904	AAA	Hyatt Sarasota	◆◆◆	$135-$265 SAVE	914
11 / p. 904		AmericInn Hotel & Suites - see color ad p 969	◆◆◆	$189-$249	910
12 / p. 904		The Ritz-Carlton, Sarasota	◆◆◆◆◆	$539	915
13 / p. 904		The Cypress, A Bed & Breakfast Inn	◆◆◆	$220-$270	911
14 / p. 904	AAA	Best Western Midtown - see color ad p 913	◆◆	$109-$149 SAVE	910
15 / p. 904	AAA	Holiday Inn-Lido Beach - see color ad p 914	◆◆◆	$262-$289 SAVE	914
16 / p. 904	AAA	Lido Beach Resort - see color ad p 915	◆◆◆	$238-$482 SAVE	915
17 / p. 904	AAA	Coquina on the Beach Resort - see color ad p 913	◆◆	$189-$259 SAVE	911
18 / p. 904		The Helmsley Sandcastle Hotel	◆◆	$189-$309	912
19 / p. 904		Hampton Inn I-75/Bee Ridge	◆◆◆	$129-$199	911
20 / p. 904	AAA	Country Inn & Suites By Carlson	◆◆◆	$99-$189 SAVE	911
21 / p. 904	AAA	Comfort Inn, Sarasota I-75	◆◆	$119-$159 SAVE	911
22 / p. 904		The Tides Inn	◆	Failed to provide	917
23 / p. 904	AAA	Hibiscus Suites Inn - see color ad p 912	◆◆◆	$179-$429 SAVE	912
24 / p. 904		The Sunset Lodge Motel	◆◆	Failed to provide	917

Spotter/Map Page Number	OA	**SARASOTA - Restaurants**	Diamond Rating	Rate Range High Season	Listing Page
1 / p. 904		The Lazy Lobster Restaurant	◇◇	$11-$21	919
2 / p. 904		Cafe of the Arts	◇◇◇	$17-$33	918
3 / p. 904		Scalini	◇◇◇	$8-$21(L)	920
4 / p. 904		Da Ru Ma Japanese Steak & Seafood Restaurant	◇◇	$14-$38	919
5 / p. 904		Vernona	◇◇◇◇	$24-$45	921
6 / p. 904		The Ca d'zan Bar	◇◇◇◇	$10-$36	918
7 / p. 904	AAA	**The Bijou Cafe**	◇◇◇	$17-$35	918
8 / p. 904		Zoria	◇◇◇	$19-$32	921
9 / p. 904		Tropical Thai Restaurant	◇◇	$6-$20	920
10 / p. 904		First Watch Restaurant	◇◇	$3-$8(L)	919
11 / p. 904		Barnacle Bill's Seafood Restaurant & Market	◇◇	$8-$25	918
12 / p. 904		Patrick's Restaurant & Tavern	◇◇	$8-$22	920
13 / p. 904		Bayou Bleu	◇◇	$12-$30	918
14 / p. 904		Two Senoritas	◇◇	$7-$14	921
15 / p. 904		Silver Cricket	◇◇◇	$12-$17	920
16 / p. 904	AAA	**Pino's 100 Central**	◇◇	$13-$23	920
17 / p. 904		Marina Jack	◇◇	$9-$39	919
18 / p. 904		Uva Rara Ristorante	◇◇◇	$16-$25	921
19 / p. 904	AAA	**Michael's On East**	◇◇◇◇	$19-$32	920
20 / p. 904		Columbia Restaurant	◇◇	$15-$26	919
21 / p. 904		Chef Caldwell's Restaurant	◇◇◇	$16-$28	918
22 / p. 904		Crab & Fin	◇◇	$8-$54	919
23 / p. 904	AAA	**Hemingway's Retreat**	◇◇	$16-$39	919
24 / p. 904		Tommy Bahama's Tropical Cafe	◇◇	$15-$23	920
25 / p. 904		Cosimo's Brick Oven	◇◇	$7-$22	919
26 / p. 904		Bella Cucina Italian Buffet	◇	$12	918
27 / p. 904		Mel's Diner	◇◇	$4-$13	920
28 / p. 904		Mi Pueblo El Restaurante Mexicana	◇◇	$7-$12	920
29 / p. 904		Sugar & Spice	◇◇	$4-$14	920
30 / p. 904		Cafe Baci	◇◇	$11-$23	918
31 / p. 904	AAA	**Madfish Grill**	◇◇	$8-$28	919
32 / p. 904	AAA	**Marie's Italian Kitchen**	◇◇	$7-$18	919
33 / p. 904		Big Kitchen	◇◇	$8-$18	918
34 / p. 904		Coasters on the Water	◇◇	$8-$19	918
35 / p. 904		Waterfront Restaurant	◇◇	$8-$27	921
36 / p. 904		J Ryan's on the Grill	◇◇◇	$8-$21	919
37 / p. 904		Roessler's Restaurant	◇◇◇	$15-$31	920
		ELLENTON - Lodgings			
27 / p. 904		Hampton Inn	◇◇◇	$129-$159	321
28 / p. 904		Sleep Inn & Suites Riverfront	◇◇	$99-$199	321

Spotter/Map Page Number	OA	ELLENTON - Lodgings (continued)	Diamond Rating	Rate Range High Season	Listing Page
29 / p. 904		GuestHouse International Inn	◇◇	$90-$110	320
		ELLENTON - Restaurants			
40 / p. 904		Beef'O'Brady's	◇◇	$6-$9	321
41 / p. 904		Peach's	◇◇	$4-$8(L)	321
42 / p. 904	AAA	**Roaring 20's Pizza and Pipes**	◇	$5-$16	321
43 / p. 904		Ruby Tuesday	◇◇	$8-$18	321
44 / p. 904		Lee's Crab Trap II	◇◇	$9-$30	321
45 / p. 904		Hickory Hollow	◇	$7-$17	321
46 / p. 904		Big L Restaurant	◇	$2-$7(L)	321
		HOLMES BEACH - Lodgings			
32 / p. 904	AAA	**Haley's Motel**	◇	$109-$259 SAVE	461
33 / p. 904	AAA	**Harrington House Beachfront Bed & Breakfast**	◇◇◇	$189-$329 SAVE	461
		HOLMES BEACH - Restaurants			
58 / p. 904		Beach Bistro	◇◇◇	$36-$61	461
59 / p. 904		Ooh La La!	◇◇	$18-$36	461
		BRADENTON - Lodgings			
36 / p. 904	AAA	**Holiday Inn-Riverfront - see color ad p 263**	◇◇◇	$129-$199 SAVE	263
37 / p. 904		Days Inn I-75	◇◇	$110	262
38 / p. 904	AAA	**Holiday Inn Express**	◇◇◇	$109-$199 SAVE	262
39 / p. 904	AAA	**Comfort Inn-Bradenton**	◇◇◇	$100-$140 SAVE	262
40 / p. 904		Motel 6 #678	◇◇	$54-$70	263
41 / p. 904		Quality Inn & Suites	◇◇	Failed to provide	263
42 / p. 904		Days Inn Bradenton	◇◇	$89-$149	262
43 / p. 904		Shorewalk Vacation Villas Resort	◇◇	$133-$135	263
44 / p. 904	AAA	**Howard Johnson Express Inn**	◇◇	$74-$124 SAVE	263
45 / p. 904		Econo Lodge Airport	◇◇	Failed to provide	262
		BRADENTON - Restaurants			
62 / p. 904		Bart's Family Diner	◇	$5-$13	264
63 / p. 904		Sonny's Real Pit Bar-B-Q	◇◇	$7-$13	264
64 / p. 904		Miller's Dutch Kitch'n	◇◇	$5-$14	264
65 / p. 904		Anna Maria Oyster Bar	◇◇	$5-$25	264
66 / p. 904		R.J. Gators Hometown Grill & Bar	◇◇	$7-$16	264
67 / p. 904		D'Aritino's Pasta & Pizza	◇◇	$6-$12	264
68 / p. 904	AAA	**Anna Maria Oyster Bar**	◇◇	$5-$25	264
		BRADENTON BEACH - Lodgings			
48 / p. 904	AAA	**Tradewinds Resort**	◇◇◇	$205-$325 SAVE	264
49 / p. 904	AAA	**Tortuga Inn Beach Resort**	◇◇◇	$155-$270 SAVE	264
		BRADENTON BEACH - Restaurants			
71 / p. 904		Beach House Restaurant	◇◇	$7-$20	265
72 / p. 904		Bridge Tender Inn	◇◇	$5-$30	265

Spotter/Map Page Number	OA	LONGBOAT KEY - Lodgings	Diamond Rating	Rate Range High Season	Listing Page
52 / p. 904	AAA	**Harbour Villa Club**	◆◆◆	$1895(W) [SAVE]	519
53 / p. 904	AAA	**Riviera Beach Resort**	◆◆	$913-$1258(W) [SAVE]	520
54 / p. 904		Hilton Longboat Key Beachfront Resort	◆◆◆	$295-$345	519
55 / p. 904		Diplomat Resort	◆◆	$1077-$1784(W)	519
56 / p. 904		The Colony Beach & Tennis Resort	◆◆◆	$195-$1175	519
57 / p. 904	AAA	**Longboat Key Club & Resort**	◆◆◆◆	$350-$1160 [SAVE]	520
		LONGBOAT KEY - Restaurants			
75 / p. 904		Mar Vista Dockside Restaurant & Pub	◆◆	$15-$20	520
76 / p. 904		Harry's Continental Kitchens	◆◆◆	$20-$32	520
77 / p. 904		Euphemia Haye Restaurant	◆◆◆	$21-$44	520
78 / p. 904		Maureen Palm Grille	◆◆◆	$11-$29	520
79 / p. 904		Cafe on the Bay	◆◆	$18-$30	520
80 / p. 904		The Colony Dining Room	◆◆◆	$20-$38	520
		SIESTA KEY - Lodgings			
60 / p. 904	AAA	**Tropical Breeze Resort & Spa of Siesta Key**	◆◆	$103-$398 [SAVE]	924
61 / p. 904	AAA	**Sunsets on the Key**	◆◆◆	$229-$339 [SAVE]	924
62 / p. 904	AAA	**Siesta Beach Resort and Suites** - see color ad p 916	◆◆	$184-$345 [SAVE]	923
63 / p. 904	AAA	**Crescent Royale Condos**	◆◆	$747-$1314(W) [SAVE]	923
64 / p. 904	AAA	**Palm Bay Club** - see color ad p 913	◆◆◆	$135-$800 [SAVE]	923
65 / p. 904	AAA	**Tropical Shores Beach Resort** - see color ad p 910	◆◆◆	$169-$495 [SAVE]	924
66 / p. 904	AAA	**Sara Sea on Siesta Key** - see color ad p 917	◆◆	$159-$429 [SAVE]	923
67 / p. 904	AAA	**Siesta Key Inn** - see color ad p 916	◆◆◆	$229-$449 [SAVE]	923
68 / p. 904		Turtle Beach Resort	◆◆◆	$340-$435	924
		SIESTA KEY - Restaurants			
83 / p. 904		Village Cafe	◆◆	$5-$10(L)	924
84 / p. 904	AAA	**Turtles on Little Sarasota Bay**	◆◆	$7-$21	924
85 / p. 904	AAA	**Ophelia's on the Bay**	◆◆◆	$20-$32	924
		PALMETTO - Restaurants			
49 / p. 904		Lee's Crab Trap 1	◆◆	$9-$39	855
50 / p. 904		Kojak's Palmetto Ribhouse	◆	$6-$19	855
51 / p. 904		A La Mode Ice Cream Parlour & Sandwich Shoppe	◆	$5-$9	855
		ANNA MARIA - Restaurants			
54 / p. 904		Bistro at Island's End	◆◆◆	$8-$27	247
55 / p. 904		Sandbar	◆◆	$11-$21	247

SARASOTA pop. 52,715   (See map and index starting on p. 904)

———— WHERE TO STAY ————

AMERICINN HOTEL & SUITES   *Book at aaa.com*   Phone: (941)342-8778   **11**

▼▼▼▼
Small-scale Hotel

2/1-4/15	1P: $189-$249
12/24-1/31	1P: $139-$199
12/1-12/23 & 4/16-11/30	1P: $99-$179

Location: I-75, exit 210, 0.4 mi w, just n on N Cattlemen Rd, then just e on Commercial Way. 5931 Fruitville Rd 34232. Fax: 941/342-8668. **Facility:** 111 units. 99 one-bedroom standard units, some with whirlpools. 12 one-bedroom suites, some with whirlpools. 4 stories, interior corridors. *Bath:* combo or shower only. **Parking:** on-site. **Amenities:** high-speed Internet, dual phone lines, voice mail, irons, hair dryers. **Pool(s):** heated outdoor. **Leisure Activities:** whirlpool, exercise room. **Guest Services:** valet and coin laundry. **Business Services:** meeting rooms, business center. **Cards:** AX, CB, DC, DS, MC, VI. *(See color ad p 969)*

SOME UNITS

ASK ⬛ ⬛ ⬛ ⬛ ⬛ ⬛ ⬛ ⬛ ⬛ / ⬛

BEST WESTERN GOLDEN HOST RESORT   *Book at aaa.com*   Phone: 941/355-5141   **8**

ⒶⒶⒶ SAVE
▼▼ ▼▼
Motel

3/1-3/31 [ECP]	1P: $139-$149	2P: $139-$149	XP: $10	F12
12/1-2/28 & 4/1-4/30 [ECP]	1P: $119-$129	2P: $119-$129	XP: $10	F12
5/1-11/30 [ECP]	1P: $79-$89	2P: $79-$89	XP: $10	F12

Location: On US 41, 0.6 mi s of jct University Pkwy. 4675 N Tamiami Tr 34234. Fax: 941/355-9286. **Facility:** 80 one-bedroom standard units, some with efficiencies. 2 stories, exterior corridors. **Parking:** on-site. **Terms:** age restrictions may apply, cancellation fee imposed, package plans. **Amenities:** irons, hair dryers. *Some:* high-speed Internet. **Dining:** 6:30 am-2 & 5-8:30 pm, wine/beer only. **Pool(s):** heated outdoor. **Leisure Activities:** sun deck, shuffleboard. **Guest Services:** coin laundry. **Business Services:** fax (fee). **Cards:** AX, DC, DS, MC, . VI. **Special Amenities:** free expanded continental breakfast and free local telephone calls.

SOME UNITS

⬛ ⬛ ⬛ ⬛ ⬛ ⬛ / ⬛ ⬛ ⬛

BEST WESTERN MIDTOWN   *Book at aaa.com*   Phone: 941/955-9841   **14**

ⒶⒶⒶ SAVE
▼▼ ▼▼
Motel

2/1-4/30	1P: $109-$149	2P: $109-$149	XP: $10	F18
12/1-1/31	1P: $89-$119	2P: $89-$119	XP: $10	F18
5/1-11/30	1P: $59-$109	2P: $59-$109	XP: $10	F18

Location: On US 41, jct Prospect St. Located just n of Sarasota Memorial Hospital. 1425 S Tamiami Tr 34239. Fax: 941/954-8948. **Facility:** 100 one-bedroom standard units. 2-3 stories, exterior corridors. **Parking:** on-site. **Amenities:** high-speed Internet, voice mail, irons, hair dryers. **Pool(s):** heated outdoor. **Leisure Activities:** barbecue area, sun deck. **Guest Services:** coin laundry. **Business Services:** meeting rooms, fax (fee). **Cards:** AX, CB, DC, DS, JC, MC, VI. **Special Amenities:** free local telephone calls and free newspaper. *(See color ad p 913)*

SOME UNITS

⬛ ⬛ ⬛ ⬛ ⬛ ⬛ ⬛ / ⬛ ⬛ ⬛

COMFORT INN SARASOTA AIRPORT   *Book at aaa.com*   Phone: (941)351-7734   **7**

ⒶⒶⒶ SAVE
▼▼▼▼
Small-scale Hotel

1/16-4/15 [ECP]	1P: $110-$140	2P: $120-$150	XP: $10	F18
12/21-1/15 [ECP]	1P: $80-$110	2P: $90-$120	XP: $10	F18
12/1-12/20 & 4/16-11/30 [ECP]	1P: $60-$90	2P: $70-$100	XP: $10	F18

Location: On US 41, just s of jct University Pkwy. 5000 N Tamiami Tr 34234. Fax: 941/351-8820. **Facility:** 96 one-bedroom standard units. 3 stories, exterior corridors. **Parking:** on-site. **Terms:** pets ($10 extra charge). **Amenities:** video games (fee), high-speed Internet, voice mail, irons, hair dryers. **Pool(s):** heated outdoor. **Leisure Activities:** exercise room. **Guest Services:** valet and coin laundry. **Business Services:** meeting rooms, fax (fee). **Cards:** AX, CB, DC, DS, JC, MC, VI. **Special Amenities:** free expanded continental breakfast and free newspaper.

SOME UNITS

⬛ ⬛ ⬛ ⬛ ⬛ ⬛ ⬛ ⬛ ⬛ / ⬛ ⬛ /
FEE   FEE

(See map and index starting on p. 904)

COMFORT INN, SARASOTA I-75
Book at aaa.com Phone: (941)921-7750 **21**

AAA SAVE ◆◆◆

1/16-4/23	1P: $119-$159	2P: $119-$159	XP: $10	F
12/22-1/15	1P: $99-$129	2P: $99-$129	XP: $10	F
12/1-12/21	1P: $89-$119	2P: $89-$119	XP: $10	F
4/24-11/30	1P: $79-$119	2P: $79-$119	XP: $10	F

Small-scale Hotel **Location:** I-75, exit 205, just w on SR 72. 5778 Clark Rd 34233. Fax: 941/925-2474. **Facility:** 63 one-bedroom standard units. 3 stories, interior corridors. *Bath:* combo or shower only. **Parking:** on-site. **Amenities:** irons, hair dryers. **Pool(s):** heated outdoor. **Leisure Activities:** whirlpool. **Guest Services:** valet and coin laundry. **Business Services:** meeting rooms, fax (fee). **Cards:** AX, CB, DC, DS, JC, MC, VI. **Special Amenities:** free expanded continental breakfast and free newspaper.

SOME UNITS

COMFORT SUITES UNIVERSITY PARK
Book at aaa.com Phone: (941)360-2626 **3**

AAA SAVE ◆◆◆

12/1-4/16 [ECP]	1P: $99-$189	2P: $99-$189	XP: $10	F18
4/17-11/30 [ECP]	1P: $89-$169	2P: $89-$169	XP: $10	F18

Small-scale Hotel **Location:** I-75, exit 213, 0.4 mi w on University Pkwy, then just n. 8305 Tourist Center Dr 34201. Fax: 941/360-1876. **Facility:** 82 one-bedroom suites. 3 stories, interior corridors. *Bath:* combo or shower only. **Parking:** on-site. **Terms:** package plans. **Amenities:** high-speed Internet, dual phone lines, voice mail, irons, hair dryers. **Pool(s):** heated outdoor. **Leisure Activities:** whirlpool, exercise room. **Guest Services:** coin laundry. **Business Services:** meeting rooms, fax (fee). **Cards:** AX, CB, DC, DS, MC, VI. **Special Amenities:** free expanded continental breakfast and free newspaper.

SOME UNITS

COQUINA ON THE BEACH RESORT
Phone: 941-388-2141 **17**

AAA SAVE ◆◆◆

2/1-4/30	1P: $189-$259	2P: $189-$259	XP: $20	F18
5/1-5/31	1P: $119-$189	2P: $119-$189	XP: $20	F18
12/1-1/31	1P: $89-$189	2P: $89-$189	XP: $20	F18
6/1-11/30	1P: $99-$159	2P: $99-$159	XP: $20	F18

Motel **Location:** Oceanfront. On St. Armands Key of Lido Beach, 0.9 mi s of St. Armands Circle. 1008 Benjamin Franklin Dr 34236. Fax: 941/388-3017. **Facility:** 34 units. 26 one-bedroom standard units with efficiencies. 7 one- and 1 two-bedroom suites ($189-$359) with kitchens. 2 stories, exterior corridors. *Bath:* combo or shower only. **Parking:** on-site. **Terms:** pets ($30 extra charge). **Pool(s):** heated outdoor. **Leisure Activities:** barbecues, beach loungers. **Guest Services:** coin laundry. **Business Services:** fax (fee). **Cards:** AX, CB, DC, DS, JC, MC, VI. **Special Amenities:** free newspaper.
(See color ad p 913)

SOME UNITS
FEE

COUNTRY INN & SUITES BY CARLSON
Book at aaa.com Phone: (941)925-0631 **20**

AAA SAVE ◆◆◆

2/1-4/16	1P: $99-$189	2P: $99-$189	XP: $10	F17
12/20-1/31	1P: $99-$179	2P: $99-$179	XP: $10	F17
12/1-12/19 & 4/17-11/30	1P: $79-$179	2P: $79-$179	XP: $10	F17

Small-scale Hotel **Location:** I-75, exit 205, 0.3 mi w on SR 72 (Clark Rd), then just n. 5730 Gantt Rd 34233. Fax: 941/925-0752. **Facility:** 100 units. 56 one-bedroom standard units, some with whirlpools. 44 one-bedroom suites ($99-$210). 4 stories, interior corridors. *Bath:* combo or shower only. **Parking:** on-site. **Terms:** cancellation fee imposed, [CP] meal plan available. **Amenities:** high-speed Internet, voice mail, safes, irons, hair dryers. **Pool(s):** heated outdoor. **Leisure Activities:** whirlpool, exercise room. **Guest Services:** coin laundry. **Business Services:** meeting rooms, fax (fee). **Cards:** AX, DC, DS, MC, VI. **Special Amenities:** free continental breakfast and free local telephone calls.

SOME UNITS

THE CYPRESS, A BED & BREAKFAST INN
Phone: 941-955-4683 **13**

◆◆◆◆

12/15-4/30 [BP]		2P: $220-$270	XP: $25
5/1-11/30 [BP]		2P: $160-$190	XP: $25
12/1-12/14 [BP]		2P: $150-$180	XP: $25

Bed & Breakfast **Location:** Just n on Palm Ave from jct US 41; or just n on Palm Ave, just s on Palm Ave. 621 Gulfstream Ave S 34236. Fax: 941/906-8952. **Facility:** The themes of the rooms at this B&B next to a marina and park include Victorian, Key West, floral and French elegance; a garden enhances the grounds. Designated smoking area. 4 units. 3 one-bedroom standard units, some with whirlpools. 1 one-bedroom suite. 2 stories, interior corridors. *Bath:* combo or shower only. **Parking:** on-site. **Terms:** 2 night minimum stay - seasonal and/or weekends, age restrictions may apply, 14 day cancellation notice-fee imposed. **Amenities:** irons, hair dryers. *Some:* DVD players. **Leisure Activities:** bicycles. *Fee:* massage. **Guest Services:** complimentary evening beverages. **Business Services:** fax. **Cards:** AX, DS, MC, VI.

SOME UNITS

HAMPTON INN I-75/BEE RIDGE
Book at aaa.com Phone: (941)371-1900 **19**

◆◆◆

1/1-4/15	1P: $129-$199	2P: $129-$199	
4/16-11/30	1P: $89-$129	2P: $89-$129	
12/1-12/31	1P: $109-$119	2P: $109-$119	

Small-scale Hotel **Location:** I-75, exit 207, just w on Bee Ridge Rd (SR 758), then just n. 5995 Cattleridge Rd 34232. Fax: 941/371-0241. **Facility:** 121 one-bedroom standard units. 5 stories, interior corridors. *Bath:* combo or shower only. **Parking:** on-site. **Terms:** check-in 4 pm, cancellation fee imposed. **Amenities:** video games (fee), high-speed Internet, voice mail, irons, hair dryers. **Pool(s):** heated outdoor. **Leisure Activities:** whirlpool, exercise room. **Guest Services:** valet and coin laundry. **Business Services:** meeting rooms, fax. **Cards:** AX, DC, DS, MC, VI.

SOME UNITS

(See map and index starting on p. 904)

THE HELMSLEY SANDCASTLE HOTEL — *Book at aaa.com* — **Phone:** (941)388-2181 — 🔟8

| | 2/3-4/23 | 1P: $189-$309 | 2P: $189-$309 | XP: $10 | F18 |
| | 12/1-2/2 & 4/24-11/30 | 1P: $119-$219 | 2P: $119-$219 | XP: $10 | F18 |

Small-scale Hotel — **Location:** Oceanfront. On St. Armand's Key of Lido Beach; 1.3 mi s of St. Armand's Circle. 1540 Benjamin Franklin Dr 34236. Fax: 941/388-2655. **Facility:** 179 units. 176 one-bedroom standard units, some with whirlpools. 3 one-bedroom suites ($399-$499) with whirlpools. 1-4 stories, exterior corridors. *Bath:* combo or shower only. **Parking:** on-site. **Amenities:** voice mail, safes, irons, hair dryers. *Some:* high-speed Internet (fee). **Pool(s):** 2 heated outdoor. **Leisure Activities:** rental boats, fishing, recreation programs, exercise room, horseshoes, shuffleboard, volleyball. *Fee:* sailboats, bicycles, massage, game room. **Guest Services:** gift shop, valet and coin laundry, area transportation. **Business Services:** conference facilities. *Fee:* PC, fax. **Cards:** AX, CB, DC, DS, JC, MC, VI.

SOME UNITS

HIBISCUS SUITES INN — **Phone:** (941)921-5797 — 2️⃣3️⃣

	12/1-4/15	1P: $179-$429	2P: $179-$429	XP: $20	F14
	6/6-9/5	1P: $149-$319	2P: $149-$319	XP: $20	F14
	4/16-6/5 & 9/6-11/30	1P: $129-$289	2P: $129-$289	XP: $20	F14

Motel — **Location:** On SR 72, 0.3 mi sw of jct US 41. 1735 Stickney Point Rd 34231. Fax: 941/922-1284. **Facility:** Smoke free premises. 27 units. 1 one-bedroom standard unit. 24 one-, 1 two- and 1 three-bedroom suites with kitchens. 2 stories, exterior corridors. **Parking:** on-site. **Terms:** office hours 7 am-10 pm, 3 day cancellation notice, small pets only ($25 fee). **Amenities:** high-speed Internet, voice mail, irons, hair dryers. **Pool(s):** heated outdoor. **Leisure Activities:** gas barbecue grill. **Guest Services:** coin laundry. **Business Services:** fax. **Cards:** AX, DS, MC, VI. **Special Amenities:** free local telephone calls and free newspaper. *(See color ad below)*

FEE — FEE

HILTON GARDEN INN SARASOTA-BRADENTON AIRPORT — **Phone:** (941)552-1100 — 2️⃣

	1/1-4/30	1P: $179-$199	2P: $179-$199	
	12/1-12/31 & 10/1-11/30	1P: $129-$149	2P: $129-$149	
	5/1-9/30	1P: $109-$129	2P: $109-$129	

Small-scale Hotel — **Location:** On US 41, 1 mi n of jct University Pkwy. 8270 N Tamiami Tr 34243. Fax: 941/552-1111. **Facility:** 115 units. 105 one-bedroom standard units. 10 one-bedroom suites. 4 stories, interior corridors. *Bath:* combo or shower only. **Parking:** on-site. **Amenities:** video games (fee), high-speed Internet, dual phone lines, voice mail, irons, hair dryers. **Pool(s):** heated outdoor. **Leisure Activities:** whirlpool, exercise room. **Guest Services:** sundries, valet and coin laundry, area transportation. **Business Services:** meeting rooms, business center. **Cards:** AX, DC, DS, MC, VI.

SOME UNITS

HOLIDAY INN LAKEWOOD RANCH — *Book at aaa.com* — **Phone:** (941)782-4400 — 4️⃣

| | 1/1-4/30 | 1P: $149-$189 | 2P: $149-$189 | XP: $10 | F19 |
| | 12/1-12/31 & 5/1-11/30 | 1P: $109-$129 | 2P: $109-$129 | XP: $10 | F19 |

Small-scale Hotel — **Location:** I-75, exit 213, just e on University Pkwy. 6231 Lake Osprey Dr 34240. Fax: 941/782-4401. **Facility:** 128 units. 124 one-bedroom standard units. 4 one-bedroom suites ($229-$299), some with whirlpools. 5 stories, interior corridors. *Bath:* combo or shower only. **Parking:** on-site. **Terms:** [BP] meal plan available, package plans. **Amenities:** video games (fee), high-speed Internet, dual phone lines, voice mail, irons, hair dryers. **Pool(s):** heated outdoor. **Leisure Activities:** whirlpool, exercise room. **Guest Services:** valet and coin laundry. **Business Services:** conference facilities, business center. **Cards:** AX, CB, DC, DS, JC, MC, VI.

SOME UNITS

(See map and index starting on p. 904)

HOLIDAY INN-LIDO BEACH   *Book at aaa.com*   Phone: (941)388-5555   **15**

(AAA) (SAVE)   1/18-5/2   1P: $262-$289   2P: $262-$289
▼▼▼   12/1-1/17 & 5/3-11/30   1P: $161-$188   2P: $161-$188
              Location: On St. Armands Key of Lido Beach; 0.4 mi s of St. Armands Circle. 233 Ben Franklin Dr 34236.
Small-scale Hotel   Fax: 941/388-4321. **Facility:** 135 units. 131 one-bedroom standard units. 4 one-bedroom suites with
              whirlpools. 7 stories, interior corridors. *Bath:* combo or shower only. **Parking:** on-site. **Amenities:** video
              games (fee), voice mail, safes, irons, hair dryers. *Some:* CD players. **Dining:** 7:30 am-2 & 5-10 pm,
cocktails. **Pool(s):** heated outdoor. **Leisure Activities:** beach access, beach chairs & umbrellas, exercise room. *Fee:* bicycles.
Guest Services: gift shop, valet and coin laundry, area transportation-within 3 mi. **Business Services:** meeting rooms, fax
(fee). **Cards:** AX, DC, DS, MC, VI. **Special Amenities:** free local telephone calls and free newspaper.
(See color ad below)

SOME UNITS
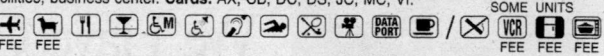
FEE   FEE

HYATT SARASOTA   *Book at aaa.com*   Phone: (941)953-1234   **10**

(AAA) (SAVE)   All Year   1P: $135-$265   2P: $135-$265   XP: $25   **F18**
▼▼▼▼   **Location:** Just w of jct US 41. 1000 Blvd of the Arts 34236. Fax: 941/952-1987. **Facility:** 294 units. 290 one-
              bedroom standard units. 4 one-bedroom suites. 10 stories, interior corridors. *Bath:* combo or shower only.
              Parking: on-site (fee) and valet. **Terms:** cancellation fee imposed, pets ($150 fee). **Amenities:** voice mail,
Large-scale Hotel   irons, hair dryers. *Fee:* video games, high-speed Internet. *Some:* dual phone lines, fax, honor bars. *Fee:*
              DVD players. **Dining:** 6:30 am-midnight, cocktails, also, Scalini, see separate listing. **Pool(s):** heated
outdoor. **Leisure Activities:** whirlpool, exercise room. *Fee:* marina, charter fishing, cruising boats, scuba boat, air hockey,
bicycles, massage, game room. **Guest Services:** gift shop, valet and coin laundry, area transportation (fee)-within 3 mi.
Business Services: conference facilities, business center. **Cards:** AX, CB, DC, DS, JC, MC, VI.

SOME UNITS

(See map and index starting on p. 904)

LIDO BEACH RESORT *Book at aaa.com*   Phone: (941)388-2161 [16]

[AAA] [SAVE]

	2/10-4/22	1P: $238-$482	2P: $238-$482	XP: $13	F16
	5/29-11/30	1P: $128-$482	2P: $128-$482	XP: $13	F16
	4/23-5/28	1P: $162-$374	2P: $162-$374	XP: $13	F16
	12/1-2/9	1P: $128-$374	2P: $128-$374	XP: $13	F16

Large-scale Hotel **Location:** Oceanfront. 0.8 mi s of St. Armands Circle; on St. Armands Key of Lido Beach. 700 Ben Franklin Dr 34236. Fax: 941/388-3175. **Facility:** 222 units. 166 one-bedroom standard units, some with efficiencies or kitchens. 46 one- and 10 two-bedroom suites ($212-$758) with kitchens. 4-12 stories, interior/exterior corridors. *Bath:* combo or shower only. **Parking:** on-site. **Terms:** check-in 4 pm, 2-3 night minimum stay - seasonal and/or weekends, package plans. **Amenities:** video games (fee), high-speed Internet, dual phone lines, voice mail, safes, irons, hair dryers. **Dining:** 2 restaurants, 6:30 am-10 pm, cocktails, entertainment. **Pool(s):** 2 heated outdoor. **Leisure Activities:** whirlpools, fishing, recreation programs, exercise room, volleyball. *Fee:* body boards, cabanas, personal watercraft. **Guest Services:** gift shop, valet and coin laundry, area transportation-St. Armands Circle. **Business Services:** conference facilities, business center. **Cards:** AX, CB, DC, DS, MC, VI. **Special Amenities:** free local telephone calls and free newspaper. *(See color ad below)*

SOME UNITS

[icons]

THE RITZ-CARLTON, SARASOTA *Book at aaa.com*   Phone: (941)309-2000 [12]

	12/1-4/30 & 9/29-11/30	1P: $539	2P: $539	XP: $25	F17
	5/1-6/1	1P: $399	2P: $399	XP: $25	F17
	6/2-9/28	1P: $349	2P: $349	XP: $25	F17

Large-scale Hotel **Location:** On US 41, jct John Ringling Blvd. 1111 Ritz-Carlton Dr 34236. Fax: 941/309-2100. **Facility:** This hotel offers first class and very luxurious accommodations. You may not be a world leader, but you will be treated like one. 266 units. 235 one-bedroom standard units. 31 one-bedroom suites, some with whirlpools. 9 stories, interior corridors. *Bath:* combo or shower only. **Parking:** on-site (fee) and valet. **Terms:** cancellation fee imposed, package plans, 10% service charge, small pets only ($125 fee). **Amenities:** video library, DVD players, video games (fee), CD players, high-speed Internet, dual phone lines, voice mail, safes, honor bars, irons, hair dryers. *Some:* fax. **Dining:** The Ca d'zan Bar, Vernona, see separate listings. **Pool(s):** 2 heated outdoor. **Leisure Activities:** saunas, whirlpools, steamrooms, fishing, 4 lighted tennis courts, recreation programs, spa, volleyball. *Fee:* canoes, sailboats, windsurfing, snorkeling, charter fishing, bicycles. **Guest Services:** gift shop, valet laundry, area transportation, beauty salon. **Business Services:** conference facilities, business center. **Cards:** AX, CB, DC, DS, JC, MC, VI.

SOME UNITS

[ASK] [icons] FEE FEE

(See map and index starting on p. 904)

SARASOTA/BRADENTON COURTYARD BY MARRIOTT   *Book at aaa.com*

▼▼▼
Small-scale Hotel

Phone: 941/355-3337   **5**

Property failed to provide current rates

Location: Just e of jct US 41. 850 University Pkwy 34234. Fax: 941/355-5518. **Facility:** 81 units. 78 one-bedroom standard units, some with whirlpools. 3 one-bedroom suites with kitchens. 3 stories, interior corridors. *Bath:* combo or shower only. **Parking:** on-site. **Amenities:** high-speed Internet, voice mail, irons, hair dryers. **Pool(s):** heated outdoor. **Leisure Activities:** whirlpool, exercise room. **Guest Services:** sundries, valet and coin laundry. **Business Services:** meeting rooms, business center.

SOME UNITS
[icons]

SARASOTA CAY CLUB RESORT MARINA

(AAA) (SAVE)
▼▼▼
Motel

Phone: (941)355-2781   **1**

1/1-4/30	1P: $89-$189	2P: $89-$189	XP: $10	F17
5/1-11/30	1P: $79-$169	2P: $79-$169	XP: $10	F17
12/1-12/31	1P: $69-$129	2P: $69-$129	XP: $10	F17

Location: On US 41, 2.4 mi n of jct University Pkwy. 7150 N Tamiami Tr 34243. Fax: 941/355-4149. **Facility:** 178 units. 173 one-bedroom standard units. 4 one- and 1 two-bedroom suites ($99-$350). 2 stories, interior/exterior corridors. *Bath:* combo or shower only. **Parking:** on-site. **Terms:** 3 day cancellation notice, [AP], [BP], [CP], [ECP] & [MAP] meal plans available, package plans. **Amenities:** high-speed Internet, dual phone lines, voice mail, irons, hair dryers. **Dining:** 6:30 am-10 pm, cocktails. **Pool(s):** heated outdoor. **Leisure Activities:** exercise room. *Fee:* marina, charter fishing, 100 boat slips. **Guest Services:** valet and coin laundry, airport transportation-Sarasota Airport. **Business Services:** meeting rooms, business center. **Cards:** AX, CB, DC, DS, JC, MC, VI.

SOME UNITS
[icons]
FEE

SLEEP INN   *Book at aaa.com*

(AAA) (SAVE)
▼▼
Small-scale Hotel

Phone: (941)359-8558   **6**

1/16-4/30	1P: $109	2P: $109	XP: $10	F18
12/1-1/15 & 5/1-11/30	1P: $79	2P: $79	XP: $10	F18

Location: Just e of jct US 41; in Airport Business Park. 900 University Pkwy 34234. Fax: 941/359-8558. **Facility:** 80 units. 76 one-bedroom standard units. 4 one-bedroom suites. 3 stories, interior corridors. *Bath:* combo or shower only. **Parking:** on-site. **Amenities:** safes (fee), irons, hair dryers. **Pool(s):** outdoor. **Guest Services:** valet and coin laundry. **Business Services:** meeting rooms, PC, fax. **Cards:** AX, DC, DS, MC, VI. **Special Amenities:** free continental breakfast and free newspaper.

SOME UNITS
[icons]

(See map and index starting on p. 904)

SOUTHLAND INN MOTEL AND APARTMENTS

AAA **SAVE** ▽▽▽▽ Motel

Phone: 941/954-5775 **9**

1/15-4/15	1P: $59-$149	2P: $69-$149	XP: $10	F7
12/1-1/14	1P: $49-$109	2P: $59-$109	XP: $10	F7
4/16-11/30	1P: $39-$99	2P: $49-$99	XP: $10	F7

Location: On US 41, 1.8 mi s of jct University Pkwy. 2229 N Tamiami Tr 34234. Fax: 941/364-8329. **Facility:** 30 units. 21 one-bedroom standard units, some with efficiencies. 9 one-bedroom suites ($149-$199) with kitchens. 2 stories, exterior corridors. *Bath:* combo or shower only. **Parking:** on-site. **Terms:** 3 day cancellation notice. **Amenities:** *Some:* irons, hair dryers. **Pool(s):** outdoor. **Leisure Activities:** sun deck. **Guest Services:** coin laundry. **Business Services:** fax (fee). **Cards:** AX, DS, MC, VI.

SOME UNITS

THE SUNSET LODGE MOTEL

▽▽▽▽ Motel

Phone: 941/925-1151 **24**

Property failed to provide current rates

Location: 0.3 mi sw of jct US 41 on SR 72, just s on Ave C, then just w. 1765 Dawn St 34231. Fax: 941/925-8168. **Facility:** Designated smoking area. 6 one-bedroom standard units with efficiencies. 1 story, exterior corridors. *Bath:* shower only. **Parking:** on-site. **Terms:** office hours 8 am-6 pm, small pets only (in designated units). **Amenities:** irons, hair dryers. **Pool(s):** outdoor. **Leisure Activities:** bicycles, shuffleboard. **Guest Services:** coin laundry. **Business Services:** fax.

THE TIDES INN

▽▽ Motel

Phone: 941/924-7541 **22**

Property failed to provide current rates

Location: On SR 72, 0.3 mi sw of jct US 41. 1800 Stickney Point Rd 34231. Fax: 941/923-6445. **Facility:** 12 units. 10 one-bedroom standard units with efficiencies. 2 one-bedroom suites with kitchens. 1 story, exterior corridors. *Bath:* combo or shower only. **Parking:** on-site. **Terms:** office hours 8:30 am-7:30 pm, pets (in designated units, with prior approval). **Amenities:** *Some:* irons, hair dryers. **Pool(s):** heated outdoor. **Leisure Activities:** horseshoes, shuffleboard. *Fee:* bicycles. **Business Services:** fax (fee).

SOME UNITS

(See map and index starting on p. 904)

──────── WHERE TO DINE ────────

BARNACLE BILL'S SEAFOOD RESTAURANT & MARKET   **Lunch:** $6-$14   **Dinner:** $8-$25   **Phone:** 941/365-6800   ⑪

Seafood

Location: Just e of jct Central Ave; downtown. 1526 Main St 34234. **Hours:** 11:30 am-9 pm, Fri & Sat-10 pm. Closed: 1/1, 11/23, 12/25; also Super Bowl Sun. **Features:** As its name suggests, the laid-back restaurant builds its theme around seafood. Service is friendly and efficient, and the food is good. The menu lists such signature dishes as stuffed flounder, crab cakes and shrimp Creole, as well as pasta, stir fry and steak items. Casual dress. **Parking:** street. **Cards:** AX, DS, MC, VI.

BAYOU BLEU   **Lunch:** $12-$30   **Dinner:** $12-$30   **Phone:** 941/917-0003   ⑬

Cajun

Location: Just e of jct US 41; downtown. 1359 1/2 Main St 34236. **Hours:** 11:30 am-10 pm, Fri & Sat-11 pm. **Features:** The second-floor restaurant overlooks shops and boutiques and can be accessed via an elevator. The cafe-esque surroundings evoke a New Orleans feel, with Mardi Gras colors and items on the walls. Menu choices include crawfish etouffee, andouille with red beans and rice, chicken with tasso, shrimp Creole, jambalaya, steaks, seafood, salads and such appetizers as oyster Bienville and boiled crawfish. Casual dress; cocktails. **Parking:** street. **Cards:** AX, CB, DC, DS, MC, VI.   🚗M

BELLA CUCINA ITALIAN BUFFET   **Lunch:** $7   **Dinner:** $12   **Phone:** 941/379-8158   ㉖

Italian

Location: I-75, exit 207, just w on Bee Ridge Rd. 3811 Kenny Dr 34232. **Hours:** 11:30 am-9 pm, Sun 10:30 am-8 pm; Sunday brunch. Closed: 12/25. **Features:** An extensive buffet feast awaits patrons of the laid-back restaurant. Among the some 40 choices are Italian roast pork, chicken Florentine and chicken marsala. Sundays usher in a popular brunch and classic car show. Casual dress; beer & wine only. **Parking:** on-site. **Cards:** AX, DS, MC, VI.   🚗M

BIG KITCHEN   **Lunch:** $8-$18   **Dinner:** $8-$18   **Phone:** 941/925-3675   ㉝

American

Location: Just e of jct Beneva Rd; in Lakeshore Village Shopping Center. 3900 Clark Rd 34233. **Hours:** 11 am-9 pm, Sun from 5 pm. Closed: Mon. **Features:** The casual eatery has an extensive menu with a multitude of choices—steaks, seafood, soul food, smoked fish platters, veggie specials, fish, chicken and many delicatessen sandwiches. Homemade bakery items are a highlight, with a variety of breads and desserts made on the premises. Casual dress; cocktails. **Parking:** on-site. **Cards:** AX, DS, MC, VI.   🚗M 🍸

THE BIJOU CAFE   *Menu on aaa.com*   **Lunch:** $9-$17   **Dinner:** $17-$35   **Phone:** 941/366-8111   ⑦

AAA

Continental

Location: Between Cocoanut and Pineapple aves; downtown. 1287 1st St 34236. **Hours:** 11:30 am-2 & 5-9:30 pm, Fri from 5 pm, Sat 5 pm-10 pm, Sun 5 pm-9 pm. Closed: 1/1, 7/4, 12/25; also Sun 6/1-12/31. **Reservations:** suggested. **Features:** In the heart of the theater and arts district, the stylish, upscale bistro draws diners in search of romance. Bijou pepper steak, pan-sizzled in a spicy hot sauce, and rack of lamb are outstanding examples on a winning menu. Dressy casual; cocktails. **Parking:** on-site and valet. **Cards:** AX, CB, DC, DS, MC, VI.   🍸

THE CA D'ZAN BAR   **Dinner:** $10-$36   **Phone:** 941/309-2000   ⑥

American

Location: On US 41 at John Ringling Blvd; in The Ritz-Carlton, Sarasota. 1111 Ritz-Carlton Dr 34236. **Hours:** 4 pm-midnight, Fri & Sat-2 am. **Reservations:** accepted. **Features:** Named in honor of John Ringling, the circus mogul and long-ago resident of Sarasota, the restaurant offers limited entree selection, however the lighter fare offers a wider array of wonderfully prepared delights and may include lemon dill cured Atlantic salmon, Florida crab spring roll or chicken satay. A specialty martini menu includes fabulous dessert concoctions and more. Casual dress; cocktails. **Parking:** on-site (fee) and valet. **Cards:** AX, CB, DC, DS, JC, MC, VI.   🚗M

CAFE BACI   **Lunch:** $7-$10   **Dinner:** $11-$23   **Phone:** 941/924-0963   ㉚

Northern Italian

Location: On US 41, just s of jct Bee Ridge Rd. 4001 S Tamiami Tr 34231. **Hours:** 11:30 am-2:30 & 4:30-10 pm, Fri-11 pm, Sat 4:30 pm-11 pm, Sun 4:30 pm-10 pm. Closed: 12/25. **Features:** Settle into a comfortable chair and relish the lovely upscale setting. Authentic Italian dishes are tastefully presented, including the excellent shrimp cocktail loaded with huge, fresh shrimp. Also, for a hearty taste of the ocean, try the seafood pasta. Dressy casual; cocktails. **Parking:** on-site. **Cards:** AX, DC, DS, MC, VI.   🍸

CAFE OF THE ARTS   **Lunch:** $8-$15   **Dinner:** $17-$33   **Phone:** 941/351-4304   ②

French

Location: On US 41, just s of jct University Pkwy. 5230 N Tamiami Tr 34234. **Hours:** Open 12/1-5/31 & 10/1-11/30; 11 am-3 & 5-9 pm. Closed: 1/1, 12/25. **Reservations:** suggested. **Features:** Varied courses are offered in intimate, sociable surroundings with a French theme. A wonderful concoction is a French loaf filled with seafood, ratatouille and rice in a flavorful cream sauce. Kudos to the staff for outstanding, attentive service. Casual dress; cocktails. **Parking:** on-site. **Cards:** AX, DS, MC, VI.   🍸

CHEF CALDWELL'S RESTAURANT   **Lunch:** $4-$10   **Dinner:** $16-$28   **Phone:** 941/957-1300   ㉑

Continental

Location: Just e of jct US 41; downtown. 1435 Main St 34236. **Hours:** 11 am-2:30 & 5-close, Sat from 5 pm. **Reservations:** suggested. **Features:** On St. Armands Circle, the popular eatery is a showcase for Chef Caldwell's signature selections, including crispy duckling, filet mignon and pecan-crusted snapper. Casual dress; beer & wine only. **Parking:** no self-parking. **Cards:** AX, MC, VI.

COASTERS ON THE WATER   **Lunch:** $8-$19   **Dinner:** $8-$19   **Phone:** 941/925-0300   ㉞

Seafood

Location: On SR 72, 0.6 mi sw of jct US 41; in Boatyard Village. 1500 Stickney Point Rd 34231. **Hours:** 11 am-10 pm. **Reservations:** not accepted. **Features:** Relax and enjoy either waterfront or patio dining. You'll find an array of health-conscious items as well as an extensive menu of pork, poultry and steak choices. The delicious grilled salmon tastes like they just plucked it from the water. Casual dress; cocktails. **Parking:** on-site. **Cards:** AX, CB, DC, DS, MC, VI.

(See map and index starting on p. 904)

COLUMBIA RESTAURANT Lunch: $9-$15 Dinner: $15-$26 Phone: 941/388-3987 ⑳
Spanish
Location: On St. Armands Key at St. Armands Circle. 411 St Armands Cir 34236. **Hours:** 11 am-11 pm, Sun noon-10 pm. **Reservations:** suggested, in season. **Features:** Colorful hand-painted tiles contribute to the Spanish motif that weaves through the cozy restaurant. Such dishes as the 1905 salad in garlic dressing and the snapper Alicante brim with flavor. Diners can unwind either in the indoor dining room or on the airy patio, where they can watch the shoppers of St. Armands pass by. Casual dress; cocktails. **Parking:** street. **Cards:** AX, MC, VI.

COSIMO'S BRICK OVEN Lunch: $7-$22 Dinner: $7-$22 Phone: 941/363-0211 ㉕
Italian
Location: US 41, jct Bee Ridge Rd; in Westfield Shopping Town Southgate. 3501 S Tamiami Tr 34239. **Hours:** 11 am-10 pm, Sun noon-8 pm. **Reservations:** accepted. **Features:** In trendy Southgate Plaza, this restaurant offers a comfortable dining setting. The varied menu offers such treats as wood-fired brick oven pizzas, signature pasta dishes and such hearty-appetite goodies as herb-roasted chicken and grilled veal chop. Casual dress; cocktails. **Parking:** on-site. **Cards:** AX, CB, DC, DS, MC, VI.

CRAB & FIN Lunch: $8-$24 Dinner: $8-$54 Phone: 941/388-3964 ㉒
Seafood
Location: On St. Armands Key, just s of jct John Ringling Blvd. 420 St. Armands Cir 34236. **Hours:** 11:30 am-10 pm, Fri & Sat-10:30 pm, Sun noon-10 pm. Closed: 11/23, 12/25. **Reservations:** suggested, for dinner. **Features:** Extensive menu offerings of homemade pasta, rack of veal, domestic lamb shank and many varieties of fresh fish, flown in daily, make it difficult to narrow down a choice. Casual dress; cocktails; entertainment. **Parking:** street. **Cards:** AX, CB, DC, MC, VI.

DA RU MA JAPANESE STEAK & SEAFOOD RESTAURANT Dinner: $14-$38 Phone: 941/951-2440 ④
Japanese
Location: US 41, jct Fruitville Rd; in Sarasota Quay. 318 Sarasota Quay 34236. **Hours:** 5 pm-10 pm. **Features:** The restaurant provides diners a Japanese experience via its traditional tableside service and teppan-style cooking. The food is creative. Casual dress; cocktails. **Parking:** on-site. **Cards:** MC, VI.

FIRST WATCH RESTAURANT Lunch: $3-$8 Phone: 941/954-1395 ⑩
American
Location: Corner of Main St and Pineapple Ave; downtown. 1395 Main St 34236. **Closed:** 11/23, 12/25. **Features:** "Eggsellent" culinary experimentation results in such light specialties as crepes, pancakes, omelets, sandwiches and salads. The classic Reuben is served with fried potatoes, salad and a small bowl of fresh fruit wedges. Service is friendly and attentive. Casual dress. **Parking:** street. **Cards:** AX, DS, MC, VI.

HEMINGWAY'S RETREAT Lunch: $8-$14 Dinner: $16-$39 Phone: 941/388-3948 ㉓
American
Location: On St. Armands Key at St. Armands Circle. 325 John Ringling Blvd 34236. **Hours:** 11:30 am-10 pm, Fri-11 pm, Sat 10 am-11 pm, Sun 10 am-10 pm. **Reservations:** accepted. **Features:** Key West decor helps to make the restaurant a nice, casual spot for lunch or dinner. The pleasant wait staff is a plus. Guests might start a relaxing meal with a bowl of chowder and then enjoy a mouthwatering rainbow trout dinner. Casual dress; cocktails. **Parking:** on-site and street. **Cards:** AX, DC, DS, MC, VI.

J RYAN'S ON THE GRILL Lunch: $8-$21 Dinner: $8-$21 Phone: 941/923-3200 ㊱
American
Location: On US 41, jct Club; in South Square. 8389 S Tamiami Tr 34238. **Hours:** 11:30 am-9 pm, Fri & Sat-10 pm. Closed: 12/25; also Super Bowl Sun. **Features:** The friendly spot has cozy decor, an inviting atmosphere and good food. Entree choices include such items as sauteed flounder piccata, grilled or poached salmon and mojo pork chops, all of which are served with tasty scallion mashed potatoes. Casual dress; cocktails. **Parking:** on-site. **Cards:** AX, DC, DS, MC, VI.

THE LAZY LOBSTER RESTAURANT Lunch: $11-$21 Dinner: $11-$21 Phone: 941/351-5515 ①
Seafood
Location: 0.9 mi n of jct University Pkwy; jct Tallevast Rd; in Lockwood Village Plaza. 7602 N Lockwood Ridge Rd 34243. **Hours:** 11:30 am-9 pm, Sun-8 pm. **Features:** Patrons can't go wrong with one of the restaurant's seafood or lobster specialties, such as macadamia nut grouper and lobster Thermidor. Casual dress; beer & wine only. **Parking:** on-site. **Cards:** AX, DS, MC, VI.

MADFISH GRILL Lunch: $8-$28 Dinner: $8-$28 Phone: 941/377-3474 ㉛
Seafood
Location: I-75, exit 207, just w on SR 758 (Bee Ridge Rd), then just s. 4059 Cattlemen Rd 34233. **Hours:** 11:30 am-10 pm, Sun 10 am-9 pm. Closed: 11/23, 12/25. **Reservations:** accepted. **Features:** Seafood with a Caribbean twist from Chef Gaddy. Enjoy anything from yellowfin tuna, grouper, mahi mahi and rainbow trout to chargrilled filet mignon or top sirloin. There are also various sandwiches, wraps, steamed shellfish, seafood platters and house specialties such as the madfish jambalaya or the potato crusted grouper. On Sundays, enjoy their weekly brunch. Catering is available as well. Casual dress; cocktails. **Parking:** on-site. **Cards:** AX, DC, DS, MC, VI.

MARIE'S ITALIAN KITCHEN *Menu on aaa.com* Lunch: $5-$7 Dinner: $7-$18 Phone: 941/923-1000 ㉜
Italian
Location: I-75, exit 205, 3 mi w on SR 72. 5767 Beneva Rd 34233. **Hours:** 11:30 am-2:30 & 4:30-9 pm. Closed major holidays; also Sun. **Reservations:** accepted. **Features:** Located in a strip mall, this small eatery features Brooklyn home-style Italian cooking. All of the traditional, classic Italian choices can be found on the menu. The lasagna and tiramisu are house specialties. Casual dress; beer & wine only. **Parking:** on-site. **Cards:** AX, DC, MC, VI.

MARINA JACK Lunch: $9-$39 Dinner: $9-$39 Phone: 941/365-4232 ⑰
Seafood
Location: Just w of jct US 41; downtown. 2 Marina Plaza 34236. **Hours:** 11:30 am-11 pm. Closed: 12/25. **Features:** In the downtown marina area, the casual establishment seats patrons inside or on the patio. Either way, they're treated to great views of the sunset and the many boats in the harbor. The varied menu centers on great seafood. Casual dress; cocktails. **Parking:** on-site. **Cards:** AX, MC, VI.

(See map and index starting on p. 904)

MEL'S DINER
American
Lunch: $4-$13   Dinner: $4-$13   Phone: 941/923-6070   27
Location: On SR 758, just e of jct Beneva Rd. 3740 Bee Ridge Rd 34233. **Hours:** 6:30 am-10 pm. Closed: 12/25. **Features:** Friendly service awaits at this throwback to a '60s-style establishment. Guests can't go wrong with a breakfast dish, such as a fresh omelet, or yummy open-faced platter. Also suggested are the hot and cold sandwiches, chili and burgers. Casual dress. **Parking:** on-site. **Cards:** AX, DS, MC, VI.

MICHAEL'S ON EAST
Continental
Lunch: $8-$19   Dinner: $19-$32   Phone: 941/366-0007   19
Location: On US 41; in Midtown Plaza, east entrance, jct Bahia Vista Dr. 1212 East Ave S 34239. **Hours:** 11:30 am-2 & 5:30-close, Sat from 6 pm. Closed: Sun. **Reservations:** suggested. **Features:** Creative dishes awaken taste buds in the upscale restaurant. Spicy seafood gumbo whets diners' appetites for larger catches such as grilled salmon, attractively presented with a colorful vegetable medley. Dressy casual; cocktails; entertainment. **Parking:** on-site and valet. **Cards:** AX, DC, DS, MC, VI.

MI PUEBLO EL RESTAURANTE MEXICANA
Mexican
Lunch: $7-$12   Dinner: $7-$12   Phone: 941/379-2880   28
Location: I-75, exit 207, 1.6 mi w; jct McIntosh Rd; in Palm Plaza. 4436 Bee Ridge Rd 34232. **Hours:** 11 am-9 pm, Fri & Sat-10 pm, Sun noon-8 pm. Closed: 1/1, 12/25; also 12/31. **Features:** The small, Mexican-themed eatery offers reliably good food. Anything from burritos to quesadillas to combination platters can be found on the menu, which lists chiles rellenos as a house specialty. Casual dress; beer & wine only. **Parking:** on-site. **Cards:** AX, MC, VI.

PATRICK'S RESTAURANT & TAVERN
American
Lunch: $5-$10   Dinner: $8-$22   Phone: 941/952-1170   12
Location: Downtown; in Kress International Plaza at Pineapple Ave. 1400 Main St 34236. **Hours:** 11 am-midnight. Closed: 12/25. **Reservations:** not accepted. **Features:** A chicken Vesuvio that erupts with flavor is the highlight of this upscale sports bar with a nice roadside appeal. Pull in for a variety of entree choices such as steak, pasta, pizza and burgers. Fresh flowers and cloth napkins add a nice touch. Casual dress; cocktails. **Parking:** valet and street. **Cards:** AX, DC, DS, MC, VI.

PINO'S 100 CENTRAL
Italian
Lunch: $7-$14   Dinner: $13-$23   Phone: 941/955-3739   16
Location: Jct US 780 (Fruitville Rd), just s on US 41 (Tamiami Tr) to Gulfstream Ave, then just e. 1301 Main St 34236. **Hours:** 11 am-10:30 pm, Sat-11 pm, Sun 4 pm-9:30 pm. Closed: 11/23, 12/25. **Reservations:** suggested. **Features:** Located just across from the downtown marina, the bistro setting is the perfect foil for the eye-pleasing and flavorful dishes brought to you by the friendly staff. Dressy casual; beer & wine only. **Parking:** street. **Cards:** AX, CB, DC, DS, MC, VI.

ROESSLER'S RESTAURANT
Continental
Dinner: $15-$31   Phone: 941/966-5688   37
Location: 0.8 mi s of Sarasota Square Mall, just e of jct US 41. 2033 Vamo Way 34238. **Hours:** 5 pm-close. **Reservations:** suggested. **Features:** In an elegant estate setting beside an ornamental pond, the romantic restaurant offers splendid entrees of duck, veal, lamb and seafood. Outside dining and casual menu available. Service is exemplary. Semi-formal attire; cocktails. **Parking:** on-site. **Cards:** AX, DS, MC, VI.

SCALINI
American
Lunch: $8-$21   Phone: 941/363-2615   3
Location: Just w of jct US 41; in Hyatt Sarasota. 1000 Blvd of the Arts 34236. **Hours:** 6:30-11 am, Sun 10:30 am-2 pm. **Features:** On the first floor of the Hyatt, the restaurant overlooks the grounds and the waterway. Clam chowder is a wonderful start to an intimate dining experience. Follow it up with fresh salmon. For a real treat, opt for the sinful chocolate lava cake as a finishing touch. Casual dress. **Parking:** on-site (fee) and valet. **Cards:** AX, DC, DS, JC, MC, VI.

SILVER CRICKET
Continental
Dinner: $12-$17   Phone: 941/955-9179   15
Location: Just w of jct Washington; downtown. 1923 Ringling Blvd 34236. **Hours:** 5 pm-10 pm. **Features:** The fusion style is evident in the downtown restaurant's signature dishes, which include Oriental paella, bronzed ahi tuna, wok-flashed lobster tail and peppercorn rack of lamb. Dressy casual; cocktails. **Parking:** street. **Cards:** DC, DS, MC, VI.

SUGAR & SPICE
American
Lunch: $4-$14   Dinner: $4-$14   Phone: 941/342-1649   29
Location: I-75, exit 207, just w on Bee Ridge Rd, then just s. 4000 Cattleman Rd 34233. **Hours:** 11 am-9 pm. Closed major holidays; also Sun. **Features:** Experience Amish-style cooking in a homey setting. The staff is dressed in conservative attire and dish up such good, hearty meals as fried chicken with mashed potatoes, green beans and a basket of bread. This enormously popular eatery is well worth any wait. Casual dress. **Parking:** on-site. **Cards:** DS, MC, VI.

TOMMY BAHAMA'S TROPICAL CAFE
Caribbean
Lunch: $8-$10   Dinner: $15-$23   Phone: 941/388-2888   24
Location: On St. Armands Key; at The Circle of St. Armands. 300 John Ringling Blvd 34236. **Hours:** 11 am-11 pm, Fri & Sat-midnight. Closed: 11/23, 12/25. **Features:** Expect a wait at this extremely popular spot, but it will be well worth it. A Caribbean flair punctuates the tropically decorated dining room. Among the wonderful food choices are island pasta, boca chica chicken, Trinidad tuna, Martinique mahi, quiche, salmon and ribs. Not too hungry? Select from many salads, sandwiches and appetizers. Casual dress; cocktails. **Parking:** street. **Cards:** AX, MC, VI.

TROPICAL THAI RESTAURANT
Thai
Lunch: $6-$7   Dinner: $6-$20   Phone: 941/364-5775   9
Location: 0.5 mi e of jct US 41; downtown. 1420 Main St 34236. **Hours:** 11:30 am-2:30 & 4-9:30 pm, Fri & Sat-10:30 pm. Closed: 11/23, 12/25; also Super Bowl Sun. **Features:** Authentic Thai cuisine is served in an intimate, nicely decorated dining room. Vegetable lovers will enjoy the sweet and sour shrimp, which is loaded with fresh vegetables and comes with a perfectly cooked bowl of rice. Service is gracious and welcoming. Casual dress; beer & wine only. **Parking:** street. **Cards:** AX, MC, VI.

(See map and index starting on p. 904)

TWO SENORITAS
Mexican

Lunch: $7-$14 **Dinner:** $7-$14 **Phone:** 941/366-1618 ⑭

Location: Just w of jct Central Ave; downtown. 1355 Main St 34236. **Hours:** 11:30 am-10:30 pm, Fri & Sat-midnight, Sun noon-10 pm. Closed major holidays. **Features:** A festive Mexican theme and great food are draws here. Specialties of the house include enchiladas, fajitas, chiles rellenos and quesadillas. Also on the menu are combination platters, steaks, chicken and seafood. Casual dress; cocktails. **Parking:** street. **Cards:** AX, MC, VI.

UVA RARA RISTORANTE
Italian

Dinner: $16-$25 **Phone:** 941/362-9006 ⑱

Location: Just w of jct S Orange Ave and Dolphin Ln. 443 Burns Ct 34236. **Hours:** 5 pm-10 pm. Closed: 1/1, 11/23, 12/25. **Reservations:** suggested. **Features:** This "rare grape" is located just off the charming Burns Court and is a local favorite for inspired Italian dining. Tantalizing fresh preparations, homemade pastas and fine wine nourish an intimate experience designed for the most discriminating appetite. Dressy casual; cocktails. **Parking:** valet and street. **Cards:** AX, CB, DC, DS, MC, VI.

VERNONA
Mediterranean

Lunch: $12-$22 **Dinner:** $24-$45 **Phone:** 941/309-2008 ⑤

Location: On US 41, jct John Ringling Blvd; in The Ritz-Carlton, Sarasota. 1111 Ritz-Carlton Dr 34236. **Hours:** 6:30-11 am, 11:30-2:30 & 5-10 pm; Sunday brunch. **Reservations:** suggested. **Features:** Verona features luxurious fine dining, a refined menu and a very knowledgeable staff. A large variety of bread and dessert and a distinctive European flair. Dressy casual; cocktails. **Parking:** valet. **Cards:** AX, CB, DC, DS, JC, MC, VI.

WATERFRONT RESTAURANT
Steak & Seafood

Dinner: $8-$27 **Phone:** 941/921-1916 ㉟

Location: On US 41, 1.3 mi s of jct SR 72. 7660 S Tamiami Tr 34231. **Hours:** 4 pm-10 pm, Fri & Sat-11 pm. Closed: 12/25, 6/1-10/1. **Features:** The casual atmosphere and pleasant views over the marina enhance dishes like lobster, chicken teriyaki, barbecue baby back ribs and daily fresh fish. Casual dress; cocktails. **Parking:** on-site. **Cards:** AX, DS, MC, VI.

ZORIA
Continental

Lunch: $9-$14 **Dinner:** $19-$32 **Phone:** 941/955-4457 ⑧

Location: Just w of jct US 301; downtown. 1991 Main St 34236. **Hours:** 11:30 am-2:30 & 5-10:30 pm, Sat from 5 pm, Sun 5 pm-9:30 pm. Closed: 11/23, 12/25. **Features:** The four-course tasting menu is a palate-pleaser, as are such interesting preparations as pepper-crusted ranch antelope. Dressy casual; cocktails. **Parking:** street. **Cards:** AX, DS, MC, VI.

SATELLITE BEACH pop. 9,577

——— WHERE TO STAY ———

DAYS INN
Motel

Book at aaa.com **Phone:** (321)777-3552

All Year 1P: $70-$200 2P: $70-$200 XP: $5 F17

Location: 0.3 mi s of jct SR 404. 180 SR A1A 32937. **Fax:** 321/777-1090. **Facility:** 104 one-bedroom standard units, some with whirlpools. 2 stories, exterior corridors. **Bath:** combo or shower only. **Parking:** on-site. **Terms:** 2-3 night minimum stay - seasonal and/or weekends, cancellation fee imposed, [ECP] meal plan available, small pets only ($10 extra charge). **Amenities:** hair dryers. **Pool(s):** outdoor. **Leisure Activities:** whirlpool, shuffleboard, volleyball. **Guest Services:** coin laundry. **Cards:** AX, CB, DC, DS, MC, VI. **Special Amenities:** free expanded continental breakfast and free newspaper.

SOME UNITS

RAMADA INN OCEANFRONT RESORT HOTEL
Small-scale Hotel

(fyi)

Phone: 321/777-7200

Property failed to provide current rates

Under major renovation, scheduled to be completed August 2005. **Last rated:** ▼▼▼ **Location:** On SR A1A, 2 mi s of jct SR 404. 1035 Hwy A1A 32937. **Fax:** 321/773-4608. **Facility:** 108 one-bedroom standard units, some with kitchens. 7 stories, interior corridors. **Parking:** on-site. **Amenities:** video library (fee), dual phone lines, voice mail, irons, hair dryers. **Pool(s):** heated outdoor. **Leisure Activities:** lighted tennis court. **Business Services:** meeting rooms, fax (fee).

SOME UNITS

——— WHERE TO DINE ———

THE DOVE RESTAURANT
Italian

Lunch: $6-$10 **Dinner:** $13-$30 **Phone:** 321/777-5817

Location: 4 mi s of jct SR 404. 1790 SR A1A 32937. **Hours:** 11:30 am-2 & 5-9 pm, Fri & Sat-10 pm. Closed: 1/1, 11/23, 12/25; also Sun. **Reservations:** suggested. **Features:** Both the signature Sophia sauce (light cream) and the tangy pepper sauce are favorites at this delightful Italian spot. A "doggie box" may be necessary, as traditional pasta specialties are heaped on an oversized dish. The knowledgeable and adept wait staff brings an air of refinement to the otherwise casual experience. Dressy casual; cocktails. **Parking:** on-site. **Cards:** AX, CB, DC, DS, MC, VI.

THE PHOENIX
Continental

Lunch: $8-$12 **Dinner:** $17-$25 **Phone:** 321/777-8414

Location: On SR A1A, 3.3 mi s of jct SR 404. 1550 Hwy A1A 32937. **Hours:** 11:30 am-2 & 5-9 pm, Sat from 5 pm; Sunday champagne brunch. Closed: 12/25; also Mon. **Reservations:** suggested. **Features:** Elegant without being stuffy, the neoclassic restaurant exudes intimacy, with dim lighting and cozy seating. Among the traditional entrees are rack of lamb with a rosemary honey mustard crust, shrimp madras and calf liver with onions and apples. Semi-formal attire; cocktails. **Parking:** on-site. **Cards:** AX, CB, DC, MC, VI.

SEASIDE

——— WHERE TO STAY ———

JOSEPHINE'S FRENCH COUNTRY INN   **Phone:** (850)231-1940
▼▼▼▼▼
All Year   2P: $235-$250   XP: $50
Country Inn
Location: Jct SR 395, 0.5 mi w on SR 30A, just n on Quincy Cir. 38 Seaside Ave 32459 (PO Box 4767). **Fax:** 850/231-2446. **Facility:** Close to boutique shops and the ocean, this property is in an area of beach cottages and Victorian-replica homes. Smoke free premises. 9 one-bedroom standard units. 2 stories, interior corridors. *Bath:* combo or shower only. **Parking:** on-site. **Terms:** check-in 4 pm, 2 night minimum stay, age restrictions may apply, 14 day cancellation notice-fee imposed, [BP] meal plan available, package plans. **Amenities:** irons. **Business Services:** meeting rooms. **Cards:** AX, MC, VI.

(ASK) (S/D) (Y1) (X) (VCR) (☆) (DATA PORT) 🖥 🖨 🖵

SEBASTIAN pop. 16,181

——— WHERE TO STAY ———

BEST WESTERN SEBASTIAN HOTEL & SUITES   **Phone:** 772/388-9300
(fyi)
12/15-5/31   1P: $109-$149   2P: $109-$149   XP: $10   F17
12/1-12/14 & 6/1-11/30   1P: $89-$119   2P: $89-$119   XP: $10   F17
Small-scale Hotel **Too new to rate. Location:** I-95, exit 156 (Fellsmere Rd/CR 512), e to US 1, then 1 mi n. 1655 US Hwy 1 32958. **Fax:** 772/388-8290. **Amenities:** 54 units, coffeemakers, microwaves, refrigerators, pool. **Terms:** cancellation fee imposed. **Cards:** AX, CB, DC, DS, JC, MC, VI.

KEY WEST INN AT CAPT HIRAM'S *Book at aaa.com*   **Phone:** (772)388-8588
(AAA) (SAVE)
2/3-5/27   1P: $129-$229   XP: $10   F17
12/1-2/2 & 5/28-7/29   1P: $119-$219   XP: $10   F17
▼▼▼▼
7/30-11/30   1P: $109-$209   XP: $10   F17
Small-scale Hotel **Location:** I-95, exit 156, 7.5 mi e, then 0.5 mi n. 1580 US 1 32958. **Fax:** 772/388-3118. **Facility:** 70 units. 65 one-bedroom standard units, some with whirlpools. 5 one-bedroom suites with efficiencies. 3 stories, interior/exterior corridors. *Bath:* combo or shower only. **Parking:** on-site. **Amenities:** DVD players, voice mail, irons, hair dryers. *Some:* video games, dual phone lines. **Dining:** 11:30 am-10 pm, cocktails, entertainment. **Pool(s):** heated outdoor. **Leisure Activities:** *Fee:* marina, charter fishing. **Guest Services:** coin laundry. **Business Services:** meeting rooms, fax (fee). **Cards:** AX, CB, DC, DS, MC, VI. **Special Amenities:** free continental breakfast and free local telephone calls.

SOME UNITS
(Y1) (Y) (&M) (&) (☆) (➷) (➔) (☆) (DATA PORT) 🖥 / (X) (VCR) 🖥 🖨 /
FEE

SEBRING pop. 9,667

——— WHERE TO STAY ———

THE CHATEAU ELAN HOTEL & SPA *Book at aaa.com*   **Phone:** (863)655-6252
▼▼▼▼
All Year   1P: $99   2P: $99
Small-scale Hotel **Location:** From US 27, 2.2 mi e on SR 98; at entrance to Sebring International Raceway. 150 Midway Dr 33870. **Fax:** 863/655-6303. **Facility:** 81 one-bedroom standard units. 4 stories, interior corridors. *Bath:* combo or shower only. **Parking:** on-site. **Terms:** 3 day cancellation notice-fee imposed, weekly rates available, package plans, pets ($50 fee). **Amenities:** high-speed Internet (fee), voice mail, irons, hair dryers. **Pool(s):** outdoor. **Leisure Activities:** whirlpool, exercise room, spa. **Guest Services:** gift shop, valet laundry, area transportation. **Business Services:** meeting rooms, business center. **Cards:** AX, CB, DC, DS, MC, VI.

SOME UNITS
(ASK) (S/D) (➔) (🐾) (Y1) (Y) (&) (➷) (➔) (X) (☆) (DATA PORT) 🖥 / (X) 🖥 /
FEE   FEE

INN ON THE LAKES   **Phone:** 863/471-9400
(AAA) (SAVE)
1/1-4/30   1P: $89-$109   2P: $89-$109
12/1-12/31 & 5/1-11/30   1P: $79-$99   2P: $79-$99
▼▼▼▼
Small-scale Hotel **Location:** On US 27, 1.5 mi n of jct SR 17. 3100 Golfview Rd 33870. **Fax:** 863/471-9400. **Facility:** 159 units. 158 one-bedroom standard units. 1 one-bedroom suite ($99-$160). 2-3 stories, interior/exterior corridors. **Parking:** on-site. **Terms:** cancellation fee imposed, package plans, small pets only ($40 fee). **Amenities:** voice mail, irons, hair dryers. **Dining:** 6:30 am-10 pm, Sun-9 pm, cocktails. **Pool(s):** outdoor. **Leisure Activities:** golf privileges, exercise room. *Fee:* massage. **Guest Services:** valet and coin laundry. **Business Services:** meeting rooms, fax (fee). **Cards:** AX, DC, DS, MC, VI.

SOME UNITS
(S/D) (🐾) (Y1) (Y) (➔) (☆) (DATA PORT) 🖥 / (X) 🖥 🖨 /
FEE   FEE

KENILWORTH LODGE *Book at aaa.com*   **Phone:** (863)385-0111
(AAA) (SAVE)
12/30-4/2 [ECP]   1P: $80-$160   2P: $80-$160   XP: $10   F12
12/1-12/29 & 4/3-11/30 [ECP]   1P: $60-$120   2P: $60-$120   XP: $10   F12
▼▼▼▼
Location: US 27, 1 mi e on SR 17. 1610 Lakeview Dr 33870. **Fax:** 863/385-4686. **Facility:** Begun in 1916, the
Historic
resort is listed on the National Register of Historic Places. There are various unit styles, including lodge
Small-scale Hotel rooms and cottages. 110 units. 75 one-bedroom standard units. 7 one-bedroom suites ($90-$160), some with efficiencies. 2 vacation homes and 26 cottages ($80-$110). 1-3 stories, interior/exterior corridors. **Parking:** on-site. **Terms:** 3 day cancellation notice-fee imposed, package plans, pets ($15 extra charge). **Amenities:** high-speed Internet, voice mail, irons. **Pool(s):** heated outdoor. **Leisure Activities:** billiards, foosball, table tennis, basketball, horseshoes, shuffleboard, volleyball. **Guest Services:** valet and coin laundry. **Business Services:** meeting rooms, business center. **Cards:** AX, DC, DS, MC, VI. **Special Amenities:** free expanded continental breakfast and free local telephone calls.

SOME UNITS
(S/D) (🐾) (Y1+) (➔) (➔) (X) (☆) (DATA PORT) 🖥 / (X) 🖨 🖥 /
FEE

QUALITY INN & SUITES CONFERENCE CENTER *Book at aaa.com*

Phone: (863)385-4500

AAA SAVE ◇◇

Small-scale Hotel

12/1-3/31 & 10/1-11/30	1P: $90-$100	2P: $90-$100
4/1-9/30	1P: $70-$80	2P: $70-$80

Location: On US 27, 7 mi n of jct SR 17. 6525 US 27 N 33870. **Fax:** 863/382-4793. **Facility:** 149 one-bedroom standard units. 2 stories (no elevator), exterior corridors. **Parking:** on-site. **Terms:** check-in 4 pm, cancellation fee imposed, weekly rates available, package plans, pets ($25 fee). **Amenities:** safes (fee), irons, hair dryers. **Dining:** 4:30 pm-9 pm, cocktails. **Pool(s):** outdoor. **Leisure Activities:** volleyball. **Guest Services:** valet and coin laundry. **Business Services:** conference facilities, fax (fee). **Cards:** AX, CB, DC, DS, JC, MC, VI. **Special Amenities:** free continental breakfast and free local telephone calls.

SOME UNITS

(icons) FEE FEE FEE

SEFFNER —See Tampa Bay p. 1045.

SEMINOLE —See Tampa Bay p. 1045.

SIESTA KEY pop. 7,150   (See map and index starting on p. 904)

---------- WHERE TO STAY ----------

CRESCENT ROYALE CONDOS

Phone: 941/349-7766 **63**

AAA SAVE ◇◇

Condominium

All Year Wkly	1P: $747-$1314	2P: $747-$1314
		XP: $25

Location: Just s of jct Avenida del Mare. 777 Beach Rd 34242. **Fax:** 941/349-8960. **Facility:** Designated smoking area. 71 units. 20 one-, 50 two- and 1 three-bedroom suites with kitchens. 5-7 stories, exterior corridors. **Parking:** on-site. **Terms:** office hours 9 am-5 pm, 7 night minimum stay, cancellation fee imposed. **Amenities:** voice mail, irons. *Some:* DVD players, CD players, hair dryers. **Pool(s):** heated outdoor. *Fee:* bicycles. **Leisure Activities:** saunas, beach access, recreation room, exercise room, shuffleboard. **Guest Services:** coin laundry. **Business Services:** meeting rooms, fax (fee). **Cards:** MC, VI. **Special Amenities:** free local telephone calls.

SOME UNITS

(icons) / (icons) /

PALM BAY CLUB

Phone: 941/349-1911 **64**

AAA SAVE ◇◇

Condominium

All Year	1P: $135-$800	2P: $135-$800

Location: Oceanfront. On SR 758, 0.8 mi n of jct SR 72. 5960 Midnight Pass Rd 34242. **Fax:** 941/349-1034. **Facility:** Buildings are set on the gulf or bay at this property where all units have a private, screened patio. 145 units. 61 one- and 84 two-bedroom suites with kitchens. 3-11 stories, interior/exterior corridors. **Parking:** on-site. **Terms:** office hours 9 am-5 pm. **Amenities:** high-speed Internet (fee), voice mail, irons, hair dryers. *Some:* DVD players, CD players. **Pool(s):** 2 heated outdoor. **Leisure Activities:** saunas, whirlpool, fishing, cabanas, fishing pier, 2 lighted tennis courts, recreation room, barbecue grills, exercise room. *Fee:* marina, boat slips, billiards, table tennis, game room. **Guest Services:** sundries, valet and coin laundry. **Business Services:** meeting rooms, fax (fee). **Cards:** AX, CB, DC, DS, JC, MC, VI. **Special Amenities:** free newspaper and early check-in/late check-out. *(See color ad p 913)*

SOME UNITS

(icons) / (icons) /

SARA SEA ON SIESTA KEY

Phone: (941)349-3244 **66**

AAA SAVE ◇◇◇

Motel

2/1-4/30	1P: $159-$429	2P: $159-$429	XP: $15	F12
5/1-11/30	1P: $99-$369	2P: $99-$369	XP: $15	F12
12/1-1/31	1P: $89-$359	2P: $89-$359	XP: $15	F12

Location: Just w of jct Midnight Pass Rd. 6760 Sara Sea Cir 34242. **Fax:** 941/349-5658. **Facility:** Designated smoking area. 22 units. 20 one-bedroom standard units with efficiencies. 2 one-bedroom suites ($169-$429) with kitchens. 1 story, exterior corridors. *Bath:* combo or shower only. **Parking:** on-site. **Terms:** office hours 9 am-9 pm, 2-3 night minimum stay - seasonal and/or weekends, 30 day cancellation notice-fee imposed, package plans. **Amenities:** video library (fee), voice mail, irons, hair dryers. *Some:* dual phone lines. **Leisure Activities:** beach access, fishing, pool privileges, beach chairs, umbrellas, gas barbecue grill, picnic area, shuffleboard. *Fee:* sailboats, catamaran, water bikes, kayaks, roller blades, scooters, bicycles. **Guest Services:** coin laundry. **Business Services:** meeting rooms, fax. **Cards:** AX, DS, MC, VI. **Special Amenities:** free room upgrade and preferred room (each subject to availability with advance reservations). *(See color ad p 917)*

(icons)

SIESTA BEACH RESORT AND SUITES *Book at aaa.com*

Phone: (941)349-3211 **62**

AAA SAVE ◇◇◇

Motel

2/1-4/30	1P: $184-$345	2P: $184-$345	XP: $15	F
12/21-1/31	1P: $145-$245	2P: $145-$245	XP: $15	F
12/1-12/20 & 5/1-11/30	1P: $105-$216	2P: $105-$216	XP: $15	F

Location: Jct Beach Rd; in Siesta Village. 5311 Ocean Blvd 34242. **Fax:** 941/349-7915. **Facility:** Designated smoking area. 51 units. 40 one-bedroom standard units, some with efficiencies. 9 one- and 2 two-bedroom suites with kitchens, some with whirlpools. 2 stories, exterior corridors. *Bath:* combo or shower only. **Parking:** on-site. **Terms:** 7 day cancellation notice, package plans. **Amenities:** voice mail, irons, hair dryers. *Some:* CD players. **Pool(s):** heated outdoor. **Leisure Activities:** whirlpool. **Guest Services:** coin laundry. **Business Services:** fax (fee). **Cards:** AX, CB, DC, DS, JC, MC, VI. **Special Amenities:** free local telephone calls and early check-in/late check-out. *(See color ad p 916)*

SOME UNITS

(icons) / (icons)

SIESTA KEY INN

Phone: (941)349-4999 **67**

AAA SAVE ◇◇◇

Motel

12/1-5/1	1P: $229-$449	2P: $229-$449	XP: $15	D12
5/2-11/30	1P: $169-$349	2P: $169-$349	XP: $15	D12

Location: Just sw of jct Midnight Pass Rd. 1017 Point of Rocks Rd 34242. **Fax:** 941/349-0700. **Facility:** Designated smoking area. 8 units. 5 one-, 2 two- and 1 three-bedroom suites with kitchens. 2 stories, exterior corridors. *Bath:* combo or shower only. **Parking:** on-site. **Terms:** office hours 9 am-9 pm, 3-7 night minimum stay - seasonal and/or weekends, 30 day cancellation notice-fee imposed, weekly rates available, package plans. **Amenities:** video library (fee), voice mail, irons, hair dryers. **Pool(s):** heated outdoor. **Leisure Activities:** whirlpool, beach access, fishing, beach chairs & umbrellas, gas barbecue grill, inline skates, scooters. *Fee:* sailboats, catamaran, kayaks, water bikes. **Guest Services:** coin laundry. **Business Services:** fax. **Cards:** AX, DS, MC, VI. **Special Amenities:** free local telephone calls and preferred room (subject to availability with advance reservations). *(See color ad p 916)*

(icons)

(See map and index starting on p. 904)

SUNSETS ON THE KEY

Phone: 941/312-9797 [61]

(AAA) [SAVE]

12/17-4/30	1P: $229-$339	2P: $229-$339
5/1-11/30	1P: $149-$209	2P: $149-$209
12/1-12/16	1P: $119-$169	2P: $119-$169

Motel

Location: Just w of Ocean Blvd via Avenida Messina; in Siesta Village. 5203 Avenida Navarra 34242. **Fax:** 941/312-9105. **Facility:** Designated smoking area. 9 units. 2 one-bedroom standard units with kitchens. 2 one- and 5 two-bedroom suites with kitchens. 2 stories, exterior corridors. *Bath:* combo or shower only. **Parking:** on-site. **Terms:** office hours 9 am-9 pm, 30 day cancellation notice-fee imposed, weekly rates available. **Amenities:** CD players, voice mail, irons, hair dryers. **Leisure Activities:** beach access, beach chairs, umbrellas, barbecue grill, deck/patio area, gazebo. **Guest Services:** coin laundry. **Business Services:** fax. **Cards:** DS, MC, VI. **Special Amenities: free local telephone calls and free room upgrade (subject to availability with advance reservations).**

TROPICAL BREEZE RESORT & SPA OF SIESTA KEY *Book at aaa.com*

Phone: (941)349-1125 [60]

(AAA) [SAVE]

1/16-4/30 Wkly [CP]	1P: $937-$2935	2P: $937-$2935	XP: $15	F14
12/1-1/15 & 5/1-11/30 Dly [CP]	1P: $103-$398	2P: $103-$398	XP: $15	F14

Motel

Location: Jct Avenida Messina; in Siesta Village. 5150 Ocean Blvd 34242. **Fax:** 941/349-0057. **Facility:** Designated smoking area. 69 units. 13 one-bedroom standard units, some with efficiencies. 44 one-, 9 two- and 3 three-bedroom suites, some with whirlpools. 1-2 stories, exterior corridors. *Bath:* combo or shower only. **Parking:** on-site. **Terms:** office hours 8 am-10 pm, 2-7 night minimum stay - seasonal and/or weekends, 14 day cancellation notice-fee imposed, daily & weekly rates available, package plans, pets ($50 extra charge). **Amenities:** video library (fee), voice mail, irons, hair dryers. **Pool(s):** 3 heated outdoor. **Leisure Activities:** beach access, sun deck, recreation programs, barbecue grills, yoga deck, exercise room, shuffleboard. *Fee:* kayaks, hobie cat, beach chair, pilates, tai chi, bicycles, massage. **Guest Services:** coin laundry. **Business Services:** meeting rooms. *Fee:* PC, fax. **Cards:** AX, DS, MC, VI. **Special Amenities: free continental breakfast and preferred room (subject to availability with advance reservations).**

TROPICAL SHORES BEACH RESORT *Book at aaa.com*

Phone: (941)349-3330 [65]

(AAA) [SAVE]

2/1-4/23	1P: $169-$495	2P: $169-$495	XP: $15	F21
12/1-1/31 & 4/24-11/30	1P: $89-$395	2P: $89-$395	XP: $15	F21

Motel

Location: S of jct SR 72 on Midnight Pass Rd, just w. 6717 Sara Sea Cir 34242. **Fax:** 941/346-0025. **Facility:** Designated smoking area. 30 units. 24 one-bedroom standard units with efficiencies, some with whirlpools. 5 one- and 1 two-bedroom suites with kitchens, some with whirlpools. 2 stories, exterior corridors. *Bath:* combo or shower only. **Parking:** on-site. **Terms:** office hours 7 am-10 pm, 14 day cancellation notice-fee imposed, package plans. **Amenities:** voice mail, irons, hair dryers. *Some:* DVD players, CD players. **Leisure Activities:** beach access, pool privileges,, barbecue grills, gazebo, shuffleboard, volleyball. *Fee:* aqua sport. **Guest Services:** valet and coin laundry. **Business Services:** PC, fax. **Cards:** AX, DS, MC, VI. *(See color ad p 910)*

SOME UNITS

TURTLE BEACH RESORT

Phone: (941)349-4554 [68]

12/1-4/30	2P: $340-$435	XP: $25	F21
5/1-11/30	2P: $295-$350	XP: $25	F21

Motel

Location: 2.8 mi s of jct SR 72. 9049 Midnight Pass Rd 34242. **Fax:** 941/349-9034. **Facility:** Designated smoking area. 10 units. 2 one-bedroom standard units, some with efficiencies. 2 one- and 6 two-bedroom suites with kitchens. 1 story, exterior corridors. *Bath:* combo or shower only. **Parking:** on-site. **Terms:** 2-7 night minimum stay - seasonal and/or weekends, 60 day cancellation notice-fee imposed, $20 service charge, pets (10% surcharge). **Amenities:** DVD players, CD players, irons, hair dryers. **Pool(s):** heated outdoor. **Leisure Activities:** boating, canoeing, paddleboats, fishing, bicycles. *Fee:* boat dock. **Guest Services:** complimentary laundry. **Cards:** DS, MC, VI.

——— **WHERE TO DINE** ———

OPHELIA'S ON THE BAY

Dinner: $20-$32 **Phone:** 941/349-2212 [85]

(AAA)

American

Location: 2.8 mi s of jct SR 72. 9105 Midnight Pass Rd 34242. **Hours:** 5 pm-10 pm. Closed: 12/25. **Reservations:** suggested. **Features:** Set on Little Sarasota Bay, this intimate restaurant offers varied dishes of duckling, veal, lamb, pasta and seafood, most notably the house specialty pompano wrapped in parchment paper. The atmosphere is gracious, as are the attentive servers. Casual dress; cocktails. **Parking:** valet. **Cards:** AX, DC, DS, MC, VI.

TURTLES ON LITTLE SARASOTA BAY

Lunch: $6-$9 **Dinner:** $7-$21 **Phone:** 941/346-2207 [84]

(AAA)

American

Location: 2.7 mi s of jct SR 72; opposite Turtle Beach. 8875 Midnight Pass Rd 34242. **Hours:** 11:30 am-10 pm. **Features:** Potato-crusted mahi mahi and snapper New Orleans are among exquisite seafood entrees at the tropical restaurant, which also serves chicken, pork and steak. Lots of windows overlook the bay for indoor dining, or enjoy the crisp air on the outdoor deck. Nightly entertainment is available in season. Casual dress; cocktails; entertainment. **Parking:** on-site. **Cards:** AX, DS, MC, VI.

VILLAGE CAFE

Lunch: $5-$10 **Phone:** 941/349-2822 [83]

American

Location: Center; in Siesta Village. 5133 Ocean Blvd 34242. **Hours:** 7 am-2:30 pm. Closed: 12/25. **Features:** Centrally located in a small strip mall in the village, the popular cafe is basically decorated and has a friendly wait staff. Menu options include many breakfast items, salads and sandwiches. Try the turkey club with its fresh crisp ingredients. Casual dress; beer & wine only. **Parking:** on-site. **Cards:** DS, MC, VI.

SILVER SPRINGS

―――― **WHERE TO STAY** ――――

DAYS INN   *Book at aaa.com*   **Phone:** (352)236-2891

(AAA) (SAVE)

| | 1/1-3/31 | 1P: $85 | 2P: $85 | XP: $5 | F17 |
| | 12/1-12/31 & 4/1-11/30 | 1P: $65 | 2P: $65 | XP: $5 | F17 |

Motel   **Location:** SR 40, 0.5 mi w of jct CR 35. 5001 E Silver Springs 34488. Fax: 352/236-3546. **Facility:** 56 one-bedroom standard units. 2 stories, exterior corridors. **Parking:** on-site. **Terms:** age restrictions may apply, pets ($7 extra charge). **Amenities:** hair dryers. **Pool(s):** outdoor. **Leisure Activities:** playground. **Guest Services:** coin laundry. **Business Services:** fax (fee). **Cards:** AX, DC, DS, MC, VI. **Special Amenities:** free continental breakfast and free newspaper.

SOME UNITS

HOLIDAY INN-SILVER SPRINGS   **Phone:** (352)236-2575

| | All Year | 1P: $69-$99 | 2P: $69-$99 | XP: $6 | F18 |

Small-scale Hotel   **Location:** SR 40. Located across from Silver Springs entrance. 5751 E Silver Springs Blvd 34488 (PO Box 156, 34489). Fax: 352/236-2576. **Facility:** 103 units. 101 one-bedroom standard units. 1 one- and 1 two-bedroom suites ($150-$250), some with whirlpools. 2 stories, exterior corridors. **Parking:** on-site. **Terms:** cancellation fee imposed, package plans. **Amenities:** high-speed Internet, safes, irons, hair dryers. **Pool(s):** outdoor, wading. **Leisure Activities:** exercise room. **Guest Services:** valet laundry. **Business Services:** meeting rooms, fax (fee). **Cards:** AX, CB, DC, DS, JC, MC, VI.

SOME UNITS

SUN PLAZA MOTEL   **Phone:** 352/236-2343

(AAA) (SAVE)

| | All Year | 1P: $50-$70 |

Motel   **Location:** SR 40, jct CR 35. 5461 E Silver Springs Blvd 34488. Fax: 352/236-1214. **Facility:** 47 one-bedroom standard units, some with efficiencies. 1 story, exterior corridors. *Bath:* combo or shower only. **Parking:** on-site. **Terms:** weekly rates available, [CP] meal plan available, pets ($10 extra charge). **Pool(s):** outdoor. **Leisure Activities:** playground, shuffleboard. **Guest Services:** coin laundry. **Business Services:** fax. **Cards:** AX, DS, MC, VI.

SOME UNITS

SOUTH DAYTONA   pop. 13,177   (See map and index starting on p. 285)

―――― **WHERE TO STAY** ――――

SUNSET INN   **Phone:** 386/767-0661   **46**

(AAA) (SAVE)

	12/1-4/14	1P: $39-$129	2P: $45-$155	XP: $5	D11
	6/26-11/30	1P: $39-$129	2P: $45-$149	XP: $5	D11
	4/15-6/25	1P: $35-$55	2P: $39-$59	XP: $5	D11

Motel   **Location:** US 1, 1 mi s of SR 400. 2425 S Ridgewood Ave 32119. Fax: 386/761-9766. **Facility:** 22 one-bedroom standard units, some with efficiencies. 1 story, exterior corridors. *Bath:* combo or shower only. **Parking:** on-site. **Terms:** 3-8 night minimum stay - seasonal, 14 day cancellation notice, weekly rates available. **Pool(s):** outdoor. **Leisure Activities:** shuffleboard. **Guest Services:** coin laundry. **Cards:** AX, DS, MC, VI.

SOME UNITS

―――― **WHERE TO DINE** ――――

MARIA BONITA   **Lunch:** $4-$12   **Dinner:** $8-$14   **Phone:** 386/767-9512   **32**

Mexican   **Location:** Just s of SR 400. 1784 S Ridgewood Ave 32119. **Hours:** 11:30 am-9 pm. Closed: 1/1, 11/23, 12/25; also Super Bowl Sun. **Features:** Everything is authentic about the Mexican cuisine served at this local favorite. From the crisp, flaky chips to the crispy fried pork (Lechon asado), rice beans and plantains, your taste buds will be very pleased. Casual dress; cocktails. **Parking:** on-site. **Cards:** AX, CB, DC, DS, JC, MC, VI.

SOUTH MIAMI —*See Miami-Miami Beach p. 614.*

SOUTH PALM BEACH   pop. 699—*See PALM BEACH.*

SOUTH PASADENA —*See Tampa Bay p. 1045.*

SPRING HILL pop. 69,078

—— WHERE TO STAY ——

HAMPTON INN
▼▼▼
Small-scale Hotel
Phone: 352/684-5000
All Year   1P: $95-$135   2P: $100-$160
Location: On US 19, 0.4 mi s of CR 574 (Spring Hill Rd). 1344 Commercial Way 34606. Fax: 352/684-5075. **Facility:** 72 one-bedroom standard units, some with whirlpools. 3 stories, interior corridors. **Bath:** combo or shower only. **Parking:** on-site. **Terms:** cancellation fee imposed, [ECP] meal plan available. **Amenities:** high-speed Internet, dual phone lines, voice mail, irons, hair dryers. **Pool(s):** outdoor. **Leisure Activities:** exercise room. **Business Services:** meeting rooms, fax (fee). **Cards:** AX, CB, DC, DS, MC, VI.

SOME UNITS
(ASK) (S/D) (T+) (&) (pool) (fridge) (film) (DATA PORT) (□) / (X) (■) (□) /
                                                                    FEE FEE

—— WHERE TO DINE ——

BEEF 'O' BRADY'S
▼▼
American
Lunch: $5-$9   **Dinner:** $5-$9   **Phone: 352/666-1831**
Location: On US 19, jct Lake In Woods Dr/Forest Oaks Blvd; in Forest Oaks Plaza. 7285 Forest Oaks Blvd 34606. **Hours:** 11 am-10:30 pm, Fri & Sat-1 am. **Features:** The restaurant is a fun dining spot, especially for those who enjoy watching sports. Monitors placed strategically around the dining room show varied events at any given time. Most entrees are of the sandwich and finger-food variety. Grilled grouper salad is a must-try, as are the chicken wings for which this place is known. Casual dress; cocktails. **Parking:** on-site. **Cards:** MC, VI.

(& M)

CODY'S ORIGINAL ROADHOUSE
▼▼
American
Lunch: $7-$20   **Dinner:** $7-$20   **Phone: 352/683-8909**
Location: On US 19 at jct Pine Forest; in Spring Hill Shopping Center. 3101 Commercial Way 34606. **Hours:** 3:30 pm-10 pm, Fri & Sat-11 pm, Sun noon-10 pm. **Features:** Lending to the fun roadhouse atmosphere are buckets full of peanuts and the shells of their downed comrades all over the floor. On the menu are rib, pork chop, rotisserie chicken, grilled shrimp, grouper, salmon and steak dishes, as well as combination platters. The must-try Caribbean tuna is coated with lime and spices, grilled and topped with garlic-lemon butter. Casual dress; cocktails. **Parking:** on-site. **Cards:** AX, DS, MC, VI.

(& M) (Y)

MY DANTE'S BISTRO RESTAURANT
▼▼
Italian
Lunch: $5-$8   **Dinner:** $6-$19   **Phone: 352/683-8420**
Location: On US 19, 0.8 mi n of jct CR 574 (Spring Hill Rd); in Village at Timber Pines Shopping Center. 2410 Commercial Way 34606. **Hours:** 11 am-10 pm, Sat & Sun from noon. **Reservations:** suggested. **Features:** Lovely touches—such as chandeliers, candlesticks, linen napkins and tablecloths—add romantic elegance to this small dining room. The outdoor cafe is an equally inviting spot to enjoy such entrees as chicken cordon bleu with roasted potatoes. Casual dress; beer & wine only. **Parking:** on-site.

UNCLE KEITH'S CONEY ISLAND
▼
American
Lunch: $2-$15   **Dinner:** $2-$15   **Phone: 352/597-5669**
Location: On US 19, 0.5 mi n of jct Berkeley Manor Blvd; in Winchester South. 5130 Commercial Way 34606. **Hours:** 6 am-11 pm. Closed: 11/23, 12/25; also Sun. **Features:** A local favorite, the casual spot serves more than a dozen hot dog preparations, such as Coney Dog New England style, Chicago dog, New York dog, Wisconsin dog, pizza dog, German dog and junkyard dog. Other offerings include submarine sandwiches, soups and various yummy desserts. Casual dress; beer & wine only. **Parking:** on-site. **Cards:** AX, DS, MC, VI.

STARKE pop. 5,593

—— WHERE TO STAY ——

BEST WESTERN MOTOR INN
(AAA) (SAVE)
▼▼
Small-scale Hotel
Book at aaa.com
All Year [CP]   1P: $69-$125   2P: $69-$125   XP: $10   F12
Phone: (904)964-6744
Location: 1 mi n on US 301 from jct SR 100. 1290 N Temple Ave 32091. Fax: 904/964-3355. **Facility:** 51 one-bedroom standard units. 2 stories, exterior corridors. **Parking:** on-site. **Terms:** 14 day cancellation notice, pets ($11 extra charge). **Amenities:** irons, hair dryers. **Pool(s):** outdoor. **Business Services:** fax (fee). **Cards:** AX, CB, DC, DS, MC, VI. **Special Amenities:** free continental breakfast and free local telephone calls.

SOME UNITS
(S/D) (↓) (T+) (pool) (film) (DATA PORT) (□) / (X) (■)
     FEE

DAYS INN *Book at aaa.com* **Phone:** (904)964-7600

AAA SAVE

Small-scale Hotel

2/16-3/31	1P: $57-$129	2P: $62-$149	XP: $7 F12
12/1-2/15 & 4/1-11/30	1P: $57-$80	2P: $62-$95	XP: $5 F12

Location: 10 mi s of jct SR 16. 1101 N Temple Ave 32091. **Fax:** 904/964-4554. **Facility:** 93 one-bedroom standard units, some with whirlpools. 2 stories, exterior corridors. *Bath:* combo or shower only. **Parking:** on-site. **Terms:** 7 day cancellation notice, pets ($10 extra charge). **Amenities:** irons, hair dryers. **Dining:** 24 hours. **Pool(s):** outdoor. **Guest Services:** coin laundry. **Cards:** AX, CB, DC, DS, JC, MC, VI.

SOME UNITS

------ **WHERE TO DINE** ------

LAREDO MEXICAN RESTAURANT   **Lunch:** $4-$7   **Dinner:** $5-$10   **Phone:** 904/966-2323

Southwest Mexican

Location: 0.5 mi n on US 301. 800 N Temple Ave 32091. **Hours:** 11 am-10 pm. Closed major holidays; also Sun. **Reservations:** suggested. **Features:** A must for the best food and service south of the border. Colorful flower beds and a bright, attractive decor create an inviting setting. Try the chalupa, a thick, toasty tortilla topped with hot beans, lettuce, tomato and a generous scoop of guacamole. Casual dress; cocktails. **Parking:** on-site. **Cards:** AX, DS, MC, VI.

STEINHATCHEE

------ **WHERE TO STAY** ------

STEINHATCHEE LANDING RESORT   *Book at aaa.com*   **Phone:** (352)498-3513

Condominium

6/1-11/30	2P: $200-$425
12/1-5/31	2P: $132-$338

Location: SR 51, 8 mi w of jct US 19/98: SR 51 N 32359 (PO Box 789). **Fax:** 352/498-2346. **Facility:** Southern-style cottages in a secluded, oak-shaded, riverside compound are the appeal here. 30 units. 14 one- and 12 two-bedroom standard units with kitchens. 4 three-bedroom suites with kitchens. 2 stories, exterior corridors. **Parking:** on-site. **Terms:** check-in 4 pm, 2 night minimum stay - weekends, 14 day cancellation notice-fee imposed, [CP] meal plan available, 2% service charge, pets ($100 deposit, in designated units). **Amenities:** irons, hair dryers. **Pool(s):** outdoor. **Leisure Activities:** whirlpool, canoeing, boat dock, fishing, lighted tennis court, bicycles, playground, exercise room, basketball, volleyball. **Guest Services:** complimentary laundry. **Business Services:** meeting rooms, fax (fee). **Cards:** AX, MC, VI.

SOME UNITS

STEINHATCHEE RIVER INN   **Phone:** (352)498-4049

Motel

5/21-11/30	1P: $84-$89	2P: $84-$89	XP: $10 F3
12/1-5/20	1P: $60-$84	2P: $60-$84	XP: $10 F3

Location: Center. Located across from the marina. 1111 Riverside Dr 32359 (PO Box 828). **Fax:** 352/498-0654. **Facility:** 17 one-bedroom standard units, some with kitchens. 2 stories, exterior corridors. **Parking:** on-site. **Terms:** 14 day cancellation notice-fee imposed, pets ($10 extra charge, small dogs only). **Pool(s):** outdoor. **Cards:** AX, DS, MC, VI.

SOME UNITS

THE SUNSET PLACE RESORT MOTEL   **Phone:** 352/498-0860

Small-scale Hotel

All Year	1P: $85-$150	2P: $85-$150

Location: SR 51, 12 mi w of jct US 98. 115 1st St SW 32359 (PO Box 975). **Fax:** 352/498-0840. **Facility:** 29 units. 15 one- and 14 two-bedroom standard units with kitchens. 3 stories (no elevator), exterior corridors. **Parking:** on-site. **Terms:** 3 night minimum stay - seasonal, 14 day cancellation notice, package plans. **Amenities:** *Some:* DVD players. **Pool(s):** outdoor. **Leisure Activities:** *Fee:* boat dock. **Business Services:** fax. **Cards:** AX, DS, MC, VI.

SOME UNITS

------ **WHERE TO DINE** ------

ROY'S   **Lunch:** $6-$14   **Dinner:** $10-$18   **Phone:** 352/498-5000

Spanish

Location: Just w of town center; on gulf. Hwy 51 32359. **Hours:** 11 am-9 pm. Closed: 12/24, 12/25. **Reservations:** accepted. **Features:** A lovely gulf view and superbly prepared food explain why this restaurant has been serving for 30 years. Here you will find the tastiest shrimp in the region along with other ocean fare that is fried, broiled or steamed, and served with great hushpuppies. Casual dress. **Parking:** on-site. **Cards:** MC, VI.

STUART pop. 14,633

------ **WHERE TO STAY** ------

HOLIDAY INN-DOWNTOWN STUART   *Book at aaa.com*   **Phone:** (772)287-6200

Small-scale Hotel

2/1-4/30	1P: $169-$239	2P: $169-$239
12/1-1/31 & 11/1-11/30	1P: $129-$199	2P: $129-$199
5/1-10/31	1P: $119-$189	2P: $119-$189

Location: On US 1, 0.5 mi s of jct SR 76. 1209 S Federal Hwy 34994 (PO Box 566-34997). **Fax:** 772/600-2002. **Facility:** 120 units. 119 one-bedroom standard units. 1 one-bedroom suite with whirlpool. 2 stories, exterior corridors. *Bath:* combo or shower only. **Parking:** on-site. **Amenities:** video games (fee), high-speed Internet, voice mail, irons, hair dryers. **Pool(s):** heated outdoor. **Leisure Activities:** exercise room. **Guest Services:** valet and coin laundry. **Business Services:** meeting rooms, fax (fee). **Cards:** AX, CB, DC, DS, MC, VI.

SOME UNITS

HOWARD JOHNSON HOTEL   *Book at aaa.com*

Phone: (772)287-3171

AAA [SAVE]

	1/1-3/31 [CP]	1P: $139-$200	2P: $139-$200	XP: $10	F18
	12/1-12/31 [CP]	1P: $92-$129	2P: $92-$129	XP: $10	F18
	4/1-11/30 [CP]	1P: $82-$129	2P: $82-$129	XP: $10	F18

Location: On US 1, just s of jct SR 76. 950 S Federal Hwy 34994. Fax: 772/220-3594. **Facility:** 81 one-bedroom
Small-scale Hotel standard units. 2 stories, interior corridors. **Parking:** on-site. **Amenities:** irons, hair dryers. **Dining:** 11 am-
12:30 am, cocktails. **Pool(s):** outdoor. **Guest Services:** valet and coin laundry. **Business Services:**
meeting rooms, fax (fee). **Cards:** AX, DC, DS, MC, VI.

SOME UNITS

[icons] FEE

HUTCHINSON ISLAND MARRIOTT BEACH RESORT
& MARINA   *Book at aaa.com*

Phone: (772)225-3700

	1/1-4/29	1P: $269-$379
	12/1-12/31	1P: $179-$259
Resort	4/30-5/31	1P: $179-$249
Large-scale Hotel	6/1-11/30	1P: $139-$249

Location: 4 mi ne on SR A1A; south end of Hutchinson Island at east end of causeway. 555 NE Ocean Blvd 34996.
Fax: 772/225-0003. **Facility:** This plantation-style hotel on the river features large hotel-room units as well as waterfront
housekeeping apartments with balconies. 280 units. 220 one-bedroom standard units, some with efficiencies. 53 one- and
two-bedroom suites ($249-$599), some with efficiencies, kitchens and/or whirlpools. 4 stories, interior/exterior corridors. *Bath:*
combo or shower only. **Parking:** on-site and valet. **Terms:** 3 day cancellation notice-fee imposed, package plans, pets ($75
fee). **Amenities:** voice mail, irons, hair dryers. *Some:* high-speed Internet (fee). **Pool(s):** 3 heated outdoor. *Leisure*
Activities: whirlpools, fishing, recreation programs, rental bicycles, playground, exercise room, spa, volleyball. *Fee:* marina,
charter fishing, golf-18 holes, 13 tennis courts (5 lighted), game room. **Guest Services:** gift shop, valet and coin laundry, area
transportation. **Business Services:** conference facilities, business center. **Cards:** AX, CB, DC, DS, JC, MC, VI.

SOME UNITS

[icons] FEE FEE   VCR FEE

PIRATES COVE RESORT & MARINA

Phone: 772/287-2500

AAA [SAVE]

	12/1-4/18	1P: $190-$220	2P: $190-$220	XP: $10	F18
	4/19-5/31 & 11/1-11/30	1P: $165-$195	2P: $165-$195	XP: $10	F18
	6/1-10/31	1P: $145-$170	2P: $145-$170	XP: $10	F18

Location: 0.3 mi e of SR A1A. 4307 SE Bayview St 34997. Fax: 772/220-2704. **Facility:** 50 one-bedroom
Small-scale Hotel standard units. 3-4 stories, exterior corridors. *Bath:* combo or shower only. **Parking:** on-site. **Terms:** check-
in 4 pm, cancellation fee imposed, [CP] meal plan available, pets ($20 extra charge). **Amenities:** voice mail,
irons, hair dryers. **Dining:** Pirate's Loft Restaurant, see separate listing, entertainment. **Pool(s):** heated outdoor. *Leisure*
Activities: *Fee:* marina, fishing, charter fishing, rack storage for boats. **Guest Services:** gift shop, valet and coin laundry.
Business Services: meeting rooms, fax (fee). **Cards:** AX, CB, DC, DS, MC, VI. **Special Amenities:** free continental
breakfast.

SOME UNITS

[icons] FEE   FEE

PLANTATION BEACH CLUB AT INDIAN RIVER
PLANTATION

Phone: (772)225-0074

| | All Year | 2P: $180-$350 |

Location: 0.5 mi se of SR A1A, via McArthur Blvd, just ne on NE Plantation Rd to NE Tradewind Ln, follow signs; in
Condominium Indian River Plantation Resort. 329 NE Tradewind Ln 34996. Fax: 772/225-6318. **Facility:** The property offers
large, fully equipped lodgings, all with large screened porches and water views. 30 units. 10 one- and 20
two-bedroom suites with kitchens and whirlpools. 1-4 stories, exterior corridors. **Parking:** on-site. **Terms:** 2 night minimum stay,
30 day cancellation notice. **Amenities:** video library (fee), CD players, voice mail, irons, hair dryers. **Pool(s):** heated outdoor.
Leisure Activities: sauna, whirlpool, fishing, exercise room. **Guest Services:** complimentary laundry, area transportation.
Business Services: meeting rooms, fax (fee). **Cards:** AX, DS, MC, VI.

[icons]

RAMADA INN   *Book at aaa.com*

Phone: (772)287-6900

	2/1-3/31	1P: $119-$189	2P: $119-$189	XP: $8	F18
	1/1-1/31	1P: $99-$169	2P: $99-$169	XP: $8	F18
	12/1-12/31	1P: $79-$149	2P: $79-$149	XP: $8	F18
Small-scale Hotel	4/1-11/30	1P: $89-$139	2P: $89-$139	XP: $8	F18

Location: On US 1, 0.5 mi s of jct SR 76. 1200 S Federal Hwy 34994. Fax: 772/286-8188. **Facility:** 118 units. 114 one-bedroom
standard units, some with whirlpools. 4 one-bedroom suites ($139-$189). 2 stories, exterior corridors. *Bath:* combo or shower
only. **Parking:** on-site. **Terms:** check-in 4 pm, 3 day cancellation notice, [ECP] meal plan available. **Amenities:** voice mail,
irons, hair dryers. **Pool(s):** heated outdoor. **Leisure Activities:** *Fee:* game room. **Guest Services:** valet and coin laundry.
Business Services: meeting rooms, business center. **Cards:** AX, CB, DC, DS, JC, MC, VI.

SOME UNITS

[icons]

SUBURBAN EXTENDED STAY HOTEL-STUART   *Book at aaa.com*

Phone: (772)286-1010

AAA [SAVE]

| | All Year | 1P: $69-$99 | 2P: $69-$99 | XP: $10 | F18 |

Location: On US 1, 2 mi s of jct SR 76. 1900 S Federal Hwy 34994. Fax: 772/286-6488. **Facility:** 126 one-
bedroom standard units with efficiencies. 3 stories, exterior corridors. *Bath:* combo or shower only. **Parking:**
Small-scale Hotel on-site. **Terms:** 10 day cancellation notice-fee imposed, weekly rates available. **Amenities:** voice mail.
Guest Services: coin laundry. **Business Services:** fax (fee). **Cards:** AX, DC, DS, MC, VI.

SOME UNITS

[icons]

————— **WHERE TO DINE** —————

THE ASHLEY RESTAURANT & BAR

Lunch: $8-$17   Dinner: $10-$27   Phone: 772/221-9476

Location: Downtown historic area by the waterfront. 61 SW Osceola St 34994. **Hours:** 11:30 am-2:30 & 5-midnight,
Continental Sun 10 am-2:30 pm. Closed: 1/1. **Reservations:** accepted. **Features:** In a historic, circa 1900 building, the
restaurant is eclectic in menu and decor and offers dishes at moderate prices. Casual dress; cocktails.
Parking: street. **Cards:** AX, DC, MC, VI.

ATLANTA BREAD COMPANY   Lunch: $4-$7   Dinner: $4-$7   Phone: 772/781-5121

♦♦♦
American

Location: On US 1, just n of jct SR 76. 2000 SE Federal Hwy (US 1) 34994. **Hours:** 7 am-9 pm, Sat 8 am-8 pm, Sun 8 am-6 pm. Closed major holidays. **Features:** The quick-serve eatery prepares sandwiches and fresh baked goods. Also on the menu are specialty coffees, smoothies and "cafechillos". Casual dress. **Parking:** on-site. **Cards:** AX, MC, VI.

DON RAMON RESTAURANT   Lunch: $4-$7   Dinner: $6-$19   Phone: 772/221-7711

♦♦♦ ♦♦♦
Cuban

Location: Jct of SR 76 and Monterey Rd. 2220 SE Ocean Blvd 34996. **Hours:** 11:30 am-9 pm, Fri & Sat-10 pm. Closed: 1/1, 7/4, 12/25. **Reservations:** required. **Features:** Warm ambience fills the dining room and the airy patio of the comfortable restaurant, a favorite with the locals. On the enticing menu are chicken, fish and shredded pork dishes, as well as sweet fried plantains and black beans with rice. Casual dress; beer & wine only. **Parking:** on-site. **Cards:** AX, DC, DS, MC, VI.

DRAGONFLY CAFE   Lunch: $6-$12   Dinner: $6-$12   Phone: 772/219-3555

♦♦♦
American

Location: I-95, exit 101, 3 mi n on SR 76 (Kanner Hwy), then 0.3 mi e; located in Willoughby Center. 900 SE Indian St 34997. **Hours:** 11 am-9 pm. Closed major holidays; also Sun. **Features:** This cafe provides high quality organic and all-natural foods in a comfortable and cozy atmosphere. Grilled paninis, marketplace sandwiches, wraps, salads and items off the grill are offered. Casual dress; beer & wine only. **Parking:** on-site. **Cards:** AX, DS, MC, VI.

EL TORO MEXICAN FOOD & CANTINA   Lunch: $6-$15   Dinner: $6-$15   Phone: 772/287-8161

♦♦♦ ♦♦♦
Mexican

Location: On US 1, 2 mi s of SR 76. 1602 SE Federal Hwy 34994. **Hours:** 11 am-10 pm, Sun from noon. Closed major holidays. **Features:** The family-owned eatery serves traditional food in a festive and fun atmosphere. Casual dress; cocktails. **Parking:** on-site. **Cards:** AX, DS, MC, VI.

THE FLAGLER GRILL   Dinner: $14-$25   Phone: 772/221-9517

♦♦♦ ♦♦♦
Regional American

Location: Just e of US 1; in historic downtown area. 47 SW Flagler Ave 34994. **Hours:** 5 pm-9:30 pm. Closed: 1/1, 12/25. **Reservations:** suggested. **Features:** In a turn-of-the-20th-century building, the cozy, friendly restaurant is noted for excellent service and innovative cuisine. Fresh ingredients and international seasonings contribute to the food's great taste; a well-balanced wine list enhances it. Casual dress; cocktails. **Parking:** street. **Cards:** AX, DS, MC, VI.

GIUSEPPE'S ITALIAN GRILL   Lunch: $8-$35   Dinner: $8-$35   Phone: 772/283-8281

♦♦♦ ♦♦♦
Italian

Location: I-95, exit 101, 3 mi n on SR 76 (Kanner Hwy), then 0.3 mi e; located in Willoughby Center. 840 SE Indian St 34997. **Hours:** 11 am-10 pm, Fri & Sat-11 pm, Sun 3 pm-10 pm. Closed major holidays. **Features:** On the restaurant's menu is a traditional selection of well-prepared and moderately priced items. Families are welcomed in the straightforward and relaxed environment. Tables are well-spaced. Casual dress; entertainment. **Parking:** on-site. **Cards:** AX, DS, MC, VI.

MARIO'S ITALIAN RESTAURANT   Dinner: $6-$15   Phone: 772/283-6660

♦♦♦ ♦♦♦
Italian

Location: On US 1, 1 mi s of jct SR 76; in Federal Plaza Shops. 1924 S Federal Hwy 34994. **Hours:** 2 pm-10 pm. Closed major holidays; also Mon. **Features:** Although the decor is plain and simple, the food is far from it. The owner/chef shares time-tested family recipes and freshly baked desserts, such as cheesecake, tiramisu and cannoli. Generous portions and a friendly staff add to the experience. Casual dress; beer & wine only. **Parking:** on-site. **Cards:** AX, MC, VI.

PIRATE'S LOFT RESTAURANT   *Menu on aaa.com*   Lunch: $6-$12   Dinner: $10-$22   Phone: 772/223-5048

AAA
♦♦♦
Seafood

Location: 0.3 mi e of SR A1A; in Pirates Cove Resort & Marina. 4307 SE Bayview St 34997. **Hours:** 11:30 am-10 pm, Sun from 10:30 am. **Reservations:** suggested. **Features:** Fish nets and nautical decorations set the mood in the restaurant, which overlooks the marina. The menu features surf and turf specials and such specialties as the seafood sampler, which includes crab cake, scallops, shrimp and the fresh catch. Casual dress; cocktails; entertainment. **Parking:** on-site. **Cards:** AX, CB, DC, DS, MC, VI.

RIVERWALK CAFE AND RAW BAR   Lunch: $5-$9   Dinner: $11-$20   Phone: 772/221-1511

♦♦♦ ♦♦♦
Regional American

Location: Just e of US 1; in historic downtown area, close to the river. 201 SW St Lucie Ave 34994. **Hours:** 11:30 am-2 & 5:30-9 pm, Fri-10 pm, Sat 5:30 pm-10 pm. Closed major holidays; also Sun. **Reservations:** accepted. **Features:** Although the menu changes regularly at the small, gourmet cafe, diners can always count on innovative, well-presented cuisine that samples intricate flavors from around the world. Created in the bistro style, the restaurant bustles with activity. Casual dress; beer & wine only. **Parking:** street. **Cards:** AX, DS, MC, VI.

THE TWISTED GRILLE   Lunch: $7-$13   Dinner: $9-$21   Phone: 772/287-1140

♦♦♦ ♦♦♦
American

Location: Jct Monteray Rd; in Smithfield Plaza. 2111 E Ocean Blvd 34996. **Hours:** 11:30 am-2:30 & 4:30-9:30 pm, Sat & Sun from 4:30 pm. Closed: 11/23, 12/25. **Reservations:** suggested. **Features:** In a plaza with plenty of parking, this comfortably decorated restaurant offers a variety of contemporary American dishes, each with its own "twist." Sauteed shrimp crab cakes with Creole-spiced mustard sauce are tasty. Servings are ample. Casual dress; cocktails. **Parking:** on-site. **Cards:** AX, CB, DC, DS, MC, VI.

SUN CITY CENTER —*See Tampa Bay p. 1046.*

SUNNY ISLES BEACH —*See Miami-Miami Beach p. 615.*

SUNRISE —*See Fort Lauderdale p. 423.*

SURFSIDE —*See Miami-Miami Beach p. 617.*

TALLAHASSEE pop. 150,624

———— WHERE TO STAY ————

BEST WESTERN SEMINOLE INN   *Book at aaa.com*   Phone: (850)656-2938

(AAA) [SAVE]   All Year   1P: $65-$150   2P: $70-$150

▼▼ ▼▼   **Location:** I-10, exit 209A, just w on US 90. Located in a quiet rural area. 6737 Mahan Dr 32308. Fax: 850/656-6380.
Motel   **Facility:** 60 one-bedroom standard units. 2 stories, exterior corridors. **Parking:** on-site. **Terms:** 7 day
cancellation notice, pets ($5 extra charge). **Amenities:** irons, hair dryers. **Pool(s):** outdoor. **Guest
Services:** coin laundry. **Business Services:** business center. **Cards:** AX, DC, DS, MC, VI.
Special Amenities: free expanded continental breakfast and free local telephone calls.

SOME UNITS

[S⟋D] [▥] [⟿] [🐾] [DATA PORT] [🛢] [⟶] / [✕]
FEE

CABOT LODGE-NORTH   *Book at aaa.com*   Phone: (850)386-8880

▼▼▼▼   All Year [ECP]   1P: $66-$71   2P: $66-$71

▼▼▼▼   **Location:** I-10, exit 199, 0.3 mi s on US 27. Located in a quiet area. 2735 N Monroe St 32303. Fax: 850/386-4254.
Small-scale Hotel   **Facility:** 160 one-bedroom standard units. 2 stories, exterior corridors. **Parking:** on-site. **Amenities:** high-
speed Internet, voice mail, irons, hair dryers. **Guest Services:** complimentary evening
beverages, valet laundry. **Business Services:** PC, fax. **Cards:** AX, DC, DS, MC, VI.

SOME UNITS

[ASK] [S⟋D] [¶✦] [⌀] [⟿] [🐾] [🐾] [DATA PORT] / [✕] [🛢] [⟶]
FEE

CABOT LODGE-THOMASVILLE RD   *Book at aaa.com*   Phone: (850)386-7500

▼▼▼▼   All Year [CP]   1P: $91-$155

Location: I-10, exit 203, 0.4 mi se. 1653 Raymond Diehl Rd 32308. Fax: 850/386-1136. **Facility:** 135 units. 134
Small-scale Hotel   one-bedroom standard units. 1 one-bedroom suite ($125-$195) with whirlpool. 5 stories, interior corridors.
Bath: combo or shower only. **Parking:** on-site. **Amenities:** high-speed Internet, voice mail, irons, hair
dryers. *Some:* dual phone lines. **Pool(s):** outdoor. **Guest Services:** coin laundry. **Business Services:** meeting rooms, PC, fax.
Cards: AX, DC, DS, MC, VI.

SOME UNITS

[ASK] [S⟋D] [¶✦] [⌀M] [⌀] [⟿] [🐾] [🐾] [DATA PORT] / [✕] [VCR] [🛢] [⟶] [⟶] /

COMFORT INN   *Book at aaa.com*   Phone: (850)562-7200

▼▼▼▼   All Year   1P: $59-$259   2P: $59-$259   XP: $5   F18

▼▼   **Location:** I-10, exit 199, just n. 2727 Graves Rd 32303. Fax: 850/562-6335. **Facility:** 100 one-bedroom standard
Small-scale Hotel   units, some with whirlpools. 3 stories, interior corridors. *Bath:* combo or shower only. **Parking:** on-site.
Amenities: high-speed Internet, voice mail, irons, hair dryers. **Pool(s):** outdoor. **Guest Services:** valet and
coin laundry. **Business Services:** fax (fee). **Cards:** AX, CB, DC, DS, JC, MC, VI.

SOME UNITS

[ASK] [S⟋D] [¶✦] [⌀] [⟿] [🐾] [DATA PORT] [⟶] / [✕] [🛢]

COMFORT SUITES   *Book at aaa.com*   Phone: (850)224-3200

▼▼▼▼   All Year [ECP]   1P: $79-$199   2P: $79-$199   XP: $10   F18

Location: 1 mi se on US 27. 1026 Apalachee Pkwy 32301. Fax: 850/216-0558. **Facility:** Smoke free premises.
Small-scale Hotel   64 one-bedroom standard units, some with whirlpools. 3 stories, interior corridors. *Bath:* combo or shower
only. **Parking:** on-site. **Terms:** 2-3 night minimum stay - seasonal and/or weekends, 7 day cancellation
notice-fee imposed, $1 service charge. **Amenities:** high-speed Internet, dual phone lines, voice mail, safes, irons, hair dryers.
Pool(s): outdoor. **Leisure Activities:** exercise room. **Guest Services:** valet and coin laundry. **Business Services:** meeting
rooms, business center. **Cards:** AX, DC, DS, MC, VI.

[ASK] [S⟋D] [¶✦] [⌀M] [⌀] [⟿] [✕] [🐾] [DATA PORT] [🛢] [⟶] [⟶]

COURTYARD BY MARRIOTT   *Book at aaa.com*   Phone: (850)222-8822

(AAA) [SAVE]   1/16-5/31   1P: $189-$289

▼▼▼▼   6/1-11/30   1P: $139-$229

   12/1-1/15   1P: $139-$229   2P: $139-$229

Small-scale Hotel   **Location:** 1 mi se on US 27. 1018 Apalachee Pkwy 32301. Fax: 850/561-0354. **Facility:** 154 units. 142 one-
bedroom standard units. 12 one-bedroom suites. 3-4 stories, interior corridors. *Bath:* combo or shower only.
Parking: on-site. **Amenities:** high-speed Internet, dual phone lines, voice mail, irons, hair dryers.
Dining: 6:30-10 am, Sat & Sun 7-11 am. **Pool(s):** heated outdoor. **Leisure Activities:** whirlpool, exercise room. **Guest
Services:** coin laundry. **Business Services:** meeting rooms, business center. **Cards:** AX, CB, DC, DS, JC, MC, VI.
Special Amenities: free newspaper.

SOME UNITS

[S⟋D] [¶] [⊟] [⟿] [🐾] [DATA PORT] [⟶] / [✕] [🛢] [⟶] /

DAYS INN   *Book at aaa.com*   Phone: (850)222-3219

(AAA) [SAVE]   4/21-5/10 [CP]   1P: $70-$199   2P: $70-$199   XP: $10   F17

   5/11-11/30 [CP]   1P: $60-$199   2P: $70-$199   XP: $10   F17

▼▼ ▼▼   12/1-12/31 [CP]   1P: $60-$149   2P: $70-$159   XP: $10   F17

   1/1-4/20 [CP]   1P: $60-$90   2P: $70-$100   XP: $10   F17

Small-scale Hotel   **Location:** 1.6 mi w of US 27. 1350 W Tennessee St 32304. Fax: 850/222-6645. **Facility:** 47 one-bedroom
standard units. 2 stories (no elevator), interior corridors. **Parking:** on-site. **Terms:** 1-3 night minimum stay -
seasonal, cancellation fee imposed, pets ($5-$10 extra charge). **Amenities:** safes (fee), hair dryers. **Pool(s):** outdoor. **Guest
Services:** coin laundry. **Cards:** AX, DC, DS, MC, VI. **Special Amenities: free continental breakfast and free local telephone
calls.**

SOME UNITS

[S⟋D] [🐾] [⟿] [🐾] / [✕] [🛢] [⟶]
FEE

DOUBLETREE HOTEL TALLAHASSEE   *Book at aaa.com*   Phone: 850/224-5000

▼▼▼▼   Property failed to provide current rates

Location: Jct Adams St and Park Ave; downtown. Located opposite the courthouse. 101 S Adams St 32301.
Large-scale Hotel   Fax: 850/224-1168. **Facility:** 243 units. 236 one-bedroom standard units. 7 one-bedroom suites. 16 stories,
interior corridors. *Bath:* combo or shower only. **Parking:** on-site (fee). **Terms:** check-in 3:30 pm.
Amenities: voice mail, irons, hair dryers. **Pool(s):** outdoor. **Guest Services:** gift shop, valet laundry. **Business Services:**
meeting rooms, business center.

SOME UNITS

[✈] [¶] [⊟] [⌀M] [⌀] [⌀] [⟿] [🐾] [🐾] [DATA PORT] [⟶] / [✕] [🛢] [⟶]
FEE

ECONO LODGE · *Book at aaa.com* · Phone: (850)385-6155

Motel

All Year · 1P: $47-$109 · 2P: $52-$109 · XP: $5 · F18
Location: I-10, exit 199, 0.5 mi s. 2681 N Monroe St 32303. Fax: 850/385-6155. **Facility:** 81 one-bedroom standard units. 2 stories, exterior corridors. **Parking:** on-site. **Terms:** [CP] meal plan available, small pets only ($10 fee). **Cards:** AX, CB, DC, DS, MC, VI. **Special Amenities:** free continental breakfast and free local telephone calls.

SOME UNITS

FAIRFIELD INN BY MARRIOTT · *Book at aaa.com* · Phone: (850)562-8766

Small-scale Hotel

All Year · 1P: $82-$189
Location: I-10, exit 199, just n. 3211 N Monroe St 32303. Fax: 850/562-2194. **Facility:** 79 one-bedroom standard units. 3 stories, interior corridors. *Bath:* combo or shower only. **Parking:** on-site. **Terms:** cancellation fee imposed. **Amenities:** irons, hair dryers. **Pool(s):** heated indoor. **Leisure Activities:** whirlpool, exercise room. **Guest Services:** valet laundry. **Business Services:** fax. **Cards:** AX, CB, DC, DS, JC, MC, VI.

SOME UNITS

GOVERNORS INN · Phone: (850)681-6855

Classic Historic Small-scale Hotel

All Year · 1P: $139-$219 · 2P: $139-$229 · XP: $10 · F
Location: Just n of state capitol; center. 209 S Adams St 32301. Fax: 850/222-3105. **Facility:** This service-oriented boutique hotel features pine paneling and an antique mahogany bar. 40 units. 39 one-bedroom standard units. 1 one-bedroom suite with whirlpool. 3 stories (no elevator), interior corridors. **Terms:** cancellation fee imposed, package plans. **Guest Services:** complimentary evening beverages: Mon-Sat, valet laundry. **Business Services:** meeting rooms, fax (fee). **Cards:** AX, DC, DS, MC, VI. **Special Amenities:** free continental breakfast and free newspaper.

SOME UNITS

HAMPTON INN · *Book at aaa.com* · Phone: (850)562-4300

Small-scale Hotel

2/1-4/30 [BP] · 1P: $119-$199 · 2P: $119-$259 · XP: $10 · F18
5/1-8/31 [BP] · 1P: $109-$199 · 2P: $109-$259 · XP: $10 · F18
9/1-11/30 [BP] · 1P: $89-$199 · 2P: $89-$259 · XP: $10 · F18
12/1-1/31 [BP] · 1P: $89-$189 · 2P: $99-$239 · XP: $10 · F18
Location: I-10, exit 199, just n. 3210 N Monroe St 32303. Fax: 850/562-6735. **Facility:** 93 units. 92 one-bedroom standard units. 1 one-bedroom suite ($149-$259) with whirlpool. 2 stories, exterior corridors. *Bath:* combo or shower only. **Parking:** on-site. **Amenities:** high-speed Internet, voice mail, irons, hair dryers. **Pool(s):** outdoor. **Guest Services:** valet laundry. **Business Services:** fax (fee). **Cards:** AX, CB, DC, DS, JC, MC, VI.

SOME UNITS

HAMPTON INN & SUITES I-10/THOMASVILLE RD · *Book at aaa.com* · Phone: (850)574-4900

Small-scale Hotel

12/1-5/25 & 7/16-11/15 · 1P: $149 · 2P: $149 · XP: $5 · F
5/26-7/15 & 11/16-11/30 · 1P: $129 · 2P: $129 · XP: $5 · F
Location: I-10, exit 203, 0.3 mi e on Raymond Diehl Rd. 3388 Lonnbladh Rd 32308. Fax: 850/574-4918. **Facility:** 122 one-bedroom standard units. 5 stories, interior corridors. *Bath:* combo or shower only. **Parking:** on-site. **Terms:** cancellation fee imposed, package plans. **Amenities:** high-speed Internet, voice mail, irons, hair dryers. **Pool(s):** outdoor. **Leisure Activities:** limited exercise equipment. **Guest Services:** complimentary evening beverages: Mon-Thurs, valet and coin laundry. **Business Services:** meeting rooms, business center. **Cards:** AX, DS, MC, VI.

SOME UNITS

HAMPTON INN TALLAHASSEE CENTRAL · *Book at aaa.com* · Phone: (850)309-1300

Small-scale Hotel

3/1-4/30 [BP] · 1P: $79-$139 · 2P: $79-$139
8/1-11/30 [BP] · 1P: $69-$119 · 2P: $69-$119
12/1-2/28 & 5/1-7/31 [BP] · 1P: $69-$109 · 2P: $69-$109
Location: US 27, 3.5 mi s. 2979 Apalachee Pkwy 32301. Fax: 850/309-0111. **Facility:** 78 one-bedroom standard units. 4 stories, interior corridors. *Bath:* combo or shower only. **Parking:** on-site. **Terms:** 10 day cancellation notice. **Amenities:** video games, dual phone lines, voice mail, irons, hair dryers. **Pool(s):** heated outdoor. **Leisure Activities:** exercise room. **Guest Services:** valet laundry. **Business Services:** meeting rooms, fax (fee). **Cards:** AX, CB, DC, DS, MC, VI.

SOME UNITS

HILTON GARDEN INN TALLAHASSEE · *Book at aaa.com* · Phone: (850)385-3553

Small-scale Hotel

All Year · 1P: $99-$179 · 2P: $104-$184
Location: I-10, exit 203, just s. 3333 Thomasville Rd 32308. Fax: 850/385-4242. **Facility:** 99 units. 93 one-bedroom standard units. 6 one-bedroom suites ($134-$224). 4 stories, interior corridors. *Bath:* combo or shower only. **Parking:** on-site. **Terms:** cancellation fee imposed, [BP] & [CP] meal plans available. **Amenities:** dual phone lines, voice mail, irons, hair dryers. **Pool(s):** outdoor. **Leisure Activities:** whirlpool, exercise room. **Guest Services:** coin laundry. **Business Services:** meeting rooms, business center. **Cards:** AX, CB, DC, DS, JC, MC, VI.

SOME UNITS

HOLIDAY INN CAPITAL EAST · *Book at aaa.com* · Phone: (850)877-3171

Small-scale Hotel

3/1-5/3 · 1P: $99-$189 · 2P: $99-$189 · XP: $10 · F
12/1-2/28 & 5/4-11/30 · 1P: $79-$189 · 2P: $79-$189 · XP: $10 · F
Location: 1.3 mi se on US 27. 1355 Apalachee Pkwy 32301. Fax: 850/877-3257. **Facility:** 149 one-bedroom standard units. 4 stories, interior corridors. *Bath:* combo or shower only. **Parking:** on-site. **Terms:** 1-2 night minimum stay - seasonal, cancellation fee imposed, [BP] & [CP] meal plans available, package plans, 18% service charge. **Amenities:** high-speed Internet, dual phone lines, voice mail, irons, hair dryers. **Pool(s):** outdoor. **Leisure Activities:** exercise room. **Guest Services:** coin laundry. **Business Services:** conference facilities, PC, fax. **Cards:** AX, CB, DC, DS, MC, VI.

SOME UNITS

HOLIDAY INN-NORTHWEST   *Book at aaa.com*   Phone: 850/562-2000

Small-scale Hotel

Property failed to provide current rates

Location: I-10, exit 199, just n. 2714 Graves Rd 32303. Fax: 850/562-8519. **Facility:** 178 one-bedroom standard units. 2 stories, exterior corridors. **Parking:** on-site. **Amenities:** video games, voice mail, irons, hair dryers. **Pool(s):** outdoor. **Guest Services:** valet and coin laundry. **Business Services:** meeting rooms, fax.

SOME UNITS

HOLIDAY INN SELECT DOWNTOWN CAPITAL HILL   *Book at aaa.com*   Phone: (850)222-9555

Small-scale Hotel

4/16-11/30	1P: $69-$300	2P: $69-$300
3/2-4/15	1P: $99-$179	2P: $99-$179
12/1-3/1	1P: $79-$149	2P: $79-$149

Location: Just w of US 27; downtown. 316 W Tennessee St 32301. Fax: 850/224-8410. **Facility:** 164 units. 153 one-bedroom standard units. 11 one-bedroom suites ($109-$300). 12 stories, interior corridors. *Bath:* combo or shower only. **Parking:** on-site. **Terms:** 2 night minimum stay - seasonal, cancellation fee imposed, [AP], [BP] & [CP] meal plans available. **Amenities:** video games, high-speed Internet, voice mail, irons, hair dryers. *Some:* dual phone lines. **Pool(s):** outdoor. **Leisure Activities:** exercise room. **Guest Services:** valet laundry, area transportation. **Business Services:** conference facilities, business center. **Cards:** AX, DC, DS, MC, VI.

SOME UNITS

HOMEWOOD SUITES BY HILTON   *Book at aaa.com*   Phone: (850)402-9400

Small-scale Hotel

All Year   1P: $89-$299   2P: $89-$299   XP: $10   F18

Location: US 27, 3.5 mi s. 2987 Apalachee Pkwy 32301. Fax: 850/402-9405. **Facility:** 94 units. 90 one- and 4 two-bedroom standard units with kitchens. 5 stories, interior corridors. *Bath:* combo or shower only. **Parking:** on-site. **Terms:** 2-5 night minimum stay - seasonal and/or weekends, small pets only ($50 fee). **Amenities:** video games, dual phone lines, voice mail, irons, hair dryers. **Pool(s):** heated outdoor. **Leisure Activities:** exercise room, sports court, basketball. **Guest Services:** complimentary evening beverages: Mon-Thurs, coin laundry. **Business Services:** meeting rooms, business center. **Cards:** AX, DC, DS, MC, VI.

SOME UNITS

HOWARD JOHNSON EXPRESS INN   *Book at aaa.com*   Phone: (850)386-5000

Motel

All Year [ECP]   1P: $49-$79   2P: $49-$79   XP: $5   F16

Location: I-10, exit 199, 0.5 mi s. 2726 N Monroe St 32303. Fax: 850/386-5000. **Facility:** 51 one-bedroom standard units. 2 stories, exterior corridors. **Parking:** on-site. **Terms:** pets ($10 extra charge). **Amenities:** high-speed Internet, voice mail, irons, hair dryers. **Business Services:** fax (fee). **Cards:** AX, CB, DC, DS, JC, MC, VI. **Special Amenities:** free expanded continental breakfast and early check-in/late check-out.

SOME UNITS

LA QUINTA INN TALLAHASSEE (NORTH)

Book at aaa.com
Phone: (850)385-7172

3/1-4/30	1P: $91-$115	2P: $97-$121	XP: $6	F18
5/1-11/30	1P: $78-$105	2P: $84-$111	XP: $6	F18
12/1-2/28	1P: $78-$98	2P: $84-$104	XP: $6	F18

Location: I-10, exit 199, just s on US 27. 2905 N Monroe St 32303-3636. **Fax:** 850/422-2463. **Facility:** 154 units. 153 one-bedroom standard units. 1 one-bedroom suite. 2-3 stories, exterior corridors. **Parking:** on-site. **Terms:** [ECP] meal plan available, small pets only. **Amenities:** video games, voice mail, irons, hair dryers. **Pool(s):** outdoor. **Leisure Activities:** picnic area. **Business Services:** fax (fee). **Cards:** AX, CB, DC, DS, MC, VI. **Special Amenities:** free expanded continental breakfast and free local telephone calls.

Small-scale Hotel

LA QUINTA INN TALLAHASSEE (SOUTH)

Book at aaa.com
Phone: (850)878-5099

3/1-5/31	1P: $99-$119	2P: $105-$125	XP: $6	F18
6/1-11/30	1P: $73-$99	2P: $79-$105	XP: $6	F18
12/1-2/28	1P: $73-$93	2P: $79-$99	XP: $6	F18

Location: 3 mi se on US 27. 2850 Apalachee Pkwy 32301-4400. **Fax:** 850/878-6665. **Facility:** 134 units. 133 one-bedroom standard units. 1 one-bedroom suite. 3-4 stories, exterior corridors. **Bath:** combo or shower only. **Parking:** on-site. **Terms:** [ECP] meal plan available, small pets only. **Amenities:** video games, voice mail, irons, hair dryers. **Pool(s):** outdoor. **Guest Services:** valet laundry. **Business Services:** fax. **Cards:** AX, CB, DC, DS, MC, VI. **Special Amenities:** free expanded continental breakfast and free local telephone calls.

Small-scale Hotel

MICROTEL INN & SUITES

Book at aaa.com
Phone: (850)562-3800

All Year	1P: $55-$100	2P: $65-$125

Location: I-10, exit 199, just n. 3216 N Monroe St 32303. **Fax:** 850/562-8611. **Facility:** 91 one-bedroom standard units. 3 stories, interior corridors. **Bath:** combo or shower only. **Parking:** on-site. **Terms:** weekly rates available, [CP] meal plan available. **Amenities:** voice mail. *Some:* irons, hair dryers. **Guest Services:** valet laundry. **Business Services:** fax (fee). **Cards:** AX, DC, DS, MC, VI.

Small-scale Hotel

MOTEL 6 #1073

Book at aaa.com
Phone: 850/877-6171

All Year	1P: $39-$49	2P: $45-$55	XP: $3	F17

Location: 1 mi se on US 27. 1027 Apalachee Pkwy 32301. **Fax:** 850/656-6120. **Facility:** 100 one-bedroom standard units, some with efficiencies (no utensils). 2 stories, exterior corridors. **Bath:** combo or shower only. **Parking:** on-site. **Pool(s):** outdoor. **Guest Services:** coin laundry. **Business Services:** meeting rooms. **Cards:** AX, CB, DC, DS, MC, VI.

Small-scale Hotel

MOTEL 6 #1191

Book at aaa.com
Phone: 850/386-7878

12/1-12/31 & 1/21-11/30	1P: $35-$45	2P: $41-$51	XP: $3	F17
1/1-1/20	1P: $33-$43	2P: $39-$49	XP: $3	F17

Location: I-10, exit 199, just s on US 27. 2738 N Monroe St 32303. **Fax:** 850/385-5616. **Facility:** 101 one-bedroom standard units, some with efficiencies (no utensils). 4 stories, exterior corridors. **Bath:** combo or shower only. **Parking:** on-site. **Pool(s):** outdoor. **Guest Services:** coin laundry. **Cards:** AX, CB, DC, DS, MC, VI.

Small-scale Hotel

MOTEL 6 - 420

Book at aaa.com
Phone: 850/668-2600

7/1-11/30	1P: $41-$51	2P: $47-$57	XP: $3	F17
12/1-12/31 & 1/28-6/30	1P: $39-$49	2P: $45-$55	XP: $3	F17
1/1-1/27	1P: $37-$47	2P: $43-$53	XP: $3	F17

Location: I-10, exit 203, just n, then w. Located next to the Market Square Shopping Center. 1481 Timberlane Rd 32308. **Fax:** 850/894-3104. **Facility:** 131 one-bedroom standard units. 2 stories, exterior corridors. **Bath:** combo or shower only. **Parking:** on-site. **Terms:** small pets only. **Pool(s):** outdoor. **Guest Services:** coin laundry. **Business Services:** fax (fee). **Cards:** AX, CB, DC, DS, MC, VI.

Motel

QUALITY INN & SUITES

Book at aaa.com
Phone: (850)877-4437

12/1-4/30	1P: $69-$130	2P: $69-$130	XP: $10	F18
5/1-11/30	1P: $59-$99	2P: $59-$99	XP: $10	F18

Location: 2.2 mi s on US 27. 2020 N Monroe St 32301. **Fax:** 850/878-9964. **Facility:** 90 units. 80 one-bedroom standard units. 10 one-bedroom suites ($89-$250), some with whirlpools. 3 stories, interior corridors. **Bath:** combo or shower only. **Parking:** on-site. **Terms:** cancellation fee imposed, package plans. **Amenities:** voice mail, irons, hair dryers. *Some:* high-speed Internet. **Pool(s):** outdoor. **Guest Services:** complimentary evening beverages: Mon-Thurs, valet and coin laundry. **Business Services:** meeting rooms, business center. **Cards:** AX, CB, DC, DS, MC, VI. **Special Amenities:** free local telephone calls and free newspaper.

Small-scale Hotel

RAMADA INN & CONFERENCE CENTER

Book at aaa.com
Phone: 850/386-1027

Property failed to provide current rates

Location: I-10, exit 199, just s. 2900 N Monroe St 32303. **Fax:** 850/422-1025. **Facility:** 182 units. 179 one-bedroom standard units. 3 one-bedroom suites. 2-4 stories, interior/exterior corridors. **Bath:** combo or shower only. **Parking:** on-site. **Terms:** pets ($10 extra charge). **Amenities:** *Some:* dual phone lines. **Pool(s):** outdoor. **Guest Services:** valet laundry, area transportation. **Business Services:** conference facilities, fax.

Large-scale Hotel

WINGATE INN
Book at aaa.com
Phone: 850/553-4400

All Year   1P: $99-$149   2P: $99-$149

Small-scale Hotel

Location: I-10, exit 199, 0.4 mi s. 2516 W Lakeshore Dr 32303. Fax: 850/553-4410. **Facility:** 116 units. 113 one-bedroom standard units. 3 one-bedroom suites with whirlpools. 3 stories, interior corridors. *Bath:* combo or shower only. **Parking:** on-site. **Terms:** 3 day cancellation notice-fee imposed. **Amenities:** video games, high-speed Internet, dual phone lines, voice mail, safes, irons, hair dryers. **Pool(s):** heated outdoor. **Leisure Activities:** whirlpool, exercise room. **Guest Services:** complimentary evening beverages: Mon-Thurs, valet and coin laundry, area transportation. **Business Services:** meeting rooms, business center. **Cards:** AX, CB, DC, DS, MC, VI.

SOME UNITS

(ASK) [icons] / X /

WHERE TO DINE

ALBERT'S PROVENCE   Lunch: $7-$14   Dinner: $15-$30   Phone: 850/894-9003

French

Location: I-10, exit 203, 0.3 mi n, then w; in Market Square. 1415 Timberlane Rd 32312. **Hours:** 11:30 am-2 & 6-9:30 pm, Fri-10 pm, Sat 6 pm-10 pm. Closed major holidays; also Sun. **Reservations:** suggested. **Features:** Enjoy classic French Mediterranean cuisine in an intimate dining room with well-trained service. Hailing from France, Albert delights diners with his fabulous lobster bisque and locals rave over his crab cakes a l'aubergine. Choose from a wide variety of wine, many available by the glass. The homemade pate changes daily. Always leave room to make a selection from the dessert tray. For those wishing a more casual experience, sit at the cafe de artiste to the rear of the dining room. Casual dress; cocktails. **Parking:** on-site. **Cards:** AX, DS, MC, VI.

ANOTHER BROKEN EGG CAFE   Lunch: $4-$12   Phone: 850/907-3447

American

Location: I-10, exit 203, 5 mi n, then just w. 3500 Kinhega Dr 32312. **Hours:** 7 am-2 pm. Closed: Mon. **Features:** Enjoy a breakfast experience you will not soon forget; huge cinnamon buns, Popeye's omelette and fruit and nut pancakes or french toast are some of the menu specialties. Casual dress. **Parking:** on-site. **Cards:** MC, VI.

BARNACLE BILL'S   Lunch: $5-$9   Dinner: $11-$19   Phone: 850/385-8734

American

Location: I-10, exit 196, 2 mi s. 1830 N Monroe St 32303. **Hours:** 11 am-11 pm, Fri & Sat-midnight. Closed: 11/23, 12/24, 12/25. **Features:** A popular local gathering spot, it features Florida seafood, pasta and an oyster bar with seasonal outdoor seating. The efficient wait staff excels at keeping guests happy. A close cousin of jambalaya, the shrimp skillet is a nice mix of rice and sausage. Casual dress; cocktails. **Parking:** on-site. **Cards:** AX, DC, DS, MC, VI.

CAFE CABERNET   Dinner: $18-$35   Phone: 850/224-1175

American

Location: Just n of downtown. 1019 N Monroe St 32303. **Hours:** 5 pm-midnight. Closed: 1/1, 12/25; also Sun. **Reservations:** accepted. **Features:** Experience traditional Italian cuisine in a authentic and comfortable setting. Casual dress; cocktails. **Parking:** on-site. **Cards:** AX, DS, MC, VI.

CARLOS' CUBAN CAFE   Lunch: $5-$13   Dinner: $10-$30   Phone: 850/222-8581

Cuban

Location: Downtown. 402 E Tennessee St 32301. **Hours:** 11 am-2 & 5-9 pm, Fri & Sat-10 pm. Closed major holidays; also Sun. **Features:** The busy downtown eatery serves such Cuban favorites as roasted chicken, yuca with mojo and Cuban ground beef with peppers, onions and tomato. All entrees are served with rice and beans. Casual dress; cocktails. **Parking:** on-site. **Cards:** AX, CB, MC, VI.

CHEZ PIERRE RESTAURANT   Lunch: $5-$13   Dinner: $13-$32   Phone: 850/222-0936

French

Location: Corner of Thomasville Rd and 6th Ave, just e of Monroe St; center. 1215 Thomasville Rd 32303. **Hours:** 11 am-2:30 & 5:30-10 pm, Fri & Sat-11 pm, Sun-9 pm; Sunday brunch. Closed major holidays. **Reservations:** suggested. **Features:** A romantic atmosphere popular with couples, the restaurant features such intimate touches as fresh flowers, French artwork and a deck bedecked with tiny white lights. Sample from creatively presented specials or from a sinful selection of pastries. Dressy casual; cocktails. **Parking:** on-site. **Cards:** AX, DC, DS, MC, VI.

JENNY'S LUNCHBOX   Lunch: $4-$8   Phone: 850/942-9766

American

Location: Jct Mahan Dr. 295 N Magnolia Dr 32301. **Hours:** 6:30 am-2:30 pm. **Features:** The walls of the popular breakfast and lunch eatery are decorated with lunchboxes from the past. Those who want a hearty breakfast of biscuits and gravy or buttermilk pancakes will not be disappointed. For lunch, a BLT or juicy burger will hit the spot. Casual dress. **Parking:** on-site. **Cards:** MC, VI.

LUCY HO'S ORIENTAL BISTRO   Lunch: $5-$12   Dinner: $6-$20   Phone: 850/893-4128

Chinese

Location: I-10, exit 203, 0.3 mi n on SR 61, then just e on Capitol Cir; in Oak Lake Village. 1700 Halstead Blvd, Suite 5 32309. **Hours:** 11:30 am-2 & 4:45-10 pm, Fri & Sat-11 pm. **Reservations:** accepted. **Features:** A professional staff will gladly help you select from the many entrees featured on this Chinese-Japanese menu. Crab ragoons are delicious with huge pieces of crab prepared with a light peanut oil. Large portions and a sushi bar will please every appetite. Casual dress; cocktails. **Parking:** on-site. **Cards:** AX, DC, DS, MC, VI.

MANNA RESTAURANT & CATERING   Lunch: $6-$13   Dinner: $8-$20   Phone: 850/668-1968

American

Location: I-10, exit 203, 0.5 mi n. 3507 Thomasville Rd 32309. **Hours:** 10:30 am-9 pm, Fri & Sat-10 pm. Closed: 11/23, 12/25; also Sun. **Features:** Manna means "food from heaven," and this restaurant comes awfully close. The house salad has mixed greens, granola, raisins, bean sprouts and cucumbers. Casual dress; beer & wine only. **Parking:** on-site. **Cards:** AX, MC, VI.

THE MELTING POT   Dinner: $15-$30   Phone: 850/386-7440

Fondue

Location: I-10, exit 199, 0.4 mi s on US 27. 2727 N Monroe St 32303. **Hours:** 5 pm-11 pm, Fri & Sat-midnight. Closed major holidays. **Reservations:** suggested. **Features:** Offering fondue prepared right at your table, this restaurant is good for group fun or a romantic night out for couples. Dressy casual; cocktails. **Parking:** on-site. **Cards:** AX, CB, DC, DS, JC, MC, VI.

NINO - A RESTAURANT

Italian

Dinner: $9-$18

Phone: 850/878-8141

Location: 7 mi e of the Capitol Building on US 27. 6497 Apalachee Pkwy 32311. **Hours:** 5 pm-10 pm. Closed major holidays; also Sun, Mon & week of July 4th. **Reservations:** suggested, weekends. **Features:** An intimate, cozy atmosphere derives from candlelit tables, lace-curtained windows and charming, old farmhouse decor. Enjoy an excellent variety of veal and seafood entrees, as well as tasty Bavarian favorites such as Wiener Schnitzel. Dressy casual; cocktails. **Parking:** on-site. **Cards:** AX, DC, DS, MC, VI.

REANGTHAI RESTAURANT

Thai

Lunch: $6-$8   **Dinner: $15-$40**   **Phone: 850/386-7898**

Location: 1.6 mi n of Apalachee Pkwy. 2747B Capital Cir NE 32308. **Hours:** 11 am-2 & 5-10 pm, Mon & Sat from 5 pm. **Closed:** 11/23, 12/25; also Sun. **Reservations:** accepted. **Features:** The restaurant offers taste of Thailand in a dining room with traditional decor. Specialties include seafood, curries, vegetarian and non-spicy dishes. Casual dress; cocktails. **Parking:** on-site. **Cards:** MC, VI.

SILVER SLIPPER

Steak & Seafood

Dinner: $12-$25   **Phone: 850/386-9366**

Location: I-10, exit 199, 1.3 mi s on US 27, then 0.3 mi e on John Knox, just s. 531 Silver Slipper Ln 32303. **Hours:** 5 pm-11 pm. **Closed:** 1/1, 11/23, 12/25; also Sun. **Reservations:** suggested. **Features:** The restaurant has lots of history and once was a hot spot for an impressive list of celebrity and political guests. It's still a good place to enjoy steaks and seafood and delicious baklava. Low lighting and greenery sets the table for romance. Casual dress; cocktails; entertainment. **Parking:** on-site. **Cards:** AX, CB, DC, DS, MC, VI.

SMOKEY BONES BAR-B-Q

Barbecue

Lunch: $5-$12   **Dinner: $9-$16**   **Phone: 850/386-2480**

Location: I-10, exit 203, 0.5 mi e, then 0.5 mi s. 3131 Capitol Cir NE 32308. **Hours:** 11 am-10 pm, Fri & Sat-11 pm. **Closed:** 11/23, 12/25. **Features:** The eatery combines a sports bar feel with the great taste of barbecue; the pulled pork sandwich is worth a try, as are the homemade donuts. Casual dress; cocktails. **Parking:** on-site. **Cards:** AX, CB, DC, DS, JC, MC, VI.

SONNY'S REAL PIT BBQ

Barbecue

Lunch: $5-$9   **Dinner: $6-$15**   **Phone: 850/878-1185**

Location: 2 mi se on Apalachee Pkwy. 2527 Apalachee Pkwy 32301. **Hours:** 11 am-9 pm, Fri & Sat-10 pm. **Closed:** 1/1, 11/23, 12/25. **Features:** The country themed restaurant offers slow-cooked barbecue, daily all-you-can-eat specials and a salad bar. Casual dress. **Parking:** on-site. **Cards:** AX, DS, MC, VI.

SONNY'S REAL PIT BBQ

Barbecue

Lunch: $5-$10   **Dinner: $5-$10**   **Phone: 850/385-2167**

Location: I-10, exit 199, 1.2 mi s. 2707 N Monroe St 32308. **Hours:** 11 am-9:30 pm. **Closed:** 11/23, 12/25. **Features:** The country themed restaurant offers slow-cooked barbecue, daily all-you-can-eat specials and a salad bar. Casual dress; beer only. **Parking:** on-site. **Cards:** AX, MC, VI.

TAMARAC —See Fort Lauderdale p. 424.

TAMPA —See Tampa Bay p. 969.

Destination Tampa Bay including St. Petersburg, Tampa and Clearwater

Tampa pop. 303,447
St. Petersburg pop. 248,232

Sunshine Skyway Bridge, St. Petersburg.
A colorful sailboard mimics the elegant
lines of the graceful Sunshine Skyway
Bridge. (See listing page 222)

*A*lthough often considered as one, Tampa, St. Petersburg, Clearwater and their neighboring beach communities are distinct entities. Taken collectively or individually, though, these cities by the bay are liberally sprinkled with enticements.

*W*hile Tampa is more oriented toward business and industry, St. Petersburg and Clearwater and their sister sun-dappled beaches appeal to those seeking a resort atmosphere. The worlds of work and play come together in the Tampa Bay area, and the combination is hard to beat.

Visit Florida

Sportfishing, Tampa Bay area. Charter a fishing boat in coastal communities and head for the open water.

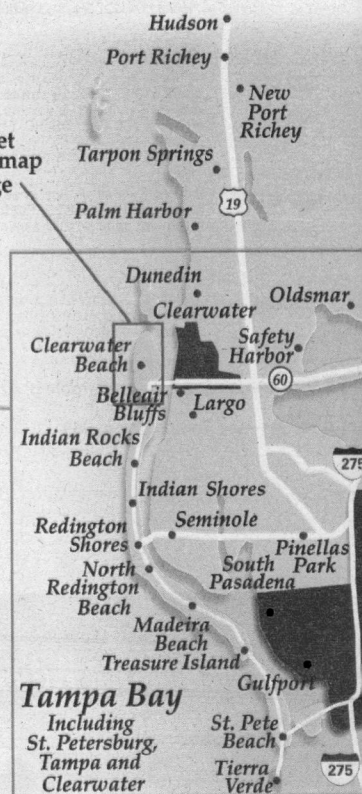

See Inset on map page 939

See map page 939

Hudson •
Port Richey •
• New Port Richey
Tarpon Springs
Palm Harbor   [19]
Dunedin
Clearwater   Oldsmar •
Clearwater   Safety Harbor
Clearwater Beach •   [60]
Belleair Bluffs   Largo
Indian Rocks Beach   [275]
Indian Shores
Redington Shores •   Seminole
North Redington Beach   Pinellas South Park Pasadena
Madeira Beach
Treasure Island
Tampa Bay   Gulfport
Including St. Petersburg, Tampa and Clearwater   St. Pete Beach
Tierra Verde•   [275]

*P*laces included in this AAA Destination Area:

Dining, Tampa Bay area.
Great ingredients for sumptuous
meals abound just offshore.

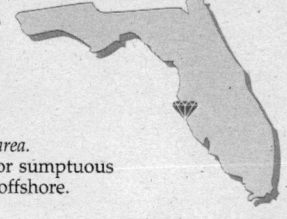

The Pier, St. Petersburg.
It's hard to tell who is
having the most fun
here. (See listing
page 219)

Dade City

75 Wesley
    Chapel   301

54

Zephyrhills

275

301   39

75   Plant
          City

Temple   4
Terrace   Seffer

60

Brandon

Tampa   Riverview
              Lithia

St.
Petersburg

Apollo
Beach

Sun City
Center

Wimauma

Ruskin

75

**See Vicinity
map pages 950 & 951**

Golfing in Greater Tampa.
Palm trees compete with the golf ball
for a place on the horizon when you
tee off at coastal courses.

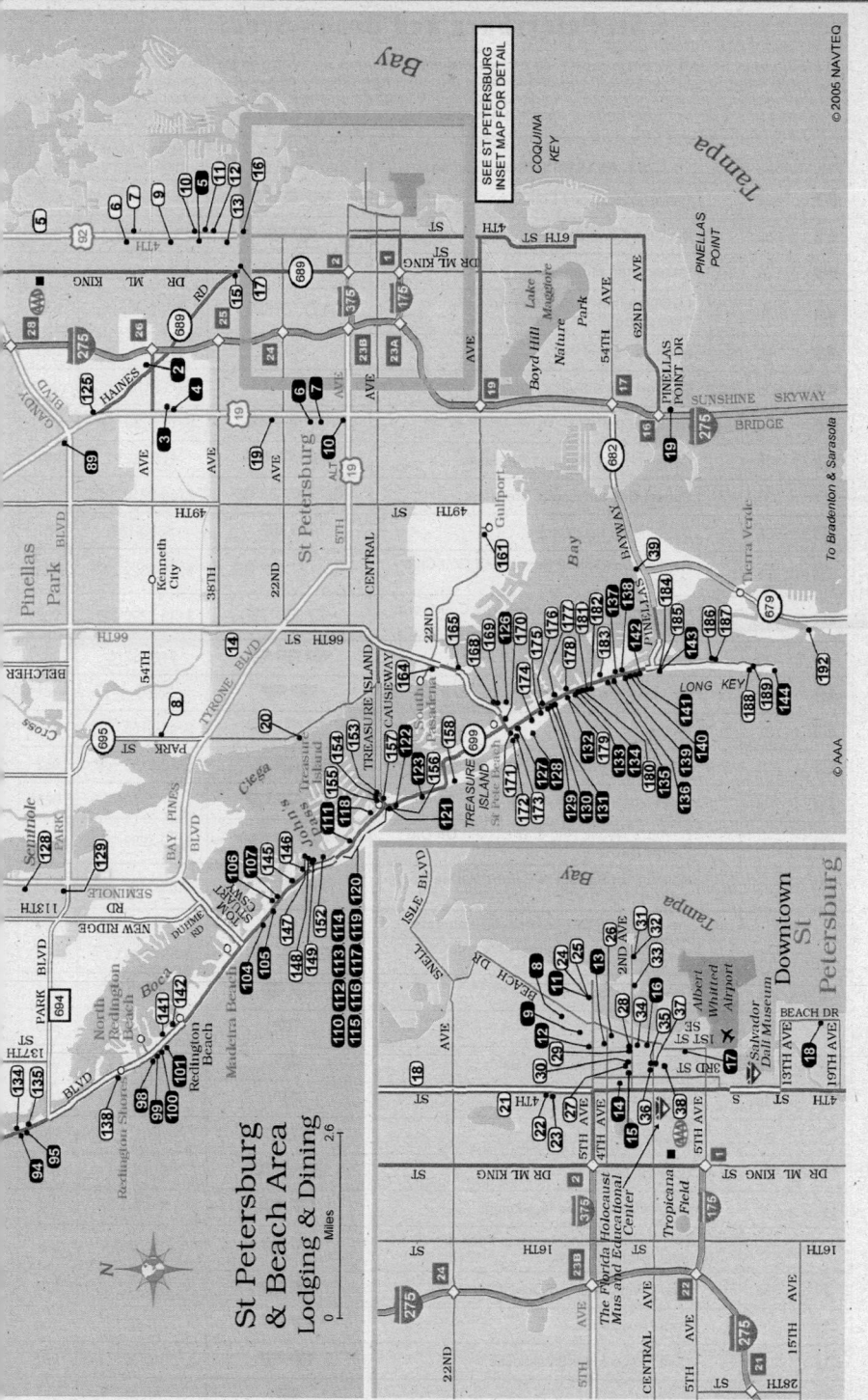

© 2005 NAVTEQ

SEE ST PETERSBURG INSET MAP FOR DETAIL

St Petersburg & Beach Area
Lodging & Dining

Downtown
St Petersburg

The Florida Holocaust
Museum and Educational
Center

Salvador Dali Museum

Albert Whitted Airport

Tropicana Field

St. Petersburg and Beach Area

This index helps you "spot" where approved accommodations and restaurants are located on the corresponding detailed maps. Lodging rate ranges are for comparison only and show the property's high season; rates are per night, unless only weekly (W) rates are available. Restaurant rate range is for dinner, unless only lunch (L) is served. Turn to the listing page for more detailed rate information and consult display ads for special promotions.

Spotter/Map Page Number	OA	ST. PETERSBURG - Lodgings	Diamond Rating	Rate Range High Season	Listing Page
1 / p. 938		Radisson Hotel and Conference Center	▽▽▽	$189-$199	964
2 / p. 938		Days Inn Tropicana Field North	▽▽	$59-$79	961
3 / p. 938	AAA	Ramada Inn Mirage	▽▽	$95-$130 SAVE	964
4 / p. 938	AAA	La Quinta Inn Tampa Bay Area (St. Petersburg) - see color ad p 982	▽▽ ▽	$79-$99 SAVE	963
5 / p. 938	AAA	Kentucky Motel	▽	$36-$53 SAVE	963
6 / p. 938	AAA	Comfort Inn & Suites	▽▽	$95-$115 SAVE	961
7 / p. 938	AAA	Hampton Inn	▽▽	$119-$189 SAVE	962
8 / p. 938		Dickens House Bed and Breakfast	▽▽▽	$120-$210	961
9 / p. 938	AAA	Sunset Bay Inn Bed & Breakfast	▽▽▽	$150-$210 SAVE	965
10 / p. 938		Days Inn St. Pete Central	▽▽	$69-$139	961
11 / p. 938	AAA	Renaissance Vinoy Resort and Golf Club - see color ad p 964	▽▽▽▽	$279-$329 SAVE	965
12 / p. 938	AAA	Mansion House B & B and The Courtyard on Fifth	▽▽▽	$149-$220 SAVE	963
13 / p. 938		Inn at the Bay Bed & Breakfast	▽▽▽	$125-$270	962
14 / p. 938		Best Inns Lee Manor Inn	▽▽	$59-$149	961
15 / p. 938	AAA	Pier Hotel	▽▽▽	$148-$158 SAVE	963
16 / p. 938	AAA	Hampton Inn & Suites - see color ad p 962	▽▽▽	$148-$186 SAVE	962
17 / p. 938		St. Petersburg Bayfront Hilton	▽▽▽	$179-$209	965
18 / p. 938	AAA	Bayboro House Bed & Breakfast On Old Tampa Bay	▽▽▽	$149-$299 SAVE	961
19 / p. 938	AAA	Holiday Inn SunSpree Resort Marina Cove - see color ad p 963	▽▽▽	$159-$189 SAVE	962
		ST. PETERSBURG - Restaurants			
1 / p. 938		Bellarte Restaurant	▽▽▽	$13-$41	965
2 / p. 938		Cody's Original Roadhouse	▽▽	$7-$20	966
3 / p. 938		Crab Shack	▽	$6-$18	966
4 / p. 938		Cool Moe's Restaurant & Bar	▽	$7-$15	966
5 / p. 938		Marbo of 4th Street	▽	$8-$9	967
6 / p. 938		Paisano's Pizza & Pasta	▽▽	$6-$19	968
7 / p. 938		Bonefish Grill	▽▽▽	$14-$19	965
8 / p. 938		Carmelita's Mexican Restaurant	▽▽	$8-$11	966
9 / p. 938		Red Mesa Regional Mexican Food & Southwestern Flavors	▽▽	$12-$20	968
10 / p. 938		Fred's Famous Bar-B-Que and Brewery	▽▽	$5-$17	967
11 / p. 938		Pepin Restaurant	▽▽	$6-$22	968
12 / p. 938		Durango Oak Fire Steakhouse	▽▽	$10-$21	967
13 / p. 938		El Cap	▽	$3-$7	967

Spotter/Map Page Number	OA	ST. PETERSBURG - Restaurants (continued)	Diamond Rating	Rate Range High Season	Listing Page
(14) / p. 938		Arigato Japanese Steak House Restaurant	◆◆	$7-$30	965
(15) / p. 938		Casual Clam Restaurant	◆	$5-$14	966
(16) / p. 938		Westshore Pizza XXVIII	◆	$5-$17	969
(17) / p. 938		Siam Garden Thai Restaurant	◆◆	$10-$20	968
(18) / p. 938		Evos St. Petersburg	◆	$5-$8	967
(19) / p. 938		Texas Cattle Company	◆◆	$11-$30	969
(20) / p. 938		Saffron's Caribbean Cuisine at Jungle Prada	◆◆	$7-$18	968
(21) / p. 938		The Limey's Pub	◆◆	$9-$18	967
(22) / p. 938		4th Street Shrimp Store	◆	$4-$21	965
(23) / p. 938		Tijuana Flats	◆	$5-$8	969
(24) / p. 938		Terrace Room	◆◆◆	$11-$29	968
(25) / p. 938		Marchand's Bar & Grill	◆◆◆	$17-$32	967
(26) / p. 938		The Moon Under Water	◆◆	$7-$17	968
(27) / p. 938		Gratzzi Ristorante	◆◆◆	$14-$28	967
(28) / p. 938		Mattison's An American Bistro & Catering Company	◆◆	$16-$28	968
(29) / p. 938		Dan Marino's Fine Food & Spirits	◆◆	$8-$28	966
(30) / p. 938		dish	◆◆	$16-$18	966
(31) / p. 938		Captain Al's Waterfront Grill & Bar	◆◆	$10-$21	966
(32) / p. 938		Columbia Restaurant	◆◆	$15-$26	966
(33) / p. 938		Cha Cha Coconuts	◆	$6-$10	966
(34) / p. 938		Lonni's Sandwiches, etc.	◆	$7-$10(L)	967
(35) / p. 938		The Garden Restaurant	◆◆	$10-$16	967
(36) / p. 938		Redwoods Restaurant	◆◆◆	$19-$29	968
(37) / p. 938		Jo-Jo's in Citta	◆◆	$9-$17	967
(38) / p. 938		Midtown Sundries Restaurant & Bar	◆◆	$7-$18	968
(39) / p. 938		Caspy's Waterside Restaurant	◆◆	$11-$22	966
		OLDSMAR - Lodgings			
(22) / p. 938		Holiday Inn Express Hotel & Suites	◆◆◆	$119-$189	1030
(23) / p. 938	(AAA)	**Courtyard by Marriott Tampa-Oldsmar**	◆◆◆	$149 [SAVE]	1030
		OLDSMAR - Restaurant			
(42) / p. 938		Winners Sports Grill	◆◆	$7-$17	1030
		DUNEDIN - Lodgings			
(26) / p. 938		Holiday Inn Express Hotel & Suites Clearwater North/Dunedin	◆◆◆	$139-$179	1022
(27) / p. 938		Best Western Yacht Harbor Inn	◆◆◆	$129-$149	1022
		DUNEDIN - Restaurants			
(45) / p. 938		Bon Appetit Restaurant & Marina Cafe	◆◆◆	$12-$15	1022
(46) / p. 938		Sea Sea Rider's Restaurant	◆◆	$6-$19	1023

Spotter/Map Page Number	OA	**DUNEDIN - Restaurants (continued)**	Diamond Rating	Rate Range High Season	Listing Page
47 / p. 938		Cafe Alfresco	◆◆	$8-$16	1023
48 / p. 938		"Kelly's For Just About...Anything!"	◆◆	$12-$22	1023
		SAFETY HARBOR - Lodgings			
30 / p. 938	AAA	**Safety Harbor Resort and Spa on Tampa Bay** - see color ad p 1036	◆◆◆	$234-$284 [SAVE]	1036
		SAFETY HARBOR - Restaurant			
51 / p. 938		Enver's Paradise Restaurant	◆◆	$5-$12	1036
		CLEARWATER BEACH - Lodgings			
33 / p. 938		Palm Pavilion Inn	◆◆	$110-$180	1019
34 / p. 938	AAA	**East Shore Resort Apartment Motel**	◆◆	$110-$150 [SAVE]	1017
35 / p. 938	AAA	**Hilton Clearwater Beach Resort** - see color ad p 1018	◆◆◆	$109-$500 [SAVE]	1018
36 / p. 938	AAA	**Howard Johnson Beachview Resort**	◆◆	$115-$130 [SAVE]	1019
37 / p. 938		Tropical Breeze Motel	◆◆	$90-$174	1020
38 / p. 938		Travelodge Beachview Resort	◆◆	Failed to provide	1020
39 / p. 938	AAA	**Pelican Pointe Condominium Resort**	◆◆	$79-$159 [SAVE]	1019
41 / p. 938		Clearwater Beach Gulfview Resort - see color ad p 1015 & p 1016	◆◆	$149-$399	1016
42 / p. 938	AAA	**Shephard's Beach Resort** - see color ad p 1019	◆◆	$142-$202 [SAVE]	1019
43 / p. 938		Chart House Suites on Clearwater Bay - see color ad p 1015 & p 1016	◆◆◆	$110-$299	1016
44 / p. 938	AAA	**Econo Lodge** - see color ad p 1017	◆◆	$119-$239 [SAVE]	1017
45 / p. 938	AAA	**Quality Hotel On The Beach**	◆◆	$89-$229 [SAVE]	1019
46 / p. 938	AAA	**Best Western Sea Wake Beach Resort** - see color ad p 1015	◆◆	$179-$219 [SAVE]	1015
47 / p. 938	AAA	**Holiday Inn SunSpree Resort & Conference Center** - see color ad p 1018	◆◆◆	$199-$329 [SAVE]	1018
48 / p. 938	AAA	**Clearwater Beach Marriott Suites on Sand Key** - see color ad p 1016	◆◆◆	$299-$459 [SAVE]	1017
49 / p. 938	AAA	**Sheraton Sand Key Resort**	◆◆◆◆	$249-$299 [SAVE]	1020
		CLEARWATER BEACH - Restaurants			
54 / p. 938		Frenchy's Rockaway Grill	◆◆	$5-$16	1021
55 / p. 938		Frenchy's Cafe	◆	$6-$8	1021
56 / p. 938		Waterfront Restaurant	◆	$6-$18	1022
57 / p. 938		Bob Heilman's Beachcomber	◆◆◆	$13-$30	1020
58 / p. 938		Bobby's Bistro & Wine Bar	◆◆	$7-$31	1020
59 / p. 938		Cooters Raw Bar & Restaurant	◆◆	$7-$23	1021
60 / p. 938		Frenchy's Saltwater Cafe	◆◆	$6-$30	1021
61 / p. 938		Crabby Bill's	◆	$7-$21	1021
62 / p. 938		Britt's Laguna Grill	◆◆	$8-$25	1021
63 / p. 938		Alex Family Restaurant	◆	$5-$24	1020
64 / p. 938		Frenchy's South Beach Cafe	◆◆	$7-$17	1021
65 / p. 938		Post Corner Pizza Restaurant	◆	$7-$15	1021
66 / p. 938	AAA	**Shephard's Waterfront Restaurant** - see color ad p 1019	◆◆	$14-$24	1022
67 / p. 938		Bonsai Japanese Cuisine-Sushi Bar	◆◆	$7-$13	1020

Spotter/Map Page Number	OA	**CLEARWATER BEACH -** Restaurants (continued)	Diamond Rating	Rate Range High Season	Listing Page
68 / p. 938		Big Ben British Restaurant & Pub	◈◈	$7-$16	1020
69 / p. 938		Gondolier Italian Restaurant and Pizza	◈◈	$5-$19	1021
70 / p. 938		Shells Seafood Restaurant	◈◈	$7-$21	1022
71 / p. 938		Rusty's Bistro	◈◈◈	$16-$26	1021
72 / p. 938		Columbia Restaurant	◈◈	$15-$26	1021
73 / p. 938		Backwater's On Sand Key	◈◈	$9-$31	1020
74 / p. 938		Cabana Grill and Bar	◈◈◈	$16-$36	1021
		CLEARWATER - Lodgings			
52 / p. 938		Howard Johnson Inn & Suites	◈◈	$75-$96	1011
53 / p. 938		Comfort Inn Clearwater North - see color ad p 1008	◈◈◈	$89-$149	1008
54 / p. 938	AAA	**Comfort Suites Clearwater Bay**	◈◈◈	$119-$169 SAVE	1008
55 / p. 938		La Quinta Clearwater Central	◈◈◈	Failed to provide	1011
56 / p. 938		Econo Lodge Clearwater Central	◈◈	$90	1009
57 / p. 938		Hampton Inn Clearwater Central	◈◈◈	$110-$140	1009
58 / p. 938		Radisson Hotel Clearwater Central	◈◈◈	$89	1011
59 / p. 938		Fairfield Inn & Suites Clearwater/Bayside	◈◈◈	$159-$209	1009
60 / p. 938		Holiday Inn Express Hotel & Suites - see color ad p 948	◈◈◈	$159-$209	1010
61 / p. 938		Days Inn-Clearwater Central	◈◈	$55-$85	1008
62 / p. 938	AAA	**Quality Inn Clearwater Central**	◈◈	$89-$159 SAVE	1011
63 / p. 938	AAA	**Belleview Biltmore Resort & Spa - see color ad p 1007**	◈◈◈	$169-$179 SAVE	1007
64 / p. 938	AAA	**Holiday Inn Express - see color ad p 1010**	◈◈◈	$109-$139 SAVE	1010
65 / p. 938	AAA	**Courtyard by Marriott**	◈◈◈	$119-$199 SAVE	1008
66 / p. 938	AAA	**La Quinta Inn Tampa Bay (Clearwater-Airport) - see color ad p 982**	◈◈◈	$85-$105 SAVE	1011
67 / p. 938		St. Petersburg/Clearwater Fairfield Inn by Marriott	◈◈◈	$109-$129	1011
68 / p. 938		Holiday Inn Select-St. Pete/Clearwater Int'l Airport	◈◈◈	$99-$129	1010
69 / p. 938		Homewood Suites by Hilton	◈◈◈	Failed to provide	1010
70 / p. 938		Homestead Studio Suites Hotel-Tampa/Clearwater	◈◈	$44-$69	1010
71 / p. 938		Hampton Inn-Clearwater/St. Petersburg Airport	◈◈◈	$109	1009
72 / p. 938	AAA	**Residence Inn by Marriott**	◈◈◈	$199-$229 SAVE	1011
73 / p. 938	AAA	**Comfort Inn Executive Center Clearwater**	◈◈	$69-$135 SAVE	1008
74 / p. 938	AAA	**Days Inn-St. Pete/Clearwater Airport**	◈◈	$89-$114 SAVE	1009
75 / p. 938		Candlewood Suites Clearwater-St Petersburg	◈◈◈	$99-$139	1007
76 / p. 938	AAA	**Super 8 Clearwater/St. Petersburg Airport**	◈◈	$79-$129 SAVE	1012
77 / p. 938		TownePlace Suites by Marriott St. Petersburg/Clearwater	◈◈◈	$149-$199	1012
78 / p. 938		Wingate Inn Clearwater	◈◈◈	Failed to provide	1012
		CLEARWATER - Restaurants			
77 / p. 938		First Watch	◈◈	$5-$7(L)	1013
78 / p. 938		Arigato Japanese Steak House	◈◈	$7-$30	1012

Spotter/Map Page Number	OA	CLEARWATER - Restaurants (continued)	Diamond Rating	Rate Range High Season	Listing Page
79 / p. 938		Durango Steakhouse	◆◆	$7-$20	1013
80 / p. 938		Lenny's	◆	$4-$8(L)	1013
81 / p. 938		Harrison's Grill & Bar	◆◆	$7-$15	1013
82 / p. 938		Park Place Grill & Tavern	◆◆	$8-$16	1014
83 / p. 938	AAA	**Oriental Super Buffet**	◆	$10-$11	1014
84 / p. 938		Roadhouse Grill	◆◆	$7-$19	1014
85 / p. 938		Tio Pepe Restaurante	◆◆	$14-$30	1015
86 / p. 938		Pete & Shorty's Tavern	◆	$4-$13	1014
87 / p. 938		Joe's Crab Shack	◆◆	$10-$25	1013
88 / p. 938		Capogna's Dugout	◆	$6-$18	1013
89 / p. 938	AAA	**Asian Chef Japanese & Chinese Buffet**	◆	$13-$14	1012
90 / p. 938		O'Keefe's Tavern & Restaurant	◆	$8-$13	1014
91 / p. 938		Egg Platter of Clearwater	◆◆	$5-$8	1013
92 / p. 938		Pronto International Food Market	◆	$5-$19	1014
93 / p. 938		Palm Grille	◆◆◆	$16-$25	1014
94 / p. 938		Sam Seltzer's Steakhouse	◆◆	$11-$21	1014
95 / p. 938		Alfano's Restaurant	◆◆◆	$12-$25	1012
96 / p. 938		Carmelita's Mexican Restaurant	◆◆	$9-$13	1013
97 / p. 938		Tucson's Cantina & Grill	◆◆	$6-$23	1015
98 / p. 938		Cafe Ponte	◆◆◆	$10-$36	1013
99 / p. 938		Saute' Cafe	◆◆◆	$10-$19	1014
100 / p. 938		Panera Bread Cafe	◆	$4-$7	1014
101 / p. 938		Bascom's Chop House	◆◆◆	$17-$29	1013
102 / p. 938		Lonni's Sandwiches, etc	◆	$6-$9(L)	1013
103 / p. 938		Antonio's Pasta Grille	◆◆	$8-$22	1012
104 / p. 938		Primo's Pasta-Ribs	◆◆	$6-$16	1014
		INDIAN ROCKS BEACH - Lodgings			
81 / p. 938		Sea Star Motel & Apartments	◆◆	$70-$110	1024
82 / p. 938	AAA	**Holiday Inn Hotel & Suites-Harbourside -** see color ad p 1023	◆◆◆	$189-$399 [SAVE]	1023
		INDIAN ROCKS BEACH - Restaurants			
110 / p. 938		Thai Pan Alley & Bamboo Beach Bar	◆◆	$8-$10	1024
111 / p. 938	AAA	**Guppy's on the Beach**	◆◆	$10-$25	1024
112 / p. 938		PJ's Oyster Bar & Seafood Restaurant	◆◆	$6-$28	1024
113 / p. 938		Jimmy Guana's Bar & Grill	◆◆	$7-$19	1024
		LARGO - Lodgings			
85 / p. 938		Suburban Lodge	◆◆	$55-$65	1025
		LARGO - Restaurants			
116 / p. 938		Pappas Mediterranean Bistro	◆◆	$14-$21	1026
117 / p. 938		Carmelita's Mexican Restaurant	◆◆	$9-$13	1025
118 / p. 938		Egg Platter III	◆	$5-$8	1026

Spotter/Map Page Number	OA	LARGO - Restaurants (continued)	Diamond Rating	Rate Range High Season	Listing Page
(119) / p. 938		Atlanta Bread Company	◆	$6-$7	1025
(120) / p. 938		Angellino's Italian Restaurant	◆◆	$9-$17	1025
(121) / p. 938		Chicago Pizza & Pasta Co.	◆◆	$8-$24	1026
(122) / p. 938		The Gathering Restaurant	◆	$5-$9(L)	1026
		PINELLAS PARK - Lodgings			
(88) / p. 938	AAA	**Econo Lodge Inn & Suites Clearwater**	◆◆	$80-$160 [SAVE]	1032
(89) / p. 938	AAA	**La Quinta Inn Tampa (Pinellas Park/Clearwater) - see color ad p 982**	◆◆◆	$85-$105 [SAVE]	1032
		PINELLAS PARK - Restaurant			
(125) / p. 938		Pin-Park Egg Platter	◆◆	$5-$8	1032
		INDIAN SHORES - Lodgings			
(92) / p. 938		Sand Castle III	◆◆	$1355-$1435(W)	1024
(93) / p. 938		Sand Castle II	◆◆	$1300-$1432(W)	1024
(94) / p. 938		Sea Gate	◆◆	$1275-$1340(W)	1025
(95) / p. 938		Beach Cottage III	◆◆	$1025-$1385(W)	1024
		INDIAN SHORES - Restaurants			
(132) / p. 938		The Pub Waterfront Restaurant & Lounge	◆◆	$8-$16	1025
(133) / p. 938		Fathom's	◆◆	$6-$23	1025
(134) / p. 938		The Tropical Grill	◆◆	$7-$18	1025
(135) / p. 938		Salt Rock Grill	◆◆◆	$10-$40	1025
		NORTH REDINGTON BEACH - Lodgings			
(98) / p. 938		Far Horizons Motel	◆◆	Failed to provide	1029
(99) / p. 938	AAA	**RamSea - see color ad p 1029**	◆◆	$690-$1500(W) [SAVE]	1029
(100) / p. 938		Doubletree Beach Resort-Tampa Bay/North Redington Beach	◆◆◆	$139-$499	1029
(101) / p. 938		Sails Resort Motel	◆◆	$75-$175	1030
		NORTH REDINGTON BEACH - Restaurants			
(141) / p. 938		The Frog Pond	◆	$4-$11(L)	1030
(142) / p. 938		Conch Republic	◆◆	$7-$24	1030
		MADEIRA BEACH - Lodgings			
(104) / p. 938	AAA	**Shoreline Island Resort - see color ad p 1027**	◆◆	$121-$265 [SAVE]	1027
(105) / p. 938		Shawnee's Island Gulf Resort	◆◆	Failed to provide	1027
(106) / p. 938	AAA	**Sea Dawn Motel**	◆	$65-$85 [SAVE]	1027
(107) / p. 938	AAA	**Snug Harbor Inn Waterfront Bed & Breakfast**	◆◆	$100-$116 [SAVE]	1027
		MADEIRA BEACH - Restaurants			
(145) / p. 938		Dockside Dave's Bar & Grill	◆	$5-$15	1028
(146) / p. 938		Courtyard Cafe	◆	$5-$8	1028
(147) / p. 938		De Losa's Pizzeria	◆	$5-$10	1028
(148) / p. 938		Scully's Boardwalk Restaurant	◆◆	$8-$21	1028
(149) / p. 938		Friendly Fisherman Waterfront Seafood Restaurant	◆◆	$5-$22	1028

Spotter/Map Page Number	OA	TREASURE ISLAND - Lodgings	Diamond Rating	Rate Range High Season	Listing Page
110 / p. 938		Gulf Sounds on Treasure Island	◆◆	$95-$140	1049
111 / p. 938		Mardi Gras Motel	◆	$60-$70	1050
112 / p. 938		Holiday Inn-Treasure Island Beach	◆◆◆	Failed to provide	1049
113 / p. 938	AAA	**The Sea Chest**	◆◆	$83-$139 (SAVE)	1050
114 / p. 938		Jamaican on the Gulf	◆◆	$750-$930(W)	1049
115 / p. 938	AAA	**Trails End Resort Motel** - see color ad p 1051	◆	$69-$159 (SAVE)	1051
116 / p. 938		South Beach Condo-Hotel	◆◆◆	Failed to provide	1050
117 / p. 938	AAA	**Tahitian Resort** - see color ad p 1051	◆◆	$95-$155 (SAVE)	1051
118 / p. 938		Best Western Treasure Island - see color ad p 1038	◆◆	$80-$180	1048
119 / p. 938	AAA	**Best Western Sea Castle Suites**	◆◆	$159-$195 (SAVE)	1048
120 / p. 938	AAA	**Thunderbird Beach Resort** - see color ad p 1051	◆◆	$129-$199 (SAVE)	1051
121 / p. 938	AAA	**Bilmar Beach Resort**	◆◆◆	$229-$425 (SAVE)	1048
122 / p. 938	AAA	**Page Terrace Motel** - see color ad p 1038	◆◆	$78-$108 (SAVE)	1050
123 / p. 938		The Jefferson Motel Apts.	◆◆		1049
		TREASURE ISLAND - Restaurants			
152 / p. 938		Gators Cafe & Saloon	◆	$6-$16	1052
153 / p. 938		The Floridian Cuban Sandwiches	◆	$4-$7	1052
154 / p. 938		Foxy's Cafe	◆◆	$7-$14	1052
155 / p. 938		Cafe Berlin	◆◆	$7-$14	1052
156 / p. 938		Sloppy Joe's On The Beach	◆◆	$10-$21	1052
157 / p. 938		VIP Sports Bar & Mexican Restaurant	◆	$5-$17	1052
158 / p. 938		Caddy's Waterfront Beach BBQ & Seafood Restaurant	◆	$6-$14	1052
		ST. PETE BEACH - Lodgings			
126 / p. 938	AAA	**Pasa Tiempo "A Private Waterfront Resort"**	◆◆◆◆	$175-$275 (SAVE)	1041
127 / p. 938	AAA	**Lamara Motel Apartments**	◆	$75-$100 (SAVE)	1040
128 / p. 938		Caprice Condominiums on St. Pete Beach	◆◆	Failed to provide	1039
129 / p. 938		Howard Johnson Lodge St. Pete Beach Resort Inn	◆◆	$95-$350	1040
130 / p. 938	AAA	**TradeWinds Sandpiper Hotel & Suites** - see color ad p 1042	◆◆◆	$169-$259 (SAVE)	1042
131 / p. 938	AAA	**Alden Beach Resort** - see color ad p 1037	◆◆◆	$199-$283 (SAVE)	1037
132 / p. 938	AAA	**TradeWinds Island Grand Beach Resort** - see color ad p 1042	◆◆◆◆	$229-$369 (SAVE)	1042
133 / p. 938	AAA	**Sirata Beach Resort & Conference Center** - see color ad p 1041	◆◆◆	$229-$399 (SAVE)	1041
134 / p. 938		Holiday Inn Hotel & Suites Beachfront Resort & Conference Center	◆◆◆	$178-$358	1040
135 / p. 938	AAA	**Gulf Strand Beach Resort**	◆◆	$130-$200 (SAVE)	1040
136 / p. 938	AAA	**Plaza Beach Resort Motel**	◆◆	$89-$199 (SAVE)	1041
137 / p. 938	AAA	**Bayview Plaza Waterfront Resort** - see color ad p 1038	◆◆	$75-$159 (SAVE)	1038
138 / p. 938		Bay Palm Resort	◆◆	$79-$109	1037

Spotter/Map Page Number	OA	ST. PETE BEACH - Lodgings (continued)	Diamond Rating	Rate Range High Season	Listing Page
139 / p. 938	AAA	Vistas On the Gulf	◇◇◇	$125-$300 [SAVE]	1042
140 / p. 938	AAA	Beach House Suites By The Don Cesar	◇◇◇	$289-$454 [SAVE]	1039
141 / p. 938	AAA	Palm Crest Resort Motel	◇◇	$89-$132 [SAVE]	1040
142 / p. 938	AAA	Long Key Beach Resort	◇◇	$49-$139 [SAVE]	1040
143 / p. 938	AAA	Don CeSar Beach Resort, A Loews Hotel - see color ad p 1039	◇◇◇◇	$294-$524 [SAVE]	1039
144 / p. 938	AAA	Island's End Resort	◇◇	$149-$290 [SAVE]	1040
		ST. PETE BEACH - Restaurants			
168 / p. 938		Bridgeview Waterfront Grill & Bar	◇◇	$5-$13	1043
169 / p. 938		Johnny Leverock's Seafood House	◇◇	$8-$24	1043
170 / p. 938		Der Eisenhut	◇◇	$9-$15	1043
171 / p. 938		Emperor's Palace Chinese Restaurant	◇	$7-$25	1043
172 / p. 938		Ferg's Beach Shack	◇	$6-$14	1043
173 / p. 938		Philthy Phil's Waterfront Bar & Grill	◇◇	$7-$18	1043
174 / p. 938		The Reef	◇◇	$6-$15	1044
175 / p. 938		Shells of St. Pete Beach	◇◇	$7-$19	1044
176 / p. 938		The Caribbean Bay Cafe	◇	$6-$7(L)	1043
177 / p. 938		Skidder's Restaurant	◇◇	$10-$24	1044
178 / p. 938		Silas Dent's Steakhouse	◇◇	$11-$21	1044
179 / p. 938		Palm Court Restaurant	◇◇◇	$16-$25	1043
180 / p. 938		Spinners Rooftop Revolving Lounge & Bistro	◇◇	$16-$40	1044
181 / p. 938		Starlite Diner	◇	$6-$13	1044
182 / p. 938		Crabby Bill's	◇	$7-$15	1043
183 / p. 938		Bounxou Thai Restaurant	◇	$8-$10	1043
184 / p. 938		Sea Porch Cafe	◇◇◇	$9-$21	1044
185 / p. 938		Maritana Grille	◇◇◇◇	$28-$42	1043
186 / p. 938		Sea Critters Cafe	◇◇	$6-$17	1044
187 / p. 938	AAA	The Wharf Seafood Restaurant	◇◇	$5-$16	1044
188 / p. 938		Hurricane Seafood Restaurant	◇◇	$15-$24	1043
189 / p. 938		Seahorse Restaurant	◇	$4-$10(L)	1044
		BELLEAIR BLUFFS - Restaurant			
107 / p. 938	AAA	E & E Stakeout Grill	◇◇	$10-$25	1001
		SEMINOLE - Restaurants			
128 / p. 938		Andre's Capo de Monte Italian Deli	◇	$6-$8	1045
129 / p. 938		Beef 'O'Brady's	◇	$6-$10	1045
		REDINGTON SHORES - Restaurant			
138 / p. 938	AAA	The Lobster Pot Restaurant	◇◇◇	$11-$40	1034
		GULFPORT - Restaurant			
161 / p. 938		Habana Cafe	◇◇	$5-$18	1023

Spotter/Map Page Number	OA	SOUTH PASADENA - Restaurants	Diamond Rating	Rate Range High Season	Listing Page
⟨164⟩ / p. 938		Horse & Jockey British Restaurant & Bar	▽▽	$7-$11	1045
⟨165⟩ / p. 938		Pasadena Steak House	▽▽	$11-$22	1046
		TIERRA VERDE - Restaurant			
⟨192⟩ / p. 938	AAA	Billy's Stone Crab & Steakhouse	▽	$10-$40	1048

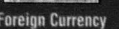

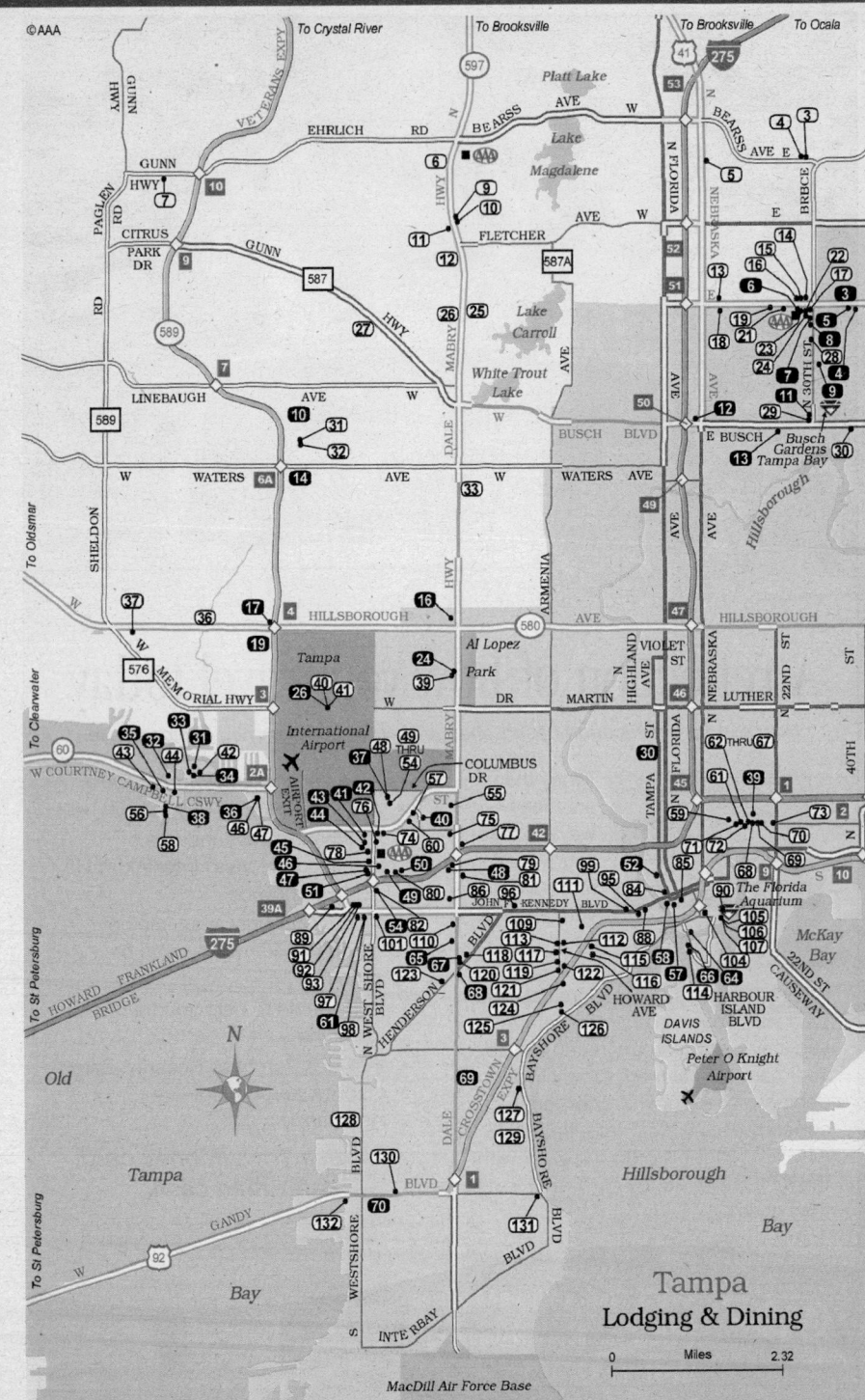

©AAA

Tampa
Lodging & Dining

0   Miles   2.32

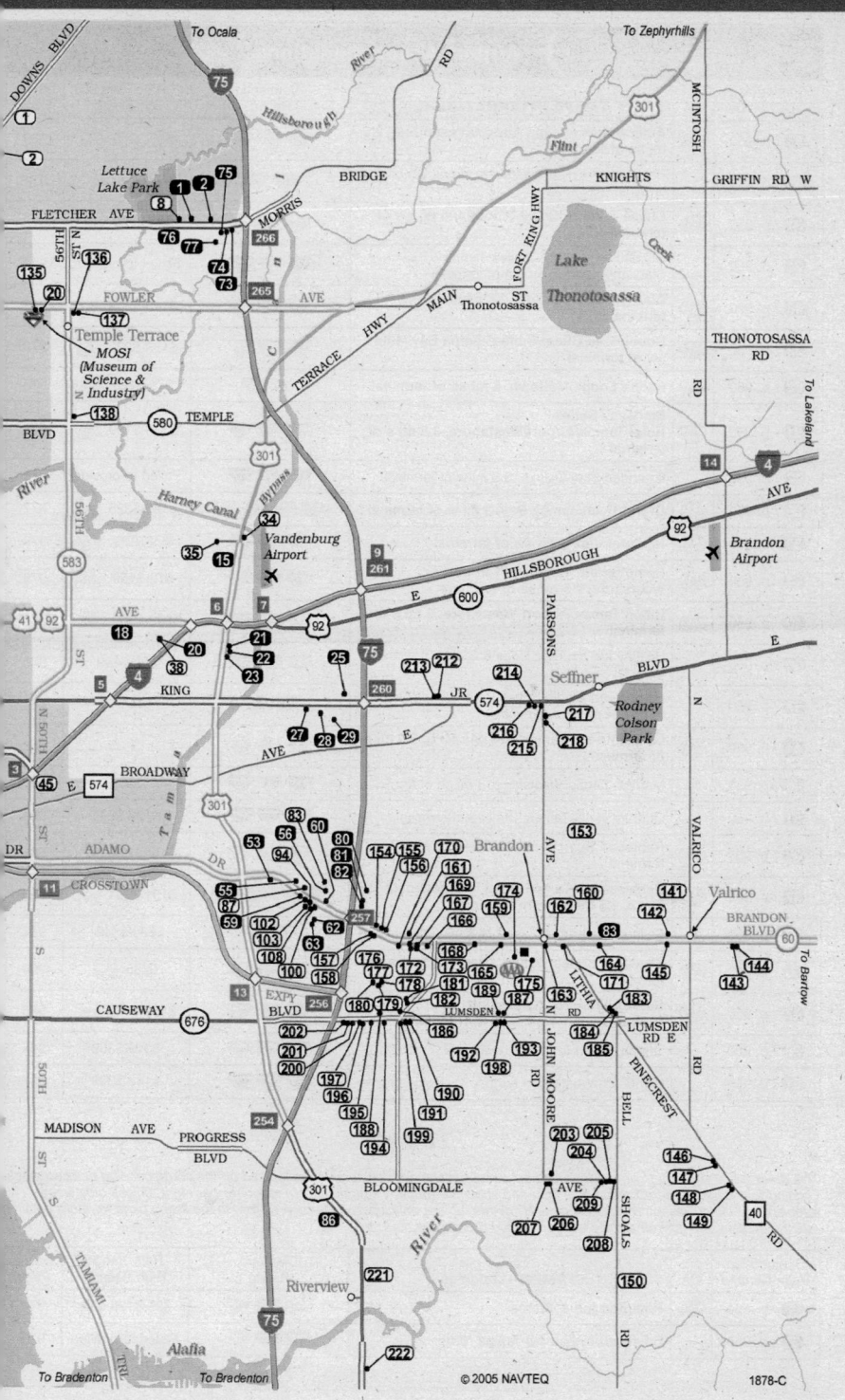

1878-C

✈ Airport Accommodations

Spotter/Map Page Number	OA	TAMPA INTERNATIONAL	Diamond Rating	Rate Range High Season	Listing Page
43 / p. 950	AAA	AmeriSuites (Tampa Airport/Westshore), 2.5 mi se of terminal	◈◈◈	$99-$200 (SAVE)	969
45 / p. 950		Best Western-The Westshore Hotel, 2.5 mi n of terminal	◈◈	$109-$139	971
31 / p. 950	AAA	Chase Suite Hotel by Woodfin, 4 mi sw of terminal	◈◈◈	$99-$229 (SAVE)	972
24 / p. 950	AAA	Comfort Inn Hotel & Suites Tampa Stadium/Airport, 5.3 mi n of terminal	◈◈◈	Failed to provide	972
48 / p. 950	AAA	Courtyard by Marriott, 3.5 mi se of the terminal	◈◈◈	$149-$219 (SAVE)	972
32 / p. 950	AAA	DoubleTree Guest Suites Tampa Bay, 4 mi sw of terminal	◈◈◈	$139-$229 (SAVE)	973
68 / p. 950	AAA	Econo Lodge Midtown, 5 mi se of terminal	◈◈	$75-$125 (SAVE)	975
54 / p. 950	AAA	Embassy Suites Hotel-Tampa/Airport/Westshore, 3.5 mi s of terminal	◈◈◈	$139-$199 (SAVE)	975
42 / p. 950		Extended Stay Deluxe, 3.5 mi w of terminal	◈◈◈	Failed to provide	976
36 / p. 950	AAA	Grand Hyatt Tampa Bay, 3 mi w of terminal	◈◈◈◈	$125-$325 (SAVE)	977
33 / p. 950	AAA	Hampton Inn, 4 mi sw of terminal	◈◈◈	$99-$189 (SAVE)	978
44 / p. 950	AAA	Hampton Inn Tampa Int'l Airport - Westshore, 2.5 mi se of terminal	◈◈◈	$79-$159 (SAVE)	979
40 / p. 950	AAA	Hilton Tampa Airport Westshore, 2 mi e of terminal	◈◈◈	$99-$309 (SAVE)	980
34 / p. 950		Holiday Inn Express Hotel & Suites, 4 mi sw of terminal	◈◈◈	$99-$199	980
17 / p. 950		Homestead Studio Suites Hotel-Tampa/North Airport, 4 mi w of terminal	◈◈	$44-$69	981
41 / p. 950	AAA	La Quinta Inn Tampa Bay (Airport), 2.5 mi n of terminal	◈◈◈	$115-$135 (SAVE)	982
46 / p. 950		Marriott-Tampa Westshore, 3 mi se of terminal	◈◈◈	$299	983
51 / p. 950		Quorum Hotel-Tampa, 3 mi se of terminal	◈◈◈	$129-$299	984
35 / p. 950	AAA	Radisson Bay Harbor Hotel, 4.3 mi w of terminal	◈◈◈	$99-$199 (SAVE)	984
37 / p. 950	AAA	Renaissance Tampa Hotel International Plaza, 1.5 mi se from terminal	◈◈◈◈	$161-$294 (SAVE)	985
38 / p. 950		Sailport Waterfront Resort, 4.8 mi w of terminal	◈◈	$86-$149	986
50 / p. 950	AAA	Sheraton Suites Tampa Airport, 3.5 mi se of terminal	◈◈◈	$285 (SAVE)	986
47 / p. 950	AAA	SpringHill Suites by Marriott Tampa/Westshore, 2.6 mi n of terminal	◈◈◈	$159-$179 (SAVE)	986
26 / p. 950		Tampa Airport Marriott, in terminal	◈◈◈	$319-$359	986
61 / p. 950		Wyndham Westshore-Tampa, 3 mi s of terminal	◈◈◈	$169-$309	987

Tampa

This index helps you "spot" where approved accommodations and restaurants are located on the corresponding detailed maps. Lodging rate ranges are for comparison only and show the property's high season; rates are per night, unless only weekly (W) rates are available. Restaurant rate range is for dinner, unless only lunch (L) is served. Turn to the listing page for more detailed rate information and consult display ads for special promotions.

Spotter/Map Page Number	OA	TAMPA - Lodgings	Diamond Rating	Rate Range High Season	Listing Page
1 / p. 950	AAA	Hampton Inn & Suites	◈◈◈	$99-$129 (SAVE)	978
2 / p. 950		Courtyard by Marriott Tampa North	◈◈◈	Failed to provide	973

Spotter/Map Page Number	OA	TAMPA - Lodgings (continued)	Diamond Rating	Rate Range High Season	Listing Page
3 / p. 950	AAA	Embassy Suites Hotel USF/Near Busch Gardens - see color ad p 976	◇◇◇	$109-$209 SAVE	976
4 / p. 950	AAA	Wingate Inn-USF Near Busch Gardens	◇◇◇	$116-$125 SAVE	987
5 / p. 950	AAA	La Quinta Inn & Suites Tampa Bay (U.S.F./Near Busch Gardens) - see color ad p 982	◇◇◇	$89-$119 SAVE	982
6 / p. 950	AAA	Holiday Inn Tampa Near Busch Gardens	◇◇◇	$89-$179 SAVE	981
7 / p. 950	AAA	AmeriSuites (Tampa near Busch Gardens)	◇◇◇	$119-$149 SAVE	969
8 / p. 950	AAA	DoubleTree Guest Suites Tampa/Busch Gardens - see color ad p 974	◇◇◇	$89-$169 SAVE	974
9 / p. 950	AAA	Best Western All Suites Hotel Near USF Behind Busch Gardens - see color ad p 971	◇◇◇	$119-$129 SAVE	971
10 / p. 950		Holiday Inn Express Hotel & Suites	◇◇◇	$129-$159	980
11 / p. 950	AAA	Baymont Inn & Suites Tampa/near Busch Gardens - see color ad p 970	◇◇◇	$89-$109 SAVE	970
12 / p. 950	AAA	Comfort Inn and Conference Center Near Busch Gardens	◇◇◇	$99-$109 SAVE	972
13 / p. 950		Red Roof Inn	◇◇	$55-$75	984
14 / p. 950		Hampton Inn Veterans Expressway	◇◇◇	$129-$149	979
15 / p. 950		Motel 6 #1192	◇	$39-$55	983
16 / p. 950	AAA	Microtel Inn & Suites	◇◇	$59-$109 SAVE	983
17 / p. 950		Homestead Studio Suites Hotel-Tampa/North Airport	◇◇	$44-$69	981
18 / p. 950	AAA	East Lake Inn	◇	$65-$70 SAVE	974
19 / p. 950		Mainsail Suites Hotel & Conference Center - see color ad p 983	◇◇◇	$149-$229	983
20 / p. 950		Hard Rock Seminole Casino & Hotel	◇◇◇	$152-$305	979
21 / p. 950		Red Roof Inn-Fairgrounds	◇◇	$53-$79	985
22 / p. 950	AAA	Holiday Inn Express Hotel & Suites Tampa-Fairgrounds	◇◇◇	$89-$169 SAVE	981
23 / p. 950	AAA	Baymont Inn Tampa-Fairgrounds - see color ad p 970	◇◇	$59-$79 SAVE	970
24 / p. 950		Comfort Inn Hotel & Suites Tampa Stadium/Airport	◇◇◇	$70-$269	972
25 / p. 950		Hilton Garden Inn Tampa East/Brandon	◇◇◇	$109-$169	979
26 / p. 950		Tampa Airport Marriott	◇◇◇	$319-$359	986
27 / p. 950		Residence Inn by Marriott Sabal Park	◇◇◇	$144-$149	985
28 / p. 950	AAA	AmeriSuites (Tampa/Sabal Corporate Park)	◇◇◇	$99-$189 SAVE	969
29 / p. 950		Crowne Plaza Tampa East	◇◇◇	$119-$214	973
30 / p. 950		Gram's Place BnB GuestHouses Hostel & Music	◇◇	$80-$95	977
31 / p. 950	AAA	Chase Suite Hotel by Woodfin	◇◇◇	$99-$229 SAVE	972
32 / p. 950	AAA	DoubleTree Guest Suites Tampa Bay	◇◇◇	$139-$229 SAVE	973
33 / p. 950	AAA	Hampton Inn - see color ad p 978	◇◇◇	$99-$189 SAVE	978
34 / p. 950		Holiday Inn Express Hotel & Suites - see color ad p 978	◇◇◇	$99-$199	980
35 / p. 950	AAA	Radisson Bay Harbor Hotel - see color ad p 984	◇◇◇	$99-$199 SAVE	984
36 / p. 950	AAA	Grand Hyatt Tampa Bay	◇◇◇◇	$125-$325 SAVE	977
37 / p. 950	AAA	Renaissance Tampa Hotel International Plaza - see color ad p 985	◇◇◇◇	$161-$294 SAVE	985

Spotter/Map Page Number	OA	TAMPA - Lodgings (continued)	Diamond Rating	Rate Range High Season	Listing Page
38 / p. 950		Sailport Waterfront Resort	◆◆	$86-$149	986
39 / p. 950		Hilton Garden Inn/Tampa Ybor City Historic District	◆◆◆	$159-$189	979
40 / p. 950	AAA	**Hilton Tampa Airport Westshore** - see color ad p 980	◆◆◆	$99-$309 [SAVE]	980
41 / p. 950	AAA	**La Quinta Inn Tampa Bay (Airport)** - see color ad p 982	◆◆◆	$115-$135 [SAVE]	982
42 / p. 950		Extended Stay Deluxe	◆◆◆	Failed to provide	976
43 / p. 950	AAA	**AmeriSuites (Tampa Airport/Westshore)**	◆◆◆	$99-$200 [SAVE]	969
44 / p. 950	AAA	**Hampton Inn Tampa Int'l Airport - Westshore**	◆◆◆	$79-$159 [SAVE]	979
45 / p. 950		Best Western-The Westshore Hotel	◆◆	$109-$139	971
46 / p. 950		Marriott-Tampa Westshore	◆◆◆	$299	983
47 / p. 950	AAA	**SpringHill Suites by Marriott Tampa/Westshore** - see color ad p 986	◆◆◆	$159-$179 [SAVE]	986
48 / p. 950	AAA	**Courtyard by Marriott**	◆◆◆	$149-$219 [SAVE]	972
49 / p. 950	AAA	**Doubletree Hotel Tampa Airport-Westshore**	◆◆◆	$139-$219 [SAVE]	974
50 / p. 950	AAA	**Sheraton Suites Tampa Airport** - see color ad p 8	◆◆◆	$285 [SAVE]	986
51 / p. 950		Quorum Hotel-Tampa - see color ad p 984	◆◆◆	$129-$299	984
52 / p. 950		Courtyard by Marriott-Downtown Tampa	◆◆◆	Failed to provide	973
53 / p. 950	AAA	**Best Western Brandon Hotel & Conference Center**	◆◆	$89-$109 [SAVE]	971
54 / p. 950	AAA	**Embassy Suites Hotel-Tampa/Airport/Westshore**	◆◆◆	$139-$199 [SAVE]	975
55 / p. 950	AAA	**Comfort Suites**	◆◆◆	$107-$199 [SAVE]	972
56 / p. 950	AAA	**Baymont Inn & Suites Tampa-Brandon** - see color ad p 970	◆◆◆	$89-$109 [SAVE]	970
57 / p. 950	AAA	**Hyatt Regency Tampa**	◆◆◆	$115-$209 [SAVE]	981
58 / p. 950		Tampa Riverwalk Hotel	◆◆◆	$159-$219	987
59 / p. 950	AAA	**Days Inn/State Fairgrounds**	◆◆	$89 [SAVE]	973
60 / p. 950		Hampton Inn-Tampa/Brandon	◆◆	$109-$129	978
61 / p. 950		Wyndham Westshore-Tampa	◆◆◆	$169-$309	987
62 / p. 950		Courtyard by Marriott-Brandon/Tampa	◆◆◆	$109-$179	973
63 / p. 950		Fairfield Inn by Marriott-Brandon/Tampa	◆◆◆	$99-$139	977
64 / p. 950		Tampa Marriott Waterside Hotel & Marina	◆◆◆	Failed to provide	987
65 / p. 950	AAA	**Tahitian Inn**	◆◆◆	$119-$219 [SAVE]	986
66 / p. 950	AAA	**Wyndham Harbour Island**	◆◆◆	$189-$289 [SAVE]	987
67 / p. 950		Best Western Tampa	◆◆	$99-$119	971
68 / p. 950	AAA	**Econo Lodge Midtown** - see color ad p 975	◆◆	$75-$125 [SAVE]	975
69 / p. 950	AAA	**Howard Johnson Express Inn & Suites**	◆◆	$65-$95 [SAVE]	981
70 / p. 950		La Quinta Inn Tampa South	◆◆◆	$110-$150	982
		TAMPA - Restaurants			
1 / p. 950		Thai Ruby	◆◆	$11-$24	999
2 / p. 950		Tampa Brickyard Grill	◆◆	$8-$16	999
3 / p. 950		Remington's Steakhouse	◆◆	$9-$21	997

Spotter/Map Page Number	OA	**TAMPA** - Restaurants (continued)	Diamond Rating	Rate Range High Season	Listing Page
④ / p. 950		Beef 'O' Brady's	▽▽	$6-$9	989
⑤ / p. 950	◬	**Skipper's Smokehouse Restaurant & Oyster Bar**	▽	$6-$16	998
⑥ / p. 950		Pita's	▽	$4-$7	996
⑦ / p. 950		Bally Hoo Grill	▽▽	$8-$20	988
⑧ / p. 950		Lenny's Sub Shop	▽	$5-$10	994
⑨ / p. 950		Arigato Japanese Steak House	▽▽	$10-$22	988
⑩ / p. 950		Vallarto's Restaurante Mexicano	▽▽	$6-$11	1000
⑪ / p. 950		Jasmine Thai Restaurant	▽▽	$6-$19	993
⑫ / p. 950		Windy City Pizza	▽▽	$6-$19	1000
⑬ / p. 950		Woody's Bar-B-Que	▽▽	$6-$15	1000
⑭ / p. 950		Taj Indian Cuisine	▽	$9-$17	999
⑮ / p. 950		First Watch	▽▽	$5-$7(L)	992
⑯ / p. 950		Firehouse Subs	▽	$5-$8	991
⑰ / p. 950		La Cocina Latin Cafe	▽▽	$5-$10	994
⑱ / p. 950		Hops Restaurant Bar & Brewery	▽▽	$7-$17	993
⑲ / p. 950		Mel's Diner	▽▽	$8-$13	995
⑳ / p. 950		Pita's	▽	$4-$7	996
㉑ / p. 950		Saigon Bay Vietnamese Restaurant	▽▽	$7-$17	997
㉒ / p. 950		Tia's Tex Mex	▽▽	$7-$15	999
㉓ / p. 950		China First Buffet	▽▽	$4-$13	990
㉔ / p. 950		Tijuana Flats	▽	$5-$9	999
㉕ / p. 950		Buca di Beppo	▽▽	$20-$28	989
㉖ / p. 950		Mimis Cafe	▽▽	$7-$16	995
㉗ / p. 950		Good Fellas	▽▽	$6-$9	992
㉘ / p. 950		Shells of North Tampa	▽▽	$7-$19	997
㉙ / p. 950		Busch's Family Sports Bar & Grill	▽▽	$9-$17	989
㉚ / p. 950		Westshore Pizzeria Tampa	▽	$4-$17	1000
㉛ / p. 950		Logan's Roadhouse	▽▽	$6-$19	994
㉜ / p. 950		Tusca Bella Grill	▽▽	$8-$19	999
㉝ / p. 950		Sukhothai Restaurant	▽▽	$6-$20	998
㉞ / p. 950		Mike's BBQ	▽	$5-$18	995
㉟ / p. 950		Frontier Steak House	▽▽	$9-$33	992
㊱ / p. 950		Pipo's & Son Restaurant	▽	$6-$10	996
㊲ / p. 950		Pita's	▽	$4-$7	996
㊳ / p. 950		Floyd's Restaurant & Night Club	▽▽▽	$15-$27	992
㊴ / p. 950		Sam Seltzer's Steakhouse	▽▽	$10-$19	997
㊵ / p. 950		CK's Restaurant	▽▽▽	$18-$38	990
㊶ / p. 950		Cafe' Elise	▽▽▽	$7-$18(L)	989
㊷ / p. 950		Bahama Breeze	▽▽	$10-$24	988

Spotter/Map Page Number	OA	**TAMPA** - Restaurants (continued)	Diamond Rating	Rate Range High Season	Listing Page
43 / p. 950		The Castaway	◆◆	$11-$20	990
44 / p. 950		Landry's Seafood House	◆◆	$14-$28	994
45 / p. 950		Brocato's Sandwich Shop	◆	$5-$8(L)	989
46 / p. 950		Armani's	◆◆◆◆	$23-$37	988
47 / p. 950		Oystercatchers	◆◆◆	$12-$30	996
48 / p. 950		Pelagia Trattoria	◆◆◆	$11-$29	996
49 / p. 950		Todai Restaurant	◆◆	$19-$21	999
50 / p. 950		The Bamboo Club	◆◆◆	$8-$23	988
51 / p. 950		Gallery Eclectic Bistro	◆◆◆	$8-$30	992
52 / p. 950		Kahunaville	◆◆	$12-$19	993
53 / p. 950		Champps Restaurant & Bar	◆◆	$5-$18	990
54 / p. 950		The Cheesecake Factory	◆◆◆	$8-$25	990
55 / p. 950	AAA	**Crazy Buffet**	◆◆	$20-$24	991
56 / p. 950		Crawdaddy's	◆◆	$16-$36	991
57 / p. 950		Lee Roy Selmon's	◆◆	$9-$20	994
58 / p. 950		The Rusty Pelican	◆◆◆	$18-$28	997
59 / p. 950		The Spaghetti Warehouse Restaurant	◆◆	$7-$15	998
60 / p. 950		Roy's Hawaiian Fusion Tampa	◆◆◆	$11-$35	997
61 / p. 950		J. Mallory Bistro and Bar	◆◆	$15-$30	993
62 / p. 950		Fresh Mouth	◆	$3-$7	992
63 / p. 950		Jax Grill at Gameworks	◆◆	$8-$18	993
64 / p. 950		Big City Tavern	◆◆◆	$11-$29	989
65 / p. 950		Barley Hoppers International Alehouse & Grill	◆◆	$7-$20	988
66 / p. 950		Samurai Blue Sushi and Sake Bar	◆◆	$8-$21	997
67 / p. 950		Dish Centro Ybor	◆◆	$16	991
68 / p. 950		Bernini	◆◆◆	$10-$25	989
69 / p. 950		Carmine's	◆	$8-$12	990
70 / p. 950		La Tropicana Cafe	◆	$6-$8(L)	994
71 / p. 950		Tampa Bay Brewing Company	◆◆	$8-$17	999
72 / p. 950		Deli Plus	◆	$3-$7	991
73 / p. 950		Columbia Restaurant Ybor City	◆◆◆	$18-$27	991
74 / p. 950		Moe's Southwest Grill	◆	$4-$9	995
75 / p. 950		Sweet Tomatoes Tampa	◆	$9	998
76 / p. 950		Houlihan's	◆◆	$8-$20	993
77 / p. 950		Tia's Tex-Mex	◆◆	$9-$16	999
78 / p. 950		La Bamba	◆	$5-$7(L)	994
79 / p. 950		Johnny Carino's	◆◆	$7-$14	993
80 / p. 950		Charley's Steakhouse	◆◆◆	$15-$40	990
81 / p. 950		J. Alexander's Restaurant	◆◆	$6-$20	993
82 / p. 950		Bay Cafe	◆◆	$10-$20	988

Spotter/Map Page Number	OA	**TAMPA** - Restaurants (continued)	Diamond Rating	Rate Range High Season	Listing Page
⑧③ / p. 950		Tapas Spanish Cafe	◈◈	$4-$11	999
⑧④ / p. 950		First Watch	◈◈	$5-$7(L)	992
⑧⑤ / p. 950		Lonni's Sandwiches, Etc	◈	$7-$9(L)	995
⑧⑥ / p. 950		Donatello	◈◈◈	$16-$29	991
⑧⑦ / p. 950		Sonny's Real Pit Bar-B-Q	◈◈	$9-$17	998
⑧⑧ / p. 950		Cafe European	◈◈	$10-$19	989
⑧⑨ / p. 950		The Fox Restaurant	◈◈◈	$10-$17	992
⑨⓪ / p. 950	◬	**Yacht Starship**	◈◈◈	$70	1000
⑨① / p. 950		P.F. Chang's China Bistro	◈◈	$6-$19	996
⑨② / p. 950		Maggiano's Little Italy Restaurant	◈◈	$12-$31	995
⑨③ / p. 950		Evos Westshore	◈	$5-$8	991
⑨④ / p. 950		Villa Rina's	◈	$5-$20	1000
⑨⑤ / p. 950		Mise en Place	◈◈◈	$15-$26	995
⑨⑥ / p. 950		Miguel's Mexican Restaurant	◈◈	$8-$15	995
⑨⑦ / p. 950		Le Petit Bistro West	◈	$6-$8	994
⑨⑧ / p. 950		Shula's Steakhouse	◈◈◈	$17-$66	998
⑨⑨ / p. 950		Valencia Garden	◈◈	$10-$17	1000
①⓪⓪ / p. 950		First Choice Bar-B-Que	◈	$4-$15	991
①⓪① / p. 950		Panera Bread Cafe	◈	$4-$7	996
①⓪② / p. 950		Sweet Tomatoes Brandon	◈	$7	998
①⓪③ / p. 950		Cherry's	◈◈	$6-$14	990
①⓪④ / p. 950		Newk's Lighthouse Cafe	◈◈	$5-$12	995
①⓪⑤ / p. 950		Stumps Supper Club	◈◈	$10-$21	998
①⓪⑥ / p. 950		grille 29	◈◈◈	$8-$28	992
①⓪⑦ / p. 950		Margarita Mama's	◈◈	$5-$9	995
①⓪⑧ / p. 950		Tokai Restaurant	◈◈	$5-$13	999
①⓪⑨ / p. 950		Mangroves Seafood Grille & Bar	◈◈	$16-$26	995
①①⓪ / p. 950		Fred Flemings Famous Bar-B-Que	◈◈	$7-$18	992
①①① / p. 950		The Rack	◈◈◈	$4-$10	996
①①② / p. 950		42nd Street The Bistro	◈◈	$7-$18	988
①①③ / p. 950		Ho Ho Windows	◈◈	$6-$12	992
①①④ / p. 950	◬	**Jackson's Bistro-Bar & Sushi**	◈◈◈	$13-$21	993
①①⑤ / p. 950		The Wine Exchange Bistro & Wine Bar	◈◈	$8-$10	1000
①①⑥ / p. 950		Samba Room	◈◈	$9-$25	997
①①⑦ / p. 950		717 South	◈◈	$15-$27	988
①①⑧ / p. 950		Bonefish Grill	◈◈◈	$15-$22	989
①①⑨ / p. 950		Royal Palace Thai Restaurant	◈◈	$10-$18	997
①②⓪ / p. 950		Pita's	◈	$4-$7	996
①②① / p. 950		Hugo's Spanish Restaurant	◈◈	$4-$12	993
①②② / p. 950		SideBern's	◈◈◈	$26-$40	998

Spotter/Map Page Number	OA	TAMPA - Restaurants (continued)	Diamond Rating	Rate Range High Season	Listing Page
(123) / p. 950		Lauro Ristorante Italiano	◆◆	$13-$28	994
(124) / p. 950		Bern's Steak House	◆◆◆	$23-$40	989
(125) / p. 950		St. Barts Island House Restaurant	◆◆◆	$12-$27	997
(126) / p. 950		Ceviche'	◆◆◆	$18-$31	990
(127) / p. 950		The Colonnade	◆◆	$6-$21	991
(128) / p. 950		Westshore Pizza & Cheesesteaks I	◆	$4-$17	1000
(129) / p. 950		Caffe Paradiso	◆◆◆	$8-$24	990
(130) / p. 950		Egg Platter	◆◆	$5-$8	991
(131) / p. 950		Kojaks House of Ribs Bar-B-Que	◆	$6-$24	994
(132) / p. 950		Jimmy Mac's Waterfront Restaurant	◆◆	$7-$25	993
		TEMPLE TERRACE - Lodgings			
(73) / p. 950		Extended StayAmerica	◆◆	$85-$115	1047
(74) / p. 950		Fairfield Inn Tampa North	◆◆	Failed to provide	1047
(75) / p. 950	◆◆◆	**Sleep Inn Temple Terrace USF Near Busch Gardens**	◆◆	$80 (SAVE)	1047
(76) / p. 950		Residence Inn by Marriott Tampa North	◆◆◆	Failed to provide	1047
(77) / p. 950		Hilton Garden Inn Tampa North	◆◆◆	$89-$189	1047
		TEMPLE TERRACE - Restaurants			
(135) / p. 950		Beef 'O' Brady's	◆◆	$6-$9	1048
(136) / p. 950		Tokyo Japanese Restaurant & Sushi Bar	◆◆	$7-$16	1048
(137) / p. 950		Clubhouse Sports Cafe	◆	$6-$10	1048
(138) / p. 950		Vallarto's Restaurante Mexicano	◆◆	$6-$11	1048
		BRANDON - Lodgings			
(80) / p. 950		Holiday Inn Express-Brandon	◆◆◆	$129-$139	1001
(81) / p. 950	◆◆◆	**La Quinta Inn & Suites Tampa Bay (Brandon)** - see color ad p 982	◆◆◆	$129-$149 (SAVE)	1001
(82) / p. 950		Homestead Studio Suites Hotel-Tampa/Brandon	◆◆	$54-$74	1001
(83) / p. 950	◆◆◆	**Brandon Motor Lodge**	◆◆	$59-$89 (SAVE)	1001
		BRANDON - Restaurants			
(153) / p. 950		Westshore Pizza & Cheesesteaks	◆	$4-$17	1006
(154) / p. 950		Wizeguyz Pizzeria	◆	$5-$14	1006
(155) / p. 950		Chicago's Maxwell Street Grill	◆	$4-$7	1003
(156) / p. 950		Moe's Southwest Grill	◆	$3-$9	1004
(157) / p. 950		Smokey Bone's Barbeque & Grill	◆◆	$7-$18	1005
(158) / p. 950		Tia's Tex Mex	◆◆	$7-$15	1006
(159) / p. 950		Babe's Pizza	◆◆	$7-$18	1002
(160) / p. 950		Ben's Family Restaurant	◆◆	$6-$14	1002
(161) / p. 950		Hao One Chinese Restaurant	◆	$6-$12	1003
(162) / p. 950		Estela's Mexican Restaurant	◆◆	$5-$10	1003
(163) / p. 950		Shells of Brandon	◆◆	$8-$15	1005
(164) / p. 950		Chop Stix Chinese Restaurant	◆	$5-$14	1003

Spotter/Map Page Number	OA	**BRANDON** - Restaurants (continued)	Diamond Rating	Rate Range High Season	Listing Page
165 / p. 950		Roadhouse Grill	◆◆	$7-$18	1005
166 / p. 950		Miller's Brandon Ale House & Raw Bar	◆◆	$6-$13	1004
167 / p. 950		Chili's Brandon	◆◆	$7-$22	1003
168 / p. 950		Rib City Grill Brandon	◆◆	$5-$20	1005
169 / p. 950		Sushi House	◆◆	$9-$14	1006
170 / p. 950		Buddy Freddy's	◆	$10-$13	1002
171 / p. 950		Oaks Bar & Grill	◆◆	$7-$21	1004
172 / p. 950		Ploy Thai Restaurant	◆◆◆	$9-$21	1005
173 / p. 950		Firehouse Subs	◆	$4-$8	1003
174 / p. 950		Della's Delectables	◆	$12-$19	1003
175 / p. 950		Cauldron Jamaican Restaurant & American Cuisine	◆◆	$9-$13	1002
176 / p. 950		Panera Bread Cafe	◆	$4-$7	1005
177 / p. 950		Ruby Tuesday	◆◆	$8-$18	1005
178 / p. 950		The American Cafe	◆◆	$8-$14	1001
179 / p. 950		Nature's Table	◆	$5-$8	1004
180 / p. 950		Steak Escape	◆	$5-$8	1006
181 / p. 950		Buffalo Wild Wings Grill & Bar	◆◆	$6-$12	1002
182 / p. 950		Mimis Cafe Brandon	◆◆	$7-$16	1004
183 / p. 950		Jo-To Japanese Steak House	◆◆	$12-$25	1004
184 / p. 950		Tadpoles	◆◆	$5-$8	1006
185 / p. 950		Joey's Famous Philly Steaks	◆	$6-$8	1004
186 / p. 950		Barnacles	◆◆	$6-$17	1002
187 / p. 950		Shrimp Boat Grill	◆◆	$11-$18	1005
188 / p. 950		Hops Grillhouse & Brewery	◆◆	$9-$20	1003
189 / p. 950		Yokohama Japanese Restaurant Sushi Bar	◆◆	$11-$21	1006
190 / p. 950		Jasmine Thai & Sushi Bar	◆◆	$7-$24	1003
191 / p. 950		Chick-N-Bones Cafe	◆	$4-$8	1003
192 / p. 950		Brandon Brew House	◆◆	$7-$19	1002
193 / p. 950		La Cubanita Cafe	◆	$7	1004
194 / p. 950		Pita's	◆	$4-$7	1005
195 / p. 950		Lin's Garden Chinese Restaurant	◆	$5-$13	1004
196 / p. 950		Cheddar's Casual Cafe	◆◆	$5-$13	1002
197 / p. 950		Buca di Beppo Brandon	◆◆	$18-$29	1002
198 / p. 950		O'Brien's Irish Pub	◆◆	$8-$17	1004
199 / p. 950		Bonefish Grill	◆◆◆	$16-$24	1002
200 / p. 950		Crispers	◆	$5-$8	1003
201 / p. 950		Tropical Smoothie Cafe	◆	$5-$7	1006

Spotter/Map Page Number	OA	BRANDON - Restaurants (continued)	Diamond Rating	Rate Range High Season	Listing Page
(202) / p. 950		Tijuana Flats	◆	$5-$9	1006
(203) / p. 950		Country Kitchen	◆◆	$6-$10	1003
(204) / p. 950		Simply Thai	◆◆	$7-$14	1005
(205) / p. 950		Cherry's	◆◆	$6-$13	1002
(206) / p. 950		Westshore Pizza VI	◆	$4-$17	1006
(207) / p. 950		Peck's Flame Broiled Chicken	◆	$6-$27	1005
(208) / p. 950		NY's Times Square Pizza	◆	$6-$19	1004
(209) / p. 950		Latin Cafe 2000	◆◆	$8-$12	1004
		RIVERVIEW - Lodgings			
(86) / p. 950		Bianchi Motel	◆	Failed to provide	1034
		RIVERVIEW - Restaurants			
(221) / p. 950		ABC Pizza	◆◆	$5-$16	1035
(222) / p. 950		Beef 'O' Brady's	◆◆	$6-$9	1035
		VALRICO - Restaurants			
(141) / p. 950	AAA	**Willie's The Place For Seafood**	◆◆	$8-$15	1057
(142) / p. 950		Ruby Tuesday	◆◆	$8-$18	1057
(143) / p. 950		China-Fuji Restaurant	◆◆	$7-$19	1057
(144) / p. 950		Beef'O'Brady's	◆◆	$6-$10	1056
(145) / p. 950		China Palace Super Buffet	◆◆	$10-$18	1057
(146) / p. 950		Raccoon's	◆	$5-$7	1057
(147) / p. 950		Panda World Chinese Restaurant	◆	$4-$15	1057
(148) / p. 950		Pacific Grill An Asian Bistro	◆◆	$8-$18	1057
(149) / p. 950		Panera Bread	◆	$6-$7	1057
(150) / p. 950		Beef O'Brady's Family Sports Pub	◆◆	$6-$8	1057
		SEFFNER - Restaurants			
(212) / p. 950		China Wok Chinese Food	◆	$4-$12	1045
(213) / p. 950		Latin Cuisine	◆	$4-$7	1045
(214) / p. 950		Stacey's Homestyle Buffet	◆	$8	1045
(215) / p. 950		Young Bin Chinese Restaurant	◆◆	$5-$12	1045
(216) / p. 950		Beef O'Brady's of Seffner	◆◆	$4-$9	1045
(217) / p. 950		Pot Bellies B-B-Que	◆◆	$6-$16	1045
(218) / p. 950	AAA	**JR's Floribbean Outpost**	◆	$6-$16	1045

ST. PETERSBURG pop. 248,232 (See map and index starting on p. 938)

──────── WHERE TO STAY ────────

BAYBORO HOUSE BED & BREAKFAST ON OLD TAMPA BAY

Phone: 727/823-4955 [18]

12/1-5/31 [BP]	1P: $149-$299 2P: $149-$299 XP: $25
6/1-11/30 [BP]	1P: $129-$279 2P: $129-$279 XP: $25

AAA SAVE
Historic Bed & Breakfast

Location: I-275, exit 22, e to 4th St S, 0.5 mi s to 22nd Ave S, 0.4 mi e, then 0.3 mi n; in Old Southeast area. 1719 Beach Dr SE 33701. Fax: 727/822-2341. **Facility:** On Tampa Bay, this 1907 Victorian home offers individually themed units, each with a view of the bay; age restrictions are imposed in the main house. Designated smoking area. 8 units. 6 one-bedroom standard units, some with whirlpools. 1 one- and 1 two-bedroom suites, some with whirlpools. 2 stories, interior corridors. *Bath:* combo or shower only. **Parking:** on-site. **Terms:** 2-3 night minimum stay - seasonal and/or weekends, 14 day cancellation notice-fee imposed, package plans. **Amenities:** video library, hair dryers. *Some:* DVD players, irons. **Pool(s):** small heated outdoor. **Leisure Activities:** whirlpool, kayak, gas barbecue, bicycles. **Guest Services:** complimentary evening beverages. **Business Services:** meeting rooms, PC, fax. **Cards:** AX, DS, MC, VI. **Special Amenities:** free full breakfast and free room upgrade (subject to availability with advance reservations).

SOME UNITS

BEST INNS LEE MANOR INN   *Book at aaa.com*

Phone: (727)894-3248 [14]

12/1-3/31 [CP]	1P: $59-$139 2P: $69-$149
11/1-11/30 [CP]	1P: $59-$129 2P: $69-$139
4/1-5/31 [CP]	1P: $49-$119 2P: $49-$119
6/1-10/31 [CP]	1P: $45-$119 2P: $45-$119

Motel

Location: Jct 4th St N; downtown. 342 3rd Ave N 33701. Fax: 727/895-8759. **Facility:** Designated smoking area. 19 one-bedroom standard units, some with efficiencies. 2 stories, interior corridors. *Bath:* combo or shower only. **Parking:** on-site. **Terms:** 1-2 night minimum stay - seasonal, cancellation fee imposed. **Amenities:** high-speed Internet, voice mail, hair dryers. *Some:* irons. **Guest Services:** complimentary evening beverages. **Business Services:** fax. **Cards:** AX, DC, DS, MC, VI.

SOME UNITS
FEE

COMFORT INN & SUITES   *Book at aaa.com*

Phone: 727/323-3100 [6]

3/1-4/15	1P: $95-$115 2P: $95-$115 XP: $7 F18
2/1-2/28	1P: $80-$95 2P: $80-$95 XP: $7 F18
12/1-1/31 & 4/16-11/30	1P: $70-$85 2P: $70-$85 XP: $7 F18

AAA SAVE

Small-scale Hotel

Location: I-275, exit 24, 1.2 mi w on 22nd Ave N, then 0.5 mi s on US 19. 1400 34th St N 33713. Fax: 727/327-5792. **Facility:** 75 units. 57 one-bedroom standard units. 18 one-bedroom suites ($95-$125). 3 stories, exterior corridors. *Bath:* combo or shower only. **Parking:** on-site. **Terms:** [CP] meal plan available. **Amenities:** high-speed Internet, irons, hair dryers. **Pool(s):** heated outdoor. **Leisure Activities:** whirlpool, sun deck, exercise room. **Guest Services:** coin laundry. **Business Services:** meeting rooms, fax. **Cards:** AX, DC, DS, MC, VI. **Special Amenities:** free continental breakfast and free local telephone calls.

SOME UNITS

DAYS INN ST. PETE CENTRAL   *Book at aaa.com*

Phone: (727)321-2958 [10]

12/1-4/30	1P: $69-$129 2P: $74-$139 XP: $7 F
8/1-9/30	1P: $79-$99 2P: $89-$109 XP: $7 F
5/1-7/31 & 10/1-11/30	1P: $49-$89 2P: $54-$99 XP: $7 F

Motel

Location: I-275, exit 24, 1.2 mi w on 22nd Ave N, then 1 mi s on US 19. 650 34th St N 33713. Fax: 727/327-1625. **Facility:** 28 one-bedroom standard units, some with efficiencies. 2 stories, exterior corridors. **Parking:** on-site. **Terms:** [AP] & [CP] meal plans available. **Amenities:** hair dryers. *Some:* irons. **Pool(s):** heated outdoor. **Leisure Activities:** whirlpool. **Guest Services:** coin laundry. **Business Services:** fax (fee). **Cards:** AX, DC, DS, MC, VI.

SOME UNITS

DAYS INN TROPICANA FIELD NORTH   *Book at aaa.com*

Phone: (727)522-3191 [2]

1/16-4/15	1P: $59-$79 2P: $59-$79 XP: $5 F12
12/1-1/15 & 4/16-11/30	1P: $54-$74 2P: $54-$74 XP: $5 F12

Motel

Location: I-275, exit 26; exit 26B northbound, 0.3 mi w. 2595 54th Ave N 33714. Fax: 727/527-6120. **Facility:** 135 one-bedroom standard units. 2 stories, exterior corridors. *Bath:* combo or shower only. **Parking:** on-site. **Terms:** pets ($25 extra charge). **Amenities:** safes (fee), hair dryers. **Pool(s):** outdoor, wading. **Leisure Activities:** playground, shuffleboard. **Guest Services:** coin laundry. **Business Services:** meeting rooms, fax. **Cards:** AX, DC, DS, JC, MC, VI.

SOME UNITS
FEE

DICKENS HOUSE BED AND BREAKFAST   *Book at aaa.com*

Phone: (727)822-8622 [8]

12/24-4/30	1P: $120-$210 2P: $120-$210 XP: $20
12/1-12/23 & 11/1-11/30	1P: $110-$178 2P: $110-$178 XP: $20
5/1-10/31	1P: $105-$168 2P: $105-$168 XP: $20

Historic Bed & Breakfast

Location: Just w of jct Beach Dr NE; downtown; in Old Northeast area. 335 8th Ave NE 33701. Fax: 727/822-6312. **Facility:** The restored house features several tastefully decorated rooms and the owner makes you feel right at home; a bountiful breakfast awaits. Designated smoking area. 5 units. 3 one- and 2 two-bedroom standard units, some with whirlpools. 3 stories (no elevator), interior corridors. **Parking:** street. **Terms:** 10 day cancellation notice-fee imposed. **Amenities:** video library, DVD players, high-speed Internet, voice mail, irons, hair dryers. **Guest Services:** complimentary evening beverages, complimentary laundry. **Business Services:** business center. **Cards:** AX, DS, MC, VI.

(See map and index starting on p. 938)

HAMPTON INN   *Book at aaa.com*   Phone: (727)322-0770   **7**

AAA SAVE
WWW

	1/16-4/1 [CP]	1P: $119-$189	2P: $119-$189
	4/2-6/1 [CP]	1P: $109-$119	2P: $109-$119
	12/1-1/15 [CP]	1P: $94-$119	2P: $94-$119
	6/2-11/30 [CP]	1P: $99-$109	2P: $99-$109

Small-scale Hotel **Location:** I-275, exit 24, 1.2 mi w on 22nd Ave N, then 0.6 mi s on US 19. 1200 34th St N 33713. Fax: 727/322-0378. **Facility:** 130 units. 126 one-bedroom standard units. 4 one-bedroom suites with efficiencies (no utensils). 4 stories, interior corridors. *Bath:* combo or shower only. **Parking:** on-site. **Terms:** check-in 4 pm, cancellation fee imposed. **Amenities:** video games (fee), high-speed Internet, dual phone lines, voice mail, irons, hair dryers. **Pool(s):** heated outdoor. **Leisure Activities:** exercise room. **Guest Services:** valet and coin laundry. **Business Services:** meeting rooms, PC, fax (fee). **Cards:** AX, DC, DS, MC, VI. *(See color ad p 948)*

SOME UNITS

🔊 📶 🍴 🛗 📶 📷 🏊 📱 DATA PORT 🔌 💻 / ✕ 📠 /

HAMPTON INN & SUITES   *Book at aaa.com*   Phone: (727)892-9900   **16**

AAA SAVE
WWW

	1/1-4/30		2P: $148-$186	XP: $10	F18
	5/1-11/30		2P: $139-$169	XP: $10	F18
	12/1-12/31		2P: $134-$166	XP: $10	F18

Small-scale Hotel **Location:** Jct 1 Ave NE; downtown. 80 Beach Dr NE 33701. Fax: 727/892-9205. **Facility:** 91 one-bedroom standard units. 4 stories, interior corridors. *Bath:* combo or shower only. **Parking:** on-site (fee) and valet. **Amenities:** video library (fee), DVD players, CD players, high-speed Internet, dual phone lines, voice mail, irons, hair dryers. **Pool(s):** heated outdoor. **Leisure Activities:** exercise room. *Fee:* massage. **Guest Services:** sundries, valet and coin laundry. **Business Services:** meeting rooms, PC, fax (fee). **Cards:** AX, CB, DC, DS, JC, MC, VI. **Special Amenities:** free expanded continental breakfast and free newspaper. *(See color ad below)*

SOME UNITS

🔊 📶 🍴 🛗 📷 🏊 📱 DATA PORT 🔌 💻 / ✕ /

HOLIDAY INN EXPRESS HOTEL & SUITES   Phone: 813/490-1000

fyi

| | 12/1-4/15 [ECP] | 1P: $100-$150 | 2P: $100-$150 | XP: $10 | F18 |
| | 4/16-11/30 [ECP] | 1P: $85-$125 | 2P: $85-$125 | XP: $10 | F18 |

Small-scale Hotel Too new to rate. **Location:** I-275, exit 26 southbound; exit 26B northbound, just e. 2171 54th Ave N 33714. Fax: 813/490-1004. **Amenities:** 76 units, coffeemakers, microwaves, refrigerators, pool. **Cards:** AX, CB, DC, DS, MC, VI.

HOLIDAY INN SUNSPREE RESORT MARINA COVE   *Book at aaa.com*   Phone: (727)867-1151   **19**

AAA SAVE
WWW

| | 2/10-4/22 | 1P: $159-$189 | 2P: $159-$189 | XP: $10 | F18 |
| | 12/1-2/9 & 4/23-11/30 | 1P: $99-$139 | 2P: $99-$139 | XP: $10 | F18 |

Resort Motel **Location:** I-275, exit 16, just e on Pinellas Point Dr, then just s. 6800 Sunshine Skyway Ln 33711. Fax: 727/864-4494. **Facility:** Many recreational activities are available at this 18-acre resort on Old Tampa Bay; an on-site restaurant has a submarine theme. Weekend entertainment. 156 units. 145 one-bedroom standard units. 11 one-bedroom suites ($169-$219) with efficiencies. 2 stories, interior/exterior corridors. *Bath:* combo or shower only. **Parking:** on-site. **Terms:** cancellation fee imposed, package plans. **Amenities:** high-speed Internet, dual phone lines, voice mail, safes, irons, hair dryers. *Some:* video games. **Dining:** 2 restaurants, 7 am-10 pm, cocktails. **Pool(s):** outdoor, heated outdoor. **Leisure Activities:** whirlpool, fishing, 5 lighted tennis courts, recreation programs, playground, exercise room, shuffleboard, volleyball. *Fee:* marina, charter fishing, beach cruisers, fishing equipment, personal watercraft, sailing school, water bike, tennis instruction, surreys, trikes, 4 wheel bikes, massage, game room. **Guest Services:** gift shop, valet and coin laundry. **Business Services:** meeting rooms, business center. **Cards:** AX, CB, DC, DS, MC, VI. **Special Amenities:** free local telephone calls and free newspaper. *(See color ad p 963)*

SOME UNITS

🔊 📶 🍴 🍷 🛗 📷 🏊 🚫 📱 DATA PORT 🔌 💻 / ✕ VCR 📠 /
FEE

INN AT THE BAY BED & BREAKFAST   *Book at aaa.com*   Phone: 727/822-1700   **13**

WWW

| | All Year [BP] | 1P: $125-$270 | 2P: $125-$270 | XP: $20 |

Historic Bed & Breakfast **Location:** Just e of jct 2nd St N; downtown. 126 4th Ave NE 33701. Fax: 727/896-7412. **Facility:** In-room whirlpools enhance many accommodations at this service-oriented inn, which is close to shops, restaurants and the pier. Designated smoking area. 12 one-bedroom standard units, some with whirlpools. 3 stories (no elevator), interior corridors. *Bath:* combo or shower only. **Parking:** on-site. **Terms:** office hours 10 am-8 pm, age restrictions may apply, 10 day cancellation notice-fee imposed. **Amenities:** DVD players, CD players, high-speed Internet, voice mail, irons, hair dryers. **Guest Services:** complimentary evening beverages, valet laundry. **Business Services:** meeting rooms, PC, fax. **Cards:** AX, CB, DC, DS, MC, VI.

SOME UNITS

🍴 🐾 ✕ 📱 DATA PORT 💻 / 🔌 /

(See map and index starting on p. 938)

KENTUCKY MOTEL

AAA SAVE

Motel

All Year   1P: $36-$46   2P: $40-$53   XP: $10
Phone: 727/526-7373   **5**
XP: $10   F10

Location: I-275, exit 26 southbound; exit 26B northbound, 1.4 mi e on 54th Ave N, then 0.7 mi s on US 92. 4246 4th St N 33703. Fax: 727/526-2698. **Facility:** 10 one-bedroom standard units. 1 story, exterior corridors. *Bath:* combo or shower only. **Parking:** on-site. **Terms:** 3 day cancellation notice, package plans. **Amenities:** *Some:* irons, hair dryers. **Cards:** AX, DS, MC, VI.

SOME UNITS

LA QUINTA INN TAMPA BAY AREA (ST. PETERSBURG)   *Book at aaa.com*

AAA SAVE

Motel

All Year   1P: $79-$99   Phone: (727)527-8421   **4**
XP: $7   F18

Location: I-275, exit 26; exit 26B northbound, just w on 54th Ave N, then just s on US 19. 4999 34th St N 33714. Fax: 727/527-8851. **Facility:** 120 one-bedroom standard units. 2 stories, exterior corridors. *Bath:* combo or shower only. **Parking:** on-site. **Terms:** [ECP] meal plan available, small pets only. **Amenities:** voice mail, irons, hair dryers. *Some:* video games, high-speed Internet. **Pool(s):** heated outdoor. **Leisure Activities:** exercise room. **Guest Services:** valet and coin laundry. **Business Services:** meeting rooms, fax. **Cards:** AX, CB, DC, DS, MC, VI. **Special Amenities:** free expanded continental breakfast and free local telephone calls. *(See color ad p 982)*

SOME UNITS
FEE   FEE

MANSION HOUSE B & B AND THE COURTYARD ON FIFTH   *Book at aaa.com*

AAA SAVE

Historic Bed & Breakfast

12/1-5/1 & 10/1-11/30 [BP]   1P: $149-$220   2P: $149-$220   Phone: (727)821-9391   **12**
5/2-9/30 [BP]   1P: $119-$220   2P: $119-$220

Location: 0.5 mi n at 1st St N; downtown. 105 5th Ave NE 33701. Fax: 727/821-6906. **Facility:** This refurbished turn-of-the-20th-century home offers a picturesque garden area with both a pool and a whirlpool. Designated smoking area. 12 units. 11 one-bedroom standard units. 1 cottage with whirlpool. 2 stories, interior/exterior corridors. *Bath:* combo or shower only. **Parking:** street. **Terms:** 2-3 night minimum stay - weekends, 14 day cancellation notice-fee imposed, package plans, small pets only (in designated units). **Amenities:** high-speed Internet, hair dryers. *Some:* irons. **Leisure Activities:** whirlpool, 2 TV/library rooms with CD, VCR, lending library. *Fee:* boat cruises. **Guest Services:** complimentary evening beverages, valet and coin laundry. **Business Services:** meeting rooms, PC, fax (fee). **Cards:** AX, CB, DC, DS, MC, VI.

SOME UNITS

PIER HOTEL   *Book at aaa.com*

AAA SAVE

Small-scale Hotel

12/31-11/30   1P: $148-$158   2P: $148-$158   Phone: (727)822-7500   **15**
12/1-12/30   1P: $108-$118   2P: $108-$118   XP: $10   F16
XP: $10   F16

Location: Jct 3rd St N; downtown. 253 2nd Ave N 33701. Fax: 727/822-0200. **Facility:** Designated smoking area. 31 units. 29 one-bedroom standard units. 2 one-bedroom suites ($138-$198). 3 stories (no elevator), interior corridors. *Bath:* combo or shower only. **Parking:** valet and street. **Terms:** cancellation fee imposed, [ECP] meal plan available. **Amenities:** high-speed Internet, voice mail, hair dryers. *Some:* irons. **Guest Services:** complimentary evening beverages, valet laundry. **Business Services:** meeting rooms, fax. **Cards:** AX, DC, DS, MC, VI. **Special Amenities:** free expanded continental breakfast and early check-in/late check-out.

SOME UNITS

(See map and index starting on p. 938)

RADISSON HOTEL AND CONFERENCE CENTER   *Book at aaa.com*   Phone: (727)572-7800   **1**
▼▼▼   All Year   1P: $189-$199   2P: $189-$199   XP: $15   F18
Large-scale Hotel   **Location:** I-275, exit 30, 0.7 mi w on SR 686. 12600 Roosevelt Blvd 33716. **Fax:** 727/572-5700. **Facility:** 205 units. 198 one-bedroom standard units. 7 one-bedroom suites ($279-$299). 9 stories, interior corridors. *Bath:* combo or shower only. **Parking:** on-site and valet. **Terms:** check-in 4 pm, [AP], [BP] & [CP] meal plans available, package plans. **Amenities:** dual phone lines, voice mail, safes, irons, hair dryers. *Fee:* video games, high-speed Internet. *Some:* CD players. **Dining:** Bellarte Restaurant, see separate listing. **Pool(s):** heated outdoor. **Leisure Activities:** sauna, exercise room. **Guest Services:** gift shop, valet and coin laundry. **Business Services:** conference facilities, business center. **Cards:** AX, CB, DC, DS, JC, MC, VI.

SOME UNITS
(ASK) (S/D) ✈ 🍴 📺 🔊M 🎿 ⊘ 🏊 📹 (DATA PORT) 🔌 💻 / ✖ 📠 /

RAMADA INN MIRAGE   *Book at aaa.com*   Phone: (727)525-1181   **3**
ⒶⒶⒶ (SAVE)   2/1-4/30   1P: $95-$130   2P: $95-$130   XP: $5   F
▼▼▼   1/1-1/31   1P: $85-$110   2P: $85-$110   XP: $5   F
Motel   12/31-12/31 & 5/1-11/30   1P: $65-$89   2P: $65-$89   XP: $5   F
Location: I-275, exit 26; exit 26B northbound, just w on 54th Ave N, then just s on US 19. 5005 34th St N 33714. **Fax:** 727/522-4505. **Facility:** 170 one-bedroom standard units, some with efficiencies. 2 stories, exterior corridors. **Parking:** on-site. **Terms:** pets ($25 fee). **Amenities:** high-speed Internet, voice mail, safes (fee), irons, hair dryers. **Dining:** 2 restaurants, 7-10 am, 11-2 & 5-10 pm, Fri & Sat-11 pm, Sun 7-10 am, 11-3 & 5-10 pm, cocktails. **Pool(s):** heated outdoor, wading. **Leisure Activities:** exercise room. **Guest Services:** valet and coin laundry. **Business Services:** meeting rooms, business center. **Cards:** AX, DC, DS, MC, VI. **Special Amenities:** free local telephone calls and free newspaper.

SOME UNITS
(S/D) 🛏 🍴 📺 🎿 📹 (DATA PORT) 🔌 📠 💻 / ✖ /
FEE

(See map and index starting on p. 938)

RENAISSANCE VINOY RESORT AND GOLF CLUB   *Book at aaa.com*   Phone: (727)894-1000   **11**

AAA SAVE

	1/1-4/3	1P: $279-$329	2P: $279-$329	XP: $25	F18
	9/7-11/30	1P: $229-$289	2P: $229-$289	XP: $25	F18
	12/1-12/31	1P: $219-$269	2P: $219-$269	XP: $25	F18
	4/4-9/6	1P: $189-$269	2P: $189-$269	XP: $25	F18

Resort
Large-scale Hotel

Location: 1.8 mi e on 4th Ave, just n on Beach Dr; downtown. 501 5th Ave NE 33701. Fax: 727/822-2785. **Facility:** Originally opened in 1925 as a haven for the rich and famous, this hotel has been restored and modernized but retains its historical grandeur. 360 units. 353 one-bedroom standard units, some with whirlpools. 7 one-bedroom suites ($319-$1200). 7 stories, interior corridors. *Bath:* combo or shower only. **Parking:** on-site (fee) and valet. **Terms:** check-in 4 pm, 3 day cancellation notice-fee imposed, package plans. **Amenities:** dual phone lines, voice mail, honor bars, irons, hair dryers. *Fee:* video games, high-speed Internet, safes. **Dining:** 5 restaurants, 6 am-11 pm, cocktails, also, Marchand's Bar & Grill, Terrace Room, see separate listings, entertainment. **Pool(s):** 2 heated outdoor. **Leisure Activities:** saunas, whirlpools, steamrooms, fishing, recreation programs, aerobics, jogging, spa. *Fee:* sailboats, marina, charter fishing, sailing instructions, golf-18 holes, driving range, 12 lighted tennis courts, bicycles. **Guest Services:** gift shop, valet and coin laundry, airport transportation (fee)-Tampa International & St Pete/Clearwater airports, area transportation-within 5 mi, beauty salon. **Business Services:** conference facilities, business center. **Cards:** AX, CB, DC, DS, JC, MC, VI.
(See color ad p 964)

SOME UNITS

$\boxed{\text{S}_\text{D}}$ $\boxed{\leftarrow}$ $\boxed{\mathsf{1}\mathsf{1}}$ $\boxed{24\top}$ $\boxed{\top}$ $\boxed{\text{fit}}$ $\boxed{\text{&}}$ $\boxed{\text{image}}$ $\boxed{\text{image}}$ $\boxed{\text{image}}$ $\boxed{\times}$ $\boxed{\text{image}}$ $\boxed{\text{DATA PORT}}$ $\boxed{\text{image}}$ / $\boxed{\times}$ $\boxed{\text{VCR}}$
FEE   FEE

ST. PETERSBURG BAYFRONT HILTON   *Book at aaa.com*   Phone: (727)894-5000   **17**

	12/1-4/30	1P: $179-$209	2P: $179-$209	XP: $10	F
	10/1-11/30	1P: $149-$209	2P: $149-$209	XP: $10	F
	5/1-9/30	1P: $149-$179	2P: $149-$179	XP: $10	F

Large-scale Hotel

Location: I-275, exit 22, 1.5 mi s on 5th Ave, then just e. Located across from the Al Lang Stadium. 333 1st 33701 (333 1st St S). Fax: 727/823-4797. **Facility:** 333 units. 330 one-bedroom standard units. 3 one-bedroom suites. 15 stories, interior corridors. *Bath:* some combo or shower only. **Parking:** on-site (fee) and valet. **Terms:** cancellation fee imposed, package plans. **Amenities:** high-speed Internet, dual phone lines, voice mail, irons, hair dryers. **Pool(s):** heated outdoor. **Leisure Activities:** whirlpool, spa. **Guest Services:** gift shop, valet laundry, area transportation. **Business Services:** conference facilities, business center. **Cards:** AX, CB, DC, DS, MC, VI.

SOME UNITS

$\boxed{\mathsf{1}\mathsf{1}}$ $\boxed{\top}$ $\boxed{\text{fit}}$ $\boxed{\text{&M}}$ $\boxed{\text{&}}$ $\boxed{\text{image}}$ $\boxed{\text{image}}$ $\boxed{\text{image}}$ $\boxed{\text{image}}$ $\boxed{\text{DATA PORT}}$ $\boxed{\text{image}}$ / $\boxed{\times}$ $\boxed{\text{image}}$
FEE

SUNSET BAY INN BED & BREAKFAST   Phone: (727)896-6701   **9**

AAA SAVE

	12/1-4/30 [BP]	1P: $150-$210	2P: $150-$210	XP: $50
	10/1-11/30 [BP]	1P: $140-$200	2P: $140-$200	XP: $50
	5/1-9/30 [BP]	1P: $130-$190	2P: $130-$190	XP: $50

Historic Bed
& Breakfast

Location: Just w of Beach Dr via 6th Ave NE; downtown. 635 Bay St NE 33701. Fax: 727/898-5311. **Facility:** This service-oriented inn set in a restored home dating from 1910 features tastefully decorated rooms, each with a theme. Designated smoking area. 8 units. 7 one-bedroom standard units, some with whirlpools. 1 one-bedroom suite ($240-$280) with whirlpool. 3 stories (no elevator), interior/exterior corridors. **Parking:** street. **Terms:** 2-4 night minimum stay - seasonal and/or weekends, 14 day cancellation notice-fee imposed, weekly rates available, package plans. **Amenities:** video library, DVD players, CD players, high-speed Internet, dual phone lines, voice mail, irons, hair dryers. **Leisure Activities:** bicycles. **Guest Services:** complimentary evening beverages, valet laundry. **Business Services:** meeting rooms, PC, fax. **Cards:** AX, DC, DS, MC, VI. **Special Amenities:** free full breakfast and free room upgrade **(subject to availability with advance reservations).**

SOME UNITS

$\boxed{\mathsf{1}\mathsf{1}+}$ $\boxed{\text{image}}$ $\boxed{\times}$ $\boxed{\text{VCR}}$ $\boxed{\text{image}}$ $\boxed{\text{DATA PORT}}$ / $\boxed{\text{image}}$ $\boxed{\text{image}}$ $\boxed{\text{image}}$ /

--------- **WHERE TO DINE** ---------

4TH STREET SHRIMP STORE   Lunch: $4-$21   Dinner: $4-$21   Phone: 727/822-0325   **22**

Seafood

Location: 0.7 mi n, jct 10th Ave N. 1006 4th St N 33701. **Hours:** 11 am-9 pm. Closed: 4/16, 11/23, 12/25. **Features:** A bright, nautical decor with colorful knickknacks will put you in the mood for fresh, delicious seafood. An extensive menu of sandwiches, chowder, fish and shrimp is served on throwaway plates and paper place mats for a no-fuss, no-muss meal. Casual dress; cocktails. **Parking:** on-site. **Cards:** MC, VI.

$\boxed{\top}$

ARIGATO JAPANESE STEAK HOUSE RESTAURANT   Dinner: $7-$30   Phone: 727/343-5200   **14**

Ethnic

Location: Just s of jct 38th Ave N. 3600 66th St N 33710. **Hours:** 5 pm-10 pm, Sun 4 pm-9 pm. Closed: 1/1, 7/4, 11/23; also 12/24. **Reservations:** suggested. **Features:** Diners should come for the show as entertaining chefs prepare Japanese specialties right at the table. The ichiban lets you sample shrimp, chicken and filet with piquant oils and spices. This is a popular place, so expect to wait on groupings at the hibachi table. Casual dress; cocktails. **Parking:** on-site. **Cards:** AX, CB, DC, DS, MC, VI.

$\boxed{\top}$

BELLARTE RESTAURANT   Lunch: $9-$18   Dinner: $13-$41   Phone: 727/561-7332   **1**

Italian

Location: I-275, exit 30, 0.7 mi w on SR 686; in Radisson Hotel and Conference Center. 12600 Roosevelt Blvd 33716. **Hours:** 6:30 am-10 pm. **Reservations:** accepted. **Features:** Located in a commercial area, this pleasant dining room offers a nice variety of traditional Italian favorites as well as some comfort foods. Casual dress; cocktails. **Parking:** on-site. **Cards:** AX, DC, MC, VI.

$\boxed{\top}$

BONEFISH GRILL   Dinner: $14-$19   Phone: 727/521-3434   **7**

American

Location: I-275, exit 26 southbound; exit 26B northbound, 1.4 mi e on 54th Ave N, then 0.5 mi n on US 92. 5901 4th St N 33703. **Hours:** 4 pm-10:30 pm, Fri & Sat-11:30 pm. Closed: 11/23, 12/25. **Features:** Upscale surroundings and a professional wait staff make for an enjoyable dining experience. The creative menu's components range from fontina chops to portobello pasta to the tasty pistachio Parmesan-crusted rainbow trout. No matter what their choice, diners are in for a treat. Dressy casual; cocktails. **Parking:** on-site. **Cards:** AX, DC, DS, MC, VI.

(See map and index starting on p. 938)

CAPTAIN AL'S WATERFRONT GRILL & BAR   **Lunch:** $7-$10   **Dinner:** $10-$21   **Phone:** 727/898-5800   31
Seafood   **Location:** 1st floor of The Pier; downtown. 800 2nd Ave NE 33701. **Hours:** 11 am-midnight. **Reservations:** accepted. **Features:** All seats offer a waterfront view of Old Tampa Bay at the busy spot. The relaxing locale is right on the pier. The menu lists specialty sandwiches, burgers, salads, yummy appetizers and heartier entrees, including such goodies as the seafood sampler, gulf grouper, snow crab legs, steak, poultry and varied pasta dishes. Casual dress; cocktails. **Parking:** on-site. **Cards:** AX, DS, MC, VI.

CARMELITA'S MEXICAN RESTAURANT   **Lunch:** $5-$8   **Dinner:** $8-$11   **Phone:** 727/545-2956   8
Mexican   **Location:** Just s of jct 54th Ave N; 0.6 mi n of jct Tyrone Blvd. 5211 Park St N 33709. **Hours:** 11 am-9:30 pm, Fri & Sat-10 pm. Closed major holidays; also for dinner 12/24. **Reservations:** not accepted. **Features:** A wide variety of entrees are featured like the Del Ray burrito, a good mixture of seasoned ground beef, tomatoes, onion and cheese. A live mariachi band performs on Tuesday nights. Casual dress; beer & wine only. **Parking:** on-site. **Cards:** AX, DC, DS, MC, VI.

CASPY'S WATERSIDE RESTAURANT   **Lunch:** $6-$10   **Dinner:** $11-$22   **Phone:** 727/906-0086   39
Continental   **Location:** On SR 686, 0.5 mi e of Pinellas Bayway; in Isla Shoppers Village. 5901 Sun Blvd 33706. **Hours:** 11:15 am-1 am. Closed: Sun. **Features:** The waterside restaurant's many entree choices include the signature chicken, curry dishes and a good selection of seafood preparations. Casual dress; cocktails. **Parking:** on-site. **Cards:** MC, VI.

CASUAL CLAM RESTAURANT   **Lunch:** $5-$11   **Dinner:** $5-$14   **Phone:** 727/895-2526   15
Seafood   **Location:** I-275, exit 25, 0.9 mi e on 38th Ave N, then 0.3 mi s. 3336 9th St N 33704. **Hours:** 11 am-9 pm, Thurs-Sat to 10 pm. Closed: 11/23, 12/25. **Features:** A popular neighborhood hangout, this light and airy eatery has the feel of rustic New England. Steamed clams, fish and chips, snow crab and shrimp scampi are among menu specialties. Pleasant servers in T-shirts and shorts add to the casual mood. Casual dress; beer & wine only. **Parking:** on-site. **Cards:** MC, VI.

CHA CHA COCONUTS   **Lunch:** $6-$10   **Dinner:** $6-$10   **Phone:** 727/822-6655   33
American   **Location:** Just e; at The Pier; downtown. 800 2nd Ave NE 33701. **Hours:** 11 am-10 pm, Fri & Sat-1 am. **Features:** The casual restaurant is known for its location atop The Pier, a local landmark. Views of Old Tampa Bay are spectacular. Also adding to this place's popularity are a friendly wait staff, and great burgers and sandwiches from its limited menu. Casual dress; cocktails. **Parking:** on-site (fee) and valet. **Cards:** AX, CB, DC, DS, MC, VI.

CODY'S ORIGINAL ROADHOUSE   **Dinner:** $7-$20   **Phone:** 727/577-7730   2
American   **Location:** I-275, exit 32 southbound; exit 28 northbound, 1.2 mi s on US 92; in Bayview Center. 11270 4th St N 33716. **Hours:** 3:30 pm-10:30 pm, Fri & Sat-11 pm, Sun noon-10 pm. Closed: 12/25. **Features:** As the name suggests, the casual restaurant nurtures the mood of a roadhouse in part through its rustic decor. Favorites on the varied menu include flavorful baby back ribs and fajitas. The service staff is friendly. Casual dress; cocktails. **Parking:** on-site. **Cards:** AX, DS, MC, VI.

COLUMBIA RESTAURANT   **Lunch:** $7-$16   **Dinner:** $15-$26   **Phone:** 727/822-8000   32
Spanish   **Location:** 4th floor of The Pier; downtown. 800 2nd Ave NE 33701. **Hours:** 11 am-10 pm, Fri & Sat-11 pm. **Reservations:** suggested. **Features:** Many of the tables afford a spectacular view of Tampa Bay and the St. Petersburg skyline. Traditional Spanish and Cuban cuisine is prepared with chicken, beef and Florida seafood. Try the arroz con pollo, baked chicken with yellow rice and pepper strips. Casual dress; cocktails. **Parking:** on-site (fee) and valet. **Cards:** AX, DC, DS, MC, VI.

COOL MOE'S RESTAURANT & BAR   **Lunch:** $7-$15   **Dinner:** $7-$15   **Phone:** 727/579-1145   4
American   **Location:** Just e of jct 4th St N. 10056 Gandy Blvd 33702. **Hours:** 11 am-10:30 pm. **Features:** The menu lists everything from raw bar items to sandwiches to the tasty New York strip steak. Even Mexican items make an appearance. Karaoke is a fun event on Friday and Saturday nights. Casual dress; cocktails. **Parking:** on-site. **Cards:** AX, MC, VI.

CRAB SHACK   **Lunch:** $6-$18   **Dinner:** $6-$18   **Phone:** 727/576-7813   3
Seafood   **Location:** 0.6 mi e of jct 4th St N. 11400 Gandy Blvd 33702. **Hours:** 11 am-9:30 pm, Fri & Sat-10:30 pm, Sun 1 pm-9:30 pm. Closed: 11/23, 12/25. **Features:** Just as the name suggests, a rustic crab shack setting—with picnic-table seating in the main dining room and small tables in the bar—awaits you here. Among menu selections are more than two dozen appetizers, three dozen entrees and a wide array of sandwiches. Landlubbers may prefer the steak and chicken choices. Casual dress; cocktails. **Parking:** on-site. **Cards:** DS, MC, VI.

DAN MARINO'S FINE FOOD & SPIRITS   **Lunch:** $8-$12   **Dinner:** $8-$28   **Phone:** 727/822-4413   29
American   **Location:** Jct 2nd St N, in Baywalk; downtown. 121 2nd Ave N, Bldg C #206 33701. **Hours:** 11 am-10 pm, Fri & Sat-1 am. Closed: 11/23, 12/25. **Reservations:** accepted. **Features:** The restaurant's namesake is the former Miami Dolphins quarterback. This place appeals to patrons with its trendy, upscale look, a bit of sports nostalgia and creative dishes along the lines of chicken skewers marinated Tokyo style in a sweet mahogany sauce or nut-crusted baked mahi mahi coated with assorted nuts and served over vanilla rum butter sauce, sauteed spinach and smashed potatoes. Casual dress; cocktails. **Parking:** on-site (fee). **Cards:** AX, MC, VI.

DISH   **Lunch:** $8-$12   **Dinner:** $16-$18   **Phone:** 727/894-5700   30
American   **Location:** Downtown; on 2nd floor of Baywalk. 192 2nd Ave N 33701. **Hours:** 11:30 am-close, Sun from noon. Closed: 11/23, 12/25. **Features:** This is a unique restaurant. Follow the tables around choosing the items that you want prepared from salad items, to sauces, to meats, to vegetables and take it to the center round where it is prepared before your eyes. Casual dress; cocktails. **Parking:** valet and street. **Cards:** AX, DC, DS, MC, VI.

(See map and index starting on p. 938)

DURANGO OAK FIRE STEAKHOUSE **Lunch:** $6-$11 **Dinner:** $10-$21 **Phone:** 727/823-2411 ⑫

Steak House

Location: On US 92, jct 39th Ave N. 3901 4th St N 33703. **Hours:** 11 am-10 pm, Fri & Sat-11 pm, Sun noon-9 pm. **Features:** Guests can savor a great oak-fire grilled steak or some mouthwatering barbecue baby back ribs. Among other choices are Atlantic salmon, bacon-wrapped shrimp and sizzling fajitas. With its great food, welcoming service and casual, rustic theme, the steakhouse is a treat. Casual dress; cocktails. **Parking:** on-site. **Cards:** MC, VI.

EL CAP **Lunch:** $3-$7 **Dinner:** $3-$7 **Phone:** 727/521-1314 ⑬

American

Location: Jct 35th Ave N. 3500 4th St N 33704. **Hours:** 11 am-11 pm. Closed major holidays; also 12/24 & 12/31. **Reservations:** not accepted. **Features:** Munch on the best burgers around at this basic sports bar where you'll also find subs, sandwiches, chili fries and jalapeno poppers. Expect good stick-to-your-ribs food served in a no-frills atmosphere. Patio dining and a carry-out window are available. Casual dress; beer & wine only. **Parking:** on-site and street. **Cards:** CB, DS, MC, VI.

EVOS ST. PETERSBURG **Lunch:** $5-$8 **Dinner:** $5-$8 **Phone:** 727/571-3867 ⑱

American

Location: Jct 27th Ave N. 2631 4th St N 33704. **Hours:** 11 am-10 pm. Closed major holidays. **Reservations:** not accepted. **Features:** Vegans are in for a treat at the quick-serve establishment. Representative of heart-healthy food are various wraps, healthy burgers and "air fries." The trendy spot is a must for those watching their calories. Casual dress. **Parking:** on-site. **Cards:** AX, DC, DS, MC, VI.

FRED'S FAMOUS BAR-B-QUE AND BREWERY **Lunch:** $5-$17 **Dinner:** $5-$17 **Phone:** 727/822-3733 ⑩

American

Location: I-275, exit 26B southbound; 1.8 mi e on 54th Ave N, then 1 mi s on US 92. 4351 4th St N 33703. **Hours:** 11 am-10 pm, Fri & Sat-11 pm. Closed: 11/23, 12/25. **Features:** The contemporary restaurant is a good place to go for great Southern barbecue. Beef and pork dinners, smoked chicken and hickory-grilled filet mignon or porterhouse are flavorfully prepared. Lighter appetites have plenty of sandwiches, salads and appetizers from which to choose. Casual dress; beer & wine only. **Parking:** on-site. **Cards:** AX, DS, MC, VI.

THE GARDEN RESTAURANT **Lunch:** $5-$8 **Dinner:** $10-$16 **Phone:** 727/896-3800 ㉟

Mediterranean

Location: Just e of jct 2nd St S; downtown. 217 Central Ave 33701. **Hours:** 11:30 am-10:30 pm, Fri & Sat-midnight. Closed: 11/23, 12/25. **Features:** The setting reflects the style of a bistro, with cozy indoor seating and a comfortable garden dining area. Mediterranean stylings, with bright colors and lots of plants, punctuate the surroundings. The on-site chef de cuisine prepares such wonderful entrees as fennel-crusted tuna or grilled lamb steak. Enjoy live jazz Friday and Saturday evenings. Casual dress; cocktails. **Parking:** street. **Cards:** AX, DS, MC, VI.

GRATZZI RISTORANTE **Lunch:** $10-$12 **Dinner:** $14-$28 **Phone:** 727/822-7769 ㉗

Italian

Location: Jct 2nd St N; in Baywalk; downtown. 199 2nd Ave N 33701. **Hours:** 11:30 am-10 pm, Fri & Sat-11 pm, Sun noon-9 pm. Closed: 12/25. **Reservations:** accepted. **Features:** On the second floor of the Baywalk is this trendy and upscale dining establishment. The menu emphasizes northern Italian cuisine, including ably prepared and pleasantly presented selections of pasta, fish, meat, fowl, veal and chicken. Dressy casual; cocktails. **Parking:** on-site (fee). **Cards:** AX, DC, DS, MC, VI.

JO-JO'S IN CITTA **Lunch:** $5-$10 **Dinner:** $9-$17 **Phone:** 727/894-0075 ㊲

Italian

Location: Jct 3rd St S; downtown; in Bank of America Tower. 200 Central Ave 33701. **Hours:** 11 am-9 pm, Fri & Sat-10 pm. Closed: Sun. **Reservations:** accepted. **Features:** Hearty portions of pasta, pizza and calzones are some of the dishes served in the fresh and modern cafe-style dining room. Guests on Friday and Saturday evenings are treated to live entertainment. Dressy casual; cocktails. **Parking:** on-site and street. **Cards:** AX, DC, MC, VI.

THE LIMEY'S PUB **Lunch:** $6-$7 **Dinner:** $9-$18 **Phone:** 727/895-2049 ㉑

English

Location: I-275, exit 24, 1.4 mi e on 22nd Ave N, then just s. 1492 4th St N 33704. **Hours:** 4 pm-1:30 am, Fri-Sun from 11:30 am. **Features:** The ambience of an English pub is pervasive in these down-to-earth surroundings. Fresh air makes the deck a comfy place to dine. The beef in Guinness pie-steak marinated in hearty beer and baked with chunks of pastry-satisfies the hungries. Cozy deck dining and a kiddie playland are on-site. Casual dress; cocktails. **Parking:** on-site. **Cards:** AX, CB, DC, MC, VI.

LONNI'S SANDWICHES, ETC. **Lunch:** $7-$10 **Phone:** 727/894-1944 ㉞

American

Location: Just w of jct 2nd Ave NE; in The Women's Tennis Association (WTA) Building; downtown. 133 1st St NE 33701. **Hours:** 9 am-4 pm. Closed: Sat & Sun. **Features:** In the lower level of the Women's Tennis Association (W.T.A.) building, the popular delicatessen piles made-to-order sandwiches high with fresh ingredients. Other choices include soups, salads and homemade muffins and cookies. Casual dress. **Parking:** street. **Cards:** AX, DS, MC, VI.

MARBO OF 4TH STREET **Lunch:** $6 **Dinner:** $8-$9 **Phone:** 727/578-3080 ⑤

Chinese

Location: I-275, exit 19 southbound; exit 15 northbound, 1.2 mi w on US 92. 8123 4th St N 33702. **Hours:** 11:30 am-9:30 pm, Fri & Sat-10 pm. Closed: 11/23. **Features:** The all-you-can-eat buffet lays out more than 100 choices ranging from Chinese seafood and Japanese sushi to spicy Thai and Mongolian grill items. Casual dress; beer & wine only. **Parking:** on-site. **Cards:** MC, VI.

MARCHAND'S BAR & GRILL **Lunch:** $8-$20 **Dinner:** $17-$32 **Phone:** 727/894-1000 ㉕

Mediterranean

Location: 1.8 mi e on 4th Ave, just n on Beach Dr; downtown; in Renaissance Vinoy Resort and Golf Club. 501 5th Ave NE 33701. **Hours:** 11:30 am-2:30 & 5:30-10 pm, Sun noon-2 & 5:30-10 pm; Sunday brunch. **Reservations:** suggested. **Features:** Marchand's occupies half of the original main dining room in the Vinoy, built in 1925 and restored in 1992. The hotel is a short distance from The Pier and several museums and theaters. Much of the opulence of the original dining room has been preserved. The menu is Mediterranean, with such specialties as seafood bouillabaisse, pan-roasted chicken and braised lamb shank. Starters range from roasted eggplant soup to beef carpaccio. Grilled meats and fish are also featured. Dressy casual; cocktails; entertainment. **Parking:** valet. **Cards:** AX, CB, DC, DS, JC, MC, VI.

(See map and index starting on p. 938)

MATTISON'S AN AMERICAN BISTRO & CATERING
COMPANY   **Lunch:** $5-$12   **Dinner:** $16-$28   **Phone:** 727/895-2200   28

American

Location: Jct 1st St N; in Plaza Tower Courtyard Shops; downtown. 111 2nd Ave NE 33701. **Hours:** 11 am-9 pm, Fri-10 pm, Sat 5 pm-10 pm. Closed: 12/25; also Sun. **Reservations:** suggested. **Features:** The modestly elegant bistro is on the second-floor mezzanine of a shopping complex. Patrons can start the meal with wonderful French onion soup or an Asian tuna salad, then savor one of Chef Paul's entrees. A favorite is veal Batiato—pine-nut-crusted veal tenderloin medallions topped with prosciutto Fontinella. A delectable finish is the chocolate Chambord torte. Dressy casual; cocktails. **Parking:** on-site. **Cards:** AX, DC, DS, MC, VI.

MIDTOWN SUNDRIES RESTAURANT & BAR   **Lunch:** $7-$8   **Dinner:** $7-$18   **Phone:** 727/502-0222   38

American

Location: Just s of jct Central Ave; downtown. 200 1st Ave S 33701. **Hours:** 11 am-11:30 pm, Fri & Sat-2 am. Closed: 4/16, 11/23, 12/25. **Features:** The neat eatery serves casual fare, including great finger foods and such choices as the yummy potato skins appetizer and the tasty club sandwich. Service is friendly. Casual dress; cocktails. **Parking:** street. **Cards:** AX, CB, DC, DS, MC, VI.

THE MOON UNDER WATER   **Lunch:** $7-$17   **Dinner:** $7-$17   **Phone:** 727/896-6160   26

British

Location: Just s of jct 4th Ave N; downtown. 322 Beach Dr NE 33701. **Hours:** 11:30 am-10 pm, Sun from 9 am. Closed: 1/1, 11/23, 12/25. **Reservations:** accepted. **Features:** This restaurant has the look and feel of a British pub. Lunch features sandwiches and salads, with the Philly cheese steak as the standout. Tiered patio dining and excellent service make for a pleasant meal. Dressy casual; cocktails. **Parking:** street. **Cards:** AX, DC, DS, MC, VI.

PAISANO'S PIZZA & PASTA   **Lunch:** $6-$19   **Dinner:** $6-$19   **Phone:** 727/521-2656   6

Italian

Location: I-275, exit 26, exit 26B northbound, 1.4 mi e on 54th Ave N, then 0.4 mi n on US 92. 6000 4th St N 33703. **Hours:** 11 am-10 pm, Fri & Sat-11 pm, Sun noon-10 pm. Closed: 11/23, 12/25. **Features:** In business since 1974, this popular eatery is a true local favorite. It's known for its gourmet pizzas, calzones, stromboli, pasta dishes and a tempting lunch buffet. Casual dress; cocktails. **Parking:** on-site. **Cards:** AX, DS, MC, VI.

PEPIN RESTAURANT   **Lunch:** $6-$22   **Dinner:** $6-$22   **Phone:** 727/821-3773   11

Spanish

Location: I-275, exit 26B southbound; exit 26 northbound, then 1.8 mi e on 54th Ave N, then 7 mi s on US 92. 4125 4th St N 33703. **Hours:** 11:30 am-10 pm, Fri-11 pm, Sat 5 pm-11 pm, Sun 5 pm-10 pm. Closed major holidays; also Super Bowl Sun. **Reservations:** accepted. **Features:** Dali and Picasso prints appeal to an artistic eye, while a concert pianist fascinates a musical ear. The friendly restaurant serves up a splendid salad as well as steak, seafood and dishes with a delightfully piquant Spanish influence. Casual dress; cocktails. **Parking:** on-site. **Cards:** AX, MC, VI.

RED MESA REGIONAL MEXICAN FOOD &
SOUTHWESTERN FLAVORS   **Lunch:** $7-$10   **Dinner:** $12-$20   **Phone:** 727/527-8728   9

Mexican

Location: I-275, exit 26, 1.4 mi e on 54th Ave N, then just s. 4912 4th St N 33703. **Hours:** 11 am-9:30 pm, Fri & Sat-10:30 pm, Sun 9 am-9 pm. Closed: 11/23, 12/25; also Super Bowl Sun. **Reservations:** suggested. **Features:** Latin flavors spice up such intricate dishes as honey-marinated tuna, which is cured with sugar cane, oven roasted and served with black bean puree and roasted potatoes. The theme carries over into the colorful dining room as well as in the music. Casual dress; beer & wine only. **Parking:** on-site. **Cards:** AX, CB, DC, DS, MC, VI.

REDWOODS RESTAURANT   **Dinner:** $19-$29   **Phone:** 727/896-5118   36

American

Location: Just w of jct 3rd St N; downtown. 247 Central Ave 33701. **Hours:** 5:30 pm-10 pm, Fri & Sat-11 pm, Sun-9 pm. Closed major holidays; also Mon. **Reservations:** suggested. **Features:** At the base of many menu offerings is a profound Pacific Rim influence, with "lau lau" banana leaf cooking. A bakery and sushi bar are on the premises. Casual dress; cocktails. **Parking:** street. **Cards:** AX, DS, MC, VI.

SAFFRON'S CARIBBEAN CUISINE AT JUNGLE
PRADA   **Lunch:** $5-$11   **Dinner:** $7-$18   **Phone:** 727/345-6400   20

Caribbean

Location: Jct Tyrone Blvd, 1.5 mi s. 1700 Park St N 33710. **Hours:** 11 am-9:30 pm, Fri-Sun to 10 pm. Closed: 5/29, 9/4. **Reservations:** suggested. **Features:** Ample portions of Caribbean cuisine are served in a comfortable setting on the Intercoastal Waterway. Jamaican jerk chicken is colorfully displayed with plantains, cabbage and yellow rice. Casual dress; cocktails. **Parking:** on-site. **Cards:** AX, DC, DS, MC, VI.

SIAM GARDEN THAI RESTAURANT   **Lunch:** $10-$20   **Dinner:** $10-$20   **Phone:** 727/822-0613   17

Thai

Location: I-275, exit 24, 1 mi e on 22nd Ave N, then 0.7 mi n. 3125 9th St N 33704. **Hours:** 11 am-3 & 5-10 pm, Sun from 4 pm. **Features:** The little eatery's casual surroundings make for a relaxing lunch or dinner. The Thai-influenced menu lists such choices as spring rolls, panang curry and prug king. Casual dress. **Parking:** on-site. **Cards:** MC, VI.

TERRACE ROOM   **Lunch:** $7-$16   **Dinner:** $11-$29   **Phone:** 727/894-1000   24

American

Location: 1.8 mi e on 4th Ave, just n on Beach Dr; downtown; in Renaissance Vinoy Resort and Golf Club. 501 5th Ave NE 33701. **Hours:** 6:30 am-2:30 & 5:30-10 pm, Sun 6:30 am-2 & 5:30-10 pm; Sunday brunch. **Reservations:** suggested. **Features:** The restaurant occupies half of the original main dining room in the Vinoy, built in 1925 and restored in 1992. Much of the opulence of the original was preserved. The menu is diverse, and the atmosphere casually elegant. Start with duck confit spring rolls, then move to a mixed greens or spinach salad. Interesting main courses include macadamia nut grouper with citrus-papaya salsa or grilled strip sirloin with blue cheese butter. Service is friendly and attentive. Dressy casual; cocktails. **Parking:** on-site and valet. **Cards:** AX, MC, VI.

(See map and index starting on p. 938)

TEXAS CATTLE COMPANY

Steak House

Dinner: $11-$30

Location: I-275, exit 24, 1.2 mi w on 22nd Ave N, then just n on US 19. 2600 34th St N 33713. **Phone:** 727/527-3335   ⑲ **Hours:** 5 pm-10 pm, Fri & Sat-11 pm, Sun-9:30 pm. Closed: 11/23, 12/25. **Features:** Wood accents convey a decidedly Western aura in this rustic steakhouse. Sure, you'll find a juicy filet mignon, but the menu also includes fresh fish, chicken and tasty rock lobster. Try not to giggle when ordering the Charlie Brownie ice cream pie. Casual dress; cocktails. **Parking:** on-site. **Cards:** AX, MC, VI.

TIJUANA FLATS

Mexican

Lunch: $5-$8   **Dinner:** $5-$8   **Phone:** 727/823-5882   ㉓

Location: Jct 9th Ave N. 944 4th St N 33701. **Hours:** 11 am-10 pm, Fri & Sat-11 pm. Closed major holidays. **Features:** The Mexican-themed eatery's specialty is burritos, but patrons also can try chimichangas, enchiladas, quesadillas, tacos or nachos. Casual dress. **Parking:** on-site. **Cards:** MC, VI.

WESTSHORE PIZZA XXVIII

Pizza

Lunch: $5-$17   **Dinner:** $5-$17   **Phone:** 727/895-5506   ⑯

Location: On US 92, jct 32nd Ave N; in 4th St Center. 3187 4th St N 33704. **Hours:** 11 am-10 pm, Fri & Sat-11 pm. Closed: 11/23, 12/25. **Features:** This place is a favorite of those who love pizza, calzones and Philly grinders. The atmosphere is relaxed, and servers are friendly. Meals are cooked to order. Casual dress. **Parking:** on-site. **Cards:** MC, VI.

TAMPA pop. 303,447   (See map and index starting on p. 950)

———— WHERE TO STAY ————

AMERISUITES (TAMPA AIRPORT/WESTSHORE)   *Book at aaa.com*   **Phone:** (813)282-1037   ㊸

Small-scale Hotel

All Year	1P: $99-$200 2P: $99-$200	XP: $10 F17

Location: I-275, exit 40A, 0.5 mi n on Westshore Blvd; exit 39A northbound, 1 mi e on Kennedy Blvd, 1 mi s on Westshore Blvd, then just w. 4811 W Main St 33607. Fax: 813/282-1148. **Facility:** 126 one-bedroom suites with efficiencies (no utensils). 6 stories, interior corridors. *Bath:* combo or shower only. **Parking:** on-site. **Terms:** small pets only. **Amenities:** high-speed Internet, voice mail, irons, hair dryers. *Some:* dual phone lines. **Pool(s):** heated outdoor. **Leisure Activities:** exercise room. **Guest Services:** valet and coin laundry. **Business Services:** meeting rooms, fax (fee). **Cards:** AX, CB, DC, DS, MC, VI. **Special Amenities:** free full breakfast.

SOME UNITS

AMERISUITES (TAMPA NEAR BUSCH GARDENS)   *Book at aaa.com*   **Phone:** (813)979-1922   ❼

Small-scale Hotel

2/1-4/15	1P: $119-$149	2P: $119-$149	XP: $10 F18
12/1-1/31	1P: $109-$139	2P: $109-$139	XP: $10 F18
4/16-11/30	1P: $99-$119	2P: $99-$119	XP: $10 F18

Location: I-275, exit 51, 1.8 mi e on SR 582, then just s. 11408 N 30th St 33612-6446. Fax: 813/979-1926. **Facility:** 127 one-bedroom suites. 6 stories, interior corridors. *Bath:* combo or shower only. **Parking:** on-site. **Terms:** package plans, pets ($10 extra charge). **Amenities:** high-speed Internet, dual phone lines, voice mail, safes (fee), irons, hair dryers. **Pool(s):** heated outdoor. **Leisure Activities:** exercise room. **Guest Services:** valet and coin laundry. **Business Services:** meeting rooms, fax. **Cards:** AX, DC, DS, MC, VI. **Special Amenities:** free full breakfast.

SOME UNITS
FEE

AMERISUITES (TAMPA/SABAL CORPORATE PARK)   *Book at aaa.com*   **Phone:** (813)622-8557   ㉘

Motel

12/1-4/30 [ECP]	1P: $99-$189	2P: $99-$189	XP: $10 F
5/1-11/30 [ECP]	1P: $79-$159	2P: $79-$159	XP: $10 F

Location: I-75, exit 260 southbound; exit 260B northbound, 0.5 mi w on SR 574 (Dr. Martin Luther King Jr Blvd), just s on Falkenburg Rd, then just w; in Sabal Corporate Park. 10007 Princess Palm Ave 33619. Fax: 813/620-4866. **Facility:** 59 units. 27 one-bedroom standard units. 32 one-bedroom suites. 2 stories, interior corridors. *Bath:* combo or shower only. **Parking:** on-site. **Terms:** small pets only. **Amenities:** dual phone lines, voice mail, irons, hair dryers. *Fee:* video games, high-speed Internet, safes. **Pool(s):** heated outdoor. **Leisure Activities:** jogging, exercise room. **Guest Services:** complimentary evening beverages, valet and coin laundry. **Business Services:** meeting rooms, fax. **Cards:** AX, CB, DC, DS, JC, MC, VI. **Special Amenities:** free full breakfast.

SOME UNITS

(See map and index starting on p. 950)

BAYMONT INN & SUITES TAMPA-BRANDON *Book at aaa.com* Phone: (813)684-4007   56

 SAVE   All Year   1P: $89-$109   XP: $7   F18
◇◇◇◇   **Location:** I-75, exit 257, just w on SR 60, then just n. 602 S Falkenburg Rd 33619. **Facility:** 100 units. 92 one-bedroom standard units. 6 one- and 2 two-bedroom suites. 3 stories, interior corridors. **Parking:** on-site. **Terms:** [ECP] meal plan available, small pets only. **Amenities:** video games, voice mail, irons, hair dryers. *Some:* dual phone lines. **Pool(s):** outdoor. **Guest Services:** coin laundry.
Small-scale Hotel **Business Services:** fax. **Cards:** AX, CB, DC, DS, MC, VI. **Special Amenities:** free expanded continental breakfast and free local telephone calls. *(See color ad below)*

SOME UNITS

BAYMONT INN & SUITES TAMPA/NEAR BUSCH
GARDENS *Book at aaa.com* Phone: (813)930-6900 11

◇◇◇ SAVE   1/16-4/30   1P: $89-$109   XP: $7   F18
◇◇◇◇   5/1-10/31   1P: $75-$95   XP: $7   F18
        11/1-11/30   1P: $75-$85   XP: $7   F18
        12/1-1/15   1P: $69-$79   XP: $7   F18
Small-scale Hotel **Location:** I-275, exit 50, 2 mi e on SR 580, then just n. 9202 N 30th St 33612. Fax: 813/930-0563. **Facility:** 143 units. 134 one-bedroom standard units. 9 one-bedroom suites. 3 stories, exterior corridors. *Bath:* combo or shower only. **Parking:** on-site. **Terms:** [ECP] meal plan available, small pets only. **Amenities:** video games (fee), voice mail, irons, hair dryers. **Pool(s):** outdoor. **Leisure Activities:** *Fee:* game room. **Guest Services:** valet and coin laundry. **Business Services:** meeting rooms, fax. **Cards:** AX, CB, DC, DS, MC, VI. **Special Amenities:** free expanded continental breakfast and free local telephone calls. *(See color ad below)*

SOME UNITS

BAYMONT INN TAMPA-FAIRGROUNDS *Book at aaa.com* Phone: (813)626-0885 23

◇◇◇ SAVE   All Year   1P: $59-$79   XP: $7   F18
◇◇◇◇   **Location:** I-4, exit 6 westbound; exit 6A eastbound, just se. 4811 US 301 N 33610. Fax: 813/623-3321. **Facility:** 101 one-bedroom standard units. 3 stories, interior corridors. **Parking:** on-site. **Terms:** [ECP] meal plan available, small pets only ($10 extra charge). **Amenities:** video games (fee), voice mail, irons, hair dryers.
Motel   **Pool(s):** outdoor. **Guest Services:** coin laundry. **Business Services:** fax. **Cards:** AX, CB, DC, DS, MC, VI. **Special Amenities:** free expanded continental breakfast and free local telephone calls.
(See color ad below)

SOME UNITS

(See map and index starting on p. 950)

BEST WESTERN ALL SUITES HOTEL NEAR USF BEHIND BUSCH GARDENS *Book at aaa.com*

Phone: (813)971-8930 ⑨

12/26-4/22 [BP]	1P: $119-$129	2P: $119-$129	XP: $7	F17
4/23-11/30 [BP]	1P: $89-$99	2P: $89-$99	XP: $7	F17
12/1-12/25 [BP]	1P: $99	2P: $99	XP: $7	F17

Small-scale Hotel **Location:** I-275, exit 51, 1.8 mi e on SR 582 (Fowler Ave), then 0.5 mi s on N 30th St. 3001 University Center Dr 33612. Fax: 813/971-8935. **Facility:** 150 one-bedroom suites. 3 stories, exterior corridors. **Parking:** on-site. **Terms:** 2 night minimum stay - seasonal and/or weekends, cancellation fee imposed, package plans, pets ($10 extra charge). **Amenities:** video games (fee), dual phone lines, voice mail, irons, hair dryers. **Dining:** 4:30 pm-9:30 pm. **Pool(s):** heated outdoor. **Leisure Activities:** whirlpool, sun deck, billiards, table tennis. **Guest Services:** sundries, valet and coin laundry. **Business Services:** meeting rooms, PC, fax (fee). **Cards:** AX, DC, DS, MC, VI. **Special Amenities:** free full breakfast and free local telephone calls. *(See color ad below)*

SOME UNITS

BEST WESTERN BRANDON HOTEL & CONFERENCE CENTER *Book at aaa.com*

Phone: (813)621-5555 ㊾

	1P: $89-$109	2P: $89-$109
1/1-4/30 [CP]	1P: $89-$109	2P: $89-$109
12/1-12/31 & 5/1-11/30 [CP]	1P: $79-$99	2P: $79-$99

Motel **Location:** I-75, exit 257, 1.2 mi w on SR 60. 9331 Adamo Dr 33619. Fax: 813/626-6032. **Facility:** 119 one-bedroom standard units. 2 stories, exterior corridors. *Bath:* combo or shower only. **Parking:** on-site. **Terms:** pets ($25 fee). **Amenities:** voice mail, irons, hair dryers. *Some:* high-speed Internet. **Pool(s):** outdoor. **Leisure Activities:** exercise room. **Guest Services:** valet and coin laundry. **Business Services:** conference facilities, PC, fax. **Cards:** AX, CB, DC, DS, MC, VI. **Special Amenities:** free continental breakfast and free local telephone calls.

SOME UNITS

BEST WESTERN TAMPA *Book at aaa.com*

Phone: (813)490-2378 ㊻

	1P: $99-$119	2P: $99-$119	XP: $10	F16
12/1-4/30	1P: $99-$119	2P: $99-$119	XP: $10	F16
5/1-11/30	1P: $79-$99	2P: $79-$99	XP: $10	F16

Small-scale Hotel **Location:** I-275, exit 41A, 1.4 mi sw on US 92. 734 S Dale Mabry Hwy 33609. Fax: 813/490-2380. **Facility:** 51 units. 49 one- and 1 two-bedroom standard units, some with whirlpools. 1 one-bedroom suite with whirlpool. 3 stories, interior corridors. *Bath:* combo or shower only. **Parking:** on-site. **Terms:** cancellation fee imposed, [CP] meal plan available. **Amenities:** safes (fee), irons, hair dryers. **Pool(s):** outdoor. **Leisure Activities:** exercise room. **Guest Services:** coin laundry. **Business Services:** meeting rooms, fax (fee). **Cards:** AX, CB, DC, DS, JC, MC, VI.

SOME UNITS

BEST WESTERN-THE WESTSHORE HOTEL *Book at aaa.com*

Phone: (813)282-3636 ㊺

1/16-4/20	1P: $109-$139	2P: $109-$139	XP: $10	F
12/1-1/15 & 10/1-11/30	1P: $99-$119	2P: $99-$119	XP: $10	F
4/21-9/30	1P: $89-$109	2P: $89-$109	XP: $10	F

Large-scale Hotel **Location:** I-275, exit 40A, 0.4 mi n; exit 39A northbound, 0.5 mi e on Kennedy Blvd, then 1.2 mi n. 1200 N Westshore Blvd 33607. Fax: 813/282-0055. **Facility:** 237 units. 235 one-bedroom standard units. 2 one-bedroom suites. 5 stories, exterior corridors. **Parking:** on-site. **Terms:** cancellation fee imposed, package plans, pets ($45 extra charge, limit 3). **Amenities:** high-speed Internet, voice mail, safes (fee), irons, hair dryers. **Pool(s):** outdoor. **Leisure Activities:** exercise room. **Guest Services:** gift shop, valet and coin laundry, area transportation. **Business Services:** conference facilities, PC, fax (fee). **Cards:** AX, CB, DC, DS, JC, MC, VI.

SOME UNITS

(See map and index starting on p. 950)

CHASE SUITE HOTEL BY WOODFIN   *Book at aaa.com*

Phone: (813)281-5677   **31**

AAA SAVE

WWW (Motel)

| All Year | 1P: $99-$229 | XP: $10 | F16 |

Location: I-275, exit 39 southbound; exit 39B northbound, 3 mi w on SR 60, then just n; in Rocky Point Harbor. 3075 N Rocky Point Dr 33607. Fax: 813/289-0266. **Facility:** 176 units. 130 one- and 46 two-bedroom suites with kitchens. 2 stories, exterior corridors. *Bath:* combo or shower only. **Parking:** on-site. **Terms:** package plans, 12% service charge, pets ($50 fee, $5 extra charge). **Amenities:** video library, high-speed Internet, voice mail, irons, hair dryers. **Dining:** noon-8 pm. **Pool(s):** heated outdoor. **Leisure Activities:** whirlpool, boat dock, fishing, barbecue area, sports court. **Guest Services:** gift shop, complimentary evening beverages, valet and coin laundry, area transportation-within 5 mi. **Business Services:** meeting rooms, business center. **Cards:** AX, CB, DC, DS, MC, VI. **Special Amenities: free expanded continental breakfast and free newspaper.**

SOME UNITS

[icons]

COMFORT INN AND CONFERENCE CENTER NEAR
BUSCH GARDENS   *Book at aaa.com*

Phone: (813)933-4011   **12**

AAA SAVE

WWWW

Small-scale Hotel

2/1-4/15 [CP]	1P: $99-$109	2P: $99-$109	XP: $10	F18
1/1-1/31 & 4/16-11/30 [CP]	1P: $89-$99	2P: $89-$99	XP: $10	F18
12/1-12/31 [CP]	1P: $79-$89	2P: $79-$89	XP: $10	F18

Location: I-275, exit 50, just e on SR 580. 820 E Busch Blvd 33612. Fax: 813/932-1784. **Facility:** 257 units. 251 one-bedroom standard units. 6 one-bedroom suites. 2-4 stories, interior/exterior corridors. *Bath:* combo or shower only. **Parking:** on-site. **Terms:** cancellation fee imposed, package plans, pets ($25 fee). **Amenities:** high-speed Internet, voice mail, safes (fee), irons, hair dryers. **Dining:** 7 am-10 & 5-10 pm, cocktails. **Pool(s):** heated outdoor, heated indoor. **Leisure Activities:** whirlpools, 4 lighted tennis courts, exercise room. *Fee:* game room. **Guest Services:** gift shop, valet and coin laundry. **Business Services:** conference facilities, business center. **Cards:** AX, DC, DS, MC, VI. **Special Amenities: free continental breakfast and preferred room (subject to availability with advance reservations).**

SOME UNITS

[icons]

COMFORT INN HOTEL & SUITES TAMPA
STADIUM/AIRPORT

Phone: 813/874-6700   **24**

WWW (Motel)

| All Year | 1P: $70-$269 | 2P: $70-$269 | XP: $10 | F18 |

Location: I-275, exit 41B, 2 mi n. 4732 N Dale Mabry Hwy 33614. Fax: 813/876-1531. **Facility:** 186 units. 180 one-bedroom standard units. 6 one-bedroom suites, some with kitchens and/or whirlpools. 2 stories, exterior corridors. *Bath:* combo or shower only. **Parking:** on-site. **Terms:** [ECP] meal plan available, package plans, pets ($25 extra charge). **Amenities:** dual phone lines, voice mail, irons, hair dryers. **Pool(s):** outdoor. **Leisure Activities:** jogging, exercise room. **Guest Services:** valet and coin laundry, area transportation (fee). **Business Services:** conference facilities, business center. **Cards:** AX, CB, DC, DS, JC, MC, VI.

SOME UNITS

[icons]

COMFORT SUITES   *Book at aaa.com*

Phone: (813)630-4444   **55**

AAA SAVE

WWW

Small-scale Hotel

| 12/29-4/30 | 1P: $107-$189 | 2P: $117-$199 | XP: $10 | F18 |
| 12/1-12/28 & 5/1-11/30 | 1P: $89-$107 | 2P: $99-$117 | XP: $10 | F18 |

Location: I-75, exit 257, 0.5 mi w on SR 60. 9932 E Adamo Dr 33619. Fax: 813/630-2093. **Facility:** 67 units. 66 one-bedroom standard units with whirlpools. 1 one-bedroom suite with kitchen and whirlpool. 4 stories, interior corridors. *Bath:* combo or shower only. **Parking:** on-site. **Amenities:** high-speed Internet, dual phone lines, voice mail, irons, hair dryers. **Pool(s):** heated outdoor. **Leisure Activities:** exercise room. **Guest Services:** gift shop, valet and coin laundry. **Business Services:** meeting rooms, fax (fee). **Cards:** AX, CB, DC, DS, MC, VI. **Special Amenities: free expanded continental breakfast and free newspaper.**

SOME UNITS

[icons]

COURTYARD BY MARRIOTT   *Book at aaa.com*

Phone: (813)874-0555   **48**

AAA SAVE

WWWW

Small-scale Hotel

1/2-5/21	1P: $149-$219	XP: $10	F18
12/1-1/1 & 9/5-11/30	1P: $129-$199	XP: $10	F18
5/22-9/4	1P: $109-$174	XP: $10	F18

Location: I-275, exit 41A, just e on US 92 (Dale Mabry Hwy), then just sw. 3805 W Cypress St 33607. Fax: 813/870-0685. **Facility:** 145 units. 134 one-bedroom standard units. 11 one-bedroom suites. 4 stories, interior corridors. *Bath:* combo or shower only. **Parking:** on-site. **Terms:** check-in 4 pm. **Amenities:** high-speed Internet, dual phone lines, voice mail, irons, hair dryers. **Dining:** 6-10:30 am, Sat & Sun 7 am-noon. **Pool(s):** heated outdoor. **Leisure Activities:** whirlpool, exercise room. **Guest Services:** sundries, valet and coin laundry, area transportation-local mall. **Business Services:** meeting rooms, business center. **Cards:** AX, CB, DC, DS, MC, VI. **Special Amenities: free newspaper.**

SOME UNITS

[icons]

(See map and index starting on p. 950)

COURTYARD BY MARRIOTT-BRANDON/TAMPA   Book at aaa.com   Phone: (813)661-9559   62

▽▼▽▼▽▼
Small-scale Hotel

| 12/1-4/30 | 1P: $109-$179 | 2P: $109-$179 |
| 5/1-11/30 | 1P: $99-$169 | 2P: $99-$169 |

Location: I-75, exit 257, just w on SR 60, just s on Falkenburg Rd, then just e. 10152 Palm River Rd 33619. Fax: 813/661-4583. **Facility:** 90 units. 87 one-bedroom standard units, some with whirlpools. 3 one-bedroom suites. 3 stories, interior corridors. *Bath:* combo or shower only. **Parking:** on-site. **Terms:** [BP] meal plan available. **Amenities:** video games (fee), high-speed Internet, dual phone lines, voice mail, irons, hair dryers. **Pool(s):** heated indoor. **Leisure Activities:** whirlpool, exercise room. **Guest Services:** valet and coin laundry. **Business Services:** meeting rooms, business center. **Cards:** AX, CB, DC, DS, JC, MC, VI.

SOME UNITS

(ASK) [S/D] [⫟] [♿] [⫯M] [♨] [▨] [⇌] [≍] [☆] [DATA PORT] [▣] / [✕] [🔋] [📠] /

COURTYARD BY MARRIOTT-DOWNTOWN TAMPA   Book at aaa.com   Phone: 813/229-1100   52

▽▼▽▼▽▼
Small-scale Hotel

Property failed to provide current rates

Location: I-275, exit 44, 0.6 mi sw via Tampa St; downtown. 102 E Cass St 33602. Fax: 813/224-9200. **Facility:** 141 units. 136 one-bedroom standard units, some with whirlpools. 5 one-bedroom suites. 6 stories, interior corridors. *Bath:* combo or shower only. **Parking:** valet. **Terms:** check-in 4 pm. **Amenities:** high-speed Internet, dual phone lines, voice mail, irons, hair dryers. **Pool(s):** heated outdoor. **Leisure Activities:** whirlpool, exercise room. **Guest Services:** sundries, valet and coin laundry. **Business Services:** meeting rooms, business center.

SOME UNITS

[⫟] [Ⓨ] [⫯M] [♨] [▨] [⇌] [≍] [☆] [DATA PORT] [▣] / [✕] [🔋] [📠] /

COURTYARD BY MARRIOTT TAMPA NORTH   Book at aaa.com   Phone: 813/978-9898   2

▽▼▽▼▽▼
Small-scale Hotel

Property failed to provide current rates

Location: I-75, exit 266, 0.5 mi w on CR 582A (Fletcher Ave). Located at Hidden River Corporate Park. 13575 Cypress Glen Ln 33637. Fax: 813/978-1835. **Facility:** 81 units. 78 one-bedroom standard units, some with whirlpools. 3 one-bedroom suites with kitchens. 3 stories, interior corridors. *Bath:* combo or shower only. **Parking:** on-site. **Amenities:** high-speed Internet, dual phone lines, voice mail, irons, hair dryers. **Pool(s):** heated outdoor. **Leisure Activities:** whirlpool, exercise room. **Guest Services:** valet and coin laundry. **Business Services:** meeting rooms, PC, fax.

SOME UNITS

[⫯M] [♨] [▨] [⇌] [≍] [☆] [DATA PORT] [▣] [🔋] [📠] /

CROWNE PLAZA TAMPA EAST   Book at aaa.com   Phone: (813)623-6363   29

▽▼▽▼▽▼
Large-scale Hotel

1/1-4/30	1P: $119-$204	2P: $129-$214	XP: $10	F18
9/5-11/30	1P: $109-$194	2P: $119-$204	XP: $10	F18
5/1-9/4	1P: $115-$184	2P: $125-$194	XP: $10	F18
12/1-12/31	1P: $99-$184	2P: $109-$194	XP: $10	F18

Location: I-75, exit 260 southbound; exit 260B northbound, just w on SR 574 (Dr. Martin Luther King Blvd); in the Sabal Corporate Park. 10221 Princess Palm Ave 33610. Fax: 813/621-7224. **Facility:** 269 units. 228 one-bedroom standard units. 41 one-bedroom suites ($194-$550), some with kitchens and/or whirlpools. 5 stories, interior corridors. *Bath:* combo or shower only. **Parking:** on-site. **Terms:** [BP] meal plan available, package plans. **Amenities:** video games (fee), CD players, high-speed Internet, dual phone lines, voice mail, irons, hair dryers. **Pool(s):** heated outdoor. **Leisure Activities:** whirlpool, lighted tennis court, jogging, exercise room, basketball. **Guest Services:** gift shop, valet and coin laundry, area transportation. **Business Services:** conference facilities, business center. **Cards:** AX, CB, DC, DS, JC, MC, VI.

SOME UNITS

(ASK) [S/D] [✈] [⫟] [Ⓨ] [⫯M] [♨] [▨] [⇌] [≍] [☆] [DATA PORT] [▣] / [✕] [🔋] /

DAYS INN/STATE FAIRGROUNDS   Book at aaa.com   Phone: (813)623-5121   59

AAA (SAVE)
▽▼▽▼▽▼
Motel

1/2-2/28 [ECP]	1P: $89	2P: $89	XP: $10	D18
3/1-4/30 [ECP]	1P: $79	2P: $79	XP: $10	D18
12/1-1/1 & 5/1-11/30 [ECP]	1P: $59	2P: $59	XP: $10	D18

Location: I-75, exit 257, 0.5 mi w on SR 60. 9942 Adamo Dr 33619. Fax: 813/628-4989. **Facility:** 100 units. 99 one-bedroom standard units. 1 one-bedroom suite with kitchen. 2 stories, interior corridors. **Parking:** on-site. **Terms:** $1 service charge. **Amenities:** safes (fee), hair dryers. *Some:* irons. **Pool(s):** outdoor. **Guest Services:** coin laundry. **Business Services:** meeting rooms, fax. **Cards:** AX, CB, DC, DS, JC, MC, VI. **Special Amenities:** free expanded continental breakfast and free local telephone calls.

SOME UNITS

[S/D] [⫟] [♨] [⇌] [⇄] [☆] / [✕] [DATA PORT] [🔋] [📠] /
FEE   FEE FEE

DOUBLETREE GUEST SUITES TAMPA BAY   Book at aaa.com   Phone: (813)888-8800   32

AAA (SAVE)
▽▼▽▼▽▼
Large-scale Hotel

12/31-4/30	1P: $139-$229	2P: $139-$229	XP: $20	F17
12/1-12/30	1P: $109-$219	2P: $109-$219	XP: $20	F17
10/1-11/30	1P: $109-$209	2P: $109-$209	XP: $20	F17
5/1-9/30	1P: $99-$199	2P: $99-$199	XP: $20	F17

Location: I-275, exit 39 southbound; exit 39B northbound, 3 mi w on SR 60, then just n; in Rocky Point Harbour. 3050 N Rocky Point Dr W 33607. Fax: 813/888-8743. **Facility:** 203 one-bedroom suites ($99-$399). 7 stories, interior corridors. **Parking:** on-site. **Terms:** [BP] & [CP] meal plans available, package plans. **Amenities:** video games (fee), voice mail, irons, hair dryers. *Some:* high-speed Internet. **Dining:** 6:30-10 am, 11:30-2 & 5-10 pm, Sat & Sun 6:30-11 am, 11:30-2 & 5-10 pm, cocktails. **Pool(s):** heated outdoor. **Leisure Activities:** sauna, whirlpool, boat dock, jogging, exercise room. *Fee:* personal watercraft, water skis. **Guest Services:** gift shop, valet and coin laundry, area transportation-within 3 mi. **Business Services:** meeting rooms, PC, fax (fee). **Cards:** AX, CB, DC, DS, JC, MC, VI. **Special Amenities:** free newspaper.

SOME UNITS

[✈] [⫟] [Ⓨ] [♨] [▨] [⇌] [≍] [☆] [DATA PORT] [🔋] [▣] / [✕] [VCR] [📠] /
FEE

(See map and index starting on p. 950)

DOUBLETREE GUEST SUITES TAMPA/BUSCH
GARDENS   *Book at aaa.com*

Phone: (813)971-7690   **8**

(AAA) [SAVE]

▽▽▽▽

Small-scale Hotel

All Year   1P: $89-$159   2P: $99-$169   XP: $10   F18

Location: I-275, exit 51, 1.8 mi e on SR 582, then just s. 11310 N 30th St 33612. **Fax:** 813/972-5525. **Facility:** 129 one-bedroom suites. 3 stories, exterior corridors. *Bath:* combo or shower only. **Parking:** on-site. **Terms:** cancellation fee imposed. **Amenities:** video games (fee), high-speed Internet, dual phone lines, voice mail, irons, hair dryers. **Pool(s):** heated outdoor. **Leisure Activities:** whirlpool. **Guest Services:** valet and coin laundry, area transportation-within 5 mi. **Business Services:** meeting rooms, fax. **Cards:** AX, CB, DC, DS, JC, MC, VI. **Special Amenities:** free newspaper. *(See color ad below)*

SOME UNITS

[S/D] [📶] [🍴⁺] [🛗M] [😊⁺] [🌀] [🏊] [🅿️⁺] [🎥] [DATA PORT] [🗄] [🖥] [🖳] / [⊠] [VCR] /
FEE

DOUBLETREE HOTEL TAMPA
AIRPORT-WESTSHORE   *Book at aaa.com*

Phone: (813)879-4800   **49**

(AAA) [SAVE]

▽▽▽▽

Large-scale Hotel

12/1-4/30	1P: $139-$219	2P: $139-$219	XP: $10 F18
10/1-11/30	1P: $109-$199	2P: $109-$199	XP: $10 F18
5/1-9/30	1P: $99-$169	2P: $99-$169	XP: $10 F18

Location: I-275, exit 40A southbound; exit 39A northbound, just w on Westshore Blvd, then just n. 4500 W Cypress St 33607. **Fax:** 813/873-2401. **Facility:** 485 units. 467 one-bedroom standard units. 18 one-bedroom suites. 5-10 stories, interior corridors. *Bath:* combo or shower only. **Parking:** on-site. **Terms:** cancellation fee imposed. **Amenities:** video games (fee), CD players, high-speed Internet, dual phone lines, voice mail, irons, hair dryers. **Dining:** 6:30 am-midnight, cocktails, also, Charley's Steakhouse, see separate listing. **Pool(s):** heated outdoor. **Leisure Activities:** whirlpool, sun deck, exercise room. *Fee:* game room. **Guest Services:** gift shop, valet and coin laundry, area transportation-within 2 mi & local malls. **Business Services:** conference facilities, business center. **Cards:** AX, CB, DC, DS, JC, MC, VI. **Special Amenities:** free newspaper and preferred room (subject to availability with advance reservations).

SOME UNITS

[S/D] [✈] [🍴⁺] [🍸] [♿] [🛗M] [😊⁺] [🏊] [✂] [🎥] [DATA PORT] [🖳] / [⊠] [🖥] [🗄] /

EAST LAKE INN

Phone: 813/622-8339   **18**

(AAA) [SAVE]

▽

Motel

10/15-11/30	1P: $65	2P: $70	XP: $5
12/1-4/15	1P: $60	2P: $65	XP: $5
4/16-10/14	1P: $55	2P: $60	XP: $5

Location: I-4, exit 7, 2.2 mi w on US 92. 6529 E Hillsborough Ave 33610. **Fax:** 813/622-8339. **Facility:** 26 one-bedroom standard units. 2 stories, exterior corridors. **Parking:** on-site. **Terms:** 3-5 night minimum stay, 3 day cancellation notice-fee imposed. **Guest Services:** coin laundry. **Business Services:** fax. **Cards:** AX, DS, MC, VI.

SOME UNITS

[🍴⁺] [🎥] [🗄] / [DATA PORT] [🖳] /

(See map and index starting on p. 950)

ECONO LODGE MIDTOWN   *Book at aaa.com*   Phone: (813)254-3005   68

2/1-4/17	1P: $75-$125	2P: $75-$125	XP: $6	F16
12/30-1/31	1P: $65-$110	2P: $65-$110	XP: $6	F16
4/18-11/30	1P: $65-$95	2P: $65-$95	XP: $6	F16
12/1-12/29	1P: $56-$85	2P: $56-$85	XP: $6	F16

Motel   **Location:** I-275, exit 41A, 1.5 mi s on US 92. 1020 S Dale Mabry Hwy 33629. Fax: 813/253-2909. **Facility:** 74 one-bedroom standard units. 2 stories, exterior corridors. *Bath:* combo or shower only. **Parking:** on-site. **Terms:** [ECP] meal plan available. **Amenities:** high-speed Internet, voice mail, hair dryers. *Some:* irons. **Pool(s):** heated outdoor. **Guest Services:** coin laundry. **Business Services:** PC, fax. **Cards:** AX, CB, DC, DS, JC, MC, VI. **Special Amenities:** free continental breakfast and free local telephone calls.

SOME UNITS

FEE

EMBASSY SUITES
HOTEL-TAMPA/AIRPORT/WESTSHORE   *Book at aaa.com*   Phone: (813)875-1555   54

1/1-4/30 [BP]	1P: $139-$199	XP: $20	F18
12/1-12/31 [BP]	1P: $119-$199	XP: $20	F18
5/1-11/30 [BP]	1P: $129-$189	XP: $20	F18

Large-scale Hotel   **Location:** I-275, exit 40A southbound, just e; exit 39A northbound, 1 mi n on Kennedy Blvd, then 0.5 mi w. 555 N Westshore Blvd 33609. Fax: 813/287-3664. **Facility:** 221 units. 195 one- and 26 two-bedroom suites ($119-$199), some with kitchens. 16 stories, interior corridors. *Bath:* combo or shower only. **Parking:** on-site and valet. **Terms:** package plans. **Amenities:** high-speed Internet, voice mail, honor bars, irons, hair dryers. **Dining:** Bay Cafe, see separate listing. **Pool(s):** heated outdoor. **Leisure Activities:** whirlpool, exercise room. **Guest Services:** sundries, complimentary evening beverages, valet and coin laundry, airport transportation-Tampa International Airport, area transportation-within 3 mi. **Business Services:** conference facilities, business center. **Cards:** AX, DC, DS, MC, VI. **Special Amenities:** free full breakfast and preferred room (subject to availability with advance reservations).

SOME UNITS

FEE

(See map and index starting on p. 950)

EMBASSY SUITES HOTEL USF/NEAR BUSCH
GARDENS   *Book at aaa.com*

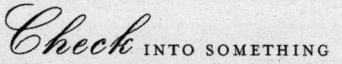

12/1-4/30 [BP]	1P: $109-$199	2P: $119-$209	XP: $10	F17
6/1-11/30 [BP]	1P: $109-$179	2P: $119-$189	XP: $10	F17
5/1-5/31 [BP]	1P: $99-$179	2P: $109-$189	XP: $10	F17

Phone: (813)977-7066   ③

Location: I-275, exit 51, 2.2 mi e on CR 582A; on USF campus. 3705 Spectrum Blvd 33612. Fax: 813/977-7933. **Facility:** 247 one-bedroom suites. 8 stories, interior corridors. *Bath:* combo or shower only. **Parking:** on-site. **Terms:** cancellation fee imposed, package plans. **Amenities:** dual phone lines, voice mail, irons, hair dryers. *Fee:* video games, high-speed Internet. **Dining:** 11 am-2 & 5-10 pm, cocktails. **Pool(s):** heated outdoor. **Leisure Activities:** sauna, whirlpool, exercise room. *Fee:* game room. **Guest Services:** gift shop, complimentary evening beverages, valet and coin laundry, area transportation-within 5 mi. **Business Services:** conference facilities, business center. **Cards:** AX, DC, DS, MC, VI. **Special Amenities:** free full breakfast and free newspaper. *(See color ad below)*

Large-scale Hotel

SOME UNITS / FEE

EMBASSY SUITES TAMPA-DOWNTOWN
CONVENTION CENTER

[fyi]

Small-scale Hotel

Phone: 813/769-8300

Under construction, scheduled to open June 2006. **Location:** 1513 S Florida Ave 33602. Fax: 813/769-8310. **Planned Amenities:** restaurant, coffeemakers, microwaves, refrigerators, pool. *(See color ad below)*

EXTENDED STAY DELUXE   *Book at aaa.com*

Small-scale Hotel

Phone: 813/637-8990   ㊷

Property failed to provide current rates

Location: I-275, exit 40A southbound, 0.5 mi n; exit 39A northbound, 0.5 mi e on Kennedy Blvd, then 1.3 mi n. 1805 N Westshore Blvd 33607. Fax: 813/637-8991. **Facility:** 133 one-bedroom suites with kitchens. 3 stories, interior corridors. *Bath:* combo or shower only. **Parking:** on-site. **Terms:** small pets only ($10 extra charge). **Amenities:** video games (fee), high-speed Internet, dual phone lines, voice mail, safes, irons, hair dryers. **Pool(s):** outdoor. **Leisure Activities:** exercise room. **Guest Services:** valet and coin laundry. **Business Services:** meeting rooms, fax.

SOME UNITS / FEE

(See map and index starting on p. 950)

FAIRFIELD INN BY MARRIOTT-BRANDON/TAMPA
Book at aaa.com   **Phone:** (813)661-9719   63

12/1-4/30 [ECP]	1P: $99-$139	2P: $99-$139
5/1-11/30 [ECP]	1P: $89-$129	2P: $89-$129

Small-scale Hotel   **Location:** I-75, exit 257, just w on SR 60, just s on Falkenburg Rd, then just e. 10150 Palm River Rd 33619. **Fax:** 813/661-0416. **Facility:** 107 one-bedroom standard units, some with whirlpools. 3 stories, interior corridors. *Bath:* combo or shower only. **Parking:** on-site. **Amenities:** video games (fee), high-speed Internet, irons, hair dryers. **Pool(s):** heated outdoor. **Leisure Activities:** exercise room. **Guest Services:** valet and coin laundry. **Business Services:** PC, fax. **Cards:** AX, CB, DC, DS, JC, MC, VI.

SOME UNITS

(ASK) (S□) (TI+) (&M) (✦) (⌂) (➤) (⚗) (DATA PORT) (🖵) / (✕) (🛏) (📷) /

GRAM'S PLACE BNB GUESTHOUSES HOSTEL & MUSIC
Phone: (813)221-0596   30

12/1-4/30 [CP]	1P: $80-$95	2P: $80-$95
5/1-11/30 [CP]	1P: $65-$80	2P: $65-$80

Bed & Breakfast   **Location:** I-275, exit 46B, 0.6 mi w on SR 574 (E Dr Martin Luther King Jr Blvd), then 0.6 mi s; jct W Plymouth St. Located in a residential area. 3109 N Ola Ave 33603. **Fax:** 813/221-0596. **Facility:** Designated smoking area. 7 one-bedroom standard units. 1 story, interior/exterior corridors. *Bath:* some shared or private, combo or shower only. **Parking:** street. **Terms:** office hours 3 pm-midnight, 7-day cancellation notice-fee imposed. **Leisure Activities:** whirlpool. **Guest Services:** coin laundry. **Business Services:** PC, fax. **Cards:** AX, MC, VI.

(ASK) (S□) (✕)

GRAND HYATT TAMPA BAY
Book at aaa.com   **Phone:** (813)874-1234   36

All Year	1P: $125-$325	2P: $125-$325	XP: $25 F18

(AAA) (SAVE)

Large-scale Hotel   **Location:** SR 60, east end of Courtney Campbell Cswy. Located in an office park area. 290 Bay Port Plaza 33607. **Fax:** 813/207-6790. **Facility:** This property is next to an ecologically protected salt marsh and overlooks Old Tampa Bay; rooms offer city and bay views. 445 units. 435 one-bedroom standard units, some with whirlpools. 10 one-bedroom suites, some with whirlpools. 1-13 stories, interior/exterior corridors. *Bath:* combo or shower only. **Parking:** on-site and valet. **Terms:** cancellation fee imposed. **Amenities:** high-speed Internet (fee), dual phone lines, voice mail, safes, honor bars, irons, hair dryers. *Some:* DVD players, CD players, fax. **Dining:** 6:30 am-10 pm, cocktails, also, Armani's, Oystercatchers, see separate listings, entertainment. **Pool(s):** 2 heated outdoor. **Leisure Activities:** saunas, whirlpools, 2 lighted tennis courts, nature preserve, nature walk & observation deck, basketball. **Fee:** massage. **Guest Services:** gift shop, valet laundry, airport transportation-Tampa International Airport. **Business Services:** conference facilities, business center. **Cards:** AX, CB, DC, DS, JC, MC, VI.

SOME UNITS

(✈) (TI) (Y) (⌂) (&M) (✦) (⌂) (➤) (✦) (✕) (⚗) (DATA PORT) (🖵) / (✕) (VCR) (🛏) (📷) /

(See map and index starting on p. 950)

HAMPTON INN   *Book at aaa.com*   Phone: (813)289-6262   **33**

AAA SAVE

2/1-4/30	1P: $99-$189	2P: $99-$189	XP: $10 F18
12/1-1/31 & 5/1-11/30	1P: $79-$159	2P: $79-$159	XP: $10 F18

Small-scale Hotel   **Location:** I-275, exit 39 southbound; exit 39B northbound, 3 mi w on SR 60, then just n; in Rocky Point Harbor. 3035 N Rocky Point Dr 33607. Fax: 813/287-9363. **Facility:** 70 one-bedroom standard units. 5 stories, interior corridors. *Bath:* combo or shower only. **Parking:** on-site. **Amenities:** video games (fee), high-speed Internet, dual phone lines, voice mail, irons, hair dryers. **Pool(s):** heated outdoor. **Guest Services:** valet and coin laundry, area transportation-within 4 mi. **Business Services:** fax. **Cards:** AX, DC, DS, MC, VI. **Special Amenities:** free expanded continental breakfast and free newspaper. *(See color ad below)*

SOME UNITS

HAMPTON INN & SUITES   *Book at aaa.com*   Phone: (813)903-6000   **1**

AAA SAVE

1/15-11/30 [ECP]	1P: $99-$129	2P: $99-$129
12/1-1/14 [ECP]	1P: $69-$89	2P: $69-$89

Location: I-75, exit 266, 0.8 mi w on CR 582A (Fletcher Ave). Located at Hidden River Corporate Park. 8210 Hidden River Pkwy 33637. Fax: 813/977-3343. **Facility:** 127 units. 89 one-bedroom standard units. 38 one-bedroom
Small-scale Hotel   suites ($99-$169) with kitchens. 4 stories, interior corridors. *Bath:* combo or shower only. **Parking:** on-site. **Terms:** package plans. **Amenities:** video games (fee), high-speed Internet, dual phone lines, voice mail, irons, hair dryers. **Pool(s):** outdoor. **Leisure Activities:** exercise room. **Guest Services:** sundries, complimentary evening beverages: Mon-Thurs, valet and coin laundry. **Business Services:** meeting rooms, fax. **Cards:** AX, CB, DC, DS, MC, VI. **Special Amenities:** free expanded continental breakfast and free local telephone calls.

SOME UNITS

HAMPTON INN-TAMPA/BRANDON   *Book at aaa.com*   Phone: (813)661-8888   **60**

12/1-4/30 [ECP]	1P: $109-$129	2P: $109-$129 XP: $5 F18
5/1-11/30 [ECP]	1P: $89-$109	2P: $89-$109 XP: $5 F18

Small-scale Hotel   **Location:** I-75, exit 257, just w on SR 60, then just n on Falkenburg Rd. 10110 Horace Ave 33619. Fax: 813/661-2828. **Facility:** 80 one-bedroom standard units. 3 stories, interior corridors. *Bath:* combo or shower only. **Parking:** on-site. **Amenities:** high-speed Internet, voice mail, irons, hair dryers. **Leisure Activities:** exercise room. **Guest Services:** valet and coin laundry. **Business Services:** meeting rooms, fax (fee). **Cards:** AX, CB, DC, DS, JC, MC, VI.

SOME UNITS

(See map and index starting on p. 950)

HAMPTON INN TAMPA INT'L AIRPORT - WESTSHORE   *Book at aaa.com*   Phone: (813)287-0778   **44**

AAA SAVE
WWW

Small-scale Hotel

All Year   1P: $79-$139   2P: $99-$159   XP: $10   F18

Location: I-275, exit 40A, 0.5 mi n on Westshore Blvd; exit 39A northbound, 1 mi e on Kennedy Blvd, 1 mi n on Westshore Blvd, then just w. 4817 W Laurel St 33607. Fax: 813/287-0882. Facility: 133 one-bedroom standard units. 6 stories, interior corridors. Parking: on-site. Terms: cancellation fee imposed, package plans. Amenities: video games (fee), high-speed Internet, voice mail, irons, hair dryers. Some: dual phone lines. Pool(s): outdoor. Leisure Activities: exercise room. Guest Services: valet laundry, area transportation-within 2 mi. Business Services: meeting rooms, business center. Cards: AX, CB, DC, DS, MC, VI. Special Amenities: free expanded continental breakfast and free local telephone calls.

SOME UNITS
[icons] FEE

HAMPTON INN VETERANS EXPRESSWAY   *Book at aaa.com*   Phone: (813)901-5900   **14**

WWW

Small-scale Hotel

12/26-4/30 [ECP]   1P: $129-$139   2P: $139-$149
5/1-11/30 [ECP]   1P: $99-$129   2P: $109-$139
12/1-12/25 [ECP]   1P: $99-$119   2P: $109-$129

Location: SR 589 (Veteran's Expwy), exit 6A, just e on CR 584. 5628 W Waters Ave 33634. Fax: 813/901-5910. Facility: 86 one-bedroom standard units. 5 stories, interior corridors. Bath: combo or shower only. Parking: on-site. Terms: pets ($35 deposit). Amenities: video games, high-speed Internet, dual phone lines, voice mail, irons. Some: CD players. Pool(s): outdoor. Leisure Activities: exercise room. Guest Services: sundries, valet and coin laundry. Business Services: meeting rooms, PC, fax (fee). Cards: AX, CB, DC, DS, JC, MC, VI.

SOME UNITS
[icons] FEE

HARD ROCK SEMINOLE CASINO & HOTEL   *Book at aaa.com*   Phone: (813)627-7625   **20**

WWW

Large-scale Hotel

12/1-5/31   1P: $152-$305   2P: $152-$305   XP: $30   F18
6/1-11/30   1P: $134-$305   2P: $134-$305   XP: $30   F18

Location: I-4, exit 6, just w. 5223 N Orient Rd 33610. Fax: 813/627-7655. Facility: 250 units. 248 one-bedroom standard units, some with whirlpools. 2 one-bedroom suites with whirlpools. 12 stories, interior corridors. Bath: combo or shower only. Parking: on-site (fee) and valet. Terms: 3 day cancellation notice-fee imposed, package plans, small pets only ($50 fee). Amenities: video games (fee), CD players, high-speed Internet, dual phone lines, voice mail, safes, honor bars, irons, hair dryers. Some: DVD players. Dining: Floyd's Restaurant & Night Club, see separate listing. Pool(s): heated outdoor. Leisure Activities: whirlpools, steamrooms, exercise room, spa, horseshoes, volleyball. Guest Services: gift shop, valet laundry. Business Services: conference facilities, fax (fee). Cards: AX, CB, DC, DS, MC, VI.

SOME UNITS
[icons] FEE

HILTON GARDEN INN TAMPA EAST/BRANDON   *Book at aaa.com*   Phone: (813)626-6700   **25**

WWW

Small-scale Hotel

1/1-4/30 & 10/1-11/30   1P: $109-$169   2P: $109-$169   XP: $10   F18
5/1-9/30   1P: $99-$159   2P: $99-$159   XP: $10   F18
12/1-12/31   1P: $89-$159   2P: $89-$159   XP: $10   F18

Location: I-75, exit 260 southbound; exit 260B northbound, just w on SR 574 (Dr. Martin Luther King Blvd), just n on Park Oaks Blvd, then just e; in Highland Oaks. 10309 Highland Manor Dr 33610. Fax: 813/626-6755. Facility: 152 units. 144 one-bedroom standard units. 8 one-bedroom suites ($179-$379), some with whirlpools. 6 stories, interior corridors. Bath: combo or shower only. Parking: on-site. Terms: [BP] & [CP] meal plans available, package plans. Amenities: video games (fee), high-speed Internet, dual phone lines, voice mail, irons, hair dryers. Some: DVD players, CD players. Pool(s): heated outdoor. Leisure Activities: whirlpool, exercise room. Guest Services: sundries, valet and coin laundry, area transportation. Business Services: meeting rooms, business center. Cards: AX, CB, DC, DS, MC, VI.

SOME UNITS
[icons]

HILTON GARDEN INN/TAMPA YBOR CITY HISTORIC DISTRICT   *Book at aaa.com*   Phone: (813)769-9267   **39**

WWW

Small-scale Hotel

12/1-4/30   1P: $159-$189   2P: $159-$189   XP: $10   F18
5/1-11/30   1P: $129-$189   2P: $129-$189   XP: $10   F18

Location: I-4, exit 1, just s on 21st St, then just w. 1700 E 9th Ave 33605. Fax: 813/769-3299. Facility: 95 units. 84 one-bedroom standard units. 11 one-bedroom suites ($169-$249). 4 stories, interior corridors. Bath: combo or shower only. Parking: on-site (fee). Terms: [AP], [BP] & [CP] meal plans available, package plans. Amenities: video games (fee), high-speed Internet, dual phone lines, voice mail, irons, hair dryers. Pool(s): heated outdoor. Leisure Activities: whirlpool, exercise room. Guest Services: sundries, valet and coin laundry, area transportation. Business Services: meeting rooms, business center. Cards: AX, CB, DC, DS, JC, MC, VI.

SOME UNITS
[icons]

(See map and index starting on p. 950)

HILTON TAMPA AIRPORT WESTSHORE   *Book at aaa.com*   Phone: (813)877-6688   40

AAA SAVE
All Year   1P: $99-$299   2P: $109-$309   XP: $10   F18
Location: I-275, exit 40B, 0.8 mi n. 2225 N Lois Ave 33607. Fax: 813/879-3264. **Facility:** 238 units. 237 one-bedroom standard units. 1 one-bedroom suite with whirlpool. 12 stories, interior corridors. *Bath:* combo or shower only. **Parking:** on-site. **Terms:** cancellation fee imposed. **Amenities:** dual phone lines, voice mail,
Large-scale Hotel   irons, hair dryers. *Fee:* video games, high-speed Internet. **Dining:** 6:30 am-10 pm, cocktails. **Pool(s):** heated outdoor. **Leisure Activities:** whirlpool, lighted tennis court, exercise room. **Guest Services:** gift shop, valet laundry, airport transportation-Tampa International Airport, area transportation-within 3 mi. **Business Services:** conference facilities, business center. **Cards:** AX, CB, DC, DS, JC, MC, VI. **Special Amenities:** free newspaper.
(See color ad below)

SOME UNITS

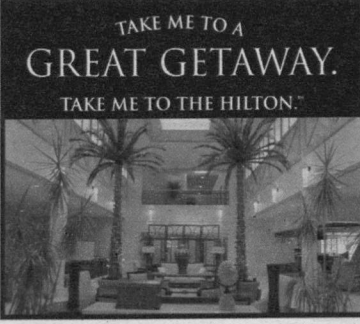

HOLIDAY INN EXPRESS & SUITES   *Book at aaa.com*   Phone: (813)910-7171

AAA SAVE
All Year [ECP]   1P: $89-$169   2P: $89-$169   XP: $10   F16
Location: I-75, exit 270, 0.3 mi n on CR 581 (Bruce B Downs Blvd), just w on Highwoods Preserve Pkwy, then just n; in Highwoods Preserve. 8310 Galbraith Rd 33647. Fax: 813/910-3310. **Facility:** 100 units. 94 one-bedroom standard units. 3 one- and 2 two-bedroom suites ($129-$309) with whirlpools. 4 stories, interior corridors.
Small-scale Hotel   *Bath:* combo or shower only. **Parking:** on-site. **Terms:** package plans, pets ($50 fee). **Amenities:** video games (fee), high-speed Internet, voice mail, irons, hair dryers. **Pool(s):** heated outdoor. **Leisure Activities:** putting green, exercise room. **Guest Services:** valet and coin laundry. **Business Services:** meeting rooms, business center. **Cards:** AX, CB, DC, DS, JC, MC, VI. **Special Amenities:** free expanded continental breakfast and free local telephone calls.

SOME UNITS

HOLIDAY INN EXPRESS HOTEL & SUITES   Phone: 813/877-6061

fyi
12/1-3/31   1P: $119-$189   2P: $119-$189
4/1-11/30   1P: $109-$139   2P: $109-$139
Small-scale Hotel   Too new to rate. **Location:** I-275, exit 41B, 2 mi n. 4750 N Dale Mabry Hwy 33614. **Amenities:** 146 units, coffeemakers. **Cards:** AX, DC, DS, MC, VI.

HOLIDAY INN EXPRESS HOTEL & SUITES   Phone: 813/835-7747

fyi
Property failed to provide current rates
Small-scale Hotel   Too new to rate. **Location:** I-4, exit 6 westbound; exit 6A eastbound, just se. US 301 N 33610. **Amenities:** 110 units.

HOLIDAY INN EXPRESS HOTEL & SUITES   *Book at aaa.com*   Phone: (813)885-3700   10

1/1-4/30 [ECP]   1P: $129-$159   2P: $129-$159
12/1-12/31 & 5/1-11/30 [ECP]   1P: $109-$129   2P: $109-$129
Small-scale Hotel   **Location:** SR 589 (Veteran's Expwy), exit 6B, just e; in Westlake Corporate Center. 9402 Corporate Lake Dr 33634. Fax: 813/885-1799. **Facility:** 85 units. 46 one-bedroom standard units. 39 one-bedroom suites. 4 stories, interior corridors. *Bath:* combo or shower only. **Parking:** on-site. **Terms:** cancellation fee imposed, pets ($35 fee). **Amenities:** video games (fee), high-speed Internet, dual phone lines, voice mail, irons, hair dryers. *Some:* CD players. **Pool(s):** outdoor. **Leisure Activities:** exercise room. **Guest Services:** sundries, valet and coin laundry. **Business Services:** meeting rooms, business center. **Cards:** AX, CB, DC, DS, JC, MC, VI.

SOME UNITS

HOLIDAY INN EXPRESS HOTEL & SUITES   *Book at aaa.com*   Phone: (813)287-8585   34

2/1-4/30   1P: $99-$199   2P: $99-$199   XP: $10   F18
12/1-1/31 & 5/1-11/30   1P: $89-$169   2P: $89-$169   XP: $10   F18
Small-scale Hotel   **Location:** I-275, exit 39 southbound; exit 39B northbound, 3 mi w on SR 60, then just n; in Rocky Point Harbour. 3025 N Rocky Point Dr 33607. Fax: 813/287-8484. **Facility:** 88 units. 52 one-bedroom standard units. 36 one-bedroom suites. 4 stories, interior corridors. *Bath:* combo or shower only. **Parking:** on-site. **Amenities:** high-speed Internet, dual phone lines, voice mail, irons, hair dryers. **Pool(s):** heated outdoor. **Leisure Activities:** exercise room. **Guest Services:** valet and coin laundry, area transportation. **Business Services:** meeting rooms, fax. **Cards:** AX, CB, DC, DS, JC, MC, VI.
(See color ad p 978)

SOME UNITS

(See map and index starting on p. 950)

HOLIDAY INN EXPRESS HOTEL & SUITES
TAMPA-FAIRGROUNDS   *Book at aaa.com*

(AAA) (SAVE) All Year   1P: $89-$169   2P: $89-$169   **Phone:** (813)490-1000   [22]
▽▽▽▽   XP: $15   F17
Location: I-4, exit 7, just se on US 301. Located across the street from Florida State Fairgrounds. 8610 Elm Fair Blvd
Small-scale Hotel 33610. Fax: 813/490-1004. **Facility:** 76 one-bedroom standard units, some with whirlpools. 4 stories, interior
corridors. *Bath:* combo or shower only. **Parking:** on-site. **Terms:** [ECP] meal plan available.
Amenities: high-speed Internet, voice mail, irons, hair dryers. **Pool(s):** heated outdoor. **Leisure**
Activities: exercise room. **Guest Services:** sundries, valet and coin laundry. **Business Services:** meeting
rooms, business center. **Cards:** AX, CB, DC, DS, MC, VI. **Special Amenities:** free expanded continental breakfast and free
newspaper.

SOME UNITS

[S/D] [▮▯] [占M] [占] [⨀] [🔲] [🐾] [🎥] [DATA PORT] [🔲] [🔲] [💻] / [⊠] /

HOLIDAY INN TAMPA NEAR BUSCH GARDENS   *Book at aaa.com*   **Phone:** (813)971-4710   [6]

(AAA) (SAVE) 2/1-4/30   2P: $89-$179   XP: $10   F18
           12/1-1/31   2P: $79-$159   XP: $10   F18
▽▽▽▽   5/1-11/30   2P: $69-$159   XP: $10   F18
Location: I-275, exit 51, 1.5 mi e on SR 582. 2701 E Fowler Ave 33612. Fax: 813/910-8038. **Facility:** 406 units.
Small-scale Hotel 405 one-bedroom standard units, some with whirlpools. 1 one-bedroom suite ($109-$199) with kitchen. 2
stories, interior/exterior corridors. *Bath:* combo or shower only. **Parking:** on-site. **Terms:** check-in 4 pm, [BP]
meal plan available, package plans, small pets only ($25 extra charge). **Amenities:** video games (fee), high-speed Internet,
voice mail, irons, hair dryers. *Some:* CD players, dual phone lines. **Dining:** 2 restaurants, 6 am-1 am, cocktails. **Pool(s):** heated
outdoor, wading. **Leisure Activities:** exercise room. *Fee:* game room. **Guest Services:** gift shop, valet and coin laundry, area
transportation-within 2.5 mi. **Business Services:** conference facilities. *Fee:* PC, fax. **Cards:** AX, DS, MC, VI.
Special Amenities: free newspaper.

SOME UNITS

[S/D] [🐕] [▮▯] [🍸] [占M] [占] [⨀] [🔲] [🎥] [DATA PORT] [💻] / [⊠] [VCR] / [🔲] [🔲] /
      FEE   FEE FEE

HOMESTEAD STUDIO SUITES
HOTEL-TAMPA/NORTH AIRPORT   *Book at aaa.com*   **Phone:** (813)243-1913   [17]

▽▽▽ ▽▽▽   All Year   1P: $44-$64   2P: $49-$69   XP: $15   F17
Motel **Location:** SR 589 (Veterans Expwy), exit 4, just w on SR 580. 5401 Beaumont Ctr Blvd 33634. Fax: 813/243-1813.
Facility: 121 one-bedroom standard units with efficiencies. 2 stories, interior/exterior corridors. *Bath:* combo
or shower only. **Parking:** on-site. **Terms:** office hours 6:30 am-10 pm, pets ($75 extra charge).
Amenities: voice mail, irons. *Some:* hair dryers. **Guest Services:** valet and coin laundry. **Business Services:** fax. **Cards:** AX,
DC, DS, MC, VI.

SOME UNITS

[ASK] [S/D] [🐕] [▮▯] [占M] [占] [⨀] [🔲🔲] [🎥] [DATA PORT] [🔲] [🔲] [💻] / [⊠] /
            FEE

HOWARD JOHNSON EXPRESS INN & SUITES   *Book at aaa.com*   **Phone:** (813)832-4656   [69]

(AAA) (SAVE) 12/1-4/15 [CP]   1P: $65-$95   2P: $65-$95   XP: $5   F18
           4/16-11/30 [CP]   1P: $55-$75   2P: $55-$75   XP: $5   F18
▽▽ ▽▽   **Location:** I-275, exit 41A, 2.5 mi s on US 92. 3314 S Dale Mabry Hwy 33629. Fax: 813/832-5454. **Facility:** 80
units. 78 one-bedroom standard units, some with kitchens. 2 one-bedroom suites with kitchens and
Small-scale Hotel whirlpools. 2 stories, exterior corridors. *Bath:* combo or shower only. **Parking:** on-site. **Amenities:** high-
speed Internet, voice mail, irons, hair dryers. *Some:* DVD players. **Pool(s):** heated outdoor. **Guest**
Services: valet and coin laundry. **Business Services:** meeting rooms, fax (fee). **Cards:** AX, CB, DC, DS, MC, VI.
Special Amenities: free continental breakfast and early check-in/late check-out.

SOME UNITS

[S/D] [▮▯] [占] [🔲] [🔲🔲] [🎥] [DATA PORT] [🔲] [🔲] [💻] / [⊠] [VCR] /
           FEE

HYATT REGENCY TAMPA   *Book at aaa.com*   **Phone:** (813)225-1234   [57]

(AAA) (SAVE) All Year   1P: $115-$209   2P: $115-$209   XP: $25   F18
▽▽▽▽   **Location:** I-275, exit 44, 0.8 mi s on Ashley St to Jackson St, then just e on Tampa St. Connects to downtown office and
shopping complex. 211 N Tampa St 33602. Fax: 813/273-0234. **Facility:** 521 units. 503 one-bedroom standard
units. 18 one-bedroom suites. 17 stories, interior corridors. *Bath:* combo or shower only. **Parking:** on-site
Large-scale Hotel (fee) and valet. **Terms:** cancellation fee imposed. **Amenities:** high-speed Internet (fee), dual phone lines,
voice mail, safes, irons, hair dryers. *Some:* CD players. **Dining:** 6:30 am-11 pm, cocktails. **Pool(s):** heated
outdoor. **Leisure Activities:** whirlpool, exercise room. **Guest Services:** gift shop, valet laundry, airport transportation (fee)-
Tampa International Airport. **Business Services:** conference facilities, business center. **Cards:** AX, CB, DC, DS, JC, MC, VI.

SOME UNITS

[🔲] [▮▯] [🍸] [占M] [占] [⨀] [🔲] [🎥] [DATA PORT] [💻] / [⊠] [VCR] [🔲] [🔲] /
FEE   FEE FEE

(See map and index starting on p. 950)

LA QUINTA INN & SUITES TAMPA BAY
(U.S.F./NEAR BUSCH GARDENS)   *Book at aaa.com*   Phone: (813)910-7500   **5**

Small-scale Hotel

All Year   1P: $89-$119   XP: $7   F18

Location: I-275, exit 51, 2.2 mi e on SR 582. 3701 E Fowler 33612. Fax: 813/910-7600. **Facility:** 109 units. 105 one-bedroom standard units. 4 one-bedroom suites ($125-$155). 4 stories, interior corridors. *Bath:* combo or shower only. **Parking:** on-site. **Terms:** [ECP] meal plan available, small pets only. **Amenities:** video games (fee), high-speed Internet, dual phone lines, voice mail, irons, hair dryers. **Pool(s):** heated outdoor. **Leisure Activities:** whirlpool, exercise room. **Guest Services:** valet and coin laundry. **Business Services:** meeting rooms, fax. **Cards:** AX, CB, DC, DS, MC, VI. **Special Amenities:** free expanded continental breakfast and free local telephone calls. *(See color ad below)*

SOME UNITS

LA QUINTA INN TAMPA BAY (AIRPORT)   *Book at aaa.com*   Phone: (813)287-0440   **41**

Motel

2/1-4/30   1P: $115-$135   XP: $7   F18
12/1-1/31   1P: $89-$109   XP: $7   F18
5/1-11/30   1P: $79-$95   XP: $7   F18

Location: I-275, exit 40A, 0.7 mi w on Westshore Blvd; exit 39A, 1 mi n on Kennedy Blvd, 1.2 mi w on Westshore Blvd, then just s. 4730 Spruce St 33607-1497. Fax: 813/286-7399. **Facility:** 122 one-bedroom standard units. 2 stories, exterior corridors. **Parking:** on-site. **Terms:** [ECP] meal plan available, small pets only. **Amenities:** video games, high-speed Internet, voice mail, irons, hair dryers. **Guest Services:** valet laundry. **Business Services:** meeting rooms, fax. **Cards:** AX, CB, DC, DS, MC, VI. **Special Amenities:** free expanded continental breakfast and free local telephone calls. *(See color ad below)*

SOME UNITS

FEE   FEE FEE

LA QUINTA INN TAMPA SOUTH   *Book at aaa.com*   Phone: (813)835-6262   **70**

Small-scale Hotel

All Year [CP]   1P: $110-$130   2P: $120-$150   XP: $10   F16

Location: Just e of jct S West Shore Blvd. 4620 W Gandy Blvd 33611. Fax: 813/835-6888. **Facility:** 54 one-bedroom standard units, some with kitchens and/or whirlpools. 3 stories, interior corridors. *Bath:* combo or shower only. **Parking:** on-site. **Terms:** $1 service charge. **Amenities:** high-speed Internet, voice mail, safes (fee), irons, hair dryers. **Pool(s):** heated outdoor. **Leisure Activities:** exercise room. **Guest Services:** coin laundry. **Business Services:** meeting rooms. **Fee:** PC, fax. **Cards:** AX, DS, MC, VI.

SOME UNITS

(See map and index starting on p. 950)

MAINSAIL SUITES HOTEL & CONFERENCE CENTER *Book at aaa.com*

▼▼▼▼

Small-scale Hotel

1/1-4/30	1P: $149-$229	2P: $149-$229
10/1-11/30	1P: $139-$179	2P: $139-$179
12/1-12/31	1P: $129-$169	2P: $129-$169
5/1-9/30	1P: $119-$169	2P: $119-$169

Phone: (813)243-2600 **19**

Location: SR 589 (Veteran's Expwy), exit 4, just w on SR 580; main entrance on Hillsborough Ave. 5108 Eisenhower Blvd 33634. Fax: 813/243-2601. **Facility:** 360 units. 96 one- and 264 two-bedroom suites with kitchens. 3 stories (no elevator), exterior corridors. *Bath:* combo or shower only. **Parking:** on-site. **Terms:** package plans. **Amenities:** high-speed Internet, dual phone lines, voice mail, irons, hair dryers. *Some:* DVD players. **Pool(s):** heated outdoor. **Leisure Activities:** lighted tennis court, basketball, volleyball. *Fee:* personal trainers. **Guest Services:** sundries, valet and coin laundry, area transportation. **Business Services:** conference facilities, fax. **Cards:** AX, CB, DC, DS, JC, MC, VI. *(See color ad below)*

SOME UNITS
ASK ⎡SⒹ⎤ ✈ ❤ ⛶ ⛟ ⛼ ⎘ ⛱ ⛇ ✕ ❦ 🅟 🄳 🅿 ⎘ / ✕ ⎘ VCR /

MARRIOTT-TAMPA WESTSHORE *Book at aaa.com*

▼▼▼▼

Large-scale Hotel

1/1-5/15	1P: $299	2P: $299
9/1-11/30	1P: $249	2P: $249
5/16-8/31	1P: $229	2P: $229
12/1-12/31	1P: $219	2P: $219

Phone: (813)287-2555 **46**

Location: I-275, exit 40A, just w; exit 39A northbound, 1 mi n on Kennedy Blvd, then 0.9 mi w. 1001 N Westshore Blvd 33607. Fax: 813/289-5464. **Facility:** 310 one-bedroom standard units. 13 stories, interior corridors. *Bath:* combo or shower only. **Parking:** on-site. **Terms:** check-in 4 pm, cancellation fee imposed, [AP] meal plan available. **Amenities:** high-speed Internet (fee), dual phone lines, voice mail, irons, hair dryers. **Pool(s):** heated indoor/outdoor. **Leisure Activities:** saunas, whirlpool, exercise room. *Fee:* massage. **Guest Services:** gift shop, valet and coin laundry, area transportation. **Business Services:** conference facilities, business center. **Cards:** AX, CB, DC, DS, JC, MC, VI.

SOME UNITS
ASK ⎡SⒹ⎤ ✈ ❤ ⛶ ⛼ ⛇ ✕ ⎘ / ✕ 🅟 🄳 /

MICROTEL INN & SUITES *Book at aaa.com*

Ⓐ SAVE

▼▼▼▼

Small-scale Hotel

All Year	1P: $59-$109

Phone: (813)739-2244 **16**
XP: $10 F12

Location: I-275, exit 30B, 3.3 mi n on Dale Mabry Hwy, just w on Hillsborough Ave, then just n. 5405 N Church Ave 33614. Fax: 813/739-2250. **Facility:** 63 units. 40 one-bedroom standard units. 23 one-bedroom suites. 3 stories, interior corridors. *Bath:* combo or shower only. **Parking:** on-site. **Amenities:** voice mail, safes (fee), irons, hair dryers. **Pool(s):** outdoor. **Guest Services:** coin laundry. **Business Services:** meeting rooms, fax (fee). **Cards:** AX, DC, DS, MC, VI.

SOME UNITS
SⒹ ⎚ ⛶ ⛇ ⛼ ⛱ 🄳 / ✕ 🅟 🄳 🅿 /

MOTEL 6 #1192 *Book at aaa.com*

▼

Motel

2/4-4/16	1P: $39-$49	2P: $45-$55
12/1-2/3 & 4/17-11/30	1P: $36-$46	2P: $42-$52

Phone: 813/628-0888 **15**
XP: $3 F17
XP: $3 F17

Location: I-4, exit 6 westbound; exit 6B eastbound, 0.7 mi n. 6510 US 301 N 33610. Fax: 813/620-4899. **Facility:** 108 one-bedroom standard units. 3 stories, exterior corridors. *Bath:* combo or shower only. **Parking:** on-site. **Terms:** small pets only. **Pool(s):** heated outdoor. **Guest Services:** coin laundry. **Cards:** AX, CB, DC, DS, MC, VI.

SOME UNITS
SⒹ ⛺ ⛼ ⛱ ⛇ 🄳 / ✕ /

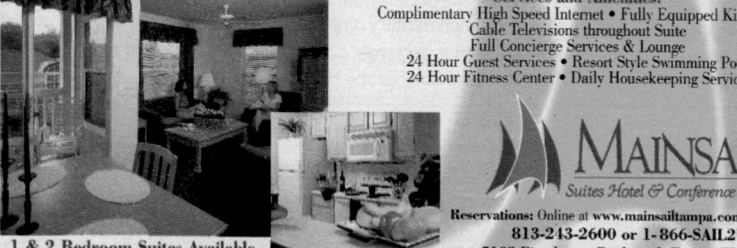

(See map and index starting on p. 950)

QUORUM HOTEL-TAMPA *Book at aaa.com* Phone: (813)289-8200 **51**

	1/1-4/12 & 9/11-11/30	1P: $129-$299	2P: $129-$299
	12/1-12/31	1P: $119-$269	2P: $119-$269
	4/13-9/10	1P: $109-$259	2P: $109-$259

Large-scale Hotel **Location:** I-275, exit 40A southbound; exit 39A northbound, 1 mi n on Kennedy Blvd, then 0.9 mi w. 700 N Westshore Blvd 33609. Fax: 813/227-4466. **Facility:** 272 units. 266 one-bedroom standard units. 6 one-bedroom suites ($249-$499). 11 stories, interior corridors. *Bath:* combo or shower only. **Parking:** on-site and valet. **Amenities:** CD players, dual phone lines, voice mail, irons, hair dryers. **Fee:** video games, high-speed Internet. **Pool(s):** outdoor. **Leisure Activities:** whirlpool, exercise room. **Guest Services:** gift shop, complimentary evening beverages: Mon-Fri, valet laundry, area transportation. **Business Services:** conference facilities, business center. **Cards:** AX, CB, DC, DS, MC, VI. *(See color ad below)*

SOME UNITS

(ASK) (S⬦) (📠) (🍴) (Ⓨ) (🎱) (💺) (🏊) (🐾) (DATA PORT) (🖥) / (✕) (🔒) /

RADISSON BAY HARBOR HOTEL *Book at aaa.com* Phone: (813)281-8900 **35**

	1/1-3/31	1P: $99-$199	2P: $99-$199	XP: $10	F
	4/1-5/31	1P: $89-$189	2P: $89-$189	XP: $10	F
	12/1-12/31 & 6/1-11/30	1P: $79-$179	2P: $79-$179	XP: $10	F

Large-scale Hotel **Location:** I-275, exit 39 southbound; exit 39B northbound, 3 mi w on SR 60. 7700 Courtney Campbell Cswy 33607. Fax: 813/281-0189. **Facility:** 257 units. 250 one-bedroom standard units. 7 one-bedroom suites. 6 stories, interior corridors. *Bath:* combo or shower only. **Parking:** on-site. **Terms:** cancellation fee imposed, package plans. **Amenities:** video games (fee), high-speed Internet, dual phone lines, voice mail, irons, hair dryers. *Some:* fax. **Dining:** 6:30 am-midnight, Fri & Sat 7 am-1 am, cocktails. **Pool(s):** heated outdoor. **Leisure Activities:** boat dock, fishing, exercise room. **Fee:** personal watercraft. **Guest Services:** gift shop, valet and coin laundry, area transportation-within 3 mi. **Business Services:** conference facilities, business center. **Cards:** AX, CB, DC, DS, MC, VI. **Special Amenities:** free newspaper and free room upgrade (subject to availability with advance reservations). *(See color ad below)*

SOME UNITS

(S⬦) (📠) (🍴) (Ⓨ) (🎱) (💺) (🏊) (✕) (🐾) (DATA PORT) (🖥) / (✕) (VCR) (🔒) /
FEE FEE

RED ROOF INN *Book at aaa.com* Phone: (813)932-0073 **13**

	1/29-4/2	1P: $55-$75	2P: $61-$75	XP: $6	F18
	1/1-1/28 & 4/3-11/30	1P: $43-$62	2P: $49-$62	XP: $6	F18
	12/1-12/31	1P: $38-$57	2P: $44-$57	XP: $6	F18

Motel **Location:** I-275, exit 50, 1.4 mi e on SR 580. 2307 E Busch Blvd 33612. Fax: 813/933-5689. **Facility:** 108 one-bedroom standard units. 2 stories, exterior corridors. **Parking:** on-site. **Terms:** small pets only. **Amenities:** video games, voice mail. *Some:* irons, hair dryers. **Pool(s):** outdoor. **Leisure Activities:** whirlpool. **Business Services:** fax. **Cards:** AX, CB, DC, DS, MC, VI.

SOME UNITS

(🐾) (🍴) (🐾) (🏊) (DATA PORT) / (✕) /

(See map and index starting on p. 950)

RED ROOF INN-FAIRGROUNDS   *Book at aaa.com*   Phone: (813)623-5245   21

▼▼▼▼
Motel

1/1-4/16	1P: $53-$79	2P: $53-$79
12/1-12/31	1P: $55-$70	2P: $55-$70
4/17-11/30	1P: $48-$57	2P: $48-$57

Location: I-4, exit 7 westbound; exit 7A eastbound, just se. 5001 N US 301 33610. Fax: 813/623-5240. **Facility:** 108 one-bedroom standard units. 2 stories, exterior corridors. *Bath:* combo or shower only. **Parking:** on-site. **Terms:** small pets only. **Amenities:** video games (fee), voice mail. *Some:* irons, hair dryers. **Business Services:** fax. **Cards:** AX, CB, DC, DS, MC, VI.

SOME UNITS

🛏️ 📶 📷 🎦 DATA PORT / ✕ 🖥️ 🖨️ /

RENAISSANCE TAMPA HOTEL INTERNATIONAL
    PLAZA   *Book at aaa.com*   Phone: (813)877-9200   37

AAA SAVE
▼▼▼▼
Large-scale Hotel

1/16-5/16	1P: $161-$294	2P: $161-$294
12/1-1/15	1P: $142-$275	2P: $142-$275
5/17-11/30	1P: $113-$218	2P: $113-$218

Location: At International Plaza. 4200 Jim Walter Blvd 33607. Fax: 813/877-3000. **Facility:** A world away from the norm at this property with elegantly decorated rooms and public areas that feel like a Spanish courtyard or a Cuban palazzo. 293 units. 289 one-bedroom standard units. 4 one-bedroom suites, some with whirlpools. 8 stories, interior corridors. *Bath:* combo or shower only. **Parking:** on-site (fee) and valet. **Terms:** check-in 4 pm. **Amenities:** CD players, dual phone lines, voice mail, safes, irons, hair dryers. *Fee:* video games, high-speed Internet. *Some:* DVD players. **Dining:** 21 restaurants, 6 am-11 pm, cocktails, also, Pelagia Trattoria, see separate listing. **Pool(s):** heated outdoor. **Leisure Activities:** whirlpool, exercise room. *Fee:* massage. **Guest Services:** gift shop, valet laundry, area transportation-within 2 mi, beauty salon. **Business Services:** conference facilities, business center. **Cards:** AX, DC, MC, VI. *(See color ad below)*

SOME UNITS

✈️ 🍴 24↑ 🍸 🏋️ 🏊 ✕ 🎦 DATA PORT 🖥️ / ✕ VCR 🖨️ /

RESIDENCE INN BY MARRIOTT SABAL PARK   *Book at aaa.com*   Phone: (813)627-8855   27

▼▼▼
Small-scale Hotel

1/9-11/30	1P: $144-$149	2P: $144-$149
12/1-1/8	1P: $114-$119	2P: $114-$119

Location: I-75, exit 260 southbound; exit 260B northbound, just w on SR 574 (Dr. Martin Luther King Jr Blvd), just s on Falkenburg Rd, then 0.4 mi w; in Sabal Corporate Center. 9719 Princess Palm Ave 33619. Fax: 813/627-8899. **Facility:** 102 units. 42 one-bedroom standard units with kitchens. 42 one- and 18 two-bedroom suites with kitchens. 3 stories, interior corridors. *Bath:* combo or shower only. **Parking:** on-site. **Terms:** small pets only ($125 fee). **Amenities:** high-speed Internet, dual phone lines, voice mail, irons, hair dryers. **Pool(s):** heated outdoor. **Leisure Activities:** whirlpool, exercise room, sports court, volleyball. **Guest Services:** complimentary evening beverages: Mon-Thurs, valet and coin laundry. **Business Services:** meeting rooms, fax. **Cards:** AX, CB, DC, DS, JC, MC, VI.

SOME UNITS

ASK S/D 🛏️ 🍴 📶 📷 🏊 ✕ 🎦 DATA PORT 🖨️ 🖥️ 🖥️ / ✕ VCR /
        FEE

(See map and index starting on p. 950)

SAILPORT WATERFRONT RESORT   *Book at aaa.com*   Phone: (813)281-9599   **38**

♦♦ ♦♦

Condominium

All Year   1P: $86-$149   2P: $86-$149
Location: I-275, exit 39 southbound; exit 39B northbound, 3 mi w on SR 60, then just s. 2506 Rocky Point Dr 33607. Fax: 813/281-9510. **Facility:** Designated smoking area. 211 units. 188 one- and 23 two-bedroom suites ($86-$149) with kitchens. 4 stories, interior/exterior corridors. **Parking:** on-site. **Terms:** 3 day cancellation notice, [CP] meal plan available, package plans. **Amenities:** video library, CD players, high-speed Internet, voice mail, irons, hair dryers. **Pool(s):** heated outdoor. **Leisure Activities:** fishing, lighted tennis court. **Guest Services:** sundries, valet and coin laundry, area transportation (fee). **Business Services:** meeting rooms, administrative services, fax (fee). **Cards:** AX, CB, DC, DS, JC, MC, VI.

(ASK) (SD) ✈ (†¶) 🏊 (†+) ✕ (VCR) ✤ (DATA PORT) 🛏 🖨

SHERATON SUITES TAMPA AIRPORT   *Book at aaa.com*   Phone: (813)873-8675   **50**

(AAA) (SAVE)

♦♦♦♦

Large-scale Hotel

All Year   1P: $285   2P: $285
Location: I-275, exit 40B, n to Cypress St, then 0.3 mi w. 4400 W Cypress St 33607. Fax: 813/877-6766. **Facility:** 260 one-bedroom suites. 8 stories, interior corridors. *Bath:* combo or shower only. **Parking:** on-site. **Terms:** cancellation fee imposed, package plans. **Amenities:** CD players, high-speed Internet (fee), dual phone lines, voice mail, irons, hair dryers. **Dining:** 6 am-10 pm, Sat from 7 am, cocktails. **Pool(s):** heated indoor. **Leisure Activities:** sauna, whirlpool, exercise room. **Guest Services:** gift shop, valet and coin laundry, airport transportation-Tampa International Airport, area transportation-within 3 mi. **Business Services:** conference facilities, business center. **Cards:** AX, CB, DC, DS, JC, MC, VI. **Special Amenities:** free newspaper. (See color ad p 8)

SOME UNITS

(SD) ✈ 🐑 (†) (†¶) ✤ (𝄞) 🏊 ✕ ✤ (DATA PORT) 🛏 🖨 🖵 /✕/

SPRINGHILL SUITES BY MARRIOTT TAMPA/WESTSHORE   *Book at aaa.com*   Phone: (813)639-9600   **47**

(AAA) (SAVE)

♦♦♦

Small-scale Hotel

12/26-4/30   1P: $159-$179   2P: $159-$179
5/1-11/30   1P: $135-$159   2P: $135-$159
12/1-12/25   1P: $105-$135   2P: $105-$135
Location: I-275, exit 40A, just n on Westshore Blvd, then just w; exit 39A, 1 mi e on Kennedy Blvd, 0.9 mi n on Westshore Blvd, then just w. 4835 W Cypress St 33607. Fax: 813/639-9700. **Facility:** 149 one-bedroom suites. 6 stories, interior corridors. *Bath:* combo or shower only. **Parking:** on-site. **Terms:** [ECP] meal plan available. **Amenities:** video games (fee), high-speed Internet, dual phone lines, voice mail, irons, hair dryers. **Pool(s):** heated outdoor. **Leisure Activities:** whirlpool, exercise room. **Guest Services:** valet and coin laundry, airport transportation-Tampa International Airport. **Business Services:** meeting rooms, business center. **Cards:** AX, CB, DC, DS, JC, MC, VI. **Special Amenities:** free expanded continental breakfast and free local telephone calls. (See color ad below)

SOME UNITS

(SD) ✈ (†¶) (𝄞M) ✤ (𝄞) 🏊 ✤ (DATA PORT) 🛏 🖨 🖵 /✕/

TAHITIAN INN   *Book at aaa.com*   Phone: (813)877-6721   **65**

(AAA) (SAVE)

♦♦♦

Motel

1/1-4/30   1P: $119-$219   2P: $119-$219
12/1-12/31 & 5/1-11/30   1P: $109-$199   2P: $109-$199
Location: I-275, exit 41A, 1.1 mi s. 601 S Dale Mabry Hwy 33609. Fax: 813/877-6218. **Facility:** 80 units. 72 one-bedroom standard units. 8 one-bedroom suites ($159-$209). 2-3 stories, interior/exterior corridors. *Bath:* combo or shower only. **Parking:** on-site. **Terms:** weekly rates available, package plans, pets ($25 extra charge, in designated units). **Amenities:** high-speed Internet, voice mail, irons, hair dryers. *Some:* DVD players, CD players. **Dining:** 7 am-10 pm, Sun-3 pm, cocktails. **Pool(s):** heated outdoor. **Leisure Activities:** barbecue grill, exercise room, spa. **Guest Services:** coin laundry. **Business Services:** meeting rooms, business center. **Cards:** AX, DC, DS, MC, VI. **Special Amenities:** free local telephone calls and early check-in/late check-out.

SOME UNITS

(SD) 🐑 (†¶) 🏊 ✕ ✤ (DATA PORT) 🛏 🖨 🖵 /✕/ (VCR)
FEE

TAMPA AIRPORT MARRIOTT   *Book at aaa.com*   Phone: (813)879-5151   **26**

♦♦♦

Large-scale Hotel

12/1-5/13   1P: $319-$349   2P: $329-$359   XP: $10   F18
9/10-11/30   1P: $239-$269   2P: $249-$279   XP: $10   F18
5/14-9/9   1P: $199-$269   2P: $209-$279   XP: $10   F18
Location: I-275, exit 39 southbound; exit 39B northbound, 2 mi w on SR 60. Tampa International Airport 33607. Fax: 813/873-0945. **Facility:** 296 units. 292 one-bedroom standard units. 4 one-bedroom suites. 8 stories, interior corridors. *Bath:* combo or shower only. **Parking:** on-site and valet. **Terms:** package plans. **Amenities:** high-speed Internet (fee), dual phone lines, voice mail, irons, hair dryers. *Some:* video games (fee). **Dining:** Cafe' Elise, CK's Restaurant, see separate listings. **Pool(s):** heated outdoor. **Leisure Activities:** exercise room. *Fee:* massage. **Guest Services:** gift shop, valet and coin laundry. **Business Services:** conference facilities, business center. **Cards:** AX, DC, DS, MC, VI.

SOME UNITS

(ASK) ✈ (†) (24†) (Y) (𝄞M) 🏊 ✤ (DATA PORT) 🖵 /✕/

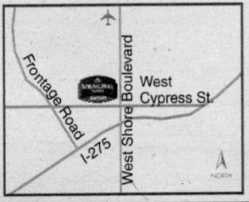

(See map and index starting on p. 950)

TAMPA MARRIOTT WATERSIDE HOTEL & MARINA   *Book at aaa.com*   **Phone:** 813/221-4900   64

Property failed to provide current rates

Large-scale Hotel

Location: I-275, exit 44 (downtown), 2.2 mi e on Ashley Dr to Platt/Channelside Dr, then just n. Located opposite the convention center. 700 S Florida Ave 33602. Fax: 813/221-0923. **Facility:** 717 units. 698 one-bedroom standard units. 19 one-bedroom suites, some with whirlpools. 27 stories, interior corridors. *Bath:* combo or shower only. **Parking:** valet. **Terms:** check-in 4 pm. **Amenities:** dual phone lines, voice mail, safes, irons, hair dryers. *Fee:* video games, high-speed Internet. **Pool(s):** heated outdoor. **Leisure Activities:** saunas, whirlpool, boat dock, spa. **Guest Services:** gift shop, valet and coin laundry, area transportation (fee), beauty salon. **Business Services:** conference facilities, business center.

SOME UNITS

TAMPA RIVERWALK HOTEL   *Book at aaa.com*   **Phone:** (813)223-2222   58

1/1-4/10 [CP]	1P: $159-$219	2P: $159-$219	XP: $10	F17
9/11-11/30 [CP]	1P: $149-$219	2P: $149-$219	XP: $10	F17
4/11-9/10 [CP]	1P: $139-$219	2P: $139-$219	XP: $10	F17
12/1-12/31 [CP]	1P: $119-$219	2P: $119-$219	XP: $10	F17

Large-scale Hotel

Location: I-275, exit 44, 0.8 mi s; downtown. 200 N Ashley Dr 33602. Fax: 813/273-0839. **Facility:** 282 units. 277 one-bedroom standard units. 5 one-bedroom suites ($295-$450). 6 stories, interior corridors. **Parking:** valet. **Terms:** 3 day cancellation notice, [AP], [BP], [ECP] & [MAP] meal plans available, package plans. **Amenities:** video games (fee), dual phone lines, voice mail, irons, hair dryers. **Pool(s):** outdoor. **Leisure Activities:** sauna, boat dock, exercise room. *Fee:* charter fishing, massage. **Guest Services:** gift shop, valet and coin laundry, area transportation. **Business Services:** conference facilities. **Cards:** AX, DC, DS, JC, MC, VI.

SOME UNITS

WINGATE INN-TAMPA NORTH   *Book at aaa.com*   **Phone:** (813)971-7676   58

All Year [BP]	1P: $89-$199	2P: $89-$199	XP: $10 F16

Small-scale Hotel

Location: I-75, exit 270, just n on CR 581 (Bruce B Downs Blvd). 17301 Dona Michelle Dr 33647. Fax: 813/910-0950. **Facility:** 85 units. 82 one-bedroom standard units. 3 one-bedroom suites ($109-$299) with whirlpools. 4 stories, interior corridors. *Bath:* combo or shower only. **Parking:** on-site. **Amenities:** video games (fee), high-speed Internet, dual phone lines, voice mail, safes, irons, hair dryers. **Pool(s):** outdoor. **Leisure Activities:** whirlpool, exercise room. *Fee:* spa privileges. **Guest Services:** complimentary evening beverages: Mon-Thurs, valet and coin laundry, area transportation. **Business Services:** meeting rooms, business center. **Cards:** AX, CB, DC, DS, JC, MC, VI.

SOME UNITS

WINGATE INN-USF NEAR BUSCH GARDENS   *Book at aaa.com*   **Phone:** (813)979-2828   4

All Year	1P: $116-$125	2P: $116-$125	XP: $10 F17

Small-scale Hotel

Location: I-275, exit 51, 2.2 mi e on SR 582. 3751 E Fowler Ave 33612. Fax: 813/977-1818. **Facility:** 85 units. 82 one-bedroom standard units. 3 one-bedroom suites with whirlpools. 4 stories, interior corridors. *Bath:* combo or shower only. **Parking:** on-site. **Terms:** [BP] & [ECP] meal plans available, pets ($40 extra charge, 1st floor units). **Amenities:** video games (fee), high-speed Internet, dual phone lines, voice mail, safes, irons, hair dryers. **Pool(s):** outdoor. **Leisure Activities:** whirlpool, picnic area, exercise room. **Guest Services:** valet and coin laundry, area transportation-within 5 mi. **Business Services:** meeting rooms, business center. **Cards:** AX, CB, DC, DS, JC, MC, VI. **Special Amenities:** free full breakfast and free local telephone calls.

SOME UNITS

WYNDHAM HARBOUR ISLAND   *Book at aaa.com*   **Phone:** (813)229-5000   66

1/1-4/30 & 10/1-11/30	1P: $189-$269	2P: $189-$289	XP: $20 F17
5/1-9/30	1P: $159-$219	2P: $159-$239	XP: $20 F17
12/1-12/31	1P: $149-$199	2P: $149-$219	XP: $20 F17

Large-scale Hotel

Location: I-275, exit 44, just e, then 2 mi s on Tampa St, follow signs to Convention Center and Harbour Island. Located in an upscale office/commercial area. 725 S Harbour Island Blvd 33602. Fax: 813/229-5322. **Facility:** 299 units. 279 one-bedroom standard units. 20 one-bedroom suites ($199-$300). 12 stories, interior corridors. *Bath:* combo or shower only. **Parking:** on-site (fee) and valet. **Amenities:** dual phone lines, voice mail, honor bars, irons, hair dryers. *Fee:* video games, high-speed Internet. *Some:* CD players. **Dining:** 2 restaurants, 6:30 am-11 pm, cocktails. **Pool(s):** heated outdoor. **Leisure Activities:** exercise room. *Fee:* boat dock, charter fishing, massage, spa privileges. **Guest Services:** gift shop, valet laundry, airport transportation-Tampa International Airport, area transportation-within 5 mi. **Business Services:** conference facilities, business center. **Cards:** AX, CB, DC, DS, JC, MC, VI.

SOME UNITS

WYNDHAM WESTSHORE-TAMPA   *Book at aaa.com*   **Phone:** (813)286-4400   61

1/1-4/30	1P: $169-$289	2P: $189-$309	XP: $20 F17
9/11-11/30	1P: $149-$249	2P: $169-$269	XP: $20 F17
5/1-9/10	1P: $139-$219	2P: $159-$239	XP: $20 F17
12/1-12/31	1P: $125-$215	2P: $145-$235	XP: $20 F17

Large-scale Hotel

Location: I-275, exit 40A, 0.5 mi s; jct SR 60 and Westshore Blvd. 4860 W Kennedy Blvd 33609-2591. Fax: 813/286-4053. **Facility:** 322 units. 320 one-bedroom standard units. 2 one-bedroom suites ($175-$439). 11 stories, interior corridors. **Parking:** on-site and valet. **Terms:** pets ($50 extra charge). **Amenities:** dual phone lines, voice mail, irons, hair dryers. *Fee:* video games, high-speed Internet. *Some:* CD players. **Dining:** Shula's Steakhouse, see separate listing. **Pool(s):** heated outdoor. **Leisure Activities:** exercise room. *Fee:* massage. **Guest Services:** gift shop, valet laundry, area transportation. **Business Services:** conference facilities, business center. **Cards:** AX, DC, DS, MC, VI.

SOME UNITS

(See map and index starting on p. 950)

——— WHERE TO DINE ———

42ND STREET THE BISTRO
American

Lunch: $7-$18   **Dinner:** $7-$18   **Phone:** 813/253-0042   (112)
Location: I-275, exit 42, 1 mi s on Armenia Ave, just e on Azeele, then 0.6 mi s. 516 S Howard Ave 33606.
Hours: 11:30 am-11 pm, Tues & Wed-midnight, Thurs & Fri-1 am, Sat noon-1 am. Closed major holidays; also Sun. **Features:** A New York Broadway theme and city library appearance give life to the trendy, upscale establishment. The well-thought-out menu offers "show stoppers," gourmet pizza, salad and a variety of flavorful entrees. Casual dress; cocktails. **Parking:** on-site. **Cards:** AX, DC, DS, MC, VI.

717 SOUTH
Italian

Lunch: $8-$12   **Dinner:** $15-$27   **Phone:** 813/250-1661   (117)
Location: I-275, exit 42, 1 mi son Armenia Ave, just e on Azeele, then 0.5 mi s. 717 S Howard Ave 33606.
Hours: 11:30 am-2:30 & 5-10 pm, Sat from 5 pm. Closed: Sun. **Features:** This upscale eatery is located in the SoHo district and offers both Italian food and culinary themes from the Pacific Rim. Items such as espresso seared sirloin, veal and wild mushroom meat loaf, miso and sake cured catch of the day and smoked duck breast are but a few of the tasty offerings found on the extensive menu. The surroundings are very inviting with an art deco flair and the service staff is professional and knowledgeable. Casual dress; cocktails. **Parking:** on-site. **Cards:** MC, VI.

ARIGATO JAPANESE STEAK HOUSE
Japanese

Dinner: $10-$22   **Phone:** 813/960-5050   (9)
Location: On US 92, just w of jct Fletcher Ave. 13755 N Dale Mabry Hwy 33618. **Hours:** 5 pm-10 pm, Sun 4 pm-9 pm. Closed major holidays; also 12/24. **Features:** Traditional floor seating lends an air of authenticity as diners enjoy the showmanship of professional tableside chefs. Expect a wait for group seating, but Japanese entrees—such as ichiban, a spicy mix of shrimp, chicken and beef—are well worth it. Casual dress; cocktails. **Parking:** on-site. **Cards:** AX, DC, DS, MC, VI.

ARMANI'S
Northern Italian

Dinner: $23-$37   **Phone:** 813/207-6800   (46)
Location: SR 60, east end of Courtney Campbell Cswy; in Grand Hyatt Tampa Bay; on the 14th Floor. 2900 Bayport Dr 33607. **Hours:** 5:30 pm-9:30 pm, Fri & Sat-10:30 pm. Closed: 12/25; also Sun. **Reservations:** required.
Features: Overlooking Old Tampa Bay, the romantic, upscale Italian restaurant is on the top floor of the hotel. Veal is the house specialty. Diners can order antipasto directly from the chef or let the waiter help. Depending on the night and the clientele, the restaurant can be bustling. Service is always prompt, and servers efficient and well-mannered. Some selections are prepared tableside. Servers are more than willing to have valet claim checks validated. Dressy casual; cocktails; entertainment. **Parking:** on-site and valet. **Cards:** AX, CB, DC, DS, JC, MC, VI.

BAHAMA BREEZE
Caribbean

Lunch: $9-$20   **Dinner:** $10-$24   **Phone:** 813/289-7922   (42)
Location: Just n of jct SR 60; in Rocky Point Harbor. 3045 N Rocky Point Dr E 33607. **Hours:** 11 am-11:30 pm, Fri & Sat-1:30 am. Closed: 11/23, 12/25. **Features:** Patrons of the popular restaurant are enveloped in a tropical, festive setting with a Caribbean feel. Known for its fun atmosphere, this place offers great Caribbean-themed dishes, such as Jamaican jerk pork, Bahamian kebabs and the well-loved Trinidad seafood pasta. Casual dress; cocktails. **Parking:** on-site. **Cards:** AX, CB, DC, DS, MC, VI.

BALLY HOO GRILL
American

Lunch: $8-$20   **Dinner:** $8-$20   **Phone:** 813/926-2149   (7)
Location: Veteran's Hwy (SR 589), exit 10, 0.4 mi w at jct Gunn Hwy. 7604 Ehrlich Rd 33634. **Hours:** 11 am-10 pm, Fri & Sat-11 pm. Closed: 1/1, 11/23, 12/25. **Features:** Guests can unwind in the casual nautical setting and sample fresh, tasty food. Choices include oak-grilled delights, as well as Cajun, steamed and fried goodies. Casual dress; cocktails. **Parking:** on-site. **Cards:** MC, VI.

THE BAMBOO CLUB
Pacific Rim

Lunch: $8-$23   **Dinner:** $8-$23   **Phone:** 813/353-0326   (50)
Location: I-275, exit 21 southbound; exit 20A northbound; 0.9 mi w on West Shore Blvd; in International Plaza and Bay Street. 2223 N West Shore Blvd, B-212 33607. **Hours:** 11:30 am-11 pm, Fri & Sat-midnight, Sun noon-9 pm. Closed: 11/23, 12/25. **Reservations:** accepted. **Features:** Touches of the jungle lend character to the trendy, upscale dining room, where patrons mingle over plates of Pacific Rim, Asian and Far Eastern cuisine. Portions are abundant, so guests should arrive hungry. Casual dress; cocktails. **Parking:** on-site. **Cards:** AX, DC, DS, MC, VI.

BARLEY HOPPERS INTERNATIONAL ALEHOUSE & GRILL
American

Lunch: $7-$20   **Dinner:** $7-$20   **Phone:** 813/242-6680   (65)
Location: I-4, exit 1, just s to 8th Ave, then just w to Centro Ybor; in Ybor City. 1600 E 8th Ave, Suite E200 33605. **Hours:** 11:30 am-10 pm, Fri & Sat-11 pm, Sun noon-4 pm. Closed: 11/23, 12/25. **Features:** On the second floor of the popular Centro Ybor complex, the lively restaurant invites diners to unwind on the patio, which overlooks the complex, or in the busy dining room, where they can watch programming on TV monitors around the room. Representative of basic fare are various sandwiches, salads, appetizers and the popular ribs. Casual dress; cocktails. **Parking:** on-site (fee). **Cards:** AX, MC, VI.

BAY CAFE
American

Lunch: $8-$13   **Dinner:** $10-$20   **Phone:** 813/875-1555   (82)
Location: I-275, exit 40A southbound, just e; exit 39A northbound, 1 mi n on Kennedy Blvd, then 0.5 mi w; in Embassy Suites Hotel-Tampa/Airport/Westshore. 555 N Westshore Blvd 33609. **Hours:** 11:30 am-2 & 5-10 pm. **Reservations:** suggested, weekends. **Features:** An extensive menu offers many choices from such favorites as surf and turf to chicken and shrimp with pasta. Fresh flowers on every table and contemporary paintings contribute to the tropical theme, with mahogany wood. The atrium is a delightful dining getaway. Casual dress; cocktails. **Parking:** on-site. **Cards:** AX, CB, DC, DS, MC, VI.

(See map and index starting on p. 950)

BEEF 'O' BRADY'S
American

Lunch: $6-$9   **Dinner:** $6-$9   **Phone:** 813/910-7705   ④
Location: I-75, exit 266, 3.8 mi w on Fletcher, 0.5 mi n on Bruce B. Downs, then just w. 2802 E Bearss Ave 33613. **Hours:** 10 am-11 pm. **Features:** The restaurant is a fun dining spot, especially for those who enjoy watching sports. Monitors placed strategically around the dining room show varied events at any given time. Most entrees are of the sandwich and finger-food variety. Grilled grouper salad is a must-try, as are the chicken wings for which this place is known. Casual dress; cocktails. **Parking:** on-site. **Cards:** MC, VI. &M

BERNINI
Italian

Lunch: $7-$18   **Dinner:** $10-$25   **Phone:** 813/248-0099   ⑥⑧
Location: Jct 17th St; in Ybor City. 1702 E 7th Ave 33607. **Hours:** 11:30 am-10 pm, Thurs & Fri-11:30 pm, Sat & Sun 4 pm-10 pm. **Features:** The casually upscale restaurant features examples of fine and innovative Italian cuisine, such as carpaccio of salmon, crispy duck with a balsamic glaze finish and Caribbean stuffed lobster. Dessert choices are plentiful. Casual dress; cocktails. **Parking:** street. **Cards:** MC, VI. Y

BERN'S STEAK HOUSE
Steak House

Dinner: $23-$40   **Phone:** 813/251-2421   ⑫④
Location: I-275, exit 42, 1 mi s on Armenia Ave, just e on Azeele, then 0.8 mi s, under overpass. 1208 S Howard Ave 33606. **Hours:** 5 pm-10:30 pm, Fri & Sat-11 pm. Closed: 9/4, 12/25. **Reservations:** suggested. **Features:** A local landmark, it is renowned for its beef entrees. Guests are invited to tour the kitchen and wine cellar before dinner. A comprehensive wine list and a separate dessert lounge make the visit enjoyable. A 12% gratuity is added in the dining room. Dressy casual; cocktails. **Parking:** valet. **Cards:** AX, CB, DC, DS, MC, VI. Y

BIG CITY TAVERN
Italian

Dinner: $11-$29   **Phone:** 813/247-3000   ⑥④
Location: I-4, exit 1, just s to 8th Ave, just w; at Centro Ybor; in Ybor City. 1600 E 8th Ave, Suite C201 33605. **Hours:** 5 pm-10 pm, Wed & Thurs-11 pm, Fri & Sat-midnight. Closed: 11/23, 12/25. **Features:** On the second level of the Centro Ybor complex, the trendy, upscale establishment prepares such menu offerings as roasted salmon, veal saltimbocca and grilled tuna with sushi handroll. Presentations are outstanding. Dressy casual; beer & wine only. **Parking:** on-site (fee). **Cards:** AX, MC, VI. &M

BONEFISH GRILL
Seafood

Dinner: $15-$22   **Phone:** 813/876-3535   ⑪⑧
Location: I-275, exit 41A, 1.4 mi sw on US 92 (Dale Mabry Hwy); just n at jct W Inman/W Lykes Ave. 3665 Henderson Blvd 33609. **Hours:** 4 pm-10:30 pm, Fri & Sat-11:30 pm, Sun-10 pm. **Features:** The dining experience is casual yet upscale. Patrons settle into inviting surroundings as the professional service staff meets their needs. Although this place is known for its grilled fish, such as Atlantic salmon and Chilean sea bass, it also prepares such specialties as tenderloin portabella piccata, fontina chops, chicken Marsala and varied steak and pasta dishes. Casual dress; cocktails. **Parking:** on-site and valet. **Cards:** AX, DC, DS, MC, VI. &M Y

BROCATO'S SANDWICH SHOP

Deli/Subs
Sandwiches

Lunch: $5-$8   **Phone:** 813/248-9977   ④⑤
Location: I-4, exit 3, just n on 50th St. 5021 E Columbus Dr 33619. **Hours:** 8 am-5 pm, Sat-3 pm. Closed: Sun. **Features:** Established in 1948, the local favorite has been family-owned-and-operated since its opening. Among offerings are various homemade soups, salads and sandwiches. The Cuban sandwich, deviled crab and fried plantains are popular dishes. Casual dress. **Parking:** on-site. **Cards:** MC, VI.

BUCA DI BEPPO
Italian

Dinner: $20-$28   **Phone:** 813/962-6673   ②⑤
Location: On US 92, 0.5 mi s of jct Fletcher Ave. 11511 N Dale Mabry Hwy 33618. **Hours:** 4 pm-10 pm, Fri-11 pm, Sat noon-11 pm. Closed: 12/25. **Features:** Patrons should come with hearty appetites to savor giant portions of fabulous Southern Italian cuisine. This place is noted for "Neapolitan pizzas as big as bathmats," as well as other well-known dishes. The decor is eclectic. Casual dress; cocktails. **Parking:** on-site. **Cards:** MC, VI. &M Y

BUSCH'S FAMILY SPORTS BAR & GRILL
American

Dinner: $9-$17   **Phone:** 813/935-4535   ②⑨
Location: Jct N 30th St. 2920 E Busch Blvd 33612. **Hours:** 4 pm-9 pm, Fri & Sat-10 pm. Closed major holidays. **Features:** Casual is the mode at this sports-themed restaurant. The menu lists such goodies as buffalo wings to start and burgers and sandwiches as main courses. Guests can watch a sporting event on one of the strategically placed television monitors. Casual dress; cocktails. **Parking:** on-site. **Cards:** AX, DC, MC, VI. Y

CAFE' ELISE
American

Lunch: $7-$18   **Phone:** 813/998-3706   ④①
Location: I-275, exit 39 southbound; exit 39B northbound, 2 mi w on SR 60; on lobby level of Tampa Airport Marriott. Tampa International Airport 33607. **Hours:** 6 am-2 pm. **Reservations:** accepted. **Features:** On the lobby level of the Tampa Airport Marriott, the restaurant is convenient to the terminals. Diners can relax in a pleasant setting and savor well-prepared dishes. Casual dress; cocktails. **Parking:** on-site (fee) and valet. **Cards:** AX, CB, DC, DS, JC, MC, VI. &M Y

CAFE EUROPEAN
Continental

Lunch: $7-$8   **Dinner:** $10-$19   **Phone:** 813/254-9458   ⑧⑧
Location: Just s of jct Kennedy Blvd (SR 60); opposite entrance to University of Tampa. 113 Hyde Park Ave 33606. **Hours:** 11 am-2 & 5:30-9 pm, Fri-11 pm, Sat 5:30 pm-11 pm. Closed: 4/16, 12/25; also Sun. **Reservations:** suggested. **Features:** This family-operated restaurant dedicates itself to preparing traditional foods with a European flair. Good, basic meals in a pleasant cafe setting include delicious fish and chips served hot and fast. Kids may choose from an available children's menu. Casual dress; beer & wine only. **Parking:** street. **Cards:** AX, MC, VI.

(See map and index starting on p. 950)

CAFFE PARADISO

Dinner: $8-$24   **Phone:** 813/835-6622   [129]

Northern Italian

Location: 0.5 mi w of jct W Gandy Blvd; in St. Croix's Plaza. 4205 S MacDill 33611. **Hours:** 5:30 pm-10:30 pm. Closed major holidays; also Sun. **Features:** Elegant, chic and intimate, this ristorante is the place to go on special occasions. You will find traditional appetizers, whole or half orders of pasta, red snapper and veal piccata, all nicely done and expertly served by a trained and cordial staff. Dressy casual; cocktails. **Parking:** on-site. **Cards:** AX, CB, DC, DS, MC, VI.

CARMINE'S

Lunch: $8-$12   **Dinner:** $8-$12   **Phone:** 813/248-3834   [69]

Spanish

Location: I-4, exit 1, just s to 7th Ave, then just w; in Ybor City. 1802 7th Ave 33605. **Hours:** 11 am-11 pm, Fri & Sat-midnight, Sun & Mon-6 pm. **Features:** On the main drag in Ybor City, the restaurant presents an extensive menu of Cuban and Spanish fare. The atmosphere is casual, and the service is friendly. Casual dress. **Parking:** street. **Cards:** MC, VI.

THE CASTAWAY

Lunch: $6-$12   **Dinner:** $11-$20   **Phone:** 813/281-0770   [43]

Seafood

Location: I-275, exit 39A northbound; exit 39 southbound, 3.3 mi w on SR 60. 7720 Courtney Campbell Cswy 33607. **Hours:** 11 am-10:30 pm, Sun 9:30 am-2:30 & 5-10 pm. **Features:** Bright Caribbean decor enlivens the breezy, bayfront setting. The Thai-style whole snapper, drenched in a spicy yet sweet chili sauce and served with a head and tail, gets your taste buds jumping. The rich tiramisu settles them back down. Casual dress; cocktails. **Parking:** on-site. **Cards:** AX, CB, DC, DS, MC, VI.

CEVICHE'

Dinner: $18-$31   **Phone:** 813/250-0203   [126]

Spanish

Location: Jct S Howard Ave; in Soho District; in Bayshore Royal Condominium Building, lower level. 2109 Bayshore Blvd 33629. **Hours:** 5 pm-midnight, Fri & Sat-2 am, Sun & Mon-10 pm. Closed major holidays. **Features:** On the menu are some 45 offerings of tapas frias or tapas calientes, as well as paella, prime New York strip and many desserts. Casual dress; cocktails. **Parking:** street. **Cards:** AX, MC, VI.

CHAMPPS RESTAURANT & BAR

Lunch: $5-$18   **Dinner:** $5-$18   **Phone:** 813/353-0200   [53]

American

Location: I-275, exit 40A southbound; exit 39A northbound; 0.9 mi w on Westshore Blvd; in International Plaza and Bay Street. 2223 N Westshore Blvd, #B221 33607. **Hours:** 11 am-10 pm, Fri & Sat-1 am, Sun-midnight. **Features:** Guests often stop at the casual eatery after a long shopping day for a little fun while they dine. Sporting events are shown on strategically placed television monitors. Such items as chicken chopsticks, walnut-crusted chicken, baby back ribs, grilled fajitas, French onion soup and grilled cobb salad find space on the varied menu. Casual dress; cocktails. **Parking:** on-site. **Cards:** MC, VI.

CHARLEY'S STEAKHOUSE

Dinner: $15-$40   **Phone:** 813/353-9706   [80]

Steak House

Location: I-275, exit 40A southbound; exit 39A northbound, just w on Westshore Blvd, then just n; in Doubletree Hotel Tampa Airport-Westshore. 4444 W Cypress St 33607. **Hours:** 5 pm-10 pm, Sat & Sun-11 pm. Closed: 11/23, 12/25; also Super Bowl Sun. **Features:** Patrons can treat themselves to mouthwatering filet mignon or a 32-ounce lobster. The steakhouse has a fine-dining flair. Although the prices can be a bit steep, they're worth it for the exceptional food and service. Dressy casual; cocktails. **Parking:** on-site and valet. **Cards:** AX, MC, VI.

THE CHEESECAKE FACTORY

Lunch: $8-$25   **Dinner:** $8-$25   **Phone:** 813/353-4200   [54]

American

Location: I-275, exit 40A southbound; exit 39A northbound, 0.9 mi w; in International Plaza and Bay Street. 2223 N Westshore Blvd 33607. **Hours:** 11 am-11 pm, Fri & Sat-12:30 am, Sun 10 am-11 pm. Closed: 11/23, 12/25. **Features:** In the trendy Bay Street area of restaurants at International Plaza is this nifty and popular place, which is known, fittingly, for its fabulous cheesecakes. The extensive multipage menu lists items to satisfy nearly any palate. Casual dress; cocktails. **Parking:** on-site and valet. **Cards:** MC, VI.

CHERRY'S

Lunch: $6-$14   **Dinner:** $6-$14   **Phone:** 813/685-3465   [103]

American

Location: I-75, exit 257, 0.4 mi w on SR 60; in Brandon Crossings. 10033 E Adamo Dr 33619. **Hours:** 11 am-11 pm, Sun-10 pm. Closed: 1/1, 4/16, 12/25. **Features:** Enjoy your favorite sporting event on one of the many television monitors placed about the dining room in this trendy little establishment. The menu offers various sandwiches and burgers, and the buffalo wings and chili cheese fry appetizers are "must-try" selections. Casual dress; cocktails. **Parking:** on-site. **Cards:** AX, MC, VI.

CHINA FIRST BUFFET

Lunch: $4-$13   **Dinner:** $4-$13   **Phone:** 813/903-8709   [23]

Chinese

Location: I-275, exit 51, 1.5 mi e on SR 582. 2811 E Fowler Ave 33612. **Hours:** 11 am-10 pm, Fri & Sat-11 pm. **Features:** A favorite choice of hungry diners, the restaurant sets up a huge buffet that incorporates at least 150 items, including appetizers, salad fixings, fruit, entrees, ice cream and desserts. Numerous ingredients are fresh. Casual dress. **Parking:** on-site. **Cards:** DS, MC, VI.

CK'S RESTAURANT

Dinner: $18-$38   **Phone:** 813/878-6500   [40]

Continental

Location: I-275, exit 39 southbound; exit 39B northbound, 2 mi w on SR 60; in Tampa Airport Marriott. **Hours:** 5 pm-9 pm, Fri & Sat-10 pm. **Reservations:** suggested, weekends. **Features:** The revolving, rooftop restaurant affords panoramic views of Tampa Bay, the airport and the downtown skyline. Try a nice presentation from the raw bar, fresh fish or certified Angus steak. Casual dress; cocktails. **Parking:** on-site. **Cards:** AX, CB, DC, DS, JC, MC, VI.

CODY'S ORIGINAL ROADHOUSE

Dinner: $7-$20   **Phone:** 813/855-2787

Steak House

Location: Jct Memorial Hwy, 1.9 mi w on SR 580; in Silver Mill Plaza. 11202 W Hillsborough Ave 33635. **Hours:** 4 pm-11 pm, Fri & Sat-midnight, Sun noon-10 pm. Closed: 12/25. **Features:** The use of lots of hardwoods and old nostalgic signs gives the lively restaurant a rustic roadhouse feel. The welcoming and efficient staff assists in creating a nice dining experience. On the menu are ribs, steaks, chicken, chops, burgers and sandwiches, as well as the fantastic fajitas, a real experience. Casual dress; cocktails. **Parking:** on-site. **Cards:** AX, DS, MC, VI.

(See map and index starting on p. 950)

THE COLONNADE   **Lunch:** $6-$21   **Dinner:** $6-$21   **Phone:** 813/839-7558   ⑫⑦
Seafood
Location: I-275, exit 41A, 4.2 mi s, 1.2 mi e on W Gandy, then 1.3 mi n. 3401 Bayshore Blvd 33629. **Hours:** 11 am-10 pm, Fri & Sat-11 pm. Closed: 11/23, 12/25. **Features:** Established in 1935, the warm and friendly atmosphere makes this a comfy place to savor a meal while enjoying panoramas of downtown Tampa from across the bay. The shrimp sampler platter is a favorite, as is the delectable chocolate bourbon pecan pie.
Casual dress; cocktails. **Parking:** on-site. **Cards:** AX, DC, DS, MC, VI.

COLUMBIA RESTAURANT YBOR CITY   **Lunch:** $10-$19   **Dinner:** $18-$27   **Phone:** 813/248-4961   ⑺⑶
Spanish
Location: I-4, exit 1; between 21st and 22nd sts; in Ybor City. 2117 E 7th Ave 33605. **Hours:** 11 am-10 pm, Fri & Sat-11 pm, Sun noon-9 pm. **Features:** This original Columbia Restaurant was established in 1905. Clubs and shops surround the popular tourist destination. Delicious Spanish and Cuban dishes are offered. Flamenco dancing and entertainment are offered every night except Sunday. Casual dress; cocktails; entertainment. **Parking:** on-site (fee) and valet. **Cards:** AX, DC, DS, MC, VI. **Historic**

CRAWDADDY'S   **Dinner:** $16-$36   **Phone:** 813/281-0407   ⑤⑥
American
Location: From east end of Courtney Campbell Cswy (SR 60), just s. 2500 Rocky Point Dr 33607. **Hours:** 5 pm-10 pm, Fri & Sat-11 pm. **Reservations:** suggested. **Features:** In the spirit of the roaring '20s, this feisty fish camp dishes up spicy jambalaya and smashed bourbon sweet potatoes, both of which boast a decidedly New Orleans flavor. The menu features steak, poultry and seafood. Enjoy great views of Old Tampa Bay.
Casual dress; cocktails. **Parking:** on-site. **Cards:** AX, DC, DS, MC, VI.

CRAZY BUFFET   **Lunch:** $14-$23   **Dinner:** $20-$24   **Phone:** 813/998-9228   ⑤⑤

Japanese
Location: I-275, exit 41B, 1.5 mi w. 2702 N Dale Mabry Hwy 33607. **Hours:** 11:30 am-2:30 & 5-9 pm, Fri-10 pm, Sat noon-4 & 5-10 pm, Sun noon-4 & 5-9 pm. Closed: 11/23. **Features:** The trendy, upscale establishment lines up a colorful and attractive buffet of mouthwatering Japanese food. Sushi lovers are in for a treat. Patrons can request cooked-to-order items at the hibachi grill. Casual dress; cocktails. **Parking:** on-site. **Cards:** AX, MC, VI.

DELI PLUS   **Lunch:** $3-$7   **Dinner:** $3-$7   **Phone:** 813/241-9526   ⑺⑵
American
Location: I-4, exit 1, just s to 7th Ave, then just w; in Ybor City. 1605 E 7th Ave 33605. **Hours:** 10 am-8 pm, Fri-Sun to 5 am. **Features:** Located right in the center of Ybor City and across from the popular Centro Ybor, this local deli offers fresh yet typical deli fare such as pastrami on rye, Italian hoagies, submarines and even Gyro pitas and the locally popular Cuban sandwich. Casual dress. **Parking:** street. **Cards:** AX, CB, DC, DS, MC, VI.

DISH CENTRO YBOR   **Lunch:** $11   **Dinner:** $16   **Phone:** 813/241-8300   ⑹⑺
American
Location: I-4, exit 1, just s to 8th Ave, then just w to Centro Ybor; in Ybor City. 1600 E 8th Ave, Suite E202 33605. **Hours:** 11:30 am-9 pm, Fri & Sat-11 pm. Closed: 11/23, 12/25. **Features:** Meals are prepared before diners' eyes on the center round cooking table. After choosing ingredients from the vast assortment of meats, sauces and vegetables, patrons present their selections to the preparer. Casual dress; cocktails. **Parking:** on-site (fee). **Cards:** AX, DC, DS, MC, VI.

DONATELLO   **Lunch:** $9-$18   **Dinner:** $16-$29   **Phone:** 813/875-6660   ⑻⑹
Northern
Italian
Location: I-275, exit 23 northbound; exit 23B southbound, 0.5 mi s on SR 92 (N Dale Mabry). 232 N Dale Mabry Hwy 33609. **Hours:** 11:30 am-2:30 & 6-11 pm, Sat & Sun from 6 pm. Closed major holidays; also Sun 6/1-10/1. **Reservations:** suggested. **Features:** Homemade pasta and veal specialties prepared with varied sauces are highlights on the restaurant's menu. Signature dishes include Florentine oysters and linguine lobster. Also appealing are the decadent desserts. Dressy casual; cocktails; entertainment. **Parking:** on-site and valet. **Cards:** AX, DC, DS, MC, VI.

EGG PLATTER   **Lunch:** $5-$8   **Dinner:** $5-$8   **Phone:** 813/839-8849   ⑬⓪
American
Location: On US 92, 0.5 mi e of jct S Westshore Blvd. 4403 W Gandy Blvd 33611. **Hours:** 24 hours. **Features:** Enjoy home-style cooking at this casual eating establishment. Known locally as a favorite for, as their name suggests, their egg dishes, the eatery also offers a wide variety of sandwiches and dinner items. Casual dress. **Parking:** on-site. **Cards:** AX, DC, DS, MC, VI.

EVOS WESTSHORE   **Lunch:** $5-$8   **Dinner:** $5-$8   **Phone:** 813/226-3867   ⑼⑶
American
Location: I-275, exit 40A, 0.4 mi s. 157 Westshore Plaza 33609. **Hours:** 10 am-9 pm. **Features:** In the Westshore shopping complex food court, the restaurant is a good stop after a long day of shopping. The menu centers on such low-fat, health-conscious items as gourmet wraps, smoothies, garden salads, veggie burgers and soy burgers. Casual dress. **Parking:** on-site. **Cards:** MC, VI.

FIREHOUSE SUBS   **Lunch:** $5-$8   **Dinner:** $5-$8   **Phone:** 813/849-1640   ⑯
American
Location: I-275, exit 51, 1.5 mi e on SR 582; in University Collections. 2710 E Fowler Ave 33612. **Hours:** 11 am-9 pm. **Features:** This deli style eatery offers hot or cold subs such as the "fully involved" with all of the extras— oven-baked meatball, smoked turkey, New York steamer, "firehouse" steak, Italian with genoa salami; or try a steamer such as the corned beef brisket, roast beef, pastrami, Virginia honey ham or the smoked turkey sub any one of which are a treat. This is a neat spot to dine in with the firehouse memorabilia about on the walls. Casual dress. **Parking:** on-site. **Cards:** MC, VI.

FIRST CHOICE BAR-B-QUE   **Lunch:** $4-$15   **Dinner:** $4-$15   **Phone:** 813/621-7434   ⑩⓪
American
Location: I-75, exit 257, 0.5 mi w on SR 60. 10113 Adamo Dr 33619. **Hours:** 11 am-9 pm. Closed: 11/23, 12/25; also Sun. **Features:** The sound of meat sizzling over an open-pit grill is a nice treat for the senses, but even nicer is the delicious Southern barbecue that perks up the taste buds. Locals flock here for succulent beef, pork, chicken, turkey, ham and sausage. Casual dress. **Parking:** on-site. **Cards:** AX, CB, DC, DS, MC, VI.

(See map and index starting on p. 950)

FIRST WATCH
American
Lunch: $5-$7   **Phone:** 813/307-9006   (84)
Location: Jct Twiggs St; downtown. 520 Tampa St 33602. **Hours:** 7 am-2:30 pm. Closed: 11/23, 12/25. **Features:** Pancakes and crepes fill the plates and are only two types of varied breakfast entrees that make regulars out of first-time guests. Fruit and salad options for the health-conscious and sandwiches you need both hands to hold please the lunch crowd. Casual dress. **Parking:** on-site (fee). **Cards:** AX, DS, MC, VI.

FIRST WATCH
American
Lunch: $5-$7   **Phone:** 813/975-1718   (15)
Location: I-275, exit 51, 1.5 mi e on Fowler Ave (SR 582); in University Collection. 2726 E Fowler Ave 33618. **Hours:** 7 am-2:30 pm. Closed: 11/23, 12/25. **Features:** Smooth service and an excellent breakfast menu make this a family favorite. Hefty portions of waffles, eggs, crepes and omelets are served during the morning hours, and salad, soups and sandwiches round out the lunch menu. Healthy options are listed, too. Casual dress. **Parking:** on-site. **Cards:** AX, DS, MC, VI.

FLOYD'S RESTAURANT & NIGHT CLUB
American
Dinner: $15-$27   **Phone:** 813/235-6937   (38)
Location: I-4, exit 6, just w; in Hard Rock Seminole Casino & Hotel. 5223 N Orient Rd 33610. **Hours:** 5 pm-11 pm. **Features:** Fabulous meals reflect creative and artistic presentation at the trendy, exciting establishment. Patrons can choose anything from New Zealand rack of lamb to albacore tuna. This is a great place to take a break from the casino action. Dressy casual; cocktails; entertainment. **Parking:** on-site. **Cards:** AX, DC, DS, MC, VI.

THE FOX RESTAURANT
American
Lunch: $6-$9   **Dinner:** $10-$17   **Phone:** 813/289-8446   (89)
Location: I-275, exit 40A southbound, 0.4 mi e on Westshore Blvd, then 0.6 mi s; exit 39B northbound, just n. 5401 W Kennedy Blvd, Suite 101 33609. **Hours:** 11 am-3 am. **Features:** The snazzy jazz club serves fabulous food ranging from oysters Rockefeller to escargot pie. After topping off the meal with a yummy slice of chocolate fudge cheesecake, patrons are set to enjoy some dancing and great jazz music. The more casual lunch menu lists varied sandwiches. Dressy casual; cocktails; entertainment. **Parking:** on-site. **Cards:** MC, VI.

FRED FLEMINGS FAMOUS BAR-B-QUE
Barbecue
Lunch: $7-$18   **Dinner:** $7-$18   **Phone:** 813/875-3733   (110)
Location: I-275, exit 41A, 0.5 mi se on US 92. 217 S Dale Mabry Hwy 33629. **Hours:** 10:30 am-10 pm, Fri & Sat-11 pm. Closed: 11/23, 12/25. **Features:** "Gourmet barbecue" is the claim here, and guests can't go wrong with any of the numerous choices. Among offerings are gourmet pizzas, barbecue dinners, burgers, steak, pork wraps and the signature rib dinners. Visitors should come with an appetite. Casual dress; cocktails. **Parking:** on-site. **Cards:** AX, DS, MC, VI.

FRESH MOUTH
American
Lunch: $3-$7   **Dinner:** $3-$7   **Phone:** 813/241-8845   (62)
Location: I-4, exit 1, just s; in Centro Ybor. 1600 E 8th Ave, #1010 33605. **Hours:** 11 am-11 pm, Fri & Sat-2 am. Closed: 11/23, 12/25. **Features:** In the heart of Centro Ybor, the fun spot is great for a yummy milk shake and excellent burger. Families can stop in for a relaxing meal after browsing the nearby shops of historic Ybor City. Casual dress. **Parking:** on-site (fee) and street. **Cards:** AX, MC, VI.

FRONTIER STEAK HOUSE
Steak House
Dinner: $9-$33   **Phone:** 813/621-3050   (35)
Location: I-4, exit 7, 0.9 mi n on US 301, then just w. 8602 E Sligh Ave 33610. **Hours:** 4 pm-10 pm. Closed major holidays. **Features:** Don't expect quick service at the comfortable restaurant, a local favorite, but enjoy the wonderful steaks. This place is famous for the "six-pound challenge." If you're craving something less weighty, choose from chicken, chops, ribs, lobster tail and varied salads, appetizers and desserts. Casual dress; cocktails; entertainment. **Parking:** on-site. **Cards:** AX, DC, DS, MC, VI.

GALLERY ECLECTIC BISTRO
American
Lunch: $7-$16   **Dinner:** $8-$30   **Phone:** 813/353-3838   (51)
Location: I-275, exit 40A northbound; exit 39A northbound, 0.9 mi w; in International Plaza and Bay Street. 2223 N Westshore Blvd, Suite 206-B 33607. **Hours:** 11 am-9:30 pm, Fri & Sat-11 pm, Sun noon-10 pm. **Features:** New American cuisine makes up the trendy, upscale establishment's menu. Anything from vegetarian pasta to oven-baked pizza to maple leaf duck can be found among the offerings. There are also several wood-grilled items. Desserts are out of this world. Casual dress; cocktails. **Parking:** on-site. **Cards:** AX, DS, MC, VI.

GOOD FELLAS
American
Lunch: $6-$9   **Dinner:** $6-$9   **Phone:** 813/963-6644   (27)
Location: 2 mi e of jct Dale Mabry Hwy; jct Plantation Blvd. 4802 Gunn Hwy 33624. **Hours:** 1 pm-3 am, Sat & Sun from noon. **Features:** A fun setting for casual dining, this place offers a menu with varied salads, burgers, sandwiches, soups, old-fashioned pizza and nachos. Also offered are heartier selections: New York strip, chicken and ribs, pasta and grouper. Casual dress; cocktails. **Parking:** on-site. **Cards:** AX, MC, VI.

GRILLE 29
American
Dinner: $8-$28   **Phone:** 813/221-2929   (106)
Location: Just e of jct Morgan St; in Channelside. 615 Channelside Dr, Suite 123 33602. **Hours:** 5 pm-10 pm. **Features:** In the popular Channelside complex, the trendy and upscale dining spot presents a menu of such interesting choices as salmon brulee, portobello and polenta Napoleon, sesame-seared tuna mignon and mushroom-stuffed chicken. The atmosphere is inviting and the service excellent. Dressy casual; cocktails. **Parking:** on-site (fee). **Cards:** MC, VI.

HO HO WINDOWS
Chinese
Lunch: $5-$12   **Dinner:** $6-$12   **Phone:** 813/254-9557   (113)
Location: I-275, exit 42, 1 mi s on Armenia Ave, just e on Azeele, then 0.4 mi s; in Whaley's Market Place. 533 S Howard Ave 33606. **Hours:** 11:30 am-10 pm, Fri-11 pm, Sat & Sun 4 pm-9:45 pm. Closed: 7/4, 11/23, 12/25. **Features:** The contemporary, inviting decor welcomes you to enjoy yourself at this Oriental restaurant. The expansive menu lists at least 75 choices, such as Mandarin beef, General Tso's chicken, spicy vegetable, dragon in the nest and honey chicken. Casual dress; beer & wine only. **Parking:** on-site. **Cards:** AX, DC, DS, MC, VI.

(See map and index starting on p. 950)

HOPS RESTAURANT BAR & BREWERY   **Lunch:** $7-$17   **Dinner:** $7-$17   **Phone:** 813/632-0717   ⑱
American   **Location:** I-275, exit 51, 0.5 mi e on SR 582. 1241 E Fowler Ave 33612. **Hours:** 11 am-10:30 pm, Fri & Sat-midnight, Sun-9:30 pm. Closed: 11/23, 12/25. **Features:** Although the restaurant is famous for its on-site microbrewery, its fresh-from-scratch menu items are no shrinking violets. Enjoy well-prepared filet mignon, rib-eye, pork chops, prime rib and top sirloin, as well as flavorful baby back ribs, grilled chicken, pasta dishes, burgers and sandwiches. Casual dress; cocktails. **Parking:** on-site. **Cards:** AX, DC, DS, MC, VI.

HOULIHAN'S   **Lunch:** $8-$20   **Dinner:** $8-$20   **Phone:** 813/287-8441   ⑰
American   **Location:** I-275, exit 40A southbound, 0.5 mi n; exit 39A northbound, 0.5 mi e on Kennedy Blvd, then 1.3 mi n. 1801 N Westshore Blvd 33607. **Hours:** 11 am-1 am, Fri & Sat-2 am, Sun-midnight. Closed: 11/23, 12/25. **Features:** The restaurant has a fun, casual atmosphere. Specialties are baby back barbecue ribs, steaks and combination platters, but the menu also lists good burgers, sandwiches and salads. Casual dress; cocktails. **Parking:** on-site. **Cards:** AX, DC, MC, VI.

HUGO'S SPANISH RESTAURANT   **Lunch:** $4-$12   **Dinner:** $4-$12   **Phone:** 813/251-2842   ⑫①
Spanish   **Location:** I-275, exit 42, 1 mi s on Armenia Ave, just e on Azeele, then 0.6 mi s; jct W Morrison Ave. 931 S Howard Ave 33606. **Hours:** 7:30 am-9 pm. Closed: Sun. **Features:** A fixture of the Hyde Park area since 1975, the casual restaurant is known for its Cuban sandwiches and black beans and rice. Other menu favorites include steak and chicken choices, Italian dishes and sandwiches. Casual dress; beer & wine only. **Parking:** on-site. **Cards:** AX, DS, MC, VI.

JACKSON'S BISTRO-BAR & SUSHI   **Lunch:** $7-$12   **Dinner:** $13-$21   **Phone:** 813/277-0339   ⑪④
American   **Location:** I-275, exit 44, 2 mi e on Tampa St to Harbour Island; in Knights Point. 601 S Harbour Island Blvd, Suite 100 33602. **Hours:** 11:30 am-2:30 & 5-10 pm, Fri & Sat-11 pm. Closed: 12/25. **Features:** Set on the waterfront in a trendy complex of shops and businesses, the decidedly upscale restaurant is beautifully decorated. Trained chefs expertly prepare many enticing dishes. Dessert is a must, especially the absolutely scrumptious raspberry macadamia nut pie. Dressy casual; cocktails; entertainment. **Parking:** on-site. **Cards:** AX, DC, DS, MC, VI.

J. ALEXANDER'S RESTAURANT   **Lunch:** $6-$20   **Dinner:** $6-$20   **Phone:** 813/354-9006   ⑧①
American   **Location:** I-275, exit 41A, just ne on US 92. 913 N Dale Mabry Hwy 33609. **Hours:** 11 am-10 pm, Fri & Sat-11 pm. Closed: 11/23, 12/25. **Features:** The upscale restaurant employs a professional service staff and tempts patrons with some wonderful choices. Try a bite of tender, mouthwatering filet mignon with garlic smashed potatoes. Dressy casual; cocktails. **Parking:** on-site. **Cards:** AX, DC, DS, MC, VI.

JASMINE THAI RESTAURANT   **Lunch:** $6-$9   **Dinner:** $6-$19   **Phone:** 813/968-1501   ⑪
Thai   **Location:** On US 92 at Fletcher Ave; in Village Center. 13248 N Dale Mabry Hwy 33618. **Hours:** 11:30 am-9:30 pm, Fri & Sat-11 pm, Sun-10 pm. Closed: 11/23. **Features:** Thai cuisine is served in very attractive surroundings by a pleasant wait staff. Try the duck mixed with mushroom caps, corn and broccoli and garnished with a butterfly-shaped carrot. You will find several nice touches during this excellent meal. Casual dress; beer & wine only. **Parking:** on-site. **Cards:** AX, DS, MC, VI.

JAX GRILL AT GAMEWORKS   **Lunch:** $8-$18   **Dinner:** $8-$18   **Phone:** 813/241-9675   ⑥③
American   **Location:** I-4, exit 1, just s, then just w; at Centro Ybor; in Ybor City. 1600 8th Ave E, Suite A147 33605. **Hours:** 11 am-midnight, Fri & Sat-2 am. **Features:** Trendy, upscale decor characterizes the restaurant's dining room. On the menu are such choices as the chicken quesadilla appetizer and the roast chicken entree. Casual dress; cocktails. **Parking:** street. **Cards:** AX, MC, VI.

JIMMY MAC'S WATERFRONT RESTAURANT   **Lunch:** $7-$25   **Dinner:** $7-$25   **Phone:** 813/839-3449   ⑬②
Seafood   **Location:** At east end of Gandy Bridge, 0.5 mi w of jct West Shore Blvd. 5000 W Gandy Blvd 33611. **Hours:** 11 am-11 pm, Fri & Sat-midnight. Closed: 11/23, 12/25. **Features:** The beautiful marina setting affords great views of boats and sunsets. Decor is nautical with lots of wood enhancements. On the extensive menu is something for everyone: appetizers, raw bar items, steamers, salads, soups, sandwiches, burgers, fresh fish, steak and chicken. Casual dress; cocktails. **Parking:** on-site. **Cards:** AX, DC, DS, MC, VI.

J. MALLORY BISTRO AND BAR   **Dinner:** $15-$30   **Phone:** 813/248-5632   ⑥①
Continental   **Location:** I-4, exit 1, just s to 8th Ave, then just w; in Ybor City. 1811 B N 15th St 33605. **Hours:** 5 pm-10 pm. Closed: Sun & Mon. **Features:** Convenient to the many shops and night spots of Ybor City, the bistro welcomes local jazz artists nightly. The chef creates such temptations as seared ahi tuna coated with black pepper and served with ginger-wasabi sauce and pan-seared Chilean sea bass topped with caviar and served over black bean puree. Salmon Napoleon, with layers of salmon, goat cheese, spinach, tomatoes and lump crab, is the signature dish. Dressy casual; cocktails; entertainment. **Parking:** on-site (fee) and street. **Cards:** MC, VI.

JOHNNY CARINO'S   **Lunch:** $7-$14   **Dinner:** $7-$14   **Phone:** 813/673-8700   ⑦⑨
Italian   **Location:** I-275, exit 41A, just sw on US 92. 1102 N Dale Mabry Hwy 33607. **Hours:** 11 am-10 pm, Fri & Sat-11 pm. Closed: 11/23, 12/25. **Features:** A wide selection of traditional Southern Italian fare—including pizza, pasta and parmigiana dishes—makes the restaurant a terrific spot for families. Casual dress; cocktails. **Parking:** on-site. **Cards:** AX, DS, MC, VI.

KAHUNAVILLE   **Lunch:** $12-$19   **Dinner:** $12-$19   **Phone:** 813/348-2011   ⑤②
American   **Location:** I-275, exit 40A southbound; exit 39A northbound, 0.9 mi w on West Shore Blvd; in International Plaza and Bay Street. 2223 N West Shore Blvd, Suite B-210 33607. **Hours:** 11 am-10 pm, Fri & Sat-11 pm. Closed: 11/23, 12/25. **Features:** The tropical jungle setting is complete with a dancing water show that diners can watch as they eat. Spectacular meals are served in huge, colorfully presented portions. Choices center on steak, fish and pasta, while other favorites include wraps. Casual dress; cocktails. **Parking:** on-site. **Cards:** MC, VI.

(See map and index starting on p. 950)

KOJAKS HOUSE OF RIBS BAR-B-QUE Lunch: $6-$24 Dinner: $6-$24 Phone: 813/837-3774 (131)
Barbecue
Location: Just w of jct Bayshore Blvd. 2808 Gandy Blvd 33611. **Hours:** 11 am-9:30 pm, Fri & Sat-10 pm, Sun noon-9 pm. Closed: Mon. **Features:** A local favorite since 1978, the restaurant is known for its Oklahoma-style barbecue. It offers some great pork spareribs, as well as sandwiches and combination dinners. Casual dress; beer & wine only. **Parking:** on-site. **Cards:** MC, VI.

LA BAMBA Lunch: $5-$7 Phone: 813/287-2575 (78)
Cuban
Location: I-275, exit 40A southbound, 0.5 mi w on Westshore; exit 39A northbound (Kennedy Blvd), 1 mi w on Westshore, then 0.3 mi s. 4815 W Laurel St 33607. **Hours:** 7 am-3 pm. Closed major holidays; also Sat & Sun. **Features:** Authentic Cuban cuisine is offered at this basic cafeteria-style eatery. It's not much for decor but the food is good and fresh. Items such as palomilla steak, fried grouper, their popular Cuban sandwiches and shrimp grouper creole are just a few of the available items. Catering, take out and a pick-up window are also available. Casual dress. **Parking:** on-site.

LA COCINA LATIN CAFE Lunch: $5-$10 Dinner: $5-$10 Phone: 813/979-9077 (17)
Latino
Location: I-275, exit 51, 1.5 mi e on SR 582. 2716 E Fowler Ave 33612. **Hours:** 11 am-8 pm. Closed major holidays; also Sun. **Features:** Latin American cuisine in the tradition of Old Tampa is the claim at this cafe. Friendly servers and yummy food offerings make for a great lunch or dinner stop after a day of shopping at the nearby mall. Among favorites are the popular Cuban sandwich, breaded palomilla steak, merluza a la Rusa, ropa vieja and masitas de Puerto fritas. Casual dress. **Parking:** on-site. **Cards:** AX, DC, DS, MC, VI.

LANDRY'S SEAFOOD HOUSE Lunch: $10-$21 Dinner: $14-$28 Phone: 813/289-7773 (44)
Seafood
Location: I-275, exit 39 southbound; exit 39B northbound, 3 mi w on SR 60, then just s. 7616 W Courtney Campbell Cswy 33607. **Hours:** 11 am-10 pm, Fri & Sat-11 pm, Sun 10:30 am-10 pm. Closed: 12/25. **Features:** On Old Tampa Bay, the 1940s-style seafood house affords wonderful water views. Among savory offerings are grilled mahi mahi, select rib-eye and shrimp etouffee. Casual dress; cocktails. **Parking:** on-site. **Cards:** DC, MC, VI.

LA TROPICANA CAFE Lunch: $6-$8 Phone: 813/247-4040 (70)
Spanish
Location: I-4, exit 1, just s to 7th Ave, then just w; in Ybor City. 1822 E 7th Ave 33605. **Hours:** 7 am-3 pm. Closed major holidays; also Sun. **Features:** In popular Ybor City, the restaurant offers some of the best in Cuban dishes. In addition to the signature Cuban sandwich, menu choices include tamales, Spanish fries and delicious black bean soup. Casual dress. **Parking:** on-site.

LAURO RISTORANTE ITALIANO Lunch: $8-$10 Dinner: $13-$28 Phone: 813/281-2100 (123)
Northern Italian
Location: I-275, exit 41A southbound, 1.5 mi w to Henderson Blvd, then just s. 3915 Henderson Blvd 33629. **Hours:** 11:30 am-2 & 5:30-10 pm, Fri & Sat-11 pm. Closed: 1/1; also Sun. **Features:** Private parties are welcome in this quaint eatery. A wide selection of pasta, fish and meat dishes is served by a staff that is well-trained to meet guests' needs. Fresh, crisp salads served with sliced bread will really whet your appetite. Dressy casual; cocktails; entertainment. **Parking:** on-site. **Cards:** AX, CB, DC, DS, MC, VI.

LEE ROY SELMON'S Lunch: $8-$20 Dinner: $8-$20 Phone: 813/977-3287
American
Location: I-75, exit 270, just e on CR 581 (Bruce B Downs Blvd); in Big Bear Crossing. 17508 Donna Michelle Dr 33647. **Hours:** 4 pm-10:30 pm, Fri-11:30 pm, Sat noon-11:30 pm, Sun noon-10 pm. **Features:** A fun place for sports buffs, the restaurant features numerous monitors strategically placed about the dining room with any number of sporting events to be seen. The homestyle food is wonderful with "southern comforts" as the theme — "Mama Selmon's southern kitchen" offers some of the best meatloaf, fried chicken, slow smoked pork ribs and fresh barbecued salmon that you can find. Casual dress; cocktails. **Parking:** on-site. **Cards:** MC, VI.

LEE ROY SELMON'S Lunch: $9-$20 Dinner: $9-$20 Phone: 813/871-3287 (57)
Southern
Location: Just w of Dale Mabry Hwy, jct Lois Ave. 4302 Boy Scout Blvd 33607. **Hours:** 11:15 am-10:30 pm, Fri & Sat-11:30 pm, Sun-10 pm. Closed: 11/23, 12/25. **Features:** Sports fans can gaze at sports memorabilia and articles of the Tampa Bay Buccaneers, including former star Lee Roy Selmon. Good home cooking—including Down South seafood, Mama Selmon's Southern kitchen, smokehouse specialties, steaks and barbecue—is prepared Southern style. Guests should come with a hearty appetite, as the portions are generous. Casual dress; cocktails. **Parking:** on-site. **Cards:** AX, DC, DS, MC, VI.

LENNY'S SUB SHOP Lunch: $5-$10 Dinner: $5-$10 Phone: 813/903-8678 (8)
Deli/Subs Sandwiches
Location: I-75, exit 266, 0.7 mi w on Fletcher Ave (CR 582A). 8225 Park Edge Dr 33637. **Hours:** 10:30 am-9 pm. **Features:** Near several office parks, the popular submarine shop prepares such items as hot and cold submarine sandwiches, salads, children's meals and box lunches. Guests can relax at comfortable patio seating or get their food to go. Casual dress. **Parking:** on-site. **Cards:** MC, VI.

LE PETIT BISTRO WEST Lunch: $6-$8 Dinner: $6-$8 Phone: 813/286-9198 (97)
American
Location: I-275, exit 40A, 0.4 mi s. 250 Westshore Plaza 33609. **Hours:** 10 am-9 pm. **Features:** In the Westshore shopping complex, the food court spot prepares tasty gourmet-type foods. Health-conscious diners will find all kinds of freshly made salads and pasta dishes on display. Casual dress. **Parking:** on-site. **Cards:** MC, VI.

LOGAN'S ROADHOUSE Lunch: $6-$19 Dinner: $6-$19 Phone: 813/884-5229 (31)
Steak House
Location: Just s of jct Linebaugh. 9218 Anderson Rd 33634. **Hours:** 11 am-10 pm, Fri & Sat-11 pm. Closed: 12/25. **Features:** Rustic effects enhance this replica of an old roadhouse. The atmosphere is relaxed, and the friendly staff is eager to help. Enjoy chicken, ribs, burgers, sandwiches, salads, appetizers and desserts, as well as signature steaks, including the noteworthy porterhouse. Casual dress; cocktails. **Parking:** on-site. **Cards:** AX, CB, DC, DS, JC, MC, VI.

(See map and index starting on p. 950)

LONNI'S SANDWICHES, ETC
American
Lunch: $7-$9   **Phone:** 813/223-2333   85
Location: Just n of jct Tampa St; downtown. 513 E Jackson St 33602. **Hours:** 9 am-4 pm. Closed major holidays; also Sat & Sun. **Features:** This local favorite offers a variety of sandwiches, salads and soups in a sandwich shop setting. Casual dress. **Parking:** street. **Cards:** AX, DS, MC, VI.

MAGGIANO'S LITTLE ITALY RESTAURANT
Italian
Lunch: $9-$15   **Dinner:** $12-$31   **Phone:** 813/288-9000   92
Location: I-275, exit 40A southbound, 0.5 mi s; exit 39A northbound (Kennedy Blvd), just n; in Westshore Plaza. 203 Westshore Plaza 33609. **Hours:** 11 am-9:45 pm. **Features:** Take a trip to Little Italy for your lunch hour or dinner pleasure; it feels so much like you've strolled into an Italian cafe when you walk through the doors. The restaurant offers authentic pasta, seafood dishes and steak, all made fresh from scratch with old world recipes. Nightly entertainment is offered in the piano bar. Casual dress; cocktails. **Parking:** on-site. **Cards:** MC, VI.

MANGROVES SEAFOOD GRILLE & BAR
Seafood
Cards: MC, VI.
Dinner: $16-$26   **Phone:** 813/258-3302   109
Location: I-275, exit 42, 1 mi s on Armenia Ave, just e on Azeele St, then just n at W Cleveland St. 208 S Howard Ave 33606. **Hours:** 5 pm-10 pm, Fri & Sat-11 pm. **Features:** Diners can enjoy a trendy, upscale establishment. The chef prepares such creations as wasabi-rubbed rack of lamb and pistachio-crusted jumbo lump crab cakes. Dressy casual; cocktails. **Parking:** on-site.

MARGARITA MAMA'S
Mexican
Lunch: $5-$9   **Dinner:** $5-$9   **Phone:** 813/228-7300   107
Location: Just s of jct SR 60; in Channelside. 615 Channelside Dr 33602. **Hours:** 11:30 am-midnight, Fri & Sat-3 am. **Closed:** 11/23, 12/25. **Features:** A festive theme and good food await at the popular spot in the Channelside area of shops. The menu lists typical fare, such as fajitas, burritos and nachos. Service is friendly and welcoming. Casual dress; cocktails. **Parking:** on-site (fee). **Cards:** DS, MC, VI.

MEL'S DINER
American
MC, VI.
Lunch: $5-$13   **Dinner:** $8-$13   **Phone:** 813/977-5777   19
Location: I-275, exit 54, 1.3 mi e at jct N 22nd St. 2101 E Fowler Ave 33612. **Hours:** 6:30 am-11 pm, Fri & Sat-midnight. **Closed:** 12/25. **Features:** Friendly service awaits at this throwback to a '60s-style establishment. Guests can't go wrong with a breakfast dish, such as a fresh omelet, or yummy open-faced platter. Also suggested are the hot and cold sandwiches, chili and burgers. Casual dress. **Parking:** on-site. **Cards:** AX, MC, VI.

MIGUEL'S MEXICAN RESTAURANT
Mexican
Cards: MC, VI.
Lunch: $8-$15   **Dinner:** $8-$15   **Phone:** 813/876-2587   96
Location: On SR 60; jct McDill. 3035 W Kennedy Blvd 33609. **Hours:** 11 am-10 pm, Fri-11 pm, Sat noon-11 pm, Sun noon-9 pm. **Features:** Basic decor characterizes the locally favorite Mexican restaurant, which offers diners a multitude of freshly prepared specialties along the lines of burritos, tacos and nachos. For a casual meal and good food, this place won't disappoint. Casual dress; beer & wine only. **Parking:** on-site.

MIKE'S BBQ
Barbecue
Lunch: $5-$18   **Dinner:** $5-$18   **Phone:** 813/626-5222   34
Location: On US 301, 1.8 mi n of jct Martin Luther King. 7117 US Hwy 301 N 33610. **Hours:** 11 am-3 pm; Tues-Thurs to 8 pm, Fri & Sat-9 pm. **Closed:** Sun. **Features:** The family-owned-and-operated eatery prepares Southern-style barbecue at its best. Owner Mike and his staff offer friendly, down-home service. Try one of the many specialty sauces, from hot to mild to classic. Pulled pork and smoked sausage are musts. Casual dress; beer & wine only. **Parking:** on-site. **Cards:** MC, VI.

MIMIS CAFE
American
Lunch: $7-$16   **Dinner:** $7-$16   **Phone:** 813/265-4460   26
Location: 0.7 mi s of jct Fletcher Ave W; in Main Street Plaza. 11702 N Dale Mabry Hwy 33618. **Hours:** 7 am-11 pm, Mon-Wed to 10 pm. **Closed:** 12/25. **Features:** With the feel of a New Orleans cafe, the eatery offers festive and colorful surroundings as well as friendly and professional service while patrons dine on bountiful meals with shades of home cooking. The menu is extensive, offering anything from yummy Pot Roast to pasta jambalaya to apple cider glazed pork chops. Casual dress; cocktails. **Parking:** on-site. **Cards:** AX, DS, MC, VI.

MISE EN PLACE
American
Cards: AX, CB, DC, DS, MC, VI.
Lunch: $6-$13   **Dinner:** $15-$26   **Phone:** 813/254-5373   95
Location: I-275, exit 44, 0.4 mi s on Ashley, then 0.3 mi w on Kennedy; in Grand Central Place; opposite University of Tampa. 442 W Kennedy Blvd 33606. **Hours:** 11:30 am-2:30 & 5:30-10 pm, Fri-11 pm, Sat 5:30 pm-11 pm. Closed major holidays; also Sun & Mon. **Reservations:** accepted. **Features:** The trendy bistro features expertly created dishes that reflect a Mediterranean flair. The interesting grilled grouper chili with a cheese-filled pasta base is wonderfully presented. An appealing lunch menu also is offered. Dressy casual; cocktails. **Parking:** street.

MOE'S SOUTHWEST GRILL
Mexican
Lunch: $4-$9   **Dinner:** $4-$9   **Phone:** 813/289-6637   74
Location: I-275, exit 40A southbound; exit 39A northbound, 0.8 mi w on Westshore Blvd; in Westshore Commons Plaza. 4614 W Boy Scout Blvd 33607. **Hours:** 11 am-9 pm. **Features:** The trendy, popular spot serves fresh burrito dishes, as well as fajitas, quesadillas, tacos and salad items. Casual dress; beer only. **Parking:** on-site. **Cards:** MC, VI.

NEWK'S LIGHTHOUSE CAFE
American
Parking: on-site. **Cards:** MC, VI.
Lunch: $5-$12   **Dinner:** $5-$12   **Phone:** 813/307-6395   104
Location: Just e; adjacent to The Ice Palace; downtown. 514 Channelside Dr 33602. **Hours:** 11 am-9 pm, Fri-midnight, Sat-10 pm, Sun-6 pm, Mon-3 pm. **Closed:** 1/1, 11/23, 12/25; also for dinner 12/24 & Sun 2/1-9/30. **Features:** Before heading off to the Ice Palace, guests can stop at this casual spot for a great sandwich, gourmet pasta or fried shrimp. Desserts are tasty, too, particularly the Mississippi mud pie. Casual dress.

(See map and index starting on p. 950)

OYSTERCATCHERS   Lunch: $8-$12   Dinner: $12-$30   Phone: 813/207-6815   (47)
Seafood
Location: SR 60, east end of Courtney Campbell Cswy; in Grand Hyatt of Tampa Bay. 6200 Courtney Campbell Cswy 33607. **Hours:** 11:30 am-2:30 & 6-10 pm, Fri & Sat-10:45 pm; Sunday brunch 10:30 am-2:30 pm. Closed: 12/25. **Reservations:** suggested. **Features:** Nestled on a point that juts into Old Tampa Bay and built low among coastal shrubbery is this upscale seafood restaurant. The three-tiered dining room affords views of the bay through many bay windows. White painted furniture, bright floral prints and staff attired in tropical whites contribute to the bright openness of the restaurant. An open kitchen adds atmosphere, as well as a measure of noise. Several tables occupy an outdoor patio. Casual dress; cocktails; entertainment. **Parking:** valet. **Cards:** AX, CB, DC, DS, JC, MC, VI.

PANERA BREAD   Lunch: $6-$7   Dinner: $6-$7   Phone: 813/979-6981
American
Location: I-75, exit 270, 0.5 mi n on Bruce B Downs Blvd. 18001 Highwoods Preserve Pkwy 33647. **Hours:** 7 am-9:30 pm, Sun-9 pm. Closed: 11/23, 12/25. **Features:** Indoor and outdoor seating can be requested at the inviting, relaxing cafe. In addition to freshly baked breads and pastries, choices include a variety of freshly made salads, soups, hot panini and signature sandwiches. Casual dress. **Parking:** on-site. **Cards:** AX, MC, VI.

PANERA BREAD CAFE   Lunch: $4-$7   Dinner: $4-$7   Phone: 813/286-7119   (101)
American
Location: Jct SR 60 (Kennedy Blvd). 112 Westshore Blvd 33609. **Hours:** 6 am-9:30 pm, Sun from 7 am. Closed major holidays. **Features:** Indoor and outdoor seating can be requested at the inviting, relaxing cafe. In addition to freshly baked breads and pastries, choices include a variety of freshly made salads, soups, hot panini and signature sandwiches. Casual dress. **Parking:** on-site. **Cards:** AX, MC, VI.

PELAGIA TRATTORIA   Lunch: $10-$19   Dinner: $11-$29   Phone: 813/313-3235   (48)
Mediterranean
Location: I-275, exit 40A southbound, At International Plaza; in Renaissance Tampa Hotel International Plaza. 4200 Jim Walter Blvd 33607. **Hours:** 6:30-10:30 am, 11-3 & 5:30-10 pm. **Features:** This restaurant with its upscale surroundings and knowledgeable, professional service staff offers a wonderful dining experience. The menu offers Northern Italian cuisine with a touch of Asian and Mediterranean flavors. Items such as grilled grouper, seared wild salmon, pistaccio crusted rack of lamb, pan seared sea scallops and potato sage gnocchi are popular entree choices. Dressy casual; cocktails. **Parking:** on-site (fee) and valet. **Cards:** AX, CB, DC, DS, JC, MC, VI.

P.F. CHANG'S CHINA BISTRO   Lunch: $6-$19   Dinner: $6-$19   Phone: 813/289-8400   (91)
Chinese
Location: I-275, exit 40A, 0.4 mi s. 219 Westshore Plaza 33609. **Hours:** 11 am-11 pm, Fri & Sat-midnight. **Features:** An inviting atmosphere and some fabulous Chinese cuisine await at the trendy dining spot just outside of the Westshore shopping complex. Shoppers might spend the day browsing then treat themselves to lunch or dinner at this great place. Among the numerous creations are wok-seared lamb, orange peel beef, mu shu pork, lemon-pepper shrimp, Cantonese roasted duck and various noodle dishes. Those with a craving for Chinese food are sure to satisfy it here. Casual dress; cocktails. **Parking:** on-site. **Cards:** MC, VI.

PIPO'S & SON RESTAURANT   Lunch: $6-$10   Dinner: $6-$10   Phone: 813/882-0184   (36)
Spanish
Location: Jct Hanley Rd. 7233 W Hillsborough 33634. **Hours:** 9 am-8:30 pm. Closed: Sun. **Features:** Guests can savor Spanish cuisine in the family-owned and operated establishment. The atmosphere is casual, but the food is more than worth the stop. Paella is an excellent dinner choice. Casual dress; beer & wine only. **Parking:** on-site. **Cards:** AX, DS, MC, VI.

PITA'S   Lunch: $4-$7   Dinner: $4-$7   Phone: 813/960-4976   (6)
American
Location: On SR 597, 1.1 mi w of jct W Fletcher Ave; in Village French Quarter. 14614 N Dale Mabry Hwy 33618. **Hours:** 11 am-9 pm. **Features:** Known for its "naturally nutritious" menu offerings, the restaurant prepares foods to be low in saturated fat and calories, in part by vertically broiling meats. Among choices are low-carbohydrate pockets and hot or cold pitas. Casual dress. **Parking:** on-site. **Cards:** MC, VI.

PITA'S   Lunch: $4-$7   Dinner: $4-$7   Phone: 813/988-4976   (20)
American
Location: I-75, exit 265, 3.2 mi w on SR 582. 5105 E Fowler Ave 33617. **Hours:** 11 am-9 pm. **Features:** Known for its "naturally nutritious" menu offerings, the restaurant prepares foods to be low in saturated fat and calories, in part by vertically broiling meats. Among choices are low-carbohydrate pockets and hot or cold pitas. Casual dress. **Parking:** on-site. **Cards:** MC, VI.

PITA'S   Lunch: $4-$7   Dinner: $4-$7   Phone: 813/879-4976   (120)
American
Location: I-275, exit 41A, 1.4 mi s on US 92. 808 S Dale Mabry Hwy 33609. **Hours:** 11 am-9 pm. **Features:** Known for its "naturally nutritious" menu offerings, the restaurant prepares foods to be low in saturated fat and calories, in part by vertically broiling meats. Among choices are low-carbohydrate pockets and hot or cold pitas. Casual dress. **Parking:** on-site. **Cards:** MC, VI.

PITA'S   Lunch: $4-$7   Dinner: $4-$7   Phone: 813/885-4976   (37)
American
Location: Jct Memorial Hwy; in Ross Plaza. 8412 W Hillsborough Ave 33615. **Hours:** 11 am-9 pm. **Features:** Known for its "naturally nutritious" menu offerings, the restaurant prepares foods to be low in saturated fat and calories, in part by vertically broiling meats. Among choices are low-carbohydrate pockets and hot or cold pitas. Casual dress. **Parking:** on-site. **Cards:** MC, VI.

THE RACK   Dinner: $4-$10   Phone: 813/250-1595   (111)
American
Location: I-275, exit 42, 1 mi s on Armenia, then just e. 1809 W Platt St 33606. **Hours:** 4 pm-3 am. **Reservations:** suggested. **Features:** Menu specialties at the eclectic trattoria include eggplant souffle cheesecake and brandy-spiked tiramisu. Don't miss the chance to try lobster Popsicles. Casual dress; cocktails. **Parking:** on-site. **Cards:** AX, DC, DS, MC, VI.

(See map and index starting on p. 950)

REMINGTON'S STEAKHOUSE   **Dinner:** $9-$21   **Phone:** 813/972-1646   ③
Steak House
Location: I-75, exit 266, 3.8 mi w on Fletcher, 0.5 mi n on Bruce B Downs, then just w. 2836 E Bearss Ave 33613. **Hours:** 3 pm-10 pm, Fri & Sat-11 pm. Closed: 12/25. **Features:** Diners who stroll past the attractive landscaping and enter the restaurant, which resembles a weathered barn, experience a rustic interior design that evokes the ambience of a Western town. On the varied menu are choices such as steak, ribs, chicken, pork chops and fajitas, as well as an array of appetizers, salads and desserts. Casual dress; cocktails. **Parking:** on-site. **Cards:** AX, DC, DS, MC, VI.

ROYAL PALACE THAI RESTAURANT   **Lunch:** $7-$18   **Dinner:** $10-$18   **Phone:** 813/258-5893   ⑲
Thai
Location: I-275, exit 42, 1 mi s on Armenia Ave, just e on Azeele, then 0.7 mi s. 811 S Howard Ave 33606. **Hours:** 11:30 am-2:30 & 4:30-10:30 pm. Closed major holidays; also Mon. **Features:** The beautifully decorated restaurant is a welcoming Thai-themed setting. The menu builds on this theme, with an extensive variety of authentic Thai cuisine and numerous chef specialties. The charming staff makes for a delightful meal. Casual dress; beer & wine only. **Parking:** on-site. **Cards:** MC, VI.

ROY'S HAWAIIAN FUSION TAMPA   **Dinner:** $11-$35   **Phone:** 813/873-7697   ⑥⓪
American
Location: I-275, exit 40B, 0.9 mi n, then just w. 4342 W Boy Scout Blvd 33607. **Hours:** 5:30 pm-10 pm, Fri & Sat-10:30 pm. Closed: 11/23, 12/25. **Features:** Aloha-style service is evident from the moment you enter the deliciously different restaurant. Innovative Hawaiian fusion cuisine includes all the classic favorites. Casual dress; cocktails. **Parking:** on-site. **Cards:** AX, DC, DS, MC, VI.

THE RUSTY PELICAN   **Lunch:** $5-$14   **Dinner:** $18-$28   **Phone:** 813/281-1943   ⑤⑧
Seafood
Location: 0.5 mi s of east end of Courtney Campbell Cswy (SR 60). 2425 Rocky Point Dr 33607. **Hours:** 11 am-3 & 5-10 pm, Fri & Sat-11 pm. **Reservations:** suggested, weekends. **Features:** Tableside cooking is just one enticement at this intimate restaurant. Fireplace parlors offer Tampa Bay panoramas. Holiday brunches are special treats and beautifully prepared dessert, such as bananas foster and cherries jubilee, is a fitting final touch. Banquet facilities from 20 to 460 may be accommodated. Dressy casual; cocktails. **Parking:** on-site and valet. **Cards:** AX, DC, DS, MC, VI.

SAIGON BAY VIETNAMESE RESTAURANT   **Lunch:** $7-$17   **Dinner:** $7-$17   **Phone:** 813/971-0854   ㉑
Vietnamese
Location: I-275, exit 51, 1.5 mi e; in Fowler Plaza South. 2373 E Fowler Ave 33612. **Hours:** 11 am-9:30 pm, Fri & Sat-10:30 pm. Closed: 11/23, 12/25. **Features:** Traditional artwork and decor characterizes this intimate Vietnamese restaurant. A lunch buffet features such tasty favorites as chicken wings, white rice, pork, fried squash and puffed sugar pastry. Or make a selection from the full menu. Casual dress; beer & wine only. **Parking:** on-site. **Cards:** AX, DS, MC, VI.

ST. BARTS ISLAND HOUSE RESTAURANT   **Dinner:** $12-$27   **Phone:** 813/251-0367   ⑫⑤
French
Location: I-275, exit 42, 1 mi s on Armenia Ave, just e on Azeele, then 1 mi s. 1502 S Howard Ave 33606. **Hours:** 5:30 pm-midnight. Closed: 1/1, 12/25; also Mon. **Features:** Cozy, romantic appointments characterize the classy bistro. The menu lists freshly prepared and artfully displayed entrees, such as roast duckling, baby lamb, veal chops, grilled sole, bouillabaisse a la Marseilles and salmon dishes. Dressy casual; cocktails; entertainment. **Parking:** valet. **Cards:** AX, DC, MC, VI.

SAMBA ROOM   **Lunch:** $8-$20   **Dinner:** $9-$25   **Phone:** 813/254-5870   ⑪⑥
Latino
Location: Jct N Dakota Ave; in Olde Hyde Park Village. 1610 W Swann Ave 33606. **Hours:** 11:30 am-11 pm, Thurs-Sun to midnight. Closed: 12/25. **Features:** Offered in a cafe-style setting, an eclectic menu displays a distinctly European influence. Start with fried pita chips covered with feta cheese and an avocado-scallion dip; then for a moist, tender entree, select the salmon prepared in parchment paper. Casual dress; cocktails. **Parking:** on-site. **Cards:** AX, CB, DC, DS, MC, VI.

SAM SELTZER'S STEAKHOUSE   **Lunch:** $8-$19   **Dinner:** $10-$19   **Phone:** 813/873-7267   ㉟
Steak & Seafood
Location: I-275, exit 41B, 2.1 mi n. 4744 N Dale Mabry Hwy 33614. **Hours:** 4 pm-10 pm, Fri-11 pm, Sat 3:30 pm-11 pm, Sun 1 pm-10 pm. Closed: 11/23, 12/25. **Reservations:** suggested. **Features:** Old family portraits and Western knickknacks adorn the wood walls of the rustic restaurant. Hearty portions of mostly steak and chicken entrees satisfy the biggest of appetites. Sam's Napoleon custard cream in a graham-cracker crust is a sweet treat. Casual dress; cocktails. **Parking:** on-site. **Cards:** AX, DC, DS, MC, VI.

SAMURAI BLUE SUSHI AND SAKE BAR   **Lunch:** $8-$21   **Dinner:** $8-$21   **Phone:** 813/242-6688   ⑥⑥
Japanese
Location: I-4, exit 1, just s to 8th Ave, then just w at Centro Ybor; in Ybor City. 1600 E 8th Ave #C208 33605. **Hours:** 11:30 am-2 & 5-11 pm, Wed & Thurs-midnight, Fri-1 am, Sat 5 pm-1 am, Sun 5 pm-11 pm. Closed: 11/23, 12/25. **Features:** On the second level of the Centro Ybor complex, the trendy, upscale establishment is popular for its extensive sushi offerings but also presents other options, including Japanese-themed dishes, on its varied menu. Casual dress; beer & wine only. **Parking:** on-site (fee). **Cards:** AX, MC, VI.

SHELLS OF NORTH TAMPA   **Lunch:** $7-$10   **Dinner:** $7-$19   **Phone:** 813/977-8456   ㉘
Seafood
Location: 1.2 mi n of jct SR 580 (Busch Blvd). 11010 N 30th St 33618. **Hours:** 11:30 am-10 pm. **Features:** Popular throughout Florida for more than 15 years, the restaurant prepares some of the freshest seafood to be found in the state. Guests can expect a relaxing nautical setting, friendly service and a menu that lists combination platters, sandwiches, grilled items, pasta dishes and even king crab. Those who love Maine lobster shouldn't miss "Lobster Tuesday.". Casual dress; cocktails. **Parking:** on-site. **Cards:** MC, VI.

(See map and index starting on p. 950)

SHULA'S STEAKHOUSE
Steak House
Lunch: $17-$33 **Dinner:** $17-$66 **Phone:** 813/286-4366 (98)
Location: I-275, exit 40A, 0.5 mi s; jct SR 60 and Westshore Blvd; in Wyndham Westshore-Tampa. 4860 W Kennedy Blvd 33609. **Hours:** 11:30 am-2 & 5:30-10 pm, Fri-10:30 pm, Sat 5:30 pm-10:30 pm, Sun 5:30 pm-9:30 pm. **Reservations:** suggested. **Features:** Although predominantly a steakhouse, the restaurant also offers fish, chicken, chops and lobster. Presentations are elegant, and the a la carte side dishes are large enough to share. For dessert, splurge on the decadent seven-layer chocolate cake. Classy decor intermingles with football memorabilia from Coach Don Shula's Dolphins in their "glory years." At dinner, the menu is printed on a football, and the theme promotes a bit of rowdiness among guests. Casual dress; cocktails; entertainment. **Parking:** valet. **Cards:** AX, CB, DC, DS, JC, MC, VI.

SIDEBERN'S
Continental
Dinner: $26-$40 **Phone:** 813/258-2233 (122)
Location: I-275, exit 42, 1 mi s on Armenia Ave, just e on Azeele, then 0.6 mi s on Howard Ave. 2208 W Morrison Ave 33606. **Hours:** 6 pm-10 pm. Closed major holidays; also Sun. **Features:** This exceptional restaurant has a well trained service staff, upscale urban surroundings and a sophisticated global menu with wonderful offerings from areas of the world such as Asia, France, Africa, Latin America and the Mediterranean. The dim sum is a popular specialty of the restaurant as well as such items as foie gras, mangrove snapper, cocoa cinnamon day boat scallops and pistachio goat cheese crusted rack of lamb. Dessert is a must; the Valrhona degustation is a delight. Dressy casual; cocktails. **Parking:** on-site. **Cards:** AX, DC, DS, MC, VI.

SKIPPER'S SMOKEHOUSE RESTAURANT & OYSTER BAR
Seafood
Menu on aaa.com **Lunch:** $6-$16 **Dinner:** $6-$16 **Phone:** 813/971-0666 (5)
Location: I-275, exit 51, just e on Fletcher Ave, 0.8 mi n on Nebraska Ave, then just e. 910 Skipper Rd 33613. **Hours:** 11 am-midnight, Sat from noon, Sun 1 pm-10 pm. Closed: 12/25; also Mon. **Features:** The casual Key West-style restaurant and oyster bar serves Florida fare with Caribbean and Louisiana accents. Menu selections include alligator, crab, shrimp, wings, ribs and conch chowder. Live entertainment invigorates the atmosphere outdoors. Casual dress; beer & wine only; entertainment. **Parking:** on-site. **Cards:** AX, MC, VI.

SONNY'S REAL PIT BAR-B-Q
Barbecue
Lunch: $5-$17 **Dinner:** $9-$17 **Phone:** 813/621-8784 (87)
Location: I-75, exit 257, 0.5 mi w on SR 60. 10010 Adamo Dr 33619. **Hours:** 11 am-9:30 pm, Fri & Sat-10 pm. **Features:** Popular throughout the South, the restaurant is known for its barbecue dishes, which can be ordered by the pound or in combination platters. Try pork three ways, which includes pulled pork, sliced pork and St. Louis spare ribs, as well as coleslaw, garlic bread and a potato dish. Several varieties of yummy barbecue sauce await on the table. Casual dress. **Parking:** on-site. **Cards:** MC, VI.

THE SPAGHETTI WAREHOUSE RESTAURANT
Italian
Lunch: $7-$15 **Dinner:** $7-$15 **Phone:** 813/248-1720 (59)
Location: I-4, exit 1, just w to 8th Ave, then just w; in Ybor Square; in Ybor City. 1911 13th St 33605. **Hours:** 11 am-10 pm, Fri & Sat-11 pm, Sun noon-10 pm. **Features:** In historic Ybor City since the 1980s, the popular spot prepares pasta and spaghetti dishes. The atmosphere in the former 1900s cigar factory is extremely nice. Various antiques contribute to the decor, as does an original Tampa trolley car that now is used as a dining car. Casual dress; cocktails. **Parking:** on-site (fee) and street. **Cards:** MC, VI.

STONEWOOD GRILL & TAVERN
American
Dinner: $10-$23 **Phone:** 813/978-0388
Location: I-75, exit 270, just s on Bruce B Downs Blvd, then just w on Tampa Palms Blvd; in The Pointe at Tampa Palms. 17050 Palm Pointe Dr 33647. **Hours:** 5 pm-10 pm, Fri & Sat 4 pm-11 pm. **Features:** Distinguishing this place are the atmosphere and market-fresh seafood items. Among suggestions to try are such oak-grilled items as grilled Maui chicken; chef specialties including Pacific Cliffs salmon; and such house favorites as jambalaya, chicken pasta, pesto chicken and the pot roast platter. Casual dress; cocktails. **Parking:** on-site. **Cards:** MC, VI.

STUMPS SUPPER CLUB
American
Dinner: $10-$21 **Phone:** 813/226-2261 (105)
Location: Just s of jct SR 60; in Channelside. 615 Channelside Dr 33602. **Hours:** 4 pm-11 pm, Fri-3 am, Sat 11 am-3 am, Sun 11 am-10 pm. Closed: 11/23, 12/25. **Features:** The interesting dining spot treats guests to "Southern cooking and deep-fried dancing" in a replicated '50s supper club atmosphere. The menu lists such choices as fried chicken, pork chops, meatloaf and other home-style meals. Casual dress; cocktails; entertainment. **Parking:** on-site (fee). **Cards:** MC, VI.

SUKHOTHAI RESTAURANT
Thai
Lunch: $5-$8 **Dinner:** $6-$20 **Phone:** 813/933-7990 (33)
Location: I-275, exit 41B, 4.8 mi n. 8201-A N Dale Mabry Hwy 33614. **Hours:** 11 am-10 pm, Sat & Sun from 5 pm. Closed major holidays; also Super Bowl Sun. **Features:** Pictures, writings and dolls decorate the dimly lit, cozy restaurant. For the most authentic experience, journey upstairs, where you'll sit on the floor to enjoy such dishes as the spicy seafood platter or stir-fried chicken in a three-spice sauce. Casual dress; beer & wine only. **Parking:** on-site. **Cards:** AX, CB, DC, DS, MC, VI.

SWEET TOMATOES BRANDON
American
Lunch: $7 **Dinner:** $7 **Phone:** 813/661-0803 (102)
Location: I-75, exit 257, 0.5 mi w on SR 60. 10017 Adamo Dr 33619. **Hours:** 11 am-9 pm, Fri & Sat-10 pm. Closed: 11/23, 12/25. **Features:** The contemporary, open and airy dining room contains buffet lines with colorful displays of goodies. On one bar are salad fixings with a variety of dressings, and other lines have fresh-baked muffins and bread, soup, chili, hot pasta and dessert, including frozen yogurt. Casual dress. **Parking:** on-site. **Cards:** DC, DS, MC, VI.

SWEET TOMATOES TAMPA
American
Lunch: $7 **Dinner:** $9 **Phone:** 813/874-6566 (75)
Location: I-275, exit 41B, 0.4 mi e on US 92. 1902 N Dale Mabry Hwy 33607. **Hours:** 11 am-9 pm, Fri & Sat-10 pm. Closed: 11/23, 12/24, 12/25. **Features:** Fresh salads are in abundance at the casual, self-serve eatery. Patrons can make up a hearty meal from the fresh salad ingredients, made-from-scratch soups, pizza focaccia, hot pasta and yummy muffins. Casual dress. **Parking:** on-site. **Cards:** DC, DS, MC, VI.

(See map and index starting on p. 950)

TAJ INDIAN CUISINE   Lunch: $9   Dinner: $9-$17   Phone: 813/971-8483   [14]
Indian
Location: I-275, exit 51, 1.3 mi e; in University Collection Shops. 2734B E Fowler Ave 33612. **Hours:** 11:30 am-2:30 & 5-10 pm. Closed: 11/23, 12/25; also Mon. **Features:** Instrumental music plays in the background of this quiet, contemporary setting. Taste such specialties as pulao rice and curried chicken from the lunch buffet. The a la carte dinner menu features a good variety, including many vegetarian dishes. Casual dress; beer & wine only. **Parking:** on-site. **Cards:** AX, MC, VI.

TAMPA BAY BREWING COMPANY   Lunch: $8-$17   Dinner: $8-$17   Phone: 813/247-1422   [71]
American
Location: I-4, exit 1, 0.3 mi s on 21st, 0.6 mi w on 7th Ave, then just n. 1812 N 15th St 33605. **Hours:** 11:30 am-2 am, Sun 1 pm-midnight, Mon & Tues 11:30 am-midnight. Closed: 12/25. **Features:** In lively and historic Ybor City, the popular establishment is famous for its variety of house brewed beers, all made on site. The varied menu lists many choices—from delicious fried calamari to burgers, seafood, poultry and steaks. Casual dress; cocktails. **Parking:** street. **Cards:** DS, MC, VI.

TAMPA BRICKYARD GRILL   Lunch: $8-$16   Dinner: $8-$16   Phone: 813/971-1787   [2]
American
Location: I-75, exit 270, 3.6 mi s; in Oak Ramble. 14947 Bruce B Downs Blvd N 33647. **Hours:** 11 am-3 am, Sun from 9 am. **Features:** Patrons savor some great eats at the popular spot. The setting is casual yet inviting with its use of dark woods. On the menu are all types of appetizers, salads, sandwiches and burgers. Fried grouper is a must-try. Finish the meal with a piece of chocolate cake. Casual dress; cocktails. **Parking:** on-site. **Cards:** MC, VI.

TAPAS SPANISH CAFE   Lunch: $4-$11   Dinner: $4-$11   Phone: 813/662-6660   [83]
Spanish
Location: I-75, exit 257, just w on SR 60, 0.3 mi n. 509 S Falkenburg Rd 33619. **Hours:** 6 am-4 pm, Sat from 8 am. Closed: Sun. **Features:** Spanish cuisine is served at the family-owned-and-operated restaurant. The staff is gracious and the surroundings cozy. Daily dinners include paella a la castellana, ropa vieja, bistec empanizado, while lunch choices include empanada and tossed salad, tamal with rice and beans, croquetas, deviled crab and stuffed potatoes. Casual dress. **Parking:** on-site. **Cards:** MC, VI.

THAI RUBY   Lunch: $8-$24   Dinner: $11-$24   Phone: 813/558-0570   [1]
Thai
Location: I-75, exit 270, 2.9 mi w on Bruce B Downs Blvd (CR 581), then just s; in the Shoppes of Amberly. 15319 Amberly Dr 33647. **Hours:** 11 am-3 & 4:30-10 pm. Closed: 11/23, 12/25. **Features:** A nice spot for a good Thai meal, the restaurant uses varied herbs, curries and spices in its meat, fish and vegetarian preparations. Casual dress; beer & wine only. **Parking:** on-site. **Cards:** AX, DS, MC, VI.

TIA'S TEX-MEX   Lunch: $6-$16   Dinner: $9-$16   Phone: 813/877-5000   [77]
Mexican
Location: I-275, exit 41B; exit 41A northbound, just n. 1503 N Dale Mabry Hwy 33607. **Hours:** 11 am-10 pm, Fri & Sat-midnight. Closed: 12/25. **Features:** Enjoy a wonderful meal in a festive Mexican cantina setting. Try any of the Tex-Mex classics—burritos, tacos, enchiladas, chalupas, quesadillas and fajitas—or something off the mesquite wood grill, such as delicious ribs. Platters satisfy hearty appetites, while salads are a tempting representative of lighter fare. Casual dress; cocktails. **Parking:** on-site. **Cards:** AX, DC, DS, MC, VI.

TIA'S TEX MEX   Lunch: $7-$15   Dinner: $7-$15   Phone: 813/972-7737   [22]
Mexican
Location: I-275, exit 51, 1.6 mi e on SR 582. 2815 Fowler Ave E 33612. **Hours:** 11 am-10 pm, Fri & Sat-11 pm. Closed: 12/25. **Features:** This cantina rocks with live entertainment on Wednesday nights, and features mesquite-grilled Tex-Mex items served with a playful, fun attitude by caring servers. Save room for dessert and indulge in the fried ice cream for a chilling taste sensation. Casual dress; cocktails. **Parking:** on-site. **Cards:** AX, DC, DS, MC, VI.

TIJUANA FLATS   Lunch: $5-$9   Dinner: $5-$9   Phone: 813/975-0800   [24]
Mexican
Location: I-275, exit 51, 1.4 mi e on SR 582. 2782 E Fowler Ave 33612. **Hours:** 11 am-10 pm, Fri & Sat-10:30 pm, Sun-9 pm. Closed major holidays. **Features:** The neat little Mexican-themed eatery's specialty is burritos, but guests also can try chimichangas, enchiladas, quesadillas, tacos or nachos. Casual dress; beer & wine only. **Parking:** on-site. **Cards:** MC, VI.

TODAI RESTAURANT   Lunch: $11-$13   Dinner: $19-$21   Phone: 813/872-8725   [49]
Japanese
Location: I-275, exit 40A, 0.9 mi n on Westshore Blvd; exit 39A northbound, 1 mi e on Kennedy Blvd, then 1.3 mi n; in International Plaza. 2223 N Westshore Blvd, #187 33607. **Hours:** 11:30 am-2:30 & 5:30-9 pm, Sat 11:45 am-2:45 & 5:30-9:30 pm, Sun 11:45 am-2:45 & 5-9 pm. **Features:** In trendy International Plaza, the restaurant is popular for its sushi bar, which offers some 40 kinds, and its seafood buffet, which includes lobster, crab legs, cocktail shrimp, half-shell scallops, 15 salads and 20 desserts. Casual dress; beer & wine only. **Parking:** on-site. **Cards:** MC, VI.

TOKAI RESTAURANT   Lunch: $5-$13   Dinner: $5-$13   Phone: 813/621-3332   [108]
Japanese
Location: I-75, exit 257, 0.5 mi w on SR 60; in Brandon Crossings. 10115 Adamo Dr 33619. **Hours:** 11:30 am-2:30 & 5:30-9:30 pm, Fri-10 pm, Sat 5 pm-10 pm. **Features:** The Japanese-themed restaurant is known for its extensive sushi menu, which lists some 130 choices. Limited hot-cooked items are available. Casual dress. **Parking:** on-site. **Cards:** MC, VI.

TUSCA BELLA GRILL   Dinner: $8-$19   Phone: 813/290-7744   [32]
Italian
Location: Just s of jct Linebaugh. 9212 Anderson Rd 33634. **Hours:** 5 pm-10 pm, Fri-Sun 4 pm-11 pm. Closed: 11/23, 12/25. **Features:** Representative of the restaurant's offerings are Tuscan wood stone pizzas, chicken gorgonzola and grouper Stepheno. Diners can't miss with the many choices and the comfortable and trendy atmosphere. Casual dress; cocktails. **Parking:** on-site. **Cards:** AX, DC, MC, VI.

(See map and index starting on p. 950)

VALENCIA GARDEN Lunch: $6-$8 Dinner: $10-$17 Phone: 813/253-3773 (99)
Spanish
Location: I-275, exit 44, 0.7 mi w on Ashley Dr, then 0.5 mi s. 811 W Kennedy Blvd 33606. **Hours:** 11 am-10 pm, Sat from 5 pm. Closed major holidays; also Sun & 7/5. **Reservations:** suggested, weekends. **Features:** Established in 1927, the restaurant details its vivid history in old murals, tiles and decorations. Each dining room carries its own theme, ranging from romantic to raucous. The chicken with yellow rice, garnished with red pepper, is delightfully spicy. Casual dress; cocktails. **Parking:** on-site. **Cards:** AX, DC, DS, MC, VI.

VALLARTO'S RESTAURANTE MEXICANO Lunch: $6-$11 Dinner: $6-$11 Phone: 813/264-7691 (10)
Mexican
Location: On US 92, just s of jct Fletcher Ave. 13731-37 N Dale Mabry Hwy 33618. **Hours:** 11 am-10 pm. **Features:** Authentic Mexican cuisine served in decorative Southwestern surroundings. The menu is extensive, with at least 60 items to choose from. The burritos and taco combo platter are quite good or try the chihuahua cheese. Casual dress; beer & wine only. **Parking:** on-site. **Cards:** MC, VI.

VILLA RINA'S Lunch: $5-$20 Dinner: $5-$20 Phone: 813/654-6449 (94)
Italian
Location: I-75, exit 257, 0.5 mi w on SR 60; in Brandon Crossings. 10073 Adamo Dr 33619. **Hours:** 10 am-10 pm, Fri & Sat-10:30 pm. Closed: 1/1, 12/25; also Sun. **Features:** Friendly servers circulate through the casual spot, which prepares tasty pizza and pasta dishes, as well as stromboli, calzones and several sandwiches. Casual dress; beer & wine only. **Parking:** on-site. **Cards:** AX, CB, DC, DS, MC, VI.

WESTSHORE PIZZA & CHEESESTEAKS I Lunch: $4-$17 Dinner: $4-$17 Phone: 813/832-5331 (128)
Pizza
Location: Jct of W Bay Court Ave. 3900 S Westshore Blvd 33611. **Hours:** 11 am-10 pm, Fri & Sat-11 pm. **Features:** This place is a favorite of those who love pizza, calzones and Philly grinders. The atmosphere is relaxed, and servers are friendly. Meals are cooked to order. Casual dress. **Parking:** on-site. **Cards:** MC, VI.

WESTSHORE PIZZERIA TAMPA Lunch: $4-$17 Dinner: $4-$17 Phone: 813/989-3050 (30)
Pizza
Location: Jct N 40th St. 3719 E Busch Blvd 33612. **Hours:** 11 am-10 pm, Fri & Sat-11 pm, Sun-9 pm. **Features:** This place is a favorite of those who love pizza, calzones and Philly grinders. The atmosphere is relaxed, and servers are friendly. Meals are cooked to order. Casual dress. **Parking:** on-site. **Cards:** MC, VI.

WINDY CITY PIZZA Lunch: $6-$19 Dinner: $6-$19 Phone: 813/960-1400 (12)
American
Location: Jct Fletcher; in Cascades Center. 12908 N Dale Mabry 33618. **Hours:** 11:30 am-10 pm, Fri & Sat-11 pm, Sun 4 pm-10 pm. Closed: 9/4, 11/23, 12/25. **Features:** A subtle Chicago sports theme is at the heart of the restaurant's contemporary decor. Gourmet pizza featuring over 15 toppings, garden fresh salad and hearty pasta entrees with homemade sauces are menu mainstays. Casual dress; beer & wine only. **Parking:** on-site. **Cards:** AX, DS, MC, VI.

THE WINE EXCHANGE BISTRO & WINE BAR Lunch: $8-$10 Dinner: $8-$10 Phone: 813/254-9463 (115)
Italian
Location: Jct Snow Ave; in Old Hyde Park Village. 1611 W Swann Ave 33606. **Hours:** 11:30 am-10 pm, Fri & Sat-11 pm, Sun 11 am-10 pm. Closed major holidays. **Features:** Dine among Greek ruins at this upscale, cafe-style restaurant. An Italian-influenced menu features many different dishes ranging from filet mignon served with mushrooms to traditional pasta and pizza. Smoking is allowed on the patio area only. Casual dress; beer & wine only. **Parking:** street. **Cards:** AX, CB, DC, DS, JC, MC, VI.

WOODY'S BAR-B-QUE Lunch: $6-$15 Dinner: $6-$15 Phone: 813/978-9132 (13)
American
Location: I-275, exit 51, just e. 1120 E Fowler Ave 33612. **Hours:** 11 am-9 pm, Fri & Sat-10 pm. Closed: 11/23, 12/25. **Features:** Vintage movie posters and bright colors pique your senses in this rustic diner. Wood-smoked pork, beef, ribs and chicken are topped with a distinctive hickory barbecue sauce and served in record time by a khaki-clad staff. Southern style quality barbecue. Casual dress; beer & wine only. **Parking:** on-site. **Cards:** AX, DC, DS, MC, VI.

YACHT STARSHIP Lunch: $70 Dinner: $70 Phone: 813/223-7999 (90)
Continental
Location: Just s of jct SR 60; at Channelside; downtown. 223 S 12th St 33602. **Hours:** hours vary. **Reservations:** required. **Features:** This popular dining establishment offers an attraction and dining all in one. A fine dining experience is just one of the draws to this yacht which offers panoramic views of downtown Tampa as you cruise Old Tampa Bay while dining and being treated by their hospitable staff. There is also live music on the top deck to dance to. Dressy casual; cocktails; entertainment. **Parking:** on-site (fee). **Cards:** MC, VI.

The Tampa Vicinity

APOLLO BEACH pop. 7,444

——— WHERE TO STAY ———

RAMADA INN ON TAMPA BAY Phone: 813/641-2700
Motel
Property failed to provide current rates
Location: I-75, exit 246, 1.8 mi w on CR 672, 1.8 mi s on US 41, then 2.4 mi w on Apollo Beach Blvd. 6414 Surfside Blvd 33572. Fax: 813/645-9294. **Facility:** 102 one-bedroom standard units. 2 stories, exterior corridors. **Parking:** on-site. **Terms:** check-in 4 pm, pets ($15 extra charge). **Amenities:** voice mail, safes (fee), irons, hair dryers. **Pool(s):** heated outdoor. **Leisure Activities:** fishing, bicycles, volleyball. **Guest Services:** valet and coin laundry. **Business Services:** meeting rooms, fax (fee).

SOME UNITS
FEE

——— WHERE TO DINE ———

BEEF O'BRADY'S   Lunch: $5-$7   Dinner: $5-$7   Phone: 813/641-1989
American
Location: I-75, exit 246, 1.8 mi w on CR 672, then 1.8 mi s on US 41. 205 Apollo Beach Blvd, Suite 108 33572. **Hours:** 11 am-11 pm, Sun 12:30 pm-10 pm. Closed: 11/23, 12/25. **Features:** Big screen TVs keep this spot hopping on game days. A bustling family sports pub that cooks up a variety of traditional burgers, sandwiches, salads and wings, it features a terrific Philly cheese steak served with french fries and a pickle spear. Casual dress; beer & wine only. **Parking:** on-site. **Cards:** AX, MC, VI.

BELLEAIR BLUFFS pop. 2,243 (See map and index starting on p. 938)

——— WHERE TO DINE ———

E & E STAKEOUT GRILL   Lunch: $10-$25   Dinner: $10-$25   Phone: 727/585-6399   [107]
American
Location: Jct Indian Rocks Rd and West Bay; in The Plaza. 100 N Indian Rocks Rd 33770. **Hours:** 11:30 am-close. Closed: 12/25. **Reservations:** suggested. **Features:** Located in strip mall of galleries and upscale boutiques, this Southwestern themed restaurant gives you the feel of New Mexico with kokopelli, the mischievous spirit, the mascot. Choices include steak, seafood, poultry and appetizers. Dessert is a must. Casual dress. **Parking:** on-site. **Cards:** AX, DC, DS, MC, VI.

BRANDON pop. 77,895 (See map and index starting on p. 950)

——— WHERE TO STAY ———

BRANDON MOTOR LODGE   Phone: (813)689-1261   [83]
Motel
2/1-4/20	1P: $59-$79	2P: $69-$89	XP: $10 F12
12/1-1/31	1P: $59-$69	2P: $69-$79	XP: $10 F12
4/21-11/30	1P: $49-$55	2P: $59-$65	XP: $10 F12

Location: I-75, exit 257, 4.1 mi e on SR 60. 906 E Brandon Blvd 33511. Fax: 13/685-0975. **Facility:** 35 one-bedroom standard units. 2 stories, exterior corridors. *Bath:* combo or shower only. **Parking:** on-site. **Amenities:** hair dryers. *Some:* irons. **Pool(s):** outdoor. **Guest Services:** coin laundry. **Business Services:** fax (fee). **Cards:** AX, DC, DS, MC, VI.

SOME UNITS

HOLIDAY INN EXPRESS-BRANDON   *Book at aaa.com*   Phone: (813)643-3800   [80]
Small-scale Hotel
1/31-4/30 [ECP]	1P: $129-$139	2P: $129-$139	XP: $10 F17
12/1-1/30 [ECP]	1P: $99-$109	2P: $99-$109	XP: $10 F17
5/1-11/30 [ECP]	1P: $89-$99	2P: $89-$99	XP: $10 F17

Location: I-75, exit 257, just e on SR 60, then 0.6 mi n; in Regency Office Park. 510 Grand Regency Blvd 33510. Fax: 813/643-5888. **Facility:** 119 units. 112 one-bedroom standard units. 7 one-bedroom suites ($129-$159) with whirlpools. 4 stories, interior corridors. *Bath:* combo or shower only. **Parking:** on-site. **Terms:** cancellation fee imposed, [CP] meal plan available. **Amenities:** high-speed Internet, voice mail, irons, hair dryers. **Pool(s):** outdoor. **Leisure Activities:** exercise room. **Guest Services:** valet and coin laundry. **Business Services:** meeting rooms, business center. **Cards:** AX, CB, DC, DS, JC, MC, VI.

SOME UNITS

HOMESTEAD STUDIO SUITES
HOTEL-TAMPA/BRANDON   *Book at aaa.com*   Phone: (813)643-5900   [82]
Motel
All Year	1P: $54-$69	2P: $59-$74	XP: $5 F17

Location: I-75, exit 257, just e on SR 60, then 0.4 mi n; in Regency Office Park. 330 Grand Regency Blvd 33510. Fax: 813/643-4343. **Facility:** 142 one-bedroom standard units with efficiencies. 2 stories, exterior corridors. *Bath:* combo or shower only. **Parking:** on-site. **Terms:** office hours 6:30 am-11 pm, pets ($25-$75 extra charge). **Amenities:** high-speed Internet (fee), voice mail, irons. *Some:* hair dryers. **Guest Services:** valet and coin laundry. **Business Services:** fax. **Cards:** AX, DC, DS, MC, VI.

SOME UNITS
FEE

LA QUINTA INN & SUITES TAMPA BAY (BRANDON)   *Book at aaa.com*   Phone: (813)643-0574   [81]
Small-scale Hotel
2/1-4/30	1P: $129-$149	XP: $7 F18
5/1-11/30	1P: $95-$105	XP: $7 F18
12/1-1/31	1P: $89-$99	XP: $7 F18

Location: I-75, exit 257, just e on SR 60, then 0.5 mi n; in Regency Office Park. 310 Grand Regency Blvd 33510. Fax: 813/643-5408. **Facility:** 128 units. 123 one-bedroom standard units. 5 one-bedroom suites ($125-$189). 5 stories, interior corridors. *Bath:* combo or shower only. **Parking:** on-site. **Terms:** [ECP] meal plan available, small pets only. **Amenities:** video games (fee), high-speed Internet, dual phone lines, voice mail, irons, hair dryers. **Pool(s):** heated outdoor. **Leisure Activities:** whirlpool, gazebo, exercise room. **Guest Services:** valet and coin laundry. **Business Services:** meeting rooms, fax (fee). **Cards:** AX, CB, DC, DS, MC, VI. **Special Amenities:** free expanded continental breakfast and free local telephone calls. (See color ad p 982)

SOME UNITS

——— WHERE TO DINE ———

THE AMERICAN CAFE   Lunch: $7-$11   Dinner: $8-$14   Phone: 813/681-8891   [178]
American
Location: I-75, exit 257, just e on SR 60, then just s; in Brandon Town Center Mall. 504 Brandon Town Center 33511. **Hours:** 11 am-10 pm, Fri & Sat-11 pm, Sun-9 pm. Closed: 11/23, 12/25. **Features:** The restaurant offers a variety of tasty treats—poultry, steak and seafood dishes, as well as burgers and sandwiches. Soups and house salads are tasty starts. It's hard to go wrong with the hearty pot roast. Casual dress; cocktails. **Parking:** on-site. **Cards:** AX, DC, DS, MC, VI.

(See map and index starting on p. 950)

BABE'S PIZZA
▽▽ ◇◇
Pizza
Dinner: $7-$18   **Phone:** 813/689-2282   [159]
Location: Just n of jct SR 60. 107 N Kings Ave 33510. **Hours:** 5 pm-10 pm, Sun-9:30 pm. Closed major holidays.
Features: The local favorite has been around for years. Lending to the casual atmosphere is a circling "choo choo." The popular double-decker pizza is smothered with lots of goodies. Casual dress; beer & wine only. **Parking:** on-site. **Cards:** MC, VI.

BARNACLES
▽▽ ◇◇
Seafood
Lunch: $6-$17   **Dinner:** $6-$17   **Phone:** 813/653-0959   [186]
Location: Jct Lumsden Rd. 926 Providence Rd 33511. **Hours:** 11 am-2 am, Thurs-Sat to 3 am, Sun-1 am.
Features: At least 100 television sets line the walls inside and outside of the sports bar and restaurant, and diners can keep up with nearly any sport imaginable. The extensive menu includes such house specialties as shrimp Malibu or steak Napoleon. The pasta also is tasty. For a lighter meal, try one of the many salads, soups, chicken sandwiches, po'boy subs or gourmet burgers. The andouille sausage sub is a good choice. Casual dress; cocktails. **Parking:** on-site. **Cards:** AX, DC, DS, MC, VI.

BEN'S FAMILY RESTAURANT
▽▽ ▽▽
American
Lunch: $6-$14   **Dinner:** $6-$14   **Phone:** 813/685-5501   [160]
Location: I-75, exit 257, 3.3 mi e on SR 60; jct Ridgewood Ave. 704 E Brandon Blvd 33510. **Hours:** 7:30 am-9 pm. Closed: 11/23, 12/25; also Mon & Tues. **Features:** Relax in this comfortable, family style restaurant with country decor and a nautical touch. A variety of home cooked entrees such as steak, chicken, pork and sandwiches are available. Try one of their many homemade desserts. Casual dress. **Parking:** on-site.
Cards: DS, MC, VI.

BONEFISH GRILL
▽▽ ▽▽ ▽▽
Seafood
Dinner: $16-$24   **Phone:** 813/571-5553   [199]
Location: Jct Causeway Blvd. 1015 Providence Rd 33511. **Hours:** 4 pm-10:30 pm, Fri & Sat-11:30 pm, Sun-10 pm. Closed: 11/23, 12/25. **Features:** Upscale surroundings and a professional wait staff contribute to an enjoyable dining experience. The creative menu's components range from fontina chops to portobello pasta to the tasty pistachio Parmesan-crusted rainbow trout. No matter what they choose, diners are in for a treat. Dressy casual; cocktails. **Parking:** on-site. **Cards:** AX, DS, MC, VI.   🔄Ⓜ 🍸

BRANDON BREW HOUSE
▽▽ ▽▽
American
Lunch: $7-$19   **Dinner:** $7-$19   **Phone:** 813/655-0511   [192]
Location: Jct of Kings Ave; in Oak Park Plaza. 779 W Lumsden Rd 33511. **Features:** A local favorite serving up casual fare such as burgers, sandwiches, steaks and chicken dishes. The service is friendly in this local eatery. A comedy club is on site offering local entertainers for a fun night out. Casual dress; cocktails. **Parking:** on-site. **Cards:** AX, MC, VI.

BUCA DI BEPPO BRANDON
▽▽ ▽▽
Italian
Dinner: $18-$29   **Phone:** 813/681-8462   [197]
Location: Jct Gornto Lake Rd. 11105 Causeway Blvd 33511. **Hours:** 4 pm-10 pm, Fri-11 pm, Sat noon-11 pm, Sun noon-9 pm. Closed: 11/23, 12/25. **Features:** Guests should come with a hearty appetite to take advantage of huge portions of fabulous Southern Italian cuisine. The restaurant is noted for "Neapolitan pizzas as big as bathmats" and other well-known favorites. The eclectic decor incorporates hundreds of wall-to-wall pictures and artifacts. Casual dress; cocktails. **Parking:** on-site. **Cards:** MC, VI.   🍸

BUDDY FREDDY'S
▽▽
American
Lunch: $8-$10   **Dinner:** $10-$13   **Phone:** 813/661-6005   [170]
Location: I-75, exit 257, 0.7 mi e on SR 60, then just s. 134 S Gornto Lake Rd 33511. **Hours:** 7 am-9 pm, Sun-8 pm. **Features:** This is good, old-fashioned home cooking dished up in a country decor. An excellent lunch and dinner buffet is offered with an a la carte menu for added variety. Bring the whole family, and take advantage of early bird specials and senior discounts. Casual dress. **Parking:** on-site. **Cards:** DS, MC, VI.   🔄Ⓜ

BUFFALO WILD WINGS GRILL & BAR
▽▽ ▽▽
American
Lunch: $6-$12   **Dinner:** $6-$12   **Phone:** 813/571-1045   [181]
Location: Just n of jct Lumsden Rd on Providence Rd. 2055 Badlands Dr 33511. **Hours:** 11 am-2 am, Sun noon-midnight, Mon 11 am-1 am. **Features:** The casual spot is great for joining friends for a fun dinner, especially for those who like large-screened TVs; this place has several of at least 10 feet by 10 feet, and the main screen is even larger. On the menu are various appetizers and finger foods, as well as salads, burgers, quesadillas, fish and chicken items. Casual dress; cocktails. **Parking:** on-site. **Cards:** MC, VI.   🔄Ⓜ 🍸

CAULDRON JAMAICAN RESTAURANT &
   AMERICAN CUISINE
▽▽ ▽▽
Jamaican
Lunch: $9-$13   **Dinner:** $9-$13   **Phone:** 813/689-1959   [175]
Location: Just e of jct Kings. 230 Oakfield Dr 33511. **Hours:** 11 am-9 pm. Closed: Sun. **Features:** This is the spot to try for those who enjoy Jamaican food, including ackee and saltfish, the country's national dish. Also on the menu are jerk pork and chicken; curry goat, shrimp or chicken; and oxtail smothered in brown island sauce. Casual dress. **Parking:** on-site. **Cards:** MC, VI.

CHEDDAR'S CASUAL CAFE
▽▽ ▽▽
American
Lunch: $5-$13   **Dinner:** $5-$13   **Phone:** 813/653-7770   [196]
Location: Just w of jct Providence Rd. 11135 Causeway Blvd 33511. **Hours:** 11 am-10 pm, Fri & Sat-11 pm. Closed: 11/23, 12/25. **Features:** Key West-themed dining rooms incorporate contemporary yet rustic influences. Representative of the great food are such choices as the sandwich board, gourmet burgers and the signature honey barbecue baby back ribs. Also available are combination plates, steaks and seafood and poultry items. Casual dress; cocktails. **Parking:** on-site. **Cards:** AX, DS, MC, VI.   🔄Ⓜ 🍸

CHERRY'S
▽▽ ▽▽
American
Lunch: $6-$13   **Dinner:** $6-$13   **Phone:** 813/662-1500   [205]
Location: Jct Bell Shoals Rd; in Bloomingdale Square. 903 E Bloomingdale Ave 33511. **Hours:** 11 am-11 pm. **Features:** Visitors can watch their favorite sporting event on one of the many television monitors placed about the dining room. The trendy establishment's menu lists sandwiches and burgers, as well as the must-try buffalo wings and chili cheese fries. Casual dress; cocktails. **Parking:** on-site. **Cards:** MC, VI.   🍸

(See map and index starting on p. 950)

CHICAGO'S MAXWELL STREET GRILL
American
Lunch: $4-$7 **Dinner:** $4-$7 **Phone:** 813/681-6725 (155)
Location: I-75, exit 257, just w on SR 60; in Regency Square. 2490 W Brandon Blvd 33511. **Hours:** 11 am-8 pm, Fri & Sat-10 pm, Sun noon-7 pm. Closed: 4/16, 11/23, 12/25. **Features:** Adjacent to a popular movie theater, the grill serves quick sandwiches, pitas, burgers or hot dogs. It's a great place to pop in before or after catching a movie or shopping in one of several shops in the strip mall. Casual dress. **Parking:** on-site. **Cards:** MC, VI.

CHICK-N-BONES CAFE
American
Lunch: $4-$8 **Dinner:** $4-$8 **Phone:** 813/689-9531 (191)
Location: Jct Providence Rd; in Brandon Centre South. 1953 W Lunsden Rd 33511. **Hours:** 11 am-9 pm, Sat-8 pm. Closed: Sun. **Features:** A homey feel characterizes the casual spot, which incorporates chickens and roosters into its decor. Flame-broiled chicken and ribs are the claim, but the menu also lists pitas, tortilla wraps, sandwiches and salads. Casual dress. **Parking:** on-site. **Cards:** AX, DS, MC, VI.

CHILI'S BRANDON
American
Lunch: $7-$22 **Dinner:** $7-$22 **Phone:** 813/681-8479 (167)
Location: I-75, exit 257, 0.5 mi e on SR 60; in Providence Square Plaza. 1949 W Brandon Blvd 33511. **Hours:** 11 am-11 pm, Fri & Sat-midnight. **Features:** A fun setting and welcoming staff make this a great spot to stop for a yummy lunch or dinner. Items on the menu include Hawaiian steak, sizzling fajitas, Monterey chicken and tasty baby back ribs and chicken. Casual dress; cocktails. **Parking:** on-site. **Cards:** MC, VI.

CHOP STIX CHINESE RESTAURANT
Chinese
Lunch: $5-$14 **Dinner:** $5-$14 **Phone:** 813/654-5195 (164)
Location: On SR 60, just w of jct Mt Carmel. 801 E Brandon Blvd 33511. **Hours:** 11 am-10:30 pm, Fri-11 pm, Sun noon-10 pm. Closed: 12/25. **Features:** Although seating is limited in this small restaurant, the food is worth the wait and is some of the best authentic Chinese food you'll find in these parts. The menu is extensive. Casual dress. **Parking:** on-site. **Cards:** MC, VI.

COUNTRY KITCHEN
American
Lunch: $6-$10 **Dinner:** $6-$10 **Phone:** 813/643-4449 (203)
Location: Just w of jct John Moore Rd; in Bloomingdale Plaza. 174 E Bloomingdale Ave 33511. **Hours:** 7 am-8 pm, Sun-3 pm. Closed: 11/23, 12/25; also Mon. **Features:** Fans of good old country cooking are in for a treat here. Anything from a country breakfast of potato pancakes to a daily special of chicken and dumplings will tickle the patron's fancy. Casual dress. **Parking:** on-site. **Cards:** MC, VI.

CRISPERS
American
Lunch: $5-$8 **Dinner:** $5-$8 **Phone:** 813/654-9940 (200)
Location: Just w of jct Providence Rd. 11019 Causeway Blvd 33511. **Hours:** 10:30 am-9 pm. **Features:** The contemporary decor incorporates a bit of an art deco flair. Guests can unwind in the relaxing spot with a salad or delicatessen-style sandwich. The food is prepared when it's ordered. Casual dress. **Parking:** on-site. **Cards:** MC, VI.

DELLA'S DELECTABLES
American
Lunch: $5-$8 **Dinner:** $12-$19 **Phone:** 813/684-3354 (174)
Location: Just s of jct SR 60, just e. 608 Oakfield Dr 33511. **Hours:** 7 am-3 pm, Thurs & Fri also 5 pm-10 pm, Sat 9 am-2 & 5-10 pm. **Features:** Enjoy freshly made deli sandwiches and bakery goods at this casual eatery and coffee bar setting. Casual dress; beer & wine only. **Parking:** on-site. **Cards:** MC, VI.

ESTELA'S MEXICAN RESTAURANT
Mexican
Lunch: $3-$6 **Dinner:** $5-$10 **Phone:** 813/657-1421 (162)
Location: I-75, exit 257, 3 mi e on SR 60, jct Kings Ave. 312 E Brandon Blvd 33511. **Hours:** 11 am-10 pm, Fri & Sat-11 pm. **Features:** The quaint Mexican cantina setting offers a relaxed ambience for a casual meal. The menu offers many choices, such as chimichangas, nachos, fajitas, huevos rancheros and quesadillas. Casual dress; beer & wine only. **Parking:** on-site. **Cards:** MC, VI.

FIREHOUSE SUBS
American
Lunch: $4-$8 **Dinner:** $4-$8 **Phone:** 813/849-0057 (173)
Location: I-75, exit 257, 0.5 mi e on SR 60; in Providence Square Plaza. 1921 W Brandon Blvd 33511. **Hours:** 10:30 am-9 pm, Fri & Sat-10:30 pm. **Features:** This is an enjoyable place to relax and have a freshly made hot or cold sub, soup, salad or any one of their many "old fashioned sandwiches" made from such meats as Virginia honey ham, smoked turkey breast or corned beef brisket. Featuring a steaming method on their meats and cheeses combined with the toasting of the rolls, the subs and sandwiches are a real treat. Casual dress. **Parking:** on-site. **Cards:** MC, VI.

HAO ONE CHINESE RESTAURANT
Chinese
Lunch: $6-$12 **Dinner:** $6-$12 **Phone:** 813/685-6381 (161)
Location: I-75, exit 257, 0.6 mi e on SR 60. 2020 W Brandon Blvd, Suite 145 33511. **Hours:** 11 am-10 pm. Closed: 11/23. **Features:** Chinese food in all its variety is the focus at this relaxing, Asian-themed restaurant. The lo mein, beef and broccoli, and General Tso's chicken are particularly tasty, and an extensive buffet is available. Casual dress; beer & wine only. **Parking:** on-site. **Cards:** AX, DS, MC, VI.

HOPS GRILLHOUSE & BREWERY
American
Lunch: $8-$20 **Dinner:** $9-$20 **Phone:** 813/661-1717 (188)
Location: Jct Providence Rd. 11310 Causeway Blvd 33619. **Hours:** 11 am-11 pm, Fri & Sat-11:30 pm, Sun-10 pm. **Features:** Tempting microbrews share top billing with the good food, which includes choices ranging from delicious Jamaican top sirloin—a 12-ounce sirloin marinated in a tropical blend of pineapple, soy and ginger—to baby back ribs and the chicken-chili burrito. For a treat, finish the meal with a slice of baked apple crunch topped with a scoop of vanilla bean ice cream. Casual dress; cocktails. **Parking:** on-site. **Cards:** MC, VI.

JASMINE THAI & SUSHI BAR
Thai
Lunch: $6-$10 **Dinner:** $7-$24 **Phone:** 813/662-3635 (190)
Location: Jct Providence Rd; in Brandon Centre South. 1947 W Lumsden Rd 33511. **Hours:** 11:30 am-2:30 & 4-9:30 pm, Fri & Sat-10:30 pm. Closed: 11/23. **Features:** The popular dinner spot serves some of the best Thai food around. Patrons who unwind in the nice, cozy surroundings are in for a fine-dining treat. The service staff is professional, and the setting is as exceptional as is the food. Casual dress; cocktails. **Parking:** on-site. **Cards:** AX, DS, MC, VI.

(See map and index starting on p. 950)

JOEY'S FAMOUS PHILLY STEAKS **Lunch:** $6-$8   **Dinner:** $6-$8   **Phone:** 813/662-5300   (185)
American
Location: Jct Lumsden. 921 S Lithia Pinecrest Rd 33511. **Hours:** 10:30 am-8 pm, Fri & Sat-8:30 pm, Sun 11 am-6 pm. Closed major holidays. **Features:** Diners who order one of the signature Philly cheese steaks are in for a delicious treat. The small eatery offers some of the best of the Northeast, with a variety of subs and sandwich offerings. Casual dress. **Parking:** on-site. **Cards:** MC, VI.

JO-TO JAPANESE STEAK HOUSE   **Dinner:** $12-$25   **Phone:** 813/684-0221   (183)
Japanese
Location: 1.1 mi s of jct SR 60; in Lithia Square. 905 Lithia Pinecrest Rd 33511. **Hours:** 5 pm-9:30 pm, Fri & Sat-10:30 pm. Closed: 7/4, 11/23, 12/25; also Super Bowl Sun. **Features:** Appreciate traditional Japanese cuisine prepared with the Teppan-yaki method of cooking. Choose from seafood, steak and chicken teriyaki or tempura dishes. Watch the cooks practice their craft table-side, or sample delicacies from the sushi bar.
Casual dress; cocktails. **Parking:** on-site. **Cards:** AX, CB, DC, MC, VI.

LA CUBANITA CAFE   **Lunch:** $7   **Dinner:** $7   **Phone:** 813/661-2253   (193)
Cuban
Location: Jct S Kings Ave; in Oak Park Plaza. 723A W Lumsden Rd 33511. **Features:** In a popular strip mall, the restaurant prepares numerous Cuban entrees; the pressed Cuban is a favorite. Service is friendly, and the surroundings are relaxed and casual. Casual dress. **Parking:** on-site. **Cards:** MC, VI.

LATIN CAFE 2000   **Lunch:** $4-$8   **Dinner:** $8-$12   **Phone:** 813/643-9475   (209)
Spanish
Location: Jct Bell Shoals Rd; in Bloomingdale Square. 829 E Bloomingdale Ave 33594. **Hours:** 7 am-9 pm, Fri & Sat-10 pm. Closed: 11/23, 12/25. **Features:** The decor is trendy in the upscale restaurant. Breakfast options are plentiful, and the main menu offers sandwiches, meat dishes, soup, chicken, seafood, salad and dessert, all prepared with a zippy Latin flair. Casual dress; beer & wine only. **Parking:** on-site. **Cards:** AX, DS, MC, VI.

LIN'S GARDEN CHINESE RESTAURANT   **Lunch:** $5-$13   **Dinner:** $5-$13   **Phone:** 813/689-6868   (195)
Chinese
Location: Jct Brandon Town Center Dr; in Lake Brandon Plaza. 11237 Causeway Blvd 33511. **Hours:** 11 am-10 pm, Fri & Sat-10:30 pm, Sun noon-9:30 pm. Closed: 11/23, 12/25. **Features:** Dine in or take out, the small, ultra-casual restaurant specializes in more than 100 choices of "New York-style" Chinese food. Casual dress. **Parking:** on-site. **Cards:** MC, VI.

MILLER'S BRANDON ALE HOUSE & RAW BAR   **Lunch:** $6-$13   **Dinner:** $6-$13   **Phone:** 813/643-0511   (166)
Seafood
Location: I-75, exit 257, 2.4 mi e on SR 60. 1817 W Brandon Blvd 33511. **Hours:** 11 am-2 am. Closed: 11/23. **Features:** This sports-themed restaurant will impress many fans with 40 TV monitors and four satellite dishes. Catch the big game and enjoy a variety of sandwiches, pasta and seafood. Casual dress; cocktails. **Parking:** on-site. **Cards:** AX, DC, DS, MC, VI.

MIMIS CAFE BRANDON   **Lunch:** $7-$16   **Dinner:** $7-$16   **Phone:** 813/684-1184   (182)
American
Location: Just ne of jct Lumsden Rd. 804 Providence Rd 33511. **Hours:** 7 am-11 pm. Closed: 12/25. **Features:** With the feel of a New Orleans cafe, the eatery offers festive and colorful surroundings as well as friendly and professional service while patrons dine on bountiful meals with shades of home cooking. The menu is extensive, offering anything from yummy pot roast to pasta jambalaya to apple cider glazed pork chops. Casual dress; cocktails. **Parking:** on-site. **Cards:** AX, MC, VI.

MOE'S SOUTHWEST GRILL   **Lunch:** $3-$9   **Dinner:** $3-$9   **Phone:** 813/681-0955   (156)
Mexican
Location: I-75, exit 257, just e on SR 60; in Regency Square. 2338 W Brandon Blvd 33511. **Hours:** 11 am-10 pm, Sun-9 pm. Closed: 11/23, 12/25. **Features:** At the neat little spot, guests can sample a freshly made fajita, taco, burrito or quesadilla that was prepared to order as they make their way down the service line. Hearty portions satisfy big appetites. Casual dress; beer & wine only. **Parking:** on-site. **Cards:** AX, MC, VI.

NATURE'S TABLE   **Lunch:** $5-$8   **Dinner:** $5-$8   **Phone:** 813/685-2766   (179)
American
Location: I-75, exit 257, just e on SR 60, then just s; in Westfield Shoppingtown. 505 Brandon Town Center Dr 33511. **Hours:** 10 am-9 pm. **Features:** In the popular Westfield Shoppingtown food court area, the eatery focuses its menu on low-carbohydrate and low-calorie options. Fresh delicatessen meats, pita breads, wheat rolls and salad fixings are prepared as patrons watch. Casual dress. **Parking:** on-site. **Cards:** MC, VI.

NY'S TIMES SQUARE PIZZA   **Lunch:** $6-$19   **Dinner:** $6-$19   **Phone:** 813/651-0122   (208)
Italian
Location: Jct Bell Shoals Rd; in Bloomingdale Square. 927 E Bloomingdale Ave 33511. **Hours:** 11 am-9 pm, Fri & Sat-midnight. **Features:** The casual eatery offers great pizzas, calzones and pasta dishes. Seating is limited, so guests should arrive early to secure a spot for good food. Casual dress. **Parking:** on-site. **Cards:** MC, VI.

OAKS BAR & GRILL   **Lunch:** $7-$21   **Dinner:** $7-$21   **Phone:** 813/685-5257   (171)
American
Location: Just s of jct SR 60. 108 S Lithia-Pinecrest Rd 33511. **Hours:** 11 am-midnight, Sun noon-9 pm, Mon & Tues 11 am-10 pm. Closed: 1/1, 11/23, 12/25. **Features:** Touches of Key West accent the decor, and live entertainment on Fridays and Saturdays keeps the mood jovial. Enjoy fresh seafood, sandwiches and steaks, including a savory seafood gumbo with a generous helping of fish in a seasoned tomato broth.
Casual dress; cocktails. **Parking:** on-site. **Cards:** AX, DS, MC, VI.

O'BRIEN'S IRISH PUB   **Lunch:** $8-$17   **Dinner:** $8-$17   **Phone:** 813/661-9688   (198)
Irish
Location: Jct Kings; in Oak Plaza Shops. 701 W Lumsden Rd 33511. **Hours:** 11 am-3 am. Closed: Sun 2/1-9/1. **Features:** A comfortable, casual setting is the scene for a wonderful Irish experience. Guests can try anything from shepherd's pie to Irish stew to bangers and mash. Casual dress; cocktails. **Parking:** on-site. **Cards:** MC, VI.

(See map and index starting on p. 950)

PANERA BREAD CAFE   Lunch: $4-$7   Dinner: $4-$7   Phone: 813/653-3837   176

American

Location: 0.5 mi s of jct SR 60; in Westfield Crossings. 364 Brandon Town Center 33511. **Hours:** 7 am-9 pm, Sun 9 am-6 pm. **Closed:** 11/23, 12/25. **Features:** Indoor and outdoor seating can be requested at the inviting, relaxing cafe. In addition to freshly baked breads and pastries, choices include a variety of freshly made salads, soups, hot panini and signature sandwiches. Casual dress. **Parking:** on-site. **Cards:** AX, MC, VI.

PECK'S FLAME BROILED CHICKEN   Lunch: $6-$27   Dinner: $6-$27   Phone: 813/643-3867   207

American

Location: Just w of jct John Moore Rd; in Bloomingdale Plaza. 127 E Bloomingdale Ave 33511. **Hours:** 11 am-9 pm. Closed major holidays; also Sun. **Features:** Diners who love the taste of flame-broiled chicken and ribs might give the casual eatery a visit. Among cooked-to-order dishes are chicken barbecue, salads and sandwich items. Casual dress. **Parking:** on-site. **Cards:** MC, VI.

PITA'S   Lunch: $4-$7   Dinner: $4-$7   Phone: 813/661-9299   194

Natural/Organic

Location: Jct Providence Rd; in Lake Brandon Plaza. 11329 Causeway Blvd 33511. **Hours:** 11 am-9 pm. **Features:** Known for its "naturally nutritious" menu offerings, the restaurant prepares foods to be low in saturated fat and calories, in part by vertically broiling meats. Among choices are low-carbohydrate pockets and hot or cold pitas. Casual dress. **Parking:** on-site. **Cards:** MC, VI.

PLOY THAI RESTAURANT   Lunch: $7-$8   Dinner: $9-$21   Phone: 813/684-5007   172

Thai

Location: I-75, exit 257, 0.5 mi e on SR 60; in Providence Square Plaza. 1941 W Brandon Blvd 33511. **Hours:** 11 am-2:30 & 4:30-10 pm, Sat noon-2:30 & 4:30-10:30 pm. Closed: Sun. **Features:** Authentic Thai cuisine and a very attractively decorated dining room replicating an elegant Thai restaurant are just the beginning of a wonderful dining experience. The staff is adorned in traditional Thai garb and offer gracious service. The food is outstanding with such choices as Tamarind duck or Thai lobster, and the Panang curry is a must try. Dressy casual. **Parking:** on-site. **Cards:** MC, VI.

RIB CITY GRILL BRANDON   Lunch: $5-$20   Dinner: $5-$20   Phone: 813/655-0023   168

Barbecue

Location: I-75, exit 257, 2.7 mi e on SR 60. 1215 W Brandon Blvd 33511. **Hours:** 11 am-9 pm, Fri & Sat-10 pm. **Features:** Known for its yummy slow-cooked baby back ribs and the variety of sauces that punctuate them, the cozy country spot is a great spot in which to relax. Popular combination platters might include baby back ribs, barbecue chicken, sliced beef or pork, the mainstay. Add a couple of side dishes, such as a fresh garden salad or sliced tomatoes, and enjoy the treat. Casual dress; beer & wine only. **Parking:** on-site. **Cards:** MC, VI.

ROADHOUSE GRILL   Lunch: $7-$18   Dinner: $7-$18   Phone: 813/657-9892   165

Steak House

Location: I-75, exit 257, 2.8 mi e on SR 60. 775 W Brandon Blvd 33511. **Hours:** 11 am-10 pm, Fri & Sat-11 pm. Closed: 11/23, 12/25. **Features:** As the name says, the restaurant gives you the feel of stepping into an old Texas roadhouse. Grab peanuts from a pail, and after you pop the nut in your mouth, toss the shell on the floor. Savory steaks are at the heart of a menu that also includes ribs, chicken and mesquite-grilled pork chops. Casual dress; cocktails. **Parking:** on-site. **Cards:** AX, DC, DS, MC, VI.

RUBY TUESDAY   Lunch: $8-$18   Dinner: $8-$18   Phone: 813/685-2615   177

American

Location: I-75, exit 257, just e on SR 60, then just s; in Westfield Commons. 450 Brandon Town Center Dr 33511. **Hours:** 11 am-11 pm, Fri & Sat-midnight, Sun-9 pm. **Features:** After a harried day of trolling the many mall stores, shoppers can stop in for a pick-me-up. The eatery offers an extensive salad bar, burgers, sandwiches, ribs, combination platters, fajitas and steaks. Casual dress; cocktails. **Parking:** on-site. **Cards:** MC, VI.

SHELLS OF BRANDON   Lunch: $8-$15   Dinner: $8-$15   Phone: 813/684-4190   163

Seafood

Location: On SR 60, jct Parsons Ave. 115 E Brandon Blvd 33511. **Hours:** 11:30 am-10 pm, Fri & Sat-11 pm, Sun noon-10 pm. **Features:** Guests can enjoy great seafood at the casual establishment, which carries out a bright, colorful nautical theme. Wall displays feature replicated historical photos of old-time Florida. The menu centers on fresh seafood, including combination platters, shrimp and seafood pasta. Casual dress; beer & wine only. **Parking:** on-site. **Cards:** MC, VI.

SHRIMP BOAT GRILL   Lunch: $11-$18   Dinner: $11-$18   Phone: 813/546-1911   187

Seafood

Location: Jct King St; in La Viva Plaza. 716 W Lumsden Rd 33511. **Hours:** 11 am-10 pm, Fri & Sat-11 pm, Sun-9 pm. **Features:** With a fun nautical theme and great menu, the grill is a neat place to dine. Such items as grilled salmon, chicken Marsala, pan-seared grouper and grilled tuna steak are found on the menu. Shrimp-lovers can choose from among all kinds of variations: marinara, Marsala, scampi, patties, beer-battered, garlic, cocktail and so on. Casual dress; cocktails. **Parking:** on-site. **Cards:** AX, MC, VI.

SIMPLY THAI   Dinner: $7-$14   Phone: 813/681-4470   204

Thai

Location: Jct Bell Shoals Rd; in Bloomingdale Square. 875 E Bloomingdale Ave 33511. **Hours:** 4 pm-9 pm, Fri-9:30 pm. Closed: 11/23, 12/25; also Mon. **Features:** Oriental surroundings characterize this friendly Thai establishment, which serves up an enticing array of traditional entrees. Casual dress; beer & wine only. **Parking:** on-site. **Cards:** MC, VI.

SMOKEY BONE'S BARBEQUE & GRILL   Lunch: $5-$18   Dinner: $7-$18   Phone: 813/655-3400   157

Barbecue

Location: I-75, exit 257, just e on SR 60. 136 Brandon Towne Center Dr 33511. **Hours:** 11 am-10 pm, Fri & Sat-11 pm. Closed: 11/23, 12/25. **Features:** A lodgelike setting contributes to the restaurant's rustic appeal. Guests can savor great barbecue dinners while watching sports on television sets around the dining room. Casual dress; cocktails. **Parking:** on-site. **Cards:** AX, MC, VI.

(See map and index starting on p. 950)

STEAK ESCAPE
American

Lunch: $5-$8   Dinner: $5-$8   Phone: 813/661-9889   **180**

Location: I-75, exit 257, just e on SR 60, then just s; in Westfield Shoppingtown. 509 Brandon Town Center Dr 33511. **Hours:** 9 am-9 pm. **Features:** In the popular Westfield Shoppingtown food court area, the eatery prepares grilled sandwiches, 13 types of smashed potatoes and 12 salads. The vegetarian sandwich with onions, mushrooms, green peppers and provolone and Swiss cheeses is a popular choice. This place offers a great respite after a long day of shopping. Casual dress. **Parking:** on-site. **Cards:** MC, VI.

SUSHI HOUSE
Japanese
Cards: MC, VI.

Lunch: $7-$11   Dinner: $9-$14   Phone: 813/651-1038   **169**

Location: I-75, exit 257, 1 mi e on SR 60. 2020 W Brandon Blvd 33511. **Hours:** 11:30 am-10 pm, Fri-10:30 pm, Sat noon-10:30 pm, Sun 5 pm-9:30 pm. **Features:** Sushi lovers can indulge their passion with some 55 sushi choices ranging from the popular California roll to the raw fish roll. Other offerings include sashimi and sake specials, udon, donburi and tempura items. Casual dress; beer & wine only. **Parking:** on-site.

TADPOLES
American

Lunch: $5-$8   Dinner: $5-$8   Phone: 813/685-8908   **184**

Location: Jct Lumsdon; in Lithia Square Shopping Center. 913 Lithia Pinecrest Rd 33511. **Hours:** 11 am-3 am, Sun from noon. **Features:** Kids love the sports-themed local favorite for its small game room, while adults enjoy watching their favorite sporting event. The menu lists a multitude of appetizers, salads, burgers and sandwiches. Casual dress; cocktails. **Parking:** on-site. **Cards:** AX, DS, MC, VI.

TIA'S TEX MEX
Mexican

Lunch: $7-$15   Dinner: $7-$15   Phone: 813/681-7716   **158**

Location: I-75, exit 257, just e on SR 60; in Brandon Town Center. 144 Brandon Town Center Dr 33511. **Hours:** 11 am-10 pm, Fri & Sat-11 pm. Closed: 11/23, 12/25. **Features:** Tex-Mex and mesquite-grilled dishes are served in a Mexican-style cantina setting complete with a courtyard dining area. Fresh, hearty portions mean flavorful choices with burritos, tacos, fajitas and the chalupa tortilla. Casual dress; cocktails. **Parking:** on-site. **Cards:** AX, DC, DS, MC, VI.

TIJUANA FLATS
Mexican

Lunch: $5-$9   Dinner: $5-$9   Phone: 813/643-3020   **202**

Location: Just w of jct Providence Rd. 11007 Causeway Blvd 33511. **Hours:** 11 am-10 pm, Sun 10 am-9 pm. **Features:** The fun spot presents a menu of good, typical Mexican fare, including quesadillas, nachos, chimichangas, enchiladas, taquitos, burritos, tacos and flautas. The decor is fun and festive, and service is relaxed. Casual dress; beer & wine only. **Parking:** on-site. **Cards:** MC, VI.

TROPICAL SMOOTHIE CAFE
American

Lunch: $5-$7   Dinner: $5-$7   Phone: 813/684-1962   **201**

Location: Just w of jct Providence Rd. 11011 Causeway Blvd 33511. **Hours:** 10 am-9 pm, Sun 11 am-8 pm. Closed: 12/25. **Features:** The cafe is known for its low-fat, power, smart, weight-gain and dessert smoothies but also prepares fresh and delicious gourmet wraps, tortizzas, specialty sandwiches, soups and salads. Casual dress. **Parking:** on-site. **Cards:** AX, DS, MC, VI.

WESTSHORE PIZZA & CHEESESTEAKS
Pizza

Lunch: $4-$17   Dinner: $4-$17   Phone: 813/661-2424   **153**

Location: 1.6 mi n of jct SR 60; in Kash N Karry Shopping Center. 1279 Kingsway Rd 33510. **Hours:** 11 am-10 pm, Fri & Sat-11 pm. **Features:** This place is a favorite of those who love pizza, calzones and Philly grinders. The sports-themed atmosphere is relaxed. Patrons can catch a favorite game on the large-screen monitor while eating freshly cooked food. Casual dress. **Parking:** on-site. **Cards:** DS, MC, VI.

WESTSHORE PIZZA VI
Italian

Lunch: $4-$17   Dinner: $4-$17   Phone: 813/662-9800   **206**

Location: Just w of jct John Moore Rd; in Bloomingdale Plaza. 133 E Bloomingdale Ave 33511. **Hours:** 11 am-10 pm, Fri & Sat-11 pm. **Features:** This place is a favorite of those who love pizza, calzones and Philly grinders. The sports-themed atmosphere is relaxed. Patrons can catch a favorite game on the large-screen monitor while eating freshly cooked food. Casual dress; beer & wine only. **Parking:** on-site. **Cards:** MC, VI.

WIZEGUYZ PIZZERIA
Italian

Lunch: $5-$14   Dinner: $5-$14   Phone: 813/643-1200   **154**

Location: I-75, exit 257, just w on SR 60; in Regency Square. 2498 W Brandon Blvd 33511. **Hours:** 11 am-10 pm, Fri & Sat-11 pm. Closed: 12/25. **Features:** The casual New York pizzeria setting is the place to go for some of the best Italian food around. Dishes are freshly prepared after you step up to the window to order. On the menu are sandwiches and pizza by the slice and by the pie, as well as such entrees as lasagna, spaghetti, baked ziti and parmesan dishes. Casual dress; beer only. **Parking:** on-site. **Cards:** MC, VI.

YOKOHAMA JAPANESE RESTAURANT SUSHI BAR
Japanese

Dinner: $11-$21   Phone: 813/684-3485   **189**

Location: Jct King St; in La Viva Plaza. 760 W Lumsden Rd 33511. **Hours:** 5 pm-10 pm, Sun-9 pm. Closed major holidays. **Features:** This is a cozy, intimate restaurant with a varied menu of freshly prepared, artistically decorated entrees. Try the tempura, sashimi, eel, beef, poultry, lobster, soup and various appetizers. There is also a wide variety of sushi choices. Very gracious service. Casual dress; beer & wine only. **Parking:** on-site. **Cards:** DS, MC, VI.

CLEARWATER pop. 108,787 (See map and index starting on p. 938)

───── **WHERE TO STAY** ─────

BELLEVIEW BILTMORE RESORT & SPA *Book at aaa.com* Phone: (727)373-3000 63

AAA **SAVE**
▽▽▽▽▽

1/16-4/30	1P: $169-$179
12/1-1/15 & 5/1-7/31	1P: $159-$179
8/1-11/30	1P: $149-$169

Classic Historic
Small-scale Hotel
Location: 2 mi s on US Alternate 19 (Ft Harrison Ave); from jct SR 60; 0.5 mi w. 25 Belleview Blvd 33756. Fax: 727/441-4173. **Facility:** This historic resort was built in 1897; on Old Clearwater Bay, it offers 47 room types. 246 units. 208 one-bedroom standard units. 37 one- and 1 three-bedroom suites ($189-$229), some with kitchens and/or whirlpools. 4 stories, interior corridors. *Bath:* combo or shower only. **Parking:** on-site (fee) and valet. **Terms:** package plans, $10 service charge, small pets only ($25 deposit). **Amenities:** dual phone lines, voice mail, irons, hair dryers. *Fee:* video games, high-speed Internet. *Some:* DVD players (fee), CD players, safes. **Dining:** 2 restaurants, cocktails, also, Palm Grille, see separate listing. **Pool(s):** 2 outdoor, heated indoor. **Leisure Activities:** saunas, whirlpools, steamrooms, water aerobics, beach area located at Beach Club (Gulf front), 4 tennis courts, recreation programs, aerobics, tai chi, historical museum on-site, hotel tour, playground, exercise room, spa, horseshoes, volleyball. *Fee:* boat dock, boat slip, golf-18 holes, mystery dinner theater, pilates, yoga, bicycles, game room. **Guest Services:** gift shop, valet laundry, area transportation-beach & golf club. **Business Services:** conference facilities, business center. **Cards:** AX, DC, DS, MC, VI. **Special Amenities:** free room upgrade and preferred room (each subject to availability with advance reservations). *(See color ad below)*

SOME UNITS
[icons] FEE FEE / FEE

CANDLEWOOD SUITES CLEARWATER-ST PETERSBURG *Book at aaa.com* Phone: (727)573-3344 75

▽▽▽
All Year   1P: $99-$129   2P: $109-$139

Small-scale Hotel
Location: I-275, exit 31 southbound; exit 30 northbound, 3 mi w on SR 688, then just s. 13231 49th St N 33762. Fax: 727/573-3074. **Facility:** 104 units. 80 one-bedroom standard units with efficiencies. 24 one-bedroom suites ($119-$149) with kitchens. 3 stories, interior corridors. *Bath:* combo or shower only. **Parking:** on-site. **Terms:** office hours 7 am-11 pm, cancellation fee imposed. **Amenities:** video library, CD players, high-speed Internet, dual phone lines, voice mail, irons, hair dryers. **Pool(s):** heated outdoor. **Leisure Activities:** exercise room. **Guest Services:** sundries, valet and coin laundry. **Business Services:** fax. **Cards:** AX, CB, DC, DS, JC, MC, VI.

SOME UNITS
[icons]

(See map and index starting on p. 938)

COMFORT INN CLEARWATER NORTH *Book at aaa.com* Phone: (727)796-1234 **53**

2/15-3/31 [ECP] 1P: $89-$119 2P: $89-$149 XP: $10 F17
12/1-2/14 & 4/1-11/30 [ECP] 1P: $79-$99 2P: $79-$119 XP: $10 F17
Small-scale Hotel **Location:** On US 19; just s of jct SR 580 at Countryside Blvd. Across from Countryside Mall. 26508 US 19 N 33761. Fax: 727/796-0452. **Facility:** 124 units. 120 one-bedroom standard units. 4 one-bedroom suites. 5 stories, interior corridors. *Bath:* combo or shower only. **Parking:** on-site. **Amenities:** high-speed Internet, voice mail, safes, irons, hair dryers. **Dining:** Arigato Japanese Steak House, see separate listing. **Pool(s):** outdoor. **Leisure Activities:** whirlpool, exercise room. **Guest Services:** valet and coin laundry. **Business Services:** meeting rooms, fax (fee). **Cards:** AX, DC, DS, MC, VI. *(See color ad below)*

SOME UNITS

COMFORT INN EXECUTIVE CENTER CLEARWATER *Book at aaa.com* Phone: (727)573-1171 **73**

12/1-4/15 1P: $69-$135 2P: $69-$135 XP: $10 F16
4/16-11/30 1P: $49-$79 2P: $49-$79 XP: $10 F16
Small-scale Hotel **Location:** I-275, exit 31 southbound; exit 30 northbound, 1.9 mi w on SR 688. 3580 Ulmerton Rd 33762. Fax: 727/572-8736. **Facility:** 115 one-bedroom standard units. 3 stories, interior corridors. **Parking:** on-site. **Terms:** check-in 4 pm. **Amenities:** voice mail, irons, hair dryers. *Some:* high-speed Internet. **Dining:** Primo's Pasta-Ribs, see separate listing. **Pool(s):** heated outdoor. **Leisure Activities:** whirlpool. **Guest Services:** valet and coin laundry, airport transportation-Clearwater & Tampa airports. **Business Services:** meeting rooms, fax (fee). **Cards:** AX, CB, DC, DS, MC, VI. **Special Amenities:** free expanded continental breakfast and free local telephone calls.

SOME UNITS

COMFORT SUITES CLEARWATER BAY *Book at aaa.com* Phone: 727/489-5000 **54**

12/1-5/5 1P: $119-$169 2P: $119-$169 XP: $10 F16
5/6-11/30 1P: $99-$129 2P: $99-$129 XP: $10 F16
Small-scale Hotel **Location:** On US Alternate 19, just n of Sunset Point. 1941 Edgewater Dr 33755. Fax: 727/489-5002. **Facility:** 40 units. 31 one-bedroom standard units. 1 one- and 8 two-bedroom suites ($129-$169), some with kitchens (no utensils) and/or whirlpools. 3 stories, interior corridors. *Bath:* combo or shower only. **Parking:** on-site. **Terms:** cancellation fee imposed. **Amenities:** high-speed Internet, voice mail, safes, irons, hair dryers. **Pool(s):** heated outdoor. **Leisure Activities:** whirlpool, exercise room. **Guest Services:** coin laundry. **Business Services:** meeting rooms, fax (fee). **Cards:** AX, CB, DC, DS, MC, VI. **Special Amenities:** free continental breakfast and free local telephone calls.

SOME UNITS

COURTYARD BY MARRIOTT *Book at aaa.com* Phone: (727)572-8484 **65**

1/16-5/25 1P: $119-$199
9/15-11/30 1P: $99-$189
12/1-1/15 1P: $99-$179
5/26-9/14 1P: $99-$169
Small-scale Hotel **Location:** I-275, exit 31 southbound; exit 30 northbound, 1.6 mi w on SR 688; in The Centres Office Park. 3131 Executive Dr 33762. Fax: 727/572-6991. **Facility:** 149 units. 137 one-bedroom standard units. 12 one-bedroom suites. 3 stories, interior corridors. *Bath:* combo or shower only. **Parking:** on-site. **Terms:** package plans. **Amenities:** video games (fee), high-speed Internet, voice mail, irons, hair dryers. **Pool(s):** heated outdoor. **Leisure Activities:** whirlpool, exercise room. **Guest Services:** sundries, valet and coin laundry. **Business Services:** meeting rooms, business center. **Cards:** AX, CB, DC, DS, MC, VI. **Special Amenities:** free newspaper.

SOME UNITS

DAYS INN-CLEARWATER CENTRAL Phone: (727)799-0100 **61**

All Year 1P: $55-$85 2P: $55-$85 XP: $6 F11
Motel **Location:** On SR 60, 0.8 mi e of jct US 19. 2940 Gulf-to-Bay Blvd 33759. Fax: 727/726-6569. **Facility:** 90 one-bedroom standard units, some with efficiencies. 2 stories, exterior corridors. **Parking:** on-site. **Terms:** [CP] meal plan available. **Amenities:** hair dryers. *Some:* irons. **Pool(s):** heated outdoor. **Leisure Activities:** whirlpool, playground, shuffleboard. **Guest Services:** coin laundry. **Business Services:** meeting rooms, fax (fee). **Cards:** AX, CB, DC, DS, JC, MC, VI.

SOME UNITS

(See map and index starting on p. 938)

DAYS INN-ST. PETE/CLEARWATER AIRPORT   *Book at aaa.com*   Phone: (727)573-3334   **74**

AAA [SAVE]
▼▼▼
Small-scale Hotel

2/16-4/30	1P: $89-$109	2P: $94-$114
12/1-2/15 & 5/1-11/30	1P: $79-$99	2P: $84-$109

Location: I-275, exit 31 southbound; exit 30 northbound, 2 mi w on SR 688. 3910 Ulmerton Rd 33762. Fax: 727/572-4845. **Facility:** 117 one-bedroom standard units. 4 stories, interior corridors. *Bath:* combo or shower only. **Parking:** on-site. **Terms:** small pets only ($20 fee, 1st floor units). **Amenities:** hair dryers. *Fee:* video games, safes. *Some:* irons. **Pool(s):** heated outdoor. **Guest Services:** valet and coin laundry, airport transportation-Tampa International and St. Pete/Clearwater airports, area transportation-within 5 mi. **Business Services:** meeting rooms, fax (fee). **Cards:** AX, CB, DC, DS, MC, VI. **Special Amenities:** free expanded continental breakfast.

SOME UNITS
[S/D] [parking] [pet] [food] [M] [accessible] [refrigerator] [pool] [exercise] [DATA PORT] [PC] / [X] [microwave] [coffee] /
FEE

ECONO LODGE CLEARWATER CENTRAL   *Book at aaa.com*   Phone: (727)799-1569   **56**

▼▼▼
Motel

2/8-4/30	1P: $90	2P: $90	XP: $10	F17
5/1-11/30	1P: $66	2P: $66	XP: $10	F17
12/1-2/7	1P: $60	2P: $60	XP: $10	F17

Location: On US 19, just n of jct SR 60. 21252 US 19 N 33765. Fax: 727/796-3165. **Facility:** 119 one-bedroom standard units. 2 stories, exterior corridors. **Parking:** on-site. **Terms:** cancellation fee imposed. **Amenities:** irons, hair dryers. **Pool(s):** heated outdoor. **Leisure Activities:** 2 tennis courts, horseshoes, shuffleboard. **Guest Services:** valet and coin laundry. **Business Services:** meeting rooms, fax (fee). **Cards:** AX, CB, DC, DS, MC, VI.

SOME UNITS
[ASK] [S/D] [food] [refrigerator] [pool] [tennis] [X] [camera] [DATA PORT] [PC] / [X] [coffee] [microwave] /

FAIRFIELD INN & SUITES CLEARWATER/BAYSIDE   *Book at aaa.com*   Phone: (727)724-6223   **59**

▼▼▼
Small-scale Hotel

1/16-4/12 [CP]	1P: $159-$209	2P: $159-$209
6/1-11/30 [CP]	1P: $109-$209	2P: $109-$209
4/13-5/31 [CP]	1P: $119-$199	2P: $119-$199
12/1-1/15 [CP]	1P: $99-$199	2P: $99-$199

Location: On SR 60, jct CR 611 (McMullen Booth Rd). 3070 Gulf-to-Bay Blvd 33759. Fax: 727/724-3413. **Facility:** 127 units. 111 one-bedroom standard units, some with whirlpools. 16 one-bedroom suites. 5 stories, interior corridors. *Bath:* combo or shower only. **Parking:** on-site. **Terms:** package plans. **Amenities:** video games (fee), high-speed Internet, dual phone lines, voice mail, irons, hair dryers. *Some:* CD players. **Pool(s):** heated outdoor. **Leisure Activities:** whirlpool, exercise room. **Guest Services:** valet and coin laundry. **Business Services:** meeting rooms, business center. **Cards:** AX, DC, DS, MC, VI.

SOME UNITS
[ASK] [S/D] [M] [accessible] [refrigerator] [pool] [camera] [DATA PORT] [PC] / [X] [coffee] [microwave] /

HAMPTON INN CLEARWATER CENTRAL   Phone: (727)797-8173   **57**

▼▼▼
Small-scale Hotel

1/16-4/15	1P: $110	2P: $140	XP: $5	F17
4/16-11/30	1P: $79	2P: $130	XP: $5	F17
12/1-1/15	1P: $76	2P: $120	XP: $5	F17

Location: On US 19, just n of jct SR 60. 21030 US 19 N 33765. Fax: 727/791-7759. **Facility:** 174 units. 158 one-bedroom standard units. 16 one-bedroom suites. 2 stories, exterior corridors. *Bath:* combo or shower only. **Parking:** on-site. **Terms:** check-in 4 pm, cancellation fee imposed. **Amenities:** video games (fee), high-speed Internet, voice mail, irons, hair dryers. **Pool(s):** heated outdoor, wading. **Leisure Activities:** whirlpool, putting green, playground, exercise room. **Guest Services:** valet and coin laundry. **Business Services:** meeting rooms, business center. **Cards:** AX, CB, DC, DS, JC, MC, VI.

SOME UNITS
[ASK] [S/D] [food] [M] [accessible] [refrigerator] [pool] [X] [camera] [DATA PORT] [PC] / [X] [coffee] [microwave] /

HAMPTON INN-CLEARWATER/ST. PETERSBURG AIRPORT   *Book at aaa.com*   Phone: (727)577-9200   **71**

▼▼▼
Motel

12/1-2/28 [BP]	1P: $109
3/1-4/30 [BP]	1P: $99
5/1-9/1 [BP]	1P: $89
9/2-11/30 [BP]	1P: $79

Location: I-275, exit 31 southbound; exit 30 northbound, 1.8 mi w on SR 688. 3655 Hospitality at Ulmerton Rd 33762. Fax: 727/572-8931. **Facility:** 118 one-bedroom standard units. 2 stories, exterior corridors. **Parking:** on-site. **Terms:** pets ($25 fee, in designated units). **Amenities:** video games (fee), high-speed Internet, dual phone lines, voice mail, irons, hair dryers. **Pool(s):** outdoor. **Leisure Activities:** sauna, whirlpool, exercise room. **Guest Services:** valet and coin laundry. **Business Services:** meeting rooms, fax. **Cards:** AX, DC, DS, MC, VI.

SOME UNITS
[ASK] [S/D] [parking] [pet] [food] [refrigerator] [pool] [X] [camera] [DATA PORT] [PC] / [X]
FEE

(See map and index starting on p. 938)

HOLIDAY INN EXPRESS *Book at aaa.com*   Phone: (727)536-7275   64

AAA SAVE   All Year   1P: $109-$139
Location: 0.5 mi e of jct US 19; just n of Ulmerton Rd (SR 688); in Icot Center Business Park. 13625 Icot Blvd 33760.
WWWW   Fax: 727/530-3053. **Facility:** 127 units. 101 one-bedroom standard units. 26 one-bedroom suites, some
with whirlpools. 3 stories, interior corridors. *Bath:* combo or shower only. **Parking:** on-site.
Small-scale Hotel **Terms:** cancellation fee imposed, [CP] meal plan available, package plans. **Amenities:** high-speed Internet,
dual phone lines, voice mail, irons, hair dryers. **Pool(s):** heated outdoor. **Leisure Activities:** whirlpool.
Guest Services: valet and coin laundry, airport transportation-St. Petersburg-Clearwater International Airport, area
transportation-within 5 mi. **Business Services:** meeting rooms, business center. **Cards:** AX, DC, DS, MC, VI.
Special Amenities: free expanded continental breakfast and free newspaper. *(See color ad below)*

SOME UNITS

HOLIDAY INN EXPRESS HOTEL & SUITES   Phone: (727)797-6300   60

WWWW   12/22-4/15 [ECP]   1P: $159-$209   2P: $159-$209   XP: $10   F17
12/1-12/21 & 4/16-11/30 [ECP]   1P: $129-$179   2P: $129-$179   XP: $10   F17
Small-scale Hotel **Location:** On SR 60. 2580 Gulf-To-Bay Blvd 33765. Fax: 727/797-4900. **Facility:** 79 units. 76 one-
bedroom standard units. 3 one-bedroom suites ($179-$209). 4 stories, interior corridors. *Bath:* combo or
shower only. **Parking:** on-site. **Amenities:** high-speed Internet, dual phone lines, voice mail, irons, hair dryers. **Pool(s):** heated
outdoor. **Leisure Activities:** exercise room. **Guest Services:** valet and coin laundry. **Business Services:** meeting rooms. *Fee:*
PC, fax. **Cards:** AX, CB, DC, DS, JC, MC, VI. *(See color ad p 948)*

SOME UNITS

HOLIDAY INN SELECT-ST. PETE/CLEARWATER INT'L AIRPORT *Book at aaa.com*   Phone: (727) 577-9100   68

WWWW   12/1-5/31   1P: $99-$129
6/1-11/30   1P: $79-$99
Large-scale Hotel **Location:** I-275, exit 31 southbound; exit 30 northbound, 1.8 mi w on SR 688. 3535 Ulmerton Rd 33762.
Fax: 727/573-5022. **Facility:** 173 units. 171 one-bedroom standard units. 2 one-bedroom suites. 5 stories,
interior corridors. **Parking:** on-site. **Amenities:** high-speed Internet, dual phone lines, voice mail, irons, hair dryers. *Some:* CD
players. **Pool(s):** heated outdoor. **Leisure Activities:** whirlpool, 2 lighted tennis courts, exercise room. **Guest Services:** valet
and coin laundry. **Business Services:** conference facilities, business center. **Cards:** AX, DC, DS, JC, MC, VI.

SOME UNITS

FEE

HOMESTEAD STUDIO SUITES HOTEL-TAMPA/CLEARWATER *Book at aaa.com*   Phone: (727)572-4800   70

WWWW   All Year   1P: $44-$64   2P: $49-$69   XP: $5   F17
Motel **Location:** I-275, exit 31 southbound; exit 30 northbound, 1.3 mi w on SR 688. 2311 Ulmerton Rd 33762.
Fax: 727/572-1200. **Facility:** 114 one-bedroom standard units with efficiencies. 2 stories, exterior corridors.
Bath: combo or shower only. **Parking:** on-site. **Terms:** office hours 6:30 am-10 pm, pets ($75 fee).
Amenities: high-speed Internet (fee), voice mail, irons. *Some:* hair dryers. **Pool(s):** outdoor. **Guest Services:** valet and coin
laundry. **Business Services:** fax (fee). **Cards:** AX, DC, DS, MC, VI.

SOME UNITS

FEE

HOMEWOOD SUITES BY HILTON *Book at aaa.com*   Phone: 727/573-1500   69

WWWW   Property failed to provide current rates
Location: I-275, exit 31 southbound; exit 30 northbound, 1.3 mi w on SR 688. 2233 Ulmerton Rd 33762.
Small-scale Hotel **Fax:** 727/573-5950. **Facility:** 112 units. 104 one- and 8 two-bedroom suites with kitchens. 2 stories, interior
corridors. *Bath:* combo or shower only. **Parking:** on-site. **Terms:** pets ($150 fee, in designated units).
Amenities: DVD players, video games (fee), CD players, high-speed Internet, voice mail, irons, hair dryers. **Pool(s):** heated
outdoor. **Leisure Activities:** exercise room. **Guest Services:** sundries, complimentary evening beverages: Mon-Thurs, valet
and coin laundry. **Business Services:** meeting rooms, business center.

SOME UNITS

FEE

(See map and index starting on p. 938)

HOWARD JOHNSON INN & SUITES   *Book at aaa.com*   **Phone:** (727)796-0135   **52**

▼▼▼▼ ▼▼▼▼
Motel

	12/16-4/15	1P: $75-$96	2P: $75-$96	XP: $5	F16
	4/16-11/30	1P: $75-$86	2P: $75-$86	XP: $5	F16
	12/1-12/15	1P: $60-$75	2P: $60-$75	XP: $5	F16

Location: On US 19, 0.6 mi n of jct SR 580. 27988 US Hwy 19 N 33761. **Fax:** 727/796-7597. **Facility:** 72 one-bedroom standard units. 2 stories, exterior corridors. **Bath:** combo or shower only. **Parking:** on-site. **Terms:** pets ($10 extra charge). **Amenities:** high-speed Internet, voice mail, irons, hair dryers. **Pool(s):** heated outdoor. **Leisure Activities:** whirlpool. **Guest Services:** coin laundry. **Business Services:** meeting rooms, fax (fee). **Cards:** AX, DC, DS, MC, VI.

SOME UNITS

(ASK) (S▢) 🐾 🛎 (¶†) (📧) 🛋 🚫 🎦 (DATA PORT) 🔲 🖥 📺 / (✕) /
FEE

LA QUINTA CLEARWATER CENTRAL   *Book at aaa.com*   **Phone:** 727/799-1565   **55**

▼▼▼▼
Motel

Property failed to provide current rates

Location: On US 19, just n of jct SR 60. 21338 US 19 N 33765. **Fax:** 727/797-6801. **Facility:** Designated smoking area. 128 units. 113 one-bedroom standard units. 15 one-bedroom suites. 2 stories, interior corridors. **Parking:** on-site. **Amenities:** video games (fee), high-speed Internet, voice mail, irons, hair dryers. **Pool(s):** heated outdoor. **Leisure Activities:** whirlpool, volleyball. **Guest Services:** valet and coin laundry. **Business Services:** conference facilities, fax.

SOME UNITS

(¶†) 🛋 🚫 ✕ 🎦 (DATA PORT) 🔲 🖥 📺 / (🖥) /

LA QUINTA INN TAMPA BAY   *Book at aaa.com*   **Phone:** (727)572-7222   **66**
(CLEARWATER-AIRPORT)

(AAA) (SAVE)
▼▼▼▼
Small-scale Hotel

| | All Year | 1P: $85-$105 | | XP: $7 | F18 |

Location: I-275, exit 31 southbound; exit 30 northbound, 1.7 mi w on SR 688; in The Centres Office Park. 3301 Ulmerton Rd 33762. **Fax:** 727/572-0076. **Facility:** 115 one-bedroom standard units. 3 stories, interior corridors. **Bath:** combo or shower only. **Parking:** on-site. **Terms:** [ECP] meal plan available. **Amenities:** video games (fee), high-speed Internet, voice mail, irons, hair dryers. **Pool(s):** heated outdoor. **Leisure Activities:** sauna, whirlpool, sun deck with barbecue grill, exercise room. **Guest Services:** valet and coin laundry, airport transportation-St. Petersburg/Clearwater Airport. **Business Services:** meeting rooms, fax (fee). **Cards:** AX, CB, DC, DS, MC, VI. **Special Amenities:** free expanded continental breakfast and free local telephone calls. *(See color ad p 982)*

SOME UNITS

(🛬) 🐾 (¶†) (📧) 🛋 🚫 ✕ 🎦 (DATA PORT) 🔲 🖥 📺 / (✕) /

QUALITY INN CLEARWATER CENTRAL   *Book at aaa.com*   **Phone:** (727)799-6133   **62**

(AAA) (SAVE)
▼▼▼
Small-scale Hotel

	3/1-4/16 [ECP]	1P: $89-$159	2P: $89-$159	XP: $10	F18
	12/31-2/28 [ECP]	1P: $79-$149	2P: $79-$149	XP: $10	F18
	12/1-12/30 & 4/17-11/30 [ECP]	1P: $64-$99	2P: $64-$99	XP: $10	F18

Location: On US 19, just s of jct SR 60; jct Druid. 20162 US Hwy 19 N 33764. **Fax:** 727/726-6564. **Facility:** 76 one-bedroom standard units. 3 stories, interior/exterior corridors. **Bath:** combo or shower only. **Parking:** on-site. **Terms:** cancellation fee imposed. **Amenities:** voice mail, irons, hair dryers. **Pool(s):** heated outdoor. **Leisure Activities:** whirlpool, sun deck, grill & picnic area, exercise room. **Guest Services:** coin laundry. **Business Services:** meeting rooms, fax. **Cards:** AX, DC, DS, MC, VI. **Special Amenities:** free expanded continental breakfast and free local telephone calls.

SOME UNITS

(S▢) (¶†) (📧) 🛋 🚫 ✕ 🎦 (DATA PORT) 🔲 🖥 / (✕) (🖥) /

RADISSON HOTEL CLEARWATER CENTRAL   **Phone:** (727)799-1181   **58**

▼▼▼
Small-scale Hotel

| | 2/2-4/15 | 1P: $89 | 2P: $89 | XP: $10 | F |
| | 12/1-2/1 & 4/16-11/30 | 1P: $75 | 2P: $75 | XP: $10 | F |

Location: On US 19, just n of jct SR 60. 20967 US 19 N 33765. **Fax:** 727/712-8404. **Facility:** 148 units. 114 one-bedroom standard units. 34 one-bedroom suites, some with whirlpools. 3 stories, interior/exterior corridors. **Bath:** combo or shower only. **Parking:** on-site. **Terms:** check-in 4 pm, cancellation fee imposed, pets ($50 fee). **Amenities:** video games (fee), high-speed Internet, voice mail, irons, hair dryers. **Pool(s):** heated outdoor, wading. **Leisure Activities:** sauna, whirlpool, exercise room. **Guest Services:** valet and coin laundry. **Business Services:** meeting rooms. *Fee:* PC, fax. **Cards:** AX, DC, DS, JC, MC, VI.

SOME UNITS

(ASK) (S▢) 🐾 (¶) (🍸) (♿M) (📧) 🛋 🚫 ✕ 🎦 (DATA PORT) (📺) / (✕) 🔲 🖥 /
FEE

RESIDENCE INN BY MARRIOTT   *Book at aaa.com*   **Phone:** (727)573-4444   **72**

(AAA) (SAVE)
▼▼▼▼
Small-scale Hotel

| | 12/1-5/15 [BP] | 1P: $199-$229 |
| | 5/16-11/30 [BP] | 1P: $159-$199 |

Location: On SR 688, 1 mi e of jct US 19. 5050 Ulmerton Rd 33760. **Fax:** 727/572-4446. **Facility:** 88 units. 59 one-bedroom standard units with efficiencies. 7 one- and 22 two-bedroom suites with kitchens. 2 stories, exterior corridors. **Bath:** combo or shower only. **Parking:** on-site. **Terms:** pets ($150 fee). **Amenities:** high-speed Internet, voice mail, irons, hair dryers. *Some:* DVD players. **Pool(s):** heated outdoor. **Leisure Activities:** whirlpool, 2 gazebos, exercise room, sports court. **Guest Services:** complimentary evening beverages: Mon-Thurs, valet and coin laundry. **Business Services:** meeting rooms, fax. **Cards:** AX, CB, DC, DS, MC, VI. **Special Amenities:** free full breakfast and free newspaper.

SOME UNITS

🐾 (📧) 🛋 🚫 ✕ 🎦 (DATA PORT) 🔲 🖥 📺 / (✕) (VCR) /
FEE

ST. PETERSBURG/CLEARWATER FAIRFIELD INN   **Phone:** (727)572-4400   **67**
BY MARRIOTT   *Book at aaa.com*

▼▼▼▼
Small-scale Hotel

	1/2-4/30	1P: $109-$129	2P: $109-$129
	5/1-5/30	1P: $89-$99	2P: $89-$99
	12/1-1/1 & 5/31-11/30	1P: $79-$89	2P: $79-$89

Location: I-275, exit 31 southbound; exit 30 northbound, 1.6 mi w on SR 688; in The Centres Office Park. 3211 Executive Dr 33762. **Fax:** 727/572-8500. **Facility:** 83 one-bedroom standard units. 3 stories, interior corridors. **Bath:** combo or shower only. **Parking:** on-site. **Terms:** 2-4 night minimum stay - seasonal, [CP] meal plan available. **Amenities:** high-speed Internet, irons, hair dryers. **Pool(s):** outdoor. **Leisure Activities:** whirlpool, exercise room. **Guest Services:** sundries, valet laundry. **Business Services:** PC, fax. **Cards:** AX, CB, DC, DS, JC, MC, VI.

SOME UNITS

(ASK) (¶†) (♿M) (📧) 🛋 🎦 (DATA PORT) 📺 / (✕) 🔲 🖥 /

(See map and index starting on p. 938)

SUPER 8 CLEARWATER/ST. PETERSBURG AIRPORT

Phone: (727)572-8881 **76**

(AAA) [SAVE]

2/1-4/30	1P: $79-$119	2P: $89-$129	XP: $10	F15
12/1-1/31 & 5/1-11/30	1P: $59-$79	2P: $69-$89	XP: $10	F15

Small-scale Hotel **Location:** I-275, exit 31 southbound; exit 30 northbound, 1.8 mi w on SR 688 (Ulmerton Rd), then just s. 13260 34th St N 33762. Fax: 727/572-6962. **Facility:** 71 one-bedroom standard units. 3 stories, interior corridors. **Parking:** on-site. **Terms:** 2-3 night minimum stay - seasonal, cancellation fee imposed, package plans, pets ($10 extra charge, in designated units). **Amenities:** safes. *Some:* DVD players, CD players, high-speed Internet, irons, hair dryers. **Pool(s):** heated outdoor. **Guest Services:** valet and coin laundry. **Business Services:** meeting rooms. *Fee:* PC, fax. **Cards:** AX, CB, DC, DS, JC, MC, VI. **Special Amenities: free continental breakfast and free local telephone calls.**

SOME UNITS

[icons] FEE

TOWNEPLACE SUITES BY MARRIOTT ST. PETERSBURG/CLEARWATER *Book at aaa.com*

Phone: (727)299-9229 **77**

1/10-4/30	1P: $149-$179	2P: $169-$199	
12/1-1/9 & 5/1-11/30	1P: $129-$159	2P: $149-$169	

Small-scale Hotel **Location:** I-275, exit 31 southbound; exit 30 northbound, 3 mi w on SR 688, then just s; in Turtle Creek. 13200 49th St N 33762. Fax: 727/299-0926. **Facility:** 95 units. 68 one-bedroom standard units with kitchens. 4 one- and 23 two-bedroom suites with kitchens. 3 stories, interior corridors. *Bath:* combo or shower only. **Parking:** on-site. **Terms:** [CP] meal plan available, pets ($75 fee). **Amenities:** high-speed Internet, voice mail, irons, hair dryers. **Pool(s):** heated outdoor. **Leisure Activities:** exercise room. **Guest Services:** valet and coin laundry. **Business Services:** business center. **Cards:** AX, DC, DS, MC, VI.

SOME UNITS

[ASK] [icons] FEE

WINGATE INN CLEARWATER *Book at aaa.com*

Phone: 727/299-9800 **78**

Property failed to provide current rates

Small-scale Hotel **Location:** On US 19, 2.3 mi s of jct SR 688 (Ulmerton Rd). 5000 Lake Blvd 33760. Fax: 727/299-0088. **Facility:** 84 units. 81 one-bedroom standard units. 3 stories, interior corridors. *Bath:* combo or shower only. **Parking:** on-site. **Amenities:** video games (fee), high-speed Internet, dual phone lines, voice mail, safes, irons, hair dryers. **Pool(s):** outdoor. **Leisure Activities:** whirlpool, exercise room. **Guest Services:** valet and coin laundry, area transportation. **Business Services:** meeting rooms, business center.

SOME UNITS

[icons] FEE

———— **WHERE TO DINE** ————

ALFANO'S RESTAURANT

Lunch: $6-$10   Dinner: $12-$25   Phone: 727/584-2125 **95**

Italian **Location:** On Alternate Rt US 19, 1.2 mi n of jct West Bay Dr; in Belleair Place. 1702 Clearwater-Largo Rd 33756. **Hours:** 11:30 am-2 & 5-close, Sat & Sun from 5 pm. Closed: 12/25; also Sun 5/14-12/31. **Reservations:** suggested. **Features:** The striking interior design is marked by gorgeous use of fabric and elements that give the room the feel of an Italian villa. Wall tapestries and artifacts are distinctive. The menu is well-rounded, with pasta and unusual dishes prepared by the trained chef. Dressy casual; cocktails. **Parking:** on-site. **Cards:** AX, DS, MC, VI.

ANTONIO'S PASTA GRILLE

Lunch: $7-$10   Dinner: $8-$22   Phone: 727/572-5566 **103**

Italian **Location:** I-275, exit 31B southbound; exit 30 northbound, 1.6 mi w. 2755 Ulmerton Rd 33762. **Hours:** 11 am-10 pm, Sat from 5 pm, Sun from 4 pm. Closed major holidays. **Features:** The popular restaurant offers Italian fare in a casual setting. On the menu are numerous choices, including such favorites as shrimp scampi, veal piccata, eggplant rolletini and delicious gourmet pizzas. Casual dress; cocktails. **Parking:** on-site. **Cards:** AX, MC, VI.

ARIGATO JAPANESE STEAK HOUSE

Dinner: $7-$30   Phone: 727/799-0202 **78**

Japanese **Location:** On US 19; just s of jct SR 580 at Countryside Blvd; in Comfort Inn Clearwater North. 26508 US 19 N 33761. **Hours:** 5 pm-10 pm, Sun 4 pm-9 pm. Closed: 1/1, 7/4, 11/23; also 12/24. **Reservations:** suggested. **Features:** Japanese cuisine is prepared table-side by strikingly fast chefs with a flare for showmanship. A good place to meet new people, the hibachi tables have different parties seated together. Order the chicken, filet and shrimp combo for a spicy feast. Casual dress; cocktails. **Parking:** on-site. **Cards:** AX, DC, DS, MC, VI.

ASIAN CHEF JAPANESE & CHINESE BUFFET

Lunch: $8-$11   Dinner: $13-$14   Phone: 727/466-6668 **89**

(AAA)

Japanese **Location:** On SR 60, jct S Pegasus Ave; just e of jct Keene Rd. 1849 Gulf-to-Bay Blvd 33765. **Hours:** 11 am-3 & 5-9 pm, Fri-Sun to 10 pm. **Features:** Patrons should come hungry, as the fabulous buffet lines up an extensive array of choices. From fresh salads to many entrees to a finishing touch of ice cream, diners are in for a filling meal. There is fresh sushi and a hibachi grill where items are made on the spot. Casual dress. **Parking:** on-site. **Cards:** MC, VI.

ATLANTA BREAD COMPANY BAKERY CAFE

Lunch: $5-$7   Dinner: $5-$7   Phone: 727/786-9447

American **Location:** On US 19, 1.3 mi n of jct SR 580 at Curlew Rd. 30200 US 19 N 33761. **Hours:** 6:30 am-8 pm, Fri-9 pm, Sat & Sun 7:30 am-8 pm. Closed: 4/16, 11/23, 12/25. **Features:** At the trendy spot, patrons can nurse an espresso or cappuccino while enjoying one of the many bakery items or freshly made delicatessen-style sandwiches. Casual dress. **Parking:** on-site. **Cards:** AX, MC, VI.

(See map and index starting on p. 938)

BASCOM'S CHOP HOUSE
▼▼▼▼
American
Lunch: $7-$20   **Dinner:** $17-$29   **Phone:** 727/573-3363   101
Location: I-275, exit 31B, 1.8 mi w on SR 688. 3665 Ulmerton Rd 33762. **Hours:** 11:30 am-2:30 & 5-10 pm, Sat from 5 pm, Sun 4 pm-9 pm. **Closed:** 11/23, 12/25. **Reservations:** suggested. **Features:** Diners can treat themselves in elegant surroundings with a pampering service staff. The varied menu lists seafood and steak items, all of which are pleasing to the eye and the taste buds. Dressy casual; cocktails. **Parking:** on-site.
Cards: AX, DC, DS, MC, VI.

CAFE PONTE
▼▼▼▼
Mediterranean
Lunch: $8-$14   **Dinner:** $10-$36   **Phone:** 727/538-5768   98
Location: 0.5 mi e of US 19; in Icot Center. 13505 Icot Blvd, Suite 214 33760. **Hours:** 11:30 am-2 & 5:30-close, Mon-2 pm, Sat from 5:30 pm. **Closed:** Sun. **Features:** A fine-dining experience awaits at the trendy, upscale establishment. Artistic, colorful presentations are a pleasure to both the eye and palate. Among temptations are walnut-crusted rack of lamb and Muscovite duck breast. For dessert, splurge on chocolate bombe cake or a fabulous Key lime tart. Dressy casual; cocktails. **Parking:** on-site. **Cards:** AX, DS, MC, VI.

CAPOGNA'S DUGOUT
▼▼▼
Italian
Lunch: $6-$18   **Dinner:** $6-$18   **Phone:** 727/441-4791   88
Location: On SR 60 at jct S Keyston Ave; just w of Duncan Ave. 1653 Gulf-To-Bay Blvd 33756. **Hours:** 11 am-11 pm, Fri-midnight, Sat noon-11 pm, Sun 11 am-10 pm. **Closed:** 11/23, 12/25. **Features:** Sports fans will enjoy this dining spot. On the walls are hundreds of pictures of sports heroes, some autographed, and all kinds of sports memorabilia. The menu lists such Italian dishes as fettuccine Alfredo, manicotti and yummy chicken parmigiana, as well as pizza, hoagies, burgers and finger foods, including chicken wings and cheese poppers. There is something for almost everyone. Casual dress; cocktails; entertainment. **Parking:** on-site. **Cards:** MC, VI.

CARMELITA'S MEXICAN RESTAURANT
▼▼▼ ▼▼▼
Mexican
Lunch: $7-$9   **Dinner:** $9-$13   **Phone:** 727/524-8226   96
Location: Jct US 19 and SR 686; in TriCity Plaza. 5042 E Bay Dr 33764. **Hours:** 11 am-9:30 pm, Fri & Sat-10 pm. Closed major holidays. **Features:** The large, friendly restaurant serves a wide variety of authentic, made-to-order choices, ranging from grilled chicken quesadillas to a hearty taco salad. Colorful wall decorations and servers in Mexican dress contribute to the south-of-the-border feel. Casual dress; cocktails. **Parking:** on-site. **Cards:** AX, DS, MC, VI.

DURANGO STEAKHOUSE
▼▼▼ ▼▼▼
Steak & Seafood
Lunch: $6-$10   **Dinner:** $7-$20   **Phone:** 727/726-7735   79
Location: US 19, just n of jct SR 60; in Campus Walk Plaza. 2571 Drew St 33765. **Hours:** 11:30 am-10 pm, Fri & Sat-11 pm, Sun noon-9 pm. **Closed:** 11/23, 12/25. **Features:** A welcoming staff adds to the inviting feel of the decidedly Southwestern-themed restaurant. Oak-grilled ribs, steak and chicken melt in your mouth, while such dishes as burritos and fajitas cater to other cravings. Also on the menu are several appetizers, salads, sandwiches and desserts. Casual dress; cocktails. **Parking:** on-site. **Cards:** AX, DC, DS, MC, VI.

EGG PLATTER OF CLEARWATER
▼▼▼ ▼▼▼
American
Lunch: $5-$8   **Dinner:** $5-$8   **Phone:** 727/535-4700   91
Location: On US 19, 1 mi s of jct SR 60. 19042 US Hwy 19 N 33764. **Hours:** 24 hours. **Features:** Open 24 hours, the popular casual spot serves good home cooking. Choices range from hearty breakfasts to ample lunch and dinner selections. Casual dress. **Parking:** on-site. **Cards:** AX, DC, DS, MC, VI.

FIRST WATCH
▼▼▼ ▼▼▼
American
Lunch: $5-$7   **Phone:** 727/712-8769   77
Location: Just e on Enterprise Rd from jct US 19, just n; in Countryside Square. 2569 Countryside Blvd 33761. **Hours:** 7 am-2:30 pm. **Closed:** 11/23, 12/25. **Features:** High-quality omelets practically overflow the plates, and a wide array of breakfast and lunch items including pancakes, eggs, salad and sandwiches tempt the taste buds. Clean and attractive, this is a popular spot with a short wait to be expected. Casual dress. **Parking:** on-site. **Cards:** AX, DS, MC, VI.

HARRISON'S GRILL & BAR
▼▼▼ ▼▼▼
American
Lunch: $5-$10   **Dinner:** $7-$15   **Phone:** 727/447-8880   81
Location: Just s of jct SR 60; downtown. 401 S Ft Harrison Ave 33756. **Hours:** 11 am-9 pm. **Closed:** Sun. **Reservations:** required. **Features:** The interesting train section of this diner-style restaurant now has a second life as a bar area. The menu features a wide variety of sandwiches, steaks, ribs and poultry dishes. Casual dress; cocktails. **Parking:** on-site and street. **Cards:** AX, CB, DC, MC, VI.

JOE'S CRAB SHACK
▼▼▼ ▼▼▼
Seafood
Lunch: $10-$25   **Dinner:** $10-$25   **Phone:** 727/799-8530   87
Location: On SR 60, just e of jct US 19. 2730 Gulf To Bay Blvd 33759. **Hours:** 11 am-10 pm, Fri & Sat-11 pm. **Closed:** 11/23, 12/25. **Features:** Bright lights and vivid colors enhance the eclectic and festive atmosphere of this fish camp/shanty-themed restaurant. Varied menu selections include appetizers, salads, sandwiches, pasta, seafood and grilled items. The fisherman's platter is superb and the stuffed crab a plus. Casual dress; cocktails. **Parking:** on-site. **Cards:** AX, DC, DS, MC, VI.

LENNY'S
▼▼▼
American
Lunch: $4-$8   **Phone:** 727/799-0402   80
Location: On US 19, 0.3 mi n of SR 60. 21220 US 19 N 33765. **Hours:** 6 am-3 pm. **Closed:** Yom Kippur & Rosh Hashanah. **Features:** Sensory overload is what you get in this eclectic sports diner. Memorabilia competes for your eyes; a noisy atmosphere conveys an energetic personality; and unusual specialties, such as alligator omelet, pique the attention of your nose and taste buds. Casual dress. **Parking:** on-site.
Cards: MC, VI.

LONNI'S SANDWICHES, ETC
▼▼▼
Deli/Subs Sandwiches
Lunch: $6-$9   **Phone:** 727/572-0557   102
Location: I-275, exit 31 southbound; exit 30 northbound, 1.6 mi w on SR 688; in Feather Sound Place. 2657 Ulmerton Rd 33762. **Hours:** 9 am-4 pm. **Closed:** Sat & Sun. **Features:** In business since 1987, the locally established chain prepares some of the best sandwiches around. Whether they try egg salad, a custom vegetarian sandwich or anything in between, diners are in for a treat. Also on the menu are numerous homemade soups, such as wild rice and chicken pasta, and salads, including stuffed tomato, rainbow pasta and Santa Fe ravioli. Desserts are homemade. Casual dress. **Parking:** on-site. **Cards:** AX, DS, MC, VI.

(See map and index starting on p. 938)

O'KEEFE'S TAVERN & RESTAURANT Lunch: $5-$8 Dinner: $8-$13 Phone: 727/442-9034 [90]
American
Location: 1 mi s of jct SR 60, jct Jefford St. 1530 S Evergreen Ave 33756. **Hours:** 11 am-2 am, Sun from 10:30 am; Sunday brunch. **Closed:** 11/23, 12/25. **Reservations:** accepted. **Features:** A local favorite and in operation since 1961, this family-run business is the place to find fresh eats. Popular for various classic dishes such as Mulligan stew and shepherd's pie, the menu features other goodies as well, like baby back ribs, porkloin, twisted chicken and even jambalaya. Casual dress; cocktails. **Parking:** on-site. **Cards:** AX, DC, DS, MC, VI.

ORIENTAL SUPER BUFFET Lunch: $6-$7 Dinner: $10-$11 Phone: 813/725-2083 [83]
Chinese
Location: On SR 60, just w of jct US 19. 2456 Gulf-To-Bay Blvd 33765. **Hours:** 11 am-3 & 4-9:30 pm, Fri & Sat-10:30 pm. **Closed:** 11/23. **Reservations:** accepted. **Features:** The popular restaurant's extensive Chinese buffet lays out more than 130 items each day, including sushi, snow crab legs, mussels, shrimp, egg rolls, salads, fruit and sweet treats from the dessert bar. Casual dress; beer & wine only. **Parking:** on-site. **Cards:** AX, MC, VI.

PALM GRILLE Lunch: $6-$24 Dinner: $16-$25 Phone: 727/373-3000 [93]
American
DS, JC, MC, VI.
Location: 2 mi s on US Alternate 19 (Ft Harrison Ave); from jct SR 60; 0.5 mi w; in Belleview Biltmore Resort & Spa. 25 Belleview Blvd 33756. **Hours:** 7 am-10 pm. **Reservations:** accepted. **Features:** Delightful repasts of steak, seafood, chicken and pasta are served in the historic dining room or on the more casual verandah. Lunch affords a more relaxed experience. Casual dress; cocktails. **Parking:** on-site and valet. **Cards:** AX, CB, DC,

PANERA BREAD CAFE Lunch: $4-$7 Dinner: $4-$7 Phone: 727/592-9690 [100]
American
Cards: AX, DS, MC, VI.
Location: I-275, exit 31B southbound; exit 30 northbound, 1.4 mi w on SR 688. 2285 Ulmerton Rd 33762. **Hours:** 6:30 am-9 pm, Sun 7 am-8 pm. **Closed:** 11/23, 12/25. **Features:** Indoor and outdoor seating can be requested at this inviting, relaxing cafe. In addition to freshly baked breads and pastries, choices include a variety of freshly made salads, soups, hot panini and signature sandwiches. Casual dress. **Parking:** on-site.

PARK PLACE GRILL & TAVERN Dinner: $8-$16 Phone: 727/796-7867 [82]
American
Location: Just n of jct SR 60; in Park Place. 420 Park Place Blvd 33759. **Hours:** 4 pm-2 am, Sun from 6 pm. **Features:** The sports-themed establishment offers a friendly wait staff and lots of fun. On the varied menu are "designer burgers," quesadillas, delicatessen sandwiches, Cajun chicken and the house specialty, mouthwatering barbecue ribs. Casual dress; cocktails. **Parking:** on-site. **Cards:** AX, DS, MC, VI.

PETE & SHORTY'S TAVERN Lunch: $4-$13 Dinner: $4-$13 Phone: 727/799-0580 [86]
American
Cards: AX, MC, VI.
Location: On SR 60, 0.5 mi e of jct US 19. 2820 Gulf-To-Bay Blvd 33759. **Hours:** 11 am-midnight, Thurs-Sat to 2 am, Sun noon-midnight. **Closed:** 11/23, 12/25. **Features:** A casual favorite with the locals, the tavern presents a menu of such fare as the popular "Shorty burger," specialty sandwiches and various entrees such as grouper, pot roast, pork chops or rib-eye steak. Casual dress; cocktails. **Parking:** on-site.

PRIMO'S PASTA-RIBS Dinner: $6-$16 Phone: 727/573-7656 [104]
Italian
Parking: on-site. Cards: AX, MC, VI.
Location: I-275, exit 31 southbound; exit 30 northbound, 1.9 mi w on SR 688; in Comfort Inn Executive Center Clearwater. 3580 Ulmerton Rd 33762. **Hours:** 3:30 pm-1 am. **Features:** Located near the local airport and many lodgings, the casual restaurant is decorated in contemporary style with Italian touches. Pasta dishes factor heavily on a menu that also includes steak, seafood and sandwiches. Casual dress; cocktails.

PRONTO INTERNATIONAL FOOD MARKET Lunch: $5-$19 Dinner: $5-$19 Phone: 727/536-0057 [92]
Italian
Location: On CR 501, 6 mi s of jct SR 60 (Gulf-To-Bay Blvd). 1443 S Belcher Rd 33764. **Hours:** 8 am-8 pm. Closed major holidays; also Sun. **Features:** The family-owned-and-operated Italian delicatessen and food market serves a variety of hot and cold submarine sandwiches, gourmet pizzas, salads and such traditional dishes as lasagna, manicotti, baked ziti and veal parmigiana. The market offers imported Italian meats and cheeses, freshly baked bread, focaccia, stuffed bread, and homemade Italian cakes and pastries. Casual dress; beer & wine only. **Parking:** on-site. **Cards:** AX, DC, DS, MC, VI.

ROADHOUSE GRILL Lunch: $7-$19 Dinner: $7-$19 Phone: 727/712-3222 [84]
Steak House
Monterey. Casual dress; cocktails. Parking: on-site. Cards: AX, DC, DS, MC, VI.
Location: On SR 60; jct US 19. 2630 Gulf To Bay Blvd 33759. **Hours:** 11 am-10 pm, Fri & Sat-11 pm. **Closed:** 11/23, 12/25. **Features:** As guests might guess, the decor here is set around a roadhouse theme and the atmosphere is fun and relaxed. The menu is varied, with numerous choices of appetizers, salads, burgers, sandwiches, beef and chops, combination platters and such favorites as the baby back ribs and chicken

SAM SELTZER'S STEAKHOUSE Dinner: $11-$21 Phone: 727/519-7267 [94]
Steak House
site. Cards: AX, DC, DS, MC, VI.
Location: On US 19, 1.5 mi s of SR 60. 18409 US Hwy 19 N 33764. **Hours:** 4 pm-10 pm, Fri-11 pm, Sat 3:30 pm-11 pm, Sun 1 pm-10 pm. **Closed:** 11/23, 12/25. **Features:** Ample portions of chicken, pork and various steak choices are what make this busy chain so popular. Any wait is worthwhile for a good steak, cooked to order. Meals are accompanied by hot rolls, choice of side items and salad. Casual dress; cocktails. **Parking:** on-

SAUTE' CAFE Lunch: $8-$13 Dinner: $10-$19 Phone: 727/573-9177 [99]
Continental
Location: I-275, exit 31 southbound; exit 30 northbound, 1.5 mi w on SR 688 (Ulmerton Rd); in Feather Sound Square. 2325 Feather Sound Square, Suite 3 33762. **Hours:** 11 am-10 pm, Fri-11 pm, Sat 3 pm-11 pm. **Closed:** 1/1, 12/25; also Sun. **Features:** The trendy spot prepares items with a sauteed, stone-baked or oak fire-grilled flair. Among numerous choices are sauteed pasta dishes, oak fire-grilled chops and Pacific Rim chicken. Guests are urged to try one of the signature dishes: coco-pecan grouper, pork roulade or Polynesian chicken stir fry. The food is good, as is the service. Dressy casual; cocktails. **Parking:** on-site. **Cards:** AX, DS, MC, VI.

(See map and index starting on p. 938)

TIO PEPE RESTAURANTE
Spanish

Lunch: $7-$13   Dinner: $14-$30   Phone: 727/799-3082   [85]

Location: On SR 60, 0.8 mi e of jct US 19. 2930 Gulf To Bay Blvd 33759. **Hours:** 11 am-2:30 & 5-11 pm, Fri-11:30 pm, Sat 5 pm-11:30 pm, Sun 4 pm-10 pm. Closed: 11/23, 12/25; also Mon. **Reservations:** suggested. **Features:** Servers crush fruit and blend in brown sugar to make a one-of-a-kind table-side sangria. Ample portions of Spanish cuisine make for a satisfying meal. For something unique, try the pork in an apple-prune sauce; then indulge in rich chocolate mousse cake. Casual dress; cocktails. **Parking:** on-site. **Cards:** AX, MC, VI.

TUCSON'S CANTINA & GRILL
American

Lunch: $6-$23   Dinner: $6-$23   Phone: 727/530-0637   [97]

Location: On SR 688, just e of jct US 19; in Icot Center. 13563 Icot Blvd 33760. **Hours:** 11 am-midnight, Sun noon-10 pm. Closed: 1/1, 11/23, 12/25. **Reservations:** accepted. **Features:** Oak-grilled steaks and seafood stand out on a menu that features Southwest-themed dishes such as enchiladas, chimichangas, fajitas, pasta and salad. The breezy patio has a casual bar and dining area. Casual dress; cocktails. **Parking:** on-site. **Cards:** AX, DC, DS, MC, VI.

CLEARWATER BEACH   (See map and index starting on p. 938)

——— WHERE TO STAY ———

BEST WESTERN SEA WAKE BEACH RESORT   *Book at aaa.com*   Phone: (727)443-7652   [46]
Small-scale Hotel

2/1-4/24	1P: $179-$219	2P: $179-$219	XP: $10 F17
4/25-11/30	1P: $139-$179	2P: $139-$179	XP: $10 F17
12/1-1/31	1P: $129-$169	2P: $129-$169	XP: $10 F17

Location: Oceanfront. 0.9 mi s of jct SR 60 (roundabout). 691 S Gulfview Blvd 33767. Fax: 727/461-2836. **Facility:** 110 one-bedroom standard units. 6 stories, interior corridors. **Bath:** combo or shower only. **Parking:** on-site. **Terms:** check-in 4 pm. **Amenities:** high-speed Internet, dual phone lines, voice mail, safes, irons, hair dryers. **Dining:** 7 am-2 pm, cocktails. **Pool(s):** heated outdoor. **Leisure Activities:** fishing, sun deck, recreation programs in summer, playground. **Guest Services:** valet and coin laundry, area transportation (fee)-trolley. **Business Services:** meeting rooms, fax. **Cards:** AX, DS, MC, VI. **Special Amenities:** free local telephone calls and free newspaper.
(See color ad below)

SOME UNITS

(See map and index starting on p. 938)

CHART HOUSE SUITES ON CLEARWATER BAY   *Book at aaa.com*   Phone: (727)449-8007 **43**
All Year   1P: $110-$299   2P: $110-$299   XP: $10   F18
Motel   Location: 1.3 mi s of jct roundabout via Gulf View Blvd. 850 Bayway Blvd 33767 (401 Second St, INDIAN ROCKS BEACH, 33785). Fax: 727/443-6081. **Facility:** 26 units. 16 one-bedroom standard units. 9 one- and 1 two-bedroom suites ($199-$499) with kitchens, some with whirlpools. 4 stories, interior/exterior corridors.
Parking: on-site. **Terms:** office hours 8 am-9 pm, check-in 4 pm, weekly rates available. **Amenities:** voice mail, irons, hair dryers. **Pool(s):** heated outdoor. **Leisure Activities:** fishing. *Fee:* marina. **Guest Services:** valet and coin laundry. **Business Services:** fax. **Cards:** AX, DS, MC, VI. *(See color ad below)*

SOME UNITS
(ASK) (SD) (TI+) (⊇) (DATA PORT) (⊟) (⊡) (⊑) / (⊠) (VCR)

CLEARWATER BEACH GULFVIEW RESORT   *Book at aaa.com*   Phone: 727/447-6461 **41**
2/1-4/30   1P: $149-$399
12/1-1/31 & 5/1-11/30   1P: $79-$229
Small-scale Hotel   **Location:** Oceanfront. 0.7 mi s of jct SR 60 at Hamden Dr. 521 S Gulfview Blvd 33767. Fax: 727/443-5888. **Facility:** 63 one-bedroom standard units. 7 stories, interior corridors. **Parking:** on-site. **Terms:** check-in 4 pm, 1-3 night minimum stay - seasonal, 3 day cancellation notice-fee imposed, $6 service charge. **Amenities:** voice mail, safes, irons, hair dryers. *Fee:* video games, high-speed Internet. **Pool(s):** heated outdoor, wading. **Leisure Activities:** *Fee:* game room. **Guest Services:** gift shop, valet and coin laundry. *Fee:* beauty salon. **Business Services:** meeting rooms, administrative services, fax. **Cards:** AX, DC, DS, JC, MC, VI. *(See color ad below)*

SOME UNITS
(ASK) (SD) (TI) (Y) (⊊M) (⊡) (⊘) (⊇) (++) (★) (DATA PORT) (⊑) / (⊠) (⊟) (⊡) /

(See map and index starting on p. 938)

CLEARWATER BEACH MARRIOTT SUITES ON SAND KEY

Book at aaa.com

AAA SAVE

Resort
Large-scale Hotel

Phone: (727)596-1100 **48**

2/13-4/7	1P: $299-$459	2P: $299-$459	XP: $10 · F17
4/8-8/12	1P: $269-$459	2P: $269-$459	XP: $10 · F17
12/1-2/12 & 8/13-11/30	1P: $229-$459	2P: $229-$459	XP: $10 · F17

Location: On SR 699, just s of Clearwater Pass Bridge. 1201 Gulf Blvd 33767. Fax: 727/595-4292. **Facility:** A blue-and-gold macaw named Lisa greets guests at this property. 220 one-bedroom suites. 10 stories, exterior corridors. **Parking:** on-site (fee) and valet. **Terms:** check-in 4 pm, 3 day cancellation notice-fee imposed, package plans. **Amenities:** voice mail, irons, hair dryers. *Fee:* video games, high-speed Internet. **Dining:** 3 restaurants, 6:30 am-10 pm, cocktails, entertainment. **Pool(s):** heated outdoor, wading. **Leisure Activities:** whirlpool, kayaks, waverunners, recreation programs, kid's activities club, playground, exercise room, spa, volleyball. *Fee:* paddleboats, parasailing, jet ski, tennis instruction, art gallery cabanas, bicycles. **Guest Services:** gift shop, valet and coin laundry, area transportation (fee)-trolley. **Business Services:** conference facilities, business center. **Cards:** AX, DC, DS, JC, MC, VI. **Special Amenities:** free newspaper. *(See color ad p 1016)*

SOME UNITS

EAST SHORE RESORT APARTMENT MOTEL

AAA SAVE

Motel

Phone: (727)442-3636 **34**

12/1-4/30	1P: $110-$150	2P: $110-$150	XP: $10
4/1-11/30	1P: $80-$110	2P: $80-$110	XP: $7

Location: Just n on E Shore Dr from jct SR 60 (causeway). 473 E Shore Dr 33767. Fax: 727/449-8302. **Facility:** 10 units. 8 one- and 2 two-bedroom suites with kitchens. 1-2 stories, exterior corridors. **Parking:** on-site. **Terms:** office hours 9 am-5 pm, 3-7 night minimum stay - seasonal, 30 day cancellation notice-fee imposed, weekly rates available. **Amenities:** voice mail, irons, hair dryers. *Some:* DVD players, CD players, safes. **Pool(s):** heated outdoor. **Leisure Activities:** boat dock, fishing, cabana, floats & beach chairs, fishing poles, barbecue grill & patio area, bicycles. *Fee:* boat slips. **Guest Services:** complimentary laundry. **Business Services:** meeting rooms, fax. **Cards:** MC, VI.

SOME UNITS

ECONO LODGE

Book at aaa.com

AAA SAVE

Small-scale Hotel

Phone: (727)446-3400 **44**

2/1-4/30	1P: $119-$239	2P: $119-$239	XP: $10 · F17
5/1-11/30	1P: $79-$199	2P: $79-$199	XP: $10 · F17
12/1-1/31	1P: $69-$199	2P: $69-$199	XP: $10 · F17

Location: Oceanfront. 0.8 mi s of jct SR 60 (roundabout). 625 S Gulfview Blvd 33767. Fax: 727/446-4615. **Facility:** 64 one-bedroom standard units, some with efficiencies or kitchens. 5 stories, interior corridors. *Bath:* combo or shower only. **Parking:** on-site. **Terms:** 3 day cancellation notice, [CP] meal plan available. **Amenities:** voice mail, safes. *Some:* irons, hair dryers. **Pool(s):** heated outdoor. **Leisure Activities:** whirlpool, fishing. **Guest Services:** valet and coin laundry. **Business Services:** fax (fee). **Cards:** AX, CB, DC, DS, JC, MC, VI. **Special Amenities:** free continental breakfast and early check-in/late check-out. *(See color ad below)*

SOME UNITS

Navigate Life's Roads Safely

AAA Roadwise Review helps older drivers keep tabs on skills associated with crash risk. Perfect for the home computer, the easy, self-paced sessions provide feedback on important safety measures. Available at local AAA offices.

For more information, visit www.aaapublicaffairs.com.

(See map and index starting on p. 938)

HILTON CLEARWATER BEACH RESORT *Book at aaa.com* Phone: (727)461-3222 **35**
All Year 1P: $109-$500 2P: $109-$500 XP: $10 F18
Location: Oceanfront. Jct SR 60 (Clearwater Pass Bridge). 400 Mandalay Ave 33767. Fax: 727/461-0610. **Facility:** Designated smoking area. 425 units. 413 one-bedroom standard units. 12 one-bedroom suites ($400-$600). 9 stories, interior corridors. *Bath:* combo or shower only. **Parking:** on-site (fee) and valet.
Large-scale Hotel **Terms:** check-in 4 pm, 3 day cancellation notice-fee imposed, package plans. **Amenities:** dual phone lines, voice mail, safes, irons, hair dryers. *Fee:* video games, high-speed Internet. **Dining:** 2 restaurants, 6:30 am-10 pm, cocktails, entertainment. **Pool(s):** 2 heated outdoor. **Leisure Activities:** whirlpool, recreation programs, supervised kids camp, bicycles, exercise room, volleyball. *Fee:* sailboats, cabanas, hydro bikes, personal watercraft, beach & water aerobics, massage, game room. **Guest Services:** gift shop, valet and coin laundry. **Business Services:** conference facilities, business center. **Cards:** AX, CB, DC, DS, JC, MC, VI. **Special Amenities:** free newspaper. *(See color ad below)*

SOME UNITS

HOLIDAY INN SUNSPREE RESORT &
CONFERENCE CENTER *Book at aaa.com* Phone: (727)447-9566 **47**
2/10-4/29 1P: $199-$329 2P: $199-$329 XP: $10 F19
4/30-6/1 1P: $179-$329 2P: $179-$329 XP: $10 F19
12/1-2/9 1P: $139-$289 2P: $139-$289 XP: $10 F19
Location: Oceanfront. 1 mi s of jct SR 60 (roundabout) northbound; at Clearwater Pass Bridge. 715 S Gulfview Blvd
Large-scale Hotel 33767. Fax: 727/446-4978. **Facility:** 216 units. 213 one-bedroom standard units. 3 one-bedroom suites ($399-$499), some with kitchens. 2-10 stories, interior/exterior corridors. *Bath:* combo or shower only.
Parking: on-site. **Terms:** open 12/1-6/1, check-in 4 pm, 3 day cancellation notice-fee imposed, [BP] meal plan available, package plans. **Amenities:** video library, video games (fee), voice mail, safes, irons, hair dryers. *Some:* dual phone lines.
Dining: 6:30 am-10 pm, cocktails, entertainment. **Pool(s):** heated outdoor, wading. **Leisure Activities:** whirlpool, fishing, sun deck, putting green, recreation programs, activities center, lending library, playground, exercise room, shuffleboard, volleyball.
Fee: waterskiing, jet skis, parasailing, game room. **Guest Services:** gift shop, complimentary evening beverages: Wed, valet and coin laundry, area transportation (fee)-trolley. **Business Services:** conference facilities. *Fee:* PC, fax. **Cards:** AX, DC, DS, MC, VI. **Special Amenities:** free local telephone calls and free newspaper. *(See color ad below)*

SOME UNITS

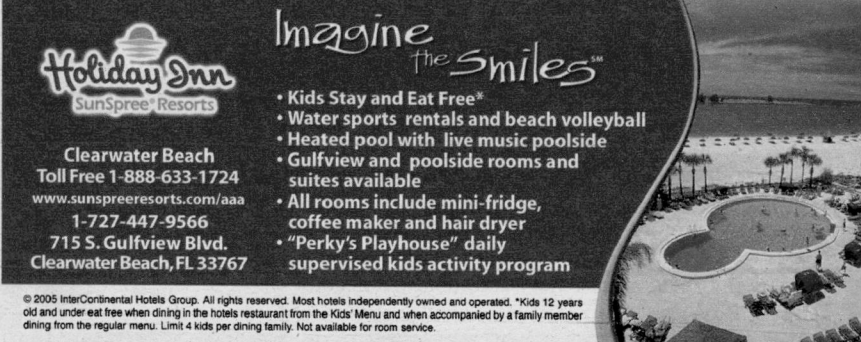

(See map and index starting on p. 938)

HOWARD JOHNSON BEACHVIEW RESORT   *Book at aaa.com*   Phone: (727)461-7695   **36**

AAA (SAVE)

3/1-4/30 [CP]	1P: $115-$130	2P: $115-$130	XP: $10	F18
5/1-8/31 [CP]	1P: $72-$125	2P: $72-$125	XP: $10	F18
9/11-11/30 [CP]	1P: $70-$110	2P: $70-$110	XP: $10	F18
12/1-2/28 [CP]	1P: $75-$90	2P: $75-$90	XP: $10	F18

Small-scale Hotel **Location:** 0.5 mi s of jct SR 60 (roundabout). 325 S Gulfview Blvd 33767. Fax: 727/442-9983. **Facility:** 64 units. 32 one-bedroom standard units, some with efficiencies. 32 one-bedroom suites ($87-$170) with kitchens. 5 stories, exterior corridors. **Parking:** on-site. **Terms:** 3 day cancellation notice. **Amenities:** voice mail, safes (fee), irons, hair dryers. **Pool(s):** heated outdoor. **Leisure Activities:** sun deck. **Guest Services:** gift shop. **Business Services:** meeting rooms, fax (fee). **Cards:** AX, DS, MC, VI. **Special Amenities:** free continental breakfast and free newspaper.

SOME UNITS
⟦S/D⟧ ⟦🍴⟧ ⟦🏊⟧ ⟦📷⟧ ⟦DATA PORT⟧ ⟦💻⟧ / ⟦✕⟧ ⟦🛗⟧ ⟦📠⟧ /

PALM PAVILION INN   Phone: (727)446-6777   **33**

▼▼▼ ▼▼▼

2/12-5/6	1P: $110-$180	2P: $110-$180	XP: $10	F16
12/1-1/1	1P: $90-$180	2P: $90-$180	XP: $10	F16
1/2-2/11 & 5/7-11/30	1P: $90-$145	2P: $90-$145	XP: $10	F16

Small-scale Hotel **Location:** 0.6 mi n of jct SR 60 (roundabout), just w. 18 Bay Esplanade 33767. Fax: 727/461-0355. **Facility:** 29 units. 24 one-bedroom standard units. 5 one-bedroom suites with kitchens. 3 stories, interior/exterior corridors. *Bath:* combo or shower only. **Parking:** on-site. **Terms:** 2 night minimum stay - weekends, 14 day cancellation notice. **Amenities:** voice mail, safes, hair dryers. *Some:* irons. **Pool(s):** heated outdoor. **Leisure Activities:** beach access. **Guest Services:** gift shop. **Business Services:** meeting rooms, fax (fee). **Cards:** AX, DC, DS, MC, VI.

SOME UNITS
⟦ASK⟧ ⟦S/D⟧ ⟦🍴⟧ ⟦🍷⟧ ⟦🏊⟧ ⟦📷⟧ ⟦DATA PORT⟧ / ⟦✕⟧ ⟦🛗⟧ ⟦📠⟧ /

PELICAN POINTE CONDOMINIUM RESORT   *Book at aaa.com*   Phone: (727)441-4902   **39**

AAA (SAVE)

▼▼▼

Condominium

All Year   1P: $79-$159   2P: $79-$159   XP: $10   F15

Location: 0.5 mi s of SR 60 (roundabout). 445 S Gulfview Blvd 33767. Fax: 727/446-4105. **Facility:** Just across the street from the Gulf, each unit offers all of the modern conveniences with equipped kitchens, large bedrooms and adequate living areas. Designated smoking area. 61 units. 35 one-bedroom standard units. 26 one-bedroom suites. 4 stories, interior/exterior corridors. **Parking:** on-site. **Terms:** 1-7 night minimum stay - seasonal and/or weekends, age restrictions may apply, weekly rates available, package plans. **Amenities:** dual phone lines, voice mail, safes, irons, hair dryers. **Pool(s):** heated outdoor. **Guest Services:** valet and coin laundry. **Business Services:** fax. **Cards:** AX, DS, MC, VI.

SOME UNITS
⟦S/D⟧ ⟦🍴⟧ ⟦🏊⟧ ⟦✕⟧ ⟦📷⟧ ⟦DATA PORT⟧ ⟦🛗⟧ ⟦📠⟧ ⟦💻⟧

QUALITY HOTEL ON THE BEACH   *Book at aaa.com*   Phone: (727)442-7171   **45**

AAA (SAVE)

▼▼▼

Small-scale Hotel

All Year   1P: $89-$229   2P: $89-$229

Location: Oceanfront. 0.8 mi s of jct SR 60 (roundabout). 655 S Gulfview Blvd 33767. Fax: 727/446-7177. **Facility:** 94 one-bedroom standard units. 5 stories, interior/exterior corridors. *Bath:* combo or shower only. **Parking:** on-site. **Terms:** cancellation fee imposed. **Amenities:** voice mail, safes, irons, hair dryers. **Dining:** 24 hours; seasonal entertainment, cocktails. **Pool(s):** heated outdoor. **Leisure Activities:** beach beds (chaises), sun deck, playground. **Fee:** parasailing, personal watercraft. **Guest Services:** valet and coin laundry. **Business Services:** administrative services, fax. **Cards:** AX, CB, DC, DS, JC, MC, VI. **Special Amenities:** free local telephone calls and free newspaper.

SOME UNITS
⟦S/D⟧ ⟦🍴⟧ ⟦🍷⟧ ⟦🏊⟧ ⟦♿⟧ ⟦📷⟧ ⟦DATA PORT⟧ ⟦🛗⟧ ⟦📠⟧ ⟦💻⟧ / ⟦✕⟧ /

SHEPHARD'S BEACH RESORT   *Book at aaa.com*   Phone: (727)442-5107   **42**

AAA (SAVE)

▼▼▼

2/1-4/30	1P: $142-$202	2P: $142-$202	XP: $10	F17
5/1-11/30	1P: $132-$172	2P: $132-$172	XP: $10	F17
12/1-1/31	1P: $112-$152	2P: $112-$152	XP: $10	F17

Small-scale Hotel **Location:** 1 mi s of jct SR 60 (roundabout). 619 S Gulfview Blvd 33767. Fax: 727/446-4238. **Facility:** 96 units. 40 one-bedroom standard units. 53 one- and 2 two-bedroom suites ($297-$397), some with kitchens and/or whirlpools. 2-6 stories, interior/exterior corridors. *Bath:* combo or shower only. **Parking:** on-site. **Terms:** 2-7 night minimum stay - seasonal and/or weekends, 7 day cancellation notice-fee imposed, 7% service charge. **Amenities:** video games (fee), high-speed Internet, voice mail, safes, irons, hair dryers. **Dining:** Shephard's Waterfront Restaurant, see separate listing, nightclub, entertainment. **Pool(s):** heated outdoor. **Leisure Activities:** whirlpool, exercise room. **Fee:** personal watercraft, parasailing, game room. **Guest Services:** gift shop, valet and coin laundry. **Business Services:** meeting rooms, business center. **Cards:** AX, DS, MC, VI. **Special Amenities:** free room upgrade (subject to availability with advance reservations). *(See color ad below)*

SOME UNITS
⟦S/D⟧ ⟦🍴⟧ ⟦🍷⟧ ⟦♿⟧ ⟦🎬⟧ ⟦🏊⟧ ⟦✕⟧ ⟦📷⟧ ⟦DATA PORT⟧ ⟦🛗⟧ ⟦📠⟧ ⟦💻⟧ / ⟦✕⟧ / ⟦VCR⟧
FEE

(See map and index starting on p. 938)

SHERATON SAND KEY RESORT *Book at aaa.com*
Phone: (727)595-1611 **49**

AAA SAVE

1/1-4/30	1P: $249-$299	2P: $249-$299	XP: $10 F18
12/1-12/31 & 5/1-11/30	1P: $219-$269	2P: $219-$269	XP: $10 F18

Resort
Large-scale Hotel

Location: Oceanfront. 2 mi s on SR 699; at south end of Clearwater Pass Bridge. 1160 Gulf Blvd 33767. **Fax:** 727/596-8488. **Facility:** On a 1,000-foot-wide beach just west of the Gulf of Mexico, the resort offers bright, cheery rooms, all with patios or decks. 390 units. 375 one-bedroom standard units. 15 one-bedroom suites ($364-$414). 9 stories, interior corridors. *Bath:* combo or shower only. **Parking:** on-site. **Terms:** package plans, pets (dogs only, with prior approval). **Amenities:** dual phone lines, voice mail, safes, irons, hair dryers. *Fee:* video games, high-speed Internet. **Dining:** 2 restaurants, 7 am-11 pm, cocktails, also, Rusty's Bistro, see separate listing, entertainment. **Pool(s):** heated outdoor, wading. **Leisure Activities:** saunas, whirlpool, rental paddleboats, fishing, 3 lighted tennis courts, tennis pro, recreation programs, playground, volleyball. *Fee:* sailboats, windsurfing, cabanas, personal watercraft, massage, game room. **Guest Services:** gift shop, valet and coin laundry, area transportation (fee)-trolley. **Business Services:** conference facilities, business center. **Cards:** AX, DC, DS, JC, MC, VI. **Special Amenities: free newspaper.**

TRAVELODGE BEACHVIEW RESORT *Book at aaa.com*
Phone: 727/446-8305 **38**

Property failed to provide current rates

Small-scale Hotel

Location: 0.5 mi s of jct SR 60 (roundabout). 401 S Gulfview Blvd 33767. **Fax:** 727/447-5293. **Facility:** 53 one-bedroom standard units, some with efficiencies. 4 stories, exterior corridors. *Bath:* combo or shower only. **Parking:** on-site. **Amenities:** safes (fee), irons, hair dryers. **Pool(s):** heated outdoor. **Business Services:** fax.

TROPICAL BREEZE MOTEL
Phone: (727)442-6865 **37**

2/1-4/26	1P: $90-$174	2P: $90-$174	XP: $8 F7
12/1-1/31 & 4/27-9/7	1P: $65-$121	2P: $65-$121	XP: $5 F7
9/8-11/30	1P: $61-$113	2P: $61-$113	XP: $5 F7

Motel

Location: 0.5 mi s on Coronado, just e on Brightwater. 333 Hamden Dr 33767. **Fax:** 727/443-4371. **Facility:** 20 one-bedroom standard units, some with kitchens. 2 stories, exterior corridors. **Parking:** on-site. **Terms:** 30 day cancellation notice-fee imposed, weekly rates available. **Amenities:** safes (fee), irons. *Some:* hair dryers. **Pool(s):** heated outdoor. **Leisure Activities:** boat dock, fishing, shuffleboard. **Guest Services:** coin laundry. **Business Services:** fax (fee). **Cards:** AX, DS, MC, VI.

------ **WHERE TO DINE** ------

ALEX FAMILY RESTAURANT
Lunch: $4-$8   **Dinner:** $5-$24   **Phone:** 727/447-4560 **63**

American

Location: 0.5 mi s of SR 60 (roundabout). 305 Coronado Dr 33767. **Hours:** 7 am-10 pm. Closed: 12/25; also 12/31 & 11/26-12/10. **Features:** The casual, diner-type establishment offers a friendly wait staff and good home-cooked food. Among the numerous menu items are sandwiches, steaks, chops, seafood and the ever-popular breakfast items, including daily specials and various omelets. Casual dress. **Parking:** on-site. **Cards:** AX, DS, MC, VI.

BACKWATER'S ON SAND KEY
Lunch: $9-$31   **Dinner:** $9-$31   **Phone:** 727/517-7383 **73**

Steak & Seafood

Location: On SR 699, just s of Clearwater Pass Bridge; in Shoppes on Sand Key. 1261 Gulf Blvd 33767. **Hours:** 11:30 am-9 pm. Closed: 11/23, 12/25. **Features:** Directly on Clearwater Bay, the inviting dining spot offers mouthwatering black Angus steak and jumbo shrimp. Seasonal stone crab claws are a favorite, and the view is beautiful. Casual dress; cocktails. **Parking:** on-site. **Cards:** DS, MC, VI.

BIG BEN BRITISH RESTAURANT & PUB
Lunch: $7-$16   **Dinner:** $7-$16   **Phone:** 727/446-8809 **68**

English

Location: 1 mi s of jct SR 60 (causeway) via Gulfview Blvd; in Bay Bazaar. 731 Bayway Blvd 33767. **Hours:** 9 am-2 am. **Features:** The feel of an authentic British pub invites you to ease on in to the restaurant. The traditional menu delivers such favorites as Lords roast, fish and chips, Cornish pastry, bangers and mash, shepherd's pie and kidney pie. If you're feeling less adventurous, there are plenty of sandwich, salad, steak, chop, dessert and side dish choices. Casual dress; beer & wine only. **Parking:** on-site. **Cards:** AX, CB, DC, DS, MC, VI.

BOBBY'S BISTRO & WINE BAR
Dinner: $7-$31   **Phone:** 727/446-9463 **58**

Continental

Location: Just n of jct SR 60 (roundabout). 447 Mandalay Ave 33767. **Hours:** 5 pm-midnight. Closed: 4/16, 11/23, 12/25. **Features:** The restaurant is known for its expansive selection of wines from such regions as the Napa Valley, Australia, France, Germany and Italy. Patrons can relax in a cozy bistro setting to sample such specialties as herb-rubbed veal chop, pepper-crusted salmon fillet and hand-made house-rolled ravioli. Salads also are a popular draw, with California pear, pecan and pepper Montrachet, Chicago chophouse steak salad and grilled chicken campeche being favorites. Casual dress; cocktails. **Parking:** on-site. **Cards:** AX, DC, DS, MC, VI.

BOB HEILMAN'S BEACHCOMBER
Lunch: $5-$15   **Dinner:** $13-$30   **Phone:** 727/442-4144 **57**

Seafood

Location: Just n of jct SR 60 (roundabout). 447 Mandalay Ave 33767. **Hours:** 11:30 am-close. **Reservations:** suggested. **Features:** Seafood specialties head the menu with steak and chops. Grouper five ways and back-to-back farm fried chicken are favorites. Meals are served in a spacious, well-lighted dining room beside a cozy, intimate lounge area. Excellent desserts round out the meal. Casual dress; cocktails; entertainment. **Parking:** valet. **Cards:** AX, DC, DS, MC, VI.

BONSAI JAPANESE CUISINE-SUSHI BAR
Dinner: $7-$13   **Phone:** 727/446-9452 **67**

Japanese

Location: 0.8 mi s of jct SR 60 (causeway). 656 S Gulfview Blvd 33767. **Hours:** 5 pm-10 pm, Fri-Sun to 11 pm. Closed: 11/23, 12/25. **Features:** The surroundings are basic but comfortable. Although the main menu is limited to a few entrees, the sushi choices are abundant: ikura, kappamaki, tekka maki, temaki, salmon, skin roll, sake, hamachi, unagi, hotategemi, ebi, saba and amaebiare. Casual dress; beer & wine only. **Parking:** on-site. **Cards:** AX, DC, DS, MC, VI.

(See map and index starting on p. 938)

BRITT'S LAGUNA GRILL
Lunch: $5-$11   **Dinner:** $8-$25   **Phone:** 727/445-1755   62
American
Location: Just s of jct SR 60 (causeway). 309 S Gulfview Blvd 33767. **Hours:** 11 am-midnight, Fri-Sun to 1 am. **Reservations:** not accepted. **Features:** Across from the beach, the comfy restaurant affords great views of the gulf. Seating is cozy, both indoors and on the outdoor deck. Menu choices include appetizers, salads, pasta dishes, seafood entrees, sandwiches and steaks. Casual dress; cocktails; entertainment. **Parking:** on-site and valet. **Cards:** AX, DC, DS, MC, VI.

CABANA GRILL AND BAR
Lunch: $8-$15   **Dinner:** $16-$36   **Phone:** 727/595-1807   74
American
Location: On the beach; in Belleview Biltmore Beach Club. 1590 Gulf Blvd 33767. **Hours:** 11:30 am-3 & 5-10 pm, Fri & Sat-11 pm. **Reservations:** suggested. **Features:** The upscale gulfside restaurant affords fabulous sunset views. On the menu are seafood, steaks, pork and an interesting open-faced lobster ravioli. Casual dress; cocktails; entertainment. **Parking:** on-site and valet. **Cards:** AX, CB, DC, DS, JC.

COLUMBIA RESTAURANT
Lunch: $7-$16   **Dinner:** $15-$26   **Phone:** 727/596-8400   72
Spanish
Location: On SR 699, just s of Clearwater Pass Bridge. 1241 Gulf Blvd 33767. **Hours:** 11:30 am-10 pm. **Reservations:** suggested, evenings. **Features:** This very elegant Spanish eatery overlooks Tampa Bay and specializes in Cuban favorites like chicken and rice with black beans. The cigar bar and the cocktail bar are perfect for relaxing after a leisurely meal overseen by a gracious, professional staff. Casual dress; cocktails. **Parking:** on-site. **Cards:** AX, MC, VI.

COOTERS RAW BAR & RESTAURANT
Lunch: $7-$23   **Dinner:** $7-$23   **Phone:** 727/462-2668   59
Seafood
Location: Just n of jct SR 60 (roundabout). 423 Poinsettia Ave 33767. **Hours:** 11:30 am-11 pm, Fri & Sat-midnight. Closed: 11/23, 12/25. **Features:** The popular local spot has the look of a rustic sea shanty. Among the many menu choices are salads, gumbo, chowder, grouper sandwiches, po'boys, burgers, New York strip, ribeye and baby back ribs, as well as plenty of entrees from the seafood family: grouper, mahi mahi, shrimp, snow crab and crab cakes. Casual dress; cocktails. **Parking:** on-site. **Cards:** AX, MC, VI.

CRABBY BILL'S
Lunch: $7-$21   **Dinner:** $7-$21   **Phone:** 727/210-1313   61
Seafood
Location: On SR 60, just e of jct Gulfview at roundabout. 37 Causeway Blvd 33767. **Hours:** 11:30 am-10 pm, Fri & Sat-11 pm. Closed: 4/16, 11/23, 12/25. **Features:** In the marina area and within walking distance of the beach, the casual eatery presents a menu that focuses on seafood. Food is fresh and tasty. Casual dress; cocktails. **Parking:** on-site (fee). **Cards:** AX, DS, MC, VI.

FRENCHY'S CAFE
Lunch: $6-$8   **Dinner:** $6-$8   **Phone:** 727/446-3607   55
Seafood
Location: 0.4 mi n on Mandalay Ave from jct SR 60 (roundabout), just e. 41 Baymont St 33767. **Hours:** 11:30 am-11 pm, Fri & Sat-midnight, Sun 10:30 am-11 pm. Closed: 11/23, 12/25. **Features:** The beachlike establishment has a Key West theme and an appropriately laid-back atmosphere, both in the dining room and on the breezy deck. On the menu are such offerings as sandwiches, burgers, appetizers and a limited selection of entrees. Casual dress; beer & wine only. **Parking:** on-site. **Cards:** AX, MC, VI.

FRENCHY'S ROCKAWAY GRILL
Lunch: $5-$16   **Dinner:** $5-$16   **Phone:** 727/446-4844   54
American
Location: Jct SR 60 (causeway), 0.4 mi n on Mandalay Ave, then just w. 7 Rockaway St 33767. **Hours:** 11 am-midnight, Fri & Sat-1 am. Closed: 11/23, 12/24, 12/25. **Reservations:** not accepted. **Features:** A variety of salads, burgers, sandwiches and seafood with Caribbean flair is offered in a festive beachfront setting. Pleasant servers bring entrees in plastic baskets with french fries and coleslaw. Try the stuffed grouper with crabmeat. Casual dress; cocktails; entertainment. **Parking:** on-site. **Cards:** AX, MC, VI.

FRENCHY'S SALTWATER CAFE
Lunch: $6-$30   **Dinner:** $6-$30   **Phone:** 727/461-6295   60
Seafood
Location: Just n of jct SR 60 (roundabout). 419 Poinsetta Ave 33767. **Hours:** 11 am-11 pm, Sun from noon. Closed: 11/23, 12/25. **Features:** You'll get the feeling you're at a Key West fish camp in this casual cafe, which offers indoor and outdoor dining areas with mainly picnic table seating. Fresh catches, boiled shrimp and Key lime pie are yummy. Casual dress; cocktails. **Parking:** on-site. **Cards:** AX, MC, VI.

FRENCHY'S SOUTH BEACH CAFE
Lunch: $7-$17   **Dinner:** $7-$17   **Phone:** 727/441-9991   64
Seafood
Location: 0.5 mi s of jct SR 60 (roundabout). 351 S Gulfview Blvd 33767. **Hours:** 11 am-10 pm, Fri & Sat-11 pm. Closed: 11/23, 12/25. **Features:** A tropical Key West theme punctuates the lively restaurant, which has a charming deck dining area directly across from the beach and gulf. While taking in a breathtaking sunset, feast on well-prepared entrees of shellfish, fish, steak, chicken or pork, as well as surf and turf specials and several other goodies. Casual dress; beer & wine only. **Parking:** on-site. **Cards:** AX, MC, VI.

GONDOLIER ITALIAN RESTAURANT AND PIZZA
Lunch: $5-$19   **Dinner:** $5-$19   **Phone:** 727/441-3353   69
Italian
Location: 0.9 mi s of jct SR 60 (causeway). 674 S Gulfview Blvd 34630. **Hours:** 8 am-midnight. **Features:** An Italian theme and decor is pervasive in the relaxed restaurant. The pleasant wait staff eagerly serves items from an extensive menu of some 100 specialty and standard items. Casual dress; beer & wine only. **Parking:** on-site. **Cards:** AX, DS, MC, VI.

POST CORNER PIZZA RESTAURANT
Lunch: $7-$15   **Dinner:** $7-$15   **Phone:** 727/461-7795   65
American
Location: 0.5 mi s of jct SR 60 (causeway). 431 Gulfview Blvd 33767. **Hours:** 7:30 am-10 pm; to 11 pm 2/28-10/1. **Features:** A local landmark for many years, the restaurant prepares pizza, sandwiches, wings and even Greek items. This place is right across from the beach. Casual dress. **Parking:** on-site. **Cards:** AX, DS, MC, VI.

RUSTY'S BISTRO
Dinner: $16-$26   **Phone:** 727/593-6000   71
American
Location: 2 mi s on SR 699; at south end of Clearwater Pass Bridge; in Sheraton Sand Key Resort. 1160 Gulf Blvd 33767. **Hours:** 6 pm-10 pm. **Reservations:** accepted. **Features:** A popular gathering spot for a refreshing beverage and a wide variety of tasty snack and comfort foods. Casual dress; cocktails. **Parking:** on-site. **Cards:** AX, DC, DS, MC, VI.

(See map and index starting on p. 938)

SHELLS SEAFOOD RESTAURANT　　　**Lunch:** $7-$21　　**Dinner:** $7-$21　　**Phone:** 727/446-5884　　⑦⓪

Seafood

Location: North end of Clearwater Pass Bridge. 551 Gulf Blvd 33767. **Hours:** 11 am-10 pm, Fri & Sat-11 pm. Closed: 11/23, 12/25. **Features:** Well established and centrally located near the end of the Clearwater Pass Bridge, the restaurant offers a wide range of seafood choices; enjoy the seafood platter or some yummy peel-and-eat shrimp while enjoying views of boats passing by on the Gulf of Mexico. Casual dress; cocktails. **Parking:** on-site. **Cards:** AX, DS, MC, VI.

SHEPHARD'S WATERFRONT RESTAURANT　　　**Lunch:** $7-$9　　**Dinner:** $14-$24　　**Phone:** 727/441-6875　　⑥⑥

Seafood

Location: 1 mi s of jct SR 60 (roundabout); in Shephard's Beach Resort. 619 S Gulfview Blvd 33767. **Hours:** 8-11 am, 11:30-3 & 4-10 pm. **Features:** Known for its seafood and prime rib buffet, the waterfront family restaurant offers views of the sparkling Gulf of Mexico from nearly every seat. A colorful and casual atmosphere is enhanced by live entertainment with a Caribbean flavor. Casual dress; cocktails; entertainment. **Parking:** on-site. **Cards:** AX, DS, MC, VI. *(See color ad p 1019)*

WATERFRONT RESTAURANT　　　**Lunch:** $6-$18　　**Dinner:** $6-$18　　**Phone:** 727/442-3684　　⑤⑥

American

Location: 0.5 mi n of jct SR 60 (roundabout). 490 Mandalay Ave 33767. **Hours:** 7 am-10 pm; to 11 pm in season. **Features:** The basic restaurant is a good stop at any time of day. The breakfast menu is expansive, lunch choices include appetizers, soups, salads, sandwiches and pasta dishes, and dinner offerings center on steaks, pork chops, chicken, ribs and seafood. Casual dress; cocktails. **Parking:** on-site. **Cards:** AX, MC, VI.

DADE CITY pop. 6,188

——— **WHERE TO DINE** ———

KAFE KOKOPELLI　　　**Lunch:** $5-$10　　**Dinner:** $10-$27　　**Phone:** 352/523-0055

American

Location: Just e of jct US 98/301; downtown. 37940 Live Oak Ave 33523. **Hours:** 11 am-9 pm, Fri & Sat-10 pm. Closed: Sun & Mon. **Features:** Rudiments of the pulley system still hang from the rafters, as do other added items, in the now-restored remnants of a Model T service center downtown. Guests eat on antique doors as tables. Entrees range from sizzling filet mignon to skewered grilled shrimp to popular pasta and Southwestern dishes. Casual dress; cocktails. **Parking:** street. **Cards:** AX, DS, MC, VI.

LUNCH ON LIMOGES　　　**Lunch:** $10-$14　　**Phone:** 352/567-5685

American

Location: Center; opposite the Court House in Williams Department Store. 14139 7th St 33525. **Hours:** 11:30 am-2:30 pm. Closed major holidays; also Sun, Mon 5/1-10/31. **Reservations:** suggested. **Features:** Located in an historic department store near the courthouse, the small cafe features excellent Southern cooking with nice touches like a basket of delectable homemade muffins. The varied menu changes daily, making fine use of market-fresh ingredients. Dressy casual; beer & wine only. **Parking:** street. **Cards:** AX, CB, DC, DS, MC, VI.

DUNEDIN pop. 35,691 (See map and index starting on p. 938)

——— **WHERE TO STAY** ———

BEST WESTERN YACHT HARBOR INN　　*Book at aaa.com*　　　**Phone:** (727)733-4121　　②⑦

Motel

2/1-4/15 [ECP]	1P: $129-$149	2P: $129-$149	XP: $10	F12
12/21-1/31 [ECP]	1P: $99-$119	2P: $99-$119	XP: $10	F12
12/1-12/20 & 4/16-11/30 [ECP]	1P: $89-$109	2P: $89-$109	XP: $10	F12

Location: Jct US Alternate Rt 19 and gulf end of Main St, 0.5 mi s of SR 580. Located across from the marina. 150 Marina Plaza 34698. **Fax:** 727/736-4365. **Facility:** Designated smoking area. 55 units. 54 one-bedroom standard units. 1 two-bedroom suite. 2 stories, exterior corridors. *Bath:* combo or shower only. **Parking:** on-site. **Terms:** 3 day cancellation notice-fee imposed. **Amenities:** high-speed Internet, dual phone lines, voice mail, irons, hair dryers. *Some:* honor bars. **Dining:** Bon Appetit Restaurant & Marina Cafe, see separate listing. **Pool(s):** heated outdoor. **Leisure Activities:** whirlpool, exercise room, shuffleboard. **Guest Services:** sundries, valet and coin laundry. **Business Services:** meeting rooms, PC, fax (fee). **Cards:** AX, DC, DS, MC, VI.

SOME UNITS

HOLIDAY INN EXPRESS HOTEL & SUITES CLEARWATER NORTH/DUNEDIN　　*Book at aaa.com*　　　**Phone:** (727)450-1200　　②⑥

Small-scale Hotel

12/1-4/20 [CP]	1P: $139-$179	XP: $5	F19
4/21-11/30 [CP]	1P: $109-$159	XP: $5	F19

Location: On US Alternate Rt 19, jct SR 580. 975 Broadway 34698. **Fax:** 727/734-1202. **Facility:** 76 units. 70 one-bedroom standard units. 6 one-bedroom suites. 3 stories, interior corridors. *Bath:* combo or shower only. **Parking:** on-site. **Terms:** check-in 4 pm, cancellation fee imposed. **Amenities:** high-speed Internet, dual phone lines, voice mail, irons, hair dryers. **Pool(s):** heated outdoor. **Leisure Activities:** whirlpool, exercise room. **Guest Services:** valet and coin laundry. **Business Services:** meeting rooms, business center. **Cards:** AX, DC, DS, JC, MC, VI.

SOME UNITS

——— **WHERE TO DINE** ———

BON APPETIT RESTAURANT & MARINA CAFE　　**Lunch:** $7-$14　　**Dinner:** $12-$15　　**Phone:** 727/733-2151　　④⑤

Continental

Location: Jct US Alternate Rt 19 and gulf end of Main St, 0.5 mi s of SR 580; in Best Western Yacht Harbor Inn. 148 Marina Plaza 34698. **Hours:** 11:30 am-10 pm. **Reservations:** suggested. **Features:** Overlooking the Intracoastal Waterway, the restaurant is a great spot for creative bistro cuisine. Seagoers can dock at the inn and dine in the outdoor cafe. Professional service and attentiveness are key to a grand, enchanting meal. Casual dress; cocktails. **Parking:** on-site. **Cards:** AX, CB, DC, DS, MC, VI.

(See map and index starting on p. 938)

CAFE ALFRESCO   Lunch: $8-$16   Dinner: $8-$16   Phone: 727/736-4299   47

Italian   **Location:** Just w of jct Douglas Ave; downtown. 344 Main St 34698. **Hours:** 11 am-10 pm, Sat & Sun from 10 am. **Features:** Patrons of the relaxed bistro have a choice of outdoor or indoor seating. The menu has some great choices, including various pasta dishes, swordfish, salmon, steak and chicken. An extensive brunch is offered weekends from 10 am to 2 pm, and Wednesday is pasta night. Casual dress; cocktails. **Parking:** street. **Cards:** MC, VI.

"KELLY'S FOR JUST ABOUT...ANYTHING!"   Lunch: $7-$10   Dinner: $12-$22   Phone: 727/736-5284   48

American   **Location:** Just e of jct US Alternate Rt 19; center. 319 Main St 34698. **Hours:** 8 am-9:30 pm, Fri & Sat-10:30 pm, Sun-9 pm. Closed: 12/25. **Reservations:** suggested. **Features:** An eclectic menu runs the gamut from simple to sublime, with a dining room decor that is as creative as the food. Professional and attentive service follows an "anything goes" philosophy. Try the grilled chicken sandwich for a light lunch. Casual dress; cocktails; entertainment. **Parking:** street. **Cards:** AX, MC, VI.

SEA SEA RIDER'S RESTAURANT   Lunch: $6-$8   Dinner: $6-$19   Phone: 727/734-1445   46

American   **Location:** Jct Main St and US Alternate Rt 19; center. 221 Main St 34698. **Hours:** 11 am-10 pm, Fri & Sat-11 pm, Sun-9 pm. Closed: 11/23, 12/25. **Reservations:** accepted. **Features:** Veranda and inside seating both provide for a pleasant and relaxing experience at this 1906 Florida cracker house. Flavorful coconut shrimp, sauteed chicken and mahi-mahi whet the appetite, while artwork by state denizens adds to the tropical decor. Casual dress; cocktails. **Parking:** on-site. **Cards:** AX, MC, VI.

GULFPORT pop. 12,527   (See map and index starting on p. 938)

———— **WHERE TO DINE** ————

HABANA CAFE   Lunch: $5-$18   Dinner: $5-$18   Phone: 727/321-8855   161

Cuban   **Location:** I-275, exit 19, 1.9 mi w on 22nd Ave S, jct 54th St S. 5402 Gulfport Blvd S 33707. **Hours:** 11 am-9 pm. Closed major holidays; also Sun. **Reservations:** accepted. **Features:** Emphasizing Cuban cuisine, the cafe serves salads, sandwiches and entrees that include picadillo, chuletas de puerco and camarones borracho. Patrons should arrive with an appetite. Casual dress; beer & wine only. **Parking:** on-site. **Cards:** AX, DC, DS, MC, VI.

HUDSON pop. 12,765

———— **WHERE TO DINE** ————

SAM'S BEACH BAR RESTAURANT   Lunch: $6-$13   Dinner: $6-$13   Phone: 727/868-1971

Seafood   **Location:** 0.8 mi w of jct US 19; at Hudson Beach. 6325 Clark St 34667. **Hours:** 7 am-midnight. **Features:** Guests of the open-air restaurant can take in a casual lunch or dinner while viewing the many happenings on the waterway. Seating is all on the deck. The mood is relaxed, and the seafood is good. Casual dress; beer & wine only. **Parking:** on-site. **Cards:** MC, VI.

INDIAN ROCKS BEACH pop. 5,072   (See map and index starting on p. 938)

———— **WHERE TO STAY** ————

HOLIDAY INN HOTEL & SUITES-HARBOURSIDE   *Book at aaa.com*   Phone: (727)595-9484   82

AAA SAVE

	1P: $189-$399	2P: $189-$399	XP: $15	F18
2/1-4/30				
12/1-1/31 & 5/1-11/30	1P: $129-$299	2P: $129-$299	XP: $10	F18

Small-scale Hotel   **Location:** Just e of jct SR 699; just s of jct SR 688 (Walsingham Rd). 401 2nd St 33785. Fax: 727/596-4825. **Facility:** 164 units. 82 one-bedroom standard units, some with efficiencies. 82 one-bedroom suites with kitchens, some with whirlpools. 3 stories, exterior corridors. *Bath:* combo or shower only. **Parking:** on-site. **Terms:** check-in 4 pm, cancellation fee imposed, package plans. **Amenities:** voice mail, irons, hair dryers. *Some:* dual phone lines. **Dining:** 7 am-11 pm, Fri & Sat-2 am, cocktails, also, Jimmy Guana's Bar & Grill, see separate listing, entertainment. **Pool(s):** 2 heated outdoor. **Leisure Activities:** whirlpool, waterslide, fishing, tennis court, inline skates, motor scooters, dockmaster, playground, exercise room, volleyball. *Fee:* boats, sailboats, windsurfing, marina, waterskiing, charter fishing, personal watercraft, massage, game room. **Guest Services:** gift shop, valet and coin laundry. **Business Services:** meeting rooms. *Fee:* administrative services, PC, fax. **Cards:** AX, CB, DC, DS, MC, VI. **Special Amenities:** free local telephone calls and free newspaper. *(See color ad below)*

SOME UNITS

(See map and index starting on p. 938)

SEA STAR MOTEL & APARTMENTS

Phone: (727)596-2525 **81**

1/1-4/30	1P: $70-$110	2P: $70-$110	XP: $10	F
12/1-12/31 & 5/1-11/30	1P: $60-$80	2P: $60-$80	XP: $10	F

Motel

Location: On SR 699, 1.2 mi n of jct SR 688 (Walsingham Rd). 1805 Gulf Blvd 33785. Fax: 727/596-2525. **Facility:** Designated smoking area. 13 units. 7 one-bedroom standard units with efficiencies. 4 one- and 1 two-bedroom suites ($430-$560) with kitchens. 1 cottage ($430-$560). 1-2 stories, exterior corridors. *Bath:* combo or shower only. **Parking:** on-site. **Terms:** 3 night minimum stay - seasonal and/or weekends, 30 day cancellation notice, weekly rates available, pets ($10 extra charge). **Amenities:** video library. *Some:* irons, hair dryers. **Leisure Activities:** whirlpool, bicycles, shuffleboard. **Guest Services:** coin laundry. **Business Services:** fax. **Cards:** AX, DS, MC, VI.

SOME UNITS

(ASK) 🐾 (¶¶→) ⊠ ⊠ ☎ 🖪 🖵 🖂 / (VCR)
FEE

——————— **WHERE TO DINE** ———————

GUPPY'S ON THE BEACH

Lunch: $10-$25   Dinner: $10-$25   Phone: 727/593-2032 **111**

Seafood

Location: On SR 699, 1 mi n of jct SR 688 (Walsingham Rd). 1701 Gulf Blvd 33785. **Hours:** 11:30 am-close. Closed: 11/23, 12/25. **Features:** Enjoy the gulf breeze with patio dining. This diner offers an excellent variety of seafood, steak and sandwich choices with a gorgeous sunset view. The fried shrimp is fresh and served with herbed wild rice and delicate vegetables. Casual dress; cocktails. **Parking:** on-site and valet. **Cards:** AX, DC, DS, MC, VI.

JIMMY GUANA'S BAR & GRILL

Lunch: $7-$19   Dinner: $7-$19   Phone: 727/595-8356 **113**

American

Location: Just e of jct SR 699; just s of jct SR 688 (Walsingham Rd); in Holiday Inn Hotel & Suites-Harbourside. 401 2nd St 33785. **Hours:** 7 am-10 pm, Fri & Sat-11 pm. **Reservations:** accepted. **Features:** This is a fun spot to visit for lunch or dinner after a long day at the beach or a day of sailing the Intracoastal Waterway. Slips are available. The seafood lover's platter is a hit, as is tropic pasta. Fridays bring the all-you-can-eat grouper fish fry. Casual dress; cocktails; entertainment. **Parking:** on-site. **Cards:** AX, CB, DC, DS, MC, VI.

(க.M) (Υ) (◣)

PJ'S OYSTER BAR & SEAFOOD RESTAURANT

Lunch: $6-$28   Dinner: $6-$28   Phone: 727/596-5898 **112**

Seafood

Location: Just e of jct SR 699. 500 First St 33785. **Hours:** 11 am-11 pm, Sun 1 pm-10 pm. **Reservations:** not accepted. **Features:** Hearty seafood dinners lure guests to the casual eatery. The service staff is friendly, and the decor is basic with a nautical flair. Casual dress. **Parking:** on-site. **Cards:** AX, MC, VI.

THAI PAN ALLEY & BAMBOO BEACH BAR

Lunch: $8-$10   Dinner: $8-$10   Phone: 727/593-3663 **110**

Thai

Location: On SR 699, 1.5 mi n of jct SR 688; in Western Plaza. 2300 Gulf Blvd 33785. **Hours:** 11 am-3 & 5-9 pm, Fri-10 pm, Sat 11 am-10 pm, Sun 4 pm-9 pm. Closed major holidays. **Features:** Hearty portions of rice and noodle dishes coated with sauces from mild to eye-watering spicy characterize the restaurant's cuisine. Dine inside amid Thai decorations that lend the air of the Orient or head out to the colorful beach bar setting. Beer & wine only. **Parking:** on-site. **Cards:** DC, DS, MC, VI.

(Υ)

INDIAN SHORES pop. 1,705   (See map and index starting on p. 938)

——————— **WHERE TO STAY** ———————

BEACH COTTAGE III

Phone: (727)595-7586 **95**

2/11-4/21 Wkly	1P: $1025-$1385	2P: $1025-$1385
12/1-2/10 Wkly	1P: $925-$1275	2P: $925-$1275
4/22-9/8 Wkly	1P: $850-$1125	2P: $850-$1125
9/9-11/30 Wkly	1P: $625-$900	2P: $625-$900

Condominium

Location: Oceanfront. On SR 699, 0.4 mi s of jct CR 694. 18450 Gulf Blvd 33785 (417 1st St, INDIAN ROCKS BEACH). Fax: 727/595-4104. **Facility:** 15 units. 1 one-, 1 two- and 13 three-bedroom suites with kitchens. 6 stories, exterior corridors. **Parking:** on-site. **Terms:** office hours 9 am-7 pm, off-site registration, check-in 4 pm, 7 night minimum stay, 45 day cancellation notice-fee imposed, $100 service charge. **Amenities:** irons. **Pool(s):** heated outdoor. **Guest Services:** complimentary laundry. **Business Services:** fax. **Cards:** DS, MC, VI.

SOME UNITS

(ASK) (S☐) (¶¶→) (🏊) (VCR) 🖪 🖵 / (⊠)

SAND CASTLE II

Phone: (727)595-7586 **93**

2/11-4/21 Wkly	1P: $1300-$1432	2P: $1300-$1432
12/1-2/10 Wkly	1P: $1225-$1349	2P: $1225-$1349
4/22-9/8 Wkly	1P: $1075-$1128	2P: $1075-$1128
9/9-11/30 Wkly	1P: $850-$910	2P: $850-$910

Condominium

Location: Oceanfront. On SR 699, 1.2 mi s of jct SR 688 (Walsingham Rd). 20002 Gulf Blvd 33785 (417 1st St, INDIAN ROCKS BEACH). Fax: 727/595-4104. **Facility:** Designated smoking area. 7 three-bedroom suites with kitchens. 10 stories, exterior corridors. **Parking:** on-site. **Terms:** office hours 9 am-7 pm, off-site registration, check-in 4 pm, 3-7 night minimum stay, 45 day cancellation notice-fee imposed, $100 service charge. **Amenities:** irons. **Pool(s):** outdoor, heated outdoor. **Leisure Activities:** whirlpool. **Guest Services:** complimentary laundry. **Business Services:** fax. **Cards:** DS, MC, VI.

(ASK) (S☐) (¶¶→) (🏊) (⊠) (VCR) 🖪 🖵

SAND CASTLE III

Phone: (727)595-7586 **92**

2/11-4/21 Wkly	1P: $1355-$1435	2P: $1355-$1435
12/1-2/10 Wkly	1P: $1250-$1380	2P: $1250-$1380
4/22-9/8 Wkly	1P: $1100-$1212	2P: $1100-$1212
9/9-11/30 Wkly	1P: $875-$920	2P: $875-$920

Condominium

Location: Oceanfront. On SR 699, 1.2 mi s of SR 688 (Walsingham Rd). 20040 Gulf Blvd 33785 (417 1st St, INDIAN ROCKS BEACH). Fax: 727/595-4104. **Facility:** 16 three-bedroom suites with kitchens. 6 stories, exterior corridors. **Parking:** on-site. **Terms:** office hours 9 am-7 pm, off-site registration, check-in 4 pm, 3-7 night minimum stay, 45 day cancellation notice-fee imposed, $100 service charge. **Amenities:** irons. **Pool(s):** heated outdoor. **Leisure Activities:** whirlpool. **Guest Services:** complimentary laundry. **Business Services:** fax. **Cards:** DS, MC, VI.

SOME UNITS

(ASK) (S☐) (¶¶→) (🏊) (VCR) 🖪 🖵 / (⊠)

(See map and index starting on p. 938)

SEA GATE   *Book at aaa.com*   Phone: (727)595-7586   94

	2/11-4/21 Wkly	1P: $1275-$1340	2P: $1275-$1340
	12/1-2/10 Wkly	1P: $1175-$1260	2P: $1175-$1260
Condominium	4/22-9/8 Wkly	1P: $1050-$1215	2P: $1050-$1215
	9/9-11/30 Wkly	1P: $850-$920	2P: $850-$920

Location: Oceanfront. On SR 699, 2.4 mi s of jct SR 688 (Walsingham Rd). 19418 Gulf Blvd 33785 (417 1st St, INDIAN ROCKS BEACH). **Fax:** 727/595-4104. **Facility:** Designated smoking area. 4 three-bedroom suites with kitchens. 6 stories, exterior corridors. **Parking:** on-site. **Terms:** office hours 9 am-7 pm, off-site registration, check-in 4 pm, 7 night minimum stay, 45 day cancellation notice-fee imposed, $100 service charge. **Amenities:** irons. **Pool(s):** heated outdoor. **Guest Services:** complimentary laundry. **Business Services:** fax. **Cards:** DS, MC, VI.

--------- WHERE TO DINE ---------

FATHOM'S   **Lunch:** $5-$23   **Dinner:** $6-$23   Phone: 727-596-2453   133

Seafood

Location: 1.3 mi n of Park Blvd Cswy (CR 694). 19915 Gulf Blvd 33785. **Hours:** 11:30 am-10 pm. Closed: 11/23, 12/25. **Features:** This local landmark serves peel-and-eat shrimp with a unique cocktail sauce on a bed of lettuce. Try the catfish fillets for a fresh local catch. Seafood and meat specialties complete the menu choices. The service is prompt and pleasant. Casual dress; cocktails. **Parking:** on-site. **Cards:** MC, VI.

THE PUB WATERFRONT RESTAURANT & LOUNGE   **Lunch:** $5-$10   **Dinner:** $8-$16   Phone: 727-595-3172   132

American

Location: On SR 699, 1.2 mi s of jct SR 688 (Walsingham Rd). 20025 Gulf Blvd 33785. **Hours:** 11 am-midnight, Sat & Sun from 8 am. Closed: 12/25. **Reservations:** accepted. **Features:** The great Intracoastal Waterway location affords beautiful views of the dock from the outdoor patio as well as the cozy inside dining area. The piano bar and dance floor add to the ambience. Listed on the extensive menu are numerous steak, seafood, pasta, rib, burger and sandwich selections, as well as salads, appetizers and desserts. Casual dress; cocktails; entertainment. **Parking:** on-site and street. **Cards:** AX, DC, DS, MC, VI.

SALT ROCK GRILL   **Dinner:** $10-$40   Phone: 727-593-7625   135

Swiss

Location: On SR 699, 0.5 mi n of jct Park Blvd Cswy (CR 694). 19325 Gulf Blvd 33785. **Hours:** 4 pm-10 pm, Fri & Sat-11 pm. Closed: 12/25. **Features:** An extremely trendy and upscale setting—a remake of "Le Pompano"—awaits the diner here. Beautiful artwork and objects abound, and the decor is tastefully done. The menu offers open-pit citrus- and oak-fired steaks and seafood prepared by trained chefs. Dressy casual; cocktails. **Parking:** on-site. **Cards:** AX, DC, DS, MC, VI.

THE TROPICAL GRILL   **Lunch:** $7-$18   **Dinner:** $7-$18   Phone: 727-595-4088   134

American

Location: On SR 699, 0.5 mi n of jct CR 694; in Indian Pass Shopping Center. 19455 Gulf Blvd 33785. **Hours:** 11:30 am-9 pm. Closed major holidays; also Sun. **Features:** The lunchtime spot serves good fried grouper sandwiches. After a long day at the beach, sun lovers can stop in for such specialties as Jamaican jerk chops, chicken cordon bleu or the popular burrito combination platters. The menu lists a multitude of choices. Casual dress; cocktails. **Parking:** on-site. **Cards:** MC, VI.

LARGO pop. 69,371   (See map and index starting on p. 938)

--------- WHERE TO STAY ---------

SUBURBAN LODGE   *Book at aaa.com*   Phone: (727)532-4800   85

	All Year	1P: $55-$65	2P: $55-$65	XP: $5 F18

Small-scale Hotel

Location: On SR 688, just w of jct US 19. 6500 Ulmerton Rd 33771. **Fax:** 727/507-8527. **Facility:** 132 one-bedroom standard units with efficiencies. 3 stories, exterior corridors. **Bath:** combo or shower only. **Parking:** on-site. **Terms:** office hours 8:30 am-7 pm, check-in 4 pm, cancellation fee imposed, weekly rates available. **Amenities:** high-speed Internet, voice mail. *Some:* irons, hair dryers. **Guest Services:** valet and coin laundry. **Business Services:** fax (fee). **Cards:** AX, DS, MC, VI.

SOME UNITS

--------- WHERE TO DINE ---------

ANGELLINO'S ITALIAN RESTAURANT   **Lunch:** $8-$11   **Dinner:** $9-$17   Phone: 727-595-8382   120

Italian

Location: On SR 688, 1.2 mi e of jct SR 699. 13883 Walsingham Rd 33774. **Hours:** 11:30 am-9 pm. Closed: 11/23, 12/25. **Features:** The casual, relaxing spot urges families to visit for a great Italian meal. On the menu are seafood, veal, chicken and pasta dishes, including such specialties as penne Angelo and linguine Capriati. Casual dress; cocktails. **Parking:** on-site. **Cards:** MC, VI.

ATLANTA BREAD COMPANY   **Lunch:** $6-$7   **Dinner:** $6-$7   Phone: 727-581-4621   119

American

Location: On SR 688, just e of jct Seminole Blvd; in Largo Mall. 10500 Ulmerton Rd 33771. **Hours:** 6:30 am-9 pm, Sat from 7:30 am, Sun 8 am-4 pm. Closed: 1/1, 11/23, 12/25. **Features:** The trendy breakfast, lunch and dinner spot serves fresh soups, sandwiches and salads. Homemade bakery items are displayed in eye-catching fashion. Casual dress. **Parking:** on-site. **Cards:** AX, MC, VI.

CARMELITA'S MEXICAN RESTAURANT   **Lunch:** $7-$9   **Dinner:** $9-$13   Phone: 727-533-8555   117

Mexican

Location: On SR 688, jct Belches; in Plaza de Sunus. 7705 Ulmerton Rd 33771. **Hours:** 11 am-9 pm, Fri & Sat-9:30 pm. Closed: Sun. **Features:** The Lopez family, which owns the popular establishment, prepares tasty Mexican fare. Anything from Mexican pizza to flautas to chiles rellenos to combination platters can be found on the menu. Fried ice cream for dessert is a must-try. Casual dress; beer & wine only. **Parking:** on-site. **Cards:** AX, DS, MC, VI.

(See map and index starting on p. 938)

CHICAGO PIZZA & PASTA CO. Dinner: $8-$24 Phone: 727/593-1300 121

Italian

Location: On SR 688, 1.6 mi e of jct SR 699. 12881 Walsingham Rd 33774. **Hours:** 4 pm-10 pm, Fri & Sat-11 pm, Sun 3 pm-10 pm. Closed: 12/25; also Mon. **Features:** On the menu are fresh pasta dishes, gourmet pizza, calzones, sandwiches, tortilla wraps and many appetizers. Servers are friendly and welcoming, and the food is great. Casual dress; cocktails. **Parking:** on-site. **Cards:** DS, MC, VI.

EGG PLATTER III Lunch: $5-$8 Dinner: $5-$8 Phone: 727/539-7420 118

American

Location: On SR 688, 2 mi w of jct SR 693 (66th St), jct Starkey. 8870 Ulmerton Rd 33771. **Hours:** 24 hours. **Features:** Open 24 hours, the popular casual spot serves good home cooking. Choices range from hearty breakfasts to ample lunch and dinner selections. Casual dress. **Parking:** on-site. **Cards:** AX, DC, DS, MC, VI.

THE GATHERING RESTAURANT Lunch: $5-$9 Phone: 727/593-1600 122

American

Location: On SR 688, 1 mi e of jct SR 699; in Sabala Plaza. 14100 Walsingham Rd 33774. **Hours:** 6:30 am-2 pm. **Features:** Bright and airy with lots of room, the restaurant offers up lighter fare, ranging from omelets and eggs Benedict to corned beef sandwiches on rye bread. The Belgian waffles are pretty tasty, too. The servers are polite and prompt. Casual dress. **Parking:** on-site. **Cards:** MC, VI.

PAPPAS MEDITERRANEAN BISTRO Lunch: $7-$13 Dinner: $14-$21 Phone: 727/538-4273 116

Mediterranean

Location: Just n of jct SR 688; in Summit Office Building at Icot Center. 13575 58th St N 33760. **Hours:** 11 am-9 pm. Closed: Sun. **Features:** On the lower level of an office complex building, the trendy bistro is casual with a touch of sophistication. Patio dining is a breezy and relaxed experience. Among Greek specialties are souvlaki, gyros and spanakopita. Dressy casual; cocktails. **Parking:** on-site. **Cards:** AX, DS, MC, VI.

LITHIA

———— WHERE TO DINE ————

BEEF O'BRADY'S Lunch: $6-$10 Dinner: $6-$10 Phone: 813/651-0388

American

Location: Jct Lithia Pinecrest Rd; in Fishhawk Plaza. 16773 Fishhawk Blvd 33547. **Hours:** 11 am-11 pm, Sun noon-10 pm. Closed: 11/23, 12/25. **Features:** Patrons can watch a favorite sports program on one of many television monitors strategically placed around the dining room. Buffalo wings and Philly cheese steaks are popular menu items. Casual dress; beer & wine only. **Parking:** on-site. **Cards:** AX, DS, MC, VI.

CHINA STAR CHINESE RESTAURANT Lunch: $5-$15 Dinner: $5-$15 Phone: 813/684-8382

Chinese

Location: Jct Lithia Pinecrest Rd; in Fishhawk Plaza. 16733 Fishhawk Blvd 33547. **Hours:** 11 am-10 pm, Fri & Sat-10:30 pm, Sun noon-10 pm. Closed: 11/23. **Features:** The small restaurant has limited seating, so arrive early and with an appetite. Menu choices include more than 160 preparations of good Chinese food. Casual dress. **Parking:** on-site. **Cards:** MC, VI.

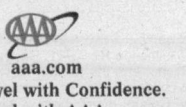

MADEIRA BEACH pop. 4,511   (See map and index starting on p. 938)

──────── **WHERE TO STAY** ────────

SEA DAWN MOTEL

			Phone: 727/391-7500	**106**
AAA SAVE	12/1-3/31	1P: $65-$85	2P: $65-$85	XP: $8
	4/1-4/30	1P: $60-$80	2P: $60-$80	XP: $8
◆◆	5/1-11/30	1P: $50-$70	2P: $50-$70	XP: $8

Motel

Location: On SR 699, 0.7 mi s of Tom Stuart Cswy. 13733 Gulf Blvd 33708. Fax: 727/398-2179. **Facility:** 8 one-bedroom standard units, some with efficiencies or kitchens. 2 stories, exterior corridors. **Parking:** on-site. **Terms:** 3 night minimum stay, 30 day cancellation notice-fee imposed, weekly rates available. **Amenities:** *Some:* irons. **Pool(s):** small outdoor. **Leisure Activities:** boat dock, fishing, sun deck, lending library. **Business Services:** fax. **Cards:** AX, MC, VI.

SOME UNITS

SHAWNEE'S ISLAND GULF RESORT

Phone: 727/398-6786   **105**

Property failed to provide current rates

◆◆◆

Condominium

Location: Oceanfront. On SR 699, 0.8 mi s of jct SR 666 (Tom Stuart Cswy). 13912 Gulf Blvd 33708. Fax: 727/397-4308. **Facility:** 15 units. 12 one- and 3 three-bedroom suites with kitchens. 4 stories, interior corridors. **Parking:** on-site. **Terms:** office hours 8 am-3 pm, check-in 4 pm. **Amenities:** irons, hair dryers. **Leisure Activities:** whirlpool. **Guest Services:** complimentary laundry. **Business Services:** fax (fee).

SHORELINE ISLAND RESORT

			Phone: (727)397-6641	**104**
AAA SAVE	1/26-4/26	1P: $121-$265	2P: $121-$265	XP: $10
	12/18-1/25 & 4/27-11/30	1P: $83-$194	2P: $83-$194	XP: $10
◆◆◆	12/1-12/17	1P: $79-$147	2P: $79-$147	XP: $10

Small-scale Hotel

Location: Oceanfront. On SR 699, 0.5 mi s of Tom Stuart Cswy. 14200 Gulf Blvd 33708. Fax: 727/393-9157. **Facility:** 71 units. 51 one-bedroom standard units, some with efficiencies. 16 one- and 4 two-bedroom suites ($79-$265) with kitchens. 2-5 stories, exterior corridors. **Parking:** on-site. **Terms:** office hours 8 am-9 pm, age restrictions may apply, 7 day cancellation notice-fee imposed. **Amenities:** video library, hair dryers. *Some:* irons. **Pool(s):** heated outdoor. **Leisure Activities:** sun deck, shuffleboard. **Guest Services:** coin laundry. **Business Services:** fax (fee). **Cards:** AX, DS, MC, VI. *(See color ad below)*

SOME UNITS

SNUG HARBOR INN WATERFRONT BED & BREAKFAST

			Phone: (727)395-9256	**107**
AAA SAVE	1/1-4/30 [ECP]	1P: $100-$116	2P: $100-$116	XP: $11	F4
	5/1-8/15 [ECP]	1P: $90-$105	2P: $90-$105	XP: $11	F4
◆◆◆	12/1-12/31 & 8/16-11/30 [ECP]	1P: $65-$90	2P: $65-$90	XP: $11	F4

Motel

Location: On SR 699, 0.9 mi s of jct Tom Stuart Cswy. 13655 Gulf Blvd 33708. Fax: 877/379-6704. **Facility:** 8 one-bedroom suites ($130-$202) with kitchens. 2 stories, exterior corridors. **Parking:** on-site. **Terms:** 28 day cancellation notice, weekly rates available, package plans. **Amenities:** *Some:* irons, hair dryers. **Pool(s):** heated outdoor. **Leisure Activities:** boat dock, fishing, 6 boat slips, 120-foot dock on Boca Ciega Bay, gas barbecue grill, bicycles. **Guest Services:** coin laundry. **Business Services:** fax (fee). **Cards:** AX, DC, DS, MC, VI. **Special Amenities:** free expanded continental breakfast and free local telephone calls.

SOME UNITS

(See map and index starting on p. 938)

——— WHERE TO DINE ———

COURTYARD CAFE **Lunch:** $5-$8   **Dinner:** $5-$8   **Phone:** 727/320-0751   (146)
▼▼▼   **Location:** On SR 699; in John's Pass Village. 13015 Village Blvd 33708. **Hours:** 10 am-8 pm. **Features:** The
American   outdoor eatery is a favorite spot to gather after a day of beach activities or shopping at John's Pass Village. Among favorites are made-to-order delicatessen classics, including wraps and submarine sandwiches. Also on site are a coffee bar, bakery and ice cream and candy counter where guests can satisfy a sweet craving.
Casual dress. **Parking:** on-site (fee). **Cards:** MC, VI.

DE LOSA'S PIZZERIA **Lunch:** $5-$10   **Dinner:** $5-$10   **Phone:** 727/398-4657   (147)
▼▼▼   **Location:** Just e of jct SR 699; in John's Pass Village. 12800 Village Blvd 33708. **Hours:** 11 am-2 am. **Features:** At
Pizza   the popular John's Pass Village of shops, the casual eatery prepares yummy pizzas, calzones and made-to-order sandwiches. Casual dress. **Parking:** on-site (fee). **Cards:** AX, MC, VI.

DOCKSIDE DAVE'S BAR & GRILL **Lunch:** $5-$15   **Dinner:** $5-$15   **Phone:** 727/392-9399   (145)
▼▼▼   **Location:** On SR 699, just n of jct 132nd Ave. 13203 Gulf Blvd 33708. **Hours:** 11 am-10 pm, Sun from noon.
Seafood   Closed: 4/16, 11/23, 12/25. **Reservations:** not accepted. **Features:** A favorite spot of locals, the restaurant prepares a yummy chargrilled black grouper sandwich that is a must-try. Other popular menu offerings include shrimp or scallop Martinique, pork loin, seafood bisque and grouper chowder. Casual dress.
Parking: on-site and street. **Cards:** MC, VI.

FRIENDLY FISHERMAN WATERFRONT SEAFOOD
   RESTAURANT **Lunch:** $4-$10   **Dinner:** $5-$22   **Phone:** 727/391-6025   (149)
▼▼ ▼▼   **Location:** At John's Pass Village; 1.4 mi s of jct Madeira Cswy. 150 Johns Pass Boardwalk 33708. **Hours:** 7 am-
Seafood   11:30 & 11:40-10 pm, Sun 7 am-10 pm. Closed: 12/25. **Reservations:** not accepted. **Features:** This rustic boardwalk eatery offers an array of seafood choices. Peel-and-eat shrimp is fresh and light. You will be treated to prompt, detail-oriented service during your seafood meal. Enjoy the waterfront view and shop the boardwalk after dinner. Casual dress; cocktails; entertainment. **Parking:** on-site. **Cards:** AX, DS, MC, VI.   ⊻

SCULLY'S BOARDWALK RESTAURANT **Lunch:** $8-$21   **Dinner:** $8-$21   **Phone:** 727/393-7749   (148)
▼▼▼ ▼▼▼   **Location:** At John's Pass Village, 1.4 mi s of jct Tom Stuart Cswy. 190 Johns Pass Boardwalk 33708. **Hours:** 11 am-
Seafood   10 pm. **Features:** A nice view of the Intracoastal Waterway can be enjoyed at this rustic and comfortable sea shanty, which offers boardwalk dining and is decorated in a nautical theme. Menu choices range from seafood to sandwiches to burgers. Casual dress; beer & wine only. **Parking:** on-site. **Cards:** MC, VI.

NEW PORT RICHEY pop. 16,117

——— WHERE TO STAY ———

BEST WESTERN NEW PORT RICHEY   *Book at aaa.com*   **Phone:** (727)842-6800
(AAA) [SAVE]   12/1-3/31   1P: $79-$89
   4/1-6/30   1P: $69-$79
▼▼▼ ▼▼▼   7/1-11/30   1P: $59-$69
Motel   **Location:** On US 19, 0.5 mi n of jct Main St. 6826 US 19 N 34652. Fax: 727/842-5072. **Facility:** 66 one-bedroom standard units, some with efficiencies (no utensils). 2 stories, exterior corridors. **Parking:** on-site.
   Terms: check-in 4 pm, 3-5 night minimum stay - seasonal and/or weekends, cancellation fee imposed, package plans. **Amenities:** *Some:* irons, hair dryers. **Pool(s):** heated outdoor. **Leisure Activities:** whirlpool, steamroom. **Guest Services:** coin laundry. **Business Services:** meeting rooms, fax. **Cards:** AX, DS, MC, VI. **Special Amenities:** free continental breakfast and free local telephone calls.
   SOME UNITS
   [S][D] [♦] [⌕] [⇌] [♦] [⌖] [DATA PORT] / [✕] [▮] [▤] [▭] /

ECONO LODGE   *Book at aaa.com*   **Phone:** (727)845-4990
(AAA) [SAVE]   2/1-4/20 [CP]   1P: $70-$120   2P: $70-$120
   1/1-1/31 & 4/21-11/30 [CP]   1P: $60-$100   2P: $65-$100
▼▼▼ ▼▼▼   12/1-12/31 [CP]   1P: $55-$90   2P: $60-$100
Motel   **Location:** On US 19, 0.8 mi n of jct Main St. 7631 US 19 34652. Fax: 727/849-1424. **Facility:** 105 one-bedroom standard units, some with efficiencies. 1 story, exterior corridors. **Parking:** on-site. **Terms:** 7 day cancellation notice, small pets only ($6 extra charge, limit 1). **Amenities:** high-speed Internet. *Some:* irons, hair dryers. **Pool(s):** heated outdoor. **Leisure Activities:** picnic and barbecue area. **Guest Services:** coin laundry. **Business Services:** fax (fee). **Cards:** AX, CB, DC, DS, JC, MC, VI. **Special Amenities:** free continental breakfast and free local telephone calls.
   SOME UNITS
   [S][D] [▥] [♦] [⇌] [⌖] [DATA PORT] / [✕] [▮] [▤] [▭]
   FEE

QUALITY INN & SUITES CONFERENCE CENTER   *Book at aaa.com*   **Phone:** (727)847-9005
(AAA) [SAVE]   1/16-4/30   2P: $94-$104   XP: $10   F
   9/15-11/30   2P: $89-$97   XP: $10   F
▼▼▼ ▼▼▼   12/1-1/15   2P: $82-$97   XP: $10   F
   5/1-9/14   2P: $84-$94   XP: $10   F
Small-scale Hotel   **Location:** 1 mi n of jct SR 54. 5316 US Hwy 19 34652. Fax: 727/844-3360. **Facility:** 150 units. 139 one-bedroom standard units. 11 one-bedroom suites ($119-$159). 2 stories, exterior corridors. *Bath:* combo or shower only. **Parking:** on-site. **Amenities:** video games (fee), dual phone lines, irons, hair dryers. **Dining:** 7 am-9 pm, cocktails. **Pool(s):** heated outdoor, wading. **Leisure Activities:** whirlpool, exercise room. **Guest Services:** valet and coin laundry. **Business Services:** meeting rooms, business center. **Cards:** AX, DC, DS, MC, VI. **Special Amenities:** free newspaper and free room upgrade (subject to availability with advance reservations).
   SOME UNITS
   [S][D] [♦] [⊻] [⌕] [⌖] [⇌] [⌖] [DATA PORT] [▮] [▭] / [✕] [▤]

─────── **WHERE TO DINE** ───────

BREW CITY
American

Lunch: $7-$13   **Dinner:** $7-$13   **Phone:** 727/816-9433
Location: On US 19, jct Cross Bayou Blvd. 5711 US 19 N 34652. **Hours:** 11:30 am-midnight. Closed: 12/25. **Features:** Rustic surroundings and a casual atmosphere help to add up to an enjoyable experience. Patrons can savor hearty portions of steak, ribs, sandwiches and burgers. There's great service to boot. Casual dress; cocktails. **Parking:** on-site. **Cards:** AX, DS, MC, VI.

CAFE GRAND
American

Lunch: $5-$7   **Dinner:** $12-$22   **Phone:** 727/848-7098
Location: Just s of Main St; downtown. 6238 Grand Blvd 34652. **Hours:** 11 am-9:30 pm, Fri 11 am-2:30 & 5-10 pm, Sat 5 pm-10 pm. Closed: 1/1, 12/25; also Sun. **Features:** In an established area of downtown, the restaurant sits opposite the theater in two storefront sections of a historic building. Operated by California transplants, the cafe uses the freshest products and ingredients, purchased daily, to create interesting pork, chicken, beef and seafood dishes. The owner's mother prepares sinful desserts. The decor is artsy and distinctive. Dressy casual; cocktails. **Parking:** on-site. **Cards:** AX, DC, DS, MC, VI.

LEVEROCKS WATERFRONT GRILL
Seafood
DS, MC, VI.

Lunch: $7-$21   **Dinner:** $9-$21   **Phone:** 727/849-8000
Location: On US 19, 1 mi n of jct SR 54. 4927 US 19 S 34652. **Hours:** 11 am-10 pm. Closed: 11/23, 12/25. **Features:** The nautically decorated restaurant, with large windows and multiple dining levels, affords views of the yacht basin from many flattering angles. With its own fleet of fishing boats, the restaurant boasts: "If it's fresher than Leverocks, it's still swimming". Casual dress; cocktails. **Parking:** on-site. **Cards:** AX, DC,

NORTH REDINGTON BEACH pop. 1,474   (See map and index starting on p. 938)

─────── **WHERE TO STAY** ───────

DOUBLETREE BEACH RESORT-TAMPA BAY/NORTH REDINGTON BEACH   *Book at aaa.com*
Large-scale Hotel

All Year   1P: $139-$499   2P: $139-$499   XP: $25   **Phone:** (727)391-4000   **100**   F18
Location: On SR 699, 2 mi n of Tom Stuart Cswy. 17120 Gulf Blvd 33708. Fax: 727/397-0699. **Facility:** 125 units. 124 one-bedroom standard units. 1 one-bedroom suite. 6 stories, interior corridors. **Parking:** on-site. **Terms:** 3 day cancellation notice, package plans. **Amenities:** high-speed Internet (fee), dual phone lines, voice mail, irons, hair dryers. **Pool(s):** heated outdoor. **Leisure Activities:** rental boats, volleyball. **Fee:** sailboats, windsurfing. **Guest Services:** valet laundry. **Business Services:** meeting rooms, fax (fee). **Cards:** AX, DC, DS, MC, VI.

SOME UNITS

FAR HORIZONS MOTEL
Condominium

Phone: 727/393-8791   **98**
Property failed to provide current rates
Location: Oceanfront. On SR 699, 1.5 mi s of jct Park Blvd (CR 694). 17248 Gulf Blvd 33708. Fax: 727/391-3980. **Facility:** 24 one-bedroom suites with efficiencies. 2 stories, exterior corridors. **Parking:** on-site. **Terms:** office hours 8 am-5 pm. **Amenities:** *Some:* irons, hair dryers. **Pool(s):** heated outdoor. **Leisure Activities:** shuffleboard. **Guest Services:** coin laundry. **Business Services:** fax.

SOME UNITS

RAMSEA   ⬤ [SAVE]
Condominium

All Year Wkly   2P: $690-$1500   **Phone:** (727)397-0441   **99**
Location: Oceanfront. On SR 699, 1.6 mi s of jct Park Blvd (CR 694). 17200 Gulf Blvd 33708. Fax: 727/397-8894. **Facility:** 68 units. 6 one-, 19 two- and 43 three-bedroom suites with kitchens. 6-7 stories, exterior corridors. **Parking:** on-site. **Terms:** office hours 9 am-8 pm, check-in 4 pm, 7 night minimum stay, 30 day cancellation notice-fee imposed, [AP] meal plan available, $100 service charge. **Amenities:** voice mail, safes (fee), irons. *Some:* DVD players. **Pool(s):** heated outdoor. **Leisure Activities:** whirlpool. **Fee:** aquacycles, cabanas, catamaran, personal watercraft. **Guest Services:** coin laundry. **Business Services:** fax (fee). **Cards:** AX, DS, MC, VI. **Special Amenities:** free newspaper. *(See color ad below)*

SOME UNITS

(See map and index starting on p. 938)

SAILS RESORT MOTEL
Phone: 727/391-6000   **101**

Motel

2/1-4/28	1P: $75-$175	2P: $75-$175	XP: $15	F3
4/29-5/31	1P: $70-$145	2P: $70-$145	XP: $10	F3
12/1-1/31	1P: $66-$139	2P: $66-$139	XP: $10	F3
6/1-11/30	1P: $65-$131	2P: $65-$131	XP: $10	F3

Location: Oceanfront. On SR 699, 2 mi n of Tom Stuart Cswy. 17004 Gulf Blvd 33708. **Fax:** 727/391-6000. **Facility:** 24 units. 2 one-bedroom standard units with efficiencies. 22 one-bedroom suites with kitchens. 2 stories, exterior corridors. *Bath:* combo or shower only. **Parking:** on-site. **Terms:** office hours 9 am-10 pm, 21 day cancellation notice-fee imposed. **Amenities:** *Some:* irons, hair dryers. **Pool(s):** heated outdoor. **Leisure Activities:** shuffleboard. **Guest Services:** coin laundry. **Business Services:** fax. **Cards:** DS, MC, VI.

--------- **WHERE TO DINE** ---------

CONCH REPUBLIC
Lunch: $7-$24   **Dinner:** $7-$24   Phone: 727/320-0536   **142**

American

Location: On SR 699, 1.8 mi n of Tom Stuart Cswy. 16699 Gulf Blvd 33708. **Hours:** 8 am-10 pm, Sat & Sun-11 pm. Closed: 11/23, 12/25. **Features:** An inviting nautical setting lures patrons to the casual dining establishment. Among choices are all kinds of fresh seafood, as well as oak-grilled steak, chicken, ribs and tasty pasta. Casual dress; cocktails. **Parking:** on-site. **Cards:** AX, MC, VI.

THE FROG POND
Lunch: $4-$11   Phone: 727/392-4117   **141**

American

Location: On SR 699, 2 mi n on Tom Stuart Cswy. 16909 Gulf Blvd 33708. **Hours:** 7 am-2 pm, Sun from 8 am. Closed: 11/23, 12/25. **Features:** The decor dabbles equally in comfortable country and bright tropical at the local-favorite restaurant. Select from a wide variety of omelets, eggs Benedict and other breakfast staples, as well as burgers, sandwiches, soups and salads. Casual dress. **Parking:** on-site. **Cards:** DS, MC, VI.

OLDSMAR pop. 11,910   (See map and index starting on p. 938)

--------- **WHERE TO STAY** ---------

COURTYARD BY MARRIOTT TAMPA-OLDSMAR
Book at aaa.com   Phone: (813)925-8887   **23**

Small-scale Hotel

1/16-4/15	1P: $149	2P: $149
12/1-1/15 & 10/2-11/30	1P: $119	2P: $119
4/16-10/1	1P: $109	2P: $109

Location: On SR 580, jct St. Pete Dr. 4014 Tampa Rd 34677. **Fax:** 813/814-7884. **Facility:** 99 units. 94 one-bedroom standard units. 5 one-bedroom suites. 4 stories, interior corridors. *Bath:* combo or shower only. **Parking:** on-site. **Terms:** cancellation fee imposed, [BP] meal plan available. **Amenities:** video games (fee), high-speed Internet, dual phone lines, voice mail, irons, hair dryers. **Dining:** 6:30 am-10 am, Sat & Sun from 7 am. **Pool(s):** heated outdoor. **Leisure Activities:** whirlpool, exercise room. **Guest Services:** sundries, complimentary evening beverages, valet and coin laundry. **Business Services:** meeting rooms, business center. **Cards:** AX, CB, DC, DS, JC, MC, VI. **Special Amenities:** free newspaper and early check-in/late check-out.

SOME UNITS

HOLIDAY INN EXPRESS HOTEL & SUITES
Book at aaa.com   Phone: (813)854-5080   **22**

Small-scale Hotel

1/2-4/30	1P: $119-$189	2P: $119-$189	XP: $10	F
12/1-1/1 & 5/1-11/30	1P: $99-$159	2P: $99-$159	XP: $10	F

Location: On SR 580, jct St. Pete Dr. 3990 Tampa Rd 34677. **Fax:** 813/854-5189. **Facility:** 81 units. 78 one- and 3 two-bedroom standard units. 4 stories, interior corridors. *Bath:* combo or shower only. **Parking:** on-site. **Terms:** cancellation fee imposed. **Amenities:** high-speed Internet, dual phone lines, voice mail, irons, hair dryers. **Pool(s):** heated outdoor. **Leisure Activities:** exercise room. **Guest Services:** valet and coin laundry, beauty salon. **Business Services:** meeting rooms, business center. **Cards:** AX, DC, DS, JC, MC, VI.

SOME UNITS

--------- **WHERE TO DINE** ---------

WINNERS SPORTS GRILL
Lunch: $7-$17   **Dinner:** $7-$17   Phone: 813/925-3133   **42**

American

Location: On SR 580, jct St. Pete Dr; in Oldsmar Town Center. 3980 Tampa Rd 34677. **Hours:** 11 am-11 pm. Closed: 4/16, 11/23, 12/25. **Features:** Patrons of the neat, sports-themed restaurant can dine and catch a favorite sporting event on any one of many television monitors strategically placed around the dining room. The menu sports everything from steaks to pasta bowls to shepherd's pie. Buffalo wings are a great starter, and the chili is some of the best. Casual dress; cocktails. **Parking:** on-site. **Cards:** AX, DS, MC, VI.

PALM HARBOR pop. 59,248

--------- **WHERE TO STAY** ---------

BEST WESTERN PALM HARBOR HOTEL
Book at aaa.com   Phone: (727)942-0358

Small-scale Hotel

12/25-4/30	1P: $93-$185	2P: $93-$185	XP: $10	F12
12/1-12/24 & 5/1-11/30	1P: $79-$170	2P: $89-$175	XP: $10	F12

Location: On US 19, 3 mi s of jct SR 582. 37611 US 19 N 34684. **Fax:** 727/938-9826. **Facility:** 97 one-bedroom standard units, some with whirlpools. 4 stories, exterior corridors. **Parking:** on-site. **Terms:** cancellation fee imposed, pets ($10 extra charge). **Amenities:** high-speed Internet, voice mail, irons, hair dryers. **Dining:** 4 pm-10 pm, cocktails. **Pool(s):** heated outdoor. **Leisure Activities:** whirlpool, fishing, fishing poles, putting green, exercise room. **Fee:** boats, boat dock, massage. **Guest Services:** gift shop, valet and coin laundry. **Business Services:** meeting rooms, business center. **Cards:** AX, DC, DS, MC, VI. **Special Amenities:** free continental breakfast and free local telephone calls.

FEE

SOME UNITS

KNIGHTS INN-CLEARWATER/PALM HARBOR — Book at aaa.com

Phone: 727/789-2002

◆ Motel

All Year — 2P: $45-$119

Location: On US 19, 1.8 mi n of CR 752 (Tampa Rd). 34106 US 19 N 34684. Fax: 727/784-6206. **Facility:** 114 one-bedroom standard units, some with efficiencies. 1 story, exterior corridors. **Parking:** on-site. **Terms:** weekly rates available, small pets only ($10 extra charge). **Amenities:** safes (fee). *Some:* irons, hair dryers. **Pool(s):** heated outdoor. **Guest Services:** coin laundry. **Business Services:** fax (fee). **Cards:** AX, CB, DC, DS, MC, VI.

SOME UNITS
(A$K) (S/D) 🛏️ (🍴) 🏊 🎥 💻 / ✕ (DATA PORT) 📠 📶 / FEE

RED ROOF INN — Book at aaa.com

Phone: 727/786-2529

AAA SAVE · ◆◆ / ◆◆ Motel

2/9-4/6	1P: $69-$93	2P: $75-$99	XP: $6
12/1-2/8 & 4/7-4/30	1P: $50-$66	2P: $56-$72	XP: $6
5/1-11/30	1P: $45-$57	2P: $45-$57	XP: $6

Location: On US 19, 0.4 mi s of jct CR 752 (Tampa Rd). 32000 US 19 N 34684. Fax: 727/786-7462. **Facility:** 100 one-bedroom standard units, some with efficiencies. 2 stories, exterior corridors. *Bath:* combo or shower only. **Parking:** on-site. **Terms:** package plans. **Amenities:** voice mail. *Some:* irons. **Pool(s):** heated outdoor. **Business Services:** fax (fee). **Cards:** AX, DC, DS, MC, VI.

SOME UNITS
(S/D) 🛏️ (🍴) 🔊 📷 🏊 🎥 (DATA PORT) / ✕ VCR 📠 📶 💻 /

THE WESTIN INNISBROOK GOLF RESORT — Book at aaa.com

Phone: (727)942-2000

AAA SAVE · ◆◆◆◆ Resort Condominium

12/1-4/9	1P: $219-$239	2P: $219-$239	XP: $20 · F17
4/10-5/24 & 9/28-11/30	1P: $169-$199	2P: $169-$199	XP: $20 · F17
5/25-9/27	1P: $109-$139	2P: $109-$139	XP: $20 · F17

Location: On US 19, 2.8 mi s of jct SR 582. 36750 US Hwy 19 N 34684. Fax: 727/942-5576. **Facility:** This golf resort is a complex of 25 buildings on 1,000 manicured acres. 618 units. 129 one-bedroom standard units, some with whirlpools. 487 one- and 2 two-bedroom suites with kitchens. 3 stories (no elevator), interior corridors. *Bath:* combo or shower only. **Parking:** on-site. **Terms:** 3 day cancellation notice-fee imposed, pets ($50 fee). **Amenities:** dual phone lines, voice mail, irons, hair dryers. *Fee:* video games, high-speed Internet. *Some:* CD players, honor bars. **Dining:** 5 restaurants, 6 am-midnight, cocktails. **Pool(s):** 6 heated outdoor. **Leisure Activities:** whirlpools, waterslide, fishing, miniature golf, night driving range, kids activity program, nature walk, wallyball, rental bicycles, jogging, playground, basketball, volleyball. *Fee:* fishing equipment, water aerobics, golf-72 holes, golf instruction & equipment, 11 tennis courts (7 lighted), racquetball courts, tennis instruction & equipment, massage, game room. **Guest Services:** gift shop, area transportation-beach. **Business Services:** conference facilities, business center. **Cards:** AX, CB, DC, DS, JC, MC, VI.

(See color ad p 8)

SOME UNITS
(S/D) ✈️ 🛏️ (🍴) 🏊 🏇 ✕ 🎥 (DATA PORT) 💻 / ✕ 📠 📶 / FEE FEE

——— WHERE TO DINE ———

AUNT CHILADAS CANTINA

Lunch: $8-$16 · Dinner: $8-$16 · Phone: 727/789-4979

◆◆ Mexican

Location: 0.3 mi s of jct Alderman Rd; in The Fountains. 34718 US 19 34684. **Hours:** 11:30 am-9:30 pm, Fri & Sat-11 pm. **Features:** Festive Mexican surroundings enhance this casual eatery. There are numerous items on their extensive menu, including tacos, burritos, chimichangas, quesadillas, fajitas and other typical Mexican fare. Casual dress; cocktails. **Parking:** on-site. **Cards:** DS, MC, VI. 🍸

THE BLUE HERON

Dinner: $17-$28 · Phone: 727/789-5176

◆◆◆ Seafood

Location: On CR 752 (Tampa Rd), 1 mi e of jct US 19; in Shoppes at Cloverplace. 3285 Tampa Rd 34684. **Hours:** 5 pm-10 pm, Fri & Sat-11 pm. Closed major holidays; also Sun. **Reservations:** accepted. **Features:** Gracious service and elegant, intimate surroundings make entree choices such as snapper, salmon, grouper, duck and chicken that much more enjoyable. All dishes are well-prepared and nicely presented with a salad of mixed greens. The creative desserts are a must. Dressy casual; cocktails. **Parking:** on-site. **Cards:** AX, DC, DS, MC, VI. 🍸

OLDE SCHOOLHOUSE RESTAURANT

Lunch: $6-$9 · Dinner: $11-$19 · Phone: 727/784-2585

◆◆ Continental

Location: On US Alternate Rt 19, 0.5 mi n of jct Alderman Rd. 3419 Alternate Hwy 19 N 34683. **Hours:** 11 am-3:30 & 5-9 pm, Fri & Sat-10 pm; Sunday brunch. Closed: 1/1, 11/23, 12/24, 12/25. **Features:** In a restored 1910 schoolhouse, the restaurant prepares good country cooking. Tempting choices include pasta primavera, stir-fry chicken and roast pork loin. Casual dress; cocktails. **Parking:** on-site. **Cards:** MC, VI. 🍸

SAINT LARRY'S

Dinner: $12-$30 · Phone: 727/786-0077

◆◆◆ Steak & Seafood

Location: Just s of jct Alderman Rd; in The Fountains. 34980 US 19 N 34684. **Hours:** 5 pm-10 pm. Closed: 1/1, 12/25; also Sun. **Features:** Reminiscent of Greenwich Village, the upscale setting features original paintings by local artists and a carpet by surrealist Salvador Dali. Large portions of certified Angus beef, fresh seafood and quality produce have pleased the local community for many years. Casual dress; cocktails. **Parking:** on-site. **Cards:** AX, DC, DS, MC, VI. 🍸

THAI NANA RESTAURANT

Lunch: $5-$7 · Dinner: $7-$25 · Phone: 727/787-0189

AAA · ◆◆ Thai

Location: US Alternate 19, jct Alderman Rd; in Crystal Beach Plaza. 2880 Alt 19 N 34683. **Hours:** 11 am-3 & 4:30-10 pm, Sat from 4:30 pm, Sun 4 pm-9 pm. **Reservations:** accepted. **Features:** Spicy, stir-fried dishes are the mainstay of this traditional Thai restaurant. Fresh ingredients can be found in all the entrees, especially Thai salad with peanut dressing, pad Thai noodle and panang curry. Casual dress; beer & wine only. **Parking:** on-site. **Cards:** DS, MC, VI.

THIRSTY MARLIN GRILL & BAR

Lunch: $5-$18 · Dinner: $5-$18 · Phone: 727/784-3469

◆◆ American

Location: Just e of jct US Alternate 19. 1023 Florida Ave 34683. **Hours:** 11:30 am-11 pm. **Features:** The charming setting features various rooms scattered about a renovated old home, as well as outdoor seating, where live entertainment is offered on occasion. The seafood-themed menu lists numerous choices, as well as sandwiches. Casual dress; cocktails. **Parking:** on-site. **Cards:** MC, VI. 🍸

PINELLAS PARK pop. 45,658 (See map and index starting on p. 938)

———— WHERE TO STAY ————

ECONO LODGE INN & SUITES CLEARWATER   *Book at aaa.com*   Phone: (727)572-4929 [88]

(AAA) (SAVE)

| | 1/16-4/15 | 1P: $80-$160 | 2P: $80-$160 | XP: $5 | F17 |
| | 12/1-1/15 & 4/16-11/30 | 1P: $60-$120 | 2P: $60-$120 | XP: $5 | F17 |

Motel

Location: On US 19, 1.6 mi s of jct SR 688 (Ulmerton Rd). 11333 US Hwy 19 N 33764-7404. **Fax:** 727/573-6051. **Facility:** 70 units. 68 one-bedroom standard units, some with efficiencies. 2 one-bedroom suites ($65-$180), some with kitchens. 2 stories, exterior corridors. **Parking:** on-site. **Terms:** $1 service charge. **Amenities:** high-speed Internet, voice mail, safes (fee), irons, hair dryers. **Pool(s):** heated outdoor. **Leisure Activities:** whirlpool, steamroom, sun deck, barbecue, basketball, shuffleboard. **Guest Services:** coin laundry. **Business Services:** fax. **Cards:** AX, CB, DC, DS, JC, MC, VI.

SOME UNITS

⬛ 🛏️ 🍴 🏊 ✖️ 📷 🔌 💻 / ✖️ 🔋 /

**LA QUINTA INN TAMPA (PINELLAS
PARK/CLEARWATER)**   *Book at aaa.com*   Phone: (727)545-5611 [89]

(AAA) (SAVE)

| | 12/1-4/30 | 1P: $85-$105 | | XP: $7 | F18 |
| | 5/1-11/30 | 1P: $75-$90 | | XP: $7 | F18 |

Small-scale Hotel

Location: I-275, exit 28, 1.4 mi s on Gandy Blvd (SR 694), then just n. 7500 US Hwy 19 N 33781. **Fax:** 727/544-4202. **Facility:** 116 units. 115 one-bedroom standard units. 1 one-bedroom suite. 3 stories, interior/exterior corridors. **Parking:** on-site. **Terms:** small pets only. **Amenities:** video games (fee), voice mail, irons, hair dryers. **Pool(s):** heated outdoor. **Guest Services:** valet and coin laundry. **Business Services:** meeting rooms, fax. **Cards:** AX, CB, DC, DS, MC, VI. **Special Amenities:** free expanded continental breakfast and free local telephone calls.** (See color ad p 982)*

SOME UNITS

🐕 🍴 🔥M 📅 🏊 📷 🔌 💻 / ✖️ 🔋

FEE

———— WHERE TO DINE ————

PIN-PARK EGG PLATTER   **Lunch:** $5-$8   **Dinner:** $5-$8   **Phone:** 727/531-0111 [125]

American

Location: On US 19, 0.5 mi s of jct Gandy Blvd. 6767 US 19 N 33764. **Hours:** 24 hours. **Features:** Open 24 hours, the popular casual spot serves good home cooking. Choices range from hearty breakfasts to ample lunch and dinner selections. Casual dress. **Parking:** on-site. **Cards:** AX, DC, DS, MC, VI.

PLANT CITY pop. 29,915

———— WHERE TO STAY ————

COMFORT INN OF PLANT CITY   *Book at aaa.com*   Phone: (813)707-6000

(AAA) (SAVE)

| | All Year [ECP] | 1P: $69-$194 | 2P: $69-$194 | XP: $10 | F17 |

Small-scale Hotel

Location: I-4, exit 22, just e. 2003 S Frontage Rd 33566. **Fax:** 813/707-6081. **Facility:** 61 units. 52 one-bedroom standard units. 9 one-bedroom suites. 3 stories, interior corridors. *Bath:* combo or shower only. **Parking:** on-site. **Terms:** cancellation fee imposed. **Amenities:** high-speed Internet, dual phone lines, voice mail, irons, hair dryers. **Pool(s):** heated outdoor. **Leisure Activities:** whirlpool. **Guest Services:** valet and coin laundry. **Business Services:** meeting rooms, business center. **Cards:** AX, CB, DC, DS, JC, MC, VI. **Special Amenities:** free expanded continental breakfast and free room upgrade (subject to availability with advance reservations).

SOME UNITS

⬛ 🍴 🔥M 🏊 📷 🔌 / ✖️ VCR 🔋 📺 💻 /

RAMADA INN PLANTATION HOUSE   *Book at aaa.com*   Phone: (813)752-3141

(AAA) (SAVE)

| | All Year | 1P: $49-$169 | 2P: $69-$189 | XP: $20 | F17 |

Motel

Location: I-4, exit 21, just se on SR 39. 2011 N Wheeler St 33563. **Fax:** 813/759-0847. **Facility:** 136 units. 101 one-bedroom standard units. 34 one- and 1 two-bedroom suites ($109-$349). 2 stories, exterior corridors. *Bath:* combo or shower only. **Parking:** on-site. **Terms:** package plans, pets ($25 extra charge, in limited units). **Amenities:** high-speed Internet, voice mail, irons, hair dryers. *Some:* DVD players, CD players, honor bars. **Dining:** 7 am-10 pm, cocktails, entertainment. **Pool(s):** heated outdoor. **Leisure Activities:** exercise room. *Fee:* golf privileges, massage. **Guest Services:** valet and coin laundry. **Business Services:** conference facilities, business center. **Cards:** AX, DS, MC, VI.

SOME UNITS

⬛ 🛏️ 🍴 🍷 🏋️ 🔥M 📷 🏊 📅 🔌 / ✖️ VCR 🔋 📺 /

FEE   FEE

———— WHERE TO DINE ————

ABC PIZZA HOUSE   **Lunch:** $7-$18   **Dinner:** $7-$18   **Phone:** 813/752-5146

American

Location: Jct W Reynolds St. 114 N Alexander 33566. **Hours:** 11 am-11 pm, Fri & Sat-midnight. Closed: 11/23, 12/25. **Features:** This pizza and sub restaurant has a casual, easy decor to match its simple menu of pizzas, grinders, pasta dishes, seafood entrees, sandwiches, gyros and numerous appetizers. Casual dress; beer & wine only. **Parking:** on-site. **Cards:** MC, VI.

APPLE TREE RESTAURANT   **Lunch:** $4-$7   **Phone:** 813/707-8109

American

Location: On SR 39, jct Alexander St; in Walden Woods. 2218 Jim Redman Pkwy 33566. **Hours:** 6 am-2:30 pm, Sat-2 pm. Closed: Sun. **Features:** The casual establishment serves good home cooking for breakfast and lunch. Daily specials might include fried chicken, New York strip steak, shrimp or chopped sirloin. Among other offerings are an all-you-can-eat salad bar, sandwiches and numerous breakfast items. Casual dress. **Parking:** on-site.

BEEF 'O'BRADY'S   **Lunch:** $5-$7   **Dinner:** $5-$7   **Phone:** 813/757-0300

American

Location: On SR 39, jct Alexander St; in Walden Village Shopping Center. 2418 Jim Redman Pkwy 33566. **Hours:** 11 am-11 pm, Sun noon-10 pm. Closed: 11/23, 12/25. **Features:** Big-screen televisions keep this family sports pub hopping on game days. The bustling spot cooks up traditional burgers, sandwiches, salads and wings. It features a terrific Philadelphia cheese steak served with fries and a pickle spear. Casual dress; beer & wine only. **Parking:** on-site. **Cards:** DS, MC, VI.

BRANCH RANCH DINING ROOM   Lunch: $6-$9   Dinner: $7-$18   Phone: 813/752-1957

Location: I-4, exit 17, 0.9 mi n on Branch Forbes Rd, then just e. 5121 W Thonotosassa Rd 33565. **Hours:** 11:30 am-9:30 pm. Closed: Mon, Tues & 12/18-12/25. **Features:** Southern food served family-style has been the trademark of this family restaurant since 1956. Fried green tomatoes, homemade buttermilk biscuits with orange-pineapple marmalade or strawberry preserves and Southern fried chicken complement the blackboard specials. Casual dress; cocktails. **Parking:** on-site. **Cards:** AX, DS, MC, VI.

American

BUDDY FREDDY'S RESTAURANT   Lunch: $8   Dinner: $11   Phone: 813/754-5120

Location: I-4, exit 19, 0.4 mi s on SR 566. 1101 Goldfinch Dr 33566. **Hours:** 7 am-9 pm. **Features:** A congenial atmosphere fills the popular, family-operated establishment. A flexible menu of home-style food allows for easy substitutions like replacing mashed potatoes with grits. Try the catfish for a real Florida feast. Also popular is the extensive buffet. Casual dress. **Parking:** on-site. **Cards:** DS, MC, VI.

American

CATFISH COUNTRY   Lunch: $5-$17   Dinner: $5-$17   Phone: 813/752-0126

Location: On SR 39, 1 mi s. 712 S Collins Ave 33566. **Hours:** 7 am-9 pm, Fri & Sat-10 pm, Sun-8:30 pm. Closed: 12/25. **Features:** Guests can savor huge portions of food served in a homey-feeling fish shanty-type setting. Friendly servers lend to a "welcome home" feeling, but it is the food that is fantastic. A hearty appetite is a must. Casual dress; beer & wine only. **Parking:** on-site. **Cards:** AX, DS, MC, VI.

Seafood

CHANCY'S CATFISH SHACK   Lunch: $3-$16   Dinner: $7-$16   Phone: 813/754-3433

Location: I-4, exit 22, just n. 2509 N Park Rd 33566. **Hours:** 7 am-9 pm, Fri & Sat-10 pm. Closed: Sun & Mon. **Features:** Lines of hungry patrons eager for a taste of good, reasonably priced food snake outside the door of this family-owned local favorite. Bring your appetite: whopping portions can easily overwhelm. Try the catfish fillets or the fried seaman's platter. Casual dress; beer & wine only. **Parking:** on-site.

Seafood

CHERRY'S   Lunch: $6-$13   Dinner: $6-$13   Phone: 813/764-8818

Location: 1 mi w of jct SR 39. 1701 Alexander St 33567. **Hours:** 11 am-10 pm, Fri-midnight, Sun-11 pm. **Features:** Diners can enjoy their favorite sports event on one of many television monitors in the dining room of the trendy little establishment. Among selections are sandwiches, burgers, buffalo wings and the chili-cheese fries appetizer. Casual dress; cocktails. **Parking:** on-site. **Cards:** AX, MC, VI.

American

FRED'S FARMERS MARKET RESTAURANT   Lunch: $6-$8   Dinner: $6-$8   Phone: 813/752-7763

Location: 1 mi w on Dr Martin Luther King Jr Blvd, jct S Alexander St. 1401 Dr Martin Luther King Jr Blvd 33707. **Hours:** 6 am-8:30 pm. Closed major holidays; also Sun, for breakfast & lunch 12/24. **Features:** Good home cooking, such as the popular fried catfish, is served for lunch or dinner. A slice of pecan pie is a perfect meal-ender. The buffet lines up a variety of goodies. Casual dress. **Parking:** on-site. **Cards:** AX, DS, MC, VI.

American

GRANDPA JOHNSON'S BARBEQUE   Lunch: $4-$15   Dinner: $4-$15   Phone: 813/759-0009

Location: 1 mi w at Alexander St. 1407 W Dr Martin Luther King Jr Blvd 33563. **Hours:** 11 am-8:30 pm, Mon-Wed to 3 pm. Closed major holidays; also Sun. **Features:** Outstanding country barbecue is served at the popular family-owned-and-operated establishment. The staff is pleasant, and the surroundings offer a cozy country feel. Casual dress. **Parking:** on-site. **Cards:** MC, VI.

Barbecue

KAZBOR'S GRILLE   Lunch: $7-$15   Dinner: $7-$15   Phone: 813/752-2700

Location: On SR 39, jct W Maki St; in Walden Woods Shopping Center. 2212 Jim Redman Pkwy 33566. **Hours:** 11 am-10 pm, Fri & Sat-midnight. Closed: 11/23, 12/25. **Features:** The sports bar is noted for great service and good casual food. Wings are a great starter, with the chicken chimichanga being a great entree choice. Finish the meal with a super sundae. Casual dress; cocktails. **Parking:** on-site. **Cards:** AX, DS, MC, VI.

American

LA ESPERANZA MEXICAN RESTAURANT   Lunch: $6-$13   Dinner: $7-$13   Phone: 813/659-3940

Location: Just w of jct SR 39. 113 W Prosser Dr 33563. **Hours:** 11 am-9:30 pm. **Features:** The casual establishment prepares some good Mexican cooking. Anything from enchiladas to entomatadas to chiles rellenos can be found on the menu. The service staff is friendly. Casual dress; beer & wine only. **Parking:** on-site. **Cards:** MC, VI.

Mexican

MI CASA MEXICAN RESTAURANT   Lunch: $7-$14   Dinner: $7-$14   Phone: 813/752-0057

Location: I-4, exit 19, 0.4 mi s on SR 566. 2613 Thonotosassa Rd 33563. **Hours:** 11 pm-9 pm, Fri & Sat-11 pm. **Features:** The festively colored decor, which includes murals and assorted artifacts, contributes to the feeling of having stepped into a Mexican village. Fabulous food offerings include enchiladas, chimichangas, burritos, grilled fajitas, steak and chicken dishes. House specials are particularly good. Casual dress; beer & wine only. **Parking:** on-site. **Cards:** AX, DS, MC, VI.

Mexican

PESO'S MEXICAN RESTAURANT   Lunch: $5-$11   Dinner: $7-$11   Phone: 813/752-8841

Location: Jct N Lemon St. 2006 W Reynolds St, Suite 1 33567. **Hours:** 11 am-8:30 pm, Fri & Sat-9 pm. Closed: 1/1, 11/23, 12/25. **Features:** The surroundings may be simple, but the food is simply excellent. Savor burritos, flautas, fajitas, chimichangas and combination platters. Casual dress; beer & wine only. **Parking:** on-site. **Cards:** AX, DS, MC, VI.

Mexican

THE RED ROSE DINING ROOM   Lunch: $7-$10   Dinner: $15-$30   Phone: 813/752-3141

Location: I-4, exit 21, just s. 2011 N Wheeler St 33563. **Hours:** 7-10 am, 11-2 & 5-10 pm. Closed: Sun & Mon. **Reservations:** accepted. **Features:** Dance to the big band under the stars and enjoy a variety of Mediterranean and Italian dishes at this upscale dining room. The soft and chewy Italian bread is made onsite as is the gnocchi and many of the desserts; the most popular is the Italian wedding cake with its "cool" center frosting. Dressy casual; cocktails; entertainment. **Parking:** on-site. **Cards:** AX, CB, DC, DS, JC, MC, VI.

Mediterranean

SHANGHAI CHINESE RESTAURANT
Chinese
Lunch: $5   **Dinner:** $7-$10   **Phone:** 813/759-0518
Location: On SR 39; at E Alsobrook St. 805 S Collins St 33566. **Hours:** 11 am-9 pm. **Features:** An Oriental theme weaves through the dining room of this relaxed restaurant. A Mongolian grill is central to the buffet area, a tempting alternative to the main menu. Its extensive offerings include some 80 selections. Casual dress. **Parking:** on-site. **Cards:** AX, DC, MC, VI.

SNELLGROVES
American
Lunch: $6-$10   **Dinner:** $6-$10   **Phone:** 813/752-3652
Location: On SR 39; downtown. 109 S Collins St 33566. **Hours:** 6 am-8 pm, Fri & Sat-9 pm. Closed major holidays; also Sun. **Features:** Reminiscent of the early '60s, this basic restaurant offers blue-plate meals, a salad bar and such home-cooked favorites as fried chicken, liver and onions, meatloaf and pork chops. Casual dress. **Parking:** street. **Cards:** DS, MC, VI.

WHISTLE STOP CAFE
American
Lunch: $6-$7   **Dinner:** $6-$7   **Phone:** 813/752-7340
Location: On US 39 at jct Arden Mays; downtown. 102 S Collins 33566. **Hours:** 10:30 am-3 & 5-9 pm; also 1st and 3rd Sat of each month. Closed: Sun. **Features:** After a long day of shopping in the many antique shops for which the city is known, hungry folks can stop in for a yummy root beer float with a freshly made salad or sandwich. In the historic downtown section of town, the cafe is a neat spot with lots of history. Casual dress. **Parking:** street. **Cards:** MC, VI.

WOODY'S BARBECUE
American
Lunch: $5-$8   **Dinner:** $7-$16   **Phone:** 813/754-3229
Location: Just s of jct SR 39; in Lake Walden Square. 203 W Alexander 33566. **Hours:** 11 am-9 pm, Fri & Sat-10 pm. Closed major holidays. **Features:** Forget the formality of tablecloths, and eat with a laid-back attitude. Take in the rustic decor and enjoy down-home barbecue chicken, ribs and pork. Hearty portions are coated in a tasty sauce and served with coleslaw, baked beans and garlic toast. Casual dress; beer & wine only. **Parking:** on-site. **Cards:** AX, DS, MC, VI.

PORT RICHEY pop. 3,021

---------- **WHERE TO STAY** ----------

COMFORT INN
Motel

Book at aaa.com   **Phone:** (727)863-3336

1/16-4/15	1P: $80-$90	XP: $10 F18
4/16-11/30	1P: $72-$82	XP: $10 F18
12/1-1/15	1P: $70-$80	XP: $10 F18

Location: On US 19, just s of jct SR 52. 11810 US 19 34668. Fax: 727/863-3336. **Facility:** 98 one-bedroom standard units. 2 stories, exterior corridors. **Parking:** on-site. **Terms:** check-in 4 pm, pets ($6 extra charge). **Amenities:** voice mail, irons, hair dryers. **Pool(s):** heated outdoor. **Guest Services:** valet and coin laundry. **Business Services:** fax (fee). **Cards:** AX, CB, DC, DS, JC, MC, VI.

SOME UNITS
(ASK) (S▢) (🛏) (📶) (🍴) (⊘) (🏊) (⊞FEE) (🐾) (DATA PORT) (💻) / (🚫) (🔒) (📼) /

HOLIDAY INN EXPRESS HOTEL & SUITES
Small-scale Hotel
Book at aaa.com   **Phone:** (727)869-9999

2/1-3/31	1P: $90
12/1-1/31 & 4/1-11/30	1P: $70

Location: On US 19, 1 mi s of SR 52. 10826 US 19 N 34668. Fax: 727/861-0941. **Facility:** 110 units. 103 one-bedroom standard units, some with efficiencies. 7 one-bedroom suites with kitchens. 2 stories, exterior corridors. Bath: combo or shower only. **Parking:** on-site. **Terms:** check-in 4 pm; weekly rates available. **Amenities:** video games (fee), voice mail, irons, hair dryers. **Pool(s):** heated outdoor. **Leisure Activities:** whirlpool, steamroom, playground, exercise room. **Guest Services:** valet and coin laundry. **Business Services:** meeting rooms, fax (fee). **Cards:** AX, CB, DC, DS, MC, VI.

SOME UNITS
(ASK) (🍴) (🔊M) (🛏) (⊘) (🏊) (🚫) (🐾) (DATA PORT) / (🚫) (🔒) (📼) (💻) /

---------- **WHERE TO DINE** ----------

CATCHES WATERFRONT GRILLE
Seafood
Lunch: $8-$14   **Dinner:** $16-$36   **Phone:** 727/849-2208
Location: Just s on US 19, just w on River Gulf Dr. 7811 Bay View Ave 34668. **Hours:** 11:30 am-10 pm. Closed: 12/25. **Features:** On the Pithlachascotee River, the restaurant treats guests to a relaxing atmosphere and a menu of fresh seafood. Among choices are combination platters, shrimp dishes, shellfish and surf and turf. Casual dress; cocktails. **Parking:** on-site. **Cards:** AX, MC, VI.
(🔊M)

REDINGTON SHORES pop. 2,338   (See map and index starting on p. 938)

---------- **WHERE TO DINE** ----------

THE LOBSTER POT RESTAURANT
Seafood
Dinner: $11-$40   **Phone:** 727/391-8592   [138]
Location: On SR 699; 1 mi s of jct Park Blvd (CR 694). 17814 Gulf Blvd 33708. **Hours:** 4:30 pm-close, Sun from 4 pm. Closed major holidays. **Reservations:** suggested. **Features:** A block from the gulf, this popular restaurant offers a fine dining experience in a rustic setting with formal touches. Select from a wide variety of dishes including fresh seafood, lobster and steak. The lobster bisque is superb, and bouillabaisse Marseille is a must try. Dressy casual; cocktails. **Parking:** on-site and valet. **Cards:** AX, CB, DC, DS, MC, VI.

RIVERVIEW pop. 12,035   (See map and index starting on p. 950)

---------- **WHERE TO STAY** ----------

BIANCHI MOTEL
Motel
Phone: 813/677-1829   [86]
Property failed to provide current rates
Location: I-75, exit 254 southbound, 3.1 mi n; exit northbound, 1.6 mi s. 6425 US 301 S 33569. Fax: 813/677-6550. **Facility:** 15 one-bedroom standard units, some with efficiencies. 1 story, exterior corridors. Bath: shower only. **Parking:** on-site. **Terms:** office hours 8 am-11 pm. **Pool(s):** outdoor.

SOME UNITS
(🏊) (📼) (🔒) / (🚫) (💻) (📺) /

(See map and index starting on p. 950)

──────── **WHERE TO DINE** ────────

ABC PIZZA
Lunch: $5-$16   Dinner: $5-$16   Phone: 813/677-8465   [221]
American
Location: 0.5 mi n of jct Riverview Dr. 7210 SR 301 33569. **Hours:** 11 am-10 pm, Fri-11 pm. Closed: 11/23, 12/25; also Sun. **Features:** The pizza and sub restaurant has a casual, easy decor to match its simple menu of pizzas, grinders, pasta dishes, seafood entrees, sandwiches, gyros and numerous appetizers. Casual dress; cocktails. **Parking:** on-site. **Cards:** MC, VI.

BEEF 'O' BRADY'S
Lunch: $6-$9   Dinner: $6-$9   Phone: 813/672-9464   [222]
American
Location: On US 301, jct Gibsonton Rd. 9622 US 301 S 33569. **Hours:** 11 am-11 pm, Sun noon-10 pm. Closed: 11/23, 12/25. **Features:** Dozens of TVs and favorite sports bar foods like burgers, sandwiches and wings make this a locals' hangout. Casual dining from plastic baskets is the norm, so feel free to dress down. Try the Philly cheese steak paired with a hearty order of onion rings. Casual dress; beer & wine only. **Parking:** on-site. **Cards:** AX, DC, DS, MC, VI.

KAZBOR'S GRILLE
Lunch: $7-$16   Dinner: $7-$16   Phone: 813/677-1673
American
Location: Jct Gibsonton Dr. 9992 US Hwy 301 S 33569. **Hours:** 11 am-10 pm, Fri & Sat-midnight, Sun noon-10 pm. Closed: 11/23, 12/25. **Features:** The neat little sports-bar-type restaurant offers great service and good casual food. The wings are a great starter, with the chicken chimichanga being a great entree choice. Finish the meal with a super sundae. Casual dress; cocktails. **Parking:** on-site. **Cards:** AX, DS, MC, VI.

WESTSHORE PIZZA & CHEESESTEAKS
Lunch: $4-$17   Dinner: $4-$17   Phone: 813/672-2828
Pizza
Location: Jct McMullen Rd; in Goolsby Pointe. 11643 Boyette Rd 33569. **Hours:** 11 am-10 pm, Fri & Sat-11 pm. **Features:** This place is a favorite of those who love pizza, calzones and Philly grinders. The sports-themed atmosphere is relaxed. Patrons can catch a favorite game on the large-screen monitor while eating freshly cooked food. Casual dress. **Parking:** on-site. **Cards:** MC, VI.

RUSKIN pop. 8,321

──────── **WHERE TO STAY** ────────

HOLIDAY INN EXPRESS   *Book at aaa.com*   Phone: (813)641-3437

1/24-4/29	1P: $93	2P: $93
12/1-1/23	1P: $78	2P: $78
4/30-11/30	1P: $72	2P: $72

Motel
Location: I-75, exit 240B, just w, jct 33rd St SE. 3113 College Ave 33570. Fax: 813/641-3213. **Facility:** 55 one-bedroom standard units. 3 stories, interior corridors. *Bath:* combo or shower only. **Parking:** on-site. **Terms:** cancellation fee imposed, [CP] meal plan available. **Amenities:** dual phone lines, voice mail, safes, irons, hair dryers. **Pool(s):** outdoor. **Guest Services:** valet and coin laundry. **Business Services:** meeting rooms, business center. **Cards:** AX, DC, DS, MC, VI. **Special Amenities:** free continental breakfast and free local telephone calls.

SOME UNITS

THE INN AT LITTLE HARBOR   *Book at aaa.com*   Phone: (813)645-3291

1/29-4/22	1P: $109-$189	2P: $109-$189	XP: $10 F17
4/23-7/4	1P: $99-$189	2P: $99-$189	XP: $10 F17
12/1-1/28 & 7/5-11/30	1P: $89-$189	2P: $89-$189	XP: $10 F17

Resort
Condominium
Location: 3.5 mi w of US 41 via Shell Point Rd, follow signs. Located in rural area on Old Tampa Bay. 611 Destiny Dr 33570. Fax: 813/641-1589. **Facility:** Set on several acres, the resort overlooks water activities and sunsets on Old Tampa Bay. Designated smoking area. 94 units. 92 one-bedroom standard units, some with efficiencies or kitchens. 2 one-bedroom suites ($169-$249) with kitchens and whirlpools. 2 stories, interior/exterior corridors. *Bath:* combo or shower only. **Parking:** on-site. **Terms:** 7 day cancellation notice-fee imposed, package plans, $5 service charge, pets ($25 deposit, with prior approval). **Amenities:** voice mail, irons, hair dryers. **Dining:** 2 restaurants, 8 am-9 pm, Fri & Sat-10 pm, cocktails, also, Tropics Restaurant, see separate listing. **Pool(s):** 2 heated outdoor, wading. **Leisure Activities:** whirlpool, fishing, fishing pier, 5 tennis courts (3 lighted), tennis club, helicopter pad, picnic area, playground, exercise room, basketball, horseshoes, shuffleboard, volleyball. *Fee:* marina, tennis instruction, massage. **Guest Services:** sundries, coin laundry. **Business Services:** meeting rooms. *Fee:* PC, fax. **Cards:** AX, DC, DS, MC, VI. **Special Amenities:** free local telephone calls and free newspaper.

FEE

SOUTHERN COMFORT BED & BREAKFAST   Phone: (813)645-6361

12/1-6/1 [BP]	1P: $95-$129	2P: $95-$125	XP: $20 D16
11/1-11/30 [BP]	1P: $95-$125	2P: $95-$125	XP: $20 D16
6/2-10/31 [BP]	1P: $75-$105	2P: $75-$105	XP: $20 D16

Bed & Breakfast
Location: Jct US 41, 1.1 mi sw on 1st St, just w on 24th Ave SW, then just s. Located in a quiet rural residential area. 2409 Ravine Dr W 33570. Fax: 813/645-6361. **Facility:** This 6,800-square-foot country home shaded by large trees features a tennis court and putting green. Designated smoking area. 5 units. 4 one-bedroom standard units, some with efficiencies. 1 two-bedroom suite ($155-$175) with kitchen. 1 story, interior/exterior corridors. *Bath:* combo or shower only. **Parking:** on-site. **Terms:** 30 day cancellation notice-fee imposed, weekly rates available, package plans. **Amenities:** *Some:* irons, hair dryers. **Pool(s):** outdoor. **Leisure Activities:** sauna, whirlpool, putting green, lighted tennis court, bicycles, limited exercise equipment. **Guest Services:** complimentary laundry. **Business Services:** meeting rooms, PC, fax. **Cards:** MC, VI.

SOME UNITS

──────── **WHERE TO DINE** ────────

BUDDY FREDDY'S COUNTRY BUFFET
Lunch: $5-$7   Dinner: $5-$8   Phone: 813/641-2241
American
Location: I-75, exit 240 northbound; exit 240B southbound, just w; in Sun Point. 3074 College Ave 33570. **Hours:** 8 am-8 pm. **Features:** The atmosphere is casual and contemporary at the congenial restaurant. The food is all-you-can-eat home-style cooking: fried chicken, meatloaf, liver, fresh vegetables, homemade mashed potatoes, salad bar fixings and a dessert bar with cake, pie and ice cream. Casual dress. **Parking:** on-site. **Cards:** AX, DS, MC, VI.

THE GOLDEN BUDDHA

▼
Chinese

Lunch: $6-$15   **Dinner:** $7-$15   **Phone:** 813/645-7730

Location: 1 mi s of jct Apollo Beach Blvd. 5813 US 41 N 33570. **Hours:** 11 am-3 am. Closed: 7/4, 11/23, 12/25. **Features:** Basic but welcoming and friendly service is offered at this small local favorite. The all-you-can-eat Chinese buffet is a popular attraction, but a standard menu—which includes chicken, beef, seafood and pork items—is also available. Peking duck is a favorite selection, as is General Tso's chicken in a spicy, flavorful sauce. Casual dress; cocktails. **Parking:** on-site. **Cards:** AX, DC, MC, VI.

TROPICS RESTAURANT

◆◆◆ ◆◆◆
American

Lunch: $5-$9   **Dinner:** $11-$16   **Phone:** 813/645-3291

Location: 3.5 mi w of US 41 via Shell Point Rd, follow signs; in The Inn at Little Harbor. 611 Destiny Dr 33570. **Hours:** 11 am-10 pm, Fri & Sat-11 pm; Sunday brunch. **Features:** Diners who patronize this locally favorite restaurant on Old Tampa Bay are in for a treat. This place is noted for its Wednesday and Friday night seafood buffets, its Saturday night prime rib buffet and its Sunday brunch. An a la carte menu also is available. Casual dress; cocktails. **Parking:** on-site. **Cards:** AX, DC, DS, MC, VI.

SAFETY HARBOR pop. 17,203   (See map and index starting on p. 938)

──────── **WHERE TO STAY** ────────

SAFETY HARBOR RESORT AND SPA ON TAMPA BAY

Book at aaa.com

Phone: (727)726-1161   **30**

1/1-4/30	1P: $234-$284	2P: $234-$284	XP: $10	F17
12/1-12/31 & 5/1-11/30	1P: $209-$260	2P: $209-$260	XP: $10	F17

◆◆ ◆◆
Resort
Small-scale Hotel

Location: Jct SR 590 (Main St); downtown. 105 N Bayshore Dr 34695. Fax: 727/726-4268. **Facility:** On extensive, manicured grounds facing Tampa Bay, this property offers a spa, a fitness studio and recreational facilities. 189 units. 185 one-bedroom standard units. 4 one-bedroom suites with whirlpools. 3-6 stories, interior corridors. *Bath:* combo or shower only. **Parking:** on-site (fee) and valet. **Terms:** 3 day cancellation notice-fee imposed, [AP] & [BP] meal plans available, $12 service charge, small pets only ($35 extra charge). **Amenities:** dual phone lines, voice mail, irons, hair dryers. *Fee:* video games, high-speed Internet. **Dining:** 7 am-1 am, cocktails. **Pool(s):** 2 heated outdoor, heated indoor. **Leisure Activities:** saunas, whirlpools, steamrooms, fishing, 9 tennis courts (6 lighted), recreation programs, bicycles, playground, spa, volleyball. *Fee:* tennis & golf academy, driving range, mineral springs, theater, hammock park. **Guest Services:** gift shop, valet and coin laundry, area transportation (fee), beauty salon. **Business Services:** conference facilities, business center. **Cards:** AX, CB, DC, DS, MC, VI. **Special Amenities:** free room upgrade (subject to availability with advance reservations). *(See color ad below)*

SOME UNITS

🆂🅳 ➰ 🐾 🍴 🍽 &M 📷 ⊘ ➹ 🛁 ✂ 🎥 DATA PORT ▭ / ✕ VCR 🔌 /
       FEE FEE   FEE

──────── **WHERE TO DINE** ────────

ENVER'S PARADISE RESTAURANT

◆◆ ◆◆
American

Lunch: $5-$12   **Dinner:** $5-$12   **Phone:** 727/725-1208   **51**

Location: On SR 590 (Main St); downtown. 443 Main St 34695. **Hours:** 7 am-9 pm, Sun 7:30 am-8 pm. Closed: 11/23, 12/25. **Features:** This family-oriented restaurant features an eclectic menu that includes sandwiches, burgers, steaks, seafood and such Greek favorites as moussaka and grape leaves. Desserts, particularly the bread and rice pudding, are a treat. Casual dress; beer & wine only. **Parking:** on-site. **Cards:** MC, VI.

ST. PETE BEACH pop. 9,929   (See map and index starting on p. 938)

———— WHERE TO STAY ————

ALDEN BEACH RESORT   *Book at aaa.com*   Phone: (727)360-7081   **131**

2/10-4/23	1P: $199-$283	2P: $199-$283	XP: $10	F12
4/24-8/5	1P: $139-$209	2P: $139-$209	XP: $10	F12
12/1-2/9	1P: $115-$187	2P: $115-$187	XP: $10	F12
8/6-11/30	1P: $121-$179	2P: $121-$179	XP: $10	F12

Resort
Small-scale Hotel

Location: Oceanfront. On SR 699, 1.7 mi n of Pinellas Bayway. 5900 Gulf Blvd 33706. Fax: 727/360-5957. **Facility:** Located directly on the Gulf of Mexico on five lushly landscaped acres, this property offers covered parking and 10 types of accommodations. 143 one-bedroom suites with kitchens. 1-6 stories, exterior corridors. **Parking:** on-site. **Terms:** check-in 4 pm, cancellation fee imposed. **Amenities:** dual phone lines, voice mail, safes, irons, hair dryers. *Fee:* video games, high-speed Internet. **Pool(s):** 2 heated outdoor. **Leisure Activities:** whirlpools, 2 lighted tennis courts, deck with gas barbecue grills, ping pong, playground, basketball, shuffleboard, volleyball. *Fee:* sailboats, charter fishing, cabanas, kayak, water trikes, parasailing, game room. **Guest Services:** valet and coin laundry. **Business Services:** meeting rooms, fax (fee). **Cards:** AX, DC, DS, MC, VI. **Special Amenities:** free newspaper. *(See color ad below)*

SOME UNITS

BAY PALM RESORT   Phone: (727)360-7642   **138**

2/1-4/30	1P: $79-$109	2P: $79-$109	XP: $5
12/1-1/31	1P: $65-$95	2P: $65-$95	XP: $5
5/1-9/1	1P: $65-$89	2P: $65-$89	XP: $5
9/2-11/30	1P: $59-$85	2P: $59-$85	XP: $5

Motel

Location: On SR 699, 0.5 mi n of Pinellas Bayway. 4237 Gulf Blvd 33706. Fax: 727/360-6517. **Facility:** Designated smoking area. 14 one-bedroom standard units, some with efficiencies or kitchens. 2 stories, exterior corridors. *Bath:* combo or shower only. **Parking:** on-site. **Terms:** office hours 9 am-7 pm, 2-3 night minimum stay - seasonal and/or weekends, 14 day cancellation notice, pets ($7 extra charge). **Amenities:** voice mail. *Some:* irons, hair dryers. **Pool(s):** heated outdoor. **Leisure Activities:** boat dock, fishing. **Guest Services:** coin laundry, area transportation (fee). **Cards:** AX, DS, MC, VI.

SOME UNITS

FEE

(See map and index starting on p. 938)

BAYVIEW PLAZA WATERFRONT RESORT *Book at aaa.com* **Phone:** (727)367-1387 137

AAA [SAVE]

2/1-4/24 1P: $75-$159 2P: $75-$159
4/25-9/5 1P: $59-$109 2P: $59-$109
12/1-1/31 & 9/6-11/30 1P: $45-$109 2P: $45-$109

Motel

Location: On SR 699; 0.8 mi n of Pinellas Bayway. 4321 Gulf Blvd 33706 (4506 Gulf Blvd). Fax: 727/367-3620. **Facility:** Designated smoking area. 8 one-bedroom standard units with kitchens. 2 stories, exterior corridors. *Bath:* combo or shower only. **Parking:** on-site. **Terms:** office hours 8 am-11 pm, off-site registration, check-in 4 pm, 5-7 night minimum stay - seasonal, 14 day cancellation notice-fee imposed, pets ($10 fee). **Amenities:** DVD players, CD players, high-speed Internet, hair dryers. *Some:* irons. **Leisure Activities:** fishing, sun deck, fishing pier, fishing pole rental, barbecue grills. **Guest Services:** coin laundry. **Cards:** DS, MC, VI. **Special Amenities:** free local telephone calls and early check-in/late check-out. *(See color ad below)*

FEE   FEE

(See map and index starting on p. 938)

BEACH HOUSE SUITES BY THE DON CESAR   *Book at aaa.com*   Phone: (727)363-0001   **140**

	1P: $289-$454	2P: $289-$454	XP: $15	F18
2/18-4/30	1P: $289-$454	2P: $289-$454	XP: $15	F18
12/1-2/17	1P: $169-$424	2P: $169-$424	XP: $15	F18
10/1-11/30	1P: $169-$379	2P: $169-$379	XP: $15	F18
5/1-9/30	1P: $169-$374	2P: $169-$374	XP: $15	F18

Small-scale Hotel **Location:** Oceanfront. On SR 699, 0.4 mi n of jct Pinellas Bayway. 3860 Gulf Blvd 33706. Fax: 727/363-5055. **Facility:** 70 one-bedroom suites with kitchens. 6 stories, exterior corridors. **Terms:** check-in 4 pm, 5 day cancellation notice-fee imposed, package plans, $10 service charge, pets ($25 fee). **Amenities:** voice mail, safes, irons, hair dryers. *Some:* DVD players, video games, CD players. **Pool(s):** heated outdoor. **Leisure Activities:** whirlpool, sun deck, picnic area, shuffleboard, volleyball. *Fee:* windsurfing, scuba diving, charter fishing, banana boat, cabanas, kayaks, sailing instruction, hobie cats, massage. **Guest Services:** gift shop, complimentary laundry, area transportation. **Business Services:** meeting rooms, fax (fee). **Cards:** AX, CB, DC, DS, JC, MC, VI.

SOME UNITS

CAPRICE CONDOMINIUMS ON ST. PETE BEACH   Phone: 727/360-6199   **128**

Property failed to provide current rates

Condominium **Location:** Just w of Gulf Blvd (SR 699), jct 70th Ave. 6950 Beach Plaza 33706. Fax: 727/363-8707. **Facility:** 33 units. 10 one- and 23 two-bedroom suites with kitchens. 6 stories, exterior corridors. **Parking:** on-site. **Terms:** office hours 9 am-5 pm. **Amenities:** video library, voice mail, irons. *Some:* DVD players, CD players, safes, hair dryers. **Pool(s):** heated outdoor. **Leisure Activities:** exercise room, volleyball. **Guest Services:** coin laundry. **Business Services:** fax.

SOME UNITS

DON CESAR BEACH RESORT, A LOEWS HOTEL   *Book at aaa.com*   Phone: (727)360-1881   **143**

2/18-4/30	1P: $294-$524	2P: $294-$524	XP: $15	F18
12/1-2/17	1P: $174-$424	2P: $174-$424	XP: $15	F18
10/1-11/30	1P: $174-$389	2P: $174-$389	XP: $15	F18
5/1-9/30	1P: $164-$389	2P: $164-$389	XP: $15	F18

Resort Large-scale Hotel **Location:** Oceanfront. On SR 699, jct Pinellas Bayway. 3400 Gulf Blvd 33706. Fax: 727/367-6952. **Facility:** Set on the gulf, the resort boasts large, lavishly decorated public areas, rooms with a gulf view and numerous specialty boutiques. 277 units. 257 one-bedroom standard units. 18 one- and 2 two-bedroom suites ($289-$3000). 10 stories, interior corridors. *Bath:* combo or shower only. **Parking:** on-site (fee) and valet. **Terms:** check-in 4 pm, 5 day cancellation notice-fee imposed, package plans, $10 service charge. **Amenities:** CD players, dual phone lines, voice mail, safes, honor bars, irons, hair dryers. *Fee:* video games, high-speed Internet. **Dining:** 7 am-10 pm, cocktails, also, Maritana Grille, Sea Porch Cafe, see separate listings, entertainment. **Pool(s):** 2 heated outdoor. **Leisure Activities:** sauna, whirlpools, steamroom, rental paddleboats, water aerobics, recreation programs, playground, spa, aerobic & yoga instruction, volleyball. *Fee:* sailboats, windsurfing, cabana, water bikes, catamarans, parasails, personal watercraft, golf & tennis privileges, game room. **Guest Services:** gift shop, valet and coin laundry, area transportation-golf course & charters. **Business Services:** conference facilities, business center. **Cards:** AX, CB, DC, DS, JC, MC, VI. *(See color ad below)*

SOME UNITS

(See map and index starting on p. 938)

GULF STRAND BEACH RESORT

Phone: (727)367-2878 `135`

AAA SAVE

Condominium

12/1-4/30	1P: $130-$200	2P: $130-$200	XP: $20	F18
5/1-9/30	1P: $100-$150	2P: $100-$150	XP: $20	F18
10/1-11/30	1P: $85-$100	2P: $85-$100	XP: $20	F18

Location: On SR 699, 0.7 mi n of Pinellas Bayway. 4510 Gulf Blvd 33706. Fax: 727/360-5364. **Facility:** 34 one-bedroom suites with kitchens. 6 stories, exterior corridors. **Parking:** on-site. **Terms:** office hours 9 am-5 pm, 3-7 night minimum stay, 30 day cancellation notice-fee imposed, weekly rates available. **Amenities:** voice mail, irons. *Some:* DVD players, CD players, hair dryers. **Pool(s):** heated outdoor. **Leisure Activities:** whirlpool, gas grills, shuffleboard. **Guest Services:** complimentary laundry. **Business Services:** fax (fee). **Cards:** AX, DS, MC, VI.

HOLIDAY INN HOTEL & SUITES BEACHFRONT
RESORT & CONFERENCE CENTER *Book at aaa.com*

Phone: (727)360-1811 `134`

Large-scale Hotel

2/10-4/22	1P: $178-$358	2P: $178-$358	XP: $20	F19
12/1-2/9 & 4/23-11/30	1P: $158-$328	2P: $158-$328	XP: $10	F19

Location: Oceanfront. On SR 699, 1 mi n of Pinellas Bayway. 5250 Gulf Blvd 33706. Fax: 727/360-6919. **Facility:** 156 units. 147 one-bedroom standard units. 9 one-bedroom suites ($248-$388), some with whirlpools. 11 stories, interior corridors. *Bath:* combo or shower only. **Parking:** on-site. **Terms:** check-in 4 pm, 3 day cancellation notice-fee imposed, package plans. **Amenities:** voice mail, safes, irons, hair dryers. **Dining:** Spinners Rooftop Revolving Lounge & Bistro, see separate listing. **Pool(s):** heated outdoor. **Leisure Activities:** exercise room, volleyball. *Fee:* sailboats, windsurfing, waterskiing, snorkeling, charter fishing, game room. **Guest Services:** gift shop, valet and coin laundry. **Business Services:** meeting rooms. *Fee:* PC, fax. **Cards:** AX, CB, DC, DS, JC, MC, VI.

SOME UNITS
FEE

HOWARD JOHNSON LODGE ST. PETE BEACH
RESORT INN *Book at aaa.com*

Phone: (727)360-7041 `129`

Small-scale Hotel

All Year	1P: $95-$350	2P: $95-$350	XP: $25	F13

Location: On SR 699, 1.8 mi n of Pinellas Bayway. 6100 Gulf Blvd 33706. Fax: 727/360-8941. **Facility:** 133 units. 123 one- and 10 two-bedroom standard units, some with kitchens (no utensils) and/or whirlpools. 5 stories, interior corridors. **Parking:** on-site. **Terms:** 3 day cancellation notice-fee imposed. **Amenities:** safes (fee), irons, hair dryers. **Pool(s):** heated outdoor, wading. **Leisure Activities:** shuffleboard. *Fee:* game room. **Guest Services:** gift shop, valet and coin laundry. **Business Services:** meeting rooms. **Cards:** AX, DC, DS, MC, VI.

SOME UNITS

ISLAND'S END RESORT

Phone: 727/360-5023 `144`

AAA SAVE

Cottage

1/1-5/31 [CP]	1P: $149-$290	2P: $149-$290	XP: $22	
6/1-9/14 [CP]	1P: $132-$290	2P: $132-$290	XP: $22	
12/1-12/31 & 9/15-11/30 [CP]	1P: $116-$290	2P: $116-$290	XP: $22	

Location: South end of island, 2 mi s of Pinellas Bayway. Located in Pass-A-Grille section on Intercoastal Waterway. 1 Pass-A-Grille Way 33706. Fax: 727/367-7890. **Facility:** 6 cottages. 1 story, exterior corridors. **Parking:** on-site. **Terms:** office hours 8:30 am-5 pm, check-in 4 pm, cancellation fee imposed, weekly rates available. **Amenities:** video library (fee), DVD players, voice mail, safes, irons, hair dryers. **Leisure Activities:** fishing, sun deck, private fishing pier, gas barbecue grills, gazebo. **Guest Services:** coin laundry. **Business Services:** fax. **Cards:** MC, VI. **Special Amenities:** free continental breakfast and free local telephone calls.

LAMARA MOTEL APARTMENTS

Phone: (727)360-7521 `127`

AAA SAVE

Motel

12/1-4/30	1P: $75-$100	2P: $75-$100	XP: $8	F5
5/1-11/30	1P: $55-$75	2P: $55-$75	XP: $8	F5

Location: Just w of Gulf Blvd (SR 699). 520 73rd Ave 33706. Fax: 727/363-0193. **Facility:** Designated smoking area. 16 one-bedroom standard units, some with efficiencies or kitchens. 2 stories, exterior corridors. *Bath:* combo or shower only. **Parking:** on-site. **Terms:** office hours 9 am-6 pm, 7 day cancellation notice, 30 day 1/1-4/30-fee imposed, small pets only. **Amenities:** *Some:* irons, hair dryers. **Pool(s):** heated outdoor. **Leisure Activities:** barbecue grill, shuffleboard. **Guest Services:** coin laundry. **Business Services:** fax (fee). **Cards:** DS, MC, VI.

LONG KEY BEACH RESORT

Phone: (727)360-1748 `142`

AAA SAVE

Motel

All Year	1P: $49-$139	2P: $49-$139	XP: $5	F

Location: Oceanfront. On SR 699, 0.3 mi n of jct Pinellas Bayway. 3828 Gulf Blvd 33706. Fax: 727/367-9026. **Facility:** Designated smoking area. 16 units. 1 one-bedroom standard unit. 15 one-bedroom suites with kitchens. 1-2 stories, exterior corridors. **Parking:** on-site. **Terms:** office hours 8 am-8 pm, 30 day cancellation notice. **Amenities:** hair dryers. *Some:* irons. **Pool(s):** heated outdoor. **Leisure Activities:** whirlpool, sun deck, shuffleboard. **Guest Services:** coin laundry. **Business Services:** fax. **Cards:** AX, MC, VI.

SOME UNITS

PALM CREST RESORT MOTEL

Phone: (727)360-9327 `141`

AAA SAVE

Motel

2/1-4/30	1P: $89-$132	2P: $89-$132	XP: $6	F5
12/1-1/31 & 5/1-9/7	1P: $64-$94	2P: $64-$94	XP: $6	F5
9/8-11/30	1P: $54-$84	2P: $54-$84	XP: $6	F5

Location: On SR 699, 0.5 mi n of Pinellas Bayway. 3848 Gulf Blvd 33706. Fax: 727/367-1073. **Facility:** 18 one-bedroom standard units with efficiencies. 2 stories, exterior corridors. **Parking:** on-site. **Terms:** office hours 9 am-9 pm, 1-3 night minimum stay - weekends, 14 day cancellation notice-fee imposed. **Amenities:** *Some:* irons, hair dryers. **Pool(s):** heated outdoor. **Leisure Activities:** gas grill, shuffleboard. **Guest Services:** coin laundry. **Business Services:** fax. **Cards:** AX, DS, MC, VI.

(See map and index starting on p. 938)

PASA TIEMPO "A PRIVATE WATERFRONT RESORT"

Book at aaa.com — Phone: (727)367-9907 `126`

AAA [SAVE]
🔻🔻🔻 🔻🔻🔻

12/28-5/31	1P: $175-$275	2P: $175-$275	XP: $35
12/1-12/27 & 10/1-11/30	1P: $175-$255	2P: $175-$255	XP: $35
6/1-9/30	1P: $155-$215	2P: $155-$215	XP: $35

Bed & Breakfast

Location: Jct SR 699, just e on 72nd Ave. 7141 Bay St 33706. Fax: 727/367-9906. **Facility:** Attractive Mediterranean villa-style architecture, beautifully decorated rooms and a lush tropical setting are this property's strong points; it overlooks the Intracoastal Waterway. Designated smoking area. 10 units. 2 one-bedroom standard units. 8 one-bedroom suites, some with kitchens and/or whirlpools. 2 stories, exterior corridors. *Bath:* combo or shower only. **Parking:** on-site. **Terms:** check-in 4 pm, age restrictions may apply, 7 day cancellation notice-fee imposed, package plans. **Amenities:** CD players, dual phone lines, voice mail, irons, hair dryers. *Some:* DVD players. **Pool(s):** heated outdoor. **Leisure Activities:** boat dock, patio. **Guest Services:** complimentary evening beverages, valet laundry. **Business Services:** meeting rooms, PC, fax. **Cards:** AX, DS, MC, VI. **Special Amenities: free expanded continental breakfast and free local telephone calls.**

SOME UNITS
🍽️➕ 🏊 ✖️ 🎦 DATA PORT 💾 💻 / VCR 📷 /

PLAZA BEACH RESORT MOTEL

Book at aaa.com — Phone: (727)367-2791 `136`

AAA [SAVE]
🔻🔻 🔻🔻

2/1-4/24	1P: $89-$199	2P: $89-$199	XP: $7	F5
4/25-9/5	1P: $79-$139	2P: $79-$139	XP: $7	F5
12/1-1/31 & 9/6-11/30	1P: $49-$129	2P: $49-$129	XP: $7	F5

Motel

Location: Oceanfront. On SR 699, 0.7 mi n of Pinellas Bayway. 4506 Gulf Blvd 33706. Fax: 727/367-3620. **Facility:** Designated smoking area. 39 units. 37 one-bedroom standard units with kitchens. 2 one-bedroom suites with kitchens. 2 stories, exterior corridors. **Parking:** on-site. **Terms:** office hours 8 am-11 pm, 5-7 night minimum stay - seasonal, 14 day cancellation notice-fee imposed. **Amenities:** high-speed Internet, voice mail, irons, hair dryers. *Some:* DVD players (fee). **Pool(s):** heated outdoor. **Leisure Activities:** fishing pole rental, miniature golf, barbecue grill, foosball, human checkerboard, shuffleboard. *Fee:* cabanas, parasailing, personal watercraft, water bikes. **Guest Services:** coin laundry. **Business Services:** meeting rooms, business center. **Cards:** DS, MC, VI. **Special Amenities: free local telephone calls and early check-in/late check-out.**

SOME UNITS
[S/D] ✈️ 🍽️➕ 🏊 👥➕ ✖️ ✖️ 🎦 DATA PORT 💾 📟 💻 / VCR /
FEE   FEE

SIRATA BEACH RESORT & CONFERENCE CENTER

Book at aaa.com — Phone: (727)363-5100 `133`

AAA [SAVE]
🔻🔻🔻 🔻🔻🔻

2/1-4/30	1P: $229-$399	2P: $229-$399	XP: $15	F13
12/25-1/31	1P: $229-$389	2P: $229-$389	XP: $15	F13
12/1-12/24 & 5/1-11/30	1P: $169-$299	2P: $169-$299	XP: $15	F13

Resort
Large-scale Hotel

Location: Oceanfront. On SR 699, 1.2 mi n of Pinellas Bayway. 5300 Gulf Blvd 33706. Fax: 727/363-5161. **Facility:** This contemporary resort's decor includes tile and pickled woods appropriate to the beach setting; guest rooms with computers are available. 380 units. 210 one-bedroom standard units, some with kitchens. 170 one-bedroom suites with kitchens, some with whirlpools. 2-8 stories, interior/exterior corridors. *Bath:* combo or shower only. **Parking:** on-site. **Terms:** check-in 4 pm, cancellation fee imposed. **Amenities:** video games (fee), CD players, high-speed Internet, voice mail, safes, irons, hair dryers. *Some:* DVD players, dual phone lines. **Dining:** 2 restaurants, 7 am-10 pm, cocktails, entertainment. **Pool(s):** 3 heated outdoor. **Leisure Activities:** whirlpools, fishing, miniature golf, playground, exercise room, volleyball. *Fee:* charter fishing, aqua trikes, boat tours, cabanas, parasailing, personal watercraft, massage, game room. **Guest Services:** gift shop, valet and coin laundry. **Business Services:** conference facilities, business center. **Cards:** AX, DS, MC, VI. **Special Amenities: free newspaper.** *(See color ad below)*

SOME UNITS
[S/D] 🍽️ 🍸 🏋️ ♿ 📶 🏊 ✖️ 🎦 DATA PORT 💾 📟 💻 / ✖️ 📷 /

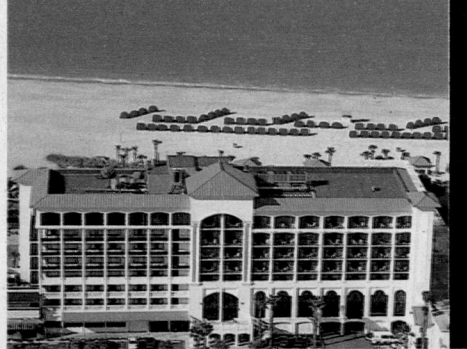

(See map and index starting on p. 938)

TRADEWINDS ISLAND GRAND BEACH RESORT

Book at aaa.com   **Phone: (727)363-2200**   **132**

(AAA) (SAVE)

2/1-4/30	1P: $229-$369	2P: $229-$369	XP: $15	F12
12/1-1/31 & 5/1-11/30	1P: $199-$299	2P: $199-$299	XP: $15	F12

Location: Oceanfront. On SR 699, 1 mi n of Pinellas Bayway. 5500 Gulf Blvd 33706. Fax: 727/363-2275. **Facility:** A winding stream, complete with gondolas, circles the gulfside property, which is highlighted by a tropical courtyard. 585 units. 378 one-bedroom standard units. 158 one-, 42 two- and 7 three-bedroom suites ($255-$459), some with efficiencies, kitchens and/or whirlpools. 2-7 stories, interior/exterior corridors. *Bath:* combo or shower only. **Parking:** on-site and valet. **Terms:** check-in 4 pm, package plans, $12 service charge. **Amenities:** CD players, voice mail, safes, honor bars, irons, hair dryers. *Fee:* video games, high-speed Internet. **Dining:** 4 restaurants, 7 am-10 pm, cocktails, also, Palm Court Restaurant, see separate listing, entertainment. **Pool(s):** 4 heated outdoor, wading. **Leisure Activities:** sauna, whirlpools, paddleboats, cabanas, water tricycles, putting green, golf privileges, 4 lighted tennis courts, playground, aeorbic instruction, sports court, volleyball. *Fee:* snorkeling, charter fishing, swimming instruction, tennis instruction, massage. **Guest Services:** gift shop, valet and coin laundry, beauty salon. **Business Services:** conference facilities, business center. **Cards:** AX, DC, DS, MC, VI. *(See color ad below)*

Resort
Large-scale Hotel

SOME UNITS

TRADEWINDS SANDPIPER HOTEL & SUITES

Book at aaa.com   **Phone: (727)360-5551**   **130**

(AAA) (SAVE)

2/1-4/30	1P: $169-$259	2P: $169-$259	XP: $15	F12
12/1-1/31 & 5/1-11/30	1P: $139-$199	2P: $139-$199	XP: $15	F12

Location: Oceanfront. On SR 699, 1.8 mi n of Pinellas Bayway. 6000 Gulf Blvd 33706. Fax: 727/363-2367. **Facility:** Trendy architecture and manicured grounds add upscale roadside appeal to this beachfront property. 209 units. 94 one-bedroom standard units. 110 one- & 5 two-bedroom suites ($199-$369) with efficiencies. 7 stories, interior/exterior corridors. *Bath:* combo or shower only. **Parking:** on-site. **Terms:** check-in 4 pm, package plans, $12 service charge. **Amenities:** high-speed Internet (fee), voice mail, safes, honor bars, irons, hair dryers. **Dining:** 7 am-10 pm, cocktails. **Pool(s):** 2 heated outdoor. **Leisure Activities:** recreation programs, children's program privileges, shuffleboard. *Fee:* charter fishing, cabanas, parasailing, exercise room, massage. **Guest Services:** gift shop. **Business Services:** meeting rooms, business center. **Cards:** AX, DC, DS, MC, VI. *(See color ad below)*

Resort
Large-scale Hotel

SOME UNITS

VISTAS ON THE GULF

Phone: (727)367-2534   **139**

(AAA) (SAVE)

All Year	1P: $125-$275	2P: $135-$300	XP: $10	F15

Location: On SR 699, 0.5 mi n of jct Pinellas Bayway. 4000 Gulf Blvd 33706. Fax: 727/360-9298. **Facility:** Located on the Gulf of Mexico, each condominium unit is individually decorated and offers modern amenities. Designated smoking area. 41 one-bedroom suites with kitchens. 5 stories, exterior corridors. **Parking:** on-site. **Terms:** office hours 9 am-5 pm, 3-7 night minimum stay - seasonal and/or weekends, 30 day cancellation notice-fee imposed, weekly rates available, package plans. **Amenities:** irons, hair dryers. *Some:* DVD players, CD players. **Pool(s):** heated outdoor. **Leisure Activities:** whirlpool, exercise room. **Guest Services:** complimentary laundry. **Business Services:** fax (fee). **Cards:** AX, DS, MC, VI.

Condominium

(See map and index starting on p. 938)

———— **WHERE TO DINE** ————

BOUNXOU THAI RESTAURANT **Lunch:** $8-$10 **Dinner:** $8-$10 **Phone:** 727/363-0307 (183)
Thai
Location: On SR 699, 0.4 mi n of jct Pinellas Bayway; in Dolphin Village. 4755 Gulf Blvd 33706. **Hours:** 11 am-10 pm. **Features:** Fresh Thai food is on the menu of the nice little spot. The buffet tempts those with hearty appetites. Casual dress. **Parking:** on-site. **Cards:** MC, VI.

BRIDGEVIEW WATERFRONT GRILL & BAR **Lunch:** $5-$13 **Dinner:** $5-$13 **Phone:** 727/368-0782 (168)
Seafood
Location: 0.4 mi e of jct SR 699; on Boca Ciega Bay. 69 Corey Ave 33706. **Hours:** 11 am-2 am. **Features:** On the Intracoastal Waterway, the casual outdoor dining spot serves seafood, sandwiches and fresh salads. Casual dress; cocktails. **Parking:** on-site. **Cards:** AX, CB, DC, MC, VI.

THE CARIBBEAN BAY CAFE **Lunch:** $6-$7 **Phone:** 727/367-0814 (176)
American
Location: On SR 699, 2 mi n of Pinellas Bayway. 6203 Gulf Blvd 33706. **Hours:** 8 am-3 pm. **Features:** Just a short walk from the beach, the cafe lures folks who spent the morning briskly walking along the shore for a fresh delicatessen-style sandwich with a bowl of homemade chicken soup. Casual dress. **Parking:** on-site. **Cards:** MC, VI.

CRABBY BILL'S **Lunch:** $7-$15 **Dinner:** $7-$15 **Phone:** 727/360-8858 (182)
Seafood
Location: Just w of jct SR 699. 5100 Gulf Blvd 33706. **Hours:** 11:30 am-10 pm, Fri & Sat-11 pm. Closed: 12/25. **Features:** Right on the gulf, the casual restaurant lets diners take in great sunset views while dining on seafood, including the house specialty crabs. Also on the menu are numerous appetizers, sandwiches, salads, pasta and platters. Guests are urged to come with an appetite, as the portions are hearty. Casual dress; cocktails. **Parking:** on-site. **Cards:** MC, VI.

DER EISENHUT **Dinner:** $9-$15 **Phone:** 727/367-6495 (170)
German
Location: Just e of SR 699. 357 Corey Ave 33706. **Hours:** 4 pm-10 pm. Closed major holidays; also 12/24, Sun, Mon & Mother's Day. **Features:** Relax in the cozy bistro setting and savor an excellent variety of ethnic dishes, ranging from German and French to Hungarian and Russian. European antiques, paintings, crystal chandeliers and assorted imports give this restaurant an air of authenticity. Casual dress; beer & wine only. **Parking:** street. **Cards:** MC, VI.

EMPEROR'S PALACE CHINESE RESTAURANT **Lunch:** $7-$25 **Dinner:** $7-$25 **Phone:** 727/360-0992 (171)
Chinese
Location: On SR 699 at Corey Ave; in Beach Plaza. 7390 Gulf Blvd 33706. **Hours:** 11:30 am-10 pm, Fri & Sat-11 pm, Sun 4 pm-10 pm. **Features:** The casual restaurant's lengthy menu lists more than 120 Chinese delights. Among choices are chow mein, lo mein, combination platters and chicken, beef, pork and vegetable dishes. Peking duck and subgum wor bar are representative of house specialties. Casual dress. **Parking:** on-site. **Cards:** MC, VI.

FERG'S BEACH SHACK **Lunch:** $6-$14 **Dinner:** $6-$14 **Phone:** 727/367-5556 (172)
Seafood
Location: Just w of jct SR 699. 677 75th Ave 33706. **Hours:** 11 am-11 pm. **Features:** Enjoy a relaxed setting on the water as you feast on shrimp, fresh stone crab claws, grouper, and burgers that have a backyard-barbecue flavor. Casual dress; cocktails. **Parking:** on-site. **Cards:** AX, MC, VI.

HURRICANE SEAFOOD RESTAURANT **Lunch:** $15-$24 **Dinner:** $15-$24 **Phone:** 727/360-9558 (188)
Seafood
Location: On Pass-A-Grille; jct 9th Ave. 809 Gulf Way 33706. **Hours:** 8 am-2 am. **Features:** The restaurant is a local favorite for watching beautiful sunsets from the rooftop. Dining is casual on the rustic first floor and slightly more upscale in the trendy second floor area, which becomes a popular dance bar after hours. Casual dress; cocktails; entertainment. **Parking:** on-site. **Cards:** AX, DS, MC, VI.

JOHNNY LEVEROCK'S SEAFOOD HOUSE **Lunch:** $6-$9 **Dinner:** $8-$24 **Phone:** 727/367-4588 (169)
Steak & Seafood
Location: West end of St Petersburg Beach Cswy (75th Ave); on Boca Ciega Bay. 10 Corey Ave 33706. **Hours:** 11:30 am-10 pm. Closed: 11/23, 12/25. **Features:** An Old Florida decor complete with hardwood floors, antiques, nautical memorabilia and big picture windows gives the bayfront restaurant its personality. Grilled mahi coconut shrimp, fresh clam chowder and onion-crusted salmon bring the menu to life. Casual dress; cocktails. **Parking:** on-site. **Cards:** AX, DC, DS, MC, VI.

MARITANA GRILLE **Dinner:** $28-$42 **Phone:** 727/360-1882 (185)
American
Location: On SR 699, jct Pinellas Bayway; in Don CeSar Beach Resort, A Loews Hotel. 3400 Gulf Blvd 33706. **Hours:** 5:30 pm-10 pm, Fri & Sat-11 pm. **Reservations:** suggested. **Features:** Resort-casual dining with artistic creations like swirled mashed potatoes that add charm to any plate. A private dining room and chef's table are available. For a light and tasty appetizer, try the lobster spring roll. Smoking is permitted in the bar only. Dressy casual; cocktails. **Parking:** on-site. **Cards:** AX, DC, DS, MC, VI.

PALM COURT RESTAURANT **Lunch:** $7-$12 **Dinner:** $16-$25 **Phone:** 727/367-6461 (179)
American
Location: SR 699, 1 mi n of Pinellas Bayway; in TradeWinds Island Grand Beach Resort. 5500 Gulf Blvd 33706. **Hours:** 11:30 am-2 & 5:30-10 pm, Sun from 10 am. **Features:** A quaint atmosphere features indoor and outdoor seating amid resort surroundings. Order the seafood pasta and you will find a thick marinara sauce filled with clams, shrimp, fish, scallops and mussels. The rich raspberry cake is artistically swirled and the chocolate cake is the highlight. Casual dress; cocktails. **Parking:** on-site and valet. **Cards:** AX, CB, DC, DS, MC, VI.

PHILTHY PHIL'S WATERFRONT BAR & GRILL **Lunch:** $7-$9 **Dinner:** $7-$18 **Phone:** 727/367-9977 (173)
Seafood
Location: Just w of jct SR 699 (Gulf Blvd). 678 75th Ave 33706. **Hours:** 11 am-10 pm, Sun from noon. **Features:** Across the street from the Blind Pass waterfront, the casual eatery affords great views of the waterway. Guests can top off a meal of fried grouper or baked salmon with a tempting slice of Key lime cheesecake. Casual dress; cocktails; entertainment. **Parking:** on-site. **Cards:** AX, MC, VI.

(See map and index starting on p. 938)

THE REEF
American
Lunch: $4-$15   **Dinner:** $6-$15   **Phone:** 727/367-5577   (174)
Location: On SR 699 at 68th Ave. 6712 Gulf Blvd 33706. **Hours:** 11 am-11 pm. **Features:** Within walking distance of the beach, the restaurant serves a fabulous fried grouper meal, as well as sandwiches, burgers, panini and fajitas. Casual dress; cocktails. **Parking:** on-site. **Cards:** AX, MC, VI.

SEA CRITTERS CAFE
Seafood
Lunch: $6-$17   **Dinner:** $6-$17   **Phone:** 727/360-3706   (186)
Location: On SR 699, 1 mi s of Pinellas Bayway, jct 21st Ave. 2007 Pass-A-Grille Way 33706. **Hours:** 11:30 am-9 pm, Fri & Sat-10 pm. Closed: 11/23. **Features:** Key West-style food. Experience dockside dining on the Intracoastal Waterway at Vina Del Mar Bridge. The seafood platter gives a sampling of fried clams, shrimp, squid, crab cake grouper nuggets and onion rings. Casual dress; cocktails. **Parking:** on-site. **Cards:** AX, DC, DS, MC, VI.

SEAHORSE RESTAURANT
Seafood
Lunch: $4-$10   **Phone:** 727/360-1734   (189)
Location: On SR 699, 1.5 mi s of jct Pinellas Bayway. 800 Pass-a-Grille Way 33706. **Hours:** 8 am-2:30 pm. Closed: 12/25; also Tues. **Reservations:** not accepted. **Features:** A no-frills eatery dating back to 1937, it boasts a breezy courtyard reminiscent of Old Florida homes. Well-seasoned black beans are a signature favorite along with specialty sandwiches such as Cajun chicken and grouper served on grilled Cuban bread. Casual dress; cocktails. **Parking:** on-site. **Cards:** DS, MC, VI.

SEA PORCH CAFE
American
Lunch: $8-$12   **Dinner:** $9-$21   **Phone:** 727/360-1884   (184)
Location: On SR 699, jct Pinellas Bayway; in Don CeSar Beach Resort, A Loews Hotel. 3400 Gulf Blvd 33706. **Hours:** 7 am-11, noon-4 & 5-11 pm. **Reservations:** suggested, for dinner. **Features:** Bright and colorful, the decor of the waterfront restaurant is unmistakably tropical. Strong flavor characterizes the rosemary chicken with homemade gravy and the Key lime pie. Light, crisp breezes drift across the outdoor boardwalk. Casual dress; cocktails; entertainment. **Parking:** valet. **Cards:** AX, CB, DC, DS, MC, VI.

SHELLS OF ST. PETE BEACH
Seafood
Lunch: $7-$19   **Dinner:** $7-$19   **Phone:** 727/360-0889   (175)
Location: On SR 699, 2 mi n of Pinellas Bayway. 6330 Gulf Blvd 33706. **Hours:** 7:30 am-10:30 & 11:30-10 pm, Sat & Sun 7:30 am-10:30 & noon-11 pm. **Features:** Popular throughout Florida for more than 15 years, the restaurant prepares some of the freshest seafood to be found in the state. Guests can expect a relaxing nautical setting, friendly service and a menu that lists combination platters, sandwiches, grilled items, pasta dishes and even king crab. Those who love Maine lobster shouldn't miss "Lobster Tuesday.". Casual dress; cocktails. **Parking:** on-site. **Cards:** MC, VI.

SILAS DENT'S STEAKHOUSE
Steak House
Dinner: $11-$21   **Phone:** 727/360-6961   (178)
Location: SR 699, 1 mi n of Pinellas Bayway; in Bayside Shores. 5501 Gulf Blvd 33706. **Hours:** 5 pm-10 pm, Fri & Sat-11 pm. Closed: 12/25. **Reservations:** suggested. **Features:** On the Intracoastal Waterway, the restaurant has an inviting patio area that overlooks the water. The original Silas Dent—the name of which ties to much history—was established in 1979, and this newer version carries on the tradition. The menu has a wide variety of salad, seafood, surf and turf fare, smokehouse items and steak. Casual dress; cocktails. **Parking:** on-site. **Cards:** AX, DS, MC, VI.

SKIDDER'S RESTAURANT
American
Lunch: $4-$9   **Dinner:** $10-$24   **Phone:** 727/360-1029   (177)
Location: SR 699, 1 mi n of Pinellas Bayway. 5799 Gulf Blvd 33706. **Hours:** 7 am-11 pm. **Reservations:** suggested. **Features:** Very popular locally, the restaurant has a contemporary design and welcoming staff. On the menu are a good variety of breakfast items—omelets, waffles and croissants—as well as numerous lunch and dinner entrees, home-cooked selections and Greek specialties. Casual dress; cocktails. **Parking:** on-site. **Cards:** AX, DC, DS, MC, VI.

SPINNERS ROOFTOP REVOLVING LOUNGE & BISTRO
American
Lunch: $8-$20   **Dinner:** $16-$40   **Phone:** 727/360-1811   (180)
Location: On SR 699, 1 mi n of Pinellas Bayway; in Holiday Inn Hotel & Suites Beachfront Resort & Conference Center. 5250 Gulf Blvd 33706. **Hours:** 6:30 am-11 pm. **Reservations:** not accepted, required 4/16, 5/14, 11/23, 12/25. **Features:** The revolving rooftop location affords great views of the city, Intracoastal Waterway and gulf sunsets. On the menu are steaks, chicken, pork, pasta and seafood dishes, as well as surf and turf. Casual dress; cocktails. **Parking:** on-site. **Cards:** AX, DC, DS, MC, VI.

STARLITE DINER
American
Lunch: $6-$13   **Dinner:** $6-$13   **Phone:** 727/363-0434   (181)
Location: On SR 699, 2.1 mi n of Pinellas Bayway. 5200 Gulf Blvd 33706. **Hours:** 7 am-9 pm. Closed: 12/25. **Features:** A '50s-style diner, complete with red vinyl upholstery and vintage signs, features mainly sandwiches, but you'll find selections like pork chops, mashed potatoes and vegetables, too. So put on your poodle skirt and bobby socks and sip on a Coke float. Casual dress. **Parking:** on-site. **Cards:** MC, VI.

THE WHARF SEAFOOD RESTAURANT
Seafood
Lunch: $5-$16   **Dinner:** $5-$16   **Phone:** 727/367-9469   (187)
Location: On SR 699, 0.9 mi s of Pinellas Bayway; in Historic Pass-A-Grille. 2001 Pass-A-Grille Way 33706. **Hours:** 11 am-11 pm. Closed: 12/25; also 9/5-9/8. **Features:** A weathered exterior lends to the rustic appeal of the casual, nautically themed restaurant, which affords great views from its location on the Intracoastal Waterway. Dine on the deck and sample choices from the oyster bar. Seafood is the menu's primary focus. Casual dress; cocktails. **Parking:** on-site. **Cards:** AX, DS, MC, VI.

SEFFNER pop. 5,467   (See map and index starting on p. 950)

——— WHERE TO DINE ———

BEEF O'BRADY'S OF SEFFNER
American
Lunch: $4-$9   **Dinner:** $4-$9   **Phone:** 813/661-7343   (216)
Location: Jct Parsons Ave. 812 Dr Martin Luther King Jr Blvd W 33584. **Hours:** 11 am-11 pm, Sun noon-10 pm. **Closed:** 4/16, 11/23, 12/25. **Features:** Patrons can watch sports programs on the many television monitors strategically placed around the dining room. Buffalo wings and Philly cheese steak are favorite choices. Casual dress; cocktails. **Parking:** on-site. **Cards:** AX, DS, MC, VI.

CHINA WOK CHINESE FOOD
Chinese
Lunch: $4-$12   **Dinner:** $4-$12   **Phone:** 813/653-9998   (212)
Location: I-75, exit 260, 1.2 mi e on SR 574, jct Lakewood Dr. 11212 E Martin Luther King Jr Blvd 33584. **Hours:** 10:30 am-10 pm, Fri & Sat-10:30 pm, Sun noon-10 pm. **Features:** With literally 200 items listed, the menu offers something for almost everyone. Among dishes are seafood delight, sweet and sour chicken, mu shu beef, moo goo gai pan, Gen. Tso's chicken, pepper steak and lo mein. Casual dress. **Parking:** on-site. **Cards:** MC, VI.

JR'S FLORIBBEAN OUTPOST
Barbecue
Lunch: $6-$16   **Dinner:** $6-$16   **Phone:** 813/655-1760   (218)
Location: Just s of jct Martin Luther King Jr Blvd. 1001 US Hwy 92 33584. **Hours:** 11 am-9 pm. **Closed:** Mon. **Features:** Southern and jerk-style ribs, pork, beef, chicken and steaks are among offerings at the cozy little eatery. The on-site "Hot Sauce Emporium" offers a choice of hundreds of hot sauces. Casual dress. **Parking:** on-site. **Cards:** MC, VI.

LATIN CUISINE
Spanish
Lunch: $4-$7   **Dinner:** $4-$7   **Phone:** 813/662-3611   (213)
Location: I-75, exit 260, 1.2 mi e on SR 574, jct Lakewood Dr. 11204 E Martin Luther King Jr Blvd 33584. **Hours:** 8:30 am-8 pm, Sat 10 am-7 pm, Mon 8:30 am-7 pm. **Closed:** Sun. **Features:** Spanish breakfast, lunch and dinner items are served at the family-owned-and-operated restaurant. Meal choices include palomilla steak, arroz con pollo and pollo picante; sides of mofongo, platanos and yuca enhance the meal. Casual dress. **Parking:** on-site. **Cards:** MC, VI.

POT BELLIES B-B-QUE
Barbecue
Lunch: $6-$16   **Dinner:** $6-$16   **Phone:** 813/657-6242   (217)
Location: Just s of jct Martin Luther King Jr Blvd. 2006 N Parsons Ave 33584. **Hours:** 10:30 am-9 pm. **Closed:** Mon. **Features:** A friendly, down-home service staff awaits at the rustic little spot known for its barbecue dinners. Choices include barbecue sliced pork, smoked ham, pork chops, baby back ribs, St. Louis ribs, fried grouper, flounder, catfish and various steaks. Add a couple of side dishes—such as fried green tomatoes, fried okra, grits or black eyed peas—for a good ol' country meal. Casual dress. **Parking:** on-site. **Cards:** MC, VI.

STACEY'S HOMESTYLE BUFFET
American
Lunch: $6   **Dinner:** $8   **Phone:** 813/657-6446   (214)
Location: Jct Parsons Ave; in Parsons Village Square. 790 Martin Luther King Jr Blvd 33584. **Hours:** 11 am-8 pm, Fri & Sat-8:30 pm. **Features:** The staff is friendly and the surroundings comfy at the buffet-style restaurant. Diners serve themselves heaping helpings of fried chicken, meatloaf, fried catfish and even pizza, along with many types of vegetables. An ample salad bar appeals to those who love a good salad. Plentiful desserts range from pie to cake to soft-serve ice cream. Casual dress. **Parking:** on-site. **Cards:** MC, VI.

YOUNG BIN CHINESE RESTAURANT
Chinese
Lunch: $5-$12   **Dinner:** $5-$12   **Phone:** 813/685-5458   (215)
Location: Jct Parsons Ave; in Parsons Village Square. 720 Martin Luther King Jr Blvd 33584. **Hours:** 11:30 am-10 pm, Sun from noon. **Features:** Cozy surroundings and pleasant service characterize this spot in a popular strip mall. With nearly 200 choices, the expansive menu is bound to feed any Chinese craving. Among dishes are chow mein, lo mein, chop suey, mu shu and such noteworthy chef specialties as orange beef, Gen. Tso's chicken, bourbon chicken and seafood delight. Casual dress. **Parking:** on-site. **Cards:** MC, VI.

SEMINOLE pop. 10,890   (See map and index starting on p. 938)

——— WHERE TO DINE ———

ANDRE'S CAPO DE MONTE ITALIAN DELI
Italian
Lunch: $6-$8   **Dinner:** $6-$8   **Phone:** 727/394-7800   (128)
Location: On US Alternate Rt 19, just n of jct of Park Blvd. 8400 Seminole Blvd 33772. **Hours:** 10 am-7 pm, Sat-3 pm, Mon-6 pm. **Closed:** 1/1, 11/23, 12/25; also Sun. **Features:** The family-owned-and-operated delicatessen prepares fresh salads, hot and cold submarine sandwiches and cheese steak, as well as such classics as baked lasagna, ziti, manicotti, ravioli and meatballs or sausage. There is also a small grocery area where imported Italian items are sold. Catering is a specialty, and all types of Italian meat and cheese trays are available. Casual dress; beer & wine only. **Parking:** on-site. **Cards:** AX, MC, VI.

BEEF 'O'BRADY'S
American
Lunch: $6-$10   **Dinner:** $6-$10   **Phone:** 727/393-2880   (129)
Location: Jct Seminole Blvd. 10799 Park Blvd 33772. **Hours:** 11 am-11 pm, Sun noon-10 pm. **Closed:** 4/16, 11/23, 12/25. **Features:** Patrons can watch sports programs on the many television monitors strategically placed around the dining room. Buffalo wings and Philly cheese steak are favorite choices. Casual dress; beer & wine only. **Parking:** on-site. **Cards:** AX, DC, DS, MC, VI.

SOUTH PASADENA pop. 5,778   (See map and index starting on p. 938)

——— WHERE TO DINE ———

HORSE & JOCKEY BRITISH RESTAURANT & BAR
English
Lunch: $5-$7   **Dinner:** $7-$11   **Phone:** 727/345-4995   (164)
Location: Just s of jct Gulfport Blvd; in Pasadena Square. 1155 Pasadena Ave S 33707. **Hours:** 11 am-10 pm, Sat from 4 pm, Sun noon-9 pm. **Closed:** 7/4, 12/25. **Features:** Fresh British specialties are served along with American favorites in pub-style surroundings. Order the fish 'n' chips in a tasty batter, bangers and mash, or cottage pie. Dine at ease with professional servers who provide knowledgeable, observant care. Casual dress; beer & wine only. **Parking:** on-site. **Cards:** AX, DS, MC, VI.

(See map and index starting on p. 938)

PASADENA STEAK HOUSE   **Lunch:** $5-$8   **Dinner:** $11-$22   **Phone:** 727/341-1711   (165)
▼▼▼ ▼▼▼   **Location:** Jct Huffman Way. 1530 Pasadena Ave S 33707. **Hours:** 11 am-10 pm. **Reservations:** accepted.
    Features: Great steaks are the draw at the popular steakhouse, which employs an eager-to-please staff.
Steak House   Casual dress; cocktails. **Parking:** on-site. **Cards:** AX, CB, DC, DS, MC, VI.

SUN CITY CENTER

━━━━━━━━━ **WHERE TO STAY** ━━━━━━━━━

COMFORT INN-SUN CITY CENTER   **Book at aaa.com**   **Phone:** (813)633-3318

(AAA) (SAVE)	1/16-4/30 [ECP]	1P: $100-$109	2P: $119-$129	XP: $10	F12
	12/16-1/15 [ECP]	1P: $80-$90	2P: $85-$95	XP: $10	F12
▼▼ ▼▼▼	12/1-12/15 [ECP]	1P: $70-$80	2P: $75-$85	XP: $10	F12
Motel	5/1-11/30 [ECP]	1P: $60-$70	2P: $65-$75	XP: $10	F12

Location: I-75, exit 240A southbound; exit 240 northbound, 0.5 mi e on SR 674. 718 Cypress Village Blvd 33573.
Fax: 813/633-2747. **Facility:** 74 units. 67 one-bedroom standard units. 7 one-bedroom suites ($159-$179)
with efficiencies (no utensils). 2 stories, exterior corridors. **Bath:** combo or shower only. **Parking:** on-site. **Terms:** 7 day
cancellation notice. **Amenities:** irons, hair dryers. **Pool(s):** outdoor. **Leisure Activities:** whirlpool. **Guest Services:** coin
laundry. **Business Services:** fax (fee). **Cards:** AX, DC, DS, MC, VI. **Special Amenities:** free expanded continental breakfast
and free local telephone calls.

SOME UNITS

━━━━━━━━━ **WHERE TO DINE** ━━━━━━━━━

BEEF 'O'BRADY'S   **Lunch:** $5-$8   **Dinner:** $5-$8   **Phone:** 813/633-2333
▼▼ ▼▼   **Location:** I-75, exit 240A southbound; exit 240 northbound, 0.5 mi e on SR 674. 723 Cypress Village Blvd 33573.
    Hours: 11 am-11 pm, Sun noon-10 pm. **Features:** Established in 1985, the popular sports-themed
American   restaurant is known for its great burgers, sandwiches, baskets, soups, salads and the favorite buffalo wings.
Patrons can savor a meal while watching a sports program on any one of the strategically placed TVs.
Casual dress; cocktails. **Parking:** on-site. **Cards:** MC, VI.

SONNY'S REAL PIT BAR-B-Q   **Lunch:** $5-$18   **Dinner:** $5-$18   **Phone:** 813/642-0907
▼▼ ▼▼   **Location:** I-75, exit 240A southbound; exit 240 northbound, 0.5 mi e on SR 674. 724 Cypress Village Blvd 33573.
    Hours: 11 am-9:30 pm, Fri & Sat-10 pm, Sun-9 pm. **Features:** Around since 1968, the restaurant prepares
Barbecue   outstanding barbecue, including dinner plates, combination platters and mouthwatering baby back ribs. It's
hard to go wrong with any of the choices. The extensive salad bar lines up all types of fresh fruits,
vegetables, soups and fixings. Casual dress. **Parking:** on-site. **Cards:** MC, VI.

TARPON SPRINGS pop. 21,003

━━━━━━━━━ **WHERE TO STAY** ━━━━━━━━━

BAVARIAN INN   **Phone:** 727/939-0850

(AAA) (SAVE)	12/1-4/30 & 10/31-11/30 [BP]	1P: $80-$135	2P: $80-$135	XP: $20
▼▼ ▼▼	5/1-10/30 [BP]	1P: $60-$100	2P: $60-$100	XP: $20

Historic Bed   **Location:** SR 582, 0.6 mi w of jct US 19; in historic district. 427 E Tarpon Ave 34689. Fax: 727/945-8647.
& Breakfast   **Facility:** The inn, built in 1904, combines American elegance with European charm to create a friendly,
relaxing atmosphere, including a porch area and a sundeck. Designated smoking area. 9 one-bedroom
standard units. 2 stories, interior corridors. **Bath:** combo or shower only. **Parking:** on-site. **Terms:** weekly
rates available. **Amenities:** video library. Some: DVD players, hair dryers. **Leisure Activities:**
Fee: massage. **Guest Services:** gift shop, coin laundry. **Business Services:** meeting rooms, fax. **Cards:** MC, VI.
Special Amenities: free full breakfast and free local telephone calls.

FEE

HOLIDAY INN HOTEL & SUITES   **Book at aaa.com**   **Phone:** (727)934-5781

▼▼ ▼▼▼	12/1-6/1	1P: $99-$149	2P: $99-$149
	6/2-11/30	1P: $79-$129	2P: $79-$129

Small-scale Hotel   **Location:** On US 19, jct Klosterman Rd. 38724 US Hwy 19 N 34689. Fax: 727/934-1755. **Facility:** 110 units. 79
one-bedroom standard units. 31 one-bedroom suites. 1-3 stories, interior/exterior corridors. **Bath:** combo or
shower only. **Parking:** on-site. **Terms:** check-in 4 pm. **Amenities:** video games (fee), high-speed Internet, dual phone lines,
voice mail, irons. Some: hair dryers. **Pool(s):** heated outdoor. **Leisure Activities:** whirlpool, exercise room. **Guest Services:**
valet and coin laundry. **Business Services:** meeting rooms, fax (fee). **Cards:** AX, CB, DC, DS, JC, MC, VI.

SOME UNITS

━━━━━━━━━ **WHERE TO DINE** ━━━━━━━━━

BRIDIE GANNON'S IRISH PUB & EATERY   **Lunch:** $4-$18   **Dinner:** $6-$18   **Phone:** 727/942-3011
▼▼ ▼▼   **Location:** Jct Stafford; downtown. 200 Tarpon Ave 34689. **Hours:** 11 am-midnight, Fri & Sat-2 am, Sun 1 pm-
    midnight. Closed: 1/1, 11/23, 12/25. **Features:** The Irish-themed eatery offers a relaxing atmosphere and
Irish   friendly service. Representative of the many traditional dishes are corned beef and cabbage, fish and chips,
bangers and mash and shepherd's pie. Among other choices are soups, salads, burgers, sandwiches and
even filet mignon. Live entertainment is on hand Thursday through Saturday. Casual dress; cocktails. **Parking:** street.
Cards: AX, DS, MC, VI.

COSTA'S RESTAURANT **Lunch:** $5-$14 **Dinner:** $5-$14 **Phone:** 727/938-6890
▼▼▼ ▼▼▼ **Location:** At Sponge Docks; 0.5 mi w on Dodecanese Blvd from jct Alternate US 19, just s. 521 Athens St 34689.
Greek **Hours:** 11 am-10 pm. **Closed:** 12/25. **Features:** Imagine what the sponge divers ate after a day in the sun, and you'll find these authentic Greek dishes and seafood specialties all the more intriguing. Snapper that is char-broiled and seasoned with garlic and sauteed in olive oil brings new meaning to the word "tasty.".
Casual dress; beer & wine only. **Parking:** on-site. **Cards:** AX, DC, DS, MC, VI.

HELLA'S RESTAURANT & BAKERY **Lunch:** $6-$10 **Dinner:** $6-$22 **Phone:** 727/943-2400
▼▼▼ ▼▼▼ **Location:** Center; at Sponge Docks. 785 Dodecanese Blvd 34689. **Hours:** 11 am-10 pm, Fri & Sat-11 pm.
Greek **Reservations:** suggested. **Features:** A family operation since 1970, the restaurant offers a wide range of authentic Greek and Mediterranean fare from fFeta cheese to gyros, spanakopita, dolmades, fresh local seafood and lamb dishes. An extensive list of Greek desserts are made on the premises. Dressy casual;
cocktails. **Parking:** street. **Cards:** AX, CB, DC, DS, MC, VI.

TASTE OF GREECE **Lunch:** $5-$15 **Dinner:** $5-$15 **Phone:** 727/938-0088
▼▼▼ ▼▼▼ **Location:** Center; at Sponge Docks. 709 Dodecanese Blvd 34689. **Hours:** 9 am-9 pm. **Features:** The Greek
Greek restaurant is a comfortable retreat from shopping amid the many favorite haunts. The menu boasts such items as souvlaki, moussaka, pastitsio, dolmades, tiropite or spanakopita. The popular chicken kebab is a must. Homemade desserts are beautifully displayed and enticing. Casual dress; cocktails. **Parking:** street.
Cards: AX, DC, DS, MC, VI.

TEMPLE TERRACE pop. 20,918 (See map and index starting on p. 950)

——— WHERE TO STAY ———

EXTENDED STAYAMERICA *Book at aaa.com* **Phone:** (813)989-2264 **73**
▼▼ ▼▼
1/16-5/1	1P: $85-$110	2P: $90-$115
5/2-11/30	1P: $70-$90	2P: $75-$95
12/1-1/15	1P: $60-$80	2P: $65-$85

Small-scale Hotel **Location:** I-75, exit 266, just w on Fletcher Ave (CR 582A). 12242 Morris Bridge Rd 33637. **Fax:** 813/989-1184.
Facility: 101 one-bedroom standard units with efficiencies. 3 stories, interior corridors. *Bath:* combo or shower only. **Parking:** on-site. **Terms:** office hours 7 am-11 pm, cancellation fee imposed, pets ($25-$75 extra charge, limit 1). **Amenities:** voice mail, irons. *Some:* hair dryers. **Guest Services:** coin laundry. **Business Services:** fax (fee). **Cards:** AX, CB, DC, DS, MC, VI.

SOME UNITS
(ASK) (SD) 🐾 (¶↓) (&M) 🛏 🔽 📷 (DATA PORT) 🛢 🖬 🖵 /⊠/
FEE

FAIRFIELD INN TAMPA NORTH *Book at aaa.com* **Phone:** 813/989-0007 **74**
▼▼ ▼▼ Property failed to provide current rates
Small-scale Hotel **Location:** I-75, exit 266, just w on Fletcher Ave (CR 582A). 12260 Morris Bridge Rd 33637. **Fax:** 813/988-0255.
Facility: 83 one-bedroom standard units. 3 stories, interior corridors. *Bath:* combo or shower only. **Parking:** on-site. **Amenities:** high-speed Internet, irons, hair dryers. **Pool(s):** outdoor. **Leisure Activities:** whirlpool,
exercise room. **Guest Services:** valet laundry. **Business Services:** fax.

SOME UNITS
(¶↓) (&M) 🛏 🔽 🐦 📷 (DATA PORT) 🖵 /⊠/ 🛢 🖬 /

HILTON GARDEN INN TAMPA NORTH *Book at aaa.com* **Phone:** (813)342-5000 **77**
▼▼▼ ▼▼▼
1/16-5/15	1P: $89-$189	2P: $89-$189	XP: $10	F18
5/16-11/30	1P: $89-$139	2P: $89-$139	XP: $10	F18
12/1-1/15	1P: $79-$129	2P: $79-$129	XP: $10	F18

Small-scale Hotel **Location:** I-75, exit 266, just w on Fletcher Ave (CR 582A), then just s on Morris Bridge Rd; in Tampa Oaks Office Park.
13305 Tampa Oaks Blvd 33637. **Fax:** 813/342-6000. **Facility:** 148 units. 126 one-bedroom standard units. 22 one-bedroom suites ($89-$239). 6 stories, interior corridors. *Bath:* combo or shower only. **Parking:** on-site. **Terms:** check-in 4 pm, cancellation fee imposed, package plans. **Amenities:** video games (fee), high-speed Internet, dual phone lines, voice mail, irons, hair dryers. **Pool(s):** heated outdoor. **Leisure Activities:** whirlpool, exercise room. *Fee:* game room. **Guest Services:** sundries, valet and coin laundry. **Business Services:** meeting rooms, business center. **Cards:** AX, CB, DC, DS, JC, MC, VI.

SOME UNITS
(ASK) (¶↓) 🍷 (&M) 🛏 🔽 🐦 ⊠ 📷 (DATA PORT) 🛢 🖬 🖵 /⊠/

RESIDENCE INN BY MARRIOTT TAMPA NORTH *Book at aaa.com* **Phone:** 813/972-4400 **76**
▼▼▼ ▼▼▼ Property failed to provide current rates
Small-scale Hotel **Location:** I-75, exit 266, 1.1 mi w on Fletcher Ave (CR 582A); in Telecom Tampa Park. 13420 N Telecom Pkwy 33637.
Fax: 813/972-3376. **Facility:** 78 units. 66 one- and 12 two-bedroom suites with kitchens. 3 stories, interior corridors. *Bath:* combo or shower only. **Parking:** on-site. **Terms:** pets ($125 fee). **Amenities:** high-speed Internet, voice mail, irons, hair dryers. **Pool(s):** heated outdoor. **Leisure Activities:** whirlpool, exercise room, sports court. **Guest Services:** complimentary evening beverages, valet and coin laundry. **Business Services:** meeting rooms, business center.

SOME UNITS
🐾 (¶↓) (&M) 🛏 🔽 🐦 ⊠ 📷 (DATA PORT) 🛢 🖬 🖵 /⊠/
FEE

SLEEP INN TEMPLE TERRACE USF NEAR BUSCH
GARDENS *Book at aaa.com* **Phone:** (813)988-4048 **75**
(AAA) (SAVE)
1/16-4/15	1P: $80	2P: $80	XP: $10	F16
12/1-1/15 & 4/16-11/30	1P: $75	2P: $75	XP: $10	F16

▼▼▼ ▼▼▼ **Location:** I-75, exit 266, just w on Fletcher Ave (CR 582A). 12282 Morris Bridge Rd 33637. **Fax:** 813/989-1659.
Small-scale Hotel **Facility:** 83 units. 81 one-bedroom standard units. 2 one-bedroom suites ($99-$130). 4 stories, interior corridors. *Bath:* combo or shower only. **Parking:** on-site. **Terms:** weekly rates available. **Amenities:** high-speed Internet. *Some:* irons, hair dryers. **Pool(s):** heated outdoor. **Leisure Activities:** basketball. **Guest Services:** valet and coin laundry. **Business Services:** meeting rooms, fax. **Cards:** AX, DC, DS, MC, VI. **Special Amenities:** free continental breakfast and free local telephone calls.

SOME UNITS
(SD) (¶↓) (&M) 🛏 🔽 🐦 ⊠ 📷 (DATA PORT) /⊠/ 🛢 🖬 🖵 /

(See map and index starting on p. 950)

———— WHERE TO DINE ————

BEEF 'O' BRADY'S
◆◆◆ ◆◆
American
Lunch: $6-$9   **Dinner:** $6-$9   **Phone:** 813/989-9125   (135)
Location: I-75, exit 265, 2.8 mi w; in People's Plaza. 5025 E Fowler Ave 33617. **Hours:** 11 am-11 pm, Fri & Sat-midnight. **Features:** The restaurant is a fun dining spot, especially for those who enjoy watching sports. Monitors placed strategically around the dining room show varied events at any given time. Most entrees are of the sandwich and finger-food variety. Grilled grouper salad is a must-try, as are the chicken wings for which this place is known. Casual dress; cocktails. **Parking:** on-site. **Cards:** MC, VI.

CLUBHOUSE SPORTS CAFE
◆
American
Lunch: $6-$10   **Dinner:** $6-$10   **Phone:** 813/914-7779   (137)
Location: I-75, exit 265, 2 mi w on SR 582, jct N 56th St; in Terrace Walk. 5621 E Fowler Ave 33617. **Hours:** 11 am-11 pm, Sun from noon. Closed: 4/16, 11/23, 12/25. **Features:** The cafe is a fun spot to stop for a sandwich, burger, salad or any one of the many appetizers. Well-placed TV monitors show sporting events. Casual dress; cocktails. **Parking:** on-site. **Cards:** AX, MC, VI.
(⎕M)

TOKYO JAPANESE RESTAURANT & SUSHI BAR
◆◆◆ ◆◆
Japanese
Lunch: $7-$16   **Dinner:** $7-$16   **Phone:** 813/983-1822   (136)
Location: I-75, exit 265, 2 mi w on SR 582 at N 56th St; in Terrace Walk. 5711 E Fowler Ave 33617. **Hours:** 11 am-2:30 & 5:30-9:30 pm, Fri-10:30 pm, Sat 5 pm-10:30 pm, Sun 5:30 pm-10 pm. Closed: 11/23, 12/25. **Features:** The staff is professional and welcoming, and their graciousness is a plus. Although the menu incorporates several hot, cooked items, the emphasis is on fresh sushi. Casual dress. **Parking:** on-site. **Cards:** AX, DS, MC, VI.

VALLARTO'S RESTAURANTE MEXICANO
◆◆◆ ◆◆
Mexican
Lunch: $6-$11   **Dinner:** $6-$11   **Phone:** 813/987-2720   (138)
Location: Just s of jct Busch Blvd. 9255 N 54th St 33617. **Hours:** 11 am-10 pm. **Features:** More than 60 preparations of authentic cuisine are served in decorative Southwestern surroundings. Chihuahua cheese is excellent with chips, and fajitas are a sizzling temptation. A colorful Mexican flair punctuates the dining room. Casual dress; beer & wine only. **Parking:** on-site. **Cards:** MC, VI.

TIERRA VERDE pop. 3,574 (See map and index starting on p. 938)

———— WHERE TO DINE ————

BILLY'S STONE CRAB & STEAKHOUSE
(AAA)
◆
Seafood
Menu on aaa.com
Lunch: $6-$22   **Dinner:** $10-$40   **Phone:** 727/866-2115   (192)
Location: 1 mi s. 1 Collany Rd 33715. **Hours:** 11:30 am-11 pm, Sun also 9-11 am. Closed: 11/23, 12/25. **Reservations:** accepted. **Features:** Diners can take in views of the marina while filling up on tasty seafood. Those who don't try the specialty stone crabs can choose from fried shrimp, oysters Rockefeller, gator nuggets or any of a number of other seafood favorites. For the landlubber, there are aged steaks and chicken dishes. Casual dress; cocktails; entertainment. **Parking:** on-site. **Cards:** AX, DC, MC, VI.
(Y)(◇)

TREASURE ISLAND pop. 7,450 (See map and index starting on p. 938)

———— WHERE TO STAY ————

BEST WESTERN SEA CASTLE SUITES   *Book at aaa.com*   **Phone:** (727)367-2704   (119)

(AAA) (SAVE)	2/10-4/22	1P: $159-$195	2P: $159-$195	XP: $10 F18
	4/23-8/10	1P: $99-$169	2P: $99-$169	XP: $10 F18
◆◆◆ ◆◆	12/1-2/9	1P: $79-$145	2P: $79-$145	XP: $10 F18
Motel	8/11-11/30	1P: $85-$129	2P: $85-$129	XP: $10 F18

Location: Oceanfront. On SR 699, jct Treasure Island Cswy. 10750 Gulf Blvd 33706. **Fax:** 727/360-2492. **Facility:** Designated smoking area. 41 one-bedroom suites with kitchens. 2-3 stories (no elevator), exterior corridors. **Parking:** on-site. **Terms:** [AP] meal plan available, package plans, small pets only ($50 deposit). **Amenities:** irons, hair dryers. **Pool(s):** heated outdoor. **Leisure Activities:** fishing, sun deck, barbecue grills, playground, shuffleboard. **Guest Services:** coin laundry. **Business Services:** fax (fee). **Cards:** AX, CB, DC, DS, MC, VI. **Special Amenities:** free local telephone calls and preferred room (subject to availability with advance reservations).
SOME UNITS
(SD) (🐾) (FEE) (🍴) (≋) (⊠) (✕) (🛎) (DATA PORT) (🔒) (▣) (/🖨/) (FEE)

BEST WESTERN TREASURE ISLAND   *Book at aaa.com*   **Phone:** (727)360-6971   (118)

◆◆◆ ◆◆	All Year	1P: $80-$180	2P: $80-$180	XP: $10 F17
Motel				

Location: On SR 699, just n of jct Treasure Island Cswy. 11125 Gulf Blvd 33706. **Fax:** 727/360-9014. **Facility:** 84 one-bedroom standard units. 3 stories, interior corridors. *Bath:* combo or shower only. **Parking:** on-site. **Terms:** cancellation fee imposed. **Amenities:** high-speed Internet, safes (fee), irons, hair dryers. **Pool(s):** heated outdoor. **Leisure Activities:** boat dock, fishing, playground. **Guest Services:** valet and coin laundry. **Business Services:** meeting rooms, fax. **Cards:** AX, CB, DC, DS, MC, VI. *(See color ad p 1038)*
SOME UNITS
(ASK) (SD) (🍴) (⎕M) (🐾) (≋) (⊠) (✕) (🛎) (DATA PORT) (🔒) (▣) (/✕/)

BILMAR BEACH RESORT   *Book at aaa.com*   **Phone:** (727)360-5531   (121)

(AAA) (SAVE)	2/13-4/22	1P: $229-$425	2P: $229-$425	XP: $10 F18
	12/24-2/12 & 4/23-11/30	1P: $169-$310	2P: $169-$310	XP: $10 F18
◆◆◆ ◆◆	12/1-12/23	1P: $139-$295	2P: $139-$295	XP: $10 F18
Condominium				

Location: Oceanfront. On SR 699, jct Treasure Island Cswy. 10650 Gulf Blvd 33706. **Fax:** 727/360-2915. **Facility:** Located directly on the Gulf, this expansive property offers lovely guest rooms with such conveniences as kitchens, full baths and large living areas. Designated smoking area. 166 units. 159 one-bedroom standard units, some with efficiencies. 6 one- and 1 two-bedroom suites ($300-$600), some with kitchens. 3-8 stories, interior/exterior corridors. *Bath:* combo or shower only. **Parking:** on-site. **Terms:** 3 day cancellation notice, package plans. **Amenities:** CD players, dual phone lines, voice mail, safes (fee), irons, hair dryers. **Dining:** 7 am-10 pm, cocktails, also, Sloppy Joe's On The Beach, see separate listing, entertainment. **Pool(s):** 2 heated outdoor. **Leisure Activities:** whirlpool, fishing, sun deck, jogging, exercise room, volleyball. *Fee:* cabanas, bicycles. **Guest Services:** gift shop, valet and coin laundry. **Business Services:** conference facilities, fax (fee). **Cards:** AX, CB, DC, DS, JC, MC, VI. **Special Amenities:** preferred room (subject to availability with advance reservations).
(SD) (🍴) (Y) (♿) (🐾) (≋) (⊠) (✕) (🛎) (DATA PORT) (🔒) (▣) (🖨)

(See map and index starting on p. 938)

GULF SOUNDS ON TREASURE ISLAND

Phone: (727)363-6114   **110**

2/1-4/30	1P: $95-$140	2P: $95-$140	XP: $8	F12
12/1-1/31	1P: $85-$115	2P: $85-$115	XP: $8	F12
5/1-8/31	1P: $75-$105	2P: $75-$105	XP: $8	F12
9/1-11/30	1P: $65-$95	2P: $65-$95	XP: $8	F12

Condominium

Location: On SR 699, 0.6 mi s of Johns Pass. 12240 Gulf Blvd 33706. **Fax:** 727/363-8041. **Facility:** Designated smoking area. 5 units. 1 one-bedroom standard unit with efficiency. 4 two-bedroom suites with kitchens. 1-2 stories, exterior corridors. **Parking:** on-site. **Terms:** office hours 9 am-9 pm, 30 day cancellation notice-fee imposed, weekly rates available. **Amenities:** voice mail. *Some:* irons, hair dryers. **Leisure Activities:** beach access. **Guest Services:** coin laundry. **Business Services:** fax. **Cards:** AX, DS, MC, VI.

(ASK) (SA) (111) (X) (DATA PORT) (■) (■) (■)

HOLIDAY INN-TREASURE ISLAND BEACH   *Book at aaa.com*

Phone: 727/367-2761   **112**

Property failed to provide current rates

Large-scale Hotel

Location: On SR 699, 0.8 mi n of jct Treasure Island Cswy. 11908 Gulf Blvd 33706. **Fax:** 727/367-9446. **Facility:** 117 one-bedroom standard units. 9 stories, interior corridors. **Parking:** on-site. **Terms:** check-in 4 pm. **Amenities:** voice mail, irons, hair dryers. **Pool(s):** heated outdoor. **Leisure Activities:** whirlpool, exercise room. *Fee:* game room. **Guest Services:** valet and coin laundry. **Business Services:** fax (fee).

SOME UNITS

(111) (Y) (2) (2) (X) (F) (DATA PORT) (■) / (X) (■) / FEE

JAMAICAN ON THE GULF

Phone: 727/360-6981   **114**

All Year Wkly   1P: $750-$930

Condominium

Location: Oceanfront. On SR 699 (Tom Stuart Cswy), 0.5 mi n of jct Treasure Island Cswy. 11660 Gulf Blvd 33706. **Fax:** 727/367-3749. **Facility:** 34 units. 22 one- and 12 two-bedroom suites with kitchens and whirlpools. 6 stories, exterior corridors. **Parking:** on-site. **Terms:** office hours 9 am-5 pm, 7 night minimum stay, 30 day cancellation notice-fee imposed. **Amenities:** irons, hair dryers. *Some:* CD players. **Pool(s):** heated outdoor. **Leisure Activities:** whirlpool, shuffleboard. **Guest Services:** complimentary laundry. **Business Services:** fax (fee). **Cards:** MC, VI.

(111) (2) (VCR) (DATA PORT) (■) (■)

THE JEFFERSON MOTEL APTS.

Phone: 727/360-5826   **123**

2/1-4/30 Wkly	1P: $798	2P: $798	XP: $10
12/1-1/31 & 5/1-9/5 Wkly	1P: $602	2P: $602	XP: $10
9/6-11/30 Wkly	1P: $553	2P: $553	XP: $10

Motel

Location: Oceanfront. On SR 699, 0.6 mi s of jct Treasure Island Cswy. 10116 Gulf Blvd 33706. **Fax:** 727/367-9396. **Facility:** 14 one-bedroom suites with kitchens. 2-3 stories, exterior corridors. **Parking:** on-site. **Terms:** 28 day cancellation notice-fee imposed. **Amenities:** voice mail. *Some:* irons. **Pool(s):** heated outdoor. **Leisure Activities:** snorkeling, fishing, bicycles, horseshoes, shuffleboard, volleyball. **Cards:** MC, VI.

SOME UNITS

(2) (X) (DATA PORT) (■) (■) / (X) (VCR) /

(See map and index starting on p. 938)

MARDI GRAS MOTEL

Phone: 727/367-1621　**111**

◆ (diamond)

Motel

2/1-4/15	1P: $60-$70	2P: $60-$70	XP: $6	F12
12/1-1/31	1P: $55-$65	2P: $55-$65	XP: $6	F12
4/16-11/30	1P: $45-$55	2P: $45-$55	XP: $6	F12

Location: On SR 699, 0.7 mi n of jct Treasure Island Cswy. 11965 Gulf Blvd 33706. Fax: 727/360-5910. **Facility:** Designated smoking area. 10 one-bedroom standard units, some with efficiencies or kitchens. 2 stories, exterior corridors. **Parking:** on-site. **Terms:** office hours 9 am-10 pm, 3 night minimum stay - weekends, 14 day cancellation notice, weekly rates available. **Pool(s):** heated outdoor. **Cards:** DS, MC, VI.

PAGE TERRACE MOTEL

Phone: 727/367-1997　**122**

AAA SAVE ◆◆◆

Motel

2/1-4/23	2P: $78-$108	XP: $8	F5
12/1-1/31 & 4/24-9/3	2P: $66-$86	XP: $8	F5
9/4-11/30	2P: $52-$74	XP: $8	F5

Location: Oceanfront. On SR 699, just s of jct Treasure Island Cswy. 10500 Gulf Blvd 33706. Fax: 727/360-7179. **Facility:** 36 units. 31 one-bedroom standard units, some with efficiencies. 5 one-bedroom suites with kitchens. 3 stories (no elevator), interior/exterior corridors. **Parking:** on-site. **Terms:** office hours 8 am-11 pm, 14 day cancellation notice. **Amenities:** voice mail. *Some:* irons, hair dryers. **Pool(s):** heated outdoor. **Leisure Activities:** shuffleboard. **Guest Services:** coin laundry. **Business Services:** fax. **Cards:** AX, DS, MC, VI. **Special Amenities: early check-in/late check-out and free room upgrade (subject to availability with advance reservations).** *(See color ad p 1038)*

THE SEA CHEST

Phone: (727) 360-5501　**113**

AAA SAVE ◆◆◆

Motel

1/15-4/30	1P: $83-$139	2P: $83-$139	XP: $6
12/1-1/14	1P: $62-$106	2P: $62-$106	XP: $6
5/1-9/5	1P: $59-$97	2P: $59-$97	XP: $6
9/6-11/30	1P: $49-$83	2P: $49-$83	XP: $6

Location: Oceanfront. On SR 699, 0.5 mi n of jct Treasure Island Cswy. 11780 Gulf Blvd 33706. Fax: 727/360-8453. **Facility:** 21 one-bedroom standard units, some with efficiencies or kitchens. 2 stories, interior/exterior corridors. **Parking:** on-site. **Terms:** office hours 8 am-9 pm, 3 night minimum stay - seasonal and/or weekends, 30 day cancellation notice-fee imposed. **Amenities:** *Some:* irons, hair dryers. **Pool(s):** heated outdoor. **Leisure Activities:** gas barbecue, picnic area, table tennis, shuffleboard. **Guest Services:** coin laundry. **Cards:** AX, MC, VI.

SOUTH BEACH CONDO-HOTEL

Phone: 727/367-1991　**116**

◆◆◆

Condominium

Property failed to provide current rates

Location: Oceanfront. On SR 699, 0.5 mi n of Treasure Island Cswy. 11360 Gulf Blvd 33706. Fax: 727/368-0096. **Facility:** Enjoy wonderful sunset views at this condominium located on the Gulf of Mexico. Units are comfortable and offer all modern amenities. 40 units. 30 one- and 10 two-bedroom suites with kitchens. 6 stories, exterior corridors. **Bath:** combo or shower only. **Parking:** on-site. **Terms:** office hours 7 pm-5 pm. **Amenities:** high-speed Internet, dual phone lines, voice mail, safes, irons, hair dryers. **Pool(s):** heated outdoor. **Leisure Activities:** whirlpool, exercise room, horseshoes, shuffleboard, volleyball. *Fee:* massage. **Guest Services:** complimentary laundry. **Business Services:** PC, fax (fee).

SOME UNITS

(See map and index starting on p. 938)

TAHITIAN RESORT   Phone: 727/360-6264   **117**

(AAA) (SAVE)	2/1-4/23	1P: $95-$155	2P: $95-$155	XP: $10	F17
	4/24-8/6	1P: $65-$149	2P: $65-$149	XP: $10	F17
◇◇◇ ◇◇◇	12/1-1/31	1P: $59-$135	2P: $59-$135	XP: $10	F17
	8/7-11/30	1P: $59-$129	2P: $59-$129	XP: $10	F17

Motel **Location:** Oceanfront. On SR 699, 0.4 mi n of jct 107th Ave (Central Ave). 11320 Gulf Blvd 33706. Fax: 727/363-0070. **Facility:** 52 units. 26 one-bedroom standard units, some with efficiencies or kitchens. 24 one- and 2 two-bedroom suites with kitchens. 2 stories, exterior corridors. **Bath:** combo or shower only. **Parking:** on-site. **Terms:** office hours 8 am-10 pm, package plans. **Amenities:** *Some:* irons, hair dryers. **Pool(s):** heated outdoor. **Leisure Activities:** kids pool, barbecue grill, sun deck, playground, shuffleboard, volleyball. **Guest Services:** coin laundry. **Business Services:** PC, fax (fee). **Cards:** AX, DS, MC, VI. *(See color ad below)*

SOME UNITS

THUNDERBIRD BEACH RESORT   ***Book at aaa.com***   Phone: (727)367-1961   **120**

(AAA) (SAVE)	2/10-4/22	1P: $129-$199	2P: $129-$199	XP: $10	F17
	4/23-8/6	1P: $99-$189	2P: $99-$189	XP: $10	F17
◇◇◇ ◇◇◇	8/7-11/30	1P: $89-$155	2P: $89-$155	XP: $10	F17
	12/1-2/9	1P: $79-$155	2P: $79-$155	XP: $10	F17

Motel **Location:** Oceanfront. On SR 699, jct Treasure Island Cswy. 10700 Gulf Blvd 33706. Fax: 727/367-1961. **Parking:** on-site. **Amenities:** voice mail, safes, irons, hair dryers. **Dining:** 7 am-9 pm, Fri & Sat-10 pm. **Pool(s):** heated outdoor. **Leisure Activities:** whirlpool, volleyball. **Business Services:** meeting rooms, PC, fax. **Cards:** AX, DC, DS, MC, VI.
(See color ad below)

SOME UNITS

TRAILS END RESORT MOTEL   Phone: (727)360-5541   **115**

(AAA) (SAVE)	12/1-1/31	1P: $69-$159	XP: $10
	2/1-4/30	1P: $89-$149	XP: $10
◇◇◇	5/1-9/30	1P: $79-$129	XP: $10
	10/1-11/30	1P: $79-$128	XP: $10

Motel **Location:** Oceanfront. On SR 699, 0.5 mi n of jct Treasure Island Cswy. 11500 Gulf Blvd 33706. Fax: 727/360-1508. **Facility:** 54 one-bedroom standard units, some with efficiencies or kitchens. 1-2 stories, exterior corridors. **Bath:** combo or shower only. **Parking:** on-site. **Terms:** 2-7 night minimum stay - seasonal and/or weekends, 30 day cancellation notice-fee imposed. **Amenities:** *Some:* irons, hair dryers. **Pool(s):** heated outdoor. **Leisure Activities:** fishing, barbecue grills, shuffleboard. **Guest Services:** coin laundry. **Business Services:** fax (fee). **Cards:** AX, CB, DC, DS, JC, MC, VI.
(See color ad below)

SOME UNITS

(See map and index starting on p. 938)

WHERE TO DINE

CADDY'S WATERFRONT BEACH BBQ & SEAFOOD RESTAURANT
Seafood

Lunch: $6-$14   **Dinner:** $6-$14   **Phone:** 727/360-4993   (158)
Location: Just w of jct SR 699 at Sunset Beach. 9000 W Gulf Blvd 33706. **Hours:** 11 am-11 pm. Closed: 12/25. **Features:** On the Gulf of Mexico, the casual, open-air restaurant beckons to patrons to come in and relax. Guests can enjoy fabulous sunset views while dining on such favorites as clam chowder and the fresh and tasty seafood basket. Casual dress; cocktails. **Parking:** on-site. **Cards:** AX, MC, VI.

CAFE BERLIN
German

Lunch: $3-$10   **Dinner:** $7-$14   **Phone:** 727/367-2495   (155)
Location: Just e of jct SR 699 (Gulf Blvd); in Treasure Island Shopping Plaza. 124 107th Ave 33706. **Hours:** 11:30 am-10 pm. Closed: 11/23, 12/25. **Features:** Pull up a chair in this authentic German diner and enjoy a night in Germany and a great selection of Bavarian dishes to choose from, including an all-time favorite, Sauerbraten. Casual dress; beer & wine only. **Parking:** on-site. **Cards:** MC, VI.

THE FLORIDIAN CUBAN SANDWICHES
American

Lunch: $4-$7   **Dinner:** $4-$7   **Phone:** 727/367-6662   (153)
Location: Just e of jct SR 699. 230 107th Ave 33706. **Hours:** 11 am-7 pm. Closed major holidays. **Reservations:** not accepted. **Features:** A short walk from the beach, the restaurant is a great spot for award-winning Cuban sandwiches. Among other offerings are roast turkey and spiced pork Cuban sandwiches. Add a bowl of black beans and yellow rice for a treat. Casual dress; beer only. **Parking:** on-site and street. **Cards:** AX, CB, DC, DS, MC, VI.

FOXY'S CAFE
American

Lunch: $4-$7   **Dinner:** $7-$14   **Phone:** 727/363-3699   (154)
Location: Just e of jct SR 699 (Gulf Blvd); in Treasure Island Shopping Plaza. 160 107th Ave 33706. **Hours:** 7 am-midnight, Fri & Sat to 3 am. **Reservations:** not accepted. **Features:** Enjoy fabulous large and hearty breakfasts cooked to your preference. A friendly staff will make you feel at home and will keep you coming back to this place where the locals meet. Casual dress. **Parking:** on-site. **Cards:** AX, MC, VI.

GATORS CAFE & SALOON
American

Lunch: $6-$16   **Dinner:** $6-$16   **Phone:** 727/367-8951   (152)
Location: 1 mi n of Treasure Island Cswy on SR 699, just e. 12754 Kingfish Dr 33706. **Hours:** 11 am-10 pm. **Features:** Great seafood meals and hearty sandwiches are menu favorites at the popular dining spot. Across from John's Pass on the Intracoastal Waterway, this spot affords views of the pass and its numerous boats or a great sunset. Indoor seating is limited, as the lengthy deck tends to entice most diners. Casual dress; cocktails; entertainment. **Parking:** on-site. **Cards:** MC, VI.

SLOPPY JOE'S ON THE BEACH
American

Lunch: $10-$21   **Dinner:** $10-$21   **Phone:** 727/367-1600   (156)
Location: On SR 699, jct Treasure Island Cswy; in Bilmar Beach Resort. 10650 Gulf Blvd 33706. **Hours:** 11 am-1 am. **Features:** Named after the famous Key West eatery visited by Ernest "Papa" Hemingway, the restaurant carries on the tradition with its menu choices, including "original Sloppy Joe's sandwiches" and macadamia nut-crusted grouper. Lovely views of the gulf and gorgeous sunsets can't be beat. Casual dress; cocktails; entertainment. **Parking:** on-site. **Cards:** AX, DS, MC, VI.

VIP SPORTS BAR & MEXICAN RESTAURANT
Mexican

Lunch: $5-$17   **Dinner:** $5-$17   **Phone:** 727/360-5062   (157)
Location: On SR 699, jct 107th Ave (Central Ave). 10625 Gulf Blvd 33706. **Hours:** 11 am-10:30 pm, Fri & Sat-11 pm, Sun 1 pm-10:30 pm. Closed: 11/23, 12/25. **Features:** Patrons can nosh on good Mexican fare while watching sporting events on well-placed television monitors. The small strip-mall eatery employs friendly servers. A must-try is the wet burrito, a specialty here. Casual dress; cocktails. **Parking:** on-site. **Cards:** AX, DS, MC, VI.

WESLEY CHAPEL pop. 5,691

WHERE TO STAY

BEST WESTERN SUMMER CREST
(fyi)
Small-scale Hotel

2/1-3/31	1P: $75-$89	2P: $75-$89	XP: $10	F18
12/1-1/31	1P: $67-$79	2P: $67-$79	XP: $10	F18
4/1-11/30	1P: $63-$74	2P: $63-$74	XP: $10	F18

Phone: 813/345-2000
Too new to rate. **Location:** I-75, exit 279, just w on SR 54, then just n. 5639 Oakley Blvd 33543. Fax: 813/345-2001. **Amenities:** 72 units, coffeemakers, microwaves, refrigerators, pool. **Cards:** AX, CB, DC, DS, MC, VI.

HOLIDAY INN EXPRESS   *Book at aaa.com*
AAA SAVE
Small-scale Hotel

1/21-4/18	1P: $85-$99	2P: $85-$99	
12/1-1/20 & 6/1-11/30	1P: $79-$89	2P: $79-$89	
4/19-5/31	1P: $69-$79	2P: $69-$79	

Phone: (813)907-1379
Location: I-75, exit 279, just w. 27615 SR 54 W 33543. Fax: 813/907-8421. **Facility:** 82 units. 80 one-bedroom standard units. 2 one-bedroom suites. 4 stories, interior corridors. *Bath:* combo or shower only. **Parking:** on-site. **Terms:** cancellation fee imposed, [CP] meal plan available. **Amenities:** high-speed Internet, dual phone lines, voice mail, safes, irons, hair dryers. **Pool(s):** outdoor. **Guest Services:** valet laundry. **Business Services:** meeting rooms, business center. **Cards:** AX, DC, DS, MC, VI. **Special Amenities: free continental breakfast and free local telephone calls.**

SOME UNITS

MASTERS INN TAMPA NORTH   *Book at aaa.com*   Phone: (813)973-0155
AAA SAVE
All Year   1P: $49-$63   XP: $4   F18
Location: I-75, exit 279, just w. 27807 SR 54 W 33543. Fax: 813/973-0210. Facility: 119 one-bedroom standard units. 2 stories, exterior corridors. Parking: on-site. Terms: pets ($10 extra charge). Dining: 24 hours. Pool(s): outdoor. Leisure Activities: barbecue grill. Guest Services: coin laundry. Business Services: meeting rooms, fax. Cards: AX, CB, DC, DS, MC, VI. Special Amenities: free local telephone calls.

Motel

SOME UNITS

SADDLEBROOK RESORT TAMPA   Phone: 813/973-1111

[fyi]   Property failed to provide current rates
Under major renovation, scheduled to be completed April 2006. Last rated: Location: I-75, exit 279, 1.2 mi e on SR 54. 5700 Saddlebrook Way 33543. Fax: 813/973-4504. Facility: The resort offers large, hotel-style rooms as well as clusters of suites with kitchens, all on spacious, manicured grounds. 547 units. 133 one-bedroom standard units. 160 one- and 254 two-bedroom suites with kitchens, some with whirlpools. 2 stories, exterior corridors. Bath: combo or shower only. Parking: on-site (fee) and valet. Amenities: high-speed Internet, dual phone lines, voice mail, honor bars, irons, hair dryers. Some: CD players. Pool(s): 3 heated outdoor. Leisure Activities: saunas, whirlpools, steamrooms, fishing, recreation programs, rental bicycles, jogging, playground, spa, basketball, volleyball. Fee: golf-36 holes, 45 tennis courts (5 lighted). Guest Services: gift shop, valet and coin laundry, area transportation (fee). Business Services: conference facilities, business center.

Resort Condominium

SOME UNITS

SLEEP INN   *Book at aaa.com*   Phone: (813)973-1665
AAA SAVE
12/1-4/30   1P: $69-$125   2P: $69-$125   XP: $6   F18
5/1-11/30   1P: $59-$95   2P: $59-$95   XP: $6   F18
Location: I-75, exit 279, just w on SR 54, then just n. 5703 Oakley Blvd 33544. Fax: 813/973-1665. Facility: 78 one-bedroom standard units. 3 stories, interior corridors. Bath: shower only. Parking: on-site.

Small-scale Hotel   Terms: cancellation fee imposed. Amenities: high-speed Internet, voice mail. Some: irons, hair dryers. Pool(s): heated outdoor. Guest Services: coin laundry. Business Services: meeting rooms, fax (fee). Cards: AX, CB, DC, DS, JC, MC, VI. Special Amenities: free expanded continental breakfast and free local telephone calls.

SOME UNITS

—— WHERE TO DINE ——

BEEF O'BRADY'S   Lunch: $5-$8   Dinner: $5-$8   Phone: 813/994-1511
Location: I-75, exit 279, just w; in Town Centre at Wesley Chapel. 27315 SR 54 33543. Hours: 11 am-10 pm, Fri & Sat-11 pm, Sun noon-10 pm. Closed: 4/16, 11/23, 12/25. Features: This ever popular sports-themed restaurant was established in 1985. Enjoy watching a favorite sports program on one of the several monitors set about the dining room while feasting on one of their tasty sandwiches, a burger or their famous O'Brady's buffalo-style chicken wings. Casual dress; beer & wine only. Parking: on-site. Cards: AX, DS, MC, VI.

American

LOS VALLARTA MEXICAN RESTAURANT   Lunch: $5-$12   Dinner: $5-$12   Phone: 813/907-5161
Location: I-75, exit 279, just e on SR 54; in Village Market of Wesley Chapel. 5335 Village Mark 33543. Hours: 11 am-10 pm, Sun from noon. Features: Festive surroundings enhance the casual eatery, where patrons can choose from at least 70 items on the extensive menu. From 30 combination platters to specials of the house, the offerings are made to satisfy hearty appetites and cravings for good Mexican food. Casual dress; cocktails. Parking: on-site. Cards: MC, VI.

Mexican

REMINGTON'S STEAKHOUSE   Lunch: $6-$20   Dinner: $6-$20   Phone: 813/973-1208
Location: I-75, exit 279, just w. 27405 SR 54 33543. Hours: 3 pm-10 pm, Fri & Sat-11 pm, Sun noon-10 pm. Closed: 12/25. Features: Known for their signature steaks, enjoy the cowboy theme and the rustic look to this restaurant while enjoying a hearty 16-ounce T-bone or how about a combo dish with some wonderful BBQ rotisserie chicken and ribs! Casual dress; cocktails. Parking: on-site. Cards: AX, DC, DS, MC, VI.

Steak House

WINNER'S SPORTS GRILL   Lunch: $6-$14   Dinner: $6-$14   Phone: 813/973-7474
Location: I-75, exit 279, just e on SR 54; in Village Market of Wesley Chapel. 5429 Village Mart 33543. Hours: 11 am-11 pm. Closed: 4/16, 11/23, 12/25. Features: At the sports-themed restaurant, guests can taste steaks, pasta bowls and shepherd's pie while catching sporting events on television monitors strategically placed around the dining room. Casual dress; cocktails. Parking: on-site. Cards: MC, VI.

American

WIMAUMA pop. 4,246

—— WHERE TO DINE ——

ANA'S RESTAURANT   Lunch: $6-$10   Dinner: $6-$10   Phone: 813/634-3721
Location: On SR 674, jct 6th St. 5705 SR 674 33573. Hours: 6:30 am-5 pm, Fri & Sat-8 pm. Closed: Sun. Features: Although the decor is basic and the locale out of the way, folks come for miles to dine on Ana's home-cooked Mexican specialties. Popular with the locals, the restaurant has limited seating, so guests should be sure to come early. Casual dress. Parking: on-site.

Mexican

COPPER PENNY RESTAURANT   Lunch: $6-$17   Dinner: $6-$17   Phone: 813/634-5476
Location: On US 301, just s of jct SR 674. 16701 US Hwy 301 S 33598. Hours: 11 am-9 pm, Sun noon-8 pm. Closed: 12/25. Features: A local landmark for many years, the restaurant is run by the Nugent family. Among offerings of good-old, down-home cooking are preparations of beef, ribs, seafood, poultry and pasta, as well as Southwestern dishes and salads. Casual dress; cocktails. Parking: on-site. Cards: AX, DS, MC, VI.

American

MC, VI.

ZEPHYRHILLS pop. 10,833

―――――― WHERE TO STAY ――――――

BEST WESTERN ZEPHYRHILLS　Book at aaa.com　　　　　　　　　Phone: (813)782-5527

▽▽▽▽
Motel

2/1-4/30 [CP]	1P: $89-$99	2P: $89-$99	XP: $5　F12
12/1-1/31 & 11/15-11/30 [CP]	1P: $69-$79	2P: $69-$79	XP: $5　F12
5/1-11/14 [CP]	1P: $59-$69	2P: $59-$69	XP: $5　F12

Location: On US 301, 0.5 mi n of jct SR 54. 5734 Gall Blvd 33542. Fax: 813/783-7102. **Facility:** 52 one-bedroom standard units. 2 stories, exterior corridors. **Parking:** on-site. **Amenities:** irons, hair dryers. *Some:* high-speed Internet. **Pool(s):** outdoor. **Business Services:** meeting rooms, fax (fee). **Cards:** AX, CB, DC, DS, MC, VI.

SOME UNITS

(ASK) (S/D) (▦+) (⌖) (⇄) (DATA PORT) (▯) (▤) (▱) / (✕) /

QUALITY INN & SUITES　Book at aaa.com　　　　　　　　　　Phone: 813/762-2000

(AAA) (SAVE)
▽▽▽▽
Motel

All Year　　　　　　　　　　1P: $59-$109　　　　　XP: $10　　　　F18

Location: On US 301, just n of Eiland Blvd (CR 54). 6815 Gall Blvd 33542. Fax: 813/762-0030. **Facility:** 71 units. 60 one-bedroom standard units. 11 one-bedroom suites. 2 stories, interior corridors. *Bath:* combo or shower only. **Parking:** on-site. **Amenities:** high-speed Internet, dual phone lines, voice mail, safes (fee), irons, hair dryers. **Pool(s):** outdoor. **Leisure Activities:** exercise room. **Guest Services:** valet laundry. **Business Services:** meeting rooms, business center. **Cards:** AX, CB, DC, DS, JC, MC, VI. **Special Amenities:** free expanded continental breakfast and free local telephone calls.

SOME UNITS

(S/D) (▦+) (⌖M) (❄) (⌖) (⇄) (✦) (DATA PORT) (▯) (▤) (▱) / (✕) /

―――――― WHERE TO DINE ――――――

BEEF'O'BRADY'S　　　　　　　**Lunch:** $5-$10　　　　**Dinner:** $5-$10　　　　Phone: 813/780-7931

◈
American

Location: On SR 301, just n of jct SR 54; in Merchants Square. 7337 Gall Blvd 33541. **Hours:** 11 am-11 pm, Sun noon-10 pm. Closed: 4/16, 11/23, 12/25. **Features:** Big-screen televisions keep this family sports pub hopping on game days. The bustling spot cooks up traditional burgers, sandwiches, salads and wings. It features a terrific Philadelphia cheese steak served with fries and a pickle spear. Casual dress; beer & wine only. **Parking:** on-site. **Cards:** AX, DS, MC, VI.

YOUNG LIFE HEALTH FOODS　　　**Lunch:** $6-$8　　　　**Dinner:** $6-$8　　　　Phone: 813/788-7772

◈
American
Cards: MC, VI.

Location: On US 301, 0.8 mi n of jct SR 54. 5914 Gall Blvd 33540. **Hours:** 9 am-6 pm. **Features:** The casual spot prepares some great health foods, including frozen yogurt, garden salads, freshly made delicatessen sandwiches and juice-bar creations. Also on site is a market area supplied with health foods and vitamins. There is seating inside and out, and the staff is friendly and inviting. Casual dress. **Parking:** on-site.

Sunshine Skyway Bridge, St. Petersburg / © Robert Harding World Imagery / Alamy

**This ends listings for the Tampa Bay Vicinity.
The following page resumes the alphabetical listings of cities in Florida.**

TARPON SPRINGS —*See Tampa Bay p. 1046.*

TAVARES —*See Orlando p. 833.*

TEMPLE TERRACE —*See Tampa Bay p. 1047.*

TEQUESTA pop. 5,273

─────── **WHERE TO STAY** ───────

JUPITER WATERFRONT INN   Phone: (561)747-9085
[AAA] [SAVE] 12/16-4/15 [CP]   1P: $159-$229   2P: $159-$229
             12/1-12/15 & 4/16-11/30 [CP] 1P: $79-$129   2P: $79-$129
Motel   **Location:** 1.5 mi n of SR 811, on US 1. 18903 SE Federal Hwy 33469. **Fax:** 561/575-3374. **Facility:** Smoke free premises. 38 one-bedroom standard units, some with whirlpools. 2 stories (no elevator), exterior corridors. *Bath:* combo or shower only. **Parking:** on-site. **Terms:** cancellation fee imposed, weekly rates available. **Amenities:** hair dryers. **Pool(s):** heated outdoor. **Leisure Activities:** whirlpool, fishing. **Guest Services:** coin laundry. **Cards:** AX, DS, MC, VI. **Special Amenities:** free continental breakfast.

─────── **WHERE TO DINE** ───────

CAFE HEIDELBERG   **Lunch:** $8-$20   **Dinner:** $15-$20   Phone: 561/746-0014
German   **Location:** Just n of Tequesta and Waterway drs; in Fashion Mall Shopping Center. 150 N US Hwy 1 33469. **Hours:** noon-9 pm, Fri-10 pm, Sat 5 pm-10 pm, Sun 5 pm-9 pm. **Closed:** Mon. **Reservations:** accepted. **Features:** Polkas and marches play in the background as diners wait for such German indulgences as wursts and schnitzels. The chef prepares all food, including the specialties, to order, which means a wait is unavoidable on busy nights. Casual dress; cocktails. **Parking:** on-site. **Cards:** AX, DS, MC, VI.

TIERRA VERDE —*See Tampa Bay p. 1048.*

TITUSVILLE pop. 40,670

─────── **WHERE TO STAY** ───────

BEST WESTERN SPACE SHUTTLE INN KENNEDY
SPACE CENTER *Book at aaa.com*   Phone: (321)269-9100
[AAA] [SAVE] 2/1-4/16 [ECP]   1P: $109-$169   2P: $109-$169
             12/1-1/31 & 10/1-11/30 [ECP] 1P: $79-$169   2P: $79-$169
             4/17-9/30 [ECP]   1P: $69-$169   2P: $69-$169
Small-scale Hotel **Location:** I-95, exit 215, just e on SR 50. 3455 Cheney Hwy 32780. **Fax:** 321/383-4674. **Facility:** 129 units. 125 one-bedroom standard units, some with whirlpools. 4 one-bedroom suites ($129-$209). 2 stories, exterior corridors. **Parking:** on-site. **Terms:** package plans, pets ($5 extra charge, in smoking units). **Amenities:** irons, hair dryers. **Dining:** 11 am-11 pm, cocktails. **Pool(s):** heated outdoor. **Leisure Activities:** sauna, fishing, picnic area, playground, limited exercise equipment, basketball, horseshoes, shuffleboard, volleyball. **Guest Services:** valet and coin laundry. **Business Services:** meeting rooms, PC. **Cards:** AX, CB, DC, DS, JC, MC, VI. **Special Amenities:** free expanded continental breakfast and free local telephone calls.
SOME UNITS

CASA COQUINA   Phone: (321)268-4653
             All Year   1P: $79-$109   2P: $79-$109   XP: $10
Bed & Breakfast **Location:** I-95, exit 215 (SR 50), 1 mi e, 0.4 mi n on US 1, then just w. 4010 Coquina Ave 32780. **Fax:** 321/268-3959. **Facility:** Smoke free premises. 5 one-bedroom standard units, some with whirlpools. 2 stories (no elevator), interior corridors. *Bath:* combo or shower only. **Parking:** on-site. **Terms:** age restrictions may apply, 10 day cancellation notice, package plans, no pets allowed (owner's pet on premises). **Amenities:** video library, hair dryers. **Leisure Activities:** whirlpool. **Guest Services:** complimentary evening beverages. **Cards:** AX, CB, DC, DS, JC, MC, VI.
SOME UNITS

DAYS INN-KENNEDY SPACE CENTER   *Book at aaa.com*   Phone: (321)269-4480
[AAA] [SAVE] 12/1-4/10   1P: $79-$125   XP: $10   F
             4/11-11/30   1P: $59-$125   XP: $10   F
Small-scale Hotel **Location:** I-95, exit 215 (SR 50). 3755 Cheney Hwy 32780. **Fax:** 321/383-0646. **Facility:** 149 units. 148 one-bedroom standard units. 1 one-bedroom suite with efficiency (no utensils) and whirlpool. 2 stories, exterior corridors. **Parking:** on-site. **Terms:** weekly rates available, pets ($10 extra charge). **Amenities:** hair dryers. *Some:* irons. **Pool(s):** outdoor, wading. **Leisure Activities:** exercise room, shuffleboard. **Guest Services:** valet and coin laundry. **Business Services:** meeting rooms, fax (fee). **Cards:** AX, DC, DS, MC, VI. **Special Amenities:** free local telephone calls and free newspaper.
SOME UNITS

HAMPTON INN TITUSVILLE/KENNEDY SPACE
CENTER *Book at aaa.com*   Phone: (321)383-9191
[AAA] [SAVE] All Year [ECP]   1P: $89-$189   2P: $89-$189
Small-scale Hotel **Location:** I-95, exit 215, just w. 4760 Helen Hauser Blvd 32780. **Fax:** 321/383-9166. **Facility:** 86 one-bedroom standard units, some with whirlpools. 4 stories, interior corridors. *Bath:* combo or shower only. **Parking:** on-site. **Terms:** cancellation fee imposed, pets ($25 fee). **Amenities:** high-speed Internet, voice mail, irons, hair dryers. **Pool(s):** outdoor. **Leisure Activities:** exercise room. **Guest Services:** valet and coin laundry. **Business Services:** meeting rooms, business center. **Cards:** AX, DC, DS, MC, VI. **Special Amenities:** free expanded continental breakfast and early check-in/late check-out.
SOME UNITS

RAMADA INN & SUITES-KENNEDY SPACE CENTER *Book at aaa.com*   Phone: (321)269-5510

(AAA) (SAVE)

| 12/1-4/2 | 1P: $69-$99 | 2P: $69-$109 |
| 4/3-11/30 | 1P: $59-$89 | 2P: $59-$89 |

Location: I-95, exit 215, just e on SR 50. 3500 Cheney Hwy 32780. Fax: 321/269-3796. **Facility:** 124 units. 96 one-bedroom standard units. 28 one-bedroom suites, some with efficiencies. 2 stories (no elevator), interior corridors. **Parking:** on-site. **Terms:** [AP] & [BP] meal plans available, small pets only ($25 fee). **Amenities:** voice mail, irons, hair dryers. **Dining:** 24 hours, cocktails. **Pool(s):** heated outdoor. **Leisure Activities:** sauna, whirlpool, playground, limited exercise equipment. *Fee:* game room. **Guest Services:** valet and coin laundry. **Business Services:** meeting rooms. **Cards:** AX, DC, DS, MC, VI. **Special Amenities:** free local telephone calls.

Small-scale Hotel

SOME UNITS

--------- WHERE TO DINE ---------

DIXIE CROSSROADS *Menu on aaa.com*   **Lunch:** $6-$14   **Dinner:** $10-$14   Phone: 321/268-5000

(AAA)

Seafood

Location: I-95, exit 220, 2 mi e; 1 mi w of jct US 1. 1475 Garden St 32796. **Hours:** 11 am-9 pm, Fri & Sat-10 pm. Closed: 11/23, 12/24, 12/25. **Features:** Stroll through the butterfly garden or stand on the bridge over the fish pond on the grounds of this large and homey family restaurant. Ample servings of such favorites as rock shrimp make up a menu of mostly seafood and steak choices. Casual dress; cocktails. **Parking:** on-site. **Cards:** AX, CB, DC, DS, MC, VI.

DOGS 'R' US   **Lunch:** $2-$13   **Dinner:** $2-$13   Phone: 321/269-9050

American

Location: US 1, 0.7 mi n of jct SR 50. 4200 S Washington Ave 32780. **Hours:** 11 am-midnight. Closed major holidays. **Features:** Specializing in grilled items, the beachside eatery presents a menu of burgers, sandwiches and hot dogs. Casual dress; cocktails. **Parking:** on-site.

EL LEONCITO   **Lunch:** $5-$11   **Dinner:** $5-$15   Phone: 321/267-1159

Cuban

Location: US 1, 1 mi n of jct SR 50. 3800 S Washington Ave 32780. **Hours:** 11 am-10 pm. Closed: 7/4, 11/23, 12/25. **Features:** Just off A1A, the Mexican and Cuban restaurant affords a wonderful view of the Vehicle Assembly Building at Kennedy Space Center. Tacos, enchiladas, Cuban sandwiches, chalupas and shredded beef casserole are a few menu offerings. Casual dress; cocktails. **Parking:** on-site. **Cards:** AX, DS, MC, VI.

PASCAL'S DOWNTOWN BISTRO   **Lunch:** $5-$7   **Dinner:** $14-$20   Phone: 321/385-9005

French

Location: Jct South St and Washington Ave, 3 blks n. 336 S Washington Ave 32796. **Hours:** 11 am-2:30 & 5-close, Sat from 5 pm. Closed: Sun. **Reservations:** suggested. **Features:** Nicely varied menu selections—including steak, rack of lamb, poultry, pork and seafood dishes—are prepared in the French tradition. The atmosphere reflects a bistro feel. Dressy casual; cocktails. **Parking:** on-site and street. **Cards:** AX, CB, DC, MC, VI.

PUMPERNICKEL'S DELI   **Lunch:** $4-$10   **Dinner:** $12-$17   Phone: 321/268-5160

German

Location: I-95, exit 215, 1 mi e on SR 50; just w of US 1. 2850 S Hopkins Ave 32780. **Hours:** 8 am-9 pm, Sun-2 pm. Closed major holidays. **Features:** The authentic, German-style deli lets patrons choose from a variety of moderately priced favorites: bratwurst, weisswurst, knockwurst, potato pancakes, Wiener schnitzel and Jaeger schnitzel. A sweet tooth can be soothed with homemade pastries or desserts. Senior portions and hot lunch and dinner buffet bars are available. Casual dress; beer & wine only. **Parking:** on-site. **Cards:** AX, DC, DS, MC, VI.

TREASURE ISLAND —*See Tampa Bay p. 1048.*

TRENTON pop. 1,617

--------- WHERE TO DINE ---------

THE OLDE BOARDING HOUSE   **Lunch:** $4-$8   **Dinner:** $6-$13   Phone: 352/463-8494

American

Location: Just n of SR 26. 115 NW First St 32693. **Hours:** 6 am-9 pm, Fri & Sat-10 pm, Sun 10 am-4 pm. Closed: 12/25. **Reservations:** accepted. **Features:** This historical building has found new life offering country style comfort food in a casual down-home setting. The buffet bar is a bargain, or order from the menu. Casual dress; beer & wine only. **Parking:** on-site. **Cards:** MC, VI.

USEPPA ISLAND

--------- WHERE TO DINE ---------

THE COLLIER INN   **Lunch:** $9-$14   **Dinner:** $10-$31   Phone: 239/283-1061

American

Cards: MC, VI.

Location: MM 63; at Useppa Island Club. Mile Marker 63 33922. **Hours:** 11:30 am-3 & 5-9 pm. **Features:** On a gorgeous tropical island steeped in history, the extremely nice dining establishment is a great stop after a stroll along a botanical trail of picturesque cottages. Such popular dishes as gulf shrimp seviche and chili-honey-glazed baked salmon are a true treat for the palate. Dressy casual; cocktails. **Parking:** on-site.

VALRICO pop. 6,582   (See map and index starting on p. 950)

--------- WHERE TO DINE ---------

BEEF'O'BRADY'S   **Lunch:** $6-$10   **Dinner:** $6-$10   Phone: 813/655-1055   (144)

American

Location: On SR 60, just e of jct Miller Rd. 2561 E SR 60 33594. **Hours:** 11 am-11 pm, Sun noon-10 pm. Closed: 4/16, 11/23, 12/25. **Features:** Patrons can watch a favorite sports program on one of many television monitors strategically placed around the dining room. Buffalo wings and Philly cheese steaks are popular menu items. Casual dress; beer & wine only. **Parking:** on-site. **Cards:** AX, DS, MC, VI.

(See map and index starting on p. 950)

BEEF O'BRADY'S FAMILY SPORTS PUB   Lunch: $6-$8   Dinner: $6-$8   Phone: 813/653-1888   (150)
American
Location: 1 mi s of jct Bloomingdale Rd. 4330 Bell Shoals Rd 33594. **Hours:** 11 am-11 pm, Sun-10 pm. Closed: 4/16, 11/23, 12/25. **Features:** Established in 1985, the popular sports-themed restaurant is known for its great burgers, sandwiches, baskets, soups, salads and the favorite, buffalo wings. Patrons can savor a meal while watching a sports program on any one of the strategically placed TVs. Casual dress; cocktails.
Parking: on-site. **Cards:** 5 MC, VI.

CHINA-FUJI RESTAURANT   Lunch: $5-$6   Dinner: $7-$19   Phone: 813/662-2997   (143)
Chinese
Location: On SR 60, jct Miller Rd; in Kash n Karry Shopping Center. 2519 E Hwy 60 33594. **Hours:** 11 am-9 pm, Fri & Sat-9:30 pm, Sun noon-9 pm. **Features:** The casual little spot serves some wonderful sushi, as well as hot Chinese and Japanese items. The menu lists some 100 choices. Casual dress; cocktails. **Parking:** on-site. **Cards:** AX, DS, MC, VI.

CHINA PALACE SUPER BUFFET   Lunch: $7-$18   Dinner: $10-$18   Phone: 813/661-1888   (145)
Chinese
Location: On SR 60, jct Morningside Dr. 1807 Hwy 60 E 33594. **Hours:** 11 am-10 pm, Fri & Sat-11 pm. **Features:** Diners serve themselves from lunch and dinner buffets that line up more than 100 choices—from seafood, beef, chicken, pork and sushi to salad fixings and desserts. A good appetite is welcomed. Casual dress. **Parking:** on-site. **Cards:** MC, VI.

PACIFIC GRILL AN ASIAN BISTRO   Lunch: $8-$18   Dinner: $8-$18   Phone: 813/657-8744   (148)
Asian
Location: Just s of jct Bloomingdale Ave; in Lithia Crossing. 3452 Litha Pinecrest Rd 33594. **Hours:** 11:30 am-3 & 5-9 pm, Fri-10 pm, Sat & Sun 5 pm-10 pm. **Features:** The cozy eatery is in an upscale strip of shops. Sophisticated surroundings enhance the dining experience. Extensive preparations of sushi center on eel, octopus, smelt roe, squid, wasabi tobiko, quail egg, California rolls, spider rolls and spicy tuna rolls. Also on the menu are such choices as Thai coconut curry, basil tofu, black bean garlic chicken, pan-seared salmon and seafood tempura. Casual dress; beer & wine only. **Parking:** on-site. **Cards:** MC, VI.

PANDA WORLD CHINESE RESTAURANT   Lunch: $4-$15   Dinner: $4-$15   Phone: 813/655-2888   (147)
Chinese
Location: Jct Bloomingdale Ave. 3244 Lithia Pinecrest Rd 33594. **Hours:** 11 am-10 pm, Fri & Sat-11 pm, Sun noon-10 pm. **Features:** With nearly 200 choices, the menu is bound to satisfy any craving for a good Chinese meal. Such typical items as happy family, shrimp lo mein, mu shu pork, moo goo gai pan and Gen. Tso's chicken are just a hint of what can be found on the expansive menu. Casual dress. **Parking:** on-site.
Cards: AX, DS, MC, VI.

PANERA BREAD   Lunch: $6-$7   Dinner: $6-$7   Phone: 813/661-4449   (149)
American
Location: At jct Bloomingdale; in Lithia Crossings. 3482 Lithia Pinecrest Rd 33594. **Hours:** 6:30 am-9:30 pm, Fri & Sat-10 pm, Sun 7 am-9 pm. **Features:** Fresh soups, sandwiches and salads are popular offerings at the trendy spot, which is open for breakfast, lunch and dinner. Eye-catching displays boost the temptation factor on homemade bakery items. Casual dress. **Parking:** on-site. **Cards:** MC, VI.

RACCOON'S   Lunch: $5-$7   Dinner: $5-$7   Phone: 813/689-5079   (146)
American
Location: Jct Bloomingdale; in Royal Oaks Plaza. 3240 Lithia Pinecrest Rd 33594. **Hours:** 9 am-3 am, Sun from 1 pm. Closed: 12/25. **Features:** The fun restaurant serves great sandwiches and hot and spicy wings. Guests can catch a sporting event on varied TV monitors. Among themed event nights is Wednesday bike night, in which pretty show bikes are displayed. Casual dress; cocktails. **Parking:** on-site. **Cards:** AX, DS, MC, VI.

RUBY TUESDAY   Lunch: $8-$18   Dinner: $8-$18   Phone: 813/849-0070   (142)
American
Location: On SR 60, just w of jct Valrico Rd. 1812 E SR 60 33594. **Hours:** 11 am-midnight, Sun-11 pm. **Features:** The popular chain-style establishment is known for its extensive salad bar offering and beautiful Victorian replicated decor. Among the many menu choices are Sonora chicken pasta, pad Thai pasta, low-carbohydrate selections, ribs, steaks, fresh catch and chicken dishes. There is something for everyone, even finger foods for lighter appetites, soups and specially made salads. Casual dress; cocktails. **Parking:** on-site.
Cards: MC, VI.

WILLIE'S THE PLACE FOR SEAFOOD   *Menu on aaa.com*   Dinner: $8-$15   Phone: 813/571-7630   (141)
Seafood
Location: Jct SR 60, 0.7 mi n on Valrico Rd, 0.3 mi w on Front St. 1912 Main St 33594. **Hours:** 4:30 pm-9 pm, Fri & Sat-10 pm. Closed: 11/23, 12/25; also Sun & Mon. **Features:** Willie didn't get fat sitting in the corner. He was too busy cooking up great tasting seafood, chicken, and steak. Specialties such as catfish, gator bites, grouper and crawfish fit in perfectly with the tin-roofed shanty setting. Casual dress; beer & wine only. **Parking:** on-site. **Cards:** MC, VI.

VENICE pop. 17,764

—————— **WHERE TO STAY** ——————

BANYAN HOUSE HISTORIC BED & BREAKFAST   Phone: 941/484-1385

1/1-4/30	2P: $129-$159	XP: $30
5/1-5/31 & 10/1-11/30	2P: $119-$149	XP: $20

Historic Bed & Breakfast
Location: 0.7 mi s of jct Venice Ave W; downtown. Located in a residential area. 519 Harbor Dr S 34285. **Fax:** 941/484-8032. **Facility:** Each guest room has its own theme in this European-style home built in 1926 and each is decorated with Victorian-style furnishings. Smoke free premises. 5 units. 4 one-bedroom standard units, some with efficiencies. 1 one-bedroom suite with efficiency. 2 stories, interior corridors. **Bath:** combo or shower only. **Parking:** on-site. **Terms:** open 1/1-5/31 & 10/1-11/30, 2 night minimum stay - seasonal and/or weekends, age restrictions may apply, 21 day cancellation notice-fee imposed, weekly rates available. **Amenities:** irons, hair dryers. **Pool(s):** heated outdoor. **Leisure Activities:** whirlpool, bicycles. **Guest Services:** coin laundry. **Business Services:** PC, fax. **Cards:** MC, VI.

SOME UNITS

BEST WESTERN AMBASSADOR SUITES

Book at aaa.com

	1P: $129-$199	2P: $129-$199	XP: $10	F17
1/27-4/16 [ECP]	1P: $99-$179	2P: $99-$179	XP: $10	F17
12/1-1/26 & 4/17-5/4 [ECP]	1P: $79-$159	2P: $79-$159	XP: $10	F17
5/5-11/30 [ECP]				

Phone: (941)480-9898

Small-scale Hotel **Location:** I-75, exit 193, just w. 400 Commercial Ct 34292. Fax: 941/488-6692. **Facility:** Designated smoking area. 83 units. 80 one-bedroom standard units. 3 one-bedroom suites with whirlpools. 3 stories, interior corridors. *Bath:* combo or shower only. **Parking:** on-site. **Terms:** 3 night minimum stay - seasonal and weekends, cancellation fee imposed, package plans. **Amenities:** high-speed Internet, dual phone lines, irons, hair dryers. **Pool(s):** heated outdoor. **Leisure Activities:** exercise room. **Guest Services:** valet and coin laundry. **Business Services:** meeting rooms, business center. **Cards:** AX, CB, DC, DS, MC, VI. **Special Amenities:** free expanded continental breakfast and free local telephone calls.

HAMPTON INN & SUITES

Book at aaa.com

12/22-4/30	1P: $99-$199	2P: $99-$199	XP: $10	F
5/1-11/30	1P: $89-$169	2P: $89-$169	XP: $10	F
12/1-12/21	1P: $89	2P: $169	XP: $10	F

Phone: (941)488-5900

Small-scale Hotel **Location:** Just e of US 41, jct US Business 41. 881 Venetia Bay Blvd 34292. Fax: 941/488-6746. **Facility:** 110 units. 76 one-bedroom standard units. 34 one-bedroom suites with kitchens. 3 stories, interior corridors. *Bath:* combo or shower only. **Parking:** on-site. **Amenities:** high-speed Internet, voice mail, irons, hair dryers. *Some:* DVD players (fee), dual phone lines. **Pool(s):** heated outdoor. **Leisure Activities:** whirlpool, jogging, exercise room. **Guest Services:** sundries, valet and coin laundry. **Business Services:** meeting rooms, fax (fee). **Cards:** AX, CB, DC, DS, JC, MC, VI. **Special Amenities:** free expanded continental breakfast and free newspaper. *(See color ad below)*

SOME UNITS

HOLIDAY INN VENICE

2/1-4/30	1P: $109-$169	2P: $109-$169
1/1-1/31	1P: $89-$139	2P: $89-$139
12/1-12/31 & 5/1-11/30	1P: $69-$109	2P: $69-$109

Phone: (941)485-5411

Motel **Location:** 0.5 mi s of jct US 41. 455 US 41 Bypass N 34285. Fax: 941/484-6193. **Facility:** 158 units. 155 one-bedroom standard units. 3 one-bedroom suites ($99-$189) with kitchens. 2 stories, interior/exterior corridors. *Bath:* combo or shower only. **Parking:** on-site. **Terms:** [AP], [BP] & [CP] meal plans available, pets ($30 fee). **Amenities:** high-speed Internet, dual phone lines, voice mail, irons, hair dryers. **Dining:** 7 am-10:30 & 5-9 pm, cocktails. **Pool(s):** heated outdoor. **Leisure Activities:** whirlpool, exercise room, basketball, shuffleboard, volleyball. **Guest Services:** valet and coin laundry. **Business Services:** meeting rooms, business center. **Cards:** AX, CB, DC, DS, MC, VI. **Special Amenities:** free newspaper and early check-in/late check-out.

SOME UNITS
FEE

HORSE AND CHAISE INN A BED & BREAKFAST

Bed & Breakfast

Phone: 941/488-2702

2/1-3/31	1P: $149-$169	2P: $149-$169	XP: $10	F10
12/1-1/31 & 4/1-11/30	1P: $125-$145	2P: $125-$145	XP: $10	F10

Location: Just s of jct Venice Ave on Nassau St, just sw; downtown. Located in a residential area. 317 Ponce de Leon 34285. Fax: 941/484-3467. **Facility:** This lovely property offers individually themed rooms and is just a short walk from historic downtown Venice and its many shops and restaurants. Designated smoking area. 8 units. 6 one-bedroom standard units. 2 one-bedroom suites. 2 stories, interior corridors. *Bath:* combo or shower only. **Parking:** on-site. **Terms:** 3 day cancellation notice, package plans, pets ($10 extra charge). **Amenities:** video library, DVD players, irons, hair dryers. **Leisure Activities:** beach chairs & towels, bicycles. **Guest Services:** complimentary laundry. **Business Services:** business center. **Cards:** MC, VI. **Special Amenities:** free full breakfast and free local telephone calls.

FEE

INN AT THE BEACH RESORT   *Book at aaa.com*

Motel

Phone: (941)484-8471

2/10-4/22 [ECP]	1P: $227-$357	2P: $227-$357	XP: $8	F16
12/1-2/9 [ECP]	1P: $107-$273	2P: $107-$273	XP: $8	F16
4/23-5/28 [ECP]	1P: $145-$257	2P: $145-$257	XP: $8	F16
5/29-11/30 [ECP]	1P: $107-$212	2P: $107-$212	XP: $8	F16

Location: At Venice Beach, jct The Esplanade, 725 W Venice Ave 34285. Fax: 941/484-0593. **Facility:** 49 units. 35 one-bedroom standard units, some with efficiencies. 10 one- and 4 two-bedroom suites ($165-$519) with kitchens. 2 stories, exterior corridors. **Parking:** on-site. **Terms:** check-in 4 pm, 2-3 night minimum stay - seasonal and/or weekends, 10 day cancellation notice. **Amenities:** high-speed Internet, voice mail, safes, irons, hair dryers. **Pool(s):** heated outdoor. **Leisure Activities:** whirlpool, beach access. **Guest Services:** coin laundry. **Business Services:** fax (fee). **Cards:** AX, DC, DS, MC, VI. **Special Amenities:** free expanded continental breakfast and free local telephone calls.

(See color ad below)

SOME UNITS

KON-TIKI MOTEL

Motel

Phone: 941/485-9696

All Year	1P: $59-$99	2P: $59-$99	XP: $15	F12

Location: On US 41 business route; just n of jct Center St. 1487 S Tamiami Tr 34285. **Facility:** 10 one-bedroom standard units with efficiencies. 1 story, exterior corridors. **Parking:** on-site. **Terms:** office hours 9 am-9 pm, 3 day cancellation notice, weekly rates available. **Pool(s):** outdoor. **Leisure Activities:** barbecue area. **Cards:** DS, MC, VI.

SOME UNITS

MOTEL 6 - 364   *Book at aaa.com*

Motel

Phone: 941/485-8255

1/7-4/2	1P: $59-$69	2P: $65-$75	XP: $3	F17
4/3-5/29	1P: $49-$59	2P: $55-$65	XP: $3	F17
12/1-1/6 & 5/30-11/30	1P: $39-$49	2P: $45-$55	XP: $3	F17

Location: Just n of jct Venice Ave. 281 US 41 Bypass N 34292. Fax: 941/488-3005. **Facility:** 103 one-bedroom standard units. 2 stories, exterior corridors. *Bath:* shower only. **Parking:** on-site. **Terms:** small pets only. **Amenities:** *Some:* irons. **Pool(s):** heated outdoor. **Guest Services:** coin laundry. **Business Services:** fax (fee). **Cards:** AX, CB, DC, DS, MC, VI.

SOME UNITS

QUARTERDECK RESORT CONDOMINIUMS   Phone: 941/488-0449

2/1-3/31 Wkly	1P: $1218-$1491 2P: $1218-$1491
12/1-1/31 & 4/1-4/30 Wkly	1P: $919-$1491 2P: $919-$1491
5/1-11/30 Wkly	1P: $683-$718 2P: $719-$953

Location: Oceanfront. 0.4 mi n of jct Venice Ave on The Esplanade, just w. 1275 Tarpon Center Dr 34285.
Condominium   **Fax:** 941/485-7288. **Facility:** Designated smoking area. 30 units. 5 one- and 25 two-bedroom suites with kitchens. 2 stories, exterior corridors. **Parking:** on-site. **Terms:** check-in 4 pm, 7 night minimum stay - seasonal, 30 day cancellation notice-fee imposed. **Amenities:** video library, irons, hair dryers. *Some:* CD players. **Pool(s):** heated outdoor. **Leisure Activities:** fishing, recreation programs, volleyball. **Guest Services:** coin laundry. **Business Services:** fax (fee). **Cards:** MC, VI. **Special Amenities:** free local telephone calls and early check-in/late check-out.

━━━━━━━ **WHERE TO DINE** ━━━━━━━

BRITISH OPEN PUB & RESTAURANT   **Lunch:** $8-$14   **Dinner:** $8-$14   **Phone:** 941/492-9227
British   **Location:** On US 41, jct Alligator Dr. 2053 S Tamiami Tr 34293. **Hours:** 11:30 am-9:30 pm. Closed: 1/1, 11/23, 12/25. **Features:** As the name suggests, the restaurant occupies a comfortable British pub setting. The menu centers on authentic food, beer and ale, including such selections as the house specialty fish and chips and the well-prepared shepherd's pie. Casual dress; cocktails. **Parking:** on-site. **Cards:** MC, VI.

CROW'S NEST MARINA RESTAURANT   *Menu on aaa.com*   **Lunch:** $8-$15   **Dinner:** $14-$28   **Phone:** 941/484-9551
Seafood   **Location:** S Jetty Venice Inlet, 0.9 mi w of US 41 via Venice Ave, 0.4 mi n on The Esplanade, then 0.5 mi nw. 1968 Tarpon Center Dr 34285. **Hours:** 11:30 am-3 & 4:30-10 pm, Sun noon-9 pm. Closed: 11/23, 12/25; also 9/4-9/14. **Reservations:** suggested. **Features:** This bustling restaurant on Venice Inlet gives off a casual ambience. Rich flavors enhance the grouper Key Largo served with scallops, shrimp, crabmeat, mushrooms and hollandaise sauce and the tart Key lime pie. The wine cellar is extensive. Dressy casual; cocktails. **Parking:** on-site. **Cards:** AX, DC, DS, MC, VI.

LEFT COAST SEAFOOD COMPANY   **Lunch:** $6-$13   **Dinner:** $6-$13   **Phone:** 941/485-5064
Seafood   **Location:** On US 41 Bypass, just s of jct US 41. 750 US 41 Bypass N 34285. **Hours:** 11 am-close. **Reservations:** accepted. **Features:** Enjoy fresh seafood as well as steak, pasta and stir fry dishes at this nautically-themed restaurant. A popular spot for steamed oysters, mussels and clams as well as fish chowder or a bowl of New England clam chowder. Casual dress; cocktails. **Parking:** on-site. **Cards:** AX, DS, MC, VI.

LUNA RISTORANTE   **Lunch:** $8-$19   **Dinner:** $8-$19   **Phone:** 941/496-9090
Italian   **Location:** On US 41, jct Jacaranda Blvd; in Venice Village Shops. 4191 S Tamiami Tr 34293. **Hours:** 11 am-9 pm, Fri & Sat-10 pm, Sun noon-9 pm. Closed major holidays. **Features:** Diners who have eaten one of the specialties here understand the popularity of this sports-themed restaurant. Hearty portions of chicken, veal, pasta and various baked dishes are loaded onto 16-inch plates. Spicy seafood marinara is full of shrimp, clams, mussels, scallops and fish. Casual dress; beer & wine only. **Parking:** on-site.

MI PUEBLO EL RESTAURANTE MEXICANA   **Lunch:** $7-$12   **Dinner:** $7-$12   **Phone:** 941/486-0005
Mexican   **Location:** Jct Gulf Coast Blvd; in Brick Yard Plaza. 530 US 41 Bypass S 34285. **Hours:** 11 am-2 & 5-9 pm, Fri & Sat-10 pm, Sun noon-3 & 5-9 pm. Closed: 1/1, 12/24, 12/25. **Features:** A festive theme and great food are draws here. House specialties include bisteck tampico, pollo zaragoza and chiles rellenos. Also on the menu are combination platters, burritos and quesadillas. Casual dress; cocktails. **Parking:** on-site. **Cards:** AX, MC, VI.

MYAKKA RIVER OYSTER BAR   **Lunch:** $6-$15   **Dinner:** $6-$15   **Phone:** 941/423-9616

Seafood   **Location:** On US 41, just s of jct River Rd, enter via Myakka Dr. 121 Playmore Dr 34293. **Hours:** 11 am-9 pm, Sun-8 pm. Closed: 4/16, 11/23, 12/25. **Features:** Diners can look out onto the scenic Myakka River—home to manatees, osprey and alligators—while enjoying dishes ranging from fried seafood to steak to sandwiches. Spicy gumbo is a treat. Casual dress; cocktails. **Parking:** on-site. **Cards:** AX, MC, VI.

SHARKY'S ON THE PIER   **Lunch:** $8-$10   **Dinner:** $9-$29   **Phone:** 941/488-1456
Seafood   **Location:** On US 41 business route, 0.5 mi w via Venice Ave, 2 mi s; at the Venice Fishing Pier. 1600 S Harbor Dr 34285. **Hours:** 11:30 am-3 & 4-10 pm. Closed: 11/23, 12/25. **Features:** Fish mounted on the walls and maritime decorations convey a fitting theme in this busy, gulf-front restaurant. Market fresh fish can be broiled, blackened, grilled or fried. Summer treats include children's crab races and calypso sundaes. Outside dining on a deck features a separate menu and a Tiki bar. Casual dress; cocktails; entertainment. **Parking:** on-site. **Cards:** AX, DS, MC, VI.

T J CARNEY'S   **Lunch:** $7-$20   **Dinner:** $7-$20   **Phone:** 941/480-9244

American   **Location:** Just w of jct US 41; downtown. 231 W Venice Ave 34285. **Hours:** 11 am-midnight. Closed: 4/16. **Features:** Located in the heart of historic downtown Venice, you'll find this casual eatery, a popular spot for locals. Dine inside or sidewalk cafe style; either way you are in for a treat with a varied menu and friendly service. Casual dress; cocktails. **Parking:** street. **Cards:** AX, DC, MC, VI.

VERO BEACH pop. 20,362

——— WHERE TO STAY ———

AQUARIUS OCEAN FRONT RESORT MOTEL

Phone: 772-231-5218

(AAA) (SAVE)

Motel

2/1-4/24	1P: $109-$169	2P: $109-$169	XP: $5	F11
12/21-1/31	1P: $99-$149	2P: $99-$149	XP: $5	F11
4/25-11/30	1P: $79-$139	2P: $79-$139	XP: $5	F11
12/1-12/20	1P: $79-$129	2P: $79-$129	XP: $5	F11

Location: 1.8 mi s; just e of SR A1A on south beach; just s of 17th St Causeway Bridge (E Causeway Blvd, SR 656). 1526 S Ocean Dr 32963. Fax: 772/231-5218. **Facility:** 26 one-bedroom standard units, some with kitchens. 2 stories, exterior corridors. **Parking:** on-site. **Terms:** 14 day cancellation notice. **Amenities:** voice mail. **Pool(s):** heated outdoor. **Leisure Activities:** limited beach access, tiki huts & grills beachside, shuffleboard. **Guest Services:** coin laundry. **Business Services:** fax (fee). **Cards:** AX, DC, DS, MC, VI. **Special Amenities:** free newspaper.

BEST WESTERN VERO BEACH   *Book at aaa.com*

Phone: (772)567-8321

(AAA) (SAVE)

Small-scale Hotel

12/27-4/1	1P: $180	2P: $180	XP: $10	F12
12/1-12/26	1P: $121	2P: $121	XP: $10	F12
4/2-11/30	1P: $111	2P: $111	XP: $10	F12

Location: I-95, exit 147 (SR 60), 1 mi e. 8797 20th St 32966. Fax: 772/569-8558. **Facility:** 115 one-bedroom standard units. 2 stories, exterior corridors. *Bath:* combo or shower only. **Parking:** on-site. **Terms:** cancellation fee imposed. **Amenities:** high-speed Internet, voice mail, irons, hair dryers. *Some:* safes. **Dining:** 11 am-9 pm, cocktails. **Pool(s):** heated outdoor, wading. **Leisure Activities:** exercise room. **Guest Services:** coin laundry. **Business Services:** meeting rooms, business center. **Cards:** AX, DC, DS, MC, VI. **Special Amenities:** free local telephone calls and free newspaper.

COMFORT INN   *Book at aaa.com*

Phone: (772)569-0900

▽▽▽

Small-scale Hotel

12/15-4/15 [ECP]	1P: $89-$199	2P: $89-$199	XP: $5	F12
12/1-12/14 [ECP]	1P: $59-$149	2P: $59-$149	XP: $5	F12
4/16-11/30 [ECP]	1P: $59-$129	2P: $59-$129	XP: $5	F12

Location: US 1, 1.3 mi s of jct SR 60. 950 US Hwy 1 32960. Fax: 772/569-5502. **Facility:** 66 one-bedroom standard units. 2 stories, exterior corridors. *Bath:* combo or shower only. **Parking:** on-site. **Terms:** 3 day cancellation notice-fee imposed. **Amenities:** irons, hair dryers. **Pool(s):** heated outdoor. **Guest Services:** coin laundry. **Business Services:** fax (fee). **Cards:** AX, CB, DC, DS, MC, VI.

DISNEY'S VERO BEACH RESORT   *Book at aaa.com*

Phone: (772)234-2000

(AAA)

Resort
Large-scale Hotel

1/1-5/31	1P: $169-$660	2P: $169-$660	
12/1-12/31	1P: $165-$640	2P: $165-$640	
6/1-8/26	1P: $215-$425	2P: $215-$425	
8/27-11/30	1P: $169-$335	2P: $169-$335	

Location: 7 mi n of Vero Beach; SR A1A, at CR 510; jct I-95, exit 156, 11 mi e via CR 512 and 510. 9250 Island Grove Terrace 32963. Fax: 772/234-2030. **Facility:** Nestled among sea grass and palm trees, this Florida-themed resort offers a variety of accommodations, all with a porch or balcony. 205 units. 151 one-bedroom standard units. 36 one- and 18 two-bedroom suites. 4 stories, interior corridors. *Bath:* combo or shower only. **Parking:** on-site. **Terms:** check-in 4 pm, 6 day cancellation notice-fee imposed, package plans. **Amenities:** voice mail, safes, irons, hair dryers. **Dining:** 2 restaurants, 7-11 am, 11:30-3 & 5-10 pm, cocktails, entertainment. **Pool(s):** heated outdoor. **Leisure Activities:** sauna, whirlpool, waterslide, limited beach access, fishing, personal watercraft, miniature golf, 2 lighted tennis courts, recreation programs, camp fires, lawn croquet, jogging, playground, exercise room, basketball, horseshoes, shuffleboard, volleyball. *Fee:* charter fishing, bicycles, massage, game room. **Guest Services:** gift shop, valet and coin laundry. **Business Services:** meeting rooms, business center. **Cards:** AX, DC, DS, JC, MC, VI.

HAMPTON INN VERO BEACH   *Book at aaa.com*

Phone: (772)770-4299

▽▽▽

Small-scale Hotel

All Year	1P: $101-$130	2P: $101-$130

Location: I-95, exit 147, just w. 9350 19th Ln 32966. Fax: 772/770-3549. **Facility:** 63 one-bedroom standard units. 3 stories, interior corridors. *Bath:* combo or shower only. **Parking:** on-site. **Amenities:** high-speed Internet, voice mail, irons, hair dryers. **Pool(s):** outdoor. **Guest Services:** valet laundry. **Business Services:** fax (fee). **Cards:** AX, CB, DC, DS, JC, MC, VI.

HOWARD JOHNSON EXPRESS INN   *Book at aaa.com*

Phone: (772)778-1985

(AAA) (SAVE)

Motel

2/1-4/5	1P: $89-$105	2P: $89-$105	XP: $10	F16
1/1-1/31	1P: $75-$99	2P: $75-$99	XP: $10	F16
12/1-12/31 & 4/6-11/30	1P: $60-$85	2P: $60-$85	XP: $5	F16

Location: I-95, exit 147 (SR 60), just se. 1985 90th Ave 32966. Fax: 772/778-1998. **Facility:** 58 one-bedroom standard units. 2 stories, exterior corridors. *Bath:* combo or shower only. **Parking:** on-site. **Terms:** [CP] meal plan available. **Amenities:** voice mail, irons, hair dryers. **Pool(s):** outdoor. **Guest Services:** coin laundry. **Business Services:** fax (fee). **Cards:** AX, CB, DC, DS, MC, VI. **Special Amenities:** free continental breakfast and free local telephone calls.

HOWARD JOHNSON INN-DOWNTOWN   *Book at aaa.com*

Phone: 772-567-5171

(AAA) (SAVE)

Motel

12/1-4/1	1P: $79-$109	2P: $99-$129	XP: $10	F17
11/1-11/30	1P: $69-$99	2P: $89-$119	XP: $10	F17
4/2-7/31	1P: $59-$89	2P: $79-$109	XP: $10	F17
8/1-10/31	1P: $54-$79	2P: $69-$89	XP: $10	F17

Location: 0.3 mi s of jct SR 60. 1725 US Hwy 1 32960. Fax: 772/567-5194. **Facility:** 51 one-bedroom standard units. 2 stories, interior/exterior corridors. **Parking:** on-site. **Amenities:** voice mail, irons, hair dryers. **Pool(s):** outdoor. **Business Services:** fax (fee). **Cards:** AX, DC, DS, MC, VI. **Special Amenities:** free expanded continental breakfast and free local telephone calls.

THE ISLANDER INN
Phone: 772/231-4431

Motel

DS, MC, VI.

All Year   1P: $99-$135   2P: $99-$135   XP: $10   F

Location: Just s of SR 60. 3101 Ocean Dr 32963. Fax: 772/231-4431. **Facility:** 16 one-bedroom standard units, some with efficiencies or kitchens. 2 stories, exterior corridors. *Bath:* combo or shower only. **Parking:** on-site. **Terms:** 7 day cancellation notice-fee imposed, weekly rates available. **Pool(s):** outdoor. **Cards:** AX, DS, MC, VI.

PALM COURT RESORT HOTEL
Phone: 772/231-2800

[fyi]

Small-scale Hotel

Property failed to provide current rates

Under major renovation, scheduled to be completed January 2006. **Last rated:** ▼▼▼ **Location:** Just s of SR 60. 3244 Ocean Dr 32963. Fax: 772/231-3446. **Facility:** 106 units. 104 one-bedroom standard units, some with efficiencies. 2 one-bedroom suites with efficiencies. 5 stories, interior corridors. *Bath:* combo or shower only. **Parking:** on-site. **Amenities:** voice mail, irons, hair dryers. **Pool(s):** heated outdoor. **Leisure Activities:** exercise room. *Fee:* charter fishing. **Guest Services:** valet and coin laundry. **Business Services:** meeting rooms, fax (fee).

SOME UNITS
FEE FEE

THE VERO BEACH HOTEL & CLUB
Phone: 772/231-5666

▼▼▼

Small-scale Hotel

Property failed to provide current rates

Location: Just n of SR 60. 3500 Ocean Dr 32963. Fax: 772/234-4866. **Facility:** 54 units. 40 one- and 14 two-bedroom standard units. 5 stories, interior/exterior corridors. **Parking:** on-site. **Amenities:** video library (fee), voice mail, irons, hair dryers. **Pool(s):** heated outdoor, wading. **Leisure Activities:** whirlpool. **Guest Services:** valet and coin laundry. **Business Services:** meeting rooms. *Fee:* administrative services, fax.

SOME UNITS

——— **WHERE TO DINE** ———

BIG APPLE PIZZA
Italian

Lunch: $5-$12   Dinner: $5-$12   **Phone: 772/569-8900**

Location: I-95, exit 68 (SR 60), 4 mi e. 5970 20th St 32966. **Hours:** 11 am-10 pm, Sun noon-9 pm. Closed major holidays. **Features:** In a busy commercial shopping area, the restaurant prepares such dishes as ziti, stuffed shells and veal parmigiana. Hand-tossed pizzas are baked on a stone deck oven. Casual dress; beer & wine only. **Parking:** on-site. **Cards:** AX, MC, VI.

CAFE' DU SOIR
French

Dinner: $22-$39   **Phone: 772/569-4607**

Location: 2 mi e of jct US 1 and SR 603 (Indian River Blvd). 21 Royal Palm Point 32960. **Hours:** 6 pm-10 pm. Closed: 1/1, 12/25; also Sun & Mon off season. **Reservations:** suggested. **Features:** The second-floor restaurant, with a terrace that looks out onto the Indian River, is a great place for cozy, romantic dining. Attentive servers often go out of their way to make your experience memorable. Enjoy the snapper for two or the rack of lamb. Semi-formal attire; beer & wine only. **Parking:** on-site. **Cards:** AX, DC, MC, VI.

CHARLEY'S SOUTH BEACH GRILLE
Steak & Seafood

Dinner: $15-$32   **Phone: 772/231-6311**

Location: SR A1A, 0.3 mi s of jct SR 656. 1410 Hwy A1A 32963. **Hours:** 5 pm-9:30 pm, Fri & Sat-10 pm. Closed: 7/4, 12/25; also Super Bowl Sun. **Reservations:** accepted. **Features:** A popular spot for retirees, this established restaurant is known for well-prepared entrees of fresh fish, steaks, Danish ribs and chicken. The prime rib is slow-cooked and served au jus. The tropical garden setting contributes to the relaxing atmosphere. Casual dress; cocktails. **Parking:** on-site. **Cards:** AX, CB, DC, DS, MC, VI.

LOBSTER SHANTY
Seafood

DC, DS, MC, VI.

Lunch: $8-$15   Dinner: $12-$26   **Phone: 772/562-1941**

Location: SR 60; 1 mi w of jct SR A1A. 1 Royal Palm Pointe 32960. **Hours:** 11:30 am-9 pm, Fri & Sat-10 pm. Closed: 12/25. **Features:** When there's a wait, you can guess the reason. Tourists and locals flock to this casual dining room overlooking the Indian River. Chicken, seafood and beef specialties are the best in town, and the salad is one of the crispiest concoctions ever. Casual dress; cocktails. **Parking:** on-site. **Cards:** AX,

OCEAN GRILL
Steak & Seafood

Lunch: $8-$12   Dinner: $18-$30   **Phone: 772/231-5409**

Location: E of SR A1A, at end of SR 60. 1050 Sexton Plaza 32963. **Hours:** 11:30 am-2:30 & 5-10 pm, Sat & Sun from 5 pm; hour vary off season. Closed: 7/4, 11/23; also Super Bowl Sun. **Features:** A dramatic oceanfront view and a rustic dining room serving great food translates to a popular, busy eatery. Broiled salmon with a particularly good dill sauce is definitely worth any wait. A courteous and knowledgeable staff attend your every need. Casual dress; cocktails. **Parking:** on-site. **Cards:** AX, CB, DC, DS, MC, VI.

TANGOS
Regional American

Dinner: $24-$38   **Phone: 772/231-1550**

Location: Jct SR A1A and Beachland, just e to Cardinal Dr, s to Bougainvillea, then just e. 3001 Ocean Dr, Suite 107 32963. **Hours:** 5 pm-10 pm. Closed: 11/23, 12/25; also Sun; also Mon 6/1-12/31. **Reservations:** suggested. **Features:** The chef/owner's creative touch enlivens the cuisine, which include selections of prime cuts of meat, fresh seafood, pasta and breads and desserts made on the premises. Choose from a wide variety of wines, several available by the glass. Casual dress; cocktails. **Parking:** street. **Cards:** AX, CB, DC, DS, MC, VI.

VILANO BEACH pop. 2,533 (See map and index starting on p. 874)

——— **WHERE TO STAY** ———

CLARION COLLECTION CASA DEL MAR
Small-scale Hotel

Book at aaa.com   **Phone: (904)827-9797**   [46]

2/2-9/8	1P: $179-$269	2P: $179-$269	XP: $10	F18
9/9-11/30	1P: $129-$179	2P: $129-$179	XP: $10	F18
12/1-2/1	1P: $119-$169	2P: $119-$169	XP: $10	F18

Location: Just s of Vilano Bridge; s of SR A1A. 95 Vilano Rd 32084. Fax: 904/824-1599. **Facility:** 94 units. 84 one-bedroom standard units. 10 one-bedroom suites with whirlpools. 3 stories, interior corridors. *Bath:* combo or shower only. **Parking:** on-site. **Terms:** cancellation fee imposed. **Amenities:** video games (fee), high-speed Internet, dual phone lines, voice mail, safes, irons, hair dryers. **Pool(s):** heated outdoor. **Leisure Activities:** whirlpool, exercise room. **Guest Services:** sundries, valet and coin laundry. **Business Services:** meeting rooms, PC. **Cards:** AX, CB, DC, DS, MC, VI.

SOME UNITS

(See map and index starting on p. 874)

OCEAN SANDS BEACH INN *Book at aaa.com* Phone: (904)824-1112 **45**
AAA SAVE All Year 1P: $49-$149 XP: $10 F
Location: 2 mi ne at Vilano Bridge on SR A1A. Located across the street from beach. 3465 Coastal Hwys (A1A N)
Motel 32084. Fax: 904/824-1119. **Facility:** 29 one-bedroom standard units, some with whirlpools. 2 stories, interior
corridors. *Bath:* combo or shower only. **Parking:** on-site. **Terms:** 3 day cancellation notice.
Amenities: video library (fee), irons, hair dryers. *Some:* DVD players (fee). **Pool(s):** heated outdoor.
Cards: AX, DS, MC, VI. **Special Amenities:** free expanded continental breakfast and free local
telephone calls. *(See color ad p 886)*

──────── WHERE TO DINE ────────

FIDDLER'S GREEN Dinner: $12-$25 Phone: 904/824-8897 **41**
AAA **Location:** Just e of SR A1A where SR A1A turns n, 0.5 mi e of Vilano Beach Bridge. 2750 Anahma Dr 32084. **Hours:** 5
pm-9 pm; to 10 pm in summer. Closed: 11/23; also 12/19-12/26 & Super Bowl Sun.
Reservations: suggested. **Features:** Sink into large rattan chairs and take in the lovely ocean view. Fresh
American local seafood is used in many of the entrees, including a creative medley of lobster, shrimp and scallops in a
white cream sauce. Twice-baked potatoes make a tasty side dish. Casual dress; cocktails. **Parking:** on-site.
Cards: AX, DC, DS, MC, VI.

WAKULLA SPRINGS

──────── WHERE TO STAY ────────

WAKULLA SPRINGS LODGE Phone: (850)224-5950
All Year 1P: $85-$105
Location: Jct SR 61 and 267; in Wakulla Springs State Park. 550 Wakulla Park Dr 32305. Fax: 850/561-7251.
Small-scale Hotel **Facility:** 27 one-bedroom standard units. 2 stories, interior corridors. **Parking:** on-site. **Terms:** 3 day
cancellation notice. **Dining:** The Ball Room, see separate listing. **Leisure Activities:** recreation programs.
Guest Services: gift shop. **Business Services:** meeting rooms, fax (fee). **Cards:** AX, CB, DC, DS, JC, MC, VI.

SOME UNITS

──────── WHERE TO DINE ────────

THE BALL ROOM Lunch: $6-$12 Dinner: $9-$20 Phone: 850/224-5950
Location: Jct SR 61 and 267; in Wakulla Springs State Park; in Wakulla Springs Lodge. 550 Wakulla Park Dr 32327.
Hours: 7:30-10 am, 11:30-2 & 6-8 pm. **Reservations:** suggested. **Features:** Freshly prepared meals with a
Regional American strong Southern accent, including pecan-crusted grouper, veal chops and excellent fried oysters from
Apalachicola Bay, are the key to the restaurant's appeal. Gaze out over lovely and scenic Wakulla Springs.
Casual dress; beer & wine only. **Parking:** on-site. **Cards:** AX, DS, MC, VI.

WEEKI WACHEE pop. 12

──────── WHERE TO STAY ────────

BEST WESTERN WEEKI WACHEE RESORT *Book at aaa.com* Phone: (352)596-2007
AAA SAVE 12/18-4/16 [CP] 1P: $75-$109 2P: $75-$109
4/17-9/3 [CP] 1P: $75-$99 2P: $75-$99
12/1-12/17 & 9/4-11/30 [CP] 1P: $65-$89 2P: $65-$89
Motel **Location:** On US 19, jct SR 50 (Cortez Blvd). 6172 Commercial Way 34606. Fax: 352/596-0667. **Facility:** 122 one-
bedroom standard units. 2 stories, exterior corridors. **Parking:** on-site. **Amenities:** high-speed Internet,
voice mail, irons, hair dryers. **Pool(s):** outdoor, wading. **Leisure Activities:** shuffleboard. **Guest Services:**
coin laundry. **Business Services:** meeting rooms, fax (fee). **Cards:** AX, DC, DS, MC, VI. **Special Amenities:** free local
telephone calls and free newspaper. *(See color ad p 926)*

SOME UNITS

──────── WHERE TO DINE ────────

NELLIE'S RESTAURANT Lunch: $5-$7 Dinner: $5-$11 Phone: 352/596-8321
Location: On SR 50, just e of jct US 19; in Weeki Wachee Village Shops. 6234 Commercial Way 34613. **Hours:** 6
am-8:30 pm. Closed: 12/25. **Features:** A savory Yankee pot roast and homemade mashed potatoes are
American highlights of this homey eatery. Freshly-prepared dishes of poultry, steaks and seafood complete the menu.
Don't leave without a piece of the coconut cream pie and a cup of coffee. Casual dress; beer & wine only.
Parking: on-site. **Cards:** AX, DS, MC, VI.

WELLINGTON pop. 38,216 (See map and index starting on p. 843)

──────── WHERE TO DINE ────────

THE PLAYER'S CLUB Dinner: $21-$39 Phone: 561/795-0080 **50**
Location: Florida Tpke, exit 93, 5.6 mi w on SR 802 (Lake Worth Rd), 2 mi n on South Shore Dr, then just e to Polo
Club Rd. 13410 South Shore Blvd 33414. **Hours:** 5 pm-10 pm, Fri-Sun to 11 pm. Closed: 9/4.
Reservations: suggested. **Features:** The large windows will allow you a view of the polo fields. Inside you
Continental will feel the club atmosphere. The menu features seafood items, meats and some pasta entrees. All of the
foods are artfully presented. Dressy dress; cocktails; entertainment. **Parking:** on-site and valet. **Cards:** AX, MC, VI.

SMOKEY BONES Lunch: $7-$21 Dinner: $7-$21 Phone: 561/383-8240 **49**
Location: Corner of US 441/SR 7; in Wellington Mall area side shops. 10260 Forest Hill Blvd 33414. **Hours:** 11 am-
10 pm, Fri & Sat-11 pm. Closed: 11/23, 12/25. **Features:** Families are welcomed in the sports-oriented
Barbecue environment. Speakers at each table allow guests to listen to the activity on the many TVs around the dining
area. The menu lists ribs and a variety of barbecue meats. Casual dress; cocktails. **Parking:** on-site.
Cards: AX, CB, DC, DS, JC, MC, VI.

WESLEY CHAPEL —*See Tampa Bay p. 1052.*

WEST MELBOURNE pop. 9,824—*See also MELBOURNE.*

———— WHERE TO STAY ————

HAMPTON INN MELBOURNE   *Book at aaa.com*   **Phone:** (321)956-6200

1/1-5/15 [ECP]	1P: $115-$135	2P: $125-$145	XP: $10	F18
5/16-11/30 [ECP]	1P: $105-$125	2P: $115-$135	XP: $10	F18
12/1-12/31 [ECP]	1P: $100-$120	2P: $110-$130	XP: $10	F18

Small-scale Hotel   **Location:** I-95, exit 180, just ne. 194 Dike Rd 32904. **Fax:** 321/956-3230. **Facility:** 66 one-bedroom standard units, some with whirlpools. 3 stories, interior corridors. *Bath:* combo or shower only. **Parking:** on-site. **Amenities:** dual phone lines, voice mail, irons, hair dryers. **Pool(s):** outdoor. **Leisure Activities:** exercise room. **Guest Services:** valet and coin laundry. **Business Services:** meeting rooms. **Cards:** AX, CB, DC, DS, MC, VI.

SOME UNITS
(A$K) (🍽️) (&M) (🛗) (🎧) (🛍️) (🎬) (DATA PORT) (💻) / (🛏️) (🍳) /
                                  FEE   FEE

HOLIDAY INN EXPRESS MELBOURNE   *Book at aaa.com*   **Phone:** (321)724-2050

All Year   1P: $79-$129

Location: I-95, exit 180, just e. 4510 W New Haven Ave 32904. **Fax:** 321/724-9882. **Facility:** 68 one-bedroom standard units. 5 stories, interior corridors. *Bath:* combo or shower only. **Parking:** on-site. **Terms:** [CP] meal plan available. **Amenities:** dual phone lines, voice mail, irons, hair dryers. **Guest Services:** valet and coin laundry. **Business Services:** meeting rooms. **Cards:** AX, CB, DC, DS, MC, VI.

Small-scale Hotel

SOME UNITS
(S/D) (🍽️) (🛗) (🎧) (🏊) (🎬) (DATA PORT) (💻) / (✖️) (🛏️) (🍳) /

HOWARD JOHNSON   *Book at aaa.com*   **Phone:** (321)768-8439

All Year   1P: $70-$110   2P: $70-$110   XP: $6   F18

Location: I-95, exit 180, just e on US 192. 4431 W New Haven Ave 32904. **Fax:** 321/768-8666. **Facility:** 116 one-bedroom standard units. 2 stories, exterior corridors. *Bath:* combo or shower only. **Parking:** on-site. **Terms:** small pets only ($20 extra charge). **Amenities:** voice mail, safes (fee), irons, hair dryers. **Pool(s):** outdoor. **Guest Services:** coin laundry. **Business Services:** meeting rooms. **Cards:** AX, DC, DS, MC, VI.

Small-scale Hotel

SOME UNITS
(S/D) (🛏️) (🍽️) (🎧) (🛍️) (🎬) (DATA PORT) (💻) / (✖️) (🛏️) (🍳) /
    FEE   FEE   FEE

WESTON —*See Fort Lauderdale p. 426.*

WEST PALM BEACH pop. 82,103   (See map and index starting on p. 843)—*See also PALM BEACH.*

─────── **WHERE TO STAY** ───────

BEST WESTERN PALM BEACH LAKES INN   *Book at aaa.com*   Phone: (561)683-8810   **6**
AAA SAVE   1/15-4/14 [ECP]   1P: $105-$110   2P: $105-$110   XP: $10   F17
WWW   12/1-1/14 & 4/15-11/30 [ECP] 1P: $79-$85   2P: $79-$85   XP: $10   F17
Small-scale Hotel **Location:** I-95, exit 71, just e. Located facing Palm Beach Mall. 1800 Palm Beach Lakes Blvd 33401. Fax: 561/687-0013. **Facility:** 135 units. 134 one-bedroom standard units. 1 one-bedroom suite ($150). 2 stories (no elevator), interior/exterior corridors. **Parking:** on-site. **Terms:** 14 day cancellation notice. **Amenities:** voice mail, irons, hair dryers. *Some:* high-speed Internet. **Pool(s):** heated outdoor. **Leisure Activities:** shuffleboard. **Guest Services:** coin laundry. *Fee:* airport transportation-Palm Beach International Airport, area transportation-within 4 mi. **Business Services:** meeting rooms. **Cards:** AX, DC, DS, MC, VI. **Special Amenities:** free expanded continental breakfast and free local telephone calls.

SOME UNITS

COMFORT INN-PALM BEACH LAKES   *Book at aaa.com*   Phone: (561)689-6100   **8**
AAA SAVE   12/1-4/15   1P: $119-$159   2P: $119-$159
WWW   4/16-11/30   1P: $109-$139   2P: $109-$139
Motel   **Location:** I-95, exit 71, just w. 1901 Palm Beach Lakes Blvd 33409. Fax: 561/686-6177. **Facility:** 162 one-bedroom standard units. 6 stories, interior corridors. **Parking:** on-site. **Terms:** 2 night minimum stay - seasonal and/or weekends, small pets only ($25 fee, $10 extra charge). **Amenities:** voice mail, irons, hair dryers. *Fee:* video games, safes. *Some:* high-speed Internet. **Pool(s):** heated outdoor. **Guest Services:** valet and coin laundry. **Business Services:** meeting rooms. **Cards:** AX, CB, DC, DS, JC, MC, VI. **Special Amenities:** early check-in/late check-out. *(See color ad below)*

SOME UNITS

COURTYARD BY MARRIOTT-WEST PALM BEACH   *Book at aaa.com*   Phone: 561/640-9000   **1**
AAA SAVE   12/1-4/30   1P: $249   2P: $249
WWW   5/1-5/28 & 10/2-11/30 1P: $169   2P: $169
             5/29-10/1   1P: $129   2P: $129
Small-scale Hotel **Location:** I-95, exit 74 (45th St), just w on CR 702; in Northpoint Corporate Park. 600 Northpoint Pkwy 33407. Fax: 561/471-0122. **Facility:** 149 units. 137 one-bedroom standard units. 12 one-bedroom suites. 3 stories, interior corridors. *Bath:* combo or shower only. **Parking:** on-site. **Amenities:** high-speed Internet, voice mail, irons, hair dryers. **Dining:** 6:30-11 am, Sat & Sun from 7 am. **Pool(s):** heated outdoor. **Leisure Activities:** whirlpool, exercise room. **Guest Services:** valet and coin laundry. **Business Services:** meeting rooms, PC. **Cards:** AX, CB, DC, DS, JC, MC, VI. **Special Amenities:** free newspaper.

SOME UNITS

COURTYARD BY MARRIOTT WEST PALM BEACH AIRPORT   *Book at aaa.com*   Phone: (561)207-1800   **14**
WWW   All Year   1P: $79-$329   2P: $79-$329
Small-scale Hotel **Location:** I-95, exit 69, 0.5 mi w on Belvedere Rd, 0.5 mi n on Australian Ave, then e. 1800 Centrepark Dr E 33401. Fax: 561/207-1818. **Facility:** 103 units. 99 one-bedroom standard units, some with whirlpools. 4 one-bedroom suites. 4 stories, interior corridors. *Bath:* combo or shower only. **Parking:** on-site. **Terms:** 1-9 night minimum stay - seasonal and/or weekends, [BP] meal plan available, package plans. **Amenities:** video games (fee), high-speed Internet, dual phone lines, voice mail, irons, hair dryers. **Pool(s):** small heated outdoor. **Leisure Activities:** whirlpool, exercise room. **Guest Services:** sundries, valet and coin laundry, area transportation. **Business Services:** meeting rooms, business center. **Cards:** AX, CB, DC, DS, JC, MC, VI.

SOME UNITS

(See map and index starting on p. 843)

CROWNE PLAZA HOTEL AND RESORT WEST PALM BEACH   *Book at aaa.com*

Phone: (561)689-6400   **15**

1/1-5/7	1P: $209-$309	2P: $209-$309
10/1-11/30	1P: $159-$259	2P: $159-$259
12/1-12/31	1P: $139-$239	2P: $139-$239
5/8-9/30	1P: $109-$209	2P: $109-$209

Large-scale Hotel **Location:** I-95, exit 69, 0.5 mi w at Australian Ave. 1601 Belvedere Rd 33406. Fax: 561/683-7150. **Facility:** 219 units. 115 one-bedroom standard units. 104 one-bedroom suites. 15 stories, interior corridors. *Bath:* combo or shower only. **Parking:** on-site. **Terms:** check-in 4 pm, cancellation fee imposed. **Amenities:** dual phone lines, voice mail, irons, hair dryers. **Dining:** 6:30 am-2 & 5-10 pm, cocktails. **Pool(s):** heated outdoor. **Leisure Activities:** saunas, whirlpool, 2 lighted tennis courts, exercise room. **Guest Services:** gift shop, valet laundry, airport transportation-Palm Beach International Airport, area transportation-within 5 mi. **Business Services:** meeting rooms, business center. **Cards:** AX, DC, DS, MC, VI.

SOME UNITS

HAMPTON INN WEST PALM BEACH AT EMERALD DUNES GOLF COURSE   *Book at aaa.com*

Phone: 561/682-9990   **9**

Property failed to provide current rates

Small-scale Hotel **Location:** Florida Tpke, exit 99 (SR 704/Okeechobee Blvd), just w to Vista Pkwy. 2025 Vista Pkwy 33411. Fax: 561/682-9446. **Facility:** 110 one-bedroom standard units. 4 stories, interior corridors. *Bath:* combo or shower only. **Parking:** on-site. **Amenities:** video games (fee), dual phone lines, voice mail, irons, hair dryers. **Pool(s):** heated outdoor. **Leisure Activities:** limited exercise equipment. **Guest Services:** sundries, complimentary evening beverages: Mon-Thurs, valet and coin laundry. **Business Services:** meeting rooms, business center.

SOME UNITS

HIBISCUS HOUSE BED & BREAKFAST

Phone: (561)863-5633   **5**

12/1-4/30 [BP]	1P: $125-$210	2P: $125-$210	XP: $10	F14
5/1-11/30 [BP]	1P: $95-$150	2P: $95-$150	XP: $10	F14

Historic Bed & Breakfast **Location:** 1.2 mi n on Flagler Dr from jct Palm Beach Lakes Blvd, 0.3 mi w. 501 30th St 33407. Fax: 561/863-5633. **Facility:** A secluded tropical garden enhances this restored home which was built for the local mayor in 1922; guest rooms have period furnishings. Smoke free premises. 5 one-bedroom standard units, some with whirlpools. 2 stories (no elevator), interior corridors. *Bath:* combo or shower only. **Parking:** on-site. **Terms:** 14 day cancellation notice-fee imposed, small pets only. **Amenities:** irons, hair dryers. **Pool(s):** small heated outdoor. **Cards:** AX, DS, MC, VI.

SOME UNITS

HILTON PALM BEACH AIRPORT   *Book at aaa.com*

Phone: 561/684-9400   **18**

12/1-4/30	1P: $179-$259	2P: $189-$269	XP: $10
5/1-11/30	1P: $129-$199	2P: $139-$209	XP: $10

Large-scale Hotel **Location:** I-95, exit 68, 0.3 mi w; at Australian Ave and Southern Blvd. 150 Australian Ave 33406. Fax: 561/689-9421. **Facility:** 247 units. 245 one-bedroom standard units. 2 one-bedroom suites (S425-$625). 10 stories, interior corridors. *Bath:* combo or shower only. **Parking:** on-site and valet. **Terms:** cancellation fee imposed. **Amenities:** video games (fee), dual phone lines, voice mail, safes, irons, hair dryers. **Dining:** 6:30 am-11 pm, cocktails. **Pool(s):** heated outdoor. **Leisure Activities:** whirlpool, fishing, 2 lighted tennis courts, exercise room. **Guest Services:** gift shop, valet laundry, airport transportation-Palm Beach International Airport, area transportation-City Place. **Business Services:** conference facilities, business center. **Cards:** AX, CB, DC, DS, MC, VI. **Special Amenities:** free newspaper.

SOME UNITS

FEE

HOLIDAY INN PALM BEACH AIRPORT   *Book at aaa.com*

Phone: (561)659-3880   **16**

1/1-4/29	1P: $109-$139	2P: $109-$139
12/1-12/31 & 4/30-11/30	1P: $79-$109	2P: $79-$109

Large-scale Hotel **Location:** I-95, exit 69, just w. 1301 Belvedere Rd 33405. Fax: 561/833-9218. **Facility:** 199 one-bedroom standard units. 11 stories, interior corridors. **Parking:** on-site. **Terms:** 3 day cancellation notice-fee imposed. [AP] & [BP] meal plans available, package plans. **Amenities:** voice mail, irons, hair dryers. **Dining:** 6:30 am-2 & 5-10 pm, cocktails. **Pool(s):** heated outdoor. **Leisure Activities:** saunas, exercise room. **Guest Services:** valet laundry, airport transportation-Palm Beach International Airport, area transportation-within 5 mi. **Business Services:** meeting rooms. **Cards:** AX, CB, DC, DS, MC, VI. **Special Amenities:** free newspaper and free room upgrade (subject to availability with advance reservations).

SOME UNITS

HOTEL BIBA   *Book at aaa.com*

Phone: (561)832-0094   **17**

12/1-4/15 [CP]	1P: $170-$200	2P: $170-$200	XP: $20	F
4/16-11/30 [CP]	1P: $109-$129	2P: $109-$129	XP: $20	F

Classic Motel **Location:** I-95, exit 69, 0.8 mi e; corner of US 1 and Olive Rd. 320 Belvedere Rd 33405. Fax: 561/833-7848. **Facility:** Designed in a Modern Bahamain-style inside and out. Rooms with a vivid room colors and custom made furniture. Relaxing courtyards, too. 43 units. 42 one-bedroom standard units. 1 two-bedroom suite ($175-$350). 2 stories (no elevator), interior/exterior corridors. *Bath:* combo or shower only. **Parking:** on-site (fee). **Terms:** package plans. **Amenities:** CD players, voice mail. **Pool(s):** heated outdoor. **Business Services:** meeting rooms, business center. **Cards:** AX, DC, MC, VI.

SOME UNITS

(See map and index starting on p. 843)

LA QUINTA INN *Book at aaa.com* Phone: (561)697-3388 **10**

	1P: $109-$129	2P: $109-$129
1/1-3/31	1P: $109-$129	2P: $109-$129
4/1-11/30	1P: $99-$109	2P: $99-$109
Motel	12/1-12/31	1P: $89-$99	2P: $89-$99

Location: SR 704, at east side of Florida Tpke, exit 99. 5981 Okeechobee Blvd 33417. Fax: 561/697-2834. **Facility:** 114 one-bedroom standard units. 4 stories, exterior corridors. *Bath:* combo or shower only. **Parking:** on-site. **Terms:** small pets only. **Amenities:** voice mail, safes, irons, hair dryers. **Pool(s):** outdoor. **Guest Services:** valet and coin laundry. **Cards:** AX, DC, DS, MC, VI.

SOME UNITS

PARKVIEW MOTOR LODGE Phone: (561)833-4644 **19**

1/10-4/15	1P: $90-$95	2P: $95-$105	XP: $10	F17
12/1-1/9 & 4/16-11/30	1P: $59-$75	2P: $59-$75	XP: $10	F17

Location: On US 1, 0.5 mi s of US 98 and SR 80. Located in a commercial area. 4710 S Dixie Hwy 33405. Fax: 561/833-4644. **Facility:** 28 units. 27 one-bedroom standard units. 1 one-bedroom suite ($118-$210). 1-2 stories (no elevator), exterior corridors. *Bath:* combo or shower only. **Parking:** on-site. **Terms:** weekly rates available, package plans. **Cards:** AX, DS, MC, VI. **Special Amenities:** free continental breakfast.

SOME UNITS

RADISSON HOTEL PALM BEACH AIRPORT *Book at aaa.com* Phone: (561)689-6888 **12**

1/1-4/30	1P: $149-$209	2P: $149-$209	XP: $10	F12
5/1-11/30	1P: $109-$159	2P: $109-$159	XP: $10	F12
12/1-12/31	1P: $99-$149	2P: $99-$149	XP: $10	F12

Location: I-95, exit 69, 0.5 mi w on Belvedere Rd, then 0.5 mi n. 1808 Australian Ave S 33409. Fax: 561/683-5783. **Facility:** 175 units. 127 one-bedroom standard units, 48 one-bedroom suites. 6 stories, interior corridors. **Parking:** on-site. **Terms:** cancellation fee imposed. **Amenities:** dual phone lines, voice mail, irons, hair dryers. **Dining:** 6:30 am-2 & 5-10 pm, Sat & Sun from 7 am, cocktails. **Pool(s):** heated outdoor. **Leisure Activities:** whirlpool, exercise room. **Guest Services:** valet laundry, airport transportation-Palm Beach International Airport, area transportation-within 3 mi. **Business Services:** meeting rooms, business center. **Cards:** AX, CB, DC, DS, MC, VI. **Special Amenities:** free newspaper and early check-in/late check-out.

SOME UNITS

RED ROOF INN-WEST PALM BEACH *Book at aaa.com* Phone: (561)697-7710 **2**

12/1-12/31	1P: $80-$95	2P: $85-$100		
1/1-3/25	1P: $74-$95	2P: $79-$100	XP: $5	F18
3/26-11/30	1P: $60-$71	2P: $66-$76	XP: $5	F18

Location: I-95, exit 74 (45th St), just w on CR 702; in Metrocenter Corporate Park. 2421 Metrocenter Blvd E 33407. Fax: 561/697-1728. **Facility:** 129 one-bedroom standard units. 3 stories, interior/exterior corridors. *Bath:* combo or shower only. **Parking:** on-site. **Terms:** small pets only. **Amenities:** video games (fee), voice mail. **Pool(s):** heated outdoor. **Guest Services:** valet laundry. **Cards:** AX, CB, DC, DS, MC, VI.

SOME UNITS
FEE FEE

RESIDENCE INN BY MARRIOTT WEST PALM BEACH *Book at aaa.com* Phone: 561/687-4747 **3**

1/1-4/30 [BP]	1P: $189-$359	2P: $189-$359
10/1-11/30 [BP]	1P: $149-$299	2P: $149-$299
12/1-12/31 [BP]	1P: $139-$289	2P: $139-$289
5/1-9/30 [BP]	1P: $119-$269	2P: $119-$269

Location: I-95, exit 74, just w on 45th St; in Metrocenter Corporate Park. 2461 Metrocenter Blvd 33407. Fax: 561/697-3633. **Facility:** 78 units. 33 one-bedroom standard units with efficiencies. 33 one- and 12 two-bedroom suites, some with efficiencies or kitchens. 3 stories, interior corridors. *Bath:* combo or shower only. **Parking:** on-site. **Terms:** small pets only ($75 fee). **Amenities:** dual phone lines, voice mail, irons, hair dryers. **Pool(s):** heated outdoor. **Leisure Activities:** whirlpool, exercise room, sports court, basketball, volleyball. **Guest Services:** complimentary evening beverages: Mon-Thurs, valet and coin laundry. **Business Services:** meeting rooms. **Cards:** AX, CB, DC, DS, JC, MC, VI.

SOME UNITS
FEE

STUDIO 6 EXTENDED STAY #6026 *Book at aaa.com* Phone: 561/640-3335 **13**

1/6-3/30	1P: $79-$89	2P: $83-$93	XP: $4	F17
12/1-1/5	1P: $65-$75	2P: $69-$79	XP: $4	F17
3/31-11/30	1P: $59-$69	2P: $63-$73	XP: $4	F17

Location: I-95, exit 69 (Belvedere Rd), w to Australian Ave, n to Centrepark Dr, then e straight ahead. 1535 Centrepark Dr N 33401. Fax: 561/640-3374. **Facility:** 137 one-bedroom standard units with efficiencies. 2 stories, exterior corridors. *Bath:* combo or shower only. **Parking:** on-site. **Terms:** weekly rates available, small pets only ($10 extra charge). **Amenities:** voice mail, irons. **Guest Services:** coin laundry. **Cards:** AX, CB, DC, DS, MC, VI.

SOME UNITS
FEE

TROPICAL GARDENS BED & BREAKFAST Phone: (561)848-4064 **4**

12/1-4/30 [BP]	1P: $110-$160	2P: $110-$160
5/1-11/30 [BP]	1P: $90-$135	2P: $90-$135

Location: Palm Beach Lakes Blvd, 1.2 mi n on N Dixie Hwy, then just w. Located in a quiet area. 419 32nd St 33407-4809. Fax: 561/848-2422. **Facility:** Decorated in a Key West theme, this B&B features a courtyard surrounded by tropical foliage with a pool in the center. Smoke free premises. 4 units. 3 one-bedroom standard units. 2 cottages. 1 story. *Bath:* combo or shower only. **Parking:** on-site. **Terms:** 2 night minimum stay - seasonal and/or weekends, age restrictions may apply, 14 day cancellation notice-fee imposed, package plans. **Amenities:** hair dryers. *Some:* DVD players, CD players, irons. **Pool(s):** small heated outdoor. **Leisure Activities:** bicycles. **Business Services:** PC. **Cards:** AX, MC, VI.

SOME UNITS

(See map and index starting on p. 843)

WELLESLEY INN (WEST PALM BEACH)   *Book at aaa.com*   Phone: 561/689-8540   7

[AAA] [SAVE] | 1/1-4/30 | 1P: $89-$159 | 2P: $99-$159 | XP: $10 | F12
| 5/1-8/31 | 1P: $79-$159 | 2P: $89-$159 | XP: $10 | F12
◇◇◇ ◇◇◇ | 12/1-12/31 & 9/1-11/30 | 1P: $69-$139 | 2P: $79-$139 | XP: $10 | F12

Location: I-95, exit 71, just w. 1910 Palm Beach Lakes Blvd 33409. Fax: 561/687-8090. **Facility:** 103 one-
Small-scale Hotel bedroom standard units. 6 stories, interior corridors. *Bath:* combo or shower only. **Parking:** on-site.
Terms: cancellation fee imposed, small pets only. **Amenities:** video games (fee), voice mail, irons, hair
dryers. **Pool(s):** heated outdoor. **Guest Services:** valet and coin laundry. **Business Services:** meeting rooms. **Cards:** AX, DC,
DS, MC, VI. **Special Amenities:** free expanded continental breakfast and free newspaper. *(See color ad below)*

SOME UNITS

[icons] / FEE FEE

WEST PALM BEACH MARRIOTT   *Book at aaa.com*   Phone: 561/833-1234   11

◇◇◇ ◇◇◇   Property failed to provide current rates

Location: I-95, exit 70, 0.8 mi e on Okeechobee Blvd E. 1001 Okeechobee Blvd 33401. Fax: 561/833-4689.
Large-scale Hotel **Facility:** 352 units. 341 one-bedroom standard units. 11 one-bedroom suites. 10 stories, interior corridors.
Bath: combo or shower only. **Parking:** on-site. **Amenities:** high-speed Internet (fee), dual phone lines, voice
mail, safes, irons, hair dryers. **Pool(s):** heated outdoor. **Leisure Activities:** whirlpool, exercise room. **Guest Services:** gift
shop, valet and coin laundry, area transportation. **Business Services:** conference facilities, business center.

SOME UNITS

[icons] / FEE FEE

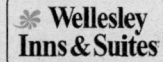

(See map and index starting on p. 843)

———— **WHERE TO DINE** ————

391ST BOMB GROUP   **Lunch:** $8-$12   **Dinner:** $12-$29   **Phone:** 561/683-3919   ⑨
💎💎💎   **Location:** I-95, exit 68, 2 mi w on US 98. 3989 Southern Blvd 33406. **Hours:** 11:30 am-10 pm, Fri-11 pm, Sat
American   noon-11 pm, Sun 10 am-2:30 & 4:30-10 pm. Closed: for lunch Sat 6/1-9/30. **Reservations:** suggested.
Features: The runway lights of Palm Beach International Airport create a romantic mood in this dining room.
World War II memorabilia decorates the walls, and there are some replica aircraft outside. Casual dress;
cocktails. **Parking:** on-site. Cards: AX, CB, DC, DS, MC, VI.   🍸

BREWZZI ITALIAN AMERICAN BISTRO &
MICROBREWERY   **Lunch:** $9-$24   **Dinner:** $9-$24   **Phone:** 561/366-9753   ⑤
💎💎💎   **Location:** I-95, exit 70A, 1.1 mi e to Florida Ave, then n; in City Place, 2nd level. 700 S Rosemary Ave, Suite 212
Italian   33401. **Hours:** 11:30 am-10:30 pm, Fri & Sat-11:30 pm, Sun-10 pm. Closed: 11/23. **Reservations:** not
accepted. **Features:** Award-winning beer is produced at this brew pub along with an excellent bistro menu
featuring American and Italian dishes, including fish n' chips, beer-battered coconut shrimp, steamed
mussels, tuna melt, turkey wraps, salads, roasted chicken, baby back ribs, steaks, pasta, Angus beef burgers, paninis and
pizza. Casual dress; cocktails. **Parking:** on-site. Cards: AX, MC, VI.   🍸

CHEEBURGER CHEEBURGER   **Lunch:** $6-$12   **Dinner:** $6-$12   **Phone:** 561/833-1997   ②
💎💎   **Location:** Jct Fern St; in City Place. 460 S Rosemary Ave 33401. **Hours:** 11 am-9 pm. **Features:** Diners can step
American   back into the past and reminisce at the '50s- style burger joint. Fun oldies music plays in the background as
patrons chomp down on specialty hamburgers. Polishing off one of the famous 20-ounce belly-bustin'
Cards: MC, VI.   "pounder" burgers is the way to earn a picture on the wall of fame. Casual dress. **Parking:** on-site.

CITY CELLAR WINE BAR & GRILL   **Lunch:** $10-$30   **Dinner:** $10-$30   **Phone:** 561/366-0071   ⑥
💎💎💎   **Location:** I-95, exit 70A, 1.1 mi e to Florida Ave, then n; in City Place, 2nd level. 700 S Rosemary Ave, Suite 218
American   33401. **Hours:** 11:30 am-11:30 pm, Fri & Sat-midnight. Closed: 11/23, 12/25. **Reservations:** accepted.
Features: This casual eatery features a varied menu that includes cashew crusted crabcakes, mussels,
escargots, Thai-style seared tuna, pizzas, ricotta gnocchi, Atlantic salmon, mahi-mahi sandwich, Chilean
sea bass, gulf shrimp, sea scallops, sirloin steak, veal saltimboca, New York cut steak, surf n' turf, broiled lobster tails, burgers,
sandwiches, calamari and entree salads. Casual dress; cocktails. **Parking:** on-site. Cards: AX, DC, DS, MC, VI.   🍸 ⑤

IL BELLAGIO AT CITY PLACE   **Lunch:** $8-$15   **Dinner:** $9-$27   **Phone:** 561/659-6160   ④
💎💎💎   **Location:** I-95, exit 70A, 1.1 mi e to S Rosemary Ave; next to fountains in the square of City Place. 600 S Rosemary
Regional   Ave, Suite 170 33401. **Hours:** 11:30 am-11 pm, Fri & Sat-midnight. Closed: 11/23, 12/25. **Features:** Right in
Italian   front of the fountains in the heart of "City Place," the setting derives some of its relaxed feel from the patio
seating. The dining room has a trendy atmosphere. Sharing menu space with brick-oven pizzas is a variety
of Italian favorites. Dressy casual; cocktails. **Parking:** on-site and valet. Cards: AX, MC, VI.
                                                                                                ♿Ⓜ 🍸 ⑤

MARK'S CITY PLACE   **Dinner:** $18-$38   **Phone:** 561/514-0770   ⑪
💎💎💎   **Location:** I-95, exit 70A, 1.1 mi e to Florida Ave, then n; in City Place, 2nd level. 700 S Rosemary Ave, #228 33401.
Regional American   **Hours:** 6 pm-11 pm, Fri & Sat-midnight, Sun-10:30 pm. **Reservations:** suggested. **Features:** Decor in the
busy "City Place" restaurant is soft with wrought iron accents and indirect lighting along with the wall
treatments. Memorable food reflects Mark Militello's twist on fresh seafood and American favorites. Dressy
casual; cocktails. **Parking:** on-site. Cards: AX, DC, DS, MC, VI.   ♿Ⓜ 🍸

ORCHIDS OF SIAM   **Lunch:** $6-$9   **Dinner:** $10-$19   **Phone:** 561/969-2444   ⑩
💎💎   **Location:** I-95, exit 66, 1.3 mi w on Forest Hill Blvd (SR 882); jct Forest Hill Blvd and Congress Ave; in Forest Hill
Thai   Center. 3027 Forest Hill Blvd 33406. **Hours:** 11:30 am-2:30 & 4:30-10 pm, Sat & Sun from 4:30 pm. Closed:
6/30-7/4. **Reservations:** suggested. **Features:** Lining the menu are traditional Thai favorites prepared with
varying degrees of spiciness. Soft decor colors offer comfort, and one dining room nurtures a tropical feel
with live orchids all around. Dressy casual; cocktails. **Parking:** on-site. Cards: AX, DC, MC, VI.   🍸 ⑤

PALM BEACH ALE HOUSE   **Lunch:** $7-$18   **Dinner:** $7-$18   **Phone:** 561/683-3777   ①
💎   **Location:** I-95, exit 71, 0.5 mi w. 2161 Palm Beach Lakes Blvd 33409. **Hours:** 11:30 am-2 am, Fri & Sat 11 am-4
American   am. Closed: 11/23, 12/25. **Features:** Sports aficionados can view events on 128 screens while noshing on
big food—including burgers, ribs and some seafood. Beer choices are plentiful. Casual dress; cocktails.
Parking: on-site. Cards: AX, MC, VI.   ⑤

PIPPENELLA'S   **Lunch:** $7-$10   **Dinner:** $10-$19   **Phone:** 561/833-9244   ⑧
💎💎   **Location:** On US 1, 0.6 mi s of Belvedere Rd. 3400 S Dixie Hwy 33405. **Hours:** 11 am-2 & 5-10 pm, Sat & Sun
Italian   from 5 pm. **Features:** Although the restaurant and dining room are unpretentious, the kitchen turns out
excellently prepared dishes. Much, including the pasta, is made in house, and some specialty ingredients
are imported to ensure their quality. Selections include chicken, veal and fish, as well as pasta, calzones
and gourmet pizza. Casual dress; beer & wine only. **Parking:** on-site. Cards: MC, VI.

RAIN DANCER STEAK HOUSE   **Dinner:** $15-$40   **Phone:** 561/684-2811   ③
💎💎💎   **Location:** I-95, exit 71, 0.8 mi w. 2300 Palm Beach Lakes Blvd, Suite 109 33409. **Hours:** 5 pm-10 pm, Fri & Sat-
Steak & Seafood   10:30 pm, Sun-9:30 pm. Closed: 11/23, 12/25. **Features:** An Old World decor sets the tone in the cozy,
rustic restaurant, where servers handle the busy tempo without missing a beat. A balanced selection of
wines complement succulent top-grade steak, such as a juicy 22-ounce porterhouse. Dressy casual;
cocktails. **Parking:** on-site. Cards: AX, CB, DC, DS, MC, VI.   🍸

(See map and index starting on p. 843)

TSUNAMI RESTAURANT   **Dinner:** $25-$35   Phone: 561/835-9696   ⑦
▼▼▼
                Location: I-95, exit 70A, 1.1 mi e; jct Okeechobee Blvd and Service Rd; in City Place. 651 Okeechobee Blvd 33401.
Asian   **Hours:** 5 pm-10:30 pm, Thurs-11 pm, Fri & Sat-midnight. **Reservations:** suggested. **Features:** This new
                eatery features high-tech lighting, a touch of the Orient and a menu offering the freshest of seafood
                combined with spices and flavors of the Far East. Dressy casual; cocktails. **Parking:** on-site and valet.
Cards: AX, DC, DS, MC, VI.

&M Ⓨ

─────── *The following restaurants have not been evaluated by AAA* ───────
but are listed for your information only.

FLANIGAN'S SEAFOOD BAR & GRILL   Phone: 561/659-3129
[fyi]   Not evaluated. **Location:** 330 Southern Blvd 33405. **Features:** The family-friendly restaurant is known for its
                baby back ribs, burgers and seafood.

LEGAL SEA FOODS   Phone: 561/838-9000
[fyi]   Not evaluated. **Location:** 550 S Rosemary Ave 33401. **Features:** New England style seafood has arrived,
                experience the clam chowder and the New England Clam Bake as well as other favorites.

WILBUR-BY-THE-SEA   (See map and index starting on p. 285)

─────── **WHERE TO DINE** ───────

BOONDOCKS   *Menu on aaa.com*   **Lunch:** $5-$15   **Dinner:** $5-$15   Phone: 386/760-9001   ㊴
AAA   **Location:** 1.3 mi s of Dunlawton Ave. 3948 S Peninsula Dr 32127. **Hours:** 11 am-10 pm. **Features:** Near a marina
▼▼   on the Halifax River, the restaurant offers casual outdoor dining and good views. Fresh seafood stands out
                on a menu that also includes tasty burgers, chowders and salads. The spot is a favorite with locals and
Seafood   tourists alike. Casual dress; cocktails. **Parking:** on-site. **Cards:** MC, VI.

Ⓨ Ⓚ

WILLISTON pop. 2,297

─────── **WHERE TO STAY** ───────

WILLISTON MOTOR INN   Phone: 352/528-4801
▼▼   All Year   1P: $38   2P: $38
                Location: 0.5 mi n on US 27 alternate route. 606 W Noble Ave 32696. Fax: 352/528-4650. **Facility:** 44 one-
Motel   bedroom standard units, some with kitchens. 1 story, exterior corridors. *Bath:* combo or shower only.
                Parking: on-site. **Terms:** cancellation fee imposed, small pets only ($6 extra charge). **Pool(s):** outdoor.
Guest Services: coin laundry. **Business Services:** fax (fee). **Cards:** DS, MC, VI.

SOME UNITS
🐴 ¶ 🛌 📡 DATA PORT / ⊠ 🖥 🖎 🖵 /
FEE

─────── **WHERE TO DINE** ───────

DRIFTWOOD GRILL   **Lunch:** $3-$13   Phone: 352/528-5074
▼▼   **Location:** Just e of town center. 515 E Noble Ave 32696. **Hours:** 6 am-2 pm, Sun from 7 am. **Features:** The
                eatery offers a variety of comfort food for a good value, including chicken wings, egg salad sandwich, and
American   blueberry cobbler. Casual dress. **Parking:** on-site. **Cards:** MC, VI.

WIMAUMA —*See Tampa Bay p. 1053.*

WINTER GARDEN —*See Orlando p. 834.*

WINTER HAVEN pop. 26,487

——— WHERE TO STAY ———

BEST WESTERN ADMIRAL'S INN   *Book at aaa.com*   Phone: (863)324-5950

| | 2/1-4/23 & 11/1-11/30 | 1P: $114-$249 | 2P: $114-$249 | XP: $6 | F18 |
| | 12/1-1/31 & 4/24-10/31 | 1P: $98-$249 | 2P: $98-$249 | XP: $6 | F18 |

Location: SR 540, 3 mi e of jct US 17; 3.9 mi w of jct US 27. 5665 Cypress Gardens Blvd 33884. Fax: 863/324-2376. **Facility:** 174 units. 171 one-bedroom standard units. 3 one-bedroom suites ($159-$249), some with whirlpools. 3-5 stories, interior/exterior corridors. *Bath:* combo or shower only. **Parking:** on-site. **Terms:** cancellation fee imposed, package plans, small pets only ($15 extra charge). **Amenities:** voice mail, safes, irons, hair dryers. **Dining:** 6:30 am-10:30 & 11-10 pm, cocktails, entertainment. **Pool(s):** outdoor. **Leisure Activities:** whirlpool, barbecue grills, exercise room. *Fee:* miniature golf, game room. **Guest Services:** valet and coin laundry. **Business Services:** meeting rooms, business center. **Cards:** AX, DC, DS, MC, VI. **Special Amenities:** free local telephone calls and free newspaper. *(See color ad below)*

Small-scale Hotel

SOME UNITS

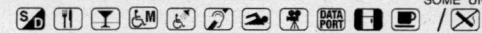

FEE

HAMPTON INN   *Book at aaa.com*   Phone: (863)299-9251

| All Year | 1P: $109-$159 | 2P: $109-$159 |

Location: On SR 540, 0.3 mi e of jct US 17. 202 Cypress Gardens Blvd 33880. Fax: 863/401-9388. **Facility:** 54 one-bedroom standard units. 3 stories, interior corridors. *Bath:* combo or shower only. **Terms:** [CP] meal plan available. **Amenities:** high-speed Internet, dual phone lines, voice mail, irons, hair dryers. **Pool(s):** small heated outdoor. **Leisure Activities:** exercise room. **Guest Services:** valet laundry. **Business Services:** business center. **Cards:** AX, CB, DC, DS, MC, VI.

Small-scale Hotel

SOME UNITS

HOLIDAY INN CYPRESS GARDENS-WINTER HAVEN   *Book at aaa.com*   Phone: (863)294-4451

| | 3/1-3/31 | 1P: $107 | 2P: $107 |
| | 12/1-2/28 & 4/1-11/30 | 1P: $71 | 2P: $71 |

Location: 0.8 mi s on US 17. 1150 Third St SW 33880. Fax: 863/293-9829. **Facility:** 227 one-bedroom standard units. 2 stories, exterior corridors. *Bath:* combo or shower only. **Parking:** on-site. **Amenities:** high-speed Internet, voice mail, irons, hair dryers. **Dining:** 6:30 am-2 & 5-8 pm, cocktails. **Pool(s):** heated outdoor, wading. **Leisure Activities:** golf privileges, exercise room. **Guest Services:** valet and coin laundry. **Business Services:** meeting rooms, fax (fee). **Cards:** AX, CB, DC, DS, JC, MC, VI.

Small-scale Hotel

SOME UNITS

───── **WHERE TO DINE** ─────

CHRISTY'S SUNDOWN RESTAURANT **Lunch:** $5-$10 **Dinner:** $12-$27 **Phone:** 863/293-0069

American

Location: 0.8 mi s on US 17. 1100 3rd St 33882. **Hours:** 11 am-10 pm, Sat from 5 pm. Closed major holidays; also Sun. **Reservations:** accepted. **Features:** Although the restaurant specializes in prime rib, its menu selections also incorporate seafood, veal, pasta and chicken dishes. The quiet dining room is a favorite of major-league baseball players during spring training. Casual dress; cocktails. **Parking:** on-site. **Cards:** AX, DS, MC, VI.

SAY AMEN CAFE **Lunch:** $4-$11 **Dinner:** $4-$11 **Phone:** 863/318-8877

American

Location: Jct SR 17 and Cypress Gardens Rd, just n. 3009 Cypress Gardens Rd 33884. **Hours:** 11 am-7 pm, Fri & Sat-8 pm, Sun noon-4 pm. Closed major holidays. **Features:** The family-owned and -operated restaurant serves up Southern comfort food with daily specials such as "Cajun Doug's Jammin Jambalaya", chicken and cumplings, fish fry or "Mom's Meat Loaf". Casual dress. **Parking:** on-site. **Cards:** AX, MC, VI.

SCHACK'S BBQ **Lunch:** $3-$18 **Dinner:** $3-$18 **Phone:** 863/324-1537

Barbecue

Location: Jct SR 17 and Cypress Gardens Rd, just n. 3000 Cypress Gardens Rd 33884. **Hours:** 6:30 am-9 pm, Sun from 8:30 am. Closed major holidays. **Features:** The family style restaunat serves barbecue favorites with popular side dishes and homestyle breakfast for early birds. Casual dress; beer only. **Parking:** on-site. **Cards:** MC, VI.

WINTER PARK —See Orlando p. 834.

WINTER SPRINGS —See Orlando p. 838.

YEEHAW JUNCTION

───── **WHERE TO DINE** ─────

DESERT INN RESTAURANT **Lunch:** $4-$12 **Dinner:** $4-$12 **Phone:** 407/436-1054

American

Location: Florida Tpke, exit 193, just w. 5570 S Kenansville Rd 34972. **Hours:** 8 am-9:30 pm, Fri & Sat-11 pm. Closed: 11/23, 12/25. **Features:** Located just off the Florida Turnpike, this casual eatery grills up tasty burgers and bakes homemade fruit pies served warm out of the oven. Casual dress; cocktails. **Parking:** on-site. **Cards:** MC, VI.

YULEE —See Jacksonville p. 506.

ZEPHYRHILLS —See Tampa Bay p. 1054.

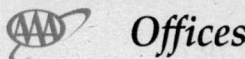

Offices

Cities with main offices are listed in **BOLD TYPE** and toll-free member service numbers in *ITALIC TYPE*. All are closed Saturdays, Sundays and holidays unless otherwise indicated.

The type of service provided is designated below the name of the city where the office is located:

✛ Auto travel services, including books/maps, marked maps and on-demand Triptik maps
● Auto travel services, including books/maps, marked maps, but no on-demand Triptik maps
■ Provides books/maps only. No marked maps or on-demand Triptik maps available
▲ Travel agency services

NATIONAL OFFICE: 1000 AAA DRIVE, HEATHROW, FLORIDA 32746-5063, (407) 444-7000

FLORIDA

BELLEAIR BLUFFS—AAA AUTO CLUB SOUTH, 100 N INDIAN ROCKS RD, 33770. MON-FRI 8:30-5:30. (727) 584-7678. ✛▲

BOCA RATON—AAA AUTO CLUB SOUTH, 2200 W GLADES RD STE 701, 33431. MON-FRI 8:30-5:30, SAT 9-1. (561) 395-8687. ✛▲

BRADENTON—AAA AUTO CLUB SOUTH, 11531 PALMBRUSH TRL, 34202. MON-FRI 8:30-5:30. (941) 756-0606. ✛▲

BRADENTON—AAA AUTO CLUB SOUTH, 6210 MANATEE AVE W, 34209. MON-FRI 8:30-5:30, SAT 9-1. (941) 798-2221. ✛▲

BRANDON—AAA AUTO CLUB SOUTH, 415 W ROBERTSON ST, 33511. MON-FRI 8:30-5:30, SAT 9-1. (813) 681-5761. ✛▲

CLEARWATER—AAA AUTO CLUB SOUTH, 2170 RAINBOW DR, 33765. MON-FRI 8:30-5:30, SAT 9-1. (727) 448-2600. ✛▲

DAYTONA BEACH—AAA AUTO CLUB SOUTH, 2525 INTNL SPEEDWAY BLVD, 32114. MON-FRI 8:30-5:30, SAT 9-1. (386) 252-0531. ✛▲

DELRAY BEACH—AAA AUTO CLUB SOUTH, 14539 MILITARY TRL #A, 33484. MON-FRI 8:30-5:30, SAT 9-1. (561) 865-1400. ✛▲

FORT MYERS—AAA AUTO CLUB SOUTH, 2516 COLONIAL BLVD, 33907. MON-FRI 8:30-5:30, SAT 9-1. (239) 939-6500. ✛▲

FORT PIERCE—AAA AUTO CLUB SOUTH, 1971 S US HWY #1, 34950. MON-FRI 8:30-5:30, SAT 9-1. (772) 461-6972. ✛▲

GAINESVILLE—AAA AUTO CLUB SOUTH, 1201 NW 13TH ST, 32601. MON-FRI 8:30-5:30, SAT 9-1. (352) 373-7801. ✛▲

HEATHROW—AAA AUTO CLUB SOUTH, 1000 AAA DR #28, 32746. MON-FRI 8:30-5:30. (407) 444-4240. ✛▲

HOLIDAY—AAA AUTO CLUB SOUTH, 4740 MILE STRETCH DR, 34690. MON-FRI 8:30-5:30. (727) 938-3794. ✛▲

JACKSONVILLE—AAA AUTO CLUB SOUTH, 4320 DEERWOOD LK PKY #109, 32216. MON-FRI 8:30-5:30, SAT 9-1. (904) 565-7722. ✛▲

KISSIMMEE—AAA AUTO CLUB SOUTH, 204 W OAK ST, 34741. MON-FRI 8:30-5:30. (407) 944-0866. ✛▲

LAKE WORTH—AAA AUTO CLUB SOUTH, 4075 SR 7 STE F1, 33467. MON-FRI 8:30-5:30. (561) 357-3475. ✛

LAKELAND—AAA AUTO CLUB SOUTH, 1457 E MEMORIAL BLVD, 33801. MON-FRI 8:30-5:30, SAT 9-1. (863) 688-7921. ✛▲

LAUDERHILL—AAA AUTO CLUB SOUTH, 4800 N UNIVERSITY DR, 33351. MON-FRI 8:30-5:30, SAT 9-1. (954) 748-2700. ✛▲

LEESBURG—AAA AUTO CLUB SOUTH, 1107 W NORTH BLVD #16, 34748. MON-FRI 8:30-5:30. (352) 787-8800. ✛▲

MARY ESTHER—AAA AUTO CLUB SOUTH, SANTA ROSA MALL STE #16, 32569. MON-FRI 8:30-5:30. (850) 244-3126. ✛▲

MELBOURNE—AAA AUTO CLUB SOUTH, 3578 N HARBOR CITY BLVD, 32935. MON-FRI 8:30-5:30, SAT 9-1. (321) 253-9100. ✛▲

MIAMI—AAA AUTO CLUB SOUTH, 6101 SUNSET DR SW, 33143. MON-FRI 8:30-5:30. (305) 661-6131. ✛▲

MIAMI—AAA AUTO CLUB SOUTH, 5044 SW 117 AVE, 33183. MON-FRI 8:30-5:30, SAT 9-1. (305) 270-6450. ✛▲

MIAMI—AAA AUTO CLUB SOUTH, 790 IVES DAIRY RD, 33179. MON-FRI 8:30-5:30. (305) 493-8700. ✛▲

NAPLES—AAA AUTO CLUB SOUTH, 5401 AIRPORT PULLING RD N, 34109. MON-FRI 8:30-5:30, SAT 9-1. (239) 594-5006. ✛▲

OCALA—AAA AUTO CLUB SOUTH, 3033 SW COLLEGE RD, 34474. MON-FRI 8:30-5:30, SAT 9-1. (352) 237-6251. ✛▲

ORANGE PARK—AAA AUTO CLUB SOUTH, 555 BLANDING BLVD, 32073. MON-FRI 8:30-5:30. (904) 272-2010. ✛▲

ORLANDO—AAA AUTO CLUB SOUTH, 4300 E COLONIAL DR, 32803. MON-FRI 8:30-5:30, SAT 9-1. (407) 894-3333. ✛▲

PALM BEACH GARDENS—AAA AUTO CLUB SOUTH, 9123 N MILITARY TRL #110, 33410. MON-FRI 8:30-5:30, SAT 9-1. (561) 694-9090. ✛▲

PALM HARBOR—AAA AUTO CLUB SOUTH, 32050 US HWY 19 N, 34684. MON-FRI 8:30-5:30, SAT 9-1. (727) 789-7850. ✛▲

PENSACOLA—AAA AUTO CLUB SOUTH, 540 BRENT LN, 32503. MON-FRI 8:30-5:30, SAT 9-1. (850) 477-6860. ✛▲

POMPANO BEACH—AAA AUTO CLUB SOUTH, 601 E ATLANTIC BLVD, 33060. MON-FRI 8:30-5:30. (954) 942-5450. ✛▲

PONTE VEDRA BEACH—AAA AUTO CLUB SOUTH, 840 A1A N #180, 32082. MON-FRI 8:30-5:30. (904) 280-8181. ✛▲

PORT CHARLOTTE—AAA AUTO CLUB SOUTH, 21229-A OLEAN BLVD, 33952. MON-FRI 8:30-5:30, SAT 9-1. (941) 627-1544. ✛▲

PORT RICHEY—AAA AUTO CLUB SOUTH, 10532 DEVCO DR, 34668. MON-FRI 8:30-5:30, SAT 9-1. (727) 868-9523. ✛▲

SARASOTA—AAA AUTO CLUB SOUTH, 258 RINGLING SHOPPING CTR, 34237. MON-FRI 8:30-5:30. (941) 362-2500. ✛▲

SARASOTA—AAA AUTO CLUB SOUTH, 3844 BEE RIDGE RD, 34233. MON-FRI 8:30-5:30, SAT 9-1. (941) 929-2299. ✛▲

SEMINOLE—AAA AUTO CLUB SOUTH, 9200 SEMINOLE BLVD, 33772. MON-FRI 8:30-5:30, SAT 9-1. (727) 398-3120. ✛▲

SPRING HILL—AAA AUTO CLUB SOUTH, 1410 PINEHURST DR, 34606. MON-FRI 8:30-5:30, SAT 9-1. (352) 683-3446. ✛▲

ST. PETERSBURG—AAA AUTO CLUB SOUTH, 7787 MLK JR ST N, 33702. MON-FRI 8:30-5:30, SAT 9-1. (727) 577-5282. ✛▲

ST. PETERSBURG—AAA AUTO CLUB SOUTH, 800 SECOND AVE S, 33701. MON-FRI 8:30-5:30. (727) 826-3600. ✛▲

STUART—AAA AUTO CLUB SOUTH, 1610 SE FEDERAL HWY, 34994. MON-FRI 8:30-5:30, SAT 9-1. (772) 287-5300. ✛▲

SUN CITY CENTER—AAA AUTO CLUB SOUTH, 717 CORTARO DR, 33573. MON-FRI 8:30-5:30. (813) 633-4880. ✛▲

TALLAHASSEE—AAA AUTO CLUB SOUTH, 1205 APALACHEE PKY, 32301. MON-FRI 8:30-5:30. (850) 878-6000. ✛▲

TAMPA—AAA AUTO CLUB SOUTH, 1515 N WESTSHORE BLVD, 33607. MON-FRI 8:30-5:30. (813) 289-5000. ✛▲

TAMPA—AAA AUTO CLUB SOUTH, 14755 N DALE MABRY, 33618. MON-FRI 8:30-5:30, SAT 9-1. (813) 963-2121. ✛▲

TAMPA—AAA AUTO CLUB SOUTH, 2335 E FOWLER AVE, 33612. MON-FRI 8:30-5:30. (813) 971-4900. ✛▲

THE VILLAGES—AAA AUTO CLUB SOUTH, 955 BICHARA BLVD, 32159. MON-FRI 8:30-5:30, SAT 9-1. (352) 753-2500. ✛▲

VENICE—AAA AUTO CLUB SOUTH, 2100 S TAMIAMI TRL, 34293. MON-FRI 8:30-5:30. (941) 493-2100. ✛▲

VERO BEACH—AAA AUTO CLUB SOUTH, 6650 20TH ST, 32966. MON-FRI 8:30-5:30. (772) 770-3400. ✛▲

WINTER HAVEN—AAA AUTO CLUB SOUTH, 601 W CENTRAL AVE, 33880. MON-FRI 8:30-5:30. (863) 293-3151. ✛▲

GOLDEN PASSPORTS

Golden Passports, available in three types, offer benefits and significant savings to individuals who plan to visit federal recreation sites.

The *Golden Eagle Passport*, available for a **$65** annual fee, is valid for entrance only to all federal recreation areas that have an entrance fee. Sites include those operated by the National Forest Service, National Park Service, Bureau of Land Management and the U.S. Fish and Wildlife Service. The passport admits all occupants of a private vehicle at locations where entrance is on a per vehicle basis. At locations where a per person fee is charged, the pass covers the pass holder, spouse, parents and children.

Citizens or permanent residents of the United States who are 62 and older can obtain *Golden Age Passports* for a one-time **$10** fee. Proof of age is required.

Golden Access Passports are free to citizens or permanent residents of the United States (regardless of age) who are medically blind or permanently disabled. Medical documention is required.

Both *Golden Age* and *Golden Access Passports* cover entrance fees for the holder and accompanying private party to all national parks and sites managed by the U.S. Fish and Wildlife Service, the U.S. Forest Service and the Bureau of Land Management, plus a 50% discount on federal recreation use fees. When a per person fee is imposed, the pass covers the pass holder, spouse and children. Apply in person at a federally operated area where an entrance fee is charged.

NATIONAL PARKS PASS

The *National Parks Pass*, valid for 1 year from its first use in a park, allows unlimited admissions to all U.S. national parks. The **$50** pass covers all occupants of a private vehicle at parks where the entrance fee is per vehicle. At parks with individual entry fees, the pass covers the pass holder, spouse, parents and children.

As a result of a partnership with the National Park Foundation, AAA members may purchase the pass for **$48**, either through AAA's internet site (www.aaa.com) or by visiting a participating AAA office. Members may also phone the National Park Foundation at **(888) 467-2757** or purchase the pass online at www.nationalparks.org. Non-members may purchase the pass through participating AAA offices for the full **$50** price or online at www.nationalparks.org.

For an upgrade fee of **$15**, a Golden Eagle Hologram sticker can be added to a *National Parks Pass*. The hologram covers entrance fees not just at national parks, but at any federal recreation area that has an admission fee. Valid for the duration of the *National Parks Pass* to which it is affixed, the Golden Eagle hologram is available at National Park Service, Fish and Wildlife Service and Bureau of Land Management fee stations.

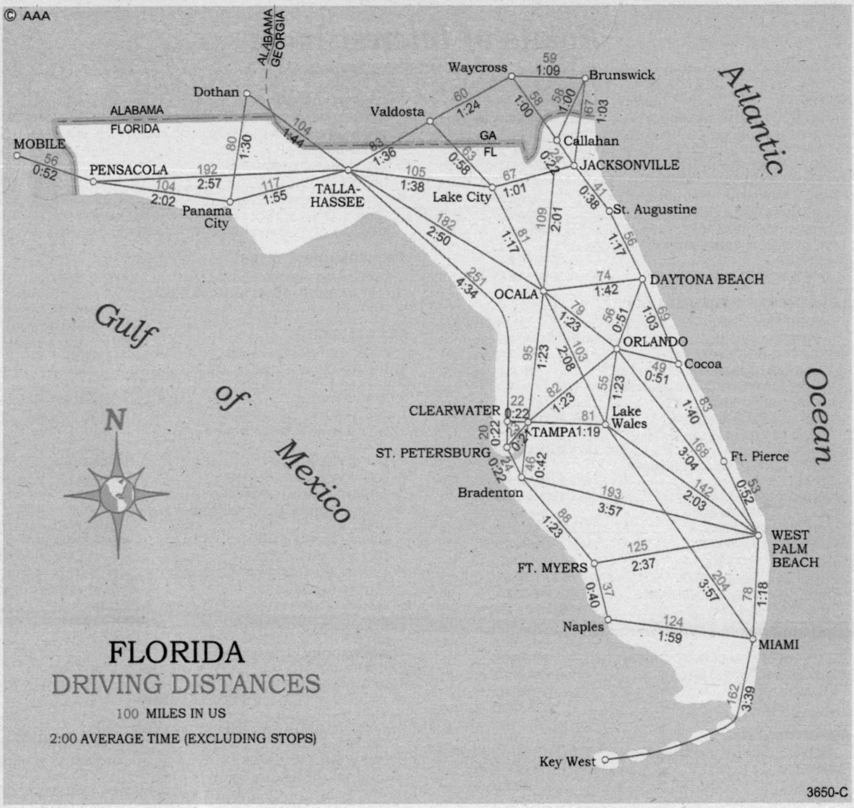

© AAA

FLORIDA
DRIVING DISTANCES
100 MILES IN US
2:00 AVERAGE TIME (EXCLUDING STOPS)

Atlantic

Ocean

Gulf

of

Mexico

N

ALABAMA
GEORGIA

Waycross
59
1:09
Brunswick

Dothan

60
1:24

ALABAMA
FLORIDA

Valdosta

104
80
1:30

83
1:36

Callahan

GA
FL

JACKSONVILLE

St. Augustine

MOBILE
56
0:52

PENSACORA

192
2:57

117
1:55

TALLA-
HASSEE

105
1:38

Lake City
67
1:01

109
2:01

Daytona Beach
74
1:42

104
2:02

Panama
City

182
2:50

251
4:34

OCALA

ORLANDO

Cocoa

CLEARWATER

TAMPA 1:19

Lake
Wales

Ft. Pierce

ST. PETERSBURG

Bradenton

193
3:57

WEST
PALM
BEACH

FT. MYERS

125
2:37

Naples
124
1:59

MIAMI

Key West

3650-C

Official Auto Club

aaa.com

DAYTONA INTERNATIONAL SPEEDWAY

MICHIGAN INTERNATIONAL SPEEDWAY

CALIFORNIA SPEEDWAY

TEXAS MOTOR SPEEDWAY

PHOENIX INTERNATIONAL RACEWAY

HOMESTEAD MIAMI SPEEDWAY

Watkins Glen NEW YORK'S Thunder Road

MARTINSVILLE SPEEDWAY

TALLADEGA SUPERSPEEDWAY

DARLINGTON too tough to tame

RICHMOND INTERNATIONAL RACEWAY

KANSAS SPEEDWAY

Points of Interest Index

Index Legend

NB. . . . . national battlefield	NR. . . . . national river
NBP. . . . . national battlefield park	NS. . . . . national seashore
NC. . . . . national cemetery	NWR. . . . . national wildlife refuge
NF. . . . . national forest	PHP. provincial historic(al) park
NHM. . . . . national historic(al) monument	PHS. . . . . provincial historic(al) site
NHP. . . . . national historic(al) park	PP. . . . . provincial park
NHS. . . . . national historic(al) site	SF. . . . . state forest
NL. . . . . national lakeshore	SHM. . . . . state historic(al) monument
NME. . . . . national memorial	SHP. state historic(al) park
NMO. . . . . national monument	SHS. . . . . state historic(al) site
NMP. . . . . national military park	SME. . . . . state memorial
NP. . . . . national park	SP. . . . . state park
NRA. . . . . national recreation area	SRA. state recreation area

⬙ GEM: Points of Interest Offering a *Great Experience for Members*®

FORT LAUDERDALE AIR & SEA SHOW......FORT LAUDERDALE, FL   84
FORT LAUDERDALE INTERNATIONAL BOAT
   SHOW.................................FORT LAUDERDALE, FL   84
MIAMI INTERNATIONAL BOAT SHOW..........MIAMI BEACH, FL   132
OCEAN FEST...............................FORT LAUDERDALE, FL   84
SUN 'N FUN EAA FLY-IN.........................LAKELAND, FL   107
WALT DISNEY WORLD FESTIVAL OF THE
   MASTERS......................................ORLANDO, FL   164
WINTER PARK SIDEWALK ART FESTIVAL.............ORLANDO, FL   163

EVENTS-SPORTS

12 HOURS OF SEBRING ENDURANCE RACE...........SEBRING, FL   206
BAY HILL INVITATIONAL..........................ORLANDO, FL   164
CAPITAL ONE BOWL...............................ORLANDO, FL   163
CELEBRITY GOLF CHAMPIONSHIP................MIAMI BEACH, FL   132
DANIA JAI-ALAI..............................DANIA BEACH, FL   84
DISNEY GOLF CLASSIC AT WALT DISNEYWORLD......ORLANDO, FL   164
DISNEY'S WIDE WORLD OF SPORTS
   COMPLEX...............................LAKE BUENA VISTA, FL   170
FLORIDA DERBY..............................FORT LAUDERDALE, FL   84
GASPARILLA DISTANCE CLASSIC.......................TAMPA, FL   230
GATE RIVER RUN............................JACKSONVILLE, FL   103
GATOR BOWL................................JACKSONVILLE, FL   103
GREATER JACKSONVILLE KINGFISH
   TOURNAMENT............................JACKSONVILLE, FL   103
JUNIOR ORANGE BOWL INTERNATIONAL YOUTH
   FESTIVAL...................................MIAMI BEACH, FL   131
MARION EDWARDS JR. MEMORIAL RACE.......MIAMI BEACH, FL   132
MID-WINTER SAILING REGATTA................MIAMI BEACH, FL   132
NASCAR BUSCH AND CRAFTSMAN TRUCK
   SERIES....................................MIAMI BEACH, FL   132
NASCAR NEXTEL CUP CHAMPIONSHIP........MIAMI BEACH, FL   132
OCEAN FEST...............................FORT LAUDERDALE, FL   84
ORANGE BOWL................................MIAMI BEACH, FL   131
ORANGE BOWL 5K/10K.........................MIAMI BEACH, FL   131
ORLANDO-SEMINOLE JAI-ALAI FRONTON............ORLANDO, FL   159
THE OUTBACK BOWL.................................TAMPA, FL   230
OUTBACK STEAKHOUSE PRO-AM.......................TAMPA, FL   230
THE PLAYERS CHAMPIONSHIP..................JACKSONVILLE, FL   103
POMPANO FISHING RODEO.................FORT LAUDERDALE, FL   84
ROYAL CARIBBEAN CLASSIC....................MIAMI BEACH, FL   132
ST. ANTHONY'S TAMPA BAY TRIATHLON.............TAMPA, FL   230
SARASOTA SKI-A-REES..........................SARASOTA, FL   201
SWAMP BUGGY RACES...............................NAPLES, FL   135
TAMPA BAY POLO CLUB........................PLANT CITY, FL   234
TARPON ROUND-UP.................................TAMPA, FL   230

EXHIBITS & COLLECTIONS-GENERAL

⚑ THE BAILEY-MATTHEWS SHELL MUSEUM.............SANIBEL, FL   200
FANTASY OF FLIGHT............................POLK CITY, FL   191
FLORIDA STATE CIVILIAN CONSERVATION CORPS
   MUSEUM..SEBRING, FL   206
FOREST CAPITAL MUSEUM SP..........................PERRY, FL   190
THE MUSEUM OF MAN IN THE SEA......PANAMA CITY BEACH, FL   188
NAVY SEAL MUSEUM..........................FORT PIERCE, FL   91
RIPLEY'S BELIEVE IT OR NOT! ORIGINAL MUSEUM.............ST.
   AUGUSTINE, FL   198
RIPLEY'S BELIEVE IT OR NOT! ORLANDO
   ODDITORIUM...................................ORLANDO, FL   154
ST. AUGUSTINE LIGHTHOUSE AND MUSEUM...................ST.
   AUGUSTINE, FL   198
SOLOMON'S CASTLE..................................ONA, FL   140
SOUTHEAST MUSEUM OF PHOTOGRAPHY.............DAYTONA
   BEACH, FL   56
WORLD CHESS HALL OF FAME AND SIDNEY SAMOLE
   MUSEUM...MIAMI, FL   124

EXHIBITS & COLLECTIONS-ANIMALS & BIRDS

ANN KOLB NATURE CENTER.....................HOLLYWOOD, FL   86
AUDUBON OF FLORIDA...........................MAITLAND, FL   182
BIG CYPRESS VISITOR CENTER.............BIG CYPRESS NATIONAL
   PRESERVE, FL   45
⚑ BUTTERFLY WORLD...........................COCONUT CREEK, FL   84
CLEARWATER MARINE AQUARIUM...............CLEARWATER, FL   231
THE CONSERVANCY NATURE CENTER..................NAPLES, FL   136
⚑ THE FLORIDA AQUARIUM........................TAMPA, FL   223
GREEN MEADOWS PETTING FARM.................KISSIMMEE, FL   166
GULF SPECIMEN MARINE LABORATORY..............PANACEA, FL   187
GULFARIUM.............................FORT WALTON BEACH, FL   92
JUNGLE ADVENTURES..........................CHRISTMAS, FL   165
KONGER TARPON SPRINGS AQUARIUM......TARPON SPRINGS, FL   235
LEE COUNTY MANATEE PARK...................FORT MYERS, FL   88
MANATEE OBSERVATION AND EDUCATION
   CENTER......................................FORT PIERCE, FL   91
MANATEE VIEWING CENTER...................APOLLO BEACH, FL   231
MIAMI MUSEUM OF SCIENCE & PLANETARIUM..........MIAMI, FL   123
MUSEUMS AND NATURE CENTER OF CRANE POINT
   HAMMOCK.....................................MARATHON, FL   75
OCTAGON WILDLIFE SANCTUARY..............PUNTA GORDA, FL   191
PEACE RIVER WILDLIFE CENTER..............PUNTA GORDA, FL   191
PELICAN MAN'S BIRD SANCTUARY..................SARASOTA, FL   205
SAWGRASS RECREATION PARK............FORT LAUDERDALE, FL   81

⚑ SOUTH FLORIDA MUSEUM........................BRADENTON, FL   47
SUNCOAST SEABIRD SANCTUARY..............INDIAN SHORES, FL   233

EXHIBITS & COLLECTIONS-AVIATION

AIR FORCE ARMAMENT MUSEUM.....FORT WALTON BEACH, FL   92
⚑ ASTRONAUT HALL OF FAME.........KENNEDY SPACE CENTER, FL   107
FANTASY OF FLIGHT............................POLK CITY, FL   191
⚑ FLORIDA AIR MUSEUM AT SUN 'N FUN............LAKELAND, FL   108
⚑ KENNEDY SPACE CENTER VISITOR COMPLEX.....KENNEDY SPACE
   CENTER, FL   107
MILITARY HERITAGE & AVIATION MUSEUM....PUNTA GORDA, FL   192
⚑ NATIONAL MUSEUM OF NAVAL AVIATION.......PENSACOLA, FL   190
ST. PETERSBURG MUSEUM OF HISTORY.......ST. PETERSBURG, FL   222
VALIANT AIR COMMAND WARBIRD AIR
   MUSEUM.......................................TITUSVILLE, FL   236
WINGS OVER MIAMI..............................MIAMI, FL   124

EXHIBITS & COLLECTIONS-CIVIL WAR HISTORY

MUSEUM OF SCIENCE AND HISTORY...........JACKSONVILLE, FL   102
MUSEUM OF SOUTHERN HISTORY.............JACKSONVILLE, FL   102
OLUSTEE BATTLEFIELD HISTORIC SP................OLUSTEE, FL   140

EXHIBITS & COLLECTIONS-DOLLS & TOYS

ELLIOTT MUSEUM.................................STUART, FL   207
FLORIDA HERITAGE MUSEUM................ST. AUGUSTINE, FL   198
⚑ THE MORIKAMI MUSEUM AND JAPANESE
   GARDENS..................................DELRAY BEACH, FL   58
PIONEER FLORIDA MUSEUM AND VILLAGE.........DADE CITY, FL   232
THE TEDDY BEAR MUSEUM OF NAPLES.................NAPLES, FL   138

EXHIBITS & COLLECTIONS-HISTORICAL

AMELIA ISLAND MUSEUM OF HISTORY............FERNANDINA
   BEACH, FL   104
⚑ ASTRONAUT HALL OF FAME.........KENNEDY SPACE CENTER, FL   107
BOCA RATON HISTORICAL SOCIETY.............BOCA RATON, FL   46
BREVARD MUSEUM OF HISTORY AND SCIENCE........COCOA, FL   50
⚑ CASTILLO DE SAN MARCOS NMO..............ST. AUGUSTINE, FL   193
CEDAR KEY HISTORICAL SOCIETY MUSEUM.......CEDAR KEY, FL   50
CEDAR KEY SP MUSEUM........................CEDAR KEY, FL   50
CENTRO YBOR MUSEUM..............................TAMPA, FL   223
CHARLOTTE COUNTY HISTORICAL
   CENTER................................CHARLOTTE HARBOR, FL   50
COLLIER COUNTY MUSEUM..........................NAPLES, FL   136
⚑ COLONIAL SPANISH QUARTER..................ST. AUGUSTINE, FL   195
CONSTITUTION CONVENTION MUSEUM SP........PORT ST. JOE, FL   191
DE LEON SPRINGS SP.......................DE LEON SPRINGS, FL   58
DE SOTO NME...FL   58
THE DEPOT—LAKE WALES MUSEUM AND CULTURAL
   CENTER....................................LAKE WALES, FL   109
DUNEDIN HISTORICAL SOCIETY AND MUSEUM.......DUNEDIN, FL   232
EAST MARTELLO MUSEUM AND GALLERY..........KEY WEST, FL   74
ELLIOTT MUSEUM.................................STUART, FL   207
⚑ FLAGLER MUSEUM...........................PALM BEACH, FL   187
FLAGLER STATION OVER-SEA RAILWAY
   HISTOREUM....................................KEY WEST, FL   72
FLAMINGO GARDENS..............................DAVIE, FL   85
FLORIDA CENTER FOR POLITICAL HISTORY AND
   GOVERNANCE.................................TALLAHASSEE, FL   209
FLORIDA HERITAGE MUSEUM................ST. AUGUSTINE, FL   198
⚑ THE FLORIDA HOLOCAUST MUSEUM........ST. PETERSBURG, FL   218
FLORIDA MUSEUM OF NATURAL HISTORY........GAINESVILLE, FL   92
FOREST CAPITAL MUSEUM SP..........................PERRY, FL   190
FORT CHRISTMAS HISTORICAL PARK............CHRISTMAS, FL   164
GAMBLE PLANTATION HISTORIC SP AND JUDAH P.
   BENJAMIN CONFEDERATE MEMORIAL.............ELLENTON, FL   59
GILBERT'S BAR HOUSE OF REFUGE MUSEUM..........STUART, FL   207
GOLD COAST RAILROAD MUSEUM......................MIAMI, FL   120
⚑ GOVERNMENT HOUSE MUSEUM................ST. AUGUSTINE, FL   195
GULF BEACHES HISTORICAL MUSEUM........ST. PETE BEACH, FL   234
HALIFAX HISTORICAL SOCIETY AND
   MUSEUM....................................DAYTONA BEACH, FL   56
HENRY A. DeLAND HOUSE MUSEUM..............DeLAND, FL   58
HENRY B. PLANT MUSEUM...........................TAMPA, FL   224
HERITAGE VILLAGE................................LARGO, FL   233
HISTORIC SPANISH POINT.........................OSPREY, FL   186
HISTORICAL MUSEUM OF SOUTHERN FLORIDA........MIAMI, FL   122
THE HOLOCAUST MEMORIAL RESOURCE AND EDUCATION
   CENTER OF FLORIDA..........................MAITLAND, FL   182
INTERNATIONAL SWIMMING HALL OF FAME................FORT
   LAUDERDALE, FL   77
JACKSONVILLE HISTORICAL CENTER...........JACKSONVILLE, FL   100
JOHN GORRIE MUSEUM SP....................APALACHICOLA, FL   44
JUNIOR MUSEUM OF BAY COUNTY...........PANAMA CITY, FL   187
KEY WEST LIGHTHOUSE MUSEUM...................KEY WEST, FL   72
KEY WEST MUSEUM OF ART & HISTORY AT THE CUSTOM
   HOUSE..KEY WEST, FL   72
KINGSLEY PLANTATION......................JACKSONVILLE, FL   102
⚑ LIGHTNER MUSEUM.........................ST. AUGUSTINE, FL   195
LOXAHATCHEE RIVER HISTORICAL MUSEUM..........JUPITER, FL   106
MAY STRINGER HERITAGE MUSEUM............BROOKSVILLE, FL   48
McLARTY TREASURE MUSEUM...................VERO BEACH, FL   236

SIGHTSEEING-AIRCRAFT RIDES & TOURS

SIGHTSEEING TOURS

SIGHTSEEING TOURS-BOATS

SIGHTSEEING TOURS-RAFTING & CANOEING

SPORTS ARENAS

💾 *Attraction Admission Discount Index*

Bed & Breakfast Lodgings Index

Some bed and breakfasts listed below might have historical significance. Those properties are also referenced in the Historical index. The indication that continental [CP] or full breakfast [BP] is included in the room rate reflects whether a property is a Bed-and-Breakfast facility.

Country Inns Index

Some of the following country inns can also be considered as bed-and-breakfast operations. The indication that continental [CP] or full breakfast [BP] is included in the room rate reflects whether a property is a Bed-and-Breakfast facility.

Historical Lodgings & Restaurants Index

Some of the following historical lodgings can also be considered as bed-and-breakfast operations. The indication that continental [CP] or full breakfast [BP] is included in the room rate reflects whether a property is a Bed-and-Breakfast facility.

Resorts Index

Many establishments are located in resort areas; however, the following places have extensive on-premises recreational facilities:

Resorts (cont'd)

Comprehensive City Index

Here is an alphabetical list of all cities appearing in this TourBook® guide. Cities are presented by state/province. Page numbers under the POI column indicate where points of interest text begins. Page numbers under the L&R column indicate where lodging and restaurant listings begin.

Comprehensive City Index (cont'd)

Comprehensive City Index (cont'd)

Crossword Puzzle

ACROSS

2
4
5
8
9
11
12
13
14

DOWN

1
3
6
7
10

Which two are the same?

Towty is a trademark of AAA

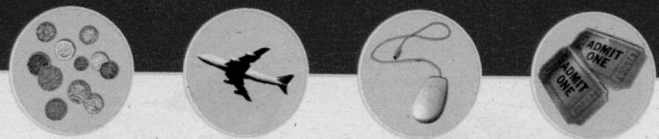